GW00360800
For further details please contact us on 01732 781000 or visit our website: www.az.co.uk
A-Z HERTFORDSHIRE COUNTY ATLAS
A-Z ESSEX COUNTY ATLAS
A-Z KENT COUNTY ATLAS
TO LONDON STANSTED AIRPORT
KEY TO MAP PAGES
Greater London Boundary
SCALE
0 1 2 3 Miles
0 1 2 3 4 Kilometres
ESSEX
KENT
HODDESDON
Broxbourne
Lower Nazeing
HARLOW
Fyfield
Thornwood Common
Epping Upland
North Weald Bassett
High Ongar
Chipping Ongar
CHESHUNT
Waltham Cross
Holyfield
WALTHAM ABBEY
EPPING
Coopersale
Copthall Green
Theydon Bois
Hobbs Cross
Stapleford Tawney
Stondon Massey
Doddinghurst
Kelvedon Hatch
Mountnessing
Enfield Wash
High Beech
Debden Green
Sewardstone
Epping Forest
Debden
LOUGHTON
Abridge
Passingford Bridge
Navestock
Navestock Side
Pilgrims Hatch
Hutton
Shenfield
Billericay
Ponders End
CHINGFORD
CHIGWELL
Chigwell Row
Lambourne End
Stapleford Abbotts
Havering-atte-Bower
Noak Hill
South Weald
BRENTWOOD
South Green
Wickford
EDMONTON
Buckhurst Hill
Grange Hill
Woodford Green
WOODFORD
Hainault
Collier Row
Harold Hill
Brook Street
Warley
Ingrave
Great Warley
Herongate
TOTTENHAM
WALTHAMSTOW
Snaresbrook
Barkingside
Chadwell Heath
Gidea Park
Harold Wood
ROMFORD
West Horndon
Laindon
North Benfleet
BASILDON
WANSTEAD
Leytonstone
LEYTON
ILFORD
Goodmayes
Becontree
HORNCHURCH
UPMINSTER
Langdon Hills
Bulphan
Manor Park
Elm Park
North Ockendon
HACKNEY
STRATFORD
BETHNAL GREEN
WEST HAM
EAST HAM
BARKING
DAGENHAM
South Hornchurch
Horndon on the Hill
Balstonia
Corringham
Coryton
STEPNEY
POPLAR
Beckton
Creekmouth
LONDON CITY AIRPORT
River Thames
Thamesmead
Rainham
South Ockendon
THURROCK
North Stifford
Orsett
Stanford-le-Hope
Thames Haven
Blackwall Tunnel
Ferry
Abbey Wood
Wennington
Aveley
Chafford Hundred
Chadwell St. Mary
East Tilbury
BERMONDSEY
WOOLWICH
Belvedere
Purfleet
THURROCK Lakeside
GRAYS
ERITH
DEPTFORD
GREENWICH
Charlton
Plumstead
DARTFORD-THURROCK RIVER CROSSING (DART CHARGE)
West Thurrock
South Stifford
West Tilbury
Cliffe
Blackheath
Kidbrooke
Welling
Slade Green
Greenhithe
TILBURY
LEWISHAM
ELTHAM
BEXLEYHEATH
Crayford
DARTFORD
Stone
Swanscombe
GRAVESEND
Lee
Blackfen
BEXLEY
Old Bexley
Bluewater
Northfleet
Chalk
CATFORD
New Eltham
Dulwich
Sydenham
Grove Park
Mottingham
SIDCUP
Wilmington
Hawley
Bean
Betsham
Higham
Wainscott
Crystal Palace
North Cray
Hextable
South Darenth
Southfleet
Istead Rise
Shorne
Strood
South Norwood
Penge
BECKENHAM
BROMLEY
CHISLEHURST
St. Paul's Cray
Swanley
Sutton at Hone
Horton Kirby
Longfield
New Barn
Sole Street
Cobham
ROCHESTER
St. Mary Cray
Petts Wood
Hayes
Crockenhill
Farningham
Fawkham Green
Hartley
Longfield Hill
Meopham Station
Meopham
Cuxton
CHATHAM
Addiscombe
Shirley
West Wickham
ORPINGTON
Eynsford
CROYDON
Addington
Keston
Farnborough
Green Street Green
Chelsfield
Well Hill
West Kingsdown
New Ash Green
Halling
New Addington
Sanderstead
Selsdon
Leaves Green
Downe
Pratt's Bottom
Halstead
Badgers Mount
Shoreham
Stansted
Culverstone Green
Vigo Village
Snodland
Farleigh
Chelsham
Biggin Hill
Berry's Green
Cudham
Knockholt
Otford
Kemsing
Wrotham
Fairseat
Aylesford
Larkfield
WARLINGHAM
Woldingham
Tatsfield
Chevening
Dunton Green
Chipstead
Seal
Borough Green
Ightham
St. Marys Platt
Wrotham Heath
West Malling
East Malling
MAIDSTONE
CLACKET LANE
Brasted
Sundridge
SEVENOAKS
Ivy Hatch
Plaxtol
Kings Hill
Barming
Limpsfield
Westerham
Oxted
Godstone
Tandridge
Hurst Green
Crockham Hill
Ide Hill
Sevenoaks Weald
Shipbourne
Hadlow
Loose
Coxheath
South Godstone
Marlpit Hill
Four Elms
Hildenborough
Edenbridge
TONBRIDGE
LONDON GATWICK AIRPORT
19 20 21 22 23
33 34 35 36 37 38 39 40 41
51 52 53 54 55 56 57 58 59
71 72 73 74 75 76 77 78 79
91 92 93 94 95 96 97 98 99 100 101
113 114 115 116 117 118 119 120 121 122 123
135 136 137 138 139 140 141 142 143 144 145
157 158 159 160 161 162 163 164 165
177 178 179 180 181 182 183 184 185
197 198 199 200 201 202 203 204 205
209 210 211
M25
M11
M20
M26
M2
A1169
A414
A10
A1170
B181
B184
A113
A128
A12
A129
A130
A132
A176
A127
A1235
A13
B1007
B1420
A1014
A226
A228
B2000
A2
A227
A229
A20
A26
A21
A225
B2042
B2026
B269
B2016
B2163
A22

MASTER ATLAS OF GREATER LONDON

CONTENTS

Key to Map Pages	Inside Front Cover
Map Pages @ approx: 3⅓" to 1 mile	2-211
Congestion Charging Zone Map	212
Large Scale Map Pages @ 9" to 1 mile	213-231
West End Cinemas & Theatres Maps	232
Road Map Pages @ 3 miles to 1"	233-241
Postcode Map Pages	242-243
Low Emission Zone Map	244-245
Index to Streets, Places & Areas and selected Places of Interest	246-425
Index to Hospitals etc.	426-430
Index to Stations	431-433
London Railway Connections Map	434-435
Underground Railway Map	436
Administrative Boundary Map	Inside Back Cover

EDITION 15 2017

Telephone : 01732 781000 (Enquiries & Trade Sales)
01732 783422 (Retail Sales)

Every possible care has been taken to ensure that, to the best of our knowledge, the information contained in this atlas is accurate at the date of publication. However, we cannot warrant that our work is entirely error free and whilst we would be grateful to learn of any inaccuracies, we do not accept responsibility for loss or damage resulting from reliance on information contained within this publication.

The representation on the maps of a road, track or footpath is no evidence of the existence of a right of way.

Safety camera information supplied by www.PocketGPSWorld.com
Speed Camera Location Database Copyright 2016 © PocketGPSWorld.com

PocketGPSWorld.com's CamerAlert is a self-contained speed and red light camera warning system for SatNavs and Android or Apple iOS smartphones/tablets. Visit www.cameralert.com to download.

Safety camera locations are publicised by the Safer Roads Partnership who operate them in order to encourage drivers to comply with speed limits at these sites. It is the drivers absolute responsibility to be aware of and to adhere to speed limits at all times.

By showing this safety camera information it is the intention of Geographers' A-Z Map Company Ltd., to encourage safe driving and greater awareness of speed limits and vehicle speed.
Data accurate at time of printing.

The publishers are deeply grateful for the ready co-operation and valuable help given to them in the production of this atlas. They would like to record their obligation to: The Engineers and Surveyors Departments and Planning Offices of all the Local Authorities covered in this atlas, The Department for Transport, Highways Agency, Transport for London, The Post Office, Police Authorities, Fire Brigades, Taxi Drivers, members of the public.

www./az.co.uk

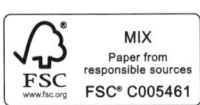

80 years
of
Geographers'
A-Z Map Company

2016 marks another milestone in the history of Britain's leading independent map publisher as we mark 80 years of map production, a journey that Phyllis Pearsall referred to as being 'From Bedsitter To Household Name'.

Although the Company's story doesn't commence until 1936, the real story begins in 1879 with the birth of Alexander Grosz, in Csurog, at the time a part of Austria-Hungary. Alexander moved to London in 1900, aged 21, and stayed in an Islington rooming-house. His motives were twofold – firstly to find his fortune and secondly to avoid conscription.

In 1901, Alexander met Isabelle (Bella) Crowley in a Creamery near Elephant & Castle. Despite resistance from her family, the couple eloped and married 2 years later in Gretna Green. The following year, in 1904, the couple moved to Court Lane Gardens in Dulwich. In 1905, Anthony (Tony) was born, followed by Phyllis Isobella on the 25th September 1906. 100 years later, a Blue Plaque was unveiled at the house to commemorate Phyllis.

In 1908, Alexander and Bella founded their first map company, Geographia Ltd, and so began Alexander's 50 years in the mapping business, in an office in John Street, just off The Strand.

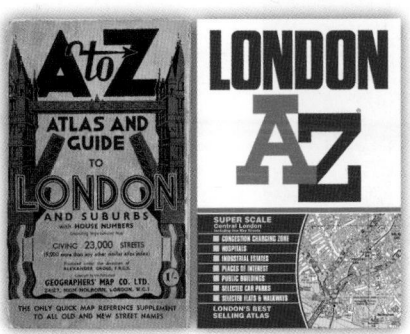

The couple were keen on travelling - Alexander liked to take annual trips to Budapest and to see his mother whenever possible, and it was during one of these trips in 1909 that Phyllis contracted Scarlet Fever. At the time this was potentially a very serious illness for any child to have, but Phyllis went on to make a full recovery, fortunately with no ill effect.

Alexander also developed a keen interest in developing aviation maps, and consequently, regularly visited Hendon Aerodrome. During a visit in 1910, one of the pilots offered to give Phyllis and Tony a quick trip in his plane, but Alexander refused to allow them to go, much to their frustration. After having them lifted from the plane they watched in horror as the plane crashed on take-off, and was consumed by fire.

With the business growing, Alexander changed offices from John Street to Fleet Street, and the family moved to North End Road. Bella wrote a play which was performed at the Savoy Theatre in 1913. After the outbreak of the First World War, Alexander built a relationship with the Telegraph, and regularly produced war maps for them. With this increase in business, the family moved out of London to Claygate.

In 1916, Phyllis started school at Rodean. Bella continued with her writing, and had a number of

Alexander Gross 1936

children's books published. In 1918, Alexander was granted The Freedom Of The City Of London, the highest honour the City can bestow. With some foresight, but little awareness of how

in Fecamp, France, both as a pupil and a teacher. It was whilst visiting Tony that Phyllis met his friend, Richard Pearsall. Richard had previously fought in the First World War as a Lieutenant in the King's Liverpool Regiment (where he had been awarded an MBE), had left service in 1921, and was now studying art with Tony.

important this was to become, Alexander registered the Geographia name in New York in 1919, leaving it dormant at this stage.

1924 portrait of Isabelle by Alfred Orr

Alexander and Bella's marriage came to an end after 17 years in 1920. Bella was badly injured in a riding accident at a similar time, and the strain between the couple was showing. The home in Claygate was sold, and Alexander moved to St James' Court in London. Bella began divorce proceedings, and in response, Alexander removed her as a Director of Geographia Ltd. This proved to be a tough time for Alexander – he authorised the purchase of a printing company by Geographia Ltd, and then the production of a World Atlas. The first edition sold well, but a second and third printing struggled. Following on from this, Alexander was voted off Geographia's board. Geographia was then sold to the bank for a paltry £1,000.

Now single, Bella met the artist Alfred Orr, and in 1921 they moved in together. Alexander, with no income, moved to Chicago, and began teaching English to pay his way. As a result of Alexander's move, and Bella's new partner, Phyllis had no place in London to call home as Alfred couldn't stand having anyone other than Bella around him. She took a position at the College de Jeunes Filles

Alexander was removed as a Fellow of the Royal Geographical Society, due to his declaring bankruptcy. Phyllis spent some of 1923 with him in Chicago before returning to Paris in 1924 to study at the Sorbonne. She initially slept rough under the Pont St Michel, until she eventually had the money for a room in an apartment in the Street Of Gallows – her fellow guests included Nabokov. She paid the rent as a translator in a department store, and also through English lessons. By the end of the year, she had her very first one-man exhibition in Orleans, the first of many through the years. At this time, Bella and Alfred were living in Chelsea, and spent two years here before moving to 31 Tite Street, previously home to John Sargent, the famous American portrait artist.

In 1926, Phyllis married Richard. Their first home was his studio in Clapham, although they were to spend many of their years travelling, initially around Belgium, and then on to Spain, mostly for

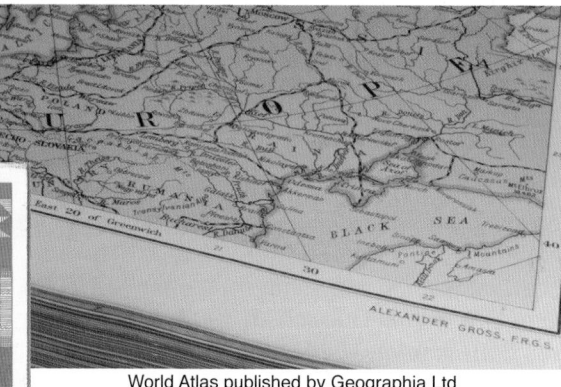
World Atlas published by Geographia Ltd

the warmer climate. Alexander returned to London in 1929 in an attempt to rescue his name and reputation and to take legal action regarding the sale of Geographia Ltd. Failing to make headway, he returned to New York and activated the previously dormant US business, Geographia Map Co Inc., at 11 John Street, NY.

Published by Geographia Map Co. Inc

1936 – – – – – – – – – – – – – – – – **1946**

25.8.1936
Geographers' Map Company founded
Formed by Alexander Gross with his children Phyllis and Anthony as shareholders

Vintage company letter stamps

The first AtoZ atlases were delivered on a borrowed wheelbarrow

War Years
Detailed street maps not published during war years. Mrs Pearsall paints portraits of officers to meet costs and travels Britain to draw women conscripted into War work

In 1934, Phyllis' first book, Castilian Ochre was published. The book covered her time travelling in Spain with Richard. In 1936, Phyllis returned to London from Europe, without Richard, having left him. She moved to Astral House in New Street. Alexander came to London at the same time, and set up Geographers' Map Company on the 25th August, issuing the shares equally between Tony

in 1940, for national safety, the government ordered the removal of all the A-Z London Maps from sale. Taking the lead from her father, Phyllis found work for the business producing war maps for the newspapers. Phyllis was also commissioned to produce drawings of women working on the war effort.

Using a double ruling pencil

Mixing indian ink

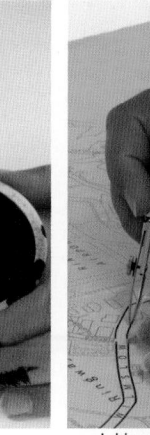

Inking linework with ruling pen

Hand lettering

and Phyllis. This newly formed Company had its first offices in Napier House, 24-27 High Holborn. The first publication to go on sale was Alexander's Map Of The World, with plans made to produce 3 London publications, including the 'OK' atlas.

Phyllis took on the responsibility for compiling the street information, and walked each day for hours on end cataloguing the house numbers, junctions and streets. This led to the publication of her first London map, and Phyllis changed the name at the last minute to the 'A to Z'. The first maps were sold to W.H. Smith and Sons. They were all hand drawn, and would take a skilled cartographer around 12 weeks to produce.

Sadly, Bella was certified and passed away in 1937. She was shortly followed by Alfred. Soon after, Richard and Phyllis' marriage was dissolved. Richard remarried in 1939, and passed away in 1971 whilst living in California.

In 1938, mixing business with her continued love of art, Phyllis held an exhibition at the Goupil gallery in London. By now, A-Z were publishing 12 titles, 6 of which being London guides. The following year, war broke out around Europe, and

As war raged on, Phyllis moved to a role working in censorship, and then on to home intelligence. At the end of the war, with the restriction on map sales lifted, the A-Z business again began to flourish. Phyllis turned down a senior civil service job to focus on the business, which now expanded to 21 Gray's Inn Road, taking time out only to visit her father in New York upon hearing of him being unwell.

Phyllis was then involved in an incredibly tragic event. In November 1946, on her return journey to the UK from the Netherlands, Phyllis was in a plane that lost its bearings in fog. The plane crashed into a hill in Surrey, and Phyllis was badly injured, with a fractured skull and spinal injuries.

London Office and Shop 1953

1949
4 Sheet Greater London map series

1951
Premier Glasgow published

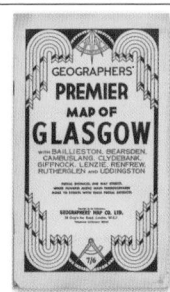

Office move
In 1953 the business moved from High Holborn to 24 Gray's Inn Road and again in 1959 to number 28

1953
First edition A-Z Birmingham

1958
Alexander Gross dies while travelling to England from New York on RMS Queen Mary

1956

Undeterred, Phyllis continued with her work, and the Company grew. In 1948, Alexander had visa issues in the US, so Phyllis spent months in New York running Geographia Map Co Inc. In her absence, Tony took on the role of Chairman of A-Z. Eventually, all visa issues resolved, Phyllis returned to London.

Despite the success of the Company, Alexander often did not agree with how Phyllis was running the business. In 1950, the same year that the Company was to publish its first street maps covering cities outside of London (Leeds, Birmingham and Manchester), Alexander wrote to Tony to tell him to take control of the Company. When this letter came to Phyllis' hands, she was to suffer a stroke and briefly lost her eyesight, leading to a period of convalescence. Alexander never saw the

War maps produced to replace loss of prohibited street maps

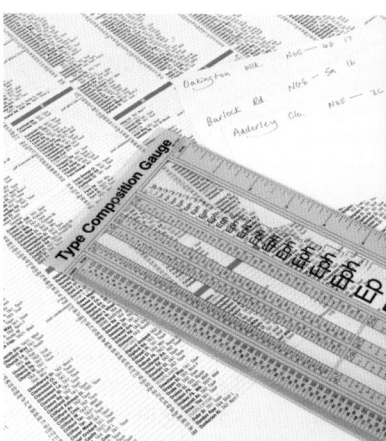

A pictorial map published 1946 illustrates areas destroyed during the London blitz

moved to 24 Gray's Inn Road. By now A-Z had over 30 publications covering cities from London to Glasgow. During her recuperation, Phyllis was able to continue to focus on both her art and writing, and in 1955 had two articles published in the New Yorker.

Souvenir route map for The Queen's coronation 1953

threat through, and Phyllis spent time in Cyprus recuperating properly for the first time since the plane crash 4 years previously.

In 1952, Phyllis and Alexander finally reconciled their differences, and Phyllis moved in to a rest home in Sussex. The following year the business

Then followed a quieter period for all, until 1958. Alexander, now almost 80, had continued in his role with Geographia Map Co Inc, and also continued to have an ongoing interest in the fortunes of A-Z. Whilst travelling over to England from New York by ship, he sadly passed away. Phyllis made her way to New York to run Geographia Map Co Inc. Realising she would not be able to manage both businesses, she turned down the management role there, and the business was sold. On returning to the UK, she then moved to Cavendish Avenue, London, and A-Z moved to 28 Gray's Inn Road.

Index cards and points ruler, tools used in compiling gazetteers for maps and atlases

1966

Office move
In 1962 the Office moved to Sevenoaks retaining a shop and London store at 28 Gray's Inn Road

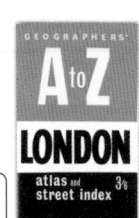
1960's A-Z London cover

A to Z MANCHESTER
BOLTON·ROCHDALE·ALTRINCHAM·OLDHAM
RINGWAY·STOCKPORT·STALYBRIDGE·BURY
atlas and street index 6/-

1963
First edition A-Z Manchester

1965
Plans for a Map Trust formulated by Mrs Pearsall to safeguard the future of the business

1967
Geographers' covers Greater London with the Master Atlas

Master atlas of GREATER LONDON

1972
A-Z London featured the new company logo designed by Roy Dewer

LONDON

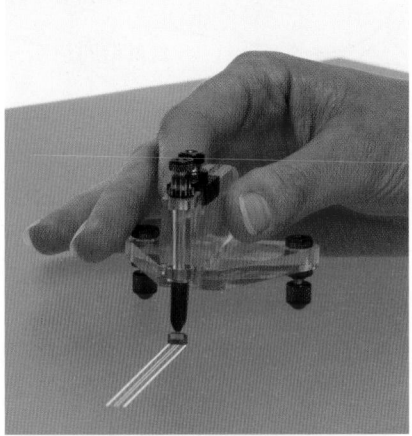
Scribing tool, dual carriageway

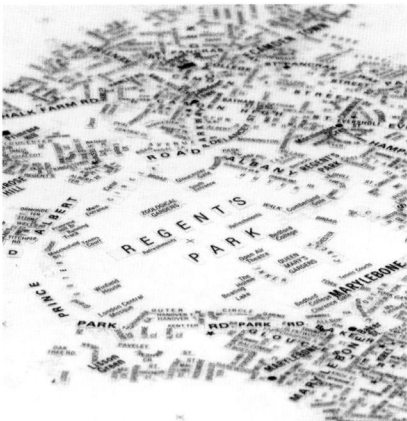
Adding stripping film type

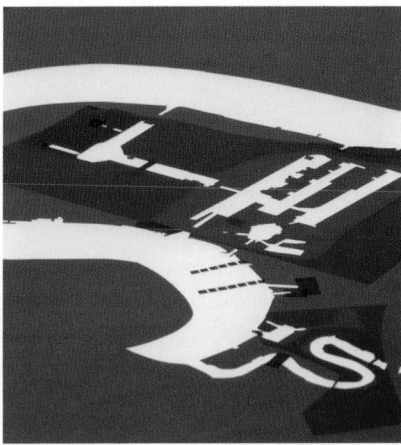
Peel coat mask for colour infills

In 1962, with larger premises and a warehouse required, the business moved out of London to Vestry Road, Sevenoaks. By 1964, the Company was publishing over 50 maps and atlases. The 1960s saw changes to road map production methods with the move away from traditional tracing paper sheets and Indian ink to scribing. Street map revision moved to Astrafoil but the process for both was still slow and fiddly.

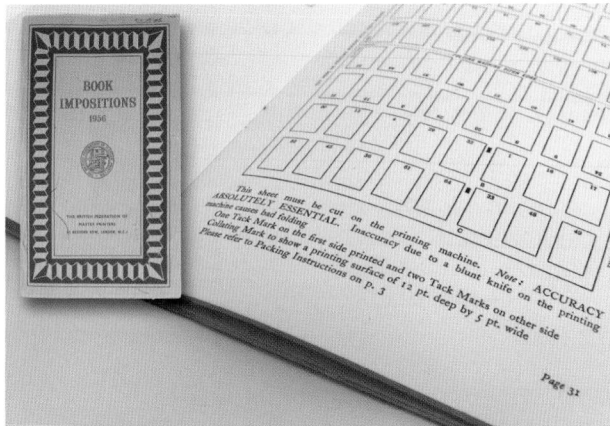
Book impositions page layout guide

With Phyllis acutely aware of her own mortality, and with her overriding concern for the welfare of the staff at A-Z, her thoughts turned to what would become of the business in the event of her death. She was keen that the business should not be taken out of the hands of those that had helped to build it so she took the extraordinary and unselfish step of placing the ownership of the business into a Trust. Therefore, in 1965, the Geographers' Map Trust was created, and both her and Tony's shares

were purchased by the Trust. In the same year, at age 59, Phyllis passed her driving test.

Phyllis' involvement with the Company lessened. In 1967, Fred Bond took on the role of Joint Managing Director, and the Company flourished under his steady hand. It wasn't until 1973 that the 'A-Z' was added to the Company title. Drawing methods also changed around this time with a move to photo typesetting, with cartographers taking turns at the typesetter to print out the letters they needed to make up the names on the map. These letters would then be added one at a time

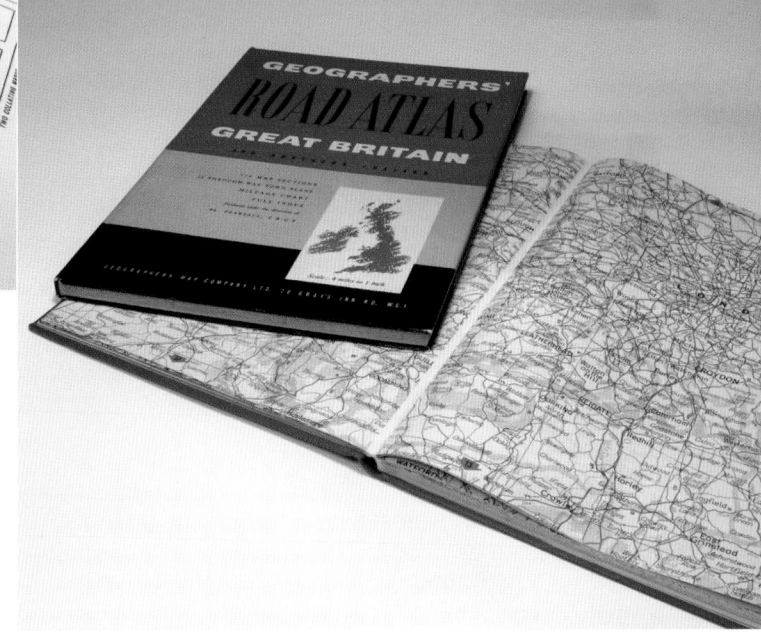
The first Geographers' Great Britain Road Atlas, 1961

1976

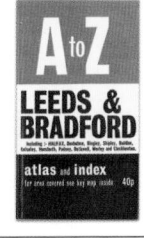
1973
The company incorporates 'A-Z' into its registered name becoming Geographers' A-Z Map Company Ltd

1973
First edition
A-Z Leeds & Bradford

1979
First edition
A-Z Newcastle

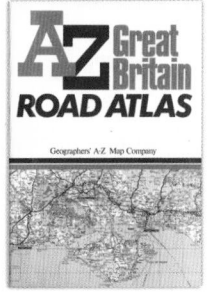

1984
Anthony Gross RA, dies

1985
First colour edition
A-Z London

1984
First large format
A-Z Road Atlas

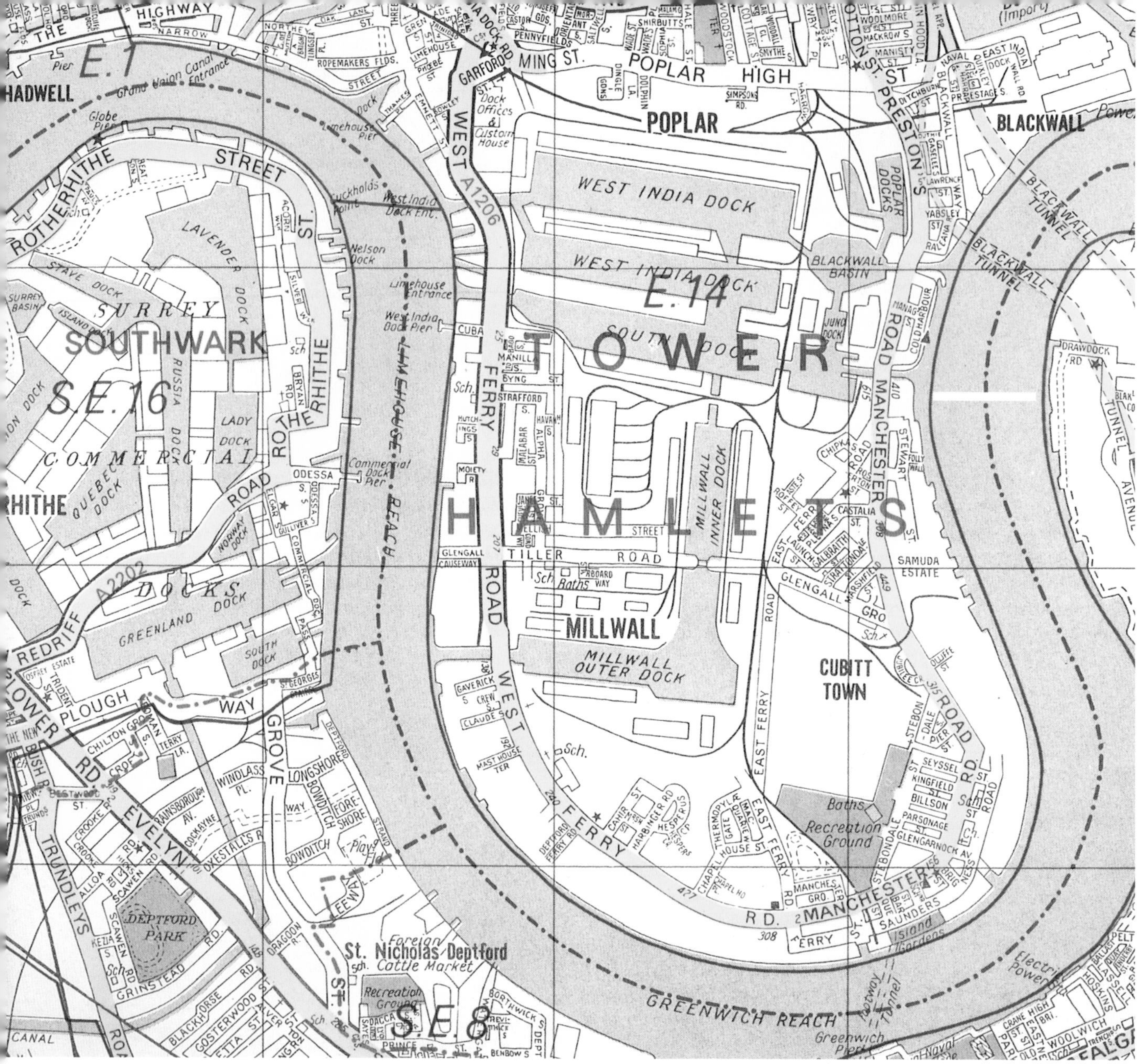

Docklands map 1967

to the sheets. Although a quicker method than previously, time could be lost as cartographers tried to find replacements from their colleagues for missing or damaged letters.

In the 1980s, mapping production was further improved by the latest innovation in scribing tools which could be used for street mapping for the first time. An additional drawing office was opened in Lancing, West Sussex in 1979, and Tony was

awarded a CBE in 1982, before passing away in 1984. In 1983, Phyllis' book, 'Fleet Street, Tite Street, Queer Street' detailing her relationship with her parents, up to her father's death, was released. In 1986, on the 50th anniversary of the Company, Phyllis was awarded the MBE, and the following year she became Chairman of the Trust.

During the late 80s, computer typesetting replaced photo typesetting, with two dedicated operators

1986

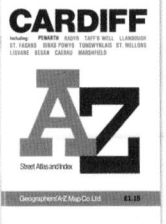

1986
First edition
A-Z Cardiff

1986
Mrs Pearsall awarded MBE

1987
First edition
A-Z Sheffield

1988
First edition
A-Z Edinburgh

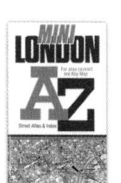
1991
First mini format
Street Atlas

1991
Computers first
introduced into the
map drawing process

Office move
A-Z moves to a new
purpose built office
and warehouse in
Borough Green 1992

Docklands map 2016

now taking on the responsibility for the letter production. The greatest production revolution was to occur in 1990 as the first CAD/CAM Unix computers arrived. Even in the early days, the advantages were obvious, and very quickly this evolved into windows based PCs using drawing software. One of the new challenges was to use this technology to create the map whilst still retaining the style that made the A-Z so unique and easy to read from the very beginning.

In 1990 Phyllis released her next book, 'From Bedsitter To Household Name' detailing her story with A-Z. With strong sales, and a solid management team, the Company then flourished, building success upon success for many years. In 1992, the Company moved to brand new premises in Borough Green, designed to the requirements of A-Z. It was shortly after celebrating the 60th anniversary of A-Z at Disneyland Paris, and 28 days short of her 90th birthday that Phyllis passed

1996

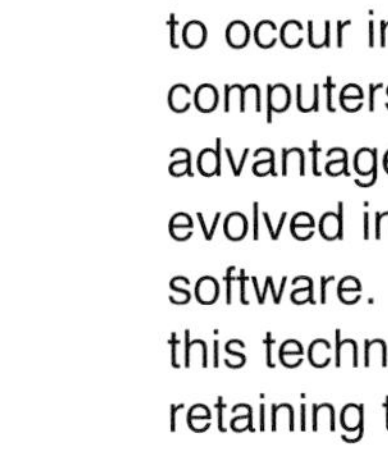

1996
First electronic A-Z street mapping of London published on CD-Rom

1996
Mrs Pearsall dies following a short illness

2001
Mapping for Windows Pocket PC based PDAs and mobile phones

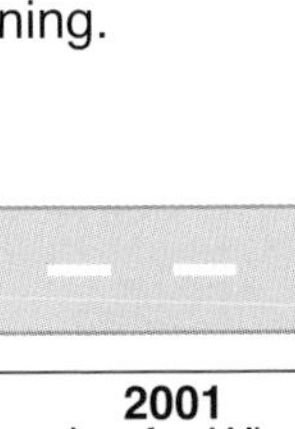

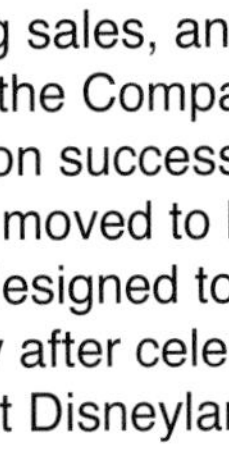

2005
Symbian based smartphone featuring A-Z mapping

2001
A-Z map catalogue exceeds 300 titles covering all regions of Great Britain

Office move
A-Z closes its London premises, retail sales transfered to Borough Green 2004

Due to the change in the market brought about by advancements in technology, printed mapping sales began to slow, and by 2013 the Company had seen significant changes. With this in mind, the Trust established in 1965 handed control of the business to a new 2013 Trust keeping to the same principals. In 2014, the business moved to Dunton Green, with the focus now on maintaining sales in the traditional market as well as producing a digital A-Z of the UK and a move to more modern methods of creating and selling mapping. As Phyllis was fond of saying, 'On we go'.

Map revision using CAD software in 1999

away on the 28th August 1996, almost exactly 60 years since Geographers' had begun.

By this time the London sheet maps were (and still are) extensively referred to by students learning "The Knowledge" in preparation for becoming a London black cab driver. Taking between two and four years, applicants for The Knowledge exams (or appearances) need to have a working knowledge of the 25,000 streets, 320 routes (runs) and 20,000 points of interest within a six mile radius of Charing Cross. Taxi drivers refer to the Oranges and Lemons – these are the A and B road colours on the A-Z maps.

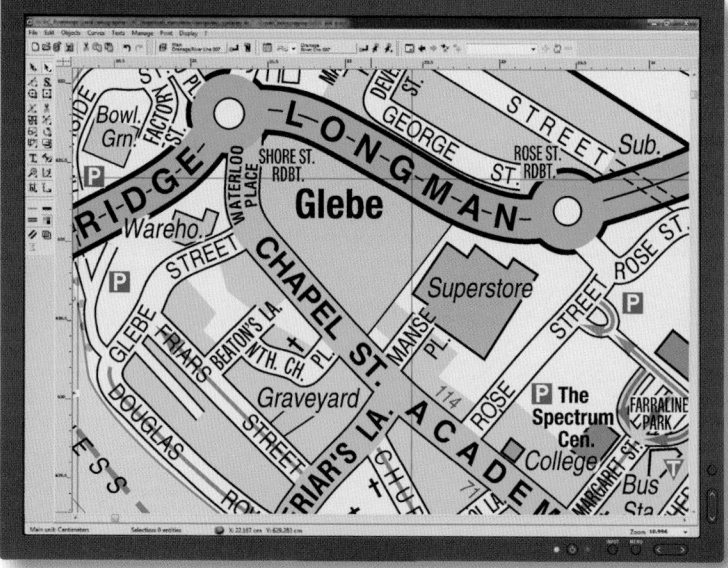

Map revision using LorikCartographer in 2016

Computer-to-plate was the next step forward, again advancing production significantly. Using this method, the drawing office managed to send out 164 jobs in a single year in 2005. In 2012 A-Z produced the mapping for the London 2012 games, and in the same year released the Adventure Atlas series, putting the familiar OS walking mapping into a book format – this series expanded to over 30 books by 2016.

The text has been compiled from a number of sources, but mostly from the books 'Fleet Street, Tite Street, Queer Street' and 'From Bedsitter To Household Name'. Additional information has been supplied from public records, and also from interview material. Some information is conflicting, in which case the most reliable source has been used. Wherever possible, the details have been taken from Phyllis Pearsall's own recollections. We have used the names Phyllis herself gave those involved, retaining her style as much as possible.

2006

2016

2006
A Blue Plaque is unveiled on Mrs Pearsall's childhood home in Dulwich

2006
First Sat Nav to include A-Z London mapping

2008
First iPhone app featuring A-Z London mapping

2012
A-Z selected official map publisher for the London 2012 Olympics

2012
The new innovative Adventure Atlas launched

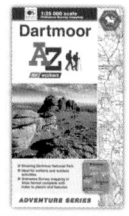

2016
A-Z celebrates 80 years

Office move
A-Z moves to Dunton Green 2014

REFERENCE

Motorway	M1	Map Continuation	56 Large Scale Map Pages 214
A Road	A2	Airport	✈
Tunnel		Car Park (selected)	P
B Road	B408	Church or Chapel	†
Dual Carriageway		Fire Station	■
One-way Street Traffic flow on A Roads is also indicated by a heavy line on the drivers' left.		Hospital	H
Road Under Construction Opening dates are correct at the time of publication.		House Numbers (A & B Roads only)	51 19 22 48
Proposed Road		Information Centre	i
Junction Name	MARBLE ARCH	National Grid Reference	530
Restricted Access		Park and Ride	Windsor (Home Park) P+R
Pedestrianized Road		Police Station	▲
Track / Footpath		Post Office	★
Residential Walkway		River Bus Stop	R
Congestion Charging Zone		Safety Camera with Speed Limit Fixed cameras and long term road works cameras. Symbols do not indicate camera direction.	30 V
Low Emission Zone			

Railway   Tunnel   Level Crossing

Stations: National Rail Network   ≷
          Crossrail   ✄
          Docklands Light Railway   DLR
          Overground   ⊖
          Underground   ●

London Tramlink   Tunnel   Stop
The boarding of Tramlink trams at stops may be
limited to a single direction, indicated by the arrow.

		Toilet:
		  without facilities for the Disabled
		  with facilities for the Disabled
		  Disabled use only
			▽
			▽
			▼

Built-up Area	BANK STREET	Educational Establishment	▭
Local Authority Boundary		Hospital or Healthcare Building	▭
Post Town and London Postal District Boundaries		Industrial Building	▭
		Leisure or Recreational Facility	▭
		Place of Interest	▭
		Public Building	▭
Postcode Boundary (within Post Town)		Shopping Centre or Market	▭
		Other Selected Buildings	▭

SCALE

Map Pages 2-211
1:19,000
3⅓ inches (8.47 cm) to 1 mile
5.26 cm to 1 km

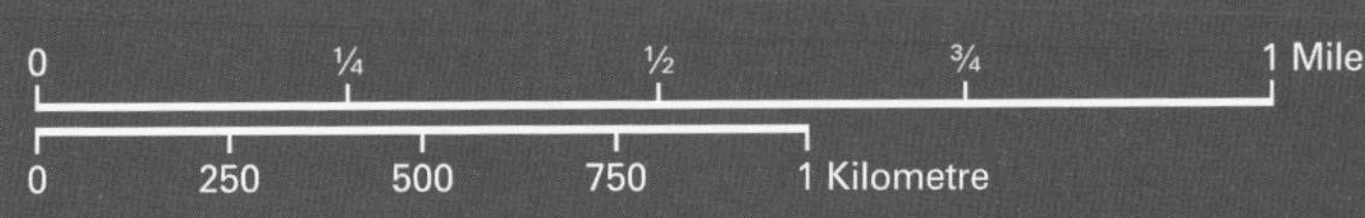

2
Berkhamsted
BERKHAMSTED
HP4
HP1
Little Heath
Fields End
Gutteridge Wood
Roseheath Wood
Littleheath Great Farm
Lower Little Heath Farm
Little Heath Farm
Fields End Farm
Bullbeggars Wood
Warners End
Bankmill Bridge
Sewage Works
River Bulbourne
Grand Union Canal
Pouchen End Hall
Pouchen End Farm
Pouchen End
Chaulden
Winkwell
Long Green
Broadway Farm
Pix Farm
The Cedars
Broadway Orchard
Cress Farm
War Mem.
Motel
Shear Meadow
Swing Bridge
Bottom Farm
Keepers Cottage
Bourne Gutter
BOURNE END LANE INDUSTRIAL ESTATE
Saw Mill
Bourne End
Snook's Grave
Moorend Farm
The Larches
Vale Orchard
Services
Lower Farm
Vale Farm
DACORUM
Green Croft
Mount's Hill
Hanging Wood
Westbrook Hay Prep. School
Great Wood
Hay Wood
Golf Driving Range
Club House
LITTLE HAY GOLF COURSE
Coleshill Wood
Ramacre Wood
Gorsefield Wood
Bury Wood
Strawberry Wood
Reservoir (covered)
Water Tower
Longcroft Farm
Berry Farm
BOVINGDON AIRFIELD (disused)
WHELPLEY HILL PARK
Whelpley Hill
Rainhill Spring
Highcroft
HIGHCROFT TRAILER GDNS
Rainhill Dell
Kingshill Dell
Chesham
HP5
CHILTERN
HMP THE MOUNT
Duckhall Farm
Honours Fm.
Pastures
Vicarage
Random Farm
Homefield Spring
Shortridge Wood
Little Colyers
Prim. Sch.
Bury Farm
Lodge
Nuffield Farm
Lane Farm
Pocket's Dell
Whelpley Ash Farm
Whitehart Cross
BOVINGDON
Ten Oaks
Copse Hill House
Bovington Lodge
Street Farm
Bulstrode
Greinan Farm
Brickworks
Bovingdon Grange
Grange Farm
Football Ground
Pudds Cross
Bovingdon Green
Clay Pit
Green Farm
Nursery
10
LONDON ROAD
BERKHAMSTED ROAD
KINGS LANGLEY BYPASS
BOX LANE
HEMPSTEAD ROAD
CHESHAM ROAD
A4251
A41
B4505

3
H
J
K
L
M
N
P
1
2
3
4
5
6
7
8
9
10
HP2
HP3
WD4
Hemel Hempstead
Kings Langley
HEMEL HEMPSTEAD
KINGS LANGLEY
Gadebridge
Highfield
Adeyfield
Counters End
Hammerfield
Green End
Boxmoor
Corner Hall
Bennetts End
Two Waters
Frogmore End
Apsley
Felden
Nash Mills
RUCKLERS LANE
Paradise
Playing Fields
Gadebridge Park
St. Cuthbert Mayne Catholic Sch.
Gade Valley Jun. Mixed & Inf. Sch.
The Cavendish Sch.
The Old Town Hall Arts Cen.
West Herts College
Northridge Park
Shrub Hill Common
Gravelhill Spring
Lockers Pk. Sch.
Adeyfield School
Broadfield Prim. Sch.
HEMEL HEMPSTEAD GENERAL HOSPITAL
St. Rose's Catholic Inf. Sch.
The Hemel Hempstead School
Sportspace
Rugby Ground
Watercress Beds
Cricket Grd.
Hemel Hempstead
Roughdown Common
Roman Fields Sch.
Tudor Prim. Sch.
Lime Wlk. Prim. Sch.
The Snow Centre
Sportspace Athletics Track
Belswains Prim. Sch.
Nash Mills C of E Prim. Sch.
Two Waters Prim. Sch.
PRIORY HOSPITAL HEMEL HEMPSTEAD
Felden Barns
Howe's Retreat
Hyde Farm Bungalows
Tower Farm
Felden Grange
Felden Manor
Felden Orchard
Felden Ash
Felden Ridge
Valley Farm
New Farm
Old Dean
Threefields
Mast
Cock's Head Wood
SHENDISH MANOR GOLF COURSE
Apsley Manor Farm
Club House
Shendish Manor
Great Wood
Phasels Wood
Stony Dene
The Bungalow
Pavilion
Works
Nash Mills Recreation Centre
Shafford Cottages
The Lodge
High Oak
Rucklers Wood
The Hangings
Merceys Wood
Barnes Lodge
Dark Wood
The Nucket
Barnes Farm
Badgerdell
Badgerdell Wood
Scatterdells Wood
Kielder
Fairydell Farm
The Grove
Hill Farm
Playing Field
Kings Langley School
Kings Langley Prim. Sch.
Kings Langley Common
A4146
A414
A4251
A41
B487
LEIGHTON BUZZARD ROAD
QUEENSWAY
ST. ALBANS RD.
STATION ROAD
LONDON ROAD
TWO WATERS WAY
TWO WATERS RD.
KINGS LANGLEY BY-PASS
LANGLEY BY-PASS
ROAD HEMPSTEAD
HIGH ROAD
Grand Union Canal
River Bulbourne
River Gade
RUCKLERS LANE
BARNES LANE
FEATHERBED LANE
LANE BULSTRODE
VICARAGE ROAD
The 11

MAYLANDS AVENUE
A4147
BREAKSPEAR WAY
A414
M1 MOTORWAY
Junction 8
M1
Buncefield Terminal
Maylands Wood
Woodwells Caravan Park
Woodwells Cemetery
Lucas Aerospace Sports Ground
Virgin Active Health Club
Breakspears
Depot
Hotel
Works
Kentish Wood
Adeyfield
Hobletts Manor Schs.
Council Offs.
Hemel Hempstead Town FC (Vauxhall Rd.)
Adeyfield School
The Reith Flds.
Ed. Support Cen.
HP2
Leverstock Green
Football Ground
Leverstock Green C of E Primary School
LEVERSTOCK GREEN RD.
ST. ALBANS RD.
HEMEL HEMPSTEAD
DACORUM
Westwick Farm
Westwick Cottage
Westwick Row Farm
Westwick Hall Cottage
Westwick Warren
Westwick House
Corner Farm Cottage
Water Tower
Beechtree Cottages
ST.
Planet Ice
Empire Cin.
Leis. World
Aquasplash
Bowl. Alley
Logandene EMI Unit
Prim. Sch.
Hobbs Hill Wood Prim. School
Tennis Courts
Sportspace
Longdean School
Chambersbury Prim. Sch.
Bennetts End
Belswains Prim. Sch.
George Wood
Bunkers Park Open Space
Bunkers Farm
Well Farm
Well Farm Cottages
Blackwater Wood
Hemel Hempstead
Great Furzefield Wood
Longdean House
Highwood Hall Farm
Pimlico
High Herts Farm
Potters Crouch Plantations
Long Deans Nature Reserve
HP3
Grove Cottages
Bedmond Hill
Rose Acre
THREE RIVERS
Nash Mills C of E Prim. Sch.
Langley Tennis Club
Abbot's Hill School
The Lodge
Tennis Courts
Nash Mills
Nash Mills Recreation Centre
Shafford Cottages
Works
LONDON RD.
HEMPSTEAD ROAD
A4251
Mast
Wireless Station
Hyde Meadow Farm
Hydelane Spring
Hyde Springs
Verulam Nursery
Heath View
Verulam Farm
Homefield Farm
Twychells Farm
Deadman Wood
Newlands Park Caravan Site
Bedmond Wood
Abbots
Piecorner Wood
New Plantation
Pimlico House
Hyde Farm
Hyde Lane Farm
Harthall Farm
Little Abbots
Hart Hall
White House Farm
Harthall Cottages
Woodlands Poultry Farm
Old Farm
Leewood Farm
Coal Yard
Poultry Fm.
High View Park
Hilltop Farm
Moor Wood
Pav. Sports Grd.
Primary School
BEDMOND
Ninnings Farm
Poultry Farm
Longspring Wood Nature Reserve
Kings Langley
WD4
Benmore Farm
Denree
Nursery
Great Notley
Kings Langley Prim. Sch.
Play. Fld.
Kings Langley Common
KINGS LANGLEY
Cricket Grd.
Happy Valley Industrial Estate
Canal
Grand Union Canal
Railway
Subway
M25 MOTORWAY
Ovaltine Dairy Farm
Stowes Wood
12

Windmillhill Wood
Wildness
Chalk Dell
Garden Cottage
Gilpins
Gorhambury House
Bruce's Plantation
Shepherds Cottages
Churchyard Meadow
Cattle Grid
Townsend
REDBOURN
A5183
River Ver
Old Gorhambury Ho. (remains of)
Oak Wood
Cypress Wood
Temple Cottage
Temple Wood
Gorham Block
Fosse
Roman Wall (course of)
Roman Theatre
Verulamium Roman Town
Lord Bacon's Mount
PRAE WOOD
Fish Ponds
Settlement
AL3
Stud Cottages
Square Wood
Prae Wood House
Praewood Farm
BLUEHOUSE HILL
A4147
The Roman Mosaic & Hypocaust
ST. ALBANS
VERULAMIUM PARK
ABBEY VIEW GOLF COURSE
Hill End Cottage
Hill End Farm
ALBANS
St. Albans
HEMEL HEMPSTEAD ROAD
A414
Madam's Wood
Birch Wood
Windridge Farm Cott.
Windridge Farm
St. Stephens Recreation Ground
Longfield Spring
Maidens Crouch Farm
M1 MOTORWAY
Little Furzefield Wood
Appspond Cottage
Appspond Wood
POTTERSCROUCH
Long Spring
Park Wood
Westfield's Farm
New Cotts.
Potters Crouch
Potters Crouch East Farm
Potters Crouch Farm
Square Wood
Scrubs Wood
Wimbushes
Cuckman's Farm
Recreation Ground
Killigrew Prim. Sch.
St. Julian's Wood
CHISWELL GREEN
GREENWOOD PARK
Greenwood Park Leisure Centre
Plaistowes Farm
Wellfield Spring
Bone Hill
The Gardens of the Rose
Daneswick
Little Daneswick
AL2
Sergehill
Serge Hill
Langley
Whitehouse Farm
The Conifers
Wayside
Plaistowes Wood
Noke Farm
NOKE LANE BUSINESS CENTRE
Otium Leisure Club
Burston Manor Fm.
HOW WOOD
Birchwood Farm
Birch Wood
Hanging Wood
Junction 6a (M1)
Holt Wood
Holt Farm
Moat
Searches Farm
Millhouse Farm
Burston Nurseries
Spielplatz
The Spinney
M25
M25 MOTORWAY
Junction 21 (M25)
Junction 21a
Tenterden House
Kettlewell Farm
Tenements Farm
NORTH ORBITAL ROAD
A405
Winch Hill Wood
Bricket Wood Sports & Country Club
Bricket Wood Paintball Centre
WATLING STREET
A5183
B4630

6
A
B
C
D
E
F
G
14
15
16
17
1
2
3
4
5
6
7
8
9
10
Townsend
Rennie Gro. Hospice
ST. ALBANS CITY HOSPITAL
MIU
SANDRIDGE ROAD
HARPENDEN ROAD
FAIRCROSS WAY
SANDPIT LANE
FOLLY LANE
A4147
VERULAM ROAD
CATHERINE ST.
JENNINGS ROAD
GAINSBOROUGH AV.
Verulam School
Fleetville
Museum of St. Albans
St. Albans City FC (Clarence Pk.)
Clarence Park
Sports Grd.
Islamic Cen.
A1057
HATFIELD ROAD
Superstore
Fleetville Jun. Sch.
Cemetery
Verulamium Pav. Mus.
Darrowfield Ho.
Pavilion
Tennis Courts
AL3
VICTORIA STREET
Alban Arena
B691
St. Albans
STATION WAY
STANHOPE RD.
Cathedral
St. Albans Sch.
The Lake
VERULAMIUM PARK
ABBEY VIEW GOLF COURSE
Westminster Lodge Athletic Track
ST. ALBANS
HOLYWELL HILL
LONDON ROAD
A1081
Cunningham Hill Playing Fields
CUNNINGHAM HILL
The Camp
Sub Aqua Club
Cottonmill Bridge
St. Peter's Sch.
Sopwell Nunnery (rems.)
Works
Club House
Quality Living Leisure Club
Foxcroft Play. Fld.
St. Albans Abbey
Abbey Thtre.
Lei. Cen.
St. Columba's College
ST. STEPHEN'S HILL
WATLING STREET
St. Stephens
Recreation Ground
Superstore
Gasholders
Sopwell Mill Farm
VERULAM GOLF COURSE
Samuel Ryder Academy
Nuffield Fitness Cen.
Playing Field
HIGHFIELD PARK DRIVE
The Marlborough Science Academy
St. Julians
Recreation Ground
Sopwell
New Barnes Mill
The Lodge
Mandeville Prim. Sch.
A5183
B4630
WATFORD ROAD
Playing Field
Sopwell Ho. Hotel
VERULAM GOLF COURSE
North Orbital Fields
Birklands Meadow
Cemy.
A414
NORTH ORBITAL ROAD
NAPSBURY LA.
B5378
Killigrew Prim. Sch.
St. Julian's Wood
Chalkdell Wood
Flint Cottages
Nursery
Farm House
Rugby Ground
Cricket Ground
Football Grd.
Greenwood Park Leisure Centre
WATLING STREET CARAVAN PARK
Hedges Farm
SHENLEY LANE
A405
ORBITAL ROAD
Park Street
Park Street
AL2
Conolly Ho.
Napsbury
Recreation Ground
Park Street C of E Prim. School
HOW WOOD
Birchwood Farm
Birch Wood
How Wood
Piggery
Playing Field
Football Pitch
South Farm Cottages
South Lodge
Barley-Mo-Farm
The Vicarage
FROGMORE
FROGMORE BUS. PK.
RADLETT RD.
PARK STREET
14
Works
All Saints Pastoral Centre (convent)

St. Albans Campus
Smallford
Wilkins Green
Ellenbrook
Hatfield
Nast Hyde
AL10
Junction 3
WELWYN HATFIELD
Roehyde
Sleapshyde
St. Albans
Tyttenhanger
ALBANS
Park Corner
COLNEY HEATH
Roestock
AL4
Willows Lakes
Tyttenhanger Park
HERTSMERE
NORTH MYMMS PARK
LONDON COLNEY
Junction 22
M25 MOTORWAY
AL9
Broad Colney
Broad Colney Lakes Nature Reserve
COLNEY FIELDS SHOPPING PARK
HATFIELD ROAD
NORTH ORBITAL ROAD
LONDON COLNEY BY-PASS
A1057
A414
A1081
A1(M)
B556

8
A
B
C
D
E
F
G
1
2
3
4
5
6
7
8
9
10
21
22
23
24
08
07
06
05
04
03
HATFIELD
HATFIELD PARK
Ellenbrook
Nast Hyde
Roehyde
South Hatfield
Oxlease
AL10
Junction 3
University of Hertfordshire (College Lane Campus)
Halls of Residence
Hazel Grove
Hatfield Leisure Cen.
Oxleys
COOMBE WOOD
Cemetery
Merrows Cottages
Lime Cottages
New Gardens
Home Farm
Orchard Ho.
Dairy Cott.
Dairy Lodges
New Cottages
Bunnyfield House
Buttfield Cottage
Howe Dell
Oak View Prim. sch.
Bishop Hatfield Girls' Sch.
Halfwayoak Pond
MILLWARD'S PARK
COMET WAY
ROEHYDE WAY
NTH. ORBITAL ROAD
A1001
A1(M)
A1000
GREAT NORTH ROAD
SOUTH WAY
Roehyde Farm
Johnson's Spring
The Bungalow
ST. ALBANS
Bullen's Green
Roundhouse Farm
COLNEY HEATH
Roestock
Colney Heath Farm
Junction 2
Hertfordshire University Park & Ride
Angerland Cmn.
Cemetery
Southfield School
New Barnfield (Herts County Council)
Factory
Warehouse
Playing Field
Nurseries
Marshmoor
Caravan Park
Welham Green
The Rookery
Depot
Works
ALPHA BUS. PK
WINGATE BUSINESS CENTRE
Dellsome Bottom
DELLSOME LANE
Electricity Sub Station
Tollgate Wood
Tollgate Farm
St. Albans
Park Cottage
Frederick's Wood
St. Mary's C of E Prim. School
Recreation Grnd.
BUSH WOOD
WELHAM GREEN
WELWYN
Skimpans Bridge
Skimpans Farm
Community Cen.
Potterells Farm
Nurseries
Pig Farm
Moat
Kennels
AL4
The Osierbeds
River Colne
NORTH MYMMS PARK
Red Lodge
War Mem.
East Lodge
Vicarage
North Mymms
Fish Pond
Grave Yard
Church Cottage
Teakettle Bri.
Home Fm. Cotts.
Cricket Gd.
The Gables
North Mymms Park
Pumping Tower
WALSINGHAM WOOD
Water Tower
Water Splash Cottages
Swallow Hole
Potterells
Swallow Holes
Water End
PEPLIN'S WOOD
Primary School
Library
Brookmans Park
Brick Kiln Wood
Abdale House
Pumping Station
Reservoir (covered)
Cobs Ash
Cangsley Grove
HERTSMERE
Round Wood
Swallow Holes
New Cottages
The Royal Veterinary Coll. (Hawkshead Campus)
Hawkshead Bridge
Blue Bridge
Sports Ground
Oak Lodge
Hawkshead Wood
Pilvage Wood
Mimmshall Brook
HAWKSHEAD ROAD
16

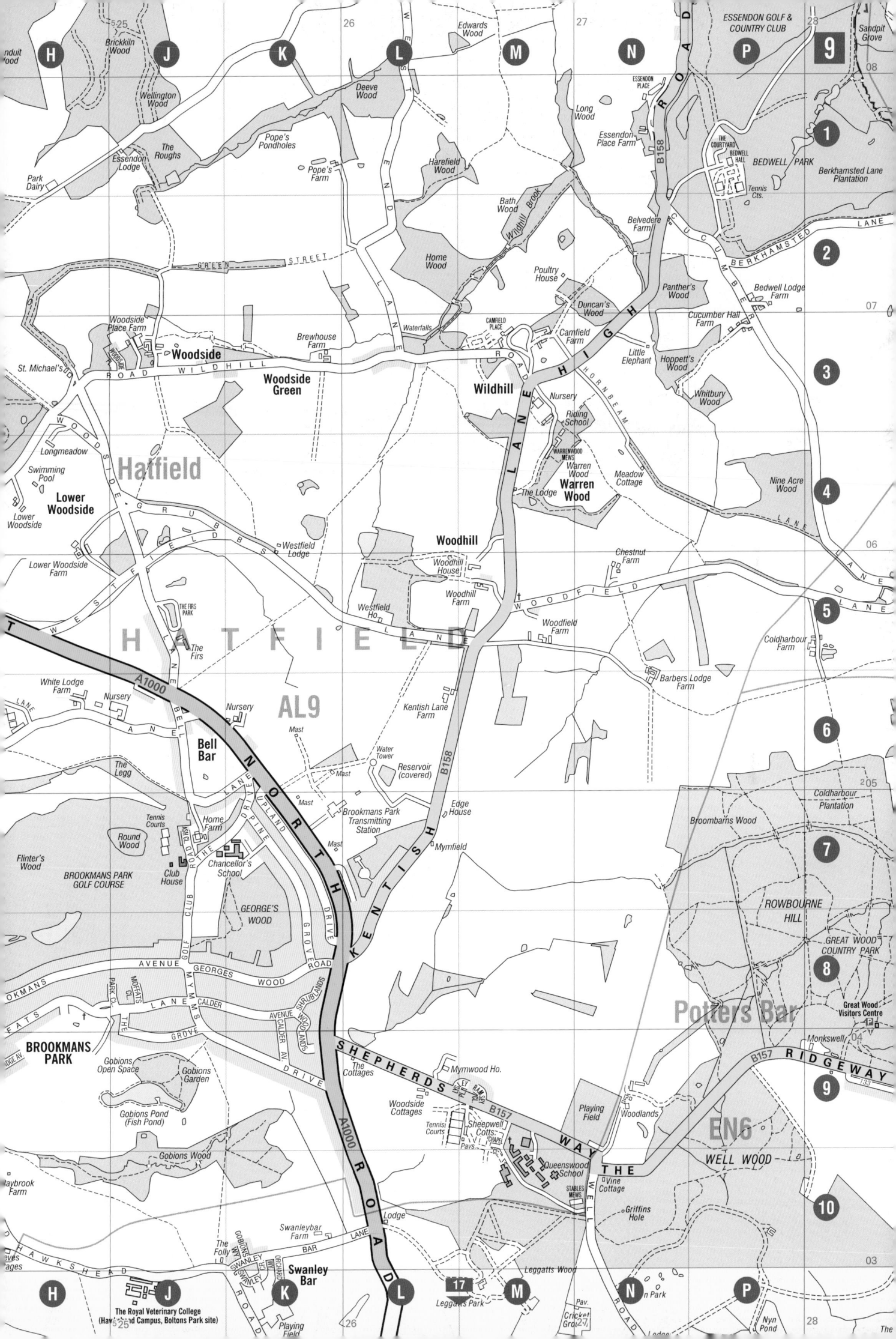
9
Essendon Golf & Country Club
Sandpit Grove
Brickkiln Wood
Wellington Wood
Edwards Wood
Deeve Wood
Long Wood
Essendon Place
Essendon Place Farm
Bedwell Park
Berkhamsted Lane Plantation
The Roughs
Essendon Lodge
Park Dairy
Pope's Pondholes
Pope's Farm
Harefield Wood
Bath Wood
Belvedere Farm
Home Wood
Green Street
Poultry House
Panther's Wood
Bedwell Lodge Farm
Duncan's Wood
Cucumber Hall Farm
Woodside Place Farm
Woodside
Brewhouse Farm
Waterfalls
Camfield Place
Camfield Farm
Little Elephant
Hoppett's Wood
St. Michael's
Wildhill Road
Woodside Green
Wildhill
High Lane
Nursery
Riding School
Whitbury Wood
Longmeadow
Hatfield
Swimming Pool
Lower Woodside
Warren Wood
Meadow Cottage
Nine Acre Wood
The Lodge
Woodhill
Woodhill House
Woodhill Farm
Westfield Lodge
Lower Woodside Farm
Chestnut Farm
Woodfield Lane
Westfield Ho.
Woodfield Farm
Coldharbour Farm
The Firs Park
Hatfield
The Firs
Barbers Lodge Farm
White Lodge Farm
Nursery
A1000
AL9
Kentish Lane Farm
Bell Bar
Mast
Water Tower
Reservoir (covered)
The Legg
Coldharbour Plantation
Brookmans Park Transmitting Station
Edge House
Broombarns Wood
Tennis Courts
Home Farm
Round Wood
Mymfield
Flinter's Wood
Brookmans Park Golf Course
Club House
Chancellor's School
Rowbourne Hill
George's Wood
Great Wood Country Park
Georges Wood Road
Potters Bar
Great Wood Visitors Centre
Monkswell
Brookmans Park
Gobions Open Space
Gobions Garden
The Cottages
Mymwood Ho.
Shepherds Way
The Ridgeway
Woodside Cottages
Playing Field
Woodlands
EN6
Sheepwell Cotts.
Gobions Pond (Fish Pond)
Gobions Wood
Well Wood
Queenswood School
Vine Cottage
Griffins Hole
Raybrook Farm
Stables Mews
Swanleybar Farm
Lodge
The Folly
Hawkshead Road
Swanley Bar
Leggatts Wood
Leggatts Park
The Royal Veterinary College (Hawkshead Campus, Boltons Park site)
Playing Field
Cricket Ground
Nyn Pond
B158
B157
A1000
17

10
Bovingdon
Bovingdon Green
Pudds Cross
Maple Hill
Venus Hill
Hogpits Bottom
Hemel Hempstead
Flaunden
HP3
Chesham
HP5
Latimer
Chenies Bottom
Chenies
Chiltern
Amersham
HP6
Rickmansworth
WD3
Bulstrode
Rosehall Green
Sarratt Bottom
Baldwin's Wood
Mount Wood
Woodman's Wood
West Wood Park
Amersham Road
A404
2
24

Kings Langley
WD4
CHIPPERFIELD
Chapel Croft
KINGS LANGLEY
Chipperfield Common
CHIPPERFIELD COMMON
Commonwood
COMMONWOOD COMMON
Bucks Hill
Sarratt Hall
SARRATT
Micklefield Green
Church End
Chandler's Cross
THREE RIVERS
Scatterdells Wood
The Grove
The Wings
Meggacres Farm
Whippendell Farm
Whippendell House
Whippendell Bottom
Rookery Wood
Ballspond Farm
Langley Lodge Farm
Kings Langley Lodge
Middle Farm
Manor House
Topcommon
Hunterswood
Little Callipers
Callipers Hall
Callipers Hall Farm
Quickmoor Farm
Baytree Farm
BERRYBUSHES WOOD
Model Farm
Sheepcote Spring
Lukes Journey Dell
Hawk Spring
Beechen Bottom
Juniper Hill
Templepan Wood
Templepan Farm
Conveyors
Westwood
Birch Spring
Cartpath Wood
The Grove Lodge
Blackets Wood
Great Wood
Great Wood Cottages
Potten's Farm
Sheepyard Spring
Chandler's Farm
Coltyard Spring
Coltspring Riding Stables
Cottage Farm
Potten Farm Cottage
Sawpit Spring
Tenements Farm
Playing Field
Frenches Farm
Chipperfield House
Braziers Farm
Football Ground
Rose Farm
Belsize Farm
Hillmeads Farm
Old Plough House
Debardine Wood
Plough Wood
Hillmeads Spring
Dellfield
Commonwood House
Sarratt Hall
Daniel's Spring
Red Lion Farm
Poultry Houses
Newhall Farm
Little Westwood Farm
Great Westwood Farm
Paddock Cott.
Oldhouse Cott.
Bucks Hill House
Bucks Hill Farm
Ainsworth Cottage
Briar Cottage
High Spring
Hill View
The Nook
Buckshill Bottom
White Cottage
By the Way
Apiary
White House
Yew Court Farm
Glenview
Dawes Common
White Oaks Farm
Sandfield Wood
Old Rectory
Rectory
GREEN END BUSINESS CENTRE
Wood Walks
Micklefield Green Farm
New Model Farm
Goldingtons
Park Cottages
Sarrattmill Cottage
Scrubbs Wood
Blunts Wood
Willow Wood
North Lodge
HARROCKS WOOD
Kennels
Dellshot Spring
Junction 19
M25 MOTORWAY
A41 KINGS LANGLEY BY-PASS
Kings Langley School
Kings Langley Common
Rudolf Steiner School
Priory (rems. of)
Hill Farm
Cricket Grd.
St. Paul's C of E Prim. Sch.
Sarratt C of E Sch.
Riding School
Highcroft
Longfield
Nursery
Vicarage
Pale Farm
Tennis Courts
Lodge
Penmans
Long Beeches
Wayside Fm.
11
3
25
12

12
Q
R
S
T
U
V
W
4
11
26
1
2
3
4
5
6
7
8
9
10
KINGS LANGLEY
DACORUM
Kings Langley
ABBOTS LANGLEY
Abbots Langley
THREE RIV
LEAVESDEN GREEN
Leavesden
WD5
WD4
WD17
WD3
Rickmansworth
Hunton Bridge
Langleybury
Junction 20
Junction 19
M25 MOTORWAY
M25
M25 MOTORWAY
KINGS LANGLEY BY-PASS
HEMPSTEAD RD.
A4251 ST.
WATFORD ROAD
HEMPSTEAD ROAD
NORTH WESTERN AV.
KINGSWAY
LEAVESDEN FILM STUDIOS
Warner Bros. Studios Leavesden
HUNTON BRIDGE
Leavesden Country Park
YMCA Leavesden Country Pk.
Ovaltine Dairy Farm
Ovaltine Egg Farm
Long Wood
Round Wood
Manor House Grounds
Tanners Wood
Hunton Park
The Grove & Club House
THE GROVE GOLF COURSE
THE GROVE PARK
WHIPPENDELL WOOD
Harebreaks Recreation Ground
Cherry Tree Prim. Sch.
Holy Rood Catholic Prim. Sch.
St. Paul's C of E Prim. Sch.
Benmore Farm
Great Notley
Little Notley
Stowes Wood
Mansion House Farm
Broadfield Farm
Moat Farm
Clapgate Farm
Middle Farm
North Grove Wood
Crabtree Dell
Dellshot Spring
Kennels
Sheepcote Spring
Lukes Journey Dell
Beechen Bottom
Juniper Hill
Brickfield Spring
Heath Wood
Clarendon Park Farm
Timber Yard Cotts.
Walled Garden
Westwood Quarry
Birch Spring
Cartpath Wood
The Grove Lodge
Blackets Wood
Leeswood Cotts.
LEES WOOD
Deer Spring
Charlotte's Vale
Rough Wood
Sports Ground
Herts Bowling Club
Playing Field
Cheslyn Gdns.
Beechfield Playgrd.
Callowland Rec. Grd.

13
M25
Junction 21 (M25)
Junction 6a (M1)
Junction 21a
M25 MOTORWAY
M1 MOTORWAY
NORTH ORBITAL ROAD
Winch Hill Wood
Waterdell
Waterdale
Coles Farm
Fortunes Farm
BLOOM WOOD
WATERDALE
The Thomas Parmiter Sports Centre
Parmiter's Sch.
High Elms Manor School
West Hertfordshire Crematorium
Brookdell Transport Depot
Sports Ground
St. Michael's Catholic High Sch. & Specialist College
Francis Combe Academy
Garston Manor Sch.
St. Catherine of Siena Catholic Prim. Sch.
Woodside Stadium
Watford Leisure Cen.
WOODSIDE
Albans Wood
Woodside Playing Fields
Hollywood Bowl Watford
Vue Cinema
Gambado
ORBITAL
Kingswood
GARSTON
NORTH WATFORD CEMETERY
Stanborough Park
Lea Farm Rec. Grd.
Berrygrove Academy
THE DOME
Superstore
Library
Parkgate Inf. Sch.
NORTH WATFORD
Watford North
COLNE WAY
NORTH-WESTERN AV.
Garston
MERIDEN
Meriden Pk.
GARSTON PARK
Bus Depot
TopGolf
Colne Bri.
Busheymill Bridge
Bushey Hall Farm
Junction 5
BERRYGROVE
OTTERSPOOL WAY
A4008 WAY
STEPHENSON
27
Mount Pleasant Lane Junior Mixed & Infant Sch.
Junction 6
BRICKET WOOD
Building Research Station
St. Albans
ST. ALBANS
Mobile Home Park
Black Grn. Rec. Grd.
HOW WOOD
Bricket Wood Sports & Country Club
Bricket Wood Paintball Centre
Blackgreen Wood
Smug Oak
Ashdale Rec. Grd.
Bricket Wood
Nottlers Wood
Nottlers House
Management Training College
Pumping Station
Jack William's Wood
New Plantation
Fords
BRICKET WOOD COMMON
Mutchetts Wood
Woodbine Cottage
Little Munden Farm
Crab Wood
Four Acre Plantation
Munden
Peartree Wood
Coldharbour Plantation
Home Farm
Munden House
Munden Spring
WD25
RIVER COLNE
Binghams
Otterspool
Otterspool Farm
HERTSMERE
ALDENHAM GOLF COURSE
ALDENHAM
Berrygrove
Playing Field
Red House
Sounding Well
Club Ho.
B462
RADLETT ROAD
Blackbirds Farm
Pond
Edge
WD24
Tenements Farm
Tenterden House
Kettlewell Farm
Spielplatz
The Spinney
14

14
How Wood
Frogmore
6
St. Albans
AL2
M25 Motorway
Radlett Road
Watling Street
A5183
Colney Street
Smug Oak
St. Albans
River Colne
Harper Lane
B556
Turning Circle
Radlett Golf Academy
Hound's Wood
Kingsley Green
Nine Acres
Wild Farm
Monks Wood
Porters Park Golf Course
Radlett
Munden
13
Blackbirds Lane
Sewage Works
Watford
WD25
Kemprow
Aldenham
High Cross
Round Bush
Battlers Green
Letchmore Heath
Delrow
28
Aldenham Road
Watford Road
Radlett Lane
Cobden Hill
Hill Street
Theobald Street
Shenley Hill
Kendal Wood
Newberries Primary Sch.
Hertsmere Jewish Prim. Sch.
Radlett Prep. Sch.
Little Kendals Wood
Moses Dell
Cobden Hill
Rugby Football Ground
Cricket Ground
Ea Fa Ga Ha Ja Ka La
14 15 16 17

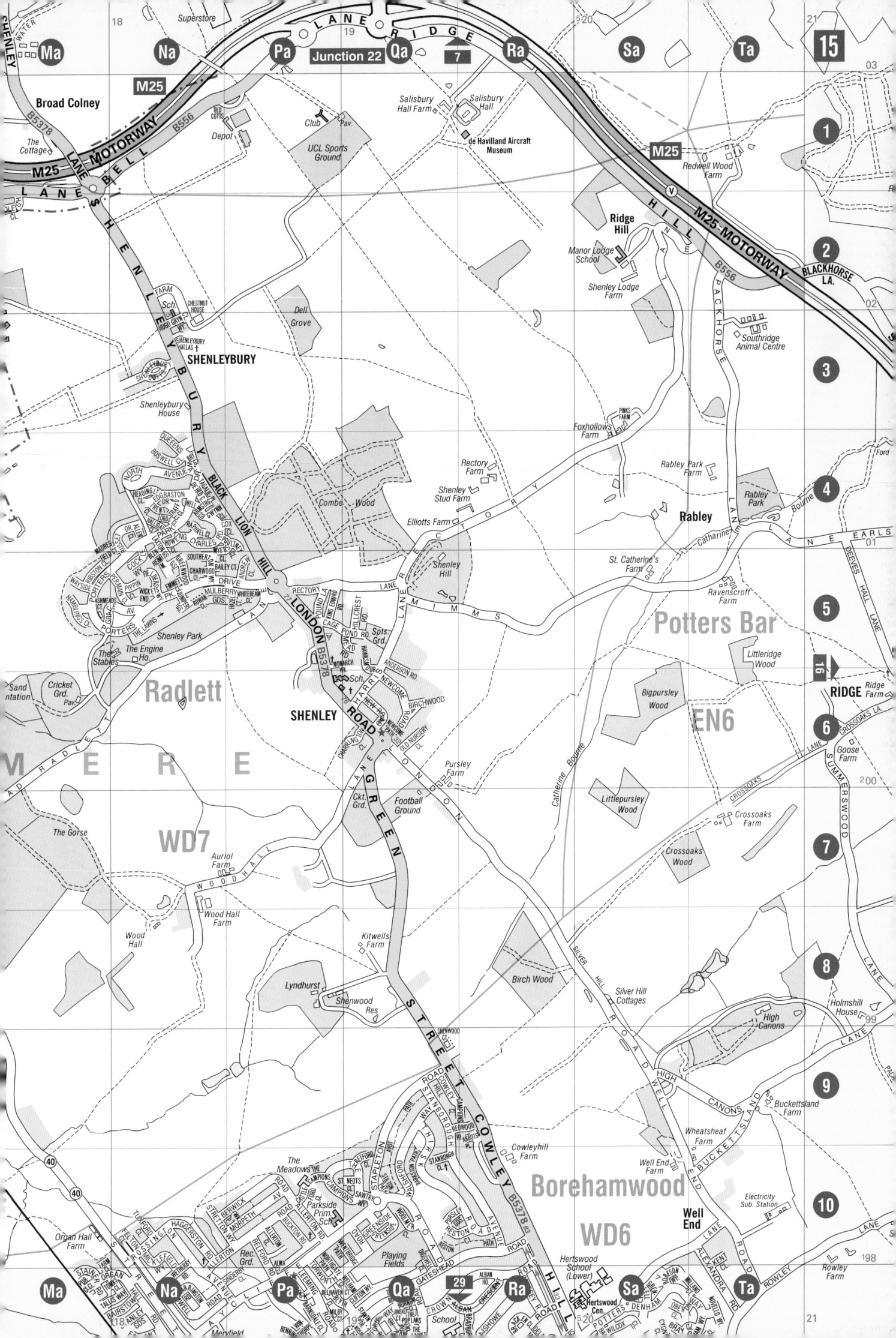

Broad Colney
Junction 22
M25 MOTORWAY
Salisbury Hall Farm
Salisbury Hall
de Havilland Aircraft Museum
UCL Sports Ground
Club
Depot
Redwell Wood Farm
Ridge Hill
Manor Lodge School
Shenley Lodge Farm
Southridge Animal Centre
BLACKHORSE LA.
SHENLEYBURY
Shenleybury House
Dell Grove
Foxhollows Farm
Rectory Farm
Shenley Stud Farm
Elliotts Farm
Combe Wood
Rabley Park Farm
Rabley Park
Rabley
St. Catherine's Farm
Ravenscroft Farm
Shenley Hill
Potters Bar
Littleridge Wood
Bigpursley Wood
EN6
RIDGE
Ridge Farm
Goose Farm
Radlett
Shenley Park
The Engine Ho.
The Stables
Cricket Grd.
SHENLEY
Pursley Farm
Football Ground
Ckt. Grd.
Littlepursley Wood
Crossoaks Farm
Crossoaks Wood
The Gorse
WD7
Auriol Farm
Wood Hall Farm
Wood Hall
Kitwells Farm
Birch Wood
Silver Hill Cottages
Lyndhurst
Shenwood Res.
High Canons
Holmshill House
Bucketsland Farm
Wheatsheaf Farm
Well End Farm
Cowleyhill Farm
Borehamwood
The Meadows
Parkside Prim. Sch.
Electricity Sub. Station
Well End
WD6
Organ Hall Farm
Rec. Grd.
Playing Fields
Hertswood School (Lower)
Hertswood Cen.
Rowley Farm
School

16
Ua
Va
Wa
Xa
Ya
Za
Ab
8
30
15
Round Wood
Swallow Holes
Hawkshead Bridge
Sports Ground
Pilvage Wood
Redwell Wood
Oak Lodge
Hawkshead Wood
Flint Cottage
Mymmshall Wood
The Grange
Woodhill Farm
BLACKHORSE LA.
Southridge Animal Centre
M25
ST. ALBANS
Town Farm
CECIL ROAD
B556
A1(M) MOTORWAY
M25 MOTORWAY
Warrengate Farm
Mimms Hall
Windmore Hall
Furzefield Wood
King George V Playing Field
Furzefield Centre
Tennis Courts
The Wroxham School
Potters Bar
EN6
Rabley Park
Catharine Bourne
EARLS LANE
SOUTH MIMMS
St. Giles C of E Prim. Sch.
Earls Farm
Ludlow's Lake
Bridgefoot Farm
Bridgefoot Ho.
Dugdale Hill
HERTS
Dame Alice Owen's Sch.
Playing Field
Littleridge Wood
Junction 1 A1(M)
Bignell's Corner
Church Fm.
Ridge Farm
RIDGE
Imperial Cancer Research Centre
Blanche Lane Farm
BIGNELL'S CORNER
South Mimms Service Area
Goose Farm
Crossoaks Farm
Junction 23 (M25)
Summerswood Farm
Dancershill Farm
Norfolk Lodge Farm
Laurel House
Laurel Lodge
Dancers Hill
Borehamwood
WD6
Dyrham Park Farm
Holmshill House
High Canons
EN5
A1081
Bettsland Farm
DYRHAM PARK GOLF COURSE
Dyrham Park Country Club & Club House
Knightsland Farm
Lower Kitt's End Farm
Kitt's End
Valentine's Farm
DYRHAM PARK
Strangeways Farm
Little Dyrham
THE SHIRE LONDON GOLF COURSE
Rowley Farm
BARNET BY-PASS
OLD FOLD MANOR GOLF COURSE

WELWYN HATFIELD
Swanley Bar
The Royal Veterinary College (Hawkshead Campus, Boltons Park site)
Swanleybar Farm
The Folly
Leggatts Wood
Leggatts Park
Griffins Hole
Nyn Park
Nyn Pond
Cricket Ground
Playing Field
Osborne House Farm
Little Heath Farm Cottage
LITTLE HEATH
Football Field
POTTERS BAR GOLF COURSE
Mount Grace School
Club House
Old Owens Sports Ground
Springfield
West Lodge
Northaw House
Stud Farm
Northaw C of E Prim. Sch.
NORTHAW
The Cottage
Fish Pond
HOOK WOOD
Morvan Park
Stormont Sch.
Chequers Mead Ho.
Riding Stables
Northaw Park
Oshwal Centre
The Hook
Five Acre Wood
Fir Wood
Parkfield Open Space
Parkfield
Bus Garage
Potters Bar FC
Library
Oakmere Park
Oakmere
Oakmere Prim. Sch.
Youth & Comm. Cen.
Potters Bar
Superstore
Cricket Grd.
Pope Paul Catholic Prim. Sch.
POTTERS BAR
POTTERS BAR COMM. HOSP.
Pond Wood
New Cottage
The Lodge
New Cottage Farm
St. John's Prep. Sch.
Stagg Ridge
Nursery
Junction 24
M25 MOTORWAY
M25
Chase Farm
Fenny Slade Hill
Chase Wood
Elm Farm
Bentleyheath Farm
Works
Bentley Heath
Ganwick Corner
Ganwick
Fir Wood
Hornbeam Hills
Three Oak Hill
Wrotham Park
North Lodge Farm
North Lodge Cottages
Plumridge Hill
Plumridge Wood
ENFIELD
Plumridge Farm
Spoilbank Wood
Cockshot Hill
Ganwick Farm
The Cottages
Deadman's Bottom
Salmon's Brook
Slopers Hill Farm
Park View Cottages
Barnet
Bartram's Quash
Hadley Wood Prim. Sch.
Hadley Wood
Hadley Wood Lawn Tennis Club
Playing Field
HADLEY WOOD
West Lodge Park (Hotel)
The Beale Arboretum
ENFIELD CHASE
Great Broadgates Hill
Club House
Ferny Hill Farm
Fernyhill Wood
GREAT NORTH ROAD
NORTH ROAD
HATFIELD ROAD
HIGH STREET
SOUTHGATE RD.
BARNET ROAD
COCKFOSTERS ROAD
STAGG HILL
THE RIDGEWAY
WAGON ROAD
JUDGE'S HILL
NORTHAW RD. WEST
THE CAUSEWAY
COOPER'S LANE
DARKES LANE
MOUNT GRACE ROAD

18
Jb
Kb
Lb
Mb
Nb
Pb
Qb
1
2
3
4
5
6
7
8
9
10
28
29
530
31
03
02
01
200
99
198
17
32
Potters Bar
EN6
WELWYN HATFIELD
EN2
EN4
Barnet
ENFIELD CHASE
ENFI
CUFFLEY
NORTHAW
BOTANY BAY
Cattlegate
Cuffley
Crews Hill
Thornton's Farm
High Willows
Vineyard Bridge
The Vineyard
VINEYARD HILL
HEMPS HILL
Northaw C of E Prim. Sch.
VINEYARDS
CHURCH
VICARAGE LA.
Playing Field
NORTHAW ROAD WEST
B156
The Cottage
PARK RD
LANE
Park Farm
Fish Pond
COLES HILL
Colesdale Farm
Hill View Farm
CATTLEGATE COTTAGES
CATTLEGATE ROAD
(CATTLEGATE HILL)
Northaw Park
WOOD CLOSE
HOOK LA.
FIRS
Oshwal Centre
The Hook
Northaw Valley
Northaw Brook
BARVIN PARK
WOODGATE AVENUE
OAK WELL DR
COOPERS LANE
Cattlegate Wood
Robin Hill
Woodhurst
Woodhurst Farm Cottages
Woodhurst Farm
Cattlegate Farm
BARVIN HILL
HOOKE HILL
Pond Wood
Turkey Brook
M25-MOTORWAY
M25
Owls Hall Farm
Owls Hall
Crews Hill Paddocks
Tilekiln Osiers
Crews Hill Piggeries
Garden Centre
Nurseries
Sub.
SOUTH HILL
Holly Hill Farm
Golf Cottages
Club House
(CREWS HILL)
ROAD
North Lodge Farm
North Lodge Cottages
South Barvin Farm
Sch.
ST. NICHOLAS HOUSES
THE DRIVE
Lodge
THE RIDGEWAY
A1005
Windrush
Holyhill Brook
LODGE
CREWS HILL GOLF COURSE
BEECH AV.
CYPRESS AV.
GOLF RIDE
ASHRIDGE
ROSEWOOD
TINGEYS
Vault Hill
Vault Hill Wood
Parting Hill
Cricket Ground
Cricket Grd.
Pav.
EAST
East Lodge
King's Oak Plain
Little Beechhill Wood
Botany Bay Farm
Plumridge Farm
Roundhedge Hill
Salmon's Brook
Duncan's Wood
Ash Wood
The Cottage
Parkside House
Park Farm
Park Farm Cottages
Camlet Moat
Reservoir
Cuckolds Hill
Parkside Farm
Pumping Station
FERNY HILL
HADLEY
Ferny Hill Cottage
Ferny Hill Farm
Obelisk
Moat Wood
Picnic Area
Camlet Hill
TRENT PARK (COUNTRY PARK)
Fernyhill Wood
Rough Lot
RECTORY FARM RD.
The Red House
Rectory Farm
Rendlesham Viaduct
KING'S OAK BMI HOSPITAL
CHASE FARM HOSPITAL
UCC
KINGFISHER CL.
HIGH OAKS
OAK AV.
RIDGE CREST
LAVENDER
FARORNA WK.
Wells Farm
Pumping Station
Waterworks Cottages
Hempshill Brook
Northaw & Cuffley Lawn Tennis Club
Sports Ground
Bowling Grn.
Soper's Viaduct
Nursery Plantation
Burnt Farm Cottages
Cuffley Brook
Cuffley Hills Farm
THE RIDGEWAY
B157
EAST RIDGEWAY
PLOUGH HILL
EAST
STATION RD
CUFFLEY
CRANFIELD CRESCENT
KING JAMES' AV.
CHURCH CL.
KINGSWELL RIDE
BURLEIGH WAY
KINGS WAY
COLESDALE
THEOBALDS
VALE CL.
SOUTH DR.
GREENFIELDS
Cuffley School
LAMBS CL.
SOPERS RD
Youth & Comm. Cen.
Works
Brook Farm
Ford
MEADWAY
TOLMERS RD
STARLING LA.
OAK LA.
ACORN
KINGSMEAD
HILL RISE
DRIVEWAY
SUTHERLAND WAY
ROWBOURNE PL.
LEEFE WAY
CANDAVIA
THE

19
GOFF'S OAK
CHURCHGATE
BURY GREEN
CHESHUNT
EN7
EN8
EN1
BROXBOURNE
Waltham Cross
Enfield
CREWS HILL
WHITEWEBBS WOOD
WHITEWEBBS PARK
WHITEWEBBS GOLF COURSE
CLAY HILL
HILLY FIELDS PARK
FORTY HILL
Forty Hall Country Park
BULLS CROSS
Turkey Street
M25-MOTORWAY
M25
Junction 25
GOFF'S LANE
B156
B198
LIEUTENANT ELLIS WAY
GREAT CAMBRIDGE ROAD
A10
WHITEWEBBS ROAD
OLD PARK RIDE
BULLSMOOR LA.
Theobalds Park Farm
Theobalds Pk. Conference Centre
Theobalds Manor
Capel Manor College
Lee Valley Park Information Centre
Myddelton House Gardens
Whitewebbs Museum of Transport
St. Mary's C of E High Sch.
Enfield Crematorium
Forty Hall
St. Ignatius College
Western Cemetery (Jewish)
Rb
Sb
Tb
Ub
Vb
Wb
Xb
1
2
3
4
5
6
7
8
9
10
20
33

20
19
34
Yb
Zb
Ac
Bc
Cc
Dc
Ec
1
2
3
4
5
6
7
8
9
10
35
36
37
38
CHESHUNT
Cheshunt
Turnford Sch. Playing Field
Sailing Club
Seventy Acres
Hayes Hill
Hayes Hill Cotts.
Stubbings Cottages
Woodside
Fishers Green
Holyfield Farm
Monkhams Hall
HOLYFIELD
CROOKED
Cheshunt Lake
Herts Young Mariners Base
Turnershill Marsh
Hooks Marsh
Youth Hostel
Brookland Inf. & Jun. Schs.
Works
Timber Yard
Cheshunt Junction
Thistly Marsh
Waltham Cross
Bowyer's Water
LEE VALLEY REGIONAL PARK
RIVER LEE NAVIGATION
ROYAL GUNPOWDER MILLS
Royal Gunpowder Mills
Hall Marsh
Powdermill Cut
Arboretum
Tree Nursery
Nurseries
Eagle Lodge
Abbey Fish Ponds
Waltham Marsh
HORSEMILL STREAM
Marsh Bridge
Cheshunt Marsh
Lee Valley White Water Centre
Waltham's Lock
Harold's Bri.
Waltham Abbey
WALTHAM ABBEY
Town Mead
Hazelmere Marina
MERIDIAN
WALTHAM CROSS
Holdbrook
HOLMESDALE TUNNEL
M25 MOTORWAY
M25
Junction 25
Cheshunt School
Playing Field
Tennis Courts
Albury Farm
Rifle Range
Cheshunt FC (The Stadium)
Holy Trinity C of E Prim. Sch.
Downfield Prim. Sch.
Grundy Pk Leisure Cen.
Grundy Park
THEOBALDS
LIEUTENANT ELLIS WAY
Rush Lodge
The Cedars Park
Theobalds Grove
WINSTON CHURCHILL WAY
A121
A10
B198
B176
B194
GREAT CAMBRIDGE ROAD
CROSSBROOK ST.
HIGH ST.
ELEANOR CROSS RD.
STATION RD.
HIGHBRIDGE S.
Theobald's Park Farm
PARK PLAZA
Gala Bingo
Superstore
Warehouses
BULLSMOOR LANE
MOLLISON AVENUE
Bullsmoor
Cobbins Brook
Warehouse
MERIDIAN BUSINESS PARK
Meridian Park
GUNPOWDER PARK
RAMMEY MARSH
Rammey Marsh Flood Relief Channel
Cattlegate Flood Relief Channel
Enfield
FREEZY WATER
Keys Meadow Prim. Sch.
Oasis Academy Enfield
EN3
EN8
Turkey St.
Turkey Street
Turkey Brook
Garden of Remembrance
Enfield Crematorium
Cemy.
HERTFORD ROAD
A1010
A1055
Enfield Lock
Prince of Wales Prim. Sch.
ENFIELD LOCK
ENFIELD WASH
Albany Leisure Cen.
Sports Hall
Oasis Academy Hadley
ALBANY PARK
ENFIELD ISLAND VILLAGE
Enfield Island Village
Overflow Channel
Pumping Station
SEWARDSTONE
Sewardstone Hall
Kingsfield Nurseries
Barnfield Riding Stables
Hannah Nursery
Durants
Nursery
RIVER LEE NAVIGATION
Small River Lee or Lea

21
HOLYFIELD
North Lodge Farm
Homefield Wood
Stable Lodge
Kennel Wood
Galley Wood House
Aimes Green
Broadgate Springs
Brayshill Spring
Monkhams Cottage
Aimesgreen Farm
Scatterbushes Wood
Stocking Grove
Longcroft Grove
Cobbinsend Farm
Maynards Farm
Maple Springs
Playground
BREACH BARNS MOBILE HOME PARK
Playing Field
Poultry Farm
Nursery
Fernhall Farm
Fernhall Wood
Willows
Brookmeadow Wood
Dallance Farm
Waltham Abbey
Galley Hill
EN9
Magic Lakes
Cobbin Pond
WARLIES PARK
Obelisk
Nicholls Farm
Home Farm
Obelisk Farm
Oaklands Farm
Nurseries
Warlies Gardens
Warlies Park House
The Temple
Burgess Farm
West Hill
Temple Hill
Nursing Home
Pickhill Farm
EPPING FOREST
Cricket Ground
Warlie's Lodge
UPSHIRE
Upshire Prim. Sch.
Sergeants Green
Warlies Park Farm
COPTHALL GREEN
Oxleys Wood
Spts. Cen.
King Harold Academy
Tennis Courts
Playing Field
Jun. & Inf. Schs.
Hazelwood Children's Cen.
Prim. Sch.
Play-ground
Comm. Cen.
Recreation Ground
Superstore
Football Ground
Cemetery
Rec. Grd.
The Leverton Infant & Junior Sch.
Honeylands
Waltham Abbey Swim. Pool
King George's Field
Woodgreen Farm
Woodgreen Potteries
Southend Farm
Upshire Hall
Potkiln Wood
Bramblу Shaw
WOOD GREEN
Woodredon House
Conybury Wood
Woodredon Farm
Stable Shaw
Sudbury Farm
WOODBINE CLOSE CARAVAN PARK
Junction 26
Skillet Hill Farm
M25 MOTORWAY
M25
Quinton Hill Farm
DOWDING WAY
A121
HONEY LANE
WOODRIDDEN HILL
Inner Lodge
Lord Padgets Wood
Poplar Shaw
Prayer Halls
Cemetery
Honey Lane Plain
Round Hills
The Downing Nursery
Beechview Nursery
BEECH HILL PARK
Tile Hill Farm
Honey Lane Quarters
Sunshine Plain
Riding School
AVEY LANE
Felicia Nursery
Kennels
Portulaca
Providence Nursery
Normandy Nursery
Aveylane Farm
The Rookery
HIGH BEECH GOLF COURSE
Club House
Wake Valley Pond
Wake Valley
EPPING FOREST
High Beech Nurseries
Kennels
Piggery
Pynest Green
Avey Cottages
Riding School
Rushey Plain
Great Monk Wood
Sewardstone Nursery
Handlers Farm
Mott Street Nursery
Thompson's Wood
Loughton
IG10
Bowling Green
Youth Hostel
Mount Pleasant
Beechside Nursery
E4
Manor Farm
High Beech C of E Primary Sch
Manor House
HIGH BEECH
Hall
Res.
Epping Forest Field Centre
Little Monk Wood
EPPING NEW ROAD
A104
A112
Oak Farm
Wallsgrove
Paul's Nursery
MOTT STREET
35
Fc
Gc
Hc
Jc
Kc
Lc
Mc
1
2
3
4
5
6
7
8
9
10

Gills Plantation
Cobbin's Brook
Cobbinsend Farm
COBBINSEND ROAD
Spratt's Hedgerow Wood
Spratt's Hedgerow
Bury Farm
BURY
Pond Field Plantation
Jenkins's Plantation
Fernhall Farm
Little Rookery Wood
LONG STREET
FERNHALL LA.
Rookery Wood
Fitches Plantation
Newhouse Farm
Obelisk
Nicholls Farm
Lodge Farm
Copped Hall
Copped Hall Gardens
THE HALL BARNS
Home Farm
Wood House
Paris Hall
New Farm
Griffin's Wood
Epping
CM16
Obelisk Farm
Burgess Farm
Copped Hall Green
The Temple
Temple Hill
Griffin's Wood
Bell Common
New House Farm
Ladderstile Farm
Millhouse Farm
UPSHIRE
The Selvage
CROWN HILL
M25
M25-MOTORWAY
Park Cottages
Bowlands Meadow
COPTHALL GREEN
Raveners Farm
Oxleys Wood
Warren Wood
The Warren
E P P I N G
EPPING THICKS
Great Gregories Farm
Brambly Shaw
Crown Hill Farm
Waltham Abbey
LODGE ROAD
HIGH ROAD
Ambresbury Banks
Club House
Little Gregories
Woodredon House
EN9
St. Thomas's Quarters
Long Running
PIERCING HILL
Piercing Hill
THEYDON BOIS GOLF COURSE
Woodredon Farm
Stable Shaw
Forest Lodge
Riding School
Genesis Slade
WOODRIDDEN HILL
A121
B172
Jack's Hill
Oak Hill
COPPICE ROW
Theydon Plain
The Coppice
Wake Arms Roundabout
Oak Hill Farm
Birch Hall
Birch Hall Farm
Theydon Bois Prim. Sch.
Sunshine Plain
WAKE ROAD
Dulsmead Hollow
Copley Plain
Cricket Ground
THEYDON BOIS
NEW ROAD
A104
GOLDINGS HILL
Loughton
Wake Valley Pond
Deershelter Plain
Redoak Wood
Birch Wood
Furze Ground
Wake Valley
IG10
Debden House Camp Site
Gaunt's Wood
DEBDEN GREEN
Ripley Grange
The Boundary
Broadstrood Plain
Great Monk Wood
EPPING FOREST
Mount Pleasant
Court Hill
Golding's Hill Ponds
LOUGHTON GOLF COURSE
Davenant Foundation School
Bellringer's Hollow
Little Monk Wood
Playing Field
Home Mead Local Nature Reserve
Blackweir Pond
36

EPPING
COOPERSALE
COOPERSALE STREET
FIDDLERS HAMLET
Steward's Green
Mount End
Ivy Chimneys
Theydon Garnon
Hobbs Cross
Theydon Bois
Theydon Mount
M11 MOTORWAY
M25 MOTORWAY
Junction 27 (M25)
Junction 6 (M11)
EPPING GOLF COURSE
HOBBS CROSS GOLF COURSE
ABRIDGE GOLF COURSE
Romford
RM4
FOREST

24
10
42
CHENIES
Amersham
HP6
LITTLE CHALFONT
CHORLEYWOOD WEST
Chorleywood
CHORLEYWOOD
CHORLEYWOOD COMMON
CHORLEYWOOD GOLF COURSE
Chorleywood Bottom
CHILTERN
Chalfont St. Giles
HP8
The Swillet
Heronsgate
Junction 17
M25
M25–MOTORWAY
Gerrards Cross
SL9
A404
B4442
A412
AMERSHAM ROAD
CHENIES ROAD
RICKMANSWORTH ROAD
NIGHTINGALES LANE
SHIRE LANE
CHALFONT LANE
LONG WALK
LODGE LANE
BURTON'S LANE
ROUGHWOOD LANE
CHESHAM LANE
GORELANDS LANE
Whitelands Wood
Carpenter's Wood
Hillas Wood
Crosslane Wood
Philipshill Wood
Newland Gorse
Shrubs Wood
Bottom Wood
Pollardshill Wood
Ladywalk Wood
Chiltern Open Air Museum
Newland Park
The Russell School
St. Clement Danes School
Shortenills Environmental Studies Centre
Field Study Centre
Five Plantation
Rowan Nurseries
Heronsgate
Ladywalk

25
H
J
K
L
M
N
P
11
Chandler's Cross
New Model Farm
Park Cottages
Scrubbs Wood
Blunts Wood
Sarratmill Bri.
Mead Spring
Fisheries
Power House
Willow Wood
North Lodge
Lower Lodge
WELLING GROVE
Sawpit Spring
Coltyard Spring
Coltspring Riding Stables
Cottage Farm
HARROCKS WOOD
Redhall Farm
Nursery
Merlin's Wood
M25
Flint Cottages
New Cotts.
Micklefield Hall
The Bungalow
Beechen Hill
CHORLEYWOOD HOUSE ESTATE
Dell Cottage
Keepers Cott.
BEECHENGROVE WOOD
Long Spring
Round Spring
Oak Farm
York House School
Model Farm
The Farmhouse
The Hut
Waterdell Spring
Round New Spring
Thick Spring
Cherry Tree Lodge
M25 - MOTORWAY
Trout Farm
Millfield Plantation
Upper Plantation
Round Spring Farm
LOUDWATER
Redheath Nursery
Little Green
Riding Stables
Thurlwood House
Croxley House
Killingdown Farm
Little Lady's Wood
Junction 18
The House
Walden Lodge
Parrot's Dell
Croxley Green
Skate Park
Baldwins La. Play. Fld.
CHORLEYWOOD
Loudwater Farm
Copthorne Wood
Little Gillions
Home Wood
Rasehill Farm
Playing Fields
Pavilion
CROXLEY GREEN
Applegarth
Yorke Mead Prim. Sch.
Round Spring
The Fringe
R I V E R S
Solomon's Wood
Charlotte House Preparatory Sch.
The Royal Masonic School for Girls
Nurseries
The Screen
West Herts Riding Sch.
Pheasant's Wood
Rickmansworth
Arnett Hills Sch.
Tennis Courts
Play. Fields
Scotsbridge Mill
Football Grd.
Sports Ground
Harvey Prim. Sch.
Rickmansworth Sch.
WATFORD ROAD
A404
A412
Cem.
Playing Field
Priory
Fortune Common
Playing Fields
Croxleyhall Wood
WD3
Rickmansworth Park
Superstore
Coun. Offs.
Mus.
Lib.
Th.
St. Joan of Arc Catholic School
RICKMANSWORTH
Croxleyhall Farm
Lot Mead Lock
Leisure Centre
Bowling Green
Tennis Courts
St. John's Catholic Prim. Sch.
Day Cen.
Comm. Cen.
Mill End
School
Playing Field
Prim. Sch.
Moneyhill
Ebury Pleasure Grd.
Boat Ho.
RIVERSIDE DRIVE
GRAND UNION CANAL
Hampton Hall Farm
Batchworth Lake
Recycling Cen.
Batchworth Lock Canal Cen.
MOOR LANE
A4145
Club House
RICKMANSWORTH GOLF COURSE
THE AQUADROME NATURE RESERVE
Bury Lake
Bury Lake Young Mariners
Colne Valley Trail
Superstore
The Grove
BATCHWORTH
MOOR PARK
UXBRIDGE ROAD
Drayton Ford
Depot
Stocker's Lake (Nature Reserve)
Stocker's Lock
Stocker's Farm
St. Mary's C of E Primary Sch.
Fairfield
Club House
Driving Range
BATCHWORTH HILL
LONDON ROAD
MOOR PARK GOLF COURSE
Watercress Beds
Froghall Farm
Garrett Wood
High Wood
Juniper Hill
Andrews Ley Farm
Juniper Dell
Greenbroom Spring
BATCHWORTH PARK GOLF COURSE
Chalk Pit
Cemetery
Sandfield
43
Springwell Lock
Springwell Lake
Quarry Farm
HERTFORD PLACE
MAPLE CROSS IND. EST.
Sixteen Acre
Pipers

Q
R
S
T
U
V
W
11
12
13
14
15
16
17
18
19
20
12
25
44
LEES WOOD
Deer Spring
Blackets Wood
Leeswood Cotts.
Nursery
ROCKS WOOD
WHIPPENDELL WOOD
JACOTTS HILL
Merlin's Wood
Newland's Spring
Merlin's Spring
ROUSEBARN LANE
WEST HERTS GOLF COURSE
Round Newland's Spring
Dell Wood
Waterdell Spring
The Hut
Long Newland's Spring
Thick Spring
Rickmansworth
Little Green
LITTLE GREEN LANE
Croxley House
Little Green Jun. Sch.
Killingdown Farm
Playing Fields
Rough Wood
Sports Ground
Playing Field
Herts Bowling Club
Cassiobury Infant Sch.
Cassiobury Junior Sch.
Watercress Beds
Iron Bridge Lock
GRAND UNION CANAL
Boating Pond
CASSIOBURY PARK
RIVER GADE
WD17
WD3
WD18
HEMPSTEAD ROAD
A411
West Herts College
WATFORD
Watford
CASSIOBURY PARK AVENUE
Watford Grammar Sch. for Boys
RICKMANSWORTH ROAD
A412
Cassio Bridge Lock
Fish Pond
Marina
KENILWORTH DRIVE
Skate Park
Baldwins La. Play. Fld.
Copthorne Wood
Little Gillions
Applegarth
Yorke Mead Prim. Sch.
CROXLEY GREEN
Sports
Youth Centre
Rec. Grd.
Tennis Courts
Inf. Sch.
WATFORD ROAD
Croxley
Harvey Rd. Prim. Sch.
Rickmansworth Sch.
SCOTS HILL
Playing Fields
Croxleyhall Wood
Long Valley Wood
Croxley Centre
HOLYWELL
Westfield Community Sports Cen.
St. Anthony's Catholic Prim. Sch.
Westfield Academy
Mail Centre
Playing Field
Harwoods Rec. Grd.
Watford Hosp.
WEST WATFORD
Croxley Common Moor Local Nature Reserve
Common Moor
Moor Park Crossing
TOLPITS LANE
A4145
King George V Playing Fields
Brightwells Farm Cotts.
Electricity Transmission Station
Croxleyhall Farm
Lot Mead Lock
Tolpits Ho.
RIVER COLNE
Brightwells Spring
Moat
THREE RIVERS
Tolpits Plantation
Running Track
Merchant Taylors' School
Playing Fields
Pumping Station
Lake
Hampton Hall Farm
MOOR LANE
The Withey Beds Local Nature Reserve
Northwood Prep. Sch.
Manor of the Rose
HAMPERMILL LANE
Hampermill Wood
Club House
SANDY LODGE ROAD
Northwood
RICKMANSWORTH GOLF COURSE
MOOR PARK
Moor Park
Club House
Farm Cottage
Round Spring
Hampermill Spring
Big Wood
HA6
SANDY LODGE GOLF COURSE
Tennis Courts
The Mansion
MOOR PARK GOLF COURSE
MOOR PARK
The Roughs
Old Furze Field
Young Hanging
SANDY LANE
A4125
LONDON ROAD
A404
BATCHWORTH HILL
Home Farm
EASTBURY
Old Hanging
Oxhey Wood Local Nature Reserve
07
08
09
510
93
94
95
96
97
98

X
Y
Z
Aa
Ba
Ca
Da
BERRYGROVE
Junction 5
13
M1 MOTORWAY
WD25
WD24
WD23
WD19
Watford Junction
Watford
Watford High St
Bushey
BUSHEY
OXHEY
The Rookery
Riverside Park
OXHEY PARK
Watford Heath
Merry Hill
CARPENDERS PARK
Carpenders Park
HERTSMERE
BUSHEY HALL GOLF COURSE
BUSHEY GOLF COURSE
OXHEY PARK GOLF COURSE
HARTSBOURNE GOLF COURSE
Little Hartsbourne Wood
Hartsbourne Country Club (Club House)
Bushey Jewish Cemetery
Bushey Hall Farm
Scotts Wood
Icedale Wood
Sherwoods Wood
Woodlands
Brick Works
Oxhey Grange
Margeholes Wood
Front Lodge
The Purcell School
Queens' School (North Site)
Queens' School (South Site)
Sports Club Metropolitan Police Sports Ground
Powerleague Soccer Centre (Watford)
Football Pitches
The Lincolnsfield Centre
Farmyard Funworld
Bushey Grove Leisure Centre
David Lloyd Leisure
Warehouse
Hartspring Cotts.
Patchetts Equestrian Cen.
Delrow Ho.
Holland Farm
Gullimore Farm
Kennels
Cemetery
Bushey Manor Junior School
The Bushey Academy
Sacred Heart Catholic Prim. Sch.
Bournehall Prim. Sch.
Moat Field
Bushey Meads School
Ashfield Jun. Sch.
St. Margaret's Sch.
St. Margaret's Sports Centre
Merry Hill House
Driving Range
Bushey House
Club House
Reservoir
Riding School
Nursery
Bromet Prim. Sch.
Watford FC (Vicarage Rd. Stadium)
WATFORD GENERAL HOSP.
WATFORD HEALTH CAMPUS
Highwood Prim. Sch.
Knutsford Sch.
Busneymill Bridge
Colne Rec. Grd.
Playing Field
Wacky Warehouse
Ox Pasture Spring
South Oxhey Playing Fields
Warren Dell
St. Joseph's Catholic Primary School
Little Furze Field
Pond Wood
Black Mason's Wood
St. Meryl Sch.
Woodwalks
Carpenders Park Cemetery
Carpenders Park Farm
Mutton Wood
Valley View Farm
Sandpit Wood
Levels Wood
Grim's Ditch
Grim's Dyke
Harrow Weald Common
CHALK HILL
LONDON ROAD
HIGH STREET
SPARROWS HERNE
PINNER ROAD
OXHEY LANE
PRESTWICK ROAD
EASTBURY ROAD
WIGGENHALL ROAD
STEPHENSON WAY
WATERFIELDS WAY
HARTSPRING LANE
ELTON WAY
OTTERSPOOL WAY
A41 (NORTH WESTERN AV.)
A411
A4008
A4125
A4178
A412
B462
B4542
11
12
13
14
15
16
17
18
19
20

28
Watford
WD25
Bushey
WD23
BUSHEY
BUSHEY HEATH
Stanmore
HA7
HA3
Delrow
Patchetts Green
LETCHMORE HEATH
ELSTREE AERODROME
HILFIELD PARK RESERVOIR
ALDENHAM COUNTRY PARK
ALDENHAM RESERVOIR
ALDENHAM PARK
Caldecote Hill
ROYAL NATIONAL ORTHOPAEDIC HOSPITAL
Stanmore Common Local Nature Reserve
HARTSBOURNE GOLF COURSE
H E R T S
H A R R O W
M1
A41
A411
A409
A4140
A5183
WATLING
TYLERS WAY
M1 MOTORWAY
ELSTREE ROAD
WATFORD ROAD
WATFORD BY-PASS
HIGH ROAD
HEATHBOURNE ROAD
COMMON ROAD
THE COMMON
STANMORE HILL
BROCKLEY HILL
ALDENHAM ROAD
HILFIELD LANE
BUSHEY LANE
ELTON WAY
SPARROWS HERNE
The Haberdashers' Aske's Boys' Sch.
The Haberdashers' Aske's School for Girls
Bushey Meads School
Immanuel College
Hartsbourne Prim. Sch.
Bentley Priory Mus.
Bentley Priory
Kestrel Grove (Offices)
The Princess Alexandra Home
Little Hartsbourne Wood
Levels Wood
Grim's Dyke
Grimsdyke Open Space
Harrow Weald Common
Heriot's Wood
Old Barn
Deer Park
Bentley Priory Local Nature Reserve
Cloisters Wood
Pear Wood
Elstree Hill Open Space
LISMIRRANE INDUSTRIAL PARK
CENTENNIAL PARK
Aldenham Country Pk. Rare Breeds Farm
Aldenham Sailing Club
Sports Ground
Laboratories
Sewage Works
Pumping Station
Flying School
Flying Club
Page's Farm
Ham Farm
Letchmore Lodge
Slades Farm
Moats
Medburn House
Medburn Bri.
Little Kendals Farm
Little Kendals Wood
Hertsmere Jewish Prim. Sch.
Radlett Prep. Sch.
Aldenham School
Boydens Hill
Playing Field
Aldenham Grange
Aldenham Cottage
Holland Farm House
Holland Farm
Bhaktivedanta Manor School
Four Want Ways
Electricity Transforming Station
Kennels
Gullimore Farm
Bushey Jewish Cemetery
Cemetery
Hilfield Farm
Hilfield Castle
Boat House
Lodge
Tyler's Farm
Hart's Farm
Caravan Site
Caldecote Farm
Rosary Priory
BUSHEY SPIRE HOSP.
Belswood Cottage
Heath House
King George Rec. Grd.
Stanmore Hall
Limes House
Cricket Ground
Fish Pond
Grove Field Pavilion
Heriots
Brockley Hill Farm
Brockley Hill Ho.
ASPIRE
Tykes Water
Home Farm
Boathouse
STANMORE COMMON (Local Nature Reserve)
Margaret's Sports Centre
Club House
Tennis Courts
Nurseries
HARROW WEALD COMMON
14 15 16 17
98 97 96 95 94 93
11 12 13 14 15 16 17 18 19 20
Ea Fa Ga Ha Ja Ka La
27 46 14 50 30

29
Well End
Hertswood School (Lower)
Hertswood Cen.
Rowley Farm
Meryfield Prim. Sch.
Cowley Hill Sch.
Meadow Park
Boreham Wood FC (Meadow Pk.)
The Ark Theatre
Hertswood Sch. (Upper)
The Venue (Leisure Cen.)
Borehamwood Ind. Park
Sports Ground
RADLETT PARK GOLF COURSE
Golf Driving Range
Club House
Parkfields Open Space
South Medburn Farm
BBC Elstree
ELSTREE STUDIOS
BOREHAMWOOD
Borehamwood Shopping Park
The Point
Superstore
King George's Field
Kenilworth Prim. Sch.
Playing Field
Yavneh Coll.
Elstree & Borehamwood
Rowley Lane Sports Grd.
Ripon Park
Recycling Centre
Cemetery
St. Nicholas Elstree C of E Prim. Sch.
ELSTREE
Woodcock Farm
Deacons Hill
The Chantry
Deacons Hill Open Space
Stirling Corner
Froghall Wood
Scratch Wood
Scratchwood Open Space
Boys Hill Wood
Thistle Wood
Hill House
Edgwarebury Ho. Farm
The Leys
Elstree Manor
Penniwells Farm
The Dower House
Elstree Open Space
Hyver Hall
Hyver Manor
Tanglewood
M1 MOTORWAY
Junction 4
Depot
Target Wood
The Shrub
Clump of Trees Wood
BARNET
Edgware Bury
Bury Farm
London Gateway Service Area
NW7
MILL HILL GOLF COURSE
Edgware
Gate Cottages
Nursery Cottage
Edgwarebury Cemetery
Nut Wood
Hemmings Wood
Stoney Wood Lake
Broadfields Prim. Sch.
Fairway Prim. Sch.
Northway Sch.
Mill Hill High Sch.
HA8
EDGWAREBURY PARK
Newlands
Driving Range
Stanmore and Edgware Golf Centre
London Academy
Apex Corner
A1 BARNET BY-PASS
A41 WATFORD BY-PASS
A5 WATLING STREET
ELSTREE WAY
SHENLEY ROAD
ALLUM LANE
BARNET LANE
WOODCOCK HILL
DEACONS HILL
EDGWARE WAY

30
Borehamwood
WD6
HERTSMERE
EN5
NW7
DYRHAM PARK
THE SHIRE LONDON GOLF COURSE
OLD FOLD MANOR GOLF COURSE
HIGH BARNET
CHIPPING BARNET
TOTTERIDGE
ARKLEY
Saffron Green
Rowley Green
Barnet Gate
Highwood Hill
Ducks Island
Borehamwood Ind. Park
Strangeways Farm
Rowley Farm
Fold Farm
Sports Ground
Shooting Ground
Galley Lane Farm
Poor Clare Monastery
Arkley Lane Open Space
Woodlands Farm
A1 Golf Driving Range
Club Ho.
Club House
Playing Field
Burial Ground
Electricity Transformer Sta.
Christ Church Primary School
Queen Elizabeth's School
Kenilworth Prim. Sch.
Rowley Lane Sports Grd.
Rowley Green Farm
ARKLEY GOLF COURSE
Arkley Rise Estate Open Space
Rowley Green Common Nature Reserve
ROWLEY LANE GOLF COURSE
Arkley Manor
Rowley Bank Nurseries
Reservoir
Nursing Home
Whalebone Park
UCC BARNET HOSPITAL
Psychiatric Unit
Cemy.
Whitings Hill Prim. Sch.
Whitings Hill Open Space
Schools
Windmill
Tennis Courts
Stirling Corner
Elstree Park
Hyver Hall
Hyver Farm
Hyver Manor
Barnet Gate Wood
Gravel Pit Wood
Tanglewood
Thistle Wood
(Old Elizabethans) Playing Field
Brent Lodge Farm
Allendale
Cottage Farm
Recreation Ground
East Barnet Old Grammarians Playing Field
Grange Playing Fields
Grange Avenue Open Space
Totteridge Park Open Space
Dollis Brook
Hendon Wood Lane Open Space
Fairlight Cottage
Hillsborough Cottage
Target Wood
The Shrubbery
Moat Mount Open Space
Moat Mount Camp Site
Leg of Mutton Pond
Clump of Trees Wood
Totteridge Fields Local Nature Reserve
Totteridge Park
Redings
Hillsdown
Montebello
Burnhams
Chestnut Cottages
Abattoir
St. Edward's
Mote End Farm
Boundary House
Farmleigh
Oak Lodge
Ellern Mede Centre
Ellern Mede Farm
Totteridge Common
The Warren
The Lynch House
Fairlawn
Nut Wood
White Lodge
Mote Mount
Hendon Park
Mill Hill High Sch.
Beech Wood
Highwood Park
The Barn
Highwood Ho.
Highwood
Highwood Hill Cottage
Holcombe Dale
Holcombe Hill
Folly Brook
Folly Brook & Darland's Lake Nature Reserve
Folly Farm
Riding School
Playing Field
Pool
Schools
Holcombe Ho.
Belmont Farm
Sports Ground
Cricket Club
Cemetery
Nursery
Burtonhole Lane Farm Estate
Burtonhole Farm
St. Paul's C of E Prim. Sch.
The Mill Field
Lawrence Green
Apex Corner
Northway Sch.
A1 BARNET BY-PASS
A5135
A411
A5109
A1081
B552
BARNET ROAD
ROWLEY LANE
ARKLEY LANE
GALLEY LANE
WOOD STREET
BARNET ROAD
HENDON WOOD LANE
BARNET GATE LANE
MAYS LANE
TOTTERIDGE COMMON
TOTTERIDGE LANE
HIGHWOOD HILL
MARSH LANE
THE RIDGEWAY
ST. ALBANS ROAD
WATFORD WAY
BARNET WAY
ELSTREE WAY
ROWLEY GREEN RD.
GRANVILLE RD.
RAVENSCROFT PK.
WEST END LA.
LEECROFT RD.
CEDAR LAWN AV.
RIVERSIDE
DOLLIS BROOK WK.
16
48
21
22
23
24
98
97
96
95
94
93
Ua
Va
Wa
Xa
Ya
Za
Ab
11
12
13
14
15
16
17
18
19
20
29

Bb
Cb
Db
Eb
Fb
Gb
Hb
17
49
25
26
27
28
97
96
95
94
93
HADLEY WOOD
COCKFOSTERS ROAD
Great Broadgates Hill
WEST CRESCENT
LANCASTER AVENUE
Club House
BEECH HILL PARK
HADLEY WOOD GOLF COURSE
ENFIELD
Fish Pond
Fernyhill Wood
Ferny Hill Farm
Rectory Farm
St. Martha's Senior School
Monken Hadley C of E Prim. Sch.
CAMLET WAY
Bournwell Hill
MONKEN HADLEY COMMON
Hadley Wood Nature Reserve
Sewits Hill
MONKEN HADLEY
HADLEY GREEN
NORTH (HADLEY) HIGHSTONE ROAD
A1000
Barnet
Priddeon's Hill
Newmans Hill
Beech Hill Lake
COMMON
HADLEY WOOD RD.
EAST BARNET GOLF COURSE
Tudor Sports Ground
Club House
Jewish Comm. Sec. Sch.
Playing Field
Play. Fld.
Livingstone Prim. Sch.
Water Tower
Oak Wood
Reservoir (covered)
Go Ape
Monument
FAIRGREEN
Playing Fields
Cemetery
HADLEY
King George's Field
BARNET
Cromer Road Prim. Sch.
NEW BARNET
Recreation Ground
Depot
Pymmes
COCKFOSTERS
Cockfosters
PLEASANT WAY
Queen Elizabeth's Girls' Sch.
Hospice
High Barnet
BARNET HILL
GREAT NORTH ROAD
STATION ROAD
A110
EAST BARNET RD.
BROOKHILL RD.
CAT HILL
New Barnet
Barnet Vale
Lyonsdown
EN4
Pleasure Ground
EAST BARNET
East Barnet Sch.
Underhill Playing Fields
Odeon Cin.
The Rainbow Cen.
LONGMORE AV.
B193
Grasvenor Avenue Inf. Sch.
KING GEORGE PLAYING FIELDS
Oak Hill Woods Nature Reserve
Oaktree Sch.
Wyatts Farm Open Space
Oakleigh Park
OAK HILL PARK
Bandstand
Playground
Miniature Golf Course
Monkfrith Prim. Sch.
Bowling Green
Pavilion
N20
Recreation Ground
SOUTH HERTS GOLF COURSE
Brook Farm Open Space
Focus School
Pupil Referral Unit
Pavilion Study Centre
Oak Hill Campus
South Barnet
Warehouses
Sports Grd.
Club House
Totteridge and Whetstone
OAKLEIGH PARK
OSIDGE LANE
TOTTERIDGE VILLAGE
TOTTERIDGE LANE
A5109
OAKLEIGH ROAD
A109
RUSSELL ROAD
B1453
Waverley
Windyridge
Dell House
The Croft
Cricket Ground
Superstore
WHETSTONE
Tennis Club
Sports Ground
N11
Swan Lane Open Space
FRIERN BARNET LANE
B550
HIGH ROAD
A1000
NORTH MIDDLESEX GOLF COURSE
Club House
BRUNSWICK PARK
Laurel Farmhouse
N12
Woodridge Prim. Sch.
North London Hospice
High Sch.
Sports Ground
Woodside Park Club
Bethune Park
Recreation Ground
NORTH OAKLEIGH
Cricket Ground
MAYFIELD AVENUE
FRIERN WATCH

32
18
50
31
TRENT PARK (COUNTRY PARK)
Trent Park
TRENT PARK GOLF COURSE
Barnet
EN4
EN2
N14
N11
BARNET
COCKFOSTERS
Cockfosters
Oakwood
OAKWOOD
OAKWOOD PARK
Highlands Village
World's End
GROVELANDS PARK
Southgate
SOUTHGATE
OSIDGE
South Barnet
BRUNSWICK PARK
PALMERS GREEN
Palmers Green
OAK HILL PARK
NEW SOUTHGATE CEMETERY
ENFIELD ROAD
SLADES ROAD
COCKFOSTERS ROAD
CHASE SIDE
BRAMLEY ROAD
CAT HILL
BOURNE HILL
THE BOURNE
HIGH STREET
CANNON HILL
ALDERMANS HILL
WATERFALL ROAD
OAKLEIGH RD. SOUTH
GREEN LANES
HADLEY ROAD
FERNY HILL
Chase Farm Hospital
North London Priory Hospital
Southgate Hockey Centre
Chickenshed Theatre
Oak Hill Theological College

33
Rb
Sb
Tb
Ub
Vb
Wb
Xb
19
51
34
Gordon Hill
Chase Side
ENFIELD TOWN
Enfield Chase
Enfield Town
ENFIELD
Enfield
GRANGE PARK
Grange Park
BUSH HILL PARK GOLF COURSE
BUSH HILL PARK
Bush Hill Park
WINCHMORE HILL
Winchmore Hill
N21
N13
N9
LOWER EDMONTON
EDMONTON
Edmonton Green
Southbury
EDMONTON CEMETERY
Firs Farm Playing Fields
JUBILEE PARK
PYMMES PARK
Playing Fields
David Lloyd Leisure
Enfield Town FC (Queen Elizabeth II Stadium)
Southbury Leisure Centre
Kingsmead School
Cineworld Cinema
Gala Bingo
Bishop Stopford's School
Suffolks Primary School
MARTIN DALE INDUSTRIAL ESTATE
ENFIELD RETAIL PK.
MARTINBRIDGE TRADING ESTATE
HASLEMERE BUSINESS CENTRE
Heron Hall Academy
The College of Haringey, Enfield & NE London
Enfield Grammar School (Lower)
ST. MICHAEL'S HOSP
Chace Com. Sch. & Spts. Cen.
Edmonton Sch. (Upper Site)
Aspire Sport & Fitness Cen.
Churchfield Prim. Sch.
Starks Field Prim. Sch.
The Latymer School
West Lea Sch.
Hazelbury Jun. & Inf. Schs.
Firs Farm Prim. Sch.
Winchmore Sch.
City Amenity Site
Clowes Sports Grd.
Nth. London Hospice
The Paulin Ground
Hazelwood Sports Club
Tottenham Park Cemetery
Federation Cemetery (Jewish)
Montagu Rec. Grd.
Aylward Academy
Hollywood Gardens
Recreation Ground
Galliard Prim. Sch.
Miniature Golf Course
Pymmes Park
Salmon's Brook
WINDMILL A110 HILL
CHURCH ST.
SOUTHBURY
A110 ROAD
GREAT CAMBRIDGE ROAD
A10
LONDON ROAD
A105
VILLAGE RD.
RIDGE A105 AV.
GREEN LANES
CHURCH STREET
B154
HERTFORD ROAD
A1010
FORE ST.
NIGHTINGALE ROAD
LANCASTER ROAD
CARTERHATCH LANE
DONKEY LANE
NEW RIVER

34
20
52
Yb
Zb
Ac
Bc
Cc
Dc
Ec
11
12
13
14
15
16
17
18
19
20
ENFIELD HIGHWAY
BRIMSDOWN
PONDERS END
SEWARDSTONE
CHINGFORD
ENFIELD
Southbury
Brimsdown
Ponders End
KING GEORGE'S
RESERVOIR
WILLIAM
GIRLING
RESERVOIR
LEE VALLEY GOLF COURSE
Odeon Cinema
Lee Valley Athletics Centre
Athletics Track
Power Station
Overflow Channel
Pumping Station
Brimsdown Sports & Social Club
Brimsdown Prim. Sch.
BRIMSDOWN INDUSTRIAL ESTATE
WATERMILL BUSINESS CENTRE
PLAZA BUSINESS CENTRE
SOVEREIGN BUSINESS CENTRE
LEASIDE BUSINESS CENTRE
MILL RIVER TRADING ESTATE
CENTENARY TRADING ESTATE
PONDERS END INDUSTRIAL ESTATE
Warehouses
Depot
Weir
South Marsh
Gas Works
Boundary Ditch
Durants Park
Kingfisher Hall Prim. Acad.
The College of Haringey, Enfield & NE London
Heron Hall Academy
Academies
Woodpecker Hall Prim. Acad.
Nightingale Academy
Montagu Rec. Grd.
Tottenham Cemetery
Federation Cemetery (Jewish)
Sewage Works
Refuse Incineration Plant
Teamsport Karting
Pickett's Lock
River Lee Navigation
River Lee Diversion
King George's Sailing Club
Chingford Golf Range
Playground
Mansfield Park
Chingford Foundation Sch.
Ridgeway Putting Park Green
Chingford Mount Cemetery
Yardley Hill
Hawkswood PRU
Yardley Prim. Sch.
Pole Obelisk
The Hawk Wood
Pitch & Putt
Kingsfield Nursery
Barnfield Riding Stables
Hannah Nursery
Fouracres Nursery
Northfield Nursery
Northcroft Nursery
Chapelfield Nursery
Marshfield Nursery
Luthers Farm
Amesbury Mead Farm
Woodlands Nursery
Caravan Park
Sewardstone Lodge
Picks Farm
Oasis Academy Hadley
Suffield Hatch
Chingford Fitness Cen.
A10
A110
A1010
A1055
A112
A1037
A1009
B137
B169
SEWARDSTONE ROAD
NAGS HEAD RD.
LEA VALLEY ROAD
MOLLISON AVENUE
MERIDIAN WAY
HERTFORD ROAD
HIGH STREET
NIGHTINGALE ROAD
MONTAGU ROAD
WALTHAM WAY
OLD CHURCH ROAD
MANSFIELD HILL
KINGS HEAD HILL
NEW ROAD
HALL LANE
ALBANY PARK
CARTERHATCH LANE
DURANTS ROAD
WHARF ROAD
PICKETTS LOCK LANE
EN3
N9
35
36
37
38
93
94
95
96
97
98

Mott Street Nursery
Thompson's Wood
Beechside Nursery
Manor Farm
High Beech C of E Primary School
HIGH BEECH
Youth Hostel
Epping Forest Field Centre
Little Monk Wood
Manor House
Oak Farm
Wallsgrove House
Cricket Ground
Pav.
Aldergrove Wood
Paul's Nursery
Blackweir Hill
Barn Hill
The Vicarage
Dairy Farm
Scout Camp Site
Kate's Cellar
Shelleys Hill
Loughton Camp
Riding School
Day's Farm
Equestrian Centre
Debden Slade
Woodbury Hollow
EPPING FOREST
Fernhill Wood
Pipers Farm
Field Study Centre
Hill Wood
Police Training Camp
Three Horseshoes Farm
Loughton
Springfield Farm
Lippittshill Lodge
Whitehouse Plain
Carrolls Farm
Strawberry Hill Ponds
Fairmead Pond
Round Thicket
Gilwell Park
Club Ho.
WEST ESSEX GOLF COURSE
Ludgate Water
Caravan Site
North Long Hills
Fairmead Bottom
LOUGHTON
Ludgate House
Almshouse Plain
IG10
Reservoir (covered)
Nursery
Bury Wood
Long Hills
Tennis Courts
Ludgate Plain
Sewardstonebury
Peartree Plain
Roding Valley High Sch.
Bury Farm
Palmer's Bridge
Superstore
Woodman's Glade
Cuckoo Pits
Bury Wood
The Hawk Wood
Grimston's Oak
Riding School
Oaklands Sch.
Buttonseed Corner
Warren Hill
Magpie Hill
Connaught Water
Warren Hill Ho.
ROYAL EPPING FOREST & CHINGFORD GOLF COURSE
Chingford Plain
Recreation Ground
Club Ho.
Queen Elizabeth's Hunting Lodge
Powell's Forest
Albany Ho.
Hill Fm.
Oak Hall
The Warren
The Connaught Club
Tennis Courts
Bowl. Grn.
Warren Pond
Barn Hoppet
Chingford
Linder's Field Local Nature Reserve
St.John's C of E Prim. School
Buckhurst Hill
CHINGFORD GREEN
Cricket Ground
Club
Whitehall Plain
Tennis Courts
Play. Fld.
Bluehouse Grove
Pimp Hall Nature Reserve
Pimp Hall Park
Friday Hill
Playing Field
Hatch Grove
Hatch Forest
Reed's Forest
Schools
HOLLY HOUSE HOSP.
BUCKHURST HILL
Buckhurst Hill
Buckhurst Hill Prim. Sch.
LORD'S BUSHES
Knighton Wood
Woodford Green IG8
Football Ground
WOODFORD GOLF COURSE
WOODFORD WELLS
Roding Valley
Rugby Football Ground
The Lops
A104
A1069
A121
A110
B160
B146
B170
EPPING NEW ROAD
RANGER'S ROAD
WHITEHALL RD
HIGH ROAD
MANOR ROAD
RODING LA.
STATION RD
HATCH LA.
PALMERSTON RD

36
DEBDEN GREEN
LOUGHTON GOLF COURSE
Loughton
IG10
LOUGHTON
DEBDEN
Debden
EPPING
M11 MOTORWAY
Junction 5
WOOLSTON MANOR GOLF COURSE
Buckhurst Hill
BUCKHURST HILL
IG9
Chigwell
CHIGWELL
IG7
Roding Valley Meadows Nature Reserve
David Lloyd Leisure
22
35
54

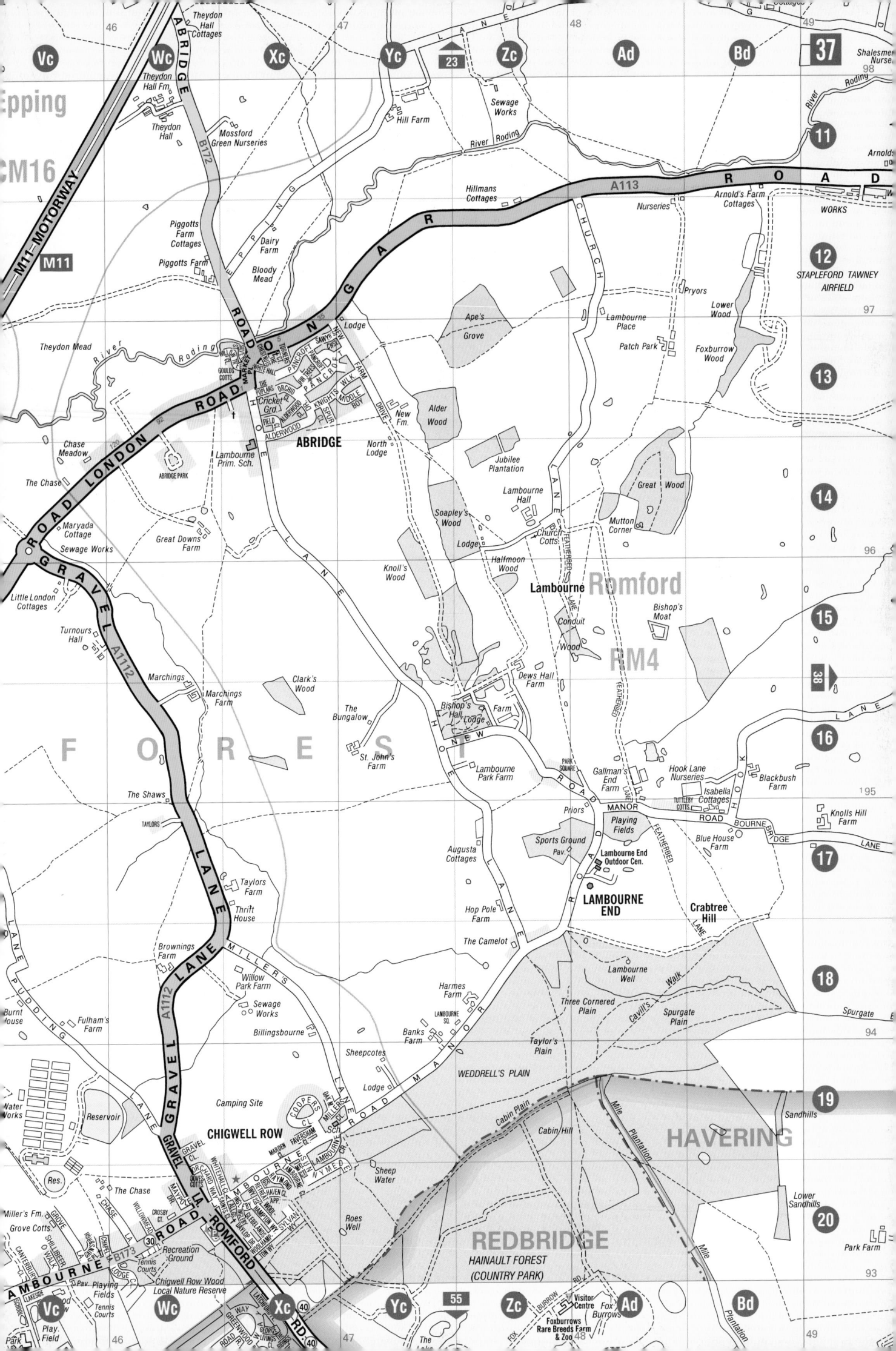
37
Epping
CM16
M11 MOTORWAY
M11
Theydon Hall Cottages
Theydon Hall Fm.
Theydon Hall
Mossford Green Nurseries
Hill Farm
Sewage Works
River Roding
Hillmans Cottages
A113
Piggotts Farm Cottages
Piggotts Farm
Dairy Farm
Bloody Mead
Theydon Mead
ABRIDGE
Lambourne Prim. Sch.
Chase Meadow
The Chase
Maryada Cottage
Sewage Works
Great Downs Farm
Little London Cottages
Turnours Hall
Marchings
Marchings Farm
A1112
FOREST
The Shaws
Taylors Farm
Thrift House
Brownings Farm
Willow Park Farm
Sewage Works
Billingsbourne
Fulham's Farm
Reservoir
Camping Site
CHIGWELL ROW
The Chase
Recreation Ground
Chigwell Row Wood Local Nature Reserve
Playing Fields
Tennis Courts
Ape's Grove
Alder Wood
Jubilee Plantation
Soapley's Wood
Knoll's Wood
Halfmoon Wood
Lambourne Hall
Church Cotts.
Lambourne
Romford
RM4
Conduit Wood
Dews Hall Farm
Bishop's Hall
Clark's Wood
The Bungalow
St. John's Farm
Lambourne Park Farm
Gallman's End Farm
Hook Lane Nurseries
Isabella Cottages
Blackbush Farm
Knolls Hill Farm
Blue House Farm
Sports Ground
Playing Fields
Lambourne End Outdoor Cen.
LAMBOURNE END
Crabtree Hill
Augusta Cottages
Hop Pole Farm
The Camelot
Lambourne Well
Harmes Farm
Three Cornered Plain
Spurgate Plain
Banks Farm
Sheepcotes
Taylor's Plain
WEDDRELL'S PLAIN
Cabin Plain
Cabin Hill
Mile Plantation
HAVERING
Sandhills
Lower Sandhills
Park Farm
Sheep Water
Roes Well
REDBRIDGE
HAINAULT FOREST (COUNTRY PARK)
Visitor Centre
Fox Burrows
Foxburrows Rare Breeds Farm & Zoo
Nurseries
Arnold's Farm Cottages
WORKS
STAPLEFORD TAWNEY AIRFIELD
Pryors
Lower Wood
Lambourne Place
Patch Park
Foxburrow Wood
Great Wood
Mutton Corner
Bishop's Moat
ABRIDGE ROAD
ONGAR ROAD
LONDON ROAD
GRAVEL LANE
MILLERS LANE
MANOR ROAD
LAMBOURNE ROAD
ROMFORD ROAD
CHURCH LANE
FEATHERBED LANE
HOOK LANE
PUDDING LANE
Spurgate
23
55
38

38
49
50
51
52
98
97
96
95
94
93
Cd
Dd
Ed
Fd
Gd
Hd
Jd
11
12
13
14
15
16
17
18
19
20
EPPING RD.
MOUNT RD.
Railmead Plantation
Mitchells Farm
River Roding
Shalesmere Nursery
Shalesmere Cottage
River Roding
TAWNEY LANE
M25 MOTORWAY
LONDON RD
LONDON ROAD
A113
Passingford Bridge
Suttons Manor
Suttons
Sutton's Farm
Playing Field
Howle Hall
Arnolds Farm
Little Arnolds
Mill House
ONGAR ROAD
A113
Arnold's Farm Cottages
Warehouse
Passingford Bridge Mill
WORKS
Passingford Bridge
M25
Waters Farm
ALBYNS LANE
River Roding
STAPLEFORD TAWNEY AIRFIELD
The Lodge
North East Lodge
Lower Wood
Burrow Wood
ROAD
B175
Rookery Wood
Green Farm Cotts.
Green Farm
Grafton Farm
ALBYNS LA.
Hammonds
Bons Farm
Church Wood
Albyns Manor
Albyns Hall
Lady Abdy's Walk
Curtismill Green
Curtismill Green
Landend Cottage
Thatched Cottage
Rose Cottages
Willow Cottage
MILL LANE
Woodside Farm
CHURCH TERRACE
CHURCH LA.
Kirton's Fm.
Gordon Cotts.
Deerbarn Wood
Bourne Brook
Brook
Church Farm
Bentleyfield Wood
CURTIS MILL LANE
Old Rectory Farm
Horsemans Lodge
STAPLEFORD ROAD
EPPING FOREST
Battles Hall
LANE
The Harrow
Curtis Mill Cottage
Stapleford Abbotts Prim. Sch.
STAPLEFORD ABBOTTS
Belmont Fm.
37
Grove House
Stapleford Hall Fm.
Tyseahill Farm
Spring Farm
Rose Cottage
High House Farm
GUTTERIDGE LA.
Olives Farm
RM4
THE PADDOCKS
Mitchell's Farm
Brook
Woodlands Fm.
B175
Blackbush Farm
High Willows
Ashwood Farm
HAVERING ROAD
Knolls Hill Farm
Bourne
Stocks Farm
Tysea Hill
Nursery
THE DRIVE
Brook Farm
Stapleford Farm
Twinoaks Farm
Nuper's Hatch
Nuper's Farm
Club House
Skips
Pinchback Bridge
TYSEA HILL
BOURNEBRIDGE LANE
Lyngs Farm
Asheton Fm.
Bournebridge Farm
LANE
OAK HILL ROAD
Stapleford Common
Crown Park Farm
KENSINGTON PK.
TOWNLEY COTTS.
TYSEA
Bourne Bridge
Butcher's Farm
Boyland's Oak Farm
Romford
Spencers Farm
Bournebridge
Nursery
Greenacres Farm
Straights Plantation
Lodge
Palace Plantation
Sandpits Plantation
Spurgate Brook
Hilly Park
Home Farm
Witch Hill Plantation
Horseshoe Farm
Osier Bed
Sandhills
Wilderness
Play. Fld.
Bower Farm
BOWER FARM
Dame Tipping C of E Prim. School
HAVERING
South Park Plantation
PYRGO PARK
Foreberry Wood North
Lower Sandhills
Pheasant Wood
SAMANTHA M.
ROWLAND WLK
Round House Farm
Park Farm
HAVERING-ATTE-BOWER
Riding Stables
St. Francis Hospice
Avenue Wood
AVENUE
WELLINGTONIA
NORTH ROAD
The Round House
BROXHILL
Ckt. Grd.
Pav.
WELLINGTONIA
CLOCKHOUSE
HAVERING COUNTRY PARK
56
ORANGE TREE HILL
Country Farm
Orange Tree Inn
Bower Farm
Foreberry Wood South
Pine Wood
PINEWOOD ROAD
Field

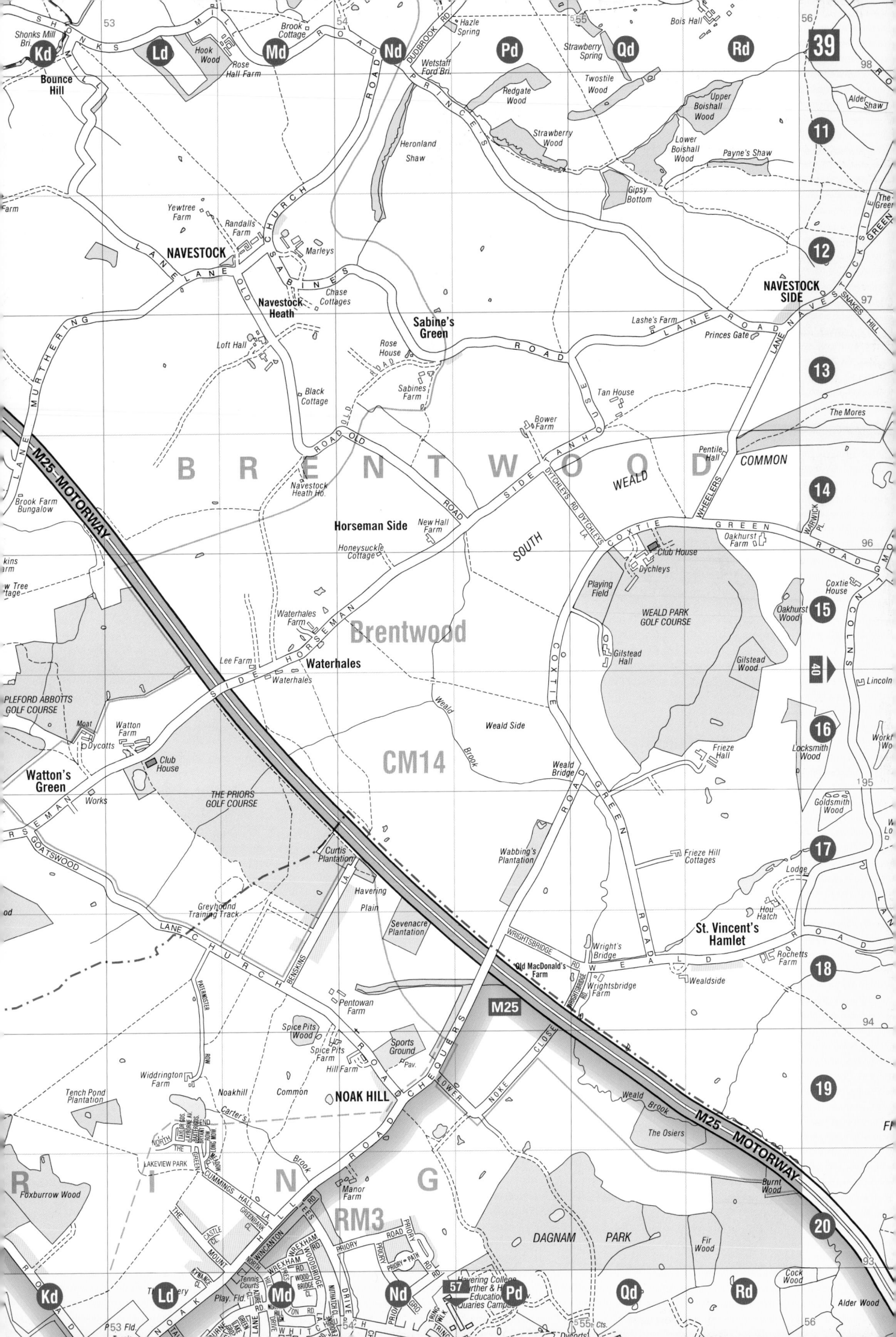

39
Bounce Hill
Hook Wood
Rose Hall Farm
Brook Cottage
Hazle Spring
Wetstaff Ford Bri.
Redgate Wood
Strawberry Spring
Twostile Wood
Strawberry Wood
Bois Hall
Upper Boishall Wood
Lower Boishall Wood
Payne's Shaw
Alder Shaw
Gipsy Bottom
Heronland Shaw
Yewtree Farm
Randalls Farm
NAVESTOCK
Marleys
Navestock Heath
Chase Cottages
Sabine's Green
NAVESTOCK SIDE
Lashe's Farm
Princes Gate
Loft Hall
Rose House
Sabines Farm
Black Cottage
Tan House
Bower Farm
The Mores
Pentile Hall
COMMON
WEALD
BRENTWOOD
Navestock Heath Ho.
Brook Farm Bungalow
Horseman Side
New Hall Farm
Honeysuckle Cottage
SOUTH
Club House
Dychleys
Oakhurst Farm
Playing Field
WEALD PARK GOLF COURSE
Coxtie House
Oakhurst Wood
Waterhales Farm
Brentwood
Gilstead Hall
Gilstead Wood
Lee Farm
Waterhales
40
Lincoln
Weald Side
Weald Brook
CM14
Watton Farm
Moat
Dycotts
Club House
Watton's Green
Works
THE PRIORS GOLF COURSE
Weald Bridge
Frieze Hall
Locksmith Wood
Goldsmith Wood
Wabbing's Plantation
Frieze Hill Cottages
Curtis Plantation
Havering Plain
Greyhound Training Track
Sevenacre Plantation
Lodge
Hou Hatch
St. Vincent's Hamlet
Wright's Bridge
Old MacDonald's Farm
Wrightsbridge Farm
Wealdside
Rochetts Farm
M25
M25 MOTORWAY
Pentowan Farm
Spice Pits Wood
Spice Pits Farm
Sports Ground
Pav.
Hill Farm
Widdrington Farm
Tench Pond Plantation
Noakhill
Common
NOAK HILL
The Osiers
Weald Brook
Carter's Brook
LAKEVIEW PARK
Foxburrow Wood
Manor Farm
RM3
DAGNAM PARK
Fir Wood
Burnt Wood
Cock Wood
Alder Wood
Havering College
Quaries Campus
57
Play. Fld.
Tennis Courts

40
Kelvedon Common
Fox Hatch
Doddinghurst Common
NAVESTOCK SIDE
BENTLEY
BENTLEY GOLF COURSE
Crow Green
COMMON
Coxtie Green
PILGRIMS HATCH
CM14
Vincent's Hamlet
WEALD COUNTRY PARK
SOUTH WEALD
BRENTWOOD
ST. FAITH'S COUNTRY PARK
FRONT PARK
M25 MOTORWAY
ONGAR ROAD
BRENTWOOD BY-PASS
LONDON ROAD
HIGH ROAD
39
58

41
MOUNTNESSING
HUTTON
SHENFIELD
HUTTON MOUNT
Brentwood
CM15
CM13
PARK WOOD
Pettit's Farm
America Farm
Long Wood
Fox Earth Wood
Heard's Farm
Icehouse Wood
Fitzwalter's
Moat
HOME WOOD
Chelmwood Farm
Thoby Farm
Bakers Farm
Drury's Farm
Hillrise Farm
Mountnessing Windmill
Mountnessing C of E Prim. Sch.
Master John's Farm
Holbrooks Cottages
Chain Bridge
Chainbridge Farm
Junction 12
Marylands
MARYLANDS INTERCHANGE
Arnold's Farm
Arnold's Shaw
Arnold's Wood
Brickley Shaw
Palmer's Farm
Palmer's Farm Cottages
Howe's Farm
Blue House
Brick House Farm
Greytoni Farm
Keepers Cottage
Canterbury Tye Spring
Wynbarns Farm
Shenfield High Sch. & Sports Centre
Long Ridings Prim. Sch.
Shenfield Hall
Shenfield Hall Farm
Hall Wood
MERRYMEADE COUNTRY PARK
St. Mary's C of E Prim. Sch.
Shenfield
Fire Brigade HQ
Willowbrook Prim. Sch.
Hutton Rec. Grd.
Sports Ground
St. Martin's School
Playing Field
South Hove
Brindles Farm
Hall Wood
Sewage Works
Ingrave Hall
Sutton Shaw
Scout Camp
Thriftwood International Scout Activity Centre
Hogarth Prim. Sch.
The Endeavour Sch.
BRENTWOOD NUFFIELD HEALTH HOSPITAL
BRENTWOOD COMMUNITY HOSPITAL
Brentwood Prep. Sch.
Sports Ground Brentwood Sch. Track
Brentwood Sch.
Brentwood High Sch.
Shenfield Common
Three Arch Bridge
Seven Arch Bridge
Ingrave Common
Birches Wood
High School Play. Fld.
St. Helens RC Jun. & Inf. Schs.
Sion Community
A12
A1023
A129
A128
B1002
B186
WOOD
MOUNTNESSING
A12-BY-PASS
ROMAN ROAD
CHELMSFORD ROAD
RAYLEIGH ROAD
HUTTON ROAD
SHENFIELD ROAD
INGRAVE ROAD
Zd Ae Be Ce De Ee Fe
11 12 13 14 15 16 17 18 19 20
59

42
24
62
CHALFONT COMMON
THE NATIONAL SOCIETY FOR EPILEPSY
CHILTERN
THREE
MAPLE CROSS
Horn Hill
Gravel Hill
WEST HYDE
Gerrards Cross
SL9
CHALFONT ST. PETER
HOGTROUGH WOOD
GERRARDS CROSS GOLF COURSE
AUSTENWOOD
GERRARDS CROSS
NOCKHILL WOOD
JUNIPER WOOD
THE MARISH
OAKEND WOOD
SOUTH BUCKS
DENHAM AERODROME
DENHAM GOLF COURSE
M25 MOTORWAY
AMERSHAM ROAD A413
GRAVEL HILL
CHALFONT ST. PETER BY-PASS
DENHAM (NORTH ORBITAL ROAD) A412
OXFORD RD. A40
Denham Golf Club

43
25
44
63
Rickmansworth
WD3
THREE RIVERS
RIVERS
HILLINGDON
Uxbridge
UB9
Batchworth Heath
Woodcock Hill
Hill End
HAREFIELD
Mount Pleasant
SOUTH HAREFIELD
BROADWATER
Denham Garden Village
DENHAM GREEN
Newyears Green
HAREFIELD HOSPITAL
BATCHWORTH PARK GOLF COURSE
BAYHURST WOOD COUNTRY PARK
Harefield United FC (Preston Park)
Rickmansworth Sailing Club
Hillingdon Outdoor Activities Centre
The Harefield Academy
Dews Farm Sand Pits Nature Reserve
Old Park Wood Nature Reserve
PARK WOOD
GRAND UNION CANAL
DENHAM WAY
(NORTH ORBITAL ROAD)
A412
A404
RICKMANSWORTH LONDON RD.
RICKMANSWORTH ROAD
BREAKSPEAR ROAD NORTH
HAREFIELD RD.
WOODCOCK HILL
SHRUBS RD.
WHITE HILL
NEW YEARS GREEN LANE
MOORHALL ROAD
PARK LANE
CHURCH HILL
HIGH ST.
Bishop's Wood
Park Wood
Cooks Wood
Pearson's Wood
Ashain Spring
Scarlet Spring
Long Spring
Sixteen Acre Spring
Watercress Beds
Springwell Lake
Lynsters Lake
Weybeards Farm
White Heath Farm
Colney Farm
Knightscote Farm
Langley Farm
Bourne Farm
Middle Lodge
Park Lodge Farm
Park Lodge Cottage
Savay Farm
Dewes Farm
Highway Farm
Pylon Farm
Braemar Farm
Reservoir (covered)
Harefield Reservoir (covered)
Battlers Wells Farm
Battlers Wells Wood
Furzefield
Deadman's Grove
Kiln Pond
Claypits
Dell
Gravel Pit
Sand & Gravel Works
Widewater Lock
Black Jacks Lock
Black Jack's Mill
Springwell Lock
Sewage Works
Watts Common
Taylors Meadow Sports Ground
Harefield Jun. & Inf. Schs.
Denham Laboratories
Moorhall Cottages
Halfway House
Pumping Station
Harefield Moor
Lower Lodge
The Bungalow
Dewes Farm Cottages
Newyears Green Covert
Battlesford Wood
Ranston Covert
Nightingale Wood
Wadley Covert
West Hyde House
Troy Mill Flats
Pipers Farm
Bush Spring
Woodcock Hill Barns
Wellingrove House
Sandfield Spring
Greenbroom Spring
Poorfield
Lockwell Wood
Howard Spring
Whipping Spring
Shepherds Hill Farm
Shepherds Hill House
Waterfall
Harefield Grove
Slaley
Sikora
French Grove
Badminton Shooting Ground
Warren Farm
Cripp's Farm
Quarry Farm
Garrett Wood
High Wood
Chalk Pit
Juniper Dell
Andrews Ley Farm
Cemetery
Driving Range
Nursing Home
Parkwood Farm Kennels
Sports Ground
One Tree Hill
Broadwater Farm
War Meml.
Nursery
Horse Shoe Bay
Maplelodge Farm
Mapple Lodge Nature Reserve
Gravel Pit
Weybeards Cotts.
El Sub Sta.
WYATT'S COVERT
Denham
04
05
06
07
88
89
90
91
92
93
H
J
K
L
M
N
P
21
22
23
24
25
26
27
28
29
30

44
26
43
64
Q
R
S
T
U
V
W
21
22
23
24
25
26
27
28
29
30
07
08
09
510
93
92
91
90
89
88
MOOR PARK
SANDY LODGE GOLF COURSE
MOOR PARK GOLF CO
Rickmansworth
Batchworth Heath
LONDON (BATCHWORTH HEATH HILL)
A404
WD3
Home Farm
Bathend Clump
Howard Spring
Batchworth Heath Farm
Whipping Spring
Park Wood
White Hill
Poorfield
Lockwell Wood
Lockwell
BISHOPS WOOD BMI HOSP.
MIU
MOUNT VERNON HOSPITAL
Hospice
Reservoir (covered)
Harefield Reservoir (covered)
Battlers Wells Farm
Battlers Wells Wood
French Grove
Northwood Health & Racquets Club (Virgin Active)
Tennis Courts
THREE RIVERS
EASTBURY
HMS Warrior
Pretty Corner
NORTHWOOD
St. Helen's School
St. Helen's Swim. & Fitness Club
Northwood
Northwood College
London Sch. of Theology
Holy Trinity C of E Sch.
St. Martin's Sch.
Playing Field
RICKMANSWORTH ROAD
WATFORD
GREEN LANE
HA6
NORTHWOOD GOLF COURSE
Club House
Denville Hall
The Gravel Pits
DUCK'S HILL ROAD
A4180
A4125
Furzefield
Deadman's Grove
Duck's Hill Farm
Ducks Hill Grange
Duck's Hill
Scarlet Spring
Raveners Spring
Badminton Shooting Ground
Ashby Cottages
Ashby Farm
Dell
HILLINGDON
Uxbridge
COPSE WOOD
RUISLIP WOODS (National Nature Reserve)
Miniature Rifle Range
HASTE HILL GOLF COURSE
Haste Hill
Poor's Field
YOUNG WOOD
MAD BESS WOOD
NORTH RIDING WOOD
Warren Farm
BREAKSPEAR ROAD
BAYHURST WOOD COUNTRY PARK
UB9
Willow Tree Centre
Willow Tree Farm
Mad Bess Wood Cottage
RUISLIP COMMON
Breakspear Crematorium (Ruislip)
Football Ground
Playing Field
Ruislip Lido Railway
Waters Edge
RUISLIP LIDO
Ruislip Lido Woodlands Centre
Woody Bay
PARK WOOD
Cannons Bridge Farm
Hillingdon Athletic Club
Ruislip
HA4
NORTHWOOD HILLS
Northwood Hills
LA Fitness
Northwood FC
Cemetery
PINNER ROAD
JOEL STREET
Haydon School
Joel Street Farm
Playing Field
Nurseries
Grangewood School
Coteford Junior Sch.
Kings College Playing Fields
Eastcote Hockey & Badminton Club
King's Coll. Play. Flds. Track
Pinn River
Oak Cottage
FINE BUSH LA
St. Leonard's Farm
NEW YEARS GREEN LANE
Newyears Green
Pylon Farm
Elm Tree Farm
High View Fm.
Braemar Farm
Crows Nest Farm
Old Clack Farm
Whiteheath Jun. & Inf. Schs.
BURY STREET
Winston Churchill Hall
Manor Farm
Highgrove Swim. Pool
EASTCOTE ROAD
B466
B469
B472

GOLF COURSE
Carpenders Park
St. Joseph's Catholic Primary School
Little Furze Field
Beck Mason's Wood
OXHEY WOODS
SOUTH OXHEY
Mutton Wood
Carpenders Park Cemetery
Sandpit Wood
Woodhall Prim. Sch.
Valley View Farm
GRIM'S DYKE GOLF COURSE
Club House
Weald Wood
Stony Wood
Grim's Ditch
Grim's Dyke
OXHEY LANE
LITTLE OXHEY LANE
B4542
PRESTWICK ROAD
Sir James Altham Pool
Nature Reserve
Nanscot Wood
Oxheylane Farm
A4008
Grimswood Lodge
Grimswood House
Highcroft
The Lodge
Harrow HA3
Birchanger
Reservoir (covered)
Pinnerwood House
Pinnerwood Farm
Pinnerwood Cottage
Grimsdyke Sch.
Saddlers Mead
Hatch End Lawn Ten. Club
Playing Fields
Bannister Sports Centre
Pinner Wood
PINNER HILL GOLF COURSE
Shaftesbury Playing Fields
Cricket Club
Hatch End
UXBRIDGE ROAD
A410
Superstore
Harrow Arts Cen.
Hatch End Play. Flds.
HATCH END
Hatch End High Sch.
Pinnerwood Park
HARROW
Rugby Football Ground
Bedford Coll. Sports Grd.
Headstone Lane
Pinner Wood Sch.
PINNER GREEN
Montesole Play. Flds.
A404
DR. GEORGE V AVENUE
PINNER PARK
Pinner Park Farm
Pinner Lawn Tennis Club
Headstone Lane Sports Grd.
RICKMANSWORTH RD.
Little Common
Paine's Br.
Cemetery
Play Fld.
Pinner Pk. Schs.
Sports Ground
Harlyn Primary Sch.
CUCKOO HILL
Cuckoo Hill
NHS Walk-in
Hlth Club
Pinner Village Hall
Pinner Memorial Park
Pinner
Superstore
Nower Hill
Pinner New Cemetery
Nower Hill High Sch.
Headstone Manor Recreation Ground
Harrow Museum
Yeading Brook
West Lodge Prim. Sch.
HA5
PINNER
Reddiford Sch.
Harrow
HEADSTONE
Woodlands Open Space
Mosque
EASTCOTE VILLAGE
Eastcote Ho. Gs.
Pinner Village Gardens
North Harrow
Yeading Brook Open Space
A4090
NORTH HARROW
HA2
Longfield Prim. Sch.
The Croft
Play. Fld.
Cannon Lane Prim. Sch.
Heathfield Sch. for Girls
Streamside Rec. Grd.
IMPERIAL DRIVE
Vaughan Prim. Sch.
West Harrow
EASTCOTE
PINNER ROAD
65
46
27
X Y Z Aa Ba Ca Da
21 22 23 24 25 26 27 28 29 30

46
Ea
Fa
Ga
Ha
Ja
Ka
La
GOLF COURSE
Bentley Priory Mus.
Bentley Priory
28
HARROW WEALD
COMMON
Levels Wood
The Princess Alexandra Home
Bentley Priory Local Nature Reserve
Stanmore Hall
STANMORE COUNTRY PARK (Local Nature Reserve)
Grim's Ditch
Grim's Dyke
Nurseries
Grimsdyke Open Space
Harrow Weald Common
The Old Barn
Heriot's Wood
Deer Park
Heriots
21
Weald Wood
REDDING
COMMON ROAD
BROOKSHILL
Hertfordshire & Middlesex Country Club
Copse Farm
Priory House
Lower Priory Farm
Nursery
Stony Wood
22
Grimswood House
Highcroft
Hermitage Cottages
Hermitage Gate
Bentley Wood High Sch.
Boot Pond
St. John's C of E Sch.
STANMORE HILL
A4140
A409
A410
LONDON ROAD
THE BROADWAY
CHURCH RD.
MARSH
Stanmore Rec. Grd.
Harrow Weald Cemetery
Woodland Hall
Brockhurst Cnr.
Harrow Coll. (Harrow Weald Campus)
Play. Fld.
STANMORE
Stanmore College
Temple Pond
Club House
OXHEY LA.
A4008
23
Playing Fields
Bannister Sports Centre
UXBRIDGE ROAD
HIGH ROAD
The Cedars
24
STANMORE GOLF COURSE
Sports Ground
HARROW WEALD
Superstore
Bus Depot
Harrow Weald Lawn Tennis Club
Recreation Ground
Cedars Manor Sch.
Hatch End High Sch.
Weald Schs.
Stanburn Schs.
25
Prim. Sch.
Headstone Lane
26
Headstone Lane Sports Grd.
Salvatorian Coll.
BELMONT
Belmont Sch.
HA3
Play Field
Priestmead Rec. Grd.
Pinner Pk. Schs.
27
Sports Ground
Works
ST. GEORGE'S WAY
GANGE WAY
Open Air Theatre
Headstone Manor
Harrow Museum
Harrow Crown Court
Harrow & Wealdstone
WEALDSTONE
Byron Recreation Ground
Cemetery
Harrow Leisure Centre
Harrow Driving, Cycling and Road Safety Centre
Headstone Manor Recreation Ground
Yeading Brook
28
HEADSTONE
Sports Grd.
HA1
Civic Centre
STATION ROAD
Elmgrove Prim. Sch.
Kenton Recreation Ground
KENTON
Bowling Green
29
Old Lyonian Sports Club
Harrow Recreation Ground
GREENHILL
Superstore
Harrow Cemetery
Rec. Grd.
GREENHILL WAY
A4005
A404
PINNER ROAD
SHEEPCOTE ROAD
A4006
KENTON ROAD
30
H HARROW
Vaughan Prim. Sch.
West Harrow
LOWLANDS
Harrow-on-the-Hill
Bus Sta.
66
St. Ann's Shopping Cen.
Sports Cen.
Halls of Residence
University of Westminster (Harrow Campus)
Harrow Sports Hall
HARROW HILL GOLF COURSE
Northwick Park
Kenton
HARROW

47
Ma
Na
Pa
Qa
Ra
Sa
Ta
29
EDGWARE WAY
EDGWARE (WATFORD BY-PASS)
A41
BROCKLEY HILL
A5
SPUR ROAD
Stanmore
A410
Stonegrove
London Academy
St. Mary's Convent
DEANS LANE
HALE LANE
SELVAGE LANE
A5109
MOTORWAY
M1
WATFORD WY.
APEX CORNER
21
22
23
24
25
26
27
28
29
30
The Hale
A5100
Mill Hill Broadway
Lyndhurst Park
Mill Hill Old Railway Nature Reserve
STONEGROVE
HIGH STREET
STATION ROAD
Edgware
Edgware Bus Sta.
Bus Depot
EDGWARE
Stonegrove Park
The Basin
Lake Grove Rec. Grd
The Lake
North London Collegiate School
King George V Memorial Gdns.
CANONS PARK
Canons Park
WHITCHURCH
B461
DEANSBROOK
BURNT OAK
Burnt Oak
EDGWARE COMM HOSP.
Watling
WATLING PARK
Chandos Recreation Grd.
LITTLE STANMORE
HA8
Barnet FC & London Broncos RLFC (The Hive)
The Hive Football & Fitness Centre
Prince Edward Playing Field
Canons High Sch.
QUEENSBURY
Queensbury
HONEYPOT LANE
A4140
BROADWAY
EDGWARE ROAD
Montrose Recreation Ground
National Blood Service
COLINDALE
Colindale
Mecca Burnt Oak
Silk Stream Park
Eton Grove Open Space
Roe Green
NW9
Kingsbury High Sch.
Roe Green Park
Kingsbury Manor
Kingsbury Manor Studio
Queensbury Park
St Bernadette's Catholic Prim. Sch.
KENTON ROAD
A4006
Kingsbury
KINGSBURY ROAD
FRYENT WAY
St. Luke's Hospice
WOODCOCK PARK
Recreation Ground
Kingsbury Grn. Prim. Sch.
St. Robert Southwell RC Prim. Sch.
JFS School
CHURCH LANE
B454
Kingsbury Green
FRYENT COUNTRY PARK
KINGSBURY
Silver Jubilee Park
Kingsbury Town FC Grd.
67
FRYENT COUNTRY PARK (Local Nature Reserve)
Mt. Stewart Jun. & Inf. Sch.
WOODCOCK
18
19
520
21

48
Ua
Va
Wa
Xa
Ya
Za
Ab
21
22
23
24
25
26
27
28
29
30
47
68
M1
Junction 2
FIVEWAYS CORNER
APEX CORNER
MILL HILL CIRCUS
MILL HILL
NW7
NW4
NW9
Mill Hill Broadway
The Hale
Edgware
Grahame Park
Colindale
COLINDALE
HENDON
Hendon Central
THE HYDE
Brent Cross
Holders Hill
Mill Hill East
Folly Farm
Burtonhole Lane Farm Estate
Burtonhole Farm
National Centre for Medical Research
Mill Hill Sub. Sta.
London Equestrian Centre
Partingdale Manor
Oakfield House
Wentworth Hall
Drivers Hill
The Mount Sch.
Watch Tower House
Mill Hill Cemetery
Bittacy Hill Park
Inglis Barracks
Featherstone Hill
Arrandene Open Space
Mill Hill School
Belmont Farm
Lawrence Green
The Mill Field
Holcombe Ho.
Copthall Leisure Centre
Saracens RFC (Allianz Park)
Shaftesbury Barnet Harriers
Metro Golf Centre
BARNET COPTHALL SPORTS CENTRE
HENDON GOLF COURSE
Hendon Crematorium
HENDON CEMETERY
Rugby Club
Chase Lodge Playing Fields
Powerleague Soccer Cen.
Dollis Jun. & Inf. Schs.
SUNNY HILL PARK
RAF Museum London
Battle of Britain Hall
Peel Centre (Metropolitan Police Training Establishment)
THE GARDEN BMI HOSP
Middlesex University
Windsor Open Space
Lyndhurst Park
Woodcroft Park
Colindale Park
National Blood Service
Rushgrove Park
HENDON PARK
BRENT CROSS INTERCHANGE
Brent Cross Shopping Centre
WEST HENDON PLAYING FIELDS
Kingsbury Town FC Grd.
Youth Sailing Base
Cool Oak Bridge
Silver Jubilee Park
WATFORD WAY
THE RIDGEWAY
M1 MOTORWAY
GREAT NORTH WAY (BARNET BY-PASS)
EDGWARE ROAD
THE HYDE
WEST HENDON BROADWAY
HENDON WAY
STATION ROAD
FINCHLEY LANE
BRENT STREET
HOLDERS HILL ROAD
NORTH CIRCULAR ROAD
GOLDERS GREEN ROAD
COLINDEEP LANE
KINGSBURY ROAD
QUEENS ROAD
THE BURROUGHS
CHURCH RD.
PARSON STREET
BITTACY HILL
PARTINGDALE LANE
DAWS LANE
THE BROADWAY
HALE LANE
DEANSBROOK ROAD
AERODROME ROAD
GRAHAME PARK WAY
A1
A41
A5
A406
A502
A504
A5100
A5150
A4006
B552
B1461
B551

49
31
50
69
Bb
Cb
Db
Eb
Fb
Gb
Hb
21
22
23
24
25
26
27
28
29
30
Woodside Park
Woodside Park Club
FINCHLEY GOLF COURSE
Frith Manor Prim. Sch.
West Finchley
Finchley Central
FINCHLEY
NORTH FINCHLEY
Tally Ho Corner
Fallow Corner
FINCHLEY MEM. HOSP.
NORTH MIDDLESEX GOLF COURSE
Friary Park
FRIERN BARNET
Bethune Park
Recreation Ground
COLNEY HATCH
Coppetts Wood & Glebelands Local Nature Reserve
Rugby Football Ground
Cricket & Football Grounds
Glebe Land Open Space
Great North Leisure Park
Strawberry Vale
Islington Crematorium
ST. PANCRAS & ISLINGTON CEM.
Muswell Hill Spts. Grd.
COLDFALL WOOD
Powerleague Soccer Cen.
Victoria Park
Avenue House Grounds
Sports Ground
Pentland Centre
St. Marylebone Crematorium
EAST FINCHLEY CEMETERY
Christ's College Finchley
EAST FINCHLEY
East Finchley
Cherry Tree Wood Rec. Grd.
FORTIS GREEN
Fortismere Sch. (North Wing)
Fortismere Sch. (South Wing)
Big Wood
Little Wood
Mutton Brook
HAMPSTEAD GARDEN SUBURB
HAMPSTEAD GOLF COURSE
HAMPSTEAD HEATH
Bunkers Hill
HARINGEY
HIGHGATE GOLF COURSE
HIGHGATE
HIGHGATE HOSPITAL
HIGHGATE WOOD
Jewish Cemetery
Golders Green Crematorium
GOLDERS GREEN
HENLYS CORNER
N20
N12
N3
N2
N10
N6
NW11
HIGH ROAD
BALLARDS LANE
REGENTS PARK ROAD
FINCHLEY ROAD
GREAT NORTH ROAD
NORTH CIRCULAR ROAD
FALLODEN WAY
LYTTELTON ROAD
AYLMER ROAD
ARCHWAY RD.
EAST END ROAD
FORTIS GREEN
WOODHOUSE RD
FRIERN BARNET LANE
FRIERN BARNET ROAD
COLNEY HATCH LA.
BOBBY MOORE WAY
A1000
A598
A406
A504
A1003
A1
B550

50
NEW SOUTHGATE CEMETERY
Crematorium
ARNOS PARK
Arnos Grove
Palmers Green
ALDERMANS HILL
Broomfield Park
Sports Ground
NEW SOUTHGATE
New Southgate
COLNEY HATCH
Coppetts Wood & Glebelands Local Nature Reserve
NORTH CIRCULAR ROAD
PINKHAM WAY
BOUNDS GREEN RD.
Bounds Green
Bowes Park
BOWES ROAD
TELFORD RD.
MUSWELL HILL GOLF COURSE
Alexandra Park School
Albert Road Rec. Grd.
DURNSFORD RD.
ALEXANDRA PALACE
Alexandra Palace
WOOD GREEN
Wood Green
ALEXANDRA PARK
Pitch & Putt Course
The Lake
MUSWELL HILL
FORTIS GREEN
N10
N11
N14
N22
N8
N6
Cranley Gardens
HIGHGATE WOOD
QUEEN'S WOOD
Highgate
HIGHGATE
ARCHWAY RD
PRIORY RD
PARK ROAD
CROUCH END
HORNSEY
Hornsey
HORNSEY VALE
STROUD GREEN
Harringay
TOTTENHAM LA
TURNPIKE LA.
HIGH RD.
LORDSHIP LA
Park Road Leisure Centre
Hornsey Cricket Club
Priory Park
70
32
49

EDMONTON
UPPER EDMONTON
PYMMES PARK
Silver Street
NORTH MIDDLESEX UNIVERSITY HOSPITAL
GREAT CAMBRIDGE JUNCTION
NORTH CIRCULAR ROAD
STERLING WAY
ANGEL
Angel Rd.
CONDUIT LANE
MONTAGU RD.
FORE ST.
GREAT CAMBRIDGE ROAD
TOTTENHAM
TOTTENHAM CEMETERY
White Hart Lane
Tottenham Hotspur FC (White Hart Lane)
Northumberland Park
BRUCE CASTLE PARK
Bruce Castle Mus.
LORDSHIP LANE
LORDSHIP RECREATION GROUND
The Moselle
Bruce Grove
BRUCE GROVE
HIGH ROAD
TOTTENHAM HALE
Tottenham Hale
FERRY LANE
FOREST RD.
MONUMENT WAY
HALE RD.
WATERMEAD WAY
Tottenham Marshes
LOCKWOOD RESERVOIR
LOW MAYNARD RESERVOIR
Lee Valley Park
River Lee Navigation
DOWNHILLS PARK
WEST GREEN
WEST GREEN ROAD
PHILIP LANE
BROAD LANE
Seven Sisters
South Tottenham
SOUTH TOTTENHAM
ST. ANN'S ROAD
ST. ANN'S HOSPITAL
SEVEN SISTERS RD.
Markfield Beam Engine & Museum
Markfield Recreation Ground
WARWICK RESERVOIR (EAST)
WARWICK RESERVOIR (WEST)
RESERVOIR No.1
RESERVOIR No.2
RESERVOIR No.3
Harringay Green Lanes
GRAND PARADE
GREEN LANES
Stamford Hill
AMHURST PK.
CLAPTON
Copper Mills Junction
Walthamstow Marsh Nature Reserve
Coppermill Bridge
N17
N18
N9
N15
N16
E17

52
Yb
Zb
Ac
Bc
Cc
Dc
Ec
34
72
21
22
23
24
25
26
27
28
29
30
Tottenham Park Cemetery
Federation Cemetery (Jewish)
Montagu Rec. Grd.
MERIDIAN WAY
A1055
Teamsport Karting
ENFIELD
Refuse Incineration Plant
Works
Pumping Station
River Lee Navigation
River Lee Diversion
CONDUIT LANE
Angel Rd.
ANGEL ROAD
A406
LEA VALLEY VIADUCT
SOUTHEND ROAD
NORTH CIRCULAR ROAD
HALL LANE
A1009
WALTHAM WAY
CHINGFORD MOUNT
NEW ROAD
A1009
OLD CHURCH RD.
Suffield Hatch
Chingford Fitness Cen.
Chingford Leisure Centre
Larkswood Playing Fields
Larks Wood
Larkswood Park
Larkswood Club
Chase Lane Park
SOUTH CHINGFORD
CHINGFORD MOUNT RD.
A112
CHINGFORD RD.
Ainslie Wood Nature Reserve
Rolls Sports Grd.
HIGHAMS PARK
Foundation School
Playing Field
Peter May Sports Cen.
WINCHESTER RD.
Superstore
Works
Powerleague Soccer Cen.
Northumberland Park
HARINGEY
LEE VALLEY PARK
BANBURY RESERVOIR
Valve Tower
Chalk Bridge
Golf Driving Range
Playing Field
Sports Ground
Britannia Sports Grd.
Walthamstow Academy
CROOKED BILLET
SOUTHEND ROAD
Recreation Ground
N17
Rec. Ground
William Morris Sch.
Stonebridge Locks
LOCKWOOD RESERVOIR
Lee Flood Relief Channel
BILLET ROAD
B179
Higham Hill Park
Whittingham Prim. Acad.
HIGHAM HILL
BLACKHORSE LANE
Chapel End
Hillyfield Prim. Sch.
LLOYD PARK
WALTHAMSTOW
Town Hall
Civic Cen.
College
Waltham Forest Pool & Track
Chestnuts Sports Ground
FULBOURNE ROAD
FOREST ROAD
THE BELL
THORPE COOMBE HOSP.
WOOD STREET
LOW MAYNARD RESERVOIR
HIGH MAYNARD RESERVOIR
Warehouses
WATERMEAD WAY
Lee Valley Park
FERRY LA.
FOREST ROAD
A503
Blackhorse Rd.
College
BLACKHORSE RD.
A1006
HOE STREET
Walthamstow Central
Walthamstow Queens Rd.
Bus Sta.
RESERVOIR No. 4
RESERVOIR No. 2
RESERVOIR No. 3
RESERVOIR No. 1
RESERVOIR No. 5
Douglas Eyre Playing Fields
Douglas Eyre Sports Centre
Games Court
WARWICK RESERVOIR (EAST)
St. James St.
ST. JAMES'S ST.
MARKHOUSE RD.
Queens Road Cemetery
ST. JAMES'S PARK
Walthamstow Leisure Cen.
WATER WORKS
Filter Beds
Playing Field
Low Hall Sports Ground
Copper Mill Junct.
Walthamstow Marsh Nature Reserve
Coppermill Bridge
High Bri.
LEYTON LINK ESTATE
FOREST BUSINESS PARK
LEA BRIDGE ROAD
A104
LEYTON GRN. RD.
HIGH STREET
Bus Depot

53
WOODFORD WELLS
Knighton Wood
WOODFORD GOLF COURSE
Football Ground
The Lops
Roding Valley
Rugby Football Ground
Chigwell Sewage Works
Woodford Side
HATCH LA.
CHINGFORD LANE
A1009
The Highams Park
Boating Lake
Highams Park
WOODFORD GREEN
Sports Ground
HIGHAMS PARK
HALE END
Haven Ho. Hospice
Rugby Football Grd.
Woodford High Sch. for Girls
Ashton Playing Fields
James Leal Cen.
Ray Park
Ray Lodge Prim. Sch.
M11 MOTORWAY
Woodford Green Athletic Cen.
Woodford
WOODFORD
BROADMEAD ROAD
EPPING FOREST
NEW WOODFORD ROAD
A104
HIGH ROAD WOODFORD GREEN
Hotel
Woodbridge High Sch.
Playing Field
Winn Bridge
Daisy Lake
Cemetery
Sports Ground
A406
WATERWORKS CORNER
Walthamstow Forest
Reservoir (covered)
Junction 4
SOUTHEND ROAD
A1199
NORTH CIRCULAR ROAD
Superstore
CHARLIE BROWN'S ROUNDABOUT
South Woodford
SOUTH WOODFORD
E18
A503
Hyland Ho. School
Gilbert's Slade
Abbeydale
Boating Pond
Community Hall
Sports Ground
RODING SPIRE HOSPITAL
Hatton School
PDSA (Veterinary Centre)
Beal High Sch.
Sylvestrian Leisure Cen.
Forest Sch.
UPPER WALTHAMSTOW
Round Pond
SNARESBROOK ROAD
Eagle Pond
SNARESBROOK
Snaresbrook Crown Court
Snaresbrook
Hollow Pond (Boating Lake)
WHIPPS CROSS ROAD
A114
WHIPPS CROSS UNIV. HOSP.
WOODBURY UNIT
Margaret Centre
Epping Temple Forest
HOLLYBUSH HILL
WANSTEAD
E11
Recreation Grd.
REDBRIDGE ROUNDABOUT
EASTERN AVENUE
A12
Leisure Cen.
Wanstead High School
Wanstead
Pumping Station
Golf Course
SOUTH WOODFORD TO BARKING RELIEF ROAD
Redbridge
REDBRIDGE
Ilford
IG4
IG8
IG9
The Heronry
Lincoln Island
CAMBRIDGE PARK
A106
BLAKE HALL RD.
73
35
54

CHIGWELL
Chigwell
Library
Old Loughtonians Hockey Club
New Barns Farm
Rugby Football Ground
Luxborough
Playing Fields
Chigwell Sewage Works
M11 MOTORWAY
M11
EPPING FOREST
West Hatch High School
Club House
CHIGWELL GOLF COURSE
Cemetery
Hill House
Ashton Playing Fields
Roding Valley Park
Sports Grd.
Woodford Green Athletic Cen. (Running Track)
Ray Lodge Prim. Sch.
St. John's RC Sch.
Lodge
Convent
Limes Farm Inf. & Jun. Schools
GRANGE HILL
Grange Hill
Hainault
HAINAULT ROAD
MANOR ROAD
HIGH ROAD
CHIGWELL ROAD
FENCEPIECE ROAD
TOMSWOOD ROAD
Redbridge
Woodford Green
IG8
WOODFORD BRIDGE
Roding Prim. Sch.
Repton Park
Health Club
Hospital Hill Wood
Hospital Hill
Cocked Hat Plantation
Egg Clump
Ash Plantation
Daisy Lake
Cuthbert Lake
Sports Ground
Playing Field
IG6
Ilford & Redbridge Hockey Club
Playing Field
Old Parkonians
The Jean Brown Indoor Arena
FAIRLOP
Forest Farm
Forest Farm Cottages
Redbridge Sports & Leisure Cen.
Fairlop
Oakfield Playing Field
Fairlop Lodge
Club House
FAIRLOP WATERS GOLF COURSE
New Rush Hall Sch.
Fairlop Prim. Sch.
FULLWELL CROSS
Ilford Jewish Prim. Sch.
King Solomon High Sch.
Playing Field
Ilford High Sch.
Fitness Cen.
High Sch.
IG5
CLAYHALL
Garden of Rest
Cemetery
Green Elms Barkingside Rec. Grd.
BARKINGSIDE
Barkingside
Redbridge FC (Oakside Stadium)
Avanti Court Primary School
Superstore
Fullwood Prim. Sch.
Sports Ground
PDSA (Veterinary Centre)
Beal High Sch.
Recreation Ground
Playground
CLAYHALL PARK
Tennis Courts
WOODFORD AVENUE
IG4
GANTS HILL
Gants Hill
CRANBROOK ROAD
EASTERN AVENUE
A12
REDBRIDGE
Redbridge
Jack Carter Centre
Sports Ground
Cranbrook Prim. Sch.
Cranbrook Castle Ten. Club
Valentines High Sch.
Valentines Mansion & Gardens
74
Ilford
Oaks Park High Sch.
NEWBURY PARK
Newbury Park
Aldborough Ho. Farm
STH. WOODFORD-TO-BARKING-RELIEF-ROAD
53
Nc
Pc
Qc
Rc
Sc
Tc
Uc
21
22
23
24
25
26
27
28
29
30
42
43
44
45

37
Vc
Wc
Xc
Yc
Zc
Ad
Bd
HAINAULT FOREST (COUNTRY PARK)
The Lake
Visitor Centre
Fox Burrows
Foxburrows Rare Breeds Farm & Zoo
Chigwell Row Wood Local Nature Reserve
Playing Fields
Tennis Courts
Wood View
Play. Field
Fairview
Old Hainault Oak
Dog Kennel Hill
HAINAULT FOREST GOLF COURSE
Nursery
Riding School
Reservoirs (covered)
Club Ho.
Golf Driving Range
Hainault Lodge Local Nature Reserve
Hog Hill
Redbridge Cycling Centre
Coppice Prim. Sch.
Forest Academy
HAINAULT
Cemetery
Forest Park Crematorium
Gardens of Peace (Muslim Cemetery)
Elmbridge Sports Ground
Club House
Skate Park
Forest Road Playing Field
Hainault Recreation Ground
Club House
Fairlop Oak Recreation Ground
Powerleague Soccer Cen.
Fairlop Sailing Centre
Fairlop Lake
FAIRLOP WATERS COUNTRY PARK
Lagoon
Farm Cottages
Hainault Works
Hainault Farm
Romford
BARKING and DAGENHAM
RM5
RM6
RM7
IG3
Marks Gate
Furze Cottage
Furze House Farm
The City Pavilion
Whites Farm
Mill Farm
Forest Farm Equestrian Centre
Cold Blow Farm
Gobions Farm
Football Grd.
Havering Park
Havering Lodge
Willoughby's Hill
Lower Park Farm
Park Farm
Sandhills
Plantation
ROMFORD ROAD
WHALEBONE LANE NORTH
HAINAULT ROAD
PAINTERS ROAD
FOREST ROAD
EASTERN AVENUE
A12
A1112
A118
B174
B177
Aldborough Hall Farm
ALDBOROUGH HATCH
Red House Farm
Hainault House
Willow Farm
Playing Field
Little Heath Sch.
Sports Ground
Chadwell Heath Cemetery
Jun. Sch.
Infant Sch.
Moat
Warren Farm
MOBY DICK
Moby Golf
Driving Range
Golf Kingdom
Warren Sports Centre
Warren Jun. Sch.
Playing Field
Golf Course
Crown Farm
Crown Cottages
KING GEORGE HOSPITAL
UCC
North Residence
South Residence
Redbridge College
Grove Prim. Sch.
Newbridge Sch.
LITTLE HEATH
GOODMAYES HOSPITAL
Bowling Green
Sports Ground
Club House
Sports Ground
Playing Field
SEVEN KINGS PARK
Farnham Green Prim. Sch.
Chadwell Millennium Green
ST. CHAD'S PARK
CHADWELL HEATH
Mecca Bingo
75
West Ham FC Training Grd.
St. Edward's C of E Sch.
Westlands Playing
Whalebone Bri.
56
21
22
23
24
25
26
27
28
29
30
46
47
48
49
88
89
90
91
92
93

HAVERING-ATTE-BOWER
St. Francis Hospice
Round House Farm
HAVERING COUNTRY PARK
Pine Wood
Foreberry Wood South
Lower Park Farm
Churchpath Plantation North
Kiln Wood
Poultry Farm
Orange Tree Inn
Bower Farm
Bower House
Bower Wood
Nursery
RM4
Willoughby's Hill
Havering Park
Larch Wood
Deer Park
Bedfords
BEDFORDS PARK
Bower Park School
CHASE CROSS
Community Centre
Clockhouse Primary School
RM5
Romford
Havering Lodge
COLLIER ROW
Sunnyside Farm
RISEBRIDGE GOLF COURSE
Club House
Gobions Farm
Lawns Rec. Grd.
RISE PARK
Football Grd.
The City Pavilion
Whites Farm
Crownfield Jun. & Inf. Schs.
Marshalls Park School
RAPHAEL PARK
Fish Ponds
Mawney
Warehouse
King Georges Field
MAWNEY PARK
RM7
RM1
Bus Depot
Romford County Ct.
Town Hall
LODGE FARM PARK
Park Lake
EASTERN AVENUE
A12
RM6
Golf Course
Crown Farm
Warren Sports Centre
Sports Ground
Cottons Park
Crown Cottages
St. Edward's C of E Sch.
Romford Stadium (Greyhound)
ROMFORD
Westlands Playing Field
West Ham FC Training Grd.
Crowlands
Gas Works
QUEEN'S HOSPITAL
HEATH PARK
HIGH RD.
LONDON ROAD
A118
A125
B174
B175
B1459
MOBY DICK

57
Kd
Ld
Md
Nd
Pd
Qd
Rd
39
77
58
DAGNAM PARK
Fir Wood
Cock Wood
Alder Wood
MAYLANDS GOLF COURSE
Havering College of Further & Higher Education (Quaries Campus)
Hatters Wood
Drapers' Academy
Dycorts Sch.
Pyrgo Priory Sch.
Duck Wood Community Nature Reserve
Club House
Maylands
Maylands Cottage
Maylands Field
Putwell Bridge
Central Park Leisure Centre
Central Park
HAROLD HILL
Long Wood
Sage Wood
Min. Golf Course
The Nursery
St. Ursula's Catholic Infant School
St. Ursula's Catholic Junior School
Hilldene Prim. Sch.
Mead Prim. Sch.
HAROLD PARK
Harold Court Prim. Sch.
ELMS INDUSTRIAL ESTATE
BATES INDUSTRIAL ESTATE
THE OLD BRICKWORKS INDUSTRIAL ESTATE
Harold Court Woods
Garden Centre
The Chase
HAROLD WOOD
Harold Wood
Cissbury Lodge Farm
Cockabourne Bridge
Miniature Golf Course
Pages Farm
Harold Wood Park
Pavilion
NHS Walk-in Cen.
Four Wantz
Emanuel Cottage
PAGES WOOD
Upminster
RM14
Harold Wood Prim. Sch.
Prospect Farm
Ingrebourne Farm
Redden Court Sch.
Sports Ground
Gallows Corner Sports Ground
GALLOWS CORNER
Superstore
GIDEA PARK
RM2
Gidea Park
Squirrel's Heath
David Lloyd Gidea Park
College
The Campion School
Playing Field
Hotel
Mount Pleasant Farm
ARDLEIGH GREEN
Miniature Golf Course
HAYNES PARK
Drill Roundabout
Hornchurch
RM11
The Rosary
Grasslands
Lillyputts Equestrian Centre
EMERSON PARK
Goodrington Sch.
HYLANDS PARK
Towers Inf. Sch.
Towers Jun. Sch.
Emerson Pk.
Emerson Park Sch.
Upminster Court
Cornlands Farm
COLCHESTER ROAD
A12
EAST
SOUTHEND ARTERIAL ROAD
A127
A118
21
22
23
24
25
26
27
28
29
30
53
54
55
56
88
89
90
91
92
93

M25 MOTORWAY
Junction 11 (A12)
Junction 28 (M25)
BROOK STREET INTERCHANGE
COLCHESTER ROAD
A12
BRENTWOOD BY-PASS
BROOK STREET
A1023
LONDON RD.
BROOK STREET
Alder Wood
Cock Wood
The Oaks
Lower Vicarage Wood
Hotel
Works
MAYLANDS GOLF COURSE
Grove Farm
The Grove
Weald Brook
Putwell Bridge
Maylands
Maylands Cottage
Maylands Field
Warley Country Park
Holly Trees Prim. Sch.
Brentwood Mus.
The Duchess of Kent Social Centre
Spts. Grd.
Mascalls Cottages
Mascalls
WARLEY
LA Fitness (Brentwood)
Sports Grd.
Warley Woods
Lower Belt
CM14
Lodge
Bachelor's Walk
Boyles Court
Boyles Court Farm
Ursuline Prep. Sch.
HARTSWOOD SPIRE HOSP.
Sewage Disposal Works
Ingrebourne River
Top Plantation
Gibblings Shaw
Tylers Shaw
Harold Court Woods
Warley Lea
Lodge
Pond
Warley Place Nature Reserve
Brentwood Park Ski & Snowboarding Centre
Headley Common
Brentford Karting
Stoney Hall Cottage
Holden's Wood
Warley Lea Farm
Tennis Court
Rustlings
The Chase
Garden Centre
Tylers Hall
Wormwalk Shaw
Jermains Wood
Jackson's Wood
GREAT WARLEY
Pump Farm
TYLERS COMMON
Stonyhills Farm
Stonyhills House
Ivy Lodge Farm
Ely Cott.
Tylers Wood
Barrack Reservoir (disused)
Tooks Farm
Clapgate
Pav. Cricket Ground
The Squirrels Nursing Home
SHEPHERDS HILL
Montrose
Tomkyns Manor
Burnside
Great Readings
Tylers Croft
Coombe
Coombe Green
Foxburrow Wood
Foxburrows
Coombe Wood
Goldings
Brentwood
Fairstead
Pages Farm
Four Wantz Works
Riding Stables
Four Wantz Cottages
Emanuel Cottage
Chalkfield
Greathouse
Beredens Cotts.
HAVERING
Warley Elms
Rectory
Sutton's Farm
Common Farm
Ashprington
Hole Farm
Normans
Normans Cottages
Tyes Cottage
Cornlands Farm
Cricket Ground
Pavilion
Great Tomkyns Farm
Great Tomkyns
Folkes Lane Woodland
Parker's Shaw
Works
Upminster
Howard Farm
Emery Farm
Upminster Lodge
Grays Cottages
RM14
Upminster Lodge Farm
Home Meadow
Nursery
Latchet's Shaw
SOUTHEND ARTERIAL ROAD
A127
Rosary
Grasslands
Codham Hall Cottages
Hazle's Pottery Barn
Codham Hall
Hulmers
Woodcroft Farm Woodlands
Codham Hall Wood
Chapmans Farm
PANTILE COTTS.
BROOKMANS PARK DR.
Tabrams Farm
Folkes Farm
Oak Royal Nurseries
Junction 29
Jax Folly
Hobbs Hole
M25
Play. Fld.
Sch.
Emerson Park School
Playing Field
Upminster Court
Upminster Hall Playing Fields
Tennis Courts
Pav.
Museum
CRANHAM
UPMINSTER
Sd Td Ud Vd Wd Xd Yd
21 22 23 24 25 26 27 28 29 30
56 57 58 59
40
57
78
B186

INGRAVE
Ingrave Common
HERONGATE
LITTLE WARLEY
Childerditch
WEST HORNDON
EAST HORNDON
THORNDON COUNTRY PARK
Thorndon Country Park North
Thorndon Country Park South
THORNDON PARK GOLF COURSE
BRENTWOOD GOLF COURSE
WARLEY PARK GOLF COURSE
BRENTWOOD ROAD
A128
A127
SOUTHEND ARTERIAL ROAD
CM13
Kent's Wood
Barrack Wood
Harts Wood
Donkey Lane Plantation
Long Plantation
Menagerie Plantation
Mill Wood
Childerditch Wood
Thorndon Countryside Centre
Chantry Chapel & Mausoleum
Thorndon Hall
Clearview Health & Racquets Club
West Horndon

High Wycombe
Beaconsfield
HP10
HP9
SL1
SL2
SOUTH
Dipple Wood
Dipple Lodge
Woodlands Farm
Hollybush Wood
Hangings Wood
Downey Bottom
Jennings Wood
Jennings Farm
Bower Wood
Hillmotts Farm
Hillmotts
Furze
Beaconsfield Common Lane
Green Common Lane
Broomhill Coppice
Hicknaham Plantation
Hicknaham Farm
Ashen Coppice
Bristles Wood
Homer Wood
Woodburn Common Road
Heathfield Rd.
Hollybush Wood
Dropmore Inf. Sch.
Dropmore Park
Dropmore House
Sewage Works
Dropmore
Abbey Wood
Brook End Farm
Lower Brook End
The Lambourne Golf Course
Club House
Lambournes Wood
Nashdom Lane
Nursery
Chalk Pit Lane
Lower Lambournes Wood
Council Depot
Archery Range
Dropmore Road
Littleworth Road
Littleworth Common
Littleworth Corner
Reservoir (covered)
Horseshoe Hill
Boveney Wood Lane
Boveney Wood Farm
Boveney Wood
Twelve Acre Wood
Dorney Common
Dorney Wood
Dorney Wood Road
Kilnwood
Scout Camp
Curriers Lane
Ship Road
Harehatch Lane
Little Jennings Farm
Akroyd Cottages
Akroyd Place
Abbey Park Farm
Abbey Park Cottage
Abbey Park Lane
Healy's Gorse
Water Tower
Summerlins Wood
Little Burnt Coppice
Heathfield Wood
Staplefurze Wood
Egypt Woods
Whitespark Wood
Nine Acre Wood
Moat
McAuliffe Drive
Halse Drive
Morton Dr.
Crabtree Heath
Dukes Drive
Fleet Wood
Tower Wood
Towerwood
Burnham Beeches
Great Burnt Coppice
Egypt
Egypt Lane
Lord Mayors Drive
Burnham Beeches National Nature Reserve
Upper Pond
Seven Ways Plain
Juniper Grove
East Burnham Common
Middle Pond
Pumpkin Hill
Pumpkin Lane
Dorney Wood
Home Close
Kiln Wood
Hawthorn Lane
Nightingale Pk.
Orchard Bungalows
Swilly Fm.
Swilly Pond
Thompkins Lane
Thompkin's Wood
East Burnham
East Burnham Ho.
East Burnham Lane
Stoney La.
Woodview
Crow Piece Lane
Allerds Road
Lock's Bottom
Hunts Wood Fm.
Hunt's Wood
Burnham Beeches Golf Course
Snowball Farm
Longmead La.
Green Lane
Club House
Burnham Grove
Greenfields Farm
Cant's Hill
Nursery
Grove Wood
Hotel
Bottom Waltons
Bottom Waltons Caravan Site
Walton Lane
Elm Cottages
Deepwood
The Spinney
Cherry Orchard
Recreation Ground
Crown Lane
Garden Centre
Allerds Farm
Nursery
Playing Field
Caldicott Sch.
Scotlands Dr.
Farnham Common
Blackpond Lane
Beaconsfield Road
Windsor Rd.
Dorney Hill South
Collinswood Road
A355
Dorney Bottom
Pennlands Wood
Pennlands Farm
Little Wood
Parish Lane
Andrew Hill Lane
Ponds
Hollybush Corner
Wood
Christmas Lane
Kiln
Moll Hay Wood
School Wood
Norfolk Ho.
Collinswood
Egypt
Stewart's Drive
Cages Wood Dr.
Inf. Sch.
Jun. Sch.
Playing Field
Sports Ground
Tennis Courts
Mount
Holly
Avenue
Beeches Dr.
Scott Cl.
Myers Dr.
Beeches Rd
Bedford Drive
Rosewood Way
Frensham
Victoria Rd.
Lib.
Forge Dr.
Elm Cl.
Parsonage Lane
Long
Spring La.
Cherry Tree Rd.
Purton Ct.
Farnham Lane
Bybend Cl.
Highfield Ct.
Dair House School
Slough Community Club
Tennis Courts
Fairfield La.
Montague
Farnham Royal
Sports Field
Tennis Courts
Home Meadow
Park
Stoke Park Av.
Rectory Cl.
Ckt. Grd.
Sch.
Beechwood & Arbour Vale Schools
Kiderminster Rd.
Doddsfield Road
Wentworth Av.
Lib.
Rokesby
Calbroke
Mascoll Pth.
Ham La.
Cress.
Farnham
Court
Britwell
Kimbers Drive
Fairway
The Fairway
Hazelhurst Rd.
Bentley Pk.
Linkswood
Pipers Cl.
Greenway
Youth Cen.
Day Cen.
Gore
Tockley Rd.
Clonmel Way
Ashcroft Ct.
Pink Lane
Poyle
Bowmans Cl.
Dorneywood Cl.
Lane
Road
Almond Rd.
Wyndham Cr.
Oxford Av.
Meadow
Baldwin
Youth Cen.
80

61
GERRARDS CROSS
Gerrards Cross
SL9
BULSTRODE PARK
Grove Plantation
Menagerie Wood
Crab Hill
FORT
Bulstrode Cotts.
Moat Farm Cotts.
Hedgerley Green
Manor Farm
Coppathorne
Sherley Close
Bloomfield Cottage
Leith Grove
Church Wood Reserve
Sutton's Wood
HEDGERLEY
Court Farm
Hanging Wood
Hedgerley Hill
HEDGERLEY
PARK
Black Grove
Park House
Mounthill Wood
Mount Hill Farm
Duke's Orchard
Riding Stables
High Meadows
Ponders
Subway
M40
M40 MOTORWAY
WINDSOR ROAD
B416
Parkside Cemetery
Pickeridge Wood
Tara
Hedgerley Park Farm
One Pin Farm
Reservoir (Covered)
Reservoir (covered)
TIMBER WOOD
Stoke Wood
Templemead
Slough
Stoke Common
STOKE COMMON
Pickeridge Farm
Kestrel Farm
Low Farm
Hay's Wood
Fish Pond
FULMER
SL3
Fulmer Hall
Church Farm
Fulmer House
Fulmer Infant Sch.
62
Penn Wood
Fernacres Farm
King George's Field
Black Firs
Oakwood House
Frame Wood
Mill House Fm.
Framewood Manor
Fulmer Court
Teikyo Sch.
Home Wood
Eight Acres Fm.
Eight Acres
Woodlands
Little Orchard
WEXHAM SPRINGS
Dogkennel Field
Burners Cottage
Upton Wood
Upton Lake
Upton Farm
Twin Trees Farm
Sandhole Wood
Rowley Wood
Gallions Wood
Rowley Slip
BUCKS
Brockhurst Wood
Duffield Fm.
LARCHMOOR PARK
GERRARDS CROSS ROAD
Stoke Park
Stoke Court
Old Orchard Wood
Old Orchard Ho.
THE SOUTH BUCKINGHAMSHIRE GOLF COURSE
Yew Place
FARNHAM PARK GOLF COURSE
Club Ho.
Tithe Fm.
STOKE POGES GOLF COURSE
Stoke Park Fm.
Manor House
Gray's Field
STOKE POGES
BELLS HILL
GRAYS PARK ROAD
Tennis Court
Rec. Grd.
Sports Grd.
Tennis Courts
Khalsa Sec. Academy
Hockley Hole
The Clock Ho.
WEXHAM PARK GOLF COURSE
Nuffield Health Fitness & Wellbeing Cen.
Berry Farm
THAMES VALLEY SPIRE HOSPITAL
WEXHAM STREET
War Mem.
Club House
Driving Range
WEXHAM PARK GOLF COURSE
Grotes Wood
Spring Wood
Hollybush Wood
Pinewood
Appletons
HAMPDEN CL.
81
H
J
K
L
M
N
P
1
2
3
4
5
6
7
8
9
10
97
98
99
500
83
84
85
86
87
88

GERRARDS CROSS
62
A
B
C
D
E
F
G
Memorial Cen.
Gerrards Cross Common
Greenacre
Collsels
Club House
Bailey Hill
42
AMERSHAM
Denham Golf Club
DOGGETTS FARM
MIDDLE
UPPER ROAD
The Gerrards Cross C of E School
Mill Wood
Gallows Wood
Gerrards Cross
Woodhill
Works
LOWER
Higher Denham
Tom William's Wood
El Sub Sta.
Sewage Works
Gasholder Station
Sluice
Weir
Comm. Cen.
Bradbury's Island
Moorhouse Farm
A413
A40
OXFORD ROAD
M25
Little Gallows Wood
HEUSDEN WAY
WINDSOR ROAD
MANOR
Cricket Grd.
Pav.
Tennis Cts.
MEADWAY
PARK
DUKES
31
32
33
34
35
36
37
38
39
40
The Rancho
Gas Pipeline Station
Caps Wood
Baker's Wood
Baker's Wd.
Hedgerows Poultry Farm
Council Offs.
CAPSWOOD BUSINESS CENTRE
CONWAY CT.
FULMER CORNER
Works
Tatling End
Felbrigg
St. Huberts
SL9
BIRCHDALE
BEECHES
HIGH
HOWARDS
DRIVE
St. Hubert's Home Farm
Prestwick Place
Little Prestwick
Old Prestwick
Prestwick Cottage
Naboth
Hollybush Cottages
Hollybush Farm
Mount Farm
RED HILL
Redhill Farm
Huntwyk
BLACKSMITHS LANE
Council Depot
Denham Mount
Maltmas Green
M25-MOTORWAY
Fulmerfields
Grayleigh
The Barn
Alderbourne Manor
Gladwins Wood
Fish Pond
The Oldhouse Farm
Alderbrook
Hawk's Wood
Hawkswood
Holly Bush
FROGGY
Hay's Wood
M40
M40-MOTORWAY
Furzeney
Broadspring Wood
86
FULMER
Fish Pond
Furzeney Wood
Junction 16 (M25)
BRADBURY GDNS.
Fulmer House
Furzeney Wood
Orchard Cottage
M40 MOTORWAY
Fulmer Hall
NORTH ROW
SOUTH ROW
Fulmer Infant Sch.
Fulmer House Farm
Alderbourne Arches
Junction 1a (M40)
Rush Green
Gossams Wood
Rush Hill Farm
Smallhoe
Durham House
Church Farm
61
ALDERBOURNE
Watersplash Farm
Ford
Alder Bourne
HAWKSWOOD
Slough
Penn Wood
Brown's Wood
Field End Farm
Ways Farm
Oldhouse Wood
Fernacres Farm
West Hill
Fulmer Rise Manor
The Spinney
The Thatched Cott.
Glen Erica
Parkspring Wood
Alderbourne Farm
Springfield Cottages
SOUTH
Home Farm
Saul's Farm
Cherry Orchard Farm
Blanchards Farm
Caravan Park
Kennels
Belle Farm
B
Alder Bourne
Home Wood
Penn Wood
Mount Fidget
Mount Fidget Wood
Woodland Court
Upton Ho.
Tennis Cts.
SL3
FULMER RISE
Fulmer Common Ho.
Black Firs
Oakwood House
Fernacres Cottage
Langley Corner
Convent
HAWKSWOOD GRO.
CHERRY TREE LANE
SEVEN HILLS ROAD
PINEWOOD ROAD
Long Coppice
Taidswood
Sevenhills Farm
Dromenagh
Playing Field
Dromenagh Farm
The Clump
WEXHAM PL.
Fulmer Common
COMMON
Langley Common
Strawberry Wood
Heathfield Plantation
Pinewood Film Studios
SOUTHLANDS ROAD
Blacketts
M25
Iver
Upton Lake
Upton Farm
Upton Plantation
Bowlers Plantation
QUEEN'S
BOND CL.
HEATHERDEN HO.
PINEWOOD GRN.
GREEN
SL0
LAUREL CT.
M25-MOTORWAY
84
Upton Wood
Spruce Wood
Sycamore Wood
Heatherden Hall
CEDAR
FIRS CL.
ASHFORD
Broom Warren
DENHAM ROAD
Dellfield Fm.
Park Lodge Farm
Brackenwood
THORNBRIDGE
Ensbys
ROWLEY LANE
Cuckoo Pen
Sandhole Wood
BLACK COUNTRY PARK
BLACK PARK ROAD
DRIVE
PEACE ROAD
Heathlands
HEATHERDEN GRN.
PARKWAY
LONGSTONE
AYSGARTH PL.
ST DAVID'S CL.
IVER HEATH
Rowley Wood
Park Lodge
Diamond Wood
Club Ho.
Rec. Grd.
Go Ape
Bowl. Gm.
ANSLOW
Rowleyfield Larches
QUEEN'S DR.
Warren Lodge
A412
Chandlers Hill
Gallions Wood
Rowley Slip
Walk Wood
Blackpark Lake
Warren House
Lib.
Play. Sch. Fld.
Ancoats Lodge
83
Black Park Countryside Cen.
CHURCH ROAD
Club
Warren Ho.
SLOUGH ROAD
MEAD HO.
30
South Lodge
Spring Wood
Hollybush Wood
Sawmill Cottages
82
UXBRIDGE ROAD
Five Points
THE CLOSE
WHITEHOUSE WAY
POTTERS CROSS
BANGORS RD. STH.
Rowley
500
01
02
03
87
85
88

63
HILLINGDON
Uxbridge
UXBRIDGE
DENHAM
ICKENHAM
WILLOWBANK
NEW DENHAM
UXBRIDGE MOOR
UB9
UB10
Denham
Newyears Green
BUCKINGHAMSHIRE GOLF COURSE
DENHAM COUNTRY PARK
UXBRIDGE GOLF COURSE
HILLINGDON GOLF COURSE
HILLINGDON COURT PARK (Recreation Ground)
Frays Valley Local Nature Reserve
Hillingdon Outdoor Activities Centre
Colne Valley Park Cen.
Uxbridge Moor Nature Reserve
Hillingdon Athletics Stadium
Hillingdon Sports & Leisure Complex
Uxbridge Lido
Uxbridge Coll. (Uxbridge Campus)
The John Locke Acad.
RAF Uxbridge, Battle of Britain Bunker
ACS Hillingdon International Sch.
Vyners School
West Middlesex College
Uxbridge High Sch.
Junction 1
DENHAM ROUNDABOUT
SWAKELEYS ROUNDABOUT
WESTERN AVENUE
A40
A412
A4020
A4007
A408
B467
B483
M25
DENHAM AVENUE
DENHAM ROAD
OXFORD ROAD
HAREFIELD ROAD
PARK ROAD
HILLINGDON ROAD
ST JOHN'S RD.
ROCKINGHAM R.
COWLEY ROAD
HIGH ST.
SWAKELEYS DRIVE
BREAKSPEAR ROAD
NEW YEARS GREEN LANE
HARVIL ROAD
SKIP LANE
MILL ROAD
THE GREENWAY
River Colne
Grand Union Canal
River Misbourne
Shire Ditch
Fray's River
Alder Bourne
River Pinn
Denham Lock
Uxbridge Lock
Copthall Covert
Newyears Green Covert
Altcar Covert
Widows Cruise Covert
Research Farm
Brackenbury Barn
Copthall Farm
Harvil Farm
Harefield Place
Highway Farm
Dewes Farm
Dewes Farm Cottages
The Alders
Gravel Pit
Savay Farm
Court Farm
Denham Mill
Denham Place
Priory Covert
Playing Field
Sports Ground
Cricket Ground
Common Plantation
The Clump
Uxbridge Common
Clare House
Ivy House Farm
Oxford Road Nursery
Brickfield Farm
Southlands Manor
Quarry
Field Cottage
Warehouse
Watergate Fm.
Electricity Sub Station
Mansfield Farm
Woodlands Park
Stables
Depot
Civic Cen.
Odeon Cin.
Superstore
Bus Sta.
Recreation Ground
Stratford Bri.
Hillingdon Cem.
Halls of Residence
43
83
64
31
32
33
34
35
36
37
38
39
40
H
J
K
L
M
N
P

Q
R
S
T
U
V
W
44
84
63
07
08
09
510
88
87
86
185
84
83
UB9
UB10
Uxbridge
Hayes
Newyears Green
Pylon Farm
Elm Tree Farm
High View Farm
St. Leonard's Farm
Braemar Farm
Crows Nest Farm
Old Clack Farm
The Corner
Tile Kiln
Grays Cottages
Dunster Cottage
Research Farm
Gatemead Farm
Brackenbury Barn
Moat
Coptha Farm
NEW YEARS GREEN LA.
BREAKSPEAR ROAD
BREAKSPEAR ROAD NTH.
BREAKSPEAR ROAD SOUTH
TILE KILN LANE
Whiteheath Jun. & Inf. Schs.
LADYGATE LANE
GLOVERS GROVE
Prim. Sch.
Youth Cen.
Play. Fld.
Winston Churchill Hall
Manor Farm
Lib.
Bowl. Grn.
Pav.
Church Field Gdns.
King's Coll. Play. Flds. Track
Eastcote Hockey & Badminton Club
River Pinn
PARK AV.
MEAD WAY
SHERWOOD AV.
APPROACH
BURY ST.
A4180
HIGH STREET
EASTCOTE ROAD
B466
EVELYN AV.
WEST HATCH MNR.
MIDCROFT
KING EDWARD'S ROAD
KINGSEND
Warrender Prim. Sch.
Ruislip Manor
Highgrove Swim. P.
RUISLIP
Ruislip
Super store
Pav.
Sports Grd.
Wealdstone FC (St. George's Stadium)
Rec. Grd.
Lib.
Syn.
RUISLIP MANOR
Playground
RUISLIP GOLF COURSE
WEST RUISLIP
Golf Driving Range
Club Ho.
West Ruislip
ICKENHAM ROAD
HIGH ROAD
Playing Field
Cricket Ground
Pav.
Schs.
Ruislip Rugby Club
Sacred Heart Catholic Primary School
WEST END ROAD
A4180
Works
Playing Field
Ruislip High Sch.
RUISLIP GARDENS
Ruislip Gardens Primary School
Ruislip Gardens
SWAKELEYS ROAD
B467
ICKENHAM
Compass Theatre
Ickenham
Community Cen.
Lib.
Play. Fld.
Harrington House
Swakeleys
Sports Ground
Ten. Cts.
Bowl. Grn.
The Clump
Vyners School
Adult Learning Centre
Sch.
Glebe Primary School
Ickenham Manor Play. Flds.
Tennis Courts
Moat
Long Lane Farm
Park Wood
HILL FARM ROAD
Weir
Ickenham Marsh
Yeading Brook
Canal Feeder
RAF NORTHOLT AERODROME
WESTERN AVENUE
A40
Hillingdon
HILLINGDON CIRCUS
Sub. Sta.
LONG LANE
Playing Field
Playing Fields
River Pinn
Freezeland Covert
Rec. Grd.
Yeading Brook
Cutthroat Wood
Gutteridge Wood
HILLINGDON COURT PARK (Recreation Ground)
Pav.
Coll.
Bowling Green
Tennis Courts
Playground
Play. Fld.
Playgrd.
Schs.
A437
30
ACS Hillingdon International Sch.
NORTH HILLINGDON
Playing Field
Ryefield Primary Sch.
Ten Acres
The Gorse
Recreation Ground
Rugby Ground
Hare Plantation
Recreation Ground
Westways Fm.
Lane Covert
Sports Grd.
Pav.
Liby.
Prim. Sch.
Playing Fld.
Home Covert
Tennis Courts
Playground
Club Ho.
HILLINGDON COURSE
Swakeleys School for Girls
Abbotsfield School
Playing Field
Children's Cen.
Comm. Cen.
Charville Prim. Sch.
Hedgewood School
Grosvenor Playing Field
Play. Fld.
Prim. Sch.
Coney Green
UXBRIDGE ROAD
HILLINGDON HILL

X
Y
Z
Aa
Ba
Ca
Da
45
EASTCOTE
Eastcote
Pinner
HA5
Roxborough Rough
Rayners Lane
RAYNERS LANE
WEST HARROW
West Harrow
Harrow
HARROW
Whitmore High Sch.
Grange Prim. Sch.
Cavendish Recreation Ground
Bessingby Playing Fields
Miniature Railway
Roxbourne Park
Roxbourne Prim. Sch.
Recreation Ground
Field End Jun. & Inf. Schs.
Newton Farm Jun. & Inf. Schs.
Newton Park West
Newton Ecology Park
Roxbourne Complex
HA2
Ruislip
HA4
SOUTH RUISLIP
South Ruislip
Deane Park
Queensmead Sports Cen.
Goals Soccer Centre
Hendon FC, Harrow Borough FC (Earlsmead Stadium)
ALEXANDRA PARK
ROXETH
South Harrow
SOUTH HARROW
Northolt Pk.
Wood End
Solid Waste Transfer Station
NORTHOLT PARK
Northolt High Sch.
Lord Halsbury Memorial Playing Flds.
Willow Tree Prim. Sch.
NORTHOLT
Northolt
Islip Manor Park
POLISH WAR MEMORIAL
C&L GOLF COURSE
LIME TREES PARK GOLF COURSE
John Chilton Sch.
Alec Reed Academy
TARGET ROUNDABOUT
Belvue Park
GREENFORD INDUSTRIAL ESTATE
LA Fitness (Northolt)
Lime Tree Park
West End
Downe Barns Fm.
West London Shooting Grounds
NORTHALA FIELDS
NORTHOLT GOLF COURSE
Gifford Primary Sch.
Smith's Farm
Greenford
UB6
RECTORY PARK (Recreation Ground)
GREENFORD
WESTERN AVENUE
A40
A4090
A312
A4180
B455
ALEXANDRA AVENUE
NORTHOLT ROAD
MANDEVILLE ROAD
CHURCH ROAD
WEST END ROAD
RUISLIP ROAD
85

66
HARROW
WEST HARROW
HARROW ON THE HILL
ROXETH
SOUTH HARROW
NORTH WEMBLEY
Northwick Park
NORTHWICK PARK
SUDBURY
Sudbury Hill Harrow
Sudbury Hill
Sudbury & Harrow Road
Sudbury Town
Northolt
Wood End
Greenford Green
Greenford
GREENFORD
PERIVALE
Perivale
South Greenford
Kenton
South Kenton
West Harrow
South Harrow
Harrow-on-the-Hill
PINNER RD.
LOWLANDS RD.
KENTON RD.
WATFORD ROAD
LOWER RD.
BESSBOROUGH RD.
ROXETH HILL
LONDON RD.
SUDBURY HILL
SUDBURY COURT DR.
HARROW ROAD
WHITTON AVENUE WEST
WHITTON AVENUE EAST
EAST LANE
BRIDGEWATER RD.
GREENFORD ROAD
WESTERN AVENUE
GREENFORD ROUNDABOUT
NORTHOLT RD.
HORSENDEN LANE NORTH
HORSENDEN LANE SOUTH
TEIGNMOUTH GDNS.
ARGYLE RD.
GRAND UNION CANAL
GRAND UNION CANAL (PADDINGTON BRANCH)
A404
A4005
A4127
A312
A4088
A4090
A40
B452
University of Westminster (Harrow Campus)
NORTHWICK PARK HOSPITAL
ST. MARK'S HOSP.
Harrow School Playing Fields
Harrow School Farm
Harrow Sch. Golf Course
School Lake
THE CLEMENTINE CHURCHILL BMI HOSPITAL
HARROW CYGNET HOSPITAL
Northwick Park Playgolf
Driving Range
Vale Farm Sports Centre
Wembley FC
Sudbury Hill Play. Flds.
Maybank Open Space
David Lloyd Leisure
Ealing Northern Sports Centre
Berkeley Fields
HORSENDEN HILL GOLF COURSE
Horsenden Hill
Horsenden Wood
SUDBURY GOLF COURSE
Perivale Wood Local Nature Reserve
Nature Reserve
Horsenden Farm
Cayton Road Sports Ground
Selborne Prim. Sch.
Perivale Park Athletics Track
EALING GOLF COURSE
Whitmore Sports Cen.
Whitmore High Sch.
Cricket Ground
Orley Farm Sch.
Harrow Ckt. Club
Toll Gate
Roxeth Rec. Grd.
Welldon Park Inf. Sch.
HA1
HA2
UB5
UB6
Ea
Fa
Ga
Ha
Ja
Ka
La
31
32
33
34
35
36
37
38
39
40
46
65
86
14
15
16
17
88
87
86
85
84
83

67
Ma
Na
Pa
Qa
Ra
Sa
Ta
47
87
KINGSBURY
Kingsbury Green
FRYENT COUNTRY PARK (Local Nature Reserve)
FRYENT WAY A4140
Barn Hill Open Space
Barn Hill
Preston Road
PRESTON
Preston Park Recreation Ground
John Billam Playing Fields
Forty Farm Sports Grd.
Preston Manor High Sch.
Stanmore Junction
FORTY AVENUE A4088
FORTY LANE
SALMON STREET
BLACKBIRD HILL
NEASDEN LA.
Wembley Park
Ark Academy
BRIDGE RD.
North Wembley
WEMBLEY PARK DR.
WEMBLEY HILL RD.
Wembley Prim. Sch.
Wembley
KING EDWARD VII PARK
WEMBLEY PARK
Brent Civic Cen.
SSE Arena
Wembley Stadium
Livingwell Health Club
LONDON DESIGNER OUTLET
Market
HA9
HA3
NW9
NW10
FIFTH WY.
FOURTH WY.
FIRST WY.
Depot
GREAT CENTRAL WAY B4557
SOUTH WAY B4557
Railway Works
Neasden Depot
NEASDEN JUNCTION
BRENT RESERVOIR
Wembley Sailing Club
Seahorse Sailing Club
Field Study Centre
Chalkhill Park
Chalkhill Prim. Sch.
St. Margaret Clitherow RC Prim. Sch.
Phoenix Arch Sch.
Superstores
Sherrans Farm Open Space
Oakington Mnr. Prim. Sch.
TOKYNGTON
HIGH RD.
A404
ROAD
Wembley Central
WEMBLEY
Playing Fld.
Youth & Comm. Cen.
Elsley Prim. Sch.
HARROW ROAD
EALING ROAD A4089
NORTH CIRCULAR A406
Wembley Brook Depot
Carriage Shed
Stonebridge Park
HARROW ROAD
Brent Junction
Bridge Park
Royal Mail Depot
STONEBRIDGE
Stonebridge Rec. Grd.
BRENTFIELD
HILLSIDE
CRAVEN PK.
CHURCH END
Mandir Hindu Temple
Alperton
Bus Garage
ALPERTON
One Tree Hill Rec. Grd.
Metropolitan Police Traffic Unit
Alperton Sports Grd.
HANGER LANE
Open Space
NORTHFIELDS INDUSTRIAL ESTATE
PARK ROYAL JUNCTION
PREMIER PARK
GRAND UNION CANAL (Paddington Branch)
Lower Place
Harlesden
PARK ROYAL
CENTRAL MIDDLESEX HOSPITAL
Twyford Abbey Prim. Sch.
MANHATTAN BUSINESS PARK
Power Station
Grand Union Canal
Harrow School
18
19
20
21

68
Ua
Va
Wa
Xa
Ya
Za
Ab
48
88
67
31
32
33
34
35
36
37
38
39
40
21
22
23
24
NW9
NW2
NW10
WEST HENDON PLAYING FIELDS
Silver Jubilee Park
Kingsbury Town FC Grd.
Cool Oak Bridge
WEST HENDON
WOODFIELD PARK
Sports Ground
Rifle Range
Woodfield Sch.
BRENT RESERVOIR
Welsh Harp (Brent Reservoir) Nature Reserve
Wembley Sailing Club
Seahorse Sailing Club
Neasden Recreation Ground
BRENT CROSS INTERCHANGE
Brent Cross
Brent Cross Bus Sta.
Junc. 1
M1
MOTORWAY
BROADWAY
HENDON WAY
STAPLES CORNER
Cineworld Cinema
Clitterhouse Recreation Ground
Brent Sidings
CRICKLEWOOD
Cricklewood
Virgin Active
NEASDEN
NEASDEN JUNCTION
Neasden
Neasden Depot
GT. CENTRAL WAY
Superstores
DOLLIS HILL
Dollis Hill
Dollis Hill House
GLADSTONE PARK
Reservoir (Covered)
Dudding Hill Junction
Water Works
DUDDEN HILL
Willesden Green
CHURCH END
WILLESDEN
WILLESDEN NEW CEMETERY
Jewish Cemy.
ROUNDWOOD PARK
WILLESDEN GREEN
Willesden Sports Stadium
Willesden Sports Cen.
King Edward VII Recreation Ground
Capital City Academy
Willesden Cen. for Health & Care
BRENT OLDER PEOPLE DAY HOSP.
HARLESDEN
Harlesden
BRONDESBURY PARK
Brondesbury Park
Queens Park Comm. Sch.
QUEENS PARK
Queens Park
KENSAL RISE
Kensal Rise
KENSAL GREEN
KILBURN
MORTIMER
Willesden Junction
Freightliner Depot
Power Station
Playing Field
A406
A407
A5
A41
A404
A4003
A4088
B4557
B453
B451
B4492
CIRCULAR
NORTH CIRCULAR ROAD
EDGWARE ROAD
CRICKLEWOOD BROADWAY
CHICHELE RD.
WALM LANE
WILLESDEN LANE
HIGH ROAD
CHURCH RD.
CRAVEN PK.
HARLESDEN RD.
HARROW RD.
TUBBS RD.
ACTON LANE

69
HAMPSTEAD HEATH
HAMPSTEAD
HIGHGATE
HARINGEY
GOLDERS GREEN
CHILD'S HILL
WEST HAMPSTEAD
SOUTH HAMPSTEAD
KILBURN
BRONDESBURY
PRIMROSE HILL
REGENT'S PARK
ST. JOHN'S WOOD
HAMPSTEAD GOLF COURSE
HIGHGATE GOLF COURSE
GOLDERS HILL PARK
PARLIAMENT HILL
VALE OF HEALTH
NORTH END
SWISS COTTAGE
FINCHLEY ROAD
HAVERSTOCK HILL
ROSSLYN HILL
FITZJOHN'S AVENUE
WEST END LANE
KILBURN HIGH ROAD
MAIDA VALE
ABBEY ROAD
WELLINGTON RD.
PRINCE ALBERT RD.
SPANIARDS ROAD
HAMPSTEAD LANE
N2
N6
NW3
NW5
NW6
NW8
NW1
NW11
ROYAL FREE HOSPITAL
Kenwood House
Golders Green Crematorium
Leg of Mutton Pond
Hampstead Ponds
Highgate Ponds
London Zoo
Middlesex CCC (Lord's)
London Central Mosque
49
89
214
215

70
Jb
Kb
Lb
Mb
Nb
Pb
Qb
50
31
32
33
34
35
36
37
38
39
40
69
215
216
217
90
HIGHGATE
Highgate
HIGHGATE HOSPITAL
CROUCH END
STROUD GREEN
Crouch Hill
HAMPSTEAD LANE
SOUTHWOOD LANE
NORTH HILL
HIGHGATE HIGH ST.
HORNSEY ROAD
HORNSEY RISE
CROUCH HILL
STROUD GREEN RD.
ARCHWAY RD.
Archway
HOLLOWAY RD.
Upper Holloway
UPPER HOLLOWAY
DARTMOUTH PARK
Whittington Park
WHITTINGTON HOSPITAL
Highgate Mental Health Centre
HIGHGATE CEMETERY
WATERLOW PARK
Lauderdale House
Finsbury Park
Park Theatre
Isledon Village
Arsenal
Arsenal FC (Emirates Stadium)
Drayton Pk.
Holloway Rd.
LOWER HOLLOWAY
HOLLOWAY
NAG'S HEAD
SEVEN SISTERS RD.
TOLLINGTON
TUFNELL PARK AV.
Tufnell Pk.
Gospel Oak
GOSPEL OAK
KENTISH TOWN
Kentish Town
Kentish Town W.
KENTISH TOWN RD.
FORTESS RD.
JUNCTION RD.
BRECKNOCK RD.
CAMDEN RD.
CAMDEN PARK RD.
YORK WAY
CALEDONIAN RD.
Caledonian Rd.
Caledonian Rd & Barnsbury
BARNSBURY
HMP PENTONVILLE
LIVERPOOL RD.
Chalk Farm
CHALK FARM RD.
ADELAIDE RD.
MALDEN RD.
HAVERSTOCK HILL
PRIMROSE HILL
Camden Town
CAMDEN TOWN
Camden Rd.
PRINCE ALBERT RD.
PARKWAY
DELANCEY ST.
CAMDEN HIGH ST.
ALBANY ST.
REGENT'S PARK
London Zoo
Gloucester Gate
Cumberland Gate
Mornington Cres.
HAMPSTEAD RD.
EVERSHOLT ST.
PANCRAS WAY
ST. PANCRAS HOSPITAL
KING'S CROSS
ST. PANCRAS INTERNATIONAL
Francis Crick Institute
British Library
SOMERS TOWN
EUSTON
COPENHAGEN ST.
PENTONVILLE RD.
PENTONVILLE
ANGEL
FINSBURY
Parliament Hill Fields
Parliament Hill School
Hampstead Heath Educ. Centre
William Ellis Sch.
Lido
Highgate Ponds
Men's Bathing Pond
Highgate School Playing Field
Lewis Cubitt Pk.
Gasholder Pk.
Islington Ten. Cen.
Caledonian Park
Barnard Park
Sobell Leisure Cen.

Rb
Sb
Tb
Ub
51
Vb
Wb
Xb
71
Harringay Green Lanes
Stamford Hill
WARWICK (WEST) RESERVOIR
Walthamstow Marsh Nature Reserve
Coppermill Bridge
Horse Shoe Point
Copper Mills Junction
Clapton Junction
31
32
33
34
35
36
37
38
39
40
AMHURST
PARK
CLAPTON
COMMON
UPPER CLAPTON
SPRINGFIELD PARK
Springfield Marina
EAST RESERVOIR
WEST RESERVOIR
West Reservoir Centre
The Castle Climbing Cen.
Manor House
FINSBURY PARK
SEVEN SISTERS
STAMFORD HILL
STOKE NEWINGTON
Stoke Newington
Abney Park Cemetery (Local Nature Reserve)
LORDSHIP PARK
MANOR ROAD
BROWNSWOOD PARK
CLISSOLD PARK
Clissold Leisure Cen.
Paddling Pool
STOKE NEWINGTON CHURCH
NORTHWOLD
RECTORY ROAD
Rectory Road
Clapton
North Millfield Recreation Ground
LEA BRIDGE RD.
LOWER CLAPTON
HACKNEY DOWNS
Mossbourne Community Academy
SHACKLEWELL
HIGHBURY
HIGHBURY PARK
GREEN LANES
ALBION ROAD
Canonbury
CANONBURY
ST. PAUL'S ROAD
BALLS POND ROAD
Dalston Kingsland
Dalston Junc.
DALSTON
GRAHAM ROAD
Hackney Downs
Hackney Cen.
HACKNEY
London Fields
LONDON FIELDS
KINGSLAND
KINGSLAND ROAD
QUEENSBRIDGE
DE BEAUVOIR TOWN
Haggerston
HAGGERSTON
Regent's Canal
ISLINGTON
Essex Rd.
NEW NORTH ROAD
ESSEX ROAD
SOUTHGATE
Britannia Centre
HOXTON
Hoxton
Hackney City Farm
HACKNEY ROAD
MARE STREET
CAMBRIDGE HEATH
Cambridge Heath
St. Agnes Gate
WELL ST.
E8
E9
218
219
91
Rb
Sb
Tb
Ub
Vb
Wb
Xb
SHOREDITCH
COLUMBIA RD.
OLD BETHNAL GRN. RD.

72
52
92
Yb
Zb
Ac
Bc
Cc
Dc
Ec
31
32
33
34
35
36
37
38
39
40
WATER WORKS
Filter Beds
Playing Field
Copper Mills Junction
Walthamstow Marsh Nature Reserve
WALTHAMSTOW
Horse Shoe Point
Horse Shoe Bri.
SPRINGFIELD PARK
UPPER CLAPTON
Clapton Junction
MARSHES
Low Hall Sports Ground
Walthamstow Leisure Cen.
Civic Amenity Site
LEYTON INDUSTRIAL VILLAGE
FOREST BUSINESS PARK
LEYTON LINK ESTATE
Works
Playground
Leyton Marshes
Lea Valley Riding Centre
Lea Bridge
Lee Valley Ice Centre
Waterworks Vis. Cen.
Waterworks Golf Course (Nature Reserve)
North Millfields Recreation Ground
Lea Bri.
RIVER LEA or LEE
Middlesex Filter Beds Nature Reserve
LEA BRIDGE
SOUTH MILL FIELDS
South Millfields Rec. Grd.
Clapton
Cow Bridge
Changing Rooms
HACKNEY MARSH
RECREATION GROUND
River Lee Navigation
Playing Fields
Mountain Bike Trail
Hackney Marshes Cen.
Temple Mills Bri.
CLAPTON PARK
HACKNEY
LEYTON
Leyton Stadium
Gala Bingo
The Lammas Sch. & Sports College
Leyton Jubilee Pk.
Manor Lodge
Marsh Lane Cottage
Playing Fields
Dagenham Brook
Running Track
Play Fld.
Leyton Midland Rd.
Brooks Farm
The Davis Cen.
Leyton Orient FC
The Score Complex
Waste Management Centre
Football Pitch
NEW SPITALFIELDS MARKET
MARKET PAVILION
Temple Mills
Lee Valley Hockey & Tennis Centre
Eton Manor
Mountain Bike Trail
All Weather Pitches
Superstore
LEA INTERCHANGE
RUCKHOLT ROAD
EAST CROSS ROUTE
EASTWAY
Marshgate Bri.
Wick Woodland
Hackney Cut
BMX Track
Lee Valley VeloPark
Velodrome
Chobham Manor
East Village
Hopkin's Fields
Road Cycle Circuit
Knights Bridge
Alfred's Meadow
Dane's Walk
Eastcross Bridge
HERE EAST
Copper Box Arena
HACKNEY WICK
Hackney Wick
Stratford International
WESTFIELD STRATFORD CITY SHOPPING CENTRE
The International Quarter
QUEEN ELIZABETH OLYMPIC PARK
London Aquatics Centre
London Stadium
West Ham Utd. FC
The Orbit
The Slide
STRATFORD
Pudding Mill Lane
BOW INTERCHANGE
OLD FORD
HOMERTON
Homerton
HOMERTON HIGH ST.
HOMERTON UNIVERSITY HOSP.
CITY & HACKNEY UCC
Recreation Ground
Football Ground
Mabley Green
HACKNEY WICK
SOUTH HACKNEY
WELL STREET COMMON
VICTORIA PARK
Victoria Park Athletics Arena
Victoria Fountain
Bandstand
Three Colt Bridge
Royal Gate East
Crown Gate East
Crown Gate West
St. Agnes Gate
Gore Gate
Bonner Hall Bri.
Skew Bridge
Cadogan Gate
Mitford Bri.
Tennis Courts
Bowling Green
GROVE ROAD
OLD FORD ROAD
TOWER HAMLETS
LONDON CHEST HOSP.
BOW
GLOBE TOWN
Bow Church
Bow Rd.
Mile End Park
Bus Garage
Cambridge Heath
Hackney Cen.
GRAHAM RD.
MARE ST.
London Fields
DALSTON
LOWER CLAPTON RD.
LEA BRIDGE ROAD
LEYTON HIGH RD.
HIGH ST.
A12
A104
A106
A102
A107
A112
A1006
A1205
A11
B112
B113
B118
B127
B161

73
REDBRIDGE
WANSTEAD
Wanstead
George Green
Wanstead High School
Golf Course
Pumping Station
53
GREEN MAN ROUNDABOUT
BUSH ROAD
A114
A12
A1008
BLAKE HALL ROAD
CAMBRIDGE PK.
HOLLYBUSH HL.
GAINSBOROUGH RD.
Leytonstone
LEYTONSTONE
Leytonstone High Rd.
The Basin (Fish Pond)
Sports Ground
WANSTEAD GOLF COURSE
WANSTEAD PARK
The Heronry
Lincoln Island
Rook Island
The Temple
Keepers Lodge
Reservoir Wood
Shoulder of Mutton Pond
Heronry Pond
Perch Pond
Bush Wood
ALDERSBROOK
ALDERSBROOK
CITY OF LONDON CEMETERY
City of London Crematorium
WANSTEAD FLATS
Playing Field
Horse Ride
CENTRE ROAD
WOODFORD ROAD
DAMES ROAD
HARROW ROAD
St. Patrick's RC Cemetery
Langthorne Park
Cann Hall
West Ham Cemetery
THE MANOR PARK CEMETERY
Manor Park Crem.
MANOR PARK
Manor Park
FOREST DRIVE
Wanstead Pk.
Forest Gate
FOREST GATE
WOODGRANGE RD.
ROMFORD ROAD
Woodgrange Park
Woodgrange Park Cemetery
Maryland
Stratford New Town
Stratford High St.
BROADWAY
WEST HAM LA.
Public Gardens
WEST HAM PARK
PORTWAY
Football Ground
UPTON
UPTON LANE
Upton Park
UPTON PARK
PLASHET
Plashet Jewish Cemy.
PLASHET
GREEN STREET
HIGH STREET NORTH
WEST HAM
Plaistow
PLAISTOW
Abbey Road
Jubilee Line Depot
Gas Depot
Pumping Station
Mill Meads
Prescott Channel
Channelsea
West Ham
East London Crematorium
EAST LONDON CEMETERY
Memorial Recreation Ground
BARKING ROAD
93
Fc
Gc
Hc
Jc
Kc
Lc
Mc
31
32
33
34
35
36
37
38
39
40
E7
E12
E13
E15
39
40
41
42

74
REDBRIDGE
WANSTEAD
Nc
Pc
Qc
Rc
Sc
Tc
Uc
54
EASTERN AVENUE
CRANBROOK RD.
BEEHIVE LA.
Valentines Mansion & Gardens
VALENTINES PARK
NORTH CIRCULAR ROAD
SOUTH WOODFORD TO BARKING RELIEF ROAD
WANSTEAD PARK
Keepers Lodge
Perch Pond
ILFORD GOLF COURSE
River Roding
CITY OF LONDON CEMETERY
City of London Crematorium
CRANBROOK
Ilford
Seven Kings
HIGH ROAD
GREEN LANE
ILFORD HILL
WINSTON WAY
ILFORD
SOUTH PARK
ALDERSBROOK RD.
MANOR PARK
Manor Park
ROMFORD ROAD
HIGH STREET NORTH
LITTLE ILFORD
E12
LOXFORD
BARKING PARK
FAIR CROSS
LONGBRIDGE RD.
FANSHAWE AV.
PLASHET
73
NORTHERN RELIEF RD.
Barking
BARKING
EAST AV.
East Ham
E6
Wallend
HIGHBRIDGE RD.
ABBEY RD.
RIPPLE RD.
Barking Abbey
The Curfew Tower
UPTON PARK
BARKING ROAD
EAST HAM
CENTRAL PARK
RANCLIFFE RD.
94
Refuse & Sewage Works
Showcase Cinema
The Discovery
ALFRED'S WAY
EAST HAM & BARKING BY-PASS
A406
A13
A123
A118
A124
A117
A116
A1083
31
32
33
34
35
36
37
38
39
40

75
SEVEN KINGS
SEVEN KINGS PARK
Chadwell Heath
CHADWELL HEATH
Goodmayes
GOODMAYES
GOODMAYES PARK
Mayfield Sch.
Play. Field
Superstore
Warehouse
Works
Depot
ELDENWALL INDUSTRIAL ESTATE
CHADWELL HEATH IND. PARK
West Ham FC Training Grd.
Whalebone Bri.
BEACONTREE HEATH
Robert Clack Leisure
Robert Clack Sch.
All Saints Cen. Cath. Sch. & Tech. Coll.
Valence Ho. Mus.
VALENCE PARK
BECONTREE
Becontree
Dagenham
DAGENHAM
Dagenham Heathway
PARSLOES PARK
The Sydney Russell Sch.
Leisure Centre
Barking FC
Mayesbrook Park Arena
Indoor Sports Cen.
MAYESBROOK PARK
Boating Lake
Cemetery
Barking Abbey Sch.
Leisure Centre
Manor Jun. & Inf. Schs.
Upney
LODGE AVENUE FLYOVER JUNC.
Eastbury Manor Ho.
CASTLE GREEN
Castle Green Leisure Cen.
Goals Soccer Cen.
Jo Richardson Comm. Sch.
Goresbrook Park
Vue Cinema
Mecca Bingo
Rippleside
Ripple Lane Sidings
Newlands Park
Scrattons Farm Eco-Park
High Speed 1
GORESBROOK INTERCHANGE
HEATHWAY
Dagenham Dock
Thames View Jun. Sch.
Thames View Inf. Sch.
Youth Centre
Library
A118
A12
A1083
A124
A1153
A1240
A1112
A13
A1306
B177
B178
RM8
RM9
RM6
IG3
HIGH ROAD
GREEN LANE
LONGBRIDGE ROAD
WOOD LANE
RIPPLE ROAD
PORTERS AVENUE
LODGE AVENUE
BENNETT'S CASTLE LANE
VALENCE AVENUE
HEATHWAY
WHALEBONE LANE SOUTH
THAMES ROAD
GOODMAYES LANE
BARLEY LANE
BECONTREE AVENUE
GATEWAY
Vc
Wc
Xc
Yc
Zc
Ad
Bd
55
95
31
32
33
34
35
36
37
38
39
40
46
47
48
49
88
87
86
85
84
83

76
56
75
96
ROMFORD
Romford
Crowlands
Westlands Playing Field
West Ham FC Training Grd.
Romford Cemetery
Crowlands Sports Ground
Gas Works
QUEEN'S HOSPITAL
Oldchurch Park
RUSH GREEN
RUSH GREEN ROAD
HORNCHURCH ROAD
BEACONTREE HEATH
CROWLANDS HEATH GOLF COURSE
Fords Sports Ground
Miniature Golf Course
Dagenham Civic Centre
CENTRAL PARK
Barking & Dagenham Coll.
EASTBROOKEND COUNTRY PARK
BARKING and DAGENHAM
White Hart Lakes
Eastbrook End Cemetery
The Chase Local Nature Reserve
The Millennium Centre
Eastbrook Comp. Sch.
Dagenham & Redbridge FC (Victoria Road)
Gas Transmission Station
Dagenham East
Dagenham
DAGENHAM
Dagenham Heathway
Bretons Outdoor Recreation Centre
Scargill Jun. & Inf. Schools
The Brittons Academy
OLD DAGENHAM PARK
Dagenham Park Leisure Cen.
THE LEYS
BEAM VALLEY COUNTRY PARK
SOUTH HORNCHURCH
Newtons Corner
Rainham
Dagenham Dock
RM7
RM8
RM9
RM10
RM13
HEATHWAY
NORTH RAINHAM ROAD
RAINHAM ROAD
SOUTH DAGENHAM RD.
BALLARDS ROAD
NEW ROAD
RIPPLE RD.
WOOD LANE
HIGH RD.
WHALEBONE LA. SOUTH
UPPER RAINHAM RD.
Cd
Dd
Ed
Fd
Gd
Hd
Jd
31
32
33
34
35
36
37
38
39
40

HORNCHURCH
Hornchurch
UPMINSTER
Upminster
ELM PARK
RAINHAM
HACTON
CORBETS TEY
St. Leonards Hamlet
EMERSON PARK
Emerson Pk.
Upminster Bridge
Hornchurch
HORNCHURCH COUNTRY PARK
Upminster Golf Course
UPMINSTER PARK
Berwick Glades
Berwick Wood
Bonnetts Wood
Airfield Wood
Flightway Wood
Farmhouse Wood
Runway Wood
Abbey Wood
Berwick Pond
Landfill Site
Refuse Transfer Station
Sand & Gravel Pits
Suttons Parkway
Hacton Parkway
Ingrebourne River
RM11
RM12
RM14
HIGH STREET
UPMINSTER ROAD
ST. MARY'S LANE
A124
B1421
57
97
78

78
Junction 29
M25
M25-MOTORWAY
CRANHAM
UPMINSTER
Upminster
RM14
HAVERING
NORTH OCKENDON
SOUTH OCKENDON
CORBETS TEY
UPMINSTER GOLF COURSE
UPMINSTER PARK
CRANHAM GOLF COURSE
Upminster Hall Playing Fields
Hall Mead School
Hall Lane Miniature Golf Course
Cranham Brickfields Local Nature Reserve
Franks Wood
Franks Farm
Westbury Farm
Cranham Court
Club House
The James Oglethorpe Prim. Sch.
Coopers' Company & Coborn Sch.
Thames Chase Forest Centre
Cranham Hall
Cranham Marsh Local Nature Reserve
Spring Wood
Middle Wood
Bonus Wood
Hobbs Hole
Clay Tye Hill
Claynes House
Clay Tye Farm
Puddle Dock
Jax Folly
Kennels
White Post Farm
Cranham Place
Bridge Cottages
Remembrance Cottages
Rectory
Hall Farm
Manor Farm
Manor Farm Cottages
Elec. Sub. Sta.
Gaynes School Language College
South Essex Crematorium
Upminster Cemetery
Redcrofts Farm
Great Sunnings
Gay's Cottages
Sullens Farm
Russells Lake
Stubbers Lodge
Stubbers Adventure Centre
Coys Lake
Caravan Site
Dennises Cottages
Bush Farm
Bramble Farm
Freeman's Shaw
Sand & Gravel Pit
Kemps Farm
Hunt's Hill Cottages
Hunt's Hill Farm
Cockhide
Damyn's Hall
Damyn's Hall Cotts.
Greenacres
Llantrisant Oaks
New House
Central Farm
The Lodge
Oakfields Montessori Sch.
Parklands School
Weir Open Space
Warwick Wood
White Post Wood
Benyon Prim. Sch.
Ockendon
Emerson Park School
Playing Field
Museum
Club House
Upminster Windmill
Grove Farm Cot
ST. MARY'S LANE
OCKENDON ROAD
B187
B1421
B186
98
58
Sd Td Ud Vd Wd Xd Yd
31 32 33 34 35 36 37 38 39 40
56 57 58 59
88 87 86 85 84 83

Zd   Ae   Be   Ce   De   Ee   Fe

Farm
Smallholding
Engineering
Works

560   61   62   63

Abattoir

HORNDON
INDUSTRIAL
PARK

WEST HORNDON

Little Warley Hall Lane
Orchard
Farm

CHILDERDITCH LANE

59

West
Horndon

Lower
Shaw

88

31

B186 STREET

MARY'S

ST.

LANE

ST. MARY'S

Brentwood

32

Monks
Farm

Little
Tillingham
Hall

Field House

Old England

DUNNINGS

Moat

Clay Tye
Wood

Tillingham
Hall

CM13

87

Sewage
Works

33

Bury Farm

I   N   G

Grid Sta.

Slough
House

CHINA

34

Fairplay Farm

86

Hatch Farm

Bullens & Herds

LANE   LANE

35

Blankets
Farm

Mar   Dyke

Caylock's
Farm

Home Farm

Stone Hall

36

The
Orchard

LANE

Corner
Farm

FEN   LANE

LANE   FEN

THARROW

LANE

Mar   Dyke

185

Club
House

TOP MEADOW
GOLF COURSE

Judds Farm

Moat

37

The Downes

FEN

Mar

Fen Farm

Bulphan   Fen

LANE

ne Farm
ottage

T   H   U   R   R   O   C   K

edcrofts

Groves
Cottages

Mar

Dyke

Stringcock Fen

38

84

Groves
Barns

ROAD

The
Wilderness

South Ockendon

39

B186

RM15

ORSETT   FEN

40

South Ockendon
Hall

LANE

Mar   Dyke

Moat

Reservoir

83

GREEN

Cemetery
Bowling
Green
Tennis
Courts

Zd   Ae   Be   Ce   De   Ee   Fe

Rec.
Grd.

560   61   62   63

99

bletts

80
60
102
FARNHAM ROYAL
BURNHAM
Burnham Park
LENT
LENT RISE
LYNCH HILL
BRITWELL
CIPPENHAM
Slough
Maidenhead
SL6
SL1
SL4
SOUTH BUCKS
LAKE END
DORNEY
ETON WICK
Windsor
Burnham Abbey
Pondleys Cottage
MAIDENHEAD HUNTERCOMBE HOSPITAL
Junction 7
Junction 6
M4 MOTORWAY
M4
BATH ROAD
A4
A355
A332
B3026
B3026
FARNHAM ROAD
BRITWELL ROAD
BURNHAM LANE
LAKE END ROAD
DORNEY COMMON
DORNEY LAKE
Dorney Lake Park & Nature Reserve
ETON WICK ROAD
COMMON ROAD
VILLAGE ROAD
TUNS LANE
ELIZABETH WY.
ETON LITTLE COMMON
ETON GREAT COMMON
NORTH FIELD
SOUTH FIELD
JUBILEE RIVER
Roundmoor Ditch
Sludge Beds
Filter Beds
Water Pollution Control Works
Pipe Line Station
Weir
SLOUGH TRADING ESTATE
SLOUGH INDUSTRIAL ESTATE
BATH ROAD RETAIL PARK
WESTGATE RETAIL PK.
SLOUGH RETAIL PK.
Superstore
Burnham Grammar Sch.
Claycots School
Beechwood & Arbour Vale Schools
St. Anthony's Catholic Prim. Sch.
The Westgate Sch.
Montem Primary Sch.
Burnham Pk. E-ACT Academy
Kennedy Park Rec. Grnd.
Cippenham Green
Mercian Way Rec. Grd.
Eton Wick Rec. Grd.
Cocksherd Wood
Grenville Court
Britwell House
Court Farm
Recreation Ground
Cherry Orchard
Burnham
ROYAL WINDSOR

81
61
103
82
H
J
K
L
M
N
P
1
2
3
4
5
6
7
8
9
10
SOUTH BUCKS
SL2
SL3
STOKE POGES GOLF COURSE
Spa SPC
Stoke Park Hotel
Club House
Stoke Park Fm.
Manor House
Gray's Field
Monument
Gardens of Remembrance
Sports Ground
Tennis Courts
Duffield Ho.
Stoke Ho.
STOKE GREEN
Park View
Cricket Grd.
Stoke Place
The Clock
Appletons
Nuffield Health Fitness & Wellbeing Cen.
Berry Farm
WEXHAM PARK
GOLF COURSE
Grotes Wood
Pinewood Nurseries
Green Acres
Bell Fm.
WEXHAM PARK HOSPITAL
John Lister Postgraduate Centre
Wexham
Wexham Sch.
Wexham Court
Spring Wood
Hollybush Wood
Jubilee Plantation
Rowley Lake
Rowleyfield
Walk Wood
Gallions Wood
Stone's Wood
Langley Furze
MANOR PARK
Wood School
Oakwood Ho.
Broom Ho.
Little Haven
Pinehurst
Alderbourne
THE SOUTH BUCKINGHAMSHIRE ACADEMY
Driving Range
Club House
Stokeplace Farm
The Park Driving Range
Wexham Park Stadium
Khalsa Prim. Sch.
Slough Crematorium
CEMETERY
Granville Playing Field
Baylis Court Sch.
Godolphin Playing Field
West Wing Arts Cen.
Football Pitches
Slough Town FC (Arbour Pk.)
James Elliman Prim. Academy
Baylis Grds.
Bowyer Play. Fld.
Thomas Gray Cen.
Primary Schools
GRAND UNION CANAL
GEORGE GREEN
Masons Fm.
Home Farm
The Manor House
Grove Fm.
Lavender Farm
Nursery
Wildcroft
MIDDLE GREEN
Langley Hall Prim. Academy
Recreation Ground
Salt Hill
Salt Hill Park
Absolutely Ten Pin
Ditton Pk. Academy
Slough
SLOUGH
Superstore
Bus Sta.
WELLINGTON
Town Hall
Gala Bingo
Montem Leisure Cen.
Queensmere Shop. Cen.
Empire Cin.
Sorting Office
The Observatory Shop. Cen.
easyGym
Gas Works
The Business Village
County & Mag. Ct.
Upton Hosp.
St. Bernard's Prep. Sch.
Playing Field
CHALVEY
College
Powerleague Soccer Centre
Upton Park
Herschel Park
The Mere
UPTON
Lascelles Playing Fields
Spring Cott.
Upton Ct.
Upton Court Farm
Long Close Sch.
Kedermister Park
Sports Field
Agars Plough
Agars Plough (Playing Fields)
Tennis Courts
Broadbent House
Beggar's Bri.
Cricket Ground
ETON
Fifteen Arch Bri.
Sixpenny or The Field
Pocock's Pond
Cricket Ground
Playing Fields
Boathouse Cott.
Boat Ho.
Landing Stage
Running Track
Thames Valley Athletics Cen.
Myrke
UPTON COURT PARK
Pumping Station
Hockey Pitch
Recreation Ground
Longmead Bridge
Datchet Mead Cottage
Reservoir (covered)
Black Potts Weir
Windsor (Home Pk.)
THE HOME PARK
Gibraltar Bridge
DITTON PARK
King's Oak
Offices
Evans Cott.
Langley Gate
M4 MOTORWAY
A4
A412
A332
B416
B3026
B376
B3022
WINDSOR RD.
UXBRIDGE RD.
LONDON RD.
SLOUGH RD.
DATCHET RD.
STOKE POGES LA.
STOKE RD.
WEXHAM RD.
PARK RD.
CHURCH LA.
FARNHAM RD.
BATH RD.
HIGH ST.
ALBERT ST.
ST. LAURENCE WY.
MIDDLEGREEN RD.
LANGLEY RD.
ELLIMAN AV.
BAYLIS RD.
SHAGGY CALF LA.
NORTHERN RD.
BEECHWOOD RD.
FIR TREE AVENUE
STOKE GREEN
WEXHAM PARK LANE
ETON
MAIDENHEAD

BLACK PARK COUNTRY PARK
LANGLEY PARK COUNTRY PARK
SOUTH BUCKS
IVER HEATH
SHREDING GREEN
GEORGE GREEN
Slough
SL3
MIDDLE GREEN
Iver
SL0
RICHINGS PARK
LANGLEY
Langley
GRAND UNION CANAL (SLOUGH ARM)
IVER GOLF COURSE
RICHINGS PARK GOLF COURSE
Sutton
DITTON PARK
Junction 5
LANGLEY ROUNDABOUT
M4 MOTORWAY
UXBRIDGE ROAD
SLOUGH ROAD
LANGLEY PARK ROAD
LONDON ROAD
STATION RD.
HIGH STREET
A412
A4007
A4
B470
62
81
104

83
63
84
105
H
J
K
L
M
N
P
Middlesex College
Woodlands Park
Stables
Moorwards Cottage
M25
M25 MOTORWAY
Palmer's Moor Farm
Delaford Manor
Coppins Fm.
Delaford Gds.
Lower Delaford
Iver Lodge
Delaford Park
Bridgefoot Ho.
Graveyard
Delaford Ho.
North Lodge
HUNTSMOOR PARK
Huntsmoor Park Fm.
Yacht Club
Farlows Lake
Sewage Works
Aqueduct
Airport Parking
Iver Water Treatment Works
Iver
THORNEY PARK GOLF COURSE
Club Ho.
THORNEY
Mercers Farm
THORNEY COUNTRY PARK
Thorney Pool
Junction 15 (M25)
M4-MOTORWAY
Old Slade Lake
Junction 4b (M4)
New Wood
Iver South SDW
Arboretum
Great Barn
Picnic Area
Home Farm
Manor Court
Warehouses
UXBRIDGE
COWLEY
Cowley Lake
Little Britain
Little Britain Lake
Old Mill Fm.
Riverdale
Cowley Rec. Ground
Airport Parking
Halls of Residence
Brunel University (Uxbridge Campus)
Athletics Centre
Uxbridge UB8
Hillingdon Cem.
Uxbridge Cem.
HILLINGDON GOLF COURSE
Brunel Uni. Sports Park
The Grove Nature Reserve
Bishopshalt School
Tudor Cott.
Pield Heath House RC Sch.
Garden Centre
PIELD HEATH
COWLEY PEACHEY
Meadow High Sch.
HILLINGDON HOSPITAL
COLHAM GREEN
Colham Manor Prim. Sch.
Moorcroft Sch.
Stockley Academy
Rabbsfarm Prim. Sch.
YIEWSLEY
GRAND UNION CANAL
Packet Boat Dock
STOCKLEY COUNTRY PARK
Recreation Ground
Uxbridge FC
Stockley Park
HILLINGDON
West Drayton
Horton Bridge
Warehouses
West Drayton Prim. Sch.
UB7
Frays Island & Mabey's Meadow Nature Reserve
Oxeney
Mayfield Caravan Park
Drayton Hall Comm. Cen.
The Closes Rec. Grd.
St. Georges Meadow
WEST DRAYTON
Cemetery
Laurel Lane Prim. Sch.
Cricket Grd.
Playing Field
Cherry La. Prim. Sch.
Recreation Ground
Hotel
M4
A408
A4020
A3044
B470
HILLINGDON HILL
FALLING LANE
HARMONDSWORTH
HOLLOWAY
SIPSON RD.
Nursery
Heathrow Primary School
41
42
43
44
45
46
47
48
49
50

84
64
83
106
Q
R
S
T
U
V
W
07
08
09
510
HILLINGDON
HILLINGDON HEATH
COLHAM GREEN
HAYES END
WOOD END GREEN
WOOD END
HAYES
HAYES TOWN
WEST DRAYTON
Goulds Green
West Drayton
Hayes
Uxbridge
HARLINGTON
CRANFORD PARK
UB10
UB8
UB4
UB3
UB7
UB11
UXBRIDGE ROAD
HARLINGTON ROAD
STOCKLEY ROAD
DRAYTON ROAD
DAWLEY ROAD
NORTH HYDE ROAD
STATION ROAD
HIGH STREET
M4 MOTORWAY
Junction 4
A4020
A437
A408
A3044
B465
Hillingdon Hospital
Bishopshalt School
Hedgewood School
Grosvenor Playing Field
Hayes Shrub
Hayes Park
Yeading Brook Nature Reserve
Grange Park Jun. & Inf. Schs.
Rosedale College
Barra Hall
Town Hall Park
Stockley Country Park
Stockley Park Golf Course
Stockley Park
Uxbridge FC
Recreation Ground
Heathpark Golf Course
Lake Farm Country Park
Grand Union Canal
Hayes & Harlington
Harlington Community Sch.
Pinkwell Park
Cranford Park Academy
Harlington Hospice
Little Harlington Field
Sports Ground
Heathrow Express Rail Link
Cherry Lane Roundabout
Frogs Ditch Farm
Goals Soccer Centre Heathrow
Burial Ground
Crane Meadows
Gravel Works
Heathrow Primary School
Sipson Meadow

85
Northolt
GREENFORD
YEADING
SOUTHALL
Southall
DORMER'S WELLS
NORWOOD GREEN
OSTERLEY PARK
Hounslow
MINET COUNTRY PARK
RECTORY PARK
(Recreation Ground)
RUISLIP ROAD
B455
THE PARKWAY
A312
UXBRIDGE ROAD
THE BROADWAY
HIGH ST.
A4020
SOUTH ROAD
A3005
MERRICK ROAD
NORWOOD ROAD
TENTELOW LANE
A4127
GREENFORD ROAD
M4 MOTORWAY
Junction 3
Heston Service Area
AIRLINKS GOLF COURSE
GRAND UNION CANAL
(PADDINGTON BRANCH)
WEST MIDDLESEX GOLF COURSE
GREENFORD PARK CEMETERY
Jubilee Park
Southall Park
King George's Field
Public Open Space
Playing Field
Willowtree Marina
Glade Lane Canalside Park
Hillingdon Cycling Circuit
Goals Soccer Centre (Hayes)
Hayes & Yeading Utd. FC (The Warren)
Havelock Cemetery
Southall Grn.
Featherstone Sports Cen.
Norwood Green
Barnes Farm
David Lloyd Leisure
Golf Driving Range
WESTERN INTERNATIONAL MARKET
Osterley Sports Club
Sports Ground
UB1
UB2
UB5
UB6
TW5
X
Y
Z
Aa
Ba
Ca
Da
41
42
43
44
45
46
47
48
49
50
65
98
107

86
66
85
108
Ea
Fa
Ga
Ha
Ja
Ka
La
41
42
43
44
45
46
47
48
49
50
GREENFORD
GREENFORD ROUNDABOUT
WESTERN AVENUE
A40
M4
M4 MOTORWAY
RAVENOR PARK
RUISLIP ROAD
UB6
UB1
UB2
TW7
W7
W13
PERIVALE PARK
PERIVALE PARK GOLF COURSE
South Greenford
Perivale Park Athletics Track
Gurnell Leisure Cen.
EALING GOLF COURSE
Pitshanger Park
Elthorne Heights
GREENFORD PARK CEMETERY
DORMER'S WELLS
WEST MIDDLESEX GOLF COURSE
BRENT VALLEY GOLF COURSE
Brent Lodge Park
Millennium Maze
Hanwell
HANWELL
Hanwell Community Centre
Drayton Green
Castle Bar Pk
Cleveland Park
SCOTCH COMMON
CASTLEBAR HILL
EALING
West Ealing
WEST EALING
UXBRIDGE ROAD
UXBRIDGE RD.
BROADWAY
NORTHFIELD AVENUE
Kensington Cemetery
City of Westminster Cemetery
EALING HOSP
ST. BERNARD'S HOSPITAL
Southall
Hanwell Locks
GRAND UNION CANAL
Glade Lane Canalside Park
Warren Farm Sports Centre
Osterley Sports Club
OSTERLEY
HOUNSLOW
Isleworth
PARK
Osterley Park House
Osterley Park Farm
WYKE GREEN GOLF COURSE
Elthorne Park
Northfields
Northfields Depot
Blondin Pk. & Nature Area
Boston Manor
Boston Manor Park
Boston Manor House
BOSTON MANOR ROAD
BOSTON ROAD
A3002
A4020
A4127
B455
B452
B454
WINDMILL LANE
TENTELOW LANE
GREENFORD ROAD
ARGYLE ROAD
OSTERLEY LANE
WALPOLE PARK
LAMMAS PARK
The Questors Theatre
Gunnersbury Catholic Sch.

87
67
109
Ma
Na
Pa
Qa
Ra
Sa
Ta
41
42
43
44
45
46
47
48
49
50
PARK ROYAL
Park Royal
Hanger Lane
Hanger Hill
West Acton
Nth. Ealing
NORTH ACTON
North Acton
Acton Main Line
ACTON
Acton Central
EAST ACTON
SOUTH ACTON
South Acton
Acton Town
ACTON GREEN
Ealing Broadway
Ealing Common
EALING COMMON
Little Ealing
GUNNERSBURY
Gunnersbury
GUNNERSBURY PARK
HOUNSLOW
BEDFORD PARK
SOUTHFIELD
Chiswick Pk.
TURNHAM GREEN
Kew Bridge
Junc. 1
Junc. 2
M4 MOTORWAY
WESTERN AVENUE
HANGER LANE
GUNNERSBURY LANE
UXBRIDGE ROAD
HIGH STREET
THE VALE
CHISWICK HIGH ROAD
GT. WEST RD.
CEDARS RD.
W3
W5

88
Ua
Va
Wa
Xa
Ya
Za
Ab
68
87
110
41
42
43
44
45
46
47
48
49
50
NW10
W10
W12
NORTH ACTON
North Acton
EAST ACTON
East Acton
Acton Central
ACTON PARK
SOUTHFIELD
BEDFORD PK.
TURNHAM GREEN
Turnham Green
CHISWICK
HOGARTH
KENSAL RISE
Kensal Rise
KENSAL GREEN
Kensal Green
KENSAL GREEN CEMETERY
COLLEGE PARK
Willesden Junction
NORTH KENSINGTON
Ladbroke Gro.
Latimer Rd.
WHITE CITY
White City
Wood La.
SHEPHERD'S BUSH
Shepherd's Bush
Shepherd's Bush Mkt.
Goldhawk Rd.
HAMMERSMITH
Hammersmith
Ravenscourt Park
Stamford Brook
WEST KENSINGTON
Barons Court
Kensington Olympia
Olympia
OLD OAK COMMON
WORMWOOD SCRUBS PARK
(Local Nature Reserve)
HMP WORMWOOD SCRUBS
HAMMERSMITH HOSP. QUEEN CHARLOTTE'S & CHELSEA HOSP. (Imperial College London)
Linford Christie Stadium
North Pole International Depot
Old Oak Common Sidings
Grand Union Canal
ST. MARY'S R.C. CEMETERY
West London Crematorium
ST. CHARLES HOSPITAL
BBC Studios
QPR FC (Loftus Rd.)
Ravenscourt Park
Hammersmith Cemetery
Riverside Studios
CHARING CROSS HOSP.
RIVER THAMES
HARROW ROAD
SCRUBS LANE
WOOD LANE
OLD OAK LANE
VICTORIA ROAD
WESTERN AVENUE
WESTWAY
UXBRIDGE ROAD
THE VALE
GOLDHAWK ROAD
KING ST.
HAMMERSMITH ROAD
HAMMERSMITH FLYOVER
TALGARTH ROAD
GREAT WEST ROAD
FULHAM PALACE RD.
SHEPHERD'S BUSH ROAD
WEST CROSS ROUTE
HOLLAND ROAD
LADBROKE GROVE
ST. QUINTIN AV.
CAMBRIDGE GDNS.
PADDENSWICK RD.
ASKEW RD.
A4020
A40
A219
A402
A315
A4
A3220
A404
A4000
B451
B412
B408
B409
B491

89
REGENT'S PARK
MARYLEBONE
St. John's Lodge
QUEEN MARY'S GARDENS
Boating Lake
The Holme
London Central Mosque
Winfield House
The Hub
Regent's Univ. London
Baker St.
Madame Tussaud's
Wallace Collection
Marble Arch
OXFORD ST.
HYDE PARK
WESTMINSTER
THE SERPENTINE
Speakers Corner
Reformers Tree
Parks Police
Serpentine Sackler Gallery
Norwegian War Mem.
The Long Water
Peter Pan Statue
Speke's Monument
The Fountains
Round Pond
KENSINGTON GARDENS
Kensington Palace
The Orangery
Physical Energy Statue
Temple Lodge
Queen Victoria Statue
Bandstand
Princess of Wales Memorial Fountain
Serpentine Gallery
Albert Memorial
Royal Albert Hall
KNIGHTSBRIDGE
Knightsbridge
Harrods
Hyde Park Corner
Science Museum
Natural History Mus.
Victoria & Albert Museum
Brompton Oratory
BROMPTON
Sth. Kensington
SOUTH KENSINGTON
Gloucester Rd.
CROMWELL ROAD
Earl's Court
EARL'S COURT
West Kensington
West Brompton
Brompton Cemetery
CHELSEA
Saatchi Gallery
Sloane Sq.
PIMLICO
Royal Hospital Chelsea
CHELSEA EMBANKMENT
KENSINGTON
HOLLAND PARK
Holland Park
High St. Kensington
KENSINGTON ROAD
BAYSWATER ROAD
Notting Hill Gate
NOTTING HILL
Queensway
Bayswater
BAYSWATER
Lancaster Gate
Paddington
PADDINGTON
Paddington Basin
Edgware Rd.
Marylebone
MARYLEBONE
LISSON GROVE
Royal Oak
Westbourne Park
WESTBOURNE GREEN
WESTWAY
Warwick Av.
Little Venice
MAIDA VALE
Maida Vale
ST. JOHN'S WOOD
Middlesex CCC (Lord's)
WEST KILBURN
MAIDA HILL
Queens Park
CARLTON VALE
Paddington Rec. Grd.
Paddington Sports Club
WELLINGTON RD.
EDGWARE RD.
PARK LANE
BROMPTON ROAD
FULHAM ROAD
KING'S ROAD
SLOANE ST.

REGENT'S PARK
QUEEN MARY'S GARDENS
MARYLEBONE
Baker St.
Regent's Pk.
Gt. Portland St.
Warren St.
Euston Sq.
EUSTON
SOMERS TOWN
British Library
ST. PANCRAS INTERNATIONAL
KING'S CROSS
PENTONVILLE
FINSBURY
ST. PANCRAS
CLERKENWELL
Russell Sq.
BLOOMSBURY
British Museum
Goodge St.
Tottenham Ct. R.
Oxford Circus
Bond St.
Marble Arch
SOHO
Holborn
HOLBORN
Chancery La.
Covent Gdn.
Temple
Leicester Sq.
Piccadilly Circus
MAYFAIR
Green Park
Hyde Park Corner
HYDE PARK
GREEN PARK
ST. JAMES'S PARK
ST. JAMES'S
Buckingham Palace
Charing Cross
Embankment
Westminster
WATERLOO
Waterloo East
Lambeth Nth.
St. James's Park
Victoria
VICTORIA
Knightsbridge
BELGRAVIA
Sloane Square
PIMLICO
Pimlico
WESTMINSTER
LAMBETH
Vauxhall
KENNINGTON
RIVER THAMES
Houses of Parliament
Big Ben

Rb
Sb
Tb
Ub
Vb
Wb
Xb
HOXTON
SHOREDITCH
Hoxton
Old Street
ST. LUKE'S
Barbican
Moorgate
LIVERPOOL ST
Shoreditch High St.
SPITALFIELDS
BETHNAL GREEN
Bethnal Grn.
Whitechapel
WHITECHAPEL
Aldgate East
Aldgate
CITY
Bank
St. Paul's
City Thameslink
Mansion Ho.
Monument
Tower Hill
Tower Gateway
Shadwell
SHADWELL
BLACKFRIARS
SOUTHWARK
CANNON STREET
LONDON BRIDGE
THE BOROUGH
Borough
The Tower of London
Tower Millennium Pier
HMS Belfast
City Hall
Tate Modern
WAPPING
Wapping
BERMONDSEY
Bermondsey
NEWINGTON
Elephant & Castle
WALWORTH
Kennington
41
42
43
44
45
46
47
48
49
50
71
92
113
219
225
230
231

92
72
114
Yb
Zb
Ac
Bc
Cc
Dc
Ec
BOW
GLOBE TOWN
Bethnal Grn.
MILE END
Mile End
Bow Church
Bow Rd.
Bromley-by-Bow
BROMLEY
Devons Rd.
BOW COMMON
TOWER HAMLETS CEMETERY PARK
Stepney Green
STEPNEY
Whitechapel
RATCLIFF
LIMEHOUSE
Limehouse
Limehouse Basin
Westferry
POPLAR
Poplar
All Saints
Langdon Pk.
Shadwell
SHADWELL
Wapping
West India Quay
Canary Wharf
WEST INDIA DOCKS
Heron Quays
South Quay
ISLE OF DOGS
Crossharbour
CUBITT TOWN
MILLWALL
Mudchute
MUDCHUTE PARK
Island Gds.
Rotherhithe
ROTHERHITHE
Canada Water
Surrey Quays
South Bermondsey
Surrey Canal (Proposed)
DEPTFORD
DEPTFORD PARK
Cutty Sark for Maritime Greenwich
LIMEHOUSE REACH
GREENWICH REACH
COMMERCIAL RD.
EAST INDIA DOCK RD.
THE HIGHWAY
CABLE ST.
MILE END RD.
BURDETT RD.
GROVE RD.
BLACKWALL TUNNEL NORTHERN APP.
EVELYN ST.
LOWER RD.
REDRIFF RD.
SALTER RD.
WESTFERRY RD.
MANCHESTER RD.
PLOUGH WAY
GROVE ST.

93
Fc
Gc
Hc
Jc
Kc
Lc
Mc
41
42
43
44
45
46
47
48
49
50
West Ham
Plaistow
PLAISTOW
East London Crematorium
EAST LONDON CEMETERY
Memorial Recreation Ground
NEWHAM UNIVERSITY HOSPITAL
Cumberland School
Newham College
Newham Leisure Centre
North Beckton
Star La.
Canning Town
CANNING TOWN
CUSTOM HOUSE
West Beckton
King George V Park
LEAMOUTH
East India
Royal Victoria
Custom House for ExCeL
Prince Regent
ExCeL
ROYAL VICTORIA DOCK
ROYAL ALBERT DOCK
LONDON CITY AIRPORT
Terminal Building
London Regatta Centre
Millennium Mill
Pontoon Dock
SILVERTOWN
Thames Barrier Park
West Silvertown
NORTH WOOLWICH ROAD
NEWHAM WAY
BARKING ROAD
VICTORIA DOCK RD.
LOWER LEA CROSSING
SILVERTOWN VIADUCT
SILVERTOWN WY.
CONNAUGHT BRIDGE
ROYAL ALBERT WY.
The O2
Up at The O2
IndigO2
North Greenwich
North Greenwich Pier
Emirates Air Line Cable Car
Emirates Greenwich Peninsula
Emirates Royal Docks
Royal Victoria Docks Watersports Cen.
Thames Wharf London City Airport Pier
Blackwall
Blackwall Point
BLACKWALL TUNNEL
Virginia Quay
Manhattan Wharf
WOOLWICH REACH
THAMES BARRIER
Thames Barrier Yacht Club Marina
Thames Barrier Info. Cen.
Greenwich Yacht Club
Greenwich Peninsula Ecology Park
Greenwich Millennium Village
GREENWICH
SE10
SE7
New Charlton
Charlton
Charlton Athletic FC (The Valley)
Westcombe Park
Maze Hill
MARYON WILSON PARK
Maryon Park
WOOLWICH ROAD
BLACKWALL TUNNEL SOUTHERN APPROACH
TRAFALGAR RD.
CHARLTON
115

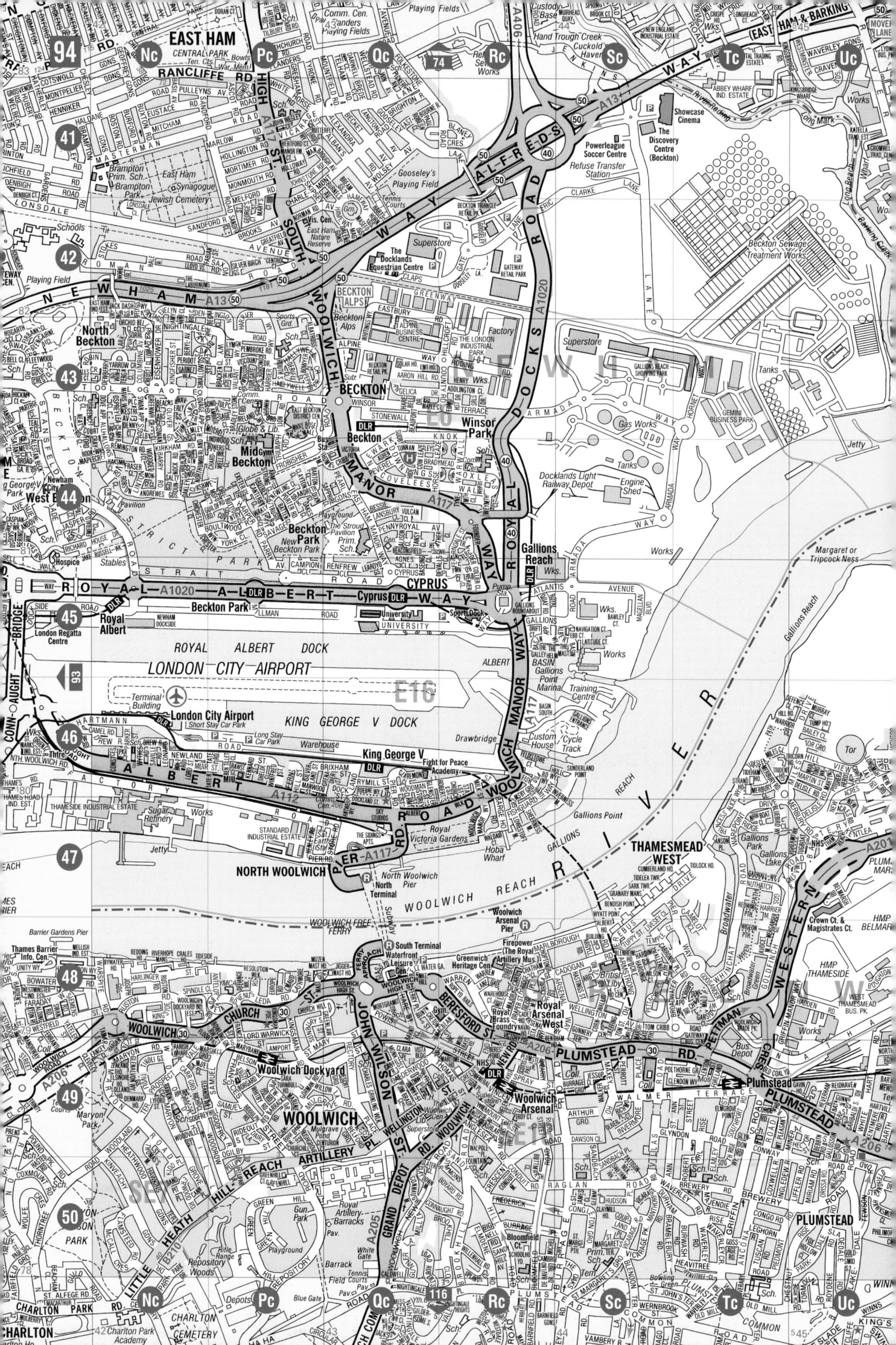
94
EAST HAM
CENTRAL PARK
RANCLIFFE RD.
HIGH ST.
Playing Fields
74
Hand Trough Creek
Cuckold's Haven
EAST HAM & BARKING
NEW ENGLAND INDUSTRIAL ESTATE
ABBEY WHARF IND. ESTATE
Showcase Cinema
The Discovery Centre (Beckton)
Powerleague Soccer Centre
Refuse Transfer Station
Brampton Prim. Sch.
Brampton Park
East Ham Synagogue
Jewish Cemetery
Gooseley's Playing Field
Vis. Cen.
East Ham Nature Reserve
The Docklands Equestrian Centre
Superstore
GATEWAY RETAIL PARK
BECKTON TRIANGLE RETAIL PK.
Beckton Sewage Treatment Works
ALFRED'S WAY
A13
NEWHAM WAY
ROYAL DOCKS ROAD
A1020
North Beckton
BECKTON ALPS
Beckton Alps
ALPINE BUSINESS CENTRE
THE LONDON INDUSTRIAL PARK
Factory
GALLIONS REACH SHOPPING PARK
GEMINI BUSINESS PARK
Tanks
Gas Works
Docklands Light Railway Depot
Engine Shed
Jetty
BECKTON
DLR Beckton
Winsor Park
E6
Mid Beckton
Globe & Lib.
West Beckton
Newham City Farm
Beckton Park
New Beckton Park
The Stroud Pavilion
Gallions Reach
Margaret or Tripcock Ness
Works
CYPRUS
Cyprus
ROYAL ALBERT WAY
A1020
Beckton Park
Royal Albert
London Regatta Centre
UNIVERSITY
ROYAL ALBERT DOCK
LONDON CITY AIRPORT
93
Terminal Building
London City Airport
Short Stay Car Park
Long Stay Car Park
KING GEORGE V DOCK
E16
Warehouse
King George V
Fight for Peace Academy
ALBERT BASIN
Gallions Point Marina
Training Centre
Custom House
Cycle Track
Drawbridge
WOOLWICH MANOR WAY
A117
ALBERT ROAD
A112
THAMESIDE INDUSTRIAL ESTATE
Sugar Refinery
Works
STANDARD INDUSTRIAL ESTATE
Royal Victoria Gardens
Hoba Wharf
Gallions Point
GALLIONS REACH
RIVER
THAMESMEAD WEST
NORTH WOOLWICH
North Woolwich Pier
North Terminal
WOOLWICH REACH
WOOLWICH FREE FERRY
Subway
Woolwich Arsenal Pier
Thames Barrier Info. Cen.
Barrier Gardens Pier
South Terminal
Waterfront Leisure Cen.
Greenwich Heritage Cen.
Firepower (The Royal Artillery Mus.)
Royal Arsenal West
Royal Brass Foundry
British Liby.
WOOLWICH CHURCH ST.
Woolwich Dockyard
JOHN WILSON ST.
BERESFORD ST.
PLUMSTEAD RD.
A206
Woolwich Arsenal
WOOLWICH
Plumstead
PLUMSTEAD
Crown Ct. & Magistrates Ct.
HMP THAMESIDE
HMP BELMARSH
WEST THAMESMEAD BUS. PK.
WESTERN WAY
Gallions Park
Gallions Lake
Broadwater
Maryon Park
PARK
Royal Artillery Barracks
Gun Park
Rifle Range
Repository Woods
White Gate
Barrack Field
GRAND DEPOT RD.
A205
ARTILLERY PL.
HILL REACH
HEATH
LITTLE HEATH
B210
Bloomfield Cl.
CHARLTON PARK
CHARLTON
Charlton Park Academy
CHARLTON CEMETERY
Blue Gate
116
Nc
Pc
Qc
Rc
Sc
Tc
Uc
41
42
43
44
45
46
47
48
49
50

95
Dagenham Dock
THAMES GATEWAY
A13
High Speed 1
75
Barking Riverside
The Ripple Nature Reserve
BARKING and DAGENHAM
RM9
Horse Shoe Corner
Power Station (disused)
George Carey C of E Prim. Sch.
Barking
CREEKMOUTH
Barking Riverside Resource Centre
Barking Riverside Recycling Park
Dagenham Sunday Market
IG11
Oil Storage Depot
Power Station
Landing Stage
THAMES
BARKING REACH
Barking or False Point
Cross Ness
Abbey Sluice
Thamesmead North
Driving Range
The Crossness Pumping Station
THAMESVIEW GOLF COURSE
SEWAGE WORKS
SE28
Thamesmere Leisure Cen.
Twin Tumps
THAMESMEAD CENTRAL
Woolwich Polytechnic School
THAMESMEAD
Birchmere Park
Football Ground
Playing Field
THAMESMEAD SOUTH
Southmere Lake
Lakeside Centre
Erith
BEXLEY
ERITH MARSHES
DA18
THAMESMEAD EAST
The Business Academy, Bexley
EASTERN WAY
A2016
A2041
HARROW MANOR WAY
Thamesmead South West
White Hart Triangle
Abbey Wood Park
ABBEY WOOD
Abbey Wood
ABBEY ROAD
B213
GILBERT RD.
Lesnes Abbey (Ruins)
Belvedere
DA17
LESNES ABBEY WOODS (Nature Reserve)
Plumstead Gdns.
McLEOD RD
BOSTALL HEATH
Greenwich & Bexley Community Hospice
Cooperative Woods
WICKHAM LA.
A209
A206
BOSTALL WOODS
WOOLWICH ROAD
HILL
KNEE HILL
WEST HEATH
Clam Field Recreation Ground
Bowling Green
117
Vc
Wc
Xc
Yc
Zc
Ad
Bd
41
42
43
44
45
46
47
48
49
50

96
Dagenham Dock
Cd
Dd
Ed
Fd
Gd
Hd
Jd
76
NEW ROAD
A1306
A13
THAMES GATEWAY
BARKING and DAGENHAM
Dagenham Breach
Motor Works
Power Station
Depot
Works
FORD INDUSTRIAL PARK
Dagenham
HORNCHURCH MARSHES
Car Compound
RM9
Beam River
Thames Gateway College (CEME)
BASEPOINT BUSINESS CENTRE
Sewage Works
Havering Coll. (Rainham Campus)
Rainham
DOVERS CORNER
Rainham Steel Mills
SUTTONS BUSINESS PARK
BEAM REACH BUSINESS PARK
Superstore
Red Bridge
Rainham Hall
ALBRIGHT INDUSTRIAL ESTATE
DENVER INDUSTRIAL ESTATE
FERRY LANE
RAINHAM
A125
B1335
BLACKWATER CL.
STAR BUSINESS CENTRE
THAMESVIEW BUS. CEN.
Timber Yard
Hornchurch Shoot
Old Man's Head
Frog Island
Jetty
Landing Stage
RM13
HAV
COLDHARBOUR LANE
FREIGHTMASTER ESTATE
EASTER INDUSTRIAL PARK
Warehouse
RIVER THAMES
ERITH REACH
Jenningtree Point
Lighthouse
Coldharbour Point
Pier
Pier (disused)
SEWAGE WORKS
Crossness
Nature Reserve
Erith
Power Station
EASTERN WAY
A2016
THAMESMEAD EAST
DA18
BEXLEY
BRONZE AGE WAY
MANORWAY
PICARDY
B253
Belvedere
Indoor Bowls Club
Sikh Temple
BELVEDERE
HILLSIDE
FRANK'S PARK
DA17
LESSNESS HEATH
ERITH ROAD
A206
FRASER ROAD
Bexley Coll.
Open Space
Erith DA8
ERITH
HAMLET INTERNATIONAL IND. EST.
EUROPA TRAD. EST.
Chalk Farm Wharf
Garden Wharf
A220
BEXLEY RD.
QUEEN'S
118
41
42
43
44
45
46
47
48
49
50
95
Concrete Works

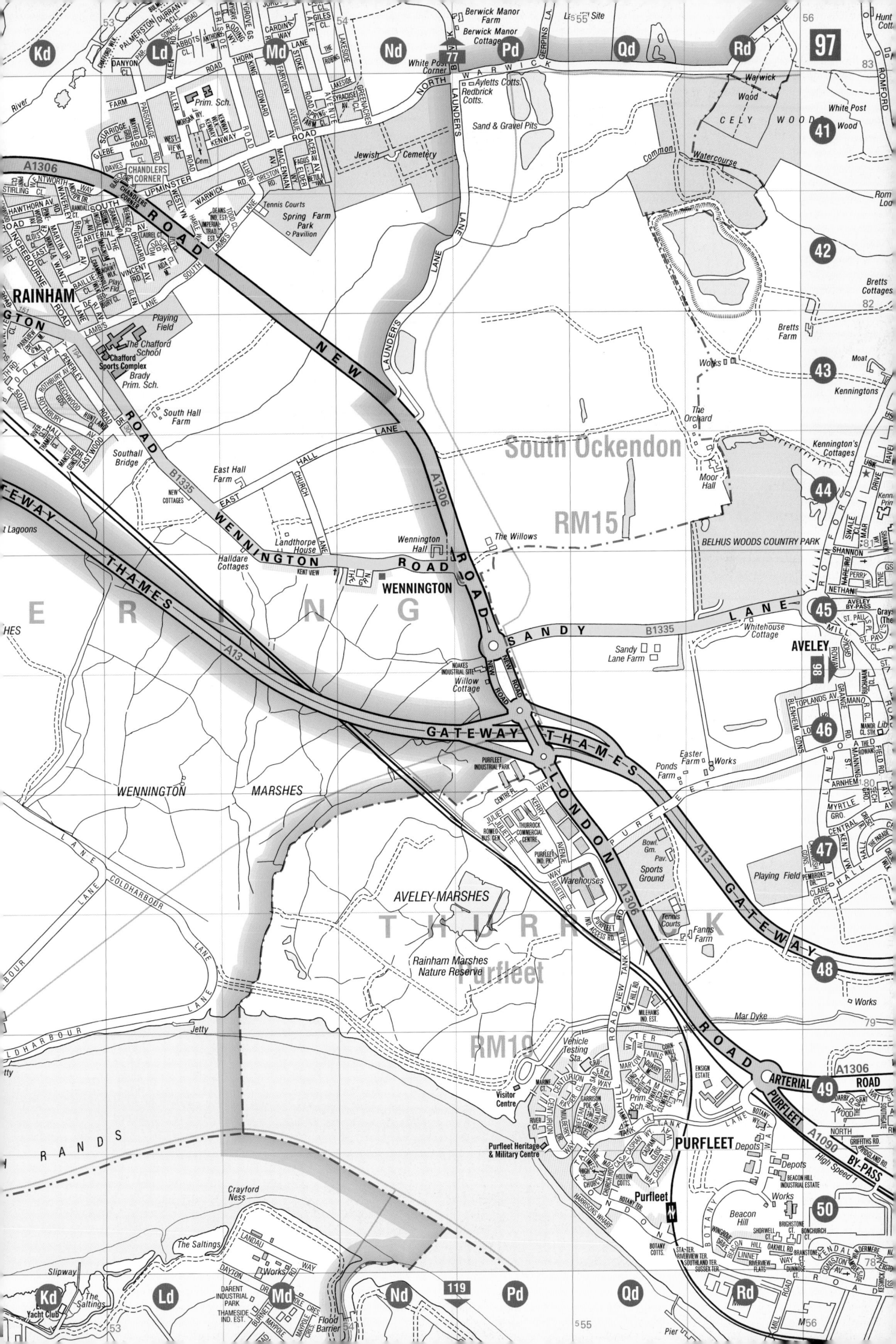
RAINHAM
South Ockendon
RM15
WENNINGTON
AVELEY
PURFLEET
Purfleet
RM19
THURROCK
WENNINGTON MARSHES
AVELEY MARSHES
Rainham Marshes Nature Reserve
BELHUS WOODS COUNTRY PARK
CELY WOODS
Warwick Wood
White Post Wood
Berwick Manor Farm
Berwick Manor Cottage
White Post Corner
Ayletts Cotts.
Redbrick Cotts.
Sand & Gravel Pits
Jewish Cemetery
Spring Farm Park
Tennis Courts
Pavilion
CHANDLERS CORNER
Prim. Sch.
The Chafford School
Chafford Sports Complex
Brady Prim. Sch.
Playing Field
South Hall Farm
Southall Bridge
East Hall Farm
Landthorpe House
Halldare Cottages
Wennington Hall
The Willows
Noakes Industrial Site
Willow Cottage
Sandy Lane Farm
Whitehouse Cottage
Moor Hall
The Orchard
Works
Bretts Farm
Bretts Cottages
Kenningtons
Kennington's Cottages
Easter Farm
Ponds Farm
Purfleet Industrial Park
Thurrock Commercial Centre
Warehouses
Bowl. Grn.
Sports Ground
Tennis Courts
Fanns Farm
Playing Field
Mar Dyke
Vehicle Testing Sta.
Visitor Centre
Purfleet Heritage & Military Centre
Milehams Ind. Est.
Ensign Estate
Depots
Beacon Hill Industrial Estate
Beacon Hill
Crayford Ness
The Saltings
Slipway
Yacht Club
Darent Industrial Park
Thameside Ind. Est.
Flood Barrier
Pier
Jetty
NEW ROAD
A1306
A13
THAMES GATEWAY
WENNINGTON ROAD
B1335
SANDY LANE
LONDON ROAD
ARTERIAL ROAD
PURFLEET BY-PASS
A1090
High Speed 1
COLDHARBOUR LANE
LAUNDER'S LANE
NORTH ROAD
GERPINS LA.
WARWICK LANE
ROMFORD ROAD
Kd
Ld
Md
Nd
Pd
Qd
Rd
41
42
43
44
45
46
47
48
49
50
77
98
119

98
97
78
120
South Ockendon
RM15
HAVERING
Upminster
RM14
BELHUS WOODS COUNTRY PARK
BELHUS PARK
BELHUS PARK GOLF COURSE
M25
M25 MOTORWAY
Junction 30
Junction 31
AVELEY
SOUTH OCKENDON
Thurrock Service Area
Thurrock Lakeside
INTU LAKESIDE (THURROCK LAKESIDE)
LAKESIDE RETAIL PARK
Alexandra Lake
Chafford Hundred
WEST THURROCK
RM20
RM19
Purfleet
Arena Essex Raceway
Speedway Circuit
Motor Sports Complex
Lakeside Karting
MARDYKE VALLEY
Davy Down Riverside Park
Davy Down (Information Cen.)
Ockendon
Factory
Industrial Estate
Ockendon Leisure Centre
The Ockendon Academy
Ormiston Park Academy
Aveley Prim. Sch.
Kenningtons Prim. Sch.
Dilkes Prim. Sch.
Shaw Prim. Sch.
Holy Cross Catholic Prim. Sch.
Bonnygate Prim. Sch.
Beacon Hill Sch.
Impulse Leisure, Belhus Park Club House
Golf Driving Range
Grays Athletic FC (The Mill Field)
Thurrock FC
QED - QUEEN ELIZABETH DISTRIBUTION PARK
Royal Opera Ho. Production Workshop
ARTERIAL ROAD
A1306
A13
A126
A1090
A282
B186
B1335
STIFFORD ROAD
GATEWAY
AVELEY BY-PASS
PURFLEET BY-PASS
THAMES
STONEHOUSE LA.
CANTERBURY WAY
THURROCK WAY
WEST THURROCK WAY
LONDON RD.
Sd
Td
Ud
Vd
Wd
Xd
Yd
41
42
43
44
45
46
47
48
49
50
56
57
58
59

ORSETT FEN
79
100
121
Reservoir
Hobletts
Cemetery
Bowling Green
Rec. Grd.
Tennis Courts
Comm. Cen.
Moat
Depot
Little Mollands Farm
Lake Alexandria
Great Mollands
Works
Grange Farm
MOLLANDS LANE
GREEN LANE
Old Rectory
Whitfields
STIFFORD CLAYS ROAD
Orsett Smock Mill
Grangewaters Outdoor Education Centre
BUCKLES LANE
Little Palmer's Shaw
Great Palmer's Shaw
Mar Dyke
Stifford Clays
A13
A1089
RM16
Bloomfields Farm
William Edwards School
Playing Field
Little Wellhouse Farm
Greygoose Farm Cottage
Greygoose Farm
Hill Fm.
Club Ho.
MARDYKE VALLEY GOLF COURSE
Hotel
Stifford Bri.
STIFFORD HILL
NORTH STIFFORD
Rec. Grd.
Stifford Clays Jun. & Inf. Schs.
THURROCK COMMUNITY HOSPITAL
Deneholm Prim. Sch.
Thurrock Rugby Club
Playing Fields
Tennis Courts
Thurrock Athletics Stadium
King George's Field
Civic Hall
Impulse Leisure, Blackshots
DANEHOLES ROUNDABOUT
A1013
STANFORD RD.
Hangmans Wood
LODGE LA.
WOODLANDS CL.
ARTERIAL ROAD
A1306
A1012
ELIZABETH RD.
HOGG LANE
A126
Caravan Park
Play Fld.
Prim. Sch.
Essex Fire Mus.
Chafford Gorges Visitor Centre
Warren Gorge
CHAFFORD HUNDRED
Chafford Gorges Nature Park
FROBISHER GARDENS
Grays
The Grays Sch. Media Arts College
Play. Field
GRAYS
Little Thurrock Prim. Sch.
St. Thomas of Canterbury Catholic Primary Sch.
Playing Field
Quarry Hill Prim. Sch.
Grays Convent High Sch.
Grays New Cemetery
LITTLE THURROCK
CHADWELL RD.
Palmer's Sports & Fitness Ce
Oil Depot
Lion Gorge
DEVONSHIRE ROAD
TITAN INDUSTRIAL ESTATE
AR Centre
Stifford Prim. Sch.
Sports Ground
LAWRENCE TRADING ESTATE
SOUTHEND ROAD
PALMERS AV.
ORSETT RD.
CLARENCE R.
DOCK RD.
Grays
Council Offs.
Mus.
Thtre.
Grays Pk.
Rec. Grd.
MARSHFOOT RD.
LONDON ROAD
THURROCK ENTERPRISE CEN.
WALSHAM ENTERPRISE CEN.
E. THURROCK ROAD
Zd
Ae
Be
Ce
De
Ee
Fe
41
42
43
44
45
46
47
48
49
50
60
61
62
63
83
82
81
80
79
78

ORSETT FEN
Reservoir
Hobletts
Snake Spinney
New Covert
Sticking Hill
Sticking Hill Covert
Long Covert
Home Farm
Fox Holes
Well Wood
ORSETT PARK
Cherry Orchard Farm
The Decoy
Orsett Hall
Linsteads Farm
Orsett Fruit Farm
Cholley's Farm
Old Hall Farm
Poplars Farm
Orsett House
ORSETT
Old Rectory
Loft Hall Farm
Larch Plantation
Whitfields
Barringtons Farm
Mill House
Orsett C of E Prim. Sch.
Baker Street
Orsett Smock Mill
Foxhound Riding School
CRITON INDUSTRIAL ESTATE
Southfields
Old Kennels Farm
Club Ho.
Mucking Heath
Five Chimney Cottages
RM16
ORSETT GOLF COURSE
Whitecroft's
Heath Place
Walnut Tree Cottages
Thurrock Rugby Club
Playing Fields
Thurrock Athletics Stadium
Brook Farm
Old House Wood
Rainbow Wood
Ashen Shaw
ORSETT HEATH
Grays
Treetops School
Civic Hall
Impulse Leisure, Blackshots
Subway Recreation Ground
Hangmans Wood
Terrels Heath Woodside Prim. Sch.
High House
Herringham Primary Sch.
CHADWELL ST. MARY
Becksland
Mill House
Palmer's Sports & Fitness Cen.
Palmer's College
LITTLE THURROCK
RM17
Chadwell Place
Works
Holford Farm
Shrove Hill Wood
Poultry Farm
Bretts Farm
The Gateway Academy & Prim. Free Sch.
Hobhill Farm
WEST TILBURY
West Tilbury Hall
Gunhill Farm
Biggin
A13
A128
A1013
A1089
A126
B149
B188
STANFORD ROAD
BRENTWOOD ROAD
MARSHFOOT ROAD
DOCK APPROACH ROAD
CHADWELL BY-PASS
MUCKINGFORD ROAD

99
122

HORNDON ON THE HILL
BALSTONIA
STANFORD-LE-HOPE
Stanford-le-Hope
SS17
The Billet
MUCKING
LINFORD
MUCKINGFORD
East Tilbury
EAST TILBURY
Tilbury
RM18
MUCKING MARSHES
EAST TILBURY MARSHES
RIVER THAMES
ROCK
ARTERIAL RD.
THE MANORWAY
A1014
A1013
A13
B1007
St. Clere's Hall Golf Course
Stanford Warren Nature Reserve
Linford Wood Local Nature Reserve
Thames Haven Junction
Heronrys Shaw
Gobians Quarry
Bluehouse Farm
The Hall
Mucking Creek
Active Workings
Jetty
Stanhope Industrial Park
Stanford Le Hope Marshes
Thames Industrial Park
Sports Ground
Factory
Old Counter Wall
Sewage Works
Hassenbrook School
St. Joseph's Catholic Prim. Sch.
St. Clere's School
Abbots Hall Primary Sch.
Thomas Bata Mem. Pk.
East Tilbury Jun. & Inf. Schs.
Cemetery
Driving Range
Mayland
Sutton's Farm
Turners Farm
Walton Hall Campsite
Merrie Loots Farm
Horndon House
The Gables
Saffron Garden Cottages
Saffron Gardens
Oak Farm
Great Garlands Farm
West Cotts.
Nursery
Works
H J K L M N P
1 2 3 4 5 6 7 8 9 10
67 68 69 570
78 79 80 81 82 83
123

80
124
A
B
C
D
E
F
G
1
2
3
4
5
6
7
8
9
10
93
94
95
96
78
77
76
75
74
73
SOUTH BUCKS
BRACKNELL FOREST
WINDSOR and
Stamford
Cress
Brook
BOVENEY ROAD
ROASTHILL LANE
Eton Wick
Rec.Grd.
Ditch
ETON
The Bungalow
BUNCES
WAY
WICK
B3026
Folly Bri.
Cemy.
SOUTH FIELD
MEADOW
SOUTH FIELD
Games Ct.
Masters' Field
College
Recreation Ground
Viaduct
ETON
SOUTH MEADOW
DORNEY LAKE
Boveney Court Farm
LOCK PATH
Boveney
Boveney Court
Boveney Weir Lock
Water Jump
Athens
ROYAL WINDSOR RACECOURSE
Long Bri.
Upper Hope
Cuckoo Weir
Parade Ring
Grandstand
Stables
Racecourse Marina
Eton College Rowing Centre
RIVER THAMES
Mill Stream
Ferry
Service
Clewer St. Andrew
Bird Sanctuary
The Brocas
Elizabeth Bri.
Pleasure Grd.
Leisure Cen.
Boat Ho.
Deadwater Ait
Windsor Marina
Bullock's Hatch Bri.
Cemy
WINDSOR ROAD
A308
MAIDENHEAD ROAD
Works
Clewer Park
CLEWER VILLAGE
Mill Stream
Clewer St. Stephen
Play. Fld.
Alexandra Gds.
Windsor & Eton Centr
Meadow Lane Farm
GREEN ROAD
B3383
THE HAND CLINIC
Bishops Farmhouse
Nursery
Fair Acres Farm
OAKLEY GREEN
OAKLEY LANE
DEDWORTH ROAD
B3024
DEDWORTH
Playing Field
Schools
Superstore
Dedworth Green
Windsor
Clewer Green
Clewer New Town
Clewer Hill
SL4
Comm. Cen.
Alexander First Sch.
Gale House Farm
Tarbay Farm
Thames Hospicecare
Windsor Girls' Sch.
Youth Cen.
Comm. Cen.
Rec. Grd.
Schs.
Cemy.
Windsor Lawn Ten. Club
Fitness Club
CLARENCE RD.
VALE ROAD
B3025
IMPERIAL ROAD
B3173
QUEEN ELIZABETH WAY
A332
GOSLAR WAY
A308
Clewer Within
Sports Ground
Spts. Cen.
Arts Cen.
OSBORNE RD.
FRANCES
HOSP.
ST. LEONARD'S ROAD
B3022
CEMETERY
Windsor FC (Stag Meadow)
Spital
Bourne Ditch
Moat
Tennis Cts.
Playing Fld.
Sch.
Queen Mary's Plantation
Park Pale
Nightingale Corner
St. Leonard's Farm
Reservoirs (covered)
Water Tower
St. Leonardshill
Ash Plantation
Withy Cover
Lodge
St. Leonard's
LEGOLAND
Main Entrance
Government Lodge
Crown Cotts.
Lodge
P+R Windsor (Legoland)
Miniature Rifle Range
Diningroom Close
Spital Meadow
Cavalry Exercise Grounds
Paddockhill Copse
New Cover
Palatine Gate
DRIVE
DARKHOLE
Queen Victoria's Tree
High Standinghill Woods
Forbe's Fields
QUEEN ADELAIDE'S RIDE
ST. LEONARD'S ROAD
Fish Pond
Forest Park
Flemish Farm
CONSORT'S
PRINCE
Bromley Hill
Star Clump
Park Pale
High Standing Hill
Badgers Bridge
BADGERS BRIDGE
WINDSOR FOREST
School Allotment
Northstreet Bridge
SCHOOL ALLOTMENT RIDE
DRIFT ROAD
PRINCE CONSORT'S DRIVE
Flemish Farm
WINKFIELD ROAD
B3022
PARK RIDE
Devil's Gap
CRANBOURNE WOOD
CRANBOURNE CHASE
WINDSOR GREAT PARK
Cranbourne Cover
Buck Paddocks
SHEET STREET ROAD
A332
Sir Andrew Cope's Clump
Battle Bourne
Sandy Arch
QUEEN ANNE'S RIDE
Cranbourne Hall
CRANBOURNE
NORTH ST.
PLAIN RIDE
FOREST ROAD
CRANBOURNE PARK
Cranbourne Tower
Reservoir (covered)
Brook's Corner
Pickleherring Pond
Ranger's Gate
Ranger's Lodge
Beehive Plantation
Beehive Hill
Seymours Plantation
Fiddle Covert
Russel's Pond
Russel's Plantation
MOUNTS HILL
B383
PRINCE CONSORT'S DRIVE

M4
81
M4
125
104
H
J
K
L
M
N
P
1
2
3
4
5
6
7
8
9
10
97
98
99
500
78
77
76
75
74
73
Recreation Ground
Thames Valley Athletics Cen.
Fifteen Arch Bri.
Sixpenny or The
Cricket Grd.
Willow Brook
The Playing Fields
Fellow's Pond
College Field
ETON
LANE
Boat Ho
Landing Stage
Reservoir (Covered)
Datchet Mead Cottage
SLOUGH ROAD
Longmead Bridge
DITTON PARK
Gibraltar Bridge
Canal
King's Oak
Offices
Langley Gate
Fish Pond
Evans Cott.
RIDING COURT FARM
Riding Court House
Slough
M4 MOTORWAY
COURT ROAD
B470 ROAD
FARM
MAJORS
LONDON ROAD
B470
HIGH STREET
SLOUGH
Mus.
Works
Windsor (Home Pk.)
P+R
Tennis Courts
THE HOME PARK
(Public Recreation Ground)
Pav.
Lodge
Black Potts Weir
Eton End School
B3026
DATCHET GOLF COURSE
CASTLE AV.
AGARS PL.
ELLESMERE CL.
ETON CL.
GABLES CL.
RUSCOMBE GS.
WHITES LA.
B376
KING EDWARD VII AV.
B470
WINDSOR
Datchet Border
Victoria Bri.
Sumptermead Ait
Churchmead C of E Sch.
Play. Fld.
Cricket Grd.
Datchet Ho.
DEEP FLD.
HIGH PARK
Slopes Lodge
Broad Water
Windsor & Eton Riverside
Theatre
St.Georges Chapel
Windsor Castle
CASTLE HILL
East Ter. Gdn.
East Lawn
South Slopes
QUEEN
ADELAIDE
VICTORIA
LIME AVENUE
Bathing Pool
DUTCH ELM AV.
Club Ho.
BUCCLEUCH
QUEENS RD.
THE GREEN
Datchet
HORTON
LONDON
FAIRFIELD
MONTROSE
JUBILEE
LAWN CL.
LINK RD.
THE CEDARS
LINCHFIELD RD.
SL3
Cemy.
DITTON ROAD
B376
PENN
FLEETBROOK HO.
THE QUEEN MOTHER RESERVOIR
Lib.
Tens. Cts.
DATCHET
Recreation Ground
THE MONTAGU
PADDOCK
THE DRIVE
TALBOT
WALK
HOLMLEA RD.
COBB CL.
MARSHFIELD
Mus.
Guildhall
PARK ST.
Riding Sch.
WINDSOR
Tennis Cts.
Cambridge Gate
ROYAL HOUSEHOLD GOLF COURSE
FROGMORE
Municipal Offs.
BROOK ST.
Victoria Barracks
SHEET ST.
KING'S
King's Pavilion
Long Walk Gate
Cricket Ground
Pav.
Adelaide Cottage
Adelaide Lodge
THE
QUEEN ELIZABETH'S WALK
Golf Cottage
HOME PARK
Double Cottages
Jetties
Jetty
PRINCE ALBERT'S WALK
Boat Ho.
Woollacombe
Sandlea Court
B3021
ROAD
SOUTHLEA
BEAULIEU
SAFFRON CL.
ELM CROFT
CLOSE
Water Intake
Southlea
Datchet Common
MILL PL.
MILL PLACE CARAVAN PARK
The Mill House
Pumping Station
B376
ROAD
DAGMAR RD.
DEVEREUX RD.
PRINCE CONSORT COTTS.
ADELAIDE SQ.
GLOUCESTER PL.
EDINBURGH
Sch.
HOSP.
OSBORNE RD.
QUEENS TER.
Frogmore
Frogmore Cott.
Frogmore House
Royal Mausoleum
Mausoleum
CORONATION
MULBERRY AV.
Prince Consort's Home Farm
The Aviary
Tea Room
Southlea Farm
MONASTERY
Monastery Cottages
Welly Farm
NEW WINDSOR
Jubilee Mount
Frogmore Lake
FROGMORE BORDER
AVENUE
EVERGREEN OAK AV.
RIVER
Albert Bridge
THAMES
Old Windsor Weir
Nickcroft Ait
Sludge Area
Bird Sanctuary
HAM FIELDS
Lagoons
Sewage Works
Sunnymeads
Nursy.
Welley Bri.
THE AVENUE
ACACIA AV.
WELLEY AV.
Shaw Farm
Shaw Farm
Windsor Hall
ROYAL GARDENS
Kingfisher
NEW CUT
Bridge Ho.
HAM LANE
Ham Island
Sunnymeads
Club
Gravel Pit Lake
Bryn Brith
Queen Anne's Cottage
ALBERT
A308
A332
KING'S ROAD
HOG COMMON
Lodge
Shawfarm Gate
Crown Cottages
Albert Lodge
North Lodge
Crown Cottages
Moram Lodge
DATCHET RD.
Manor Farm
Fairview
Ham Bridge
ENGLISH GS.
PARK AV.
THE DRIVE
QUEENS GATE COTTAGES
Garrison Sports Ground
Park Pale
Bourne
Battle
ROAD
STRAIGHT
Library
TAPESTRIES HALL
OLD WINDSOR LOCK
Boat Ho.
Remenham House
Remenham Park
MAIDENHEAD
CLAYHALL LANE
ALBANY
TYLE PL.
Clayhall Farm
Moat
CHURCH ROAD
Cemy.
GLEBE RD.
THE AVENUE
CELL FARM AV.
MEADOW CL.
POLLARD CL.
THE GRANGE
HAM
The Manor
Church Ho.
WHITE HERMITAGE
The Priory
KINGSWOOD CREEK
Hunting Lodge
CREEK DRIVE
Wraysbury Lake Sailing Club
HOLLY DRIVE
South Lodge
Tileplace Farm
MILLERS LANE
ST. ANDREW'S
ST. LUKE'S RD.
ST. PETER'S RD.
LYNWOOD
QUEEN'S
ROBIN WILLIS WY.
Rec. Grd.
OLD WINDSOR
MEADOW
RICARDO
FOLLETT CL.
SAXON
FRIARY
FERRY LA.
OLD FERRY DRIVE
Old Ferry Ho.
HILL VIEW RD.
Friary Island
FRIARY ISLAND
OLD FERRY
WAYLANDS
Coach Ho.
Petershill Copse
Peter's Hill
St. Peter's C of E Mid. Sch.
CROFT
CORNWELL
Playgrd
GREGORY DR.
PARKER
A308
40
Staines
Manor Farm Estate
FAIRFIELD
NURSERY WY.
FAIRFIELD RD.
POULCOTT
WINDSOR ROAD
Newmeadow Plantation
Play. Fld.
Mount Place
NEWTONSIDE ORCHARD
BURFIELD
KINGSBURY
ASHBROOK
ORCHARD
MILLS SPUR
MALT HOUSE CL.
THE FRIARY
Moat
Crimp Hill Cemetery
CRIMP
Bear's Rails
Bear's Rails Gate
Sch.
HARWOOD GDS.
WALPOLE
GROVE CL.
WHARF ROAD
RIVERSIDE
OUSELEY
TW19
WRAYSBURY
GARSON
Rush Pond
Bear's Rails Pond
Scout Camp
BEARS RAILS PARK
Woodside Farm
AYLESWORTH SPUR
BRINKWORTH PL.
KEPPEL SPUR
TUDOR LA.
OUSELEY LODGE
ROAD
THE EMBANKMENT
Prince of Wales Pond
Old Windsor Wood
Dower House
PELLING HILL
WINDSOR
Runnymede House
Pats Croft Eyot
MEDE CL.
MAGNA CARTA LA.
Withy Bed
Woodside
Beaumont House
A328
HILL
Priest Hill House
A308
Duke of York Plantation
Liddell Plantation
Old Covert
Playing Field
Runnymede
RUNNYMEDE
Magna Carta Island
Sultan Plantation
Wild Enclosure
Ten. Cts.
Play. Fld.
PRIEST
South Lodge Farm
John F. Kennedy Memorial
ROAD

M4 MOTORWAY
Junction 5
LANGLEY ROUNDABOUT
COLNBROOK
Brands Hill
Datchet Watersports Centre
THE QUEEN MOTHER RESERVOIR
WINDSOR and MAIDENHEAD
Slough
SL3
HORTON
POYLE
Sunnymeads
WRAYSBURY RESERVOIR
WRAYSBURY
Wraysbury
Wraysbury Lake Sailing Club
Wraysbury Dive Cen.
Arthur Jacob Nature Reserve
Colnbrook C of E Primary School
Gravel Pit Lake
HERON LAKE
British Disabled Water-Ski Association
Junction 13
M25 MOTORWAY
Staines
TW19
Ankerwycke Farm
The Moor
126
103

Old Slade Lake
Junction 15 (M25)
Junction 4b (M4)
New Wood
Arboretum
Nursery
Heathrow Primary School
The Great Barn
Picnic Area
Home Farm
Manor Court
HARMONDSWORTH MOOR WATERSIDE
Scotchlake Farm
Visitor Centre
Comm. Cen.
Harmondsworth Prim. Sch.
Rec. Grd.
Computer Centre
Tennis Cts.
Harmondsworth Immigration Detention Centre
HARMONDSWORTH
West Drayton
UB7
SIPSON
HOLLOWAY LANE
HATCH LANE
A3044
HARMONDSWORTH LANE
LAKESIDE IND. EST.
Works
Depot
M25 MOTORWAY
COLNBROOK BY-PASS
A4
BATH ROAD
MOOR JUNCTION
Recreation Ground
Tennis Cts.
Playgrd.
Summit Cen.
POLAR PARK
Hotel
Warehouses
ARGONAUT PARK
COLN TRADING EST.
Mad Bridge
Longford Roundabout
LONGFORD
Longford Bri.
Longfordmoor
Moor Bri.
Elbow Meadow
PERIMETER ROAD
NORTHERN PERIMETER ROAD
HILLINGDON
LONDON HEATHROW AIRPORT
TERMINAL 5A
Heathrow Terminal 5
TERMINAL 5B
TERMINAL 5C
Hounslow
Control Tower
TERMINAL 3
Airside Road Tunnel
Heathrow Express Rail Link
TW6
POLYGON BUSINESS CENTRE
POYLE INDUSTRIAL ESTATE
Bedfont Court Estate
River Colne
Nurseries
Junction 14
AIRPORT WAY
A3113
Airport Parking
Reservoir
The Mill
Weir
Recreation Ground
Hithermoor Lake
Southern Fm.
STANWELL MOOR
Hithermoor Farm
Pumping Sta.
STANWELL MOOR ROAD
Gravel Pit
SOUTHERN PERIMETER ROAD
Cargo Terminal
CARGO POINT
B378
PARK ROAD
TOWN LANE
STANWELL
Stanwell Fields C of E Prim. Sch.
Rec. Grd.
Cemetery
Prim. Sch.
Play Fld.
Tennis Cts.
Recreation Ground
WEST BEDFONT
Ashford Town FC
Westview Cotts.
Sports Ground
Playing Field
Nurseries
Club
Ashford Cemetery
Homers Farm
Superstore
LONDON ROAD
A30
SPELTHORNE
KING GEORGE VI RESERVOIR
STAINES RESERVOIRS
THE CAMGATE CENTRE
SPROGGIT IND. EST.
Depot
Works
106
127
04
05
06
07

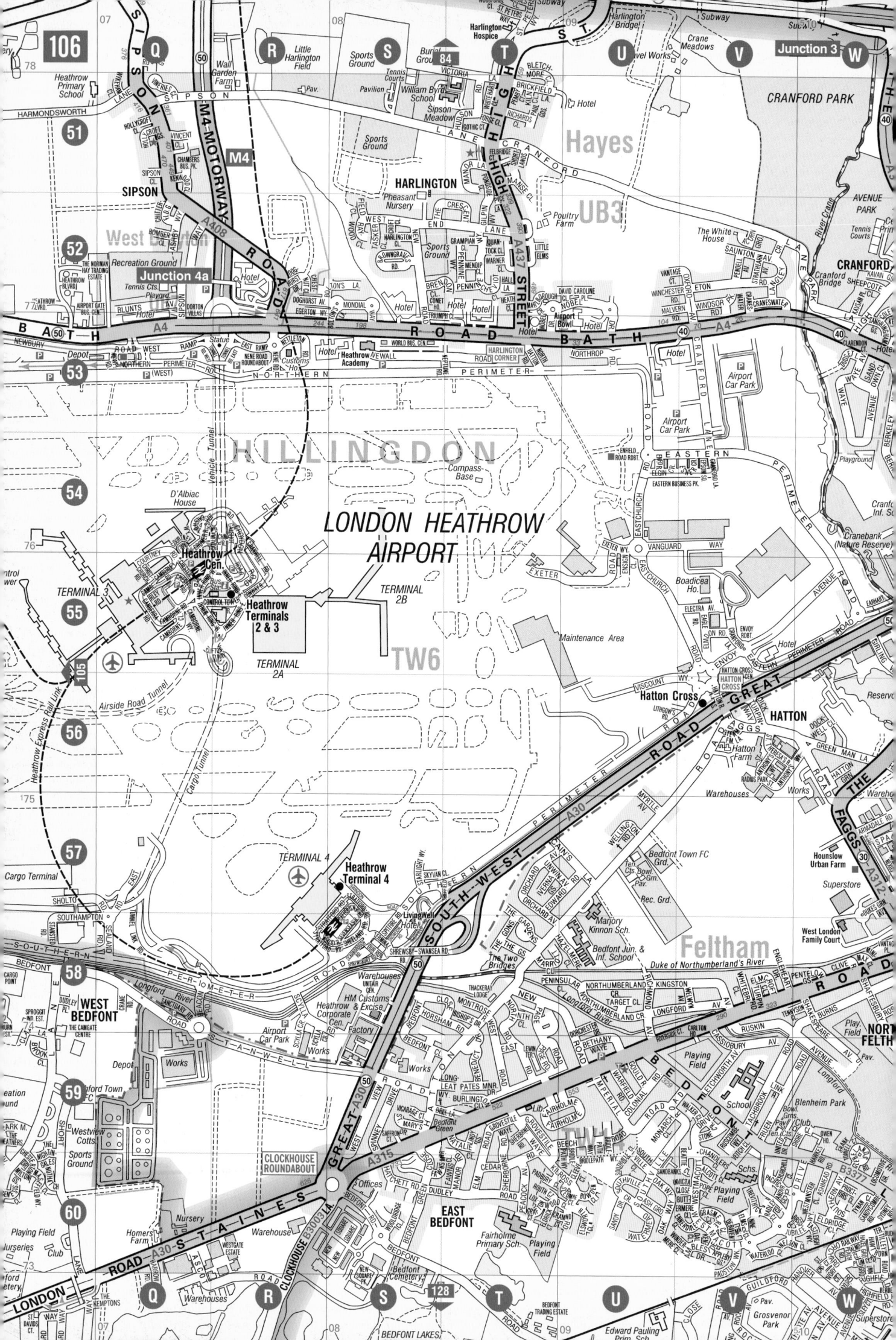

106
Junction 3
Junction 4a
CRANFORD PARK
Hayes
HARLINGTON
SIPSON
West Drayton
UB3
M4-MOTORWAY
M4
A408
A437
HIGH STREET
SIPSON LANE
CRANFORD LANE
HARMONDSWORTH
Heathrow Primary School
Little Harlington Field
Sports Ground
William Byrd School
Sipson Meadow
Harlington Hospice
Harlington Bridge
Crane Meadows
Pheasant Nursery
Poultry Farm
The White House
Recreation Ground
AVENUE PARK
CRANFORD
Cranford Bridge
BATH ROAD
A4
NORTHERN PERIMETER RD.
Heathrow Academy
Customs Ho.
HARLINGTON CORNER
Airport Car Park
HILLINGDON
LONDON HEATHROW AIRPORT
Compass Base
D'Albiac House
Heathrow Cen.
Heathrow Terminals 2 & 3
TERMINAL 3
TERMINAL 2B
TERMINAL 2A
Vehicle Tunnel
Airside Road Tunnel
Cargo Tunnel
Heathrow Express Rail Link
Maintenance Area
TW6
EASTERN PERIMETER
EASTERN BUSINESS PK.
VANGUARD WAY
Boadicea Ho.
Cranebank (Nature Reserve)
Hatton Cross
HATTON
Hatton Farm
Warehouses
Hounslow Urban Farm
Superstore
West London Family Court
GREAT SOUTH-WEST ROAD
A30
TERMINAL 4
Heathrow Terminal 4
Cargo Terminal
SOUTHERN PERIMETER ROAD
Bedfont Town FC Grd.
Rec. Grd.
Marjory Kinnon Sch.
Bedfont Jun. & Inf. School
Feltham
Duke of Northumberland's River
Longford River
HM Customs & Excise
Heathrow Corporate Cen.
WEST BEDFONT
THE CAMGATE CENTRE
STANWELL ROAD
Westview Cotts.
Sports Ground
Playing Field
CLOCKHOUSE ROUNDABOUT
LONDON ROAD
STAINES ROAD
A315
Homers Farm
Nursery
Warehouse
EAST BEDFONT
Fairholme Primary Sch.
Bedfont Cemetery
BEDFONT ROAD
BEDFONT LAKES
Edward Pauling Prim. Sch.
Grosvenor Park
Blenheim Park
NORTH FELTHAM
GUILDFORD AVENUE
128

107
AIRLINKS GOLF COURSE
Heston Service Area
M4
M4-MOTORWAY
Sports Ground
Concorde Centre
Thorncliffe House (Hotel)
HESTON PARK
Heston Pool
OSTERLEY PARK
Playing Field
Heston Comm. Sports Hall
HESTON
TW5
WAGGONERS ROUNDABOUT
HENLYS ROUNDABOUT
BATH RD.
GREAT WEST ROAD
A4
Sutton Playing Field
Lampton Academy
Lampton Sports Cen.
Civic Centre
LAMPTON PARK
SPRING GROVE
LAMPTON RD.
Hounslow East
Hounslow West
Bowls Club
Sports Grd.
Beaversfield Park
HOUNSLOW WEST
Cavalry Barracks
Hounslow Central
Hounslow Manor Sch.
Treaty Centre
HOUNSLOW
Maswell Park
Hounslow
CAUSEWAY
PARKWAY
A312
A30
A3006
A3063
A3005
A315
A314
B361
Rifle Range
Sports Ground
Reservoir
Warehouse
PROLOGIS PARK
TW4
CENTRAL PARK ESTATE
Heath Nurseries
Golf Course
NORTH FELTHAM TRADING ESTATE
Club House
HOUNSLOW HEATH GOLF COURSE
HOUNSLOW HEATH
Hounslow Heath Nature Reserve
STAINES RD.
The Heathland School
Mosque
WELLINGTON ROAD SOUTH
NELSON ROAD
HOSPITAL BRIDGE
Sports Ground
WHITTON
Hounslow Cemy.
HEATHROW GATEWAY
Bridge Farm Nursery
Cemetery
Recreation Grd.
Heathfield Jun. & Inf. Schs.
TW13
South West Middlesex Crematorium
De Brome Building
Playing Field
HANWORTH RD.
HARLINGTON RD. EAST
UXBRIDGE RD.
Twickenham Cemetery
CHERTSEY RD.
A316
Crane Park Island Nature Reserve
Feltham Community College
Gala Bingo
Cineworld
FELTHAM
Feltham
X
Y
Z
Aa
Ba
Ca
Da
85
129
51
52
53
54
55
56
57
58
59
60
13
14

109
Junc. 2
Junc. 1
Kew Bridge
WELLESLEY
TURNHAM GREEN
CEDARS RD.
ELLESMERE RD.
HOGARTH LA.
CHISWICK
HOUNSLOW
Brentford FC (Griffin Pk.)
Brentford Ait
Botanical Library
Kew Palace
Kew Green
Strand on the Green
Oliver's Island
Old Brentford
The National Archives
Chiswick
W4
GROVE PARK
Chiswick House & Gardens
KEW
ROYAL BOTANIC GARDENS
GARDENS
DEER PARK
MID-SURREY GOLF COURSE
Kew Gds.
NORTH SHEEN
Mortlake Crematorium
DUKE'S MEADOWS
Barnes Bri.
MORTLAKE
Mortlake
LOWER RICHMOND RD.
CLIFFORD AV.
CHALKER'S CORNER
North Sheen
RICHMOND
Richmond
RICHMOND CIRCUS
UPPER RICHMOND RD.
EAST SHEEN
SW14
SHEEN
COMMON
RICHMOND PARK
THAMES
Petersham Meadows
PETERSHAM
Pen Ponds
White Lodge Museum
The Royal Ballet Lower School
SIDMOUTH WOOD
SPANKERS HILL WOOD
(Open during daylight hours only)
131

110
TURNHAM GREEN
CHISWICK
Chiswick House & Gardens
W4
Sports Ground
Riverside Lands
Playing Fields
DUKE'S MEADOWS
Barnes Bridge
MORTLAKE HIGH ST.
UPPER RICHMOND RD. W.
EAST SHEEN
ROEHAMPTON PRIORY HOSP.
ROEHAMPTON GOLF COURSE
ROEHAMPTON
RICHMOND PARK
RICHMOND PARK GOLF COURSE
Kingsfarm Plantation
Putney Vale Crematorium
KINGSTON ROAD
PUTNEY HEATH
Tibbet's Corner
PUTNEY
SW15
FULHAM
Fulham FC (Craven Cottage)
Fulham Palace
Putney Pier
BARNES
SW13
LONDON WETLAND CENTRE
Barn Elms Playing Fields
Castelnau
Hammersmith Pier
The Harrodian Sch.
Leg O'Mutton Local Nature Reserve
RIVER THAMES
Barnes Common Nature Reserve
Roehampton University
QUEEN MARY'S HOSPITAL ROEHAMPTON
Chiswick Eyot
St. Pauls School
CHARING CROSS HOSP.
Barons Court
Hurlingham Yacht Club
88
109
132

111
Bb
Cb
Db
Eb
Fb
Gb
Hb
89
CHELSEA
West Brompton
WEST BROMPTON
Brompton Cemetery
Earls Court (Proposed)
Royal Hospital Chelsea
Chelsea FC (Stamford Bridge)
Fulham Broadway
EMBANKMENT
CHEYNE WALK
CHELSEA
THAMES
RIVER
Cadogan Pier
CHELSEA REACH
Peace Pagoda
Children's Zoo
Pump House Gallery
BATTERSEA PARK
General Games Ground
BATTERSEA
SANDS END
Imperial Wharf
WALHAM GREEN
Parsons Grn.
PARSONS GRN
SOUTH PARK
HURLINGHAM PARK
Hurlingham
The Hurlingham Club
Chelsea Harbour Pier
Cremorne Riverside Centre
Cremorne Gardens
Chelsea Creek
Chelsea Wharf
THE LONDON HELIPORT
Lensbury Wharf
Plantation Wharf Pier
Fulham Wharf
Hurlingham Wharf
Trinidad Wharf
Wandsworth Riverside Quarter Pier
CLAPHAM JUNCTION
Falcon Park
Wandsworth Town
WANDSWORTH GYRATORY
WANDSWORTH
King George's Park
West Hill
Spencer Park
Emanuel School
WANDSWORTH COMMON
Wandsworth Common
HMP WANDSWORTH
WANDSWORTH CEMETERY
EARLSFIELD
Earlsfield
SOUTHFIELDS
Southfields
Southfields Academy
Mecca Bingo
CLAPHAM COMMON
THE AVENUE
NIGHTINGALE LANE
BELLEVUE RD.
BURNTWOOD
133
51
52
53
54
55
56
57
58
59
60

112
Jb
Kb
Lb
Mb
Nb
Pb
Qb
51
52
53
54
55
56
57
58
59
60
90
111
134
GROSVENOR ROAD
CHELSEA EMBANKMENT
RIVER THAMES
CHELSEA REACH
Grosvenor Bridge
Vauxhall
VAUXHALL CROSS
St. George Wharf Pier
KENNINGTON
Surrey CCC (The Oval)
Oval
VAUXHALL
NINE ELMS
NINE ELMS LANE
US Embassy From 2017
Battersea Power Station Development
Power Sta. Pk.
Battersea Dogs' Home
Battersea Park
BATTERSEA PARK
BATTERSEA
Peace Pagoda
Children's Zoo
Millennium Arena
Pump House Gallery
Boating Lake
General Games Ground
Sun Gate
QUEENSTOWN RD.
Queenstown Rd. (Battersea)
NEW COVENT GARDEN MARKET
Fruit & Vegetable Market
SOUTH LAMBETH
SOUTH LAMBETH ROAD
Larkhall Park
Stockwell
STOCKWELL
STOCKWELL ROAD
Platanos College
Angell Town
Wandsworth Rd.
WANDSWORTH ROAD
Clapham High St.
Clapham North
Lambeth Hospital
CLAPHAM
CLAPHAM ROAD
CLAPHAM HIGH ST.
Trinity Hospice
Clapham Comn.
CLAPHAM COMMON
CLAPHAM COMMON NORTH SIDE
CLAPHAM COMMON SOUTH SIDE
LONG RD.
CLAPHAM PARK RD.
ACRE LANE
BRIXTON
Brixton
COLDHARBOUR LANE
BRIXTON HILL
Lambeth Academy
CLAPHAM PARK
Sports Ground
HMP BRIXTON
Windmill Gdns.
Eagle Pond
Mount Pond
Long Pond
Bandstand
Clapham Sth.
CAVENDISH RD.
POYNDERS RD.
KINGS AVENUE
BEDFORD RD.
LAVENDER HILL
CEDARS RD.
NIGHTINGALE LANE
Wandsworth Common
BALHAM
Balham
BALHAM HIGH ROAD
BEDFORD HILL
STREATHAM HILL
STREATHAM PL.
CHRISTCHURCH ROAD
TULSE HILL
Leisure Cen.
Football Pitch

CAMBERWELL
PECKHAM
EAST DULWICH
DULWICH VILLAGE
HERNE HILL
NORTH DULWICH
TULSE HILL
NUNHEAD
PECKHAM RYE COMMON
PECKHAM RYE PARK
DULWICH PARK
RUSKIN PARK
BROCKWELL PARK
SE22
SE24
SE21
SE23
CAMBERWELL GREEN
Burgess Park
Playing Fields
Camberwell Old Cemetery
Horniman Museum
Horniman Gardens
DULWICH & SYDENHAM HILL GOLF COURSE
KINGS COLLEGE HOSPITAL
THE MAUDSLEY HOSP.
DULWICH COMMUNITY HOSP.
Dulwich Picture Gallery
Dulwich College
Dulwich Hamlet FC (Champion Hill Stadium)
Herne Hill Stadium
Loughborough Junc.
Denmark Hill
Peckham Rye
East Dulwich
Queens Rd. (Peckham)
West Dulwich
PECKHAM ROAD
PECKHAM HIGH ST.
QUEEN'S RD.
SOUTHAMPTON WAY
CAMBERWELL NEW RD.
ALBANY RD.
OLD KENT ROAD
DENMARK HILL
HERNE HILL
LORDSHIP LA.
EAST DULWICH ROAD
DULWICH COMMON
LONDON ROAD
HALF MOON LA.
VILLAGE WAY
CROXTED ROAD
NORWOOD ROAD
RYE LANE
NUNHEAD LA.
EVELINA RD.
COLDHARBOUR LA.
MILKWOOD ROAD
DOG KENNEL HILL
GROVE VALE
BARRY RD.
FOREST HILL ROAD
THURLOW PARK ROAD
Rb
Sb
Tb
Ub
Vb
Wb
Xb
91
135
114
51
52
53
54
55
56
57
58
59
60

114
Yb
Zb
Ac
Bc
Cc
Dc
Ec
92
136
113
51
52
53
54
55
56
57
58
59
60
Bermondsey
Millwall FC (The Den)
Surrey Canal (Proposed)
DEPTFORD PARK
RIVER THAMES
GREENWICH REACH
DEPTFORD
Cutty Sark for Maritime Greenwich
Greenwich
Deptford
Deptford Bri.
New Cross
New Cross Gate
NEW CROSS GATE
NEW CROSS
Goldsmiths College
Queens Rd. (Peckham)
OLD KENT RD.
NEW CROSS RD.
NEW CROSS ROAD
LEWISHAM WAY
BROCKLEY RD.
DRAKEFELL RD.
LOAMPIT VALE
LOAMPIT HILL
BLACKHEATH RD.
BROOKMILL ROAD
DEPTFORD CHURCH ST.
CREEK RD.
EVELYN ST.
ST. JOHNS
St. Johns
Elverson Rd.
Lewisham
LEWISHAM
Nunhead
NUNHEAD CEMETERY
NUNHEAD
SOUTHWARK
Nunhead Cemetery Nature Reserve
Telegraph Hill Park
SE15
SE4
SE22
SE23
Brockley
BROCKLEY
HILLY FIELDS
Crofton Park
Ladywell
LADYWELL
Ladywell Fields
University Hospital Lewisham
Lewisham Park
PECKHAM RYE PARK
Newlands
Honor Oak Crematorium
Honor Oak Park
HONOR OAK PARK
HONOR OAK
One Tree Hill Local Nature Reserve
Blythe Hill Fields
Blythe Hill
Catford Bridge
Catford
CATFORD
STANSTEAD ROAD
FOREST HILL
Forest Hill
Horniman Museum
LONDON RD.
RUSHEY GRN.
BROMLEY RD.
CATFORD HILL
ADELAIDE ROAD
MOLESWORTH ST.
LEWISHAM HIGH ST.

Fc
Gc
Hc
Jc
Kc
Lc
Mc
WOOLWICH
Westcombe Park
93
MARYON WILSON PARK
TRAFALGAR
Maze Hill
National Maritime Museum
GREENWICH
GREENWICH PARK
Prime Meridian Line
Royal Observatory Greenwich
Peter Harrison Planetarium
The Wilderness (Deer Park)
Ranger's House
CHARLTON
Charlton Ho.
CHARLTON PARK
SE7
Blackheath RUFC (Rectory Fld.)
QUEEN ELIZABETH HOSPITAL
SHOOTERS HILL
OLD DOVER ROAD
BLACK HEATH
Blackheath Vale
KIDBROOKE
Morden College (Almshouses)
Corelli College
BLACKHEATH
Blackheath
SE3
Thomas Tallis Sch.
Kidbrooke
BLACKHEATH PARK
LEE
Hither Green
HITHER GREEN
Lee
SE12
Horn Park
SUTCLIFFE PARK
Sutcliffe Park Athletics Track
ELTHAM
SE9
BROMLEY
MOTTINGHAM
HITHER GREEN CEMETERY
137
116
51
52
53
54
55
56
57
58
59
60
A2
A20
A205
A210
A2213
A2212
A102
A207
B210
B212
B220

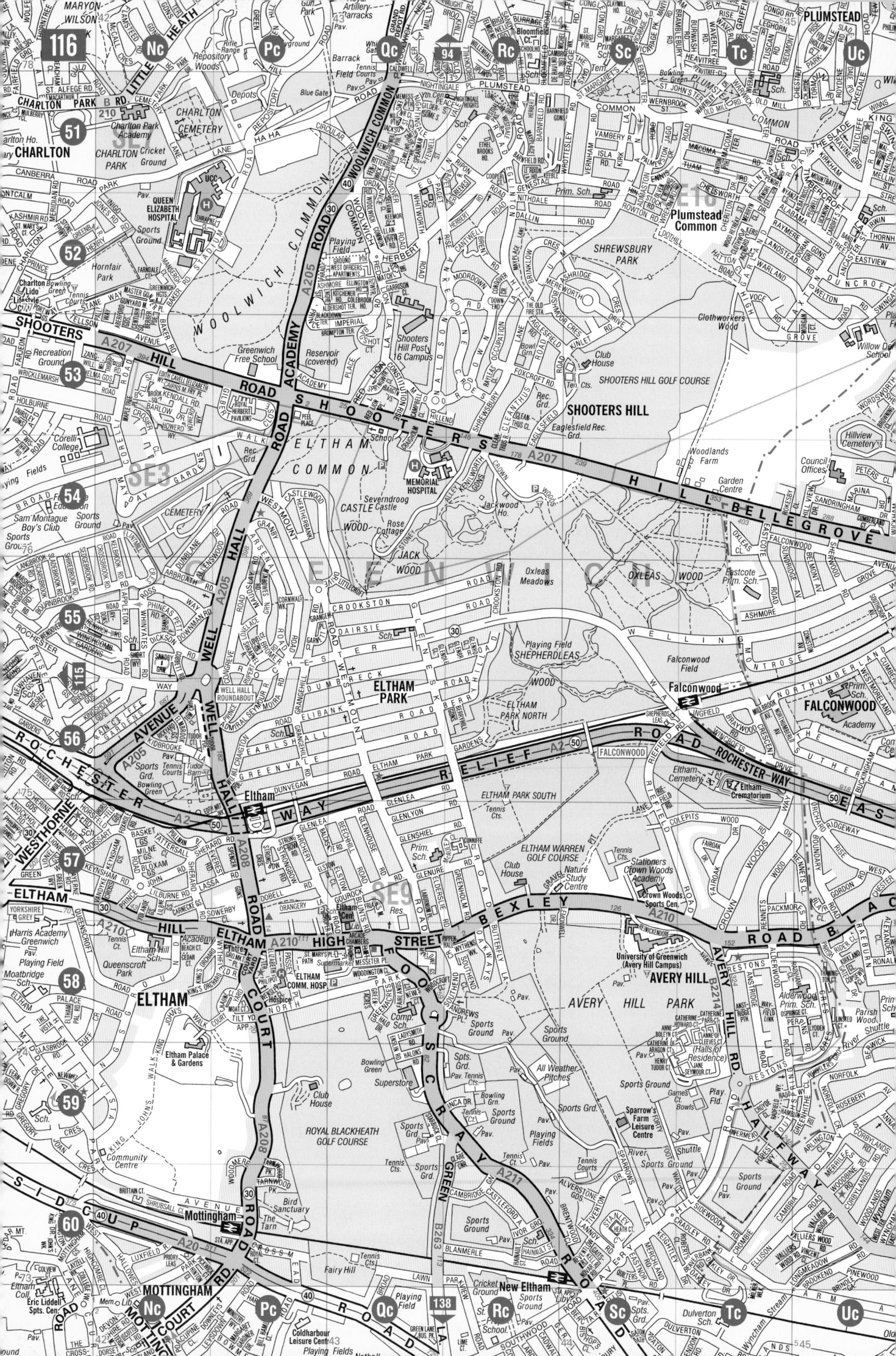
116
Nc
Pc
Qc
Rc
Sc
Tc
Uc
94
PLUMSTEAD
CHARLTON
CHARLTON PARK
Charlton Park Academy
CHARLTON CEMETERY
Repository Woods
Rifle Range
Artillery Barracks
Barrack Field
Blue Gate
Depots
QUEEN ELIZABETH HOSPITAL
UCC
Sports Ground
Hornfair Park
Charlton Lido
Charlton Ho.
Plumstead Common
SHREWSBURY PARK
Clothworkers Wood
Willow Dene School
WOOLWICH COMMON
Woolwich Common
Playing Field
Reservoir (covered)
Shooters Hill Post 16 Campus
Greenwich Free School
SHOOTERS HILL
SHOOTERS HILL GOLF COURSE
Club House
Eaglesfield Rec. Grd.
Woodlands Farm
Hillview Cemetery
Council Offices
Garden Centre
MEMORIAL HOSPITAL
ELTHAM COMMON
CASTLE WOOD
Severndroog Castle
Rose Cottage
JACK WOOD
Jackwood Ho.
Recreation Ground
Corelli College
SE3
Sam Montague Boy's Club
Sports Ground
CEMETERY
GREENWICH
Oxleas Meadows
OXLEAS WOOD
Eastcote Prim. Sch.
Playing Field
SHEPHERDLEAS WOOD
Falconwood Field
Falconwood
FALCONWOOD
ELTHAM PARK
ELTHAM PARK NORTH
ELTHAM PARK SOUTH
WELL HALL ROUNDABOUT
Eltham
Eltham Cemetery
Eltham Crematorium
ELTHAM WARREN GOLF COURSE
Stationers Crown Woods Academy
Crown Woods Sports Cen.
Nature Study Centre
SE9
University of Greenwich (Avery Hill Campus)
AVERY HILL
AVERY HILL PARK
Halls of Residence
All Weather Pitches
Sports Ground
Sparrow's Farm Leisure Centre
Harris Academy Greenwich
Queenscroft Park
Moatbridge Sch.
ELTHAM
Eltham Palace & Gardens
ELTHAM COMM. HOSP.
Hospice
Superstore
Club House
ROYAL BLACKHEATH GOLF COURSE
Community Centre
Bird Sanctuary
The Tarn
Mottingham
MOTTINGHAM
Eric Liddell Spts. Cen.
Eltham Coll.
Fairy Hill
Playing Field
Coldharbour Leisure Centre
New Eltham
Dulverton Sch.
Parish Wood
138
SHOOTERS HILL ROAD
WOOLWICH COMMON
ACADEMY ROAD
WELL HALL ROAD
ROCHESTER WAY RELIEF ROAD
BEXLEY ROAD
ELTHAM HIGH STREET
ELTHAM HILL
COURT ROAD
SIDCUP ROAD
FOOTSCRAY ROAD
AVERY HILL RD.
HALFWAY
BELLEGROVE
A2
A20
A205
A207
A208
A210
A211
B263
B2214

117
95
118
139
Vc
Wc
Xc
Yc
Zc
Ad
Bd
51
52
53
54
55
56
57
58
59
60
BOSTALL HEATH
HILL WOOLWICH ROAD
A206
BOSTALL WOODS
SE2
Greenwich & Bexley Community Hospice
BELVEDERE PRIVATE HOSP.
Clam Field Recreation Ground
Heathview Day Centre
WEST HEATH
Bedonwell Jun. & Inf. Schs.
Woolwich Cemetery
The William Barefoot Gdn.
PLUMSTEAD CEMETERY
Hill Grove
East Wickham Open Space
EAST WICKHAM
Stevens Park
WICKHAM LANE
UPPER WICKHAM LA.
A209
E. Wickham Prim. Acad.
Welling Sch.
Welling
WELLING
NORTHDOWN ROAD
Bexleyheath Station
Brampton Prim. Acad.
Bexleyheath
DA7
DA16
DA6
DA5
DA15
WELLING HIGH ST.
PARK VIEW RD.
A207
CROOK LOG BROADWAY
BEXLEYHEATH
Bexleyheath Academy
Goals Soccer Cen.
Welling United FC (Park View Road)
Bexleyheath Sports Club
Danson House
DANSON PARK
THE LAKE
Danson Park Watersports Centre
Bexley Grammar Sch.
Crook Log Leisure Cen.
Upton
Red House
BEXLEYHEATH GOLF COURSE
Upton Prim. Sch.
Grammar Sch.
ALBION ROAD
DANSON ROAD
A221
ROCHESTER ROAD
ROCHESTER WAY
A2
A210
Sidcup
Blackfen Sch. for Girls
Sherwood Park Prim. Sch.
BLACKFEN
Days Lane Prim. Sch.
Hollyoak Wood Park
PENHILL PARK
PENHILL RD.
BLENDON RD.
Blendon
BRIDGEN RD.
Bridgen
Bexley Park Wood
Bexley
SIDCUP GOLF COURSE
Lamorbey
Chatsworth Inf. Sch.
Rose Theatre
Rose Bruford College
Hurtsmere School
HURST ROAD
A222
Old Bexley C of E Prim. Sch.
Cricket Ground
Upper College Farm
Sidcup Leisure Centre
Albany Park
Abbeyhill Park
46
47
48
49

118
Erith
ERITH
Northumberland Heath
NORTHUMBERLAND HEATH
North End
Slade Green
SLADE GREEN
Barnehurst
BARNEHURST
Bexleyheath
BEXLEYHEATH
Crayford
CRAYFORD
Bexley
BEXLEY
OLD BEXLEY
Maypole
Coldblow
Bowmans
DARTFORD HEATH
DA5
DA6
DA7
DA8
A2
A206
A207
A220
A221
A222
A223
A2000
A2018
A2174
B2186
B2210
ROCHESTER WAY
BOURNE ROAD
WATLING ST.
BEXLEY ROAD
NORTHEND ROAD
QUEEN'S ROAD
PERRY STREET
THAMES ROAD
BROADWAY
GRAVEL HILL
NORTH CRAY RD.
DARTFORD RD.
OLD BEXLEY LA.
SHEPHERDS LANE
DARTFORD HEATH
BLACK PRINCE INTERCHANGE
Hall Place
Hall Place Gardens
Barnehurst Golf Course
Crayford Stadium (Greyhound)
Erith & Dist. Hosp.
Erith Leisure Centre
Erith Stadium
Bursted Wood
Bursted Wood Prim. Sch.
Martens Grove Park
Russell Park
Recreation Ground
Churchfield Wood
Upper College Farm
Perry Street Farm
Pinewood Cottage
The Old Orchard
Recycling Centre
Pumping Station
Sports Field
96
117
140

RIVER THAMES
LONG REACH
PURFLEET
THURROCK
RM16
DARTFORD SALT MARSHES
Dartford Clay Shooting Club
CRAYFORD MARSHES
RIVER DARENT
RIVER CRAY
Dartford
DARTFORD FRESH MARSHES
JOYCE GREEN
Temple Hill
New Town
DARTFORD
The Bridge
LITTLEBROOK BUSINESS CENTRE
Power Station (Disused)
Joyce Green Farm
Howbury Farm
Erith Yacht Club
The Saltings
Flood Barrier
DARENT INDUSTRIAL PARK
THAMESIDE IND. EST.
BOB DUNN WAY
A206
A2026
VICTORIA RD.
BURNHAM ROAD
A226
WEST HILL
EAST HILL
THE BRENT
LONDON RD.
WATLING STREET
PRINCES ROAD
A225
A2018
B2174
B2500
A296
A282
DARTFORD TUNNEL APPROACH RD.
CROSSWAYS
Junction 1a
LITTLEBROOK INTERCHANGE
Junc.1b
PRINCES RD. INTERCHANGE
DA2
Central Park Arena
Fairfield Pool & Leisure Cen.
Dartford Grammar Sch. for Girls
Dartford Science & Technology College
DARTFORD GOLF COURSE
Brooklands Lake
David Lloyd Leisure
Dartford FC (Princes Pk.)
The Leigh Academy
Goals Soccer Cen.
PRINCES PARK GOLF COURSE
Fleetdown Primary Sch.
Miskin Theatre
LITTLE BROOK HOSP.
GREENACRES
Kd
Ld
Md
Nd
Pd
Qd
Rd
97
141
120
51
52
53
54
55
56
57
58
59
60

120
Sd
Td
Ud
Vd
Wd
Xd
Yd
Purfleet
RM19
Royal Opera Ho. Production Workshop
PURFLEET BY-PASS
STONEHOUSE LA.
LONDON RD.
A1090
A282
WEST THURROCK
West Thurrock Prim. Sch.
Cemetery
Superstore
WEST THURROCK WAY
STONENESS ROAD
A126
LONDON ROAD
HEDLEY
THURROCK TRADE PARK
OLIVER CL.
OLIVER ROAD
Warehouse
Depot
RM20
West Thurrock Marshes
Oil Storage Depot
OLIVER CLOSE IND. EST.
BURNLEY RD.
WATSON CL.
Tunnel Wharf
Jetty
Pier
LONG REACH
Power Station (Disused)
Works
DARTFORD-THURROCK RIVER CROSSING (Dart Charge)
www.gov.uk/pay-dartford-crossing-charge
QUEEN ELIZABETH II BRIDGE
CANTERBURY WAY
DARTFORD TUNNEL
Stone Ness
Lighthouse
RIVER
STONE MARSHES
Offices
DA1
BOB DUNN WAY
EDISON'S PARK
CLIPPER BLVD. W.
Hotel
A206 BOULEVARD
CROSSWAYS BOULEVARD
Dartford
CROSSWAYS 25 BUSINESS PARK
Johnson's Wharf
Causeway
Ingress Park
Superstore
HIGH B255 ST.
THE AVENUE
Ingress Abbey
LivingWell Health Club
COTTON LANE
Junction 1a
LITTLEBROOK INTERCHANGE
St. MARY'S ROAD
CHARLES STREET
Stone Crossing
STONE
ELIZABETH ST.
Playing Field
Greenhithe for Bluewater
LONDON ROAD
GREENHITHE
Knockhall Academy
Knockhall
ST. CLEMENTS LAKES DEVELOPMENT
HORNS CROSS
Greenhithe
DA9
Recreation Ground
Dartford Judo Club
Bowls & Social Club
LITTLE BROOK HOSP.
GREENACRES
A226
LONDON ROAD
Stone Recreation Ground
CHALK PIT (DISUSED)
John's Hole
Stone Prim. Sch.
Coach Park
BLUEWATER PARKWAY
Western Village
BLUEWATER SHOPPING CENTRE
Pirate Cove
Eastern Village
Bluewater
Showcase Cinema
Southern Village
Events Centre
Bluewater Bus Sta.
DA2
Junc.1b
PRINCES RD. INTERCHANGE
WATLING STREET
B2500
PRINCES ROAD
A296
WATLING ST.
Blackshole Farm
Helipad
Buses only
DARENT VALLEY HOSPITAL
Village Green
Play. Fld.
Western Cross
CHALK PIT
Washmills
ST. CLEMENTS WAY
B255
BEAN LA.
FLEET DOWNS
Fleetdown Primary Sch.
Downs Farm
Ightham Cotts.
Nursery
142
56
57
58
59

121
Zd
Ae
Be
Ce
De
Ee
Fe
GRAYS
Grays
Sports Ground
Stifford Prim. Sch.
LAWRENCE TRADING ESTATE
CLARENCE R.
THURROCK RD.
DOCK
A126
ROAD
SOUTH STIFFORD
Works
(Proposed)
Jetty
S. Essex College (Thurrock Campus)
Council Offs.
Thurrock Yacht Club
Boating Pool
Grays Beach Riverside Park
Thameside Prim. Sch.
Playing Field
Warehouse
Superstore
Tilbury North Junction
Rail Container Terminal
THURROCK PARK
CAPSTAN CENTRE
A1089 ROAD
DOCK
ST. ANDREW'S RD.
51
52
53
54
55
56
57
58
59
60
THAMES
REACH
Lighthouse
Causeway
Mills
Mill
Grain Terminal
TILBURY DOCKS
Warehouses
No. 1 Gate Main Entrance
Tilbury
RM18
Northfleet Hope Container Terminal
Aggregates Terminal
NORTHFLEET HOPE
Broadness Salt Marshes
Pier
Bell Wharf
Swanscombe Marshes
Sewage Works
Botany Marshes
Depot
Wharf
TOWER WHARF
High Speed 1
MANOR WAY
122
TILBURY FREE PORT
Rolling Lift Bridge
Tilbury Ness
Swing B.
Jetty
NORTHFLEET INDUSTRIAL ESTATE
LOWER ROAD
MANOR WAY BUS. PK.
SWANSCOMBE BUSINESS CEN.
KENT KRAFT IND. EST.
NORTHFLEET IND. EST.
Warehouses
Ebbsfleet Utd. FC (Stonebridge Rd.)
Lighthouse Jetty
A226
GALLEY HILL ROAD
GALLEY HILL INDUSTRIAL ESTATE
Swanscombe
Gravesend
Northfleet
GRAVESHAM
HIGH STREET
B2175
THE HILL
LONDON ROAD
Mills
Warehouse
STONEBRIDGE RD.
THAMES WAY
Huggens College
Prim. Sch.
Swanscombe Leisure Cen.
Swanscombe Heritage Park
SWANSCOMBE
Swanscombe Skull Site National Nature Reserve
Recreation Ground
Rec. Grd.
Cemy.
Lib.
The Ebbsfleet Academy
Manor Primary Sch.
Alkerden
Swanscombe
DA10
Ebbsfleet Valley
Castle Hill
Fastrack Bus Route
The Observatory
Weldon
EBBSFLEET GREEN
Ebbsfleet International
EBBSFLEET
INTERNATIONAL WAY
A2260 EBBSFLEET GATEWAY
Sewage Works
SPRINGHEAD ENTERPRISE PARK
SPRINGHEAD RD.
B262
Recreation Ground
Northfleet Urban Country Park
Depot
Cemy.
Club Recreation Ground
Northfleet Technology College
Play. Field
Wombwell Park
Pitch
Sports Grnd.
Cygnet Leis. Cen.
Social Cen.
PERRY STREET
DOVER RD.
Acad.
Nursery
SOUTHFLEET RD.
CRESSFIELD
143
Northfleet West Grid Sub Sta.

122
100
121
144
Grays
RM17
RM16
RM18
Biggin
TILBURY MARSHES
Tilbury Town
TILBURY
Tilbury
TILBURY DOCKS
TILBURY FREE PORT
Tilbury Fort
Tilbury Landing Stage
LONDON INTERNATIONAL CRUISE TERMINAL
Tilbury Power Sta
West Tilbury Marshes
Walton Common
West Tilbury Hall
WEST TILBURY
Fort Road Common
Hallhill Common
Parsonage Common
Shrove Hill Wood
Chadwell Place
The Gateway Academy & Prim. Free Sch.
Tilbury FC Ground
Playing Field
Tilbury Manor Jun. Sch. & Manor Inf. Sch.
King George's Field
LONDON DISTRIBUTION PARK
RIVERSIDE RAIL FREIGHT TERMINAL
FORTRESS DISTRIBUTION PARK
Bulk Metal Terminal
Cement Terminal
Aggregates Terminal
Bill Meroy Creek
Sewage Works
Foot Ferry
RIVER
THAMES
GRAVESEND
Gravesend
Northfleet
ROSHERVILLE
MILTON
PERRY STREET
Wombwell Park
Royal Terrace Pier
Gravesend Sailing Club
Chantry Heritage Cen.
Bronte School
Copperfield Academy
Northfleet Urban Country Park
Northfleet Technology College
St. John's Catholic Prim. Sch.
St. John's Catholic Comp. Sch.
Cold Harbour Gravesend Woodlands Park
A126
A1089
A226
A227
B2175
B261
B256
ST. ANDREW'S ROAD
FERRY ROAD
MONTREAL RD.
ST. CHADS ROAD
DOCK APPROACH RD.
MARSHFOOT ROAD
CHADWELL BY-PASS
DOCK ROAD
OVERCLIFFE
LONDON ROAD
WROTHAM RD.
MILTON RD.
ROCHESTER RD.
DOVER RD.
EAST OLD ROAD
WEST OLD ROAD

123
INDUSTRIAL PARK
Sports Ground
Factory
101
EAST TILBURY
EAST TILBURY MARSHES
West Cotts.
Industrial Estate
Street
STATION ROAD
Goshem's Farm
Barvills Farm
PRINCESS MARGARET ROAD
LOW STREET LANE
COAL ROAD
GRASS RD.
LOVE LANE
Buckland
Bowaters Farm
R O C K
UNLEY CL.
GORDON CL.
Mariner Cotts.
Church Green
Coalhouse Fort & Thameside Aviation Museum
East Tilbury Marshes
Valve Compound
Water Tower
Coalhouse Point
Jetty
Wharf
THE LOWER HOPE
THAMES
GRAVESEND REACH
Higham Saltings
Rochester ME3
Causeway
Shornmead Fort
SHORNE MARSHES
Jetty
London Port Health Authority
North West Kent College
Warehouse
Milton Rifle Range
EASTCOURT MARSHES
Sewage Works
Thames & Medway Canal (disused)
LION BUSINESS PARK
Gravesend
Westcourt Marshes
Great Clane Lane Marshes
FILBOROUGH MARSHES
NURALITE IND. CEN.
S H A M
DALEFIELD WAY
APEX BUSINESS PARK
Fish Pond
Hoo Junction
DA12
Sports Ground
QUEEN'S FARM
Queen's Farm Cotts.
HIGHAM ROAD
Eastcourt Cotts.
Filborough Farm
Piggery
LOWER ROAD
QUEEN'S FARM ROAD
King's Farm
CHALK
145
East Court Manor
CHURCH LA.
WESTCOURT
ROAD
H J K L M N P
1 2 3 4 5 6 7 8 9 10
67 68 69 570
78 77 76 175 74 73

CRANBOURNE PARK
CRANBOURNE
Windsor
WINDSOR
The Village
SL4
BRACKNELL FOREST
SOUTH FOREST
GREAT WINDSOR and PARK
Woodside
Wood End
Sunninghill Park
CHEAPSIDE
Buckhurst Hill
ROYAL ASCOT GOLF COURSE
Ascot
SL5
Imperial College London (Silwood Park Campus)
SILWOOD PARK
ASCOT
SUNNINGHILL
Blacknest
Beggar's Bush
SHEET STREET ROAD
WINDSOR ROAD
SUNNINGHILL ROAD
BUCKHURST ROAD
LONDON ROAD
LOVEL LANE
Queen Elizabeth II Coronation Grove
Queen's Diamond Jubilee Plantation 1897
Royal Ascot Racecourse
102
146

Runnymede
Englefield Green
Egham
TW20
Bishops Gate
Dell Park
Egham Wick
Runnymede
Virginia Water
GU25
Royal Holloway (University of London)
Cooper's Hill Slopes
The Savill Garden
Smith's Lawn (Polo & Equestrian Grounds)
Guards Polo Club
The Valley Gardens
Windsor Road
Priest Hill
St. Jude's Road
Egham Hill
London Road
Christchurch Road
Blacknest Road
A30
A328
A308
A329
B389
103
147
126

126
104
125
148
WINDSOR and MAIDENHEAD
RUNNYMEDE
TW19
TW20
GU25
EGHAM
Egham
EGHAM HYTHE
HYTHE END
THORPE
THORPE LEA
Pooley Green
Glanty
Church Lammas
The Moor
Eastly End
Stroude
VIRGINIA WATER
Virginia Water
Ripley Springs
Thorpe Green
COOPER'S HILL
COOPER'S HILL SLOPES
RUNNYMEDE PARK
Runnymede Pleasure Ground
River Thames
Junction 13
Junction 12 (M25)
Junction 2 (M3)
M25 MOTORWAY
M3 MOTORWAY
A30
A308
B376
B388
B389
B3376
B3407
STAINES ROAD
WINDSOR ROAD
EGHAM HILL
EGHAM BY-PASS
HIGH ST
THE CAUSEWAY
WRAYSBURY ROAD
VICARAGE ROAD
THORPE LEA ROAD
THORPE BY-PASS
MILL HOUSE LANE
CHRISTCHURCH ROAD
SANDHILLS LANE
Royal Holloway (University of London)
Halls of Residence
Egham Leisure Centre
Egham Town FC (Runnymede Stadium)
Manorcroft Prim. Sch.
Strode's Coll.
British Disabled Water-Ski Association
Thorpe Hay Meadow Nature Reserve
Great Fosters
Longside Lake
Manor Lake
St. Ann's Lake
St. Ann's Heath
Frank Muir Memorial Field
Water Gardens
John Battleday Water Ski Cen.
Cemetery
Thorpe Ind. Park
Air Forces Memorial
Magna Carta Island
Ankerwycke Farm
Queensmead Lake
Hollyhock Island
Gas Works
Superstore
Rusham Crossing
Stroude Crossing
Milton Park Cottages
Crown Cottages
Whitehall Farm
Great Wood
The Dell
Research Laboratories
Sports Centre

127
105
128
149
KING GEORGE VI RESERVOIR
STAINES RESERVOIRS
QUEEN MARY RESERVOIR
ASHFORD
Ashford
STAINES-UPON-THAMES
KNOWLE GREEN
Birch Green
Ashford Park
SPELTHORNE
LALEHAM
Laleham Reach
Penton Hook
Chertsey KT16
Shepperton TW17
SHEPPERTON GREEN
TW15
TW18
CROOKED BILLET ROUNDABOUT
FORDBRIDGE ROUNDABOUT
HMP BRONZEFIELD
ASHFORD MANOR GOLF COURSE
LALEHAM GOLF COURSE
Shepperton Film Studios
Staines Town FC (Wheatsheaf Pk.)
Penton Hook Marina
Penton Hook Yacht Club
Penton Hook Lock
Penton Hook Island
Laleham Park
Abbey Lake
Beomonds Farm
Mountbatten Pavilion
Laleham Nurseries
Laleham C of E Primary School
Buckland Primary School
The Matthew Arnold Sch.
Riverbridge Prim. Sch.
Thomas Knyvett College
Brooklands College
St. James Independent Schools (Senior Boys)
Ashford Park Primary School
Shortwood Common
Shortwood Farm
Shortwood Pond
Hengrove Farm
Intake Channel
Pumping Station
Round Copse
LONDON ROAD
STAINES BYPASS
KINGSTON ROAD
STAINES ROAD
SHEPPERTON ROAD
LALEHAM ROAD
ASHFORD ROAD
CHURCH ROAD
STANWELL MOOR ROAD
A30
A308
A3044
A320
B376
B377
B378
River Thames
H J K L M N P
61 62 63 64 65 66 67 68 69 70
04 05 06 07
170

EAST BEDFONT
106
TW14
BEDFONT LAKES COUNTRY PARK
HMYOI FELTHAM
LOWER FELTHAM
ASHFORD
CHATTERN HILL
FELTHAMHILL
ASHFORD COMMON
SUNBURY COMMON
Littleton Common
Sunbury Cross
QUEEN MARY RESERVOIR
Upper Halliford
CHARLTON
LITTLETON
Shepperton
SHEPPERTON GREEN
TW17
TW15
TW16
UPPER HALLIFORD
SUNBURY GOLF COURSE
LALEHAM
127
150
STAINES ROAD
LONDON ROAD
KINGSTON ROAD
FELTHAM ROAD
ASHFORD ROAD
CHERTSEY ROAD
CLOCKHOUSE LANE
SCHOOL ROAD
CONVENT RD.
WINDMILL ROAD
UPPER HALLIFORD ROAD
UPPER HALLIFORD BY-PASS
HIGH ROAD
CHARLTON ROAD
NEW ROAD
M3 MOTORWAY
A30
A308
A244
B377
B378
B3003
B376
Junc.1
Shepperton Film Studios
Staines Reservoirs Aqueduct
SCHOOL ROAD JUNCTION
Q
R
S
T
U
V
W
61
62
63
64
65
66
67
68
69
70

129
HANWORTH PARK
Hanworth Park House
HANWORTH
TW13
Feltham Community College
Hanworth Air Park Leisure Centre
De Brome Building
Crane Park Island Nature Reserve
HOUNSLOW ROAD
A314
UXBRIDGE ROAD
A312
HAMPTON RD. WEST
GREAT CHERTSEY ROAD
A316
STAINES RD.
TWICKENHAM RD.
APEX CORNER
Fulwell Park
HAMPTON GOLF COURSE
FULWELL GOLF COURSE
David Lloyd Centre
HOSPITAL BRIDGE ROUNDABOUT
HAMPTON HILL
Hampton Academy
The Lady Eleanor Holles Sch.
Hampton School
Hampton
Kempton Nature Reserve
Staines Reservoirs Aqueduct
Half Moon Covert
Marling Park
Hatherop Park
Kempton Park
KEMPTON PARK RACECOURSE
Grandstand
Reservoir
Football Ground
Hydes Field
Portlane Bridge
UPPER SUNBURY ROAD
A308
Stain Hill West Reservoir
Stain Hill East Reservoir
Grand Junction Reservoir
Kenton Court Meadow
Sunbury Court
HAMPTON
Hampton & Richmond Borough FC (Beveree Stadium)
Garrick's Ait
Hurst Park Open Space
HURST PARK
Platt's Eyot
Sunnyside Reservoir
RIVER THAMES
Grand Junction Isle
Rivermead Island
Sunbury Locks
SUNBURY
Walton-on-Thames
KT12
ELMBRIDGE
MOLESEY RESERVOIRS
BESSBOROUGH RESERVOIR
KNIGHTS RESERVOIR
HURST ROAD
A3050
WALTON RD.
West Molesey
Molesey Hurst Rec. Grd.
Hurst Pool
East & West Molesey Cemy.
Grovelands Rec. Grd.
WEST MOLESEY
The Pav. Sports & Fitness Club
Apps Court Farm
Rivernook Farm

130
Ea
Fa
Ga
Ha
Ja
Ka
La
TWICKENHAM
Twickenham
HAM
Ham House & Garden
Ham Lands Nature Reserve
Ham Riverside Lands
Radnor Gardens
Strawberry Hill
STRAWBERRY HILL
St. Mary's University College
STRAWBERRY HILL GOLF COURSE
St. James's Catholic Primary School
Waldegrave Sch. for Girls
Fulwell
FULWELL GOLF COURSE
Fulwell Park
Hampton
HAMPTON HILL
TEDDINGTON
Teddington
Teddington Lock
Teddington Studios
Teddington Weir
National Phy. Lab.
Canal Plantation
Upper Lodge
Pantile Bridge
The Brew House
TW12
Hampton Open Air Pool
Bartons Cottage
Cricket Ground
Bushy House
Round Plantation
BUSHY PARK
Broom Clumps
The Pheasantry Welcome Centre
Willow Plantation
River Lodge
Waterhouse Woodland Garden
Waterhouse Pond
Fisher's Pond
Red Brick Bridge
Deer Pen
Heron Pond
Hawthorn Lodge
Warren Plantation
Half Moon Plantation
Leg-of-Mutton Pond
Oval Plantation
Diana Fountain
HAMPTON WICK
Hampton Wick Royal Cricket Ground
The King's Field
The Royal Paddocks
Bushy Lodge
Hampton Court House Sch.
Hampton Court Gate
Hampton Court Green
Hampton Court Gardens
Maze
HAMPTON COURT
Hampton Court Palace
Privy Garden
Cigarette Island Park
Hampton Court
HAMPTON COURT PARK
The Long Water
Farm Cottages
Stud House
The Rick Pond
HAMPTON COURT PALACE GOLF COURSE
HAMPTON
Hampton & Richmond Borough FC
Garrick's Ait
RIVER THAMES
HURST PARK
Terrace Gardens
Hurst Park
Ash Island
Molesey Hurst Rec. Grd.
East Molesey
EAST MOLESEY
LAMBRIDGE
HAMPTON COURT RD.
BUSHY PARK
STAINES ROAD
HAMPTON ROAD
HAMPTON COURT ROAD
HURST ROAD
WALTON ROAD
BRIDGE RD.
KINGSTON ROAD
HIGH STREET
BROAD ST.
WALDEGRAVE ROAD
STRAWBERRY VALE
TWICKENHAM RD.
SANDY LANE
PARK RD.
CHESTNUT AVENUE
152
129
108
61
62
63
64
65
66
67
68
69
70

131
PETERSHAM
SIDMOUTH WOOD
Petersham Gate
King Henry VIII
White Lodge Museum
The Royal Ballet Lower School
Queen Mothers Copse
Pen Ponds
Leg of Mutton Pond
Queen Elizabeth's Plantation
Lawn Plantation
Treebox Wood
SPANKERS HILL WOOD
DEER PARK
King George V Jubilee Plantation
Pond Plantation
Oak Lodge
Pembroke Lodge (Cafeteria)
PETERSHAM PARK
SUDBROOK PARK
Sudbrook Park Club House
The Wilderness
RICHMOND GOLF COURSE
White Ash Lodge
HORNBEAM WALK
Horse Ride
(Open during daylight hours only)
R I C H M O N D
P A R K
Richmond
T H A M E S
Pond Slade
(National Nature Reserve)
Tercentenary Plantation
Prince Charles's Spinney
Gibbet Wood
Isabella Plantation Garden
Ham Cross Plantation
Ham Bottom
Peg's Pond
Thomson's Pond
Broomfield Hill
Broomfield Hill Wood
ISABELLA PLANTATION
Ham Cross
Ham Gate
Ham Dip
High Wood
Still Pond
Deer Fold
HAM GATE AVENUE
HAM COMMON (Nature Reserve)
TW10
B352
KINGSTON VALE
KINGSTON HILL
A308
Walkden Hall
Robin Hood Prim. Sch.
Kingston University (Kingston Hill Campus)
KINGSTON BY-PASS
Coronation Plantation
The Flat
Dann's Pond
Ladderstile Gate
Gallows Pond
King's Clump
Canbury Sch.
Warren House
COOMBE HILL GOLF COURSE
COOMBE WOOD GOLF COURSE
COOMBE
Club House
Holy Cross Preparatory RC Sch.
Marymount International School
Coombe Hill Jun. & Inf. Schools
Coombe Girls' Sch.
UPPER HAM RD.
PETERSHAM RD.
A307
RICHMOND ROAD
CASSEL HOSP.
ST. GEORGE'S INDUSTRIAL ESTATE
YMCA Sports Grd.
The Tiffin Girls' Sch.
Tiffin Girls Comm. Spts. Cen.
Fern Hill Prim. Sch.
KT2
Latchmere Sch.
RC Prim. Sch.
Sports Ground
Kingston Gate
QUEENS ROAD
B351
Park Hill Sch.
KINGSTON HOSPITAL
Recreation Ground
Steven's Eyot
Canbury Gardens
Virgin Active Superstore
Kingston
The Rotunda Cen.
CROMWELL R.
FAIRFIELD N.
LONDON ROAD
A308
COOMBE ROAD
A238
Norbiton
NORBITON
CAMBRIDGE RD.
The Fairfield Sch. Recreation Ground
Kingston Hall
Kingston Univ.
KINGSTON UPON THAMES
Kingston Cemetery
Kingston Crematorium
Athletics Centre
Indoor Bowls Club
AFC Wimbledon & Kingstonian FC (Kingsmeadow)
Comm. Cen.
Sludge Beds
Recreation Ground
Hogsmill River
Waste Disposal Centre
Sewage Works
Surbiton Cemetery
Surbiton
KT5
Berrylands
KT3
New Malden
Islamic Cen.
Corpus Christi Catholic Prim. School
Retail Park
A2043
KINGSTON ROAD
WEST LANE
TRAPS LANE
COOMBE LANE
Club House
Recreation Ground
Pavilion
PORTSMOUTH ROAD
A307
HIGH ST.
PENRHYN RD.
A240
SURBITON RD.
SURBITON HILL RD.
132
109
153
Ma
Na
Pa
Qa
Ra
Sa
Ta
61
62
63
64
65
66
67
68
69
70

132
WANDSWORTH
WIMBLEDON COMMON
PUTNEY HEATH
PUTNEY VALE
KINGSTON VALE
WIMBLEDON
COPSE HILL
Cottenham Park
Raynes Park
RAYNES PARK
NEW MALDEN
New Malden
WEST BARNES
Wimbledon Chase
KINGSTON upon THAMES
Kingston upon Thames
Richmond
SW15
SW19
SW20
KT3
TW10
RICHMOND PARK GOLF COURSE
ROYAL WIMBLEDON GOLF COURSE
WIMBLEDON COMMON GOLF COURSE
LONDON SCOTTISH GOLF COURSE
COOMBE HILL GOLF COURSE
SPANKERS HILL WOOD
Putney Vale Cemetery
Putney Vale Crematorium
Kingston University (Roehampton Vale Centre)
Wimbledon Windmill Museum
Caesar's Camp
Cannizaro Park
Beverley Meads & Fishpond Woods Nature Reserve
Wolfson Neurorehab. Centre
Wimbledon Coll.
New Victoria Hospital
Parkside Hosp.
Wimbledon All England Lawn Tennis & Croquet Club
Buddhist Temple
Prince George's Playing Field
Bushey Mead
David Lloyd Leisure & Lloyds Lanes Raynes Park
Joseph Hood Recreation Ground
Messines Playing Field
CANNON HILL COMMON (Recreation Ground)
World of Golf Driving Range & Jurassic Encounter
Emanuel School Playing Field
KINGSTON VALE A3
ROEHAMPTON VALE
ROBIN HOOD WAY (KINGSTON BY-PASS) A3
BEVERLEY WAY A3 (KINGSTON BY-PASS)
COOMBE LANE A238
COOMBE LANE WEST A238
KINGSTON ROAD A238
BUSHEY ROAD A298
WIMBLEDON PARKSIDE A219
HIGH ST.
DURHAM ROAD B281
GRAND DRIVE B279
WEST BARNES LANE
TRAPS LANE B283
COOMBE LANE
HIGH ST. B283
BURLINGTON RD. B282
MALDEN WAY A3
WORPLE ROAD
MARTIN WAY
SHANNON CORNER
ROBIN HOOD
STAG LANE
ROEHAMPTON LANE
COOMBE LANE
131
154
Ua Va Wa Xa Ya Za Ab
61 62 63 64 65 66 67 68 69 70
21 22 23 24
73 72 71 70 69 68

133
EARLSFIELD
Earlsfield
BALHAM
Tooting Bec
WANDSWORTH
STREATHAM CEMETERY
UPPER TOOTING
SPRINGFIELD UNIVERSITY HOSPITAL
CENTRAL LONDON GOLF COURSE
Burntwood School
Garratt Green
Garratt Park
SUMMERSTOWN
Wimbledon Stadium (Greyhound)
Lambeth Crematorium
LAMBETH CEMETERY
Wimbledon Cemetery
Wimbledon Park
WIMBLEDON PARK
Tooting Broadway
St. George's Uni. of London
ST. GEORGE'S HOSPITAL
TOOTING
Haydons Road
Wandle Meadow Nature Park
TOOTING GRAVENEY
SOUTH WIMBLEDON
Wimbledon
South Wimbledon
Colliers Wood
COLLIER'S WOOD
Wandle Park
Tooting
MERTON
MERTON PARK
Merton Park
South Merton
Morden
MORDEN
Morden South
MORDEN HALL PARK
Morden Hall
Morden Lodge
Ravensbury Park
Mitcham
MITCHAM
Cricket Green
Canons Leisure Centre
Lavender Park
Deen City Farm
John Innes Park
NELSON HOSP.
Mostyn Gardens
Kendor Gardens
Beehive Bridge
Blue Houses Bridge
Wilson Hospital
Phipps Bridge
Belgrave Wlk.
Tooting Leisure Cen.
MERTON HIGH STREET
THE BROADWAY
MERANTUN WAY
WESTERN ROAD
LONDON ROAD
MORDEN ROAD
MORDEN HALL RD
COMMONSIDE WEST
CRANMER RD.
MITCHAM LANE
TOOTING HIGH STREET
UPPER TOOTING ROAD
TRINITY ROAD
BURNTWOOD LANE
GARRATT LANE
DURNSFORD RD.
HAYDONS ROAD
PLOUGH LANE
GAP ROAD
ALEXANDRA RD.
HARTFIELD ROAD
KINGSTON ROAD
CENTRAL ROAD
A24 A217 A218 A219 A214 A236 A238 A239 A297 B235 B285 B286 B229
SW18
Bb Cb Db Eb Fb Gb Hb
61 62 63 64 65 66 67 68 69 70
111
134
155

134
BALHAM
Balham
Jb
Kb
Lb
Mb
Nb
Pb
Qb
112
STREATHAM HILL
Streatham Hill
SW2
SW12
SW17
SW16
TOOTING BEC COMMON
Tooting Bec
Tooting Bec Lido
Tooting Bec Athletic Track
Tooting Graveney Common
WANDSWORTH
BEC ROAD
A214
STREATHAM PARK
STREATHAM
Streatham
Streatham Hub
STREATHAM COMMON NORTH
Streatham Common
STREATHAM COMMON
The Rookery
Norwood Grove Recreation Ground
FURZEDOWN
Furzedown School
Tooting
133
STREATHAM VALE
Streatham Vale Park
Lonesome
MITCHAM ROAD
A216
MERTON
Mitcham Eastfields
South London Crematorium
Streatham Park Cemetery
Jewish Cemetery
Harris Academy Merton
William Morris Primary Sch.
NORBURY
Norbury
NORBURY PARK
Norbury Hall
Norbury Manor Business & Enterprise Coll. for Girls
Hermitage Bridge
LONDON ROAD
A23
Pollards Hill
Donnelly Green
Sherwood Park
MITCHAM
MITCHAM COMMON
Blue Houses Bridge
Beehive Bridge
Canons Leisure Centre
Wilson Hospital NHS Walk-In
Mitcham Golf Course
Playing Fields
156
Gonville Academy
Keith Tuckey
Thornton
61
62
63
64
65
66
67
68
69
70
28
29
30
31

135
Rb
Sb
Tb
Ub
Vb
Wb
Xb
TULSE HILL
Tulse Hill
West Dulwich
WEST DULWICH
DULWICH COMMON
Dulwich College
DULWICH & SYDENHAM HILL GOLF COURSE
SOUTHWARK
DULWICH
FOREST HILL
Sydenham Hill Local Nature Reserve
Dulwich Wood
SE21
Kingsdale Foundation Sch.
Sydenham Hill
West Norwood Crematorium
Cemetery
West Norwood
WEST NORWOOD
UPPER SYDENHAM
LEWISHAM
Sydenham Wells Park
NORWOOD PARK
Gipsy Hill
CRYSTAL PALACE PARK
TV Transmitter
Crystal Palace National Sports Centre
CRYSTAL PALACE
Crystal Palace Museum
Crystal Palace Athletics Stadium
Crystal Palace
Crystal Palace Dinosaurs
SYDENHAM
Sydenham
Penge East
Penge West
NORWOOD NEW TOWN
NORWOOD
UPPER NORWOOD
Recreation Ground
BROMLEY
SE20
PENGE
Anerley
ANERLEY
David Livingstone Prim. Acad.
Grangewood Park
South Norwood Lake
Croydon Sailing Club
SOUTH NORWOOD
Birkbeck
Beckenham Crematorium
SOUTH NORWOOD COUNTRY PARK
Thornton Heath
THORNTON HEATH
Crystal Palace FC (Selhurst Park)
SE25
Norwood Junc.
Croydon Sports Arena
113
157
136
61
62
63
64
65
66
67
68
69
70
A205
A2199
A215
A212
A214
A234
A213
A2216
B266
B273

136
STANSTEAD
CATFORD
FOREST HILL
Forest Hill
SE23
SE6
Bellingham
BELLINGHAM
BELL GREEN
LOWER SYDENHAM
SYDENHAM
Sydenham
Lwr. Sydenham
SOUTHEND
SOUTHEND LA.
BROMLEY RD.
BECKENHAM HILL RD.
Beckenham Hill
NEW BECKENHAM
New Beckenham
BECKENHAM PLACE PARK
BECKENHAM PLACE PARK GOLF COURSE
Beckenham Place Park Local Nature Reserve
Penge East
Penge West
PENGE
SE20
ANERLEY
Kent House
Beckenham Road
Clock Ho.
Beckenham Junc.
BECKENHAM
Beckenham
BR3
Birkbeck
Beckenham Crematorium
Elmers End
ELMERS END
EDEN PARK
Kelsey Park
SE25
SOUTH NORWOOD COUNTRY PARK
CROYDON
PARK LANGLEY
HAYES
114
135
158
30
A212
A2218
A2015
A213
A234
A222
A214
B227
Yb
Zb
Ac
Bc
Cc
Dc
Ec
61
62
63
64
65
66
67
68
69
70

137
115
138
159
MOTTINGHAM
SE9
SE12
GROVE PARK
HITHER GREEN CEMETERY
Hither Green Crematorium
Grove Park Nature Reserve
DOWNHAM
Downham Health & Leisure Centre
Churchdown Christian Centre
FORSTER MEMORIAL PARK
BR1
BR2
BR7
PLAISTOW
SUNDRIDGE
Sundridge Park
SUNDRIDGE PARK GOLF COURSE
Sundridge Park Manor
ELMSTEAD WOOD
ELMSTEAD
Elmstead Woods
Chinbrook Meadows
Grove Park Cemetery
Marvels Wood
Lower Marvels Wood
SHORTLANDS GOLF COURSE
BROMLEY PARK
Shortlands
SHORTLANDS
BROMLEY
Bromley
Bromley Civic Centre
Bromley Nth.
Bromley South
Widmore Green
WIDMORE
BICKLEY
Ravensbourne
Eltham Coll.
Eric Liddell Spts. Cen.
Hadlow Coll. (Mottingham Campus)
Bannatyne Health Club
King's Meadow Playing Grd.
Bromley Hill Cemy.
Martin's Hill
Queen's Mead
Churchill Theatre
Highfield Jun. Sch.
Harris Prim. Acad.
Bromley Trust Academy
Nuffield Health Fitness & Wellbeing
Virgin Active Health Club
Whitehall Pleasure Ground
Recreation Ground
BARING ROAD
BURNT ASH LANE
CHINBROOK ROAD
GROVE PARK ROAD
LONDON ROAD
BROMLEY ROAD
BECKENHAM LANE
WIDMORE ROAD
BICKLEY ROAD
MASONS HILL
BROMLEY COMMON
HAYES ROAD
WESTMORELAND ROAD
HAYES LANE
A21
A222
A2212
B226
B228
B251
B265
B2212

MOTTINGHAM
NEW ELTHAM
LONGLANDS
ELMSTEAD
CHISLEHURST WEST
CHISLEHURST
BICKLEY
SOUTHBOROUGH
PETTS WOOD
ELMSTEAD WOOD
CAMDEN PARK
CHISLEHURST GOLF COURSE
SUNDRIDGE PARK GOLF COURSE
JUBILEE COUNTRY PARK
Chislehurst Common
Elmstead Woods
Chislehurst
Bickley
Coldharbour Leisure Centre
World of Golf at Sidcup
Kemnal Park Cemetery
Foxbury
Darul Uloom London
Farringtons School
Hawkwood Estate
Bromley High School
Petts Wood Junction
Chislehurst Junction
St. Mary Cray Junction
Bickley Junc.
SIDCUP ROAD
MAIN ROAD
WHITE HORSE HILL
RED HILL
HIGH ST.
CENTRE COMN. RD.
ROYAL PDE.
ST. PAUL'S CRAY ROAD
PERRY LANE
BROMLEY RD.
WATTS LA.
MANOR PARK RD.
OLD HILL
SUMMER HILL
BICKLEY PARK ROAD
BICKLEY RD.
ORPINGTON RD.
COURT ROAD
MOTTINGHAM LANE
GREEN LA.
FOOTS CRAY ROAD
A20
A208
A211
A222
B263
B264
B265
SE9
BR1
BR2
116
137
160

139
SIDCUP
Sidcup
Albany Park
Chislehurst & Sidcup Grammar Sch.
Sidcup Leisure Centre
Rose Theatre
Rose Bruford College
Lamorbey Park
All Weather Pitch
Abbeyhill Park
King George's Rec. Grd.
HURST ROAD
STATION ROAD
CHISLEHURST RD
SIDCUP HIGH ST.
SIDCUP HILL
MAIDSTONE RD.
MAIDSTONE ROAD
NORTH CRAY ROAD
SIDCUP BY-PASS
A20 BY PASS
EDGINGTON WY.
SEVENOAKS WAY
CRAY AVENUE
A222
A211
A223
A224
A2001
B2173
B258
Birkbeck Prim. Sch.
Waring Park
Royal Park Prim. Sch.
The Alders
Cleeve Pk. Sch.
North Cray Woods
FOOTS CRAY MEADOWS (Nature Reserve)
Five Arch Bri.
Stable Meadow
Foots Cray Place
Dower House
David Lloyd Leisure
Cray Youth & Community Centre
Catholic Prim. Sch.
Sidcup Place Park
Sidcup Place
Christ The King (St Mary's) Sixth Form College
QUEEN MARY'S HOSPITAL
Frognal Ho.
Chestnut Ho.
FROGNAL CORNER
Orchard Prim. Sch.
Football Grd.
FOOTS CRAY
Foots Cray Bri.
SIDCUP TECHNOLOGY CENTRE
FIVE ARCHES BUSINESS PARK
Sports Ground
Woollett Hall Farm
Crayzee Barn
Loring Hall
Bunkers Hill
Pond Farm
Home Wood
Gattons Wood
NORTH CRAY
Manor Cotts.
Manor Farm
North Cray Poultry Farm
Ruxley Corner
RUXLEY
RUXLEY WOOD
Ruxley Manor Garden Centre
Upper Ruxley
Caravan Site
SCADBURY PARK (Nature Reserve)
Bank's Shaw
Little Wood
Irish Plantation
Spring Shaw
Kemnal Tech. College
CRITTALLS CORNER
Midfield Prim. Sch.
Grays Farm Cottages
Gray's Farm Prim. Acad.
Bromley Ski Centre
LA Fitness (Orpington)
RUXLEY PARK GOLF COURSE
Home Farm Cotts.
Driving Range
Club House
CRAY VALLEY GOLF COURSE
CRAYFIELDS INDUSTRIAL PARK
Riverside Sch.
Recreation Ground
Garland Hill
The Lodge
Pilgrim Manor
Holly Cottage
The Gardens
Chestnut Cottage
Barnfield Bank
Lower Hockenden Farm
Simon's Field Shaw
PAULS CRAY HILL PARK
The Small House
Highlands Wood
HOCKENDEN WOOD
ST. PAUL'S CRAY
Recreation Ground
Fairmile Ho.
Leesons Prim. Sch.
St. Paul's Cray C of E Prim. Sch.
St. Mary Cray
ST. MARY CRAY
POVEREST
Poverest Prim. Sch.
BLACKSMITH'S LANE
Cemetery
The Warren
Manor Oak Primary Sch.
Sheepcote Farm
Child's Wood
117
161
140

140
Maypole
Coldblow
Old Bexley La.
Dartford Heath
Leyton Cross
The Bracton Centre
Heath Side
Hook Green
Joydens Wood
Joydens Wood (Woodland Trust)
DA5
Bexley
BEXLEY
Sidcup
DA14
Chalk Wood
Birchwood Park Golf Course
Stonehill Green
Puddledock
Hextable
Hextable Heritage Centre & Gardens
Upper Ruxley
Sidcup By-Pass
Maidstone Road
London Road
Swanley
Swanley Park
Cray Valley Golf Course
Hockenden
BROMLEY
Bourne Wood
SWANLEY
BR8
Sevenoaks
Cd
Dd
Ed
Fd
Gd
Hd
Jd
61
62
63
64
65
66
67
68
69
70
118
139
162

Dartford
WILMINGTON
HAWLEY
DARENTH
SUTTON AT HONE
SOUTH DARENTH
Clement Street
SWANLEY VILLAGE
HORTON KIRBY
FARNINGHAM WOOD
DARTFORD GOLF COURSE
PRINCES PARK GOLF COURSE
DARENTH INTERCHANGE
Junction 2
Junction 3 (M25)
Junction 1 (M20)
M25 MOTORWAY
DARTFORD BY-PASS
DA1
DA2
DA4
Farningham Road
Canada Heights Motorcycle Circuit
Parkwood Hall Co-Operative Academy
The Olympic Golf Driving Range
North West Kent College of Technology
Miskin Theatre
Sutton-at-Hone C of E Prim. Sch.
St. Paul's C of E Prim. Sch.
St. John's Jerusalem
Wilmington Prim. Sch.
Oakfield Prim. Sch.
119
142
163

142
120
164
141
FLEET DOWNS
DARENT VALLEY HOSPITAL
WATLING
Western Cross
CHALK PIT
Washmills
A296 STREET
A2 BY-PASS
DARENTH COUNTRY PARK
DARENTH INTERCHANGE
DARTFORD A2
M25 MOTORWAY
Junction 2
DARENTH WOOD
LADIES WOOD
LORDS WOOD
BEACON WOOD COUNTRY PARK
DA2
DA4
BEAN
Lane End
DARENTH
GREEN STREET GREEN
St. Margarets
SUTTON AT HONE
SOUTH DARENTH
HORTON KIRBY
Dean Bottom
Pinden
Grubb Street
Dartford
DARTFORD
SEVENOA

143
121
144
165
Swanscombe
DA10
Weldon
The Observatory
CRESSFIELD
Northfleet West Grid Sub Sta.
WATLING STREET
A2
Wombwell Park
Northfleet Technology College
NEW HOUSE
Pepper Hill
DA11
Gravesend
GRAVESHAM
BETSHAM
STATION ROAD
B262
Northend
Warwick House
Betsham House
Highfield Farm
Manor House Farm
Orchard House
FORD
SOUTHFLEET
DA13
Village Hall
Haydon Cross
The Mount
Court Hill Cottages
Chapter Farm
Broadditch Farm
Redstreet
Northfleet Green
Northfleet Green Farm
Madam Wood
Hook Green Farm
Hook Green
Hook Place Fm.
Westwood Farm
Westwood
WESTWOOD ROAD
WHITEHILL ROAD
B255
Thomas's Cottages
Brakefield Cottage
Court Wood
ISTEAD RISE
Willerby Farm
Elmlands Shaw
Rose Farm
Walnut Wood
Thirty Acre Shaw
Bushfield Shaw
Longfield
LONGFIELD
Mile End Green
Playing Field
DA3
MAIN ROAD
B260
Longfield Academy
Rowhill School
Langafel C of E Prim. Sch.
NEW BARN
Reservoirs (covered)
Nurstead Hall
LONGFIELD HILL
Gorse Wood
Cobham Valleys
HARTLEY
Hartley Green
HARTLEY WOOD
Steephill School
Bramblefield Wood
Dean Bottom Farm
Cricket Ground
Manor Farm
Skinners Hill
LONGFIELD RD.
61
62
63
64
65
66
67
68
69
70
71
560
Zd
Ae
Be
Ce
De
Ee
Fe

144
122
143
A
B
C
D
E
F
G
1
2
3
4
5
6
7
8
9
10
Wombwell Park
NEW HOUSE
Northfleet Sch. for Girls
Sports Grnd
Cygnet Leis. Cen.
Nursing Home
Club Sports Grd.
Cemetery
OLD ROAD W.
OLD ROAD EAST
B261
Cold War Bunker Gravesend
Woodlands Park
St. George's C of E Sch.
DA11
WROTHAM ROAD
A227
A2
MID KENT GOLF COURSE
Club House
KINGS FARM
Kings Farm Prim. Sch.
Parrock Farm
Christian Fields
Riverview Jun. & Inf. Schs.
SINGLEWELL
Sports & Social Club
Playing Field
Reservoir (Covered)
Singlewell Prim. Sch.
Superstore
Cyclopark
BMX Track
Ellenor Lions Hospice
High Speed 1
Claylane
ISTEAD RISE
Recreation Ground
Comm. Cen.
Chalk Hole Shaw
G R A V
Ifield
Ifield Court
Hever Court Farm
New Cottages
DA13
Huntdown Wood
Marlboro Boarding Kennels
Stamford House
Castle Shaw
Willerby Farm
Elmlands Shaw
Rose Farm
Prim. Sch.
DA3
Pigstles Shaw
Walnut Wood
Thirty Acre Shaw
Water Works
Nash Street
The Grove
Cozendon Wood
Tollingtrough Green
HENHURST
Winstead Hill
Henhurst Lake
Jeskyns Cotts.
Dabbs Place Farm
Jeskyns Farm
Burleigh
Priestfield Shaw
Nurstead Wood
Nurstead
Nurstead Court
THE PARK
Millhill Shaw
Mill Hill
Foxbury Spring
Blackhorse Cottage
Eden Cottage
Round Street
Millfield Shaw
Cobham Valleys
Gorse Wood
Southdown Wood
Southdown Shaw
Nurstead Hall
Dark Sallows
Broadfield Shaw
Lordscroft Shaw
Waterditch Wood
Meopham
MEOPHAM STATION
Sallows Shaw
SOLE STREET
Gold Street
The White Ho.
Danes Place
LONGFIELD R.
63
64
565
66
72
71
170
69
68

CHALK
WESTCOURT
HIGHAM
ROCHESTER ROAD
A226
Eastcourt Cotts.
123
Piggery
Queen's Farm Cotts.
LOWER ROAD
King's Farm
East Court Manor
Polperro
Piggery
CHURCH LANE
GREEN FARM LANE
The Cottage
Green Farm Cotts.
Longten's Cotts.
Chalkpit Cotts.
Green Farm
ROAD GRAVESEND ROAD
New Cotts.
Homelea Farm
Golden Knob
Robinson's Cotts.
Lower Shorne
BURDETT AV.
COUTTS AV.
Chilton Hills
Shorne Ho.
Courtlands
The Manor House
Thamesview Sch.
Playing Field
GRAVESEND GOLF CENTRE
Driving Range
Club Ho.
Sports Ground
Miniature Railway
Ten. Cts.
Cascades Leisure Centre
Club House
SOUTHERN VALLEY GOLF COURSE
MUGGINS LANE
DA12
Smith's Farm
The Warren
SHORNE
Prim. Sch.
Shorne Hill
COURT WOOD
RIVERVIEW PARK
Harts Hill
Cats Wood
Ifield Farm
SHORNE IFIELD ROAD
Orchard Lea Farm
WARREN VIEW
Gravesend
Westwood Farm
Brummelhill Wood
Fenn Wood
THONG
SHORNE RIDGEWAY
Starmore Wood
Cole Wood
Deglan
Cheneys Farm
Randall Bottom
Randall Heath
Pear Tree House
RIDGEWAY BUNGALOWS
PEAR TREE LANE
Dunbar's Wood
GREAT CRABBLES WOOD
RANDALL WOOD
Thong Lodge
SHORNE WOODS COUNTRY PARK
Furzy Leas Wood
Shorne Woods Country Park Visitor Cen.
Furze Bank
BOWESDEN LANE
Rec. Grd.
New Fish Pond
Gravelhill Wood
Old Fish Pond
Hotel
Puckle Hill
BREWERS WOOD
BREWERS ROAD
Twenty Acre Wood
The Square
WATLING STREET
Junction 1
A2
M2 MOTORWAY
M2
HASTED R.
Scalers Hill House
Scalers Hill
Chambers Hill Wood
The Mount
Fish Pond
Reservoir (covered)
Well Shaw
Ashenbank Wood (Ancient Woodland)
High Speed 1
Cole Wood
Peggy Taylor's Hill
Brick Kiln Ponds
WEST PARK
ROCHESTER AND COBHAM PARK GOLF COURSE
Rochester
Cobham Hall
Cobham Hall School
Tennis Courts
Club Ho.
Knightsplace Farm Equestrian Centre
Battle Street
ME2
COBHAM PARK
GREAT WOOD
Rec. Grd.
Prim. Sch.
Deer Park
COBHAM
STREET
LODGE LANE
War Mem.
Lodge Farm
Darnley Mausoleum (Cobham Mausoleum)
New College of Cobham
Cobhambury House
Cobhambury Farm
Home Farm Cottage
The Vineyard
Norwood Grove
MEDWAY
Birch Wood
Winterham Hill
Lodge Wood
COBHAMBURY ROAD
Warren Plain
Nor Wood
Middlefield Shaw

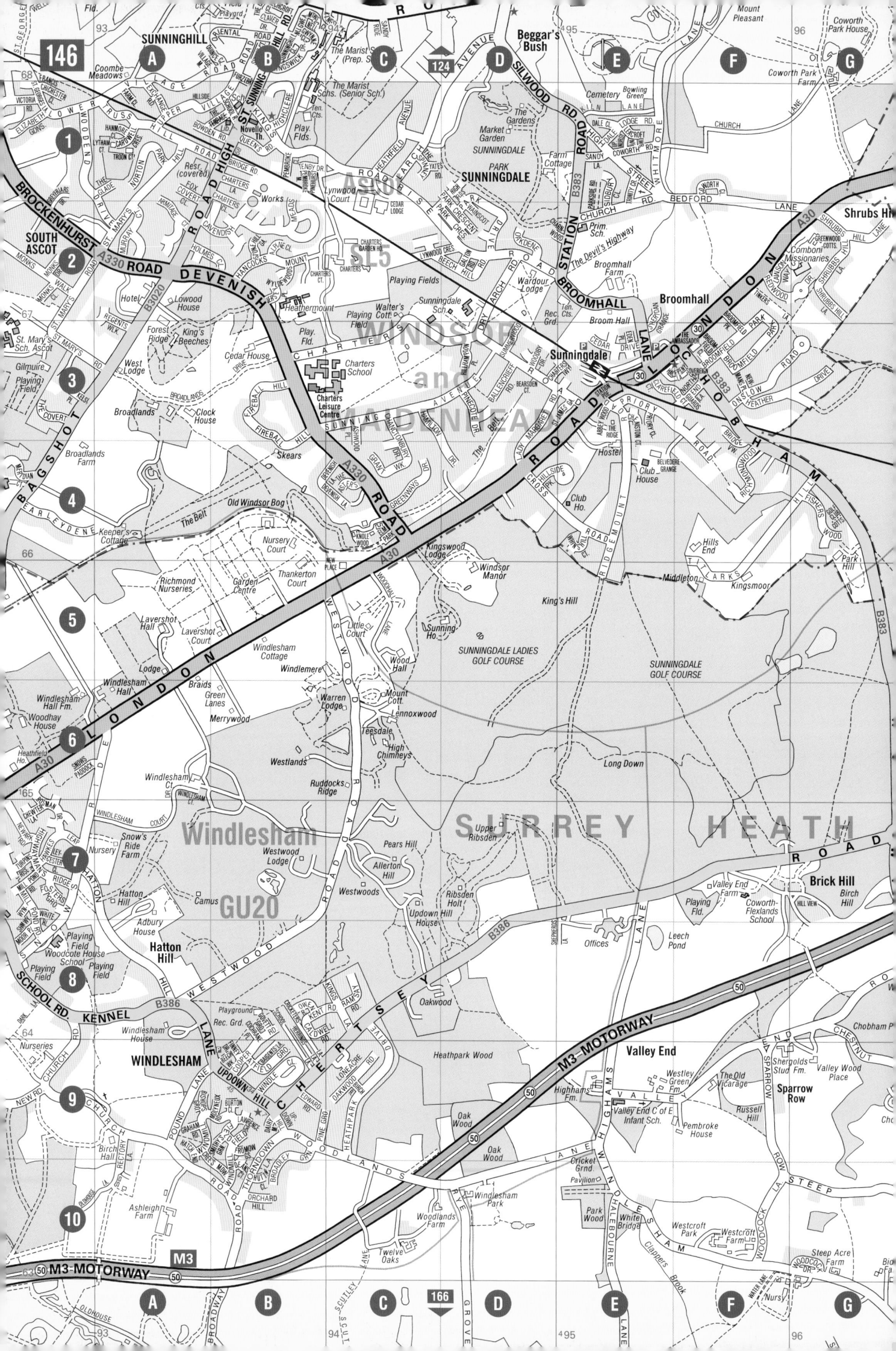
SUNNINGHILL
Coombe Meadows
South Ascot
St. Mary's Sch. Ascot
Gilmuire
Broadlands
Broadlands Farm
Clock House
West Lodge
Forest Ridge
King's Beeches
Lowood House
Hotel
Cedar House
Heathermount
Charters School
Charters Leisure Centre
Walter's Cott.
Sunningdale Sch.
Playing Fields
Lynwood Court
Cedar Lodge
Ascot
SL5
The Marist Schs. (Senior Sch.)
The Marist Prep. Sch.
Beggar's Bush
Mount Pleasant
Coworth Park House
Coworth Park Farm
Cemetery
Bowling Green
The Gardens
Market Garden
SUNNINGDALE PARK
SUNNINGDALE
Farm Cottage
Prim. Sch.
The Devil's Highway
Broomhall Farm
Broomhall
Broom Hall
Sunningdale
Shrubs Hill
Comboni Missionaries
Wardour Lodge
Rec. Grd.
WINDSOR and MAIDENHEAD
Skears
Old Windsor Bog
The Belt
Keeper's Cottage
Nursery Court
Thankerton Court
Garden Centre
Richmond Nurseries
Kingswood Lodge
Windsor Manor
King's Hill
Hills End
Middleton
Kingsmoor
Park Hill
Laversholt Hall
Lavershot Court
Windlesham Cottage
Windlemere
Little Court
Wood Hall
Sunning Ho.
SUNNINGDALE LADIES GOLF COURSE
SUNNINGDALE GOLF COURSE
Lodge
Windlesham Hall
Windlesham Hall Fm.
Woodhay House
Heathfield Ho.
Braids
Green Lanes
Merrywood
Warren Lodge
Mount Cott.
Lennoxwood
Teesdale
High Chimneys
Westlands
Ruddocks Ridge
Long Down
Windlesham Ct.
Windlesham
SURREY HEATH
Upper Ribsden
Snow's Ride Farm
Nursery
Westwood Lodge
Pears Hill
Allerton Hill
Westwoods
Hatton Hill
Camus
GU20
Ribsden Holt
Updown Hill House
Adbury House
Hatton Hill
Playing Field
Woodcote House School
Valley End Farm
Coworth-Flexlands School
Brick Hill
Birch Hill
Playing Fld.
Offices
Leech Pond
Oakwood
Playground
Rec. Grd.
Windlesham House
Nurseries
WINDLESHAM
Heathpark Wood
M3 MOTORWAY
Valley End
Highams Fm.
Westley Green Fm.
Valley End C of E Infant Sch.
Pembroke House
The Old Vicarage
Russell Hill
Shergolds Stud Fm.
Valley Wood Place
Sparrow Row
Chobham P
Oak Wood
Birch Hall
Ashleigh Farm
Cricket Grnd.
Pavilion
Windlesham Park
Woodlands Farm
Park Wood
White Bridge
Westcroft Park
Westcroft Farm
Steep Acre Farm
Twelve Oaks
Clappers Brook
Nurs.
A30
A330
B3020
B383
B386
M3
LONDON ROAD
DEVENISH ROAD
BROCKENHURST ROAD
BAGSHOT ROAD
HIGH STREET
STATION ROAD
BROOMHALL LANE
CHOBHAM ROAD
CHERTSEY ROAD
WESTWOOD ROAD
KENNEL LANE
SCHOOL RD.
CHURCH ROAD
UPDOWN HILL
WOODLANDS LANE
WINDLESHAM ROAD
HIGHAMS LANE
HALEBOURNE LANE
BEDFORD LANE
CHURCH ROAD
SILWOOD RD
RIDGEMOUNT ROAD
SUNNINGDALE
A B C D E F G
1 2 3 4 5 6 7 8 9 10
93 94 95 96
63 64 65 66 67 68

124
166

147
125
148
167
Virginia Water
Wentworth
GU25
Knowle Hill
Trumps Green
RUNNYMEDE
Longcross
LONGCROSS
Chertsey
KT16
Woking
GU24
CHOBHAM COMMON
Burrowhill
Clearmount
Stanners Hill
Stonehill
M3 MOTORWAY
WENTWORTH GOLF COURSE (WEST COURSE)
WENTWORTH GOLF COURSE (EAST COURSE)
WENTWORTH GOLF COURSE (EDINBURGH COURSE)
BARROW HILLS GOLF COURSE
CHOBHAM COMMON National Nature Reserve
Race Track
Burnt Hill
Ship Hill
Long Arm
Little Arm
Oystershell Hill
Staple Hill
Chickabiddy Hill
Albury Bottom
The Bee Garden
Roundpond Clump
Round Pond
Little Fir Clump
Langshot Bog
Gracious Pond
Gracious Pond Farm
Butts Hill
Livery Stables
Ram Bridge
Mossat Farm
Westways Farm
Little Manor Farm
Chobham Park House
Old Slade
Bee Garden (Earthwork)
Childown Farm Cottage
Fish Pond
Stannershill Farm
Pipers Green Stud
The Homestead
The Lodge
Upper Childown
Childown
North Lodge
Childown Lodge
Fern Hill
Stanyards
Greenacres
Chertsey Common
Hersham Farm
Dicken's Wood
Grangewood
Smith's Cotts.
Poultry Farm
Hillside
Flutters Hill
Lily Pond Farm
Longcross House
Bog Wood
Knowle Grove
Trumps Farm
Beech Wood
Westwood
Fairway
Great Wood
The Dormy House
Orchard Cottage
Podenhale
Broom Hill
Wentworth Pond
Wentworth Club (Club House)
The Wentworth Tennis & Health Club
Wellington Bridge
Duke's Copse
General's Copse
Virginia Wood
Belvedere Fort
Riverside Walk Local Nature Reserve
King George V Playing Field
Trumps Green Inf. Sch.
Waterloo Bri.
CHRISTCHURCH ROAD
CHERTSEY ROAD
LONGCROSS ROAD
GRACIOUS POND ROAD
STAPLE HILL
ACCOMMODATION ROAD
STONEHILL ROAD
WEST DRIVE
EAST DRIVE
WELLINGTON AVENUE
TRUMPSGREEN ROAD
A30
B386
B383
B389
M3

VIRGINIA WATER
Virginia Water
Thorpe Green
St. Ann's Park
SANDHILLS
M3-MOTORWAY
Junction 2 (M3)
Junction 12 (M25)
MILL HOUSE LANE
St. Ann's Lake
John Battleday Water Ski Cen.
Trumps Green
Sewage Disposal Works
Community Recycling Centre
Lyne Farm
LYNE CROSSING ROAD
RUXBURY ROAD
Chertsey
KT16
Lyne Place Manor
Trumps House
Trumps Farm
The Rough
Merrywood Farm
Almner Priory
Almners Farm
HARDWICK LANE
M25-MOTORWAY
Great Cockcrow Railway
Hersham Copse
LYNE
Fan Grove
Lynwood Farm
Playing Field
Hardwick Court Farm
Chertsey Common
Hersham Farm
Angel Farm
Lyne & Long Cross C of E Inf. Sch.
LONGCROSS ROAD
HOLLOWAY HILL
ABRAHAM COWLEY UNIT
RUNNYMEDE BMI HOSP.
ST. PETER'S HOSPITAL
Chertsey South
GUILDFORD RD.
FOXHILLS GOLF COURSE
Foxhills Country Club
Botleys Mansion
Homewood Park
ST. PETER'S WAY
A320
ACCOMMODATION ROAD
The Homestead
The Lodge
Upper Childown
Childown
Fish Pond
Dower House
Budds Cottage
North Lodge
Kitchenride Corner
Penny Farthing Cottage
Ether Hill
Memorial Fields
OTTERSHAW
MURRAY ROAD
Great Grove Farm
Stonehill Cottage
Stone Hill
Ten Acres
Coach House
QUEENWOOD GOLF COURSE
Childown Lodge
Merlewood
Stonehill
Queenwood House
The Paddock
Club House
Chaworth Copse
Ottershaw C of E Inf. & Jun. Schs.
Meath School
Ottershaw Chase
Timber Hill
The Common
Bousley Farm
Otterhill Nursery
Stanners Hill
Woking GU24
SURREY HEATH
Fern Hill
Hawks Hill
Hawks Hill Cottage
CHOBHAM ROAD
Playing Field
The Mansion
Ottershaw Park
Brox
Southern Wood Farm
Greenacres
Timber Hill Cotts.
Miniature Rifle Range
Long Copse
Bramshill
Brox Wood
Bourne Rise Farm
126
147
168

LALEHAM
BURWAY
Laleham Park
Staines
TW18
SPELTHORNE
Shepperton
TW17
Pool End
M3 MOTORWAY
Gravel Pit
Pumping Station
ABBEY MEAD
Abbey Chase Farm
CHERTSEY
Chertsey Lock
Chertsey Bridge
CHERTSEY BRIDGE RD.
CHERTSEY ROAD
RENFREE WY.
Riversleigh Farm
Mead Farm
The Range
DOCKETT EDDY LANE
Chertsey Meads Local Nature Reserve
Chertsey Meads
Dockett Point
Eastworth
EASTWORTH ROAD
GUILDFORD ST.
LONDON ST.
WINDSOR ST.
ST. ANN'S ROAD
FORDWATER RD.
WEIR RD.
HANWORTH TRADING ESTATE
Playing Field
Pannells Farm
Addlestone Moor
ABBEY MOOR GOLF COURSE
Conference Centre
Philip Southcote Sch.
Woburn Park Farm
Woburn Park
WOBURN HILL
WOBURN PARK
St. George's College
Hamm Court Farm
Weybridge
KT13
WEY
Junc. 11
M25
A317
A318
CHERTSEY RD.
HIGH ST.
STATION ROAD
CHURCH ROAD
WEYBRIDGE RD.
Addlestone
Ham Moor
WEYBRIDGE
ADDLESTONE
Addlestone Leisure Centre
St. Paul's C of E Prim. School
Crockford Bridge Farm
RIVER WEY NAVIGATION
WEY MEADOWS
Playing Fields
Heathside School
Brooklands College (Weybridge Campus)
ELMBRIDGE
Addlestone Junction
Coxes Lock
Mill Pond
Sayes Court Open Space
KT15
Garden Centre
NEW HAW ROAD
Rowhill
Coombelands Farm
ROW TOWN
Moated Farm
TopGolf Surrey
Driving Range
Golf Course
Wey Manor Farm
Nine Arches Bridge
Seven Arches Bridge
The London Bus Museum
Brooklands Museum
NEW HAW
Hall's Farm
H
J
K
L
M
N
P
04
05
06
07
127
169
150
71
72
73
74
75
76
77
78
79
80

SHEPPERTON GREEN
Q
R
S
T
U
V
W
128
SUNBURY GOLF COURSE
UPPER HALLIFORD
Sunbury-on-Thames
TW16
LALEHAM ROAD
M3 MOTORWAY
Pool End
Sheepwalk Lake
Funky Footprints Nature Reserve
Shepperton
SHEPPERTON
Staines Road Farm
Nurseries
River Ash
Gaston Bridge
Watersplash Farm
UP. HALLIFORD BY-PASS
GASTON BRIDGE ROAD
WALTON BRIDGE RD.
The Bradbury Cen.
Thamesmead School
The Swan Sanctuary
River Ash Estate
Riverhouse Gdns.
Riverhouse Barn
Marina
Gravel Pit
RENFREE WAY
RUSSELL RD.
CHERTSEY RD.
Halliford Mere Lake
Cemetery
Lower Halliford
Bishop Duppas Pk.
Las Palmas Estate
Cricket Ground
Desborough Sailing Club
DESBOROUGH ISLAND
Playing Field
Thames Meadow
Cowey Sale
WALTON BRIDGE
NEW ZEALAND AV.
HEPWORTH WY.
CHURCH TERRACE
TW17
Mead Farm
Desborough Channel
Shepperton Lock
Sailing Club
Tennis Club
Pharaoh's Island
Hamhaugh Island
Hamhaugh Point
Thames Lock
Hamm Court Farm
149
Engine River
Greenlands Farm
Broadwater Farm
PORTMORE PARK
Broad Water
Golf Course
St. James C of E Prim. Sch.
Ashley Park
Cricket Ground
WALTON-ON-THAMES
OATLANDS PARK
OATLANDS DRIVE
A3050
ASHLEY ROAD
B365
Cleves School
The Bull Dogs
WEYBRIDGE
Weybridge
Churchfields Rec. Grd.
Weybridge Lock
MONUMENT HILL
HIGH ST.
QUEENS ROAD
A317
Oatlands Sch.
Walton Leigh Sch.
Burwood Park
Walton Common
HEATH ROAD
Heathside School
Brooklands College (Weybridge Campus)
Cemetery
HANGER HILL
ST. GEORGE'S AVENUE
The Heath
KT13
Weybridge Junc.
Conduit Hill
Works
Seven Arches Bridge
The London Bus Museum
Brooklands Museum
Mercedes-Benz World
BROOKLANDS ROAD
Tennis Courts
Club
Warren Pond
SEVEN HILLS ROAD
Sports Ground
Recreation Ground
Upper Common
Rabbit Lane House
BURHILL GOLF COURSE
BURWOOD ROAD
170
71
72
73
74
75
76
77
78
79
80

151
QUEEN ELIZABETH II
RESERVOIR
KNIGHTS
RESERVOIR
BESSBOROUGH
RESERVOIR
ISLAND BARN
RESERVOIR
WEST MOLESEY
West Molesey
KT8
Molesey Heath
Local Nature Reserve
Fieldcommon
Walton-on-Thames
KT12
Rydens
HERSHAM
Hersham
Hersham Green
HERSHAM GOLF COURSE
Esher RUFC
(Molesey Rd.)
Esher Water Pollution
Control Works
Hersham
Water Pollution
Control Works
Lower
Green
SANDOWN PARK
RACECOURSE
SANDOWN PARK
GOLF COURSE
ESHER
Esher
KT10
WEST END
MOORE PLACE
GOLF COURSE
Claremont Park
Claremont
Landscape
Garden
WEST END
COMMON
(Local Nature Reserve)
Burhill
River Mole
A244
A307
A3050
B369
HURST ROAD
WALTON ROAD
MOLESEY ROAD
HERSHAM BY-PASS
ESHER ROAD
LAMMAS LA.
PORTSMOUTH ROAD
STONY HILL
COPSEM LANE
129
152
171

152
Ea
Fa
Ga
Ha
Ja
Ka
La
WALTON ROAD
Hampton Court
130
HAMPTON COURT PARK
East Molesey KT8
HAMPTON COURT PALACE GOLF COURSE
KT1
RICHMOND upon THAMES
The Rick Pond
Club House
Ditton Field
Pavilion
Grist Memorial Sports Ground
EAST MOLESEY
Nielson Playing Field
Sports Ground
Sailing Club
West Molesey KT8
ISLAND BARN RESERVOIR
Metropolitan Police FC (Imber Ct.)
Imber Court
EMBER COURT RD.
THAMES DITTON
Thames Ditton
Sports Ground
Seething Wells
STATION RD.
Playing Field
Esher College
Long Ditton Recreation Ground
LONG DITTON
Giggshill
Miniature Railway
Cranmere Primary School
WESTON GREEN
Sports Ground
GOLF COURSE
THAMES DITTON & ESHER
Esher
GOLF COURSE
Yew Tree Cottages
Ditton Common
SANDOWN PARK GOLF COURSE
SANDOWN PARK RACECOURSE
Lower Green
151
Club House
Daytona Sandown Park
Grandstand
Sandown Sports Club
Ski Slope
SCILLY ISLES
A307
A309
B364
B3379
PORTSMOUTH ROAD
KINGSTON BY-PASS
Hinchley Wood
HINCHLEY WOOD
Hinchley Wood Sch. & Sixth Form Centre
Hinchley Wood Prim. Sch.
Stokes Field (Local Nature Reserve)
Cemetery
Cricket Grd.
Littleworth Common
E L M B R I D G E
ESHER
Civic Centre
The Waffrons
SURBITON GOLF COURSE
Club House
Chessington Equestrian
Five Acres Farm
Playing Field
Claygate Ho.
Bowling Green
Harelane Grn.
Esher KT10
Slough Farm
Wingham Court
Manor Farm House
Lower Wood
Manor Farm
Elm Farm
Lovelace Prim. Sch.
Community Cen.
Loseberry
Loseberry Farm
Milbourne Lodge Prep. School
Claygate
Claygate Prim. Sch.
Recreation Ground
CLAYGATE
Rowan Prep. Sch.
CLAYGATE COMMON (Local Nature Reserve)
Oak Cottage
Claremont Park
Stable Pond
Arbrook Common
Barwell Farm
Winey Hill
ESHER BY-PASS
A3
A244
COPSEM LANE
172
71
72
73
74
75
76
77
78
79
80
14
15
16
17
63
64
65
66
67
68

153
131
173
Berrylands
BERRYLANDS
Surbiton
SURBITON
KT6
KT5
KT3
KT4
KT9
KT19
New Malden
Malden Manor
OLD MALDEN
TOLWORTH
Tolworth
TOLWORTH JUNCTION
KINGSTON upon THAMES
SOUTHBOROUGH
HOOK
Chessington
CHESSINGTON
Chessington North
Chessington South
Worcester Park
EPSOM
EWELL
WEST EWELL
HORTON PARK GOLF COURSE
HORTON COUNTRY PARK
Hogsmill Local Nature Reserve
Castle Hill Local Nature Reserve
Bonesgate Open Space Local Nature Reserve
Butcher's Grove
Alexandra Millennium Green
Recreation Ground
Playing Field
Sports Ground
Tolworth Court Bridge
Jubilee Way Training Track
King George's Field
Hollywood Bowl
Surbiton Raceway
Richard Challoner School
Grand Avenue Prim. Sch.
Knollmead Prim. Sch.
Tolworth Hosp.
Tolworth Rec. Cen.
Epsom & Ewell High Sch.
Hogsmill River
KINGSTON BY-PASS
A3
A240
A243
B284
HOOK ROAD
EWELL ROAD
CHESSINGTON ROAD
RUXLEY LANE
KINGSTON ROAD
MALDEN ROAD

154
MALDEN
Comm. Cen.
SHANNON CORNER
KINGSTON
BURLINGTON
WEST BARNES
132
Ua
Va
Wa
Xa
Ya
Za
Ab
71
72
73
74
75
76
77
78
79
80
Cannon Hill
Cherry Wood
Raynes Park Playing Fields
SW20
Coombe Boys Sch.
Motspur Pk.
Sports Ground
St. John Fisher RC Prim. Sch.
Old Blues Rugby Football Grd.
University of London Athletic Ground
New Malden
Nursery
North East Surrey Crematorium
The Sir Joseph Hood Memorial Playing Fields
BBC Sports Ground
MOTSPUR PARK
Gas Works
MORDEN CEMETERY
MORDEN PARK
Hatfeild Prim. Sch.
KINGSTON upon THAMES
Playing Fields
Beverley Brook
Merton & Sutton Joint Cemetery
Aragon Prim. Sch.
King George's Field
ASM Ten. Cen.
MANOR PARK
Green Lane Prim. Sch.
Refuse Destructor
Mayflower Park
Richard Challoner School
Malden Manor Prim. Sch.
Malden Manor
Sports Centre
OLD MALDEN
Malden Green
Worcester Park
Worcester Park
Dorchester Prim. Sch.
ST. ANTHONY'S HOSP.
St. Raphael's Hospice
Playing Field
Maori Sports Ground
Nursery
KT4
Cemy.
Shadbolt Park
WORCESTER PARK
Linden Bridge School
Wandgas Athletics Ground
Dancer 'Dick' Wood
Cuddington Prim. Sch.
King George's Field
Auriol Park
Schools
Cuddington Recreation Ground
Beverley Brook
Goals Soccer Cen.
NORTH CHEAM
Superstore
QUEEN VICTORIA
Cheam Leisure Cen.
SM3
Epsom
LA Fitness
Sports Ground
STONELEIGH
Stoneleigh
Meadow Prim. Sch.
Cheam High Sch.
Sports Hall
Oak Plantation
London Road Plantation
Cheam Recreation Ground
Hogsmill Local Nature Reserve
Ewell Ct. Park
KT19
BEGGAR'S HILL
KT17
NONSUCH PARK
Mansion House
CHEAM PARK
CHEAM
EPSOM and EWELL
WEST EWELL
Chamber Mead
Hogsmill River
The Harriers Running Track
Playing Field
EWELL
London Rd. Rec. Grd.
ORGAN CROSSROADS
David Lloyd Leisure Cen.
Nonsuch High Sch.
Harefield Rd.
Playing Field
Warren Fm.
174
Ewell West
Bourne Hall Mus.
A3
A2043
A24
A240
A232
B279
B284
B2200
KINGSTON BY-PASS
CENTRAL ROAD
CHEAM COMMON RD.
LONDON ROAD
MALDEN ROAD
STONECOT HILL
EWELL BY-PASS

155
MORDEN
Morden South
Morden Park Pools
South Thames College (Merton College)
Recreation Ground
Risley Sports Grd.
St. Helier
Mitcham
Mitcham Junction
River Wandle
Watermeads
Tooting & Mitcham United FC (Imperial Fields)
Poulter Park
Bennett's Hole
Harris Academy Morden
Moreton Green
Playing Fields
Open Space
ST. HELIER
Sutton Arena Leisure Centre
St. Helier Open Space
ROSEHILL
Rosehill Park East
Greenshaw Wood
ST. HELIER HOSPITAL
QUEEN MARY'S HOSPITAL FOR CHILDREN
ROSE HILL ROUNDABOUT
Mecca Bingo
Rosehill Recreation Ground
The Sports Village
Sutton Tennis Academy
Sutton Cemetery
Glenthorne High Sch.
Sutton Common
Superstore
BENHILTON
Royston Park
THE WRYTHE
Rushy Meadow Prim. Sch.
Muschamp Prim. Sch.
Carshalton Coll.
Wrythe Rec. Grd.
Carshalton Athletic FC (War Memorial Sports Ground)
Carshalton
CARSHALTON
Westcroft Leisure Cen.
Council Offices
Studio Thtre.
The Frying Pan
CARSHALTON PARK
Benhill Rec. Grd.
Collingwood Road Recreation Ground
Sutton United FC (Borough Sports Grd.)
West Sutton
SUTTON
Perrett's Field
Sutton Cmty. Grd.
Fitness4Less (Sutton)
Secombe Thtre.
Civic Cen.
Manor Park
Sutton
Carshalton Beeches
Stanley Pk. Rec. Grd.
CARSHALTON ON THE HILL
CARSHALTON BEECHES
Overton Grange Sch.
Overton Park
Resrs (covered)
Nature Reserves
Wilderness Island
Wandle Bri.
HACKBRIDGE
LONDON ROAD
CARSHALTON ROAD
BISHOPSFORD ROAD
ST. HELIER AVENUE
REIGATE AVENUE
CENTRAL ROAD
LONDON ROAD
COMMON ROAD
OLDFIELDS ROAD
ROSE HILL
ANGEL HILL
WRYTHE LANE
CARSHALTON ROAD
CHEAM ROAD
BRIGHTON ROAD
BEECHES AV.
NIGHTINGALE RD.
A217
A24
A297
A239
A232
A237
B278
B2230
B279
B271
133
156
175

156
MITCHAM COMMON
MERTON
MITCHAM GOLF COURSE
Club House
Mitcham Junction
CROYDON ROAD
WINDMILL RD.
Playing Fields
Keith Tuckey Stadium
Croydon Crematorium
CROYDON CEMETERY
Gonville Academy
Thornton Heath Pond
The Archbishop Lanfranc Sch.
Beddington Lane
Traq Motor Racing
Hundred Acre Bridge
Mill Green
Mitcham
Sand Plant
CR4
Sludge Beds
BEDDINGTON CORNER
Irrigation Bridge
Beddington Sewage Treatment Works
Therapia Lane
Ampere Way
LOMBARD ROUNDABOUT
Canterbury Rec. Grd.
Bus Depot
PIONEERS INDUSTRIAL PARK
BEDDINGTON TRADING ESTATE
VALLEY LEISURE PARK
Vue Cinema
Superstores
Waddon Marsh
Mile Road Bridge
Hackbridge
HACKBRIDGE
FELNEX TRADING ESTATE
SUTTON
Tennis Courts
Sports Ground
Pavilion
BEDDINGTON PARK
River Wandle
Wilderness Island
Wandle Bri.
Carew Manor & Dovecote
Carew Academy
The Grange
Boating Lake
Manor Gdn.
Grammar Sch.
Electricity Switching Station
BEDDINGTON
Superstore
Warehouse
WADDON
Waddon Ponds
Waddon
CARSHALTON
Westcroft Leisure Cen.
Council Offices
Studio Thtre.
WALLINGTON GRN
CROYDON ROAD
A232
Wallington
Bandon Hill Cemetery
Bandonhill
FIVEWAYS CORNER
Retail Park
Playing Field
SM6
WALLINGTON
Mellows Park
The Frying Pan
CARSHALTON PARK
Carshalton
Carshalton Beeches
SM5
STAFFORD ROAD
SOUTH BEDDINGTON
Wilson's Sch.
Powerleague Soccer Centre (Croydon)
Foresters Prim. Sch.
Phoenix Cen.
Roundshaw
Virgin Active The Surrey Health & Racquets Club
Amy Johnson Prim. Sch.
Roundshaw Park (Playing Fields)
Roundshaw Downs Local Nature Reserve
Kidspace Health Club
WOODCOTE ROAD
PURLEY WAY
155
176
134

THORNTON HEATH
Norwood Junc.
SOUTH NORWOOD COUNTRY PARK
Croydon Sports Arena
Croydon FC Grd.
SELHURST
Selhurst
WOODSIDE
Broad Green
CROYDON
West Croydon
East Croydon
ADDISCOMBE
Addiscombe
Queen's Rd. Cemy.
Lloyd Park
LLOYD PARK
COOMBE PARK
Coombe Farm
SHIRLEY
SHIRLEY PARK GOLF COURSE
Trinity School Playing Field
South Croydon
SOUTH CROYDON
HALING PARK
HALING GROVE
CROHAM HURST
CROHAM HURST GOLF COURSE
Breakneck Hill
Thrift Wood
Bramley Bank Nature Reserve
Royal Russell School
Old Ballards Cottage
Ballards Plantation
Coombe Wood
Addington Hills
LITTLEHEATH WOOD
Sanderstead
Harris Academy Purley
St. Giles School
Whitgift Sch.
FLYOVER
WELLESLEY ROAD
ST. JAMES'S ROAD
WINDMILL RD.
LOWER ADDISCOMBE ROAD
MORLAND ROAD
ADDISCOMBE ROAD
COOMBE ROAD
COOMBE LANE
SHIRLEY ROAD
SPRING LANE
PORTLAND ROAD
WOODSIDE GREEN
SELHURST ROAD
WHITEHORSE ROAD
NORTHCOTE RD.
BRIGHTON ROAD
SOUTH END
UPPER SELSDON ROAD
PARK LANE
WARHAM ROAD
ROMAN WAY
OLD TOWN
CROYDON
Rb
Sb
Tb
Ub
Vb
Wb
Xb
71
72
73
74
75
76
77
78
79
80
135
158
177

158
SOUTH NORWOOD COUNTRY PARK
ELMERS END
EDEN PARK
PARK LANGLEY
Croydon Sports Arena
Croydon FC Grd.
Oasis Academy Arena
World of Golf Centre
Long Lane Wood
Bird Sanctuary
David Lloyd Leisure
Langley Court (Research Labs)
Beckenham
Langley Park School for Boys
Langley Park School for Girls
Langley Park Sports Centre
UPPER ELMERS END
Crouch Oak Wood
UPPER ELMERS END ROAD
ELMERS END ROAD
SOUTH EDEN PARK RD.
BECKENHAM ROAD
LINKS WAY
Monks Orchard Prim. Sch.
Glade Wood
MONKS ORCHARD
Edenham High Sch.
Sports Grd.
Bethlem & Maudsley Hospital Sch.
BETHLEM ROYAL HOSPITAL
High Broom Wood
Cold Shaw
Whitley House
Denis Hill Unit
Chelsham House
River House
Garavan Park
Wickham Park House
Ashburton Playing Fields
Oasis Academy Shirley Park (Seniors)
SHIRLEY OAKS BMI HOSPITAL
Shirley Oaks
Playing Field
Parkfields Recreation Ground
WEST WICKHAM
West Wickham
Oak Lodge Prim. Sch.
Blake Recreation Ground
SHIRLEY ROAD
ADDISCOMBE ROAD
WICKHAM ROAD
HIGH STREET
Trinity Sch.
SHIRLEY
Croydon
CR0
SPRING PARK
Forest Acad.
Harris Prim. Academy, Benson
Spring Park Pond
Miller's Pond
SHIRLEY PARK GOLF COURSE
Colma Convent Girls' Sch.
Shirley High School Performing Arts College
Shirley Windmill
Foxes Wood
Pinewoods
Wychwood
Kennel Wood
CROYDON
UPPER SHIRLEY
THE ADDINGTON GOLF COURSE
Club House
The Bungalow
Addington Hills
Threehalfpenny Wood
Pumping Station
Rugby Ground
Foxhill Shaw
COOMBE LANE
Reservoir (covered)
Coombe Lane
Bandy Mount
Royal Russell School
ADDINGTON
ADDINGTON VILLAGE RD.
SPRING PARK
ADDINGTON PALACE GOLF COURSE
Addington Palace
ADDINGTON PARK
Addington Village
Rowdown Fields
Time Bridge Community Centre
Applegarth Academy
Castle Hill Academy
BIRCH WOOD
GRAVEL HILL
Heathfield (Train. Cen.)
Heathfield Farm
Bramley Bank Nature Reserve
South Croydon
Gilbert Scott Primary School & Red Gates School
The Quest Academy
John Ruskin College
SELSDON PARK ROAD
KENT GATE WAY
Fieldway
ADDINGTON COURT GOLF COURSE
Addington Well Pumping Sta.
LITTLEHEATH WOOD
CR2
BR3
178
136
157

159
137
179
Fc
Gc
Hc
Jc
Kc
Lc
Mc
71
72
73
74
75
76
77
78
79
80
Bromley
HAYES
BR2
BROMLEY COMMON
NORMAN PARK
HAYES COMMON
CONEY HALL
KESTON MARK
KESTON
Keston
NASH
NEW ADDINGTON
BROMLEY
BR4
Wickham
PARK
WESTMORELAND RD.
PICKHURST LANE
HAYES LANE
HAYES ROAD
BROMLEY COMMON
CROYDON ROAD
WESTERHAM ROAD
OAKLEY ROAD
BASTON ROAD
COMMONSIDE
HEATHFIELD
Nuffield Health Fitness & Wellbeing Centre
Bromley FC & Cray Wanderers FC (Courage Stadium)
Norman Park Athletics Track
Bromley College of Further & Higher Education
Bromley Trust Academy
Hayes Street Farm
Hayes Prim. Sch.
Hayes Sch.
HAYES GROVE PRIORY HOSP.
Nash College
West Wickham Common
Coney Hall Rec. Grd.
The Emmaus Centre
Wickham Court Farm
Keston Court Riding School
Keston Windmill
KESTON COMMON
Keston C of E Prim. Sch.
Ravens Wood Sch.
Oakley House
Caesars Camp
Holwood
The Temple (Roman Mausoleum)
Wilberforce Oak
Metropolitan Police Dog Training Establishment
Electricity Sub Station
Scrogginhall Wood
Mazzards Wood
Woodcock Grove
Brook Wood
Barnet Wood
Padmall Wood
Cooper's Wood
James's Wood
Well Wood
Bradmanshill Wood
Long Shaw
Fishers Wood
Cupola Wood
Recreation Ground
Pickhurst Jun. & Inf. Schs.
Hawes Down Jun.& Inf. Schs.
Glebe Sch.
Hayes
A232
A233
A21
B265
B251
A2022

SOUTHBOROUGH
JUBILEE COUNTRY PARK
Bromley High School
Petts Wood Junction
Thornet Wood
Jubilee Country Park Sydney Shaw Local Nature Reserve
PETTS WOOD
Petts Wood
Southborough Prim. Sch.
St. James' RC Prim. Sch.
Southborough Open Space (Rec. Grd.)
Playing Field
Parkfield Recreation Ground
BROMLEY GOLF COURSE
Bromley College Further & Higher Education
Bridgeways
Cemetery
BROMLEY COMMON
Driving Range
Bishop Justus C of E School
Princes Plain Prim. Sch.
Prince's Plain
Bromley
Scrubs Farm
BR2
Sparrow Wood
Sparrow Common
Roundabout Wood
Crofton Heath
Clay Wood
Petts Wood Recreation Ground
Crofton Jun. Sch.
Crofton Inf. Sch.
ORPINGTON
CROFTON
Gumping Common
Oakley House
Oakley Farm
Ravens Bourne
Bus Depot
Nursery
Nobody's Wood
Pokeridden Wood
Knowlehill Wood
Knowlehill Farm
Hollydale Recreation Grounds
Ravens Wood Sch.
LOCKSBOTTOM
PRINCESS ROYAL UNIVERSITY HOSP. UCC
Superstore
Farnborough Pav. Recreation Ground
Darrick Wood Swimming Pool
Darrick Wood School
Darrick Wood Sports Cen.
Darrick Wood Jun. & Inf. Schs.
Darrick Wood
Newstead Wood School
Newstead Wood
Bromley Tennis Centre
Playing Field
Tubbenden Prim. Sch.
CROYDON ROAD
A232
A21
A233
KESTON MARK
Keston
THE FANTAIL
FARNBOROUGH COMMON
FARNBOROUGH HIGH STREET
FARNBOROUGH
Farnborough Prim. Sch.
The Manse
Scouts Hall
Club Sports Ground
Ninhams Wood
SOUTH PARK
Lake Wood
Keston C of E Prim. Sch.
Forest Lodge
KESTON COMMON
Caesars Camp
Broom Bank
Woodlands Poultry Farm
The Larches
Mill Hill
Church Field Plantation
Holwood
HOLWOOD ESTATE
THE COURTYARD
Sevenoaks Lodge
SHIRE LANE
Lower Hook Farm
LOWER HOOK BUSINESS PARK
North End Farm
North End Farm Cotts.
Blacklands
BOGEY LANE
WESTERHAM ROAD
Westerham Lodge
Holwood Farm
Scout Camp
Tennis Court
GLEBE FARM BUSINESS PARK
PADDOCK MOBILE HOME PARK
Farthing Street
Farthing
HIGH ELMS COUNTRY PARK (Local Nature Reserve)
Bromley Environmental Education Centre at High Elms (BEECHE)
The Lodge
Woodpiece
Club House
High Elms Clockhouse
The Rookery
HIGH ELMS GOLF COURSE
Whitelands Wood
Cocksett Plantation
Cocksett Hill
Ramus Wood
GREEN STREET GREEN
138
180
159

161
St. Mary Cray
POVEREST
ST. MARY CRAY
BLACKSMITH'S LANE
CROCKENHILL
KEVINGTON
Derry Downs
The Warren
Sheepcote Farm
Child's Wood
Manor Oak Primary Sch.
Kent House Hospital
Kevington Manor
Kynaston Wood
Little Kevington
Waldens Farm
Crouch Farm
Walden Manor
Waldens Bungalow
Lark Rise
Heather's Holding
Bleak House Farm
East Hall Cottage
Green Cedar
Eastwood
Griff's Wood Cottage
Griff's Wood
Piggery
Piggeries
Orchard View
Lone Barn Farm
Brambles
Byways Nursery
Sage Wents
Fairfield
Cookham Hill Farm
Cookham Farm
Feathercot
Woods
Micklewood Farm
BR5
Covet Wood
Recreation Ground
Perry Hall Prim. Sch.
PERRY HALL RD.
Broom Hill
Priory Gardens
Grave Yard
RAMSDEN
The Priory School
Priory Sports Cen.
Playing Field
Grassmeade Recreation Ground
Hillside Primary School
Sports Ground
Leisure Cen.
Bowl. Alley
Super-store
STATION ROAD
SPUR ROAD
A232
Orpington
Blenheim Prim. Sch. & Nursery
Burwood School
GODDINGTON
Goddington Park
Rounds Smallams
The Lodge
Orpington Sports Club
Lilly's Wood
Black Bush Wood
St. Olave's & St. Saviour's Grammar Sch.
Ontario Centre
BR6
Hospice
ORPINGTON HOSPITAL
COURT ROAD
A224
(ORPINGTON BY-PASS)
The Highway Prim. Sch.
CHELSFIELD
Chelsfield
Chelsfield Village
CHELSFIELD PARK BMI HOSPITAL
Brown's School
Court Lodge Farm
Court Lodge
Bucks Cross Farm
Maypole
Glentrammon Rec. Grd.
High Beeches
Sports Ground
Pecks Cotts.
Chelsfield Riding School
Julian Brimstone
Club House
Driving Range
CHELSFIELD LAKES GOLF COURSE
Eleven Oaks
Chelsfield Hill Wood
Chelsfield Hall
Rounds Wood
Hewitts
HEWITTS ROUNDABOUT
Knockholt
Broke Lodge
Goss Bush
PRATT'S BOTTOM
SEVENOAKS ROAD
A21
ORPINGTON
M25
181
162

162
SWANLEY
CROCKENHILL
Swanley
BR8
BROMLEY
Orpington
BR6
BR5
Sevenoaks
TN14
WELL HILL
Maypole
Hulberry
Hulberry Farm
Baldwins Cottages
M25 MOTORWAY
M25
Junction 4
A20
B258
B2173
SWANLEY BY PASS
LONDON ROAD
CRAY ROAD
EYNSFORD ROAD
WESTED ROAD
GOLDSEL RD.
SKEET HILL LANE
PARKGATE ROAD
REDMANS LANE
HILL REDMANS
COCKERHURST ROAD
FIRMINGERS ROAD
GORSE ROAD
HAWSTEAD LANE
MAYPOLE ROAD
SHOREHAM ROAD
CHELSFIELD LANE
HEWITTS ROAD
ORPINGTON ROAD
HEWITTS ROUNDABOUT
Quarry
Hook Spring
Tile Kilns Wood
Marwood Ho. Caravan & Camping Site
Football Ground
Nursery
Sheepcote Farm
Waldens Farm
Crouch Farm
Crouch Farm House
Crouch Farm Cottages
Felma House
Walden Manor
Middle Farm Nursery
Willow Farm
Fleetfoot Fm.
Prim. Sch.
Peartrees
Cemetery
Cherry Orchard
Gosenhill Farm
Wested Farm Cotts.
Little Wested House
Wested Meadows
Wested Farm
Cacketshill Wood
Industrial Estate
Bleak House Farm
East Hall Cottage
Piggery
Orchard View
The Oaks
Lone Barn Farm
Brambles
Highcroft Hall
Heathfield Shaw
Horncross Shaw
Pollard
Fairfield
Crown Wood
Crown Wood Fm.
Woodside
Cookham Farm
Feathercot
Micklewood Farm
Playing Field
Skeet Hill Farm
Davidson House
Snow White Cottages
Park Gate House
Club House
Roughet
LULLINGSTONE PARK GOLF COURSE
LULLINGSTONE PARK
LULLINGSTONE COUNTRY PARK
Driving Range
UPPER BEECHEN WOOD
LOWER BEECHEN WOOD
HOME WOOD
Doctor's Wood
OWEN WOOD
Bucks Cross Farm
Reservoir
Goat Hill
Westwood Cottage
Great Cockerhurst
Ridge Farm
Homewood Farm
Westwood Farm
WEST WOOD
Pascalls Wood
Hewitts
Coneyearth Wood
HOLLOWS WOOD
Brent Farm
Dalhanna
Longspring Wood
Goss Bushes
Keepers Cottage
Coombe Hollow Cottage

163
Junction 3 (M25)
Junction 1 (M20)
M25 MOTORWAY
M20 MOTORWAY
SWANLEY INTERCHANGE
LONDON ROAD
FARNINGHAM WOOD
The Folly
Franks Hall
Little Franks
Abington
Driving Range
Club House
Reservoir (covered)
Pedham Place Farm
PEDHAM PLACE GOLF COURSE
Coldharbour Farm
The Beacon
Mill House
The Manor Ho.
FARNINGHAM
Cricket Grd.
Charton Manor
Charton Farm
Eglantine Villa
Eglantine Farm
Riseley Hall
EGLANTINE LANE
GORSE HILL (MAIN ROAD)
DARTFORD ROAD
MAIN ROAD
Polly Shaw
The Little House
Fountain Hoy
Eynsford Hill
Sunfield
Sunhurst
Mount Eagle
Tabsfield
The Anthony Roper Prim. Sch.
Eynsford Castle
Furlongs Farm
Riverside Nursy.
Tills Cottage
Hall
Beesfield Farm
Cresset Cottage
DONKEY LANE
Firpound Shaw
Alchin's Wood
Dartford DA4
EYNSFORD
Recreation Ground
Glyndel
Eagle Heights Wildlife Park
Viaduct
Home Farm
Ford
Olivers Shaw
Gorse Hill Nursery
164
SEVENOAKS
Lullingstone Roman Villa
Newbarn Farm
Lullingstone Park Farm
Eynsford
STATION ROAD
HIGH STREET
MAPLESCOMBE LANE
Sandhole Shaw
Lullingstone
World Garden
Lullingstone Castle
Weir
Higham
Park House Farm
Black Cottage
Chalkhurst Wood
Lower Park Wood
MAPLESCOMBE
Maplescombe Farm
Adder Bank Shaw
Courtfield Shaw
Reservoir
The Rookery
Lower Austin Lodge
AUSTIN LODGE ROAD
BOWER LANE
Bower Park Farm
Hartnips Wood
Maplebank Poultry Farm
Sevenoaks TN15
The Strikes
SHOREHAM ROAD
The Birches
Coombe Firs
Hog Wood
Upper Austin Lodge
183
Preston Hill Plantation
Kd Ld Md Nd Pd Qd Rd
71 72 73 74 75 76 77 78 79 80

164
142
163
184
HORTON KIRBY
Horton Kirby Environmental Education Centre
Reynolds Place Farm
Franks
Cricket Grd.
Eglantine Villa
Mussenden Cottage
Mussenden Farm
Blue Cottages
Riseley Hall
Eglantine Farm
Beeches Farm
Canada Farm
Hill Barn Farm
Lone Oak Farm
Scudder Farm
Wickhams
The Grange
Dartford
DA4
M20-MOTORWAY
M20
Liberty Farm
THE GROVE CRAFT WORKSHOPS
Grove Farm
Fawkham
Fawkham C of E Prim. Sch.
HORTON WOOD
Hopkins Spring Wood
Parkfield Wood
FAWKHAM MANOR BMI HOSPITAL
Hatchfield Wood
Fawkham Manor Farm
Cresset Cottage
Speedgate Farm
Speedgate House
White House Farm
Speedgate
Alchin's Wood
Paygate Cottage
Gabrielspring Wood
Choaks Farm
Choaks Wood
FAWKHAM GREEN
Gorse Hill Nursery
Hazlewood
Birchgrove
Greenlands
Cherrywood
The Haven
Springfield
Rowanhurst
Ashen Grove
Brands Hatch Place
Saxten's Wood
Cage's Wood
Sandhole Shaw
Shetley Shaws
Grandstand
Vineyard Shaw
Hotel
Offices
Eastwood
Rogers Wood
Woodlands
Gallows Wood
Little Haven
Billet Wood
BRANDS HATCH MOTOR RACING CIRCUIT
Lower Park Wood
MAPLESCOMBE
Kingsdown Farm
Cowless Shaw
Battersea at Brands Hatch
Maplescombe Farm
Bank Shaw
Grove Wood
BLUE CHALET INDUSTRIAL PARK
Courtfield Shaw
Maplebank Nursery
Westfield Cotts.
THE LONDON GOLF COURSE
Maplebank Poultry Farm
To the Woods Caravan & Camping Site
FLORENCE FARM MOBILE HOME PK.
Broomfield Wood
Mace Wood
Birtley House School
CHURCH WOOD
Springham's Cotts.
Rec. Grd.
Sidehilly Wood
WEST KINGSDOWN
Crowhurst Farm
Club House
HIGH CASTLE WOOD
Sports Ground
Lib.
WEST KINGSDOWN INDUSTRIAL EST.
Ashen Shaw
Richardson's Farm
THE LONDON GOLF COURSE
GORSE HILL (MAIN ROAD)
A20
LONDON ROAD
FAWKHAM ROAD
SCHOOL LANE
MUSSENDEN LANE
GABRIEL SPRING ROAD
SPEEDGATE HILL
VALLEY ROAD
BILLET LANE
ROGERS WOOD LANE
SEVE

HARTLEY
Hartley Green
Longfield
LONGFIELD HILL
DA3
GRAVESHAM
Hartley Hill
NEW ASH GREEN
West Yoke
Gravesend
DA13
ASH
Sevenoaks
TN15
RIDLEY
New Street
TONBRIDGE and MALLING
HODSOLL STREET
Pettings
CORINTHIAN GOLF COURSE
Milestone Academy
Redlibbets Wood
Foxbrough Wood
Nine Horse Wood
Hartley Wood
Hartley Manor
Middleton Cottages
Middleton Farm
Hartley Bottom Farm
Northdown Farm
Southdown Farm
Idleigh Farm
Idleigh Court
Cuckolds Corner
White Ash Wood
Middle Wood
Grubb Wood
Eldridge Shaw
Elbows Wood
Viney Wood
Dunmery Grove
Ridley Wood
Ridley Court Farm
Ridley Farm
Pond Farm
Pilgrim Corner
Newlands Shaw
Jub's Hill Wood
Pettings Wood
Pettings Court Farm
Haven Wood
Haven Manor
The Roughets
Baker's Shaw
Baker's Wood
Pumping Station
The Old Malt Ho.
Holywell Park Farm
Dairy House Farm
Holywell Farm
Greenfields
Rumney Farm
Rumney Farm Cottages
Pease Hill Cottages
Hilly Field Shaw
Goss Wood
Galsmead
Ash Place Farm
Swan Farm
Landway Farm
Oliver's Farm
Swan Meadows Farm
Orange Hill
Broom Wood
Rabbit Wood
Shipley Hills Shaw
Millfield Shaw
Langley Grove
Millers Wood
Selbyfield Shaw
Ten Acre Shaw
Eight Acre Wood
Ashplat Wood
Oxens Shaw
Long Bottom Wood
Carlows Wood
Lion Wood
Sheeplands Shaw
Eldridge Cottage
Orchard Cottage
New Street Farm
New Street Farm Cottages
Redsteadle Wood
Dell Wood
Feathercot
Court View
Larksfield
Sunnymead
Sunnydale
Skinners Hill
Nurstead Hall
Manor Farm
Cricket Ground
Hartley Dell
Bridelands Wood
Goldsmiths Shaw
Bowes Wood
Recreation Ground
North Lands Shaw
Chapel Wood
Corinthian Sports Club
Football Ground
B260
143
185
Zd Ae Be Ce De Ee Fe
71 72 73 74 75 76 77 78 79 80
560 61 62 63
68 67 66 165 64 63

166
146
186
M3 MOTORWAY
M3
Lightwater
LIGHTWATER
GU18
GU24
SURREY
WEST END
BISLEY
KNAPHILL
Donkey Town
Lucas Green
Staffordlake
Penny Pot
Reidon Hill
LIGHTWATER BY-PASS
GUILDFORD ROAD
BAGSHOT ROAD
A322
A319
B311
Ashleigh Farm
Woodlands Farm
Park Wood
White Bridge
Westcroft Park
Westcroft Farm
Steep Acre Farm
Old House Farm
Broadwaygreen Farm
Lee Lane Farm
Rectory Farm
Halebourne Copse
Manor Farm Wood
Manor Farm Cottages
Sewage Works
Brooklands Farm
Halebourne House
Higher Park Farm
Shrubb's Farm
Nurseries
Hookstone Farm
Hookstone Green
WINDLEMERE GOLF COURSE
Driving Range
Club Ho.
Playing Field
Pankhurst Farm
Brook Place
Turf Hill
The Laurels
Holly Farm
Gordon's School
New England
Sandpit Hill
Holy Trinity C of E Primary School
Greyspot Hill
Cuckoo Hill
Mortar Range DANGER AREA
The Oaks
Hatchgate Farm
Beldam Bridge Farm
Beldam Bri.
Lovelands Farm
Rounce Farm
Fenns Fm.
Rosedene Farm
Dog Hill
Trulley Brook
Lucas Green Manor
Trulleys
The Bourne
New Bridge
Scott's Farm
CHOBHAM GOLF COURSE
Sports Ground
Hawk Farm
Springfield Fm.
Nursery Cottages
Ford Farm
Tennis Courts
White Cottage Farm
Pine Grove Farm
Lucas Green Farm
Rec. Grd.
Bisley Green
Brock Hill
Peatmoor Pond
Works
Hill Place Farm
Hill Place
The Mews
Bayfield Piggery
Ashgrove Nursery
Furze Farm
Bullhousen Farm
WOKING PRIORY HOSPITAL
Hillview Poultry Farm
BISLEY COMMON
DANGER AREA
HMP COLDINGLEY
Ramsbrook Farm
Long Siberia Range
Miles Green
Therapy Centre
Hangmoor Copse
Stickle Down
High Hoglees
Short Siberia Range
Strawberry Farm
Stickledown Range
Bisley Ranges
Polledoak Slade
Chaseley
Staffordlake Farm
Princess Christian Homes & Training Centre
Stafford Lake
Hog Lees
Century Range
Wisdom Farm
Wisdom Corner
Clock Tower
Ranges
Grindstone Handle Corner
Shrubb's Copse
Superstore
Knaphill Sch.
Lower Sch.

167
Burrowhill
Stanners Hill
Mossat Farm
Westways Farm
Paradise Farm
Stannershill Farm
Little Heath
Woods Farm
Henage Corner
Chobham Park House
Partridge Farm
Chobham Park Farm
Greenacres
Stanyards
Stanyards Cottage
Stanyards Farm
Nursery
Nurseries
Wishmore Cross Academy
Larkenshaw
Larkenshaw Farm
Fishpool Bridge
Sowmoor Plantation
CHERTSEY ROAD
A319
Copyhold
Sow Moor
Mill Bourne
Millbourne Bridge
Chobham Mus.
CHOBHAM
Riverside Nursery
Emmetts Mill
Brooklands Farm
Burnside Nursery
Sunfield Farm
Little Goldbridge Farm
Willow Farm
Cricket Field
Recreation Ground
Grant's Bridge
Broadford
Broadford Farm
HEATH
STATION ROAD
A3046
Highfield
SANDPIT HALL ROAD
Milford Green
CASTLE GREEN
Sewage Works
Cox Hill
MIMBRIDGE
Milford House
Milford Farm
White Lodge Farm
Wapshott Farm
Horsell Common
Heather Farm
Milbrook Animal Centre
Woking
Coxhill Green
Border Farm
Shaw's Farm
Scotchers Farm Cotts.
Surrey Rose Farms
Deep Pool Farm
CHOBHAM ROAD
Mim Br.
Knaphill Manor Farm
Beetle Cottage
Knaphill Manor
Graylands Farm
Willow View Farm
Parley Brook
Wesbury Farm
LITTLEWICK ROAD
HORSELL COMMON ROAD
Littlewick Common
Parley Brook Farm
Woking High Sch.
WOKING
Knapwood House
LITTLEWICK
Mizens Railway
Knap Hill Nursery
Parley Bridge
Games Courts
Tracious Copse
Goldsworth Park
Recreation Ground
GOLDSWORTH PARK TRADING ESTATE
HORSELL
St. Andrew's Sch.
WATERERS PARK
Beaufort Prim. Sch.
GOLDSWORTH PARK
Horsell Moor
LOCKFIELD DRIVE
A324
Fitness
Surrey History Cen.
Goldsworth
Superstore
WOKING
Sports Cen.
HERMITAGE ROAD
Woking Crematorium
ST. JOHNS
MOUNT HERMON
147
168
187

168
148
167
188
A
B
C
D
E
F
G
81
82
83
84
85
86
87
88
89
90
Stanners Hill
Hawks Hill
Timber Hill
Timber Hill Cotts.
Stanyards
Greenacres
Stanyards Cott.
Stanyards Farm
Chobham Business Centre
Berwin Park
SURREY HEATH
FAIROAKS AIRPORT
GU24
Copyhold
Riverside Nursery
Brooklands Farm
Burnside Nursery
Sunfield Farm
The Bourne
Young Stroat Farm
Scotchers Farm
Scotchers Farm Cotts.
Shaw's Farm
Horsell Common
HORSELL COMMON
Bonseys Cotts.
Danewell Hill
Anthonys
New Houses
Pinewood Cotts.
Works
McLAREN TECHNOLOGY CENTRE
Bonsey's Bridge
Samson's Wood
Long Copse
Miniature Rifle Range
Play. Fld.
Tennis Courts
The Mansion
Ottershaw Park
Playing Field
Little Blackmole Pond
Beech Hill Clump
Great Blackmole Pond
The Wey Farm
Decoy Plantation
Dunford Ho.
Dunford Bridge
Old Farm
Bridge House
Sandpit Plantation
Bramshill
Hill Crest
Brox
Chertsey
Gable Cottage
Great Wood
KT16
Halls
The Warren
Thatch Cottage
Ware Copse
Anningsley Park
ANNINGSLEY PARK
Brox Copse
Brox Wood
Holly Farm
Beyond
Bourne Rise Farm
Southern Wood
Rodwell
Holme Farm
Grovers Farm
Birch Wood
The Cottage
Hoyt Wood
The Larches
The Hoyte
Hoyte Lodge
Club House
NEW ZEALAND GOLF COURSE
Tennis Courts
Durnford Farm
Timber Yard
Community Recycling Centre
Danewell House
SHEERWATER
Sheerwater Recreation Ground
The Bishop David Brown Sch.
Broadmere Prim. Sch.
Youth Club
WEST BYFLEET GOLF COURSE
Monument Bridge
Britannia Wharf
Playing Field
New Monument School
Woking
WOKING
MAYBURY
Horsell Moor
Goldsworth
Surrey History Cen.
Shey Copse
Piggery
HOEBRIDGE GOLF COURSE
Fox Hill
THE ROUGH
Pyrford Common
Driving Range
Roundbridge
Sports Ground
MOUNT HERMON
WOKING PARK
CHERTSEY ROAD
GUILDFORD ROAD
A320
A319
A245
A3046
A324
B385
B382
WOODHAM LANE
SHORES ROAD
CHOBHAM RD.
VICTORIA WAY
LOCKFIELD DR.
SHEERWATER
OLD WOKING ROAD

ROW TOWN
NEW HAW
Addlestone
WOODHAM
KT15
M25 MOTORWAY
BROOKLANDS
Weybridge
KT13
Byfleet & New Haw
West Byfleet
Dartnell Park
WEST BYFLEET
BYFLEET
Sanway
RIDGWAY
PYRFORD
WISLEY
GU22
GU23
PYRFORD GREEN
PYRFORD VILLAGE
GUILDFORD
RHS Garden Wisley
WISLEY COMMON
Brooklands Museum
Mercedes-Benz World
PARVIS ROAD
OYSTER LANE
PORTSMOUTH ROAD

170
150
Q
R
S
T
U
V
W
The London Bus Museum
Mercedes-Benz World
Brooklands Museum
BROOKLANDS
Weybridge
ST. GEORGE'S HILL
KT13
ST. GEORGE'S HILL GOLF COURSE
GOLF COURSE
Club House
David Lloyd Leisure
Blue Barn Farm
WHITELEY VILLAGE
Walton-on-Thames
KT12
BURHILL GOLF COURSE
Burhill Park
Club House
Dick Turpin's Cottage
Strawberry Hill
Beards Hill
Notre Dame Preparatory & Senior Schools
Burwood Park
Seven Hills Estate
Walton Firs Scout Camp
Manor Pond
PAINSHILL
SEVEN HILLS ROAD
B365
BYFLEET ROAD
A245
ESHER ROAD
PORTSMOUTH ROAD
A3
Silvermere
SILVERMERE GOLF COURSE
Driving Range
Thirty Acre Wood
Silvermere Farm Estate
St. George's Nursing Home
Hotel
Feltonfleet Sch.
Cobham Bridge
Pains Hill
PAINSHILL PARK
Gothic Temple
The Lake
Heyswood Girl Guide Camp
The Broom
Wood Hill
Education Cen.
Lodge Cottages
Cobham Court Farm
West Byfleet
BYFLEET
KT14
Byfleet Mill
Bluegates Hole
Foxholm Covert
Home Farm
The Hangers
Queen Anne's Cottage
Queen Anne's Hills
Manor House
The Island
Park Barn Farm
River Wey
Nursery
Long Orchard Farm
Highlands Farm
Foxwarren Park
Red Hill
Gothic Tower
Tower Hill
Waterwheel
Wheel Island
Buxton Wood
Clearmount
Oak Pollard
M25 MOTORWAY
WISLEY INTERCHANGE
Junction 10
Wisley Common
Woolger's Wood
Pond Farm
Cockcrow Hill
Redhill Bottom
Chatley Wood
Sandpit Hill
Chatley Farm
River Mole
GUILDFORD
WISLEY COMMON
Woking
GU23
Hut Hill Cottage
Hut Hill
Currie's Clump
OCKHAM COMMON
Chatley Cott.
The Bogs
Breach Hill Wood
Chatley Heath
Telegraph Hill
Chatley Heath Semaphore Tower
Wisley Common, Ockham & Chatley Heath Nature Reserve
Bolder Mere
Hatchford Wood
Woodside Cottage
Elm Cottage
HATCHFORD MANOR
Hatchford Park
Lodge Copse
Bramble Wood
Bramble Cottage
Halfpenny Cross
Wrens Nest Cottage
Pointers Green
Poynters Farm
Brickfield Copse
Little Brickfield Copse
Pondtail Farm
Highfield Farm
Nurseries
Oakham Village Green
Fellside Cottages
ELM CORNER
Wilderness Farm
Hatchford End
Hatchford
190
169
81
82
83
84
85
86
87
88
89
90
07
08
09
510
63
62
61
60
59
58

171
151
191
172
Claremont Park
Claremont Landscape Garden
WEST END COMMON (Local Nature Reserve)
Horseshoe Clump
Claremont Lake
Esher
ESHER COMMON (Local Nature Reserve)
KT10
Black Pond
Winterdown Wood
The Homewood
Winterdown
ACS Cobham International School
RIVER MOLE
Burhill
Riverside Farm
Southwood Manor Farm
BURHILL GOLF COURSE
Hollybush Cottages
Fairmile Golf Range
The Fairmile
Chippings Farm
Hook's Corner
Old Common (Local Nature Reserve)
Randalls Cotts.
Old Common
FAIRMILE COMMON
Middle Pond
Fairmile
Reed's Sch.
Cricket Ground
OXSHOTT HEATH
Leatherhead
KT22
Oxshott
Cobham
KT11
COBHAM
Cobham Mill
Knowle Hill
Little Heath
Littleheath Common
Polyapes Scout Camp
The Furze
Lower Cobham Tilt
Rose Lodge Wood
Pyports
Elm Farm
Upper Cobham Tilt
Cemetery
Ash Ford
Pav. Recreation Ground
STOKE D'ABERNON
Lower Farm
Cobham & Stoke D'Abernon
Tennis Courts
Chelsea Football Academy
Manor Farm
Nursery
COBHAM PARK
Big Roundabout
Little Roundabout
Park Wood
Cobham Park Nursery
Cobham Stud
Cossins Farm
Cobham Lodge
Downside Farm Cottage
Downside Saw Mill
Downside Farm
Downside Common
Downside
Rye Salters
Wrens Hill Wood
Parkside Sch.
South Lodge
Old Parks Copse
Old Parks
Old Parks Cottage
Little Park
WOODLANDS PARK
Woodlands Park
Manor Farm
Pine Trees
M25 MOTORWAY
Stoke D'Abernon Bri.
Little Slyfield
Slyfield House
Heathfield Copse
ESHER BY-PASS
A3
A307
A245
A244
ROAD
COPSEM LANE
WARREN LANE
BLACKHILLS
SANDY LANE
FAIRMILE LANE
OXSHOTT ROAD
STOKE ROAD
HIGH ST.
MILL RD.
WOODLANDS LANE
DOWNSIDE ROAD
DOWNSIDE BRIDGE ROAD
DOWNSIDE COMMON RD
COBHAM PARK RD.
BLUNDEL LANE
BLUE BELL LANE
BRIDLE LANE
LITTLEHEATH ROAD
EATON PARK ROAD
Tennis Courts
Sports Ground
Rec. Grd
X Y Z Aa Ba Ca Da
81 82 83 84 85 86 87 88 89 90

Esher
KT10
CLAYGATE
CLAYGATE COMMON (Local Nature Reserve)
ESHER COMMON
Arbrook Common
ESHER BY-PASS
A3
COPSEM LANE
A244
Birchwood
Holroyd's Plantation
Great Oaks
Sixty Acre Wood
Chessington World of Adventures
KINGSTON
Milbournehold Plantation
Limekiln Wood
Jubilee Wood
Old Carpenters Plantation
MALDEN RUSHETT
Stokesheath Farm Cottages
The Heckets
Brickyard Plantation
The Milbournehold Wood
NEW WOOD
FAIROAK LANE
B280
ELMBRIDGE
Leatherhead
OXSHOTT
KT22
Stoke Wood
Jessop's Well
Bunkers Hill
Rushett Farm
PRINCE'S COVERTS
Adecroft Furze Field
Telegraph Hill
Reservoir (covered)
D'Abernon Chase Cottage
Eleven Acres
Danes Hill School
Horns Hill
D'Abernon Ho.
LEATHERHEAD GOLF COURSE
Oxshott Flat
Knott Park
Clouds Hill Farm
Oxshott Mead
Pachesham Lake
LEATHERHEAD COMMON
Club House
Pachesham Park
Little Brook Park
Crab Apple Court
Ashley Court
Paddock Lodge Stables
Hillthorpe
The Oaks
KINGSTON ROAD
A243
LEATHERHEAD ROAD
OXSHOTT ROAD
MOLE VALLEY
Woodlands Farm
Manor Farm
Pine Trees
WOODLANDS LANE
Woodlands Park
Cobham
KT11
WOODLANDS PARK
Queen Elizabeth's Foundation
Tyrwhitt House
Junction 9
M25 MOTORWAY
Dorincourt
Teazle Wood
Golf Course
Club Ho.
Driving Range
PACHESHAM PARK GOLF COURSE
Superstore
Rowhurst Forge
Heathfield Copse
West Orchard
Brook Willow Farm
Pachesham Farm
The Mounts
Research Laboratories
LEATHERHEAD COMMON
West Hill Sch.
Sewage Works
RANDALLS RD.
A245
OAKLAWN ROAD
B2430
Barnett Wood
LOWER ASHTEAD

152
171
192

173
153
193
174
HORTON PARK GOLF COURSE
Horton Country Park Local Nature Reserve
HORTON COUNTRY PARK
Four Acre Wood
Pond Wood
Park Farm
Acre Hill Farmhouse
Chessington & Hook United FC
BARWELL BUSINESS PARK
KT9
KT19
KT18
KT21
HORTON
Horton Park Children's Farm
David Lloyd Leisure
Polo Ground
Equus Equestrian Centre
West Park Farm
NEW EPSOM & EWELL COTTAGE HOSPITAL
Laundry Cott.
Hollywood Lodge
Glanmire Farm
CHRIST CHURCH ROAD
B280
ROAD WEST
Stamford Green
Stamford Green Prim. Sch.
Southfield Park Prim. Sch.
Sports Ground
St. Ebba's Farm Cottage
ST. EBBA'S
Cemetery
Playing Field
CHESSINGTON ROAD
B2200
B284
HOOK ROAD
Stew Pond
Great Stew Pond
Epsom Common Local Nature Reserve
EPSOM COMMON
Newton Wood
THE FOREST
The Wells
EPSOM
Epsom
Rosebery Park
EPSOM GENERAL HOSPITAL
St. Josephs Catholic Prim. Sch.
Rosebery Sch.
DORKING ROAD
A24
WOODCOTE
Woodcote Stud Farm
Epsom Common
Woodcote Park
Woodcote Park (Club House)
Halfmoon Clump
Fish Pond
Crockingham Wood
RAC GOLF COURSE
Ridgecourt
The Durdans
The Grove
Woodcote Grove
Racing Stables
EPSOM DOWNS
Langley Bottom Wood
Ashtead
ASHTEAD
ASHTEAD PARK
ASHTEAD PARK (Local Nature Reserve)
The Cottage in the Park
Island Pond
Ashtead House
Nursery
Wood Field
The Rye
THE STREET
City of London Freemen's Sch.
William III Gate
Playing Field
Greenside
Fairways
Little Copse
Spinney's
Meridan
Spindles

174
154
194
173
EWELL
EPSOM
EAST EWELL
Ewell West
Ewell East
Epsom Downs
KT19
KT17
KT18
KT20
E P S O M
and
E W E L L
Epsom
R E I G A T
NORK
NORK PARK
Tadworth
North Looe
CUDDINGTON GOLF COURSE
GOLF COURSE
EPSOM DOWNS RACECOURSE
E P S O M   D O W N S
THE HILL
RAC GOLF COURSE
Great Burgh
TATTENHAM CORNER
BURGH HEATH
EPSOM DOWNS
Langley Vale
Howell Hill Nature Reserve
Sports Ground
NESCOT (North East Surrey College of Technology)
Nescot Sports Centre
Bourne Hall Mus.
Hatch Furlong
Rugby Football Grd.
Priest Hill
Reservoir (covered)
North Looe Farm
The Downs Farm
DRIFT BRIDGE
Epsom College
Epsom College Fitness Cen.
Rifle Range
Racing Stables
Crockingham Wood
Queen's Stand
Grandstand
Tattenham Corner
Nork Park Farm
Park Wood
Round Wood
Warren Mead Jun. & Inf. Schs.
Tattenham Way Recreation Ground
CHESSINGTON
HOOK
Rainbow Leisure Centre
Glyn School
Wallace Fields Jun. Sch.
Alexandra Rec. Grd.
Gibraltar Rec. Grd.
David Lloyd Leisure Cen.
Nonsuch High Sch.
ORGAN CROSSROADS
EWELL BY-PASS
LONDON RD.
HIGH ST.
REIGATE ROAD
CHEAM RD.
EPSOM RD.
EAST ST.
UP. HIGH ST.
ALEXANDRA ROAD
COLLEGE ROAD
ASHLEY RD.
ST. BURGH
DOWNS RD.
THE DOWNS
LONGDOWN LANE SOUTH
FIR TREE RD.
YEW TREE BOTTOM RD.
TATTENHAM CORNER
TATTENHAM CR.
GREAT TATTENHAMS
TATTENHAM WAY
FIR TREE RD. A2022
HIGH CUDDINGTON
GRANDSTAND RD.
A24
A240
A232
A2022
B2200
B284
B288
B289
B290
B291
B2221
A217
21
22
23
24
59
81
82
83
84
85
86
87
88
89
90
Ua
Va
Wa
Xa
Ya
Za
Ab

BELMONT
CARSHALTON BEECHES
CARSHALTON ON THE HILL
Sutton
SM2
SM5
Carshalton
BANSTEAD DOWNS
BANSTEAD DOWNS GOLF COURSE
HMP HIGH DOWN
HMP DOWNVIEW
OAKS SPORTS CENTRE GOLF COURSE
OAKS PARK
LITTLE WOODCOTE
Banstead
BANSTEAD
SM7
WOODMANSTERNE
PARK DOWNS
BANSTEAD WOOD
CHIPSTEAD
CHIPSTEAD GOLF COURSE
SUTTON HOSPITAL
THE ROYAL MARSDEN HOSP. (SUTTON)
WINKWORTH ROAD
CROYDON LANE
BRIGHTON ROAD
WOODMANSTERNE LANE
HOLLY LANE
HIGH STREET
Great Solom's Wood
Scratch Wood
Chipstead
Coulsdon
CR5

176
CARSHALTON ON THE HILL
Jb
Kb
Lb
Mb
Nb
Pb
Qb
156
Roundshaw
Roundshaw Park (Playing Fields)
Croydon
Roundshaw Downs Local Nature Reserve
CR0
Sports Ground
Roundshaw Park
Amy Johnson Prim. Sch.
Wallington
Carshalton
SM5
SM6
SUTTON
81
82
83
84
85
86
87
88
89
90
Stanley Park High Sch.
Running Track
Diamond Riding Centre
High Sch. for Girls
WOODCOTE GREEN
Play. Fields
Nursery
The John Fisher School
Peaks Hill
Laleham Lea School
Purley Ckt. Club
Sports Grd.
Margaret Roper Cath. Prim. Sch.
Thomas More Cath. Sch.
PURLEY
PURLEY CROSS
Superstore
OAKS PARK
LITTLE WOODCOTE
Little Woodcote Farm
Little Woodcote Fm. Cotts.
Old Lodge Farm
Lower Pillory Down
WOODCOTE PARK GOLF COURSE
Caravan Park
Hylands Nurseries
Ruffet Wood
Big Wood
175
Sports Ground
Hillside Cotts.
Woodmansterne Primary Sch.
Manor Cottage Farm
The Manor Ho.
The Old Sch.
WOODMANSTERNE
New Lodge Farm
Woodcote Grove House
Orford Ho.
Woodcote Grove
Woodcote Grove Farm
Club House
CLOCK HOUSE
Recreation Ground
Woodcote High Sch.
Playing Field
Woodcote Primary School
Upper Woodcote Ho.
WOODCOTE
Purley
Model Village
CR8
Reedham
Coun. Offices
Reedham Park Sch.
Prim. Sch.
Tennis Courts
Prospect Plantation
Woodmansterne
Coulsdon Town
Smitham Prim. Sch.
COULSDON
St. Aidan's Cath. Prim. Sch.
Twiners Shaw
Coulsdon South
Postern Wood
CANE HILL DEVELOPMENT
War Mem.
Rec. Grd.
Oasis Academy (Byron)
Stonyfield Shaw
COULSDON COURT GOLF COURSE
Coulsdon Court Club House
Chipstead Valley Prim. Sch.
Playing Fld.
REIGATE and BANSTEAD
Page Hill
White Hill
HOW HILLS
CHIPSTEAD GOLF COURSE
Woodlands Deer Stock Farm
Recreation Ground
Chipstead
Club House
West Ridge
How Green
Marlfield Shaw
CHIPSTEAD
196
FARTHING OR FAIRDEAN DOWNS
HAPPY VALLEY
AR Centre
Bowling Green
Rec. Grd.
Coulsdon Coll. Playing Field
Keston Prim. Sch.
A23
A237
A2022
B272
B2030
B2032
B276
B278
BRIGHTON ROAD
WOODCOTE ROAD
FOXLEY LANE
SMITHAM BOTTOM LA.
SMITHAM DOWNS RD.
WOODCOTE GROVE ROAD
WOODMANSTERNE LA.
LITTLE WOODCOTE LA.
CHIPSTEAD VALLEY ROAD
FARTHING WAY
COULSDON ROAD
MARLPIT LANE
OUTWOOD LANE
RECTORY LANE
CARSHALTON ROAD
PURLEY WAY
PLOUGH LANE
BRIGHTON ROAD
28
29
530
31

177
157
178
197
Rb
Sb
Tb
Ub
Vb
Wb
Xb
81
82
83
84
85
86
87
88
89
90
32
33
34
35
Sanderstead
Purley Oaks
Riddlesdown
Kenley
KENLEY
Whyteleafe
WHYTELEAFE
Whyteleafe South
Upper Warlingham
SANDERSTEAD
SELSDON
HAMSEY GREEN
South Croydon
Kenley
Warlingham
Whyteleafe
TANDRIDGE
CR2
CR3
CR6
CR8
PURLEY DOWNS GOLF COURSE
SELSDON PARK HOTEL GOLF COURSE
CROHAM HURST GOLF COURSE
KENLEY COMMON
KENLEY AERODROME
MITCHLEY WOOD
KINGS WOOD
Riddlesdown Collegiate
Atwood Prim. Academy
Gresham Prim. Sch.
Ridgeway Prim. Sch.
Kenley Prim. Sch.
Hamsey Green Prim. Sch.
Warlingham Sch.
Kingswood Secondary School
Croydon High School
Croydon High Sports Club
Dollypers Hill Nature Reserve
Betts Mead Recreation Ground
Sanderstead Plantation
Littleshaws
Barnfield Shaw
Ansley Berry Shaw
Dipsley's Shaw
Ragged Grove
Coombes Wood
Hook's Hill
Breakneck Hill
Thrift Wood
Littleheath Wood
Selsdon Hill
Joysons Hill
Bryngwyn Farm
Sunnycroft Farm
Elm Grove Farm
Kenley House
Warlingham Court Farm
Batts Farm
Tithepit Shaw
Foxes Wood
Whyteleafe Rec. Grd.
Whyteleafe FC Grd.
Purley Beeches
Halls Wettern Tree Gdn.
Cumnor House Sch.
LIMPSFIELD ROAD
ADDINGTON ROAD
SELSDON ROAD
UPPER SELSDON ROAD
SANDERSTEAD ROAD
SANDERSTEAD HILL
MITCHLEY AVENUE
COURT ROAD
GODSTONE ROAD
HILLBURY ROAD
KINGS ROAD
HAYES LANE
A22
A23
A235
A2022
B269
B270
B275

178
SELSDON
FORESTDALE
ADDINGTON COURT GOLF COURSE
SELSDON PARK HOTEL GOLF COURSE
FARLEIGH COURT GOLF COURSE
FARLEIGH
TANDRIDGE
HAMSEY GREEN
Warlingham
WARLINGHAM
CHELSHAM
CR2
CR6
158
177
198

Electricity Sub Station
Rushfield Shaw
Broomfieldbank Shaw
159
The Temple (Roman Mausoleum)
Keston Court Farm
Wilberforce Oak
Scout Camp
Metropolitan Police Dog Training Establishment
Milchdene
CHURCH
LANE
WESTERHAM RD.
Westerham Lodge
DOWNE
ROAD
Pitch & Putt Golf Course
ROWDOWN WOOD
NEW ADDINGTON
GLEBE FARM BUSINESS PARK
PADOCK MOBILE HOME PARK
BLACKNESS
ORCHARD PL.
A233
Layham's Farm Cottage
Layham's Farm
Longlands Nurseries
KIMBERLEY BUSINESS PARK
VULCAN BUSINESS CENTRE
ADDINGTON BUSINESS CENTRE
MERIDIAN CENTRE
Furze Bottom
Rowdown Primary School
Warehouses
Vale Farm
GREEN
ROAD
Keston
BR2
Sports Ground
Hoppershatch Shaw
Greyhound Training Kennels
Ten. Cts.
Bowling Green
Milne Park
Higham's Hill
LEAVES
The Green
Greenacres Riding Sch.
ROSE COTTAGES
Bradmoor
High House Farm
Ashmore Farm
LEAVES GREEN
Milking Lane Farm
West Wickham Res. (covered)
Club House
Play. Fld.
Club
Tennis Courts
Gushybank Shaw
Fairchildes Prim. Sch.
Meridian High Sch.
Terminal
LONDON BIGGIN HILL AIRPORT
SHEEPBARN LANE
HIGHAMS HILL
JEWELS HILL
Babington Place
Saltbox Hill Nature Reserve
Playing Field
Fairchildes Cotts.
JEWELS WOOD
MAIN
SALTBOX
HILL
Bograms Wood
North Lodge
South Lodge
Blackmans Cotts.
BLACKMAN'S LA.
Fairchildes Farm
Coxs Cottages
PARK ROAD
BROMLEY
FICKLESHOLE
Fickleshole Farm
Fickleshole Farm Cotts.
Cudham Lodge Woods
South London Aero Club
180
AIRPORT INDUSTRIAL ESTATE
BIGGIN HILL BUSINESS PARK
CONCORDE BUSINESS PK.
Skid Hill House
Skid Hill Farm
Greathill Shaw
Midgley Shaws
Westerham
Jugg Hill
Costains Farm
Honeyoak Wood
Oaklands Prim. Sch.
TN16
CROWN
ROAD
Norheads Farm
Cemetery
Recreation Ground
Biggin Hill Memorial Pool
Church Cotts.
BIGGIN HILL
Norheads Farm Cotts.
Long Coppice
MOLLARDS WOOD
Hall
Jerry Reddins Shaw
Broom Lodge Farm
Chelsham Court Farm
Chelsham Court
Owls Wood
CHELSHAM COURT ROAD
BEDDLESTEAD LANE
Cony Crook
White Bank
Long Coppice
Parsons Shaw
Farley Kennels
Cowyard Shaw
Milbury Cott.
Round Wood
199
Beddlestead House
Kingscote
Isle Shaw
Home

180
160
179
200
Nc
Pc
Qc
Rc
Sc
Tc
Uc
42
43
44
45
58
59
61
62
63
81
82
83
84
85
86
87
88
89
90
Wilberforce Oak
Westerham Lodge
GLEBE FARM BUSINESS PARK
LOWER HOOK BUSINESS PARK
North End Farm
North End Farm Cotts.
HIGH ELMS COUNTRY PARK (Local Nature Reserve)
Whitelands Wood
Club House
High Elms Clockhouse
The Rookery
HIGH ELMS GOLF COURSE
Rec. Grd.
Holwood Farm
PADDOCK MOBILE HOME PARK
Farthing Street Farm
Farthing Street
Farthings
Orange Court
Meadow Cott.
Downe Court Riding Centre
Green Acres
Blacklands
Keston
BR2
Hazels
Little Crowhill
CROWHILL
ROOKERY VILLAS
Rookery Cotts.
Cuckoo Lodge
CUCKOO WOOD
Gorringes
Great Molloms Wood
Burnt Gorse
The Shack
White Earth
Endsleigh
Snag Farm
Southfields
Long Acre
Play Fld.
Rec. Grd.
Cemy.
Sch.
DOWNE
Avondale Farm
LEAVES GREEN
Milking Lane Farm
Petleys Farm
Petleys
Downe Hall
Downe Hall Farm
Christmas Tree Farm
HAZELWOOD
Hang Grove Farm
Rose Cott.
Club House
Downe Lodge
The Vicarage
Green Hill
Thompson Wood
Square Shaw
Hazel Wood
The Oaks
BROMLEY
Down House
Downe Court
Oak Lodge
Snag Lane Fm.
Millfield Wood
LONDON BIGGIN HILL AIRPORT
WEST KENT GOLF COURSE
Lordfield Shaw
Downe Bank Nature Reserve
The Shaws (Girl Guides' Camp)
Mace Farm
Mace Farm Cotts.
Cricket Grd.
Pav.
Overshaws
Hostye Lodge
Hang Grove
Shaws Cott.
Hostye Fm.
Hostye Bungalow
SOW WOOD
Beechwood
Fairways
The Boundary
Granada Ho.
Holmleigh
Snotsdale Wood
Cudham Lodge Woods
Spencers Grove
Luxted
Flora Cottage
Brownsea Hut (Boy Scouts)
Greenacres
Church Hill Farm
Foxbury Wood
South London Aero Club
Ladies Wood
Spencers Grove
Luxted Fm.
Twenty Acre Shaw
Downe Camp
Clock Twr.
Angas Home (Site)
Hook Wood
Leasons Wood
Bird House Wood
Great Southfield Shaw
Single Street
Bottom Barn Farm
Cudham Ct. Farm
Rec. Grd.
Bromley Croft
CUDHAM
BIGGIN HILL
St. Julians Farm
Playing Fld.
Darwin Sports Centre
Cudham Hall
The Lodge
Costains Farm
Strakes Shaw
Bertrey Cotts.
LORD DARBY MEWS
Cacket's Cotts.
Charles Darwin School
Barn Farm
Cudham C of E Prim. Sch.
Parkfield Fm.
Primrose Farm
Hall
RESTAVON CARAVAN SITE
Vicarage
Cemetery
Homeleigh Farm
BERRY'S GREEN
Parsonage Fm.
Golden Acres
Westerham
Blackbush Shaw
Underhill Farm
Westbrook Farm
Maple Farm
Biggin Hill Prim. Sch.
Recreation Ground
Littlewood Farm
Grubb Grounds Farm
Brickyard Farm
Corkers Fm.
Rosehaugh Farm
Biggin Hill Memorial Pool
Piggeries
Lib.
Warren Farm
CHERRY LODGE GOLF COURSE
Oak Farm
Foal Farm Animal Rescue Centre
Club House
Valley View
Nurseries
TN16
Pimlico Wood
Aperfield
Laurel Farm
The Grove
New Barn Farm
Cedar Cott.
Homelands Hall
Thrift Farm
HORNS GREEN
A233
Barn End
Park Farm
Silver Beech Fm.
Farley Kennels
Buckhurst Farm
Cudham Frith
CUDHAM FRITH
Baverstock Farm
St43 Farm
Withins Wood
N
O

181
161
201
182
Orpington
BR6
Sevenoaks
TN14
SEVENOAKS
DOWNS
PRATT'S BOTTOM
HALSTEAD
KNOCKHOLT POUND
KNOCKHOLT
LETT'S GREEN
CHEVENING
Knockholt
SEVENOAKS ROAD
A21
A224
M25
ORPINGTON BY-PASS RD.
HEWITTS ROUNDABOUT
CHELSFIELD LAKES GOLF COURSE
BROKE HILL GOLF COURSE
Club House
Broke Lodge
Eleven Oaks
Chelsfield Hill Wood
Rounds Wood
Yew Tree Cottage
Charmwood Farm
Little Molloms Wood
Charm Wood
Homefield Spring
Norsted Manor Farm
Sumachs
Broom Wood
High Wood
Kangles Wood
NEWYEARS WOOD
Fairtrough Farm
Lower Brooms Wood
Upper Brooms Wood
The Washneys
Hayman's Wood
Newlands Wood
Birches Croft
Long Bottoms Shaw
Jockey's Wood
Cophall Wood
Shelleys
Pratts Bottom Wood
Hook Wood
Lattice Coppice
Beech Cott.
Perry Wood
Lower Randle's Wood
Piece Wood
Hawfield Wood
Blueberry Farm
The Spinney Nurseries
Garden Centre
Knockholt Village Centre
Play. Fields
Homefield
Pratt's Grove
RUSHMORE HILL WOOD
Birthday Wood
Hillside Farm
Works
Rock-Field Shaw
Stonehouse Farm
Garden Cen.
Closeheath Wood
Park Farm
New Stables Farm
Stud Farm
Widmore Farm
Deerleap Wood
Warren Court Farm
Curry Wood Farm
Curry Farm
Halstead Primary Sch.
Chalkhurst Wood
Woodvale Cott.
Kangles Farm
Broomfield Cottage
Broomfield Wood
Watercrofts
Cemetery
Goss Bushes
Chapel Croft
Aldwyn Lodge
Ivy Farm
Lees Wood
Dutchmans Wood
Ashfield Wood
Minny Wood
The Keyhole
Lord Chatham's Ride
Park House
Sand Banks
Summerhouse Wood
Coalhearth Cottage
The Spinney
Pilgrims' Way (course of)
Cooper's Wood
Ash Platt
Knockholt Lodge
Knockholt Beeches
Keepers Cottage
PARK WOOD
Sundridge Hill Farm
Roughfields Wood
Hagbush Wood
Chevening House
St. Katharine's Knockholt C of E Prim. Sch.
Crittleshaw
WT Sta. Masts
Highfield House
Baston Wood
Wood Farm
Knockholt Wood
Bowman's Orchard
High Land
Burwood
Mountross Farm
Poultry Hos.
The Mount
Minquintin
Hazlet Wood Farm
Pilgrims Ho.
Witherfield
Burlings
SINGLES CROSS
SINGLES CROSS LA
POUND LA
BOND ST
HARROW RD
LONDON ROAD
STAR HILL
OTFORD ROAD
SHOREHAM ROAD
CHURCH LANE
STATION ROAD
CADLOCKS
WATERCROFT
KNOCKHOLT LA
HALSTEAD ROAD
RUSHMORE HILL
HOOKWOOD ROAD
NORSTED LANE
FAIRTROUGH RD
PERRYS LA
STUBBS HILL
WASHNEYS LANE
NEW YEARS LANE
SHELLEYS LANE
BLUEBERRY LANE
RANDLES LANE
KNOCKHOLT ROAD
MAIN ROAD
SUNDRIDGE LANE
MOUNT ROAD
CHEVENING LANE
BRASTED
STONEINGS LANE
BURLINGS LANE
ROYAL OAK
CHARMWOOD LANE
THE CHASE
STONEHOUSE ROAD
ORCHARD ROAD
BROKE FARM DRIVE
TURNPIKE DR.
BUDGIN'S HILL
PORT HILL
Vc Wc Xc Yc Zc Ad Bd
46 47 48 49
63 62 61 60 59 58
81 82 83 84 85 86 87 88 89 90

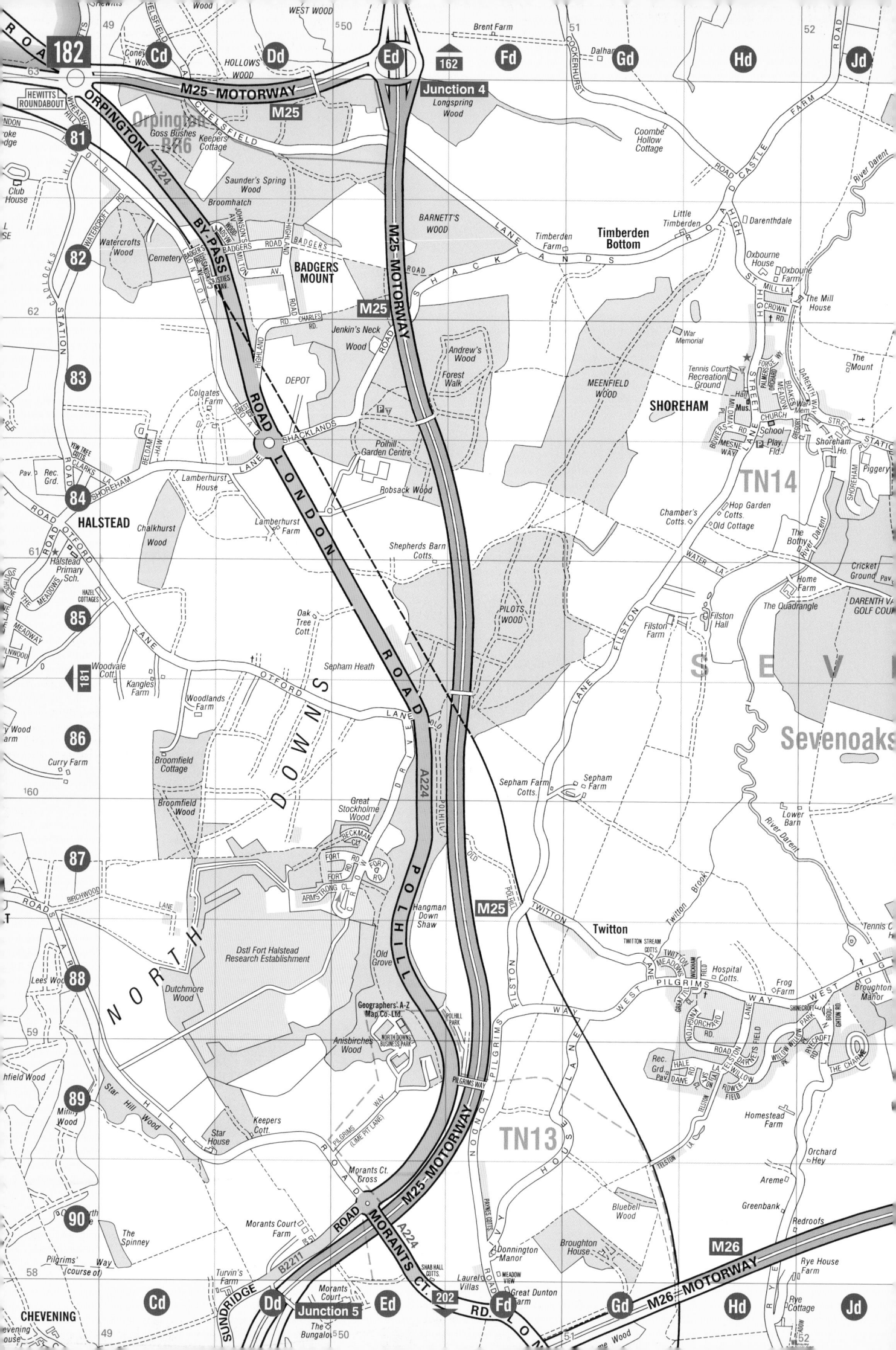

182
M25 MOTORWAY
Junction 4
HEWITTS ROUNDABOUT
ORPINGTON BY-PASS
Orpington BR6
Longspring Wood
Coombe Hollow Cottage
Saunder's Spring Wood
Broomhatch
BARNETT'S WOOD
Timberden Farm
Timberden Bottom
Little Timberden
Darenthdale
Oxbourne House
Oxbourne Farm
The Mill House
BADGERS MOUNT
Watercrofts Wood
Cemetery
Jenkin's Neck Wood
Andrew's Wood
Forest Walk
DEPOT
War Memorial
MEENFIELD WOOD
The Mount
SHOREHAM
Colgates Farm
Polhill Garden Centre
Robsack Wood
Lamberhurst House
HALSTEAD
Chalkhurst Wood
Lamberhurst Farm
Shepherds Barn Cotts.
Chamber's Cotts.
Hop Garden Cotts.
Old Cottage
TN14
Halstead Primary Sch.
PILOTS WOOD
Filston Farm
Filston Hall
Home Farm
The Quadrangle
DARENTH VALLEY GOLF COURSE
Oak Tree Cott.
Sepham Heath
Woodvale Cott.
Kangles Farm
Woodlands Farm
Sevenoaks
Curry Farm
Broomfield Cottage
Broomfield Wood
Sepham Farm Cotts.
Sepham Farm
Great Stockholme Wood
Lower Barn
River Darent
NORTH DOWNS
Hangman Down Shaw
Twitton
Dstl Fort Halstead Research Establishment
Old Grove
Hospital Cotts.
Frog Farm
Broughton Manor
Dutchmore Wood
Geographers' A-Z Map Co. Ltd.
NORTH DOWNS BUSINESS PARK
Anisbirches Wood
Star Hill Wood
Keepers Cott.
Star House
Homestead Farm
TN13
Orchard Hey
Morants Ct. Cross
Areme
Greenbank
Redroofs
Bluebell Wood
Morants Court Farm
The Spinney
Pilgrims' Way (course of)
Donnington Manor
Broughton House
Rye House Farm
M26 MOTORWAY
Turvin's Farm
Laurel Villas
Great Dunton Farm
Morants Court
Junction 5
Rye Cottage
CHEVENING
202

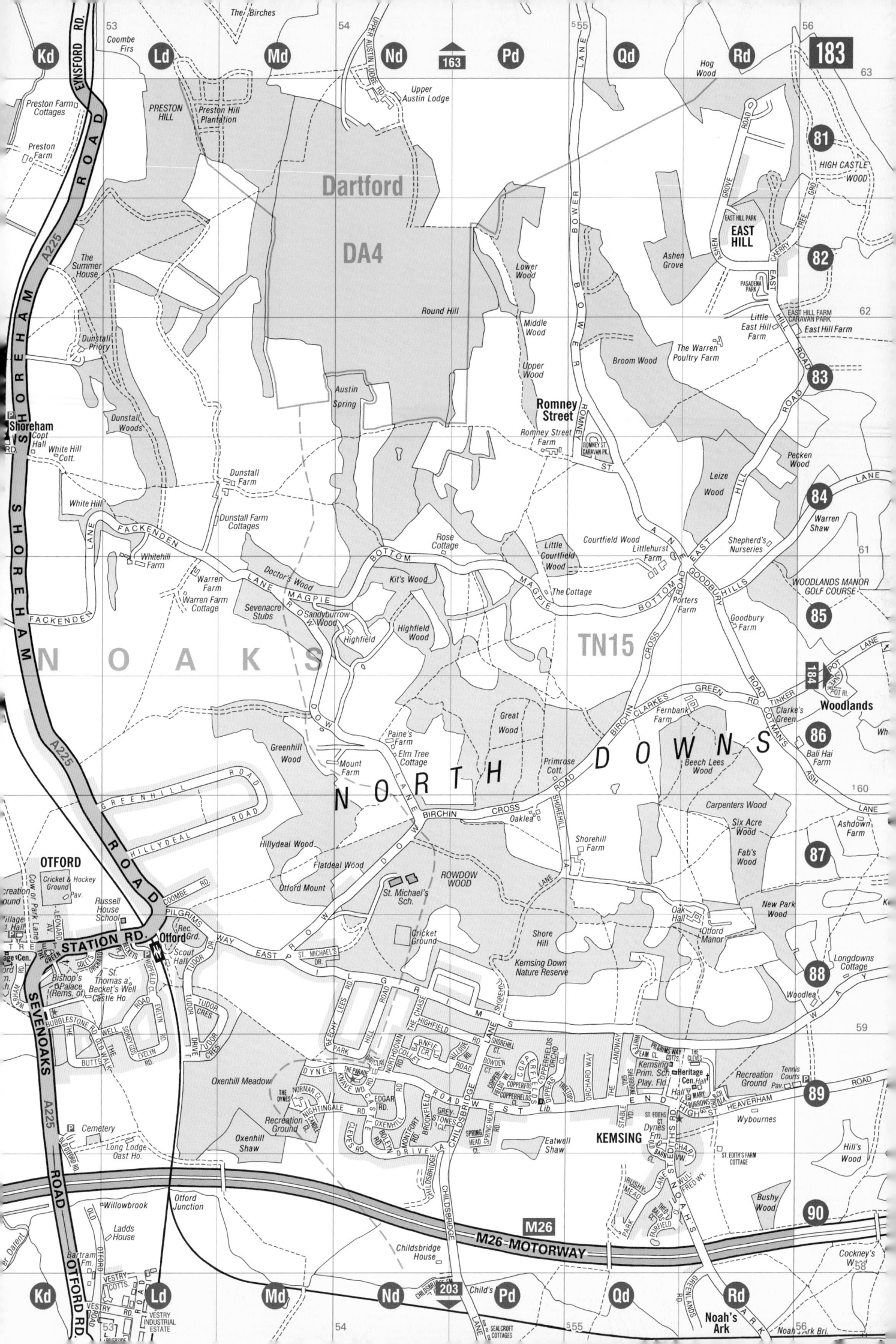

Dartford
DA4
TN15
NORTH DOWNS
SEVENOAKS
Preston Farm Cottages
Preston Farm
PRESTON HILL
Preston Hill Plantation
Coombe Firs
The Birches
Upper Austin Lodge
Hog Wood
East Hill
East Hill Park
Ashen Grove
High Castle Wood
The Summer House
Round Hill
Lower Wood
Middle Wood
Upper Wood
Dunstall Priory
Dunstall Woods
Austin Spring
Romney Street
Romney Street Farm
Romney St. Caravan Pk.
Little East Hill Farm
East Hill Farm
East Hill Farm Caravan Park
The Warren Poultry Farm
Broom Wood
Shoreham
Copt Hall
White Hill Cott.
Dunstall Farm
Dunstall Farm Cottages
White Hill
Whitehill Farm
Warren Farm
Warren Farm Cottage
Doctor's Wood
Sevenacre Stubs
Sandyburrow Wood
Highfield
Highfield Wood
Kit's Wood
Rose Cottage
Little Courtfield Wood
Courtfield Wood
Littlehurst Farm
The Cottage
Porters Farm
Leize Wood
Pecken Wood
Warren Shaw
Shepherd's Nurseries
Woodlands Manor Golf Course
Goodbury Farm
Woodlands
Clarke's Green
Fernbank Farm
Great Wood
Paine's Farm
Elm Tree Cottage
Mount Farm
Greenhill Wood
Primrose Cott.
Beech Lees Wood
Bali Hai Farm
Carpenters Wood
Six Acre Wood
Ashdown Farm
Fab's Wood
Oaklea
Shorehill Farm
Hillydeal Wood
Flatdeal Wood
Otford Mount
Rowdow Wood
St. Michael's Sch.
Cricket Ground
Shore Hill
Kemsing Down Nature Reserve
Oak Hall
Otford Manor
New Park Wood
Longdowns Cottage
Woodlea
OTFORD
Cricket & Hockey Ground
Pav.
Russell House School
Otford
Rec. Grd.
Scout Hall
Bishop's Palace (Rems. of)
St. Thomas a Becket's Well
Castle Ho.
Oxenhill Meadow
Recreation Ground
Oxenhill Shaw
Cemetery
Long Lodge Oast Ho.
Kemsing Prim. Sch.
Play. Fld.
Heritage Cen.
Hall
Recreation Ground
Tennis Courts
Wybournes
KEMSING
Dynes Fm.
Eatwell Shaw
St. Edith's Farm Cottage
Hill's Wood
Bushy Wood
Willowbrook
Otford Junction
Ladds House
Bartram Fm.
Childsbridge House
Child's
Noah's Ark
Noah's Ark Bri.
Cockney's Wood
Vestry Industrial Estate
Sealcroft Cottages
Lib.
SHOREHAM ROAD
EYNSFORD RD.
A225
STATION RD.
SEVENOAKS
OTFORD RD.
PILGRIMS WAY
PILGRIMS WAY EAST
PILGRIMS WAY WEST
FACKENDEN LANE
MAGPIE BOTTOM
ROWDOW LANE
BIRCHIN CROSS ROAD
CLARKE'S GREEN RD.
COTMAN'S ASH LANE
TINKER POT LANE
GOODBURY HILLS
EAST HILL ROAD
BOWER LANE
ROMNEY ST.
GREENHILL ROAD
HILLYDEAL ROAD
COOMBE RD.
SHOREHILL LANE
HEAVERHAM ROAD
HIGH ST.
WEST END
CHILDSBRIDGE LANE
CHILDSBRIDGE WAY
NOAH'S ARK
M26 MOTORWAY
M26
Kd
Ld
Md
Nd
Pd
Qd
Rd
163
184
203
53
54
55
56
58
59
60
61
62
63
81
82
83
84
85
86
87
88
89
90

Sd
Td
Ud
Vd
Wd
Xd
Yd
164
WEST KINGSDOWN
Sidehilly Wood
Springham's Cotts.
Crowhurst Farm
Crowhurst Lane
KINGSWOOD CL.
CHANCEL CL.
CHURCH CL.
CLEARWAYS CARAVAN PK.
RUSHETTS
KAYSLAND PK.
LONDON ROAD
A20
SOUTHFIELDS
WAR LAND RD.
BAKERS
KINGSINGFIELD CL.
KINGSINGFIELD ROAD
Pav.
Lib.
Skate Pk.
Hall
Sports Ground
Ten. Cts.
WEST KINGSDOWN INDUSTRIAL EST.
ASH TREE
MEADOW BANK
BIRCHWAY
POUND BANK CL.
DRIVE
BLACKTHORN
THE GRANGE
ASH TREE CL.
VERNON CL.
ST. EDMUND'S CT.
BEACON ROW
FAWKHAM ROAD
PORTOBELLO PDE
Prim. Academy
Richardson's Farm
MEWS
MEADOW
HAZELDEN CL.
FORGE LA.
MILLVIEW PARK
Ashen Shaw
Inges Shaw
M20
M20 MOTORWAY
Southfield Shaw
THE LONDON GOLF COURSE
Little Boutshole Shaw
Hatch Wood
Bouts Corner
81
82
83
84
85
86
87
88
89
90
HIGH CASTLE WOOD
CHERRY TREE GRO.
GROVE ROAD
ASHEN
EAST HILL
EAST HILL PARK
Blooming Wood
PASADENA PARK
EAST HILL
Little East Hill Farm
EAST HILL FARM CARAVAN PARK
East Hill Farm
HILL ROAD
Leize Wood
EAST HILL
Pecken Wood
Warren Shaw
Shepherd's Nurseries
HILLS
Goodbury Farm
Goodbury
WOODLANDS MANOR GOLF COURSE
KNATTS VALLEY
KNATTS VALLEY ROAD
KNATTS VALLEY CARAVAN PARK
Kingsingfield Shaw
West Kingsdown Smockmill
THE GROVE
Mill Farm
STANSTED
LONDON ROAD
Rose Cottage
Abbott's Wood
Noah's Rough
Pells Farm
PELLS LANE
Stacklands Wood
HOLLYWOOD LA.
SEVENOAKS
KNATTS
Knatts Farm
MANOR ROAD
SCHOOL LANE
Subway
Depot
Kent Firefighting Museum
Garden Cen.
BENNETTS AV.
ASH ROAD
Peckham Wood Corner
Water Wood
Knockmill
ST. CLERE HILL
Gravelpit Wood
PECKHAM WOOD
Knockmill Wood
Barn Gate
TINKERPOT LANE
Tinkerpot Shaw
WOODLANDS MANOR GOLF COURSE
KNATTS
Club House
WOODLANDS
183
POT RI.
TINKER POT LANE
GREEN RD.
Clarke's Green
Bali Hai Farm
Whitehill Wood
Drane Farm
KNOCK MILL LANE
BIRCHES WOOD
Arboretum
Terry's Lodge Farm
TERRY'S LODGE ROAD
EXEDOWN ROAD
EXEDOWN
WT St.
NORTH
Lees Wood
COTMAN'S ASH LANE
Carpenters Wood
Six Acre Wood
Fab's Wood
Ashdown Farm
Cotman's Ash
Summeryards Wood
Shoulder of Mutton
Chalk Pit Wood
White Hill
Pilgrims' Way
New Park Wood
Kester
Cotmans Ash
Otford Manor
ASH
Downlands
OLD WAY
KEMSING ROAD
Longdowns Cottage
PILGRIMS WAY
Woodlea
The Wilderness
The Bothy
ST. CLERE
KEMSING ROAD
Coney Shaw
ST. EDITH COTTS.
FEN POND ROAD
EXEDOWN ROAD
Recreation Ground
Tennis Courts
HEAVERHAM ROAD
Crowdleham
Crowdleham House
LANE
Heaverham
Manor House
Chequers
Lower St. Clere
West Yaldham Farm
YALDHAM MANOR DR.
Yaldham Manor
Wybournes
ST. EDITH'S FARM COTTAGE
Hill's Wood
Martin Spring Wood
Broughton Cottages
Bushy Wood
M26
M26 MOTORWAY
Cockney's Wood
Spindles
FEN POND COTTS.
FEN MEADOW
POND
CHAUCER BUSINESS PARK
WATERY LANE
204
Hook Wood
Rumley Wood
Noah's Ark
Noah's Ark Bri.
Kemsing
56
57
58
59
63
62
61
60
59
58

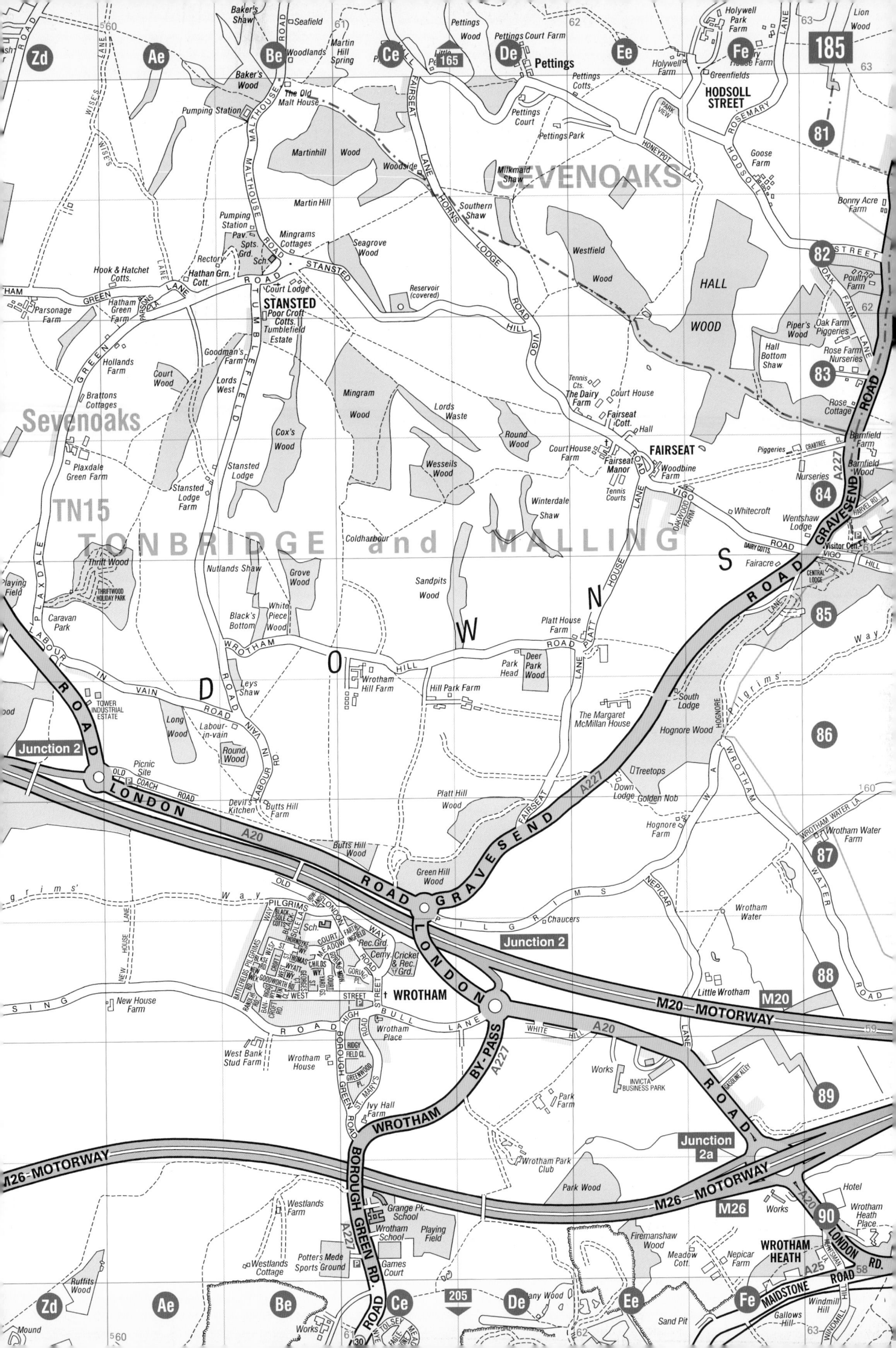
SEVENOAKS
TONBRIDGE and MALLING
Sevenoaks
TN15
HODSOLL STREET
STANSTED
FAIRSEAT
WROTHAM
WROTHAM HEATH
DOWNS
M20 MOTORWAY
M26 MOTORWAY
Junction 2
Junction 2a
LONDON ROAD
GRAVESEND ROAD
WROTHAM BY-PASS
BOROUGH GREEN RD.
MAIDSTONE ROAD
Martinhill Wood
HALL WOOD
Mingram Wood
Westfield Wood
Park Wood
Pettings
165
205

166
Princess Christian Homes & Training Centre
Staffordlake
Wisdom Farm
Wisdom Corner
Century Range
Hog Lees
Clock Tower
Shorts Range
Stafford Lake
Nursery
Grindstone Handle Corner
Brookwood Farm
Superstore
KNAPHILL
Brookwood Country Park
Cow Moor
No 4 Range
BISLEY CAMP (National Rifle Association)
Bisley Camp
Shrubb's Copse
Sheet's Heath
Recreation Ground
BROOKWOOD
Cowshot Common
Lord Roberts Centre
Running Track
Sports Ground
Pirbright Camp
Ten. Cts.
Sports Ground
Parade Gd.
Alexander Barracks
PIRBRIGHT CAMP
Cowshot Hill
Victoria Farm
Basingstoke Canal
Connaught Hall
Prim. Sch.
CONNAUGHT ROAD
A324
BROOKWOOD ROAD
A322
BAGSHOT ROAD
Club House
Brookwood
Pirbright Bridge
The Slade
Cowshot Manor Bri.
B3012 ROAD
Basingstoke Canal
New Pond
Memorial
Military Cemetery
Woking
The Cottage
Works
PIRBRIGHT COMMON
PIRBRIGHT GOLF COURSE
Club Ho.
GAPEMOUTH RD.
GOLE
B3012
Stanley Pool
Manyuema
MODEL COTTS.
THE CEDARS
Causeway Farm
Dawney's Hill
DAWNEY HILL
Furzehill Place
Aruwimi Wood
Furze Hill
Mazamboni Farm
Holy Island
Ruwenzori Hill
STANLEY HILL
GRANGE ROAD
B3405
SCHOOL LANE
Cook's Green
Pirbright Village Prim. School
Wickham's Farm
Sch.
West Heath
Burrow Hill
PIRBRIGHT
BROOKWOOD CEMETERY
CEMETERY PALES
CHAPEL LANE
CHURCH LANE
West Hall Farm
GU24
Grove Farm Nurseries
No. 1 Range
The Manor House
Mill Ho.
Manor Farm
Cove Bri.
PIRBRIGHT GRN.
GUILDFORD RD.
Vines Farm
Hazelacre Hill
Pirbright Lodge
Crammond House
Nursery
White's Farm
Hogleys Farm
PIRBRIGHT COMMON
No. 2 Range
Piggery
Burner's Heath
GUILDFORD LANE
LONG HOUSES
Bowling Hill
Rowe Lane Farm
Ardeley
Furzefield Copse
Admiral's Walk
Heatherwood
GUILDFORD
Gorselands
B3032
Chair Hill
Bush Bottom
Track End
Newbridge Common
Bullswater Common
BULLSWATER COMMON
Bullswater Bridge
Fox Corner
Fox Corner Community Wildlife Area
Kiln Hill
ADMIRAL'S
Berrylands Farm
Upper Stanford Bridge
Bakersgate
B380 ROAD
ASH
The Bungalow
Rails Farm
Stream Farm
Stanford Farm
Lower Stanford Bridge
Sludge Lagoons
Filter Beds
Sewage Disposal Works
PIRBRIGHT COMMON
Oldfield Wood
Peat Moor
Stanford Common
Stanford Brook
STANFORD COMMON
The Animal Virus Research Institute
Sludge Beds
Westwind
Peatmoor Pond
HENLEY
Henley Park Ranges
Henleypark Lake
Standinghill Wood
ALDERSHOT ROAD
COBBETTHILL COMMON
MERRIST WOOD
Wireless Station (Disused)
NORMANDY BUSINESS PARK
COBBETT HILL
Guildford College of Further & Higher Education (Merrist Wood Campus)
GU3
Guildford College of Further & Higher Education (Merrist Wood Campus- Equine Centre)
Leapingbar Copse
Mercury Lodge
Deyrolles
Park Farm
MERRIST WOOD GOLF COURSE
Slyfield Wood
PIRBRIGHT ROAD
Finavon
Club House
The Glen
HENLY BUSINESS PARK
Henley Pk. Fm.
HENLEY PARK
Clasford Bridge
Island Copse
Clasford Common
Littlefield Common
Littlefield Cottages
FAIROAKS CARAVAN PARK
A323

WOKING
MOUNT HERMON
ST. JOHNS
HOOK HEATH
WOKING GOLF COURSE
HOOK HEATH
GU22
W O K I N G
WORPLESDON GOLF COURSE
MAYFORD
Prey Heath
Worplesdon
PYLE HILL
Sutton Green Golf Course
Guildford
Whitmoor Common
JORDAN HILL
WORPLESDON
Whitmoor & Rickford Commons
Local Nature Reserve
WHITMOOR COMMON
GU4
JACOBS WELL
PITCH PLACE
Stringers Common
HERMITAGE ROAD
HERMITAGE RD.
ST. JOHN'S HILL ROAD
HOOK HEATH ROAD
SAUNDERS LANE
SMART'S HEATH LANE
MAYFORD GREEN
EGLEY ROAD
GUILDFORD ROAD
WESTFIELD
PREY HEATH ROAD
BURDENSHOTT ROAD
RYE
GOOSE RYE
WORPLESDON ROAD
SALT BOX ROAD
WOKING ROAD
CLAY LANE
A324
A320
A322
B380
Woking Crematorium
Club House
Football Ground
Recreation Ground
Freemantle School
Barnsbury Primary School
Westfield Prim. Sch.
Kemishford Bridge
Burdenshott Hill
Bonnieshott Wood Farm
Bridley Manor
Bridley Copse
Rickford Mill
Rye Farm
Gooserye
Whitmoor Pond
Poor Jack's Wood
Whitmoor Wood
Britten's Pond
Mount Pleasant
Hurst View
Willow Grange
Frog Lane Farm
Cox's Farm
Field Research Sta.
Tangley Place Farm
Perry Hill
Maryland
Sudpre
Pinewood House
Crastock Farm
Crastock Manor
Berryhill Nursery
Fisher's Hill House
Brook Farm
Havering Farm
Wingstone
167
188

188
168
187
A
B
C
D
E
F
G
91
92
93
94
95
96
97
98
99
100
WOKING
MOUNT HERMON
KINGFIELD
OLD WOKING
WESTFIELD
MAYFORD
CARTBRIDGE
SUTTON GREEN
SEND
PYLE HILL
JACOBS WELL
Crickets Hill
Sutton Park
FRITHY
GU22
GU4
Guildford
WOKING
HOEBRIDGE GOLF COURSE
SUTTON GREEN GOLF COURSE
SUTTON PARK
Pool in the Park
Woking Leisure Cen.
WOKING PARK
White Rose Lane Local Nature Reserve
Hoe Bridge Sch. (Pre-Preparatory)
St. John the Baptist School
Woking College
Woking FC (Kingfield Stadium)
David Lloyd Leisure
Kingfield Green
Barnsbury Primary School
Westfield Prim. Sch.
Westfield Common
Sewage Works
Site of Woking Palace
Oldhall Copse
River Wey
Broad Mead
Broadmead Cut
River Wey Navigation
Lancaster Hall
Ashburton House
Worsfold Gates
Cartbridge House
Fisher's Farm
Runtley Wood
Lower Westfield Farm
Runtleywood Farm
Triggs Lock Bridge
Triggs Lock
Wareham's Farm
Cricketshill Farm
Cricket Ground
Sendholme
St. Bede's C of E Jun. Sch.
Send C of E First Sch.
Send Hill
Cemetery
Send Hill Riding Stables
Sendcourt Farm
Send Grove
Fell Hill
Woodhill Cottage
Old Woodhill Cottage
Woodhill Farm Cottage
Woodhill House Farm
Sendhurst Grange
Old Timbers
Old Timbers Cottage
Nutbourne Fruit Farm
Three Fords
Ford Cottage
Whitehouse Farm
Nuthill Farm
Broadoak Br.
Bower's Lock
Burpham Court Farm
Sutton Place
Statue
Ladygrove Farm
Sutton Park House
Stables Cottage
The Bungalow
The Pavilion
Manor House
Sutton Green House
Elm Nursery
Tadpole House
Sunridge House
Whitmoor House
Whitmoor Wood
Whitmoor Farm
Cox's Farm
Oak House
Vine Cottage
St. Edward's Well
Frog Lane Farm
Loampits Farm
Elm Trees Farm
Mayford Meadows Local Nature Reserve
Hillside Farm
Riverdale Farm
Wokingpark Farm
Roundbridge Farm
Monument Hill
Club House
HIGH STREET
BROADMEAD ROAD
SEND ROAD
SEND BARNS
LONDON ROAD
A3
A247
A320
B380
B381
B382
B368
B2215
GUILDFORD ROAD
WESTFIELD ROAD
KINGFIELD ROAD
VICARAGE RD.
OLD WOKING RD.
CARTERS LANE
ROBIN HOOD LANE
RUNTLEY WOOD LA.
SUTTON GREEN
VICARAGE LANE
WOODHILL
POTTERS LANE
SEND LANE
MOOR LANE
PYLE HILL
EGLEY

189
169
190
PYRFORD VILLAGE
Vicarage
The Prae
Wheelers Farm
The Bourne
Abbey Stream Bri.
Abbey Stream
Newark Priory (Remains of)
Newark New Bri.
Wey Navigation
Newark Lock
Irish Hole
Mill House
Mill Stream
Ockham Mill Stream
WARREN FARM MOBILE HOME PARK
Sludge Bed
Walsham Plantation
Walsham Lock
RIVER WEY
Walsham Meadow
Ockham Mill
Ockham Mill Farm
Nursery
Rock Garden
RHS Garden Wisley
Garden Cen.
Battleston Hill
PORTSMOUTH RD.
A3
Stratford Bridge
Wisley Airfield (Disused)
El. Sub. Sta.
Dunsborough Farm
Dunsborough Park
Bridgefoot Farm
Cricket Grd.
Sewage Works
BARATARIA PARK
Homewood Farm
Lodge
B367
HIGH STREET PORTSMOUTH RD.
B2215
Ripley Green
RIPLEY
Mus.
Sch.
Hall
Chapel Farm
Ripley Ct. Sch.
Tennis Court
Buckingham Lodge
Tankards
Chimneys
OCKHAM ROAD
B2039
Old Rectory Farm
Church End
Chestnut Farm
OCKHAM ROAD NORTH
Ockham Park
OCKHAM PARK
Park Wood
Guileshill Lodge
Guileshill Farm
Devonia Farm
Hurst Farm
Works
Papercourt Sailing Club
Woking
Industrial Estate
RIPLEY BY-PASS
GUILDFORD
Willow Farm
GROVE HEATH ROAD
Grove Heath Farm
Grove Heath
GU23
SEND MARSH
Loveland's Copse
Ryde Farm
Roborow
Roborow Wood
Bachelor's Copse
Romer Cottage
The Old Cottage
Russets
Hungry Hill Cottage
Hungry Hill
Hangover Ho.
Garlick's Arch Copse
Garlick's Arch
BURNTCOMMON
Oldlands
Oldlands Copse
Three Bridges
GAMBLES LANE
The Paddocks
Nursery
Sheppardsgrove Copse
Brambleride Copse
Jury Farm
Brambleride
Depot
Tithe Barns
Tythebarns Farm
TITHEBARNS LANE
Cedarwood
Oak Ride Farm
Sussex Farm
Holride Farm
August Hill
Blendon
Highcotts Wood
The Oaks
Hazelhurst Cottage
Nursery
HMP SEND
Furze Copse
Southernwood
Guildford
A247
CLANDON ROAD
GREEN LANE
Humphreys Copse
Lower Hammond's Farm
Dedswell Manor Farm House
GU4
Dedswell Manor Farm
Nursery
Fish Pond
Roam Wells
Martin Furze
Gason Wood
WEST CLANDON
THE STREET
Birch Farm
Buttinham Copse
Clandon
CROCKERY LANE
LONG WALK
KINGSTON LANE

190
ELM CORNER
Hatchford End
Hatchford
MARTYR'S GREEN
May's Green
Cobham
Bridge End
OCKHAM
Church End
Woking
GU23
KT11
Effingham Junction
DRIFT GOLF COURSE
BARNSTHORNS WOOD
EFFINGHAM COMMON
Effingham Common
Horsley
KT24
WEST HORSLEY
EAST HORSLEY
M25
B2039
Wisley Airfield (disused)
The Forest Nature Reserve
The Raleigh School
Nomad Theatre
Horsley Towers
189
170
91
92
93
94
95
96
97
98
99
100

191
ELMBRIDGE
Downside
Downside Common
Downside Farm Cottage
Downside Saw Mill
Downside Farm
Rye Salters
M25 MOTORWAY
M25
Cobham Service Area
Bull Riding Farm
Withy Bed
Peaked Rough
Muggeridge Wood
Wrens Hill Wood
Thornets Wood
Spring Meadow Wood
Down Wood
Chasemore Wood
Chasemoor Farm
New Barn Wood
Newmarsh Farm
North Surrey Gun Club
Hundred Pound Bridge Wood
Hundred Pound Bridge
Hill Farm
Bank's Common
Bank's Farm
Bushy Thicket
Thicket Copse
Little Mornshill Wood
Banks Way House
Mornshill Farm
GREAT MORNSHILL WOOD
Little Bookham Common
GREAT BOOKHAM COMMON
The Common
Merritt's Farm
Manor Cottage
Oak Tree Cottage
The White House
Sewage Works
Beehive Farm
Bookham
Leatherhead
Slater's Oak
Norwood Farm
Long Maddox Farm
Herons Reach
Pikes Pool
Mallards Mere
Lower Farm
Little Bookham
OAKEN WOOD
MOLE VALLEY
KT22
KT23
GREAT BOOKHAM
Jun. Sch.
Inf. Sch.
Keswick
Merrylands Farm
Yehudi Menuhin Hall
Yehudi Menuhin School
Bookham Lodge Stud
Bookham Lodge
Gardeners Cottage
Gate Lodge
Slyfield House
Little Slyfield
Little Wood
Slyfield Farm
Slyfield Cotts.
Sheepbell Farm
Bushy Copse
Cattle Grid
The Birches
Nursery
Godstone Ho.
Ashspring Copse
Barracks Farm
Monksgree Farm
D'Abernon Bri.
Weir
Heathfield
Indian Farm
Moat
Upper Leewood Farm
GREATLEE WOOD
THORNET WOOD
Littlelee Wood
Great Ridings Plantation
Cook's Coppice
Effingham Lodge Farm
The Vineries
Preston Farm
Preston Cross
The Grange (Training Centre)
Manor House Sch.
Manor Farm
Sports Centre
Howard of Effingham School
King George's Field
EFFINGHAM
Hall
Rolls Farm
The Old Rectory
Nursery
Prim. Sch.
Club
Orestan Farm
Parrott's Coppice
Home Farm
The Nook Farm
Works
The Short Wood
Floriana Farm
Club House
Tennis Courts
EFFINGHAM GOLF COURSE
Goldstone Farm
Rec. Grd.
The Dawnay Sch.
Bowling Green
Polesden Lacey Infant Sch.
Kenilworth Riding Stables
Phoenice Park Cottage
Connicut Wood
North Lodge
GUILDFORD ROAD
LEATHERHEAD ROAD
A246
171
192
X
Y
Z
Aa
Ba
Ca
Da
91
92
93
94
95
96
97
98
99
100
11
12
13
14
53
54
55
56
57
58

192
Ea
Fa
Ga
Ha
Ja
Ka
La
172
191
91
92
93
94
95
96
97
98
99
100
PACHESHAM PARK
GOLF COURSE
Pachesham
Farm
Heathfield
Copse
West Orchard
Brook Willow
Farm
Sewage
Works
Refuse
Composting
Plant
Household
Waste
Recycling Site
River Mole
Local Nature Reserve
Slyfield
Farm
Bushy
Copse
Research
Laboratories
The
Mounts
Bushy
Platt
Gutter's
Bri.
LEATHERHEAD
COMMON
West
Hill Sch.
Therfield
Sch.
Randalls Park
Crematorium
(Leatherhead)
Randalls Park Lawn
Cemetery
Barracks
Farm
Monksgreen
Farm
Nursery
Nurseries
Sports Field
Ashspring Copse
RANDALLS
WOODLANDS RD.
A245
ROAD
Leatherhead
Randalls
Research
Park
Fairfield
Play
Fld.
Leatherhead
Trinity Prim.
Sch.
M25 MOTORWAY
M25
Junc. 9
BY-PASS RD.
KT22
Nature Reserve
LEATHERHEAD
Leatherhead FC
(Fetcham Grove)
Thorncroft
Manor
Leatherhead
Leisure
Centre
Rifle
Range
Elmer Water
Works
Cherry
Orchard
Farm
Hawk's Hill
Leatherhead
FETCHAM
Fetcham
Village
Inf. Sch.
Oakfield
Jun. Sch.
COBHAM ROAD
CANNON WAY
CANNONSIDE
HIGHLANDS RD.
B2033
LEATHERHEAD
COMMUNITY
HOSP.
Woodlands
Sch.
Vale
Lodge
Downside
Farm
Reservoir
(covered)
Downside
Naomi
Acres
MOLE
River Mole
Local Nature Reserve
YOUNG STREET
A246
GUILDFORD
GUILDFORD RD.
B2122
(HAWK'S HILL)
Bocketts Farm
Park
DORKING ROAD
B2450
A24
BY-PASS
Coronation
Glen
Oakwood
Court
Seven
Gables
Givons Grove
GREAT
BOOKHAM
LEATHERHEAD
ROAD
The
Junipers
The Hazels
The Crown
of the Hill
Roaringhouse
Farm
Fetcham
Downs
Denshire
Hill
The Scrubs
Updown
Wood
Walnut Tree
Clump
Pressforward
Cotts.
Lilac Cottage
Icehouse Combe
Norbury Park
Farm
The
Priory
Nursery
Norbury
Park
Dorking
Norbury
Tunnel
Polesden Lacey
Infant Sch.
Kenilworth
Riding Stables
KT23
Saw
Mill
Norbury Park
NORBURY PARK
Bookham
Wood
Druids
Grove
MICKLEHAM
MICKLEHAM BY-PASS
Mole
Cott.
Box Hill
Sch.
MICKLEHAM
Swanworth
Farm
RH5
Mickleham
Hall
Charley
Mount
LONDON ROAD
B2209
Juniperhill
JUNIPERHILL
WOOD
Lodge Farm
Cowslip
Fm.
Cowslip
Cottage
Beechy
Wood
Phoenice Park
Cottage
Phoenice Farm
Connicut
Wood
North Lodge
CHAPEL LANE
POLESDEN
14
15
16
17
53
54
55
56
57
58

ASHTEAD PARK
ASHTEAD
Ashtead
KT21
RAC GOLF COURSE
EPSOM DOWNS
Langley Vale
Langley Bottom
Langley Bottom Wood
EPSOM and EWELL
Epsom
KT18
Langley Bottom Farm
Gillette Cottages
Nohome Farm
City of London Freemen's Sch.
William III Gate
Playing Field
Sports Hall
Pitch
Larch Field
Tudor Croft
Ermyn Lodge
Thirty Acres Barn
Chase Farm Stud
Ashtead Hosp.
Prim. Sch.
Offices
Addlestead Wood
Addlestead Farm
North Lodge
Loretta Lodge
Fourfield Close
Walton Hurst Farm
The Hurst
Little Hurst Wood
Edes Barn Cottages
M25 MOTORWAY
M25
Highdale
Highlands Farm
Reservoir (covered)
Hambleton Wood
Play. Fld.
Headley Court Rehabilitation Cen.
Headley Park Farm
Headley Park
Hook Wood
GREAT HURST WOOD
Tyrrell's Wood
Club House
Round Wood
Pignut Wood
Court Farm
Lee Green
Shepherds Close
TYRRELLS WOOD GOLF COURSE
VALLEY
NOWER WOOD
Oyster Hill
Great Hurst Wood
Costal Wood
Subway
Tumber House
Golf Course
Paddock Cottage
Radio Bungalow
Leatherhead Downs
The Garden Ho.
Wellbottom Cottage
Cherkley Court
CHERKLEY WOOD
Tunbarr
Tot Hill
Hayes Cotts.
HEADLEY
Rectory
Kingsbarns
Manor House
Heath Farm
Goodman's Furze
Cricket Ground
Great Hayes
White Lodge
Mickleham Downs
Garden Cottage
Dean Wood
Cockshoot Wood
CKLEHAM DOWNS
Cockshoot Cottage
White Hill
Warren Farm
Warren Farm Cottages
High Ashurst (Camping Site)
HEADLEY HEATH
Headley Grove Farm
Headley Grove
Herring Grove
Junipers
Whitehill Cottage
Middlehill Wood
Bullen Wood
Headley Plantation
Headley Reservoir (covered)
Pebble Coombe
Fraser Heath
HEADLEY COMMON ROAD
B2033
REIGATE ROAD
MILL WAY
LEECH LA.
LODGEBOTTOM LANE
HEADLEY DRIVE
HEADLEY ROAD
WALTON ROAD
LANGLEY VALE ROAD
HURST LANE
CHURCH LANE
SLOUGH LANE
TUMBER STREET
Stane Street
LEATHERHEAD ROAD
A24
194
Ma Na Pa Qa Ra Sa Ta
91 92 93 94 95 96 97 98 99 100

EPSOM DOWNS
THE HILL
EPSOM DOWNS RACECOURSE
Tattenham Corner
Tattenham Cnr.
174
TATTENHAM CORNER
EPSOM DOWNS
Downs House
Racing Stables
Langley Vale
Langley Bottom
The Warren
The Warren Rec. Grd.
EPSOM and EWELL
WALTON DOWNS
Nohome Farm
Epsom
KT18
Downs View Wood
Round Wood
Little Hurst Wood
The Hurst
Edes Barn Cottages
Twistwood
Wingfield Stud Farm
Wildwoods Riding Centre
Wildwoods
GREAT HURST WOOD
SANDHILL WOOD
Great Hurst Wood
M25
M25 MOTORWAY
WALTON PARK WOOD
Subway
Rectory
Manor House
Heath Farm
Great Hayes
White Lodge
Herring Grove
Headley Grove Farm
Headley Grove
Queen's Wood
LITTLE HEATH
Little Heath Cottages
HEADLEY COMMON
Pebble Coombe
Headley Reservoir
Frith Park
Frith Park Farm
Hedgecroft
Walton Heath
PRIORY HOSPITAL STURT GRANGE
Walton Oaks
The Hermitage
Round Wood
206
193
Ebbisham Farm
Walton Manor
Walton Manor Farm
Bramley Sch.
Recreation Ground
WALTON ON THE HILL
Prim. Sch.
Comm. Cen.
Club House
Recreation Ground
Works
Pav.
Heath Farm
Mere Pond
Priests' Mere Pond
Hedge Corner
REIGATE and BANSTEAD
Castle House
Dowding Lodge
BANSTEAD HEATH
The Gallops
WALTON HEATH GOLF COURSE
WALTON HEATH
Chussex Plain
Hockey Ground
Sports Ground
Workhouse Pond
Rookery Cottages
Natural Gas Pressure Reducing Station
Mogador Cottages
MOGADOR
Wayside Farm
Red Lodge Mobile Home Park
Stables
TADWORTH
Tadworth
KT20
Tadworth Park
Tadworth Prim. Sch.
THE CHILDREN'S TRUST
Millennia Ho.
Garden Farm
Kingswood Park
Tadworth Roundabout
BURGH HEATH
Lonesome Ponds
Superstore
Marbles Pond
Banstead Athletic FC Grd.
Tadworth Leis. & Comm. Centre
Epsom Downs Prim. Sch. & Children's Cen.
Play. Fld.
Pit Wood
Lothian Wd.
B290 LANE
EPSOM LANE NORTH
ASHURST ROAD
B2220 STREET
MERE RD.
NEW ROAD
MILL ROAD
DORKING ROAD
B2032
B2033
CHEQUERS LANE
BRIGHTON ROAD
A217
A240 REIGATE RD.
BONSOR
Ua
Va
Wa
Xa
Ya
Za
Ab
91
92
93
94
95
96
97
98
99
100
21
22
23
24
58
57
56
155
54
53

BANSTEAD WOOD
Banstead SM7
Perrotts Farm
Lunch Wood
Canons Farm Cottages
Canons Farm
Reads Rest Cottages
Ambrose Cottages
Fames Rough
Sports Ground
Chiphouse Wood
Well Copse
Little Manor
Training Cen.
Kingswood
Furze Hill
Chipstead Bottom
Old School House
Outwood Shaw
Lawn Tennis Club
Out Wood
SURREY DOWNS GOLF COURSE
Woodcot Cottages
Eyhurst Farm Lodge
Club Ho.
Eyhurst Farm
Eyhurst Farm House
The Lodge
Warren Cotts.
Cornerways
Windlestraw
KINGSWOOD GOLF COURSE
Longcroft Shaw
Kingswood Warren
KINGSWOOD
Club House
SMUGGLERS PIT PLANTATION
Coulsdon
Poorfield Wood
Porters Wood
Shabden Park
South Lodge
The Belt
Hog's Cross
The Long Plantation
Northdean Shaw
CR5
Pigeonhouse Farm
Top Shaw
Tickners Wood
Round Wood
Northfield Shaw
Field View
Reeves Rest
Homefield Shaws
Penlan
Wellfield Shaw
Southerns Farm
May Cottages
Old Farm House
April Cottage
Merton
Vean
Sandy Crest
Sports Ground
Beechen Copse
Millfield Wood
Mill House
Parson's Green
Old Rectory
Orchard Cottage
MUGSWELL
Corner Cottage
Lilac Cottage
Long Wood
Little Wood
Marksland
Park Farm
KINGSWOOD FIELDS BUSINESS PARK
High Bank
Furzefield Copse
Keepers Cottage
UPPER GATTON WOOD
Pilgrims
Grub Wood
Gatwick Wood
Colts Bushes
Dell Wood
UPPER GATTON PARK
Reigate
Home Field Farm
Upper Gatton Park
Colts Lodge
Lovelands Mead
LOWER KINGSWOOD
Old Mint House
The Old Forge
RH2
Upper Gatton
Ishstar Gate
Park Shaw
Jubilee Plantations
Council Yard
Tennis Courts
Recreation Ground
KINGSWOOD GRANGE
The Crossways
Crossways Farm
Majority Plantation
Manships Shaw
Kingswood Hill
Kingswood Manor
Kingswood Knoll
Kingswood Prim. Sch.
Grove Shaw
Glebe Shaw
Gatlands Shaw
Gatton East
Catsbrain Field Shaw
Catsbrain Shaw
MARGERY
NORTH DOWNS
M25 MOTORWAY
Junc. 8
BANSTEAD
CHIPSTEAD
CHIPSTEAD GOLF COURSE
Club Ho.
West Ridge
How Green
Starrock Farm
Vincents Grn.
Chipstead Meads (Recreation Ground)
Longshaw
Courtyard Theatre
Elmore
Elmore Pond
Club
The Rectory
Embers Shaw
Ley Cottage
Court Lodge
Church Green
Noke Farm
The Grove
Fairdene
Tennis Courts
Fourteen Acre Shaw
The Ruffett
Round Wood
Ruffetts Wood
Prior's Field
South Manor
Sopers Cottage
Bugspit Shaw
Woodfield Place
Boars Green Shaw
Boars Green Farm
Mawingo
Lodge Fm.
Furzefield Shaw
Markedge Shaw
Ashtead Hill
Jubilee Plantations
Whitehall Farm
REIGATE HILL GOLF COURSE
North Lodge
GATTON
Tower Wood
High Beeches
Royal Alexandra & Albert School
GATTON PARK
East Lodge Farm

196
Jb
Kb
Lb
Mb
Nb
Pb
Qb
176
208
195
28
29
30
31
58
57
56
155
54
53
CHIPSTEAD
West Ridge
How Green
Club House
HOLLYMEAD
HOLLYMEAOK
BOUVERIE
ISSOMS RD.
PORTNALLS RD.
WOODFIELD
Hooley Farm
WOODPLACE
THE NETHERLANDS
WILHELMINA AV
FARTHING OR FAIRDEAN DOWNS
CHALDON WAY
HAPPY VALLEY
Keston Prim. Sch.
Coulsdon Coll.
Playing Field
PLACEHOUSE LA.
CROSSWAYS
THORNTON CRES.
Driftway
KESTON
KERRILL AV
COULSDON
CROYDON
Lacey Green
Playing Field
Tollers Farm
Parson's Pightle
GOODENOUGH
ELLIS CL.
B2030
A23
BRIGHTON ROAD
Star Shaw
Starrock Farm
Starrock Wood
STARROCK LANE
COULSDON LA.
HOW LANE
Vincents Grn.
Chipstead Meads (Recreation Ground)
Club
Elmore Pond
ELMORE ROAD
91
92
93
94
95
96
97
98
99
100
The Rectory
Ley Cottage
Embers Shaw
HOOLEY
Hooley Lodge
Community Centre
Court Lodge
Church Green
Church Shaw
STAR LA.
CHURCH LANE
Noke Farm
The Grove
HOGSCROSS
Fairdene
Tennis Courts
The Ruffett
Ruffetts Wood
Fourteen Acre Shaw
BROAD WALK
GARDEN WLK.
Rec. Grd.
Woodplace Farm
Coulsdon
Club
Football Ground
CR5
Three Cornered Shaw
Star Bridge
Petershole Shaw
Boxers Wood
Ditches Shaw
Devilsden Wood
The Devil's Den
Sparklie Wood
Netherne-on-the-Hill
Netherne House
Netherne Leisure Cen.
Forge Bridge
Lower Lodge
The Gullet
Figgs Wood
Netherne Wood
Sports Ground
Bowling Green
Grasscuts Shaw
Lord's Wood
REIGATE and BANSTEAD
Dean Farm
Coldroast Shaw
Sparticles Shaw
Sparticles Wood
Prior's Field
Hedgefield Shaw
Coldroast Shaw
Harps Wood
ALDERSTEAD HEATH CARAVAN SITE
Furzefield Wood
Alderstead Heath
PILES WOOD
THE BRIDLEPATH
Church Green
Court Farm
DOCTORS
CHURCH LANE
Glebe House
The Rookery
CHALDON
DEAN LANE
ROOK
B2031
Cold Blow
Alderstead Heath
Sopers Cottage
Bugspit Shaw
Mersham Tunnel
Junction 7
NORTH
Tollsworth Cottages
Tollsworth Manor
Six Brothers Field
Uplands Farm
Woodfield Place
Fox Shaw
HARPS OAK LANE
Boars Green Shaw
Mawingo
Field End
Harps Oak
Harps Oak Shaw
Boars Green Farm
Lodge Fm.
The Shrubbery
Alderstead Fort (Disused)
Reservoir (covered)
Ridge Ho.
Alderstead Farm
ALDERSTEAD HILL
BEECH RD
Five Pillars
Hoaths Farm House
LONDON ROAD
SHEPHERD'S HILL
Hilltop Farm
PILGRIMS LANE
The Beacon
Pilgrims Way
Rest Harrow
HILLTOP
Furzefield Shaw
Marling Glen Wood
Gatton Bottom
Church Hill
Marling Glen
Beech Wood
Church Hill Covert
Wellhead Wood
Redhill
M23 MOTORWAY
Subway
M23
Ockley Hill
Ockley Wood
Hawthorns
Ashtead Hill
Denehole
RH1
Brambleside
North Lodge
Grave Yard
ROCKSHAW ROAD
Tennis Cts.
Bedlams Bank
Meadshaw
Pilgrim Hill
M25
The Glade House
BOTTOM
GATTON BOTTOM
RH2
Heronswood Mere
Junction 7 (M25)
Withy Shaw
Greenacres
Junction 8 (M23)
Sarmans
Rockshaw House
Sunacre
Orchard Cottage
REIGATE HILL GOLF COURSE
Whitehall Farm
Cricket Ground
Pav.
M25 MOTORWAY
Weavers
Club House
MERSTHAM
Merstham
Playgrd.
Rec. Grd.
Furzefield Wood
Playing Field
Sch.
Playing Field
CHESTERTON DR
The Oakley Youth Club
GATTON
Middle Lodge
GATTON PARK
Royal Alexandra & Albert School
The Bushetts
BUSHETTS
East Lodge Farm
LONDON RD.
NORTH HIGH ST.
The Grove
NUTFIELD CTR.
BLETCHINGLEY ROAD
WORSTED
MANOR
Lib.
GREEN
Coppice
WARWICK WOLD
Warwick Wold Fm.
Yew Tree Cott.
Warwick Wold

197
177
198
209
KENLEY AERODROME
Kenley
CR8
WHYTELEAFE
Whyteleafe
CR3
Whyteleafe South
OLD COULSDON
Oasis Academy Coulsdon
Windmill Farm Kennels
COULSDON COMMON
Warlingham
CR6
Manor Park
WAPSES LODGE ROUNDABOUT
Woldingham Road
Caterham-on-the-Hill
CATERHAM
Caterham
CR3
Queens Park
Surrey National Golf Course
Dean Hill
Rifle Ranges
Club House
Public Open Space
Westway Common
St. Francis' Catholic Prim. Sch.
Sunnydown School
de Stafford School
de Stafford Sports Cen.
Audley Prim. Sch.
Recreation Ground
North Downs Private Hosp.
Caterham School
Caterham Preparatory School
Oakhyrst Grange Sch.
St. John's C of E Prim. Sch.
Valley Sports Ground
Eight Acre Wood
Upwood Gorse
TANDRIDGE
DOWNS
Oldpark Wood
White Hill
Quarry Hangers
Gravelly Hill
Ten Acre Shaw
Tupwood Scrubs
Fosterdown Wood
Pilgrim Fort
The Roughets
Godstone RH9
GODSTONE INTERCHANGE
Junc. 6
M25 MOTORWAY
Caterham By-Pass
Godstone Road
Banstead Road
Chaldon Road
Stites Hill
Birch Wood
Stony Hill
Tillingdown Farm
Reservoir (cov.)
Park Shaw
Paddock Wood
Ockley Wood
The Devils Hole
Pendell Wood
Black Bushes
Little Park Hill
White Rose Farm
War Coppice House
The Mound
Arthur's Seat
Whitehill Tower
Willey Park Farm
Roverdene (Scout Camp Site)
Green Hollows
Fryern Farm
Rook Hill
Round Wood
Bulstaff Cottage
Five Acres
Grubs Wood
Quarry Cottages
Quarry Hall Farm
Spring Bottom
Rocky Shaw
Rb Sb Tb Ub Vb Wb Xb
91 92 93 94 95 96 97 98 99 100
32 33 34 535
53 54 55 56 57 58

WARLINGHAM
WOLDINGHAM GOLF COURSE
LIMPSFIELD ROAD
WOLDINGHAM GARDEN VILLAGE
Caterham
CR3
WOLDINGHAM
Woldingham
Marden Park
MARDEN PARK
NORTH DOWNS GOLF COURSE
NORTH
Godstone
RH9
CATERHAM BY-PASS
A22
M25 MOTORWAY
GODSTONE INTERCHANGE
Junction 6
Woldingham School
Godstone Vineyards
Green Dragons Airsports
Nore Hill Pinnacle (Local Nature Reserve)
Oxted Tunnel
B269
Yb
Zb
Ac
Bc
Cc
Dc
Ec
178
197
210

199
179
200
211
Warlingham
CR6
BROMLEY
Westerham
TN16
TATSFIELD
Tatsfield Green
RH8
Oxted
OXTED
LIMPSFIELD
TITSEY
Cheverells
Titsey Place & Gardens
TITSEY PARK
TITSEY PLANTATION
PITCHERS WOOD
Lumberdine Wood
Kitchen Grove
Ashen Shaw
Beaver Water World
Tatsfield Primary School
Clacket Lane Service Area
Hookwood Park
M25 MOTORWAY
M25
A25
B269
B2024
B2025
NORTH DOWNS
RIDGE
CLARKS LANE
TITSEY ROAD
TITSEY HILL
PILGRIMS WAY
WESTERHAM ROAD
St. Mary's C of E Jun. Sch.
Downs Way Sch.
Limpsfield Grange Sch.
Park Wood Golf Course
Hill Park (Local Nature Reserve)
TITSEY WOOD

200
180
199
Farley Kennels
TATSFIELD
Gorsey Down Farm
Manor House
Tatsfield Green
Park Farm
Colegates
RAG HILL
The Hermitage
Painter's Wood
Ashen Shaw
Leecroft
Baverstock Farm
Stud Farm
SOUTH STREET
Little South Street Farm
Great South Street Farm
WESTERHAM HILL
Withins Wood
Park Farm
Barn End
Silver Beech F.
Buckhurst Farm
Southwood Farm
Southwood
Buckhurst
Shellem Wood
Piggeries
Bombers Lodge
Bombers Farm
Bombers Cott.
Squirrel Wood
CUDHAM FRITH
Cudham Frith Farm
Cudham Grange
Woodlands
Joelands
Silverstead
Gray's Farm
NORTH DOWNS
BROMLEY
Sheepshed Cott.
Tor Croft
Westerham Riding School
Hawley's Corner
Broomcocks Wood
Westerham Heights
Heights View
Fort Cotts.
Deepdale
Deepdale Cott.
Pilgrim House
Play. Fld.
PARK WOOD GOLF COURSE
Park Wood
Club House
Compton Chase
Homestead
Little Betsom's Farm
Round Shaw
BETSOM'S HILL
Whitelands Shaw
Highfield
Lime Villa
Whitlands
Hill Park (Local Nature Reserve)
Cerne Easter
Halston
Rysted
Tatsfield Court Farm
The Old Rectory
The Old Rectory Lodge
Betsoms
Playing Field
Pav.
Hill Park
REDWOOD HO.
Betsomhill Farm
SEV
TANDRIDGE
Westerham
Force Green Farm Cottages
Force Green Farm
Green Leas
Force Green
Gaysham
Rowtye Wood
Hartley Wood
WESTERHAM WOOD
Church Wood
Clacket Wood
Clacket Green
Cupids Coppice
Gaysham Cottages
Roughfield Shaw
Square Wood
M25-MOTORWAY
M25
TN16
Tennis Court
Churchill C of E Prim. Sch.
Playing Field
Court Lodge
Wet Wood
Devil of Kent
Clacket Lane Service Area
TITSEY WOOD
Green Croft Farm
Greencroft Cotts.
Farley Common
Farley Grange
Gotley
Squerryes Sand Pit
Westwood Farm
King George's Field
Quebec Ho.
WESTERHAM
High Cottage
Bower Cottage
Hosey Trees
Hosey Shaw
Broomlands Farm
Ashen Coppice
Oxted
Works
Moorhouse Sand Pits
Moorhouse
Covers Farm
New Winterton
Park Lodge
Lodge
Squerryes
Lodges Wood
Squerryes Home Farm
Spring Shaw
Red Eaves
Glebe House
Packway
Croft Cott.
Beech Cott.
Whitefriars
Hosey Croft
Deane Cott.
Hoseyridge
Hosey Hill
The Mead
Chart's Edge
Thrift Wood
RH8
The Rips
The Birches
Grey Timbers
Moorhouse Farm
Moorhouse Bank
Moor House
Moorhouse Bank Common
Rooks Nest
Loampit Wood
Watts Hill
Cronklands
SQUERRYES PARK
R. Darent
TOWER WOOD
A233
A25
B2024
B2026
CLARKS LANE
PILGRIMS WAY
CROYDON ROAD
WESTERHAM HILL
LONDON ROAD
MAIN ROAD
BEGGARS LANE
HIGH STREET
WESTERHAM ROAD
BRASTED
HOSEY HILL
HOSEY COMMON RD.
CHESTNUT AVENUE
GRAYS ROAD
CLACKET LANE
BROOMLANDS LANE
FORCE GREEN
STOCK LANE
GOODLEY
MOORHOUSE RD.
Nc Pc Qc Rc Sc Tc Uc
91 92 93 94 95 96 97 98 99 100
42 43 44 45
58 57 56 155 54 53

Sevenoaks
CHEVENING
CHEVENING PARK
SUNDRIDGE
BRASTED
Brasted Chart
French Street
M25 MOTORWAY
M25
A25
A233
B2211
TN14
181
202
Home Wood
Combebank Wood
Combe Wood
Shootfield Wood
Roughfields Wood
Hagbush Wood
The Nower
Hogtrough Hill
Park Wood
Holywell Shaw
Valence Wood
Westerham Golf Course
Birchfield Wood
Great Wood
Quornden Wood
Round Wood
Chevening House
Combe Bank Sch.
Recreation Ground
High Street
Main Road
Westerham Road
Pilgrims Way
Chevening Road
Ovenden Road
Brasted Hill
Rectory La.
Church Road
Pipers Lane
Chart Lane
Pipers Green Rd.
Little Norman St.
Brasted Place
The Rookeries
Sundridge Place Farm
Hill Water Bottom Wood
Chapman's Wood
Phillipines Shaw
Ebor Wood

CHEVENING
DUNTON GREEN
CHIPSTEAD
RIVERHEAD
SUNDRIDGE
Sevenoaks
Longford
Bessels Green
Dryhill
Dibden
Cross Keys
Kippington
Fig Street
Whitley Row
M25 MOTORWAY
M26 MOTORWAY
Junction 5 (M25)
MORANTS CT. RD.
LONDON ROAD
SUNDRIDGE ROAD
WESTERHAM ROAD
SEVENOAKS BY-PASS
COLD ARBOR RD.
BRADBOURNE
AMHERST HILL
MAIN ROAD
TN13
TN14
Chevening (St. Botolph's) C of E Prim. Sch.
Chipstead Sailing Club
Chipstead Lake Cheshire Home
Sevenoaks Wildlife Reserve
Knole Academy Sports & Leisure Centre
Jeffery Harrison Visitor Centre
Dryhill Local Nature Reserve
Montreal Park
Holmesdale Sports Grd.
Riverhead Infants' School
Council Refuse Transfer Cen.
Dunton Green
Superstore
Home Wood
Alder Shaw
Edward Shaw
Rakefield Wood
Claypit Shaw
Cold Arbor Wood
Ash Platt Wood
Obelisk Wood
Salters Heath
Little Britain's Wood
Great Britain's Wood
Red Grove
Greenlane Wood
Furzefield Wood
Willow Wood
Hawks Wood
Mildridge Wood
Mill Bank Wood
Whitley Forest
Middlings Wood
Longspring Wood
Hill Water Bottom Wood
Lodge Barn Farm
Manor Farm
Greenlane Farm
Greenlane Farm Cotts.
Dibden Farm
Brittains Farm
Fig Street Farm
Dryhill Farm
Wellers Farm
Warren Farm
Froghall Farm
Windmill Farm
Great Dunton Farm
Morants Court Farm
Turvin's Farm
Grove House
Broughton House
Rye House Farm
Redroofs
Coalhearth Cottage
The Spinney
The Warren
Sundridge Place Farm
Old Rectory
Brook Place Cotts.
Brook Place
Little Norman Street Farm
The Bungalow
Mackerels Plain
Nightingale Cott.
Seven Wents
The Woodman
Rustwood
Tennis Courts
Greystones
Goldsmith's Bottom
Shrubs Corner
Pollard's Barn
Whitley
Nursery
Cods Corner
The New Beacon Sch.
Sevenoaks Mag. Ct.
182
201
91
92
93
94
95
96
97
98
99
100
Cd
Dd
Ed
Fd
Gd
Hd
Jd

M26 MOTORWAY
TN14
TN15
SEVENOAKS
SEAL
St. John's
Bat & Ball
Greatness
Wildernesse
Godden Green
Noah's Ark
Fullers Hill
SEAL CHART
Carter's Hill
Sevenoaks Common
Fawke Common
KNOLE PARK
KNOLE PARK GOLF COURSE
WILDERNESSE GOLF COURSE
CHANCE WOOD
RAMBLES WOOD
FAWKE COMMON
DEER PARK
Knole
Otford Junction
Child's Bridge
Seal Chase
Penfield
Tanners Cross
Money Shaw
Wildwood
Waterden
Weald of Kent Grammar Sch. (Sevenoaks Annexe)
Trinity Sch.
Summerhouse Wood
Dorton College of Further Education
Dorton House School
Sevenoaks Leisure Centre
Sevenoaks Rugby Club
Sevenoaks School
CYGNET HOSPITAL GODDEN GREEN
Knole Development Centre
Sevenoaks Prep. Sch.
Walthamstow Hall
Hollybush Spts. Complex
Echo Mount
Birdhouse
Cedarholme
The Wilderness
Running Track
The Seven Oaks
Rumshott Wood
Badcock Wood
Redlands Wood
Chestnut Plantation
Clacketts Wood
Weald Cottage
Broadfield Shaw
A25
A225
A224
B2019
B2020
SEAL ROAD
HIGH STREET
MAIDSTONE ROAD
DARTFORD RD.
TONBRIDGE ROAD
HOLLOW LANE
PARK LANE
FAWKE COMMON ROAD
ST. JULIAN ROAD
WOODLAND RISE
BLACKHALL LANE
STONE STREET
HONEY POT LANE
WATERY LANE
CHILDSBRIDGE LANE
183
204
91
92
93
94
95
96
97
98
99
100

M26 MOTORWAY
184
Spindles
CHAUCER BUSINESS PARK
The Rises
Kemsing
Noah's Ark
Cockney's Wood
HONEY POT LANE
Pumping Station
Osier Bed Wood
Hook Wood
Rumleys Wood
Clay Pits
Patchgrove Wood
Tanners Cross
Stonepitts Cott.
Stonepitts Farm
Stonepitts Manor
North Lodge
Broomsleigh Farm
Broomsleigh
Money Shaw
Fullers Hill
SEVENOAKS
Chart Farm
Manor Farm Cottages
Manor Farm House
Heron Shaw Wood
Oldbury Farm House
Oldbury
WATERY LANE
Waterden
Broadoak Cottages
Chart Lodge
Fern Villa
The Nuttery
The Broom
Styants Bottom
OLDBURY HILL
Oldbury Hillfort (Remains)
Ightham Prim. Sch.
Recreation Ground
Tennis Court
Oldbury Place
The Rectory
The Old Rectory
Petham
MAIDSTONE ROAD / SEVENOAKS ROAD
A25
Vildwood
Chart Warren
Saxbys
The Grove
Lodge
Larchwood Farm
OLDBURY HILL CAMPING & CARAVANNING CLUB SITE
OLDBURY WOOD
Redwell
Copt Hall
The Grange
Oak Bank Hall
Playing Field
REDHILL WOOD
Styants Wood
Picnic Site
SEAL CHART
Seal Chart
Chapel Wood
Frankfield Ho.
Little Frankfield
Crown Point
COPT HALL ROAD
IGHTHAM COMMON
Mainfield
Flanes Wood
Hanger Wood
Flaneswood
Fish Ponds Wood
Crown Point Nurseries
Lower Frankfield
Apps's Wood
Hall Place
Little Roger's Wood
Godden Green
St. Lawrence C of E Prim. Sch.
TONBRIDGE
Hall Wood
Blakes Green
RASPIT HILL
Merry Mead Fm.
War Mem.
Raspit Hill
Nursery
CYGNET HOSPITAL GODDEN GREEN
Medlars Mead Cotts.
Great Roger's Wood
Foxbury Fm.
The Little House
STONE STREET
Greens Cotts.
Beechwood
Lord's Spring Farm
Broomfield Wood
Broomfield Cottages
Foxbury Bungalow
Barnfield Cottage
Court Farm
Colebank
Lord's Spring Wood
Perry Hill Quarry
Daintshatch Wood
Bitchet Farm
Ivy Hatch Court
IVY HATCH
Paxton Farm
Bitchet Green
Baker's Wood
South Field Shaw
Lower Bitchet
BROADHOATH
Sports Grd.
Cricket Grd.
Pav.
Tennis Cts.
HIGH CROSS ROAD
High Cross House
Watlynge
East Bank Wood
Lower Fawke Farm
Nether Fawke
Mare Reeds Fawke Fm.
Little Fawke Farm
Mote Cotts.
Scathes Wood
Fawke House
Fawke Common Cotts.
BITCHET COMMON
Burnt Wood
Broadhoath Wood
Scatheswood House
The Mount Cotts.
East Mote
North Lodge
Martins Wood
Ightham Mote
Fairlawne
Front Lodge
Starvecrow House
The Red Cottage
White Cottage
Rooks Hill House
One Tree Hill
Mote Farm
Tonbridge TN11
Plantation Farm
Rookery
Carter's Hill
White Rocks
Rooks Hill
Shingle Hill
Wilmot Hill
Barnfield Wood
Stone Cott.
Cinderfield Wood
Alders Shaw
Orchard Shaw
Shingle Hill Wood
Greybury Wood
Elders Wood
Fatting Pen
The White House
White Rocks
Tudor Ho.
Carter's Hill Cott.
Wilmot Cott.
Cinderfield Shaw
South Seers Shaw
South Seers Wood
Crane Shaw
Sports Ground
Rock Robin
Stonecroft
Budd's Dell
IGHTHAM ROAD
TONBRIDGE ROAD
A227
203

WROTHAM HEATH
Borough Green & Wrotham
BOROUGH GREEN
ST. MARYS PLATT
Comp
Basted
CROUCH
Claygate Cross
Sheet Hill
Yopps Green
PLAXTOL
Plaxtol Spoute
Dunk's Green
Roughway
Gover Hill
Sevenoaks
and
MALLING
TN15
MEREWORTH WOODS
HURST WOOD
MAIDSTONE ROAD
BOROUGH GREEN RD.
BY - PASS
WROTHAM ROAD
A227
A25
Platt Industrial Estate
Stangate Hill
Basted House
Long Wood
Haw's Wood
Mill Pond
Butlers Wood
Longbrook Wood
Sewage Works (Disused)
Long Bottom Wood
Kingshill Farm
Landway Farm
Claygate House
Claygate Cross Farm
Crouch Cottage
Winfield Farm
Hatcham's Wood
Pondbottom Wood
Hatcham House
Hurst Wood Farm
Rye Field Cott.
Bourne Farm
Sheet Hill Farm
Brookside Farm
Golding Hop Farm
Boot Wood
Lady's Wood
Bourne Hill Farm
Yopps Green Farm
Bartons Farm
Dux Farm
Duck's Farm
Cage House
Old Soar Oast
Old Soar Manor
Old Soar Farm
Old Soar Cotts.
Broadfield Shaw
Broadfield Farm
Oast House
Quarry Wood
Marsh Cottage
Keeper's Cottage
Spinners Wents
Sedgebrook Cotts.
Brook Farm
Rec. Grd.
Allen's House
Little Allen's
Old Allen's
Allen's Farm
Mill Shaw
Roughway Mills
Roughway Farm
Roughway Farm Cottage
Roundels
Upper Farm
Ivy Cottage
Rats Castle
Roughway Cottage
Well House
The White Cott.
Crooked Chimneys
Gover Hill
Plaxtol Primary School
Cricket Ground
FAIRLAWNE PARK
The Wilderness
Plaxtol Lane Cottages
Home Coverts
Brakybank Wood
Well Shaw
Barton Cotts.
Crowhurst Farm
Kings Cotts.
Goddens Cotts.
Reservoir
Warren Farm
Ash Tree Fm.
Trycewell Farm
Stangate Bri.
Gracelands Park
Dark Hill Farm
Brick Works
Cricketts Farm
Ashplat Wood
Mound
Ruffits Wood
West Cottage
Potters Mede Sports Ground
Wrotham School
Playing Field
Works
West Bank
The Dene
Botany Wood
Firemanshaw Wood
Meadow Cott.
Nepicar Farm
Sand Pit
Windmill Hill
Gallows Hill
Valley Wood
WROTHAM HEATH GOLF COURSE
Windmill House
Ingleborough Farm
High Haugh
Mays Cottages
Potter's Hole
Platt Wood
Rough Acres
Great Comp Garden
The Pavilion
Paddock Orchard
Potash Farm
Beechin Wood Farm
Green Acres
Comp Shoot Cottages
Beechin Oast
Napps Farm
Birchin Napps Farm
Gowles Farm
The Napps
Platt Farm
King George's Field
Bracken Hill
Rowan Wood
Stone House Farm
Playing Field
Staddles Wood
Pine Close
SWANTON LANE
PECKHAM HURST RD.
GOVER HILL
OXENHOATH RD.
ROUGHWAY LANE
HURST ROAD
SOAR ROAD
LONG MILL LANE
CROUCH LANE
BASTED HILL
PLOUGH HILL
WINFIELD
CROWHURST LANE
BASTED LANE
BOURNE LANE
DUX HILL
GRANGE HILL
THE STREET
BROOK LANE
OLD LANE
ALLENS LANE
COMP LANE
BEECHIN WOOD LANE
WINDMILL HILL
SCHOOL LANE
Be
Ce
De
Ee
Fe
Zd
Ae
185
91
92
93
94
95
96
97
98
99
100
155
560
61
62
63
58
57
56
55
54
53

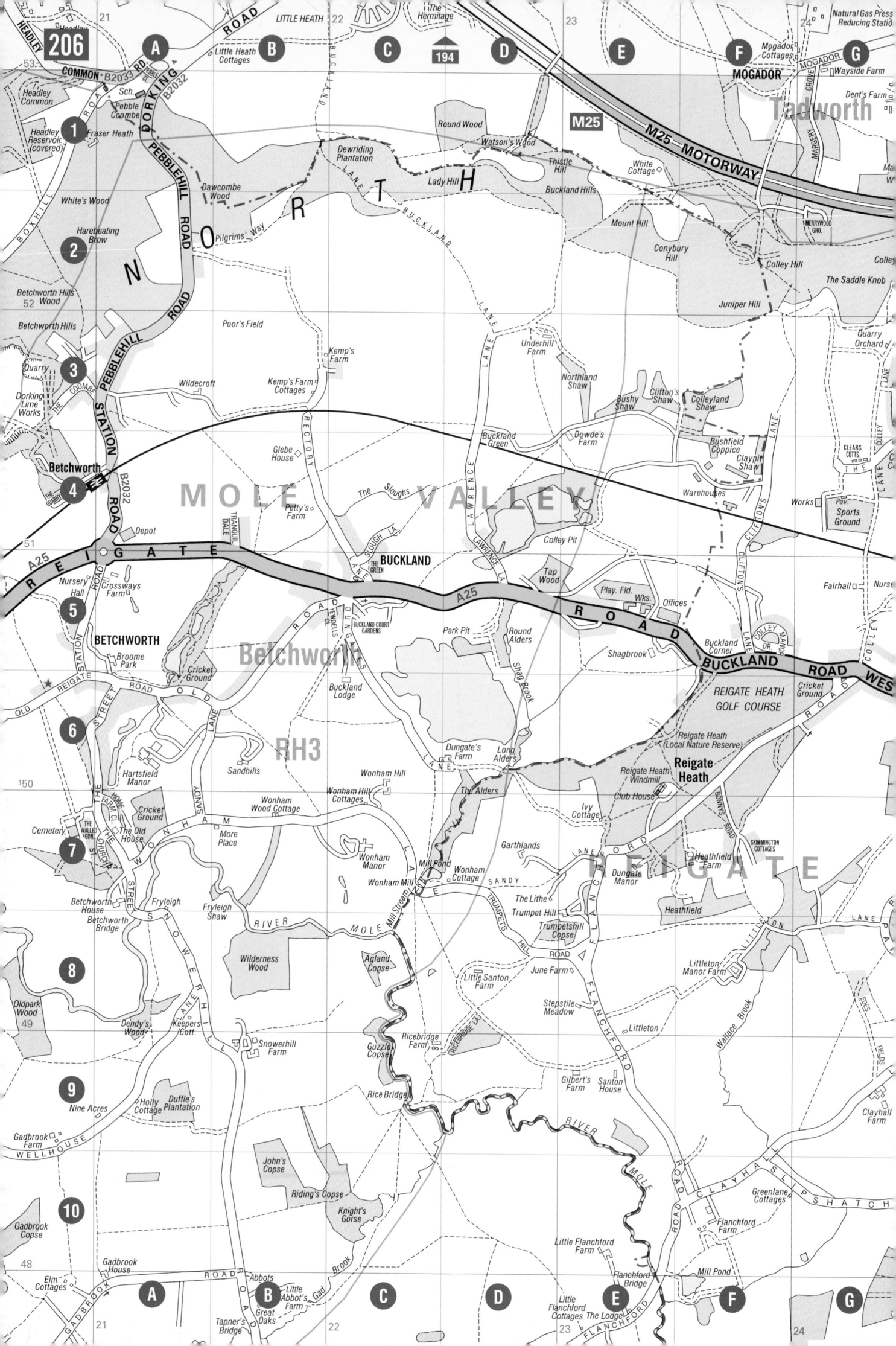

194
NORTH
MOLE VALLEY
Betchworth
RH3
REIGATE
BETCHWORTH
BUCKLAND
MOGADOR
Tadworth
Reigate Heath
M25
M25 MOTORWAY
A25
REIGATE ROAD
BUCKLAND ROAD
DORKING ROAD
PEBBLEHILL ROAD
STATION ROAD
B2032
B2033
HEADLEY COMMON RD.
Headley Common
Headley Reservoir (covered)
Fraser Heath
Pebble Coombe
White's Wood
Harebeating Brow
Betchworth Hills Wood
Betchworth Hills
Dorking Lime Works
Quarry
Wildecroft
Poor's Field
Kemp's Farm
Kemp's Farm Cottages
Glebe House
Petty's Farm
The Sloughs
Depot
Little Heath Cottages
LITTLE HEATH
The Hermitage
Round Wood
Watson's Wood
Dewriding Plantation
Dawcombe Wood
Pilgrims' Way
Lady Hill
Thistle Hill
Buckland Hills
White Cottage
Mount Hill
Conybury Hill
Colley Hill
The Saddle Knob
Juniper Hill
Underhill Farm
Northland Shaw
Bushy Shaw
Clifton's Shaw
Colleyland Shaw
Buckland Green
Dowde's Farm
Bushfield Coppice
Claypit Shaw
Warehouses
Colley Pit
Tap Wood
Play. Fld.
Wks.
Offices
Park Pit
Round Alders
Shagbrook
Shag Brook
Buckland Corner
REIGATE HEATH GOLF COURSE
Cricket Ground
Reigate Heath (Local Nature Reserve)
Reigate Heath Windmill
Club House
Natural Gas Press Reducing Station
Mogador Cottages
Wayside Farm
Dent's Farm
Quarry Orchard
Works
Sports Ground
Fairhall
Nursery Hall
Crossways Farm
Broome Park
Buckland Lodge
BUCKLAND COURT GARDENS
Dungate's Farm
Long Alders
The Alders
Sandhills
Hartsfield Manor
Wonham Hill
Wonham Hill Cottages
Wonham Wood Cottage
More Place
The Old House
Cemetery
Wonham Manor
Mill Pond
Wonham Mill
Wonham Cottage
Mill Stream
Garthlands
Ivy Cottage
Dungate Manor
Heathfield Farm
Heathfield
The Lithe
Trumpet Hill
Trumpetshill Copse
SKIMMINGTON COTTAGES
Betchworth House
Betchworth Bridge
Fryleigh
Fryleigh Shaw
RIVER MOLE
Wilderness Wood
Agland Copse
Little Santon Farm
June Farm
Stepstile Meadow
Littleton
Littleton Manor Farm
Wallace Brook
Oldpark Wood
Dendy's Wood
Keepers Cott.
Snowerhill Farm
Ricebridge Farm
Guzzle Copse
Gilbert's Farm
Santon House
Rice Bridge
Nine Acres
Holly Cottage
Duffle's Plantation
Gadbrook Farm
WELLHOUSE
John's Copse
Riding's Copse
Knight's Gorse
Greenlane Cottages
Flanchford Farm
Clayhall Farm
Gadbrook Copse
Little Flanchford Farm
Flanchford Bridge
Mill Pond
Gadbrook House
Elm Cottages
Abbots
Little Abbot's Farm
Gad Brook
Great Oaks
Tapner's Bridge
Little Flanchford Cottages
The Lodge
FLANCHFORD ROAD
CLAYHALL LANE
SLIPSHATCH
SNOWERHILL
SANDY LANE
WONHAM LANE
TRUMPETS HILL ROAD
LAWRENCE LANE
RECTORY LANE
DUNGATES LANE
CLIFTON'S LANE
COLLEY LANE
COLLEY MANOR DR.
BONNY'S ROAD
LONGFORD
MARGERY GROVE
MERRYWOOD GRO.
CLEARS COTTS
THE CLEARS
OLD REIGATE ROAD
THE COOMBE
THE QUARRY
TRANQUIL DALE
SLOUGH LA.
THE GREEN
YEWELLS CL.
HOME FARM CL.
THE WALLED GDN.
CHURCH ST.
BOXHILL
GADBROOK ROAD
ABBOTS ROAD
A B C D E F G
1 2 3 4 5 6 7 8 9 10
21 22 23 24
48 49 150 51 52 53

207
GATTON
MARGERY
KT20
M25 MOTORWAY
Junction 8
REIGATE HILL INTERCHANGE
GATTON PARK
Royal Alexandra & Albert School
THE LAKE
Reigate
RH2
REIGATE
COLES MEADS
REDHILL
Redhill
Wray Common
STATION RD.
A25
A242
A217
A23
REIGATE ROAD
CROYDON ROAD
GATTON ROAD
PARK ROAD
LONDON ROAD
HIGH ST.
BLACKBOROUGH ROAD
REDSTONE HILL
Priory Museum
Reigate Priory Playing Fields
REIGATE PARK
REDHILL COMMON
MEAD VALE
EARLSWOOD
Earlswood
WOODHATCH
SOUTH PARK
EARLSWOOD COMMON (Local Nature Reserve)
REDHILL & REIGATE GOLF COURSE
Boating Lake
Earlswood Lakes
Rushetts Farm
DOVERSGREEN
Petridge Wood Common
Household Waste Recycling Centre
Redhill Football Club
Recreation Ground
Felland Copse
WOODHATCH ROAD
A2044
CROYDON
BRIGHTON ROAD
COCKSHOT HILL
The Cutting
HORLEY ROAD
REIGATE and BANSTEAD

208
GATTON
MERSTHAM
Merstham
Club House
Middle Lodge
REIGATE HILL GOLF COURSE
Furzefield Wood
Playing Field
Junction 9 (M25)
The Oakley Youth Club
Junction 8 (M23)
196
Reigate
RH2
GATTON PARK
East Lodge Farm
The Bushetts
Royal Alexandra & Albert School
THE LAKE
Boat Ho.
Jetty
Temple Wood
Temple Lodge
Gatton Point
LONDON ROAD
A23
GATTON PARK RD.
A242
The Grove
Woodfield Sch.
St. Nicholas Sch.
SOUTH MERSTHAM
Coppice Lea
Poultry Houses
Warwick Wold Farm
WARWICK WOLD
Yew Tree Cottage
North Lodge
Residential Caravan Park
M23 MOTORWAY
Mercers West
Spynes Mere Nature Reserve
Sewage Works
Redhill
Mercers Country Park
Mercers Farm
East Surrey Coll. (Gatton Point North)
East Surrey Coll. (Gatton Point S.)
HOLMETHORPE
Holmethorpe Lagoons Nature Reserve
The Moors
The Moors Nature reserve
Ford Bri.
Nutfield Marsh
Ckt. Grd.
Marsh Cotts.
Glebe Lake
Redhill
REIGATE and BANSTEAD
Chilmead Farm
REDHILL
Redhill Tennis Club
The Warwick Sch.
Sandpit
RH1
Pimlico Hill
Park Wood
Sports Grd.
NUTFIELD
Robert Denholm House
Capenor Nursery
Kennedys Wood
Works
Patteson Court
Cemy.
Adlington Cotts.
Fox Hole
North Park
NUTFIELD ROAD
HIGH ST. BLETCHINGLEY ROAD
A25
207
Redstone Hall
Nutfield Lodge
Byes Wood
Hillsbrow
Nutfield Priory Hotel
Playing Field
Furze Hill
Kingfisher House
Nursery Cottage
Steners Hill
Stockers Hill
Priory Farm
Ride The Hill, Mountainboarding Centre
Redstone Hill
Nutfield Priory Lake
Bowerhill Wood
Little Cormongers Farm
High Beech
Cemetery
RNIB Redhill College
Bower Hill
Bower Hill Farm
Bray's Farm
Rec. Grd.
Nutfield Church C of E Primary School
Lyttel Hall
EARLSWOOD
Earlswood
Playing Field
Sports Ground
Old Gladstone's House
Nutfield
SOUTH NUTFIELD
Maple Farm
King's Mill
Cricket Grd.
YMCA Sports Centre
Old Garston's House
Garston's Wood
Thepps Shaw
Nutfield Park
Ketwin's Wood
Crab Hill House
Thepsswood Hse.
REDHILL GOLF COURSE
Driving Range
Club Ho.
Ridge Green
Redhill Football Club
EAST SURREY HOSPITAL
Robin Cooks Farm
Warehouse
Depot
Staplehurst Farm
Hale Farm
Crab Hill Farm
Crab Hill
Nutfield Nurseries
Tennis Courts
Eugene Bann Indoor Tennis Centre
White Bushes
Hazelhurst Farm
Helicopter Landing Square
The Rookery
REDHILL AERODROME AND HELIPORT
Perimeter Cotts.
HORLEY ROAD
A23
BRIGHTON ROAD

209
197
210
M25
M25 MOTORWAY
M23
Junc. 6
GODSTONE INTERCHANGE
A25
B2235
B2236
BLETCHINGLEY
GODSTONE
Tyler's Green
Stratton
White Post
South Park
TANDRIDGE
Godstone RH9
The Roughets
Roughets House
Whitehill Roughets
White Hill House
Rose Farm
Little Park Hill
Quarry Hall Farm
Black Bushes
Conduit Shaw
Kitchen Copse
Big Pickle
The Orpheus Centre
Place Farm
The Hawthorns School Sports Centre
The Hawthorns Sch.
Pendell Farm
Brewerstreet Farm
The Old Rectory
DAIRY BUSINESS PARK
Dormers Farm
BLETCHINGLEY GOLF COURSE
Club House
Court Lodge Farm
Cemetery
Bletchingley Comm. Learning Cen.
Castle Place
Castle Hill
Bletchingley Castle
Stanley's Wood
Castlehill Farm
Poor Man's Shaw
Play. Flds.
School
Sandhills
Sandhills Farm
Oakbarn Cotts.
Crookedfield Shaw
Gravelhill Wood
Mitchener's Bank
Coldharbour House
Coldharbour Farm
Springfield Shaw
Snatts Hill
Pound Farm
Harlings Shaw
Garston Park
Tilburstowhill or Tilbusterhill Plantation
Tilburstow or Tilbuster Hill
Penduck Shaw
Eleven Acre Shaw
Moors Wood
Long Shaw
Tilburstowhill Farm
Blackvent Wood
Wychcroft
Prickloves Farm
Hawksnest Ghyll
Norbryghts Hole
Furze Wood
Maple Wood
Tye Copse
Fountains Cotts.
Cucksey's Farm
South Park Farm
Bletchingley Tunnel
Kennels Farm
Cinderhill Wood
Four Acre Wood
Poundhill Wood
Bransland Wood
Temple Wood
The Park
Henhaw Farm
LAMBS BUSINESS PARK
Prickle Shaw
Birchen Coppice
Nash's Farm
Salfords Stream
Nutfield Brook
Redhill Brook
Cockley Plantation
Ivy Mill Farm
Stangrave Hall
Garden Centre
Water House Farm
Dell Cotts.
Eden Brook
Elm Platt
Orchard Cotts.
North Park Cotts.
East Reservoir
Nature Reserve
Little Place Fm.
Bay Pond
Old Garston Farmhouse
Godstone Green
Freer Farm
Castle View
Kennel Shaw
Godstone Inn & Playbarn
Surrey Crest
Dinmore
L'Etac
The Yews
Green Croft
War Coppice House
The Mound
Roman Road
CASTLE STREET
HIGH ST.
GODSTONE ROAD
BLETCHINGLEY RD.
OXTED RD.
EAST HILL
TILBURSTOW HILL
HEATH ROAD
OUTWOOD LANE
SOUTH PARK LANE
NORTH PARK LANE
WHITE HILL LANE
PLACE FARM ROAD
BREWER STREET
STYCHENS LANE
LITTLE COMMON LANE
BIG COMMON LANE
CHURCH LANE
GREEN LANE
ROUGHETS LANE
WATERHOUSE LANE
IVY MILL LANE
CUCKSEYS LANE
TERRACOTTA RD.
CONEYBURY
1 2 3 4 5 6 7 8 9 10
H J K L M N P
32 33 34 35
48 49 50 51 52 53

210
Junction 6
M25 MOTORWAY
M25
198
209
GODSTONE INTERCHANGE
Godstone Vineyards
Kennel Shaw
Castle View
Generals Grove
Flint Hall Farm
Hanging Wood
Nixon's Pit
Primrose Bank
Tandridge Hill Farm
Robins Grove Wood
Barrow Green Court
THE ABBEYS
North Model Farm
Barrow Green Farm
Barrow Green Farm Cotts.
Buttersgreen Shaw
Palmer's Wood
Palmers Wood Oilfield
The Firs
Greenacres
Priory Shaw
Flower Wood
Duckpit Wood
Kennels
Coney Hill Sand Pit
Tandridge Priory Farm
Tyler's Green
GODSTONE HILL
GODSTONE ROAD
A22
B2235
Flower Farm
Works
Club House
Oxted Sand Pit
Rooks Nest
GODSTONE GOLF COURSE
School Plantation
East Reservoir
Nature Reserve
OXTED ROAD
A25
Depot
GODSTONE
Garden Centre
Nags Hall
Furzefield Plantation
Bushey Croft Rec. Grd.
Club House
BLETCHINGLEY RD.
Little Place Fm.
Bay Pond
TANDRIDGE GOLF COURSE
Godstone Green
Old Garston Farmhouse
Moore's Shaw
Glebe Water
Church Town
The Rectory
BULLBEGGARS LANE
Windmillstadle Wood
The Birches
The Glebe House
Tennis Court
Little Court Farm
Flowergarden Plantation
Beechwood Hill
Oxted Place
New Bustons Wood
The Mount
Stratton
Godstone Farm & Playbarn
The Old Pack House
Castlehill Wood
The Lodge
Tandridge Court
Bustons Wood
Stonepit Shaw
Leigh Place
Leigh Place Pond
Oldpark Wood
Tandridge Court Fm.
Round Wood
Maizenhill Shaw
Garston Park
Castlehill Wood
Leigh Mill House
Stratton Brook
ST. EASTBOURNE
B2236
Roman Road
Taylors Hill Depot
TANDRIDGE
Southlands
TANDRIDGE PARK
Refuse Tips
Dean Shaw Cottages
Dean Shaw
St. Peter's C of E Inf. Sch.
Redding Wood
Tilburstowhill or Tilbusterhill Common
Smokey Hollow
Mereland Wood
Sewage Works
Gibbs Brook
Tandridge Hall
Southlands Shaws
Tilburstowhill or Tilbusterhill Plantation
Hopgarden Wood
GODSTONE BY-PASS
Southlands Lodge
Beechwood Plantation
Godstone
RABIES HEATH ROAD
Tilburstow or Tilbuster Hill
RH1
Southlands Wood
Eleven Acre Shaw
Brakey Hill
RH9
EASTBOURNE ROAD
Wonham Pl.
Long Shaw
Slurry Lagoons
Stow Coppice
Tilburstowhill Farm
Orme House
Newhouse Farm
HARTS LANE
MILES
NEW ROAD
Blackvent Wood
Steadmanshill Wood
Paygate Wood
Brook Farm
Piper's Wood
Nash's Farm
New Zealand Cottages
Hawksnest Ghyll
Barnfield Shaw
Park Pale
Postern Gate Farm
Lagham Wood
Gibbs Brook
Furze Wood
St. Stephen's C of E Prim.Sch.
SOUTH GODSTONE
Chathill
HUNTERS CHASE
Chathill Park Farm
LAMBS BUSINESS PARK
BROOKSIDE ROAD
Godstone
STATION RD.
LAGHAM CT.
Pav.
Playing Field
Old Hall Farm
RUSHTON AV.
Wks.
ST. JOHNS CT.
Lagham Park Farm
Prickle Shaw
Oakhurst Court
WATER LANE
RSPCA Animal Cen.
Lagham Manor
Crowhurst Lane End
CROWHURST LANE END
Drewsherne Farm
Brickmakers' Wood
Kings Farm
Moat
Birchen Coppice
Works
Lingfield
A B C D E F G
1 2 3 4 5 6 7 8 9 10
53 52 51 50 49 48
535 36 37 38

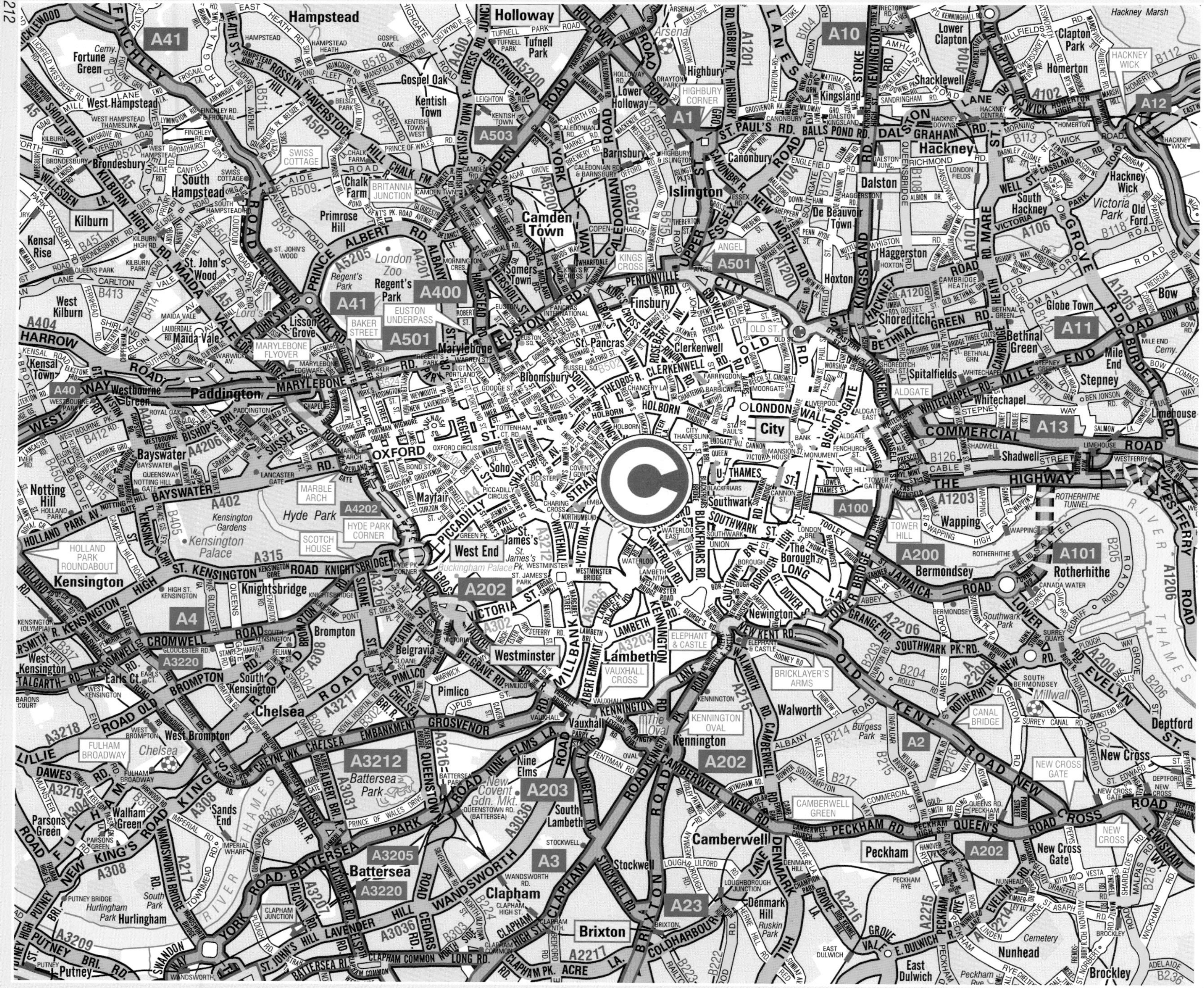

Congestion Charging Zone

The daily charge applies Mon.-Fri. 7-00am to 6-00pm excluding English bank and public holidays and designated non-charging days.

Payment of the daily charge allows you to drive in, around, leave and re-enter the charging zone as many times as required.

Payment must be made before or on the day of travel by midnight. Drivers who forget to pay the charge for the previous day's journey can pay a late payment charge the next day up until midnight by telephone or online and avoid a Penalty Charge.

You can pay using Congestion Charging Auto Pay (registration required), online (www.cclondon.com), by telephone (0343 222 2222), by SMS text message (registration required) or by post (10 days in advance).

Exemptions include motorcycles, mopeds and bicycles.
Registration for discount schemes, including Congestion Charging Auto Pay, Fleet Auto Pay, Blue Badge holders, residents & Ultra Low Emission Vehicles, is available from Transport for London.

Penalty charge for non-payment of the daily charge by midnight on the day after the day of travel.

This information is correct at the time of publication.

For further information www.tfl.gov.uk

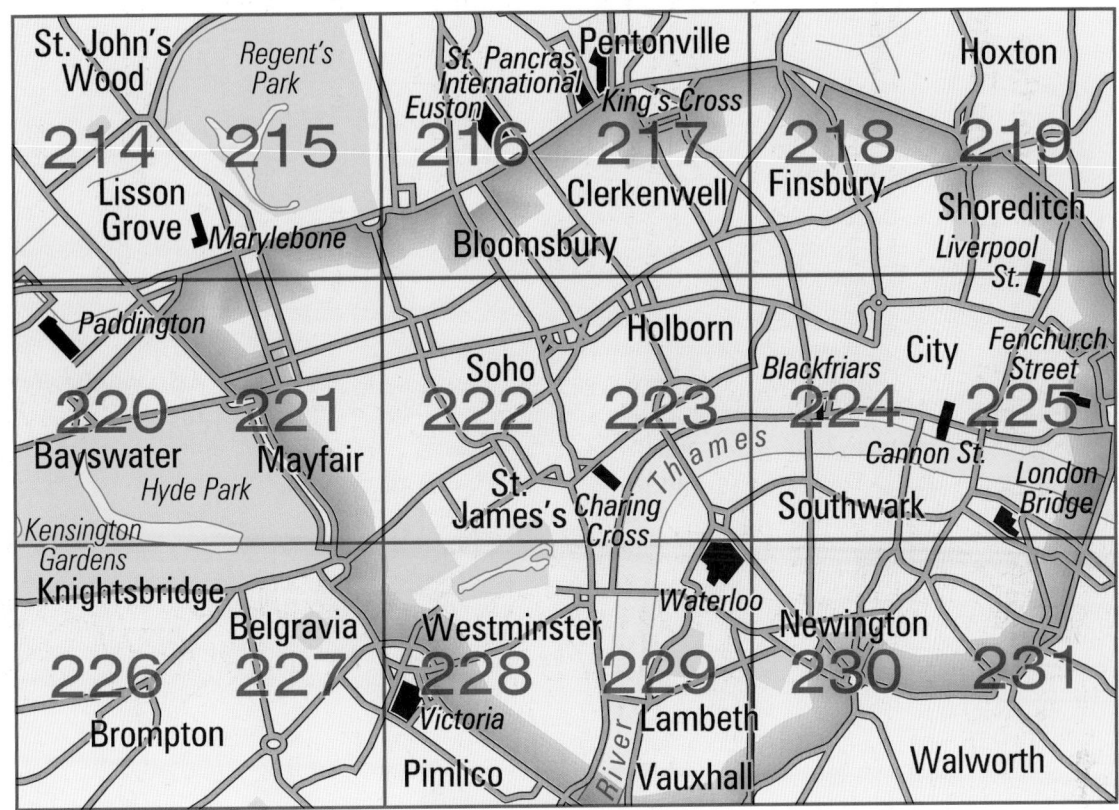

The map shows the following areas with page grid numbers:

- St. John's Wood **214** — Regent's Park **215** — St. Pancras International, Euston **216** — Pentonville, King's Cross **217** — Finsbury **218** — Hoxton **219**
- Lisson Grove, Marylebone, Paddington — Clerkenwell, Bloomsbury — Holborn — Shoreditch, Liverpool St.
- Bayswater **220** — Mayfair **221** — Soho **222** — **223** — Blackfriars, City **224** — Fenchurch Street **225**
- Hyde Park, Kensington Gardens — St. James's, Charing Cross — Thames — Cannon St., Southwark — London Bridge
- Knightsbridge — Belgravia **226**/**227** — Westminster **228** — Waterloo, Lambeth **229** — Newington **230** — **231**
- Brompton — Victoria — Pimlico — Vauxhall — Walworth
- River Thames

REFERENCE

A Road	`A10`	
B Road	`B326`	
Dual Carriageway		
One-way Street		
Road Under Construction — Opening Dates are correct at the time of publication.		
Proposed		
Inner Ring Road	`R`	
Junction Name	`MARBLE ARCH`	
Restricted Access		
Pedestrianized Road		
Congestion Charging Zone		
Railway Station		
Railway Station Entrance: National Rail Network / Crossrail / Docklands Light Railway (DLR) / Overground / Underground		
Local Authority Boundary		

Postal Boundary		
Map Continuation `69` / Large Scale Map Pages `222`		
Car Park (selected)	`P`	
Cinema		
Cycle Hire Docking Station		
Fire Station		
Hospital	`H`	
House Numbers (A & B Roads only)	`34` / `62`	
Information Centre		
National Grid Reference	`179`	
Park and Ride	Windsor (Home Park) `P+R`	
Police Station	▲	
Post Office	★	
Red Light Camera		
River Boat Trip		
River Bus Stop		

Safety Camera with Speed Limit — Fixed and long term road works cameras only. Symbols do not indicate direction of camera.	`30`
Theatre	
Toilet: without facilities for the Disabled / with facilities for the Disabled / Disabled use only	
Educational Establishment	
Hospital or Healthcare Building	
Industrial Building	
Leisure or Recreational Facility	
Office Building	
Place of Interest - Public Access	
Place of Interest - no Public Access	
Place of Worship	
Public Building	
Residential Building	
Shopping Centre or Market	
Other Selected Buildings	

SCALE

Pages 214-231
1:7,040
9 inches
(22.7cm) to 1 mile
14.2cm to 1km

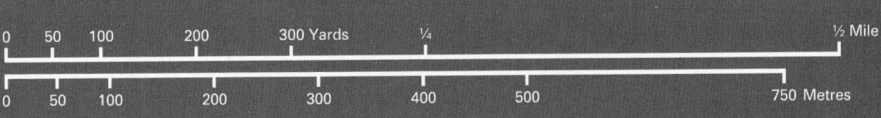

0 50 100 200 300 Yards ¼ ½ Mile

0 50 100 200 300 400 500 750 Metres

214
A
B
C
D
E
1
2
3
4
5
6
7
69
68
220
ST. JOHN'S WOOD
MAIDA VALE
LISSON GROVE
NW8
W9
W2
PADDINGTON
ST. JOHN'S WOOD
WARWICK AVENUE
EDGWARE ROAD
MARYLEBONE FLYOVER
Quintin Kynaston Sch.
St. John's Wood Barracks
Robinsfield Inf. Sch.
TOWNSHEND EST.
BARROW HILL EST.
Barrow Hill Jun. Sch.
The American School in London
New London Synagogue
Arnold House Sch.
St. John's Wood Syn.
Hospital of St John & St. Elizabeth
St. John's Hospice
Convent of Mercy
The Wellington Hosp.
The Wellington Hospital
South Sudan Hlth. Cen.
Abercorn Sch.
Recording Studio
St. Mark's Ch.
Violet Hill Gdns.
St. John's Wood Church Gardens
St. John the Baptist's Ch. & Sch.
Middlesex County Cricket Club & Marylebone CC
Lord's Cricket Ground
MCC Cricket Museum & Tours
Media Cen.
The Liberal Jewish Synagogue
Church of Our Lady
Electricity Transformer Station
London Central Mosque
CLOSED Midnight - 7am
REGENT'S CANAL
St. Joseph's R.C. Prim. Sch.
LISSON GREEN ESTATE
Gateway Academy
Lisson Green
Cockpit
Abingdon House Sch.
St. Edward's RC Prim. Sch. & Convent
CHURCH ST. EST.
Broadley Gdns.
King Solomon Academy
Nightingale Hospital
Paddington Green Prim. Sch.
Catholic Apostolic Ch.
Little Venice Sports Cen.
St. Mary's Gardens
City of Westminster College
St. David's Ch.
St. Mary's Ch.
St. Saviour's Ch.
Warwick Gdns.
Little Venice
Fire Sta.
Police Sta.
Cet Prim. Sch.
Nuffield Fitness Cen.
Blind Veterans UK
A41
A5
B507
A5205
A501
A40
B413
B525
FINCHLEY ROAD
WELLINGTON ROAD
ST. JOHN'S WOOD ROAD
PRINCE ALBERT ROAD
EDGWARE ROAD
MAIDA VALE
HAMILTON TERRACE
GROVE END ROAD
ABBEY ROAD
LISSON GROVE
HARROW ROAD
MARYLEBONE ROAD
CLIFTON GARDENS
WARWICK AVENUE
BLOMFIELD ROAD
PARK ROAD

215
216
REGENT'S PARK
CAMDEN
NW1
W1
MARYLEBONE
Regent's Canal
Prince Albert Road
Outer Circle
Inner Circle
Chester Road
Marylebone Road
Baker Street
Gloucester Place
Park Square Gardens
Park Crescent
Crescent Gardens
Cumberland Basin
Primrose Hill Bri.
Running Track
Snowdon Aviary
Entrance
London Zoo
Playground
Car & Coach Park
CLOSED Midnight - 7am
Cricket Ground
The Hub
Refreshments
Cumberland Gate
St. John's Lodge
Frazer Lodge
Parks Department
Lodge
Nursery
Regent's Park Open Air
Chester Road Gates
Queen Mary's Gardens
The Holme
Boating Lake
Children's Boating Pond
Bandstand
Jubilee Gates
New Lodge
Avenue Gdns.
English Gdns.
Chester Walk Gate
Tennis Courts
Regent's University London
Clarence Gate
London Business Sch.
Royal Coll. of Obstetricians & Gynaecologists
Francis Holland Sch.
St. Cyprian's Ch.
The Sherlock Holmes Mus.
Lost Property Off.
Madame Tussaud's
Ryl. Academy of Music Mus.
International Comm. Sch.
Harley House
The London Clinic
Central London Civil Justice Centre
St. Marylebone Ch.
University of Westminster (Marylebone Campus)
The Princess Grace Sch. Hosp.
The St. Marylebone Sch.
King Edward VII's Hosp.
The Harley St. Clinic
The Heart Hospital
Royal College of Physicians
Holy Trinity Ch.
Central London Co. Ct.
The Portland Hosp.
Ryl. Natl. Orthopaedic Hosp.
RIBA
Portland Pl. Sch.
Central Synagogue
Franco-Anglaise Sch.
PureGym
BBC Broadcasting House
Town Hall
Lib.
St. Mary's Prim. Sch.
St. Mary's Ch.
Everyman Baker St.
Paddington Street Gdns.
West London Coll.
Danish Ch.
Regent's Park Barracks
Christ Ch. C of E Prim. Sch.
Nash Ho.
Richmond Ho.
Camberley Ho.
Cath.
Windermere
Thirlmere
Grasmere
Wasdale
Troutbeck
Tilehurst
Swallowfield
Colosseum Ter.
The White Ho.
Nth. Bri. Ho. Prep. Sch.
Holyrood Ct.
Delancey Street
Mornington
Albany Street
Gloucester Gate
Park Village West
Cambridge Gate
St. Andrews Pl.
Ulster Ter.
York Gate
Devonshire Place
Harley Street
Wimpole St.
Portland Place
Great Portland St.
Regent's Park
Baker St.
Marylebone
A41
A501
A4201
A5205
B524
B506
69
70
221

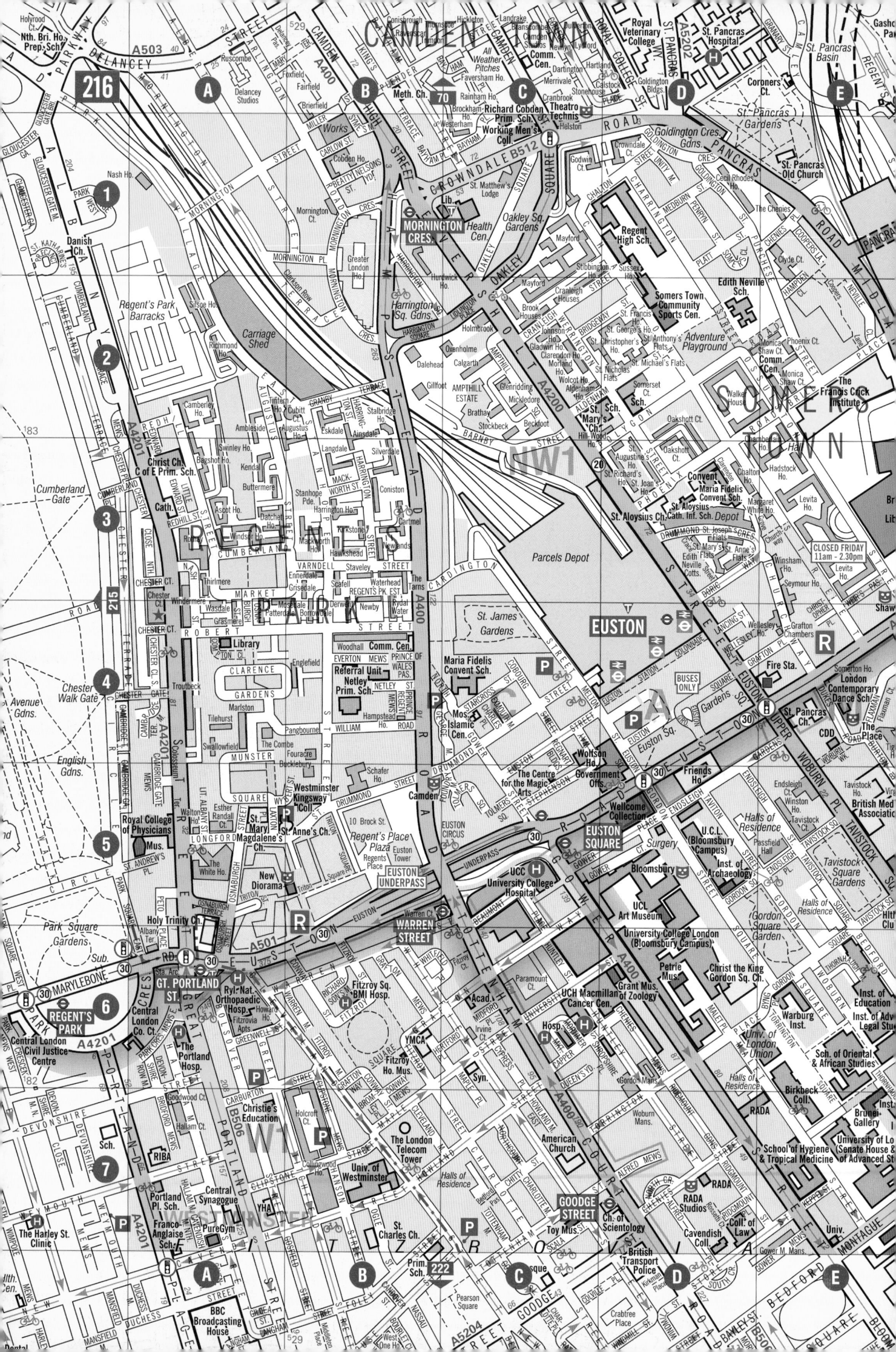

216
CAMDEN TOWN
A
B
C
D
E
Royal Veterinary College
St. Pancras Hospital
St. Pancras Basin
Coroners Ct.
St. Pancras Gardens
St. Pancras Old Church
Delancey Studios
Meth. Ch.
70
Richard Cobden Prim. Sch.
Working Men's Coll.
Theatre Technis
Goldington Cres. Gdns.
CROWNDALE ROAD
PANCRAS ROAD
MORNINGTON CRES.
Greater London Ho.
Oakley Sq. Gardens
Health Cen.
Regent High Sch.
Somers Town Community Sports Cen.
Edith Neville Sch.
Adventure Playground
Regent's Park Barracks
Carriage Shed
Harrington Sq. Gdns.
AMPTHILL ESTATE
EVERSHOLT STREET
The Francis Crick Institute
SOMERS TOWN
NW1
Parcels Depot
EUSTON
St. James Gardens
Christ Ch. C of E Prim. Sch.
REGENT'S PARK
Library
Comm. Cen.
Referral Unit
Netley Prim. Sch.
Maria Fidelis Convent Sch.
Convent
Maria Fidelis Convent Sch.
CLOSED FRIDAY 11am - 2.30pm
Fire Sta.
London Contemporary Dance Sch.
BUSES ONLY
Euston Sq.
Cumberland Gate
Chester Walk Gate
Avenue Gdns.
English Gdns.
Royal College of Physicians
Mus.
Westminster Kingsway Coll.
St. Mary Magdalene's Ch.
St. Anne's Ch.
Camden
The Centre for the Magic Arts
Wolfson Ho.
Government Offs.
Friends Ho.
Wellcome Collection
EUSTON SQUARE
Regent's Place Plaza
EUSTON UNDERPASS
EUSTON CIRCUS
UCC University College Hospital
Bloomsbury
U.C.L. (Bloomsbury Campus)
Inst. of Archaeology
Halls of Residence
Tavistock Square Gardens
Gordon Square Garden
New Diorama
Holy Trinity Ch.
Park Square Gardens
WARREN STREET
UCL Art Museum
University College London (Bloomsbury Campus)
Petrie Mus.
Christ the King Gordon Sq. Ch.
Grant Mus. of Zoology
UCH Macmillan Cancer Cen.
British Medical Association
Inst. of Education
Warburg Inst.
Univ. of London Union
Sch. of Oriental & African Studies
Birkbeck Coll.
RADA
Brunei Gallery
University of London (Senate House & Inst. of Advanced St.)
School of Hygiene & Tropical Medicine
GT. PORTLAND ST.
REGENT'S PARK
Central London Civil Justice Centre
Ryl. Nat. Orthopaedic Hosp.
The Portland Hosp.
Fitzroy Sq. BMI Hosp.
YMCA
Fitzroy Ho. Mus.
Syn.
American Church
Christie's Education
W1
The London Telecom Tower
Univ. of Westminster
RIBA
Portland Pl. Sch.
Central Synagogue
PureGym
Franco-Anglaise Sch.
The Harley St. Clinic
St. Charles Ch.
GOODGE STREET
Ch. of Scientology
Toy Mus.
British Transport Police
RADA Studios
Cavendish Coll.
Coll. of Law
Univ.
222
BBC Broadcasting House
FITZROVIA
TOTTENHAM COURT ROAD
EUSTON ROAD
MARYLEBONE ROAD
PARK CRESCENT
A4201
A400
A501
A5204
Pearson Square
Crabtree Place

KING'S CROSS
PENTONVILLE
ISLINGTON
ST. PANCRAS
CLERKENWELL
BLOOMSBURY
HOLBORN
217
218
223
KING'S CROSS ST. PANCRAS
ST. PANCRAS INTERNATIONAL
KING'S CROSS
CHANCERY LANE
RUSSELL SQ.
Western Transit Shed
UAL Central Saint Martins
West Handyside Canopy
E. Handyside Canopy
Midland Goods Shed
House of Illustration
Granary Square
Regents Canal
Thornhill Bridge
Kings Place
London Canal Mus.
Pancras Sq. Leisure Cen.
Pancras Square
The Gymnasium
Copenhagen Prim. Sch.
Blessed Sacrament Cath. Prim. Sch.
Young Actors Theatre Sch.
Vittoria Prim. Sch.
Winton Prim. Sch.
Priory Green Estate
Joseph Grimaldi Park
Elizabeth Garrett Anderson School
The Gower Sch.
White Lion Cen.
Utd. Reformed Ch.
Crafts Council
Angel Building
Reservoir
Myddleton House
Police Sta.
Superstore
N1 Shopping Centre
Peel Cen.
Sch. of Oriental & African Studies
Baptist Ch.
Royal National Throat, Nose & Ear Hosp.
Nuffield Cen.
King's Cross Mission Ch.
Town Hall
Argyle Prim. Sch.
St. Mark's Ch.
Baptist Chap.
Clerkenwell Parochial C of E Prim. Sch.
The Nautilus Bldg.
New River Head
Holy Cross Ch.
St. Mary's German Ch.
Halls of Residence
RNIB
Westminster Kingsway Coll. (Kings Cross Cen.)
Eastman Dental Hosp. & Institute
St. Andrews Gdns.
Mount Pleasant Sorting Office
The Postal Museum (2017)
Ch. of Our Most Holy Redeemer
London Metropolitan Archives
Lumen Utd. Ref. Ch.
St. George's Gdns.
Thomas Coram Early Childhood Cen.
The Foundling Mus.
Sch. of Pharmacy
The Wolfson Assessment Cen.
Mecklenburgh Square Gardens
Coram's Fields
Brunswick Centre
Curzon
Nuffield Fitness Cen.
The Charles Dickens Mus.
Independent Television News
St. Peter's Ch.
The National Hospital for Neurology and Neurosurgery
Gt. Ormond Street Hospital for Children
Royal London Hospital for Integrated Medicine
St. George the Martyr C of E Prim. Sch.
Buddhist Cen. London
St. Giles Coll. London Central
Russell Square Gardens
Mary Ward Cen.
PureGym
Pol. Sta.
Library
Gray's Inn Gardens
Gray's Inn
St. Alban's C of E Prim. Sch.
Islamic Cen.
Conway Hall
The Old School
British Museum
College
Le Cordon Bleu
Bloomsbury Square Gdns.
St. Etheldreda
A5200
A5203
A501
A201
A401
A5201
A4200
B502
B504
B515
B521
A40
A5202

218
224
217
70
71
A
B
C
D
E
1
2
3
4
5
6
7
ISLINGTON
FINSBURY
CLERKENWELL
CAMDEN
CITY OF LONDON
EC1
N1
ANGEL
FARRINGDON
BARBICAN
Business Design Centre
N1 Shop. Centre
Vue Cin.
Superstore
Islington Tunnel
Police Sta.
White Lion Cen.
Utd. Reformed Ch.
Crafts Council
Reservoir
Angel Building
St. Mark's Ch.
Baptist Chap.
Sadler's Wells
Sixth Form College
Old Red Lion
Virgin Active
Fitness First (Angel)
RNIB
City University London (Northampton Sq. Campus)
Hugh Myddelton Prim. Sch.
The Urdang
Ch. of Our Most Holy Redeemer
London Metropolitan Archives
Dania Sch.
Spa Fields Open Space
Woodbridge Chapel
St. James's Church
Church of St. John
Mus. St. John's Gate
St. John's Gdns.
Queen Mary University of London (Charterhouse Square)
Charterhouse
The Italia Conti
Saddlers Sports Cen.
County Court
Finsbury Leisure Cen.
Ironmonger Row Baths
LSO St. Lukes
King Square Gardens
Moreland Prim. Sch.
St. Clement with St. Barnabas & St. Matthew Ch.
Stem Academy
City Road Lock
City Road Basin
Wenlock Basin
Shepherdess Walk
Packington St. Br.
Regent's Canal
Works
Hanover Prim. Sch.
Polish Catholic Ch.
Convent St. John's Ch.
St. John Prim. Sch.
City of London Academy-Islington
Richard Cloudesley Sch.
Holy Trinity Ch.
London Coll. of Fashion
City of London Prim. Acad.
Leisure Cen.
Fortune St. Pk.
Schools Golden La. Campus
Jewin Ch.
Barbican Arts Cen.
City of London Sch. for Girls
Guildhall Sch. of Music
St. Giles
Ironmongers Hall
Barber Surgeon's Hall
Museum of London
St. Bartholomew the Great Ch.
Central Markets
(Smithfield)
Haberdashers
St. Etheldreda's Ch.
Islamic Cen.
St. Alban's C of E Prim. Sch.
St. Peter's Ch.
PENTONVILLE ROAD
CITY ROAD
GOSWELL ROAD
ST. JOHN STREET
ROSEBERY AVENUE
FARRINGDON ROAD
CLERKENWELL ROAD
OLD STREET
ALDERSGATE STREET
UPPER STREET
LIVERPOOL ROAD
ISLINGTON HIGH ST.
A1
A401
A501
A5201
A201
B502
B501
B515
B521
B500
B144
A104
A5200

HOXTON
HACKNEY
HAGGERSTON
SHOREDITCH
SPITALFIELDS
EC2
E1
E2
SHOREDITCH PARK
Play Park
Tennis Courts
Britannia Leisure Centre
Whitmore Prim. Sch.
St. Annes with St. Columba Ch.
Burbage Prim. Sch.
Trust HQ & Hlth. Cen.
Randal Cremer Prim. Sch.
St. Mary's Community Garden
Haggerston Sch.
Bridge Academy
Geffrye Mus.
Geffrye's Gdns.
HOXTON
Hoxton Hall
St. Chad's Ch.
True Jesus Ch.
St. John the Baptist C of E Prim. Sch.
St. John the Baptist Ch.
Hackney Comm. Coll. (Shoreditch Campus)
Univ. Tech. College
St. Monica's RC Prim. Sch.
St. Monica's RC Church
Aske Gdns.
Mildmay Hosp.
Columbia Mkt. Nursy. Sch.
Ravenscroft Park
Sports Cen.
Tech. College
Moorfields Eye Hosp.
Shoreditch Town Hall
St. Leonard's Ch.
Boundary Gdns.
ARNOLD CIRCUS
OLD STREET
Fire Sta.
Central Foundation Boys' Sch.
Wesley's Chapel & Mus.
Bunhill Fields Burial Ground
Armoury House
Virgin Active
HAC Ground
The College of Law
London Coll. of Fashion
Holywell Cen.
The Lyceum Sch.
Government Offices
Army Reserve Cen.
SHOREDITCH HIGH STREET
Dennis Severs House
Old Spitalfields Market
Exchange Building
Broadgate Tower
Broadgate Ice Rink
Exchange Square
LIVERPOOL STREET
Chapel of the Open Book
St. Mary Moorfields Ch.
Broadgate Circle
Milton Ct. Concert Hall
MOORGATE
Christ Ch.
Christ Church Prim. Sch.
Pol. Sta.
Mosque
CITY ROAD
OLD STREET
GREAT EASTERN STREET
COMMERCIAL STREET
KINGSLAND ROAD
SHOREDITCH HIGH STREET
BISHOPSGATE
NORTON FOLGATE
HACKNEY ROAD
BETHNAL GREEN
BRICK LANE
FINSBURY PAVEMENT
CURTAIN ROAD
A10
A1202
A5201
A501
A1200
A1208
A1209
B100
B101
B118
B122
B134
B144
219
71
91
225

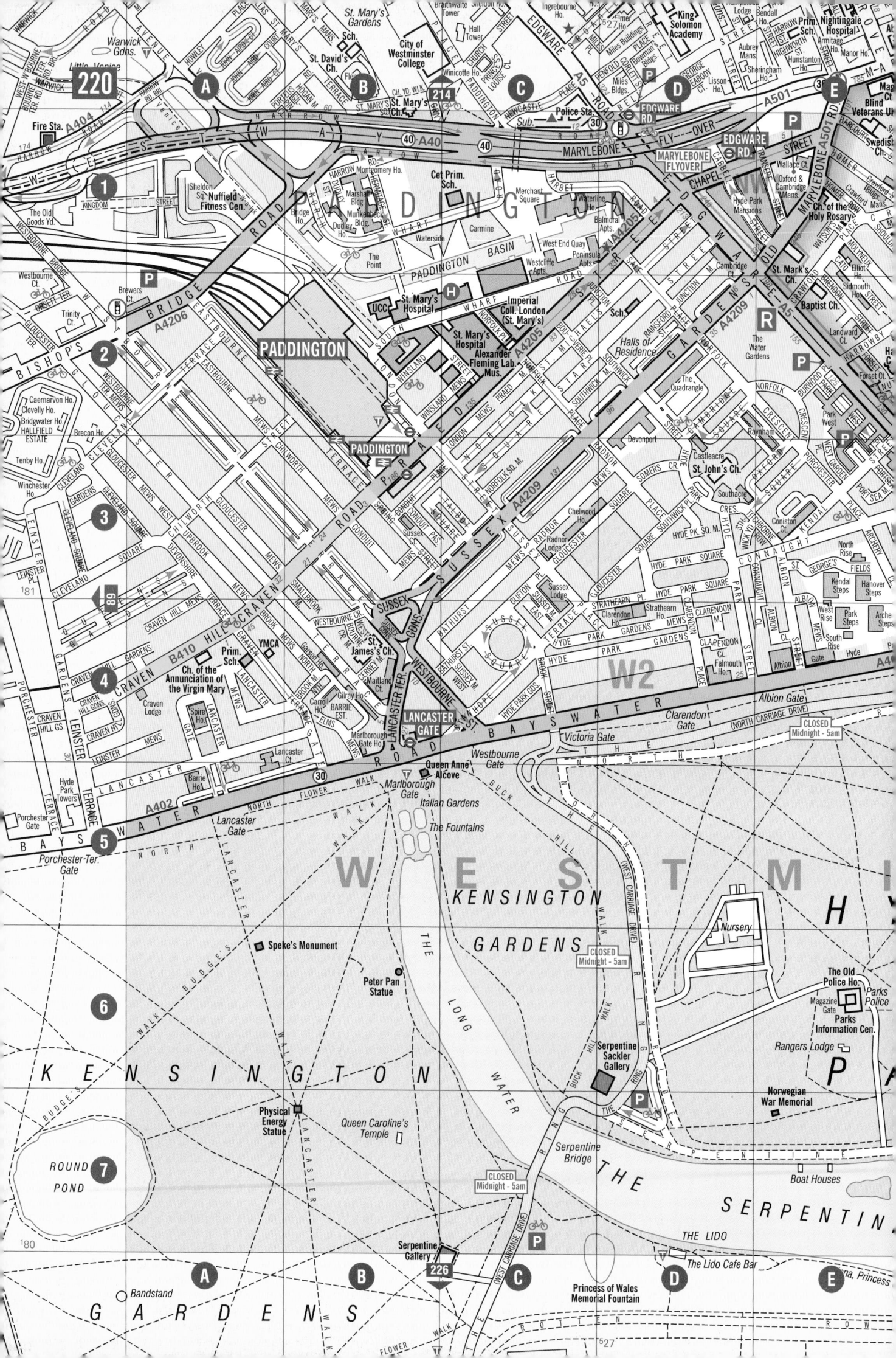
220
214
226
PADDINGTON
W2
WESTMINSTER
KENSINGTON GARDENS
THE SERPENTINE
HYDE PARK
PADDINGTON BASIN
St. Mary's Hospital
Paddington
Lancaster Gate
Edgware Rd.
Marylebone Flyover
Round Pond
Peter Pan Statue
Speke's Monument
Physical Energy Statue
Queen Caroline's Temple
Serpentine Gallery
Serpentine Sackler Gallery
Serpentine Bridge
The Long Water
Italian Gardens
The Fountains
The Lido
Princess of Wales Memorial Fountain
Norwegian War Memorial
Bayswater Road
Sussex Gardens
Praed Street
Edgware Road
Westway

221
222
F
G
H
J
K
R
1
2
3
4
5
6
7
Town Hall
Lib.
Bickenhall Mansions
Everyman Baker St.
Paddington Street Gdns.
St. Andrews Mans.
Meth. Ch.
York Mans.
Luxborough Tower
Newcastle Ho. Luxborough Ho.
King Edward VII's Hosp.
Basildon Ct.
Tenby Mans.
215
RIBA
Sch.
Central Synagogue
PureGym
The Heart Hospital
Hlth. Cen.
The Clinic
BBC Broadcasting House
All Souls Ch.
St. Mary's Prim. Sch.
St. Mary's Ch.
Sch.
Clarewood Ct.
Princess Ct.
Sherwood Ct.
Harrowby Ho.
Sylvia Young Theatre Sch.
Wetherby Prep. Sch.
Cumberland Mans.
Bryanston Ct.
Halcyon London International Sch.
Stourcliffe Cl.
Dudley Ct.
Bilton Towers
Portman Towers
Syns.
Ch. of the Annunciation
Cumberland Ct.
Grosvenor Ct. Mans.
Lanchester Ct.
Connaught Ho. School
Tyburn Tree (Site of)
Marble Arch
MARBLE ARCH
Speakers' Corner
Stanhope Place Gate
ENTRANCE TO UNDERGROUND CAR PARK
Fitness First
Wendover Ho.
West London Coll.
St. Vincent's Cath. Sch.
St. James's Ch. in Spanish Pl.
Admiral Ct.
Wallace Collection
St. Paul's Ch.
Fitzhardinge Ho.
Orchard Ct.
Selfridges
Primark
Virgin Active
Park House
North Row Bldgs.
Lees Ct.
Avenfield Ho.
Upper Feilde
Animals in War Memorial
Coll.
Clarendon Flats
Montessori Centre International
Chesham Flats
Kings Weigh Ho. Ch.
BOND ST.
West One Shop. Cen.
HMV
AR Cen.
Mus.
Hinde Ho.
Meth. Ch.
College
BDA Dental Museum
London Welbeck Hospital
Queen's Coll.
London Eye Hosp.
Chapel
Convent
Coll.
Wigmore Hall
Welbeck Ho.
Harcourt Ho.
St. Peter's Ch.
Disney
Univ. of Westminster (Regent Camp.)
ENTRANCE TO UNDERGROUND CAR PARK
London Coll. of Fashion
John Lewis
Regent
Buses & Taxis only Mon. - Sat. 11am- 7pm
Hanover Square Gdns.
Roosevelt Mem.
American Embassy Until 2017
Grosvenor Hill Ct.
Chap.
Connaught Ho.
Fitness First
W1
M A Y F A I R
W E S T M I N S T E R
Library
St. George's Gdns.
Grosvenor Chapel
St. George's (Hanover Sq.) Prim. Sch.
Ch. of the Immaculate Conception
Fountain Ho.
Aldford Ho.
Rosebery Ct.
Third Ch. of Christ Scientist
Chesterfield Ho.
Curzon
Carrington Ho.
Garrick Ho.
Christ Ch.
Mos.
Park Towers
Refreshment Kiosk
Parade Ground
Reformers Tree
ENTRANCE TO UNDERGROUND CAR PARK
Joy of Life Fountain
The Lookout Education Cen.
Reservoir
Diana, Princess of Wales Memorial Walk
7/7 Memorial
Bandstand
The Serpentine Bar & Kitchen
Boating Lake
Cavalry Memorial
Achilles Statue
Queen Elizabeth Gate
Nannies Lawn
Fishermans Keep
Holocaust Memorial
The Holocaust Memorial Garden
The Dell
Rose Garden
Memorial Walk
Pier
227
Apsley Ho. (Wellington Museum)
HYDE PARK CORNER
New Zealand War Meml.
RAF Bomber Command Memorial
Wellington Mon.
Apsley Ga.
HYDE PARK
GREEN PARK
Canada
H Y D E P A R K
A41
A5204
A5
A40
A4202
A4201
A4
B524
B406
MARYLEBONE HIGH ST.
BAKER ST.
GLOUCESTER PLACE
PORTMAN SQUARE
WIGMORE STREET
OXFORD STREET
CAVENDISH SQ.
PORTLAND PLACE
NEW BOND STREET
GROSVENOR SQUARE
BERKELEY SQUARE
PARK LANE
PICCADILLY
CURZON STREET
MANCHESTER SQUARE
MONTAGU SQUARE
BRYANSTON SQUARE
SEYMOUR PLACE
EDGWARE ROAD
NORTH AUDLEY STREET
SOUTH AUDLEY STREET
DUKE STREET
JAMES STREET
MANDEVILLE PL.
WELBECK ST.
HARLEY ST.
WIMPOLE ST.
MARYLEBONE LANE
BROOK STREET
MOUNT STREET
UPPER BROOK STREET
UPPER GROSVENOR STREET
NORTH ROW
SOUTH STREET
SOUTH MOLTON STREET
DAVIES STREET
CARLOS PLACE
NORTH AUDLEY ST.
HERTFORD STREET
DOWN STREET
HAMILTON PLACE
OLD PARK LANE
ROTTEN ROW
CUMBERLAND GATE
GREAT CUMBERLAND PL.
BRYANSTON STREET
SEYMOUR STREET
GEORGE STREET
BLANDFORD STREET
DORSET STREET
PADDINGTON STREET
CRAWFORD STREET
YORK STREET
MONTAGU PLACE
HENRIETTA PLACE
QUEEN ANNE STREET
NEW CAVENDISH STREET
DUCHESS ST.
MANSFIELD ST.
HARLEY ST.
WEYMOUTH ST.
DEVONSHIRE ST.
NOTTINGHAM ST.
MADDOX STREET
BRUTON STREET
DAVIES ST.
HILL STREET
CHARLES STREET
CHESTERFIELD HILL
HAY'S MEWS
FARM STREET
CLARGES STREET
HALF MOON STREET
WHITE HORSE ST.
SHEPHERD STREET
BOLTON STREET
STRATTON STREET

222
RIBA
Telecom Tower
Univ. of Westminster
Halls of Residence
Church
School of Hygiene & Tropical Medicine
Senate House
RADA
RADA Studios
GOODGE STREET
Ch. of Scientology
Toy Mus.
216
St. Charles Ch.
Prim. Sch.
Mosque
British Transport Police
Cavendish Coll.
Coll. of Law
The Harley St. Clinic
Sch.
Syn.
YHA
Gym
BBC Broadcasting House
All Souls' Ch.
Pearson Square
Crabtree Place
Queen's Coll.
Dental Museum
Univ. of Westminster
Furnival Mans.
West One Ho.
Univ.
St. Andrews Cham.
Architectural Association
Odeon
Harmont Ho.
Chapel
Convent
London Eye Hosp.
Coll.
Cavendish Ho.
All Saints Ch.
Temple
Sorting Office
Academy
Central YMCA
Dominion
Wigmore Hall
CAVENDISH SQ.
Univ. of Westminster (Regent Campus)
Welsh Baptist Chapel
Buses & Taxis only Mon. - Sat. 7am- 7pm
The Plaza Shop. Cen.
TOTTENHAM COURT ROAD
Primark
Centrepoint
Harcourt Ho.
ENTRANCE TO UNDERGROUND CAR PARK
OXFORD CIRCUS
London Coll. of Fashion
Tem.
French Protestant Ch.
St. Peter's Ch.
John Lewis
W1
Photographers' Gallery
Youth Hostel
St. Patrick's Ch.
Disney
Regent Hall
Buses & Taxis only Mon. - Sat. 7am- 7pm
Fitness First
London Palladium
College of Beauty Therapy
Soho
NHS Cen.
Phoenix
HMV
Hanover Square Gdns.
Marshall St. Leisure Cen.
Prince Edward
Adult Ed. Cen.
SOHO
221
Mus.
Fitness First
Westminster Kingsway Coll.
Curzon
Palace
Fire Sta.
St. George's Ch.
Pol. Sta.
St. Anne's Ch.
St. James Residences
Sch.
Queen's
Gielgud
Apollo
Lyric
China Town
Prince Charles
Leicester Sq.
Vue
Empire
Ch.
Piccadilly
Picturehouse
London Trocadero
London Pav.
PICCADILLY CIRCUS
Eros
Criterion
Prince of Wales
Comedy Store
Leicester Fields
Odeon
Cen. Ref. Lib.
Chap.
Connaught Ho.
Fitness First
Royal Institution Mus.
The Faraday Mus.
Royal Academy of Arts (Burlington Ho.)
Jermyn St.
Vue (Apollo)
Harold Pinter
Haymarket Theatre Royal
Cineworld
PureGym
Her Majesty's
Ch. of the Immaculate Conception
Rosebery Ct.
St. James's Ch.
Canada Ho.
National Gallery (Sainsbury Wing)
Third Ch. of Christ Scientist
London Library
SW1
ST. JAMES'S
HQ of the Inst. of Directors
Royal Marines Meml.
Mall Galleries
ICA
Curzon
Garrick Ho.
Carrington Ho.
Arlington Ho.
GREEN PARK
Waterloo Gdns.
RAC
Duke of York Column
Old Admiralty Offices
Spencer Ho.
Marlborough House (Commonwealth Conference Centre)
King George VI & Queen Mother Memorials
Queen's Chapel
Chapel Royal
St. James's Palace
CLOSED SUNDAY
Guards Mem.
Park Towers
GREEN PARK
228
Clarence Ho.
Lancaster Ho.
Stable Yard Gate
Refreshments
ST. JAMES'S PARK
Duck Island
RAF Bomber Command Memorial
Canada Memorial

223
217
224
229
F
G
H
J
K
1
2
3
4
5
6
7
WC1
WC2
EC1
EC4
SE1
HOLBORN
COVENT GARDEN
LAMBETH
Bloomsbury Square Gdns.
Gray's Inn Gardens
Gray's Inn
Lincoln's Inn Fields
Lincoln's Inn Library
Lincoln's Inn Hall
Royal Courts of Justice
Royal Coll. of Surgeons
The Hunterian Mus.
Old Curiosity Shop
Sir John Soane's Museum
London School of Economics
Royal Opera House
The Royal Ballet Sch.
The Market
London Transport Mus.
Film Mus.
Jubilee Hall Gym
St. Paul's Ch.
Somerset House
Courtauld Gallery
King's Coll. (Strand Campus)
Embankment Galleries
Bush Ho.
India Ho.
Australia Ho.
Inland Revenue
St. Mary-le-Strand Ch.
St. Clement Danes Ch.
Temple Bar
Temple Ch.
Inner Temple Hall
Mid. Temple Hall
Inner Temple Garden
Victoria Embankment Gardens
Charing Cross Underground Shop. Cen.
St. Martin-in-the-Fields Ch.
Cleopatra's Needle
Savoy Pier
Embankment Pier
Festival Pier
Hungerford Bridge
The Golden Jubilee Bridges
RS Hispaniola
PS Tattershall Castle
HQS Wellington
HMS President
Lifeboat Station
Temple Pier
St. Katharine
Garden Bridge (Proposed)
RIVER THAMES
Kings Reach
Stamford Wharf
OXO TOWER WHARF
Gabriels Wharf
The London Television Centre
BFI Southbank
National Theatre
Purcell Room
Queen Elizabeth Hall
Hayward Gallery
Southbank Centre
Royal Festival Hall
Rambert
King's College London (Waterloo Campus)
King's College London
IMAX
Jubilee Gardens
London Eye
London Eye Millennium Pier
RAF Memorial
Whitehall Stairs
Old War Office
Ministry of Defence
Banqueting House
Dept. for Energy
Scotland Office
Wales Office
Shell Centre
Whitehouse Apartments
The Warehouse
St. John's Ch.
Bernie Spain Gardens
PEABODY ESTATE
HOLBORN
CHANCERY LANE
TEMPLE
EMBANKMENT
CHARING CROSS
COVENT GARDEN
WATERLOO
WATERLOO EAST
LEICESTER SQ.
A40
A4200
A401
A5200
B400
B402
B401
A4
A3211
A301
A3200
A3212
B308
B521
HIGH HOLBORN
KINGSWAY
STRAND
ALDWYCH
FLEET STREET
WATERLOO BRIDGE
VICTORIA EMBANKMENT
NORTHUMBERLAND AV.
WHITEHALL
HORSE GUARDS AVENUE
STAMFORD ST.
UPPER GROUND
LONG ACRE
GREAT QUEEN STREET
DRURY LANE
SOUTHAMPTON ROW
THEOBALD'S ROAD
GRAY'S INN ROAD
CHANCERY LANE
FETTER LANE
NEW FETTER LANE
SHAFTESBURY AV.
BLOOMSBURY WAY
NEW OXFORD STREET

224
223
218
230
A
B
C
D
E
1
2
3
4
5
6
7
FARRINGDON
BARBICAN
CHANCERY LA.
CITY THAMESLINK
ST. PAUL'S
MANSION HO.
BLACKFRIARS
SOUTHWARK
WATERLOO EAST
WATERLOO
EC1
EC4
SE1
LAMBETH
SOUTHWARK
RIVER
HOLBORN
HOLBORN CIRCUS
HOLBORN VIADUCT
FLEET STREET
NEWGATE STREET
CHARTERHOUSE ST.
FARRINGDON ROAD
FARRINGDON STREET
NEW BRIDGE STREET
BLACKFRIARS BRIDGE
BLACKFRIARS ROAD
QN. VICTORIA ST.
VICTORIA EMBANKMENT
UPPER THAMES STREET
SOUTHWARK STREET
SOUTHWARK BRIDGE
SOUTHWARK BRIDGE RD.
STAMFORD STREET
UPPER GROUND
UNION STREET
ALDERSGATE
ST. MARTIN'S LE GRAND
KING EDWARD ST.
LONDON WALL
CHEAPSIDE
CANNON STREET
FETTER LANE
NEW FETTER LANE
SMITHFIELD
LUDGATE HILL
LUDGATE CIRCUS
A40
A201
A4
A1
A3200
A3211
A300
A301
B500
B521
B400
B300
Central Markets
(Smithfield)
Museum of London
St. Bartholomew's Hospital
Central Criminal Ct.
Old Bailey
St. Paul's Cathedral
London Stock Exchange
British Telecom Centre
Postmans Park
Tate Modern
Shakespeare's Globe & Exhibition
Bankside Gallery
Millennium Bridge
Blackfriars Millennium Pier
Bankside Pier
HMS President
HQS Wellington
Garden Bridge (Proposed)
OXO TOWER WHARF
The London Television Centre
The London Nautical Sch.
The Young Vic
Nelson Sq. Gdn.
Blackfriars Crown Court
London Fire Brigade Museum
The Rose Thtre. (site of)
Menier Chocolate Factory
City of London Sch.
Salvation Army HQ
Temple Ch.
Inner Temple Garden
Middle Temple Garden
Temple Bar
Barbican Arts Cen.
City of London Sch. for Girls

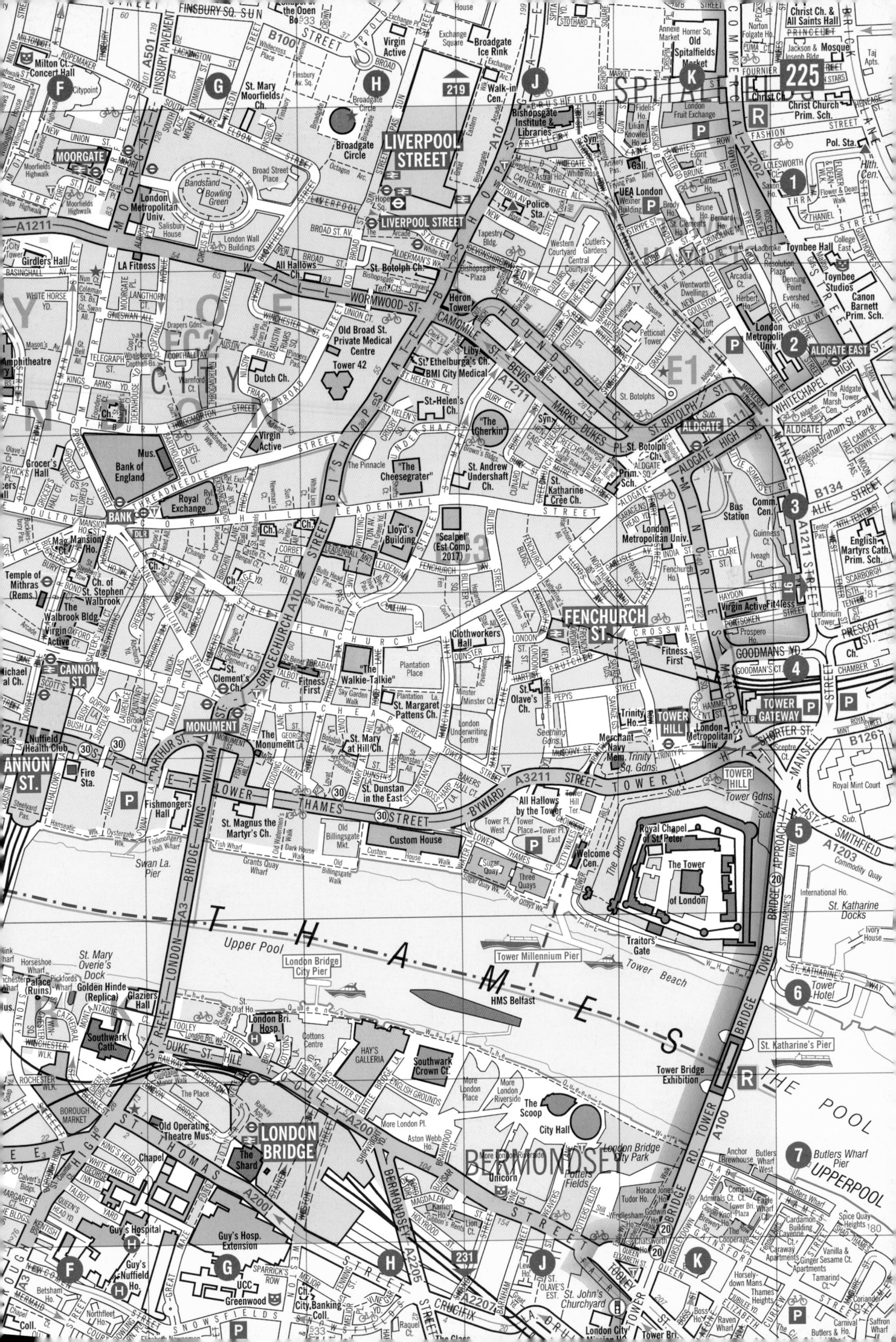

225
219
231
Milton Ct. Concert Hall
MOORGATE
London Metropolitan Univ.
St. Mary Moorfields Ch.
Broadgate Circle
Virgin Active
Exchange Square
Broadgate Ice Rink
LIVERPOOL STREET
Bishopsgate Institute & Libraries
Old Spitalfields Market
London Fruit Exchange
Christ Ch. & All Saints Hall
Christ Church Prim. Sch.
SPITALFIELDS
Bandstand Bowling Green
FINSBURY CIRCUS
All Hallows Ch.
LA Fitness
Girdlers Hall
WORMWOOD ST.
St. Botolph Ch.
Heron Tower
Police Sta.
UEA London Wexner Building
Toynbee Hall
Toynbee Studios
Canon Barnett Prim. Sch.
EC2
CITY OF LONDON
Old Broad St. Private Medical Centre
Tower 42
Dutch Ch.
St. Ethelburga's Ch.
BMI City Medical
St. Helen's Ch.
"The Gherkin"
HOUNDSDITCH
E1
St. Botolphs
ALDGATE EAST
ALDGATE
WHITECHAPEL HIGH ST.
Braham St. Park
Bank of England
Mus.
Royal Exchange
BANK
LEADENHALL STREET
The Pinnacle
"The Cheesegrater"
St. Andrew Undershaft Ch.
St. Katharine Cree Ch.
Lloyd's Building
"Scalpel" (Est Comp. 2017)
EC3
Bus Station
English Martyrs Cath. Prim. Sch.
Mag.Mansion Ho.
Temple of Mithras (Rems.)
Ch. of St. Stephen Walbrook
The Walbrook Bldg
Virgin Active
CANNON ST.
FENCHURCH ST
Clothworkers Hall
"The Walkie-Talkie"
Plantation Place
Fitness First
St. Margaret Pattens Ch.
St. Olave's Ch.
London Metropolitan Univ.
Virgin Active
Fit4less
GOODMANS YD.
TOWER GATEWAY
TOWER HILL
Trinity Ho.
Merchant Navy Mem.
Trinity Sq. Gdns.
Royal Mint Court
MONUMENT
The Monument
St. Mary at Hill Ch.
St. Dunstan in the East
London Underwriting Centre
Nuffield Health Club
Fire Sta.
CANNON ST.
Fishmongers Hall
St. Magnus the Martyr's Ch.
LOWER THAMES STREET
Custom House
Old Billingsgate Mkt.
All Hallows by the Tower
Welcome Cen.
Tower Gdns.
Royal Chapel of St. Peter
The Tower of London
Traitors Gate
International Ho.
St. Katharine Docks
Swan La. Pier
Upper Pool
London Bridge City Pier
Tower Millennium Pier
Tower Beach
HMS Belfast
THAMES
St. Katharine's Pier
Tower Bridge Exhibition
Tower Hotel
THE POOL
St. Mary Overie's Dock
Palace (Ruins)
Golden Hinde (Replica)
Glaziers Hall
Southwark Cath.
London Bri. Hosp.
Cottons Centre
HAY'S GALLERIA
Southwark Crown Ct.
More London Place
More London Riverside
The Scoop
City Hall
BOROUGH MARKET
Old Operating Theatre Mus.
LONDON BRIDGE
The Shard
Guy's Hospital
Guy's Hosp. Extension
Guy's Nuffield Ho.
UCC
Greenwood
BERMONDSEY
London Bridge City Park
Potters Fields
Unicorn
Butlers Wharf Pier
UPPER POOL
TOWER BRIDGE RD.
St. John's Churchyard
City Banking Coll.
London City
Coll.

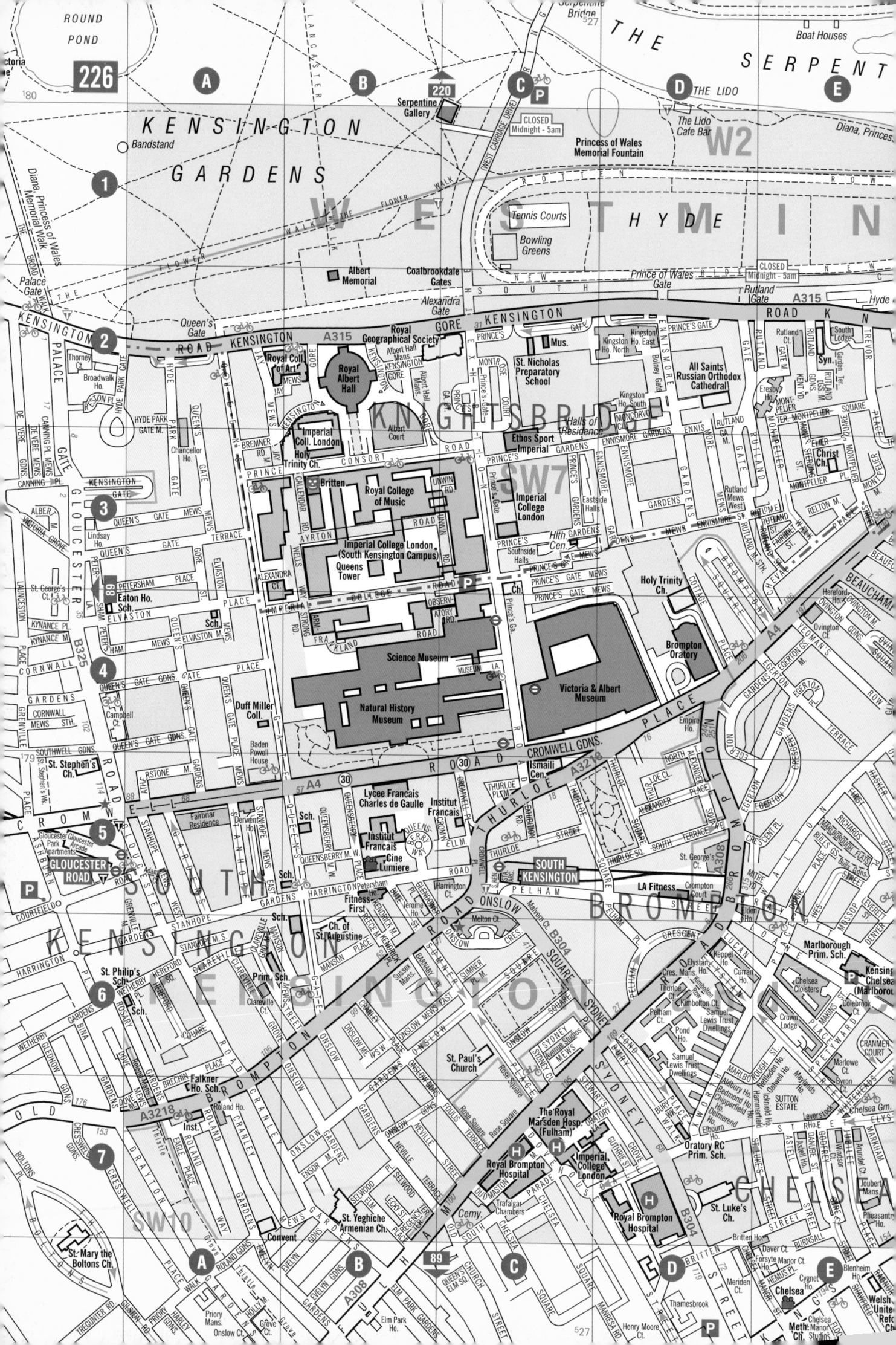

ROUND POND
226
A
B
C
D
E
220
Serpentine Gallery
Serpentine Bridge
THE SERPENTINE
Boat Houses
THE LIDO
The Lido Cafe Bar
KENSINGTON GARDENS
Bandstand
Diana, Princess of Wales Memorial Walk
CLOSED Midnight - 5am
WEST CARRIAGE DRIVE
Princess of Wales Memorial Fountain
W2
Diana, Princess
1
THE FLOWER WALK
ROTTEN ROW
WESTMINSTER
HYDE PARK
Tennis Courts
Bowling Greens
Albert Memorial
Coalbrookdale Gates
Alexandra Gate
Prince of Wales Gate
Rutland Gate
Palace Gate
THE BROAD WALK
Queen's Gate
2
KENSINGTON ROAD
KENSINGTON GORE
A315
Royal Geographical Society
Royal Coll. of Art
Royal Albert Hall
Albert Hall Mans.
Mus.
St. Nicholas Preparatory School
All Saints Russian Orthodox Cathedral
Syn.
KNIGHTSBRIDGE
Imperial Coll. London
Holy Trinity Ch.
Albert Court
Halls of Residence
Ethos Sport Imperial
PRINCE CONSORT ROAD
PRINCE'S GARDENS
ENNISMORE GARDENS
Christ Ch.
SW7
Britten
Royal College of Music
Imperial College London
Imperial College London (South Kensington Campus)
Queens Tower
3
KENSINGTON GATE
QUEEN'S GATE TERRACE
GLOUCESTER ROAD
Holy Trinity Ch.
Brompton Oratory
Eaton Ho. Sch.
68
ELVASTON PLACE
IMPERIAL COLLEGE ROAD
Science Museum
Natural History Museum
Victoria & Albert Museum
EXHIBITION ROAD
4
B325
QUEEN'S GATE GDNS.
CORNWALL GARDENS
Duff Miller Coll.
Baden Powell House
BROMPTON ROAD
BEAUCHAMP PLACE
A4
St. Stephen's Ch.
CROMWELL ROAD
CROMWELL GDNS.
Ismaili Cen.
A3218
THURLOE PLACE
Lycee Francais Charles de Gaulle
Institut Francais
Fairbriar Residence
5
GLOUCESTER ROAD
Institut Francais Cine Lumiere
SOUTH KENSINGTON
LA Fitness
Fitness First
HARRINGTON ROAD
ONSLOW
Ch. of St. Augustine
BROMPTON
Malborough Prim. Sch.
St. Philip's Sch.
6
Prim. Sch.
B304
SOUTH KENSINGTON
St. Paul's Church
Rose Square
Falkner Ho. Sch.
The Royal Marsden Hosp. (Fulham)
Royal Brompton Hospital
Imperial College London
Royal Brompton Hospital
Oratory RC Prim. Sch.
Sutton Estate
7
OLD BROMPTON ROAD
Convent
St. Yeghiche Armenian Ch.
SW10
St. Mary the Boltons Ch.
THE BOLTONS
89
A308
St. Luke's Ch.
CHELSEA
FULHAM ROAD
Chelsea

227
221
228
89
90
Pier
Boating Lake
The Serpentine Bar & Kitchen
Bandstand
Cavalry Memorial
Achilles Statue
Queen Elizabeth Gate
Nannies Lawn
Holocaust Memorial
The Holocaust Memorial Garden
Fishermans Keep
The Dell
Rose Garden
Memorial Walk
CLOSED Midnight - 5am
Apsley Ho. (Wellington Museum)
HYDE PARK CORNER
Apsley Ga.
New Zealand War Meml.
RAF Bomber Command Memorial
Wellington Mon.
Wellington Arch
Australian War Meml.
CLOSED SUNDAY
Diana, Princess of Wales Memorial Walk
Commonwealth Memorial Gates
CONSTITUTION HILL
GREEN PARK
PALACE GARDENS
Canada
Buckingham Palace
The Royal Mews
Royal Mews
SERPENTINE
ROTTEN ROW
'Pan' (Epstein)
One Hyde Park
KNIGHTSBRIDGE
SCOTCH HOUSE
Albert Gate
The Knightsbridge Apartments
Park Mans.
Lincoln Ho.
Washington Ho.
Harrods
Marland Ho.
Hugo Ho.
Lowndes Ct.
Carlton Twr. Pl.
Thorburn Ho.
Greville Ho.
St. Paul's Ch.
Belgravia Ho.
Lowndes Lodge
Montrose Ho.
St. Peter's Ch.
Instituto Cervantes
BELGRAVIA
SW1
Clunie Ho.
Denbigh Ho.
St. Saviour's Ch.
Chase Ct.
More Ho. Sch.
Sch.
St. Columba's Ch.
Knightsbridge Sch.
Walton Ho.
Pembroke Ho.
Dorchester Ct.
Fordie Ho.
Oakley Ho.
St. Simon Zelotes Ch.
Sussex Ho.Sch.
Cadogan Hall
Holy Trinity Ch.
Sloane Ter. Mans.
Prim. Sch.
Inchbald Sch.
Eaton Mans.
SLOANE SQ.
Royal Ct.
St. Mary's Ch.
St. Thomas More Language Coll. & St. Joseph RC Prim. Sch.
Cadogan Mans.
Wyndham Ho.
Tambrook Ct.
St. Mary's Ch.
Francis Holland School
Carmel Hall
Kilmuir Ho.
St. Michael's Ch.
Victoria Coach Sta. (Arrivals)
Chester Ho.
Liby.
Victoria Coach Sta. (Departures)
Police Sta.
National Audit Office
St. Peter's Prim. Sch.
Belgravia Ct.
Chantrey Ho.
VICTORIA
Victoria Place Shop. Cen.
Fountain Square
Station
Coach
Inchbald Sch. of Design
St. Barnabas C of E Prim. Sch
Church of St. Barnabas
The Old Chapel
Saatchi Gallery
Duke of York Square
Frederick Court
Garden Ho. Sch.
Whitelands Ho.
Royal Av. Ho.
KINGS WALK SHOP. CEN.
Mitre Ho.
Courtyard Square
Atlantic Ct.
Chelsea Affiliated Synagogue
St. Leonard's Studios
Burton's Court
Royal Hospital Chelsea
Mus.
Chap.
LIGHT HORSE CT.
RANELAGH GARDENS
Ebury Bri. Cen.
Carriage Shed
PIMLICO
CHELSEA BRIDGE ROAD
BUCKINGHAM PALACE ROAD
GROSVENOR PLACE
BELGRAVE SQUARE
EATON SQUARE
Eaton Square Gardens
CHESHAM STREET
PONT STREET
SLOANE STREET
SLOANE SQUARE
CADOGAN PLACE
HOBART PL.
ECCLESTON STREET
ELIZABETH STREET
CHESTER SQUARE
LOWER SLOANE STREET
ROYAL HOSPITAL ROAD
KINGS ROAD
A4
A4202
A302
A3216
A3217
A3213
A3214
B310
B319
B302
B312
B313
F
G
H
J
K
1
2
3
4
5
6
7

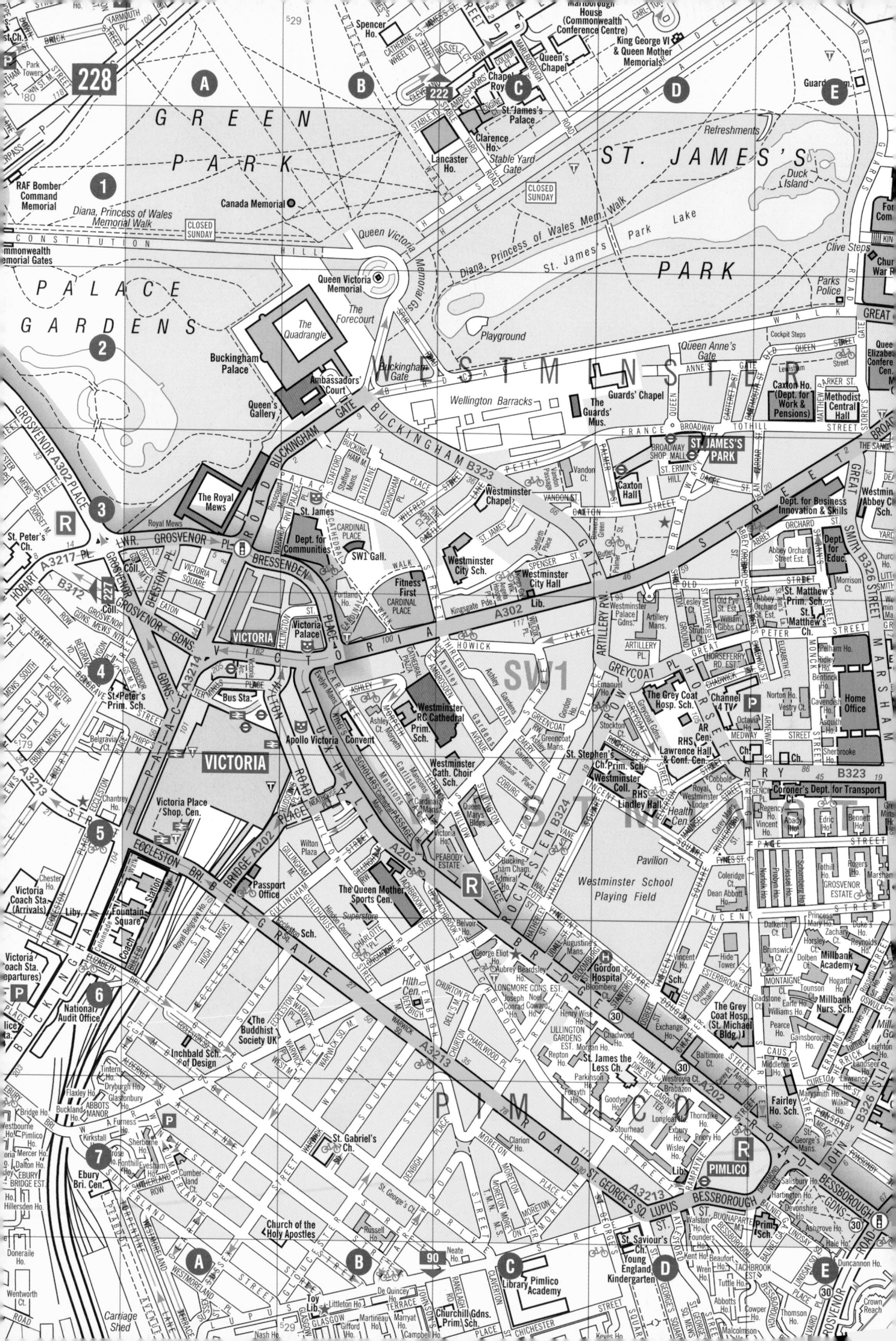
228
GREEN PARK
RAF Bomber Command Memorial
Canada Memorial
Diana, Princess of Wales Memorial Walk
CLOSED SUNDAY
CONSTITUTION HILL
Commonwealth Memorial Gates
PALACE GARDENS
Buckingham Palace
The Quadrangle
Queen Victoria Memorial
The Forecourt
Ambassadors' Court
Queen's Gallery
The Royal Mews
Spencer Ho.
Marlborough House (Commonwealth Conference Centre)
King George VI & Queen Mother Memorials
Queen's Chapel
Chapel Royal
St. James's Palace
Clarence Ho.
Lancaster Ho.
Stable Yard Gate
222
ST. JAMES'S PARK
St. James's Park Lake
Duck Island
Refreshments
Clive Steps
Parks Police
Playground
Queen Anne's Gate
WESTMINSTER
Wellington Barracks
Guards' Chapel
The Guards' Mus.
Caxton Ho. (Dept. for Work & Pensions)
Methodist Central Hall
ST. JAMES'S PARK
Broadway Shop. Mall
Caxton Hall
Westminster Chapel
Westminster City Sch.
Westminster City Hall
Dept. for Business Innovation & Skills
Dept. for Communities
SW1 Gall.
Fitness First
VICTORIA
Victoria Palace
Apollo Victoria
Bus Sta.
Victoria Place Shop. Cen.
Westminster RC Cathedral
Westminster Cath. Choir Sch.
SW1
The Grey Coat Hosp. Sch.
Channel 4 TV
Home Office
Dept. for Educ.
St. Matthew's Prim. Sch.
Coroner's Dept. for Transport
RHS Lawrence Hall & Conf. Cen.
RHS Lindley Hall
Westminster Coll.
Westminster School Playing Field
Pavilion
Passport Office
The Queen Mother Sports Cen.
Gordon Hospital
Millbank Academy
The Grey Coat Hosp. (St. Michael Bldg.)
Fairley Ho. Sch.
PIMLICO
Victoria Coach Sta. (Arrivals)
Victoria Coach Sta. (Departures)
National Audit Office
Inchbald Sch. of Design
The Buddhist Society UK
St. Gabriel's Ch.
Church of the Holy Apostles
St. Saviour's Ch.
Young England Kindergarten
Library
Pimlico Academy
Churchill Gdns. Prim. Sch.
Ebury Bri. Cen.
90
227
A B C D E
1 2 3 4 5 6 7

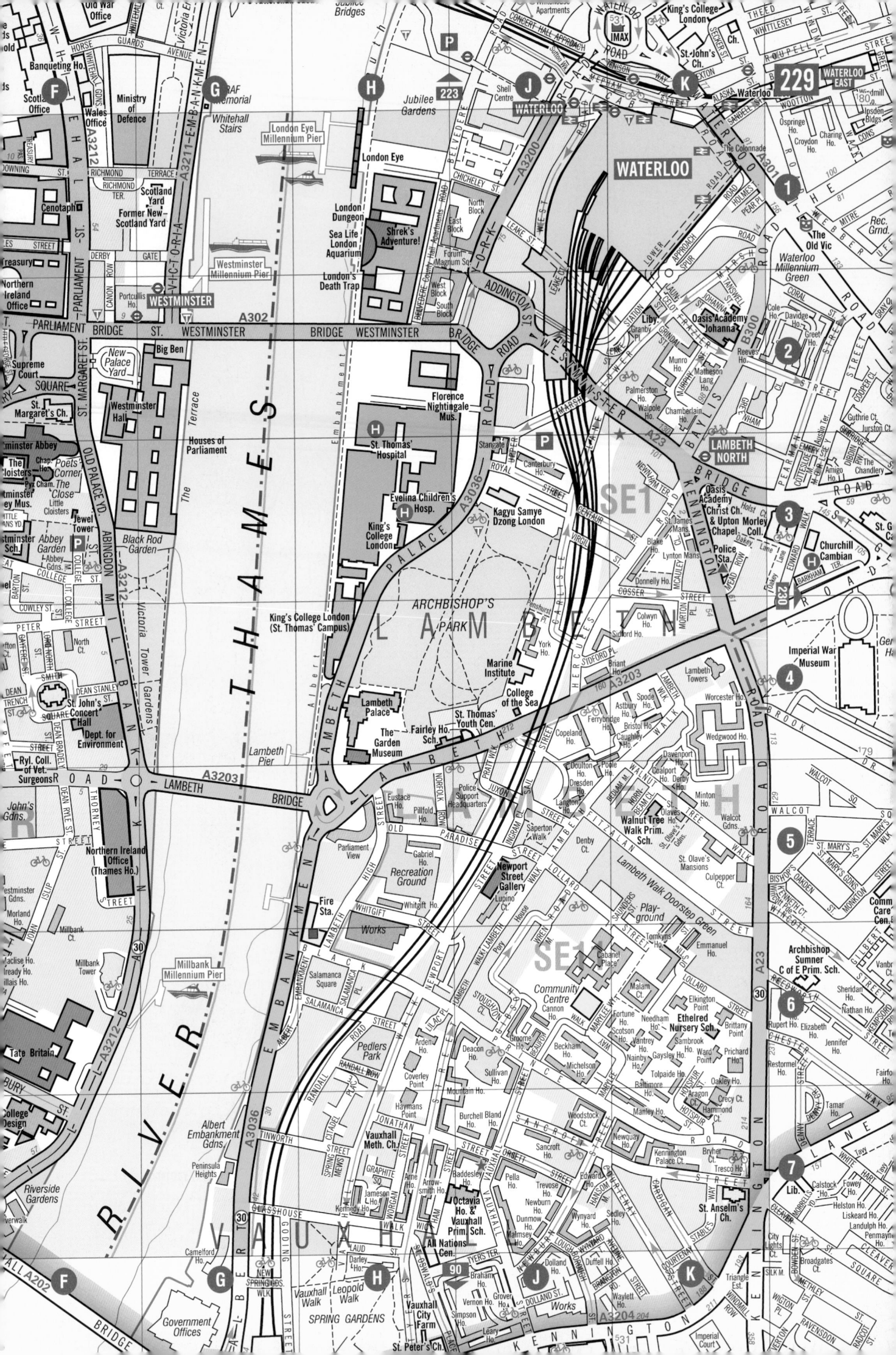
229
WATERLOO EAST
223
230
90
WATERLOO
WESTMINSTER
LAMBETH NORTH
RIVER THAMES
LAMBETH
SE1
SE11
VAUXHALL
ARCHBISHOP'S PARK
Jubilee Gardens
Jubilee Bridges
London Eye
London Eye Millennium Pier
Westminster Millennium Pier
Millbank Millennium Pier
Lambeth Pier
London Dungeon
Sea Life London Aquarium
Shrek's Adventure!
London's Death Trap
Shell Centre
IMAX
King's College London
St. John's Ch.
The Old Vic
Waterloo Millennium Green
Oasis Academy Johanna
Florence Nightingale Mus.
St. Thomas' Hospital
Evelina Children's Hosp.
King's College London
King's College London (St. Thomas' Campus)
Kagyu Samye Dzong London
Marine Institute
College of the Sea
St. Thomas' Youth Cen.
Lambeth Palace
The Garden Museum
Fairley Ho. Sch.
Imperial War Museum
Oasis Academy
Christ Ch. & Upton Chapel
Morley Coll.
Police Sta.
Churchill Cambian
Old War Office
Banqueting Ho.
Scotland Office
Wales Office
Ministry of Defence
RAF Memorial
Whitehall Stairs
Scotland Yard
Former New Scotland Yard
Cenotaph
Treasury
Northern Ireland Office
Portcullis Ho.
Big Ben
New Palace Yard
Westminster Hall
Houses of Parliament
Supreme Court
St. Margaret's Ch.
Westminster Abbey
Poets' Corner
The Cloisters
Black Rod Garden
Victoria Tower Gardens
Jewel Tower
Abbey Garden
St. John's Concert Hall
Dept. for Environment
Ryl. Coll. of Vet. Surgeons
Northern Ireland Office (Thames Ho.)
Millbank Tower
Tate Britain
College of Design
Riverside Gardens
Albert Embankment Gdns.
Peninsula Heights
Government Offices
Parliament View
Recreation Ground
Fire Sta.
Works
Newport Street Gallery
Police Support Headquarters
Walnut Tree Walk Prim. Sch.
Lambeth Walk Doorstep Green
Play-ground
Community Centre
Ethelred Nursery Sch.
Pedlers Park
Vauxhall Meth. Ch.
Octavia Ho. & Vauxhall Prim. Sch.
All Nations Cen.
Vauxhall City Farm
Vauxhall Walk
Leopold Walk
SPRING GARDENS
St. Peter's Ch.
St. Anselm's Ch.
Archbishop Sumner C of E Prim. Sch.
Lib.
Imperial Court
WESTMINSTER BRIDGE
LAMBETH BRIDGE
VAUXHALL BRIDGE
ALBERT EMBANKMENT
MILLBANK
LAMBETH PALACE ROAD
KENNINGTON ROAD
KENNINGTON LANE
LAMBETH ROAD
WATERLOO ROAD
YORK ROAD
BAYLIS ROAD
A23
A302
A3036
A3203
A3212
A3200
A3204
A202
A301
B300

230
SOUTHWARK
King's College London
WATERLOO EAST
WATERLOO
Waterloo East
St. John's Ch.
The Colonnade
The Young Vic
Lewisham Coll. (Waterloo Cen.)
The Old Vic
Waterloo Millennium Green
Oasis Academy Johanna
St. Andrews Ch.
Nelson Sq. Gdn.
NELSON SQUARE
UNION
224
B300
Union
Palestra Ho.
Fire Brigade HQ
Jerwood Space Art Gallery
Blackfriars Crown Court
London Fire Brigade Museum
Great Guildford Business Square
Menier Chocolate Factory
Precious Blood Ch.
The Cathedral of St. Saviour & St. Mary Overie
St. Joseph Cath. Prim. Sch.
Lit. Dorrit Park
BOROUGH
THE BOROUGH
Charles Dickens Prim. Sch.
Moonraker Point
Sports Grd.
Youth & Community Cen.
Friars Primary Foundation Sch.
Teacher Training Cen.
Theatre Rites
Rec. Grnd.
LAMBETH NORTH
WESTMINSTER BRIDGE ROAD
A3202
ST. GEORGE'S ROAD
BOROUGH ROAD
BLACKFRIARS ROAD
A201
A301
A300
A3
London South Bank University
London Sth. Bank Univ.
London South Bank Univ. Technopark
Deeper Life Bible Ch.
Inner London Crown Court (Sessions House)
Police Sta.
Court Annexe
The Henry Wood Hall
Mosque
Newington Gardens
Southwark Playhouse
St. George's RC Cathedral
Notre Dame School
Oasis Academy Christ & Upton Chapel
Morley Coll.
Churchill Cambian
Police Sta.
229
A3203
Imperial War Museum
Geraldine Mary Harmsworth Park
Siobhan Davis Dance Studios
Charlotte Sharman Foundation Prim. Sch.
West Sq. Gdn.
Imperial War Mus. (All Saints Annexe)
ELEPHANT & CASTLE
NEWINGTON
Metro Central Heights
Perry Lib.
London College of Communication
Metropolitan Tabernacle
Coronet Theatre
Elephant & Castle Shopping Centre
Palace Bingo Superbowl
Elephant & Castle Leisure Cen.
One The Elephant
St. Mary's Churchyard
Comm. Cen.
St. Matthews Ch.
Brotherhood of the Cross & Star Church
Halls of Residence
Crossway Ch.
Castle Ind. Est.
NEW KENT ROAD
WALWORTH ROAD
SE11
LAMBETH
Comm. Care Cen.
Archbishop Sumner C of E Prim. Sch.
Jamyang Buddhist Centre
Ethelred Nursery Sch.
Walk Doorstep Green
A3204
KENNINGTON LANE
NEWINGTON BUTTS
KENNINGTON PARK ROAD
KENNINGTON ROAD
Pedlars Acre
Guinness Trust Bldgs.
Crampton Prim. Sch.
Newington Ind. Est.
Dashwood Studios
Police Station
Tibetan Buddhist Cen.
Depot
St. John's Ch.
St. John's Prim. Sch.
WALWORTH
A215
St. Anselm's Ch.
KENNINGTON
St. Mary's Ch.
Alberta Estate
AR Cen.
Walworth Gdn. Farm
London Art Sch.
Tel. Ex.
90
91
30
Keyworth Prim. Sch.
Pasley Park
Imperial Court

231
225
91
London Bridge City Park
The Shard
LONDON BRI.
Guy's Hospital
Guy's Hosp. Extension
Guy's Nuffield Ho.
ST. THOMAS STREET
A200
CRUCIFIX
A2207
TOOLEY STREET
JAMAICA RD.
St. John's Churchyard
London City Mission HQ
Tower Bri. Prim. Sch.
Snowsfields Prim. Sch.
Guy St. Park
Community Park
Leathermarket Gdns.
The Glass Art Gallery
Fashion & Textile Mus.
Bermondsey Pgrd.
St. Mary Magdalen Ch.
Churchyard
New Caledonian Mkt.
Shortwave
A2198
LONG LANE
A2205
BERMONDSEY STREET
A100
TOWER BRIDGE ROAD
B202
Beormund Sch.
Tabard Gardens
TABARD GARDEN ESTATE
A2
DOVER
GREAT DOVER STREET
Globe Academy Sec. Sch.
Mayflower Gdns.
St. Saviour's & St. Olave's Sch.
BRICKLAYER'S ARMS
Haddon Hall Baptist Ch.
Grange Prim. Sch.
The Green
GRANGE ROAD
A2206
Kagyu Samye Dzong London
Bermondsey Spa Gardens (Recreation Ground)
Playground
Boutcher C of E Prim. Sch.
Kintore Wy. Children's Cen.
Harris Academy Bermondsey
SOUTHWARK PK RD.
NECKINGER ESTATE
ARNOLD ESTATE
Paragon Gdns.
Lady Margaret's Ch.
SE17
Townsend Prim. Sch.
Depots
Depot
BRICKLAYERS ARMS DISTRIBUTION CENTRE
Warehouse
OLD KENT ROAD
Lib.
St. Christopher's Ch.
English Martyrs Ch.
English Martyrs RC Prim. Sch.
Nursery Row Park
UAE Academy
Surgery
Surrey Square Primary Sch.
All Saint's Ch.
Surrey Square Park
Superstore
SOUTHERNWOOD RETAIL PARK
MANDELA WAY
B203
B204
B214
Walworth Academy (Upper Sch.)
Methodist Ch.
Fire Sta.
B215
St. Peter's C of E Prim. Sch.
Faraday Gdns.
Michael Faraday House

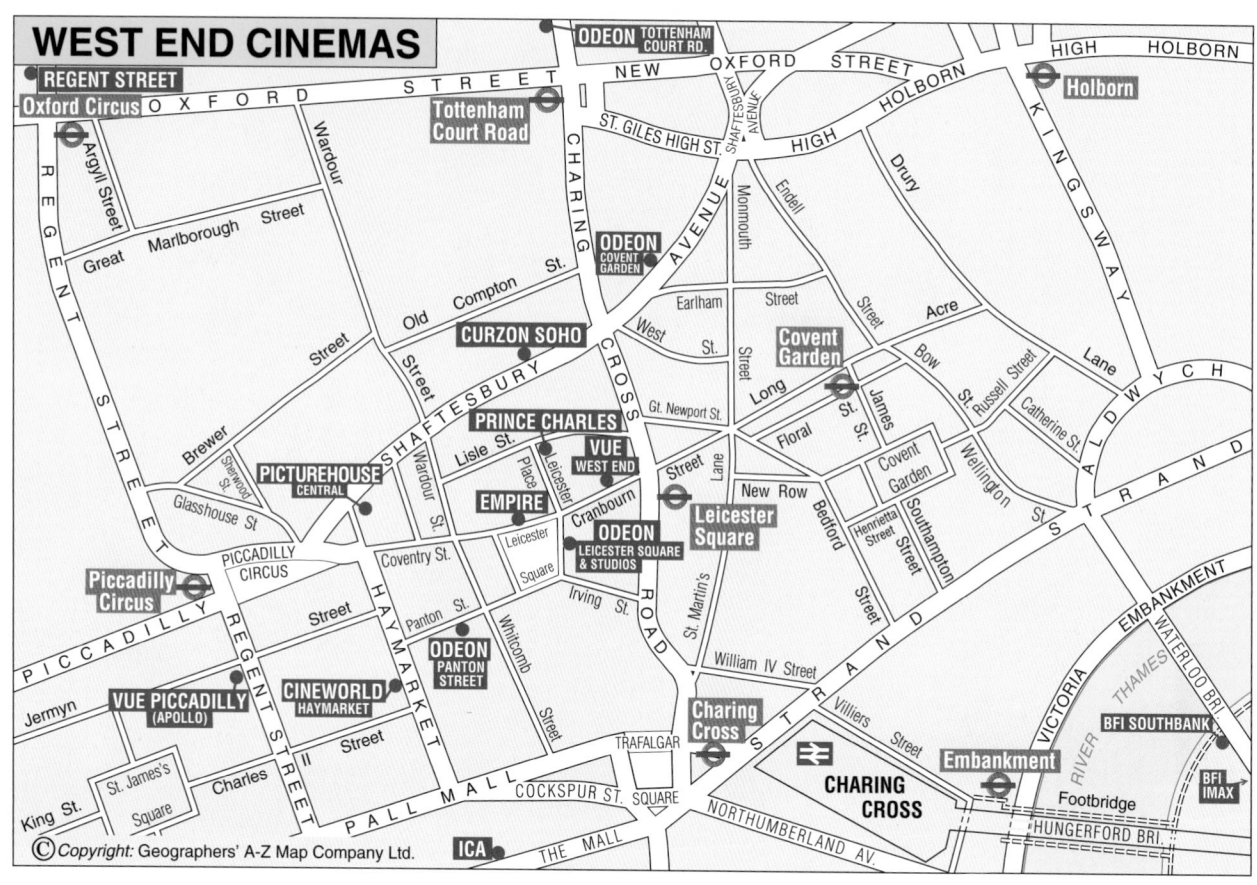

WEST END CINEMAS

REGENT STREET
Oxford Circus
OXFORD STREET
Argyll Street
Great Marlborough Street
Wardour Street
Brewer Street
Sherwood Street
Glasshouse St.
REGENT STREET
PICCADILLY CIRCUS
Piccadilly Circus
PICCADILLY
VUE PICCADILLY (APOLLO)
Jermyn
King St.
St. James's Square
Charles Street
CINEWORLD HAYMARKET
HAYMARKET
PALL MALL
ODEON TOTTENHAM COURT RD.
NEW OXFORD STREET
HIGH HOLBORN
Holborn
Tottenham Court Road
ST. GILES HIGH ST.
SHAFTESBURY AVENUE
HIGH HOLBORN
KINGSWAY
Drury
Monmouth
Endell Street
CHARING CROSS ROAD
ODEON COVENT GARDEN
Compton St.
Earlham Street
Acre
Bow
St. Russell Street
Lane
ALDWYCH
CURZON SOHO
Old Compton Street
Lisle St.
West St.
Covent Garden
Long
James St. St.
Catherine St.
PRINCE CHARLES
Gt. Newport St.
New Row
Covent Garden
Wellington St.
STRAND
VUE WEST END
Cranbourn
Floral
Bedford
Henrietta Street
Southampton Street
PICTUREHOUSE CENTRAL
EMPIRE
Leicester
ODEON LEICESTER SQUARE & STUDIOS
Leicester Square
Street
Coventry St.
Panton St.
Whitcomb Street
Irving St.
St. Martin's
William IV Street
Leicester Square
ODEON PANTON STREET
Charing Cross
STRAND
Villiers Street
EMBANKMENT
WATERLOO BRI.
VICTORIA
RIVER THAMES
BFI SOUTHBANK
Embankment
TRAFALGAR SQUARE
COCKSPUR ST.
CHARING CROSS
NORTHUMBERLAND AV.
Footbridge
HUNGERFORD BRI.
BFI IMAX
© Copyright: Geographers' A-Z Map Company Ltd.
ICA
THE MALL

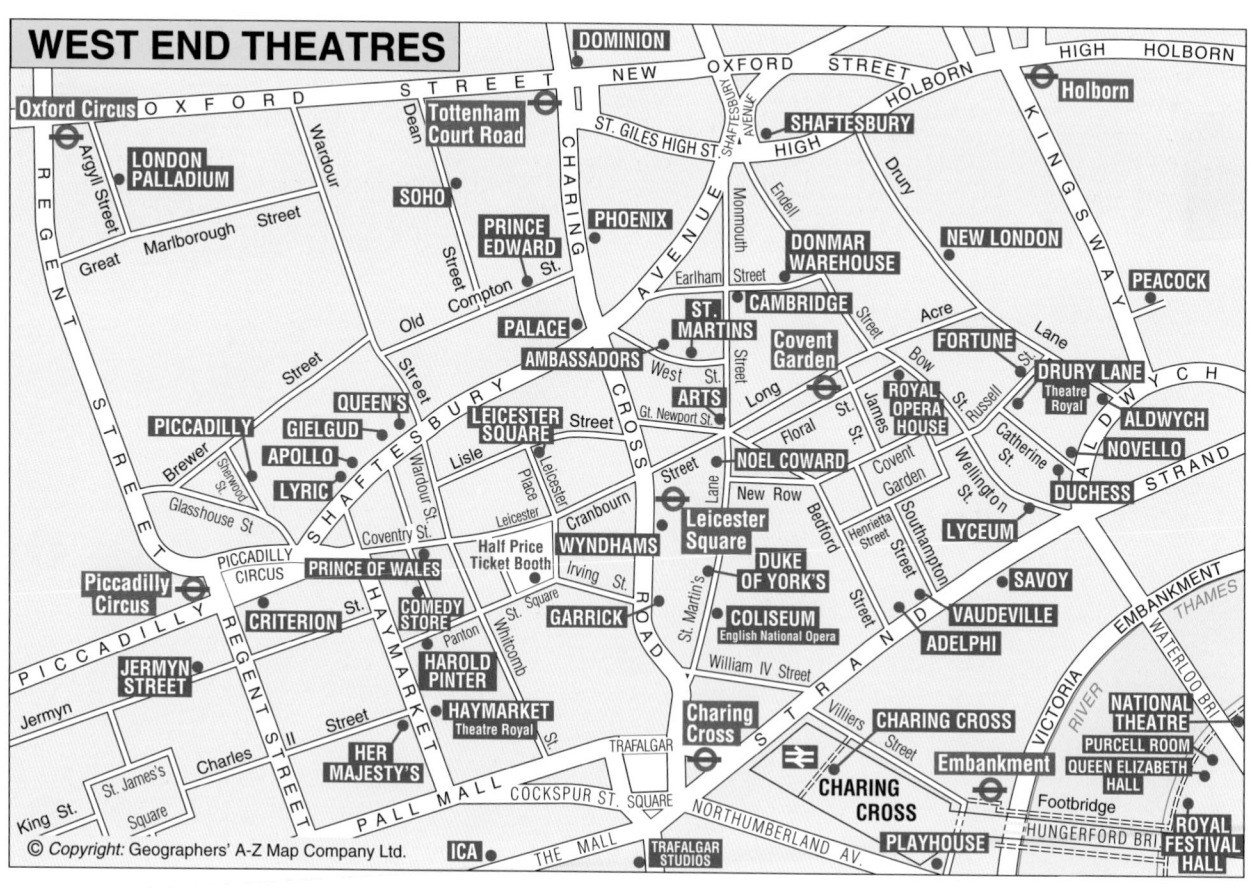

WEST END THEATRES

DOMINION
Oxford Circus
OXFORD STREET
Argyll Street
LONDON PALLADIUM
Great Marlborough Street
Wardour Street
Dean Street
Street
Old Compton Street
SOHO
PRINCE EDWARD
Compton St.
NEW OXFORD STREET
HIGH HOLBORN
SHAFTESBURY
Holborn
Tottenham Court Road
ST. GILES HIGH ST.
SHAFTESBURY AVENUE
HIGH HOLBORN
KINGSWAY
Drury
Monmouth
Endell Street
CHARING CROSS ROAD
PHOENIX
DONMAR WAREHOUSE
NEW LONDON
PEACOCK
Earlham Street
CAMBRIDGE
Acre
Lane
ST. MARTINS
FORTUNE
Bow
Russell St.
DRURY LANE
Theatre Royal
ALDWYCH
PALACE
AMBASSADORS
West St.
Covent Garden
Long
James St.
Catherine St.
NOVELLO
ARTS
Gt. Newport St.
ROYAL OPERA HOUSE
Floral
St. St.
Covent Garden
Wellington St.
DUCHESS
STRAND
QUEEN'S
GIELGUD
LEICESTER SQUARE
Street
NOEL COWARD
New Row
Bedford
Henrietta Street
Southampton Street
LYCEUM
PICCADILLY
APOLLO
Brewer
Sherwood Street
Lisle
Cranbourn
Leicester
LYRIC
Glasshouse St.
Coventry St.
Half Price Ticket Booth
WYNDHAMS
Leicester Square
DUKE OF YORK'S
SAVOY
Piccadilly Circus
PICCADILLY CIRCUS
PRINCE OF WALES
Panton St.
Whitcomb Street
Irving St.
St. Martin's
COLISEUM English National Opera
VAUDEVILLE
ADELPHI
REGENT STREET
COMEDY STORE
GARRICK
CRITERION
St.
William IV Street
EMBANKMENT
WATERLOO BRI.
VICTORIA
RIVER THAMES
JERMYN STREET
HAROLD PINTER
Charing Cross
CHARING CROSS
NATIONAL THEATRE
Jermyn
HAYMARKET Theatre Royal
Villiers Street
Street
Embankment
PURCELL ROOM
QUEEN ELIZABETH HALL
King St.
St. James's Square
Charles Street
HER MAJESTY'S
TRAFALGAR SQUARE
COCKSPUR ST.
CHARING CROSS
NORTHUMBERLAND AV.
Footbridge
HUNGERFORD BRI.
ROYAL FESTIVAL HALL
PALL MALL
© Copyright: Geographers' A-Z Map Company Ltd.
ICA
THE MALL
TRAFALGAR STUDIOS
PLAYHOUSE

ROAD MAPS

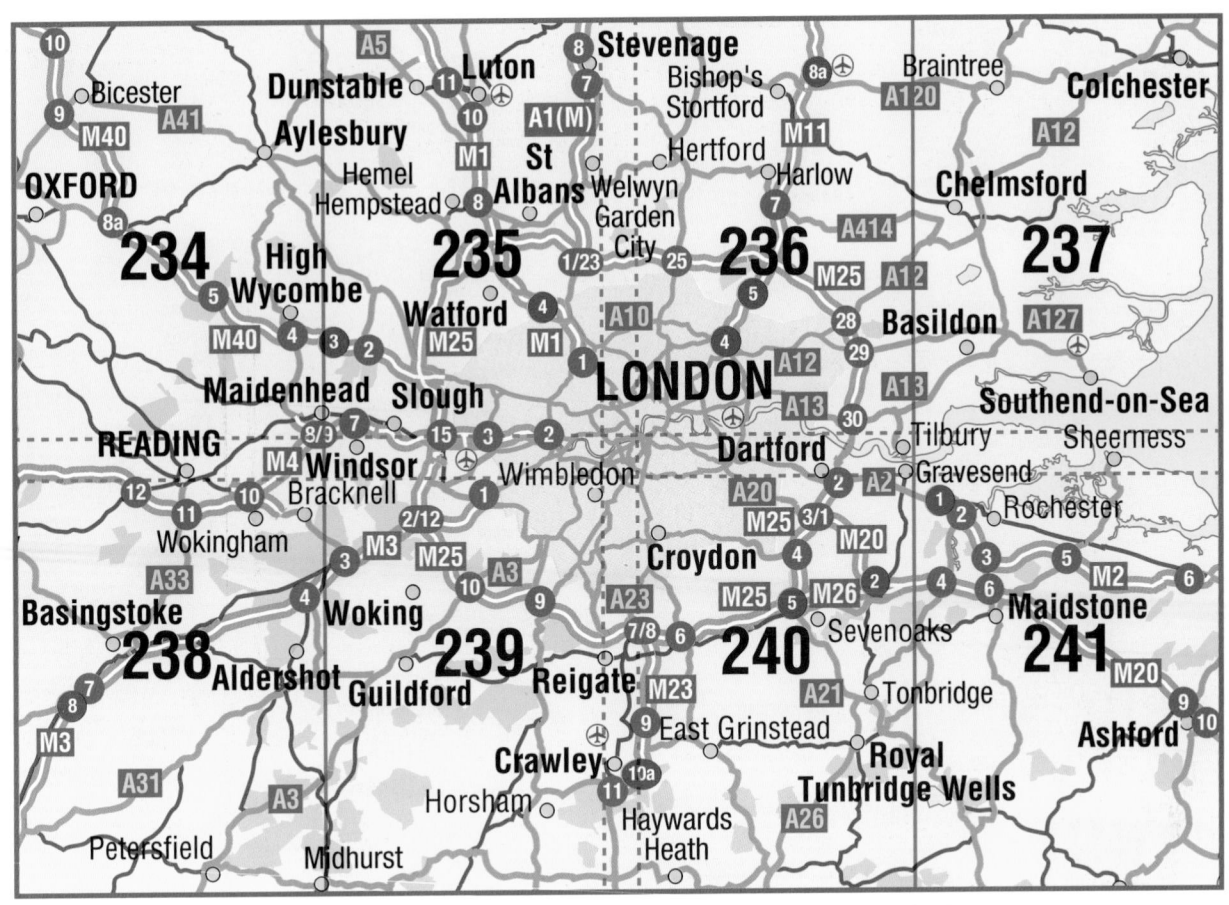

REFERENCE AND TOURIST INFORMATION

Motorway	≡M1≡	
Motorway Under Construction		
Motorway Proposed		
Motorway Junctions with Numbers	4	
Unlimited Interchange	4	
Limited Interchange	5	5
Motorway Service Area with access from one carriageway only	HESTON ≡S≡ / ≡S≡	
Major Road Service Area with 24 hour facilities	PEASE POTTAGE ≡S≡ / ≡S≡	
Major Road Junctions	Detailed 4	
	Other	
Primary Route	A12	
Primary Route Junction with Number	5	
Primary Route Destination	ENFIELD	

Dual Carriageways (A & B roads)		
Class A Road	A129	
Class B Road	B177	
Narrow Major Road (passing places)		
Major Roads Under Construction		
Major Roads Proposed		
Safety Cameras with Speed Limits Single Camera	30	
Multiple Cameras	50	
Single & Multiple Variable Speed Cameras	V / V	
Gradient 1:7 (14%) & steeper	» »	
Toll	Toll	
Dart Charge www.gov.uk/pay-dartford-crossing-charge	C	
Park & Ride	P+R	
Mileage between markers	8	

Airport	✈	
Airfield	+	
Heliport	Ⓗ	
Ferry (vehicular, sea) (vehicular, river) (foot only)		
Railway and Station		
Level Crossing and Tunnel		
River or Canal		
County or Unitary Authority Boundary		
Built-up Area		
Town, Village or Hamlet	o	
Wooded Area		
Spot Height in Feet	813 ·	
Relief above 400' (122m)		
National Grid Reference (kilometres)	600	
Page Continuation	234	

Abbey, Church, Friary, Priory	†	
Animal Collection		
Aquarium		
Arboretum, Botanical Garden	♣	
Aviary, Bird Garden		
Battle Site and Date	1066 ⚔	
Blue Flag Beach		
Bridge		
Castle (open to public)		
Castle with Garden (open to public)		
Cathedral	†	
Cidermaker		
Country Park	ᴪ	
Distillery		
Farm Park, Open Farm		
Fortress, Hill Fort	※	

Garden (open to public)	❊	
Golf Course	▷	
Historic Building (open to public)	⌂	
Historic Building with Garden (open to public)		
Horse Racecourse		
Industrial Monument	☼	
Leisure Park, Leisure Pool		
Lighthouse		
Mine, Cave		
Monument		
Motor Racing Circuit		
Museum, Art Gallery	M	
National Park		
National Trust Property		
Nature Reserve or Bird Sanctuary		

Nature Trail or Forest Walk		
Picnic Site		
Place of Interest	Craft Centre ·	
Prehistoric Monument		
Railway, Steam or Narrow Gauge		
Roman Remains		
Theme Park		
Tourist Information Centre (All year)	i	
(Summer season only)	i	
Viewpoint (360 degrees)		
(180 degrees)		
Vineyard		
Visitor Information Centre	V	
Wildlife Park		
Windmill		
Zoo or Safari Park		

SCALE 1:200,000

0 1 2 3 4 5 ... 10 miles
0 1 2 3 4 5 ... 10 ... 15 kilometres

Map Pages 234-241
3.156 miles to 1 inch
2kms to 1 cm

234
Fritwell
Baynard's Green
Hardwick
Hethe
Stoke Lyne
Fringford
A4421
Chetwode
Preston Bissett
Hillesden
Adstock
Addington
A413
B4033
Winslow
Mursley
Drayton Parslow
A4146
Fewcott
Ardley
CHERWELL VALLEY
Upper Heyford
Bainton
Stratton Audley
Twyford
Steeple Claydon
Claydon Brook
Middle Claydon
Shipton
Swanbourne
B4032
Stewkley Dean
Hollingdon
Soulbury
Bucknell
M40
Caversfield
Poundon
Grebe Lake
Claydon
East Claydon
Granborough
Hoggeston
Stewkley
B4030
Caulcott
Bicester
Charndon
Calvert
Botolph Claydon
Dunton
Littlecote
Burcot
Middleton Stoney
Woodfield
Bicester
Launton
Marsh Gibbon
Edgcott
North Marston
Cublington
A4095
Chesterton
A4421
Grendon Underwood
BUCKINGHAMSHIRE
Oving
Wing
A41
Kirtlington
Weston-on-the-Green
Wendlebury
Ambrosden
Blackthorn
Kingswood
Quainton
Pitchcott
Whitchurch
Aston Abbotts
A418
Crafton
Buckinghamshire Railway Centre
Hardwick
Wingrave
Bletchingdon
B4027
Merton
R. Ray
Lower Arncott
Ludgershall
Weedon
Rowsham
Hampton Poyle
Charlton-on-Otmoor
Fencott
Upper Arncott
Piddington
The Lake
Wotton House
Wotton Underwood
Westcott
Waddesdon
A413
Hulcott
A34
Murcott
Duck Decoy
Waddesdon Manor
A41
Watermead
Long Marston
Kidlington
Islip
Oddington
Boarstall
Brill
Ashendon
Upper Winchendon
Quarrendon
Bierton
Puttenham
Gosford
DANGER AREA
OT MOOR
Boarstall Tower
Little London
Dorton
AYLESBURY
County
Grand Union Canal
Wilstone
P+R
A4260
Noke
Horton-cum-Studley
Pollicott
Nether Winchendon
River Thame
A41
Buckland
OXFORD PEARTREE
Woodeaton
Beckley
B4027
M40
Oakley
B4011
Chilton
Nether Winchendon House
A418
Stone
Upton
Southcourt
Aston Clinton
A40
Sunnymead
Elsfield
Stanton St John
Easington
Chearsley
Cuddington
Gibraltar
Dinton
Bishopstone
B4443
A413
Weston Turville
RAF Halton
Marston
OXFORD
Forest Hill
Worminghall
Long Crendon
Courthouse
Aylesbury (Thame)
Westlington
Haddenham
Ford
Stoke Mandeville
Bucks Goat Centre
Halton
Parktown
Barton
Sandhills
Ickford
Shabbington
Tiggywinkles Wildlife Hospital
Aston Sandford
Kimble Wick
Marsh
North Lee
A4010
Nash Lee
Terrick
B4009
Wendover
Headington
P+R
A40
Holton
Waterperry
North Weston
Thame
A4129
Kingsey
Owlswick
Meadle
Little Kimble
Ellesborough
Coombe Hill Monument
A420
Light Infantry
Shotover
Wheatley
Waterstock
Draycot
A418
Towersey
Ilmer
Longwick
Askett
Great Kimble
Chequers
Dunsmore
Kingsash
Grandpont
A4142
Horspath
Tiddington
Rycote Chapel
Moreton
A329
Monks Risborough
Whiteleaf Cross
South Hinksey
P+R
Iffley
Cowley
OXFORD
Cuddesdon
Milton Common
A40
B4012
B4445
Skittle Green
Pitch Green
Princes Risborough
Little Hampden
Kennington
Littlemore
Garsington
Denton
Great Milton
Great Haseley
M40
Tetsworth
Sydenham
Emmington
Henton
Horsenden
Chinnor & Princes Risborough
Great Hampden
Hampden Monument
Bayworth
Sandford-on-Thames
Toot Baldon
B480
Little Milton
A329
Latchford
Kingston Stert
Chinnor
Bledlow
Saunderton
Loosley Row
Lacey Green
Prestwood
Bryant's Bottom
A34
A4074
Marsh Baldon
Little Haseley
Stoke Talmage
Adwell
Postcombe
Kingston Blount
Bledlow Cross
Saunderton Lee
Speen
Great Missenden
Radley
Nuneham Courtenay
Chiselhampton
R. Thame
B4015
Chalgrove
Aston Rowant
B4009
Horse Trust
A4010
Rout's Green
Great Kingshill
Northcourt
A4183
ABINGDON-ON-THAMES
Harcourt
Stadhampton
Chalgrove 1643
Easington
South Weston
Lewknor
A40
Radnage
Walter's Ash
Upper North Dean
A4128
County Hall
Clifton Hampden
B4015
Berinsfield
Drayton St Leonard
Chalgrove
Newington
B480
B4009
The City
Bledlow Ridge
Bradenham
Hughenden Valley
Widmer End
Naphill
Cryers Hill
Culham
A415
Burcot
Dorchester on Thames
A329
Brightwell Baldwin
Cuxham
Pyrton
Shirburn
Stokenchurch
West Wycombe
Downley
Hell-Fire Caves
Hughenden Manor
Appleford
Pendon
Little Wittenham
Abbey
Warborough
Berrick Salome
Watlington
Beacon's Bottom
Piddington
West Wycombe Park
Tylers Green
Sutton Courtenay
Long Wittenham
Christmas Common
White Mark
Ibstone
B482
M40
HIGH WYCOMBE
Wycombe Marsh
A4130
Shillingford
Rokemarsh
Roke
B4009
Britwell Salome
B480
Cadmore End
Railway
Benson
Ewelme
Greenfield
Northend
Turville Heath
Lane End
Booker
P+R
A40
Didcot
A4130
Slade End
Brightwell-cum-Sotwell
Benson
A4074
Cookley Green
Turville
Fingest
B4493
R. Thames
Castle
Crowmarsh Gifford
Pishill
Skirmett
Frieth
Handy Cross
Flackwell Heath
Northbourne
Coscote
East Hagbourne
North Moreton
Wallingford
A4130
Nuffield Place
B481
Park Corner
Russell's Water
Maidensgrove
Stonor
Stonor
Parmoor
Chisbridge Cross
A404
Marlow Bottom
A4155
West Hagbourne
South Moreton
Winterbrook
Cholsey & Wallingford Railway
Old Kiln
B480
Rockwell End
Lower Woodend
Pheasants Hill
B482
Bovingdon Green
Little Marlow
Upton
Blewbury
B4016
Aston Upthorpe
Cholsey
Nuffield
Nettlebed
Crocker End
Fawley
Middle Assendon
Marlow Common
MARLOW
Cookham Dean
Stanley Spencer
Aston Tirrold
A329
North Stoke
Ipsden
Highmoor
Bix
Lower Assendon
Hambleden
Mill End
A4155
Bisham
B4493
A417
Moulsford
B4009
Maharajah's Well
Witheridge Hill
Highmoor Cross
Shepherd's Green
Greys Court
Aston
Remenham
Medmenham
Hurley
Cookham Rise
A4074
South Stoke
Checkendon
Stoke Row
Satwell
HENLEY-ON-THAMES
A4130
A308
B4447
Streatley
Cleeve
Woodcote
Exlade Street
Wyfold
Rotherfield Peppard
Rotherfield Greys
Remenham Hill
Cockpole Green
Burchett's Green
Pinkneys Green
Compton
Goring
B4526
Gallowstree Common
Sonning Common
Harpsden
River & Rowing
Warren Row
MAIDENHEAD
Aldworth
Cray's Pond
The Herb Farm
Lower Shiplake
A321
Crazies Hill
A4
A34
A329
Beale Park
Whitchurch Hill
Goring Heath
Cane End
Kidmore End
B481
Binfield Heath
Wargrave
Knowl Hill
Littlewick Green
A404(M)
Lower Basildon
Whitchurch-on-Thames
A4074
Dunsden Green
Shiplake
B477
Hare Hatch
Kiln Green
White Waltham
Waltham Place
Woodlands Park
The Living Rainforest
Hampstead Norreys
Ashampstead
Quick's Green
Basildon Park
Pangbourne
Toll
Mapledurham
Mapledurham House
Caversham Heights
Tokers Green
Emmer Green
A4155
Sonning Eye
A4
Charvil
A3032
Ruscombe
St Lawrence
B3024
Maidenhead
Bothampstead
Upper Basildon
Purley on Thames
A329
Caversham
Play Hatch
B478
Twyford
West End
Paley Street
Touchen-end
Eling
Yattendon
Burnt Hill
Tidmarsh
A340
R. Thames
238
B3345
Sonning
Whistley Green
Shurlock Row
M4
Hawthorn Hill
A330
Oare
Hermitage
Frilsham
M4
Sulham
Tilehurst
READING
Berkshire Aviation
B3030
Hurst
A321
B3018
A3095
Wellhouse
Bradfield
Englefield
North Street
Woodley
Rural
Dinton
Warfield

235
CENTRAL BEDS
HERTFORDSHIRE
Toddington
Heath and Reach
Leighton Buzzard
Houghton Regis
DUNSTABLE
LUTON
HITCHIN
STEVENAGE
Stanbridge
Totternhoe
Eaton Bray
Edlesborough
Kensworth
Whipsnade
Studham
Markyate
Flamstead
Caddington
Harpenden
Wheathampstead
Redbourn
Ivinghoe
Tring
Wigginton
Aldbury
Little Gaddesden
Great Gaddesden
Berkhamsted
Northchurch
Potten End
HEMEL HEMPSTEAD
Kings Langley
Abbots Langley
Chiswell Green
ST ALBANS
London Colney
HATFIELD
WELWYN GARDEN CITY
Welwyn
Knebworth
Codicote
Kimpton
Great Offley
Lilley
Stopsley
Potters Bar
South Mimms
Brookmans Park
Chesham
Chesham Bois
Amersham
Bovingdon
Chipperfield
Sarratt
Chorleywood
WATFORD
Bushey
Radlett
Shenley
Borehamwood
Elstree
Barnet
East Barnet
Rickmansworth
Northwood
Harefield
Ruislip
Pinner
Harrow
Stanmore
Edgware
Finchley
Hendon
Kenton
Wembley
Northolt
Uxbridge
Hillingdon
Hayes
Southall
Greenford
Ealing
Acton
Willesden
Hampstead
LONDON
Camden Town
Marylebone
Paddington
Kensington
Westminster
Chelsea
Hammersmith
Chiswick
Fulham
Barnes
Battersea
Putney
Wandsworth
Clapham
Richmond
Twickenham
Isleworth
Hounslow
Brentford
Feltham
Heathrow
Harmondsworth
West Drayton
Yiewsley
Iver Heath
Denham
Gerrards Cross
Chalfont St Peter
Chalfont St Giles
Beaconsfield
Farnham Common
Stoke Poges
Burnham
Slough
Eton
Windsor
Datchet
Colnbrook
Staines
Wraysbury
Old Windsor
Cranbourne
Stanwell
239
236
M1
M25
M4
M40
A1(M)

236
Weston
Throcking
Buntingford
Great Hormead
Berden
Rickling Green
Quendon
Holder's Green
Luffenhall
Cromer
Cottered
A507
Aspenden
Hare Street
Little Hormead
Furneux Pelham
Stocking Pelham
Ugley
M11
Woodend Green
Monk Street
Henham
Ardeley
Westmill
Dassels
Hay Street
Mallows Green
Manuden
Ugley Green
Pledgdon Green
Broxted
Duton Hill
Walkern
Bassus Green
Cherry Green
Patmore Heath
Farnham Green
Stansted Mountfitchet
Elsenham
Molehill Green
Great Easton
STEVENAGE
A1155
Aston End
Clay End
Wood End
Braughing
Clapgate
Albury
Upwick Green
Farnham
Tye Green
Little Easton
Easton Lodge
Benington
Great Munden
Nasty
Shephall
Aston
Haultwick
Levens Green
Puckeridge
Standon
A10
A120
Burton End
LONDON STANSTED
Bamber's Green
B184
Green End
Hebing End
Wellpond Green
Little Hadham
BISHOP'S STORTFORD
Birchanger
Great Dunmow
Bragbury End
A602
HERTFORDSHIRE
Colliers End
Hadham Ford
Smith's Green
Takeley
Knebworth
Hook's Cross
Dane End
Standon Green End
Bromley
Bury Green
Start Hill
B1256
Takeley Street
Little Canfield
Latchford
Rhodes
BIRCHANGER GREEN
Bedlar's Green
Hatfield Forest
Datchworth
Sacombe
Barwick
Hopleys
Much Hadham
Thorley Street
Great Hallingbury
Puttock's End
Bacon End
Watton at Stone
High Cross
Forge
Thorley
Little Hallingbury
Great Canfield
Woolmer Green
Bull's Green
Wadesmill
Tonwell
Hadham Cross
Perry Green
Green Tye
Spellbrook
Wright's Green
Hatfield Broad Oak
Taverners Green
Bishop's Green
Burnham Green
Stapleford
A119
Chapmore End
Thundridge
Babbs Green
High Roding
Harmer Green
Bramfield
Wareside
Widford
Allen's Green
A1184
Hatfield Heath
Digswell
Tewin
Waterford
WARE
Sawbridgeworth
THE RODINGS
Roundbush Green
Leaden Roding
High Easter
Hunsdon
High Wych
Sheering
A1060
HERTFORD
WELWYN GARDEN CITY
A414
Great Amwell
Hunsdonbury
Pye Corner
Gibberd
M11
White Roding
Good Easter
Hatfield Hyde
Cole Green
Hertingfordbury
Hertford Heath
Stanstead Abbotts
Eastwick
Matching
Nether Street
Margaret Roding
St Margarets
HARLOW
Matching Green
Abbess Roding
Letty Green
Hailey
Roydon
Mark Hall
Matching Tye
Chalk End
Church Langley
Beauchamp Roding
A1025
Hare Street
Rye House Gatehouse
Essendon
Little Berkhamsted
Bayford
HODDESDON
A1170
Great Parndon
Potter Street
Foster Street
High Laver
Little Laver
Birds Green
Shellow Bowells
Broxbourne Wood
Lowewood
Hatfield House
West End
Broxbourne
Roydon Hamlet
A1169
Magdalen Laver
Moreton
Fyfield
Woodside
Redwings
Hastingwood
Epping Green
Lower Nazeing
Nazeing
Broadley Common
B1393
A414
Willingale
A1000
Paradise
Newgate Street
Hammond Street
Wormley
Bumble's Green
Epping Green
Tyler's Green
Bovinger
Bobbingworth
Norton Mandeville
Norton Heath
Brookmans Park
Great Wood
Turnford
Holyfield Hall Farm
Epping Upland
Thornwood Common
North Weald Airfield
North Weald Bassett
High Ongar
Loves Green
Cuffley
Goff's Oak
Hayes Hill Farm
Holyfield
Lee Valley Pk.
Coopersale
Greensted Green
Epping Ongar Railway
POTTERS BAR
Northaw
B156
CHESHUNT
Gunpowder Mills
Harold's Bridge
Waltham Cross
EPPING
Coopersale Street
Toot Hill
Saxon Wooden Church
Chipping Ongar
Nine Ashes
Elkins Green
Beggar Hill
Upshire
Epping Forest
Tunnel
Fiddlers Hamlet
Stanford Rivers
A113
Stondon Massey
Blackmore
M25
Crews Hill
Capel Manor
WALTHAM ABBEY
Copthall Green
Theydon Bois
Little End
A128
Fryerning
Bentley Heath
A111
Transport
Enfield Wash
A121
Sewardstone
Stapleford Tawney
Wyatt's Green
Botany Bay
Forty Hill
A1055
A104
Hobbs Cross
Secret Nuclear Bunker
Fox Hatch
Doddinghurst
Monken Hadley
Hadley Wood
Trent Park
ENFIELD
A1010
High Beech
Epping Forest
Debden Green
A113
Kelvedon Hatch
Mountnessing
Cockfosters
A110
A112
Stapleford Abridge
Passingford Bridge
Navestock
Crow Green
A12
Winchmore Hill
A105
LOUGHTON
Queen's Lodge
Navestock Side
Pilgrims Hatch
EAST BARNET
Ponders End
Buckhurst Hill
CHIGWELL
Lambourne End
Stapleford Abbotts
Old MacDonald's Farm
Hutton
SOUTHGATE
Whetstone
A598
FRIERN BARNET
A406
EDMONTON
CHINGFORD
Grange Hill
A1112
Hainault Forest
Chigwell Row
Noak Hill
Weald
South Weald
Shenfield
A129
BRENTWOOD
Woodford Green
Havering
Havering-Atte-Bower
Harold Hill
Brook Street
A128
Ingrave
Bruce Castle
TOTTENHAM
Hainault
A123
Great Warley
Thorndon
Herongate
Muswell Hill
WOOD GREEN
HORNSEY
Vestry
A503
WOODFORD
A1400
Gants Hill
Barkingside
Collier Row
Gidea Park
Harold Wood
Little Warley
WALTHAMSTOW
A127
Cranham
West Horndon
Golders Green
Highgate
Beam
LEYTON
WANSTEAD
Chadwell Heath
ROMFORD
Nostalgia
Kenwood
STOKE NEWINGTON
A118
Goodmayes
A124
UPMINSTER
LONDON
Leytonstone
Manor Park
Eastbrookend
HORNCHURCH
Thames Chase
North Ockendon
Bulphan
A400
HAMPSTEAD
ISLINGTON
HACKNEY
Olympic Park
ILFORD
Valence
Becontree
Elm Park
STRATFORD
A124
A1240
A125
A5
A41
CAMDEN TOWN
FINSBURY
BETHNAL GREEN
BARKING
DAGENHAM
South Hornchurch
Belhus Woods
MARYLEBONE
SHOREDITCH
Holborn
WEST HAM
EAST HAM
Eastbury Ho.
Creekmouth
A1306
Rainham
South Ockendon
Orsett
PADDINGTON
WEST END
CITY
STEPNEY
POPLAR
A13
A1020
Beckton
Wennington
B1335
North Stifford
Baker Street
KENSINGTON
Hyde Park
Blackwall Tunnel
LONDON CITY
Thamesmead
A2016
A13
Aveley
THURROCK
Little Thurrock
WESTMINSTER
LAMBETH
BERMONDSEY
A102
Barrier
Abbey Wood
Belvedere
Thames
A1090
Chafford Hundred
CHELSEA
DEPTFORD
GREENWICH
Charlton
WOOLWICH
ERITH
Purfleet
South Stifford
CAMBERWELL
A23
Plumstead
A206
Slade Green
Dartford-Thurrock River Crossing
Dart Charge
West Thurrock
GRAYS
BATTERSEA
Blackheath
Kidbrooke
A207
A209
Welling
Bexleyheath
A282
A1089
CLAPHAM
BRIXTON
LEWISHAM
A20
Lee
Danson Pk.
Red Ho.
Crayford
DARTFORD
Greenhithe
Northfleet
WANDSWORTH
Horniman
A205
ELTHAM
Blackfen
Bexley
Hall Place
Stone
A226
Swanscombe
Ebbsfleet
A218
STREATHAM
Dulwich
CATFORD
A21
Mottingham
New Eltham
A211
SIDCUP
Old Bexley
Bluewater
240
235

237
COLCHESTER
CHELMSFORD
BRAINTREE
WITHAM
MALDON
BILLERICAY
BASILDON
RAYLEIGH
SOUTHEND-ON-SEA
SHEERNESS
GRAVESEND
Halstead
Gosfield
Greenstead Green
Earls Colne
White Colne
Wakes Colne
Chappel
Hemp's Green
West Bergholt
Fordham
Fordham Heath
Ardleigh
Shalford
Shalford Church End
Great Bardfield Cottage
Bardfield Saling
Beazley End
Bocking Churchstreet
High Garrett
Panfield
Great Saling
Stebbing Green
Rayne
Felsted
Coggeshall
Stisted
Pattiswick
Bradwell
Stockstreet
Feering
Kelvedon
Marks Tey
Great Tey
Eight Ash Green
Stanway
Copford
Copford Green
Wivenhoe
Rowhedge
Fingringhoe
Layer-de-la-Haye
Abberton
Abberton Resr.
Peldon
MERSEA ISLAND
West Mersea
Virley Channel
Tollesbury
Tolleshunt D'Arcy
Tolleshunt Major
Tolleshunt Knights
Tiptree
Great Totham North
Great Totham South
Goldhanger
Heybridge
Heybridge Basin
Osea Island
RIVER BLACKWATER
Northey Island
Bradwell-on-Sea
Bradwell Waterside
Sales Point
St Peter's Chapel
Tillingham
St Lawrence
Steeple
Mayland
Maylandsea
Asheldham
Dengie
Southminster
Burnham-on-Crouch
Holliwell Point
Foulness Point
FOULNESS ISLAND
Wallasea Island
Potton Island
Maplin Sands
Great Wakering
Shoeburyness
SHOEBURY NESS
Rochford
Hockley
Ashingdon
Hullbridge
Thundersley
Hadleigh
Leigh-on-Sea
Westcliff-on-Sea
CANVEY ISLAND
Corringham
Stanford-le-Hope
Thames
Great Baddow
Danbury
Galleywood
Margaretting
Stock
Wickford
Laindon
South Woodham Ferrers
North Fambridge
Isle of Grain
Thamesport
Minster
Queenborough
Cliffe
High Halstow
Allhallows-on-Sea
Warden Point
Blythe Sands
Coryton
MEDWAY

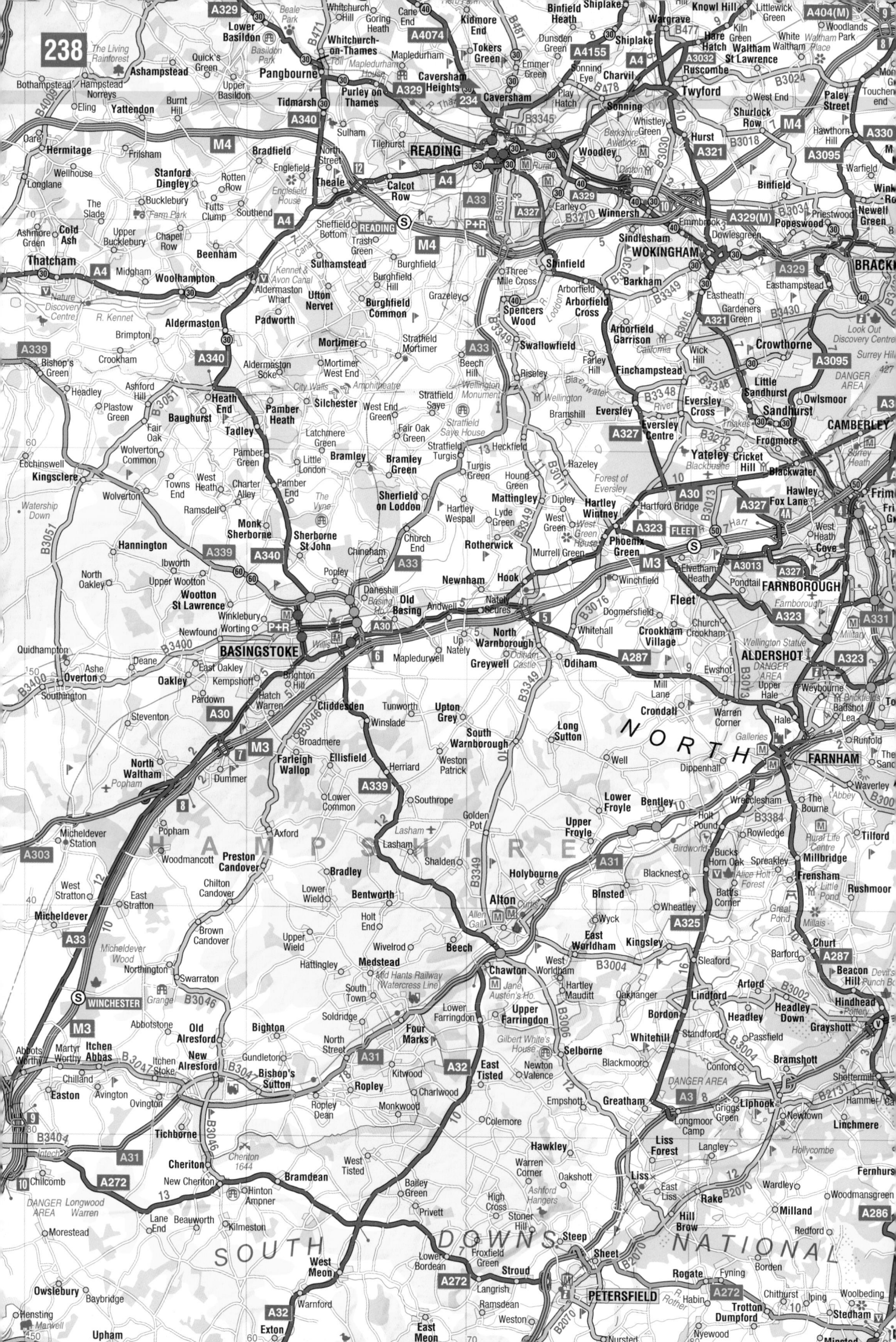

238
The Living Rainforest
Ashampstead
Bothampstead
Hampstead Norreys
Eling
Yattendon
Burnt Hill
Quick's Green
Upper Basildon
Lower Basildon
Basildon Park
Beale Park
Pangbourne
Whitchurch
Whitchurch Hill
Whitchurch-on-Thames
Goring Heath
Cane End
Kidmore End
Tokers Green
Mapledurham
Mapledurham House
Purley on Thames
Caversham Heights
Caversham
Tidmarsh
Sulham
Tilehurst
READING
Binfield Heath
Shiplake
Dunsden Green
Emmer Green
Sonning Eye
Charvil
Play Hatch
Sonning
Wargrave
Knowl Hill
Hare Hatch
Kiln Green
Littlewick Green
Woodlands Park
White Waltham
Waltham St Lawrence
Ruscombe
Twyford
West End
Shurlock Row
Paley Street
Touchen end
Hawthorn Hill
Whistley Green
Berkshire Aviation
Woodley
Dinton
Hurst
Warfield
Binfield
Hermitage
Oare
Frilsham
Wellhouse
Longlane
Bradfield
Englefield
Englefield House
North Street
Theale
Calcot Row
Stanford Dingley
Rotten Row
Bucklebury
Tutts Clump
Southend
Farm Park
The Slade
Cold Ash
Ashmore Green
Upper Bucklebury
Chapel Row
Beenham
Thatcham
Midgham
Woolhampton
Nature Discovery Centre
R. Kennet
Kennet & Avon Canal
Aldermaston Wharf
Sheffield Bottom
Trash Green
Sulhamstead
Burghfield
Burghfield Hill
Burghfield Common
Ufton Nervet
Grazeley
Padworth
Aldermaston
Brimpton
Crookham
Three Mile Cross
Shinfield
Spencers Wood
Arborfield
Arborfield Cross
Earley
Winnersh
Sindlesham
WOKINGHAM
Emmbrook
Dowlesgreen
Barkham
Eastheath
Gardeners Green
Easthampstead
Priestwood
Popeswood
Newell Green
BRACK
Look Out Discovery Centre
Surrey Hill
Crowthorne
Arborfield Garrison
California
Finchampstead
Wick Hill
Little Sandhurst
Sandhurst
Owlsmoor
CAMBERLEY
Mortimer
Stratfield Mortimer
Mortimer West End
Aldermaston Soke
Beech Hill
Wellington Monument
Swallowfield
Farley Hill
Riseley
Wellington
Blackwater
Bramshill
Eversley
Eversley Cross
Eversley Centre
Yateley
Cricket Hill
Blackbushe
Frogmore
Blackwater
Bishop's Green
Headley
Ashford Hill
Plastow Green
Heath End
Baughurst
Tadley
Pamber Heath
Silchester
City Walls
Amphitheatre
West End Green
Stratfield Saye
Stratfield Saye House
Fair Oak Green
Latchmere Green
Little London
Bramley
Bramley Green
Stratfield Turgis
Turgis Green
Heckfield
Hazeley
Forest of Eversley
Hound Green
Mattingley
Ecchinswell
Kingsclere
Wolverton
Wolverton Common
Fair Oak
Pamber Green
Pamber End
Towns End
West Heath
Charter Alley
Ramsdell
The Vyne
Sherfield on Loddon
Hartley Wespall
Lyde Green
Dipley
Hartley Wintney
West Green
West Green House
Hartford Bridge
Hawley
Fox Lane
Watership Down
Hannington
Monk Sherborne
Sherborne St John
Chineham
Church End
Rotherwick
Murrell Green
Phoenix Green
FLEET
Hart
West Heath
Cove
North Oakley
Ibworth
Upper Wootton
Wootton St Lawrence
Popley
Daneshill
Basing Ho.
Old Basing
Newnham
Hook
Winchfield
Elvetham Heath
Pondtail
FARNBOROUGH
Farnborough
Winklebury
Worting
Newfound
BASINGSTOKE
Andwell
Nately Scures
Up Nately
North Warnborough
Odiham Castle
Greywell
Mapledurwell
Dogmersfield
Whitehall
Odiham
Crookham Village
Church Crookham
Fleet
Wellington Statue
ALDERSHOT
Quidhampton
Ashe
Overton
Southington
Deane
East Oakley
Oakley
Kempshott
Pardown
Brighton Hill
Hatch Warren
Cliddesden
Tunworth
Winslade
Upton Grey
South Warnborough
Long Sutton
Mill Lane
Crondall
Ewshot
Warren Corner
Upper Hale
Weybourne
Badshot Lea
Hale
Galleries
Steventon
Broadmere
Farleigh Wallop
Ellisfield
Herriard
Weston Patrick
Well
Dippenhall
FARNHAM
Runfold
Waverley Abbey
North Waltham
Dummer
Popham
Lower Common
Southrope
Golden Pot
Lower Froyle
Bentley
Wrecclesham
The Bourne
Holt Pound
Rowledge
Tilford
Micheldever Station
Woodmancott
Axford
Lasham
Upper Froyle
Birdworld
Bucks Horn Oak
Spreakley
Millbridge
Rural Life Centre
HAMPSHIRE
Preston Candover
Shalden
Holybourne
Blacknest
Alice Holt Forest
Frensham
Rushmoor
Little Pond
West Stratton
East Stratton
Chilton Candover
Bradley
Lower Wield
Bentworth
Alton
Curtis
Allen Gall.
Binsted
Wheatley
Batt's Corner
Great Pond
Millais
Micheldever
Brown Candover
Holt End
Upper Wield
Wivelrod
Beech
Wyck
East Worldham
Kingsley
Churt
Micheldever Wood
Northington
Hattingley
Medstead
Chawton
West Worldham
Sleaford
Barford
Beacon Hill
Devil's Punch Bowl
Swarraton
Grange
Mid Hants Railway (Watercress Line)
South Town
Jane Austen's Ho.
Hartley Mauditt
Oakhanger
Lindford
Arford
Headley
Headley Down
Hindhead
Grayshott
WINCHESTER
Abbotstone
Soldridge
Lower Farringdon
Upper Farringdon
Bordon
Passfield
Standford
Old Alresford
Bighton
North Street
Four Marks
Gilbert White's House
Whitehill
Bramshott
Abbots Worthy
Martyr Worthy
Itchen Abbas
Itchen Stoke
New Alresford
Gundleton
Bishop's Sutton
Kitwood
East Tisted
Newton Valence
Selborne
Blackmoor
Conford
Shottermill
Chilland
Avington
Easton
Ovington
Ropley
Charlwood
Ropley Dean
Monkwood
Empshott
Greatham
DANGER AREA
Liphook
Griggs Green
Newtown
Hammer
Tichborne
Colemore
Longmoor Camp
Linchmere
Intech
Cheriton
Cheriton 1644
West Tisted
Hawkley
Warren Corner
Liss Forest
Langley
Hollycombe
Chilcomb
New Cheriton
Bramdean
Oakshott
Liss
Fernhurst
Hinton Ampner
Bailey Green
High Cross
Ashford Hangers
East Liss
Rake
Wardley
Woodmansgreen
Longwood Warren
Lane End
Beauworth
Privett
Stoner Hill
Milland
Morestead
Kilmeston
Hill Brow
Redford
SOUTH DOWNS NATIONAL
Steep
Sheet
West Meon
Lower Bordean
Froxfield Green
Stroud
Rogate
Fyning
Borden
Owslebury
Baybridge
Langrish
PETERSFIELD
Habin
R. Rother
Chithurst
Iping
Woolbeding
Trotton
Dumpford
Stedham
Hensting
Marwell
Warnford
Ramsdean
Weston
Nyewood
Upham
Exton
East Meon
Nursted
Minsted
M4
M3
A329
A4074
B471
B481
A4155
A4
A3032
B477
A404(M)
B3024
B4009
A340
B3345
B478
B3030
B3018
A321
A330
A3095
A33
B3031
A327
A329(M)
B3034
B3349
B3030
B3016
A3095
B3430
A339
B3051
B3348
B3272
A30
B3013
A323
A3013
A327
A331
B3011
B3016
A287
B3400
B3046
B3349
A303
A31
B3384
A325
B3004
B3006
B3002
A32
B3047
B3404
A272
A3
B2131
B2070
A286

239
WINDSOR
Eton
SOUTHALL
HESTON
Brentford
CHISWICK
HAMMERSMITH
FULHAM
CHELSEA
BATTERSEA
ISLEWORTH
RICHMOND
PUTNEY
WANDSWORTH
CLAPHAM
HOUNSLOW
FELTHAM
TWICKENHAM
WIMBLEDON
STREATHAM
WINDSOR GREAT PARK
EGHAM
ASHFORD
STAINES-UPON-THAMES
TEDDINGTON
MERTON
MITCHAM
KINGSTON UPON THAMES
NEW MALDEN
MORDEN
SUNBURY
Shepperton
CHERTSEY
WALTON-ON-THAMES
SURBITON
CARSHALTON
WEYBRIDGE
ESHER
SUTTON
WALLINGTON
EWELL
EPSOM
Addlestone
Woodham
Byfleet
Cobham
BANSTEAD
WOKING
LEATHERHEAD
Ashtead
Fetcham
Great Bookham
GUILDFORD
DORKING
REIGATE
REDHILL
HORLEY
GODALMING
Cranleigh
CRAWLEY
HORSHAM
Haslemere
Billingshurst
Petworth
NORTH DOWNS
SURREY
WEST SUSSEX
ST LEONARDS FOREST
LONDON HEATHROW
LONDON GATWICK

Kent map — Medway Towns, Maidstone, Ashford, Sheppey and Romney Marsh area.

Towns and places: GRAVESEND, STROOD, ROCHESTER, CHATHAM, GILLINGHAM, Rainham, Sittingbourne, Faversham, SHEERNESS, Queenborough, Minster, Eastchurch, Leysdown-on-Sea, Warden, Grain, Allhallows, Cliffe, High Halstow, Lower Stoke, Stoke, Snodland, Halling, Aylesford, Larkfield, West Malling, MAIDSTONE, Bearsted, Leeds, Harrietsham, Lenham, Charing, Westwell, ASHFORD, Sevington, Kingsnorth, Mersham, Wye, Sheldwich, Doddington, Newnham, Teynham, Ospringe, Boughton Lees, Challock, Paddock, Hothfield, Pluckley, Egerton, Headcorn, Staplehurst, Marden, Paddock Wood, Brenchley, Horsmonden, Goudhurst, Cranbrook, Sissinghurst, Biddenden, Tenterden, High Halden, Woodchurch, Appledore, Hamstreet, Brookland, Newchurch, Lydd, Rye, Peasmarsh, Northiam, Bodiam, Robertsbridge, Ticehurst, Hawkhurst, Flimwell, Hurst Green, Etchingham, Burwash.

Regions: ISLE OF SHEPPEY, Isle of Harty, Elmley Island, Isle of Grain, NORTH DOWNS, THE WEALD, LOW WEALD, ROMNEY MARSH, WALLAND MARSH, SUSSEX.

Rivers/water: R. Medway, R. Swale, River Beult, River Rother, Bewl Water.

Roads: M2, M20, A2, A20, A21, A26, A28, A226, A228, A229, A249, A250, A251, A252, A259, A262, A268, A274, A278, A289, A299, A2070, A2500, B2004, B2067, B2080, B2099, B2165, B2231.

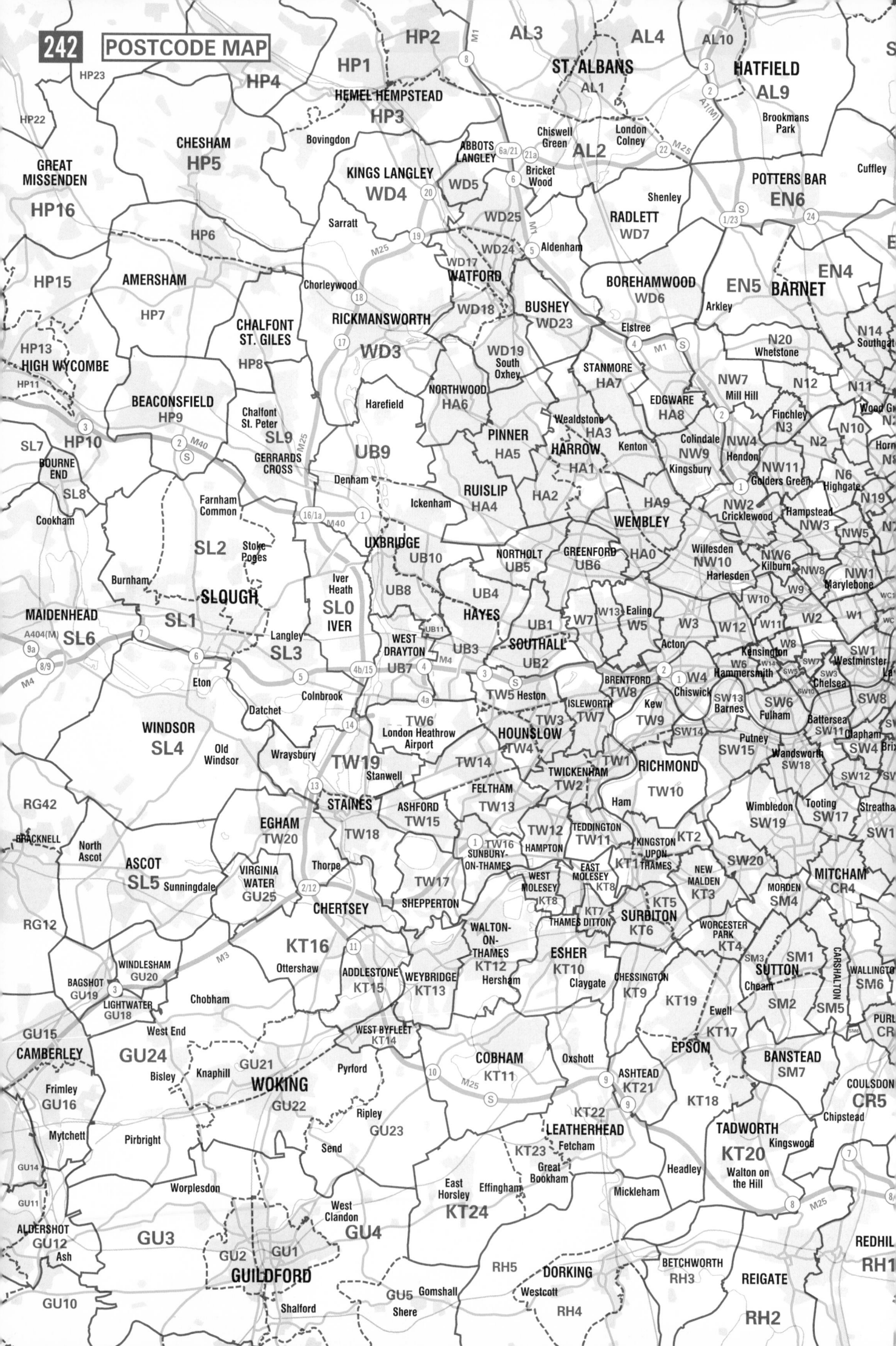

HP2
HP1
AL3
AL4
AL10
HATFIELD
AL9
ST. ALBANS
AL1
HP23
HP4
HEMEL HEMPSTEAD
HP3
HP22
CHESHAM
HP5
Bovingdon
ABBOTS LANGLEY
Chiswell Green
London Colney
AL2
Brookmans Park
GREAT MISSENDEN
HP16
KINGS LANGLEY
WD4
WD5
Bricket Wood
POTTERS BAR
EN6
Cuffley
Shenley
RADLETT
WD7
HP6
Sarratt
WD25
WD24
Aldenham
HP15
AMERSHAM
WD17
WATFORD
BOREHAMWOOD
WD6
EN5
BARNET
EN4
Chorleywood
HP7
CHALFONT ST. GILES
RICKMANSWORTH
WD3
WD18
BUSHEY
WD23
Arkley
Elstree
N20
Whetstone
N14
Southgate
HP13
HIGH WYCOMBE
HP8
WD19
South Oxhey
STANMORE
HA7
NW7
Mill Hill
N12
N11
HP11
BEACONSFIELD
HP9
Chalfont St. Peter
SL9
Harefield
NORTHWOOD
HA6
EDGWARE
HA8
Finchley
N3
Wood Green
N10
HP10
SL7
BOURNE END
SL8
GERRARDS CROSS
UB9
PINNER
HA5
Wealdstone
HA3
HARROW
HA1
Kenton
Colindale
NW9
NW4
Hendon
N2
Kingsbury
NW11
Golders Green
N6
Highgate
Denham
Farnham Common
Cookham
Ickenham
RUISLIP
HA4
HA2
HA9
WEMBLEY
NW2
Cricklewood
Hampstead
NW3
N19
NW5
SL2
Stoke Poges
UXBRIDGE
UB10
NORTHOLT
UB5
GREENFORD
UB6
HA0
Willesden
NW10
NW6
Kilburn
NW8
NW1
Marylebone
Burnham
SLOUGH
Iver Heath
SL0
IVER
UB8
UB4
HAYES
Harlesden
MAIDENHEAD
SL1
SL6
A404(M)
Langley
SL3
UB11
WEST DRAYTON
UB7
UB3
SOUTHALL
UB1
UB2
W7
W13
Ealing
W5
W3
W10
W9
W12
W11
W2
W1
Acton
Kensington
W8
SW1
Westminster
Eton
Colnbrook
Datchet
TW5
Heston
BRENTFORD
TW8
W4
Chiswick
W6
Hammersmith
SW7
SW5
SW3
Chelsea
SW10
SW8
ISLEWORTH
TW7
TW6
London Heathrow Airport
TW3
HOUNSLOW
TW4
Kew
TW9
SW13
Barnes
SW6
Fulham
Battersea
SW11
Clapham
WINDSOR
SL4
Old Windsor
Wraysbury
TW19
Stanwell
TW14
TW1
RICHMOND
SW14
Putney
SW15
Wandsworth
SW18
SW4
TWICKENHAM
TW2
FELTHAM
TW13
Ham
TW10
SW12
RG42
STAINES
ASHFORD
TW15
EGHAM
TW20
TW18
TW12
HAMPTON
TEDDINGTON
TW11
Wimbledon
SW19
Tooting
SW17
Streatham
BRACKNELL
North Ascot
TW16
SUNBURY-ON-THAMES
KINGSTON UPON THAMES
KT2
KT1
SW20
ASCOT
SL5
Sunningdale
VIRGINIA WATER
GU25
Thorpe
TW17
SHEPPERTON
WEST MOLESEY
KT8
EAST MOLESEY
NEW MALDEN
KT3
MITCHAM
CR4
MORDEN
SM4
CHERTSEY
KT7
THAMES DITTON
KT5
SURBITON
KT6
RG12
KT16
WALTON-ON-THAMES
KT12
Hersham
ESHER
KT10
Claygate
WORCESTER PARK
KT4
SM3
SM1
SUTTON
Cheam
SM2
CARSHALTON
SM5
WALLINGTON
SM6
WINDLESHAM
GU20
BAGSHOT
GU19
LIGHTWATER
GU18
Ottershaw
ADDLESTONE
KT15
WEYBRIDGE
KT13
CHESSINGTON
KT9
KT19
Ewell
Chobham
West End
GU15
CAMBERLEY
GU24
WEST BYFLEET
KT14
EPSOM
KT17
COBHAM
KT11
Oxshott
BANSTEAD
SM7
GU21
Knaphill
Bisley
Pyrford
WOKING
GU22
ASHTEAD
KT21
KT18
COULSDON
CR5
Frimley
GU16
Ripley
GU23
KT22
LEATHERHEAD
Chipstead
TADWORTH
KT20
Kingswood
Mytchett
Pirbright
Send
KT23
Fetcham
Great Bookham
Headley
Walton on the Hill
GU14
Worplesdon
East Horsley
Effingham
Mickleham
GU11
West Clandon
KT24
ALDERSHOT
GU12
Ash
GU3
GU2
GU1
GU4
GUILDFORD
RH5
DORKING
Westcott
BETCHWORTH
RH3
REIGATE
REDHILL
RH1
GU10
GU5
Gomshall
Shere
Shalford
RH4
RH2
M1
M25
M40
M4
M3
A1(M)

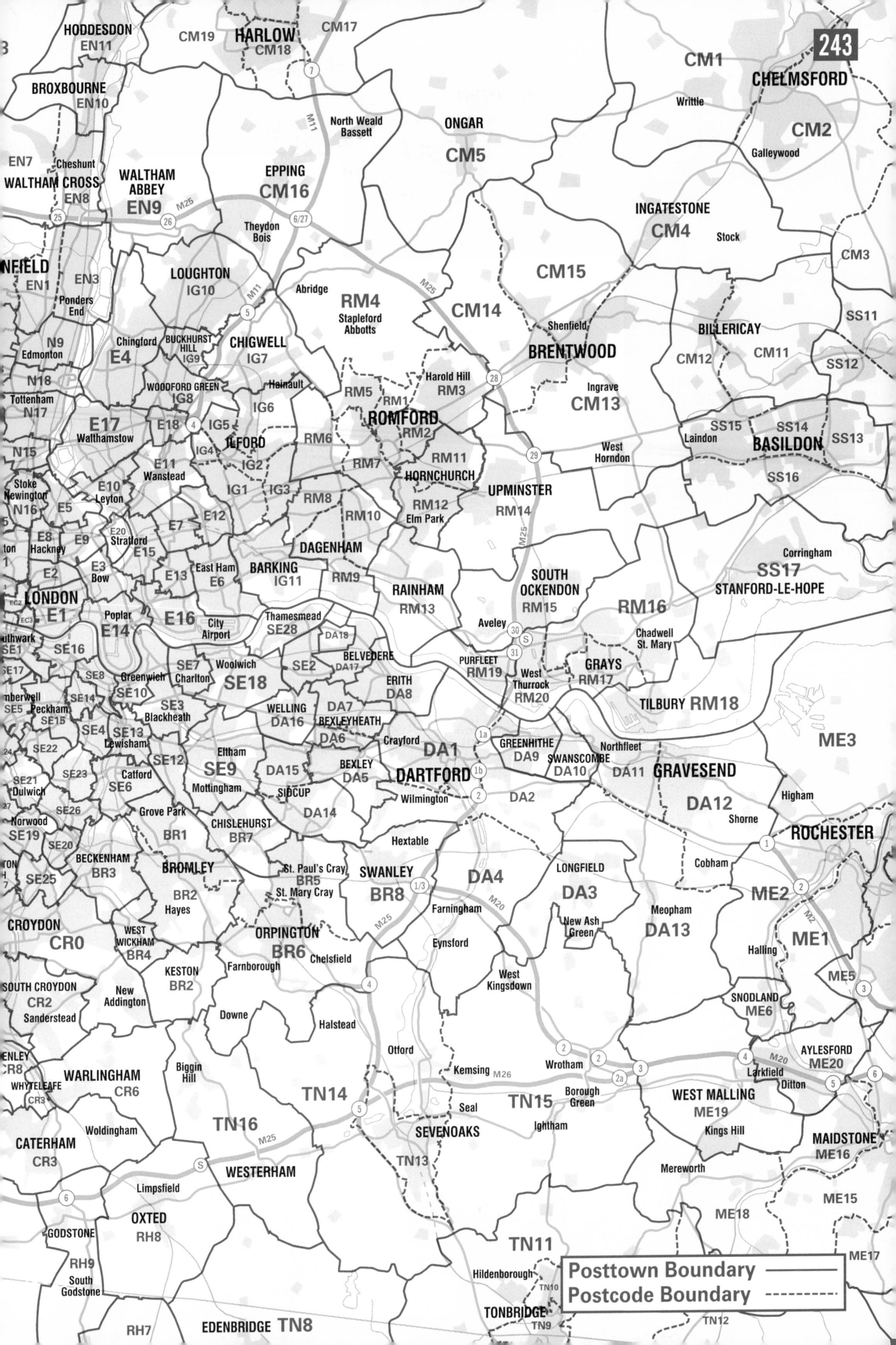
HODDESDON
EN11
CM19
HARLOW
CM18
CM17
CM1
CHELMSFORD
BROXBOURNE
EN10
Writtle
North Weald
Bassett
ONGAR
CM5
CM2
Galleywood
EN7
Cheshunt
WALTHAM CROSS
EN8
WALTHAM
ABBEY
EN9
EPPING
CM16
M25
M11
Theydon
Bois
INGATESTONE
CM4
Stock
CM3
ENFIELD
EN1
EN3
Ponders
End
LOUGHTON
IG10
Abridge
RM4
Stapleford
Abbotts
CM14
CM15
Shenfield
BRENTWOOD
BILLERICAY
CM11
CM12
SS11
SS12
N9
Edmonton
Chingford
E4
BUCKHURST
HILL
IG9
CHIGWELL
IG7
Hainault
Harold Hill
RM3
Ingrave
CM13
N18
Tottenham
N17
WOODFORD GREEN
IG8
IG6
RM5
RM1
ROMFORD
RM2
E17
Walthamstow
E18
IG5
ILFORD
IG4
IG2
RM6
RM7
RM11
HORNCHURCH
West
Horndon
SS15
Laindon
SS14
BASILDON
SS13
SS16
N15
E11
Wanstead
IG1
IG3
UPMINSTER
RM14
Stoke
Newington
N16
E10
Leyton
E5
RM8
RM10
RM12
Elm Park
E20
Stratford
E8
Hackney
E9
E7
E12
E15
DAGENHAM
Corringham
SS17
STANFORD-LE-HOPE
E2
E3
Bow
E13
East Ham
E6
BARKING
IG11
RM9
SOUTH
OCKENDON
RM15
RM16
EC2
LONDON
E1
EC3
Poplar
E14
E16
City
Airport
Thamesmead
SE28
RAINHAM
RM13
Aveley
Chadwell
St. Mary
Southwark
SE1
SE16
DA18
BELVEDERE
DA17
SE2
PURFLEET
RM19
West
Thurrock
RM20
GRAYS
RM17
TILBURY
RM18
SE17
SE8
Greenwich
SE7
Charlton
Woolwich
SE18
ERITH
DA8
Camberwell
SE5
Peckham
SE15
SE14
SE10
SE3
Blackheath
WELLING
DA16
DA7
BEXLEYHEATH
DA6
Crayford
DA1
GREENHITHE
DA9
SWANSCOMBE
DA10
Northfleet
DA11
GRAVESEND
ME3
SE4
SE13
Lewisham
SE22
SE12
Eltham
SE9
Mottingham
DA15
BEXLEY
DA5
DARTFORD
SIDCUP
Wilmington
DA2
DA12
Shorne
Higham
SE21
Dulwich
SE23
Catford
SE6
SE26
Grove Park
CHISLEHURST
BR7
DA14
Hextable
Norwood
SE19
SE20
BR1
ROCHESTER
BECKENHAM
BR3
BROMLEY
St. Paul's Cray
BR5
St. Mary Cray
SWANLEY
BR8
DA4
LONGFIELD
DA3
Cobham
ME2
SE25
BR2
Hayes
Farningham
M20
Meopham
DA13
New Ash
Green
ME1
M2
CROYDON
CR0
WEST
WICKHAM
BR4
ORPINGTON
BR6
Chelsfield
Eynsford
Halling
Farnborough
KESTON
BR2
West
Kingsdown
ME5
SOUTH CROYDON
CR2
Sanderstead
New
Addington
Downe
Halstead
SNODLAND
ME6
Otford
Kemsing
M26
Wrotham
AYLESFORD
ME20
KENLEY
CR8
WARLINGHAM
CR6
WHYTELEAFE
CR3
Biggin
Hill
TN14
Larkfield
Ditton
Seal
TN15
Borough
Green
WEST MALLING
ME19
TN16
Woldingham
SEVENOAKS
Ightham
Kings Hill
MAIDSTONE
ME16
CATERHAM
CR3
WESTERHAM
TN13
Mereworth
Limpsfield
ME15
OXTED
RH8
ME18
GODSTONE
TN11
RH9
South
Godstone
Hildenborough
TN10
ME17
TONBRIDGE
TN9
TN12
RH7
EDENBRIDGE
TN8
Posttown Boundary
Postcode Boundary

Chiswell Green
Bovingdon
Kings Langley
London Colney
Brookmans Park
Chesham
Abbots Langley
Bricket Wood
South Mimms
Potters Bar
Radlett
AMERSHAM
WATFORD
Borehamwood
Cockfosters
Chorleywood
Bushey
Elstree
BARNET
Rickmansworth
LONDON GATEWAY
Chalfont St. Giles
South Oxhey
Mill Hill
Stanmore
Edgware
Northwood
Finchley
BEACONSFIELD
Chalfont St. Peter
Harefield
Pinner
Wealdstone
HARROW
Hendon
Gerrards Cross
Ruislip
Highgate
Denham
Cricklewood
Neasden
Hampstead
Sudbury
Wembley
Uxbridge
Northolt
Willesden
Stoke Poges
Hillingdon
Harlesden
Kilburn
Burnham
Greenford
Iver
Hayes
EALING
Acton
Paddington
Yiewsley
SLOUGH
Southall
Hanwell
Shepherds Bush
Kensington
Langley
West Drayton
Eton
Harmondsworth
Harlington
HESTON
Hammersmith
Chelsea
Windsor
Datchet
Colnbrook
Brentford
Kew
Chiswick
Fulham
Battersea
Poyle
LONDON HEATHROW AIRPORT
HOUNSLOW
Isleworth
Barnes
RICHMOND
Putney
Wandsworth
Wraysbury
Stanwell
Feltham
Twickenham
Englefield Green
Egham
Ashford
STAINES-UPON-THAMES
Teddington
Tooting
Wimbledon
Hampton
Virginia Water
Sunbury
KINGSTON UPON THAMES
New Malden
Merton
Ascot
Sunningdale
West Molesey
East Molesey
Morden
Shepperton
Surbiton
Chertsey
Worcester Park
Walton-on-Thames
Windlesham
Weybridge
Esher
Addlestone
Chessington
SUTTON
Carshalton
Chobham
Ewell
Cheam
Lightwater
West End
Bisley
West Byfleet
Byfleet
Oxshott
Cobham
EPSOM
Banstead
WOKING
COBHAM
Ashtead
Chipstead
Ripley
LEATHERHEAD
Tadworth
Pirbright
Fetcham
Kingswood
Walton on the Hill
East Horsley
Great Bookham
GUILDFORD
DORKING
REIGATE
Redhill
SCALE
0 1 2 3 Miles
0 1 2 3 4 5 Kilometres

LOW EMISSION ZONE

The Low Emission Zone (LEZ) is a specified area of Greater London within which the most polluting diesel-engined vehicles are required to meet specific emissions standards. If they do not they will need to pay a daily charge. The LEZ operates 24 hours a day, 365 days a year.
The LEZ emissions standards are based on Euro standards for the emission of particulate matter (PM). Larger vans and minibuses need to meet the Euro 3 emissions standard for particulate matter and lorries, buses and coaches need to meet Euro IV.
A small number of vehicles are entitled to an exemption from the LEZ.
For more information contact Transport for London (www.tfl.gov.uk/roadusers/lez)

INDEX

Including Streets, Places & Areas, Industrial Estates,
Selected Flats & Walkways, Junction Names & Service Areas and Selected Places of Interest.

HOW TO USE THIS INDEX

1. Each street name is followed by its Postcode District (or, if outside the London Postcodes, by its Locality Abbreviation(s)) and then by its map reference; e.g. **Abbey Av.** HA0: Wemb . . . . 40Na **67** is in the HA0 Postcode District and the Wembley Locality and is to be found in square 40Na on page **67**. The page number being shown in bold type.

2. A strict alphabetical order is followed in which Av., Rd., St., etc. (though abbreviated) are read in full and as part of the street name; e.g. **Alder M.** appears after **Aldermere Av.** but before **Aldermoor Rd.**

3. Streets and a selection of flats and walkways that cannot be shown on the mapping, appear in the index with the thoroughfare to which they are connected shown in brackets; e.g. **Abbey Ct.** *AL1: St A . . . .3B* ***6*** *(off Holywell Hill)*

4. Addresses that are in more than one part are referred to as not continuous.

5. Places and areas are shown in the index in **BLUE TYPE** and the map reference is to the actual map square in which the town centre or area is located and not to the place name shown on the map; e.g. **ABBEY WOOD 49Yc 95**

6. An example of a selected place of interest is **Barnet Mus. 14Ab 30**

7. Park & Ride are shown in the index in **Blue Type**; e.g. **Windsor, Home Park (Park & Ride) 1J 103**

8. Junction names and Service Areas are shown in the index in **BOLD CAPITAL TYPE**; e.g. **ANGEL EDMONTON 22Wb 51**

9. Map references for entries that appear on large scale pages **214-231** are shown first, with small scale map references shown in brackets; e.g. **Abbey Gdns.** NW8 . . . .2A **214** (40Eb **69**)

GENERAL ABBREVIATIONS

All. : Alley
App. : Approach
Arc. : Arcade
Av. : Avenue
Bk. : Back
Blvd. : Boulevard
Bri. : Bridge
B'way. : Broadway
Bldg. : Building
Bldgs. : Buildings
Bungs. : Bungalows
Bus. : Business
Cvn. : Caravan
C'way. : Causeway
Cen. : Centre
Chu. : Church
Chyd. : Churchyard
Circ. : Circle
Cir. : Circus
Cl. : Close
Coll. : College
Comn. : Common
Cnr. : Corner
Cott. : Cottage
Cotts. : Cottages
Ct. : Court
Cres. : Crescent
Cft. : Croft
Dpt. : Depot
Dr. : Drive
E. : East
Emb. : Embankment
Ent. : Enterprise
Est. : Estate
Fld. : Field
Flds. : Fields
Gdn. : Garden
Gdns. : Gardens
Gth. : Garth
Ga. : Gate
Gt. : Great
Grn. : Green
Gro. : Grove
Hgts. : Heights
Ho. : House
Ho's. : Houses
Ind. : Industrial
Info. : Information
Intl. : International
Junc. : Junction
La. : Lane
Lit. : Little
Lwr. : Lower
Mnr. : Manor
Mans. : Mansions
Mkt. : Market
Mdw. : Meadow
Mdws. : Meadows
M. : Mews
Mt. : Mount
Mus. : Museum
Nth. : North
Pal. : Palace
Pde. : Parade
Pk. : Park
Pas. : Passage
Pav. : Pavilion
Pl. : Place
Pct. : Precinct
Prom. : Promenade
Quad. : Quadrant
Res. : Residential
Ri. : Rise
Rd. : Road
Rdbt. : Roundabout
Shop. : Shopping
Sth. : South
Sq. : Square
Sta. : Station
St. : Street
Ter. : Terrace
Twr. : Tower
Trad. : Trading
Up. : Upper
Va. : Vale
Vw. : View
Vs. : Villas
Vis. : Visitors
Wlk. : Walk
W. : West
Yd. : Yard

LOCALITY ABBREVIATIONS

Abbots Langley: WD5 . . . . Ab L
Abridge: CM16,IG7,RM4 . . . . Abr
Addington: BR4,CR0 . . . . Addtn
Addlestone: KT15 . . . . Add
Aldenham: WD25 . . . . A'ham
Arkley: EN5 . . . . Ark
Ascot: SL5 . . . . Asc
Ash: TN15 . . . . Ash
Ashford: TW15 . . . . Ashf
Ashtead: KT21,KT22 . . . . Asht
Aveley: RM14,RM15,RM19 . . . . Avel
Badger's Mount: TN14 . . . . Bad M
Banstead: CR5,KT17,SM2,SM7 . . . . Bans
Barking: IG3,IG11,RM9 . . . . Bark
Barnet: EN4,EN5 . . . . Barn
Beaconsfield: HP9 . . . . Beac
Bean: DA2 . . . . Bean
Beckenham: BR3 . . . . Beck
Beddington: CR0,SM6 . . . . Bedd
Bedfont: TW14 . . . . Bedf
Bedmond: WD5 . . . . Bedm
Belvedere: DA7,DA17,DA18 . . . . Belv
Berkhamsted: HP4 . . . . Berk
Bessels Green: TN13 . . . . Bes G
Betchworth: RH3 . . . . Bet
Bexley: DA1,DA5,DA15 . . . . Bexl
Bexleyheath: DA5,DA6,DA7 . . . . Bex
Biggin Hill: TN16 . . . . Big H
Bisley: GU24 . . . . Bisl
Bletchingley: CR3,RH1 . . . . Blet
Bluewater: DA2,DA9 . . . . Bluew
Bookham: KT23 . . . . Bookh
Borehamwood: WD6 . . . . Bore
Borough Green: TN15 . . . . Bor G
Bovingdon: HP3 . . . . Bov
Box Hill: KT20 . . . . Box H
Brasted: TN16 . . . . Bras
Brasted Chart: TN16 . . . . B Char
Brentford: TW7,TW8 . . . . Bford
Brentwood: CM13,CM14,CM15 . . . . B'wood
Bricket Wood: AL2 . . . . Brick W
Brimsdown: EN3 . . . . Brim
Bromley: BR1,BR2 . . . . Brom
Brookmans Park: AL9 . . . . Brk P
Brookwood: GU21,GU24 . . . . Brkwd
Buckhurst Hill: IG8,IG9 . . . . Buck H
Buckland: RH3 . . . . Bkld
Bucks Hill: WD3,WD4 . . . . Bucks
Bulphan: RM14 . . . . Bulp
Burnham: SL1,SL2 . . . . Burn
Burpham: GU4 . . . . Burp
Bushey: WD23,WD24 . . . . Bush
Bushy Heath: WD23 . . . . B Hea
Byfleet: KT14 . . . . Byfl
Carshalton: CR4,SM5 . . . . Cars
Caterham: CR3 . . . . Cat'm
Chadwell Heath: IG7,RM6,RM7 . . . . Chad H
Chafford Hundred: RM16,RM20 . . . . Chaf H
Chalfont St Giles: HP8 . . . . Chal G
Chalfont St Peter: SL9,WD3 . . . . Chal P
Chandler's Cross: WD3 . . . . Chan C
Cheam: KT17,SM2,SM3 . . . . Cheam
Chelsfield: BR6 . . . . Chels
Chenies: WD3 . . . . Chen
Chertsey: KT16 . . . . Chert
Cheshunt: EN7,EN8 . . . . Chesh
Chessington: KT9 . . . . Chess
Chevening: TN14 . . . . Chev
Chigwell: IG6,IG7 . . . . Chig
Chipperfield: WD3,WD4 . . . . Chfd
Chipstead: CR5,TN13,TN14 . . . . Chip
Chislehurst: BR7 . . . . Chst
Chiswell Green: AL2 . . . . Chis G
Chobham: GU24 . . . . Chob
Chorleywood: WD3 . . . . Chor
Claygate: KT10 . . . . Clay
Cobham: DA12,DA13,KT11,KT12 . . . . Cobh
Cockfosters: EN4,EN5 . . . . Cockf
Collier Row: RM5,RM6,RM7 . . . . Col R
Colnbrook: SL3 . . . . Coln
Colney Heath: AL4 . . . . Col H
Colney Street: AL2 . . . . Col S
Coopersale: CM16 . . . . Coop
Corringham: SS17 . . . . Corr
Coulsdon: CR3,CR5,RH1 . . . . Coul
Cowley: UB8 . . . . Cowl
Cranford: TW4,TW5,TW6,UB3 . . . . Cran
Crayford: DA1 . . . . Cray
Crews Hill: EN2 . . . . Crew H
Crockenhill: BR8 . . . . Crock
Crouch: TN15 . . . . Crou
Crowhurst: RH7,RH8 . . . . C'rst
Croxley Green: WD3 . . . . Crox G
Croydon: CR0 . . . . C'don
Cudham: TN14,TN16 . . . . Cud
Cuffley: EN6,EN7 . . . . Cuff
Dagenham: IG11,RM6,RM8-9,RM10 . . . . Dag
Darenth: DA2 . . . . Daren
Dartford: DA1,DA2,DA3,DA5,DA9,RM20 . . . . Dart
Datchet: SL3 . . . . Dat
Denham: SL0,UB9 . . . . Den
Doddinghurst: CM15 . . . . Dodd
Dorney: SL4 . . . . Dor
Dorney Reach: SL6 . . . . Dor R
Downe: BR6 . . . . Downe
Downside: KT11 . . . . D'side
Dunk's Green: TN11 . . . . Dun G
Dunton Green: TN13,TN14 . . . . Dun G
East Barnet: EN4 . . . . E Barn
East Clandon: GU4 . . . . E Clan
Eastcote: HA4,HA5 . . . . Eastc
East Horsley: KT24 . . . . E Hor
East Molesey: KT8,TW12 . . . . E Mos
East Tilbury: RM18,SS17 . . . . E Til
Ebbsfleet: DA10 . . . . Ebbs
Edenbridge: TN8 . . . . Eden
Edgware: HA8 . . . . Edg
Effingham: KT24 . . . . Eff
Effingham Junction: KT24 . . . . Eff J
Egham: TW20 . . . . Egh
Elstree: WD6 . . . . E'tree
Enfield: EN1-2 . . . . Enf
Enfield Highway: EN3 . . . . Enf H
Enfield Lock: EN3 . . . . Enf L
Enfield Wash: EN3 . . . . Enf W
Englefield Green: TW20 . . . . Eng G
Epping: CM16,EN9 . . . . Epp
Epsom: KT17,KT18-19 . . . . Eps
Epsom Downs: KT17,KT18 . . . . Eps D
Erith: DA1,DA7,DA8,DA17-18 . . . . Erith
Esher: KT10 . . . . Esh
Essendon: AL9 . . . . Ess
Eton: SL4 . . . . Eton
Eton Wick: SL4 . . . . Eton W
Ewell: KT17,KT19,SM2 . . . . Ewe
Eynsford: BR8,DA4,TN14 . . . . Eyns
Fairseat: TN15 . . . . Fair
Farnborough: BR5,BR6 . . . . Farnb
Farnham Common: SL1,SL2 . . . . Farn C
Farnham Royal: SL2 . . . . Farn R
Farningham: BR8,DA4 . . . . Farni
Fawkham: DA3 . . . . Fawk
Feltham: TW13,TW14 . . . . Felt
Fetcham: KT22,KT23 . . . . Fet
Fiddlers Hamlet: CM16 . . . . Fidd H
Flaunden: HP3,HP5 . . . . Flau
Frogmore: AL2 . . . . F'mre
Fulmer: SL3 . . . . Ful
George Green: SL3 . . . . Geor G
Gerrards Cross: SL2,SL9 . . . . Ger X
Godden Green: TN15 . . . . God G
Godstone: RH8,RH9 . . . . G'stone
Goff's Oak: EN7 . . . . G Oak
Gravesend: DA11,DA12 . . . . Grav'nd
Grays: RM16-17,RM18,RM20 . . . . Grays
Great Warley: CM13,CM14,RM14 . . . . Gt War
Greenford: UB6 . . . . G'frd
Greenhithe: DA2,DA9,DA10 . . . . Ghithe
Green Street Green: DA2 . . . . G St G
Guildford: GU2-3,GU4 . . . . Guild
Hadley Wood: EN4 . . . . Had W
Halstead: TN14 . . . . Hals
Ham: TW10 . . . . Ham
Hampton: TW12 . . . . Hamp
Hampton Hill: TW12 . . . . Hamp H
Hampton Wick: KT1,TW11 . . . . Hamp W
Hanworth: TW13 . . . . Hanw
Harefield: UB9,WD3 . . . . Hare
Harlington: UB3,UB7 . . . . Harl
Harmondsworth: UB7 . . . . Harm
Harold Wood: RM3,RM11 . . . . Hrld W
Harrow: HA1-2,HA3 . . . . Harr
Harrow Weald: HA3 . . . . Hrw W
Hartley: DA3,TN15 . . . . Hartl
Hatch End: HA5 . . . . Hat E
Hatfield: AL9,AL10 . . . . Hat
Havering-Atte-Bower: RM1,RM4 . . . . Have B
Hawley: DA2 . . . . Hawl
Hayes: BR2,BR4,UB3,UB4 . . . . Hayes
Headley: KT18 . . . . Head
Hedgerley: SL2 . . . . Hedg
Hemel Hempstead: HP1-2,HP3 . . . . Hem H
Herongate: CM13 . . . . Heron
Heronsgate: WD3 . . . . Herons
Hersham: KT10,KT12 . . . . Hers
Heston: TW5 . . . . Hest
Hextable: BR8 . . . . Hext
Higham: DA12,ME2-3 . . . . High'm
High Beech: EN9,IG10 . . . . H Beech
Hillingdon: UB4,UB8,UB10 . . . . Hil
Hinchley Wood: KT10 . . . . Hin W
Hodsoll Street: TN15 . . . . Hod S
Hornchurch: RM2,RM11,RM12,RM13 . . . . Horn
Horndon-on-the-Hill: SS17 . . . . Horn H
Horton: SL3 . . . . Hort
Horton Kirby: DA3,DA4 . . . . Hort K
Hounslow: TW3,TW4,TW7,TW14 . . . . Houn
Hunton Cross: WD4,WD25 . . . . Hunt C
Hutton: CM13,CM15 . . . . Hut
Ickenham: UB10 . . . . Ick
Ide Hill: TN14 . . . . Ide H
Ightham: TN15 . . . . Igh
Ilford: IG1-3,IG4-5,IG6,IG7,IG8,RM6 . . . . Ilf
Ingatestone: CM4 . . . . Inga
Ingrave: CM13 . . . . Ingve
Isleworth: TW1,TW3,TW5,TW7 . . . . Isle
Istead Rise: DA3,DA11,DA13 . . . . Ist R
Iver: SL0 . . . . Iver
Iver Heath: SL0 . . . . Iver H
Ivy Hatch: TN15 . . . . Ivy H
Jacobs Well: GU4 . . . . Jac W
Kelvedon Common: CM14 . . . . Kel C
Kelvedon Hatch: CM14,CM15 . . . . Kel H
Kemsing: TN15 . . . . Kems'g
Kenley: CR3,CR8 . . . . Kenley
Kenton: HA3,HA7,HA9 . . . . Kenton
Keston: BR2 . . . . Kes
Kew: TW9 . . . . Kew
Kings Langley: WD4 . . . . K Lan
Kingston upon Thames: KT1,KT2 . . . . King T
Kingswood: CR5,KT20 . . . . Kgswd
Knaphill: GU21 . . . . Knap
Knatts Valley: TN15 . . . . Knat
Knockholt: TN14 . . . . Knock
Laleham: TW18 . . . . Lale
Langley: SL3 . . . . L'ly
Langleybury: WD4 . . . . Lang
Latimer: HP5 . . . . Lat
Leatherhead: KT9,KT11,KT18,KT22 . . . . Lea
Leigh: RH2 . . . . Leigh
Letchmore Heath: WD25 . . . . Let H
Ley Hill: HP5 . . . . Ley H
Lightwater: GU18 . . . . Light
Limpsfield: RH8,TN8 . . . . Limp
Linford: SS17 . . . . Linf
Little Chalfont: HP6-7 . . . . L Chal
Little Warley: CM13 . . . . L War
London Colney: AL2 . . . . Lon C
London Heathrow Airport: TW6 . . . . H'row A
Longcross: KT16 . . . . Longc
Longfield: DA3,DA13 . . . . Lfield
Longfield Hill: DA3 . . . . Long H
Longford: TW6,UB7 . . . . Lford
Loudwater: WD3 . . . . Loud
Loughton: CM16,EN9,IG7,IG9-10 . . . . Lough
Lower Kingswood: KT20 . . . . Lwr K
Lyne: KT16 . . . . Lyne
Maple Cross: HP8,WD3 . . . . Map C
Mawney: RM7 . . . . Mawney
Meopham: DA13 . . . . Meop
Merstham: RH1 . . . . Mers
Mickleham: RH5 . . . . Mick
Mitcham: CR0,CR4 . . . . Mitc
Morden: SM4 . . . . Mord
Mountnessing: CM13,CM15 . . . . Mount
Navestock: CM14,RM4 . . . . Nave
Navestockside: CM14,RM4 . . . . N'side
New Addington: CR0 . . . . New Ad
New Ash Green: DA3,TN15 . . . . Nw A G
New Barnet: EN5 . . . . New Bar
Newgate Street: SG13 . . . . New S
New Haw: KT15 . . . . New H
New Malden: KT3 . . . . N Mald
Noak Hill: RM4 . . . . Noak H
Normandy: GU3 . . . . Norm
Northaw: EN6 . . . . N'thaw
Northfleet: DA10,DA11 . . . . Nflt
Northfleet Green: DA13 . . . . Nflt G
North Mymms: AL9 . . . . N Mym
North Ockendon: RM14,RM15 . . . . N Ock
Northolt: UB4,UB5 . . . . N'olt
North Stifford: RM15,RM16 . . . . N Stif
North Weald: CM16 . . . . N Weald
Northwood: HA6 . . . . Nwood
Nutfield: RH1 . . . . Nutf
Oakley Green: SL4 . . . . Oak G
Ockham: GU23 . . . . Ock
Old Windsor: SL4,TW20 . . . . Old Win
Orpington: BR5,BR6 . . . . Orp
Orsett: RM16,SS17 . . . . Ors
Otford: TN13,TN14 . . . . Otf
Ottershaw: KT16 . . . . Ott
Oxshott: KT10,KT11,KT22 . . . . Oxs
Oxted: RH8 . . . . Oxt
Park Street: AL2 . . . . Park
Petts Wood: BR5,BR6 . . . . Pet W
Pilgrims Hatch: CM14,CM15 . . . . Pil H
Pinner: HA5,HA6,WD19 . . . . Pinn
Pirbright: GU24 . . . . Pirb
Platt: TN15 . . . . Plat
Plaxtol: TN11,TN15 . . . . Plax
Ponders End: EN3 . . . . Pond E
Potten End: HP4 . . . . Pott E
Potters Bar: EN5,EN6 . . . . Pot B
Potters Crouch: AL2 . . . . Pot C
Poyle: SL3 . . . . Poyle
Pratts Bottom: BR6,TN14 . . . . Prat B
Purfleet: RM15,RM19 . . . . Purf
Purley: CR5,CR8 . . . . Purl
Pyrford: GU22 . . . . Pyr
Radlett: WD7,WD25 . . . . R'lett
Rainham: RM9,RM12,RM13,RM14 . . . . Rain
Ranmore Common: KT24 . . . . Ran C
Redhill: RH1 . . . . Redh
Reigate: KT20,RH2 . . . . Reig
Richings Park: SL0,SL3 . . . . Rich P
Richmond: TW9-10 . . . . Rich
Rickmansworth: UB9,WD3 . . . . Rick
Ridge: EN6 . . . . Ridge
Ripley: GU23 . . . . Rip
Riverhead: TN13 . . . . Riv
Romford: CM14,RM1,RM2,RM3, RM5,RM7,RM11 . . . . Rom
Roughway: TN11 . . . . Roug
Ruislip: HA4 . . . . Ruis
Rush Green: RM1,RM7,RM10 . . . . Rush G
St Albans: AL1,AL2,AL3,AL4 . . . . St A
St Mary Cray: BR5,BR6 . . . . St M Cry
St Pauls Cray: BR5 . . . . St P
Sanderstead: CR2 . . . . Sande
Sarratt: WD3 . . . . Sarr
Seal: TN15 . . . . Seal
Selsdon: CR0,CR2 . . . . Sels
Send: GU23 . . . . Send
Sevenoaks: TN13,TN14,TN15,TN16 . . . . S'oaks
Shenfield: CM15 . . . . Shenf
Shenley: WD7 . . . . Shenl
Shepperton: TW17,TW18 . . . . Shep
Shipbourne: TN11,TN15 . . . . S'brne
Shoreham: TN14 . . . . S'ham
Shorne: DA12 . . . . Shorne
Sidcup: BR5,BR7,DA14,DA15 . . . . Sidc
Sipson: UB7 . . . . Sip
Slough: SL1-2,SL3 . . . . Slou
Smallford: AL4 . . . . S'ford
Sole Street: DA12,DA13 . . . . Sole S
Southall: UB1-2 . . . . S'hall
South Croydon: CR2 . . . . S Croy
South Darenth: DA4 . . . . S Dar
Southfleet: DA2,DA13 . . . . Sflt
South Godstone: RH9 . . . . S God
South Mimms: EN6 . . . . S Mim
South Nutfield: RH1 . . . . S Nut
South Ockendon: RM15 . . . . S Ock
South Weald: CM14 . . . . S Weald
Staines: TW18,TW19 . . . . Staines
Stanford-le-Hope: SS17 . . . . Stan H
Stanmore: HA3,HA7 . . . . Stan
Stansted: TN15 . . . . Stans
Stanwell: TW6,TW19 . . . . Stanw
Stanwell Moor: TW19 . . . . Stanw M
Stapleford Abbotts: RM4 . . . . Stap A
Stapleford Tawney: RM4 . . . . Stap T
Stockley Park: UB11 . . . . Stock P
Stoke D'Abernon: KT11 . . . . Stoke D
Stoke Poges: SL2,SL3 . . . . Stoke P
Strood: DA12,ME2 . . . . Strood
Sunbury: TW16 . . . . Sun
Sundridge: TN14 . . . . Sund
Sunningdale: SL5 . . . . S'dale
Sunninghill: SL5 . . . . S'hill
Surbiton: KT1,KT5-6,KT10 . . . . Surb
Sutton: SM1,SM2,SM3 . . . . Sutt
Sutton at Hone: DA2,DA4 . . . . Sut H
Sutton Green: GU4 . . . . Sut G
Swanley: BR5,BR8,DA4,DA14 . . . . Swan
Swanscombe: DA10 . . . . Swans
Tadworth: KT18,KT20 . . . . Tad
Tandridge: RH8 . . . . Tand
Taplow: SL6 . . . . Tap
Tatsfield: TN16 . . . . Tats
Tattenham Corner: KT18 . . . . Tatt C
Teddington: TW1,TW11 . . . . Tedd
Thames Ditton: KT7,KT10 . . . . T Ditt
Theydon Bois: CM16,EN9 . . . . They B
Theydon Garnon: CM16 . . . . They G
Theydon Mount: CM16 . . . . They M
Thorney: SL0 . . . . Thorn
Thornton Heath: CR7 . . . . Thor H
Thorpe: TW20 . . . . Thorpe
Tilbury: RM18 . . . . Tilb
Titsey: RH8,TN16 . . . . T'sey
Trottiscliffe: ME19 . . . . Tros
Twickenham: TW1,TW2,TW7,TW13 . . . . Twick
Underriver: TN15 . . . . Under
Upminster: CM13,CM14,RM11, RM12,RM14 . . . . Upm
Uxbridge: UB8,UB10 . . . . Uxb
Virginia Water: GU25,KT16,SL5 . . . . Vir W
Waddon: CR0 . . . . Wadd
Wallington: SM5-6 . . . . Wall
Waltham Abbey: CM16,EN9 . . . . Walt A
Waltham Cross: EN2,EN7,EN8-9 . . . . Walt C
Walton-on-Thames: KT12 . . . . Walt T
Walton on the Hill: KT18,KT20 . . . . Walt H
Warley: CM13,CM14 . . . . W'ley
Warlingham: CR3,CR6 . . . . W'ham
Water Oakley: SL4 . . . . Wat O
Watford: WD3,WD17-24,WD25 . . . . Wat
Wealdstone: HA3 . . . . W'stone
Welham Green: AL9 . . . . Wel G
Well Hill: BR6 . . . . Well H
Welling: DA16 . . . . Well
Wembley: HA0,HA9 . . . . Wemb
Wennington: RM13,RM15 . . . . Wenn
West Byfleet: KT14 . . . . W Byf
West Clandon: GU4 . . . . W Cla
West Drayton: UB7 . . . . W Dray
West End: GU24 . . . . W End
Westerham: RH8,TN16 . . . . Westrm
West Horndon: CM13 . . . . W H'dn
West Horsley: KT24 . . . . W Hor
Westhumble: KT23 . . . . Westh
West Hyde: WD3 . . . . W Hyd
West Kingsdown: TN15 . . . . W King
West Molesey: KT8 . . . . W Mole
West Thurrock: RM19,RM20 . . . . W Thur
West Tilbury: RM16,RM18 . . . . W Til
West Wickham: BR4 . . . . W W'ck
Wexham: SL2,SL3 . . . . Wex
Weybridge: KT13 . . . . Weyb
Whelpley Hill: HP5 . . . . Whel H
Whiteley Village: KT12 . . . . W Vill
Whitton: TW2 . . . . Whitt
Whyteleafe: CR3 . . . . Whyt
Wilmington: DA2 . . . . Wilm
Windlesham: GU20 . . . . W'sham
Windsor: SL4 . . . . Wind
Winkfield: SL4 . . . . Wink
Wisley: GU23 . . . . Wis
Woking: GU21,GU22,GU24 . . . . Wok
Woldingham: CR3,CR6 . . . . Wold
Woodford Green: IG4,IG8,IG9 . . . . Wfd G
Woodham: KT15 . . . . Wdhm
Worcester Park: KT4,SM3 . . . . Wor Pk
Worplesdon: GU3 . . . . Worp
Wraysbury: TW19 . . . . Wray
Wrotham: TN15 . . . . Wro
Wrotham Heath: TN15 . . . . Wro H
Yeading: UB4 . . . . Yead
Yiewsley: UB7,UB8 . . . . Yiew

2 Temple Place—Adam Cl.

2 Temple Place 4K 223
2 Willow Road 35Gb 69
7/7 Memorial 7J 221 (46Jb 90)
10 Brock St. NW1 5B 216
18 Stafford Terrace
The Sambourne Family Home 48Cb 89
(off Stafford Ter.)
60 St Martins La. WC2 4F 223
198 Contemporary Arts and Learning 58Rb 113
(off Railton Rd.)
201 Bishopsgate EC2 7J 219

A

A1 Golf Driving Range 13Ua 30
Aaron Hill Rd. E6 43Qc 94
Aashiana Ct. WD18: Wat 16W 26
Abady Ho. SW1 5E 228
Abberley M. SW4 55Kb 112
Abberton Wlk. RM13: Rain 39Hd 76
Abbess Cl. E6 43Nc 94
SW2 60Rb 113
Abbess Ct. IG10: Lough 13Rc 36
Abbess Ter. IG10: Lough 13Qc 36
Abbeville M. SW4 56Mb 112
Abbeville Rd. N8 29Mb 50
SW4 58Lb 112
Abbey Av. AL3: St A 5N 5
HA0: Wemb 40Na 67
Abbey Chase KT16: Chert 73K 149
Abbey Cl. BR6: Chels 77Xc 161
E5 35Wb 71
GU22: Pyr 88G 168
HA5: Pinn 27X 45
RM1: Rom 30Jd 56
SL1: Slou 5C 80
SW8 53Mb 112
UB3: Hayes 46X 85
UB5: N'olt 41Ba 85
Abbey Ct. AL1: St A 3B 6
(off Holywell Hill)
EN9: Walt A 6Dc 20
KT16: Chert 73K 149
NW8 1A 214
SE6 58Cc 114
SE17 50Sb 91
(off Macleod St.)
TW12: Hamp 66Ca 129
TW18: Lale 70L 127
Abbey Cres. DA17: Belv 49Cd 96
Abbeydale Rd. HA0: Wemb 39Pa 67
Abbey Dr. DA2: Wilm 61Gd 140
SW17 64Jb 134
TW18: Lale 69L 127
WD5: Ab L 4W 12
Abbey Est. NW8 39Db 69
Abbeyfield Cl. CR4: Mitc 68Gb 133
Abbeyfield Est. SE16 49Yb 92
Abbeyfield Rd. SE16 49Yb 92
(not continuous)
Abbeyfields KT16: Chert 73M 149
Abbeyfields Cl. NW10 41Qa 87
Abbey Gdns. BR7: Chst 67Qc 138
KT16: Chert 72J 149
NW8 2A 214 (40Eb 69)
SE16 49Wb 91
SW1 3F 229
TW15: Ashf 64R 128
W6 51Ab 110
Abbey Gateway AL3: St A 2A 6
Abbey Grn. KT16: Chert 72J 149
Abbey Gro. SE2 49Xc 95
Abbeyhill Rd. DA15: Sidc 61Yc 139
Abbey Ho. E15 40Gc 73
(off Baker's Row)
NW8 3A 214
Abbey Ind. Est. CR4: Mitc 71Hb 155
HA0: Wemb 39Pa 67
Abbey La. BR3: Beck 66Cc 136
E15 40Ec 72
(not continuous)
Abbey La. Commercial Est. E15 40Gc 73
Abbey Leisure Cen. 39Sc 74
Abbey Life Ct. E16 43Kc 93
Abbey Lodge NW8 4E 214
Abbey Mansion M. SE24 57Rb 113
Abbey Mead Ind. Est. EN9: Walt A 7Ec 20
Abbey Mead Ind. Pk. EN9: Walt A 6Dc 20
Abbey Mdws. KT16: Chert 73L 149
Abbey M. AL1: St A 3B 6
(off Holywell Hill)
E17 29Cc 52
TW7: Isle 53Ka 108
TW18: Lale 70L 127
Abbey Mill End AL3: St A 3A 6
Abbey Mill La. AL3: St A 3A 6
Abbey Moor Golf Course 76J 149
Abbey Mt. DA17: Belv 50Bd 95
Abbey Orchard St. SW1 3D 228 (48Mb 90)
Abbey Orchard St. Est.
SW1 3E 228 (48Mb 90)
(not continuous)
Abbey Pde. SW19 66Eb 133
(off Merton High St.)
W5 41Pa 87
Abbey Pk. BR3: Beck 66Cc 136
Abbey Pk. Ind. Est. IG11: Bark 40Sc 74
Abbey Pk. La. SL1: Burn 3C 60
Abbey Pl. DA1: Dart 57Md 119
KT16: Chert 69J 127
Abbey Retail Pk. IG11: Bark 38Rc 74
Abbey Rd. CR0: C'don 76Rb 157
CR2: Sels 82Zb 178
DA7: Bex 56Ad 117
DA9: Ghithe 57Yd 120
DA12: Grav'nd 10Ge 123
DA17: Belv 49Zc 95
E15 40Fc 73
EN1: Enf 15Ub 33
EN8: Walt C 6Ac 20
GU21: Wok 9N 167
GU25: Vir W 1P 147
IG2: Ilf 29Tc 54
IG11: Bark 39Rc 74
KT16: Chert 73K 149
NW6 38Db 69
NW8 1A 214 (38Db 69)
NW10 39Ra 67
SE2 49Zc 95
SW19 66Eb 133
TW17: Shep 74Q 150
Abbey Rd. Apartments NW8 2A 214
Abbey Sports Cen. 39Sc 74
Abbey St. E13 42Jc 93
SE1 3J 231 (48Ub 91)
SE16 48Wb 91
Abbey Ter. SE2 49Yc 95
Abbey Theatre 4A 6
Abbey Trad. Est. SE26 64Bc 136
Abbey Vw. AL1: St A 4B 6
EN9: Walt A 5Dc 20
NW7 20Va 30
WD7: R'lett 7Ha 14
WD25: Wat 8Z 13
Abbey View Golf Course 4A 6
Abbey Vw. Rd. AL3: St A 2A 6
Abbey Wlk. KT8: W Mole 69Da 129
Abbey Wharf Ind. Est. IG11: Bark 41Tc 94
ABBEY WOOD 49Yc 95
Abbey Wood SL5: S'dale 3E 146
Abbey Wood Cvn. Club Site SE2 49Yc 95
Abbey Wood La. RM13: Rain 40Md 77
Abbey Wood Rd. SE2 49Xc 95
Abbot Cl. HA4: Ruis 34Z 65
KT14: Byfl 82M 169
TW18: Staines 66M 127
Abbot Ct. SW8 52Nb 112
(off Hartington Rd.)
Abbot Ho. E14 45Dc 92
(off Smythe St.)
Abbots Av. AL1: St A 5C 6
KT19: Eps 83Qa 173
Abbots Av. W. AL1: St A 5B 6
Abbotsbury NW1 38Mb 70
(off Camley St.)
Abbotsbury Cl. E15 40Ec 72
W14 47Ab 88
Abbotsbury Ct. WD25: Wat 4X 13
Abbotsbury Gdns. HA5: Eastc 31Y 65
Abbotsbury Ho. W14 47Ab 88
Abbotsbury M. SE15 55Yb 114
Abbotsbury Rd. BR2: Hayes 75Hc 159
SM4: Mord 71Db 155
W14 47Ab 88
Abbots Bus. Pk. WD4: K Lan 10A 4
Abbots Cl. BR5: Farnb 74Sc 160
CM15: Shenf 18Ce 41
RM13: Rain 40Ld 77
Abbots Ct. RM3: Hrld W 25Pd 57
(off Queen's Pk. Rd.)
W8 47Db 89
(off Thackeray St.)
Abbots Dr. GU25: Vir W 1M 147
HA2: Harr 33Ca 65
Abbots Fld. DA12: Grav'nd 5E 144
Abbotsford Av. N15 28Sb 51
Abbotsford Cl. GU22: Wok 89C 168
Abbotsford Gdns. IG8: Wfd G 24Jc 53
Abbotsford Rd. IG3: Ilf 33Wc 75
Abbots Gdns. N2 28Fb 49
Abbots Grn. CR0: Addtn 79Zb 158
Abbotshade Rd. SE16 46Zb 92
Abbotshall Av. N14 20Lb 32
Abbotshall Rd. SE6 60Fc 115
Abbots Hill HP3: Hem H 7A 4
Abbot's Ho. W14 48Bb 89
(off St Mary Abbot's Ter.)
Abbots La. CR8: Kenley 88Sb 177
ABBOTS LANGLEY 3U 12
Abbotsleigh Cl. SM2: Sutt 80Db 155
Abbotsleigh Rd. SW16 63Lb 134
Abbots Mnr. SW1 7K 227 (49Kb 90)
(not continuous)
Abbots Pk. AL1: St A 4E 6
SW2 60Qb 112
Abbot's Pl. NW6 39Db 69
Abbots Pl. WD6: Bore 9Ra 15
Abbots Ri. RH1: Redh 4A 208
WD4: K Lan 8P 3
Abbot's Rd. E6 39Mc 73
Abbots Rd. HA8: Edg 24Sa 47
WD5: Ab L 3S 12
Abbots Ter. N8 30Nb 50
Abbotstone Rd. SW15 55Ya 110
Abbot St. E8 37Vb 71
Abbots Vw. WD4: K Lan 9P 3
Abbots Wlk. SL4: Wind 4C 102
W8 48Db 89
Abbots Way BR3: Beck 71Ac 158
KT16: Chert 73H 149
Abbotswell Rd. SE4 57Bc 114
Abbotswood KT13: Weyb 76V 150
Abbotswood Cl. DA17: Belv 48Ad 95
Abbotswood Dr. KT13: Weyb 82T 170
Abbotswood Gdns. IG5: Ilf 27Pc 54
Abbotswood Rd. SE22 56Ub 113
SW16 62Mb 134
Abbotswood Way UB3: Hayes 46X 85
Abbott Av. SW20 67Za 132
Abbott Cl. TW12: Hamp 65Aa 129
UB5: N'olt 37Ba 65
Abbott Rd. E14 43Ec 92
(not continuous)
TN15: Bor G 92Be 205
Abbott's Cl. UB8: Cowl 43M 83
Abbotts Cl. BR8: Swan 70Jd 140
N1 37Sb 71
RM7: Mawney 27Dd 56
SE28 45Yc 95
Abbotts Cres. E4 21Fc 53
EN2: Enf 12Rb 33
Abbotts Dr. EN9: Walt A 5Jc 21
HA0: Wemb 33Ka 66
SS17: Stan H 1M 101
Abbotts Hall Chase SS17: Stan H 1N 101
Abbotts Ho. SW1 7D 228
Abbotts Mead TW10: Ham 63Ma 131
Abbottsmede Cl. TW1: Twick 61Ha 130
Abbotts Pk. Rd. E10 31Ec 72
Abbotts Rd. CR4: Mitc 70Lb 134
EN5: New Bar 14Db 31
SM3: Cheam 77Ab 154
UB1: S'hall 46Aa 85
Abbott's Tilt KT12: Hers 76Aa 151
Abbott's Wlk. DA7: Bex 52Zc 117
Abbotts Wlk. CR3: Cat'm 94Xb 197
Abbotts Way SL1: Slou 6B 80
Abbott's Wharf E14 44Cc 92
(off Stainsby Pl.)
Abbotts Wharf Moorings E14 44Cc 92
(off Stainsby Rd.)
Abbs Cross RM12: Horn 32Ld 77
Abbs Cross Gdns. RM12: Horn 32Ld 77
Abbs Cross Health & Fitness Club 34Ld 77
Abbs Cross La. RM12: Horn 34Ld 77
Abchurch La. EC4 4G 225 (45Tb 91)
(not continuous)
Abchurch Yd. EC4 4F 225 (45Tb 91)
Abdale La. AL9: N Mym 9D 8
Abdale Rd. W12 46Xa 88
Abelard Pl. W5 48Ma 87
Abel Cl. HP2: Hem H 2A 4
Abel Ho. SE11 51Qb 112
(off Kennington Rd.)
Abelia Cl. GU24: W End 5C 166
Abell Ct. KT15: Add 78K 149
Abenberg Way CM13: Hut 19De 41
Abenglen Ind. Est. UB3: Hayes 47T 84
Aberavon Rd. E3 41Ac 92
Abercairn Rd. SW16 66Lb 134
Aberconway Rd. SM4: Mord 70Db 133
Abercorn Cl. CR2: Sels 85Zb 178
NW7 24Ab 48
NW8 2A 214 (41Eb 89)
Abercorn Commercial Cen.
HA0: Wemb 39Ma 67
Abercorn Cotts. NW8 3A 214
Abercorn Cres. HA2: Harr 32Da 65
Abercorn Dell WD23: B Hea 19Ea 28
Abercorn Gdns. HA3: Kenton 31Ma 67
RM6: Chad H 30Xc 55
Abercorn Gro. HA4: Ruis 28T 44
Abercorn Mans. NW8 2A 214
Abercorn M. TW10: Rich 56Pa 109
Abercorn Pl. NW8 3A 214 (41Eb 89)
Abercorn Rd. HA7: Stan 24La 46
NW7 24Ab 48
Abercorn Wlk. NW8 3A 214 (41Eb 89)
Abercorn Way GU21: Wok 10L 167
SE1 50Wb 91
Abercrombie Dr. EN1: Enf 11Wb 33
Abercrombie Rd. E20 36Dc 72
Abercrombie St. SW11 54Gb 111
Aberdale Ct. SE16 47Zb 92
(off Garter Way)
Aberdale Gdns. EN6: Pot B 4Bb 17
Aberdare Cl. BR4: W W'ck 75Ec 158
Aberdare Gdns. NW6 38Db 69
NW7 24Za 48
Aberdare Rd. EN3: Pond E 14Yb 34
Aberdeen Av. SL1: Slou 5E 80
Aberdeen Cotts. HA7: Stan 24La 46
Aberdeen Ct. W9 6B 214
Aberdeen La. N5 36Sb 71
Aberdeen Mans. WC1 5F 217
Aberdeen Pde. N18 22Xb 51
(off Aberdeen Rd.)
Aberdeen Pk. N5 36Sb 71
Aberdeen Pl. NW8 6B 214 (42Fb 89)
Aberdeen Rd. CR0: C'don 77Sb 157
HA3: W'stone 26Ha 46
N5 35Sb 71
N18 22Wb 51
(not continuous)
NW10 36Va 68
Aberdeen Sq. E14 46Bc 92
Aberdeen Ter. SE3 54Fc 115
Aberdeen Way GU21: Knap 1F 186
Aberdeen Wharf E1 46Xb 91
(off Wapping High St.)
Aberdour Rd. IG3: Ilf 34Xc 75
Aberdour St. SE1 4H 231 (49Ub 91)
Aberfeldy Ho. SE5 52Rb 113
(not continuous)
Aberfeldy St. E14 43Ec 92
(not continuous)
Aberford Gdns. SE18 53Nc 116
Aberford Rd. WD6: Bore 12Qa 29
Aberfoyle Rd. SW16 65Mb 134
(not continuous)
Abergeldie Rd. SE12 58Kc 115
Abernethy Ho. EC1 1D 224
(off Bartholomew Cl.)
Abernethy Rd. SE13 56Gc 115
Abersham Rd. E8 36Vb 71
Abery St. SE18 49Uc 94
Abigail M. RM3: Hrld W 26Pd 57
Ability Pl. E14 47Dc 92
Ability Plaza E8 38Vb 71
(off Arbutus St.)
Ability Towers EC1 3D 218
Abingdon W14 49Bb 89
(off Kensington Village)
Abingdon Cl. GU21: Wok 10N 167
KT4: Wor Pk 76Xa 154
NW1 37Mb 70
SE1 49Vb 91
(off Bushwood Dr.)
SW19 65Eb 133
UB10: Hil 39P 63
Abingdon Ct. EN8: Walt C 5Ac 20
(off High St.)
GU22: Wok 90B 168
W8 48Cb 89
(off Abingdon Vs.)
Abingdon Gdns. W8 48Cb 89
Abingdon Ho. BR1: Brom 66Kc 137
E2 5K 219
Abingdon Lodge BR2: Brom 68Hc 137
(off Beckenham La.)
W8 48Cb 89
Abingdon Mans. W8 48Cb 89
(off Pater St.)
Abingdon Pl. EN6: Pot B 4Db 17
Abingdon Rd. N3 26Eb 49
SW16 68Nb 134
W8 48Cb 89
Abingdon St. SW1 3F 229 (48Nb 90)
Abingdon Vs. W8 48Bb 89
Abingdon Way BR6: Chels 77Xc 161
Abinger Av. SM2: Cheam 81Ya 174
Abinger Cl. BR1: Brom 69Nc 138
CR0: New Ad 79Ec 158
IG11: Bark 35Wc 75
SM6: Wall 78Nb 156
Abinger Ct. SM6: Wall 78Nb 156
(off Abinger Cl.)
W5 45La 86
Abinger Dr. RH1: Redh 8N 207
Abinger Gdns. TW7: Isle 55Ga 108
Abinger Gro. SE8 51Bc 114
Abinger Ho. SE1 2F 231
Abinger M. W9 42Cb 89
Abinger Rd. W4 48Ua 88
Abington Ct. RM14: Upm 32Sd 78
Ablett St. SE16 50Yb 92
Abney Gdns. N16 33Vb 71
Abney Pk. Cemetery
(Local Nature Reserve) 33Ub 71
Abney Pk. Ter. N16 33Vb 71
(off Cazenove Rd.)
Aborfield NW5 36Lb 70
Aboyne Dr. SW20 68Wa 132
Aboyne Rd. NW10 34Ua 68
SW17 62Fb 133
Abraham Cl. WD19: Wat 21X 45
Abraham Ct. RM14: Upm 33Qd 77
Abraham Fisher Ho. E12 36Qc 74
ABRIDGE 13Xc 37
Abridge Cl. EN8: Walt C 7Zb 20
Abridge Gdns. RM5: Col R 23Cd 56
Abridge Golf Course 9Bd 23
Abridge Pk. RM4: Abr 14Wc 37
Abridge Rd.
CM16: Abr, Lough, They B 9Vc 23
IG7: Abr, Chig 16Tc 36
RM4: Abr 9Vc 23
Absolutely Ice 6H 81
Absolutely Ten Pin 6H 81
Abyssinia Cl. SW11 56Gb 111
Abyssinia Ct. N8 29Pb 50
Abyssinia Rd. SW11 56Gb 111
Acacia Av. GU22: Wok 2P 187
HA4: Ruis 32W 64
HA9: Wemb 36Na 67
N17 24Tb 51
RM12: Horn 33Hd 76
TW8: Bford 52Ka 108
TW17: Shep 71Q 150
TW19: Wray 56A 104
UB3: Hayes 44V 84
UB7: Yiew 45P 83
Acacia Bus. Cen. E11 34Gc 73
Acacia Cl. BR5: Pet W 71Tc 160
HA7: Stan 23Ga 46
KT15: Wdhm 82H 169
SE8 49Ac 92
SE20 68Wb 135
Acacia Ct. DA11: Grav'nd 9C 122
EN9: Walt A 6Jc 21
(off Lamplighters Cl.)
HA1: Harr 29Da 45
Acacia Dr. KT15: Wdhm 82H 169
RM14: Upm 35Qd 77
SM3: Sutt 74Bb 155
SM7: Bans 86Za 174
Acacia Fitness 59Nd 119
Acacia Gdns. BR4: W W'ck 75Ec 158
NW8 1C 214 (40Fb 69)
RM14: Upm 31Vd 78
Acacia Gro. KT3: N Mald 69Ta 131
SE21 61Tb 135
Acacia Hall 59Nd 119
Acacia Ho. N22 25Qb 50
(off Douglas Rd.)
SL9: Chal P 25A 42
Acacia M. UB7: Harm 51M 105
Acacia Pl. NW8 1C 214 (40Fb 69)
Acacia Rd. BR3: Beck 69Bc 136
CR4: Mitc 69Jb 134
DA1: Dart 60Md 119
DA9: Ghithe 58Ud 120
E11 33Gc 73
E17 30Ac 52
EN2: Enf 11Tb 33
N22 25Qb 50
NW8 1C 214 (40Fb 69)
SW16 67Nb 134
TW12: Hamp 65Ca 129
TW18: Staines 64K 127
W3 45Sa 87
Acacias, The EN4: E Barn 15Fb 31
Acacia St. AL10: Hat 3C 8
Acacia Wlk. BR8: Swan 68Fd 140
SW10 52Eb 111
(off Tadema Rd.)
Acacia Way DA15: Sidc 60Vc 117
Academia Way N17 23Ub 51
Academy, The
Middlesex County Cricket Club 26Db 49
Academy, The SW8 51Pb 112
Academy Apartments E8 36Xb 71
(off Dalston La.)
Academy Bldgs. N1 3H 219
Academy Ct. AL2: Lon C 8F 6
DA5: Bexl 61Gd 140
(off Beaconsfield Rd.)
E2 41Yb 92
(off Kirkwall Pl.)
NW6 39Cb 69
RM8: Dag 35Wc 75
WD6: Bore 14Qa 29
Academy Flds. Cl. RM2: Rom 29Jd 56
Academy Flds. Rd. RM2: Rom 29Kd 57
Academy Gdns. CR0: C'don 74Vb 157
UB5: N'olt 40Z 65
W8 47Cb 89
Academy Ho. E3 43Cc 92
(off Violet Rd.)
WD6: Bore 14Qa 29
(off Academy Ct.)
Academy Pl. SE18 53Pc 116
TW7: Isle 53Ga 108
Academy Rd. SE18 53Pc 116
Academy Way E17 25Cc 52
RM8: Dag 35Wc 75
Acanthus Dr. SE1 50Wb 91
Acanthus Rd. SW11 55Jb 112
Access Bus. Pk. KT14: Byfl 83M 169
Accommodation La. UB7: Harm 51L 105
UB7: Lford 53J 105
Accommodation Rd. E4 20Fc 35
(off Ashwood Rd.)
KT16: Longc 6P 147
KT17: Ewe 78Wa 154
NW11 32Bb 69
AC Court KT7: T Ditt 72Ja 152
Accrington Ho. RM3: Rom 22Md 57
(off Montgomery Cres.)
Ace Pde. KT9: Chess 76Na 153
Acer Av. RM13: Rain 41Md 97
UB4: Yead 43Aa 85
Acer Cl. KT19: Eps 81Sa 173
SM7: Bans 87Za 174
Acer Ct. EN3: Enf H 13Ac 34
(off Enstone Rd.)
Acer Dr. GU24: W End 5D 166
Acer Rd. E8 38Vb 71
TN16: Big H 88Mc 179
Acers AL2: Park 10A 6
BR7: Chst 66Nc 138
Aces Ct. TW3: Houn 54Ea 108
Acfold Rd. SW6 53Db 111
Achilles Cl. HP2: Hem H 1P 3
SE1 50Wb 91
Achilles Ho. E2 40Xb 71
(off Old Bethnal Grn. Rd.)
Achilles Pl. GU21: Wok 9N 167
Achilles Rd. NW6 36Cb 69
Achilles Statue 7J 221 (46Jb 90)
Achilles St. SE14 52Ac 114
Achilles Way W1 7J 221 (46Jb 90)
Acklam Rd. W10 43Bb 88
(not continuous)
Acklington Dr. NW9 25Ua 48
Ackmar Rd. SW6 53Cb 111
Ackroyd Dr. E3 43Bc 92
Ackroyd Rd. SE23 59Zb 114
Acland Cl. SE18 52Tc 116
Acland Cres. SE5 55Tb 113
Acland Ho. SW9 53Pb 112
Acland Rd. NW2 37Xa 68
Acle Cl. IG6: Ilf 24Rc 54
Acme Rd. WD24: Wat 10W 12
Acme Studios E14 43Ec 92
(Gillender St.)
E14 43Ec 92
(off Leven Rd.)
Acock Gro. UB5: N'olt 35Da 65
Acol Ct. NW6 38Cb 69
Acol Cres. HA4: Ruis 36X 65
Acol Rd. NW6 38Cb 69
Aconbury Rd. RM9: Dag 39Xc 75
Acorn Cen., The IG6: Ilf 23Xc 55
Acorn Cl. BR7: Chst 64Sc 138
E4 22Dc 52
EN2: Enf 11Rb 33
HA7: Stan 24Ka 46
RM1: Rom 26Gd 56
SL3: L'ly 50D 82
SM7: Bans 87Ab 174
TW12: Hamp 65Da 129
Acorn Ct. AL2: Lon C 9F 6
E3 40Cc 72
(off Morville St.)
E6 38Nc 74
EN8: Walt C 5Zb 20
IG2: Ilf 30Uc 54
Acorn Gdns. SE19 67Vb 135
W3 43Ta 87
Acorn Gro. GU22: Wok 93A 188
HA4: Ruis 35V 64
KT20: Kgswd 96Bb 195
UB3: Harl 52V 106
Acorn Ho. BR8: Swan 68Hd 140
(off Squirrels Cl.)
Acorn Ind. Pk. DA1: Cray 57Jd 118
Acorn La. EN6: Cuff 1Nb 18
Acorn Pde. SE15 52Xb 113
Acorn Pl. WD24: Wat 9W 12
Acorn Production Cen. N7 38Nb 70
Acorn Rd. DA1: Cray 57Hd 118
HP3: Hem H 3A 4
Acorns, The AL4: St A 2H 7
IG7: Chig 21Uc 54
TN13: S'oaks 95Jd 202
Acorns Way KT10: Esh 78Ea 152
Acorn Trad. Est.
RM20: Grays 51Zd 121
Acorn Wlk. SE16 46Ac 92
Acorn Way BR3: Beck 71Ec 158
BR6: Farnb 77Rc 160
SE23 62Zb 136
Acqua Ho. TW9: Kew 52Ra 109
Acre Dr. SE22 56Wb 113
Acrefield Ho. NW4 28Za 48
(off Belle Vue Est.)
Acrefield Rd. SL9: Chal P 27A 42
Acre Gro. GU22: Wok 92A 188
Acre La. SM5: Cars 77Jb 156
SM6: Wall 77Jb 156
SW2 56Nb 112
Acre Pas. SL4: Wind 3H 103
Acre Path UB5: N'olt 37Aa 65
(off Arnold Rd.)
Acre Rd. KT2: King T 67Na 131
RM10: Dag 38Dd 76
SW19 65Fb 133
Acres, The SS17: Stan H 1P 101
Acres Gdns. KT20: Tad 91Za 194
Acre Vw. RM11: Horn 28Nd 57
Acre Way HA6: Nwood 25V 44
Acrewood HP2: Hem H 3N 3
Acrewood Pk. AL4: St A 2K 7
Acrewood Way AL4: St A 2K 7
Acris St. SW18 57Eb 111
Acropolis Ho. KT1: King T 69Pa 131
(off Winery La.)
ACTON 46Sa 87
Acton Apartments N1 39Tb 71
(off Branch Pl.)
Acton Central Ind. Est. W3 46Ra 87
Acton Cl. EN8: Chesh 3Ac 20
N9 19Wb 33
ACTON GREEN 48Sa 87
Acton Hill M. W3 46Ra 87
Acton Ho. E8 39Vb 71
(off Lee St.)
W3 44Sa 87
Acton La. NW10 41Sa 87
W3 47Sa 87
W4 49Sa 87
(not continuous)
Acton M. E8 39Vb 71
Acton Pk. Est. W3 47Ta 87
Acton St. WC1 4H 217 (41Pb 90)
Acton Swimming Baths 46Sa 87
(off Salisbury St.)
Acton Va. Ind. Pk. W3 47Va 88
Acuba Rd. SW18 61Db 133
Acworth Cl. N9 17Yb 34
Acworth Ho. SE18 51Rc 116
(off Barnfield Rd.)
Acworth Pl. DA1: Dart 58Ld 119
Ada Cl. N11 20Hb 31
Ada Ct. N1 39Sb 71
(off Packington St.)
W9 4A 214 (41Eb 89)
Ada Gdns. E14 44Fc 93
E15 39Hc 73
Adagio Point SE8 51Dc 114
(off Copperas St.)
Ada Ho. E2 39Wb 71
(off Ada Pl.)
Adair Cl. SE25 69Xb 135
Adair Gdns. CR3: Cat'm 93Sb 197
Adair Ho. SW3 51Gb 111
(off Oakley St.)
Adair Rd. W10 42Ab 88
Adair Twr. W10 42Ab 88
(off Appleford Rd.)
Adair Wlk. GU24: Brkwd 3A 186
Ada Kennedy Ct. SE10 52Ec 114
(off Greenwich Sth. St.)
Ada Lewis Ho. HA9: Wemb 35Pa 67
Adam & Eve Ct. W1 2C 222
Adam & Eve M. W8 48Cb 89
Ada Maria Ct. E1 44Xb 91
(off James Voller Way)
Adam Cl. NW7 23Za 48
SE6 63Bc 136
SL1: Slou 6E 80

Adam Ct.—Albert Ct. Ga.

Adam Ct. DA2: Wilm 63Ld 141
SE11 6B 230
SW7 5A 226
Adamfields NW3 38Fb 69
(off Adamson Rd.)
Adam Rd. E4 23Bc 52
Adams Bri. Bus. Cen.
HA9: Wemb 36Ra 67
Adams Cl. KT5: Surb 72Pa 153
N3 24Cb 49
NW9 33Ra 67
RM5: Col R 25Ed 56
Adams Ct. E17 30Ac 52
EC2 2G 225 (44Ub 91)
WD25: Wat 8Z 13
Adams Cft. GU24: Brkwd 2A 186
Adams Gdns. Est. SE16 47Yb 92
Adams Ho. E14 44Fc 93
(off Aberfeldy St.)
Adamsley Rd. SS17: Stan H 3K 101
Adams M. N22 24Pb 50
SW17 61Hb 133
Adamson Ct. N2 27Gb 49
Adamson Rd. E16 44Jc 93
NW3 38Fb 69
Adamson Way BR3: Beck 71Ec 158
Adams Pl. E14 46Dc 92
(off The Nth. Colonnade)
N7 36Pb 70
Adams Quarter TW8: Bford 52La 108
Adamsrill Cl. EN1: Enf 16Tb 33
Adamsrill Rd. SE26 63Zb 136
Adams Rd. BR3: Beck 71Ac 158
N17 26Tb 51
SS17: Stan H 2N 101
Adam's Row W1 5J 221 (45Jb 90)
Adams Sq. DA6: Bex 55Ad 117
Adams Ter. E3 41Cc 92
(off Rainhill Way)
Adam St. WC2 5G 223 (45Nb 90)
Adams Wlk. KT1: King T 68Na 131
Adams Way CR0: C'don 72Vb 157
SE25 71Xb 157
Adam Wlk. SW6 52Ya 110
Adana SE13 54Ec 114
Ada Pl. E2 39Wb 71
Adare Wlk. SW16 62Pb 134
Ada Rd. HA0: Wemb 34Ma 67
SE5 52Ub 113
Adastral Ho. WC1 7H 217
Adastra Way SM6: Wall 79Nb 156
Ada St. E8 39Xb 71
Adcock Wlk. BR6: Orp 77Vc 161
Adderley Gdns. SE9 63Qc 138
Adderley Gro. SW11 57Jb 112
Adderley Rd. HA3: W'stone 25Ha 46
Adderley St. E14 44Ec 92
Addey Ho. SE8 52Bc 114
ADDINGTON 78Cc 158
Addington Bus. Cen.
CR0: New Ad 82Gc 179
Addington Cl. SL4: Wind 5E 102
Addington Ct. SW14 55Ta 109
Addington Court Golf Course 81Cc 178
Addington Dr. N12 23Fb 49
Addington Golf Course, The 77Bc 158
Addington Gro. SE26 63Ac 136
Addington Hgts. CR0: New Ad 83Ec 178
Addington Ho. SW9 54Pb 112
(off Stockwell Rd.)
Addington Lofts SE5 52Sb 113
(off Bethwin Rd.)
Addington Palace Golf Course 79Ac 158
Addington Rd. BR4: W W'ck 77Ec 158
CR0: C'don 74Qb 156
CR2: Sande, Sels 83Wb 177
E3 41Cc 92
E16 42Gc 93
N4 30Qb 50
Addington Sq. SE5 51Tb 113
(not continuous)
Addington St. SE1 2J 229 (47Pb 90)
Addington Village Rd.
CR0: Addtn 79Bc 158
(not continuous)
Addis Cl. EN3: Enf H 11Zb 34
ADDISCOMBE 74Wb 157
Addiscombe Av. CR0: C'don 74Wb 157
Addiscombe Cl. HA3: Kenton 29La 46
Addiscombe Ct. Rd. CR0: C'don 74Ub 157
Addiscombe Gro. CR0: C'don 75Ub 157
Addiscombe Rd. CR0: C'don 75Tb 157
(not continuous)
WD18: Wat 14X 27
Addis Ho. E1 43Yb 92
(off Lindley St.)
Addisland Ct. W14 47Ab 88
(off Holland Vs. Rd.)
Addison Av. N14 16Kb 32
TW3: Houn 53Ea 108
W11 46Ab 88
Addison Bri. Pl. W14 49Bb 89
Addison Cl. BR5: Pet W 73Sc 160
CR3: Cat'm 94Tb 197
HA6: Nwood 25W 44
SL0: Iver 45G 82
Addison Ct. CM16: Epp 3Wc 23
NW6 39Cb 69
(off Brondesbury Rd.)
Addison Cres. W14 48Ab 88
(not continuous)
Addison Dr. SE12 57Kc 115
Addison Gdns. KT5: Surb 70Pa 131
RM17: Grays 49Ee 99
W14 48Za 88
Addison Gro. W4 48Ua 88
Addison Ho. NW8 3B 214
Addison Pk. Mans. W14 48Za 88
(off Richmond Way)
Addison Pl. SE25 70Wb 135
UB1: S'hall 45Ca 85
W11 46Ab 88
Addison Rd. BR2: Brom 71Lc 159
CR3: Cat'm 93Tb 197
E11 30Jc 53
E17 29Dc 52
EN3: Enf H 11Yb 34
GU21: Wok 89B 168
IG6: Ilf 25Sc 54
SE25 70Wb 135
TW11: Tedd 65Ka 130
W14 47Ab 88
Addisons Cl. CR0: C'don 75Bc 158
Addison Ter. W4 49Sa 87
(off Chiswick Rd.)
Addison Way HA6: Nwood 25V 44
NW11 28Bb 49
UB3: Hayes 44W 84
Addle Hill EC4 3C 224 (44Rb 91)
ADDLESTONE 77L 149
Addlestone Ho. KT15: Add 76K 149
W10 43Ya 88
(off Sutton Way)
Addlestone Leisure Cen. 77J 149
ADDLESTONE MOOR 75K 149
Addlestone Moor KT15: Add 75L 149
Addlestone Pk. KT15: Add 78K 149
Addlestone Rd. KT13: Weyb 77N 149
KT15: Add 77N 149
Addle St. EC2 1E 224 (44Sb 91)
Addy Ho. SE16 49Yb 92
Adecroft Way KT8: W Mole 69Ea 130
Adela Av. KT3: N Mald 71Xa 154
Adela Ho. W6 50Ya 88
(off Queen Caroline St.)
Adelaide Av. SE4 56Bc 114
Adelaide Cl. EN1: Enf 10Ub 19
HA7: Stan 21Ja 46
SL1: Slou 7E 80
SW9 56Qb 112
Adelaide Ct. BR3: Beck 66Cc 136
E9 36Ac 72
(off Kenworthy Rd.)
NW8 2A 214
W7 47Ha 86
Adelaide Gdns. RM6: Chad H 29Ad 55
Adelaide Gro. W12 46Wa 88
Adelaide Ho. E15 40Hc 73
E17 26Bc 52
SE5 54Ub 113
W11 44Bb 89
(off Portobello Rd.)
Adelaide Pl. KT13: Weyb 77T 150
Adelaide Rd. BR7: Chst 64Rc 138
E10 34Dc 72
IG1: Ilf 33Rc 74
KT6: Surb 71Na 153
KT12: Walt T 76W 150
NW3 38Fb 69
RM18: Tilb 3B 122
SL4: Wind 3K 103
SW18 57Cb 111
TW5: Hest 53Aa 107
TW9: Rich 56Pa 109
TW11: Tedd 65Ha 130
TW15: Ashf 64M 127
UB2: S'hall 49Aa 85
W13 46Ja 86
Adelaide Sq. SL4: Wind 4H 103
Adelaide St. AL3: St A 1B 6
WC2 5F 223 (45Nb 90)
(not continuous)
Adelaide Ter. TW8: Bford 50Ma 87
Adela St. W10 42Ab 88
Adelina Gro. E1 43Yb 92
Adelina M. SW12 60Mb 112
Adelina Yd. E1 43Yb 92
(off Adelina Gro.)
Adeline Pl. WC1 1E 222 (43Mb 90)
Adeliza Cl. IG11: Bark 38Sc 74
Adelphi Ct. E8 38Vb 71
(off Celandine Dr.)
SE16 47Zb 92
(off Garter Way)
W4 51Ta 109
Adelphi Cres. RM12: Horn 33Jd 76
UB4: Hayes 41U 84
Adelphi Gdns. SL1: Slou 7J 81
Adelphi Rd. KT17: Eps 85Ta 173
Adelphi Ter. WC2 5G 223 (45Nb 90)
Adelphi Theatre 5G 223
Adelphi Way UB4: Hayes 41V 84
Adeney Cl. W6 51Za 110
Aden Gro. N16 35Tb 71
Adenmore Rd. SE6 59Cc 114
Aden Rd. EN3: Brim 14Ac 34
IG1: Ilf 31Sc 74
Aden Ter. N16 35Tb 71
ADEYFIELD 2A 4
Adeyfield Gdns. HP2: Hem H 1P 3
Adeyfield Ho. EC1 4G 219
Adeyfield Rd. HP2: Hem H 2N 3
Adhara Rd. HA6: Nwood 22W 44
Adie Rd. W6 48Ya 88
Adine Rd. E13 42Kc 93
Adler Ind. Est. UB3: Hayes 47T 84
Adler St. E1 44Wb 91
Adley St. E5 36Ac 72
Adlington Cl. N18 22Tb 51
Admark Ho. KT18: Eps 87Ra 173
Admaston Rd. SE18 52Sc 116
Admiral Cl. BR5: St P 70Zc 139
KT13: Weyb 75U 150
Admiral Ct. IG11: Bark 40Xc 75
SE5 53Ub 113
(off Havil St.)
SM5: Cars 74Gb 155
SW10 53Eb 111
(off Admiral Sq.)
W1 1H 221
Admiral Hood Ho. SL9: Chal P 21A 42
Admiral Ho. SW1 5C 228
TW11: Tedd 63Ja 130
Admiral Hyson Ind. Est. SE16 50Xb 91
Admiral M. SW19 66Eb 133
W10 42Za 88
Admiral Pl. N8 28Rb 51
SE16 46Ac 92
Admirals Cl. AL4: Col H 5A 8
E18 28Kc 53
Admirals Ct. E6 44Rc 94
(off Trader Rd.)
HA6: Nwood 22W 44
SE1 7K 225
Admiral Seymour Rd. SE9 56Pc 116
Admiral's Ga. SE10 53Dc 114
Admirals Lodge RM1: Rom 28Hd 56
Admiral Sq. SW10 53Eb 111
Admiral's Rd. GU24: Pirb 7A 186
Admirals Rd. KT22: Fet 98Fa 192
KT23: Bookh 100Ea 192
Admiral Stirling Ct. KT13: Weyb 77P 149
Admiral's Twr. SE10 51Dc 114
(off Dowells St.)
Admiral St. SE8 54Cc 114
Admirals Wlk. AL1: St A 4E 6
CR5: Coul 92Pb 196
DA9: Ghithe 57Xd 120
NW3 34Eb 69
Admirals Way DA12: Grav'nd 8F 122
E14 47Cc 92
Admiralty & Commercial Court
2K 223 (44Qb 90)
Admiralty Arch 6E 222 (46Mb 90)
Admiralty Bldg. KT2: King T 67Ma 131
(off Down Hall Rd.)
Admiralty Cl. SE8 52Cc 114
UB7: W Dray 47N 83
Admiralty Rd. TW11: Tedd 65Ha 130
Admiralty Way TW11: Tedd 65Ha 130
Admiral Wlk. W9 43Cb 89
Adnams Wlk. RM13: Rain 37Jd 76
Adolf St. SE6 63Dc 136
Adolphus Rd. N4 33Rb 71
Adolphus St. SE8 52Bc 114
Adomar Rd. RM8: Dag 34Ad 75
Adpar St. W2 7B 214 (43Fb 89)
Adrian Av. NW2 32Xa 68
Adrian Boult Ho. E2 41Xb 91
(off Mansford St.)
Adrian Cl. EN5: Barn 16Za 30
HP1: Hem H 3K 3
UB9: Hare 25M 43
Adrian Ho. E15 38Fc 73
(off Jupp Rd.)
N1 1J 217
SW8 52Nb 112
(off Wyvil Rd.)
Adrian M. SW10 51Db 111
Adrian Rd. WD5: Ab L 3U 12
Adrians Wlk. SL2: Slou 6K 81
Adriatic Apartments E16 45Jc 93
(off Western Gateway)
Adriatic Bldg. E14 45Ac 92
(off Horseferry Rd.)
Adriatic Ho. E1 42Zb 92
(off Ernest St.)
Adrienne Av. UB1: S'hall 42Ba 85
Adrienne Bus. Cen. UB1: S'hall 41Ba 85
Adron Ho. SE16 49Yb 92
(off Millender Wlk.)
Adstock Ho. N1 38Rb 71
(off The Sutton Est.)
Adstock M. SL9: Chal P 25A 42
Adstock Way RM17: Grays 49Ce 99
Advance Rd. SE27 63Sb 135
Adventure Kingdom 68Kc 137
(off Stockwell Cl.)
Adventurers Ct. E14 45Fc 93
(off Newport Av.)
Adventure World 8H 7
Advent Way N18 22Yb 52
Advice Av. RM16: Grays 47Ce 99
Adys Lawn NW2 37Xa 68
Ady's Rd. SE15 55Vb 113
Aegean Apartments E16 45Jc 93
(off Western Gateway)
Aegon Ho. E14 48Dc 92
(off Lanark Sq.)
Aerodrome Rd. NW4 26Va 48
NW9 26Va 48
Aerodrome Way TW5: Hest 51Y 107
WD25: Wat 6V 12
Aeroville NW9 26Ua 48
AFC Hornchurch 33Qd 77
AFC Wimbledon 69Qa 131
Affleck St. N1 2J 217 (40Pb 70)
Afghan Rd. SW11 54Gb 111
Afsil Ho. EC1 1A 224
Aftab Ter. E1 42Xb 91
(off Tent St.)
Afton Dr. RM15: S Ock 44Xd 98
Agamemnon Rd. NW6 35Bb 69
Agar Cl. KT6: Surb 75Pa 153
Agar Gro. NW1 38Lb 70
Agar Gro. Est. NW1 38Mb 70
Agar Ho. KT1: King T 69Na 131
(off Denmark Rd.)
Agar Pl. NW1 38Lb 70
Agars Pl. SL3: Dat 1L 103
Agar St. WC2 5F 223 (45Nb 90)
Agate Cl. E16 44Mc 93
NW10 41Qa 87
Agate Rd. W6 48Ya 88
Agates La. KT21: Asht 90Ma 173
Agatha Cl. E1 46Xb 91
Agaton Path SE9 61Sc 138
Agaton Rd. SE9 61Sc 138
Agave Rd. NW2 35Ya 68
Agdon St. EC1 5B 218 (42Rb 91)
Ager Av. RM8: Dag 32Zc 75
Agincourt SL5: Asc 9A 124
Agincourt Rd. NW3 35Hb 69
Agister Rd. IG7: Chig 22Wc 55
Agnes Av. IG1: Ilf 35Qc 74
Agnes Cl. E6 45Qc 94
Agnesfield Cl. N12 23Gb 49
Agnes Gdns. RM8: Dag 35Zc 75
Agnes George Wlk. E16 46Mc 93
Agnes Ho. W11 45Za 88
(off St Ann's Rd.)
Agnes Rd. W3 46Va 88
Agnes Scott Ct. KT13: Weyb 76R 150
(off Palace Dr.)
Agnes St. E14 44Bc 92
Agnew Rd. SE23 59Zb 114
Agricola Ct. E3 39Bc 72
(off Parnell Rd.)
Agricola Pl. EN1: Enf 15Vb 33
Agua Ho. KT16: Chert 73L 149
Ahoy Cen., The SE8 50Cc 92
(off Stretton Mans.)
Aida M. RM13: Rain 42Ld 97
Aidan Cl. RM8: Dag 35Ad 75
Aigburth Mans. SW9 52Qb 112
(off Mowll St.)
Ailantus Ct. HA8: Edg 22Pa 47
Aileen Wlk. E15 38Hc 73
Ailsa Av. TW1: Twick 57Ja 108
Ailsa Ho. E16 45Qc 94
(off University Way)
Ailsa Rd. TW1: Twick 57Ka 108
Ailsa St. E14 43Ec 92
Ailsa Wlk. E14 47Cc 92
(off Alpha Gro.)
AIMES GREEN 1Hc 21
Ainger M. NW3 38Hb 69
(off Ainger Rd.)
Ainger Rd. NW3 38Hb 69
Ainsdale NW1 2B 216
Ainsdale Cl. BR6: Orp 74Tc 160
Ainsdale Cres. HA5: Pinn 27Ca 45
Ainsdale Dr. SE1 50Wb 91
Ainsdale Rd. W5 42Ma 87
WD19: Wat 20Y 27
Ainsdale Way GU21: Wok 10L 167
Ainsley Av. RM7: Rom 30Dd 56
Ainsley Cl. N9 18Ub 33
Ainsley St. E2 41Xb 91
Ainslie Ct. HA0: Wemb 40Na 67
Ainslie Wlk. SW12 59Kb 112
Ainslie Wood Cres. E4 22Dc 52
Ainslie Wood Gdns. E4 21Dc 52
Ainslie Wood Nature Reserve 22Dc 52
Ainslie Wood Rd. E4 22Cc 52
Ainsty Est. SE16 47Zb 92
Ainsty St. SE16 47Yb 92
Ainsworth Cl. NW2 34Wa 68
SE15 54Ub 113
Ainsworth Ct. NW10 41Xa 88
(off Plough Cl.)
Ainsworth Ho. NW8 39Db 69
(off Ainsworth Way)
W10 41Ab 88
(off Kilburn La.)
Ainsworth Rd. CR0: C'don 74Rb 157
E9 38Yb 72
Ainsworth Way NW8 39Eb 69
Aintree Av. E6 39Nc 74
Aintree Cl. DA12: Grav'nd 2D 144
SL3: Poyle 53G 104
UB8: Hil 44R 84
Aintree Cres. IG6: Ilf 26Sc 54
Aintree Est. SW6 52Ab 110
Aintree Gro. RM14: Upm 34Pd 77
Aintree Rd. UB6: G'frd 40Ka 66
Aintree St. SW6 52Ab 110
Airbourne Ho. SM6: Wall 77Lb 156
(off Maldon Rd.)
Air Call Bus. Cen. NW9 27Ta 47
Airco Cl. NW9 27Ta 47
Aird Ho. SE1 4D 230
Airdrie Cl. N1 38Pb 70
UB4: Yead 43Aa 85
Airedale Av. W4 49Va 88
Airedale Av. Sth. W4 50Va 88
Airedale Cl. DA2: Dart 60Sd 120
Airedale Rd. SW12 59Hb 111
W5 48La 86
Airedale Wlk. E15 38Gc 73
(off Maiden Rd.)
Aire Dr. RM15: S Ock 42Xd 98
Airey Neave Ct. RM17: Grays 47Ce 99
Airfield Pathway RM12: Horn 38Ld 77
Airfield Way RM12: Horn 37Kd 77
Air Forces Memorial 3P 125
Airlie Gdns. IG1: Ilf 32Rc 74
W8 46Cb 89
Airlinks Golf Course 50Y 85
Air Links Ind. Est. TW13: Hanw 62Aa 129
Airlinks Ind. Est. TW5: Cran 50Y 85
Air Pk. Way TW13: Felt 61X 129
Airport Bowl 53U 106
Airport Ga. Bus. Cen. UB7: Sip 52P 105
Airport Ind. Est. TN16: Big H 86Mc 179
Airport Way TW19: Stanw M 56H 105
Air Sea M. TW2: Twick 62Ea 130
Air St. W1 5C 222 (45Lb 90)
Airthrie Rd. IG3: Ilf 33Xc 75
Aisgill Av. W14 50Bb 89
(not continuous)
Aisher Rd. SE28 45Yc 95
Aisher Way TN13: Riv 93Gd 202
Aislibie Rd. SE12 56Gc 115
Aisselle Pl. KT10: Esh 77Da 151
Aiten Pl. W6 49Wa 88
Aithan Ho. E14 44Bc 92
(off Copenhagen Pl.)
Aitken Cl. CR4: Mitc 73Hb 155
E8 39Wb 71
HA4: Eastc 30W 44
Aitken Rd. EN5: Barn 15Ya 30
SE6 61Dc 136
Aitman Dr. TW8: Bford 50Qa 87
Aitons Ho. TW8: Bford 50Na 87
Aits Vw. KT8: W Mole 69Da 129
Ajax Av. NW9 27Ua 48
SL1: Slou 5F 80
Ajax Ho. E2 40Xb 71
(off Old Bethnal Grn. Rd.)
Ajax Rd. NW6 35Bb 69
Akabusi Cl. CR0: C'don 72Wb 157
Akbar Ho. E14 49Dc 92
(off Cahir St.)
Akehurst La. TN13: S'oaks 97Jd 203
Akehurst St. SW15 58Wa 110
Akeman Cl. AL3: St A 4M 5
Akenside Rd. NW3 36Fb 69
Akerman Rd. KT6: Surb 72La 152
SW9 54Rb 113
Akers Ct. EN8: Walt C 4Ac 20
Akers La. WD3: Chor 16F 24
Akintaro Ho. SE8 51Bc 114
(off Alverton St.)
Alabama St. SE18 52Tc 116
Alacross Rd. W5 47La 86
Alamaro Lodge SE10 48Hc 93
(off Teal St.)
Alamein Gdns. DA2: Dart 59Td 120
Alamein Rd. DA10: Swans 58Zd 121
Alana Hgts. E4 17Dc 34
Alanbrooke DA12: Grav'nd 9E 122
Alanbrooke Cl. GU21: Knap 10G 166
Alan Cl. DA1: Dart 56Ld 119
Alan Coren Cl. NW2 35Ya 68
Alandale Dr. HA5: Pinn 25X 45
Aland Ct. SE16 48Ac 92
Alander M. E17 28Ec 52
Alan Dr. EN5: Barn 16Ab 30
Alan Gdns. RM7: Rush G 31Cd 76
Alan Hilton Ct. KT16: Ott 79F 148
(off Cheshire Cl.)
Alan Hocken Way E15 40Gc 73
Alan Preece Ct. NW6 38Za 68
Alan Rd. SW19 64Ab 132
Alanthus Cl. SE12 58Jc 115
Alan Way SL3: Geor G 44A 82
Alaska Apartments E16 45Jc 93
(off Western Gateway)
Alaska Bldg. SE13 53Dc 114
(off Deal's Gateway)
Alaska Bldgs. SE1 4K 231 (48Ub 91)
Alaska St. SE1 7K 223 (46Qb 90)
Alastor Ho. E14 48Ec 92
(off Strattondale Ho.)
Alba Cl. UB4: Yead 42Z 85
Albacore Cres. SE13 58Dc 114
Albacore Way UB3: Hayes 45V 84
Alba Gdns. NW11 30Ab 48
Albain Cres. TW15: Ashf 61N 127
Alba M. SW18 61Cb 133
Alban Arena (Theatre & Cinema) 2B 6
Alban Av. AL3: St A 1B 6
Alban Ct. AL1: St A 2F 6
(off Burleigh Rd.)
Alban Cres. DA4: Farni 74Qd 163
WD6: Bore 11Ra 29
Alban Highwalk EC2 1E 224
(not continuous)
Alban Ho. WD6: Bore 11Ra 29
Albanian Ct. AL1: St A 3E 6
Alban Pk. AL4: St A 2K 7
Albans Vw. WD25: Wat 5X 13
Albanwood WD25: Wat 5X 13
Albany, The 52Cc 114
Albany N12 23Db 49
W1 5B 222 (45Lb 90)
Albany, The IG8: Wfd G 21Hc 53
Albany Cl. DA5: Bexl 59Yc 117
KT10: Esh 81Ca 171
N15 28Rb 51
RH2: Reig 3J 207
SW14 56Ra 109
UB10: Ick 36Q 64
WD23: Bush 16Fa 28
Albany Ct. CM16: Epp 2Vc 23
E1 44Wb 91
(off Plumber's Row)
E4 16Cc 34
(Chelwood Cl.)
E4 22Bc 52
(Westward Rd.)
E10 31Cc 72
HA8: Edg 25Ta 47
KT13: Weyb 77R 150
(Hillcrest)
KT13: Weyb 75U 150
(Oakhill Gdns.)
NW8 2B 214
NW10 41Xa 88
(off Trenmar Gdns.)
TW15: Ashf 66S 128
TW20: Egh 64D 126
Albany Courtyard W1 5C 222 (45Lb 90)
Albany Cres. HA8: Edg 24Qa 47
KT10: Clay 79Ga 152
Albany Ga. AL1: St A 3B 6
Albany Hgts. RM17: Grays 50Ce 99
(off Hogg La.)
Albany Leisure Cen. 10Zb 20
Albany Mans. SW11 52Gb 111
Albany M. AL2: Chis G 9N 5
(off Nth. Orbital Rd.)
BR1: Brom 65Jc 137
KT2: King T 65Ma 131
N1 38Qb 70
SE5 51Sb 113
SM1: Sutt 78Db 155
Albany Pde. TW8: Bford 51Na 109
Albany Pk. SL3: Coln 53F 104
Albany Pk. Av. EN3: Enf W 11Yb 34
Albany Pk. Rd. KT2: King T 65Ma 131
KT22: Lea 91Ja 192
Albany Pas. TW10: Rich 57Na 109
Albany Pl. TW8: Bford 51Ma 109
TW20: Egh 63D 126
Albany Reach KT7: T Ditt 71Ha 152
Albany Rd. BR7: Chst 64Rc 138
CM15: Pil H 16Xd 40
DA5: Bexl 59Yc 117
DA17: Belv 51Bd 117
E10 31Cc 72
E12 35Mc 73
E17 30Ac 52
EN3: Enf W 9Zb 20
KT3: N Mald 70Ta 131
KT12: Hers 77Z 151
N4 30Qb 50
N18 22Yb 52
RM6: Chad H 30Bd 55
RM12: Horn 32Jd 76
RM18: Tilb 3C 122
SE5 7J 231 (51Tb 113)
SL4: Old Win 7L 103
SL4: Wind 4H 103
SW19 64Db 133
TW8: Bford 51Ma 109
TW10: Rich 57Pa 109
W13 45Ka 86
Albany St. NW1 1K 215 (40Kb 70)
Albany Ter. NW1 6A 216
TW10: Rich 57Pa 109
(off Albany Pas.)
Albany Vw. IG9: Buck H 18Jc 35
Albany Way TW18: Staines 65M 127
Albany Works E3 39Ac 72
(off Gunmakers La.)
Alba Pl. W11 44Bb 89
Albatross NW9 26Va 48
Albatross Cl. E6 43Pc 94
Albatross Gdns. CR2: Sels 83Zb 178
Albatross St. SE18 52Uc 116
Albatross Way SE16 47Zb 92
Albemarle SW19 61Za 132
Albemarle App. IG2: Ilf 30Rc 54
Albemarle Av. EN6: Pot B 5Db 17
TW2: Whitt 60Ba 107
Albemarle Cl. RM17: Grays 47Ce 99
Albemarle Ct. N17 27Xb 51
(off Perkyn Sq.)
Albemarle Gdns. IG2: Ilf 30Rc 54
KT3: N Mald 70Ta 131
Albemarle Ho. SE8 49Bc 92
(off Foreshore)
Albemarle Pk. BR3: Beck 67Dc 136
HA7: Stan 22La 46
Albemarle Rd. BR3: Beck 67Dc 136
EN4: E Barn 17Gb 31
Albemarle St. W1 5A 222 (45Kb 90)
Albemarle Wlk. SW9 55Qb 112
Albemarle Way EC1 6B 218 (42Rb 91)
Alberon Gdns. NW11 28Bb 49
Alberta Av. SM1: Sutt 77Ab 154
Alberta Est. SE17 7C 230
Alberta Ho. UB4: Yead 41X 85
(off Ayles Rd.)
Alberta Rd. DA8: Erith 53Ed 118
EN1: Enf 16Vb 33
Alberta St. SE17 7B 230 (50Rb 91)
Albert Av. E4 21Cc 52
KT16: Chert 69J 127
SW8 52Pb 112
Albert Barnes Ho. SE1 4D 230
Albert Basin Way E16 45Sc 94
Albert Bigg Point E15 40Ec 72
(off Godfrey St.)
Albert Bri. SW3 51Gb 111
Albert Bri. Rd. SW11 52Gb 111
Albert Carr Gdns. SW16 64Nb 134
Albert Cl. E9 39Xb 71
N22 25Mb 50
RM16: Grays 8C 98
SL1: Slou 8K 81
Albert Cotts. E1 43Wb 91
(off Deal St.)
Albert Ct. E7 35Jc 73
EN8: Walt C 6Bc 20
(off Holdbrook Sth.)
SW7 2B 226 (48Fb 89)
Albert Ct. Ga. SW1 2F 227

Albert Cres.—Alfred Gdns.

Albert Cres. E4 21Cc 52
Albert Dane Cen. UB2: S'hall 48Aa 85
Albert Dr. GU21: Wok 87D 168
SW19 61Ab 132
TW18: Staines 64H 127
Albert Emb. SE1 4H 229 (48Pb 90)
(Lambeth Pal. Rd.)
SE1 7G 229 (50Nb 90)
(Vauxhall Bri.)
Albert Gdns. E1 44Zb 92
Albert Ga. SW1 1G 227 (47Hb 89)
Albert Gray Ho. SW10 52Fb 111
(off Worlds End Est.)
Albert Gro. SW20 67Za 132
Albert Hall Mans. SW7 2B 226 (47Fb 89)
Albert Ho. E18 27Kc 53
(off Albert Rd.)
SE28 48Sc 94
Albertine Cl. KT17: Eps D 88Xa 174
Albert Mans. CR0: C'don 74Tb 157
(off Lansdowne Rd.)
SW11 53Hb 111
(off Albert Bri. Rd.)
Albert Memorial
Knightsbridge 2B 226 (47Fb 89)
Albert M. E14 45Ac 92
(off Northey St.)
N4 32Pb 70
RH1: Redh 9A 208
SE4 56Ac 114
UB9: Den 29H 43
W8 3A 226 (48Eb 89)
Albert Murray Cl. DA12: Grav'nd 9E 122
Albert Pal. Mans. SW11 53Kb 112
(off Lurline Gdns.)
Albert Pl. N3 25Cb 49
N17 27Vb 51
SL4: Eton W 10E 80
W8 48Db 89
Albert Rd. BR2: Brom 71Mc 159
BR5: St M Cry 72Xc 161
BR6: Chels 78Wc 161
CR4: Mitc 69Hb 133
CR6: W'ham 89Bc 178
DA2: Wilm 62Ld 141
DA5: Bexl 58Cd 118
DA10: Swans 58Be 121
DA17: Belv 50Bd 95
E10 33Ec 72
E16 46Nc 94
E17 29Cc 52
E18 27Kc 53
EN4: E Barn 14Eb 31
HA2: Harr 27Ea 46
IG1: Ilf 34Rc 74
IG9: Buck H 19Mc 35
KT1: King T 68Pa 131
KT3: N Mald 70Va 132
KT15: Add 76M 149
KT17: Eps 85Va 174
KT21: Asht 90Pa 173
N4 32Pb 70
N15 30Ub 51
N22 25Lb 50
NW4 28Za 48
NW6 40Bb 69
NW7 22Va 48
RH1: Mers 1C 208
RM1: Rom 29Hd 56
RM8: Dag 32Cd 76
SE9 62Nc 138
SE20 65Zb 136
SE25 70Wb 135
SL4: Old Win, Wind 5H 103
SM1: Sutt 78Fb 155
TW1: Twick 60Ha 108
TW3: Houn 56Ca 107
TW10: Rich 57Na 109
TW11: Tedd 65Ha 130
TW12: Hamp H 64Ea 130
TW15: Ashf 64P 127
TW20: Eng G 5P 125
UB2: S'hall 48Z 85
UB3: Hayes 48U 84
UB7: Yiew 46N 83
W5 42Ka 86
Albert Rd. Est. DA17: Belv 50Bd 95
Albert Rd. Nth. RH2: Reig 5H 207
WD17: Wat 13X 27
Albert Rd. Sth. WD17: Wat 13X 27
Alberts Ct. NW1 5E 214
Albert Sleet Ct. N9 20Xb 33
(off Colthurst Dr.)
Albert Sq. E15 36Gc 73
SW8 52Pb 112
Albert Starr Ho. SE8 49Zb 92
(off Haddonfield)
Albert St. AL1: St A 3B 6
CM14: W'ley 22Yd 58
N12 22Eb 49
NW1 1A 216 (39Kb 70)
SL1: Slou 8K 81
(not continuous)
SL4: Wind 3F 102
Albert Studios SW11 53Hb 111
Albert Ter. IG9: Buck H 19Nc 36
NW1 39Jb 70
NW10 39Sa 67
W5 42Ka 86
W6 50Wa 88
(off Beavor La.)
Albert Ter. M. NW1 39Jb 70
Albert Victoria Ho. N22 25Qb 50
Albert Wlk. E16 47Qc 94
Albert Way SE15 52Xb 113
Albert Westcott Ho.
SE17 7C 230 (50Rb 91)
Albert Whicher Ho. E17 28Ec 52
Albert Yd. SE19 65Vb 135
Albery Ct. E8 38Vb 71
(off Middleton Rd.)
Albion Av. N10 25Jb 50
SW8 54Mb 112
Albion Bldgs. N1 2G 217
Albion Cl. RM7: Rom 30Fd 56
SL2: Slou 6L 81
W2 4E 220 (45Gb 89)
Albion Ct. SE10 49Gc 93
(off Azof St.)
SM2: Sutt 80Fb 155
W6 49Xa 88
(off Albion Pl.)
Albion Dr. E8 38Vb 71
Albion Est. SE16 47Zb 92
Albion Gdns. W6 49Xa 88
Albion Ga. W2 4E 220
(not continuous)
Albion Gro. N16 35Ub 71
Albion Hill HP2: Hem H 3M 3
IG10: Lough 15Lc 35
Albion Ho. E16 46Rc 94
(off Church St.)
GU21: Wok 89B 168
SE8 52Cc 114
(off Watsons St.)
Albion M. N1 39Qb 70
NW6 38Bb 69
W2 3E 220 (45Gb 89)
W6 49Xa 88
Albion Pde. DA12: Grav'nd 8F 122
N16 35Tb 71
Albion Pk. IG10: Lough 15Mc 35
Albion Pl. EC1 7B 218 (43Rb 91)
EC2 1G 225 (43Tb 91)
SL4: Wind 4E 102
W6 49Xa 88
Albion Riverside Bldg. SW11 52Gb 111
Albion Rd. AL1: St A 2D 6
DA6: Bex 56Bd 117
DA12: Grav'nd 9E 122
E17 27Ec 52
KT2: King T 67Sa 131
N16 35Tb 71
N17 26Wb 51
RH2: Reig 7L 207
SM2: Sutt 79Fb 155
TW2: Twick 60Ga 108
TW3: Houn 56Ca 107
UB3: Hayes 44U 84
Albion Sq. E8 38Vb 71
(not continuous)
Albion St. CR0: C'don 74Rb 157
SE16 47Yb 92
W2 3E 220 (44Gb 89)
Albion Ter. DA12: Grav'nd 8E 122
E4 14Dc 34
E8 38Vb 71
Albion Vs. Rd. SE26 62Yb 136
Albion Wlk. N1 2G 217
Albion Way EC1 1D 224 (43Sb 91)
HA9: Wemb 34Qa 67
SE13 56Ec 114
Albion Yd. E1 43Xb 91
N1 2G 217 (40Nb 70)
Albon Ho. SW18 58Db 111
(off Neville Gill Cl.)
Albright Ind. Est. RM13: Rain 42Hd 96
Albrighton Rd. SE22 55Ub 113
Albuhera Cl. EN2: Enf 11Qb 32
Albuhera M. NW7 22Za 48
Albury Av. DA7: Bex 54Ad 117
SM2: Cheam 81Ya 174
TW7: Isle 52Ha 108
Albury Cl. KT16: Longc 6L 147
KT19: Eps 81Ra 173
TW12: Hamp 65Da 129
Albury Ct. CR0: C'don 77Sb 157
(off Tanfield Rd.)
CR4: Mitc 68Fb 133
SE8 51Cc 114
(off Albury St.)
SM1: Sutt 77Eb 155
UB5: N'olt 41Y 85
(off Canberra Dr.)
Albury Dr. HA5: Pinn 25Y 45
Albury Gro. Rd. EN8: Chesh 2Zb 20
Albury Ho. SE1 2C 230
Albury M. E12 33Lc 73
Albury Pl. KT10: Clay 79Ga 152
RH1: Mers 1C 208
Albury Ride EN8: Chesh 3Zb 20
Albury Rd. KT9: Chess 78Na 153
KT12: Hers 79U 150
RH1: Mers 1C 208
Albury St. SE8 51Cc 114
Albury Wlk. EN8: Chesh 2Yb 20
(not continuous)
Albyfield BR1: Brom 70Pc 138
Albyn Ho. HP2: Hem H 2M 3
Albyn Rd. SE8 53Cc 114
Albyns Cl. RM13: Rain 38Jd 76
Albyns La. RM4: Stap T, Nave 12Ed 38
Alcester Ct. SM6: Wall 77Kb 156
Alcester Cres. E5 33Xb 71
Alcester Ho. RM3: Rom 22Md 57
(off Northallerton Way)
Alcester Rd. SM6: Wall 77Kb 156
Alcock Cl. SM6: Wall 80Mb 156
Alcock Cres. DA1: Cray 57Jd 118
Alcock Rd. TW5: Hest 52Z 107
Alcocks Cl. KT20: Tad 92Ab 194
Alcocks La. KT20: Kgswd, Tad 93Ab 194
Alconbury DA6: Bex 57Dd 118
Alconbury Cl. WD6: Bore 11Pa 29
Alconbury Rd. E5 33Wb 71
Alcorn Cl. SM3: Sutt 75Cb 155
Alcott Cl. TW14: Felt 60V 106
W7 43Ha 86
Alcuin Ct. HA7: Stan 24La 46
Aldam Pl. N16 33Vb 71
Aldborough Ct. IG2: Ilf 29Vc 55
(off Aldborough Rd. Nth.)
ALDBOROUGH HATCH 28Vc 55
Aldborough Rd. RM10: Dag 37Ed 76
RM14: Upm 33Pd 77
Aldborough Rd. Nth.
IG2: Ilf 29Vc 55
Aldborough Rd. Sth. IG3: Ilf 32Uc 74
Aldborough Spur SL1: Slou 4J 81
Aldbourne Rd. SL1: Burn 3A 80
W12 46Va 88
Aldbridge St. SE17 7J 231 (50Ub 91)
Aldburgh M. W1 2J 221 (44Jb 90)
Aldbury Av. HA9: Wemb 38Ra 67
Aldbury Cl. WD25: Wat 8Z 13
Aldbury Ho. SW3 6D 226
Aldbury M. N9 17Tb 33
Aldbury Rd. WD3: Rick 17H 25
Aldebert Ter. SW8 52Nb 112
Aldeburgh Cl. E5 33Xb 71
Aldeburgh Pl. IG8: Wfd G 21Jc 53
SE10 49Jc 93
(off Aldeburgh St.)
Aldeburgh St. SE10 50Jc 93
Alden Av. E15 41Hc 93
Alden Ct. CR0: C'don 76Ub 157
ALDENHAM 10Da 13
Aldenham Av. WD7: R'lett 8Ja 14
Aldenham Cl. SL3: L'ly 8P 81
Aldenham Country Pk. 15Ka 28
Aldenham Country Pk. Rare Breeds Farm
15Ka 28
Aldenham Dr. UB8: Hil 42R 84
Aldenham Golf Course 10Da 13
Aldenham Gro. WD7: R'lett 6Ka 14
Aldenham Ho. NW1 2C 216
Aldenham Rd. WD6: E'tree 13Ja 28
WD7: R'lett 7Ja 14
WD19: Wat 16Aa 27
WD23: Bush 16Aa 27
WD25: Let H 11Ga 28
Aldenham Sailing Club 15La 28
Aldenham St. NW1 2C 216 (40Lb 70)
Aldenholme KT13: Weyb 79U 150
Alden Ho. E8 39Xb 71
(off Duncan Rd.)
Alden Mead HA5: Hat E 23Ca 45
(off The Avenue)
Aldensley Rd. W6 48Xa 88
Alden Vw. SL4: Wind 3B 102
Alder Av. RM14: Upm 35Pd 77
Alderbourne La. SL0: Iver H 5P 61
SL3: Ful 5P 61
Alderbrook Rd. SW12 58Kb 112
Alderbury Rd. SL3: L'ly 47B 82
SW13 51Wa 110
Alderbury Rd. W. SL3: L'ly 47B 82
Alder Cl. AL2: Park 10P 5
DA18: Erith 47Bd 95
SE15 51Vb 113
SL1: Slou 6D 80
TW20: Eng G 64A 126
Aldercombe La. CR3: Cat'm 99Ub 197
Alder Ct. E7 36Jc 73
N11 23Lb 50
Alder Cft. CR5: Coul 88Pb 176
Alder Dr. RM15: S Ock 42Yd 98
Alderglade Nature Reserve, The 36M 63
Alder Gro. NW2 33Wa 68
Aldergrove Gdns. TW3: Houn 54Aa 107
Aldergrove Wlk. RM12: Horn 37Ld 77
Alder Ho. E3 39Bc 72
(off Hornbeam Sq.)
NW3 37Hb 69
SE4 55Cc 114
SE15 51Vb 113
(off Alder Cl.)
Alder Lodge SW6 53Ya 110
Alderman Av. IG11: Bark 41Wc 95
Aldermanbury EC2 2E 224 (44Sb 91)
Aldermanbury Sq. EC2 1E 224 (43Sb 91)
Alderman Cl. AL9: Wel G 6E 8
DA1: Cray 59Gd 118
Alderman Judge Mall
KT1: King T 68Na 131
(off Eden St.)
Aldermans Hill N13 21Nb 50
Aldermans Ho. E9 36Ac 72
(off Ward La.)
Aldermans Wlk. EC2 1H 225 (43Ub 91)
Aldermary Rd. BR1: Brom 67Jc 137
Aldermere Av. EN8: Chesh 1Yb 20
Alder M. N19 33Lb 70
Aldermoor Rd. SE6 62Bc 136
Alderney Av. TW5: Hest, Isle 52Da 107
Alderney Ct. SE10 51Fc 115
(off Trafalgar Rd.)
Alderney Gdns. UB5: N'olt 38Ba 65
Alderney Ho. EN3: Enf W 10Zb 20
N1 37Sb 71
(off Arran Wlk.)
WD18: Wat 16V 26
Alderney M. SE1 3F 231 (48Tb 91)
Alderney Rd. DA8: Erith 52Jd 118
E1 42Zb 92
Alderney St. SW1 6A 228 (49Kb 90)
Alder Rd. DA14: Sidc 62Vc 139
SL0: Iver H 40F 62
SW14 55Ta 109
UB9: Den 37L 63
Alders, The BR4: W W'ck 74Dc 158
KT14: W Byf 84L 169
N21 16Qb 32
SW16 63Lb 134
TW5: Hest 51Ba 107
TW13: Hanw 63Aa 129
UB9: Den 37L 63
Alders Av. IG8: Wfd G 23Gc 53
ALDERSBROOK 33Kc 73
Aldersbrook Av. EN1: Enf 12Ub 33
Aldersbrook Dr. KT2: King T 65Pa 131
Aldersbrook La. E12 34Pc 74
Aldersbrook Rd. E11 33Kc 73
E12 33Kc 73
Alders Cl. E11 33Kc 73
HA8: Edg 22Sa 47
W5 48Ma 87
Aldersey Gdns. IG11: Bark 37Tc 74
Aldersford Cl. SE4 57Zb 114
Aldersgate Ct. EC1 1D 224
Aldersgate St. EC1 7D 218 (43Sb 91)
Alders Gro. KT8: E Mos 71Fa 152
Aldersgrove EN9: Walt A 6Gc 21
Aldersgrove Av. SE9 62Mc 137
Aldershot Rd. GU24: Pirb 9B 186
NW6 39Bb 69
Aldershot Ter. SE18 52Qc 116
Alderside Wlk. TW20: Eng G 64A 126
Aldersmead Av. CR0: C'don 72Zb 158
Aldersmead Rd. BR3: Beck 66Ac 136
Alderson Pl. UB2: S'hall 46Ea 86
Alderson St. W10 42Ab 88
Alders Rd. HA8: Edg 22Sa 47
RH2: Reig 4K 207
ALDERSTEAD HEATH 97Mb 196
Alderstead Heath Cvn. Site
RH1: Mers 96Mb 196
Alderstead La. RH1: Mers 97Mb 196
Alderton Cl. CM15: Pil H 15Xd 40
IG10: Lough 14Qc 36
NW10 34Ta 67
Alderton Ct. KT8: W Mole 70Ba 129
(off Dunstable Rd.)
Alderton Cres. NW4 29Xa 48
Alderton Hall La. IG10: Lough 14Qc 36
Alderton Hill IG10: Lough 15Nc 36
Alderton M. IG10: Lough 14Qc 36
Alderton Ri. IG10: Lough 14Qc 36
Alderton Rd. CR0: C'don 73Vb 157
RM16: Ors 4G 100
SE24 55Sb 113
Alderton Way IG10: Lough 15Pc 36
NW4 29Xa 48
Alderville Rd. SW6 54Bb 111
Alder Wlk. IG1: Ilf 36Sc 74
WD25: Wat 7X 13
Alder Way BR8: Swan 68Fd 140
Alderwick Ct. N7 37Pb 70
(off Cornelia St.)
Alderwick Dr. TW3: Houn 55Fa 108
Alderwood Cl. CR3: Cat'm 97Ub 197
RM4: Abr 13Xc 37
Alderwood Dr. RM4: Abr 13Xc 37
Alderwood Ho. WD19: Wat 20Y 27
Alderwood M. EN4: Had W 10Eb 17
Alderwood Rd. SE9 58Tc 116
Aldford Ho. W1 6H 221
Aldford St. W1 6H 221 (46Jb 90)
ALDGATE 3K 225
Aldgate E1 44Vb 91
(off Whitechapel High St.)
EC3 3K 225 (44Vb 91)
Aldgate Av. E1 2K 225 (44Vb 91)
Aldgate Barrs E1 2K 225
Aldgate High St. EC3 3K 225 (44Vb 91)
Aldgate Pl. E1 44Vb 91
Aldgate Sq. EC3 3K 225 (44Vb 91)
Aldgate Twr. E1 2K 225 (44Vb 91)
Aldham Dr. RM15: S Ock 43Yd 98
Aldham Ho. SE4 54Bc 114
(off Malpas Rd.)
Aldin Av. Nth. SL1: Slou 7L 81
Aldin Av. Sth. SL1: Slou 7L 81
Aldine Ct. W12 47Ya 88
(off Aldine St.)
Aldine Pl. W12 47Ya 88
Aldine St. W12 47Ya 88
Aldingham Ct. RM12: Horn 36Kd 77
(off Easedale Dr.)
Aldingham Gdns.
RM12: Horn 36Jd 76
Aldington Cl. RM8: Dag 32Yc 75
Aldington Ct. E8 38Wb 71
(off London Flds. W. Side)
Aldington Rd. SE18 48Mc 93
Aldis M. EN3: Enf L 9Cc 20
SW17 64Gb 133
Aldis St. SW17 64Gb 133
Aldred Rd. NW6 36Cb 69
Aldren Rd. SW17 62Eb 133
Aldrich Cres. CR0: New Ad 81Ec 178
Aldriche Way E4 23Ec 52
Aldrich Gdns. SM3: Cheam 76Bb 155
Aldrich Ter. SW18 61Eb 133
Aldrick Ho. N1 1J 217
Aldridge Av. EN3: Enf L 10Cc 20
HA4: Ruis 33Y 65
HA7: Stan 25Na 47
HA8: Edg 20Ra 29
Aldridge Ct. W11 43Bb 89
(off Aldridge Rd. Vs.)
Aldridge Pl. SL2: Stoke P 8K 61
Aldridge Ri. KT3: N Mald 73Ua 154
Aldridge Rd. SL2: Slou 2E 80
Aldridge Rd. Vs. W11 43Bb 89
Aldridge Wlk. N14 17Nb 32
Aldrin Cl. SS17: Stan H 1N 101
Aldrington Rd. SW16 64Lb 134
Aldsworth Cl. W9 42Db 89
Aldwick AL1: St A 4F 6
Aldwick Cl. SE9 62Tc 138
Aldwick Ct. AL1: St A 4F 6
Aldwick Rd. CR0: Bedd 76Pb 156
Aldworth Gro. SE13 58Ec 114
Aldworth Rd. E15 38Gc 73
Aldwych WC2 4H 223 (44Pb 90)
Aldwych Av. IG6: Ilf 28Sc 54
Aldwych Bldgs. WC2 2G 223
Aldwych Cl. RM12: Horn 33Jd 76
Aldwych Ct. E8 38Vb 71
(off Middleton Rd.)
Aldwych Theatre 3H 223
Aldwyck Ct. HP1: Hem H 1L 3
Aldwyn Ho. SW8 52Nb 112
(off Davidson Gdns.)
Aldwyn Pl. TW20: Eng G 5M 125
Aldykes AL10: Hat 1B 8
Alers Rd. DA6: Bex 57Zc 117
Alesia Cl. N22 24Nb 50
Alestan Beck Rd. E16 44Mc 93
Alexa Ct. SM2: Sutt 79Cb 155
W8 49Cb 89
Alexander Av. NW10 38Xa 68
Alexander Cl. BR2: Hayes 74Jc 159
DA15: Sidc 58Uc 116
EN4: E Barn 14Fb 31
TW2: Twick 61Ga 130
UB2: S'hall 46Ea 86
Alexander Ct. BR3: Beck 67Ec 137
EN8: Chesh 2Zb 20
HA7: Stan 27Pa 47
TW16: Sun 65V 128
Alexander Cres. CR3: Cat'm 93Sb 197
Alexander Evans M. SE23 61Zb 136
Alexander Fleming Laboratory Mus.
2C 220 (44Fb 89)
Alexander Godley Cl. KT21: Asht 91Pa 193
Alexander Ho. E14 48Cc 92
(off Tiller Rd.)
KT2: King T 67Na 131
(off Seven Kings Way)
RM14: Upm 30Ud 58
SE15 54Xb 113
(off Godman Rd.)
Alexander La. CM13: Hut 16De 41
CM15: Shenf 15Ce 41
Alexander M. SW16 64Lb 134
W2 44Db 89
Alexander Pl. RH8: Oxt 100Gc 199
SW7 5D 226 (49Gb 89)
Alexander Raby Mill KT15: Add 78N 149
(off Bourneside Rd.)
Alexander Rd. AL2: Lon C 7G 6
BR7: Chst 65Rc 138
CR5: Coul 87Kb 176
DA7: Bex 54Zc 117
DA9: Ghithe 57Yd 120
N19 34Nb 70
RH2: Reig 9J 207
TW20: Egh 64E 126
Alexander Sq. SW3 5D 226 (49Gb 89)
Alexander St. W2 44Cb 89
Alexander Studios SW11 56Fb 111
(off Haydon Way)
Alexanders Wlk.
CR3: Cat'm 98Vb 197
Alexander Ter. SE2 50Xc 95
Alexandra Av. CR6: W'ham 89Bc 178
HA2: Harr 32Ba 65
N22 25Mb 50
SM1: Sutt 76Cb 155
SW11 53Jb 112
UB1: S'hall 45Ba 85
W4 52Ta 109
Alexandra Cl. BR8: Swan 68Gd 140
HA2: Harr 34Ca 65
KT12: Walt T 75W 150
RM16: Grays 7D 100
SE8 51Bc 114
TW15: Ashf 66T 128
TW18: Staines 65M 127
Alexandra Cotts. SE14 53Bc 114
Alexandra Ct. HA9: Wemb 35Pa 67
N14 15Lb 32
SE5 51Sb 113
(off Urlwin St.)
SL4: Wind 4H 103
(off Alexandra Rd.)
SW7 3A 226
TW3: Houn 54Da 107
TW15: Ashf 65T 128
UB6: G'frd 40Da 65
W2 45Db 89
(off Moscow Rd.)
W9 5A 214
WD24: Wat 12Y 27
Alexandra Cres. BR1: Brom 65Hc 137
Alexandra Dr. KT5: Surb 73Qa 153
SE19 64Ub 135
Alexandra Gdns. GU21: Knap 10G 166
N10 28Kb 50
SM5: Cars 80Jb 156
TW3: Houn 54Da 107
W4 52Ua 110
Alexandra Gro. N4 32Rb 71
N12 22Db 49
Alexandra Ho. E16 46Kc 93
(off Wesley Av.)
IG8: Wfd G 24Qc 54
W6 50Ya 88
(off Queen Caroline St.)
Alexandra Lodge KT13: Weyb 77R 150
(off Monument Hill)
Alexandra Mans. KT17: Eps 85Va 174
(off Alexandra Rd.)
SW3 51Fb 111
(off King's Rd.)
W12 46Ya 88
(off Stanlake Rd.)
Alexandra M. N2 27Hb 49
N4 33Rb 71
SW19 65Bb 133
WD17: Wat 12W 26
Alexandra Palace 26Mb 50
Alexandra Pal. Way N8 28Lb 50
N22 28Lb 50
Alexandra Pde. HA2: Harr 35Da 65
Alexandra Pk. Rd. N10 26Kb 50
N22 25Lb 50
Alexandra Pl. CR0: C'don 74Ub 157
NW8 39Eb 69
SE25 71Tb 157
Alexandra Plaza SL1: Slou 7H 81
(off Chalvey Rd. W.)
Alexandra Rd. AL1: St A 2C 6
CM14: B'wood 20Yd 40
CR0: C'don 74Ub 157
CR4: Mitc 66Gb 133
CR6: W'ham 89Bc 178
DA8: Erith 51Hd 118
DA12: Grav'nd 9G 122
E6 41Qc 94
E10 34Ec 72
E17 30Bc 52
E18 27Kc 53
EN3: Pond E 14Zb 34
HP2: Hem H 1M 3
KT2: King T 66Qa 131
KT7: T Ditt 71Ha 152
KT15: Add 77M 149
(not continuous)
KT17: Eps 85Va 174
N8 27Qb 50
N9 17Xb 33
N10 24Kb 50
N15 29Tb 51
NW4 28Za 48
NW8 39Eb 69
RM1: Rom 30Hd 56
RM6: Chad H 30Ad 55
RM13: Rain 39Hd 76
RM18: Tilb 4B 122
SE26 65Zb 136
SL1: Slou 8H 81
SL4: Wind 4H 103
SW14 55Ta 109
SW19 65Bb 133
TN16: Big H 91Kc 199
TW1: Twick 58La 108
TW3: Houn 54Da 107
TW8: Bford 51Ma 109
TW9: Kew 54Pa 109
TW15: Ashf 66T 128
TW20: Eng G 5N 125
UB8: Uxb 40M 63
W4 47Ta 87
WD3: Sarr 8J 11
WD4: Chfd 2J 11
WD4: K Lan 1Q 12
WD6: Bore 10Ta 15
WD17: Wat 12W 26
Alexandra Rd. Ind. Est.
EN3: Pond E 14Zb 34
Alexandra Sq. SM4: Mord 71Cb 155
Alexandra St. E16 43Jc 93
SE14 52Ac 114
Alexandra Ter. DA1: Dart 58Md 119
E14 50Dc 92
(off Westferry Rd.)
Alexandra Wlk. DA4: S Dar 68Ud 142
SE19 64Ub 135
Alexandra Way EN8: Walt C 6Bc 20
KT19: Eps 83Qa 173
RM18: E Til 9K 101
Alexandra Wharf E2 39Xb 71
(off Darwen Pl.)
Alexandra Yd. E9 39Zb 72
Alexandria Apartments SE17 5H 231
Alexandria Rd. W13 45Ja 86
Alex Ct. HP2: Hem H 1M 3
Alex Guy Gdns. RM8: Dag 32Dd 76
Alexia Sq. E14 48Dc 92
Alexis St. SE16 49Wb 91
Alfan La. DA2: Wilm 64Fd 140
Alfearn Rd. E5 35Yb 72
Alford Ct. N1 2E 218
(not continuous)
Alford Grn. CR0: New Ad 79Fc 159
Alford Ho. N6 30Lb 50
Alford Pl. N1 2E 218 (40Sb 71)
Alford Rd. DA8: Erith 50Ed 96
Alfoxton Av. N15 28Rb 51
Alfreda St. SW11 53Kb 112
Alfred Cl. W4 49Ta 87
Alfred Ct. SE16 49Xb 91
(off Bombay St.)
Alfred Dickens Ho. E16 44Hc 93
(off Hallsville Rd.)
Alfred Finlay Ho. N22 26Rb 51
Alfred Gdns. UB1: S'hall 45Aa 85

Alfred Ho.—Ambrose St.

Alfred Ho. DA11: Nflt 10B 122
E9 36Ac 72
(off Homerton Rd.)
E12 38Nc 74
(off Tennyson Av.)
Alfred M. W1 7D 216 (43Mb 90)
Alfred Nunn Ho. NW10 39Va 68
Alfred Pl. DA11: Nflt 10B 122
WC1 7D 216 (43Mb 90)
Alfred Prior Ho. E12 35Qc 74
Alfred Rd. CM14: B'wood 19Zd 41
DA2: Hawl 63Nd 141
DA11: Grav'nd 1D 144
DA17: Belv 50Bd 95
E15 36Hc 73
IG9: Buck H 19Mc 35
KT1: King T 69Na 131
RM15: Avel 46Sd 98
SE25 71Wb 157
SM1: Sutt 78Eb 155
TW13: Felt 61Y 129
W2 43Cb 89
W3 46Sa 87
Alfred Salter Ho. SE1 6K 231
Alfred's Gdns. IG11: Bark 40Uc 74
Alfred St. E3 41Bc 92
RM17: Grays 51Ee 121
Alfreds Way IG11: Bark 41Rc 94
Alfreds Way Ind. Est.
IG11: Bark 40Wc 75
Alfred Vs. E17 28Ec 52
Alfreton Cl. SW19 62Za 132
Alfriston KT5: Surb 72Pa 153
Alfriston Av. CR0: C'don 73Nb 156
HA2: Harr 30Ca 45
Alfriston Cl. DA1: Cray 58Gd 118
KT5: Surb 71Pa 153
Alfriston Rd. SW11 57Hb 111
Algar Cl. HA7: Stan 22Ha 46
TW7: Isle 55Ja 108
Algar Ho. SE1 2B 230
Algar Rd. TW7: Isle 55Ja 108
Algarve Rd. SW18 60Db 111
Algernon Rd. NW4 30Wa 48
NW6 39Cb 69
SE13 56Dc 114
Algers Cl. IG10: Lough 15Mc 35
Algers Mead IG10: Lough 15Mc 35
Algers Rd. IG10: Lough 15Mc 35
Algiers Rd. SE13 56Cc 114
Alibon Gdns. RM10: Dag 36Cd 76
Alibon Rd. RM9: Dag 36Bd 75
RM10: Dag 36Bd 75
Alice Cl. EN5: New Bar 14Eb 31
(off Station App.)
Alice Gilliatt Ct. W14 51Bb 111
(off Star Rd.)
Alice La. E3 39Bc 72
Alice M. TW11: Tedd 64Ha 130
Alice Owen Technology Cen. EC1 3B 218
Alice Ruston Pl. GU22: Wok 1N 187
Alice Shepherd Ho. E14 47Ec 92
(off Manchester Rd.)
Alice St. SE1 4H 231 (48Ub 91)
(not continuous)
Alice Thompson Cl. SE12 61Lc 137
Alice Walker Cl. SE24 56Rb 113
Alice Way TW3: Houn 56Da 107
Alicia Av. HA3: Kenton 28Ka 46
Alicia Cl. HA3: Kenton 28La 46
Alicia Gdns. HA3: Kenton 28Ka 46
Alicia Ho. DA16: Well 53Xc 117
Alie St. E1 3K 225 (44Vb 91)
Alington Cres. NW9 31Sa 67
Alington Gro. SM6: Wall 81Lb 176
Alison Cl. CR0: C'don 74Zb 158
E6 44Qc 94
GU21: Wok 87A 168
HA5: Eastc 30X 45
Alison Ct. HP2: Hem H 1C 4
Aliwal M. SW11 56Gb 111
Aliwal Rd. SW11 56Gb 111
ALKERDEN 59Zd 121
Alkerden La. DA9: Ghithe 58Yd 120
DA10: Swans 58Yd 120
Alkerden Rd. W4 50Ua 88
Alkham Rd. N16 33Vb 71
Allan Barclay Cl. N15 30Vb 51
Allan Cl. KT3: N Mald 71Ta 153
Allandale AL3: St A 5P 5
HP2: Hem H 1M 3
Allandale Av. N3 27Ab 48
Allandale Cres.
EN6: Pot B 4Ab 16
Allandale Pl. BR6: Chels 76Zc 161
Allandale Rd. EN3: Enf W 8Zb 20
RM11: Horn 31Hd 76
Allan Ho. CR8: Purl 83Pb 176
Allanson Ct. E10 33Cc 72
(off Leyton Grange Est.)
Allan Way W3 43Sa 87
Allard Cl. BR5: Orp 73Yc 161
Allard Cres. WD23: B Hea 18Ea 28
Allard Gdns. SW4 57Mb 112
Allard Ho. NW9 26Va 48
(off Boulevard Dr.)
Allardyce St. SW4 56Pb 112
Allbrook Cl. TW11: Tedd 64Ga 130
Allcroft Rd. NW5 36Jb 70
Allder Way CR2: S Croy 80Rb 157
Alldicks Rd. HP3: Hem H 4P 3
Allenby Av. CR2: S Croy 81Sb 177
Allenby Cl. UB6: G'frd 41Ca 85
Allenby Cres. RM17: Grays 50Ee 99
Allenby Dr. RM11: Horn 32Nd 77
Allenby Rd. SE23 62Ac 136
SE28 48Sc 94
TN16: Big H 89Nc 180
UB1: S'hall 41Ca 85
Allen Cl. CR4: Mitc 67Kb 134
TW16: Sun 67X 129
WD7: Shenl 4Na 15
Allen Ct. AL10: Hat 2D 8
E17 30Cc 52
(off Yunus Khan Cl.)
UB6: G'frd 36Ha 66
Allendale Av. UB1: S'hall 44Ca 85
Allendale Cl. DA2: Dart 60Td 120
SE5 54Tb 113
SE26 64Zb 136
Allendale Rd. HA0: Wemb 37Ka 66
UB6: G'frd 37Ka 66
Allen Edwards Dr. SW8 53Nb 112
Allenford Ho. SW15 58Va 110
(off Tunworth Cres.)
Allen Ho. W8 48Cb 89
(off Allen St.)
Allen Ho. Pk. GU22: Wok 2N 187
Allen Mans. W8 48Cb 89
(off Allen St.)
Allen Rd. BR3: Beck 68Zb 136
CR0: C'don 74Qb 156
E3 40Bc 72
KT23: Bookh 98Da 191
N16 35Ub 71
RM13: Rain 40Ld 77
TW16: Sun 67X 129
Allensbury Pl. NW1 38Mb 70
Allens La. TN15: Plax 100Ce 205
Allens Mead
DA12: Grav'nd 10H 123
Allens Rd. EN3: Pond E 15Yb 34
Allen St. W8 48Cb 89
Allensway SS17: Stan H 1P 101
Allenswood SW19 60Ab 110
Allenswood Rd. SE9 55Nc 116
Allen Way SL3: Dat 3N 103
Allerds Rd. SL2: Farn R 9D 60
Allerford Ct. HA2: Harr 29Ea 46
Allerford Rd. SE6 62Dc 136
Allerton Cl. WD6: Bore 10Pa 15
Allerton Ho. N1 3F 219
Allerton Rd. N16 33Sb 71
WD6: Bore 10Na 15
Allerton St. N1 3G 219 (41Tb 91)
Allerton Wlk. N7 33Pb 70
Allestree Rd. SW6 52Ab 110
Alleyn Cres. SE21 61Tb 135
Alleyndale Rd.
RM8: Dag 33Yc 75
Alleyn Ho. SE1 4G 231
Alleyn Pk. SE21 61Tb 135
UB2: S'hall 50Ca 85
Alleyn Rd. SE21 62Tb 135
Alleys, The HP2: Hem H 1M 3
Alley Way UB8: Uxb 38M 63
Allfarthing La. SW18 58Db 111
Allgood Cl. SM4: Mord 72Za 154
Allgood St. E2 40Vb 71
Allhallows La.
EC4 5F 225 (45Tb 91)
All Hallows Rd. N17 25Ub 51
Allhallows Rd. E6 43Nc 94
Allhusen Gdns. SL3: Ful 35A 62
Alliance Cl. HA0: Wemb 35Ma 67
TW4: Houn 57Ba 107
Alliance Ct. TW15: Ashf 63S 128
W3 43Ra 87
Alliance Rd. E13 43Lc 93
SE18 51Wc 117
W3 42Ra 87
Allianz Pk. 24Ya 48
Allied Ct. N1 38Ub 71
(off Enfield Rd.)
Allied Ind. Est. W3 47Ua 88
Allied Way W3 47Ua 88
Allingham Cl. W7 45Ha 86
Allingham Ct. BR2: Brom 70Hc 137
Allingham M. N1 1D 218
Allingham Rd. RH2: Reig 9J 207
Allingham St. N1 1D 218 (40Sb 71)
Allington Av. N17 23Ub 51
TW17: Shep 69U 128
Allington Cl. DA12: Grav'nd 10H 123
SW19 64Za 132
UB6: G'frd 38Ea 66
Allington Ct. CR0: C'don 72Yb 158
(off Chart Cl.)
EN3: Pond E 15Zb 34
SL2: Slou 4K 81
SW8 54Lb 112
Allington Rd. BR6: Orp 75Tc 160
HA2: Harr 29Ea 46
NW4 29Xa 48
W10 41Ab 88
Allingtons RH2: Reig 3J 207
Allington St. SW1 4B 228 (48Kb 90)
Allison Cl. EN9: Walt A 4Jc 21
SE10 53Ec 114
Allison Gro. SE21 60Ub 113
Allison Rd. N8 29Qb 50
W3 44Sa 87
Alliston Ho. E2 41Vb 91
(off Gibraltar Wlk.)
Allistonway SS17: Stan H 1P 101
Allitsen Rd. NW8 2D 214 (40Gb 69)
(not continuous)
Allium Ri. DA1: Dart 56Md 119
Allkins Ct. SL4: Wind 4H 103
All Nations Ho. E8 38Xb 71
(off Martello St.)
Allnutts Rd. CM16: Epp 5Wc 23
Allnutt Way SW4 57Mb 112
Alloa Rd. IG3: Ilf 33Wc 75
SE8 50Zb 92
Allom Ho. W11 45Ab 88
(off Clarendon Rd.)
Allonby Dr. HA4: Ruis 31R 64
Allonby Gdns. HA9: Wemb 32La 66
Allonby Ho. E14 43Ac 92
(off Aston St.)
Allotment La. TN13: S'oaks 94Ld 203
Allotment Way NW2 34Za 68
Alloway Cl. GU21: Wok 10M 167
Alloway Rd. E3 41Ac 92
Allport Ho. SE5 55Tb 113
(off Champion Pk.)
Allport M. E1 42Yb 92
(off Hayfield Pas.)
All Saints Cl. DA10: Swans 57Be 121
IG7: Chig 20Xc 37
N9 19Wb 33
SW8 53Nb 112
All Saint's Ct. TW5: Hest 53Z 107
(off Springwell Rd.)
All Saints Ct. E1 45Yb 92
(off Johnson St.)
SW11 52Kb 112
(off Prince of Wales Dr.)
All Saints Cres. WD25: Wat 5Z 13
All Saints Dr. CR2: Sande 84Vb 177
SE3 54Gc 115
(not continuous)
All Saints Ho. W11 43Bb 89
(off All Saints Rd.)
All Saints La. WD3: Crox G 16Q 26
All Saints M. HA3: Hrw W 23Ga 46
All Saints Pas. SW18 57Cb 111
All Saints Rd. DA11: Nflt 10B 122
GU18: Light 2A 166
SM1: Sutt 76Db 155
SW19 66Eb 133
(not continuous)
W3 48Sa 87
W11 43Bb 89
All Saints St. N1 1H 217 (40Pb 70)
Allsop Pl. NW1 6G 215 (42Hb 89)
All Souls Av. NW10 40Xa 68
All Souls' Pl.
W1 1A 222 (43Kb 90)
Allum Gro. KT20: Tad 93Xa 194
Allum La. WD6: E'tree 15Ma 29
Allum Way N20 18Eb 31
Alluvium Ct. SE1 3H 231
(off Long La.)
Allwood Cl. SE26 63Zb 136
Allyn Cl. TW18: Staines 65H 127
Alma, The DA12: Grav'nd 4H 145
Alma Av. E4 24Ec 52
RM12: Horn 35Nd 77
Alma Barn M. BR6: Orp 75Zc 161
Alma Birk Ho. NW6 38Ab 68
Almack Rd. E5 35Yb 72
Alma Cl. GU21: Knap 10H 167
N10 25Kb 50
Alma Ct. CR3: Cat'm 93Sb 197
(off Coulsdon Rd.)
EN6: Pot B 2Eb 17
HA2: Harr 33Fa 66
SL1: Burn 1A 80
WD6: Bore 10Pa 15
Alma Cres. SM1: Sutt 78Ab 154
Alma Cut AL1: St A 3C 6
Alma Gro. SE1 49Vb 91
Alma Ho. N9 21Wb 51
TW8: Bford 51Na 109
Almanza Pl. IG11: Bark 40Xc 75
Alma Pl. CR7: Thor H 71Qb 156
NW10 41Xa 88
SE19 66Vb 135
WD25: Wat 8Aa 13
Alma Rd. AL1: St A 3C 6
BR5: Orp 75Zc 161
DA10: Swans 57Be 121
DA14: Sidc 62Wc 139
EN3: Enf H, Pond E 15Ac 34
KT10: Esh 74Ga 152
N10 24Kb 50
RH2: Reig 5K 207
SL4: Eton W 9D 80
SL4: Wind 4G 102
SM5: Cars 78Gb 155
SW18 56Eb 111
UB1: S'hall 45Aa 85
Alma Rd. Ind. Est.
EN3: Pond E 14Zb 34
Alma Row HA3: Hrw W 25Fa 46
Alma Sq. NW8 2A 214 (40Eb 69)
Alma St. E15 37Fc 73
NW5 37Kb 70
Alma Ter. E3 39Bc 72
(off Beale Rd.)
SW18 59Fb 111
W8 48Cb 89
Almeida St. N1 39Rb 71
Almeida Theatre 39Rb 71
(off Almeida St.)
Almeric Rd. SW11 56Hb 111
Almer Rd. SW20 66Wa 132
Almington St. N4 32Pb 70
Almners Rd. KT16: Lyne 74C 148
(not continuous)
Almond Av. GU22: Wok 3P 187
SM5: Cars 75Hb 155
UB7: W Dray 48Q 84
UB10: Ick 34R 64
W5 48Ma 87
Almond Cl. BR2: Brom 73Qc 160
E17 28Ac 52
HA4: Ruis 34V 64
RM16: Grays 8C 100
SE15 54Wb 113
SL4: Wind 4F 102
TW13: Felt 60W 106
TW17: Shep 68S 128
TW20: Eng G 5M 125
UB3: Hayes 45U 84
Almond Dr. BR8: Swan 68Fd 140
Almond Gro. TW8: Bford 52Ka 108
Almond Ho. E15 41Gc 93
(off Teasel Way)
Almond Rd. DA2: Dart 59Sd 120
KT19: Eps 83Ta 173
N17 24Wb 51
SE16 49Xb 91
SL1: Burn 1A 80
Almonds, The AL1: St A 6F 6
Almonds Av. IG9: Buck H 19Jc 35
Almond Wlk. AL10: Hat 3C 8
Almond Way BR2: Brom 73Qc 160
CR4: Mitc 71Mb 156
HA2: Harr 26Da 45
WD6: Bore 14Ra 29
Almons Way SL2: Slou 3M 81
Almorah Rd. N1 38Tb 71
TW5: Hest 53Z 107
Alms Heath GU23: Ock 93R 190
Almshouse La. EN1: Enf 9Xb 19
KT9: Chess 81La 172
Alms Ho's., The IG11: Bark 37Sc 74
Almshouses IG10: Lough 11Pc 36
KT16: Chert 73J 149
Almshouses, The
EN8: Chesh 2Zb 20
(off Turner's Hill)
Alms Row TN16: Bras 96Xc 201
Alnmouth Ct. UB1: S'hall 44Ea 86
(off Fleming Rd.)
Alnwick N17 24Xb 51
Alnwick Ct. DA2: Dart 58Rd 119
(off Osbourne Rd.)
Alnwick Gro. SM4: Mord 70Db 133
Alnwick Rd. E16 44Lc 93
SE12 58Kc 115
ALPERTON 40Na 67
Alperton La. HA0: Wemb 41La 86
UB6: G'frd 41La 86
Alperton St. W10 42Bb 89
Alphabet Gdns. SM5: Cars 72Fb 155
Alphabet Sq. E3 43Cc 92
Alpha Bus. Cen. E17 29Bc 52
Alpha Bus. Pk. AL9: Wel G 5E 8
Alpha Cl. NW1 4E 214 (42Gb 89)
Alpha Ct. CR3: Whyt 90Wb 177
WD17: Wat 13Y 27
(off Grosvenor Rd.)
Alpha Est. UB3: Hayes 47U 84
Alpha Gro. E14 47Cc 92
Alpha Ho. NW6 40Cb 69
NW8 6D 214
SW4 56Pb 112
Alpha Pl. NW6 40Cb 69
SM4: Mord 74Za 154
SW3 51Gb 111
Alpha Rd. CM13: Hut 16Fe 41
CR0: C'don 74Ub 157
E4 20Cc 34
EN3: Pond E 14Ac 34
GU22: Wok 88D 168
GU24: Chob 2K 167
KT5: Surb 72Pa 153
N18 23Wb 51
SE14 53Bc 114
TW11: Tedd 64Fa 130
UB10: Hil 42R 84
Alpha St. SE15 54Wb 113
Alpha St. Nth. SL1: Slou 7L 81
Alpha St. Sth. SL1: Slou 8K 81
Alpha Way TW20: Thorpe 67E 126
Alphea Cl. SW19 66Gb 133
Alpine Av. KT5: Surb 75Sa 153
Alpine Bus. Cen. E6 43Qc 94
Alpine Cl. CR0: C'don 76Ub 157
KT19: Ewe 78Sa 153
RM3: Rom 21Nd 57
SL5: S'hill 2B 146
Alpine Copse BR1: Brom 68Qc 138
Alpine Gro. E9 38Yb 72
Alpine Rd. E10 33Dc 72
KT12: Walt T 73W 150
NW9 28Qa 47
RH1: Redh 3A 208
SE16 50Zb 92
Alpine Vw. SM5: Cars 78Gb 155
Alpine Wlk. HA7: Stan 19Ga 28
Alpine Way E6 43Qc 94
Alric Av. KT3: N Mald 69Ua 132
NW10 38Ta 67
Alroy Rd. N4 31Qb 70
Alsace Rd. SE17 7H 231
Alsager KT22: Lea 91Ja 192
(off Clements Mead)
Alscot Rd. SE1 5K 231 (49Vb 91)
Alscot Way SE1 5K 231 (49Vb 91)
Alsford Pl. SL3: L'ly 9P 81
Alsike Rd. DA18: Erith 48Zc 95
SE2 48Zc 95
Alsom Av. KT4: Wor Pk 77Wa 154
Alsop Cl. AL2: Lon C 9J 7
Alston Cl. KT6: Surb 73Ka 152
Alstonfield KT10: Esh 78Ea 152
Alston Rd. EN5: Barn 13Ab 30
HP1: Hem H 3J 3
N18 22Xb 51
SW17 63Fb 133
Alston Works EN5: Barn 12Ab 30
Altair Cl. N17 23Vb 51
Altair Way HA6: Nwood 21V 44
Altamont CR6: W'ham 91Xb 197
Altash Way SE9 61Pc 138
Altenburg Av. W13 48Ka 86
Altenburg Gdns. SW11 56Hb 111
Alterton Cl. GU21: Wok 9L 167
Alt Gro. SW19 66Bb 133
Altham Ct. HA2: Harr 25Da 45
Altham Gdns. WD19: Wat 21Z 45
Altham Rd. HA5: Pinn 24Aa 45
Altham Way WD19: Wat 22Aa 45
Althea St. SW6 54Db 111
Althorne Gdns. E18 28Hc 53
Althorne Rd. RH1: Redh 8A 208
Althorne Way RM10: Dag 33Cd 76
Althorp Cl. EN5: Ark 17Wa 30
Althorpe M. SW11 53Fb 111
Althorpe Rd. HA1: Harr 29Ea 46
Althorp Rd. AL1: St A 1D 6
SW17 60Hb 111
Altima Ct. SE22 56Wb 113
(off E. Dulwich Rd.)
Altior Ct. N6 30Lb 50
Altissima Ho. SW8 52Kb 112
Altitude Apartments CR0: C'don 76Tb 157
(off Altyre Rd.)
Altius Apartments E3 40Cc 72
(off Wick La.)
Altius Ct. E4 23Ec 52
Altius Wlk. E20 37Ec 72
Altmore Av. E6 38Pc 74
Alton Av. HA7: Stan 24Ha 46
Altona Way SL1: Slou 4F 80
Alton Cl. DA5: Bexl 60Ad 117
TW7: Isle 54Ha 108
Alton Cotts. DA4: Eyns 74Nd 163
Alton Ct. TW18: Staines 67G 126
Alton Gdns. BR3: Beck 66Cc 136
TW2: Whitt 59Fa 108
Alton Ho. E3 41Dc 92
(off Bromley High St.)
RH1: Redh 4A 208
Alton Rd. CR0: Wadd 76Qb 156
N17 27Tb 51
SW15 60Wa 110
TW9: Rich 56Na 109
Alton St. E14 43Dc 92
Altura Twr. SW11 54Fb 111
Altus Ho. SE6 63Ec 136
Altwood Cl. SL1: Slou 3C 80
Altyre Cl. BR3: Beck 71Bc 158
Altyre Rd. CR0: C'don 75Tb 157
Altyre Way BR3: Beck 71Bc 158
Aluna Ct. SE15 55Yb 114
Aluric Cl. RM16: Grays 9D 100
Alvanley Gdns. NW6 36Db 69
Alva Way WD19: Wat 19Z 27
Alverstoke Rd. RM3: Rom 24Nd 57
Alverstone Av. EN4: E Barn 17Gb 31
SW19 61Cb 133
Alverstone Gdns. SE9 60Sc 116
Alverstone Ho. SE11 51Qb 112
Alverstone Rd. E12 35Qc 74
HA9: Wemb 32Pa 67
KT3: N Mald 70Ua 132
NW2 38Ya 68
Alverston Gdns. SE25 71Ub 157
Alverton St. SE8 50Bc 92
(not continuous)
Alveston Av. HA3: Kenton 27Ka 46
Alveston Sq. E18 26Jc 53
Alvey St. SE17 7H 231 (50Ub 91)
Alvia Gdns. SM1: Sutt 77Eb 155
Alvington Cres. E8 36Vb 71
Alvista Av. SL6: Tap 4A 80
Alway Av. KT19: Ewe 78Ta 153
Alwen Gro. RM15: S Ock 43Xd 98
Alwin Pl. WD18: Wat 14U 26
Alwold Cres. SE12 58Kc 115
Alwyn Av. W4 50Ta 87
Alwyn Cl. CR0: New Ad 80Dc 158
WD6: E'tree 16Pa 29
Alwyne Av. CM15: Shenf 16Ce 41
Alwyne Cl. GU21: Wok 88A 168
Alwyne La. N1 38Rb 71
Alwyne Pl. N1 37Sb 71
Alwyne Rd. N1 38Sb 71
SW19 65Bb 133
W7 45Ga 86
Alwyne Sq. N1 37Sb 71
Alwyne Vs. N1 38Rb 71
Alwyn Gdns. NW4 28Wa 48
W3 44Ra 87
Alwyns Cl. KT16: Chert 72J 149
Alwyns La. KT16: Chert 72H 149
Alyth Gdns. NW11 30Cb 49
Alzette Ho. E2 40Zb 72
(off Mace St.)
Amalgamated Dr. TW8: Bford 51Ka 108
Amanda Cl. IG7: Chig 23Tc 54
Amanda Ct. SL3: L'ly 8P 81
TW15: Ashf 61P 127
(off Edward Way)
Amanda M. RM7: Rom 29Ed 56
Amar Ct. SE18 49Vc 95
Amar Deep Ct. SE18 50Vc 95
Amarelle Apartments
CR0: C'don 74Tb 157
(off Cherry Orchard Rd.)
Amazon Bldg. N8 28Pb 50
Amazon St. E1 44Wb 91
Ambassador, The SL5: S'dale 3F 146
Ambassador Cl. TW3: Houn 54Aa 107
Ambassador Gdns. E6 43Pc 94
Ambassador Ho. NW8 1A 214 (39Eb 69)
Ambassadors Cinema
Woking 89A 168
(off Victoria Way)
Ambassador's Ct. SW1 7C 222
Ambassadors Ct. E8 38Vb 71
(off Holly St.)
Ambassador Sq. E14 49Dc 92
Ambassadors Theatre 3E 222
Amber Av. E17 25Ac 52
Amber Cl. EN5: New Bar 16Db 31
KT17: Eps D 87Xa 174
Amber Ct. CR0: C'don 74Ub 157
E15 39Ec 72
(off Warton Rd.)
KT5: Surb 73Pa 153
N7 37Qb 70
(off Bride St.)
TW18: Staines 64H 127
(off Laleham Rd.)
Ambercroft Way CR5: Coul 91Rb 197
Amberden Av. N3 27Cb 49
Ambergate St. SE17 7C 230 (50Rb 91)
Amber Gro. NW2 32Za 68
Amber Ho. E1 44Zb 92
(off Aylward St.)
Amber La. IG6: Ilf 24Rc 54
Amberley Cl. BR6: Chels 78Vc 161
GU23: Send 97H 189
HA5: Pinn 27Ba 45
Amberley Ct. BR3: Beck 66Bc 136
DA14: Sidc 64Yc 139
Amberley Dr. KT15: Wdhm 82H 169
Amberley Gdns. EN1: Enf 17Ub 33
KT19: Ewe 77Va 154
Amberley Gro. CR0: C'don 73Vb 157
SE26 64Xb 135
Amberley Pl. SL4: Wind 3H 103
(off Peascod St.)
Amberley Rd. E10 31Cc 72
EN1: Enf 17Vb 33
IG9: Buck H 18Lc 35
N13 19Pb 32
SE2 51Zc 117
SL2: Slou 3C 80
W9 43Cb 89
Amberley Ter. WD19: Wat 16Aa 27
(off Villiers Rd.)
Amberley Way RM7: Mawney 28Dd 56
SM4: Mord 73Bb 155
TW4: Houn 57Y 107
UB10: Uxb 40N 63
Amberlith Ho. CR7: Thor H 71Qb 156
(off Thornton Rd.)
Amber M. N22 27Qb 50
(off High Rd.)
Amberside Cl. TW7: Isle 58Fa 108
Amberside Ct. HP3: Hem H 5K 3
Amber Way W3 47Ua 88
Amber Wharf E2 1K 219
Amberwood Cl. SM6: Wall 78Nb 156
Amberwood Ri. KT3: N Mald 72Ua 154
Amblecote KT11: Cobh 83Aa 171
Amblecote Cl. SE12 62Kc 137
Amblecote Mdws. SE12 62Kc 137
Amblecote Rd. SE12 62Kc 137
Ambler Rd. N4 34Rb 71
Ambleside BR1: Brom 65Fc 137
CM16: Epp 3Wc 23
NW1 2A 216
RM19: Purf 50Sd 98
SW19 60Ab 110
Ambleside Av. BR3: Beck 71Ac 158
KT12: Walt T 74Y 151
RM12: Horn 36Kd 77
SW16 63Mb 134
Ambleside Cl. E9 36Yb 72
E10 31Dc 72
N17 27Vb 51
RH1: Redh 10B 208
Ambleside Cres. EN3: Enf H 13Zb 34
Ambleside Dr. TW14: Felt 60V 106
Ambleside Gdns. CR2: Sels 81Zb 178
HA9: Wemb 32Ma 67
IG4: Ilf 28Nc 54
SM2: Sutt 79Eb 155
SW16 64Mb 134
Ambleside Point SE15 52Yb 114
(off Tustin Est.)
Ambleside Rd. DA7: Bex 54Cd 118
GU18: Light 3A 166
NW10 38Va 68
Ambleside Wlk. UB8: Uxb 39M 63
Ambrey Way SM6: Wall 81Mb 176
Ambridge Ho. CR3: Cat'm 95Tb 197
Ambrooke Rd. DA17: Belv 48Cd 96
Ambrosden Av. SW1 4C 228 (48Lb 90)
Ambrose Av. NW11 31Ab 68
Ambrose Cl. BR6: Orp 76Vc 161
DA1: Cray 56Hd 118
E6 43Pc 94
Ambrose Ct. N18 23Vb 51
(off Cannon Rd.)
Ambrose Cres. CM16: Epp 2Uc 22
Ambrose Ho. E14 43Cc 92
(off Selsey St.)
Ambrose M. SW11 54Hb 111
Ambrose St. SE16 49Xb 91

Ambrose Wlk.—Appleby Cl.

Ambrose Wlk. E3 40Cc 72
Ambulance Rd. E11 29Fc 53
AMC Bus. Cen. NW10 41Ra 87
Amelia Cl. W3 46Ra 87
Amelia Ho. NW9 26Va 48
(off Boulevard Dr.)
TW9: Kew 52Ra 109
W6 50Ya 88
(off Queen Caroline St.)
Amelia Mans. E20 37Dc 72
(off Olympic Pk. Av.)
Amelia St. SE17 7C 230 (50Sb 91)
Amelle Gdns. RM3: Hrld W 23Rd 57
Amen Corner EC4 3C 224 (44Rb 91)
SW17 65Hb 133
Amen Ct. EC4 3C 224 (44Rb 91)
Amenity Way SM4: Mord 73Ya 154
Amerara Ct. DA3: Lfield 69Be 143
(off Harrison Av.)
Amerden Way SL1: Slou 7E 80
American International University
in London, The
Kensington Campus -
Ansdell Street 48Db 89
(off Ansdell St.)
St Albans Grove 48Db 89
Young Street 47Db 89
Richmond Hill Campus 58Na 109
American University of London, The
34Pb 70
America Sq. EC3 4K 225 (45Vb 91)
America St. SE1 7D 224 (46Sb 91)
Amerland Rd. SW18 57Bb 111
Amersham Av. N18 23Tb 51
Amersham Cl. RM3: Rom 23Pd 57
Amersham Dr. RM3: Rom 23Nd 57
Amersham Gro. SE14 52Bc 114
Amersham Ho. WD18: Wat 17U 26
(off Chenies Way)
Amersham Rd. CR0: C'don 72Sb 157
HP6: L Chal 11A 24
RM3: Rom 23Nd 57
SE14 53Bc 114
SL9: Chal P 21A 42
SL9: Ger X 30C 42
UB9: Den 30C 42
WD3: Chen 11A 24
Amersham Va. SE14 52Bc 114
Amersham Wlk. RM3: Rom 23Pd 57
Amersham Way HP6: L Chal 11A 24
Amery Gdns. NW10 39Ya 68
RM2: Rom 27Md 57
Amery Ho. SE17 7J 231
Amery Rd. HA1: Harr 33Ja 66
Amesbury EN9: Walt A 4Jc 21
Amesbury Av. SW2 61Nb 134
Amesbury Cl. CM16: Epp 3Vc 23
KT4: Wor Pk 74Ya 154
Amesbury Ct. EN2: Enf 12Qb 32
Amesbury Dr. E4 16Dc 34
Amesbury Rd. BR1: Brom 69Mc 137
CM16: Epp 3Vc 23
RM9: Dag 38Zc 75
SL1: Slou 7D 80
TW13: Felt 61Z 129
Amesbury Twr. SW8 54Lb 112
Ames Cotts. E14 43Ac 92
(off Maroon St.)
Ames Ho. E2 40Zb 72
(off Mace St.)
Ames Rd. DA10: Swans 58Ae 121
Amethyst Cl. N11 24Mb 50
Amethyst Ct. BR6: Chels 78Uc 160
(off Farnborough Hill)
DA8: Erith 52Jd 118
EN3: Enf H 13Ac 34
(off Enstone Rd.)
Amethyst Rd. E15 35Fc 73
Amey Dr. KT23: Bookh 96Ea 192
AMF Bowling
Gravesend 8C 122
Amherst Av. W13 44La 86
Amherst Cl. BR5: St M Cry 70Xc 139
Amherst Dr. BR5: St M Cry 70Vc 139
Amherst Gdns. W13 44La 86
(off Amherst Rd.)
Amherst Hill TN13: Riv 95Hd 202
Amherst Ho. SE16 47Zb 92
(off Wolfe Cres.)
Amherst Pl. TN13: Riv 94Hd 202
Amherst Rd. TN13: S'oaks 94Kd 203
W13 44La 86
Amhurst Cl. EN3: Enf W 9Ac 20
Amhurst Gdns. TW7: Isle 54Ja 108
Amhurst Pde. N16 31Vb 71
(off Amhurst Pk.)
Amhurst Pk. N16 31Tb 71
Amhurst Pas. E8 35Wb 71
Amhurst Rd. E8 36Xb 71
N16 35Vb 71
Amhurst Ter. E8 35Wb 71
Amhurst Wlk. SE28 46Wc 95
Amias Dr. HA8: Edg 21Na 47
Amias Ho. EC1 5D 218
Amicia Gdns. SL2: Stoke P 9K 61
Amidas Gdns. RM8: Dag 35Xc 75
Amiel St. E1 42Yb 92
Amies St. SW11 55Hb 111
Amigo Ho. SE1 3A 230
Amina Way SE16 48Wb 91
Amiot Ho. NW9 26Va 48
(off Heritage Av.)
Amis Av. KT15: New H 82J 169
KT19: Ewe 79Ra 153
Amisha Ct. SE1 4K 231
Amis Rd. GU21: Wok 1J 187
Amity Ct. DA9: Ghithe 56Wd 120
Amity Gro. SW20 67Xa 132
Amity Rd. E15 38Hc 73
Ammanford Grn. NW9 30Ua 48
Ammonite Ho. E15 38Hc 73
Amner Rd. SW11 58Jb 112
Amor Rd. W6 48Ya 88
Amory Ho. N1 1J 217
Amott Rd. SE15 55Wb 113
Amoy Pl. E14 45Cc 92
(not continuous)
Ampere Way CR0: Wadd 73Nb 156
Amphlett Cl. DA13: Sflt 65Ce 143
Ampleforth Cl. BR6: Chels 77Yc 161
Ampleforth Rd. SE2 47Xc 95
Amport Pl. NW7 23Ab 48
Ampthill Est. NW1 2C 216 (40Lb 70)
Ampthill Ho. RM3: Rom 22Md 57
(off Montgomery Cres.)
Ampthill Sq. NW1 2C 216 (40Lb 70)
Ampton Pl. WC1 4H 217 (41Pb 90)
Ampton St. WC1 4H 217 (41Pb 90)
Amroth Cl. SE23 60Xb 113
Amroth Grn. NW9 30Ua 48
Amstel Ct. SE15 52Vb 113
Amstel Way GU21: Wok 10K 167
Amsterdam Rd. E14 48Ec 92
Amundsen Ct. E14 50Cc 92
(off Napier Av.)
Amundsen Ho. NW10 38Ta 67
(off Stonebridge Pk.)
Amwell Cl. EN2: Enf 15Tb 33
WD25: Wat 7Aa 13
Amwell Ct. EN9: Walt A 5Hc 21
Amwell Ct. Est. N4 33Sb 71
Amwell Ho. WC1 3K 217
Amwell St. EC1 3K 217 (41Qb 90)
Amwell Vw. IG6: Chig, Ilf 22Xc 55
Amyand Cotts. TW1: Twick 58Ka 108
Amyand La. TW1: Twick 59Ka 108
Amyand Pk. Gdns. TW1: Twick 59Ka 108
Amyand Pk. Rd. TW1: Twick 59Ja 108
Amy Cl. SM6: Wall 80Nb 156
Amy Johnson Ct. HA8: Edg 26Ra 47
Amy Rd. RH8: Oxt 1J 211
Amyruth Rd. SE4 57Cc 114
Amy Warne Cl. E6 42Nc 94
Anarth Ct. KT13: Weyb 74U 150
Anastasia M. N12 22Db 49
Anatola Rd. N19 33Lb 70
Anayah Apartments SE8 50Zb 92
(off Trundleys Rd.)
Ancaster Cres. KT3: N Mald 72Wa 154
Ancaster M. BR3: Beck 69Zb 136
Ancaster Rd. BR3: Beck 69Zb 136
Ancaster St. SE18 52Uc 116
Anchor SW18 56Db 111
Anchorage Cl. SW19 64Cb 133
Anchorage Ho. E14 45Fc 93
(off Clove Cres.)
Anchorage Point E14 47Bc 92
(off Cuba St.)
Anchorage Point Ind. Est. SE7 48Lc 93
Anchor & Hope La. SE7 48Kc 93
Anchor Bay Ind. Est. DA8: Erith 51Jd 118
Anchor Blvd. DA2: Dart 56Sd 120
Anchor Brewhouse SE1 7K 225 (46Vb 91)
Anchor Bus. Cen. CR0: Bedd 76Nb 156
Anchor Cl. IG11: Bark 41Xc 95
Anchor Ct. DA8: Erith 52Hd 118
EN1: Enf 15Ub 33
RM17: Grays 52De 121
SW1 6D 228
Anchor Cres. GU21: Knap 9H 167
Anchor Dr. N15 28Ub 51
RM13: Rain 41Kd 97
Anchor Hill GU21: Knap 9H 167
Anchor Ho. E16 43Hc 93
(off Barking Rd.)
E16 44Lc 93
(off Prince Regent La.)
EC1 5D 218
SW10 51Fb 111
(off Cremorne Est.)
Anchor La. HP1: Hem H 4K 3
(not continuous)
Anchor M. N1 37Ub 71
SW12 58Kb 112
Anchor Retail Pk. E1 42Yb 92
Anchor St. SE16 49Xb 91
Anchor Ter. E1 42Yb 92
SE1 6E 224
Anchor Wharf E3 43Dc 92
(off Yeo St.)
Anchor Yd. EC1 5E 218 (42Sb 91)
Ancient Almshouses EN8: Chesh 2Zb 20
(off Turner's Hill)
Ancill Cl. W6 51Ab 110
Ancona Rd. NW10 40Wa 68
SE18 50Tc 94
Andace Pk. Gdns. BR1: Brom 68Lc 137
Andalus Rd. SW9 55Nb 112
Ander Cl. HA0: Wemb 35Ma 67
Andermans SL4: Wind 3B 102
Anderson Cl. KT19: Eps 84Ra 173
N21 15Pb 32
SM3: Sutt 74Cb 155
UB9: Hare 25J 43
W3 44Ta 87
Anderson Ct. NW2 32Ya 68
RH1: Redh 9A 208
Anderson Dr. TW15: Ashf 63S 128
Anderson Hgts. SW16 68Pb 134
Anderson Ho. AL4: St A 3H 7
E14 45Ec 92
(off Woolmore St.)
IG11: Bark 39Tc 74
SW17 64Fb 133
Anderson Pl. TW3: Houn 56Da 107
Anderson Rd. E9 37Zb 72
IG8: Wfd G 27Mc 53
KT13: Weyb 76T 150
WD7: Shenl 5Qa 15
Andersons SS17: Stan H 1P 101
Anderson Sq. N1 39Rb 71
(off Gaskin St.)
Anderson St. SW3 7F 227 (50Hb 89)
Anderson Way DA17: Belv 47Dd 96
Anderton Cl. SE5 55Tb 113
Anderton Ct. N22 26Mb 50
Andora Ct. NW6 38Ab 68
(off Brondesbury Pk.)
Andora Ho. E10 32Ac 72
Andorra Ct. BR1: Brom 67Lc 137
Andover Av. E16 44Mc 93
Andover Cl. KT19: Eps 83Ta 173
TW14: Felt 60V 106
UB6: G'frd 42Da 85
UB8: Uxb 40K 63
Andover Ct. E2 42Xb 91
(off Thee Colts La.)
TW19: Stanw 59M 105
Andover Pl. NW6 40Db 69
Andover Rd. BR6: Orp 74Tc 160
N7 33Pb 70
TW2: Twick 60Fa 108
Andoversford Ct. SE15 51Ub 113
(off Bibury Cl.)
Andover Ter. W6 49Xa 88
(off Raynham Rd.)
Andrea Av. RM16: Grays 47Ce 99
Andreck Ct. BR3: Beck 68Ec 136
(off Crescent Rd.)
Andre St. E8 36Wb 71
Andrew Cl. DA1: Cray 57Fd 118
IG6: Ilf 23Tc 54
WD7: Shenl 4Pa 15
Andrew Ct. SE23 61Zb 136
Andrewes Gdns. E6 44Nc 94
Andrewes Highwalk EC2 1E 224
Andrewes Ho. EC2 1E 224
SM1: Sutt 77Cb 155
Andrew Gibb Memorial, The 53Hc 115
Andrew Hill La. SL2: Hedg 3G 60
Andrew Pl. SW8 52Mb 112
Andrew Reed Ct. WD24: Wat 12Y 27
(off Keele Cl.)
Andrew Reed Ho. SW18 59Ab 110
(off Linstead Way)
Andrew's Cl. BR5: St P 68Zc 139
KT17: Eps 86Va 174
Andrews Cl. HA1: Harr 31Fa 66
HP2: Hem H 1M 3
IG9: Buck H 19Lc 35
KT4: Wor Pk 75Ya 154
Andrews Crosse WC2 3K 223
Andrews Ga. TW17: Shep 68S 128
Andrew's Ho. CR2: S Croy 79Sb 157
Andrews Ho. NW3 38Hb 69
(off Fellows Rd.)
Andrews's La. EN7: Chesh, G Oak 1Vb 19
Andrews Pl. DA2: Wilm 61Gd 140
SE9 58Rc 116
Andrew's Rd. E8 39Xb 71
Andrew St. E14 44Ec 92
Andrews Wlk. SE17 51Rb 113
Andringham Lodge BR1: Brom 67Kc 137
(off Palace Gro.)
Andromeda Ct. RM3: Rom 24Ld 57
Andrula Ct. N22 25Rb 51
Andwell Cl. SE2 47Xc 95
Anelle Ri. HP3: Hem H 6P 3
ANERLEY 67Xb 135
Anerley Gro. SE19 66Vb 135
Anerley Hill SE19 65Vb 135
Anerley Pk. SE20 66Wb 135
Anerley Pk. Rd. SE20 66Wb 135
Anerley Rd. SE19 66Wb 135
SE20 66Wb 135
Anerley Sta. Rd. SE20 67Xb 135
Anerley Va. SE19 66Vb 135
Aneurin Bevan Ct. NW2 33Xa 68
Aneurin Bevan Ho. N11 24Mb 50
Anfield Cl. SW12 59Lb 112
Angas Ct. KT13: Weyb 78S 150
ANGEL 2A 218 (40Qb 70)
Angela Carter Cl. SW9 55Qb 112
Angela Davies Ind. Est. SE24 56Rb 113
Angela Hooper Pl. SW1 3C 228
Angel All. E1 44Vb 91
(off Whitechapel High St.)
Angel Bldg. N1 2A 218 (40Qb 70)
Angel Cl. N18 22Vb 51
TW12: Hamp H 64Ea 130
Angel Cnr. Pde. N18 21Wb 51
Angel Ct. E15 37Fc 73
EC2 2G 225 (44Tb 91)
SW1 7C 222 (46Lb 90)
ANGEL EDMONTON 22Wb 51
Angelfield TW3: Houn 56Da 107
Angel Ga. EC1 3C 218 (41Rb 91)
(not continuous)
Angel Hill SM1: Sutt 76Db 155
Angel Hill Dr. SM1: Sutt 76Db 155
Angel Ho. E3 41Cc 92
(off Campbell Rd.)
Angelica Cl. UB7: Yiew 44N 83
Angelica Dr. E6 43Qc 94
Angelica Gdns. CR0: C'don 74Zb 158
Angelica Ho. E3 39Bc 72
(off Sycamore Av.)
Angelica Rd. GU24: Bisl 7E 166
Angelina Ho. SE15 53Wb 113
(off Goldsmith Rd.)
Angelis Apartments N1 2C 218
Angel La. E15 37Fc 73
EC4 5F 225 (45Tb 91)
UB3: Hayes 43T 84
Angell Pk. Gdns. SW9 55Qb 112
Angell Rd. SW9 55Qb 112
ANGELL TOWN 53Qb 112
Angell Town Est. SW9 54Qb 112
Angel M. E1 45Xb 91
N1 2A 218 (40Qb 70)
SW15 59Wa 110
Angel M. SW16 69Pb 134
Angelo's SL4: Eton 10H 81
(off Common La.)
Angel Pl. N18 21Wb 51
RH2: Reig 9K 207
SE1 1F 231 (47Tb 91)
Angel Rd. HA1: Harr 30Ga 46
KT7: T Ditt 73Ja 152
N18 22Wb 51
Angel Rd. Works N18 22Yb 52
Angel Sq. EC1 2B 218 (40Rb 71)
Angel St. EC1 2D 224 (44Sb 91)
Angel Wlk. W6 49Ya 88
Angel Way RM1: Rom 29Gd 56
Angel Wharf N1 1E 218 (40Sb 71)
Angel Yd. N6 32Jb 70
Angerstein Bus. Pk. SE10 49Jc 93
Angerstein La. SE3 53Hc 115
Angie M. DA1: Dart 54Pd 119
Anglais M. NW9 28Ua 48
(off Colin Cl.)
Anglebury W2 44Cb 89
(off Talbot Rd.)
Angle Cl. UB10: Hil 39Q 64
Angle Grn. RM8: Dag 32Yc 75
Angle Rd. RM20: Grays 51Zd 121
Anglers, The KT1: King T 69Ma 131
(off High St.)
Anglers Cl. TW10: Ham 63La 130
Angler's La. NW5 37Kb 70
Anglers Reach KT6: Surb 71Ma 153
Anglesea Av. SE18 49Rc 94
Anglesea Ho. KT1: King T 70Ma 131
(off Anglesea Rd.)
Anglesea M. SE18 49Rc 94
Anglesea Pl. DA11: Grav'nd 8D 122
(off New Rd.)
Anglesea Rd. BR5: St M Cry 72Yc 161
KT1: King T 70Ma 131
SE18 49Rc 94
Anglesea Ter. W6 48Xa 88
(off Wellesley Av.)
Anglesey Cl. TW15: Ashf 62Q 128
Anglesey Ct. Rd. SM5: Cars 79Jb 156
Anglesey Dr. RM13: Rain 42Jd 96
Anglesey Gdns. SM5: Cars 79Jb 156
Anglesey Ho. E14 44Cc 92
(off Lindfield St.)
Anglesey Rd. EN3: Pond E 14Xb 33
WD19: Wat 22Y 45
Anglesmede Cres. HA5: Pinn 27Ca 45
Anglesmede Way HA5: Pinn 27Ca 45
Angles Rd. SW16 63Nb 134
Anglia Cl. N17 24Xb 51
Anglia Ct. RM8: Dag 32Zc 75
(off Spring Cl.)
Anglia Ho. E14 44Ac 92
(off Salmon La.)
Anglian Cl. WD24: Wat 12Y 27
Anglian Ind. Est. IG11: Bark 42Vc 95
Anglian Rd. E11 34Fc 73
Anglia Wlk. E6 39Qc 74
(off Napier Rd.)
Anglia Way RM15: S Ock 42Xd 98
Anglo Rd. E3 40Bc 72
Angrave Ct. E8 39Vb 71
(off Scriven St.)
Angrave Pas. E8 39Vb 71
Angus Cl. KT9: Chess 78Qa 153
Angus Dr. HA4: Ruis 35Y 65
Angus Gdns. NW9 25Ta 47
Angus Ho. SW2 59Mb 112
Angus Rd. E13 41Lc 93
Angus St. SE14 52Ac 114
Anhalt Rd. SW11 52Gb 111
Anise Ct. DA11: Nflt 59Fe 121
Ankerdine Cres. SE18 52Rc 116
Anlaby Rd. TW11: Tedd 64Ga 130
Anley Rd. W14 47Za 88
Anmer Cl. KT20: Tad 92Xa 194
Anmersh Gro. HA7: Stan 25Ma 47
Annabel Cl. E14 44Dc 92
Annabell Av. RM16: Ors 4F 100
Annabels M. W5 42Ma 87
Annables Ct. AL1: St A 2C 6
(off Victoria St.)
Anna Cl. E8 39Vb 71
Annadale Ct. RH1: Redh 5P 207
(off Warwick Rd.)
Annalee Gdns. RM15: S Ock 43Xd 98
Annalee Rd. RM15: S Ock 43Xd 98
Annaleigh Pl. KT12: Hers 77Z 151
Annandale Gro. UB10: Ick 34S 64
Annandale Rd. CR0: C'don 75Wb 157
DA15: Sidc 59Uc 116
SE10 51Hc 115
W4 50Ua 88
Annan Dr. SM5: Cars 81Jb 176
Anna Neagle Cl. E7 35Jc 73
Annan Way RM1: Rom 25Gd 56
Anne Boleyn Ct. SE9 58Sc 116
Anne Boleyn's Wlk. KT2: King T 64Na 131
SM3: Cheam 80Za 154
Anne Case M. KT3: N Mald 69Ta 131
Anne Compton M. SE12 59Hc 115
Anne Goodman Ho. E1 44Yb 92
(off Jubilee St.)
Anne Heart Cl. RM16: Chaf H 49Zd 99
Anne Matthews Ct. E14 43Cc 92
(off Selsey St.)
Anne M. IG11: Bark 38Sc 74
Anne Nastri Ct. RM2: Rom 29Kd 57
(off Heath Pk. Rd.)
Anne of Cleeves Ct. SE9 58Tc 116
Anne of Cleves Rd. DA1: Dart 57Md 119
Anners Cl. TW20: Thorpe 69E 126
Annes Ct. NW1 5E 214
Annesley Av. NW9 27Ta 47
Annesley Cl. NW10 34Ua 68
Annesley Dr. CR0: C'don 76Bc 158
Annesley Ho. SW9 53Qb 112
Annesley Pl. BR2: Brom 72Nc 160
Annesley Rd. SE3 53Kc 115
Annesley Wlk. N19 33Lb 70
Annesmere Gdns. SE3 55Mc 115
Anne St. E13 42Jc 93
Anne Sutherland Ho. BR3: Beck 66Ac 136
Anne's Wlk. CR3: Cat'm 92Ub 197
Annett Cl. TW17: Shep 70U 128
Annette Cl. HA3: W'stone 26Ga 46
Annette Cres. N1 38Sb 71
Annette Rd. N7 34Pb 70
(not continuous)
Annett Rd. KT12: Walt T 73W 150
Annetts Hall TN15: Bor G 91Ce 205
Anne Way IG6: Ilf 23Sc 54
KT8: W Mole 70Da 129
Annexe Mkt. E1 7K 219
Annie Besant Cl. E3 39Bc 72
Annie Brookes Cl. TW18: Staines 62F 126
Annie Taylor Ho. E12 35Qc 74
(off Walton Rd.)
Annifer Way RM15: S Ock 43Xd 98
ANNINGSLEY PARK 82E 168
Anningsley Pk. KT16: Ott 82D 168
Anning St. EC2 5J 219 (42Ub 91)
Annington Rd. N2 27Hb 49
Annis Rd. E9 37Ac 72
Ann La. SW10 51Fb 111
Ann Moss Way SE16 48Yb 92
Ann's Cl. SW1 2G 227
Ann's Pl. E1 1K 225
Ann St. N1 1D 218 (39Sb 71)
SE18 50Sc 94
(not continuous)
Ann Stroud Ct. SE12 57Jc 115
Anns Wlk. RH1: Blet 5K 209
Annsworthy Av. CR7: Thor H 69Tb 135
Annsworthy Cres. SE25 68Tb 135
Ansar Gdns. E17 29Bc 52
Ansculf Rd. SL2: Slou 1E 80
Ansdell Rd. SE15 54Yb 114
Ansdell St. W8 48Db 89
Ansdell Ter. W8 48Db 89
Ansell Gro. SM5: Cars 74Jb 156
Ansell Ho. E1 43Yb 92
(off Mile End Rd.)
Ansell Rd. SW17 62Gb 133
Anselm Cl. CR0: C'don 76Vb 157
Anselm Rd. HA5: Hat E 24Ba 45
SW6 51Cb 111
Ansford Rd. BR1: Brom 64Ec 136
Ansleigh Pl. W11 45Za 88
Ansley Cl. CR2: Sande 86Xb 177
Anslow Gdns. SL0: Iver H 40F 62
Anslow Pl. SL1: Slou 3A 80
Anson Cl. AL1: St A 4F 6
HP3: Bov 9B 2
RM7: Mawney 26Dd 56
Anson Ho. E1 42Ac 92
(off Shandy St.)
SW1 51Lb 112
(off Churchill Gdns.)
Anson M. SW19 66Cb 133
Anson Pl. SE28 47Tc 94
Anson Rd. N7 35Lb 70
NW2 35Xa 68
Anson Ter. UB5: N'olt 37Da 65
Anson Wlk. HA6: Nwood 21S 44
Anstead Dr. RM13: Rain 40Jd 76
Anstey Ct. W3 47Ra 87
Anstey Ho. E9 39Yb 72
(off Templecombe Rd.)
Anstey Rd. SE15 55Wb 113
Anstey Wlk. N15 28Rb 51
Anstice Cl. W4 52Ua 110
Anstridge Path SE9 58Tc 116
Anstridge Rd. SE9 58Tc 116
Antelope Av. RM16: Grays 48Ce 99
Antelope Rd. SE18 48Pc 94
Antelope Wlk. KT6: Surb 71Ma 153
Antenor Ho. E2 40Xb 71
(off Old Bethnal Grn. Rd.)
Anthems Way E20 37Dc 72
Anthony Cl. NW7 21Ua 48
TN13: Dun G 92Gd 202
WD19: Wat 18Y 27
Anthony Cope Ct. N1 3G 219
Anthony Ct. W3 47Ua 88
Anthony Ho. CR5: Coul 94Mb 196
NW8 6D 214
Anthony La. BR8: Swan 67Jd 140
Anthony M. RM13: Rain 40Ld 77
Anthony Rd. DA16: Well 53Wc 117
SE25 72Wb 157
UB6: G'frd 41Ga 86
WD6: Bore 12Pa 29
ANTHONYS 84C 168
Anthony St. E1 44Xb 91
Anthony Way N18 23Zb 52
SL1: Slou 5B 80
Anthorne Cl. EN6: Pot B 3Db 17
Anthus M. HA6: Nwood 24U 44
Antigua M. E13 41Kc 93
Antigua Wlk. SE19 64Tb 135
Antila Ct. E1 5K 219
Antilles Bay E14 47Ec 92
Antill Rd. E3 41Ac 92
N15 28Wb 51
Antill Ter. E1 44Zb 92
Antlers Hill E4 15Dc 34
Antoinette Ct. WD5: Ab L 1V 12
Antoinette M. NW2 37Wa 68
Anton Cres. SM1: Sutt 76Cb 155
Antoneys Cl. HA5: Pinn 26Z 45
Antonine Ga. AL3: St A 3N 5
Antonine Hgts. SE1 2H 231
Anton Pl. HA9: Wemb 34Ra 67
Anton Rd. RM15: S Ock 43Xd 98
Anton St. E8 36Wb 71
Antony Ho. SE16 49Yb 92
(off Raymouth Rd.)
Antrim Gro. NW3 37Hb 69
Antrim Rd. NW3 37Hb 69
Antrobus Cl. SM1: Sutt 78Bb 155
Antrobus Rd. W4 49Sa 87
Antwerp Way E16 47Qc 94
Anvil Cl. HP3: Bov 10D 2
SW16 66Lb 134
Anvil Ct. SL3: L'ly 49C 82
Anvil La. KT11: Cobh 86W 170
Anvil M. RM13: Rain 39Hd 76
Anvil Pl. AL2: Chis G 8N 5
Anvil Rd. TW16: Sun 69W 128
Anvil Ter. DA2: Wilm 61Gd 140
Anworth Cl. IG8: Wfd G 23Kc 53
Anyards Rd. KT11: Cobh 85X 171
Anzio Gdns. CR3: Cat'm 93Sb 197
Apeldoorn Dr. SM6: Wall 81Nb 176
Aperdele Rd. KT22: Lea 90Ja 172
APERFIELD 89Nc 180
Aperfield Rd. DA8: Erith 51Hd 118
TN16: Big H 89Nc 180
Aperfields TN16: Big H 89Nc 180
Apers Av. GU22: Wok 93B 188
Apex Bus. Pk.
DA12: Grav'nd 9P 123
Apex Cl. BR3: Beck 67Dc 136
APEX CORNER
Feltham 62Ba 129
Mill Hill 21Ua 48
Apex Ct. KT14: W Byf 84K 169
W13 45Ja 86
Apex Ho. BR5: St M Cry 70Yc 139
(off Ridge Pl.)
E1 5K 219
Apex Ind. Est. NW10 42Va 88
Apex Pde. NW7 21Ta 47
(off Selvage La.)
Apex Point AL9: Wel G 4E 8
Apex Retail Pk. TW13: Hanw 62Ba 129
Aphrodite Ct. E14 49Cc 92
(off Homer Dr.)
E15 39Ec 72
(off Warton Rd.)
Apley Rd. RH2: Reig 9J 207
Aplin Way TW7: Isle 53Ga 108
Apollo Av. BR1: Brom 67Kc 137
HA6: Nwood 22W 44
Apollo Bldg. E14 49Cc 92
Apollo Bus. Cen. SE8 50Zb 92
Apollo Cl. RM12: Horn 33Kd 77
Apollo Ct. E1 45Wb 91
(off Thomas More St.)
E15 39Ec 72
(off High St.)
SW9 53Qb 112
(off Southey Rd.)
Apollo Ho. E2 40Xb 71
(off St Jude's Rd.)
E3 40Cc 72
(off Garrison Rd.)
N6 31Hb 69
SW10 52Fb 111
(off Milman's St.)
Apollo Pl. E11 34Gc 73
GU21: Wok 1L 187
SW10 52Fb 111
Apollo Theatre
Soho 4D 222
Apollo Victoria Theatre 4B 228
Apollo Way DA8: Erith 49Fd 96
SE28 48Tc 94
Apostle Ct. SE20 66Zb 136
Apostles, The SE23 61Zb 136
(off Church Ri.)
Apostle Way CR7: Thor H 68Rb 135
Apothecary St. EC4 3B 224 (44Rb 91)
Appach Rd. SW2 57Qb 112
Appian Ct. E3 40Bc 72
(off Parnell Rd.)
Apple Barn Ct. TN15: Crou 94Ee 205
Apple Blossom Ct. SW8 52Mb 112
(off Pascal St.)
Appleby Cl. BR5: Pet W 73Uc 160
E4 23Ec 52
N15 29Tb 51
TW2: Twick 61Fa 130
UB8: Hil 44S 84

Arnhem Av.—Ashleigh Rd.

Arnhem Av. RM15: Avel .46Sd 98
Arnhem Dr. CR0: New Ad .83Fc 179
Arnhem Pl. E14 .48Cc 92
Arnhem Way SE22 .57Ub 113
Arnhem Wharf E14 .48Bc 92
Arnison Rd. KT8: E Mos .70Fa 130
Arnold Av. E. EN3: Enf L .10Cc 20
Arnold Av. W. EN3: Enf L .10Bc 20
Arnold Bennett Way N8 .27Qb 50
Arnold Cir. E2 .4K 219 (41Vb 91)
Arnold Cl. HA3: Kenton .31Pa 67
Arnold Ct. N22 .24Nb 50
Arnold Cres. TW7: Isle .57Fa 108
Arnold Dr. KT9: Chess .79Ma 153
Arnold Est. SE1 .2K 231 (47Vb 91)
(not continuous)
Arnold Gdns. N13 .22Rb 51
Arnold Ho. *SE3* .52Lc 115
(off Shooters Hill Rd.)
SE17 .7C 230
Arnold Mans. *W14* .51Bb 111
(off Queen's Club Gdns.)
Arnold Pl. RM18: Tilb .3E 122
Arnold Rd. DA12: Grav'nd .1F 144
E3 .41Cc 92
EN9: Walt A .7Ec 20
GU21: Wok .87D 168
N15 .27Vb 51
RM9: Dag .38Bd 75
RM10: Dag .38Bd 75
SW17 .66Hb 133
TW18: Staines .66L 127
UB5: N'olt .37Z 65
Arnolds Av. CM13: Hut .15Ee 41
Arnolds Cl. CM13: Hut .15Ee 41
Arnolds Farm La. CM13: Mount .13Fe 41
Arnold's La. DA4: Sut H .65Pd 141
Arnold Ter. HA7: Stan .22Ha 46
Arnold Way KT19: Eps .84Pa 173
Arnos Gro. N14 .21Mb 50
Arnos Gro. Ct. *N11* .22Lb 50
(off Palmer's Rd.)
Arnos Rd. N11 .22Lb 50
Arnos Swimming Pool .22Mb 50
Arnot Ho. *SE5* .52Sb 113
(off Comber Gro.)
Arnott Cl. SE28 .46Yc 95
W4 .49Ta 87
Arnould Av. SE5 .56Tb 113
Arnsberg Way DA6: Bex .56Cd 118
DA7: Bex .56Cd 118
Arnside Gdns. HA9: Wemb .32Ma 67
Arnside Ho. *SE17* .51Tb 113
(off Arnside St.)
Arnside Rd. DA7: Bex .53Cd 118
Arnside St. SE17 .51Tb 113
Arnulf St. SE6 .63Dc 136
Arnulls Rd. SW16 .65Rb 135
Arnwil Dr. RM3: Rom .22Ld 57
Arodene Rd. SW2 .58Pb 112
Arona Ho. BR3: Beck .68Ec 136
Arosa Rd. TW1: Twick .58Ma 109
Arpley Sq. *SE20* .66Yb 136
(off High St.)
Arragon Gdns. BR4: W W'ck .76Dc 158
SW16 .66Nb 134
Arragon Rd. E6 .39Mc 73
SW18 .60Cb 111
TW1: Twick .59Ja 108
Arran Cl. DA8: Erith .51Fd 118
HP3: Hem H .4C 4
SM6: Wall .77Kb 156
Arran Ct. NW9 .26Va 48
NW10 .34Ta 67
Arran Dr. E12 .32Mc 73
Arran Grn. WD19: Wat .21Z 45
Arran Ho. *E14* .46Ec 92
(off Raleana Rd.)
WD18: Wat .16W 26
Arran M. W5 .46Pa 87
Arranmore Ct. WD23: Bush .14Aa 27
Arran Rd. SE6 .61Dc 136
Arran Wlk. N1 .38Sb 71
Arran Way KT10: Esh .75Da 151
Arras Av. SM4: Mord .71Eb 155
Arretine Cl. AL3: St A .4M 5
Arreton Mead GU21: Wok .86B 168
Arrol Ho. SE1 .4E 230 (48Sb 91)
Arrol Rd. BR3: Beck .69Yb 136
Arrow Ct. *SW5* .49Cb 89
(off W. Cromwell Rd.)
Arrowhead Quay E14 .47Cc 92
Arrow Ho. N1 .1J 219
Arrow Rd. E3 .41Dc 92
Arrowscout Wlk. *UB5: N'olt* .41Aa 85
(off Argus Way)
Arrows Ho. *SE15* .52Yb 114
(off Clifton Way)
Arrowsmith Cl. IG7: Chig .22Vc 55
Arrowsmith Ho. SE11 .7H 229
Arrowsmith Path IG7: Chig .22Vc 55
Arrowsmith Rd. IG7: Chig .22Uc 54
Arsenal FC .35Qb 70
Arsenal Rd. SE9 .54Pc 116
Arsenal Way SE18 .48Sc 94
Arta Ho. *E1* .44Yb 92
(off Devonport St.)
Artbrand Ho. SE1 .2H 231
Artemis SW11 .54Hb 111
Artemis Cl. DA12: Grav'nd .9G 122
Artemis Ct. *E14* .49Cc 92
(off Homer Dr.)
Artemis Pl. SW18 .59Bb 111
Arterberry Rd. SW20 .66Ya 132
Arterial Av. RM13: Rain .42Kd 97
Arterial Rd. RM16: N Stif .47Zd 99
RM19: Purf, W Thur .49Rd 97
RM20: W Thur .48Vd 98
SS17: Stan H .1L 101
Artesian Cl. NW10 .38Ta 67
RM11: Horn, Rom .30Hd 56
Artesian Gro. EN5: New Bar .14Eb 31
Artesian Ho. SE1 .4K 231
Artesian Rd. W2 .44Cb 89
Artesian Wlk. E11 .34Gc 73
Arthaus Apartments *E8* .37Xb 71
(off Richmond Rd.)
Arthingworth St. E15 .39Gc 73
Arthouse
Crouch End .29Nb 50
Arthur Barnes Ct. RM16: Grays .8E 100
Arthur Ct. *CR0: C'don* .76Ub 157
(off Fairfield Path)
SW11 .53Jb 112
W2 .44Db 89
(off Queensway)
W10 .44Za 88
(off Silchester Rd.)
Arthur Deakin Ho. *E1* .43Wb 91
(off Hunton St.)
Arthurdon Rd. SE4 .57Cc 114
Arthur Gro. SE18 .49Sc 94
Arthur Henderson Ho.
SW6 .54Bb 111
(off Fulham Rd.)
Arthur Horsley Wlk. *E7* .36Hc 73
(off Tower Hamlets Rd.)
Arthur Ho. *N1* .39Ub 71
(off Halcomb St.)
Arthur Jacob Nature Reserve .55E 104
Arthur Lovell Ct. *E14* .44Bc 92
(off Lovat Cl.)
Arthur Newton Ho. *SW11* .55Fb 111
(off Winstanley Est.)
Arthur Rd. AL1: St A .2F 6
E6 .40Pc 74
KT2: King T .66Qa 131
KT3: N Mald .71Xa 154
N7 .35Pb 70
N9 .19Vb 33
RM6: Chad H .30Yc 55
SL1: Slou .7H 81
SL4: Wind .3G 102
SW19 .64Bb 133
TN16: Big H .87Lc 179
Arthur's Bri. Rd.
GU21: Wok .9N 167
Arthur's Bri. Wharf
GU21: Wok .9P 167
Arthur St. DA8: Erith .52Hd 118
DA11: Grav'nd .9C 122
EC4 .4G 225 (45Tb 91)
RM17: Grays .51Ee 121
WD23: Bush .14Z 27
Arthur St. W.
DA11: Grav'nd .9C 122
Arthur Toft Ho.
RM17: Grays .51De 121
(off New Rd.)
Arthur Wade Ho. E2 .3K 219
Arthur Wallis Ho. *E12* .34Qc 74
(off Grantham Rd.)
Artichoke Dell WD3: Chor .14G 24
Artichoke Hill E1 .45Xb 91
Artichoke M. *SE5* .53Tb 113
(off Artichoke Pl.)
Artichoke Pl. SE5 .53Tb 113
Artichoke Wlk. *TW9: Rich* .57Ma 109
(off Red Lion St.)
Artillery Bldg., The *E1* .1J 225
(off Artillery La.)
Artillery Cl. IG2: Ilf .30Sc 54
Artillery Ho. *E3* .39Ac 72
(off Barge La.)
E15 .37Gc 73
SE18 .50Qc 94
(off Connaught M.)
Artillery La. E1 .1J 225 (43Ub 91)
W12 .44Wa 88
Artillery Mans. SW1 .4D 228
Artillery Pas. E1 .1J 225
Artillery Pl. HA3: Hrw W .24Ea 46
SE18 .49Pc 94
SW1 .4D 228 (48Mb 90)
Artillery Row
DA12: Grav'nd .9E 122
SW1 .4D 228 (48Lb 90)
Artillery Sq. *SE18* .48Rc 94
(off No 1 St.)
Artington Cl. BR6: Farnb .77Sc 160
Artisan Cl. E6 .44Rc 94
Artisan Ct. E8 .37Wb 71
Artisan Cres. AL3: St A .1A 6
(not continuous)
Artisan M. *NW10* .41Za 88
(off Warfield Rd.)
Artisan Pl. HA3: W'stone .26Ga 46
Artisan Quarter *NW10* .41Za 88
(off Wellington Rd.)
Artizan St. E1 .2J 225
Art School Yd. *AL1: St A* .2B 6
(off Victoria St.)
Arts Depot .22Eb 49
Arts La. SE16 .4K 231 (48Vb 91)
Arts Sq. E1 .42Ac 92
Arts Theatre .4F 223
Arun RM18: E Til .9L 101
Arun Ct. SE25 .71Wb 157
Arundale *KT1: King T* .70Ma 131
(off Anglesea Rd.)
Arundel Av. CR2: Sande .82Wb 177
KT17: Ewe .82Xa 174
SM4: Mord .70Bb 133
Arundel Bldgs.
SE1 .4J 231 (48Ub 91)
Arundel Cl. CR0: Wadd .76Rb 157
DA5: Bexl .58Bd 117
E15 .35Gc 73
EN8: Chesh .1Yb 20
HP2: Hem H .1B 4
SW11 .57Gb 111
TW12: Hamp H .64Da 129
Arundel Ct. BR2: Brom .68Gc 137
HA2: Harr .35Ca 65
N12 .23Gb 49
N17 .25Wb 51
SE16 .50Xb 91
(off Verney Rd.)
SL3: L'ly .9P 81
SW3 .7E 226
SW13 .51Xa 110
(off Arundel Ter.)
W11 .45Bb 89
(off Arundel Gdns.)
Arundel Dr. BR6: Chels .78Xc 161
HA2: Harr .35Ba 65
IG8: Wfd G .24Jc 53
WD6: Bore .14Sa 29
Arundel Gdns. HA8: Edg .24Ta 47
IG3: Ilf .33Wc 75
N21 .18Qb 32
W11 .45Bb 89
Arundel Gt. Ct.
WC2 .4J 223 (45Pb 90)
Arundel Gro. N16 .36Ub 71
Arundel Ho. *CR0: C'don* .78Tb 157
(off Heathfield Rd.)
E17 .25Bc 52
UB8: Cowl .42L 83
W3 .47Ra 87
(off Park Rd. Nth.)
WD6: Bore .14Sa 29
(off Arundel Dr.)
Arundel Mans. *SW6* .53Bb 111
(off Kelvedon Rd.)
Arundel Pl. N1 .37Qb 70
Arundel Rd. CR0: C'don .72Tb 157
DA1: Dart .56Ld 119
EN4: Cockf .13Gb 31
KT1: King T .68Ra 131
RM3: Hrld W .24Pd 57
SM2: Cheam, Sutt .80Bb 155
(not continuous)
TW4: Houn .55Y 107
UB8: Uxb .40K 63
WD5: Ab L .4W 12
Arundel Sq. N7 .37Qb 70
Arundel St. WC2 .4J 223 (45Pb 90)
Arundel Ter. SW13 .51Xa 110
Arun Ho. KT2: King T .67Ma 131
Arvon Rd. N5 .36Qb 70
(not continuous)
Asa Ct. UB3: Harl .48V 84
Asbaston Ter. IG1: Ilf .37Sc 74
Asbridge Ct. *W6* .48Xa 88
(off Dalling Rd.)
Asbury Ct. *N21* .15Nb 32
(off Pennington Dr.)
Ascalon Ho. *SW8* .52Lb 112
(off Thessaly Rd.)
Ascalon St. SW8 .52Lb 112
Ascension Rd. RM5: Col R .23Ed 56
Ascensis Twr. SW18 .56Eb 111
Ascent Ho. *KT13: Weyb* .78U 150
(off Ellesmere Rd.)
NW9 .26Va 48
(off Boulevard Dr.)
Ascham Dr. E4 .24Dc 52
Ascham End E17 .25Ac 52
Ascham St. NW5 .36Lb 70
Aschurch Rd. CR0: C'don .73Vb 157
ASCOT .9A 124
Ascot Cl. IG6: Ilf .23Uc 54
TN15: Bor G .92De 205
UB5: N'olt .36Ca 65
WD6: E'tree .15Qa 29
Ascot Ct. DA5: Bexl .59Bd 117
NW8 .4B 214
WD3: Crox G .16R 26
Ascot Gdns. EN3: Enf W .9Yb 20
RM12: Horn .35Nd 77
UB1: S'hall .42Ba 85
Ascot Ho. NW1 .3A 216
SL4: Wind .3D 102
(off Paddock Cl.)
W9 .42Cb 89
(off Harrow Rd.)
Ascot Lodge NW6 .39Db 69
Ascot M. SM6: Wall .81Lb 176
Ascot Pl. HA7: Stan .22La 46
Ascot Rd. BR5: St M Cry .70Vc 139
DA12: Grav'nd .2D 144
E6 .41Pc 94
N15 .29Tb 51
N18 .21Wb 51
SW17 .65Jb 134
TW14: Bedf .60Q 106
WD18: Wat .15U 26
Ascott Av. W5 .47Na 87
Ascott Ct. HA5: Eastc .28W 44
ASH .78Ae 165
Ashanti M. E8 .36Yb 72
Ashbeam Cl. CM13: Gt War .23Yd 58
Ashbee Ho. *E2* .41Yb 92
(off Portman Pl.)
Ashbourne AL2: Brick W .3Ba 13
Ashbourne Av. DA7: Bex .52Ad 117
E18 .28Kc 53
HA2: Harr .33Fa 66
N20 .19Hb 31
NW11 .29Bb 49
Ashbourne Cl. CR5: Coul .90Lb 176
N12 .21Db 49
W5 .43Qa 87
Ashbourne Ct. AL4: St A .5G 6
E5 .35Ac 72
N12 .21Db 49
(off Ashbourne Cl.)
Ashbourne Gro. NW7 .22Ta 47
SE22 .56Vb 113
W4 .50Ua 88
Ashbourne Ho. SL1: Slou .7J 81
Ashbourne Pde. NW11 .28Bb 49
W5 .42Pa 87
Ashbourne Ri. BR6: Orp .77Uc 160
Ashbourne Rd. CR4: Mitc .66Jb 134
RM3: Rom .21Ld 57
W5 .42Pa 87
Ashbourne Sq. HA6: Nwood .23U 44
Ashbourne Ter. SW19 .66Bb 133
Ashbourne Way NW11 .28Bb 49
Ashbridge Rd. E11 .31Gc 73
Ashbridge St. NW8 .6D 214 (42Gb 89)
Ashbrook HA8: Edg .23Pa 47
Ashbrook Rd. N19 .32Mb 70
RM10: Dag .34Dd 76
SL4: Old Win .9M 103
Ashburn Gdns. SW7 .49Eb 89
Ashburnham Av. HA1: Harr .30Ha 46
Ashburnham Cl. N2 .27Fb 49
TN13: S'oaks .99Ld 203
WD19: Wat .20W 26
Ashburnham Ct. BR3: Beck .68Ec 136
Ashburnham Dr. WD19: Wat .20W 26
Ashburnham Gdns. HA1: Harr .30Ha 46
RM14: Upm .32Rd 77
Ashburnham Gro. SE10 .52Dc 114
Ashburnham Mans. *SW10* .52Eb 111
(off Ashburnham Rd.)
Ashburnham Pk. KT10: Esh .77Ea 152
Ashburnham Pl. SE10 .52Dc 114
Ashburnham Retreat SE10 .52Dc 114
Ashburnham Rd. DA17: Belv .49Ed 96
NW10 .41Ya 88
SW10 .52Eb 111
TW10: Ham .62Ka 130
Ashburnham Twr. *SW10* .52Fb 111
(off Worlds End Est.)
Ashburn Pl. SW7 .5A 226 (49Eb 89)
Ashburton Av. CR0: C'don .74Xb 157
IG3: Ilf .36Uc 74
Ashburton Cl. CR0: C'don .74Wb 157
Ashburton Ent. Cen. SW15 .58Ya 110
Ashburton Gdns. CR0: C'don .75Wb 157
ASHBURTON GROVE .35Qb 70
Ashburton Ho. *W9* .42Bb 89
(off Fernhead Rd.)
Ashburton Memorial Homes
CR0: C'don .73Xb 157
Ashburton Rd. CR0: C'don .75Wb 157
E16 .44Jc 93
HA4: Ruis .33W 64
Ashburton Ter. E13 .40Jc 73
Ashburton Triangle N5 .35Qb 70
Ashbury Cl. AL10: Hat .1A 8
Ashbury Dr. UB10: Ick .34R 64
Ashbury Gdns. RM6: Chad H .29Zc 55
Ashbury Pl. SW19 .65Eb 133
Ashbury Rd. SW11 .55Hb 111
Ashby Av. KT9: Chess .79Qa 153
Ashby Cl. BR4: W W'ck .76Fc 159
RM11: Horn .32Qd 77
RM16: Ors .4G 100
Ashby Ct. NW8 .5C 214
Ashby Gdns. AL1: St A .6B 6
Ashby Gro. N1 .38Sb 71
(not continuous)
Ashby Ho. *N1* .38Sb 71
(off Essex Rd.)
SW9 .54Rb 113
UB5: N'olt .42Ba 85
(off Waxlow Way)
Ashby M. SE4 .54Bc 114
SW2 .57Nb 112
(off Prague Pl.)
Ashby Rd. N15 .29Wb 51
SE4 .54Bc 114
WD24: Wat .10W 12
Ashbys Ct. *E3* .40Bc 72
(off Centurion La.)
Ashby St. EC1 .4C 218 (41Rb 91)
Ashby Wlk. CR0: C'don .72Sb 157
Ashby Way UB7: Sip .52Q 106
Ashchurch Gro. W12 .48Wa 88
Ashchurch Pk. Vs. W12 .48Wa 88
Ashchurch Ter. W12 .48Wa 88
Ash Cl. AL9: Brk P .7J 9
BR5: Pet W .71Tc 160
BR8: Swan .68Ed 140
CM15: Pil H .15Vd 40
DA14: Sidc .62Xc 139
GU22: Pyr .87J 169
GU22: Wok .92A 188
HA7: Stan .23Ja 46
HA8: Edg .21Sa 47
KT3: N Mald .68Ta 131
RH1: Mers .2C 208
RM5: Col R .24Dd 56
SE20 .68Yb 136
SL3: L'ly .48D 82
SM5: Cars .75Hb 155
SM7: Bans .87Ab 174
TW7: Isle .53Ha 108
UB9: Hare .25M 43
WD5: Ab L .4T 12
WD25: Wat .7X 13
Ashcombe Av. KT6: Surb .73Ma 153
Ashcombe Cl. TW15: Ashf .62N 127
Ashcombe Ct. TW15: Ashf .61P 127
Ashcombe Gdns. HA8: Edg .21Qa 47
Ashcombe Ho. *E3* .41Dc 92
(off Bruce Rd.)
EN3: Pond E .13Zb 34
Ashcombe Pde. *GU22: Wok* .92C 188
(off Kingfield Rd.)
Ashcombe Pk. NW2 .34Ua 68
Ashcombe Rd. RH1: Mers .99Lb 196
SM5: Cars .79Jb 156
SW19 .64Cb 133
Ashcombe Sq. KT3: N Mald .69Sa 131
Ashcombe St. SW6 .54Db 111
Ashcombe Ter. KT20: Tad .92Xa 194
Ash Copse AL2: Brick W .3Ba 13
Ash Ct. KT15: Add .78K 149
KT19: Ewe .77Sa 153
KT22: Lea .92Ha 192
N11 .23Lb 50
SW19 .66Ab 132
Ashcroft HA5: Hat E .23Ca 45
N14 .19Mb 32
Ashcroft Av. DA15: Sidc .58Wc 117
Ash Cft. Ct. DA3: Nw A G .76Ae 165
Ashcroft Ct. DA1: Dart .59Qd 119
N20 .19Fb 31
SL1: Burn .10A 60
Ashcroft Cres. DA15: Sidc .58Wc 117
Ashcroft Dr. UB9: Den .30H 43
Ashcroft Ho. *SW8* .53Lb 112
(off Wadhurst Rd.)
Ashcroft Pk. KT11: Cobh .84Aa 171
Ashcroft Pl. KT22: Lea .93La 192
Ashcroft Ri. CR5: Coul .88Nb 176
Ashcroft Rd. KT9: Chess .76Pa 153
Ashcroft Sq. W6 .49Ya 88
Ashcroft Theatre
Croydon .76Tb 157
(within Fairfield Halls)
Ashdale KT23: Bookh .98Ea 192
Ashdale Cl. TW2: Whitt .59Ea 108
TW19: Stanw .61N 127
Ashdale Gro. HA7: Stan .23Ha 46
Ashdale Ho. N4 .31Tb 71
Ashdale Rd. SE12 .60Kc 115
Ashdales AL1: St A .6B 6
Ashdale Way TW2: Whitt .59Da 107
Ashdene HA5: Pinn .27Y 45
SE15 .52Xb 113
Ashdene Cl. TW15: Ashf .66S 128
Ashdene Ho. TW20: Eng G .5N 125
Ashdon Cl. CM13: Hut .16Ee 41
IG8: Wfd G .23Kc 53
RM15: S Ock .44Xd 98
Ashdon Rd. NW10 .39Va 68
WD23: Bush .13Z 27
Ashdown *W13* .43Ka 86
(off Clivedon Ct.)
Ashdown Cl. BR3: Beck .68Dc 136
DA5: Bexl .59Ed 118
GU22: Wok .90A 168
RH2: Reig .10K 207
Ashdown Ct. E17 .26Ec 52
IG11: Bark .37Rc 74
SM2: Sutt .79Eb 155
Ashdown Cres. EN8: Chesh .1Ac 20
NW5 .36Jb 70
Ashdown Dr. WD6: Bore .12Pa 29
Ashdowne Ct. N17 .25Wb 51
Ashdown Gdns. CR2: Sande .87Xb 177
Ashdown Pl. KT7: T Ditt .73Ja 152
KT17: Ewe .80Va 154
Ashdown Rd. EN3: Enf H .12Yb 34
KT1: King T .68Na 131
KT17: Eps .85Va 174
RH2: Reig .10K 207
UB10: Hil .40Q 64
Ashdown Wlk. E14 .49Cc 92
RM7: Mawney .25Dd 56
Ashdown Way SW17 .61Jb 134
Ash Dr. AL10: Hat .3C 8
RH1: Redh .8A 208
Ashe Ho. TW1: Twick .58Ma 109
Ashen E6 .44Qc 94
Ashenbank Wood (Ancient Woodland)
.8J 145
Ashenden Rd. E5 .36Ac 72
Ashenden Wlk. SL2: Farn C .5H 61
Ashen Dr. DA1: Dart .58Jd 118
Ashen Gro. SW19 .62Cb 133
Ashen Gro. Rd. TN15: Knat .82Rd 183
Ashentree Ct. EC4 .3A 224
Ashen Va. CR2: Sels .81Zb 178
Asher Loftus Way N11 .23Hb 49
Asher Way E1 .45Wb 91
Ashfield Av. TW13: Felt .60X 107
WD23: Bush .16Da 27
Ashfield Cl. BR3: Beck .66Cc 136
KT21: Asht .91Na 193
TW10: Ham .60Na 109
Ashfield Ct. *SW9* .54Nb 112
(off Clapham Rd.)
Ashfield Ho. *W14* .50Bb 89
(off W. Cromwell Rd.)
Ashfield La. BR7: Chst .65Rc 138
(not continuous)
Ashfield Pde. N14 .18Mb 32
Ashfield Rd. N4 .30Sb 51
N14 .20Lb 32
W3 .46Va 88
Ashfields IG10: Lough .12Pc 36
WD25: Wat .7V 12
Ashfields Ct. RH2: Reig .4K 207
Ashfield St. E1 .43Xb 91
(not continuous)
Ashfield Yd. E1 .43Yb 92
Ashflower Dr. RM3: Hrld W .25Nd 57
ASHFORD .63P 127
Ashford Av. CM14: B'wood .20Xd 40
N8 .28Nb 50
TW15: Ashf .65R 128
UB4: Yead .44Z 85
Ashford Bus. Complex
TW15: Ashf .64S 128
Ashford Cl. E17 .30Bc 52
TW15: Ashf .63N 127
ASHFORD COMMON .66T 128
Ashford Ct. HA8: Edg .20Ra 29
KT19: Eps .84Pa 173
NW2 .35Za 68
RM17: Grays .50Fe 99
Ashford Cres. EN3: Enf H .12Yb 34
TW15: Ashf .62N 127
Ashford Gdns. KT11: Cobh .88Z 171
Ashford Grn. WD19: Wat .22Z 45
Ashford Ho. SE8 .51Bc 114
SW9 .56Rb 113
Ashford Ind. Est. TW15: Ashf .63S 128
Ashford La. SL4: Dor .7A 80
Ashford Manor Golf Course .65P 127
Ashford M. N17 .25Wb 51
ASHFORD PARK .63M 127
Ashford Pas. NW2 .35Za 68
Ashford Rd. E6 .38Qc 74
E18 .26Kc 53
NW2 .35Za 68
SL0: Iver H .39E 62
TW13: Felt .63T 128
TW15: Ashf .66S 128
TW18: Lale, Staines .68L 127
Ashford St. N1 .3H 219 (41Ub 91)
Ashford Tennis Club .63M 127
Ash Grn. UB9: Den .37K 63
Ash Gro. BR4: W W'ck .75Ec 158
E8 .39Xb 71
(not continuous)
EN1: Enf .17Ub 33
HA0: Wemb .35Ja 66
HP3: Hem H .6P 3
N10 .28Kb 50
N13 .20Sb 33
NW2 .35Za 68
SE12 .60Jc 115
SE20 .68Yb 136
SL2: Stoke P .8K 61
TW5: Hest .53Z 107
TW14: Felt .60U 106
TW18: Staines .65L 127
UB1: S'hall .43Ca 85
UB3: Hayes .45T 84
UB7: Yiew .45P 83
UB9: Hare .25M 43
W5 .47Na 87
Ashgrove TN14: Knock .87Ad 181
Ashgrove Ct. *W9* .43Cb 89
(off Elmfield Way)
Ashgrove Ho. SW1 .7E 228
Ashgrove Rd. BR1: Brom .65Fc 137
IG3: Ilf .32Vc 75
TN13: S'oaks .99Jd 202
TW15: Ashf .64S 128
Ash Hill Cl. WD23: Bush .18Da 27
Ash Hill Dr. HA5: Pinn .27Y 45
Ash Ho. DA3: Nw A G .75Ae 165
E14 .47Ec 92
(off E. Ferry Rd.)
SE1 .6K 231
TW18: Staines .63H 127
W10 .42Ab 88
(off Heather Wlk.)
Ashingdon Cl. E4 .20Ec 34
Ashington Ho. *E1* .42Xb 91
(off Barnsley St.)
Ashington Rd. SW6 .54Bb 111
Ash Island KT8: E Mos .69Fa 130
Ashlake Rd. SW16 .63Nb 134
Ashland Pl. W1 .7H 215 (43Jb 90)
Ashlands Ct. RM18: E Til .8L 101
Ash La. RM1: Rom .23Jd 56
RM11: Horn .28Qd 57
SL4: Wind .4B 102
TN15: Ash, W King .84Yd 184
Ashlar Pl. SE18 .49Rc 94
Ashlea Ct. CR6: W'ham .90Wb 177
Ashlea Rd. SL9: Chal P .26A 42
Ashleigh Av. TW20: Egh .66E 126
Ashleigh Commercial Est.
SE7 .48Lc 93
Ashleigh Ct. EN9: Walt A .6Jc 21
N14 .17Lb 32
W5 .49Ma 87
(off Murray Rd.)
WD3: Rick .17M 25
WD17: Wat .13Y 27
(off Loates La.)
Ashleigh Gdns. RM14: Upm .34Td 78
SM1: Sutt .75Db 155
Ashleigh M. *SE15* .55Vb 113
(off Oglander Rd.)
Ashleigh Point SE23 .62Zb 136
Ashleigh Rd. SE20 .69Xb 136
SW14 .55Ua 110

Ashley Av.—Auckland Hill

Ashley Av. IG6: Ilf 26Rc 54
KT18: Eps 85Ta 173
SM4: Mord 71Cb 155
Ashley Cen. KT18: Eps 85Ta 173
Ashley Cl. HA5: Pinn 26X 45
HP3: Hem H 4P 3
KT12: Walt T 74V 150
KT23: Bookh 97Ba 191
NW4 26Ya 48
TN13: S'oaks 96Kd 203
Ashley Ct. EN5: New Bar 15Eb 31
GU21: Wok 10K 167
KT18: Eps 85Ta 173
NW4 26Ya 48
SW1 4B 228
UB5: N'olt 39Aa 65
Ashley Cres. N22 26Qb 50
SW11 55Jb 112
Ashley Dr. KT12: Walt T 76W 150
SM7: Bans 86Cb 175
TW2: Whitt 59Da 107
TW7: Isle 51Ga 108
WD6: Bore 15Sa 29
Ashley Gdns. BR6: Orp 78Uc 160
HA9: Wemb 33Na 67
N13 21Sb 51
RM16: Grays 46Ee 99
SW1 4C 228 (48Lb 90)
(not continuous)
TW10: Ham 61Ma 131
Ashley Gro. IG10: Lough 13Nc 36
Ashley La. CR0: Wadd 77Rb 157
NW4 26Ya 48
ASHLEY PARK 76W 150
Ashley Pk. Av. KT12: Walt T 75V 150
Ashley Pk. Cres. KT12: Walt T 74W 150
Ashley Pk. Rd. KT12: Walt T 75W 150
Ashley Pl. KT12: Walt T 75W 150
(off Ashley Rd.)
SW1 4B 228 (48Lb 90)
(not continuous)
Ashley Ri. KT12: Walt T 77W 150
Ashley Rd. AL1: St A 2G 6
CR7: Thor H 70Pb 134
E4 23Cc 52
E7 38Lc 73
EN3: Enf H 12Yb 34
GU21: Wok 10K 167
KT7: T Ditt 72Ha 152
KT12: Walt T 77V 150
KT18: Eps, Eps D 85Ta 173
N17 27Wb 51
N19 32Nb 70
SW19 65Db 133
TN13: S'oaks 96Kd 203
TW9: Rich 55Na 109
TW12: Hamp 67Ca 129
UB8: Uxb 40K 63
Ashleys WD3: Rick 17H 25
Ashley Sq. KT18: Eps 85Ta 173
(off South St.)
Ashley Wlk. NW7 24Ya 48
Ashley Way GU24: W End 5B 166
Ashling Rd. CR0: C'don 74Wb 157
Ashlin Rd. E15 35Fc 73
Ash Lodge KT12: Walt T 74W 150
TW16: Sun 66V 128
(off Forest Dr.)
Ashlone Rd. SW15 55Ya 110
Ashlyn Cl. WD23: Bush 14Aa 27
Ashlyn Ct. WD23: Bush 14Aa 27
Ashlyn Gro. RM11: Horn 27Md 57
Ashlyns Pk. KT11: Cobh 85Aa 171
Ashlyns Rd. CM16: Epp 2Vc 23
Ashlyns Way KT9: Chess 79Ma 153
Ashmead N14 15Lb 32
Ashmead Bus. Cen. E16 42Fc 93
Ashmead Cl. TW15: Ashf 66S 128
Ashmead Ct. DA9: Ghithe 58Xd 120
Ashmead Dr. UB9: Den 33J 63
Ashmead Ga. BR1: Brom 67Lc 137
Ashmead Ho. E9 36Ac 72
(off Homerton Rd.)
W13 46Ja 86
(off Tewkesbury Rd.)
Ashmead La. UB9: Den 33J 63
Ashmead M. SE8 54Cc 114
Ashmead Rd. SE8 54Cc 114
TW14: Felt 60W 106
Ashmeads IG10: Lough 13Pc 36
Ashmeads Ct. WD7: Shenl 5Ma 15
Ashmere Av. BR3: Beck 68Fc 137
Ashmere Cl. SM3: Cheam 78Za 154
Ashmere Gro. SW2 56Nb 112
Ash M. CR3: Cat'm 95Tb 197
KT18: Eps 85Ua 174
NW5 36Lb 70
Ashmill St. NW1 7D 214 (43Gb 89)
Ashmole Pl. SW8 51Pb 112
Ashmole St. SW8 51Pb 112
Ashmore NW1 38Mb 70
(off Agar Gro.)
Ashmore Cl. SE15 52Vb 113
Ashmore Ct. N11 23Hb 49
TW5: Hest 51Ca 107
Ashmore Gdns. DA11: Nflt 62Fe 143
HP3: Hem H 3B 4
Ashmore Gro. DA16: Well 55Tc 116
Ashmore Ho. W14 48Ab 88
(off Russell Rd.)
Ashmore La. BR2: Kes 83Lc 179
Ashmore Rd. SE18 52Pc 116
W9 40Bb 69
Ashmount Cres. SL1: Slou 7E 80
Ashmount Est. N19 31Mb 70
Ashmount Rd. N15 29Vb 51
N19 31Lb 70
Ashmount Ter. W5 49Ma 87
Ashmour Gdns. RM1: Rom 26Fd 56
Ashneal Gdns. HA1: Harr 34Fa 66
Ashness Gdns. UB6: G'frd 37Ka 66
Ashness Rd. SW11 57Hb 111
Ashpark Ho. E14 44Bc 92
(off Norbiton Rd.)
Ash Platt, The TN15: Seal 92Nd 203
Ash Platt Rd. TN15: Seal 93Nd 203
Ash Ride EN2: Crew H 7Qb 18
Ashridge Cl. HA3: Kenton 30La 46
HP3: Bov 10B 2
Ashridge Ct. N3 27Cb 49
N14 15Lb 32
UB1: S'hall 44Ea 86
(off Redcroft Rd.)
Ashridge Cres. SE18 52Sc 116
Ashridge Dr. AL2: Brick W 2Aa 13
WD19: Wat 22Y 45
Ashridge Gdns. HA5: Pinn 28Aa 45
N13 22Mb 50
Ashridge Ho. WD18: Wat 17U 26
(off Chenies Way)
Ashridge Way SM4: Mord 69Bb 133
TW16: Sun 65W 128
Ash Rd. BR6: Chels 80Vc 161
CR0: C'don 75Cc 158
DA1: Dart 60Md 119
DA2: Hawl 63Pd 141
DA3: Hartl, Lfield, Nw A G 69Ae 143
DA12: Grav'nd 3E 144
E15 36Gc 73
GU22: Wok 2P 187
GU24: Pirb 8D 186
IG7: Chig 21Tc 54
SM3: Sutt 73Ab 154
TN15: Ash, Nw A G 77Zd 165
TN16: Westrm 97Tc 200
TW17: Shep 70Q 128
Ash Row BR2: Brom 73Qc 160
ASHTEAD 90Pa 173
Ashtead Common (National Nature Reserve) 87La 172
Ashtead Gap KT22: Lea 88Ka 172
ASHTEAD PARK 90Qa 173
Ashtead Pk. (Local Nature Reserve) 89Qa 173
Ashtead Rd. E5 31Wb 71
Ashtead Woods Rd. KT21: Asht 89La 172
Ashton Cl. KT12: Hers 79X 151
SM1: Sutt 77Cb 155
Ashton Ct. E4 20Gc 35
HA1: Harr 34Ha 66
Ashton Gdns. RM6: Chad H 30Ad 55
TW4: Houn 56Ba 107
Ashton Ga. RM3: Rom 24Md 57
Ashton Hgts. SE23 60Yb 114
Ashton Ho. SE11 7B 230
SW9 52Qb 112
Ashton Pl. KT10: Clay 80Ha 152
Ashton Reach SE16 49Ac 92
Ashton Rd. E15 36Fc 73
EN3: Enf W 8Ac 20
GU21: Wok 9K 167
RM3: Rom 24Md 57
Ashton St. E14 45Ec 92
Ashtree Av. CR4: Mitc 68Fb 133
Ash Tree Cl. CR0: C'don 72Ac 158
KT6: Surb 75Na 153
TN15: W King 81Vd 184
Ashtree Cl. BR6: Farnb 77Rc 160
Ash Tree Ct. TN15: W King 81Vd 184
TW15: Ashf 64R 128
(off Feltham Hill Rd.)
Ashtree Ct. AL1: St A 2D 6
EN9: Walt A 6Jc 21
(off Horseshoe Cl.)
Ash Tree Dell NW9 29Sa 47
Ash Tree Dr. TN15: W King 80Vd 164
Ash Tree Ho. SE5 52Sb 113
(off Pitman St.)
Ash Tree Rd. WD24: Wat 8X 13
Ash Tree Way CR0: C'don 71Zb 158
Ashtree Way HP1: Hem H 3J 3
Ashurst KT18: Eps 86Ta 173
Ashurst Cl. CR8: Kenley 87Tb 177
DA1: Cray 55Hd 118
HA6: Nwood 24U 44
KT22: Lea 93Ja 192
SE20 67Xb 135
Ashurst Dr. IG2: Ilf 30Rc 54
IG6: Ilf 29Sc 54
TW17: Shep 71N 149
Ashurst Gdns. SW2 60Qb 112
Ashurst Pk. SL5: S'hill 9C 124
Ashurst Rd. EN4: Cockf 15Hb 31
KT20: Tad 93Xa 194
N12 22Gb 49
Ashurst Wlk. CR0: C'don 75Xb 157
Ash Va. WD3: Map C 22F 42
Ashvale Ct. E3 40Cc 72
(off Matilda Gdns.)
Ashvale Dr. RM14: Upm 33Ud 78
Ashvale Gdns. RM5: Col R 22Fd 56
RM14: Upm 33Ud 78
Ashvale Rd. SW17 64Hb 133
Ashview Apartments N4 31Sb 71
(off Katherine Cl.)
Ashview Cl. TW15: Ashf 64N 127
Ashview Gdns. TW15: Ashf 64N 127
Ashville Rd. E11 33Fc 73
Ash Wlk. HA0: Wemb 35La 66
RM15: S Ock 41Zd 99
Ashwater Rd. SE12 60Jc 115
Ash Way IG8: Wfd G 26Mc 53
Ashway Cen., The KT2: King T 67Na 131
Ashwell Cl. E6 44Nc 94
Ashwell Ct. TW15: Ashf 61N 127
Ashwell Pl. WD24: Wat 9W 12
Ashwells Rd. CM15: Pil H 13Td 40
Ashwell St. AL3: St A 1B 6
Ashwick Cl. CR3: Cat'm 96Wb 197
Ashwindham Ct.
GU21: Wok 10K 167
Ashwin St. E8 37Vb 71
Ashwood CR6: W'ham 92Yb 198
Ashwood Av. RM13: Rain 42Kd 97
UB8: Hil 44Q 84
Ashwood Gdns. CR0: New Ad 79Ec 158
UB3: Harl 49V 84
Ashwood Ho. HA5: Hat E 23Ca 45
(off The Avenue)
NW4 28Ya 48
(off Belle Vue Est.)
Ashwood M. AL1: St A 4B 6
Ashwood Pk. GU22: Wok 90C 168
KT22: Fet 95Ea 192
Ashwood Pl. DA2: Bean 62Xd 142
GU22: Wok 90C 168
SL5: S'dale 3C 146
Ashwood Rd. E4 20Fc 35
EN6: Pot B 5Db 17
GU22: Wok 90B 168
TW20: Eng G 5M 125
Ashworth Av. TN15: W King 80Td 164
(off London Rd.)
Ashworth Cl. SE5 54Tb 113
Ashworth Est. CR0: Bedd 74Nb 156
Ashworth Mans. W9 41Db 89
(off Elgin Av.)
Ashworth Rd. W9 41Db 89
Aske Ho. N1 3H 219
Asker Ho. N7 35Nb 70
Askern Cl. DA6: Bex 56Zc 117
Aske St. N1 3H 219 (41Ub 91)
Askew Bldg., The EC1 1D 224
Askew Cres. W12 47Va 88
Askew Est. W12 46Va 88
(off Uxbridge Rd.)
Askew Rd. HA6: Nwood 19T 26
W12 47Va 88
Askews Farm La.
RM17: Grays 50Ae 99
Askham Ct. W12 46Wa 88
Askham Rd. W12 46Wa 88
Askill Dr. SW15 57Ab 110
Askwith Rd. RM13: Rain 41Fd 96
Asland Rd. E15 39Gc 73
Aslett St. SW18 59Db 111
Aslin Ct. AL1: St A 2C 6
(off Hatfield Rd.)
Asman Ho. N1 1B 218
Asmara Rd. NW2 36Ab 68
Asmar Cl. CR5: Coul 87Nb 176
Asmuns Hill NW11 29Cb 49
Asmuns Pl. NW11 29Bb 49
Asolando Dr.
SE17 6E 230 (49Sb 91)
Aspasia Cl. AL1: St A 3D 6
Aspdin Rd. DA11: Nflt 62Fe 143
Aspect Ct. E14 47Ec 92
(off Manchester Rd.)
SW6 54Eb 111
Aspects SM1: Sutt 78Db 155
Aspects Ct. SL1: Slou 7J 81
Aspen Cl. AL2: Brick W 2Aa 13
BR6: Chels 78Wc 161
BR8: Swan 67Fd 140
KT1: Hamp W 67La 130
KT11: Stoke D 88Aa 171
KT19: Eps 81Ta 173
N19 33Lb 70
SL2: Slou 3F 80
TW18: Staines 62H 127
UB7: Yiew 46P 83
W5 47Pa 87
Aspen Copse BR1: Brom 68Pc 138
Aspen Ct. CM13: B'wood 20Ce 41
DA1: Dart 58Qd 119
GU25: Vir W 70A 126
NW4 26Ab 48
Aspen Dr. HA0: Wemb 34Ja 66
Aspen Gdns. CR4: Mitc 71Jb 156
TW15: Ashf 64S 128
W6 50Xa 88
Aspen Grn. DA18: Erith 48Bd 95
Aspen Gro. HA5: Eastc 27V 44
RM14: Upm 35Qd 77
Aspen Ho. CR6: W'ham 87Dc 178
DA15: Sidc 61Wc 139
E15 41Gc 93
(off Teasel Way)
SE15 51Yb 114
(off Sharratt St.)
Aspen La. UB5: N'olt 41Aa 85
Aspenlea Rd. W6 51Za 110
Aspen Lodge W8 48Db 89
(off Abbots Wlk.)
Aspen M. SE20 65Yb 136
Aspen Pk. Dr. WD25: Wat 7X 13
Aspen Pl. WD23: B Hea 17Ga 28
Aspens, The EN9: Walt A 7Lc 21
(within Woodbine Cl. Caravan Pk.)
Aspens Pl. HP1: Hem H 5H 3
Aspen Sq. KT13: Weyb 76T 150
Aspen Va. CR3: Whyt 89Vb 177
Aspen Way E14 45Dc 92
EN3: Enf W 7Zb 20
RM15: S Ock 41Zd 99
SM7: Bans 86Za 174
TW13: Felt 62X 129
Aspern Gro. NW3 36Gb 69
Aspinall Rd. SE4 55Zb 114
(not continuous)
Aspinden Rd. SE16 49Xb 91
ASPIRE National Training Cen. 19Ka 28
Aspire Sport & Fitness Cen. 18Ub 33
Aspland Gro. E8 37Xb 71
Aspley Rd. SW18 57Db 111
Asplins Rd. N17 25Wb 51
Asprey Gro. CR3: Cat'm 96Wb 197
Asprey M. BR3: Beck 71Bc 158
Asprey Pl. BR1: Brom 68Nc 138
Asquith Cl. RM8: Dag 32Yc 75
Asquith Ho. SM7: Bans 87Bb 175
(off Dunnymans Rd.)
SW1 4E 228
Assam St. E1 44Wb 91
(off White Church La.)
Assata M. N1 37Rb 71
Assembly Apartments
SE15 53Yb 114
(off York Gro.)
Assembly Pas. E1 43Yb 92
Assembly Wlk. SM5: Cars 73Gb 155
Assher Rd. KT12: Hers 76Aa 151
Ass Ho. La. HA3: Hrw W 21Da 45
Astall Cl. HA3: Hrw W 25Ga 46
Astbury Bus. Pk. SE15 53Yb 114
Astbury Ho. SE11 4K 229
Astbury Rd. SE15 53Yb 114
Astede Pl. KT21: Asht 90Pa 173
Astell Ho. SW3 7E 226
Astell Rd. SE3 56Lc 115
Astell St. SW3 7E 226 (50Gb 89)
Asten Way RM7: Mawney 26Dd 56
Aster Ct. E5 33Yb 72
(off Woodmill Rd.)
Asterid Hgts. E20 36Ec 72
(off Liberty Bri. Rd.)
Aster Pl. E9 38Yb 72
(off Frampton Pk. Rd.)
Asters, The EN7: G Oak 1Tb 19
SL5: S'dale 4C 146
Aste St. E14 47Ec 92
Astey's Row N1 38Sb 71
Asthall Gdns. IG6: Ilf 28Sc 54
Astins Ho. E17 28Dc 52
Astleham Rd.
TW17: Shep 69N 127
Astle St. SW11 54Jb 112
Astley RM17: Grays 51Be 121
Astley Av. NW2 36Ya 68
Astley Ho. SE1 7K 231
SW13 51Xa 110
(off Wyatt Dr.)
W2 43Cb 89
(off Alfred Rd.)
Astley Rd. HP1: Hem H 2L 3
Aston Av. HA3: Kenton 31La 66
Aston Cl. DA14: Sidc 62Wc 139
HP3: Hem H 6M 3
KT21: Asht 90La 172
WD23: Bush 16Ea 28
WD24: Wat 12Y 27
Aston Ct. IG8: Wfd G 23Jc 53
Aston Grn. TW4: Cran 54Y 107
Aston Ho. EC4 1K 223
RM8: Dag 35Wc 75
SW8 53Mb 112
W11 45Bb 89
(off Westbourne Gro.)
Aston Mead SL4: Wind 3C 102
Aston M. RM6: Chad H 31Yc 75
W10 41Za 88
Aston Pl. SW16 65Rb 135
Aston Rd. KT10: Clay 78Ga 152
SW20 68Ya 132
W5 44Ma 87
Astons Rd. HA6: Nwood 20S 26
Aston St. E14 43Ac 92
Aston Ter. SW12 58Kb 112
Astonville St. SW18 60Cb 111
Aston Way EN6: Pot B 4Fb 17
KT18: Eps 87Va 174
Aston Webb Ho. SE1 7H 225
Astor Av. RM7: Rom 30Ed 56
Astor Cl. KT2: King T 65Ra 131
KT15: Add 77M 149
Astor Ct. E16 44Lc 93
(off Ripley Rd.)
SW6 52Eb 111
(off Maynard Cl.)
Astoria Ct. CR8: Purl 83Rb 177
(off High St.)
E8 38Vb 71
(off Queensbridge Rd.)
Astoria Ho. NW9 26Va 48
(off Boulevard Dr.)
Astoria Mans. SW16 62Nb 134
Astoria Wlk. SW9 55Qb 112
Astor Rd. TN15: W King 79Ud 164
Astra Cl. RM12: Horn 37Kd 77
Astra Ct. WD18: Wat 15V 26
Astra Dr. DA12: Grav'nd 4G 144
Astra Ho. E3 41Bc 92
(off Alfred St.)
SE14 51Bc 114
(off Arklow Rd.)
Astral Ho. E1 1J 225
SE6 63Ec 136
Astrid Ho. TW13: Felt 61Y 129
Astrop M. W6 48Ya 88
Astrop Ter. W6 47Ya 88
Astwood Cl. RM11: Horn 31Pd 77
Astwood M. SW7 49Eb 89
Asylum Arch Rd. RH1: Redh 9P 207
Asylum Rd. SE15 52Xb 113
Atalanta Cl. CR8: Purl 82Qb 176
Atalanta St. SW6 52Za 110
Atbara Rd. TW11: Tedd 65Ka 130
Atcham Rd. TW3: Houn 56Ea 108
Atcost Rd. IG11: Bark 43Wc 95
Atcraft Cen. HA0: Wemb 39Na 67
Atelier Ct. SE8 52Cc 114
(off Watson's St.)
Atelier Ct. Central E14 43Ec 92
(off Leven Rd.)
Atelier Ct. Nth. E14 43Ec 92
(off Leven Rd.)
Atelier Ct. Sth. E14 43Ec 92
(off Leven Rd.)
Atfield Gro. GU20: W'sham 9B 146
Atheldene Rd. SW18 60Db 111
Athelney St. SE6 62Cc 136
Athelstan Cl. RM3: Hrld W 26Pd 57
Athelstane Gro. E3 40Bc 72
Athelstane M. N4 32Qb 70
Athelstan Gdns. NW6 38Ab 68
Athelstan Ho. E9 36Bc 72
(off Homerton Rd.)
KT1: King T 70Pa 131
(off Athelstan Rd.)
Athelstan Pl. TW2: Twick 60Ga 108
Athelstan Rd. HP3: Hem H 5P 3
KT1: King T 70Pa 131
RM3: Hrld W 25Pd 57
Athelstan Way BR5: St P 67Wc 139
Athelstone Rd. HA3: W'stone 26Fa 46
Athena Cl. HA2: Harr 33Fa 66
KT1: King T 69Pa 131
Athena Ct. SE1 2H 231
Athenaeum Ct. N5 35Sb 71
Athenaeum Pl. N10 27Kb 50
Athenaeum Rd. N20 18Eb 31
Athena Pl. HA6: Nwood 25V 44
Athene Pl. EC4 2A 224
Athenia Cl. EN7: G Oak 1Rb 19
Athenia Ho. E14 44Fc 93
(off Blair St.)
Athenlay Rd. SE15 57Zb 114
Athens Gdns. W9 42Cb 89
(off Harrow Rd.)
Atherden Rd. E5 35Yb 72
Atherfield Ho. RH2: Reig 9L 207
(off Atherfield Rd.)
Atherfield Rd. RH2: Reig 9L 207
Atherfold Rd. SW9 55Nb 112
Atherley Way TW4: Houn 59Ba 107
Atherstone Ct. W2 43Db 89
(off Delamere Ter.)
Atherstone M. SW7 5A 226 (49Eb 89)
Atherton Cl. TW19: Stanw 58M 105
Atherton Ct. SL4: Eton 2H 103
Atherton Dr. SW19 63Za 132
Atherton Gdns. RM16: Grays 9E 100
Atherton Hgts. HA0: Wemb 38La 66
Atherton Ho. RM3: Rom 24Nd 57
(off Leyburn Cres.)
Atherton Leisure Cen. 37Hc 73
Atherton M. E7 37Hc 73
Atherton Pl. HA2: Harr 27Fa 46
UB1: S'hall 45Ca 85
Atherton Rd. E7 37Hc 73
IG5: Ilf 26Nc 54
SW13 52Wa 110
Atherton St. SW11 54Gb 111
Athill Ct. TN13: S'oaks 94Ld 203
Athlone KT10: Clay 79Ga 152
Athlone Cl. E5 36Xb 71
WD7: R'lett 8Ja 14
Athlone Ct. E17 27Fc 53
Athlone Ga. W10 43Ab 88
Athlone Ho. E1 44Yb 92
(off Sidney St.)
Athlone Pl. W10 43Ab 88
(off Athlone Ga.)
Athlone Rd. SW2 59Pb 112
Athlone Sq. SL4: Wind 3G 102
Athlone St. NW5 37Jb 70
Athlon Ind. Est. HA0: Wemb 39Ma 67
Athlon Rd. HA0: Wemb 40Ma 67
Athol Cl. HA5: Pinn 25X 45
Athole Gdns. EN1: Enf 15Ub 33
Athol Gdns. HA5: Pinn 25X 45
Atholl Ho. W9 4A 214
Atholl Rd. IG3: Ilf 31Wc 75
Athol Rd. DA8: Erith 50Ed 96
Athol Sq. E14 44Ec 92
Athol Way UB10: Hil 41Q 84
Atkin Bldg. WC1 7J 217
Atkins Cl. GU21: Wok 10L 167
TN16: Big H 84Lc 179
Atkins Ct. E3 39Bc 72
(off Willow Tree Cl.)
Atkins Dr. BR4: W W'ck 75Fc 159
Atkins Lodge BR6: Orp 73Wc 161
(off High St.)
W8 47Cb 89
(off Thornwood Gdns.)
Atkinson Cl. BR6: Chels 78Wc 161
SW20 66Wa 132
WD23: Bush 17Ga 28
Atkinson Ct. E10 31Dc 72
(off Kings Cl.)
Atkinson Ho. E2 40Wb 71
(off Pritchards Rd.)
E13 42Hc 93
(off Sutton Rd.)
SE17 6G 231
SW11 53Jb 112
(off Austin Rd.)
Atkinson Morley Av. SW17 62Fb 133
Atkinson Rd. E16 43Lc 93
Atkins Rd. E10 30Dc 52
SW12 59Lb 112
Atkins Sq. E5 36Xb 71
Atlanta Blvd. RM1: Rom 30Gd 56
Atlanta Bldg. SE13 53Dc 114
(off Deal's Gateway)
Atlanta Ct. CR7: Thor H 69Sb 135
Atlanta Ho. SE16 48Ac 92
(off Brunswick Quay)
Atlantic Apartments E16 45Jc 93
(off Seagull La.)
Atlantic Cl. DA10: Swans 57Ae 121
Atlantic Ct. E14 45Fc 93
(off Jamestown Way)
SW3 7F 227 (50Hb 89)
Atlantic Rd. SW9 56Qb 112
Atlantic Wharf E1 45Zb 92
Atlantis Av. E16 45Rc 94
Atlantis Cl. IG11: Bark 41Xc 95
Atlas Bus. Cen. NW2 32Xa 68
Atlas Cres. HA8: Edg 19Ra 29
Atlas Gdns. SE7 49Lc 93
Atlas M. E8 37Vb 71
N7 37Pb 70
SE13 56Fc 115
Atlas Rd. DA1: Dart 55Pd 119
E13 40Jc 73
HA9: Wemb 35Sa 67
N11 24Jb 50
NW10 41Ua 88
Atlas Trade Pk. DA8: Erith 50Fd 96
Atlas Wharf E9 37Cc 72
Atlip Rd. HA0: Wemb 39Na 67
Atlitude E1 44Wb 91
(off Alie St.)
Atney Rd. SW15 56Ab 110
Atria Rd. HA6: Nwood 22W 44
Atrium, The IG9: Buck H 19Mc 35
W12 46Za 88
Atrium Apartments N1 39Tb 71
(off Felton St.)
Atrium Hgts. SE8 51Dc 114
(off Creekside)
Atrium Ho. SE8 52Bc 114
Attel Cl. KT15: Add 80J 149
Attenborough Cl. WD19: Wat 20Aa 27
Atterbury Cl. TN16: Westrm 98Tc 200
Atterbury Rd. N4 30Qb 50
Atterbury St. SW1 6F 229 (49Nb 90)
Attewood Av. NW10 34Ua 68
Attewood Rd. UB5: N'olt 37Aa 65
Attfield Cl. N20 19Fb 31
Attfield Ct. KT1: King T 68Pa 131
(off Albert Rd.)
Attilburgh Ho. SE1 3K 231
Attleborough Ct. SE23 61Wb 135
Attle Cl. UB10: Hil 40Q 64
Attlee Cl. CR7: Thor H 71Sb 157
UB4: Yead 41X 85
UB5: N'olt 41X 85
Attlee Ct. RM17: Grays 48Ce 99
Attlee Dr. DA1: Dart 57Qd 119
Attlee Rd. SE28 45Xc 95
UB4: Yead 41W 84
Attlee Ter. E17 28Ec 52
Attneave St. WC1 4K 217 (41Qb 90)
Attock M. E17 29Dc 52
Attwood Cl. CR2: Sande 86Xb 177
Attwood Pl. Yd. TN15: Ash 78Zd 165
Atunbi Ct. NW1 38Lb 70
(off Farrier St.)
Atwater Cl. SW2 60Qb 112
Atwell Cl. E10 30Dc 52
Atwell Pl. KT7: T Ditt 74Ha 152
Atwell Rd. SE15 54Wb 113
Atwood KT23: Bookh 96Aa 191
Atwood Av. TW9: Kew 54Qa 109
Atwood Ho. W14 49Bb 89
(off Beckford Cl.)
Atwood Rd. W6 49Xa 88
Atwoods All. TW9: Kew 53Qa 109
Aube Ho. SE6 63Ec 136
Aubers Ridge Ct. E3 40Bc 72
(off Festubert Pl.)
Aubert Ct. N5 35Rb 71
Aubert Pk. N5 35Rb 71
Aubert Rd. N5 35Rb 71
Aubretia Cl. RM3: Hrld W 25Nd 57
Aubrey Av. AL2: Lon C 8G 6
Aubrey Beardsley Ho. SW1 6C 228
Aubrey Mans. NW1 7D 214
Aubrey Moore Point E15 40Ec 72
(off Abbey La.)
Aubrey Pl. NW8 2A 214 (40Eb 69)
Aubrey Rd. E17 27Cc 52
N8 29Nb 50
W8 46Bb 89
Aubrey's Rd. HP1: Hem H 3G 2
Aubrey Wlk. W8 46Bb 89
Auburn Cl. SE14 52Ac 114
Aubyn Hill SE27 63Sb 135
Aubyn Sq. SW15 57Wa 110
Auckland Av. RM13: Rain 41Hd 96
Auckland Cl. EN1: Enf 9Xb 19
RM18: Tilb 4C 122
SE19 67Vb 135
Auckland Ct. UB4: Yead 42Y 85
Auckland Gdns. SE19 67Ub 135
Auckland Hill SE27 63Sb 135

Auckland Ho.—Babbage Ct.

Auckland Ho. KT12: Walt T 74W 150
W12 45Xa 88
(off White City Est.)
Auckland Ri. SE19 67Ub 135
Auckland Rd. CR3: Cat'm 94Ub 197
E10 34Dc 72
EN6: Pot B 4Ab 16
IG1: Ilf 32Rc 74
KT1: King T 70Pa 131
SE19 67Vb 135
SW11 56Gb 111
Auckland St. SE11 50Pb 90
Audax NW9 26Va 48
Auden Dr. WD6: Bore 15Qa 29
Auden Pl. NW1 39Jb 70
SM3: Cheam 77Ya 154
Audleigh Pl. IG7: Chig 23Qc 54
Audley Cl. KT15: Add 78K 149
N10 24Kb 50
SW11 55Jb 112
WD6: Bore 13Qa 29
Audley Ct. E18 28Hc 53
HA5: Pinn 26Y 45
TW2: Twick 62Fa 130
UB5: N'olt 41Y 85
Audley Dr. CR6: W'ham 87Yb 178
E16 46Kc 93
Audley Firs KT12: Hers 77Y 151
Audley Gdns. EN9: Walt A 6Ec 20
IG3: Ilf 33Vc 75
IG10: Lough 12Sc 36
(not continuous)
Audley Ho. KT15: Add 78K 149
Audley Pl. SM2: Sutt 80Db 155
Audley Rd. EN2: Enf 12Rb 33
NW4 29Wa 48
TW10: Rich 57Pa 109
W5 43Pa 87
Audley Sq. W1 6J 221 (46Jb 90)
Audley Wlk. BR5: St M Cry 72Yc 161
Audrey Cl. BR3: Beck 72Dc 158
Audrey Gdns. HA0: Wemb 33Ka 66
Audrey Rd. IG1: Ilf 34Rc 74
Audrey St. E2 40Wb 71
Audric Cl. KT2: King T 67Qa 131
Audwick Cl. EN8: Chesh 1Ac 20
Augur Cl. TW18: Staines 64H 127
Augurs La. E13 41Kc 93
Augusta Cl. KT8: W Mole 69Ba 129
Augusta Rd. SS17: Stan H 3K 101
TW2: Twick 61Ea 130
Augustas La. N1 38Qb 70
Augusta St. E14 44Dc 92
Augusta Wlk. W5 43Ma 87
August End SL3: Geor G 44A 82
Augustine Bell Twr. E3 40Cc 72
(off Pancras Way)
Augustine Cl. SL3: Poyle 55G 104
Augustine Ct. EN9: Walt A 5Dc 20
Augustine Rd. BR5: St P 69Zc 139
DA12: Grav'nd 9E 122
(not continuous)
HA3: Hrw W 25Da 45
W14 48Za 88
Augustus Bldg. E1 44Xb 91
(off Tarling St.)
Augustus Cl. AL3: St A 4N 5
HA7: Stan 20Ma 29
TW8: Bford 52La 108
W12 47Xa 88
Augustus Ct. SE1 5H 231
SW16 61Mb 134
TW13: Hanw 63Ba 129
Augustus Ho. NW1 2B 216
Augustus La. BR6: Orp 75Wc 161
Augustus Rd. SW19 60Za 110
Augustus St. NW1 2A 216 (40Kb 70)
Aulay Ho. SE16 48Vb 91
Aultone Way SM1: Sutt 75Db 155
SM5: Cars 76Hb 155
Aultone Yd. Ind. Est. SM5: Cars 76Hb 155
Aulton Pl. SE11 50Qb 90
Aura Ct. SE15 56Xb 113
Aura Ho. TW9: Kew 53Ra 109
Aurelia Gdns. CR0: C'don 71Pb 156
Aurelia Ho. E20 36Ec 72
(off Sunrise Cl.)
Aurelia Rd. CR0: C'don 72Nb 156
Auriel Av. RM10: Dag 37Fd 76
Auriga M. N1 36Tb 71
Auriol Cl. KT4: Wor Pk 76Ua 154
Auriol Dr. UB6: G'frd 38Fa 66
UB10: Hil 37Q 64
Auriol Ho. W12 46Xa 88
(off Ellerslie Rd.)
Auriol Mans. W14 49Ab 88
(off Edith Rd.)
Auriol Pk. Rd. KT4: Wor Pk 76Ua 154
Auriol Rd. W14 49Ab 88
Aurora Apartments EC1 3D 218
SW18 57Cb 111
(off Buckhold Rd.)
Aurora Bldg. E14 46Ec 92
(off Blackwall Way)
Aurora Bldg., The N1 2G 219
Aurora Cl. WD25: Wat 6Y 13
Aurora Ct. DA12: Grav'nd 8E 122
(off Romulus Rd.)
Aurora Ho. E14 44Dc 92
(off Kerbey St.)
SE6 63Ec 136
Ausden Pl. WD17: Wat 15Y 27
(off Pumphouse Cres.)
Austell Gdns. NW7 20Ua 30
Austell Hgts. NW7 20Ua 30
(off Austell Gdns.)
Austen Apartments
SE20 68Xb 135
Austen Cl. DA9: Ghithe 58Yd 120
IG10: Lough 13Tc 36
RM18: Tilb 4E 122
SE28 46Xc 95
Austen Ct. KT22: Lea 93Ja 192
(off Highbury Dr.)
Austen Gdns. DA1: Dart 56Pd 119
Austen Ho. NW6 41Cb 89
(off Cambridge Rd.)
SW17 62Fb 133
(off St George's Gro.)
Austen Rd. DA8: Erith 52Dd 118
HA2: Harr 33Da 65
Austen Vw. SL3: L'ly 51B 104
Austen Way SL3: L'ly 51B 104
Austenway SL9: Chal P 27A 42
AUSTENWOOD 28A 42
Austenwood La.
SL9: Chal P 26A 42, 27A 42
Austin Av. BR2: Brom 71Nc 160
Austin Cl. CR5: Coul 90Rb 177
SE23 59Ac 114
TW1: Twick 57La 108
Austin Ct. E6 39Lc 73
EN1: Enf 15Ub 33
SE15 55Wb 113
(off Peckham Rye)
WD3: Rick 19K 25
Austin Friars EC2 2G 225 (44Tb 91)
Austin Friars Pas. EC2 2G 225
Austin Friars Sq. EC2 2G 225
Austin Ho. SE14 52Bc 114
(off Achilles St.)
Austin Pl. KT13: Weyb 75U 150
Austin Rd. BR5: St M Cry 72Wc 161
DA11: Nflt 10B 122
SW11 53Jb 112
UB3: Hayes 47V 84
Austin's La. HA4: Ruis 35T 64
UB10: Ick 34S 64
Austins Mead HP3: Bov 10D 2
Austins Pl. HP2: Hem H 1M 3
Austin St. E2 4K 219 (41Vb 91)
Austin Ter. SE1 3A 230
Austin Vs. WD25: Wat 3X 13
Austin Waye UB8: Uxb 39L 63
Austral Cl. DA15: Sidc 62Vc 139
Austral Dr. RM11: Horn 31Md 77
Australian War Memorial 1J 227
Australia Rd. SL1: Slou 7M 81
W12 45Xa 88
Austral St. SE11 5B 230 (49Rb 91)
Austyn Gdns. KT5: Surb 74Ra 153
Austyns Pl. KT17: Ewe 81Wa 174
Autumn Cl. EN1: Enf 11Wb 33
SL1: Slou 6D 80
SW19 65Eb 133
Autumn Dr. SM2: Sutt 81Db 175
Autumn Glades HP3: Hem H 4C 4
Autumn Gro. BR1: Brom 65Kc 137
Autumn Lodge CR2: S Croy 77Ub 157
(off South Pk. Hill Rd.)
Autumn St. E3 39Cc 72
Autumn Way UB7: W Dray 47P 83
Avalon Cl. BR6: Chels 76Zc 161
EN2: Enf 12Qb 32
SW20 68Ab 132
W13 43Ja 86
WD25: Wat 4Aa 13
Avalon Ct. CR0: C'don 73Vb 157
WD25: A'ham 11Ca 27
Avalon Rd. BR6: Chels 75Yc 161
SW6 53Db 111
W13 42Ja 86
Avante KT1: King T 69Ma 131
Avantgarde Pl. E1 5K 219
Avantgarde Twr. E1 5K 219
Avard Gdns. BR6: Farnb 77Sc 160
Avarn Rd. SW17 65Hb 133
Avebury SL1: Slou 5E 80
Avebury Ct. N1 1F 219
SE16 49Yb 92
(off Debnams Rd.)
Avebury Pk. KT6: Surb 73Ma 153
Avebury Rd. BR6: Orp 76Tc 160
E11 32Fc 73
SW19 67Bb 133
Avebury St. N1 39Tb 71
AVELEY 46Td 98
Aveley By-Pass RM15: Avel 45Sd 98
Aveley Cl. DA8: Erith 51Hd 118
RM15: Avel 46Td 98
Aveley Mans. IG11: Bark 38Rc 74
(off Whiting Av.)
Aveley Rd. RM1: Rom 28Fd 56
RM14: Avel, Upm 37Rd 77
Aveline St. SE11 7K 229 (50Qb 90)
Aveling Cl. CR8: Purl 85Pb 176
Aveling Pk. Rd. E17 26Cc 52
Avelon Rd. RM5: Col R 23Fd 56
RM13: Rain 39Jd 76
Ave Maria La. EC4 3C 224 (44Rb 91)
Avenell Mans. N5 35Rb 71
Avenell Rd. N5 34Rb 71
Avenfield Ho. W1 4G 221
Avening Rd. SW18 59Cb 111
Avening Ter. SW18 59Cb 111
Avenons Rd. E13 42Jc 93
Aventine Av. CR4: Mitc 69Kb 134
Aventine Ct. AL1: St A 3B 6
(off Holywell Hill)
Avenue, The BR1: Brom 69Mc 137
BR2: Kes 77Mc 159
BR3: Beck 67Dc 136
BR4: W W'ck 73Ec 158
BR5: St P 66Xc 139
BR6: Orp 75Vc 161
CM13: B'wood 23Ae 59
CM15: Kel H 11Ud 40
CR0: C'don 76Ub 157
CR3: Whyt 91Wb 197
CR5: Coul 87Mb 176
DA5: Bexl 59Zc 117
DA9: Ghithe 56Xd 120
DA11: Grav'nd 10C 122
DA12: Cobh 10K 145
E3 42Dc 92
(off Devas St.)
E4 23Fc 53
E11 30Kc 53
EC2 2J 225 (44Ub 91)
EN5: Barn 13Ab 30
EN6: Pot B 2Bb 17
GU3: Worp 9J 187
GU24: Chob 1L 167
HA3: Hrw W 25Ha 46
HA5: Hat E 23Ba 45
HA5: Pinn 30Ba 45
HA6: Nwood 23S 44
HA9: Wemb 32Na 67
HP1: Hem H 1G 2
IG9: Buck H 19Lc 35
IG10: Lough 16Mc 35
KT4: Wor Pk 75Va 154
KT5: Surb 72Pa 153
KT10: Clay 79Ga 152
KT15: New H 82J 169
KT17: Ewe 80Xa 154
KT20: Tad 94Xa 194
KT22: Oxs 83Ha 172
N3 26Cb 49
N8 27Qb 50
N10 26Lb 50
N11 22Kb 50
N17 27Tb 51
NW6 39Za 68
RH1: S Nut 9E 208
RM1: Rom 28Fd 56
Avenue, The RM12: Horn 33Ld 77
SE10 52Fc 115
SL2: Farn C 5F 60
SL3: Dat 3M 103
SL4: Old Win 7M 103
SM2: Cheam 81Bb 175
SM3: Cheam 80Ya 154
SM5: Cars 80Jb 156
SW4 56Jb 112
SW18 59Gb 111
TN15: Bor G 91Ce 205
TN16: Tats, Westrm 94Pc 200
TW1: Twick 57Ka 108
TW3: Houn 57Da 107
TW5: Cran 52W 106
TW9: Kew 54Pa 109
TW12: Hamp 65Ba 129
TW16: Sun 67X 129
TW18: Staines 67K 127
TW19: Wray 5P 103
TW20: Egh 63D 126
UB8: Cowl 42M 83
UB10: Ick 35Q 64
W4 48Ua 88
W13 44Ka 86
WD7: R'lett 5Ja 14
WD17: Wat 12W 26
WD23: Bush 14Ba 27
Avenue App. WD4: K Lan 2Q 12
Avenue C KT15: Add 76N 149
Avenue Cl. KT20: Tad 94Xa 194
N14 16Lb 32
NW8 1E 214 (39Gb 69)
(not continuous)
RM3: Hrld W 24Pd 57
TW5: Cran 53X 107
UB7: W Dray 48M 83
Avenue Ct. IG5: Ilf 27Nc 54
KT20: Tad 95Xa 194
N14 16Lb 32
NW2 34Bb 69
SW3 6F 227
Avenue Cres. TW5: Cran 53X 107
W3 47Ra 87
Avenue de Cagny GU24: Pirb 4D 186
Avenue Elmers KT6: Surb 71Na 153
Avenue Gdns. SE25 68Wb 135
SW14 55Ua 110
TW5: Cran 52X 107
TW11: Tedd 66Ha 130
W3 47Ra 87
Avenue Ga. IG10: Lough 16Lc 35
Avenue Ho. NW6 38Ab 68
(off The Avenue)
NW8 2D 214
NW10 40Xa 68
(off All Souls Av.)
Avenue Ind. Est. E4 23Cc 52
RM3: Hrld W 26Md 57
Avenue Lodge NW8 38Fb 69
(off Avenue Rd.)
RM17: Grays 50Ee 99
Avenue Mans. NW3 36Db 69
(off Finchley Rd.)
Avenue M. N10 27Kb 50
Avenue One KT15: Add 77N 149
Avenue Pde. N21 17Tb 33
TW16: Sun 69X 129
Avenue Pk. Rd. SE27 61Rb 135
Avenue Ri. WD23: Bush 15Ca 27
Avenue Rd. AL1: St A 1C 6
BR3: Beck 68Zb 136
CM14: W'ley 21Yd 58
CM16: They B 9Tc 22
CR3: Cat'm 94Tb 197
DA7: Bex 55Ad 117
DA8: Erith 52Ed 118
DA17: Belv, Erith 49Ed 96
E7 35Kc 73
HA5: Pinn 27Aa 45
IG8: Wfd G 23Lc 53
KT1: King T 69Na 131
KT3: N Mald 70Ua 132
KT11: Cobh 88Z 171
KT18: Eps 86Ta 173
N6 31Lb 70
N12 21Eb 49
N14 17Lb 32
N15 29Tb 51
NW3 38Fb 69
NW8 1D 214 (38Fb 69)
NW10 40Va 68
RM3: Hrld W 24Pd 57
RM6: Chad H 31Xc 75
SE20 67Yb 136
SE25 68Vb 135
SM2: Sutt 82Cb 175
SM6: Wall 80Lb 156
SM7: Bans 87Db 175
SW16 68Mb 134
SW20 68Xa 132
TN13: S'oaks 96Ld 203
TN16: Tats 92Nc 200
TW7: Isle 53Ha 108
TW8: Bford 50La 86
TW11: Tedd 66Ja 130
TW12: Hamp 67Da 129
TW13: Felt 62V 128
TW18: Staines 64F 126
UB1: S'hall 46Ba 85
W3 47Ra 87
Avenue Sth. KT5: Surb 73Qa 153
Avenue Studios SW3 6C 226
Avenue Ter. KT3: N Mald 69Sa 131
WD19: Wat 16Aa 27
Avenue Three KT15: Add 76N 149
Avenue Two KT15: Add 77N 149
Avenue Vs. RH1: Mers 1C 208
Averil Ct. SL6: Tap 4A 80
Averil Gro. SW16 65Rb 135
Averill St. W6 51Za 110
Avern Gdns. KT8: W Mole 70Da 129
Avern Rd. KT8: W Mole 70Da 129
Avershaw Ho. SW15 57Za 110
Avery Cl. BR3: Beck 65Bc 136
Avery Farm Row SW1 6K 227 (49Jb 90)
Avery Gdns. IG2: Ilf 29Pc 54
AVERY HILL 58Tc 116
Avery Hill Rd. SE9 58Tc 116
Avery Row W1 4K 221 (45Kb 90)
Avery Way DA1: Dart 61Pd 141
Avey La. EN9: Lough, Walt A 8Fc 21
IG10: H Beech, Lough 10Hc 21
Avia Cl. HP3: Hem H 6M 3
Avian Av. AL2: F'mre 10C 6
Aviary Cl. E16 43Hc 93
Aviary Rd. GU22: Pyr 88J 169
Aviation Dr. NW9 26Wa 48
Aviator Pk. KT15: Add 77M 149
Aviemore Cl. BR3: Beck 71Bc 158
Aviemore Way BR3: Beck 71Ac 158
Avigdor M. N16 33Tb 71
Avignon Rd. SE4 55Zb 114
Avingdor Ct. W3 46Sa 87
(off Horn La.)
Avington Ct. SE1 6J 231
Avington Gro. SE20 66Yb 136
Avion Cres. NW9 25Wa 48
Avior Dr. HA6: Nwood 21V 44
Avis Sq. E1 44Zb 92
Avoca Rd. SW17 63Jb 134
Avocet Cl. SE1 50Wb 91
Avocet M. SE28 48Tc 94
Avocet Rd. HP3: Hem H 7L 3
Avon Cl. DA12: Grav'nd 1F 144
KT4: Wor Pk 75Wa 154
KT15: Add 79J 149
SL1: Slou 5C 80
SM1: Sutt 77Eb 155
UB4: Yead 42Y 85
WD25: Wat 6Y 13
Avon Ct. E4 18Ec 34
HA5: Hat E 24Ca 45
(off The Avenue)
IG9: Buck H 18Kc 35
N12 22Db 49
SW15 57Ab 110
UB6: G'frd 42Da 85
W9 43Cb 89
(off Elmfield Way)
Avondale Av. EN4: E Barn 18Hb 31
KT4: Wor Pk 74Va 154
KT10: Hin W 76Ja 152
N12 22Db 49
NW2 34Ua 68
TW18: Staines 66H 127
Avondale Cl. IG10: Lough 17Pc 36
KT12: Hers 78Y 151
Avondale Ct. AL1: St A 2C 6
E11 32Gc 73
E16 43Gc 93
E18 25Kc 53
SM2: Sutt 80Eb 155
(off Brighton Rd.)
Avondale Cres. EN3: Enf H 13Ac 34
IG4: Ilf 29Mc 53
Avondale Dr. IG10: Lough 17Pc 36
UB3: Hayes 46W 84
Avondale Gdns. TW4: Houn 57Ba 107
Avondale High CR3: Cat'm 93Xb 197
Avondale Ho. SE1 50Wb 91
(off Avondale Sq.)
Avondale Mans. SW6 53Bb 111
(off Rostrevor Rd.)
Avondale Pk. Gdns. W11 45Ab 88
Avondale Pk. Rd. W11 45Ab 88
Avondale Pavement SE1 50Wb 91
Avondale Ri. SE15 55Vb 113
Avondale Rd. BR1: Brom 65Gc 137
CR2: S Croy 79Sb 157
DA16: Well 54Yc 117
E16 43Gc 93
E17 31Cc 72
HA3: W'stone 27Ha 46
N3 25Eb 49
N13 19Qb 32
N15 29Rb 51
SE9 61Nc 138
SW14 55Ua 110
SW19 64Db 133
TW15: Ashf 62M 127
Avondale Sq. SE1 50Wb 91
Avonfield Ct. E17 27Fc 53
Avon Grn. RM15: S Ock 44Xd 98
Avongrove Ct. EC1 3E 218
Avon Ho. KT2: King T 67Ma 131
RM14: Upm 31Ud 78
W8 48Cb 89
(off Allen St.)
W14 49Bb 89
(off Kensington Village)
Avonhurst Ho. NW2 38Ab 68
Avonley Rd. SE14 52Yb 114
Avonmead GU21: Wok 10N 167
Avon M. HA5: Hat E 24Ba 45
Avonmore Gdns. W14 49Bb 89
Avonmore Mans. W14 49Ab 88
(off Avonmore Rd.)
Avonmore Pl. W14 49Ab 88
Avonmore Rd. W14 49Ab 88
Avonmor M. GU23: Rip 94K 189
Avonmouth Apartments SW11 56Gb 111
(off Monarch Sq.)
Avonmouth Rd. DA1: Dart 57Md 119
Avonmouth St. SE1 3D 230 (48Sb 91)
Avon Path CR2: S Croy 79Sb 157
Avon Pl. SE1 2E 230 (47Sb 91)
Avon Rd. E17 27Fc 53
RM14: Upm 30Td 58
SE4 55Cc 114
TW16: Sun 66V 128
UB6: G'frd 42Ca 85
Avonstowe Cl. BR6: Farnb 76Sc 160
Avontar Ct. RM15: S Ock 42Xd 98
Avontar Rd. RM15: S Ock 42Xd 98
Avon Ter. IG10: Lough 16Pc 36
Avon Way E18 27Jc 53
Avonwick Rd. TW3: Houn 54Da 107
Avril Way E4 22Ec 52
Avro Ct. E9 36Ac 72
(off Mabley St.)
Avro Ho. NW9 26Va 48
(off Boulevard Dr.)
SW8 52Kb 112
(off Havelock Ter.)
Avro Pl. TW5: Hest 52Y 107
Avro Way KT13: Weyb 82N 169
SM6: Wall 80Nb 156
Awberry Ct. WD18: Wat 16T 26
Awlfield Av. N17 25Tb 51
Awliscombe Rd. DA16: Well 54Vc 117
Axe St. IG11: Bark 39Sc 74
(not continuous)
Axholme Av. HA8: Edg 25Qa 47
Axiom Apartments
BR2: Brom 70Kc 137
(off Masons Hill)
RM1: Rom 28Hd 56
(off Mercury Gdns.)
Axio Way E3 43Cc 92
Axis Apartments E1 5K 219
(off Sclater St.)
Axis Ct. SE10 51Gc 115
(off Woodland Cres.)
SE16 47Wb 91
(off East La.)
Axis Ho. SE13 56Ec 114
(off Lewisham High St.)
Axis Pk. SL3: L'ly 50D 82
Axminster Cres. DA16: Well 53Yc 117
Axminster Rd. N7 34Nb 70
Axon Pl. IG1: Ilf 33Sc 74
Axtaine Rd. BR5: St M Cry 73Zc 161
Axtane DA13: Sflt 66Be 143
Axtane Cl. DA4: S Dar 68Sd 142
Axwood KT18: Eps 87Sa 173
Aybrook St. W1 1H 221 (43Jb 90)
Aycliffe Cl. BR1: Brom 70Pc 138
Aycliffe Ho. SE17 51Tb 113
(off Portland St.)
Aycliffe Rd. W12 46Wa 88
WD6: Bore 11Na 29
Ayebridges Av.
TW20: Egh 66E 126
Ayelands DA3: Nw A G 75Ae 165
Ayelands La. DA3: Nw A G 76Ae 165
Ayerst Ct. E10 31Ec 72
Aylands Cl. HA9: Wemb 33Na 67
Aylands Rd. EN3: Enf W 8Yb 20
Aylesbury Cl. E7 37Hc 73
Aylesbury Ct. SM1: Sutt 76Eb 155
Aylesbury Cres. SL1: Slou 4H 81
Aylesbury Ho. HA0: Wemb 39Na 67
(off Hatton Rd.)
SE15 51Wb 113
(off Friary Est.)
Aylesbury Rd. BR2: Brom 69Jc 137
SE17 7G 231 (50Tb 91)
Aylesbury St. EC1 6B 218 (42Rb 91)
NW10 34Ta 67
Aylesford Av. BR3: Beck 71Ac 158
Aylesford Ho. SE1 2G 231
Aylesford St. SW1 7D 228 (50Mb 90)
Aylesham Cen. SE15 53Wb 113
Aylesham Cl. NW7 24Wa 48
Aylesham Rd. BR6: Orp 73Vc 161
Ayles Rd. UB4: Yead 41X 85
Aylestone Av. NW6 38Za 68
Aylesworth Av. SL2: Slou 1E 80
Aylesworth Spur SL4: Old Win 9M 103
Aylett Rd. RM14: Upm 33Sd 78
SE25 70Xb 135
TW7: Isle 54Ga 108
Ayley Cft. EN1: Enf 15Wb 33
Ayliffe Cl. KT1: King T 68Qa 131
Aylmer Cl. HA7: Stan 21Ja 46
Aylmer Ct. N2 29Hb 49
Aylmer Dr. HA7: Stan 21Ja 46
Aylmer Ho. SE10 50Fc 93
Aylmer Pde. N2 29Hb 49
Aylmer Rd. E11 32Hc 73
N2 29Gb 49
RM8: Dag 34Ad 75
W12 47Va 88
Ayloffe Rd. RM9: Dag 37Bd 75
Ayloffs Cl. RM11: Horn 28Md 57
Ayloffs Wlk. RM11: Horn 29Md 57
Aylsham Dr. UB10: Ick 33S 64
Aylsham La. RM3: Rom 21Ld 57
Aylton Est. SE16 47Yb 92
Aylward Rd. SE23 61Zb 136
SW20 68Bb 133
Aylwards Ri. HA7: Stan 21Ja 46
Aylward St. E1 44Yb 92
(Jamaica St.)
E1 44Yb 92
(Jubilee St.)
Aylwin Est. SE1 3J 231 (48Ub 91)
Aymer Cl. TW18: Staines 67G 126
Aymer Dr. TW18: Staines 67G 126
Aynhoe Mans. W14 49Za 88
(off Aynhoe Rd.)
Aynhoe Rd. W14 49Za 88
Aynho St. WD18: Wat 15X 27
Aynscombe Angle BR6: Orp 73Wc 161
Aynscombe Path SW14 54Sa 109
Ayot Path WD6: Bore 9Qa 15
Ayr Ct. W3 43Qa 87
Ayres Cl. E13 41Jc 93
Ayres St. SE1 1E 230 (47Sb 91)
Ayr Grn. RM1: Rom 25Gd 56
Ayron Rd. RM15: S Ock 42Xd 98
Ayrsome Rd. N16 34Ub 71
Ayrton Gould Ho. E2 41Zb 92
(off Roman Rd.)
Ayrton Rd. SW7 3B 226 (48Fb 89)
Ayr Way RM1: Rom 25Gd 56
Aysgarth Ct. SM1: Sutt 76Db 155
Aysgarth Pl. SL0: Iver H 39F 62
Aysgarth Rd. SE21 59Ub 113
Ayston Ho. SE16 49Zb 92
(off Plough Way)
Aytoun Pl. SW9 54Pb 112
Aytoun Rd. SW9 54Pb 112
Azalea Cl. AL2: Lon C 9F 6
IG1: Ilf 36Rc 74
W7 46Ha 86
Azalea Ct. GU22: Wok 1P 187
IG8: Wfd G 23Gc 53
W7 46Ha 86
Azalea Dr. BR8: Swan 70Fd 140
Azalea Ho. SE14 52Bc 114
(off Achilles St.)
TW13: Felt 60X 107
Azalea Wlk. HA5: Eastc 29X 45
Azalea Way SL3: Geor G 44A 82
Azania M. NW5 37Kb 70
Azenby Rd. SE15 54Vb 113
Azof St. SE10 49Gc 93
Azov Ho. E1 42Ac 92
(off Commodore St.)
Aztec Ho. IG1: Ilf 33Tc 74
IG6: Ilf 25Sc 54
Azura Ct. E15 39Ec 72
(off Warton Rd.)
Azure Bldg. E15 38Fc 73
(off Gt. Eastern Rd.)
Azure Cl. RM3: Rom 21Md 57
Azure Ct. NW9 29Qa 47
Azure Ho. E2 41Wb 91
(off Buckfast St.)
Azure Pl. TW3: Houn 56Da 107

B

Baalbec Rd. N5 36Rb 71
Babbacombe Cl. KT9: Chess 78Ma 153
Babbacombe Gdns. IG4: Ilf 28Nc 54
Babbacombe Ho. BR1: Brom 67Jc 137
(off Babbacombe Rd.)
Babbacombe Rd. BR1: Brom 67Jc 137
Babbage Ct. SE17 51Rb 113
(off Cook's Rd.)

Babell Ho. N1 . . . 37Rb 71
(off Canonbury Rd.)
Baber Bri. Cvn. Site TW14: Felt . . . 57Y 107
Baber Bri. Pde. TW14: Felt . . . 58Y 107
Baber Dr. TW14: Felt . . . 58Y 107
Babington Ct. WC1 . . . 7H 217
Babington Ho. SE1 . . . 1E 230
Babington Ri. HA9: Wemb . . . 37Qa 67
Babington Rd. NW4 . . . 28Xa 48
RM8: Dag . . . 36Yc 75
RM12: Horn . . . 32Kd 77
SW16 . . . 64Mb 134
Babmaes St. SW1 . . . 5D 222 (45Mb 90)
Babylon La. KT20: Lwr K . . . 99Cb 195
Bacchus Wlk. N1 . . . 2H 219
Bachelors Acre SL4: Wind . . . 3H 103
Bachelors La. GU23: Ock . . . 96P 189
Bache's St. N1 . . . 3G 219 (41Tb 91)
Back All. EC3 . . . 3J 225
Bk. Church La. E1 . . . 44Wb 91
Back Grn. KT12: Hers . . . 79Y 151
Back Hill EC1 . . . 6A 218 (42Qb 90)
Backhouse Pl. SE17 . . . 6J 231 (49Ub 91)
Back La. DA5: Bexl . . . 59Cd 118
HA8: Edg . . . 25Sa 47
IG9: Buck H . . . 19Mc 35
N8 . . . 29Nb 50
NW3 . . . 35Eb 69
NW9 . . . 26Ta 47
RH2: Reig . . . 1M 207
RM6: Chad H . . . 31Zc 75
RM16: N Stif . . . 47Yd 98
RM19: Purf . . . 48Ud 98
RM20: W Thur . . . 48Xd 98
TN13: Bes G . . . 100Dd 202
TN14: Ide H . . . 100Dd 202
TN15: God G . . . 96Qd 203
TN15: Igh . . . 96Yd 204
TW8: Bford . . . 51Ma 109
TW10: Ham . . . 62La 130
WD3: Chen . . . 10D 10
WD25: Let H . . . 11Ga 28
Backley Gdns. SE25 . . . 72Wb 157
Back of High St. GU24: Chob . . . 3J 167
Back Pas. EC1 . . . 7C 218
Back Path RH1: Blet . . . 5J 209
Back Rd. DA14: Sidc . . . 63Wc 139
E17 . . . 28Ec 52
TW11: Tedd . . . 66Ga 130
Bacon Gro. SE1 . . . 4K 231 (48Vb 91)
Bacon La. HA8: Edg . . . 25Qa 47
NW9 . . . 28Ra 47
(not continuous)
Bacon Link RM5: Col R . . . 23Dd 56
Bacon's College Sports Cen. . . . 46Ac 92
Bacons Dr. EN6: Cuff . . . 1Nb 18
Bacons La. N6 . . . 32Jb 70
Baconsmead UB9: Den . . . 33J 63
Bacon St. E1 . . . 5K 219 (42Vb 91)
E2 . . . 5K 219 (42Vb 91)
Bacon Ter. RM8: Dag . . . 36Xc 75
Bacton NW5 . . . 36Jb 70
Bacton St. E2 . . . 41Yb 92
Badburgham Ct. EN9: Walt A . . . 5Hc 21
Baddeley Cl. EN3: Enf L . . . 9Cc 20
Baddeley Ho. KT8: W Mole . . . 71Ca 151
(off Down St.)
Baddesley Ho. SE11 . . . 7J 229
Baddow Cl. IG8: Wfd G . . . 23Lc 53
RM10: Dag . . . 39Cd 76
Baddow Wlk. N1 . . . 39Sb 71
(off New North Rd.)
Baden Cl. TW18: Staines . . . 66K 127
Baden Dr. E4 . . . 14Dc 34
Baden Pl. SE1 . . . 1F 231 (47Tb 91)
Baden Powell Cl. KT6: Surb . . . 75Pa 153
RM9: Dag . . . 39Ad 75
Baden Powell Ho. DA17: Belv . . . 48Cd 96
(off Ambrooke Rd.)
SW7 . . . 4A 226
Baden Powell Rd. TN13: Riv . . . 93Gd 202
Baden Rd. IG1: Ilf . . . 36Rc 74
N8 . . . 28Mb 50
Bader Cl. CR8: Kenley . . . 87Tb 177
Bader Ct. NW9 . . . 26Va 48
(off Runway Cl.)
Bader Gdns. SL1: Slou . . . 7E 80
Bader Wlk. DA11: Nflt . . . 2B 144
Bader Way RM13: Rain . . . 37Jd 76
SW15 . . . 58Wa 110
UB10: Uxb . . . 38N 63
Badgemore Path SE18 . . . 50Tc 94
(off Tuscan Rd.)
Badger Cl. IG2: Ilf . . . 30Sc 54
TW4: Houn . . . 55Y 107
TW13: Felt . . . 62X 129
Badger Ct. NW2 . . . 34Ya 68
Badgersbridge Ride SL4: Wink . . . 9A 102
Badgers Cl. EN2: Enf . . . 13Rb 33
GU21: Wok . . . 10N 167
HA1: Harr . . . 30Fa 46
TW15: Ashf . . . 64P 127
UB3: Hayes . . . 45U 84
WD6: Bore . . . 12Pa 29
Badgers Copse BR6: Orp . . . 75Vc 161
KT4: Wor Pk . . . 75Va 154
Badger's Ct. KT17: Eps . . . 85Ua 174
Badgers Ct. WD25: Wat . . . 6V 12
Badgers Cft. HP2: Hem H . . . 3D 4
N20 . . . 17Ab 30
SE9 . . . 62Qc 138
Badgers Dell WD3: Chor . . . 14D 24
Badgers Hill GU25: Vir W . . . 1N 147
Badgers Hole CR0: C'don . . . 77Zb 158
Badgers La. CR6: W'ham . . . 92Yb 198
Badgers Lodge KT17: Eps . . . 85Ua 174
BADGERS MOUNT . . . 82Dd 182
Badgers Mt. RM16: Ors . . . 7B 100
Badger's Ri. TN14: Bad M . . . 82Cd 182
Badgers Rd.
TN14: Bad M, S'ham . . . 82Dd 182
Badgers Wlk. CR3: Whyt . . . 90Vb 177
CR8: Purl . . . 83Lb 176
KT3: N Mald . . . 68Ua 132
WD3: Chor . . . 14H 25
Badgers Wood CR3: Cat'm . . . 97Tb 197
SL2: Farn C . . . 6G 60
Badger Wlk. GU3: Norm . . . 10A 186
Badger Way AL10: Hat . . . 2D 8
Badingham Dr. KT22: Fet . . . 95Ga 192
Badlis Rd. E17 . . . 27Cc 52
Badlow Cl. DA8: Erith . . . 52Gd 118
Badma Cl. N9 . . . 20Yb 34
Badminton Cl. HA1: Harr . . . 28Ga 46
UB5: N'olt . . . 37Ca 65
WD6: Bore . . . 12Qa 29
Badminton Ho. WD24: Wat . . . 12Y 27
(off Anglian Cl.)
Badminton M. E16 . . . 46Jc 93
Badminton Rd. SW12 . . . 58Jb 112
Badric Ct. SW11 . . . 54Fb 111
Badsworth Rd. SE5 . . . 53Sb 113
Baffin Rd. DA12: Grav'nd . . . 3E 144
Baffin Way E14 . . . 46Ec 92
Bafton Ga. BR2: Hayes . . . 74Kc 159
Bagenal Ho. WD5: Ab L . . . 4V 12
Bagley Cl. UB7: W Dray . . . 47N 83
Bagley's La. SW6 . . . 53Db 111
Bagleys Spring RM6: Chad H . . . 28Ad 55
Bagnigge Ho. WC1 . . . 4K 217
(off Ruthin Cl.)
Bagot Cl. KT21: Asht . . . 88Pa 173
Bagshot Ct. SE18 . . . 53Qc 116
Bagshot Ho. NW1 . . . 3A 216
Bagshot Rd. EN1: Enf . . . 17Vb 33
GU3: Worp . . . 10F 166
GU21: Knap . . . 10F 166
GU22: Wok . . . 10F 166
GU24: Brkwd, Wok . . . 10F 166
GU24: Chob, W End . . . 4C 166
SL5: Asc, S'hill . . . 4A 146
TW20: Eng G . . . 6N 125
Bagshot St. SE17 . . . 7J 231 (50Ub 91)
Bahram Ct. E2 . . . 42Xb 91
(off Three Colts La.)
Bahram Rd. KT19: Eps . . . 82Ta 173
Baigents La. GU20: W'sham . . . 9B 146
Baildon E2 . . . 40Yb 72
(off Cyprus St.)
Baildon St. SE8 . . . 52Bc 114
Bailes Pl. BR3: Beck . . . 67Ac 136
Bailey Cl. E4 . . . 21Ec 52
N11 . . . 24Mb 50
RM19: Purf . . . 49Td 98
SE28 . . . 46Uc 94
SL4: Wind . . . 4E 102
Bailey Cotts. E14 . . . 43Ac 92
(off Maroon St.)
Bailey Ct. NW9 . . . 27Ua 48
(off Lingard Av.)
Bailey Cres. KT9: Chess . . . 80Ma 153
Bailey Ho. E3 . . . 41Dc 92
(off Talwin St.)
SW10 . . . 52Db 111
(off Coleridge Gdns.)
Bailey M. SW2 . . . 57Qb 112
W4 . . . 51Ra 109
Bailey Pl. N16 . . . 36Ub 71
SE26 . . . 65Zb 136
Baileys M. HP1: Hem H . . . 1M 3
(off High St.)
Bailey Twr. E1 . . . 45Xb 91
Baillie Cl. RM13: Rain . . . 42Kd 97
Baillie M. KT16: Ott . . . 79F 148
Baillies Wlk. W5 . . . 47Ma 87
Bainbridge Cl. TW10: Ham . . . 64Na 131
Bainbridge Rd. RM9: Dag . . . 35Bd 75
Bainbridge St. WC1 . . . 2E 222 (44Mb 90)
Baines Cl. CR2: S Croy . . . 78Tb 157
Bainton Mead GU21: Wok . . . 9L 167
Baird Av. UB1: S'hall . . . 45Da 85
Baird Cl. E10 . . . 32Cc 72
NW9 . . . 30Sa 47
SL1: Slou . . . 7F 80
WD23: Bush . . . 16Da 27
Baird Gdns. SE19 . . . 63Ub 135
Baird Ho. W12 . . . 45Xa 88
(off White City Est.)
Baird Memorial Cotts. N14 . . . 19Mb 32
(off Balaams La.)
Baird Rd. EN1: Enf . . . 13Xb 33
Baird St. EC1 . . . 5E 218 (42Sb 91)
Bairny Wood App. IG8: Wfd G . . . 23Kc 53
Bairstow Cl. WD6: Bore . . . 11Na 29
Baizdon Rd. SE3 . . . 54Gc 115
Bakeham La. TW20: Eng G . . . 6P 125
Bakehouse M. TW12: Hamp . . . 66Ca 129
Baker Beal Ct. DA7: Bex . . . 55Dd 118
Baker Boy La. CR0: Sels . . . 85Ac 178
Baker Ct. WD6: Bore . . . 12Ra 29
Baker Cres. DA1: Dart . . . 59Ld 119
Baker Hill Cl. DA11: Nflt . . . 3B 144
Baker Ho. E3 . . . 41Dc 92
(off Bromley High St.)
W7 . . . 46Ha 86
WC1 . . . 6G 217
Baker La. CR4: Mitc . . . 68Jb 134
Baker Pas. NW10 . . . 39Ua 68
Baker Pl. KT19: Ewe . . . 79Sa 153
Baker Rd. NW10 . . . 39Ua 68
SE18 . . . 52Nc 116
Bakers Av. E17 . . . 30Dc 52
TN15: W King . . . 80Ud 164
Bakers Cl. AL1: St A . . . 3E 6
CR8: Kenley . . . 86Sb 177
Bakers Ct. CM14: B'wood . . . 20Yd 40
RH1: Redh . . . 7P 207
SE25 . . . 69Ub 135
UB8: Uxb . . . 38M 63
Bakers End SW20 . . . 68Ab 132
Baker's Fld. N7 . . . 35Mb 70
Bakersfield Cl. KT19: Ewe . . . 81Ta 173
Bakers Gdns. SM5: Cars . . . 75Gb 155
Bakersgate Courtyard GU24: Pirb . . . 8E 186
Bakersgate Gdns. GU24: Pirb . . . 7E 186
Bakers Hall Ct. EC3 . . . 5J 225
Bakers Hill E5 . . . 32Yb 72
EN5: New Bar . . . 12Db 31
Bakers Ho. W5 . . . 46Ma 87
(off The Grove)
Bakers La. CM16: Epp . . . 2Vc 23
N6 . . . 30Hb 49
Bakers Mead RH9: G'stone . . . 2A 210
Baker's M. W1 . . . 2H 221 (44Jb 90)
Bakers M. BR6: Chels . . . 79Vc 161
Bakers Pas. NW3 . . . 35Eb 69
(off Heath St.)
Baker's Rents E2 . . . 3K 219 (41Vb 91)
Bakers Rd. EN7: Chesh . . . 2Xb 19
UB8: Uxb . . . 38M 63
Baker's Row E15 . . . 40Gc 73
EC1 . . . 6K 217 (42Qb 90)
BAKER STREET . . . 4A 100
BAKER STREET . . . 7G 215 (43Hb 89)
Baker St. EN1: Enf . . . 13Tb 33
EN6: Pot B . . . 7Ab 16
KT13: Weyb . . . 77Q 150
NW1 . . . 6G 215 (42Hb 89)
RM16: Ors . . . 4A 100
W1 . . . 6G 215 (42Hb 89)
Bakers Vs., The CM16: Epp . . . 2Vc 23
BAKER'S WOOD . . . 32F 62
Bakers Wood UB9: Den . . . 33F 62
Bakers Yd. EC1 . . . 6K 217
Bakers Yd. UB8: Uxb . . . 38M 63
Bakery Cl. SW9 . . . 52Pb 112
Bakery M. KT6: Surb . . . 74Qa 153
Bakery Path HA8: Edg . . . 22Ra 47
(off St Margaret's Rd.)
Bakery Pl. SW11 . . . 56Hb 111
Bakewell Way KT3: N Mald . . . 68Ua 132
Balaam Ho. SM1: Sutt . . . 77Cb 155
Balaam Leisure Cen. . . . 42Jc 93
Balaams La. N14 . . . 19Mb 32
Balaam St. E13 . . . 42Jc 93
Balaclava Rd. KT6: Surb . . . 73La 152
SE1 . . . 6K 231 (49Vb 91)
Bala Grn. NW9 . . . 30Ua 48
(off Ruthin Cl.)
Balcaskie Rd. SE9 . . . 57Pc 116
Balchen Rd. SE3 . . . 54Mc 115
Balchier Rd. SE22 . . . 58Xb 113
Balcombe Cl. DA6: Bex . . . 56Zc 117
Balcombe Ho. NW1 . . . 5E 214
Balcombe St. NW1 . . . 5F 215 (42Hb 89)
Balcon Ct. W5 . . . 44Pa 87
Balcon Way WD6: Bore . . . 11Sa 29
Balcony, The W12 . . . 46Za 88
Balcorne St. E9 . . . 38Yb 72
Balder Ri. SE12 . . . 61Kc 137
Balderton Flats W1 . . . 3J 221
Balderton St. W1 . . . 3J 221 (44Jb 90)
Baldewyne Ct. N17 . . . 25Wb 51
Baldocks Rd. CM16: They B . . . 7Uc 22
Baldock St. E3 . . . 40Dc 72
Baldock Way WD6: Bore . . . 11Pa 29
Baldrey Ho. SE10 . . . 50Hc 93
(off Blackwall La.)
Baldry Gdns. SW16 . . . 65Nb 134
Baldwin Cres. SE5 . . . 53Sb 113
Baldwin Gdns. TW3: Houn . . . 53Ea 108
Baldwin Ho. SW2 . . . 60Qb 112
Baldwin Rd. SL1: Burn . . . 1A 80
SW11 . . . 58Jb 112
WD17: Wat . . . 10W 12
Baldwin's Bec SL4: Eton . . . 1H 103
(off Baldwin's Shore)
Baldwins Gdns. EC1 . . . 7K 217 (43Qb 90)
Baldwins Hill IG10: Lough . . . 12Pc 36
Baldwin's La. WD3: Crox G . . . 14Q 26
Baldwin's Shore SL4: Eton . . . 1H 103
Baldwin St. EC1 . . . 4F 219 (41Tb 91)
Baldwin Ter. N1 . . . 1D 218 (40Sb 71)
Baldwyn Gdns. W3 . . . 45Ta 87
Baldwyn's Pk. DA5: Bexl . . . 61Fd 140
Baldwyn's Rd. DA5: Bexl . . . 61Fd 140
Balearic Apartments E16 . . . 45Jc 93
(off Western Gateway)
Bale Rd. E1 . . . 43Ac 92
Bales Ter. N9 . . . 20Vb 33
Balfern Gro. W4 . . . 50Ua 88
Balfern St. SW11 . . . 54Gb 111
Balfe St. N1 . . . 1G 217 (40Nb 70)
Balfont Cl. CR2: Sande . . . 85Wb 177
Balfour Av. GU22: Wok . . . 94A 188
W7 . . . 46Ha 86
Balfour Bus. Cen. UB2: S'hall . . . 48Y 85
Balfour Ct. RM17: Grays . . . 49Fe 99
Balfour Gro. N20 . . . 20Hb 31
Balfour Ho. KT13: Weyb . . . 77Q 150
(off Balfour Rd.)
SW11 . . . 53Jb 112
(off Forfar Rd.)
W10 . . . 43Za 88
(off St Charles Sq.)
Balfour M. HP3: Bov . . . 9C 2
N9 . . . 20Wb 33
W1 . . . 6J 221 (46Jb 90)
Balfour Pl. SW15 . . . 56Xa 110
W1 . . . 5J 221 (45Jb 90)
Balfour Rd. BR2: Brom . . . 71Mc 159
HA1: Harr . . . 29Fa 46
IG1: Ilf . . . 33Rc 74
KT13: Weyb . . . 77Q 150
N5 . . . 35Sb 71
RM17: Grays . . . 49Ee 99
SE25 . . . 71Wb 157
SM5: Cars . . . 80Hb 155
SW19 . . . 66Db 133
TW3: Houn . . . 55Da 107
UB2: S'hall . . . 48Z 85
W3 . . . 43Sa 87
W13 . . . 47Ja 86
Balfour St. SE17 . . . 5F 231 (49Tb 91)
Balfour Ter. N3 . . . 26Db 49
Balfron Twr. E14 . . . 44Ec 92
Balgonie Rd. E4 . . . 18Fc 35
Balgores Cres. RM2: Rom . . . 27Kd 57
Balgores La. RM2: Rom . . . 27Kd 57
Balgores Sq. RM2: Rom . . . 28Kd 57
Balgove Ct. NW10 . . . 37Xa 68
(off Eden Gro.)
Balgowan Cl. KT3: N Mald . . . 71Ua 154
Balgowan Rd. BR3: Beck . . . 69Ac 136
Balgowan St. SE18 . . . 49Vc 95
BALHAM . . . 60Jb 112
Balham Continental Mkt.
SW12 . . . 60Kb 112
(off Shipka Rd.)
Balham Gro. SW12 . . . 59Jb 112
Balham High Rd. SW12 . . . 62Jb 134
SW17 . . . 62Jb 134
Balham Hill SW12 . . . 59Kb 112
Balham Leisure Cen. . . . 61Kb 134
Balham New Rd. SW12 . . . 59Kb 112
Balham Pk. Rd. SW12 . . . 60Hb 111
Balham Rd. N9 . . . 19Wb 33
Balham Sta. Rd. SW12 . . . 60Kb 112
Balin Ho. SE1 . . . 1F 231
Balkan Wlk. E1 . . . 45Xb 91
Balladier Wlk. E14 . . . 43Dc 92
Ballamore Rd. BR1: Brom . . . 62Jc 137
Ballance Rd. E9 . . . 37Zb 72
Ballands Nth., The KT22: Fet . . . 94Ga 192
Ballands Sth., The KT22: Fet . . . 95Ga 192
Ballantine St. SW18 . . . 56Eb 111
Ballantrae Ho. NW2 . . . 35Bb 69
Ballantyne Cl. SE9 . . . 63Nc 138
Ballantyne Dr. KT20: Kgswd . . . 93Bb 195
Ballard Cl. KT2: King T . . . 66Ta 131
Ballard Grn. SL4: Wind . . . 2C 102
Ballard Ho. SE10 . . . 51Dc 114
(off Thames St.)
Ballards Cl. RM10: Dag . . . 39Dd 76
Ballards Farm Rd.
CR0: C'don . . . 79Xb 157
CR2: S Croy . . . 79Wb 157
Ballards Grn. KT20: Tad . . . 91Ab 194
Ballards La. N3 . . . 25Cb 49
N12 . . . 25Cb 49
RH8: Limp . . . 1N 211
Ballards M. HA8: Edg . . . 23Qa 47
Ballards Ri. CR2: Sels . . . 79Wb 157
Ballards Rd. NW2 . . . 33Wa 68
RM10: Dag . . . 40Dd 76
Ballards Way CR0: C'don . . . 79Wb 157
CR2: Sels . . . 79Wb 157
Ballast Quay SE10 . . . 50Fc 93
Ballater Cl. WD19: Wat . . . 21Y 45
Ballater Rd. CR2: S Croy . . . 78Vb 157
SW2 . . . 56Nb 112
Ball Ct. EC3 . . . 3G 225
Ballencrieff Rd. SL5: S'dale . . . 3D 146
Balletica Apartments WC2 . . . 3G 223
Ball Ho. NW9 . . . 27Va 48
(off Aerodrome Rd.)
Ballina St. SE23 . . . 59Zb 114
Ballin Ct. E14 . . . 47Ec 92
(off Stewart St.)
Ballingdon Rd. SW11 . . . 58Jb 112
Ballinger Ct. WD18: Wat . . . 13X 27
Ballinger Point E3 . . . 41Dc 92
(off Bromley High St.)
Ballinger Way UB5: N'olt . . . 42Aa 85
Balliol Av. E4 . . . 21Gc 53
Balliol Rd. DA16: Well . . . 54Xc 117
N17 . . . 25Ub 51
W10 . . . 44Ya 88
Balloch Rd. SE6 . . . 60Fc 115
Ballogie Av. NW10 . . . 35Ua 68
Balloon Cnr. AL9: Wel G . . . 5D 8
Ballow Cl. SE5 . . . 52Ub 113
Balls Pond Pl. N1 . . . 37Tb 71
Balls Pond Rd. N1 . . . 37Tb 71
Balmain Cl. W5 . . . 46Ma 87
Balmain Ct. TW3: Houn . . . 53Da 107
Balmain Lodge KT5: Surb . . . 70Na 131
(off Cranes Pk. Av.)
Balman Ho. SE16 . . . 49Zb 92
(off Rotherhithe New Rd.)
Balmer Rd. E3 . . . 40Bc 72
Balmes Rd. N1 . . . 39Tb 71
Balmoral Apartments W2 . . . 1D 220
Balmoral Av. BR3: Beck . . . 70Ac 136
N11 . . . 23Jb 50
Balmoral Cl. AL2: Park . . . 10A 6
SL1: Slou . . . 4C 80
SW15 . . . 58Za 110
Balmoral Ct. BR3: Beck . . . 67Ec 136
(off The Avenue)
HA9: Wemb . . . 34Pa 67
KT4: Wor Pk . . . 75Xa 154
NW8 . . . 1B 214
SE12 . . . 63Kc 137
SE16 . . . 46Zb 92
(off King & Queen Wharf)
SE17 . . . 50Tb 91
(off Merrow St.)
SE27 . . . 63Sb 135
SM2: Sutt . . . 80Cb 155
Balmoral Cres. KT8: W Mole . . . 69Ca 129
Balmoral Dr. GU22: Wok . . . 88E 168
UB1: S'hall . . . 42Ba 85
UB4: Hayes . . . 42U 84
WD6: Bore . . . 15Ta 29
Balmoral Gdns. CR2: Sande . . . 82Tb 177
DA5: Bexl . . . 59Bd 117
IG3: Ilf . . . 32Vc 75
SL4: Wind . . . 5H 103
W13 . . . 48Ja 86
Balmoral Gro. N7 . . . 37Pb 70
Balmoral Ho. E14 . . . 48Dc 92
(off Lanark Sq.)
E16 . . . 46Kc 93
(off Keats Av.)
W14 . . . 49Ab 88
(off Windsor Way)
Balmoral M. W12 . . . 48Va 88
Balmoral Rd. CM15: Pil H . . . 16Xd 40
DA4: Sut H . . . 66Rd 141
E7 . . . 35Lc 73
E10 . . . 33Dc 72
EN3: Enf W . . . 8Zb 20
HA2: Harr . . . 35Ca 65
KT1: King T . . . 70Pa 131
KT4: Wor Pk . . . 76Xa 154
NW2 . . . 37Xa 68
RM2: Rom . . . 29Kd 57
RM12: Horn . . . 34Md 77
WD5: Ab L . . . 4W 12
WD24: Wat . . . 10Y 13
Balmoral Trad. Est. IG11: Bark . . . 43Vc 95
Balmoral Way SM2: Sutt . . . 82Cb 175
Balmore Cl. E14 . . . 44Ec 92
Balmore Cres. EN4: Cockf . . . 15Jb 32
Balmore St. N19 . . . 33Kb 70
Balmuir Gdns. SW15 . . . 56Ya 110
Balnacraig Av. NW10 . . . 35Ua 68
Balniel Ga. SW1 . . . 7E 228 (50Mb 90)
Balquhain Cl. KT21: Asht . . . 89Ma 173
Balsam Ho. E14 . . . 45Dc 92
(off E. India Dock Rd.)
BALSTONIA . . . 1N 101
Baltic Apartments E16 . . . 45Jc 93
(off Western Gateway)
Baltic Av. TW8: Bford . . . 50Ma 87
Baltic Cl. SW19 . . . 66Fb 133
Baltic Ct. E1 . . . 46Yb 92
(off Clave St.)
SE16 . . . 47Zb 92
Baltic Ho. SE5 . . . 54Sb 113
Baltic Pl. N1 . . . 39Ub 71
Baltic St. E. EC1 . . . 6D 218 (42Sb 91)
Baltic St. W. EC1 . . . 6D 218 (42Sb 91)
Baltic Wharf DA11: Grav'nd . . . 7C 122
Baltimore Cl. DA17: Belv . . . 47Dd 96
Baltimore Ct. SW1 . . . 6D 228
Baltimore Ho. SE11 . . . 6K 229
SW18 . . . 55Eb 111
Baltimore Pl. DA16: Well . . . 54Vc 117
Baltimore Twr. E14 . . . 47Dc 92
Baltimore Wharf E14 . . . 48Dc 92
Balvaird Pl. SW1 . . . 7E 228 (50Mb 90)
Balvernie Gro. SW18 . . . 59Bb 111
Balvernie M. SW18 . . . 59Cb 111
Bamber Ho. IG11: Bark . . . 39Sc 74
Bamber Rd. SE15 . . . 53Vb 113
Bamborough Gdns. W12 . . . 47Ya 88
Bamburgh N17 . . . 24Xb 51
Bamford Av. HA0: Wemb . . . 39Pa 67
Bamford Rd. BR1: Brom . . . 64Ec 136
IG11: Bark . . . 37Sc 74
Bamford Way RM5: Col R . . . 22Dd 56
Bampfylde Cl.
SM6: Wall . . . 76Lb 156
Bampton Ct. W5 . . . 44Ma 87
Bampton Dr. NW7 . . . 24Wa 48
Bampton Rd. RM3: Rom . . . 22Pd 58
SE23 . . . 62Zb 136
Bampton Way GU21: Wok . . . 10L 167
Banavie Gdns. BR3: Beck . . . 67Ec 136
Banbury Av. SL1: Slou . . . 3D 80
Banbury Cl. EN2: Enf . . . 11Rb 33
Banbury Ct. SM2: Sutt . . . 80Cb 155
WC2 . . . 4F 223
Banbury Ho. E9 . . . 38Zb 72
Banbury Rd. E9 . . . 38Zb 72
E17 . . . 24Zb 52
Banbury St. SW11 . . . 54Gb 111
WD18: Wat . . . 15W 26
Banbury Vs. DA13: Sflt . . . 65Be 143
Banbury Wlk. UB5: N'olt . . . 40Ca 65
(off Brabazon Rd.)
Banchory Rd. SE3 . . . 52Kc 115
Bankside DA3: Hartl . . . 70Ae 143
Bancroft Av. IG9: Buck H . . . 19Jc 35
N2 . . . 29Gb 49
Bancroft Chase RM12: Horn . . . 33Hd 76
Bancroft Cl. TW15: Ashf . . . 64Q 128
Bancroft Ct. RH2: Reig . . . 6K 207
SW8 . . . 52Nb 112
(off Allen Edwards Dr.)
UB5: N'olt . . . 39Y 65
Bancroft Gdns. BR6: Orp . . . 74Vc 161
HA3: Hrw W . . . 25Ea 46
Bancroft Ho. E1 . . . 42Yb 92
(off Cephas St.)
Bancroft Rd. E1 . . . 41Yb 92
HA3: Hrw W . . . 26Ea 46
RH2: Reig . . . 6J 207
TN15: Wro . . . 88Be 185
Band La. TW20: Egh . . . 64B 126
Bandon Cl. UB10: Uxb . . . 40P 63
BANDONHILL . . . 78Mb 156
Bandon Ri. SM6: Wall . . . 78Mb 156
Banfield Rd. SE15 . . . 55Xb 113
Banfor Ct. SM6: Wall . . . 78Lb 156
Bangalore St. SW15 . . . 55Ya 110
Bangays Way TN15: Bor G . . . 93Ae 205
Bangla Ho. E8 . . . 39Vb 71
(off Clarissa St.)
Bangor Cl. UB5: N'olt . . . 36Da 65
Bangors Cl. SL0: Iver . . . 44G 82
Bangors Pk. SL0: Iver H . . . 42G 82
Bangors Rd. Nth. SL0: Iver H . . . 39F 62
Bangors Rd. Sth. SL0: Iver, Iver H . . . 41G 82
Banim St. W6 . . . 49Xa 88
Banister Ho. E9 . . . 36Zb 72
SW8 . . . 53Lb 112
(off Wadhurst Rd.)
W10 . . . 41Ab 88
(off Bruckner St.)
Banister M. NW6 . . . 38Db 69
Banister Rd. W10 . . . 41Za 88
Bank, The N6 . . . 32Kb 70
Bank Av. CR4: Mitc . . . 68Fb 133
Bank Bldgs. E4 . . . 23Fc 53
(off The Avenue)
Bank Ct. DA1: Dart . . . 58Nd 119
E17 . . . 28Ec 52
HP1: Hem H . . . 3L 3
Bank End SE1 . . . 6E 224 (46Sb 91)
Bankfoot RM17: Grays . . . 50Be 99
Bankfoot Rd. BR1: Brom . . . 63Gc 137
Bank Ho. KT15: Add . . . 77K 149
Bankhurst Rd. SE6 . . . 59Bc 114
Bank La. KT2: King T . . . 66Na 131
SW15 . . . 57Ua 110
Bank M. SM1: Sutt . . . 79Eb 155
Bank Mill HP4: Berk . . . 1A 2
Bank Mill La. HP4: Berk . . . 2A 2
Bank of England . . . 3F 225 (44Tb 91)
Bank of England Mus. . . . 3G 225
Bank of England Sports Cen. . . . 57Ua 110
Bank Pl. CM14: B'wood . . . 19Yd 40
Banks Ho. SE1 . . . 4D 230
Banksian Wlk. TW7: Isle . . . 53Ga 108
Banksia Rd. N18 . . . 22Zb 52
Bankside CR2: S Croy . . . 79Vb 157
DA11: Nflt . . . 58Ee 121
EN2: Enf . . . 11Rb 33
GU21: Wok . . . 10M 167
(not continuous)
KT17: Eps D . . . 88Ya 174
SE1 . . . 5D 224 (45Sb 91)
(not continuous)
TN13: Dun G . . . 93Fd 202
UB1: S'hall . . . 46Z 85
Bankside Av. SE13 . . . 55Ec 114
UB5: N'olt . . . 40W 64
Bankside Cl. DA5: Bexl . . . 63Fd 140
SM5: Cars . . . 79Gb 155
TN16: Big H . . . 90Lc 179
TW7: Isle . . . 56Ha 108
UB9: Hare . . . 23J 43
Bankside Down WD3: Rick . . . 16L 25
Bankside Dr. KT7: T Ditt . . . 74Ka 152
Bankside Gallery . . . 5C 224 (45Rb 91)
Bankside Lofts SE1 . . . 6C 224
Bankside Mix SE1 . . . 6D 224 (46Sb 91)
Bankside Pk. IG11: Bark . . . 41Wc 95
Bankside Pl. N4 . . . 30Sb 51
Bankside Rd. IG1: Ilf . . . 36Sc 74
Bankside Way SE19 . . . 65Ub 135
Bank's La. KT24: Eff J . . . 95W 190
Banks La. CM16: Fidd H, They M . . . 5Ad 23
DA6: Bex . . . 56Bd 117
Bank Spur SL1: Slou . . . 7F 80
Banks Rd. WD6: Bore . . . 12Sa 29
Bank St. DA12: Grav'nd . . . 8D 122
E14 . . . 46Dc 92
TN13: S'oaks . . . 97Ld 203
Banks Way E12 . . . 35Qc 74
Banks Yd. TW5: Hest . . . 51Ba 107
Bankton Rd. SW2 . . . 56Qb 112
Bankwell Rd. SE13 . . . 56Gc 115
Bannatyne Health Club
Chafford Hundred . . . 48Yd 98
Chingford . . . 23Cc 52
Grove Park . . . 61Kc 137
Maida Vale . . . 40Db 69
(off Greville Rd.)
Russell Square . . . 5E 216
Bann Cl. RM15: S Ock . . . 45Xd 98
Banner Cl. RM19: Purf . . . 49Td 98
Banner Ct. SE16 . . . 49Yb 92
(off Rotherhithe New Rd.)
Banner Ho. EC1 . . . 6E 218
Banner La. RM8: Dag . . . 32Ad 75
Bannerman Ho. SW8 . . . 51Pb 112
Banner St. EC1 . . . 6E 218 (42Sb 91)
Banning St. SE10 . . . 50Gc 93
Bannister Cl. SL3: L'ly . . . 47A 82
SW2 . . . 60Qb 112
UB6: G'frd . . . 36Fa 66
Bannister Dr. CM13: Hut . . . 16Ee 41
Bannister Gdns. BR5: St P . . . 69Yc 139
Bannister Ho. HA3: W'stone . . . 27Ga 46
(off Headstone Dr.)
SE14 . . . 51Zb 114
(off John Williams Cl.)

Bannister Sports Cen.—Barr Rd.

Bannister Sports Cen. 23Ea 46
Bannockburn Rd. SE18 . . . . 49Uc 94
Bannon Ct. SW6 . . . . 53Db 111
(off Michael Rd.)
Bannow Cl. KT19: Ewe 77Ua 154
Banqueting House 7F 223 (46Nb 90)
BANSTEAD 87Db 175
Banstead Ct. W12 . . . . 45Va 88
Banstead Downs Golf Course 83Cb 175
Banstead Gdns. N9 . . . . 20Ub 33
Banstead Rd. CR3: Cat'm 93Tb 197
CR8: Purl 83Qb 176
KT17: Ewe 82Xa 174
SM5: Cars 81Fb 175
SM7: Bans 82Xa 174
Banstead Rd. Sth. SM2: Sutt 83Eb 175
Banstead St. SE15 . . . . 55Yb 114
Banstead Way SM6: Wall 78Nb 156
Banstead Wood SM7: Bans 90Eb 175
Banstock Rd. HA8: Edg 23Ra 47
Bantam Ho. NW9 . . . . 26Va 48
(off Heritage Av.)
Banting Dr. N21 . . . . 15Pb 32
Banting Ho. NW2 . . . . 34Wa 68
Bantock Ho. W10 . . . . 41Ab 88
(off Third Av.)
Banton Cl. EN1: Enf 12Xb 33
Bantry Ho. E1 . . . . 42Zb 92
(off Ernest St.)
Bantry Rd. SL1: Slou 7D 80
Bantry St. SE5 . . . . 52Tb 113
Banwell Rd. DA5: Bexl 58Zc 117
Banyard Rd. SE16 . . . . 48Xb 91
Banyards RM11: Horn 28Nd 57
Baptist Gdns. NW5 . . . . 37Jb 70
Baquba SE13 . . . . 54Dc 114
Barandon Rd. W11 . . . . 45Za 88
(off Grenfell Rd.)
Barandon Wlk. W11 . . . . 45Za 88
Barataria Pk. GU23: Rip 93H 189
Barbanel Ho. E1 . . . . 42Yb 92
(off Cephas St.)
Barbara Brosnan Ct.
NW8 . . . . 2B 214 (40Fb 69)
Barbara Castle Cl. SW6 . . . . 51Bb 111
Barbara Cl. TW17: Shep 71R 150
Barbara Hucklesby Cl. N22 . . . . 26Rb 51
Barbauld Rd. N16 . . . . 34Ub 71
Barbel Cl. EN8: Walt C 6Cc 20
Barber Beaumont Ho. E1 . . . . 41Zb 92
(off Bancroft Rd.)
Barber Cl. N21 . . . . 17Qb 32
Barberry Cl. RM3: Rom 24Ld 57
Barberry Ct. E15 . . . . 37Gc 73
Barberry Rd. HP1: Hem H 2J 3
Barbers All. E13 . . . . 41Kc 93
Barbers Rd. E15 . . . . 40Dc 72
Barbican EC2 . . . . 43Sb 91
(off Silk St.)
Barbican Arts Cen. 7E 218 (43Sb 91)
Barbican Cinema
Beech St. 7E 218
Whitecross St. 7E 218
Barbican Rd. UB6: G'frd 44Da 85
Barbican Theatre
Silk St. 7E 218
Barb M. W6 . . . . 48Ya 88
Barbon All. EC2 . . . . 2J 225
Barbon Cl. WC1 . . . . 7G 217 (43Pb 90)
Barbot Cl. N9 . . . . 20Wb 33
Barchard St. SW18 . . . . 57Db 111
Barchester Cl. UB8: Cowl 42L 83
W7 . . . . 46Ha 86
Barchester Rd. HA3: Hrw W 26Fa 46
SL3: L'ly 47B 82
Barchester St. E14 . . . . 43Dc 92
Barcino Ho. AL1: St A 3D 6
Barclay Cl. KT22: Fet 95Da 191
SW6 . . . . 52Cb 111
WD18: Wat 16W 26
Barclay Fld. TN15: Kems'g 89Nd 183
Barclay Ho. E9 . . . . 38Yb 72
(off Well St.)
Barclay Oval IG8: Wfd G 21Jc 53
Barclay Path E17 . . . . 29Ec 52
Barclay Rd. CR0: C'don 76Tb 157
E11 . . . . 32Hc 73
E13 . . . . 42Lc 93
E17 . . . . 29Ec 52
N18 . . . . 23Tb 51
SW6 . . . . 52Cb 111
Barclay Way RM20: W Thur 50Vd 98
Barcombe Av. SW2 . . . . 61Nb 134
Barcombe Cl. BR5: St P 69Vc 139
Bardell Ho. SE1 . . . . 47Wb 91
(off Parkers Row)
Barden Cl. UB9: Hare 24L 43
Barden St. SE18 . . . . 52Uc 116
Bardeswell Cl. CM14: B'wood 19Yd 40
Bardfield Av. RM6: Chad H 27Zc 55
Bardney Rd. SM4: Mord 70Db 133
Bardolph Av. CR0: Sels 81Ac 178
Bardolph Rd. N7 . . . . 35Nb 70
TW9: Rich 55Pa 109
Bardon Wlk. GU21: Wok 9M 167
Bard Rd. W10 . . . . 45Za 88
Bards Cnr. HP1: Hem H 1K 3
Bards Ct. RM3: Rom 24Kd 57
Bardsey Pl. E1 . . . . 42Yb 92
Bardsey Wlk. N1 . . . . 37Sb 71
(off Douglas Rd. Nth.)
Bardsley Cl. CR0: C'don 76Vb 157
Bardsley Ho. SE10 . . . . 51Ec 114
(off Bardsley La.)
Bardsley La. SE10 . . . . 51Ec 114
Bardwell Ct. AL1: St A 3B 6
(off Bardwell Rd.)
Bardwell Rd. AL1: St A 3B 6
Barents Ho. E1 . . . . 42Zb 92
(off White Horse La.)
Barfett St. W10 . . . . 42Bb 89
Barfield DA4: Sut H 67Rd 141
Barfield Av. N20 . . . . 19Hb 31
Barfield Ct. RH1: Redh 4A 208
Barfield Rd. BR1: Brom 69Qc 138
E11 . . . . 32Hc 73
Barfields IG10: Lough 14Qc 36
RH1: Blet 5H 209
Barfields Gdns. IG10: Lough 14Qc 36
Barfields Path IG10: Lough 14Qc 36
Barfleur La. SE8 . . . . 49Bc 92
Barfolds AL9: Wel G 5E 8
Barford Cl. NW4 . . . . 26Wa 48
Barford Ho. E3 . . . . 40Bc 72
(off Tredegar Rd.)
Barford St. N1 . . . . 1A 218 (39Qb 70)
Barforth Rd. SE15 . . . . 55Xb 113
Barfreston Way SE20 . . . . 67Xb 135
Bargate Cl. KT3: N Mald 73Wa 154
SE18 . . . . 50Vc 95
Barge Cl. DA9: Ghithe 56Yd 120
Barge Dr. UB2: S'hall 48Da 85
Barge Ho. HP3: Hem H 6P 3
Barge Ho. Rd. E16 . . . . 47Rc 94
Barge Ho. St. SE1 . . . . 6A 224 (46Qb 90)
Barge La. E3 . . . . 39Ac 72
Bargery Rd. SE6 . . . . 60Dc 114
Barge Wlk. KT1: Hamp W 69Ma 131
KT1: King T 67Ma 131
KT8: E Mos 72Ja 152
(Boyle Farm Island)
KT8: E Mos 69Fa 130
(Hampton Ct. Cres.)
SE10 . . . . 48Hc 93
Bargrove Av. HP1: Hem H 3J 3
Bargrove Cl. SE20 . . . . 66Wb 135
Bargrove Cres. SE6 . . . . 61Bc 136
Barham Av. WD6: E'tree 13Pa 29
Barham Cl. BR2: Brom 74Nc 160
BR7: Chst 64Rc 138
DA12: Grav'nd 10H 123
HA0: Wemb 37Ka 66
KT13: Weyb 77S 150
RM7: Mawney 26Dd 56
Barham Ct. CR2: S Croy 77Sb 157
(off Barham Rd.)
Barham Ho. SE17 . . . . 7J 231
Barham Rd. BR7: Chst 64Rc 138
CR2: S Croy 77Sb 157
DA1: Dart 59Qd 119
SW20 . . . . 66Wa 132
Baring Cl. SE12 . . . . 61Jc 137
Baring Ct. N1 . . . . 39Tb 71
(off Baring St.)
Baring Ho. E14 . . . . 44Cc 92
(off Canton St.)
Baring Rd. CR0: C'don 74Wb 157
EN4: Cockf 14Fb 31
SE12 . . . . 59Jc 115
Baring St. N1 . . . . 39Tb 71
Baritone Ct. E15 . . . . 39Hc 73
(off Church St.)
Bark Burr Rd. RM16: Chaf H 47Be 99
Barker Cl. HA6: Nwood 24V 44
KT3: N Mald 70Ra 131
KT16: Chert 73G 148
TW9: Kew 54Ra 109
Barker Dr. NW1 . . . . 38Lb 70
Barker Flds. DA13: Sflt 65Ce 143
Barker Ho. SE17 . . . . 6H 231
Barker M. SW4 . . . . 56Kb 112
Barker Rd. KT16: Chert 73G 148
Barkers Arc. W8 . . . . 47Db 89
Barker St. SW10 . . . . 51Eb 111
Barker Wlk. SW16 . . . . 62Mb 134
Barkham Rd. N17 . . . . 24Tb 51
Barkham Ter. SE1 . . . . 3A 230
Bark Hart Rd. BR6: Orp 74Xc 161
BARKING 38Sc 74
Barking Abbey 39Sc 74
Barking Abbey School Leisure Cen.
. . . . 37Wc 75
Barking Bus. Cen. IG11: Bark 41Wc 95
Barking Ind. Pk. IG11: Bark 39Vc 75
Barking Northern Relief Rd.
IG11: Bark 38Rc 74
BARKING RIVERSIDE 41Xc 95
Barking Rd. E6 . . . . 43Hc 93
E13 . . . . 43Hc 93
E16 . . . . 43Gc 93
BARKINGSIDE 27Sc 54
Barking Splash Pk. 36Tc 74
Barkis Ho. W11 . . . . 46Za 88
Bark Pl. W2 . . . . 45Db 89
Barkston Gdns. SW5 . . . . 49Db 89
Barkston Path WD6: Bore 10Qa 15
Barkway Ct. N4 . . . . 33Sb 71
Barkway Dr. BR6: Farnb 77Qc 160
Barkwith Ho. SE14 . . . . 51Zb 114
(off Cold Blow La.)
Barkwood Cl. RM7: Rom 29Ed 56
Barkworth Rd. SE16 . . . . 50Xb 91
Barlborough St. SE14 . . . . 52Zb 114
Barlby Gdns. W10 . . . . 42Za 88
Barlby Rd. W10 . . . . 43Ya 88
Barlee Cres. UB8: Cowl 43L 83
Barle Gdns. RM15: S Ock 44Xd 98
Barley Brow WD25: Wat 3X 13
Barley Cl. HA0: Wemb 35Ma 67
WD23: Bush 15Da 27
Barleycorn Way E14 . . . . 45Bc 92
(not continuous)
RM11: Horn 30Pd 57
Barley Ct. E5 . . . . 33Yb 72
RM13: Rain 40Fd 76
(off Lwr Mardyke Av.)
Barley Cft. HP2: Hem H 2C 4
Barleyfields Cl. RM6: Chad H 30Xc 55
Barley La. IG3: Ilf 31Wc 75
RM6: Chad H 31Wc 75
Barley Mow Cvn. Site AL4: St A 4K 7
Barley Mow Cl. GU21: Knap 9H 167
Barley Mow La. AL4: St A 5J 7
GU21: Knap 8G 166
Barley Mow Pas. EC1 . . . . 1C 224
W4 . . . . 50Ta 87
Barley Mow Rd. TW20: Eng G 4N 125
Barley Mow Way TW17: Shep 70Q 128
Barley Shotts Bus. Pk. W10 . . . . 43Bb 89
Barling NW1 . . . . 37Kb 70
(off Castlehaven Rd.)
Barlow Cl. SM6: Wall 79Nb 156
Barlow Dr. SE18 . . . . 53Nc 116
Barlow Ho. N1 . . . . 3F 219
SE16 . . . . 49Xb 91
(off Rennie Est.)
W11 . . . . 45Ab 88
(off Walmer Rd.)
Barlow Pl. W1 . . . . 5A 222 (45Kb 90)
Barlow Rd. NW6 . . . . 37Bb 69
TW12: Hamp 66Ca 129
W3 . . . . 46Ra 87
Barlow St. SE17 . . . . 6G 231 (49Tb 91)
Barlow Way RM13: Rain 43Fd 96
Barmeston Rd. SE6 . . . . 61Dc 136
Barmor Cl. HA2: Harr 26Da 45
Barmouth Av. UB6: G'frd 40Ha 66
Barmouth Rd. CR0: C'don 75Zb 158
SW18 . . . . 58Eb 111
Barn, The RM17: Grays 49De 99
Barnabas Ct. EN2: Enf 14Qb 32
Barnabas Ho. EC1 . . . . 4D 218
Barnabas Lodge SW8 . . . . 53Nb 112
(off Guildford Rd.)
Barnabas Rd. E9 . . . . 36Zb 72
Barnaby Cl. HA2: Harr 33Ea 66
Barnaby Ct. NW9 . . . . 27Ua 48
SE16 . . . . 47Wb 91
(off Scott Lidgett Cres.)
Barnaby Ho. SE15 . . . . 51Yb 114
Barnaby Pl. SW7 . . . . 6B 226
Barnaby Way IG7: Chig 20Rc 36
Barnacre Cl. UB8: Cowl 44M 83
Barnacres Rd. HP3: Hem H 7P 3
Barnard Cl. BR7: Chst 67Tc 138
SE18 . . . . 48Qc 94
SM6: Wall 80Mb 156
TW16: Sun 66X 129
Barnard Ct. DA2: Dart 58Rd 119
(off Osbourne Rd.)
GU21: Wok 10J 167
Barnard Gdns. KT3: N Mald 70Wa 132
UB4: Yead 42X 85
Barnard Gro. E15 . . . . 38Hc 73
Barnard Hill N10 . . . . 25Kb 50
Barnard Ho. E2 . . . . 41Xb 91
(off Ellsworth St.)
Barnard Lodge EN5: New Bar 14Eb 31
W9 . . . . 43Cb 89
(off Admiral Wlk.)
Barnard M. SW11 . . . . 56Gb 111
Barnardo Dr. IG6: Ilf 28Sc 54
Barnardo Gdns. E1 . . . . 45Zb 92
Barnardo St. E1 . . . . 44Zb 92
Barnardos Village IG6: Ilf 27Sc 54
Barnardo Village Wlk. IG6: Ilf 27Sc 54
Barnard Rd. CR4: Mitc 69Jb 134
CR6: W'ham 91Dc 198
EN1: Enf 12Xb 33
SW11 . . . . 56Gb 111
Barnards Ho. SE16 . . . . 47Bc 92
(off Wyatt Cl.)
Barnard's Inn EC1 . . . . 2A 224
Barnards Pl. CR2: S Croy 81Rb 177
Barnard Way HP3: Hem H 3N 3
Barnato Cl. KT14: Byfl 84N 169
Barnbrough NW1 . . . . 39Lb 70
(off Camden St.)
Barnby Cl. KT21: Asht 89La 172
Barnby Rd. GU21: Knap 9H 167
Barnby Sq. E15 . . . . 39Gc 73
Barnby St. E15 . . . . 39Gc 73
NW1 . . . . 2C 216 (40Lb 70)
Barn Cl. HP3: Hem H 5P 3
KT18: Eps 87Sa 173
NW5 . . . . 36Mb 70
(off Torriano Av.)
SL2: Farn C 5F 60
SM7: Bans 87Fb 175
TW15: Ashf 64R 128
UB5: N'olt 40Y 65
WD7: R'lett 7Ja 14
Barn Cres. CR8: Purl 85Tb 177
HA7: Stan 23La 46
Barncroft Cl. IG10: Lough 15Qc 36
UB8: Hil 43R 84
Barncroft Grn. IG10: Lough 15Qc 36
Barncroft Rd. IG10: Lough 15Qc 36
Barncroft Way AL1: St A 3E 6
Barndale Ct. DA12: Shorne 4N 145
Barneby Cl. TW2: Twick 60Ga 108
BARNEHURST 55Ed 118
Barnehurst Av. DA7: Bex 53Ed 118
DA8: Erith 53Ed 118
Barnehurst Cl. DA8: Erith 53Ed 118
Barnehurst Golf Course 55Fd 118
Barnehurst Rd. DA7: Bex 54Ed 118
Barn Elms Athletics Track 54Xa 110
Barn Elms Cl. KT4: Wor Pk 76Va 154
Barn Elms Pk. SW15 . . . . 55Ya 110
Barn End Dr. DA2: Wilm 64Ld 141
Barn End La. DA2: Wilm 65Ld 141
BARNES 54Va 110
Barnes All. TW12: Hamp 68Ea 130
Barnes Av. SW13 . . . . 52Wa 110
UB2: S'hall 49Ba 85
Barnes Bri. W4 . . . . 54Ua 110
Barnes Cl. E12 . . . . 35Mc 73
HA8: Edg 21Pa 47
Barnes Common Nature Reserve
. . . . 55Wa 110
Barnes Ct. CR7: Thor H 69Sb 135
E16 . . . . 43Lc 93
EN5: New Bar 14Db 31
IG8: Buck H, Wfd G 22Mc 53
N1 . . . . 38Qb 70
BARNES CRAY 56Jd 118
Barnes Cray Rd. DA1: Cray 56Jd 118
Barnesdale Cres.
BR5: St M Cry 72Wc 161
Barnes End KT3: N Mald 71Wa 154
Barnes High St. SW13 . . . . 54Va 110
Barnes Ho. E2 . . . . 40Yb 72
(off Wadeson St.)
IG11: Bark 39Tc 74
SE14 . . . . 51Zb 114
(off John Williams Cl.)
Barnes La. WD4: K Lan 9K 3
Barnes Pikle W5 . . . . 45Ma 87
Barnes Ri. WD4: K Lan 9P 3
Barnes Rd. IG1: Ilf 36Sc 74
N18 . . . . 21Yb 52
Barnes St. E14 . . . . 44Ac 92
Barnes Ter. SE8 . . . . 50Bc 92
Barnes Wallis Cl. KT24: Eff 99Z 191
Barnes Wallis Ct. HA9: Wemb 34Sa 67
Barnes Wallis Dr. KT13: Weyb 83N 169
Barnes Way EN9: Walt A 4Jc 21
SL0: Iver 45H 83
BARNET 13Ab 30
Barnet Burnt Oak Leisure Cen. 25Ta 47
Barnet Bus. Cen. EN5: Barn 13Ab 30
Barnet By-Pass NW4 . . . . 26Ya 48
NW7 . . . . 23Va 48
Barnet By-Pass Rd.
EN5: Ark, Barn 13Ua 30
WD6: Bore 16Ta 29
Barnet Copthall Sports Cen. 25Xa 48
Barnet Dr. BR2: Brom 75Nc 160
Barnet FC 25Na 47
BARNET GATE 16Va 30
Barnet Ga. La. EN5: Ark 16Va 30
Barnet Gro. E2 . . . . 41Wb 91
Barnet Hill EN5: Barn 14Bb 31
Barnet Ho. N20 . . . . 19Eb 31
Barnet La. EN5: Barn 18Bb 31
N20 . . . . 18Bb 31
WD6: Bore, E'tree 16Ma 29
(not continuous)
Barnet Mus. 14Ab 30
Barnet Rd. AL2: Lon C 9J 7
EN5: Ark 16Ta 29
EN5: Barn, Pot B 8Cb 17
EN6: Pot B 5Db 17
Barnett Cl. DA8: Erith 54Hd 118
KT22: Lea 91Ka 192
Barnett Row GU4: Jac W 10P 187
Barnetts Ct. HA2: Harr 34Da 65
Barnett's Shaw RH8: Oxt 99Fc 199
Barnett St. E1 . . . . 44Xb 91
Barnetts Way RH8: Oxt 99Fc 199
Barnett Wood La.
KT21: Asht 90La 172
KT22: Lea 92Ka 192
BARNET VALE 15Db 31
Barnet Way NW7 . . . . 20Ta 29
Barnet Wood Rd. BR2: Brom 75Lc 159
Barney Cl. SE7 . . . . 50Lc 93
Barn Fld. NW3 . . . . 36Hb 69
Barnfield CM16: Epp 1Wc 23
DA11: Grav'nd 1C 144
HP3: Hem H 5P 3
KT3: N Mald 72Ua 154
SL0: Iver 44G 82
SL1: Slou 6B 80
SM7: Bans 86Db 175
Barnfield Av. CR0: C'don 75Yb 158
CR4: Mitc 70Kb 134
KT2: King T 63Ma 131
Barnfield Cl. BR8: Crock 73Ed 162
CR5: Coul 91Sb 197
DA3: Lfield 69Fe 143
DA9: Ghithe 58Vd 120
N4 . . . . 31Nb 70
SW17 . . . . 62Fb 133
Barnfield Cres.
TN15: Kems'g 89Nd 183
Barnfield Gdns. KT2: King T 63Na 131
SE18 . . . . 51Rc 116
Barnfield Pk. TN15: Ash 78Zd 165
Barnfield Pl. E14 . . . . 49Cc 92
Barnfield Rd. BR5: St P 69Zc 139
CR2: Sande 81Ub 177
DA17: Belv 51Bd 117
HA8: Edg 25Sa 47
SE18 . . . . 51Rc 116
(not continuous)
TN13: Riv 95Gd 202
TN16: Tats 92Mc 199
W5 . . . . 42La 86
Barnfield Wlk. RM2: Rom 28Ld 57
Barnfield Way RH8: Oxt 5L 211
Barnfield Wood Cl. BR3: Beck 72Fc 159
Barnfield Wood Rd. BR3: Beck 72Fc 159
Barnham Dr. SE28 . . . . 46Vc 95
(not continuous)
Barnham Rd. UB6: G'frd 41Ea 86
Barnham St. SE1 . . . . 1J 231 (47Ub 91)
Barn Hill HA9: Wemb 32Qa 67
Barnhill HA5: Eastc 29Y 45
Barnhill Av. BR2: Brom 71Hc 159
Barnhill La. UB4: Yead 41X 85
Barnhill Rd. HA9: Wemb 34Sa 67
UB4: Yead 41X 85
Barnhurst Path WD19: Wat 22Y 45
Barningham Way NW9 . . . . 30Ta 47
Barn Lea WD3: Rick 18J 25
Barnlea Cl. TW13: Hanw 61Aa 129
Barn Mead CM16: They B 8Uc 22
Barnmead GU24: Chob 2K 167
Barnmead Ct. RM9: Dag 36Bd 76
Barnmead Gdns. RM9: Dag 36Bd 75
Barnmead Mdw. RM16: Grays 8B 100
Barn Mdw. La. KT23: Bookh 96Ba 191
Barnmead Rd. BR3: Beck 67Zb 136
RM9: Dag 36Bd 75
Barn M. HA2: Harr 34Ca 65
Barnock Cl. DA1: Cray 59Gd 118
Barn Ri. HA9: Wemb 32Qa 67
BARNSBURY 38Pb 70
Barnsbury Cl. KT3: N Mald 70Sa 131
Barnsbury Cres. KT5: Surb 74Sa 153
Barnsbury Est. N1 . . . . 1J 217 (39Pb 70)
(not continuous)
Barnsbury Farm Est. GU22: Wok 2P 187
Barnsbury Gro. N7 . . . . 38Pb 70
Barnsbury Ho. SW4 . . . . 58Mb 112
Barnsbury La. KT5: Surb 75Ra 153
Barnsbury Pk. N1 . . . . 38Qb 70
Barnsbury Rd. N1 . . . . 1K 217 (40Qb 70)
Barnsbury Sq. N1 . . . . 38Qb 70
Barnsbury St. N1 . . . . 38Qb 70
Barnsbury Ter. N1 . . . . 38Pb 70
Barnscroft SW20 . . . . 69Xa 132
Barnsdale Av. E14 . . . . 49Dc 92
Barnsdale Cl. WD6: Bore 11Pa 29
Barnsdale Rd. W9 . . . . 42Bb 89
Barnsfield Pl. UB8: Uxb 39L 63
Barnsford Cres. GU24: W End 5E 166
Barnsley Rd. RM3: Rom 24Pd 57
Barnsley St. E1 . . . . 42Xb 91
Barnstable La. SE13 . . . . 56Ec 114
Barnstaple Ho. SE10 . . . . 52Dc 114
(off Devonshire Dr.)
SE12 . . . . 57Hc 115
(off Taunton Rd.)
Barnstaple Path RM3: Rom 22Ld 57
Barnstaple Rd. HA4: Ruis 34Y 65
RM3: Rom 22Ld 57
Barnston Wlk. N1 . . . . 39Sb 71
(off Popham St.)
Barnston Way CM13: Hut 15Ee 41
Barn St. N16 . . . . 33Ub 71
Barnsway WD4: K Lan 10N 3
Barn Theatre, The
Oxted 100Gc 199
Sidcup 60Wc 117
West Molesey 70Ca 129
Barn Way HA9: Wemb 32Qa 67
Barnway TW20: Eng G 4N 125
Barnwell Cl. HA8: Edg 21Pa 47
Barnwell Ho. SE5 . . . . 53Ub 113
(off St Giles Rd.)
Barnwell Rd. DA1: Dart 55Pd 119
SW2 . . . . 57Qb 112
Barnwood Cl. HA4: Ruis 33T 64
N20 . . . . 18Bb 31
W9 . . . . 42Db 89
Barnyard, The KT20: Walt H 96Wa 194
Baron Cl. N1 . . . . 1K 217 (40Qb 70)
N11 . . . . 22Jb 50
SM2: Sutt 82Db 175
Baroness Rd. E2 . . . . 3K 219 (41Vb 91)
Baronet Gro. N17 . . . . 25Wb 51
Baronet Rd. N17 . . . . 25Wb 51
Baron Gdns. IG6: Ilf 27Sc 54
Baron Gro. CR4: Mitc 70Gb 133
Baron Ho. SW19 . . . . 67Fb 133
Baron Rd. RM8: Dag 32Zc 75
Barons, The TW1: Twick 58Ka 108
Baronsclere Ct. N6 . . . . 31Lb 70
BARONS COURT 50Ab 88
Barons Ct. IG1: Ilf 33Tc 74
NW9 . . . . 30Ta 47
SM6: Bedd 76Mb 156
Baron's Ct. Rd. W14 . . . . 50Ab 88
Barons Court Theatre 50Ab 88
(off Comeragh Rd.)
Baronsfield Rd. TW1: Twick 58Ka 108
Barons Ga. EN4: E Barn 16Gb 31
W4 . . . . 48Sa 87
Baron's Hurst KT18: Eps 88Sa 173
Barons Keep W14 . . . . 50Ab 88
Barons Lodge E14 . . . . 49Fc 93
(off Manchester Rd.)
Barons Mead HA1: Harr 28Ga 46
Baronsmead Rd. SW13 . . . . 53Wa 110
Baronsmede W5 . . . . 47Pa 87
Baronsmere Ct. EN5: Barn 14Ab 30
Baronsmere Rd. N2 . . . . 28Gb 49
Baron's Pl. SE1 . . . . 2A 230 (47Qb 90)
Baron St. N1 . . . . 1K 217 (40Qb 70)
Baron's Wlk. CR0: C'don 72Ac 158
Baron's Way RH2: Reig 10J 207
Barons Way TW20: Egh 65F 126
Barons Wood TW20: Eng G 4P 125
Baron Wlk. CR4: Mitc 70Gb 133
E16 . . . . 43Hc 93
Baroque Ct. TW3: Houn 55Da 107
Baroque Gdns. SE8 . . . . 49Ac 92
(off Grand Canal Av.)
Barque M. SE8 . . . . 51Cc 114
Barquentine Hgts. SE10 . . . . 48Jc 93
Barrack La. SL4: Wind 3H 103
Barrack Path GU21: Wok 10J 167
(not continuous)
Barrack Rd. TW4: Houn 56Z 107
Barrack Row DA11: Grav'nd 8D 122
Barracks La. EN5: Barn 13Ab 30
Barra Cl. HP3: Hem H 5C 4
Barracouta Ho. SE18 . . . . 51Vc 117
Barra Hall Cir. UB3: Hayes 45U 84
Barra Hall Rd. UB3: Hayes 45U 84
Barra Ho. WD18: Wat 16V 26
(off Scammell Way)
Barrass Cl. EN3: Enf L 9Cc 20
Barratt Av. N22 . . . . 26Pb 50
Barratt Ho. N1 . . . . 38Rb 71
(off Sable St.)
Barratt Ind. Est. UB1: S'hall 47Ca 85
Barratt Ind. Pk. E3 . . . . 42Ec 92
Barratt Way HA3: W'stone 26Fa 46
Barra Wood Cl. UB3: Hayes 44U 84
Barrenger Rd. N10 . . . . 25Hb 49
Barrens Brae GU22: Wok 90C 168
Barrens Cl. GU22: Wok 91C 188
Barrens Pk. GU22: Wok 90C 168
Barret Ho. NW6 . . . . 39Cb 69
SW9 . . . . 55Pb 112
(off Benedict Rd.)
Barrett Cl. RM3: Rom 24Kd 57
Barrett Ct. SE5 . . . . 52Tb 113
(off Dobson Wlk.)
Barrett Ho. SE17 . . . . 7E 230
Barrett Rd. E17 . . . . 28Ec 52
KT22: Fet 96Fa 192
Barrett's Grn. Rd. NW10 . . . . 41Sa 87
Barrett's Gro. N16 . . . . 36Ub 71
Barretts Rd. TN13: Dun G 92Fd 202
Barrett St. W1 . . . . 3J 221 (44Jb 90)
Barrett Way RM15: Avel 45Td 98
Barrhill Rd. SW2 . . . . 61Nb 134
Barricane GU21: Wok 1M 187
Barrie Cl. CR5: Coul 88Lb 176
Barrie Ct. EN5: New Bar 15Eb 31
(off Lyonsdown Rd.)
Barriedale SE14 . . . . 54Ac 114
Barrie Est. W2 . . . . 4B 220 (45Fb 89)
Barrie Ho. KT15: Add 80J 149
NW8 . . . . 1F 215
W2 . . . . 5A 220
Barrier App. SE7 . . . . 48Mc 93
Barrier Point Rd. E16 . . . . 46Lc 93
Barringers Ct. HA4: Ruis 31T 64
Barringer Sq. SW17 . . . . 63Jb 134
Barrington Cl. IG5: Ilf 25Pc 54
IG10: Lough 13Sc 36
NW5 . . . . 36Jb 70
Barrington Ct. CM13: Hut 17Ee 41
N10 . . . . 26Jb 50
RH1: Redh 4A 208
SW4 . . . . 54Nb 112
TW18: Staines 65H 127
(off Thameside)
W3 . . . . 47Ra 87
(off Cheltenham Pl.)
Barrington Dr. KT22: Fet 97Fa 192
UB9: Hare 24J 43
Barrington Grn. IG10: Lough 14Sc 36
Barrington Lodge KT13: Weyb 78S 150
Barrington Pk. Gdns. HP8: Chal G 18A 24
Barrington Rd. CR8: Purl 84Lb 176
DA7: Bex 54Zc 117
E12 . . . . 37Qc 74
IG10: Lough 14Sc 36
N8 . . . . 29Mb 50
SM3: Sutt 75Cb 155
SW9 . . . . 55Rb 113
Barrington Vs. SE18 . . . . 53Qc 116
Barrington Wlk. SE19 . . . . 65Ub 135
Barrow Av. SM5: Cars 80Hb 155
Barrow Cl. N21 . . . . 20Rb 33
Barrow Ct. SE6 . . . . 60Hc 115
(off Cumberland Pl.)
Barrowdene Cl. HA5: Pinn 26Aa 45
Barrowell Grn. N21 . . . . 19Rb 33
Barrowfield Cl. N9 . . . . 20Xb 33
Barrow Gdns. RH1: Redh 4B 208
Barrowgate Rd. W4 . . . . 50Sa 87
Barrow Grn. Rd. RH8: Oxt 2E 210
Barrow Hall Ho. RM16: Grays 8B 100
Barrow Hedges Cl. SM5: Cars 80Gb 155
Barrow Hedges Way SM5: Cars 80Gb 155
Barrow Hill KT4: Wor Pk 75Ua 154
Barrow Hill Cl. KT4: Wor Pk 75Ua 154
Barrow Hill Est. NW8 . . . . 2D 214
Barrow Hill Rd. NW8 . . . . 2D 214 (40Gb 69)
Barrow Hills Golf Course 5N 147
Barrow La. EN7: Chesh, G Oak 2Vb 19
(not continuous)
Barrow Lodge SL2: Slou 2G 80
Barrow Point Av. HA5: Pinn 26Aa 45
Barrow Point La. HA5: Pinn 26Aa 45
Barrow Rd. CR0: Wadd 78Qb 156
SW16 . . . . 65Mb 134
Barrowsfield CR2: Sande 84Vb 177
Barrow Store Ct. SE1 . . . . 3H 231
Barrow Wlk. TW8: Bford 51La 108
Barr Rd. DA12: Grav'nd 1H 145
EN6: Pot B 5Eb 17

Barrsbrook Farm Rd.—Beardell St.

Barrsbrook Farm Rd. KT16: Chert 74G 148
Barrsbrook Hall KT16: Chert 74G 148
Barr's La. GU21: Knap 8H 167
(not continuous)
Barr's Rd. SL6: Tap 4A 80
Barrs Rd. NW10 38Ta 67
Barry Av. DA7: Bex 52Ad 117
N15 30Vb 51
SL4: Wind 2G 102
Barry Blandford Way E3 42Dc 92
Barry Cl. AL2: Chis G 7P 5
BR6: Orp 76Uc 160
RM16: Grays 8C 100
Barry Ct. RM5: Col R 22Fd 56
WD18: Wat 15Y 27
(off Cardiff Rd.)
Barrydene N20 18Fb 31
Barry Ho. SE16 49Xb 91
(off Rennie Est.)
Barry Pde. SE22 57Wb 113
Barry Rd. E6 44Nc 94
NW10 38Sa 67
SE22 58Wb 113
Barry Ter. TW15: Ashf 61P 127
(off Orchard Way)
Barset Rd. SE15 55Yb 114
(not continuous)
Barson Cl. SE20 66Yb 136
Barstable Rd. SS17: Stan H 1M 101
Barston Rd. SE27 62Sb 135
Barstow Cres. SW2 60Pb 112
Bartel Cl. HP3: Hem H 4D 4
Bartelotts Rd. SL2: Slou 2B 80
Barter St. WC1 1G 223 (43Nb 90)
Barters Wlk. HA5: Pinn 27Aa 45
Barth M. SE18 49Uc 94
Bartholomew Cl. EC1 1C 224 (43Sb 91)
(not continuous)
SW18 56Eb 111
Bartholomew Ct. E14 45Fc 93
(off Newport Av.)
EC1 5E 218
HA8: Edg 24Ma 47
Bartholomew Dr. RM3: Hrld W 26Md 57
Bartholomew Ho. EN3: Enf W 9Ac 20
IG8: Wfd G 24Rc 54
W10 42Ab 88
(off Appleford Rd.)
Bartholomew La. EC2 3G 225 (44Tb 91)
Bartholomew Pl. EC1 1D 224
Bartholomew Rd. NW5 37Lb 70
Bartholomew Sq. E1 42Xb 91
EC1 4E 218 (41Sb 91)
Bartholomew St. SE1 4G 231 (48Tb 91)
Bartholomew Vs. NW5 37Lb 70
Bartholomew Way BR8: Swan 69Gd 140
Barth Rd. SE18 49Uc 94
Bartle Av. E6 40Nc 74
Bartle Rd. W11 44Ab 88
Bartlett Cl. E14 44Cc 92
Bartlett Ct. EC4 2A 224 (44Qb 90)
Bartlett Ho. KT4: Wor Pk 75Va 154
(off The Avenue)
Bartlett Ho's. RM10: Dag 38Dd 76
(off Vicarage Rd.)
Bartlett M. E14 50Dc 92
Bartlett Rd. DA11: Grav'nd 10C 122
TN16: Westrm 98Sc 200
Bartletts Hillside Cl. SL9: Chal P 24A 42
Bartletts Pas. EC4 2A 224
Bartlett St. CR2: S Croy 78Tb 157
Bartlow Gdns. RM5: Col R 25Fd 56
Bartok Ho. W11 46Bb 89
(off Lansdowne Wlk.)
Barton, The KT11: Cobh 84Z 171
Barton Av. RM7: Rush G 32Dd 76
Barton Cl. DA6: Bex 57Ad 117
E6 44Pc 94
E9 36Yb 72
GU21: Knap 10G 166
IG7: Chig 19Sc 36
KT15: Add 79J 149
NW4 29Wa 48
SE15 55Xb 113
TW17: Shep 72R 150
Barton Ct. CR3: W'ham 91Wb 197
(off Godstone Rd.)
W14 50Ab 88
(off Baron's Ct. Rd.)
Barton Friars IG7: Chig 19Sc 36
Barton Grn. KT3: N Mald 68Ta 131
Barton Ho. E3 41Dc 92
(off Bow Rd.)
N1 38Rb 71
(off Sable St.)
SW6 55Db 111
(off Wandsworth Bri. Rd.)
Barton Mdws. IG6: Ilf 28Rc 54
Barton M. E14 47Dc 92
SW19 65Eb 133
Barton Rd. DA4: Sut H 67Rd 141
DA14: Sidc 65Ad 139
RM12: Horn 32Jd 76
SL3: L'ly 47B 82
W14 50Ab 88
Bartons, The WD6: E'tree 16Ma 29
Barton St. SW1 3F 229 (48Nb 90)
Barton Way WD3: Crox G 15R 26
WD6: Bore 12Qa 29
Bartonway NW8 1B 214
Bartram Cl. UB8: Hil 42R 84
Bartram Rd. SE4 57Ac 114
Bartrams La. EN4: Had W 10Eb 17
Bartrip St. E9 37Bc 72
Barts Cl. BR3: Beck 71Cc 158
Barville Cl. SE4 56Ac 114
Barwell Bus. Pk. KT9: Chess 80Ma 153
Barwell Ct. KT9: Chess 80Ka 152
Barwell Cres. TN16: Big H 84Lc 179
Barwell Ho. E2 42Wb 91
(off Menotti St.)
Barwell La. KT9: Chess 80La 152
Barwick Dr. UB8: Hil 43R 84
Barwick Ho. W3 47Sa 87
(off Strafford Rd.)
Barwick Rd. E7 35Kc 73
Barwood Av. BR4: W W'ck 74Dc 158
Baryta Cl. SS17: Stan H 2L 101
Bascombe Gro. DA1: Bexl, Cray 59Gd 118
Bascombe St. SW2 58Qb 112
Basden Gro. TW13: Hanw 61Ca 129
Basden Ho. TW13: Hanw 61Ca 129
Basedale Rd. RM9: Dag 38Xc 75
Baseing Cl. E6 45Qc 94
Baseline Bus. Studios W11 45Za 88
(off Barandon Wlk.)
Basepoint Bus. Cen. RM13: Rain 42Fd 96
Basevi Way SE8 51Dc 114
Basford Way SL4: Wind 5B 102
Bashley Rd. NW10 42Ta 87
Basil Av. E6 41Nc 94
Basildene Rd. TW4: Houn 55Z 107
Basildon Av. IG5: Ilf 25Qc 54
Basildon Cl. SM2: Sutt 81Db 175
WD18: Wat 16S 26
Basildon Ct. HP3: Hem H 7P 3
W1 7J 215
Basildon Rd. SE2 50Wc 95
Basil Gdns. CR0: C'don 74Zb 158
SE27 64Sb 135
Basil Ho. E1 44Wb 91
(off Henriques St.)
SW8 52Nb 112
(off Wyvil Rd.)
Basilica Pl. E3 40Bc 72
Basil Mans. SW3 2F 227
Basilon Rd. DA7: Bex 54Ad 117
Basil Spence Ho. N22 25Pb 50
Basil St. SW3 3F 227 (48Hb 89)
Basin App. E14 44Ac 92
E16 45Rc 94
Basing Cl. KT7: T Ditt 73Ha 152
Basing Ct. SE15 53Vb 113
Basingdon Way SE5 56Tb 113
Basing Dr. DA5: Bexl 58Bd 117
Basingfield Rd. KT7: T Ditt 73Ha 152
Basinghall Av. EC2 1F 225 (44Tb 91)
Basinghall Gdns. SM2: Sutt 81Db 175
Basinghall St. EC2 1E 224 (44Tb 91)
Basing Hill HA9: Wemb 33Pa 67
NW11 32Bb 69
Basing Ho. Yd. E2 3J 219
Basing Pl. E2 3J 219 (41Ub 91)
Basing Rd. SM7: Bans 86Bb 175
WD3: Rick 18H 25
Basing St. W11 44Bb 89
Basing Way KT7: T Ditt 73Ha 152
N3 27Cb 49
Basin Mill Apartments E2 1K 219
Basin Sth. E16 46Rc 94
Basire St. N1 39Sb 71
Baskerville Gdns. NW10 35Ua 68
Baskerville Rd. SW18 59Gb 111
Basket Gdns. SE9 57Nc 116
Baslow Cl. HA3: Hrw W 25Fa 46
Baslow Wlk. E5 35Zb 72
Basnett Rd. SW11 55Jb 112
Basque Ct. SE16 47Zb 92
(off Garter Way)
Bassano St. SE22 57Vb 113
Bassant Rd. SE18 51Vc 117
Bass Ct. E15 39Hc 73
(off Plaistow Rd.)
Bassein Pk. Rd. W12 47Va 88
Basset Cl. KT15: New H 82K 169
Bassett Cl. SM2: Sutt 81Db 175
Bassett Dr. RH2: Reig 5J 207
Bassett Gdns. TW7: Isle 52Ea 108
Bassett Ho. SW19 64Db 133
Bassett Rd. GU22: Wok 88E 168
UB8: Uxb 38L 63
W10 44Za 88
Bassetts TN16: Tats 93Lc 199
Bassett's Cl. BR6: Farnb 77Rc 160
Bassett St. NW5 37Jb 70
Bassett's Way BR6: Farnb 77Rc 160
Bassett Way SL2: Slou 2C 80
UB6: G'frd 44Da 85
Bassil Rd. HP2: Hem H 3M 3
Bassingbourn Ho. N1 38Qb 70
(off The Sutton Est.)
Bassingham Rd. HA0: Wemb 37Ma 67
SW18 59Eb 111
Bassishaw Highwalk EC2 1F 225
Bass M. SE22 56Wb 113
Basswood Cl. SE15 55Xb 113
Bastable Av. IG11: Bark 40Uc 74
BASTED 95Be 205
Basted La. TN15: Crou 95Ce 205
Basted Mill TN15: Bor G 93Ae 205
Basterfield Ho. EC1 6D 218
Bastion Highwalk EC2 1E 224
Bastion Ho. EC2 1D 224
Bastion Rd. SE2 50Wc 95
Baston Mnr. Rd.
BR2: Hayes, Kes 76Kc 159
Baston Rd. BR2: Hayes 75Kc 159
Bastwick St. EC1 5C 218 (42Sb 91)
Basuto Rd. SW6 53Cb 111
Bata Av. RM18: E Til 10K 101
Bataleur Ct. RM11: Horn 30Md 57
BAT & BALL 93Ld 203
Bat & Ball Ent. Cen.
TN14: S'oaks 93Ld 203
Bat & Ball Rd. TN14: S'oaks 93Ld 203
Batavia Cl. TW16: Sun 67X 129
Batavia Ho. SE14 52Ac 114
(off Batavia Rd.)
Batavia M. SE14 52Ac 114
Batavia Rd. SE14 52Ac 114
TW16: Sun 67X 129
Batchelor St. N1 1A 218 (39Qb 70)
Batchwood Dr. AL3: St A 1P 5
Batchwood Grn. BR5: St P 69Wc 139
BATCHWORTH 19N 25
BATCHWORTH HEATH 21Q 44
Batchworth Heath WD3: Rick 21R 44
Batchworth Heath Hill WD3: Rick 21Q 44
Batchworth Hill WD3: Rick 19N 25
(not continuous)
Batchworth La. HA6: Nwood 22S 44
Batchworth Lock Canal Cen. 18N 25
Batchworth Pk. Golf Course 20N 25
BATCHWORTH RDBT. 18N 25
Bateman Cl. IG11: Bark 37Sc 74
Bateman Ho. SE17 51Rb 113
(off Otto St.)
Bateman M. SW4 58Mb 112
Bateman Rd. E4 23Cc 52
WD3: Crox G 16Q 26
Bateman's Bldgs. W1 3D 222
Batemans M. CM14: W'ley 22Xd 58
Bateman's Row EC2 5J 219 (42Ub 91)
Bateman St. W1 3D 222 (44Mb 90)
Bates Bus. Cen. RM3: Hrld W 24Qd 57
Bates Cl. SL3: Geor G 44A 82
Bates Cres. CR0: Wadd 78Qb 156
SW16 66Lb 134
Bates Hill TN15: Igh 94Yd 204
Bates Ind. Est. RM3: Hrld W 24Qd 57
Bateson Dr. WD25: Wat 5V 12
Bateson St. SE18 49Uc 94
Bateson Way GU21: Wok 86E 168
Bates Point E13 39Jc 73
(off Pelly Rd.)
Bates Rd. RM3: Hrld W 24Qd 57
Bate St. E14 45Bc 92
Bates Wlk. KT15: Add 79L 149
Bat Gdns. KT2: King T 65Pa 131
Bath Cl. SE15 52Xb 113
Bath Ct. EC1 4F 219
(St Luke's Est.)
EC1 6K 217
(Warner St.)
SE26 62Wb 135
(off Droitwich Cl.)
Bathgate Ho. SW9 53Rb 113
(off Lothian Rd.)
Bathgate Rd. SW19 62Za 132
Bath Gro. E2 40Wb 71
(off Horatio St.)
Bath Ho. E2 42Wb 91
(off Ramsey St.)
IG11: Bark 38Sc 74
SE1 3D 230
Bath Ho. Rd. CR0: Bedd 74Nb 156
Bath Pas. KT1: King T 68Ma 131
Bath Pl. EC2 4H 219 (41Ub 91)
EN5: Barn 13Bb 31
W6 50Ya 88
(off Peabody Est.)
Bath Rd. DA1: Dart 59Kd 119
E7 37Mc 73
N9 19Xb 33
RM6: Chad H 30Ad 55
SL1: Slou 4A 80
SL3: Coln 52E 104
SL3: Coln, Poyle 53G 104
SL6: Tap 4A 80
TW3: Houn 55Da 107
TW4: Houn 54Z 107
TW5: Cran 53Y 107
TW6: H'row A 53U 106
UB3: Harl 53U 106
UB7: Lford, Harm, Sip 53K 105
W4 49Ua 88
Bath Rd. Retail Pk. SL1: Slou 4D 80
Baths Ct. W12 47Xa 88
Baths Rd. BR2: Brom 70Mc 137
Bath St. DA11: Grav'nd 8D 122
EC1 4E 218 (41Sb 91)
Bath Ter. SE1 4D 230 (48Sb 91)
Bathurs Sq. N15 28Ub 51
Bathurst Av. SW19 67Db 133
Bathurst Cl. SL0: Rich P 47H 83
Bathurst Gdns. NW10 40Xa 68
Bathurst Ho. W12 45Xa 88
(off White City Est.)
Bathurst M. W2 4C 220 (44Fb 89)
Bathurst Rd. IG1: Ilf 32Rc 74
Bathurst St. W2 4C 220 (45Fb 89)
Bathurst Wlk. SL0: Rich P 47G 82
Bathway SE18 49Qc 94
Batley Cl. CR4: Mitc 73Hb 155
Batley Pl. N16 34Vb 71
Batley Rd. EN2: Enf 11Sb 33
N16 34Vb 71
Batman Cl. W12 46Xa 88
Baton Cl. RM19: Purf 49Td 98
Batoum Gdns. W6 48Ya 88
Batsford Ho. SW19 63Db 133
(off Durnsford Rd.)
Batson Ho. E1 44Wb 91
(off Fairclough St.)
Batson St. W12 47Wa 88
Batsworth Rd. CR4: Mitc 69Fb 133
Batten Av. GU21: Wok 1J 187
Battenberg Wlk. SE19 65Ub 135
Batten Cl. E6 44Pc 94
Batten Cotts. E14 43Ac 92
(off Maroon St.)
Batten Ho. SW4 57Lb 112
W10 41Ab 88
(off Third Av.)
Batten St. SW11 55Gb 111
Battersby Rd. SE6 61Fc 137
BATTERSEA 53Jb 112
Battersea Arts Cen. 55Hb 111
(off Lavender Hill)
Battersea at Brands Hatch 78Xd 164
Battersea Bri. SW3 52Fb 111
Battersea Bri. Rd. SW11 52Gb 111
Battersea Bus. Cen. SW11 55Jb 112
Battersea Bus. Pk. SW8 53Lb 112
Battersea Church Rd. SW11 53Fb 111
Battersea Dogs' Home 52Kb 112
Battersea High St. SW11 53Fb 111
(not continuous)
BATTERSEA PARK 52Kb 112
Battersea Pk. 52Hb 111
Battersea Pk. Children's Zoo 52Jb 112
Battersea Pk. Rd. SW8 54Gb 111
SW11 54Gb 111
Battersea Power Station Development
SW8 51Kb 112
Battersea Ri. SW11 57Gb 111
Battersea Roof Gdns. SW8 52Kb 112
Battersea Sports Cen. 55Fb 111
Battersea Sq. SW11 53Fb 111
Battery Rd. SE28 47Uc 94
Battilion Ho. NW9 26Va 48
(off Heritage Av.)
Battis, The RM1: Rom 30Gd 56
Battishill St. N1 38Rb 71
Battlebridge Ct. N1 1G 217
Battle Bri. La. SE1 7H 225 (46Ub 91)
Battlebridge La. RH1: Mers, Redh 2B 208
Battle Cl. SW19 65Eb 133
Battledean Rd. N5 36Rb 71
Battlefield Rd. AL1: St A 1D 6
Battlefields Rd. TN15: Wro 88Be 185
Battle Ho. SE15 51Wb 113
(off Haymerle Rd.)
Battle Rd. DA8: Erith 49Ed 96
DA17: Belv, Erith 49Ed 96
BATTLERS GREEN 8Ga 14
Battlers Grn. Dr. WD7: R'lett 9Ga 14
BATTLE STREET 9H 145
Battle St. DA12: Cobh 9H 145
Batts Hill RH1: Redh 4N 207
RH2: Reig 4M 207
Batt's Rd. DA12: Cobh, Sole S 10J 145
Batty St. E1 44Wb 91
Batwa Ho. SE16 50Xb 91
Baudwin Rd. SE6 61Gc 137
Baugh Rd. DA14: Sidc 64Yc 139
Baulk, The SW18 59Cb 111
Bavant Rd. SW16 68Nb 134
Bavaria Rd. N19 33Nb 70
Bavdene M. NW4 28Xa 48
(off The Burroughs)
Bavent Rd. SE5 54Sb 113
Bawdale Rd. SE22 57Vb 113
Bawdsey Av. IG2: Ilf 28Vc 55
Bawley Ct. E16 45Sc 94
Bawley Ter. E15 39Fc 73
(off Rick Roberts Way)
Bawtree Cl. SM2: Sutt 82Eb 175
Bawtree Rd. SE14 52Ac 114
UB8: Uxb 37M 63
Bawtry Rd. N20 20Hb 31
Baxendale N20 19Eb 31
Baxendale St. E2 41Wb 91
Baxter Av. RH1: Redh 6P 207
Baxter Cl. BR1: Brom 69Rc 138
SL1: Slou 8J 81
UB2: S'hall 48Da 85
UB10: Hil 41R 84
Baxter Gdns. RM3: Rom 19Ld 39
Baxter Ho. E3 41Dc 92
(off Bromley High St.)
Baxter Rd. E16 44Lc 93
IG1: Ilf 36Rc 74
N1 37Tb 71
N18 21Xb 51
WD24: Wat 8W 12
Baxter Wlk. SW16 61Mb 134
Bayard Ct. DA6: Bex 56Dd 118
Bayards CR6: W'ham 90Yb 178
Bay Ct. E1 42Zb 92
(off Frimley Way)
W5 48Na 87
Baycroft Cl. HA5: Eastc 27Y 45
Baydon Ct. BR2: Brom 69Hc 137
Bayer Ho. EC1 6D 218
Bayes Cl. SE26 64Yb 136
Bayes Ct. NW3 38Hb 69
(off Primrose Hill Rd.)
Bayes Ho. N1 38Qb 70
(off Augustas La.)
Bayeux KT20: Tad 94Za 194
Bayfield Ho. SE4 56Zb 114
(off Coston Wlk.)
Bayfield Pl. BR6: Orp 75Zc 161
Bayfield Rd. SE9 56Mc 115
Bayford M. E8 38Xb 71
(off Bayford St.)
Bayford Rd. NW10 41Za 88
Bayford St. E8 38Xb 71
Bayford St. Bus. Cen. E8 38Xb 71
(off Sidworth St.)
Baygrove M. KT1: Hamp W 67La 130
Bayham Pl. NW1 1B 216 (39Lb 70)
Bayham Rd. SM4: Mord 70Db 133
TN13: S'oaks 95Ld 203
W4 48Ta 87
W13 45Ka 86
Bayham St. NW1 1B 216 (39Lb 70)
Bayhurst Dr. HA6: Nwood 23V 44
Bayhurst Wood Country Pk. 29P 43
Bayleaf Cl. TW12: Hamp H 64Fa 130
Bayley Mead HP1: Hem H 4K 3
Bayleys Mead CM13: Hut 19Ee 41
Bayley St. WC1 1D 222 (43Mb 90)
Bayley Wlk. SE2 51Ad 117
Baylie Ct. HP2: Hem H 1N 3
Baylie La. HP2: Hem H 1N 3
Baylis Bus. Cen. SL1: Slou 5H 81
Baylis M. TW1: Twick 59Ja 108
Baylis Pde. SL1: Slou 4J 81
Baylis Pl. BR1: Brom 69Nc 138
Baylis Rd. SE1 2K 229 (47Qb 90)
SL1: Slou 5H 81
Bayliss Av. SE28 45Zc 95
Bayliss Cl. N21 15Nb 32
UB1: S'hall 44Da 85
(off Whitecote Rd.)
Bayly Rd. DA1: Dart 58Qd 119
Bay Mnr. La. RM20: W Thur 51Vd 120
Baymans Wood CM15: Shenf 19Be 41
Bayne Cl. E6 44Pc 94
Baynes Cl. EN1: Enf 11Wb 33
Baynes M. NW3 37Fb 69
Baynes St. NW1 38Lb 70
Baynham Cl. DA5: Bexl 58Bd 117
Baynton Rd. GU22: Wok 92D 188
Bayonne Rd. W6 51Ab 110
Bay Path RH9: G'stone 3A 210
Bays Ct. HA8: Edg 22Ra 47
Bays Farm Ct. UB7: Lford 53L 105
Bayshill Ri. UB5: N'olt 37Da 65
Baysixty6 Skate Pk. 43Bb 89
(off Acklam Rd.)
Bayston Rd. N16 34Vb 71
BAYSWATER 45Eb 89
Bayswater Cl. N13 21Rb 51
Bayswater Rd. W2 5A 220 (45Db 89)
Baythorne Ho. E16 44Hc 93
(off Turner St.)
Baythorne St. E3 43Bc 92
Bayton Ct. E8 38Wb 71
(off Lansdowne Dr.)
Bay Tree Av. KT22: Lea 92Ja 192
Bay Tree Cl. AL2: Park 10A 6
BR1: Brom 67Mc 137
IG6: Ilf 24Rc 54
Baytree Cl. DA15: Sidc 60Vc 117
Baytree Ct. SL1: Burn 1A 80
Baytree Ct. SW2 56Pb 112
Bay Tree Ho. EC1 6K 217
Baytree Ho. E4 17Dc 34
Baytree M. SE17 5F 231 (49Tb 91)
Baytree Rd. SW2 56Pb 112
Bay Trees RH8: Oxt 5M 211
Baytrees SL9: Ger X 28B 42
Baytree Shop. Cen., The
CM14: B'wood 19Yd 40
Baytree Wlk. WD17: Wat 10V 12
Baywillow Av. SM5: Cars 74Hb 155
Baywood Sq. IG7: Chig 21Xc 55
Bazalgette Cl. KT3: N Mald 71Ta 153
Bazalgette Gdns. KT3: N Mald 71Ta 153
Bazalgette Ho. NW8 5C 214
Bazalgette Way SE2 46Yc 95
Bazeley Ho. SE1 2B 230
Bazely St. E14 45Ec 92
Bazes Shaw DA3: Nw A G 75Be 165
(not continuous)
Bazile Rd. N21 16Qb 32
BBC Broadcasting House
1A 222 (43Kb 90)
BBC Elstree 13Qa 29
BBC Maida Vale Studios 42Db 89
(off Delaware Rd.)
BBC Studios W12 46Ya 88
BBC Worldwide W12 45Ya 88
BDA Dental Mus. 1K 221 (43Kb 90)
Beacham Cl. SE7 50Mc 93
Beachborough Rd. BR1: Brom 63Ec 136
Beach Ct. SE9 58Nc 116
Beachcroft Av. UB1: S'hall 46Aa 85
Beachcroft Rd. E11 34Gc 73
Beachcroft Way N19 32Mb 70
Beach Gro. TW13: Hanw 61Ca 129
Beach Ho. SW5 50Cb 89
(off Philbeach Gdns.)
TW13: Hanw 61Ca 129
Beach's Ho. TW18: Staines 64J 127
Beachy Rd. E3 38Cc 72
Beacon Bingo
Cricklewood 35Za 68
Streatham 61Nb 134
Beacon Cl. SL9: Chal P 24A 42
SM7: Bans 88Za 174
UB8: Uxb 36M 63
Beacon Ct. SL3: Coln 52E 104
Beacon Dr. DA2: Bean 62Xd 142
Beaconfield Av. CM16: Epp 1Vc 23
Beaconfield Rd. CM16: Epp 1Vc 23
Beaconfields TN13: S'oaks 98Hd 202
Beaconfield Way CM16: Epp 1Vc 23
Beacon Ga. SE14 55Zb 114
Beacon Gro. SM5: Cars 77Jb 156
Beacon Hill GU21: Wok 1N 187
N7 36Nb 70
RM19: Purf 50Rd 97
Beacon Hill Ind. Est. RM19: Purf 50Rd 97
Beacon Ho. AL1: St A 2D 6
E14 50Dc 92
(off Burrells Wharf Sq.)
SE5 52Ub 113
(off Southampton Way)
Beacon Pl. CR0: Bedd 76Nb 156
Beacon Point SE10 51Dc 114
(off Dowells St.)
Beacon Ri. TN13: S'oaks 98Jd 202
Beacon Rd. DA8: Erith 52Kd 119
SE13 58Fc 115
TW6: H'row A 58Q 106
Beacon Row TN15: W King 81Vd 184
Beacons, The IG10: Lough 10Qc 22
Beacons Cl. E6 43Nc 94
Beaconsfield WC1 1H 223
Beaconsfield Cl. N11 22Jb 50
SE3 51Jc 115
W4 50Sa 87
Beaconsfield Comn. La. HP9: Beac 1G 60
Beaconsfield Ct. WD25: Wat 4X 13
(off Horseshoe La.)
Beaconsfield Gdns. KT10: Clay 80Ga 152
Beaconsfield Pde. SE9 63Nc 138
Beaconsfield Pl. KT17: Eps 84Ua 174
Beaconsfield Rd. AL1: St A 2C 6
BR1: Brom 69Mc 137
CR0: C'don 72Tb 157
DA5: Bexl 61Gd 140
E10 33Ec 72
E16 42Hc 93
E17 30Bc 52
EN3: Enf W 9Zb 20
GU22: Wok 92B 188
KT3: N Mald 68Ta 131
KT5: Surb 73Pa 153
KT10: Clay 80Ga 152
KT18: Eps D 91Ta 193
N9 20Wb 33
N11 20Jb 32
N15 28Ub 51
NW10 37Va 68
SE3 52Hc 115
SE9 63Nc 138
SE17 7H 231 (50Tb 91)
SL2: Farn C, Farn R 10G 60
TW1: Twick 58Ka 108
UB1: S'hall 46Z 85
UB4: Yead 46Y 85
W4 48Ta 87
W5 47La 86
Beaconsfield St. N1 39Nb 70
Beaconsfield Ter. RM6: Chad H 30Zc 55
Beaconsfield Ter. Rd. W14 48Ab 88
Beaconsfield Wlk. E6 44Qc 94
SW6 53Bb 111
Beacontree Av. E17 25Fc 53
BEACONTREE HEATH 32Cd 76
Beacontree Rd. E11 32Hc 73
Beacon Way SM7: Bans 88Za 174
WD3: Rick 17J 25
Beacon Wood Country Pk. 63Xd 142
Beadle Pl. DA8: Erith 52Hd 118
Beadles La. RH8: Oxt 2H 211
Beadle's Pde. RM10: Dag 37Ed 76
Beadlow Cl. SM5: Cars 72Fb 155
Beadman Pl. SE27 63Rb 135
Beadman St. SE27 63Rb 135
Beadnell Ct. E1 45Wb 91
(off Cable St.)
Beadnell Rd. SE23 60Zb 114
Beadon Rd. BR2: Brom 70Jc 137
W6 49Ya 88
Beads Hall La. CM15: Pil H 14Xd 40
Beaford Gro. SW20 69Ab 132
Beagle Cl. TW13: Felt 63X 129
WD7: R'lett 9Ha 14
Beagles Cl. BR5: Orp 75Zc 161
Beak St. W1 4B 222 (45Lb 90)
Beal Cl. DA16: Well 53Wc 117
Beale Arboretum, The 10Hb 17
Beale Cl. N13 22Rb 51
Beale Pl. E3 40Bc 72
Beale Rd. E3 39Bc 72
Beales La. KT13: Weyb 76R 150
Beales Rd. KT23: Bookh 99Da 191
Beal Rd. IG1: Ilf 33Qc 74
Beam Av. RM10: Dag 39Dd 76
Beames Rd. NW10 39Ta 67
Beaminster Gdns. IG6: Ilf 26Rc 54
Beaminster Ho. SW8 52Pb 112
(off Dorset Rd.)
Beamish Dr. WD23: B Hea 18Ea 28
Beamish Ho. SE16 49Xb 91
(off Rennie Est.)
Beamish Rd. BR5: Orp 73Yc 161
N9 18Wb 33
Beam Reach Bus. Pk. RM13: Rain 41Fd 96
Beam Valley Country Pk. 39Ed 76
Beamway RM10: Dag 38Fd 76
BEAN 62Xd 142
Beanacre Cl. E9 37Bc 72
Beane Cft. DA12: Grav'nd 10H 123
Bean Hill Cotts. DA2: Bean 63Yd 142
(not continuous)
Bean La. DA2: Bean 61Xd 142
Bean Rd. DA6: Bex 56Zc 117
DA9: Ghithe 57Xd 120
Beanshaw SE9 63Qc 138
Beansland Gro. RM6: Chad H 27Ad 55
Bear All. EC4 2B 224 (44Rb 91)
Bear Cl. RM7: Rom 30Dd 56
Beardell St. SE19 65Vb 135

Beardow Gro.—Beechfield Gdns.

Beardow Gro. N14 16Lb 32
Beard Rd. KT2: King T 64Pa 131
Beardsfield E13 40Jc 73
Beard's Hill TW12: Hamp 67Ca 129
Beard's Hill Cl.
TW12: Hamp 67Ca 129
Beardsley Ter. *RM8: Dag* 36Xc 75
(off Stonard Rd.)
Beardsley Way W3 47Ta 87
Beard's Rd. TW15: Ashf 65U 128
Bearfield Rd. KT2: King T 66Na 131
Bear Gdns. SE1 6D 224 (46Sb 91)
Bearing Cl. IG7: Chig 21Wc 55
Bearing Way IG7: Chig 21Wc 55
Bear La. SE1 6C 224 (46Rb 91)
Bear Pit Apartments SE1 6D 224
Bear Rd. TW13: Hanw 63Z 129
Bears Den KT20: Kgswd 94Bb 195
Bearsden Ct. SL5: S'dale 3D 146
Bears Rails Pk. SL4: Old Win 9K 103
Bearstead Ri. SE4 57Bc 114
Bearsted Ter. BR3: Beck 67Cc 136
Bear St. WC2 4E 222 (45Mb 90)
Bearwood Cl. EN6: Pot B 3Fb 17
KT15: Add 79J 149
Bearwood Rd. SS17: Stan H 3K 101
Beasley's Ait TW16: Sun 72V 150
Beasley's Ait La. TW16: Sun 72V 150
Beaton Cl. DA9: Ghithe 57Xd 120
SE15 53Vb 113
Beatrice Av. HA9: Wemb 36Na 67
SW16 69Pb 134
Beatrice Cl. E13 42Jc 93
HA5: Eastc 28W 44
Beatrice Ct. IG9: Buck H 19Mc 35
Beatrice Gdns. DA11: Nflt 1A 144
Beatrice Ho. *W6* 50Ya 88
(off Queen Caroline St.)
Beatrice Pl. W8 48Db 89
Beatrice Rd. E17 29Cc 52
N4 31Qb 70
N9 17Yb 34
RH8: Oxt 1J 211
SE1 49Wb 91
TW10: Rich 57Pa 109
UB1: S'hall 46Ba 85
Beatrice Webb Ho. *E3* 40Ac 72
(off Chisenhale Rd.)
Beatrice Wilson Flats
TN13: S'oaks 97Kd 203
Beatrix Apartments *E3* 42Bc 92
(off English St.)
Beatrix Ho. *SW5* 50Db 89
(off Old Brompton Rd.)
Beatson Wlk. SE16 46Ac 92
(not continuous)
Beattie Cl. KT23: Bookh 96Ba 191
TW14: Felt 59V 106
Beattie Ho. SW8 53Lb 112
Beattock Ri. N10 28Kb 50
Beatty Ho. *E14* 47Cc 92
(off Admirals Way)
SW1 50Lb 90
(off Dolphin Sq.)
Beatty Rd. EN8: Walt C 6Bc 20
HA7: Stan 23La 46
N16 35Ub 71
Beatty St. NW1 1B 216 (40Lb 70)
Beattyville Gdns. IG6: Ilf 28Qc 54
Beauchamp Cl. W4 48Sa 87
Beauchamp Ct. *EN5: Barn* 14Bb 31
(off Victors Way)
HA7: Stan 22La 46
Beauchamp Gdns. WD3: Rick 18J 25
Beauchamp Pl. SW3 3E 226 (48Gb 89)
Beauchamp Rd. E7 38Kc 73
KT8: W Mole, E Mos 71Da 151
SE19 67Tb 135
SM1: Sutt 77Cb 155
SW11 56Gb 111
TW1: Twick 59Ja 108
Beauchamp St. EC1 1K 223 (43Qb 90)
Beauchamp Ter. SW15 55Xa 110
Beauclare Cl. KT22: Lea 92Ma 193
Beauclerc Ct. TW16: Sun 68Y 129
Beauclerc Rd. W6 48Xa 88
Beauclere Ho. SM2: Sutt 79Eb 155
Beauclerk Cl. TW13: Felt 60X 107
Beauclerk Ho. SW16 62Nb 134
Beau Ct. *HA7: Stan* 24Ma 47
(off Hitchin La.)
Beaudesert M. UB7: W Dray 47N 83
Beaufort E6 43Qc 94
Beaufort Av. HA3: Kenton 28Ja 46
Beaufort Cl. E4 23Dc 52
GU22: Wok 88E 168
RH2: Reig 5H 207
RM7: Mawney 28Ed 56
RM16: Chaf H 48Be 99
SW15 59Xa 110
W5 43Pa 87
Beaufort Ct. *E14* 47Cc 92
(off Admirals Way)
EN5: New Bar 15Eb 31
N11 22Kb 50
(off The Limes Av.)
SW6 51Cb 111
TW10: Ham 63La 130
Beaufort Dr. NW11 28Cb 49
Beaufort Gdns. E1 43Zb 92
IG1: Ilf 32Qc 74
NW4 30Ya 48
SW3 3E 226 (48Gb 89)
SW16 66Pb 134
TW5: Hest 53Aa 107
Beaufort Ho. *E16* 46Kc 93
(off Fairfax M.)
SW1 7D 228
SW3 51Fb 111
(off Beaufort St.)
Beaufort Mans. SW3 51Fb 111
Beaufort M. GU21: Wok 10P 167
SW6 51Bb 111
Beaufort Pk. NW11 28Cb 49
Beaufort Pl. BR5: St P 68Yc 139
Beaufort Rd. GU22: Wok 88E 168
HA4: Ruis 33T 64
KT1: King T 70Na 131
RH2: Reig 5H 207
TW1: Twick 59La 108
TW10: Ham 63La 130
W5 43Pa 87
Beauforts TW20: Eng G 4N 125
Beaufort Sq. NW9 26Wa 48
Beaufort St. SW3 51Fb 111
Beaufort Ter. *E14* 50Ec 92
(off Ferry St.)
Beaufort Way KT17: Ewe 80Wa 154
Beaufoy Ho. SE27 62Rb 135
SW8 52Pb 112
(off Rita Rd.)
Beaufoy Rd. N17 24Ub 51
(not continuous)
Beaufoy Wlk. SE11 6J 229 (49Pb 90)
Beaulieu Av. E16 46Kc 93
SE26 63Xb 135
Beaulieu Cl. CR4: Mitc 67Jb 134
NW9 28Ua 48
SE5 55Tb 113
SL3: Dat 3M 103
TW1: Twick 58Ma 109
TW4: Houn 57Ba 107
WD19: Wat 18Y 27
Beaulieu Ct. W5 43Na 87
Beaulieu Dr. EN9: Walt A 5Dc 20
HA5: Pinn 30Z 45
Beaulieu Gdns. N21 17Sb 33
Beaulieu Hgts. SE25 67Ub 135
Beaulieu Lodge *E14* 48Fc 93
(off Schooner Cl.)
Beaulieu Pl. W4 48Sa 87
Beauly Way RM1: Rom 25Gd 56
Beaumanor Gdns. SE9 63Qc 138
Beaumanor Mans. *W2* 45Db 89
(off Queensway)
Beaumans Dr. E17 25Bc 52
Beaumaris Ct. SL2: Slou 3F 80
Beaumaris Dr. IG8: Wfd G 24Mc 53
Beaumaris Gdns. SE19 66Sb 135
Beaumaris Grn. NW9 30Ua 48
Beaumaris Twr. *W3* 47Ra 87
(off Park Rd. Nth.)
Beaumayes Cl.
HP1: Hem H 3K 3
Beaumonds AL1: St A 2C 6
Beaumont *W14* 49Bb 89
(off Kensington Village)
Beaumont Av. AL1: St A 1F 6
HA0: Wemb 36La 66
HA2: Harr 30Da 45
TW9: Rich 55Pa 109
W14 50Bb 89
Beaumont Bldgs. WC2 3G 223
Beaumont Cen. EN8: Chesh 2Zb 20
Beaumont Cl. KT2: King T 66Qa 131
N2 28Gb 49
RM2: Rom 26Ld 57
Beaumont Ct. E1 41Zb 92
E5 34Xb 71
HA0: Wemb 36La 66
NW1 39Mb 70
NW9 26Va 48
(off Cherry Cl.)
W1 7J 215
W4 50Sa 87
Beaumont Cres. RM13: Rain 37Jd 76
W14 50Bb 89
Beaumont Dr. DA11: Nflt 9A 122
KT4: Wor Pk 73Xa 154
TW15: Ashf 64T 128
Beaumont Gdns. CM13: Hut 16Ee 41
NW3 34Cb 69
Beaumont Ga. *WD7: R'lett* 7Ja 14
(off Shenley Hill)
Beaumont Gro. E1 42Zb 92
Beaumont Ho. *E10* 31Dc 72
(off Skelton's La.)
W9 41Bb 89
(off Fernhead Rd.)
Beaumont Lodge *E8* 37Wb 71
(off Greenwood Rd.)
Beaumont M. HA5: Pinn 27Aa 45
NW5 36Mb 70
(off Charlton King's Rd.)
W1 7J 215 (43Jb 90)
Beaumont Pl. EN5: Barn 11Bb 31
TW7: Isle 57Ha 108
UB10: Ick 36Q 64
W1 5C 216 (42Lb 90)
WD18: Wat 15W 26
Beaumont Ri. N19 32Mb 70
Beaumont Rd. BR5: Pet W 72Tc 160
CR8: Purl 85Qb 176
E10 31Dc 72
(not continuous)
E13 41Kc 93
SE19 65Sb 135
SL2: Slou 2H 81
SL4: Wind 4G 102
SW19 59Ab 110
W4 48Sa 87
Beaumont Sq. E1 43Zb 92
Beaumont St. W1 7J 215 (43Jb 90)
Beaumont Ter. *SE13* 59Gc 115
(off Wellmeadow Rd.)
Beaumont Wlk. NW3 38Hb 69
Beaumont Works *AL1: St A* 2F 6
(off Hedley Rd.)
Beaumore Pl. SL9: Ger X 28B 42
Beauvais Ter. UB5: N'olt 41Z 85
Beauvale *NW1* 38Jb 70
(off Ferdinand St.)
Beauval Rd. SE22 58Vb 113
Beaux Arts Bldg., The N7 34Nb 70
Beaverbank Rd. SE9 60Tc 116
BEAVERBROOK RDBT. 95Ma 193
Beaver Cl. SE20 66Wb 135
SM4: Mord 73Ya 154
TW12: Hamp 67Da 129
Beaver Ct. BR3: Beck 66Dc 136
Beaver Gro. UB5: N'olt 41Aa 85
Beaver Ind. Est. UB2: S'hall 48Ba 85
Beaver Rd. IG6: Ilf 22Yc 55
Beavers Cres. TW4: Houn 56Y 107
Beavers La. TW4: Houn 54Y 107
Beavers La. Campsite TW4: Houn 56Z 107
Beavers Lodge DA14: Sidc 63Vc 139
Beaver Water World 94Kc 199
Beaverwood Rd. BR7: Chst 65Uc 138
Beavor Gro. *W6* 50Wa 88
(off Beavor La.)
Beavor La. W6 50Wa 88
Bebbington Rd. SE18 49Uc 94
Beblets Cl. BR6: Chels 78Vc 161
Beccles Dr. IG11: Bark 37Uc 74
Beccles St. E14 44Bc 92
Bec Cl. HA4: Ruis 34Z 65
Bechervaise Ct. *E10* 32Dc 72
(off Leyton Grange Est.)
Bechtel Ho. *W6* 49Za 88
(off Hammersmith Rd.)
Beck Cl. SE13 53Dc 114
Beck Ct. BR3: Beck 69Zb 136
BECKENHAM 68Cc 136
Beckenham Bus. Cen.
BR3: Beck 65Ac 136
Beckenham Crematorium
BR3: Beck 69Yb 136
Beckenham Gdns. N9 20Ub 33
Beckenham Gro. BR2: Brom 68Fc 137
Beckenham Hill Est. BR3: Beck 64Dc 136
Beckenham Hill Rd.
BR3: Beck 65Dc 136
SE6 65Dc 136
Beckenham La. BR2: Brom 68Gc 137
Beckenham Pl. Pk. BR3: Beck 66Dc 136
Beckenham Place Pk. Golf Course 65Dc 136
Beckenham Place Pk. Local Nature Reserve 65Ec 136
Beckenham Rd. BR3: Beck 67Zb 136
BR4: W W'ck 73Dc 158
Beckenham Theatre Cen., The 68Dc 136
Beckenshaw Gdns.
SM7: Bans 87Gb 175
Beckers, The N16 35Wb 71
Becket Av. E6 41Qc 94
Becket Cl. CM13: Gt War 23Yd 58
IG5: Ilf 25Nc 54
SE25 72Wb 157
SW19 67Db 133
(off High Path)
Becket Fold HA1: Harr 29Ha 46
Becket Ho. *E16* 46Kc 93
(off Constable Av.)
SE1 2F 231
WC1 4G 217
Becket Rd. N18 21Yb 52
Beckets Pl. TN14: Otf 88Ld 183
Beckets Sports Cen. 58Ld 119
Becket St. SE1 3F 231 (48Tb 91)
Beckett Av. CR8: Kenley 87Rb 177
Beckett Chase SL3: L'ly 50B 82
Beckett Cl. DA17: Belv 48Bd 95
NW10 37Ua 68
SW16 61Mb 134
Beckett Ho. *E1* 43Yb 92
(off Jubilee St.)
SW9 54Nb 112
Beckett M. DA12: Grav'nd 3F 144
Beckett Rd. CR5: Coul 94Mb 196
Becketts Cl. BR6: Orp 76Vc 161
DA5: Bexl 60Ed 118
TW14: Felt 58X 107
Becketts Ho. IG1: Ilf 34Qc 74
Becketts Pl. KT1: Hamp W 67Ma 131
Becketts Wharf
KT1: Hamp W 67Ma 131
(off Lwr. Teddington Rd.)
Beckett Wlk. BR3: Beck 65Ac 136
Beckfoot NW1 2C 216
Beckford Cl. W14 49Bb 89
Beckford Dr. BR5: Orp 73Tc 160
Beckford Ho. N16 36Ub 71
Beckford Pl. SE17 7E 230 (50Sb 91)
Beckford Rd. CR0: C'don 72Vb 157
Beckham Ho. SE11 6J 229 (49Pb 90)
Beckhaven Ho. SE11 5A 230
Beck Ho. *N18* 22Xb 51
(off Upton Rd.)
Beckingham Metro *TW20: Egh* 64C 126
(off Station Rd.)
Beck La. BR3: Beck 69Zb 136
Beckley Cl. DA12: Grav'nd 1K 145
Beckley Ho. *E3* 42Bc 92
(off Hamlets Way)
Becklow Gdns. *W12* 47Wa 88
(off Becklow Rd.)
Becklow M. *W12* 47Wa 88
(off Becklow Rd.)
Becklow Rd. W12 47Va 88
Beckman Cl. TN14: Hals 87Ed 182
Beck River Pk. BR3: Beck 67Bc 136
Beck Rd. CR4: Mitc 72Hb 155
E8 39Xb 71
Becks Rd. DA14: Sidc 62Wc 139
Beck Theatre, The 44V 84
BECKTON 43Qc 94
BECKTON ALPS 42Pc 94
BECKTON PARK 44Pc 94
Beckton Retail Pk. E6 43Qc 94
Beckton Rd. E16 43Hc 93
Beckton Triangle Retail Pk. E6 42Rc 94
Beck Way BR3: Beck 69Bc 136
Beckway Rd. SW16 68Mb 134
Beckway St. SE17 6G 231 (49Ub 91)
(not continuous)
Beckwell Rd. SL1: Slou 7G 80
Beckwith Cl. EN2: Enf 11Rb 33
Beckwith Ho. *E2* 40Xb 71
(off Wadeson St.)
Beckwith Rd. SE24 57Tb 113
Beclands Rd. SW17 65Jb 134
Becmead Av. HA3: Kenton 29Ka 46
SW16 63Mb 134
Becondale Rd. SE19 64Ub 135
BECONTREE 35Zc 75
Becontree Av. RM8: Dag 35Xc 75
Becontree Heath Leisure Cen. 33Cd 76
Becquerel Ct. *SE10* 48Hc 93
(off West Parkside)
Bective Pl. SW15 56Bb 111
Bective Rd. E7 35Jc 73
SW15 56Bb 111
Becton Pl. DA8: Erith 53Dd 118
Bedale Rd. EN2: Enf 10Sb 19
RM3: Rom 22Qd 57
Bedale St. SE1 7F 225 (46Tb 91)
Bedale Wlk. DA2: Dart 60Rd 119
Beddalls Farm Ct. E6 43Mc 93
BEDDINGTON 77Nb 156
BEDDINGTON CORNER 73Jb 156
Beddington Cross CR0: Bedd 73Mb 156
Beddington Farm Rd.
CR0: Bedd, Wadd 73Nb 156
Beddington Gdns. SM5: Cars 79Jb 156
SM6: Wall 79Jb 156
Beddington Grn. BR5: St P 67Vc 139
Beddington Gro. SM6: Wall 78Mb 156
Beddington La.
CR0: Bedd, C'don 71Lb 156
Beddington Pk. 76Kb 156
Beddington Pk. Cotts.
SM6: Bedd 76Mb 156
Beddington Path BR5: St P 67Vc 139
Beddington Rd. BR5: St P 68Uc 138
IG3: Ilf 31Vc 75
Beddington Ter. CR0: C'don 73Pb 156
Beddington Trad. Est.
CR0: Bedd 74Nb 156
Beddlestead La.
CR6: W'ham 89Hc 179
Bede Cl. HA5: Pinn 25Z 45
Bedefield WC1 4G 217 (41Nb 90)
Bede Ho. *SE14* 53Bc 114
(off Clare Rd.)
Bedens Rd. DA14: Sidc 65Ad 139
Bede Rd. RM6: Chad H 30Yc 55
Bede Sq. *E3* 42Bc 92
(off Joseph St.)
Bedevere Rd. N9 20Wb 33
Bedfont Cl. CR4: Mitc 68Jb 134
TW14: Bedf 58S 106
Bedfont Ct. TW19: Stanw M 55J 105
Bedfont Ct. Est.
TW19: Stanw M 56K 105
Bedfont Grn. Cl. TW14: Bedf 60S 106
Bedfont Ind. Pk. TW15: Ashf 62S 128
Bedfont Ind. Pk. Nth.
TW15: Ashf 62S 128
Bedfont Lakes Country Pk. 61S 128
Bedfont Lakes Country Pk. Vis. Cen. 62R 128
Bedfont La. TW13: Felt 59U 106
TW14: Felt 59U 106
Bedfont Rd. TW13: Felt 60S 106
TW14: Bedf 60S 106
TW19: Stanw 58N 105
Bedfont Trad. Est.
TW14: Bedf 61T 128
Bedford Av. EN5: Barn 15Bb 31
HP6: L Chal 11A 24
SL1: Slou 4D 80
UB4: Yead 44X 85
WC1 1E 222 (43Mb 90)
Bedfordbury WC2 4F 223 (45Nb 90)
(not continuous)
Bedford Cl. GU21: Wok 7N 167
N10 24Jb 50
W4 51Ua 110
WD3: Chen 10D 10
Bedford Cnr. *W4* 49Ua 88
(off South Pde.)
Bedford Ct. *CR0: C'don* 74Tb 157
(off Tavistock Rd.)
WC2 5F 223 (45Nb 90)
Bedford Ct. Mans. WC1 1E 222
Bedford Cres. EN3: Enf W 7Ac 20
Bedford Dr. SL2: Farn C 6F 60
Bedford Gdns. RM12: Horn 33Ld 77
W8 46Cb 89
Bedford Gdns. Ho. *W8* 46Cb 89
(off Bedford Gdns.)
Bedford Hill SW12 60Kb 112
SW16 61Kb 134
Bedford Ho. CR0: C'don 73Rb 157
SW4 56Nb 112
(off Solon New Rd. Est.)
Bedford La. SL5: S'dale 1F 146
Bedford M. N2 27Gb 49
SE6 61Dc 136
BEDFORD PARK 48Ta 87
Bedford Pk. CR0: C'don 74Sb 157
Bedford Pk. Cnr. W4 49Ua 88
Bedford Pk. Mans. W4 49Ta 87
Bedford Pk. Rd. AL1: St A 2C 6
Bedford Pas. *SW6* 52Ab 110
(off Dawes Rd.)
W1 7C 216 (43Lb 90)
Bedford Pl. CR0: C'don 74Tb 157
WC1 7F 217 (43Nb 90)
Bedford Rd. AL1: St A 3C 6
BR6: Orp 75Xc 161
DA1: Dart 59Qd 119
DA11: Nflt 1B 144
DA15: Sidc 62Uc 138
E6 39Qc 74
E17 26Cc 52
E18 26Jc 53
HA1: Harr 30Ea 46
HA4: Ruis 35V 64
HA6: Nwood 20S 26
IG1: Ilf 34Rc 74
KT4: Wor Pk 75Ya 154
N2 27Gb 49
N8 30Mb 50
N9 17Xb 33
N15 28Ub 51
N22 26Nb 50
NW7 19Ua 30
RM17: Grays 50De 99
SW4 56Nb 112
TW2: Twick 62Fa 130
W4 48Ta 87
W13 45Ka 86
Bedford Row SE1 3E 230 (48Sb 91)
WC1 7J 217 (43Pb 90)
Bedford Sq. DA3: Lfield 69Zd 143
WC1 1E 222 (43Mb 90)
Bedford St. HP4: Berk 1A 2
WC2 4F 223 (45Nb 90)
WD24: Wat 11X 27
Bedford Ter. SM2: Sutt 79Eb 155
SW2 57Nb 112
Bedford Way
WC1 6E 216 (42Mb 90)
Bedgebury Ct. E17 26Ec 52
Bedgebury Gdns. SW19 61Ab 132
Bedgebury Rd. SE9 56Mc 115
Bedivere Rd. BR1: Brom 62Jc 137
Bedlam M. SE11 5K 229
Bedlow Way CR0: Bedd 77Pb 156
BEDMOND 9F 4
BEDMOND HILL 7E 4
Bedmond Ho. SW3 7D 226
Bedmond La. AL2: Pot C 8G 4
AL3: St A 4M 5
WD5: Bedm 8G 4
Bedmond Rd. HP3: Hem H 3C 4
WD5: Ab L, Bedm 1V 12
Bedonwell Rd.
DA7: Belv, Bex, Erith 51Bd 117
DA17: Belv 51Ad 117
SE2 51Ad 117
Bedser Cl. CR7: Thor H 69Sb 135
GU21: Wok 88C 168
SE11 51Pb 112
Bedser Dr. UB6: G'frd 36Fa 66
Bedster Gdns.
KT8: W Mole 68Da 129
Bedwardine Rd. SE19 66Ub 135
Bedwell Cl. CR0: C'don 71Tb 157
Bedwell Ct. *RM6: Chad H* 31Zc 75
(off Chapel La.)
Bedwell Gdns. UB3: Harl 50U 84
(not continuous)
Bedwell Hall AL9: Ess 1P 9
Bedwell Ho. SW9 54Qb 112
Bedwell Pk. 1P 9
Bedwell Rd. DA17: Belv 50Cd 96
N17 25Ub 51
Beeby Rd. E16 43Kc 93
Beech Av. BR8: Swan 70Hd 140
CM13: B'wood 20Be 41
CR2: Sande 83Tb 177
DA15: Sidc 59Wc 117
EN2: Crew H 7Qb 18
HA4: Ruis 32X 65
IG9: Buck H 19Kc 35
KT24: Eff 100Z 191
N20 18Gb 31
RM14: Upm 34Rd 77
TN16: Tats 91Mc 199
TW8: Bford 52Ka 108
W3 46Ua 88
WD7: R'lett 5Ja 14
Beech Cl. AL10: Hat 1C 8
IG10: Lough 13Rc 36
KT11: Cobh 84Ca 171
KT12: Hers 77Y 151
KT14: Byfl 84N 169
KT24: Eff 100Z 191
N9 16Wb 33
RM12: Horn 34Kd 77
SE8 51Cc 114
SM5: Cars 75Hb 155
SW15 59Wa 110
SW19 65Ya 132
TW15: Ashf 64T 128
TW16: Sun 68Z 129
TW19: Stanw 59M 105
UB7: W Dray 48Q 84
Beech Cl. Ct. KT11: Cobh 83Ba 171
Beech Copse BR1: Brom 67Pc 138
CR2: S Croy 78Ub 157
Beech Ct. *BR1: Brom* 67Hc 137
(off Blyth Rd.)
BR3: Beck 66Bc 136
DA1: Dart 58Qd 119
E17 27Fc 53
IG1: Ilf 34Qc 74
(off Riverdene Rd.)
KT6: Surb 73Ma 153
UB5: N'olt 39Aa 65
W9 43Cb 89
(off Elmfield Way)
Beech Cres. Ct. N5 35Rb 71
Beechcroft BR7: Chst 66Qc 138
KT21: Asht 91Pa 193
Beechcroft Av. CR8: Kenley 87Tb 177
DA7: Bex 53Fd 118
HA2: Harr 31Ca 65
KT3: N Mald 67Sa 131
NW11 31Bb 69
SS17: Linf 9J 101
WD3: Crox G 16S 26
Beechcroft Cl. BR6: Orp 77Tc 160
SL5: S'hill 10B 124
SW16 64Pb 134
TW5: Hest 52Aa 107
Beechcroft Ct. N12 21Db 49
NW11 31Bb 69
(off Beechcroft Av.)
Beechcroft Farm Industries
TN15: Ash 76Zd 165
Beechcroft Gdns. HA9: Wemb 34Pa 67
Beechcroft Ho. W5 43Na 87
Beechcroft Lodge SM2: Sutt 80Eb 155
Beechcroft Mnr. KT13: Weyb 76T 150
Beechcroft Pl. *HA6: Nwood* 22V 44
(off Eastbury Av.)
Beechcroft Rd. BR6: Orp 77Tc 160
E18 26Kc 53
KT9: Chess 76Pa 153
SW14 55Sa 109
SW17 61Gb 133
WD23: Bush 15Aa 27
Beechdale N21 19Pb 32
Beechdale Rd. SW2 58Pb 112
Beech Dell BR2: Kes 77Pc 160
Beechdene KT20: Tad 94Xa 194
SE15 53Xb 113
(off Carlton Gro.)
Beech Dr. GU23: Rip 96J 189
KT20: Kgswd 94Bb 195
N2 26Hb 49
RH2: Reig 6M 207
WD6: Bore 12Pa 29
Beechen Cliff Way
TW7: Isle 54Ha 108
Beechen Gro. HA5: Pinn 27Ba 45
WD17: Wat 13X 27
Beechen La. KT20: Kgswd 97Bb 195
Beechenlea La. BR8: Swan 70Jd 140
Beechen Pl. SE23 61Zb 136
Beechen Wood
WD3: Map C 22F 42
Beechers Cft. TN16: Big H 89Lc 179
Beeches, The AL2: Park 9B 6
BR8: Hext 66Hd 140
CM14: B'wood 20Xd 40
CR2: S Croy 78Tb 157
(off Blunt Rd.)
DA3: Lfield 68Ee 143
DA13: Sole S 10F 144
E12 38Nc 74
EN9: Walt A 1Lc 21
(within Woodbine Cl. Caravan Pk.)
KT22: Fet 96Ga 192
RM18: Tilb 4D 122
SL2: Slou 1D 80
SM7: Bans 88Cb 175
TW3: Houn 53Da 107
TW18: Staines 64J 127
WD3: Chor 15H 25
WD18: Wat 13X 27
(off Halsey Rd.)
Beeches Av. SM5: Cars 80Gb 155
Beeches Cl. KT20: Kgswd 95Cb 195
SE20 67Yb 136
Beeches Dr. KT23: Bookh 97Da 191
Beeches Rd. SL2: Farn C 6F 60
SM3: Sutt 74Ab 154
SW17 62Gb 133
Beeches Wlk. SM5: Cars 81Fb 175
Beeches Wood KT20: Kgswd 94Cb 195
Beechey Ho. *E1* 46Xb 91
(off Watts St.)
Beech Farm Rd. CR6: W'ham 92Ec 198
Beechfield KT13: Weyb 77R 150
SM7: Bans 85Db 175
WD4: K Lan 2P 11
Beechfield Cl. WD6: Bore 12Na 29
Beechfield Cotts. BR1: Brom 67Lc 137
Beechfield Ct. *CR2: S Croy* 77Sb 157
(off Bramley Hill)
WD17: Wat 11W 26
Beechfield Gdns.
RM7: Rush G 31Ed 76

Beechfield Rd.—Benbow Cl.

Beechfield Rd. BR1: Brom 68Lc 137
DA8: Erith 52Gd 118
HP1: Hem H 3K 3
N4 ....30Sb 51
SE6 ....60Bc 114
Beechfield Wlk. EN9: Walt A 7Fc 21
Beech Gdns. EC2 ....7D 218
GU21: Wok 87A 168
RM10: Dag 38Ed 76
W5 ....47Na 87
Beech Gro. CR3: Cat'm 98Ub 197
CR4: Mitc 71Mb 156
GU22: Wok 5P 187
GU24: Brkwd 2A 186
(not continuous)
IG6: Ilf 23Uc 54
KT3: N Mald 69Ta 131
KT15: Add 77K 149
KT18: Tatt C 89Xa 174
KT23: Bookh 99Ca 191
RM15: Avel 47Sd 98
Beech Hall KT16: Ott 80E 148
Beech Hall Cres. E4 ....24Fc 53
Beech Hall Rd. E4 ....24Ec 52
Beech Haven Ct. *DA1: Cray* *57Fd 118*
(off London Rd.)
Beech Hill EN4: Had W 10Fb 17
GU22: Wok 5P 187
Beech Hill Av. EN4: Had W 11Eb 31
Beech Hill Ct. HP4: Berk 1A 2
Beech Hill Gdns.
EN9: Walt A 9Kc 21
Beech Hill Rd. SL5: S'dale 2D 146
Beechhill Rd. SE9 ....57Qc 116
Beech Holt KT22: Lea 94La 192
Beech Ho. CM13: Hut 16Ee 41
CR0: New Ad 79Dc 158
KT15: Add *77M 149*
(off Victory Pk. Rd.)
SE16 ....*47Yb 92*
(off Ainsty Est.)
Beech Ho. Rd. CR0: C'don 76Tb 157
Beech Hurst Cl. BR7: Chst 67Sc 138
Beeching Ct. *W3* *48Sa 87*
(off Bollo Bri. Rd.)
Beechin Wood La. TN15: Plat 94Ee 205
Beechlands Cl. DA3: Hartl 71Ce 165
Beech La. IG9: Buck H 19Kc 35
Beech Lawns N12 ....22Fb 49
Beechlee SM6: Wall 82Lb 176
Beech Lodge TW18: Staines 64G 126
Beechmeads KT11: Cobh 85Z 171
Beechmont Av. GU25: Vir W 1P 147
Beechmont Cl. BR1: Brom 64Gc 137
Beechmore Gdns. SM3: Cheam 75Za 154
Beechmore Rd. SW11 ....53Hb 111
Beechmount Av. W7 ....43Fa 86
Beecholme N12 ....22Db 49
SM7: Bans 86Ab 174
Beecholme Av. CR4: Mitc 67Kb 134
Beecholme Est. E5 ....34Xb 71
Beecholme M. SW12 ....58Jb 112
Beechpark Way WD17: Wat 9U 12
Beech Pl. CM16: Epp 3Vc 23
Beech Rd. BR6: Chels 80Wc 161
DA1: Dart 60Md 119
KT13: Weyb 77T 150
KT17: Eps 87Va 174
N11 ....23Nb 50
RH1: Mers 98Lb 196
RH2: Reig 3J 207
SL3: L'ly 47A 82
SW16 ....68Nb 134
TN13: S'oaks 97Kd 203
TN16: Big H 91Kc 199
TW14: Bedf 59U 106
WD24: Wat 9W 12
Beechrow TW10: Ham 63Ma 131
Beech St. EC2 ....7D 218 (43Sb 91)
RM7: Rom 28Ed 56
Beech Ter. IG10: Lough 14Nc 36
Beechtree Av. TW20: Eng G 5M 125
Beech Tree Cl. HA7: Stan 22La 46
KT23: Fet 97Fa 192
N1 ....38Qb 70
Beech Tree Glade E4 ....18Hc 35
Beech Tree La. TW18: Lale 68K 127
Beechtree La. AL3: St A 4H 5
Beech Tree Pl. SM1: Sutt 78Db 155
Beechvale *GU22: Wok* *90B 168*
(off Hill Vw. Rd.)
Beechvale Cl. N12 ....22Gb 49
Beech Wlk. DA1: Cray 56Jd 118
GU20: W'sham 9B 146
KT17: Ewe 83Wa 174
N17 ....27Vb 51
NW7 ....23Ua 48
Beech Way CR2: Sels 85Zb 178
KT17: Eps 87Va 174
NW10 ....38Ta 67
TW2: Twick 62Ca 129
Beechway DA5: Bexl 58Zc 117
Beech Waye SL9: Ger X 31B 62
Beechwood CR3: Cat'm 96Wb 197
Beechwood Av. AL1: St A 1F 6
BR6: Chels 78Uc 160
CR5: Coul 87Kb 176
CR7: Thor H 70Rb 135
EN6: Pot B 5Db 17
HA2: Harr 34Da 65
HA4: Ruis 33V 64
KT13: Weyb 77U 150
KT20: Kgswd 93Cb 195
N3 ....27Bb 49
TW9: Kew 53Qa 109
TW16: Sun 65W 128
TW18: Staines 65K 127
UB3: Hayes 45T 84
UB6: G'frd 41Da 85
UB8: Hil 44Q 84
WD3: Chor 14D 24
Beechwood Cen., The
BR2: Brom *74Pc 160*
(off Lwr. Gravel Rd.)
Beechwood Circ. HA2: Harr 34Da 65
Beechwood Cl. GU21: Knap 9J 167
KT6: Surb 73La 152
KT13: Weyb 77U 150
N2 ....27Hb 49
NW7 ....22Ua 48
Beechwood Cotts. WD3: Chor 16E 24
Beechwood Ct.
KT12: Walt T *76W 150*
(off Station Av.)
SM5: Cars 77Hb 155
TW16: Sun 65W 128
W4 ....51Ta 109
Beechwood Cres. DA7: Bex 55Zc 117
Beechwood Dr. BR2: Kes 77Mc 159
IG8: Wfd G 22Hc 53
KT11: Cobh 83Ca 171
Beechwood Gdns. CR3: Cat'm 94Wb 197
HA2: Harr 34Da 65
IG5: Ilf 29Pc 54
NW10 ....41Pa 87
RM13: Rain 43Kd 97
SL1: Slou 7J 81
Beechwood Gro. KT6: Surb 73La 152
W3 ....45Ua 88
Beechwood Hall KT20: Kgswd 95Eb 195
N3 ....27Bb 49
Beechwood Ho. *E2* *40Wb 71*
(off Teale St.)
Beechwood La. CR6: W'ham 91Zb 198
Beechwood Mnr. KT13: Weyb 77U 150
Beechwood M. N9 ....19Wb 33
Beechwood Pk. E18 ....27Jc 53
HP3: Hem H 5H 3
KT22: Lea 94La 192
WD3: Chor 14H 25
Beechwood Ri. BR7: Chst 63Rc 138
WD24: Wat 8X 13
Beechwood Rd. CR2: Sande 82Ub 177
CR3: Cat'm 94Wb 197
E8 ....37Vb 71
GU21: Knap 9J 167
GU25: Vir W 3L 147
N8 ....28Mb 50
SL2: Slou 3H 81
Beechwoods Ct. SE19 ....64Vb 135
Beechworth NW6 ....38Ab 68
Beechworth Cl. NW3 ....33Cb 69
Beechy Lees Rd. TN14: Otf 89Md 183
Beecot La. KT12: Walt T 75Y 151
Beecroft La. SE4 ....57Ac 114
Beecroft M. SE4 ....57Ac 114
Beecroft Rd. SE4 ....57Ac 114
Beehive Cl. E8 ....38Vb 71
UB10: Uxb 38P 63
WD6: E'tree 16Ma 29
Beehive Ct. HA8: Edg 22Ra 47
IG1: Ilf 30Pc 54
RM3: Hrld W 24Pd 57
Beehive La. IG1: Ilf 29Pc 54
IG4: Ilf 29Pc 54
Beehive Pas. EC3 ....3H 225
Beehive Pl. SW9 ....55Qb 112
Beehive Rd. TW18: Staines 64H 127
Beehive Way RH2: Reig 10K 207
Beeken Dene BR6: Farnb 77Sc 160
Beeleigh Rd. SM4: Mord 70Db 133
Beemans Row SW18 ....61Eb 133
Beesfield La. DA4: Farni 73Qd 163
Beesons Yd. WD3: Rick 18M 25
Beeston Cl. E8 ....36Wb 71
WD19: Wat 21Z 45
Beeston Ct. *DA2: Dart* *58Rd 119*
(off Hardwick Cres.)
Beeston Ho. SE1 ....4F 231
Beeston Pl. SW1 ....4A 228 (48Kb 90)
Beeston Rd. EN4: E Barn 16Fb 31
Beeston Way TW14: Felt 58Y 107
Beethoven Rd. WD6: E'tree 16La 28
Beethoven St. W10 ....41Ab 88
Beeton Cl. HA5: Hat E 24Ca 45
Beeton Way SE27 ....63Tb 135
Begbie Rd. SE3 ....53Lc 115
BEGGAR'S BUSH 10D 124
Beggars Bush La. WD18: Wat 15T 26
BEGGAR'S HILL **79Va 154**
Beggar's Hill KT17: Ewe 80Va 154
Beggars Hollow EN2: Enf 9Tb 19
Beggars La. GU24: Chob 3G 166
TN16: Westrm 97Tc 200
Beggars Roost La. SM1: Sutt 79Cb 155
Begonia Cl. E6 ....43Pc 94
Begonia Pl. TW12: Hamp 65Ca 129
Begonia Wlk. W12 ....44Va 88
Beira St. SW12 ....59Kb 112
Bejun Ct. EN5: New Bar 14Eb 31
Beken Ct. WD25: Wat 7Y 13
Bekesbourne St. E14 ....44Ac 92
Bekesbourne Twr. *BR5: Orp* *74Zc 161*
(off Wichling Cl.)
Belcroft Cl. BR1: Brom 66Hc 137
Beldam Bri. Rd.
GU24: Chob, W End 5E 166
Beldam Haw TN14: Hals 84Cd 182
Beldam Way TW3: Houn 55Ba 107
Beldanes Lodge NW10 ....38Wa 68
Beldham Gdns. KT8: W Mole 68Da 129
Belfairs Dr. RM6: Chad H 31Yc 75
Belfairs Grn. WD19: Wat 22Z 45
Belfast Av. SL1: Slou 4G 80
Belfast Rd. N16 ....33Vb 71
SE25 ....70Xb 135
Belfield Rd. KT19: Ewe 81Ta 173
Belfont Wlk. N7 ....35Nb 70
(not continuous)
Belford Gro. SE18 ....49Qc 94
Belford Ho. E8 ....39Vb 71
Belford Rd. WD6: Bore 10Pa 15
Belfort Rd. SE15 ....54Yb 114
Belfry, The RH1: Redh 5P 207
WD24: Wat 11Y 27
Belfry Av. UB9: Hare 24J 43
Belfry Cl. BR1: Brom 70Rc 138
SE16 ....50Xb 91
Belfry La. WD3: Rick 18L 25
Belgrade Rd. N16 ....35Ub 71
TW12: Hamp 67Da 129
Belgrave Av. RM2: Rom 27Ld 57
WD18: Wat 15V 26
Belgrave Cl. BR5: St M Cry 70Yc 139
KT12: Hers 77X 151
N14 ....15Lb 32
NW7 ....22Ta 47
W3 ....47Ra 87
Belgrave Ct. *E2* *40Xb 71*
(off Temple St.)
E13 ....42Lc 93
E14 ....*45Bc 92*
(off Westferry Cir.)
SW8 ....*52Lb 112*
(off Ascalon St.)
W4 ....50Sa 87
Belgrave Cres. TW16: Sun 67X 129
Belgrave Dr. WD4: K Lan 10C 4
Belgrave Gdns. HA7: Stan 22La 46
N14 ....15Mb 32
NW8 ....39Db 69
Belgrave Hgts. E11 ....32Jc 73
Belgrave Ho. SW9 ....52Qb 112
Belgrave Mnr. GU22: Wok 91A 188
Belgrave Mans. *NW8* *39Db 69*
(off Belgrave Gdns.)
Belgrave M. UB8: Cowl 42M 83
Belgrave M. Nth.
SW1 ....3H 227 (47Jb 90)
Belgrave M. Sth. SW1 ....3J 227 (48Jb 90)
Belgrave M. W.
SW1 ....3H 227 (48Jb 90)
Belgrave Pde. *SL1: Slou* *5J 81*
(off Stoke Poges La.)
Belgrave Pl. SL1: Slou 7L 81
SW1 ....3J 227 (48Jb 90)
Belgrave Rd. CR4: Mitc 69Fb 133
E10 ....32Ec 72
E11 ....33Jc 73
E13 ....42Lc 93
E17 ....29Cc 52
IG1: Ilf 32Pc 74
SE25 ....70Vb 135
SL1: Slou 5J 81
SW1 ....5A 228 (49Kb 90)
SW13 ....52Va 110
TW4: Houn 55Ba 107
TW16: Sun 67X 129
Belgrave Sq. SW1 ....3H 227 (48Jb 90)
Belgrave St. E1 ....43Zb 92
Belgrave Ter. IG8: Wfd G 20Jc 35
Belgrave Wlk. CR4: Mitc 69Fb 133
Belgrave Yd. SW1 ....4K 227
BELGRAVIA 4J 227 (48Jb 90)
Belgravia Cl. EN5: Barn 13Bb 31
Belgravia Ct. SW1 ....4K 227
Belgravia Gdns. BR1: Brom 65Gc 137
Belgravia Ho. SW1 ....3H 227
SW4 ....58Mb 112
Belgravia M. KT1: King T 70Ma 131
Belgravia Workshops *N19* *33Nb 70*
(off Marlborough Rd.)
Belgrove St. WC1 ....3G 217 (41Nb 90)
Belham Rd. WD4: K Lan 10P 3
Belham Wlk. SE5 ....53Tb 113
Belhaven Ct. WD6: Bore 11Pa 29
Belhus Av. RM15: Avel 45Td 98
Belhus Pk. 44Td 98
Belhus Pk. Golf Course 44Ud 98
Belhus Vw. RM15: Avel 46Ud 98
Belhus Woods Country Pk.
Romford Road 41Td 98
Sandy Lane 44Rd 97
Belhus Woods Country Pk. Vis. Cen.
....41Td 98
Belinda Rd. SW9 ....55Rb 113
Belitha Vs. N1 ....38Pb 70
BELL, THE **27Cc 52**
Bella Best Ho. *SW1* *7A 228*
(off Westmoreland Ter.)
Bellamy Cl. E14 ....47Cc 92
HA8: Edg 19Sa 29
UB10: Ick 34Q 64
W14 ....50Bb 89
WD17: Wat 11W 26
Bellamy Ct. HA7: Stan 25Ka 46
Bellamy Dr. HA7: Stan 25Ka 46
Bellamy Ho. SW17 ....63Fb 133
TW5: Hest 51Ca 107
Bellamy Rd. E4 ....23Dc 52
EN2: Enf 12Tb 33
EN8: Chesh 1Ac 20
Bellamy's Ct. *SE16* *46Zb 92*
(off Abbotshade Rd.)
Bellamy St. SW12 ....59Kb 112
Bel La. TW13: Hanw 62Aa 129
Bellarmine Cl. SE28 ....46Vc 95
Bellasis Av. SW2 ....61Nb 134
Bell Av. RM3: Rom 25Kd 57
UB7: W Dray 49P 83
BELL BAR 6J 9
Bell Bri. Rd. KT16: Chert 74H 149
Bell Brook Ri. N11 ....21Kb 50
Bellchambers Cl. AL2: Lon C 8G 6
Bell Cl. DA9: Ghithe 57Vd 120
HA4: Ruis 34V 64
HA5: Pinn 26Y 45
SL2: Slou 3M 81
WD5: Bedm 9F 4
Bellclose Rd. UB7: W Dray 47N 83
BELL COMMON 4Tc 22
Bell Comn. CM16: Epp 4Uc 22
Bell Cnr. KT16: Chert 73H 149
RM14: Upm 33Sd 78
Bell Ct. NW4 ....28Ya 48
Bell Cres. CR5: Coul 93Kb 196
Bell Dr. SW18 ....59Ab 110
Bellefield SL1: Slou 7D 80
Bellefield Rd. BR5: St M Cry 71Xc 161
Bellefields Rd. SW9 ....55Pb 112
Bellegrove Cl. DA16: Well 54Vc 117
Bellegrove Pde. DA16: Well 55Vc 117
Bellegrove Rd. DA16: Well 54Tc 116
Bellenden Rd. SE15 ....53Vb 113
Bellenden Rd. Retail Pk. SE15 ....53Wb 113
Bellestaines Pleasaunce E4 ....19Cc 34
Belleville Ho. *SE10* *52Dc 114*
(off Norman Rd.)
Belleville Rd. SW11 ....57Gb 111
Belle Vue UB6: G'frd 39Fa 66
Belle Vue Cl. TW18: Staines 67J 127
Bellevue Ct. TW3: Houn 56Ca 107
Belle Vue Est. NW4 ....28Za 48
Belle Vue La. WD23: B Hea 18Fa 28
Bellevue M. N11 ....22Jb 50
Bellevue Pde. SW17 ....60Hb 111
Belle Vue Pk. CR7: Thor H 69Sb 135
Bellevue Pl. E1 ....42Yb 92
Belle Vue Rd. BR6: Downe 82Qc 180
E17 ....26Fc 53
NW4 ....28Ya 48
RM5: Col R 23Ed 56
Bellevue Rd. DA6: Bex 57Bd 117
KT1: King T 69Na 131
(not continuous)
N11 ....21Jb 50
RM11: Horn 32Pd 77
SW13 ....54Wa 110
SW17 ....60Gb 111
W13 ....42Ka 86
Bellevue Ter. UB9: Hare 24J 43
Bellew St. SW17 ....62Eb 133
Bell Farm Av. RM10: Dag 34Ed 76
Bell Farm Cotts. CM16: Epp 4Uc 22
Bellfield CR0: Sels 81Ac 178
Bellfield Av. HA3: Hrw W 23Fa 46
Bellfield Cl. SE3 ....52Kc 115
Bellflower Cl. E6 ....43Nc 94
Bellflower Path RM3: Rom 24Ld 57
Bell Gdns. BR5: St M Cry 71Yc 161
E10 ....*32Cc 72*
(off Church Rd.)
Bellgate M. NW5 ....35Kb 70
BELL GREEN 63Bc 136
Bell Grn. HP3: Bov 9D 2
SE26 ....63Bc 136
Bell Grn. La. SE26 ....64Bc 136
Bell Grn. Retail Pk. SE6 ....62Bc 136
Bell Grn. Trade City SE6 ....62Bc 136
Bellhaven E15 ....37Fc 73
Bell Hill CR0: C'don 75Sb 157
Bell Ho. HA9: Wemb 34Ma 67
RM17: Grays 51Be 121
SE10 ....*51Ec 114*
(off Haddo St.)
Bellhouse Cotts.
UB3: Hayes 45U 84
Bellhouse La. CM14: Pil H 15Ud 40
Bell Ho. Rd. RM7: Rush G 32Ed 76
Bellina M. NW5 ....35Kb 70
Bell Ind. Est. W4 ....49Sa 87
Bellingdon WD19: Wat 20Aa 27
BELLINGHAM 62Dc 136
Bellingham *N17* *24Xb 51*
(off Park La.)
Bellingham Ct. IG11: Bark 41Xc 95
Bellingham Dr. RH2: Reig 6H 207
Bellingham Grn. SE6 ....62Cc 136
Bellingham Leisure & Lifestyle Cen.
....62Dc 136
Bellingham Rd. SE6 ....62Dc 136
Bellingham Trad. Est.
SE6 ....62Dc 136
Bell Inn Yd. EC3 ....3G 225 (44Tb 91)
Bell La. AL2: Lon C 1Na 15
AL9: Brk P 6J 9
E1 ....1K 225 (43Vb 91)
E16 ....46Hc 93
EN3: Enf H, Enf W 10Zb 20
HA9: Wemb 33Ma 67
KT22: Fet 95Fa 192
NW4 ....28Za 48
SL4: Eton W 9D 80
TW1: Twick 60Ja 108
TW14: Bedf 59T 106
WD5: Bedm 9F 4
Bell La. Cl. KT22: Fet 95Fa 192
Bellmaker Ct. E3 ....43Cc 92
Bellman Av. DA12: Grav'nd 10G 122
Bellman Cl. SL1: Slou 7M 81
Bellmarsh Rd. KT15: Add 77K 149
Bell Mdw. RH9: G'stone 4P 209
SE19 ....64Ub 135
Bell Moor NW3 ....34Eb 69
Bellmount Wood Av. WD17: Wat 11U 26
Bello Cl. SE24 ....59Rb 113
Bellot Gdns. *SE10* *50Gc 93*
(off Bellot St.)
Bellot St. SE10 ....50Gc 93
Bellows La. TN15: Bor G 92Ae 205
Bell Pde. BR4: W W'ck 75Ec 158
SL4: Wind 4D 102
Bellreeves Cl. SS17: Stan H 1L 101
Bellring Cl. DA17: Belv 51Cd 118
Bell Rd. EN1: Enf 11Tb 33
KT8: E Mos 71Fa 152
TW3: Houn 55Da 107
Bell Rdbt., The AL2: Lon C 9L 7
Bells All. SW6 ....54Cb 111
Bellsfield Ct. *SL4: Eton W* *9D 80*
(off Bell La.)
Bells Hill EN5: Barn 15Za 30
SL2: Stoke P 9L 61
Bells Hill Grn. SL2: Stoke P 8L 61
Bellsize Ct. NW3 ....36Fb 69
Bells La. SL3: Hort 55D 104
Bell St. NW1 ....7D 214 (43Gb 89)
RH2: Reig 6J 207
SE18 ....53Nc 116
Bellswood La. SL0: Iver 43D 82
Bell Ter. DA1: Dart 55Pd 119
Belltrees Gro. SW16 ....64Pb 134
Bell Vw. AL4: St A 2H 7
SL4: Wind 5D 102
Bell Vw. Cl. SL4: Wind 4D 102
Bell Vw. Mnr. HA4: Ruis 31T 64
Bell Vue Pl. SL1: Slou 8K 81
Bell Water Ga. SE18 ....48Qc 94
Bellway Ho. RH1: Mers 100Lb 196
Bell Weir Cl. TW19: Staines 61D 126
Bell Wharf La. EC4 ....5E 224 (45Sb 91)
Bellwood Rd. SE15 ....56Zb 114
Bell Yd. WC2 ....3K 223 (44Qb 90)
Bell Yd. M. SE1 ....2J 231 (47Ub 91)
Belmarsh Rd. SE28 ....47Uc 94
BELMONT
HA3 ....26Ja 46
SM2 ....82Cb 175
Belmont KT13: Weyb 79S 150
SL2: Slou 3E 80
Belmont Av. DA16: Well 55Uc 116
EN4: Cockf 15Hb 31
HA0: Wemb 39Pa 67
KT3: N Mald 71Wa 154
N9 ....18Wb 33
N13 ....22Pb 50
N17 ....27Sb 51
RM14: Upm 33Pd 77
UB2: S'hall 48Aa 85
Belmont Circ. HA3: Kenton 25Ka 46
Belmont Cl. E4 ....22Fc 53
EN4: Cockf 14Hb 31
IG8: Wfd G 21Kc 53
N20 ....18Db 31
SW4 ....55Lb 112
UB8: Uxb 37M 63
Belmont Cotts. *SL3: Coln* *52E 104*
(off High St.)
Belmont Ct. AL1: St A 3B 6
N5 ....35Sb 71
NW11 ....29Bb 49
Belmont Gro. SE13 ....55Fc 115
W4 ....49Ta 87
Belmont Hall Ct. SE13 ....55Fc 115
Belmont Hill AL1: St A 3B 6
SE13 ....55Fc 115
Belmont La. BR7: Chst 64Sc 138
HA7: Stan 25La 46
Belmont Lodge
HA3: Hrw W 24Fa 46
Belmont M. SW19 ....61Za 132
Belmont Pde. BR7: Chst 64Sc 138
NW11 ....29Bb 49
Belmont Pk. SE13 ....56Fc 115
Belmont Pk. Cl. SE13 ....56Gc 115
Belmont Pk. Rd. E10 ....30Dc 52
Belmont Ri. SM2: Sutt 79Bb 155
Belmont Rd. BR3: Beck 68Ac 136
BR7: Chst 64Rc 138
DA8: Erith 52Cd 118
HA3: W'stone 27Ha 46
HP3: Hem H 5N 3
Belmont Rd. IG1: Ilf 34Sc 74
KT22: Lea 94Ja 192
N15 ....28Sb 51
N17 ....28Sb 51
RH2: Reig 7L 207
RM12: Horn 34Md 77
RM17: Grays 51Be 121
SE25 ....71Xb 157
SM2: Sutt 82Cb 175
SM6: Wall 78Kb 156
SW4 ....55Lb 112
TW2: Twick 61Fa 130
UB8: Uxb 38M 63
W4 ....49Ta 87
WD23: Bush 15Aa 27
Belmont St. NW1 ....38Jb 70
Belmont Ter. W4 ....49Ta 87
Belmor WD6: E'tree 16Qa 29
Belmore Av. GU22: Pyr 88F 168
UB4: Hayes 44W 84
Belmore Ho. N7 ....36Mb 70
Belmore La. N7 ....36Mb 70
Belmore St. SW8 ....53Mb 112
Beloe Cl. SW15 ....56Wa 110
Belsham St. E9 ....37Yb 72
BELSIZE 4H 11
Belsize Av. N13 ....23Pb 50
NW3 ....37Fb 69
W13 ....48Ka 86
Belsize Cl. HP3: Hem H 3A 4
Belsize Cotts. WD3: Chfd 5G 10
Belsize Ct. SM1: Sutt 77Db 155
Belsize Ct. Garages *NW3* *36Fb 69*
(off Belsize La.)
Belsize Cres. NW3 ....36Fb 69
Belsize Gdns. SM1: Sutt 77Db 155
Belsize Grange KT16: Chert 73L 149
Belsize Gro. NW3 ....37Gb 69
Belsize La. NW3 ....37Fb 69
Belsize M. NW3 ....37Fb 69
Belsize Pk. NW3 ....37Fb 69
Belsize Pk. Gdns. NW3 ....37Fb 69
Belsize Pk. M. NW3 ....37Fb 69
Belsize Pl. NW3 ....36Fb 69
Belsize Rd. HA3: Hrw W 24Fa 46
HP3: Hem H 3A 4
NW6 ....39Db 69
Belsize Sq. NW3 ....37Fb 69
Belsize Ter. NW3 ....37Fb 69
Belson Rd. SE18 ....49Pc 94
Belswains Grn. HP3: Hem H 5N 3
Belswains La. HP3: Hem H 5N 3
Beltana Dr. DA12: Grav'nd 3G 144
Beltane Dr. SW19 ....62Za 132
Belthorn Cres. SW12 ....59Lb 112
Beltinge Rd. RM3: Hrld W 26Pd 57
Belton Rd. DA14: Sidc 63Wc 139
E7 ....38Kc 73
E11 ....35Gc 73
N17 ....27Ub 51
NW2 ....37Wa 68
Belton Way E3 ....43Cc 92
Beltran Rd. SW6 ....54Db 111
Beltwood Rd. DA17: Belv 49Ed 96
BELVEDERE 49Cd 96
Belvedere, The *SW10* *53Eb 111*
(off Chelsea Harbour)
Belvedere Av. IG5: Ilf 26Rc 54
SW19 ....64Ab 132
Belvedere Bldgs. SE1 ....2C 230 (47Rb 91)
Belvedere Bus. Pk. DA17: Belv 47Dd 96
Belvedere Cl. DA12: Grav'nd 10E 122
KT10: Esh 78Da 151
KT13: Weyb 78Q 150
TW11: Tedd 64Ga 130
Belvedere Ct. DA17: Belv 48Bd 95
N1 ....*39Ub 71*
(off De Beauvoir Cres.)
N2 ....29Fb 49
NW2 ....*37Za 68*
(off Willesden La.)
RH1: Redh 2A 208
SW15 ....56Ya 110
WD19: Wat 16Aa 27
Belvedere Dr. SW19 ....64Ab 132
Belvedere Gdns. AL2: Chis G 9N 5
KT8: W Mole 71Ba 151
Belvedere Grange SL5: S'dale 4E 146
Belvedere Gro. SW19 ....64Ab 132
Belvedere Ho. KT13: Weyb 78R 150
TW13: Felt *60W 106*
(off Lemon Gro.)
Belvedere Ind. Est. DA17: Belv 46Ed 96
Belvedere Link Bus. Pk.
DA8: Erith 48Ed 96
Belvedere Mans. SL1: Slou 7H 81
Belvedere M. SE3 ....52Kc 115
SE15 ....55Yb 114
Belvedere Pl. SE1 ....2C 230 (47Rb 91)
SW2 ....56Pb 112
Belvedere Rd.
CM14: B'wood 20Vd 40
DA7: Bex 55Bd 117
E10 ....32Ac 72
SE1 ....2H 229 (47Pb 90)
SE19 ....66Vb 135
TN16: Big H 90Pc 180
W7 ....48Ha 86
Belvederes, The RH2: Reig 8K 207
Belvedere Sq. SW19 ....64Ab 132
Belvedere Way HA3: Kenton 30Na 47
Belvoir Cl. SE9 ....62Nc 138
Belvoir Ho. SW1 ....6C 228 (49Lb 90)
Belvoir Rd. SE22 ....59Wb 113
Belvue Bus. Cen. UB5: N'olt 38Da 65
Belvue Cl. UB5: N'olt 38Ca 65
Belvue Rd. UB5: N'olt 38Ca 65
Belz Dr. N15 ....28Ub 51
Belz Ter. E5 ....31Wb 71
Bembridge Cl. NW6 ....38Ab 68
Bembridge Ct. SL1: Slou 7K 81
Bembridge Gdns. HA4: Ruis 33T 64
Bembridge Ho. *KT2: King T* *68Qa 131*
(off Coombe Rd.)
SE8 ....*49Bc 92*
(off Longshore)
SW18 ....*58Db 111*
(off Iron Mill Rd.)
Bembridge Pl. WD25: Wat 5W 12
Bemersyde Point *E13* *41Kc 93*
(off Dongola Rd. W.)
Bemerton Est. N1 ....38Nb 70
Bemerton St. N1 ....39Pb 70
Bemish Rd. SW15 ....55Za 110
Bempton Dr. HA4: Ruis 33X 65
Bemsted Rd. E17 ....27Bc 52
Benares Rd. SE18 ....49Vc 95
Benbow Cl. AL1: St A 4F 6

Benbow Ct.—Besson St.

Benbow Ct. W6 48Ya 88
(off Benbow Rd.)
Benbow Ho. SE8 51Cc 114
(off Benbow St.)
Benbow M. E3 41Bc 92
(off Tredegar Sq.)
Benbow Moorings UB8: Cowl 43L 83
Benbow Rd. W6 48Xa 88
Benbow St. SE8 51Cc 114
Benbow Waye UB8: Cowl 43L 83
Benbury Cl. BR1: Brom 64Ec 136
Bence, The TW20: Thorpe 69D 126
Bence Ho. SE8 49Ac 92
(off Rainsborough Av.)
Bench, The TW10: Ham 62La 130
Bench Fld. CR2: S Croy 79Vb 157
Benchleys Rd. HP1: Hem H 4H 3
Bencombe Rd. CR8: Purl 86Qb 176
Bencroft Rd. HP2: Hem H 2N 3
SW16 66Lb 134
Bencurtis Pk. BR4: W W'ck 76Fc 159
Bendall Ho. NW1 7E 214
Bendall M. NW1 7E 214
Bendemeer Rd. SW15 55Za 110
Benden Ho. SE13 57Ec 114
(off Monument Gdns.)
Bendish Point SE28 47Sc 94
Bendish Rd. E6 38Nc 74
Bendmore Av. SE2 50Wc 95
Bendon Valley SW18 59Db 111
Bendysh Rd. WD23: Bush 13Aa 27
Benedict Cl. BR6: Orp 76Uc 160
DA17: Belv 48Ad 95
Benedict Ct. RM6: Chad H 30Bd 55
Benedict Dr. TW14: Bedf 59T 106
Benedict Ho. AL3: St A 1B 6
(off Adelaide St.)
Benedictine Pl. AL1: St A 2B 6
(off London Rd.)
Benedict Rd. CR4: Mitc 69Fb 133
SW9 55Pb 112
Benedicts Wharf IG11: Bark 39Rc 74
Benedict Way N2 27Eb 49
Benedict Wharf CR4: Mitc 69Gb 133
Benenden Grn. BR2: Brom 71Jc 159
Benenden Ho. SE17 7J 231
Benen-Stock Rd. TW19: Stanw M 57J 105
Benets Rd. RM11: Horn 32Qd 77
Benett Gdns. SW16 68Nb 134
Ben Ezra Ct. SE17 6E 230
Benfleet Cl. KT11: Cobh 84Aa 171
SM1: Sutt 76Eb 155
Benfleet Ct. E8 39Vb 71
Benfleet Way N11 19Jb 32
Bengal Ct. EC3 3G 225
Bengal Rd. IG1: Ilf 35Rc 74
Bengarth Dr. HA3: Hrw W 26Fa 46
Bengarth Rd. UB5: N'olt 39Aa 65
Bengeo Gdns. RM6: Chad H 30Yc 55
Bengeworth Rd. HA1: Harr 33Ja 66
SE5 55Sb 113
Ben Hale Cl. HA7: Stan 22Ka 46
Benham Cl. CR5: Coul 90Rb 177
KT9: Chess 79La 152
SW11 55Fb 111
Benham Gdns. TW4: Houn 57Ba 107
Benham Ho. SW10 52Db 111
(off Coleridge Gdns.)
Benham Rd. W7 43Ga 86
Benham's Pl. NW3 35Eb 69
Benhill Av. SM1: Sutt 77Db 155
(not continuous)
Benhill Rd. SE5 52Tb 113
SM1: Sutt 76Eb 155
Benhill Wood Rd. SM1: Sutt 76Eb 155
BENHILTON 75Db 155
Benhilton Gdns. SM1: Sutt 76Db 155
Benhurst Av. RM12: Horn 35Kd 77
Benhurst Cl. CR2: Sels 82Zb 178
Benhurst Ct. SW16 64Qb 134
Benhurst Gdns. CR2: Sels 82Yb 178
Benhurst La. SW16 64Qb 134
Benina Cl. IG2: Ilf 29Vc 55
Beningfield Dr. AL2: Lon C 9E 6
Benin Ho. WC1 1H 223
Benin St. SE13 59Fc 115
Benison Ct. SL1: Slou 8K 81
Benjafield Cl. N18 21Xb 51
Benjamin Cl. E8 39Wb 71
RM11: Horn 30Jd 56
Benjamin Ct. DA17: Belv 51Bd 117
TW15: Ashf 66S 128
Benjamin Franklin House 6F 223
(off Craven St.)
Benjamin La. SL3: Wex 2M 81
Benjamin M. SW12 59Lb 112
Benjamin St. EC1 7B 218 (43Rb 91)
Benjamin Truman Cl. E1 42Wb 91
Ben Jonson Ct. N1 1J 219 (40Ub 71)
Ben Jonson Ho. EC2 7E 218
Ben Jonson Pl. EC2 7E 218
Ben Jonson Rd. E1 43Zb 92
Benkart M. SW15 58Wa 110
Benledi Rd. E14 44Fc 93
Benlow Works UB3: Hayes 47V 84
(off Silverdale Rd.)
Ben More SL9: Ger X 29B 42
Benn Cl. RH8: Oxt 6L 211
Benneck Ho. WD18: Wat 16U 26
Bennelong Cl. W12 45Xa 88
Benner La. GU24: W End 4D 166
Bennerley Rd. SW11 57Gb 111
Bennet Cl. KT1: Hamp W 67La 130
Bennet M. N19 34Mb 70
(off Wedmore St.)
Bennets Courtyard SW19 67Eb 133
Bennets Fld. Rd. UB11: Stock P 46R 84
Bennet's Hill EC4 4C 224 (45Sb 91)
Bennets Lodge EN2: Enf 13Rb 33
Bennet St. SW1 6B 222 (46Lb 90)
Bennett Cl. DA16: Well 54Wc 117
HA6: Nwood 24V 44
KT11: Cobh 85W 170
TW4: Houn 57Aa 107
Bennett Ct. N7 34Pb 70
Bennett Gro. SE13 53Dc 114
Bennett Ho. DA11: Nflt 2B 144
SW1 5E 228
Bennett Pk. SE3 55Hc 115
Bennett Pl. DA1: Dart 55Pd 119
Bennett Rd. E13 42Lc 93
N16 35Ub 71
RM6: Chad H 30Ad 55
SW9 54Qb 112
Bennetts Av. CR0: C'don 75Ac 158
TN15: W King 84Yd 184
UB6: G'frd 39Ga 66
Bennett's Castle La. RM8: Dag 33Yc 75
Bennetts Cl. AL4: Col H 5P 7
CR4: Mitc 67Kb 134
N17 23Vb 51
SL1: Slou 6E 80
Bennetts Copse BR7: Chst 65Nc 138
BENNETTS END 4A 4
Bennetts End Cl. HP3: Hem H 4P 3
Bennetts End Rd. HP3: Hem H 3P 3
Bennetts Farm Pl. KT23: Bookh 97Ba 191
Bennetts Fld. WD23: Bush 14Aa 27
Bennetts Ga. HP3: Hem H 5A 4
Bennett St. W4 51Ua 110
Bennetts Way CR0: C'don 75Ac 158
Bennett's Yd. SW1 4E 228 (48Mb 90)
UB8: Uxb 38L 63
Bennett Way DA2: Daren 63Td 142
GU4: W Cla 100J 189
Benning Cl. SL4: Wind 5B 102
Benning Dr. RM8: Dag 32Ad 75
Benningholme Rd. HA8: Edg 23Ua 48
Bennington Dr. WD6: Bore 11Pa 29
Bennington Rd. IG8: Wfd G 24Gc 53
N17 25Ub 51
Bennions Cl. RM12: Horn 37Md 77
Bennison Dr. RM3: Hrld W 26Md 57
Benn's All. TW12: Hamp 68Da 129
Benn St. E9 37Ac 72
Benns Wlk. TW9: Rich 56Na 109
(off Michelsdale Dr.)
Benrek Cl. IG6: Ilf 25Sc 54
Bensbury Cl. SW15 59Xa 110
Bensham Cl. CR7: Thor H 70Sb 135
Bensham Gro. CR7: Thor H 68Sb 135
Bensham La. CR0: C'don 73Rb 157
CR7: Thor H 71Rb 157
Bensham Mnr. Rd. CR7: Thor H 70Sb 135
Bensham Mnr. Rd. Pas.
CR7: Thor H 70Sb 135
Benskin Rd. WD18: Wat 15W 26
Benskins La. RM4: Noak H 18Md 39
Bensley Cl. N11 22Hb 49
Ben Smith Way SE16 48Wb 91
Benson Av. E6 40Lc 73
Benson Cl. EN5: Barn 15Bb 31
SL2: Slou 6L 81
TW3: Houn 56Ca 107
UB8: Hil 43N 83
Benson Ct. SW8 53Nb 112
(off Hartington Rd.)
Benson Ho. E2 5K 219
SE1 7A 224
W14 49Bb 89
(off Radnor Ter.)
Benson Quay E1 45Yb 92
Benson Rd. CR0: Wadd 76Qb 156
RM17: Grays 51Ee 121
SE23 60Yb 114
Bentall Cen., The KT1: King T 68Ma 131
Bentfield Gdns. SE9 62Mc 137
Bentfield Ho. NW9 27Va 48
(off Heritage Av.)
Benthall Gdns. CR8: Kenley 89Sb 177
Benthal Rd. N16 33Wb 71
Bentham Av. GU21: Wok 87E 168
Bentham Ct. N1 38Sb 71
(off Ecclesbourne Rd.)
Bentham Ho. SE1 3F 231
SE18 48Rc 94
Bentham Rd. E9 37Zb 72
SE28 45Xc 95
Bentham Wlk. NW10 36Sa 67
Ben Tillet Cl. E16 46Pc 94
IG11: Bark 38Wc 75
Ben Tillet Ho. N15 27Rb 51
Bentinck Cl. NW8 2E 214 (40Gb 69)
Bentinck Ho. SW1 4E 228
W12 45Xa 88
(off White City Est.)
WD17: Wat 15Y 27
(off Pumphouse Cres.)
Bentinck Mans. W1 2J 221
Bentinck M. W1 2J 221 (44Jb 90)
Bentinck Rd. UB7: Yiew 46M 83
Bentinck St. W1 2J 221 (44Jb 90)
Bentine La. WD18: Wat 13X 27
BENTLEY 12Td 40
Bentley Cl. DA3: Lfield 69Ee 143
SW19 62Cb 133
W7 46Ha 86
Bentley Ct. SE13 56Ec 114
(off Whitburn Rd.)
Bentley Crematorium CM15: Pil H 14Vd 40
Bentley Dr. IG2: Ilf 30Sc 54
KT13: Weyb 81Q 170
NW2 34Bb 69
Bentley Golf Course 11Ud 40
BENTLEY HEATH 7Bb 17
Bentley Heath La. EN5: Barn 6Ab 16
Bentley Ho. E3 42Cc 92
(off Wellington Way)
SE5 53Ub 113
(off Peckham Rd.)
Bentley Lodge WD23: B Hea 19Ga 28
Bentley M. EN1: Enf 16Tb 33
Bentley Pk. SL1: Burn 10B 60
Bentley Pl. KT13: Weyb 77R 150
(off Baker St.)
Bentley Priory Local Nature Reserve
21Ga 46
Bentley Priory Mus. 20Ga 28
Bentley Rd. N1 37Ub 71
SL1: Slou 6E 80
Bentley's Mdw. TN15: Seal 92Pd 203
Bentley St. DA12: Grav'nd 8E 122
Bentley St. Ind. Est. DA12: Grav'nd 8E 122
Bentley Way EN5: New Bar 14Eb 31
HA7: Stan 22Ja 46
IG8: Buck H, Wfd G 19Jc 35
Benton Rd. IG1: Ilf 32Tc 74
WD19: Wat 22Z 45
Bentons La. SE27 63Sb 135
Benton's Ri. SE27 64Tb 135
Bentry Cl. RM8: Dag 33Ad 75
Bentry Rd. RM8: Dag 33Ad 75
Bentworth Ct. E2 42Wb 91
(off Granby St.)
Bentworth Rd. W12 44Xa 88
Ben Uri Gallery 39Db 69
Benville Ho. SW8 52Pb 112
(off Dorset Rd.)
Benwell Cen. TW16: Sun 67W 128
Benwell Ct. TW16: Sun 67W 128
Benwell Rd. GU24: Brkwd 1D 186
N7 35Qb 70
Benwick Cl. SE16 49Xb 91
Benwick M. SE20 67Yb 136
Benwood Ct. SM1: Sutt 76Eb 155
Benworth St. E3 41Bc 92
Benyon Ct. N1 39Ub 71
(off De Beauvoir Est.)
Benyon Ho. EC1 3A 218
Benyon Path RM15: S Ock 41Yd 98
Benyon Rd. N1 39Tb 71
Benyon Wharf E8 39Ub 71
(off Kingsland Rd.)
Beomonds KT16: Chert 73J 149
Beomonds Row KT16: Chert 73J 149
Berberis Ct. IG1: Ilf 37Rc 74
Berberis Ho. E3 43Cc 92
(off Gale St.)
TW13: Felt 61W 128
Berberis Wlk. UB7: W Dray 49N 83
Berber Pde. SE18 53Nc 116
Berber Pl. E14 45Cc 92
Berber Rd. SW11 57Hb 111
Berberry Cl. HA8: Edg 21Sa 47
Berceau Wlk. WD17: Wat 11U 26
Bercta Rd. SE9 61Sc 138
Berebinder Ho. E3 40Bc 72
(off Tredegar Rd.)
Bere Cl. DA9: Ghithe 57Yd 120
Beredens La.
CM13: Gt War 27Vd 58
Beregaria Ct. SE11 51Qb 112
(off Kennington Pk. Rd.)
Berengers Ct. RM6: Chad H 31Bd 75
(off Whalebone La. Sth.)
Berengers Pl. RM9: Dag 37Xc 75
Berenger Twr. SW10 52Fb 111
(off Worlds End Est.)
Berenger Wlk. SW10 52Fb 111
(off Worlds End Est.)
Berens Ct. DA14: Sidc 63Vc 139
Berens Rd. BR5: St M Cry 71Zc 161
NW10 41Za 88
Berens Way BR7: Chst 69Vc 139
Beresford Av. HA0: Wemb 39Pa 67
KT5: Surb 74Ra 153
N20 19Hb 31
SL2: Slou 5N 81
TW1: Twick 58La 108
W7 43Fa 86
Beresford Ct. E9 36Ac 72
(off Mabley St.)
Beresford Dr. BR1: Brom 69Nc 138
IG8: Wfd G 21Lc 53
Beresford Gdns. EN1: Enf 14Ub 33
RM6: Chad H 29Ad 55
TW4: Houn 57Ba 107
Beresford Rd. AL1: St A 3F 6
DA11: Nflt 9A 122
E4 18Gc 35
E17 25Dc 52
HA1: Harr 29Fa 46
KT2: King T 67Pa 131
KT3: N Mald 70Sa 131
N2 27Gb 49
N5 36Tb 71
N8 29Qb 50
SM2: Sutt 80Bb 155
UB1: S'hall 46Z 85
WD3: Rick 18H 25
Beresford Sq. SE18 49Rc 94
Beresford St. SE18 48Rc 94
Beresford Ter. N5 36Sb 71
Berestede Rd. W6 50Va 88
Bere St. E1 45Zb 92
Bergen Ho. SE5 54Sb 113
(off Carew St.)
Bergenia Ct. GU24: W End 5C 166
Bergenia Ho. TW13: Felt 60W 106
Bergen Sq. SE16 48Ac 92
Berger Cl. BR5: Pet W 72Tc 160
Berger Rd. E9 37Zb 72
Berghem M. W14 48Za 88
Bergholt Av. IG4: Ilf 29Nc 54
Bergholt Cres. N16 31Ub 71
Bergholt M. NW1 38Mb 70
Berglen Ct. E14 44Ac 92
Bergman Ho. E17 28Cc 52
(off Hoe St.)
Bering Sq. E14 50Cc 92
Bering Wlk. E16 44Mc 93
Berisford M. SW18 58Eb 111
Berkeley Av. DA7: Bex 53Zc 117
IG5: Ilf 26Qc 54
RM5: Col R 24Ed 56
TW4: Cran 53W 106
UB6: G'frd 37Fa 66
(not continuous)
Berkeley Cl. BR5: Pet W 73Uc 160
EN6: Pot B 4Ab 16
HA4: Ruis 34W 64
KT2: King T 66Na 131
RM11: Horn 33Rd 77
TW19: Staines 61F 126
WD5: Ab L 4V 12
WD6: E'tree 15Qa 29
Berkeley Ct. BR2: Brom 70Kc 137
BR8: Swan 69Gd 140
CR0: C'don 77Tb 157
(off Coombe Rd.)
KT6: Surb 73Ma 153
KT13: Weyb 75T 150
KT21: Asht 90Pa 173
N3 25Db 49
N14 16Lb 32
NW1 6G 215
NW10 35Ua 68
NW11 31Bb 69
(off Ravenscroft Av.)
SM6: Wall 76Lb 156
W5 45La 86
WD3: Crox G 15T 26
Berkeley Cres. DA1: Dart 60Pd 119
EN4: E Barn 15Fb 31
Berkeley Dr. KT8: W Mole 69Ba 129
RM11: Horn 32Qd 77
SL4: Wink 10A 102
Berkeley Gdns. KT10: Clay 79Ja 152
KT12: Walt T 73V 150
KT14: W Byf 86H 169
N21 17Tb 33
W8 46Cb 89
Berkeley Ho. E3 41Cc 92
(off Wellington Way)
SE8 50Bc 92
(off Grove St.)
TW8: Bford 51Ma 109
(off Albany Rd.)
Berkeley M. AL1: St A 3F 6
SL1: Slou 4B 80
TW16: Sun 69Y 129
W1 3G 221 (44Hb 89)
Berkeley Pl. KT18: Eps 87Ta 173
SW19 65Za 132
Berkeley Rd. E12 36Nc 74
N8 29Mb 50
N15 30Tb 51
NW9 28Qa 47
SW13 53Wa 110
UB10: Hil 38S 64
Berkeleys, The KT22: Fet 96Ga 192
SE25 70Wb 135
Berkeley Sq. W1 5K 221 (45Kb 90)
Berkeley St. W1 5A 222 (45Kb 90)
Berkeley Ter. RM18: Tilb 2C 122
Berkeley Twr. E14 46Bc 92
(off Westferry Cir.)
Berkeley Wlk. N7 33Pb 70
(off Durham Rd.)
Berkeley Waye TW5: Hest 51Z 107
Berkhampstead Rd. DA17: Belv 50Cd 96
BERKHAMSTED 1A 2
Berkhamsted Av. HA9: Wemb 37Pa 67
Berkhamsted By-Pass
HP1: Hem H 3A 2
HP4: Berk 3A 2
Berkhamsted La. AL9: Ess 2P 9
Berkhamsted Rd.
HP1: Hem H 1G 2
Berkley Av. EN8: Walt C 6Zb 20
Berkley Cl. TW2: Twick 62Ga 130
(off Wellesley Rd.)
Berkley Cres. DA12: Grav'nd 8E 122
Berkley Gro. NW1 38Jb 70
Berkley Pl. EN8: Walt C 6Zb 20
Berkley Rd. DA12: Grav'nd 8D 122
NW1 38Hb 69
Berks Hill WD3: Chor 15E 24
Berkshire Av. SL1: Slou 4F 80
Berkshire Cl. CR3: Cat'm 94Tb 197
Berkshire Ct. W7 42Ha 86
(off Copley Cl.)
Berkshire Gdns. N13 23Qb 50
N18 22Xb 51
Berkshire Ho. SE6 63Cc 136
Berkshire Rd. E9 37Bc 72
Berkshire Way CR4: Mitc 70Nb 134
RM11: Horn 29Qd 57
Berkshire Yeomanry Mus. 6H 103
Berley Rd. E17 25Bc 52
Berlin Ter. E15 36Gc 73
Berman's Cl. CM13: Hut 19De 41
Bermans Way NW10 35Ua 68
Bermer Rd. WD24: Wat 11Y 27
BERMONDSEY 7J 225 (47Wb 91)
Bermondsey Exchange SE1 2J 231
Bermondsey Sq. SE1 3J 231 (48Ub 91)
Bermondsey St. SE1 7H 225 (46Ub 91)
Bermondsey Trad. Est. SE16 50Yb 92
Bermondsey Wall E. SE16 47Wb 91
Bermondsey Wall W. SE16 47Wb 91
Bermuda Rd. RM18: Tilb 4C 122
Bermuda Way E1 43Ac 92
(off Dongola Rd.)
Bernal Cl. SE28 45Zc 95
Bernard Angell Ho. SE10 51Fc 115
(off Trafalgar Rd.)
Bernard Ashley Dr. SE7 50Kc 93
Bernard Av. W13 48Ka 86
Bernard Cassidy St. E16 43Hc 93
Bernard Gdns. SW19 64Bb 133
Bernard Gro. EN9: Walt A 5Dc 20
Bernard Hegarty Lodge E8 38Wb 71
(off Lansdowne Dr.)
Bernard Ho. E1 1K 225
Bernard Mans. WC1 6F 217
Bernard Myers Ho. SE5 52Ub 113
(off Havil St.)
Bernard Pl. KT17: Ewe 82Ya 174
Bernard Rd. N15 29Vb 51
RM7: Rush G 31Ed 76
SM6: Wall 77Kb 156
Bernards Cl. IG6: Ilf 24Tc 54
Bernard Shaw Ct. NW1 38Lb 70
(off St Pancras Way)
Bernard Shaw Ho. NW10 39Ta 67
(off Knatchbull Rd.)
Bernard St. AL3: St A 1B 6
DA12: Grav'nd 8D 122
WC1 6F 217 (42Nb 90)
Bernard Sunley Ho. SW9 52Qb 112
(off Sth. Island Pl.)
Bernays Cl. HA7: Stan 23La 46
Bernays Gro. SW9 56Pb 112
Bernel Dr. CR0: C'don 76Bc 158
Berne Rd. CR7: Thor H 71Sb 157
Berners Cl. SL1: Slou 5C 80
Berners Dr. AL1: St A 5C 6
W13 45Ja 86
Berners Ho. N1 1K 217
Berners M. W1 1C 222 (43Lb 90)
Berners Pl. W1 2C 222 (44Lb 90)
Berners Rd. N1 1B 218 (39Rb 71)
N22 25Qb 50
Berners St. W1 1C 222 (43Lb 90)
Berner Ter. E1 44Wb 91
(off Fairclough St.)
Berney Ho. BR3: Beck 71Ac 158
Berney Rd. CR0: C'don 73Tb 157
Bernhard Baron Ho. E1 44Wb 91
(off Henriques St.)
Bernhardt Cres. NW8 5D 214 (42Gb 89)
Bernhart Cl. HA8: Edg 24Sa 47
Bernice Cl. RM13: Rain 42Ld 97
Bernie Grant Arts Cen. 28Vb 51
Bernville Way HA3: Kenton 29Pa 47
Bernwelle Av. RM3: Rom 23Nd 57
Bernwell Rd. E4 20Gc 35
Berridge Grn. HA8: Edg 24Qa 47
Berridge M. NW6 36Cb 69
Berridge Rd. SE19 64Tb 135
Berriman Rd. N7 34Pb 70
Berrington Dr. KT24: E Hor 96V 190
Berrington Ho. W2 45Cb 89
(off Herrington Rd.)
Berrington M. SL1: Slou 6D 80
Berriton Rd. HA2: Harr 32Ba 65
Berry Av. WD24: Wat 8X 13
Berrybank Cl. E4 19Ec 34
Berry Cl. N21 18Rb 33
RM10: Dag 36Cd 76
RM12: Horn 36Ld 77
WD3: Rick 17K 25
Berry Cotts. E14 44Ac 92
(off Maroon St.)
Berry Ct. TW4: Houn 57Ba 107
Berrydale Rd. UB4: Yead 42Aa 85
Berryfield SL2: Slou 4N 81
Berryfield Cl. BR1: Brom 67Nc 138
E17 28Dc 52
Berryfield Rd. SE17 7C 230 (50Rb 91)
BERRYGROVE 10Ba 13
Berry Gro. La. WD25: A'ham 10Aa 13
(Otterspool La.)
WD25: A'ham 11Ca 27
(Otterspool Way)
Berry Hill HA7: Stan 21Ma 47
Berryhill SE9 56Rc 116
Berryhill Gdns. SE9 56Rc 116
Berry Ho. E1 42Xb 91
(off Headlam St.)
SW11 54Hb 111
(off Culvert Rd.)
BERRYLANDS 72Qa 153
Berrylands BR6: Chels 76Yc 161
DA3: Hartl 72Ce 165
KT5: Surb 72Pa 153
SW20 69Ya 132
Berrylands Rd. KT5: Surb 72Pa 153
Berry La. GU3: Worp 7G 186
(not continuous)
GU22: Wok 6H 187
KT12: Hers 78Z 151
(off New Berry La.)
SE21 63Tb 135
WD3: Chor, Rick 16F 24
Berryman Cl. RM8: Dag 34Yc 75
Berryman's La. SE26 63Zb 136
Berrymead HP2: Hem H 1P 3
Berry Meade KT21: Asht 89Pa 173
Berry Meade Cl. KT21: Asht 89Pa 173
Berrymead Gdns. W3 46Sa 87
Berrymede Rd. W4 48Ta 87
Berry Pl. EC1 4C 218 (41Rb 91)
Berrys Ct. KT14: Byfl 83M 169
Berryscroft Ct. TW18: Staines 66L 127
Berryscroft Rd. TW18: Staines 66L 127
BERRY'S GREEN 88Rc 180
Berry's Grn. Rd. TN16: Big H 88Rc 180
Berry's Hill TN16: Big H 88Rc 180
Berryside Apartments N4 32Sb 71
(off Swan La.)
Berry's La. KT14: Byfl 83M 169
Berry St. EC1 5C 218 (42Rb 91)
Berry Wlk. KT21: Asht 91Pa 193
Berry Way W5 48Na 87
WD3: Rick 17K 25
Bersham La. RM17: Grays 49Be 99
Bertal Rd. SW17 63Fb 133
Bertelli Pl. TW13: Felt 60X 107
Bertha Hollamby Ct. DA14: Sidc 64Yc 139
(off Sidcup Hill)
Bertha James Ct. BR2: Brom 70Kc 137
Berther Rd. RM11: Horn 31Md 77
Berthold M. EN9: Walt A 5Dc 20
Berthons Gdns. E17 29Fc 53
(off Wood St.)
Berthon St. SE8 52Cc 114
Bertie Rd. NW10 37Wa 68
SE26 65Zb 136
Bertram Cotts. SW19 66Cb 133
Bertram Rd. EN1: Enf 14Wb 33
KT2: King T 66Qa 131
NW4 30Wa 48
Bertram St. N19 33Kb 70
Bertrand Ho. E16 44Kc 93
(off Russell Rd.)
SW16 62Nb 134
(off Leigham Av.)
Bertrand St. SE13 55Dc 114
Bertrand Way SE28 45Xc 95
Bert Rd. CR7: Thor H 71Sb 157
Bert Way EN1: Enf 14Vb 33
Berwick Av. SL1: Slou 5F 80
UB4: Yead 44Z 85
Berwick Cl. EN8: Walt C 6Cc 20
HA7: Stan 23Ha 46
TW2: Whitt 60Ca 107
Berwick Ct. SE1 2E 230
Berwick Cres. DA15: Sidc 59Uc 116
Berwick Gdns. SM1: Sutt 76Eb 155
Berwick Ho. BR6: Orp 74Wc 161
N2 26Fb 49
Berwick Pond Cl. RM13: Rain 40Md 77
Berwick Pond Rd. RM13: Rain 40Nd 77
RM14: Rain, Upm 38Pd 77
Berwick Rd. DA16: Well 53Xc 117
E16 44Kc 93
N22 25Rb 51
RM13: Rain 40Md 77
WD6: Bore 10Pa 15
Berwick St. W1 2C 222 (44Lb 90)
Berwick Way BR6: Orp 74Wc 161
TN14: S'oaks 92Kd 203
Berwyn Av. TW3: Houn 53Da 107
Berwyn Rd. SE24 60Rb 113
TW10: Rich 56Ra 109
Beryl Av. E6 43Nc 94
Beryl Ho. SE18 50Vc 95
(off Spinel Cl.)
Beryl Rd. W6 50Za 88
Berystede KT2: King T 66Ra 131
Besant Cl. NW2 34Ab 68
Besant Ct. N1 36Tb 71
SE28 46Xc 95
(off Titmuss Av.)
Besant Ho. NW8 39Eb 69
(off Boundary Rd.)
WD24: Wat 12Z 27
Besant Pl. SE22 56Vb 113
Besant Rd. NW2 35Ab 68
Besant Wlk. N7 33Pb 70
Besant Way NW10 36Sa 67
Besford Ho. E2 40Wb 71
(off Pritchard's Rd.)
Besley St. SW16 65Lb 134
Bessant Dr. TW9: Kew 53Ra 109
Bessborough Gdns.
SW1 7E 228 (50Mb 90)
Bessborough Ho. DA9: Ghithe 56Yd 120
(off Carmichael Av.)
Bessborough Pl. SW1 7D 228 (50Mb 90)
Bessborough Rd. HA1: Harr 32Fa 66
SW15 60Wa 110
Bessborough St. SW1 7D 228 (50Mb 90)
BESSELS GREEN 96Fd 202
Bessels Grn. Rd. TN13: Bes G 95Fd 202
Bessels Mdw. TN13: Bes G 96Fd 202
Bessels Way TN13: Bes G 96Fd 202
Bessemer Cl. SL3: L'ly 50B 82
Bessemer Ct. NW1 38Lb 70
(off Rochester Sq.)
Bessemer Pk. Ind. Est. SE24 56Rb 113
Bessemer Pl. SE10 48Hc 93
Bessemer Rd. SE5 54Sb 113
Bessie Lansbury Cl. E6 44Qc 94
Bessingby Rd. HA4: Ruis 33X 65
Bessingham Wlk. SE4 56Zb 114
(off Aldersford Cl.)
Besson St. SE14 53Yb 114

Bessy St.—Birdwood Sq.

Bessy St. E2 .41Yb 92
Bestobell Rd. SL1: Slou .4G 80
Best Ter. BR8: Crock .72Ed 162
Bestwood St. SE8 .49Zb 92
Beswick M. NW6 .37Db 69
Beta Ct. CR0: C'don .74Tb 157
(off Sydenham Rd.)
Betam Rd. UB3: Hayes .47T 84
Beta Pl. SW4 .56Pb 112
Beta Rd. GU22: Wok .88D 168
GU24: Chob .2K 167
Beta Way TW20: Thorpe .67E 126
BETCHWORTH .6A 206
Betchworth Cl. SM1: Sutt .78Fb 155
Betchworth Rd. IG3: Ilf .33Uc 74
Betchworth Way
CR0: New Ad .81Ec 178
Betenson Av. TN13: S'oaks .94Hd 202
Betham Rd. UB6: G'frd .41Fa 86
Bethany Cl. RM12: Horn .33Ld 77
Bethany Pl. GU21: Wok .10P 167
Bethany Waye TW14: Bedf .59U 106
Bethecar Rd. HA1: Harr .29Ga 46
Bethel Cl. NW4 .29Za 48
Bethell Av. E16 .42Hc 93
IG1: Ilf .31Qc 74
Bethel Rd. DA16: Well .55Yc 117
TN13: S'oaks .95Ld 203
Bethersden Cl. BR3: Beck .66Bc 136
Bethersden Ho. SE17 .7J 231
Bethlehem Cl. UB6: G'frd .40La 66
Bethlehem Ho. E14 .45Bc 92
(off Limehouse C'way.)
BETHNAL GREEN .41Xb 91
Bethnal Green Cen. For Sports &
Performing Arts .4K 219 (41Vb 91)
Bethnal Grn. Rd. E1 .5K 219 (42Vb 91)
E2 .5K 219 (42Vb 91)
Bethune Av. N11 .21Hb 49
Bethune Rd. N16 .31Tb 71
NW10 .42Ta 87
Bethwin Rd. SE5 .52Rb 113
Betjeman Cl. CR5: Coul .89Pb 176
HA5: Pinn .28Ca 45
Betjeman Ct. UB7: Yiew .46M 83
Betjeman Gdns. WD3: Chor .14F 24
Betjeman M. N5 .35Sb 71
Betjeman Way HP1: Hem H .1K 3
Betley Ct. KT12: Walt T .76X 151
Betony Cl. CR0: C'don .74Zb 158
Betony Rd. RM3: Rom .23Ld 57
Betoyne Av. E4 .21Gc 54
BETSHAM .63Be 143
Betsham Ho. SE1 .1F 231
Betsham Rd. DA8: Erith .52Hd 118
DA10: Swans .59Ae 121
DA13: Sflt .64Zd 143
Betstyle Cir. N11 .21Kb 50
Betstyle Ho. N10 .24Jb 50
Betstyle Rd. N11 .21Kb 50
Bettenson Cl. BR7: Chst .64Pc 138
Better Gym
Greenwich .41Gc 93
Betterton Dr. DA14: Sidc .61Ad 139
Betterton Ho. WC2 .3G 223
Betterton Rd. RM13: Rain .41Gd 96
Betterton St. WC2 .3F 223 (44Nb 90)
Bettles Cl. UB8: Uxb .40L 63
Bettons Pk. E15 .39Gc 73
Bettridge Rd. SW6 .54Bb 111
Betts Cl. BR3: Beck .68Ac 136
Betts Ho. E1 .45Xb 91
(off Betts St.)
Betts M. E17 .30Bc 52
Betts Rd. E16 .45Kc 93
Betts St. E1 .45Xb 91
Betts Way KT6: Surb .74Ka 152
SE20 .67Xb 135
Betty Brooks Ho. E11 .34Fc 73
Betty Entwistle Ho. AL1: St A .5B 6
Betty May Gray Ho. E14 .49Ec 92
(off Pier St.)
Betty Paterson Ho. HP1: Hem H .2L 3
(off Astley Rd.)
Betula Cl. CR8: Kenley .87Rb 177
Betula Wlk. RM13: Rain .41Md 97
Between Streets KT11: Cobh .86W 170
Beulah Av. CR7: Thor H .68Sb 135
Beulah Cl. HA8: Edg .20Ra 29
Beulah Cres. CR7: Thor H .68Sb 135
Beulah Gro. CR0: C'don .72Sb 157
Beulah Hill SE19 .65Rb 135
Beulah Path E17 .29Ec 52
Beulah Pl. EN9: Walt A .5Nc 22
Beulah Rd. CM16: Epp .1Wc 23
CR7: Thor H .69Sb 135
E17 .29Dc 52
RM12: Horn .34Ld 77
SM1: Sutt .77Cb 155
SW19 .66Bb 133
Beulah Wlk. CR3: Wold .92Ac 198
Beult Rd. DA1: Cray .56Jd 118
Bevan Av. IG11: Bark .38Wc 75
Bevan Cl. HP3: Hem H .4M 3
Bevan Ct. CR0: Wadd .78Qb 156
E3 .40Cc 72
(off Tredegar Rd.)
Bevan Ho. IG11: Bark .38Xc 75
N1 .1H 219
(off Halcomb St.)
RM16: Grays .47Fe 99
TW1: Twick .58Ma 109
WC1 .7G 217
WD24: Wat .12Z 27
Bevan M. W12 .47Wa 88
Bevan Pk. KT17: Ewe .82Va 174
Bevan Pl. BR8: Swan .70Hd 140
Bevan Rd. EN4: Cockf .14Hb 31
SE2 .50Xc 95
Bevans Cl. DA9: Ghithe .58Yd 120
Bevans Ho. SW18 .56Eb 111
(off Eltringham St.)
Bevan St. N1 .1E 218 (39Sb 71)
Bevan Way RM12: Horn .35Pd 77
Bev Callender Cl. SW8 .55Kb 112
Bevenden St. N1 .3G 219 (41Tb 91)
Bevercote Wlk. DA17: Belv .51Bd 117
(off Osborne Rd.)
Beveree Stadium .67Da 129
Beveridge Ct. N21 .15Nb 32
(off Pennington Dr.)
SE28 .45Xc 95
(off Saunders Way)
Beveridge M. E1 .43Yb 92
Beveridge Rd. NW10 .38Ua 68
Beverley Av. DA15: Sidc .59Vc 117
SW20 .67Va 132
TW4: Houn .56Ba 107
Beverley Cl. EN1: Enf .14Ub 33
KT9: Chess .77La 152
KT13: Weyb .75U 150
KT15: Add .78M 149
KT17: Ewe .83Ya 174
N21 .18Sb 33
RM11: Horn .31Pd 77
RM16: Ors .4F 100
SW11 .56Fb 111
SW13 .54Wa 110
Beverley Cotts. SW15 .62Ua 132
Beverley Ct. HA2: Harr .27Fa 46
HA3: Kenton .28La 46
N2 .28Hb 49
(off Western Rd.)
N14 .17Lb 32
NW6 .38Eb 69
(off Fairfax Rd.)
SE4 .55Bc 114
(not continuous)
SL1: Slou .7M 81
TW4: Houn .56Ba 107
W4 .50Sa 87
Beverley Cres. IG8: Wfd G .25Kc 53
Beverley Dr. HA8: Edg .27Qa 47
Beverley Gdns. EN7: Chesh .2Wb 19
HA7: Stan .25Ja 46
HA9: Wemb .32Pa 67
KT4: Wor Pk .74Wa 154
NW11 .31Ab 68
RM11: Horn .31Pd 77
SW13 .55Va 110
Beverley Hgts. RH2: Reig .4K 207
Beverley Ho. BR1: Brom .64Fc 137
(off Brangbourne Rd.)
Beverley Hyrst CR0: C'don .75Vb 157
Beverley La. KT2: King T .66Ua 132
SW15 .62Va 132
Beverley Meads & Fishpond Woods
Nature Reserve .65Va 132
Beverley M. E4 .23Fc 53
Beverley Path SW13 .54Va 110
Beverley Rd. BR2: Brom .75Nc 160
CR3: Whyt .88Ub 177
CR4: Mitc .70Mb 134
DA7: Bex .54Ed 118
E4 .23Fc 53
E6 .41Mc 93
HA4: Ruis .33W 64
KT1: Hamp W .67La 130
KT3: N Mald .70Wa 132
KT4: Wor Pk .75Ya 154
RM9: Dag .35Ad 75
SE20 .68Xb 135
SW13 .55Va 110
TW16: Sun .67V 128
UB2: S'hall .49Aa 85
W4 .50Va 88
Beverley Trad. Est. SM4: Mord .73Za 154
Beverley Way KT3: N Mald .67Va 132
SW20 .67Va 132
Beversbrook Rd. N19 .34Mb 70
Beverstone Rd. CR7: Thor H .70Qb 134
SW2 .57Pb 112
Beverston M. W1 .1F 221
Bevile Ho. RM17: Grays .52De 121
Bevill Allen Cl. SW17 .64Hb 133
Bevill Cl. SE25 .69Wb 135
Bevin Cl. SE16 .46Ac 92
Bevin Ct. WC1 .3J 217 (41Pb 90)
Bevington Path SE1 .2K 231
Bevington Rd. BR3: Beck .68Dc 136
W10 .43Ab 88
Bevington St. SE16 .47Wb 91
Bevin Ho. E2 .41Yb 92
(off Butler St.)
E3 .41Cc 92
(off Alfred St.)
Bevin Rd. UB4: Yead .41W 84
Bevin Sq. SW17 .62Hb 133
Bevin Wlk. SS17: Stan H .1M 101
Bevin Way WC1 .3K 217 (40Qb 70)
Bevis Cl. DA2: Dart .59Sd 120
Bevis Marks EC3 .2J 225 (44Ub 91)
Bewcastle Gdns. EN2: Enf .14Nb 32
Bew Ct. SE22 .59Wb 113
Bewdley St. N1 .38Qb 70
Bewick M. SE15 .52Xb 113
Bewick St. SW8 .54Kb 112
Bewley Cl. EN8: Chesh .3Zb 20
Bewley Ho. E1 .45Xb 91
(off Bewley St.)
Bewley La. TN15: Bor G, Plax .97Yd 204
Bewley St. E1 .45Yb 92
SW19 .65Eb 133
Bewlys Rd. SE27 .64Rb 135
Bexhill Cl. TW13: Felt .61Aa 129
Bexhill Dr. RM17: Grays .51Ae 121
Bexhill Rd. N11 .22Mb 50
SE4 .58Bc 114
SW14 .55Sa 109
Bexhill Wlk. E15 .39Gc 73
BEXLEY .59Cd 118
Bexley Cl. DA1: Cray .57Gd 118
Bexley Cotts. DA4: Hort K .70Rd 141
Bexley Ct. TN14: Dun G .92Hd 202
(off Campion Sq.)
Bexley Gdns. N9 .20Tb 33
RM6: Chad H .29Xc 55
BEXLEYHEATH .56Cd 118
Bexleyheath Golf Course .57Ad 117
Bexleyheath Sports Club .56Yc 117
Bexley High St. DA5: Bexl .59Cd 118
Bexley Ho. SE4 .56Ac 114
Bexley La. DA1: Cray .57Gd 118
DA14: Sidc .63Yc 139
Bexley Lawn Tennis, Squash &
Racketball Club .59Cd 118
Bexley Mus. Collection, The .58Ed 118
Bexley Music & Dance Cen. .63Wc 139
(off Station Rd.)
Bexley Rd. DA8: Erith .52Ed 118
(not continuous)
SE9 .57Rc 116
Bexley St. SL4: Wind .3G 102
Beynon Rd. SM5: Cars .78Hb 155
Bezier Apartments EC2 .5G 219 (42Tb 91)
BFI Southbank .6J 223
Bianca Ho. N1 .2H 219
Bianca Rd. SE15 .51Wb 113
Bibsworth Rd. N3 .26Bb 49
Bibury Cl. SE15 .51Ub 113
(not continuous)
Bicester Rd. TW9: Rich .55Qa 109
Bickels Yd. SE1 .2J 231 (47Ub 91)
Bickenhall Mans. W1 .7G 215
(not continuous)
Bickenhall St. W1 .7G 215 (43Hb 89)
Bickersteth Rd. SW17 .65Hb 133
Bickerton Ho. WD17: Wat .14Y 27
(off Pumphouse Cres.)
Bickerton Rd. N19 .33Lb 70
BICKLEY .69Nc 138
Bickley Cres. BR1: Brom .70Nc 138
Bickley Pk. Rd. BR1: Brom .69Nc 138
Bickley Rd. BR1: Brom .68Mc 137
E10 .31Dc 72
Bickley St. SW17 .64Gb 133
Bicknell Ho. E1 .44Wb 91
(off Ellen St.)
Bicknell Rd. SE5 .55Sb 113
Bickney Way KT22: Fet .94Ea 192
Bicknoller Cl. SM2: Sutt .82Db 175
Bicknoller Rd. EN1: Enf .11Ub 33
Bicknor Rd. BR6: Orp .73Uc 160
Bicycle M. SW4 .55Mb 112
Bidborough Cl. BR2: Brom .71Hc 159
Bidborough St. WC1 .4F 217 (41Nb 90)
Biddenden Way DA13: Ist R .6A 144
SE9 .63Qc 138
Biddenham Ho. SE16 .49Zb 92
(off Plough Way)
Biddenham Turn WD25: Wat .7Y 13
Bidder St. E16 .43Gc 93
(not continuous)
Biddesden Ho. SW3 .6F 227
Biddestone Rd. N7 .35Pb 70
Biddles Cl. SL1: Slou .6C 80
Biddulph Ho. SE18 .49Pc 94
Biddulph Mans. W9 .41Db 89
(off Elgin Av.)
Biddulph Rd. CR2: S Croy .82Sb 177
W9 .41Db 89
Bideford Av. UB6: G'frd .40Ka 66
Bideford Cl. HA8: Edg .25Qa 47
RM3: Rom .25Ld 57
TW13: Hanw .62Ba 129
Bideford Gdns. EN1: Enf .17Ub 33
Bideford Rd. BR1: Brom .62Hc 137
DA16: Well .52Xc 117
EN3: Enf L .10Bc 20
HA4: Ruis .34X 65
Bideford Spur SL2: Slou .1F 80
Bidhams Cres. KT20: Tad .93Ya 194
Bidwell Gdns. N11 .24Lb 50
Bidwell St. SE15 .53Xb 113
Bield, The RH2: Reig .8J 207
Big Apple, The
Woking .89B 168
Big Ben .2G 229 (47Nb 90)
Bigbury Cl. N17 .24Tb 51
Big Comn. La. RH1: Blet .5H 209
Biggerstaff Rd. E15 .39Ec 72
Biggerstaff St. N4 .33Qb 70
BIGGIN .1D 122
Biggin Av. CR4: Mitc .67Hb 133
BIGGIN HILL .89Mc 179
Biggin Hill SE19 .66Rb 135
BIGGIN HILL AIRPORT .84MC 179
Biggin Hill Bus. Pk.
TN16: Big H .87Mc 179
Biggin Hill Cl. KT2: King T .64La 130
Biggin Hill Memorial Pool .88Mc 179
Biggin La. RM16: Grays .1D 122
Biggin Way SE19 .66Rb 135
Bigginwood Rd. SW16 .66Rb 135
Biggs Ct. NW9 .26Ua 48
(off Harvey Cl.)
Biggs Row SW15 .55Za 110
Biggs Sq. E9 .37Bc 72
Big Hill E5 .32Xb 71
Bigland St. E1 .44Xb 91
Bignell Rd. SE18 .50Rc 94
BIGNELL'S CORNER .5Xa 16
BIGNELL'S CORNER .6Wa 16
Bignells Cnr. EN6: S Mim .6Xa 16
Bignold Rd. E7 .35Jc 73
Bigsworth Ct. SE20 .67Xb 135
Bigwood Ct. NW11 .29Db 49
Bigwood Rd. NW11 .29Db 49
Bike Shed, The IG11: Bark .38Sc 74
(off Ripple Rd.)
Biko Cl. UB8: Cowl .44L 83
Bilberry Ho. E3 .43Cc 92
(off Watts Gro.)
Billericay Rd. CM13: Heron .24Fe 59
BILLET, THE .2P 101
Billet Cl. RM6: Chad H .27Zc 55
Billet Hill TN15: Ash .77Yd 164
Billet La. RM11: Horn .32Md 77
SL0: Iver H .41D 82
SL3: L'ly .45D 82
SS17: Stan H .2M 101
Billet Rd. E17 .25Zb 52
RM6: Chad H .27Xc 55
TW18: Staines .62J 127
Billets Hart Cl. W7 .47Ga 86
Bill Hamling Cl. SE9 .61Pc 138
Billing Cl. RM9: Dag .38Yc 75
Billingford Cl. SE4 .56Zb 114
Billing Ho. E1 .44Zb 92
(off Bower St.)
Billingley NW1 .39Lb 70
(off Pratt St.)
Billing Pl. SW10 .52Db 111
Billing Rd. SW10 .52Db 111
Billingsgate Market .46Dc 92
Billings Hill Shaw DA3: Hartl .72Be 165
Billing St. SW10 .52Db 111
Billington M. W3 .46Ra 87
(off High St.)
Billington Rd. SE14 .52Zb 114
Billinton Hill CR0: C'don .75Tb 157
Billiter Sq. EC3 .3J 225
Billiter St. EC3 .3J 225 (44Ub 91)
Bill Nicholson Way N17 .24Vb 51
(off High Rd.)
Billockby Cl. KT9: Chess .79Pa 153
Billson St. E14 .49Ec 92
Bill Voisey Ct. E14 .44Ac 92
(off Repton St.)
Billy Lows La. EN6: Pot B .3Cb 17
Bilsby Gro. SE9 .63Mc 137
Bilsby Lodge HA9: Wemb .34Sa 67
(off Chalklands)
Bilton Cen. KT22: Lea .91Ha 192
Bilton Cen., The UB6: G'frd .39Ka 66
Bilton Cl. SL3: Poyle .54G 104
Bilton Rd. DA8: Erith .52Jd 118
UB6: G'frd .39Ja 66
Bilton Towers W1 .3G 221
Bilton Way EN3: Enf L .11Ac 34
UB3: Hayes .47X 85
Bina Gdns. SW5 .6A 226 (49Eb 89)
Binbrook Ho. W10 .43Ya 88
(off Sutton Way)
Bincote Rd. EN2: Enf .13Pb 32
Binden Rd. W12 .48Va 88
Bindon Grn. SM4: Mord .70Db 133
Binfield Cl. KT14: Byfl .84P 169
Binfield Rd. CR2: S Croy .78Vb 157
KT14: Byfl .84N 169
SW4 .53Nb 112
Bingfield St. N1 .39Nb 70
(not continuous)
Bingham Cl. RM15: S Ock .44Yd 98
Bingham Ct. N1 .38Rb 71
(off Halton Rd.)
Bingham Dr. GU21: Wok .10K 167
TW18: Staines .66M 127
Bingham Pl. W1 .6H 215 (43Jb 90)
Bingham Point SE18 .49Rc 94
(off Wilmount St.)
Bingham Rd.
CR0: C'don .74Wb 157
Bingham St. N1 .37Tb 71
Bingley Rd. E16 .44Lc 93
TW16: Sun .66W 128
UB6: G'frd .42Ea 86
Binley Ho. SW15 .58Wa 110
Binnacle Ho. E1 .46Xb 91
(off Cobblestone Sq.)
Binney St. W1 .3J 221 (44Jb 90)
Binnie Ho. SE1 .4D 230
Binnie Rd. DA1: Dart .54Nd 119
Binnington Twr.
BR2: Brom .72Nc 160
Binns Rd. W4 .50Ua 88
Binns Ter. W4 .50Ua 88
Binsey Wlk. SE2 .47Yc 95
(not continuous)
Binstead Cl. UB4: Yead .44Aa 85
Binyon Cres. HA7: Stan .22Ha 46
Bioko Ct. E1 .43Ac 92
(off Ocean Est.)
Biraj Ho. E6 .39Pc 74
Birbetts Rd. SE9 .61Pc 138
Bircham Path SE4 .56Zb 114
(off Aldersford Cl.)
Birchanger Rd. SE25 .71Wb 157
Birch Av. CR3: Cat'm .96Tb 197
KT22: Lea .92Ha 192
N13 .20Sb 33
UB7: Yiew .45N 83
Birch Cl. DA3: Lfield .68Ee 143
DA4: Eyns .76Md 163
E16 .43Gc 93
GU21: Wok .1N 187
GU23: Send .97H 189
IG9: Buck H .20Mc 35
KT15: New H .81M 169
N19 .33Lb 70
RM7: Mawney .27Dd 56
RM15: S Ock .42Zd 99
SE15 .54Wb 113
SL0: Iver H .40F 62
SM7: Bans .86Ab 174
TN13: S'oaks .95Kd 203
TW3: Houn .54Fa 108
TW8: Bford .52Ka 108
TW11: Tedd .64Ja 130
TW17: Shep .68U 128
Birch Copse AL2: Brick W .2Aa 13
Birch Ct. HA6: Nwood .23S 44
KT22: Lea .92Ha 192
N12 .21Db 49
RM6: Chad H .30Yc 55
SM1: Sutt .77Eb 155
SM6: Wall .77Kb 156
Birch Cres. RM11: Horn .28Nd 57
RM15: S Ock .41Zd 99
UB10: Uxb .39P 63
Birchcroft Cl. CR3: Cat'm .97Sb 197
Birchdale SL9: Ger X .2P 61
Birchdale Cl. KT14: W Byf .83L 169
Birchdale Gdns.
RM6: Chad H .31Zc 75
Birchdale Rd. E7 .36Lc 73
Birchdene Dr. SE28 .46Wc 95
Birchdown Ho. E3 .41Dc 92
(off Rainhill Way)
Birch Dr. AL10: Hat .1C 8
WD3: Map C .22F 42
Birchen Cl. NW9 .33Ta 67
Birchend Cl. CR2: S Croy .79Tb 157
Birchen Gro. NW9 .33Ta 67
Birches, The AL2: Lon C .9G 6
BR2: Brom .70Hc 137
(off Durham Rd.)
BR6: Farnb .77Qc 160
BR8: Swan .68Gd 140
CM13: B'wood .20Ae 41
E12 .35Nc 74
EN9: Walt A .6Hc 21
GU22: Wok .90B 168
HP3: Hem H .5H 3
KT24: E Hor .98U 190
N21 .16Pb 32
SE5 .54Ub 113
SE7 .51Kc 115
TW4: Houn .59Ba 107
WD23: Bush .15Ea 28
Birches Cl. CR4: Mitc .69Hb 133
HA5: Pinn .29Aa 45
KT18: Eps .87Ua 174
Birchfield RM16: N Stif .46Zd 99
TN14: Sund .99Ad 201
Birchfield Cl. CR5: Coul .88Pb 176
KT15: Add .77K 149
Birchfield Ct. KT12: Walt T .73X 151
(off Grove Cres.)
Birchfield Gro. KT17: Ewe .82Ya 174
Birchfield Ho. E14 .45Cc 92
(off Birchfield St.)
Birchfield Rd. EN8: Chesh .1Xb 19
Birchfield St. E14 .45Cc 92
Birch Gdns. RM10: Dag .34Ed 76
BIRCH GREEN .63J 127
Birch Grn. HP1: Hem H .1H 3
NW9 .24Ua 48
TW18: Staines .63H 127
Birch Gro. DA16: Well .56Wc 117
E11 .35Gc 73
EN6: Pot B .4Cb 17
GU22: Pyr .87F 168
KT11: Cobh .86Y 171
KT20: Kgswd .96Ab 194
SE12 .59Hc 115
SL2: Slou .3F 80
SL4: Wind .6B 102
TW17: Shep .68U 128
W3 .46Qa 87
Birchgrove Ho. TW9: Kew .52Ra 109
Birch Hill CR0: C'don .78Zb 158
Birch Ho. N22 .25Qb 50
(off Acacia Rd.)
SE14 .53Bc 114
SW2 .58Qb 112
UB7: W Dray .47P 83
(off Park Lodge Av.)
W10 .42Ab 88
(off Droop St.)
Birchin Cross Rd. TN15: Knat .87Nd 183
Birchington Cl. BR5: Orp .74Yc 161
DA7: Bex .53Dd 118
Birchington Ct. NW6 .39Db 69
(off West End La.)
Birchington Ho. E5 .36Xb 71
Birchington Rd. KT5: Surb .73Pa 153
N8 .30Mb 50
NW6 .39Cb 69
SL4: Wind .4E 102
Birchin La. EC3 .3G 225 (44Tb 91)
Birchlands Av. SW12 .59Hb 111
Birch La. CR8: Purl .83Nb 176
GU24: W End .4B 166
HP3: Flau .5D 10
Birch Mead BR6: Farnb .75Qc 160
Birchmead WD17: Wat .10V 12
Birchmead Av. HA5: Pinn .28Y 45
Birchmere Bus. Pk. SE28 .47Wc 95
Birchmere Lodge SE16 .50Xb 91
(off Sherwood Gdns.)
Birchmere Row SE3 .54Hc 115
Birchmore Hall N5 .34Sb 71
Birchmore Wlk. N5 .34Sb 71
(not continuous)
Birch Pk. HA3: Hrw W .24Ea 46
Birch Pl. DA9: Ghithe .58Ud 120
TN13: S'oaks .96Jd 202
Birch Platt GU24: W End .5B 166
Birch Rd. GU20: W'sham .9C 146
RM7: Mawney .27Dd 56
TW13: Hanw .64Z 129
Birch Row BR2: Brom .73Qc 160
Birch Tree Av. BR4: W W'ck .78Hc 159
Birch Tree Wlk. WD17: Wat .9V 12
Birch Tree Way CR0: C'don .75Xb 157
Birch Va. KT11: Cobh .84Ca 171
Birch Va. Ct. NW8 .5C 214
Birch Vw. CM16: Epp .1Xc 23
HA1: Harr .29Fa 46
Birchville Ct. WD23: B Hea .18Ga 28
Birch Wlk. CR4: Mitc .67Kb 134
DA8: Erith .51Ed 118
IG3: Ilf .35Uc 74
(off Loxford La.)
KT14: W Byf .84J 169
(not continuous)
WD6: Bore .11Qa 29
Birch Way AL2: Lon C .9H 7
CR6: W'ham .90Ac 178
RH1: Redh .8B 208
Birchway TN15: W King .81Vd 184
UB3: Hayes .46W 84
Birchwood EN9: Walt A .6Gc 21
WD7: Shenl .6Qa 15
Birchwood Apartments N4 .31Sb 71
(off Woodberry Gro.)
Birchwood Av. BR3: Beck .70Bc 136
DA14: Sidc .61Xc 139
N10 .27Jb 50
SM6: Wall .76Jb 156
Birchwood Cl. CM13: Gt War .23Yd 58
SM4: Mord .70Db 133
Birchwood Ct. HA8: Edg .26Sa 47
KT13: Weyb .78S 150
N13 .22Rb 51
Birchwood Dr. DA2: Wilm .63Gd 140
GU18: Light .2A 166
KT14: W Byf .84J 169
NW3 .34Db 69
Birchwood Gro. TW12: Hamp .65Ca 129
Birchwood La. CR3: Cat'm .97Rb 197
KT10: Esh .81Fa 172
KT22: Oxs .81Fa 172
TN14: Dun G .87Bd 181
Birchwood Pde. DA2: Wilm .63Gd 140
Birchwood Pk. Av. BR8: Swan .69Gd 140
Birchwood Pk. Golf Course .66Ed 140
Birchwood Rd. BR5: Pet W .70Tc 138
BR8: Swan .67Ed 140
DA2: Wilm .64Gd 140
KT14: W Byf .84J 169
SW17 .64Kb 134
Birchwood Way AL2: Park .10P 5
Birdbrook Cl. CM13: Hut .16De 41
RM10: Dag .38Ed 76
Birdbrook Ho. N1 .38Sb 71
(off Popham Rd.)
Birdbrook Rd. SE3 .56Lc 115
Birdcage Wlk. SW1 .2B 228 (47Lb 90)
Birdham Cl. BR1: Brom .71Nc 160
Birdhouse La. BR6: Downe .87Qc 180
Birdhurst Av. CR2: S Croy .77Tb 157
Birdhurst Ct. SM6: Wall .80Lb 156
(off Woodcote Av.)
Birdhurst Gdns. CR2: S Croy .77Tb 157
Birdhurst Ri. CR2: S Croy .78Ub 157
Birdhurst Rd. CR2: S Croy .78Ub 157
SW18 .57Eb 111
SW19 .65Gb 133
Bird in Bush BMX Track .52Xb 113
(off Bird in Bush Rd.)
Bird in Bush Rd. SE15 .52Wb 113
Bird in Hand La. BR1: Brom .68Mc 137
Bird-in-Hand M. SE23 .61Yb 136
(off Bird-in-Hand Pas.)
Bird-in-Hand Pas. SE23 .61Yb 136
Bird in Hand Path CR0: C'don .73Tb 157
(off Sydenham Rd.)
Bird in Hand Yd. NW3 .35Eb 69
Bird La. CM13: Gt War, L War .27Yd 58
RM14: Upm .29Td 58
UB9: Hare .26L 43
Birdsall Ho. SE5 .55Ub 113
Birds Farm Av. RM5: Col R .24Dd 56
Birdsfield La. E3 .39Bc 72
Birds Gro. GU21: Knap .10F 166
Birds Hill Dr. KT22: Oxs .85Fa 172
Birds Hill Ri. KT22: Oxs .85Fa 172
Birds Hill Rd. KT22: Oxs .84Fa 172
Birdsmouth Ct. N15 .28Ub 51
(off Bathurst Sq.)
Bird St. W1 .3J 221 (44Jb 90)
Birdswood Dr. GU21: Wok .1J 187
Bird Wlk. TW2: Whitt .60Ba 107
Birdwood Av. DA1: Dart .54Pd 119
SE13 .58Fc 115
Birdwood Cl. CR2: Sels .83Yb 178
TW11: Tedd .63Ga 130
Birdwood Sq. DA1: Dart .54Qd 119

Birkbeck Av.—Blenheim Cl.

Birkbeck Av. UB6: G'frd 39Ea 66
W3 45Sa 87
Birkbeck Ct. W3 46Ta 87
Birkbeck Gdns. IG8: Wfd G 19Jc 35
Birkbeck Gro. W3 47Ta 87
Birkbeck Hill SE21 60Rb 113
Birkbeck M. E8 36Vb 71
W3 46Ta 87
Birkbeck Pl. SE21 61Sb 135
Birkbeck Rd. BR3: Beck 68Yb 136
CM13: Hut 16Fe 41
DA14: Sidc 62Wc 139
E8 36Vb 71
EN2: Enf 11Tb 33
IG2: Ilf 29Tc 54
N8 28Nb 50
N12 22Eb 49
N17 25Vb 51
NW7 22Va 48
RM7: Rush G 32Fd 76
SW19 64Db 133
W3 46Ta 87
W5 49La 86
Birkbeck St. E2 41Xb 91
Birkbeck Way UB6: G'frd 39Fa 66
Birkdale Av. HA5: Pinn 27Ca 45
RM3: Hrld W 24Pd 57
Birkdale Cl. BR6: Orp 73Tc 160
SE16 50Xb 91
SE28 44Zc 95
Birkdale Ct. *UB1: S'hall 44Ea 86*
(off Redcroft Rd.)
Birkdale Gdns. CR0: C'don 77Zb 158
WD19: Wat 20Z 27
Birkdale Rd. SE2 49Wc 95
W5 42Na 87
Birkenhead Av. KT2: King T 68Pa 131
Birkenhead St. WC1 3G 217 (41Nb 90)
Birken M. HA6: Nwood 22R 44
Birkett Way HP8: Chal G 13A 24
Birkhall Rd. SE6 60Fc 115
Birkheads Rd. RH2: Reig 5J 207
Birkin Ct. KT14: Byfl 83M 169
Birklands La. AL1: St A 6F 6
Birklands Pk. AL1: St A 6F 6
Birkwood Cl. SW12 59Mb 112
Birley Lodge NW8 1C 214
Birley Rd. N20 19Eb 31
SL1: Slou 4H 81
Birley St. SW11 54Jb 112
Birling Rd. DA8: Erith 52Fd 118
Birnam Cl. GU23: Rip 96J 189
Birnam Rd. N4 33Pb 70
Birnbeck Ct. EN5: Barn 14Za 30
NW11 29Bb 49
Birrell Ho. *SW9 54Pb 112*
(off Stockwell Rd.)
Birse Cres. NW10 34Ua 68
Birstal Grn. WD19: Wat 21Z 45
Birstall Rd. N15 29Ub 51
Birtrick Dr. DA13: Meop 10B 144
(not continuous)
Birtwhistle Ho. *E3 39Bc 72*
(off Parnell Rd.)
Biscay Ho. *E1 42Zb 92*
(off Mile End Rd.)
Biscayne Av. E14 46Fc 93
Biscay Rd. W6 50Za 88
Biscoe Cl. TW5: Hest 51Ca 107
Biscoe Way SE13 55Fc 115
Biscott Ho. E3 42Dc 92
Bisenden Rd. CR0: C'don 75Ub 157
Bisham Cl. SM5: Cars 74Hb 155
Bisham Ct. *SL1: Slou 7K 81*
(off Park St.)
Bisham Gdns. N6 32Jb 70
Bishams Ct. CR3: Cat'm 96Vb 197
Bishop Butt Cl. BR6: Orp 76Vc 161
Bishop Ct. TW9: Rich 55Na 109
Bishop Duppas Pk. TW17: Shep 73U 150
Bishop Fox Way KT8: W Mole 70Ba 129
Bishop Ken Rd. HA3: W'stone 26Ha 46
Bishop King's Rd. W14 49Ab 88
Bishop Ramsey Cl. HA4: Ruis 31V 64
Bishop Rd. N14 17Kb 32
Bishop's Av. E13 39Kc 73
SW6 54Za 110
Bishops Av. BR1: Brom 68Lc 137
HA6: Nwood 21U 44
RM6: Chad H 30Yc 55
WD6: E'tree 15Pa 29
Bishops Av., The N2 31Fb 69
Bishop's Bri. Rd. W2 2A 220 (44Db 89)
Bishop's Cl. CR5: Coul 90Qb 176
N19 34Lb 70
SE9 61Sc 138
SM1: Sutt 76Cb 155
Bishops Cl. AL10: Hat 1B 8
E17 28Dc 52
EN1: Enf 12Xb 33
EN5: Barn 16Za 30
TW10: Ham 62Ma 131
UB10: Hil 40Q 64
W4 50Sa 87
Bishop's Ct. EC4 2B 224
WC2 2K 223
Bishops Ct. CR0: C'don 75Vb 157
DA9: Ghithe 57Vd 120
EN8: Chesh 2Yb 20
HA0: Wemb 35Ka 66
N2 29Gb 49
RM16: Ors 3C 100
W2 44Db 89
(off Bishop's Bri. Rd.)
WD5: Ab L 3V 12
Bishopsdale Ho. *NW6 39Cb 69*
(off Kilburn Vale)
Bishop's Dr. TW14: Bedf 58T 106
Bishops Dr. UB5: N'olt 39Aa 65
Bishops Farm Cl. SL4: Oak G 4A 102
Bishopsford Ho. SM5: Cars 72Gb 155
Bishopsford Rd. SM4: Mord 73Eb 155
BISHOPS GATE 2L 125
Bishopsgate EC2 3H 225 (44Ub 91)
Bishopsgate Arc. EC2 1J 225
Bishopsgate Chyd. EC2 2H 225 (43Ub 91)
Bishopsgate Institute & Libraries 1J 225
Bishopsgate Plaza EC3 2J 225
Bishopsgate Rd. TW20: Eng G 2K 125
Bishops Grn. BR1: Brom 67Lc 137
Bishop's Gro. TW12: Hamp 63Ba 129
Bishops Gro. GU20: W'sham 9A 146
KT20: Tad 94Xa 194
N2 30Gb 49
Bishops Gro. Cvn. Site
TW12: Hamp, Hamp H 63Ca 129
Bishop's Hall KT1: King T 68Ma 131
Bishop's Hall Rd. CM15: Pil H 16Xd 40
Bishops Hill KT12: Walt T 73W 150
Bishops Ho. *SW8 52Nb 112*
(off Sth. Lambeth Rd.)
Bishop's Mans. SW6 54Za 110
Bishops Mead HP1: Hem H 4K 3
SE5 52Sb 113
(off Camberwell Rd.)
Bishopsmead Cl.
KT19: Ewe 82Ta 173
KT24: E Hor 100U 190
Bishopsmead Ct. KT19: Ewe 82Ua 174
Bishopsmead Dr. KT24: E Hor 100V 190
Bishopsmead Pde.
KT24: E Hor 100U 190
Bishops Orchard SL2: Farn R 1F 80
Bishop's Pk. Rd. SW6 54Za 110
Bishops Pk. Rd. SW16 67Nb 134
Bishops Pl. SM1: Sutt 78Eb 155
Bishops Ri. AL10: Hat 1B 8
Bishop's Rd. CR0: C'don 73Rb 157
SW11 52Gb 111
UB3: Hayes 44S 84
Bishops Rd. N6 30Jb 50
SL1: Slou 7L 81
SS17: Stan H 1P 101
SW6 53Ab 110
W7 47Ga 86
Bishops Sq. E1 7J 219 (43Ub 91)
Bishop's Ter. SE11 5A 230 (49Qb 90)
Bishopsthorpe Rd. SE26 63Zb 136
Bishop St. N1 39Sb 71
Bishops Vw. Ct. N10 28Kb 50
Bishops Wlk. BR7: Chst 67Sc 138
CR0: Addtn 78Zb 158
HA5: Pinn 27Aa 45
Bishop's Way E2 40Xb 71
Bishops Way TW20: Egh 65F 126
Bishops Wharf Ho. *SW11 52Gb 111*
(off Parkgate Rd.)
Bishops Wood GU21: Wok 9K 167
Bishops Wood Almshouses *E5 35Xb 71*
(off Lwr. Clapton Rd.)
Bishopswood Rd. N6 31Hb 69
Bishop Wlk. CM15: Shenf 19Be 41
Bishop Wilfred Wood Cl. SE15 54Wb 113
Bishop Wilfred Wood Ct. *E13 40Lc 73*
(off Pragel St.)
Biskra WD17: Wat 11W 26
BISLEY 7D 166
BISLEY CAMP 1B 186
Bisley Cl. EN8: Walt C 5Zb 20
KT4: Wor Pk 74Ya 154
Bisley Grn. GU24: Bisl 8D 166
Bison Ct. TW14: Felt 59X 107
Bispham Rd. NW10 41Pa 87
Bissagos Ct. *E1 43Ac 92*
(off Ocean Est.)
Bissextile Ho. SE13 54Dc 114
Bisson Rd. E15 40Ec 72
Bisterne Av. E17 27Fc 53
BITCHET GREEN 98Td 204
Bittacy Bus. Cen. NW7 24Ab 48
Bittacy Cl. NW7 23Za 48
Bittacy Ct. NW7 24Ab 48
Bittacy Hill NW7 23Za 48
Bittacy Pk. Av. NW7 22Za 48
Bittacy Ri. NW7 23Ya 48
Bittacy Rd. NW7 23Za 48
Bittams La. KT16: Chert 77F 148
Bittern Cl. HP3: Hem H 7P 3
UB4: Yead 43Z 85
Bittern Ct. NW9 26Ua 48
SE8 51Cc 114
Bitterne Dr. GU21: Wok 9K 167
Bittern Ho. SE1 2D 230
UB7: Yiew 45M 83
(off Wraysbury Dr.)
Bittern Pl. N22 26Pb 50
Bittern St. SE1 2D 230 (47Sb 91)
Bittoms, The KT1: King T 69Ma 131
Bittoms Ct. KT1: King T 69Ma 131
Bixley Cl. UB2: S'hall 49Ba 85
Bkackthorn Cl. KT17: Eps D 88Xa 174
Blackacre Rd. CM16: They B 9Uc 22
Blackall St. EC2 5H 219 (42Ub 91)
Blackberry Cl. E17 27Dc 52
TW17: Shep 70U 128
Blackberry Ct. HA9: Wemb 31Na 67
Blackberry Farm Cl. TW5: Hest 52Aa 107
Blackberry Fld. BR5: St P 67Wc 139
Blackberry Way HP2: Hem H 2D 4
Blackbird Ct. NW9 34Ta 67
Blackbird Hill NW9 33Sa 67
Blackbirds La. WD25: A'ham 6Ea 14
Blackbird Yd. E2 41Vb 91
Blackborne Rd. RM10: Dag 37Cd 76
Blackborough Cl. RH2: Reig 6L 207
Blackborough Ho. *IG9: Buck H 19Mc 35*
(off Beatrice Ct.)
Blackborough Rd. RH2: Reig 7L 207
Black Boy La. N15 29Sb 51
Black Boy Wood AL2: Brick W 2Ca 13
Blackbridge Rd. GU22: Wok 1P 187
Blackbrook La. BR1: Brom 71Pc 160
BR2: Brom 71Pc 160
Black Bull Yd. EC1 7K 217
Blackburn NW9 26Va 48
Blackburn, The KT23: Bookh 96Ba 191
Blackburne's M. W1 4H 221 (45Jb 90)
Blackburn Rd. NW6 37Db 69
Blackburn Trad. Est.
TW19: Stanw 58P 105
Blackburn Way TW4: Houn 57Aa 107
Blackbury Cl. EN6: Pot B 3Eb 17
Blackbush Av. RM6: Chad H 29Zc 55
Blackbush Cl. SM2: Sutt 80Db 155
Black Bush La. SS17: Horn H 1F 100
Black Cut AL1: St A 3C 6
Blackdown Av. GU22: Pyr 87G 168
Blackdown Cl. GU22: Pyr 88E 168
N2 26Eb 49
Blackdown Ter. SE18 53Pc 116
Black Eagle Cl. TN16: Westrm 99Sc 200
Black Eagle Dr. DA11: Nflt 57Ce 121
Black Eagle Sq. TN16: Westrm 99Sc 200
Blackett Apartments *E3 42Bc 92*
(off Hamlets Way)
Blackett Cl. TW18: Staines 68G 126
Blackett St. SW15 55Za 110
Blacketts Wood Dr. WD3: Chor 15D 24
Black Fan Cl. EN2: Enf 11Sb 33
BLACKFEN 58Wc 117
Blackfen Pde. DA15: Sidc 58Wc 117
Blackfen Rd. DA15: Sidc 57Uc 116
Blackford Cl. CR2: S Croy 81Rb 177
Blackford Rd. WD19: Wat 22Z 45
Blackford's Path SW15 59Wa 110
Blackfriars Bri. EC4 4B 224 (45Rb 91)
Blackfriars Ct. *AL1: St A 1C 6*
(off Newsom Pl.)
EC4 4B 224
Black Friars La. EC4 4B 224 (44Rb 91)
(not continuous)
Blackfriars Pas. EC4 4B 224 (45Rb 91)
Blackfriars Rd. SE1 6B 224 (47Rb 91)
Blackfriars Underpass
EC4 4B 224 (45Qb 90)
Black Gates HA5: Pinn 27Ba 45
Black Grn. Wood Cl.
AL2: Park 1Da 13
Blackhall La.
TN15: God G, S'oaks 95Md 203
BLACKHEATH 54Hc 115
Blackheath Av. SE10 52Fc 115
Blackheath Bus. Cen. SE10 53Ec 114
Blackheath Bus. Est. *SE10 53Ec 114*
(off Blackheath Hill)
Blackheath Concert Halls 55Hc 115
Blackheath Gro. SE3 54Hc 115
Blackheath Hill SE10 53Ec 114
BLACKHEATH PARK 55Jc 115
Blackheath Pk. SE3 55Hc 115
Blackheath Ri. SE13 54Ec 114
(not continuous)
Blackheath Rd. SE10 53Dc 114
Blackheath RUFC 52Kc 115
BLACKHEATH VALE 54Hc 115
Blackheath Va. SE3 54Gc 115
Blackheath Village SE3 54Hc 115
Blackhills KT10: Esh 81Ba 171
Black Horse Cl. SL4: Wind 4B 102
Black Horse Ct.
SE1 3G 231 (48Tb 91)
Blackhorse La. CR0: C'don 73Wb 157
E17 26Zb 52
EN6: S Mim 2Ua 16
KT20: Lwr K 1K 207
Black Horse M. TN15: Bor G 92Ce 205
Blackhorse M. E17 27Zb 52
Black Horse Pde. HA5: Eastc 29X 45
Black Horse Pl. UB8: Uxb 39K 63
BLACKHORSE ROAD 28Zb 52
Blackhorse Rd. DA14: Sidc 63Wc 139
E17 28Zb 52
GU22: Wok 2H 187
SE8 51Ac 114
Black Horse Yd. SL4: Wind 3H 103
UB8: Uxb 39K 63
Black Lake Cl. TW20: Egh 67C 126
Blacklands Dr. UB4: Hayes 42S 84
Blacklands Mdw. RH1: Nutf 5E 208
Blacklands Rd. SE6 63Ec 136
Blacklands Ter. SW3 6F 227 (49Hb 89)
Blackley Cl. WD17: Wat 9V 12
Black Lion Hill WD7: Shenl 4Na 15
Black Lion La. W6 49Wa 88
Black Lion M. W6 49Wa 88
Blackmans Cl. DA1: Dart 60Ld 119
Blackman's La. CR6: W'ham 86Gc 179
Blackmans Yd. E2 42Wb 91
Blackmead TN13: Riv 93Gd 202
Blackmoor La. WD18: Wat 15T 26
Blackmore Av. UB1: S'hall 46Fa 86
Blackmore Cl. RM17: Grays 50De 99
Blackmore Ct. EN9: Walt A 5Jc 21
Blackmore Cres. GU21: Wok 87E 168
Blackmore Dr. NW10 38Ra 67
Blackmore Ho. N1 1J 217
Blackmore Rd. IG9: Buck H 17Nc 36
Blackmore's Gro. TW11: Tedd 65Ja 130
Blackmore Way UB8: Uxb 37M 63
Blackness La. BR2: Kes 81Mc 179
GU22: Wok 91A 188
BLACKNEST 9F 124
Blacknest Ga. Rd. SL5: S'hill 9F 124
Blacknest Rd. GU25: Vir W 9H 125
SL5: S'hill 9H 125
Black Pk. Country Pk. 39C 62
Black Pk. Countryside Cen. 40B 62
Black Pk. Rd. SL3: Ful, Wex 40A 62
Black Path E10 31Ac 72
Blackpond La. SL2: Farn C, Farn R 7F 60
Blackpool Gdns. UB4: Hayes 42U 84
Blackpool Rd. SE15 54Xb 113
Black Prince Cl. KT14: Byfl 85P 169
BLACK PRINCE INTERCHANGE 58Dd 118
Black Prince Rd. SE1 6H 229 (49Pb 90)
SE11 6H 229 (49Pb 90)
Black Prince St. SE18 51Wc 117
Black Rd. E11 30Gc 53
Black Robins La. HP3: Flau 4D 10
Black Rod Cl. UB3: Hayes 48V 84
Blackshaw Rd. SW17 63Eb 133
Blackshots La. RM16: Grays 45Ee 99
Blacksmith Cl. KT21: Asht 91Pa 193
Blacksmith Row HP3: Hem H 3C 4
Blacksmiths Cl. SL3: L'ly 49C 82
Blacksmiths Cl. RM6: Chad H 30Yc 55
Blacksmiths Hill CR2: Sande 85Wb 177
Blacksmiths Ho. *E17 28Cc 52*
(off Gillards M.)
Blacksmith's La. BR5: St M Cry 71Yc 161
RM13: Rain 39Hd 76
Blacksmiths La. AL3: St A 2P 5
KT16: Chert 73J 149
TW18: Lale 69K 127
UB9: Den 33E 62
Blacksole Cotts. TN15: Wro 87Be 185
Blacksole La. TN15: Wro 88Be 185
Blacksole Rd. TN15: Wro 88Be 185
Blacks Rd. W6 50Ya 88
Blackstock M. N4 33Rb 71
Blackstock Rd. N4 33Rb 71
N5 33Rb 71
Blackstone Cl. RH1: Redh 7N 207
Blackstone Est. E8 38Wb 71
Blackstone Hill RH1: Redh 7M 207
Blackstone Ho. *SW1 50Lb 90*
(off Churchill Gdns.)
Blackstone Rd. NW2 36Ya 68
Blackstroud La. E. GU18: Light 3A 166
Blackstroud La. W. GU18: Light 3B 166
Black Swan Yd. SE1 1H 231 (47Ub 91)
Black's Yd. *TN13: S'oaks 97Ld 203*
(off Bank St.)
Blackthorn Av. N7 37Qb 70
UB7: W Dray 49Q 84
Blackthorn Cl. RH2: Reig 8L 207
RH9: G'stone 2A 210
TN15: W King 81Vd 184
WD25: Wat 7Z 13
Blackthorn Ct. *E15 35Fc 73*
(off Hall Rd.)
TW5: Hest 52Aa 107
Blackthorne Av. CR0: C'don 74Yb 158
Blackthorne Cl. AL10: Hat 3B 8
Blackthorne Ct. *SE15 52Vb 113*
(off Cator St.)
TW15: Ashf 66S 128
UB1: S'hall 46Da 85
(off Dormer's Wells La.)
Blackthorne Cres. SL3: Poyle 54G 104
Blackthorne Dell SL3: L'ly 8N 81
Blackthorne Dr. E4 21Fc 53
Blackthorne Ind. Est.
SL3: Poyle 55G 104
Blackthorne Rd. KT23: Bookh 98Ea 192
SL3: Poyle 55G 104
Blackthorn Gro.
BR5: St M Cry 72Xc 161
DA7: Bex 55Ad 117
Blackthorn Ho. *SE16 47Ac 92*
(off Blondin Way)
Blackthorn Rd. CR3: Cat'm 95Tb 197
IG1: Ilf 36Tc 74
RH2: Reig 8L 207
RM16: Grays 46De 99
TN16: Big H 88Mc 179
Blackthorn St. E3 42Cc 92
Blackthorn Way CM14: W'ley 22Zd 59
Blacktree M. SW9 55Qb 112
BLACKWALL 46Ec 92
Blackwall La. SE10 50Gc 93
Blackwall Trad. Est. E14 43Fc 93
Blackwall Tunnel E14 46Fc 93
(not continuous)
Blackwall Tunnel App. E14 45Ec 92
Blackwall Tunnel Northern App.
E3 41Ec 92
E14 41Ec 92
Blackwall Tunnel Southern App.
SE10 48Gc 93
Blackwall Way E14 46Ec 92
Blackwater CM14: B'wood 18Xd 40
Blackwater Cl. E7 35Hc 73
RM13: Rain 43Fd 96
Blackwater Ho. NW8 7C 214
Blackwater La. HP3: Hem H 5E 4
Blackwater St. SE22 57Vb 113
Blackwell Cl. E5 35Zb 72
HA3: Hrw W 24Fa 46
N21 15Nb 32
Blackwell Dr. WD19: Wat 16Y 27
Blackwell Gdns. HA8: Edg 21Qa 47
Blackwell Ho. SW4 58Mb 112
Blackwell Rd. WD4: K Lan 1Q 12
Blackwood Av. N18 22Zb 52
Blackwood Cl.
KT14: W Byf 84L 169
Blackwood Ho. *E1 42Xb 91*
(off Collingwood St.)
Blackwood St. SE17 7F 231 (50Tb 91)
Blade Ct. RM7: Rush G 30Gd 56
Blade M. SW15 56Bb 111
Bladen Cl. KT13: Weyb 79T 150
Bladen Ho. *E1 44Zb 92*
(off Dunelm St.)
Blades Cl. KT22: Lea 92Ma 193
Blades Ct. SW15 56Bb 111
W6 50Xa 88
(off Lower Mall)
Blades Ho. *SE11 51Qb 112*
(off Kennington Oval)
Bladindon Dr. DA5: Bexl 59Yc 117
Bladon Ct. SW16 65Nb 134
Bladon Gdns. HA2: Harr 30Da 45
Blagdens Cl. N14 19Mb 32
Blagdens La. N14 19Lb 32
Blagdon Ct. W7 45Ga 86
Blagdon Rd. KT3: N Mald 70Va 132
SE13 58Dc 114
Blagdon Wlk. TW11: Tedd 65La 130
Blagrove Cres. HA4: Eastc 29X 45
Blagrove Rd. TW11: Hamp W 66Ka 130
W10 43Ab 88
Blair Av. KT10: Esh 75Ea 152
NW9 31Ua 68
Blair Cl. DA15: Sidc 57Uc 116
N1 37Sb 71
UB3: Harl 49W 84
Blair Ct. BR3: Beck 67Dc 136
NW8 39Fb 69
SE6 60Hc 115
Blairderry Rd. SW2 61Nb 134
Blair Dr. TN13: S'oaks 95Kd 203
Blairgowrie Ct. *E14 44Fc 93*
(off Blair St.)
Blairhead Dr. WD19: Wat 20X 27
Blair Ho. SW9 54Pb 112
Blair Rd. SL1: Slou 6J 81
Blair St. E14 44Ec 92
Blake Av. IG11: Bark 39Uc 74
Blakeborough Dr. RM3: Hrld W 26Nd 57
Blake Bldg. N8 27Pb 50
Blake Cl. AL1: St A 5E 6
DA16: Well 53Uc 116
RM13: Rain 39Hd 76
SM5: Cars 74Gb 155
UB4: Hayes 40T 64
W10 43Ya 88
Blake Ct. KT19: Eps 84Pa 173
N21 15Pb 32
NW6 41Cb 89
(off Malvern Rd.)
SE16 50Xb 91
(off Stubbs Dr.)
Blakeden Dr. KT10: Clay 79Ha 152
Blakefield Gdns. CR5: Coul 90Pb 176
Blake Gallery, The
DA12: Grav'nd 9D 122
(off Woodville Pl.)
Blake Gdns. DA1: Dart 56Pd 119
SW6 53Db 111
Blake Hall Cres. E11 32Jc 73
Blake Hall Rd. E11 31Jc 73
Blakehall Rd. SM5: Cars 79Hb 155
Blake Ho. *E14 47Cc 92*
(off Admirals Way)
SE1 3K 229 (48Qb 90)
SE8 51Cc 114
(off New King St.)
Blake M. TW9: Kew 53Qa 109
Blakemore Gdns. SW13 51Xa 110
Blakemore Rd.
CR7: Thor H 71Pb 156
SW16 62Nb 134
Blakemore Way DA17: Belv 48Ad 95
Blakeney Av. BR3: Beck 67Bc 136
Blakeney Cl. E8 36Wb 71
KT19: Eps 83Ta 173
N20 18Eb 31
NW1 38Mb 70
Blakeney Rd. BR3: Beck 66Bc 136
Blakenham Rd. SW17 63Hb 133
Blaker Ct. SE7 52Lc 115
(not continuous)
Blake Rd. CR0: C'don 75Ub 157
CR4: Mitc 69Gb 133
E16 42Hc 93
N11 24Lb 50
Blaker Rd. E15 40Ec 72
Blakes Av. KT3: N Mald 71Va 154
Blakes Ct. KT16: Chert 74J 149
BLAKES GREEN 97Td 204
Blake's Grn. BR4: W W'ck 74Ec 158
Blakes La. KT3: N Mald 71Va 154
Blakesley Av. W5 44La 86
Blakesley Ho. *E12 34Qc 74*
(off Grantham Rd.)
Blakesley Wlk. SW20 68Bb 133
Blake's Rd. SE15 52Ub 113
Blakes Ter. KT3: N Mald 71Wa 154
Blakesware Gdns. N9 17Tb 33
Blake Twr. EC2 7D 218
Blake Way *RM18: Tilb 4E 122*
(off Coleridge Rd.)
Blakewood Cl. TW13: Hanw 63Y 129
Blakewood Ct. *SE20 66Xb 135*
(off Anerley Pk.)
Blanchard Cl. SE9 62Nc 138
Blanchard Dr. WD18: Wat 14U 26
Blanchard Gro. EN3: Enf L 10Dc 20
Blanchard Ho. *TW1: Twick 58Ma 109*
(off Clevedon Rd.)
Blanchard M. RM3: Hrld W 24Pd 57
Blanchards Hill
GU4: Jac W, Sut G 100A 188
Blanchard Way E8 37Wb 71
Blanch Cl. SE15 52Yb 114
Blanchedowne SE5 56Tb 113
Blanche La. EN6: S Mim 4Wa 16
Blanche St. E16 42Hc 93
Blanchland Rd.
SM4: Mord 71Db 155
Blanchman's Rd.
CR6: W'ham 90Ac 178
Blandfield Rd. SW12 59Jb 112
Blandford Av. BR3: Beck 68Ac 136
TW2: Whitt 60Da 107
Blandford Cl. CR0: Bedd 76Nb 156
GU22: Wok 89D 168
N2 28Eb 49
RM7: Mawney 28Dd 56
SL3: L'ly 8P 81
Blandford Ct. *N1 38Ub 71*
(off St Peter's Way)
NW6 38Za 68
SL3: L'ly 8P 81
Blandford Cres. E4 17Ec 34
Blandford Ho. *SW8 52Pb 112*
(off Richborne Ter.)
Blandford Rd. AL1: St A 2E 6
BR3: Beck 68Yb 136
TW11: Tedd 64Fa 130
UB2: S'hall 49Ca 85
W4 48Ua 88
W5 47Ma 87
Blandford Rd. Nth. SL3: L'ly 8P 81
Blandford Rd. Sth. SL3: L'ly 8P 81
Blandford Sq.
NW1 6E 214 (42Gb 89)
Blandford St. W1 2G 221 (44Hb 89)
Blandford Waye UB4: Yead 44Y 85
Bland Ho. SE11 7J 229
Bland St. SE9 56Mc 115
Blaney Cres. E6 41Rc 94
Blanford M. RH2: Reig 6M 207
Blanford Rd. RH2: Reig 7L 207
Blanmerle Rd. SE9 60Rc 116
Blann Cl. SE9 58Mc 115
Blantyre St. SW10 52Fb 111
Blantyre Twr. *SW10 52Fb 111*
(off Blantyre St.)
Blantyre Wlk. *SW10 52Fb 111*
(off Worlds End Est.)
Blashford *NW3 38Hb 69*
(off Adelaide Rd.)
Blashford St. SE13 59Fc 115
Blashill Ct. *E14 45Ec 92*
(off Bullivant St.)
Blasker Wlk. E14 50Dc 92
Blatchford Cl.
KT12: Walt T 75W 150
Blattner Cl. WD6: E'tree 14Na 29
Blaven Path E16 42Hc 93
Blawith Rd. HA1: Harr 28Ga 46
Blaxland Ho. *W12 45Xa 88*
(off White City Est.)
Blaydon Cl. HA4: Ruis 31U 64
N17 24Xb 51
Blaydon Ct. UB5: N'olt 37Ca 65
Blaydon Wlk. N17 24Xb 51
Blays Cl. TW20: Eng G 5N 125
Blay's La. TW20: Eng G 6M 125
Blazer Ct. NW8 4C 214
Bleak Hill La. SE18 51Vc 117
Bleak Ho. La. *W4 50Ta 87*
(off Chiswick High Rd.)
Blean Gro. SE20 66Yb 136
Bleasdale Av. UB6: G'frd 40Ja 66
Blechynden Ho. *W10 44Za 88*
(off Kingsdown Cl.)
Blechynden St. W10 45Za 88
Bledlow Cl. NW8 6C 214 (42Fb 89)
SE28 45Yc 95
Bledlow Ri. UB6: G'frd 40Ea 66
Bleeding Heart Yd. EC1 1A 224
Blegborough Rd. SW16 65Lb 134
Blemundsbury WC1 7H 217
Blencarn Cl. GU21: Wok 8K 167
BLENDON 58Zc 117
Blendon Dr. DA5: Bexl 58Zc 117
Blendon Path BR1: Brom 66Hc 137
Blendon Rd. DA5: Bexl 58Zc 117
Blendon Row SE17 6F 231
Blendon Ter. SE18 50Sc 94
Blendworth Point SW15 60Xa 110
Blenheim Av. IG2: Ilf 29Pc 54
Blenheim Bus. Cen. *CR4: Mitc 68Hb 133*
(off London Rd.)
Blenheim Cen., The TW3: Houn 55Da 107
Blenheim Cl. DA1: Dart 58Ld 119
KT14: W Byf 85H 169
N21 18Sb 33
RM7: Mawney 28Ed 56
RM14: Upm 32Ud 78
SE12 60Kc 115
SL3: L'ly 46B 82
SM6: Wall 80Lb 156
SW20 69Ya 132
UB6: G'frd 40Fa 66
WD19: Wat 17Y 27

Blenheim Ct.—Boreham Wood FC

Blenheim Ct. BR2: Brom ...70Hc 137
DA14: Sidc ...62Tc 138
HA3: Kenton ...30Ja 46
IG8: Wfd G ...24Kc 53
N7 ...37Nb 70
N19 ...33Nb 70
RM12: Horn ...36Ld 77
RM13: Rain ...*40Fd 76*
(off Lowen Rd.)
SE10 ...*50Jc 93*
(off Denham St.)
SE16 ...*46Zb 92*
(off King & Queen Wharf)
SM2: Sutt ...79Eb 155
TW18: Staines ...63F 126
Blenheim Cres. CR2: S Croy ...80Sb 157
HA4: Ruis ...33T 64
W11 ...45Ab 88
Blenheim Dr. DA16: Well ...53Vc 117
Blenheim Gdns. CR2: Sande ...84Wb 177
GU22: Wok ...1M 187
HA9: Wemb ...34Na 67
KT2: King T ...66Ra 131
NW2 ...37Ya 68
RM15: Avel ...46Rd 97
SM6: Wall ...79Lb 156
SW2 ...58Pb 112
Blenheim Gro. DA12: Grav'nd ...9E 122
SE15 ...54Wb 113
Blenheim Ho. *E16* ...*46Kc 93*
(off Constable Av.)
SE18 ...48Sc 94
SW3 ...7E 226
TW3: Houn ...55Ca 107
Blenheim M. WD7: Shenl ...5Na 15
Blenheim Pde. UB10: Hil ...42R 84
Blenheim Pk. Rd. CR2: S Croy ...81Sb 177
Blenheim Pas. NW8 ...1A 214 (40Eb 69)
Blenheim Pl. TW11: Tedd ...64Ha 130
Blenheim Ri. N15 ...28Vb 51
Blenheim Rd. AL1: St A ...1D 6
BR1: Brom ...70Nc 138
BR6: Orp ...75Yc 161
CM15: Pil H ...16Wd 40
DA1: Dart ...58Ld 119
DA15: Sidc ...60Yc 117
E6 ...41Mc 93
E15 ...35Gc 73
E17 ...27Zb 52
EN5: Barn ...13Za 30
HA2: Harr ...30Da 45
KT19: Eps ...83Ta 173
NW8 ...1A 214 (40Eb 69)
SE20 ...66Yb 136
SL3: L'ly ...9P 81
SM1: Sutt ...76Cb 155
SW20 ...69Ya 132
UB5: N'olt ...37Da 65
W4 ...48Ua 88
WD5: Ab L ...4W 12
Blenheim Shop. Cen. SE20 ...66Yb 136
Blenheim St. W1 ...3K 221 (44Kb 90)
Blenheim Ter. NW8 ...1A 214 (40Eb 69)
Blenheim Twr. *SE14* ...*52Ac 114*
(off Batavia Rd.)
Blenheim Way TW7: Isle ...53Ja 108
Blenkarne Rd. SW11 ...58Hb 111
Bleriot Av. KT15: Add ...80J 149
Bleriot Rd. TW5: Hest ...52Y 107
Blessbury Rd. HA8: Edg ...25Sa 47
Blessington Cl. SE13 ...55Fc 115
Blessington Rd. SE13 ...55Fc 115
Blessing Way IG11: Bark ...41Yc 95
BLETCHINGLEY ...5J 209
Bletchingley Cl. CR7: Thor H ...70Rb 135
RH1: Mers ...1C 208
Bletchingley Golf Course ...5K 209
Bletchingley Rd. RH1: Mers ...1C 208
RH1: Nutf ...5G 208
RH9: G'stone ...3N 209
Bletchley Ct. *HA7: Stan* ...*24Na 47*
(off Hitchin Way)
N1 ...2F 219
Bletchley St. N1 ...2E 218 (40Tb 71)
Bletchmore Cl. UB3: Harl ...50T 84
Bletsoe Wlk. N1 ...1E 218 (40Sb 71)
Blewbury Ho. SE2 ...47Yc 95
(not continuous)
Blewitts Cotts. *RM13: Rain* ...*41Hd 96*
(off Dunedin Rd.)
Blick Ho. *SE16* ...*48Yb 92*
(off Neptune St.)
Bligh Rd. DA11: Grav'nd ...8C 122
Bligh's Ct. *TN13: S'oaks* ...*97Ld 203*
(off Bligh's Rd.)
Bligh's Mdw. *TN13: S'oaks* ...*97Ld 203*
(off High St.)
Bligh's Rd. TN13: S'oaks ...97Ld 203
Bligh's Wlk. *TN13: S'oaks* ...*97Kd 203*
(off Bligh's Rd.)
Blincoe Cl. SW19 ...61Za 132
Blinco La. SL3: Geor G ...44A 82
Blind La. EN9: Walt A ...5Lc 21
GU24: Chob ...2D 166
IG10: Lough ...12Gc 35
RH8: Oxt ...2J 211
SM7: Bans ...87Gb 175
Blindman's La. EN8: Chesh ...2Zb 20
Bliss Cres. SE13 ...54Dc 114
Blissett St. SE10 ...53Ec 114
Bliss Ho. EN1: Enf ...10Wb 19
Bliss M. W10 ...41Ab 88
Blisworth Cl. UB4: Yead ...42Aa 85
Blisworth Ho. *E2* ...*39Wb 71*
(off Whiston Rd.)
Blithbury Rd. RM9: Dag ...37Xc 75
Blithdale Rd. SE2 ...49Wc 95
Blithehale Ct. *E2* ...*41Xb 91*
(off Withan St.)
Blithfield St. W8 ...48Db 89
Blockhouse Rd. RM17: Grays ...51Ee 121
Blockley Rd. HA0: Wemb ...33Ka 66
Block Wharf *E14* ...*47Cc 92*
(off Cuba St.)
Bloemfontein Av. W12 ...46Xa 88
Bloemfontein Rd. W12 ...45Xa 88
Bloemfontein Way W12 ...46Xa 88
Blomfield Ct. W9 ...5A 214
Blomfield Mans. *W12* ...*46Ya 88*
(off Stanlake Rd.)
Blomfield Rd. W9 ...7A 214 (43Db 89)
Blomfield St. EC2 ...1G 225 (43Tb 91)
Blomfield Vs. W2 ...43Db 89
Blomville Rd. RM8: Dag ...34Ad 75
Blondell Cl. UB7: Harm ...51M 105
Blondel St. SW11 ...54Jb 112
Blondin Av. W5 ...49La 86
Blondin Pk. & Nature Area ...49Ka 86
Blondin St. E3 ...40Cc 72
Blondin Way SE16 ...47Ac 92
Bloomberg Arc. EC4 ...3E 224 (44Tb 91)
Bloomberg Ct. SW1 ...6D 228
Bloomburg St. SW1 ...6C 228 (49Mb 90)
Bloomfield Cl. GU21: Knap ...9J 167
Bloomfield Ct. *E10* ...*34Dc 72*
(off Brisbane Rd.)
N6 ...30Jb 50
Bloomfield Cres. IG2: Ilf ...30Rc 54
Bloomfield Ho. *E1* ...*43Wb 91*
(off Old Montague St.)
Bloomfield Pl. W1 ...4A 222
Bloomfield Rd. BR2: Brom ...71Mc 159
KT1: King T ...70Na 131
N6 ...30Jb 50
SE18 ...51Rc 116
Bloomfield Ter. SW1 ...7J 227 (50Jb 90)
TN16: Westrm ...97Tc 200
Bloomfield Wlk. RM16: Ors ...3C 100
Bloom Gro. SE27 ...62Rb 135
Bloomhall Rd. SE19 ...64Tb 135
Bloom Pk. Rd. SW6 ...52Bb 111
BLOOMSBURY ...7G 217 (43Nb 90)
Bloomsbury Cl. KT19: Eps ...82Ta 173
NW7 ...24Wa 48
W5 ...45Pa 87
Bloomsbury Ct. HA5: Pinn ...27Ba 45
TW5: Cran ...53X 107
WC1 ...1G 223
Bloomsbury Ho. SW4 ...58Mb 112
Bloomsbury Mans. *BR1: Brom* ...*67Kc 137*
(off Widmore Rd.)
Bloomsbury M. IG8: Wfd G ...23Nc 54
Bloomsbury Pl. SW18 ...57Eb 111
WC1 ...7G 217 (43Nb 90)
Bloomsbury Sq. WC1 ...1G 223 (43Nb 90)
Bloomsbury St. WC1 ...1E 222 (43Mb 90)
Bloomsbury Theatre ...5D 216
Bloomsbury Way WC1 ...2F 223 (43Nb 90)
Blore Cl. SW8 ...53Mb 112
Blore Ct. W1 ...4D 222
Blore Ho. *SW10* ...*52Db 111*
(off Coleridge Gdns.)
Blossom Av. HA2: Harr ...33Da 65
Blossom Cl. CR2: S Croy ...78Vb 157
RM9: Dag ...39Bd 76
W5 ...47Na 87
Blossom Dr. BR6: Orp ...75Vc 161
Blossom La. EN2: Enf ...11Sb 33
Blossom Pl. SE28 ...45Sc 94
Blossom St. E1 ...6J 219 (42Ub 91)
Blossom Way UB7: W Dray ...49Q 84
UB10: Hil ...38P 63
Blossom Waye TW5: Hest ...51Aa 107
Blount M. UB10: Uxb ...40N 63
Blount St. E14 ...44Ac 92
Bloxam Gdns. SE9 ...57Nc 116
Bloxhall Rd. E10 ...32Bc 72
Bloxham Cres. TW12: Hamp ...66Ba 129
Bloxworth Cl. SM6: Wall ...76Lb 156
Blucher Rd. SE5 ...52Sb 113
Blue Anchor All. TW9: Rich ...56Na 109
Blue Anchor La. RM18: W Til ...9F 100
SE16 ...49Wb 91
Blue Anchor Yd. E1 ...45Wb 91
Blue Ball La. TW20: Egh ...64B 126
Blue Ball Yd. SW1 ...7B 222 (46Lb 90)
Blue Barn La. KT13: Weyb ...83Q 170
Bluebell Apartments *N4* ...*32Sb 71*
(off Swan La.)
Bluebell Av. E12 ...36Mc 73
Bluebell Cl. AL2: Park ...9A 6
BR6: Farnb ...75Sc 160
E9 ...39Yb 72
HP1: Hem H ...3G 2
RM7: Rush G ...33Gd 76
SE26 ...63Vb 135
SM6: Wall ...74Kb 156
UB5: N'olt ...37Ba 65
Bluebell Ct. GU22: Wok ...1P 187
NW9 ...*25Ua 48*
(off Heybourne Cres.)
Bluebell Dr. EN7: G Oak ...1Tb 19
WD5: Bedm ...9F 4
Bluebell Ho. *SE16* ...*47Ac 92*
(off Bondin Way)
Blue Bell La. KT11: Stoke D ...89Ca 171
Bluebell La. KT24: E Hor ...100U 190
Bluebell M. RM17: Grays ...50De 99
Bluebell Ter. UB7: W Dray ...47P 83
Bluebell Wlk. HP2: Hem H ...2D 4
Bluebell Way IG1: Ilf ...37Rc 74
Blueberry Cl. IG8: Wfd G ...23Jc 53
WD19: Wat ...17Y 27
Blueberry Gdns. CR5: Coul ...88Pb 176
Blueberry La. TN14: Knock ...88Yc 181
Bluebird Cl. SW20 ...68Ya 132
Bluebird Ho. IG11: Bark ...41Vc 95
Bluebird La. RM10: Dag ...38Cd 76
Bluebird Way AL2: Brick W ...2Ba 13
SE28 ...47Tc 94
Bluebridge Av. AL9: Brk P ...9H 9
Bluebridge Rd. AL9: Brk P ...8G 8
Blue Bldg. *SE10* ...*50Hc 93*
(off Glenforth St.)
Blue Cedars SM7: Bans ...86Za 174
Blue Cedars Pl. KT11: Cobh ...84Z 171
Blue Chalet Ind. Pk.
TN15: W King ...78Td 164
Blue Ct. *N1* ...*39Tb 71*
(off Sherborne St.)
Blue Elephant Theatre ...52Sb 113
(off Bethwin Rd.)
Bluefield Cl. TW12: Hamp ...64Ca 129
Blue Fin Bldg. SE1 ...6C 224
Bluegate M. E1 ...45Xb 91
Bluegate Pk. CM14: B'wood ...20Xd 40
Bluegates KT17: Ewe ...80Wa 154
Blue Ho. Cotts. DA2: Bean ...62Zd 143
Bluehouse Gdns. RH8: Oxt ...100Jc 199
Bluehouse Hill AL3: St A ...3N 5
Bluehouse La. RH8: Limp, Oxt ...100Gc 199
Bluehouse Rd. E4 ...19Gc 35
Blue Leaves Av. CR5: Coul ...93Mb 196
Blue Lion Pl. SE1 ...3H 231 (48Ub 91)
Blueprint Apartments *SW12* ...*59Kb 112*
(off Balham Gro.)
Blue Riband Ind. Est.
CR0: C'don ...75Rb 157
Blues St. E8 ...37Vb 71
Bluett Rd. AL2: Lon C ...9H 7
BLUEWATER ...60Vd 120
Blue Water SW18 ...56Db 111
Bluewater Parkway
DA9: Bluew, Ghithe ...59Vd 120
Bluewater Shop. Cen.
DA9: Bluew ...59Vd 120
Blumenthal Cl. TW7: Isle ...52Fa 108
Blumfield Ct. SL1: Slou ...2B 80
Blumfield Cres. SL1: Slou ...2B 80
Blundel La. KT11: Stoke D ...88Ba 171
Blundell Cl. BR5: St M Cry ...72Yc 161
E8 ...36Wb 71
Blundell Rd. HA8: Edg ...25Ta 47
Blundell St. N7 ...38Nb 70
Blunden Cl. RM8: Dag ...32Yc 75
Blunden Ct. *SW6* ...*52Cb 111*
(off Farm La.)
Blunden Dr. SL3: L'ly ...49D 82
Blunesfield EN6: Pot B ...3Fb 17
Blunt Rd. CR2: S Croy ...78Tb 157
Blunts Av. UB7: Sip ...52Q 106
Blunts La. AL2: Pot C ...6K 5
WD5: Bedm ...9K 5
Blunts Rd. SE9 ...57Qc 116
Blurton Rd. E5 ...35Yb 72
Blydon Ct. *N21* ...*15Pb 32*
(off Chaseville Pk. Rd.)
Blyth Cl. E14 ...49Fc 93
TW1: Twick ...58Ha 108
WD6: Bore ...11Pa 29
Blyth Ct. *BR1: Brom* ...*67Hc 137*
(off Blyth Rd.)
Blythe Cl. SE6 ...59Bc 114
SL0: Iver ...44H 83
BLYTHE HILL ...59Bc 114
Blythe Hill BR5: St P ...67Vc 139
SE6 ...59Bc 114
Blythe Hill La. SE6 ...59Bc 114
Blythe Hill Pl. SE23 ...59Ac 114
Blythe Ho. SE11 ...51Qb 112
SL1: Slou ...6B 80
Blythe M. W14 ...48Za 88
Blythendale Ho. *E2* ...*40Wb 71*
(off Mansford St.)
Blythe Rd. W14 ...48Za 88
Blythe St. E2 ...41Xb 91
Blytheswood HP3: Hem H ...5J 3
Blytheswood Pl. SW16 ...63Pb 134
Blythe Va. SE6 ...60Bc 114
Blyth Hill Pl. *SE23* ...*59Ac 114*
(off Brockley Pk.)
Blyth Ho. DA8: Erith ...50Gd 96
Blyth Rd. BR1: Brom ...67Hc 137
E17 ...31Bc 72
SE28 ...45Yc 95
UB3: Hayes ...47U 84
Blyth's Wharf E14 ...45Ac 92
Blythswood Rd. IG3: Ilf ...32Wc 75
Blyth Wlk. RM14: Upm ...30Ud 58
Blyth Wood Pk. BR1: Brom ...67Hc 137
Blythwood Rd. HA5: Pinn ...25Z 45
N4 ...31Nb 70
Boades M. NW3 ...35Fb 69
Boadicea Cl. SL1: Slou ...6C 80
Boadicea St. N1 ...39Pb 70
Boakes Cl. NW9 ...28Sa 47
Boakes Mdw. TN14: S'ham ...83Hd 182
Boar Cl. IG7: Chig ...22Wc 55
Boardman Av. E4 ...15Dc 34
Boardman Cl. EN5: Barn ...15Ab 30
Boardman Pl. CM14: B'wood ...20Xd 40
Board School Rd. GU21: Wok ...88B 168
Boardwalk Pl. E14 ...46Ec 92
Boarlands Cl. SL1: Slou ...5D 80
Boarlands Path SL1: Slou ...5D 80
Boarley Ho. SE17 ...6H 231
Boars Head Yd. TW8: Bford ...52Ma 109
Boatemah Wlk. *SW9* ...*54Qb 112*
(off Peckford Pl.)
Boathouse, The E14 ...44Cc 92
Boathouse Cen., The *W10* ...*42Za 88*
(off Canal Cl.)
Boathouse Wlk. SE15 ...52Vb 113
(not continuous)
Boat La. E2 ...1K 219 (39Vb 71)
Boat Lifter Way SE16 ...49Ac 92
Boat Quay E16 ...45Lc 93
Boatyard Apartments E14 ...50Dc 92
Bob Anker Cl. E13 ...41Jc 93
Bobbin Cl. SW4 ...55Lb 112
Bobby Moore Way IG11: Bark ...39Sc 74
N10 ...24Hb 49
Bob Dunn Way DA1: Dart ...56Ld 119
Bob Hope Theatre, The ...58Pc 116
Bob Marley Way SE24 ...56Qb 112
Bobs La. RM1: Rom ...24Jd 56
Bocketts Farm Pk. ...97Ha 192
Bocketts La. KT22: Fet ...96Ha 192
Bockhampton Rd. KT2: King T ...66Pa 131
Bocking St. E8 ...39Xb 71
Boddicott Cl. SW19 ...61Ab 132
Boddington Gdns. W3 ...47Qa 87
Boddington Ho. *SE14* ...*53Yb 114*
(off Pomeroy St.)
SW13 ...*51Xa 110*
(off Wyatt Dr.)
Bodell Cl. RM16: Grays ...48De 99
Bodeney Ho. *SE5* ...*53Ub 113*
(off Peckham Rd.)
Boden Ho. *E1* ...*43Wb 91*
(off Woodseer St.)
Bodiam Cl. EN1: Enf ...12Ub 33
Bodiam Rd. SW16 ...66Mb 134
Bodiam Way NW10 ...41Pa 87
Bodicea M. TW4: Houn ...58Ba 107
Bodington Ct. W12 ...47Za 88
Bodium Ct. *E17* ...*25Bc 52*
(off Thornbury Way)
Bodle Av. DA10: Swans ...59Ae 121
Bodleian Ho. SE20 ...67Wb 135
Bodley Cl. CM16: Epp ...2Vc 23
KT3: N Mald ...71Ua 154
Bodley Ho. SL0: Iver H ...40F 62
Bodley Mnr. Way SW2 ...59Qb 112
Bodley Rd. KT3: N Mald ...72Ta 153
Bodmin Av. SL2: Slou ...3E 80
Bodmin Cl. BR5: Orp ...74Yc 161
HA2: Harr ...34Ba 65
Bodmin Ct. RM3: Rom ...25Md 57
Bodmin Gro. SM4: Mord ...71Db 155
Bodmin St. SW18 ...60Cb 111
Bodnant Gdns. SW20 ...69Wa 132
Bodney Rd. E8 ...36Xb 71
Bodwell Cl. HP1: Hem H ...1J 3
Boeing Way UB2: S'hall ...48X 85
Boevey Path DA17: Belv ...50Bd 95
Bogart Ct. *E14* ...*45Cc 92*
(off Premiere Pl.)
Bogey La. BR6: Downe ...80Qc 160
Bognor Gdns. WD19: Wat ...22Y 45
Bognor Rd. DA16: Well ...53Zc 117
Bohemia HP2: Hem H ...1N 3
Bohemia Pl. E8 ...37Yb 72
Bohn Rd. E1 ...43Ac 92
Bohun Gro. EN4: E Barn ...16Gb 31
Boileau Pde. *W5* ...*44Pa 87*
(off Boileau Rd.)
Boileau Rd. SW13 ...52Wa 110
W5 ...44Pa 87
Bois Hall Rd. KT15: Add ...78M 149
Boisseau Ho. *E1* ...*43Yb 92*
(off Stepney Way)
Boissy Cl. AL4: St A ...3J 7
Bolanachi Bldg. SE16 ...48Vb 91
Bolander Gro. Nth. *SW6* ...*51Cb 111*
(off Seagrave Rd.)
Bolander Gro. Sth. *SW6* ...*51Cb 111*
(off Seagrave Rd.)
Bolberry Rd. RM5: Col R ...22Fd 56
Bolden St. SE8 ...54Dc 114
Boldero Pl. NW8 ...6D 214
Bolderwood Way
BR4: W W'ck ...75Dc 158
Bolding Ho. La.
GU24: W End ...5D 166
Boldmere Rd. HA5: Eastc ...31Y 65
Bold's Ct. SL2: Stoke P ...8L 61
Boleyn Av. EN1: Enf ...11Xb 33
KT17: Ewe ...82Xa 174
Boleyn Cl. E17 ...28Cc 52
IG10: Lough ...16Nc 36
RM16: Chaf H ...48Be 99
TW18: Staines ...64G 126
Boleyn Ct. *GU21: Knap* ...*10G 166*
(off Tudor Way)
IG9: Buck H ...18Jc 35
KT8: E Mos ...*70Fa 130*
(off Bridge Rd.)
RH1: Redh ...*5A 208*
(off St Anne's Ri.)
Boleyn Dr. AL1: St A ...4B 6
HA4: Ruis ...33Z 65
KT8: W Mole ...69Ba 129
Boleyn Gdns. BR4: W W'ck ...75Dc 158
CM13: B'wood ...20Ce 41
RM10: Dag ...38Ed 76
Boleyn Gro. BR4: W W'ck ...75Ec 158
Boleyn Ho. *E16* ...*46Jc 93*
(off Southey M.)
Boleyn Rd. E6 ...40Mc 73
E7 ...38Jc 73
N16 ...36Ub 71
TN15: Kems'g ...89Nd 183
Boleyn Row CM16: Epp ...1Yc 23
Boleyn Wlk. KT22: Lea ...92Ha 192
Boleyn Way DA10: Swans ...59Ae 121
EN5: New Bar ...13Eb 31
IG6: Ilf ...23Sc 54
Bolina Rd. SE16 ...50Yb 92
Bolingbroke Cl. EN4: Cockf ...13Hb 31
Bolingbroke Gro. SW11 ...56Gb 111
Bolingbroke Rd. W14 ...48Za 88
Bolingbroke Wlk. SW11 ...53Fb 111
Bolingbroke Way UB3: Hayes ...46T 84
Bolliger Ct. NW10 ...42Sa 87
Bollinder Pl. EC1 ...3D 218 (41Sb 91)
Bollo Bri. Rd. W3 ...48Ra 87
Bollo La. W3 ...47Ra 87
W4 ...49Sa 87
Bolney Ga. SW7 ...2D 226 (47Gb 89)
Bolney St. SW8 ...52Pb 112
Bolney Way TW13: Hanw ...62Aa 129
Bolsover Gro. RH1: Mers ...1E 208
Bolsover St. W1 ...6A 216 (42Kb 90)
Bolstead Rd. CR4: Mitc ...67Kb 134
Bolster Gro. N22 ...24Mb 50
Bolt Cellar La. CM16: Epp ...2Uc 22
Bolt Ct. EC4 ...3A 224 (44Qb 90)
Bolters La. SM7: Bans ...86Bb 175
Bolt Ho. N1 ...1J 219
Boltmore Cl. NW4 ...27Za 48
Bolton Av. SL4: Wind ...5G 102
Bolton Cl. KT9: Chess ...79Ma 153
SE20 ...68Wb 135
Bolton Cres. SE5 ...52Rb 113
SE11 ...52Qb 112
SL4: Wind ...5G 102
Bolton Dr. SM4: Mord ...73Eb 155
Bolton Gdns. BR1: Brom ...65Hc 137
NW10 ...40Za 68
SW5 ...50Db 89
TW11: Tedd ...65Ja 130
Bolton Gdns. M. SW10 ...50Eb 89
Bolton Ho. *SE10* ...*50Gc 93*
(off Trafalgar Rd.)
SE11 ...5B 230
Bolton Pl. *NW8* ...*39Db 69*
(off Bolton Rd.)
Bolton Rd. E15 ...37Hc 73
HA1: Harr ...28Ea 46
KT9: Chess ...79Ma 153
N18 ...22Vb 51
NW8 ...39Db 69
NW10 ...39Ua 68
SL4: Wind ...5G 102
W4 ...52Sa 109
Boltons, The HA0: Wemb ...35Ha 66
IG8: Wfd G ...21Jc 53
SW10 ...7A 226 (50Eb 89)
Boltons Cl. GU22: Pyr ...88J 169
Boltons Ct. *SW5* ...*50Db 89*
(off Old Brompton Rd.)
Bolton's La. UB3: Harl ...53S 106
Boltons La. GU22: Pyr ...88J 169
Boltons Pl. SW5 ...7A 226 (50Eb 89)
Bolton St. W1 ...6A 222 (46Kb 90)
Bolton Studios SW10 ...50Eb 89
Bolton Wlk. *N7* ...*33Pb 70*
(off Durham Rd.)
Bombay Ct. *SE16* ...*47Yb 92*
(off St Marychurch St.)
Bombay St. SE16 ...49Xb 91
Bombers La. TN16: Westrm ...91Tc 200
Bomer Cl. UB7: Sip ...52Q 106
Bomore Rd. W11 ...45Ab 88
Bonaly Ho. RH8: Oxt ...3G 210
Bonar Pl. BR7: Chst ...66Nc 138
Bonar Rd. SE15 ...52Wb 113
Bonaventure Ct. DA12: Grav'nd ...10C 122
Bonchester Cl. BR7: Chst ...66Qc 138
Bonchurch Cl. SM2: Sutt ...80Db 155
Bonchurch Ct. RM19: Purf ...50Sd 98
Bonchurch Rd. W10 ...43Ab 88
W13 ...46Ka 86
Bond Cl. SL0: Iver H ...38D 62
TN14: Knock ...87Zc 181
UB7: Yiew ...44P 83
Bond Ct. EC4 ...3F 225 (45Tb 91)
Bondfield Av. UB4: Yead ...41W 84
Bondfield Rd. E6 ...43Pc 94
Bondfield Wlk. DA1: Dart ...56Pd 119
Bond Gdns. SM6: Wall ...77Lb 156
Bond Ho. *NW6* ...*40Bb 69*
(off Rupert Rd.)
SE14 ...*52Ac 114*
(off Goodwood Rd.)
TW8: Bford ...50Ma 87
Bonding Yd. Wlk. SE16 ...48Ac 92
Bond Rd. CR4: Mitc ...68Gb 133
CR6: W'ham ...90Zb 178
KT6: Surb ...75Pa 153
Bond St. E15 ...36Gc 73
RM17: Grays ...51Ee 121
TN14: Knock ...87Ad 181
TW20: Eng G ...4M 125
W4 ...49Ta 87
W5 ...45Ma 87
Bondway SW8 ...51Nb 112
Boneashe La. TN15: Plat ...93Fe 205
Bone Mill La. RH9: G'stone ...6C 210
Bonesgate Open Space Local Nature Reserve ...79Qa 153
Boneta Rd. SE18 ...48Pc 94
Bonfield Rd. SE13 ...56Ec 114
Bonham Cl. DA17: Belv ...50Bd 95
Bonham Dr. RM16: Ors ...3C 100
Bonham Gdns. RM8: Dag ...33Zc 75
Bonham Ga. *KT12: Walt T* ...*74V 150*
(off New Zealand Av.)
Bonham Ho. *W11* ...*46Bb 89*
(off Boyne Ter. M.)
Bonham Rd. RM8: Dag ...33Zc 75
SW2 ...57Pb 112
Bonham Way DA11: Nflt ...60Ee 121
Bonheur Rd. W4 ...47Ta 87
Bonhill St. EC2 ...6G 219 (42Tb 91)
Boniface Gdns. HA3: Hrw W ...24Da 45
Boniface Rd. UB10: Ick ...34R 64
Boniface Wlk. HA3: Hrw W ...24Da 45
Bonington Ho. EN1: Enf ...15Wb 33
Bonington Rd. RM12: Horn ...36Md 77
Bonita M. SE4 ...55Zb 114
Bon Marche Ter. M. *SE27* ...*63Ub 135*
(off Gypsy Rd.)
Bonner Hill Rd. KT1: King T ...68Pa 131
Bonner Rd. E2 ...40Yb 72
Bonners Cl. GU22: Wok ...94B 188
Bonnersfield Cl. HA1: Harr ...30Ha 46
Bonnersfield La. HA1: Harr ...30Ha 46
(not continuous)
Bonner St. E2 ...40Yb 72
Bonner Wlk. RM16: Chaf H ...48Be 99
Bonnett M. RM11: Horn ...32Nd 77
Bonneville Gdns. SW4 ...58Lb 112
Bonney Gro. EN7: Chesh ...2Wb 19
Bonney Way BR8: Swan ...68Gd 140
Bonnington Ct. *UB5: N'olt* ...*40Z 65*
(off Gallery Gdns.)
Bonnington Ho. N1 ...2H 217 (40Pb 70)
Bonningtons CM13: B'wood ...20De 41
Bonnington Sq. SW8 ...51Pb 112
Bonnys Rd. RH2: Reig ...7F 206
Bonny St. NW1 ...38Lb 70
Bonser Rd. TW1: Twick ...61Ha 130
Bonsey Cl. GU22: Wok ...93A 188
Bonsey La. GU22: Wok ...93A 188
Bonseys La. GU24: Chob ...81B 168
Bonsey's Yd. UB8: Uxb ...38M 63
Bonsor Dr. KT20: Kgswd ...94Ab 194
Bonsor Ho. SW8 ...53Lb 112
Bonsor St. SE5 ...52Ub 113
Bonville Gdns. NW4 ...28Xa 48
Bonville Rd. BR1: Brom ...64Hc 137
Bookbinders Cott. Homes N20 ...20Hb 31
Bookbinders Ct. *E1* ...*42Xb 91*
(off Cudworth St.)
Booker Cl. E14 ...43Bc 92
Booker Rd. N18 ...22Wb 51
Bookham Comn. Rd.
KT23: Bookh ...93Aa 191
Bookham Ct. CR4: Mitc ...69Fb 133
KT23: Bookh ...95Ba 191
Bookham Gro. KT23: Bookh ...98Da 191
Bookham Ind. Est. KT23: Bookh ...95Ba 191
Bookham Rd. KT11: D'side ...91Y 191
Book Ho. N1 ...3D 218 (40Sb 71)
Boomes Ind. Est. RM13: Rain ...42Hd 96
Boone Ct. N9 ...20Yb 34
Boones Rd. SE13 ...56Gc 115
Boone St. SE13 ...56Gc 115
Boord St. SE10 ...48Gc 93
Boot All. *AL3: St A* ...*2B 6*
(off Chequer St.)
Boothby Ct. E4 ...20Ec 34
Boothby Rd. N19 ...33Mb 70
Booth Cl. E9 ...39Xb 71
SE28 ...46Xc 95
Booth Ct. SE13 ...55Dc 114
Booth Dr. TW18: Staines ...65M 127
Booth Ho. *TW8: Bford* ...*52La 108*
(off High St.)
Booth La. EC4 ...4D 224
Boothman Ho. HA3: Kenton ...27Ma 47
Booth Rd. CR0: C'don ...75Rb 157
E16 ...47Lc 93
NW9 ...26Ta 47
Booths Cl. AL9: Wel G ...6F 8
Booth's Ct. CM13: Hut ...16Ee 41
Booth's Pl. W1 ...1C 222 (43Lb 90)
Boot Pde. *HA8: Edg* ...*23Qa 47*
(off High St.)
Boot St. N1 ...4H 219 (41Ub 91)
Bordars Rd. W7 ...43Ga 86
Bordars Wlk. W7 ...43Ga 86
Bordeaux Ho. *E15* ...*36Gc 73*
(off Luxembourg M.)
Borden Av. EN1: Enf ...16Tb 33
Border Cres. SE26 ...64Xb 135
Border Gdns. CR0: C'don ...77Dc 158
Bordergate CR4: Mitc ...67Hb 133
Border Rd. SE26 ...64Xb 135
Borders Cres. *IG10: Lough* ...*14Rc 36*
(off Border's La.)
Borderside SL2: Slou ...4L 81
Border's La. IG10: Lough ...14Qc 36
Borders Wlk. *IG10: Lough* ...*14Qc 36*
(off Border's La.)
Bordesley Rd. SM4: Mord ...71Db 155
Bordeston Ct. *TW8: Bford* ...*52La 108*
(off The Hermitage)
Bordon Wlk. SW15 ...59Wa 110
Boreas Wlk. N1 ...2C 218
Boreham Av. E16 ...44Jc 93
Boreham Cl. E11 ...32Ec 72
Boreham Holt WD6: E'tree ...14Pa 29
Boreham Rd. N22 ...26Sb 51
BOREHAMWOOD ...13Qa 29
Borehamwood Ent. Cen.
WD6: Bore ...13Pa 29
Boreham Wood FC ...12Ra 29

Borehamwood Ind. Pk.—Brabourn Gro.

Borehamwood Ind. Pk. WD6: Bore . . .12Ta 29
Borehamwood Shop. Pk.
WD6: Bore 13Qa 29
Boreman Ho. SE10 . . . . .51Ec 114
(off Thames St.)
Borgard Rd. SE18 . . . . .49Pc 94
Borkwood Pk. BR6: Orp 77Vc 161
Borkwood Way BR6: Orp 77Uc 160
Borland Cl. DA9: Ghithe 57Wd 120
Borland Rd. SE15 . . . . .56Yb 114
TW11: Tedd 66Ka 130
Borley Ct. RM16: Ors 4F 100
TW19: Stanw 60N 105
Bornedene EN6: Pot B 3Ab 16
Borneo St. SW15 . . . . .55Ya 110
BOROUGH, THE 2E 230 (47Tb 91)
Borough Grange CR2: Sande 84Wb 177
BOROUGH GREEN 92Be 205
Borough Grn. Rd.
TN15: Bor G, Igh 93Zd 205
(not continuous)
TN15: Wro 89Ce 185
Borough High St. SE1 . . . . .2E 230 (47Sb 91)
Borough Hill CR0: Wadd 76Rb 157
Borough Mkt. SE1 . . . . .7F 225
Borough Rd. CR4: Mitc 68Gb 133
KT2: King T 67Qa 131
SE1 . . . . .3B 230 (48Rb 91)
TN16: Tats 93Mc 199
TW7: Isle 53Ga 108
Borough Sports Ground 77Cb 155
Borough Sq. SE1 . . . . .2D 230
Borough Way EN6: Pot B 4Ab 16
Borrett Cl. SE17 . . . . .7D 230 (50Sb 91)
Borrodaile Rd. SW18 . . . . .58Db 111
Borromeo Way CM14: B'wood 18Xd 40
Borrowdale NW1 . . . . .4B 216
Borrowdale Av. HA3: W'stone 26Ja 46
Borrowdale Cl. CR2: Sande 85Vb 177
IG4: Ilf 28Nc 54
N2 . . . . .26Eb 49
TW20: Egh 66D 126
Borrowdale Ct. EN2: Enf 11Sb 33
Borrowdale Dr. CR2: Sande 84Vb 177
Borthwick M. E15 . . . . .35Gc 73
Borthwick Rd. E15 . . . . .35Gc 73
NW9 .30Va 48
Borthwick St. SE8 . . . . .50Cc 92
Borwick Av. E17 . . . . .27Bc 52
Bosanquet Cl. UB8: Cowl 42M 83
Bosbury Rd. SE6 . . . . .62Ec 136
Boscastle Rd. NW5 . . . . .34Kb 70
Boscobel Cl. BR1: Brom 68Pc 138
Boscobel Ho. E8 . . . . .37Xb 71
Boscobel Pl. SW1 . . . . .5J 227 (49Jb 90)
Boscobel St. NW8 . . . . .6C 214 (42Fb 89)
Bosco Cl. BR6: Orp 77Vc 161
Boscombe Av. E10 . . . . .31Fc 73
RM11: Horn 31Md 77
RM17: Grays 49Fe 99
Boscombe Cir. NW9 . . . . .25Ta 47
Boscombe Cl. E5 . . . . .36Ac 72
TW20: Egh 67E 126
Boscombe Gdns. SW16 . . . . .65Nb 134
Boscombe Ho. CR0: C'don 74Tb 157
(off Sydenham Rd.)
Boscombe Rd. KT4: Wor Pk 74Ya 154
SW17 . . . . .65Jb 134
SW19 . . . . .67Db 133
W12 .46Wa 88
Bose Cl. N3 . . . . .25Ab 48
Bosgrove E4 . . . . .19Ec 34
Boshers Gdns. TW20: Egh 65B 126
Bosman Dr. GU20: W'sham 7A 146
Boss Ho. SE1 . . . . .1K 231
Boss St. SE1 . . . . .1K 231 (47Vb 91)
Bostall Hill SE2 . . . . .50Wc 95
Bostall La. SE2 . . . . .49Xc 95
Bostall Mnr. Way SE2 . . . . .49Xc 95
Bostall Pk. Av. DA7: Bex 52Ad 117
Bostall Rd. BR5: St P 66Xc 139
Bostock Ho. TW5: Hest 51Ca 107
Boston Bus. Pk. W7 . . . . .48Ga 86
Boston Ct. SE25 . . . . .70Vb 135
SM2: Sutt 80Eb 155
Boston Gdns. TW8: Bford 49Ja 86
W4 . . . . .51Ua 110
W7 . . . . .49Ja 86
Boston Gro. HA4: Ruis 30S 44
SL1: Slou 4G 80
Boston Ho. SW5 . . . . .49Db 89
(off Collingham Rd.)
BOSTON MANOR 49Ja 86
Boston Manor House 50Ka 86
Boston Mnr. Rd. TW8: Bford 49Ka 86
Boston Pde. W7 . . . . .48Ja 86
Boston Pk. Rd. TW8: Bford 50La 86
Boston Pl. NW1 . . . . .6F 215 (42Hb 89)
Boston Rd. CR0: C'don 72Pb 156
E6 . . . . .41Nc 94
E17 . . . . .30Cc 52
HA8: Edg 24Sa 47
W7 . . . . .46Ga 86
Bostonthorpe Rd. W7 . . . . .47Ga 86
Boston Va. W7 . . . . .49Ja 86
Bosun Cl. E14 . . . . .47Cc 92
Bosville Av. TN13: S'oaks 95Jd 202
Bosville Dr. TN13: S'oaks 95Jd 202
Bosville Rd. TN13: S'oaks 95Jd 202
Boswell Cl. BR5: Orp 72Yc 161
WD7: Shenl 4Na 15
Boswell Ct. KT2: King T 67Pa 131
(off Clifton Rd.)
NW9 .26Ua 48
(off Charcot Rd.)
W14 .48Za 88
(off Blythe Rd.)
WC1 . . . . .7G 217 (43Nb 90)
Boswell Ho. WC1 . . . . .7G 217
Boswell Path UB3: Harl 49V 84
Boswell Rd. CR7: Thor H 70Sb 135
Boswell Row CR3: Cat'm 94Wb 197
Boswell St. WC1 . . . . .7G 217 (43Nb 90)
Boswood Ct. TW3: Houn 55Ba 107
Bosworth Cl. E17 . . . . .25Bc 52
Bosworth Ct. SL1: Slou 5A 80
Bosworth Cres. RM3: Rom 23Ld 57
Bosworth Ho. DA8: Erith 50Gd 96
(off Saltford Cl.)
W10 .42Ab 88
(off Bosworth Rd.)
Bosworth Rd. EN5: New Bar 13Cb 31
N11 .23Mb 50
RM10: Dag 34Cd 76
W10 .42Ab 88
BOTANY BAY 8Mb 18
Botany Bay La. BR7: Chst 69Sc 138
Botany Cl. EN4: E Barn 14Gb 31
Botany Cotts. RM19: Purf 50Qd 97
Botany Rd. DA11: Nflt 56Ce 121
Botany Ter. RM19: Purf 50Qd 97
Botany Way RM19: Purf 49Rd 97
Boteley Cl. E4 . . . . .19Fc 35
Botery's Cross RH1: Blet 5H 209
Botham Cl. HA8: Edg 24Sa 47
Botham Dr. SL1: Slou 8J 81
Botha Rd. E13 . . . . .43Kc 93
Bothwell Cl. E16 . . . . .43Hc 93
Bothwell Rd. CR0: New Ad 82Ec 178
Bothwell St. W6 . . . . .51Za 110
Bothy, The GU22: Pyr 89H 169
SM7: Bans 90Eb 175
Botolph All. EC3 . . . . .4H 225
Botolph La. EC3 . . . . .5H 225 (45Ub 91)
Botsford Rd. SW20 . . . . .68Ab 132
Botsom La. TN15: W King 79Sd 164
Bottle Cotts. TN13: S'oaks 94Jd 202
Bottom La. WD3: Bucks 7K 11
WD4: Bucks 7K 11
Bottom Waltons Cvn. Site
SL2: Farn R 10C 60
Bott Rd. DA2: Hawl 63Pd 141
Botts M. W2 . . . . .44Cb 89
Botwell Comn. Rd. UB3: Hayes 45T 84
Botwell Cres. UB3: Hayes 44U 84
Botwell Green Sports & Leisure Cen.
. . . . .46V 84
Botwell La. UB3: Hayes 45U 84
Boucher Cl. TW11: Tedd 64Ha 130
Boucher Dr. DA11: Nflt 2B 144
Bouchier Ho. N2 . . . . .26Fb 49
(off The Grange)
Bouchier Wlk. RM13: Rain 37Jd 76
Boughton Beech Ct. EN3: Enf W 9Zb 20
Boughton Av. BR2: Hayes 73Hc 159
Boughton Hall Av. GU23: Send 96H 189
Boughton Ho. SE1 . . . . .1F 231
Boughton Rd. SE28 . . . . .48Uc 94
Boulcott St. E1 . . . . .44Zb 92
Boulevard, The DA9: Ghithe 56Yd 120
IG8: Wfd G 23Qc 54
SW6 .53Eb 111
SW17 . . . . .61Jb 134
SW18 . . . . .56Db 111
WD18: Wat 15T 26
Boulevard 25 WD6: Bore 13Qa 29
Boulevard Dr. NW9 . . . . .26Va 48
Boulevard Walkway E1 . . . . .44Wb 91
(off Piazza Wlk.)
Boulmer Rd. UB8: Cowl 41L 83
Boulogne Ho. SE1 . . . . .3K 231
Boulogne Rd. CR0: C'don 72Sb 157
Boulter Cl. BR1: Brom 69Qc 138
Boulter Gdns. RM13: Rain 37Jd 76
Boulter Ho. SE14 . . . . .53Yb 114
(off Kender St.)
Boulters Cl. SL1: Slou 6E 80
Boulthurst Way RH8: Oxt 4M 211
Boulton Ho. TW8: Bford 50Na 87
Boulton Rd. RM8: Dag 33Ad 75
Boultwood Rd. E6 . . . . .44Pc 94
Bounce, The HP2: Hem H 1M 3
BOUNCE HILL 11Kd 39
Bounces La. N9 . . . . .19Xb 33
Bounces Rd. N9 . . . . .19Xb 33
Boundaries Rd. SW12 . . . . .61Hb 133
TW13: Felt 60Y 107
Boundary Av. E17 . . . . .31Bc 72
Boundary Bus. Cen. GU21: Wok 87C 168
Boundary Bus. Ct. CR4: Mitc 69Fb 133
Boundary Cl. EN5: Barn 11Bb 31
IG3: Ilf 35Uc 74
KT1: King T 69Ra 131
SE20 .68Wb 135
UB2: S'hall 50Ca 85
Boundary Cotts. HP3: Bov 1F 10
Boundary Ct. CM16: Epp 4Tc 22
N18 . . . . .23Vb 51
(off Snells Pk.)
Boundary Dr. CM13: Hut 17Fe 41
Boundary Ho. DA11: Nflt 10B 122
(off Victoria Rd.)
EN8: Chesh 4Zb 20
SE5 . . . . .52Sb 113
W11 .46Za 88
(off Queensdale Cres.)
Boundary La. E13 . . . . .41Mc 93
SE17 .51Sb 113
Boundary Pk. HP2: Hem H 1C 4
KT13: Weyb 76U 150
Boundary Pas. E2 . . . . .5K 219 (42Vb 91)
Boundary Rd. AL1: St A 1C 6
DA15: Sidc 57Uc 116
E13 . . . . .40Lc 73
E17 . . . . .31Bc 72
GU21: Wok 88C 168
HA5: Eastc 31Z 65
HA9: Wemb 34Na 67
IG11: Bark 39Tc 74
(King Edwards Rd.)
IG11: Bark 40Sc 74
(The Clarksons)
N2 . . . . .25Fb 49
N9 . . . . .16Yb 34
N22 .27Rb 51
NW8 .39Db 69
RM1: Rom 30Jd 56
RM14: Upm 34Qd 77
SM5: Cars 79Kb 156
SM6: Wall 79Kb 156
SW19 . . . . .65Fb 133
TW15: Ashf 64L 127
Boundary Row SE1 . . . . . . .1B 230 (47Rb 91)
Boundary St. DA8: Erith 52Hd 118
E2 . . . . .4K 219 (41Vb 91)
Boundary Way CR0: Addtn 78Cc 158
GU21: Wok 87C 168
HP2: Hem H 1C 4
WD25: Wat 4X 13
Boundfield Rd. SE6 . . . . .62Gc 137
BOUNDS GREEN 23Mb 50
Bounds Grn. Ct. N11 . . . . .23Mb 50
(off Bounds Grn. Rd.)
Bounds Grn. Ind. Est. N11 . . . . .23Lb 50
Bounds Grn. Rd. N11 . . . . .23Lb 50
N22 .23Lb 50
Bourbon Ho. SE6 . . . . .64Ec 136
Bourbon La. W12 . . . . .46Za 88
Bourbon Rd. SW9 . . . . .53Qb 112
Bourchier Cl. TN13: S'oaks 98Kd 203
Bourchier St. W1 . . . . .4D 222 (45Mb 90)
Bourdon Pl. W1 . . . . .4A 222
Bourdon Rd. SE20 . . . . .68Yb 136
Bourdon St. W1 . . . . .4A 222 (45Kb 90)
Bourke Cl. NW10 . . . . .37Ua 68
SW4 .58Nb 112
Bourke Hill CR5: Chip 90Hb 175
Bourlet Cl. W1 . . . . .1B 222 (43Lb 90)
Bourn Av. EN4: E Barn 15Fb 31
N15 .28Tb 51
UB8: Hil 42Q 84
Bournbrook Rd. SE3 . . . . .55Mc 115
Bourne, The HP3: Bov 9C 2
KT16: Chert 73J 149
(off Guildford St.)
N14 .18Mb 32
Bourne Av. HA4: Ruis 36Y 65
KT16: Chert 69J 127
N14 .19Nb 32
SL4: Wind 5G 102
UB3: Harl 48S 84
BOURNEBRIDGE 18Dd 38
Bournebridge Cl. CM13: Hut 17Fe 41
Bournebridge La. RM4: Stap A 17Bd 37
Bournebrook Gro. RM7: Rush G 30Fd 56
Bourne Bus. Pk. KT15: Add 77N 149
Bourne Cir. UB3: Harl 48S 84
Bourne Cl. KT7: T Ditt 75Ha 152
KT14: W Byf 85K 169
TW7: Isle 55Ga 108
Bourne Ct. CR3: Cat'm 95Wb 197
HA4: Ruis 36X 65
IG8: Wfd G 23Kc 53
W4 . . . . .51Sa 109
Bourne Dr. CR4: Mitc 68Fb 133
BOURNE END 4E 2
Bourne End RM11: Horn 31Qd 77
Bourne End La. HP1: Hem H 7C 2
Bourne End La. Ind. Est. HP1: Hem H . . .4D 2
Bourne End Rd. HA6: Nwood 21U 44
Bourne Ent. Cen. TN15: Bor G 91Ce 205
Bourne Est. EC1 . . . . .7K 217 (43Qb 90)
Bournefield Rd. CR3: Whyt 90Wb 177
Bourne Gdns. E4 . . . . .21Dc 52
Bourne Gro. KT21: Asht 91Ma 193
Bournehall WD23: Bush 16Ca 27
Bournehall Av. WD23: Bush 15Ca 27
Bournehall La. WD23: Bush 16Ca 27
Bourne Hall Mus. 81Va 174
Bournehall Rd. WD23: Bush 16Ca 27
Bourne Hill N13 . . . . .19Nb 32
Bourne Hill Cl. N13 . . . . .19Pb 32
Bourne Ho. IG9: Buck H 20Mc 35
TW15: Ashf 64Q 128
Bourne Ind. Pk. DA1: Cray 57Gd 118
Bourne La. CR3: Cat'm 93Tb 197
TN15: Plax 98Be 205
Bourne Mead DA5: Bexl 57Fd 118
Bournemead WD23: Bush 16Da 27
Bournemead Av. UB5: N'olt 40W 64
Bournemead Cl. UB5: N'olt 40W 64
Bourne Mdw. TW20: Thorpe 70D 126
Bournemead Way UB5: N'olt 40X 65
Bourne M. RH9: G'stone 2A 210
W1 . . . . .2J 221 (44Jb 90)
Bournemouth Cl. SE15 . . . . .54Wb 113
Bournemouth Rd. SE15 . . . . .54Wb 113
SW19 . . . . .67Cb 133
Bourne Pde. DA5: Bexl 59Dd 118
Bourne Pk. Cl. CR8: Kenley 88Ub 177
Bourne Pl. KT16: Chert 74K 149
W4 . . . . .50Ta 87
Bourne Rd. BR2: Brom 70Mc 137
DA1: Cray 58Ed 118
DA5: Bexl, Dart 59Dd 118
DA12: Grav'nd 1H 145
E7 . . . . .34Hc 73
GU25: Vir W 1P 147
N8 . . . . .30Nb 50
RH1: Mers 2C 208
SL1: Slou 7G 80
WD23: Bush 15Ca 27
Bournes Ho. N15 . . . . .30Ub 51
(off Chisley Rd.)
Bourneside GU25: Vir W 3L 147
Bourneside Cres. N14 . . . . .18Mb 32
Bourneside Gdns. SE6 . . . . .64Ec 136
Bourneside Rd. KT15: Add 77M 149
Bourne St. CR0: C'don 75Rb 157
SW1 . . . . .6H 227 (49Jb 90)
Bourne Ter. W2 . . . . .43Db 89
Bourne Va. BR2: Hayes 74Hc 159
TN15: Plax 99Ce 205
Bournevale Rd. SW16 . . . . .63Nb 134
Bourne Vw. CR8: Kenley 87Tb 177
UB6: G'frd 37Ha 66
Bourneville Rd. SE6 . . . . .59Cc 114
Bourne Way BR2: Hayes 75Hc 159
BR8: Swan 69Ed 140
GU22: Wok 4P 187
KT15: Add 78L 149
KT19: Ewe 77Sa 153
SM1: Sutt 78Bb 155
Bournewood Gro. CR6: W'ham 91Yb 198
Bournewood Rd. BR5: Orp 73Yc 161
SE18 .52Wc 117
Bournwell Cl. EN4: Cockf 13Hb 31
Bourton Cl. UB3: Hayes 46W 84
Bousfield Rd. SE14 . . . . .54Zb 114
Bousley Ri. KT16: Ott 79F 148
Boutflower Rd. SW11 . . . . .56Gb 111
Boutique Hall SE13 . . . . .56Ec 114
Bouton Pl. N1 . . . . .38Rb 71
(off Waterloo Ter.)
Bouverie Gdns. CR8: Purl 86Pb 176
HA3: Kenton 30Ma 47
Bouverie M. N16 . . . . .33Ub 71
Bouverie Pl. W2 . . . . .2C 220 (44Fb 89)
Bouverie Rd. CR5: Chip 90Jb 176
HA1: Harr 30Ea 46
N16 .33Ub 71
Bouverie St. EC4 . . . . .3A 224 (44Qb 90)
Bouverie Way SL3: L'ly 50A 82
Bouvier Rd. EN3: Enf W 10Yb 20
BOVENEY 1B 102
Boveney Cl. SL1: Slou 7E 80
Boveney New Rd. SL4: Eton W 9C 80
Boveney Rd. SE23 . . . . .59Zb 114
SL4: Dor 9A 80
Boveney Wood La. SL1: Burn 4B 60
Bovet Ct. E1 . . . . .43Ac 92
(off Ocean Est.)
Bovey Way RM15: S Ock 43Xd 98
Bovill Rd. SE23 . . . . .59Zb 114
BOVINGDON 9C 2
Bovingdon Av. HA9: Wemb 37Qa 67
Bovingdon Cl. N19 . . . . .33Lb 70
Bovingdon Ct. HP3: Bov 10C 2
WD23: Bush 15Da 27
(off Farrington Av.)
Bovingdon Cres. WD25: Wat 6Z 13
BOVINGDON GREEN 1C 10
Bovingdon Grn. HP3: Bov 1C 10
Bovingdon La. NW9 . . . . .25Ua 48
Bovingdon Rd. SW6 . . . . .53Db 111
Bovril Ct. SW6 . . . . .52Db 111
(off Fulham Rd.)
BOW 41Bc 92
Bow Arrow La. DA1: Dart 58Qd 119
DA2: Dart 58Qd 119
Bowater Cl. NW9 . . . . .29Ta 47
SW2 .58Nb 112
Bowater Gdns. TW16: Sun 68Y 129
Bowater Ho. EC1 . . . . .6D 218
Bowater Pl. SE3 . . . . .52Kc 115
Bowater Ridge KT13: Weyb 82T 170
Bowater Rd. HA9: Wemb 34Ra 67
SE18 .48Mc 93
Bow Bell Twr. E3 . . . . .39Cc 72
(off Pancras Way)
Bow Bri. Est. E3 . . . . .41Dc 92
Bow Brook, The E2 . . . . .40Zb 72
(off Mace St.)
Bow Chyd. EC4 . . . . .3E 224
BOW COMMON 43Cc 92
Bow Comn. La. E3 . . . . .42Bc 92
Bow Creek Ecology Pk. 44Gc 93
Bowden Cl. TW14: Bedf 60U 106
Bowden Ct. TN15: Kems'g 89Pd 183
Bowden Dr. RM11: Horn 32Nd 77
Bowden Ho. E3 . . . . .41Dc 92
(off Rainhill Way)
Bowden Rd. SL5: S'hill 1A 146
Bowden St. SE11 . . . . .7A 230 (50Qb 90)
Bowditch SE8 . . . . .49Bc 92
Bowdon Rd. E17 . . . . .31Cc 72
Bowen Ct. SE16 . . . . .49Yb 92
(off Debnams Rd.)
Bowen Dr. SE21 . . . . .62Ub 135
Bowen Rd. HA1: Harr 31Ea 66
Bowen St. E14 . . . . .44Dc 92
Bowens Wood CR0: Sels 81Bc 178
Bowen Way CR5: Coul 94Mb 196
Bower Av. SE10 . . . . .53Gc 115
Bower Cl. RM5: Col R 24Fd 56
UB5: N'olt 40Y 65
Bower Ct. CM16: Epp 4Wc 23
E4 . . . . .18Ec 34
(off The Ridgeway)
GU22: Wok 88D 168
SL1: Slou 5D 80
Bowerdean St. SW6 . . . . .53Db 111
Bowerden Ct. NW10 . . . . .40Xa 68
Bower Farm Rd. RM4: Have B 20Ed 38
Bower Hill CM16: Epp 3Wc 23
Bower Hill Cl. RH1: S Nut 9E 208
Bower Hill Ind. Est. CM16: Epp 4Wc 23
Bower Hill La. RH1: S Nut 7D 208
Bower La. DA4: Eyns 75Nd 163
TN15: Knat 82Qd 183
Bowerman Av. SE14 . . . . .51Ac 114
Bowerman Ct. N19 . . . . .33Mb 70
(off St John's Way)
Bowerman Rd. RM16: Grays 9C 100
Bower Rd. BR8: Hext 66Jd 140
Bowers RM11: Horn 29Md 57
Bowers Av. DA11: Nflt 3B 144
Bowers Rd. TN14: S'ham 83Hd 182
Bower St. E1 . . . . .44Zb 92
Bowers Wlk. E6 . . . . .44Pc 94
Bower Ter. CM16: Epp 4Wc 23
Bower Va. CM16: Epp 4Wc 23
Bower Way SL1: Slou 5C 80
Bowery Ct. RM10: Dag 37Dd 76
Bowes Cl. DA15: Sidc 58Xc 117
Bowes Ct. DA2: Dart 58Rd 119
(off Osbourne Rd.)
Bowesden La.
DA12: Shorne, Strood 6N 145
Bowe's Ho. IG11: Bark 38Rc 74
Bowes Lyon Cl. SL4: Wind 3G 102
(off Mountbatten Sq.)
Bowes-Lyon Hall E16 . . . . .46Jc 93
(off Wesley Av.)
Bowes Lyon M. AL3: St A 2B 6
BOWES PARK 23Nb 50
Bowes Rd. KT12: Walt T 75X 151
N11 .22Lb 50
N13 .22Lb 50
RM8: Dag 35Yc 75
TW18: Staines 64G 126
W3 . . . . .45Ua 88
Bowes Wood DA3: Nw A G 76Be 165
Bow Exchange E3 . . . . .43Dc 92
(off Yeo St.)
Bow Fair E3 . . . . .40Cc 72
(off Fairfield Rd.)
Bowfell Rd. W6 . . . . .51Ya 110
Bowford Av. DA7: Bex 53Ad 117
Bowgate AL1: St A 1C 6
Bowhay CM13: Hut 19De 41
Bowhill Cl. SW9 . . . . .52Qb 112
Bow Ho. N1 . . . . .1H 219
Bowie Cl. SW4 . . . . .59Mb 112
BOW INTERCHANGE 40Dc 72
Bowland Rd. IG8: Wfd G 23Lc 53
SW4 .56Mb 112
Bowland Yd. SW1 . . . . .2G 227
Bow La. EC4 . . . . .3E 224 (44Sb 91)
N12 .24Eb 49
SM4: Mord 72Ab 154
Bowlby Ho. SE4 . . . . .56Zb 114
(off Frendsbury Rd.)
Bowl Ct. EC2 . . . . .6J 219 (42Ub 91)
Bowlers Grn. WD7: Shenl 2La 14
Bowles Ct. N12 . . . . .24Gb 49
Bowles Grn. EN1: Enf 8Xb 19
Bowles Rd. SE1 . . . . .51Wb 113
Bowley Cl. SE19 . . . . .65Vb 135
Bowley Ho. SE16 . . . . .48Wb 91
Bowley La. SE19 . . . . .64Vb 135
Bowline Ct. SE10 . . . . .49Gc 93
TW8: Bford 51La 108
Bowling, The KT12: Walt T 73W 150
Bowling Cl. UB10: Uxb 39P 63
Bowling Ct. WD18: Wat 14W 26
Bowling Grn. Cl. SW15 . . . . .59Xa 110
Bowling Grn. Ct. HA9: Wemb 33Pa 67
Bowling Grn. Ho. SW10 . . . . .52Fb 111
(off Riley St.)
Bowling Grn. La. EC1 . . . . .5A 218 (42Qb 90)
Bowling Grn. Pl. SE1 . . . . .1F 231 (47Tb 91)
Bowling Grn. Rd. GU24: Chob 1J 167
Bowling Grn. Row SE18 . . . . .48Pc 94
Bowling Grn. St. SE11 . . . . .51Qb 112
Bowling Grn. Wlk. N1 . . . . .3H 219 (41Ub 91)
Bow Locks E3 . . . . .42Ec 92
Bowls, The IG7: Chig 20Uc 36
Bowls Cl. HA7: Stan 22Ka 46
Bowman Av. E16 . . . . .45Hc 93
Bowman M. SW18 . . . . .60Bb 111
BOWMANS 59Hd 118
Bowman's Bldgs. NW1 . . . . .7D 214
Bowmans Cl. EN6: Pot B 4Fb 17
SL1: Burn 9A 60
W13 .46Ka 86
Bowmans Grn. WD25: Wat 8Aa 13
Bowmans Lea SE23 . . . . .59Yb 114
Bowmans Mdw. SM6: Wall 76Kb 156
Bowman's M. E1 . . . . .44Wb 91
N7 . . . . .34Nb 70
Bowman's Pl. N7 . . . . .34Nb 70
Bowman's Rd. DA1: Dart 59Hd 118
Bowman Trad. Est. NW9 . . . . .27Qa 47
Bowmead SE9 . . . . .61Pc 138
Bowmont Cl. CM13: Hut 16De 41
Bowmore Wlk. NW1 . . . . .38Mb 70
Bown Cl. RM18: Tilb 5D 122
Bowness Cl. E8 . . . . .37Vb 71
(off Beechwood Rd.)
Bowness Cres. SW15 . . . . .64Ua 132
Bowness Dr. TW4: Houn 56Aa 107
Bowness Ho. SE15 . . . . .52Yb 114
(off Hillbeck Cl.)
Bowness Rd. DA7: Bex 54Dd 118
SE6 . . . . .59Dc 114
Bowness Way RM12: Horn 36Jd 76
Bowood Rd. EN3: Enf H 12Zb 34
SW11 . . . . .57Jb 112
Bowring Grn. WD19: Wat 22Y 45
Bow Rd. E3 . . . . .41Bc 92
Bowrons Av. HA0: Wemb 38Ma 67
Bowry Dr. TW19: Wray 58B 104
Bowry Ho. E14 . . . . .43Bc 92
(off Wallwood St.)
Bowsley Ct. TW13: Felt 61W 128
Bowsprit, The KT11: Cobh 87Y 171
Bowsprit Point E14 . . . . .48Cc 92
(off Westferry Rd.)
Bow St. E15 . . . . .36Gc 73
WC2 . . . . .3G 223 (44Nb 90)
Bow Triangle Bus. Cen. E3 . . . . .42Cc 92
(not continuous)
Bowyer Cl. E6 . . . . .43Pc 94
Bowyer Ct. EN8: Walt C 5Bc 20
Bowyer Cres. UB9: Den 30H 43
Bowyer Dr. SL1: Slou 6C 80
Bowyer Ho. N1 . . . . .1J 219
Bowyer Pl. SE5 . . . . .52Sb 113
Bowyers HP2: Hem H 1M 3
Bowyers Cl. KT21: Asht 90Pa 173
Bowyers Ct. TW1: Isle 56Ka 108
Bowyer St. SE5 . . . . .52Sb 113
Boxall Rd. SE21 . . . . .58Ub 113
Boxall Way SL3: L'ly 10N 81
Boxelder Cl. HA8: Edg 22Sa 47
Boxford Cl. CR2: Sels 84Zb 178
Boxgrove Rd. SE2 . . . . .48Xc 95
Boxhill Rd. KT20: Box H . . .100Ta 193, 2A 206
Box La. HP3: Hem H 7E 2
IG11: Bark 40Xc 75
Boxley Rd. SM4: Mord 70Eb 133
Boxley St. E16 . . . . .46Kc 93
BOXMOOR .4K 3
Boxmoor Ho. E2 . . . . .39Wb 71
(off Whiston Rd.)
W11 . . . . .46Za 88
(off Queensdale Cres.)
Boxmoor Playhouse Theatre 4L 3
Boxmoor Rd. HA3: Kenton 28Ka 46
RM5: Col R 22Ed 56
Boxoll Rd. RM9: Dag 35Bd 75
Box Ridge Av. CR8: Purl 84Pb 176
Boxted Cl. IG9: Buck H 18Nc 36
Boxted Rd. HP1: Hem H 1H 3
Box Tree Ho. SE8 . . . . .51Ac 114
Boxtree La. HA3: Hrw W 25Ea 46
Boxtree Rd. HA3: Hrw W 24Fa 46
Box Tree Wlk. BR5: Orp 74Zc 161
RH1: Redh 9L 207
Boxwood Cl. UB7: W Dray 47P 83
Boxwood Way CR6: W'ham 89Zb 178
Boxworth Cl. N12 . . . . .22Fb 49
Boxworth Gro. N1 . . . . .39Pb 70
Boyard Rd. SE18 . . . . .50Rc 94
Boyce Cl. WD6: Bore 11Na 29
Boyce Ct. WD17: Wat 11W 26
(off Lockhart Rd.)
Boyce Ho. SW16 . . . . .64Lb 134
W10 . . . . .41Bb 89
(off Bruckner St.)
Boyce Rd. SS17: Stan H 1L 101
Boyce Way E13 . . . . .42Jc 93
Boycroft Av. NW9 . . . . .30Sa 47
Boyd Av. UB1: S'hall 46Ba 85
Boyd Carpenter Ho. SL9: Chal P 22B 42
Boyd Cl. KT2: King T 66Qa 131
RM14: Upm 33Ud 78
Boydell Ct. NW8 . . . . .38Fb 69
(not continuous)
Boyden Ho. E17 . . . . .27Ec 52
Boyd Rd. SW19 . . . . .65Fb 133
Boyd St. E1 . . . . .44Wb 91
Boyd Way SE3 . . . . .56Lc 115
Boyes Cres. AL2: Lon C 8F 6
Boyfield St. SE1 . . . . .2C 230 (47Rb 91)
Boyland Rd. BR1: Brom 64Hc 137
Boyle Av. HA7: Stan 23Ja 46
Boyle Cl. UB10: Uxb 40P 63
Boyle Farm Island KT7: T Ditt 72Ja 152
Boyle Farm Rd. KT7: T Ditt 72Ja 152
Boyle St. W1 . . . . .4B 222 (45Lb 90)
Boyne Av. NW4 . . . . .28Za 48
Boyne Rd. RM10: Dag 34Cd 76
SE13 . . . . .55Ec 114
Boyne Ter. M. W11 . . . . .46Bb 89
Boyseland Ct. HA8: Edg 19Sa 29
Boyson Rd. SE17 . . . . .51Sb 113
(not continuous)
Boyson Wlk. SE17 . . . . .51Tb 113
Boyton Cl. E1 . . . . .42Yb 92
N8 . . . . .27Nb 50
Boyton Ho. NW8 . . . . .1C 214
Boyton Rd. N8 . . . . .27Nb 50
Brabant Ct. EC3 . . . . .4H 225
Brabant Rd. N22 . . . . .26Pb 50
Brabazon Av. SM6: Wall 80Nb 156
Brabazon Ct. SW1 . . . . .7D 228
Brabazon Rd. TW5: Hest 52Y 107
UB5: N'olt 40Ca 65
Brabazon St. E14 . . . . .44Dc 92
Brabiner Gdns. CR0: New Ad 82Fc 179
Brabner Ho. E2 . . . . .41Wb 91
(off Wellington Row)
Brabourne Cl. SE19 . . . . .64Ub 135
Brabourne Cres. DA7: Bex 51Bd 117
Brabourne Hgts. NW7 . . . . .20Ua 30
Brabourne Ri. BR3: Beck 71Ec 158
Brabourn Gro. SE15 . . . . .54Yb 114

Brabrook Ct. SM6: Wall 77Kb **156**
Brabstone Ho. UB6: G'frd 40Ha **66**
Bracer Ho. N1 . . . . .1J **219**
Bracewell Av. UB6: G'frd 36Ha **66**
Bracewell Rd. W10 . . . . .43Ya **88**
Bracewood Gdns. CR0: C'don 76Vb **157**
Bracey M. N4 . . . . .33Nb **70**
Bracey St. N4 . . . . .33Nb **70**
Bracken, The E4 . . . . .19Ec **34**
Bracken Av. CR0: C'don 76Dc **158**
SW12 . . . . .58Jb **112**
Brackenbridge Dr. HA4: Ruis 34Z **65**
Brackenbury *N4* *32Qb* **70**
(off Osborne Rd.)
Brackenbury Gdns. W6 . . . . .48Xa **88**
Brackenbury Rd. N2 . . . . .27Eb **49**
W6 . . . . .48Xa **88**
Bracken Cl. E6 . . . . .43Pc **94**
GU22: Wok 90B **168**
IG10: Lough 11Rc **36**
KT23: Bookh 96Ba **191**
SL2: Farn C 5H **61**
TW2: Whitt 59Ca **107**
TW16: Sun 65V **128**
WD6: Bore 11Ra **29**
Bracken Ct. IG6: Ilf 23Vc **55**
Brackendale EN6: Pot B 5Cb **17**
N21 . . . . .19Pb **32**
Brackendale Cl. TW3: Houn 53Da **107**
TW20: Eng G 5N **125**
Brackendale Gdns. RM14: Upm 35Sd **78**
Brackendene AL2: Brick W 2Ba **13**
DA2: Wilm 63Gd **140**
Brackendene Cl. GU21: Wok 87C **168**
Bracken Dr. IG7: Chig 23Rc **54**
Bracken End TW7: Isle 57Fa **108**
Brackenfield Cl. E5 . . . . .34Xb **71**
Brackenforde SL3: L'ly 7N **81**
Bracken Gdns. SW13 . . . . .54Wa **110**
Brackenhill HA4: Ruis 35Aa **65**
KT11: Cobh 84Da **171**
Bracken Hill Cl. BR1: Brom 67Hc **137**
HA6: Nwood 22W **44**
Bracken Hill La. BR1: Brom 67Hc **137**
Bracken Ho. *E3* *43Cc* **92**
(off Devons Rd.)
Bracken Ind. Est. IG6: Ilf 24Uc **54**
Bracken M. E4 . . . . .18Ec **34**
RM7: Rom 30Dd **56**
Bracken Path KT18: Eps 85Ra **173**
Brackens BR3: Beck 66Cc **136**
Brackens, The BR6: Chels 78Wc **161**
EN1: Enf 17Ub **33**
HP2: Hem H 1M **3**
TN13: S'oaks 95Ld **203**
Brackens Dr. CM14: W'ley 22Yd **58**
Bracken Way GU24: Chob 2K **167**
Brackenwood TW16: Sun 67W **128**
Brackenwood Lodge
EN5: New Bar *14Cb* **31**
(off Prospect Rd.)
Brackenwood Rd. GU21: Wok 1H **187**
Brackley KT13: Weyb 78T **150**
Brackley Av. SE15 . . . . .55Yb **114**
Brackley Cl. SM6: Wall 80Nb **156**
Brackley Ct. NW8 . . . . .5B **214**
Brackley Rd. BR3: Beck 66Bc **136**
W4 . . . . .50Ua **88**
Brackley Sq. IG8: Wfd G 24Mc **53**
Brackley St. EC1 . . . . .7E **218** (42Sb **91**)
Brackley Ter. W4 . . . . .50Ua **88**
Brackley Wlk. HA8: Edg 24Ra **47**
Bracklyn Ct. N1 . . . . .1F **219** (40Tb **71**)
(not continuous)
Bracklyn St. N1 . . . . .1F **219** (40Tb **71**)
Bracknell Cl. N22 . . . . .25Qb **50**
Bracknell Gdns. NW3 . . . . .35Db **69**
Bracknell Ga. NW3 . . . . .36Db **69**
Bracknell Way NW3 . . . . .35Db **69**
Bracondale KT10: Esh 78Ea **152**
Bracondale Av. DA13: Ist R 7B **144**
Bracondale Rd. SE2 . . . . .49Wc **95**
Bracton La. DA2: Wilm 61Hd **140**
Bradbeer Ho. *E2* *41Yb* **92**
(off Cornwall Av.)
Bradbery WD3: Map C 22F **42**
Bradbourne Ct. TN13: S'oaks 94Kd **203**
Bradbourne Pk. Rd.
TN13: S'oaks 95Jd **202**
Bradbourne Rd. DA5: Bexl 59Cd **118**
RM17: Grays 51De **121**
TN13: S'oaks 94Kd **203**
Bradbourne St. SW6 . . . . .54Cb **111**
Bradbourne Va. Rd.
TN13: S'oaks 94Hd **202**
Bradbrook Dr. DA3: Lfield 69Be **143**
Bradbury Cl. UB2: S'hall 49Ba **85**
WD6: Bore 11Ra **29**
Bradbury Ct. DA11: Nflt 10B **122**
Bradbury Gdns. SL3: Ful 5P **61**
Bradbury M. N16 . . . . .36Ub **71**
Bradbury St. N16 . . . . .36Ub **71**
Bradby Ho. *NW8* *40Db* **69**
(off Hamilton Ter.)
Bradby's *HA1: Harr* *32Ga* **66**
(off High St.)
Bradcaster Gro. KT22: Lea 93Na **193**
Bradd Cl. RM15: S Ock 41Yd **98**
Braddock Cl. RM5: Col R 23Ed **56**
TW7: Isle 54Ha **108**
Braddon Ct. EN5: Barn 13Ab **30**
Braddon Rd. TW9: Rich 55Pa **109**
Braddyll St. SE10 . . . . .50Gc **93**
Bradenham Av. DA16: Well 56Wc **117**
Bradenham Cl. SE17 . . . . .51Tb **113**
Bradenham Rd. HA3: Kenton 28Ka **46**
UB4: Hayes 41U **84**
Bradenhurst Cl. CR3: Cat'm 98Vb **197**
Braden St. W9 . . . . .42Db **89**
Bradfield Cl. GU22: Wok 90A **168**
Bradfield Ct. *NW1* *38Kb* **70**
(off Hawley Rd.)
RM19: Purf *50Rd* **97**
(off Linnet Way)
Bradfield Dr. IG11: Bark 36Wc **75**
Bradfield Ho. IG8: Wfd G 23Qc **54**
Bradfield Rd. E16 . . . . .47Jc **93**
HA4: Ruis 36Aa **65**
Bradford Cl. BR2: Brom 74Pc **160**
N17 . . . . .23Vb **51**
SE26 . . . . .63Xb **135**
Bradford Dr. KT19: Ewe 79Va **154**
Bradford Ho. *W14* *48Za* **88**
(off Spring Va. Ter.)
Bradford Rd. IG1: Ilf 32Tc **74**
SL1: Slou 4E **80**
W3 . . . . .47Ua **88**
WD3: Herons 17E **24**
Bradfords Cl. IG9: Buck H 21Mc **53**
Bradgate Rd. SE6 . . . . .58Dc **114**
Brading Cres. E11 . . . . .33Kc **73**
Brading Rd. CR0: C'don 72Pb **156**
SW2 . . . . .59Pb **112**
Brading Ter. W12 . . . . .48Wa **88**
Bradiston Rd. W9 . . . . .41Bb **89**
Bradleigh Av. RM17: Grays 50Ee **99**
Bradley Cl. N7 . . . . .37Nb **70**
SM2: Sutt 82Cb **175**
Bradley Ct. *EN3: Enf L* *10Ac* **20**
(off Bradley Rd.)
Bradley Gdns. W13 . . . . .44Ka **86**
Bradley Ho. *E3* *41Dc* **92**
(off Bromley High St.)
IG8: Wfd G 24Jc **53**
SE16 . . . .*49Yb* **92**
(off Raymouth Rd.)
Bradley M. SW17 . . . . .60Hb **111**
Bradley Rd. EN3: Enf L 10Ac **20**
EN9: Walt A 7Ec **20**
N22 . . . . .26Pb **50**
SE19 . . . . .65Sb **135**
SL1: Slou 5H **81**
Bradley's Cl. N1 . . . . .1A **218** (40Qb **70**)
Bradley Stone Rd. E6 . . . . .43Pc **94**
Bradman Ho. *NW8* *41Eb* **89**
(off Abercorn Pl.)
Bradman Row HA8: Edg 24Sa **47**
Bradmead SW8 . . . . .52Kb **112**
Bradmore Ct. *EN3: Enf H* *13Ac* **34**
(off Enstone Rd.)
BRADMORE GREEN **90Pb 176**
Bradmore Grn. AL9: Brk P 8G **8**
CR5: Coul 90Pb **176**
Bradmore La. AL9: N Mym 9E **8**
Bradmore Pk. Rd. W6 . . . . .49Xa **88**
Bradmore Way AL9: Brk P 8G **8**
CR5: Coul 89Nb **176**
Bradshaw Cl. SL4: Wind 3C **102**
SW19 . . . . .65Cb **133**
Bradshaw Cotts. *E14* *44Ac* **92**
(off Repton St.)
Bradshaw Dr. NW7 . . . . .24Za **48**
Bradshawe Rd. RM16: Grays 46Ce **99**
Bradshawe Waye UB8: Hil 43P **83**
Bradshaw Rd. WD24: Wat 11Y **27**
Bradshaws AL10: Hat 4B **8**
Bradshaws Cl. SE25 . . . . .69Wb **135**
Bradstock Ho. E9 . . . . .38Zb **72**
Bradstock Rd. E9 . . . . .37Zb **72**
KT17: Ewe 78Wa **154**
Brad St. SE1 . . . . .7A **224** (46Qb **90**)
Bradwell Av. RM10: Dag 33Cd **76**
Bradwell Cl. E18 . . . . .28Hc **53**
RM12: Horn 37Kd **77**
Bradwell Ct. *CM13: Hut* *16Ee* **41**
(off Bradwell Grn.)
CR3: Whyt *91Wb* **197**
(off Godstone Rd.)
Bradwell Grn. CM13: Hut 16Ee **41**
Bradwell Ho. *NW6* *39Db* **69**
(off Mortimer Cres.)
Bradwell M. N18 . . . . .21Wb **51**
Bradwell Rd. IG9: Buck H 17Nc **36**
Bradwell St. E1 . . . . .41Zb **92**
Brady Av. IG10: Lough 12Sc **36**
Brady Ct. RM8: Dag 32Zc **75**
Brady Dr. BR1: Brom 69Qc **138**
Brady Ho. *SW8* *53Lb* **112**
(off Corunna Rd.)
Bradymead E6 . . . . .44Qc **94**
Brady St. E1 . . . . .42Xb **91**
Braeburn Ct. *BR6: Orp* *75Vc* **161**
(off Blossom Dr.)
EN4: E Barn 14Fb **31**
RM13: Rain *40Fd* **76**
(off Broadis Way)
Brae Ct. KT2: King T 67Qa **131**
Braemar SW15 . . . . .58Za **110**
Braemar Av. CR2: S Croy 82Sb **177**
CR7: Thor H 69Qb **134**
DA7: Bex 56Ed **118**
HA0: Wemb 38Ma **67**
N22 . . . . .25Nb **50**
NW10 . . . . .34Ta **67**
SW19 . . . . .61Cb **133**
Braemar Cl. *SE16* *50Xb* **91**
(off Masters Dr.)
Braemar Ct. *SE6* *60Hc* **115**
(off Cumberland Pl.)
WD23: Bush 16Ca **27**
Braemar Gdns. BR4: W W'ck 74Ec **158**
DA15: Sidc 62Tc **138**
NW9 . . . . .25Ta **47**
RM11: Horn 30Qd **57**
SL1: Slou 7E **80**
Braemar Ho. W9 . . . . .4A **214**
Braemar Mans. *SW7* *48Db* **89**
(off Cornwall Gdns.)
Braemar Rd. E13 . . . . .42Hc **93**
KT4: Wor Pk 76Xa **154**
N15 . . . . .29Ub **51**
TW8: Bford 51Ma **109**
Braeside BR3: Beck 64Cc **136**
KT15: New H 83K **169**
Braeside Av. SW19 . . . . .67Ab **132**
TN13: S'oaks 96Hd **202**
Braeside Cl. HA5: Hat E 24Ca **45**
TN13: S'oaks 95Hd **202**
Braeside Cres. DA7: Bex 56Ed **118**
Braeside Rd. SW16 . . . . .66Lb **134**
Braes Mead RH1: S Nut 7E **208**
Braes St. N1 . . . . .38Rb **71**
Braesyde Cl. DA17: Belv 49Bd **95**
Brafferton Rd. CR0: C'don 77Sb **157**
Braganza St.
SE17 . . . . .7B **230** (50Rb **91**)
Bragg Cl. RM8: Dag 37Xc **75**
Bragmans La. WD3: Sarr 6E **10**
Braham Ct. *E2* *42Xb* **91**
(off Three Colts La.)
Braham Cres. WD25: Wat 5V **12**
Braham Ho. SE11 . . . . .7J **229** (50Pb **90**)
Braham St. E1 . . . . .3K **225** (44Vb **91**)
Braid Av. W3 . . . . .44Ua **88**
Braid Cl. TW13: Hanw 61Ba **129**
Braidwood Pas. EC1 . . . . .7D **218**
Braidwood Rd. SE6 . . . . .60Fc **115**
Braidwood St. SE1 . . . . . .7H **225** (46Ub **91**)
Brailsford Cl. CR4: Mitc 66Gb **133**
Brailsford Rd. SW2 . . . . .57Qb **112**
Brainton Av. TW14: Felt 59X **107**
Braintree Av. IG4: Ilf 28Nc **54**
Braintree Ho. *E1* *42Yb* **92**
(off Malcolm Rd.)
Braintree Rd. HA4: Ruis 35X **65**
RM10: Dag 34Cd **76**
Braintree St. E2 . . . . .41Yb **92**
Braithwaite Av.
RM7: Rush G 31Cd **76**
Braithwaite Ct. WD17: Wat 10W **12**
Braithwaite Gdns. HA7: Stan 25La **46**
Braithwaite Ho. EC1 . . . . .5F **219**
Braithwaite Rd.
EN3: Brim 13Bc **34**
Braithwaite St. E1 . . . . . . .6K **219** (42Vb **91**)
Braithwaite Twr. W2 . . . . .7B **214**
Brakefield Rd. DA13: Sflt 65De **143**
Brakes Pl.
TN15: W King 79Ud **164**
Brakey Hill RH1: Blet 6L **209**
Bramah Grn. *SW9* *53Qb* **112**
Bramah Ho. SW1 . . . . .7K **227** (50Kb **90**)
Bramah Rd. SW9 . . . . .53Qb **112**
Bramalea Cl. N6 . . . . .30Jb **50**
Bramall Cl. E15 . . . . .36Hc **73**
Bramall Ct. *N7* *37Pb* **70**
(off Watkinson Rd.)
Bramber WC1 . . . . .4F **217**
Bramber Cl. KT20: Tad 95Xa **194**
Bramber Ct. *DA2: Dart* *58Rd* **119**
(off Bow Arrow La.)
SL1: Slou 6E **80**
TW8: Bford 49Na **87**
W14 . . . .*51Bb* **111**
(off Bramber Rd.)
Bramber Ho. *KT2: King T* *67Na* **131**
(off Seven Kings Way)
Bramber Rd. N12 . . . . .22Gb **49**
W14 . . . . .51Bb **111**
Bramber Way CR6: W'ham 88Bc **178**
Brambleacres Cl.
SM2: Sutt 80Cb **155**
Bramble Av. DA2: Bean 62Yd **142**
Bramble Banks
SM5: Cars 81Jb **176**
Bramblebury Rd. SE18 . . . . .50Sc **94**
Bramble Cl. BR3: Beck 71Ec **158**
CR0: C'don 77Cc **158**
HA7: Stan 24Ma **47**
IG7: Chig 18Sc **36**
N15 . . . . .28Wb **51**
RH1: Redh 8A **208**
RH8: Oxt 5M **211**
SE19 . . . . .67Tb **135**
SL9: Chal P 23A **42**
TW17: Shep 69T **128**
UB8: Hil 44P **83**
WD25: Wat 6W **12**
Bramble Ct. IG6: Ilf 23Vc **55**
Bramble Cft. DA8: Erith 49Ed **96**
Brambledene Cl.
GU21: Wok 10N **167**
Brambledown DA3: Hartl 70Be **143**
TW18: Staines 67K **127**
Brambledown Cl.
BR4: W W'ck 71Gc **159**
Brambledown Rd.
CR2: Sande 80Ub **157**
SM5: Cars 80Jb **156**
SM6: Wall 80Jb **156**
Bramblefield Cl. DA3: Lfield 69Zd **143**
Bramble Gdns. W12 . . . . .45Va **88**
Bramble Ho. *E3* *43Cc* **92**
(off Devons Rd.)
Bramble La. RM14: Upm 39Sd **78**
TN13: S'oaks 100Kd **203**
TW12: Hamp 65Ba **129**
Bramble M. DA12: Grav'nd 3F **144**
Bramble Ri. KT11: Cobh 87Y **171**
Bramble Rd. AL10: Hat 1P **7**
Brambles, The AL1: St A 4B **6**
EN8: Chesh 3Zb **20**
IG7: Chig 23Sc **54**
SM1: Sutt 75Fb **155**
SW19 . . . .*64Bb* **133**
(off Woodside)
UB7: W Dray 49M **83**
Brambles Cl. CR3: Cat'm 94Ub **197**
TW7: Isle 52Ka **108**
Brambles Farm Dr. UB10: Hil 41Q **84**
Brambletye Pk. Rd. RH1: Redh 8P **207**
Bramble Wlk. KT18: Eps 86Ra **173**
RH1: Redh 8A **208**
Bramble Way GU23: Rip 96H **189**
Bramblewood RH1: Mers 1B **208**
Bramblewood Cl. SM5: Cars 74Gb **155**
Brambling Cl. DA9: Ghithe 58Wd **120**
WD23: Bush 14Aa **27**
Brambling Ct. *SE8* *51Bc* **114**
(off Abinger Gro.)
Bramblings, The E4 . . . . .21Fc **53**
Bramcote Av. CR4: Mitc 70Hb **133**
Bramcote Ct. *CR4: Mitc* *70Hb* **133**
(off Bramcote Av.)
Bramcote Gro. SE16 . . . . .50Yb **92**
Bramcote Ho. KT13: Weyb 77S **150**
Bramcote Rd. SW15 . . . . .56Xa **110**
Bramdean Cres. SE12 . . . . .60Jc **115**
Bramdean Gdns. SE12 . . . . .60Jc **115**
Bramerton *NW6* *38Za* **68**
(off Willesden La.)
Bramerton Rd. BR3: Beck 69Bc **136**
Bramerton St. SW3 . . . . .51Gb **111**
Bramfield WD25: Wat 6Aa **13**
Bramfield Ct. *N4* *33Sb* **71**
(off Queen's Dr.)
Bramfield Rd. SW11 . . . . .58Gb **111**
Bramford Ct. N14 . . . . .19Mb **32**
Bramford Rd. SW18 . . . . .56Eb **111**
Bramham Ct. HA6: Nwood 23U **44**
Bramham Gdns.
KT9: Chess 77Ma **153**
SW5 . . . . .50Db **89**
Bramhope La. SE7 . . . . .51Kc **115**
Bramlands Cl. SW11 . . . . .55Gb **111**
Bramleas WD18: Wat 14V **26**
Bramley Av. CR5: Coul 87Lb **176**
TW17: Shep 69U **128**
Bramley Bank Nature Reserve 79Yb **158**
Bramley Cl. BR6: Farnb 74Rc **160**
BR8: Swan 70Gd **140**
CR2: S Croy 78Sb **157**
DA13: Ist R 6B **144**
E17 . . . . .26Ac **52**
HA5: Eastc 27V **44**
IG8: Wfd G 24Lc **53**
KT16: Chert 74K **149**
N14 . . . . .15Kb **32**
NW7 . . . . .20Ua **30**
RH1: Redh 8N **207**
TW2: Whitt 58Ea **108**
TW18: Staines 65L **127**
UB3: Hayes 45W **84**
Bramley Ct. *BR6: Orp* *75Vc* **161**
(off Blossom Dr.)
CR4: Mitc 68Fb **133**
DA16: Well 53Xc **117**
E4 . . . .*18Ec* **34**
(off The Ridgeway)
EN4: E Barn 14Gb **31**
GU24: Bisl 9F **166**
RH1: Redh 4N **207**
RM13: Rain *40Fd* **76**
(off Broadis Way)
UB1: S'hall *45Ea* **86**
(off Haldane Rd.)
WD25: Wat 4X **13**
Bramley Cres. IG2: Ilf 30Qc **54**
SW8 . . . . .52Mb **112**
Bramley Gdns. WD19: Wat 23Y **45**
Bramley Gro. KT21: Asht 91Na **193**
Bramley Hill CR2: S Croy 78Rb **157**
Bramley Ho. RH1: Redh 7A **208**
SW15 . . . .*58Va* **110**
(off Tunworth Cres.)
TW4: Houn 56Ba **107**
W10 . . . . .44Za **88**
Bramley Ho. Ct. EN2: Enf 9Tb **19**
Bramley Hyrst CR2: S Croy 78Sb **157**
Bramley Lodge HA0: Wemb 35Ma **67**
Bramley Pde. N14 . . . . .14Mb **32**
Bramley Pl. DA1: Cray 56Jd **118**
Bramley Rd. N14 . . . . .15Kb **32**
SM1: Sutt 78Fb **155**
SM2: Cheam 81Za **174**
W5 . . . . .48La **86**
W10 . . . . .44Za **88**
Bramleys SS17: Stan H 1M **101**
Bramley Shaw EN9: Walt A 5Hc **21**
Bramley Sports Ground 15Jb **32**
Bramley Way AL4: St A 3G **6**
BR4: W W'ck 75Dc **158**
KT21: Asht 89Pa **173**
TW4: Houn 57Ba **107**
Brammas Cl. SL1: Slou 8G **80**
Brampton WC1 . . . . .1H **223**
Brampton Cl. E5 . . . . .33Xb **71**
EN7: Chesh 1Wb **19**
Brampton Ct. NW4 . . . . .28Xa **48**
RM7: Rush G *30Fd* **56**
(off Union Rd.)
Brampton Gdns. KT12: Hers 78Y **151**
Brampton Gro. HA3: Kenton 28Ja **46**
HA9: Wemb 32Qa **67**
NW4 . . . . .28Xa **48**
Brampton Ho. *SE16* *47Yb* **92**
(off Albatross Way)
Brampton La. NW4 . . . . .28Ya **48**
Brampton Pk. Rd. N22 . . . . .27Qb **50**
Brampton Rd. AL1: St A 1E **6**
CR0: C'don 73Vb **157**
DA7: Bex 55Zc **117**
E6 . . . . .41Mc **93**
N15 . . . . .29Sb **51**
NW9 . . . . .28Qa **47**
SE2 . . . . .51Yc **117**
UB10: Hil 40R **64**
WD19: Wat 20W **26**
Brampton Ter. *WD6: Bore* *10Qa* **15**
(off Stapleton Rd.)
Bramshaw Gdns. WD19: Wat 22Z **45**
Bramshaw Ri. KT3: N Mald 72Ua **154**
Bramshaw Rd. E9 . . . . .37Zb **72**
Bramshill Cl. IG7: Chig 22Uc **54**
Bramshill Gdns. NW5 . . . . .34Kb **70**
Bramshill Rd. NW10 . . . . .40Va **68**
Bramshot Av. SE7 . . . . .51Jc **115**
Bramshot Way WD19: Wat 19W **26**
Bramshurst *NW8* *39Db* **69**
(off Abbey Rd.)
Bramston Cl. IG6: Ilf 23Vc **55**
Bramston Rd. NW10 . . . . .40Wa **68**
SW17 . . . . .62Eb **133**
Bramwell Cl. TW16: Sun 68Z **129**
Bramwell Ho. SE1 . . . . . . .4E **230** (48Sb **91**)
SW1 . . . .*50Lb* **90**
(off Churchill Gdns.)
Bramwell M. N1 . . . . .39Pb **70**
Bramwell Way E16 . . . . .46Lc **93**
Brancaster Dr. NW7 . . . . .24Wa **48**
Brancaster Ho. *E1* *41Zb* **92**
(off Moody St.)
Brancaster La. CR8: Purl 82Sb **177**
Brancaster Pl. IG10: Lough 13Pc **36**
Brancaster Rd. E12 . . . . .35Pc **74**
IG2: Ilf .30Uc **54**
SW16 . . . . .62Nb **134**
Brancepeth Gdns. IG9: Buck H 19Jc **35**
Branch Hill NW3 . . . . .34Eb **69**
Branch Hill Ho. NW3 . . . . .34Db **69**
Branch Pl. N1 . . . . .39Tb **71**
Branch Rd. AL2: Park 9B **6**
AL3: St A 1P **5**
E14 . . . . .45Ac **92**
IG6: Ilf .22Xc **55**
Branch St. SE15 . . . . .52Ub **113**
Brancker Rd. HA3: Kenton 27Ma **47**
Brancroft Way EN3: Brim 11Ac **34**
Brand Av. UB10: Uxb 40N **63**
Brand Cl. N4 . . . . .32Rb **71**
Brandesbury Sq. IG8: Wfd G 24Qc **54**
Brandlehow Rd. SW15 . . . . .56Bb **111**
Brandon Cl. RM16: Chaf H 47Be **99**
Brandon Ct. E16 . . . . .42Hc **93**
Brandon Est. SE17 . . . . .51Rb **113**
Brandon Groves Av. RM15: S Ock . . .41Yd **98**
Brandon Ho. *BR3: Beck* *64Dc* **136**
(off Beckenham Hill Rd.)
Brandon Mans. *W14* *51Ab* **110**
(off Queen's Club Gdns.)
Brandon M. EC2 . . . . .1F **225**
SE17 . . . . .6E **230**
Brandon Mobile Home Pk. AL4: St A . . .2H **7**
Brandon Rd. DA1: Dart 59Qd **119**
E17 . . . . .28Ec **52**
N7 . . . . .38Nb **70**
SM1: Sutt 77Db **155**
UB2: S'hall 50Ba **85**
Brandon St. DA11: Grav'nd 9D **122**
SE17 . . . . .6E **230** (49Sb **91**)
(not continuous)
Brandram M. *SE13* *56Gc* **115**
(off Brandram Rd.)
Brandram Rd. SE13 . . . . .55Gc **115**
Brandrams Wharf SE16 . . . . .47Yb **92**
Brandreth Ct. HA1: Harr 30Ha **46**
Brandreth Rd. E6 . . . . .44Pc **94**
SW17 . . . . .61Kb **134**
Brandries, The SM6: Bedd 76Mb **156**
Brands Hatch Motor Racing Circuit
. . . . .78Ud **164**
Brands Hatch Pk. DA3: Fawk 77Vd **164**
Brands Hatch Rd. DA3: Fawk 76Wd **164**
BRANDS HILL **51D 104**
Brands Ho. *NW6* *39Bb* **69**
(off Lincoln M.)
Brandsland RH2: Reig 10K **207**
Brands Rd. SL3: L'ly 51D **104**
Brand St. SE10 . . . . .52Ec **114**
Brandville Gdns. IG6: Ilf 28Rc **54**
Brandville Rd. UB7: W Dray 47N **83**
Brandy Way SM2: Sutt 80Cb **155**
Branfill Rd. RM14: Upm 33Rd **77**
Brangbourne Rd. BR1: Brom 64Ec **136**
Brangton Rd. SE11 . . . . . .7J **229** (50Pb **90**)
Brangwyn Ct. *W14* *48Ab* **88**
(off Blythe Rd.)
Brangwyn Cres. SW19 . . . . .67Eb **133**
Branham Ho. SE18 . . . . .50Rc **94**
Branksea St. SW6 . . . . .52Ab **110**
Branksome *KT13: Weyb* *79T* **150**
(off Gower Rd.)
Branksome Av. N18 . . . . .23Vb **51**
Branksome Cl. HP2: Hem H 1A **4**
KT12: Walt T 75Z **151**
TW11: Tedd 63Fa **130**
Branksome Ho. *SW8* *52Pb* **112**
(off Meadow Rd.)
Branksome Rd. SW2 . . . . .57Nb **112**
SW19 . . . . .67Cb **133**
Branksome Way HA3: Kenton 30Pa **47**
KT3: N Mald 67Sa **131**
Branksone Ct. N2 . . . . .27Eb **49**
Brannigan Way HA8: Edg 21Pa **47**
Bransby Rd. KT9: Chess 79Na **153**
Branscombe NW1 . . . . .1C **216**
Branscombe Ct. BR2: Brom 71Hc **159**
Branscombe Gdns. N21 . . . . .17Qb **32**
Branscombe Ho. WD24: Wat 9W **12**
Branscombe St. SE13 . . . . .55Dc **114**
Bransdale Cl. NW6 . . . . .39Cb **69**
Bransell Cl. BR8: Crock 72Ed **162**
Bransgrove Rd. HA8: Edg 25Pa **47**
Branston Cl. WD19: Wat 17Y **27**
Branston Cres. BR5: Pet W 74Tc **160**
Branstone Ct. RM19: Purf 50Rd **97**
Branstone Rd. TW9: Kew 53Pa **109**
Branton Rd. DA9: Ghithe 58Vd **120**
Brants Wlk. W7 . . . . .42Ga **86**
Brantwood Av. DA8: Erith 52Ed **118**
TW7: Isle 56Ja **108**
Brantwood Cl. E17 . . . . .27Dc **52**
KT14: W Byf 85J **169**
Brantwood Ct. *KT14: W Byf* *85H* **169**
(off Brantwood Dr.)
Brantwood Dr. KT14: W Byf 85H **169**
Brantwood Gdns. EN2: Enf 14Nb **32**
IG4: Ilf .28Nc **54**
KT14: W Byf 85H **169**
Brantwood Ho. *SE5* *52Sb* **113**
(off Wyndam Est.)
Brantwood Rd. CR2: S Croy 81Sb **177**
DA7: Bex 54Dd **118**
N17 . . . . .23Wb **51**
SE24 . . . . .57Sb **113**
Brantwood Way BR5: St P 69Xc **139**
Branxholme Ct. *BR1: Brom* *67Hc* **137**
(off Highland Rd.)
Braque Bldg. SE1 . . . . .7D **224**
Brasenose Dr. SW13 . . . . .51Ya **110**
Brasher Cl. UB6: G'frd 36Fa **66**
Brassett Point *E15* *39Gc* **73**
(off Abbey Rd.)
Brassey Cl. RH8: Oxt 1L **211**
TW14: Felt 60W **106**
Brassey Hill RH8: Oxt 2L **211**
Brassey Ho. *E14* *49Dc* **92**
(off Cahir St.)
Brassey Rd. NW6 . . . . .37Bb **69**
RH8: Oxt 2K **211**
Brassey Sq. SW11 . . . . .55Jb **112**
Brassie Av. W3 . . . . .44Ua **88**
Brass Talley All. SE16 . . . . .47Zb **92**
BRASTED **96Yc 201**
BRASTED CHART **100Xc 201**
Brasted Cl. BR6: Orp 75Wc **161**
DA6: Bex 57Zc **117**
SE26 . . . . .63Yb **136**
SM2: Sutt 82Cb **175**
Brasted Hill TN14: Knock, Sund 91Wc **201**
Brasted Hill Rd. TN16: Bras 93Xc **201**
Brasted La. TN14: Knock 91Wc **201**
Brasted Lodge BR3: Beck 66Cc **136**
Brasted Rd. DA8: Erith 52Gd **118**
TN16: Westrm 98Uc **200**
Brathay NW1 . . . . .2C **216**
Brathway Rd. SW18 . . . . .59Cb **111**
Bratley St. E1 . . . . .42Wb **91**
Bratten Ct. CR0: C'don 72Tb **157**
Brattle Wood TN13: S'oaks 100Ld **203**
Braund Av. UB6: G'frd 42Da **85**
Braundton Av. DA15: Sidc 60Vc **117**
Braunston Dr. UB4: Yead 42Aa **85**
Braunston Ho. HA0: Wemb 39Na **67**
Bravington Cl. TW17: Shep 71P **149**
Bravington Pl. W9 . . . . .42Bb **89**
Bravington Rd. W9 . . . . .40Bb **69**
Bravingtons Wlk. N1 . . . . .2G **217**
Brawlings La. SL9: Chal P 21C **42**
Brawne Ho. *SE17* *51Rb* **113**
(off Brandon Est.)
Braxfield Rd. SE4 . . . . .56Ac **114**
Braxted Pk. SW16 . . . . .65Pb **134**
Bray NW3 . . . . .38Gb **69**
Brayards Rd. SE15 . . . . .54Xb **113**
Brayards Rd. Est. *SE15* *54Xb* **113**
(off Caulfield Rd.)
Braybourne Cl. UB8: Uxb 37L **63**
Braybourne Dr. TW7: Isle 52Ha **108**
Braybrooke Gdns. SE19 . . . . .66Ub **135**
Braybrook St. W12 . . . . .43Va **88**
Brayburne Av. SW4 . . . . .54Lb **112**
Bray Cl. WD6: Bore 11Sa **29**
Bray Ct. *E2* *41Zb* **92**
(off Meath Cres.)
SW16 . . . . .64Nb **134**
Braycourt Av. KT12: Walt T 73X **151**
Bray Cres. SE16 . . . . .47Zb **92**
Braydon Rd. N16 . . . . .32Wb **71**
Bray Dr. E16 . . . . .45Hc **93**
Brayfield Ter. N1 . . . . .38Qb **70**
Brayford Sq. E1 . . . . .44Yb **92**
Bray Gdns. GU22: Pyr 88G **168**
Bray Pas. E16 . . . . .45Jc **93**
Bray Pl. SW3 . . . . .6F **227** (49Hb **89**)
Bray Rd. KT11: Stoke D 88Aa **171**
NW7 . . . . .23Za **48**
Bray Springs EN9: Walt A 6Gc **21**
Brayton Gdns. EN2: Enf 14Mb **32**

Braywood Av.—Bridle End

Braywood Av. TW20: Egh 65B 126
Braywood Rd. SE9 56Tc 116
Brazier Cres. UB5: N'olt 42Ba 85
Brazil Cl. CR0: Bedd 73Nb 156
Breach Barns La. EN9: Walt A 2Hc 21
Breach Barns Mobile Home Pk.
EN9: Walt A 2Kc 21
Breach La. RM9: Dag 41Cd 96
Breach Rd. RM20: W Thur 51Vd 120
Bread St. EC4 4E 224 (44Sb 91)
(not continuous)
Breakfield CR5: Coul 88Nb 176
Breakneck Hill DA9: Ghithe 57Xd 120
Breakspear Av. AL1: St A 3D 6
Breakspear Ct. WD5: Ab L 2V 12
Breakspear Crematorium (Ruislip)
HA4: Ruis 29S 44
Breakspeare Cl. WD24: Wat 10X 13
Breakspeare Rd. WD5: Ab L 3U 12
Breakspear Ho. UB9: Hare 27N 43
Breakspear M. UB9: Hare 27M 43
Breakspear Path UB9: Hare 27M 43
Breakspear Pl. WD5: Ab L 2V 12
Breakspear Rd. HA4: Ruis 31R 64
Breakspear Rd. Nth. UB9: Hare 25L 43
Breakspear Rd. Sth. UB9: Hare 34P 63
UB10: Ick 34P 63
Breakspears Dr. BR5: St P 67Wc 139
Breakspears M. SE4 54Bc 114
Breakspears Rd. SE4 56Bc 114
(not continuous)
Breakspear Way HP2: Hem H 2C 4
Breakwell Ct. W10 42Ab 88
(off Wornington Rd.)
Bream Cl. N17 28Xb 51
Bream Gdns. E6 41Qc 94
Breamore Cl. SW15 60Wa 110
Breamore Ct. IG3: Ilf 33Wc 75
Breamore Ho. SE15 52Wb 113
(off Friary Est.)
Breamore Rd. IG3: Ilf 33Vc 75
Bream's Bldgs. EC4 2K 223 (44Qb 90)
Bream St. E3 38Cc 72
Breamwater Gdns. TW10: Ham 62Ka 130
Brearley Cl. HA8: Edg 24Sa 47
UB8: Uxb 37N 63
Breasley Cl. SW15 56Xa 110
Breasy Pl. NW4 28Xa 48
(off Burroughs Gdns.)
Brechin Pl. SW7 7A 226 (49Eb 89)
Brecknock Rd. N7 36Mb 70
N19 35Lb 70
Brecknock Rd. Est. N19 35Lb 70
Breckonmead BR1: Brom 68Lc 137
Brecon Cl. CR4: Mitc 69Nb 134
KT4: Wor Pk 75Ya 154
Brecon Ct. SL1: Slou 7G 80
Brecon Grn. NW9 30Ua 48
Brecon Ho. E3 40Bc 72
(off Ordell Rd.)
UB5: N'olt 41Ba 85
(off Taywood Rd.)
W2 2A 220
Brecon Lodge UB7: W Dray 47P 83
Brecon M. N7 36Mb 70
Brecon Rd. EN3: Pond E 14Yb 34
W6 51Ab 110
Brecons, The KT13: Weyb 77T 150
Brede Cl. E6 41Qc 94
Bredel Ho. E14 43Cc 92
(off St Paul's Way)
Bredgar SE13 57Dc 114
Bredgar Rd. N19 33Lb 70
Bredhurst Cl. SE20 65Yb 136
Bredinghurst SE22 59Wb 113
Bredin Ho. SW10 52Db 111
(off Coleridge Gdns.)
Bredle Way RM15: Avel 46Ud 98
Bredon Rd. CR0: C'don 73Vb 157
Bredune CR8: Kenley 87Tb 177
Breech La. KT20: Walt H 96Wa 194
Breer St. SW6 55Db 111
Breezers Ct. E1 45Wb 91
(off The Highway)
Breezer's Hill E1 45Wb 91
Breeze Ter. EN8: Chesh 1Zb 20
Brember Rd. HA2: Harr 33Ea 66
Bremer M. E17 28Dc 52
Bremer Rd. TW18: Staines 62J 127
Bremner Cl. BR8: Swan 70Jd 140
Bremner Rd. SW7 3A 226 (48Eb 89)
Brenchley Av. DA11: Grav'nd 4D 144
Brenchley Cl. BR2: Brom 72Hc 159
BR7: Chst 67Qc 138
Brenchley Gdns. SE23 58Yb 114
Brenchley Rd. BR5: St P 68Vc 139
Bren Ct. EN3: Enf L 9Cc 20
(off Colgate Pl.)
Brendans Cl. RM11: Horn 32Nd 77
Brenda Rd. SW17 61Hb 133
Brenda Ter. DA10: Swans 59Ae 121
Brende Gdns. KT8: W Mole 70Da 129
Brendon Av. NW10 35Ua 68
Brendon Cl. DA8: Erith 53Gd 118
KT10: Esh 79Ea 152
UB3: Harl 52S 106
Brendon Ct. UB2: S'hall 49Da 85
WD7: R'lett 6Ka 14
Brendon Dr. KT10: Esh 79Ea 152
Brendon Gdns. HA2: Harr 35Da 65
IG2: Ilf 29Uc 54
Brendon Gro. N2 26Eb 49
Brendon Rd. RM8: Dag 32Bd 75
SE9 61Tc 138
Brendon St. W1 2E 220 (44Gb 89)
Brendon Vs. N21 18Sb 33
Brendon Way EN1: Enf 17Ub 33
Brenley Cl. CR4: Mitc 69Jb 134
Brenley Gdns. SE9 56Mc 115
Brenley Ho. SE1 1F 231
Brennand Ct. N19 34Lb 70
Brennan Rd. RM18: Tilb 4D 122
Brent, The DA1: Dart 59Qd 119
DA2: Dart 59Qd 119
Brent Cl. DA2: Dart 58Rd 119
DA5: Bexl 60Ad 117
Brentcot Cl. W13 42Ka 86
Brent Ct. NW11 31Za 68
W7 45Fa 86
Brent Cres. NW10 40Pa 67
BRENT CROSS 31Ya 68
Brent Cross Fly-Over NW2 31Za 68
NW4 31Za 68
Brent Cross Gdns. NW4 30Za 48
BRENT CROSS INTERCHANGE 30Ya 48
Brent Cross Shop. Cen. NW4 31Ya 68
Brentfield NW10 38Ra 67
Brentfield Cl. NW10 37Ta 67
Brentfield Gdns. NW2 31Za 68
Brentfield Ho. NW10 38Ta 67
Brentfield Rd. DA1: Dart 58Qd 119
NW10 37Ta 67
BRENTFORD 51Ma 109
Brentford Bus. Cen.
TW8: Bford 52La 108
Brentford Cl. UB4: Yead 42Z 85
BRENTFORD END 52Ka 108
Brentford FC 51Ma 109
Brentford Fountain Leisure Cen. 50Pa 87
Brentford Ho. TW1: Twick 59Ka 108
Brentford Karting 24Yd 58
Brent Grn. NW4 29Ya 48
Brent Grn. Wlk. HA9: Wemb 34Sa 67
Brentham Club 41La 86
Brentham Way W5 42Ma 87
Brent Ho. E9 37Yb 72
(off Brenthouse Rd.)
Brenthouse Rd. E9 38Yb 72
Brenthurst Rd. NW10 37Va 68
Brentlands Dr. DA1: Dart 60Qd 119
Brent La. DA1: Dart 59Pd 119
Brent Lea TW8: Bford 52La 108
Brentleigh Ct.
CM14: B'wood 20Wd 40
Brentmead Cl. W7 45Ga 86
Brentmead Gdns. NW10 40Pa 67
Brentmead Pl. NW11 30Za 48
Brentmoor Rd. GU24: W End 5A 166
Brent New Ent. Cen. NW10 37Va 68
Brenton Ct. E9 36Ac 72
(off Mabley St.)
Brenton St. E14 44Ac 92
Brent Pk. Ind. Est. UB2: S'hall 48X 85
Brent Pk. Rd. NW4 31Xa 68
NW9 31Xa 68
Brent Pl. EN5: Barn 15Bb 31
Brent Rd. CR2: Sels 81Xb 177
E16 44Jc 93
SE18 52Rc 116
TW8: Bford 51La 108
UB2: S'hall 48Y 85
Brent Side TW8: Bford 51La 108
Brentside Cl. W13 42Ja 86
Brentside Executive Cen.
TW8: Bford 51Ka 108
Brent Sth. Shop. Pk. NW2 32Ya 68
Brent St. NW4 28Ya 48
Brent Ter. NW2 32Ya 68
(not continuous)
Brent Trad. Cen. NW10 36Ua 68
Brentvale Av. HA0: Wemb 39Pa 67
UB1: S'hall 46Fa 86
Brent Valley Golf Course 45Ga 86
Brent Vw. Rd. NW9 30Wa 48
Brentwaters Bus. Pk.
TW8: Bford 52La 108
Brent Way DA2: Dart 58Rd 119
HA9: Wemb 37Ra 67
N3 23Cb 49
TW8: Bford 52Ma 109
Brentwick Gdns.
TW8: Bford 49Na 87
BRENTWOOD 19Zd 41
Brentwood By-Pass
CM14: B'wood, Pil H, S Weald
21Td 58
CM15: B'wood, Pil H, Shenf 16Yd 40
Brentwood Camping & Caravaning Site
CM15: Dodd 12Vd 40
Brentwood Cathedral 19Zd 41
Brentwood Cen., The 16Yd 40
Brentwood Cl. SE9 60Sc 116
Brentwood Ct. KT15: Add 77K 149
Brentwood Golf Course 21Ae 59
Brentwood Ho. SE18 52Mc 115
(off Portway Gdns.)
Brentwood Leisure Pk.
CM13: Gt War 24Yd 58
Brentwood Lodge NW4 29Za 48
(off Holmdale Gdns.)
Brentwood Mus. 21Yd 58
Brentwood Pk. Ski & Snowboarding Cen.
24Xd 58
Brentwood Pl. CM15: B'wood 18Zd 41
Brentwood Rd.
CM13: Heron, Ingve, W H'dn 21Ce 59
RM1: Rom 30Hd 56
RM2: Rom 30Kd 57
RM16: Grays, Ors 1E 100
Brentwood School Sports Cen. 19Zd 41
Brentwood Theatre 18Zd 41
Brereton Ct. HP3: Hem H 4N 3
Brereton Rd. N17 24Vb 51
Bressay Dr. NW7 24Wa 48
Bressenden Pl. SW1 3A 228 (48Kb 90)
Bressey Av. EN1: Enf 11Wb 33
Bressey Gro. E18 26Hc 53
Bresslaw Ct. E3 43Bc 92
(off Wager St.)
Bretlands Rd. KT16: Chert 75G 148
Breton Highwalk EC2 7E 218
Breton Ho. EC2 7E 218
SE1 3K 231
Bretons Outdoor Recreation Cen.
37Hd 76
Brett Cl. N16 33Ub 71
UB5: N'olt 41Z 85
Brett Ct. N9 19Yb 34
Brettell St. SE17 7G 231 (50Tb 91)
Brettenham Av. E17 25Cc 52
Brettenham Rd. E17 26Cc 52
N18 21Wb 51
Brett Gdns. RM9: Dag 38Ad 75
Brettgrave KT19: Eps 82Sa 173
Brett Ho. EN8: Chesh 1Zb 20
Brett Ho. Cl. SW15 59Za 110
Brettinghurst SE1 50Wb 91
(off Avondale Sq.)
Brett Pas. E8 36Xb 71
Brett Pl. WD24: Wat 9W 12
Brett Rd. E8 36Xb 71
EN5: Barn 15Ya 30
Brevet Cl. RM19: Purf 49Td 98
Brewers Bldgs. EC1 3B 218
Brewers Ct. W2 2A 220 (43Eb 89)
Brewer's Fld. DA2: Wilm 63Ld 141
Brewer's Grn. SW1 3D 228
Brewer's Hall Gdn. EC2 1E 224
Brewers La. TW9: Rich 57Ma 109
Brewers Rd. DA12: Shorne 7L 145
Brewer St. RH1: Blet 3J 209
W1 5C 222 (45Lb 90)
Brewery, The EC2 7F 219 (43Sb 91)
RM1: Rom 29Gd 56
Brewery Cl. HA0: Wemb 36Ja 66
Brewery Ind. Est., The N1 2E 218
Brewery La. KT14: Byfl 85N 169
TN13: S'oaks 97Kd 203
TW1: Twick 59Ha 108
Brewery M. Cen. TW7: Isle 55Ja 108
Brewery Rd. BR2: Brom 74Nc 160
GU21: Wok 9P 167
N7 38Nb 70
SE18 50Tc 94
Brewery Sq. EC1 5C 218 (42Rb 91)
SE1 7K 225
Brewery Wlk. RM1: Rom 29Gd 56
Brewhouse La. E1 46Xb 91
SW15 55Ab 110
Brewhouse Rd. SE18 49Pc 94
Brewhouse Wlk. SE16 46Ac 92
Brewhouse Yd.
DA12: Grav'nd 8D 122
EC1 5B 218 (42Rb 91)
Brewin Ter. UB4: Yead 43Y 85
Brewood Rd. RM8: Dag 37Xc 75
Brewster Ct. CM14: W'ley 22Xd 58
Brewster Gdns. W10 43Ya 88
Brewster Ho. E14 45Bc 92
(off Three Colt St.)
SE1 5K 231
Brewster Pl. KT1: King T 68Sa 131
Brewster Rd. E10 32Dc 72
Brian Av. CR2: Sande 84Ub 177
Brian Cl. RM12: Horn 35Kd 77
Briane Rd. KT19: Eps 82Sa 173
Brian Rd. RM6: Chad H 29Yc 55
Briant Ho. SE1 4K 229
Briants Cl. HA5: Pinn 26Ba 45
Briant St. SE14 53Zb 114
Briar Av. SW16 66Pb 134
Briarbank Rd. W13 44Ja 86
Briar Banks SM5: Cars 81Jb 176
Briarcliff HP1: Hem H 1G 2
Briar Cl. CR6: W'ham 88Cc 178
EN8: Chesh 1Yb 20
IG9: Buck H 19Mc 35
KT14: W Byf 83K 169
N2 27Db 49
N13 20Sb 33
SL6: Tap 4A 80
TW7: Isle 57Ha 108
TW12: Hamp 64Ba 129
Briar Ct. E3 40Cc 72
(off Morville St.)
GU24: Bisl 9F 166
SM3: Cheam 77Ya 154
SW15 56Xa 110
Briar Cres. UB5: N'olt 37Da 65
Briardale HA8: Edg 21Ta 47
Briardale Gdns. NW3 34Cb 69
Briarfield Av. N3 26Db 49
(not continuous)
Briarfield Cl. DA7: Bex 54Cd 118
Briar Gdns. BR2: Hayes 74Hc 159
Briar Gro. CR2: Sande 85Wb 177
Briar Hill CR8: Purl 83Nb 176
Briaris Cl. N17 24Xb 51
Briar La. BR4: Addtn 77Dc 158
SM5: Cars 81Jb 176
Briarleas Gdns. RM14: Upm 31Ud 78
Briar Rd. DA5: Bexl 62Fd 140
GU23: Send 96D 188
HA3: Kenton 29La 46
NW2 35Ya 68
RM3: Rom 24Ld 57
SW16 69Nb 134
TW2: Twick 60Ga 108
TW17: Shep 71P 149
WD25: Wat 6W 12
Briars, The CM15: Kel H 11Ud 40
EN8: Chesh 3Ac 20
SL3: L'ly 50B 82
TN15: W King 79Td 164
TW19: Stanw M 57J 105
WD3: Sarr 8J 11
WD23: B Hea 18Ea 28
Briars Ct. KT22: Oxs 86Fa 172
Briars La. AL10: Hat 1C 8
Briars Wlk. RM3: Hrld W 26Pd 57
Briars Way DA3: Hartl 71Ce 165
Briarswood EN7: G Oak 1Tb 19
Briarswood Way BR6: Chels 78Vc 161
Briar Wlk. HA8: Edg 24Sa 47
KT14: W Byf 84J 169
SW15 56Xa 110
W10 42Ab 88
Briar Way SL2: Slou 3F 80
UB7: W Dray 47Q 84
Briar Wood Cl. BR2: Brom 75Nc 160
Briarwood Cl. NW9 30Sa 47
TW13: Felt 63U 128
Briarwood Ct. KT4: Wor Pk 74Wa 154
(off The Avenue)
Briarwood Dr. HA6: Nwood 26W 44
Briarwood Rd. GU21: Wok 1H 187
KT17: Ewe 79Wa 154
SW4 57Mb 112
Briary Cl. NW3 38Gb 69
Briary Ct. DA14: Sidc 64Xc 139
E16 44Hc 93
Briary Gdns. BR1: Brom 64Kc 137
Briary Gro. HA8: Edg 26Ra 47
Briary La. N9 20Vb 33
Briary Lodge BR3: Beck 67Ec 136
Briavels Ct. KT18: Eps 87Ua 174
Brickbarn Cl. SW10 52Eb 111
(off King's Barn)
Brickbat All. KT22: Lea 93Ka 192
Brick Ct. EC4 3K 223 (44Qb 90)
RM17: Grays 51Ce 121
(off Columbia Wharf Rd.)
Brickenden Ct. EN9: Walt A 5Hc 21
Bricket Rd. AL1: St A 2B 6
Brickett Cl. HA4: Ruis 29S 44
BRICKET WOOD 2Ba 13
Bricket Wood Common 4Ca 13
Bricket Wood Paintball Cen. 1Da 13
Brick Farm Cl. TW9: Kew 53Ra 109
Brickfield AL10: Hat 3C 8
Brickfield Av. HP3: Hem H 3B 4
Brickfield Cl. E9 37Yb 72
TW8: Bford 52La 108
Brickfield Cotts. BR7: Chst 64Qc 138
SE18 51Vc 117
Brickfield Ct. AL10: Hat 3C 8
Brickfield Farm DA3: Lfield 69Ce 143
Brickfield Farm Cl. DA3: Lfield 69Be 143
Brickfield Farm Gdns.
BR6: Farnb 77Sc 160
Brickfield Ho. N1 39Ub 71
(off Hertford Rd.)
Brickfield La. EN5: Ark 16Va 30
UB3: Harl 51T 106
Brickfield M. WD19: Wat 16Aa 27
Brickfield Rd. CM16: Coop 1Zc 23
CR4: Mitc 69Gb 133
CR7: Thor H 67Rb 135
E3 42Dc 92
SW4 58Mb 112
(off Parkfield Rd.)
SW19 63Db 133
Brickfields HA2: Harr 33Fa 66
(not continuous)
Brickfields Cotts. WD6: Bore 13Pa 29
Brickfields Way UB7: W Dray 48P 83
BRICK HILL 7G 146
Brick Kiln Cl. WD19: Wat 16Aa 27
Brick Kiln La. RH8: Limp 2N 211
Brick Kiln Rd. RM3: Rom 21Ld 57
Brick Knoll Pk. AL1: St A 3G 6
Brick La. E1 5K 219 (42Vb 91)
E2 4K 219 (41Vb 91)
EN1: Enf 12Xb 33
EN3: Enf H 12Xb 33
HA7: Stan 24Ma 47
UB5: N'olt 41Ba 85
Brick Lane Music Hall 46Mc 93
BRICKLAYER'S ARMS 4G 231 (49Tb 91)
Bricklayers Arms Distribution Cen.
SE1 5J 231 (49Ub 91)
(not continuous)
Brickmakers La. HP3: Hem H 3B 4
Brickmakers Mdws. TN15: Plat 92Ee 205
Brickstock Furze CM15: Shenf 18Ce 41
Brick St. W1 7K 221 (46Kb 90)
Brickwall La. HA4: Ruis 32U 64
Brickwood Cl. SE26 62Xb 135
Brickwood Rd. CR0: C'don 75Ub 157
Brickworks Cotts. TN14: S'oaks 92Md 203
Brideale Cl. SE15 51Vb 113
Bride Ct. EC4 3B 224
Bride La. EC4 3B 224 (44Rb 91)
Bridel M. N1 1B 218
Brides M. N7 37Pb 70
Brides Pl. N1 38Ub 71
Bride St. N7 37Pb 70
Bridewain St. SE1 3K 231 (48Vb 91)
Bridewell Pl. E1 46Xb 91
EC4 3B 224 (44Rb 91)
Bridford M. W1 7A 216 (43Kb 90)
BRIDGE, THE 54Qd 119
Bridge, The HA3: W'stone 28Ha 46
SW8 52Kb 112
WD4: K Lan 1R 12
Bridge App. NW1 38Jb 70
Bridge Av. RM14: Upm 34Qd 77
W6 49Ya 88
W7 43Fa 86
Bridge Av. Mans. W6 50Ya 88
(off Bridge Av.)
Bridge Barn La. GU21: Wok 10P 167
Bridge Bus. Cen., The UB2: S'hall 47Ca 85
Bridge Cl. CM13: B'wood 20Ae 41
DA2: Dart 55Td 120
EN1: Enf 12Xb 33
GU21: Wok 9N 167
KT12: Walt T 73V 150
KT14: Byfl 84P 169
RM7: Rush G 30Gd 56
SL1: Slou 5D 80
TW11: Tedd 63Ha 130
TW18: Staines 63G 126
W10 44Za 88
Bridge Ct. E10 32Bc 72
E14 45Fc 93
(off Newport Av.)
GU21: Wok 9P 167
HA2: Harr 33Ea 66
KT12: Walt T 74V 150
(off Bridge St.)
KT13: Weyb 77R 150
KT22: Lea 94Ja 192
RM17: Grays 51De 121
(off Bridge Rd.)
WD7: R'lett 7Ka 14
Bridge Dr. N13 21Pb 50
BRIDGE END 92R 190
Bridge End E17 25Ec 52
Bridge End Cl. KT2: King T 67Qa 131
Bridgefield Cl. SM7: Bans 87Ya 174
Bridgefield Ho. W2 44Db 89
(off Queensway)
Bridgefield Rd. SM1: Sutt 79Cb 155
Bridgefields Cl. RM11: Horn 32Kd 77
Bridgefoot SE1 50Nb 90
TW16: Sun 67V 128
Bridgefoot Ho. WD7: R'lett 3Ha 14
Bridgefoot La. EN6: Pot B 5Ya 16
Bridgeford Ho. WD18: Wat 13X 27
Bridge Gdns. KT8: E Mos 70Fa 130
N16 35Tb 71
TW15: Ashf 66S 128
Bridge Ga. N21 17Sb 33
Bridgeham Cl. KT13: Weyb 78Q 150
Bridge Hill CM16: Epp 5Vc 23
Bridgehill Cl. HA0: Wemb 39Ma 67
Bridge Ho. CR0: C'don 76Sb 157
(off Surrey St.)
DA1: Dart 59Nd 119
E9 37Zb 72
(off Shepherds La.)
KT16: Chert 73L 149
NW3 38Jb 70
(off Adelaide Rd.)
NW10 40Za 68
(off Chamberlayne Rd.)
SE4 56Bc 114
SM2: Sutt 79Db 155
(off Bridge Rd.)
SW1 7K 227
UB7: W Dray 46M 83
W2 1B 220
Bridgehouse Ct. SE1 1B 230
Bridge Ho. Quay E14 46Ec 92
Bridgeland Rd. E16 45Jc 93
Bridgelands Cl. BR3: Beck 66Bc 136
Bridge La. GU25: Vir W 71A 148
NW11 28Ab 48
SW11 53Gb 111
Bridge Leisure Cen., The 63Bc 136
Bridgeman Ct. SL4: Wind 4E 102
Bridgeman Dr. SL4: Wind 4E 102
Bridgeman Ho. E9 38Yb 72
(off Frampton Pk. Rd.)
W14 49Bb 89
(off Radnor Ter.)
Bridgeman Rd. N1 38Pb 70
TW11: Tedd 65Ja 130
Bridgeman St. NW8 2D 214 (40Gb 69)
Bridge Mead GU24: Pirb 8D 186
Bridge Mdws. SE14 51Zb 114
Bridge M. GU21: Wok 9P 167
NW10 37Ua 68
Bridgemount M. N4 31Pb 70
BRIDGEN 59Ad 117
Bridgend Rd. EN1: Enf 7Yb 20
SW18 56Eb 111
Bridgenhall Rd. EN1: Enf 11Vb 33
Bridgen Ho. E1 44Xb 91
(off Nelson St.)
Bridgen Rd. DA5: Bexl 59Ad 117
Bridge Pde. N21 17Sb 33
(off Ridge Av.)
Bridgepark SW18 57Cb 111
Bridge Pk. Community Leisure Cen.
38Ra 67
Bridge Pl. CR0: C'don 74Tb 157
SW1 5A 228 (49Kb 90)
WD17: Wat 15Z 27
Bridge Point RM11: Horn 27Nd 57
Bridgepoint Ct. AL2: Brick W 2Aa 13
(off Old Watford Rd.)
Bridgepoint Lofts E7 38Lc 73
Bridgepoint Pl. N6 32Lb 70
(off Hornsey La.)
Bridgeport Pl. E1 46Wb 91
Bridger Cl. WD25: Wat 5Z 13
Bridge Rd. BR3: Beck 66Bc 136
BR5: St M Cry 72Xc 161
DA7: Bex 54Ad 117
DA8: Erith 54Hd 118
E6 38Pc 74
E11 30Fc 53
E15 38Fc 73
E17 31Bc 72
HA9: Wemb 34Qa 67
KT8: E Mos 70Fa 130
KT9: Chess 78Na 153
KT13: Weyb 77P 149
KT16: Chert 73K 149
KT17: Eps 84Va 174
N9 20Wb 33
N22 25Nb 50
NW10 37Ua 68
RM13: Rain 42Jd 96
RM17: Grays 51De 121
SL5: S'hill 1B 146
SM2: Sutt 79Db 155
SM6: Wall 78Kb 156
TW1: Twick 58Ka 108
TW3: Houn, Isle 55Fa 108
TW7: Isle 55Fa 108
UB2: S'hall 47Ba 85
UB8: Uxb 40L 63
WD4: Hunt C 5S 12
Bridge Rd. Depot E15 39Gc 73
Bridge Row CR0: C'don 74Tb 157
Bridges Ct. Rd. SW11 55Fb 111
Bridges Dr. DA1: Dart 57Rd 119
Bridges Ho. SE5 52Tb 113
(off Elmington Est.)
Bridgeside Lodge N1 1D 218
Bridges La. CR0: Bedd 77Nb 156
Bridges Pl. SW6 53Bb 111
Bridges Rd. HA7: Stan 22Ha 46
SW19 65Db 133
Bridges Rd. M. SW19 65Db 133
Bridge St. HA5: Pinn 27Aa 45
HP1: Hem H 3M 3
KT12: Walt T 74U 150
KT22: Lea 94Ja 192
SL3: Coln 52F 104
SW1 2F 229 (47Nb 90)
TW9: Rich 57Ma 109
TW18: Staines 63G 126
W4 49Ta 87
Bridges Wharf SW11 55Fb 111
Bridge Ter. E15 38Fc 73
Bridgetown Cl. SE19 64Ub 135
Bridge Vw. DA9: Ghithe 56Xd 120
SL5: S'dale 3F 146
W6 50Ya 88
Bridge Vw. Ct. SE1 4J 231
Bridgeview Ct. IG6: Ilf 23Tc 54
Bridge Vw. Ind. Est.
RM20: W Thur 51Wd 120
Bridge Wlk. IG1: Ilf 33Rc 74
(within The Exchange)
SE8 51Dc 114
(off Copperas St.)
Bridgewalk Hgts. SE1 1G 231
Bridgewater GU21: Wok 88B 168
Bridgewater Cl. BR7: Chst 69Uc 138
Bridgewater Ct. SL3: L'ly 49C 82
Bridgewater Gdns. HA8: Edg 26Pa 47
Bridgewater Highwalk EC2 7D 218
Bridgewater Rd. E15 39Ec 72
HA0: Wemb 37La 66
KT13: Weyb 79T 150
Bridgewater Sq. EC2 7D 218 (43Sb 91)
Bridgewater St. EC2 7D 218 (43Sb 91)
Bridgewater Ter. SL4: Wind 3H 103
Bridgewater Way SL4: Wind 3H 103
WD23: Bush 16Da 27
Bridge Way CR5: Chip 91Gb 195
KT11: Cobh 85V 170
N11 20Lb 32
NW11 29Bb 49
TW2: Whitt 59Ea 108
UB10: Ick 36R 64
Bridgeway HA0: Wemb 38Na 67
IG11: Bark 38Vc 75
Bridgeway St. NW1 2C 216 (40Lb 70)
Bridge Wharf E2 40Zb 72
KT16: Chert 73L 149
N1 1H 217
Bridge Wharf Rd.
TW7: Isle 55Ka 108
Bridgewood Cl. SE20 66Xb 135
Bridgewood Rd.
KT4: Wor Pk 77Wa 154
SW16 66Mb 134
Bridge Works UB8: Cowl 42L 83
Bridge Yd. SE1 6G 225 (46Tb 91)
Bridgford St. SW18 62Eb 133
Bridgland Rd. RM19: Purf 50Sd 98
Bridgman Rd. W4 48Sa 87
Bridgnorth Ho. SE15 51Wb 113
(off Friary Est.)
Bridgwater Cl. RM3: Rom 22Md 57
Bridgwater Ho. W2 2A 220
Bridgwater Rd. HA4: Ruis 35W 64
RM3: Rom 22Ld 57
Bridgwater Wlk. RM3: Rom 22Md 57
Bridle Cl. EN3: Enf L 9Bc 20
KT1: King T 70Ma 131
KT19: Ewe 78Ta 153
TW16: Sun 69W 128
Bridle End KT17: Eps 85Va 174

Bridle La.—Brockham Ho.

Bridle La. KT11: Stoke D 87Da 171
KT22: Oxs 87Da 171
TW1: Twick 58Ka 108
W1 4C 222 (45Lb 90)
WD3: Loud 13L 25
Bridle M. EN5: Barn 14Bb 31
Bridle Path CR0: Bedd 76Nb 156
WD17: Wat 12X 27
Bridle Path, The IG8: Wfd G 24Gc 53
KT17: Ewe 82Ya 174
Bridlepath, The CR3: Cat'm 95Qb 196
Bridlepath Way TW14: Bedf 59U 106
Bridle Rd. CR0: C'don 76Cc 158
CR2: Sande 81Wb 177
HA5: Eastc 30X 45
KT10: Clay 79Ka 152
KT17: Eps 85Va 174
Bridle Rd., The CR8: Purl 82Nb 176
Bridle Way BR6: Farnb 77Sc 160
CR0: C'don 78Cc 158
Bridle Way, The CR0: Sels 82Ac 178
Bridleway, The CR5: Coul 86Kb 176
SM6: Wall 77Lb 156
Bridleway Cl. KT17: Ewe 82Ya 174
Bridlington Cl. TN16: Big H 91Kc 199
Bridlington Rd. N9 17Xb 33
WD19: Wat 20Z 27
Bridlington Spur SL1: Slou 8F 80
Bridport SE17 7F 231
Bridport Av. RM7: Rom 30Dd 56
Bridport Ho. *N1* 39Tb 71
(off Bridport Pl.)
N18 22Vb 51
(off College Gdns.)
Bridport Pl. N1 1G 219 (39Tb 71)
(not continuous)
Bridport Rd. CR7: Thor H 69Qb 134
N18 22Ub 51
UB6: G'frd 39Da 65
Bridport Ter. *SW8* 53Mb 112
(off Deeley Rd.)
Bridport Way SL2: Slou 2F 80
Bridstow Pl. W2 44Cb 89
Brief St. SE5 53Rb 113
Brierfield NW1 1B 216
Brier Lea KT20: Lwr K 98Bb 195
Brierley CR0: New Ad 79Dc 158
(not continuous)
Brierley Av. N9 18Yb 34
Brierley Cl. RM11: Horn 30Ld 57
SE25 70Wb 135
Brierley Ct. W7 45Ga 86
Brierley Rd. E11 35Fc 73
SW12 61Lb 134
Brierly Gdns. E2 40Yb 72
Brier Rd. KT20: Tad 91Xa 194
Briers, The EN6: Pot B 4Db 17
Briery Ct. WD3: Chor 14J 25
Briery Fld. WD3: Chor 14J 25
Briery Way HP2: Hem H 1A 4
Brigade Cl. HA2: Harr 33Fa 66
Brigade Pl. CR3: Cat'm 94Sb 197
Brigade St. *SE3* 54Hc 115
(off Tranquil Va.)
Brigadier Av. EN2: Enf 10Sb 19
Brigadier Hill EN2: Enf 10Sb 19
Brigadier Ho. *NW9* 26Va 48
(off Heritage Av.)
Briggeford Cl. E5 33Wb 71
Briggs Cl. CR4: Mitc 67Kb 134
Briggs Ho. E2 3K 219
Brighstone Ct. RM19: Purf 50Rd 97
Bright Cl. DA17: Belv 49Zc 95
Brightfield Rd. SE12 57Gc 115
Brightlands DA11: Nflt 3A 144
Brightlands Rd. RH2: Reig 4L 207
Brightling Rd. SE4 58Bc 114
Brightlingsea Pl. E14 45Bc 92
Brightman Rd. SW18 60Fb 111
Brighton Av. E17 29Bc 52
Brighton Bldgs. SE1 4H 231
Brighton Cl. KT15: Add 78L 149
UB10: Hil 38R 64
Brighton Dr. UB5: N'olt 37Ca 65
Brighton Gro. SE14 53Ac 114
Brighton Ho. *SE5* 53Tb 113
(off Camberwell Grn.)
Brighton Rd. CR2: S Croy 78Sb 157
CR5: Coul 95Kb 196
CR8: Purl 83Qb 176
E6 41Qc 94
(not continuous)
KT6: Surb 72La 152
KT15: Add 78L 149
KT20: Kgswd, Lwr K, Tad 93Ab 194
N2 26Eb 49
N16 35Ub 71
RH1: Mers 95Kb 196
RH1: Redh 7P 207
SM2: Bans, Sutt 83Cb 175
SM7: Bans 93Ab 194
WD24: Wat 10W 12
Brighton Spur SL2: Slou 2F 80
Brighton Ter. RH1: Redh 7P 207
SW9 56Pb 112
Brights Av. RM13: Rain 42Kd 97
Brightside, The EN3: Enf H 11Zb 34
Brightside Av. TW18: Staines 66L 127
Brightside Rd. SE13 58Fc 115
Bright St. E14 43Dc 92
Brightview Cl. AL2: Brick W 1Aa 13
Brightwell Cl. CR0: C'don 74Qb 156
Brightwell Ct. *N7* 36Pb 70
(off Mackenzie Rd.)
Brightwell Cres. SW17 64Hb 133
Brightwell Rd. WD18: Wat 15W 26
Brightwen Gro. HA7: Stan 19Ja 28
Brig M. SE8 51Cc 114
Brigstock Ho. SE5 54Sb 113
Brigstock Rd. CR5: Coul 87Kb 176
CR7: Thor H 71Qb 156
DA17: Belv 49Dd 96
Brill Pl. NW1 2E 216 (40Mb 70)
Brimfield Rd. RM19: Purf 49Td 98
Brim Hill N2 28Eb 49
Brimpsfield Cl. SE2 48Xc 95
(not continuous)
BRIMSDOWN 12Bc 34
Brimsdown Av. EN3: Enf H 12Ac 34
Brimsdown Ho. E3 42Dc 92
Brimsdown Ind. Est. EN3: Brim 11Bc 34
(Lockfield Av.)
EN3: Brim 12Bc 34
(Stockingswater La.)
Brimshot La. GU24: Chob 1J 167
Brimstone Cl. BR6: Chels 80Yc 161
Brimstone Ho. *E15* 38Gc 73
(off Victoria St.)
Brind Cotts. GU24: Chob 2K 167
Brindle Ga. DA15: Sidc 60Uc 116
Brindles RM11: Horn 28Nd 57
Brindles, The SM7: Bans 89Bb 175
Brindles Cl. CM13: Hut 19Ee 41
SS17: Linf 9J 101
Brindlewick Gdns.
BR3: Beck 65Cc 136
Brindley Cl. DA7: Bex 55Dd 118
HA0: Wemb 39Ma 67
Brindley Ct. HA7: Stan 24Ma 47
Brindley Ho. *W2* 43Cb 89
(off Alfred Rd.)
WD6: E'tree 16Ma 29
Brindley St. SE14 53Bc 114
Brindley Way BR1: Brom 64Jc 137
HP3: Hem H 7P 3
UB1: S'hall 45Da 85
Brindwood Rd. E4 20Bc 34
Brine Ho. *E3* 40Ac 72
(off St Stephen's Rd.)
Brinkburn Cl. HA8: Edg 27Ra 47
SE2 49Wc 95
Brinkburn Gdns. HA8: Edg 27Qa 47
Brinkley KT1: King T 68Qa 131
Brinkley Rd. KT4: Wor Pk 75Xa 154
Brinklow Ct. AL3: St A 5P 5
Brinklow Cres. SE18 52Rc 116
Brinklow Ho. *W2* 43Db 89
(off Torquay St.)
Brinkworth Pl. SL4: Old Win 9M 103
Brinkworth Rd. IG5: Ilf 27Nc 54
Brinkworth Way E9 37Bc 72
Brinley Cl. EN8: Chesh 3Zb 20
Brinsdale Rd. NW4 27Za 48
Brinsley Ho. *E1* 44Yb 92
(off Tarling St.)
Brinsley Rd. HA3: Hrw W 26Fa 46
Brinsmead AL2: F'mre 9C 6
Brinsmead Rd. RM3: Hrld W 26Qd 57
Brinson Way RM15: Avel 45Td 98
Brinsworth Cl. TW2: Twick 60Fa 108
Brinsworth Ho. TW2: Twick 61Fa 130
Brinton Wlk. SE1 7B 224
Brion Pl. E14 43Ec 92
Brisbane Av. SW19 67Db 133
Brisbane Ho. RM18: Tilb 3C 122
W12 45Xa 88
(off White City Est.)
Brisbane Rd. E10 33Dc 72
IG1: Ilf 31Rc 74
W13 47Ja 86
Brisbane St. SE5 52Tb 113
Briscoe Cl. E11 33Hc 73
Briscoe M. TW2: Twick 61Fa 130
Briscoe Rd. RM13: Rain 40Ld 77
SW19 65Fb 133
Briset Rd. SE9 55Mc 115
Briset St. EC1 7B 218 (42Rb 91)
Briset Way N7 33Pb 70
Brisson Cl. KT10: Esh 79Ba 151
Bristol Cl. SM6: Wall 80Nb 156
TW4: Houn 59Ca 107
TW19: Stanw 58N 105
Bristol Ct. TW19: Stanw 58N 105
Bristol Gdns. SW15 59Ya 110
W9 42Db 89
Bristol Ho. *IG11: Bark* 38Wc 75
(off Margaret Bondfield Av.)
SE11 4K 229
SW1 7H 227
WC1 1G 223
WD6: Bore 12Qa 29
(off Eldon Av.)
Bristol M. W9 42Db 89
Bristol Pk. Rd. E17 28Ac 52
Bristol Rd. DA12: Grav'nd 2F 144
E7 37Lc 73
SM4: Mord 71Eb 155
UB6: G'frd 39Da 65
Bristol Wlk. *NW6* 40Cb 69
(off Alpha Pl.)
Bristol Way SL1: Slou 6K 81
Briston Gro. N8 30Nb 50
Briston M. NW7 24Wa 48
Bristow Ct. *E8* 39Xb 71
(off Triangle Rd.)
Bristowe Cl. SW2 58Qb 112
Bristowe Dr. RM16: Ors 4F 100
Bristow Rd. CR0: Bedd 77Nb 156
DA7: Bex 53Ad 117
SE19 64Ub 135
TW3: Houn 55Ea 108
Britannia Bldg. N1 3F 219
Britannia Bus. Cen. NW2 35Za 68
Britannia Bus. Pk. EN8: Walt C 7Bc 20
Britannia Cen., The IG10: Lough 14Tc 36
Britannia Cl. DA8: Erith 51Hd 118
SW4 56Mb 112
UB5: N'olt 41Z 85
Britannia Ct. *EN8: Walt C* 6Bc 20
(off Eleanor Cross Rd.)
KT2: King T 67Ma 131
(off Skerne Wlk.)
UB7: W Dray 48M 83
Britannia Dr. DA12: Grav'nd 4H 145
Britannia Ga. E16 46Jc 93
Britannia Ind. Est. SL3: Poyle 54G 104
BRITANNIA JUNC. 39Kb 70
Britannia La. TW2: Whitt 59Ea 108
Britannia Leisure Cen. 1G 219 (39Tb 71)
Britannia Rd. CM14: W'ley 22Yd 58
E14 49Cc 92
EN8: Walt C 6Bc 20
IG1: Ilf 34Rc 74
KT5: Surb 73Pa 153
N12 20Eb 31
SW6 52Db 111
Britannia Row N1 39Rb 71
Britannia St. WC1 3H 217 (41Pb 90)
Britannia Wlk. N1 2F 219 (40Tb 71)
(not continuous)
Britannia Way NW10 42Ra 87
SW6 52Db 111
(off Britannia Rd.)
TW19: Stanw 59M 105
Britannic Highwalk EC2 1F 225
British Disabled Water-Ski Association 60E 104
British Genius Site 52Jb 112
British Gro. W4 50Va 88
British Gro. Pas. W4 50Va 88
British Gro. Sth. W4 50Va 88
British Legion Rd. E4 19Hc 35
British Library 3E 216 (41Mb 90)
British Mus. 7F 217 (43Nb 90)
British St. E3 41Bc 92
British Telecom Cen. EC1 2D 224
British Wharf Ind. Est. SE14 50Zb 92
Britley Ho. *E14* 44Bc 92
(off Copenhagen Pl.)
Briton Cl. CR2: Sande 83Ub 177
Briton Cres. CR2: Sande 83Ub 177
Briton Hill Rd. CR2: Sande 82Ub 177
Brittain Ct. SE9 60Nc 116
Brittain Rd. KT12: Hers 78Z 151
RM8: Dag 34Ad 75
Brittains La. TN13: S'oaks 96Hd 202
Brittany Ho. EN2: Enf 10Sb 19
Brittany Point SE11 6K 229 (49Qb 90)
Britten Cl. NW11 32Db 69
WD6: E'tree 16Ma 29
Britten Ct. E15 40Fc 73
Brittenden Cl. BR6: Chels 79Vc 161
Brittenden Pde. BR6: Chels 79Vc 161
Britten Dr. UB1: S'hall 44Ca 85
Britten Ho. SW3 7D 226
Brittens Cl. GU2: Guild 10L 187
Britten St. SW3 7D 226 (50Gb 89)
Britten Theatre 3B 226
Brittidge Rd. NW10 38Ua 68
Britton Av. AL3: St A 2B 6
Britton Cl. SE6 59Fc 115
Britton St. EC1 6B 218 (42Rb 91)
BRITWELL 1E 80
Britwell Gdns. SL1: Burn 1B 80
Britwell Rd. SL1: Burn 1A 80
Brixham Cres. HA4: Ruis 32W 64
Brixham Gdns. IG3: Ilf 36Uc 74
Brixham Rd. DA16: Well 53Zc 117
Brixham St. E16 46Qc 94
BRIXTON 56Pb 112
Brixton Hill SW2 59Nb 112
Brixton Hill Ct. SW2 57Pb 112
Brixton Hill Pl. SW2 59Nb 112
Brixton Oval SW2 56Qb 112
Brixton Recreation Cen. 55Qb 112
(off Brixton Sta. Rd.)
Brixton Rd. SE11 51Qb 112
SW9 56Qb 112
WD24: Wat 11X 27
Brixton Sta. Rd. SW9 55Qb 112
Brixton Water La. SW2 57Pb 112
Broad Acre AL2: Brick W 2Aa 13
Broadacre TW18: Staines 64J 127
Broadacre Cl. UB10: Ick 34R 64
Broadbent Cl. N6 32Kb 70
Broadbent St. W1 4K 221 (45Kb 90)
Broadberry Ct. N18 23Xb 51
Broadbridge Cl. SE3 52Jc 115
Broad Cl. KT12: Hers 76Z 151
BROAD COLNEY 1Ma 15
Broad Colney Lakes Nature Reserve 10H 7
Broad Comn. Est. *N16* 32Wb 71
(off Osbaldeston Rd.)
Broadcoombe CR2: Sels 80Yb 158
Broad Ct. WC2 3G 223 (44Nb 90)
Broadcroft Av. HA7: Stan 26Ma 47
Broadcroft Rd. BR5: Pet W 73Tc 160
Broad Ditch Rd. DA13: Nflt G 66Ee 143
Broadeaves Cl. CR2: S Croy 78Ub 157
Broadfield NW6 37Db 69
Broadfield Cl. CR0: Wadd 75Pb 156
KT20: Tad 92Ya 194
NW2 34Ya 68
RM1: Rom 29Hd 56
Broadfield Ct. *HA2: Harr* 25Da 45
(off Broadfields)
WD23: B Hea 19Ga 28
Broadfield La. NW1 38Nb 70
Broadfield Pde. *HA8: Edg* 20Ra 29
(off Glengall Rd.)
Broadfield Rd. HP2: Hem H 2P 3
SE6 59Gc 115
Broadfields EN7: G Oak 1Rb 19
HA2: Harr 26Da 45
KT8: E Mos 72Ga 152
Broadfields Av. HA8: Edg 21Ra 47
N21 16Qb 32
Broadfields Hgts. HA8: Edg 21Ra 47
Broadfields La. WD19: Wat 18X 27
Broadfield Sq. EN1: Enf 12Xb 33
Broadfields Way NW10 36Va 68
Broadfield Way IG9: Buck H 20Lc 35
WD25: A'ham 8Da 13
Broadford Ho. *E1* 42Ac 92
(off Commodore St.)
Broadford La. GU24: Chob 4J 167
Broadgate EC2 1H 225
EN9: Walt A 5Hc 21
Broadgate Circle 1H 225 (43Ub 91)
Broadgate Circ. EC2 7H 219 (43Ub 91)
Broadgate Ice Rink 7J 219 (43Ub 91)
Broadgate Plaza EC2 7J 219 (43Ub 91)
Broadgate Rd. E16 44Mc 93
Broadgates Av. EN4: Had W 11Db 31
Broadgates Ct. SE11 7A 230
Broadgates Rd. SW18 60Fb 111
Broadgate Twr. EC2 6J 219 (42Ub 91)
BROAD GREEN 73Rb 157
Broad Grn. Av. CR0: C'don 73Rb 157
Broad Hall *AL10: Hat* 2B 8
(off Bishops Ri.)
BROADHAM GREEN 4H 211
Broadham Grn. Rd. RH8: Oxt 4H 211
Broadham Pl. RH8: Oxt 3H 211
Broadhead Strand NW9 25Va 48
Broadheath Dr. BR7: Chst 64Pc 138
Broad Highway
KT11: Cobh 86Z 171
Broadhinton Rd. SW4 55Kb 112
Broadhoath TN15: Ivy H 98Ud 204
Broadhope Av. SS17: Stan H 3L 101
Broadhurst KT21: Asht 88Na 173
Broadhurst Av. HA8: Edg 21Ra 47
IG3: Ilf 35Vc 75
Broadhurst Cl. NW6 37Eb 69
TW10: Rich 57Pa 109
Broadhurst Gdns.
HA4: Ruis 33Y 65
IG7: Chig 21Sc 54
NW6 37Db 69
RH2: Reig 9K 207
Broadhurst Wlk. RM13: Rain 37Jd 76
Broadis Way RM13: Rain 40Fd 76
Broadlake Cl. AL2: Lon C 9H 7
Broadlands E17 27Ac 52
RM17: Grays 50Be 99
TW13: Hanw 62Ca 129
Broadlands Av. EN3: Enf H 13Xb 33
SW16 61Nb 134
TW17: Shep 72S 150
Broadlands Cl. EN3: Enf H 13Yb 34
EN8: Walt C 6Yb 20
N6 31Jb 70
SW16 61Nb 134
Broadlands Ct. *TW9: Kew* 52Qa 109
(off Kew Gdns. Rd.)
Broadlands Dr. CR6: W'ham 91Yb 198
SL5: Asc, S'hill 3A 146
Broadlands Lodge N6 31Hb 69
Broadlands Rd. BR1: Brom 63Kc 137
N6 31Hb 69
Broadlands Way KT3: N Mald 72Va 154
Broad La. DA2: Wilm 63Jd 140
EC2 7H 219 (43Ub 91)
N8 29Pb 50
N15 28Vb 51
N17 28Vb 51
TW12: Hamp 66Ba 129
Broad Lawn SE9 61Qc 138
Broadlawns Ct. HA3: Hrw W 25Ha 46
Broadley Gdns. WD7: Shenl 4Na 15
Broadley Grn.
GU20: W'sham 10B 146
Broadleys SL4: Wind 2D 102
Broadley St. NW8 7C 214 (43Fb 89)
Broadley Ter. NW1 6E 214 (42Gb 89)
Broadmark Rd. SL2: Slou 5M 81
Broadmayne SE17 7F 231
Broadmead KT21: Asht 89Pa 173
RH1: Mers 100Lb 196
(off Station Rd.)
SE6 62Cc 136
W14 49Ab 88
Broadmead Av. KT4: Wor Pk 73Wa 154
Broadmead Cen. *IG8: Wfd G* 24Lc 53
(off Navestock Cres.)
Broadmead Cl. HA5: Hat E 24Aa 45
TW12: Hamp 65Ca 129
Broadmead Ct. IG8: Wfd G 23Jc 53
Broadmead Rd. GU22: Wok 94D 188
GU23: Send 94D 188
IG8: Wfd G 23Jc 53
(not continuous)
UB4: Yead 42Aa 85
UB5: N'olt 42Aa 85
Broadmeads GU23: Send 94D 188
Broad Oak IG8: Wfd G 22Kc 53
SL2: Slou 2G 80
TW16: Sun 65V 128
Broadoak Av. EN3: Enf W 7Zb 20
Broad Oak Cl. BR5: St P 68Wc 139
E4 22Cc 52
Broadoak Cl. DA4: Sut H 65Qd 141
Broad Oak Ct. SL2: Slou 2G 80
Broadoak Ct. *SW9* 55Qb 112
(off Gresham Rd.)
Broadoak Ho. *NW6* 39Db 69
(off Mortimer Cres.)
Broadoak Rd. DA8: Erith 52Fd 118
Broadoaks CM16: Epp 3Vc 23
KT6: Surb 75Ra 153
Broadoaks Cres. KT14: W Byf 85K 169
Broadoaks Way BR2: Brom 71Hc 159
Broad Platts SL3: L'ly 8P 81
Broad Rd. DA10: Swans 58Ae 121
WD24: Wat 8W 12
Broad Sanctuary SW1 2E 228 (47Mb 90)
Broadstone *NW1* 38Mb 70
(off Agar Gro.)
Broadstone Ho. *SW8* 52Pb 112
(off Dorset Rd.)
Broadstone Pl. W1 1H 221 (43Jb 90)
Broadstone Rd. RM12: Horn 33Jd 76
SS17: Stan H 3K 101
Broad St. GU24: W End 5B 166
HP2: Hem H 1M 3
RM10: Dag 38Cd 76
TW11: Tedd 65Ha 130
Broad St. Av. EC2 1H 225 (43Ub 91)
Broad St. Mkt. RM10: Dag 38Cd 76
Broad St. Pl. EC2 1G 225
Broadstrood IG10: Lough 10Qc 22
Broadview NW9 30Qa 47
Broadview Av. RM16: Grays 47Fe 99
Broadview Pl. E5 32Yb 72
Broadview Rd. SW16 66Mb 134
Broad Wlk. BR6: Chels 76Zc 161
CR3: Cat'm 94Vb 197
CR5: Coul 95Jb 196
KT18: Tatt C 91Za 194
N21 19Pb 32
NW1 1J 215 (39Jb 70)
SE3 54Lc 115
TN15: S'oaks 100Nd 203
TW5: Hest 53Z 107
TW9: Kew 52Pa 109
W1 5G 221 (45Hb 89)
Broad Wlk., The KT8: E Mos 70Ha 130
W8 1A 226 (46Db 89)
Broadwalk E18 27Hc 53
HA2: Harr 29Ca 45
Broadwalk, The HA6: Nwood 26S 44
Broadwalk Ct. *W8* 46Cb 89
(off Palace Gdns. Ter.)
Broadwalk Ho. EC2 7H 219
SW7 2A 226
Broad Wlk. La. NW11 31Bb 69
Broadwalk Nth., The
CM13: B'wood 20Ce 41
Broadwalk Shop. Cen. HA8: Edg 23Ra 47
Broadwalk Sth., The
CM13: B'wood 21Ce 59
Broadwall SE1 6A 224 (46Qb 90)
Broadwater EN6: Pot B 2Db 17
Broadwater Cl. GU21: Wok 84F 168
KT12: Hers 78W 150
TW19: Wray 59B 104
Broadwater Farm Est. N17 26Tb 51
Broadwater Gdns.
BR6: Farnb 77Rc 160
UB9: Hare 28L 43
Broadwater La. UB9: Hare 28K 43
Broadwater Pk. UB9: Den 30J 43
Broadwater Pl. KT13: Weyb 75U 150
Broadwater Rd. N17 25Ub 51
SE28 48Tc 94
SW17 63Gb 133
Broadwater Rd. Nth.
KT12: Hers 78V 150
Broadwater Rd. Sth.
KT12: Hers 78V 150
Broadway BR8: Crock 72Ed 162
DA6: Bex 56Ad 117
(not continuous)
DA7: Bex 56Dd 118
E13 40Kc 73
E15 38Fc 73
GU21: Knap 10F 166
IG11: Bark 39Sc 74
RM2: Rom 26Jd 56
RM13: Rain 42Jd 96
RM17: Grays 51Ee 121
Broadway RM18: Tilb 4B 122
SL4: Wink 10A 102
SW1 2D 228 (48Mb 90)
TW18: Staines 64K 127
UB9: Den 30J 43
W7 46Ga 86
W13 46Ja 86
Broadway, The AL1: St A 2B 6
CR0: Bedd 77Nb 156
E4 23Fc 53
EN6: Pot B 4Bb 17
(not continuous)
GU21: Wok 89B 168
HA3: W'stone 26Ga 46
HA6: Nwood 26W 44
HA7: Stan 22La 46
HA9: Wemb 34Na 67
IG8: Wfd G 23Kc 53
IG10: Lough 14Sc 36
KT7: T Ditt 74Ga 152
KT15: New H 82J 169
N8 30Nb 50
N9 20Wb 33
N11 22Hb 49
N14 18Mb 32
(off The Bourne)
N22 26Qb 50
NW7 22Ua 48
RM8: Dag 32Bd 75
RM12: Horn 35Kd 77
SL2: Farn C 7G 60
SL9: Chal P 25A 42
(off Market Pl.)
SM1: Sutt 78Eb 155
SM3: Cheam 79Ab 154
SW13 54Ua 110
SW19 65Bb 133
TW18: Lale 69L 127
UB1: S'hall 45Z 85
UB6: G'frd 42Ea 86
W3 47Qa 87
(off Ridgeway Dr.)
W5 45Ma 87
WD17: Wat 13Y 27
Broadway Arc. *W6* 49Ya 88
(off Hammersmith B'way.)
Broadway Av. CR0: C'don 71Tb 157
TW1: Twick 58Ka 108
Broadway Cen., The W6 49Ya 88
Broadway Chambers *W6* 49Ya 88
(off Hammersmith B'way.)
Broadway Cl. CR2: Sande 86Xb 177
IG8: Wfd G 23Kc 53
Broadway Ct. BR3: Beck 69Ec 136
GU21: Knap 9G 166
SW19 65Cb 133
Broadway E. UB9: Den 31J 63
Broadway Gdns. CR4: Mitc 70Gb 133
IG8: Wfd G 23Kc 53
Broadway Ho. *BR1: Brom* 64Fc 137
(off Bromley Rd.)
BR1: Brom 69Jc 137
(High St.)
E8 39Xb 71
(off Ada St.)
GU21: Knap 10G 166
Broadway Mans. *SW6* 52Cb 111
(off Fulham Rd.)
Broadway Mkt. E8 39Xb 71
(not continuous)
IG6: Ilf 25Tc 54
(not continuous)
SW17 63Hb 133
Broadway Mkt. M. E8 39Wb 71
Broadway M. E5 31Vb 71
N13 22Pb 50
N21 18Rb 33
Broadway Pde. *E4* 23Ec 52
(off The Broadway)
HA2: Harr 29Da 45
N8 30Nb 50
RM12: Horn 35Kd 77
(off The Broadway)
UB3: Hayes 46W 84
Broadway Pl. SW19 65Bb 133
Broadway Retail Pk. NW2 35Za 68
Broadway Rd. GU18: Light 2A 166
GU20: W'sham 2A 166
Broadway Shop. Cen. DA6: Bex 56Cd 118
Broadway Shop. Mall
SW1 3D 228 (48Mb 90)
Broadway Sq. DA6: Bex 56Cd 118
Broadway Theatre, The
Barking 39Sc 74
Catford 59Dc 114
Broadway W5, The W5 45Ma 87
Broadway Wlk. E14 47Cc 92
Broadwell Ct. *TW5: Hest* 53Z 107
(off Springwell Rd.)
Broadwell Pde. *NW6* 37Db 69
(off Broadhurst Gdns.)
Broadwick St. W1 4C 222 (45Lb 90)
Broadwood DA11: Grav'nd 4D 144
Broadwood Av. HA4: Ruis 30T 44
Broadwood Rd. CR5: Coul 93Mb 196
Broadwood Ter. W8 49Bb 89
Broad Yd. EC1 6B 218 (42Rb 91)
Brocas Cl. NW3 38Gb 69
Brocas St. SL4: Eton 2H 103
Brocas Ter. SL4: Eton 2H 103
Brockbridge Ho. SW15 58Va 110
Brockdene Dr. BR2: Kes 77Mc 159
Brockdish Av. IG11: Bark 36Vc 75
Brockenhurst KT8: W Mole 71Ba 151
Brockenhurst Av. KT4: Wor Pk 74Ua 154
Brockenhurst Cl. GU21: Wok 86B 168
Brockenhurst Dr. SS17: Stan H 1L 101
Brockenhurst Gdns. IG1: Ilf 36Sc 74
NW7 22Ua 48
Brockenhurst M. N18 21Wb 51
Brockenhurst Rd. CR0: C'don 73Xb 157
SL5: Asc 1A 146
Brockenhurst Way SW16 68Mb 134
Brocket Cl. IG7: Chig 21Vc 55
Brocket Ho. SW8 54Mb 112
Brockett Rd. RM16: Grays 8C 100
Brocket Way IG7: Chig 22Uc 54
Brock Grn. RM15: S Ock 44Xd 98
Brockham Cl. SW19 64Bb 133
Brockham Ct. CR2: S Croy 78Sb 157
RH1: Redh 4B 208
(off Goodworth Rd.)
Brockham Cres. CR0: New Ad 80Fc 159
Brockham Dr. IG2: Ilf 30Rc 54
SW2 59Pb 112
Brockham Ho. NW1 1C 216
SW2 59Pb 112
(off Brockham Dr.)

Brockham St.—Broughton Pl.

Brockham St. SE1 3E 230 (48Sb 91)
Brockhill GU21: Wok 9L 167
Brockhurst Cl. HA7: Stan 23Ha 46
Brockill Cres. SE4 56Ac 114
Brocklebank Ct. CR3: Whyt 90Wb 177
Brocklebank Ho. *E16* 46Qc 94
(off Glenister St.)
Brocklebank Rd. SE7 49Kc 93
SW18 59Eb 111
Brocklehurst St. SE14 52Zb 114
Brocklesbury Cl.
WD24: Wat 13Z 27
Brocklesby Rd. SE25 70Xb 135
BROCKLEY 56Zb 114
Brockley Av. HA7: Stan 20Na 29
Brockley Cl. HA7: Stan 21Na 47
Brockley Combe KT13: Weyb 77T 150
Brockley Cres. RM5: Col R 24Ed 56
Brockley Cross SE4 55Ac 114
Brockley Cross Bus. Cen.
SE4 55Ac 114
Brockley Footpath SE4 57Ac 114
(not continuous)
SE15 55Yb 114
Brockley Gdns. SE4 54Bc 114
Brockley Gro. CM13: Hut 18Ce 41
SE4 57Bc 114
Brockley Hall Rd. SE4 57Ac 114
Brockley Hill HA7: Stan 18La 28
Brockley Jack Theatre 57Ac 114
Brockley M. SE4 57Ac 114
Brockley Pk. SE23 59Ac 114
Brockley Ri. SE23 60Ac 114
Brockley Rd. SE4 55Bc 114
Brockleyside HA7: Stan 21Na 47
Brockley Vw. SE23 59Ac 114
Brockley Way SE4 57Zb 114
Brockman Ri. BR1: Brom 63Fc 137
Brockmer Ho. *E1* 45Xb 91
(off Crowder St.)
Brock Pl. E3 42Dc 92
Brock Rd. E13 43Kc 93
Brocks Dr. SM3: Cheam 76Ab 154
Brockshot Cl. TW8: Bford 50Ma 87
Brocksparkwood CM13: B'wood 20De 41
Brock St. SE15 55Yb 114
Brockton Cl. RM1: Rom 28Hd 56
Brock Way GU25: Vir W 1N 147
Brockway TN15: Bor G 92Ce 205
Brockway Cl. E11 33Gc 73
Brockweir *E2* 40Yb 72
(off Cyprus St.)
Brockwell Av. BR3: Beck 71Dc 158
Brockwell Cl. BR5: St M Cry 71Vc 161
Brockwell Ct. SW2 57Qb 112
Brockwell Ho. *SE11* 51Pb 112
(off Vauxhall St.)
Brockwell Pk. 58Rb 113
Brockwell Pk. Gdns. SE24 59Qb 112
Brockwell Pk. Lido 58Rb 113
Brockwell Pk. Row SW2 59Qb 112
Brockwell Pas. SE24 58Rb 113
Broderick Gro. KT23: Bookh 98Ca 191
Brodewater Rd. WD6: Bore 12Ra 29
Brodia Rd. N16 34Ub 71
Brodick Ho. *E3* 40Bc 72
(off Saxon Rd.)
Brodie Ho. SE1 7K 231
Brodie Rd. E4 18Ec 34
EN2: Enf 10Sb 19
Brodie St. SE1 7K 231 (50Vb 91)
Brodlove La. E1 45Zb 92
Brodrick Gro. SE2 49Xc 95
Brodrick Rd. SW17 61Gb 133
Brody Ho. E1 1K 225
Brograve Gdns. BR3: Beck 68Dc 136
Broke Farm Dr. BR6: Prat B 81Yc 181
Broke Hill Golf Course 81Bd 181
Broken Furlong SL4: Eton 10F 80
Brokengate La. UB9: Den 32E 62
Broken Wharf EC4 4D 224 (45Sb 91)
Brokes Cres. RH2: Reig 4J 207
Brokesley St. E3 41Bc 92
Brokes Rd. RH2: Reig 4J 207
Broke Wlk. E8 39Vb 71
Bromar Rd. SE5 55Ub 113
Bromborough Grn. WD19: Wat 22Y 45
Bromefield HA7: Stan 25La 46
Bromefield Ct. EN9: Walt A 5Jc 21
Bromehead St. E1 44Yb 92
Bromell's Rd. SW4 56Lb 112
Brome Rd. SE9 55Pc 116
Bromet Cl. WD17: Wat 10V 12
(not continuous)
Bromfelde Rd. SW4 55Mb 112
Bromfelde Wlk. SW4 54Mb 112
Bromfield Ct. *SE16* 48Wb 91
(off Ben Smith Way)
Bromfield St. N1 1A 218 (39Qb 70)
Bromford Cl. RH8: Oxt 5L 211
Bromhall Rd. RM8: Dag 37Xc 75
RM9: Dag 37Xc 75
Bromhead Rd. *E1* 44Yb 92
(off Jubilee St.)
Bromhedge SE9 62Pc 138
Bromholm Rd. SE2 48Xc 95
Bromleigh Ct. SE23 61Wb 135
Bromleigh Ho. SE1 3K 231
BROMLEY
BR1 68Jc 137
E3 41Dc 92
Bromley RM17: Grays 51Ce 121
Bromley Av. BR1: Brom 66Gc 137
Bromley Coll. BR1: Brom 67Jc 137
BROMLEY COMMON 73Nc 160
Bromley Comn. BR2: Brom 70Lc 137
Bromley Cres. BR2: Brom 69Hc 137
HA4: Ruis 35V 64
Bromley Environmental Education Cen.
at High Elms (BEECHE) 79Tc 160
Bromley FC 71Kc 159
Bromley Gdns. BR2: Brom 69Hc 137
Bromley Golf Course 73Nc 160
Bromley Gro. BR2: Brom 68Fc 137
Bromley Hall Rd. E14 43Ec 92
Bromley High St. E3 41Dc 92
Bromley Hill BR1: Brom 65Gc 137
Bromley Ho. *BR1: Brom* 67Jc 137
(off North St.)
Bromley Indoor Bowls Cen. 74Yc 161
Bromley Ind. Cen.
BR1: Brom 69Mc 137
Bromley La. BR7: Chst 66Sc 138
Bromley Little Theatre 67Jc 137
Bromley Mus. 73Xc 161
BROMLEY PARK 67Gc 137
Bromley Pk. BR1: Brom 67Hc 137
Bromley Pl. W1 7B 216 (43Lb 90)
Bromley Rd. BR1: Brom 60Dc 114
BR2: Brom 68Dc 136
BR3: Beck 67Dc 136
BR7: Chst 67Rc 138
E10 30Dc 52
E17 27Cc 52
N17 25Vb 51
N18 20Tb 33
SE6 60Dc 114
Bromley Ski Cen. 67Ad 139
Bromley St. E1 43Zb 92
Bromley Tennis Cen. 76Tc 160
Bromley Valley Gymnastics Cen.
68Wc 139
BROMPTON 4E 226 (48Gb 89)
Brompton Arc. SW3 2G 227
Brompton Cemetery 51Db 111
Brompton Cl. SE20 68Wb 135
TW4: Houn 57Ba 107
Brompton Cotts. *SW10* 51Eb 111
(off Hollywood Rd.)
Brompton Ct. *BR1: Brom* 67Jc 137
(off Tweedy Rd.)
Brompton Dr. DA8: Erith 52Kd 119
Brompton Gro. N2 28Gb 49
Brompton M. N12 23Eb 49
Brompton Oratory 4D 226 (48Gb 89)
Brompton Pk. Cres. SW6 51Db 111
Brompton Pl. SW3 3E 226 (48Gb 89)
Brompton Rd. SW1 5D 226 (49Gb 89)
SW3 5D 226 (49Gb 89)
SW7 49Gb 89
Brompton Sq. SW3 3D 226 (48Gb 89)
Brompton Ter. SE18 53Pc 116
Brompton Vs. *SW6* 51Cb 111
(off Lillie Rd.)
Bromwich Av. N6 33Jb 70
Bromyard Av. W3 45Ua 88
Bromyard Ho. *SE15* 52Xb 113
(off Commercial Way)
Bromycroft Rd. SL2: Slou 1E 80
Bromyward Ho. W3 46Va 88
Bron Ct. NW6 39Cb 69
BRONDESBURY 38Bb 69
Brondesbury Ct. NW2 37Za 68
Brondesbury M. NW6 38Cb 69
BRONDESBURY PARK 39Ya 68
Brondesbury Pk. NW2 37Ya 68
NW6 37Ya 68
Brondesbury Pk. Mans. *NW6* 39Ab 68
(off Salusbury Rd.)
Brondesbury Rd. NW6 40Bb 69
Brondesbury Vs. NW6 40Bb 69
Bronhill Ter. N17 25Wb 51
Bronsart Rd. SW6 52Ab 110
Bronsdon Way UB9: Den 33H 63
Bronson Rd. SW20 68Za 132
Bronte Cl. DA8: Erith 52Dd 118
E7 35Jc 73
IG2: Ilf 28Qc 54
RM18: Tilb 4E 122
SL1: Slou 7J 81
Bronte Ct. RH1: Redh 5A 208
Bronte Ct. W3 47Qa 87
W14 48Za 88
(off Girdler's Rd.)
Bronte Gro. DA1: Dart 56Pd 119
Bronte Ho. N16 36Ub 71
SW4 59Lb 112
SW17 62Fb 133
(off Grosvenor Way)
Bronte Vw. DA12: Grav'nd 10E 122
Bronti Cl. SE17 7E 230 (50Sb 91)
Bronwen Ct. NW8 4B 214
Bronze Age Way DA8: Erith 47Dd 96
DA17: Belv 47Dd 96
Bronze St. SE8 52Cc 114
Brook Av. HA8: Edg 23Ra 47
HA9: Wemb 33Pa 67
RM10: Dag 38Dd 76
Brook Bank EN1: Enf 9Xb 19
Brookbank Av. W7 43Fa 86
Brookbank Rd. SE13 55Cc 114
Brook Bus. Cen. UB8: Uxb 40K 63
Brook Cl. HA4: Ruis 31U 64
KT19: Ewe 81Ua 174
NW7 24Ab 48
RM2: Rom 25Hd 56
SW17 61Jb 134
SW20 69Xa 132
TW19: Stanw 59P 105
W3 46Qa 87
WD6: Bore 12Ra 29
Brook Ct. BR3: Beck 67Bc 136
E11 34Gc 73
E17 27Ac 52
EC4 4F 225
HA8: Edg 22Ra 47
IG11: Bark 39Vc 75
(Sebastian Ct.)
IG11: Bark 40Sc 74
(Spring Pl.)
SE12 62Lc 137
WD7: R'lett 5Ja 14
Brook Cres. E4 21Cc 52
N9 21Xb 51
SL1: Slou 4C 80
Brookdale N11 21Lb 50
Brookdale Av. RM14: Upm 34Qd 77
Brookdale Cl. RM14: Upm 34Rd 77
Brookdale Rd. DA5: Bexl 58Ad 117
E17 27Cc 52
SE6 59Dc 114
(Catford B'way.)
SE6 58Dc 114
(Medusa Rd.)
Brookdales NW11 28Ab 48
Brookdene Av. WD19: Wat 17X 27
Brookdene Dr. HA6: Nwood 24V 44
Brookdene Rd. SE18 49Uc 94
Brook Dr. HA1: Harr 28Ea 46
HA4: Ruis 31U 64
SE11 4A 230 (48Qb 90)
WD7: R'lett 5Ha 14
Brooke Av. HA2: Harr 34Ea 66
Brooke Cl. WD23: Bush 17Ea 28
Brooke Ct. *W10* 40Ab 68
(off Kilburn La.)
Brooke Dr. DA12: Grav'nd 10K 123
Brooke End RH8: Oxt 5L 211
Brooke Ho. SE14 53Ac 114
WD23: Bush 17Ea 28
Brookehowse Rd. SE6 61Cc 136
Brookend Rd. DA15: Sidc 60Uc 116
Brooke Rd. E5 34Wb 71
E17 28Ec 52
N16 34Vb 71
RM17: Grays 50Ce 99
Brooker Rd. EN9: Walt A 6Ec 20
Brookers Cl. KT21: Asht 89La 172
Brooke's Ct. EC1 1K 223 (43Qb 90)
Brooke's Mkt. EC1 7K 217
Brooke St. EC1 1K 223 (43Qb 90)
Brooke Trad. Est. RM1: Rom 31Hd 76
Brooke Way WD23: Bush 17Ea 28
Brook Farm Rd. KT11: Cobh 87Z 171
Brookfield GU21: Wok 8M 167
N6 34Jb 70
TN15: Kems'g 89Nd 183
Brookfield Av. E17 28Ec 52
NW7 23Xa 48
SM1: Sutt 77Fb 155
W5 42Ma 87
Brookfield Cl. CM13: Hut 16Ee 41
KT16: Ott 79F 148
KT21: Asht 92Na 193
NW7 23Xa 48
Brookfield Ct. N12 21Db 49
UB6: G'frd 41Ea 86
Brookfield Cres. HA3: Kenton 29Na 47
NW7 23Xa 48
Brookfield Gdns. KT10: Clay 79Ha 152
Brookfield Ho. *HP2: Hem H* 3M 3
(off Selden Hill)
Brookfield Pk. NW5 34Kb 70
Brookfield Path IG8: Wfd G 23Gc 53
Brookfield Pl. KT11: Cobh 87Aa 171
Brookfield Rd. E9 37Ac 72
N9 20Wb 33
W4 47Ta 87
Brookfields EN3: Pond E 14Zb 34
Brookfields Av. CR4: Mitc 71Gb 155
Brook Gdns. E4 21Dc 52
KT2: King T 67Sa 131
SW13 55Va 110
Brook Ga. W1 5G 221 (45Hb 89)
BROOK GREEN 49Za 88
Brook Grn. *GU24: Chob* 2K 167
(off Chertsey Rd.)
W6 48Za 88
Brook Grn. Flats *W14* 48Za 88
(off Dunsany Rd.)
Brook Hill RH8: Oxt 2G 210
Brookhill Cl. EN4: E Barn 15Gb 31
SE18 50Rc 94
Brookhill Rd. EN4: E Barn 15Gb 31
SE18 51Rc 116
Brook Ho. *E1* 45Wb 91
(off Fletcher St.)
SL1: Slou 8H 81
W6 49Ya 88
(off Shepherd's Bush Rd.)
Brookhouse Gdns. E4 21Gc 53
Brook Ho's. NW1 2C 216
Brookhurst Rd. KT15: Add 79K 149
Brook Ind. Est. UB4: Yead 46Z 85
Brook Ind. Pk. BR5: St M Cry 70Yc 139
Brooking CM14: B'wood 20Xd 40
Brooking Cl. RM8: Dag 34Yc 75
Brooking Rd. E7 36Jc 73
Brookland Cl. NW11 28Cb 49
Brookland Ct. RH2: Reig 4K 207
Brookland Gth. NW11 28Cb 49
Brookland Hill NW11 28Db 49
Brookland Ri. NW11 28Cb 49
BROOKLANDS 82P 169
Brooklands DA1: Dart 60Nd 119
Brooklands, The TW7: Isle 53Fa 108
Brooklands App. RM1: Rom 28Fd 56
Brooklands Av. DA15: Sidc 61Tc 138
SW19 61Db 133
Brooklands Bus. Pk. KT13: Weyb 83N 169
Brooklands Cl. KT11: Cobh 87Aa 171
RM7: Rom 28Fd 56
TW16: Sun 67U 128
Brooklands Ct. AL1: St A 2C 6
CR4: Mitc 68Fb 133
KT1: King T 70Ma 131
(off Surbiton Rd.)
KT15: New H 82M 169
N21 15Tb 33
NW6 38Bb 69
Brooklands Dr. KT13: Weyb 82P 169
UB6: G'frd 39La 66
Brooklands Gdns. EN6: Pot B 4Ab 16
KT10: Esh 75Da 151
RM11: Horn 30Ld 57
Brooklands Ind. Est. KT13: Weyb 82N 169
Brooklands La. KT13: Weyb 79P 149
RM7: Rom 28Fd 56
(not continuous)
Brooklands Mus. 81Q 170
Brooklands Pk. SE3 55Jc 115
Brooklands Pas. SW8 53Mb 112
Brooklands Pl. TW12: Hamp H 64Da 129
Brooklands Rd. KT7: T Ditt 74Ha 152
KT13: Weyb 84Q 170
RM7: Rom 28Fd 56
Brooklands Ter. TW16: Sun 70W 128
Brooklands Way RH1: Redh 4N 207
Brook La. BR1: Brom 65Jc 137
DA5: Bexl, Bex 58Zc 117
GU23: Send 94G 188
GU24: Chob 3H 167
SE3 54Kc 115
TN15: Plax 99Ce 205
Brook La. Bus. Cen. TW8: Bford 50Ma 87
Brook La. Nth. TW8: Bford 50Ma 87
(not continuous)
Brooklea Cl. NW9 25Ua 48
Brookleys GU24: Chob 2K 167
Brooklime Path RM3: Rom 24Ld 57
Brook Lodge *NW11* 29Za 48
(off Nth. Circular Rd.)
RM7: Rom 28Fd 56
(off Brooklands Rd.)
Brooklyn SE20 66Wb 135
Brooklyn Av. IG10: Lough 14Nc 36
SE25 70Xb 135
Brooklyn Cl. GU22: Wok 91A 188
SM5: Cars 75Gb 155
Brooklyn Ct. GU22: Wok 91A 188
IG10: Lough 14Nc 36
W12 46Ya 88
(off Frithville Gdns.)
Brooklyn Gro. SE25 70Xb 135
Brooklyn Pas. *W12* 47Ya 88
(off Lime Gro.)
Brooklyn Rd. BR2: Brom 71Mc 159
GU22: Wok 90A 168
SE25 70Xb 135
Brooklyn Way UB7: W Dray 48M 83
Brookman Ho. *E3* 40Bc 72
(off Mostyn Gro.)
Brookman's Av. RM16: Grays 46Ee 99
Brookmans Av. AL9: Brk P 8H 9
Brookmans Cl. RM14: Upm 31Ud 78
BROOKMANS PARK 8G 8
Brookmans Pk. Dr. RM14: Upm 29Ud 58
Brookmans Pk. Golf Course 7J 9
Brookmarsh Ind. Est. SE10 52Dc 114
Brook Mead KT19: Ewe 79Ua 154
Brookmead CR0: Bedd 72Lb 156
Brookmead Av. BR1: Brom 71Pc 160
Brookmead Cl. BR5: St M Cry 73Xc 161
Brookmead Ind. Est.
CR0: Bedd 72Lb 156
Brook Mdw. N12 20Db 31
Brook Mdw. Cl. IG8: Wfd G 23Gc 53
Brookmeadow Way EN9: Walt A 2Kc 21
Brookmead Rd. CR0: C'don 72Lb 156
Brookmead Way BR5: St M Cry 72Xc 161
Brook M. IG7: Chig 20Rc 36
N13 22Pb 50
WC2 3E 222 (44Mb 90)
Brook M. Nth. W2 4A 220 (45Eb 89)
Brookmill Cl. WD19: Wat 17X 27
Brookmill Rd. SE8 53Cc 114
Brook Pde. IG7: Chig 20Rc 36
Brook Pk. DA1: Dart 61Qd 141
Brook Pk. Cl. N21 15Rb 33
Brook Path IG10: Lough 14Nc 36
SL1: Slou 5D 80
(not continuous)
Brook Pl. EN5: Barn 15Cb 31
Brook Retail Pk. HA4: Ruis 36Z 65
Brook Ri. IG7: Chig 20Qc 36
Brook Rd. BR8: Swan 69Fd 140
CM14: B'wood 20Vd 40
CM16: Epp 5Wc 23
CR7: Thor H 70Sb 135
DA11: Nflt 10A 122
EN8: Walt C 6Bc 20
IG2: Ilf 30Uc 54
IG9: Buck H, Wfd G 19Jc 35
IG10: Lough 14Nc 36
KT6: Surb 75Na 153
N8 28Nb 50
N22 27Pb 50
NW2 33Va 68
RH1: Mers 1C 208
RH1: Redh 7P 207
RM2: Rom 26Hd 56
TW1: Twick 58Ja 108
WD6: Bore 11Qa 29
Brook Rd. Sth. TW8: Bford 51Ma 109
Brooks Apartments *E3* 43Cc 92
(off Geoff Cade Way)
Brooks Av. E6 42Pc 94
Brooksbank Ho. *E9* 37Yb 72
(off Retreat Pl.)
Brooksbank St. E9 37Yb 72
Brooksby Ho. *N1* 38Qb 70
(off Liverpool Rd.)
Brooksby M. N1 38Qb 70
Brooksby St. N1 38Qb 70
Brooksby's Wlk. E9 36Zb 72
Brooks Cl. KT13: Weyb 82Q 170
SE9 61Qc 138
Brooks Ct. SW8 52Lb 112
Brookscroft CR0: Sels 82Bc 178
E17 27Dc 52
Brookscroft Rd. E17 25Dc 52
(not continuous)
Brooks Farm 31Dc 72
Brookshill HA3: Hrw W 22Fa 46
Brookshill Av. HA3: Hrw W 22Fa 46
Brookshill Dr. HA3: Hrw W 22Fa 46
Brookshill Ga. HA3: Hrw W 22Fa 46
Brooks Ho. CM14: B'wood 18Yd 40
Brookside AL10: Hat 1P 7
BR6: Orp 73Vc 161
EN4: E Barn 16Gb 31
EN6: S Mim 4Wa 16
EN9: Walt A 4Gc 21
GU4: Jac W 10P 187
IG6: Ilf 23Sc 54
KT16: Chert 73G 148
N21 16Pb 32
RH9: S God 10B 210
RM11: Horn 29Nd 57
SL3: Coln 52E 104
SM5: Cars 78Jb 156
UB10: Uxb 38P 63
WD24: Wat 9Z 13
Brookside Av. TW15: Ashf 64L 127
TW19: Wray 55A 104
Brookside Caravans WD19: Wat 17X 27
Brookside Cl. EN5: Barn 16Ab 30
HA2: Harr 35Aa 65
HA3: Kenton 29Ma 47
TW13: Felt 62W 128
Brookside Cotts. WD4: Hunt C 6S 12
Brookside Cres. KT4: Wor Pk 74Wa 154
Brookside Gdns. EN1: Enf 9Xb 20
Brookside Rd. DA13: Ist R 6B 144
N9 21Xb 51
(not continuous)
N19 33Lb 70
NW11 30Ab 48
UB4: Yead 45Y 85
WD19: Wat 17X 27
Brookside Sth. EN4: E Barn 17Jb 32
Brookside Wlk. N3 27Ab 48
N12 23Cb 49
NW11 28Ab 48
Brookside Way CR0: C'don 72Zb 158
Brooks La. W4 51Qa 109
Brooks Lodge N1 1J 219 (40Ub 71)
Brook's M. W1 4K 221 (45Kb 90)
Brook Sq. SE18 53Nc 116
Brooks Rd. E13 39Jc 73
W4 50Qa 87
BROOK STREET 21Vd 58
Brook St. CM14: B'wood 22Td 58
DA8: Erith 50Dd 96
DA17: Belv, Erith 50Dd 96
KT1: King T 68Na 131
N17 26Vb 51
SL4: Wind 4H 103
W1 4J 221 (45Kb 90)
W2 4C 220 (45Fb 89)
BROOK STREET INTERCHANGE 22Td 58
Brooksville Av. NW6 39Ab 68
Brooks Way BR5: St P 68Yc 139
RM3: Rom 22Md 57
Brook Va. DA8: Erith 53Dd 118
Brookview Ct. EN1: Enf 15Ub 33
Brookview Rd. SW16 64Lb 134
Brookville Rd. SW6 52Bb 111
Brook Wlk. HA8: Edg 23Ta 47
N2 25Fb 49
Brook Way IG7: Chig 20Qc 36
KT22: Lea 90Ja 172
Brookway RM13: Rain 43Kd 97
SE3 55Jc 115
BROOKWOOD 2E 186
Brookwood Av. SW13 54Va 110
Brookwood Cl. BR2: Brom 70Hc 137
Brookwood Country Pk. 1G 186
Brookwood Farm GU21: Brkwd 10E 166
Brookwood Farm Dr. GU21: Knap 1F 186
Brookwood Ho. SE1 2C 230
Brookwood Lye Rd. GU24: Brkwd 2F 186
Brookwood Rd. SW18 60Bb 111
TW3: Houn 54Da 107
Broom Av. BR5: St P 68Xc 139
Broom Bank CR6: W'ham 91Ec 198
Broom Cl. AL10: Hat 3B 8
BR2: Brom 72Nc 160
KT10: Esh 78Da 151
TW11: Tedd 66Ma 131
Broomcroft Av. UB5: N'olt 41Y 85
Broomcroft Cl. GU22: Pyr 88F 168
Broomcroft Dr. GU22: Pyr 87F 168
Broome Cl. KT18: Head 98Sa 193
Broome Ct. KT20: Tad 91Ab 194
Broome Lodge *TW18: Staines* 64J 127
(off Kingston Rd.)
Broome Pl. RM15: Avel 46Td 98
Broome Rd. TW12: Hamp 66Ba 129
Broomer Pl. EN8: Chesh 1Yb 20
Broome Way SE5 52Tb 113
Broom Farm Est. SL4: Wind 4A 102
Broomfield AL2: Park 9A 6
E17 31Bc 72
NW1 38Jb 70
(off Ferdinand St.)
TW16: Sun 67W 128
TW18: Staines 65J 127
Broomfield Av. IG10: Lough 16Pc 36
N13 22Pb 50
Broomfield Cl. RM5: Col R 24Fd 56
SL5: S'dale 3F 146
Broomfield Ct. KT13: Weyb 79R 150
N2 28Gb 49
Broomfield Ga. SL2: Slou 2F 80
Broomfield Ho. *HA7: Stan* 20Ja 28
(off Stanmore Hill)
SE17 6H 231
Broomfield La. N13 21Nb 50
Broomfield Pk. SL5: S'dale 2F 146
Broomfield Pl. W13 46Ka 86
Broomfield Ride KT22: Oxs 84Fa 172
Broomfield Ri. WD5: Ab L 4T 12
Broomfield Rd. BR3: Beck 69Ac 136
DA6: Bex 57Cd 118
DA10: Swans 57Ae 121
KT5: Surb 74Pa 153
KT15: New H 83K 169
N13 22Nb 50
RM6: Chad H 31Zc 75
TN13: S'oaks 94Hd 202
TW9: Kew 53Pa 109
TW11: Tedd 65La 130
W13 46Ka 86
Broomfields DA3: Hartl 71Ae 165
KT10: Esh 78Ea 152
Broomfield St. E14 43Cc 92
Broom Gdns. CR0: C'don 76Cc 158
Broom Gro. WD17: Wat 10W 12
Broomgrove Gdns.
HA8: Edg 25Qa 47
Broomgrove Rd. SW9 54Pb 112
BROOMHALL 2E 146
Broom Hall KT22: Oxs 86Fa 172
Broomhall End *GU21: Wok* 88A 168
(off Broomhall La.)
Broomhall La. GU21: Wok 88A 168
SL5: S'dale 2E 146
Broomhall Rd. CR2: Sande 81Tb 177
GU21: Wok 88A 168
BROOM HILL 73Wc 161
Broom Hill HP1: Hem H 3G 2
SL2: Stoke P 8L 61
Broomhill Ct. IG8: Wfd G 23Jc 53
Broomhill Ri. DA6: Bex 57Cd 118
Broomhill Rd. BR6: Orp 73Wc 161
DA1: Dart 58Kd 119
IG3: Ilf 33Wc 75
IG8: Wfd G 23Jc 53
(not continuous)
SW18 57Cb 111
Broomhills DA13: Sflt 63Ae 143
Broomhill Wlk. IG8: Wfd G 23Hc 53
Broom Ho. SL3: L'ly 49B 82
Broomhouse La. SW6 54Cb 111
Broomhouse Rd. SW6 54Cb 111
Broomlands La.
RH8: Limp, T'sey 98Mc 199
Broom La. GU24: Chob 1J 167
Broomloan La. SM1: Sutt 75Cb 155
Broom Lock TW11: Tedd 65La 130
Broom Mead DA6: Bex 58Cd 118
Broom Pk. TW11: Tedd 66Ma 131
Broom Rd. CR0: C'don 76Cc 158
TW11: Tedd 64Ka 130
Broomsleigh Bus. Pk. SE26 64Bc 136
Broomsleigh St. NW6 36Bb 69
Broomstick Hall Rd.
EN9: Walt A 5Gc 21
Broom Water TW11: Tedd 65La 130
Broom Water W. TW11: Tedd 64La 130
Broom Way KT13: Weyb 77U 150
Broomwood Cl. CR0: C'don 71Zb 158
DA5: Bexl 61Fd 140
Broomwood Gdns.
CM15: Pil H 16Wd 40
Broomwood Rd. BR5: St P 68Xc 139
SW4 58Hb 111
SW11 58Hb 111
Broseley Gdns. RM3: Rom 21Nd 57
Broseley Gro. SE26 64Ac 136
Broseley Rd. RM3: Rom 21Nd 57
Brosse Way BR2: Brom 72Nc 160
Broster Gdns. SE25 69Vb 135
Brotherstone Wlk. TW9: Kew 53Ra 109
Brouard Ct. BR1: Brom 69Jc 137
Brougham Ct. *DA2: Dart* 58Rd 119
(off Hardwick Cres.)
Brougham Rd. E8 39Wb 71
W3 44Sa 87
Brougham St. SW11 54Hb 111
Brough Cl. KT2: King T 64Ma 131
SW8 52Nb 112
Broughinge Rd. WD6: Bore 12Ra 29
Broughton Av. N3 27Ab 48
TW10: Ham 62Ka 130
Broughton Ct. W13 45Ka 86
Broughton Dr. SW9 56Qb 112
Broughton Gdns. N6 30Lb 50
Broughton Pl. E17 25Bc 52

Broughton Rd. BR6: Orp 75Tc 160
CR7: Thor H 72Qb 156
SW6 . . . . . 54Db 111
TN14: Otf 88Jd 182
W13 . . . . . 45Ka 86
Broughton Rd. App. SW6 . . . . . 54Db 111
Broughton St. SW8 . . . . . 54Jb 112
Broughton St. Ind. Est.
SW11 . . . . . 54Jb 112
Broughton Way WD3: Rick 17J 25
Brouncker Rd. W3 . . . . . 47Sa 87
Brow, The HP8: Chal G 20A 24
WD25: Wat 5X 13
Brow Cl. BR5: Orp 73Zc 161
Brow Cres. BR5: Orp 74Yc 161
Browells La. TW13: Felt 61X 129
(not continuous)
Brown Bear Ct. TW13: Hanw 63Z 129
Brown Cl. SM6: Wall 80Nb 156
Browne Cl. CM14: B'wood 18Xd 40
GU22: Wok 92D 188
RM5: Col R 22Dd 56
Browne Ho. *SE8* *52Cc 114*
(off Deptford Chu. St.)
Brownell Pl. W7 . . . . . 47Ha 86
Brownfield Area E14 . . . . . 44Dc 92
Brownfield St. E14 . . . . . 44Dc 92
Browngraves Rd. UB3: Harl 52S 106
Brown Hart Gdns.
W1 . . . . . 4J 221 (45Jb 90)
Brownhill Rd. SE6 . . . . . 59Dc 114
Browning Apartments *E3* *42Bc 92*
(off Hamlets Way)
Browning Av. KT4: Wor Pk 74Xa 154
SM1: Sutt 77Gb 155
W7 . . . . . 44Ha 86
Browning Cl. DA16: Well 53Uc 116
E17 . . . . . 28Ec 52
RM5: Col R 24Bd 55
TW12: Hamp 63Ba 129
W9 . . . . . 6A 214 (42Eb 89)
Browning Ct. *W14* *51Bb 111*
(off Turneville Rd.)
Browning Ho. *N16* *35Ub 71*
(off Shakspeare Wlk.)
SE14 . . . . . *53Ac 114*
(off Loring Rd.)
W12 . . . . . *44Ya 88*
(off Wood La.)
Browning M. W1 . . . . . 1J 221 (43Kb 90)
Browning Rd. DA1: Dart 56Pd 119
E11 . . . . . 31Hc 73
E12 . . . . . 36Pc 74
EN2: Enf 9Tb 19
KT22: Fet 97Fa 192
Brownings, The AL2: Lon C 9F 6
Browning St. SE17 . . . . . 7E 230 (50Sb 91)
Browning Wlk. *RM18: Tilb* *4E 122*
(off Coleridge Rd.)
Browning Way TW5: Hest 53Z 107
Brownlea Gdns. IG3: Ilf 33Wc 75
Brownlow Cl. EN4: E Barn 15Fb 31
Brownlow Ct. N2 . . . . . 29Eb 49
N11 . . . . . *23Nb 50*
(off Brownlow Rd.)
Brownlow Farm Barns HP1: Hem H 1F 2
Brownlow Ho. *SE16* *47Wb 91*
(off George Row)
Brownlow M. WC1 . . . . . 5J 217 (42Pb 90)
Brownlow Rd. CR0: C'don 77Ub 157
E7 . . . . . 35Jc 73
E8 . . . . . 39Vb 71
N3 . . . . . 24Db 49
N11 . . . . . 23Nb 50
NW10 . . . . . 38Ua 68
RH1: Redh 6N 207
W13 . . . . . 46Ja 86
WD6: Bore 14Qa 29
Brownlow St. WC1 . . . . . 1J 223 (43Pb 90)
Brownrigg Rd. TW15: Ashf 63Q 128
Brown Rd. DA12: Grav'nd 10G 122
Brown's Bldgs. EC3 . . . . . 3J 225 (44Ub 91)
Browns Ct. SL1: Slou 5C 80
Brownsea Wlk. NW7 . . . . . 23Za 48
Browns La. KT24: Eff 99Z 191
NW5 . . . . . 36Kb 70
Brownspring Dr. SE9 . . . . . 63Rc 138
Brown's Rd. KT5: Surb 73Pa 153
Browns Rd. E17 . . . . . 27Cc 52
Brown St. W1 . . . . . 2F 221 (44Hb 89)
Brownswell Rd. N2 . . . . . 26Fb 49
BROWNSWOOD PARK 33Rb 71
Brownswood Rd. N4 . . . . . 34Rb 71
BROX 80E 148
Broxash Rd. SW11 . . . . . 58Jb 112
Broxbourne Av. E18 . . . . . 28Kc 53
Broxbourne Gdns. *BR6: Orp* *74Vc 161*
(off Broxbourne Rd.)
Broxbourne Ho. *E3* *42Dc 92*
(off Empson St.)
Broxbourne Rd. BR6: Orp 74Vc 161
E7 . . . . . 34Jc 73
Broxburn Ct. RM15: S Ock 45Xd 98
Broxburn Dr. RM15: S Ock 45Wd 98
Broxburn Pde. RM15: S Ock 45Xd 98
Broxhill Cen. RM4: Have B 21Kd 57
Broxhill Rd. RM4: Have B 20Gd 38
Broxholme Cl. SE25 . . . . . 70Tb 135
Broxholme Ho. *SW6* *53Db 111*
(off Harwood Rd.)
Broxholm Rd. SE27 . . . . . 62Qb 134
Brox La. KT15: Add 81F 168
KT16: Ott 80E 148
Brox M. KT16: Ott 79E 148
Brox Rd. KT16: Ott 79E 148
Broxted M. CM13: Hut 16Ee 41
Broxted Rd. SE6 . . . . . 61Bc 136
Broxwood Way
NW8 . . . . . 1E 214 (39Gb 69)
Bruce Av. RM12: Horn 33Ld 77
TW17: Shep 72S 150
Bruce Castle Ct. *N17* *25Vb 51*
(off Lordship La.)
Bruce Castle Mus. 25Ub 51
Bruce Castle Rd. N17 . . . . . 25Vb 51
Bruce Cl. DA16: Well 53Xc 117
KT14: Byfl 85M 169
KT15: Add 76L 149
SL1: Slou 6E 80
W10 . . . . . 43Za 88
Bruce Ct. DA15: Sidc 63Vc 139
Bruce Dr. CR2: Sels 81Zb 178
Bruce Gdns. N20 . . . . . 20Hb 31
Bruce Gro. BR6: Orp 74Wc 161
N17 . . . . . 25Ub 51
WD24: Wat 10Y 13
Bruce Hall M. SW17 . . . . . 63Jb 134
Bruce Ho. W10 . . . . . 43Za 88
Bruce Rd. CR4: Mitc 66Jb 134
E3 . . . . . 41Dc 92
EN5: Barn 13Ab 30
HA3: W'stone 26Ga 46
NW10 . . . . . 38Ta 67
SE25 . . . . . 70Tb 135
Bruces Wharf Rd. RM17: Grays 51Ce 121
Bruce Wlk. SL4: Wind 4B 102
Bruce Way EN8: Walt C 5Zb 20
Bruckner St. W10 . . . . . 41Ab 88
Brudenell SL4: Wind 5D 102
Brudenell Rd. SW17 . . . . . 62Hb 133
Bruffs Mdw. UB5: N'olt 37Aa 65
Bruford Ct. SE8 . . . . . 51Cc 114
Bruges Pl. *NW1* *38Lb 70*
(off Randolph St.)
Brumana Cl. KT13: Weyb 79R 150
Brumfield Rd. KT19: Ewe 78Sa 153
Brummel Cl. DA7: Bex 55Ed 118
Brune Ho. E1 . . . . . 1K 225
Brunei Gallery 7E 216 (43Mb 90)
Brunel Cl. RM1: Rom 28Gd 56
RM18: Tilb 5D 122
SE19 . . . . . 65Vb 135
TW5: Cran 52X 107
UB5: N'olt 41Ba 85
Brunel Ct. *AL1: St A* *1C 6*
(off Newsom Pl.)
HA8: Edg 21Pa 47
HP3: Hem H 4M 3
SE16 . . . . . *47Yb 92*
(off Canon Beck Rd.)
SW13 . . . . . *54Va 110*
(off Westfields Av.)
Brunel Est. W2 . . . . . 43Cb 89
Brunel Ho. *BR2: Brom* *72Nc 160*
(off Wells Vw. Dr.)
CM14: B'wood 20Yd 40
DA2: Dart *58Sd 120*
(off Stone Ho. La.)
E14 . . . . . *50Dc 92*
(off Ship Yd.)
RM8: Dag 35Wc 75
Brunel M. W10 . . . . . 41Za 88
Brunel Mus. 47Yb 92
Brunel Pl. UB1: S'hall 44Da 85
Brunel Rd. E17 . . . . . 30Ac 52
IG8: Wfd G 22Pc 54
SE16 . . . . . 47Yb 92
W3 . . . . . 43Ua 88
Brunel Science Pk. UB8: Cowl 41N 83
Brunel St. E16 . . . . . 44Hc 93
Brunel University
Indoor Athletics Cen. 41N 83
Sports Pk. 42P 83
Uxbridge Campus 41M 83
Brunel Wlk. N15 . . . . . 29Ub 51
SW10 . . . . . *52Fb 111*
(off Cheyne Rd.)
TW2: Whitt 59Ca 107
Brunel Way DA1: Dart 55Pd 119
SL1: Slou 6K 81
Brune St. E1 . . . . . 1K 225 (43Vb 91)
Brunlees Ho. SE1 . . . . . 4D 230
Brunner Cl. NW11 . . . . . 29Db 49
Brunner Ct. KT16: Ott 78E 148
Brunner Ho. SE6 . . . . . 63Ec 136
Brunner Rd. E17 . . . . . 29Ac 52
W5 . . . . . 42Ma 87
Bruno Pl. NW9 . . . . . 33Sa 67
Brunswick Av. N11 . . . . . 20Jb 32
RM14: Upm 31Ud 78
Brunswick Cen. WC1 . . . . . 5F 217 (42Nb 90)
Brunswick Cl. DA6: Bex 56Zc 117
HA5: Pinn 30Aa 45
KT7: T Ditt 74Ha 152
KT12: Walt T 75Y 151
TW2: Twick 62Fa 130
Brunswick Cl. Est. EC1 . . . . . 4B 218 (41Rb 91)
Brunswick Ct. CM14: W'ley 22Xd 58
EC1 . . . . . 4B 218
EN4: E Barn 15Fb 31
RM14: Upm 31Vd 78
SE1 . . . . . 2J 231 (47Ub 91)
SM1: Sutt 77Db 155
SW1 . . . . . 6E 228
Brunswick Cres. N11 . . . . . 20Jb 32
Brunswick Dr. GU24: Brkwd 2B 186
Brunswick Flats *W11* *44Cb 89*
(off Westbourne Gro.)
Brunswick Gdns. IG6: Ilf 24Sc 54
W5 . . . . . 42Na 87
W8 . . . . . 46Cb 89
Brunswick Gro. KT11: Cobh 85Y 171
N11 . . . . . 20Jb 32
Brunswick Ho. E2 . . . . . 1K 219
N3 . . . . . 25Bb 49
SE16 . . . . . *48Ac 92*
(off Brunswick Quay)
W6 . . . . . *50Ya 88*
(off Parrs Way)
Brunswick Ind. Pk. N11 . . . . . 21Kb 50
Brunswick Mans. WC1 . . . . . 5G 217
Brunswick M. SW16 . . . . . 65Mb 134
W1 . . . . . 2G 221 (44Hb 89)
BRUNSWICK PARK 20Hb 31
Brunswick Pk. SE5 . . . . . 53Ub 113
Brunswick Pk. Gdns. N11 . . . . . 19Jb 32
Brunswick Pk. Rd. N11 . . . . . 19Jb 32
Brunswick Pl. N1 . . . . . 4G 219 (41Tb 91)
NW1 . . . . . 6J 215 (42Jb 90)
(not continuous)
SE19 . . . . . 66Wb 135
Brunswick Quay SE16 . . . . . 48Zb 92
Brunswick Rd. DA6: Bex 56Zc 117
E10 . . . . . 32Ec 72
E14 . . . . . 44Ec 92
EN3: Enf L 10Cc 20
GU24: Brkwd 3A 186
KT2: King T 67Qa 131
N15 . . . . . 29Ub 51
SM1: Sutt 77Db 155
W5 . . . . . 42Ma 87
Brunswick Sq. N17 . . . . . 23Vb 51
WC1 . . . . . 5G 217 (42Nb 90)
(not continuous)
Brunswick St. E17 . . . . . 29Ec 52
Brunswick Ter. BR3: Beck 67Dc 136
Brunswick Vs. SE5 . . . . . 53Ub 113
Brunswick Wlk. DA12: Grav'nd 9F 122
Brunswick Way N11 . . . . . 21Kb 50
Brunton Pl. E14 . . . . . 44Ac 92
Brushfield St. E1 . . . . . 7J 219 (43Ub 91)
Brushfield Way GU21: Knap 1G 186
Brushrise WD24: Wat 8X 13
Brushwood Cl. E14 . . . . . 43Dc 92
Brushwood Dr. WD3: Chor 14E 24
Brussels Rd. SW11 . . . . . 56Fb 111
Bruton Cl. BR7: Chst 66Pc 138
Bruton La. W1 . . . . . 5A 222 (45Kb 90)
Bruton Pl. W1 . . . . . 5A 222 (45Kb 90)
Bruton Rd. SM4: Mord 70Eb 133
Bruton St. W1 . . . . . 5A 222 (45Kb 90)
Bruton Way W13 . . . . . 43Ja 86
Brutus Ct. SE11 . . . . . 6B 230
Bryan Av. NW10 . . . . . 38Xa 68
Bryan Cl. TW16: Sun 66W 128
Bryan Ho. NW10 . . . . . 38Xa 68
SE16 . . . . . 47Bc 92
Bryan Rd. SE16 . . . . . 47Bc 92
Bryan's All. SW6 . . . . . 54Db 111
Bryanston Av. TW2: Whitt 60Da 107
Bryanston Cl. UB2: S'hall 49Ba 85
Bryanston Ct. HP2: Hem H 3M 3
W1 . . . . . 2F 221
(not continuous)
Bryanstone Ct. SM1: Sutt 76Eb 155
Bryanstone Rd.
EN8: Walt C 6Bc 20
N8 . . . . . 29Mb 50
Bryanston Mans. W1 . . . . . 7F 215
Bryanston M. E. W1 . . . . . 1F 221 (43Hb 89)
Bryanston M. W. W1 . . . . . 1F 221 (43Hb 89)
Bryanston Pl. W1 . . . . . 1F 221 (43Hb 89)
Bryanston Rd. RM18: Tilb 4E 122
Bryanston Sq. W1 . . . . . 1F 221 (44Hb 89)
Bryanston St. W1 . . . . . 3F 221 (44Hb 89)
Bryan St. N1 . . . . . 1J 217 (39Pb 70)
Bryant Av. RM3: Hrld W 25Md 57
SL2: Slou 3H 81
Bryant Cl. EN5: Barn 15Bb 31
Bryant Ct. E2 . . . . . 1K 219
(not continuous)
W3 . . . . . 46Ta 87
Bryant Ho. *E3* *40Cc 72*
(off Thomas Fyre Dr.)
Bryant Rd. UB5: N'olt 41Y 85
Bryant Row RM3: Rom 19Ld 39
Bryant St. E2 . . . . . 1K 219 (39Vb 71)
E15 . . . . . 38Fc 73
Bryantwood Rd. N7 . . . . . 36Qb 70
Brycedale Cres. N14 . . . . . 21Mb 50
Bryce Ho. *SE14* *51Zb 114*
(off John Williams Cl.)
Bryce Rd. RM8: Dag 35Yc 75
Brydale Ho. *SE16* *49Zb 92*
(off Rotherhithe New Rd.)
Bryden Cl. SE26 . . . . . 64Ac 136
Brydges Pl. WC2 . . . . . 5F 223 (45Nb 90)
Brydges Rd. E15 . . . . . 36Fc 73
Brydon Wlk. N1 . . . . . 39Nb 70
Bryer Ct. EC2 . . . . . 7D 218
Bryer Pl. SL4: Wind 5B 102
Bryett Rd. N7 . . . . . 34Nb 70
Bryher Ct. SE11 . . . . . 7K 229
Brymay Cl. E3 . . . . . 40Cc 72
Brymcourt W9 . . . . . 40Db 69
Brynford Cl. GU21: Wok 87A 168
Brynmaer Rd. SW11 . . . . . 53Hb 111
Bryn-y-mawr Rd. EN1: Enf 14Vb 33
Bryony Cl. IG10: Lough 14Rc 36
UB8: Hil 43P 83
Bryony Rd. W12 . . . . . 45Wa 88
Bryony Way TW16: Sun 65W 128
Bubblestone Rd. TN14: Otf 88Kd 183
Buccleuch Rd. SL3: Dat 2L 103
Buccleugh Ho. E5 . . . . . 31Wb 71
Buchanan Cl. N21 . . . . . 15Pb 32
RM15: Avel 46Sd 98
Buchanan Ct. *SE16* *49Zb 92*
(off Worgan St.)
WD6: Bore 12Sa 29
Buchanan Gdns. NW10 . . . . . 40Xa 68
Buchanan Pl. KT17: Ewe 82Wa 174
Buchan Cl. UB8: Cowl 41L 83
Buchan Ho. *W3* *47Ra 87*
(off Hanbury Rd.)
Buchan Rd. SE15 . . . . . 55Yb 114
Bucharest Rd. SW18 . . . . . 59Eb 111
Buckbean Path RM3: Rom 24Ld 57
Buckden Cl. N2 . . . . . 28Hb 49
SE12 . . . . . 58Jc 115
Buckettsland La. WD6: Bore 10Ta 15
Buckfast Ct. *W13* *45Ja 86*
(off Romsey Rd.)
Buckfast Ho. N14 . . . . . 15Lb 32
Buckfast Rd. SM4: Mord 70Db 133
Buckfast St. E2 . . . . . 41Wb 91
Buckfield Ct. SL0: Rich P 47H 83
Buckham Thorns Rd.
TN16: Westrm 98Sc 200
Buck Hill Wlk. W2 . . . . . 5C 220 (45Fb 89)
Buckhold Rd. SW18 . . . . . 58Cb 111
Buckhurst Av. SM5: Cars 74Gb 155
TN13: S'oaks 97Ld 203
Buckhurst Cl. RH1: Redh 4N 207
Buckhurst Ct. IG9: Buck H 18Mc 35
BUCKHURST HILL
IG9 . . . . . 19Mc 35
SL5 . . . . . 7D 124
Buckhurst Hill Ho. IG9: Buck H 19Kc 35
Buckhurst Ho. N7 . . . . . 36Mb 70
Buckhurst La. SL5: S'hill 9D 124
TN13: S'oaks 97Ld 203
Buckhurst Rd. SL5: Asc, S'hill 7D 124
TN16: Westrm 93Qc 200
Buckhurst St. E1 . . . . . 42Xb 91
Buckhurst Way IG9: Buck H 21Mc 53
Buckingham Arc. WC2 . . . . . 5G 223
Buckingham Av. CR7: Thor H 67Qb 134
DA16: Well 56Uc 116
KT8: W Mole 68Da 129
N20 . . . . . 17Eb 31
SL1: Slou 4C 80
TW14: Felt 58X 107
UB6: G'frd 39Ja 66
Buckingham Av. E. SL1: Slou 4G 80
Buckingham Chambers
SW1 . . . . . 5C 228
Buckingham Cl. BR5: Pet W 73Uc 160
EN1: Enf 12Ub 33
RM11: Horn 30Md 57
TW12: Hamp 64Ba 129
W5 . . . . . 43La 86
Buckingham Ct. *AL1: St A* *1D 6*
(off Lemsford Rd.)
NW4 . . . . . 27Wa 48
SM2: Sutt 81Cb 175
TW18: Staines *63J 127*
(off Kingston Rd.)
UB5: N'olt 40Aa 65
W7 . . . . . *42Ha 86*
(off Copley Cl.)
W11 . . . . . *45Cb 89*
(off Kensington Pk. Rd.)
Buckingham Dr. BR7: Chst 63Sc 138
Buckingham Gdns.
CR7: Thor H 68Qb 134
HA8: Edg 24Na 47
KT8: W Mole 68Da 129
SL1: Slou 7K 81
Buckingham Ga. SW1 . . . . . 3B 228 (48Lb 90)
Buckingham Gro. UB10: Hil 40Q 64
WD6: Bore 14Ta 29
Buckingham Hill Rd.
SS17: Ors, Stan H 5H 101
Buckingham La. SE23 . . . . . 59Ac 114
Buckingham Mans. *NW6* *36Db 69*
(off West End La.)
Buckingham M. N1 . . . . . 37Ub 71
NW10 . . . . . 40Va 68
SW1 . . . . . 3B 228
Buckingham Palace 2A 228 (47Kb 90)
Buckingham Pal. Rd.
SW1 . . . . . 6K 227 (49Kb 90)
Buckingham Pde. HA7: Stan 22La 46
SL9: Chal P *25A 42*
(off Market Pl.)
Buckingham Pl. SW1 . . . . . 3B 228 (48Lb 90)
Buckingham Rd. CM16: Epp 2Uc 22
CR4: Mitc 70Nb 134
DA11: Nflt 59Fe 121
E10 . . . . . 34Dc 72
E11 . . . . . 29Lc 53
E15 . . . . . 36Hc 73
E18 . . . . . 25Hc 53
HA1: Harr 29Fa 46
HA8: Edg 24Pa 47
IG1: Ilf 33Tc 74
KT1: King T 70Pa 131
N1 . . . . . 37Ub 71
N22 . . . . . 25Nb 50
NW10 . . . . . 40Va 68
TW10: Ham 61Ma 131
TW12: Hamp 63Ba 129
WD6: Bore 14Ta 29
WD24: Wat 9Y 13
Buckinghamshire Golf Course 33L 63
Buckinghamshire New University
Uxbridge Campus 37L 63
Buckingham St. WC2 . . . . . 5G 223 (45Nb 90)
Buckingham Way SM6: Wall 81Lb 176
BUCKLAND 5C 206
Buckland Av. SL3: Slou 9M 81
Buckland Cl. NW7 . . . . . 21Wa 48
Buckland Ct. N1 . . . . . 1H 219
RH1: Redh 4B 208
UB10: Ick 33S 64
Buckland Ct. Gdns. RH3: Bkld 5C 206
Buckland Cres. NW3 . . . . . 38Fb 69
SL4: Wind 3D 102
Buckland Ga. SL3: Wex 1M 81
Buckland Ho. SW1 . . . . . 7K 227
Buckland La. KT20: Walt H 100Wa 194
RH3: Bkld 2C 206
Buckland Ri. HA5: Pinn 25Y 45
Buckland Rd. BR6: Orp 77Uc 160
E10 . . . . . 33Ec 72
KT9: Chess 78Pa 153
KT20: Lwr K 1H 207
RH2: Reig 5F 206
SM2: Cheam 82Ya 174
Bucklands WD19: Wat 20Z 27
Bucklands, The WD3: Rick 17J 25
Bucklands Rd. TW11: Tedd 65La 130
Buckland St. N1 . . . . . 2G 219 (40Tb 71)
Buckland's Wharf KT1: King T 68Ma 131
Buckland Wlk. SM4: Mord 70Eb 133
W3 . . . . . 47Sa 87
Buckland Way KT4: Wor Pk 74Ya 154
RM13: Rain 40Md 77
Buck La. NW9 . . . . . 29Ta 47
Bucklebury NW1 . . . . . 5B 216
Buckleigh Av. SW20 . . . . . 69Ab 132
Buckleigh Rd. SW16 . . . . . 65Mb 134
Buckleigh Way SE19 . . . . . 66Vb 135
Buckler Ct. N7 . . . . . 36Pb 70
Buckler Gdns. SE9 . . . . . 62Pc 138
Bucklers All. SW6 . . . . . 51Bb 111
Bucklersbury EC4 . . . . . 3F 225 (44Tb 91)
Bucklersbury Pas. EC4 . . . . . 3F 225 (44Tb 91)
Bucklers Ct. CM14: W'ley 22Yd 58
Buckler's Way SM5: Cars 76Hb 155
Buckles Ct. DA17: Belv 49Zc 95
Buckles La. RM15: S Ock 43Yd 98
Buckle St. E1 . . . . . 44Vb 91
Buckles Way SM7: Bans 88Ab 174
Buckley Cl. DA1: Cray 54Hd 118
SE23 . . . . . 59Xb 113
Buckley Ct. NW6 . . . . . 38Bb 69
SE1 . . . . . 4K 231 (48Vb 91)
Buckley Ho. *W14* *47Ab 88*
(off Holland Pk. Av.)
Buckley Rd. NW6 . . . . . 38Bb 69
Buckmaster Cl. *SW9* *55Qb 112*
(off Stockwell Pk. Rd.)
Buckmaster Ho. N7 . . . . . 35Pb 70
Buckmaster Rd. SW11 . . . . . 56Gb 111
Bucknalls Cl. WD25: Wat 4Aa 13
Bucknalls Dr. AL2: Brick W 3Ba 13
Bucknalls La. WD25: Wat 4Z 13
Bucknall St. WC2 . . . . . 2E 222 (44Nb 90)
Bucknall Way BR3: Beck 70Dc 136
Bucknell Cl. SW2 . . . . . 56Pb 112
Buckner Rd. SW2 . . . . . 56Pb 112
Bucknill Ho. SW1 . . . . . 7K 227
Bucknills Cl. KT18: Eps 86Sa 173
Buckrell Rd. E4 . . . . . 19Fc 35
Buckridge Ho. EC1 . . . . . 7K 217
Buck's Av. WD19: Wat 17Aa 27
Bucks Cl. KT14: W Byf 86K 169
Bucks Cross Rd. BR6: Chels 78Ad 161
DA11: Nflt 2B 144
Buckshead Ho. *W2* *43Cb 89*
(off Gt. Western Rd.)
BUCKS HILL 7M 11
Bucks Hill WD4: Bucks 5L 11
Buckston Browne Gdns.
BR6: Downe 84Pc 180
Buckstone Cl. SE23 . . . . . 58Yb 114
Buckstone Rd. N18 . . . . . 22Wb 51
Buck St. NW1 . . . . . 38Kb 70
Buckters Rents SE16 . . . . . 46Ac 92
Buckthorne Rd. SE4 . . . . . 57Ac 114
Buckthorn Ho. *DA15: Sidc* *62Vc 139*
(off Longlands Rd.)
E15 . . . . . *41Gc 93*
(off Manor Rd.)
Buckton Rd. WD6: Bore 10Pa 15
Buck Wlk. E17 . . . . . 28Fc 53
Buckwell Pl. TN13: S'oaks 100Ld 203
Buckwheat Ct. DA18: Erith 48Zc 95
Budd Cl. N12 . . . . . 21Db 49
Buddings Circ. HA9: Wemb 34Sa 67
Buddleia Ho. TW13: Felt 60W 106
Budd's All. TW1: Twick 57La 108
Budebury Rd. TW18: Staines 64J 127
Bude Cl. E17 . . . . . 29Bc 52
Budge La. CR4: Mitc 73Hb 155
Budgen Dr. RH1: Redh 3A 208
Budge's Wlk. W2 . . . . . 7A 220
Budgin's Hill BR6: Prat B 84Yc 181
Budleigh Cres. DA16: Well 53Yc 117
Budleigh Ho. *SE15* *52Wb 113*
(off Bird in Bush Rd.)
Budoch Ct. IG3: Ilf 33Wc 75
Budoch Dr. IG3: Ilf 33Wc 75
Buer Rd. SW6 . . . . . 54Ab 110
Buff Av. SM7: Bans 86Db 175
Buffers La. KT22: Lea 91Ja 192
Bug Hill CR3: Wold 92Zb 198
CR6: W'ham, Wold 92Zb 198
Bugsby's Way SE7 . . . . . 49Hc 93
SE10 . . . . . 49Hc 93
Buick Ho. *E3* *42Cc 92*
(off Wellington Way)
KT2: King T 68Pa 131
Building 50 SE18 . . . . . 48Sc 94
Bulbarrow *NW8* *39Db 69*
(off Abbey Rd.)
Bulbeggars La. RH9: G'stone 4A 210
Bulbourne Cl. HP1: Hem H 3J 3
Bulbourne Ho. *HP1: Hem H* *4L 3*
(off Cotterells)
Bulganak Rd. CR7: Thor H 70Sb 135
Bulinga St. SW1 . . . . . 6F 229
Bulkeley Av. SL4: Wind 5F 102
Bulkeley Cl. TW20: Eng G 4N 125
Bullace Cl. HP1: Hem H 1J 3
Bullace La. DA1: Dart 58Nd 119
Bullace Row SE5 . . . . . 53Tb 113
Bull All. DA16: Well 55Xc 117
Bullard's Pl. E2 . . . . . 41Zb 92
Bullbanks Rd. DA17: Belv 49Ed 96
Bullbeggars La. GU21: Wok 8M 167
HP4: Berk, Pott E 2B 2
Bull Cl. RM16: Chaf H 48Fe 99
Bulleid Way SW1 . . . . . 6A 228 (49Kb 90)
Bullen Ho. *E1* *42Xb 91*
(off Collingwood St.)
BULLEN'S GREEN 4B 8
Bullens Grn. La. AL4: Col H 4A 8
Bullen St. SW11 . . . . . 54Gb 111
Buller Cl. SE15 . . . . . 52Wb 113
Buller Rd. CR7: Thor H 68Tb 135
IG11: Bark 38Uc 74
N17 . . . . . 26Wb 51
N22 . . . . . 26Qb 50
NW10 . . . . . 41Za 88
Bullers Cl. DA14: Sidc 64Ad 139
Bullers Wood Dr. BR7: Chst 66Pc 138
Bullescroft Rd. HA8: Edg 20Qa 29
Bullfinch Cl. TN13: Riv 94Fd 202
Bullfinch Dene TN13: Riv 94Fd 202
Bullfinch Ho. *NW9* *30Va 48*
(off Perryfield Way)
Bullfinch La. TN13: Riv 94Fd 202
Bullfinch Rd. CR2: Sels 82Zb 178
Bullhead Rd. WD6: Bore 13Sa 29
Bull Hill DA4: Hort K 70Sd 142
KT22: Lea 93Ja 192
Bullingham Mans. *W8* *47Cb 89*
(off Pitt St.)
Bull Inn Ct. WC2 . . . . . 5G 223
Bullivant Cl. DA9: Ghithe 57Wd 120
Bullivant St. E14 . . . . . 45Ec 92
Bull La. BR7: Chst 66Tc 138
N18 . . . . . 22Ub 51
RM10: Dag 34Dd 76
SL9: Chal P, Ger X 27A 42
TN15: Wro 88Ce 185
Bullman Cl. DA7: Bex 55Dd 118
Bull Rd. E15 . . . . . 40Hc 73
Bullrush Cl. AL10: Hat 1D 8
CR0: C'don 72Ub 157
SM5: Cars 75Gb 155
Bullrush Gro. UB8: Cowl 42L 83
Bull's All. SW14 . . . . . 54Ta 109
Bulls Bri. Cen. UB3: Hayes 48W 84
Bullsbridge Ind. Est. UB2: S'hall 49Y 85
Bulls Bri. Rd. UB2: S'hall 49Y 85
UB3: Hayes 48X 85
Bullsbrook Rd. UB4: Yead 46Y 85
BULLS CROSS 7Wb 19
Bulls Cross EN2: Enf 7Wb 19
Bulls Cross Ride EN7: Walt C 5Wb 19
Bulls Gdns. SW3 . . . . . 5E 226 (49Gb 89)
Bulls Head Pas. EC3 . . . . . 3H 225
Bulls Head Row RH9: G'stone 3P 209
Bulls Head Yd. *DA1: Dart* *58Nd 119*
(off High St.)
Bullsland Gdns. WD3: Chor 16D 24
Bullsland La. WD3: Chor 18D 24
Bulls La. AL9: Brk P, Wel G 6F 8
BULLSMOOR 7Yb 20
Bullsmoor Cl. EN8: Walt C 7Yb 20
Bullsmoor Gdns. EN8: Walt C 7Xb 19
Bullsmoor La. EN1: Enf 7Wb 19
EN3: Enf W 7Xb 19
EN7: Walt C 7Wb 19
Bullsmoor Ride EN8: Walt C 7Yb 20
Bullsmoor Way EN8: Walt C 7Yb 20
BULLSWATER COMMON 8E 186
Bullswater Comn. Rd. GU24: Pirb 8E 186
Bullswater La. GU24: Pirb 7E 186
Bull Theatre, The 14Bb 31
Bullwell Cres. EN8: Chesh 1Ac 20
Bull Yd. SE15 . . . . . 53Wb 113
Bulmer Gdns. HA3: Kenton 31Ma 67
Bulmer M. W11 . . . . . 45Cb 89
Bulmer Pl. W11 . . . . . 46Cb 89
Bulmer Wlk. RM13: Rain 40Ld 77
Bulow Est. *SW6* *53Db 111*
(off Pearscroft Rd.)
BULSTRODE 1G 10
Bulstrode Av. TW3: Houn 54Ba 107
Bulstrode Cl. WD4: Chfd 1G 10
Bulstrode Ct. SL9: Ger X 30A 42
Bulstrode Gdns.
TW3: Houn 55Ca 107
Bulstrode La. HP3: Hem H 7J 3
WD4: Chfd, K Lan 1G 10
Bulstrode Pl. SL1: Slou 8K 81
W1 . . . . . 1J 221 (43Jb 90)
Bulstrode Rd. TW3: Houn 55Ca 107
Bulstrode St. W1 . . . . . 2J 221 (44Jb 90)
Bulstrode Way SL9: Ger X 29A 42
Bulwark Ct. *E14* *45Ec 92*
(off Parkside Sq.)
Bulwer Ct. E11 . . . . . 32Fc 73
Bulwer Ct. Rd. E11 . . . . . 32Fc 73
Bulwer Gdns. EN5: New Bar 14Eb 31

Bulwer Rd. E11 .... 31Fc **73**
EN5: New Bar 14Db **31**
N18 .... 21Ub **51**
Bulwer St. W12 .... 46Ya **88**
Bumpstead Mead RM15: Avel 46Ud **98**
Bunbury Ho. *SE15* *52Wb* ***113***
(off Fenham Rd.)
Bunbury Way KT17: Eps D 88Xa **174**
Bunby Rd. SL2: Stoke P 8K **61**
Bunce Dr. CR3: Cat'm 95Tb **197**
Buncefield La. HP2: Hem H 1C **4**
Buncefield Terminal
HP2: Hem H 1D **4**
Bunce's Cl. SL4: Eton W 10F **80**
Bunce's La. IG8: Wfd G 24Hc **53**
Bundy's Way TW18: Staines 65H **127**
Bungalow Rd. SE25 .... 70Ub **135**
Bungalows, The E10 .... 30Ec **52**
HA2: Harr 35Ba **65**
IG6: Ilf 25Uc **54**
RM20: Grays 51Zd **121**
SM6: Wall 78Kb **156**
SW16 .... 66Kb **134**
UB4: Yead 42Z **85**
Bunhill Row EC1 .... 5F **219** (42Tb **91**)
Bunhouse Pl. SW1 .... 7H **227** (50Jb **90**)
Bunkers Hill DA14: Sidc 62Bd **139**
DA17: Belv 49Cd **96**
NW11 .... 31Eb **69**
TN15: Ash 79De **165**
Bunkers La. HP3: Hem H 7A **4**
Bunning Way N7 .... 38Nb **70**
Bunns La. NW7 .... 23Ua **48**
(not continuous)
Bunny Hill DA12: Shorne 5N **145**
Bunsen Ho. *E3* *40Ac* ***72***
(off Grove Rd.)
Bunsen St. E3 .... 40Ac **72**
Bunstone Hall DA2: Dart 58Sd **120**
Bunten Meade SL1: Slou 6F **80**
Buntingbridge Rd. IG2: Ilf 29Tc **54**
Bunting Cl. CR4: Mitc 71Hb **155**
HP3: Hem H 7L **3**
N9 .... 18Zb **34**
Bunting Ct. NW9 .... 26Ua **48**
Bunting Ho. *UB10: Ick* *33S* ***64***
(off Coyle Dr.)
Bunton St. SE18 .... 48Qc **94**
Bunwell Ho. *E3* *42Bc* ***92***
(off William Whiffin Sq.)
Bunyan Ct. EC2 .... 7D **218**
Bunyan Rd. E17 .... 27Ac **52**
Bunyan's La. GU24: Chob 6G **166**
Bunyard Dr. GU21: Wok 86E **168**
Buonaparte M. SW1 .... 7D **228** (50Mb **90**)
Burbage Cl. EN8: Chesh 3Bc **20**
SE1 .... 4F **231** (48Tb **91**)
UB3: Hayes 44T **84**
Burbage Ho. N1 .... 1G **219**
SE14 .... *51Zb* ***114***
(off Samuel Cl.)
Burbage Rd. SE21 .... 58Sb **113**
SE24 .... 58Sb **113**
Burberry Cl. KT3: N Mald 68Ua **132**
Burbery Cl. UB9: Hare 26M **43**
Burbidge Rd. TW17: Shep 70Q **128**
Burbridge Rd. WD25: Wat 5V **12**
Burbridge Way N17 .... 26Wb **51**
Burcham Cl. TW12: Hamp 66Ca **129**
Burcham St. E14 .... 44Dc **92**
Burcharbro Rd. SE2 .... 51Zc **117**
Burchell Ct. WD23: Bush 17Ea **28**
Burchell Ho. SE11 .... 7J **229**
Burchell Rd. E10 .... 32Dc **72**
SE15 .... 53Xb **113**
Burcher Gale Gro. SE15 .... 52Vb **113**
Burchetts Way TW17: Shep 72R **150**
Burchett Way RM6: Chad H 30Bd **55**
Burch Rd. DA11: Nflt 8B **122**
Burchwall Cl. RM5: Col R 24Ed **56**
Burcote KT13: Weyb 79T **150**
Burcote Rd. SW18 .... 59Fb **111**
Burcott Gdns. KT15: Add 79L **149**
Burcott Rd. CR8: Purl 86Qb **176**
Burden Cl. TW8: Bford 50La **86**
Burden Ho. *SW8* *52Nb* ***112***
(off Thorncroft St.)
Burdenshot Hill GU3: Worp 7L **187**
Burdenshott Av. TW10: Rich 56Ra **109**
Burdenshott Rd. GU3: Worp 7L **187**
Burden Way E11 .... 33Kc **73**
Burder Cl. N1 .... 37Ub **71**
Burder Rd. N1 .... 37Ub **71**
Burdett Av. DA12: Shorne 3N **145**
SW20 .... 67Wa **132**
Burdett Cl. DA14: Sidc 64Ad **139**
W7 .... 46Ha **86**
Burdett M. NW3 .... 37Fb **69**
W2 .... 44Db **89**
Burdett Rd. CR0: C'don 72Tb **157**
E3 .... 42Ac **92**
E14 .... 42Ac **92**
TW9: Rich 54Pa **109**
Burdetts Rd. RM9: Dag 39Bd **75**
Burdock Cl. CR0: C'don 74Zb **158**
GU18: Light 3A **166**
Burdock Rd. N17 .... 27Wb **51**
Burdon La. SM2: Cheam 80Ab **154**
Burdon Pk. SM2: Cheam 81Bb **175**
Bure RM18: E Til 8L **101**
Bure Ct. EN5: New Bar 15Db **31**
Burfield Cl. SW17 .... 63Fb **133**
Burfield Dr. CR6: W'ham 91Yb **198**
Burfield Rd. SL4: Old Win 8L **103**
WD3: Chor 15E **24**
Burford Cl. IG6: Ilf 28Sc **54**
RM8: Dag 34Yc **75**
UB10: Ick 35N **63**
Burford Gdns. N13 .... 20Pb **32**
SL1: Slou 3A **80**
Burford Ho. KT17: Ewe 83Ya **174**
TW8: Bford 50Ma **87**
Burford La. KT17: Ewe 83Ya **174**
Burford Rd. BR1: Brom 70Nc **138**
E6 .... 41Nc **94**
E15 .... 39Fc **73**
KT4: Wor Pk 73Va **154**
SE6 .... 61Bc **136**
SM1: Sutt 75Cb **155**
TW8: Bford 50Na **87**
Burford Wlk. SW6 .... 52Eb **111**
Burford Way CR0: New Ad 79Ec **158**
Burford Wharf Apartments *E15* *39Fc* ***73***
(off Cam Rd.)
Burgate Cl. DA1: Cray 55Hd **118**
Burges Cl. RM11: Horn 30Pd **57**
Burges Gro. SW13 .... 52Xa **110**
Burges Rd. E6 .... 38Nc **74**
Burgess Av. NW9 .... 30Ta **47**
SS17: Stan H 2N **101**
Burgess Bus. Pk. SE5 .... 52Tb **113**
Burgess Cl. TW13: Hanw 63Aa **129**
Burgess Ct. CM15: B'wood 18Zd **41**
E6 .... 38Qc **74**
SE6 .... 59Cc **114**
UB1: S'hall *44Da* ***85***
(off Fleming Rd.)
WD6: Bore *10Pa* ***15***
(off Aycliffe Rd.)
Burgess Hill NW2 .... 35Cb **69**
Burgess Ho. *SE5* *52Sb* ***113***
(off Bethwin Rd.)
Burgess Lofts *SE5* *52Sb* ***113***
(off Bethwin Rd.)
Burgess M. SW19 .... 65Db **133**
Burgess Pk. 51Tb **113**
Burgess Pk. Kart Track 51Tb **113**
Burgess Rd. E6 .... 38Qc **74**
E15 .... 35Gc **73**
SM1: Sutt 77Db **155**
Burgess St. E14 .... 43Cc **92**
Burge St. SE1 .... 4G **231** (48Tb **91**)
Burges Way TW18: Staines 64J **127**
Burgett Rd. SL1: Slou 8F **80**
Burgh Cft. KT17: Eps 87Va **174**
Burghfield KT17: Eps 87Va **174**
Burghfield Rd. DA13: Ist R 6B **144**
BURGH HEATH **91Ab 194**
Burgh Heath Rd.
KT17: Eps, Eps D 86Va **174**
Burgh House 35Fb **69**
Burghill Rd. SE26 .... 63Ac **136**
Burghley Av. KT3: N Mald 67Ta **131**
WD6: Bore 15Sa **29**
Burghley Hall Cl. SW19 .... 60Ab **110**
Burghley Ho. SW19 .... 62Ab **132**
Burghley Pas. *E11* *32Gc* ***73***
(off Burghley Rd.)
Burghley Pl. CR4: Mitc 71Hb **155**
Burghley Rd. E11 .... 32Gc **73**
N8 .... 27Qb **50**
NW5 .... 35Kb **70**
RM16: Chaf H 48Yd **98**
SW19 .... 63Za **132**
Burghley Twr. W3 .... 45Va **88**
Burgh Mt. SM7: Bans 87Bb **175**
Burgh St. N1 .... 1C **218** (40Rb **71**)
Burgh Wood SM7: Bans 87Ab **174**
Burgoine Quay KT1: Hamp W 67Ma **131**
Burgon St. EC4 .... 3C **224** (44Rb **91**)
Burgos Cl. CR0: Wadd 79Qb **156**
Burgos Gro. SE10 .... 53Dc **114**
Burgoyne Ho. *TW8: Bford* *50Ma* ***87***
(off Ealing Rd.)
Burgoyne Rd. N4 .... 30Rb **51**
SE25 .... 70Vb **135**
SW9 .... 55Pb **112**
TW16: Sun 65V **128**
Burgundy Ho. *E20* *36Ec* ***72***
(off Liberty Bri. Rd.)
EN2: Enf *10Sb* ***19***
(off Bedale Rd.)
Burgundy Pl. W12 .... 46Za **88**
Burham Cl. SE20 .... 66Yb **136**
BURHILL **81X 171**
Burhill Golf Course 81W **170**
Burhill Gro. HA5: Pinn 26Aa **45**
Burhill Rd. KT12: Hers 81X **171**
Burke Cl. SW15 .... 56Ua **110**
Burke Lodge E13 .... 41Kc **93**
Burke St. E16 .... 43Hc **93**
(not continuous)
Burket Cl. UB2: S'hall 49Aa **85**
Burland Rd. CM15: B'wood 18Zd **41**
RM5: Col R 23Ed **56**
SW11 .... 57Hb **111**
Burlea Cl. KT12: Hers 78X **151**
Burleigh Av. DA15: Sidc 57Vc **117**
SM6: Wall 76Jb **156**
Burleigh Cl. KT15: Add 78K **149**
RM7: Mawney 28Dd **56**
Burleigh Ct. KT22: Lea 94Ja **192**
Burleigh Gdns. GU21: Wok 89B **168**
N14 .... 18Lb **32**
TW15: Ashf 64S **128**
Burleigh Ho. *SW3* *51Fb* ***111***
(off Beaufort St.)
W10 .... *43Ab* ***88***
(off St Charles Sq.)
WC1 .... 4G **217**
Burleigh Pde. N14 .... 18Mb **32**
Burleigh Pk. KT11: Cobh 84Aa **171**
Burleigh Pl. SW15 .... 57Za **110**
Burleigh Rd. AL1: St A 2F **6**
EN1: Enf 14Ub **33**
EN8: Chesh 4Ac **20**
HP2: Hem H 3C **4**
KT15: Add 78K **149**
SM3: Sutt 74Ab **154**
UB10: Hil 39R **64**
Burleigh St. WC2 .... 4G **223** (45Pb **90**)
Burleigh Wlk. SE6 .... 60Ec **114**
Burleigh Way EN2: Enf 13Tb **33**
EN6: Cuff 2Nb **18**
Burlescombe Ho. *RH1: Redh* *4A* ***208***
(off Burrage Rd.)
Burley Cl. E4 .... 22Cc **52**
SW16 .... 68Mb **134**
Burley Ho. *E1* *44Zb* ***92***
(off Chudleigh St.)
WD5: Ab L 4V **12**
Burley Orchard KT16: Chert 72J **149**
Burley Rd. E16 .... 44Lc **93**
BURLINGS **89Vc 181**
Burlings La. TN14: Knock 89Vc **181**
Burlington Arc. W1 .... 5B **222** (45Lb **90**)
Burlington Av. RM7: Rom 30Dd **56**
SL1: Slou 7J **81**
TW9: Kew 53Qa **109**
Burlington Cl. BR6: Farnb 75Rc **160**
E6 .... 44Nc **94**
HA5: Eastc 27X **45**
TW14: Bedf 59T **106**
W9 .... 42Cb **89**
Burlington Cnr. *NW1* *38Lb* ***70***
(off Camden Rd.)
Burlington Ct. *E1* *45Wb* ***91***
(off Cable St.)
RH1: Redh *5P* ***207***
(off Station Rd.)
SL1: Slou 7J **81**
Burlington Gdns. RM6: Chad H 31Ad **75**
SW6 .... 54Ab **110**
W1 .... 5B **222** (45Lb **90**)
W3 .... 46Sa **87**
W4 .... 50Sa **87**
Burlington Ho. *N15* *30Tb* ***51***
(off Tewkesbury Rd.)
SE16 .... *47Zb* ***92***
(off Province Dr.)
UB7: W Dray *47P* ***83***
(off Park Lodge Av.)
Burlington La. W4 .... 52Sa **109**
Burlington M. SW15 .... 57Bb **111**
W3 .... 46Sa **87**
Burlington Pl. IG8: Wfd G 20Kc **35**
RH2: Reig 5J **207**
SW6 .... 54Ab **110**
TN13: S'oaks 95Jd **202**
Burlington Ri. EN4: E Barn 18Gb **31**
Burlington Rd.
CR7: Thor H 68Sb **135**
EN2: Enf 11Tb **33**
KT3: N Mald 70Va **132**
N10 .... 27Jb **50**
N17 .... 25Wb **51**
SL1: Burn 2A **80**
SL1: Slou 7J **81**
SW6 .... 54Ab **110**
TW7: Isle 53Fa **108**
W4 .... 50Sa **87**
Burma M. N16 .... 35Tb **71**
Burman Cl. DA2: Dart 59Sd **120**
Burma Rd. GU24: Chob 6K **147**
N16 .... 35Tb **71**
Burmarsh NW5 .... 37Jb **70**
Burmarsh Ct. SE20 .... 67Yb **136**
Burma Ter. SE19 .... 64Ub **135**
Burmester Rd. SW17 .... 62Eb **133**
Burnaby Cres. W4 .... 51Sa **109**
Burnaby Gdns. W4 .... 51Ra **109**
Burnaby Rd. DA11: Nflt 9A **122**
Burnaby St. SW10 .... 52Eb **111**
Burnand Ho. *W14* *48Za* ***88***
(off Redan St.)
Burnbrae Cl. N12 .... 23Db **49**
Burnbury Rd. SW12 .... 60Lb **112**
Burn Cl. KT15: Add 77M **149**
KT22: Oxs 87Fa **172**
WD25: A'ham 13Fa **28**
Burncroft Av. EN3: Enf H 12Yb **34**
Burndell Way UB4: Yead 43Z **85**
Burne Jones Ho. W14 .... 49Ab **88**
Burnell Av. DA16: Well 54Wc **117**
TW10: Ham 64La **130**
Burnell Gdns. HA7: Stan 26Ma **47**
Burnell Ho. *E20* *36Dc* ***72***
(off Peloton Av.)
Burnelli Bldg. *SW8* *52Kb* ***112***
(off Sopwith Way)
Burnell Rd. SM1: Sutt 77Db **155**
Burnell Wlk. CM13: Gt War 23Yd **58**
SE1 .... *50Vb* ***91***
(off Cadet Dr.)
Burnels Av. E6 .... 41Qc **94**
Burness Cl. N7 .... 37Pb **70**
UB8: Uxb 40M **63**
Burne St. NW1 .... 7D **214** (43Gb **89**)
Burnet Cl. GU24: W End 5C **166**
HP3: Hem H 3N **3**
Burnet Gro. KT19: Eps 85Sa **173**
Burnett Cl. E9 .... 36Yb **72**
Burnett Ho. *SE13* *54Ec* ***114***
(off Lewisham Hill)
Burnett Rd. DA8: Erith 51Md **119**
IG6: Ilf 24Rc **54**
Burnetts Rd. SL4: Wind 3C **102**
Burney Av. KT5: Surb 71Pa **153**
Burney Cl. KT22: Fet 97Ea **192**
Burney Dr. IG10: Lough 12Rc **36**
Burney Ho. *KT22: Lea* *93Ja* ***192***
(off Highbury Dr.)
Burney St. SE10 .... 52Ec **114**
Burnfoot Av. SW6 .... 53Ab **110**
BURNHAM **1A 80**
Burnham NW3 .... 38Gb **69**
Burnham Av. UB10: Ick 35S **64**
BURNHAM BEECHES **6F 60**
Burnham Beeches Golf Course 9B **60**
Burnham Beeches National Nature Reserve
.... 7D **60**
Burnham Cl. EN1: Enf 10Ub **19**
GU21: Knap 10H **167**
HA3: W'stone 28Ja **46**
NW7 .... 24Wa **48**
SE1 .... 6K **231** (49Vb **91**)
SL4: Wind 4B **102**
Burnham Ct. *NW4* *28Ya* ***48***
(off Brent St.)
NW6 .... *38Eb* ***69***
(off Fairhazel Gdns.)
W2 .... *45Db* ***89***
(off Moscow Rd.)
Burnham Cres. DA1: Dart 56Ld **119**
E11 .... 28Lc **53**
Burnham Dr. KT4: Wor Pk 75Za **154**
RH2: Reig 5J **207**
Burnham Est. *E2* *41Yb* ***92***
(off Burnham St.)
Burnham Gdns. CR0: C'don 73Vb **157**
TW4: Cran 53X **107**
UB3: Harl 48T **84**
Burnham Hgts. SL1: Slou 4A **80**
Burnham La. SL1: Slou 3B **80**
Burnham Rd. AL1: St A 2E **6**
DA1: Dart 56Ld **119**
DA14: Sidc 61Ad **139**
E4 .... 22Bc **52**
GU21: Knap 10H **167**
RM7: Rom 27Fd **56**
RM9: Dag 38Xc **75**
SM4: Mord 70Db **133**
Burnhams Gro. KT19: Eps 83Ra **173**
Burnhams Rd. KT23: Bookh 96Aa **191**
Burnham St. E2 .... 41Yb **92**
KT2: King T 67Qa **131**
Burnham Ter. DA1: Dart 57Md **119**
Burnham Trad. Est.
DA1: Dart 56Md **119**
Burnham Way SE26 .... 64Bc **136**
W13 .... 49Ka **86**
Burnhill Cl. SE15 .... 52Xb **113**
Burnhill Ho. EC1 .... 4D **218**
Burnhill Rd. BR3: Beck 68Cc **136**
Burnley Cl. WD19: Wat 22Y **45**
Burnley Rd. NW10 .... 36Va **68**
RM20: W Thur 53Vd **120**
SW9 .... 54Pb **112**
Burnsall St.
SW3 .... 7E **226** (50Gb **89**)
Burns Av. DA15: Sidc 58Xc **117**
RM6: Chad H 31Yc **75**
TW14: Felt 58W **106**
UB1: S'hall 45Ca **85**
Burns Cl. DA8: Erith 53Hd **118**
DA16: Well 53Vc **117**
E17 .... 28Ec **52**
SM5: Cars 81Jb **176**
SW19 .... 65Fb **133**
UB4: Hayes 43V **84**
Burns Dr. SM7: Bans 86Ab **174**
Burns Ho. *E2* *41Yb* ***92***
(off Cornwall Av.)
SE17 .... *50Rb* ***91***
(off Doddington Gro.)
Burnside AL1: St A 4F **6**
KT21: Asht 90Pa **173**
Burnside Av. E4 .... 23Bc **52**
Burnside Cl. EN5: New Bar 13Cb **31**
SE16 .... 46Zb **92**
TW1: Twick 58Ja **108**
Burnside Ct. SM5: Cars 76Jb **156**
Burnside Cres.
HA0: Wemb 39Ma **67**
Burnside Ind. Est. IG6: Ilf 22Xc **55**
Burnside Rd. RM8: Dag 33Yc **75**
Burns Pl. RM18: Tilb 3D **122**
Burns Rd. HA0: Wemb 40Na **67**
NW10 .... 39Va **68**
SW11 .... 54Hb **111**
W13 .... 47Ka **86**
Burns Way CM13: Hut 17Fe **41**
TW5: Hest 54Z **107**
Burnt Ash Hgts. BR1: Brom 64Kc **137**
Burnt Ash Hill SE12 .... 58Hc **115**
Burnt Ash La. BR1: Brom 66Jc **137**
Burnt Ash Rd. SE12 .... 57Hc **115**
BURNTCOMMON **97H 189**
Burnt Comn. Cl. GU23: Rip 97H **189**
Burnt Comn. La. GU23: Rip 97J **189**
Burntfarm Ride EN2: Crew H 6Qb **18**
EN7: Walt C 5Rb **19**
Burnt Ho. La. DA1: Dart 62Pd **141**
DA2: Hawl 63Nd **141**
Burnthwaite Rd. SW6 .... 52Bb **111**
BURNT OAK **25Ra 47**
Burnt Oak Apartments *E16* *44Jc* ***93***
(off Pacific Rd.)
Burnt Oak B'way. HA8: Edg 24Qa **47**
Burnt Oak Flds. HA8: Edg 25Sa **47**
Burnt Oak La. DA15: Sidc 58Wc **117**
(not continuous)
Burnt Pollard La. GU18: Light 2C **166**
Burntwood CM14: B'wood 20Yd **40**
Burntwood Av. RM11: Horn 30Md **57**
Burntwood Cl. CM13: W H'dn 30Fe **59**
CR3: Cat'm 93Wb **197**
SW18 .... 60Gb **111**
Burntwood Dr. RH8: Oxt 3J **211**
Burntwood Grange Rd. SW18 .... 60Fb **111**
Burntwood Gro. TN13: S'oaks 99Kd **203**
Burntwood La. CR3: Cat'm 94Ub **197**
SW17 .... 62Eb **133**
Burntwood Rd. TN13: S'oaks 100Kd **203**
Burntwood Vw. SE19 .... 64Vb **135**
Burn Wlk. SL1: Burn 1A **80**
Burnway RM11: Horn 31Nd **77**
Buross St. E1 .... 44Xb **91**
Burpham Cl. UB4: Yead 43Z **85**
Burrage Ct. *SE16* *49Zb* ***92***
(off Worgan St.)
Burrage Gro. SE18 .... 49Sc **94**
Burrage Pl. SE18 .... 50Rc **94**
Burrage Rd. RH1: Redh 4B **208**
SE18 .... 50Sc **94**
Burrard Ho. *E2* *40Yb* ***72***
(off Bishop's Way)
Burrard Rd. E16 .... 44Kc **93**
NW6 .... 36Cb **69**
Burr Bank Ter. DA2: Wilm 63Ld **141**
Burr Cl. AL2: Lon C 9J **7**
DA7: Bex 55Bd **117**
E1 .... 46Wb **91**
Burreed M. RM13: Rain 40Ed **76**
Burrell Cl. CR0: C'don 72Ac **158**
HA8: Edg 19Ra **29**
Burrell Row BR3: Beck 68Cc **136**
Burrells, The KT16: Chert 74K **149**
Burrell St. SE1 .... 6B **224** (46Rb **91**)
Burrells Wharf Sq. E14 .... 50Dc **92**
Burrell Towers E10 .... 31Cc **72**
Burrfield Dr. BR5: St M Cry 71Zc **161**
Burrhill Ct. *SE16* *48Zb* ***92***
(off Worgan St.)
Burr Hill La. GU24: Chob 1K **167**
Burritt Rd. KT1: King T 68Qa **131**
Burroughs, The NW4 .... 28Xa **48**
Burroughs Club, The 28Xa **48**
Burroughs Cotts. *E14* *43Ac* ***92***
(off Halley St.)
Burroughs Dr. DA1: Dart 57Pd **119**
Burroughs Gdns. NW4 .... 28Xa **48**
Burroughs Pde. NW4 .... 28Xa **48**
Burroway Rd. SL3: L'ly 48D **82**
Burrow Cl. IG7: Chig 22Vc **55**
WD17: Wat 8V **12**
Burrow Grn. IG7: Chig 22Vc **55**
BURROW HILL **4C 186**
BURROWHILL **1J 167**
Burrow Hill Grn. GU24: Chob 1H **167**
Burrow Ho. *SW9* *54Qb* ***112***
(off Stockwell Pk. Rd.)
Burrow Rd. IG7: Chig 22Vc **55**
SE22 .... 56Ub **113**
Burrows Chase EN9: Walt A 7Fc **21**
Burrows Cl. KT23: Bookh 96Ba **191**
Burrows M. SE1 .... 1B **230** (47Rb **91**)
Burrows Rd. NW10 .... 41Ya **88**
Burrow Wlk. SE21 .... 59Sb **113**
Burr Rd. SW18 .... 60Cb **111**
Bursar St. SE1 .... 7H **225** (46Ub **91**)
Bursdon Cl. DA15: Sidc 61Vc **139**
Burses Way CM13: Hut 17De **41**
Bursland Rd. EN3: Pond E 14Zb **34**
Burslem Av. IG6: Ilf 23Wc **55**
Burslem St. E1 .... 44Wb **91**
Burstead Cl. KT11: Cobh 84Z **171**
Burstock Rd. SW15 .... 56Ab **110**
Burston Dr. AL2: Park 10A **6**
Burston Rd. SW15 .... 57Za **110**
Burston Vs. *SW15* *57Za* ***110***
(off St John's Av.)
Burstow Rd. SW20 .... 67Ab **132**
Burtenshaw Rd.
KT7: T Ditt 73Ja **152**
Burtley Cl. N4 .... 32Sb **71**
Burton Av. WD18: Wat 14W **26**
Burton Bank *N1* *38Tb* ***71***
(off Yeate St.)
Burton Cl. CR7: Thor H 69Tb **135**
GU20: W'sham 9B **146**
KT9: Chess 80Ma **153**
Burton Ct. KT7: T Ditt 72Ja **152**
SE20 .... 68Yb **136**
SW3 .... 7G **227**
(not continuous)
Burton Dr. EN3: Enf L 9Cc **20**
Burton Gdns. TW5: Hest 53Ba **107**
Burton Gro. SE17 .... 7F **231** (50Tb **91**)
Burtonhole Cl. NW7 .... 21Za **48**
Burtonhole La. N12 .... 21Ab **48**
NW7 .... 22Ya **48**
Burton Ho. *SE16* *47Xb* ***91***
(off Cherry Gdn. St.)
Burton La. EN7: G Oak 1Ub **19**
SW9 .... 54Qb **112**
(not continuous)
Burton M. SW1 .... 6J **227** (49Jb **90**)
Burton Pl. WC1 .... 5E **216** (41Mb **90**)
Burton Ridge Ct. *E3* *40Bc* ***72***
(off Festubert Pl.)
Burton Rd. DA12: Grav'nd 3E **144**
E18 .... 27Kc **53**
IG10: Lough 14Sc **36**
KT2: King T 66Na **131**
NW6 .... 38Bb **69**
SW9 .... 54Rb **113**
(Akerman Rd.)
SW9 .... 54Qb **112**
(Evesham Wlk.)
Burtons Ct. E15 .... 38Fc **73**
Burton's La. HP8: Chal G 13A **24**
WD3: Chor 15B **24**
Burton's Rd. TW12: Hamp H 63Da **129**
Burton St. WC1 .... 4E **216** (41Mb **90**)
Burton Way SL4: Wind 5C **102**
Burtonwood Ho. N4 .... 31Tb **71**
Burtop Rd. Est. SW17 .... 62Eb **133**
Burt Rd. E16 .... 46Lc **93**
Burts Wharf DA17: Belv 45Ed **96**
Burtt Ho. N1 .... 3H **219**
Burtwell La. SE27 .... 63Tb **135**
Burvale Ct. WD18: Wat 13X **27**
Burwash Ct. BR5: St M Cry 71Yc **161**
Burwash Ho. SE1 .... 2G **231**
Burwash Rd. SE18 .... 50Tc **94**
Burway Cl. CR2: S Croy 79Ub **157**
Burway Cres. KT16: Chert 70J **127**
Burwell *KT1: King T* *68Qa* ***131***
(off Excelsior Cl.)
Burwell Av. UB6: G'frd 37Ga **66**
Burwell Cl. E1 .... 44Xb **91**
Burwell Rd. E10 .... 32Ac **72**
Burwell Rd. Ind. Est. E10 .... 32Ac **72**
Burwell Wlk. E3 .... 42Cc **92**
Burwood Av. BR2: Hayes 75Kc **159**
CR8: Kenley 86Rb **177**
HA5: Eastc 29X **45**
Burwood Cl. KT6: Surb 74Qa **153**
KT12: Hers 79Y **151**
RH2: Reig 6M **207**
Burwood Gdns. RM13: Rain 41Hd **96**
Burwood Ho. SW9 .... 56Rb **113**
Burwood Pde. *KT16: Chert* *73J* ***149***
(off Guildford St.)
BURWOOD PARK
KT11 .... **84W 170**
KT12 .... **78W 150**
Burwood Pk. Rd. KT12: Hers 77X **151**
Burwood Pl. EN4: Had W 11Eb **31**
W2 .... 2E **220** (44Gb **89**)
Burwood Rd. KT12: Hers 80U **150**
Bury, The HP1: Hem H 1L **3**
WD3: Rick 18M **25**
Bury Av. HA4: Ruis 30S **44**
UB4: Hayes 40U **64**
Bury Cl. GU21: Wok 8P **167**
SE16 .... 46Zb **92**
Bury Ct. EC3 .... 2J **225** (44Ub **91**)
HP1: Hem H 2L **3**
Burydell La. AL2: Park 9B **6**
Buryfield Ct. *SE8* *49Zb* ***92***
(off Lower Rd.)
BURY GREEN **3Wb 19**
Bury Grn. HP1: Hem H 1L **3**
Bury Grn. Rd. EN7: Chesh 3Wb **19**
EN7: Walt C 4Wb **19**
Bury Gro. SM4: Mord 71Db **155**
Bury Hall Vs. N9 .... 17Vb **33**
Bury Hill HP1: Hem H 1K **3**
Bury Hill Cl. HP1: Hem H 1L **3**
Bury Lake Young Mariners 19L **25**
Bury La. CM16: Epp 1Tc **22**
GU21: Wok 8N **167**
WD3: Rick 18M **25**
Bury Mdws. WD3: Rick 18M **25**
Bury M. RM1: Rom 30Hd **56**
WD3: Rick *18M* ***25***
(off Bury La.)
Bury Pl. WC1 .... 1F **223** (43Nb **90**)
Bury Ri. HP3: Hem H 7F **2**
Bury Rd. CM16: Epp 3Uc **22**
E4 .... 13Fc **35**
HP1: Hem H 1L **3**
N22 .... 26Qb **50**
RM10: Dag 36Dd **76**
Buryside Cl. IG2: Ilf 28Vc **55**
Bury St. EC3 .... 3J **225** (44Ub **91**)
HA4: Ruis 29S **44**
N9 .... 17Vb **33**
SW1 .... 6B **222** (46Lb **90**)
Bury St. W. N9 .... 17Tb **33**
Bury Wlk. SW3 .... 6D **226** (49Gb **89**)
Busbridge Ho. *E14* *43Cc* ***92***
(off Brabazon St.)
Busby Ho. SW16 .... 63Lb **134**
Busby M. NW5 .... 37Mb **70**
Busby Pl. NW5 .... 37Mb **70**
Busch Cl. TW7: Isle 53Ka **108**
Bushbaby Cl. SE1 .... 4H **231** (48Ub **91**)
Bushbarns EN7: Chesh 1Wb **19**
Bushberry Rd. E9 .... 37Ac **72**
Bush Cl. IG2: Ilf 29Tc **54**
KT15: Add 78L **149**
Bush Cotts. SW18 .... 57Cb **111**
Bush Ct. N14 .... 18Mb **32**
W12 .... 47Za **88**
Bushell Cl. SW2 .... 61Pb **134**
Bushell Grn. WD23: B Hea 19Fa **28**
Bushell St. E1 .... 46Wb **91**
Bushell Way BR7: Chst 64Qc **138**
Bush Elms Rd.
RM11: Horn 31Jd **76**
Bushetts Gro. RH1: Mers 1B **208**
BUSHEY **16Ca 27**
Bushey Av. BR5: Pet W 73Tc **160**
E18 .... 27Hc **53**
Bushey Cl. CR8: Kenley 88Vb **177**
E4 .... 20Ec **34**
UB10: Ick 33Q **64**

Bushey Ct. DA8: Erith .53Jd 118
SW20 .69Xa 132
Bushey Cft. RH8: Oxt .2G 210
Bushey Down SW12 .61Kb 134
Bushey Golf Course .16Ca 27
Bushey Grove Leisure Cen. .13Ba 27
Bushey Gro. Rd. WD23: Bush .14Z 27
Bushey Hall Dr. WD23: Bush .14Aa 27
Bushey Hall Golf Course .14Aa 27
Bushey Hall Pk. WD23: Bush .13Aa 27
Bushey Hall Rd.
WD23: Bush .14Z 27
BUSHEY HEATH .18Fa 28
Bushey Hill Rd. SE5 .53Ub 113
Bushey La. SM1: Sutt .77Cb 155
Bushey Lees DA15: Sidc .58Vc 117
BUSHEY MEAD .68Za 132
Bushey Mill Cres.
WD24: Wat .9Y 13
Bushey Mill La. WD23: Bush .10Z 13
WD24: Wat .9Y 13
Bushey Mus. & Art Gallery .16Ca 27
Bushey Pk. WD23: Bush .16Ca 27
Bushey Rd. CR0: C'don .75Cc 158
E13 .40Lc 73
N15 .30Ub 51
SM1: Sutt .77Cb 155
(not continuous)
SW20 .69Xa 132
UB3: Harl .49U 84
UB10: Ick .33Q 64
Bushey Shaw KT21: Asht .89Ka 172
Bushey Vw. Wlk. WD24: Wat .12Z 27
Bushey Way BR3: Beck .72Fc 159
Bush Fair Ct. N14 .16Kb 32
Bushfield Cl. HA8: Edg .19Ra 29
Bushfield Cres. HA8: Edg .19Ra 29
Bushfield Dr. RH1: Redh .10A 208
Bushfield Rd. HP3: Bov .7E 2
Bushfields IG10: Lough .15Qc 36
Bushfield Wlk. DA10: Swans .58Ae 121
Bush Gro. HA7: Stan .25Ma 47
NW9 .31Sa 67
Bushgrove Rd. RM8: Dag .35Zc 75
Bush Hill N21 .17Sb 33
Bush Hill Pde. EN1: Enf .17Tb 33
N9 .17Tb 33
BUSH HILL PARK .16Vb 33
Bush Hill Pk. Golf Course .15Sb 33
Bush Hill Rd. HA3: Kenton .30Pa 47
N21 .16Tb 33
Bush Ind. Est. N19 .34Lb 70
NW10 .42Ta 87
Bush La. EC4 .4F 225 (45Tb 91)
GU23: Send .96F 188
Bushmead Cl. N15 .28Vb 51
Bushmoor Cres. SE18 .52Rc 116
Bushnell Rd. SW17 .61Kb 134
Bush Rd. E8 .39Xb 71
E11 .31Hc 73
IG9: Buck H .21Mc 53
SE8 .49Zb 92
TW9: Kew .51Pa 109
TW17: Shep .71P 149
Bush Theatre .47Ya 88
Bushway RM8: Dag .35Zc 75
Bushwood E11 .31Hc 73
Bushwood Cl. AL9: Wel G .5D 8
Bushwood Dr. SE1 .6K 231 (49Vb 91)
Bushwood Rd. TW9: Kew .51Qa 109
Bushy Cl. RM1: Rom .23Fd 56
Bushy Ct. *KT1: Hamp W .67La 130*
(off Beverley Rd.)
Bushy Pk. .66Fa 130
Bushy Pk. Gdns. TW11: Tedd .64Fa 130
Bushy Pk. Rd. TW11: Tedd .66Ka 130
(not continuous)
Bushy Rd. KT22: Fet .94Da 191
TW11: Tedd .65Ha 130
Business Cen., The RM3: Rom .24Md 57
Bus. Design Cen. N1 .1A 218
Bus. Innovation Cen., The
EN3: Enf L .8Bc 20
(off Innova Bus. Pk.)
Bus. Pk. 5 KT22: Lea .92Ha 192
Bus. Pk. 8 KT22: Lea .91Ka 192
Bus. Pk. 25 RH1: Redh .4B 208
Bus. Village, The SL2: Slou .6M 81
Buspace Studios *W10 .42Ab 88*
(off Conlan St.)
Busty La. TN15: Igh .93Zd 205
Butcher Row E14 .45Zb 92
Butchers Hill DA12: Shorne .1N 145
Butcher's La. TN15: Ash, Hartl .75Zd 165
Butchers M. *UB3: Hayes .45V 84*
(off Hemmen La.)
Butchers Rd. E16 .44Jc 93
Butchers Yd. BR6: Downe .83Qc 180
Butcher Wlk. DA10: Swans .59Ae 121
Bute Av. TW10: Ham .61Na 131
Bute Ct. SM6: Wall .78Lb 156
Bute Gdns. SM6: Wall .78Lb 156
TW10: Ham .60Na 109
W6 .49Za 88
Bute Gdns. W. SM6: Wall .78Lb 156
Bute M. NW11 .29Eb 49
Bute Rd. CR0: C'don .74Qb 156
IG6: Ilf .29Rc 54
SM6: Wall .77Lb 156
Bute St. SW7 .5B 226 (49Fb 89)
Bute Wlk. N1 .37Tb 71
Butfield Ho. *E9 .37Yb 72*
(off Stevens Av.)
Butler Av. HA1: Harr .31Fa 66
Butler Cl. HA8: Edg .26Ra 47
Butler Ct. HA0: Wemb .35Ja 66
RM8: Dag .33Cd 76
(off Gosfield Rd.)
SW11 .53Gb 111
(off Hyde La.)
Butler Dr. DA8: Erith .52Gd 118
Butler Farm Cl. TW10: Ham .63Ma 131
Butler Hall *AL10: Hat .2B 8*
(off Bishops Ri.)
Butler Ho. *E2 .41Yb 92*
(off Bacton St.)
E3 .43Bc 92
(off Geoffrey Chaucer Way)
E14 .44Bc 92
(off Burdett St.)
RM17: Grays .51De 121
(off Argent St.)
SW9 .53Rb 113
(off Lothian Rd.)
Butler Pl. SW1 .3D 228 (48Mb 90)
Butler Rd. HA1: Harr .31Ea 66
NW10 .38Va 68
RM8: Dag .35Xc 75

Butlers & Colonial Wharf SE1 .1K 231
Butlers Cl. SL4: Wind .3B 102
TW4: Houn .55Ba 107
Butlers Ct. EN8: Walt C .4Ac 20
Butlers Dene Rd. CR3: Wold .92Bc 198
Butlers Dr. E4 .10Ec 20
Butler's Pl. TN15: Ash .76Ae 165
Butler St. E2 .41Yb 92
UB10: Hil .42R 84
Butlers Wharf SE1 .7K 225 (46Vb 91)
Butlers Wharf W. SE1 .7K 225
Butler Wlk. RM17: Grays .49Fe 99
Butley Ct. *E3 .40Ac 72*
(off Ford St.)
Buttell Cl. RM17: Grays .50Fe 99
Buttercross La. CM16: Epp .2Wc 23
Buttercup Cl. RM3: Hrld W .25Md 57
UB5: N'olt .37Ba 65
Buttercup Sq. TW19: Stanw .60M 105
Butterfield Cl. N17 .23Sb 51
SE16 .47Xb 91
TW1: Twick .58Ha 108
Butterfield La. AL1: St A .6C 6
Butterfields E17 .29Ec 52
Butterfield Sq. E6 .44Pc 94
Butterfly Apartments *SW11 .56Gb 111*
(off Comyn Rd.)
Butterfly Ct. E6 .41Pc 94
N15 .28Ub 51
(off Bathurst Sq.)
NW9 .25Ua 48
Butterfly Cres. HP3: Hem H .7A 4
Butterfly La. SE9 .58Rc 116
WD6: E'tree .13Ja 28
Butterfly Wlk.
CR6: W'ham, Wold .92Yb 198
SE5 .53Tb 113
(off Denmark Hill)
Butter Hill SM5: Cars .76Jb 156
SM6: Wall .76Jb 156
Butteridges Cl. RM9: Dag .39Bd 75
Butterley M. RM3: Rom .23Nd 57
Butterly Av. DA1: Dart .61Pd 141
Buttermere NW1 .3A 216
Buttermere Av. SL1: Slou .3A 80
Buttermere Cl. AL1: St A .3F 6
DA1: Dart .55Qd 119
E15 .35Fc 73
SE1 .6K 231 (49Vb 91)
SM4: Mord .72Za 154
TW14: Felt .60V 106
Buttermere Ct. *NW8 .39Fb 69*
(off Boundary Rd.)
Buttermere Dr. SW15 .57Ab 110
Buttermere Gdns. CR8: Purl .85Tb 177
Buttermere Ho. *E3 .41Bc 92*
(off Mile End Rd.)
Buttermere Pl. WD25: Wat .5W 12
Buttermere Rd. BR5: St P .70Zc 139
Buttermere Wlk. E8 .37Vb 71
Buttermere Way TW20: Egh .66D 126
Butterscotch Row WD5: Ab L .4T 12
Butterwick W6 .49Za 88
WD25: Wat .8Aa 13
Butterworth Gdns. IG8: Wfd G .23Jc 53
Butterworth Ter. SE17 .7E 230
Buttery M. N14 .20Nb 32
Buttesland St. N1 .3G 219 (41Tb 91)
Buttfield Cl. RM10: Dag .37Dd 76
Butt Fld. Vw. AL1: St A .6A 6
Buttlehide WD3: Map C .22F 42
Buttmarsh Cl. SE18 .50Rc 94
Button Lodge E17 .28Cc 52
Button Rd. RM17: Grays .49Be 99
Buttonscroft Cl. CR7: Thor H .69Sb 135
Button St. BR8: Swan .68Ld 141
Button St. Bus. Cen. BR8: Swan .68Ld 141
Butts, The TN14: Otf .88Kd 183
TW8: Bford .51La 108
TW16: Sun .69Y 129
Buttsbury Rd. IG1: Ilf .36Sc 74
Butts Cotts TW13: Hanw .62Aa 129
Butts Cres. TW13: Hanw .62Ca 129
Butts End HP1: Hem H .1J 3
Butts Grn. Rd. RM11: Horn .30Md 57
Butts La. SS17: Stan H .2K 101
Buttsmead HA6: Nwood .24S 44
Butts Piece UB5: N'olt .40X 65
Butts Rd. BR1: Brom .64Gc 137
GU21: Wok .89A 168
SS17: Stan H .2L 101
Buxhall Cres. E9 .37Bc 72
Buxted Rd. E8 .38Vb 71
N12 .22Gb 49
SE22 .56Ub 113
Buxton Av. CR3: Cat'm .93Ub 197
Buxton Cl. IG8: Wfd G .23Mc 53
KT19: Eps .83Ra 173
N9 .19Yb 34
Buxton Ct. E11 .31Hc 73
N1 .3E 218
(not continuous)
Buxton Cres. SM3: Cheam .77Ab 154
Buxton Dr. E11 .28Gc 53
KT3: N Mald .68Ta 131
Buxton Gdns. W3 .45Ra 87
Buxton Ho. E11 .28Gc 53
Buxton La. CR3: Cat'm .92Tb 197
Buxton M. SW4 .54Mb 112
Buxton Path WD19: Wat .20Y 27
Buxton Pl. CR3: Cat'm .92Tb 197
Buxton Rd. CM16: They B .8Uc 22
CR7: Thor H .71Rb 157
DA8: Erith .52Fd 118
E4 .17Fc 35
E6 .41Nc 94
E15 .36Gc 73
E17 .28Ac 52
(not continuous)
EN9: Walt A .4Jc 21
IG2: Ilf .30Uc 54
N19 .32Mb 70
NW2 .37Xa 68
RM16: Grays .7A 100
SW14 .55Ua 110
TW15: Ashf .64M 127
Buxton St. E1 .6K 219 (42Vb 91)
Buzzard Creek Ind. Est.
IG11: Bark .43Wc 95
Byam St. SW6 .54Eb 111
Byards Ct. *SE16 .49Zb 92*
(off Worgan St.)
Byards Cft. SW16 .67Mb 134
Byas Ho. *E3 .41Bc 92*
(off Benworth St.)
Byatt Wlk. TW12: Hamp .65Aa 129
Bybend Cl. SL2: Farn R .9F 60
Bychurch End TW11: Tedd .64Ha 130

Bycliffe M. *DA11: Grav'nd .9B 122*
(off Bycliffe Ter.)
Bycliffe Ter. DA11: Grav'nd .9B 122
Bycroft Rd. UB1: S'hall .42Ca 85
Bycroft St. SE20 .66Zb 136
Bycullah Av. EN2: Enf .13Rb 33
Bycullah Rd. EN2: Enf .12Rb 33
Bye, The W3 .44Ua 88
Byegrove Rd. SW19 .65Fb 133
Byelands Cl. SE16 .46Zb 92
Byers Cl. EN6: Pot B .6Eb 17
(not continuous)
Byewaters WD18: Wat .16S 26
Bye Way, The HA3: W'stone .25Ga 46
Byeway, The SW14 .55Sa 109
WD3: Rick .19N 25
Byeways TW2: Twick .62Da 129
Byeways, The KT5: Surb .71Qa 153
Byfeld Gdns. SW13 .53Wa 110
Byfield Cl. SE16 .47Bc 92
Byfield Ct. CM13: W H'dn .30Ee 59
Byfield Rd. TW7: Isle .55Ja 108
BYFLEET .84N 169
Byfleet Ind. Est. KT14: Byfl .82M 169
WD18: Wat .18S 26
Byfleet Rd. KT11: Cobh .84Q 170
KT14: Byfl .84Q 170
KT15: New H .80M 149
Byfleet Technical Cen. KT14: Byfl .83M 169
Byford Cl. E15 .38Gc 73
Byford Ho. EN5: Barn .14Za 30
HA2: Harr .32Ca 65
Bygrove CR0: New Ad .79Dc 158
Bygrove St. E14 .44Dc 92
(not continuous)
Byland Cl. N21 .17Pb 32
SM4: Mord .73Eb 155
Bylands GU22: Wok .91C 188
Bylands Cl. SE2 .48Xc 95
Byne Rd. SE26 .65Yb 136
SM5: Cars .75Gb 155
Bynes Rd. CR2: S Croy .80Tb 157
Byng Dr. EN6: Pot B .3Cb 17
Byng Pl. WC1 .6E 216 (42Mb 90)
Byng Rd. EN5: Barn .12Za 30
Byng St. E14 .47Cc 92
Bynon Av. DA7: Bex .55Bd 117
By-Pass Rd. KT22: Lea .92Ka 192
SS17: Horn H .1J 101
Byrd Way SS17: Stan H .1L 101
Byre Rd. N14 .16Kb 32
Byrne Cl. CR0: C'don .72Sb 157
Byrne Rd. SW12 .60Kb 112
Byron SL3: L'ly .50D 82
Byron Av. CR5: Coul .87Nb 176
E12 .37Nc 74
E18 .27Hc 53
KT3: N Mald .71Wa 154
NW9 .28Ra 47
SM1: Sutt .77Fb 155
TW4: Cran .54W 106
WD6: Bore .15Qa 29
WD24: Wat .11Z 27
Byron Av. E. SM1: Sutt .77Fb 155
Byron Cl. E8 .39Wb 71
GU21: Knap .9J 167
KT12: Walt T .74Aa 151
KT23: Bookh .96Ca 191
SE20 .69Xb 135
SE26 .63Ac 136
SE28 .46Yc 95
SW16 .65Nb 134
TW12: Hamp .63Ba 129
Byron Ct. *E11 .28Kc 53*
(off Makepeace Rd.)
EN2: Enf .12Rb 33
HA1: Harr .30Ga 46
NW6 .38Eb 69
(off Fairfax Rd.)
SE22 .60Wb 113
SL4: Wind .5E 102
SW3 .6E 226
W7 .49Ja 86
(off Boston Rd.)
W9 .42Cb 89
(off Lanhill Rd.)
WC1 .5H 217
Byron Dr. DA8: Erith .52Dd 118
N2 .30Fb 49
Byron Gdns. RM18: Tilb .3E 122
SM1: Sutt .77Fb 155
Byron Hill Rd. HA2: Harr .32Fa 66
Byron Ho. DA1: Cray .57Gd 118
Byron Mans. RM14: Upm .34Sd 78
Byron M. NW3 .35Gb 69
W9 .42Cb 89
Byron Pde. UB10: Hil .42S 84
Byron Pl. KT22: Lea .94Ka 192
Byron Rd. CM13: Hut .17Fe 41
CR2: Sels .82Xb 177
DA1: Dart .56Rd 119
E10 .32Dc 72
E17 .27Cc 52
HA0: Wemb .33La 66
HA1: Harr .30Ga 46
HA3: W'stone .26Ha 46
KT15: Add .77N 149
NW2 .33Xa 68
NW7 .22Wa 48
W5 .46Pa 87
Byron St. E14 .44Ec 92
Byron Ter. N9 .16Yb 34
SE7 .52Lc 115
Byron Way RM3: Rom .25Ld 57
UB4: Hayes .42V 84
UB5: N'olt .41Aa 85
UB7: W Dray .49P 83
Bysouth Cl. IG5: Ilf .25Rc 54
N15 .28Tb 51
By the Wood WD19: Wat .19Z 27
Bythorn St. SW9 .55Pb 112
Byton Rd. SW17 .65Hb 133
Byttom Hill RH5: Mick .98La 192
Byward Av. TW14: Felt .58Y 107
Byward St. EC3 .5J 225 (45Ub 91)
Bywater Ho. SE18 .48Nc 94
Bywater Pl. SE16 .46Ac 92
Bywater St. SW3 .7F 227 (50Hb 89)
Byway E11 .29Lc 53
Byway, The EN6: Pot B .5Cb 17
KT19: Ewe .77Va 154
SM2: Sutt .81Fb 175
Byways, The KT21: Asht .90Ma 173
Bywell Pl. E16 .43Hc 93
W1 .1B 222
Bywood Av. CR0: C'don .72Yb 158
Bywood Cl. CR8: Kenley .87Rb 177
SM7: Bans .89Bb 175

By-Wood End SL9: Chal P .22C 42
Byworth Wlk. N19 .32Nb 70

C

Cabanel Pl. SE11 .6J 229 (49Pb 90)
Cabbell Pl. KT15: Add .77L 149
Cabbell St. NW1 .1D 220 (43Gb 89)
Cabborns Cres. SS17: Stan H .3M 101
Caberfeigh Cl. RH1: Redh .6M 207
Cabinet Ct. NW2 .34Va 68
Cabinet Way E4 .23Bc 52
Cable Car .47Hc 93
Cable Ct. *SE16 .49Ac 92*
(off Rope St.)
Cable Ho. WC1 .3K 217
Cable Ho. Ct. GU21: Wok .87A 168
Cable Pl. SE10 .53Ec 114
Cable St. E1 .45Wb 91
Cable Trade Pk. SE7 .49Lc 93
Cabot Cl. CR0: Wadd .76Qb 156
Cabot Ct. *SE16 .49Zb 92*
(off Worgan St.)
Cabot Sq. E14 .46Cc 92
Cabot Way E6 .39Mc 73
Cabrera Av. GU25: Vir W .2N 147
Cabrera Cl. GU25: Vir W .2P 147
Cab Rd. SE1 .7K 223
Cabul Rd. SW11 .54Gb 111
Caci Ho. *W14 .49Bb 89*
(off Kensington Village)
Cacket's La. TN14: Cud .87Tc 180
Cacketts Cotts. TN16: B Char .98Yc 201
Cactus Cl. SE15 .54Ub 113
Cactus Wlk. W12 .44Va 88
Cadbury Cl. TW7: Isle .53Ja 108
TW16: Sun .66U 128
Cadbury Rd. TW16: Sun .66U 128
Cadbury Way SE16 .48Vb 91
Caddington Cl. EN4: E Barn .15Gb 31
Caddington Rd. NW2 .34Ab 68
Caddis Cl. HA7: Stan .24Ha 46
Caddy Cl. TW20: Egh .64C 126
Cade La. TN13: S'oaks .100Ld 203
Cadell Cl. E2 .2K 219 (40Vb 71)
Cade Rd. SE10 .53Fc 115
Cader Rd. SW18 .58Eb 111
Cadet Dr. SE1 .49Vb 91
Cadet Ho. SE18 .48Rc 94
Cadiz Ct. RM10: Dag .38Fd 76
Cadiz Rd. RM10: Dag .38Fd 76
Cadiz St. SE17 .7E 230 (50Sb 91)
Cadley Ter. SE23 .61Yb 136
Cadlocks Hill TN14: Hals .82Bd 181
Cadman Cl. SW9 .52Rb 113
Cadman Ct. *W4 .50Ra 87*
(off Chaseley Dr.)
Cadmer Cl. KT3: N Mald .70Ua 132
Cadmium Sq. *E2 .41Zb 92*
(off Palmer's Rd.)
Cadmore Ct. EN8: Chesh .1Zb 20
Cadmore Ho. *N1 .38Rb 71*
(off The Sutton Est.)
Cadmore La. EN8: Chesh .1Zb 20
Cadmus Cl. SW4 .55Mb 112
Cadmus Ct. *SE16 .49Ac 92*
(off Seafarer Way)
SW9 .53Qb 112
(off Southey Rd.)
Cadnam Lodge *E14 .48Ec 92*
(off Schooner Cl.)
Cadnam Point SW15 .60Xa 110
Cadogan Av. CM13: W H'dn .30Fe 59
DA2: Dart .59Td 120
Cadogan Cl. BR3: Beck .67Fc 137
E9 .38Bc 72
HA2: Harr .35Da 65
TW11: Tedd .64Ga 130
Cadogan Ct. *E9 .38Bc 72*
(off Cadogan Ter.)
SM2: Sutt .79Db 155
SW3 .6F 227
Cadogan Ct. Gdns. SW1 .5H 227
Cadogan Gdns. E18 .27Kc 53
N3 .25Db 49
N21 .15Qb 32
SW3 .5G 227 (49Hb 89)
Cadogan Ga. SW1 .5G 227 (49Hb 89)
Cadogan Hall .5G 227
Cadogan Ho. IG8: Wfd G .24Rc 54
SW3 .51Fb 111
(off Beaufort St.)
Cadogan La. SW1 .3H 227 (48Jb 90)
Cadogan Mans. SW3 .6G 227
Cadogan Pl. CR8: Kenley .89Sb 177
SW1 .3G 227 (48Hb 89)
Cadogan Rd. KT6: Surb .71Ma 153
SE18 .48Sc 94
Cadogan Sq. SW1 .4F 227 (48Hb 89)
Cadogan St. SW3 .6F 227 (49Hb 89)
Cadogan Ter. E9 .37Bc 72
Cadoxton Av. N15 .30Vb 51
Cadwal Apartments *N1 .38Nb 70*
(off Caledonian Rd.)
Cadwallon Rd. SE9 .61Rc 138
Caedmon Rd. N7 .35Pb 70
Caelian Pl. AL3: St A .5P 5
Caenshill Ho. KT13: Weyb .80Q 150
Caenshill Pl. KT13: Weyb .80Q 150
Caenshill Rd. KT13: Weyb .80Q 150
Caenswood Hill KT13: Weyb .82Q 170
Caenwood Cl. KT13: Weyb .79Q 150
Caen Wood Rd. KT21: Asht .90La 172
Caerleon Cl. DA14: Sidc .64Yc 139
KT10: Clay .80Ka 152
Caerleon Ter. SE2 .49Xc 95
Caernafon Ho. HA7: Stan .22Ja 46
Caernarvon Cl. CR4: Mitc .69Nb 134
HP2: Hem H .2M 3
RM11: Horn .32Qd 77
Caernarvon Ct. HP2: Hem H .2M 3
Caernarvon Dr. IG5: Ilf .25Qc 54
Caernarvon Ho. *E16 .46Kc 93*
(off Audley Dr.)
W2 .2A 220
Caesar Ct. *E2 .40Zb 72*
(off Palmer's Rd.)
Caesars Ct. *AL3: St A .2B 6*
(off Verulam Rd.)
Caesars Wlk. CR4: Mitc .71Hb 155
Caesars Way TW17: Shep .72T 150
Café Gallery .48Yb 92
Cage Pond Rd. WD7: Shenl .5Pa 15
Cages Wood Dr. SL2: Farn C .5F 60
Cage Yd. RH2: Reig .6J 207
Cagney Cl. TW16: Sun .67W 128
Cahill St. EC1 .6E 218 (42Sb 91)

Cahir St. E14 .49Dc 92
Caillard Rd. KT14: Byfl .83N 169
Cain Cl. AL1: St A .4D 6
Cain Ct. *EN8: Chesh .1Zb 20*
(off Wycliffe Cl.)
W5 .43La 86
(off Castlebar M.)
Caine Ho. *W3 .47Ra 87*
(off Hanbury Rd.)
Cain's La. TW14: Felt .57U 106
Caird St. W10 .41Ab 88
Cairn Av. W5 .46Ma 87
Cairn Ct. KT17: Ewe .82Va 174
Cairncross M. N8 .30Nb 50
Cairndale Cl. BR1: Brom .66Hc 137
Cairnfield Av. NW2 .34Ua 68
Cairngorm Cl. TW11: Tedd .64Ja 130
Cairngorm Pl. SL2: Slou .2H 81
Cairns Av. IG8: Wfd G .23Nc 54
SW16 .69Lb 134
Cairns Cl. AL4: St A .3H 7
DA1: Dart .57Md 119
Cairns M. SE18 .53Nc 116
Cairns Pl. SW16 .68Lb 134
Cairns Rd. SW11 .57Gb 111
Cairn Way HA7: Stan .23Ha 46
Cairo New Rd. CR0: C'don .75Rb 157
Cairo Rd. E17 .28Cc 52
Caishowe Rd. WD6: Bore .11Ra 29
Caisson Moor Ct. *E3 .42Ec 92*
(off Navigation Rd.)
Caister Cl. HP2: Hem H .3N 3
Caister Ho. N7 .37Pb 70
Caistor Ho. *E15 .39Hc 73*
(off Caistor Pk. Rd.)
Caistor M. SW12 .59Kb 112
Caistor Pk. Rd. E15 .39Hc 73
Caistor Rd. SW12 .59Kb 112
Caithness Dr. KT18: Eps .86Ta 173
Caithness Gdns. DA15: Sidc .58Vc 117
Caithness Ho. *N1 .39Pb 70*
(off Twyford St.)
Caithness Rd. CR4: Mitc .66Kb 134
W14 .48Za 88
Calabria Rd. N5 .37Rb 71
Calais Cotts. DA3: Fawk .75Wd 164
Calais Ga. SE5 .53Rb 113
Calais St. SE5 .53Rb 113
Calbourne Av. RM12: Horn .36Kd 77
Calbourne Rd. SW12 .59Hb 111
Calbroke Rd. SL2: Slou .2D 80
Calcott Cl. CM14: B'wood .18Xd 40
Calcott Ct. *W14 .48Ab 88*
(off Blythe Rd.)
Calcott Wlk. SE9 .63Nc 138
Calcraft Ho. *E2 .40Yb 72*
(off Bonner Rd.)
Calcroft Av. DA9: Ghithe .57Yd 120
Calcutta Rd. RM18: Tilb .4B 122
Caldbeck EN9: Walt A .6Fc 21
(not continuous)
Caldbeck Av. KT4: Wor Pk .75Wa 154
Caldecot Av. EN7: Chesh .1Vb 19
Caldecote *KT1: King T .68Qa 131*
(off Excelsior Cl.)
Caldecote Gdns. WD23: Bush .17Ga 28
CALDECOTE HILL .17Ha 28
Caldecote La. WD23: Bush .16Ha 28
Caldecot Rd. SE5 .54Sb 113
Caldecott Way E5 .34Zb 72
Calder RM18: E Til .9L 101
Calder Av. AL9: Brk P .8J 9
UB6: G'frd .40Ha 66
Calder Cl. EN1: Enf .13Ub 33
Calder Ct. SE16 .46Bc 92
SL3: L'ly .50B 82
Calder Gdns. HA8: Edg .27Qa 47
Calderon Ho. NW8 .1D 214
Calderon Pl. W10 .43Ya 88
Calderon Rd. E11 .35Ec 72
Calder Rd. SM4: Mord .71Eb 155
Caldervale Rd. SW4 .57Mb 112
Calder Way SL3: Poyle .55G 104
Calderwood DA12: Grav'nd .4G 144
Calderwood Pl. EN4: Had W .11Db 31
Calderwood St. SE18 .49Qc 94
Caldew Ct. NW7 .24Wa 48
Caldew St. SE5 .52Tb 113
Caldicote Grn. NW9 .30Ua 48
Caldon Ho. UB5: N'olt .42Ba 85
Caldwell Cl. SE18 .50Qc 94
Caldwell Ho. *SW13 .52Ya 110*
(off Trinity Chu. Rd.)
Caldwell Rd. GU20: W'sham .8B 146
SS17: Stan H .2K 101
WD19: Wat .21Z 45
Caldwell St. SW9 .52Pb 112
Caldy Rd. DA17: Belv .48Dd 96
Caldy Wlk. N1 .38Sb 71
Caleb St. SE1 .1E 230 (47Sb 91)
Caledonia Ct. *IG11: Bark .40Yc 75*
(off Keel Cl.)
Caledonia Ho. *E14 .44Ac 92*
(off Salmon La.)
Caledonian Cl. IG3: Ilf .32Xc 75
Caledonian Ct. *BR2: Brom .72Nc 160*
(off Wells Vw. Dr.)
UB5: N'olt .42Aa 85
WD17: Wat .12X 27
Caledonian Rd. N1 .2G 217 (40Nb 70)
N7 .35Pb 70
Caledonian Sq. NW1 .37Mb 70
Caledonian Wharf E14 .49Fc 93
Caledonia Rd.
TW19: Stanw .60N 105
Caledonia St. N1 .2G 217 (40Nb 70)
Caledon Rd. AL2: Lon C .8G 6
E6 .39Pc 74
SM6: Wall .77Jb 156
Calendar M. KT6: Surb .72Ma 153
Cale St. SW3 .7D 226 (50Gb 89)
Calestock Way SE10 .50Hc 93
Calfstock La. DA4: Farni .70Pd 141
Calgarth NW1 .2C 216
Calgary Ct. RM7: Mawney .28Dd 56
SE16 .47Yb 92
(off Canada Est.)
Calia Ho. *E20 .37Ec 72*
(off Anthems Way)
Caliban Twr. N1 .2H 219
Calico Ct. *SE16 .48Wb 91*
(off Marine St.)
Calico Ho. *E20 .37Ec 72*
(off Mirabelle Gdns.)
EC4 .3E 224
SE1 .2H 231
Calico Row SW11 .55Eb 111
Calidore Cl. SW2 .58Pb 112

California Bldg.—Canfield Rd.

California Bldg. SE13 ... 53Dc 114
(off Deal's Gateway)
California Cl. SM2: Sutt ... 82Cb 175
California La. WD23: B Hea ... 18Fa 28
California Pl. WD23: B Hea ... 18Fa 28
(off High Rd.)
California Rd. KT3: N Mald ... 70Ra 131
Caling Cft. DA3: Nw A G ... 74Be 165
Caliph Cl. DA12: Grav'nd ... 2H 145
Callaby Ter. N1 ... 37Tb 71
Callaghan Cl. SE13 ... 56Gc 115
Callaghan Ct. HP4: Berk ... 1A 2
Callahan Cotts. E1 ... 43Yb 92
(off Lindley St.)
Callander Rd. SE6 ... 61Dc 136
Callanders, The WD23: B Hea ... 18Ga 28
Callan Gro. RM15: S Ock ... 45Xd 98
Callard Av. N13 ... 21Rb 51
Callard Cl. W2 ... 6B 214 (42Fb 89)
Callcott Ct. NW6 ... 38Bb 69
Callcott Rd. NW6 ... 38Bb 69
Callcott St. W8 ... 46Cb 89
Callendar Rd. SW7 ... 3B 226 (48Fb 89)
Callender Ct. CR0: C'don ... 72Sb 157
(off Harry Cl.)
Callender Rd. DA8: Erith ... 52Gd 118
Calley Down Cres. CR0: New Ad ... 82Fc 179
Callingham Cl. E14 ... 43Bc 92
Callington M. TW2: Twick ... 61Ga 130
Callis Farm Cl. TW19: Stanw ... 58N 105
Callisons Pl. SE10 ... 50Gc 93
Callis Rd. E17 ... 30Bc 52
Calliston Ct. E16 ... 43Jc 93
(off Hammersley Rd.)
Callonfield E17 ... 28Zb 52
Callow Fld. CR8: Purl ... 85Qb 176
Callow Hill GU25: Vir W ... 9N 125
Callowland Pl. WD24: Wat ... 10X 13
Callowlands WD24: Wat ... 11X 27
(off Leavesden Rd.)
Callow St. SW3 ... 51Fb 111
Calluna Ct. GU22: Wok ... 90B 168
Cally Swimming Pool ... 39Pb 70
Calmont Rd. BR1: Brom ... 65Fc 137
Calmore Cl. RM12: Horn ... 36Ld 77
Calne Av. IG5: Ilf ... 25Rc 54
Calonne Rd. SW19 ... 63Za 132
Calshot Av. RM16: Chaf H ... 47Be 99
Calshot Ct. DA2: Dart ... 58Rd 119
(off Osbourne Rd.)
Calshot Ho. N1 ... 1H 217
Calshot Rd. TW6: H'row A ... 54Q 106
Calshot St. N1 ... 1H 217 (40Pb 70)
Calshot Way EN2: Enf ... 13Rb 33
TW6: H'row A ... 54Q 106
Calstock NW1 ... 1D 216
Calstock Ho. SE11 ... 7A 230
Calthorpe Gdns. HA8: Edg ... 22Na 47
SM1: Sutt ... 76Eb 155
Calthorpe St. WC1 ... 5J 217 (42Pb 90)
Calton Av. SE21 ... 58Ub 113
Calton Cl. KT16: Vir W ... 5L 147
Calton Rd. EN5: New Bar ... 16Eb 31
Calverley Cl. BR3: Beck ... 65Dc 136
Calverley Ct. KT19: Ewe ... 77Ta 153
Calverley Cres. RM10: Dag ... 33Cd 76
Calverley Gdns. HA3: Kenton ... 31Ma 67
Calverley Gro. N19 ... 32Mb 70
Calverley Rd. KT17: Ewe ... 79Wa 154
Calvert Av. E2 ... 4J 219 (41Ub 91)
Calvert Cl. DA14: Sidc ... 65Ad 139
DA17: Belv ... 49Cd 96
KT19: Eps ... 82Ra 173
Calvert Ct. TW9: Rich ... 56Pa 109
Calvert Dr. DA2: Wilm ... 61Fd 140
Calvert Ho. W12 ... 45Xa 88
(off White City Est.)
Calverton SE5 ... 51Ub 113
(off Albany Rd.)
Calverton Pl. UB6: G'frd ... 37Ha 66
Calverton Rd. E6 ... 39Qc 74
Calvert Rd. EN5: Barn ... 12Za 30
KT24: Eff ... 100X 191
SE10 ... 50Hc 93
Calvert's Bldgs. SE1 ... 7F 225 (46Tb 91)
Calvert St. NW1 ... 39Jb 70
Calvin Cl. BR5: St P ... 69Zc 139
Calvin St. E1 ... 6K 219 (42Vb 91)
Calydon Rd. SE7 ... 50Kc 93
Calypso Cres. SE15 ... 52Vb 113
Calypso Way SE16 ... 48Bc 92
Camac Rd. TW2: Twick ... 60Fa 108
Camarthen Grn. NW9 ... 29Ua 48
Cambalt Rd. SW15 ... 57Za 110
Cambay Ho. E1 ... 42Ac 92
(off Harford St.)
Camber Ho. SE15 ... 51Yb 114
Camberley Av. EN1: Enf ... 14Ub 33
SW20 ... 68Xa 132
Camberley Cl. SM3: Cheam ... 76Za 154
Camberley Ho. NW1 ... 2A 216
Camberley Rd. TW6: H'row A ... 55Q 106
Cambert Way SE3 ... 56Kc 115
CAMBERWELL ... 53Tb 113
Camberwell Bus. Cen. SE5 ... 52Tb 113
Camberwell Chu. St. SE5 ... 53Tb 113
Camberwell Glebe SE5 ... 53Ub 113
CAMBERWELL GREEN ... 53Sb 113
Camberwell Grn. SE5 ... 53Tb 113
Camberwell Gro. SE5 ... 53Tb 113
Camberwell Leisure Cen. ... 53Tb 113
Camberwell New Rd. SE5 ... 51Qb 112
Camberwell Pl. SE5 ... 53Sb 113
Camberwell Rd. SE5 ... 51Sb 113
Camberwell Sta. Rd. SE5 ... 53Sb 113
Camberwell Trad. Est. SE5 ... 53Rb 113
Cambeys Rd. RM10: Dag ... 36Dd 76
Cambisgate SW19 ... 64Ab 132
Camborne Av. RM3: Rom ... 24Nd 57
W13 ... 47Ka 86
Camborne Cl. TW6: H'row A ... 55Q 106
Camborne Cres. TW6: H'row A ... 55Q 106
(off Camborne Rd.)
Camborne M. SW18 ... 59Cb 111
W11 ... 44Ab 88
Camborne Rd. CR0: C'don ... 73Wb 157
DA14: Sidc ... 62Yc 139
DA16: Well ... 54Vc 117
SM2: Sutt ... 80Cb 155
SM4: Mord ... 71Za 154
SW18 ... 59Cb 111
TW6: H'row A ... 55Q 106
Camborne Way RM3: Rom ... 24Nd 57
TW5: Hest ... 53Ca 107
TW6: H'row A ... 55Q 106
Cambourne Av. N9 ... 17Zb 34
Cambourne Ct. SE15 ... 51Vb 113
Cambourne Rd. HA8: Edg ... 21Pa 47
Cambourne Wlk. TW10: Rich ... 58Ma 109
Cambrai Ct. N13 ... 20Nb 32
Cambray Rd. BR6: Orp ... 73Vc 161
SW12 ... 60Lb 112
Cambria Cl. DA15: Sidc ... 60Tc 116
TW3: Houn ... 56Ca 107
Cambria Ct. DA9: Ghithe ... 56Wd 120
E17 ... 27Ac 52
SL3: L'ly ... 7N 81
TW14: Felt ... 59X 107
TW18: Staines ... 63G 126
Cambria Cres. DA12: Grav'nd ... 3G 144
Cambria Gdns. TW19: Stanw ... 59N 105
(not continuous)
Cambria Ho. E14 ... 44Ac 92
(off Salmon La.)
SE26 ... 63Wb 135
(off High Level Dr.)
Cambrian Av. IG2: Ilf ... 29Uc 54
Cambrian Cl. SE27 ... 62Rb 135
Cambrian Grn. NW9 ... 29Ua 48
(off Snowdon Dr.)
Cambrian Gro. DA11: Grav'nd ... 9C 122
Cambrian Rd. E10 ... 31Cc 72
TW10: Rich ... 58Pa 109
Cambria Rd. SE5 ... 55Sb 113
Cambria St. SW6 ... 52Db 111
Cambridge Arc. E9 ... 38Yb 72
Cambridge Av. DA16: Well ... 56Vc 117
KT3: N Mald ... 69Ua 132
(not continuous)
NW6 ... 40Cb 69
RM2: Rom ... 27Ld 57
SL1: Burn ... 10A 60
SL1: Slou ... 4E 80
UB6: G'frd ... 36Ha 66
Cambridge Barracks Rd.
SE18 ... 49Pc 94
Cambridge Cir. WC2 ... 3E 222 (44Mb 90)
Cambridge Cl. E17 ... 30Bc 52
EN4: E Barn ... 18Jb 32
EN8: Chesh ... 1Yb 20
GU21: Wok ... 10K 167
N22 ... 25Qb 50
NW10 ... 34Sa 67
SW20 ... 67Xa 132
TW4: Houn ... 56Aa 107
UB7: Harm ... 51M 105
Cambridge Cotts. TW9: Kew ... 51Qa 109
Cambridge Ct. E2 ... 40Xb 71
(off Cambridge Heath Rd.)
N16 ... 31Ub 71
(off Amhurst Pk.)
NW6 ... 40Cb 69
(not continuous)
W2 ... 1D 220
W6 ... 49Ya 88
(off Shepherd's Bush Rd.)
Cambridge Cres. E2 ... 40Xb 71
TW11: Tedd ... 64Ja 130
Cambridge Dr. EN6: Pot B ... 3Za 16
HA4: Ruis ... 33Y 65
SE12 ... 57Jc 115
Cambridge Gdns. EN1: Enf ... 12Wb 33
KT1: King T ... 68Qa 131
N10 ... 25Jb 50
N17 ... 24Tb 51
N21 ... 17Tb 33
NW6 ... 40Cb 69
RM16: Grays ... 9C 100
W10 ... 44Za 88
Cambridge Ga. NW1 ... 5K 215 (42Kb 90)
Cambridge Ga. M. NW1 ... 5A 216 (42Kb 90)
Cambridge Grn. SE9 ... 60Rc 116
Cambridge Gro. SE20 ... 67Xb 135
W6 ... 49Xa 88
Cambridge Gro. Rd. KT1: King T ... 69Qa 131
(not continuous)
Cambridge Heath Rd. E1 ... 43Xb 91
E2 ... 42Yb 92
Cambridge Ho. SL4: Wind ... 3G 102
W6 ... 49Xa 88
(off Cambridge Gro.)
W13 ... 44Ja 86
Cambridge Pde. EN1: Enf ... 11Wb 33
Cambridge Pk. E11 ... 30Jc 53
TW1: Twick ... 58La 108
Cambridge Pk. Ct. TW1: Twick ... 59Ma 109
Cambridge Pk. Rd. E11 ... 31Jc 73
(off Lonsdale Rd.)
Cambridge Pl. W8 ... 47Db 89
Cambridge Rd. AL1: St A ... 3F 6
BR1: Brom ... 66Jc 137
CR4: Mitc ... 69Lb 134
DA14: Sidc ... 63Uc 138
E4 ... 18Fc 35
E11 ... 30Hc 53
HA2: Harr ... 29Ca 45
IG3: Ilf ... 32Uc 74
IG11: Bark ... 38Sc 74
KT1: King T ... 68Pa 131
KT2: King T ... 68Pa 131
KT3: N Mald ... 70Ta 131
KT8: W Mole ... 70Ba 129
KT12: Walt T ... 72X 151
NW6 ... 40Cb 69
(not continuous)
SE20 ... 69Xb 135
SM5: Cars ... 79Gb 155
SW11 ... 53Hb 111
SW13 ... 54Va 110
SW20 ... 67Wa 132
TW1: Twick ... 58Ma 109
TW4: Houn ... 56Aa 107
TW9: Kew ... 52Qa 109
TW11: Tedd ... 63Ha 130
TW12: Hamp ... 66Ba 129
TW15: Ashf ... 66S 128
UB1: S'hall ... 46Ba 85
UB8: Uxb ... 37M 63
W7 ... 47Ha 86
WD18: Wat ... 14Y 27
Cambridge Rd. Nth. W4 ... 50Ra 87
Cambridge Rd. Sth. W4 ... 50Ra 87
Cambridge Row SE18 ... 50Rc 94
Cambridge Sq. RH1: Redh ... 9A 208
W2 ... 2D 220 (44Gb 89)
Cambridge St. SW1 ... 6A 228 (49Kb 90)
Cambridge Ter. HP4: Berk ... 1A 2
N9 ... 17Ub 33
NW1 ... 4K 215 (41Kb 90)
Cambridge Ter. M. NW1 ... 4A 216 (41Kb 90)
Cambridge Theatre ... 3F 223
Cambstone Cl. N11 ... 19Jb 32
Cambus Cl. UB4: Yead ... 43Aa 85
Cambus Rd. E16 ... 43Jc 93
Cam Ct. SE15 ... 51Vb 113
Camdale Rd. SE18 ... 52Vc 117
Camden Arts Cen. ... 36Db 69
Camden Av. TW13: Felt ... 60Y 107
UB4: Yead ... 45Z 85
Camden Cl. BR7: Chst ... 67Sc 138
DA11: Nflt ... 60Ee 121
RM16: Grays ... 9D 100
Camden Cotts. KT13: Weyb ... 76Q 150
Camden Ct. DA17: Belv ... 50Cd 96
NW1 ... 38Lb 70
(off Rousden St.)
Camden Gdns. CR7: Thor H ... 69Rb 135
NW1 ... 38Kb 70
SM1: Sutt ... 78Db 155
Camden Gro. BR7: Chst ... 65Rc 138
Camden High St. NW1 ... 1B 216 (38Kb 70)
Camden Hill Rd. SE19 ... 65Ub 135
Camden Ho. HP1: Hem H ... 3M 3
SE8 ... 50Bc 92
Camdenhurst St. E14 ... 44Ac 92
Camden La. N7 ... 36Mb 70
Camden Lock Market ... 38Kb 70
Camden Lock Pl. NW1 ... 38Kb 70
Camden Markets ... 38Kb 70
Camden M. NW1 ... 38Lb 70
Camden Pk. Rd. BR7: Chst ... 66Pc 138
NW1 ... 37Mb 70
Camden Pas. N1 ... 1B 218 (40Rb 71)
Camden People's Theatre ... 5B 216
Camden Rd. DA5: Bexl ... 60Ad 117
E11 ... 30Kc 53
E17 ... 30Bc 52
N7 ... 35Nb 70
NW1 ... 38Lb 70
RM16: Chaf H ... 48Ae 99
SM1: Sutt ... 78Db 155
SM5: Cars ... 77Hb 155
TN13: S'oaks ... 94Kd 203
Camden Row HA5: Pinn ... 27Y 45
SE3 ... 54Gc 115
Camden Sq. NW1 ... 38Mb 70
(not continuous)
SE15 ... 53Vb 113
Camden St. NW1 ... 1C 216 (38Lb 70)
Camden Studios NW1 ... 1C 216
Camden Ter. NW1 ... 37Mb 70
TN15: Seal ... 93Pd 203
CAMDEN TOWN ... 1C 216 (39Kb 70)
Camden Wlk. N1 ... 1B 218 (39Rb 71)
Camden Way BR7: Chst ... 66Pc 138
CR7: Thor H ... 69Rb 135
Cameford Ct. SW2 ... 59Nb 112
Camelford NW1 ... 39Lb 70
(off Royal Coll. St.)
Camelford Ct. W11 ... 44Ab 88
Camelford Ho. RM3: Rom ... 21Nd 57
(off Chudleigh Rd.)
SE1 ... 7G 229 (50Nb 90)
Camelford Wlk. W11 ... 44Ab 88
Camel Gro. KT2: King T ... 64Ma 131
Camellia Cl. CM13: W H'dn ... 30Ee 59
E10 ... 33Cc 72
RM3: Hrld W ... 25Nd 57
Camellia Ct. GU24: W End ... 5D 166
Camellia Ho. SE8 ... 52Bc 114
(off Idonia St.)
TW13: Felt ... 60W 106
(off Bedfont La.)
Camellia La. KT5: Surb ... 70Ra 131
Camellia M. TW20: Eng G ... 6N 125
Camellia Pl. TW2: Whitt ... 59Da 107
Camellia St. SW8 ... 52Nb 112
(not continuous)
Camelot Cl. SE28 ... 47Tc 94
SW19 ... 63Bb 133
TN16: Big H ... 88Lc 179
Camelot Ho. NW1 ... 37Mb 70
Camel Rd. E16 ... 46Nc 94
Camera Pl. SW10 ... 51Fb 111
Camera Press Gallery, The ... 1K 231
(off Queen Elizabeth St.)
Cameret Ct. W11 ... 47Za 88
(off Holland Rd.)
Cameron Cl. CM14: W'ley ... 21Zd 59
DA5: Bexl ... 62Gd 140
N18 ... 21Xb 51
N20 ... 19Fb 31
N22 ... 24Pb 50
Cameron Cres. HA8: Edg ... 25Ra 47
Cameron Dr. DA1: Dart ... 54Qd 119
EN8: Walt C ... 6Zb 20
Cameron Ho. BR1: Brom ... 67Hc 137
NW8 ... 1D 214
SE5 ... 52Sb 113
Cameron Pl. E1 ... 44Xb 91
SW16 ... 61Qb 134
Cameron Rd. BR2: Brom ... 71Jc 159
CR0: C'don ... 72Rb 157
IG3: Ilf ... 32Uc 74
SE6 ... 61Bc 136
Cameron Sq. CR4: Mitc ... 67Gb 133
Cameron Ter. SE12 ... 62Kc 137
Camerton Cl. E8 ... 37Vb 71
Camfield Pl. AL9: Ess ... 3M 9
Camgate Cen., The TW19: Stanw ... 58P 105
Camgate Mans. SE5 ... 51Sb 113
(off Camberwell Rd.)
Cam Grn. RM15: S Ock ... 44Xd 98
Camilla Cl. KT23: Bookh ... 97Da 191
TW16: Sun ... 65V 128
Camilla Rd. SE16 ... 49Xb 91
Camille Cl. SE25 ... 69Wb 135
Camlan Rd. BR1: Brom ... 63Hc 137
Camlet St. E2 ... 5K 219 (42Vb 91)
Camlet Way AL3: St A ... 1P 5
EN4: Barn, Had W ... 12Cb 31
Camley St. N1 ... 1E 216 (38Mb 70)
Camley Street Natural Pk.
... 1F 217 (40Nb 70)
Camley Street Natural Pk. Vis. Cen.
... 1E 216 (40Mb 70)
Camm Av. SL4: Wind ... 5C 102
Camm Cl. KT15: Add ... 76M 149
Camm Gdns. KT1: King T ... 68Pa 131
KT7: T Ditt ... 73Ha 152
Camms Ter. RM10: Dag ... 36Ed 76
(off Cambeys Rd.)
Camomile Av. CR4: Mitc ... 67Hb 133
Camomile Rd. RM7: Rush G ... 33Fd 76
Camomile St. EC3 ... 2H 225 (44Ub 91)
Camomile Way UB7: Yiew ... 44N 83
CAMP, THE ... 4F 6
Campaign Ct. W9 ... 42Bb 89
(off Chantry Cl.)
Campana Rd. SW6 ... 53Cb 111
Campania Bldg. E1 ... 45Zb 92
(off Jardine Rd.)
Campaspe Bus. Pk. TW16: Sun ... 71V 150
Campbell Av. GU22: Wok ... 93B 188
IG6: Ilf ... 28Rc 54
Campbell Cir. KT13: Weyb ... 82P 169
Campbell Cl. HA4: Ruis ... 30W 44
KT14: Byfl ... 84M 169
RM1: Rom ... 23Gd 56
SE18 ... 53Qc 116
SW16 ... 63Mb 134
TW2: Twick ... 60Fa 108
Campbell Ct. N17 ... 25Vb 51
NW9 ... 30Sa 47
SE22 ... 60Wb 113
SW7 ... 4A 226
Campbell Cft. HA8: Edg ... 22Qa 47
Campbell Gordon Way NW2 ... 35Xa 68
Campbell Ho. SW1 ... 7B 228
W2 ... 7B 214
W12 ... 45Xa 88
(off White City Est.)
Campbell Rd. CR0: C'don ... 73Rb 157
CR3: Cat'm ... 93Tb 197
DA11: Grav'nd ... 10B 122
E3 ... 41Cc 92
E6 ... 39Nc 74
E15 ... 35Hc 73
E17 ... 28Bc 52
KT8: E Mos ... 69Ga 130
KT13: Weyb ... 80Q 150
N17 ... 25Vb 51
TW2: Twick ... 61Fa 130
W7 ... 45Ga 86
Campbell Wlk. N1 ... 39Nb 70
(off Outram Pl.)
Campdale Rd. N7 ... 34Mb 70
Campden Cres. HA0: Wemb ... 34Ka 66
RM8: Dag ... 35Xc 75
Campden Gro. W8 ... 47Cb 89
Campden Hill W8 ... 47Cb 89
Campden Hill Ct. W8 ... 47Cb 89
Campden Hill Gdns. W8 ... 46Cb 89
Campden Hill Ga. W8 ... 47Cb 89
Campden Hill Mans. W8 ... 46Cb 89
(off Edge St.)
Campden Hill Pl. W11 ... 46Bb 89
Campden Hill Rd. W8 ... 46Cb 89
Campden Hill Sq. W8 ... 46Bb 89
Campden Hill Towers W11 ... 45Cb 89
Campden Ho. NW6 ... 38Fb 69
(off Harben Rd.)
W8 ... 46Cb 89
(off Sheffield Ter.)
Campden Ho. Cl. W8 ... 47Cb 89
Campden Ho's. W8 ... 46Cb 89
Campden Ho. Ter. W8 ... 46Cb 89
(off Kensington Chu. St.)
Campden Mans. W8 ... 46Cb 89
(off Kensington Mall)
Campden Rd. CR2: S Croy ... 78Ub 157
UB10: Ick ... 34P 63
Campden St. W8 ... 46Cb 89
Campden Way RM8: Dag ... 35Xc 75
Campe Ho. N10 ... 24Jb 50
Campen Cl. SW19 ... 61Ab 132
Camp End Rd. KT13: Weyb ... 84S 170
Camperdown Ho. SL4: Wind ... 4G 102
Camperdown St. E1 ... 3K 225 (44Vb 91)
Campfield Rd. AL1: St A ... 3E 6
SE9 ... 59Mc 115
Camphill Ct. KT14: W Byf ... 84J 169
Camphill Ind. Est. KT14: W Byf ... 83K 169
Camphill Rd. KT14: W Byf ... 84J 169
Campion Cl. CR0: C'don ... 77Ub 157
DA11: Nflt ... 3A 144
E6 ... 45Pc 94
HA3: Kenton ... 30Pa 47
RM7: Rush G ... 33Fd 76
UB8: Hil ... 43P 83
UB9: Den ... 34J 63
WD25: Wat ... 5W 12
Campion Ct. HA0: Wemb ... 40Na 67
RM17: Grays ... 51Fe 121
Campion Dr. KT20: Tad ... 92Xa 194
Campion Gdns. IG8: Wfd G ... 22Jc 53
Campion Gro. RM3: Rom ... 23Nd 57
Campion Ho. E14 ... 44Bc 92
(off Frances Wharf)
RH1: Redh ... 3P 207
SE16 ... 47Ac 92
(off Blondin Way)
Campion Pl. SE28 ... 46Wc 95
Campion Rd. E10 ... 31Dc 72
HP1: Hem H ... 3G 2
SW15 ... 56Ya 110
TW7: Isle ... 53Ha 108
Campions IG10: Lough ... 10Qc 22
Campions, The WD6: Bore ... 10Pa 15
Campions Cl. WD6: Bore ... 9Ra 15
Campion Sq. TN14: Dun G ... 92Hd 202
Campion Ter. NW2 ... 34Za 68
Campion Way HA8: Edg ... 21Sa 47
Cample La. RM15: S Ock ... 45Wd 98
Camplin Rd. HA3: Kenton ... 29Na 47
Camplin St. SE14 ... 52Zb 114
Camp Rd. AL1: St A ... 2D 6
CR3: Wold ... 92Ac 198
SL9: Ger X ... 1N 61
SW19 ... 64Xa 132
Campsbourne, The N8 ... 28Nb 50
Campsbourne Ho. N8 ... 28Nb 50
(off Pembroke Rd.)
Campsbourne Pde. N8 ... 28Nb 50
(off High St.)
Campsbourne Rd. N8 ... 27Nb 50
(not continuous)
Campsey Gdns. RM9: Dag ... 38Xc 75
Campsey Rd. RM9: Dag ... 38Xc 75
Campsfield Ho. N8 ... 27Nb 50
(off Campsfield Rd.)
Campsfield Rd. N8 ... 27Nb 50
Campshill Pl. SE13 ... 57Ec 114
Campshill Rd. SE13 ... 57Ec 114
Campus, The HP2: Hem H ... 1B 4
IG10: Lough ... 14Rc 36
Campus Av. RM8: Dag ... 35Wc 75
Campus Ct. IG10: Lough ... 14Qc 36
Campus Ho. TW7: Isle ... 52Ga 108
Campus Rd. E17 ... 30Bc 52
Campus Way NW4 ... 27Xa 48
Camp Vw. SW19 ... 64Xa 132
Camp Vw. Rd. AL1: St A ... 3F 6
Cam Rd. E15 ... 39Fc 73
Camrose Av. DA8: Erith ... 51Dd 118
HA8: Edg ... 26Na 47
TW13: Felt ... 63Y 129
Camrose Cl. CR0: C'don ... 73Ac 158
SM4: Mord ... 70Cb 133
Camrose St. SE2 ... 50Wc 95
Camwal Cl. CR4: Mitc ... 68Gb 133
Canada Av. N18 ... 23Sb 51
RH1: Redh ... 10A 208
Canada Cres. W3 ... 43Sa 87
Canada Dr. RH1: Redh ... 10A 208
Canada Est. SE16 ... 48Yb 92
Canada Farm Rd. DA2: G St G ... 70Wd 142
DA3: Fawk ... 70Wd 142
DA4: S Dar ... 70Wd 142
Canada Gdns. SE13 ... 57Ec 114
Canada Heights Motorcycle Circuit
... 69Md 141
Canada House ... 6E 222
Canada Ho. SE16 ... 48Ac 92
(off Brunswick Quay)
SW1 ... 46Mb 90
(off Trafalgar Sq.)
Canada Memorial ... 1A 228
Canada Pl. E14 ... 46Dc 92
(off Canada Sq.)
Canada Rd. DA8: Erith ... 52Kd 119
KT11: Cobh ... 85Y 171
KT14: Byfl ... 83M 169
SL1: Slou ... 7M 81
W3 ... 43Sa 87
Canada Sq. E14 ... 46Dc 92
Canada St. SE16 ... 47Zb 92
Canada Way W12 ... 45Xa 88
Canada Wharf SE16 ... 46Bc 92
Canadian Av. SE6 ... 60Dc 114
Canadian Memorial Av.
TW20: Eng G ... 8K 125
Canal App. SE8 ... 50Ac 92
Canal Bank KT15: Add ... 79M 149
Canal Bank M. GU21: Wok ... 89A 168
Canal Basin DA12: Grav'nd ... 8F 122
Canal Blvd. NW1 ... 37Mb 70
CANAL BRIDGE ... 51Wb 113
Canal Bri. KT15: Add ... 80M 149
Canal Bldg. N1 ... 1D 218 (40Sb 71)
Canal Cl. E1 ... 42Ac 92
W10 ... 42Za 88
Canal Cotts. E3 ... 39Bc 72
(off Parnell Rd.)
Canal Ct. HP4: Berk ... 1A 2
Canal Gro. SE15 ... 51Xb 113
Canal Ind. Pk. DA12: Grav'nd ... 8F 122
Canal Market ... 38Kb 70
(off Castlehaven Rd.)
Canal Path E2 ... 39Vb 71
Canal Reach N1 ... 39Mb 70
Canal Rd. DA12: Grav'nd ... 8E 122
Canal Side UB9: Hare ... 24J 43
Canalside RH1: Mers, Redh ... 3B 208
SE28 ... 45Zc 95
Canalside Activity Cen. ... 42Za 88
Canalside Gdns. UB2: S'hall ... 49Aa 85
Canalside Sq. N1 ... 1E 218
Canal Side Studios NW1 ... 39Mb 70
(off St Pancras Way)
Canalside Studios N1 ... 39Ub 71
(off Orsman Rd.)
Canal St. SE5 ... 51Tb 113
Canal Wlk. CR0: C'don ... 72Ub 157
E17 ... 27Zb 52
N1 ... 39Tb 71
NW10 ... 38Sa 67
(off Westend Cl.)
SE26 ... 64Yb 136
Canal Way UB9: Hare ... 23J 43
W10 ... 42Za 88
Canal Wharf E8 ... 39Ub 71
(off Kingsland Rd.)
SL3: L'ly ... 47C 82
UB6: G'frd ... 39Ja 66
Canal Wharf Ind. Est. SL3: L'ly ... 47C 82
Canary Vw. SE10 ... 51Dc 114
(off Dowells St.)
Canberra Cl. NW4 ... 27Wa 48
RM10: Dag ... 39Fd 76
RM12: Horn ... 35Ld 77
Canberra Cres. RM10: Dag ... 38Fd 76
Canberra Dr. UB4: N'olt ... 41Z 85
UB5: N'olt ... 41Y 85
Canberra Ho. AL1: St A ... 2B 6
(off London Rd.)
Canberra Path E10 ... 31Dc 72
(off Whitney Rd.)
Canberra Pl. TW9: Rich ... 55Qa 109
Canberra Rd. DA7: Bex ... 51Zc 117
E6 ... 39Pc 74
SE7 ... 51Lc 115
TW6: H'row A ... 55Q 106
W13 ... 46Ja 86
Canberra Sq. RM18: Tilb ... 4C 122
Canbury Av. KT2: King T ... 67Pa 131
Canbury Bus. Cen. KT2: King T ... 67Na 131
Canbury Bus. Pk. KT2: King T ... 67Na 131
(off Canbury Pk. Rd.)
Canbury Ct. KT2: King T ... 66Ma 131
Canbury M. SE26 ... 62Wb 135
Canbury Pk. Rd. KT2: King T ... 67Na 131
Canbury Pas. KT2: King T ... 67Ma 131
Canbury Path BR5: St M Cry ... 70Wc 139
Cancell Rd. SW9 ... 53Qb 112
Candahar Rd. SW11 ... 54Gb 111
Cander Way RM15: S Ock ... 45Xd 98
Candida Ct. NW1 ... 38Kb 70
Candid Ho. NW10 ... 41Xa 88
(off Trenmar Gdns.)
Candlefield Cl. HP3: Hem H ... 5A 4
Candlefield Rd. HP3: Hem H ... 5A 4
Candlefield Wlk. HP3: Hem H ... 5A 4
Candle Gro. SE15 ... 55Xb 113
Candlelight Ct. E15 ... 37Hc 73
(off Romford Rd.)
Candler M. TW1: Twick ... 59Ja 108
Candler St. N15 ... 30Tb 51
Candlerush Cl. GU22: Wok ... 89D 168
Candle St. E1 ... 43Ac 92
C & L Golf Course ... 38X 65
Candover Cl. UB7: Harm ... 52M 105
Candover Rd. RM12: Horn ... 32Kd 77
Candover St. W1 ... 1B 222 (43Lb 90)
Candy Cft. KT23: Bookh ... 98Da 191
Candy St. E3 ... 39Cc 72
Candy Wharf E3 ... 42Ac 92
Cane Hill RM3: Hrld W ... 26Md 57
Cane Hill Development
CR5: Coul ... 89Lb 176
Cane Hill Dr. CR5: Coul ... 89Lb 176
Caneland Ct. EN9: Walt A ... 6Hc 21
Canewdon Cl. GU22: Wok ... 91A 188
Caney M. NW2 ... 33Za 68
Canfield Dr. HA4: Ruis ... 36X 65
Canfield Gdns. NW6 ... 38Db 69
Canfield Ho. N15 ... 30Ub 51
(off Albert Rd.)
Canfield Pl. NW6 ... 37Eb 69
Canfield Rd. IG8: Wfd G ... 24Nc 54
RM13: Rain ... 39Hd 76

Canford Av.—Carmalt Gdns.

Canford Av. UB5: N'olt 39Ba 65
Canford Cl. EN2: Enf 12Qb 32
Canford Dr. KT15: Add 75K 149
Canford Gdns.
KT3: N Mald 72Ua 154
Canford Pl. TW11: Tedd 65La 130
Canford Rd. SW11 57Jb 112
Cangels Cl. HP1: Hem H 4J 3
Canham Gdns.
TW4: Houn 59Ba 107
Canham Rd. SE25 69Ub 135
W3 47Ua 88
Can Hatch KT20: Tad 90Ab 174
Canmore Gdns. SW16 66Lb 134
CANN HALL 35Gc 73
Cann Hall Rd. E11 35Gc 73
Cann Ho. W14 48Ab 88
(off Russell Rd.)
Canning Cres. N22 25Pb 50
Canning Cross SE5 54Ub 113
Canning Ho. W12 45Xa 88
(off Australia Rd.)
Canning Pas. W8 48Eb 89
Canning Pl. W8 3A 226 (48Eb 89)
Canning Pl. M. W8 3A 226
Canning Rd. CR0: C'don 75Vb 157
E15 40Gc 73
E17 28Ac 52
HA3: W'stone 27Ga 46
N5 34Rb 71
Canning Sq. EN1: Enf 11Wb 33
Cannington Rd.
RM9: Dag 37Yc 75
CANNING TOWN 44Hc 93
CANNING TOWN 43Gc 93
Cannizaro Rd. SW19 65Ya 132
Cannock Ct. E17 26Ec 52
Cannock Ho. N4 31Sb 71
Cannonbury Av. HA5: Pinn 30Z 45
Cannon Cl. SS17: Stan H 1P 101
SW20 69Ya 132
TW12: Hamp 65Da 129
Cannon Ct. EC1 5C 218
Cannon Cres. GU24: Chob 3J 167
Cannon Dr. E14 45Cc 92
Cannon Ga. SL2: Slou 5N 81
Cannon Gro. KT22: Fet 94Ga 192
Cannon Hill N14 20Nb 32
NW6 36Cb 69
Cannon Hill La. SW20 71Za 154
Cannon Hill M. N14 20Nb 32
Cannon Ho. SE11 6J 229
Cannon La. HA5: Pinn 29Aa 45
NW3 34Fb 69
Cannon M. EN9: Walt A 5Dc 20
KT22: Fet 93Ga 192
Cannon Pl. NW3 34Fb 69
SE7 50Nc 94
Cannon Retail Pk. SE28 45Wc 95
Cannon Rd. DA7: Bex 53Ad 117
N14 20Nb 32
N18 23Vb 51
WD18: Wat 15Y 27
Cannons Health Club
Richmond 56Ma 109
Cannonside KT22: Fet 94Ga 192
Cannon St. AL3: St A 1B 6
EC4 3D 224 (44Sb 91)
Cannon St. Rd. E1 44Xb 91
Cannon Trad. Est.
HA9: Wemb 35Ra 67
Cannon Wlk. DA12: Grav'nd 9E 122
(off Albert Murray Cl.)
Cannon Way KT8: W Mole 70Ca 129
KT22: Fet 93Ga 192
Cannon Wharf Bus. Cen. SE8 49Ac 92
(off Pell St.)
Cannon Wharf Development SE8 49Ac 92
(off Yeoman St.)
Cannon Workshops E14 45Cc 92
(off Cannon Dr.)
Canon All. EC4 3D 224
Canon Av. RM6: Chad H 29Yc 55
Canon Beck Rd. SE16 47Yb 92
Canonbie Rd. SE23 59Yb 114
CANONBURY 37Sb 71
Canonbury Bus. Cen. N1 39Sb 71
Canonbury Cotts. EN1: Enf 11Ub 33
Canonbury Ct. N1 38Rb 71
(off Hawes St.)
Canonbury Cres. N1 38Sb 71
Canonbury Gro. N1 38Sb 71
Canonbury Hgts. N1 37Tb 71
(off Dove Rd.)
Canonbury La. N1 38Rb 71
Canonbury Pk. Nth. N1 37Sb 71
Canonbury Pk. Sth. N1 37Sb 71
Canonbury Pl. N1 37Rb 71
(not continuous)
Canonbury Rd. EN1: Enf 11Ub 33
N1 37Rb 71
Canonbury Sq. N1 38Rb 71
Canonbury St. N1 38Sb 71
Canonbury Vs. N1 38Rb 71
Canon Mohan Cl. N14 16Jb 32
Canon Rd. BR1: Brom 69Lc 137
Canon Row SW1 2F 229 (47Nb 90)
(not continuous)
Canon's Cl. N2 31Fb 69
Canons Cl. CR4: Mitc 70Hb 133
HA8: Edg 23Pa 47
RH2: Reig 5H 207
WD7: R'lett 7Ka 14
Canons Cnr. HA8: Edg 21Na 47
Canons Ct. E15 35Gc 73
HA8: Edg 23Pa 47
Canons Dr. HA8: Edg 23Na 47
Canon's Hill
CR5: Coul, Purl 89Rb 177
Canons La. KT20: Tad 90Ab 174
Canonsleigh Rd. RM9: Dag 38Xc 75
Canons Leisure Cen.
Mitcham 70Hb 133
CANONS PARK 24Ma 47
Canons Pk. HA7: Stan 23Ma 47
Canons Pk. Cl. HA8: Edg 24Na 47
Canon St. N1 39Sb 71
Canon's Wlk. CR0: C'don 76Zb 158
Canons Yd. RH2: Reig 9K 207
Canopus Way
HA6: Nwood 21W 44
TW19: Stanw 59N 105
Canrobert St. E2 40Xb 71
Cantelowes Rd. NW1 37Mb 70
Canterbury Av. DA15: Sidc 61Xc 139
IG1: Ilf 31Nc 74
RM14: Upm 32Vd 78
SL2: Slou 2G 80
Canterbury Cl. BR3: Beck 67Dc 136
DA1: Dart 59Qd 119
E6 44Pc 94
HA6: Nwood 23V 44
IG7: Chig 20Vc 37
KT4: Wor Pk 75Za 154
SE5 54Sb 113
(off Lilford Rd.)
UB6: G'frd 43Da 85
Canterbury Ct. AL1: St A 1D 6
(off Battlefield Rd.)
CM15: Pil H 15Vd 40
CR2: S Croy 80Sb 157
(off St Augustine's Av.)
NW6 40Cb 69
(off Canterbury Rd.)
NW9 26Ua 48
SE5 52Qb 112
SE12 62Kc 137
TW15: Ashf 63P 127
Canterbury Cres. SW9 55Qb 112
Canterbury Gro. SE27 63Qb 134
Canterbury Hall KT4: Wor Pk 73Xa 154
Canterbury Ho. CR0: C'don 74Tb 157
(off Sydenham Rd.)
DA8: Erith 52Hd 118
E3 41Dc 92
(off Bow Rd.)
IG11: Bark 38Wc 75
(off Margaret Bondfield Av.)
KT19: Eps 83Qa 173
(off Queen Alexandra's Way)
RM8: Dag 35Wc 75
(off Academy Way)
SE1 3J 229 (48Pb 90)
SE8 50Cc 92
(off Wharf St.)
WD6: Bore 12Qa 29
(off Stratfield Rd.)
WD24: Wat 12Y 27
(off Anglian Cl.)
Canterbury Ind. Pk. SE15 51Yb 114
Canterbury M. KT22: Oxs 85Ea 172
SL4: Wind 4E 102
Canterbury Pde. RM15: S Ock 41Yd 98
Canterbury Pl. RM17: Grays 50Fe 99
SE17 6C 230 (50Rb 91)
Canterbury Rd. CR0: C'don 73Pb 156
DA12: Grav'nd 1E 144
E10 31Ec 72
HA1: Harr 29Da 45
HA2: Harr 29Da 45
NW6 40Bb 69
(Carlton Va.)
NW6 40Cb 69
(Princess Rd.)
SM4: Mord 73Db 155
TW13: Hanw 61Aa 129
WD6: Bore 12Qa 29
WD17: Wat 12X 27
Canterbury Ter. NW6 40Cb 69
Canterbury Way CM13: Gt War 23Yd 58
RM19: Purf 50Ud 98
RM20: W Thur 52Ud 120
WD3: Crox G 13S 26
Cantium Retail Pk. SE1 51Wb 113
Cantley Gdns. IG2: Ilf 30Sc 54
SE19 67Vb 135
Cantley Rd. W7 48Ja 86
Canto Ct. EC1 5E 218
Canton St. E14 44Cc 92
Cantrell Rd. E3 42Bc 92
Cantwell Rd. SE18 52Rc 116
Canute Gdns. SE16 49Zb 92
Canvey St. SE1 6D 224 (46Sb 91)
Capability Way DA9: Ghithe 56Yd 120
Cape Cl. IG11: Bark 38Rc 74
Cape Henry Ct. E14 45Fc 93
(off Jamestown Way)
Cape Ho. E8 37Vb 71
(off Dalston La.)
Capelands DA3: Nw A G 75Ce 165
Capel Av. SM6: Wall 78Pb 156
Capel Cl. BR2: Brom 74Nc 160
N20 20Eb 31
SS17: Stan H 1N 101
Capel Ct. EC2 3G 225
SE20 67Yb 136
Capel Cres. HA7: Stan 19Ja 28
Capel Gdns. HA5: Pinn 28Ba 45
IG3: Bark, Ilf 35Vc 75
Capel Ho. E9 38Yb 72
(off Loddiges Rd.)
WD19: Wat 21Z 45
Capella Rd. HA6: Nwood 21V 44
Capell Av. WD3: Chor 15E 24
Capell Rd. WD3: Chor 15F 24
Capell Way WD3: Chor 15F 24
Capel Manor Gdns. 7Wb 19
Capel Pl. DA2: Wilm 63Ld 141
Capel Rd. E7 35Kc 73
E12 35Kc 73
EN1: Enf 8Xb 19
EN4: E Barn 16Gb 31
WD19: Wat 16Aa 27
Capelvere Wlk. WD17: Wat 11U 26
Capener's Cl. SW1 2G 227
Capern Rd. SW18 60Eb 111
Cape Rd. AL1: St A 2F 6
N17 27Wb 51
Cape Yd. E1 46Wb 91
Capital Bus. Cen. CR2: S Croy 80Tb 157
HA0: Wemb 40Ma 67
WD24: Wat 8Z 13
Capital Bus. Pk. WD6: Bore 13Sa 29
Capital E. Apartments E16 45Jc 93
(off Western Gateway)
Capital Ho. SW15 57Ab 110
(off Plaza Gdns.)
Capital Ind. Est. CR4: Mitc 71Hb 155
DA17: Belv 48Dd 96
Capital Interchange Way
TW8: Bford 50Qa 87
Capital Mill Apartments E2 1K 219
Capital Pk. GU22: Wok 93D 188
Capital Trad. Est. IG11: Bark 40Tc 74
Capital Wharf E1 46Wb 91
Capitol Ind. Pk. NW9 27Sa 47
Capitol Sq. KT17: Eps 85Ua 174
Capitol Wlk. SE23 61Yb 136
(off London Rd.)
Capitol Way NW9 27Sa 47
Capland Ho. NW8 5C 214
Capland St. NW8 5C 214 (42Fb 89)
Caple Ho. SW10 52Eb 111
(off King's Rd.)
Caple Rd. NW10 40Va 68
Capon Cl. CM14: B'wood 18Xd 40
Capper St. WC1 6C 216 (42Lb 90)
Caprea Cl. UB4: Yead 43Z 85
Capricorn Cen. RM8: Dag 31Bd 75
Capri Ho. E17 26Bc 52
RM15: S Ock 42Xd 98
Capri Rd. CR0: C'don 74Vb 157
Capstan Cen. RM18: Tilb 52Fe 121
Capstan Cl. RM6: Chad H 30Xc 55
Capstan Ct. DA2: Dart 56Sd 120
E1 45Yb 92
(off Wapping Wall)
Capstan Dr. RM13: Rain 42Jd 96
Capstan Ho. E14 45Fc 93
(off Clove Cres.)
E14 49Ec 92
(off Stebondale St.)
Capstan M. DA11: Nflt 9A 122
Capstan Ride EN2: Enf 12Qb 32
Capstan Rd. SE8 49Bc 92
Capstan Sq. E14 47Ec 92
Capstans Wharf GU21: Wok 10K 167
Capstan Way SE16 46Ac 92
Capstone Rd. BR1: Brom 63Hc 137
Capswood Bus. Cen. UB9: Den 32E 62
Captain Cook Statue 6E 222
Captains Wlk. HP4: Berk 2A 2
Capthorne Av. HA2: Harr 32Aa 65
Capuchin Cl. HA7: Stan 23Ka 46
Capulet M. E16 46Jc 93
Capulet Sq. E3 41Dc 92
(off Talwin St.)
Capworth St. E10 32Cc 72
Caractacus Cott. Vw. WD18: Wat 17W 26
Caractacus Grn. WD18: Wat 16V 26
Caradoc Cl. W2 44Cb 89
Caradoc Evans Cl. N11 22Kb 50
(off Springfield Rd.)
Caradoc St. SE10 50Gc 93
Caradon Cl. E11 32Gc 73
GU21: Wok 10M 167
Caradon Way N15 28Tb 51
Cara Ho. N1 38Qb 70
(off Liverpool Rd.)
Caramel Ct. E3 40Dc 72
(off Taylor Pl.)
Caranday Vs. W11 46Za 88
(off Norland Rd.)
Carat Ho. E14 43Cc 92
(off Ursula Gould Way)
Cvn. La. WD3: Rick 17N 25
Cvn. Site, The RM15: Avel 48Td 98
Caravel Cl. E14 48Cc 92
RM16: Chaf H 48Be 99
Caravelle Gdns. UB5: N'olt 41Z 85
Caravel M. SE8 51Cc 114
Caraway Apartments SE1 1K 231
Caraway Cl. E13 43Kc 93
Caraway Hgts. E14 45Ec 92
(off Poplar High St.)
Caraway Pl. SM6: Wall 76Kb 156
Carberry Rd. SE19 65Ub 135
Carbery Av. W3 47Pa 87
Carbery La. SL5: Asc 9A 124
Carbis Cl. E4 18Fc 35
Carbis Rd. E14 44Bc 92
Carbrooke Ho. E9 39Yb 72
(off Templecombe Rd.)
Carbuncle Pas. N17 26Wb 51
Carburton St. W1 7A 216 (43Kb 90)
Carbury Cl. RM12: Horn 37Ld 77
Cardale St. E14 47Ec 92
Cardamon Bldg. SE1 7K 225
Carden Ct. KT8: W Mole 70Da 129
Carden Rd. SE15 55Xb 113
Cardiff Cl. RM5: Col R 24Fd 56
Cardiff Ho. SE15 51Wb 113
(off Friary Est.)
Cardiff Rd. EN3: Pond E 14Xb 33
W7 48Ja 86
WD18: Wat 15X 27
Cardiff St. SE18 52Uc 116
Cardiff Way WD5: Ab L 4W 12
Cardigan Cl. GU21: Wok 10J 167
SL1: Slou 5D 80
Cardigan Ct. W7 42Ha 86
(off Copley Cl.)
Cardigan Gdns. IG3: Ilf 33Wc 75
Cardigan Ho. RM3: Rom 22Md 57
(off Bridgwater Wlk.)
Cardigan Pl. SE3 54Fc 115
Cardigan Rd. E3 40Bc 72
SW13 54Wa 110
SW19 65Eb 133
TW10: Rich 58Na 109
Cardigan St. SE11 7K 229 (50Qb 90)
Cardigan Wlk. N1 38Sb 71
(off Ashby Gro.)
Cardinal Av. KT2: King T 64Na 131
SM4: Mord 72Ab 154
WD6: Bore 13Ra 29
Cardinal Bourne St. SE1 4G 231 (48Tb 91)
Cardinal Cap All. SE1 5D 224 (46Sb 91)
Cardinal Cl. BR7: Chst 67Uc 138
CR2: Sande 85Wb 177
HA8: Edg 24Sa 47
KT4: Wor Pk 77Wa 154
SM4: Mord 72Ab 154
Cardinal Ct. E1 45Xb 91
(off Thomas More St.)
WD6: Bore 13Qa 29
Cardinal Cres. KT3: N Mald 68Sa 131
Cardinal Dr. IG6: Ilf 23Sc 54
KT12: Walt T 74Z 151
Cardinal Gro. AL3: St A 4P 5
Cardinal Hinsley Cl. NW10 40Wa 68
Cardinal Mans. SW1 5B 228
Cardinal Pl. AL2: Park 7B 6
GU22: Wok 90A 168
SW1 3B 228 (48Lb 90)
(not continuous)
SW15 56Za 110
Cardinal Rd. HA4: Ruis 32Z 65
RM16: Chaf H 48Ae 99
TW13: Felt 60X 107
Cardinals Wlk. SL6: Tap 4A 80
TW12: Hamp 66Ea 130
TW16: Sun 65U 128
Cardinals Way N19 32Mb 70
Cardinal Wlk. SW1 4B 228
Cardinal Way HA3: W'stone 27Ga 46
RM13: Rain 40Md 77
Cardine M. SE15 52Xb 113
Cardingham GU21: Wok 9L 167
Cardington Sq. TW4: Houn 56Z 107
Cardington St. NW1 3C 216 (41Lb 90)
Cardinham Rd. BR6: Chels 77Vc 161
Cardozo Rd. N7 36Nb 70
Cardrew Av. N12 22Fb 49
Cardrew Cl. N12 22Gb 49
Cardrew Ct. N12 22Fb 49
Cardross Ho. W6 48Xa 88
(off Cardross St.)
Cardross St. W6 48Xa 88
Cardwell Cres. SL5: S'hill 1A 146
Cardwell Rd. N7 35Nb 70
Cardwell Ter. N7 35Nb 70
(off Cardwell Rd.)
Cardy Rd. HP1: Hem H 3K 3
Career Ct. SE16 47Zb 92
(off Christopher Cl.)
Carew Cl. CR5: Coul 91Rb 197
N7 33Pb 70
RM16: Chaf H 48Ae 99
Carew Ct. RM6: Chad H 30Xc 55
(off Quarles Pk. Rd.)
SE14 51Zb 114
(off Samuel Cl.)
SM2: Sutt 81Db 175
Carew Manor & Dovecote 76Lb 156
Carew Mnr. Cotts. SM6: Bedd 76Mb 156
Carew Rd. CR4: Mitc 68Jb 134
CR7: Thor H 70Rb 135
HA6: Nwood 23U 44
N17 26Wb 51
SM6: Wall 79Lb 156
TW15: Ashf 65S 128
W13 47La 86
Carew St. SE5 54Sb 113
Carew Way BR5: Orp 74Yc 161
WD19: Wat 20Ba 27
Carey Cl. SL4: Wind 5F 102
Carey Ct. DA6: Bex 57Dd 118
SE5 52Sb 113
Carey Gdns. SW8 53Lb 112
Carey La. EC2 2D 224 (44Sb 91)
Carey Mans. SW1 5D 228
Carey Pl. SW1 6D 228 (49Mb 90)
WD17: Wat 14Y 27
Carey Rd. RM9: Dag 35Ad 75
Carey's Fld. TN13: Dun G 92Gd 202
Carey St. WC2 3J 223 (44Pb 90)
Carey Way HA9: Wemb 35Ra 67
Carfax Ho. SE20 67Wb 135
Carfax Pl. SW4 56Mb 112
Carfax Rd. RM12: Horn 35Hd 76
UB3: Harl 50V 84
Carfree Cl. N1 38Qb 70
Cargill Rd. SW18 60Db 111
Cargo Point TW19: Stanw 58P 105
Cargreen Pl. SE25 70Vb 135
(off Cargreen Rd.)
Cargreen Rd. SE25 70Vb 135
Cargrey Ho. HA7: Stan 22La 46
Carholme Rd. SE23 60Bc 114
Carillon Ct. E1 43Wb 91
(off Greatorex St.)
W5 45Ma 87
Carina Ho. E20 36Ec 72
(off Cheering La.)
Carinthia Ct. SE16 49Ac 92
(off Plough Way)
Carisbrook N10 26Kb 50
Carisbrook Cl. CM16: Epp 3Wc 23
EN1: Enf 11Vb 33
Carisbrooke Av. DA5: Bexl 60Zc 117
WD24: Wat 11Z 27
Carisbrooke Cl. HA7: Stan 26Ma 47
RM11: Horn 32Qd 77
TW4: Houn 59Aa 107
Carisbrooke Ct. DA2: Dart 58Rd 119
(off Osbourne Rd.)
SL1: Slou 5K 81
SM2: Cheam 80Bb 155
UB5: N'olt 39Ba 65
(off Eskdale Av.)
W1 1J 221
W3 47Sa 87
(off Brouncker Rd.)
Carisbrooke Gdns. SE15 52Vb 113
Carisbrooke Ho. HA6: Nwood 22V 44
KT2: King T 67Na 131
(off Seven Kings Way)
TW10: Rich 57Qa 109
UB7: W Dray 47P 83
(off Park Lodge Av.)
Carisbrooke Rd. BR2: Brom 70Lc 137
CR4: Mitc 70Mb 134
E17 28Ac 52
Carisbrook Rd. AL2: Chis G 8P 5
CM15: Pil H 16Xd 40
Carker's La. NW5 36Kb 70
Carlbury Cl. AL1: St A 3F 6
Carlcott Cl. KT12: Walt T 73X 151
Carl Ekman Ho. DA11: Nflt 59Fe 121
Carleton Av. SM6: Wall 81Mb 176
Carleton Cl. KT10: Esh 74Fa 152
Carleton Gdns. N19 36Lb 70
Carleton Pl. DA4: Hort K 70Sd 142
Carleton Rd. DA1: Dart 59Qd 119
N7 36Mb 70
Carleton Vs. NW5 36Lb 70
Carlile Cl. E3 40Bc 72
Carlile Ho. SE1 4G 231
Carlile Pl. TW10: Rich 58Pa 109
Carlina Gdns. IG8: Wfd G 22Kc 53
Carlingford Gdns. CR4: Mitc 66Hb 133
Carlingford Rd. N15 27Rb 51
NW3 35Fb 69
SM4: Mord 72Za 154
Carlisle Av. AL1: St A 1B 6
AL3: St A 1B 6
EC3 3J 225 (44Ub 91)
W3 44Ua 88
Carlisle Cl. HA5: Pinn 31Aa 65
KT2: King T 67Qa 131
Carlisle Gdns. HA3: Kenton 31Ma 67
IG1: Ilf 30Nc 54
Carlisle Ho. IG1: Ilf 30Nc 54
WD6: Bore 12Qa 29
Carlisle La. SE1 4J 229 (48Pb 90)
Carlisle Mans. SW1 5B 228
Carlisle M. KT2: King T 67Qa 131
Carlisle Pl. N11 21Kb 50
SW1 4B 228 (48Lb 90)
Carlisle Rd. DA1: Dart 58Qd 119
E10 32Cc 72
N4 31Qb 70
NW6 39Ab 68
NW9 27Sa 47
RM1: Rom 29Jd 56
SL1: Slou 5H 81
SM1: Sutt 79Bb 155
TW12: Hamp 66Da 129
Carlisle St. W1 3D 222 (44Mb 90)
Carlisle Wlk. E8 37Vb 71
Carlisle Way SW17 64Jb 134
Carlos Pl. W1 5J 221 (45Jb 90)
Carlow St. NW1 1B 216 (40Lb 70)
Carlson Ct. SW15 56Bb 111
Carlton Av. CR2: S Croy 80Ub 157
DA9: Ghithe 58Ud 120
HA3: Kenton 29Ka 46
N14 15Mb 32
TW14: Felt 58Y 107
UB3: Harl 49U 84
Carlton Av. E. HA9: Wemb 33Ma 67
Carlton Av. W. HA0: Wemb 33Ka 66
Carlton Cl. GU21: Wok 86B 168
HA8: Edg 22Qa 47
KT9: Chess 79Ma 153
NW3 33Cb 69
RM14: Upm 33Rd 77
UB5: N'olt 36Ea 66
WD6: Bore 14Ta 29
Carlton Ct. IG6: Ilf 27Tc 54
N3 24Cb 49
SE20 67Xb 135
TW18: Staines 64J 127
UB8: Cowl 43M 83
W9 40Db 69
(off Maida Vale)
WD19: Wat 16Y 27
Carlton Cres. SM3: Cheam 77Ab 154
Carlton Dr. IG6: Ilf 27Tc 54
SW15 57Za 110
Carlton Gdns. SW1 6D 222 (46Mb 90)
W5 44La 86
Carlton Grn. DA14: Sidc 63Vc 139
RH1: Redh 3N 207
Carlton Gro. SE15 53Xb 113
Carlton Hill NW8 1A 214 (40Db 69)
Carlton Ho. IG10: Lough 15Mc 35
NW6 40Cb 69
(off Canterbury Ter.)
SE16 47Zb 92
(off Wolfe Cres.)
TW3: Houn 58Ca 107
TW14: Felt 58V 106
Carlton Ho. Ter. SW1 7D 222 (46Mb 90)
Carlton Lodge N4 31Qb 70
(off Carlton Rd.)
Carlton Mans. N16 32Vb 71
NW6 38Cb 69
(off West End La.)
W9 41Db 89
W14 47Ab 88
(off Holland Pk. Gdns.)
Carlton M. NW6 36Cb 69
(off West Cotts.)
Carlton Pde. BR6: St M Cry 73Xc 161
HA9: Wemb 33Na 67
TN13: S'oaks 94Ld 203
Carlton Pk. Av. SW20 68Za 132
Carlton Pl. HA6: Nwood 22R 44
KT13: Weyb 77R 150
(off Castle Vw. Rd.)
Carlton Rd. CR2: S Croy 79Tb 157
DA8: Erith 51Dd 118
DA14: Sidc 64Vc 139
DA16: Well 55Xc 117
E11 32Hc 73
E12 35Mc 73
E17 25Ac 52
GU21: Wok 86C 168
KT3: N Mald 68Ua 132
KT12: Walt T 73X 151
N4 31Qb 70
N11 22Jb 50
RH1: Redh 4M 207
RH2: Reig 4M 207
RM2: Rom 29Hd 56
RM16: Grays 7B 100
SL2: Slou 5M 81
SW14 55Sa 109
TW16: Sun 66V 128
W4 47Ta 87
W5 45La 86
Carlton Sq. E1 42Zb 92
(not continuous)
Carlton St. SW1 5D 222 (45Mb 90)
Carlton Ter. E7 38Lc 73
E11 29Kc 53
(not continuous)
N18 20Tb 33
SE26 62Yb 136
Carlton Twr. Pl.
SW1 3G 227 (48Hb 89)
Carlton Towers SM5: Cars 76Hb 155
Carlton Va. NW6 40Bb 69
Carlton Vs. SW15 57Ab 110
Carlton Works, The SE15 52Xb 113
(off Asylum Rd.)
Carlwell St. SW17 64Gb 133
Carlyle Av. BR1: Brom 69Mc 137
UB1: S'hall 45Ba 85
Carlyle Cl. KT8: W Mole 68Da 129
N2 30Eb 49
Carlyle Ct. SW6 53Db 111
(off Imperial Rd.)
SW10 53Eb 111
(off Chelsea Harbour Dr.)
Carlyle Gdns. UB1: S'hall 45Ba 85
Carlyle Ho. KT8: W Mole 71Ca 151
(off Down St.)
N16 34Ub 71
SE5 52Sb 113
(off Bethwin Rd.)
SW3 51Fb 111
(off Old Church St.)
Carlyle Mans. SW3 51Gb 111
(off Cheyne Wlk.)
W8 46Cb 89
(off Kensington Mall)
Carlyle M. E1 42Zb 92
Carlyle Pl. SW15 56Za 110
Carlyle Rd. CR0: C'don 75Wb 157
E12 35Nc 74
NW10 39Ta 67
SE28 45Xc 95
TW18: Staines 66J 127
W5 49La 86
Carlyle's House 51Gb 111
(off Cheyne Row)
Carlyle Sq. SW3 50Fb 89
Carly M. E2 41Wb 91
(off Barnet Gro.)
Carlyon Av. HA2: Harr 35Ba 65
Carlyon Cl. HA0: Wemb 39Na 67
Carlyon Rd. HA0: Wemb 40Na 67
UB4: Yead 43Y 85
(not continuous)
Carlys Cl. BR3: Beck 68Zb 136
Carmalt Gdns. KT12: Hers 78Y 151
SW15 56Ya 110

Carmarthen Ct.—Cato St.

Carmarthen Ct. W7 .....42Ha 86
(off Copley Cl.)
Carmarthen Pl. SE1 .....1H 231 (47Ub 91)
Carmarthen Rd. SL1: Slou 5J 81
Carmel Cl. GU22: Wok 90A 168
Carmel Ct. HA9: Wemb 33Ra 67
W8 .....47Db 89
(off Holland St.)
Carmelite Cl. HA3: Hrw W 25Ea 46
Carmelite Rd. HA3: Hrw W 25Ea 46
Carmelite St. EC4 .....4A 224 (45Qb 90)
Carmelite Wlk.
HA3: Hrw W 25Ea 46
Carmelite Way DA3: Hartl 71Be 165
HA3: Hrw W 26Ea 46
Carmel Lodge SW6 .....51Cb 111
(off Lillie Rd.)
Carmelo M. E1 .....43Zb 92
(off Maria Ter.)
Carmel Way TW9: Rich 54Ra 109
Carmen Ct. WD6: Bore 10Pa 15
(off Aycliffe Rd.)
Carmen St. E14 .....44Dc 92
Carmichael Av. DA9: Ghithe 56Yd 120
Carmichael Cl. HA4: Ruis 35W 64
SW11 .....55Fb 111
Carmichael Ct. SW13 .....54Va 110
(off Grove Rd.)
Carmichael Ho. E14 .....45Ec 92
(off Poplar High St.)
Carmichael M. SW18 .....59Fb 111
Carmichael Rd. SE25 .....71Vb 157
Carmine W2 .....1C 220
Carmine Ct. BR1: Brom 66Hc 137
Carmine Wharf E14 .....44Bc 92
Carminia Rd. SW17 .....61Kb 134
Carnaby St. W1 .....3B 222 (44Lb 90)
Carnach Grn. RM15: S Ock 45Wd 98
Carnac St. SE27 .....63Tb 135
Carnanton Rd. E17 .....25Fc 53
Carnarvon Av. EN1: Enf 13Vb 33
Carnarvon Dr. UB3: Harl 48S 84
Carnarvon Rd. E10 .....29Ec 52
E15 .....37Hc 73
E18 .....25Hc 53
EN5: Barn 13Ab 30
Carnation Cl. RM7: Rush G 33Gd 76
Carnation St. SE2 .....50Xc 95
Carnbrook M. SE3 .....55Mc 115
Carnbrook Rd. SE3 .....55Mc 115
Carnecke Gdns. SE9 .....57Nc 116
Carnegie Cl. EN3: Enf L 10Dc 20
KT6: Surb 75Pa 153
Carnegie Ct. SL2: Farn C 7F 60
Carnegie Pl. SW19 .....62Za 132
Carnegie Rd. HA1: Harr 31Ha 66
Carnegie St. N1 .....1J 217 (39Pb 70)
Carnell Apartments E14 .....44Bc 92
(off St Anne's Row)
Carnet Cl. DA1: Cray 59Gd 118
Carney Pl. SW9 .....56Qb 112
Carnforth Cl. KT19: Ewe 79Ra 153
Carnforth Gdns. RM12: Horn 36Hd 76
Carnforth Rd. SW16 .....66Mb 134
(not continuous)
Carnie Lodge SW17 .....62Kb 134
Carnival Ho. SE1 .....1K 231
Carnoustie Cl. SE28 .....44Zc 95
Carnoustie Dr. N1 .....38Pb 70
(not continuous)
Carnwath Rd. SW6 .....55Cb 111
Caroe Ct. N9 .....18Xb 33
Caro La. HP3: Hem H 4B 4
Carol Cl. NW4 .....28Za 48
Carole Ho. NW1 .....39Hb 69
(off Regent's Pk. Rd.)
Carolina Cl. E15 .....36Gc 73
Carolina Rd. CR7: Thor H 68Rb 135
Caroline Cl. CR0: C'don 77Ub 157
N10 .....26Kb 50
SW16 .....62Pb 134
TW7: Isle 52Fa 108
UB7: W Dray 47M 83
W2 .....45Db 89
Caroline Ct. HA7: Stan 23Ja 46
SE6 .....63Fc 137
TW15: Ashf 65R 128
Caroline Gdns. E2 .....3J 219 (41Ub 91)
SE15 .....52Xb 113
(not continuous)
Caroline Ho. W2 .....45Db 89
(off Bayswater Rd.)
W6 .....50Ya 88
(off Queen Caroline St.)
Caroline Pl. SW11 .....54Jb 112
UB3: Harl 52U 106
W2 .....45Db 89
WD19: Wat 16Aa 27
Caroline Pl. M. W2 .....45Db 89
Caroline Rd. SW19 .....66Bb 133
Caroline St. E1 .....44Zb 92
Caroline Ter. SW1 .....6H 227 (49Jb 90)
Caroline Wlk. W6 .....51Ab 110
(off Lillie Rd.)
Carol St. NW1 .....39Lb 70
Carolyn Cl. GU21: Wok 1K 187
Carolyn Dr. BR6: Chels 76Wc 161
Caronia Ct. SE16 .....49Ac 92
(off Plough Way)
Caroon Dr. WD3: Sarr 8K 11
Caro Pl. KT3: N Mald 70Va 132
Carpenders Av. WD19: Wat 20Aa 27
CARPENDERS PARK 20Z 27
Carpenter Cl. KT17: Ewe 81Va 174
Carpenter Gdns. N21 .....19Rb 33
Carpenter Ho. E1 .....43Zb 92
(off Trafalgar Gdns.)
E14 .....43Cc 92
(off Burgess St.)
NW11 .....30Eb 49
Carpenter Path CM13: Hut 15Fe 41
Carpenters Arms Apartments
SE1 .....49Wb 91
(off Welsford St.)
Carpenters Arms Path SE9 .....58Pc 116
(off Eltham High St.)
Carpenters Cl. EN5: New Bar 16Db 31
Carpenters Ct. NW1 .....39Lb 70
(off Pratt St.)
TW2: Twick 61Ga 130
Carpenters M. N7 .....36Nb 70
Carpenters Pl. SW4 .....56Mb 112
Carpenter's Rd. E15 .....38Ec 72
E20 .....37Cc 72
Carpenters Rd. EN1: Enf 8Yb 20
Carpenter St. W1 .....5K 221 (45Kb 90)
Carpenters Wood Dr. WD3: Chor 14D 24
Carpenter Way EN6: Pot B 5Eb 17
Carp Ho. E3 .....39Bc 72
(off Old Ford Rd.)
Carrack Ho. DA8: Erith 50Gd 96
(off Saltford Cl.)
Carradale Ho. E14 .....44Ec 92
(off St Leonard's Rd.)
Carraige Wlk.
RH1: Redh 8P 207
Carrara Cl. SE24 .....56Qb 112
SW9 .....56Rb 113
Carrara M. E8 .....37Wb 71
(off Dalston La.)
Carrara Wharf SW6 .....55Ab 110
Carr Cl. HA7: Stan 23Ja 46
Carre M. SE5 .....53Rb 113
(off Calais St.)
Carrera Twr. EC1 .....3D 218
Carr Gro. SE18 .....49Nc 94
Carr Ho. DA1: Cray 57Gd 118
Carriage Dr. E. SW11 .....52Jb 112
Carriage Dr. Nth. SW11 .....51Jb 112
(Carriage Dr. E.)
SW11 .....52Hb 111
(The Parade)
Carriage Dr. Sth. SW11 .....53Hb 111
(not continuous)
Carriage Dr. W. SW11 .....52Hb 111
Carriage M. IG1: Ilf 33Sc 74
Carriage Pl. N16 .....34Tb 71
SW16 .....64Lb 134
Carriage St. SE18 .....48Rc 94
Carriage Way SE8 .....52Cc 114
(off Deptford High St.)
Carriageway, The TN16: Bras 96Zc 201
Carrick Cl. TW7: Isle 55Ja 108
Carrick Dr. IG6: Ilf 25Sc 54
TN13: S'oaks 95Kd 203
Carrick Gdns. N17 .....24Ub 51
Carrick Ga. KT10: Esh 76Ea 152
Carrick Ho. N7 .....37Pb 70
(off Caledonian Rd.)
SE11 .....7B 230 (50Qb 90)
Carrick M. SE8 .....51Cc 114
Carrick Sq. TW8: Bford 52La 108
Carrigshaun KT13: Weyb 78T 150
Carrill Way DA17: Belv 48Zc 95
Carrington Av. TW3: Houn 57Da 107
WD6: Bore 15Ra 29
Carrington Cl. CR0: C'don 73Ac 158
EN5: Ark 15Wa 30
KT2: King T 64Sa 131
RH1: Redh 5P 207
WD6: Bore 15Sa 29
Carrington Ct. SW11 .....56Gb 111
(off Barnard Rd.)
Carrington Gdns. E7 .....35Jc 73
Carrington Ho. W1 .....7K 221
Carrington Pl. KT10: Esh 77Da 151
Carrington Rd. DA1: Dart 58Pd 119
SL1: Slou 5J 81
TW10: Rich 56Qa 109
Carrington Sq. HA3: Hrw W 23Ea 46
Carrington St. W1 .....7K 221 (46Kb 90)
Carrock Ct. RM7: Rush G 30Fd 56
(off Union Rd.)
Carrol Cl. NW5 .....35Kb 70
Carroll Cl. E15 .....36Hc 73
Carroll Ct. W3 .....48Ra 87
(off Osborne Rd.)
Carroll Hill IG10: Lough 13Pc 36
Carroll Ho. W2 .....4B 220
Carronade Ct. N7 .....36Pb 70
Carronade Pl. SE28 .....48Sc 94
Carron Cl. E14 .....44Dc 92
Carroun Rd. SW8 .....52Pb 112
Carroway La. UB6: G'frd 41Fa 86
Carrow Rd. KT12: Walt T 76Z 151
RM9: Dag 38Xc 75
Carr Rd. E17 .....26Bc 52
UB5: N'olt 37Ca 65
Carrs La. N21 .....15Sb 33
Carr St. E14 .....43Ac 92
CARSHALTON 77Jb 156
Carshalton Athletic FC 77Gb 155
CARSHALTON BEECHES 81Gb 175
Carshalton Gro. SM1: Sutt 77Fb 155
Carshalton Lodge KT13: Weyb 76T 150
(off Oatlands Dr.)
CARSHALTON ON THE HILL 80Jb 156
Carshalton Pk. Rd. SM5: Cars 78Hb 155
Carshalton Pl. SM5: Cars 78Jb 156
Carshalton Rd. CR4: Mitc 70Jb 134
SM1: Sutt 78Eb 155
SM5: Cars 78Eb 155
SM7: Bans 86Hb 175
Carsington Gdns. DA1: Dart 61Md 141
Carslake Rd. SW15 .....58Ya 110
Carson Rd. E16 .....42Jc 93
EN4: Cockf 14Hb 31
SE21 .....61Tb 135
Carson Ter. W11 .....46Ab 88
(off Princes Pl.)
Carstairs Rd. SE6 .....62Ec 136
Carston Cl. SE12 .....57Hc 115
Carswell Cl. CM13: Hut 16Fe 41
IG4: Ilf 28Mc 53
Carswell Rd. SE6 .....59Ec 114
CARTBRIDGE 94D 188
Cartbridge Cl. GU23: Send 95D 188
Cartel Cl. RM19: Purf 49Td 98
Carter Av. TN15: W King 80Td 164
Carter Cl. EN5: Barn 15Ab 30
NW9 .....30Ta 47
RM5: Col R 24Cd 56
SL4: Wind 4E 102
Carter Ct. EC4 .....3C 224
Carter Dr. RM5: Col R 22Dd 56
Carteret Ho. W12 .....45Xa 88
(off White City Est.)
Carteret St. SW1 .....2D 228 (47Mb 90)
Carteret Way SE8 .....49Ac 92
Carterhatch La. EN1: Enf 10Vb 19
Carterhatch Rd. EN3: Enf H 11Yb 34
Carter Ho. E1 .....1K 225
Carter La. EC4 .....3C 224 (44Rb 91)
Carter Pl. SE17 .....7E 230 (50Sb 91)
Carter Rd. E13 .....39Kc 73
SW19 .....65Fb 133
Carters Cl. KT4: Wor Pk 75Za 154
NW5 .....36Mb 70
(off Torriano Av.)
Carter's Cotts. RH1: Redh 8N 207
Cartersfield Rd. EN9: Walt A 6Ec 20
CARTER'S HILL 100Rd 203
Carter's Hill TN15: Under 100Rd 203
Carters Hill Cl. SE9 .....60Lc 115
Carters La. GU22: Wok 92E 188
SE23 .....61Ac 136
Carter Sq. E14 .....44Dc 92
(off Bowen St.)
Carters Rd. KT17: Eps 87Va 174
Carters Row DA11: Nflt 10B 122
Carter St. SE17 .....51Sb 113
Carter's Yd. SW18 .....57Cb 111
Carthew Rd. W6 .....48Xa 88
Carthew Vs. W6 .....48Xa 88
Carthouse La. GU21: Wok 6J 167
Carthusian Ct EC1 .....7D 218
Carthusian St. EC1 .....7D 218 (43Sb 91)
Cartier Circ. E14 .....46Dc 92
Carting La. WC2 .....5G 223 (45Nb 90)
Cart La. E4 .....18Gc 35
RM17: Grays 50De 99
Cart Lodge M.
CR0: C'don 74Ub 157
Cartmel NW1 .....3B 216
Cartmel Cl. N17 .....24Xb 51
RH2: Reig 4N 207
Cartmel Ct. UB5: N'olt 37Aa 65
Cartmel Gdns.
SM4: Mord 71Eb 155
Cartmel Rd. DA7: Bex 53Cd 118
Carton Ho. W11 .....45Za 88
(off St Ann's Rd.)
Cartoon Mus. 1F 223
Cart Path WD25: Wat 5Y 13
Cartridge Pl. SE18 .....48Rc 94
Cart Track, The HP3: Hem H 7P 3
Cartwright Gdns. WC1 .....4F 217 (41Nb 90)
Cartwright Ho. SE1 .....4E 230
Cartwright Rd. RM9: Dag 38Bd 75
Cartwright St. E1 .....45Vb 91
Cartwright Way SW13 .....52Xa 110
Carvel Ho. E14 .....50Ec 92
(off Manchester Rd.)
Carver Cl. W4 .....48Sa 87
Carver Rd. SE24 .....58Sb 113
Carville Cres. TW8: Bford 49Na 87
Carville St. N4 .....33Qb 70
Cary Av. SE16 .....49Ac 92
Cary Rd. E11 .....35Gc 73
Carysfort Rd. N8 .....29Mb 50
N16 .....34Tb 71
Cary Wlk. WD7: R'lett 6Ka 14
Casby Ho. SE16 .....48Wb 91
(off Marine St.)
Cascade Av. N10 .....28Lb 50
Cascade Cl. BR5: St P 69Yc 139
IG9: Buck H 19Mc 35
Cascade Ct. SW8 .....52Kb 112
Cascade Rd. IG9: Buck H 19Mc 35
Cascades CR0: Sels 82Bc 178
Cascades Ct. SW19 .....66Bb 133
Cascades Leisure Cen.
Gravesend 3J 145
Cascades Twr. E14 .....46Bc 92
Casel Ct. HA7: Stan 19Ja 28
(off Brightwen Gro.)
Caselden Cl. KT15: Add 78L 149
Casella Rd. SE14 .....52Zb 114
Casewick Rd. SE27 .....64Qb 134
Casey Av. UB5: N'olt 40Ba 65
Casey Cl. NW8 .....4D 214 (41Gb 89)
Casey Ct. SE14 .....53Zb 114
(off Besson St.)
Cashmere Ho. E8 .....39Vb 71
(off Pamela St.)
Casimir Rd. E5 .....33Yb 72
Casino Av. SE24 .....57Sb 113
Caspian Cl. RM19: Purf 49Qd 97
Caspian St. SE5 .....52Tb 113
Caspian Wlk. E16 .....44Mc 93
Caspian Way DA10: Swans 57Ae 121
RM19: Purf 50Qd 97
Caspian Wharf E3 .....43Dc 92
(off Violet Rd.)
Cassander Pl. HA5: Pinn 25Aa 45
(off Holly Gro.)
Cassandra Cl. RM13: Rain 39Hd 76
UB5: N'olt 35Fa 66
Casselden Rd. NW10 .....38Ta 67
Cassell Cl. RM16: Ors 3C 100
Cassell Ho. SW9 .....54Pb 112
(off Stockwell Gdns. Est.)
Cass Ho. E9 .....37Zb 72
(off Harrowgate Rd.)
Cassidy Rd. SW6 .....52Cb 111
(not continuous)
Cassilda Rd. SE2 .....49Wc 95
Cassilis Rd. E14 .....47Cc 92
TW1: Twick 57Ka 108
Cassini Apartments E16 .....44Jc 93
Cassio Apartments WD17: Wat 12X 27
(off Malden Rd.)
Cassiobridge Rd. WD18: Wat 14U 26
Cassiobridge Ter. WD3: Wat 15T 26
Cassiobury Av. TW14: Felt 59V 106
Cassiobury Ct. WD17: Wat 12U 26
Cassiobury Dr. WD17: Wat 10U 12
Cassiobury Pk. 13U 26
Cassiobury Pk. Av. WD18: Wat 13U 26
Cassiobury Rd. E17 .....29Ac 52
Cassio Ho. WD18: Wat 14V 26
(off Manhattan Av.)
Cassio Pl. WD18: Wat 14U 26
Cassio Rd. WD18: Wat 13X 27
Cassio Wharf WD18: Wat 15T 26
Cassis Ct. IG10: Lough 14Sc 36
Cassius Dr. AL3: St A 4P 5
Cassland Rd. CR7: Thor H 70Tb 135
E9 .....38Zb 72
Casslee Rd. SE6 .....59Bc 114
Cassocks Sq. TW17: Shep 73T 150
Casson Apartments E14 .....44Cc 92
(off Upper Nth. St.)
Casson Ho. E1 .....43Wb 91
(off Hanbury St.)
Casson St. E1 .....43Wb 91
Casstine Cl. BR8: Hext 66Hd 140
Castalia Ct. DA1: Dart 55Pd 119
Castalia Sq. E14 .....47Ec 92
Castano Ct. WD5: Ab L 3U 12
Castellain Mans. W9 .....42Db 89
(off Castellain Rd.)
Castellain Rd. W9 .....42Db 89
Castellan Av. RM2: Rom 27Kd 57
Castellane Cl. HA7: Stan 24Ha 46
Castell Ho. SE8 .....52Cc 114
Castello Av. SW15 .....57Ya 110
Castell Rd. IG10: Lough 11Sc 36
CASTELNAU 51Xa 110
Castelnau SW13 .....53Wa 110
Castelnau Gdns. SW13 .....51Xa 110
Castelnau Mans. SW13 .....51Xa 110
(off Castelnau)
Castelnau Row SW13 .....51Xa 110
Casterbridge NW6 .....39Db 69
(off Abbey Rd.)
W11 .....44Bb 89
(off Dartmouth Cl.)
Casterbridge Rd. SE3 .....55Jc 115
Casterton St. E8 .....37Xb 71
Castile Ct. EN8: Walt C 6Cc 20
Castile Gdns. WD4: K Lan 1P 11
Castile Rd. SE18 .....49Qc 94
Castillon Rd. SE6 .....61Gc 137
Castlands Rd. SE6 .....61Bc 136
Castleacre W2 .....3D 220
Castle Av. E4 .....22Fc 53
KT17: Ewe 81Wa 174
RM13: Rain 38Gd 76
SL3: Dat 1L 103
UB7: Yiew 45N 83
Castlebar Ct. W5 .....43La 86
Castlebar Hill W5 .....43La 86
Castlebar M. W5 .....43La 86
Castlebar Pk. W5 .....43Ka 86
Castlebar Rd. W5 .....43La 86
Castle Baynard St. EC4 .....4C 224 (45Rb 91)
Castlebrook Cl. SE11 .....5B 230 (49Rb 91)
Castle Bus. Cen. TW12: Hamp 67Da 129
(off Castle M.)
Castle Climbing Cen., The 33Sb 71
Castle Cl. BR2: Brom 69Gc 137
E9 .....36Ac 72
RH1: Blet 5J 209
RH2: Reig 10K 207
RM3: Rom 20Ld 39
SW19 .....62Za 132
TW16: Sun 66U 128
W3 .....47Ra 87
WD23: Bush 16Da 27
Castlecombe Dr. SW19 .....59Za 110
Castlecombe Rd. SE9 .....63Nc 138
Castle Ct. EC3 .....3G 225
SE26 .....63Ac 136
SW15 .....55Ab 110
(off Brewhouse La.)
Castleden Ho. NW3 .....38Fb 69
(off Hilgrove Rd.)
Castledine Rd. SE20 .....66Xb 135
Castle Dr. IG4: Ilf 30Nc 54
RH2: Reig 10J 207
TN15: Kems'g 89Nd 183
Castle Farm Cvn. Site SL4: Wind 4B 102
Castle Farm Rd. TN14: S'ham 81Hd 182
Castlefield Ct. RH2: Reig 6K 207
Castlefield Rd. RH2: Reig 6J 207
Castlefields DA13: Ist R 7B 144
Castleford Av. SE9 .....60Rc 116
Castleford Cl. N17 .....23Vb 51
WD6: Bore 10Pa 15
Castleford Ct. NW8 .....5C 214
Castlegate TW9: Rich 55Pa 109
CASTLE GREEN 5H 167
Castle Grn. KT13: Weyb 76U 150
Castle Green Leisure Cen. 39Zc 75
Castle Gro. Rd. GU24: Chob 5H 167
Castlehaven Rd. NW1 .....38Kb 70
Castle Hgts. RM9: Dag 39Xc 75
CASTLE HILL 59Be 121
Castle Hill DA3: Fawk, Hartl 70Zd 143
SL4: Wind 3H 103
Castle Hill Av. CR0: New Ad 81Dc 178
Castle Hill Local Nature Reserve
.....79Qa 153
Castle Hill Pde. W13 .....45Ka 86
(off The Avenue)
Castle Hill Rd. TW20: Eng G 3M 125
Castle Ho. SM2: Sutt 79Cb 155
SW8 .....52Nb 112
(off Sth. Lambeth Rd.)
Castle Ind. Est. SE17 .....5D 230 (49Sb 91)
Castle La. DA12: Grav'nd 1K 145
SW1 .....3B 228 (48Lb 90)
Castleleigh Ct. EN2: Enf 15Tb 33
Castlemaine Av. CR2: S Croy 78Vb 157
KT17: Ewe 81Xa 174
Castlemain St. E1 .....43Xb 91
Castle Mead HP1: Hem H 4K 3
SE5 .....52Sb 113
Castle M. KT13: Weyb 76U 150
N12 .....22Eb 49
NW1 .....37Kb 70
SW17 .....63Gb 133
TW12: Hamp 67Da 129
(not continuous)
Castle Pde. KT17: Ewe 80Wa 154
Castle Pl. NW1 .....37Kb 70
W4 .....49Ua 88
Castle Point E13 .....40Lc 73
(off Boundary Rd.)
Castlereagh Ho. HA7: Stan 23Ka 46
Castlereagh St. W1 .....2F 221 (44Hb 89)
Castleridge Dr. DA9: Ghithe 58Wd 120
Castle Rd. AL1: St A 2F 6
CR5: Chip 92Gb 195
DA4: Eyns 79Kd 163
DA10: Swans 58Be 121
EN3: Enf H 11Ac 34
GU21: Wok 86B 168
KT13: Weyb 76T 150
KT18: Eps 87Ra 173
N12 .....22Eb 49
NW1 .....37Kb 70
RM9: Dag 39Xc 75
RM17: Grays 51Be 121
TW7: Isle 54Ha 108
UB2: S'hall 48Ba 85
UB5: N'olt 37Da 65
Castle Row W4 .....50Ta 87
Castle Sq. RH1: Blet 5J 209
Castle St. DA9: Ghithe 57Wd 120
DA10: Swans 58Be 121
E6 .....40Lc 73
KT1: King T 68Na 131
RH1: Blet 5H 209
SL1: Slou 8K 81
Castleton Av. DA7: Bex 53Fd 118
HA9: Wemb 35Na 67
Castleton Cl. CR0: C'don 72Ac 158
SM7: Bans 87Cb 175
Castleton Dr. SM7: Bans 87Cb 175
Castleton Gdns. HA9: Wemb 34Na 67
Castleton Ho. E14 .....49Ec 92
(off Pier St.)
Castleton Rd. CR4: Mitc 70Mb 134
E17 .....26Fc 53
HA4: Ruis 32Z 65
IG3: Ilf 32Wc 75
SE9 .....63Mc 137
Castletown Rd. W14 .....50Ab 88
Castle Vw. KT18: Eps 86Ra 173
Castleview Cl. N4 .....33Sb 71
Castleview Gdns. IG1: Ilf 30Nc 54
Castleview Pde. SL3: L'ly 9P 81
Castleview Rd. KT13: Weyb 77R 150
SL3: L'ly 9N 81
Castle Wlk. RH2: Reig 6J 207
TW16: Sun 69Y 129
Castle Way KT17: Ewe 82Wa 174
SW19 .....62Za 132
TW13: Hanw 63Y 129
Castle Wharf E14 .....45Gc 93
(off Orchard Pl.)
Castlewood Dr. SE9 .....54Pc 116
Castlewood Rd. EN4: Cockf 13Fb 31
N15 .....30Wb 51
N16 .....31Wb 71
Castle Yd. N6 .....31Jb 70
SE1 .....6C 224 (46Rb 91)
TW10: Rich 57Ma 109
Castor La. E14 .....45Dc 92
Catalina Av. RM16: Chaf H 47Be 99
Catalina Ct. AL1: St A 2C 6
(off Beaconsfield Rd.)
Catalina Ho. E1 .....44Wb 91
(off Piazza Wlk.)
Catalina Rd. TW6: H'row A 54R 106
Catalin Ct. EN9: Walt A 5Fc 21
(off Howard Cl.)
Catalonia Apartments WD18: Wat 14V 26
(off Metropolitan Sta. App.)
Catalpa Ct. SE13 .....58Fc 115
Caterfield La. RH8: Oxt 10L 211
CATERHAM 96Wb 197
Caterham Av. IG5: Ilf 26Pc 54
Caterham By-Pass CR3: Cat'm 92Xb 197
Caterham Cl. GU24: Pirb 3C 186
Caterham Ct. CR3: Cat'm 96Ub 197
EN9: Walt A 6Hc 21
Caterham Dr. CR5: Coul 90Rb 177
Caterham High School Fitness Cen.
.....26Pc 54
CATERHAM-ON-THE-HILL 94Ub 197
Caterham Rd. SE13 .....55Fc 115
Catesby Ho. E9 .....38Yb 72
(off Frampton Pk. Rd.)
Catesby St. SE17 .....6G 231 (49Tb 91)
CATFORD 59Dc 114
Catford B'way. SE6 .....59Dc 114
CATFORD GYRATORY 59Dc 114
Catford Hill SE6 .....60Bc 114
Catford Island SE6 .....59Dc 114
Catford M. SE6 .....59Dc 114
Catford Rd. SE6 .....59Cc 114
Catford Trad. Est. SE6 .....61Dc 136
Cathall Rd. E11 .....33Fc 73
Catham Cl. AL1: St A 4F 6
Catharine Cl. RM16: Chaf H 47Be 99
Catharine Ho. WD19: Wat 20X 27
Cathay Ho. SE16 .....47Xb 91
Cathay St. SE16 .....47Xb 91
Cathay Wlk. UB5: N'olt 40Ca 65
(off Brabazon Rd.)
Cathcart Dr. BR6: Orp 75Uc 160
Cathcart Hill N19 .....34Lb 70
Cathcart Ho. SW10 .....50Eb 89
(off Cathcart Rd.)
Cathcart Rd. SW10 .....51Db 111
Cathcart St. NW5 .....37Kb 70
Cathedral Ct. AL3: St A 4P 5
Cathedral Lodge EC1 .....7D 218
Cathedral Mans. SW1 .....5B 228
Cathedral Piazza SW1 .....4B 228 (48Lb 90)
Cathedral Pl. CM14: B'wood 19Zd 41
Cathedral St. SE1 .....6F 225 (46Tb 91)
Cathedral Vw. AL3: St A 2B 6
(off High St.)
Cathedral Wlk. SW1 .....3B 228
Catherall Rd. N5 .....34Sb 71
Catherine Cl. CM15: Pil H 15Wd 40
IG10: Lough 16Qb 36
KT14: Byfl 86N 169
NW4 .....28Xa 48
Catherine Ct. IG2: Ilf 29Sc 54
N14 .....15Lb 32
SW3 .....51Fb 111
(off Callow St.)
SW19 .....64Bb 133
Catherine Dr. TW9: Rich 56Na 109
TW16: Sun 65V 128
Catherine Gdns. TW3: Houn 56Fa 108
Catherine Griffiths Ct. EC1 .....5A 218
Catherine Gro. SE10 .....53Dc 114
Catherine Ho. E3 .....40Cc 72
(off Thomas Fyre Dr.)
N1 .....1J 219
Catherine Howard Ct.
KT13: Weyb 76R 150
(off Old Palace Rd.)
SE9 .....58Tc 116
Catherine of Aragon Ct. SE9 .....58Sc 116
Catherine Parr Ct. SE9 .....58Tc 116
Catherine Pl. HA1: Harr 29Ha 46
SW1 .....3B 228 (48Lb 90)
Catherine Rd. EN3: Enf W 9Ac 20
KT6: Surb 71Ma 153
RM2: Rom 29Kd 57
Catherines Cl. UB7: W Dray 47M 83
Catherine St. AL3: St A 1B 6
WC2 .....4H 223 (45Pb 90)
Catherine Wheel All. E1 .....1J 225 (43Ub 91)
Catherine Wheel Rd.
TW8: Bford 52Ma 109
Catherine Wheel Yd. SW1 .....7B 222
Catherwood Ct. N1 .....2F 219
Cat Hill EN4: E Barn 16Gb 31
Cathles Rd. SW12 .....58Kb 112
Cathnor Rd. W12 .....47Xa 88
Catisfield Rd. EN3: Enf W 9Ac 20
Catkin Cl. E14 .....44Fc 93
HP1: Hem H 1K 3
Catkin Ho. RM3: Hrld W 26Nd 57
Catlin Cres. TW17: Shep 71T 150
Catlin Gdns. RH9: G'stone 2P 209
Catling Cl. SE23 .....62Yb 136
Catlin's La. HA5: Eastc 27X 45
Catlin St. HP3: Hem H 5K 3
SE16 .....50Wb 91
Cator Cl. CR0: New Ad 83Gc 179
Cator Cres. CR0: New Ad 83Gc 179
Cator La. BR3: Beck 67Bc 136
Cato Rd. SW4 .....55Mb 112
Cator Rd. SE26 .....65Zb 136
SM5: Cars 78Hb 155
Cator St. SE15 .....52Vb 113
(Commercial Way)
SE15 .....51Vb 113
(Ebley Cl.)
Cato's Hill KT10: Esh 77Da 151
Cato St. W1 .....1E 220 (43Gb 89)

Catsdell Bottom—Centre Rd.

Catsdell Bottom HP3: Hem H 5B 4
Catsey La. WD23: Bush 17Ea 28
Catsey Woods WD23: Bush 17Ea 28
Catterick Cl. N11 23Jb 50
Catterick Way WD6: Bore 11Pa 29
Cattistock Rd. SE9 64Nc 138
CATTLEGATE 5Nb 18
Cattlegate Cotts. EN6: N'thaw 3Mb 18
Cattlegate Hill
EN6: Cuff, N'thaw 4Mb 18
Cattlegate Rd. EN2: Crew H 6Nb 18
EN6: Cuff, N'thaw 3Mb 18
Cattley Cl. EN5: Barn 14Ab 30
Cattlins Cl. EN7: Chesh 1Ub 19
Catton St. WC1 1H 223 (43Pb 90)
Cattsdell HP2: Hem H 1N 3
Catwalk Pl. N15 30Tb 51
Caudwell Ter. SW18 58Fb 111
Caughley Ho. SE11 4K 229
Caulfield Ct. *NW1* *38Lb 70*
(off Baynes St.)
Caulfield Gdns. HA5: Pinn 26Y 45
Caulfield Rd. E6 39Nc 74
SE15 54Xb 113
W3 48Sa 87
Causeway, The EN6: Pot B 3Eb 17
(not continuous)
KT9: Chess 77Na 153
KT10: Clay 80Ha 152
N2 28Gb 49
SM2: Sutt 81Eb 175
SM5: Cars 76Jb 156
SW18 57Db 111
SW19 64Ya 132
TW4: Houn 56W 106
TW11: Tedd 65Ha 130
TW14: Felt, Houn 56W 106
TW18: Staines 63E 126
Causeway Cl. EN6: Pot B 3Fb 17
Causeway Corporate Cen.
TW18: Staines 63E 126
Causeway Ct. GU21: Wok 10K 167
Causeway Ho. BR6: Orp 74Wc 161
WD5: Ab L 3U 12
Causeyware Rd. N9 17Xb 34
Causton Cotts. *E14* *44Ac 92*
(off Galsworthy Av.)
Causton Ho. SE5 51Sb 113
SW9 53Pb 112
Causton Rd. N6 31Kb 70
Causton Sq. RM10: Dag 38Cd 76
Causton St. SW1 6E 228 (49Mb 90)
Cautley Av. SW4 57Lb 112
Cavalier Cl. RM6: Chad H 28Zc 55
Cavalier Ct. KT5: Surb 72Pa 153
Cavalier Gdns. UB3: Hayes 44T 84
Cavalier Ter. SE7 51Lc 115
Cavalli Apartments
WD18: Wat *14U 26*
(off Moderna M.)
Cavalry Cres. SL4: Wind 5G 102
TW4: Houn 56Z 107
Cavalry Gdns. SW15 57Bb 111
Cavalry Memorial 7H 221 (46Jb 90)
Cavalry Pl. E17 26Zb 52
Cavalry Sq.
SW3 6G 227 (50Hb 89)
Cavan Ct. AL10: Hat 1C 8
Cavan Pl. HA5: Hat E 25Ba 45
Cavatina Point *SE8* *51Dc 114*
(off Copperas St.)
Cavaye Ho. *SW10* *51Eb 111*
(off Cavaye Pl.)
Cavaye Pl. SW10 50Eb 89
Cavell Cres. DA1: Dart 56Qd 119
RM3: Hrld W 26Nd 57
Cavell Dr. EN2: Enf 12Qb 32
Cavell Ho. *N1* *39Ub 71*
(off Colville Est.)
Cavell Rd. N17 24Tb 51
Cavell St. E1 43Xb 91
Cavell Way GU21: Knap 1G 186
KT19: Eps 83Qa 173
Cavendish Av. DA8: Erith 51Ed 118
DA15: Sidc 59Wc 117
DA16: Well 55Vc 117
HA1: Harr 35Fa 66
HA4: Ruis 36X 65
IG8: Wfd G 25Kc 53
KT3: N Mald 71Wa 154
N3 26Cb 49
NW8 2C 214 (40Fb 69)
RM12: Horn 37Kd 77
TN13: S'oaks 94Jd 202
W13 43Ja 86
Cavendish Cl. N18 22Xb 51
NW6 37Bb 69
NW8 3C 214 (41Fb 89)
TW16: Sun 65V 128
UB4: Hayes 43U 84
Cavendish Ct. EC3 2J 225
HP3: Hem H 7N 3
KT13: Weyb 79S 150
KT16: Chert *74J 149*
(off Victory Rd.)
SE6 *60Dc 114*
(off Bromley Rd.)
SL3: Poyle 53G 104
SM6: Wall 79Kb 156
TW16: Sun 65V 128
WD3: Crox G 15T 26
Cavendish Cres. RM12: Horn 37Kd 77
WD6: E'tree 14Qa 29
Cavendish Dr. E11 32Fc 73
HA8: Edg 23Pa 47
KT10: Clay 78Ga 152
Cavendish Gdns. IG1: Ilf 32Qc 74
IG11: Bark 36Uc 74
RH1: Redh 5A 208
RM6: Chad H 29Ad 55
RM15: Avel 47Sd 98
SW4 58Lb 112
Cavendish Ho. *CR0: C'don* *74Tb 157*
(off Tavistock Rd.)
KT12: Hers 78Y 151
NW8 2C 214
NW9 27Va 48
SW1 4E 228
UB7: W Dray *47P 83*
(off Park Lodge Av.)
W1 1B 222
Cavendish Mans. EC1 6K 217
NW6 36Cb 69
Cavendish Meads SL5: S'hill 2B 146
Cavendish M. Nth.
W1 7A 216 (43Kb 90)
Cavendish M. Sth.
W1 1A 222 (43Kb 90)
Cavendish Pde. *SW4* *58Kb 112*
(off Clapham Comn. Sth. Side)
TW4: Houn 54Aa 107
Cavendish Pl. *AL10: Hat* *1B 8*
(off Aldykes)
BR1: Brom 70Pc 138
NW2 37Za 68
SW4 57Mb 112
W1 2A 222 (44Kb 90)
Cavendish Rd. AL1: St A 2D 6
CR0: C'don 74Rb 157
E4 23Ec 52
EN5: Barn 13Ya 30
GU22: Wok 1P 187
KT3: N Mald 70Va 132
KT13: Weyb 81R 170
N4 30Rb 51
N18 22Xb 51
NW6 38Ab 68
RH1: Redh 6A 208
SM2: Sutt 80Eb 155
SW12 58Kb 112
SW19 66Fb 133
TW16: Sun 65V 128
W4 53Sa 109
Cavendish Sq. DA3: Lfield 69Zd 143
W1 2A 222 (44Kb 90)
Cavendish St. N1 2F 219 (40Tb 71)
Cavendish Ter. E3 41Bc 92
TW13: Felt 61W 128
Cavendish Wlk. KT19: Eps 83Ra 173
Cavendish Way AL10: Hat 1B 8
BR4: W W'ck 74Dc 158
Cavenham Cl. GU22: Wok 91A 188
Cavenham Gdns. IG1: Ilf 34Tc 74
RM11: Horn 29Ld 57
Caverleigh Pl. BR1: Brom 68Lc 137
Caverleigh Way
KT4: Wor Pk 74Wa 154
Cave Rd. E13 41Kc 93
TW10: Ham 63La 130
Caversham Av. N13 20Qb 32
SM3: Cheam 75Ab 154
Caversham Ct. *N11* *20Jb 32*
(off Brunswick Pk. Rd.)
Caversham Ho.
KT1: King T *68Na 131*
(off Lady Booth Rd.)
N15 *28Sb 51*
(off Caversham Rd.)
SE15 *51Wb 113*
(off Haymerle Rd.)
Caversham M. *SW3* *51Hb 111*
(off Caversham St.)
Caversham Rd. KT1: King T 68Pa 131
N15 28Sb 51
NW5 37Lb 70
NW9 27Wa 48
Caversham St. SW3 51Hb 111
Caverswall St. W12 44Ya 88
Caveside Cl. BR7: Chst 67Qc 138
Cavesson Ho. *E20* *36Ec 72*
(off Ribbons Wlk.)
Cavour Ho. SE17 7C 230
Cawcott Dr. SL4: Wind 3C 102
Cawdor Av. RM15: S Ock 45Xd 98
Cawdor Cres. W7 49Ja 86
Cawdor Ho. CM14: W'ley 21Zd 59
Cawdor Wlk. E14 44Ec 92
Cawnpore St. SE19 64Ub 135
Cawsey Way GU21: Wok 89A 168
Cawston Ct. BR1: Brom 66Hc 137
Caxton Av. KT15: Add 79J 149
Caxton Ct. DA3: Hartl 69Be 143
Caxton Ct. EN8: Walt C 7Ac 20
SW11 54Gb 111
Caxton Dr. UB8: Uxb 40M 63
Caxton Gro. E3 41Cc 92
Caxton Hall SW1 3D 228
Caxton La. RH8: Limp 3P 211
Caxton M. TW8: Bford 51Ma 109
Caxton Pk. DA11: Nflt 61Ee 143
Caxton Pl. IG1: Ilf 34Qc 74
Caxton Ri. RH1: Redh 5A 208
Caxton Rd. N22 26Pb 50
SW19 64Eb 133
UB2: S'hall 48Z 85
W12 47Za 88
Caxtons, The *SW9* *52Rb 113*
(off Langton Rd.)
Caxton St. SW1 3C 228 (48Lb 90)
Caxton St. Nth. E16 44Hc 93
Caxton Trad. Est.
UB3: Hayes 47U 84
Caxton Wlk. WC2 3E 222 (44Mb 90)
Caxton Way RM1: Rom 28Gd 56
WD18: Wat 17T 26
Cayenne Ct. SE1 7K 225 (47Vb 91)
Caygill Cl. BR2: Brom 70Hc 137
Cayley Rd. UB2: S'hall 48Da 85
Cayton Pl. EC1 4F 219
Cayton Rd. CR5: Coul 94Lb 196
UB6: G'frd 40Ga 66
Cayton St. EC1 4F 219 (41Tb 91)
Cazenove Rd. E17 25Cc 52
N16 33Vb 71
Cearns Ho. E6 39Mc 73
Cearn Way CR5: Coul 87Pb 176
Cecil Av. EN1: Enf 14Vb 33
HA9: Wemb 36Pa 67
IG11: Bark 38Tc 74
RM11: Horn 27Nd 57
RM16: Chaf H 47Be 99
Cecil Cl. KT9: Chess 77Ma 153
TW15: Ashf 66S 128
W5 43Ma 87
Cecil Ct. CR0: C'don 75Vb 157
EN2: Enf 14Tb 33
EN5: Barn 13Za 30
EN8: Chesh 4Ac 20
NW6 38Db 69
SW10 *51Eb 111*
(off Fawcett St.)
WC2 4F 223 (45Nb 90)
Cecile Pk. N8 30Nb 50
Cecil Gro. NW8 1E 214 (39Gb 69)
Cecil Hepworth Playhouse, The
74V 150
(off Hepworth Way)
Cecil Ho. E17 25Cc 52
Cecilia Cl. N2 27Eb 49
Cecilia Rd. E8 36Vb 71
Cecil Manning Cl.
UB6: G'frd 39Ja 66
Cecil Mans. SW17 61Jb 134
Cecil Pk. HA5: Pinn 28Aa 45
Cecil Pl. CR4: Mitc 71Hb 155
Cecil Rhodes Ho. NW1 1D 216
Cecil Rd. AL1: St A 2D 6
CR0: C'don 72Nb 156
DA11: Grav'nd 10B 122
E11 34Hc 73
E13 39Jc 73
E17 25Cc 52
EN2: Enf 13Sb 33
EN6: S Mim 4Wa 16
EN8: Chesh 4Ac 20
HA3: W'stone 27Ga 46
IG1: Ilf 35Rc 74
N10 26Kb 50
N14 18Lb 32
NW9 27Ua 48
NW10 39Ua 68
RM6: Chad H 31Zc 75
SL0: Iver 44G 82
SM1: Sutt 79Bb 155
SW19 66Db 133
TW3: Houn 54Ea 108
TW15: Ashf 66S 128
W3 43Sa 87
Cecil Rosen Ct. HA0: Wemb 34Ka 66
WD23: B Hea 18Ga 28
Cecil Sharp House *39Jb 70*
(off Gloucester Av.)
Cecil St. WD24: Wat 10X 13
Cecil Way BR2: Hayes 74Jc 159
SL2: Slou 2D 80
Cedar Av. DA12: Grav'nd 3E 144
DA15: Sidc 59Wc 117
EN3: Enf H 12Yb 34
EN4: E Barn 17Gb 31
EN8: Walt C 5Zb 20
HA4: Ruis 36Y 65
KT11: Cobh 87Y 171
RM6: Chad H 29Ad 55
RM14: Upm 35Qd 77
TW2: Whitt 58Da 107
UB3: Hayes 44W 84
UB7: Yiew 45P 83
Cedar Cl. BR2: Brom 76Nc 160
BR8: Swan 68Ed 140
CM13: Hut 17Fe 41
CR6: W'ham 91Ac 198
E3 39Bc 72
EN6: Pot B 2Cb 17
IG1: Ilf 36Tc 74
IG9: Buck H 19Mc 35
KT8: E Mos 70Ga 130
KT10: Esh 79Ba 151
KT17: Eps 86Va 174
RH2: Reig 8L 207
RM7: Rom 28Ed 56
SE21 60Sb 113
SL0: Iver H 39E 62
SL1: Burn 2A 80
SM5: Cars 79Hb 155
SW15 63Ta 131
TW18: Lale 69L 127
Cedar Copse BR1: Brom 68Pc 138
Cedar Ct. AL4: St A 2H 7
CM16: Epp 3Wc 23
E11 29Kc 53
E18 25Jc 53
KT15: Add 77L 149
KT16: Ott 78E 148
KT22: Fet 94Ja 192
N1 38Sb 71
N10 26Jb 50
N11 22Lb 50
N20 18Fb 31
SE1 2J 231
SE7 51Lc 115
SE9 58Nc 116
SE13 56Fc 115
SL4: Wind 4E 102
SM2: Sutt 79Eb 155
SW19 62Za 132
TW8: Bford 51La 108
TW20: Egh 63C 126
WD25: Wat *5Z 13*
(off Lych Ga.)
Cedar Cres. BR2: Brom 76Nc 160
WD23: Bush 13Z 27
Cedarcroft Rd. KT9: Chess 77Pa 153
Cedar Dr. DA4: Sut H 68Rd 141
HA5: Hat E 23Ca 45
IG10: Lough 13Rc 36
KT22: Fet 95Ga 192
N2 28Gb 49
SL5: S'dale 3E 146
SL5: S'hill 10H 125
Cedar Gdns. GU21: Wok 10M 167
GU24: Chob 2K 167
RM14: Upm 34Sd 78
SM2: Sutt 79Eb 155
Cedar Grange EN1: Enf 15Ub 33
Cedar Gro. DA5: Bexl 58Zc 117
GU24: Bisl 7E 166
KT13: Weyb 77S 150
UB1: S'hall 43Ca 85
W5 48Na 87
Cedar Hgts. NW2 37Bb 69
TW10: Ham 60Na 109
Cedar Hill KT18: Eps 88Sa 173
Cedar Ho. CR8: Purl 84Nb 176
E2 *40Xb 71*
(off Mowlem St.)
E14 *47Ec 92*
(off Manchester Rd.)
KT22: Lea 91Ha 192
N22 *25Qb 50*
(off Acacia Rd.)
SE14 53Zb 114
SE16 *47Zb 92*
(off Woodland Cres.)
SW6 *54Eb 111*
(off Lensbury Av.)
TW9: Kew 53Ra 109
TW16: Sun *66V 128*
(off Spelthorne Gro.)
UB4: Yead 42Y 85
W8 *48Db 89*
(off Marloes Rd.)
Cedarhurst BR1: Brom 66Gc 137
Cedarhurst Cotts.
DA5: Bexl 59Cd 118
Cedarhurst Dr. SE9 57Lc 115
Cedarland Ter. SW20 66Xa 132
Cedar Lawn Av. EN5: Barn 15Ab 30
Cedar Lodge SL5: S'dale 2C 146
Cedar M. SE4 55Bc 114
SW15 57Za 110
Cedar Mt. SE9 60Mc 115
Cedarne Rd. SW6 52Db 111
Cedar Pk. CR3: Cat'm 93Ub 197
IG7: Chig 21Qc 54
Cedar Pk. Gdns. RM6: Chad H 31Zc 75
SW19 64Xa 132
Cedar Pk. Rd. EN2: Enf 10Sb 19
Cedar Pl. HA6: Nwood 23S 44
KT11: Cobh 86X 171
SE7 50Lc 93
Cedar Ri. N14 17Jb 32
RM15: S Ock 42Yd 98
Cedar Rd. AL10: Hat 1C 8
BR1: Brom 68Lc 137
CM13: Hut 16Fe 41
CR0: C'don 75Tb 157
DA1: Dart 60Md 119
DA8: Erith 53Jd 118
EN2: Enf 10Rb 19
GU22: Wok 2M 187
HP4: Berk 2A 2
KT8: E Mos 70Ga 130
KT11: Cobh 86X 171
KT13: Weyb 77Q 150
N17 25Vb 51
NW2 35Ya 68
RM7: Rom 28Ed 56
RM12: Horn 34Ld 77
RM16: Grays 8C 100
SM2: Sutt 79Eb 155
TW4: Cran 54Y 107
TW11: Tedd 64Ja 130
TW14: Bedf 60T 106
WD19: Wat 16Y 27
Cedars SM7: Bans 86Hb 175
SS17: Stan H 1N 101
Cedars, The AL3: St A 1A 6
E9 *38Zb 72*
(off Banbury Rd.)
E15 38Hc 73
EN9: Walt A *7Lc 21*
(within Woodbine Cl. Caravan Pk.)
GU24: Pirb 4B 186
HP4: Berk 1A 2
IG9: Buck H 18Jc 35
KT14: Byfl 84P 169
KT22: Lea 93Ma 193
KT23: Bookh 98Ea 192
RH2: Reig 6M 207
SL2: Slou 1D 80
SL3: Dat 3N 103
SM6: Wall 77Lb 156
TW11: Tedd 65Ha 130
W13 44La 86
WD3: Rick 17M 25
Cedars Av. CR4: Mitc 70Jb 134
E17 29Cc 52
WD3: Rick 18L 25
Cedars Cl. NW4 27Za 48
SE13 55Fc 115
SL9: Chal P 22A 42
WD6: Bore 14Ra 29
Cedars Ct. N9 19Ub 33
Cedars Dr. UB10: Hil 40P 63
Cedars Ho. E17 27Dc 52
WD3: Chor 14H 25
Cedars M. SW4 56Kb 112
(not continuous)
Cedars Rd. BR3: Beck 68Ac 136
CR0: Bedd 76Nb 156
E15 37Gc 73
KT1: Hamp W 67La 130
N9 19Wb 33
N21 19Rb 33
SM4: Mord 70Cb 133
SW4 55Kb 112
SW13 54Wa 110
W4 50Sa 87
Cedars Wlk. WD3: Chor 14H 25
Cedar Ter. TW9: Rich 56Na 109
Cedar Ter. Rd. TN13: S'oaks 95Ld 203
Cedar Tree Gro. SE27 64Rb 135
Cedar Vw. *KT1: King T* *69Ma 131*
(off Milner Rd.)
Cedarville Gdns. SW16 65Pb 134
Cedar Wlk. CR8: Kenley 88Sb 177
EN9: Walt A 6Fc 21
HP3: Hem H 4M 3
KT10: Clay 79Ha 152
KT20: Tad 92Ab 194
Cedar Way HP4: Berk 2A 2
N1 38Mb 70
SL3: L'ly 50A 82
TW16: Sun 66U 128
Cedar Way Ind. Est. N1 38Mb 70
Cedar Wood Dr. WD25: Wat 7X 13
Cedarwood Dr. AL4: St A 2H 7
Cedra Ct. N16 32Wb 71
Cedric Av. RM1: Rom 27Gd 56
Cedric Chambers NW8 5B 214
Cedric Rd. SE9 62Sc 138
Celadon Cl. EN3: Enf H 13Ac 34
Celandine Cl. E14 43Cc 92
RM15: S Ock 42Yd 98
Celandine Ct. E4 20Dc 34
Celandine Dr. E8 38Vb 71
SE28 46Xc 95
Celandine Gro. N14 15Lb 32
Celandine Rd. KT12: Hers 77Aa 151
Celandine Way E15 41Gc 93
Celbridge M. W2 43Db 89
Celebration Av. E20 36Ec 72
Celebration Way E4 23Ec 52
Celedon Cl. RM16: Chaf H 48Ae 99
Celestial Gdns. SE13 56Fc 115
Celia Av. *TN15: W King* *80Ud 164*
(off London Rd.)
Celia Cres. TW15: Ashf 65M 127
Celia Ho. N1 2H 219
Celia Johnson Ho. WD6: Bore 11Sa 29
Celia Rd. N19 35Lb 70
Cell Barnes Cl. AL1: St A 4F 6
Cell Barnes La. AL1: St A 3E 6
(not continuous)
Cell Farm Av. SL4: Old Win 7M 103
Celtic Av. BR2: Brom 69Gc 137
Celtic Farm Rd. RM13: Rain 42Jd 96
Celtic Rd. KT14: Byfl 86N 169
Celtic St. E14 43Dc 92
Cement Block Cotts.
RM17: Grays 51Ee 121
Cemetery Hill HP1: Hem H 3L 3
Cemetery La. SE7 51Nc 116
TW17: Shep 73R 150
Cemetery Pales GU24: Brkwd 4D 186
Cemetery Rd. E7 36Hc 73
N17 24Ub 51
SE2 52Xc 117
Cemetery Way E4 20Cc 34
Cemmaes Ct. Rd. HP1: Hem H 2L 3
Cemmaes Mdw. HP1: Hem H 2L 3
Cenacle Cl. NW3 34Cb 69
Cenotaph 1F 229 (47Nb 90)
Centaur Ct. TW8: Bford 50Na 87
Centaurs Bus. Pk. TW7: Isle 51Ja 108
Centaur St. SE1 3J 229 (48Pb 90)
Centaurus Sq. AL2: F'mre 9C 6
Centenary Cl. TN13: Dun G 92Gd 202
Centenary Ct. DA4: Farni 73Qd 163
RH1: Redh *5P 207*
(off Warwick Rd.)
Centenary Rd. EN3: Brim 14Bc 34
Centenary Trad. Est. EN3: Brim 13Bc 34
Centennial Av. WD6: E'tree 17Ka 28
Centennial Ct. WD6: E'tree 17La 28
Centennial Pk. WD6: E'tree 17La 28
Central Apartments HA9: Wemb 36Na 67
Central Arc. *TW15: Ashf* *63P 127*
(off Woodthorpe Rd.)
Central Av. DA12: Grav'nd 1D 144
DA16: Well 54Vc 117
E11 33Fc 73
EN1: Enf 12Xb 33
EN8: Walt C 5Ac 20
HA5: Pinn 30Ba 45
KT8: W Mole 70Ba 129
N2 26Fb 49
N9 20Ub 33
RM15: Avel 47Sd 98
RM18: Tilb 3C 122
RM20: W Thur 50Vd 98
SM6: Wall 78Nb 156
SW6 55Eb 111
SW11 52Hb 111
TW3: Houn 56Ea 108
UB3: Hayes 46V 84
Central Bus. Cen. NW10 36Ua 68
Central Cir. NW4 29Xa 48
Central Ct. KT15: Add 77L 149
Central Courtyard EC2 1J 225
Central Criminal Court
Old Bailey 2C 224 (44Rb 91)
Central Dr. AL4: St A 1G 6
RM12: Horn 34Nd 77
SL1: Slou 5D 80
Centrale Shop. Cen. CR0: C'don 75Sb 157
Central Gallery *IG1: Ilf* *33Rc 74*
(within The Exchange)
Central Gdns. SM4: Mord 71Db 155
Central Hgts. *WD18: Wat* *14V 26*
(off Manhattan Av.)
Central Hill SE19 64Tb 135
Central Ho. E15 40Dc 72
IG11: Bark 38Sc 74
Central Lodge TN15: Wro 85Fe 185
Central London Golf Course 61Fb 133
Central Mall *SW18* *58Db 111*
(within Southside Shop. Cen.)
Central Mans. *NW4* *29Xa 48*
(off Watford Way)
Central Markets (Smithfield) 1B 224
Central Pde. CR0: New Ad 82Ec 178
DA15: Sidc 62Wc 139
E17 28Cc 52
EN3: Enf H 12Yb 34
HA1: Harr 29Ha 46
IG2: Ilf 30Tc 54
KT6: Surb 72Na 153
KT8: W Mole 70Ba 129
RH1: Redh 5P 207
SE20 *66Zb 136*
(off High St.)
TW5: Hest 52Ba 107
TW14: Felt 59Y 107
UB6: G'frd 41Ja 86
W3 47Ra 87
Central Pk. NW10 41Sa 87
Central Pk. Arena 60Nd 119
Central Pk. Av. RM10: Dag 34Dd 76
Central Pk. Est. TW4: Houn 57Z 107
Central Pk. Leisure Cen. 22Nd 57
Central Pk. Rd. E6 40Mc 73
Central Pl. SE25 71Wb 157
Central Rd. DA1: Dart 57Nd 119
HA0: Wemb 36Ka 66
KT4: Wor Pk 74Wa 154
SM4: Mord 72Cb 155
SS17: Stan H 2M 101
Central St Giles Piazza WC2 2E 222
Central St Martins College of Art & Design
Byam Shaw Campus 33Mb 70
Central School Path SW14 55Sa 109
Central Sq. *HA9: Wemb* *36Na 67*
(off High Rd.)
KT8: W Mole 71Ba 151
NW11 30Db 49
Central Stores IG10: Lough 16Pc 36
Central St. EC1 3D 218 (41Sb 91)
Central Ter. BR3: Beck 69Zb 136
Central Wlk. KT19: Eps 85Ta 173
Central Walkway *N19* *35Mb 70*
(off Pleshey Rd.)
Central Way HA6: Nwood 24U 44
NW10 41Sa 87
RH8: Oxt 99Fc 199
SE28 46Wc 95
SM5: Cars 80Gb 155
TW14: Felt 57W 106
Central W. UB6: G'frd 42Ea 86
Central Wharf *E14* *44Cc 92*
(off Thomas Rd.)
Centre, The
Carpenders Pk. 20Y 27
Slough 5G 80
Centre, The KT12: Walt T 74W 150
TW3: Houn 55Da 107
TW13: Felt 60X 107
Centre Av. CM16: Epp 4Vc 23
W3 46Ta 87
Centre Cl. CM16: Epp 4Vc 23
Centre Comn. Rd.
BR7: Chst 65Sc 138
Centre Ct. Shop. Cen. SW19 65Bb 133
Centre Dr. CM16: Epp 4Vc 23
Cen. For the Magic Arts, The 5C 216
Cen. for Wildlife Gardening Vis. Cen.
55Vb 113
Centre Grn. CM16: Epp 4Vc 23
Centre Hgts. *NW3* *38Fb 69*
(off Finchley Rd.)
Cen. of the Cell *43Xb 91*
(off Newark St.)
Cen. Point SE1 50Wb 91
Centrepoint WC2 2E 222
Cen. Point Ho. WC2 2E 222
Centre Rd. DA3: Nw A G 76Ae 165
E7 33Jc 73
E11 33Jc 73
RM10: Dag 40Dd 76
SL4: Wind 2A 102

Centre Sq.—Chapman Ho.

Centre Sq. SW18 57Cb 111
(off Buckhold Rd.)
Centre St. E2 40Xb 71
Centre Vw. Apartments
CR0: C'don 76Sb 157
(off Whitgift St.)
Centre Way E17 24Ec 52
N9 19Yb 34
Centreway IG1: Ilf 33Sc 74
(off High Rd.)
Centreway Apartments IG1: Ilf 33Sc 74
(off Axon Pl.)
Centric Cl. NW1 39Jb 70
Centrillion Point CR0: C'don 77Sb 157
(off Mason's Av.)
Centrium AL1: St A 4A 6
GU22: Wok 89B 168
Centro Ct. E6 42Pc 94
Centurion Bldg. SW8 51Kb 112
Centurion Cl. N7 38Pb 70
Centurion Ct. AL1: St A 3E 6
(off Camp Rd.)
SE18 49Qc 94
SM6: Wall 75Kb 156
Centurion Ho. UB3: Hayes 44T 84
Centurion La. E3 39Bc 72
Centurion Sq. SE18 53Nc 116
Centurion Way DA18: Erith 48Bd 95
RM19: Purf 49Pd 97
(not continuous)
Centuryan Pl. DA1: Cray 56Kd 119
Century Cl. AL3: St A 1A 6
NW4 29Za 48
Century Ct. GU21: Wok 88B 168
NW8 4C 214
WD18: Wat 17S 26
Century Gdns. CR2: Sande 85Wb 177
Century Ho. HA9: Wemb 33Pa 67
SM7: Bans 87Db 175
SW15 56Za 110
Century M. E5 35Yb 72
N5 34Rb 71
(off Conewood St.)
Century Pk. WD17: Wat 15Y 27
Century Plaza HA8: Edg 23Qa 47
(off Station Rd.)
Century Rd. E17 27Ac 52
TW18: Staines 64E 126
Century Way BR3: Beck 65Bc 136
GU24: Brkwd 1B 186
Century Yd. SE23 61Yb 136
(not continuous)
Cephas Av. E1 42Yb 92
Cephas Ho. E1 42Yb 92
(off Doveton St.)
Cephas St. E1 42Yb 92
Ceres Rd. SE18 49Vc 95
Ceres Vw. TN16: Big H 86Lc 179
Cerise Apartments E3 39Ac 72
(off Gunmaker's La.)
Cerise Rd. SE15 53Wb 113
Cerne Cl. UB4: Yead 45Y 85
Cerne Rd. DA12: Grav'nd 3G 144
SM4: Mord 72Eb 155
Cerney M. W2 4B 220 (45Fb 89)
Cerotus Pl. KT16: Chert 73H 149
Cervantes Ct. HA6: Nwood 24V 44
W2 44Db 89
W11 44Ab 88
(off Rushton M.)
Cervia Way DA12: Grav'nd 2H 145
Cester St. E2 39Wb 71
Ceylon Rd. W14 48Za 88
Ceylon Wharf Apartments SE16 47Yb 92
(off St Marychurch St.)
Cezanne Rd. WD25: Wat 8Z 13
CFGS Community Performing Arts & Sports Cen. 41Bc 92
Chabot Dr. SE15 55Xb 113
Chace Av. EN6: Pot B 4Fb 17
Chadacre Av. IG5: Ilf 27Pc 54
Chadacre Ct. E15 39Jc 73
(off Vicars Cl.)
Chadacre Ho. SW9 56Rb 113
(off Loughborough Pk.)
Chadacre Rd. KT17: Ewe 79Xa 154
Chadbourn St. E14 43Dc 92
Chadbury Ct. NW7 25Wa 48
Chad Cres. N9 20Yb 34
Chadd Dr. BR1: Brom 69Nc 138
Chadd Grn. E13 39Jc 73
(not continuous)
Chadfields RM18: Tilb 2C 122
Chadston Ho. N1 38Rb 71
(off Halton Rd.)
Chadswell WC1 4G 217
Chadview Ct. RM6: Chad H 31Zc 75
Chadville Gdns. RM6: Chad H 29Zc 55
Chadway RM8: Dag 32Yc 75
Chadwell Av. EN8: Chesh 1Yb 20
RM6: Chad H 31Xc 75
Chadwell By-Pass RM16: Grays 10B 100
CHADWELL HEATH 31Zc 75
Chadwell Heath Ind. Pk.
RM8: Dag 32Zc 75
Chadwell Heath La. RM6: Chad H 28Xc 55
Chadwell Hill RM16: Grays 10D 100
Chadwell Ho. SE17 7G 231
Chadwell La. N8 27Pb 50
Chadwell Rd. RM17: Grays 49Ee 99
CHADWELL ST MARY 8D 100
Chadwell St. EC1 3A 218 (41Qb 90)
Chadwick Av. E4 21Fc 53
N21 15Pb 32
SW19 65Cb 133
Chadwick Cl. DA11: Nflt 1A 144
SW15 59Va 110
TW11: Tedd 65Ja 130
W7 43Ha 86
Chadwick Ct. E14 44Cc 92
(off Jonzen Wlk.)
Chadwick Dr. RM3: Hrld W 26Md 57
Chadwick Gdns. UB8: Uxb 38N 63
Chadwick M. W4 51Ra 109
Chadwick Pl. KT6: Surb 73La 152
Chadwick Rd. E11 30Gc 53
IG1: Ilf 34Rc 74
NW10 39Va 68
SE15 54Vb 113
SL3: L'ly 7P 81
Chadwick St. SW1 4E 228 (48Mb 90)
Chadwick Way SE28 45Zc 95
Chadwin Rd. E13 43Kc 93
Chadworth Ho. EC1 4D 218
N4 32Sb 71
Chadworth Way KT10: Clay 78Fa 152
Chaffers Mead KT21: Asht 88Pa 173
Chaffinch Av. CR0: C'don 72Zb 158
Chaffinch Bus. Pk. BR3: Beck 70Zb 136
Chaffinch Cl. CR0: C'don 71Zb 158
KT6: Surb 76Qa 153
N9 18Zb 34
Chaffinches Grn.
HP3: Hem H 6A 4
Chaffinch La. WD18: Wat 17V 26
Chaffinch Rd. BR3: Beck 67Ac 136
Chafford CM14: B'wood 18Xd 40
Chafford Gdns. CM13: W H'dn 30Fe 59
Chafford Gorges Nature Pk. 48Zd 99
Chafford Gorges Vis. Cen. 48Zd 99
CHAFFORD HUNDRED 48Be 99
Chafford Sports Complex 43Ld 97
Chafford Wlk. RM13: Rain 40Ld 77
Chafford Way RM6: Chad H 28Yc 55
RM16: Grays 46Ce 99
Chagford Ho. E3 41Dc 92
(off Talwin St.)
Chagford St. NW1 6F 215 (42Hb 89)
Chailey Av. EN1: Enf 12Vb 33
Chailey Cl. TW5: Hest 53Z 107
Chailey Ind. Est. UB3: Hayes 47W 84
Chailey Pl. KT12: Hers 77Aa 151
Chailey St. E5 34Yb 72
Chairman's Wlk. UB9: Den 29H 43
Chalbury Wlk. N1 1J 217 (40Pb 70)
Chalcombe Rd. SE2 48Xc 95
Chalcot Cl. SM2: Sutt 80Cb 155
Chalcot Cres. NW1 39Hb 69
Chalcot Gdns. NW3 37Hb 69
Chalcot M. SW16 62Nb 134
Chalcot Rd. NW1 38Jb 70
Chalcot Sq. NW1 38Jb 70
(not continuous)
Chalcott SL1: Slou 8J 81
Chalcott Gdns. KT6: Surb 74La 152
Chalcroft Rd. SE13 57Gc 115
CHALDON 96Qb 196
Chaldon Cl. RH1: Redh 8N 207
Chaldon Comn. Rd. CR3: Cat'm 96Sb 197
Chaldon Ct. SE19 68Tb 135
Chaldon Path CR7: Thor H 70Rb 135
Chaldon Rd. CR3: Cat'm 96Tb 197
SW6 52Ab 110
Chaldon Way CR5: Coul 89Nb 176
Chale Ct. SS17: Stan H 3L 101
Chale Rd. SW2 58Nb 112
Chalet Cl. DA5: Bexl 63Fd 140
TW15: Ashf 65T 128
Chalet Ct. CR7: Thor H 71Sb 157
Chalet Est. NW7 21Wa 48
Chale Wlk. SM2: Sutt 81Db 175
Chalfont Av. HA9: Wemb 37Ra 67
HP6: L Chal 11A 24
Chalfont Cen. For Epilepsy
SL9: Chal P 22B 42
CHALFONT COMMON 22B 42
Chalfont Ct. HA1: Harr 30Ha 46
(off Northwick Pk. Rd.)
NW1 6G 215
NW9 27Va 48
Chalfont Grn. N9 20Ub 33
Chalfont Ho. SE16 48Xb 91
(off Keetons Rd.)
WD18: Wat 16U 26
Chalfont La. WD3: Chor 15D 24
WD3: W Hyd 23E 42
Chalfont M. SW19 60Bb 111
UB10: Hil 38R 64
Chalfont Pk. 27B 42
Chalfont Pk. SL9: Chal P 26A 42
Chalfont Pl. AL1: St A 2C 6
Chalfont Rd. HP8: Chal G, Map C 19D 24
N9 20Ub 33
SE25 69Vb 135
UB3: Hayes 47W 84
WD3: Map C 19D 24
CHALFONT ST PETER 25A 42
Chalfont St Peter By-Pass
SL9: Chal P, Ger X 25A 42
Chalfont Wlk. HA5: Pinn 26Y 45
Chalfont Way W13 48Ka 86
Chalford NW6 37Eb 69
(off Finchley Rd.)
Chalford Cl. KT8: W Mole 70Ca 129
Chalforde Gdns. RM2: Rom 28Kd 57
Chalford Rd. SE21 63Tb 135
Chalford Wlk. IG8: Wfd G 25Mc 53
Chalgrove Av. SM4: Mord 71Cb 155
Chalgrove Cres. IG5: Ilf 26Nc 54
Chalgrove Gdns. N3 27Ab 48
Chalgrove Rd. N17 25Xb 51
SM2: Sutt 80Fb 155
Chalice Cl. SM6: Wall 79Mb 156
Chalice Ct. N2 28Gb 49
SE19 65Tb 135
Chalice Way DA9: Ghithe 57Ud 120
CHALK 10K 123
Chalk Ct. RM17: Grays 51Ce 121
(off Argent St.)
Chalkdell Hill HP2: Hem H 2N 3
Chalkdell Ho. WD25: Wat 5Y 13
Chalkenden Cl. SE20 66Xb 135
CHALKER'S CORNER 55Ra 109
CHALK FARM 38Jb 70
Chalk Farm Pde. NW3 38Jb 70
(off Adelaide Rd.)
Chalk Farm Rd. NW1 38Jb 70
Chalk Hill WD19: Wat 16Aa 27
Chalk Hill Rd. W6 49Za 88
Chalkhill Rd. HA9: Wemb 34Ra 67
Chalklands HA9: Wemb 34Sa 67
Chalk La. EN4: Cockf 13Hb 31
KT18: Eps, Eps D 87Ta 173
KT21: Asht 91Pa 193
Chalkley Cl. CR4: Mitc 68Hb 133
Chalkmead RH1: Mers 2C 208
Chalkmill Dr. EN1: Enf 13Xb 33
Chalk Paddock KT18: Eps 87Ta 173
Chalk Pit Av. BR5: St P 69Yc 139
Chalk Pit La. SL1: Burn 8A 60
Chalkpit La. CR3: Wold 97Ec 198
KT23: Bookh 99Ba 191
RH8: Oxt 97Ec 198
Chalk Pit Rd. KT18: Eps D 91Sa 193
SM7: Bans 89Cb 175
Chalk Pit Way SM1: Sutt 78Eb 155
Chalkpit Wood RH8: Oxt 99Fc 199
Chalk Rd. DA12: Grav'nd 10J 123
E13 43Kc 93
Chalkstone Cl. DA16: Well 53Wc 117
Chalkwell Ho. E1 44Zb 92
(off Pitsea St.)
Chalkwell Pk. Av. EN1: Enf 14Ub 33
Chalky Bank DA11: Grav'nd 3C 144
Chalky La. KT9: Chess 82Ma 173
Challacombe Cl. CM13: Hut 18De 41
Challenge Cl. DA12: Grav'nd 3H 145
NW10 39Ua 68
Challenge Ct. KT22: Lea 91Ka 192
TW2: Twick 59Ga 108
Challenger Ho. E14 45Ac 92
(off Victory Pl.)
Challenge Rd. TW15: Ashf 62T 128
Challice Way SW2 60Pb 112
Challin St. SE20 67Yb 136
Challis Rd. TW8: Bford 50Ma 87
Challock Cl. TN16: Big H 88Lc 179
Challoner Cl. N2 26Fb 49
Challoner Ct. BR2: Brom 68Fc 137
W14 50Bb 89
(off Challoner St.)
Challoner Cres. W14 50Bb 89
Challoner Mans. W14 50Bb 89
(off Challoner St.)
Challoners Cl. KT8: E Mos 70Fa 130
Challoner St. W14 50Bb 89
Challoner Wlk. E1 44Wb 91
(off Christian St.)
Chalmers Ct. WD3: Crox G 16P 25
Chalmers Ho. E17 29Dc 52
Chalmers Rd. SM7: Bans 87Fb 175
TW15: Ashf 64R 128
Chalmers Rd. E.
TW15: Ashf 63R 128
Chalmers Wlk. SE17 51Rb 113
(off Hillingdon St.)
Chalmers Way TW1: Isle 56Ka 108
TW14: Felt 57X 107
Chaloner Ct. SE1 1F 231
Chalsey Rd. SE4 56Bc 114
Chalton Dr. N2 30Fb 49
Chalton Ho. NW1 3D 216
Chalton St. NW1 1C 216 (40Lb 70)
(not continuous)
CHALVEY 8H 81
Chalvey Gdns. SL1: Slou 7J 81
Chalvey Gro. SL1: Slou 8F 80
Chalvey Pk. SL1: Slou 7J 81
Chalvey Rd. E. SL1: Slou 7J 81
Chalvey Rd. W. SL1: Slou 7H 81
Chamberlain Cl. IG1: Ilf 34Sc 74
KT19: Eps 82Ta 173
SE28 48Tc 94
UB3: Hayes 45V 84
Chamberlain Cotts. SE5 53Tb 113
Chamberlain Ct. SE16 49Yb 92
(off Silwood St.)
Chamberlain Cres. BR4: W W'ck 74Dc 158
Chamberlain Gdns. TW3: Houn 53Ea 108
Chamberlain Ho. E1 45Yb 92
(off Cable St.)
EC2 5H 219
NW1 2D 216
SE1 2K 229
Chamberlain La. HA5: Eastc 27W 44
Chamberlain Pl. E17 27Ac 52
Chamberlain Rd. N2 26Eb 49
W13 47Ja 86
Chamberlain St. NW1 38Hb 69
Chamberlain Wlk. TW13: Hanw 63Aa 129
Chamberlain Way HA5: Eastc 27X 45
KT6: Surb 73Na 153
Chamberlayne Av. HA9: Wemb 34Na 67
Chamberlayne Mans. NW10 41Za 88
(off Chamberlayne Rd.)
Chamberlayne Rd. NW10 39Ya 68
Chamberlens Garages W6 49Xa 88
(off Dalling Rd.)
Chambers, The SW10 53Eb 111
(off Chelsea Harbour Dr.)
Chambers Av. DA14: Sidc 65Ad 139
Chambersbury La. HP3: Hem H 7A 4
(not continuous)
Chambers Bus. Pk. UB7: Sip 51Q 106
Chambers Cl. DA9: Ghithe 57Wd 120
Chambers Gdns. N2 25Fb 49
Chambers La. NW10 38Xa 68
Chambers Pl. CR2: S Croy 80Tb 157
Chambers Rd. N7 35Nb 70
Chambers St. SE16 47Wb 91
Chamber St. E1 4K 225 (45Vb 91)
Chambers Wlk. HA7: Stan 22Ka 46
Chambers Wharf SE16 47Wb 91
Chambon Pl. W6 49Wa 88
Chambord Ho. E2 4K 219
Chambord St. E2 3K 219 (41Vb 91)
Chamomile Ct. E17 30Cc 52
(off Yunus Khan Cl.)
Champa Cl. N17 26Vb 51
Champion Cres. SE26 63Ac 136
Champion Down KT24: Eff 100Aa 191
Champion Gro. SE5 55Tb 113
Champion Hill SE5 55Tb 113
Champion Hill Est. SE5 55Ub 113
Champion Hill Stadium 56Ub 113
Champion Ho. SE7 51Lc 115
(off Charlton Rd.)
Champion Pk. SE5 54Tb 113
Champion Rd. RM14: Upm 33Rd 77
SE26 63Ac 136
Champions Wlk. E20 36Ec 72
Champions Way NW4 25Xa 48
NW7 25Xa 48
Champlain Ho. W12 45Xa 88
(off White City Est.)
Champness Cl. E17 27Zb 52
SE27 63Tb 135
Champness Rd. IG11: Bark 37Vc 75
Champney Cl. SL3: Hort 55C 104
Champneys WD19: Wat 19Aa 27
Champneys Cl. SM2: Cheam 80Bb 155
Chancel Cl. RM16: Chaf H 48Be 99
Chancel Cl. TN15: W King 80Ud 164
UB8: Uxb 40K 63
Chancel Ct. W1 4D 222
Chancel Ind. Est. NW10 36Va 68
Chancellor Gdns. CR2: S Croy 81Rb 177
Chancellor Gro. SE21 61Sb 135
Chancellor Ho. E1 46Xb 91
(off Green Bank)
SW7 3A 226
Chancellor Pas. E14 46Cc 92
Chancellor Pl. NW9 26Va 48
Chancellors Cl. BR3: Beck 73Cc 158
Chancellors Ct. WC1 7H 217
Chancellor's Rd. W6 50Ya 88
Chancellor's St. W6 50Ya 88
Chancellors Wharf W6 50Ya 88
Chancellor Way RM8: Dag 35Wc 75
TN13: S'oaks 94Jd 202
Chancelot Rd. SE2 49Xc 95
Chancel St. SE1 7B 224 (46Rb 91)
Chance Mead KT15: New H 82L 169
Chancery Bldg. SW8 51Mb 112
Chancery Bldgs. E1 45Xb 91
(off Lowood St.)
Chancery Ct. DA1: Dart 59Qd 119
Chancerygate UB7: Yiew 46Q 84
Chancerygate Bus. Cen.
HA4: Ruis 35Aa 65
SL3: L'ly 47A 82
Chancery Ga. Bus. Pk.
KT6: Surb 75Pa 153
Chancery La. BR3: Beck 68Dc 136
WC2 1J 223 (44Qb 90)
Chancery M. SW17 61Gb 133
Chance St. E1 5K 219 (42Vb 91)
E2 5K 219 (42Vb 91)
Chanctonbury Chase
RH1: Redh 6A 208
Chanctonbury Cl. SE9 62Rc 138
Chanctonbury Dr. SL5: S'dale 3C 146
Chanctonbury Gdns. SM2: Sutt 80Db 155
Chanctonbury Way N12 21Bb 49
Chandaria Ct. CR0: C'don 76Sb 157
(off Church Rd.)
Chandler Av. E16 43Jc 93
Chandler Cl. TW12: Hamp 67Ca 129
Chandler Ct. TW14: Felt 58W 106
Chandler Ho. NW6 39Eb 69
(off Willesden La.)
WC1 6G 217
Chandler Rd. IG10: Lough 11Rc 36
Chandlers Av. SE10 48Hc 93
Chandlers Cl. GU21: Wok 10K 167
(off Robin Hood Rd.)
KT8: W Mole 71Da 151
TW14: Felt 59V 106
CHANDLERS CORNER 41Ld 97
Chandlers Cnr. RM13: Rain 41Ld 97
Chandlers Ct. SE12 60Kc 115
CHANDLER'S CROSS 10P 11
Chandlers Dr. DA8: Erith 49Fd 96
Chandler's La. WD3: Chan C 8N 11
Chandlers M. DA9: Ghithe 56Yd 120
E14 47Cc 92
Chandler St. E1 46Xb 91
Chandlers Way RM1: Rom 29Gd 56
SW2 59Qb 112
Chandler Way SE15 51Ub 113
Chandlery, The SE1 3A 230
Chandlery Ho. E1 44Wb 91
(off Gower's Wlk.)
Chandon Lodge SM2: Sutt 80Eb 155
Chandos Av. E17 26Cc 52
N14 20Lb 32
N20 18Eb 31
W5 49La 86
Chandos Cl. IG9: Buck H 19Kc 35
Chandos Ct. HA7: Stan 23Ka 46
HA8: Edg 24Pa 47
N14 19Mb 32
Chandos Cres. HA8: Edg 24Pa 47
Chandos Gdns. CR5: Coul 91Rb 197
Chandos Mall SL1: Slou 7K 81
(within Queensmere Shop. Cen.)
Chandos Pde. HA8: Edg 24Pa 47
Chandos Pl. WC2 5F 223 (45Nb 90)
Chandos Rd. E15 36Fc 73
HA1: Harr 29Ea 46
HA5: Eastc 31Z 65
N2 26Fb 49
N17 26Ub 51
NW2 36Ya 68
NW10 42Ua 88
TW18: Staines 64F 126
WD6: Bore 12Pa 29
Chandos St. W1 1A 222 (43Kb 90)
Chandos Way NW11 32Db 69
Change All. EC3 3G 225 (44Tb 91)
Chanin M. NW2 36Ya 68
Chanlock Path RM15: S Ock 45Xd 98
Channel 4 TV 4D 228
Channel Cl. TW5: Hest 53Ca 107
Channel Ga. Rd. NW10 41Ua 88
Channel Ho. E14 43Ac 92
(off Aston St.)
SE16 47Zb 92
(off Water Gdns. Sq.)
Channel Islands Est. N1 37Sb 71
Channelsea Ho. E15 40Fc 73
Channelsea Path E15 39Fc 73
Channelsea Rd. E15 39Fc 73
Channing Cl. RM11: Horn 31Pd 77
Channings GU21: Wok 87A 168
Channon Ct. KT6: Surb 71Na 153
(off Maple Rd)
Chantilly Way KT19: Eps 82Ra 173
Chanton Dr. KT17: Cheam 82Ya 174
SM2: Cheam, Ewe 82Ya 174
Chantress Cl. RM10: Dag 39Fd 76
Chantrey Ho. SW1 5K 227
Chantrey Rd. SW9 55Pb 112
Chantreywood CM13: B'wood 20Ce 41
Chantry, The E4 18Ec 34
UB8: Hil 41P 83
Chantry Av. DA3: Hartl 72Ae 165
Chantry Cl. DA14: Sidc 64Ad 139
EN2: Enf 10Sb 19
HA3: Kenton 29Pa 47
KT21: Asht 91La 192
NW7 16Va 30
SE2 48Yc 95
SL4: Wind 3E 102
TW16: Sun 66W 128
UB7: Yiew 45M 83
W9 42Cb 89
WD4: K Lan 1Q 12
Chantry Ct. AL10: Hat 1C 8
DA12: Grav'nd 8E 122
SM5: Cars 76Gb 155
Chantry Cres. NW10 37Va 68
SS17: Stan H 2L 101
Chantry Heritage Cen. 8E 122
Chantry Ho. KT1: King T 70Na 131
Chantry Hurst KT18: Eps 87Ta 173
Chantry La. AL2: Lon C 8H 7
AL10: Hat 1B 8
(College La.)
AL10: Hat 1C 8
(Sparrowhawk Pl.)
BR2: Brom 71Mc 159
Chantry Pl. HA3: Hrw W 25Da 45
Chantry Rd. HA3: Hrw W 25Da 45
KT9: Chess 78Pa 153
KT16: Chert 73L 149
Chantry Sq. W8 48Db 89
Chantry St. N1 1C 218 (39Rb 71)
Chantry Way CR4: Mitc 69Fb 133
Chant Sq. E15 38Fc 73
Chant St. E15 38Fc 73
(not continuous)
Chapel, The CM14: W'ley 22Xd 58
(off The Galleries)
SW15 58Ab 110
Chapel Av. KT15: Add 77K 149
Chapel Cl. AL9: Brk P 9M 9
DA1: Cray 57Gd 118
NW10 36Va 68
RM20: W Thur 51Xd 120
WD25: Wat 6V 12
Chapel Cotts. HP2: Hem H 1M 3
Chapel Ct. DA10: Swans 58Ae 121
E10 33Dc 72
(off Rosedene Ter.)
N2 27Gb 49
RM7: Rush G 30Fd 56
SE1 1F 231 (47Tb 91)
SE18 51Wc 117
UB3: Hayes 45V 84
CHAPEL CROFT 3J 11
Chapel Cft. WD4: Chfd 3J 11
Chapel Dr. DA2: Dart 58Sd 120
CHAPEL END 25Dc 52
Chapel Farm Rd. SE9 62Pc 138
Chapel Ga. M. SW4 55Nb 112
(off Bedford Rd.)
Chapel Ga. Pl. BR7: Chst 65Rc 138
Chapel Grn. CR8: Purl 85Qb 176
Chapel Gro. KT15: Add 77K 149
KT18: Tatt C 91Ya 194
Chapel High CM14: B'wood 19Yd 40
(off High St.)
Chapel Hill DA1: Cray 57Gd 118
KT24: Eff 99Z 191
Chapel Ho. St. E14 50Dc 92
Chapelier Ho. SW18 56Cb 111
Chapel La. GU24: Pirb 4E 186
HA5: Pinn 27Z 45
IG7: Chig 20Vc 37
KT23: Bookh, Westh 100Ea 192
RM6: Chad H 31Zc 75
SL2: Stoke P 8M 61
UB8: Hil 44Q 84
Chapel Lodge RM13: Rain 41Jd 96
Chapel Mkt. N1 1K 217 (40Qb 70)
Chapel M. IG8: Wfd G 23Qc 54
RM11: Horn 31Ld 77
Chapel Mill Rd. KT1: King T 69Pa 131
Chapelmount Rd. IG8: Wfd G 23Pc 54
Chapel of St John the Evangelist 5K 225
(within The Tower of London)
Chapel of St Peter & St Paul 51Fc 115
(within University of Greenwich)
Chapel Pk. Rd. KT15: Add 77K 149
Chapel Path E11 30Kc 53
(off Woodbine Pl.)
Chapel Pl. AL1: St A 5B 6
EC2 4H 219 (41Ub 91)
N1 1A 218 (40Qb 70)
N17 24Vb 51
W1 3K 221 (44Kb 90)
Chapel Rd. CM16: Epp 2Vc 23
CR6: W'ham 90Zb 178
DA7: Bex 56Cd 118
IG1: Ilf 34Qc 74
KT20: Tad 95Ya 194
RH1: Redh 6P 207
RH8: Limp 2N 211
SE27 63Rb 135
TW1: Twick 59Ka 108
TW3: Houn 55Da 107
W13 46Ka 86
Chapel Row TN15: Igh 93Yd 204
UB9: Hare 25L 43
Chapels Cl. SL1: Slou 6C 80
Chapel Side W2 45Db 89
Chapel Sq. GU25: Vir W 70A 126
Chapel Stones N17 25Vb 51
Chapel St. EN2: Enf 13Sb 33
GU21: Wok 89B 168
HP2: Hem H 1M 3
NW1 1D 220 (43Gb 89)
SL1: Slou 7K 81
SW1 3J 227 (48Jb 90)
UB8: Uxb 39L 63
Chapel Ter. IG10: Lough 14Nc 36
Chapel Vw. CR2: Sels 79Yb 158
TN15: Igh 93Yd 204
Chapel Wlk. CR0: C'don 75Sb 157
CR5: Coul 94Mb 196
DA2: Wilm 61Gd 140
(off Pinewood Pl.)
NW4 28Xa 48
(not continuous)
Chapel Way KT18: Tatt C 91Ya 194
N7 34Pb 70
WD5: Bedm 9F 4
Chapel Wood DA3: Nw A G 74Ae 165
(not continuous)
Chapelwood Pl. DA13: Sole S 10E 144
Chapel Wood Rd. DA3: Hartl 76Ae 165
TN15: Ash 76Ae 165
Chapel Yd. SW18 57Db 111
(off Wandsworth High St.)
Chaplaincy Gdns. RM11: Horn 32Nd 77
Chaplin Cl. HA0: Wemb 37Ma 67
SE1 1A 230 (47Qb 90)
Chaplin Ct. DA4: Sut H 65Qd 141
E3 42Bc 92
(off Joseph St.)
SE14 53Zb 114
(off Besson St.)
SE17 51Rb 113
(off Royal Rd.)
Chaplin Cres. TW16: Sun 65U 128
Chaplin Ho. DA14: Sidc 63Wc 139
(off Sidcup High St.)
E17 28Cc 52
(off Hoe St.)
N1 39Tb 71
(off Shepperton Rd.)
W3 48Sa 87
(off All Saints Rd.)
Chaplin M. SL3: L'ly 50B 82
Chaplin Rd. E15 40Hc 73
HA0: Wemb 37La 66
N17 27Vb 51
NW2 37Wa 68
RM9: Dag 38Ad 75
Chaplin Sq. N12 24Fb 49
Chapman Cl. UB7: W Dray 48P 83
Chapman Ct. DA1: Dart 54Qd 119
EN8: Chesh 2Zb 20
Chapman Cres. HA3: Kenton 30Na 47
Chapman Grn. N22 25Qb 50
Chapman Hall AL10: Hat 2B 8
(off Bishops Ri.)
Chapman Ho. E1 44Xb 91
(off Bigland St.)

Chapman Pl.—Cheam Pk. Way

Chapman Pl. N4 33Rb 71
Chapman Rd. CR0: C'don 74Qb 156
DA17: Belv 50Cd 96
E9 37Bc 72
Chapmans Cl. TN14: Sund 96Ad 201
Chapman's Hill DA13: Meop 79Fe 165
Chapman's La. BR5: St P, Swan 68Zc 139
DA17: Belv 49Zc 95
SE2 49Yc 95
Chapmans Pk. Ind. Est. NW10 37Va 68
Chapman Sq. SW19 61Za 132
Chapmans Rd. TN14: Sund 96Ad 201
Chapman's Ter. N22 25Rb 51
Chapman St. E1 45Xb 91
Chapone Pl. W1 3D 222 (44Mb 90)
Chapter Chambers SW1 6D 228
Chapter Cl. UB10: Hil 38P 63
W4 48Sa 87
Chapter House 3D 224
Chapter Ho. E2 42Wb 91
(off Dunbridge St.)
Chapter M. SL4: Wind 2H 103
Chapter Rd. NW2 36Wa 68
SE17 50Rb 91
Chapter St. SW1 6D 228 (49Mb 90)
Chapter Way SW19 67Fb 133
TW12: Hamp 63Ca 129
Chara Pl. W4 51Ta 109
Charcot Ho. SW15 58Va 110
Charcot Rd. NW9 26Ua 48
Charcroft Ct. W14 47Za 88
(off Minford Gdns.)
Charcroft Gdns. EN3: Pond E 14Zb 34
Chardin Ho. SW9 53Qb 112
(off Gosling Way)
Chardin Rd. W4 49Ua 88
Chardins Cl. HP1: Hem H 1H 3
Chardmore Rd. N16 32Wb 71
Chard Rd. TW6: H'row A 54R 106
Chardwell Cl. E6 44Pc 94
Charecroft Way W12 47Za 88
W14 47Za 88
Charfield Ct. W9 42Db 89
(off Shirland Rd.)
Charford Rd. E16 43Jc 93
Chargate Cl. KT12: Hers 79V 150
Chargeable La. E13 42Hc 93
Chargeable St. E16 42Hc 93
Chargrove Cl. SE16 47Zb 92
Charing Cl. BR6: Orp 77Vc 161
Charing Ct. BR2: Brom 68Gc 137
Charing Cross SW1 6F 223
Charing Cross Rd. WC2 2E 222 (44Mb 90)
Charing Cross Sports Club 51Za 110
Charing Cross Theatre 6G 223
Charing Cross Underground Shop. Cen.
WC2 5F 223
Charing Ho. SE1 1A 230
Chariot Cl. E3 39Cc 72
Chariotts Pl. SL4: Wind 3H 103
Charis Ho. E3 41Dc 92
(off Grace St.)
Charkham M. AL9: Wel G 6E 8
Charlbert Ct. NW8 1D 214
Charlbert St. NW8 1D 214 (40Gb 69)
Charlbury Av. HA7: Stan 22Ma 47
Charlbury Cl. RM3: Rom 23Ld 57
Charlbury Cres. RM3: Rom 23Ld 57
Charlbury Gdns. IG3: Ilf 33Vc 75
Charlbury Gro. W5 44La 86
Charlbury Rd. UB10: Ick 34P 63
Charldane Rd. SE9 62Rc 138
Charlecombe Ct. TW18: Staines 64K 127
Charlecote Gro. SE26 62Xb 135
Charlecote Rd. RM8: Dag 34Ad 75
Charlemont Rd. E6 42Pc 94
Charles II Pl. SW3 7E 226 (50Hb 89)
Charles II St. SW1 6D 222 (46Mb 90)
Charles Auffray Ho. E1 43Yb 92
(off Smithy St.)
Charles Babbage Cl. KT9: Chess 80La 152
Charles Baker Pl. SW17 60Gb 111
Charles Barry Cl. SW4 55Lb 112
Charles Bradlaugh Ho. N17 24Xb 51
(off Haynes Cl.)
Charles Burton Ct. E5 36Ac 72
(off Ashenden Rd.)
Charles Chu. Wlk. IG1: Ilf 30Pc 54
Charles Cl. DA14: Sidc 63Xc 139
Charles Cobb Gdns. CR0: Wadd 78Qb 156
Charles Ct. DA8: Erith 51Gd 118
Charles Coveney Rd. SE15 53Vb 113
Charles Cres. HA1: Harr 31Fa 66
(not continuous)
Charles Curran Ho. UB10: Ick 34R 64
Charles Darwin Ho. E2 41Xb 91
(off Canrobert St.)
Charles Dickens Ho. E2 41Wb 91
(off Mansford St.)
Charles Dickens Mus., The 6J 217
Charlesfield SE9 62Lc 137
Charles Flemwell M. E16 46Jc 93
Charles Gdns. SL2: Slou 4M 81
Charles Gardner Ct. N1 3G 219
Charles Grinling Wlk. SE18 49Qc 94
Charles Gro. N14 18Lb 32
Charles Haller St. SW2 59Qb 112
Charles Harrod Ct. SW13 51Ya 110
(off Somerville Av.)
Charles Hocking Ho. W3 47Sa 87
(off Bollo Bri. Rd.)
Charles Ho. KT16: Chert 74H 149
(off Sth. Guildford St.)
N17 24Vb 51
(off Love La.)
SL4: Wind 3G 102
UB2: S'hall 47Ca 85
W14 49Bb 89
Charles Lamb Ct. N1 1C 218
Charles La. NW8 2C 214 (40Gb 69)
Charles Lesser Ho. KT9: Chess 78Ma 153
Charles Mackenzie Ho. SE16 49Wb 91
(off Linsey St.)
Charlesmere Gdns. SE28 47Uc 94
(off Thames Reach)
Charles Nex M. SE21 61Sb 135
Charles Pl. E4 17Fc 35
NW1 4C 216 (41Lb 90)
Charles Rd. E7 38Lc 73
RM6: Chad H 30Zc 55
RM10: Dag 37Fd 76
SW19 67Cb 133
TN14: Bad M 82Dd 182
TW18: Staines 65M 127
W13 44Ja 86
Charles Rowan Ho. WC1 4K 217
Charles Sevright Way NW7 22Za 48
Charles Simmons Ho. WC1 4J 217
Charles Sq. N1 4G 219 (41Tb 91)
Charles Sq. Est. N1 4G 219
Charles St. CM16: Epp 4Wc 23
CR0: C'don 76Sb 157
DA9: Ghithe 57Ud 120
(not continuous)
E16 46Lc 93
EN1: Enf 15Vb 33
HP1: Hem H 3L 3
KT16: Chert 74H 149
N19 32Nb 70
RM17: Grays 51De 121
SL4: Wind 3G 102
SW13 54Ua 110
TW3: Houn 54Ba 108
UB10: Hil 42R 84
W1 6K 221 (46Kb 90)
Charles Talbot M. SE22 60Xb 113
Charleston Cl. TW13: Felt 62W 128
Charleston St. SE17 6E 230 (49Sb 91)
Charles Townsend Ho. EC1 4B 218
Charles Uton Ct. E8 35Wb 71
Charles Whincup Rd. E16 46Kc 93
Charlesworth Cl. HP3: Hem H 4M 3
Charlesworth Ho. E14 44Cc 92
(off Dod St.)
Charlesworth Pl. SW13 55Ua 110
Charleville Cir. SE26 64Wb 135
Charleville Ct. W14 50Bb 89
(off Charleville Rd.)
Charleville Mans. W14 50Ab 88
(off Charleville Rd.)
Charleville M. TW7: Isle 56Ka 108
Charleville Rd. W14 50Ab 88
CHARLIE BROWN'S RDBT. 26Lc 53
Charlie Chaplin Wlk.
SE1 7J 223 (46Pb 90)
Charlieville Rd. DA8: Erith 52Ed 118
Charlmont Rd. SW17 65Gb 133
Charlock Way WD18: Wat 16V 26
Charlotte Av. SL2: Slou 5K 81
Charlotte Cl. AL4: St A 2J 7
DA6: Bex 57Ad 117
IG6: Ilf 25Sc 54
KT21: Asht 90Na 173
WD19: Wat 17Y 27
Charlotte Ct. IG2: Ilf 30Qc 54
KT10: Esh 78Ea 152
N8 30Mb 50
RM11: Horn 31Md 77
SE1 5H 231
W6 49Wa 88
Charlotte Despard Av. SW11 53Jb 112
Charlotte Gdns. RM5: Col R 23Dd 56
Charlotte Ho. E16 46Kc 93
(off Fairfax M.)
W6 50Ya 88
(off Queen Caroline St.)
Charlotte M. KT10: Esh 77Da 151
(off Heather Pl.)
RM13: Rain 40Md 77
W1 7C 216 (43Lb 90)
W10 44Za 88
W14 49Ab 88
Charlotte Pk. Av. BR1: Brom 69Nc 138
Charlotte Pl. NW9 29Sa 47
RM20: W Thur 51Xd 120
SW1 6B 228 (49Lb 90)
W1 1C 222 (43Lb 90)
Charlotte Rd. EC2 4H 219 (41Ub 91)
RM10: Dag 37Dd 76
SM6: Wall 79Lb 156
SW13 53Va 110
Charlotte Row SW4 55Lb 112
Charlotte Sq. TW10: Rich 58Pa 109
Charlotte St. W1 7C 216 (43Lb 90)
Charlotte Ter. KT10: Esh 79Ea 152
(off Princess Sq.)
N1 1J 217 (39Pb 70)
Charlow Cl. SW6 54Eb 111
CHARLTON
SE7 52Mc 115
TW17 69S 128
Charlton SL4: Wind 4A 102
Charlton Athletic FC 50Lc 93
Charlton Av. KT12: Hers 77X 151
Charlton Chu. La. SE7 50Lc 93
Charlton Cl. SL1: Slou 7F 80
UB10: Ick 33R 64
Charlton Ct. E2 1K 219 (39Vb 71)
NW5 36Mb 70
Charlton Cres. IG11: Bark 40Vc 75
Charlton Dene SE7 52Lc 115
Charlton Dr. TN16: Big H 89Mc 179
Charlton Gdns. CR5: Coul 90Lb 176
Charlton Ga. Bus. Pk. SE7 49Lc 93
Charlton Ho. TW8: Bford 51Na 109
Charlton Kings KT13: Weyb 76U 150
Charlton King's Rd. NW5 36Mb 70
Charlton La. SE7 49Mc 93
TW17: Shep 69S 128
(not continuous)
Charlton Lido 52Mc 115
Charlton Pk. La. SE7 52Mc 115
Charlton Pk. Rd. SE7 51Mc 115
Charlton Pl. N1 1B 218 (40Rb 71)
SL4: Wind 4A 102
(off Charlton)
Charlton Riverside Pl. SE7 49Kc 93
Charlton Rd. HA3: Kenton 28Ma 47
HA9: Wemb 32Pa 67
N9 18Zb 34
NW10 39Ua 68
SE3 52Jc 115
SE7 52Kc 115
TW17: Shep 69S 128
Charlton Row SL4: Wind 4A 102
Charlton Sq. SL4: Wind 4A 102
(off Charlton)
Charlton St. RM20: Grays 51Zd 121
Charlton Ter. SE11 51Qb 112
Charlton Wlk. SL4: Wind 4A 102
Charlton Way SE3 53Gc 115
SL4: Wind 4A 102
Charlwood CR0: Sels 81Bc 178
Charlwood Cl. HA3: Hrw W 23Ga 46
KT23: Bookh 96Da 191
Charlwood Dr. KT22: Oxs 87Fa 172
Charlwood Ho. SW1 6D 228
TW9: Kew 52Ra 109
Charlwood Ho's. WC1 4G 217
(off Midhope St.)
Charlwood Pl. RH2: Reig 6H 207
SW1 6C 228 (49Lb 90)
Charlwood Rd. SW15 56Za 110
Charlwood St. SW1 7B 228 (50Lb 90)
(not continuous)
Charlwood Ter. SW15 56Za 110
Charman Rd. RH1: Redh 6N 207
Charmans Ho. SW8 52Nb 112
(off Wandsworth Rd.)
Charmeuse Ct. E2 40Xb 71
(off Silk Weaver Way)
Charmian Av. HA7: Stan 27Ma 47
Charmian Ho. N1 2H 219
Charminster Av. SW19 68Cb 133
Charminster Ct. KT6: Surb 73Ma 153
Charminster Rd. KT4: Wor Pk 74Za 154
SE9 63Mc 137
Charmouth Ct. TW10: Rich 57Pa 109
Charmouth Ho. SW8 52Pb 112
Charmouth Rd. AL1: St A 1E 6
DA16: Well 53Yc 117
Charne, The TN14: Otf 89Jd 182
Charnwood La. BR6: Prat B 81Xc 181
Charnock BR8: Swan 70Gd 140
Charnock Ho. W12 45Xa 88
(off White City Est.)
Charnock Rd. E5 34Xb 71
Charnwood SL5: S'dale 2D 146
Charnwood Av. SW19 68Cb 133
Charnwood Cl. KT3: N Mald 70Ua 132
Charnwood Dr. E18 27Kc 53
Charnwood Gdns. E14 49Cc 92
Charnwood Pl. N20 20Eb 31
Charnwood Rd. EN1: Enf 8Xb 19
SE25 71Tb 157
UB10: Hil 40Q 64
Charnwood St. E5 33Xb 71
Charrington Cl. WD7: Shenl 6Qa 15
Charrington Ct. RM1: Rush G 30Gd 56
Charrington Pl. AL1: St A 3D 6
Charrington Rd. CR0: C'don 75Sb 157
Charrington St. NW1 1D 216 (40Mb 70)
(not continuous)
Charsley Rd. SE6 61Dc 136
Charta Rd. TW20: Egh 64E 126
Chart Cl. BR2: Brom 67Gc 137
CR0: C'don 72Yb 158
CR4: Mitc 70Hb 133
Charter Av. IG2: Ilf 32Tc 74
Charter Bldgs. SE10 53Dc 114
(off Catherine Gro.)
Charter Cl. AL1: St A 2B 6
SL1: Slou 8K 81
Charter Ct. HP2: Hem H 2M 3
KT3: N Mald 69Ua 132
N4 32Qb 70
N22 25Mb 50
UB1: S'hall 46Ca 85
Charter Cres. TW4: Houn 56Aa 107
Charter Dr. DA5: Bexl 59Ad 117
Charterhouse 6C 218
Charter Ho. SM2: Sutt 79Db 155
(off Mulgrave Rd.)
WC2 3G 223
Charterhouse Apartments
SW18 56Eb 111
Charterhouse Av. HA0: Wemb 35La 66
Charterhouse Bldgs.
EC1 6D 218 (42Sb 91)
Charterhouse Dr. TN13: S'oaks 95Jd 202
Charterhouse M. EC1 7C 218 (43Rb 91)
Charterhouse Rd. BR6: Chels 76Wc 161
E8 35Wb 71
Charterhouse Sq. EC1 7C 218 (43Rb 91)
Charterhouse St. EC1 1A 224 (43Qb 90)
Charteris Community Sports Cen.
39Cb 69
Charteris Rd. IG8: Wfd G 24Kc 53
N4 32Qb 70
NW6 39Bb 69
Charter Pl. TW18: Staines 65J 127
UB8: Uxb 38M 63
WD17: Wat 14Y 27
Charter Quay KT1: King T 68Ma 131
(off Wadbrook St.)
Charter Rd. KT1: King T 69Ra 131
SL1: Slou 5C 80
Charter Rd., The IG8: Wfd G 23Gc 53
Charters SL5: S'dale 2C 146
Charters Cl. SE19 64Ub 135
SL5: S'hill 1B 146
Charters Ct. SL5: S'hill 2B 146
Charters Gdn. Ho. SL5: S'hill 2C 146
Charters Health Club 3G 6
Charters La. SL5: S'hill 1B 146
Charters Leisure Cen. 3B 146
Charter Sq. KT1: King T 68Ra 131
Charters Rd. SL5: S'dale 3B 146
Charters Way SL5: S'dale 3D 146
Charter Way N3 28Bb 49
N14 16Lb 32
Chartes Ho. SE1 3J 231
Chartfield Av. SW15 57Xa 110
Chartfield Pl. KT13: Weyb 78R 150
Chartfield Rd. RH2: Reig 7L 207
Chartfield Sq. SW15 57Za 110
Chartham Ct. SW9 55Qb 112
(off Canterbury Cres.)
Chartham Gro. SE27 62Rb 135
Chartham Ho. SE1 3G 231
Chartham Rd. SE25 69Xb 135
Chart Hills Cl. SE28 44Ad 95
Chart Ho. CR4: Mitc 68Hb 133
E14 50Dc 92
(off Burrells Wharf Sq.)
Chart La. RH2: Reig 6K 207
TN16: Bras, B Char 100Xc 201
Chartley Av. HA7: Stan 23Ha 46
NW2 34Ua 68
Charton Cl. DA17: Belv 51Bd 117
Chartres Ct. UB6: G'frd 40Fa 66
Chartridge SE17 51Tb 113
(off Westmoreland Rd.)
WD19: Wat 19Z 27
Chartridge Cl. EN5: Ark 15Wa 30
WD23: Bush 16Ea 28
Chartridge Way HP2: Hem H 2C 4
Chart St. N1 3G 219 (41Tb 91)
Chart Vw. TN15: Kems'g 89Rd 183
Chartway RH2: Reig 5K 207
TN13: S'oaks 96Ld 203
Chartwell GU22: Wok 90A 168
(off Mt. Hermon Rd.)
Chartwell Bus. Cen. BR1: Brom 69Mc 137
Chartwell Cl. CR0: C'don 74Tb 157
EN9: Walt A 5Gc 21
SE9 61Tc 138
UB6: G'frd 39Da 65
Chartwell Ct. EN5: Barn 14Ab 30
IG8: Wfd G 24Hc 53
NW2 34Wa 68
UB3: Hayes 45V 84
Chartwell Dr. BR6: Farnb 78Tc 160
Chartwell Gdns. SM3: Cheam 77Ab 154
Chartwell Ho. W11 46Bb 89
(off Ladbroke Rd.)
Chartwell La. DA3: Lfield 69Ae 143
Chartwell Lodge
BR3: Beck 66Cc 136
Chartwell Pl. HA2: Harr 33Fa 66
KT18: Eps 86Ua 174
SM3: Cheam 77Ab 154
Chartwell Rd. HA6: Nwood 23V 44
Chartwell Way SE20 67Xb 135
Charville Ct. HA1: Harr 30Ha 46
(off Gayton Rd.)
SE10 51Fc 115
(off Trafalgar Gro.)
Charville La. UB4: Hayes 41S 84
Charville La. W. UB10: Hil 41R 84
(not continuous)
Charwood SW16 63Qb 134
Charwood Cl. WD7: Shenl 5Na 15
Chase, The BR1: Brom 69Kc 137
BR6: Prat B 84Wc 181
CM13: Ingve 22Ee 59
CM14: B'wood 20Zd 41
CM14: W'ley 21Xd 58
(Cromwell Rd.)
CM14: W'ley 22Zd 59
(Nelson Cl.)
CR5: Coul 86Lb 176
DA3: Lfield 69Be 143
DA7: Bex 55Dd 118
E12 35Mc 73
EN7: G Oak 1Rb 19
HA5: Eastc 30Y 45
HA5: Pinn 28Ba 45
HA7: Stan 23Ja 46
HA8: Edg 25Ra 47
HP2: Hem H 3N 3
IG7: Chig 21Sc 54
IG10: Lough 17Mc 35
KT20: Kgswd 94Cb 195
KT21: Asht 90La 172
KT22: Oxs 87Ea 172
KT24: E Hor 98V 190
RH2: Reig 7M 207
RM1: Rom 27Gd 56
RM6: Chad H 30Ad 55
RM7: Rush G 34Fd 76
RM13: Rain 39Kd 77
RM14: Upm 34Ud 78
RM20: Grays 51Zd 121
SM6: Wall 78Nb 156
SW4 55Kb 112
SW16 66Pb 134
SW20 67Ab 132
TN15: Kems'g 88Nd 183
TW16: Sun 67X 129
UB10: Ick 36Q 64
WD7: R'lett 7Ha 14
WD18: Wat 14U 26
Chase Bank Ct. N14 16Lb 32
(off Avenue Rd.)
Chase Cen., The NW10 41Ta 87
Chase Ct. SW3 4F 227
SW20 68Ab 132
TW7: Isle 54Ja 108
Chase Ct. Gdns. EN2: Enf 13Sb 33
CHASE CROSS 23Gd 56
Chase Cross Rd. RM5: Col R 24Ed 56
Chase End KT19: Eps 84Ta 173
Chasefield Rd. SW17 63Hb 133
Chase Gdns. E4 21Cc 52
TW2: Whitt 59Fa 108
Chase Grn. EN2: Enf 13Sb 33
EN6: Cuff 1Nb 18
Chase Grn. Av. EN2: Enf 12Rb 33
Chase Hill EN2: Enf 13Sb 33
Chase Ho. NW6 41Cb 89
(off Hansel Rd.)
Chase Ho. Gdns. RM11: Horn 29Pd 57
Chase La. IG2: Ilf 29Tc 54
IG6: Ilf 29Tc 54
IG7: Chig 20Vc 37
Chaseley Ct. KT13: Weyb 74U 150
Chaseley Dr. CR2: Sande 82Tb 177
W4 50Ra 87
Chaseley St. E14 44Ac 92
Chase Local Nature Reserve, The
34Hd 76
Chasemore Cl. CR4: Mitc 73Hb 155
Chasemore Gdns. CR0: Wadd 78Qb 156
Chasemore Ho. SW6 52Ab 110
(off Williams Cl.)
Chase Ridings EN2: Enf 12Qb 32
Chase Rd. CM14: B'wood 20Yd 40
KT19: Eps 84Ta 173
N14 15Lb 32
NW10 42Ta 87
Chase Rd. Trad. Est. NW10 42Ta 87
CHASE SIDE 11Tb 33
Chase Side EN2: Enf 13Sb 33
N14 16Jb 32
Chase Side Av. EN2: Enf 12Sb 33
SW20 67Ab 132
Chaseside Cl. RM1: Rom 23Gd 56
Chase Side Cres. EN2: Enf 11Sb 33
Chaseside Gdns. KT16: Chert 73K 149
Chase Side Pl. EN2: Enf 12Sb 33
Chase Sq. DA11: Grav'nd 8D 122
Chaseville Pde. N21 15Pb 32
Chaseville Pk. Rd. N21 15Nb 32
Chase Way N14 19Kb 32
RM20: Grays 51Zd 121
Chaseway Lodge E16 44Jc 93
(off Butchers Rd.)
Chaseways Vs. RM5: Col R 25Bd 55
Chasewood Av. EN2: Enf 12Rb 33
Chasewood Ct. NW7 22Ta 47
Chasewood Pk. HA1: Harr 34Ha 66
Chastilian Rd. DA1: Dart 59Hd 118
Chaston Pl. NW5 36Jb 70
(off Grafton Ter.)
Chater Ho. E2 41Zb 92
(off Roman Rd.)
Chatfield SL2: Slou 3E 80
Chatfield Ct. CR3: Cat'm 94Tb 197
Chatfield Rd. CR0: C'don 74Rb 157
SW11 55Eb 111
Chatham Av. BR2: Hayes 73Hc 159
Chatham Cl. NW11 29Cb 49
SE18 48Rc 94
SM3: Sutt 73Bb 155
Chatham Ct. SL1: Slou 8L 81
(off Grove Cl.)
Chatham Hill Rd.
TN14: S'oaks 93Ld 203
Chatham Ho. SM6: Wall 78Kb 156
(off Melbourne Rd.)
Chatham Pl. E9 37Yb 72
Chatham Rd. E17 27Ac 52
E18 26Hc 53
KT1: King T 68Qa 131
SW11 58Hb 111
Chatham St. SE17 5F 231 (49Tb 91)
Chatham Way CM14: B'wood 19Yd 40
CHATHILL 9F 210
Chatley Heath Semaphore Tower 90T 170
Chatsfield KT17: Ewe 82Wa 174
Chatsfield Pl. W5 44Na 87
Chats Palace Arts Cen. 36Zb 72
Chatsworth Av. BR1: Brom 63Kc 137
DA15: Sidc 60Wc 117
HA9: Wemb 36Pa 67
NW4 26Ya 48
SW20 67Ab 132
Chatsworth Cl. BR4: W W'ck 75Hc 159
NW4 26Ya 48
W4 51Sa 109
WD6: Bore 13Qa 29
Chatsworth Ct. AL1: St A 2D 6
(off Stanhope Rd.)
HA7: Stan 22La 46
SW16 69Pb 134
W8 49Cb 89
(off Pembroke Rd.)
Chatsworth Cres. TW3: Houn 56Fa 108
Chatsworth Dr. EN1: Enf 17Wb 33
Chatsworth Est. E5 35Zb 72
Chatsworth Gdns. HA2: Harr 32Da 65
KT3: N Mald 71Va 154
W3 46Ra 87
Chatsworth Ho. BR2: Brom 70Jc 137
(off Westmoreland Rd.)
E16 46Kc 93
(off Wesley Av.)
SE1 1K 231
Chatsworth Lodge W4 50Ta 87
(off Bourne Pl.)
Chatsworth M. DA14: Sidc 63Vc 139
WD24: Wat 10W 12
Chatsworth Pde. BR5: Pet W 71Sc 160
Chatsworth Pk. SM7: Bans 89Db 175
Chatsworth Pl. CR4: Mitc 69Hb 133
KT22: Oxs 85Fa 172
TW11: Tedd 63Ja 130
Chatsworth Ri. W5 42Pa 87
Chatsworth Rd. CR0: C'don 77Tb 157
DA1: Dart 57Ld 119
E5 34Yb 72
E15 36Hc 73
NW2 37Ya 68
SM3: Cheam 78Za 154
UB4: Yead 42X 85
W4 51Sa 109
W5 42Pa 87
Chatsworth Way SE27 62Rb 135
Chatteris Av. RM3: Rom 23Ld 57
CHATTERN HILL 63R 128
Chattern Hill TW15: Ashf 63R 128
Chattern Rd. TW15: Ashf 63S 128
Chatterton Ct. TW9: Kew 54Pa 109
Chatterton M. N4 34Rb 71
(off Chatterton Rd.)
Chatterton Rd. BR2: Brom 70Mc 137
N4 34Rb 71
Chatton Row GU24: Bisl 9E 166
Chatto Rd. SW11 57Hb 111
Chaucer Av. KT13: Weyb 80Q 150
TW4: Cran 54X 107
TW9: Rich 55Qa 109
UB4: Hayes 43W 84
Chaucer Bus. Pk. TN15: Kems'g 90Td 184
Chaucer Cl. N11 22Lb 50
RM18: Tilb 4E 122
SL4: Wind 5H 103
SM7: Bans 86Ab 174
Chaucer Ct. EN5: New Bar 15Db 31
N16 35Ub 71
RH1: Redh 3A 208
SW17 62Fb 133
(off Lanesborough Way)
Chaucer Dr. SE1 6K 231 (49Vb 91)
Chaucer Gdns. CR5: Coul 89Lb 176
SM1: Sutt 76Cb 155
Chaucer Grn. CR0: C'don 73Xb 157
Chaucer Gro. WD6: Bore 14Qa 29
Chaucer Ho. EN5: Barn 14Za 30
SM1: Sutt 76Cb 155
(off Chaucer Gdns.)
SW1 50Lb 90
(off Churchill Gdns.)
Chaucer Mans. W14 51Ab 110
(off Queen's Club Gdns.)
Chaucer Pk. DA1: Dart 59Pd 119
Chaucer Rd. DA11: Nflt 62Fe 143
DA15: Sidc 60Yc 117
DA16: Well 53Uc 116
E7 37Jc 73
E11 30Jc 53
E17 26Ec 52
RM3: Rom 24Kd 57
SE24 57Qb 112
SM1: Sutt 77Cb 155
TW15: Ashf 63N 127
W3 46Sa 87
Chaucer Way DA1: Dart 56Qd 119
(not continuous)
KT15: Add 79J 149
SL1: Slou 6K 81
SW19 65Fb 133
CHAULDEN 3H 3
Chaulden Ho. EC1 4G 219
Chaulden Ho. Gdns. HP1: Hem H 4H 3
Chaulden La. HP1: Hem H 4F 2
Chaulden Ter. HP1: Hem H 3H 3
Chauncey Cl. N9 20Wb 33
Chauncey Ho. WD18: Wat 16U 26
Chauncy Av. EN6: Pot B 5Eb 17
Chaundrye Cl. SE9 58Pc 116
Chauntler Cl. E16 44Kc 93
Chave Cft. KT18: Tatt C 91Ya 194
Chavecroft Ter. KT18: Tatt C 91Ya 194
Chave Rd. DA2: Wilm 62Nd 141
Chaville Ct. N11 21Jb 50
Chaville Way N3 25Cb 49
Chaworth Cl. KT16: Ott 79E 148
Chaworth Rd. KT16: Ott 79E 148
Cheadle Ct. NW8 5C 214
Cheadle Ho. E14 44Bc 92
(off Copenhagen Pl.)
CHEAM 79Ab 154
Cheam Cl. KT20: Tad 93Xa 194
Cheam Comn. Rd.
KT4: Wor Pk 75Xa 154
Cheam Leisure Cen. 77Za 154
Cheam Mans. SM3: Cheam 80Ab 154
Cheam Pk. Way SM3: Cheam 79Ab 154

Cheam Rd.—Chester Rd.

Cheam Rd. KT17: Ewe .82Wa 174
SM1: Sutt .79Bb 155
SM2: Cheam .82Xa 174
Cheam St. SE15 .55Yb 114
CHEAM VILLAGE .79Ab 154
CHEAPSIDE .7C 124
Cheapside EC2 .3D 224 (44Sb 91)
GU21: Wok .6P 167
N13 .21Tb 51
N22 .27Qb 50
Cheapside La. UB9: Den .33H 63
Cheapside Pas. EC2 .3D 224
Cheapside Rd. SL5: Asc .9A 124
Cheddar Cl. N11 .23Hb 49
Cheddar Waye UB4: Yead .44X 85
Cheddington Ho. E2 .39Wb 71
(off Whiston Rd.)
Cheddington Rd. N18 .20Ub 33
Chedworth Cl. E16 .44Hc 93
(off Wouldham Rd.)
Chedworth Ho. N15 .28Tb 51
(off West Grn. Rd.)
Cheeky Monkeys Jungle Adventure .1Wb 19
Cheelson Rd. RM15: S Ock .40Yd 78
Cheena Ho. SL9: Chal P .24B 42
Cheering La. E20 .36Ec 72
Cheesegrater, The .3H 225
Cheeseman Cl. TW12: Hamp .65Aa 129
Cheesemans Ter. W14 .50Bb 89
(not continuous)
Cheffery Ct. TW15: Ashf .65R 128
Cheldon Av. NW7 .24Za 48
Chelford Rd. BR1: Brom .64Fc 137
Chelmer Cres. IG11: Bark .40Xc 75
Chelmer Dr. CM13: Hut .16Fe 41
RM15: S Ock .45Yd 98
Chelmer Ho. RM16: Grays .10C 100
(off River Vw.)
Chelmer Rd. E9 .36Zb 72
RM14: Upm .30Td 58
RM16: Grays .10C 100
Chelmsford Av. RM5: Col R .24Fd 56
Chelmsford Cl. E6 .44Pc 94
SM2: Sutt .81Cb 175
W6 .51Za 110
Chelmsford Ct. N14 .17Mb 32
(off Chelmsford Rd.)
Chelmsford Dr. RM14: Upm .34Pd 77
Chelmsford Gdns. IG1: Ilf .31Nc 74
Chelmsford Ho. N7 .35Pb 70
(off Holloway Rd.)
Chelmsford Rd. CM15: Shenf .16Be 41
E11 .32Fc 73
E17 .30Cc 52
E18 .25Hc 53
N14 .17Lb 32
Chelmsford Sq. NW10 .39Ya 68
Chelmsine Ct. HA4: Ruis .29S 44
CHELSEA .7E 226 (50Gb 89)
Chelsea Bri. SW1 .51Kb 112
Chelsea Bri. Rd. SW1 .7H 227 (50Jb 90)
Chelsea Bri. Wharf SW8 .51Kb 112
Chelsea Cinema .7E 226 (50Gb 89)
Chelsea Cloisters SW3 .6E 226 (49Gb 89)
Chelsea Cl. HA8: Edg .26Qa 47
KT4: Wor Pk .73Wa 154
NW10 .39Ta 67
TW12: Hamp H .64Ea 130
Chelsea Ct. BR1: Brom .69Nc 138
(off Holmdene Ct.)
KT18: Eps .85Ta 173
(off Ashley Rd.)
SW3 .51Hb 111
(off Embankment Gdns.)
Chelsea Cres. NW2 .37Bb 69
SW10 .53Eb 111
Chelsea Emb. SW3 .51Gb 111
Chelsea Farm Ho. Studios
SW10 .51Fb 111
(off Cremorne Est.)
Chelsea FC .52Db 111
Chelsea Flds. SW19 .67Fb 133
Chelsea Football Academy .89Aa 171
Chelsea Gdns. SM3: Cheam .77Ab 154
SW1 .50Jb 90
W13 .43Ha 86
Chelsea Ga. SW1 .7J 227
Chelsea Harbour SW10 .53Eb 111
Chelsea Harbour Design Cen.
SW10 .53Eb 111
(off Chelsea Harbour Dr.)
Chelsea Harbour Dr. SW10 .53Eb 111
Chelsea Lodge SW3 .51Hb 111
(off Tite St.)
Chelsea Mnr. Ct. SW3 .51Gb 111
Chelsea Mnr. Gdns. SW3 .50Gb 89
Chelsea Mnr. St. SW3 .7D 226 (50Gb 89)
Chelsea Mnr. Studios SW3 .7E 226
Chelsea M. RM11: Horn .32Kd 77
Chelsea Pk. Gdns. SW3 .51Fb 111
Chelsea Physic Garden .51Hb 111
Chelsea Reach Twr. SW10 .52Fb 111
(off Worlds End Est.)
Chelsea Sports Cen. .50Gb 89
Chelsea Sq. SW3 .7C 226 (50Fb 89)
Chelsea Studios SW6 .52Db 111
(off Fulham Rd.)
Chelsea Theatre, The .52Eb 111
Chelsea Towers SW3 .51Gb 111
(off Chelsea Mnr. Gdns.)
Chelsea Village SW6 .52Db 111
(off Fulham Rd.)
Chelsea Vista SW6 .53Eb 111
Chelsea Way CM14: B'wood .18Yd 40
Chelsea Wharf SW10 .52Fb 111
(off Lots Rd.)
CHELSFIELD .78Xc 161
Chelsfield Av. N9 .17Zb 34
Chelsfield Gdns. SE26 .62Yb 136
Chelsfield Grn. N9 .17Zb 34
(not continuous)
Chelsfield Hill BR6: Chels .81Yc 181
Chelsfield Ho. SE17 .6H 231
Chelsfield Lakes Golf Course .80Ad 161
Chelsfield La. BR5: Orp .73Zc 161
BR6: Chels, Orp .75Zc 161
BR6: Well H .80Cd 162
TN14: S'ham .81Cd 182
Chelsfield Point E9 .38Zb 72
(off Penshurst Rd.)
Chelsfield Rd. BR5: St M Cry .72Yc 161
CHELSFIELD VILLAGE .78Ad 161
CHELSHAM .89Cc 178
Chelsham Cl. CR6: W'ham .90Ac 178
CHELSHAM COMMON .88Cc 178
Chelsham Comn. Rd.
CR6: W'ham .89Cc 178
Chelsham Ct. Rd.
CR6: W'ham .90Fc 179
Chelsham Rd. CR2: S Croy .80Tb 157
CR6: W'ham .90Bc 178
SW4 .55Mb 112
Chelsham Ter. CR6: W'ham .90Bc 178
Chelsing Ri. HP2: Hem H .3C 4
Chelsiter Ct. DA14: Sidc .63Vc 139
Chelston App. HA4: Ruis .33W 64
Chelston Ct. E11 .29Kc 53
Chelston Rd. HA4: Ruis .32W 64
Chelsworth Cl. RM3: Hrld W .24Pd 57
Chelsworth Dr. RM3: Hrld W .25Nd 57
SE18 .51Tc 116
Cheltenham Av. TW1: Twick .59Ja 108
Cheltenham Cl. DA12: Grav'nd .4E 144
KT3: N Mald .69Sa 131
UB5: N'olt .37Da 65
Cheltenham Ct. AL1: St A .3E 6
(off Dexter Cl.)
HA7: Stan .22La 46
(off Marsh La.)
Cheltenham Gdns. E6 .40Nc 74
IG10: Lough .16Nc 36
Cheltenham Ho. IG8: Wfd G .23Qc 54
UB3: Harl .48S 84
(off Skipton Dr.)
WD24: Wat .12Y 27
(off Exeter Cl.)
Cheltenham Pl. HA3: Kenton .28Na 47
W3 .46Ra 87
Cheltenham Rd. BR6: Chels .76Wc 161
E10 .30Ec 52
SE15 .56Yb 114
Cheltenham Ter. SW3 .7G 227 (50Hb 89)
Cheltenham Vs. TW19: Stanw M .58H 105
Chelverton Rd. SW15 .56Za 110
Chelwood N20 .19Fb 31
Chelwood Cl. CR5: Coul .91Lb 196
E4 .16Dc 34
HA6: Nwood .24S 44
KT17: Eps .84Va 174
Chelwood Ct. CR2: S Croy .78Sb 157
SW11 .53Fb 111
(off Westbridge Rd.)
Chelwood Gdns. TW9: Kew .54Qa 109
Chelwood Gdns. Pas. TW9: Kew .54Qa 109
Chelwood Ho. W2 .3C 220
Chelwood Wlk. SE4 .56Ac 114
Chenappa Cl. E13 .41Jc 93
Chenduit Way HA7: Stan .22Ha 46
Chene Dr. AL3: St A .1B 6
Chene M. AL3: St A .1B 6
Cheney Ct. SE23 .60Zb 114
Cheney Row E17 .25Bc 52
Cheneys Rd. E11 .34Gc 73
Cheney St. HA5: Eastc .28Y 45
CHENIES .10D 10
Chenies HA6: Nwood .22V 44
Chenies, The BR6: Pet W .72Uc 160
DA2: Wilm .63Gd 140
NW1 .1E 216
CHENIES BOTTOM .9C 10
Chenies Hill HP3: Flau .9D 10
HP5: Flau .9D 10
WD3: Chen .9D 10
Chenies Ho. W2 .45Db 89
(off Moscow Rd.)
W4 .52Va 110
(off Corney Reach Way)
Chenies Manor House .10C 10
Chenies M. WC1 .6D 216 (42Mb 90)
Chenies Pl. EN5: Ark .15Wa 30
NW1 .1E 216 (40Mb 70)
Chenies Rd. WD3: Chen, Chor .12F 24
Chenies St. WC1 .7D 216 (43Mb 90)
Chenies Village WD3: Chen .10D 10
Chenies Way WD18: Wat .17U 26
Cheniston Cl. KT14: W Byf .85J 169
Cheniston Ct. SL5: S'dale .3E 146
Cheniston Gdns. W8 .48Db 89
Chenla SE13 .54Dc 114
Chennells AL10: Hat .1C 8
Cheping Ho. W10 .45Za 88
(off Shalfleet Dr.)
Chepstow Av. RM12: Horn .34Nd 77
Chepstow Cl. SW15 .57Ab 110
Chepstow Cnr. W2 .44Cb 89
(off Chepstow Pl.)
Chepstow Ct. W11 .45Cb 89
(off Chepstow Vs.)
Chepstow Cres. IG3: Ilf .30Uc 54
W11 .45Cb 89
Chepstow Gdns. UB1: S'hall .44Ba 85
Chepstow Ho. RM3: Rom .22Qd 57
(off Leamington Rd.)
Chepstow Pl. W2 .44Cb 89
Chepstow Ri. CR0: C'don .76Ub 157
Chepstow Rd. CR0: C'don .76Ub 157
W2 .44Cb 89
W7 .48Ja 86
Chepstow Vs. W11 .45Bb 89
Chequers IG9: Buck H .18Kc 35
Chequers, The HA5: Pinn .27Z 45
Chequers Cl. BR5: St P .70Vc 139
DA13: Ist R .8A 144
KT20: Walt H .97Wa 194
NW9 .27Ua 48
Chequers Ct. DA17: Belv .49Cd 96
EC1 .6F 219
Chequers Ho. NW8 .5D 214
Chequers La. KT20: Walt H .97Wa 194
RM9: Dag .42Bd 95
(not continuous)
WD25: Wat .2X 13
Chequers Orchard SL0: Iver .44H 83
Chequers Pde. N13 .22Sb 51
RM9: Dag .39Bd 75
SE9 .58Pc 116
(off Eltham High St.)
Chequers Rd. CM14: N'side, Rom .19Nd 39
IG10: Lough .15Qc 36
RM3: Rom .19Nd 39
Chequers Sq. UB8: Uxb .38L 63
Chequer St. AL1: St A .2B 6
EC1 .6E 218 (42Sb 91)
(not continuous)
Chequers Wlk. EN9: Walt A .5Hc 21
Chequers Way N13 .22Rb 51
Chequer Tree Cl. GU21: Knap .8J 167
Cherbury Cl. SE28 .44Zc 95
Cherbury Ct. N1 .2G 219
Cherbury St. N1 .2G 219 (40Tb 71)
Cherchefelle M. HA7: Stan .22Ka 46
Cherimoya Gdns. KT8: W Mole .69Da 129
Cherington Rd. W7 .46Ga 86
Cheriton Av. BR2: Brom .71Hc 159
IG5: Ilf .26Pc 54
Cheriton Cl. EN4: Cockf .13Hb 31
W5 .43La 86
Cheriton Ct. KT12: Walt T .74Y 151
SE12 .59Jc 115
SE25 .71Ub 157
Cheriton Dr. SE18 .52Tc 116
Cheriton Lodge HA4: Ruis .32V 64
Cheriton Sq. SW17 .61Jb 134
Cherkley Hill KT22: Lea .98La 192
Cherries, The SL2: Slou .4M 81
Cherry Acre SL9: Chal P .21A 42
Cherry Av. BR8: Swan .70Fd 140
CM13: B'wood .20Be 41
SL3: L'ly .7P 81
UB1: S'hall .46Z 85
Cherry Bank HP2: Hem H .1M 3
(off Chapel St.)
Cherry Blossom Cl. N13 .22Rb 51
Cherry Bounce HP1: Hem H .1M 3
Cherry Cl. E17 .29Dc 52
HA0: Wemb .34Ma 67
HA4: Ruis .34V 64
NW9 .26Ua 48
SL0: Iver .45H 83
SM4: Mord .70Ab 132
SM5: Cars .75Hb 155
SM7: Bans .86Za 174
SW2 .59Qb 112
W5 .48Ma 87
Cherrycot Hill BR6: Farnb .77Sc 160
Cherrycot Ri. BR6: Farnb .77Sc 160
Cherry Cotts.
KT20: Walt H .96Xa 194
Cherry Ct. HA5: Pinn .26Z 45
IG6: Ilf .27Rc 54
W3 .46Ua 88
Cherry Cres. TW8: Bford .52Ka 108
Cherry Cft. WD3: Crox G .16R 26
Cherrycroft Gdns. HA5: Hat E .24Ba 45
Cherrydale WD18: Wat .14V 26
Cherrydown RM16: Grays .46Fe 99
Cherrydown Av. E4 .20Bc 34
Cherrydown Cl. E4 .20Cc 34
Cherrydown Rd. DA14: Sidc .61Zc 139
Cherrydown Wlk. RM7: Mawney .26Dd 56
Cherry Gdn. Ho. SE16 .47Xb 91
(off Cherry Gdn. St.)
Cherry Gdns. RM9: Dag .36Bd 75
UB5: N'olt .38Da 65
Cherry Gdn. St. SE16 .47Xb 91
Cherry Gth. TW8: Bford .50Ma 87
Cherry Grn. Cl. RH1: Redh .8B 208
Cherry Gro. UB3: Hayes .46X 85
UB8: Hil .43R 84
Cherry Hill AL2: Chis G .7N 5
EN5: New Bar .16Db 31
HA3: Hrw W .23Ha 46
WD3: Loud .13K 25
(not continuous)
Cherry Hill Gdns. CR0: Wadd .77Pb 156
Cherry Hills WD19: Wat .22Aa 45
Cherry Hollow WD5: Ab L .3V 12
Cherrylands Cl. NW9 .33Sa 67
Cherry La. UB7: W Dray .49P 83
Cherry Laurel Wlk. SW2 .58Pb 112
Cherry Lodge Golf Course .89Qc 180
Cherry Orchard KT21: Asht .90Ra 173
SE7 .51Lc 115
SL2: Stoke P .8M 61
TW18: Staines .64J 127
UB7: W Dray .47N 83
Cherry Orchard Cl.
BR5: St M Cry .71Yc 161
Cherry Orchard Gdns.
CR0: C'don .74Tb 157
KT8: W Mole .69Ba 129
Cherry Orchard Rd. BR2: Brom .75Nc 160
CR0: C'don .75Tb 157
KT8: W Mole .69Ca 129
Cherry Pk. La. E20 .38Ec 72
Cherry Red Records Stadium
(Kingsmeadow) .69Ra 131
Cherry Ri. HP8: Chal G .19A 24
Cherry Rd. EN3: Enf W .10Yb 20
Cherry St. GU21: Wok .90A 168
RM7: Rom .29Fd 56
Cherry Tree Av. AL2: Lon C .8H 7
TW18: Staines .65K 127
UB7: Yiew .44P 83
Cherry Tree Cl. E9 .39Yb 72
HA0: Wemb .35Ja 66
RM13: Rain .40Jd 76
RM17: Grays .51Fe 121
Cherry Tree Ct. CR5: Coul .90Pb 176
KT22: Lea .92Ha 192
(off Park Vw. Rd.)
NW1 .38Lb 70
(off Camden Rd.)
NW9 .28Sa 47
SE7 .51Lc 115
Cherry Tree Dr. RM15: S Ock .42Zd 99
SW16 .62Nb 134
Cherry Tree Grn. CR2: Sande .86Xb 177
Cherry Tree Grn. TN15: Knat .82Rd 183
Cherry Tree Hill N2 .29Gb 49
Cherry Tree Ho. N22 .24Nb 50
Cherry Tree La. DA2: Wilm .62Hd 140
EN6: Pot B .6Db 17
RM13: Rain .41Gd 96
SL0: Iver H .39J 63
SL3: Ful .37B 62
WD3: Herons .18E 24
Cherrytree La. SL9: Chal P .26A 42
Cherry Tree Ri. IG9: Buck H .21Lc 53
Cherry Tree Rd. E15 .36Gc 73
N2 .28Hb 49
SL2: Farn R .8G 60
WD24: Wat .8X 13
Cherry Trees DA3: Hartl .71Be 165
Cherrytrees CR5: Coul .93Mb 196
Cherry Tree Ter. SE1 .2J 231
Cherry Tree Wlk. BR3: Beck .70Bc 136
BR4: W W'ck .77Hc 159
EC1 .6E 218 (42Sb 91)
Cherry Tree Way E13 .42Mc 93
HA7: Stan .23Ka 46
Cherry Wlk. BR2: Hayes .74Jc 159
RM13: Rain .40Jd 76
RM16: Grays .8C 100
WD3: Sarr .12L 25
Cherry Way AL10: Hat .3C 8
KT19: Ewe .79Ta 153
SL3: Hort .55E 104
TW17: Shep .70T 128
Cherrywood Av. TW20: Eng G .6M 125
Cherrywood Cl. E3 .41Ac 92
KT2: King T .66Qa 131
Cherrywood Ct. TW11: Tedd .64Ja 130
Cherrywood Dr. DA11: Nflt .3A 144
SW15 .57Za 110
Cherrywood La. SM4: Mord .70Ab 132
Cherrywood Lodge SE13 .58Fc 115
(off Birdwood Av.)
Cherry Wood Way W5 .43Qa 87
Cherston Gdns. IG10: Lough .14Qc 36
Cherston Rd. IG10: Lough .14Qc 36
CHERTSEY .73J 149
Chertsey Abbey (remains) .72J 149
Chertsey Blvd. KT16: Chert .74H 149
Chertsey Bri. Rd. KT16: Chert .73L 149
Chertsey Camping & Caravanning Club
KT16: Chert .73L 149
Chertsey Cl. CR8: Kenley .87Rb 177
Chertsey Ct. SW14 .55Ra 109
Chertsey Cres. CR0: New Ad .82Ec 178
Chertsey Dr. SM3: Cheam .75Ab 154
Chertsey Ho. E2 .4K 219
(off Arnold Cir.)
KT16: Chert .74L 149
Chertsey La. KT19: Eps .84Qa 173
TW18: Staines .64G 126
CHERTSEY LOCK .73L 149
CHERTSEY MEADS .74N 149
Chertsey Meads KT16: Chert .74M 149
Chertsey Meads Local Nature Reserve .74N 149
Chertsey Mus. .72J 149
Chertsey Rd. E11 .33Fc 73
GU20: W'sham .9B 146
GU21: Wok .89B 168
GU24: Chob .2K 167
(Chobham Rd.)
GU24: Chob .7H 147
(Windsor Rd.)
IG1: Ilf .35Tc 74
KT14: Byfl .83M 169
KT15: Add .75K 149
TW1: Twick .58Ha 108
TW2: Twick .61Da 129
TW13: Felt .62U 128
TW15: Ashf .66T 128
TW16: Sun .66T 128
TW17: Shep .73N 149
CHERTSEY SOUTH .76G 148
Chertsey St. SW17 .64Jb 134
Chertsey Wlk. KT16: Chert .73J 149
Chervil Cl. TW13: Felt .62W 128
Chervil Ct. DA11: Nflt .9A 122
(off Watercress Way)
Chervil M. SE28 .46Xc 95
Chervil Rd. HP2: Hem H .2D 4
Cherwell Cl. SL3: L'ly .51D 104
WD3: Crox G .15Q 26
Cherwell Ct. KT19: Ewe .77Sa 153
Cherwell Gro. RM15: S Ock .45Xd 98
Cherwell Ho. NW8 .6C 214
Cherwell M. SW11 .56Gb 111
Cherwell Way HA4: Ruis .30S 44
Cherylls Cl. SW6 .53Db 111
Cheseman St. SE26 .62Xb 135
Chesfield Rd. KT2: King T .66Na 131
Chesham Apartments E4 .24Dc 52
Chesham Av. BR5: Pet W .72Rc 160
Chesham Cl. NW7 .21Ua 48
RM7: Rom .28Fd 56
SM2: Cheam .82Ab 174
SW1 .4H 227
Chesham Ct. HA6: Nwood .23V 44
Chesham Cres. SE20 .67Yb 136
Chesham Flats W1 .4J 221
Chesham Hgts. KT20: Kgswd .93Bb 195
Chesham Ho. KT18: Eps .85Ta 173
(off South St.)
RM3: Rom .23Nd 57
(off Leyburn Cres.)
SE8 .52Cc 114
(off Brookmill Rd.)
Chesham La. HP8: Chal G .21A 42
SL9: Chal P .21A 42
Chesham M. SW1 .3H 227
Chesham Pl. SW1 .4H 227 (48Jb 90)
(not continuous)
Chesham Rd. HP3: Bov .9A 2
HP5: Whel H .10A 2
KT1: King T .68Qa 131
SE20 .68Yb 136
SW19 .64Fb 133
Chesham St. NW10 .34Ta 67
SW1 .4H 227 (48Jb 90)
Chesham Ter. W13 .47Ka 86
Chesham Way WD18: Wat .16U 26
Cheshire Cl. CR4: Mitc .69Nb 134
E17 .25Dc 52
KT16: Ott .79F 148
RM11: Horn .29Qd 57
SE4 .54Bc 114
Cheshire Ct. EC4 .3A 224
SL1: Slou .7M 81
Cheshire Dr. WD25: Wat .6V 12
Cheshire Gdns. KT9: Chess .79Ma 153
Cheshire Ho. KT16: Ott .79F 148
(off Crawshaw Rd.)
N18 .21Xb 51
SM4: Mord .73Db 155
Cheshire Rd. N22 .24Pb 50
Cheshire St. E2 .42Vb 91
Cheshir Ho. NW4 .28Ya 48
Chesholm Rd. N16 .34Ub 71
CHESHUNT .1Zb 20
Cheshunt EN8: Chesh .1Zb 20
Cheshunt Cen., The EN8: Chesh .1Zb 20
Cheshunt Ho. NW6 .39Db 69
(off Mortimer Cres.)
Cheshunt Rd. DA17: Belv .50Cd 96
E7 .37Kc 73
Chesil Ct. E2 .40Yb 72
SW3 .51Gb 111
Chesilton Rd. SW6 .53Bb 111
Chesil Way UB4: Hayes .41V 84
Chesley Gdns. E6 .40Mc 73
Cheslyn Gdns. .9V 12
Chesney Ct. W9 .42Cb 89
(off Shirland Rd.)
Chesney Cres. CR0: New Ad .80Ec 158
Chesney Ho. SE13 .56Fc 115
(off Mercator Rd.)
Chesney St. SW11 .53Jb 112
Chesnut Gro. N17 .27Vb 51
Chesnut Rd. N17 .27Vb 51
Chesnut Row N3 .24Cb 49
(off Nether St.)
Chess Cl. HP5: Lat .8A 10
WD3: Loud .14M 25
Chessell Cl. CR7: Thor H .70Rb 135
Chessfield Pk. HP6: L Chal .11A 24
Chess Hill WD3: Loud .14M 25
Chessholme Ct. TW16: Sun .66U 128
(off Scotts Av.)
Chessholme Rd. TW15: Ashf .65S 128
Chessing Ct. N2 .27Hb 49
(off Fortis Grn.)
CHESSINGTON .78Na 153
Chessington Av. DA7: Bex .52Ad 117
N3 .27Ab 48
Chessington Cl. KT19: Ewe .79Sa 153
Chessington Ct. HA5: Pinn .28Ba 45
N3 .27Bb 49
(off Charter Way)
Chessington Hall Gdns.
KT9: Chess .80Ma 153
Chessington Hill Pk.
KT9: Chess .78Qa 153
Chessington Ho. KT17: Ewe .81Va 174
(off Spring St.)
SW8 .54Mb 112
Chessington Lodge N3 .27Bb 49
Chessington Mans. E10 .31Cc 72
E11 .31Gc 73
Chessington Pde. KT9: Chess .79Ma 153
Chessington Pk. KT9: Chess .77Qa 153
Chessington Rd. KT17: Ewe .79Ra 153
KT19: Ewe .79Qa 153
Chessington Sports Cen. .80Ma 153
Chessington Trade Pk.
KT9: Chess .77Qa 153
Chessington Way
BR4: W W'ck .75Dc 158
Chessington World of Adventures .82La 172
Chess La. WD3: Loud .14M 25
Chesson Rd. W14 .51Bb 111
Chess Va. Ri. WD3: Crox G .16P 25
Chess Way WD3: Chor .13J 25
Chesswood Ct. WD3: Rick .18M 25
Chesswood Way HA5: Pinn .26Z 45
Chestbrook Ct. EN1: Enf .15Ub 33
(off Forsyth Pl.)
Chester Av. RM14: Upm .33Ud 78
TW2: Whitt .60Ba 107
TW10: Rich .58Pa 109
Chester Cl. EN6: Pot B .1Db 17
IG10: Lough .11Sc 36
RM16: Chaf H .47Ae 99
SM1: Sutt .75Cb 155
SW1 .2K 227 (47Kb 90)
SW13 .55Xa 110
TW10: Rich .58Pa 109
TW15: Ashf .64T 128
UB8: Hil .44R 84
Chester Cl. Nth.
NW1 .3A 216 (41Kb 90)
Chester Cl. Sth. NW1 .4A 216 (41Kb 90)
Chester Cotts. SW1 .6H 227
Chester Ct. BR2: Brom .70Hc 137
(off Durham Rd.)
NW1 .3A 216 (41Kb 90)
(not continuous)
SE5 .52Tb 113
(off Lomond Gro.)
SE8 .50Zb 92
W6 .49Za 88
(off Wolverton Gdns.)
Chester Cres. E8 .36Vb 71
Chester Dr. HA2: Harr .30Ba 45
Chesterfield Cl.
BR5: St M Cry .70Ad 139
SE13 .54Fc 115
Chesterfield Ct. KT5: Surb .71Na 153
(off Cranes Pk.)
Chesterfield Dr. DA1: Dart .57Kd 119
KT10: Hin W .75Ja 152
TN13: Riv .93Fd 202
Chesterfield Flats EN5: Barn .15Za 30
(off Bells Hill)
Chesterfield Gdns. N4 .29Rb 51
SE10 .53Fc 115
W1 .6K 221 (46Kb 90)
Chesterfield Gro. SE22 .57Vb 113
Chesterfield Hill W1 .6K 221 (46Kb 90)
Chesterfield Ho. W1 .6J 221
Chesterfield Lodge N21 .17Pb 32
(off Church Hill)
Chesterfield M. N4 .29Rb 51
TW15: Ashf .63N 127
Chesterfield Rd. E10 .30Ec 52
EN3: Enf W .9Ac 20
EN5: Barn .15Za 30
KT19: Ewe .80Ta 153
N3 .23Cb 49
TW15: Ashf .63N 127
W4 .51Sa 109
Chesterfield St. W1 .6K 221 (46Kb 90)
Chesterfield Wlk. SE10 .53Fc 115
Chesterfield Way SE15 .52Yb 114
UB3: Hayes .47W 84
Chesterford Gdns. NW3 .35Db 69
Chesterford Ho. SE18 .53Mc 115
(off Tellson Av.)
Chesterford Rd. E12 .36Pc 74
Chester Gdns. EN3: Pond E .16Xb 33
SM4: Mord .72Eb 155
W13 .44Ka 86
Chester Ga. NW1 .4K 215 (41Kb 90)
Chester Gibbons Grn.
AL2: Lon C .8H 7
Chester Grn. IG10: Lough .11Sc 36
Chester Ho. N10 .26Kb 50
SE8 .51Bc 114
SW1 .5K 227
SW9 .52Qb 112
(off Cranmer Rd.)
UB8: Cowl .42L 83
Chesterman Ct. W4 .52Ua 110
(off Corney Reach Way)
Chester M. E17 .26Cc 52
SW1 .3K 227 (48Kb 90)
Chester Path IG10: Lough .11Sc 36
Chester Pl. HA6: Nwood .24U 44
(off Green La.)
NW1 .3K 215 (41Kb 90)
Chester Rd. DA15: Sidc .57Uc 116
E7 .38Mc 73
E11 .30Kc 53
E16 .42Gc 93
E17 .29Zb 52
HA6: Nwood .24U 44
IG3: Ilf .32Vc 75
IG7: Chig .20Qc 36
IG10: Lough .12Rc 36
KT24: Eff .100X 191
N9 .18Xb 33
N17 .27Tb 51
N19 .33Kb 70
NW1 .4J 215 (41Jb 90)

Chester Rd.—Chobham Common Memorial Cross

Chester Rd. SL1: Slou 4H 81
SW19 . . . . . 65Ya 132
TW4: Houn 55X 107
TW6: H'row A 55Q 106
WD6: Bore 13Sa 29
WD18: Wat 15W 26
Chester Row SW1 . . . . . 6H 227 (49Jb 90)
Chesters, The KT3: N Mald 67Ua 132
Chester Sq. SW1 . . . . . 5J 227 (49Jb 90)
Chester Sq. M. SW1 . . . . . 4K 227
Chester St. E2 . . . . . 42Wb 91
SW1 . . . . . 3J 227 (48Jb 90)
Chester Ter. IG11: Bark 37Tc 74
NW1 . . . . . 3K 215 (41Kb 90)
(not continuous)
Chesterton Cl. SW18 . . . . . 57Cb 111
UB6: G'frd 40Da 65
Chesterton Ct. *W3* *48Ra 87*
(off Bollo Bri. Rd.)
W5 . . . . . 43Ma 87
Chesterton Dr. RH1: Mers 100Nb 196
TW19: Stanw 60P 105
Chesterton Ho. *CR0: C'don* *77Tb 157*
(off Heathfield Rd.)
SW11 . . . . . *55Fb 111*
(off Ingrave St.)
W10 . . . . . *43Ab 88*
(off Portobello Rd.)
Chesterton Rd. E13 . . . . . 41Jc 93
W10 . . . . . 43Za 88
Chesterton Sq. W8 . . . . . 49Cb 89
Chesterton Ter. E13 . . . . . 41Jc 93
KT1: King T 68Qa 131
Chesterton Way *RM18: Tilb* *4E 122*
(off Brennan Rd.)
Chester Way SE11 . . . . . 6A 230 (49Qb 90)
Chesthunte Rd. N17 . . . . . 25Sb 51
Chestlands Ct. UB10: Hil 37Q 64
Chestnut All. SW6 . . . . . 51Bb 111
Chestnut Av. BR4: W W'ck 78Gc 159
CM14: S Weald 17Ud 40
DA9: Bluew 59Vd 120
E7 . . . . . 35Kc 73
GU25: Vir W 10K 125
HA0: Wemb 36Ka 66
HA6: Nwood 26V 44
HA8: Edg 23Na 47
IG9: Buck H 20Mc 35
KT8: E Mos 69Ha 130
KT10: Esh 73Fa 152
KT12: W Vill 81U 170
KT13: Weyb 80S 150
KT19: Ewe 77Ua 154
N8 . . . . . 29Nb 50
RM12: Horn 33Hd 76
RM16: Grays 47De 99
SL3: L'ly 47A 82
SW14 . . . . . 55Ta 109
TN16: Westrm 94Mc 199
TW8: Bford 49Ma 87
TW11: Tedd 68Ha 130
TW12: Hamp 66Ca 129
UB7: Yiew 45P 83
WD3: Rick 15J 25
Chestnut Av. Nth. E17 . . . . . 28Fc 53
Chestnut Av. Sth. E17 . . . . . 29Ec 52
Chestnut Cl. BR6: Chels 78Wc 161
DA11: Nflt 8B 122
DA15: Sidc 60Wc 117
GU23: Rip 97H 189
IG9: Buck H 20Mc 35
KT15: Add 78M 149
KT20: Kgswd 95Cb 195
N14 . . . . . 15Lb 32
N16 . . . . . 33Tb 71
RH1: Redh 8B 208
RM12: Horn 35Ld 77
SE6 . . . . . 64Ec 136
SE14 . . . . . 53Bc 114
SL9: Chal P 25B 42
SM5: Cars 74Hb 155
SW16 . . . . . 63Qb 134
TW15: Ashf 63R 128
TW16: Sun 65V 128
TW20: Eng G 5M 125
UB3: Hayes 45U 84
UB7: Harl, Sip 52R 106
Chestnut Copse RH8: Oxt 4M 211
Chestnut Ct. *CR2: S Croy* *77Sb 157*
(off Bramley Hill)
KT22: Lea 92Ha 192
N8 . . . . . 29Nb 50
RH1: Redh 8P 207
SW6 . . . . . 51Bb 111
TW13: Hanw 64Z 129
TW19: Stanw *60N 105*
(off Mulberry Av.)
W8 . . . . . *48Db 89*
(off Abbots Wlk.)
WD18: Wat 14U 26
Chestnut Cres. KT12: W Vill 81U 170
Chestnut Dr. AL4: St A 1F 6
DA7: Bex 55Zc 117
E11 . . . . . 30Jc 53
HA3: Hrw W 24Ha 46
HA5: Pinn 30Z 45
HP4: Berk 2A 2
SL4: Wind 6C 102
TW20: Egh 5P 125
Chestnut Glen RM12: Horn 33Hd 76
Chestnut Gro. CM14: B'wood 19Yd 40
CR2: Sels 80Xb 157
CR4: Mitc 71Mb 156
DA2: Wilm 63Fd 140
EN4: E Barn 15Hb 31
GU22: Wok 92A 188
HA0: Wemb 36Ka 66
IG6: Ilf 23Uc 54
KT3: N Mald 69Ta 131
SE20 . . . . . 66Xb 135
SW12 . . . . . 59Jb 112
TW7: Isle 56Ja 108
TW18: Staines 65L 127
W5 . . . . . 48Ma 87
Chestnut Ho. *BR8: Swan* *69Hd 140*
(off Squirrels Cl.)
E3 . . . . . *39Bc 72*
(off Sycamore Av.)
SW15 . . . . . 56Va 110
W4 . . . . . *49Ua 88*
(off The Orchard)
WD7: Shenl 2Na 15
Chestnut La. GU24: Chob 8G 146
KT13: Weyb 78R 150
N20 . . . . . 18Ab 30
TN13: S'oaks 96Kd 203
Chestnut Mnr. Cl. TW18: Staines 64K 127
Chestnut Mead RH1: Redh 5N 207
Chestnut M. SW14 . . . . . 56Sa 109
Chestnut Pl. *KT13: Weyb* *78R 150*
(off Pine Gro.)
KT17: Ewe 83Wa 174
KT21: Asht 91Na 193
SE26 . . . . . 63Vb 135
Chestnut Plaza *E20* *37Ec 72*
(within Westfield Stratford City Shop. Cen.)
Chestnut Ri. SE18 . . . . . 51Tc 116
WD23: Bush 17Da 27
Chestnut Rd. DA1: Dart 60Md 119
EN3: Enf W 8Ac 20
KT2: King T 66Na 131
SE27 . . . . . 62Rb 135
SW20 . . . . . 68Za 132
TW2: Twick 61Ga 130
TW15: Ashf 63R 128
Chestnuts CM13: Hut 18De 41
Chestnuts, The BR3: Beck 69Zb 136
HA5: Hat E 24Ba 45
HP3: Hem H 6H 3
IG10: Lough 15Mc 35
KT12: Walt T 75W 150
N5 . . . . . *35Sb 71*
(off Highbury Grange)
RM4: Abr 13Xc 37
UB10: Uxb 38N 63
Chestnut Ter. SM1: Sutt 77Db 155
Chestnut Wlk. IG8: Wfd G 22Jc 53
KT12: W Vill 81U 170
KT14: Byfl 84N 169
SL9: Chal P 24A 42
TN15: S'oaks 100Nd 203
TW17: Shep 70U 128
WD24: Wat 9W 12
Chestnut Way KT17: Eps D 88Xa 174
TW13: Felt 62X 129
Cheston Av. CR0: C'don 75Ac 158
Chestwood Gro. UB10: Hil 38P 63
Cheswick Cl. DA1: Cray 56Hd 118
Chesworth Cl. DA8: Erith 54Gd 118
Chesworth Ct. *E1* *43Yb 92*
(off Fulneck Pl.)
Chettle Cl. SE1 . . . . . 3F 231
Chettle Ct. N8 . . . . . 30Qb 50
Chetwode Dr. KT18: Tatt C 90Za 174
Chetwode Ho. NW8 . . . . . 5D 214
Chetwode Rd. KT20: Tad 91Ya 194
SW17 . . . . . 62Hb 133
Chetwood Wlk. *E6* *43Nc 94*
(off Greenwich Cres.)
Chetwynd Av. EN4: E Barn 18Hb 31
Chetwynd Dr. UB10: Hil 40P 63
Chetwynd Rd. NW5 . . . . . 35Kb 70
Chetwynd Vs. *NW5* *35Kb 70*
(off Chetwynd Rd.)
Chevalier Cl. HA7: Stan 21Na 47
Cheval Pl. SW7 . . . . . 3E 226 (48Gb 89)
Cheval St. E14 . . . . . 48Cc 92
Cheveley Cl. RM3: Hrld W 25Nd 57
Cheveley Gdns. SL1: Burn 10A 60
Cheveley Cl. CM16: Coop 1Zc 23
Cheveney Wlk. BR2: Brom 69Jc 137
CHEVENING 91Bd 201
Chevening Cross TN14: Chev 92Cd 202
Chevening La. TN14: Knock 87Ad 181
Chevening Rd. NW6 . . . . . 40Za 68
SE10 . . . . . 50Hc 93
SE19 . . . . . 65Tb 135
TN13: Chip 91Bd 201
TN14: Chev, Chip, Sund 91Bd 201
TN14: Sund 95Ad 201
Chevenings, The DA14: Sidc 62Yc 139
Cheverell Ho. *E2* *40Wb 71*
(off Pritchard's Rd.)
CHEVERELLS 94Gc 199
Cheverton Rd. N19 . . . . . 32Mb 70
Chevet St. E9 . . . . . 36Ac 72
Chevington NW2 . . . . . 37Bb 69
Chevington Pl. RM12: Horn 36Md 77
Chevington Vs. RH1: Blet 4L 209
Chevington Way RM12: Horn 35Md 77
Cheviot *N17* *24Xb 51*
(off Northumberland Gro.)
Cheviot Cl. DA7: Bex 54Gd 118
EN1: Enf 12Tb 33
SM2: Sutt 81Fb 175
SM7: Bans 87Db 175
UB3: Harl 52T 106
WD23: Bush 16Ea 28
Cheviot Ct. *SE14* *51Yb 114*
(off Avonley Rd.)
UB2: S'hall 49Da 85
Cheviot Gdns. NW2 . . . . . 33Za 68
SE27 . . . . . 63Rb 135
Cheviot Ga. NW2 . . . . . 33Ab 68
Cheviot Ho. *DA11: Nflt* *58Fe 121*
(off Laburnum Gro.)
E1 . . . . . *44Xb 91*
(off Commercial Rd.)
Cheviot Rd. RM11: Horn 31Jd 76
SE27 . . . . . 64Qb 134
SL3: L'ly 50C 82
Cheviots AL10: Hat 3C 8
Cheviot Way IG2: Ilf 28Uc 54
Chevron Cl. E16 . . . . . 44Jc 93
Chevron Ho. RM17: Grays 52De 121
Chevy Rd. UB2: S'hall 47Ea 86
Chewter La. GU20: W'sham 7A 146
Chewton Rd. E17 . . . . . 28Ac 52
Cheyham Gdns. SM2: Cheam 82Za 174
Cheyham Way SM2: Cheam 82Ab 174
Cheylesmore Ho. SW1 . . . . . 7K 227
Cheyne Av. E18 . . . . . 27Hc 53
TW2: Whitt 60Ba 107
Cheyne Cl. BR2: Brom 76Nc 160
NW4 . . . . . 29Ya 48
SL9: Ger X 32A 62
Cheyne Ct. SM7: Bans 87Db 175
SW3 . . . . . 51Hb 111
WD23: Bush 14Aa 27
Cheyne Gdns. SW3 . . . . . 51Gb 111
Cheyne Hill KT5: Surb 70Pa 131
Cheyne Ho. *SW3* *51Hb 111*
(off Chelsea Emb.)
Cheyne M. SW3 . . . . . 51Gb 111
Cheyne Pk. Dr. BR4: W W'ck 76Ec 158
Cheyne Path W7 . . . . . 43Ha 86
Cheyne Pl. SW3 . . . . . 51Hb 111
Cheyne Rd. TW15: Ashf 66T 128
Cheyne Row SW3 . . . . . 51Gb 111
Cheyne Wlk. CR0: C'don 75Wb 157
DA3: Lfield 69Zd 143
N21 . . . . . 15Rb 33
NW4 . . . . . 30Ya 48
SW3 . . . . . 52Fb 111
SW10 . . . . . 52Fb 111
Cheyneys Av. HA8: Edg 23Ma 47
Chichele Gdns. CR0: C'don 77Ub 157
Chichele Rd. NW2 . . . . . 36Za 68
RH8: Oxt 100Gc 199
Chicheley Gdns. HA3: Hrw W 24Ea 46
(not continuous)
Chicheley Rd. HA3: Hrw W 24Ea 46
Chicheley St. SE1 . . . . . 1J 229 (47Pb 90)
Chichester Av. HA4: Ruis 33T 64
Chichester Cl. E6 . . . . . 44Nc 94
RM15: Avel 46Td 98
RM16: Chaf H 49Zd 99
SE3 . . . . . 52Lc 115
TW12: Hamp 65Ba 129
Chichester Ct. HA7: Stan 27Na 47
HA8: Edg *23Qa 47*
(off Whitchurch La.)
KT17: Ewe 81Va 174
NW1 . . . . . *38Lb 70*
(off Royal Coll. St.)
SL1: Slou 8M 81
TW19: Stanw 60N 105
UB5: N'olt 39Ba 65
Chichester Dr. CR8: Purl 84Pb 176
TN13: S'oaks 97Hd 202
Chichester Gdns. IG1: Ilf 31Nc 74
Chichester Ho. *CM14: B'wood* *19Yd 40*
(off Sir Francis Way)
KT19: Eps 84Qa 173
NW6 . . . . . 40Cb 69
SW9 . . . . . *52Qb 112*
(off Cranmer Rd.)
Chichester M. SE27 . . . . . 63Qb 134
Chichester Rents WC2 . . . . . 2K 223
Chichester Ri. DA12: Grav'nd 3F 144
Chichester Rd. CR0: C'don 76Ub 157
DA9: Ghithe 58Vd 120
E11 . . . . . 34Gc 73
N9 . . . . . 18Wb 33
NW6 . . . . . 40Cb 69
W2 . . . . . 43Db 89
Chichester St. SW1 . . . . . 7C 228 (50Lb 90)
Chichester Way E14 . . . . . 49Fc 93
TW14: Felt 59Y 107
WD25: Wat 5Aa 13
Chichester Wharf DA8: Erith 50Gd 96
Chicken La. AL2: Lon C 9H 7
Chickenshed Theatre 15Jb 32
Chicksand Ho. *E1* *43Wb 91*
(off Chicksand St.)
Chicksand St. E1 . . . . . 43Vb 91
(not continuous)
Chidbrook Ho. WD18: Wat 16U 26
Chiddingfold N12 . . . . . 20Cb 31
Chiddingstone SE13 . . . . . 57Ec 114
Chiddingstone Av. DA7: Bex 52Bd 117
Chiddingstone Cl. SM2: Sutt 82Cb 175
Chiddingstone St. SW6 . . . . . 54Cb 111
Chieftain Rd. KT16: Vir W 5L 147
Chieftan Dr. RM19: Purf 49Qd 97
Chieveley Pde. DA7: Bex 55Dd 118
Chieveley Rd. DA7: Bex 56Dd 118
Chiffinch Gdns. DA11: Nflt 2A 144
Chignell Pl. W13 . . . . . 46Ja 86
CHIGWELL 20Rc 36
Chigwell Ct. *E9* *37Ac 72*
(off Ballance Rd.)
Chigwell Golf Course 21Qc 54
Chigwell Grange IG7: Chig 18Sc 36
Chigwell Hill E1 . . . . . 45Xb 91
Chigwell Hurst Ct. HA5: Pinn 27Z 45
Chigwell La. IG7: Chig, Lough 15Sc 36
IG10: Lough 15Sc 36
Chigwell Pk. IG7: Chig 21Rc 54
Chigwell Pk. Dr. IG7: Chig 21Qc 54
Chigwell Ri. IG7: Chig 19Qc 36
Chigwell Rd. E18 . . . . . 27Kc 53
IG8: Wfd G 23Pc 54
CHIGWELL ROW 20Xc 37
Chigwell Row Wood Local Nature Reserve 21Wc 55
Chigwell Vw. RM5: Col R 23Cd 56
Chilberton Dr. RH1: Mers 2C 208
Chilbolton TW20: Egh 64A 126
Chilbrook Rd. KT11: D'side 90W 170
Chilcombe Ho. *SW15* *59Wa 110*
(off Fontley Way)
Chilcot Cl. E14 . . . . . 44Dc 92
Chilcott Cl. HA0: Wemb 35La 66
Chilcott Rd. WD24: Wat 8U 12
Childebert Rd. SW17 . . . . . 61Kb 134
CHILDERDITCH 27Ce 59
Childerditch Hall Dr.
CM13: L War 27Ce 59
Childerditch Ind. Pk.
CM13: L War 27Be 59
Childerditch La.
CM13: L War, W H'dn 24Ae 59
Childerditch St. CM13: L War 26Ce 59
Childeric Rd. SE14 . . . . . 52Ac 114
Childerley *KT1: King T* *69Qa 131*
(off Burritt Rd.)
Childerley St. SW6 . . . . . 53Ab 110
Childers, The IG8: Wfd G 22Pc 54
Childers St. SE8 . . . . . 51Ac 114
Child La. SE10 . . . . . 48Hc 93
Childs Av. UB9: Hare 26L 43
Childsbridge Farm Pl.
TN15: Seal 91Nd 203
Childsbridge La.
TN15: Kems'g, Seal 90Nd 183
Childsbridge Way TN15: Seal 92Pd 203
Childs Cl. RM11: Horn 30Ld 57
Childs Ct. UB3: Hayes 45W 84
Childs Cres. DA10: Swans 58Zd 121
Childs Hall Cl. KT23: Bookh 97Ba 191
Childs Hall Dr. KT23: Bookh 97Ba 191
Childs Hall Rd. KT23: Bookh 97Ba 191
CHILD'S HILL 34Bb 69
Childs Hill Wlk. *NW2* *34Bb 69*
(off Cricklewood La.)
Child's La. SE19 . . . . . 65Ub 135
Child's M. *SW5* *49Cb 89*
(off Child's Pl.)
Child's Pl. SW5 . . . . . 49Cb 89
Child's St. SW5 . . . . . 49Cb 89
Child's Wlk. *SW5* *49Cb 89*
(off Child's St.)
Childs Way NW11 . . . . . 29Bb 49
TN15: Wro 88Be 185
Childwick Ct. HP3: Hem H 3N 3
Chilham Cl. DA5: Bexl 59Bd 117
HP2: Hem H 3N 3
UB6: G'frd 40Ja 66
Chilham Ho. SE1 . . . . . 3G 231 (48Tb 91)
SE15 . . . . . 51Yb 114
Chilham Rd. SE9 . . . . . 63Nc 138
Chilham Way BR2: Hayes 73Jc 159
Chilianwallah Memorial 51Jb 112
Chillerton Rd. SW17 . . . . . 64Jb 134
Chillingford Ho. SW17 . . . . . 63Eb 133
Chillington Dr. SW11 . . . . . 56Fb 111
Chillingworth Gdns. TW1: Twick 62Ha 130
Chillingworth Rd. N7 . . . . . 36Qb 70
Chilmans Dr. KT23: Bookh 97Da 191
Chilmark Gdns. KT3: N Mald 72Wa 154
RH1: Mers 1E 208
Chilmark Rd. SW16 . . . . . 68Mb 134
Chilmead RH1: Redh 5P 207
Chilmead La. RH1: Nutf 4D 208
Chilsey Grn. Rd. KT16: Chert 72G 148
Chiltern Av. TW2: Whitt 60Ca 107
WD23: Bush 16Ea 28
Chiltern Bus. Village UB8: Uxb 40K 63
Chiltern Cl. CR0: C'don 76Ub 157
DA7: Bex 53Gd 118
GU22: Wok 4N 187
KT4: Wor Pk 74Ya 154
TW18: Staines 64J 127
UB10: Ick 33Q 64
WD6: Bore 12Pa 29
WD18: Wat 14V 26
WD23: Bush 16Da 27
Chiltern Ct. *BR2: Brom* *75Nc 160*
(off Gravel Rd.)
EN5: New Bar 15Eb 31
HA1: Harr 29Fa 46
N10 . . . . . 26Jb 50
NW1 . . . . . 6G 215
SE14 . . . . . *52Yb 114*
(off Avonley Rd.)
SL4: Wind *3F 102*
(off Fawcett Rd.)
UB8: Hil 42R 84
Chiltern Ct. M. *SL4: Wind* *3F 102*
(off Fawcett Rd.)
Chiltern Dene EN2: Enf 14Pb 32
Chiltern Dr. KT5: Surb 72Qa 153
WD3: Rick 17H 25
Chiltern Est. WD24: Wat 11Y 27
Chiltern Gdns. BR2: Brom 70Hc 137
NW2 . . . . . 34Za 68
RM12: Horn 34Ld 77
Chiltern Hgts. *N1* *38Pb 70*
(off Caledonian Rd.)
Chiltern Hill SL9: Chal P 25A 42
Chiltern Ho. N9 . . . . . 20Wb 33
SE17 . . . . . *51Tb 113*
(off Portland St.)
W5 . . . . . 43Na 87
W10 . . . . . *43Ab 88*
(off Telford Rd.)
WD18: Wat *14Y 27*
(off King St.)
Chiltern Open Air Mus. 18B 24
Chiltern Rd. DA11: Nflt 2A 144
E3 . . . . . 42Cc 92
HA5: Eastc 29Y 45
IG2: Ilf 29Uc 54
SL1: Burn 3A 80
SM2: Sutt 81Db 175
Chilterns AL10: Hat 3C 8
Chilterns, The *BR1: Brom* *68Kc 137*
(off Murray Av.)
SM2: Sutt 81Db 175
Chiltern St. W1 . . . . . 7H 215 (43Jb 90)
Chiltern Vw. Rd. UB8: Uxb 40L 63
Chiltern Way IG8: Wfd G 20Jc 35
Chilthorne Cl. SE6 . . . . . 59Bc 114
Chilton Av. W5 . . . . . 49Ma 87
Chilton Ct. KT12: Walt T 77W 150
N22 . . . . . *24Nb 50*
(off Truro Rd.)
SL6: Tap 4A 80
Chilton Gro. SE8 . . . . . 49Zb 92
CHILTON HILLS 3P 145
Chiltonian Ind. Est. SE12 . . . . . 58Hc 115
Chiltonian M. SE13 . . . . . 57Fc 115
Chilton Rd. HA8: Edg 23Qa 47
RM16: Grays 8C 100
TW9: Rich 55Qa 109
Chiltons, The E18 . . . . . 26Jc 53
Chiltons Cl. SM7: Bans 87Db 175
Chilton St. E2 . . . . . 42Vb 91
Chilvers Cl. TW2: Twick 61Ga 130
Chilver St. SE10 . . . . . 50Hc 93
Chilwell Gdns. WD19: Wat 21Y 45
Chilwick Rd. SL2: Slou 2D 80
Chilworth Ct. SW19 . . . . . 60Za 110
Chilworth Gdns. SM1: Sutt 76Eb 155
Chilworth M. W2 . . . . . 3A 220 (44Fb 89)
Chilworth Pl. IG11: Bark 40Wc 75
Chilworth St. W2 . . . . . 3A 220 (44Eb 89)
Chimes Av. N13 . . . . . 22Qb 50
Chimes Ho. BR3: Beck 67Ac 136
Chime Sq. AL3: St A 1C 6
Chimes Shop. Cen., The UB8: Uxb 38M 63
Chimes Ter. N8 . . . . . 29Nb 50
Chimney Ct. *E1* *46Xb 91*
(off Brewhouse La.)
Chimneys, The WD23: Bush 15Ba 27
China Ct. *E1* *46Xb 91*
(off Asher Way)
China Hall M. SE16 . . . . . 48Yb 92
China La. RM14: Bulp 34Fe 79
China M. SW2 . . . . . 59Pb 112
China Town 4E 222
China Wharf SE1 . . . . . 47Wb 91
Chinbrook Cres. SE12 . . . . . 62Kc 137
Chinbrook Rd. SE12 . . . . . 62Kc 137
Chinchilla Dr. TW4: Houn 54Y 107
Chindits La. CM14: W'ley 22Yd 58
Chine, The HA0: Wemb 36Ka 66
N10 . . . . . 28Lb 50
N21 . . . . . 16Rb 33
Chine Farm Pl. TN14: Knock 88Zc 181
Ching Ct. WC2 . . . . . 3F 223
Chingdale Rd. E4 . . . . . 20Gc 35
CHINGFORD 18Ec 34
Chingford Av. E4 . . . . . 20Cc 34
Chingford Fitness & Wellbeing Cen. 21Ec 52
Chingford Golf Range 18Cc 34
CHINGFORD GREEN 18Fc 35
CHINGFORD HATCH 21Fc 53
Chingford Ind. Cen. E4 . . . . . 22Ac 52
Chingford La. IG8: Wfd G 21Gc 53
Chingford Leisure Cen. 21Ec 52
CHINGFORD MOUNT 21Cc 52
Chingford Mt. Rd. E4 . . . . . 21Cc 52
Chingford Rd. E4 . . . . . 23Cc 52
E17 . . . . . 25Dc 52
Chingley Cl. BR1: Brom 65Gc 137
Chingstone Ter. E4 . . . . . 18Ec 34
Ching Way E4 . . . . . 23Bc 52
(not continuous)
Chinnery Cl. EN1: Enf 11Vb 33
Chinnock's Wharf *E14* *45Ac 92*
(off Narrow St.)
Chinnor Cres. UB6: G'frd 40Da 65
Chinthurst M. CR5: Coul 88Jb 176
Chipka St. E14 . . . . . 47Ec 92
(not continuous)
Chipley St. SE14 . . . . . 51Ac 114
Chipmunk Gro. UB5: N'olt 41Aa 85
Chippendale All. UB8: Uxb 38M 63
Chippendale Ho. *SW1* *50Kb 90*
(off Churchill Gdns.)
Chippendale St. E5 . . . . . 34Zb 72
Chippendale Waye UB8: Uxb 38M 63
Chippenham *KT1: King T* *68Pa 131*
(off Excelsior Cl.)
Chippenham Av. HA9: Wemb 36Ra 67
Chippenham Cl. HA5: Eastc 28V 44
RM3: Rom 22Md 57
Chippenham Gdns. NW6 . . . . . 41Cb 89
Chippenham M. W9 . . . . . 42Cb 89
Chippenham Rd. RM3: Rom 23Md 57
W9 . . . . . 42Cb 89
Chippenham Wlk. RM3: Rom 23Md 57
CHIPPERFIELD 3J 11
Chipperfield Cl. RM14: Upm 32Ud 78
CHIPPERFIELD COMMON 4K 11
Chipperfield Ho. SW3 . . . . . 7D 226
Chipperfield Rd. BR5: St P 67Wc 139
(not continuous)
HP3: Bov 9D 2
HP3: Hem H 6L 3
WD4: Chfd 9D 2
WD4: K Lan 2L 11
CHIPPING BARNET 14Ab 30
Chipping Cl. EN5: Barn 13Ab 30
CHIPSTEAD
CR5 . . . . . 90Hb 175
TN13 . . . . . 94Ed 202
Chipstead Av. CR7: Thor H 70Rb 135
CHIPSTEAD BOTTOM 93Fb 195
Chipstead Cl. CR5: Coul 88Jb 176
RH1: Redh 7P 207
SE19 . . . . . 66Vb 135
SM2: Sutt 81Db 175
Chipstead Ct. GU21: Knap 9J 167
Chipstead Gdns. NW2 . . . . . 33Xa 68
Chipstead Golf Course 90Hb 175
Chipstead La. CR5: Chip, Coul 96Eb 195
KT20: Kgswd 97Bb 195
TN13: Chip, Riv 94Ed 202
Chipstead Pk. TN13: Chip 94Fd 202
Chipstead Pk. Cl. TN13: Chip 94Ed 202
Chipstead Pl. Gdns. TN13: Chip 94Ed 202
Chipstead Rd. DA8: Erith 52Gd 118
SM7: Bans 89Bb 175
Chipstead Sailing Club 94Ed 202
Chipstead Sq. TN13: Chip 94Ed 202
Chipstead Sta. Pde. CR5: Chip 90Hb 175
Chipstead St. SW6 . . . . . 53Cb 111
Chipstead Valley Rd. CR5: Coul 88Jb 176
Chipstead Way SM7: Bans 88Hb 175
Chip St. SW4 . . . . . 55Mb 112
Chirdland Ho. WD18: Wat 16U 26
Chirk Cl. UB4: Yead 42Aa 85
Chirton Wlk. GU21: Wok 10L 167
Chisenhale Rd. E3 . . . . . 40Ac 72
Chisholm Ct. W6 . . . . . 50Wa 88
Chisholm Rd. CR0: C'don 75Ub 157
TW10: Rich 58Pa 109
Chisledon Wlk. *E9* *37Bc 72*
(off Osborne Rd.)
CHISLEHURST 65Rc 138
Chislehurst Av. N12 . . . . . 24Eb 49
Chislehurst Caves 67Qc 138
Chislehurst Golf Course 66Rc 138
Chislehurst Rd. BR1: Brom 68Mc 137
BR5: Pet W 70Uc 138
BR6: Orp, Pet W, St M Cry 70Uc 138
BR7: Chst 68Mc 137
DA14: Sidc 64Wc 139
TW10: Rich 57Na 109
CHISLEHURST WEST 65Qc 138
Chislet Cl. BR3: Beck 66Cc 136
Chisley Rd. N15 . . . . . 30Ub 51
Chiswell Ct. WD24: Wat 10Y 13
CHISWELL GREEN 7N 5
Chiswell Grn. La. AL2: Chis G, Pot C 7K 5
Chiswell Sq. SE3 . . . . . 54Kc 115
Chiswell St. EC1 . . . . . 7E 218 (43Sb 91)
SE5 . . . . . *52Tb 113*
(off Edmund St.)
CHISWICK 50Ta 87
Chiswick Bri. SW14 . . . . . 54Sa 109
Chiswick Cl. CR0: Bedd 76Pb 156
Chiswick Comn. Rd. W4 . . . . . 49Ta 87
Chiswick Community Sports Hall 52Ta 109
Chiswick Ct. HA5: Pinn 27Ba 45
W4 . . . . . 49Ra 87
Chiswick High Rd. TW8: Bford 50Qa 87
W4 . . . . . 50Qa 87
Chiswick House & Gdns. 51Ua 110
Chiswick Ho. Grounds W4 . . . . . 51Ua 110
Chiswick La. W4 . . . . . 50Ua 88
Chiswick La. Sth. W4 . . . . . 51Va 110
Chiswick Lifeboat Station 52Va 110
Chiswick Mall W4 . . . . . 51Va 110
W6 . . . . . 50Wa 88
Chiswick Pk. W4 . . . . . 49Ra 87
Chiswick Plaza W4 . . . . . 51Sa 109
Chiswick Quay W4 . . . . . 53Sa 109
Chiswick Rd. N9 . . . . . 19Wb 33
W4 . . . . . 49Sa 87
CHISWICK RDBT. 50Qa 87
Chiswick Sq. W4 . . . . . 51Ua 110
Chiswick Staithe W4 . . . . . 53Sa 109
Chiswick Ter. *W4* *49Sa 87*
(off Chiswick High Rd.)
Chiswick Village W4 . . . . . 51Qa 109
Chiswick Wharf W4 . . . . . 51Va 110
Chittenden Cotts. GU23: Wis 88N 169
Chitterfield Ga. UB7: Sip 52Q 106
Chitty's La. RM8: Dag 33Zc 75
Chitty St. W1 . . . . . 7C 216 (43Lb 90)
Chivalry Rd. SW11 . . . . . 57Gb 111
Chivelston SW19 . . . . . 60Za 110
Chivenor Gro. KT2: King T 64Ma 131
Chivenor Pl. AL4: St A 4G 6
Chivers Rd. E4 . . . . . 20Dc 34
Choats Mnr. Way RM9: Dag 40Ad 75
Choats Rd. IG11: Bark 40Yc 75
RM9: Dag 40Yc 75
CHOBHAM 3J 167
Chobham Academy Sports Cen. 36Ec 72
Chobham Bus. Cen. GU24: Chob 2P 167
Chobham Cl. KT16: Ott 79D 148
Chobham Common Memorial Cross 5H 147

Chobham Common National Nature Reserve—Church Side

Chobham Common National Nature Reserve
. . . . .6H 147
Chobham Gdns. SW19 . . . . .61Za 132
Chobham Golf Course 7H 167
Chobham La. KT16: Longc 6K 147
CHOBHAM MANOR 36Dc 72
Chobham Mus. 3J 167
Chobham Pk. La. GU24: Chob 2L 167
Chobham Rd. E15 . . . . .36Fc 73
GU21: Knap, Wok 10F 166
GU21: Wok 5N 167
(Horsell Comn. Rd.)
GU21: Wok 88A 168
(Wheatsheaf Cl., not continuous)
GU24: Chob 3F 146
KT16: Ott 80C 148
SL5: S'dale 3F 146
Chocolate Factory 1, The 26Pb 50
(off Clarendon Rd.)
Chocolate Factory 2, The 26Pb 50
(off Coburg Rd.)
Chocolate Studios N1 . . . . .3F 219
Choice Vw. IG1: Ilf 33Sc 74
(off Axon Pl.)
Choir Grn. GU21: Knap 9J 167
Cholesbury WD19: Wat 19Aa 27
Cholmeley Cl. N6 . . . . .31Kb 70
Cholmeley Cres. N6 . . . . .31Kb 70
Cholmeley Lodge N6 . . . . .32Kb 70
Cholmeley Pk. N6 . . . . .32Kb 70
Cholmley Gdns. NW6 . . . . .36Cb 69
Cholmley Rd. KT7: T Ditt 72Ka 152
Cholmley Ter. KT7: T Ditt 73Ka 152
(off Portsmouth Rd.)
Cholmley Vs. KT7: T Ditt 72Ka 152
(off Portsmouth Rd.)
Cholmondeley Av. NW10 . . . . .40Wa 68
Cholmondeley Wlk. TW9: Rich 57La 108
Choppin's Ct. E1 . . . . .46Xb 91
Chopwell Cl. E15 . . . . .38Fc 73
CHORLEYWOOD 14F 24
CHORLEYWOOD BOTTOM 15F 24
Chorleywood Bottom WD3: Chor 15F 24
Chorleywood Cl. WD3: Rick 17M 25
Chorleywood Coll. Est. WD3: Chor 14H 25
Chorleywood Cres. BR5: St P 68Vc 139
Chorleywood Golf Course 14F 24
Chorleywood Ho. WD3: Chor 13G 24
Chorleywood Ho. Dr. WD3: Chor 13G 24
Chorleywood House Estate 12H 25
Chorleywood Lodge La.
WD3: Chor 13H 25
Chorleywood Rd. WD3: Rick 14J 25
CHORLEYWOOD WEST 14D 24
Choudhury Mans. N1 . . . . .38Nb 70
(off Pembroke St.)
Choumert Gro. SE15 . . . . .54Wb 113
Choumert M. SE15 . . . . .54Wb 113
Choumert Rd. SE15 . . . . .55Vb 113
Choumert Sq. SE15 . . . . .54Wb 113
Chown Ct. KT24: E Hor 100V 190
Chow Sq. E8 . . . . .36Vb 71
Chrislaine Cl. TW19: Stanw 58M 105
Chrisp Ho. SE10 . . . . .51Gc 115
(off Maze Hill)
Chrisp St. E14 . . . . .43Dc 92
(not continuous)
Chris Pullen Way N7 . . . . .37Nb 70
Christabel Cl. TW7: Isle 55Ga 108
Christabel Pankhurst Ct. SE5 . . . . .52Tb 113
(off Brisbane St.)
Christchurch Av. DA8: Erith 51Fd 118
HA0: Wemb 37Na 67
HA3: Kenton, W'stone 28Ha 46
N12 . . . . .23Eb 49
NW6 . . . . .39Za 68
RM13: Rain 40Hd 76
TW11: Tedd 64Ja 130
Christchurch Cl. AL3: St A 1A 6
EN2: Enf 12Sb 33
N12 . . . . .24Fb 49
SW19 . . . . .66Fb 133
Christ Church Ct. NW10 . . . . .39Ua 68
Christchurch Ct. EC4 . . . . .2C 224
NW6 . . . . .38Ab 68
(off Willesden La.)
UB4: Yead 42Y 85
(off Dunedin Way)
Christchurch Cres. DA12: Grav'nd 9E 122
WD7: R'lett 8Ja 14
Christchurch Flats TW9: Rich 55Na 109
Christchurch Gdns. HA3: W'stone 28Ja 46
KT19: Eps 83Ra 173
Christchurch Grn. HA0: Wemb 37Na 67
Christchurch Hill NW3 . . . . .34Fb 69
Christchurch Ho. RM8: Dag 36Xc 75
SW2 . . . . .60Pb 112
(off Christchurch Rd.)
Christchurch La. EN5: Barn 12Ab 30
Christchurch Lodge EN4: Cockf 14Hb 31
Christ Chu. Mt. KT19: Eps 84Ra 173
(not continuous)
Christchurch Pk. SM2: Sutt 80Eb 155
Christchurch Pas. EN5: Barn 12Ab 30
NW3 . . . . .34Eb 69
Christchurch Path UB3: Harl 48S 84
Christchurch Pl. KT19: Eps 83Ra 173
SW8 . . . . .54Mb 112
Christ Chu. Rd. BR3: Beck 68Cc 136
KT5: Surb 72Pa 153
KT19: Eps 84Na 173
Christchurch Rd. CR8: Purl 83Rb 177
DA1: Dart 59Ld 119
DA12: Grav'nd 10E 122
DA15: Sidc 63Vc 139
GU25: Vir W 9L 125
HP2: Hem H 1M 3
IG1: Ilf 32Rc 74
N8 . . . . .30Nb 50
RM18: Tilb 3C 122
SW2 . . . . .60Pb 112
SW14 . . . . .57Ra 109
SW19 . . . . .66Fb 133
TW6: H'row A 55Q 106
Christchurch Sq. E9 . . . . .39Yb 72
Christchurch St. SW3 . . . . .51Hb 111
Christchurch Ter. SW3 . . . . .51Hb 111
(off Christchurch St.)
Christchurch Way GU21: Wok 89B 168
SE10 . . . . .50Gc 93
Christian Ct. SE16 . . . . .46Bc 92
CHRISTIAN FIELDS 3F 144
Christian Flds. SW16 . . . . .66Qb 134
Christian Flds. Av. DA12: Grav'nd 3E 144
Christian Pl. E1 . . . . .44Wb 91
(off Burslem St.)
Christian Sq. SL4: Wind 3G 102
Christian St. E1 . . . . .44Wb 91
Christie Cl. GU18: Light 2A 166
KT23: Bookh 97Ba 191
Christie Ct. CM14: B'wood 20Yd 40
N19 . . . . .33Nb 70
WD18: Wat 15W 26
Christie Dr. CR0: C'don 71Wb 157
Christie Gdns. RM6: Chad H 30Xc 55
Christie Ho. E16 . . . . .43Jc 93
(off Hammersley Rd.)
SE10 . . . . .50Hc 93
(off Blackwall La.)
W12 . . . . .44Xa 88
(off Du Cane Rd.)
Christie Rd. E9 . . . . .37Ac 72
EN9: Walt A 7Dc 20
Christies Av. TN14: Bad M 82Cd 182
Christie Wlk. CR3: Cat'm 94Tb 197
Christina Sq. N4 . . . . .32Rb 71
Christina St. EC2 . . . . .5H 219 (42Ub 91)
Christine Ct. RM13: Rain 43Jd 96
Christine Worsley Cl. N21 . . . . .18Rb 33
Christmas La. SL2: Farn C 4G 60
Christmas Tree Farm 84Qc 180
Christopher Av. W7 . . . . .48Ja 86
Christopher Bell Twr. E3 . . . . .40Cc 72
(off Pancras Way)
Christopher Cl. DA15: Sidc 57Vc 117
RM12: Horn 35Md 77
SE16 . . . . .47Zb 92
Christopher Ct. DA15: Sidc 61Wc 139
(off Station Rd.)
E1 . . . . .44Wb 91
(off Leman St.)
HP3: Hem H 5M 3
KT20: Tad 95Ya 194
TW15: Ashf 64N 127
Christopher Gdns. RM9: Dag 36Zc 75
Christopher Pl. AL3: St A 2B 6
(off Verulam Rd.)
N22 . . . . .24Nb 50
(off Myddleton Rd.)
NW1 . . . . .4E 216 (41Mb 90)
Christopher Rd. UB2: S'hall 49X 85
Christophers M. W11 . . . . .46Ab 88
Christopher St. EC2 . . . . .6G 219 (42Tb 91)
Christy Rd. TN16: Big H 87Lc 179
Chroma Mans. E20 . . . . .37Ec 72
(off Penny Brookes St.)
Chrome Rd. DA8: Erith 52Jd 118
Chronicle Twr. N1 . . . . .3D 218 (41Sb 91)
Chryssell Rd. SW9 . . . . .52Qb 112
Chrystie La. KT23: Bookh 98Da 191
Chubworthy St. SE14 . . . . .51Ac 114
Chucks La. KT20: Walt H 96Xa 194
Chudleigh DA14: Sidc 63Xc 139
Chudleigh Cres. IG3: Ilf 35Uc 74
Chudleigh Gdns. SM1: Sutt 76Eb 155
Chudleigh Rd. NW6 . . . . .38Za 68
RM3: Rom 21Nd 57
SE4 . . . . .57Bc 114
TW2: Twick 58Ga 108
Chudleigh St. E1 . . . . .44Zb 92
Chudleigh Way HA4: Ruis 32W 64
Chulsa Rd. SE26 . . . . .64Xb 135
Chumleigh Gdns. SE5 . . . . .51Ub 113
(off Chumleigh St.)
Chumleigh St. SE5 . . . . .51Ub 113
Chumleigh Wlk. KT5: Surb 70Pa 131
Church All. CR0: C'don 74Qb 156
DA11: Grav'nd 8D 122
(off High St.)
WD25: A'ham 10Ea 14
Church App. SE21 . . . . .62Tb 135
TN14: Cud 87Sc 180
TW19: Stanw 58M 105
TW20: Thorpe 69E 126
Church Av. BR3: Beck 67Cc 136
DA14: Sidc 64Wc 139
E4 . . . . .23Fc 53
(not continuous)
HA4: Ruis 32T 64
HA5: Pinn 30Aa 45
NW1 . . . . .37Kb 70
SW14 . . . . .55Ta 109
UB2: S'hall 48Aa 85
UB5: N'olt 38Ba 65
Churchbank E17 . . . . .28Cc 52
(off Eastfield Rd.)
Churchbury Cl. EN1: Enf 12Ub 33
Churchbury Ho. EN8: Walt C 4Zb 20
(off High St.)
Churchbury La. EN1: Enf 13Tb 33
Churchbury Rd. EN1: Enf 12Ub 33
SE9 . . . . .59Mc 115
Church Cloisters EC3 . . . . .5H 225
Church Cl. CM15: Mount 11Fe 41
EN6: Cuff 1Nb 18
GU21: Wok 8P 167
GU24: Brkwd 3D 186
HA6: Nwood 24V 44
HA8: Edg 22Sa 47
IG10: Lough 12Pc 36
KT15: Add 77K 149
KT17: Eps 85Ua 174
KT20: Lwr K 99Bb 195
KT22: Fet 96Fa 192
N20 . . . . .20Gb 31
SL4: Eton 1H 103
SS17: Horn H 1H 101
TW3: Houn 54Aa 107
TW18: Lale 69L 127
UB4: Hayes 43T 84
UB7: W Dray 48N 83
UB8: Uxb 40K 63
W8 . . . . .47Db 89
WD7: R'lett 8Ja 14
Church Cotts. KT15: Add 76N 149
Church Ct. EC4 . . . . .3K 223 (44Qb 90)
KT10: Esh 79Ea 152
(off Princess Sq.)
RH2: Reig 6K 207
SE16 . . . . .47Ac 92
(off Rotherhithe St.)
TW9: Rich 57Ma 109
Church Cres. AL3: St A 1A 6
CM15: Mount 11Fe 41
E9 . . . . .38Zb 72
N3 . . . . .25Bb 49
N10 . . . . .28Kb 50
N20 . . . . .20Gb 31
RM15: S Ock 41Yd 98
Church Cft. AL4: St A 4G 6
Churchcroft Cl. SW12 . . . . .59Jb 112
Churchdown BR1: Brom 63Gc 137
Church Dr. BR4: W W'ck 76Gc 159
HA2: Harr 30Ca 45
NW9 . . . . .32Ta 67
Church Elm La. RM10: Dag 37Cd 76
CHURCH END
GU23 . . . . .93P 189
N3 . . . . .25Bb 49
NW10 . . . . .38Ua 68
WD3 . . . . .10H 11
Church End E17 . . . . .28Dc 52
NW4 . . . . .27Xa 48
Church Entry EC4 . . . . .3C 224
Church Est. Almshouses
TW9: Rich 56Pa 109
(off Sheen Rd.)
Church Farm Cl. BR8: Crock 72Ed 162
Church Farm La. SM3: Cheam 79Ab 154
Church Farm Pool 17Hb 31
Church Farm Way WD25: A'ham 10Da 13
Church Fld. CM16: Epp 1Wc 23
DA2: Wilm 61Md 141
TN13: Riv 94Hd 202
WD7: R'lett 8Ja 14
Churchfield Av. N12 . . . . .23Fb 49
Churchfield Cl. HA2: Harr 28Ea 46
UB3: Hayes 45V 84
Church Fld. Cotts. TN15: Seal 92Pd 203
Churchfield Ct. RH2: Reig 6K 207
Churchfield Ho. KT11: Cobh 86X 171
(off Lushington Dr.)
W2 . . . . .6B 214
Churchfield Mans. SW6 . . . . .54Bb 111
(off New Kings Rd.)
Churchfield M. SL2: Slou 4L 81
Churchfield Path EN8: Chesh 1Yb 20
(not continuous)
Churchfield Pl. KT13: Weyb 77Q 150
TW17: Shep 73R 150
Churchfield Rd. DA16: Well 55Wc 117
KT12: Walt T 74W 150
KT13: Weyb 77Q 150
RH2: Reig 5H 207
SL9: Chal P 25A 42
W3 . . . . .46Sa 87
W7 . . . . .47Ga 86
W13 . . . . .46Ka 86
Churchfields E18 . . . . .25Jc 53
GU21: Wok 88A 168
IG10: Lough 14Nc 36
KT8: W Mole 69Ca 129
SE10 . . . . .51Ec 114
Churchfields Av. KT13: Weyb 77R 150
TW13: Hanw 62Ba 129
Churchfields Rd. BR3: Beck 68Zb 136
WD24: Wat 8V 12
Churchfield Way N12 . . . . .23Eb 49
Church Gdns. HA0: Wemb 35Ja 66
KT22: Lea 92Ka 192
W5 . . . . .47Ma 87
Church Gth. N19 . . . . .33Mb 70
(off St John's Gro.)
CHURCHGATE 1Xb 19
Church Ga. SW6 . . . . .55Ab 110
Churchgate EN8: Chesh 1Xb 19
Churchgate Rd. EN8: Chesh 1Xb 19
Church Grn. KT12: Hers 79Y 151
KT20: Walt H 96Wa 194
SW9 . . . . .53Qb 112
UB3: Hayes 44V 84
Church Gro. HP6: L Chal 11A 24
KT1: Hamp W 67La 130
SE13 . . . . .57Dc 114
SL3: Wex 3N 81
Church Hill BR6: Orp 73Wc 161
CM16: Epp 1Wc 23
CR3: Cat'm 96Vb 197
CR8: Purl 82Nb 176
DA1: Cray 56Gd 118
DA2: Wilm 61Md 141
DA9: Ghithe 57Ud 120
E17 . . . . .28Cc 52
GU21: Wok 8P 167
GU22: Pyr 89H 169
HA1: Harr 32Ga 66
IG10: Lough 13Nc 36
N21 . . . . .17Pb 32
RH1: Mers 98Kb 196
RH1: Nutf 5F 208
SE18 . . . . .48Pc 94
SM5: Cars 78Hb 155
SS17: Stan H 2L 101
SW19 . . . . .64Bb 133
TN14: Cud 87Sc 180
TN15: Plax 99Ae 205
TN16: Tats 94Mc 199
UB9: Hare 27L 43
WD5: Bedm 7F 4
Church Hill Rd. E17 . . . . .28Dc 52
EN4: E Barn 16Gb 31
KT6: Surb 71Na 153
SM3: Cheam 76Za 154
Church Hill Wood BR5: St M Cry 71Vc 161
Church Hollow RM19: Purf 50Qd 97
Church Ho. EC1 . . . . .5C 218
SW1 . . . . .3E 228
Church Hyde SE18 . . . . .51Uc 116
Churchill Av. HA3: Kenton 30Ka 46
UB10: Hil 41R 84
Churchill Bus. Pk. TN16: Westrm 98Tc 200
Churchill Cl. CR6: W'ham 89Yb 178
DA1: Dart 60Rd 119
KT22: Fet 95Ga 192
RH1: Redh 5P 207
TW14: Felt 60V 106
UB10: Hil 41R 84
Churchill Ct. BR6: Farnb 78Sc 160
HA2: Harr 33Da 65
(Eastcote Av.)
HA2: Harr 29Da 45
(Montrose Ct.)
HA5: Hat E 25Aa 45
HA6: Nwood 23T 44
N4 . . . . .31Qb 70
N9 . . . . .18Ub 33
SE18 . . . . .49Pc 94
TN16: Westrm 98Tc 200
TW18: Staines 65K 127
UB5: N'olt 36Ca 65
(off Newmarket Av.)
W5 . . . . .42Pa 87
Churchill Cres. AL9: Wel G 6E 8
Churchill Dr. KT13: Weyb 77S 150
KT16: Vir W 5L 147
Churchill Gdns. RH8: Oxt 99Fc 199
SW1 . . . . .50Lb 90
(off Churchill Gdns. Rd.)
W3 . . . . .44Qa 87
Churchill Gdns. Rd. SW1 . . . . .50Kb 90
Churchill Ho. SM7: Bans 86Bb 175
(off Dunnymans Rd.)
Churchill Ct. TN14: Dun G 92Hd 202
Churchill Lodge IG6: Ilf 28Sc 54
Churchill Pk. DA1: Dart 57Qd 119
Churchill Pl. E14 . . . . .46Dc 92
HA1: Harr 28Ga 46
Churchill Rd. AL1: St A 1E 6
CR2: S Croy 81Sb 177
DA4: Hort K 70Sd 142
DA11: Grav'nd 10B 122
E16 . . . . .44Lc 93
HA8: Edg 23Pa 47
KT19: Eps 83Qa 173
NW2 . . . . .37Xa 68
NW5 . . . . .35Kb 70
RM17: Grays 51Fe 121
SL3: L'ly 49B 82
UB10: Uxb 40N 63
Churchills M. IG8: Wfd G 23Hc 53
Churchill Ter. E4 . . . . .21Cc 52
Churchill Theatre 68Jc 137
Churchill Wlk. E9 . . . . .36Yb 72
Churchill War Rooms 1E 228 (47Mb 90)
BR1: Brom 68Jc 137
TN16: Big H 87Mc 179
TW16: Sun 64W 128
Church Island
TW18: Staines 63F 126
CHURCH LAMMAS 63G 126
Churchlands Way
KT4: Wor Pk 75Za 154
Church La. AL4: Col H 4M 7
BR2: Brom 74Nc 160
BR7: Chst 67Sc 138
CM13: Gt War 30Zd 59
CR3: Cat'm 96Qb 196
CR5: Coul 94Jb 196
CR6: W'ham 89Zb 178
(Church Rd.)
CR6: W'ham 88Dc 178
(Ledgers Rd.)
DA12: Grav'nd 2L 145
E11 . . . . .32Gc 73
E17 . . . . .28Dc 52
EN1: Enf 13Tb 33
EN6: N'thaw 2Jb 18
EN8: Chesh 1Xb 19
GU3: Worp 9J 187
GU23: Send 98D 188
GU24: Bisl 7E 166
GU24: Pirb 4B 186
HA3: W'stone 25Ha 46
HA5: Pinn 27Aa 45
HP3: Bov 9D 2
IG10: Lough 13Pc 36
KT7: T Ditt 72Ha 152
KT9: Chess 79Pa 153
KT13: Weyb 77Q 150
KT18: Head 96Sa 193
KT18: Tad 89Za 174
N2 . . . . .27Fb 49
N8 . . . . .28Pb 50
N9 . . . . .19Wb 33
N17 . . . . .25Ub 51
NW9 . . . . .30Sa 47
RH1: Blet 5K 209
RH8: Oxt 2H 211
RH9: G'stone 4B 210
RM1: Rom 28Gd 56
RM4: Abr 12Ad 37
RM4: Stap A 14Ed 38
RM10: Dag 38Ed 76
RM13: Wenn 44Md 97
RM14: N Ock 36Xd 78
RM19: Purf 50Qd 97
SL2: Stoke P 2K 81
SL3: Wex 2M 81
SL4: Wind 3H 103
SL5: S'dale 1F 146
SL5: S'hill 10B 124
SL9: Chal P 25A 42
SM6: Bedd 76Mb 156
(not continuous)
SW17 . . . . .64Hb 133
SW19 . . . . .67Bb 133
TN15: Kems'g 89Rd 183
TW1: Twick 60Ja 108
TW10: Ham 60Na 109
TW11: Tedd 64Ha 130
UB8: Uxb 40K 63
W5 . . . . .47La 86
WD3: Rick 18J 25
WD3: Sarr 10H 11
WD4: K Lan 1Q 12
WD25: A'ham 10Da 13
Church La. Av. CR5: Coul 94Kb 196
Church La. Dr. CR5: Coul 94Kb 196
Churchley Rd. SE26 . . . . .63Xb 135
Church Manorway DA8: Erith 49Fd 96
DA17: Belv 47Ed 96
SE2 . . . . .50Wc 95
Church Mead SE5 . . . . .52Sb 113
(off Camberwell Rd.)
Churchmead Cl. EN4: E Barn 16Gb 31
Church Mdw. KT6: Surb 75La 152
Churchmead Rd. NW10 . . . . .37Wa 68
Church M. KT15: Add 77L 149
Churchmore Rd. SW16 . . . . .67Lb 134
Church Mt. N2 . . . . .29Fb 49
Church Paddock Ct. SM6: Bedd 76Mb 156
Church Pde. TW15: Ashf 63P 127
Church Pas. EC2 . . . . .2E 224
(off Gresham St.)
EN5: Barn 13Ab 30
KT6: Surb 71Na 153
TW1: Twick 60Ka 108
Church Path BR8: Swan 67Kd 141
CR0: C'don 75Sb 157
CR4: Mitc 69Gb 133
(not continuous)
CR5: Coul 90Qb 176
DA9: Ghithe 57Vd 120
DA11: Nflt 58Ee 121
E11 . . . . .29Jc 53
E17 . . . . .28Dc 52
GU21: Wok 89B 168
KT11: Cobh 86X 171
N5 . . . . .36Rb 71
N8 . . . . .29Pb 50
(off Tottenham La.)
N12 . . . . .20Eb 31
(Woodside La.)
N12 . . . . .21Eb 49
(Woodside Pk. Rd.)
N17 . . . . .24Ub 51
NW10 . . . . .38Ua 68
RH1: Mers 99Kb 196
RM1: Rom 29Gd 56
(off Market Pl.)
RM17: Grays 51Ce 121
SL5: Asc, S'hill 9C 124
Church Path SW14 . . . . .55Ta 109
(not continuous)
SW19 . . . . .68Bb 133
UB1: S'hall 46Ca 85
UB2: S'hall 48Ba 85
(not continuous)
W3 . . . . .47Sa 87
(not continuous)
W4 . . . . .48Sa 87
Church Pl. CR4: Mitc 69Gb 133
SW1 . . . . .5C 222 (45Lb 90)
UB10: Ick 34S 64
W5 . . . . .47Ma 87
Church Ri. KT9: Chess 79Pa 153
SE23 . . . . .61Zb 136
Church Rd. BR2: Brom 68Jc 137
(Edison Rd.)
BR2: Brom 69Gc 137
(Hazelwood Ho's.)
BR2: Kes 80Mc 159
BR6: Chels 80Yc 161
BR6: Farnb 78Sc 160
BR8: Crock 73Fd 162
BR8: Swan 67Md 141
CM15: Mount 11Fe 41
CR0: C'don 76Sb 157
(not continuous)
CR3: Cat'm 95Vb 197
CR3: Whyt 90Vb 177
CR3: Wold 94Zb 198
CR4: Mitc 67Fb 133
CR6: W'ham 89Zb 178
CR8: Kenley 87Tb 177
CR8: Purl 82Nb 176
DA3: Hartl, Nw A G 70Be 143
DA4: Sut H 66Nd 141
DA7: Bex 54Bd 117
DA8: Erith 50Fd 96
DA9: Ghithe 57Vd 120
DA10: Swans 58Be 121
DA12: Grav'nd 5E 144
DA13: Ist R, Cobh 6C 144
DA14: Sidc 63Wc 139
DA16: Well 54Xc 117
E10 . . . . .32Cc 72
E12 . . . . .36Nc 74
E17 . . . . .26Ac 52
EN3: Pond E 16Yb 34
EN6: Pot B 2Cb 17
GU20: W'sham 9A 146
GU21: Wok 87A 168
(Beech Gdns.)
GU21: Wok 1L 187
(St John's Hill Rd.)
GU24: W End 4D 166
HA6: Nwood 24V 44
HA7: Stan 22Ka 46
HP3: Hem H 4C 4
IG2: Ilf 30Uc 54
IG9: Buck H 18Kc 35
IG10: H Beech, Lough 13Jc 35
IG11: Bark 37Sc 74
KT1: King T 68Pa 131
KT4: Wor Pk 74Ua 154
KT6: Surb 74La 152
KT8: E Mos 70Fa 130
KT10: Clay 79Ha 152
KT14: Byfl 86N 169
KT15: Add 78J 149
KT17: Eps 84Ua 174
KT19: Ewe 80Ta 153
KT21: Asht 90Ma 173
KT22: Lea 94Ka 192
KT23: Bookh 95Ba 191
N1 . . . . .37Sb 71
N6 . . . . .30Jb 50
N17 . . . . .25Ub 51
(not continuous)
NW4 . . . . .28Xa 48
NW10 . . . . .38Ua 68
RH1: Redh 8N 207
RH2: Reig 8J 207
RM3: Hrld W 25Qd 57
RM4: Nave 12Md 39
RM4: Noak H 18Ld 39
RM18: Tilb 3B 122
RM18: W Til 1G 122
SE19 . . . . .67Ub 135
SL0: Iver H 41E 82
SL2: Farn R 1G 80
SL4: Old Win 7M 103
SL5: S'dale 2E 146
SM3: Cheam 79Ab 154
SM6: Bedd 76Mb 156
SW13 . . . . .54Va 110
SW19 . . . . .64Ab 132
(Courthorpe Rd.)
SW19 . . . . .67Fb 133
(Reynolds Cl.)
TN14: Hals 83Ad 181
TN14: Sund 99Ad 201
TN15: Ash 78Ae 165
TN15: Ivy H, Seal 95Ud 204
TN15: Seal 93Pd 203
TN15: W King 80Ud 164
TN16: Big H 89Mc 179
TN16: Bras 96Xc 201
TW5: Cran 50X 85
TW5: Hest 52Ca 107
TW7: Isle 53Fa 108
TW9: Rich 56Na 109
TW10: Ham 63Ma 131
TW10: Rich 57Na 109
TW11: Tedd 63Ga 130
TW13: Hanw 64Z 129
TW15: Ashf 62P 127
TW17: Shep 73R 150
TW20: Egh 64B 126
UB2: S'hall 48Ba 85
UB3: Hayes 46V 84
UB5: N'olt 40Z 65
UB7: W Dray 48M 83
UB8: Cowl 42M 83
UB9: Hare 27L 43
W3 . . . . .46Sa 87
W7 . . . . .45Fa 86
WD17: Wat 11W 26
Church Rd. Almshouses E10 . . . . .33Dc 72
(off Church Rd.)
Church Rd. Ind. Est. E10 . . . . .32Cc 72
Church Row BR7: Chst 67Sc 138
NW3 . . . . .35Eb 69
RM16: Ors 2C 100
(off Malting La.)
SW6 . . . . .52Db 111
(off Moore Pk. Rd.)
Church Row M. BR7: Chst 66Sc 138
Church Side KT18: Eps 85Ra 173

Churchside Cl.—Clarinet Ct.

Churchside Cl. TN16: Big H 89Lc 179
Church Sq. TW17: Shep 73R 150
Church St. AL3: St A 1B 6
CR0: C'don 76Rb 157
DA11: Grav'nd 8D 122
DA13: Sflt 64Ce 143
E15 39Gc 73
E16 46Rc 94
EN2: Enf 13Sb 33
EN9: Walt A 5Ec 20
GU22: Wok 93E 188
HP2: Hem H 1M 3
HP3: Bov 9D 2
KT1: King T 68Ma 131
KT10: Esh 77Da 151
KT11: Cobh 87X 171
KT12: Walt T 74W 150
KT13: Weyb 77Q 150
KT17: Eps 85Ua 174
KT17: Ewe 81Wa 174
KT22: Lea 94Ka 192
KT24: Eff 99Z 191
N9 17Tb 33
NW8 7C 214 (43Fb 89)
RH2: Reig 6J 207
RH3: Bet 7A 206
RM10: Dag 37Dd 76
RM17: Grays 51Ee 121
SL1: Burn 2A 80
SL1: Slou 7G 80
(Damson Gro.)
SL1: Slou 7K 81
(Osborne St.)
SL4: Wind 3H 103
SM1: Sutt 78Db 155
TN14: S'ham 83Hd 182
TN15: Seal 93Qd 203
TW1: Twick 60Ja 108
TW7: Isle 55Ka 108
TW12: Hamp 67Ea 130
TW16: Sun 69X 129
TW18: Staines 64F 126
W2 7C 214 (43Fb 89)
(not continuous)
W4 51Va 110
WD3: Rick 18N 25
WD18: Wat 14Y 27
Church St. E. GU21: Wok 89B 168
Church St. Est. NW8 6C 214 (42Fb 89)
Church St. Nth. E15 39Gc 73
Church St. Pas. E15 39Gc 73
(off Church St.)
Church St. W. GU21: Wok 89A 168
Church Stretton Rd. TW3: Houn 57Ea 108
Church Ter. NW4 27Xa 48
RM4: Stap A 14Ed 38
SE13 55Gc 115
SL4: Wind 4C 102
TW10: Rich 57Ma 109
CHURCH TOWN 4B 210
Church Trad. Est. DA8: Erith 52Jd 118
Church Va. N2 27Hb 49
SE23 61Zb 136
Church Vw. BR8: Swan 69Fd 140
RM14: Upm 33Rd 77
RM15: Avel 47Sd 98
TW10: Rich 57Na 109
Churchview Cl. CR3: Cat'm 96Wb 197
Churchview Cl. DA12: Grav'nd 1G 144
Church Vw. Gro. SE26 65Zb 136
Churchview Rd. TW2: Twick 60Fa 108
Church Vs. TN13: Riv 94Gd 202
Church Wlk. CM15: B'wood 17Xd 40
CR3: Cat'm 96Wb 197
DA2: Wilm 62Md 141
DA4: Eyns 76Nd 163
DA12: Grav'nd 10F 122
EN2: Enf 13Tb 33
KT7: T Ditt 72Ha 152
KT12: Walt T 74W 150
(not continuous)
KT13: Weyb 76Q 150
KT16: Chert 72J 149
KT22: Lea 94Ka 192
N6 34Jb 70
N16 34Tb 71
(not continuous)
NW2 34Bb 69
NW4 27Ya 48
NW9 33Ta 67
RH1: Blet 5K 209
(not continuous)
RH2: Reig 6K 207
(not continuous)
SL1: Burn 2A 80
(not continuous)
SW13 53Wa 110
SW15 57Xa 110
SW16 68Lb 134
SW20 69Ya 132
TW8: Bford 51La 108
(not continuous)
TW9: Rich 57Ma 109
UB3: Hayes 44U 84
WD23: Bush 16Ca 27
Churchward Ho. SE17 51Rb 113
(off Lorrimore Sq.)
W14 50Bb 89
(off Ivatt Pl.)
Church Way CR2: Sande 82Vb 177
EN4: Cockf 14Hb 31
HA8: Edg 23Qa 47
N20 20Gb 31
RH8: Oxt 4K 211
Churchway NW1 3E 216 (41Mb 90)
(not continuous)
Churchwell Path E9 36Yb 72
Churchwood Gdns. IG8: Wfd G 21Jc 53
SE23 59Yb 114
Church Wood Reserve 2K 61
Churchyard Pas. SE5 54Tb 113
Churchyard Row
SE11 5C 230 (49Rb 91)
Church Yd. Wlk. W2 7B 214
Churston Av. E13 39Kc 73
Churston Cl. SW2 60Qb 112
Churston Dr. SM4: Mord 71Za 154
Churston Gdns. N11 23Lb 50
Churston Mans. WC1 6J 217
Churton Pl. SW1 6C 228 (49Lb 90)
Churton St. SW1 6C 228 (49Lb 90)
Chusan Pl. E14 44Bc 92
Chute Ho. SW9 54Qb 112
(off Stockwell Pk. Rd.)
Chuter Ede Ho. SW6 51Bb 111
(off Clem Attlee Ct.)
Chuters Cl. KT14: Byfl 84N 169
Chuters Gro. KT17: Eps 84Va 174
Chyne, The SL9: Ger X 29B 42
Chyngton Cl. DA15: Sidc 62Vc 139
Chynham Pl. CR2: Sande 82Ub 177
Cibber Rd. SE23 61Zb 136
Cicada Rd. SW18 58Eb 111
Cicely Ct. CR0: Wadd 78Qb 156
Cicely Ho. NW8 2C 214
Cicely Rd. SE15 53Wb 113
Cimba Wood DA12: Grav'nd 3G 144
Cinderella Path NW11 32Db 69
Cinderford Way BR1: Brom 63Gc 137
Cinder Path GU22: Wok 1N 187
Cine Lumiere 5B 226
Cineworld Cinema
Bexleyheath 56Dd 118
Chelsea -
Fulham Rd. 50Eb 89
King's Rd. 51Fb 111
Enfield 14Wb 33
Feltham 61X 129
Haymarket 5D 222
Ilford 34Rc 74
(off Clements Rd.)
Staples Corner 32Xa 68
The O2 46Gc 93
(within The O2)
Wandsworth 57Db 111
Wembley 35Qa 67
West India Quay 45Cc 92
Wood Green 26Qb 50
(within Wood Green Shop. City)
Cinnabar Wharf Central E1 46Wb 91
(off Wapping High St.)
Cinnabar Wharf E. E1 46Wb 91
(off Wapping High St.)
Cinnabar Wharf W. E1 46Wb 91
(off Wapping High St.)
Cinnamon Cl. CR0: C'don 73Nb 156
SE15 52Vb 113
SL4: Wind 3D 102
Cinnamon M. N13 19Qb 32
Cinnamon Row SW11 55Eb 111
Cinnamon St. E1 46Xb 91
Cinnamon Wharf SE1 47Vb 91
(off Shad Thames)
Cintra Pk. SE19 66Vb 135
Cipher Ct. NW2 34Wa 68
CIPPENHAM 5C 80
Cippenham Cl. SL1: Slou 5D 80
Cippenham La. SL1: Slou 5D 80
Circa Apartments NW1 38Jb 70
Circle, The NW2 34Ua 68
NW7 23Ta 47
RM18: Tilb 3C 122
SE1 1K 231
Circle Gdns. KT14: Byfl 85P 169
SW19 68Cb 133
Circle Rd. KT12: W Vill 81U 170
Circuit Cen., The KT13: Weyb 83N 169
Circuits, The HA5: Pinn 28Y 45
Circular Rd. N17 27Vb 51
Circular Way SE18 51Pc 116
Circus, The KT22: Lea 92Ka 192
(off By-Pass Rd.)
Circus Lodge NW8 3B 214
Circus M. W1 7F 215
Circus Pl. EC2 1G 225 (43Tb 91)
Circus Rd. NW8 3B 214 (41Fb 89)
Circus Rd. E. SW8 52Kb 112
Circus Rd. W. SW8 52Kb 112
Circus St. SE10 52Ec 114
Circus W. SW8 51Kb 112
Cirencester St. W2 43Db 89
Cirrus Apartments E1 5K 219
Cirrus Cl. SM6: Wall 80Nb 156
Cirrus Cres. DA12: Grav'nd 4G 144
Cissbury Ho. SE26 62Wb 135
Cissbury Ring Nth. N12 22Bb 49
Cissbury Ring Sth. N12 22Bb 49
Cissbury Rd. N15 29Tb 51
Citadel Pl. SE11 7H 229 (50Pb 90)
Citius Apartments E3 40Cc 72
(off Tredegar La.)
Citius Ct. E4 23Ec 52
Citius Wlk. E20 37Ec 72
Citizen Ho. N7 35Qb 70
Citizen Rd. N7 35Qb 70
Citrine Apartments E3 39Ac 72
(off Gunmaker's La.)
Citrus Ho. SE8 50Bc 92
(off Alverton St.)
CITY AIRPORT 46Nc 94
City Apartments E1 44Wb 91
(off White Church La.)
City Bus. Cen. SE16 48Yb 92
City Ct. CR0: C'don 73Rb 157
City Cross Bus. Pk. SE10 49Gc 93
City E. Bldg. E1 45Xb 91
(off Cable St.)
City Forum EC1 3D 218 (41Sb 91)
City Gdn. Row N1 2C 218 (40Rb 71)
City Ga. Ho. IG2: Ilf 30Qc 54
(off Eastern Av.)
City Gateway E1 45Wb 91
(off Ensign St.)
City Hall 7J 225 (46Ub 91)
City Harbour E14 48Dc 92
(off Selsdon Way)
City Hgts. E8 39Vb 71
(off Kingsland Rd.)
City Ho. BR2: Brom 72Nc 160
City Island E14 44Gc 93
City Lights Ct. SE11 7A 230
City Mill Apartments E8 39Vb 71
(off Lovelace St.)
City Mill River Path E15 39Ec 72
CITY OF LONDON 2G 225 (44Tb 91)
City of London Almshouses
SW9 56Pb 112
City of London Crematorium
E12 34Nc 74
City of London Distillery
3B 224 (44Rb 91)
City of London Point N7 37Mb 70
(off York Way)
City of London Police Mus.
2E 224 (44Sb 91)
City of Westminster College
Paddington Green Campus 7B 214
City Pavilion, The
Marks Gate 26Bd 55
City Pav. EC1 7B 218
City Pl. Ho. EC2 1E 224
Citypoint EC2 7F 219
City Pride Development E14 46Cc 92
City Rd. EC1 2B 218 (40Rb 71)
City Twr. EC2 1F 225
SW8 51Nb 112
City University London
Goswell Pl. 4C 218 (41Rb 91)
Northampton Square Campus
4B 218 (41Rb 91)
Saddlers Sports Cen., The
5C 218 (42Rb 91)
City Vw. IG1: Ilf 33Sc 74
(off Axon Pl.)
Cityview SE7 51Lc 115
City Vw. Apartments N1 38Sb 71
(off Essex Rd.)
N4 31Tb 71
(off Devan Gro.)
City Vw. Ct. SE22 59Wb 113
City Wlk. SE1 3H 231 (47Ub 91)
City Wlk. Apartments EC1 4C 218
City Wharf Ho. KT7: T Ditt 72Ka 152
Civic Ct. AL1: St A 2B 6
Civic Sq. RM18: Tilb 4C 122
Civic Way HA4: Ruis 36Z 65
IG6: Ilf 28Sc 54
Civil and Family Courts
Barnet 25Cb 49
Civil Justice Cen.
Central London 6K 215
Clabon M. SW1 4F 227 (48Hb 89)
Clacket La. TN16: Westrm 96Nc 200
CLACKET LANE SERVICE AREA 98Nc 200
Clack La. HA4: Ruis 32S 64
Clack St. SE16 47Yb 92
Clacton Rd. E6 41Mc 93
E17 30Ac 52
N17 26Vb 51
Claigmar Gdns. N3 25Db 49
Claire C'way. DA2: Dart 56Ud 120
Claire Cl. CM13: B'wood 21Be 59
Claire Ct. EN8: Chesh 4Zb 20
HA5: Hat E 24Ba 45
N12 20Eb 31
NW2 37Ab 68
WD23: B Hea 18Fa 28
Claire Gdns. HA7: Stan 22La 46
Claire Ho. IG1: Ilf 35Rc 74
Claire Pl. E14 48Cc 92
Claireville Ct. RH2: Reig 6M 207
Clairvale RM11: Horn 31Nd 77
Clairvale Rd. TW5: Hest 53Z 107
Clairview Rd. SW16 64Kb 134
Clairville Gdns. W7 46Ga 86
Clairville Point SE23 62Zb 136
(off Dacres Rd.)
Clammas Way UB8: Cowl 43L 83
Clamp Hill HA7: Stan 21Fa 46
Clancarty Rd. SW6 54Cb 111
Clandon Av. TW20: Egh 66E 126
Clandon Cl. KT17: Ewe 79Va 154
W3 47Ra 87
Clandon Gdns. N3 27Cb 49
Clandon Ho. SE1 2C 230
Clandon Rd. GU4: W Cla 97H 189
GU23: Send 97H 189
IG3: Ilf 33Uc 74
Clandon St. SE8 54Cc 114
Clandon Ter. SW20 68Za 132
Clanricarde Gdns. W2 45Cb 89
Clapgate Rd. WD23: Bush 16Da 27
CLAPHAM 56Lb 112
CLAPHAM COMMON 56Mb 112
Clapham Comn. Nth. Side
SW4 56Hb 111
Clapham Comn. Sth. Side SW4 58Kb 112
Clapham Comn. W. Side SW4 56Hb 111
(not continuous)
Clapham Cres. SW4 56Mb 112
Clapham High St. SW4 56Mb 112
CLAPHAM JUNCTION 55Gb 111
Clapham Leisure Cen. 55Mb 112
Clapham Mnr. Ct. SW4 55Lb 112
Clapham Mnr. St. SW4 55Lb 112
CLAPHAM PARK 59Mb 112
Clapham Pk. Est. SW4 58Mb 112
Clapham Pk. Rd. SW4 56Lb 112
Clapham Pk. Ter. SW2 57Nb 112
(off Lyham Rd.)
Clapham Picturehouse 56Lb 112
Clapham Rd. SW9 55Nb 112
Clapham Rd. Est. SW4 55Nb 112
Clap La. RM10: Dag, Rush G 33Dd 76
Clappers La. GU24: Chob 3G 166
Claps Ga. La. E6 42Qc 94
Clapton Comn. E5 31Vb 71
(not continuous)
CLAPTON PARK 35Zb 72
Clapton Pk. Est. E5 35Zb 72
Clapton Pas. E5 36Yb 72
Clapton Sq. E5 36Yb 72
Clapton Ter. E5 32Wb 71
Clapton Way E5 35Wb 71
Clara Grant Ho. E14 48Cc 92
(off Mellish St.)
Clara Nehab Ho. NW11 29Bb 49
(off Leeside Cres.)
Clara Pl. SE18 49Qc 94
Clare Cl. KT14: W Byf 85J 169
N2 27Eb 49
WD6: E'tree 16Pa 29
Clare Cnr. SE9 59Rc 116
Clare Cotts. RH1: Blet 5H 209
Clare Ct. AL1: St A 3D 6
CR3: Wold 95Cc 198
EN3: Enf W 7Ac 20
HA6: Nwood 22U 44
RM15: Avel 47Sd 98
W11 45Ab 88
(off Clarendon Rd.)
WC1 4G 217
Clare Cres. KT22: Lea 90Ja 172
Claredale GU22: Wok 91A 188
Claredale Ho. E2 40Xb 71
(off Claredale St.)
Claredale St. E2 40Wb 71
Clare Dr. SL2: Farn C 5F 60
Clarefield Ct. SL5: S'dale 3E 146
Clare Gdns. E7 35Jc 73
IG11: Bark 37Vc 75
TW20: Egh 64C 126
W11 44Ab 88
Claregate EN6: Pot B 2Eb 17
Clare Hill KT10: Esh 78Da 151
Clare Ho. E3 39Bc 72
E16 45Qc 94
(off University Way)
HA8: Edg 26Sa 47
(off Burnt Oak B'way.)
SE1 7K 231
Clare La. N1 38Sb 71
Clare Lawn Av. SW14 57Ta 109
Clare Mkt. WC2 3J 223 (44Pb 90)
Clare M. SW6 52Db 111
Claremont AL2: Brick W 3Ca 13
EN7: Chesh 1Vb 19
TW17: Shep 72R 150
(off Laleham Rd.)
Claremont Av. GU22: Wok 91A 188
HA3: Kenton 29Na 47
KT3: N Mald 71Wa 154
KT10: Esh 79Ba 151
KT12: Hers 77Z 151
TW16: Sun 67X 129
Claremont Cl. BR6: Farnb 77Qc 160
CR2: Sande 87Xb 177
E16 46Qc 94
KT12: Hers 78Y 151
N1 2A 218 (40Qb 70)
RM16: Grays 48Ee 99
SW2 60Nb 112
Claremont Ct. E2 40Xb 71
(off Cambridge Heath Rd.)
E2 40Wb 71
(off Claredale St.)
W2 44Db 89
(off Queensway)
W9 40Bb 69
(off Claremont Rd.)
Claremont Cres.
DA1: Cray 56Gd 118
WD3: Crox G 15S 26
Claremont Dr. GU22: Wok 91A 188
KT10: Esh 81Ca 171
TW17: Shep 72R 150
Claremont End KT10: Esh 79Da 151
Claremont Gdns. IG3: Ilf 33Uc 74
KT6: Surb 71Na 153
RM14: Upm 32Td 78
Claremont Gro. IG8: Wfd G 23Lc 53
W4 52Ua 110
Claremont Ho. SM2: Sutt 80Db 155
WD18: Wat 16T 26
Claremont Landscape Garden 80Ba 151
Claremont La. KT10: Esh 78Da 151
Claremont M. DA1: Dart 55Qd 119
CLAREMONT PARK 80Da 151
Claremont Pk. N3 25Ab 48
Claremont Pk. Rd.
KT10: Esh 79Da 151
Claremont Pl. DA11: Grav'nd 9D 122
(off Arthur St.)
IG7: Chig 20Rc 36
KT10: Clay 79Ha 152
Claremont Rd. BR1: Brom 70Nc 138
BR8: Hext 66Gd 140
CR0: C'don 74Wb 157
E7 36Kc 73
E11 34Fc 73
E17 26Ac 52
EN4: Had W 10Eb 17
HA3: W'stone 26Ga 46
KT6: Surb 71Na 153
KT10: Clay 80Ga 152
KT14: W Byf 84J 169
N6 31Lb 70
NW2 31Za 68
RH1: Redh 3A 208
RM11: Horn 30Jd 56
SL4: Wind 4G 102
TW1: Twick 58Ka 108
TW11: Tedd 64Ha 130
TW18: Staines 64F 126
W9 40Ab 68
W13 43Ja 86
Claremont Sq. N1 2K 217 (40Qb 70)
Claremont St. E16 47Qc 94
N18 23Wb 51
SE10 51Dc 114
Claremont Ter. KT7: T Ditt 73Ka 152
Claremont Vs. SE5 52Tb 113
(off Southampton Way)
Claremont Way NW2 32Ya 68
(not continuous)
Claremont Way Ind. Est.
NW2 32Ya 68
Claremount Cl. KT18: Tatt C 89Ya 174
Claremount Gdns. KT18: Tatt C 89Ya 174
Clarence Av. BR1: Brom 70Nc 138
IG2: Ilf 30Qc 54
KT3: N Mald 68Sa 131
RM14: Upm 33Qd 77
SW4 59Mb 112
Clarence Cl. EN4: E Barn 15Fb 31
KT12: Hers 77X 151
WD23: B Hea 17Ha 28
Clarence Ct. NW7 22Ua 48
RM17: Grays 51De 121
(off Clarence Rd.)
SL3: L'ly 51D 104
SL4: Wind 3F 102
TW20: Egh 64B 126
(off Clarence St.)
W6 49Xa 88
(off Cambridge Gro.)
Clarence Cres. DA14: Sidc 62Xc 139
SL4: Wind 3G 102
SW4 58Mb 112
Clarence Dr. TW20: Eng G 3N 125
Clarence Gdns. NW1 4A 216 (41Kb 90)
Clarence Ga. IG8: Ilf, Wfd G 23Qc 54
Clarence Ga. Gdns. NW1 6G 215
Clarence House 1C 228
Clarence Ho. KT12: Hers 78X 151
(off Queens Rd.)
SE17 51Tb 113
(off Merrow St.)
Clarence La. SW15 58Ua 110
Clarence M. E5 36Xb 71
SE16 46Zb 92
SW12 59Kb 112
Clarence Pk. 2D 6
Clarence Pk. Cres. HA7: Stan 20Ga 28
Clarence Pk. M. AL1: St A 2D 6
Clarence Pl. DA12: Grav'nd 9D 122
E5 36Xb 71
KT17: Ewe 82Wa 174
Clarence Rd. AL1: St A 2D 6
BR1: Brom 69Mc 137
CM15: Pil H 16Xd 40
CR0: C'don 73Tb 157
DA6: Bex 56Ad 117
DA14: Sidc 62Xc 139
E5 35Xb 71
E12 35Lc 73
E16 42Gc 93
E17 26Zb 52
EN3: Pond E 15Xb 33
KT12: Hers 77X 151
N15 29Sb 51
N22 24Nb 50
Clarence Rd. NW6 38Bb 69
RH1: Redh 9M 207
RM17: Grays 51Ce 121
SE8 51Dc 114
SE9 61Nc 138
SL4: Wind 3E 102
SM1: Sutt 78Db 155
SM6: Wall 78Kb 156
SW19 65Db 133
TN16: Big H 90Pc 180
TW9: Kew 53Pa 109
TW11: Tedd 65Ha 130
W4 50Qa 87
Clarence Row
DA12: Grav'nd 9D 122
Clarence St. KT1: King T 68Ma 131
TW9: Rich 56Na 109
TW18: Staines 63G 126
TW20: Egh 65B 126
UB2: S'hall 48Z 85
Clarence Ter. NW1 5G 215 (42Hb 89)
TW3: Houn 56Da 107
Clarence Wlk. RH1: Redh 9M 207
SW4 54Nb 112
Clarence Way NW1 38Kb 70
RM15: S Ock 44Zd 99
Clarenden Pl. DA2: Wilm 64Gd 140
Clarendon Cl. BR5: St P 69Wc 139
E9 38Yb 72
HP2: Hem H 1M 3
W2 4D 220 (45Gb 89)
Clarendon Ct. BR3: Beck 67Dc 136
(off Albemarle Rd.)
HA6: Nwood 22V 44
NW2 38Ya 68
NW11 28Bb 49
SL2: Slou 5M 81
SL4: Wind 3F 102
TW5: Cran 53W 106
TW9: Kew 53Pa 109
W9 5A 214
Clarendon Cres. TW2: Twick 62Fa 130
Clarendon Cross W11 45Ab 88
Clarendon Dr. SW15 56Ya 110
Clarendon Flds.
WD3: Chan C 10P 11
Clarendon Flats W1 3J 221
Clarendon Gdns. DA2: Dart 59Td 120
HA9: Wemb 34Ma 67
IG1: Ilf 31Pc 74
NW4 27Wa 48
W9 6A 214 (42Eb 89)
Clarendon Ga. KT16: Ott 79F 148
Clarendon Grn. BR5: St P 70Wc 139
Clarendon Gro. BR5: St P 70Wc 139
CR4: Mitc 69Hb 133
NW1 3D 216 (41Mb 90)
Clarendon Ho. KT2: King T 67Na 131
(off Cowleaze Rd.)
NW1 2C 216
W2 4D 220
Clarendon Lodge W11 45Ab 88
(off Clarendon Rd.)
Clarendon Lofts WD17: Wat 13X 27
(off Clarendon Rd.)
Clarendon M. DA5: Bexl 60Dd 118
KT21: Asht 91Pa 193
(off Rectory La.)
W2 4D 220 (45Gb 89)
WD6: Bore 13Qa 29
Clarendon Pde. EN8: Chesh 1Zb 20
Clarendon Path BR5: St P 70Wc 139
(not continuous)
Clarendon Pl. TN13: S'oaks 97Jd 202
W2 4D 220 (45Gb 89)
Clarendon Ri. SE13 56Ec 114
Clarendon Rd. CR0: C'don 75Rb 157
DA12: Grav'nd 8E 122
E11 32Fc 73
E17 30Dc 52
E18 27Jc 53
EN8: Chesh 1Zb 20
HA1: Harr 30Ga 46
N8 27Pb 50
N15 28Sb 51
N18 23Wb 51
N22 26Pb 50
RH1: Redh 5P 207
SM6: Wall 79Lb 156
SW19 66Gb 133
TN13: S'oaks 96Jd 202
TW15: Ashf 63P 127
UB3: Hayes 47V 84
W5 41Na 87
W11 45Ab 88
WD6: Bore 13Qa 29
WD17: Wat 12X 27
Clarendon St. SW1 7A 228 (50Kb 90)
Clarendon Ter. W9 5A 214 (42Eb 89)
Clarendon Wlk. W11 44Ab 88
Clarendon Way BR5: St P 69Vc 139
BR7: Chst 69Vc 139
N21 16Sb 33
Clarens St. SE6 61Bc 136
Clare Pl. SW15 59Va 110
Clare Point NW2 32Za 68
(off Whitefield Av.)
Clare Rd. E11 30Fc 53
NW10 38Wa 68
SE14 53Bc 114
SL6: Tap 4A 80
TW4: Houn 55Ba 107
TW19: Stanw 60M 105
UB6: G'frd 37Fa 66
Clares, The CR3: Cat'm 96Wb 197
Clare St. E2 40Xb 71
Claret Gdns. SE25 69Ub 135
Claret Ho. WD17: Wat 12X 27
Clareville Ct. SW7 6A 226
Clareville Gro. SW7 6A 226 (49Eb 89)
Clareville Gro. M. SW7 6A 226 (49Eb 89)
Clareville Rd. BR5: Farnb 75Sc 160
CR3: Cat'm 96Wb 197
Clareville St. SW7 6A 226 (49Eb 89)
Clare Way DA7: Bex 53Ad 117
TN13: S'oaks 100Ld 203
Clare Wood KT22: Lea 90Ka 172
Clarewood Ct. W1 1F 221
Clarewood Wlk. SW9 56Qb 112
Clarges M. W1 6K 221 (46Kb 90)
Clarges St. W1 6A 222 (46Kb 90)
Claribel Rd. SW9 54Rb 113
Clarice Way SM6: Wall 81Nb 176
Claridge Ct. SW6 54Bb 111
Claridge Rd. RM8: Dag 32Zc 75
Clarinda Ho. DA9: Ghithe 56Yd 120
(off Clovelly Pl.)
Clarinet Ct. HA8: Edg 24Ra 47

Clarion Ho.—Clock Ho. Mead

Clarion Ho. E3 40Ac 72
(off Roman Rd.)
SW1 7C 228
W1 3D 222
Clarissa Ho. E14 44Dc 92
(off Cordela St.)
Clarissa Rd. RM6: Chad H 31Zc 75
Clarissa St. E8 39Vb 71
Clarke Cl. DA8: Erith 53Jd 118
Clarke Apartments E3 42Bc 92
(off Heath Pl.)
Clarkebourne Dr. RM17: Grays 51Fe 121
Clarke Cl. CR0: C'don 72Sb 157
Clarke Grn. WD25: Wat 7W 12
Clarke Mans. IG11: Bark 38Vc 75
(off Upney La.)
Clarke M. N9 20Xb 33
Clarke Path N16 32Wb 71
Clarkes Av. KT4: Wor Pk 74Za 154
Clarkes Dr. UB8: Hil 43N 83
Clarke's Grn. Rd. TN15: Knat 86Qd 183
Clarke's M. W1 7J 215 (43Jb 90)
Clarke Way WD25: Wat 7W 12
Clarkfield WD3: Rick 18K 25
Clark Gro. IG3: Ilf 35Uc 74
Clark Ho. SW10 52Eb 111
(off Coleridge Gdns.)
Clarks La. CM16: Epp 3Vc 23
RH8: T'sey 95Jc 199
TN14: Hals 84Bd 181
TN16: Tats, Westrm 95Jc 199
Clarks Mead WD23: Bush 17Ea 28
Clarks M. CM16: Epp 2Wc 23
Clarkson Rd. E16 44Hc 93
Clarkson Row NW1 2B 216
Clarksons, The IG11: Bark 40Sc 74
Clarkson St. E2 41Xb 91
Clarks Rd. IG1: Ilf 33Tc 74
Clark St. E1 43Xb 91
(not continuous)
Clark Way TW5: Hest 52Z 107
Clarnico Rd. E20 37Cc 72
Clarson Ho. SE5 52Rb 113
(off Midnight Av.)
SE8 51Ac 114
Classic Mans. E9 38Yb 72
Classon Cl. UB7: W Dray 47M 83
Claston Cl. DA1: Cray 56Gd 118
Claude Rd. E10 33Ec 72
E13 39Kc 73
SE15 54Xb 113
Claude St. E14 49Cc 92
Claudia Jones Ho. N17 25Sb 51
Claudia Jones Way SW2 58Nb 112
Claudian Pl. AL3: St A 3N 5
Claudian Way RM16: Grays 8D 100
Claudia Pl. SW19 60Ab 110
Claudius Cl. HA7: Stan 20Ma 29
Claughton Ct. AL4: St A 3G 6
Claughton Rd. E13 40Lc 73
Claughton Way CM13: Hut 16Fe 41
Clauson Av. UB5: N'olt 36Da 65
Clavell St. SE10 51Ec 114
Claverdale Rd. SW2 59Pb 112
Claver Dr. SL5: S'hill 10B 124
Claverhambury Rd. EN9: Walt A 2Hc 21
Clavering Av. SW13 51Xa 110
Clavering Cl. TW1: Twick 63Ja 130
Clavering Gdns. CM13: W H'dn 30Fe 59
Clavering Ho. SE13 56Fc 115
(off Blessington Rd.)
Clavering Pl. SW12 58Jb 112
Clavering Rd. E12 32Mc 73
Claverings Ind. Est. N9 19Yb 34
(off Centre Way)
Clavering Way CM13: Hut 16Ee 41
Claverley Gro. N3 25Db 49
Claverley Vs. N3 24Db 49
Claverton KT21: Asht 89Na 173
Claverton Cl. HP3: Bov 10C 2
Claverton St. SW1 7C 228 (50Lb 90)
Clave St. E1 46Yb 91
Claxton Gro. W6 50Za 88
Claxton Path SE4 56Zb 114
(off Coston Wlk.)
Clay Av. CR4: Mitc 68Kb 134
Claybank Gro. SE13 55Dc 114
Claybourne M. SE19 66Ub 135
Claybridge Rd. SE12 63Lc 137
Claybrook Cl. N2 27Fb 49
Claybrook Rd. W6 51Za 110
Clayburn Gdns. RM15: S Ock 45Xd 98
Claybury WD23: Bush 17Da 27
Claybury B'way. IG5: Ilf 27Nc 54
Claybury Hall IG8: Wfd G 24Pc 54
Claybury Rd. IG8: Wfd G 24Nc 54
Clay Cl. KT15: Add 78K 149
(off Monks Cres.)
Claycorn Ct. KT10: Clay 79Ga 152
Clay Cnr. KT16: Chert 74K 149
Clay Ct. E17 27Fc 53
SE1 3H 231
(off Long La.)
Claydon Ct. TW18: Staines 63J 127
(off Kingston Rd.)
Claydon Dr. CR0: Bedd 77Nb 156
Claydon End SL9: Chal P 27A 42
Claydon Ho. NW4 26Za 48
(off Holders Hill Rd.)
Claydon La. SL9: Chal P 27A 42
Claydon Rd. GU21: Wok 8L 167
Claydown M. SE18 50Qc 94
Clayfarm Rd. SE9 61Sc 138
CLAYGATE 79Ha 152
Claygate Cl. RM12: Horn 35Jd 76
Claygate Common (Local Nature Reserve) 80Ha 152
Claygate Cres. CR0: New Ad 79Ec 158
CLAYGATE CROSS 96Ce 205
Claygate La. EN9: Walt A 2Ec 20
KT7: T Ditt 74Ja 152
KT10: Clay, Hin W 75Ja 152
Claygate Lodge Cl. KT10: Clay 80Ga 152
Claygate Rd. W13 48Ka 86
CLAYHALL 27Nc 54
Clayhall Av. IG5: Ilf 27Nc 54
Clayhall Ct. E3 40Bc 72
(off St Stephen's Rd.)
Clayhall Ho. RH2: Reig 5J 207
(off Somers Cl.)
Clayhall La. RH2: Reig 10F 206
SL4: Old Win 7K 103
CLAY HILL 9Sb 19
Clay Hill EN2: Enf 9Sb 19
Clayhill KT5: Surb 71Qa 153
Clayhill Cres. SE9 63Mc 137
Claylands Pl. SW8 52Qb 112
Claylands Rd. SW8 51Pb 112
Clay La. GU4: Burp, Jac W 10P 187
HA3: Kenton 28Ma 47
HA8: Edg 19Qa 29
KT18: Head 96Ra 193
RH1: S Nut 7C 208
TW19: Stanw 59P 105
WD23: B Hea 17Ga 28
Claymill Ho. SE18 50Sc 94
Claymills M. HP3: Hem H 5A 4
Claymore Cl. SM4: Mord 73Cb 155
Clay Path E17 26Cc 52
Claypit Hill
EN9: H Beech, Lough, Walt A 8Lc 21
Claypole Ct. E17 29Cc 52
(off Yunus Khan Cl.)
Claypole Dr. TW5: Hest 53Aa 107
Claypole Rd. E15 40Ec 72
Clayponds Av. TW8: Bford 49Ma 87
Clayponds Gdns. W5 49Ma 87
(not continuous)
Clayponds La. TW8: Bford 50Na 87
(not continuous)
Clay Ride IG10: Lough 11Mc 35
Clayside IG7: Chig 22Sc 54
Clay's La. IG10: Lough 11Qc 36
Clay St. W1 1G 221 (43Hb 89)
Clayton Av. HA0: Wemb 38Na 67
RM14: Upm 36Rd 77
Clayton Bus. Cen. UB3: Hayes 47U 84
Clayton Cl. E6 44Pc 94
Clayton Ct. SL3: L'ly 48C 82
Clayton Cres. N1 39Nb 70
TW8: Bford 50Ma 87
Clayton Cft. Rd. DA2: Wilm 61Jd 140
Clayton Dr. HP3: Hem H 4D 4
SE8 50Ac 92
Clayton Fld. NW9 24Ua 48
Clayton Ho. E9 38Yb 72
(off Frampton Pk. Rd.)
KT7: T Ditt 74Ka 152
SW13 52Ya 110
(off Trinity Chu. Rd.)
Clayton Mead RH9: G'stone 2P 209
Clayton M. SE10 53Fc 115
Clayton Pde. EN8: Chesh 2Zb 20
Clayton Rd. KT9: Chess 77La 152
KT17: Eps 84Ua 174
RM7: Rush G 32Ed 76
SE15 53Wb 113
TW7: Isle 55Ga 108
UB3: Hayes 47U 84
Clayton St. SE11 51Qb 112
Clayton Ter. UB4: Yead 43Aa 85
Claytonville Ter. DA17: Belv 47Ed 96
Clayton Way UB8: Cowl 42M 83
Clay Tye Rd. RM14: Upm 33Yd 78
Clay Wood Cl. BR6: Orp 73Uc 160
Claywood La. DA2: Bean 62Zd 143
Clayworth Cl. DA15: Sidc 58Xc 117
Cleall Av. EN9: Walt A 6Ec 20
Cleanthus Cl. SE18 53Rc 116
Cleanthus Rd. SE18 54Rc 116
(not continuous)
Clearbrook Way E1 44Yb 92
Cleardown GU22: Wok 90D 168
Cleares Pasture SL1: Burn 1A 80
CLEARMOUNT 9J 147
Clears, The RH2: Reig 4G 206
Clears Cotts. RH2: Reig 4G 206
Clearview Health & Racquets Club 29Be 59
Clearwater Pl. KT6: Surb 72La 152
Clearwater Ter. W11 47Za 88
Clearwater Yd. NW1 39Kb 70
(off Inverness St.)
Clearway Ct. CR3: Cat'm 94Wb 197
Clearways Bus. Est.
TN15: W King 80Ud 164
Clearways Cvn. Pk.
TN15: W King 80Td 164
Clearwell Dr. W9 42Db 89
Cleave Av. BR6: Chels 79Uc 160
UB3: Harl 49U 84
Cleaveland Rd. KT6: Surb 71Ma 153
Cleave Prior CR5: Chip 91Gb 195
Cleaverholme Cl. SE25 72Xb 157
Cleaver Ho. NW3 38Hb 69
(off Adelaide Rd.)
Cleaver Sq. SE11 7A 230 (50Qb 90)
Cleaver St. SE11 7A 230 (50Qb 90)
Cleaves Almshouses
KT2: King T 68Na 131
(off London Rd.)
Cleeve Ct. TW14: Bedf 60U 106
Cleeve Hill SE23 60Xb 113
Cleeve Ho. E2 4J 219
Cleeve Pk. Gdns. DA14: Sidc 61Xc 139
Cleeve Rd. KT22: Lea 92Ha 192
Cleeves Ct. RH1: Redh 5A 208
(off St Anne's Mt.)
Cleeves Vw. DA1: Dart 58Md 119
(off Priory Pl.)
Cleeve Way SM1: Sutt 74Db 155
SW15 59Va 110
Cleeve Workshops E2 4J 219
Clegg Ho. SE16 48Yb 92
(off Moodkee St.)
Clegg St. E1 46Xb 91
E13 40Jc 73
Cleland Ho. E2 40Yb 72
(off Sewardstone Rd.)
Cleland Path IG10: Lough 11Rc 36
Cleland Rd. SL9: Chal P 26A 42
Clematis Apartments E3 41Bc 92
(off Merchant St.)
Clematis Cl. RM3: Rom 24Ld 57
Clematis Gdns. IG8: Wfd G 22Jc 53
Clematis St. W12 45Wa 88
Clem Attlee Ct. SW6 51Bb 111
Clem Attlee Pde. SW6 51Bb 111
(off North End Rd.)
Clemence Rd. RM10: Dag 39Ed 76
Clemence St. E14 43Bc 92
Clement Av. SW4 56Mb 112
Clement Cl. CR8: Purl 88Rb 177
NW6 38Ya 68
W4 49Ta 87
Clement Danes Ho. W12 44Xa 88
Clement Gdns. UB3: Harl 49U 84
Clementhorpe Rd. RM9: Dag 37Yc 75
Clement Ho. SE8 49Ac 92
W10 43Ya 88
(off Dalgarno Gdns.)
Clementina Ct. E3 42Ac 92
(off Copperfield Rd.)
Clementina Rd. E10 32Bc 72
Clementine Cl. W13 47Ka 86
Clementine Wlk. IG8: Wfd G 24Jc 53
Clementine Way HP1: Hem H 4K 3
Clement Rd. BR3: Beck 68Zb 136
SW19 64Ab 132
Clement's Av. E16 45Jc 93
Clements Cl. N12 21Db 49
SL1: Slou 7M 81
Clements Ct. IG1: Ilf 34Rc 74
TW4: Houn 56Z 107
WD25: Wat 7Y 13
Clements Ho. KT22: Lea 91Ja 192
Clement's Inn
WC2 3J 223 (44Pb 90)
Clement's Inn Pas. WC2 3J 223
Clements La. EC4 4G 225 (45Tb 91)
IG1: Ilf 34Rc 74
Clements Mead KT22: Lea 91Ja 192
Clements Pl. TW8: Bford 50Ma 87
Clement's Rd. WD3: Chor 15F 24
Clements Rd. E6 38Nc 74
IG1: Ilf 34Rc 74
KT12: Walt T 75X 151
SE16 48Wb 91
CLEMENT STREET 65Md 141
Clement St. BR8: Swan 65Md 141
DA4: Swan 65Md 141
Clement Way RM14: Upm 34Pd 77
Clemson Ho. E8 39Vb 71
Clemson M. KT17: Eps 84Va 174
Clenches Farm TN13: S'oaks 99Jd 202
Clenches Farm La. TN13: S'oaks 98Jd 202
Clenches Farm Rd. TN13: S'oaks 98Jd 202
Clendon Way SE18 49Tc 94
Clennam St. SE1 1E 230 (47Sb 91)
Clensham Ct. SM1: Sutt 75Cb 155
Clensham La. SM1: Sutt 75Cb 155
Clenston M. W1 2F 221 (44Hb 89)
Cleopatra Cl. HA7: Stan 20Ma 29
Cleopatra's Needle 6H 223 (46Nb 90)
Clephane Rd. N1 37Sb 71
Clephane Rd. Nth. N1 37Sb 71
Clere Pl. EC2 5G 219 (42Tb 91)
Clere St. EC2 5G 219 (42Tb 91)
Clerics Wlk. TW17: Shep 73T 150
CLERKENWELL 6A 218 (42Qb 90)
Clerkenwell Cl. EC1 5A 218 (42Qb 90)
(not continuous)
Clerkenwell Ct. N1 1B 218
Clerkenwell Grn. EC1 6A 218 (42Qb 90)
Clerkenwell Rd. EC1 7K 217 (42Qb 90)
Clerks Cft. RH1: Blet 5K 209
Clerk's Piece IG10: Lough 13Pc 36
Clerk's Pl. EC2 2H 225 (44Ub 91)
Clermont Rd. E9 39Yb 72
Clevedon KT13: Weyb 78T 150
Clevedon Cl. N16 34Vb 71
Clevedon Ct. CR2: S Croy 78Ub 157
SW11 53Gb 111
(off Bolingbroke Wlk.)
Clevedon Gdns. TW5: Cran 53X 107
UB3: Harl 48T 84
Clevedon Ho. SM1: Sutt 77Eb 155
Clevedon Mans. NW5 35Jb 70
Clevedon Pas. N16 33Vb 71
Clevedon Rd. KT1: King T 68Qa 131
SE20 67Zb 136
TW1: Twick 58Ma 109
Cleve Ho. NW6 38Db 69
Clevehurst Cl. SL2: Stoke P 7L 61
Cleveland Av. SW20 68Bb 133
TW12: Hamp 66Ba 129
W4 49Va 88
Cleveland Cl. KT12: Walt T 76X 151
Cleveland Ct. W13 43Ka 86
Cleveland Cres. WD6: Bore 15Sa 29
Cleveland Dr. TW18: Staines 68K 127
Cleveland Gdns. KT4: Wor Pk 75Ua 154
N4 29Sb 51
NW2 33Za 68
SW13 54Va 110
W2 3A 220 (44Eb 89)
Cleveland Gro. E1 42Yb 92
Cleveland Ho. DA11: Nflt 58Fe 121
N2 26Fb 49
(off The Grange)
Cleveland Mans. NW6 38Bb 69
(off Willesden La.)
SW9 52Qb 112
(off Mowll St.)
W9 42Cb 89
Cleveland M. W1 7B 216 (43Lb 90)
Cleveland Pk. TW19: Stanw 58N 105
Cleveland Pk. Av. E17 28Cc 52
Cleveland Pk. Cres. E17 28Cc 52
Cleveland Pl. SW1 6C 222 (46Lb 90)
Cleveland Ri. SM4: Mord 73Za 154
Cleveland Rd. DA16: Well 54Vc 117
E18 27Jc 53
HP2: Hem H 1B 4
IG1: Ilf 34Rc 74
KT3: N Mald 70Ua 132
KT4: Wor Pk 75Ua 154
N1 38Tb 71
N9 17Xb 33
SW13 54Va 110
TW7: Isle 56Ja 108
UB8: Cowl, Uxb 42M 83
W4 48Sa 87
W13 43Ja 86
Cleveland Row SW1 7B 222 (46Lb 90)
Cleveland Sq. W2 3A 220 (44Eb 89)
Cleveland St. W1 6A 216 (42Kb 90)
Cleveland Ter. W2 3A 220 (44Eb 89)
Cleveland Way E1 42Yb 92
HP2: Hem H 1B 4
Cleveley Cl. SE7 49Mc 93
Cleveley Ct. SE16 49Ac 92
(off Ashton Reach)
Cleveley Cres. W5 40Na 67
Cleveleys Rd. E5 34Xb 71
Cleve Pl. KT13: Weyb 78T 150
Cleverly Est. W12 46Wa 88
Cleve Rd. DA14: Sidc 62Zc 139
NW6 38Cb 69
Cleves, The TN15: Kems'g 89Rd 183
Cleves Av. CM14: B'wood 18Xd 40
KT17: Ewe 81Xa 174
Cleves Cl. IG10: Lough 16Nc 36
KT11: Cobh 86X 171
Cleves Ct. DA1: Dart 59Nd 119
KT17: Eps 84Va 174
SL4: Wind 5D 102
Cleves Cres. CR0: New Ad 83Ec 178
Cleves Ho. E16 46Jc 93
(off Southey M.)
Cleves Rd. E6 39Mc 73
TN15: Kems'g 89Nd 183
TW10: Ham 62La 130
Cleves Wlk. IG6: Ilf 24Sc 54
Cleves Way HA4: Ruis 32Z 65
TW12: Hamp 66Ba 129
TW16: Sun 65V 128
Cleves Wood KT13: Weyb 77U 150
Clewer Av. SL4: Wind 4E 102
Clewer Ct. E10 32Cc 72
(off Leyton Grange Est.)
Clewer Ct. Rd. SL4: Wind 2F 102
Clewer Cres. HA3: Hrw W 25Fa 46
Clewer Flds. SL4: Wind 3G 102
CLEWER GREEN 4D 102
CLEWER HILL 5C 102
Clewer Hill Rd. SL4: Wind 4C 102
Clewer Ho. SE2 47Zc 95
(off Wolvercote Rd.)
CLEWER NEW TOWN 4E 102
Clewer New Town SL4: Wind 4E 102
Clewer Pk. SL4: Wind 2E 102
CLEWER ST ANDREW 2F 102
CLEWER ST STEPHEN 2F 102
CLEWER VILLAGE 2E 102
CLEWER WITHIN 3G 102
Clew's La. GU24: Bisl 8E 166
Cley Ho. SE4 56Zb 114
Clichy Est. E1 43Yb 92
Clichy Ho. E1 43Yb 92
(off Stepney Way)
Clifden M. E5 35Zb 72
Clifden Rd. E5 36Yb 72
TW1: Twick 60Ha 108
TW8: Bford 51Ma 109
Cliffe Ho. SE10 50Hc 93
(off Blackwall La.)
Cliff End CR8: Purl 84Rb 177
Cliffe Rd. CR2: S Croy 78Tb 157
Cliffe Wlk. SM1: Sutt 78Eb 155
(off Greyhound Rd.)
Clifford Av. BR7: Chst 65Pc 138
IG5: Ilf 25Rc 54
SM6: Wall 77Lb 156
SW14 55Ra 109
Clifford Cl. UB5: N'olt 39Aa 65
Clifford Ct. W2 43Db 89
(off Westbourne Pk. Vs.)
Clifford Dr. SW9 56Rb 113
Clifford Gdns. NW10 40Ya 68
UB3: Harl 49U 84
Clifford Gro. TW15: Ashf 63Q 128
Clifford Haigh Ho. SW6 52Za 110
Clifford Ho. BR3: Beck 65Dc 136
(off Calverley Cl.)
W14 49Bb 89
(off Edith Vs.)
Clifford Rd. E16 42Hc 93
E17 26Ec 52
EN5: New Bar 13Db 31
HA0: Wemb 38Ma 67
N1 39Ub 71
N9 16Yb 34
RM16: Chaf H 47Be 99
SE25 70Wb 135
TW4: Houn 55Z 107
TW10: Ham 61Ma 131
Clifford's Inn EC4 3K 223
Clifford's Inn Pas. EC4 3K 223 (44Qb 90)
Clifford St. W1 5B 222 (45Lb 90)
Clifford Way NW10 35Va 68
Cliff Pl. RM15: S Ock 41Zd 99
Cliff Reach DA9: Bluew 58Vd 120
Cliff Rd. NW1 37Mb 70
Cliffsend Ho. SW9 53Qb 112
(off Cowley Rd.)
Cliff Ter. SE8 54Cc 114
Cliffview Rd. SE13 55Cc 114
Cliff Vs. NW1 37Mb 70
Cliff Wlk. E16 43Hc 93
Clifton Av. E17 27Zb 52
HA7: Stan 26Ka 46
HA9: Wemb 37Pa 67
N3 25Bb 49
SM2: Sutt 83Db 175
TW13: Felt 62Y 129
W12 46Va 88
Clifton Cl. BR6: Farnb 78Sc 160
CR3: Cat'm 95Tb 197
EN8: Chesh 1Ac 20
KT15: Add 75K 149
Clifton Ct. BR3: Beck 67Dc 136
HP3: Hem H 4M 3
IG8: Wfd G 23Jc 53
KT5: Surb 73Pa 153
KT19: Eps 84Pa 173
N4 33Qb 70
NW8 5B 214
SE15 52Xb 113
TW19: Stanw 58N 105
Clifton Cres. SE15 52Xb 113
Clifton Est. SE15 53Xb 113
Clifton Gdns. EN2: Enf 14Nb 32
N15 30Vb 51
NW11 30Bb 49
UB10: Hil 40R 64
W4 49Ta 87
(not continuous)
W9 6A 214 (42Eb 89)
Clifton Ga. SW10 51Eb 111
Clifton Gro. DA11: Grav'nd 9D 122
E8 37Wb 71
Clifton Hill NW8 1A 214 (40Db 69)
Clifton Hill Studios NW8 40Eb 69
Clifton Ho. E2 5K 219
E11 33Gc 73
Clifton Lodge SL4: Eton W 10E 80
Clifton Marine Pde. DA11: Grav'nd 8B 122
(not continuous)
Clifton M. SE25 70Ub 135
Clifton Pde. TW13: Felt 62Y 129
Clifton Pk. Av. SW20 68Ya 132
Clifton Pl. SE16 47Yb 92
SM7: Bans 87Cb 175
SW10 51Eb 111
(off Hollywood Rd.)
W2 3C 220 (44Fb 89)
Clifton Ri. SE14 52Ac 114
(not continuous)
SL4: Wind 3B 102
Clifton Rd. CR5: Coul 87Kb 176
DA11: Grav'nd 8C 122
DA14: Sidc 63Uc 138
DA16: Well 55Yc 117
E7 37Mc 73
E16 43Gc 93
HA3: Kenton 28Pa 47
IG2: Ilf 30Tc 54
IG10: Lough 14Nc 36
KT2: King T 66Pa 131
N1 37Sb 71
N3 25Eb 49
Clifton Rd. N8 30Mb 50
N22 25Lb 50
NW10 40Wa 68
RM11: Horn 30Jd 56
SE25 70Ub 135
SL1: Slou 7M 81
SM6: Wall 78Kb 156
SW19 65Za 132
TW7: Isle 54Ga 108
TW11: Tedd 63Ga 130
UB2: S'hall 49Aa 85
UB6: G'frd 42Ea 86
W9 5A 214 (42Eb 89)
WD18: Wat 15X 27
Clifton's La. RH2: Reig 4F 206
Clifton St. AL1: St A 1C 6
EC2 6H 219 (42Ub 91)
Clifton Ter. N4 33Qb 70
Clifton Vs. W9 43Eb 89
Cliftonville Ct. SE12 60Jc 115
Clifton Wlk. DA2: Dart 58Rd 119
W6 49Xa 88
(off King St.)
Clifton Way CM13: Hut 18Fe 41
GU21: Wok 9K 167
HA0: Wemb 39Na 67
SE15 52Xb 113
TW6: H'row A 55Q 106
WD6: Bore 11Qa 29
Climb, The WD3: Rick 16K 25
Climsland Ho. SE1 6A 224 (46Qb 90)
Cline Rd. N11 23Lb 50
Clinger Ct. N1 1H 219
Clink Prison Mus. 6F 225
Clink St. SE1 6E 224 (46Tb 91)
Clink Wharf SE1 6F 225
Clinton Av. DA16: Well 56Wc 117
KT8: E Mos 70Ea 130
Clinton Cl. GU21: Knap 10H 167
KT13: Weyb 75R 150
Clinton Cres. IG6: Ilf 23Uc 54
Clinton End HP2: Hem H 2C 4
Clinton Ho. KT6: Surb 73Ma 153
(off Lovelace Gdns)
Clinton Rd. E3 41Ac 92
E7 35Jc 73
KT22: Lea 95La 192
N15 28Tb 51
Clinton Ter. SE8 51Cc 114
(off Watergate St.)
SM1: Sutt 77Eb 155
Clipper Apartments SE10 51Ec 114
(off Welland St.)
Clipper Blvd. DA2: Dart 55Ud 120
Clipper Blvd. W. DA2: Dart 55Td 120
Clipper Cl. SE16 47Zb 92
Clipper Cres. DA12: Grav'nd 3H 145
Clipper Ho. E14 50Ec 92
(off Manchester Rd.)
Clipper Pk. RM18: Tilb 52Fe 121
Clipper Way SE13 56Ec 114
Clippesby Cl. KT9: Chess 79Pa 153
Clipstone M. W1 7B 216 (43Lb 90)
Clipstone Rd. TW3: Houn 55Ca 107
Clipstone St. W1 7A 216 (43Kb 90)
Clissold Cl. N2 27Hb 49
Clissold Ct. N4 33Sb 71
Clissold Cres. N16 34Tb 71
Clissold Leisure Cen. 34Tb 71
Clissold Rd. N16 34Tb 71
Clitheroe Av. HA2: Harr 32Ca 65
Clitheroe Gdns. WD19: Wat 20Z 27
Clitheroe Rd. RM5: Col R 22Ed 56
SW9 54Nb 112
Clitherow Av. W7 48Ja 86
Clitherow Ct. TW8: Bford 50La 86
Clitherow Pas. TW8: Bford 50La 86
Clitherow Rd. TW8: Bford 50Ka 86
Clitterhouse Cres. NW2 32Ya 68
Clitterhouse Rd. NW2 32Ya 68
Clive Av. DA1: Cray 58Hd 118
N18 23Wb 51
Clive Cl. EN6: Pot B 3Bb 17
Clive Ct. SL1: Slou 7H 81
W9 5A 214 (42Eb 89)
Cliveden Cl. CM15: Shenf 17Be 41
N12 21Eb 49
Cliveden Ho. E16 46Jc 93
(off Fitzwilliam M.)
SW1 5H 227
Cliveden Pl. SW1 5H 227 (49Jb 90)
TW17: Shep 72S 150
Cliveden Rd. SW19 67Bb 133
Clivedon Ct. W13 43Ka 86
Clivedon Rd. E4 22Gc 53
Clive Ho. SE10 51Ec 114
(off Haddo St.)
Clive Lloyd Ho. N15 29Sb 51
(off Woodlands Pk. Rd.)
Clive Lodge NW4 30Za 48
Clive Pde. HA6: Nwood 24U 44
Clive Pas. SE21 62Tb 135
Clive Rd. CM13: Gt War 24Yd 58
DA11: Grav'nd 8D 122
DA17: Belv 49Cd 96
EN1: Enf 14Wb 33
KT10: Esh 77Da 151
RM2: Rom 29Kd 57
SE21 62Tb 135
SW19 65Gb 133
TW1: Twick 63Ha 130
TW14: Felt 58W 106
Clivesdale Dr. UB3: Hayes 46X 85
Clive Way EN1: Enf 14Wb 33
WD24: Wat 11Y 27
Cloak La. EC4 4E 224 (45Sb 91)
Clochar Ct. NW10 39Va 68
Clock Ct. E11 28Kc 53
CLOCK HOUSE 86Kb 176
Clock Ho. E3 41Ec 92
E17 28Fc 53
(off Wood St.)
Clockhouse, The SW19 62Ya 132
Clockhouse Av. IG11: Bark 39Sc 74
Clock Ho. Cl. KT14: Byfl 84P 169
Clockhouse Cl. SW19 61Ya 132
Clockhouse Ct. BR3: Beck 68Ac 136
CLOCKHOUSE JUNC. 22Pb 50
Clock Ho. La. TN13: S'oaks 95Jd 202
Clockhouse La. RM4: Have B 21Dd 56
RM5: Col R 24Dd 56
RM16: Chaf H, N Stif 46Zd 99
(not continuous)
TW14: Bedf 63Q 128
TW15: Ashf 63Q 128
Clockhouse La. E. TW20: Egh 66D 126
Clockhouse La. W. TW20: Egh 66C 126
Clock Ho. Mead KT22: Oxs 86Da 171

Coles Grn.—Compass Cl.

Coles Grn. IG10: Lough 11Qc 36
WD23: B Hea 18Ea 28
Coles Grn. Ct. NW2 33Wa 68
Coles Grn. Rd. NW2 32Wa 68
Coles Hill HP1: Hem H 1J 3
Coleshill Flats SW1 6J 227
Coleshill Rd. TW11: Tedd 65Ga 130
Coles La. TN16: Bras 95Yc 201
Colesmead Rd. RH1: Redh 3P 207
COLES MEADS 3P 207
Colestown St. SW11 54Gb 111
Cole St. SE1 2E 230 (47Sb 91)
Colesworth Ho. HA8: Edg 26Sa 47
(off Burnt Oak B'way.)
Colet Cl. N13 23Rb 51
Colet Ct. W6 49Za 88
(off Hammersmith Rd.)
Colet Flats E1 44Ac 92
(off Troon St.)
Colet Gdns. W14 49Za 88
Colet Ho. SE17 50Rb 91
(off Doddington Gro.)
Colet Rd. CM13: Hut 15Ee 41
Colets Orchard TN14: Otf 88Kd 183
Colette Ct. SE16 47Zb 92
(off Eleanor Cl.)
Coley Av. GU22: Wok 90C 168
Coley St. WC1 6J 217 (42Pb 90)
Colfe & Hatcliffe Glebe
SE13 57Dc 114
(off Lewisham High St.)
Colfe Rd. SE23 60Ac 114
Colfes Leisure Cen. 58Jc 115
Colgate Pl. EN3: Enf L 9Cc 20
Colham Av. UB7: Yiew 46N 83
COLHAM GREEN 43Q 84
Colham Grn. Rd. UB8: Hil 43Q 84
Colham Mill Rd. UB7: W Dray 47M 83
Colham Rd. UB8: Hil 42P 83
COLHAM RDBT. 44Q 84
Colina M. N15 28Rb 51
Colina Rd. N15 29Rb 51
Colin Chapman Way DA3: Fawk 77Ud 164
Colin Cl. BR4: W W'ck 76Hc 159
CR0: C'don 76Bc 158
DA2: Dart 58Rd 119
NW9 28Ua 48
Colin Ct. SE6 59Bc 114
Colin Cres. NW9 28Va 48
COLINDALE 27Ta 47
Colindale Av. AL1: St A 4D 6
NW9 27Ta 47
Colindale Bus. Pk. NW9 27Sa 47
Colindale Retail Pk. NW9 28Ta 47
Colindeep Gdns. NW4 28Wa 48
Colindeep La. NW4 27Ua 48
NW9 27Ua 48
Colin Dr. NW9 29Va 48
Colinette Rd. SW15 56Ya 110
Colin Gdns. NW9 28Va 48
Colin Pde. NW9 28Ua 48
Colin Pk. Rd. NW9 28Ua 48
Colin Pond Ct. RM6: Chad H 28Zc 55
Colin Rd. CR3: Cat'm 95Wb 197
NW10 37Wa 68
Colinsdale N1 1B 218
Colinswood SL2: Farn C 4G 60
Colinton Rd. IG3: Ilf 33Xc 75
Colin Way SL1: Slou 8F 80
Colin Winter Ho. E1 42Yb 92
(off Nicholas Rd.)
Coliseum Theatre 5F 223
Coliston Pas. SW18 59Cb 111
(off Coliston Rd.)
Coliston Rd. SW18 59Cb 111
Collamore Av. SW18 60Gb 111
Collapit Cl. HA1: Harr 30Da 45
Collard Av. IG10: Lough 12Sc 36
Collard Cl. CR8: Kenley 92Tb 197
Collard Grn. IG10: Lough 12Sc 36
Collard Pl. NW1 38Kb 70
Collards Almshouses E17 29Ec 52
(off Maynard Rd.)
Collection Pl. NW8 39Db 69
(off Bolton Pl.)
College SL4: Eton 1H 103
(off Westons Yd.)
College App. SE10 51Ec 114
College Av. HA3: Hrw W 25Ga 46
KT17: Eps 86Va 174
RM17: Grays 49De 99
SL1: Slou 8J 81
TW20: Egh 65D 126
College Cl. AL9: N Mym 10F 8
E9 36Yb 72
HA3: Hrw W 24Ga 46
IG10: Lough 14Rc 36
N18 22Vb 51
RM17: Grays 49Ee 99
TW2: Twick 60Fa 108
College Ct. EN3: Pond E 15Yb 34
EN8: Chesh 2Yb 20
NW3 37Fb 69
(off College Cres.)
RM2: Rom 29Kd 57
(off Scholars Way)
SW3 50Hb 89
(off West Rd.)
W5 45Na 87
W6 50Ya 88
(off Queen Caroline St.)
College Cres. NW3 37Eb 69
RH1: Redh 3A 208
SL4: Wind 4F 102
College Cross N1 38Qb 70
College Dr. HA4: Ruis 31W 64
KT7: T Ditt 73Ga 152
College E. E1 1K 225 (43Vb 91)
College Flds. Bus. Cen. SW19 67Gb 133
College Gdns. E4 17Dc 34
EN2: Enf 11Tb 33
IG4: Ilf 29Nc 54
KT3: N Mald 71Va 154
N18 22Wb 51
SE21 60Ub 113
SW17 61Gb 133
College Grn. SE19 66Ub 135
College Gro. NW1 39Lb 70
College Hill EC4 4E 224 (45Sb 91)
College Hill Rd. HA3: Hrw W 24Ga 46
College Ho. SW15 57Za 110
TW7: Isle 52Ga 108
College La. AL10: Hat 2A 8
(not continuous)
GU22: Wok 1N 187
NW5 35Kb 70
College Mans. NW6 39Ab 68
(off Salusbury Rd.)
College M. N1 38Qb 70
(off College Cross)
SW1 3F 229
SW18 57Db 111
College of Arms 4D 224
College Pde. NW6 39Ab 68
(off Salusbury Rd.)
COLLEGE PARK 41Xa 88
College Pk. Cl. SE13 56Fc 115
College Pk. Rd. N17 23Vb 51
College Pl. AL3: St A 2A 6
CM16: They B 8Sc 22
DA9: Ghithe 56Yd 120
E17 28Gc 53
NW1 1C 216 (39Lb 70)
SW10 52Eb 111
College Point E15 37Hc 73
College Rd. AL1: St A 3F 6
BR1: Brom 67Jc 137
BR8: Hext 67Gd 140
CR0: C'don 75Tb 157
DA11: Nflt 57De 121
E17 29Ec 52
EN2: Enf 12Tb 33
EN8: Chesh 2Yb 20
GU22: Wok 88D 168
HA1: Harr 30Ga 46
HA3: Hrw W 25Ga 46
HA9: Wemb 32Ma 67
KT17: Eps 86Va 174
N17 23Vb 51
N21 19Qb 32
NW10 40Ya 68
RM17: Grays 49Ee 99
SE19 64Vb 135
SE21 59Ub 113
SL1: Slou 6D 80
SW19 65Fb 133
TW7: Isle 53Ha 108
W13 44Ka 86
WD5: Ab L 3V 12
COLLEGE RDBT. 69Na 131
College Row E9 36Zb 72
College Slip BR1: Brom 67Jc 137
College St. AL3: St A 2B 6
EC4 4E 224 (45Sb 91)
College Ter. E3 41Bc 92
N3 26Bb 49
College Vw. SE9 60Mc 115
College Wlk. KT1: King T 69Na 131
College Way
HA6: Nwood 23T 44
RM8: Dag 35Wc 75
RM16: Grays 8A 100
TW15: Ashf 63P 127
UB3: Hayes 45W 84
College Yd. AL3: St A 2B 6
(off Lwr. Dagnall St.)
NW5 35Kb 70
NW6 39Ab 68
WD24: Wat 10X 13
Collendale Rd. E17 27Zb 52
Collens Fld. GU24: Pirb 6D 186
Collent St. E9 37Yb 72
Coller Cres. DA2: Daren 64Ud 142
Collerne St. RM3: Rom 22Nd 57
Collerston Ho. SE10 50Hc 93
(off Armitage Rd.)
Colless Rd. N15 29Vb 51
Collet Rd. TN15: Kems'g 89Nd 183
Collett Rd. HP1: Hem H 2L 3
SE16 48Wb 91
Collett Way UB2: S'hall 47Da 85
Colley Hill La. SL2: Hedg 4K 61
Colley Ho. UB8: Uxb 39M 63
Colleyland WD3: Chor 14F 24
Colley La. RH2: Reig 5G 206
Colley Mnr. Dr. RH2: Reig 5F 206
Colley Way RH2: Reig 3G 206
Collier Cl. E6 45Rc 94
KT19: Ewe 79Qa 153
SL1: Slou 7D 80
Collier Ct. RM16: Grays 46De 99
Collier Dr. HA8: Edg 26Qa 47
COLLIER ROW 24Dd 56
Collier Row La. RM5: Col R 24Dd 56
Collier Row Rd. RM5: Col R 25Bd 55
Colliers CR3: Cat'm 97Wb 197
Colliers Cl. GU21: Wok 9M 167
Colliers Ct. CR0: C'don 77Tb 157
(off St Peter's Rd.)
Colliers Shaw BR2: Kes 77Mc 159
Collier St. N1 2H 217 (40Pb 70)
Colliers Water La. CR7: Thor H 71Qb 156
COLLIERS WOOD 66Fb 133
COLLIERS WOOD 66Fb 133
Collindale Av. DA8: Erith 52Dd 118
DA15: Sidc 60Wc 117
Collingbourne Rd. W12 46Xa 88
Collingham Gdns. SW5 49Db 89
Collingham Pl. SW5 49Db 89
Collingham Rd. SW5 49Db 89
Collingridge Way KT17: Ewe 82Wa 174
Collingsbourne KT15: Add 77L 149
(off High St.)
Collings Cl. N22 23Pb 50
Collington Cl. DA11: Nflt 9A 122
Collington St. SE10 50Fc 93
Collingtree Rd. SE26 63Yb 136
Collingwood Av. KT5: Surb 74Sa 153
N10 27Jb 50
Collingwood Cl. SE20 67Xb 135
TW2: Whitt 59Ca 107
Collingwood Ct. EN5: New Bar 15Db 31
W5 43Pa 87
Collingwood Dr. AL2: Lon C 7H 7
Collingwood Ho. DA9: Ghithe 57Yd 120
E1 42Xb 91
(off Darling Row)
SE16 47Xb 91
(off Cherry Gdn. St.)
SW1 50Mb 90
(off Dolphin Sq.)
W1 7B 216
Collingwood Pl. KT12: Walt T 76W 150
Collingwood Rd. CR4: Mitc 69Gb 133
E17 30Cc 52
N15 28Ub 51
RM13: Rain 40Hd 76
SM1: Sutt 76Cb 155
UB8: Hil 42R 84
Collingwood St. E1 42Xb 91
Collins Av. HA7: Stan 26Na 47
Collins Cl. SS17: Stan H 1N 101
Collins Ct. E8 37Wb 71
WD23: Bush 15Da 27
(off Lea Cl.)
Collins Dr. HA4: Ruis 33Y 65
Collins Ho. E14 45Ec 92
(off Newby Pl.)
SE10 50Hc 93
(off Armitage Rd.)
Collinson Ct. SE1 2D 230
Collinson Ho. SE3 56Kc 115
(off Wallace Ct.)
SE15 52Wb 113
(off Peckham Pk. Rd.)
Collinson St. SE1 2D 230 (47Sb 91)
Collinson Wlk. SE1 2D 230 (47Sb 91)
Collins Path TW12: Hamp 65Ba 129
Collins Rd. N5 35Sb 71
Collins Sq. SE3 54Hc 115
Collins St. SE3 54Gc 115
(not continuous)
Collinswood Rd. SL2: Farn C 2E 60
Collin's Yd. N1 39Rb 71
Collinwood Av. EN3: Enf H 13Yb 34
Collinwood Gdns. IG5: Ilf 29Pc 54
Collis All. TW2: Twick 60Ga 108
Collison Pl. N16 32Ub 71
Coll's Rd. SE15 53Yb 114
Collum Grn. Rd.
SL2: Farn C, Hedg, Stoke P 4H 61
Collyer Av. CR0: Bedd 77Nb 156
Collyer Pl. SE15 53Wb 113
Collyer Rd. AL2: Lon C 9H 7
CR0: Bedd 77Nb 156
Colman Cl. KT18: Tatt C 89Ya 174
SS17: Stan H 1M 101
Colman Ct. HA7: Stan 23Ka 46
N12 23Eb 49
Colman Ho. RH1: Redh 4P 207
Colman Pde. EN1: Enf 13Ub 33
Colman Rd. E16 43Lc 93
Colmans Wharf E14 43Dc 92
(off Morris Rd.)
Colman Way RH1: Redh 4N 207
Colmar Cl. E1 42Zb 92
Colmer Pl. HA3: Hrw W 24Fa 46
Colmer Rd. SW16 67Nb 134
Colmore M. SE15 53Xb 113
Colmore Rd. EN3: Pond E 14Yb 34
COLNBROOK 52F 104
Colnbrook By-Pass SL3: Coln, L'ly 51E 104
UB7: Harm 52K 105
Colnbrook Cl. AL2: Lon C 9J 7
Colnbrook Ct. SL3: Poyle 53H 105
Colnbrook St. SE1 4B 230 (48Rb 91)
Colndale Rd. SL3: Poyle 54G 104
Colne RM18: E Til 8L 101
Colne Av. UB7: W Dray 47L 83
WD3: Rick 19J 25
WD19: Wat 16X 27
Colne Bank SL3: Hort 55E 104
Colnebridge Cl. TW18: Staines 63G 126
Colne Bri. Retail Pk. WD17: Wat 16Z 27
Colne Cl. RM15: S Ock 45Yd 98
Colne Ct. KT19: Ewe 77Sa 153
RM18: E Til 8L 101
W7 44Fa 86
(off High La.)
Colnedale Rd. UB8: Uxb 36M 63
Colne Dr. KT12: Walt T 76Z 151
RM3: Rom 23Pd 57
Colne Gdns. AL2: Lon C 9J 7
Colne Ho. IG11: Bark 38Rc 74
NW8 6C 214
Colne Lodge WD3: Rick 18J 25
WD23: Bush 14Z 27
Colne Mead WD3: Rick 19J 25
Colne Orchard SL0: Iver 44H 83
Colne Pk. Cvn. Site UB7: W Dray 49L 83
Colne Pl. UB9: Den 31J 63
Colne Reach TW19: Stanw M 57H 105
Colne Rd. E5 35Ac 72
N21 17Tb 33
TW1: Twick 60Ga 108
TW2: Twick 60Ga 108
Colne St. E13 41Jc 93
Colne Valley RM14: Upm 30Ud 58
Colne Valley Pk. Cen. 34K 63
Colne Valley Retail Pk. WD17: Wat 15Z 27
Colne Way TW19: Staines 61D 126
WD24: Wat 8Y 13
WD25: Wat 8Y 13
Colne Way Ct. WD24: Wat 9Z 13
Colne Way Ind. Pk. WD25: Wat 8Z 13
Colney Flds. Shop. Pk. AL2: Lon C 10K 7
COLNEY HATCH 23Hb 49
Colney Hatch La. N10 24Jb 50
N11 23Hb 49
COLNEY HEATH 5P 7
Colney Heath La. AL4: St A 2H 7
Colney Rd. DA1: Dart 58Pd 119
COLNEY STREET 2Ga 14
Colnhurst Rd. WD17: Wat 11W 26
Colnmore Ct. E2 41Zb 92
(off Meath Cres.)
Coln Trad. Est. SL3: Poyle 53H 105
Cologne Rd. SW11 56Fb 111
Coloma Ct. BR4: W W'ck 77Gc 159
Colombo Rd. IG1: Ilf 32Sc 74
Colombo St. SE1 7B 224 (46Rb 91)
Colombo Street Sports & Community Cen.
7B 224
Colomb St. SE10 50Gc 93
Colonel's La. KT16: Chert 72J 149
Colonel's Wlk. EN2: Enf 13Rb 33
Colonial Av. TW2: Whitt 58Ea 108
Colonial Bus. Pk. WD24: Wat 11Y 27
Colonial Ct. N7 34Pb 70
Colonial Dr. W4 49Sa 87
Colonial Rd. SL1: Slou 7L 81
TW14: Felt 59U 106
Colonial Way WD24: Wat 11Y 27
Colonnade WC1 6F 217 (42Nb 90)
Colonnade, The AL3: St A 2B 6
(off Verulam Rd.)
SE1 1K 229
SE8 49Bc 92
Colonnades, The W2 44Db 89
Colonnades Leisure Pk., The 70Qb 156
Colonnade Wlk. SW1 6K 227 (49Kb 90)
Colonsay HP3: Hem H 4C 4
Colony Mans. SW5 50Db 89
(off Earl's Ct. Rd.)
Colony M. N1 36Tb 71
(off Mildmay Gro. Nth.)
Colorado Apartments N8 27Pb 50
(off Gt. Amwell La.)
Colorado Bldg. SE13 53Dc 114
(off Deal's Gateway)
Colosseum, The 13W 26
Colosseum Apartments E2 40Zb 72
(off Palmers Rd.)
Colosseum Ter. NW1 4A 216
Colour Ct. SW1 7C 222
Colour Ho. SE1 2J 231
Colour House Theatre
Merton 67Eb 133
Colroy Ct. NW11 29Ab 48
Colson Gdns. IG10: Lough 14Rc 36
Colson Grn. IG10: Lough 15Rc 36
Colson Path IG10: Lough 14Qc 36
Colson Rd. CR0: C'don 75Ub 157
IG10: Lough 14Rc 36
Colson Way SW16 63Lb 134
Colstead Ho. E1 44Xb 91
(off Watney Mkt.)
Colsterworth Rd. N15 28Vb 51
(not continuous)
Colston Av. SM5: Cars 77Gb 155
Colston Ct. SL9: Ger X 30A 42
SM5: Cars 77Hb 155
Colston Rd. E7 37Mc 73
SW14 56Sa 109
Coltash Ct. EC1 5E 218
Colthurst Cres. N4 33Rb 71
Colthurst Dr. N9 20Xb 33
Coltishall Rd. RM12: Horn 37Ld 77
Coltman Ho. SE10 51Ec 114
(off Welland St.)
Coltman St. E14 43Ac 92
Colt M. EN3: Enf L 9Cc 20
Coltness Cres. SE2 50Xc 95
Colton Gdns. N17 27Sb 51
Colton Rd. HA1: Harr 29Ga 46
Coltsfoot, The HP1: Hem H 3G 2
Coltsfoot Ct. RM17: Grays 51Fe 121
Coltsfoot Dr. UB7: Yiew 44N 83
Coltsfoot La. RH8: Oxt 5K 211
Coltsfoot Path RM3: Rom 24Ld 57
Coltstead DA3: Nw A G 75Ae 165
Columbas Dr. NW3 32Fb 69
Columbia Av. HA4: Ruis 32X 65
HA8: Edg 25Ra 47
KT4: Wor Pk 73Va 154
Columbia Gdns. Nth. SW6 51Cb 111
(off Rickett St.)
Columbia Gdns. Sth. SW6 51Cb 111
(off Rickett St.)
Columbia Ho. E3 42Bc 92
(off Hamlets Way)
Columbia Point SE16 48Yb 92
(off Canada Est.)
Columbia Rd. E2 3K 219 (41Vb 91)
E13 42Hc 93
Columbia Road Flower Market 3K 219
(off Columbia Rd.)
Columbia Sq. SW14 56Sa 109
Columbia Wharf EN3: Pond E 16Ac 34
Columbia Wharf Rd.
RM17: Grays 51Ce 121
Columbine Av. CR2: S Croy 80Rb 157
E6 43Nc 94
Columbine Way RM3: Hrld W 25Nd 57
SE13 54Ec 114
Columbus Ct. DA8: Erith 52Hd 118
SE16 46Yb 92
(off Rotherhithe St.)
Columbus Courtyard E14 46Cc 92
Columbus Gdns. HA6: Nwood 25W 44
Columbus Sq. DA8: Erith 51Hd 118
Colva Wlk. N19 33Kb 70
Colvern Ho. RM7: Rom 29Ed 56
Colverson Ho. E1 43Yb 92
(off Lindley St.)
Colvestone Cres. E8 36Vb 71
Colview Ct. SE9 60Mc 115
Colville Est. N1 39Ub 71
Colville Est. W. E2 41Vb 91
(off Turin St.)
Colville Gdns. GU18: Light 3A 166
W11 44Bb 89
(not continuous)
Colville Ho. E2 40Yb 72
(off Waterloo Gdns.)
Colville Ho's. W11 44Bb 89
Colville Mans. E20 36Dc 72
(off Victory Pde.)
Colville M. W11 44Bb 89
Colville Pl. W1 1C 222 (43Mb 90)
Colville Rd. E11 34Ec 72
E17 26Ac 52
N9 18Xb 33
W3 48Ra 87
W11 44Bb 89
Colville Sq. W11 44Bb 89
Colville Ter. W11 44Bb 89
Colvin Cl. SE26 64Yb 136
Colvin Gdns. E4 20Ec 34
E11 28Kc 53
EN8: Walt C 7Zb 20
IG6: Ilf 25Sc 54
Colvin Ho. W10 44Za 88
(off Kingsdown Cl.)
Colvin Rd. CR7: Thor H 71Qb 156
E6 38Nc 74
Colwall Gdns. IG8: Wfd G 22Jc 53
Colwell Rd. SE22 57Vb 113
Colwick Cl. N6 31Mb 70
Colwith Rd. W6 51Ya 110
Colwood Gdns. SW19 66Fb 133
Colworth Gro. SE17 6E 230 (49Sb 91)
Colworth Rd. CR0: C'don 74Wb 157
E11 30Gc 53
Colwyn Av. UB6: G'frd 40Ha 66
Colwyn Cl. SW16 64Lb 134
Colwyn Cres. TW3: Houn 53Ea 108
Colwyn Grn. NW9 30Ua 48
(off Snowdon Dr.)
Colwyn Ho. SE1 4K 229 (48Qb 90)
Colwyn Rd. NW2 34Xa 68
Colyer Cl. SE9 61Rc 138
Colyer Rd. DA11: Nflt 61Ee 143
Colyers Cl. DA8: Erith 53Fd 118
Colyers La. DA8: Erith 53Ed 118
Colyers Wlk. DA8: Erith 53Gd 118
Colyton Cl. DA16: Well 53Zc 117
GU21: Wok 9K 167
HA0: Wemb 37La 66
Colyton La. SW16 64Qb 134
Colyton Rd. SE22 57Xb 113
Colyton Way N18 22Wb 51
Combe, The NW1 4A 216 (41Kb 70)
Combe Av. SE3 52Hc 115
Combe Bank Dr. TN14: Sund 94Ad 201
Combedale Rd. SE10 50Jc 93
Combe Ho. W2 43Cb 89
(off Gt. Western Rd.)
WD18: Wat 16U 26
Combemartin Rd. SW18 59Ab 110
Combe M. SE3 52Hc 115
Comber Cl. NW2 34Xa 68
Comber Gro. SE5 52Sb 113
Comber Ho. SE5 52Sb 113
Combermere Cl. SL4: Wind 4F 102
Combermere Rd. SM4: Mord 72Db 155
SW9 55Pb 112
Combe Rd. WD18: Wat 16V 26
Comberton KT1: King T 68Qa 131
(off Eureka Rd.)
Comberton Rd. E5 33Xb 71
Combeside SE18 52Vc 117
Combe St. HP1: Hem H 2L 3
Combewood WD25: Wat 4Y 13
Combwell Cres. SE2 48Wc 95
Comedy Store 5D 222
Comely Bank Rd. E17 29Ec 52
Comeragh Cl. GU22: Wok 2L 187
Comeragh M. W14 50Ab 88
Comeragh Rd. W14 50Ab 88
Comer Cres. UB2: S'hall 47Ea 86
(off Windmill Av.)
Comerell Pl. SE10 50Hc 93
Comerford Rd. SE4 56Ac 114
Comer Ho. EN5: New Bar 14Eb 31
Comet Cl. E12 35Mc 73
RM19: Purf 49Qd 97
WD25: Wat 6V 12
Comet Ho. UB3: Harl 52S 106
Comet Pl. SE8 52Cc 114
(not continuous)
Comet Rd. TW19: Stanw 59M 105
Comet St. SE8 52Cc 114
Comet Way AL10: Hat 1A 8
Comforts Farm Av. RH8: Oxt 5K 211
Comfort St. SE15 51Ub 113
Comfrey Ct. RM17: Grays 51Fe 121
Commander Av. NW9 27Wa 48
Commerce Pk. CR0: Wadd 75Pb 156
Commerce Rd. N22 25Pb 50
TW8: Bford 51La 108
Commerce Way CR0: Wadd 75Pb 156
Commercial Dock Path SE16 48Bc 92
(off Gulliver St.)
Commercial Pl. DA12: Grav'nd 8E 122
Commercial Rd. E1 44Wb 91
E14 44Yb 92
N18 22Ub 51
TW18: Staines 65J 127
Commercial Rd. Ind. Est. N18 23Vb 51
Commercial St. E1 6K 219 (42Vb 91)
Commercial Way GU21: Wok 89A 168
NW10 40Ra 67
SE10 49Hc 93
SE15 52Vb 113
Commercial Wharf E8 39Ub 71
(off Kingsland Rd.)
Commerell St. SE10 50Gc 93
Commodity Quay E1 5K 225 (45Vb 91)
Commodore Ct. SE8 53Cc 114
(off Albyn Rd.)
Commodore Ho. E14 45Ec 92
(off Poplar High St.)
SW18 55Eb 111
Commodore Sq. SW10 53Eb 111
Commodore St. E1 42Ac 92
COMMON, THE 94Ba 191
Common, The E15 37Gc 73
HA7: Stan 19Ga 28
KT21: Asht 88Ma 173
UB2: S'hall 49Y 85
UB7: W Dray 49L 83
W5 45Na 87
(not continuous)
WD4: Chfd 4J 11
WD4: K Lan 10A 4
WD7: Shenl 3Ka 14
Common Cl. GU21: Wok 6P 167
Commondale SW15 54Ya 110
Commonfield La. SW17 64Gb 133
Commonfield Rd. SM7: Bans 86Cb 175
Commonfields GU24: W End 4E 166
Common Ga. Rd. WD3: Chor 15F 24
Common La. DA2: Wilm 61Jd 140
GU24: W End 7B 166
KT10: Clay 80Ja 152
KT15: New H 81L 169
SL1: Burn 4B 60
SL4: Eton 10H 81
WD4: K Lan 10P 3
WD7: R'lett 11Ga 28
WD25: Let H 11Ga 28
Common La. Ho. SL4: Eton 10H 81
(off Common La.)
Commonmeadow La.
WD25: A'ham 6Da 13
Common Mile Cl. SW4 57Mb 112
Common Rd. CM13: Ingve 22Ee 59
HA7: Stan 21Fa 46
KT10: Clay 79Ja 152
RH1: Redh 8P 207
SL3: L'ly 49C 82
SL4: Dor, Eton W 9A 80
SL4: Eton W 9D 80
SW13 55Xa 110
TN15: Igh 95Xd 204
WD3: Chor 14F 24
Common Side KT18: Eps 87Qa 173
Commonside BR2: Kes 77Lc 159
KT23: Bookh 94Ca 191
(not continuous)
Commonside Cl. CR5: Coul 92Rb 197
SM2: Sutt 83Db 175
Commonside E. CR4: Mitc 69Jb 134
Commonside W. CR4: Mitc 69Hb 133
Commons La. HP2: Hem H 1N 3
Commonwealth Av. UB3: Hayes 44T 84
W12 45Xa 88
(not continuous)
Commonwealth Ho. RM18: Tilb 4C 122
(off Montreal Rd.)
Commonwealth Rd. CR3: Cat'm 95Wb 197
N17 24Wb 51
Commonwealth Secretariat 7C 222
Commonwealth Way SE2 50Xc 95
COMMONWOOD 6K 11
Common Wood SL2: Farn C 5G 60
Community Cl. TW5: Cran 53X 107
UB10: Ick 34R 64
Community La. N7 36Mb 70
Community Rd. E15 36Fc 73
UB6: G'frd 39Ea 66
Community Wlk. KT10: Esh 77Ea 152
Community Way WD3: Crox G 15Q 26
Como Rd. SE23 61Ac 136
Como St. RM7: Rom 29Fd 56
COMP 93Fe 205
Compass Bus. Pk. KT9: Chess 77Qa 153
Compass Cl. HA8: Edg 21Pa 47
TW15: Ashf 66S 128

Compass Ct.—Cooper's Rd.

Compass Ct. SE1 .... 7K **225**
Compass Hill TW10: Rich 58Ma **109**
Compass Ho. *E1* *46Xb* ***91***
(off Raine St.)
SW18 .... 56Db **111**
Compass La. *BR1: Brom* *67Jc* ***137***
(off North St.)
Compass Point *E14* *45Bc* ***92***
(off Grenade St.)
Compass Theatre 34S 64
Compayne Gdns. NW6 .... 38Db **69**
Compayne Mans. *NW6* *37Db* ***69***
(off Fairhazel Gdns.)
Comp La. TN15: Plat, Wro H 93Ee **205**
Comport Grn. CR0: New Ad 84Gc **179**
Compter Pas. EC2 .... 3E **224**
Compton Av. CM13: Hut 18Ee **41**
E6 .... 40Mc **73**
HA0: Wemb 35La **66**
N1 .... 37Rb **71**
N6 .... 31Gb **69**
RM2: Rom 27Ld **57**
Compton Cl. E3 .... 43Cc **92**
HA8: Edg 24Sa **47**
KT10: Esh 79Fa **152**
NW1 .... 4A **216**
NW11 .... 34Za **68**
SE15 .... 52Wb **113**
W13 .... 44Ja **86**
Compton Ct. SE19 .... 65Ub **135**
SL1: Slou 4C **80**
SM1: Sutt 77Eb **155**
Compton Cres. KT9: Chess 78Na **153**
N17 .... 24Sb **51**
UB5: N'olt 39Z **65**
W4 .... 51Sa **109**
Compton Gdns. AL2: Chis G 8P **5**
KT15: Add *78K* ***149***
(off Monks Cres.)
Compton Ho. *E20* *36Dc* ***72***
(off Peloton Av.)
SW11 .... 53Gb **111**
Compton Leisure Cen. 23Gb 49
Compton Pas. EC1 ...... 5C **218** (42Rb **91**)
Compton Pl. DA8: Erith 51Hd **118**
WC1 .... 5F **217** (42Nb **90**)
WD19: Wat 20Aa **27**
Compton Ri. HA5: Pinn 29Aa **45**
Compton Rd. CR0: C'don 74Xb **157**
N1 .... 37Rb **71**
N21 .... 18Rb **33**
NW10 .... 41Za **88**
SW19 .... 65Bb **133**
UB3: Hayes 45U **84**
Compton St. EC1 .... 5B **218** (42Rb **91**)
Compton Ter. N1 .... 37Rb **71**
N21 .... 18Qb **32**
Comreddy Cl. EN2: Enf 11Rb **33**
Comus Ho. SE17 .... 6H **231**
Comus Pl. SE17 .... 6H **231** (49Ub **91**)
Comyne Rd. WD24: Wat 8V **12**
Comyn Rd. SW11 .... 56Gb **111**
Comyns, The WD23: B Hea 18Ea **28**
Comyns Cl. E16 .... 43Hc **93**
Comyns Rd. RM9: Dag 38Cd **76**
Conant Ho. *SE11* *51Rb* ***113***
(off St Agnes Pl.)
Conant M. E1 .... 45Wb **91**
Conaways Cl. KT17: Ewe 82Wa **174**
Concanon Rd. SW2 .... 56Pb **112**
Concert Hall App. SE1 ..... 7J **223** (46Pb **90**)
Concord Bus. Cen. W3 .... 42Ra **87**
Concord Cl. UB5: N'olt 41Z **85**
Concord Ct. *KT1: King T* *69Pa* ***131***
(off Winery La.)
Concorde Bus. Pk. TN16: Big H ... 87Mc **179**
Concorde Cl. TW3: Houn 54Da **107**
UB10: Uxb 40N **63**
Concorde Ct. SL4: Wind 4E **102**
Concorde Dr. E6 .... 43Pc **94**
HP2: Hem H 2M **3**
Concorde Ho. *RM12: Horn* *37Kd* ***77***
(off Cavendish Av.)
Concorde Way SE16 .... 49Zb **92**
SL1: Slou 7G **80**
Concord Ho. CR0: C'don 72Rb **157**
KT3: N Mald 69Ua **132**
N17 .... *24Vb* ***51***
(off Park La.)
Concordia Wharf *E14* *46Ec* ***92***
(off Coldharbour)
Concord Rd. EN3: Pond E 15Xb **33**
W3 .... 42Ra **87**
Concord Ter. *HA2: Harr* *33Da* ***65***
(off Coles Cres.)
Concourse, The *N9* *19Wb* ***33***
(within Edmonton Grn. Shop. Cen.)
NW9 .... *25Va* ***48***
(off Quakers Course)
Condell Rd. SW8 .... 53Lb **112**
Conder St. E14 .... 44Ac **92**
Condor Ct. WD24: Wat 10X **13**
Condor Path *UB5: N'olt* *40Ca* ***65***
(off Union Rd.)
Condor Rd. TW18: Lale 69L **127**
Condor Wlk. RM12: Horn 38Kd **77**
Condover Cres. SE18 .... 52Rc **116**
Condray Pl. SW11 .... 52Gb **111**
Conduit, The RH1: Blet 1K **209**
Conduit Av. SE10 .... 53Fc **115**
Conduit Ct. WC2 .... 4F **223**
Conduit La. CR0: C'don 78Wb **157**
CR2: S Croy 78Wb **157**
EN3: Pond E 16Ac **34**
N18 .... 22Yb **52**
SL3: L'ly 50A **82**
Conduit M. SE18 .... 50Rc **94**
W2 .... 3B **220** (44Fb **89**)
Conduit Pas. W2 .... 3B **220**
Conduit Pl. W2 .... 3B **220** (44Fb **89**)
Conduit Rd. SE18 .... 50Rc **94**
Conduit St. W1 .... 4A **222** (45Kb **90**)
Conduit Way NW10 .... 38Sa **67**
Conegar Ct. SL1: Slou 6J **81**
Conewood St. N5 .... 34Rb **71**
Coney Acre SE21 .... 60Sb **113**
Coneyberry RH2: Reig 10L **207**
Coney Burrows E4 .... 19Gc **35**
Coneybury RH1: Blet 6L **209**
Coneybury Cl.
CR6: W'ham 91Xb **197**
Coney Cl. AL10: Hat 2D **8**
Coney Gro. UB8: Hil 41Q **84**
Coneygrove Path *UB5: N'olt* *37Aa* ***65***
(off Arnold Rd.)
CONEY HALL 76Gc 159
Coney Hall Pde.
BR4: W W'ck 76Gc **159**
Coney Hill Rd.
BR4: W W'ck 75Gc **159**
Coney Way SW8 .... 51Pb **112**
Conference Cl. E4 .... 19Ec **34**
Conference Rd. SE2 .... 49Xc **95**
Confluence Plaza *SE13* *55Ec* ***114***
(off Station Rd.)
Congers Ho. SE8 .... 52Cc **114**
Congleton Gro. SE18 .... 50Sc **94**
Congo Dr. N9 .... 20Yb **34**
Congo Rd. SE18 .... 50Tc **94**
Congress Rd. SE2 .... 49Yc **95**
Congreve Ho. N16 .... 36Ub **71**
Congreve Rd.
EN9: Walt A 5Gc **21**
SE9 .... 55Pc **116**
Congreve St. SE17 ..... 5H **231** (49Ub **91**)
Congreve Wlk. *E16* *43Mc* ***93***
(off Fulmer Rd.)
Conical Cnr. EN2: Enf 12Sb **33**
Conifer Av. DA3: Hartl 72Ae **165**
RM5: Col R 22Dd **56**
Conifer Cl. BR6: Orp 77Tc **160**
EN7: Chesh 1Vb **19**
RH2: Reig 4J **207**
Conifer Ct. *TW15: Ashf* *64P* ***127***
(off The Crescent)
Conifer Dr. CM14: W'ley 22Zd **59**
Conifer Gdns. EN1: Enf 16Ub **33**
SM1: Sutt 75Db **155**
SW16 .... 62Pb **134**
Conifer Ho. *SE4* *56Bc* ***114***
(off Brockley Rd.)
Conifer La. TW20: Egh 64E **126**
Conifer Pk. KT17: Eps 83Ua **174**
Conifers KT13: Weyb 77U **150**
Conifers, The HP3: Hem H 5H **3**
WD25: Wat 7Y **13**
Conifers Cl. TW11: Tedd 66Ka **130**
Conifer Wlk. SL4: Wind 2A **102**
Conifer Way BR8: Swan 67Ed **140**
HA0: Wemb 34La **66**
UB3: Hayes 45W **84**
Coniger Rd. SW6 .... 54Cb **111**
Coningesby Dr.
WD17: Wat 11U **26**
Coningham Ct. *SW10* *52Eb* ***111***
(off King's Rd.)
Coningham M. W12 .... 46Wa **88**
Coningham Rd. W12 .... 47Xa **88**
Coningsby Av. NW9 .... 26Ua **48**
Coningsby Bank AL1: St A 6B **6**
Coningsby Cl. AL9: Wel G 6F **8**
Coningsby Cotts. W5 .... 47Ma **87**
Coningsby Ct. CR4: Mitc 68Jb **134**
WD7: R'lett 8Ha **14**
Coningsby Dr. EN6: Pot B 5Fb **17**
Coningsby Gdns. E4 .... 23Dc **52**
Coningsby Rd. CR2: S Croy 81Sb **177**
N4 .... 31Rb **71**
W5 .... 47Ma **87**
Conington Rd. SE13 .... 54Dc **114**
Conisbee Ct. N14 .... 15Lb **32**
Conisborough Ct. *DA2: Dart* *58Rd* ***119***
(off Osbourne Rd.)
Conisborough Cres. SE6 .... 62Ec **136**
Conisbrough NW1 .... 1B **216**
Coniscliffe Cl. BR7: Chst 67Qc **138**
Coniscliffe Rd. N13 .... 20Sb **33**
Conista Ct. GU21: Wok 8K **167**
Coniston NW1 .... 3B **216**
Coniston Av. DA16: Well 55Uc **116**
IG11: Bark 38Uc **74**
RM14: Upm 35Sd **78**
RM19: Purf 50Sd **98**
UB6: G'frd 41Ka **86**
Coniston Cl. DA1: Dart 60Kd **119**
DA7: Bex 53Ed **118**
DA8: Erith 52Gd **118**
HP3: Hem H 3C **4**
IG11: Bark 38Uc **74**
N20 .... 20Eb **31**
SW13 .... 52Va **110**
SW20 .... 72Za **154**
W4 .... 52Sa **109**
Coniston Ct. CM16: Epp 3Wc **23**
GU18: Light 2A **166**
KT13: Weyb 79R **150**
NW7 .... *24Ab* ***48***
(off Langstone Way)
SE16 .... *47Zb* ***92***
(off Eleanor Cl.)
SM6: Wall 77Kb **156**
TW15: Ashf 62M **127**
W2 .... 3E **220**
Coniston Cres. SL1: Slou 3A **80**
Conistone Way N7 .... 38Nb **70**
Coniston Gdns. HA5: Eastc 28W **44**
HA9: Wemb 32La **66**
IG4: Ilf 28Nc **54**
N9 .... 18Yb **34**
NW9 .... 29Ta **47**
SM2: Sutt 79Fb **155**
Coniston Ho. *E3* *42Bc* ***92***
(off Southern Gro.)
SE5 .... *52Sb* ***113***
(off Wyndham Rd.)
Coniston Lodge WD17: Wat 12W **26**
Coniston Rd. BR1: Brom 65Gc **137**
CR0: C'don 73Wb **157**
CR5: Coul 88Lb **176**
DA7: Bex 53Ed **118**
GU22: Wok 92D **188**
N10 .... 26Kb **50**
N17 .... 23Wb **51**
TW2: Whitt 58Da **107**
WD4: K Lan 10P **3**
Coniston Wlk. E9 .... 36Yb **72**
Coniston Way KT9: Chess 76Na **153**
RH2: Reig 5N **207**
RM12: Horn 36Jd **76**
TW20: Egh 66D **126**
Conlan St. W10 .... 42Ab **88**
Conley Rd. NW10 .... 37Ua **68**
Conley St. SE10 .... 50Gc **93**
Connaught Av. E4 .... 17Fc **35**
EN1: Enf 12Ub **33**
EN4: E Barn 18Hb **31**
IG10: Lough 14Mc **35**
RM16: Grays 47De **99**
SW14 .... 55Sa **109**
TW4: Houn 56Aa **107**
TW15: Ashf 63N **127**
Connaught Bri. E16 .... 46Mc **93**
Connaught Bus. Cen.
CR0: Wadd 79Pb **156**
CR4: Mitc 71Hb **155**
NW9 .... 29Va **48**
Connaught Cl. E10 .... 33Ac **72**
EN1: Enf 12Ub **33**
HP2: Hem H 1A **4**
SM1: Sutt 75Fb **155**
UB8: Hil 42S **84**
W2 .... 3E **220** (44Gb **89**)
Connaught Club, The 17Hc 35
Connaught Ct. *E17* *28Dc* ***52***
(off Orford Rd.)
W2 .... 3F **221**
Connaught Cres.
GU24: Brkwd 2D **186**
Connaught Dr. KT13: Weyb 83Q **170**
NW11 .... 28Cb **49**
Connaught Gdns. N10 .... 29Kb **50**
N13 .... 21Rb **51**
SM4: Mord 70Eb **133**
Connaught Hgts. *E16* *46Mc* ***93***
(off Agnes George Wlk.)
UB10: Hil *42S* ***84***
(off Uxbridge Rd.)
Connaught Hill IG10: Lough 14Mc **35**
Connaught Ho. *NW10* *41Xa* ***88***
(off Trenmar Gdns.)
W1 .... 5K **221**
WD23: Bush *14Ba* ***27***
(off Royal Connaught Dr.)
Connaught La. IG1: Ilf 33Sc **74**
Connaught Lodge *N4* *31Qb* ***70***
(off Connaught Rd.)
Connaught M. NW3 .... 35Gb **69**
SE18 .... 50Qc **94**
SW6 .... 53Ab **110**
Connaught Pl. IG10: Lough 14Nc **36**
W2 .... 4F **221** (45Hb **89**)
Connaught Rd. E4 .... 17Gc **35**
E11 .... 32Fc **73**
E16 .... 46Mc **93**
E17 .... 29Cc **52**
EN5: Barn 16Za **30**
GU24: Brkwd 3C **186**
HA3: W'stone 25Ha **46**
IG1: Ilf 33Tc **74**
KT3: N Mald 70Ua **132**
N4 .... 31Qb **70**
NW10 .... 39Ua **68**
RM12: Horn 34Md **77**
SE18 .... 50Qc **94**
SL1: Slou 7M **81**
SM1: Sutt 75Fb **155**
TW10: Rich 57Pa **109**
TW11: Tedd 64Fa **130**
W13 .... 45Ka **86**
CONNAUGHT RDBT. *45Mc* ***93***
(off Victoria Dock Rd.)
Connaught Sq. W2 ..... 3F **221** (44Hb **89**)
Connaught St. W2 ..... 3D **220** (44Gb **89**)
Connaught Way N13 .... 21Rb **51**
Connaught Works *E3* *39Ac* ***72***
(off Old Ford Rd.)
Connections Bus. Pk.
TN14: S'oaks 91Ld **203**
Connect La. IG6: Ilf 26Sc **54**
Connell Ct. *SE14* *51Zb* ***114***
(off Myers La.)
Connell Cres. W5 .... 42Pa **87**
Connemara Cl. WD6: Bore 16Ta **29**
Connersville Way CR0: Wadd 76Qb **156**
Connicut La. KT23: Bookh 100Da **191**
Conniffe Ct. SE9 .... 57Rc **116**
Conningham Ct. SE9 .... 57Lc **115**
Connington Cres. E4 .... 20Fc **35**
Connolly Ct. GU25: Vir W 70A **126**
RM7: Rush G *30Gd* ***56***
(off Union Rd.)
Connop Rd. EN3: Enf W 10Zb **20**
Connor Cl. E11 .... 31Gc **73**
IG6: Ilf 25Sc **54**
Connor Ct. SW11 .... 53Kb **112**
Connor Rd. RM9: Dag 35Bd **75**
Connor St. E9 .... 39Zb **72**
Conolly Dell *W7* *46Ga* ***86***
(off Conolly Rd.)
Conolly Rd. W7 .... 46Ga **86**
Conqueror Ct. RM3: Rom 24Md **57**
Conquest Rd. KT15: Add 78J **149**
Conrad Cl. RM16: Grays 47De **99**
Conrad Ct. *NW9* *26Ue* ***48***
(off Needleman Cl.)
SE16 .... *49Ac* ***92***
(off Cary Av.)
SS17: Stan H 2L **101**
Conrad Dr. KT4: Wor Pk 74Ya **154**
Conrad Gdns. RM16: Grays 47Ce **99**
Conrad Ho. E8 .... 37Wb **71**
E14 .... *45Ac* ***92***
(off Victory Pl.)
E16 .... *46Kc* ***93***
(off Wesley Av.)
N16 .... *36Ub* ***71***
(off Matthias Rd.)
SW8 .... *52Nb* ***112***
(off Wyvil Rd.)
Conrad M. DA11: Nflt 61De **143**
Conrad Rd. SS17: Stan H 1N **101**
Conrad Twr. W3 .... 48Ra **87**
Consfield Av. KT3: N Mald 70Wa **132**
Consort Cl. CM14: W'ley 22Yd **58**
Consort Ct. GU22: Wok 90A **168**
W8 .... *48Db* ***89***
(off Wright's La.)
Consort Ho. *E14* *50Dc* ***92***
(off St Davids Sq.)
SW6 .... *54Eb* ***111***
(off Lensbury Av.)
W2 .... *45Db* ***89***
(off Queensway)
Consort Lodge NW8 .... 1F **215**
Consort M. TW7: Isle 57Fa **108**
Consort Rd. SE15 .... 53Xb **113**
Cons St. SE1 .... 1A **230** (47Qb **90**)
Constable Av. E16 .... 46Kc **93**
Constable Cl. KT17: Ewe 82Wa **174**
N11 .... 22Hb **49**
NW11 .... 30Db **49**
UB4: Hayes 40S **64**
Constable Ct. *SE16* *50Xb* ***91***
(off Stubbs Dr.)
W4 .... *50Ra* ***87***
(off Chaseley Dr.)
Constable Cres. N15 .... 29Wb **51**
Constable Gdns. HA8: Edg 25Qa **47**
TW7: Isle 57Fa **108**
Constable Ho. NW3 .... 38Hb **69**
UB5: N'olt *40Z* ***65***
(off Gallery Gdns.)
Constable Ho's. *E14* *47Cc* ***92***
(off Cassilis Rd.)
Constable M. BR1: Brom 68Kc **137**
RM8: Dag 35Xc **75**
Constable Rd. DA11: Nflt 2A **144**
Constable Wlk. SE21 .... 62Ub **135**
Constance Allen Ho. *W10* *44Za* ***88***
(off Bridge Cl.)
Constance Cl. SW15 .... 63Ta **131**
Constance Cres. BR2: Hayes 73Hc **159**
Constance Gro. DA1: Dart 58Md **119**
Constance Rd. CR0: C'don 73Rb **157**
EN1: Enf 16Ub **33**
SM1: Sutt 77Eb **155**
TW2: Whitt 59Da **107**
Constance St. E16 .... 46Nc **94**
Constant Ho. *E14* *45Dc* ***92***
(off Harrow La.)
Constantine Ct. *E1* *44Wb* ***91***
(off Fairclough St.)
Constantine Ho. UB3: Hayes 44T **84**
Constantine Pl. UB10: Hil 39P **63**
Constantine Rd. NW3 .... 35Gb **69**
Constant Mdw. TN13: S'oaks 97Ld **203**
Constitution Cres.
DA12: Grav'nd *10E* ***122***
(off Constitution Hill)
Constitution Hill DA12: Grav'nd 10E **122**
GU22: Wok 91A **188**
SW1 .... 1K **227** (47Kb **90**)
Constitution Ri. SE18 .... 53Qc **116**
Consul Av. RM9: Dag, Rain 41Ed **96**
RM13: Rain 41Ed **96**
Consul Gdns. BR8: Hext 66Hd **140**
Consul Ho. *E3* *42Cc* ***92***
(off Wellington Way)
Content St. SE17 .... 6F **231** (49Tb **91**)
Contessa Cl. BR6: Farnb 78Uc **160**
Continuity Ct. DA9: Ghithe 56Wd **120**
Control Twr. Rd. TW6: H'row A 55Q **106**
Convair Wlk. UB5: N'olt 41Z **85**
Convent Cl. BR3: Beck 66Ec **136**
EN5: Barn 12Bb **31**
GU22: Wok 89D **168**
Convent Gdns. W5 .... 49La **86**
W11 .... 44Ab **88**
Convent Hill SE19 .... 65Sb **135**
Convent La. KT11: Cobh 83U **170**
Convent Rd. SL4: Wind 4D **102**
TW15: Ashf 64R **128**
Convent Way UB2: S'hall 49Y **85**
Conway Cl. BR3: Beck 67Ac **136**
HA7: Stan 23Ja **46**
RM13: Rain 38Jd **76**
Conway Ct. SL9: Ger X 32D **62**
Conway Cres. RM6: Chad H 30Yc **55**
UB6: G'frd 40Ga **66**
Conway Dr. SM2: Sutt 79Db **155**
TW15: Ashf 65S **128**
UB3: Harl 48S **84**
Conway Gdns. CR4: Mitc 70Nb **134**
EN2: Enf 10Ub **19**
HA9: Wemb 31La **66**
RM17: Grays 52De **121**
Conway Gro. W3 .... 43Ta **87**
Conway Ho. *E14* *49Cc* ***92***
(off Cahir St.)
SW3 .... *50Hb* ***89***
(off Ormonde Ga.)
WD6: Bore 14Sa **29**
Conway M. W1 .... 6B **216**
Conway Rd. N14 .... 20Nb **32**
N15 .... 29Rb **51**
NW2 .... 33Ya **68**
SE18 .... 49Tc **94**
SL6: Tap 4A **80**
SW20 .... 67Ya **132**
TW4: Houn 59Ba **107**
TW6: H'row A 55R **106**
TW13: Hanw 64Z **129**
Conways Rd. RM16: Ors 1C **100**
Conway St. W1 .... 6B **216** (42Lb **90**)
(not continuous)
Conway Wlk. TW12: Hamp 65Ba **129**
Conybeare NW3 .... 38Gb **69**
Conybury Ct. EN9: Walt A 4Jc **21**
Conyerd Rd. TN15: Bor G 92Be **205**
Conyers Cl. IG8: Wfd G 23Gc **53**
KT12: Hers 78Z **151**
Conyer's Rd. SW16 .... 64Mb **134**
Conyer St. E3 .... 40Ac **72**
Conyers Way IG10: Lough 13Rc **36**
Cooden Cl. BR1: Brom 66Kc **137**
Cook Ct. DA8: Erith 52Hd **118**
SE8 .... *50Ac* ***92***
(off Evelyn St.)
SE16 .... *46Yb* ***92***
(off Rotherhithe St.)
Cooke Cl. RM16: Chaf H 48Ae **99**
SE2 .... 48Yc **95**
Cookes Cl. E11 .... 33Hc **73**
Cookes La. SM3: Cheam 79Ab **154**
Cooke St. IG11: Bark 39Sc **74**
(not continuous)
Cookham Cl. UB2: S'hall 48Da **85**
Cookham Cres. SE16 .... 47Zb **92**
Cookham Dene Cl. BR7: Chst 67Tc **138**
Cookham Hill BR5: Orp 76Cd **162**
Cookham Ho. E2 .... 5K **219**
Cookham Rd. BR8: Swan 67Cd **140**
Cookhill Rd. SE2 .... 47Xc **95**
Cook Rd. RM9: Dag 39Ad **75**
Cook's Cl. RM5: Col R 25Ed **56**
Cooks Cl. *E14* *46Cc* ***92***
(off Cabot Sq.)
SL9: Chal P 23A **42**
Cooks Hole Rd. EN2: Enf 10Rb **19**
Cooks Mead WD23: Bush 16Da **27**
Cookson Gro. DA8: Erith 52Dd **118**
Cook Sq. DA8: Erith 52Hd **118**
Cook's Rd. E15 .... 40Dc **72**
Cooks Rd. SE17 .... 51Rb **113**
Cooks Way AL10: Hat 2D **8**
Coolfin Rd. E16 .... 44Jc **93**
Coolgardie Av. E4 .... 22Fc **53**
IG7: Chig 20Qc **36**
Coolgardie Rd. TW15: Ashf 64S **128**
Coolhurst Rd. N8 .... 30Mb **50**
Coolhurst Tennis & Squash Club ... 30Mb 50
Cool Oak La. NW9 .... 31Ua **68**
Coomassie Rd. W9 .... 42Bb **89**
COOMBE 66Sa 131
Coombe, The RH3: Bet 3A **206**
Coombe Av. CR0: C'don 77Ub **157**
TN14: S'oaks 92Kd **203**
Coombe Bank KT2: King T 67Ua **132**
Coombe Cl. HA8: Edg 26Pa **47**
SL2: Slou 2D **80**
TW3: Houn 56Ca **107**
Coombe Cnr. N21 .... 18Rb **33**
Coombe Ct. *CR0: C'don* *77Tb* ***157***
(off Coombe Rd.)
KT20: Tad 95Ya **194**
TN14: S'oaks 92Kd **203**
Coombe Cres. TW12: Hamp 66Ba **129**
Coombe Dene *BR2: Brom* *70Hc* ***137***
(off Cumberland Rd.)
Coombe Dr. HA4: Ruis 32X **65**
KT15: Add 79H **149**
Coombe End KT2: King T 66Ta **131**
Coombefield Cl. KT3: N Mald 71Ua **154**
Coombe Gdns. KT3: N Mald 70Va **132**
SW20 .... 68Wa **132**
Coombe Hill Ct. SL4: Wind 6B **102**
Coombe Hill Glade KT2: King T ... 66Ua **132**
Coombe Hill Golf Course 66Ta 131
Coombe Hill Rd. KT2: King T 66Ua **132**
WD3: Rick 17J **25**
Coombe Ho. N7 .... 36Mb **70**
Coombe Ho. Chase KT3: N Mald .. 67Ta **131**
Coombehurst Cl. EN4: Cockf 12Hb **31**
Coombelands La. KT15: Add 79J **149**
COOMBE LANE **67Va 132**
Coombe La. CR0: C'don 78Xb **157**
GU3: Worp 10G **186**
(not continuous)
KT12: W Vill 81V **170**
SL5: S'hill 10A **124**
SW20 .... 67Va **132**
Coombe La. Flyover SW20 .... 67Va **132**
Coombe La. W. KT2: King T 67Ra **131**
Coombe Lea BR1: Brom 69Nc **138**
Coombe Lodge SE7 .... 51Lc **115**
Coombe Mnr. GU24: Bisl 7E **166**
Coombe Neville KT2: King T 66Ta **131**
Coombe Pk. KT2: King T 64Sa **131**
Coombe Pl. KT2: King T 64Sa **131**
Coomber Ho. *SW6* *55Db* ***111***
(off Wandsworth Bri. Rd.)
Coombe Ridings KT2: King T 64Sa **131**
Coombe Ri. CM15: Shenf 18Be **41**
KT2: King T 67Sa **131**
SS17: Stan H 1N **101**
Coombe Rd. CR0: C'don 77Tb **157**
DA12: Grav'nd 1E **144**
KT2: King T 67Qa **131**
KT3: N Mald 68Ua **132**
N22 .... 26Qb **50**
NW10 .... 34Ta **67**
RM3: Hrld W 27Pd **57**
SE26 .... 63Xb **135**
TN14: Otf 87Ld **183**
TW12: Hamp 65Ba **129**
W4 .... 50Ua **88**
W13 .... 48Ka **86**
WD23: Bush 17Fa **28**
Coomber Way CR0: Bedd 73Mb **156**
Coombes Rd. AL2: Lon C 8G **6**
RM9: Dag 39Bd **75**
Coombe Va. SL9: Ger X 32A **62**
Coombe Wlk. SM1: Sutt 76Db **155**
Coombe Way KT14: Byfl 84P **169**
Coombewood Dr. RM6: Chad H 30Bd **55**
Coombe Wood Golf Course 66Ra 131
Coombe Wood Hill CR8: Purl 85Sb **177**
Coombe Wood Local Nature Reserve
.... 66Va 132
Coombe Wood Rd. KT2: King T 64Sa **131**
Coombfield Dr. DA2: Daren 63Td **142**
Coombrook Ct. *SE16* *47Ac* ***92***
(off Elgar St.)
Coombs St. N1 .... 2C **218** (40Rb **71**)
Coomer M. SW6 .... 51Bb **111**
Coomer Pl. SW6 .... 51Bb **111**
Coomer Rd. SW6 .... 51Bb **111**
Coopers Wlk. HA8: Edg 25Sa **47**
Coope Ct. *RM7: Rush G* *30Gd* ***56***
(off Union Rd.)
Cooperage, The SE1 .... 7K **225**
SW8 .... *52Pb* ***112***
(off Regent's Bri. Gdns.)
Cooperage Cl. N17 .... 23Vb **51**
Co-operative Ho. SE15 .... 55Wb **113**
Cooper Av. E17 .... 25Ac **52**
Cooper Cl. DA9: Ghithe 57Vd **120**
SE1 .... 2A **230** (47Qb **90**)
Cooper Ct. SE18 .... 51Rc **116**
Cooper Cres. SM5: Cars 76Hb **155**
Cooper Ho. NW8 .... 6B **214**
RM16: Grays 8B **100**
SE4 .... *57Zb* ***114***
(off St Norbert Rd.)
TW4: Houn 55Ba **107**
Cooper La. N16 .... 35Tb **71**
Cooper Rd. CR0: Wadd 77Rb **157**
GU20: W'sham 9B **146**
NW4 .... 30Za **48**
NW10 .... 36Wa **68**
Coopers, The TN14: Dun G 92Hd **202**
COOPERSALE 1Zc 23
Coopersale Cl. IG8: Wfd G 24Lc **53**
Coopersale Comn.
CM16: Coop, Epp, N Weald 1Zc **23**
Coopersale La.
CM16: They B, They G 9Wc **23**
Coopersale Rd. E9 .... 36Zb **72**
COOPERSALE STREET 3Yc 23
Coopersale St. CM16: Epp, Fidd H 4Yc **23**
Coopers Cl. DA4: S Dar 67Td **142**
E1 .... 42Yb **92**
IG7: Chig 19Xc **37**
RM10: Dag 37Dd **76**
TW18: Staines 64G **126**
Coopers Ct. *E3* *42Bc* ***92***
(off Eric St.)
TW7: Isle *54Ha* ***108***
(off Woodlands Rd.)
W3 .... *46Sa* ***87***
(off Church Rd.)
Coopers Cres. WD6: Bore 11Sa **29**
Coopers Dr. DA2: Wilm 61Gd **140**
Coopers Ga. AL4: Col H 4M **7**
Coopers Hill Dr. GU24: Brkwd 2A **186**
Coopers Hill La.
TW20: Egh, Eng G 2N **125**
Cooper's Hill Rd. RH1: Nutf, S Nut ... 6G **208**
Cooper's La. EN6: N'thaw, Pot B 3Fb **17**
SE12 .... 61Kc **137**
Coopers La. E10 .... 32Dc **72**
NW1 .... 1E **216** (40Mb **70**)
RM18: W Til 1G **122**
TW18: Staines 63J **127**
Coopers La. Rd.
EN6: N'thaw, Pot B 3Fb **17**
Coopers Lodge SE1 .... 1K **231**
Coopers M. BR3: Beck 68Cc **136**
WD25: Wat 7X **13**
Cooper's Rd. SE1 .... 7K **231** (50Vb **91**)

Coopers Rd.—Cotes Ho.

Coopers Rd. DA10: Swans 59Be 121
DA11: Nflt 10B 122
EN6: Pot B 2Eb 17
Coopers Row EC3 4K 225 (45Vb 91)
SL0: Iver H 42E 82
Coopers Shaw Rd. RM18: W Til 2F 122
Cooper St. E16 43Hc 93
Coopers Wlk. E15 36Gc 73
EN8: Chesh 1Zb 20
Cooper's Yd. SE19 65Ub 135
Coopers Yd. *N1* 38Rb 71
(off Upper St.)
Cooper Way HP4: Berk 1A 2
SL1: Slou 8F 80
Coote Gdns. RM8: Dag 34Bd 75
Coote Rd. DA7: Bex 53Bd 117
RM8: Dag 34Bd 75
Cope Ho. EC1 4E 218
Copeland Dr. E14 49Cc 92
Copeland Ho. SE11 4J 229
SW17 63Fb 133
Copeland Rd. E17 30Dc 52
SE15 54Wb 113
Copeman Cl. SE26 64Yb 136
Copeman Rd. CM13: Hut 17Fe 41
Copenhagen Ct. *SE8* 49Ac 92
(off Pell St.)
Copenhagen Gdns. W4 47Ta 87
Copenhagen Ho. N1 1J 217
Copenhagen Pl. E14 44Bc 92
(not continuous)
Copenhagen St. N1 1K 217 (39Nb 70)
Copenhagen Way KT12: Walt T 76X 151
Cope Pl. W8 48Cb 89
Copers Cope Rd. BR3: Beck 66Bc 136
Cope St. SE16 49Zb 92
Copford Cl. IG8: Wfd G 23Nc 54
Copford Wlk. *N1* 39Sb 71
(off Popham St.)
Copgate Path SW16 65Pb 134
Copinger Wlk. HA8: Edg 25Ra 47
Copland Av. HA0: Wemb 36Ma 67
Copland Cl. HA0: Wemb 36La 66
Copland M. HA0: Wemb 37Na 67
Copland Rd. HA0: Wemb 37Na 67
SS17: Stan H 2M 101
Copleigh Dr. KT20: Tad 92Ab 194
Copleston M. SE15 54Vb 113
Copleston Pas. SE5 54Vb 113
Copleston Rd. SE15 55Vb 113
Copley Cl. GU21: Wok 1J 187
RH1: Redh 4N 207
SE17 51Sb 113
W7 42Ha 86
Copley Dene BR1: Brom 67Mc 137
Copley Pk. SW16 65Pb 134
Copley Rd. HA7: Stan 22La 46
Copley St. E1 43Zb 92
Copley Way KT20: Tad 92Za 194
Copmans Wick WD3: Chor 15F 24
Coppard Gdns. KT9: Chess 79La 152
COPPED HALL 3Qc 22
Coppelia Rd. SE3 56Hc 115
Coppen Rd. RM8: Dag 31Bd 75
Copperas St. SE8 51Dc 114
Copper Beech Cl. BR5: St M Cry 71Yc 161
DA12: Grav'nd 9F 122
GU22: Wok 3M 187
HP3: Hem H 5H 3
IG5: Ilf 25Qc 54
SL4: Wind 3B 102
Copperbeech Cl. NW3 36Fb 69
Copper Beech Ct. IG10: Lough 11Qc 36
Copper Beeches Ct. TW7: Isle 53Fa 108
Copper Beech Ho. GU22: Wok 89B 168
Copper Beech Rd. RM15: S Ock 41Yd 98
Copper Box Arena 37Cc 72
Copper Cl. N17 24Xb 51
SE19 66Vb 135
Copper Ct. E5 33Yb 72
Copperdale Ct. WD18: Wat 15U 26
Copperdale Rd. UB3: Hayes 47W 84
Copperfield IG7: Chig 22Tc 54
Copperfield Av. UB8: Hil 43Q 84
Copperfield Cl. CR2: Sande 83Sb 177
DA12: Grav'nd 10J 123
Copperfield Ct. KT22: Lea 93Ja 192
Copperfield Dr. N15 28Vb 51
Copperfield Gdns. CM14: B'wood 18Xd 40
Copperfield Ho. *SE1* 47Wb 91
(off Wolseley St.)
W1 7J 215
W11 46Za 88
(off St Ann's Rd.)
Copperfield M. *E2* 40Wb 71
(off Claredale St.)
N18 21Ub 51
Copperfield Ri. KT15: Add 78H 149
Copperfield Rd. E3 42Ac 92
SE28 44Yc 95
Copperfields BR3: Beck 67Ec 136
HA1: Harr 31Ga 66
KT22: Fet 94Ea 192
TN15: Kems'g 89Pd 183
TW16: Sun 65V 128
Copperfields Cl. TN15: Kems'g 89Pd 183
Copperfields Ct. W3 47Qa 87
Copperfields Orchard
TN15: Kems'g 89Pd 183
Copperfields Shop. Cen.
DA1: Dart 58Nd 119
(off Spital St.)
Copperfield St. SE1 1C 230 (47Rb 91)
Copperfields Wlk. TN15: Kems'g 89Pd 183
Copperfields Way RM3: Hrld W 25Md 57
Copperfield Ter. *SL2: Slou* 5M 81
(off Mirador Cres.)
Copperfield Way BR7: Chst 65Sc 138
HA5: Pinn 28Ba 45
Coppergate Cl. BR1: Brom 67Kc 137
Coppergate Ct. *EN9: Walt A* 6Jc 21
(off Farthingale La.)
Copper Horse Ct. SL4: Wind 4E 102
Copperlight Apartments *SW18* 57Cb 111
(off Buckhold Rd.)
Coppermead Cl. NW2 34Ya 68
Copper M. W4 48Sa 87
Coppermill Ct. WD3: W Hyd 24H 43
Copper Mill Dr. TW7: Isle 54Ha 108
Coppermill Hgts. *N17* 27Xb 51
(off Daneland Wlk.)
Copper Mill La. SW17 63Eb 133
Coppermill La. E17 30Yb 52
UB9: Hare 24G 42
WD3: Hare, W Hyd 24G 42
Copper Mill Lock UB9: Hare 24J 43
Coppermill Rd. TW19: Wray 58C 104
Copper Ridge SL9: Chal P 22B 42
Copper Row SE1 7K 225
Copperwood Pl. SE10 53Ec 114
Copperworks, The *N1* 2G 217
(off Railway St.)
Coppetts Cen. N12 24Hb 49
Coppetts Cl. N12 24Gb 49
Coppetts Rd. N10 24Hb 49
Coppetts Wood & Glebelands
Local Nature Reserve 23Hb 49
Coppice, The DA5: Bexl 62Fd 140
EN2: Enf 14Rb 33
EN5: New Bar 16Db 31
(off Great Nth. Rd.)
HP2: Hem H 1B 4
TW15: Ashf 65R 128
UB7: Yiew 44N 83
WD19: Wat 16Y 27
Coppice Av. KT11: Cobh 86Ba 171
Coppice Cl. AL10: Hat 3B 8
BR3: Beck 70Dc 136
HA4: Ruis 30T 44
HA7: Stan 23Ha 46
SW20 69Ya 132
Coppice Dr. SW15 58Xa 110
TW19: Wray 9P 103
Coppice End GU22: Pyr 88G 168
Coppice La. RH2: Reig 4H 207
Coppice Path IG7: Chig 21Xc 55
Coppice Rd. RH2: Reig 5G 206
Coppice Row CM16: They B 8Sc 22
Coppice Wlk. N20 20Cb 31
Coppice Way E18 28Hc 53
SL2: Hedg 3H 61
Coppies Gro. N11 21Kb 50
Copping Cl. CR0: C'don 77Ub 157
Coppins, The CR0: New Ad 79Dc 158
HA3: Hrw W 23Ga 46
Coppins La. SL0: Iver 43H 83
Coppock Cl. SW11 54Gb 111
Coppsfield KT8: W Mole 69Ca 129
Copse, The CR3: Cat'm 98Wb 197
CR6: W'ham 89Ac 178
E4 18Hc 35
GU23: Send 96H 189
HP1: Hem H 1G 2
KT22: Fet 95Da 191
N2 27Hb 49
RH1: S Nut 8E 208
TN16: Tats 92Lc 199
WD23: Bush 13Z 27
Copse Av. BR4: W W'ck 75Dc 158
RM3: Hrld W 25Nd 57
Copse Bank TN15: Seal 92Pd 203
Copse Cl. HA6: Nwood 26S 44
SE7 51Kc 115
SL1: Slou 6D 80
UB7: W Dray 48M 83
Copse Edge Av. KT17: Eps 85Va 174
Copse Glade KT6: Surb 73Ma 153
COPSE HILL 66Wa 132
Copse Hill CR8: Purl 85Nb 176
SM2: Sutt 80Db 155
SW20 67Wa 132
Copsem Dr. KT10: Esh 79Da 151
Copse M. KT13: Weyb 77T 150
Copsem La. KT10: Esh, Oxs 79Ea 152
KT22: Oxs 79Ea 152
Copsem Way KT10: Esh 79Ea 152
Copsen Wood KT22: Oxs 83Ea 172
Copse Rd. GU21: Wok 10K 167
KT11: Cobh 85X 171
RH1: Redh 8L 207
Copse Side DA3: Hartl 69Ae 163
Copse Vw. CR2: Sels 81Zb 178
Copse Wood SL0: Iver H 39F 62
Copsewood Cl. DA15: Sidc 58Uc 116
Copse Wood Ct. RH2: Reig 4N 207
Copsewood Rd. WD24: Wat 11X 27
Copse Wood Way HA6: Nwood 25R 44
Coptain Ho. SW18 56Cb 111
Coptefield Dr. DA17: Belv 48Zc 95
Coptfold Rd. CM14: B'wood 19Yd 40
Copthall Av. EC2 2G 225 (44Tb 91)
(not continuous)
Copthall Bldgs. EC2 2F 225
Copthall Cl. EC2 2F 225 (44Tb 91)
SL9: Chal P 24B 42
Copthall Cnr. SL9: Chal P 24A 42
Copthall Dr. NW7 24Wa 48
Copthall Gdns. NW7 24Wa 48
TW1: Twick 60Ha 108
COPTHALL GREEN 5Nc 22
Copthall La. SL9: Chal P 24A 42
Copthall Leisure Cen. 24Xa 48
Copt Hall Rd. TN15: Igh 95Wd 204
Copthall Rd. DA13: Meop, Sole S 10D 144
Copthall Rd. E. UB10: Ick 33Q 64
Copthall Rd. W. UB10: Ick 33Q 64
Copthall Way KT15: New H 82H 169
Copt Hill La. KT20: Tad 92Ab 194
Copthorne Av. BR2: Brom 75Pc 160
IG6: Ilf 23Rc 54
SW12 59Mb 112
Copthorne Chase TW15: Ashf 63P 127
Copthorne Cl. TW17: Shep 72S 150
WD3: Crox G 15P 25
Copthorne Ct. KT22: Lea 94Ja 192
Copthorne Dr. GU18: Light 2A 166
Copthorne Gdns. RM11: Horn 29Qd 57
Copthorne M. UB3: Harl 49U 84
Copthorne Ri. CR2: Sande 85Tb 177
Copthorne Rd. KT22: Lea 92Ka 192
WD3: Crox G 16P 25
Coptic St. WC1 1F 223 (43Nb 90)
Copt Pl. NW7 23Ab 48
Copwood Cl. N12 21Fb 49
Coral Apartments *E16* 45Jc 93
(off Western Gateway)
Coral Cl. RM6: Chad H 27Zc 55
Coral Gdns. HP2: Hem H 1P 3
Coral Ho. *E1* 42Ac 92
(off Harford St.)
NW10 41Qa 87
Coraline Cl. UB1: S'hall 41Ba 85
Coralline Wlk. SE2 48Yc 95
Coral Mans. *NW6* 39Cb 69
(off Kilburn High Rd.)
Coral Row SW11 55Eb 111
Coral St. SE1 2A 230 (47Qb 90)
Coram Grn. CM13: Hut 16Fe 41
Coram Ho. *W4* 50Ua 88
(off Wood St.)
WC1 5F 217
Coram Mans. *WC1* 6H 217
(off Millman St.)
Coram St. WC1 6F 217 (42Nb 90)
Coran Cl. N9 17Zb 34
Corban Rd. TW3: Houn 55Ca 107
Corbar Cl. EN4: Had W 11Fb 31
Corbden Cl. SE15 53Vb 113
Corben M. SW8 54Lb 112
Corbet Cl. SM6: Wall 74Jb 156
Corbet Ct. EC3 3G 225 (44Tb 91)
Corbet Ho. N1 1K 217
SE5 52Sb 113
(off Wyndham Rd.)
Corbet Pl. E1 7K 219 (43Vb 91)
Corbet Rd. KT17: Ewe 82Ua 174
Corbets Av. RM14: Upm 36Rd 77
CORBETS TEY 36Sd 78
Corbets Tey Rd. RM14: Upm 35Rd 77
Corbett Cl. CR0: New Ad 84Fc 179
Corbett Ct. SE26 63Bc 136
Corbett Gro. N22 24Nb 50
Corbett Ho. *SW10* 51Eb 111
(off Cathcart Rd.)
Corbett Rd. E11 30Lc 53
E17 27Ec 52
Corbetts La. SE16 49Yb 92
(not continuous)
Corbetts Pas. *SE16* 49Yb 92
(off Corbetts La.)
Corbetts Wharf *SE16* 47Xb 91
(off Bermondsey Wall E.)
Corbett Theatre 13Rc 36
Corbicum E11 31Gc 73
Corbidge Ct. SE8 51Dc 114
Corbiere Ct. SW19 65Za 132
Corbiere Ho. *N1* 39Tb 71
(off De Beauvoir Est.)
Corbin Ho. *E3* 41Dc 92
(off Bromley High St.)
Corbins La. HA2: Harr 34Da 65
Corbould Cl. SM5: Cars 79Hb 155
Corbridge N17 24Xb 51
Corbridge Cres. E2 40Xb 71
Corbridge M. RM1: Rom 29Hd 56
Corby Cl. AL2: Chis G 7N 5
TW20: Eng G 5N 125
Corby Cres. EN2: Enf 14Nb 32
Corby Dr. TW20: Eng G 5M 125
Corbylands Rd. DA15: Sidc 59Uc 116
Corbyn St. N4 32Nb 70
Corby Rd. NW10 40Ta 67
Corby Way E3 42Cc 92
Corcorans CM15: Pil H 16Yd 40
Cordage Ho. *E1* 46Xb 91
(off Cobblestone Sq.)
Cordelia Cl. SE24 56Rb 113
Cordelia Gdns. TW19: Stanw 59N 105
Cordelia Ho. N1 1J 219
Cordelia Rd. TW19: Stanw 59N 105
Cordelia St. E14 44Dc 92
Cordell Ho. *N15* 29Vb 51
(off Newton Rd.)
Corder Cl. AL3: St A 5N 5
Corderoy Pl. KT16: Chert 72G 148
Cordingley Rd. HA4: Ruis 33T 64
Cording St. E14 43Dc 92
Cordons Cl. SL9: Chal P 25A 42
Cordrey Gdns. CR5: Coul 87Nb 176
(not continuous)
Cordrey Ho. KT15: Add 75J 149
Cordwainer Ho. E8 39Xb 71
Cordwainers Ct. *E9* 38Yb 72
(off St Thomas's Sq.)
Cordwainers Wlk. E13 40Jc 73
Cord Way E14 48Cc 92
Cordwell Rd. SE13 57Gc 115
Corefield Cl. N11 19Jb 32
Corelli Ct. SE1 49Xb 91
SW5 49Cb 89
(off W. Cromwell Rd.)
Corelli Rd. SE3 54Nc 116
Coresbrook Way GU21: Knap 10E 166
Corfe Av. HA2: Harr 35Ca 65
Corfe Cl. HP2: Hem H 3N 3
KT21: Asht 90La 172
TW4: Houn 60Aa 107
UB4: Yead 44Y 85
WD6: Bore 13Ta 29
Corfe Gdns. SL1: Slou 5E 80
Corfe Ho. *SW8* 52Pb 112
(off Dorset Rd.)
Corfe Twr. W3 47Ra 87
Corfield Rd. N21 15Pb 32
Corfield St. E2 41Xb 91
Corfton Lodge W5 43Na 87
Corfton Rd. W5 44Na 87
Coriander Av. E14 44Fc 93
Coriander Ct. SE1 1K 231
Cories Cl. RM8: Dag 33Zc 75
Corinium Cl. HA9: Wemb 35Pa 67
Corinium Ga. AL3: St A 4N 5
Corinne Rd. N19 35Lb 70
Corinthian Golf Course 72Zd 165
Corinthian Manorway DA8: Erith 49Fd 96
Corinthian Rd. DA8: Erith 49Fd 96
Corinthian Sports Club 72Zd 165
Corinthian Way TW19: Stanw 59M 105
Corkers Path IG1: Ilf 33Sc 74
Corker Wlk. N7 33Pb 70
Cork Ho. SW19 63Db 133
Corkran Rd. KT6: Surb 73Ma 153
Corkscrew Hill BR4: W W'ck 75Ec 158
Cork Sq. E1 46Xb 91
Cork St. W1 5B 222 (45Lb 90)
Cork St. M. W1 5B 222
Cork Tree Ho. *SE27* 64Rb 135
(off Lakeview Rd.)
Cork Tree Retail Pk. E4 22Ac 52
Cork Tree Way E4 22Ac 52
Corlett St. NW1 7D 214 (43Gb 89)
Cormongers La. RH1: Nutf 3D 208
Cormont Rd. SE5 53Rb 113
Cormorant Cl. E17 24Ac 52
Cormorant Ct. *SE8* 51Bc 114
(off Pilot Cl.)
Cormorant Ho. EN3: Pond E 15Zb 34
Cormorant Lodge *E1* 46Wb 91
(off Thomas More St.)
Cormorant Pl. SM1: Sutt 78Bb 155
Cormorant Rd. E7 36Hc 73
Cormorant Wlk. RM12: Horn 37Kd 77
Cornburgh Wlk. *RM3: Rom* 22Md 57
(off Quilter Way)
Cornbury Ho. *SE8* 51Bc 114
(off Evelyn St.)
Cornbury Rd. HA8: Edg 24Ma 47
Corncrake Gro. HP3: Hem H 7L 3
Cornel Ho. DA15: Sidc 62Wc 139
SL4: Wind 5H 103
Cornelia Dr. UB4: Yead 42Y 85
Cornelia Ho. *TW1: Twick* 58Ma 109
(off Denton Rd.)
Cornelia Pl. DA8: Erith 51Gd 118
Cornelia St. N7 37Pb 70
Cornelius Ho. *WD18: Wat* 14V 26
(off Chiltern Cl.)
Cornell Bldg. *E1* 44Wb 91
(off Coke St.)
Cornell Cl. DA14: Sidc 65Ad 139
Cornell Ct. EN3: Enf H 13Ac 34
Cornell Gdns. EN4: E Barn 15Jb 32
Cornell Ho. HA2: Harr 34Ba 65
Cornell Sq. SW8 53Mb 112
Cornell Way RM5: Col R 22Cd 56
Corner, The KT14: W Byf 85J 169
W5 46Na 87
Corner Ct. *E2* 42Xb 91
(off Three Colts La.)
Cornercroft *SM3: Cheam* 78Za 154
(off Wickham Av.)
Corner Farm Cl. KT20: Tad 94Ya 194
Corner Fielde SW2 60Pb 112
Corner Grn. SE3 54Jc 115
CORNER HALL 4M 3
Corner Hall HP3: Hem H 4L 3
(not continuous)
Corner Hall Av. HP3: Hem H 4M 3
Corner Ho. *NW6* 40Db 69
(off Oxford Rd.)
Corner House Arts Cen., The 74Pa 153
Corner Ho. St. WC2 6F 223
Corner Mead NW9 24Va 48
Cornerside TW15: Ashf 66S 128
Cornerstone Ho. CR0: C'don 73Sb 157
Corner Vw. AL9: Wel G 6E 8
Corney Reach Way W4 52Ua 110
Corney Rd. W4 51Ua 110
Cornfield Cl. UB8: Uxb 40M 63
Cornfield Rd. RH2: Reig 7L 207
WD23: Bush 14Da 27
Cornfields, The HP1: Hem H 3K 3
Cornflower La. CR0: C'don 74Zb 158
Cornflower Ter. SE22 58Xb 113
Cornflower Way RM3: Hrld W 25Nd 57
Cornford Cl. BR2: Brom 71Jc 159
Cornford Gro. SW12 61Kb 134
Cornhill EC3 3G 225 (44Tb 91)
Cornhill Cl. KT15: Add 75K 149
Cornhill Dr. EN3: Enf W 9Ac 20
Cornick Ho. *SE16* 48Xb 91
(off Slippers Pl.)
Cornish Ct. N9 17Xb 33
Cornish Gro. SE20 67Xb 135
Cornish Ho. *SE17* 51Rb 113
(off Brandon Est.)
TW8: Bford 50Pa 87
Cornmill EN9: Walt A 5Dc 20
Corn Mill Dr. BR6: Orp 73Wc 161
Cornmill Ho. *SE8* 50Cc 92
(off Wharf St.)
Cornmill La. SE13 55Ec 114
Cornmow Dr. NW10 36Va 68
Cornshaw Rd. RM8: Dag 32Zc 75
Cornsland CM14: B'wood 20Zd 41
Cornsland Cl. RM14: Upm 27Sd 58
Cornsland Ct. CM14: B'wood 20Yd 40
Cornthwaite Rd. E5 34Yb 72
Cornwall Av. DA16: Well 55Uc 116
E2 41Yb 92
KT10: Clay 80Ha 152
KT14: Byfl 86P 169
N3 24Cb 49
N22 25Nb 50
SL2: Slou 2G 80
UB1: S'hall 43Ba 85
Cornwall Cl. EN8: Walt C 2Ac 20
IG11: Bark 37Vc 75
RM11: Horn 28Qd 57
SL4: Eton W 10C 80
Cornwall Ct. HA5: Hat E 24Ba 45
TW18: Staines 65G 126
(off Cornwall Way)
W7 42Ha 86
(off Copley Cl.)
Cornwall Cres. W11 44Ab 88
Cornwall Dr. BR5: St P 66Yc 139
Cornwall Gdns. NW10 37Xa 68
SE25 70Vb 135
SW7 4A 226 (48Db 89)
Cornwall Gdns. Wlk. SW7 48Db 89
Cornwall Ga. RM19: Purf 49Qd 97
Cornwall Gro. W4 50Ua 88
Cornwall Ho. *SW7* 48Db 89
(off Cornwall Gdns.)
Cornwallis Av. N9 19Xb 33
SE9 61Tc 138
Cornwallis Cl. CR3: Cat'm 94Sb 197
DA8: Erith 51Hd 118
Cornwallis Ct. *SW8* 53Nb 112
(off Lansdowne Grn.)
Cornwallis Gro. N9 19Xb 33
Cornwallis Ho. *SE16* 47Xb 91
(off Cherry Gdn. St.)
W12 45Xa 88
(off India Way)
Cornwallis Rd. E17 28Zb 52
N9 19Xb 33
N19 33Nb 70
RM9: Dag 35Zc 75
SE18 48Sc 94
Cornwallis Sq. N19 33Nb 70
Cornwallis Wlk. SE9 55Pc 116
Cornwall Mans. *SW10* 52Eb 111
(off Cremorne Rd.)
W8 47Db 89
(off Kensington Ct.)
W14 48Za 88
(off Blythe Rd.)
Cornwall M. Sth. SW7 4A 226 (48Eb 89)
Cornwall M. W. SW7 48Db 89
Cornwall Pl. E4 14Dc 34
Cornwall Rd. AL1: St A 4C 6
CM15: Pil H 15Xd 40
CR0: C'don 75Rb 157
DA1: Dart 55Pd 119
HA1: Harr 30Ea 46
HA4: Ruis 34Y 64
HA5: Hat E 24Ba 45
N4 31Qb 70
N15 29Tb 51
N18 22Wb 51
SE1 6K 223 (46Qb 90)
SM2: Sutt 80Bb 155
TW1: Twick 59Ja 108
UB8: Uxb 37M 63
Cornwall Sq. SE11 7B 230
Cornwall St. E1 45Xb 91
Cornwall Ter. NW1 6G 215 (42Hb 89)
Cornwall Ter. M. NW1 6G 215
Cornwall Way TW18: Staines 65G 126
Corn Way E11 34Fc 73
Cornwell Av. DA12: Grav'nd 2E 144
Cornwell Cres. SS17: Stan H 1N 101
Cornwell Rd. SL4: Old Win 8L 103
Cornwells Gdns. E10 31Cc 72
Cornwood Cl. N2 29Fb 49
Cornwood Dr. E1 44Yb 92
Cornworthy Rd. RM8: Dag 36Yc 75
Corona Bldg. *E14* 46Ec 92
(off Blackwall Way)
Corona Rd. SE12 59Jc 115
Coronation Av. N16 35Vb 71
RM18: E Til 9K 101
SL3: Geor G 43A 82
SL4: Wind 4L 103
Coronation Cl. DA5: Bexl 58Zc 117
IG6: Ilf 28Sc 54
Coronation Ct. DA8: Erith 52Fd 118
E15 37Hc 73
KT1: King T 70Na 131
(off Surbiton Rd.)
RM18: E Til 9L 101
(off Coronation Av.)
W10 43Ya 88
(off Brewster Gdns.)
Coronation Dr. RM12: Horn 36Kd 77
Coronation Hill CM16: Epp 2Vc 23
Coronation Rd. E13 41Lc 93
NW10 41Qa 87
UB3: Harl 49V 84
Coronation Vs. NW10 42Ra 87
Coronation Wlk. TW2: Whitt 60Ca 107
Coroner's Court
City of London 4F 225 (45Tb 91)
North London 14Bb 31
Poplar 45Dc 92
(off Poplar High St.)
St Pancras 1E 216 (39Mb 70)
South London 76Tb 157
(off Barclay Rd.)
Southwark 1F 231 (47Tb 91)
West London 53Eb 111
Westminster 5E 228 (49Mb 90)
Coronet Pde. HA0: Wemb 37Na 67
Coronet St. N1 4H 219 (41Ub 91)
Coronet Theatre 4D 230
Corporate Dr. TW13: Felt 62X 129
Corporation Ho. HA3: Hrw W 25Fa 46
Corporation Av. TW4: Houn 56Aa 107
Corporation Row EC1 5A 218 (42Qb 90)
Corporation St. E15 40Gc 73
N7 36Nb 70
Corrance Rd. SW2 56Nb 112
Corran Way RM15: S Ock 45Xd 98
Corri Av. N14 21Mb 50
Corrib Ct. N13 20Pb 32
Corrib Dr. SM1: Sutt 78Gb 155
Corrie Gdns. GU25: Vir W 3N 147
Corrie Rd. GU22: Wok 92D 188
KT15: Add 77M 149
Corrigan Av. CR5: Coul 87Jb 176
Corrigan Cl. NW4 27Ya 48
Corringham Ct. AL1: St A 1D 6
NW11 31Cb 69
Corringham Ho. *E1* 44Zb 92
(off Pitsea St.)
Corringham Rd. HA9: Wemb 33Qa 67
NW11 31Cb 69
SS17: Stan H 2M 101
Corringway NW11 31Db 69
W5 42Qa 87
Corris Grn. NW9 29Ua 48
Corry Dr. SW9 56Rb 113
Corry Ho. *E14* 45Dc 92
(off Wade's Pl.)
Corry's End AL4: Col H 4A 8
Corsair Cl. TW19: Stanw 59M 105
Corsair Rd. TW19: Stanw 59N 105
Corscombe Cl. KT2: King T 64Sa 131
Corsehill St. SW16 65Lb 134
Corsellis Sq. *TW1: Isle* 56Ka 108
(off Varley Dr.)
Corsham St. N1 4G 219 (41Tb 91)
Corsica St. N5 37Rb 71
Corsley Way E9 37Bc 72
Corston Hollow *RH1: Redh* 7P 207
(off Woodlands Rd.)
Cortayne Ct. TW2: Twick 61Ga 130
Cortayne Rd. SW6 54Bb 111
Cortina Dr. RM13: Rain 40Ed 76
Cortis Rd. SW15 58Xa 110
Cortis Ter. SW15 58Xa 110
Cortland Cl. DA1: Cray 58Gd 118
IG8: Wfd G 25Lc 53
Corunna Rd. SW8 53Lb 112
Corunna Ter. SW8 53Lb 112
Corve La. RM15: S Ock 45Xd 98
Corvette Sq. SE10 51Fc 115
Corwell Gdns. UB8: Hil 44S 84
Corwell La. UB8: Hil 44S 84
Cory Dr. CM13: Hut 17De 41
Coryton Path *W9* 42Bb 89
(off Ashmore Rd.)
Cosbycote Av. SE24 57Sb 113
Cosdach Av. SM6: Wall 80Mb 156
Cosedge Cres. CR0: Wadd 78Qb 156
Cosgrove Cl. N21 19Sb 33
UB4: Yead 42Z 85
Cosgrove Ho. *E2* 39Wb 71
(off Whiston Rd.)
HA0: Wemb 39Na 67
(off Hatton Rd.)
Cosmia Ct. *WD23: Bush* 15Aa 27
(off Vale Rd.)
Cosmo Pl. WC1 7G 217 (43Nb 90)
Cosmopolitan Ct. EN1: Enf 15Wb 33
Cosmur Cl. W12 48Va 88
Cossall Wlk. SE15 54Xb 113
Cossar M. SW2 57Qb 112
Cosser St. SE1 3K 229 (48Qb 90)
Costa St. SE15 54Wb 113
Costead Mnr. Rd. CM14: B'wood 18Xd 40
Costells Mdw. TN16: Westrm 98Tc 200
Costemonger Bldg. SE16 4K 231
Costins Wlk. *HP4: Berk* 1A 2
(off Robertson Rd.)
Costons Av. UB6: G'frd 41Fa 86
Costons La. UB6: G'frd 41Fa 86
(not continuous)
Coston Wlk. SE4 56Zb 114
Cosway Mans. NW1 7E 214
Cosway St. NW1 7E 214 (43Gb 89)
Cotall St. E14 43Cc 92
Coteford Cl. HA5: Eastc 29W 44
IG10: Lough 12Rc 36
Coteford St. SW17 63Hb 133
Cotelands CR0: C'don 76Ub 157
Cotesbach Rd. E5 34Yb 72
Cotes Ho. NW8 6D 214

Cotesmore Gdns.—Craig's Ct.

Cotesmore Gdns. RM8: Dag 35Yc 75
Cotesmore Rd. HP1: Hem H 3G 2
Cotford Rd. CR7: Thor H 70Sb 135
Cotham St. SE17 6E 230 (49Sb 91)
Cotherstone KT19: Ewe 82Ta 173
Cotherstone Ct. *E2* 42Xb 91
(off Three Colts La.)
Cotherstone Rd. SW2 60Pb 112
Cotland Acres RH1: Redh 8M 207
Cotlandswick AL2: Lon C 7G 6
Cotleigh Av. DA5: Bexl 61Zc 139
Cotleigh Rd. NW6 38Cb 69
RM7: Rom 30Fd 56
Cotman Cl. NW11 30Eb 49
SW15 58Za 110
Cotmandene Cres. BR5: St P 68Wc 139
Cotman Gdns. HA8: Edg 26Qa 47
Cotman Ho. NW8 1D 214
UB5: N'olt 40Z 65
(off Academy Gdns.)
Cotman M. *RM8: Dag* 36Yc 75
(off Highgrove Rd.)
COTMAN'S ASH 87Sd 184
Cotman's Ash La.
TN15: Kems'g 86Rd 183
Cotmans Cl. UB3: Hayes 46W 84
Coton Dr. UB10: Ick 34S 64
Coton Rd. DA16: Well 55Wc 117
Cotsford Av. KT3: N Mald 71Sa 153
Cotsmoor *AL1: St A* 2D 6
(off Granville Rd.)
Cotswold Av. WD23: Bush 16Ea 28
Cotswold Cl. DA7: Bex 54Gd 118
KT2: King T 65Sa 131
KT10: Hin W 75Ha 152
N11 21Jb 50
SL1: Slou 8G 80
TW18: Staines 64J 127
UB8: Uxb 39L 63
Cotswold Ct. EC1 5D 218
UB6: G'frd 40Ha 66
(off Hodder Dr.)
Cotswold Gdns. CM13: Hut 17Fe 41
E6 41Mc 93
IG2: Ilf 31Tc 74
NW2 33Za 68
Cotswold Ga. NW2 32Ab 68
Cotswold Grn. EN2: Enf 14Pb 32
Cotswold M. SW11 53Fb 111
Cotswold Ri. BR6: St M Cry 72Vc 161
Cotswold Rd. DA11: Nflt 2A 144
RM3: Hrld W 26Pd 57
SM2: Sutt 82Db 175
TW12: Hamp 64Ca 129
Cotswolds AL10: Hat 2C 8
Cotswold St. SE27 63Rb 135
Cotswold Way EN2: Enf 13Pb 32
KT4: Wor Pk 75Ya 154
Cottage Av. BR2: Brom 74Nc 160
Cottage Cl. *E1* 42Yb 92
(off Mile End Rd.)
HA2: Harr 33Fa 66
HA4: Ruis 32T 64
KT16: Ott 79E 148
WD3: Crox G 16P 25
WD17: Wat 12V 26
Cottage Farm Way TW20: Thorpe 69E 126
Cottage Fld. Cl. DA14: Sidc 60Yc 117
Cottage Gdns. EN8: Chesh 1Zb 20
Cottage Grn. SE5 52Tb 113
Cottage Gro. KT6: Surb 72Ma 153
SW9 55Nb 112
Cottage M. RM11: Horn 28Ld 57
Cottage Pk. Rd. SL2: Hedg 3H 61
Cottage Pl. SW3 3D 226 (48Gb 89)
Cottage Rd. KT19: Ewe 80Ta 153
N7 36Pb 70
(not continuous)
Cottages, The UB10: Ick 33N 63
Cottage St. E14 45Dc 92
Cottage Wlk. N16 34Vb 71
Cottenham Dr. NW9 27Va 48
SW20 66Xa 132
Cottenham Pde. SW20 68Xa 132
COTTENHAM PARK 67Xa 132
Cottenham Pk. Rd. SW20 67Wa 132
(not continuous)
Cottenham Pl. SW20 66Xa 132
Cottenham Rd. E17 28Bc 52
Cotterells HP1: Hem H 2L 3
Cotterells Hill HP1: Hem H 2L 3
Cotterill Rd. KT6: Surb 75Na 153
Cottesbrooke Cl. SL3: Coln 53F 104
Cottesbrook St. SE14 52Ac 114
Cottesloe Cl. GU24: Bisl 8D 166
Cottesloe Ho. NW8 5D 214
Cottesloe M. SE1 3A 230
Cottesmore Av. IG5: Ilf 26Qc 54
Cottesmore Ct. *W8* 48Db 89
(off Stanford Rd.)
Cottesmore Gdns. W8 48Db 89
Cottesmore Ho. UB10: Ick 33S 64
Cottimore Av. KT12: Walt T 74X 151
Cottimore Cres. KT12: Walt T 73X 151
Cottimore La. KT12: Walt T 74X 151
Cottimore Ter. KT12: Walt T 73X 151
Cottingham Chase HA4: Ruis 34W 64
Cottingham Rd. SE20 66Zb 136
SW8 52Pb 112
Cottington Rd. TW13: Hanw 63Z 129
Cottington St. SE11 7A 230 (50Qb 90)
Cottis La. CM16: Epp 2Vc 23
Cottle Way *SE16* 47Xb 91
(off Paradise St.)
Cotton Apartments *E1* 43Zb 92
(off Killick Way)
Cotton Av. W3 44Ta 87
Cotton Cl. CR4: Mitc 69Gb 133
E11 33Gc 73
RM9: Dag 38Yc 75
Cottongrass Cl. CR0: C'don 74Zb 158
Cotton Hall Ho. *SL4: Eton* 1G 102
(off Eton Wick Rd.)
Cottonham Cl. N12 22Fb 49
Cotton Hill BR1: Brom 63Ec 136
Cotton Ho. SW2 59Nb 112
Cotton La. DA2: Dart, Ghithe 57Sd 120
DA9: Ghithe 57Sd 120
Cottonmill Cres. AL1: St A 3B 6
Cottonmill La. AL1: St A 4B 6
Cotton Rd. EN6: Pot B 3Eb 17
Cotton Row SW11 55Eb 111
Cottons App. RM7: Rom 29Fd 56
Cottons Cen. SE1 6H 225 (46Ub 91)
Cottons Ct. RM7: Rom 29Fd 56
Cotton's Gdns. E2 3J 219 (41Ub 91)
Cottons La. SE1 6G 225 (46Tb 91)
Cotton St. E14 45Ec 92
Cottrell Ct. *SE10* 49Hc 93
(off Hop St.)
Cottrill Gdns. E8 37Xb 71
Cotts Cl. W7 43Ha 86
Couchmore Av. IG5: Ilf 26Pc 54
KT10: Hin W 75Ga 152
Coulgate St. SE4 55Ac 114
COULSDON 88Mb 176
Coulsdon Common 93Sb 197
Coulsdon Court Golf Course 88Pb 176
Coulsdon Ct. Rd. CR5: Coul 88Pb 176
Coulsdon La. CR5: Chip 91Hb 195
Coulsdon Nth. Ind. Est.
CR5: Coul 88Mb 176
Coulsdon Pl. CR3: Cat'm 94Tb 197
Coulsdon Ri. CR5: Coul 89Nb 176
Coulsdon Rd. CR3: Cat'm, Coul 94Tb 197
CR5: Coul 87Pb 176
Coulson Cl. RM8: Dag 32Yc 75
Coulson Ct. AL2: Lon C 9H 7
Coulson St. SW3 7F 227 (50Hb 89)
Coulson Way SL1: Burn 3A 80
Coulter Cl. UB4: Yead 42Aa 85
Coulter Ho. DA9: Ghithe 57Yd 120
Coulter Rd. W6 48Xa 88
Coulthurst Ct. *SW16* 66Nb 134
(off Heybridge Av.)
Coulton Av. DA11: Nflt 9A 122
Council Av. DA11: Nflt 58Ee 121
Council Cotts. GU23: Wis 87M 169
GU24: W End 4D 166
Councillor St. SE5 52Sb 113
Counter Ct. SE1 7F 225
Counters Cl. HP1: Hem H 2J 3
Counters Ct. *W14* 48Ab 88
(off Holland Rd.)
COUNTERS END 2J 3
Counter St. SE1 7H 225 (46Ub 91)
Countess Cl. UB9: Hare 26L 43
Countess Rd. NW5 36Lb 70
Countisbury Av. EN1: Enf 17Vb 33
Countisbury Gdns. KT15: Add 78K 149
Country Way TW13: Hanw 65X 129
County Court
Brentford 51Ma 109
Bromley 67Jc 137
Central London 6A 216
Clerkenwell and Shoreditch
5D 218 (42Sb 91)
Croydon 75Tb 157
Dartford 58Nd 119
Edmonton 23Wb 51
Kingston upon Thames 68Ma 131
Reigate 6M 207
Romford 28Hd 56
St Albans 2C 6
Slough 7J 81
Staines upon Thames 64J 127
Uxbridge 43V 84
Wandsworth 57Ab 110
Watford 12X 27
West London 50Za 88
(off Talgarth Rd.)
Willesden 40Va 68
Woolwich 48Qc 94
County Gdns. TW7: Isle 56Fa 108
County Ga. EN5: New Bar 16Db 31
SE9 62Sc 138
County Ground, The
Beckenham 65Cc 136
County Gro. SE5 53Sb 113
County Hall Apartments SE1 1H 229
County Hall (Former) 1H 229
County Ho. BR3: Beck 67Ac 136
SW9 53Qb 112
(off Brixton Rd.)
County Pde. TW8: Bford 52Ma 109
County Rd. CR7: Thor H 68Rb 135
E6 43Rc 94
County St. SE1 4E 230 (48Sb 91)
Couper Ho. WD18: Wat 16U 26
Coupland Pl. SE18 50Sc 94
Courage Cl. RM11: Horn 30Ld 57
Courage Ct. CM13: Hut 16Ee 41
Courage Stadium 71Kc 159
Courage Wlk. CM13: Hut 16Fe 41
Courcy Rd. N8 27Qb 50
Courier Rd. RM9: Dag 42Ed 96
Courland Gro. SW8 53Mb 112
Courland Rd. KT15: Add 76K 149
Courland St. SW8 53Mb 112
Course, The SE9 62Qc 138
Coursers Rd. AL4: Col H 9L 7
Court, The CR6: W'ham 90Ac 178
HA4: Ruis 35Aa 65
Court Annexe 2E 230 (47Sb 91)
Courtauld Cl. SE28 46Wc 95
Courtauld Gallery 4H 223
Courtauld Ho. *E2* 39Wb 71
(off Goldsmiths Row)
Courtauld Rd. N19 32Nb 70
Courtaulds WD4: Chfd 2K 11
Court Av. CR5: Coul 90Qb 176
DA17: Belv 50Bd 95
RM3: Hrld W 24Qd 57
Court Bushes Rd. CR3: W'ham 91Wb 197
Court Cl. HA3: Kenton 27Na 47
NW8 38Fb 69
(off Boydell Ct.)
SM6: Wall 80Mb 156
TW2: Twick 62Da 129
Court Cl. Av. TW2: Twick 62Da 129
Court Cres. BR8: Swan 70Gd 140
KT9: Chess 78Ma 153
SL1: Slou 4H 81
Court Downs Rd. BR3: Beck 68Dc 136
Court Dr. CR0: Wadd 77Pb 156
HA7: Stan 21Na 47
SM1: Sutt 77Gb 155
UB10: Hil 39P 63
Courtenay Av. HA3: Hrw W 24Ea 46
N6 31Gb 69
SM2: Sutt 81Cb 175
Courtenay Dr. BR3: Beck 68Fc 137
RM16: Chaf H 48Be 99
Courtenay Gdns. HA3: Hrw W 26Ea 46
RM14: Upm 32Sd 78
Courtenay Ho. *CR0: C'don* 73Sb 157
(off Oakfield Rd.)
Courtenay M. E17 29Ac 52
GU21: Wok 88C 168
Courtenay Pl. E17 29Ac 52
Courtenay Rd. E11 34Hc 73
E17 28Zb 52
GU21: Wok 88C 168
HA9: Wemb 34Ma 67
KT4: Wor Pk 76Ya 154
SE20 65Zb 136
Courtenay Sq. SE11 7K 229 (50Qb 90)
Courtenay St. SE11 7J 229 (50Qb 90)
Courtens M. HA7: Stan 24La 46
Court Farm Av. KT19: Ewe 78Ta 153
Court Farm Cl. SL1: Slou 6F 80
Court Farm Gdns. KT19: Eps 83Sa 173
Court Farm La. RH8: Oxt 100Gc 199
UB5: N'olt 38Ca 65
Court Farm Pk. CR6: W'ham 88Wb 177
Court Farm Rd. CR6: W'ham 90Wb 177
SE9 61Mc 137
UB5: N'olt 38Ca 65
Courtfield W5 43La 86
Courtfield Av. HA1: Harr 29Ha 46
Courtfield Cres. HA1: Harr 29Ha 46
Courtfield Gdns. HA4: Ruis 33V 64
SW5 49Db 89
UB9: Den 34J 63
W13 44Ja 86
Courtfield Ho. EC1 7K 217
UB8: Uxb 37M 63
(off Fairfield Rd.)
Courtfield M. SW5 49Eb 89
Courtfield Ri. BR4: W W'ck 76Fc 159
Courtfield Rd. SW7 6A 226 (49Eb 89)
TW15: Ashf 65R 128
Court Gdns. N1 37Qb 70
N7 37Qb 70
RM3: Hrld W 23Qd 57
Courtgate Cl. NW7 23Va 48
Court Grn. Hgts. GU22: Wok 2N 187
Court Haw SM7: Bans 87Gb 175
Court Hill CR2: Sande 84Ub 177
CR5: Chip 90Gb 175
Courthill Rd. SE13 56Ec 114
Courthope Ho. *SE16* 48Yb 92
(off Lower Rd.)
SW8 52Nb 112
(off Hartington Rd.)
Courthope Rd. NW3 35Hb 69
SW19 64Ab 132
UB6: G'frd 40Fa 66
Courthope Vs. SW19 66Ab 132
Courthouse, The SW1 4E 228
Courthouse Gdns. N3 23Cb 49
Courthouse La. N16 35Vb 71
Court Ho. Mans. KT19: Eps 84Ta 173
Courthouse Rd. N12 23Db 49
Courtland Av. E4 19Hc 35
IG1: Ilf 33Pc 74
NW7 20Ta 29
SW16 66Pb 134
Courtland Dr. IG7: Chig 20Rc 36
Courtland Gro. SE28 44Zc 95
Courtland Rd. E6 39Nc 74
Courtlands KT12: Walt T 73W 150
TW10: Rich 57Qa 109
Courtlands Av. BR2: Hayes 74Gc 159
KT10: Esh 79Ba 151
SE12 57Kc 115
SL3: L'ly 9P 81
TW9: Kew 54Ra 109
TW12: Hamp 65Ba 129
Courtlands Cl. CR2: Sande 82Vb 177
HA4: Ruis 31V 64
WD24: Wat 7U 12
Courtlands Cres. SM7: Bans 87Cb 175
Courtlands Dr. KT19: Ewe 79Ua 154
WD17: Wat 9U 12
WD24: Wat 9U 12
Courtlands Rd. KT5: Surb 73Qa 153
Court La. KT19: Eps 85Sa 173
SE21 58Ub 113
SL0: Iver 46H 83
(not continuous)
SL1: Burn 1B 80
SL4: Dor 8A 80
Court La. Gdns. SE21 59Ub 113
Courtleas KT11: Cobh 85Ca 171
Courtleet Dr. DA8: Erith 53Dd 118
Courtleigh NW11 29Bb 49
Courtleigh Av. EN4: Had W 10Fb 17
Courtleigh Gdns. NW11 28Ab 48
Court Lodge DA12: Shorne 5N 145
DA17: Belv 50Cd 96
SW1 6H 227
(off Sloane Sq.)
Courtman Rd. N17 24Sb 51
Court Mead UB5: N'olt 41Ba 85
Courtmead Cl. SE24 58Sb 113
Court Mdw. TN15: Wro 88Be 185
Courtnell St. W2 44Cb 89
Courtney Cl. SE19 65Ub 135
Courtney Ct. N7 36Qb 70
Courtney Cres. SM5: Cars 80Hb 155
Courtney Ho. *NW4* 27Ya 48
(off Mulberry Cl.)
W14 48Ab 88
(off Russell Rd.)
Courtney Pl. CR0: Wadd 76Qb 156
KT11: Cobh 84Ba 171
Courtney Rd. CR0: Wadd 76Qb 156
N7 36Qb 70
RM16: Grays 7E 100
SW19 66Gb 133
TW6: H'row A 55Q 106
Courtney Way TW6: H'row A 54Q 106
Court Pde. HA0: Wemb 34Ka 66
Courtrai Rd. SE23 58Ac 114
Court Rd. BR6: Chels, Orp 73Xc 161
CR3: Cat'm 95Tb 197
DA2: Daren 64Ud 142
RH9: G'stone 3A 210
SE9 58Pc 116
SE25 68Vb 135
SM7: Bans 88Cb 175
UB2: S'hall 49Ba 85
UB10: Ick 36R 64
Court Royal SW15 57Ab 110
Courtside AL3: St A 1B 6
N8 30Mb 50
SE26 62Xb 135
Court St. BR1: Brom 68Jc 137
E1 43Xb 91
Courts Way RM15: Avel 45Td 98
Courtville Ho. *W10* 41Ab 88
(off Third Av.)
Court Way NW9 28Ua 48
RM3: Hrld W 26Nd 57
TW2: Twick 59Ha 108
W3 43Sa 87
Courtway IG6: Ilf 27Sc 54
IG8: Wfd G 22Lc 53
Courtway, The WD19: Wat 19Aa 27
Courtwood Dr. TN13: S'oaks 96Jd 202
Courtwood La. CR0: Sels 83Bc 178
Court Yd. SE9 58Pc 116
Courtyard SW3 7F 227
Courtyard, The AL4: St A 2K 7
AL9: Ess 1P 9
BR2: Kes 79Nc 160
CM15: B'wood 17Xd 40
CR3: Whyt 90Vb 177
E2 41Vb 91
(off Ezra St.)
EC3 3G 225
(within Royal Exchange)
HP3: Hem H 8M 3
KT14: W Byf 84J 169
KT20: Kgswd 95Eb 195
N1 38Pb 70
NW1 38Jb 70
SE14 53Zb 114
(off Besson St.)
SL3: L'ly 47C 82
SW3 51Fb 111
(off Trident Pl.)
TN16: Westrm 99Tc 200
WD3: Crox G 13R 26
Courtyard Apartments E1 5K 219
Courtyard Gdns. TN15: Wro 88Be 185
Courtyard Ho. *SW6* 54Eb 111
(off Lensbury Av.)
Courtyard M. BR5: St P 66Wc 139
DA9: Ghithe 58Wd 120
RM13: Rain 39Hd 76
Courtyards, The WD18: Wat 17T 26
Courtyard Theatre
Chipstead 92Hb 195
Shoreditch 4H 219 (41Ub 91)
Cousin La. EC4 5F 225 (45Tb 91)
Cousins Cl. UB7: Yiew 45N 83
Couthurst Rd. SE3 51Kc 115
Coutts Av. DA12: Shorne 3N 145
KT9: Chess 78Na 153
Coutt's Cres. NW5 34Jb 70
Couzens Ho. *E3* 43Bc 92
(off Weatherley Cl.)
Couzins Wlk. DA1: Dart 54Qd 119
Coval Gdns. SW14 56Ra 109
Coval La. SW14 56Ra 109
Coval Pas. SW14 56Sa 109
Coval Rd. SW14 56Ra 109
Coveham Cres. KT11: Cobh 85W 170
Covelees Wall E6 44Qc 94
Covell Ct. *EN2: Enf* 10Pb 18
(off The Ridgeway)
SE8 52Cc 114
Covell Ho. KT19: Eps 84Ra 173
Covenbrook CM13: B'wood 20De 41
COVENT GARDEN 4G 223 (45Nb 90)
Covent Garden 4G 223 (45Nb 90)
Covent Gdn. WC2 4G 223 (45Nb 90)
Coventry Cl. E6 44Pc 94
NW6 40Cb 69
Coventry Hall SW16 64Nb 134
Coventry Rd. E1 42Xb 91
E2 42Xb 91
IG1: Ilf 33Rc 74
SE25 70Wb 135
Coventry St. W1 5D 222 (45Mb 90)
Coverack Cl. CR0: C'don 73Ac 158
N14 16Lb 32
Coverdale Cl. HA7: Stan 22Ka 46
Coverdale Ct. EN3: Enf W 9Ac 20
Coverdale Gdns. CR0: C'don 76Vb 157
Coverdale Rd. N11 23Jb 50
NW2 38Za 68
W12 47Xa 88
Coverdales, The IG11: Bark 40Tc 74
Coverdale Way SL2: Slou 2C 80
Coverham Ho. *SE4* 56Zb 114
(off Billingford Cl.)
Coverley Cl. CM13: Gt War 23Yd 58
E1 43Wb 91
Coverley Point SE11 6H 229
Covert, The BR6: Pet W 72Uc 160
HA6: Nwood 25S 44
SE19 66Vb 135
(off Fox Hill)
SL5: Asc 3A 146
Coverton Rd. SW17 64Gb 133
Covert Rd. IG6: Ilf 22Vc 55
Coverts, The CM13: Hut 18Ce 41
Coverts Rd. KT10: Clay 80Ha 152
Covert Way EN4: Had W 12Eb 31
Covesfield DA11: Grav'nd 9B 122
Covet Wood Cl. BR5: St M Cry 72Vc 161
Covey Cl. SW19 68Db 133
Covey Rd. KT4: Wor Pk 75Za 154
Covington Gdns. SW16 66Rb 135
Covington Way SW16 65Pb 134
(not continuous)
Cowan Cl. E6 43Nc 94
Coward Ind. Est. RM16: Grays 10D 100
Cowbridge La. IG11: Bark 38Rc 74
Cowbridge Mdw. GU24: Pirb 5D 186
Cowbridge Rd. HA3: Kenton 28Pa 47
Cowcross St. EC1 7B 218 (43Rb 91)
Cowdenbeath Path N1 39Pb 70
Cowden Rd. BR6: Orp 73Vc 161
Cowden St. SE6 63Cc 136
Cowdray Rd. UB10: Hil 39S 64
Cowdray Way RM12: Horn 35Jd 76
WD3: Crox G 14R 26
Cowdrey Cl. EN1: Enf 12Ub 33
Cowdrey Ct. DA1: Dart 59Kd 119
Cowdrey M. SE6 63Cc 136
Cowdrey Rd. SW19 64Db 133
Cowen Av. HA2: Harr 33Fa 66
Cowgate Rd. UB6: G'frd 41Fa 86
Cowick Rd. SW17 63Hb 133
Cowings Mead UB5: N'olt 37Aa 65
Cowland Av. EN3: Pond E 14Yb 34
Cow La. UB6: G'frd 40Fa 66
WD23: Bush 16Ca 27
WD25: Wat 8Y 13
Cow Leaze E6 44Qc 94
Cowleaze Rd. KT2: King T 67Na 131
COWLEY 42M 83
Cowley Av. DA9: Ghithe 57Vd 120
KT16: Chert 73H 149
Cowley Bus. Pk. UB8: Cowl 41L 83
Cowley Cl. CR2: Sels 81Yb 178
Cowley Cres. KT12: Hers 77Y 151
UB8: Cowl 43L 83
Cowley Hill WD6: Bore 9Qa 15
(not continuous)
Cowley La. E11 34Gc 73
KT16: Chert 73H 149
Cowley Lodge KT16: Chert 73H 149
Cowley Mill Rd. UB8: Uxb 40K 63
Cowley Mill Trad. Est. UB8: Uxb 40K 63
COWLEY PEACHEY 44M 83
Cowley Pl. NW4 29Ya 48
Cowley Retail Pk. UB8: Cowl 45M 83
Cowley Rd. E11 29Kc 53
IG1: Ilf 31Pc 74
RM3: Rom 24Kd 57
SW9 53Qb 112
(not continuous)
SW14 55Ua 110
UB8: Uxb 40L 63
W3 46Va 88
Cowley St. SW1 4F 229 (48Nb 90)
Cowling Cl. W11 46Ab 88
Coworth Cl. SL5: S'dale 1F 146
Coworth Pk. 10G 124
Coworth Rd. SL5: S'dale 1E 146
Cowper Av. E6 38Nc 74
RM18: Tilb 3D 122
SM1: Sutt 77Fb 155
Cowper Cl. BR2: Brom 70Mc 137
DA16: Well 57Wc 117
KT16: Chert 72H 149
Cowper Ct. WD24: Wat 9W 12
Cowper Gdns. N14 16Kb 32
SM6: Wall 79Lb 156
Cowper Ho. SE17 7E 230
SW1 7E 228
Cowper Rd. BR2: Brom 70Mc 137
DA17: Belv 49Cd 96
HP1: Hem H 4K 3
KT2: King T 64Pa 131
N14 18Kb 32
N16 36Ub 71
N18 22Wb 51
RM13: Rain 42Jd 96
SL2: Slou 2E 80
SW19 65Eb 133
W3 46Ta 87
W7 45Ha 86
Cowper's Ct. EC3 3G 225
Cowper St. EC2 5G 219 (42Tb 91)
Cowper Ter. W10 43Za 88
COWSHOT COMMON 2C 186
Cowshot Cres. GU24: Brkwd 2B 186
Cowslip Cl. UB10: Uxb 38N 63
Cowslip La. GU21: Wok 7M 167
RH5: Mick 100Ja 192
(not continuous)
Cowslip Rd. E18 26Kc 53
Cowthorpe Rd. SW8 53Mb 112
Cox Cl. WD7: Shenl 4Pa 15
Cox Ct. EN4: E Barn 14Gb 31
Coxdean KT18: Tatt C 91Ya 194
Coxe Pl. HA3: W'stone 28Ja 46
Coxfield Cl. HP2: Hem H 3N 3
Cox Ho. *W6* 51Ab 110
(off Field Rd.)
Cox La. KT9: Chess 77Pa 153
KT19: Ewe 78Ra 153
(not continuous)
Coxley Ri. CR8: Purl 85Sb 177
Coxmount Rd. SE7 50Mc 93
Coxon Dr. RM16: Chaf H 48Ae 99
Coxs Av. TW17: Shep 69U 128
Coxson Way SE1 2K 231 (47Vb 91)
Cox's Wlk. SE21 60Wb 113
COXTIE GREEN 15Sd 40
Coxtie Grn. Rd.
CM14: Pil H, S Weald 14Qd 39
Coxwell Rd. SE18 50Tc 94
SE19 66Ub 135
Coxwold Path KT9: Chess 80Na 153
Coyle Dr. UB10: Ick 33S 64
Coyne Cl. GU18: Light 2A 166
Crabbs Cft. Cl. BR6: Farnb 78Sc 160
Crab Hill BR3: Beck 66Fc 137
Crab Hill La. RH1: S Nut 10F 208
Crab La. WD25: A'ham 7Da 13
Crabtree Av. HA0: Wemb 40Na 67
RM6: Chad H 28Zc 55
Crabtree Cl. E2 2K 219 (40Vb 71)
HP3: Hem H 4M 3
KT23: Bookh 98Ea 192
TN15: Fair 84Fe 185
WD23: Bush 15Da 27
Crabtree Ct. EN5: New Bar 14Db 31
HP3: Hem H 4N 3
Crabtree Dr. KT22: Lea 96La 192
Crabtree Hall *SW6* 52Ya 110
(off Crabtree La.)
CRABTREE HILL 17Bd 37
Crabtree La. HP3: Hem H 4M 3
KT18: Head 98Sa 193
KT23: Bookh 98Ea 192
SW6 52Ya 110
(not continuous)
Crabtree Manorway Nth.
DA17: Belv, Erith 47Ed 96
Crabtree Manorway Sth.
DA17: Belv 48Ed 96
Crabtree Office Village
TW20: Thorpe 68E 126
Crabtree Pl. W1 1D 222 (43Lb 90)
Crabtree Rd. TW20: Thorpe 68E 126
Crabtree Wlk. CR0: C'don 74Wb 157
Crabwood RH8: Oxt 100Gc 199
Crace St. NW1 3D 216 (41Mb 90)
Cracknell Cl. EN1: Enf 8Xb 19
Craddock Rd. EN1: Enf 13Vb 33
Craddocks Av. KT21: Asht 89Na 173
Craddocks Cl. KT21: Asht 88Qa 173
Craddocks Pde. KT21: Asht 89Na 173
Craddock St. NW5 37Jb 70
Cradford Ho. Nth. E2 41Zb 92
Cradford Ho. Sth. E2 41Zb 92
Cradley Rd. SE9 60Tc 116
Crafts Council & Gallery
2A 218 (40Qb 70)
Cragg Av. WD7: R'lett 8Ha 14
Cragie Ho. *SE1* 49Vb 91
(off Balaclava Rd.)
Craigdale Rd. RM11: Horn 30Hd 56
Craig Dr. UB8: Hil 44R 84
Craigen Av. CR0: C'don 74Xb 157
Craigen Gdns. IG3: Ilf 35Uc 74
Craigerne Rd. SE3 52Kc 115
Craig Gdns. E18 26Hc 53
Craigholm SE18 54Qc 116
Craig Ho. *E17* 28Cc 52
(off High St.)
Craigie Ct. DA1: Dart 59Qd 119
Craigmore Ct. HA6: Nwood 24U 44
Craigmore Twr. *GU22: Wok* 91A 188
(off Constitution Hill)
Craig Mt. WD7: R'lett 7Ka 14
Craigmuir Pk. HA0: Wemb 39Pa 67
Craignair Rd. SW2 59Qb 112
Craignish Av. SW16 68Pb 134
Craig Pk. Rd. N18 21Xb 51
Craig Rd. TW10: Ham 63La 130
Craig's Ct. SW1 6F 223 (46Nb 90)

Craigton Rd.—Crete Hall Rd.

Craigton Rd. SE9 56Pc 116
Craigweil Av. WD7: R'lett 7Ka 14
Craigweil Cl. HA7: Stan 22Ma 47
Craigweil Dr. HA7: Stan 22Ma 47
Craigwell Av. TW13: Felt 62W 128
Craigwell Cl. TW18: Staines 67G 126
Craik Ct. NW6 40Bb 69
(off Carlton Vale)
Crail Row SE17 6G 231 (49Tb 91)
Crakell Rd. RH2: Reig 7L 207
Crakers Mead WD18: Wat 13X 27
Crales Ho. SE18 48Nc 94
Cramer St. W1 1J 221 (43Jb 90)
Crammavill St. RM16: Grays 45Ce 99
Crammerville Wlk. RM13: Rain 42Kd 97
Crammond Cl. W6 51Ab 110
Cramond Ct. TW14: Bedf 60U 106
Cramonde Ct. DA16: Well 54Wc 117
Crampshaw La. KT21: Asht 91Pa 193
Crampton Ho. SW8 53Lb 112
Crampton Rd. SE20 65Yb 136
Cramptons Rd. TN14: S'oaks 92Kd 203
Crampton St. SE17 6D 230 (49Sb 91)
Cranberry Cl. UB5: N'olt 40Z 65
Cranberry Ent. Pk. N17 24Vb 51
(off White Hart La.)
Cranberry La. E16 42Gc 93
Cranborne Av. EN6: Pot B 2Ab 16
KT6: Surb 76Qa 153
UB2: S'hall 49Ca 85
Cranborne Cl. EN6: Pot B 3Ab 16
Cranborne Ct. EN3: Enf W 8Zb 20
Cranborne Cres. EN6: Pot B 3Ab 16
Cranborne Gdns. RM14: Upm 33Rd 77
Cranborne Ind. Est. EN6: Pot B 2Ab 16
(not continuous)
Cranborne Pde. EN6: Pot B 3Za 16
Cranborne Rd. EN6: Pot B 2Ab 16
EN8: Chesh 4Zb 20
IG11: Bark 39Tc 74
Cranborne Waye UB4: Yead 44X 85
(not continuous)
Cranbourn All. WC2 4E 222
CRANBOURNE 10A 102
Cranbourne NW1 38Mb 70
(off Agar Gro.)
Cranbourne Av. E11 28Kc 53
SL4: Wind 4D 102
Cranbourne Cl. KT12: Hers 79Y 151
SL1: Slou 6G 80
SW16 69Nb 134
Cranbourne Cotts. SL4: Wink 2A 124
Cranbourne Ct. SW11 52Gb 111
(off Albert Bri. Rd.)
Cranbourne Dr. HA5: Pinn 29Z 45
Cranbourne Gdns. IG6: Ilf 27Sc 54
NW11 29Ab 48
Cranbourne Hall Cotts. SL4: Wink 10A 102
(off Squirrel La.)
Cranbourne Pas. SE16 47Xb 91
Cranbourne Rd. E12 36Nc 74
E15 35Ec 72
HA6: Nwood 27V 44
N10 26Kb 50
SL1: Slou 6G 80
Cranbourn Ho. SE16 47Xb 91
(off Marigold St.)
Cranbourn St. WC2 4E 222 (45Mb 90)
CRANBROOK 32Pc 74
Cranbrook NW1 1C 216
Cranbrook Castle Tennis Club 31Pc 74
Cranbrook Cl. BR2: Hayes 72Jc 159
Cranbrook Ct. CR2: S Croy 78Ub 157
TW8: Bford 51La 108
Cranbrook Dr. AL4: St A 2J 7
KT10: Esh 74Ea 152
RM2: Rom 28Ld 57
TW2: Whitt 60Da 107
Cranbrook Est. E2 40Zb 72
Cranbrook Ho. DA8: Erith 52Hd 118
(off Boundary St.)
Cranbrook La. N11 21Kb 50
Cranbrook M. E17 29Bc 52
Cranbrook Pk. N22 25Qb 50
Cranbrook Ri. IG1: Ilf 30Pc 54
Cranbrook Rd. CR7: Thor H 68Sb 135
DA7: Bex 53Bd 117
EN4: E Barn 16Fb 31
IG1: Ilf 31Qc 74
IG2: Ilf 29Qc 54
IG6: Ilf 29Qc 54
SE8 53Cc 114
SW19 66Ab 132
TW4: Houn 56Ba 107
W4 50Ua 88
Cranbrook St. E2 40Zb 72
Cranbury Rd. SW6 54Db 111
Crandley Ct. SE8 49Ac 92
(not continuous)
Crandon Wlk. DA4: S Dar 68Ud 142
Crane Av. TW7: Isle 57Ja 108
W3 45Sa 87
Cranebank M. TW1: Twick 56Ja 108
Cranebank (Nature Reserve) 54W 106
Cranebrook TW2: Twick 61Ea 130
Crane Cl. HA2: Harr 34Ea 66
RM10: Dag 37Cd 76
Crane Ct. EC4 3A 224 (44Qb 90)
KT19: Ewe 77Sa 153
SW14 56Sa 109
Cranefield Dr. WD25: Wat 4Aa 13
Craneford Cl. TW2: Twick 59Ha 108
Craneford Way TW2: Twick 59Ga 108
Crane Gdns. UB3: Harl 49V 84
Crane Gro. N7 37Qb 70
Crane Hgts. N17 27Xb 51
(off Waterside Way)
Crane Ho. E3 40Ac 72
(off Roman Rd.)
SE15 53Vb 113
TW13: Hanw 62Ca 129
Cranell Grn. RM15: S Ock 46Xd 98
Crane Lodge Rd. TW5: Cran 51X 107
Crane Mead SE16 50Yb 92
Crane Mead Ct. TW1: Twick 59Ha 108
Crane Pk. Island Nature Reserve
61Ba 129
Crane Pk. Rd. TW2: Whitt 61Da 129
Crane Rd. TW2: Twick 60Ga 108
TW19: Stanw 58Q 106
Cranesbill Cl. NW9 27Ta 47
SW16 68Mb 134
Cranes Dr. KT5: Surb 70Na 131
Cranes Pk. KT5: Surb 70Na 131
Cranes Pk. Av. KT5: Surb 70Na 131
Cranes Pk. Cres. KT5: Surb 70Pa 131
Crane St. SE10 50Ec 93
SE15 53Vb 113
Craneswater UB3: Harl 52V 106
Craneswater Pk. UB2: S'hall 50Ba 85
Cranes Way WD6: Bore 15Sa 29
Crane Way TW2: Whitt 59Ea 108
Cranfield Ct. SE27 62Sb 135
Cranfield Ct. GU21: Wok 10L 167
W1 1E 220
Cranfield Cres. EN6: Cuff 1Nb 18
Cranfield Dr. NW9 24Ua 48
Cranfield Ho. WC1 7F 217
Cranfield Rd. SE4 55Bc 114
Cranfield Rd. E. SM5: Cars 81Jb 176
Cranfield Rd. W. SM5: Cars 81Jb 176
Cranfield Row SE1 3A 230
Cranfield Wlk. SE3 55Kc 115
CRANFORD 52W 106
Cranford Av. N13 22Nb 50
TW19: Stanw 59N 105
Cranford Cl. CR8: Purl 85Sb 177
SW20 66Xa 132
TW19: Stanw 59N 105
Cranford Community College Sports Cen.
51X 107
Cranford Cotts. E1 45Zb 92
(off Cranford St.)
Cranford Dr. SL1: Slou 7D 80
UB3: Harl 49V 84
Cranford La. TW5: Cran, Hest 52X 107
TW6: H'row A 53V 106
(Bath Rd.)
TW6: H'row A 55V 106
(Elmdon Rd.)
UB3: Cran, Harl 51T 106
Cranford M. BR2: Brom 71Nc 160
Cranford Pk. Rd. UB3: Harl 49V 84
Cranford Ri. KT10: Esh 78Ea 152
Cranford Rd. DA1: Dart 60Nd 119
Cranford St. E1 45Zb 92
Cranford Way N8 28Pb 50
CRANHAM 31Ud 78
Cranham Brickfields Local Nature Reserve
31Vd 78
Cranham Gdns. RM14: Upm 32Ud 78
Cranham Golf Course 33Wd 78
Cranham Hall M. RM14: Upm 34Ud 78
Cranham Marsh Local Nature Reserve
35Ud 78
Cranham Rd. RM11: Horn 30Kd 57
Cranhurst Rd. NW2 36Ya 68
Cranleigh W11 46Bb 89
(off Ladbroke Rd.)
Cranleigh Cl. BR6: Chels 76Wc 161
CR2: Sande 84Wb 177
DA5: Bexl 58Dd 118
EN7: Chesh 1Wb 19
SE20 68Xb 135
Cranleigh Ct. CR4: Mitc 69Fb 133
TW9: Rich 55Qa 109
UB1: S'hall 44Ba 85
Cranleigh Dr. BR8: Swan 70Gd 140
Cranleigh Gdns. CR2: Sande 84Wb 177
HA3: Kenton 29Na 47
IG10: Lough 16Pc 36
IG11: Bark 38Tc 74
KT2: King T 65Pa 131
N21 15Pb 32
SE25 69Ub 135
SM1: Sutt 75Db 155
UB1: S'hall 44Ba 85
Cranleigh Gdns. Ind. Est.
UB1: S'hall 44Ba 85
Cranleigh Ho's. NW1 2C 216
Cranleigh M. SW11 54Gb 111
Cranleigh Rd. KT10: Esh 74Ea 152
N15 29Sb 51
SW19 69Cb 133
TW13: Felt 63V 128
Cranleigh St. NW1 2C 216 (40Lb 70)
Cranley Dene Ct. N10 28Kb 50
Cranley Dr. HA4: Ruis 33V 64
IG2: Ilf 31Sc 74
CRANLEY GARDENS 28Kb 50
Cranley Gdns. N10 28Kb 50
N13 20Pb 32
SM6: Wall 81Lb 176
SW7 7A 226 (50Eb 89)
Cranley M. SW7 7A 226 (50Eb 89)
Cranley Pde. SE9 63Nc 138
(off Beaconsfield Rd.)
Cranley Pl. GU21: Knap 10H 167
SW7 6B 226 (49Fb 89)
Cranley Rd. E13 43Kc 93
IG2: Ilf 30Sc 54
KT12: Hers 78V 150
Cranmer Av. W13 48Ka 86
Cranmer Cl. CR6: W'ham 89Ac 178
EN6: Pot B 2Eb 17
HA4: Ruis 32Z 65
HA7: Stan 24La 46
KT13: Weyb 80Q 150
SM4: Mord 72Za 154
Cranmer Ct. GU21: Knap 10G 166
(off Hampton Cl.)
N3 26Ab 48
SW3 6E 226 (49Gb 89)
SW4 55Mb 112
TW12: Hamp H 64Da 129
Cranmere Ct. EN2: Enf 12Qb 32
Cranmer Farm Cl. CR4: Mitc 70Hb 133
Cranmer Gdns. CR6: W'ham 89Ac 178
RM10: Dag 35Ed 76
Cranmer Ho. SW9 52Qb 112
(off Cranmer Rd.)
SW11 53Gb 111
(off Surrey La. Est.)
Cranmer Rd. CR0: C'don 76Rb 157
CR4: Mitc 70Hb 133
E7 35Kc 73
HA8: Edg 20Ra 29
KT2: King T 64Na 131
SW9 52Qb 112
TN13: Riv 95Gd 202
TW12: Hamp H 64Da 129
UB3: Hayes 44T 84
Cranmer Ter. SW17 64Fb 133
Cranmore Av. TW7: Isle 52Ea 108
Cranmore Ct. AL1: St A 1D 6
(off Avenue Rd.)
Cranmore La.
KT24: W Hor 100R 190, 100S 190
Cranmore Rd. BR1: Brom 62Hc 137
BR7: Chst 64Pc 138
Cranmore Way N10 28Lb 50
Cranston Cl. RH2: Reig 7K 207
TW3: Houn 54Aa 107
UB10: Ick 33T 64
Cranstone Lodge HP1: Hem H 4L 3
(off Cotterells)
Cranston Est. N1 1G 219 (40Tb 71)
Cranston Gdns. E4 23Dc 52
Cranston Pk. Av. RM14: Upm 35Rd 77
Cranston Rd. SE23 60Ac 114
Cranswick Rd. SE16 50Xb 91
Crantock Rd. SE6 61Dc 136
Cranwell Cl. AL4: St A 4G 6
Cranwell Gro. TW17: Shep 70P 127
Cranwell Rd. TW6: H'row A 54R 106
Cranwells La. SL2: Farn C 4G 60
Cranwich Av. N21 17Tb 33
Cranwich Rd. N16 31Tb 71
Cranwood Ct. EC1 4G 219
Cranwood St. EC1 4G 219 (41Tb 71)
Cranworth Cres. E4 18Fc 35
Cranworth Gdns. SW9 53Qb 112
Craster Rd. SW2 59Pb 112
Crathie Rd. SE12 58Kc 115
Cravan Av. TW13: Felt 61W 128
Craven Av. UB1: S'hall 43Ba 85
W5 45La 86
Craven Cl. N16 31Wb 71
UB4: Hayes 44W 84
Craven Cottage 54Za 110
Craven Ct. NW10 39Ua 68
RM6: Chad H 30Ad 55
Craven Gdns. IG6: Ilf 26Tc 54
IG11: Bark 40Uc 74
RM3: Hrld W 23Sd 58
RM5: Col R 22Cd 56
SW19 64Cb 133
Craven Hill W2 4A 220 (45Eb 89)
Craven Hill Gdns. W2 4A 220 (45Eb 89)
(not continuous)
Craven Hill M. W2 4A 220 (45Eb 89)
Craven Ho. N2 26Fb 49
(off High Rd. E. Finchley)
Craven Lodge SW6 53Za 110
(off Harbord St.)
W2 4A 220
Craven M. SW11 55Jb 112
Craven Pk. NW10 39Ta 67
Craven Pk. M. NW10 38Ua 68
Craven Pk. Rd. N15 30Vb 51
NW10 39Ua 68
Craven Pas. WC2 6F 223
Craven Rd. BR6: Chels 76Zc 161
CR0: C'don 74Xb 157
KT2: King T 67Pa 131
NW10 39Ta 67
W2 4A 220 (45Eb 89)
W5 45La 86
Craven St. WC2 6F 223 (46Nb 90)
Craven Ter. W2 4A 220 (45Eb 89)
Craven Wlk. N16 31Wb 71
Crawford Av. DA1: Dart 58Md 119
HA0: Wemb 36Ma 67
RM16: Grays 46De 99
Crawford Bldgs. W1 1E 220
Crawford Cl. TW7: Isle 54Ga 108
Crawford Compton Cl.
RM12: Horn 37Ld 77
Crawford Ct. NW9 27Ua 48
(off Charcot Rd.)
Crawford Est. SE5 54Sb 113
Crawford Gdns. N13 20Rb 33
UB5: N'olt 41Ba 85
Crawford Mans. W1 1E 220
Crawford M. W1 1F 221 (43Hb 89)
Crawford Pas. EC1 6K 217 (42Qb 90)
Crawford Pl. W1 2E 220 (44Gb 89)
Crawford Rd. SE5 53Sb 113
Crawfords BR8: Hext 66Gd 140
Crawford St. NW10 38Ta 67
W1 1E 220 (43Gb 89)
Crawley Ct. DA11: Grav'nd 7D 122
Crawley Rd. E10 32Dc 72
EN1: Enf 17Ub 33
N22 26Sb 51
Crawshaw Rd. KT16: Ott 79F 148
Crawshay Cl. TN13: S'oaks 95Jd 202
Crawshay Rd. SW9 53Qb 112
Crawthew Gro. SE22 56Vb 113
Cray Av. BR5: St M Cry 72Xc 161
KT21: Asht 88Na 173
Craybrooke Rd. DA14: Sidc 63Xc 139
Crayburne DA13: Sflt 64Be 143
Craybury End SE9 61Sc 138
Cray Cl. DA1: Cray 56Jd 118
Craydene Rd. DA8: Erith 53Hd 118
Crayfields Bus. Pk. BR5: St P 67Yc 139
Crayfields Ind. Pk. BR5: St P 68Yc 139
CRAYFORD 57Hd 118
Crayford Cl. E6 44Nc 94
Crayford High St. DA1: Cray 57Gd 118
Crayford Ho. SE1 2G 231
Crayford Ind. Est. DA1: Cray 57Hd 118
Crayford M. N7 35Nb 70
Crayford Rd. DA1: Cray 57Hd 118
N7 35Mb 70
Crayford Stadium (Greyhound) 58Gd 118
Crayford Way DA1: Cray 57Hd 118
Cray Ho. NW8 7C 214
Crayke Hill KT9: Chess 80Na 153
Craylands BR5: St P 69Yc 139
Craylands La.
DA10: Ghithe, Swans 57Zd 121
Craylands Sq. DA10: Swans 57Zd 121
Crayle Ho. EC1 5B 218
Crayleigh Ter. DA14: Sidc 65Yc 139
Crayle St. SL2: Slou 1E 80
Craymill Sq. DA1: Cray 54Hd 118
Crayonne Cl. TW16: Sun 67U 128
Cray Rd. BR8: Crock 72Ed 162
DA1: Cray 56Jd 118
DA14: Sidc 65Yc 139
DA17: Belv 51Cd 118
Crayside Ind. Est. DA1: Cray 56Kd 119
Crayside Leisure Cen. 58Gd 118
Cray's Pde. BR5: St P 68Yc 139
Cray Valley Golf Course 68Ad 139
Cray Valley Rd. BR5: St M Cry 71Wc 161
Cray Vw. Cl. BR5: St M Cry 70Yc 139
(off Market Mdw.)
Cray Wanderers FC 71Kc 159
Crayzee Barn 61Bd 139
Crealock Gro. IG8: Wfd G 22Hc 53
Crealock St. SW18 58Db 111
Creasey Cl. RM11: Horn 33Kd 77
Creasy Cl. WD5: Ab L 3V 12
Creasy Ct. EN8: Walt C 6Zb 20
Creasy Est. SE1 4H 231 (48Ub 91)
Creative Ho. SW8 52Kb 112
(off Prince of Wales Dr.)
Creative Rd. SE8 52Dc 114
Crebor St. SE22 58Wb 113
Crecy Ct. SE11 7K 229
Credenhall Dr. BR2: Brom 74Pc 160
Credenhill Ho. SE15 52Xb 113
Credenhill St. SW16 65Lb 134
Crediton Hgts. NW10 39Za 68
(off Okehampton Rd.)
Crediton Hill NW6 36Cb 69
Crediton Rd. E16 44Jc 93
NW10 39Za 68
Crediton Way KT10: Clay 78Ja 152
Credon Rd. E13 40Lc 73
SE16 50Xb 91
Credo Way RM20: W Thur 51Xd 120
Creechurch La. EC3 3J 225 (44Ub 91)
(not continuous)
Creechurch Pl. EC3 3J 225
Creed Ct. E1 41Ac 92
EC4 3C 224
Creed La. EC4 3C 224 (44Rb 91)
Creeds Cotts. CM16: Epp 4Uc 22
Creek, The DA11: Nflt 57De 121
TW16: Sun 71W 150
Creek Cotts. KT8: E Mos 70Ga 130
(off Creek Rd.)
Creek Ho. W14 48Ab 88
(off Russell Rd.)
Creek Mill Way DA1: Dart 56Md 119
CREEKMOUTH 42Vc 95
Creekmouth Ind. Pk.
IG11: Bark 42Vc 95
Creek Rd. IG11: Bark 41Vc 95
KT8: E Mos 70Ga 130
SE8 51Cc 114
SE10 51Cc 114
Creekside RM13: Rain 42Gd 96
SE8 52Dc 114
Creekside Discovery Cen. 52Dc 114
Creekside Foyer SE8 51Dc 114
(off Stowage)
Creek Way RM13: Rain 43Gd 96
Creeland Gro. SE6 60Bc 114
Cree's Mdw. GU20: W'sham 9A 146
Cree Way KT15: Add 80J 149
RM1: Rom 24Gd 56
Crefeld Cl. W6 51Ab 110
Creffield Rd. W3 45Pa 87
W5 45Pa 87
Creighton Av. AL1: St A 6B 6
E6 40Mc 73
N2 27Gb 49
N10 27Gb 49
Creighton Cl. W12 45Wa 88
Creighton Rd. N17 24Ub 51
NW6 40Za 68
W5 48Ma 87
Cremer Bus. Cen. E2 2K 219
Cremer Ho. SE8 52Cc 114
(off Deptford Chu. St.)
Cremer St. E2 2K 219 (40Vb 71)
Cremorne Est. SW10 51Fb 111
(not continuous)
Cremorne Gdns. KT19: Ewe 82Ta 173
Cremorne Riverside Cen. 52Fb 111
Cremorne Rd. DA11: Nflt 9B 122
SW10 52Eb 111
Creon Ct. SW9 52Qb 112
(off Caldwell St.)
Crescent EC3 4K 225 (45Vb 91)
Crescent, The AL2: Brick W 2Ca 13
BR3: Beck 67Cc 136
BR4: W W'ck 72Gc 159
CM14: B'wood 20Xd 40
CM16: Epp 4Vc 23
CR0: C'don 71Tb 157
CR3: Wold 95Cc 198
DA3: Lfield 69Ae 143
DA5: Bexl 59Yc 117
DA9: Ghithe 57Yd 120
DA11: Nflt 1B 144
DA14: Sidc 63Vc 139
E17 30Ac 52
EN5: New Bar 12Db 31
HA0: Wemb 33Ka 66
HA2: Harr 32Ea 66
IG2: Ilf 30Qc 54
IG10: Lough 15Mc 35
KT3: N Mald 69Sa 131
KT6: Surb 71Na 153
KT8: W Mole 70Ca 129
KT13: Weyb 76Q 150
KT16: Chert 70J 127
KT18: Eps 86Qa 173
(not continuous)
KT22: Lea 94Ka 192
N9 19Xb 33
N11 21Hb 49
NW2 34Xa 68
RH1: Redh 9M 207
RH2: Reig 6K 207
RM14: Upm 31Ud 78
SE8 53Cc 114
(off Seager Pl.)
SL1: Slou 7J 81
(not continuous)
SM1: Sutt 78Fb 155
SM2: Sutt 83Cb 175
SW13 54Va 110
SW19 62Cb 133
TN13: S'oaks 93Md 203
TN15: Bor G 91Ce 205
TW15: Ashf 64P 127
TW17: Shep 73V 150
TW20: Egh 65A 126
UB1: S'hall 47Ba 85
UB3: Harl 52S 106
W3 44Ua 88
W12 46Ya 88
WD3: Crox G 16R 26
WD5: Ab L 2V 12
WD18: Wat 14Y 27
WD25: A'ham 10Ea 14
Crescent Arc. SE10 51Ec 114
(off Creek Rd.)
Crescent Av. RM12: Horn 33Hd 76
RM17: Grays 50Fe 99
(not continuous)
Crescent Cotts. TN13: Dun G 92Gd 202
Crescent Ct. KT6: Surb 71Ma 153
RH1: Redh 4A 208
(off Foxboro Rd.)
RM17: Grays 50Fe 99
SW4 57Mb 112
(off Park Hill)
Crescent Ct. Bus. Cen. E16 42Fc 93
Crescent Dr. BR5: Pet W 71Rc 160
CM15: Shenf 18Ae 41
Crescent E. EN4: Had W 10Eb 17
Crescent Gdns. BR8: Swan 68Ed 140
HA4: Ruis 31X 65
SW19 62Cb 133
Crescent Gro. CR4: Mitc 70Gb 133
SW4 56Lb 112
Crescent Ho. EC1 6D 218
SE13 54Dc 114
Crescent La. SW4 56Lb 112
Crescent Mans. SW3 6D 226
W11 45Ab 88
(off Elgin Cres.)
Crescent M. N22 25Nb 50
Crescent Pde. UB10: Hil 41Q 84
Crescent Pl. SW3 5E 226 (49Gb 89)
Crescent Ri. EN4: E Barn 15Gb 31
N3 25Bb 49
N22 25Mb 50
Crescent Rd. BR1: Brom 66Jc 137
BR3: Beck 68Dc 136
CM14: W'ley 21Xd 58
CR3: Cat'm 96Wb 197
DA8: Erith 53Gd 118
DA15: Sidc 62Vc 139
E4 17Gc 35
E6 39Lc 73
E10 33Dc 72
E13 39Jc 73
E18 25Lc 53
EN2: Enf 14Rb 33
EN4: E Barn 14Fb 31
HP2: Hem H 2M 3
KT2: King T 66Qa 131
N3 25Bb 49
N8 30Mb 50
N9 18Wb 33
N11 21Hb 49
N15 27Rb 51
N22 25Mb 50
RH1: Blet 5J 209
RH2: Reig 8J 207
RM10: Dag 34Dd 76
RM15: Avel 47Sd 98
SE18 50Rc 94
SW20 67Za 132
TW17: Shep 71S 150
Crescent Row EC1 6D 218 (42Sb 91)
Crescent Stables SW15 57Ab 110
Crescent St. N1 38Pb 70
Crescent Vw. IG10: Lough 16Mc 35
Crescent Wlk. RM15: Avel 47Sd 98
Crescent Way BR6: Orp 78Uc 160
N12 23Gb 49
RM15: Avel 46Td 98
SE4 55Cc 114
SW16 65Pb 134
Crescent W. EN4: Had W 11Eb 31
Crescent Wharf E16 47Kc 93
(not continuous)
Crescent Wood Rd. SE26 62Wb 135
Cresford Rd. SW6 53Db 111
Crespigny Rd. NW4 30Xa 48
Cressage Cl. UB1: S'hall 42Ca 85
Cressage Ho. TW8: Bford 51Na 109
(off Ealing Rd.)
Cressal Ho. E14 48Cc 92
(off Tiller Rd.)
Cressall Cl. KT22: Lea 92Ka 192
Cressall Mead KT22: Lea 92Ka 192
Cress Ct. TN14: S'oaks 92Kd 203
Cress End WD3: Rick 18J 25
Cresset Pl. DA1: Dart 57Md 119
Cresset Ho. E9 37Yb 72
Cresset Rd. E9 37Yb 72
Cresset St. SW4 55Mb 112
CRESSFIELD 61Ce 143
Cressfield Cl. NW5 36Jb 70
Cressida Rd. N19 32Lb 70
Cressingham Gro. SM1: Sutt 77Eb 155
Cressingham Rd. HA8: Edg 23Ta 47
SE13 55Ec 114
Cressinghams, The KT18: Eps 85Ta 173
Cressington Cl. N16 36Ub 71
Cress M. BR1: Brom 64Fc 137
Cress Rd. SL1: Slou 7F 80
Cresswell Gdns. SW5 7A 226 (50Eb 89)
Cresswell Ho. HA9: Wemb 34Na 67
TW19: Stanw 58N 105
(off Douglas Rd.)
Cresswell Pk. SE3 55Hc 115
Cresswell Pl. SW10 7A 226 (50Eb 89)
Cresswell Rd. SE25 70Wb 135
TW1: Twick 58Ma 109
TW13: Hanw 62Aa 129
Cresswell Way N21 17Qb 32
Cressy Ct. E1 43Yb 92
W6 48Xa 88
Cressy Ho. SW15 55Xa 110
Cressy Ho's. E1 43Yb 92
(off Hannibal Rd.)
Cressy Pl. E1 43Yb 92
Cressy Rd. NW3 36Hb 69
Crest, The KT5: Surb 71Qa 153
N13 21Qb 50
NW4 29Xa 48
Cresta Ct. W5 42Pa 87
Cresta Dr. KT15: Wdhm 82H 169
Cresta Ho. E3 42Cc 92
(off Dimson Cres.)
NW3 38Fb 69
(off Finchley Rd.)
Crest Av. RM17: Grays 52De 121
Crestbrook Av. N13 20Rb 33
Crestbrook Pl. N13 20Rb 33
(off Green Lanes)
Crest Cl. TN14: Bad M 83Dd 182
Crest Ct. NW4 29Xa 48
Crest Dr. EN3: Enf W 10Yb 20
Crested Ct. NW9 31Ta 68
Crestfield St. WC1 3G 217 (41Nb 90)
Crest Gdns. HA4: Ruis 34Y 65
Cresthill Av. RM17: Grays 49Ee 99
Creston Av. GU21: Knap 9J 167
Creston Way KT4: Wor Pk 74Za 154
Crest Pk. HP2: Hem H 1C 4
Crest Rd. BR2: Hayes 73Hc 159
CR2: Sels 80Xb 157
NW2 33Va 68
Crest Vw. DA9: Ghithe 56Wd 120
HA5: Pinn 28Z 45
Crest Vw. Dr. BR5: Pet W 71Rc 160
Crest Way E18 26Lc 53
Crestway SW15 58Wa 110
Crestwood Way TW4: Houn 57Aa 107
Creswell GU21: Knap 9H 167
Creswell Cnr. GU21: Knap 9H 167
Creswell Dr. BR3: Beck 71Dc 158
Creswick Ct. W3 45Ra 87
Creswick Rd. W3 45Ra 87
Creswick Wlk. E3 41Cc 92
NW11 28Bb 49
Crete Hall Rd. DA11: Nflt 58Fe 121

Creton St.—Crown Cotts.

Creton St. SE18 . . . . . 48Qc 94
Creukhorne Rd. NW10 . . . . . 38Ua 68
Crewdson Rd. SW9 . . . . . 52Qb 112
Crewe Ct. KT20: Tad 94Ya 194
Crewe Pl. NW10 . . . . . 41Va 88
Crewe's Av. CR6: W'ham 88Yb 178
Crewe's Cl. CR6: W'ham 89Yb 178
Crewe's Farm La. CR6: W'ham 88Zb 178
Crewe's La. CR6: W'ham 88Yb 178
Crewkerne Ct. *SW11* *53Fb 111*
(off Bolingbroke Wlk.)
CREWS HILL 7Rb 19
Crews Hill EN2: Crew H 6Pb 18
Crews Hill Golf Course 7Pb 18
Crews St. E14 . . . . . 49Cc 92
Crewys Rd. NW2 . . . . . 33Bb 69
SE15 . . . . . 54Xb 113
Crichton Av. SM6: Bedd 78Mb 156
Crichton Ho. DA14: Sidc 65Zc 139
Crichton Rd. SM5: Cars 79Hb 155
Crichton St. SW8 . . . . . 54Lb 112
Crick Ct. *IG11: Bark* *40Sc 74*
(off Spring Pl.)
Cricketers Arms Rd. EN2: Enf 12Sb 33
Cricketers Cl. AL3: St A 1C 6
DA8: Erith 50Gd 96
GU22: Wok 93A 188
KT9: Chess 77Ma 153
N14 . . . . . 17Lb 32
Cricketers Ct. SE11 . . . . . 6B 230
Cricketers La. CM13: Heron 23Fe 59
GU20: W'sham 8B 146
Cricketers M. SW18 . . . . . 57Db 111
Cricketers Row CM13: Heron 24Fe 59
Cricketers Ter. SM5: Cars 76Gb 155
Cricketers Wlk. SE26 . . . . . 64Yb 136
Cricket Fld. Rd. UB8: Uxb 39M 63
Cricketfield Rd. E5 . . . . . 35Xb 71
UB7: W Dray 49L 83
Cricket Grn. CR4: Mitc 69Hb 133
Cricket Ground Rd. BR7: Chst 67Rc 138
Cricket Hill RH1: S Nut 8F 208
Cricket La. BR3: Beck 65Ac 136
TW12: Hamp H 65Ea 130
CRICKETS HILL 97D 188
Cricket Vw. KT13: Weyb 78R 150
Cricket Way KT13: Weyb 75U 150
Cricklade Av. RM3: Rom 23Md 57
SW2 . . . . . 61Nb 134
Cricklefield Pl. IG1: Ilf 33Uc 74
CRICKLEWOOD 35Za 68
Cricklewood B'way. NW2 . . . . . 34Ya 68
Cricklewood La. NW2 . . . . . 35Za 68
Cridland St. E15 . . . . . 39Hc 73
Crieff Ct. TW11: Tedd 66La 130
Crieff Rd. SW18 . . . . . 58Eb 111
Criffel Av. SW2 . . . . . 61Mb 134
Crimp Hill SL4: Old Win 9K 103
TW20: Eng G 2L 125
Crimscott St. SE1 . . . . . 4J 231 (48Ub 91)
Crimson Rd. DA8: Erith 52Jd 118
Crimsworth Rd. SW8 . . . . . 53Mb 112
Crinan St. N1 . . . . . 1G 217 (40Nb 70)
Cringle Ct. EN6: Pot B 2Eb 17
Cringle St. SW8 . . . . . 52Lb 112
Crinoline M. E1 . . . . . 1K 225 (43Vb 91)
Cripplegate St. EC2 . . . . . 7E 218 (43Sb 91)
Cripps Grn. UB4: Yead 42X 85
Crispe Ho. IG11: Bark 40Tc 74
N1 . . . . . 1J 217
Crispen Rd. TW13: Hanw 63Aa 129
Crispian Cl. NW10 . . . . . 35Ua 68
Crispin Cl. CR0: Bedd 75Nb 156
KT21: Asht 90Pa 173
Crispin Ct. SE17 . . . . . 6J 231 (49Ub 91)
Crispin Cres. CR0: Bedd 76Mb 156
Crispin Ind. Cen. N18 . . . . . 22Yb 52
Crispin Lodge N11 . . . . . 22Hb 49
Crispin M. NW11 . . . . . 29Bb 49
Crispin Pl. E1 . . . . . 7K 219 (43Vb 91)
Crispin Rd. HA8: Edg 23Sa 47
Crispin St. E1 . . . . . 1K 225 (43Vb 91)
Crispin Way SL2: Farn C 5H 61
UB8: Hil 42P 83
Crisp Rd. W6 . . . . . 50Ya 88
Cristie Ct. E16 . . . . . 42Hc 93
Cristowe Rd. SW6 . . . . . 54Bb 111
Critchley Av. DA1: Dart 58Md 119
Criterion Bldgs. *KT7: T Ditt* *73Ka 152*
(off Portsmouth Rd.)
Criterion Ct. *E8* *38Vb 71*
(off Middleton Rd.)
Criterion M. N19 . . . . . 33Mb 70
SE24 . . . . . *57Rb 113*
(off Shakespeare Rd.)
Criterion Theatre 5D 222
Criton Ind. Est. RM16: Ors 4G 100
CRITTALLS CORNER 66Yc 139
Crockenhall Way DA13: Ist R 6A 144
CROCKENHILL 72Fd 162
Crockenhill La.
BR8: Crock, Eyns, Farni 73Jd 162
DA4: Eyns, Farni 73Jd 162
Crockenhill Rd. BR5: St M Cry 71Zc 161
BR8: Crock 71Zc 161
Crockerton Rd. SW17 . . . . . 61Hb 133
Crockery La. GU4: E Clan 100N 189
Crockford Cl. KT15: Add 77L 149
Crockford Pk. Rd. KT15: Add 78L 149
Crockham Way SE9 . . . . . 63Qc 138
Crocus Cl. CR0: C'don 74Zb 158
Crocus Fld. EN5: Barn 16Bb 31
Croffets KT20: Tad 93Za 194
Croft, The AL2: Chis G 7N 5
BR8: Swan 69Ed 140
CR0: C'don 76Vb 157
E4 . . . . . 19Gc 35
EN5: Barn 14Ab 30
HA0: Wemb 36La 66
HA4: Ruis 35Y 65
HA5: Pinn 31Ba 65
HA8: Edg 24Ra 47
IG10: Lough 12Qc 36
KT17: Eps 86Va 174
KT22: Fet 95Ga 192
NW10 . . . . . 40Va 68
TW5: Hest 51Aa 107
W5 . . . . . 43Na 87
Croft Av. BR4: W W'ck 74Ec 158
Croft Cl. BR7: Chst 64Pc 138
DA17: Belv 50Bd 95
NW7 . . . . . 20Ua 30
SL9: Chal P 26A 42
TN13: S'oaks 100Hd 202
UB3: Harl 52S 106
UB10: Hil 38Q 64
WD4: Chfd 2J 11
Croft Cnr. SL4: Old Win 7M 103
Croft Ct. HA4: Ruis 32V 64
SE13 . . . . . 58Ec 114
SM1: Sutt 75Fb 155
WD6: Bore 13Ta 29
Croftdown Rd. NW5 . . . . . 34Jb 70
Croft End Cl.
KT9: Chess 76Pa 153
Croft End Rd. WD4: Chfd 2J 11
Crofters SL4: Old Win 8L 103
Crofters Cl. RH1: Redh 8B 208
TW7: Isle 57Ha 108
TW19: Stanw 58L 105
Crofters Ct. *SE8* *49Ac 92*
(off Croft St.)
Crofters Mead CR0: Sels 81Bc 178
Crofters Rd. HA6: Nwood 21U 44
Crofters Way NW1 . . . . . 39Mb 70
Croft Fld. WD4: Chfd 2J 11
Croft Gdns. HA4: Ruis 32V 64
W7 . . . . . 47Ja 86
Crofthill Rd. SL2: Slou 2F 80
Croft Ho. E17 . . . . . 28Dc 52
NW9 . . . . . 27Va 48
W10 . . . . . *41Ab 88*
(off Third Av.)
Croft La. WD4: Chfd 2J 11
Croftleigh Av. CR8: Purl 88Qb 176
Croft Lodge Cl. IG8: Wfd G 23Kc 53
Croft Mdw. WD4: Chfd 2J 11
Croft M. N12 . . . . . 20Eb 31
CROFTON 75Sc 160
Crofton KT21: Asht 90Na 173
Crofton Av. BR6: Farnb 75Sc 160
DA5: Bexl 59Zc 117
KT12: Walt T 76Y 151
W4 . . . . . 52Sa 109
Crofton Cl. KT16: Ott 80E 148
Croftongate Way SE4 . . . . . 57Ac 114
Crofton Gro. E4 . . . . . 21Fc 53
Crofton Ho. *SW3* *51Gb 111*
(off Old Church St.)
Crofton La.
BR5: Farnb, Orp, Pet W 75Tc 160
BR6: Pet W 73Tc 160
CROFTON PARK 57Bc 114
Crofton Pk. Rd. SE4 . . . . . 58Bc 114
Crofton Rd.
BR6: Farnb, Orp 76Qc 160
E13 . . . . . 42Kc 93
RM16: Grays 7A 100
SE5 . . . . . 53Ub 113
Crofton Roman Villa 75Uc 160
Crofton Ter. E5 . . . . . 36Ac 72
TW9: Rich 56Pa 109
Crofton Way EN2: Enf 12Qb 32
EN5: New Bar 16Db 31
Croft Rd. BR1: Brom 65Jc 137
CR3: Wold 94Cc 198
EN3: Enf H 11Ac 34
SL9: Chal P 26A 42
SM1: Sutt 78Gb 155
SW16 . . . . . 67Qb 134
SW19 . . . . . 66Eb 133
TN16: Westrm 98Rc 200
Crofts, The HP3: Hem H 3B 4
TW17: Shep 70U 128
Crofts Ho. *E2* *40Wb 71*
(off Teale St.)
Croftside, The SE25 . . . . . 69Wb 135
Crofts La. N22 . . . . . 24Qb 50
Crofts Path HP3: Hem H 4A 4
Crofts Rd. HA1: Harr 30Ja 46
Crofts St. E1 . . . . . 45Wb 91
Croft St. SE8 . . . . . 49Ac 92
Crofts Vs. HA1: Harr 30Ja 46
Croft Way DA15: Sidc 62Uc 138
TN13: S'oaks 97Hd 202
Croftway NW3 . . . . . 35Cb 69
TW10: Ham 62Ka 130
Crogsland Rd. NW1 . . . . . 38Jb 70
Croham Cl. CR2: S Croy 80Ub 157
Croham Hurst Golf Course 79Vb 157
Croham Mnr. Rd. CR2: S Croy 80Ub 157
Croham Mt. CR2: S Croy 80Ub 157
Croham Pk. Av. CR2: S Croy 78Ub 157
Croham Rd. CR2: S Croy 78Tb 157
Croham Valley Rd. CR2: Sels 79Wb 157
Croindene Rd. SW16 . . . . . 67Nb 134
Crokesley Ho. *HA8: Edg* *26Sa 47*
(off Burnt Oak B'way.)
Cromar Ct. GU21: Wok 8N 167
Cromartie Rd. N19 . . . . . 31Mb 70
Cromarty Ct. SW2 . . . . . 57Pb 112
Cromarty Ho. *E1* *43Ac 92*
(off Ben Jonson Rd.)
Cromarty Rd. HA8: Edg 19Ra 29
Cromberdale Ct. *N17* *25Wb 51*
(off Spencer Rd.)
Crombie Cl. IG4: Ilf 29Pc 54
Crombie M. SW11 . . . . . 54Gb 111
Crombie Rd. DA15: Sidc 60Tc 116
Crome Ho. *UB5: N'olt* *40Aa 65*
(off Parkfield Dr.)
Cromer Cl. UB8: Hil 44S 84
Cromer Ct. SL1: Slou 4J 81
SW16 . . . . . 62Nb 134
Cromer Hyde SM4: Mord 71Db 155
Cromer Rd. NW10 . . . . . 37Ua 68
Cromer Pl. BR6: Orp 74Uc 160
Cromer Rd. E10 . . . . . 31Fc 73
EN5: New Bar 14Eb 31
IG8: Wfd G 21Jc 53
N17 . . . . . 26Wb 51
RM6: Chad H 30Ad 55
RM7: Rom 30Ed 56
RM11: Horn 31Md 77
SE25 . . . . . 69Xb 135
SW17 . . . . . 65Jb 134
TW6: H'row A 54Q 106
WD24: Wat 10Y 13
Cromer St. WC1 . . . . . 4F 217 (41Nb 90)
Cromer Ter. E8 . . . . . 36Wb 71
RM6: Chad H 29Xc 55
Cromer Vs. Rd. SW18 . . . . . 58Bb 111
Cromford Cl. BR6: Orp 76Uc 160
Cromford Path E5 . . . . . 35Zb 72
Cromford Rd. SW18 . . . . . 57Cb 111
Cromford Way
KT3: N Mald 67Ta 131
Cromie Cl. N13 . . . . . 20Qb 32
Cromlix Cl. BR7: Chst 68Rc 138
Crompton Ct. *BR2: Brom* *69Jc 137*
(off St Mark's Sq.)
SW3 . . . . . 5D 226 (49Gb 89)
Crompton Hall SL9: Ger X 29B 42
Crompton Ho. SE1 . . . . . 4E 230
W2 . . . . . 6B 214
Crompton Pl. EN3: Enf L 10Cc 20
Crompton St. W2 . . . . . 6B 214 (42Fb 89)
Cromwell Av. BR2: Brom 70Kc 137
EN7: Chesh 2Xb 19
KT3: N Mald 71Va 154
N6 . . . . . 32Kb 70
W6 . . . . . 50Xa 88
Cromwell Cen. IG6: Ilf 22Xc 55
IG11: Bark 41Wc 95
NW10 . . . . . 41Ta 87
Cromwell Cen., The *RM8: Dag* *31Bd 75*
(off Coppen Rd.)
Cromwell Cl. BR2: Brom 70Kc 137
E1 . . . . . 46Wb 91
KT12: Walt T 74X 151
N2 . . . . . 28Fb 49
TW18: Staines 65L 127
W3 . . . . . 46Sa 87
(not continuous)
W4 . . . . . *50Ra 87*
(off Harvard Rd.)
Cromwell Ct. EN3: Pond E 15Zb 34
GU21: Knap *1G 186*
(off Tudor Way)
Cromwell Cres. SW5 . . . . . 49Cb 89
Cromwell Dr. SL1: Slou 4J 81
Cromwell Gdns. SW7 . . . . . 4C 226 (48Fb 89)
Cromwell Gro. CR3: Cat'm 93Sb 197
W6 . . . . . 48Ya 88
Cromwell Highwalk EC2 . . . . . 7E 218
Cromwell Ho. CR0: C'don 76Rb 157
SW11 . . . . . *53Jb 112*
(off Charlotte Despard Av.)
Cromwell Ind. Est. E10 . . . . . 32Ac 72
Cromwell Lodge DA6: Bex 57Ad 117
E1 . . . . . *42Yb 92*
(off Cleveland Gro.)
IG11: Bark 36Uc 74
Cromwell Mans. *SW5* *49Cb 89*
(off Cromwell Rd.)
Cromwell M. SW7 . . . . . 5C 226 (49Fb 89)
Cromwell Pl. EC2 . . . . . 7E 218
N6 . . . . . 32Kb 70
SW7 . . . . . 5C 226 (49Fb 89)
SW14 . . . . . 55Sa 109
Cromwell Rd. BR3: Beck 68Ac 136
CM14: W'ley 21Xd 58
CR0: C'don 73Tb 157
CR3: Cat'm 93Sb 197
E7 . . . . . 38Lc 73
E17 . . . . . 29Ec 52
HA0: Wemb 40Na 67
KT2: King T 67Na 131
KT4: Wor Pk 76Ta 153
KT12: Walt T 74X 151
KT16: Vir W 5L 147
N3 . . . . . 25Eb 49
N10 . . . . . 24Jb 50
(not continuous)
RH1: Redh 6P 207
RM17: Grays 49Ce 99
SW5 . . . . . 49Cb 89
SW7 . . . . . 5A 226 (49Cb 89)
SW9 . . . . . 53Qb 112
SW19 . . . . . 64Cb 133
TW3: Houn 56Ca 107
TW11: Tedd 65Ja 130
TW13: Felt 60X 107
UB3: Hayes 44T 84
WD6: Bore 11Na 29
Cromwells Ct. SL3: L'ly 46B 82
Cromwells Mere RM1: Rom 23Fd 56
Cromwell St. TW3: Houn 56Ca 107
Cromwell Twr. EC2 . . . . . 7E 218
Cromwell Trad. Cen. IG11: Bark 41Uc 94
Cromwell Wlk. RH1: Redh 6P 207
Crondace Rd. SW6 . . . . . 53Cb 111
Crondall Ct. N1 . . . . . 2H 219
Crondall Ho. SW15 . . . . . 59Wa 110
Crondall St. N1 . . . . . 2G 219 (40Tb 71)
Crone Ct. *NW6* *40Bb 69*
(off Denmark Rd.)
Cronin St. SE15 . . . . . 52Vb 113
Cronks Hill RH1: Redh 8L 207
RH2: Reig 8L 207
Cronks Hill Cl. RH1: Redh 8M 207
Cronks Hill Rd. RH1: Redh 8M 207
CROOKED BILLET 24Cc 52
Crooked Billet SW19 . . . . . 65Ya 132
CROOKED BILLET RDBT. 63J 127
Crooked Billet Yd. E2 . . . . . 3J 219
Crooked La. DA12: Grav'nd 8D 122
Crooked Mile EN9: Walt A 1Ec 20
Crooked Usage N3 . . . . . 27Ab 48
Crooke Rd. SE8 . . . . . 50Ac 92
Crookham Rd. SW6 . . . . . 53Bb 111
Crook Log DA6: Bex 55Zc 117
Crook Log Leisure Cen. 55Zc 117
Crookston Rd. SE9 . . . . . 55Qc 116
Croombs Rd. E16 . . . . . 43Lc 93
Croom's Hill SE10 . . . . . 52Ec 114
Croom's Hill Gro. SE10 . . . . . 52Ec 114
Cropley Ct. N1 . . . . . 1F 219
(not continuous)
Cropley St. N1 . . . . . 1F 219 (40Tb 71)
Croppath Rd. RM10: Dag 35Cd 76
Cropthorne Ct. W9 . . . . . 4A 214 (41Eb 89)
Crosbie Ho. *E17* *27Ec 52*
(off Prospect Hill)
Crosby Cl. AL4: St A 5G 6
TW13: Hanw 62Aa 129
Crosby Ct. IG7: Chig 20Wc 37
SE1 . . . . . 1F 231 (47Tb 91)
Crosby Gdns. UB8: Uxb 38N 63
Crosby Ho. *BR1: Brom* *68Jc 137*
(off Elmfield Rd.)
E7 . . . . . 37Jc 73
E14 . . . . . *48Ec 92*
(off Manchester Rd.)
Crosby Rd. E7 . . . . . 37Jc 73
RM10: Dag 40Dd 76
Crosby Row SE1 . . . . . 2F 231 (47Tb 91)
Crosby Sq. EC3 . . . . . 2H 225 (44Ub 91)
Crosby Wlk. E8 . . . . . 37Vb 71
SW2 . . . . . 59Qb 112
Crosby Way SW2 . . . . . 59Qb 112
Crosfield Ct. *WD18: Wat* *15Y 27*
(off Lwr. High St.)
Crosier Cl. SE3 . . . . . 53Nc 116
Crosier Rd. UB10: Ick 35S 64
Crosier Way HA4: Ruis 34U 64
Crosland Pl. SW11 . . . . . 55Jb 112
Crossacres GU22: Pyr 88G 168
Cross Av. SE10 . . . . . 51Fc 115
Crossbones Graveyard 7E 224
Crossbow Ho. N1 . . . . . 1H 219
W13 . . . . . *46Ka 86*
(off Sherwood Cl.)
Crossbow Rd. IG7: Chig 22Vc 55
Crossbrook AL10: Hat 1A 8
Crossbrook Ct. EN8: Chesh 3Zb 20
Crossbrook Rd. SE3 . . . . . 54Nc 116
Crossbrook St. EN8: Chesh 3Zb 20
Crossby Cl. CM15: Mount 11Fe 41
Cross Cl. SE15 . . . . . 54Xb 113
Cross Ct. *SE28* *45Xc 95*
(off Titmuss Av.)
Cross Deep TW1: Twick 61Ha 130
Cross Deep Gdns.
TW1: Twick 61Ha 130
Crossett Grn. HP3: Hem H 4C 4
Crossfell Rd. HP3: Hem H 3C 4
Crossfield Ct. *W10* *44Za 88*
(off Cambridge Gdns.)
Crossfield Ho. SL9: Ger X 28A 42
W11 . . . . . *45Ab 88*
(off Mary Pl.)
Crossfield Pl. KT13: Weyb 80R 150
Crossfield Rd. N17 . . . . . 27Sb 51
NW3 . . . . . 37Fb 69
Crossfields AL3: St A 5P 5
IG10: Lough 15Rc 36
Crossfield St. SE8 . . . . . 52Cc 114
(not continuous)
Crossford St. SW9 . . . . . 54Pb 112
Cross Ga. HA8: Edg 20Qa 29
Crossgate UB6: G'frd 37Ka 66
Crossing Rd. CM16: Epp 4Wc 23
CROSS KEYS 99Jd 202
Cross Keys Cl. N9 . . . . . 19Wb 33
TN13: S'oaks 99Jd 202
W1 . . . . . 1J 221 (43Jb 90)
Cross Keys Sq. EC1 . . . . . 1D 224
Cross Lances Rd. TW3: Houn 56Da 107
Crossland Ho. *GU25: Vir W* *70A 126*
(off Holloway Dr.)
Crossland Rd. CR7: Thor H 72Rb 157
RH1: Redh 6A 208
Crosslands KT16: Chert 77G 148
WD3: Map C 21G 42
Crosslands Av. UB2: S'hall 50Ba 85
W5 . . . . . 46Pa 87
Crosslands Rd. KT19: Ewe 79Ta 153
Cross La. DA5: Bexl 59Bd 117
EC3 . . . . . 5H 225 (45Ub 91)
(not continuous)
KT16: Ott 79D 148
N8 . . . . . 27Pb 50
(not continuous)
Cross La. E. DA12: Grav'nd 1D 144
Cross Lanes SL9: Chal P 22A 42
Cross Lanes Cl. SL9: Chal P 22B 42
Cross La. W. DA11: Grav'nd 1D 144
Crossleigh Ct. *SE14* *52Bc 114*
(off New Cross Rd.)
Crosslet St. SE17 . . . . . 5G 231 (49Tb 91)
Crosslet Va. SE10 . . . . . 53Dc 114
Crossley Cl. TN16: Big H 87Mc 179
Crossley St. N7 . . . . . 37Qb 70
Crossmead SE9 . . . . . 60Pc 116
WD19: Wat 16X 27
Crossmead Av. UB6: G'frd 41Ca 85
Crossmount Ho. *SE5* *52Sb 113*
(off Bowyer St.)
Crossness Footpath DA18: Erith 46Bd 95
Crossness La. SE2 . . . . . 45Ad 95
Crossness Nature Reserve 46Cd 96
Crossness Pumping Station, The 44Ad 95
Crossness Rd. IG11: Bark 41Vc 95
Cross Oak SL4: Wind 4E 102
Crossoaks La. EN6: Ridge, S Mim 6Ua 16
WD6: Bore 7Ta 15
Crosspath, The WD7: R'lett 7Ja 14
Crosspoint Ho. *SE8* *52Cc 114*
(off Watson's St.)
Crossrail Pl. E14 . . . . . 46Dc 92
Crossrail Wlk. E14 . . . . . 46Dc 92
Cross Rd. BR2: Brom 75Nc 160
BR5: St M Cry 71Xc 161
CR0: C'don 74Tb 157
CR8: Purl 85Rb 177
DA1: Dart 58Ld 119
DA2: Hawl 63Pd 141
DA11: Nflt 8B 122
DA14: Sidc 63Xc 139
E4 . . . . . 18Fc 35
EN1: Enf 14Ub 33
EN8: Walt C 5Ac 20
HA1: Harr 28Fa 46
HA2: Harr 34Da 65
HA3: W'stone 26Ja 46
IG8: Wfd G 23Pc 54
KT2: King T 66Pa 131
KT13: Weyb 76T 150
KT20: Tad 94Ya 194
N11 . . . . . 22Kb 50
N22 . . . . . 24Qb 50
RM6: Chad H 31Yc 75
RM7: Mawney 28Cd 56
SE5 . . . . . 54Ub 113
SL5: S'dale 4D 146
SM1: Sutt 78Fb 155
SM2: Sutt 82Cb 175
SW19 . . . . . 66Cb 133
TW13: Hanw 63Aa 129
UB8: Uxb 38L 63
WD19: Wat 16Aa 27
Cross Roads IG10: H Beech 12Kc 35
Crossroads, The KT24: Eff 100Z 191
Cross St. AL3: St A 2B 6
DA8: Erith 51Gd 118
DA12: Grav'nd *8D 122*
(off Terrace St.)
N1 . . . . . 39Rb 71
N18 . . . . . 22Wb 51
SE5 . . . . . 55Tb 113
SW13 . . . . . 54Ua 110
TW12: Hamp H 64Ea 130
UB8: Uxb 38L 63
WD17: Wat 13Y 27
Cross Ter. *EN9: Walt A* *6Gc 21*
(off Stonyshotts)
Crossthwaite Av. SE5 . . . . . 56Tb 113
Crosstrees Ho. *E14* *48Cc 92*
(off Cassilis Rd.)
Crosswall EC3 . . . . . 4K 225 (45Vb 91)
Cross Way NW10 . . . . . 38Wa 68
Cross Way, The HA3: W'stone 26Ga 46
Crossway BR5: Pet W 70Tc 138
EN1: Enf 17Ub 33
HA4: Ruis 35Y 65
HA5: Pinn 26X 45
IG8: Wfd G 21Lc 53
KT12: Walt T 75X 151
N12 . . . . . 23Fb 49
N16 . . . . . 36Ub 71
NW9 . . . . . 28Va 48
RM8: Dag 34Yc 75
Crossway SE28 . . . . . 44Xc 95
SS17: Stan H 1P 101
SW20 . . . . . 70Ya 132
UB3: Hayes 46W 84
W13 . . . . . 42Ja 86
Crossway, The N22 . . . . . 24Rb 51
SE9 . . . . . 61Mc 137
UB10: Hil 40P 63
Crossway Ct. SE4 . . . . . 54Ac 114
Crossway Pde. *N22* *24Rb 51*
(off The Crossway)
Crossways CM15: Shenf 16Ce 41
CR2: Sels 80Ac 158
DA2: Dart 56Sd 120
HP3: Hem H 2B 4
IG10: Lough 15Qc 36
KT24: Eff 99Z 191
N21 . . . . . 16Sb 33
RM2: Rom 27Kd 57
SM2: Sutt 81Fb 175
TN16: Tats 92Lc 199
TW16: Sun 66V 128
TW20: Egh 65F 126
Crossways, The CR5: Coul 91Pb 196
HA9: Wemb 33Qa 67
KT5: Surb 74Ra 153
RH1: Mers 2C 208
TW5: Hest 52Ba 107
Crossways 25 Bus. Pk.
DA2: Dart 56Sd 120
Crossways Blvd. DA2: Dart 56Sd 120
DA9: Ghithe 56Ud 120
Crossways Ct. *SL4: Wind* *4G 102*
(off Osborne Rd.)
TN16: Tats 92Lc 199
Crossways Ho. KT17: Eps 84Ua 174
Crossways La. RH2: Reig 100Eb 195
(not continuous)
Crossways Rd. BR3: Beck 70Cc 136
CR4: Mitc 69Kb 134
Crossways Ter. E5 . . . . . 35Yb 72
Crosswell Cl. TW17: Shep 68S 128
Crosthwaite Way
SL1: Slou 3B 80
Croston St. E8 . . . . . 39Wb 71
Crothall Cl. N13 . . . . . 20Pb 32
CROUCH 95De 205
Crouch Av. IG11: Bark 40Xc 75
Crouch Cl.
BR3: Beck 65Cc 136
Crouch Cft. SE9 . . . . . 62Qc 138
CROUCH END 31Mb 70
Crouch End Hill N8 . . . . . 31Mb 70
Crouchfield HP1: Hem H 3K 3
Crouch Hall Ct. N19 . . . . . 32Nb 70
Crouch Hall Rd. N8 . . . . . 30Mb 50
Crouch Hill N4 . . . . . 30Nb 50
N8 . . . . . 30Nb 50
Crouch Ind. Est. KT22: Lea 91Ka 192
Crouch La. KT10: Hin W 76Ha 152
TN15: Bor G 92Ce 205
Crouchman Cl. RM16: Grays 47Ee 99
Crouchman's Cl. SE26 . . . . . 62Vb 135
Crouch Oak La. KT15: Add 77L 149
Crouch Rd. NW10 . . . . . 38Ta 67
RM16: Grays 10C 100
Crouch Valley RM14: Upm 31Ud 78
Crowborough Cl. CR6: W'ham 90Ac 178
Crowborough Dr. CR6: W'ham 90Ac 178
Crowborough Path WD19: Wat 21Z 45
Crowborough Rd. SW17 . . . . . 65Jb 134
Crowden Way SE28 . . . . . 45Xc 95
Crowder Cl. N12 . . . . . 25Eb 49
Crowder St. E1 . . . . . 45Xb 91
CROWDLEHAM 89Td 184
Crow Dr. TN14: Hals 87Ed 182
Crowfield Ho. N5 . . . . . 35Sb 71
Crowfoot Cl. E9 . . . . . 36Bc 72
SE28 . . . . . 46Uc 94
CROW GREEN 13Vd 40
Crow Grn. La. CM15: Pil H 15Wd 40
Crow Grn. Rd. CM15: Pil H 15Vd 40
Crow Hill TN15: Bor G 92Ce 205
Crowhill BR6: Downe 82Qc 180
Crow Hill Rd. TN15: Bor G 92Ce 205
Crowhurst Cl. SW9 . . . . . 54Qb 112
Crowhurst Ho. *SW9* *54Pb 112*
(off Aytoun Rd.)
Crowhurst La. RH7: C'rst 10G 210
RH8: Oxt 10G 210
TN15: Ash, W King 81Wd 184
TN15: Bor G 96Zd 205
CROWHURST LANE END 10F 210
Crowhurst La. End RH7: C'rst 10F 210
RH8: C'rst, Tand 10F 210
Crowhurst Mead RH9: G'stone 2A 210
Crowhurst Rd. TN15: Bor G 93Be 205
Crowhurst Way BR5: St M Cry 71Yc 161
Crowland Av. UB3: Harl 49U 84
Crowland Gdns. N14 . . . . . 17Nb 32
Crowland Ho. *NW8* *39Eb 69*
(off Springfield Rd.)
Crowland Rd. CR7: Thor H 70Tb 135
N15 . . . . . 29Vb 51
CROWLANDS 31Dd 76
Crowlands Av. RM7: Rom 30Dd 56
Crowlands Heath Golf Course 32Dd 76
Crowland Ter. N1 . . . . . 38Tb 71
Crowland Wlk. SM4: Mord 72Db 155
Crow La. RM7: Rush G 31Bd 75
Crowley Cres. CR0: Wadd 78Qb 156
Crowley M. SW16 . . . . . 69Lb 134
Crowline Wlk. N1 . . . . . 37Sb 71
Crowmarsh Gdns. SE23 . . . . . 59Yb 114
Crown, The TN16: Westrm 98Tc 200
Crown All. *SE9* *58Pc 116*
(off Court Yd.)
Crown Apartments HA4: Ruis 32W 64
Crown Arc. KT1: King T 68Ma 131
Crown Ash Hill TN16: Big H 86Kc 179
Crown Ash La. CR6: W'ham 88Jc 179
TN16: Big H 88Jc 179
Crownbourne Ct. *SM1: Sutt* *77Db 155*
(off St Nicholas Way)
Crown Bldgs. E4 . . . . . 18Ec 34
Crown Cl. BR6: Chels 78Wc 161
E3 . . . . . 39Cc 72
IG9: Buck H 18Kc 35
KT12: Walt T 73Y 151
N22 . . . . . 25Qb 50
NW6 . . . . . 37Db 69
NW7 . . . . . 19Va 30
SL3: Coln 52E 104
UB3: Hayes 47V 84
Crown Cl. Bus. Cen. *E3* *39Cc 72*
(off Crown Cl.)
Crown Cotts. RM5: Col R 25Cd 56
SL4: Wind 6H 103

Crown Court—Cygnet Ho. Sth.

Crown Court
Blackfriars 1C 230 (47Rb 91)
Croydon 75Tb 157
Harrow 27Fa 46
Inner London 3D 230 (48Sb 91)
Isleworth 53Ga 108
Kingston upon Thames 69Ma 131
Snaresbrook 29Hc 53
Southwark 6H 225 (46Ub 91)
Wood Green 25Qb 50
Woolwich 47Uc 94
St Albans 2C 6
Crown Ct. EC2 3E 224
N10 24Jb 50
NW8 4E 214
RM18: Tilb 4C 122
SE12 58Kc 115
WC2 3G 223 (44Nb 90)
Crown Crest Ct. TN13: S'oaks 93Ld 203
(off Seal Rd.)
Crown Dale SE19 65Rb 135
(not continuous)
Crowndale Ct. NW1 1D 216
Crowndale Pl. E17 26Ec 52
Crowndale Rd. NW1 1C 216 (40Lb 70)
Crown Dr. RM7: Rush G 30Fd 56
Crownfield Av. IG2: Ilf 30Uc 54
Crownfield Rd. E15 35Fc 73
Crownfields TN13: S'oaks 97Kd 203
Crowngate Ho. E3 40Bc 72
(off Hereford Rd.)
Crown Grn. DA12: Shorne 4N 145
Crown Grn. M. HA9: Wemb 33Na 67
Crown Hill CR0: C'don 75Sb 157
EN9: Walt A 5Nc 22
Crownhill Rd. IG8: Wfd G 24Nc 54
NW10 39Va 68
Crown Ho. KT3: N Mald 69Sa 131
NW10 40Qa 67
Crown La. BR2: Brom 71Mc 159
BR7: Chst 67Sc 138
DA12: Shorne 4N 145
GU25: Vir W 2P 147
N14 18Lb 32
SL2: Farn R 10E 60
SM4: Mord 70Cb 133
SW16 64Qb 134
Crown La. Gdns. SW16 64Qb 134
Crown La. Spur BR2: Brom 72Mc 159
Crown Lodge SW3 6E 226
Crown Mdw. SL3: Coln 52D 104
Crown Mdw. Ct. BR2: Brom 72Nc 160
Crownmead Way RM7: Mawney 28Dd 56
Crown M. E1 43Zb 92
(off White Horse La.)
E13 39Lc 73
TW13: Felt 60X 107
W6 49Wa 88
Crown Mill CR4: Mitc 71Gb 155
Crown Office Row EC4 4K 223 (45Qb 90)
Crown Pde. N14 18Lb 32
SM4: Mord 69Cb 133
Crown Pas. KT1: King T 68Ma 131
(off Church St.)
SW1 7C 222 (46Lb 90)
WD18: Wat 14Y 27
Crown Pl. EC2 7H 219 (43Ub 91)
NW5 37Kb 70
SE16 50Xb 91
Crown Point SE19 65Rb 135
Crown Point Pde. SE19 65Rb 135
(off Crown Dale)
Crown Reach SW1 7E 228 (50Mb 90)
Crown Ri. KT16: Chert 74H 149
WD25: Wat 6Y 13
Crown Rd. BR6: Chels 78Wc 161
CM14: Kel H 11Td 40
EN1: Enf 13Wb 33
GU25: Vir W 2N 147
HA4: Ruis 36Z 65
(not continuous)
IG6: Ilf 28Tc 54
KT3: N Mald 67Sa 131
N10 24Jb 50
RM17: Grays 51Ce 121
SM1: Sutt 77Db 155
SM4: Mord 70Db 133
TN14: S'ham 82Hd 182
TW1: Twick 58Ka 108
WD6: Bore 11Qa 29
Crown Sq. GU21: Wok 89B 168
(off Chertsey Rd.)
Crownstone Ct. SW2 57Qb 112
Crownstone Rd. SW2 57Qb 112
Crown St. CM14: B'wood 19Yd 40
HA2: Harr 32Fa 66
RM10: Dag 37Ed 76
(not continuous)
SE5 52Sb 113
TW20: Egh 63C 126
W3 46Ra 87
Crown Ter. N14 18Mb 32
(off Crown La.)
TW9: Rich 56Pa 109
Crown Trad. Cen. UB3: Hayes 47U 84
Crowntree Cl. TW7: Isle 51Ha 108
Crown Wlk. HA9: Wemb 34Pa 67
HP3: Hem H 6N 3
UB8: Uxb 38L 63
Crown Way UB7: Yiew 46P 83
Crown Wharf E14 46Ec 92
(off Coldharbour)
SE8 50Bc 92
(off Grove St.)
Crown Woods SE18 54Rc 116
Crown Woods Sports Cen. 57Sc 116
Crown Woods Way SE9 57Uc 116
Crown Yd. E2 40Xb 71
SW6 54Cb 111
TW3: Houn 55Ea 108
Crow Piece La. SL2: Farn R 8D 60
Crowshott Av. HA7: Stan 26La 46
Crows Rd. CM16: Epp 2Vc 23
E3 41Fc 93
E15 41Fc 93
IG11: Bark 37Rc 74
Crowstone Rd. RM16: Grays 47Ee 99
Crowther Av. TW8: Bford 49Na 87
Crowther Cl. SW6 51Bb 111
(off Bucklers All.)
Crowther Rd. SE25 71Wb 157
Crowthorne Cl. SW18 59Bb 111
Crowthorne Rd. W10 44Za 88
Croxall Ho. KT12: Walt T 72Y 151
Croxdale Rd. WD6: Bore 12Pa 29
Croxden Cl. HA8: Edg 27Qa 47
Croxden Wlk. SM4: Mord 72Eb 155
Croxford Gdns. N22 24Rb 51
Croxford Way RM7: Rush G 32Fd 76
CROXLEY CENTRE 16T 26
Croxley Cl. BR5: St P 68Xc 139
Croxley Common Moor Local Nature Reserve 17S 26
CROXLEY GREEN 16R 26
Croxley Grn. BR5: St P 67Xc 139
Croxley Green Skate Pk. 14Q 26
Croxleyhall Wood 17Q 26
Croxley Rd. HP3: Hem H 7P 3
W9 41Bb 89
Croxley Vw. WD18: Wat 16U 26
Croxted Cl. SE21 59Sb 113
Croxted M. SE24 58Sb 113
Croxted Rd. SE21 59Sb 113
SE24 59Sb 113
Croxteth Ho. SW8 54Mb 112
Croyde Av. UB3: Harl 49U 84
UB6: G'frd 41Ea 86
Croyde Cl. DA15: Sidc 59Tc 116
CROYDON 75Sb 157
Croydon N17 26Tb 51
(off Gloucester Rd.)
Croydon Airport Ind. Est.
CR0: Wadd 79Pb 156
Croydon Airport Vis. Cen. 79Qb 156
Croydon Clocktower 76Sb 157
(off Katharine St.)
Croydon Crematorium
CR0: C'don 71Pb 156
Croydon Flyover, The
CR0: C'don 77Rb 157
Croydon Gro. CR0: C'don 74Rb 157
Croydon High Sports Club 83Yb 178
Croydon Ho. SE1 1A 230
Croydon La. SM7: Bans 86Eb 175
Croydon La. Sth. SM7: Bans 86Eb 175
Croydon Rd. BR2: Hayes, Kes 76Lc 159
BR3: Beck 71Zb 158
BR4: Hayes, W W'ck 76Gc 159
CR0: Bedd, Wadd 77Kb 156
CR0: C'don 70Jb 134
CR3: Cat'm 95Wb 197
CR4: Mitc 70Jb 134
E13 42Hc 93
RH2: Reig 6K 207
SE20 68Xb 135
SM6: Bedd, Wall 77Kb 156
TN16: Westrm 95Pc 200
TW6: H'row A 54R 106
Croydon Rd. Ind. Est. BR3: Beck 70Zb 136
Croydon Sailing Club 68Vb 135
Croydon Sports Arena 71Yb 158
Croydon Valley Trade Pk.
CR0: Bedd 73Nb 156
(off Therapia La.)
Croyland Rd. N9 18Wb 33
Croylands Dr. KT6: Surb 73Na 153
Crozier Dr. CR2: Sels 82Xb 177
Crozier Ho. SW8 52Pb 112
(off Wilkinson St.)
Crozier Ter. E9 36Zb 72
(not continuous)
Crucible Cl. RM6: Chad H 30Xc 55
Crucifix La. SE1 1H 231 (47Ub 91)
Cruden Ho. E3 40Bc 72
(off Vernon Rd.)
SE17 51Rb 113
(off Brandon Est.)
Cruden Rd. DA12: Grav'nd 2H 145
Cruden St. N1 1C 218 (39Rb 71)
Cruick Av. RM15: S Ock 44Yd 98
Cruikshank Ho. NW8 1D 214
Cruikshank Rd. E15 35Gc 73
Cruikshank St. WC1 3K 217 (41Qb 90)
Crummock Cl. SL1: Slou 4A 80
Crummock Gdns. NW9 29Ua 48
Crumpsall St. SE2 49Yc 95
Crundale Av. NW9 29Qa 47
Crundale Twr. BR5: Orp 74Yc 161
(off Tintagel Rd.)
Crunden Rd. CR2: S Croy 80Tb 157
Crusader Cl. RM19: Purf 49Qd 97
Crusader Ct. DA1: Dart 57Pd 119
Crusader Gdns. CR0: C'don 76Ub 157
Crusader Ind. Est. N4 30Sb 51
Crusader Way WD18: Wat 16V 26
Crushes Cl. CM13: Hut 16Fe 41
Crusoe M. N16 33Tb 71
Crusoe Rd. CR4: Mitc 66Hb 133
DA8: Erith 50Fd 96
Crutched Friars EC3 4J 225 (45Ub 91)
Crutchfield La. KT12: Walt T 75X 151
Crutchley Rd. SE6 61Gc 137
Crypt, The 53Tb 113
Crystal, The 45Jc 93
Crystal Av. RM12: Horn 35Nd 77
Crystal Ct. E8 39Xb 71
SE19 64Vb 135
(off College Rd.)
Crystal Ho. SE18 50Vc 95
CRYSTAL PALACE 65Vb 135
Crystal Palace Athletics Stadium 65Wb 135
Crystal Palace Dinosaurs 65Wb 135
Crystal Palace FC 70Ub 135
Crystal Palace Indoor Bowling Club 67Xb 135
Crystal Palace Mus. 65Vb 135
Crystal Palace National Sports Cen. 64Wb 135
Crystal Palace Pde. SE19 65Vb 135
Crystal Palace Pk. 64Wb 135
Crystal Palace Pk. Farm 65Wb 135
Crystal Palace Pk. Rd. SE26 64Wb 135
Crystal Palace Rd. SE22 55Vb 113
Crystal Palace Sta. Rd. SE19 65Wb 135
Crystal Pl. KT4: Wor Pk 75Xa 154
Crystal Ter. SE19 65Tb 135
Crystal Vw. Ct. BR1: Brom 63Fc 137
Crystal Way HA1: Harr 29Ha 46
RM8: Dag 32Yc 75
Crystal Wharf N1 2C 218 (40Rb 71)
Cuba Dr. EN3: Enf H 12Yb 34
Cuba St. E14 47Cc 92
Cube, The
North East London Gymnastic Club 35Tb 71
Cube Ho. SE16 4K 231 (48Vb 91)
Cubitt Apartments SW11 55Eb 111
(off Chatfield Rd.)
Cubitt Bldg. SW1 50Kb 90
Cubitt Ct. NW1 2B 216
Cubitt Ho. SW4 58Lb 112
Cubitt Sq. UB2: S'hall 46Ea 86
Cubitt Steps E14 46Cc 92
Cubitt St. WC1 4J 217 (41Pb 90)
Cubitt's Yd. WC2 4G 223
Cubitt Ter. SW4 55Lb 112
CUBITT TOWN 49Ec 92
Cubitt Way GU21: Knap 10H 167
Cuckmans Dr. AL2: Chis G 7N 5
Cuckmere Way BR5: Orp 74Zc 161
Cuckoo Av. W7 42Ga 86
Cuckoo Dene W7 43Fa 86
Cuckoo Hall La. N9 17Yb 34
Cuckoo Hall Rd. N9 17Yb 34
Cuckoo Hill
HA5: Eastc, Pinn 27Y 45
Cuckoo Hill Dr. HA5: Pinn 27Y 45
Cuckoo Hill Rd. HA5: Pinn 28Y 45
Cuckoo La. GU24: W End 5B 166
RM16: N Stif 46Be 99
(not continuous)
W7 45Ga 86
Cuckoo Pound TW17: Shep 71U 150
Cuckoo Va. GU24: W End 5B 166
Cuckseys La. RH1: Blet 8K 209
Cucumber La. AL9: Ess 2N 9
SG13: New S 2N 9
Cudas Cl. KT19: Ewe 77Va 154
Cuddington Av. KT4: Wor Pk 76Va 154
Cuddington Ct. SM2: Cheam 81Za 174
Cuddington Glade
KT19: Eps 84Qa 173
Cuddington Golf Course 85Ab 174
Cuddington Pk. Cl. SM7: Bans 85Bb 175
Cuddington Pl. KT20: Tad 92Za 194
Cuddington Way
SM2: Cheam 84Za 174
CUDHAM 87Tc 180
Cudham Cl. SM2: Sutt 82Cb 175
Cudham Dr. CR0: New Ad 82Ec 178
Cudham La. Nth.
BR6: Downe 86Sc 180
TN14: Cud 86Sc 180
Cudham La. Sth.
TN14: Cud, Knock 87Sc 180
Cudham Pk. Rd. TN14: Cud 82Uc 180
Cudham Rd. BR6: Downe 83Qc 180
TN16: Tats 91Nc 200
Cudham St. SE6 59Ec 114
Cudworth Ho. SW8 53Lb 112
Cudworth St. E1 42Xb 91
Cuff Cres. SE9 58Mc 115
CUFFLEY 1Nb 18
Cuffley Av. WD25: Wat 6Z 13
Cuffley Hill EN7: Cuff, G Oak 1Qb 18
Cuffley Ho. W10 43Ya 88
(off Sutton Way)
Cuff Point E2 3K 219
Cugley Rd. DA2: Dart 59Sd 120
Culand Ho. SE17 6H 231
Culcroft DA3: Hartl 69Be 143
Culford Gdns. SW3 6G 227 (49Hb 89)
Culford Gro. N1 37Ub 71
Culford Mans. SW3 6G 227
Culford M. N1 37Ub 71
Culford Rd. N1 38Ub 71
RM16: Grays 47Ee 99
Culford Ter. N1 37Ub 71
(off Balls Pond Rd.)
Culgaith Gdns. EN2: Enf 14Nb 32
Culham Ho. E2 4K 219
W2 43Cb 89
(off Gt. Western Rd.)
Cullen Sq. RM15: S Ock 46Yd 98
Cullen Way NW10 42Sa 87
Cullera Cl. HA6: Nwood 23V 44
Cullerne Cl. KT17: Ewe 82Va 174
Cullesden Rd. CR8: Kenley 87Rb 177
Culling Rd. DA17: Belv 48Ed 96
SE16 48Yb 92
Cullings Ct. EN9: Walt A 5Hc 21
Cullington Cl. HA3: W'stone 28Ja 46
Cullingworth Rd. NW10 36Wa 68
Culloden Cl. SE7 51Kc 115
SE16 50Wb 91
Culloden Ho. SE14 52Ac 114
(off Batavia Rd.)
Culloden Rd. EN2: Enf 12Rb 33
Cullum St. EC3 4H 225 (45Ub 91)
Cullum Welch Ct. N1 3G 219
Cullum Welch Ho. EC1 6D 218
Culmington Pde. W13 46La 86
(off Uxbridge Rd.)
Culmington Rd. CR2: S Croy 81Sb 177
W13 46La 86
Culmore Rd. SE15 52Xb 113
Culmstock Rd. SW11 57Jb 112
Culpeper Cl. IG6: Ilf 23Rc 54
Culpepper Cl. N18 22Xb 51
Culpepper Ct. SE11 5K 229
Culross Cl. N15 28Sb 51
Culross Ho. W10 44Ya 88
(off Bridge Cl.)
Culross St. W1 5H 221 (45Jb 90)
Culsac Rd. KT6: Surb 75Na 153
Culverden Ct. KT13: Weyb 76T 150
(off Oatlands Dr.)
Culverden Rd. SW12 61Lb 134
WD19: Wat 20X 27
Culverden Ter. KT13: Weyb 76T 150
Culver Dr. RH8: Oxt 2J 211
Culver Gro. HA7: Stan 26La 46
Culverhay KT21: Asht 88Na 173
Culverhouse WC1 1H 223
Culverhouse Gdns. SW16 62Pb 134
Culverin Av. RM16: Grays 9B 100
Culverlands Cl. HA7: Stan 21Ka 46
Culverley Rd. SE6 60Dc 114
Culver Rd. AL1: St A 1C 6
Culvers Av. SM5: Cars 75Hb 155
Culvers Ct. DA12: Grav'nd 10H 123
Culvers Retreat SM5: Cars 74Hb 155
Culverstone Cl. BR2: Brom 72Hc 159
Culvers Way SM5: Cars 75Hb 155
Culvert Dr. E3 41Ec 92
Culvert La. UB8: Uxb 40K 63
Culvert Pl. SW11 54Jb 112
Culvert Rd. N15 29Ub 51
(not continuous)
SW11 54Hb 111
Culvey Cl. DA3: Hartl 71Ae 165
Culworth Ho. NW8 1D 214
Culworth St. NW8 2D 214 (40Gb 69)
Culzean Cl. SE27 62Rb 135
Cumberland Av.
DA12: Grav'nd 9E 122
DA16: Well 55Uc 116
GU2: Guild 10L 187
NW10 41Ra 87
RM12: Horn 34Nd 77
SL2: Slou 2G 80
Cumberland Bus. Pk.
NW10 41Ra 87
Cumberland Cl. E8 37Vb 71
HP3: Hem H 6E 4
IG6: Ilf 25Sc 54
KT19: Ewe 82Ua 174
RM12: Horn 34Nd 77
SW20 66Za 132
TW1: Twick 58Ka 108
Cumberland Ct. AL3: St A 1C 6
CR0: C'don 74Tb 157
DA16: Well 54Uc 116
HA1: Harr 27Ga 46
(off Princes Dr.)
SW1 7A 228
TN13: Dun G 92Fd 202
W1 3G 221
Cumberland Cres. W14 49Ab 88
(not continuous)
Cumberland Dr. DA1: Dart 59Pd 119
DA7: Bex 52Ad 117
KT9: Chess 76Na 153
KT10: Hin W 75Ja 152
Cumberland Gdns. NW4 26Ab 48
WC1 3K 217 (41Qb 90)
Cumberland Ga. W1 4F 221 (45Hb 89)
Cumberland Ho. E16 46Jc 93
(off Wesley Av.)
KT2: King T 66Ra 131
N9 18Yb 34
(off Cumberland Rd.)
SE28 47Sc 94
W8 47Db 89
(off Kensington Ct.)
Cumberland Mans. W1 2F 221
Cumberland Mkt. NW1 3A 216 (41Kb 90)
Cumberland M. SE11 7A 230 (50Qb 90)
Cumberland Mills Sq. E14 50Fc 93
Cumberland Obelisk 6K 125
Cumberland Pk. NW10 45Sa 87
Cumberland Pk. Ind. Est. NW10 41Wa 88
Cumberland Pl. NW1 3K 215 (41Kb 90)
SE6 60Hc 115
TW16: Sun 70W 128
Cumberland Rd. BR2: Brom 70Gc 137
E12 35Mc 73
E13 43Kc 93
E17 26Ac 52
HA1: Harr 29Da 45
HA7: Stan 27Pa 47
N9 18Yb 34
N22 26Pb 50
RM16: Chaf H 47Ae 99
SE25 72Xb 157
SW13 53Va 110
TW9: Kew 52Qa 109
TW15: Ashf 62M 127
W3 45Sa 87
W7 47Ha 86
Cumberlands CR8: Kenley 87Tb 177
Cumberland St. SW1 7A 228 (50Kb 90)
TW18: Staines 64F 126
Cumberland Ter. NW1 2K 215 (40Kb 70)
Cumberland Ter. M. NW1 2K 215
(not continuous)
Cumberland Vs. W3 45Sa 87
(off Cumberland Rd.)
Cumberland Wharf SE16 47Yb 92
(off Rotherhithe St.)
Cumberlow Av. SE25 69Vb 135
Cumberlow Pl. HP2: Hem H 3C 4
Cumbernauld Gdns. TW16: Sun 64V 128
Cumberton Rd. N17 25Tb 51
Cumbrae Cl. SL2: Slou 6L 81
Cumbrae Gdns. KT6: Surb 75Ma 153
Cumbria Ct. RH2: Reig 5M 207
Cumbrian Av. DA7: Bex 54Gd 118
Cumbrian Gdns. NW2 33Za 68
Cumbrian Way UB8: Uxb 38M 63
Cummings Hall La. RM3: Rom 20Ld 39
Cumming St. N1 2J 217 (40Pb 70)
Cumnor Cl. SW9 54Pb 112
(off Robsart St.)
Cumnor Gdns. KT17: Ewe 79Wa 154
Cumnor Ri. CR8: Kenley 89Sb 177
Cumnor Rd. SM2: Sutt 79Eb 155
Cunard Ct. HA7: Stan 19Ja 28
(off Brightwen Gro.)
Cunard Cres. N21 16Tb 33
Cunard Pl. EC3 3J 225 (44Ub 91)
Cunard Rd. NW10 41Ta 87
Cunard Wlk. SE16 49Zb 92
Cundy Rd. E16 44Lc 93
Cundy St. SW1 6J 227 (49Jb 90)
Cunio M. NW7 22Ab 48
Cunliffe Cl. KT18: Head 96Ra 193
Cunliffe Pde. KT19: Ewe 77Va 154
Cunliffe Rd. KT19: Ewe 77Va 154
Cunliffe St. SW16 65Lb 134
Cunningham Av. AL1: St A 4D 6
EN3: Enf W 8Ac 20
Cunningham Cl. BR4: W W'ck 75Dc 158
RM6: Chad H 29Yc 55
Cunningham Ct. E10 34Dc 72
(off Oliver Rd.)
W9 6A 214
Cunningham Hill Rd. AL1: St A 4D 6
Cunningham Ho. SE5 52Tb 113
(off Elmington Est.)
Cunningham Pk. HA1: Harr 29Ea 46
Cunningham Pl. NW8 5B 214 (42Fb 89)
Cunningham Rd. N15 28Wb 51
SM7: Bans 87Fb 175
Cunningham Way WD25: Wat 5V 12
Cunnington St. W4 48Sa 87
Cupar Rd. SW11 53Jb 112
Cupola Cl. BR1: Brom 64Kc 137
Curates Wlk. DA2: Wilm 62Md 141
Curchin Cl. TN16: Big H 84Lc 179
Cureton St. SW1 6E 228 (49Mb 90)
Curfew Bell Rd. KT16: Chert 73H 149
Curfew Ho. IG11: Bark 39Sc 74
Curfew Tower, The 39Sc 74
Curfew Yd. SL4: Wind 3H 103
Curie Ct. HA1: Harr 31Ka 66
Curie Gdns. NW9 26Ua 48
Curlew Cl. CR2: Sels 83Zb 178
SE28 45Zc 95
Curlew Ct. KT6: Surb 76Qa 153
W13 42Ha 86
Curlew Ho. EN3: Pond E 15Zb 34
SE4 56Ac 114
(off St Norbert Rd.)
SE15 53Vb 113
Curlews, The DA12: Grav'nd 1F 144
Curlew St. SE1 1K 231 (47Vb 91)
Curlew Way UB4: Yead 43Z 85
Curling Cl. CR5: Coul 92Pb 196
Curling La. RM17: Grays 50Be 99
Curness St. SE13 56Ec 114
Curnick's La. SE27 63Sb 135
Curo Pk. AL2: F'mre 9C 6
Curran Av. DA15: Sidc 57Vc 117
SM6: Wall 76Jb 156
Curran Cl. UB8: Cowl 42L 83
Curran Ho. SW3 6D 226
Currey Rd. UB6: G'frd 37Fa 66
Curricle St. W3 46Ua 88
Currie Hill Cl. SW19 63Bb 133
Curriers La. SL1: Burn 6B 60
Curry Ri. NW7 23Za 48
Cursitor St. EC4 2K 223 (44Qb 90)
Curtain Pl. EC2 5J 219 (41Ub 91)
Curtain Rd. EC2 4J 219 (42Ub 91)
Curthwaite Gdns. EN2: Enf 14Mb 32
Curtis Cl. WD3: Rick 18J 25
Curtis Dr. W3 44Ta 87
Curtis Fld. Rd. SW16 63Pb 134
Curtis Ho. SE17 7F 231
Curtis La. HA0: Wemb 37Na 67
Curtismill Cl. BR5: St P 69Xc 139
CURTISMILL GREEN 13Hd 38
Curtis Mill La. RM4: Nave 14Gd 38
Curtismill Way BR5: St P 69Xc 139
Curtis Rd. HP3: Hem H 3D 4
KT19: Ewe 77Sa 153
RM11: Horn 32Pd 77
TW4: Houn 59Ba 107
Curtiss Dr. WD25: Wat 6V 12
Curtiss Ho. NW9 27Va 48
Curtis St. SE1 5K 231 (49Vb 91)
Curtis Way HP4: Berk 2A 2
SE1 5K 231 (49Vb 91)
SE28 45Xc 95
Curtlington Ho. HA8: Edg 26Sa 47
(off Burnt Oak B'way.)
Curvan Cl. KT17: Ewe 82Va 174
Curve, The W12 45Wa 88
Curwen Av. E7 35Kc 73
Curwen Rd. W12 47Wa 88
Curzon Av. EN3: Pond E 15Zb 34
HA7: Stan 25Ja 46
Curzon Cinema
Bloomsbury 6G 217 (42Nb 90)
Mayfair 7K 221
Richmond 57Ma 109
Soho 4E 222
Curzon Cl. BR6: Orp 77Tc 160
KT13: Weyb 77Q 150
Curzon Ct. SW6 53Eb 111
(off Imperial Rd.)
Curzon Cres. IG11: Bark 40Vc 75
NW10 38Ua 68
Curzon Dr. RM17: Grays 52Ee 121
Curzon Ga. W1 7J 221 (46Jb 90)
Curzon Ga. Ct. WD17: Wat 11W 26
Curzon Mall SL1: Slou 7K 81
(within Queensmere Shop. Cen.)
Curzon Pl. HA5: Eastc 29Y 45
Curzon Rd. CR7: Thor H 72Qb 156
KT13: Weyb 78Q 150
N10 26Kb 50
W5 42Ka 86
Curzon Sq. W1 7J 221 (46Jb 90)
Curzon St. W1 7J 221 (46Jb 90)
Cusack Cl. TW1: Tedd 63Ha 130
Cussans Ho. WD18: Wat 16U 26
Cussons Cl. EN7: Chesh 1Wb 19
Custance Ho. N1 2F 219
Custance St. N1 3F 219 (41Tb 91)
CUSTOM HOUSE 44Lc 93
Custom Ho. EC3 5H 225 (45Ub 91)
Custom Ho. Reach SE16 47Bc 92
Custom Ho. Wlk. EC3 5H 225 (45Ub 91)
Cut, The SE1 1A 230 (47Qb 90)
SL2: Slou 2E 80
Cutbush Ho. N7 36Mb 70
Cutcombe Rd. SE5 54Sb 113
Cuthberga Cl. IG11: Bark 38Sc 74
Cuthbert Bell Twr. E3 40Cc 72
(off Pancras Way)
Cuthbert Ct. CR3: W'ham 91Wb 197
(off Godstone Rd.)
Cuthbert Gdns. SE25 69Ub 135
Cuthbert Harrowing Ho. EC1 6D 218
Cuthbert Ho. W2 7B 214
Cuthbert Rd. CR0: C'don 75Rb 157
E17 27Ec 52
N18 22Wb 51
Cuthberts Cl. EN7: Chesh 1Vb 19
Cuthbert St. W2 6B 214 (43Fb 89)
Cuthered M. CR5: Coul 89Lb 176
Cuthill Wlk. SE5 53Tb 113
Cutlers Gdns. EC2 1J 225 (43Ub 91)
Cutlers Gdns. Arc. EC2 2J 225
Cutlers Sq. E14 49Cc 92
Cutlers Ter. N1 37Ub 71
(off Balls Pond Rd.)
Cutler St. E1 2J 225 (44Ub 91)
Cutmore Dr. AL4: Col H 4M 7
Cutmore St. DA11: Grav'nd 9D 122
Cutter Ho. DA8: Erith 49Gd 96
Cutter La. SE10 47Gc 93
Cutthroat All. TW10: Ham 61La 130
Cutting, The RH1: Redh 8P 207
Cuttsfield Ter. HP1: Hem H 3H 3
Cutty Sark 51Ec 114
Cutty Sark Gdns. SE10 51Ec 114
(off King William Wlk.)
Cutty Sark Hall SE10 51Ec 114
(off Welland St.)
Cuxton BR5: Pet W 71Sc 160
Cuxton Cl. DA6: Bex 57Ad 117
Cuxton Ho. SE17 7J 231
Cyan Apartments E3 39Ac 72
(off Gunmaker's La.)
Cyclamen Cl. TW12: Hamp 65Ca 129
Cyclamen Rd. BR8: Swan 70Fd 140
Cyclamen Way KT19: Ewe 78Sa 153
Cyclopark 3B 144
Cyclops M. E14 49Cc 92
Cygnus Ct. CR8: Purl 83Rb 177
(off Brighton Rd.)
Cygnet Av. TW14: Felt 59Y 107
Cygnet Cl. BR5: St P 69Wc 139
GU21: Wok 8M 167
HA6: Nwood 23S 44
NW10 36Ta 67
WD6: Bore 11Sa 29
Cygnet Gdns. DA11: Nflt 1B 144
Cygnet Ho. DA12: Grav'nd 9D 122
(off Windmill St.)
SE15 51Wb 113
SW3 7E 226
Cygnet Ho. Nth. E14 44Dc 92
(off Chrisp St.)
Cygnet Ho. Sth. E14 44Dc 92
(off Chrisp St.)

Cygnet Leisure Cen.—Dartford By-Pass

Cygnet Leisure Cen. 1A 144
Cygnets, The TW13: Hanw 63Aa 129
TW18: Staines 64H 127
Cygnets Cl. RH1: Redh 4A 208
Cygnet St. E1 5K 219 (42Vb 91)
Cygnet Vw. RM20: W Thur 49Vd 98
Cygnet Way UB4: Yead 43Z 85
Cygnus Bus. Cen. NW10 36Va 68
Cymbeline Ct. AL3: St A 1A 6
(off The Lawns)
HA1: Harr 30Ha 46
Cynthia St. N1 2J 217 (40Pb 70)
Cyntra Pl. E8 38Xb 71
Cypress Av. EN2: Crew H 7Qb 18
TW2: Whitt 59Ea 108
Cypress Cl. E5 33Wb 71
EN9: Walt A 6Fc 21
KT19: Eps 81Ta 173
Cypress Ct. E15 35Fc 73
(off Langthorne Rd.)
GU25: Vir W 70A 126
NW9 28Qa 47
(off Alpine Rd.)
SM1: Sutt 78Cb 155
Cypress Gdns. SE4 57Ac 114
Cypress Gro. IG6: Ilf 23Uc 54
Cypress Ho. SE14 53Zb 114
SE16 47Zb 92
(off Woodland Cres.)
SL3: L'ly 50D 82
Cypress Path RM3: Rom 24Md 57
Cypress Pl. W1 6C 216 (42Lb 90)
Cypress Rd. HA3: Hrw W 26Fa 46
SE25 68Ub 135
Cypress Tree Cl. DA15: Sidc 60Vc 117
Cypress Wlk. TW20: Eng G 5M 125
WD25: Wat 7X 13
Cypress Way SM7: Bans 86Za 174
CYPRUS 45Qc 94
Cyprus Av. N3 26Ab 48
Cyprus Cl. N4 30Rb 51
Cyprus Gdns. N3 26Ab 48
Cyprus Pl. E2 40Yb 72
E6 45Qc 94
Cyprus Rd. N3 26Bb 49
N9 19Vb 33
Cyprus St. E2 40Yb 72
(not continuous)
Cyrena Rd. SE22 58Vb 113
Cyril Dumpleton Ho. AL2: Lon C 8H 7
Cyril Lodge DA14: Sidc 63Wc 139
Cyril Mans. SW11 53Hb 111
Cyril Rd. BR6: Orp 73Wc 161
DA7: Bex 54Ad 117
Cyrils Way AL1: St A 5B 6
Cyrus Ho. EC1 5C 218
Cyrus St. EC1 5C 218
Cyrus Ter. UB10: Ick 34S 64
(off Pentland Way)
Czar St. SE8 51Cc 114

D

Dabbling Cl. DA8: Erith 52Kd 119
Dabbs Hill La. UB5: N'olt 37Ba 65
(not continuous)
Dabbs La. EC1 6A 218
Dabbs Pl. DA13: Cobh 8F 144
D'Abernon Chase KT22: Oxs 86Ja 172
D'Abernon Cl. KT10: Esh 77Ca 151
D'Abernon Dr. KT11: Stoke D 88Aa 171
Dabin Cres. SE10 53Ec 114
Dacca St. SE8 51Bc 114
Dace Rd. E3 39Cc 72
Dacorum Way HP1: Hem H 2L 3
(not continuous)
Dacre Av. IG5: Ilf 26Qc 54
RM15: Avel 46Td 98
Dacre Cl. CR5: Chip 90Hb 175
IG7: Chig 21Sc 54
UB6: G'frd 40Da 65
Dacre Cres. RM15: Avel 46Td 98
Dacre Gdns. IG7: Chig 21Sc 54
SE13 56Gc 115
WD6: Bore 15Ta 29
Dacre Ho. SW3 51Fb 111
(off Beaufort St.)
Dacre Ind. Est. EN8: Chesh 1Bc 20
Dacre Pk. SE13 55Gc 115
Dacre Pl. SE13 55Gc 115
Dacre Rd. CR0: C'don 73Nb 156
E11 32Hc 73
E13 39Kc 73
Dacres Cl. EN7: Chesh 1Vb 19
Dacres Est. SE23 62Zb 136
Dacres Ho. SW4 55Kb 112
Dacres Rd. SE23 61Zb 136
Dacre St. SW1 3D 228 (48Mb 90)
Dade Way UB2: S'hall 50Ba 85
Daerwood Cl. BR2: Brom 74Pc 160
Daffodil Av. CM15: Pil H 15Xd 40
Daffodil Cl. CR0: C'don 74Zb 158
Daffodil Dr. GU24: Bisl 8E 166
Daffodil Gdns. IG1: Ilf 36Rc 74
Daffodil Pl. TW12: Hamp 65Ca 129
Daffodil St. W12 45Va 88
Dafforne Rd. SW17 62Jb 134
Da Gama Pl. E14 50Cc 92
DAGENHAM 37Cd 76
Dagenham & Redbridge FC 36Dd 76
Dagenham Av. RM9: Dag 39Ad 75
(not continuous)
Dagenham Bowl 39Ad 75
Dagenham Leisure Pk. 39Zc 75
Dagenham Pk. Leisure Cen. 38Cd 76
Dagenham Rd. E10 32Bc 72
RM7: Rush G 31Fd 76
RM10: Dag 35Ed 76
RM13: Rain 38Fd 76
Dagger La. WD6: E'tree 16Ja 28
Daggsdell Rd. HP1: Hem H 1G 2
Dagmar Av. HA9: Wemb 35Pa 67
Dagmar Ct. E14 48Ec 92
Dagmar Gdns. NW10 40Za 68
Dagmar M. UB2: S'hall 48Aa 85
(off Dagmar Rd.)
Dagmar Pas. N1 39Rb 71
(off Cross St.)
Dagmar Rd. KT2: King T 67Pa 131
N4 31Qb 70
N15 28Tb 51
N22 25Mb 50
RM10: Dag 38Ed 76
SE5 53Ub 113
SE25 71Ub 157
SL4: Wind 4H 103
UB2: S'hall 48Aa 85
Dagmar Ter. N1 39Rb 71
Dagnall Cres. UB8: Cowl 43L 83
Dagnall Pk. SE25 72Ub 157
Dagnall Rd. SE25 71Ub 157
Dagnall St. SW11 54Hb 111
Dagnam Pk. Cl. RM3: Rom 22Qd 57
Dagnam Pk. Dr. RM3: Rom 22Nd 57
Dagnam Pk. Gdns. RM3: Rom 23Qd 57
Dagnam Pk. Sq. RM3: Rom 23Rd 57
Dagnan Rd. SW12 59Kb 112
Dagobert Ho. E1 43Yb 92
(off Smithy St.)
Dagonet Gdns. BR1: Brom 62Jc 137
Dagonet Rd. BR1: Brom 62Jc 137
Dahlia Dr. BR8: Swan 68Hd 140
Dahlia Gdns. CR4: Mitc 70Mb 134
IG1: Ilf 37Rc 74
Dahlia Rd. SE2 49Xc 95
Dahomey Rd. SW16 65Lb 134
Daiglen Dr. RM15: S Ock 42Xd 98
Daimler Ho. E3 42Cc 92
(off Wellington Way)
Daimler Way SM6: Wall 80Nb 156
Dain Ct. W8 49Cb 89
(off Lexham Gdns.)
Daines Cl. E12 34Pc 74
RM15: S Ock 42Wd 98
Dainford Cl. BR1: Brom 64Fc 137
Dainton Cl. BR1: Brom 67Kc 137
Dainton Ho. W2 43Cb 89
(off Gt. Western Rd.)
Daintry Cl. HA3: W'stone 28Ja 46
Daintry Lodge HA6: Nwood 23V 44
Daintry Way E9 37Bc 72
Dairsie Ct. BR1: Brom 67Lc 137
Dairsie Rd. SE9 55Qc 116
Dairy Bus. Pk. RH1: Blet 3J 209
Dairy Cl. BR1: Brom 66Kc 137
CR7: Thor H 68Sb 135
DA4: Sut H 66Rd 141
EN3: Enf W 9Yb 20
NW10 39Wa 68
SW6 53Cb 111
UB6: G'frd 40Fa 66
Dairy Cotts. TN15: Fair 84Fe 185
Dairy Farm La. UB9: Hare 26L 43
Dairyglen Av. EN8: Chesh 3Ac 20
Dairy La. SE18 49Pc 94
Dairyman Cl. NW2 34Za 68
Dairyman's Wlk. GU4: Burp 100D 188
Dairy M. GU20: W'sham 9B 146
N2 28Gb 49
RM6: Chad H 31Zc 75
SW9 55Nb 112
WD18: Wat 15W 26
Dairy Wlk. SW19 63Ab 132
Dairy Way WD5: Ab L 1V 12
Daisy Cl. CR0: C'don 74Zb 158
NW9 33Sa 67
Daisy Dobbings Wlk. N19 31Nb 70
(off Jessie Blythe La.)
Daisy La. SW6 55Cb 111
Daisy Mdw. TW20: Egh 64C 126
Daisy Rd. E16 42Gc 93
E18 26Kc 53
Dakin Pl. E1 43Ac 92
Dakota Bldg. SE13 53Dc 114
(off Deal's Gateway)
Dakota Cl. SM6: Wall 80Pb 156
Dakota Gdns. E6 42Nc 94
UB5: N'olt 41Aa 85
Dakota Ho. CR7: Thor H 72Rb 157
Dalberg Rd. SW2 56Qb 112
(not continuous)
Dalberg Way SE2 48Zc 95
Dalby Rd. SW18 56Eb 111
Dalbys Cres. N17 23Ub 51
Dalby St. NW5 37Kb 70
Dalcross Rd. TW4: Houn 54Aa 107
Dale, The BR2: Kes 77Mc 159
EN9: Walt A 6Gc 21
Dale Av. HA8: Edg 25Pa 47
TW4: Houn 55Aa 107
Dalebury Pl. TW5: Hest 50Ca 85
Dalebury Rd. SW17 61Hb 133
Dale Cl. DA1: Cray 58Hd 118
E4 20Ec 34
EN5: New Bar 16Db 31
HA5: Pinn 25X 45
KT15: Add 78K 149
KT23: Bookh 97Ea 192
RM15: S Ock 44Wd 98
SE3 55Jc 115
SL5: S'dale 1E 146
Dale Ct. EN2: Enf 11Sb 33
KT2: King T 66Pa 131
(off York Rd.)
SL1: Slou 7G 80
WD25: Wat 5W 12
Dale Dr. UB4: Hayes 42V 84
Dale End DA1: Cray 58Hd 118
Dalefield IG9: Buck H 18Lc 35
(off Roebuck La.)
Dalefield Way DA12: Grav'nd 9H 123
Dale Gdns. IG8: Wfd G 21Kc 53
Dalegarth Gdns. CR8: Purl 85Tb 177
Dale Grn. Rd. N11 20Kb 32
Dale Gro. N12 22Eb 49
Daleham Av. TW20: Egh 65C 126
Daleham Dr. UB8: Hil 44R 84
Daleham Gdns. NW3 36Fb 69
Daleham M. NW3 37Fb 69
Dalehead NW1 2B 216
Dale Ho. N1 39Ub 71
(off Halcomb St.)
NW8 39Eb 69
(off Boundary Rd.)
SE4 56Ac 114
Dale Lodge N6 30Lb 50
Dale Lodge Rd. SL5: S'dale 1E 146
Dalemain M. E16 46Jc 93
Dale Pk. Av. SM5: Cars 75Hb 155
Dale Pk. Rd. SE19 67Sb 135
Dale Rd. BR8: Swan 68Ed 140
CR8: Purl 84Qb 176
DA1: Cray 58Hd 118
DA13: Sflt 63Ce 143
KT12: Walt T 73V 150
NW5 36Jb 70
SE17 51Rb 113
SM1: Sutt 77Bb 155
TW16: Sun 66V 128
UB6: G'frd 43Da 85
Dale Row W11 44Ab 88
Dale Side SL9: Ger X 32A 62
Daleside BR6: Chels 78Wc 161
Daleside Cl. BR6: Chels 79Wc 161
Daleside Dr. EN6: Pot B 5Bb 17
Daleside Gdns. IG7: Chig 20Sc 36
Daleside Rd. KT19: Ewe 79Ta 153
SW16 64Kb 134
Dales Path WD6: Bore 15Ta 29
Dales Rd. WD6: Bore 15Ta 29
Dalestone M. RM3: Rom 23Kd 57
Dale St. DA1: Dart 57Pd 119
W4 50Ua 88
Dale Vw. DA8: Erith 54Hd 118
GU21: Wok 10M 167
KT18: Head 95Ra 193
Dale Vw. Av. E4 19Ec 34
Dale Vw. Cres. E4 19Ec 34
Dale Vw. Gdns. E4 20Fc 35
Daleview Rd. N15 30Ub 51
Dale Wlk. DA2: Dart 60Sd 120
Dalewood Cl. RM11: Horn 31Pd 77
Dalewood Gdns.
KT4: Wor Pk 75Xa 154
Dale Wood Rd. BR6: Orp 73Uc 160
Daleworth Cl. BR3: Beck 65Cc 136
Daley Ho. W12 44Xa 88
Daley St. E9 37Zb 72
Daley Thompson Way SW8 54Kb 112
Dalgarno Gdns. W10 43Ya 88
Dalgarno Way W10 42Ya 88
Dalgleish St. E14 44Ac 92
Daling Way E3 39Ac 72
Dalkeith Ct. SW1 6E 228
Dalkeith Gro. HA7: Stan 22Ma 47
Dalkeith Ho. SW9 53Rb 113
(off Lothian Rd.)
Dalkeith Rd. IG1: Ilf 34Sc 74
SE21 60Sb 113
Dallas Rd. NW4 31Wa 68
SE26 62Xb 135
SM3: Cheam 79Ab 154
W5 43Pa 87
Dallas Ter. UB3: Harl 48V 84
Dallega Cl. UB3: Hayes 45T 84
Dallinger Rd. SE12 58Hc 115
Dalling Rd. W6 49Xa 88
Dallington Cl. KT12: Hers 79Y 151
Dallington Sq. EC1 5C 218
(off Dallington St.)
Dallington St. EC1 5C 218 (42Rb 91)
Dallin Rd. DA6: Bex 56Zc 117
SE18 52Rc 116
Dalmain Rd. SE23 60Zb 114
Dalmally Rd. CR0: C'don 73Vb 157
Dalmany Pas. CR0: C'don 73Vb 157
Dalmeny Av. N7 35Mb 70
SW16 68Qb 134
Dalmeny Cl. HA0: Wemb 37La 66
Dalmeny Cres. TW3: Houn 56Fa 108
Dalmeny Rd. DA8: Erith 53Dd 118
EN5: New Bar 16Eb 31
KT4: Wor Pk 76Xa 154
N7 34Mb 70
(not continuous)
SM5: Cars 80Jb 156
Dalmeny Way KT18: Eps 86Sa 173
Dalmeyer Rd. NW10 37Va 68
Dalmore Av. KT10: Clay 79Ha 152
Dalmore Rd. SE21 61Sb 135
Dalo Lodge E3 43Cc 92
(off Gale St.)
Dalroy Cl. RM15: S Ock 44Wd 98
Dalrymple Cl. N14 17Mb 32
Dalrymple Rd. SE4 56Ac 114
DALSTON 37Vb 71
Dalston Gdns. HA7: Stan 25Na 47
Dalston La. E8 37Vb 71
Dalston Sq. E8 37Vb 71
(not continuous)
Dalton Av. CR4: Mitc 68Gb 133
Dalton Cl. BR6: Orp 76Uc 160
CR8: Purl 84Sb 177
UB4: Hayes 42T 84
Dalton Grn. SL3: L'ly 51B 104
Dalton Ho. E3 40Ac 72
(off Ford St.)
HA7: Stan 22Ja 46
SE14 51Zb 114
(off John Williams Cl.)
SW1 7K 227
Dalton Rd. HA3: W'stone 26Fa 46
Daltons Rd. BR6: Well H 76Dd 162
BR8: Crock 76Dd 162
Daltons Shaw RM16: Ors 3C 100
Dalton St. AL3: St A 1B 6
SE27 62Rb 135
Daltons Wharf HP4: Berk 1A 2
Dalton Way WD17: Wat 15Z 27
Dalwood St. SE5 53Ub 113
Daly Dr. BR1: Brom 69Qc 138
Dalyell Rd. SW9 55Pb 112
Damascene Wlk. SE21 60Sb 113
Damask Cl. GU24: W End 5C 166
Damask Ct. SM1: Sutt 74Db 155
Damask Cres. E16 42Gc 93
Damask Grn. HP1: Hem H 3G 2
Damer Ter. SW10 52Eb 111
Dames Rd. E7 34Jc 73
Dame St. N1 1D 218 (40Sb 71)
Damien Ct. E1 44Xb 91
(off Damien St.)
Damien St. E1 44Xb 91
Damigos Rd. DA12: Grav'nd 10H 123
Damon Cl. DA14: Sidc 62Xc 139
Damory Ho. SE16 49Xb 91
(off Abbeyfield Est.)
Damsel Ho. SE4 55Ac 114
(off Dragonfly Pl.)
Damson Cl. WD24: Wat 9W 12
Damson Ct. BR8: Swan 70Fd 140
Damson Dr. UB3: Hayes 45W 84
Damson Gro. SL1: Slou 7G 80
Damson Way AL4: St A 1G 6
SM5: Cars 81Hb 175
Damsonwood Rd. UB2: S'hall 48Ca 85
Danbrook Rd. SW16 67Nb 134
Danbury Cl. CM15: Pil H 15Vd 40
RM6: Chad H 27Zc 55
Danbury Cres. RM15: S Ock 44Wd 98
Danbury Mans. IG11: Bark 38Rc 74
(off Whiting Av.)
Danbury M. SM6: Wall 77Kb 156
Danbury Rd. IG10: Lough 17Nc 36
RM13: Rain 39Hd 76
Danbury St. N1 1C 218 (40Rb 71)
Danbury Way IG8: Wfd G 23Lc 53
Danby Ct. EN2: Enf 13Sb 33
Danby Ho. E9 38Yb 72
(off Frampton Pk. Rd.)
W10 41Ab 88
(off Bruckner St.)
Danby St. SE15 55Vb 113
Dance Ho. SE4 57Zb 114
(off St Norbert Rd.)
Dancer Rd. SW6 53Bb 111
TW9: Rich 55Qa 109
DANCERS HILL 8Za 16
Dancers Hill Rd. EN5: Barn 8Ya 16
Dancers La. EN5: Barn 7Ya 16
Dancers Way SE8 51Dc 114
Dance Sq. EC1 4D 218 (41Sb 91)
Dan Ct. NW10 41Qa 87
Dandelion Cl. RM7: Rush G 33Gd 76
Dandelion Pl. RM3: Rom 24Md 57
Dandridge Cl. SE10 50Hc 93
SL3: L'ly 9P 81
Dandridge Ho. E1 7K 219
Danebury CR0: New Ad 79Ec 158
Danebury Av. SW15 58Ua 110
Daneby Rd. SE6 62Dc 136
Dane Cl. BR6: Farnb 78Tc 160
DA5: Bexl 59Cd 118
Dane Ct. GU22: Pyr 87H 169
Danecourt Gdns. CR0: C'don 76Vb 157
Danecroft Rd. SE24 57Sb 113
Danehill Wlk. DA14: Sidc 62Wc 139
DANEHOLES RDBT. 48Fe 99
Danehurst TW8: Bford 52La 108
Danehurst Cl. TW20: Egh 65A 126
Danehurst Ct. KT17: Eps 85Va 174
Danehurst Gdns. IG4: Ilf 29Nc 54
Danehurst St. SW6 53Ab 110
Daneland EN4: E Barn 16Hb 31
Daneland Wlk. N17 27Xb 51
Danemead Gro. UB5: N'olt 36Da 65
Danemere St. SW15 55Ya 110
Dane Pl. E3 40Ac 72
Dane Rd. CR6: W'ham 89Zb 178
IG1: Ilf 36Sc 74
N18 20Yb 34
SW19 67Eb 133
TN14: Otf 89Hd 182
TW15: Ashf 65S 128
UB1: S'hall 45Aa 85
W13 46La 86
Danes, The AL2: Park 10A 6
Danesbury Rd. TW13: Felt 60X 107
Danes Cl. DA11: Nflt 62Ee 143
KT22: Oxs 86Ea 172
Danescombe SE12 60Jc 115
Danes Ct. HA9: Wemb 34Ra 67
NW8 1F 215
Danescourt Cres. SM1: Sutt 75Eb 155
Danescroft NW4 29Za 48
Danescroft Av. NW4 29Za 48
Danescroft Gdns. NW4 29Za 48
Danesdale Rd. E9 37Ac 72
Danesfield GU23: Rip, Send 95H 189
SE5 51Ub 113
(off Albany Rd.)
Danesfield Cl. KT12: Walt T 76X 151
Danes Ga. HA1: Harr 27Ga 46
Danes Hill GU22: Wok 90C 168
Daneshill RH1: Redh 5N 207
Daneshill Cl. RH1: Redh 5N 207
Danes Hill School Dr. KT22: Oxs 86Ea 172
Danes Ho. W10 43Ya 88
(off Sutton Way)
Danesmead KT11: Cobh 83Ca 171
Danes Rd. RM7: Rush G 31Ed 76
Dane St. WC1 1H 223 (43Pb 90)
Danes Way CM15: Pil H 15Wd 40
KT22: Oxs 86Fa 172
Daneswood Av. SE6 62Ec 136
Daneswood Cl. KT13: Weyb 78R 150
Danethorpe Rd. HA0: Wemb 37Ma 67
Danetree Cl. KT19: Ewe 80Sa 153
Danetree Rd. KT19: Ewe 80Sa 153
Danette Gdns. RM10: Dag 33Cd 76
Daneville Rd. SE5 53Tb 113
Danewood Dr. N2 31Fb 69
Dangan Rd. E11 30Jc 53
Daniel Bolt Cl. E14 43Dc 92
Daniel Cl. N18 21Yb 52
RM16: Chaf H 47Ae 99
RM16: Grays 8D 100
SW17 65Gb 133
TW4: Houn 59Ba 107
Daniel Ct. NW9 25Ua 48
Daniel Gdns. SE15 52Vb 113
Daniel Lambert Mill KT15: Add 78N 149
(off Bourneside Rd.)
Daniell Ho. N1 1G 219
Daniell Way CR0: Wadd 74Nb 156
Daniel Pl. NW4 31Xa 68
Daniel Rd. W5 45Pa 87
Daniels La. CR6: W'ham 88Bc 178
Daniels Rd. SE15 55Yb 114
Daniel Way SM7: Bans 86Db 175
Danleigh Ct. N14 17Mb 32
Dan Leno Wlk. SW6 52Db 111
Dan Mason Dr. W4 54Sa 109
Danny Fiszman Bri. N5 35Qb 70
N7 35Qb 70
Dansey Pl. W1 4D 222
Dansington Rd. DA16: Well 56Wc 117
Danson Cres. DA16: Well 55Xc 117
Danson House 56Yc 117
DANSON INTERCHANGE 57Zc 117
Danson La. DA16: Well 56Xc 117
Danson Mead DA16: Well 55Yc 117
Danson Pk. 57Yc 117
Danson Pk. Watersports Cen. 56Yc 117
Danson Rd. DA5: Bexl, Bex 57Yc 117
DA6: Bex 57Zc 117
SE17 7C 230 (50Rb 91)
Danson Underpass DA15: Sidc 58Yc 117
Dante Pl. SE11 6C 230 (49Rb 91)
Dante Rd. SE11 5B 230 (49Rb 91)
Danube Apartments N8 27Pb 50
(off Gt. Amwell La.)
Danube Cl. N9 20Yb 34
Danube Ct. SE15 52Vb 113
(off Daniel Gdns.)
Danube St. SW3 7E 226 (50Gb 89)
Danvers Av. SW11 56Gb 111
Danvers Ho. E1 44Wb 91
(off Christian St.)
Danvers Rd. N8 28Mb 50
Danvers St. SW3 51Fb 111
Danvers Way CR3: Cat'm 95Sb 197
Danyon Cl. RM13: Rain 40Ld 77
Danziger Way WD6: Bore 11Sa 29
Dao Ct. E13 39Kc 73
Da Palma Ct. SW6 51Cb 111
(off Anselm Rd.)
Daphne Ct. KT4: Wor Pk 75Ua 154
Daphne Gdns. E4 20Ec 34
Daphne Ho. N22 25Qb 50
(off Acacia Rd.)
Daphne St. SW18 58Eb 111
Daplyn St. E1 43Wb 91
Darbishire Pl. E1 45Wb 91
(off John Fisher St.)
D'Arblay St. W1 3C 222 (44Lb 90)
Darby Cl. CR3: Cat'm 94Sb 197
RM19: Purf 49Sd 98
Darby Cres. TW16: Sun 68Y 129
Darby Dr. EN9: Walt A 5Ec 20
Darby Gdns. TW16: Sun 68Y 129
Darcy Av. SM6: Wall 77Lb 156
Darcy Cl. CM13: Hut 17De 41
CR5: Coul 91Rb 197
EN8: Chesh 3Ac 20
N20 19Fb 31
D'Arcy Dr. HA3: Kenton 28Ma 47
D'Arcy Gdns. HA3: Kenton 28Ma 47
Darcy Gdns. RM9: Dag 39Bd 75
Darcy Ho. E8 39Xb 71
(off London Flds. E. Side)
RM9: Dag 39Cd 76
D'Arcy Pl. BR2: Brom 70Jc 137
KT21: Asht 89Pa 173
D'Arcy Rd. KT21: Asht 89Pa 173
SM3: Cheam 77Za 154
Darcy Rd. SW16 68Nb 134
TW7: Isle 53Ja 108
Dare Gdns. RM8: Dag 34Ad 75
Darell Rd. TW9: Rich 55Qa 109
Darent Cl. TN13: Chip 94Ed 202
DARENTH 64Sd 142
Darenth Country Pk. 61Td 142
Darenth Dr. DA12: Grav'nd 10K 123
Darenth Gdns. TN16: Westrm 98Tc 200
Darenth Hill DA2: Daren 64Sd 142
DARENTH INTERCHANGE 62Rd 141
Darenth La. RM15: S Ock 44Wd 98
TN13: Dun G 93Gd 202
Darenth Mill La. DA2: Daren 64Rd 141
Darent Ho. BR1: Brom 64Fc 137
NW8 7C 214
Darenth Pk. Av. DA2: Dart 61Td 142
Darenth Pl. DA2: Daren 64Td 142
Darenth Rd. DA1: Dart 59Pd 119
DA16: Well 53Wc 117
N16 31Vb 71
Darenth Rd. Sth. DA2: Daren 63Rd 141
Darenth Valley Golf Course 84Jd 182
Darenth Way TN14: S'ham 83Jd 182
Darenth Wood Rd. DA2: Dart 63Ud 142
Darent Ind. Pk. DA8: Erith 51Md 119
Darent Mead DA4: Sut H 67Rd 141
Darfield NW1 39Lb 70
(off Bayham St.)
Darfield Rd. SE4 57Bc 114
Darfield Way W10 44Za 88
Darfur St. SW15 55Za 110
Dargate Cl. SE19 66Vb 135
Dariel Cl. SL1: Slou 7D 80
Darien Rd. SW11 55Fb 111
Daring Ho. E3 40Ac 72
(off Roman Rd.)
Darkes La. EN6: Pot B 4Cb 17
Dark Hill Rd. TN15: Bor G 92Ae 205
Darkhole Ride SL4: Wink 7A 102
Dark Ho. Wlk. EC3 5G 225 (45Tb 91)
Dark La. CM14: Gt War 23Vd 58
EN7: Chesh 2Wb 19
GU20: W'sham 8A 146
Darlands Dr. EN5: Barn 15Za 30
Darlan Rd. SW6 52Bb 111
Darlaston Rd. SW19 66Za 132
Darley Cl. CR0: C'don 72Ac 158
KT15: Add 78L 149
Darley Ct. AL2: Park 10P 5
Darley Dene Ct. KT15: Add 77L 149
Darley Dr. KT3: N Mald 68Ta 131
Darley Gdns. SM4: Mord 72Eb 155
Darley Ho. SE11 7H 229
Darley Rd. N9 18Vb 33
SW11 58Hb 111
Darling Ho. TW1: Twick 58Ma 109
Darling Rd. SE4 55Cc 114
Darling Row E1 42Xb 91
Darlington Ct. CM15: Pil H 16Wd 40
SE6 60Hc 115
Darlington Gdns. RM3: Rom 22Md 57
Darlington Ho. SW8 52Mb 112
(off Hemans St.)
Darlington Path RM3: Rom 22Md 57
Darlington Rd. SE27 64Rb 135
Darlton Cl. DA1: Cray 55Hd 118
Darmaine Cl. CR2: S Croy 80Sb 157
Darnall Ho. SE10 53Ec 114
(off Royal Hill)
Darnaway Pl. E14 43Ec 92
(off Aberfeldy St.)
Darnay Apartments E15 37Fc 73
Darndale Cl. E17 26Bc 52
Darnets Fld. TN14: Otf 89Hd 182
Darnhills WD7: R'lett 7Ha 14
Darnley Cl. DA15: Sidc 57Vc 117
Darnley Ct. DA11: Grav'nd 9C 122
(off Darnley Rd.)
Darnley Ho. E14 44Ac 92
(off Camdenhurst St.)
Darnley Mausoleum 10N 145
Darnley Pk. KT13: Weyb 76R 150
Darnley Rd. DA11: Grav'nd 10C 122
(not continuous)
E9 37Yb 72
IG8: Wfd G 25Jc 53
RM17: Grays 51De 121
Darnley St. DA11: Grav'nd 9C 122
Darnley Ter. W11 46Za 88
Darns Hill BR8: Crock 73Ed 162
Darrell Charles Ct. UB8: Uxb 38N 63
Darrell Cl. SL3: L'ly 49B 82
Darrell Rd. SE22 57Wb 113
Darren Cl. N4 31Pb 70
Darren Ct. N7 35Nb 70
Darrick Wood Rd. BR6: Orp 75Tc 160
Darrick Wood Sports Cen. 76Sc 160
Darrick Wood Swimming Pool 76Sc 160
Darrington Rd. WD6: Bore 11Na 29
Darris Cl. UB4: Yead 42Aa 85
Darsley Dr. SW8 53Mb 112
Dart Cl. RM14: Upm 30Td 58
SL3: L'ly 50D 82
Dartfields RM3: Rom 23Md 57
DARTFORD 58Nd 119
Dartford Av. N9 16Yb 34
Dartford Borough Mus. 59Nd 119
Dartford Bus. Pk. DA1: Dart 57Md 119
Dartford By-Pass DA1: Dart 60Gd 118
DA2: Bean, Daren, Dart, Hawl, Wilm 63Pd 141
DA5: Bexl, Dart 60Gd 118

Dartford Clay Shooting Club—Delamare Ct.

Dartford Clay Shooting Club ... 52Nd 119
Dartford Ct. KT19: Eps ... 84Na 173
Dartford FC ... 60Qd 119
Dartford Gdns. RM6: Chad H ... 29Xc 55
Dartford Golf Course ... 61Kd 141
DARTFORD HEATH ... 60Hd 118
Dartford Heath Retail Pk.
DA1: Dart ... 60Ld 119
Dartford Ho. SE1 ... 6K 231
Dartford Judo Club ... 58Sd 120
Dartford Rd. DA1: Dart ... 58Jd 118
DA4: Farni, Hort K, S Dar ... 72Pd 163
DA5: Bexl ... 60Ed 118
TN13: S'oaks ... 96Ld 203
Dartford St. SE17 ... 51Sb 113
Dartford-Thurrock River Crossing
RM20: W Thur ... 54Ud 120
Dartford Trade Pk. DA1: Dart ... 61Nd 141
Dartford Tunnel DA1: Dart ... 55Td 120
Dartford Tunnel App. Rd.
DA1: Dart ... 59Rd 119
Dart Grn. RM15: S Ock ... 43Xd 98
Dartington NW1 ... 1C 216
Dartington Ho. SW8 ... 54Mb 112
(off Union Gro.)
W2 ... 43Db 89
(off Senior St.)
Dartle Ct. SE16 ... 47Wb 91
(off Scott Lidgett Cres.)
Dartmoor Wlk. E14 ... 49Cc 92
(off Severnake Cl.)
Dartmouth Av. GU21: Wok ... 86E 168
Dartmouth Cl. W11 ... 44Bb 89
Dartmouth Ct. SE10 ... 53Ec 114
Dartmouth Grn. GU21: Wok ... 86F 168
Dartmouth Gro. SE10 ... 53Ec 114
Dartmouth Hill SE10 ... 53Ec 114
Dartmouth Ho. KT2: King T ... 67Na 131
(off Seven Kings Way)
SE10 ... 53Dc 114
(off Catherine Gro.)
DARTMOUTH PARK ... 34Kb 70
Dartmouth Pk. Av. NW5 ... 34Kb 70
Dartmouth Pk. Hill N19 ... 32Kb 70
NW5 ... 32Kb 70
Dartmouth Pk. Rd. NW5 ... 35Kb 70
Dartmouth Path GU21: Wok ... 86F 168
Dartmouth Pl. SE23 ... 61Yb 136
W4 ... 51Ua 110
Dartmouth Rd. BR2: Hayes ... 73Jc 159
HA4: Ruis ... 34W 64
NW2 ... 37Za 68
NW4 ... 30Wa 48
SE23 ... 62Xb 135
SE26 ... 62Xb 135
Dartmouth Row SE10 ... 54Ec 114
Dartmouth St. SW1 ... 2D 228 (47Mb 90)
Dartmouth Ter. SE10 ... 53Fc 115
Dartnell Av. KT14: W Byf ... 84K 169
Dartnell Cl. KT14: W Byf ... 84K 169
Dartnell Ct. KT14: W Byf ... 84L 169
Dartnell Cres. KT14: W Byf ... 84K 169
DARTNELL PARK ... 84K 169
Dartnell Pk. Rd. KT14: W Byf ... 84K 169
Dartnell Pl. KT14: W Byf ... 84K 169
Dartnell Rd. CR0: C'don ... 73Vb 157
Darton Ct. W3 ... 46Sa 87
Dartrey Twr. SW10 ... 52Eb 111
(off Worlds End Est.)
Dartrey Wlk. SW10 ... 52Eb 111
Dart St. W10 ... 41Ab 88
Dartview Cl. RM17: Grays ... 9A 100
Darvel Cl. GU21: Wok ... 8L 167
Darvell Ho. SE17 ... 7G 231
Darvells Yd. WD3: Chor ... 14F 24
Darville Rd. N16 ... 34Vb 71
Darvill's La. SL1: Slou ... 7H 81
Darwell Cl. E6 ... 40Qc 74
Darwen Pl. E2 ... 40Xb 71
Darwin Av. DA1: Dart ... 54Nd 119
Darwin Cl. BR6: Farnb ... 78Tc 160
N11 ... 20Kb 32
Darwin Ct. CR2: S Croy ... 78Rb 157
(off Warham Rd.)
E13 ... 41Kc 93
NW1 ... 39Kb 70
(not continuous)
SE17 ... 6G 231
Darwin Dr. UB1: S'hall ... 44Da 85
Darwin Gdns. WD19: Wat ... 22Y 45
Darwin Ho. SE20 ... 67Wb 135
SW1 ... 51Lb 112
(off Grosvenor Rd.)
Darwin Ri. DA11: Nflt ... 60De 121
Darwin Rd. DA16: Well ... 55Vc 117
N22 ... 25Rb 51
RM18: Tilb ... 3B 122
SL3: L'ly ... 47B 82
W5 ... 50La 86
Darwin Sports Cen. ... 87Pc 180
Darwin St. SE17 ... 5G 231 (49Tb 91)
(not continuous)
Darwood Ct. NW6 ... 38Eb 69
(off Belsize Rd.)
Daryngton Dr. UB6: G'frd ... 40Fa 66
Daryngton Ho. SE1 ... 2F 231
SW8 ... 52Nb 112
(off Hartington Rd.)
Dashwood Cl. DA6: Bex ... 57Cd 118
KT14: W Byf ... 84L 169
SL3: L'ly ... 9N 81
Dashwood Lang Rd. KT15: Add ... 77M 149
Dashwood Rd. DA11: Grav'nd ... 10C 122
N8 ... 30Pb 50
Dashwood Studios SE17 ... 6D 230
Dassett Rd. SE27 ... 64Rb 135
Data Point Bus. Cen. E16 ... 42Fc 93
Datchelor Pl. SE5 ... 53Tb 113
DATCHET ... 3M 103
DATCHET COMMON ... 3P 103
Datchet Golf Course ... 2L 103
Datchet Ho. E2 ... 4K 219
NW1 ... 3A 216
Datchet Pl. SL3: Dat ... 3M 103
Datchet Rd. SE6 ... 61Bc 136
SL3: Hort ... 55B 104
SL3: Slou ... 9K 81
SL4: Old Win ... 6L 103
SL4: Wind ... 2H 103
Datchet Watersports Cen. ... 52D 104
Datchworth Ct. EN1: Enf ... 15Ub 33
Datchworth Ho. N1 ... 38Rb 71
(off The Sutton Est.)
Datchworth Turn HP2: Hem H ... 2C 4
Date St. SE17 ... 7E 230 (50Tb 91)
Daubeney Gdns. N17 ... 24Sb 51
Daubeney Pl. TW12: Hamp ... 67Ea 130
(off High St.)
Daubeney Rd. E5 ... 35Ac 72
N17 ... 24Sb 51
Daubeney Twr. SE8 ... 50Bc 92
(off Bowditch)
Dault Rd. SW18 ... 58Eb 111
Dauncey Ho. SE1 ... 2B 230
Davall Ho. RM17: Grays ... 51De 121
(off Argent St.)
Dave Adams Ho. E3 ... 40Bc 72
(off Norman Gro.)
Davema Cl. BR7: Chst ... 67Qc 138
Davenant Ho. E1 ... 43Wb 91
(off Old Montague St.)
Davenant Rd. CR0: C'don ... 77Rb 157
N19 ... 33Mb 70
Davenant St. E1 ... 43Wb 91
Davenham Av. HA6: Nwood ... 22V 44
Davenham Pl. HA6: Nwood ... 22V 44
Davenport Cen. IG11: Bark ... 39Xc 75
Davenport Cl. TW11: Tedd ... 65Ja 130
Davenport Ct. CR0: C'don ... 73Rb 157
Davenport Ho. SE11 ... 4K 229
UB7: W Dray ... 47P 83
Davenport Lodge TW5: Hest ... 52Aa 107
Davenport Rd. DA14: Sidc ... 61Ad 139
SE6 ... 58Dc 114
Daventer Dr. HA7: Stan ... 24Ha 46
Daventry Av. E17 ... 30Cc 52
Daventry Cl. SL3: Poyle ... 53H 105
Daventry Gdns. RM3: Rom ... 22Ld 57
Daventry Grn. RM3: Rom ... 22Ld 57
Daventry Rd. RM3: Rom ... 22Ld 57
Daventry St. NW1 ... 7D 214 (43Gb 89)
Daver Ct. SW3 ... 7E 226 (50Gb 89)
W5 ... 42Ma 87
Davern Cl. SE10 ... 49Hc 93
Davey Cl. N7 ... 37Pb 70
N13 ... 22Pb 50
Davey Gdns. IG11: Bark ... 42Wc 95
Davey Rd. E9 ... 38Cc 72
Davey's Ct. WC2 ... 4F 223
Davey St. SE15 ... 51Vb 113
David Av. UB6: G'frd ... 41Ga 86
David Cl. UB3: Harl ... 52U 106
David Coffer Ct. DA17: Belv ... 49Dd 96
David Ct. E14 ... 43Dc 92
(off Hillary M.)
N20 ... 20Eb 31
David Dr. RM3: Hrld W ... 23Qd 57
Davidge Ho. SE1 ... 2A 230
Davidge St. SE1 ... 2B 230 (47Rb 91)
David Hewitt Ho. E3 ... 43Dc 92
(off Watts Gro.)
David Ho. DA15: Sidc ... 62Wc 139
SW8 ... 52Nb 112
(off Wyvil Rd.)
David Lean Cinema
Croydon ... 76Tb 157
(within Fairfield Halls)
David Lean Ct. UB9: Den ... 29H 43
(off Patrons Way W.)
David Lee Point E15 ... 39Gc 73
(off Leather Gdns.)
David Lloyd Leisure
Chigwell ... 18Pc 36
Barnet ... 24Fb 49
Beckenham ... 70Bc 136
Bushey ... 12Ca 27
Cheam ... 80Za 154
Dartford ... 60Pd 119
Enfield ... 12Wb 33
Epsom ... 82Qa 173
Fulham ... 52Cb 111
(within Fulham Broadway Shop. Cen.)
Hampton ... 62Ca 129
Hornchurch ... 27Md 57
Hounslow ... 50Y 85
Kidbrooke ... 56Kc 115
Kingston upon Thames ... 68Na 131
(within The Rotunda Cen.)
Raynes Park ... 69Za 132
Sidcup ... 64Yc 139
South Kensington ... 49Db 89
(off Point West)
Sudbury Hill ... 36Fa 66
Weybridge ... 82Q 170
Woking ... 92B 188
David M. SE10 ... 52Ec 114
W1 ... 7H 215 (43Hb 89)
David Rd. RM8: Dag ... 33Ad 75
SL3: Poyle ... 54H 105
Davidson Gdns. SW8 ... 52Nb 112
Davidson Ho. HP2: Hem H ... 1M 3
Davidson La. HA1: Harr ... 31Ha 66
Davidson Rd. CR0: C'don ... 74Ub 157
Davidson Terraces E7 ... 36Kc 73
(off Claremont Rd.)
Davidson Way RM7: Rush G ... 31Gd 76
David's Rd. SE23 ... 60Yb 114
David St. E15 ... 37Fc 73
David's Way IG6: Ilf ... 24Uc 54
David Ter. RM3: Hrld W ... 24Qd 57
David Twigg Cl. KT2: King T ... 67Na 131
David Wildman La. NW7 ... 23Ab 48
Davies Cl. CR0: C'don ... 72Wb 157
RM13: Rain ... 41Ld 97
Davies La. E11 ... 33Gc 73
Davies M. W1 ... 4K 221 (45Kb 90)
Davies St. W1 ... 3K 221 (44Kb 90)
Davies Wlk. TW7: Isle ... 53Fa 108
Da Vinci Ct. SE16 ... 50Xb 91
(off Rossetti Rd.)
WD25: Wat ... 8Z 13
Da Vinci Lodge SE10 ... 48Hc 93
(off West Parkside)
Da Vinci Torre SE13 ... 55Dc 114
(off Loampit Va.)
Davington Gdns. RM8: Dag ... 36Xc 75
Davington Rd. RM8: Dag ... 37Xc 75
Davinia Cl. IG8: Wfd G ... 23Pc 54
Davis Av. DA11: Nflt ... 10A 122
Davis Cl. TN13: S'oaks ... 94Ld 203
Davis Ct. AL1: St A ... 2C 6
Davis Ho. W12 ... 45Xa 88
(off White City Est.)
Davison Cl. KT19: Eps ... 83Ra 173
Davison Dr. EN8: Chesh ... 1Zb 20
Davison Rd. SL3: L'ly ... 50B 82
Davis Rd. KT9: Chess ... 77Qa 153
KT13: Weyb ... 82P 169
RM15: Avel ... 46Td 98
RM16: Chaf H ... 48Be 99
W3 ... 46Va 88
Davis Rd. Ind. Pk. KT9: Chess ... 77Qa 153
Davis St. E13 ... 40Kc 73
Davisville Rd. W12 ... 47Wa 88
Davis Way DA14: Sidc ... 65Ad 139
Davmor Ct. TW8: Bford ... 50La 86
Davos Cl. GU22: Wok ... 91A 188
Davy Down (Information Cen.) ... 46Yd 98
Davy Down Riverside Pk. ... 46Yd 98
Davy Ho. AL1: St A ... 3D 6
Davy's Pl. DA12: Grav'nd ... 5G 144
Dawburn Pl. TW5: Hest ... 52Z 107
Dawell Dr. TN16: Big H ... 89Lc 179
Dawes Av. RM12: Horn ... 34Md 77
TW7: Isle ... 57Ja 108
Dawes Cl. DA9: Ghithe ... 57Vd 120
UB10: Uxb ... 40N 63
Dawes Ct. KT10: Esh ... 77Da 151
Dawes East Rd. SL1: Burn ... 2A 80
Dawes Ho. SE17 ... 6F 231
Dawes La. WD3: Sarr ... 9G 10
Dawes Moor Cl. SL2: Slou ... 4N 81
Dawe's Rd. UB10: Uxb ... 40N 63
Dawes Rd. SW6 ... 52Ab 110
Dawes St. SE17 ... 7G 231 (50Tb 91)
Dawkins Ct. SE1 ... 4F 231 (48Tb 91)
Dawley Av. UB8: Hil ... 43S 84
Dawley Grn. RM15: S Ock ... 44Wd 98
Dawley Pde. UB3: Hayes ... 45S 84
Dawley Pk. UB3: Hayes ... 47T 84
Dawley Ride SL3: Poyle ... 53G 104
Dawley Rd.
UB3: Harl, Hayes ... 45S 84
Dawlish Av. N13 ... 21Nb 50
SW18 ... 61Db 133
UB6: G'frd ... 40Ja 66
Dawlish Dr. HA4: Ruis ... 33W 64
HA5: Pinn ... 29Aa 45
IG3: Ilf ... 35Uc 74
Dawlish Rd. E10 ... 32Ec 72
N17 ... 27Wb 51
NW2 ... 37Za 68
Dawlish Wlk. RM3: Rom ... 25Ld 57
Dawnay Gdns. SW18 ... 61Fb 133
Dawnay Rd. KT23: Bookh ... 98Da 191
SW18 ... 61Eb 133
Dawn Cl. TW4: Houn ... 55Aa 107
Dawn Ct. AL1: St A ... 3E 6
Dawn Cres. E15 ... 39Fc 73
Dawney Hill GU24: Pirb ... 3C 186
Dawneys Rd. GU24: Pirb ... 4C 186
Dawn Redwood Cl. SL3: Hort ... 55C 104
Dawpool Rd. NW2 ... 33Va 68
Daws Ct. SL0: Iver ... 44H 83
Daws Hill E4 ... 12Ec 34
Daws La. NW7 ... 22Va 48
Dawson Av. BR5: St P ... 68Xc 139
IG11: Bark ... 38Vc 75
Dawson Cl. SE18 ... 49Sc 94
SL4: Wind ... 4E 102
UB3: Hayes ... 43T 84
Dawson Ct. W3 ... 48Sa 87
(off Palmerston Rd.)
Dawson Dr. BR8: Hext ... 66Gd 140
RM13: Rain ... 38Kd 77
Dawson Gdns. IG11: Bark ... 38Vc 75
Dawson Ho. E2 ... 41Yb 92
(off Sceptre Rd.)
Dawson Pl. W2 ... 45Cb 89
Dawson Rd. KT1: King T ... 69Pa 131
KT14: Byfl ... 83M 169
NW2 ... 36Ya 68
Dawson St. E2 ... 2K 219 (40Vb 71)
Dawson Ter. N9 ... 17Yb 34
Daws Pl. RH1: Mers ... 3C 208
Dax Ct. TW16: Sun ... 69Y 129
Daybrook Rd. SW19 ... 68Db 133
Day Dr. RM8: Dag ... 32Zc 75
Day Ho. SE5 ... 52Sb 113
(off Bethwin Rd.)
Daylesford Av. SW15 ... 56Wa 110
Daylesford Gro. SL1: Slou ... 7D 80
Daylop Dr. IG7: Chig ... 20Xc 37
Daymer Gdns. HA5: Pinn ... 28X 45
Daymerslea Ridge KT22: Lea ... 93La 192
Daynor Ho. NW6 ... 39Cb 69
(off Quex Ho.)
Days Acre CR2: Sande ... 82Vb 177
Daysbrook Rd. SW2 ... 60Pb 112
Days La. CM15: Dodd, Pil H ... 14Wd 40
DA15: Sidc ... 59Uc 116
Daytona Sandown Pk. ... 76Ea 152
Dayton Dr. DA8: Erith ... 50Md 97
Dayton Gro. SE15 ... 53Yb 114
Deacon Cl. AL1: St A ... 6B 6
CR8: Purl ... 81Nb 176
KT11: D'side ... 91Ca 191
Deacon Ct. SL4: Wind ... 4B 102
Deaconess Ct. N15 ... 28Vb 51
(off Tottenham Grn. E.)
Deacon Estate, The E4 ... 23Bc 52
Deacon Ho. SE11 ... 6J 229
Deacon M. N1 ... 38Tb 71
Deacon Pl. CR3: Cat'm ... 95Sb 197
Deacon Rd. KT2: King T ... 67Pa 131
NW2 ... 36Wa 68
Deacons Cl. HA5: Pinn ... 26X 45
WD6: E'tree ... 14Qa 29
Deacons Ct. TW1: Twick ... 61Ha 130
Deaconsfield Rd. HP3: Hem H ... 5M 3
Deacons Hgts. WD6: E'tree ... 16Qa 29
Deacons Hill WD6: E'tree ... 16Pa 29
WD19: Wat ... 16Y 27
Deacon's Hill Rd. WD6: E'tree ... 14Pa 29
Deacons Leas BR6: Orp ... 77Tc 160
Deacon's Ri. N2 ... 31Fb 69
Deacons Ter. N1 ... 37Sb 71
(off Harecourt Rd.)
Deacons Wlk. TW12: Hamp ... 63Ca 129
Deacon Way IG8: Wfd G ... 24Pc 54
Deadhearn La. HP8: Chal G ... 18A 24
Deadman's Ash La. WD3: Sarr ... 8K 11
Deakin Cl. WD18: Wat ... 17U 26
Deakins Ter. BR6: Orp ... 73Wc 161
Deal Av. SL1: Slou ... 4D 80
Deal Ct. NW9 ... 26Va 48
(off Hazel Cl.)
UB1: S'hall ... 44Ea 86
(off Haldane Rd.)
Deal Ho. SE15 ... 51Zb 114
(off Lovelinch La.)
SE17 ... 7J 231
Deal M. W5 ... 49Ma 87
Deal Porters Wlk. SE16 ... 47Zb 92
Deal Porters Way SE16 ... 48Yb 92
Deal Rd. SW17 ... 65Jb 134
Deal's Gateway SE13 ... 53Cc 114
Deal St. E1 ... 43Wb 91
Dealtry Rd. SW15 ... 56Ya 110
Deal Wlk. SW9 ... 52Qb 112
Dean Abbott Ho. SW1 ... 5D 228
Deanacre Cl. SL9: Chal P ... 23A 42
DEAN BOTTOM ... 69Xd 142
Dean Bradley St. SW1 ... 4F 229 (48Nb 90)
Dean Cl. E9 ... 36Yb 72
GU22: Pyr ... 87G 168
SE16 ... 46Zb 92
SL4: Wind ... 5B 102
UB10: Hil ... 38P 63
Dean Ct. HA0: Wemb ... 34Ka 66
HA8: Edg ... 23Ra 47
RM7: Rom ... 29Fd 56
SW8 ... 52Nb 112
(off Thorncroft St.)
W3 ... 44Ta 87
WD25: Wat ... 5Z 13
Deancroft Rd. SL9: Chal P ... 23A 42
Deancross St. E1 ... 44Yb 92
Dean Dr. HA7: Stan ... 26Na 47
Deane Av. HA4: Ruis ... 36Y 65
Deane Ct. HA6: Nwood ... 25U 44
Deane Cft. Rd. HA5: Eastc ... 30Y 45
Deanery Cl. N2 ... 28Gb 49
Deanery M. W1 ... 6J 221
Deanery Rd. E15 ... 37Gc 73
Deanery St. W1 ... 6J 221 (46Jb 90)
Deane Way HA4: Ruis ... 30X 45
Dean Farrar St. SW1 ... 3E 228 (48Mb 90)
Dean Fld. HP3: Bov ... 9C 2
Deanfield Gdns. CR0: C'don ... 77Tb 157
Dean Gdns. E17 ... 28Fc 53
Deanhill Ct. SW14 ... 56Ra 109
Deanhill Rd. SW14 ... 56Ra 109
Dean Ho. E1 ... 44Yb 92
(off Tarling St.)
SE14 ... 52Ac 114
(off New Cross Rd.)
Dean La. RH1: Mers ... 95Kb 196
Dean Moore Cl. AL1: St A ... 3A 6
Dean Path IG11: Bark ... 35Wc 75
Dean Rd. CR0: C'don ... 77Tb 157
NW2 ... 37Ya 68
SE28 ... 46Wc 95
TW3: Houn ... 57Da 107
TW12: Hamp ... 64Ca 129
Dean Ryle St. SW1 ... 5F 229 (49Nb 90)
Deansbrook Cl. HA8: Edg ... 24Sa 47
Deansbrook Rd. HA8: Edg ... 24Ra 47
Dean's Bldgs. SE17 ... 6F 231 (49Tb 91)
Deans Cl. CR0: C'don ... 76Vb 157
HA8: Edg ... 23Sa 47
KT20: Walt H ... 96Xa 194
SL2: Stoke P ... 9M 61
W4 ... 51Ra 109
WD5: Ab L ... 4T 12
Dean's Ct. EC4 ... 3C 224 (44Rb 91)
Deans Ct. GU20: W'sham ... 10B 146
Deanscroft Av. NW9 ... 32Sa 67
Deans Dr. HA8: Edg ... 22Ta 47
N13 ... 23Rb 51
Deans Factory Est. RM13: Rain ... 42Ld 97
Deansfield CR3: Cat'm ... 97Vb 197
Deans Ga. Cl. SE23 ... 62Zb 136
Deanshanger Ho. SE8 ... 49Zb 92
(off Chilton Gro.)
Deans La. HA8: Edg ... 23Sa 47
KT20: Walt H ... 96Xa 194
RH1: Nutf ... 5G 208
W4 ... 51Ra 109
(off Deans Cl.)
Dean's M. W1 ... 2A 222 (44Kb 90)
Deans Rd. CM14: W'ley ... 21Xd 58
RH1: Mers ... 2C 208
SM1: Sutt ... 76Db 155
W7 ... 46Ha 86
Dean Stanley St. SW1 ... 4F 229 (48Nb 90)
Deanston Wharf E16 ... 47Kc 93
(not continuous)
Dean St. E7 ... 36Jc 73
W1 ... 2D 222 (44Mb 90)
Dean's Wlk. CR5: Coul ... 90Qb 176
Deans Way HA8: Edg ... 22Sa 47
Deansway HP3: Hem H ... 5P 3
N2 ... 28Fb 49
N9 ... 20Ub 33
Deanswood N11 ... 23Mb 50
Dean's Yd. SW1 ... 3E 228 (48Mb 90)
Dean Trench St. SW1 ... 4F 229 (48Nb 90)
Dean Wlk. HA8: Edg ... 23Sa 47
KT23: Bookh ... 98Da 191
Dean Way UB2: S'hall ... 47Da 85
Dearmer Ho. SL9: Chal P ... 22A 42
(off Micholls Av.)
Dearne Cl. HA7: Stan ... 22Ja 46
De'Arn Gdns. CR4: Mitc ... 69Gb 133
Dearsley Ho. RM13: Rain ... 40Fd 76
Dearsley Rd. EN1: Enf ... 13Wb 33
Death Trap, London's ... 2H 229
Deauville Ct. SE16 ... 47Zb 92
(off Eleanor Cl.)
SW4 ... 58Lb 112
De Barowe M. N5 ... 35Rb 71
Debdale Ho. E2 ... 39Wb 71
(off Whiston Rd.)
DEBDEN ... 14Sc 36
Debden N17 ... 26Tb 51
(off Gloucester Rd.)
Debden Cl. IG8: Wfd G ... 24Mc 53
KT2: King T ... 64Ma 131
NW9 ... 25Ua 48
DEBDEN GREEN ... 10Rc 22
Debden Ho. IG10: Lough ... 10Rc 22
Debden La. IG10: Lough ... 10Sc 22
Debden Rd. IG10: Lough ... 10Rc 22
Debden Wlk. RM12: Horn ... 37Kd 77
De Beauvoir Ct. N1 ... 38Tb 71
(off Northchurch Rd.)
De Beauvoir Cres. N1 ... 39Ub 71
De Beauvoir Est. N1 ... 39Ub 71
De Beauvoir Pl. N1 ... 37Ub 71
De Beauvoir Rd. N1 ... 39Ub 71
De Beauvoir Sq. N1 ... 38Ub 71
DE BEAUVOIR TOWN ... 39Ub 71
De Beauvoir Wharf N1 ... 39Ub 71
(off Hertford Rd.)
Deben RM18: E Til ... 8L 101
Debenham Ct. E8 ... 39Wb 71
(off Pownall Rd.)
EN5: Barn ... 15Ya 30
Debham Ct. NW2 ... 34Ya 68
Deblin Dr. UB10: Uxb ... 40N 63
Debnams Rd. SE16 ... 49Yb 92
De Bohun Av. N14 ... 16Kb 32
Deborah Cl. TW7: Isle ... 53Ga 108
Deborah Ct. E18 ... 27Kc 53
(off Victoria Rd.)
Deborah Cres. HA4: Ruis ... 31T 64
Deborah Lodge HA8: Edg ... 25Ra 47
Debrabant Cl. DA8: Erith ... 51Fd 118
De Brome Rd. TW13: Felt ... 60Y 107
De Bruin Ct. E14 ... 50Ec 92
(off Ferry St.)
De Burgh Gdns. KT20: Tad ... 91Za 194
De Burgh Pk. SM7: Bans ... 87Db 175
Deburgh Rd. SW19 ... 66Eb 133
Debussy NW9 ... 26Va 48
Decies Way SL2: Stoke P ... 9L 61
Decima St. SE1 ... 3H 231 (48Ub 91)
Decima Studios SE1 ... 3H 231
Decimus Cl. CR7: Thor H ... 70Tb 135
Deck Cl. SE16 ... 46Zb 92
De Coubertin St. E20 ... 37Ec 72
Decoy Av. NW11 ... 29Ab 48
De Crespigny Pk. SE5 ... 54Tb 113
Dedswell Dr. GU4: W Cla ... 100J 189
DEDWORTH ... 3C 102
Dedworth Dr. SL4: Wind ... 3D 102
DEDWORTH GREEN ... 4C 102
Dedworth Mnr. SL4: Wind ... 3D 102
Dedworth Rd. SL4: Wind ... 4A 102
Dee Cl. RM14: Upm ... 30Ud 58
Dee Ct. W7 ... 44Fa 86
(off Hobbayne Rd.)
Dee Ho. KT2: King T ... 67Ma 131
(off May Bate Av.)
Deeley Rd. SW8 ... 53Mb 112
Deena Cl. SL1: Slou ... 5C 80
W3 ... 44Pa 87
Deen City Farm ... 68Eb 133
Deepak Ho. SW17 ... 63Gb 133
Deepdale SW19 ... 63Za 132
Deepdale Av. BR2: Brom ... 70Hc 137
Deepdale Cl. N11 ... 23Jb 50
Deepdale Ct. CR2: S Croy ... 77Tb 157
(off Birdhurst Av.)
Deep Dene W5 ... 42Pa 87
Deepdene EN6: Pot B ... 3Za 16
Deepdene Av. CR0: C'don ... 76Vb 157
Deepdene Cl. E11 ... 28Jc 53
Deepdene Ct. BR2: Brom ... 69Gc 137
N21 ... 16Rb 33
Deepdene Gdns. SW2 ... 59Pb 112
Deepdene Mans. SW6 ... 53Bb 111
(off Rostrevor Rd.)
Deepdene Path IG10: Lough ... 14Qc 36
(not continuous)
Deepdene Point SE23 ... 62Zb 136
Deepdene Rd. DA16: Well ... 55Wc 117
IG10: Lough ... 14Qc 36
SE5 ... 56Tb 113
Deep Fld. SL3: Dat ... 2M 103
Deepfield Way CR5: Coul ... 88Nb 176
Deep Pool La. GU24: Wok ... 6M 167
Deepwell Cl. TW7: Isle ... 53Ja 108
Deepwood La. UB6: G'frd ... 41Fa 86
Deerbrook Rd. SE24 ... 60Rb 113
Deercote Cl. EN8: Chesh ... 2Zb 20
Deerdale Rd. SE24 ... 56Sb 113
Deere Av. RM13: Rain ... 37Jd 76
Deerfield Cl. NW9 ... 29Va 48
Deerfield Cotts. NW9 ... 29Va 48
Deerhurst Cl. DA3: Lfield ... 69Ee 143
TW13: Felt ... 63X 129
Deerhurst Ct. CR0: C'don ... 74Rb 157
(off Parson's Mead)
Deerhurst Cres. TW12: Hamp H ... 64Ea 130
Deerhurst Ho. SE15 ... 51Wb 113
(off Haymerle Rd.)
Deerhurst Rd. NW2 ... 37Za 68
SW16 ... 64Pb 134
Deering Ho. SE3 ... 56Lc 115
Deerings Dr. HA5: Eastc ... 29W 44
Deerings Rd. RH2: Reig ... 6K 207
Deerleap Gro. E4 ... 15Dc 34
Deerleap La. TN14: Knock ... 85Ad 181
Deer Mead Ct. RM1: Rom ... 29Hd 56
Dee Rd. SL4: Wind ... 4C 102
TW9: Rich ... 56Pa 109
Deer Pk. Cl. KT2: King T ... 66Ra 131
Deer Pk. Gdns. CR4: Mitc ... 70Fb 133
Deer Pk. Rd. SW19 ... 68Db 133
Deer Pk. Way BR4: W W'ck ... 75Hc 159
EN9: Walt A ... 8Dc 20
Deers Farm Cl. GU23: Wis ... 88N 169
Deerswood Av. AL10: Hat ... 2D 8
Deerswood Cl. CR3: Cat'm ... 96Wb 197
Deeside Rd. SW17 ... 62Fb 133
Dee St. E14 ... 44Ec 92
Deeves Hall La. EN6: Ridge ... 5Ua 16
Dee Way KT19: Ewe ... 82Ua 174
RM1: Rom ... 24Gd 56
Defence Cl. SE28 ... 46Uc 94
Defiance Wlk. SE18 ... 48Pc 94
Defiant Way SM6: Wall ... 80Nb 156
Defoe Av. TW9: Kew ... 52Qa 109
Defoe Cl. DA8: Erith ... 53Gd 118
SE16 ... 47Bc 92
SW17 ... 65Gb 133
Defoe Ct. KT17: Eps ... 84Ua 174
Defoe Ho. EC2 ... 7D 218
Defoe Pde. RM16: Grays ... 8D 100
Defoe Pl. EC2 ... 7D 218
SW17 ... 63Hb 133
Defoe Rd. N16 ... 34Ub 71
Defoe Way RM5: Col R ... 23Cd 56
De Frene Rd. SE26 ... 63Zb 136
Degema Rd. BR7: Chst ... 64Rc 138
Dehar Cres. NW9 ... 31Va 68
de Havilland Aircraft Mus. ... 1Ra 15
Dehavilland Cl. UB5: N'olt ... 41Z 85
De Havilland Ct. N17 ... 27Xb 51
WD7: Shenl ... 4Na 15
De Havilland Dr. KT13: Weyb ... 83N 169
SE18 ... 51Rc 116
De Havilland Rd. HA8: Edg ... 26Qa 47
TW5: Hest ... 52Y 107
Dehavilland Studios E5 ... 33Yb 72
(off Theydon Rd.)
De Havilland Way TW19: Stanw ... 58M 105
WD5: Ab L ... 4V 12
Deirdre Chapman Ho.
DA10: Swans ... 58Ae 121
(off Craylands La.)
Dekker Ho. SE5 ... 52Tb 113
(off Elmington Est.)
Dekker Rd. SE21 ... 58Ub 113
Delabole Rd. RH1: Mers ... 1E 208
Delacourt Rd. SE3 ... 52Kc 115
Delacy Ct. SM2: Sutt ... 83Cb 175
Delafield Ho. E1 ... 44Wb 91
(off Christian St.)
Delafield Rd. RM17: Grays ... 50Fe 99
SE7 ... 50Kc 93
Delaford Cl. SL0: Iver ... 44J 83
Delaford Rd. SE16 ... 50Xb 91
Delaford St. SW6 ... 52Ab 110
Delagarde Rd. TN16: Westrm ... 98Sc 200
Delahay Ho. SW3 ... 51Hb 111
(off Chelsea Emb.)
Delamare Ct. SE6 ... 62Dc 136

Delamare Cres.—Devizes Ho.

Delamare Cres. CR0: C'don 72Yb 158
Delamare Rd. EN8: Chesh 2Ac 20
Delamere Cl. SS17: Stan H 3K 101
Delamere Ct. E17 26Ec 52
Delamere Gdns. NW7 23Ta 47
Delamere Rd. RH2: Reig 10K 207
SW20 67Za 132
UB4: Yead 45Z 85
W5 47Na 87
WD6: Bore 11Ra 29
Delamere St. W2 43Db 89
Delamere Ter. W2 43Db 89
Delancey Pas. NW1 1A 216
Delancey St. NW1 1K 215 (39Kb 70)
Delancey Studios NW1 1A 216 (39Kb 70)
Delany Ho. SE10 51Ec 114
(off Thames St.)
Delaporte Cl. KT17: Eps 84Ua 174
De Lapre Cl. BR5: St M Cry 73Zc 161
De Lara Way GU21: Wok 10P 167
Delarch Ho. SE1 2B 230
Delargy Cl. RM16: Grays 8D 100
De Laune St. SE17 7B 230 (50Rb 91)
Delaware Mans. W9 42Db 89
(off Delaware Rd.)
Delaware Rd. W9 42Db 89
Delawyk Cres. SE24 58Sb 113
Delcombe Av. KT4: Wor Pk 74Ya 154
Delderfield KT22: Lea 92Ma 193
Delderfield Ho. RM1: Rom 26Fd 56
(off Portnoi Cl.)
Delft Ho. KT2: King T 66Pa 131
(off Acre Rd.)
Delft Way SE22 57Ub 113
Delhi Rd. EN1: Enf 17Vb 33
Delhi St. N1 39Nb 70
Delia St. SW18 59Db 111
Delisle Rd. SE28 46Uc 94
Delius Cl. WD6: E'tree 16La 28
Delius Gro. E15 40Fc 73
Delius Way SS17: Stan H 1L 101
Dell, The AL1: St A 1E 6
CM13: Gt War 23Xd 58
DA5: Bexl 60Gd 118
DA9: Ghithe 57Xd 120
EN9: Walt A 8Ec 20
GU21: Wok 1N 187
HA0: Wemb 36Ka 66
HA5: Pinn 26Z 45
HA6: Nwood 19U 26
IG8: Wfd G 20Kc 35
KT20: Tad 93Ya 194
RH2: Reig 5J 207
SE2 50Wc 95
SE19 67Vb 135
SL9: Chal P 23A 42
TW8: Bford 51La 108
TW14: Felt 59X 107
TW20: Eng G 2L 125
WD7: R'lett 8Ja 14
Della Path E5 34Wb 71
Dellbow Rd. TW14: Felt 57X 107
Dell Cl. E15 39Fc 73
IG8: Wfd G 20Kc 35
KT22: Fet 95Fa 192
RH5: Mick 99La 192
SL2: Farn C 6G 60
SM6: Wall 77Lb 156
Dell Ct. HA6: Nwood 24T 44
RM12: Horn 33Nd 77
Delle Gro. RM3: Rom 23Md 57
Dell Farm Rd. HA4: Ruis 29T 44
Dellfield AL1: St A 3D 6
Dellfield Cl. BR3: Beck 67Ec 136
WD7: R'lett 7Ha 14
WD17: Wat 12W 26
Dellfield Ct. WD17: Wat 12W 26
Dellfield Cres. UB8: Cowl 42M 83
Dellfield Pde. UB8: Cowl 42L 83
Dell La. KT17: Ewe 78Wa 154
Dell Mdw. HP3: Hem H 6N 3
Dellmeadow WD5: Ab L 2U 12
Dell Nature Reserve 12H 25
Dellors Cl. EN5: Barn 15Za 30
Dellow Cl. IG2: Ilf 31Tc 74
Dellow Ho. E1 45Xb 91
(off Dellow St.)
Dellow St. E1 45Xb 91
Dell Ri. AL2: Park 8P 5
Dell Rd. EN3: Enf W 10Yb 20
KT17: Ewe 79Wa 154
RM17: Grays 49De 99
UB7: W Dray 49P 83
WD24: Wat 9W 12
Dells, The HP3: Hem H 3B 4
Dells Cl. E4 17Dc 34
TW11: Tedd 65Ha 130
Dell Side WD24: Wat 9W 12
Dellside UB9: Hare 29L 43
Dell's M. SW1 6C 228
Dellsome La. AL4: Col H 5A 8
AL9: Wel G 5B 8
Dell Wlk. KT3: N Mald 68Ua 132
Dell Way W13 44La 86
Dellwood WD3: Rick 18K 25
Dellwood Gdns. IG5: Ilf 27Qc 54
Delmar Av. HP2: Hem H 3D 4
Delmare Cl. SW9 56Pb 112
Delme Cres. SE3 54Kc 115
Delmer Ct. WD6: Bore 10Pa 15
(off Aycliffe Rd.)
Delmerend Ho. SW3 7D 226
Delmey Cl. CR0: C'don 76Vb 157
Deloraine Ho. SE8 53Cc 114
Delorme St. W6 51Za 110
Delphina Ho. CM14: B'wood 19Zd 41
DELROW 11Ea 28
Delroy Ct. N20 17Eb 31
Delta Bldg. E14 44Ec 92
(off Ashton St.)
Delta Bldg., The RM7: Rush G 30Gd 56
Delta Cen. HA0: Wemb 39Pa 67
Delta Cl. GU24: Chob 2K 167
KT4: Wor Pk 76Va 154
Delta Ct. NW2 33Wa 68
SE8 51Ac 114
(off Trundleys Rd.)
Delta Gain WD19: Wat 19Z 27
Delta Gro. UB5: N'olt 41Z 85
Delta Ho. KT16: Chert 73L 149
N1 3F 219
Delta Pk. SW18 56Db 111
Delta Pk. Ind. Est.
EN3: Brim 13Bc 34
Delta Point CR0: C'don 74Sb 157
(off Wellesley Rd.)
E2 41Wb 91
(off Delta St.)
Delta Rd. CM13: Hut 16Fe 41
GU21: Wok 88C 168
GU24: Chob 2K 167
KT4: Wor Pk 76Ua 154
Delta St. E2 41Wb 91
Delta Way TW20: Thorpe 67E 126
De Luci Rd. DA8: Erith 50Ed 96
De Lucy St. SE2 49Xc 95
Delvan Cl. SE18 52Qc 116
Delvers Mead RM10: Dag 35Ed 76
Delverton Ho. SE17 7C 230
Delverton Rd. SE17 7C 230 (50Rb 91)
Delves KT20: Tad 93Za 194
Delves Cl. CR8: Purl 85Pb 176
Delvino Rd. SW6 53Cb 111
De Mel Cl. KT19: Eps 84Ra 173
Demesne Rd. SM6: Wall 77Mb 156
Demeta Cl. HA9: Wemb 34Sa 67
De Montfort Pde. SW16 62Nb 134
De Montfort Rd. SW16 62Nb 134
De Morgan Rd. SW6 55Db 111
Dempsey Ct. SE6 59Cc 114
Dempster Cl. KT6: Surb 74La 152
Dempster Rd. SW18 57Eb 111
Den, The 50Yb 92
Denbar Pde. RM7: Rom 28Ed 56
Denberry Dr. DA14: Sidc 62Xc 139
Denbigh Cl. BR7: Chst 65Pc 138
HA4: Ruis 33V 64
HP2: Hem H 3N 3
RM11: Horn 28Qd 57
SM1: Sutt 78Bb 155
UB1: S'hall 44Ba 85
W11 45Bb 89
Denbigh Ct. E6 41Mc 93
W7 43Ha 86
(off Copley Cl.)
Denbigh Dr. UB3: Harl 47S 84
Denbigh Gdns. TW10: Rich 57Pa 109
Denbigh Ho. RM3: Rom 23Nd 57
(off Kingsbridge Cir.)
SW1 3G 227
W11 45Bb 89
(off Westbourne Gro.)
Denbigh M. SW1 6B 228
Denbigh Pl. SW1 7B 228 (50Lb 90)
Denbigh Rd. E6 41Mc 93
TW3: Houn 54Da 107
UB1: S'hall 44Ba 85
W11 45Bb 89
W13 45Ka 86
Denbigh St. SW1 6B 228 (49Lb 90)
(not continuous)
Denbigh Ter. W11 45Bb 89
Denbridge Rd. BR1: Brom 68Pc 138
Denbury Ho. E3 41Dc 92
(off Talwin St.)
Denby Ct. SE11 5J 229
Denby Rd. KT11: Cobh 84Y 171
Dence Ho. E2 41Wb 91
(off Turin St.)
Denchworth Ho. SW9 54Qb 112
Dencliffe TW15: Ashf 64Q 128
Den Cl. BR3: Beck 69Fc 137
Dencora Cen., The AL1: St A 2E 6
EN3: Brim 13Ac 34
Dendridge Cl. EN1: Enf 9Xb 19
Dene, The CR0: C'don 77Zb 158
HA9: Wemb 35Na 67
KT8: W Mole 71Ba 151
SM2: Cheam 83Bb 175
TN13: S'oaks 98Kd 203
W13 43Ka 86
Dene Av. DA15: Sidc 59Xc 117
TW3: Houn 55Ba 107
Dene Cl. BR2: Hayes 74Hc 159
CR5: Chip 91Gb 195
DA2: Wilm 63Gd 140
E10 33Dc 72
KT4: Wor Pk 75Va 154
SE4 55Ac 114
Dene Ct. CR2: S Croy 78Sb 157
(off Warham Rd.)
W5 43La 86
Denecroft Cres. UB10: Hil 39R 64
Denecroft Gdns. RM17: Grays 48Fe 99
Dene Dr. BR6: Chels 76Xc 161
DA3: Lfield 68De 143
Denefield Dr. CR8: Kenley 87Tb 177
Dene Gdns. HA7: Stan 22La 46
KT7: T Ditt 75Ja 152
Dene Holm Rd. DA11: Nflt 62Fe 143
Dene Ho. N14 17Mb 32
Denehurst Gdns. IG8: Wfd G 21Kc 53
NW4 30Ya 48
TW2: Twick 59Fa 108
TW10: Rich 56Qa 109
W3 46Ra 87
Dene Lodge Cl. TN15: Bor G 92Be 205
Dene Path RM15: S Ock 44Wd 98
Dene Pl. GU21: Wok 10N 167
Dene Rd. DA1: Dart 59Pd 119
HA6: Nwood 23S 44
IG9: Buck H 18Mc 35
KT21: Asht 91Pa 193
N11 18Hb 31
Denes, The HP3: Hem H 6P 3
Denesfield Ct. TN13: Chip 95Dd 202
Denesmead SE24 57Sb 113
Dene Wlk. DA3: Lfield 69Ae 143
Denewood EN5: New Bar 15Eb 31
KT17: Eps 85Ua 174
Denewood Cl. WD17: Wat 9V 12
Denewood M. WD17: Wat 9V 12
Denewood Pl. HA6: Nwood 23T 44
Denewood Rd. N6 30Hb 49
Denford St. SE10 50Hc 93
(off Glenforth St.)
Dengie Wlk. N1 39Sb 71
(off Basire St.)
DENHAM 34H 63
Denham Aerodrome 29G 42
Denham Av. UB9: Den 33H 63
Denham Cl. DA16: Well 55Yc 117
UB9: Den 34J 63
Denham Country Pk. 32K 63
Denham Ct. NW6 38Eb 69
(off Fairfax Rd.)
SE26 62Xb 135
(off Kirkdale)
UB1: S'hall 45Ea 86
(off Baird Av.)
Denham Ct. Dr. UB9: Den 35J 63
Denham Cres. CR4: Mitc 70Hb 133
Denham Dr. IG2: Ilf 30Sc 54
DENHAM GARDEN VILLAGE 29H 43
Denham Golf Course 30F 42
DENHAM GREEN 30H 43
Denham Grn. Cl. UB9: Den 31J 63
Denham Grn. La. UB9: Den 29G 42
Denham Ho. UB7: W Dray 47P 83
(off Park Lodge Av.)
W12 45Xa 88
(off White City Est.)
Denham La. SL9: Chal P 23B 42
Denham Lodge UB9: Den 37L 63
Denham Pde. UB9: Den 34H 63
(off Oxford Gdns.)
Denham Pl. UB9: Den 32H 63
Denham Rd. KT17: Eps 84Va 174
N20 20Hb 31
SL0: Iver H 39F 62
TW14: Felt 59Y 107
TW20: Egh 63C 126
UB9: Den 36H 63
DENHAM RDBT. 35J 63
Denham St. SE10 50Jc 93
Denham Wlk. SL9: Chal P 23B 42
Denham Way IG11: Bark 39Uc 74
UB9: Den 34J 63
(Old Mill Rd.)
UB9: Den 27H 43
(Wyatt's Covert)
WD3: Map C, W Hyd 23G 42
WD6: Bore 11Sa 29
Denholme Rd. W9 41Bb 89
Denholme Wlk. RM13: Rain 37Hd 76
Denison Cl. N2 27Eb 49
Denison Ho. E14 48Dc 92
Denison Rd. SW19 65Fb 133
TW13: Felt 63V 128
W5 42La 86
Deniston Av. DA5: Bexl 60Ad 117
Denis Way SW4 55Mb 112
Denland Ho. SW8 52Pb 112
(off Dorset Rd.)
Denleigh Gdns. KT7: T Ditt 72Ga 152
N21 18Qb 32
Denley Sq. UB8: Uxb 38M 63
Denly Way GU18: Light 2A 166
Denman Dr. KT10: Clay 78Ja 152
NW11 29Cb 49
TW15: Ashf 65R 128
Denman Dr. Nth. NW11 29Cb 49
Denman Dr. Sth. NW11 29Cb 49
Denman Ho. N16 33Ub 71
Denman Pl. W1 4D 222
Denman Rd. SE15 53Vb 113
Denman St. W1 5D 222 (45Mb 90)
Denmark Av. SW19 66Ab 132
Denmark Ct. KT13: Weyb 76R 150
(off Grotto Rd.)
SM4: Mord 72Cb 155
Denmark Gdns. SM5: Cars 76Hb 155
Denmark Gro. N1 1K 217 (40Qb 70)
DENMARK HILL 55Sb 113
Denmark Hill SE5 53Tb 113
Denmark Hill Dr. NW9 27Wa 48
Denmark Hill Est. SE5 56Tb 113
Denmark Ho. SE7 49Nc 94
Denmark Lodge RM3: Hrld W 25Nd 57
Denmark Mans. SE5 54Sb 113
(off Coldharbour La.)
Denmark Path SE25 71Xb 157
Denmark Pl. E3 41Cc 92
WC2 2E 222 (44Mb 90)
Denmark Rd. BR1: Brom 67Kc 137
KT1: King T 69Na 131
N8 28Qb 50
NW6 40Bb 69
SE5 53Sb 113
SE25 71Wb 157
SM5: Cars 76Hb 155
SW19 65Za 132
TW2: Twick 62Fa 130
W13 45Ka 86
Denmark St. E11 34Gc 73
E13 43Kc 93
N17 25Xb 51
WC2 3E 222 (44Mb 90)
WD17: Wat 12X 27
Denmark Ter. N2 27Hb 49
Denmark Wlk. SE27 63Sb 135
Denmead Cl. SL9: Ger X 31A 62
Denmead Ho. SW15 58Va 110
Denmead Rd. CR0: C'don 74Rb 157
Denmore Ct. SM6: Wall 78Kb 156
Dennan Rd. KT6: Surb 74Pa 153
Dennard Way BR6: Farnb 77Rc 160
Denner Rd. E4 19Cc 34
Denne Ter. E8 39Vb 71
Dennett Rd. CR0: C'don 74Qb 156
Dennett's Gro. SE14 54Zb 114
Dennett's Rd. SE14 53Yb 114
Denning Av. CR0: Wadd 77Qb 156
Denning Cl. NW8 3A 214 (41Eb 89)
TW12: Hamp 64Ba 129
Denning M. SW12 58Jb 112
Denning Point E1 2K 225
Denning Rd. NW3 35Fb 69
Dennington Cl. E5 33Yb 72
Dennington Pk. Rd. NW6 37Cb 69
Denningtons, The KT4: Wor Pk 75Ua 154
Dennis Av. HA9: Wemb 36Pa 67
Dennis Cl. RH1: Redh 4N 207
TW15: Ashf 66T 128
Dennis Ct. AL3: St A 1B 6
Dennises La. RM14: Upm 39Ud 78
RM15: S Ock 39Wd 78
Dennis Gdns. HA7: Stan 22La 46
Dennis Ho. E3 40Bc 72
(off Roman Rd.)
SM1: Sutt 77Db 155
Dennis La. HA7: Stan 20Ka 28
Dennison Point E15 38Ec 72
Dennis Pde. N14 18Mb 32
Dennis Pk. Cres. SW20 67Ab 132
Dennis Reeve Cl. CR4: Mitc 67Hb 133
Dennis Rd. DA11: Grav'nd 2C 144
KT8: E Mos 70Ea 130
RM15: S Ock 38Wd 78
Dennis Severs' House 7J 219 (43Ub 91)
Dennis Way SL1: Slou 5B 80
SW4 55Mb 112
Denny Av. EN9: Walt A 6Fc 21
Denny Cl. E6 43Nc 94
Denny Ct. DA2: Dart 58Rd 119
(off Bow Arrow La.)
Denny Cres. SE11 7A 230 (50Qb 90)
Denny Gdns. RM9: Dag 38Xc 75
Denny Rd. N9 18Xb 33
SL3: L'ly 49B 82
Denny St. SE11 7A 230 (50Qb 90)
De Novo Pl. AL1: St A 2D 6
(off Stanhope Rd.)
Den Rd. BR2: Brom 69Fc 137
Densham Dr. CR8: Purl 86Qb 176
Densham Ho. NW8 2C 214
Densham Rd. E15 39Gc 73
Densole Cl. BR3: Beck 67Ac 136
Denstone Ho. SE15 51Wb 113
(off Haymerle Rd.)
Densworth Gro. N9 19Yb 34
Dent Cl. RM15: S Ock 44Wd 98
Dent Ho. SE17 6H 231
DENTON 9G 122
Denton NW1 37Jb 70
Denton Cl. EN5: Barn 15Ya 30
RH1: Redh 10A 208
Denton Ct. Rd. DA12: Grav'nd 9G 122
Denton Gro. KT12: Walt T 75Aa 151
Denton Ho. N1 38Rb 71
(off Halton Rd.)
WD19: Wat 20Y 27
Denton Rd. DA1: Dart 59Gd 118
DA5: Bexl 61Gd 140
DA16: Well 52Yc 117
N8 29Pb 50
N18 21Ub 51
TW1: Twick 58Ma 109
Denton St. DA12: Grav'nd 9G 122
SW18 58Db 111
Denton Ter. DA5: Bexl 61Gd 140
Denton Way E5 34Zb 72
GU21: Wok 9K 167
SL1: Slou 7M 81
Denton Wharf DA12: Grav'nd 8G 122
Dents Gro. KT20: Lwr K 100Bb 195
Dents Rd. SW11 58Hb 111
Denvale Wlk. GU21: Wok 10L 167
Denver Cl. BR6: Pet W 72Uc 160
Denver Ind. Est. RM13: Rain 43Hd 96
Denver Rd. DA1: Dart 59Jd 118
N16 31Ub 71
Denwood SE23 62Zb 136
Denyer St. SW3 6E 226 (49Gb 89)
Denys Ho. EC1 7K 217
Denziloe Av. UB10: Hil 41R 84
Denzil Rd. NW10 36Va 68
Deodar Rd. SW15 56Ab 110
Deodora Cl. N20 20Gb 31
Department for Communities 3B 228
De Pass Gdns. IG11: Bark 42Wc 95
De Paul Way CM14: B'wood 18Xd 40
Depot App. NW2 35Za 68
Depot Rd. KT17: Eps 85Ua 174
TW3: Houn 55Fa 108
W12 45Ya 88
Depot St. SE5 51Tb 113
DEPTFORD 52Cc 114
Deptford Bri. SE8 53Cc 114
Deptford B'way. SE8 53Cc 114
Deptford Bus. Pk. SE15 51Yb 114
Deptford Chu. St. SE8 51Cc 114
Deptford Creek Bri. SE8 51Dc 114
(off Creek Rd.)
Deptford Ferry Rd. E14 49Cc 92
Deptford Grn. SE8 51Cc 114
Deptford High St. SE8 51Cc 114
Deptford Pk. Bus. Cen. SE8 50Ac 92
Deptford Strand SE8 49Bc 92
Deptford Trad. Est. SE8 50Ac 92
Deptford Wharf SE8 49Bc 92
De Quincey Ho. SW1 7B 228
De Quincey M. E16 46Jc 93
De Quincey Rd. N17 25Tb 51
Derby Arms Rd. KT18: Eps D 89Va 174
Derby Av. HA3: Hrw W 25Fa 46
N12 22Eb 49
RM7: Rom 30Ed 56
RM14: Upm 34Pd 77
Derby Cl. KT18: Tatt C 91Xa 194
Derby Ga. SW1 1F 229 (47Nb 90)
(not continuous)
Derby Hill SE23 61Yb 136
Derby Hill Cres. SE23 61Yb 136
Derby Ho. HA5: Pinn 26Z 45
SE11 5K 229
WD23: Bush 14Ca 27
Derby Lodge N3 26Bb 49
WC1 3H 217
Derby Rd. CR0: C'don 74Rb 157
E7 38Mc 73
E9 39Zb 72
E18 25Hc 53
EN3: Pond E 15Xb 33
KT5: Surb 74Qa 153
N18 22Yb 52
RM17: Grays 50De 99
SM1: Sutt 79Bb 155
SW14 56Ra 109
SW19 66Cb 133
TW3: Houn 56Da 107
UB6: G'frd 39Da 65
UB8: Uxb 40L 63
WD17: Wat 13Y 27
(not continuous)
Derby Rd. Bri. RM17: Grays 51De 121
Derby Rd. Ind. Est. TW3: Houn 56Da 107
Derbyshire St. E2 41Wb 91
(not continuous)
Derby Sq., The KT19: Eps 85Ta 173
(off High St.)
Derby Stables Rd. KT18: Eps D 89Va 174
Derby St. W1 7J 221 (46Jb 90)
Dere Cl. SW6 53Ab 110
Dereham Ho. SE4 56Zb 114
(off Frendsbury Rd.)
Dereham Pl. EC2 4J 219 (41Ub 91)
RM5: Col R 23Dd 56
Dereham Rd. IG11: Bark 36Vc 75
Derek Av. HA9: Wemb 38Ra 67
KT19: Ewe 79Qa 153
SM6: Wall 77Kb 156
Derek Cl. KT19: Ewe 78Ra 153
Derek Walcott Cl. SE24 57Rb 113
Derham Gdns. RM14: Upm 34Sd 78
Deri Av. RM13: Rain 42Kd 97
Dericote St. E8 39Xb 71
Deri Dene Cl. TW19: Stanw 58N 105
Derifall Cl. E6 43Pc 94
Dering Pl. CR0: C'don 77Sb 157
Dering Rd. CR0: C'don 77Sb 157
Dering St. W1 3K 221 (44Kb 90)
Dering Way DA12: Grav'nd 9H 123
Dering Yd. W1 3A 222 (44Kb 90)
Derinton Rd. SW17 63Hb 133
Derisley Cl. KT14: Byfl 84M 169
Derley Rd. UB2: S'hall 48Y 85
Dermody Gdns. SE13 57Fc 115
Dermody Rd. SE13 57Fc 115
Deronda Rd. SE24 60Rb 113
De Ros Pl. TW20: Egh 65C 126
Deroy Cl. SM5: Cars 79Hb 155
Derrick Av. CR2: Sande 82Sb 177
Derrick Gdns. SE7 48Lc 93
Derrick Rd. BR3: Beck 69Bc 136
Derry Av. RM15: S Ock 44Wd 98
Derrycombe Ho. W2 43Cb 89
(off Gt. Western Rd.)
Derrydown GU22: Wok 3N 187
DERRY DOWNS 72Yc 161
Derry Downs BR5: St M Cry 72Yc 161
Derry Ho. NW8 6C 214
Derry M. N19 33Nb 70
Derry Rd. CR0: Bedd 76Nb 156
Derry St. W8 47Db 89
Dersingham Av. E12 35Pc 74
Dersingham Rd. NW2 34Ab 68
Derwent NW1 4B 216
Derwent Av. EN4: E Barn 18Hb 31
HA5: Hat E 23Aa 45
N18 22Tb 51
NW7 23Ta 47
NW9 29Ua 48
SW15 63Ua 132
UB10: Ick 33Q 64
Derwent Cl. DA1: Dart 60Kd 119
KT10: Clay 79Ga 152
KT15: Add 78M 149
TW14: Felt 60V 106
WD25: Wat 6Y 13
Derwent Ct. SE16 47Zb 92
(off Eleanor Cl.)
Derwent Cres. DA7: Bex 54Cd 118
HA7: Stan 26La 46
N20 20Eb 31
Derwent Dr. BR5: Pet W 73Tc 160
CR8: Purl 85Tb 177
SL1: Slou 3A 80
UB4: Hayes 43U 84
Derwent Gdns. HA9: Wemb 31La 66
IG4: Ilf 28Nc 54
Derwent Gro. SE22 56Vb 113
Derwent Ho. E3 42Bc 92
(off Southern Gro.)
KT2: King T 67Ma 131
(off May Bate Av.)
SW7 5A 226
Derwent Lodge KT4: Wor Pk 75Xa 154
TW7: Isle 54Fa 108
Derwent Pde. RM15: S Ock 44Wd 98
Derwent Point EC1 3B 218
(off Goswell Rd.)
Derwent Ri. NW9 30Ua 48
Derwent Rd. GU18: Light 3A 166
HP3: Hem H 3C 4
N13 21Pb 50
SE20 68Wb 135
SW20 72Za 154
TW2: Whitt 58Da 107
TW20: Egh 66D 126
UB1: S'hall 44Ba 85
W5 48La 86
Derwent St. SE10 50Gc 93
Derwent Wlk. SM6: Wall 80Kb 156
Derwentwater Rd. W3 46Sa 87
Derwent Way RM12: Horn 36Kd 77
Derwent Yd. W5 48La 86
(off Derwent Rd.)
De Salis Rd. UB10: Hil 42S 84
Des Barres Ct. SE10 48Jc 93
Desborough Cl. TW17: Shep 73Q 150
W2 43Db 89
Desborough Ho. W14 51Bb 111
(off North End Rd.)
Desborough Sailing Club 73R 150
Desborough St. W2 43Db 89
(off Cirencester St.)
Desenfans Rd. SE21 58Ub 113
Deseronto Trad. Est. SL3: L'ly 47A 82
Desford Rd. E16 42Gc 93
Desford Way TW15: Ashf 61P 127
Design Mus.
Kensington 48Bb 89
Desmond Ho. EN4: E Barn 16Gb 31
Desmond Rd. WD24: Wat 8V 12
Desmond St. SE14 51Ac 114
Desmond Tutu Dr. SE23 60Bc 114
Despard Rd. N19 32Lb 70
de Stafford Sports Cen. 93Vb 197
Desvignes Dr. SE13 58Fc 115
De Tany Ct. AL1: St A 3B 6
Dethick Ct. E3 39Ac 72
Detillens La. RH8: Limp 1L 211
Detling Cl. RM12: Horn 36Ld 77
Detling Ho. SE17 6H 231
Detling Rd. BR1: Brom 64Jc 137
DA8: Erith 52Fd 118
DA11: Nflt 60Fe 121
Detmold Rd. E5 33Yb 72
Dettingen Pl. IG11: Bark 40Xc 75
Deva Cl. AL3: St A 4N 5
Devalls Cl. E6 45Rc 94
Devana End SM5: Cars 76Hb 155
Devane Way SE27 62Rb 135
Devan Gro. N4 31Tb 71
Devas Rd. SW20 67Ya 132
Devas St. E3 42Dc 92
Devenay Rd. E15 38Hc 73
Devenish La. SL5: S'dale 4C 146
Devenish Rd. SE2 47Wc 95
SL5: S'dale, S'hill 2A 146
Deventer Cres. SE22 57Ub 113
Deveraux Cl. BR3: Beck 71Ec 158
De Vere Cl. SM6: Wall 80Nb 156
De Vere Cotts. W8 48Eb 89
(off Canning Pl.)
De Vere Gdns. IG1: Ilf 33Pc 74
W8 3A 226 (47Eb 89)
De Vere Leisure Club
Denham 27G 42
Deverell St. SE1 4F 231 (48Tb 91)
De Vere M. W8 3A 226
Devereux Ct. WC2 3K 223
Devereux Dr. WD17: Wat 10U 12
Devereux La. SW13 52Xa 110
Devereux Rd. RM16: Chaf H 48Be 99
SL4: Wind 4H 103
SW11 58Hb 111
De Vere Wlk. WD17: Wat 12U 26
Deverills Way SL3: L'ly 49E 82
Deveron Gdns. RM15: S Ock 43Wd 98
Deveron Way RM1: Rom 25Gd 56
Devey Cl. KT2: King T 66Va 132
Devil's La. TW18: Staines 66F 126
TW20: Egh 65E 126
Devitt Cl. KT21: Asht 88Qa 173
Devitt Ho. E14 45Dc 92
(off Wade's Pl.)
Devizes Ho. RM3: Rom 22Md 57
(off Montgomery Cres.)

Devizes St.—Doncel Ct.

Devizes St. N1 39Tb 71
Devoke Way KT12: Walt T 75Z 151
Devon Av. SL1: Slou 4G 80
TW2: Twick 60Ea 108
Devon Cl. CR8: Kenley 88Vb 177
IG9: Buck H 19Kc 35
N17 27Vb 51
UB6: G'frd 39La 66
Devon Ct. AL1: St A 3C 6
DA4: Sut H 67Rd 141
KT18: Eps 86Ua 174
(off St Martin's Av.)
TW12: Hamp 66Ca 129
W7 43Ha 86
(off Copley Cl.)
Devon Cres. RH1: Redh 6M 207
Devoncroft Gdns.
TW1: Twick 59Ja 108
Devon Gdns. N4 30Rb 51
Devon Ho. CR3: Cat'm 96Vb 197
E17 26Bc 52
N1 1B 218
Devonhurst Pl. W4 50Ta 87
Devonia Gdns. N18 23Sb 51
Devonia Rd. N1 1C 218 (40Rb 71)
Devon Mans. HA3: Kenton 29La 46
(off Woodcock Hill)
SE1 2K 231
Devon Pde. HA3: Kenton 29La 46
Devonport W2 3D 220 (44Gb 89)
Devonport Gdns. IG1: Ilf 30Pc 54
Devonport Ho. W2 43Bb 89
(off Gt. Western Rd.)
Devonport M. W12 47Xa 88
Devonport Rd. W12 46Xa 88
(not continuous)
Devonport St. E1 44Yb 92
Devon Ri. N2 28Fb 49
Devon Rd.
DA4: S Dar, Sut H 67Rd 141
IG11: Bark 39Uc 74
KT12: Hers 77Y 151
RH1: Mers 2C 208
SM2: Cheam 81Ab 174
WD24: Wat 11Z 27
Devons Est. E3 41Dc 92
Devonshire Av. DA1: Dart 58Kd 119
GU21: Wok 86E 168
SM2: Sutt 80Eb 155
Devonshire Bus. Cen. EN6: Pot B 2Ab 16
Devonshire Bus. Pk. WD6: Bore 13Ta 29
Devonshire Cl. E15 35Gc 73
N13 20Qb 32
SL2: Farn R 10F 60
W1 7K 215 (43Kb 90)
Devonshire Ct. E1 41Yb 92
(off Bancroft Rd.)
HA5: Hat E 25Ba 45
(off Devonshire Rd.)
N17 23Sb 51
TW13: Felt 61X 129
WC1 7G 217
Devonshire Cres. NW7 24Za 48
Devonshire Dr. KT6: Surb 74Ma 153
SE10 52Dc 114
Devonshire Gdns. N17 23Sb 51
N21 17Sb 33
SS17: Linf 8J 101
W4 52Sa 109
Devonshire Grn. SL2: Farn R 10F 60
Devonshire Gro. SE15 51Xb 113
Devonshire Hall E9 37Yb 72
(off Frampton Pk. Rd.)
Devonshire Hill La. N17 23Rb 51
Devonshire Ho. E14 49Cc 92
(off Westferry Rd.)
IG8: Wfd G 24Rc 54
NW6 37Bb 69
(off Kilburn High Rd.)
SE1 3D 230
SM2: Sutt 80Eb 155
SW1 7E 228
SW15 57Za 110
W2 7C 214
WD23: Bush 14Ba 27
Devonshire Ho. Bus. Cen.
BR2: Brom 70Kc 137
(off Devonshire Sq.)
Devonshire M. N13 21Qb 50
SW10 51Fb 111
(off Park Wlk.)
W4 50Ua 88
Devonshire M. Nth. W1 7K 215 (43Kb 90)
Devonshire M. Sth. W1 7K 215 (43Kb 90)
Devonshire M. W. W1 6J 215 (42Jb 90)
Devonshire Pas. W4 50Ua 88
Devonshire Pl. NW2 34Cb 69
W1 6J 215 (42Jb 90)
W8 48Db 89
Devonshire Pl. M. W1 6J 215 (43Jb 90)
Devonshire Point TW15: Ashf 62S 128
Devonshire Rd. BR6: Orp 73Wc 161
CR0: C'don 73Tb 157
DA6: Bex 56Ad 117
DA12: Grav'nd 10D 122
E16 44Kc 93
E17 30Cc 52
HA1: Harr 30Fa 46
HA5: Eastc 30Y 45
HA5: Hat E 25Ba 45
IG2: Ilf 31Uc 74
KT13: Weyb 77Q 150
N9 18Yb 34
N13 21Pb 50
N17 23Sb 51
NW7 24Za 48
RM12: Horn 33Ld 77
RM16: Chaf H, Grays 50Ae 99
SE9 61Nc 138
SE23 60Yb 114
SM2: Sutt 80Eb 155
SM5: Cars 77Jb 156
SW19 66Gb 133
TW13: Hanw 62Aa 129
UB1: S'hall 43Ca 85
W4 50Ua 88
W5 48La 86
Devonshire Road Nature Reserve 59Zb 114
Devonshire Road Nature Reserve Vis. Cen. 59Zb 114
Devonshire Row
EC2 1J 225 (43Ub 91)
Devonshire Row M. W1 6A 216
Devonshires, The
KT18: Eps 86Va 174
Devonshire Sq. BR2: Brom 70Kc 137
EC2 2J 225 (44Ub 91)
Devonshire St. W1 7J 215 (43Jb 90)
W4 50Ua 88
Devonshire Ter. W2 3A 220 (44Eb 89)
Devonshire Way
CR0: C'don 75Ac 158
UB4: Yead 44X 85
Devons Rd. E3 41Dc 92
Devon St. SE15 51Xb 113
Devon Way KT9: Chess 78La 152
KT19: Ewe 78Ra 153
UB10: Hil 40P 63
Devon Waye TW5: Hest 52Ba 107
De Walden Ho. NW8 1D 214
De Walden St. W1 1J 221 (43Jb 90)
Dewar Spur SL3: L'ly 51B 104
Dewar St. SE15 55Wb 113
Dewberry Gdns. E6 43Nc 94
Dewberry St. E14 43Ec 92
Dewey Ct. BR1: Brom 69Jc 137
Dewey La. SW2 58Qb 112
(off Tulse Hill)
Dewey Path RM12: Horn 37Ld 77
Dewey Rd. N1 1K 217 (40Qb 70)
RM10: Dag 37Dd 76
Dewey St. SW17 64Hb 133
Dewgrass Gro. EN8: Walt C 7Zb 20
Dewhurst Ct. TW3: Houn 56Ca 107
Dewhurst Rd. EN8: Chesh 1Xb 19
W14 48Za 88
Dewlands RH9: G'stone 3A 210
(not continuous)
Dewlands Av. DA2: Dart 59Rd 119
Dewlands Rd. RH9: G'stone 3A 210
Dewsbury Cl. HA5: Pinn 30Aa 45
RM3: Rom 23Nd 57
Dewsbury Ct. W4 49Sa 87
Dewsbury Gdns.
KT4: Wor Pk 76Wa 154
RM3: Rom 23Md 57
Dewsbury Rd. NW10 36Wa 68
RM3: Rom 23Md 57
Dewsbury Ter. NW1 39Kb 70
Dews Farm Sand Pits Nature Reserve 30M 43
De Wyndsor Ct. SE16 48Wb 91
(off Jamaica Rd.)
Dexter Apartments SE15 53Xb 113
(off Queen's Rd.)
Dexter Cl. AL1: St A 3E 6
RM17: Grays 48Ce 99
Dexter Ho. DA18: Erith 48Ad 95
(off Kale Rd.)
Dexter Rd. EN5: Barn 16Za 30
UB9: Hare 26L 43
Deyncourt Gdns. RM14: Upm 33Sd 78
Deyncourt Rd. N17 25Sb 51
Deynecourt Gdns. E11 28Lc 53
D'Eynsford Rd. SE5 53Tb 113
Dharam Marg
WD25: A'ham, Let H 12Ea 28
Dhonau Ho. SE1 5K 231
Diadem Ct. W1 3D 222
Dial Cl. DA9: Ghithe 57Yd 120
Dialmead EN6: Ridge 6Va 16
Dial Stone Ct. KT13: Weyb 78S 150
Dial Wlk., The W8 47Db 89
Diamedes Av. TW19: Stanw 59M 105
Diameter Rd. BR5: Pet W 73Rc 160
Diamond Cl. RM8: Dag 32Yc 75
RM16: Chaf H 48Be 99
Diamond Ct. BR5: St P 67Xc 139
RH1: Redh 5A 208
(off St Anne's Mt.)
RM11: Horn 32Jd 76
Diamond Est. SW17 62Gb 133
Diamond Gdns. E3 43Bc 92
Diamond Ho. E3 40Ac 72
(off Roman Rd.)
Diamond Jubilee Way
SM5: Cars 80Hb 155
Diamond Pl. RH2: Reig 5K 207
Diamond Rd. HA4: Ruis 35Z 65
SL1: Slou 7L 81
WD24: Wat 10W 12
Diamond St. NW10 38Ta 67
SE15 52Ub 113
Diamond Ter. SE10 53Ec 114
Diamond Way SE8 51Cc 114
Diana Cl. DA14: Sidc 61Ad 139
E18 25Kc 53
RM16: Chaf H 48Be 99
SE8 51Bc 114
SL3: Geor G 44A 82
Diana Ct. DA8: Erith 51Gd 118
Diana Gdns. KT6: Surb 75Pa 153
Diana Ho. SW13 53Va 110
Diana, Princess of Wales
Memorial Playground 46Db 89
Diana, Princess of Wales Memorial Walk 1A 226
Diana Rd. E17 27Bc 52
Dianne Ct. SE12 60Jc 115
Dianne Way EN4: E Barn 14Gb 31
Dianthus Cl. KT16: Chert 73G 148
SE2 50Xc 95
Dianthus Ct. GU22: Wok 90C 168
Diban Av. RM12: Horn 35Kd 77
Diban Ct. RM12: Horn 35Kd 77
(off The Broadway)
DIBDEN 99Gd 202
Dibden Ho. SE5 52Ub 113
Dibden La. TN14: Ide H, S'oaks 98Gd 202
Dibden St. N1 39Sb 71
Dibdin Cl. SM1: Sutt 76Cb 155
Dibdin Ho. W9 40Db 69
Dibdin Rd. SM1: Sutt 76Cb 155
Dibdin Row SE1 3A 230 (48Qb 90)
Diceland Lodge SM7: Bans 88Bb 175
(off Diceland Rd.)
Diceland Rd. SM7: Bans 88Bb 175
Dicey Av. NW2 35Ya 68
Dickens Av. DA1: Dart 56Qd 119
N3 25Eb 49
RM18: Tilb 3D 122
UB8: Hil 44R 84
Dickens Cl. AL3: St A 1B 6
DA3: Hartl 71Be 165
DA8: Erith 52Dd 118
TW10: Ham 61Na 131
UB3: Harl 49U 84
Dickens Ct. E11 28Jc 53
(off Makepeace Rd.)
SW17 62Fb 133
(off Grosvenor Way)
Dickens Dr. BR7: Chst 65Sc 138
KT15: Add 79H 149
Dickens Est. SE1 47Wb 91
SE16 48Wb 91
Dickens Ho. NW6 41Cb 89
(off Malvern Rd.)
NW8 5C 214
SE17 50Rb 91
(off Doddington Gro.)
SE19 66Ub 135
WC1 5F 217
Dickens La. N18 22Ub 51
Dickens M. EC1 7B 218
Dickenson Cl. N9 18Wb 33
Dickenson Rd. N8 31Nb 70
TW13: Hanw 64Y 129
Dickensons La. SE25 71Wb 157
(not continuous)
Dickensons Pl. SE25 72Wb 157
Dickens Pl. SL3: Poyle 53G 104
Dickens Ri. IG7: Chig 20Rc 36
Dickens Rd. DA12: Grav'nd 10G 122
E6 40Mc 73
Dickens Sq. SE1 3E 230 (48Sb 91)
Dickens St. SW8 54Kb 112
Dickens Way RM1: Rom 28Gd 56
Dickenswood Cl. SE19 66Rb 135
Dickerage La. KT3: N Mald 69Sa 131
Dickerage Rd. KT1: King T 67Sa 131
KT3: N Mald 67Sa 131
Dickinson Av. WD3: Crox G 16Q 26
Dickinson Ct. EC1 6C 218
Dickinson Quay HP3: Hem H 7N 3
Dickinson Sq. WD3: Crox G 16R 26
Dicksee Ho. NW8 6B 214
Dickson Fold HA5: Pinn 28Z 45
Dickson Ho. E1 44Xb 91
(off Philpot St.)
N1 38Qb 70
(off Drummond Way)
Dickson Rd. SE9 55Nc 116
Dick Turpin Way TW14: Felt 56V 106
Didsbury Cl. E6 39Pc 74
Digby Bus. Cen. E9 37Zb 72
(off Digby Rd.)
Digby Cres. N4 33Sb 71
Digby Gdns. RM10: Dag 39Cd 76
Digby Mans. W6 50Xa 88
(off Hammersmith Bri. Rd.)
Digby M. RM3: Rom 23Nd 57
Digby Pl. CR0: C'don 76Vb 157
Digby Rd. E9 37Zb 72
IG11: Bark 38Vc 75
Digby St. E2 41Yb 92
Digby Wlk. RM12: Horn 37Ld 77
Digby Way KT14: Byfl 84P 169
Digdens Ri. KT18: Eps 87Sa 173
Diggens Ct. IG10: Lough 13Nc 36
Diggon St. E1 43Zb 92
Dighton Ct. SE5 51Sb 113
Dighton Rd. SW18 57Eb 111
Dignum St. N1 1K 217 (40Qb 70)
Digswell Cl. WD6: Bore 10Qa 15
Digswell St. N7 37Qb 70
Dilhorne Cl. SE12 62Kc 137
Dilke St. SW3 51Hb 111
Dillon Cl. KT19: Eps 84Pa 173
Dilloway La. UB2: S'hall 47Aa 85
Dillwyn Cl. SE26 63Ac 136
Dilston Cl. UB5: N'olt 41Y 85
Dilston Gro. SE16 49Yb 92
Dilston Rd. KT22: Lea 91Ja 192
Dilton Gdns. SW15 60Wa 110
Dilwyn Ct. E17 26Ac 52
Dimes Pl. W6 49Xa 88
Dimmock Dr. UB6: G'frd 36Fa 66
Dimmocks La. WD3: Sarr 8K 11
Dimond Cl. E7 35Jc 73
Dimsdale Dr. EN1: Enf 17Wb 33
NW9 32Sa 67
SL2: Farn C 6C 60
Dimsdale Hgts. E1 44Xb 91
(off Spencer Way)
Dimsdale Wlk. E13 40Jc 73
Dimson Cres. E3 41Cc 92
Dinerman Ct. NW8 39Eb 69
Dingle, The UB10: Hil 41R 84
Dingle Cl. EN5: Ark 16Va 30
Dingle Gdns. E14 45Cc 92
Dingle Rd. TW15: Ashf 64R 128
Dingles Ct. HA5: Pinn 25Z 45
Dingley La. SW16 61Mb 134
Dingley Pl. EC1 4E 218 (41Sb 91)
Dingley Rd. EC1 3E 218 (41Sb 91)
Dingwall Av. CR0: C'don 75Sb 157
Dingwall Gdns. NW11 30Cb 49
Dingwall Rd. CR0: C'don 74Tb 157
SM5: Cars 81Hb 175
SW18 59Eb 111
Dinmont Est. E2 40Wb 71
Dinmont Ho. E2 40Wb 71
(off Pritchard's Rd.)
Dinmont St. E2 40Xb 71
Dinmore HP3: Bov 10B 2
Dinmore Ho. E9 39Yb 72
(off Templecombe Rd.)
Dinnington Ho. E1 42Xb 91
(off Coventry Rd.)
Dinsdale Cl. GU22: Wok 90C 168
Dinsdale Gdns. EN5: New Bar 15Db 31
SE25 71Ub 157
Dinsdale Rd. SE3 51Hc 115
Dinsmore Rd. SW12 59Kb 112
Dinton Ho. NW8 5D 214
Dinton Rd. KT2: King T 66Pa 131
SW19 65Fb 133
Diploma Av. N2 28Gb 49
Diploma Ct. N2 28Gb 49
Dippers Cl. TN15: Kems'g 89Pd 183
Diprose Lodge SW17 63Fb 133
Dirdene Cl. KT17: Eps 84Va 174
Dirdene Gdns. KT17: Eps 84Va 174
Dirdene Gro. KT17: Eps 84Ua 174
Dirleton Rd. E15 39Hc 73
Dirtham La. KT24: Eff 100X 191
Dirty La. SE1 6E 224 (46Sb 91)
Disbrowe Rd. W6 51Ab 110
Discover
Stratford 38Fc 73
Discover Greenwich Vis. Cen. 51Ec 114
Discovery Bus. Pk. SE16 48Wb 91
(off St James's Rd.)
Discovery Cen. (Beckton), The 41Sc 94
Discovery Dock Apartments E.
E14 47Dc 92
(off Sth. Quay Sq.)
Discovery Dock Apartments W.
E14 47Dc 92
(off Sth. Quay Sq.)
Discovery Ho. E14 45Ec 92
(off Newby Pl.)
Discovery Wlk. E1 46Xb 91
Dishforth La. NW9 24Ua 48
Disley Ct. UB1: S'hall 44Da 85
(off Howard Rd.)
Disney Pl. SE1 1E 230 (47Sb 91)
Disney St. SE1 1E 230 (47Sb 91)
Dison Cl. EN3: Enf H 11Zb 34
Disraeli Cl. SE28 46Yc 95
W4 48Ta 87
Disraeli Ct. SL3: L'ly 51D 104
Disraeli Gdns. SW15 56Bb 111
Disraeli Rd. E7 37Jc 73
NW10 40Ta 67
SW15 56Ab 110
W5 46Ma 87
Diss St. E2 2K 219 (41Vb 91)
Distaff La. EC4 4D 224 (45Sb 91)
Distillery La. W6 50Ya 88
Distillery Rd. W6 50Ya 88
Distillery Twr. SE8 53Cc 114
Distillery Wlk. TW8: Bford 51Na 109
Distillery Wharf W6 51Ya 110
Distin St. SE11 6K 229 (49Qb 90)
District Rd. HA0: Wemb 36Ka 66
Ditch All. SE13 53Dc 114
Ditchburn St. E14 45Ec 92
Ditches La. CR3: Cat'm, Coul 92Nb 196
CR5: Coul 92Nb 196
Ditches Ride, The
CM16: Lough, They B 10Qc 22
IG10: Lough 10Qc 22
Ditchfield Rd. UB4: Yead 42Aa 85
Ditchley Ct. W7 44Ha 86
(off Templeman Rd.)
Ditchling Ct. AL1: St A 2C 6
(off Bricket Rd.)
Dittisham Rd. SE9 63Nc 138
Ditton Cl. KT7: T Ditt 73Ja 152
Dittoncroft Cl. CR0: C'don 77Ub 157
Ditton Grange Cl. KT6: Surb 74Ma 153
Ditton Grange Dr. KT6: Surb 74Ma 153
Ditton Hill KT6: Surb 74La 152
Ditton Hill Rd. KT6: Surb 74La 152
Ditton Lawn KT7: T Ditt 74Ja 152
Ditton Pk. 10P 81
Ditton Pk. Rd. SL3: L'ly 51A 104
Ditton Pl. SE20 67Xb 135
Ditton Reach KT7: T Ditt 72Ka 152
Ditton Rd. DA6: Bex 57Zc 117
KT6: Surb 75Ma 153
SL3: Dat 3P 103
SL3: L'ly 50B 82
UB2: S'hall 50Ba 85
Diversity Av. RM13: Rain 40Fd 76
Divine Way UB3: Hayes 44T 84
Divis Way SW15 58Xa 110
(off Dover Pk. Dr.)
Dixon Clark Ct. N1 37Rb 71
Dixon Cl. E6 44Pc 94
Dixon Dr. KT13: Weyb 82P 169
Dixon Ho. W10 44Za 88
(off Darfield Way)
Dixon Pl. BR4: W W'ck 74Dc 158
Dixon Rd. SE14 53Ac 114
SE25 69Ub 135
Dixon's All. SE16 47Xb 91
Dixons Hill Cl. AL9: N Mym 7D 8
Dixons Hill Rd. AL9: N Mym, Wel G 7D 8
Dixon Way NW10 38Ua 68
Dobbin Cl. HA3: Kenton 26Ja 46
Dobell Rd. SE9 57Pc 116
Doble Ct. CR2: Sande 84Wb 177
Dobles Ct. CR5: Coul 87Nb 176
Dobree Av. NW10 38Xa 68
Dobson Cl. NW6 38Fb 69
Dobson Ho. SE14 51Zb 114
(off John Williams Cl.)
Dobson Rd. DA12: Grav'nd 4G 144
Dobson Wlk. SE5 52Tb 113
Doby Ct. EC4 4E 224
Dock App. Rd. RM16: Grays 1A 122
RM17: Grays 1A 122
Dock Cotts. E1 45Yb 92
(off The Highway)
Dockers Tanner Rd. E14 48Cc 92
Dockett Eddy KT16: Chert 74N 149
Dockett Eddy La. TW17: Shep 74P 149
Dockett Moorings KT16: Chert 74N 149
Dockhead SE1 2K 231 (47Vb 91)
Dockhead Wharf SE1 1K 231
Dock Hill Av. SE16 46Zb 92
Docklands Ct. E14 44Bc 92
(off Wharf La.)
Docklands Equestrian Cen., The 42Qc 94
Docklands Sailing & Watersports Cen. 48Cc 92
Dockland St. E16 46Qc 94
(not continuous)
Dockley Rd. SE16 48Wb 91
Dockley Rd. Ind. Est. SE16 48Wb 91
(off Dockley Rd.)
Dock Mdw. Reach W7 48Ga 86
Dock Offices SE16 48Yb 92
(off Surrey Quays Rd.)
Dock Rd. E16 45Hc 93
IG11: Bark 40Sc 74
RM17: Grays 51Fe 121
(not continuous)
RM18: Tilb 3A 122
TW8: Bford 52Ma 109
Dockside Ct. E5 33Yb 72
Dockside Rd. E16 45Mc 93
Dock St. E1 45Wb 91
Dock Wlk. RM3: Rom 22Ld 57
Dockwell Cl. TW14: Felt 56W 106
Dockwell's Ind. Est. TW14: Felt 57X 107
Doctor Johnson Av. SW17 62Kb 134
Dr Johnson's House 2A 224
Doctors Cl. SE26 64Yb 136
Doctors La. CR3: Cat'm 95Qb 196
Docura Ho. N7 33Pb 70
Docwra's Bldgs. N1 37Ub 71
Dodbrooke Rd. SE27 62Qb 134
Dodd Ho. SE16 49Xb 91
(off Rennie Est.)
Doddinghurst Rd.
CM15: B'wood, Dodd, Pil H 11Zd 41
Doddington Gro. SE17 7C 230 (51Rb 113)
Doddington Pl. SE17 51Rb 113
Dodd Rd. WD24: Wat 8W 12
Dodds Cres. KT14: W Byf 86K 169
Doddsfield Rd. SL2: Slou 1E 80
Dodd's La. GU22: Pyr 86J 169
Dodsley Pl. N9 20Yb 34
Dodson St. SE1 2A 230 (47Qb 90)
Dod St. E14 44Bc 92
Doebury Wlk. SE18 52Wc 117
(off Prestwood Cl.)
Doel Cl. SW19 66Eb 133
Dog & Duck Yd. WC1 7H 217
Doggett Rd. SE6 59Cc 114
Doggetts Cl. EN4: E Barn 15Gb 31
Doggett's Cnr. RM11: Horn 33Pd 77
Doggetts Farm Rd. UB9: Den 31E 62
Doggetts Way AL1: St A 4A 6
Doghurst Av. UB3: Harl 52R 106
Doghurst Dr. UB7: Sip 52R 106
Doghurst La. CR5: Chip 92Hb 195
Dog Kennel Hill SE22 55Ub 113
Dog Kennel Hill Est. SE22 55Ub 113
(off Albrighton Rd.)
Dog Kennel La. WD3: Chor 14H 25
Dog La. NW10 35Ua 68
Dogwood Cl. DA11: Nflt 3B 144
Doherty Rd. E13 42Jc 93
Dokal Ind. Est. UB2: S'hall 47Aa 85
Dolben Ct. SW1 6E 228
Dolben St. SE1 7B 224 (46Rb 91)
(not continuous)
Dolby Rd. SW6 54Bb 111
Dolland Ho. SE11 7J 229
Dolland St. SE11 7J 229 (50Pb 90)
Dollar Bay E14 47Ec 92
Dollary Pde. KT1: King T 69Ra 131
(off Kingston Rd.)
Dolliffe Cl. CR4: Mitc 68Gb 133
Dollis Av. N3 25Bb 49
Dollis Brook Wlk. EN5: Barn 16Ab 30
Dollis Cres. HA4: Ruis 32Y 65
Dolliscroft NW7 24Ab 48
DOLLIS HILL 33Xa 68
Dollis Hill Av. NW2 34Xa 68
Dollis Hill La. NW2 35Va 68
Dollis M. N3 25Cb 49
Dollis Pk. N3 25Bb 49
Dollis Rd. N3 24Ab 48
NW7 24Ab 48
Dollis Valley Dr. EN5: Barn 16Bb 31
Dollis Valley Way EN5: Barn 16Bb 31
Dollypers Hill Nature Reserve 90Rb 177
Dolman Cl. N3 26Eb 49
Dolman Rd. W4 49Ta 87
Dolman St. SW4 56Pb 112
Dolphin App. RM1: Rom 28Hd 56
Dolphin Cl. KT6: Surb 71Ma 153
SE16 47Zb 92
SE28 44Zc 95
Dolphin Ct. IG7: Chig 20Rc 36
NW11 30Ab 48
SL1: Slou 7M 81
TW18: Staines 62J 127
Dolphin Ct. Nth. TW18: Staines 62J 127
Dolphin Est. TW16: Sun 67U 128
Dolphin Ho. SW6 54Eb 111
(off Lensbury Av.)
SW18 56Db 111
Dolphin La. E14 45Dc 92
Dolphin Pk. Ind. Est. RM19: Purf 50Ud 98
Dolphin Point RM19: Purf 50Ud 98
Dolphin Rd. SL1: Slou 7M 81
TW16: Sun 67U 128
UB5: N'olt 40Ba 65
Dolphin Rd. Nth. TW16: Sun 67U 128
Dolphin Rd. Sth. TW16: Sun 67U 128
Dolphin Rd. W. TW16: Sun 67U 128
Dolphin Sq. SW1 50Lb 90
W4 52Ua 110
Dolphin St. KT1: King T 68Na 131
Dolphin Twr. SE8 51Bc 114
(off Abinger Gro.)
Dolphin Way RM19: Purf 49Ud 98
Dolphin Yd. AL1: St A 3B 6
(off Holywell Hill)
Dolphin Yard, The DA12: Grav'nd 8D 122
(off Queen St.)
Dombey Ho. SE1 47Wb 91
(off Wolseley St.)
W11 46Za 88
(off St Ann's Rd.)
Dombey St. WC1 7H 217 (43Pb 90)
(not continuous)
DOME, THE 8Y 13
Dome, The RH1: Redh 5P 207
Domecq Ho. EC1 5C 218
Dome Hill CR3: Cat'm 99Ub 197
Dome Hill Pk. SE26 63Vb 135
Dome Hill Peak CR3: Cat'm 98Ub 197
Domelton Ho. SW18 58Db 111
(off Iron Mill Rd.)
Domett Cl. SE5 56Tb 113
Dome Way RH1: Redh 5P 207
Domfe Pl. E5 35Yb 72
Domingo St. EC1 5D 218 (42Sb 91)
Dominica Cl. E13 40Mc 73
Dominic Ct. EN9: Walt A 5Dc 20
Dominion Bus. Pk. N9 19Zb 34
Dominion Cen., The UB2: S'hall 47Aa 85
Dominion Cl. TW3: Houn 54Fa 108
Dominion Ct. E8 38Vb 71
(off Middleton Rd.)
Dominion Dr. RM5: Col R 23Dd 56
SE16 47Zb 92
Dominion Ho. E14 50Dc 92
(off St Davids Sq.)
EC1 1D 224
Dominion Ind. Est. UB2: S'hall 47Aa 85
(off Feather Rd.)
Dominion Pde. HA1: Harr 29Ha 46
Dominion Rd. CR0: C'don 73Vb 157
UB2: S'hall 47Aa 85
Dominion St. EC2 7G 219 (43Tb 91)
Dominion Theatre 2E 222
Dominion Wlk. E14 45Fc 93
(off Fairmont Av.)
Dominion Way RM13: Rain 41Jd 96
Domonic Dr. SE9 63Rc 138
Domville Cl. N20 19Fb 31
Domville Ct. SE17 50Ub 91
(off Bagshott St.)
Donald Biggs Dr. DA12: Grav'nd 10E 122
Donald Dr. RM6: Chad H 29Yc 55
Donald Hunter Ho. E7 36Kc 73
(off Woodgrange Rd.)
Donald Rd. CR0: C'don 73Qb 156
E13 39Kc 73
Donaldson Rd. NW6 39Bb 69
SE18 53Qc 116
Donald Woods Gdns. KT5: Surb 75Ra 153
Donato Dr. SE15 51Ub 113
Doncaster Dr. UB5: N'olt 36Ba 65
Doncaster Gdns. N4 30Sb 51
UB5: N'olt 36Ba 65
Doncaster Grn. WD19: Wat 22Y 45
Doncaster Rd. N9 17Xb 33
Doncaster Way RM14: Upm 34Pd 77
Doncel Ct. E4 17Fc 35

Doncella Cl. RM16: Chaf H 48Zd 99
Donegal Ho. *E1* *42Xb 91*
(off Cambridge Heath Rd.)
Donegal St. N1 2J 217 (40Pb 70)
Doneraile Ho. SW1 7K 227
Doneraile St. SW6 54Za 110
Dongola Rd. E1 43Ac 92
E13 41Kc 93
N17 27Ub 51
Dongola Rd. W. E13 41Kc 93
Don Gratton Ho. *E1* *43Wb 91*
(off Old Montague St.)
Donington Av. IG2: Ilf 29Sc 54
IG6: Ilf 29Sc 54
Donkey All. SE22 59Wb 113
Donkey La. DA4: Farni 75Rd 163
EN1: Enf 12Wb 33
UB7: W Dray 49L 83
DONKEY TOWN 5B 166
Donkin Ho. *SE16* *49Xb 91*
(off Rennie Est.)
Donmar Warehouse Theatre 3F 223
Donnafields GU24: Bisl 8E 166
Donnatt's Rd. SE14 53Bc 114
Donne Ct. SE24 58Sb 113
Donnefield Av. HA8: Edg 24Na 47
Donne Gdns. GU22: Pyr 87G 168
Donne Ho. *E14* *44Cc 92*
(off Dod St.)
SE14 *51Zb 114*
(off Samuel Cl.)
Donnelly Ct. *SW6* *52Ab 110*
(off Dawes Rd.)
Donnelly Ho. SE1 3K 229
Donne Pl. CR4: Mitc 70Kb 134
SW3 5E 226 (49Gb 89)
Donne Rd. RM8: Dag 33Yc 75
Donnington Ct. *DA2: Dart* *58Rd 119*
(off Osbourne Rd.)
NW1 *38Kb 70*
(off Castlehaven Rd.)
NW10 *38Xa 68*
(off Donnington Rd.)
Donnington Mans. *NW10* *39Ya 68*
(off Donnington Rd.)
Donnington Rd.
HA3: Kenton 29Ma 47
KT4: Wor Pk 75Wa 154
NW10 38Xa 68
TN13: Dun G 92Fd 202
Donnybrook Ct. *E3* *39Bc 72*
(off Old Ford Rd.)
Donnybrook Rd. SW16 66Lb 134
Donoghue Bus. Pk. NW2 34Za 68
Donoghue Cotts. *E14* *43Ac 92*
(off Galsworthy Av.)
Donoghue Ct. *E3* *42Dc 92*
(off Barry Blandford Way)
Donovan Av. N10 26Kb 50
Donovan Cl. KT19: Eps 82Ta 173
Donovan Ct. *SW10* *50Fb 89*
(off Drayton Gdns.)
Donovan Ho. *E1* *45Yb 92*
(off Cable St.)
Donovan Pl. N21 15Pb 32
Donovan's Gdn. CM13: Heron 24Fe 59
Don Phelan Cl. SE5 53Tb 113
Dons Ct. *BR1: Brom* *67Hc 137*
(off London Rd.)
Don Way RM1: Rom 24Gd 56
Donyngs Recreation Cen. 5N 207
Doods Pk. Rd. RH2: Reig 5L 207
Doods Pl. RH2: Reig 5M 207
Doods Rd. RH2: Reig 5L 207
Doods Way RH2: Reig 5M 207
Doolittle Mdws. HP3: Hem H 7N 3
Doone Cl. TW11: Tedd 65Ja 130
Doon St. SE1 7K 223 (46Qb 90)
Dorado Gdns. BR6: Chels 76Zc 161
Dora Ho. *E14* *44Bc 92*
(off Rhodeswell Rd.)
W11 *45Za 88*
(off St Ann's Rd.)
Doral Way SM5: Cars 78Hb 155
Doran Ct. E6 40Pc 74
RH1: Redh 6M 207
RH2: Reig 6M 207
Dorando Cl. W12 45Xa 88
Doran Dr. RH1: Redh 6M 207
Doran Gdns. RH1: Redh 6M 207
Doran Gro. SE18 52Uc 116
Doran Mnr. *N2* *29Hb 49*
(off Great Nth. Rd.)
Doran Wlk. E15 38Ec 72
Dora Rd. SW19 64Cb 133
Dora St. E14 44Bc 92
Dora Way SW9 54Qb 112
Dorchester Av. DA5: Bexl 60Zc 117
HA2: Harr 30Ea 46
N13 21Sb 51
Dorchester Cl. BR5: St P 66Xc 139
DA1: Dart 59Pd 119
KT10: Hin W 75Ha 152
UB5: N'olt 36Da 65
Dorchester Ct. *AL1: St A* *3E 6*
(off Dexter Cl.)
E18 *25Hc 53*
(off Buckingham Rd.)
GU22: Wok 88C 168
N1 *38Ub 71*
(off Englefield Rd.)
N10 27Kb 50
N14 17Kb 32
NW2 34Za 68
RH2: Reig 5M 207
SE24 57Sb 113
SW1 4G 227
TW18: Staines 63J 127
WD3: Crox G 15S 26
WD19: Wat *16Aa 27*
(off Chalk Hill)
Dorchester Dr. SE24 57Sb 113
TW14: Bedf 58U 106
Dorchester Gdns. E4 21Cc 52
NW11 28Cb 49
Dorchester Gro. W4 50Ua 88
Dorchester Ho. TW9: Kew 52Ra 109
Dorchester M. KT3: N Mald 70Ta 131
KT16: Vir W 5L 147
TW1: Twick 58La 108
Dorchester Rd. DA12: Grav'nd 2F 144
KT4: Wor Pk 74Ya 154
KT13: Weyb 76R 150
SM4: Mord 73Db 155
UB5: N'olt 36Da 65
Dorchester Ter. *NW2* *34Za 68*
(off Needham Ter.)
Dorchester Way HA3: Kenton 30Pa 47
Dorchester Waye UB4: Yead 44X 85
(not continuous)
Dorcis Av. DA7: Bex 54Ad 117
Dordrecht Rd. W3 46Ua 88
Dore Av. E12 36Qc 74
Doreen Av. NW9 32Ta 67
Doreen Capstan Ho. *E11* *34Gc 73*
(off Apollo Pl.)
Dore Gdns. SM4: Mord 73Db 155
Dorell Cl. UB1: S'hall 43Ba 85
Doresa Cl. KT15: Add 78J 149
Dorey Ho. *TW8: Bford* *52La 108*
(off High St.)
Dorfman Theatre *6J 223*
(within National Theatre)
Doria Dr. DA12: Grav'nd 2G 144
Dorian Dr. SL5: Asc 7C 124
Dorian Rd. RM12: Horn 32Jd 76
Doria Rd. SW6 54Bb 111
Doric Dr. KT20: Tad 92Bb 195
Doric Ho. *E2* *40Zb 72*
(off Mace St.)
Doric Way NW1 3D 216 (41Mb 90)
Dorie M. *N12* *21Db 49*
(off Ashbourne Cl.)
Dorien Rd. SW20 68Za 132
Dorin Ct. CR6: W'ham 92Xb 197
GU22: Pyr 87G 168
Doris Ashby Cl.
UB6: G'frd 39Ja 66
Doris Av. DA8: Erith 53Ed 118
Doris Emmerton Ct. SW11 56Eb 111
Doris Rd. E7 38Jc 73
TW15: Ashf 65T 128
Dorking Cl. KT4: Wor Pk 75Za 154
SE8 51Bc 114
Dorking Ct. *N17* *25Wb 51*
(off Hampden La.)
Dorking Gdns. RM3: Rom 22Md 57
Dorking Ho. SE1 3G 231 (48Tb 91)
Dorking Ri. RM3: Rom 21Md 57
Dorking Rd. KT18: Eps 88Qa 173
KT20: Tad, Walt H 1A 206
KT22: Lea 94Ka 192
KT23: Bookh 98Da 191
RM3: Rom 22Md 57
Dorking Vs. GU21: Knap 9H 167
Dorking Wlk. RM3: Rom 21Md 57
Dorkins Way RM14: Upm 31Ud 78
Dorlcote Rd. SW18 59Gb 111
Dorling Dr. KT17: Eps 84Va 174
Dorly Cl. TW17: Shep 71U 150
Dorman Pl. N9 19Wb 33
Dormans Cl. HA6: Nwood 24T 44
Dorman Wlk. NW10 36Ta 67
Dorman Way NW8 39Fb 69
Dorma Trad. Pk. E10 32Zb 72
Dormay St. SW18 57Db 111
Dormer Cl. E15 37Hc 73
EN5: Barn 15Za 30
Dormers HP3: Bov 9G 2
Dormer's Av. UB1: S'hall 44Ca 85
Dormers Ri. UB1: S'hall 45Da 85
DORMER'S WELLS 44Ca 85
Dormer's Wells La. UB1: S'hall 44Ca 85
Dormers Wells Leisure Cen. 44Da 85
Dormstone Ho. SE17 6H 231
Dormywood HA4: Ruis 29V 44
Dornberg Cl. SE3 52Jc 115
Dornberg Rd. SE3 52Kc 115
Dorncliffe Rd. SW6 54Ab 110
Dornels SL2: Slou 4N 81
DORNEY 8A 80
Dorney NW3 38Gb 69
Dorney Gro. KT13: Weyb 75R 150
Dorney Hill Sth. HP9: Beac 1E 60
Dorney Lake 1A 102
Dorney Lake Pk. & Nature Reserve
10A 80
Dorney Pl. DA1: Dart 55Qd 119
Dorney Ri. BR5: St M Cry 70Vc 139
Dorney Way TW4: Houn 57Aa 107
Dorneywood Cl. SL1: Burn 10A 60
Dorney Wood Rd. SL1: Burn 4A 60
Dornfell St. NW6 36Bb 69
Dornford Gdns. CR5: Coul 91Sb 197
Dornoch Ho. *E3* *40Bc 72*
(off Anglo Rd.)
Dornton Rd. CR2: S Croy 78Tb 157
SW12 61Kb 134
Dorothy Av. HA0: Wemb 38Na 67
Dorothy Evans Cl. DA7: Bex 56Dd 118
Dorothy Gdns. RM8: Dag 35Xc 75
Dorothy Pettingell Ho.
SM1: Sutt *76Db 155*
(off Vermont Rd.)
Dorothy Rd. SW11 55Hb 111
Dorothy Smith La. N17 24Tb 51
Dorrell Pl. SW9 55Qb 112
Dorrien Wlk. SW16 61Mb 134
Dorrington Ct. SE25 68Ub 135
Dorrington Gdns. RM12: Horn 32Md 77
Dorrington Point *E3* *41Dc 92*
(off Bromley High St.)
Dorrington St. EC1 7K 217 (43Qb 90)
Dorrington Way BR3: Beck 71Ec 158
Dorrit Ho. *W11* *46Za 88*
(off St Ann's Rd.)
Dorrit M. N18 22Ub 51
Dorrit St. SE1 1E 230 (47Sb 91)
Dorrit Way BR7: Chst 65Sc 138
Dorrofield Cl. WD3: Crox G 15S 26
Dorryn Ct. SE26 64Zb 136
Dors Cl. NW9 32Ta 67
Dorset Av. DA16: Well 56Vc 117
RM1: Rom 28Fd 56
UB2: S'hall 49Ca 85
UB4: Hayes 41U 84
Dorset Bldgs. EC4 3B 224 (44Rb 91)
Dorset Cl. KT9: Chess 77Ma 153
NW1 7F 215 (43Hb 89)
UB4: Hayes 41U 84
Dorset Ct. HA6: Nwood 25V 44
KT17: Eps 84Va 174
N1 *38Ub 71*
(off Hertford Rd.)
UB5: N'olt 41Aa 85
W7 *43Ha 86*
(off Copley Cl.)
Dorset Cres. DA12: Grav'nd 3G 144
Dorset Dr. GU22: Wok 89D 168
HA8: Edg 23Pa 47
Dorset Gdns. CR4: Mitc 70Pb 134
HA0: Wemb 36La 66
SS17: Linf 7J 101
Dorset Ho. NW1 6G 215
Dorset Mans. *SW6* *51Za 110*
(off Lillie Rd.)
Dorset M. N3 25Cb 49
SW1 3K 227 (48Kb 90)
Dorset Pl. E15 37Fc 73
Dorset Ri. EC4 3B 224 (44Rb 91)
Dorset Rd. BR3: Beck 69Zb 136
CR4: Mitc 68Gb 133
E7 38Lc 73
HA1: Harr 30Ea 46
N15 28Tb 51
N22 25Nb 50
SE9 61Nc 138
SL4: Wind 3G 102
SM2: Sutt 82Cb 175
SW8 52Nb 112
SW19 67Cb 133
TW15: Ashf 62M 127
W5 48La 86
Dorset Sq. KT19: Ewe 82Ta 173
NW1 6F 215 (42Hb 89)
Dorset St. TN13: S'oaks 97Ld 203
W1 1G 221 (43Hb 89)
Dorset Way KT14: Byfl 82M 169
TW2: Twick 60Fa 108
UB10: Hil 40P 63
Dorset Waye TW5: Hest 52Ba 107
Dorset Wharf *W6* *52Ya 110*
(off Rainville Rd.)
Dorsey Ho. *N1* *37Rb 71*
(off Canonbury Rd.)
Dorton Cl. SE15 52Ub 113
Dorton Dr. TN15: Seal 94Pd 203
(not continuous)
Dorton Vs. UB7: Sip 52Q 106
Dorton Way GU23: Rip 93K 189
Dorville Cres. W6 48Xa 88
Dorville Rd. SE12 57Hc 115
Dothill Rd. SE18 52Sc 116
Douai Gro. TW12: Hamp 67Ea 130
Doubleday Rd. IG10: Lough 13Sc 36
Doughty Ct. *E1* *46Xb 91*
(off Prusom St.)
Doughty Ho. *SW10* *51Eb 111*
(off Netherton Gro.)
Doughty M. WC1 6H 217 (42Pb 90)
Doughty St. WC1 5H 217 (42Pb 90)
Douglas Av. E17 25Bc 52
HA0: Wemb 38Na 67
KT3: N Mald 70Xa 132
RM3: Hrld W 26Nd 57
WD24: Wat 9Z 13
Douglas Bader Ho. TW7: Isle 55Fa 108
Douglas Cl. EN4: Had W 10Fb 17
GU4: Jac W 10P 187
HA7: Stan 22Ja 46
IG6: Ilf 24Rc 54
RM16: Chaf H 48Ae 99
SM6: Wall 79Nb 156
Douglas Ct. CR3: Cat'm 94Sb 197
KT1: King T *70Na 131*
(off Geneva Rd.)
N3 26Db 49
NW6 *38Cb 69*
(off Quex Rd.)
TN16: Big H 89Nc 180
Douglas Cres. UB4: Yead 42Y 85
Douglas Dr. CR0: C'don 76Cc 158
Douglas Est. *N1* *37Sb 71*
(off Oransay Rd.)
Douglas Eyre Sports Cen. 29Zb 52
Douglas Ho. *EN8: Chesh* *1Zb 20*
(off Davison Dr.)
KT6: Surb 74Pa 153
KT23: Bookh 96Ca 191
RH2: Reig 5J 207
Douglas Johnstone Ho. *SW6* *51Bb 111*
(off Clem Attlee Ct.)
Douglas La. TW19: Wray 57B 104
Douglas Mans. TW3: Houn 55Da 107
Douglas M. NW2 34Ab 68
SM7: Bans 88Bb 175
Douglas Path *E14* *50Ec 92*
(off Manchester Rd.)
Douglas Rd. DA16: Well 53Xc 117
E4 17Gc 35
E16 43Jc 93
IG3: Ilf 31Wc 75
KT1: King T 68Ra 131
KT6: Surb 75Pa 153
KT10: Esh 75Da 151
KT15: Add 76K 149
N1 38Sb 71
N22 25Qb 50
NW6 39Bb 69
RH2: Reig 5J 207
RM11: Horn 30Hd 56
SL2: Slou 3H 81
TW3: Houn 55Da 107
TW19: Stanw 58M 105
Douglas Rd. Nth. N1 37Sb 71
Douglas Rd. Sth. N1 37Sb 71
Douglas Robinson Ct. *SW16* *66Nb 134*
(off Streatham High Rd.)
Douglas Sq. SM4: Mord 72Cb 155
Douglas St. SW1 6D 228 (49Mb 90)
Douglas Ter. E17 25Bc 52
Douglas Waite Ho. NW6 38Cb 69
Douglas Way SE8 52Bc 114
(Stanley St.)
SE8 52Cc 114
(Watsons St.)
Doug Siddons Ct. RM17: Grays 51De 121
Doulton Ho. SE11 5J 229
Doulton M. NW6 37Db 69
Doultons, The TW18: Staines 66J 127
Dounesforth Gdns. SW18 60Db 111
Dounsell Ct. CM15: Pil H 16Wd 40
Douro Pl. W8 48Db 89
Douro St. E3 40Cc 72
Douthwaite Sq. E1 46Wb 91
Dove App. E6 43Nc 94
Dove Cl. CR2: Sels 83Zb 178
RM16: Chaf H 48Ae 99
SM6: Wall 80Pb 156
UB5: N'olt 42Z 85
Dove Commercial Cen. NW5 36Lb 70
Dovecot Cl. HA5: Eastc 29Y 45
Dovecote Av. N22 27Qb 50
Dovecote Cl. KT13: Weyb 76R 150
Dovecote Gdns. SW14 55Ta 109
Dovecote Ho. *SE16* *47Zb 92*
(off Water Gdns. Sq.)
Dovecote M. UB9: Hare 27N 43
Dove Ct. AL10: Hat 1C 8
TW19: Stanw 59N 105
Dovedale Av. HA3: Kenton 30La 46
IG5: Ilf 26Qc 54
Dovedale Bus. Est. *SE15* *54Wb 113*
(off Blenheim Gro.)
Dovedale Cl. DA16: Well 54Wc 117
UB9: Hare 26L 43
Dovedale Ri. CR4: Mitc 66Hb 133
Dovedale Rd. DA2: Dart 60Sd 120
SE22 57Xb 113
Dovedon Cl. N14 19Nb 32
Dovehouse Ct. *UB5: N'olt* *41Z 85*
(off Delta Gro.)
Dove Ho. Cres. SL2: Slou 1C 80
Dove Ho. Gdns. E4 19Cc 34
Dovehouse Grn. KT13: Weyb 76T 150
Dovehouse Mead IG11: Bark 40Tc 74
Dovehouse St. SW3 7C 226 (50Fb 89)
Dove La. EN6: Pot B 6Eb 17
Dove M. SW5 6A 226 (49Eb 89)
Doveney Cl. BR5: St P 69Yc 139
Dove Pk. HA5: Hat E 24Ca 45
WD3: Chor 16D 24
Dover Cl. NW2 33Za 68
RM5: Col R 26Ed 56
Dover Ct. EC1 5B 218
N1 *38Tb 71*
(off Southgate Rd.)
Dovercourt Av. CR7: Thor H 71Qb 156
Dovercourt Est. N1 37Tb 71
Dovercourt Gdns. HA7: Stan 22Na 47
Dovercourt La. SM1: Sutt 76Eb 155
Dovercourt Rd. SE22 58Ub 113
Doverfield EN7: G Oak 1Sb 19
Doverfield Rd. SW2 59Nb 112
Dover Flats SE1 6J 231 (49Ub 91)
Dover Gdns. SM5: Cars 76Hb 155
Dover Ho. N18 22Vb 51
SE15 51Yb 114
Dover Ho. Rd. SW15 56Wa 110
Doveridge Gdns. N13 21Rb 51
Dove Rd. N1 37Tb 71
Dove Row E2 39Wb 71
Dover Pk. Dr. SW15 58Xa 110
Dover Patrol SE3 54Kc 115
Dover Rd. DA11: Nflt 59Fe 121
E12 33Lc 73
N9 19Yb 34
RM6: Chad H 30Ad 55
SE19 65Tb 135
SL1: Slou 4D 80
Dover Rd. E. DA11: Grav'nd 9A 122
DOVERS CORNER 41Jd 96
Dovers Cnr. RM13: Rain 41Jd 96
Dovers Cnr. Ind. Est. RM13: Rain 41Hd 96
DOVERSGREEN 10K 207
Dovers Grn. Rd. RH2: Reig 10K 207
Doversmead GU21: Knap 8J 167
Dover St. W1 5A 222 (45Kb 90)
Dovers Way RH2: Reig 10K 207
Dover Ter. *TW9: Rich* *54Pa 109*
(off Sandycombe Rd.)
Dover Way WD3: Crox G 14S 26
Dover Yd. W1 6B 222
Doves Cl. BR2: Brom 75Nc 160
Doves Cotts. IG7: Chig 20Wc 37
Doves Yd. N1 1A 218 (39Qb 70)
Dovet Ct. SW9 53Pb 112
Doveton Ho. *E1* *42Yb 92*
(off Doveton St.)
Doveton Rd. CR2: S Croy 78Tb 157
Doveton St. E1 42Yb 92
Dove Tree Cl. KT19: Eps 81Ta 173
Dovetree Ct. *RM3: Rom* *21Md 57*
(off North Hill Dr.)
Dove Wlk. RM12: Horn 37Kd 77
SW1 7H 227 (50Jb 90)
Dovey Lodge *N1* *38Qb 70*
(off Bewdley St.)
Dovoll Ct. *SE16* *48Wb 91*
(off Old Jamaica Rd.)
Dowanhill Rd. SE6 60Fc 115
Dowd Cl. N11 19Jb 32
Dowdeswell Cl. SW15 56Ua 110
Dowding Dr. SE9 57Lc 115
Dowding Ho. *N6* *31Jb 70*
(off Hillcrest)
Dowding Pl. HA7: Stan 23Ja 46
Dowding Rd. TN16: Big H 87Mc 179
UB10: Uxb 38P 63
Dowding Wlk. DA11: Nflt 2A 144
Dowding Way EN9: Walt A 8Fc 21
RM12: Horn 38Kd 77
WD25: Wat 6V 12
Dowdney Cl. NW5 36Lb 70
Dowe Ho. SE3 55Gc 115
Dowells St. SE10 51Dc 114
Dower Av. SM6: Wall 81Kb 176
Dower Ct. *SE16* *49Yb 92*
(off Silwood Rd.)
Dower Pk. SL4: Wind 6C 102
Dowes Ho. SW16 62Nb 134
Dowgate Hill EC4 4F 225 (45Tb 91)
Dowgate Ho. KT13: Weyb 76Q 150
Dowland Ct. SS17: Stan H 1L 101
Dowland St. W10 41Ab 88
Dowlans Cl. KT23: Bookh 99Ca 191
Dowlans Rd. KT23: Bookh 99Da 191
Dowlas St. SE5 52Ub 113
Dowler Ct. KT2: King T 67Na 131
Dowler Ho. *E1* *44Wb 91*
(off Burslem St.)
Dowlerville Rd. BR6: Chels 79Vc 161
Dowling Ct. HP3: Hem H 5M 3
Dowling Ho. DA17: Belv 48Bd 95
Dowman Cl. SW19 66Db 133
Downage NW4 27Ya 48
(not continuous)
Downage, The DA11: Grav'nd 1C 144
Downalong WD23: B Hea 18Fa 28
Downbank Av. DA7: Bex 53Fd 118
Down Barns Rd. HA4: Ruis 34Z 65
Downbarton Ho. *SW9* *53Qb 112*
(off Gosling Way)
Downbury M. SW18 57Cb 111
Down Cl. UB5: N'olt 40X 65
Downderry Rd. BR1: Brom 62Fc 137
DOWNE 83Qc 180
Downe Av. TN14: Cud 84Tc 180
Downe Bank Nature Reserve 85Rc 180
Downe Cl. DA16: Well 52Yc 117
Downedge AL3: St A 1P 5
Downend SE18 52Rc 116
Downend Ct. *SE15* *51Ub 113*
(off Bibury Cl.)
Downer Dr. WD3: Sarr 8J 11
Downe Rd. BR2: Kes 81Nc 180
CR4: Mitc 68Hb 133
TN14: Cud 85Sc 180
Downer's Cott. SW4 56Lb 112
Downesbury *NW3* *37Hb 69*
(off Steele's Rd.)
Downes Cl. TW1: Twick 58Ka 108
Downes Ct. N21 18Qb 32
Downes Ho. *CR0: Wadd* *77Rb 157*
(off Violet La.)
Downe Ter. TW10: Rich 58Na 109
Downey Ho. *E1* *42Zb 92*
(off Globe Rd.)
Downfield KT4: Wor Pk 74Va 154
Downfield Cl. W9 42Db 89
Downfield Rd. EN8: Chesh 3Ac 20
Down Hall Rd. KT2: King T 67Ma 131
DOWNHAM 64Fc 137
Downham Cl. RM5: Col R 24Cd 56
Downham Ct. *KT12: Walt T* *76Y 151*
(off Long Lodge Dr.)
N1 *38Tb 71*
(off Downham Rd.)
Downham Ent. Cen. SE6 61Hc 137
Downham Health & Leisure Cen.
63Hc 137
Downham La. BR1: Brom 64Fc 137
Downham Rd. N1 38Tb 71
Downham Way BR1: Brom 64Fc 137
Downham Wharf *N1* *39Ub 71*
(off Downham Rd.)
Downhills Av. N17 27Tb 51
Downhills Pk. Rd. N17 27Sb 51
Downhills Way N17 27Sb 51
Down House 84Qc 180
Downhurst Av. NW7 22Ta 47
Downhurst Ct. NW4 27Ya 48
Downing Cl. HA2: Harr 27Ea 46
Downing Ct. WC1 6G 217
WD6: Bore *11Pa 29*
(off Bennington Dr.)
Downing Dr. UB6: G'frd 39Fa 66
Downing Ho. *W10* *44Za 88*
(off Cambridge Gdns.)
Downing Path SL2: Slou 2C 80
Downing Rd. RM9: Dag 38Bd 75
Downings E6 44Qc 94
Downing St. SW1 1F 229 (47Nb 90)
Downings Wood
WD3: Map C 22F 42
Downland Cl. KT18: Tatt C 90Xa 174
N20 18Eb 31
Downland Ct. E11 33Gc 73
Downland Gdns. KT18: Tatt C 90Xa 174
Downlands EN9: Walt A 6Gc 21
Downlands Ct. CR5: Coul 86Kb 176
Downlands Rd. CR8: Purl 85Nb 176
Downland Way KT18: Tatt C 90Xa 174
Downleys Cl. SE9 61Nc 138
Downman Rd. SE9 55Nc 116
Down Pl. W6 49Xa 88
Down Rd. TW11: Tedd 65Ka 130
Downs, The AL10: Hat 2C 8
KT22: Lea 97La 192
SW20 66Za 132
Downs Av. BR7: Chst 64Pc 138
DA1: Dart 59Qd 119
HA5: Pinn 30Aa 45
KT18: Eps 86Ua 174
Downs Bri. Rd. BR3: Beck 67Fc 137
Downs Ct. RH1: Redh 3A 208
UB6: G'frd 41Ja 86
Downs Ct. Pde. *E8* *36Xb 71*
(off Amhurst Rd.)
Downs Ct. Rd. CR8: Purl 84Rb 177
Downsell Rd. E15 35Ec 72
Downsfield AL10: Hat 3D 8
Downsfield Rd. E17 30Ac 52
Downshall Av. IG3: Ilf 30Uc 54
Downs Hill BR3: Beck 66Fc 137
DA13: Nflt G 66Ee 143
Downs Hill Rd. KT18: Eps 86Ua 174
Downshire Hill NW3 35Fb 69
Downs Ho. TN13: S'oaks 94Ld 203
Downs Ho. Rd. KT18: Eps D 90Ua 174
DOWNSIDE 90X 171
Downside HP2: Hem H 1N 3
KT16: Chert 74H 149
KT18: Eps 86Ua 174
TW1: Twick 62Ha 130
TW16: Sun 67W 128
Downside Bri. Rd. KT11: Cobh 86X 171
Downside Cl. SW19 65Eb 133
Downside Comn. KT11: D'side 90X 171
Downside Comn. Rd.
KT11: D'side 90X 171
Downside Ct. RH1: Mers 1C 208
Downside Cres. NW3 36Gb 69
W13 42Ja 86
Downside Orchard GU22: Wok 89C 168
Downside Rd. KT11: D'side 88X 171
SM2: Sutt 79Fb 155
Downside Wlk. *TW8: Bford* *51Ma 109*
(off Windmill Rd.)
UB5: N'olt 41Ba 85
Downsland Dr. CM14: B'wood 20Yd 40
Downs La. AL10: Hat 2C 8
E5 35Xb 71
KT22: Lea 95Ka 192
Downs Lodge Ct. KT17: Eps 86Ua 174
Downs Pk. Rd. E5 36Vb 71
E8 36Vb 71
Downs Reach KT17: Eps D 89Xa 174
Downs Res. Site, The
CR3: Cat'm 99Xb 197
Downs Rd. BR3: Beck 68Dc 136
CR5: Coul 90Mb 176
CR7: Thor H 67Sb 135
CR8: Purl 83Rb 177
DA11: Ist R, Nflt 63Fe 143
DA13: Ist R, Nflt G 66Fe 143
E5 35Wb 71
EN1: Enf 14Ub 33
KT18: Eps D 92Sa 193
KT18: Eps, Eps D 87Ua 174
RH5: Mick 100La 192
SL3: L'ly 7P 81
SM2: Sutt 82Db 175
Downs Side SM2: Cheam 83Bb 175
Down St. KT8: W Mole 71Ca 151
W1 7K 221 (46Kb 90)
Down St. M. W1 7K 221 (46Kb 90)
Downs Valley DA3: Hartl 70Ae 143
Downs Vw. KT20: Tad 93Xa 194
TW7: Isle 53Ha 108
Downsview Av. GU22: Wok 93B 188
Downs Vw. Cl. BR6: Prat B 82Yc 181
Downsview Cl. BR8: Swan 69Hd 140
KT11: D'side 91X 191
Downsview Gdns. SE19 66Rb 135
Downs Vw. Rd.
KT23: Bookh 99Ea 192
Downsview Rd. SE19 66Sb 135
TN13: S'oaks 97Hd 202

Downs Way KT18: Eps ... 88Va 174
KT20: Tad ... 93Xa 194
KT23: Bookh ... 98Ea 192
RH8: Oxt ... 99Gc 199
Downsway BR6: Orp ... 78Uc 160
CR2: Sande ... 83Ub 177
CR3: Whyt ... 88Vb 177
Downsway, The SM2: Sutt ... 81Eb 175
Downsway Cl. KT20: Tad ... 93Wa 194
Downs Wood KT18: Tatt C ... 89Xa 174
Downswood RH2: Reig ... 3M 207
Downton Av. SW2 ... 61Nb 134
Downton M. DA8: Erith ... 52Gd 118
Downtown Rd. SE16 ... 47Ac 92
Down Way UB5: N'olt ... 41X 85
Downy Ho. W3 ... 46Ua 88
Dowrey St. N1 ... 39Qb 70
Dowry Wlk. WD17: Wat ... 10V 12
Dowsett Rd. N17 ... 26Vb 51
Dowson Cl. SE5 ... 56Tb 113
Dowson Ho. *E1* ... *44Zb 92*
(off Bower St.)
Doyce St. SE1 ... 1D 230 (47Sb 91)
Doyle Cl. DA8: Erith ... 53Gd 118
Doyle Gdns. NW10 ... 39Wa 68
Doyle Ho. *SW13* ... *52Ya 110*
(off Trinity Chu. Rd.)
Doyle Rd. SE25 ... 70Wb 135
Doyle Way *RM18: Tilb* ... *4E 122*
(off Coleridge Rd.)
D'Oyley St. SW1 ... 5H 227 (49Jb 90)
D'Oyly Carte Island KT13: Weyb ... 74R 150
Doynton St. N19 ... 33Kb 70
Draco Ga. SW15 ... 55Ya 110
Draco St. SE17 ... 51Sb 113
Dragmore St. SW4 ... 58Mb 112
Dragonfly Cl. E13 ... 41Kc 93
KT5: Surb ... 74Sa 153
Dragonfly Ct. *NW9* ... *25Ua 48*
(off Heybourne Cres.)
Dragonfly Pl. SE4 ... 55Ac 114
Dragon La. KT13: Weyb ... 83Q 170
Dragon Rd. SE15 ... 51Ub 113
Dragons Way EN5: Barn ... 15Bb 31
Dragon Yd. WC1 ... 2G 223 (44Nb 90)
Dragoon Rd. SE8 ... 50Bc 92
Dragor Rd. NW10 ... 42Sa 87
Drake Av. CR3: Cat'm ... 94Sb 197
SL3: L'ly ... 9P 81
TW18: Staines ... 64H 127
Drake Cl. CM14: W'ley ... 22Ae 58
IG11: Bark ... 42Wc 95
SE16 ... 47Zb 92
Drake Ct. *DA8: Erith* ... *52Hd 118*
(off Frobisher Rd.)
KT5: Surb ... *70Na 131*
(off Cranes Pk. Av.)
SE1 ... 2E 230
SE19 ... 64Vb 135
W12 ... *47Ya 88*
(off Scott's Rd.)
Drake Cres. SE28 ... 44Yc 95
Drakefell Rd. SE4 ... 54Zb 114
SE14 ... 54Zb 114
Drakefield Rd. SW17 ... 62Jb 134
Drake Hall *E16* ... *46Kc 93*
(off Wesley Av.)
Drake Ho. *E1* ... *43Yb 92*
(off Stepney Way)
E14 ... *45Ac 92*
(off Victory Pl.)
SW1 ... *51Mb 112*
(off Dolphin Sq.)
Drakeland Ho. *W9* ... *42Bb 89*
(off Fernhead Rd.)
Drakeley Ct. N5 ... 35Rb 71
Drake M. BR2: Brom ... 70Lc 137
DA12: Grav'nd ... 3F 144
RM12: Horn ... 37Jd 76
Drake Point DA8: Erith ... 50Gd 96
Drake Rd. CR0: C'don ... 73Pb 156
CR4: Mitc ... 72Jb 156
HA2: Harr ... 33Ba 65
KT9: Chess ... 78Qa 153
RM16: Chaf H ... 48Ae 99
SE4 ... 55Cc 114
Drakes, The SE8 ... 51Cc 114
Drake's Cl. KT10: Esh ... 77Ca 151
Drakes Ct. SE23 ... 60Yb 114
Drakes Courtyard NW6 ... 38Bb 69
Drakes Dr. AL1: St A ... 5F 6
HA6: Nwood ... 25R 44
Drake St. EN2: Enf ... 11Tb 33
WC1 ... 1H 223 (43Pb 90)
Drakes Wlk. E6 ... 39Pc 74
Drakes Way AL10: Hat ... 2D 8
GU22: Wok ... 4P 187
Drakewood Rd. SW16 ... 66Mb 134
Draper Cl. DA17: Belv ... 49Bd 95
RM20: Grays ... 51Zd 121
TW7: Isle ... 54Fa 108
Draper Ct. BR1: Brom ... 70Nc 138
Draper Ho. SE1 ... 5C 230
Draper Pl. *N1* ... *39Rb 71*
(off Dagmar Ter.)
Drapers Almshouses *E3* ... *41Dc 92*
(off Rainhill Way)
Drapers Cott. Homes NW7 ... 21Va 48
(not continuous)
Draper's Ct. *SW11* ... *53Jb 112*
(off Battersea Pk. Rd.)
Drapers Ct. RM12: Horn ... 33Nd 77
Drapers Cres. KT12: W Vill ... 82V 170
Drapers Gdns. EC2 ... 2G 225 (44Tb 91)
Drapers Rd. E15 ... 35Fc 73
EN2: Enf ... 12Rb 33
N17 ... 27Vb 51
Drappers Way SE16 ... 49Wb 91
Draven Cl. BR2: Hayes ... 73Hc 159
Drawell Cl. SE18 ... 50Uc 94
Drax Av. SW20 ... 66Wa 132
Draxmont SW19 ... 65Ab 132
Draycot Rd. E11 ... 30Kc 53
KT6: Surb ... 74Qa 153
Draycott Av. HA3: Kenton ... 30Ka 46
SW3 ... 5E 226 (49Gb 89)
Draycott Cl. HA3: Kenton ... 30Ka 46
NW2 ... 34Za 68
SE5 ... 52Tb 113
(not continuous)
Draycott Ct. *SW11* ... *53Gb 111*
(off Westbridge Rd.)
Draycott M. *SW6* ... *54Bb 111*
(off Laurel Bank Gdns.)
Draycott Pl. SW3 ... 6F 227 (49Hb 89)
Draycott Ter. SW3 ... 6G 227 (49Hb 89)
Dray Ct. *HA0: Wemb* ... *36Ja 66*
(off Brewery Cl.)
Drayford Cl. W9 ... 42Bb 89
Dray Gdns. SW2 ... 57Pb 112
Draymans M. SE15 ... 54Vb 113
Draymans Way TW7: Isle ... 55Ha 108
Drayside M. UB2: S'hall ... 47Ba 85
Drayson Cl. EN9: Walt A ... 4Gc 21
Drayson M. W8 ... 47Cb 89
Drayton Av. BR6: Farnb ... 74Rc 160
EN6: Pot B ... 4Ab 16
IG10: Lough ... 17Pc 36
W13 ... 45Ja 86
Drayton Bri. Rd. W7 ... 45Ha 86
W13 ... 45Ha 86
Drayton Cl. IG1: Ilf ... 32Tc 74
KT22: Fet ... 96Ga 192
TW4: Houn ... 57Ba 107
Drayton Ct. UB7: W Dray ... 49P 83
Drayton Ford WD3: Rick ... 19J 25
Drayton Gdns. N21 ... 17Rb 33
SW10 ... 7A 226 (50Eb 89)
UB7: W Dray ... 47N 83
W13 ... 45Ja 86
Drayton Grn. W13 ... 45Ja 86
Drayton Grn. Rd. W13 ... 45Ka 86
Drayton Gro. W13 ... 45Ja 86
Drayton Ho. E11 ... 32Fc 73
SE5 ... *52Tb 113*
(off Elmington Rd.)
Drayton Pk. N5 ... 35Qb 70
Drayton Pk. M. N5 ... 36Qb 70
Drayton Rd. CR0: C'don ... 75Rb 157
E11 ... 32Fc 73
N17 ... 26Ub 51
NW10 ... 39Va 68
W13 ... 45Ja 86
WD6: Bore ... 14Qa 29
Drayton Waye HA3: Kenton ... 30Ka 46
Dray Wlk. E1 ... 6K 219 (42Vb 91)
Dreadnought Cl. SW19 ... 68Fb 133
Dreadnought St. SE10 ... 48Gc 93
Dreadnought Wlk. SE10 ... 51Dc 114
Drenon Sq. UB3: Hayes ... 45V 84
Dresden Cl. NW6 ... 37Db 69
Dresden Ho. SE11 ... 5J 229
SW11 ... *54Jb 112*
(off Dagnall St.)
Dresden Rd. N19 ... 32Lb 70
Dresden Way KT13: Weyb ... 78S 150
Dressington Av. SE4 ... 58Cc 114
Drewery Ct. SE3 ... 55Gc 115
Drewett Ho. *E1* ... *44Wb 91*
(off Christian St.)
Drew Gdns. UB6: G'frd ... 37Ha 66
Drew Ho. SE8 ... 50Cc 92
SW16 ... 62Nb 134
Drew Mdw. SL2: Farn C ... 5G 60
Drew Pl. CR3: Cat'm ... 95Tb 197
Drew Rd. E16 ... 46Mc 93
(not continuous)
Drewstead La. SW16 ... 61Mb 134
Drewstead Rd. SW16 ... 61Mb 134
Drey, The SL9: Chal P ... 22A 42
Drey Ct. *KT4: Wor Pk* ... *75Wa 154*
(off The Avenue)
Driffield Ct. *NW9* ... *25Ua 48*
(off Pageant Av.)
Driffield Rd. E3 ... 40Ac 72
Drift, The BR2: Brom ... 76Mc 159
DRIFT BRIDGE ... 86Ya 174
Drift Ct. E16 ... 45Rc 94
Drift Golf Course ... 95Ua 190
Drift La. KT11: Stoke D ... 88Ba 171
Drift Rd. KT24: E Hor, Eff J ... 96T 190
SL4: Wink ... 10A 102
Drift Way SL3: Coln ... 53E 104
Driftway, The CR4: Mitc ... 67Jb 134
HP2: Hem H ... 2P 3
KT22: Lea ... 95Ka 192
(not continuous)
SM7: Bans ... 87Ya 174
Driftway Ho. *E3* ... *40Bc 72*
(off Stafford Rd.)
Driftwood Av. AL2: Chis G ... 8N 5
Driftwood Dr. CR8: Kenley ... 89Rb 177
Drill Hall Rd. KT16: Chert ... 73J 149
Drinkwater Ho. *SE5* ... *52Tb 113*
(off Picton St.)
Drinkwater Rd. HA2: Harr ... 33Da 65
Driscoll Way CR3: Cat'm ... 95Tb 197
Drive, The AL2: Lon C ... 7E 6
AL9: Brk P ... 7J 9
BR3: Beck ... 68Cc 136
BR4: W W'ck ... 73Fc 159
BR6: Orp ... 75Vc 161
BR7: Chst ... 69Vc 139
CM13: Gt War ... 22Yd 58
CR5: Coul ... 86Nb 176
CR7: Thor H ... 70Tb 135
DA3: Lfield ... 69De 143
DA5: Bexl ... 58Yc 117
DA8: Erith ... 52Dd 118
DA12: Grav'nd ... 3F 144
DA14: Sidc ... 62Xc 139
E4 ... 17Ec 35
E17 ... 27Dc 52
E18 ... 28Jc 53
EN2: Enf ... 11Tb 33
(Farr Rd.)
EN2: Enf ... 7Jb 18
(St Nicholas Ho's.)
EN5: Barn ... 13Ab 30
EN5: New Bar ... 16Eb 31
EN6: Pot B ... 5Bb 17
EN7: G Oak ... 1Rb 19
GU22: Wok ... 2M 187
GU25: Vir W ... 71B 148
HA2: Harr ... 31Ca 65
HA6: Nwood ... 26U 44
HA8: Edg ... 22Qa 47
HA9: Wemb ... 33Sa 67
IG1: Ilf ... 30Nc 54
IG9: Buck H ... 17Lc 35
IG10: Lough ... 13Nc 36
IG11: Bark ... 38Vc 75
KT2: King T ... 66Sa 131
KT6: Surb ... 73Na 153
KT10: Esh ... 74Ea 152
KT11: Cobh ... 86Aa 171
KT18: Head ... 96Pa 193
KT19: Ewe ... 79Va 154
KT20: Lwr K ... 98Bb 195
KT22: Fet ... 94Ga 192
KT22: Lea ... 95Na 193
N3 ... 24Db 49
N6 ... 29Hb 49
N7 ... 37Pb 70
(not continuous)
N11 ... 23Lb 50
Drive, The NW10 ... 39Va 68
NW11 ... 31Ab 68
RM3: Hrld W ... 25Nd 57
RM4: Stap A ... 17Ed 38
RM5: Col R ... 25Ed 56
SL3: Dat ... 3M 103
SL3: L'ly ... 47A 82
SL4: Wind ... 3D 102
SL9: Chal P ... 24A 42
SM2: Cheam ... 84Bb 175
SM4: Mord ... 71Eb 155
SM6: Wall ... 82Lb 176
SM7: Bans ... 89Ab 174
SW6 ... 54Ab 110
SW20 ... 66Ya 132
TN13: S'oaks ... 96Kd 203
TW3: Houn ... 54Fa 108
TW7: Isle ... 54Fa 108
TW14: Felt ... 59Y 107
TW15: Ashf ... 66T 128
TW19: Wray ... 7P 103
UB10: Ick ... 35N 63
W3 ... 44Sa 87
WD3: Rick ... 15K 25
WD7: R'lett ... 6Ja 14
WD17: Wat ... 9T 12
Drive Ct. HA8: Edg ... 22Qa 47
Drive Mans. *SW6* ... *54Ab 110*
(off Fulham Rd.)
Drive Mead CR5: Coul ... 86Nb 176
Drive Rd. CR5: Coul ... 92Mb 196
(not continuous)
Drive Spur KT20: Kgswd ... 93Db 195
Driveway, The *E17* ... *30Dc 52*
(off Hoe St.)
EN6: Cuff ... 1Nb 18
HP1: Hem H ... 3K 3
Droitwich Cl. SE26 ... 62Wb 135
Dromey Gdns. HA3: Hrw W ... 24Ha 46
Dromore Rd. SW15 ... 58Ab 110
Dronfield Gdns. RM8: Dag ... 36Yc 75
Dron Ho. *E1* ... *43Yb 92*
(off Adelina Gro.)
Droop St. W10 ... 41Za 88
Drop La. AL2: Brick W ... 2Da 13
Dropmore Ho. SL1: Burn ... 4A 60
Dropmore Pk. ... 4A 60
Dropmore Rd. SL1: Burn ... 5A 60
Drovers Ct. *KT1: King T* ... *68Na 131*
(off Fairfield E.)
Drovers Mead CM14: W'ley ... 21Xd 58
Drovers Pl. SE15 ... 52Yb 114
Drovers Rd. CR2: S Croy ... 78Tb 157
Drovers Way AL3: St A ... 2B 6
N7 ... 37Nb 70
Drove Way, The DA13: Ist R ... 6A 144
Droveway IG10: Lough ... 12Rc 36
Druce Rd. SE21 ... 58Ub 113
Drudgeon Way DA2: Bean ... 62Xd 142
Druids Cl. KT21: Asht ... 92Pa 193
Druid St. SE1 ... 1J 231 (47Ub 91)
(not continuous)
Druids Way BR2: Brom ... 70Fc 137
Drumaline Ridge KT4: Wor Pk ... 75Ua 154
Drum Ct. *N1* ... *38Nb 70*
(off Gifford St.)
Drummer Stagpole M. NW7 ... 22Ab 48
Drummond Av. RM7: Rom ... 28Fd 56
Drummond Cl. DA8: Erith ... 53Gd 118
Drummond Ct. CM15: B'wood ... 17Yd 40
KT19: Eps ... 84Pa 173
N12 ... 24Gb 49
W3 ... *48Sa 87*
(off Palmerston Rd.)
Drummond Cres. NW1 ... 3D 216 (41Mb 90)
Drummond Dr. HA7: Stan ... 24Ha 46
Drummond Gdns. KT19: Eps ... 83Sa 173
Drummond Ga. SW1 ... 7E 228 (50Mb 90)
Drummond Ho. *E2* ... *40Wb 71*
(off Goldsmiths Row)
N2 ... *26Eb 49*
(off Font Hills)
SL4: Wind ... *5H 103*
(off Balmoral Gdns.)
Drummond Pl. TW1: Twick ... 59Ka 108
Drummond Rd. CR0: C'don ... 75Sb 157
E11 ... 30Lc 53
RM7: Rom ... 28Fd 56
SE16 ... 48Xb 91
Drummonds, The CM16: Epp ... 2Wc 23
IG9: Buck H ... 19Kc 35
Drummonds Pl. TW9: Rich ... 56Na 109
Drummond St. NW1 ... 5B 216 (42Lb 90)
Drummond Way N1 ... 38Qb 70
Druries *HA1: Harr* ... *32Ga 66*
(off High St.)
Drury Cl. SW15 ... 58Wa 110
Drury Cres. CR0: Wadd ... 75Qb 156
Drury Ho. SW8 ... 53Lb 112
Drury La. WC2 ... 2G 223 (44Nb 90)
Drury Lane Theatre Royal ... 3H 223
Drury Rd. HA1: Harr ... 31Ea 66
Drury Way NW10 ... 36Ta 67
Drury Way Ind. Est. NW10 ... 36Sa 67
Dryad St. SW15 ... 55Za 110
Dry Arch Rd. SL5: S'dale ... 2D 146
Dryburgh Gdns. NW9 ... 27Qa 47
Dryburgh Ho. SW1 ... 7K 227
Dryburgh Rd. SW15 ... 55Xa 110
Dryden Av. W7 ... 44Ha 86
Dryden Bldg. *E1* ... *44Wb 91*
(off Commercial Rd.)
Dryden Cl. IG6: Ilf ... 23Vc 55
SW4 ... 57Mb 112
Dryden Ct. SE11 ... 6A 230 (49Qb 90)
Dryden Mans. *W14* ... *51Ab 110*
(off Queen's Club Gdns.)
Dryden Pl. RM18: Tilb ... 3D 122
Dryden Rd. DA16: Well ... 53Vc 117
EN1: Enf ... 16Ub 33
HA3: W'stone ... 25Ha 46
SW19 ... 65Eb 133
Dryden St. WC2 ... 3G 223 (44Nb 90)
Dryden Towers RM3: Rom ... 24Kd 57
Dryden Way BR6: Orp ... 74Wc 161
Dryfield Cl. NW10 ... 37Sa 67
Dryfield Rd. HA8: Edg ... 23Sa 47
Dryfield Wlk. SE8 ... 51Cc 114
DRYHILL ... 96Dd 202
Dryhill La. TN14: Sund ... 95Dd 202
Dryhill Local Nature Reserve ... 96Dd 202
Dryhill Rd. DA17: Belv ... 51Bd 117
Dryland Av. BR6: Orp ... 77Vc 161
Dryland Rd. TN15: Bor G ... 93Be 205
Drylands Rd. N8 ... 30Nb 50
Drynham Pk. KT13: Weyb ... 76U 150
Drysdale Av. E4 ... 17Dc 34
Drysdale Cl. HA6: Nwood ... 24U 44
Drysdale Dwellings *E8* ... *36Vb 71*
(off Dunn St.)
Drysdale Pl. N1 ... 3J 219 (41Ub 91)
Drysdale St. N1 ... 3J 219 (41Ub 91)
Duarte Pl. RM16: Chaf H ... 48Be 99
Dublin Av. E8 ... 39Wb 71
Dublin Ct. *HA2: Harr* ... *33Fa 66*
(off Northolt Rd.)
Dubrae Cl. AL3: St A ... 4N 5
Du Burstow Ter. W7 ... 47Ga 86
Ducaine Apartments *E3* ... *41Bc 92*
(off Merchant St.)
Ducal St. E2 ... 4K 219 (41Vb 91)
Du Cane Cl. W12 ... 44Ya 88
Du Cane Ct. SW17 ... 60Jb 112
Du Cane Rd. W12 ... 44Va 88
Ducavel Ho. SW2 ... 60Pb 112
Duchess Cl. N11 ... 22Kb 50
SM1: Sutt ... 77Eb 155
Duchess Ct. KT13: Weyb ... 76T 150
Duchess Cres. HA7: Stan ... 20Ha 28
Duchess Gro. IG9: Buck H ... 19Kc 35
Duchess M. W1 ... 1A 222 (43Kb 90)
Duchess of Bedford Ho. *W8* ... *47Cb 89*
(off Duchess of Bedford's Wlk.)
Duchess of Bedford's Wlk. W8 ... 47Cb 89
Duchess St. SL1: Slou ... 6C 80
W1 ... 1A 222 (43Kb 90)
Duchess Theatre ... 4H 223
Duchess Wlk. SE1 ... 7K 225 (46Vb 91)
Duchess' Wlk. TN15: S'oaks ... 98Nd 203
Duchy Rd. EN4: Had W ... 10Fb 17
Duchy St. SE1 ... 6A 224 (46Qb 90)
(not continuous)
Ducie St. SW4 ... 56Pb 112
Duckett M. N4 ... 30Rb 51
Duckett Rd. N4 ... 30Rb 51
Duckett's Apartments *E3* ... *38Bc 72*
(off Wick La.)
Ducketts Rd. DA1: Cray ... 57Hd 118
Duckett St. E1 ... 42Zb 92
Ducking Stool Ct. RM1: Rom ... 28Gd 56
Duck La. W1 ... 3D 222
Duck Lees La. EN3: Pond E ... 14Ac 34
Duck's Hill Rd. HA4: Ruis ... 28S 44
HA6: Nwood ... 26R 44
DUCKS ISLAND ... 16Za 30
Ducks Wlk. TW1: Twick ... 57La 108
Duck Wood Community Nature Reserve ... 22Rd 57
Duckworth Dr. KT22: Asht ... 92Ma 193
Du Cros Dr. HA7: Stan ... 23Ma 47
Du Cros Rd. W3 ... 46Ua 88
Dudbrook Rd.
CM14: Kel C, Nave ... 11Sd 40, 11Nd 39
DUDDEN HILL ... 36Xa 68
Dudden Hill La. NW10 ... 35Va 68
Dudden Hill Pde. NW10 ... 35Va 68
Duddington Cl. SE9 ... 63Mc 137
Dudley Av. EN8: Walt C ... 4Zb 20
HA3: Kenton ... 27La 46
Dudley Cl. HP3: Bov ... 9C 2
KT15: Add ... 76L 149
RM16: Chaf H ... 47Ae 99
Dudley Ct. NW11 ... 28Bb 49
SL1: Slou ... 8L 81
W1 ... 3F 221
WC2 ... 2F 223 (44Nb 90)
Dudley Dr. HA4: Ruis ... 36X 65
SM4: Mord ... 74Ab 154
Dudley Gdns. HA2: Harr ... 32Fa 66
RM3: Rom ... 23Md 57
W13 ... 47Ka 86
Dudley Gro. KT18: Eps ... 86Sa 173
Dudley Ho. HP3: Bov ... 9C 2
W2 ... 1B 220
Dudley M. SW2 ... 58Qb 112
Dudley Pl. TW19: Stanw ... 58P 105
UB3: Harl ... 49T 84
Dudley Rd. DA11: Nflt ... 9A 122
E17 ... 26Cc 52
HA2: Harr ... 33Ea 66
IG1: Ilf ... 35Rc 74
KT1: King T ... 69Pa 131
KT12: Walt T ... 72W 150
N3 ... 26Db 49
NW6 ... 40Ab 68
RM3: Rom ... 23Md 57
SW19 ... 65Cb 133
TW9: Rich ... 55Pa 109
TW14: Bedf ... 60S 106
TW15: Ashf ... 64P 127
UB2: S'hall ... 47Z 85
Dudley St. W2 ... 1B 220 (43Fb 89)
Dudley Wharf SL0: Iver ... 46E 82
Dudley Wharf Caravans SL0: Iver ... 46D 82
Dudlington Rd. E5 ... 33Yb 72
Dudmaston M. SW3 ... 7C 226
Dudrich Cl. N11 ... 23Hb 49
Dudrich M. EN2: Enf ... 11Qb 32
SE22 ... 57Vb 113
Dudsbury Rd. DA1: Dart ... 58Kd 119
DA14: Sidc ... 65Xc 139
Dudset La. TW5: Cran ... 53W 106
Duett Ct. TW5: Hest ... 52Aa 107
Duffell Ho. SE11 ... 7J 229
Dufferin Av. EC1 ... 6F 219
Dufferin Ct. EC1 ... 6F 219
Dufferin St. EC1 ... 6E 218 (42Sb 91)
Duffield Cl. HA1: Harr ... 29Ha 46
RM16: Chaf H ... 48Be 99
Duffield Dr. N15 ... 28Vb 51
Duffield La. SL2: Stoke P ... 7K 61
Duffield Pk. SL2: Stoke P ... 1K 81
Duffield Rd. KT20: Walt H ... 96Xa 194
Duffins Orchard KT16: Ott ... 80E 148
Duffins Orchard Mobile Homes
KT16: Ott ... 80E 148
Duff St. E14 ... 44Dc 92
Dufour's Pl. W1 ... 3C 222 (44Lb 90)
Dufton Dwellings *E15* ... *35Gc 73*
(off High Rd. Leyton)
Dugard Way SE11 ... 5B 230 (49Rb 91)
Dugdale Cen.
Enfield ... 14Tb 33
Dugdale Ct. *NW10* ... *41Xa 88*
(off Harrow Rd.)
DUGDALE HILL ... 5Ab 16
Dugdale Hill La. EN6: Pot B ... 5Ab 16
Dugdale Ho. *TW20: Egh* ... *64E 126*
(off Rowan Av.)
Dugdales WD3: Crox G ... 14Q 26
Duggan Dr. BR7: Chst ... 65Nc 138
Dugolly Av. HA9: Wemb ... 34Ra 67
Duke Ct. TW3: Houn ... 56Ba 107
Duke Gdns. IG6: Ilf ... 28Tc 54
Duke Humphrey Rd. SE3 ... 53Gc 115
Duke of Cambridge Cl.
TW2: Whitt ... 58Fa 108
Duke of Clarence Ct. SE17 ... 7D 230
Duke of Edinburgh Rd.
SM1: Sutt ... 75Fb 155
Duke of Wellington Av. SE18 ... 48Rc 94
Duke of Wellington Pl.
SW1 ... 2J 227 (47Jb 90)
Duke of York Column (Memorial) ... 7D 222
Duke of York Sq. SW3 ... 6G 227 (50Hb 89)
Duke of York's Theatre ... 5F 223
Duke of York St. SW1 ... 6C 222 (46Lb 90)
Duke Pl. *SL1: Slou* ... *5K 81*
(off Montague Rd.)
Duke Rd. IG6: Ilf ... 28Tc 54
W4 ... 50Ta 87
Duke's Av. HA8: Edg ... 23Pa 47
N10 ... 27Kb 50
W4 ... 50Ta 87
Dukes Av. CM16: They B ... 7Uc 22
HA1: Harr ... 28Ga 46
HA2: Harr ... 30Ba 45
KT2: King T ... 63La 130
KT3: N Mald ... 69Ua 132
N3 ... 25Db 49
RM17: Grays ... 48Ce 99
TW4: Houn ... 56Aa 107
TW10: Ham ... 63La 130
UB5: N'olt ... 38Aa 65
Dukes Cl. SL9: Ger X ... 2P 61
TW12: Hamp ... 64Ba 129
TW15: Ashf ... 63S 128
Dukes Ct. E6 ... 39Qc 74
(not continuous)
GU21: Wok ... 89B 168
KT15: Add ... 77L 149
KT19: Ewe ... 81Ua 174
SE13 ... 54Ec 114
SW14 ... 54Ta 109
W2 ... *45Db 89*
(off Moscow Rd.)
Dukes Dr. SL2: Farn C ... 6D 60
Dukes Ga. W4 ... 49Sa 87
Dukes Grn. Av. TW14: Felt ... 57W 106
Dukes Head Pas. TW12: Hamp ... 66Ea 130
Duke's Head Yd. N6 ... 32Kb 70
Dukes Hill CR3: Wold ... 92Ac 198
Duke Shore Wharf E14 ... 45Bc 92
Duke's Ho. SW1 ... 5E 228
Dukes Kiln Dr. SL9: Ger X ... 2N 61
Dukes La. SL4: Wind ... 6E 124
SL5: Asc ... 6E 124
SL9: Ger X ... 31A 62
W8 ... 47Db 89
Duke's La. Chambers *W8* ... *47Db 89*
(off Dukes La.)
Duke's La. Mans. *W8* ... *47Db 89*
(off Dukes La.)
Dukes Lodge *W8* ... *46Bb 89*
(off Holland Wlk.)
Dukes Meadow Golf & Tennis ... 54Ta 109
Duke's Meadow Golf Course ... 54Ta 109
Duke's Meadows ... 54Ta 109
Duke's M. W1 ... 2J 221
Dukes M. N10 ... 27Kb 50
Dukes Orchard DA5: Bexl ... 60Ed 118
Duke's Pas. E17 ... 28Ec 52
Duke's Pl. CM14: B'wood ... 18Yd 40
EC3 ... 3J 225 (44Ub 91)
Dukes Point *N6* ... *32Kb 70*
(off Dukes Head Yd.)
Dukes Ride SL9: Ger X ... 32A 62
UB10: Ick ... 35N 63
Duke's Rd. WC1 ... 4E 216 (41Mb 90)
Dukes Rd. E6 ... 39Qc 74
KT12: Hers ... 78Z 151
W3 ... 42Qa 87
Dukesthorpe Rd. SE26 ... 63Zb 136
Duke St. GU21: Wok ... 89B 168
SL4: Wind ... 2G 103
SM1: Sutt ... 77Fb 155
TW9: Rich ... 56Ma 109
W1 ... 2J 221 (44Jb 90)
WD17: Wat ... 13Y 27
Duke St. Hill SE1 ... 6G 225 (46Tb 91)
Duke St. Mans. W1 ... 3J 221
Duke St. St James's
SW1 ... 6C 222 (46Lb 90)
Dukes Valley SL9: Ger X ... 3M 61
Dukes Way BR4: W W'ck ... 76Gc 159
HA9: Wemb ... 36Na 67
UB8: Uxb ... 39K 63
Dukes Wood Av. SL9: Ger X ... 31A 62
Dukes Wood Dr. SL9: Ger X ... 2N 61
Duke's Yd. W1 ... 4J 221 (45Jb 90)
Dukes Yd. WD24: Wat ... 10W 12
Dulas St. N4 ... 32Pb 70
Dulcie Cl. DA9: Ghithe ... 58Ud 120
Dulford St. W11 ... 45Ab 88
Dulka Rd. SW11 ... 57Hb 111
Dullshot Grn. KT17: Eps ... 85Ua 174
Dulverton NW1 ... 1C 216
Dulverton Mans. WC1 ... 6J 217
Dulverton Rd. CR2: Sels ... 82Yb 178
HA4: Ruis ... 32W 64
RM3: Rom ... 23Md 57
SE9 ... 61Sc 138
DULWICH ... 61Ub 135
Dulwich & Sydenham Hill Golf Course ... 61Vb 135
Dulwich Bus. Cen. SE23 ... 60Zb 114
Dulwich Comn. SE21 ... 60Ub 113
SE22 ... 60Ub 113
Dulwich Hamlet FC ... 56Ub 113
Dulwich Lawn Cl. SE22 ... 57Vb 113
Dulwich Leisure Cen. ... 56Wb 113
Dulwich Oaks, The SE21 ... 62Vb 135
Dulwich Picture Gallery ... 59Tb 113
Dulwich Ri. Gdns. SE22 ... 57Vb 113
Dulwich Rd. SE24 ... 57Qb 112
Dulwich Upper Wood Nature Pk. ... 64Vb 135
DULWICH VILLAGE ... 59Ub 113
Dulwich Village SE21 ... 58Tb 113
Dulwich Way WD3: Crox G ... 15Q 26
Dulwich Wood Av. SE19 ... 63Ub 135
Dulwich Wood Pk. SE19 ... 63Ub 135
Dumain Ct. SE11 ... 6B 230
Dumas Way WD18: Wat ... 14U 26
Dumbarton Av. EN8: Walt C ... 6Zb 20
Dumbarton Ct. SW2 ... 58Nb 112
Dumbarton Rd. SW2 ... 58Nb 112
Dumbarton Way SL3: L'ly ... 10N 81
Dumbleton Cl. KT1: King T ... 67Ra 131
Dumbletons, The WD3: Map C ... 21G 42
Dumbreck Rd. SE9 ... 56Pc 116
Dumfries Cl. WD19: Wat ... 20V 26
Dumont Rd. N16 ... 34Ub 71

Dumpton Pl.—Eastbury Av.

Dumpton Pl. NW1 38Jb 70
Dumsey Eyot KT16: Chert 73N 149
Dumville Dr. RH9: G'stone 3P 209
Dunally Pk. TW17: Shep 73T 150
Dunbar Av. BR3: Beck 70Ac 136
RM10: Dag 34Cd 76
SW16 68Qb 134
Dunbar Cl. SL2: Slou 5L 81
UB4: Hayes 43X 85
Dunbar Ct. BR2: Brom 69Hc 137
(off Durham Rd.)
KT12: Walt T 74Y 151
SM1: Sutt 78Fb 155
Dunbar Gdns. RM10: Dag 36Cd 76
Dunbar Rd. E7 37Jc 73
KT3: N Mald 70Sa 131
N22 25Qb 50
Dunbar St. SE27 62Sb 135
Dunbar Twr. E8 37Vb 71
(off Dalston Sq.)
Dunbar Wharf E14 45Bc 92
(off Narrow St.)
Dunblane Cl. HA8: Edg 19Ra 29
Dunblane Rd. SE9 55Nc 116
Dunboe Pl. TW17: Shep 73S 150
Dunboyne Pl. SL4: Old Win 6L 103
Dunboyne Rd. NW3 36Hb 69
Dunbridge Ho. SW15 58Va 110
Dunbridge St. E2 42Wb 91
Duncan Cl. EN5: New Bar 14Eb 31
Duncan Ct. AL1: St A 4D 6
E14 43Ec 92
(off Teviot St.)
N21 18Rb 33
Duncan Gdns. TW18: Staines 65J 127
Duncan Gro. W3 44Ua 88
Duncan Ho. NW3 38Hb 69
(off Fellows Rd.)
SW1 50Lb 90
(off Dolphin Sq.)
Duncannon Cres. SL4: Wind 5B 102
Duncannon Ho. SW1 7E 228
Duncannon Pl. DA9: Ghithe 56Yd 120
Duncannon St. WC2 5F 223 (45Nb 90)
Duncan Rd. E8 39Xb 71
KT20: Tad 91Ab 194
TW9: Rich 56Na 109
Duncan St. N1 1B 218 (40Rb 71)
Duncans Yd. TN16: Westrm 98Tc 200
Duncan Ter. N1 2B 218 (40Rb 71)
(not continuous)
Duncan Way WD23: Bush 12Ba 27
Dunch St. E1 44Xb 91
Dunchurch Ho. RM10: Dag 38Cd 76
Duncombe Ct. RM19: Purf 50Rd 97
(off Wingrove Dr.)
TW18: Staines 66H 127
Duncombe Hill SE23 59Ac 114
Duncombe Rd. N19 32Mb 70
Duncrievie Rd. SE13 58Fc 115
Duncroft SE18 52Uc 116
SL4: Wind 5D 102
Duncroft Cl. RH2: Reig 6H 207
Duncroft Mnr. TW18: Staines 63G 126
Dundalk Ho. E1 44Yb 92
(off Clark St.)
Dundalk Rd. SE4 55Ac 114
Dundas Ct. SE10 51Dc 114
(off Dowells St.)
Dundas Gdns. KT8: W Mole 69Da 129
Dundas Ho. E2 40Yb 72
(off Bishop's Way)
Dundas M. EN3: Enf L 9Cc 20
Dundas Rd. SE15 54Yb 114
SW9 53Qb 112
Dundee Ct. E1 46Xb 91
(off Wapping High St.)
SE1 3H 231
(off Long La.)
Dundee Ho. W9 3A 214
Dundee Rd. E13 40Kc 73
SE25 71Xb 157
SL1: Slou 4D 80
Dundee St. E1 46Xb 91
Dundee Way EN3: Brim 13Ac 34
Dundee Wharf E14 45Bc 92
Dundela Gdns. KT4: Wor Pk 77Xa 154
Dundonald Cl. E6 44Nc 94
Dundonald Rd. NW10 39Za 68
SW19 66Ab 132
Dundrey Cres. RH1: Mers 1E 208
Dundry Ho. SE26 62Wb 135
Dunedin Dr. CR3: Cat'm 97Ub 197
Dunedin Ho. E16 46Pc 94
(off Manwood St.)
Dunedin M. SW2 60Nb 112
Dunedin Rd. E10 34Dc 72
IG1: Ilf 32Sc 74
RM13: Rain 41Hd 96
Dunedin Way UB4: Yead 42Y 85
Dunelm Gro. SE27 62Sb 135
Dunelm St. E1 44Zb 92
Dunfee Way KT14: Byfl 84N 169
Dunfermline Ho. WD19: Wat 20Y 27
Dunfield Gdns. SE6 64Dc 136
Dunfield Rd. SE6 64Dc 136
(not continuous)
Dunford Ct. HA5: Hat E 24Ba 45
Dunford Rd. N7 35Pb 70
Dungannon Ho. SW6 52Cb 111
(off Vanston Pl.)
Dungarvan Av. SW15 56Wa 110
Dungates La. RH3: Bkld 5C 206
Dunheved Cl. CR7: Thor H 72Qb 156
Dunheved Rd. Nth. CR7: Thor H 72Qb 156
Dunheved Rd. Sth. CR7: Thor H 72Qb 156
Dunheved Rd. W. CR7: Thor H 72Qb 156
Dunhill Point SW15 60Wa 110
Dunholme Grn. N9 20Vb 33
Dunholme La. N9 20Vb 33
Dunholme Rd. N9 20Vb 33
Dunkeld Rd. RM8: Dag 33Xc 75
SE25 70Tb 135
Dunkellin Gro. RM15: S Ock 44Wd 98
Dunkellin Way RM15: S Ock 44Wd 98
Dunkery Rd. SE9 63Mc 137
Dunkin Rd. DA1: Dart 56Qd 119
Dunkirk Cl. DA12: Grav'nd 4E 144
Dunkirk Ho. SE1 2G 231 (47Tb 91)
Dunkirk St. SE27 63Sb 135
DUNK'S GREEN 100Ce 205
Dunlace Rd. E5 35Yb 72
Dunleary Cl. TW4: Houn 59Ba 107
Dunley Dr. CR0: New Ad 80Dc 158
Dunlin Ho. SE16 49Zb 92
(off Tawny Way)
Dunloe Av. N17 27Tb 51
Dunloe Ct. E2 2K 219 (40Vb 71)
Dunloe Pas. E2 40Vb 71
(off Dunloe St.)
Dunloe St. E2 2K 219 (40Vb 71)
Dunlop Cl. DA1: Dart 55Nd 119
RM18: Tilb 4B 122
Dunlop Pl. SE16 48Vb 91
Dunlop Rd. RM18: Tilb 3B 122
Dunmail Dr. CR8: Purl 86Ub 177
Dunmore Point E2 4K 219
Dunmore Rd. NW6 39Ab 68
SW20 67Ya 132
Dunmow Cl. IG10: Lough 16Nc 36
RM6: Chad H 29Yc 55
TW13: Hanw 62Aa 129
Dunmow Dr. RM13: Rain 39Hd 76
Dunmow Gdns. CM13: W H'dn 30Fe 59
Dunmow Ho. KT14: Byfl 85N 169
SE11 7J 229
Dunmow Rd. E15 35Fc 73
Dunmow Wlk. N1 39Sb 71
(off Popham St.)
Dunnage Cres. SE16 49Ac 92
(not continuous)
Dunnell Cl. TW16: Sun 67W 128
Dunnets GU21: Knap 9J 167
Dunnett Ho. E3 40Bc 72
(off Vernon Rd.)
Dunnico Ho. SE17 7H 231
Dunning Cl. RM15: S Ock 44Wd 98
Dunningford Cl. RM12: Horn 36Hd 76
Dunnings La. CM13: W H'dn 31De 79
RM14: Bulp 31De 79
Dunn Mead NW9 24Va 48
Dunnock Cl. HP3: Hem H 7L 3
N9 18Zb 34
WD6: Bore 14Qa 29
Dunnock Ho. NW9 30Va 48
Dunnock M. E5 34Wb 71
Dunnock Rd. E6 44Nc 94
Dunnose Ct. RM19: Purf 50Rd 97
Dunn's Pas. WC1 2G 223
Dunn St. E8 36Vb 71
Dunny La. WD3: Chfd 5G 10
WD4: Chfd 5G 10
Dunnymans Rd. SM7: Bans 87Bb 175
Dunollie Pl. NW5 36Lb 70
Dunollie Rd. NW5 36Lb 70
Dunoon Gdns. SE23 59Zb 114
Dunoon Ho. N1 39Pb 70
(off Bemerton Est.)
Dunoon Rd. SE23 59Yb 114
Dunoran Home BR1: Brom 67Nc 138
Dunottar Cl. RH1: Redh 8M 207
Dunraven Dr. EN2: Enf 12Qb 32
Dunraven Rd. W12 46Wa 88
Dunraven St. W1 4G 221 (45Hb 89)
Dunsany Rd. W14 48Za 88
DUNSBOROUGH PARK 93L 189
Dunsbury Cl. SM2: Sutt 81Db 175
Dunsfold Ct. SM2: Sutt 80Db 155
(off Blackbush Cl.)
Dunsfold Ri. CR5: Coul 85Mb 176
Dunsfold Way CR0: New Ad 81Dc 178
Dunsford Way SW15 58Xa 110
Dunsmore WD19: Wat 18Z 27
Dunsmore Cl. UB4: Yead 42Z 85
WD23: Bush 16Fa 28
Dunsmore Rd. KT12: Walt T 72X 151
Dunsmore Way WD23: Bush 16Fa 28
Dunsmure Rd. N16 32Ub 71
Dunspring La. IG5: Ilf 26Rc 54
Dunstable Cl. RM3: Rom 23Md 57
Dunstable M. W1 7J 215 (43Jb 90)
Dunstable Rd. KT8: W Mole 70Ba 129
RM3: Rom 23Md 57
SS17: Stan H 1L 101
TW9: Rich 56Na 109
Dunstall Grn. GU24: Chob 1N 167
Dunstall Rd. SW20 65Xa 132
Dunstall Way KT8: W Mole 69Da 129
Dunstall Welling Est.
DA16: Well 54Xc 117
Dunstan Cl. N2 27Eb 49
Dunstan Glade BR5: Pet W 72Tc 160
Dunstan Gro. SE20 66Xb 135
Dunstan Ho's. E1 43Yb 92
(off Stepney Grn.)
Dunstan M. EN1: Enf 13Ub 33
Dunstan Rd. CR5: Coul 89Mb 176
NW11 32Bb 69
Dunstan's Gro. SE22 58Xb 113
Dunstan's Rd. SE22 59Wb 113
Dunster Av. SM4: Mord 74Za 154
Dunster Cl. EN5: Barn 14Za 30
RM5: Col R 26Ed 56
UB9: Hare 25K 43
Dunster Ct. EC3 4J 225 (45Ub 91)
WD6: Bore 13Ta 29
Dunster Cres. RM11: Horn 33Qd 77
Dunster Dr. NW9 32Sa 67
Dunster Gdns. NW6 38Bb 69
SL1: Slou 5E 80
Dunster Ho. SE6 62Ec 136
Dunsterville Way SE1 2G 231 (47Tb 91)
Dunster Way HA2: Harr 34Aa 65
SM6: Wall 74Jb 156
Dunston Ct. TW18: Staines 63J 127
Dunstone Ct. SE6 59Cc 114
Dunston Rd. E8 39Vb 71
SW11 54Jb 112
Dunston St. E8 39Ub 71
Dunton Cl. KT6: Surb 74Na 153
Dunton Ct. SE23 61Xb 135
DUNTON GREEN 92Gd 202
Dunton Rd. E10 31Dc 72
RM1: Rom 28Gd 56
SE1 7K 231 (50Vb 91)
Duntshill Rd. SW18 60Db 111
Dunvegan Cl. KT8: W Mole 70Ca 129
Dunvegan Ho. RH1: Redh 6P 207
Dunvegan Rd. SE9 56Pc 116
Dunwich Ct. RM6: Chad H 29Xc 55
(off Glandford Way)
Dunwich Rd. DA7: Bex 53Bd 117
Dunworth M. W11 44Bb 89
Duplex Ride SW1 2G 227 (47Hb 89)
Dupont Rd. SW20 68Za 132
Duppas Av. CR0: Wadd 77Rb 157
Duppas Cl. TW17: Shep 71T 150
Duppas Ct. CR0: C'don 76Rb 157
(off Duppas Hill Ter.)
Duppas Hill La. CR0: C'don 77Rb 157
Duppas Hill Rd. CR0: Wadd 77Qb 156
Duppas Hill Ter. CR0: C'don 76Rb 157
Duppas Rd. CR0: Wadd 76Qb 156
Dupre Cl. RM16: Chaf H 48Ae 99
SL1: Slou 7C 80
Dupree Rd. SE7 50Kc 93
Dura Den Cl. BR3: Beck 66Dc 136
Durand Gdns. SW9 53Pb 112
Durands Wlk. SE16 47Bc 92
Durand Way NW10 38Sa 67
Durant Rd. BR8: Hext 65Jd 140
Durants Pk. 13Yb 34
Durants Pk. Av. EN3: Pond E 14Zb 34
Durants Rd. EN3: Pond E 14Yb 34
Durant St. E2 40Wb 71
Durban Cl. E7 38Mc 73
Durban Gdns. RM10: Dag 38Ed 76
Durban Ho. W12 45Xa 88
(off White City Est.)
Durban Rd. BR3: Beck 68Bc 136
E15 41Gc 93
E17 25Bc 52
IG2: Ilf 32Uc 74
N17 23Ub 51
SE27 63Sb 135
Durban Rd. E. WD18: Wat 14W 26
Durban Rd. W. WD18: Wat 14W 26
Durbin Rd. KT9: Chess 77Na 153
Durdan Cotts. UB1: S'hall 44Ba 85
(off Denbigh Rd.)
Durdans Ho. NW1 38Kb 70
(off Farrier St.)
Durdans Rd. UB1: S'hall 44Ba 85
Durell Gdns. RM9: Dag 36Zc 75
Durell Ho. SE16 47Zb 92
(off Wolfe Cres.)
Durell Rd. RM9: Dag 36Zc 75
Durfey Pl. SE5 52Tb 113
Durfold Dr. RH2: Reig 6L 207
Durford Cres. SW15 60Xa 110
Durham Av. BR2: Brom 70Hc 137
IG8: Buck H, Wfd G 22Mc 53
RM2: Rom 28Ld 57
SL1: Slou 4E 80
TW5: Hest 50Ba 85
Durham Cl. SW20 68Xa 132
Durham Ct. KT22: Lea 94Ja 192
NW6 40Cb 69
(off Kilburn Pk. Rd.)
TW11: Tedd 63Ga 130
Durham Hill BR1: Brom 63Hc 137
Durham Ho. BR2: Brom 70Gc 137
IG11: Bark 38Wc 75
(off Margaret Bondfield Av.)
NW8 4D 214
RM10: Dag 36Ed 76
WD6: Bore 12Qa 29
(off Canterbury Rd.)
Durham Ho. St. WC2 5G 223
Durham Pl. IG1: Ilf 35Sc 74
SW3 7F 227 (50Hb 89)
Durham Ri. SE18 50Sc 94
Durham Rd. BR2: Brom 69Hc 137
DA14: Sidc 64Xc 139
E12 35Mc 73
E16 42Gc 93
HA1: Harr 29Da 45
N2 27Gb 49
N7 33Pb 70
N9 19Xb 33
RM10: Dag 36Ed 76
SW20 67Xa 132
TW14: Felt 59Y 107
W5 48Ma 87
WD6: Bore 13Sa 29
Durham Row E1 43Ac 92
Durham St. SE11 50Pb 90
Durham Ter. W2 44Db 89
Durham Wharf Dr. TW8: Bford 52La 108
Durham Yd. E2 41Xb 91
Durian Way DA8: Erith 52Kd 119
Durleston Pk. Dr. KT23: Bookh 97Ea 192
Durley Av. HA5: Pinn 31Aa 65
Durley Gdns. BR6: Chels 76Xc 161
Durley Rd. N16 31Ub 71
Durlings Orchard TN15: Igh 93Zd 205
Durlston Rd. E5 33Wb 71
KT2: King T 65Na 131
Durndale La. DA11: Nflt 3A 144
Durnell Way IG10: Lough 13Qc 36
Durnford Ho. SE6 62Ec 136
SL4: Eton 1H 103
(off Slough Rd.)
Durnford St. N15 29Ub 51
SE10 51Ec 114
Durninge Wlk. RM16: Grays 45De 99
Durning Pl. SL5: Asc 9A 124
Durning Rd. SE19 64Tb 135
Durnsford Av. SW19 61Cb 133
Durnsford Ct. EN3: Enf H 13Ac 34
(off Enstone Rd.)
Durnsford Rd. N11 25Mb 50
SW19 61Cb 133
Durrant Ct. HA3: Hrw W 26Ga 46
Durrant Ho. EC1 7G 219
Durrants Cl. RM13: Rain 40Ld 77
Durrants Dr. WD3: Crox G 13S 26
Durrants Hill Rd. HP3: Hem H 5M 3
Durrants Ho. WD3: Crox G 14R 26
Durrant Way BR6: Farnb 78Tc 160
DA10: Swans 59Ae 121
Durrell Dene DA1: Dart 54Pd 119
Durrell Rd. SW6 53Bb 111
Durrell Way TW17: Shep 72T 150
Durrels Ho. W14 49Bb 89
(off Warwick Gdns.)
Durrington Av. SW20 66Ya 132
Durrington Pk. Rd. SW20 67Ya 132
Durrington Rd. E5 35Ac 72
Durrington Twr. SW8 54Lb 112
Durrisdeer Ho. NW2 35Bb 69
(off Lyndale)
Dursley Cl. SE3 54Lc 115
Dursley Gdns. SE3 53Mc 115
Dursley Rd. SE3 54Lc 115
Durward Ho. W8 47Db 89
(off Kensington Ct.)
Durward St. E1 43Xb 91
Durweston M. W1 7G 215
Durweston St. W1 1G 221 (43Hb 89)
Dury Falls Cl. RM11: Horn 32Qd 77
Dury Falls Ct. RM5: Col R 26Ed 56
Dury Rd. EN5: Barn 11Bb 31
Dutch Barn Cl. TW19: Stanw 58M 105
Dutch Elm Av. SL4: Wind 2K 103
Dutch Gdns. KT2: King T 65Ra 131
Dutch Yd. SW18 57Cb 111
Dutton St. SE10 53Ec 114
Dutton Way SL0: Iver 44G 82
Duval Ho. N19 33Mb 70
(off Ashbrook Rd.)
Duxberry Av. TW13: Felt 62Y 129
Duxberry Cl. BR2: Brom 71Nc 160
Duxford Cl. RM12: Horn 37Ld 77
Duxford Ho. SE2 47Zc 95
(off Wolvercote Rd.)
Dux Hill TN15: Plax 98Be 205
Dux La. TN15: Plax 98Be 205
Duxons Turn HP2: Hem H 1B 4
Dwelly La. TN8: Eden 9M 211
DW Fitness
Waldorf Hotel 3H 223
Dwight Rd. WD18: Wat 17T 26
Dyas Rd. TW16: Sun 67W 128
Dye Ho. La. E3 39Cc 72
Dyer Ho. TW12: Hamp 67Da 129
Dyer's Bldgs. EC1 1K 223 (43Qb 90)
Dyers Hall Rd. E11 32Gc 73
Dyers Hill Rd. E11 33Fc 73
Dyers La. SW15 56Xa 110
Dyers Way RM3: Rom 24Kd 57
Dyke Dr. BR5: Orp 73Yc 161
Dykes Path GU21: Wok 87E 168
Dykes Way BR2: Brom 69Hc 137
Dykewood Cl. DA5: Bexl 62Fd 140
Dylan Cl. WD6: E'tree 17Ma 29
Dylan Rd. DA17: Belv 48Cd 96
SE24 56Rb 113
Dylways SE5 56Tb 113
Dymchurch Cl. BR6: Orp 77Uc 160
IG5: Ilf 26Qc 54
Dymes Path SW19 61Za 132
Dymock St. SW6 55Db 111
Dymoke Rd. RM11: Horn 31Hd 76
Dyneley Rd. SE12 62Lc 137
Dyne Rd. NW6 38Ab 68
Dynes, The
TN15: Kems'g 89Md 183
Dynes Rd.
TN15: Kems'g 89Md 183
Dynevor Rd. N16 34Ub 71
TW10: Rich 57Na 109
Dynham Rd. NW6 38Cb 69
Dyott St. WC1 2E 222 (44Mb 90)
Dyrham La. EN5: Barn 8Wa 16
Dyrham Pk.
Hertfordshire 10Wa 16
Dyrham Pk. Country Club & Golf Course 9Xa 16
Dysart Av. KT2: King T 64La 130
Dysart St. EC2 6H 219 (42Tb 91)
Dyson Cl. SL4: Wind 5F 102
Dyson Ct. HA0: Wemb 35Ja 66
NW2 32Ya 68
WD17: Wat 14Y 27
Dyson Ho. SE10 50Hc 93
(off Blackwall La.)
Dyson Rd. E11 30Gc 53
E15 37Hc 73
Dysons Cl. EN8: Walt C 5Zb 20
Dysons Rd. N18 22Xb 51
Dytchleys La. CM14: N'side 14Qd 39
Dytchleys Rd. CM14: N'side 14Pd 39

E

Eade Rd. N4 31Sb 71
Eagans Cl. N2 27Fb 49
Eagle Av. RM6: Chad H 30Ad 55
Eagle Cl. EN3: Pond E 14Yb 34
EN9: Walt A 6Jc 21
RM12: Horn 37Kd 77
SE16 50Yb 92
SM6: Wall 79Nb 156
Eagle Ct. E11 28Jc 53
EC1 7B 218 (43Rb 91)
Eagle Dr. NW9 26Ua 48
Eagle Dwellings EC1 3E 218
Eagle Hgts. SW11 55Gb 111
Eagle Heights Wildlife Pk. 75Kd 163
Eagle Hill SE19 65Tb 135
Eagle Ho. E1 42Xb 91
(off Headlam St.)
EC1 3F 219
N1 1F 219
RM17: Grays 51Be 121
Eagle Ho. M. SW4 57Lb 112
Eagle La. E11 28Jc 53
Eagle Lodge NW11 31Bb 69
Eagle Mans. N16 36Vb 71
(off Salcombe Rd.)
Eagle M. N1 37Ub 71
Eagle Pl. SW1 5C 222
SW7 7A 226 (50Eb 89)
Eagle Point EC1 4F 219
Eagle Rd. HA0: Wemb 38Ma 67
SL1: Slou 5D 80
TW6: H'row A 55V 106
Eagles Dr. TN16: Tats 90Mc 179
Eaglesfield Equestrian Cen. 76Zd 165
Eaglesfield Rd. SE18 53Rc 116
Eagles Rd. DA9: Ghithe 56Xd 120
Eaglestone Cl. TN15: Bor G 91Ce 205
Eagle St. WC1 1H 223 (43Pb 90)
Eagle Ter. IG8: Wfd G 24Kc 53
Eagle Trad. Est. CR4: Mitc 72Hb 155
Eagle Way AL10: Hat 2C 8
CM13: Gt War 23Xd 58
DA11: Nflt 57Ce 121
Eagle Wharf Ct. SE1 7K 225
Eagle Wharf E. E14 45Ac 92
(off Narrow St.)
Eagle Wharf Rd. N1 1E 218 (40Sb 71)
Eagle Wharf W. E14 45Ac 92
(off Narrow St.)
Eagle Works E. E1 6K 219
Eagle Works W. E1 6K 219
Eagling Cl. E3 41Cc 92
Ealdham Sq. SE9 56Lc 115
EALING 45Ma 87
Ealing B'way. Cen. W5 45Ma 87
Ealing Cl. WD6: Bore 11Ta 29
EALING COMMON 45Pa 87
Ealing Golf Course 41Ka 86
Ealing Grn. W5 46Ma 87
Ealing Pk. Gdns. W5 49La 86
Ealing Pk. Mans. W5 48Ma 87
(off Sth. Ealing Rd.)
Ealing Rd. HA0: Wemb 37Na 67
TW8: Bford 50Ma 87
UB5: N'olt 39Ca 65
Ealing Squash & Fitness Club 44Na 87
Ealing Studios 46Ma 87
Ealing Village W5 44Na 87
Eamont Cl. HA4: Ruis 31R 64
Eamont Ct. NW8 1E 214
Eamont St. NW8 1D 214 (40Gb 69)
Eardemont Cl. DA1: Cray 56Hd 118
Eardley Cres. SW5 50Cb 89
Eardley Point SE18 49Rc 94
(off Wilmount St.)
Eardley Rd. DA17: Belv 50Cd 96
SW16 64Lb 134
TN13: S'oaks 96Kd 203
Earhart Ho. NW9 27Wa 48
(off East Dr.)
Earhart Way
TW6: Cran, H'row A 55W 106
Earl Cl. N11 22Kb 50
Earldom Rd. SW15 56Ya 110
Earle Gdns. KT2: King T 66Na 131
Earle Ho. SW1 6E 228
Earleswood KT11: Cobh 84Aa 171
Earleswood Ct. HP3: Hem H 6M 3
Earleydene SL5: Asc 4A 146
Earlham Ct. E11 31Hc 73
Earlham Gro. E7 36Hc 73
N22 24Pb 50
Earlham St. WC2 3E 222 (44Nb 90)
Earl Ho. NW1 6E 214
Earlom Ho. WC1 4K 217
Earl Ri. SE18 50Tc 94
Earl Rd. DA11: Nflt 1A 144
SW14 56Sa 109
Earlsbrook Rd. RH1: Redh 8P 207
(not continuous)
Earlsbury Gdns. HA8: Edg 21Qa 47
Earls Cnr. EN6: S Mim 5Wa 16
EARL'S COURT 49Db 89
Earl's Ct. Gdns. SW5 49Db 89
Earl's Ct. Rd. SW5 48Cb 89
W8 48Cb 89
Earl's Ct. Sq. SW5 50Db 89
Earls Cres. HA1: Harr 28Ga 46
Earlsdown Ho. IG11: Bark 40Tc 74
Earlsferry Way N1 38Nb 70
(not continuous)
EARLSFIELD 60Eb 111
Earlsfield Ho.
KT2: King T 67Ma 131
(off Seven Kings Way)
Earlsfield Rd. SW18 60Eb 111
Earlshall Rd. SE9 56Pc 116
Earls Ho. TW9: Kew 52Ra 109
Earls La. EN6: Ridge, S Mim 4Ua 16
SL1: Slou 6D 80
Earlsmead HA2: Harr 35Ba 65
Earlsmead Rd. N15 29Vb 51
NW10 41Ya 88
Earlsmead Stadium 35Ba 65
Earl's Path IG10: Lough 12Lc 35
Earls Ter. W8 48Bb 89
Earlsthorpe M. SW12 58Jb 112
Earlsthorpe Rd. SE26 63Zb 136
Earlstoke St. EC1 3B 218 (41Rb 91)
Earlston Gro. E9 39Xb 71
Earl St. EC2 7G 219 (43Tb 91)
WD17: Wat 13Y 27
Earl's Wlk. RM8: Dag 35Xc 75
Earls Wlk. W8 48Cb 89
Earls Way SE1 1J 231
Earlswell Wlk. RM3: Rom 22Ld 57
EARLSWOOD 8P 207
Earlswood Av. CR7: Thor H 71Qb 156
Earlswood Cl. SE10 51Gc 115
Earlswood Common (Local Nature Reserve) 9M 207
Earlswood Ct. RH1: Redh 8P 207
Earlswood Gdns. IG5: Ilf 27Qc 54
Earlswood Rd. RH1: Redh 7P 207
Earlswood St. SE10 50Gc 93
Early M. NW1 39Kb 70
Early Rivers Ho. E20 36Ec 72
(off Ellis Way)
Earnshaw Ho. EC1 4C 218
Earnshaw St. WC2 2E 222 (44Mb 90)
Earsby St. W14 49Ab 88
(not continuous)
Easby Cres. SM4: Mord 72Db 155
Easebourne Rd. RM8: Dag 36Yc 75
Easedale Dr. RM12: Horn 36Jd 76
Easedale Ho. TW7: Isle 57Ha 108
Eashing Point SW15 60Xa 110
(off Wanborough Dr.)
Easington Way RM15: S Ock 43Wd 98
Easleys M. W1 2J 221 (44Jb 90)
East 10 Ent. Pk. E10 32Ac 72
EAST ACTON 45Ta 88
E. Acton Arc. W3 44Ua 88
E. Acton Ct. W3 45Ua 88
E. Acton La. W3 46Ua 88
E. Arbour St. E1 44Zb 92
East Av. E12 38Nc 74
E17 28Dc 52
KT12: W Vill 82V 170
SM6: Wall 78Pb 156
UB1: S'hall 45Ba 85
UB3: Hayes 46V 84
East Bank N16 31Ub 71
Eastbank Cl. E17 29Dc 52
Eastbank Rd. TW12: Hamp H 64Ea 130
EAST BARNET 16Gb 31
East Barnet Golf Course 13Db 31
E. Barnet Rd. EN4: E Barn 14Fb 31
E. Bay La. E20 36Cc 72
E. Beckton District Cen. E6 43Pc 94
EAST BEDFONT 59U 106
E. Block SE1 1J 229
Eastbourne Av. W3 44Ta 87
Eastbourne Gdns. SW14 55Sa 109
Eastbourne M. W2 2A 220 (44Eb 89)
Eastbourne Rd. E6 41Qc 94
(not continuous)
E15 39Gc 73
N15 30Ub 51
RH9: G'stone, S God 4A 210
SL1: Slou 1E 80
SW17 65Jb 134
TW8: Bford 50La 86
TW13: Felt 61Z 129
W4 51Sa 109
Eastbourne Ter. W2 2A 220 (44Eb 89)
Eastbournia Av. N9 20Xb 33
Eastbridge SL2: Slou 7M 81
Eastbrook Av. N9 17Yb 34
RM10: Dag 35Ed 76
Eastbrook Cl. GU21: Wok 88C 168
RM10: Dag 35Ed 76
Eastbrook Dr. RM7: Rush G 34Gd 76
Eastbrookend Country Pk. 34Fd 76
Eastbrook Rd. EN9: Walt A 5Gc 21
SE3 53Kc 115
Eastbrook Way HP2: Hem H 2N 3
EAST BURNHAM 8E 60
E. Burnham La. SL2: Farn R 9E 60
EASTBURY 21V 44
Eastbury Av. EN1: Enf 11Vb 33
HA6: Nwood 24U 44
IG11: Bark 39Uc 74

Eastbury Ct.—Edgehill Ct.

Eastbury Ct. AL1: St A 1D 6
EN5: New Bar 15Eb 31
(off Lyonsdown Rd.)
IG11: Bark 39Uc 74
WD19: Wat 17Y 27
Eastbury Farm Cl. HA6: Nwood 21U 44
Eastbury Gro. W4 .....50Ua 88
Eastbury Manor House 39Vc 75
Eastbury Pl. HA6: Nwood 22V 44
Eastbury Rd. BR5: Pet W 72Tc 160
E6 .....42Qc 94
HA6: Nwood 23U 44
KT2: King T 66Na 131
RM7: Rom 30Fd 56
WD19: Wat 17X 27
Eastbury Sq. IG11: Bark 39Vc 75
Eastbury Ter. E1 .....42Zb 92
E. Carriage Ho. SE18 .....48Rc 94
(off Royal Carriage M.)
Eastcastle St. W1 .....2B 222 (44Lb 90)
Eastcheap EC3 .....4G 225 (45Ub 91)
E. Churchfield Rd. W3 .....46Ta 87
Eastchurch Rd. TW6: H'row A 54U 106
East Cl. AL2: Chis G 7P 5
EN4: Cockf 14Jb 32
RM13: Rain 42Kd 97
UB6: G'frd 40Ea 66
W5 .....42Qa 87
Eastcombe Av. SE7 .....51Kc 115
East Comn. SL9: Ger X 30A 42
EASTCOTE 31X 65
Eastcote BR6: Orp 74Vc 161
Eastcote Av. HA2: Harr 33Da 65
KT8: W Mole 71Ba 151
UB6: G'frd 36Ja 66
Eastcote Hockey & Badminton Club 30V 44
Eastcote Ho. KT17: Eps 84Ua 174
Eastcote Ind. Est. HA4: Ruis 31Y 65
Eastcote La. HA2: Harr 35Aa 65
UB5: N'olt 36Ba 65
(not continuous)
Eastcote La. Nth. UB5: N'olt 37Ba 65
Eastcote Pl. HA5: Eastc 30X 45
Eastcote Rd. DA16: Well 54Tc 116
HA2: Harr 34Ea 66
HA4: Ruis 31U 64
HA5: Pinn 29Z 45
Eastcote St. SW9 .....54Pb 112
Eastcote Vw. HA5: Pinn 28Y 45
EASTCOTE VILLAGE 29X 45
Eastcott Cl. KT2: King T 64Sa 131
East Ct. HA0: Wemb 33La 66
East Cres. EN1: Enf 15Vb 33
N11 .....21Hb 49
SL4: Wind 3D 102
East Cres. Rd. DA12: Grav'nd 8E 122
Eastcroft SL2: Slou 2F 80
East Cft. Ho. HA2: Harr 33Ea 66
Eastcroft Rd. KT19: Ewe 80Ua 154
E. Cross Route E3 .....38Bc 72
E9 .....36Bc 72
(Crowfoot Cl.)
E9 .....38Bc 72
(Wansbeck Rd.)
E10 .....36Bc 72
Eastdean Av. KT18: Eps 85Ra 173
E. Dene Dr. RM3: Rom 22Md 57
Eastdown Ct. SE13 .....56Fc 115
Eastdown Ho. E8 .....35Wb 71
Eastdown Pk. SE13 .....56Fc 115
East Dr. AL4: St A 1J 7
BR5: St M Cry 72Xc 161
GU25: Vir W 3L 147
HA6: Nwood 19U 26
NW9 .....27Wa 48
SL2: Stoke P 1J 81
SM5: Cars 81Gb 175
WD25: Wat 8X 13
E. Duck Lees La. EN3: Pond E 14Ac 34
EAST DULWICH 56Vb 113
East Dulwich Est. SE22 .....55Ub 113
(off Albrighton Rd.)
E. Dulwich Gro. SE22 .....57Ub 113
E. Dulwich Rd. SE15 .....56Vb 113
SE22 .....56Vb 113
(not continuous)
E. End Farm HA5: Pinn 27Ba 45
E. End Rd. N2 .....27Db 49
N3 .....26Cb 49
E. End Way HA5: Pinn 27Aa 45
East Entrance RM10: Dag 40Dd 76
Easter Ind. Pk. RM13: Rain 45Gd 96
Eastern App. IG11: Bark 39Wc 75
Eastern Av. E11 .....30Kc 53
EN8: Walt C 5Bc 20
HA5: Pinn 31Z 65
IG2: Ilf 30Rc 54
IG4: Ilf 30Mc 53
KT16: Chert 69J 127
RM6: Chad H 28Wc 55
RM15: Avel 46Sd 98
RM20: W Thur 50Vd 98
Eastern Av. E. RM1: Rom 27Fd 56
RM2: Rom 27Fd 56
RM3: Rom 27Fd 56
Eastern Av. Retail Pk. RM7: Rom 28Ed 56
Eastern Av. W. RM1: Rom 28Ad 55
RM5: Rom 28Ad 55
RM6: Chad H 28Ad 55
RM7: Chad H, Mawney, Rom 28Ad 55
Eastern Bus. Pk. TW6: H'row A 54U 106
Eastern Ct. E15 .....37Gc 73
(off Gt. Eastern Rd.)
Eastern Gateway E16 .....45Lc 93
Eastern Ho. E2 .....41Xb 91
(off Bethnal Grn. Rd.)
Eastern Ind. Est.
DA18: Erith 47Cd 96
Eastern Path RM12: Horn 38Md 77
RM13: Horn, Rain 39Ld 77
Eastern Perimeter Rd.
TW6: H'row A 54V 106
Eastern Quay Apartments
E16 .....46Kc 93
(off Portsmouth M.)
Eastern Rd. E13 .....40Kc 73
E17 .....29Ec 52
N2 .....27Hb 49
N22 .....25Nb 50
RM1: Rom 29Gd 56
(not continuous)
RM17: Grays 49Fe 99
SE4 .....56Cc 114
EASTERN RDBT. 33Sc 74
Eastern Vw. TN16: Big H 89Lc 179
Easternville Gdns. IG2: Ilf 30Sc 54
Eastern Way DA17: Belv 47Wc 95
DA18: Erith 47Wc 95
RM17: Grays 51Ce 121
SE2 .....47Wc 95
SE28 .....47Wc 95
Easter Way RH9: S God 9C 210
EAST EWELL 82Ya 174
E. Ferry Rd. E14 .....49Dc 92
Eastfield Av. WD24: Wat 11Z 27
Eastfield Cl. SL1: Slou 8L 81
Eastfield Gdns. RM10: Dag 35Cd 76
Eastfield Rd. CM14: B'wood 19Zd 41
E17 .....28Cc 52
EN3: Enf W 10Zb 20
EN8: Walt C 3Bc 20
N8 .....27Nb 50
RH1: Redh 7C 208
RM9: Dag 35Bd 75
RM10: Dag 35Bd 75
Eastfields HA5: Eastc 29Y 45
Eastfields Av. SW18 .....56Cb 111
Eastfields Rd. CR4: Mitc 68Jb 134
W3 .....43Sa 87
Eastfield St. E14 .....43Ac 92
EAST FINCHLEY 28Gb 49
East Flint HP1: Hem H 1H 3
East Gdns. GU22: Wok 89E 168
SW17 .....65Gb 133
Eastgate GU22: Wok 89B 168
SM7: Bans 86Bb 175
Eastgate Bus. Pk. E10 .....32Ac 72
Eastgate Cl. SE28 .....44Zc 95
Eastglade HA5: Pinn 27Ba 45
HA6: Nwood 22V 44
East Grn. HP3: Hem H 7P 3
E. Hall La. RM13: Wenn 44Md 97
E. Hall Rd. BR5: St M Cry 73Ad 161
EAST HAM 40Pc 74
East Ham & Barking By-Pass
IG11: Bark 40Tc 74
Eastham Cl. EN5: Barn 15Ab 30
Eastham Cres. CM13: B'wood 21Ce 59
East Ham Ind. Est. E6 .....42Nc 94
East Ham Leisure Cen. 39Pc 74
East Ham Mnr. Way E6 .....44Qc 94
East Ham Nature Reserve 42Pc 94
East Ham Nature Reserve Vis. Cen. 42Pc 94
E. Handyside Canopy
N1 .....1G 217 (39Nb 70)
E. Harding St. EC4 .....2A 224 (44Qb 90)
E. Heath Rd. NW3 .....34Eb 69
EAST HILL 82Rd 183
East Hill CR2: Sande 82Ub 177
DA1: Dart 59Pd 119
DA4: S Dar 67Sd 142
GU22: Wok 88E 168
HA9: Wemb 33Qa 67
RH8: Oxt 1J 211
SW18 .....57Db 111
TN16: Big H 90Kc 179
E. Hill Ct. RH8: Oxt 2J 211
E. Hill Dr. DA1: Dart 59Pd 119
East Hill Farm Cvn. Pk.
TN15: Knat 82Rd 183
E. Hill Pk. TN15: Knat 82Rd 183
E. Hill Rd. RH8: Oxt 1J 211
TN15: Knat 82Rd 183
Eastholm NW11 .....28Db 49
East Holme DA8: Erith 53Fd 118
Eastholme UB3: Hayes 46W 84
EAST HORNDON 28Fe 59
EAST HORSLEY 100V 190
E. India Bldgs. E14 .....45Cc 92
(off Saltwell St.)
E. India Ct. SE16 .....47Yb 92
(off St Marychurch St.)
East India Dock Basin Nature Reserve 45Gc 93
E. India Dock Ho. E14 .....44Ec 92
E. India Dock Rd. E14 .....44Cc 92
E. India Way CR0: C'don 74Vb 157
E. Kent Av. DA11: Nflt 58Ee 121
Eastlake Ho. NW8 .....6C 214
Eastlake Rd. SE5 .....54Sb 113
Eastlands Cl. RH8: Oxt 99Fc 199
Eastlands Cres. SE21 .....58Vb 113
Eastlands Way RH8: Oxt 99Fc 199
East La. DA4: S Dar 68Td 142
HA0: Wemb 34Ka 66
HA9: Wemb 34Ka 66
KT1: King T 69Ma 131
KT24: W Hor 98S 190
SE16 .....47Wb 91
(Chambers St.)
SE16 .....47Wb 91
(Scott Lidgett Cres.)
WD5: Ab L, Bedm 10F 4
WD25: Wat 1W 12
East La. Bus. Pk. HA9: Wemb 33Ma 67
Eastlea Av. WD25: Wat 9Aa 13
Eastlea M. E16 .....42Gc 93
Eastleigh Av. HA2: Harr 33Da 65
Eastleigh Cl. NW2 .....34Ua 68
SM2: Sutt 80Db 155
Eastleigh Rd. DA7: Bex 55Ed 118
E17 .....26Bc 52
Eastleigh Wlk. SW15 .....59Wa 110
Eastleigh Way TW14: Felt 60W 106
East Lodge E16 .....46Jc 93
(off Wesley Av.)
E. Lodge La. EN2: Crew H, Enf 8Mb 18
E. London Crematorium E13 .....41Hc 93
East London Gymnastic Cen. 44Pc 94
EASTLY END 69G 126
East Mall RM17: Grays 51De 121
(off Grays Shop. Cen.)
TW18: Staines 63H 127
(within The Elmsleigh Cen.)
Eastman Ho. SW4 .....58Lb 112
Eastman Rd. W3 .....47Ta 87
Eastman Way KT19: Eps 82Ra 173
East Mead HA4: Ruis 34Z 65
Eastmead GU21: Wok 9M 167
Eastmead Av. UB6: G'frd 41Da 85
Eastmead Cl. BR1: Brom 68Nc 138
Eastmearn Rd. SE21 .....61Sb 135
East Mill DA11: Grav'nd 8B 122
E. Milton Rd. DA12: Grav'nd 9F 122
East Mimms HP2: Hem H 1N 3
EAST MOLESEY 70Fa 130
Eastmont Rd. KT10: Hin W 75Ga 152
Eastmoor Pl. SE7 .....48Mc 93
Eastmoor St. SE7 .....48Mc 93
East Mt. St. E1 .....43Xb 91
(not continuous)
Eastney Rd. CR0: C'don 74Rb 157
Eastney St. SE10 .....50Fc 93
Eastnor HP3: Bov 10C 2
Eastnor Cl. RH2: Reig 8H 207
Eastnor Pl. RH2: Reig 8J 207
Eastnor Rd. RH2: Reig 9J 207
SE9 .....60Sc 116
Eastone Apartments E1 .....43Vb 91
(off Lolesworth Cl.)
Easton Gdns. WD6: Bore 14Ua 30
Easton St. WC1 .....5K 217 (42Qb 90)
East Pk. Cl. RM6: Chad H 29Ad 55
East Parkside CR6: W'ham 88Cc 178
SE10 .....47Gc 93
East Pas. EC1 .....7C 218
East Pl. SE27 .....63Sb 135
East Point SE1 .....50Wb 91
E. Pole Cotts. N14 .....14Mb 32
E. Poultry Av. EC1 .....1B 224 (43Rb 91)
East Ramp TW6: H'row A 53R 106
East Ridgeway EN6: Cuff 1Nb 18
East Rd. DA16: Well 54Xc 117
E15 .....39Jc 73
EN3: Enf W 10Yb 20
EN4: E Barn 18Jb 32
HA1: Harr 31Ka 66
HA8: Edg 25Ra 47
KT2: King T 67Na 131
KT13: Weyb 80T 150
N1 .....4F 219 (41Tb 91)
RH2: Reig 5H 207
RM6: Chad H 29Ad 55
RM7: Rush G 31Fd 76
SW3 .....7H 227 (50Jb 90)
SW19 .....65Eb 133
TW14: Bedf 59T 106
UB7: W Dray 49P 83
E. Rochester Way DA5: Bexl 57Uc 116
DA15: Sidc 57Uc 116
East Row E11 .....30Jc 53
W10 .....42Ab 88
Eastry Av. BR2: Hayes 72Hc 159
Eastry Ho. SW8 .....52Nb 112
(off Hartington Rd.)
W11 .....45Ab 88
(off Walmer Rd.)
Eastry Rd. DA8: Erith 52Cd 118
EAST SHEEN 56Sa 109
E. Sheen Av. SW14 .....57Ta 109
East Shop. Cen. E7 .....38Kc 73
East Side W12 .....47Ya 88
(off Shepherd's Bush Mkt.)
Eastside Halls SW7 .....3C 226
Eastside M. E3 .....40Cc 72
(off Morville St.)
Eastside Rd. NW11 .....28Bb 49
East Smithfield E1 .....5K 225 (45Vb 91)
East Sq. E10 .....31Dc 72
East Stand N5 .....34Rb 71
East St. BR1: Brom 68Jc 137
DA7: Bex 56Cd 118
HP2: Hem H 2M 3
IG11: Bark 39Sc 74
KT17: Eps 85Ua 174
KT23: Bookh 97Da 191
RM17: Grays 51Ee 121
RM20: Grays 51Ae 121
SE17 .....7E 230 (50Sb 91)
(not continuous)
E. Surrey Gro. SE15 .....52Vb 113
East Surrey Mus. 96Vb 197
E. Tenter St. E1 .....44Vb 91
East Ter. DA12: Grav'nd 8E 122
DA15: Sidc 60Uc 116
SL4: Wind 3J 103
E. Thamesmead Bus. Pk.
DA18: Erith 47Bd 95
E. Thurrock Rd. RM17: Grays 51Ee 121
EAST TILBURY 9K 101
E. Tilbury Rd. SS17: Linf 7J 101
East Twr. E14 .....47Dc 92
(off Pan Peninsula Sq.)
East Towers HA5: Pinn 29Z 45
East Va. W3 .....46Va 88
East Vw. E4 .....22Ec 52
EN5: Barn 12Bb 31
Eastview Av. SE18 .....52Uc 116
EAST VILLAGE 36Ec 72
Eastville Av. NW11 .....30Bb 49
East Wlk. EN4: E Barn 17Jb 32
RH2: Reig 6K 207
UB3: Hayes 46W 84
East Way BR2: Hayes 73Jc 159
CR0: C'don 75Ac 158
E11 .....29Kc 53
HA4: Ruis 32W 64
UB3: Hayes 46W 84
Eastway E9 .....37Bc 72
(not continuous)
KT19: Eps 83Ta 173
SM4: Mord 71Za 154
SM6: Wall 77Lb 156
Eastway Cres. HA2: Harr 33Da 65
Eastwell Cl. BR3: Beck 66Ac 136
Eastwell Ho. SE1 .....3G 231
Eastwick Cres. WD3: Rick 19H 25
Eastwick Dr. KT23: Bookh 95Ca 191
EAST WICKHAM 53Yc 117
Eastwick Pk. Av. KT23: Bookh 96Da 191
Eastwick Rd. KT12: Hers 79X 151
KT23: Bookh 97Da 191
Eastwick Row HP2: Hem H 3A 4
East Wing DA2: Dart 58Sd 120
East Wintergarden 46Dc 92
(off Bank St.)
East Wood WD25: A'ham 8Da 13
Eastwood KT13: Weyb 79T 150
(off Bridgewater Rd.)
Eastwood Cl. E18 .....26Jc 53
N7 .....36Qb 70
N17 .....24Xb 51
Eastwood Ct. HP2: Hem H 1A 4
Eastwood Dr. RM13: Rain 44Kd 97
Eastwood Ho. DA11: Grav'nd 1E 144
(off Hither Flds.)
E3 .....40Cc 92
(off Bow Comn. La.)
Eastwood Rd. E18 .....26Jc 53
IG3: Ilf 32Wc 75
N10 .....26Jb 50
UB7: W Dray 47Q 84
East Woodside DA5: Bexl 59Ad 117
Eastwood St. SW16 .....65Lb 134
EASTWORTH 74K 149
Eastworth Rd. KT16: Chert 74J 149
easyGym
Fulham 51Bb 111
(off North End Rd.)
Slough 7L 81
Eatington Rd. E10 .....29Fc 53
Eaton Av. SL1: Slou 5A 80
Eaton Cl. HA7: Stan 21Ka 46
SW1 .....6H 227 (49Jb 90)
Eaton Ct. E18 .....26Jc 53
HA8: Edg 21Qa 47
Eaton Dr. KT2: King T 66Qa 131
RM5: Col R 24Dd 56
SW9 .....56Rb 113
Eaton Gdns. RM9: Dag 38Ad 75
Eaton Ga. HA6: Nwood 23S 44
SW1 .....5H 227 (49Jb 90)
Eaton Ho. E14 .....45Bc 92
(off Westferry Cir.)
SW11 .....53Fb 111
Eaton La. SW1 .....4A 228 (48Kb 90)
Eaton Mans. SW1 .....6H 227
Eaton M. Nth. SW1 .....5H 227 (49Jb 90)
Eaton M. Sth. SW1 .....5J 227 (49Jb 90)
Eaton M. W. SW1 .....5J 227 (49Jb 90)
Eaton Pk. KT11: Cobh 86Aa 171
Eaton Pk. Rd. KT11: Cobh 86Aa 171
N13 .....19Qb 32
Eaton Pl. CR3: Cat'm 94Tb 197
SW1 .....4H 227 (49Jb 90)
Eaton Ri. E11 .....29Lc 53
W5 .....43Ma 87
Eaton Rd. AL1: St A 2F 6
DA14: Sidc 61Zc 139
EN1: Enf 14Ub 33
NW4 .....29Ya 48
RM14: Upm 33Ud 78
SM2: Sutt 79Fb 155
TW3: Houn 56Fa 108
Eaton Row SW1 .....4K 227 (48Kb 90)
Eatons Mead E4 .....19Cc 34
Eaton Sq. DA3: Lfield 69Zd 143
SW1 .....5H 227 (49Jb 90)
Eaton Ter. E3 .....41Ac 92
SW1 .....5H 227 (49Jb 90)
Eaton Ter. M. SW1 .....5H 227
Eatonville Rd. SW17 .....61Hb 133
Eatonville Vs. SW17 .....61Hb 133
Eaton Way WD6: Bore 11Pa 29
Eaves Cl. KT15: Add 79L 149
Ebbage Ct. GU22: Wok 90A 168
Ebbas Way KT18: Eps 87Ra 173
Ebb Ct. E16 .....45Sc 94
Ebberns Rd. HP3: Hem H 5M 3
Ebbett Ct. W3 .....43Ta 87
Ebbisham Cen. KT19: Eps 85Ta 173
Ebbisham Dr. SW8 .....51Pb 112
Ebbisham La. KT20: Tad, Walt H 93Va 194
Ebbisham Rd. KT4: Wor Pk 75Ya 154
KT18: Eps 86Ra 173
Ebbisham Sports Club 83Sa 173
EBBSFLEET 59Ce 121
Ebbsfleet Bus. Pk. DA11: Nflt 57Ce 121
Ebbsfleet Ct. DA11: Nflt 58De 121
Ebbsfleet Gateway DA10: Ebbs 60Ce 121
Ebbsfleet Grn. DA10: Swans 60Be 121
Ebbsfleet Rd. NW2 .....36Ab 68
Ebbsfleet United FC 57Ce 121
EBBSFLEET VALLEY 60Zd 121
Ebbsfleet Wlk. DA11: Nflt 58De 121
Ebdon Way SE3 .....55Kc 115
Ebenezer Ho. SE11 .....6A 230 (49Rb 91)
Ebenezer Mussel Ho. E2 .....40Yb 72
(off Patriot Sq.)
Ebenezer St. N1 .....3F 219 (41Tb 91)
Ebenezer Wlk. SW16 .....67Lb 134
Ebley Cl. SE15 .....51Vb 113
Ebner St. SW18 .....57Db 111
Ebony Cres. EN4: E Barn 15Jb 32
Ebony Ho. E2 .....41Wb 91
(off Buckfast St.)
Ebor Cotts. SW15 .....62Ua 132
Ebor St. E1 .....5K 219 (42Vb 91)
Ebrington Rd. HA3: Kenton 30Ma 47
Ebsworth St. SE23 .....59Zb 114
Eburne Rd. N7 .....34Nb 70
Ebury App. WD3: Rick 18M 25
Ebury Bri. SW1 .....7K 227 (50Kb 90)
Ebury Bri. Est. SW1 .....7K 227 (50Kb 90)
Ebury Bri. Rd. SW1 .....7J 227 (50Jb 90)
Ebury Cl. BR2: Kes 76Nc 160
HA6: Nwood 22S 44
Ebury M. N5 .....34Sb 71
SE27 .....62Rb 135
SW1 .....5J 227 (49Kb 90)
Ebury M. E. SW1 .....5K 227 (48Kb 90)
Ebury Rd. WD3: Rick 18M 25
WD17: Wat 13Y 27
EBURY RDBT. 18M 25
Ebury Sq. SW1 .....6J 227 (49Jb 90)
Ebury St. SW1 .....6J 227 (49Jb 90)
Ecclesbourne Apartments N1 .....38Tb 71
(off Ecclesbourne Rd.)
Ecclesbourne Cl. N13 .....22Qb 50
Ecclesbourne Gdns. N13 .....22Qb 50
Ecclesbourne Rd. CR7: Thor H 71Sb 157
N1 .....38Sb 71
Eccleshill BR2: Brom 70Hc 137
(off Durham Rd.)
Eccles Rd. SW11 .....56Hb 111
Eccleston Bri. SW1 .....5A 228 (49Kb 90)
Eccleston Cl. BR6: Orp 74Tc 160
EN4: Cockf 14Hb 31
Eccleston Cres. RM6: Chad H 31Xc 75
Ecclestone Ct. HA9: Wemb 36Na 67
Ecclestone M. HA9: Wemb 36Na 67
Ecclestone Pl. HA9: Wemb 36Pa 67
Eccleston Ho. SW2 .....58Qb 112
Eccleston M. SW1 .....4J 227 (48Jb 90)
Eccleston Pl. SW1 .....6K 227 (49Kb 90)
Eccleston Rd. W13 .....45Ja 86
Eccleston Sq. SW1 .....6A 228 (49Kb 90)
(not continuous)
Eccleston Sq. M. SW1 .....6A 228 (49Kb 90)
Eccleston St. SW1 .....4J 227 (48Jb 90)
Echelforde Dr. TW15: Ashf 63Q 128
Echo Ct. DA12: Grav'nd 1E 144
Echo Hgts. E4 .....18Dc 34
Echo Sq. DA12: Grav'nd 1E 144
Eckford St. N1 .....1K 217 (40Qb 70)
Eckington Cl. SE14 .....52Zb 114
Eckington Ho. N15 .....30Tb 51
(off Fladbury Rd.)
Eckington La. SE14 .....52Zb 114
Eckstein Rd. SW11 .....56Gb 111
Eclipse, The KT10: Esh 75Da 151
Eclipse Bldg. N1 .....37Qb 70
(off Laycock St.)
Eclipse Ho. N22 .....26Pb 50
(off Station Rd.)
Eclipse Ind. Est. KT19: Eps 85Sa 173
Eclipse Rd. E13 .....43Kc 93
Ecology Cen. & Arts Pavilion 41Ac 92
Eco Va. SE23 .....58Xb 113
Ecton Rd. KT15: Add 77K 149
Ector Rd. SE6 .....61Gc 137
Edam Ct. DA15: Sidc 62Wc 139
Edans Ct. W12 .....47Va 88
Edar Ho. CR0: New Ad 79Dc 158
Edbrooke Rd. W9 .....42Cb 89
Eddington Ct. E16 .....43Hc 93
(off Silvertown Sq.)
Eddinton Cl. CR0: New Ad 79Ec 158
Eddisbury Ho. SE26 .....62Wb 135
Eddiscombe Rd. SW6 .....54Bb 111
Eddy Cl. RM7: Rom 30Dd 56
Eddystone Rd. SE4 .....57Ac 114
Eddystone Twr. SE8 .....50Ac 92
Eddystone Wlk. TW19: Stanw 59N 105
Ede Cl. TW3: Houn 55Ba 107
Ede Ct. KT17: Eps 84Va 174
(off East St.)
Eden Apartments E14 .....49Ec 92
(off Glengarnock Av.)
Eden Av. IG7: Chig 21Tc 54
Edenbridge Cl. BR5: St M Cry 70Zc 139
SE16 .....50Xb 91
(off Masters Dr.)
Edenbridge Rd. E9 .....38Zb 72
EN1: Enf 16Ub 33
SL2: Slou 2D 80
Eden Cl. DA5: Bexl 63Fd 140
EN3: Enf L 10Cc 20
HA0: Wemb 39Ma 67
KT15: New H 82K 169
NW3 .....33Cb 69
SL3: L'ly 50C 82
W8 .....48Cb 89
Eden Ct. IG6: Ilf 24Tc 54
Edencourt Rd. SW16 .....65Kb 134
Edendale W3 .....45Ra 87
Edendale Rd. DA7: Bex 53Fd 118
Eden Dr. HP2: Hem H 2N 3
Edenfield Gdns. KT4: Wor Pk 76Va 154
Eden Grn. RM15: S Ock 43Xd 98
Eden Gro. E17 .....29Dc 52
N7 .....36Pb 70
NW10 .....37Xa 68
Eden Gro. Rd. KT14: Byfl 85N 169
Edenhall Cl. HP2: Hem H 3D 4
RM3: Rom 22Ld 57
Edenhall Glen RM3: Rom 22Ld 57
Edenhall Rd. RM3: Rom 22Ld 57
Edenham Way W10 .....42Bb 89
Eden Ho. NW8 .....6D 214
SE8 .....52Cc 114
(off Deptford High St.)
SE16 .....47Zb 92
(off Water Gdns. Sq.)
Edenhurst TN13: S'oaks 97Jd 202
Edenhurst Av. SW6 .....55Bb 111
Eden Lodge NW6 .....38Za 68
Eden Lodges IG7: Chig 22Tc 54
Eden M. SW17 .....62Eb 133
EDEN PARK 71Cc 158
Eden Pk. Av. BR3: Beck 70Ac 136
Eden Pl. DA12: Grav'nd 9D 122
SL5: S'dale 3E 146
Eden Rd. BR3: Beck 70Ac 136
CR0: C'don 77Tb 157
DA5: Bexl 63Ed 140
E17 .....29Dc 52
SE27 .....63Rb 135
TN14: Dun G 92Gd 202
Edenside Rd. KT23: Bookh 96Ba 191
Edensor Gdns. W4 .....52Ua 110
Edensor Rd. W4 .....52Ua 110
Eden St. KT1: King T 68Ma 131
Edenvale EN7: G Oak 1Xb 19
Edenvale Cl. CR4: Mitc 66Jb 134
Edenvale Rd. CR4: Mitc 66Jb 134
Edenvale St. SW6 .....54Eb 111
Eden Wlk. KT1: King T 68Na 131
Eden Way BR3: Beck 71Bc 158
CR6: W'ham 90Ac 178
E3 .....39Bc 72
Ederline Av. SW16 .....69Pb 134
Edes Flds. RH2: Reig 8G 206
Edgar Cl. BR8: Swan 69Hd 140
Edgar Ct. KT3: N Mald 68Ua 132
Edgar Ho. E9 .....36Ac 72
(off Homerton Rd.)
E11 .....31Jc 73
SW8 .....52Nb 112
(off Wyvil Rd.)
Edgar Kail Way SE22 .....56Ub 113
Edgarley Ter. SW6 .....53Ab 110
Edgar Myles Ho. E16 .....43Hc 93
(off Ordnance Rd.)
Edgar Rd. CR2: Sande 81Tb 177
E3 .....41Dc 92
RM6: Chad H 31Zc 75
TN15: Kems'g 89Nd 183
TN16: Tats 93Mc 199
TW4: Houn 59Ba 107
UB7: Yiew 45N 83
Edgar Wallace Cl. SE15 .....52Ub 113
Edgar Wright Ct. SW6 .....52Bb 111
(off Dawes Rd.)
Edgbaston Dr. WD7: Shenl 4Na 15
Edgbaston Rd. WD19: Wat 20X 27
Edgcott Ho. W10 .....43Ya 88
(off Sutton Way)
Edge, The HP3: Hem H 5M 3
SE8 .....52Bc 114
(off Glenville Gro.)
Edge Apartments E15 .....38Fc 73
Edgeborough Way BR1: Brom 66Mc 137
Edgebury BR7: Chst 63Rc 138
Edgebury Wlk. BR7: Chst 63Sc 138
Edge Bus. Cen., The NW2 .....33Xa 68
Edge Cl. KT13: Weyb 80Q 150
Edgecombe Ho. SE5 .....54Ub 113
SW19 .....60Ab 110
Edgecoombe CR2: Sels 80Yb 158
Edgecoombe Cl.
KT2: King T 66Ta 131
Edgecote Cl. W3 .....46Sa 87
Edgecot Gro. N15 .....29Ub 51
Edgefield Av. IG11: Bark 38Vc 75
Edgefield Cl. BR3: Beck 65Cc 136
DA1: Dart 60Rd 119
RH1: Redh 10A 208
Edgefield Ct. IG11: Bark 38Vc 75
(off Edgefield Av.)
Edge Hill SE18 .....51Rc 116
SW19 .....66Za 132
Edge Hill Av. N3 .....28Cb 49
Edge Hill Ct. DA14: Sidc 63Vc 139
SW19 .....66Za 132
Edgehill Ct. KT12: Walt T 74Y 151

Eliot Dr.—Elm St.

Eliot Dr. HA2: Harr 33Da 65
Eliot Gdns. SW15 56Wa 110
Eliot Hill SE13 54Ec 114
Eliot M. NW8 2A 214 (40Eb 69)
Eliot Pk. SE13 54Ec 114
Eliot Pl. SE3 54Gc 115
Eliot Rd. DA1: Dart 57Rd 119
RM9: Dag 35Zc 75
Eliot Va. SE3 54Fc 115
Elis David Almshouses
CR0: C'don 76Rb 157
Elis Way E20 36Ec 72
Elizabethan Cl. TW19: Stanw 59M 105
Elizabethan Way TW19: Stanw 59M 105
Elizabeth Av. EN2: Enf 13Rb 33
HP6: L Chal 11A 24
IG1: Ilf 33Tc 74
N1 39Sb 71
TW18: Staines 65L 127
Elizabeth Barnes Ct. *SW6* 54Db 111
(off Marinefield Rd.)
Elizabeth Bates Ct. *E1* 43Yb 92
(off Fulneck Pl.)
Elizabeth Blackwell Ho. *N22* 25Qb 50
(off Progress Way)
Elizabeth Blount Ct. *E14* 44Ac 92
(off Carr St.)
Elizabeth Bri. SW1 6K 227 (49Kb 90)
Elizabeth Cl. E14 44Dc 92
EN5: Barn 13Za 30
RM7: Mawney 25Dd 56
RM18: Tilb 4D 122
SM1: Sutt 77Bb 155
W9 6A 214 (42Eb 89)
Elizabeth Clyde Cl. N15 28Ub 51
Elizabeth Cotts. TW9: Kew 53Pa 109
Elizabeth Ct. *BR1: Brom* 67Hc 137
(off Highland Rd.)
CR0: C'don 76Ub 157
(off The Avenue)
CR3: Cat'm 94Sb 197
CR3: Whyt 90Vb 177
DA11: Grav'nd 8C 122
E4 22Bc 52
E10 31Dc 72
IG8: Wfd G 24Lc 53
KT2: King T 67Na 131
KT13: Weyb 77T 150
NW1 5E 214
SL1: Slou 7L 81
SL4: Wind 4G 102
(off Beaumont Rd.)
SW1 4E 228
SW10 51Fb 111
(off Milman's St.)
TW11: Tedd 64Ga 130
TW16: Sun 69Y 129
(off Elizabeth Gdns.)
WD17: Wat 10V 12
Elizabeth Croll Ho. WC1 3J 217
Elizabeth Dr. CM16: They B 8Uc 22
SM7: Bans 90Eb 175
Elizabeth Fry Apartments
IG11: Bark 38Sc 74
(off Kings Rd.)
Elizabeth Fry Ho. UB3: Harl 49V 84
Elizabeth Fry M. E8 38Xb 71
Elizabeth Fry Pl. SE18 53Nc 116
Elizabeth Gdns. HA7: Stan 23La 46
SL5: Asc 1A 146
TW7: Isle 56Ja 108
TW16: Sun 69Y 129
W3 46Va 88
Elizabeth Garrett Anderson Ho.
DA17: Belv 48Cd 96
(off Ambrooke Rd.)
Elizabeth Hart Ct. KT13: Weyb 78P 149
Elizabeth Ho. CR3: Cat'm 96Wb 197
E3 41Dc 92
(off St Leonard's St.)
HP2: Hem H 1M 3
(off Chapel St.)
RM2: Rom 28Ld 57
RM16: Grays 46De 99
SE11 6A 230
SM3: Cheam 79Ab 154
(off Park La.)
SM7: Bans 90Eb 175
W6 50Ya 88
(off Queen Caroline St.)
WD24: Wat 12Y 27
Elizabeth Huggins Cotts.
DA11: Grav'nd 1D 144
Elizabeth Ind. Est. SE14 51Zb 114
Elizabeth M. *E2* 40Wb 71
(off Kay St.)
HA1: Harr 30Ga 46
NW3 37Gb 69
Elizabeth Newcomen Ho. SE1 1F 231
Elizabeth Pl. DA4: Farni 72Pd 163
N15 28Tb 51
SL4: Eton W 9D 80
Elizabeth Ride N9 17Xb 33
Elizabeth Rd. CM15: Pil H 16Xd 40
E6 39Mc 73
N15 29Ub 51
RM13: Rain 43Kd 97
RM16: Grays 47Be 99
Elizabeth Sq. *SE16* 45Ac 92
(off Sovereign Cres.)
Elizabeth St. DA9: Ghithe 57Wd 120
SW1 5J 227 (49Jb 90)
Elizabeth Ter. SE9 58Pc 116
Elizabeth Way BR5: St M Cry 71Yc 161
SE19 66Tb 135
SL2: Stoke P 9K 61
TW13: Hanw 63Y 129
Eliza Cook Cl. DA9: Ghithe 56Xd 120
Elkanette M. N20 19Eb 31
Elkington Point SE11 6K 229
Elkington Rd. E13 42Kc 93
Elkins, The RM1: Rom 26Gd 56
Elkins Rd. SL2: Hedg 3J 61
Elkstone Rd. W10 43Bb 89
Ella Cl. BR3: Beck 68Cc 136
Ellacott M. SW16 61Mb 134
Ellaline Rd. W6 51Za 110
Ella M. NW3 35Hb 69
Ellanby Cres. N18 21Xb 51
Elland Cl. EN5: New Bar 15Fb 31
Elland Ho. *E14* 44Bc 92
(off Copenhagen Pl.)
Elland Rd. KT12: Walt T 75Z 151
SE15 56Yb 114
Ella Rd. N8 31Nb 70
Ellement Cl. HA5: Pinn 29Z 45
Ellena Ct. *N14* 20Nb 32
(off Conway Rd.)
Ellenborough Ho. *W12* 45Xa 88
(off White City Est.)
Ellenborough Pl. SW15 56Wa 110
Ellenborough Rd.
DA14: Sidc 64Zc 139
N22 25Sb 51
Ellenbridge Way CR2: Sande 81Ub 177
ELLENBROOK 1P 7
Ellenbrook Cl. WD24: Wat 11Y 27
Ellenbrook Cres. AL10: Hat 1P 7
Ellenbrook La. AL10: Hat 1P 7
Ellen Cl. BR1: Brom 69Mc 137
HP2: Hem H 1P 3
Ellen Ct. *E4* 18Ec 34
(off The Ridgeway)
N9 19Yb 34
Ellen Julia Ct. *E1* 44Yb 92
(off James Voller Way)
Ellen M. HP2: Hem H 1P 3
Ellen St. E1 44Wb 91
Ellen Terry Ct. *NW1* 38Kb 70
(off Farrier St.)
Ellen Webb Dr. HA3: W'stone 27Ga 46
Ellen Wilkinson Ho. *E2* 41Zb 92
(off Usk St.)
RM10: Dag 34Cd 76
SW6 51Bb 111
(off Clem Attlee Ct.)
Elleray Rd. TW11: Tedd 65Ha 130
Ellerby St. SW6 53Za 110
Ellerdale Cl. NW3 35Eb 69
Ellerdale Rd. NW3 36Eb 69
Ellerdale St. SE13 56Dc 114
Ellerdine Rd. TW3: Houn 56Ea 108
Ellerker Gdns. TW10: Rich 58Na 109
Ellerman Av. TW2: Whitt 60Ba 107
Ellerman Rd. RM18: Tilb 4B 122
Ellerslie Ct. *DA12: Grav'nd* 9F 122
(off Copper Beech Cl.)
Ellerslie Gdns. NW10 39Wa 68
Ellerslie Rd. W12 46Xa 88
Ellerslie Sq. Ind. Est. SW2 57Nb 112
Ellerton Gdns. RM9: Dag 38Yc 75
Ellerton Lodge N3 26Cb 49
Ellerton Rd. KT6: Surb 75Pa 153
RM9: Dag 38Yc 75
SW13 53Wa 110
SW18 60Fb 111
SW20 66Wa 132
Ellery Ho. SE17 6G 231 (49Tb 91)
Ellery Rd. SE19 66Tb 135
Ellery St. SE15 54Xb 113
Ellesborough Cl. WD19: Wat 22Y 45
Ellesmere Av. BR3: Beck 68Ec 136
NW7 20Ta 29
Ellesmere Cl. E11 29Hc 53
HA4: Ruis 31S 64
SL3: Dat 1L 103
Ellesmere Ct. KT13: Weyb 79U 150
SE12 60Jc 115
W4 50Ta 87
Ellesmere Dr. CR2: Sande 86Xb 177
Ellesmere Gdns. IG4: Ilf 29Nc 54
Ellesmere Gro. EN5: Barn 15Bb 31
Ellesmere Ho. *SW10* 51Eb 111
(off Fulham Rd.)
Ellesmere Mans. *NW6* 37Eb 69
(off Canfield Gdns.)
Ellesmere Pl. KT12: Hers 78U 150
Ellesmere Rd. E3 40Ac 72
HP4: Berk 1A 2
KT13: Weyb 80U 150
NW10 36Wa 68
TW1: Twick 58La 108
UB6: G'frd 42Ea 86
W4 51Ta 109
Ellesmere St. E14 44Dc 92
Ellice Rd. RH8: Oxt 1K 211
Ellie Cl. SS17: Stan H 1L 101
Ellie M. E13 40Lc 73
Ellies M. TW15: Ashf 61N 127
Elliman Av. SL2: Slou 5J 81
Elliman Sq. *SL1: Slou* 7K 81
(within Queensmere Shop. Cen.)
Ellingfort Rd. E8 38Xb 71
Ellingham GU22: Wok 91A 188
Ellingham Cl. HP2: Hem H 1A 4
Ellingham Rd. E15 35Fc 73
HP2: Hem H 1P 3
KT9: Chess 79Ma 153
W12 47Wa 88
Ellingham Vw. DA1: Dart 55Qd 119
Ellington Ct. N14 19Mb 32
Ellington Ho. SE1 4E 230 (48Sb 91)
SE18 52Qc 116
Ellington Rd. N10 28Kb 50
TW3: Houn 54Da 107
TW13: Felt 63V 128
Ellington St. N7 37Qb 70
Ellington Way KT18: Tatt C 89Xa 174
Elliot Cl. E15 38Gc 73
IG8: Wfd G 23Mc 53
Elliot Ho. *SW17* 62Fb 133
(off Grosvenor Way)
W1 1E 220
Elliot Rd. NW4 30Xa 48
WD17: Wat 10W 12
Elliott Av. HA4: Ruis 33X 65
Elliott Cl. HA9: Wemb 34Pa 67
Elliott Gdns. RM3: Rom 25Kd 57
TW17: Shep 70Q 128
Elliott Rd. BR2: Brom 70Mc 137
CR7: Thor H 70Rb 135
HA7: Stan 23Ja 46
SW9 53Rb 113
W4 49Ua 88
Elliotts Cl. UB8: Cowl 43L 83
Elliotts La. TN16: Bras 96Yc 201
Elliott's Pl. N1 39Rb 71
Elliott Sq. NW3 38Gb 69
Elliotts Row SE11 5C 230 (49Rb 91)
Elliott St. DA12: Grav'nd 9F 122
Ellis Av. RM8: Dag 32Ad 75
RM13: Rain 43Jd 96
SL1: Slou 7J 81
SL9: Chal P 25B 42
Ellis Cl. BR8: Swan 70Fd 140
CR5: Coul 92Pb 196
HA4: Eastc 30W 44
HA8: Edg 23Ua 48
NW10 37Xa 68
RM16: Ors 4F 100
SE9 61Sc 138
Elliscombe Mt. SE7 51Lc 115
Elliscombe Rd. SE7 51Lc 115
Ellis Ct. *E1* 44Yb 92
(off James Voller Way)
W7 43Ha 86
Ellis Farm Cl. GU22: Wok 4P 187
Ellisfield Dr. SW15 59Wa 110
Ellis Franklin Ct. NW8 1A 214
Ellis Ho. AL1: St A 3D 6
SE17 7F 231
Ellison Apartments *E3* 41Cc 92
(off Merchant St.)
Ellison Cl. SL4: Wind 5D 102
Ellison Gdns. UB2: S'hall 49Ba 85
Ellison Ho. *SE13* 54Dc 114
(off Lewisham Rd.)
SL4: Wind 3H 103
(off Victoria St.)
Ellison Rd. DA15: Sidc 60Tc 116
SW13 54Va 110
SW16 66Mb 134
Ellis Rd. CR4: Mitc 72Hb 155
CR5: Coul 92Pb 196
UB2: S'hall 46Ea 86
Ellis St. SW1 5G 227 (49Jb 90)
Ellis Ter. SE11 52Qb 112
Elliston Ho. *SE18* 49Qc 94
(off Wellington St.)
Elliston Way KT21: Asht 91Na 193
Ellis Way DA1: Dart 61Pd 141
Ellmore Cl. RM3: Rom 25Kd 57
Ellora Rd. SW16 64Mb 134
Ellswood Ct. KT6: Surb 73Ma 153
Ellsworth St. E2 41Xb 91
Ellwood Ct. *W9* 42Db 89
(off Clearwell Dr.)
WD25: Wat 6X 13
Ellwood Gdns.
WD25: Wat 6Y 13
Ellwood Ho. SL9: Chal P 25A 42
Elmar Grn. SL2: Slou 1E 80
Elmar Rd. N15 28Tb 51
Elm Av. HA4: Ruis 32W 64
RM14: Upm 34Rd 77
TW19: Stanw 61N 127
W5 46Na 87
WD19: Wat 17Aa 27
Elmbank N14 17Nb 32
Elmbank Av. EN5: Barn 14Ya 30
TW20: Eng G 5M 125
Elm Bank Dr. BR1: Brom 68Mc 137
Elm Bank Gdns. SW13 54Ua 110
Elmbank Way W7 43Fa 86
Elmbourne Dr.
DA17: Belv 49Dd 96
Elmbourne Rd. SW17 62Kb 134
Elmbridge Av. KT5: Surb 71Ra 153
Elmbridge Cl. HA4: Ruis 30W 44
Elmbridge Dr. HA4: Ruis 29V 44
Elmbridge Est. GU22: Wok 91B 188
Elmbridge La. GU22: Wok 91B 188
Elmbridge Mus. 77Q 150
Elmbridge Rd. IG6: Ilf 23Wc 55
Elmbridge Sports Hub 71X 151
Elmbridge Wlk. E8 38Wb 71
Elmbridge Xcel Leisure Complex
71X 151
Elmbrook Cl. TW16: Sun 67X 129
Elmbrook Gdns. SE9 56Nc 116
Elmbrook Rd. SM1: Sutt 77Bb 155
Elm Cl. CR2: S Croy 79Ub 157
CR6: W'ham 89Zb 178
DA1: Dart 60Ld 119
E11 30Kc 53
EN9: Walt A 6Fc 21
GU21: Wok 7P 167
GU23: Rip 96J 189
HA2: Harr 30Da 45
IG9: Buck H 19Mc 35
KT5: Surb 73Sa 153
KT22: Lea 94Ka 192
N19 33Lb 70
NW4 29Za 48
RM7: Mawney 25Dd 56
SL2: Farn C 7G 60
SM5: Cars 74Hb 155
SW20 70Ya 132
TW2: Twick 61Da 129
TW19: Stanw 60M 105
UB3: Hayes 44W 84
ELM CORNER 90Q 170
Elmcote HA5: Pinn 26Z 45
Elmcote Way WD3: Crox G 16P 25
Elm Cotts. CR4: Mitc 68Hb 133
Elm Ct. CR4: Mitc 68Hb 133
EC4 3K 223
EN4: E Barn 17Gb 31
GU21: Knap 9H 167
KT8: W Mole 70Da 129
SE1 2H 231
SE13 55Fc 115
SW9 53Qb 112
(off Cranworth Gdns.)
TW16: Sun 66V 128
(off Grangewood Dr.)
W9 43Cb 89
(off Admiral Wlk.)
WD17: Wat 13X 27
Elmcourt Rd. SE27 61Rb 135
Elm Cres. KT2: King T 67Na 131
W5 46Na 87
Elm Cft. SL3: Dat 3N 103
Elmcroft *GU22: Wok* 90B 168
(off Fairview Av.)
KT23: Bookh 96Ca 191
N6 31Lb 70
N8 29Pb 50
Elmcroft Av. DA15: Sidc 59Vc 117
E11 29Kc 53
N9 16Xb 33
NW11 31Bb 69
Elmcroft Cl. E11 28Kc 53
KT9: Chess 76Na 153
TW14: Felt 58V 106
W5 44Ma 87
Elmcroft Cres. HA2: Harr 27Ca 45
NW11 31Ab 68
Elmcroft Dr. KT9: Chess 76Na 153
TW15: Ashf 64Q 128
Elmcroft Gdns. NW9 28Qa 47
Elmcroft Rd. BR6: Orp 73Wc 161
Elmcroft St. E5 35Yb 72
Elmcroft Ter. UB8: Hil 44Q 84
Elmdale Rd. N13 22Pb 50
Elmdene KT5: Surb 74Sa 153
Elmdene Av. RM11: Horn 29Pd 57
Elmdene Cl. BR3: Beck 72Bc 158
Elmdene Ct. *GU22: Wok* 91A 188
(off Constitution Hill)
Elmdene Rd. SE18 50Rc 94
Elmdon Rd. RM15: S Ock 43Wd 98
TW4: Houn 54Z 107
TW6: H'row A 55V 106
Elm Dr. AL4: St A 2G 6
AL10: Hat 1C 8
BR8: Swan 68Fd 140
EN8: Chesh 1Ac 20
GU24: Chob 2K 167
HA2: Harr 30Da 45
KT22: Lea 95Ka 192
SL4: Wink 10A 102
TW16: Sun 68Y 129
Elmer Av. RM4: Have B 20Gd 38
Elmer Cl. EN2: Enf 13Pb 32
RM13: Rain 38Jd 76
Elmer Cotts. KT22: Fet 95Ja 192
Elmer Gdns. HA8: Edg 24Ra 47
RM13: Rain 38Jd 76
TW7: Isle 55Fa 108
Elmer Ho. NW8 7D 214
Elmer M. KT22: Fet 94Ja 192
Elmer Rd. SE6 59Ec 114
Elmers Dr. TW11: Tedd 65Ka 130
ELMERS END 70Ac 136
Elmers End Rd. BR3: Beck 68Yb 136
SE20 68Yb 136
Elmerside Rd. BR3: Beck 70Ac 136
Elmers Lodge BR3: Beck 70Zb 136
Elmers Rd. SE25 73Wb 157
Elm Farm Cvn. Pk.
KT16: Lyne 73D 148
Elmfield HA1: Harr 31Ha 66
KT23: Bookh 95Ca 191
Elmfield Av. CR4: Mitc 67Jb 134
N8 29Nb 50
TW11: Tedd 64Ha 130
Elmfield Cl. DA11: Grav'nd 10D 122
EN6: Pot B 5Ab 16
HA1: Harr 33Ga 66
Elmfield Ct. DA16: Well 53Xc 117
Elmfield Ho. *N2* 26Fb 49
(off The Grange)
NW8 40Db 69
(off Carlton Hill)
W9 42Cb 89
(off Goldney Rd.)
Elmfield Pk. BR1: Brom 69Jc 137
Elmfield Rd. BR1: Brom 68Jc 137
E4 19Ec 34
E17 30Zb 52
EN6: Pot B 4Ab 16
N2 27Fb 49
SW17 61Jb 134
UB2: S'hall 48Aa 85
Elmfield Way CR2: Sande 81Vb 177
W9 43Cb 89
Elm Friars Wlk. NW1 38Mb 70
Elm Gdns. CR4: Mitc 70Mb 134
EN2: Enf 10Tb 19
KT10: Clay 79Ha 152
KT18: Tatt C 91Ya 194
N2 27Eb 49
Elmgate Av. TW13: Felt 62X 129
Elmgate Gdns. HA8: Edg 22Sa 47
Elm Grn. W3 44Ua 88
Elmgreen Cl. E15 39Gc 73
Elm Gro. BR6: Orp 74Vc 161
CR3: Cat'm 94Ub 197
DA8: Erith 52Fd 118
GU24: Bisl 8E 166
HA2: Harr 31Ca 65
IG8: Wfd G 22Hc 53
KT2: King T 67Na 131
KT12: Walt T 74W 150
KT18: Eps 86Sa 173
N8 30Nb 50
NW2 35Za 68
RM11: Horn 30Nd 57
SE15 54Vb 113
SM1: Sutt 77Db 155
SW19 66Ab 132
UB7: Yiew 45P 83
WD24: Wat 9W 12
Elmgrove Cl. GU21: Wok 1H 187
Elmgrove Cres. HA1: Harr 29Ha 46
Elmgrove Gdns. HA1: Harr 29Ja 46
Elmgrove M. KT13: Weyb 76R 150
Elm Gro. Pde. SM6: Wall 76Jb 156
Elmgrove Point SE18 49Tc 94
Elm Gro. Rd. KT11: Cobh 88Z 171
SW13 53Wa 110
W5 47Na 87
Elmgrove Rd. CR0: C'don 73Xb 157
HA1: Harr 29Ha 46
HA3: W'stone 29Ja 46
KT13: Weyb 77Q 150
Elm Hall Gdns. E11 29Kc 53
(not continuous)
Elm Hatch HA5: Hat E 24Ba 45
Elm Ho. *E3* 39Bc 72
(off Sycamore Av.)
E14 47Ec 92
(off E. Ferry Rd.)
KT2: King T 66Pa 131
(off Elm Rd.)
W10 42Ab 88
(off Briar Wlk.)
Elmhurst DA9: Ghithe 58Xd 120
DA17: Belv 51Ad 117
Elmhurst Av. CR4: Mitc 66Kb 134
N2 27Fb 49
Elmhurst Cl. WD23: Bush 14Aa 27
Elmhurst Ct. CR0: C'don 77Tb 157
Elmhurst Dr. E18 26Jc 53
RM11: Horn 32Ld 77
Elmhurst Lodge SM2: Sutt 80Eb 155
Elmhurst Mans. SW4 55Mb 112
Elmhurst Rd. E7 38Kc 73
EN3: Enf W 9Yb 20
N17 26Vb 51
SE9 61Nc 138
SL3: L'ly 48C 82
Elmhurst St. SW4 55Mb 112
Elmhurst Way IG10: Lough 17Pc 36
Elmington Cl. DA5: Bexl 58Dd 118
Elmington Est. SE5 52Tb 113
Elmington Rd. SE5 52Tb 113
Elmira St. SE13 55Dc 114
Elm La. GU23: Ock 91Q 190
KT11: Cobh 91Q 190
SE6 61Bc 136
Elm Lawn Cl. UB8: Uxb 38N 63
Elm Lawns Cl. AL1: St A 1C 6
Elmlea Dr. UB3: Hayes 43U 84
Elm Lea Trad. Est. N17 23Xb 51
Elmlee Cl. BR7: Chst 65Pc 138
Elmley Cl. E6 43Nc 94
Elmley St. SE18 50Tc 94
(not continuous)
Elm Lodge SW6 53Ya 110
Elmore Cl. HA0: Wemb 40Na 67
Elmore Ho. *N1* 38Tb 71
(off Elmore St.)
SW9 54Rb 113
Elmore Rd. CR5: Chip, Coul 93Hb 195
E11 34Ec 72
EN3: Enf W 10Zb 20
Elmores IG10: Lough 13Qc 36
Elmore St. N1 38Sb 71
Elm Pde. DA14: Sidc 63Wc 139
RM12: Horn 35Kd 77
ELM PARK 35Kd 77
Elm Pk. HA7: Stan 22Ka 46
SL5: S'dale 4C 146
SW2 58Pb 112
Elm Pk. Av. N15 29Vb 51
RM12: Horn 35Jd 76
Elm Pk. Chambers *SW10* 50Fb 89
(off Fulham Rd.)
Elm Pk. Ct. HA5: Pinn 27Y 45
Elm Pk. Gdns. CR2: Sels 82Yb 178
NW4 29Za 48
SW10 7B 226 (50Fb 89)
Elm Pk. Ho. SW10 7B 226 (50Fb 89)
Elm Pk. La. SW3 50Fb 89
Elm Pk. Mans. SW10 51Eb 111
Elm Pk. Rd. E10 32Ac 72
HA5: Pinn 26Y 45
N3 24Bb 49
N21 17Sb 33
SE25 69Vb 135
SW3 51Fb 111
Elm Pas. EN5: Barn 14Bb 31
Elm Pl. SW7 7B 226 (50Fb 89)
TW15: Ashf 64Q 128
Elm Quay Ct. SW8 51Mb 112
Elm Rd. BR3: Beck 68Bc 136
BR6: Chels 80Wc 161
CR6: W'ham 89Zb 178
CR7: Thor H 70Tb 135
CR8: Purl 85Rb 177
DA1: Dart 60Md 119
DA8: Erith 53Jd 118
DA9: Ghithe 58Ud 120
DA12: Grav'nd 2E 144
DA14: Sidc 63Wc 139
E7 37Hc 73
E11 33Fc 73
E17 29Ec 52
EN5: Barn 14Bb 31
GU21: Wok 87B 168
(Heath Rd.)
GU21: Wok 10P 167
(The Mount)
HA9: Wemb 36Na 67
KT2: King T 67Pa 131
KT3: N Mald 68Ta 131
KT9: Chess 77Na 153
KT10: Clay 79Ha 152
KT17: Ewe 79Va 154
KT22: Lea 94Ka 192
N22 25Rb 51
RH1: Redh 6N 207
RM7: Mawney 26Dd 56
RM15: Avel 46Td 98
RM17: Grays 51Ee 121
SL4: Wind 5F 102
SM6: Wall 74Jb 156
SW14 55Sa 109
TN16: Westrm 97Uc 200
TW14: Bedf 60T 106
Elm Rd. W. SM3: Sutt 73Bb 155
Elm Row NW3 34Eb 69
Elmroyd Av. EN6: Pot B 5Bb 17
Elmroyd Cl. EN6: Pot B 5Bb 17
Elms, The *CR0: C'don* 74Sb 157
(off Tavistock Rd.)
CR6: W'ham 87Yb 178
E12 37Mc 73
EN9: Walt A 7Lc 21
(within Woodbine Cl. Caravan Pk.)
IG10: Lough 12Hc 35
KT10: Clay 80Ha 152
SW13 55Va 110
TW15: Ashf 64Q 128
Elms Av. N10 27Kb 50
NW4 29Za 48
Elms Cl. RM11: Horn 31Kd 77
Elmscott Gdns. N21 16Sb 33
Elmscott Rd. BR1: Brom 64Gc 137
Elms Ct. HA0: Wemb 35Ja 66
Elms Cres. SW4 58Lb 112
Elmscroft Gdns. EN6: Pot B 4Bb 17
Elmsdale Rd. E17 28Bc 52
Elmsdene M. HA6: Nwood 23S 44
Elms Farm Rd. RM12: Horn 36Ld 77
Elms Gdns. HA0: Wemb 35Ja 66
RM9: Dag 35Bd 75
Elmshaw Rd. SW15 57Wa 110
Elmshorn KT17: Eps D 88Ya 174
Elmshott La. SL1: Slou 5C 80
Elmshurst Cres. N2 28Fb 49
Elmside CR0: New Ad 79Dc 158
Elmside Rd. HA9: Wemb 34Qa 67
Elms Ind. Est. RM3: Hrld W 24Rd 57
Elms La. HA0: Wemb 34Ja 66
Elmsleigh Av. HA3: Kenton 28Ka 46
Elmsleigh Cen., The
TW18: Staines 63H 127
Elmsleigh Ct. SM1: Sutt 76Db 155
Elmsleigh Ho. *TW2: Twick* 61Fa 130
(off Staines Rd.)
Elmsleigh Rd. TW2: Twick 61Fa 130
TW18: Staines 64H 127
Elmslie Cl. IG8: Wfd G 23Pc 54
KT18: Eps 86Sa 173
Elmslie Point *E3* 43Bc 92
(off Leopold St.)
Elms M. W2 4B 220 (45Fb 89)
Elms Pk. Av. HA0: Wemb 35Ja 66
Elms Rd. HA3: Hrw W 24Ga 46
SL9: Chal P 24A 42
SW4 57Lb 112
ELMSTEAD 65Pc 138
Elmstead Av. BR7: Chst 64Pc 138
HA9: Wemb 32Na 67
Elmstead Cl. KT19: Ewe 78Ua 154
N20 19Cb 31
TN13: Riv 94Gd 202
Elmstead Gdns. KT4: Wor Pk 76Wa 154
Elmstead Glade BR7: Chst 65Pc 138
Elmstead La. BR7: Chst 66Nc 138
Elmstead Rd. DA8: Erith 53Gd 118
IG3: Ilf 34Vc 75
KT14: W Byf 85J 169
Elmsted Cres. DA16: Well 51Yc 117
Elmstone Rd. SW6 53Cb 111
Elmstone Ter. BR5: St M Cry 70Yc 139
Elm St. WC1 6J 217 (42Pb 90)

Elmsway—Epsom Playhouse

Elmsway TW15: Ashf 64Q 128
Elmswood IG7: Chig 23Tc 54
KT23: Bookh 96Ba 191
Elmsworth Av. TW3: Houn 54Da 107
Elm Ter. HA3: Hrw W 25Fa 46
NW2 34Cb 69
NW3 35Gb 69
RM20: W Thur 51Xd 120
SE9 58Qc 116
Elmton Ct. NW8 5B 214
Elm Tree Av. KT10: Esh 73Fa 152
Elm Tree Cl. KT16: Chert 75G 148
NW8 3B 214 (41Fb 89)
TW15: Ashf 64R 128
UB5: N'olt 40Ba 65
Elmtree Cl. KT14: Byfl 85N 169
Elm Tree Ct. NW8 3B 214
SE7 51Lc 115
Elm Tree Rd. NW8 3B 214 (41Fb 89)
Elmtree Rd.
TW11: Tedd 63Ga 130
Elm Tree Wlk. WD3: Chor 13H 25
Elm Vw. Ct. UB2: S'hall 49Ca 85
Elm Vw. Ho. UB3: Harl 49T 84
Elm Wlk. BR6: Farnb 76Pc 160
NW3 33Cb 69
RM2: Rom 27Jd 56
SW20 70Ya 132
WD7: R'lett 8Ha 14
Elm Way CM14: B'wood 21Wd 58
KT4: Wor Pk 76Ya 154
KT19: Ewe 78Ta 153
N11 23Jb 50
NW10 35Ua 68
WD3: Rick 18K 25
Elmway RM16: Grays 45Ee 99
Elmwood Av. HA3: Kenton 29Ja 46
N13 22Nb 50
TW13: Felt, Hanw 61W 128
WD6: Bore 14Ra 29
Elmwood Cl. KT17: Ewe 80Wa 154
KT21: Asht 89Ma 173
SM6: Wall 75Kb 156
Elmwood Ct. E10 32Cc 72
(off Goldsmith Rd.)
HA0: Wemb 34Ja 66
KT21: Asht 89Ma 173
SW11 53Kb 112
Elmwood Cres. NW9 28Sa 47
Elmwood Dr. DA5: Bexl 59Ad 117
KT17: Ewe 79Wa 154
Elmwood Gdns. W7 44Ga 86
Elmwood Gro. HP3: Hem H 5P 3
Elmwood Ho. NW10 40Xa 68
(off All Souls Av.)
Elmwood Pk. SL9: Ger X 32A 62
Elmwood Rd. CR0: C'don 73Rb 157
CR4: Mitc 69Hb 133
GU21: Wok 1H 187
RH1: Redh 2A 208
SE24 57Tb 113
SL2: Slou 5M 81
W4 51Sa 109
Elmworth Gro. SE21 61Tb 135
Elnathan M. W9 42Db 89
Elphinstone Cl. GU24: Brkwd 3D 186
Elphinstone Ct. SW16 65Nb 134
Elphinstone Rd. E17 26Bc 52
Elphinstone St. N5 35Rb 71
Elrick Cl. DA8: Erith 51Gd 118
Elrington Rd. E8 37Wb 71
IG8: Wfd G 22Jc 53
Elruge Cl. UB7: W Dray 48M 83
Elsa Cotts. E14 43Ac 92
(off Halley St.)
Elsa Ct. BR3: Beck 67Bc 136
Elsa Rd. DA16: Well 54Xc 117
Elsa St. E1 43Ac 92
Elsdale St. E9 37Yb 72
Elsden M. E2 40Yb 72
Elsden Rd. N17 25Vb 51
Elsdon Rd. GU21: Wok 10L 167
Elsenham Rd. E12 36Qc 74
Elsenham St. SW18 60Bb 111
Elsham Rd. E11 34Gc 73
W14 47Ab 88
Elsham Ter. W14 48Ab 88
(off Elsham Rd.)
Elsiedene Rd. N21 17Sb 33
Elsie La. Ct. W2 43Cb 89
(off Westbourne Pk. Vs.)
Elsiemaud Rd. SE4 57Bc 114
Elsie Rd. SE22 56Vb 113
Elsinge Rd. EN1: Enf 8Xb 19
Elsinore Av. TW19: Stanw 59N 105
Elsinore Gdns. NW2 34Ab 68
Elsinore Ho. N1 1K 217
SE5 54Sb 113
(off Denmark Rd.)
SE7 49Nc 94
W6 50Za 88
(off Fulham Pal. Rd.)
Elsinore Rd. SE23 60Ac 114
Elsinore Way TW9: Rich 55Ra 109
Elsley Ct. HA9: Wemb 37Ra 67
Elsley Rd. SW11 55Hb 111
Elspeth Rd. HA0: Wemb 36Na 67
SW11 56Hb 111
Elsrick Av. SM4: Mord 71Cb 155
Elstan Way CR0: C'don 73Ac 158
Elstar Ct. RM13: Rain 40Fd 76
(off Lowen Rd.)
Elstead Ct. SM3: Sutt 74Ab 154
Elstead Ho. SW2 59Pb 112
(off Redlands Way)
Elsted St. SE17 6G 231 (49Tb 91)
Elstow Cl. HA4: Ruis 31Z 65
SE9 57Pc 116
(not continuous)
Elstow Gdns. RM9: Dag 39Ad 75
Elstow Grange NW6 38Za 68
Elstow Rd. RM9: Dag 39Ad 75
ELSTREE 16Ma 29
Elstree Aerodrome 13Ha 28
Elstree & Borehamwood Mus. 14Qa 29
Elstree Cl. RM12: Horn 38Kd 77
Elstree Distribution Pk.
WD6: Bore 13Ta 29
Elstree Gdns. DA17: Belv 49Ad 95
IG1: Ilf 36Sc 74
N9 18Xb 33
Elstree Ga. WD6: Bore 12Ta 29
Elstree Hill BR1: Brom 66Gc 137
Elstree Hill Nth. WD6: E'tree 15Ma 29
Elstree Hill Sth. WD6: E'tree 17La 28
Elstree Ho. WD6: Bore 12Ta 29
(off Elstree Way)
Elstree Pk. WD6: Bore 16Ta 29
Elstree Rd. WD6: E'tree 17Ha 28
WD23: B Hea 17Fa 28
Elstree Studios
WD6: Bore 13Ra 29
Elstree Twr. WD6: Bore 12Ta 29
(off Elstree Way)
Elstree Way WD6: Bore 13Ra 29
Elswick Rd. SE13 54Dc 114
Elswick St. SW6 54Eb 111
Elsworth Cl. TW14: Bedf 60U 106
Elsworthy KT7: T Ditt 72Ga 152
Elsworthy Ct. NW3 38Hb 69
(off Primrose Hill Rd.)
Elsworthy Ri. NW3 38Gb 69
Elsworthy Rd. NW3 39Gb 69
Elsworthy Ter. NW3 38Gb 69
Elsynge Rd. SW18 57Fb 111
ELTHAM 58Pc 116
Eltham Av. SL1: Slou 6C 80
Eltham Cen. 57Qc 116
Eltham Crematorium SE9 56Tc 116
Eltham Grn. SE9 57Mc 115
Eltham Grn. Rd. SE9 56Lc 115
Eltham High St. SE9 58Pc 116
Eltham Hill SE9 57Mc 115
Eltham Palace & Gdns. 59Nc 116
Eltham Pal. Rd. SE9 58Lc 115
ELTHAM PARK 56Qc 116
Eltham Pk. Gdns. SE9 56Qc 116
Eltham Rd. SE9 57Hc 115
SE12 57Hc 115
Eltham Warren Golf Course 57Rc 116
Elthiron Rd. SW6 53Cb 111
Elthorne Av. W7 47Ha 86
Elthorne Ct. TW13: Felt 60Y 107
ELTHORNE HEIGHTS 43Ga 86
Elthorne Pk. Rd. W7 47Ha 86
Elthorne Rd. N19 33Mb 70
NW9 31Ta 67
UB8: Uxb 40M 63
Elthorne Sports Cen. 48Ha 86
Elthorne Way NW9 30Ta 47
Elthruda Rd. SE13 58Fc 115
Eltisley Rd. IG1: Ilf 35Rc 74
Elton Av. EN5: Barn 15Bb 31
HA0: Wemb 36Ka 66
UB6: G'frd 37Ga 66
Elton Cl. KT1: Hamp W 66La 130
Elton Ho. E3 39Bc 72
(off Candy St.)
Elton Pk. WD17: Wat 12W 26
Elton Pl. N16 36Ub 71
Elton Rd. CR8: Purl 84Lb 176
KT2: King T 67Pa 131
Elton Way WD25: A'ham 11Ca 27
Eltringham St. SW18 56Eb 111
Eluna Apartments E1 45Xb 91
(off Wapping La.)
Elvaston M. SW7 3A 226 (48Eb 89)
Elvaston Pl. SW7 4A 226 (48Eb 89)
Elveden Cl. GU22: Pyr 89K 169
Elveden Ho. SE24 57Rb 113
Elveden Pl. GU22: Pyr 89K 169
NW10 40Qa 67
Elveden Rd. NW10 40Qa 67
Elvedon Rd. KT11: Cobh 83X 171
TW13: Felt 62V 128
Elvendon Rd. N13 23Nb 50
Elven M. SE15 53Yb 114
Elver Gdns. E2 41Wb 91
Elverson Rd. SE8 54Dc 114
Elverton St. SW1 5D 228 (49Mb 90)
Elvet Av. RM2: Rom 28Ld 57
Elvin Ct. NW9 31Sa 67
Elvin Dr. RM16: N Stif 46Zd 99
Elvington Grn. BR2: Brom 71Hc 159
Elvington La. NW9 25Ua 48
Elvino Rd. SE26 64Ac 136
Elvis Rd. NW2 37Ya 68
Elwell Cl. TW20: Egh 65C 126
Elwick Ct. DA1: Cray 56Kd 119
Elwick Rd. RM15: S Ock 44Yd 98
Elwill Way BR3: Beck 70Ec 136
DA13: Ist R 7B 144
Elwin St. E2 41Wb 91
Elwood Cl. EN5: New Bar 14Eb 31
Elwood St. N5 34Rb 71
Elworth Ho. SW8 52Pb 112
(off Oval Pl.)
Elwyn Gdns. SE12 59Jc 115
Ely Av. SL1: Slou 3G 80
Ely Cl. DA8: Erith 54Hd 118
KT3: N Mald 68Va 132
Ely Ct. EC1 1A 224
KT1: King T 68Qa 131
Ely Gdns. IG1: Ilf 31Nc 74
RM10: Dag 34Ed 76
WD6: Bore 15Ta 29
Ely Ho. SE15 52Wb 113
(off Friary Est.)
Elyne Rd. N4 30Qb 50
Ely Pl. EC1 1A 224 (43Qb 90)
IG8: Wfd G 23Qc 54
SW8 52Pb 112
Ely Rd. AL1: St A 3F 6
CR0: C'don 71Tb 157
E10 30Ec 52
TW4: Houn 55Y 107
TW6: H'row A 54V 106
(off Esher Cres.)
Elysian Av. BR5: St M Cry 72Vc 161
Elysian M. N7 37Pb 70
Elysian Pl. CR2: S Croy 80Sb 157
Elysium Apartments E1 42Yb 92
(off Theven St.)
Elysium Pl. SW6 54Bb 111
(off Elysium St.)
Elysium St. SW6 54Bb 111
Elystan Bus. Cen. UB4: Yead 45Y 85
Elystan Cl. SM6: Wall 81Lb 176
Elystan Ho. SW3 6D 226
Elystan Pl. SW3 7E 226 (50Gb 89)
Elystan St. SW3 6D 226 (49Gb 89)
Elystan Wlk. N1 1K 217 (39Qb 70)
Ely's Yd. E1 7K 219 (43Vb 91)
Emanuel Av. W3 44Sa 87
Emanuel Dr. TW12: Hamp 64Ba 129
Emanuel Ho. SW1 4D 228 (48Mb 90)
Embankment SW15 54Za 110
Embankment, The HP3: Hem H 7P 3
TW1: Twick 60Ja 108
TW19: Wray 9N 103
Embankment Galleries 5H 223
Embankment Gdns. SW3 51Hb 111
Embankment Ho. KT16: Chert 74L 149
Embankment Pl. WC2 6G 223 (46Nb 90)
Embassy Apartments SE5 54Sb 113
(off Coldharbour La.)
Embassy Ct. DA14: Sidc 62Xc 139
DA16: Well 55Xc 117
E2 42Xb 91
(off Brady St.)
N11 23Mb 50
(off Bounds Grn. Rd.)
NW8 2C 214
SM6: Wall 79Kb 156
W5 45Pa 87
Embassy Gdns. BR3: Beck 67Bc 136
Embassy Ho. NW6 38Db 69
Embassy Lodge N3 26Bb 49
(off Cyprus Rd.)
Embassy Theatre
Central School of Speech & Drama
38Fb 69
Embassy Way SW8 51Mb 112
Emba St. SE16 47Wb 91
Ember Cen. KT12: Walt T 75Aa 151
Ember Cl. BR5: Pet W 73Sc 160
KT15: Add 78N 149
Ember Ct. NW9 26Va 48
Embercourt Rd. KT7: T Ditt 72Ga 152
Ember Farm Av. KT8: E Mos 72Fa 152
Ember Farm Way
KT8: E Mos 72Fa 152
Ember Gdns. KT7: T Ditt 73Ga 152
Ember La. KT8: E Mos 73Fa 152
KT10: Esh 73Fa 152
Ember Rd. SL3: L'ly 48D 82
Emberton SE5 51Ub 113
(off Albany Rd.)
Emberton Ct. EC1 4B 218
Embleton Rd. SE13 56Dc 114
WD19: Wat 20W 26
Embleton Wlk. TW12: Hamp 64Ba 129
Embroidery World Bus. Cen.
IG8: Wfd G 26Mc 53
Embry Cl. HA7: Stan 21Ja 46
Embry Dr. HA7: Stan 23Ja 46
Embry Rd. SE9 56Lc 115
Embry Way HA7: Stan 22Ja 46
Emden Cl. UB7: W Dray 47Q 84
Emden St. SW6 53Db 111
Emerald Cl. E16 44Mc 93
Emerald Ct. CR5: Coul 87Mb 176
SL1: Slou 7J 81
WD6: Bore 10Pa 15
(off Aycliffe Rd.)
Emerald Gdns. RM8: Dag 32Cd 76
Emerald Rd. NW10 39Ta 67
Emerald Sq. SW15 57Wa 110
UB2: S'hall 48Z 85
Emerald St. WC1 7H 217 (43Pb 90)
Emerson Apartments N8 27Pb 50
Emerson Dr. RM11: Horn 31Md 77
Emerson Gdns. HA3: Kenton 30Pa 47
Emerson Ho. RM11: Horn 30Md 57
Emerson M. KT3: N Mald 70Ua 132
EMERSON PARK 31Nd 77
Emerson Pk. Ct. RM11: Horn 31Md 77
Emerson Rd. IG1: Ilf 31Qc 74
Emersons Av. BR8: Hext 66Hd 140
Emerson St. SE1 6D 224 (46Sb 91)
Emerton Cl. DA6: Bex 56Ad 117
Emerton Rd. KT22: Fet 93Ea 192
Emery Hill St. SW1 4C 228 (48Lb 90)
Emery St. SE1 3A 230 (48Qb 90)
Emery Theatre 44Dc 92
(off Annabel Cl.)
Emery Walker Trust 50Wa 88
(off Hammersmith Ter.)
Emes Rd. DA8: Erith 52Ed 118
Emilia Cl. EN3: Pond E 15Xb 33
Emily Bowes Ct. N17 27Xb 51
Emily Ct. DA2: Wilm 63Ld 141
SE1 2D 230
Emily Davison Dr. KT18: Tatt C 90Xa 174
Emily Duncan Pl. E7 35Kc 73
Emily Ho. W10 42Ab 88
(off Kensal Rd.)
Emily Jackson Cl. TN13: S'oaks 96Kd 203
Emily St. E16 44Hc 93
(off Jude St.)
Emirates Air Line 47Hc 93
Emirates Stadium 35Qb 70
Emley Rd. KT15: Add 76J 149
Emlyn Bldgs. SL4: Eton 2G 102
Emlyn Gdns. W12 47Ua 88
Emlyn La. KT22: Lea 94Ja 192
Emlyn Rd. RH1: Redh 8A 208
W12 47Ua 88
Emma Ho. RM1: Rom 28Gd 56
Emmanuel Ct. E10 31Dc 72
Emmanuel Ho. SE11 6K 229 (49Qb 90)
Emmanuel Lodge EN8: Chesh 2Yb 20
Emmanuel Rd. HA6: Nwood 24V 44
SW12 60Lb 112
Emma Rd. E13 40Hc 73
Emma St. E2 40Xb 71
Emmaus Way IG7: Chig 22Qc 54
Emmeline Ct. KT12: Walt T 73Y 151
Emmett Cl. WD7: Shenl 5Na 15
Emmetts Cl. GU21: Wok 9P 167
Emmetts La. TN14: Ide H 100Zc 201
Emminster NW6 39Db 69
(off Abbey Rd.)
Emmott Av. IG6: Ilf 29Sc 54
Emmott Cl. E1 42Ac 92
NW11 30Eb 49
Emms Pas. KT1: King T 68Ma 131
Emperor Ho. E20 36Ec 72
(off Napa Cl.)
SE4 55Ac 114
(off Dragonfly Pl.)
Emperor's Ga. SW7 48Eb 89
Empingham Ho. SE8 49Zb 92
(off Chilton Gro.)
Empire Av. N18 22Sb 51
Empire Cen. WD24: Wat 11Y 27
Empire Cinema
Bromley 68Jc 137
(off High St.)
Hemel Hempstead 3P 3
Leicester Square 4E 222
Slough 7K 81
Sutton 78Db 155
Walthamstow 28Cc 52
Empire Cl. SE7 51Kc 115
Empire Ct. HA9: Wemb 34Ra 67
Empire Ho. N18 23Tb 51
SW7 4D 226
Empire M. SW16 64Nb 134
Empire Pde. HA9: Wemb 34Qa 67
N18 23Tb 51
Empire Reach SE10 51Dc 114
(off Dowells St.)
Empire Rd. UB6: G'frd 39Ka 66
Empire Sq. N7 34Nb 70
SE1 2F 231
SE20 66Zb 136
(off High St.)
Empire Sq. E. SE1 2F 231
Empire Sq. Sth. SE1 2F 231
Empire Sq. W. SE1 2F 231
Empire Wlk. DA9: Ghithe 56Yd 120
Empire Way HA9: Wemb 35Pa 67
Empire Wharf E3 39Ac 72
(off Old Ford Rd.)
Empire Wharf Rd. E14 49Fc 93
Empress App. SW6 50Cb 89
Empress Av. E4 24Dc 52
E12 33Lc 73
IG1: Ilf 33Pc 74
IG8: Wfd G 24Hc 53
Empress Dr. BR7: Chst 65Rc 138
Empress M. SE5 54Sb 113
Empress Pde. E4 24Cc 52
Empress Pl. SW6 50Cb 89
Empress Rd. DA12: Grav'nd 9G 122
Empress State Bldg. SW6 50Cb 89
Empress St. SE17 51Sb 113
Empson St. E3 42Dc 92
Emsworth Cl. N9 18Yb 34
Emsworth Ct. SW16 62Nb 134
Emsworth Rd. IG6: Ilf 26Rc 54
Emsworth St. SW2 61Pb 134
EMT House E6 43Qc 94
Emu Rd. SW8 54Kb 112
Enard Ho. E3 40Bc 72
(off Cardigan Rd.)
Ena Rd. SW16 69Nb 134
Enborne Grn. RM15: S Ock 43Wd 98
Enbrook St. W10 41Ab 88
Enclave, The SW13 54Va 110
Enclave Ct. EC1 5C 218
Endale Cl. SM5: Cars 75Hb 155
Endeavour Ho. E14 47Cc 92
(off Cuba St.)
SE16 49Ac 92
(off Ashton Reach)
Endeavour Way CR0: Bedd 73Nb 156
IG11: Bark 40Wc 75
SW19 63Db 133
Endell St. WC2 2F 223 (44Nb 90)
Enderby St. SE10 50Fc 93
Enderley Cl. HA3: Hrw W 26Ga 46
Enderley Rd. HA3: Hrw W 25Ga 46
Endersby Rd. EN5: Barn 15Ya 30
Enders Cl. EN2: Enf 10Qb 18
Endersleigh Gdns. NW4 28Wa 48
Endlebury Rd. E4 19Ec 34
Endlesham Rd. SW12 59Jb 112
Endsleigh Cl. CR2: Sels 82Yb 178
Endsleigh Ct. WC1 5E 216
Endsleigh Gdns. IG1: Ilf 33Pc 74
KT6: Surb 72La 152
KT12: Hers 78Y 151
WC1 5D 216 (42Mb 90)
Endsleigh Ind. Est. UB2: S'hall 49Aa 85
Endsleigh Pl. WC1 5E 216 (42Mb 90)
Endsleigh Rd. RH1: Mers 1C 208
UB2: S'hall 49Aa 85
W13 45Ja 86
Endsleigh St. WC1 5D 216 (42Mb 90)
Endway KT5: Surb 73Ra 153
Endwell Rd. SE4 54Ac 114
Endymion Rd. N4 31Qb 70
SW2 58Pb 112
Energen Cl. NW10 37Ua 68
Energize Fitness Club
Hammersmith 50Ab 88
(off Gliddon Rd.)
Energy Cen., The N1 4H 219
ENFIELD 13Tb 33
Enfield Bus. Cen. EN3: Enf H 12Yb 34
Enfield Cloisters N1 3H 219
Enfield Cl. UB8: Uxb 40M 63
Enfield Crematorium EN1: Enf 9Xb 19
Enfield Golf Course 14Rb 33
ENFIELD HIGHWAY 13Yb 34
Enfield Ho. RM3: Rom 24Nd 57
(off Leyburn Cres.)
SW9 54Nb 112
(off Stockwell Rd.)
ENFIELD ISLAND VILLAGE 9Cc 20
ENFIELD LOCK 9Bc 20
Enfield Lock EN3: Enf L 10Cc 20
Enfield Mus. 14Tb 33
(off London Rd.)
Enfield Retail Pk. EN1: Enf 13Wb 33
Enfield Rd. EN2: Enf 14Mb 32
N1 38Ub 71
TW6: H'row A 54U 106
TW8: Bford 50Ma 87
W3 47Ra 87
ENFIELD ROAD RDBT. 54U 106
ENFIELD TOWN 14Tb 33
Enfield Town FC 12Vb 33
Enfield Wlk. TW8: Bford 50Ma 87
ENFIELD WASH 9Zb 20
Enford St. W1 7F 215 (43Hb 89)
Engadine Cl. CR0: C'don 76Vb 157
Engadine St. SW18 60Bb 111
Engate St. SE13 56Ec 114
Engayne Gdns. RM14: Upm 32Rd 77
Engel Pk. NW7 23Ya 48
Engine Ct. SW1 7C 222
Engineer Cl. SE18 51Qc 116
Engineers Row SE18 49Qc 94
(off Woolwich New Rd.)
Engineers Way HA9: Wemb 35Qa 67
Engineers Wharf UB5: N'olt 42Ba 85
England's La. NW3 37Hb 69
Englands La. IG10: Lough 12Qc 36
England Way KT3: N Mald 70Ra 131
Englefield NW1 4B 216
Englefield Cl.
BR5: St M Cry 71Vc 161
CR0: C'don 72Sb 157
EN2: Enf 12Qb 32
TW20: Eng G 5N 125
Englefield Cres.
BR5: St M Cry 70Vc 139
ENGLEFIELD GREEN 4N 125
Englefield Path
BR5: St M Cry 70Wc 139
Englefield Rd. GU21: Knap 9G 166
N1 38Tb 71
Engleheart Dr. TW14: Felt 58V 106
Engleheart Rd. SE6 59Dc 114
Englehurst TW20: Eng G 5N 125
Englemere Pk. KT22: Oxs 85Da 171
Englewood Rd. SW12 58Kb 112
Engliff La. GU22: Pyr 88J 169
English Gdns. TW19: Wray 6P 103
English Grounds
SE1 7H 225 (46Ub 91)
English St. E3 42Bc 92
Enid Cl. AL2: Brick W 3Ba 13
Enid St. SE16 3K 231 (48Vb 91)
Enmore Av. SE25 71Wb 157
Enmore Gdns. SW14 57Ta 109
Enmore Rd. SE25 71Wb 157
SW15 56Ya 110
UB1: S'hall 42Ca 85
Ennerdale NW1 3B 216
Ennerdale Av. HA7: Stan 27La 46
RM12: Horn 36Jd 76
Ennerdale Cl. AL1: St A 4F 6
SM1: Sutt 77Bb 155
TW14: Felt 60V 106
Ennerdale Ct. E11 31Jc 73
(off Cambridge Rd.)
Ennerdale Cres. SL1: Slou 3A 80
Ennerdale Dr. NW9 29Ua 48
WD25: Wat 5Y 13
Ennerdale Gdns. HA9: Wemb 32La 66
Ennerdale Ho. E3 42Bc 92
Ennerdale Rd. DA7: Bex 53Cd 118
TW9: Kew, Rich 54Pa 109
Ennersdale Rd. SE13 57Fc 115
Ennis Ho. E14 44Dc 92
(off Vesey Path)
Ennismore Av. UB6: G'frd 37Ga 66
W4 49Va 88
Ennismore Gdns.
KT7: T Ditt 72Ga 152
SW7 2D 226 (47Gb 89)
Ennismore Gdns. M.
SW7 3D 226 (48Gb 89)
Ennismore M. SW7 2D 226 (48Gb 89)
Ennismore St. SW7 3D 226 (48Gb 89)
Ennis Rd. N4 32Qb 70
SE18 51Sc 116
Ennor Ct. SM3: Cheam 77Ya 154
Ensbury Ho. SW8 52Pb 112
(off Carroun Rd.)
Ensham Ho. SW17 64Hb 133
Ensign Cl. CR8: Purl 82Qb 176
TW6: H'row A 55U 106
TW19: Stanw 60M 105
Ensign Dr. N13 20Sb 33
Ensign Est. RM19: Purf 49Rd 97
Ensign Ho. E14 47Cc 92
(off Admirals Way)
NW9 27Wa 48
(off East Dr.)
RM17: Grays 51Be 121
SW18 55Eb 111
Ensign St. E1 45Wb 91
SE3 56Kc 115
Ensign Way SM6: Wall 80Nb 156
TW19: Stanw 60M 105
Enslin Rd. SE9 58Qc 116
Ensor M. SW7 7B 226 (50Fb 89)
Enstone Rd. EN3: Enf H 13Ac 34
UB10: Ick 34P 63
Enterdent, The RH9: G'stone 5B 210
Enterdent Cotts.
RH9: G'stone 5B 210
Enterdent Rd. RH9: G'stone 6A 210
Enterprise Bus. Pk. E14 47Dc 92
Enterprise Cen., The
BR3: Beck 64Ac 136
(off Cricket La.)
EN6: Pot B 2Ab 16
Enterprise Cl. CR0: C'don 74Qb 156
Enterprise Ct. RH1: Redh 7P 207
(off Mill St.)
Enterprise Ho. E4 17Ec 34
E9 38Yb 72
(off Tudor Gro.)
E14 50Dc 92
(off St Davids Sq.)
IG11: Bark 41Vc 95
KT12: Walt T 73X 151
Enterprise Ind. Est. SE16 50Yb 92
Enterprise Row N15 29Vb 51
Enterprise Trad. Est. UB2: S'hall 47Da 85
Enterprise Way NW10 41Va 88
SW18 56Cb 111
TW11: Tedd 65Ha 130
Enterprize Way SE8 49Bc 92
Entertainment Av. SE10 46Gc 93
Enville Ho. WD19: Wat 20Y 27
Envoy Av. TW6: H'row A 55V 106
Envoy Ho. NW9 27Wa 48
(off East Dr.)
ENVOY RDBT. 55V 106
Eothen Cl. CR3: Cat'm 96Wb 197
Epcot M. NW10 41Za 88
Epirus M. SW6 52Cb 111
Epirus Rd. SW6 52Bb 111
EPPING 2Wc 23
Epping Cl. E14 49Cc 92
RM7: Mawney 27Dd 56
Epping Forest District Mus. 5Ec 20
Epping Glade E4 16Ec 34
Epping Golf Course 5Xc 23
Epping La.
RM4: Abr, Stap T 11Cd 38, 12Xc 37
Epping New Rd. IG9: Buck H 20Jc 35
IG10: H Beech, Lough 12Lc 35
Epping Pl. N1 37Qb 70
Epping Rd. CM16: Epp 8Pc 22
CM16: Epp, N Weald 1Yc 23
Epping Sports Cen. 3Vc 23
Epping Way E4 16Dc 34
Epple Rd. SW6 53Bb 111
EPSOM 85Ta 173
Epsom Bus. Pk. KT17: Eps 83Ua 174
Epsom Cl. DA7: Bex 55Dd 118
DA12: Grav'nd 5E 144
UB5: N'olt 36Ba 65
Epsom College Fitness Cen. 87Wa 174
Epsom Common Local Nature Reserve
85Pa 173
Epsom Ct. WD3: Rick 18K 25
EPSOM DOWNS 90Ua 174
Epsom Downs Metro Cen.
KT20: Tad 92Xa 194
Epsom Downs Racecourse 90Va 174
Epsom Gap KT9: Lea 87Ka 172
Epsom Golf Course 87Wa 174
Epsom Ho. RM3: Rom 22Nd 57
(off Dagnam Pk. Dr.)
SL4: Wind 3D 102
(off Paddock Cl.)
Epsom La. Nth.
KT18: Tad, Tatt C 90Xa 174
KT20: Tad 90Xa 174
Epsom La. Sth. KT20: Tad 93Ya 194
Epsom Playhouse 85Ta 173

Epsom Rd.—Evesham Grn.

Epsom Rd. CR0: Wadd ... 77Qb 156
E10 ... 30Ec 52
IG3: Ilf ... 30Vc 55
KT17: Ewe ... 83Va 174
KT21: Asht ... 90Pa 173
KT22: Lea ... 93Ka 192
SM3: Sutt ... 73Bb 155
SM4: Mord ... 73Bb 155
Epsom Sports Club ... 87Ta 173
Epsom Sq. TW6: H'row A ... 54V 106
Epsom Trade Pk.
KT19: Eps ... 83Ta 173
Epsom Way RM12: Horn ... 35Pd 77
Epstein Ct. N1 ... 39Rb 71
(off Gaskin St.)
Epstein Rd. SE28 ... 46Wc 95
Epstein Sq. E14 ... 44Cc 92
(off Upper Nth. St.)
Epworth Rd. TW7: Isle ... 52Ka 108
Epworth St. EC2 ... 6G 219 (42Tb 91)
Equana Apartments SE8 ... 50Ac 92
(off Evelyn St.)
Equestrian Statue George III (Copper Horse)
... 1H 125
Equiano Ho. SW9 ... 53Pb 112
(off Lett Rd.)
Equinox Ct. IG2: Ilf ... 29Rc 54
Equinox Ho. IG11: Bark ... 37Sc 74
(off Wakering Rd.)
Equinox Sq. E14 ... 44Dc 92
Equity M. W5 ... 46Ma 87
Equity Sq. E2 ... 4K 219
Equus Cl. SL9: Ger X ... 2N 61
Equus Equestrian Cen. ... 82Pa 173
Erasmus St. SW1 ... 6E 228 (49Mb 90)
Erconwald St. W12 ... 44Va 88
Erebus Dr. SE28 ... 48Sc 94
Eresby Dr. BR3: Beck ... 74Cc 158
Eresby Ho. SW7 ... 2E 226
Eresby Pl. NW6 ... 38Cb 69
Erica Cl. GU24: W End ... 5C 166
SL1: Slou ... 5C 80
Erica Ct. BR8: Swan ... 70Gd 140
GU22: Wok ... 10P 167
Erica Gdns. CR0: C'don ... 76Dc 158
Erica Ho. N22 ... 25Qb 50
(off Acacia Rd.)
SE4 ... 55Bc 114
Erica St. W12 ... 45Wa 88
Eric Clarke La. IG11: Bark ... 42Rc 94
Eric Cl. E7 ... 35Jc 73
Ericcson Cl. SW18 ... 57Cb 111
Eric Fletcher Ct. N1 ... 38Sb 71
(off Essex Rd.)
Erickson Gdns. BR2: Brom ... 72Nc 160
Eric Liddell Sports Cen. ... 61Mc 137
Eric Rd. E7 ... 35Jc 73
NW10 ... 37Va 68
RM6: Chad H ... 31Zc 75
Eric Shipman Ter. E13 ... 42Jc 93
(off Balaam St.)
Ericson Ho. SE13 ... 56Fc 115
(off Blessington Rd.)
Eric Steele Ho. AL2: Park ... 9P 5
Eric St. E3 ... 42Bc 92
(not continuous)
Eric Wilkins Ho. SE1 ... 50Wb 91
(off Old Kent Rd.)
Eridge Ct. WD25: Wat ... 8Z 13
(off Ley Farm Cl.)
Eridge Grn. Cl. BR5: Orp ... 74Yc 161
Eridge Rd. W4 ... 48Ta 87
Erin Cl. BR1: Brom ... 66Gc 137
IG3: Ilf ... 30Wc 55
SW6 ... 52Cb 111
Erindale SE18 ... 51Tc 116
Erindale Ter. SE18 ... 51Tc 116
Erin M. N22 ... 25Rb 51
Erin's Vs. SE14 ... 53Zb 114
(off New Cross Rd.)
Eriswell Cres. KT12: Hers ... 79U 150
Eriswell Rd. KT12: Hers ... 77V 150
ERITH ... 50Hd 96
Erith Ct. RM19: Purf ... 49Qd 97
Erith Cres. RM5: Col R ... 25Ed 56
Erith High St. DA8: Erith ... 50Gd 96
(not continuous)
Erith Leisure Cen. ... 51Gd 118
Erith Playhouse ... 50Hd 96
(off Erith High St.)
Erith Quarry DA8: Erith ... 51Ed 118
Erith Rd. DA7: Bex ... 56Dd 118
DA8: Erith ... 50Cd 96
(Picardy Rd.)
DA8: Erith ... 56Dd 118
(Watling St.)
DA17: Belv, Erith ... 50Cd 96
ERITH RDBT. ... 50Gd 96
Erith School Community Sports Cen.
... 52Ed 118
Erith Stadium ... 51Gd 118
Erith Yacht Club ... 51Kd 119
Erkenwald Cl. KT16: Chert ... 73G 148
Erlanger Rd. SE14 ... 53Zb 114
Erlesmere Gdns. W13 ... 48Ja 86
Erlich Cotts. E1 ... 43Yb 92
(off Sidney St.)
Ermine Cl. AL3: St A ... 3N 5
EN7: Chesh ... 3Xb 19
TW4: Houn ... 54Y 107
Ermine Ho. E3 ... 39Bc 72
(off Parnell Rd.)
N17 ... 24Vb 51
(off Moselle St.)
Ermine M. E2 ... 1K 219 (39Vb 71)
Ermine Rd. N15 ... 30Vb 51
SE13 ... 56Dc 114
Ermine Side EN1: Enf ... 15Wb 33
Ermington Rd. SE9 ... 61Sc 138
Ermyn Cl. KT22: Lea ... 93Ma 193
Ermyn Way KT22: Lea ... 93Ma 193
Ernald Av. E6 ... 40Nc 74
Ernan Cl. RM15: S Ock ... 43Wd 98
Ernan Rd. RM15: S Ock ... 43Wd 98
Erncroft Way TW1: Twick ... 58Ha 108
Ernest Av. SE27 ... 63Rb 135
Ernest Cl. BR3: Beck ... 71Cc 158
Ernest Cotts. KT17: Ewe ... 80Va 154
Ernest Gdns. W4 ... 51Ra 109
Ernest Gro. BR3: Beck ... 71Bc 158
Ernest Harriss Ho. W9 ... 42Cb 89
(off Elgin Av.)
Ernest Rd. KT1: King T ... 68Ra 131
RM11: Horn ... 30Nd 57
Ernest Shackleton Lodge
SE10 ... 49Gc 93
(off Christchurch Way)
Ernest Sq. KT1: King T ... 68Ra 131
Ernest St. E1 ... 42Zb 92
Ernle Rd. SW20 ... 66Xa 132
Ernshaw Pl. SW15 ... 57Ab 110
Ernst Bldg. SE1 ... 7C 224
Eros ... 5D 222 (45Mb 90)
Eros Ho. Shops SE6 ... 59Dc 114
(off Brownhill Rd.)
Erpingham Rd. SW15 ... 55Ya 110
Erridge Rd. SW19 ... 68Cb 133
Erriff Dr. RM15: S Ock ... 43Vd 98
Errington Cl.
RM16: Grays ... 8D 100
Errington Dr. SL4: Wind ... 3E 102
Errington Rd. W9 ... 42Bb 89
Errol Gdns. KT3: N Mald ... 70Wa 132
UB4: Yead ... 42X 85
Erroll Rd. RM1: Rom ... 28Hd 56
Errol St. EC1 ... 6E 218 (42Sb 91)
Erskine Cl. SM1: Sutt ... 76Gb 155
Erskine Cres. N17 ... 28Xb 51
Erskine Hill NW11 ... 28Cb 49
Erskine Ho. SW1 ... 50Lb 90
(off Churchill Gdns.)
TN13: S'oaks ... 97Jd 202
WD19: Wat ... 20Z 27
Erskine M. NW3 ... 38Hb 69
(off Erskine Rd.)
Erskine Rd. E17 ... 28Bc 52
NW3 ... 38Hb 69
SM1: Sutt ... 77Fb 155
Erwin Ho. NW9 ... 27Wa 48
(off Commander Av.)
Erwood Rd. SE7 ... 50Nc 94
Esam Way SW16 ... 64Qb 134
Escombe Ct. CR3: Whyt ... 91Wb 197
(off Godstone Rd.)
Escombe Dr. GU2: Guild ... 10M 187
Escot Rd. TW16: Sun ... 66U 128
Escott Gdns. SE9 ... 63Nc 138
Escott Pl. KT16: Ott ... 79E 148
Escot Way EN5: Barn ... 15Ya 30
Escreet Gro. SE18 ... 49Qc 94
Esdaile Gdns.
RM14: Upm ... 31Td 78
ESHER ... 77Da 151
Esher Av. KT12: Walt T ... 73W 150
RM7: Rom ... 30Ed 56
SM3: Cheam ... 76Za 154
Esher By-Pass KT9: Chess ... 82Ea 172
KT10: Clay ... 82Ea 172
KT10: Esh ... 82Ca 171
KT11: Cobh ... 85V 170
KT22: Oxs ... 82Ea 172
Esher Cl. DA5: Bexl ... 60Ad 117
KT10: Esh ... 78Da 151
ESHER COMMON ... 82Ea 172
Esher Common (Local Nature Reserve)
... 82Ca 171
Esher Cres. TW6: H'row A ... 54V 106
Esher Gdns. SW19 ... 61Za 132
Esher Grn. KT10: Esh ... 77Da 151
Esher Grn. Dr. KT10: Esh ... 76Ca 151
Esher M. CR4: Mitc ... 69Jb 134
Esher Pk. Av. KT10: Esh ... 77Da 151
Esher Pl. Av. KT10: Esh ... 77Ca 151
Esher Rd. IG3: Ilf ... 34Uc 74
KT8: E Mos ... 72Fa 152
KT12: Hers ... 78Z 151
Esher RUFC ... 75Aa 151
Eskdale AL2: Lon C ... 9K 7
NW1 ... 2B 216
Eskdale Av. UB5: N'olt ... 39Ba 65
Eskdale Cl. DA2: Dart ... 61Sd 142
HA9: Wemb ... 33Ma 67
Eskdale Gdns. CR8: Purl ... 86Tb 177
Eskdale Rd. DA7: Bex ... 54Cd 118
UB8: Uxb ... 40K 63
Eskdale Rd. Ind. Est. UB8: Uxb ... 40K 63
Esk Ho. E3 ... 42Bc 92
(off British St.)
Eskley Gdns. RM15: S Ock ... 43Xd 98
(not continuous)
Eskmont Ridge SE19 ... 66Tb 135
Esk Rd. E13 ... 42Jc 93
Esk Way RM1: Rom ... 24Fd 56
Esmar Cres. NW9 ... 31Wa 68
Esmat Cl. E11 ... 29Kc 53
Esmeralda Rd. SE1 ... 49Wb 91
Esmond Cl. RM13: Rain ... 38Kd 77
Esmond Ct. W8 ... 48Db 89
(off Thackeray St.)
Esmond Gdns. W4 ... 49Ta 87
Esmond Rd. NW6 ... 39Bb 69
W4 ... 49Ta 87
Esmond St. SW15 ... 56Ab 110
Esparto St. SW18 ... 59Db 111
Esparto Way DA4: S Dar ... 67Sd 142
Esprit Ct. E1 ... 1K 225
Esquiline La. CR4: Mitc ... 69Kb 134
Essan Ho. W5 ... 43Ka 86
Essence E3 ... 40Bc 72
(off Cardigan Rd.)
Essence Ct. HA9: Wemb ... 33Pa 67
Essendene Cl. CR3: Cat'm ... 95Ub 197
Essendene Rd. CR3: Cat'm ... 95Ub 197
Essenden Rd. CR2: S Croy ... 80Ub 157
DA17: Belv ... 50Cd 96
Essendine Mans. W9 ... 41Cb 89
Essendine Rd. W9 ... 41Cb 89
Essendon Golf Course ... 1P 9
Essendon Pl. AL9: Ess ... 1N 9
Essex Av. SL2: Slou ... 3G 80
TW7: Isle ... 55Ga 108
Essex Cl. E17 ... 28Ac 52
HA4: Ruis ... 32Z 65
KT15: Add ... 77L 149
RM7: Mawney ... 28Dd 56
SM4: Mord ... 73Za 154
Essex Ct. EC4 ... 3K 223
SW13 ... 54Va 110
W6 ... 48Ya 88
(off Hammersmith Gro.)
Essex Fire Mus. ... 48Ce 99
Essex Gdns. N4 ... 30Rb 51
RM11: Horn ... 29Qd 57
SS17: Linf ... 7J 101
Essex Gro. SE19 ... 65Tb 135
Essex Hall E17 ... 25Zb 52
Essex Ho. E14 ... 44Dc 92
(off Giraud St.)
Essex La. WD4: Hunt C ... 5T 12
Essex Mans. E11 ... 31Fc 73
Essex M. SE19 ... 65Ub 135
Essex Pk. N3 ... 23Db 49
Essex Pk. M. W3 ... 46Ua 88
Essex Pl. W4 ... 49Sa 87
(not continuous)
Essex Pl. Sq. W4 ... 49Ta 87
Essex Rd. DA1: Dart ... 58Md 119
(not continuous)
DA3: Lfield ... 68Zd 143
DA11: Grav'nd ... 10C 122
E4 ... 18Gc 35
E10 ... 30Ec 52
E12 ... 36Nc 74
E17 ... 30Ac 52
E18 ... 26Kc 53
EN2: Enf ... 14Tb 33
IG11: Bark ... 38Tc 74
N1 ... 1B 218 (39Rb 71)
NW10 ... 38Ua 68
RM6: Chad H ... 31Yc 75
RM7: Mawney ... 28Dd 56
RM10: Dag ... 36Dd 76
RM20: W Thur ... 51Wd 120
W3 ... 45Sa 87
W4 ... 49Ta 87
WD6: Bore ... 13Qa 29
WD17: Wat ... 12W 26
Essex Rd. Sth. E11 ... 31Fc 73
Essex St. AL1: St A ... 1C 6
E7 ... 36Jc 73
WC2 ... 3K 223 (44Qb 90)
Essex Twr. SE20 ... 67Xb 135
(off Jasmine Gro.)
Essex Vs. W8 ... 47Cb 89
Essex Way CM13: Gt War ... 23Yd 58
Essex Wharf E5 ... 33Zb 72
Essian St. E1 ... 43Ac 92
Essoldo Way HA8: Edg ... 27Pa 47
Estate Cotts. RH5: Mick ... 99Ma 193
Estate Way E10 ... 32Bc 72
Estcourt Rd. SE25 ... 72Xb 157
SW6 ... 52Bb 111
WD17: Wat ... 13Y 27
Estella Apartments E15 ... 37Fc 73
(off Grove Cres. Rd.)
Estella Av. KT3: N Mald ... 70Xa 132
Estella Ho. W11 ... 45Za 88
(off St Ann's Rd.)
Estelle Rd. NW3 ... 35Hb 69
Esterbrooke St. SW1 ... 6D 228 (49Mb 90)
Este Rd. SW11 ... 55Gb 111
Esther Anne Pl. N1 ... 39Rb 71
Esther Cl. N21 ... 17Qb 32
Esther M. BR1: Brom ... 67Kc 137
(off Freelands Rd.)
Esther Randall Ct. NW1 ... 5A 216
Esther Rd. E11 ... 31Gc 73
Estoria Cl. SW2 ... 59Qb 112
Estorick Collection of Modern Italian Art
... 37Rb 71
Estreham Rd. SW16 ... 65Mb 134
Estridge Cl. TW3: Houn ... 56Ca 107
Estuary Cl. IG11: Bark ... 41Xc 95
Estuary Ho. E16 ... 46Mc 93
(off Agnes George Wlk.)
Eswarah Ho. KT17: Eps ... 83Va 174
(off Epsom Rd.)
Eswyn Rd. SW17 ... 63Hb 133
Etal Ho. N1 ... 38Rb 71
(off The Sutton Est.)
Etcetera Theatre ... 38Kb 70
(off Camden High St.)
Etchingham Ct. N3 ... 24Db 49
Etchingham Pk. Rd. N3 ... 24Db 49
Etchingham Rd. E15 ... 35Ec 72
Eternit Wlk. SW6 ... 53Ya 110
Etfield Gro. DA14: Sidc ... 64Xc 139
Ethel Bailey Cl. KT19: Eps ... 84Qa 173
Ethelbert Cl. BR1: Brom ... 68Jc 137
Ethelbert Ct. BR1: Brom ... 69Jc 137
(off Ethelbert Rd.)
Ethelbert Gdns. IG2: Ilf ... 29Pc 54
Ethelbert Ho. E9 ... 35Ac 72
(off Homerton Rd.)
Ethelbert Rd. BR1: Brom ... 69Jc 137
BR5: St P ... 69Zc 139
DA2: Hawl ... 63Nd 141
DA8: Erith ... 52Ed 118
SW20 ... 67Za 132
Ethelbert St. SW12 ... 60Kb 112
Ethel Brooks Ho. SE18 ... 51Rc 116
Ethelburga Rd.
RM3: Hrld W ... 25Pd 57
Ethelburga St. SW11 ... 53Gb 111
Ethelburga Twr. SW11 ... 53Gb 111
(off Rosenau Rd.)
Etheldene Av. N10 ... 28Lb 50
Ethelden Rd. W12 ... 46Xa 88
Ethelred Ct. CR3: Whyt ... 91Wb 197
(off Godstone Rd.)
HA3: Kenton ... 29Qa 47
Ethel Rd. E16 ... 44Kc 93
TW15: Ashf ... 64N 127
Ethel St. SE17 ... 6E 230 (49Sb 91)
Ethel Ter. BR6: Prat B ... 81Yc 181
Ethelwine Pl. WD5: Ab L ... 2V 12
Etheridge Grn.
IG10: Lough ... 13Sc 36
Etheridge Rd. IG10: Lough ... 12Rc 36
NW4 ... 31Ya 68
(not continuous)
Etherley Rd. N15 ... 29Sb 51
Etherow St. SE22 ... 59Wb 113
Etherstone Grn. SW16 ... 63Qb 134
Etherstone Rd. SW16 ... 63Qb 134
Ethnard Rd. SE15 ... 51Xb 113
Ethorpe Cl. SL9: Ger X ... 29A 42
Ethorpe Cres. SL9: Ger X ... 29A 42
Ethorpe Ho. SL9: Ger X ... 29A 42
Ethos Sport Imperial ... 3C 226 (47Fb 89)
Ethronvi Rd. DA7: Bex ... 55Ad 117
Etloe Ho. E10 ... 32Cc 72
Etloe Rd. E10 ... 33Cc 72
Etna Rd. AL3: St A ... 1B 6
ETON ... 1H 103
Eton Av. EN4: E Barn ... 16Gb 31
HA0: Wemb ... 35Ka 66
KT3: N Mald ... 71Ta 153
N12 ... 24Eb 49
NW3 ... 38Fb 69
TW5: Hest ... 51Ba 107
Eton Cl. SL3: Dat ... 1L 103
SW18 ... 59Db 111
Eton College ... 10G 80
Eton Coll. Rd. NW3 ... 37Hb 69
Eton College Rowing Cen. ... 2B 102
Eton Ct. HA0: Wemb ... 35La 66
NW3 ... 38Fb 69
SL4: Eton ... 2H 103
TW18: Staines ... 64H 127
Eton Garages NW3 ... 37Gb 69
Eton Gro. NW9 ... 27Qa 47
SE13 ... 55Gc 115
Eton Hall NW3 ... 37Hb 69
Eton Ho. KT18: Eps ... 85Sa 173
(off Dalmeny Way)
N5 ... 35Rb 71
(off Leigh Rd.)
RH1: Redh ... 4A 208
(off Old School Cl.)
UB7: W Dray ... 47P 83
WD24: Wat ... 12Y 27
(off Anglian Cl.)
ETON MANOR ... 35Dc 72
Eton Mnr. Ct. E10 ... 33Cc 72
(off Leyton Grange Est.)
Eton Pl. NW3 ... 38Jb 70
Eton Ri. NW3 ... 37Hb 69
Eton Riverside SL4: Eton ... 2H 103
Eton Rd. BR6: Chels ... 77Xc 161
IG1: Ilf ... 35Sc 74
NW3 ... 38Hb 69
SL3: Dat ... 10K 81
UB3: Harl ... 52V 106
Eton Sq. SL4: Eton ... 2H 103
Eton St. TW9: Rich ... 57Na 109
Eton Vs. NW3 ... 37Hb 69
Eton Wlk. SL1: Slou ... 8J 81
(off Upton Pk.)
Eton Way DA1: Dart ... 56Ld 119
ETON WICK ... 9D 80
Eton Wick Rd. SL4: Eton, Eton W ... 9C 80
Etta St. SE8 ... 51Ac 114
Etton Cl. RM12: Horn ... 33Nd 77
Ettrick St. E14 ... 44Ec 92
(not continuous)
Etwell Pl. KT5: Surb ... 72Pa 153
Eucalyptus M. SW16 ... 65Mb 134
Euclid Way RM20: W Thur ... 50Vd 98
Euesden Cl. N9 ... 20Xb 33
Eugene Bann Indoor Tennis Cen. ... 10F 208
Eugene Cl. RM2: Rom ... 28Ld 57
Eugene Cotter Ho. SE17 ... 6G 231
Eugenia Rd. SE16 ... 49Yb 92
Eugenie M. BR7: Chst ... 67Rc 138
Eureka Rd. KT1: King T ... 68Qa 131
Eurobet Ho. GU21: Wok ... 89A 168
(off Church St. W.)
Euro Cl. NW10 ... 37Wa 68
Eurolink Bus. Cen. SW2 ... 56Qb 112
Europa Gym Cen. ... 57Jd 118
Europa Pk. RM20: Grays ... 50Zd 99
Europa Pl. EC1 ... 4D 218 (41Sb 91)
Europa Trade Pk. E16 ... 42Gc 93
Europa Trad. Est. DA8: Erith ... 50Fd 96
European Bus. Cen. NW9 ... 27Sa 47
(not continuous)
European Design Cen. NW9 ... 27Ta 47
Europe Rd. SE18 ... 48Pc 94
Euro Trade Cen. DA17: Belv ... 47Ed 96
Eustace Bldg. SW8 ... 51Kb 112
Eustace Ho. SE11 ... 5H 229
Eustace Pl. SE18 ... 49Pc 94
Eustace Rd. E6 ... 41Nc 94
RM6: Chad H ... 31Zc 75
SW6 ... 52Cb 111
Euston Av. WD18: Wat ... 15V 26
Euston Cir. NW1 ... 5C 216 (42Lb 90)
Euston Gro. NW1 ... 4D 216
Euston Rd. CR0: C'don ... 74Qb 156
N1 ... 4D 216 (41Mb 90)
NW1 ... 6A 216 (42Kb 90)
Euston Sq. NW1 ... 4D 216 (41Mb 90)
(not continuous)
Euston Sta. Colonnade
NW1 ... 4D 216 (41Mb 90)
Euston St. NW1 ... 5C 216 (41Lb 90)
Euston Twr. NW1 ... 5B 216 (42Lb 90)
EUSTON UNDERPASS ... 5C 216 (42Lb 90)
Eva Ct. CR2: S Croy ... 79Ub 157
Evan Cook Cl. SE15 ... 53Yb 114
Evandale Rd. SW9 ... 54Qb 112
Evangelist Ho. EC4 ... 3B 224
(off Black Friars La.)
Evangelist Rd. NW5 ... 35Kb 70
Evan Ho. E16 ... 43Jc 93
(off Exeter Rd.)
Evans Apartments E2 ... 41Zb 92
Evans Av. WD25: Wat ... 7V 12
Evans Cl. DA9: Ghithe ... 57Wd 120
E8 ... 37Vb 71
WD3: Crox G ... 15Q 26
Evansdale RM13: Rain ... 41Hd 96
Evans Gro. TW13: Hanw ... 61Ca 129
Evans Ho. SW8 ... 52Mb 112
(off Wandsworth Rd.)
TW13: Hanw ... 61Ca 129
W12 ... 45Xa 88
(off White City Est.)
Evans Rd. SE6 ... 61Gc 137
Evanston Av. E4 ... 24Ec 52
Evanston Gdns. IG4: Ilf ... 30Nc 54
Evans Wharf
HP3: Hem H ... 6N 3
Eva Rd. RM6: Chad H ... 31Yc 75
Evedon Ho. N1 ... 1H 219
(off Halcomb St.)
Evelina Mans. SE5 ... 52Tb 113
Evelina Rd. SE15 ... 55Yb 114
SE20 ... 66Yb 136
Eveline Lowe Est. SE16 ... 48Wb 91
Eveline Rd. CR4: Mitc ... 67Hb 133
Evelyn Av. HA4: Ruis ... 31U 64
NW9 ... 28Ta 47
RH8: T'sey ... 96Lc 199
Evelyn Cl. GU22: Wok ... 2P 187
TW2: Whitt ... 59Da 107
Evelyn Cotts. RH9: S God ... 9C 210
Evelyn Ct. E3 ... 43Bc 92
(off Burdett Rd.)
E8 ... 35Wb 71
N1 ... 2F 219
Evelyn Cres. TW16: Sun ... 67V 128
Evelyn Denington Ct. N1 ... 38Rb 71
(off The Sutton Est.)
Evelyn Denington Rd. E6 ... 42Nc 94
Evelyn Dr. HA5: Pinn ... 24Z 45
Evelyn Fox Ct. W10 ... 43Ya 88
Evelyn Gdns. RH9: G'stone ... 2A 210
SW7 ... 7A 226 (50Eb 89)
TW9: Rich ... 56Na 109
Evelyn Gro. UB1: S'hall ... 44Ba 85
W5 ... 46Pa 87
Evelyn Ho. SE14 ... 53Ac 114
(off Loring Rd.)
W8 ... 47Db 89
(off Hornton Pl.)
W12 ... 47Va 88
(off Cobbold Rd.)
Evelyn Mans. SW1 ... 4B 228
W14 ... 51Ab 110
(off Queen's Club Gdns.)
Evelyn Rd. E16 ... 46Jc 93
E17 ... 28Ec 52
EN4: Cockf ... 14Hb 31
SW19 ... 64Db 133
TN14: Otf ... 88Ld 183
TW9: Rich ... 55Na 109
TW10: Ham ... 62La 130
W4 ... 48Ta 87
Evelyns Cl. UB8: Hil ... 44Q 84
Evelyn Sharp Cl. RM2: Rom ... 27Md 57
Evelyn Sharp Ho. HP2: Hem H ... 3B 4
RM2: Rom ... 27Md 57
Evelyn St. SE8 ... 49Ac 92
Evelyn Ter. TW9: Rich ... 55Na 109
Evelyn Wlk. CM13: Gt War ... 23Yd 58
DA9: Ghithe ... 56Wd 120
N1 ... 2F 219 (40Tb 71)
Evelyn Way KT11: Stoke D ... 88Ba 171
KT19: Eps ... 83Qa 173
SM6: Bedd ... 77Mb 156
TW16: Sun ... 67V 128
Evelyn Yd. W1 ... 2D 222 (44Mb 90)
Evening Hill BR3: Beck ... 66Ec 136
Evenlode Ho. SE2 ... 47Yc 95
Evensyde WD18: Wat ... 16S 26
Evenwood Cl. SW15 ... 57Ab 110
Everall Cl. HP1: Hem H ... 2L 3
Everall Ct. E4 ... 23Bc 52
Everard Av. BR2: Hayes ... 74Jc 159
SL1: Slou ... 7J 81
Everard Cl. AL1: St A ... 4B 6
Everard Ct. N13 ... 20Pb 32
Everard Ho. E1 ... 44Wb 91
(off Boyd St.)
Everard La. CR3: Cat'm ... 94Xb 197
Everard Way HA9: Wemb ... 34Na 67
Everatt Cl. SW18 ... 58Bb 111
Everdon Rd. SW13 ... 51Wa 110
Everest Cl. DA11: Nflt ... 2A 144
Everest Ct. GU21: Wok ... 8J 167
Everest Pl. BR8: Swan ... 70Fd 140
E14 ... 43Ec 92
Everest Rd. SE9 ... 57Pc 116
TW19: Stanw ... 59M 105
Everest Way HP2: Hem H ... 1A 4
Everett Cl. HA5: Eastc ... 27V 44
WD23: B Hea ... 18Ga 28
Everett Ct. WD7: R'lett ... 6Ja 14
Everett Ho. SE17 ... 7G 231
Everett Wlk. DA17: Belv ... 50Bd 95
(off Osborne Rd.)
Everglade TN16: Big H ... 90Mc 179
Everglade Cl. DA3: Hartl ... 70Ae 143
Everglade Ho. E17 ... 26Bc 52
Everglades, The TW3: Houn ... 55Ea 108
Everglade Strand NW9 ... 25Va 48
Evergreen Apartments IG8: Wfd G ... 25Hc 53
(off High Rd. Woodford Grn.)
Evergreen Cl. SE20 ... 66Yb 136
Evergreen Ct. TW19: Stanw ... 59M 105
Evergreen Dr. UB7: W Dray ... 47P 83
UB10: Hil ... 40R 64
Evergreen Oak Av. SL4: Wind ... 5L 103
Evergreen Sq. E8 ... 38Vb 71
Evergreen Wlk. HP3: Hem H ... 4N 3
Evergreen Way TW19: Stanw ... 59M 105
UB3: Hayes ... 45V 84
Everilda St. N1 ... 39Pb 70
Evering Rd. E5 ... 34Vb 71
N16 ... 34Vb 71
Everington Rd. N10 ... 26Hb 49
Everington St. W6 ... 51Za 110
Everitt Rd. NW10 ... 41Ta 87
Everlands Cl. GU22: Wok ... 90A 168
Everlasting La. AL3: St A ... 1A 6
(not continuous)
Everleigh St. N4 ... 32Pb 70
Eve Rd. E11 ... 35Gc 73
E15 ... 40Gc 73
GU21: Wok ... 87D 168
N17 ... 27Ub 51
TW7: Isle ... 56Ja 108
Eversfield Gdns. NW7 ... 23Ua 48
Eversfield Rd. RH2: Reig ... 6K 207
TW9: Kew ... 54Pa 109
Evershed Ho. E1 ... 2K 225
Evershed Wlk. W4 ... 48Sa 87
Eversholt Ct.
EN5: New Bar ... 15Eb 31
Eversholt St. NW1 ... 1C 216 (40Lb 70)
Evershot Rd. N4 ... 32Pb 70
Eversleigh Ct. N3 ... 24Bb 49
Eversleigh Gdns.
RM14: Upm ... 32Td 78
Eversleigh Pl. BR3: Beck ... 65Cc 136
Eversleigh Rd. E6 ... 39Mc 73
EN5: New Bar ... 15Eb 31
N3 ... 24Bb 49
SW11 ... 55Hb 111
Eversley Av. DA7: Bex ... 54Fd 118
HA9: Wemb ... 33Qa 67
Eversley Cl. IG10: Lough ... 13Sc 36
N21 ... 16Pb 32
Eversley Cres. HA4: Ruis ... 33U 64
N21 ... 16Pb 32
TW7: Isle ... 53Fa 108
Eversley Cross DA7: Bex ... 54Gd 118
Eversley Ho. E2 ... 41Wb 91
(off Gosset St.)
Eversley Mt. N21 ... 16Pb 32
Eversley Pk. SW19 ... 65Xa 132
Eversley Pk. Rd. N21 ... 16Pb 32
Eversley Rd. KT5: Surb ... 70Pa 131
SE7 ... 51Kc 115
SE19 ... 66Tb 135
Eversley Way
CR0: C'don ... 76Cc 158
TW20: Thorpe ... 68E 126
Everthorpe Rd. SE15 ... 55Vb 113
Everton Ct. HA7: Stan ... 27Na 47
(off Honeypot La.)
Everton Dr. HA7: Stan ... 27Na 47
Everton M. NW1 ... 4B 216 (41Lb 90)
Everton Rd. CR0: C'don ... 74Wb 157
Everyman Cinema
Baker Street ... 7G 215
Belsize Pk. ... 36Gb 69
Oxted ... 1J 211
Reigate ... 6J 207
Walton-on-Thames ... 74W 150
Evesham Av. E17 ... 26Cc 52
Evesham Cl. RH2: Reig ... 5H 207
SM2: Sutt ... 80Cb 155
UB6: G'frd ... 40Da 65
Evesham Ct. TW10: Rich ... 58Pa 109
W13 ... 46Ja 86
(off Tewkesbury Rd.)
Evesham Grn. SM4: Mord ... 72Db 155

Evesham Ho.—Fairway Av.

Evesham Ho. E2 40Yb 72
(off Old Ford Rd.)
NW8 39Eb 69
(off Abbey Rd.)
SW1 7A 228
Evesham Rd. DA12: Grav'nd 1F 144
E15 38Hc 73
N11 22Lb 50
RH2: Reig 5H 207
SM4: Mord 72Db 155
Evesham Rd. Nth. RH2: Reig 5H 207
Evesham St. W11 45Za 88
Evesham Ter. KT6: Surb 72Ma 153
Evesham Wlk. SE5 54Tb 113
SW9 54Qb 112
Evesham Way IG5: Ilf 27Qc 54
SW11 55Jb 112
Evette M. IG5: Ilf 25Qc 54
Evolution WD25: Wat 6Z 13
Evreham Rd. SL0: Iver 44G 82
Evreham Sports Cen. 43F 82
Evry Rd. DA14: Sidc 65Yc 139
Ewald Rd. SW6 54Bb 111
Ewanrigg Ter. IG8: Wfd G 22Lc 53
Ewan Rd. RM3: Hrld W 26Md 57
Ewart Gro. N22 25Pb 50
Ewart Ho. HA1: Harr 29Ja 46
Ewart Pl. E3 40Bc 72
Ewart Rd. SE23 59Zb 114
Ewe Cl. N7 37Nb 70
EWELL 81Va 174
Ewell By-Pass KT17: Ewe 80Wa 154
Ewell Ct. Av. KT19: Ewe 78Ua 154
Ewell Downs Rd.
KT17: Ewe 83Wa 174
Ewell Gro. Ct. KT17: Ewe 81Va 174
(off West St.)
Ewell Ho. KT17: Ewe 82Va 174
(off Ewell Ho. Gro.)
Ewell Ho. Gro. KT17: Ewe 82Va 174
Ewell Ho. Pde. KT17: Ewe 82Va 174
(off Epsom Rd.)
Ewellhurst Rd. IG5: Ilf 26Nc 54
Ewell Pk. Gdns. KT17: Ewe 80Wa 154
Ewell Pk. Way KT17: Ewe 79Wa 154
Ewell Rd. KT6: Surb 73Ka 152
(Mount Holme)
KT6: Surb 72Na 153
(South Ter.)
SM3: Cheam 79Za 154
Ewelme Rd. SE23 60Yb 114
Ewen Cres. SW2 59Qb 112
Ewen Henderson Ct. SE14 52Ac 114
(off Goodwood Rd.)
Ewen Ho. N1 1H 217
Ewer St. SE1 7D 224 (46Sb 91)
Ewhurst Av. CR2: Sande 81Vb 177
Ewhurst Cl. E1 43Yb 92
SM2: Cheam 81Ya 174
Ewhurst Ct. CR4: Mitc 69Fb 133
Ewhurst Rd. SE4 58Bc 114
Exbury Ho. E9 38Yb 72
SW1 7D 228
Exbury Rd. SE6 61Cc 136
ExCeL 45Kc 93
Excel Ct. WC2 5E 222
Excel Marina E16 45Jc 93
Excelsior Cl. KT1: King T 68Qa 131
Excelsior Gdns. SE13 54Ec 114
Excelsior Ind. Est. SE15 51Yb 114
Excel Waterfront E16 45Kc 93
Exchange, The CR0: C'don 76Sb 157
(off Surrey St.)
GU22: Wok 89B 168
(off Oriental Rd.)
IG1: Ilf 33Rc 74
Exchange Apartments
BR2: Brom 70Kc 137
(off Sparkes Cl.)
Exchange Arc. EC2 7J 219 (43Ub 91)
Exchange Bldg. E1 6K 219
Exchange Cl. N11 19Jb 32
Exchange Ct. WC2 5G 223 (45Nb 90)
Exchange Garages N13 21Qb 50
Exchange Ho. EC2 7J 219
NW10 38Xa 68
SW1 6D 228
Exchange Mans. NW11 31Bb 69
Exchange Pl. EC2 7H 219 (43Ub 91)
Exchange Rd. SL5: S'hill 1A 146
(not continuous)
WD18: Wat 13X 27
Exchange Sq. EC2 7H 219 (43Ub 91)
Exchange St. EC1 4D 218 (41Sb 91)
RM1: Rom 29Gd 56
Exchange Wlk. HA5: Pinn 31Aa 65
Executive Pk. AL1: St A 2F 6
Exedown Rd. TN15: Wro 86Xd 184
Exeforde Av. TN15: Ashf 63Q 128
Exeter Cl. E6 44Pc 94
WD24: Wat 12Y 27
Exeter Ct. KT6: Surb 71Na 153
(off Maple Rd.)
NW6 40Cb 69
(off Cambridge Rd.)
Exeter Gdns. IG1: Ilf 32Nc 74
Exeter Ho. E14 43Ec 92
(off St Ives Pl.)
IG11: Bark 38Wc 75
(off Margaret Bondfield Av.)
N1 1H 219
(off New Era Est.)
RM8: Dag 35Wc 75
SE15 51Wb 113
(off Friary Est.)
SW15 58Ya 110
TW13: Hanw 61Ba 129
(off Watermill Way)
W2 44Eb 89
(off Hallfield Est.)
WD6: Bore 12Qa 29
Exeter Mans. NW2 37Ab 68
Exeter M. NW6 37Db 69
SW6 52Cb 111
Exeter Rd. CR0: C'don 73Ub 157
DA12: Grav'nd 2F 144
DA16: Well 54Vc 117
E16 43Jc 93
E17 29Cc 52
EN3: Pond E 13Zb 34
HA2: Harr 33Aa 65
N9 19Yb 34
N14 18Kb 32
NW2 36Ab 68
RM10: Dag 37Dd 76
TW6: H'row A 55T 106
TW13: Hanw 62Ba 129
Exeter St. WC2 4G 223 (45Nb 90)
Exeter Way SE14 52Bc 114
TW6: H'row A 54U 106
Exford Ct. SW11 53Fb 111
(off Bolingbroke Wlk.)
Exford Gdns. SE12 60Kc 115
Exford Rd. SE12 61Kc 137
Exhibition Cl. W12 45Ya 88
Exhibition Grounds HA9: Wemb 35Ra 67
Exhibition Rd. SW7 2C 226 (47Fb 89)
Exhibition Way HA9: Wemb 35Qa 67
Exit Rd. N2 26Fb 49
Exmoor Cl. IG6: Ilf 25Sc 54
Exmoor Ho. DA17: Belv 47Dd 96
E3 40Ac 72
(off Gernon Rd.)
Exmoor St. W10 42Za 88
Exmouth Ho. E14 49Dc 92
(off Cahir St.)
EC1 5K 217
Exmouth Mkt. EC1 5K 217 (42Qb 90)
Exmouth M. NW1 4C 216 (41Lb 90)
Exmouth Pl. E8 38Xb 71
Exmouth Rd. DA16: Well 53Yc 117
E17 29Bc 52
HA4: Ruis 34Y 65
RM17: Grays 51De 121
UB4: Hayes 41U 84
Exmouth St. E1 44Yb 92
Exning Rd. E16 42Gc 93
Exon Apartments RM1: Rom 28Hd 56
(off Mercury Gdns.)
Exonbury NW8 39Db 69
(off Abbey Rd.)
Exon St. SE17 6H 231 (50Ub 91)
Explorer Av. TW19: Stanw 60N 105
Explorer Dr. WD18: Wat 16V 26
Explorers Ct. E14 45Fc 93
(off Newport Av.)
Export Ho. SE1 2J 231
Express Dr. IG3: Ilf 32Xc 75
Express Ho. SE8 51Ac 114
(off Rolt St.)
Express Newspapers SE1 6B 224
Express Wharf E14 47Cc 92
(off Hutchings St.)
Exton Gdns. RM8: Dag 36Yc 75
Exton Rd. NW10 38Sa 67
Exton St. SE1 7K 223 (46Qb 90)
Eyebright Cl. CR0: C'don 74Zb 158
Eyhurst Av. RM12: Horn 34Jd 76
Eyhurst Cl. KT20: Kgswd 95Bb 195
NW2 33Wa 68
Eyhurst Pk. KT20: Kgswd 95Eb 195
Eyhurst Pl. CR5: Coul 88Kb 176
Eyhurst Spur KT20: Kgswd 96Bb 195
Eylewood Rd. SE27 64Sb 135
Eynella Rd. SE22 59Vb 113
Eynham Rd. W12 44Ya 88
EYNSFORD 75Nd 163
Eynsford Castle 75Nd 163
Eynsford Cl. BR5: Pet W 73Sc 160
Eynsford Cres. DA5: Bexl 60Yc 117
Eynsford Ho. SE1 2F 231
SE15 51Yb 114
SE17 6H 231
Eynsford Ri. DA4: Eyns 77Md 163
Eynsford Rd. BR8: Crock 72Fd 162
DA4: Eyns, Farni 74Pd 163
DA9: Ghithe 57Yd 120
IG3: Ilf 33Uc 74
TN14: Eyns, S'ham 80Kd 163
Eynsford Ter. UB7: Yiew 44P 83
Eynsham Dr. SE2 49Wc 95
Eynswood Dr. DA14: Sidc 64Xc 139
Eyot Gdns. W6 50Va 88
Eyot Grn. W4 50Va 88
Eyot Ho. SE16 48Wb 91
(off Frean St.)
Eyre Cl. RM2: Rom 28Kd 57
Eyre Ct. NW8 1B 214 (40Fb 69)
Eyre Grn. SL2: Slou 1E 80
Eyre St. Hill EC1 6K 217 (42Qb 90)
Eysham Ct. EN5: New Bar 15Db 31
Eyston Dr. KT13: Weyb 82Q 170
Eythorne Rd. SW9 53Qb 112
Ezra St. E2 41Vb 91

F

Faber Gdns. NW4 29Wa 48
Fabian Bell Twr. E3 40Cc 72
(off Pancras Way)
Fabian Rd. SW6 52Bb 111
Fabian St. E6 42Pc 94
Fable Apartments N1 2D 218 (41Sb 91)
Facade, The RH2: Reig 5J 207
SE23 61Yb 136
Fackenden La. TN14: S'ham 85Kd 183
Factory La. CR0: C'don 74Qb 156
N17 26Vb 51
Factory Rd. DA11: Nflt 58Ee 121
E16 46Mc 93
Factory Yd. W7 46Ga 86
Faesten Way DA5: Bexl 62Gd 140
Faggotts Cl. WD7: R'lett 7La 14
Faggs Rd. TW14: Felt 56V 106
Fagus Av. RM13: Rain 41Md 97
Faints Cl. EN7: Chesh 1Vb 19
Fairacre HA5: Eastc 28W 44
HP3: Hem H 6P 3
KT3: N Mald 69Ua 132
Fairacre Ct. HA6: Nwood 24U 44
Fairacre Pl. DA3: Hartl 69Ae 143
Fair Acres BR2: Brom 71Jc 159
CR0: Sels 81Bc 178
Fairacres HA4: Ruis 31V 64
KT11: Cobh 84Z 171
KT20: Tad 93Ya 194
SW15 56Va 110
Fairacres Cl. EN6: Pot B 5Bb 17
Fairacres Ind. Est. SL4: Wind 4B 102
Fairbain Grn. SW9 53Rb 113
Fairbairn Cl. CR8: Purl 85Qb 176
Fairbank Av. BR6: Farnb 75Rc 160
Fairbank Est. N1 2G 219 (40Tb 71)
Fairbanks Ct. HA0: Wemb 39Na 67
Fairbanks Lodge WD6: Bore 14Qa 29
Fairbanks Rd. N17 27Vb 51
Fairbourne KT11: Cobh 85Z 171
Fairbourne Cl. GU21: Wok 10L 167
Fairbourne Ho. UB3: Harl 48S 84
Fairbourne La. CR3: Cat'm 94Sb 197
Fairbourne Rd. N17 27Ub 51
SW4 58Mb 112
Fairbriar Ct. KT18: Eps 85Ua 174
(off Hereford Cl.)
Fairbriar Residence SW7 5A 226
Fairbridge Rd. N19 33Mb 70
Fairbrook Cl. N13 22Qb 50
Fairbrook Rd. N13 23Qb 50
Fairburn Cl. WD6: Bore 11Qa 29
Fairburn Ct. SW15 57Ab 110
Fairburn Ho. W14 50Bb 89
(off Ivatt Pl.)
Fairby Grange DA3: Hartl 72Ae 165
Fairby Ho. SE1 5K 231
Fairby La. DA3: Hartl 72Ae 165
Fairby Rd. SE12 57Kc 115
Fairchild Cl. SW11 54Fb 111
Fairchildes Av. CR0: New Ad 84Fc 179
Fairchildes La. CR6: W'ham 86Fc 179
Fairchild Ho. E2 40Xb 71
(off Cambridge Cres.)
E9 38Yb 72
(off Frampton Pk. Rd.)
N1 3H 219
N3 25Cb 49
Fairchild Pl. EC2 6J 219
Fairchild St. EC2 6J 219 (42Ub 91)
Fair Cl. WD23: Bush 17Da 27
Fairclough Cl. UB5: N'olt 42Ba 85
Fairclough St. E1 44Wb 91
Faircroft SL2: Slou 2F 80
Faircroft Ct. TW11: Tedd 65Ja 130
FAIR CROSS 36Uc 74
Faircross Av. IG11: Bark 37Sc 74
RM5: Col R 24Fd 56
Faircross Ho. WD17: Wat 13X 27
(off The Parade)
Faircross Pde. IG11: Bark 36Uc 74
Faircross Way AL1: St A 1E 6
Fairdale Gdns. SW15 56Xa 110
UB3: Hayes 47W 84
Fairdene Rd. CR5: Coul 90Mb 176
Fairey Av. UB3: Harl 49V 84
Fairfax Av. KT17: Ewe 81Xa 174
RH1: Redh 5N 207
Fairfax Cl. KT12: Walt T 74X 151
RH8: Oxt 2H 211
Fairfax Ct. DA1: Dart 58Qd 119
NW6 38Eb 69
(off Fairfax Rd.)
Fairfax Gdns. SE3 53Lc 115
Fairfax Ho. KT1: King T 69Pa 131
(off Livesey Cl.)
Fairfax Mans. NW6 38Eb 69
(off Finchley Rd.)
Fairfax M. E16 46Kc 93
N8 28Rb 51
SW15 56Ya 110
Fairfax Pl. NW6 38Eb 69
W14 48Ab 88
Fairfax Rd. GU22: Wok 92D 188
N8 28Qb 50
NW6 38Eb 69
RM17: Grays 50De 99
RM18: Tilb 3B 122
TW11: Tedd 65Ja 130
W4 48Ua 88
Fairfax Way N10 24Jb 50
FAIRFIELD 93Ka 192
Fairfield E1 43Yb 92
(off Redman's Rd.)
KT1: King T 68Pa 131
N20 17Fb 31
NW1 1B 216
Fairfield App. TW19: Wray 8P 103
Fairfield Av. HA4: Ruis 31S 64
HA8: Edg 23Ra 47
NW4 30Xa 48
RM14: Upm 34Sd 78
RM16: Grays 45Ee 99
SL3: Dat 2N 103
TW2: Whitt 60Da 107
TW18: Staines 63H 127
WD19: Wat 20Y 27
Fairfield Cl. CR4: Mitc 66Gb 133
DA15: Sidc 58Vc 117
EN3: Pond E 14Zb 34
HA6: Nwood 22S 44
KT19: Ewe 78Ua 154
N12 21Eb 49
RM12: Horn 32Jd 76
SL3: Dat 2P 103
TN15: Kems'g 90Qd 183
WD7: R'lett 9Ga 14
Fairfield Cotts. KT23: Bookh 97Da 191
Fairfield Ct. HA4: Ruis 32T 64
HA6: Nwood 26W 44
KT22: Lea 93Ka 192
(off Leret Way)
NW10 39Wa 68
Fairfield Cres. HA8: Edg 23Ra 47
Fairfield Dr. HA2: Harr 27Ea 46
SW18 57Db 111
UB6: G'frd 39La 66
Fairfield E. KT1: King T 68Na 131
Fairfield Gdns. N8 29Nb 50
Fairfield Gro. SE7 51Mc 115
Fairfield Halls
Croydon 76Tb 157
Fairfield La. GU24: W End 4E 166
SL2: Farn R 10F 60
Fairfield Nth. KT1: King T 68Na 131
Fairfield Pk. KT11: Cobh 86Z 171
Fairfield Path CR0: C'don 76Tb 157
Fairfield Pl. KT1: King T 69Na 131
Fairfield Pool & Leisure Cen. 59Nd 119
Fairfield Rd. BR1: Brom 66Jc 137
BR3: Beck 68Cc 136
BR5: Pet W 72Tc 160
CM14: B'wood 20Yd 40
CM16: Epp 1Xc 23
CR0: C'don 76Tb 157
DA7: Bex 54Bd 117
E3 40Cc 72
E17 26Ac 52
IG1: Ilf 37Rc 74
IG8: Wfd G 23Jc 53
KT1: King T 68Na 131
KT22: Lea 93Ka 192
N8 29Nb 50
N18 21Wb 51
SL1: Burn 1A 80
TN15: Bor G 91Be 205
TW19: Wray 8P 103
UB1: S'hall 44Ba 85
UB7: Yiew 45N 83
UB8: Uxb 37M 63
Fairfields DA12: Grav'nd 4G 144
KT16: Chert 74J 149
Fairfields Cl. NW9 29Sa 47
Fairfields Cres. NW9 28Sa 47
Fairfield Sth. KT1: King T 68Na 131
Fairfield Sq. DA11: Grav'nd 8C 122
Fairfields Rd. TW3: Houn 55Ea 108
Fairfield St. SW18 57Db 111
Fairfield Trade Pk. KT1: King T 69Pa 131
Fairfield Wlk. EN8: Chesh 1Ac 20
KT22: Lea 93Ka 192
(off Fairfield Rd.)
Fairfield Way CR5: Coul 86Mb 176
EN5: Barn 15Cb 31
KT19: Ewe 78Ua 154
Fairfield W. KT1: King T 68Na 131
Fairfolds WD25: Wat 8Aa 13
Fairfoot Rd. E3 42Cc 92
Fairford SE6 60Cc 114
Fairford Av. CR0: C'don 71Zb 158
DA7: Bex 53Fd 118
Fairford Cl. CR0: C'don 71Ac 158
KT14: W Byf 86H 169
RH2: Reig 4L 207
RM3: Rom 23Rd 57
Fairford Ct. SM2: Sutt 80Db 155
Fairford Gdns. KT4: Wor Pk 75Va 154
Fairford Ho. SE11 6A 230 (49Qb 90)
Fairford Way RM3: Rom 23Rd 57
Fairgreen EN4: Cockf 13Hb 31
Fairgreen Ct. EN4: Cockf 13Hb 31
Fairgreen E. EN4: Cockf 13Hb 31
Fairgreen Rd. CR7: Thor H 71Rb 157
Fairhall Ct. KT5: Surb 73Pa 153
Fairham Av. RM15: S Ock 45Wd 98
Fairhaven AL2: Park 9B 6
TW20: Egh 64B 126
Fairhaven Av. CR0: C'don 72Zb 158
Fairhaven Ct. CR2: S Croy 78Sb 157
(off Warham Rd.)
TW18: Staines 65G 126
(off Bowes Rd.)
TW20: Egh 64B 126
Fairhaven Cres. WD19: Wat 20W 26
Fairhaven Rd. RH1: Redh 2A 208
Fairhazel Gdns. NW6 37Db 69
Fairhazel Mans. NW6 38Eb 69
(off Fairhazel Gdns.)
Fairhill HP3: Hem H 6P 3
Fairholme TW14: Bedf 59T 106
Fairholme Av. RM2: Rom 29Jd 56
Fairholme Cl. N3 28Ab 48
Fairholme Ct. HA5: Hat E 23Ba 45
Fairholme Cres. KT21: Asht 89La 172
UB4: Hayes 42V 84
Fairholme Gdns. N3 27Ab 48
RM14: Upm 31Vd 78
Fairholme Rd. CR0: C'don 73Qb 156
HA1: Harr 29Ha 46
IG1: Ilf 31Pc 74
SM1: Sutt 79Bb 155
TW15: Ashf 64N 127
W14 50Ab 88
Fairholt Cl. N16 32Ub 71
Fairholt Rd. N16 32Tb 71
Fairholt St. SW7 3E 226 (48Gb 89)
Fairkytes Av. RM11: Horn 32Md 77
Fairland Ho. BR2: Brom 70Kc 137
Fairland Rd. E15 37Hc 73
Fairlands Av. CR7: Thor H 70Pb 134
IG9: Buck H 19Jc 35
SM1: Sutt 75Cb 155
Fairlands Ct. SE9 58Qc 116
Fair La. CR5: Coul 97Eb 195
Fairlane Dr. RM15: S Ock 42Xd 98
Fairlawn KT2: King T 65Sa 131
KT13: Weyb 78U 150
KT23: Bookh 96Ba 191
SE7 52Lc 115
Fairlawn Av. DA7: Bex 54Zc 117
N2 28Gb 49
W4 49Sa 87
Fairlawn Cl. KT2: King T 65Sa 131
KT10: Clay 79Ha 152
N14 16Lb 32
TW13: Hanw 63Ba 129
Fairlawn Ct. SE7 52Lc 115
(not continuous)
W4 49Sa 87
Fairlawn Dr. IG8: Wfd G 24Jc 53
RH1: Redh 8N 207
FAIRLAWNE 99Yd 204
Fairlawnes SM6: Wall 78Kb 156
Fairlawn Gdns. UB1: S'hall 45Ba 85
Fairlawn Gro. SM7: Bans 85Fb 175
W4 49Sa 87
Fairlawn Mans. SE14 53Zb 114
Fairlawn Pk. GU21: Wok 86A 168
SE26 64Ac 136
SL4: Wind 6C 102
Fairlawn Rd. SM5: Cars 83Eb 175
SM7: Bans 84Fb 175
SW19 66Bb 133
Fairlawns CM14: B'wood 20Wd 40
CM16: Epp 1Xc 23
HA5: Pinn 26Z 45
KT15: Add 78K 149
KT15: Wdhm 83H 169
TW1: Twick 58La 108
TW16: Sun 69W 128
WD17: Wat 10V 12
Fairlawns Cl. RM11: Horn 31Pd 77
TW18: Staines 65K 127
Fairlead Ho. E14 48Cc 92
(off Alpha Gro.)
Fairlea Pl. W5 42La 86
Fairley Way EN7: Chesh 1Xb 19
Fairlie Ct. E3 41Dc 92
(off Stroudley Wlk.)
Fairlie Gdns. SE23 59Yb 114
Fairlie Rd. SL1: Slou 4E 80
Fairlight TW12: Hamp H 64Da 129
Fairlight Av. E4 19Fc 35
IG8: Wfd G 23Jc 53
NW10 40Ua 68
SL4: Wind 4H 103
Fairlight Cl. E4 19Fc 35
KT4: Wor Pk 77Ya 154
Fairlight Ct. NW10 40Ua 68
UB6: G'frd 40Ea 66
Fairlight Cross DA3: Lfield 69De 143
Fairlight Dr. UB8: Uxb 37M 63
Fairlight Rd. SW17 63Fb 133
Fairline Ct. BR3: Beck 68Ec 136
FAIRLOP 25Uc 54
Fairlop Cl. RM12: Horn 37Kd 77
Fairlop Ct. E11 32Fc 73
Fairlop Gdns. IG6: Ilf 24Sc 54
Fairlop Rd. E11 31Fc 73
IG6: Ilf 26Sc 54
Fairlop Sailing Cen. 25Vc 55
Fairlop Waters Country Pk. 26Vc 55
Fairlop Waters Golf Course 25Uc 54
Fairmark Dr. UB10: Hil 37Q 64
Fairmead BR1: Brom 70Pc 138
GU21: Wok 10N 167
KT5: Surb 74Ra 153
Fairmead Cl. BR1: Brom 70Pc 138
KT3: N Mald 69Ta 131
TW5: Hest 52Z 107
Fairmead Ct. TW9: Rich 54Ra 109
Fairmead Cres. HA8: Edg 20Sa 29
Fairmead Gdns. IG4: Ilf 29Nc 54
Fairmead Ho. E9 35Ac 72
Fairmead Rd. CR0: C'don 73Pb 156
IG10: H Beech, Lough 15Kc 35
N19 34Mb 70
Fairmeads IG10: Lough 12Rc 36
KT11: Cobh 85Ba 171
Fairmeadside IG10: Lough 15Lc 35
FAIRMILE 84Ba 171
Fairmile Av. KT11: Cobh 86Aa 171
SW16 64Mb 134
Fairmile Ct. KT11: Cobh 84Aa 171
Fairmile Golf Range 83Y 171
Fairmile Ho. TW11: Tedd 63Ja 130
Fairmile La. KT11: Cobh 84Z 171
Fairmile Pk. Copse
KT11: Cobh 85Ba 171
Fairmile Pk. Rd. KT11: Cobh 85Ba 171
Fairmont Av. E14 46Fc 93
Fairmont Cl. DA17: Belv 50Bd 95
Fairmont Ho. E3 42Cc 92
(off Wellington Way)
SE16 47Zb 92
(off Needleman St.)
Fairmont M. NW2 33Cb 69
Fairmount Rd. SW2 58Pb 112
Fairoak Cl. BR5: Pet W 73Rc 160
CR8: Kenley 87Rb 177
KT22: Oxs 84Fa 172
Fairoak Dr. SE9 57Tc 116
Fairoak Gdns. RM1: Rom 26Gd 56
Fairoak La. KT9: Chess 84Ea 172
KT22: Oxs 84Ea 172
Fair Oak Pl. IG6: Ilf 26Sc 54
Fairoaks Cvn. Pk.
GU3: Worp 10E 186
Fairoaks Ct. KT15: Add 78K 149
(off Liberty La.)
Fairoaks Gro. EN3: Enf W 9Zb 20
FAIRSEAT 84Ee 185
Fairseat Cl. WD23: B Hea 19Ga 28
Fairseat La. TN15: Stans 81Ce 185
TN15: Wro 87De 185
Fairs Rd. KT22: Lea 91Ja 192
Fairstead Lodge IG8: Wfd G 23Jc 53
(off Snakes La. W.)
Fairstead Wlk. N1 39Sb 71
(off Popham St.)
Fair St. SE1 1J 231 (47Ub 91)
TW3: Houn 55Ea 108
Fairthorne Vs. SE7 50Jc 93
(off Felltram Way)
Fairthorn Rd. SE7 50Jc 93
Fairtrough Rd.
BR6: Prat B 84Xc 181
Fairview DA3: Fawk 76Xd 164
DA8: Erith 52Hd 118
EN6: Pot B 1Db 17
HA4: Ruis 35Y 65
KT17: Ewe 83Ya 174
Fairview Av. CM13: Hut 17Fe 41
GU22: Wok 90A 168
HA0: Wemb 37Ma 67
RM13: Rain 40Md 77
SS17: Stan H 2L 101
Fairview Chase SS17: Stan H 3L 101
Fairview Cl. E17 25Ac 52
GU22: Wok 90B 168
IG7: Chig 21Uc 54
SE26 64Ac 136
Fairview Ct. NW4 26Za 48
TW15: Ashf 64Q 128
Fairview Cres. HA2: Harr 32Ca 65
Fairview Dr. BR6: Orp 77Tc 160
IG7: Chig 21Uc 54
TW17: Shep 71P 149
WD17: Wat 8U 12
Fairview Est. NW10 41Sa 87
Fairview Gdns. IG8: Wfd G 25Kc 53
Fairview Ho. SW2 59Pb 112
Fairview Ind. Pk. RM13: Rain 43Fd 96
Fairview Pl. SW2 59Pb 112
Fairview Rd. DA13: Ist R, Nflt G 66Fe 143
EN2: Enf 11Qb 32
IG7: Chig 21Uc 54
KT17: Ewe 83Va 174
N15 29Vb 51
SL2: Slou 2D 80
SM1: Sutt 78Fb 155
SW16 67Pb 134
Fairviews RH8: Oxt 5L 211
Fairview Vs. E4 24Cc 52
Fairview Way HA8: Edg 21Qa 47
Fairwall Ho. SE5 53Ub 113
Fairwater Av. DA16: Well 56Wc 117
Fairwater Dr. KT15: New H 81M 169
TW17: Shep 71S 150
Fairwater Ho. TW11: Tedd 63Ja 130
Fairway BR5: Pet W 71Tc 160
DA6: Bex 57Ad 117
GU25: Vir W 2N 147
HP3: Hem H 6P 3
IG8: Wfd G 22Lc 53
KT16: Chert 74K 149
RM16: Grays 46De 99
SM5: Cars 83Eb 175
SW20 69Ya 132
Fairway, The BR1: Brom 71Pc 160
DA11: Grav'nd 1C 144
EN5: New Bar 16Db 31
GU3: Worp 6G 186
HA0: Wemb 34Ka 66
HA4: Ruis 35Y 65
HA6: Nwood 21U 44
KT3: N Mald 67Ta 131
KT8: W Mole 69Da 129
KT13: Weyb 83Q 170
KT22: Lea 90Ja 172
N13 20Sb 33
N14 16Kb 32
NW7 20Ta 29
RM14: Upm 31Sd 78
SL1: Burn 10A 60
UB5: N'olt 37Ea 66
UB10: Hil 41P 83
W3 44Ua 88
WD5: Ab L 4T 12
Fairway Av. NW9 27Ra 47
UB7: W Dray 46L 83
WD6: Bore 12Ra 29

Fairway Cl.—Feather M.

Fairway Cl. AL2: Park 9A 6
CR0: C'don 71Ac 158
GU22: Wok 1M 187
KT10: Surb 76Ka 152
KT19: Ewe 77Sa 153
NW11 31Eb 69
TW4: Houn 57Y 107
(Amberley Way)
TW4: Houn 57Z 107
(Islay Gdns.)
UB7: W Dray 46M 83
Fairway Ct. *E3* 41Ec 92
(off Culvert Dr.)
EN5: New Bar 16Db 31
HP3: Hem H 6P 3
NW7 20Ta 29
SE16 47Zb 92
(off Christopher Cl.)
Fairway Dr. DA2: Dart 59Rd 119
SE28 44Zc 95
UB6: G'frd 38Da 65
Fairway Gdns. BR3: Beck 72Fc 159
IG1: Ilf 36Sc 74
Fairway Ho. *WD6: Bore* 13Ra 29
(off Eldon Av.)
Fairways CR8: Kenley 89Sb 177
E17 28Ec 52
EN9: Walt A 6Gc 21
HA7: Stan 26Na 47
KT24: Eff J 95V 190
TW7: Isle 53Fa 108
TW11: Tedd 66Ma 131
TW15: Ashf 65R 128
Fairways, The RH1: Redh 9M 207
Fairways Bus. Pk. E10 33Ac 72
Fairway Trad. Est. TW4: Houn 57Y 107
Fairweather Cl. DA16: Well 57Wc 117
N15 28Ub 51
Fairweather Ct. N13 20Pb 32
Fairweather Ho. N7 35Nb 70
Fairweather Rd. N16 30Wb 51
Fairwell La. KT24: W Hor 100R 190
Fairwyn Rd. SE26 63Ac 136
Faith Cl. RM2: Rom 29Kd 57
Faith Ct. *E3* 40Cc 72
(off Lefevre Wlk.)
SE1 50Vb 91
(off Cooper's Rd.)
Faithfield WD23: Bush 16Aa 27
Faith M. E12 35Mc 73
Fakenham Cl. NW7 24Wa 48
UB5: N'olt 37Ba 65
Fakruddin St. E1 42Wb 91
Falaise TW20: Egh 64A 126
Falcon WC1 7G 217
Falcon Av. BR1: Brom 70Nc 138
RM15: S Ock 42Xd 98
RM17: Grays 52De 121
Falconberg M. W1 2D 222 (44Mb 90)
Falcon Bus. Cen. RM3: Rom 24Nd 57
Falcon Cl. AL10: Hat 2C 8
DA1: Dart 57Pd 119
EN9: Walt A 6Jc 21
HA6: Nwood 24U 44
W4 51Sa 109
Falcon Ct. *E18* 27Kc 53
(off Albert Rd.)
EC4 3K 223 (44Qb 90)
EN5: New Bar 14Eb 31
GU21: Wok 85E 168
HA4: Ruis 33U 64
N1 2C 218
Falcon Cres. EN3: Pond E 15Zb 34
Falcondal Ct. NW10 41Qa 87
Falcon Dr. TW19: Stanw 58M 105
Falconer Ct. *N17* 24Sb 51
(off Compton Cres.)
Falconer Rd. IG6: Ilf 22Xc 55
WD23: Bush 16Ba 27
Falconer Wlk. N7 33Pb 70
Falconet Ct. *E1* 46Xb 91
(off Wapping High St.)
Falcon Gro. SW11 55Gb 111
Falcon Highwalk EC2 1D 224
Falcon Ho. BR1: Brom 67Hc 137
E14 50Dc 92
(off St Davids Sq.)
NW6 39Db 69
(off Springfield Wlk.)
SW5 50Db 89
(off Old Brompton Rd.)
Falconhurst KT22: Oxs 87Fa 172
Falcon La. SW11 55Gb 111
Falcon Lodge *W9* 43Cb 89
(off Admiral Wlk.)
Falcon M. DA11: Nflt 10A 122
Falcon Pk. Ind. Est. NW10 35Ua 68
Falcon Point SE1 5C 224 (45Rb 91)
Falcon Rd. EN3: Pond E 15Zb 34
SW11 54Gb 111
TW12: Hamp 66Ba 129
Falconry Ct. CM16: Epp 2Vc 23
KT1: King T 69Na 131
(off Fairfield Sth.)
Falcons Cl. TN16: Big H 89Mc 179
Falcon St. E13 42Jc 93
Falcon Ter. SW11 55Gb 111
Falcon Way E11 28Jc 53
E14 49Dc 92
HA3: Kenton 29Na 47
NW9 26Ua 48
RM12: Horn 38Jd 76
TW14: Felt 57X 107
TW16: Sun 68U 128
WD25: Wat 6Aa 13
Falcon Wharf SW11 54Fb 111
FALCONWOOD 56Vc 117
FALCONWOOD 56Tc 116
Falcon Wood KT22: Lea 92Ha 192
Falconwood KT24: E Hor 96V 190
TW20: Egh 64A 126
Falconwood Av. DA16: Well 54Tc 116
Falconwood Ct. *SE3* 54Hc 115
(off Montpelier Row)
Falconwood Pde.
DA16: Well 56Uc 116
Falconwood Rd. CR0: Sels 81Bc 178
Falcourt Cl. SM1: Sutt 78Db 155
Faldo Cl. CM14: B'wood 20Xd 40
Falkirk Cl. RM11: Horn 32Qd 77
Falkirk Ct. *SE16* 46Zb 92
(off Rotherhithe St.)
Falkirk Gdns. WD19: Wat 22Z 45
Falkirk Ho. *W9* 40Db 69
(off Maida Vale)
Falkirk St. N1 2J 219 (40Ub 71)
Falkland Av. N3 24Cb 49
N11 21Kb 50
Falkland Ho. SE6 63Ec 136
W8 48Db 89
W14 50Bb 89
(off Edith Vs.)
Falkland Pk. Av. SE25 69Ub 135
Falkland Pl. NW5 36Lb 70
Falkland Rd. EN5: Barn 12Ab 30
N8 28Qb 50
NW5 36Lb 70
Fallaize Av. IG1: Ilf 35Rc 74
Falling La. UB7: Yiew 45N 83
Falloden Way NW11 28Cb 49
Fallodon Ho. *W11* 43Bb 89
(off Tavistock Cres.)
Fallow Cl. IG7: Chig 22Vc 55
FALLOW CORNER 24Eb 49
Fallow Ct. *SE16* 50Wb 91
(off Argyle Way)
Fallow Ct. Av. N12 24Eb 49
Fallowfield DA2: Bean 62Xd 142
HA7: Stan 21Ja 46
Fallowfield Cl. UB9: Hare 25L 43
Fallowfield Ct. HA7: Stan 20Ja 28
Fallow Flds. IG10: Lough 16Lc 35
Fallowfields Dr. N12 23Gb 49
Fallowhurst Path N3 24Eb 49
Fallow Pl. TW11: Tedd 64Ga 130
Fallows Cl. N2 26Fb 49
Fallsbrook Rd. SW16 65Kb 134
Falman Cl. N9 18Wb 33
Falmer Rd. E17 27Dc 52
EN1: Enf 14Ub 33
N15 29Sb 51
Falmouth Av. E4 22Fc 53
Falmouth Cl. N22 24Pb 50
SE12 57Hc 115
Falmouth Ct. AL3: St A 1A 6
Falmouth Gdns. IG4: Ilf 28Mc 53
Falmouth Ho. HA5: Hat E 24Ba 45
KT2: King T 67Ma 131
(off Skerne Rd.)
SE11 7A 230
W2 4D 220
Falmouth Rd. KT12: Hers 77Y 151
SE1 4E 230 (48Sb 91)
SL1: Slou 4E 80
Falmouth St. E15 36Fc 73
Falmouth Wlk. SW15 58Wa 110
Falmouth Way E17 29Bc 52
Falstaff Bldg. *E1* 45Xb 91
(off Cannon St. Rd.)
Falstaff Cl. DA1: Cray 59Gd 118
Falstaff Ct. SE11 6B 230
Falstaff Gdns. AL1: St A 5P 5
Falstaff Ho. N1 2H 219
Falstaff M. DA9: Ghithe 58Xd 120
TW12: Hamp H 64Fa 130
(off High St.)
Falstone GU21: Wok 10M 167
Fambridge Cl. SE26 63Bc 136
Fambridge Ct. *RM7: Rom* 29Fd 56
(off Marks Rd.)
Fambridge Rd. RM8: Dag 32Cd 76
Famet Av. CR8: Purl 85Sb 177
Famet Cl. CR8: Purl 85Sb 177
Famet Gdns. CR8: Kenley 85Sb 177
Famet Wlk. CR8: Purl 85Sb 177
Family Court
East London 46Cc 92
West London 58W 106
Fancourt M. BR1: Brom 69Qc 138
Fane St. W14 51Bb 111
Fangrove Pk. KT16: Lyne 74C 148
Fan Mus., The 52Ec 114
Fanns Ri. RM19: Purf 49Qd 97
Fann St. EC1 6D 218 (42Sb 91)
EC2 6D 218 (42Sb 91)
(not continuous)
Fanshawe Av. IG11: Bark 37Sc 74
Fanshawe Cres. RM9: Dag 36Ad 75
RM11: Horn 30Md 57
Fanshawe Rd. RM16: Grays 8C 100
TW10: Ham 63La 130
Fanshaw St. N1 3H 219 (41Ub 91)
FANTAIL, THE 76Pc 160
Fantail Cl. SE28 44Yc 95
Fantasia Ct. CM14: W'ley 22Xd 58
Fanthorpe St. SW15 55Ya 110
Faraday Av. DA14: Sidc 61Wc 139
Faraday Bldg. E14 44Gc 93
Faraday Cl. N7 37Pb 70
SL2: Slou 3F 80
WD18: Wat 16T 26
Faraday Ct. WD18: Wat 16W 26
Faraday Ho. *E14* 45Bc 92
(off Brightlingsea Pl.)
EN3: Enf L 9Bc 20
(off Velocity Way)
HA9: Wemb 34Sa 67
SE1 2F 231
W10 43Ab 88
(off Wornington Rd.)
WD18: Wat 16T 26
Faraday Lodge SE10 48Hc 93
Faraday Mans. *W14* 51Ab 110
(off Queen's Club Gdns.)
Faraday Mus., The 5B 222 (45Lb 90)
Faraday Pl. KT8: W Mole 70Ca 129
Faraday Rd. DA16: Well 55Wc 117
E15 37Hc 73
KT8: W Mole 70Ca 129
SL2: Slou 3F 80
SW19 65Cb 133
UB1: S'hall 45Da 85
W3 45Sa 87
W10 43Ab 88
Faraday Way BR5: St M Cry 70Xc 139
CR0: Wadd 74Pb 156
SE18 48Mc 93
Fardell Ct. *AL1: St A* 2D 6
(off Newsom Pl.)
Fareham Ho. HP1: Hem H 3M 3
Fareham Rd. TW14: Felt 59Y 107
Far End AL10: Hat 3D 8
Farewell Pl. CR4: Mitc 67Gb 133
Fari Cl. *E17* 28Cc 52
(off Tower M.)
Faringdon Av. BR2: Brom 73Qc 160
RM3: Rom 25Ld 57
Faringford Cl. EN6: Pot B 3Fb 17
Faringford Rd. E15 38Gc 73
Farington Acres KT13: Weyb 76T 150
Faris Barn Dr. KT15: Wdhm 84H 169
Faris La. KT15: Wdhm 83H 169
Farjeon Ho. *NW6* 38Fb 69
(off Hilgrove Rd.)
Farjeon Rd. SE3 53Mc 115
Farland Rd. HP2: Hem H 2B 4
FARLEIGH 86Bc 178
Farleigh Av. BR2: Hayes 73Hc 159
FARLEIGH COMMON 86Ac 178
Farleigh Ct. CR2: S Croy 78Sb 157
Farleigh Court Golf Course 84Cc 178
Farleigh Ct. Rd. CR6: W'ham 86Bc 178
Farleigh Dean Cres. CR0: Sels 83Dc 178
Farleigh Ho. *N1* 38Rb 71
(off Halton Rd.)
Farleigh Pl. N16 35Vb 71
Farleigh Rd. CR6: W'ham 90Zb 178
KT15: New H 83J 169
N16 35Vb 71
Farleton Cl. KT13: Weyb 79T 150
FARLEY COMMON 98Rc 200
Farley Ct. NW1 6H 215
W14 48Bb 89
Farleycroft TN16: Westrm 98Sc 200
Farley Dr. IG3: Ilf 32Uc 74
Farley Ho. SE26 62Xb 135
Farley La. TN16: Westrm 98Rc 200
Farley M. SE6 59Ec 114
Farley Nursery TN16: Westrm 99Sc 200
Farley Pk. RH8: Oxt 2H 211
Farley Pl. SE25 70Wb 135
Farley Rd. CR2: Sels 80Xb 157
DA12: Grav'nd 10H 123
SE6 59Dc 114
Farleys Cl. KT24: W Hor 98S 190
Farlington Pl. SW15 59Xa 110
Farlow Cl. DA11: Nflt 2B 144
Farlow Rd. SW15 55Za 110
Farlton Rd. SW18 60Db 111
Farman Gro. UB5: N'olt 41Z 85
Farman Ter. HA3: Kenton 28Ma 47
Farm Av. BR8: Swan 69Ed 140
HA0: Wemb 37La 66
HA2: Harr 31Ba 65
NW2 34Ab 68
SW16 63Nb 134
Farmborough Cl. HA1: Harr 31Fa 66
Farm Cl. BR4: W W'ck 76Hc 159
CM13: Hut 17Ee 41
CR5: Chip 92Hb 195
EN5: Barn 15Ya 30
EN8: Chesh 2Yb 20
GU3: Worp 10G 186
IG9: Buck H 20Lc 35
KT14: Byfl 84P 169
KT16: Lyne 72C 148
KT22: Fet 96Fa 192
KT24: E Hor 100V 190
RM10: Dag 38Ed 76
SL5: S'hill 1A 146
SM2: Sutt 80Fb 155
SM6: Wall 82Lb 176
SW6 52Db 111
TW17: Shep 73Q 150
TW18: Staines 64G 126
UB1: S'hall 45Da 85
UB10: Ick 33R 64
WD6: Bore 10Ma 15
WD7: Shenl 2Na 15
Farmcote Rd. SE12 60Jc 115
Farm Cotts. BR8: Crock 71Hd 162
Farm Ct. NW4 27Wa 48
Farm Cres. AL2: Lon C 8E 6
SL2: Slou 3M 81
Farmcroft DA11: Grav'nd 1C 144
Farmdale Rd. SE10 50Jc 93
SM5: Cars 80Gb 155
Farm Dr. CR0: C'don 75Bc 158
CR8: Purl 84Mb 176
RM16: Grays 45Ee 99
SL4: Old Win 8M 103
Farm End E4 15Gc 35
HA6: Nwood 25R 44
Farmer Rd. E10 32Dc 72
Farmers Cl. WD25: Wat 5X 13
Farmers Ct. EN9: Walt A 5Jc 21
Farmer's Rd. SE5 52Rb 113
Farmers Rd. TW18: Staines 64G 126
Farmer St. W8 46Cb 89
Farm Fld. WD17: Wat 10U 12
Farmfield Rd. BR1: Brom 64Gc 137
Farm Flds. CR2: Sande 83Ub 177
Farm Hill Rd. EN9: Walt A 5Fc 21
Farm Holt DA3: New A G 74Be 165
Farmhouse Cl. GU22: Pyr 87F 168
Farm Ho. Ct. NW7 24Wa 48
Farmhouse Rd. SW16 66Lb 134
Farmilo Rd. E17 31Bc 72
Farmington Av. SM1: Sutt 76Fb 155
Farmlands EN2: Enf 11Qb 32
HA5: Eastc 28W 44
Farmlands, The UB5: N'olt 37Ba 65
Farmland Wlk. BR7: Chst 64Rc 138
Farm La. CR0: C'don 75Bc 158
CR8: Purl 82Lb 176
GU23: Send 96E 188
KT15: Add 80J 149
KT18: Eps D 89Qa 173
KT21: Asht 89Qa 173
KT24: E Hor 100V 190
N14 17Kb 32
SL1: Slou 5H 81
SW6 51Cb 111
WD3: Loud 13L 25
Farmleigh N14 17Lb 32
Farmleigh Gro. KT12: Hers 78V 150
Farmleigh Ho. SW9 57Rb 113
Farm M. CR4: Mitc 68Kb 134
Farm Pl. DA1: Cray 56Jd 118
W8 46Cb 89
Farm Rd. AL1: St A 1F 6
CR6: W'ham 91Ac 198
GU22: Wok 92D 188
HA6: Nwood 22R 44
HA8: Edg 23Ra 47
KT10: Esh 74Da 151
N21 18Sb 33
NW10 39Ta 67
RM13: Rain 41Ld 97
RM16: Ors 7B 100
RM18: E Til 9L 101
SM2: Sutt 80Fb 155
SM4: Mord 71Db 155
TN14: S'oaks 92Ld 203
TW4: Houn 60Aa 107
TW18: Staines 65K 127
WD3: Chor 14C 24
Farmside Pl. KT19: Eps 84Pa 173
Farmstead KT19: Eps 81Qa 173
Farmstead Ct. *SM6: Wall* 78Kb 156
(off Melbourne Rd.)
Farmstead Rd. HA3: Hrw W 25Fa 46
SE6 63Dc 136
Farm St. W1 5K 221 (45Kb 90)
Farm Va. DA5: Bexl 58Dd 118
Farm Vw. KT11: Cobh 88Z 171
KT20: Lwr K 99Bb 195
Farm Wlk. NW11 29Bb 49
Farm Way HA6: Nwood 21U 44
HP2: Hem H 1P 3
IG9: Buck H 21Lc 53
KT4: Wor Pk 76Ya 154
RM12: Horn 35Ld 77
TW19: Stanw M 58H 105
WD23: Bush 14Da 27
Farmway RM8: Dag 34Yc 75
Farm Yd. SL4: Wind 2H 103
Farmyard Funworld 13Ba 27
Farnaby Dr. TN13: S'oaks 98Hd 202
Farnaby Ho. *W10* 41Bb 89
(off Bruckner St.)
Farnaby Rd. BR1: Brom 66Fc 137
BR2: Brom 66Fc 137
SE9 56Lc 115
Farnaby Way SS17: Stan H 1L 101
Farnan Av. E17 26Cc 52
Farnan Lodge SW16 64Nb 134
Farnan Rd. SW16 64Nb 134
FARNBOROUGH 78Sc 160
Farnborough Av. CR2: Sels 81Zb 178
E17 27Ac 52
Farnborough Cl. HA9: Wemb 33Ra 67
Farnborough Comn. BR6: Farnb 76Pc 160
Farnborough Cres. BR2: Hayes 74Hc 159
CR2: Sels 81Ac 178
Farnborough Hill
BR6: Chels, Farnb 78Tc 160
Farnborough Ho. SW15 60Wa 110
Farnborough Way
BR6: Chels, Farnb 78Sc 160
Farnburn Av. SL1: Slou 3F 80
Farncombe St. SE16 47Wb 91
Farndale Av. N13 19Rb 33
Farndale Ct. SE18 52Nc 116
Farndale Cres. UB6: G'frd 41Ea 86
Farndale Ho. *NW6* 39Db 69
(off Kilburn Vale)
Farne Ho. *WD18: Wat* 16V 26
(off Scammell Way)
Farnell M. KT13: Weyb 76R 150
SW5 50Db 89
Farnell Pl. W3 45Ra 87
Farnell Rd. TW7: Isle 55Fa 108
TW18: Staines 62J 127
Farnes Dr. RM2: Rom 26Ld 57
Farnfield Ct. CR2: S Croy 78Rb 157
Farnham Cl. HP3: Bov 10C 2
N20 17Eb 31
FARNHAM COMMON 7G 60
Farnham Ct. SM3: Cheam 79Ab 154
UB1: S'hall 45Ea 86
(off Redcroft Rd.)
Farnham Gdns. SW20 68Xa 132
Farnham Ho. NW1 6E 214
SE1 7D 224
Farnham La. SL2: Slou 1C 80
Farnham Pk. Golf Course
Buckinghamshire 9J 61
Farnham Pk. La. SL2: Farn R 8G 60
Farnham Pl. SE1 7C 224 (46Rb 91)
Farnham Rd. DA16: Well 54Yc 117
IG3: Ilf 31Vc 75
RM3: Rom 22Md 57
SL1: Slou 1F 80
SL2: Farn R, Slou 1F 80
FARNHAM ROYAL 1G 80
Farnham Royal SE11 50Pb 90
FARNINGHAM 73Pd 163
Farningham Ct. SW16 66Mb 134
Farningham Cres. CR3: Cat'm 95Wb 197
Farningham Hill Rd. DA4: Farni 71Ld 163
Farningham Ho. N4 31Tb 71
Farningham Rd. CR3: Cat'm 95Wb 197
N17 24Wb 51
Farnley GU21: Wok 9K 167
Farnley Ho. SW8 54Mb 112
Farnley Rd. E4 17Gc 35
SE25 70Tb 135
Farnol Rd. DA1: Dart 57Qd 119
Farnsworth Ct. *SE10* 48Hc 93
(off West Parkside)
Farnworth Ho. *E14* 49Fc 93
(off Manchester Rd.)
Faro Cl. BR1: Brom 68Qc 138
Faroe Rd. W14 48Za 88
Farorna Wlk. EN2: Enf 11Qb 32
Farquhar Rd. SE19 64Vb 135
SW19 62Cb 133
Farquharson Rd. CR0: C'don 74Sb 157
Farraline Rd. WD18: Wat 14X 27
Farrance Rd. RM6: Chad H 31Ad 75
Farrance St. E14 44Cc 92
Farrans Ct. HA3: Kenton 31Ka 66
Farrant Av. N22 26Qb 50
Farrant Cl. BR6: Chels 80Wc 161
Farrant Way WD6: Bore 11Na 29
Farr Av. IG11: Bark 40Wc 75
Farrell Ct. DA2: Wilm 62Ld 141
Farrell Ho. *E1* 44Yb 92
(off Ronald St.)
Farren Rd. SE23 61Ac 136
Farrer Ct. TW1: Twick 59Ma 109
Farrer Ho. SE8 52Cc 114
SL4: Eton 10G 80
(off Common La.)
Farrer M. N8 28Lb 50
Farrer Rd. HA3: Kenton 29Na 47
N8 28Lb 50
Farrer's Pl. CR0: C'don 77Zb 158
Farrier Cl. BR1: Brom 69Mc 137
TW16: Sun 70W 128
UB8: Hil 44Q 84
Farrier Ct. *E1* 43Zb 92
(off White Horse La.)
RM13: Rain 40Fd 76
(off Lowen Rd.)
Farrier Pl. SM1: Sutt 76Db 155
Farrier Rd. UB5: N'olt 40Ca 65
Farriers Cl. DA12: Grav'nd 10H 123
HP3: Bov 10D 2
KT17: Eps 84Ua 174
Farriers Ct. WD25: Wat 4X 13
Farriers Ho. EC1 6E 218
Farriers M. SE15 55Yb 114
Farriers Rd. KT17: Eps 83Ua 174
Farrier St. NW1 38Kb 70
Farriers Way WD6: Bore 15Ta 29
Farrier Wlk. SW10 51Eb 111
Farringdon Ho. TW9: Kew 52Ra 109
UB7: W Dray 47P 83
Farringdon La. EC1 6A 218 (42Qb 90)
Farringdon Rd. EC1 5K 217 (42Qb 90)
Farringdon St. EC4 1B 224 (43Rb 91)
Farringford Cl. AL2: Chis G 8N 5
Farrington Av. BR5: St P 69Xc 139
WD23: Bush 14Da 27
Farrington Ct. *BR1: Brom* 68Kc 137
(off Widmore Rd.)
Farrington Pl. BR7: Chst 66Tc 138
HA6: Nwood 21V 44
Farrins Rents SE16 46Ac 92
Farrow Gdns. RM16: Grays 46De 99
Farrow La. SE14 52Yb 114
Farrow Pl. SE16 48Ac 92
Farr Rd. EN2: Enf 11Tb 33
Farrs M. WD3: Rick 18M 25
Farthingale Ct. EN9: Walt A 6Jc 21
Farthingale La. EN9: Walt A 6Jc 21
Farthingale Wlk. E15 38Fc 73
Farthing All. SE1 47Wb 91
Farthing Barn La. BR6: Downe 81Qc 180
Farthing Cl. DA1: Dart 56Pd 119
WD18: Wat 15Y 27
Farthing Ct. NW7 24Ab 48
Farthingfield TN15: Wro 88Ce 185
Farthing Flds. E1 46Xb 91
Farthing Grn. La. SL2: Stoke P 10L 61
Farthings GU21: Knap 8J 167
HP8: Chal G 13A 24
Farthings, The HP1: Hem H 2K 3
KT2: King T 67Qa 131
Farthings Cl. E4 20Gc 35
HA5: Eastc 30X 45
FARTHING STREET 81Pc 180
Farthing St. BR6: Downe 80Pc 160
Farthing Way CR5: Coul 89Mb 176
Farwell Rd. DA14: Sidc 63Xc 139
Farwig La. BR1: Brom 67Hc 137
Fashion & Textile Mus. 1J 231 (47Ub 91)
Fashion St. E1 1K 225 (43Vb 91)
Fashoda Rd. BR2: Brom 70Mc 137
Fassett Rd. E8 37Wb 71
KT1: King T 70Na 131
Fassett Sq. E8 37Wb 71
Fastrack Mnr. Way DA9: Ghithe 56Zd 121
Fathom Ct. *E16* 45Rc 94
(off Basin App.)
Fauconberg Ct. *W4* 51Sa 109
(off Fauconberg Rd.)
Fauconberg Rd. W4 51Sa 109
Faulkner Cl. RM8: Dag 31Zc 75
Faulkner Ct. *AL1: St A* 1C 6
(off Boundary Rd.)
Faulkner Ho. BR7: Chst 67Tc 138
W6 51Ya 110
Faulkner M. E17 25Ac 52
Faulkners All. EC1 7B 218 (43Rb 91)
Faulkners Rd. KT12: Hers 78Y 151
Faulkner St. SE14 53Yb 114
Fauna Cl. HA7: Stan 21Ma 47
RM6: Chad H 30Yc 55
Faunce Ho. *SE17* 51Rb 113
(off Doddington Gro.)
Faunce St. SE17 50Rb 91
Favart Rd. SW6 53Cb 111
Faversham Av. E4 18Gc 35
EN1: Enf 16Tb 33
Faversham Cl. IG7: Chig 19Xc 37
Faversham Ho. NW1 1C 216
SE17 7H 231
Faversham Rd. BR3: Beck 68Bc 136
SE6 59Bc 114
SM4: Mord 72Db 155
Fawcett Cl. SW11 54Fb 111
SW16 64Qb 134
Fawcett Ct. *SW10* 51Eb 111
(off Fawcett St.)
Fawcett Est. E5 32Wb 71
Fawcett Rd. CR0: C'don 76Sb 157
NW10 38Va 68
SL4: Wind 3F 102
Fawcett St. SW10 51Eb 111
Fawcus Cl. KT10: Clay 79Ga 152
Fawe Pk. M. SW15 56Bb 111
Fawe Pk. Rd. SW15 56Bb 111
Fawe St. E14 43Dc 92
FAWKE COMMON 99Qd 203
Fawke Comn.
TN15: God G, Under 98Qd 203
Fawkes Av. DA1: Dart 61Pd 141
Fawke Wood Rd. TN15: Under 100Qd 203
FAWKHAM 73Xd 164
Fawkham Av. DA3: Lfield 69Ee 143
FAWKHAM GREEN 76Xd 164
Fawkham Grn. Rd. DA3: Fawk 76Xd 164
Fawkham Ho. SE1 6K 231
Fawkham Rd. DA3: Fawk 77Vd 164
DA3: Fawk, Lfield 70Zd 143
TN15: W King 81Wd 184
Fawley Lodge *E14* 49Fc 93
(off Millennium Dr.)
Fawley Rd. NW6 36Db 69
Fawnbrake Av. SE24 57Rb 113
Fawn Hgts. *IG9: Buck H* 19Kc 35
(off Stag La.)
Fawn Rd. E13 40Lc 73
IG7: Chig 22Vc 55
Fawns Mnr. Cl. TW14: Bedf 60S 106
Fawns Mnr. Rd. TW14: Bedf 60T 106
Fawood Av. NW10 38Sa 67
Fawsley Cl. SL3: Poyle 52G 104
Fawters Cl. CM13: Hut 16Fe 41
Fayerfield EN6: Pot B 3Fb 17
Faygate Cres. DA6: Bex 57Cd 118
Faygate Rd. SW2 61Pb 134
Fay Grn. WD5: Ab L 5T 12
Fayland Av. SW16 64Lb 134
Faymore Gdns. RM15: S Ock 44Wd 98
Fazeley Ct. *W9* 43Cb 89
(off Elmfield Way)
Fazeley Ho. *UB5: N'olt* 41Ba 85
(off Taywood Rd.)
Feacey Down HP1: Hem H 1J 3
Fearn Cl. KT24: E Hor 100U 190
Fearney Mead WD3: Rick 18J 25
Fearnley Cres. TW12: Hamp 64Aa 129
Fearnley Ho. SE5 54Ub 113
Fearnley St. WD18: Wat 14X 27
Fearns Ho. W13 46Ja 86
Fearns Mead CM14: W'ley 22Yd 58
Fearon St. SE10 50Jc 93
Featherbed La. AL2: Pot C 7K 5
CR0: Sels 80Bc 158
CR6: W'ham 80Bc 158
HP3: Hem H 7J 3
(not continuous)
RM4: Abr 14Zc 37
(not continuous)
WD5: Bedm 8H 5
Feather M. E1 43Wb 91

Feathers La.—Fillebrook Rd.

Feathers La. TW19: Wray 61C 126
Feathers Pl. SE10 51Fc 115
Featherstone Av. SE23 61Xb 135
Featherstone Ct. UB2: S'hall 48Z 85
Featherstone Gdns. WD6: Bore 14Ta 29
Featherstone Ho. UB4: Yead 43Y 85
Featherstone Ind. Est.
UB2: S'hall 48Aa 85
(off Feather Rd.)
Featherstone Rd. NW7 23Xa 48
UB2: S'hall 48Aa 85
Featherstone Sports Cen. 49Z 85
Featherstone St. EC1 5F 219 (42Tb 91)
Featherstone Ter. UB2: S'hall 48Aa 85
Featley Rd. SW9 55Rb 113
Federal Rd. UB6: G'frd 39La 66
Federal Way WD24: Wat 11Y 27
Federation Rd. SE2 49Xc 95
Fee Farm Rd. KT10: Clay 80Ha 152
Feenan Highway RM18: Tilb 2D 122
Feeny Cl. NW10 35Va 68
Felbridge Av. HA7: Stan 25Ja 46
Felbridge Cl. SM2: Sutt 81Db 175
SW16 63Qb 134
Felbridge Ct. TW13: Felt 60X 107
(off High St.)
UB3: Harl 51T 106
Felbridge Ho. SE22 55Ub 113
Felbrigge Rd. IG3: Ilf 33Vc 75
Felcott Cl. KT12: Hers 76Y 151
Felcott Rd. KT12: Hers 76Y 151
Felday Rd. SE13 58Dc 114
FELDEN 6J 3
Felden Cl. HA5: Hat E 24Aa 45
WD25: Wat 6Z 13
Felden Dr. HP3: Hem H 6J 3
Felden La. HP3: Hem H 5H 3
Felden Lawns HP3: Hem H 6J 3
Felden St. SW6 53Bb 111
Feldman Cl. N16 32Wb 71
Feldspar Ct. EN3: Enf H 13Ac 34
(off Enstone Rd.)
Feldspar M. N13 22Rb 51
Felgate M. W6 49Xa 88
Felhampton Rd. SE9 61Rc 138
Felhurst Cres. RM10: Dag 35Dd 76
Felicia Way RM16: Grays 9D 100
Feline Ct. EN4: E Barn 16Gb 31
Felipe Rd. RM16: Chaf H 48Yd 98
Felix Av. N8 30Nb 50
Felix Ct. E17 29Dc 52
NW9 26Ua 48
Felix Dr. GU4: W Cla 100J 189
Felix Ho. E16 45Qc 94
(off University Way)
Felix La. TW17: Shep 72U 150
Felix Mnr. BR7: Chst 65Uc 138
Felix Neubergh Ho. EN1: Enf 14Ub 33
Felix Pl. SW2 57Qb 112
(off Talma Rd.)
Felix Point E14 44Cc 92
(off Upper Nth. St.)
Felix Rd. KT12: Walt T 72W 150
W13 45Ja 86
Felixstowe Ct. E16 46Rc 94
Felixstowe Rd. N9 20Wb 33
N17 27Vb 51
NW10 41Xa 88
SE2 48Xc 95
Felix St. E2 40Xb 71
Felland Way RH2: Reig 10M 207
Fellbrigg Rd. SE22 57Vb 113
Fellbrigg St. E1 42Xb 91
Fellbrook TW10: Ham 62Ka 130
Fellmongers Path SE1 2K 231
Fellmongers Yd. CR0: C'don 76Sb 157
Fellowes Cl. UB4: Yead 42Z 85
WD25: Wat 8Y 13
Fellowes La. AL4: Col H 5P 7
Fellowes Rd. SM5: Cars 76Gb 155
Fellow Grn. GU24: W End 5D 166
Fellow Grn. Rd. GU24: W End 5D 166
Fellows Ct. E2 1K 219 (40Vb 71)
(not continuous)
Fellowship Cl. RM8: Dag 35Wc 75
Fellows Rd. NW3 38Fb 69
Fell Path WD6: Bore 15Ta 29
(off Clydesdale Cl.)
Fell Rd. CR0: C'don 76Sb 157
Felltram M. SE7 50Jc 93
Felltram Way SE7 50Jc 93
Fell Wlk. HA8: Edg 25Sa 47
Felmersham Cl. SW4 56Nb 112
Felmingham Rd. SE20 68Yb 136
Felnex Trad. Est. NW10 40Ta 67
SM6: Wall 75Jb 156
Felsberg Rd. SW2 58Nb 112
Fels Cl. RM10: Dag 34Dd 76
Fels Farm Av. RM10: Dag 34Ed 76
Felsham M. SW15 55Za 110
(off Felsham Rd.)
Felsham Rd. SW15 55Ya 110
Felspar Cl. SE18 50Vc 95
Felstead Av. IG5: Ilf 25Qc 54
Felstead Cl. CM13: Hut 16Ee 41
N13 22Qb 50
Felstead Gdns. E14 50Ec 92
Felstead Rd. BR6: Chels 75Wc 161
E9 37Bc 72
E11 31Jc 73
EN8: Walt C 4Ac 20
IG10: Lough 17Nc 36
KT19: Eps 83Ta 173
RM5: Col R 24Ed 56
Felstead St. E9 37Bc 72
Felstead Way SL2: Slou 2E 80
Felstead Wharf E14 50Ec 92
Felsted Rd. E16 44Mc 93
FELTHAM 60X 107
Feltham Av. KT8: E Mos 70Ga 130
Felthambrook Ind. Est.
TW13: Felt 62X 129
Felthambrook Way TW13: Felt 62X 129
Feltham Bus. Complex
TW13: Felt 61X 129
Feltham Corporate Cen.
TW13: Felt 62X 129
FELTHAMHILL 64V 128
Feltham Hill Rd. TW15: Ashf 64Q 128
Feltham Rd. CR4: Mitc 68Hb 133
RH1: Redh 10P 207
TW15: Ashf 63Q 128
Feltham Wlk. RH1: Redh 10P 207
Felton Cl. BR5: Pet W 72Rc 160
WD6: Bore 10Na 15
Felton Gdns. IG11: Bark 39Uc 74
Felton Hall Ho. SE16 47Wb 91
(off George Row)
Felton Ho. N1 39Tb 71
(off Colville Est.)
Felton Lea DA14: Sidc 64Vc 139
Felton Rd. IG11: Bark 40Uc 74
W13 47La 86
Felton St. N1 39Tb 71
Fenbridge Ct. RH1: Redh 4B 208
Fencepiece Rd. IG6: Chig, Ilf 22Sc 54
IG7: Chig 22Sc 54
Fenchurch Av. EC3 3H 225 (44Ub 91)
Fenchurch Bldgs. EC3 3J 225 (44Ub 91)
Fenchurch Ho. EC3 3K 225
Fenchurch M. E3 43Bc 92
(off St Paul's Way)
Fenchurch Pl. EC3 4J 225 (44Ub 91)
Fenchurch St. EC3 4H 225 (45Ub 91)
Fen Cl. CM15: Shenf 14Ee 41
Fen Ct. EC3 3H 225 (44Ub 91)
Fendall Rd. KT19: Ewe 76Sa 153
Fendall St. SE1 4J 231 (48Ub 91)
(not continuous)
Fendt Cl. E16 44Hc 93
Fendyke Rd. DA17: Belv 49Zc 95
Fenelon Pl. W14 49Bb 89
Fenemore Rd. CR8: Kenley 92Tb 197
Fengate Cl. KT9: Chess 79Ma 153
Fengates Rd. RH1: Redh 6N 207
Fen Gro. DA15: Sidc 57Vc 117
Fenham Rd. SE15 52Wb 113
Fenland Ho. E5 33Yb 72
Fen La. RM14: Bulp, N Ock 36Yd 78
RM16: Ors 1B 100
SW13 53Xa 110
Fenman Ct. N17 25Xb 51
Fenman Gdns. IG3: Ilf 32Xc 75
Fen Mdw. TN15: Igh 90Yd 184
Fenn Cl. BR1: Brom 65Jc 137
Fennel Apartments SE1 1K 231
Fennel Cl. CR0: C'don 74Zb 158
E16 42Gc 93
Fennells Mead KT17: Ewe 81Va 174
Fennell St. SE18 51Qc 116
Fenner Cl. SE16 49Xb 91
Fenner Ho. E1 46Xb 91
(off Watts St.)
KT12: Hers 77W 150
Fenner Rd. RM16: Chaf H 49Yd 98
Fenners Marsh DA12: Grav'nd 10H 123
Fenner Sq. SW11 55Fb 111
Fenn Ho. TW7: Isle 53Ka 108
Fennings Rd. SW4 58Mb 112
Fenning St. SE1 1H 231 (47Ub 91)
Fennscombe Ct. GU24: W End 5C 166
Fenns La. GU24: W End 5C 166
Fenn St. E9 36Zb 72
Fenns Way GU21: Wok 87A 168
Fen Pond Cotts. TN15: Igh 90Yd 184
Fen Pond Rd. TN15: Igh, Wro 88Yd 184
Fensomes All. HP2: Hem H 1M 3
Fensomes Cl. HP2: Hem H 1M 3
Fenstanton N4 32Pb 70
(off Marquis Rd.)
Fenstanton Av. N12 23Fb 49
Fen St. E16 45Hc 93
Fens Way BR8: Hext 65Jd 140
Fenswood Cl. DA5: Bexl 58Cd 118
Fentiman Rd. SW8 51Nb 112
Fentiman Way HA2: Harr 33Da 65
RM11: Horn 32Nd 77
Fenton Av. TW18: Staines 65L 127
Fenton Cl. BR7: Chst 64Pc 138
E8 37Vb 71
RH1: Redh 6A 208
SW9 54Pb 112
Fenton House 34Eb 69
(off Hampstead Gro.)
Fenton Ho. SE14 52Ac 114
TW5: Hest 51Ca 107
Fenton Pde. SE10 50Hc 93
(off Woolwich Rd.)
Fenton Rd. N17 24Sb 51
RH1: Redh 6A 208
RM16: Chaf H 48Ae 99
Fentons Av. E13 41Kc 93
Fenton St. E1 44Xb 91
Fenwick Cl. GU21: Wok 10M 167
SE18 51Qc 116
Fenwick Gro. SE15 55Wb 113
Fenwick Path WD6: Bore 10Pa 15
Fenwick Pl. CR2: S Croy 80Rb 157
SW9 55Nb 112
Fenwick Rd. SE15 55Wb 113
Ferby Ct. DA14: Sidc 63Vc 139
(off Main Rd.)
Ferdinand Ct. SE6 59Cc 114
(off Adenmore Rd.)
Ferdinand Dr. SE15 52Ub 113
Ferdinand Ho. NW1 38Jb 70
(off Ferdinand Pl.)
Ferdinand Pl. NW1 38Jb 70
Ferdinand St. NW1 38Jb 70
Ferguson Av. DA12: Grav'nd 3E 144
KT5: Surb 71Pa 153
RM2: Rom 26Ld 57
Ferguson Cen., The E17 30Ac 52
Ferguson Cl. BR2: Brom 69Fc 137
E14 49Cc 92
Ferguson Ct. RM2: Rom 26Md 57
Ferguson Dr. W3 44Ta 87
Ferguson Gro. EN8: Chesh 1Zb 20
Fergus Rd. N5 36Rb 71
Ferial Ct. SE15 52Wb 113
(off Fenham Rd.)
Fermain Ct. E. N1 39Ub 71
(off Hertford Rd.)
Fermain Ct. Nth. N1 39Ub 71
(off De Beauvoir Est.)
Fermain Ct. W. N1 39Ub 71
(off De Beauvoir Est.)
Ferme Pk. Rd. N4 29Nb 50
N8 29Nb 50
Fermor Rd. SE23 60Ac 114
Fermoy Ho. W9 42Bb 89
(off Fermoy Rd.)
Fermoy Rd. UB6: G'frd 42Da 85
W9 42Bb 89
(not continuous)
Fern Av. CR4: Mitc 70Mb 134
Fernbank DA4: Eyns 75Pd 163
IG9: Buck H 18Kc 35
Fernbank Av. HA0: Wemb 35Ha 66
KT12: Walt T 73Aa 151
RM12: Horn 35Ld 77
Fernbank M. SW12 58Lb 112
Fernbank Rd. KT15: Add 78J 149
Fernbrook Av. DA15: Sidc 57Uc 116
Fernbrook Cres. SE13 58Gc 115
(off Leahurst Rd.)
Fernbrook Dr. HA2: Harr 31Da 65
Fernbrook Rd. SE13 57Gc 115
Ferncliff Rd. E8 36Wb 71
Fern Cl. CR6: W'ham 90Ac 178
DA8: Erith 53Kd 119
N1 1H 219 (40Ub 71)
Fern Copse KT23: Bookh 97Ba 191
Fern Ct. DA7: Bex 56Cd 118
RM5: Col R 24Cd 56
RM7: Rom 29Fd 56
SE14 54Zb 114
SS17: Stan H 1M 101
Ferncroft Av. HA4: Ruis 33Y 65
N12 23Hb 49
NW3 34Cb 69
Ferndale BR1: Brom 68Lc 137
TN13: S'oaks 94Ld 203
Ferndale Av. E17 29Fc 53
KT16: Chert 76G 148
TW4: Houn 55Aa 107
Ferndale Cl. DA7: Bex 53Ad 117
Ferndale Community Sports Cen.
55Pb 112
Ferndale Cres. SM5: Cars 74Hb 155
UB8: Cowl 41L 83
Ferndale Rd. DA12: Grav'nd 1D 144
E7 38Kc 73
E11 33Gc 73
EN3: Enf W 9Ac 20
GU21: Wok 88B 168
N15 30Vb 51
RM5: Col R 26Ed 56
SE25 71Xb 157
SM7: Bans 88Bb 175
SW4 56Nb 112
SW9 56Nb 112
TW15: Ashf 64M 127
Ferndale St. E6 45Rc 94
Ferndale Ter. HA1: Harr 28Ha 46
Ferndale Way BR6: Farnb 78Tc 160
Ferndell Av. DA5: Bexl 62Fd 140
Fern Dells AL10: Hat 1B 8
Fern Dene W13 43Ka 86
Ferndene AL2: Brick W 3Ba 13
DA3: Lfield 69Fe 143
Ferndene Rd. SE24 56Sb 113
Fernden Way RM7: Rom 30Dd 56
Ferndown HA6: Nwood 26W 44
NW1 38Mb 70
(off Camley St.)
RM11: Horn 30Pd 57
Ferndown Av. BR6: Orp 74Tc 160
Ferndown Cl. HA5: Pinn 24Aa 45
SM2: Sutt 79Fb 155
SS17: Stan H 3K 101
Ferndown Ct. UB1: S'hall 44Ea 86
(off Haldane Rd.)
Ferndown Gdns. KT11: Cobh 85Y 171
Ferndown Lodge E14 48Ec 92
(off Manchester Rd.)
Ferndown Rd. SE9 59Mc 115
WD19: Wat 21Y 45
Fern Dr. HP3: Hem H 3N 3
SL6: Tap 4A 80
Fernecroft AL1: St A 5B 6
Fernery, The TW18: Staines 64G 126
Fernes Cl. UB8: Cowl 44L 83
Ferney Ct. KT14: Byfl 83M 169
Ferney Meade Way TW7: Isle 54Ja 108
Ferney Rd. EN4: E Barn 17Jb 32
KT14: Byfl 84M 169
Fern Gro. TW14: Felt 59X 107
Ferngrove Cl. KT22: Fet 95Ga 192
Fern Hall AL10: Hat 2B 8
(off Bishops Ri.)
Fernhall Dr. IG4: Ilf 29Mc 53
Fernhall La. EN9: Walt A 3Mc 21
Fernham Rd. CR7: Thor H 69Sb 135
Fernhead Rd. W9 41Bb 89
Fernheath Way DA2: Wilm 64Fd 140
Fernhill KT22: Oxs 86Fa 172
Fernhill Cl. GU22: Wok 2N 187
Fernhill Ct. E17 26Fc 53
Fernhill Gdns. KT2: King T 64Ma 131
Fernhill La. GU22: Wok 2N 187
Fernhill Pk. GU22: Wok 2N 187
Fern Hill Pl. BR6: Farnb 78Sc 160
Fernhills WD4: Hunt C 6T 12
Fernhill St. E16 46Pc 94
Fernholme Rd. SE15 57Zb 114
Fernhurst Gdns. HA8: Edg 23Qa 47
Fernhurst Rd. CR0: C'don 73Xb 157
SW6 53Ab 110
TW15: Ashf 63S 128
Fernie Cl. IG7: Chig 22Wc 55
Fernie Way IG7: Chig 22Wc 55
Fernihough Cl. KT13: Weyb 82Q 170
Fernlands Cl. KT16: Chert 76G 148
Fern La. TW5: Hest 50Ba 85
Fernlea KT23: Bookh 96Da 191
Fernlea Pl. KT11: Cobh 83Z 171
Fernlea Rd. CR4: Mitc 68Jb 134
SW12 60Kb 112
Fernleigh Cl. CR0: Wadd 77Qb 156
KT12: Walt T 76X 151
W9 41Bb 89
Fernleigh Ct. HA2: Harr 26Da 45
HA9: Wemb 33Na 67
RM7: Rom 29Ed 56
Fernleigh Rd. N21 19Qb 32
Fernly Cl. HA5: Eastc 28W 44
Ferns, The TN15: Plat 92Ee 205
Fernsbury St. WC1 4K 217 (41Qb 90)
Ferns Cl. CR2: Sande 82Xb 177
EN3: Enf W 8Ac 20
Fernshaw Cl. SW10 51Eb 111
Fernshaw Mans. SW10 51Eb 111
(off Fernshaw Rd.)
Fernshaw Rd. SW10 51Eb 111
Fernside IG9: Buck H 18Kc 35
KT7: T Ditt 74Ka 152
NW11 33Cb 69
SL2: Slou 5M 81
Fernside Av. NW7 20Ta 29
TW13: Felt 63X 129
Fernside Ct. NW4 26Za 48
Fernside Rd. SW12 60Hb 111
Fernsleigh Cl. SL9: Chal P 23A 42
Ferns Rd. E15 37Hc 73
Fern St. E3 42Cc 92
Fernthorpe Rd. SW16 65Lb 134
Ferntower Rd. N5 36Tb 71
Fern Towers CR3: Cat'm 97Wb 197
Fernville La. HP2: Hem H 2M 3
Fern Wlk. SE16 50Wb 91
TW15: Ashf 64M 127
Fern Way WD25: Wat 7X 13
Fernways IG1: Ilf 35Rc 74
Fernwood CR0: Sels 81Ac 178
SW19 60Bb 111
Fernwood Av. HA0: Wemb 37La 66
SW16 63Mb 134
Fernwood Cl. BR1: Brom 68Lc 137
Fernwood Ct. N14 17Lb 32
Fernwood Cres. N20 20Hb 31
Fernwood Pl. KT10: Hin W 75Ha 152
Ferny Hill EN4: Had W 9Gb 17
Ferranti Cl. SE18 48Mc 93
Ferraro Cl. TW5: Hest 51Ca 107
Ferrers Av. SM6: Bedd 77Mb 156
UB7: W Dray 47M 83
Ferrers Cl. SL1: Slou 6C 80
Ferrers Rd. SW16 64Mb 134
Ferrestone Rd. N8 28Pb 50
Ferrey M. SW9 54Qb 112
Ferriby Cl. N1 38Qb 70
Ferrier Ind. Est. SW18 56Db 111
(off Ferrier St.)
Ferrier Point E16 43Jc 93
(off Forty Acre La.)
Ferrier St. SW18 56Db 111
Ferriers Way KT18: Tatt C 90Ya 174
Ferring Cl. HA2: Harr 32Ea 66
Ferrings SE21 62Ub 135
Ferris Av. CR0: C'don 76Bc 158
Ferris Rd. SE22 56Wb 113
Ferron Rd. E5 34Xb 71
Ferro Rd. RM13: Rain 42Jd 96
Ferry App. SE18 48Qc 94
Ferry Av. TW18: Staines 66G 126
Ferrybridge Ho. SE11 4J 229
Ferrydale Lodge NW4 28Ya 48
(off Parson St.)
Ferryhills Cl. WD19: Wat 20Y 27
Ferry Ho. E5 32Xb 71
(off Harrington Hill)
Ferry Island Retail Pk. N17 27Wb 51
Ferry La. KT16: Chert 72J 149
N17 28Wb 51
RM13: Rain 44Gd 96
SW13 51Va 110
TW8: Bford 51Na 109
TW9: Kew 51Pa 109
TW17: Shep 74Q 150
TW18: Lale 69L 127
TW19: Wray 61D 126
Ferry La. Ind. Est. E17 28Zb 52
RM13: Rain 43Hd 96
Ferryman's Quay SW6 54Eb 111
Ferrymead Av. UB6: G'frd 41Ca 85
Ferrymead Dr. UB6: G'frd 40Ca 65
Ferrymead Gdns. UB6: G'frd 40Ea 66
Ferrymoor TW10: Ham 62Ka 130
Ferry Pl. SE18 48Qc 94
Ferry Quays TW8: Bford 51Na 109
(Ferry La.)
TW8: Bford 52Ma 109
(off Point Wharf La.)
Ferry Rd. KT7: T Ditt 72Ka 152
KT8: W Mole 69Ca 129
RM18: Tilb 5C 122
SW13 52Wa 110
TW1: Twick 60Ka 108
TW11: Tedd 64Ka 130
Ferry Sq. TW8: Bford 52Na 109
Ferry St. E14 50Ec 92
Ferry Wharf TW8: Bford 52Na 109
Ferryby Rd. RM16: Grays 8D 100
Festing Rd. SW15 55Za 110
Festival Av. DA3: Lfield 69Fe 143
Festival Cl. DA5: Bexl 60Zc 117
DA8: Erith 52Hd 118
UB10: Hil 39R 64
Festival Ct. E8 38Vb 71
(off Holly St.)
SM1: Sutt 73Db 155
Festival Wlk. SM5: Cars 77Hb 155
Festival Way E4 23Ec 52
Festive Mans. E20 36Ec 72
(off Napa Cl.)
Festoon Way E16 45Mc 93
Festubert St. E3 40Bc 72
Festuca Ho. E20 36Ec 72
(off Mirabelle Gdns.)
FETCHAM 95Fa 192
Fetcham Comn. La. KT22: Fet 93Da 191
FETCHAM DOWNS 98Fa 192
Fetcham Pk. Dr. KT22: Fet 95Ga 192
Fetherstone Cl. EN6: Pot B 4Fb 17
Fetherstone Ct. RM6: Chad H 30Bd 55
(off High Rd.)
Fetherston Rd. SS17: Stan H 1M 101
Fetherton Ct. IG11: Bark 40Sc 74
(off Spring Pl.)
Fetter La. EC4 3A 224 (44Qb 90)
Fetter La. Apartments EC4 3K 223
(off Fetter La.)
Fettes Ho. NW8 2C 214
Fews Lodge RM6: Chad H 28Zc 55
Ffinch St. SE8 52Cc 114
FICKLESHOLE 86Fc 179
Fiddicroft Av. SM7: Bans 86Db 175
Fiddler's Cl. DA9: Ghithe 56Xd 120
FIDDLERS HAMLET 4Yc 23
Fidelis Ho. E1 1K 225
Fidgeon Cl. BR1: Brom 69Qc 138
Fidler Pl. WD23: Bush 16Da 27
Field Cl. BR1: Brom 68Lc 137
CR2: Sande 86Xb 177
E4 23Dc 52
HA4: Ruis 32S 64
IG9: Buck H 20Lc 35
KT8: W Mole 71Da 151
KT9: Chess 78La 152
NW2 33Wa 68
RM4: Abr 13Xc 37
TW4: Cran 53X 107
UB3: Harl 52S 106
UB10: Ick 33R 64
FIELDCOMMON 73Ba 151
Fieldcommon La. KT12: Walt T 74Aa 151
Field Ct. DA11: Nflt 1B 144
RH8: Oxt 99Gc 199
SW19 62Cb 133
WC1 1J 223 (43Pb 90)
Field End CR5: Coul 86Mb 176
EN5: Ark 14Xa 30
GU24: W End 5D 166
HA4: Ruis 37Y 65
UB5: N'olt 37Z 65
Fieldend TW1: Twick 63Ha 130
Fld. End Cl. WD19: Wat 17Aa 27
Fld. End M. WD19: Wat 17Aa 27
Fld. End Rd. HA4: Ruis 32Z 65
HA5: Eastc 29X 45
Fieldend Rd. SW16 67Lb 134
Fielden Ter. DA11: Nflt 60Ee 121
Fielder Apartments E3 42Bc 92
(off Heath Pl.)
Fielders Cl. EN1: Enf 14Ub 33
HA2: Harr 32Ea 66
Fielders Way WD7: Shenl 5Na 15
Fieldfare Cl. HP3: Hem H 7M 3
Fieldfare La. DA9: Ghithe 59Wd 120
Fieldfare Rd. SE28 45Yc 95
Fieldfares AL2: Lon C 9H 7
Fieldgate Ct. KT11: Cobh 86W 170
Fieldgate La. CR4: Mitc 68Gb 133
Fieldgate Mans. E1 43Wb 91
(off Fieldgate St.)
Fieldgate St. E1 43Wb 91
Field Ho. NW6 41Za 88
(off Harvist Rd.)
SM4: Mord 71Db 155
(off School Ga. Dr.)
Fieldhouse Cl. E18 25Jc 53
Fieldhouse Rd. SW12 60Lb 112
Fieldhouse Vs. SM7: Bans 87Gb 175
Fieldhurst SL3: L'ly 50B 82
Fieldhurst Cl. KT15: Add 78K 149
Fielding Av. RM18: Tilb 3D 122
TW2: Twick 62Ea 130
Fielding Ct. WC2 3F 223
Fielding Gdns. SL3: L'ly 7N 81
Fielding Ho. NW8 39Eb 69
(off Ainsworth Way)
W4 51Ua 110
(off Devonshire Rd.)
Fielding La. BR2: Brom 70Lc 137
Fielding M. SW13 51Xa 110
Fielding Rd. W4 48Ta 87
W14 48Za 88
Fieldings, The GU21: Wok 8K 167
SE23 60Yb 114
SM7: Bans 89Bb 175
Fieldings Rd. EN8: Chesh 1Bc 20
Fielding St. SE17 51Sb 113
Fielding Ter. W5 45Pa 87
Fielding Wlk. W13 48Ka 86
Fielding Way CM13: Hut 16Ee 41
Field La. TW8: Bford 52La 108
TW11: Tedd 64Ja 130
Fld. Maple M. RM5: Col R 24Cd 56
Field Mead NW7 24Ua 48
NW9 24Va 48
Fieldoaks Way RH1: Mers 1C 208
Fieldpark Gdns. CR0: C'don 74Ac 158
Field Pl. KT3: N Mald 72Va 154
Field Point E7 35Jc 73
Field Rd. E7 35Hc 73
HP2: Hem H 3A 4
N17 27Tb 51
RM15: Avel 46Sd 98
TW14: Felt 58X 107
UB9: Den 35F 62
(not continuous)
W6 50Ab 88
WD19: Wat 16Aa 27
Fields, The SL1: Slou 7H 81
Fields Ct. EN6: Pot B 5Fb 17
FIELDS END 1F 2
Flds. End La. HP1: Hem H 1F 2
Fieldsend Rd. SM3: Cheam 78Ab 154
Fields Est. E8 38Wb 71
Fieldside Cl. BR6: Farnb 77Sc 160
Fieldside Rd. BR1: Brom 64Fc 137
Fields Pk. Cres. RM6: Chad H 29Zc 55
Field St. WC1 3H 217 (41Pb 90)
Fieldsway Ho. N5 36Qb 70
Field Vw. TW13: Felt 63T 128
TW20: Egh 64E 126
Fieldview SW18 60Fb 111
Field Vw. Cl. RM7: Mawney 27Cd 56
Fieldview Cotts. N14 19Mb 32
(off Balaams La.)
Fieldview Ct. TW18: Staines 64J 127
Field Vw. Ri. AL2: Brick W 1Aa 13
Field Vw. Rd. EN6: Pot B 5Cb 17
Field Way GU23: Rip 97H 189
HA4: Ruis 32S 64
HP3: Bov 9C 2
NW10 38Sa 67
UB6: G'frd 39Da 65
UB8: Cowl 42M 83
WD3: Rick 18K 25
Fieldway BR5: Pet W 72Tc 160
CR0: New Ad 80Dc 158
HP4: Berk 3A 2
RM8: Dag 34Yc 75
RM16: Grays 46Ce 99
SL9: Chal P 24A 42
Fieldway Cres. N5 36Qb 70
Fiennes Cl. RM8: Dag 32Yc 75
Fiennes Way TN13: S'oaks 99Ld 203
Fifehead Cl. TW15: Ashf 65N 127
Fife Rd. E16 43Jc 93
KT1: King T 68Na 131
N22 24Rb 51
SW14 57Sa 109
Fife Ter. N1 1J 217 (40Pb 70)
Fife Way KT23: Bookh 97Ca 191
Fifield Path SE23 62Zb 136
Fifteenth Av. KT20: Lwr K 98Bb 195
Fifth Av. E12 35Pc 74
KT20: Lwr K 97Ab 194
RM20: W Thur 51Wd 120
UB3: Hayes 46V 84
W10 41Ab 88
WD25: Wat 7Z 13
Fifth Cross Rd. TW2: Twick 61Fa 130
Fifth Way HA9: Wemb 35Ra 67
Figges Rd. CR4: Mitc 66Jb 134
Figgswood CR5: Coul 94Lb 196
Fight for Peace Academy 46Qc 94
FIG STREET 100Jd 202
Fig St. TN14: S'oaks 100Hd 202
Fig Tree Cl. NW10 39Ua 68
Figtree Hill HP2: Hem H 1M 3
Figure Ct. SW3 50Hb 89
(off West Rd.)
Filament Wlk. SW18 57Cb 111
(off Spectrum Way)
Filanco Ct. W7 46Ha 86
Filbert Cl. AL10: Hat 3B 8
Filborough Way DA12: Grav'nd 1K 145
Filby Rd. KT9: Chess 79Pa 153
Filey Av. N16 32Wb 71
Filey Cl. SM2: Sutt 80Eb 155
TN16: Big H 91Kc 199
Filey Spur SL1: Slou 7F 80
Filey Waye HA4: Ruis 33W 64
Filigree Ct. SE16 46Bc 92
Fillebrook Av. EN1: Enf 12Ub 33
Fillebrook Rd. E11 32Fc 73

Filmer Chambers SW6 ... 53Ab 110
(off Filmer Rd.)
Filmer Ho. SW6 ... 53Bb 111
(off Filmer Rd.)
Filmer La. TN14: S'oaks ... 93Nd 203
Filmer M. SW6 ... 53Bb 111
Filmer Rd. SL4: Wind ... 4B 102
SW6 ... 53Ab 110
Filston La. TN14: Otf, S'ham ... 88Fd 182
Filston Rd. DA8: Erith ... 50Ed 96
Filton Cl. NW9 ... 25Ua 48
Filton Ct. SE14 ... 52Yb 114
(off Farrow La.)
Filton Ho. WD19: Wat ... 20Z 27
Finborough Ho. SW10 ... 51Eb 111
(off Finborough Rd.)
Finborough Rd. SW10 ... 50Db 89
SW17 ... 65Hb 133
Finborough Theatre, The ... 51Db 111
(off Finborough Rd.)
Finchale Rd. SE2 ... 48Wc 95
Fincham Cl. UB10: Ick ... 34S 64
Finch Av. SE27 ... 63Tb 135
Finch Cl. AL10: Hat ... 2C 8
EN5: Barn ... 15Cb 31
GU21: Knap ... 9G 166
NW10 ... 37Ta 67
Finch Ct. DA14: Sidc ... 62Xc 139
Finchdale HP1: Hem H ... 2J 3
Finchdean Ho. SW15 ... 59Va 110
Finch Dr. TW14: Felt ... 59Z 107
Finches, The UB9: Den ... 29H 43
Finches Av. WD3: Crox G ... 13P 25
Finch Gdns. E4 ... 22Cc 52
Finch Grn. WD3: Chor ... 14H 25
Finch Ho. E3 ... 39Bc 72
(off Jasmine Sq.)
SE8 ... 52Dc 114
(off Bronze St.)
Finchingfield Av. IG8: Wfd G ... 24Lc 53
Finch La. EC3 ... 3G 225 (44Tb 91)
WD23: Bush ... 13Ba 27
FINCHLEY ... 25Cb 49
Finchley Cl. DA1: Dart ... 58Qd 119
Finchley Ct. N3 ... 23Db 49
Finchley Golf Course ... 23Bb 49
Finchley Ind. Est. N12 ... 21Eb 49
Finchley La. NW4 ... 28Ya 48
Finchley Lido ... 24Fb 49
Finchley Manor Club ... 25Bb 49
Finchley Pk. N12 ... 21Eb 49
Finchley Pl. NW8 ... 1B 214 (40Fb 69)
Finchley Rd. NW2 ... 28Bb 49
NW3 ... 35Cb 69
NW8 ... 1B 214 (39Fb 69)
NW11 ... 28Bb 49
RM17: Grays ... 51De 121
Finchley Way N3 ... 24Cb 49
Finch Lodge W9 ... 43Cb 89
(off Admiral Wlk.)
Finch M. SE15 ... 53Vb 113
Finch's Ct. E14 ... 45Dc 92
Finch's Ct. M. E14 ... 45Dc 92
(off Finch's Ct.)
Finden Rd. E7 ... 36Lc 73
Findhorn Av. UB4: Yead ... 43X 85
Findhorn St. E14 ... 44Ec 92
Findlay Ho. E3 ... 41Cc 92
(off Trevithick Way)
Findon Cl. HA2: Harr ... 34Da 65
SW18 ... 58Cb 111
Findon Ct. KT15: Add ... 78H 149
Findon Gdns. RM13: Rain ... 43Jd 96
Findon Rd. N9 ... 18Xb 33
W12 ... 47Wa 88
Fine Bush La. UB9: Hare ... 30R 44
Fingal St. SE10 ... 50Hc 93
Fingest Ho. NW8 ... 5D 214
Finglesham Cl. BR5: Orp ... 74Zc 161
Finians Cl. UB10: Uxb ... 38P 63
Finland Rd. SE4 ... 55Ac 114
Finland St. SE16 ... 48Ac 92
Finlay Gdns. KT15: Add ... 77L 149
Finlays Cl. KT9: Chess ... 78Qa 153
Finlay St. SW6 ... 53Za 110
Finley Ct. SE5 ... 52Sb 113
(off Redcar St.)
Finmere Ho. N4 ... 31Sb 71
Finnart Cl. KT13: Weyb ... 77S 150
Finnart Ho. Dr. KT13: Weyb ... 77S 150
Finnemore Ho. N1 ... 39Sb 71
(off Britannia Row)
Finney Dr. GU20: W'sham ... 9B 146
Finney La. TW7: Isle ... 53Ja 108
Finn Ho. N1 ... 3G 219
Finnis St. E2 ... 41Xb 91
Finnymore Rd. RM9: Dag ... 38Ad 75
FINSBURY ... 4A 218 (41Qb 90)
Finsbury Av. EC2 ... 1G 225 (43Tb 91)
Finsbury Av. Sq. EC2 ... 7H 219 (43Ub 91)
Finsbury Cir. EC2 ... 1G 225 (43Tb 91)
Finsbury Cotts. N22 ... 24Nb 50
Finsbury Ct. EN8: Walt C ... 6Ac 20
Finsbury Est. EC1 ... 4B 218 (41Qb 90)
Finsbury Ho. N22 ... 25Nb 50
Finsbury Leisure Cen. ... 5D 218 (41Sb 91)
Finsbury Mkt. EC2 ... 6H 219 (42Ub 91)
(not continuous)
FINSBURY PARK ... 32Qb 70
Finsbury Pk. Av. N4 ... 30Sb 51
Finsbury Pk. Rd. N4 ... 33Rb 71
Finsbury Pavement EC2 ... 7G 219 (43Tb 91)
Finsbury Rd. N22 ... 24Pb 50
(not continuous)
Finsbury Sq. EC2 ... 6G 219 (42Tb 91)
Finsbury St. EC2 ... 7F 219 (43Tb 91)
Finsbury Way DA5: Bexl ... 58Bd 117
Finsen Rd. SE5 ... 56Sb 113
Finstock Rd. W10 ... 44Za 88
Finucane Ct. TW9: Rich ... 55Pa 109
(off Lwr. Mortlake Rd.)
Finucane Dr. BR5: Orp ... 73Yc 161
Finucane Gdns. RM13: Rain ... 37Jd 76
Finucane Ri. WD23: B Hea ... 19Ea 28
Finway Ct. WD18: Wat ... 15V 26
Finwhale Ho. E14 ... 48Dc 92
(off Glengall Gro.)
Fiona Cl. KT23: Bookh ... 96Ca 191
Fiona Ct. EN2: Enf ... 13Rb 33
NW6 ... 40Cb 69
Firbank Cl. E16 ... 43Mc 93
EN2: Enf ... 14Sb 33
Firbank Dr. GU21: Wok ... 1M 187
WD19: Wat ... 17Aa 27
Firbank La. GU21: Wok ... 1M 187
Firbank Pl. TW20: Eng G ... 5M 125
Firbank Rd. RM5: Col R ... 22Ed 56
SE15 ... 54Xb 113
Fir Cl. KT12: Walt T ... 73W 150
Fircroft Cl. GU22: Wok ... 90B 168
SL2: Stoke P ... 7L 61
Fircroft Ct. GU22: Wok ... 90B 168
Fircroft Gdns. HA1: Harr ... 34Ga 66
Fircroft Rd. KT9: Chess ... 77Pa 153
SW17 ... 61Hb 133
TW20: Eng G ... 6N 125
Fir Dene BR6: Farnb ... 76Pc 160
Firdene KT5: Surb ... 74Sa 153
Fireball Hill SL5: S'dale ... 3B 146
Fire Bell All. KT6: Surb ... 72Na 153
Firecrest Cl. DA3: Lfield ... 69De 143
Firecrest Dr. NW3 ... 34Db 69
Firefly Cl. UB3: Hayes ... 45V 84
UB5: N'olt ... 41Z 85
Firefly Gdns. E6 ... 42Nc 94
Firefly Rd. KT16: Vir W ... 5L 147
Firehorn Ho. E15 ... 41Gc 93
(off Teasel Way)
Firemans Flats N22 ... 24Nb 50
Firepower (The Royal Artillery Mus.) ... 48Rc 94
Fire Station All. EN5: Barn ... 13Ab 30
Firestation Cen. for Arts & Culture, The Windsor ... 4G 102
Fire Station M. BR3: Beck ... 67Cc 136
Firestone Ho. TW8: Bford ... 50Na 87
Firethorn Cl. HA8: Edg ... 21Sa 47
Firewatch Ct. E1 ... 43Ac 92
(off Candle St.)
Firfield Rd. KT15: Add ... 77J 149
Firfields KT13: Weyb ... 79R 150
Fir Grange Av. KT13: Weyb ... 78R 150
Fir Gro. KT3: N Mald ... 72Va 154
Firgrove GU21: Wok ... 1M 187
Firgrove Ct. SE6 ... 59Cc 114
Fir Gro. Rd. SW9 ... 54Qb 112
Firham Pk. Av. RM3: Hrld W ... 24Qd 57
Firhill Rd. SE6 ... 63Cc 136
Fir Ho. W10 ... 42Ab 88
(off Droop St.)
Firlands KT13: Weyb ... 79U 150
Firle Ct. KT17: Eps ... 84Va 174
Firle Ho. W10 ... 43Ya 88
(off Sutton Way)
Firman Cl. KT3: N Mald ... 70Ua 132
Firmans Ct. E17 ... 28Fc 53
Firmingers Rd. BR6: Well H ... 78Dd 162
Firmin Rd. DA1: Dart ... 57Ld 119
Fir Rd. SM3: Sutt ... 74Bb 155
TW13: Hanw ... 64Z 129
Firs, The AL1: St A ... 6F 6
CM15: Pil H ... 16Wd 40
CR3: Cat'm ... 94Tb 197
DA5: Bexl ... 60Fd 118
DA15: Sidc ... 61Vc 139
E6 ... 38Nc 74
EN9: Walt A ... 7Lc 21
(within Woodbine Cl. Caravan Pk.)
GU24: Bisl ... 8E 166
HA8: Edg ... 21Ta 47
(off Stoneyfields La.)
IG8: Wfd G ... 24Lc 53
KT14: Byfl ... 84M 169
KT23: Bookh ... 96Ea 192
N20 ... 18Fb 31
RM16: Grays ... 46Ee 99
SE26 ... 64Xb 135
(Border Rd.)
SE26 ... 64Yb 136
(Waverley Ct.)
W5 ... 43Ma 87
Firs Av. N10 ... 27Jb 50
N11 ... 23Hb 49
SL4: Wind ... 5D 102
SW14 ... 56Sa 109
Firsby Av. CR0: C'don ... 74Zb 158
Firsby Rd. N16 ... 32Wb 71
Firs Cl. AL10: Hat ... 1D 8
CR4: Mitc ... 68Kb 134
KT10: Clay ... 79Ga 152
N10 ... 28Jb 50
SE23 ... 59Ac 114
SL0: Iver H ... 39E 62
Firscroft N13 ... 20Sb 33
Firsdene Cl. KT16: Ott ... 79F 148
Firs Dr. IG10: Lough ... 11Qc 36
SL3: L'ly ... 46B 82
TW5: Cran ... 52X 107
Firs End SL9: Chal P ... 27A 42
Firsgrove Cres. CM14: W'ley ... 21Xd 58
Firsgrove Rd. CM14: W'ley ... 21Xd 58
Firs Ho. N22 ... 25Qb 50
(off Acacia Rd.)
Firside Gro. DA15: Sidc ... 60Vc 117
Firs La. EN6: Pot B ... 5Db 17
N13 ... 20Sb 33
N21 ... 17Sb 33
Firs Pk., The AL9: Hat ... 5J 9
Firs Pk. Av. N21 ... 18Tb 33
Firs Pk. Gdns. N21 ... 18Sb 33
Firs Rd. CR8: Kenley ... 87Rb 177
First Av. DA7: Bex ... 52Yc 117
DA11: Nflt ... 10A 122
E12 ... 35Nc 74
E13 ... 41Jc 93
E17 ... 29Cc 52
EN1: Enf ... 15Vb 33
EN9: Walt A ... 1Kc 21
HA9: Wemb ... 33Ma 67
KT8: W Mole ... 70Ba 129
KT12: Walt T ... 72X 151
KT19: Ewe ... 81Ua 174
KT20: Lwr K ... 97Ab 194
N18 ... 21Yb 52
NW4 ... 28Ya 48
RM6: Chad H ... 29Yc 55
RM10: Dag ... 40Dd 76
RM20: W Thur ... 51Wd 120
SS17: Stan H ... 1M 101
SW14 ... 55Ua 110
UB3: Hayes ... 46V 84
W3 ... 46Va 88
W10 ... 42Bb 89
WD25: Wat ... 7Y 13
First Central Bus. Pk. NW10 ... 41Pa 87
First Cl. KT8: W Mole ... 69Ea 130
First Cres. SL1: Slou ... 3G 80
First Cross Rd. TW2: Twick ... 61Ga 130
First Dr. NW10 ... 38Sa 67
First Quarter KT19: Eps ... 83Ua 174
First Slip KT22: Lea ... 90Ja 172
First St. SW3 ... 5E 226 (49Gb 89)
First Way HA9: Wemb ... 35Ra 67
Firstway SW20 ... 68Ya 132
Firs Wlk. HA6: Nwood ... 23T 44
IG8: Wfd G ... 22Jc 53
Firswood Av. KT19: Ewe ... 78Ua 154
Firs Wood Cl. EN6: N'thaw ... 4Hb 17
Firth Gdns. SW6 ... 53Ab 110
Firth Ho. E2 ... 41Wb 91
(off Turin St.)
Fir Tree Av. SL2: Stoke P ... 2K 81
UB7: W Dray ... 48O 84
Firtree Av. CR4: Mitc ... 68Jb 134
Fir Tree Cl. BR6: Chels ... 78Vc 161
HP3: Hem H ... 3A 4
KT10: Esh ... 78Ea 152
KT17: Eps D ... 87Ya 174
KT19: Ewe ... 77Va 154
KT22: Lea ... 95La 192
RM1: Rom ... 27Fd 56
RM17: Grays ... 51Fe 121
SW16 ... 64Lb 134
W5 ... 44Na 87
Fir Tree Ct. WD6: E'tree ... 14Pa 29
Fir Tree Gdns. CR0: C'don ... 77Cc 158
Fir Tree Gro. SM5: Cars ... 80Hb 155
Fir Tree Hill WD3: Chan C ... 10P 11
Firtree Ho. SE13 ... 59Fc 115
(off Birdwood Av.)
Fir Tree Pl. TW15: Ashf ... 64Q 128
Fir Tree Rd. KT17: Eps D ... 88Xa 174
KT22: Lea ... 95La 192
SM7: Bans ... 86Ya 174
TW4: Houn ... 56Aa 107
Fir Trees CM16: Epp ... 1Xc 23
RM4: Abr ... 13Xc 37
Fir Trees Cl. SE16 ... 46Ac 92
Fir Tree Wlk. EN1: Enf ... 13Tb 33
RH2: Reig ... 6M 207
RM10: Dag ... 34Ed 76
Fir Wlk. SM3: Cheam ... 79Za 154
Firwood Av. AL4: St A ... 2J 7
Firwood Cl. GU21: Wok ... 1J 187
Firwood La. RM3: Hrld W ... 26Nd 57
Firwood Rd. GU25: Vir W ... 2J 147
Fisgard Ct. DA12: Grav'nd ... 8F 122
Fisher Cl. CR0: C'don ... 74Vb 157
E9 ... 36Zb 72
EN3: Enf L ... 9Dc 20
KT12: Hers ... 77X 151
SE16 ... 46Zb 92
UB6: G'frd ... 41Ca 85
WD4: K Lan ... 1Q 12
Fisher Ho. E1 ... 45Yb 92
(off Cable St.)
N1 ... 1K 217
Fisherman KT16: Chert ... 74L 149
Fisherman Cl. TW10: Ham ... 63Ka 130
Fishermans Dr. SE16 ... 47Zb 92
Fisherman's Pl. W4 ... 51Va 110
Fisherman's Wlk. E14 ... 46Cc 92
Fishermans Wlk. SE28 ... 47Uc 94
Fishermens Hill DA11: Nflt ... 57De 121
Fisher Rd. HA3: W'stone ... 26Ha 46
Fisher's Cl. SW16 ... 62Mb 134
Fishers Cl. EN8: Walt C ... 6Cc 20
WD23: Bush ... 13Aa 27
Fishers Ct. SE14 ... 53Zb 114
Fishersdene KT10: Clay ... 80Ja 152
FISHERS GREEN ... 1Dc 20
Fishers Grn. La. EN9: Walt A ... 1Dc 20
Fisher's Ind. Est. WD18: Wat ... 15Y 27
Fisher's La. W4 ... 49Ta 87
Fishers La. CM16: Epp ... 4Uc 22
Fishers Oak TN14: S'oaks ... 93Ld 203
Fisher St. E16 ... 43Jc 93
WC1 ... 1H 223 (43Pb 90)
Fishers Way DA17: Belv ... 46Ed 96
HA0: Wemb ... 36Ka 66
Fishers Wood SL5: S'dale ... 4G 146
Fisherton St. NW8 ... 6B 214 (42Fb 89)
Fishery Cotts. HP1: Hem H ... 4J 3
Fishery Pas. HP1: Hem H ... 4J 3
Fishery Rd. HP1: Hem H ... 4J 3
Fishguard Spur SL1: Slou ... 7M 81
Fishguard Way E16 ... 46Rc 94
Fishing Temple Pk. Homes TW18: Staines ... 67H 127
Fishmongers Hall Wharf EC4 ... 5G 225
Fishponds Rd. BR2: Kes ... 78Mc 159
SW17 ... 63Gb 133
Fishpool St. AL3: St A ... 2P 5
Fish St. Hill EC3 ... 5G 225 (45Tb 91)
Fish Wharf EC3 ... 5G 225 (45Tb 91)
Fisk Cl. TW16: Sun ... 65V 128
Fiske Ct. IG11: Bark ... 40Tc 74
N17 ... 25Wb 51
SM2: Sutt ... 80Eb 155
Fit4less
Tower Hill ... 4K 225
Fitch Ct. SW2 ... 57Qb 112
Fitness4Less
Canning Town ... 43Gc 93
Sutton ... 79Cb 155
Fitness First
America Square ... 4K 225
Angel ... 2B 218 (40Rb 71)
Baker Street ... 1G 221 (43Hb 89)
Beckenham ... 68Dc 136
Berkeley Square ... 5A 222 (45Kb 90)
Bloomsbury ... 6F 217
Brentwood ... 19Yd 40
(within The Baytree Centre)
Brixton ... 55Qb 112
Camden ... 39Kb 70
Chancery Lane ... 2A 224
Clapham Junction ... 56Gb 111
Covent Garden ... 5G 223
Fetter Lane ... 2A 224
Gracechurch Street ... 4H 225
Great Marlborough Street ... 3B 222
Hammersmith ... 49Ya 88
Harrow ... 30Ga 46
(within St George's Shop. & Leisure Cen.)
Highbury ... 34Rb 71
High Holborn ... 2H 223
Ilford ... 33Sc 74
Kilburn ... 39Bb 69
Kingly Street ... 4B 222
Kingsbury ... 29Qa 47
Leyton Mills ... 34Ec 72
London Bridge ... 7G 225
(off London Bri. St.)
North Finchley ... 22Eb 49
Paternoster Square ... 2C 224
Pinner ... 27Z 45
Queen Victoria Street ... 4D 224
Romford ... 30Gd 56
St Albans ... 2B 6
(off Verulam Rd.)
Fitness First
South Kensington ... 5B 226
Streatham ... 61Nb 134
Thomas More Square ... 45Wb 91
(off Thomas More Sq.)
Tooting Bec ... 62Jb 134
Victoria ... 3B 228
Walworth Road ... 50Sb 91
Wembley ... 36Na 67
FitSpace Gym ... 48Rc 94
Fittleton Gdns. E3 ... 42Cc 92
Fitzalan Ho. KT17: Ewe ... 82Va 174
Fitzalan Rd. KT10: Clay ... 80Ga 152
N3 ... 27Ab 48
Fitzalan St. SE11 ... 5J 229 (49Qb 90)
Fitzclarence Ho. W11 ... 47Ab 88
(off Holland Park Av.)
Fitzgeorge Av. KT3: N Mald ... 67Ta 131
W14 ... 49Ab 88
Fitzgerald Av. SW14 ... 55Ua 110
Fitzgerald Ct. E10 ... 32Dc 72
(off Leyton Grange Est.)
Fitzgerald Ho. E14 ... 44Dc 92
(off E. India Dock Rd.)
SW9 ... 54Qb 112
SW17 ... 62Fb 133
UB3: Hayes ... 46X 85
Fitzgerald Rd. E11 ... 29Jc 53
KT7: T Ditt ... 72Ja 152
SW14 ... 55Ta 109
Fitzhardinge Ho. W1 ... 2H 221
Fitzhardinge St. W1 ... 2H 221 (44Jb 90)
Fitzherbert Cl. IG5: Ilf ... 25Nc 54
Fitzherbert Wlk. UB1: S'hall ... 47Fa 86
Fitzhugh Gro. SW18 ... 58Fb 111
Fitzilian Av. RM3: Hrld W ... 25Pd 57
Fitzjames Av. CR0: C'don ... 75Wb 157
W14 ... 49Ab 88
Fitzjohn Av. EN5: Barn ... 15Ab 30
Fitzjohn's Av. NW3 ... 35Eb 69
Fitzmaurice Ho. SE16 ... 49Xb 91
(off Rennie Est.)
Fitzmaurice Pl. W1 ... 6A 222 (46Kb 90)
Fitzneal St. W12 ... 44Va 88
Fitzpatrick Rd. SW9 ... 53Rb 113
Fitzrobert Pl. TW20: Egh ... 65C 126
FITZROVIA ... 7A 216
Fitzrovia Apartments W1 ... 6A 216
Fitzroy Bri. NW1 ... 39Jb 70
Fitzroy Bus. Pk. BR5: St P ... 66Zc 139
Fitzroy Cl. N6 ... 32Hb 69
Fitzroy Ct. CR0: C'don ... 73Tb 157
DA1: Dart ... 60Rd 119
(off Churchill Cl.)
N6 ... 30Lb 50
W1 ... 6C 216
Fitzroy Cres. W4 ... 52Ta 109
Fitzroy Gdns. SE19 ... 66Ub 135
Fitzroy Ho. E14 ... 43Bc 92
(off Wallwood St.)
SE1 ... 50Vb 91
(off Cooper's Rd.)
Fitzroy House Mus. ... 6B 216 (42Lb 90)
Fitzroy M. W1 ... 6B 216
Fitzroy Pk. N6 ... 32Hb 69
Fitzroy Pl. RH2: Reig ... 6M 207
Fitzroy Rd. NW1 ... 39Jb 70
Fitzroy Sq. W1 ... 6B 216 (42Lb 90)
Fitzroy St. W1 ... 6B 216 (42Lb 90)
(not continuous)
Fitzroy Yd. NW1 ... 39Jb 70
Fitzstephen Rd. RM8: Dag ... 36Xc 75
Fitzwarren Gdns. N19 ... 32Lb 70
Fitzwilliam Av. TW9: Rich ... 54Pa 109
Fitzwilliam Cl. N20 ... 18Jb 32
Fitzwilliam Ct. AL1: St A ... 2C 6
(off St Peter's St.)
WD6: Bore ... 11Pa 29
(off Lyndhurst Wlk.)
Fitzwilliam Hgts. SE23 ... 61Yb 136
Fitzwilliam Ho. TW9: Rich ... 56Ma 109
Fitzwilliam M. E16 ... 46Jc 93
Fitzwilliam Rd. SW4 ... 55Lb 112
Fitz Wygram Cl. TW12: Hamp H ... 64Ea 130
Five Acre NW9 ... 26Va 48
Fiveacre Cl. CR7: Thor H ... 72Qb 156
Five Acres AL2: Lon C ... 7H 7
WD4: K Lan ... 1P 11
Five Acres Av. AL2: Brick W ... 1Ba 13
Five Arches Bus. Pk. DA14: Sidc ... 64Zc 139
Five Ash Rd. DA11: Grav'nd ... 9B 122
Five Bell All. E14 ... 44Bc 92
(off Three Colt St.)
Five Elms BR2: Hayes ... 76Kc 159
Five Elms Rd. BR2: Hayes ... 76Kc 159
RM9: Dag ... 34Bd 75
Five Flds. Cl. WD19: Wat ... 19Ba 27
Five Oaks AL10: Hat ... 3D 8
(off Sandifield)
Five Oaks Cl. GU21: Wok ... 1H 187
Five Oaks La. IG7: Chig ... 23Ad 55
Five Oaks M. BR1: Brom ... 62Jc 137
Fives Ct. SE11 ... 4B 230 (48Rb 91)
FIVEWAYS ... 61Rc 138
Five Ways Bus. Cen. TW13: Felt ... 62X 129
FIVEWAYS CORNER
Croydon ... 77Qb 156
Hendon ... 25Wa 48
Fiveways Rd. SW9 ... 54Qb 112
Five Wents BR8: Swan ... 68Jd 140
Flack Ct. E10 ... 31Dc 72
Fladbury Rd. N15 ... 30Tb 51
Fladgate Rd. E11 ... 30Gc 53
Flag Cl. CR0: C'don ... 74Zb 158
Flagon Ct. CR0: C'don ... 77Sb 157
(off St Andrew's Rd.)
Flags, The HP2: Hem H ... 2B 4
Flagstaff Cl. EN9: Walt A ... 5Dc 20
Flagstaff Rd. EN9: Walt A ... 5Dc 20
Flag Wlk. HA5: Eastc ... 30W 44
Flambard Rd. HA1: Harr ... 30Ja 46
Flamborough Cl. TN16: Big H ... 91Kc 199
Flamborough Ho. SE15 ... 53Wb 113
(off Clayton Rd.)
Flamborough Rd. HA4: Ruis ... 34W 64
Flamborough Spur SL1: Slou ... 7E 80
Flamborough St. E14 ... 44Ac 92
Flamborough Wlk. E14 ... 44Ac 92
(off Flamborough St.)
Flamingo Ct. SE8 ... 52Cc 114
(off Hamilton St.)
SE17 ... 7D 230
Flamingo Gdns. UB5: N'olt ... 41Aa 85
Flamingo Wlk. RM12: Horn ... 37Jd 76
Flamstead End Rd. EN8: Chesh ... 1Xb 19
Flamstead Gdns. RM9: Dag ... 38Yc 75
Flamstead Ho. SW3 ... 7D 226
(off Cale St.)
Flamstead Rd. RM9: Dag ... 38Yc 75
Flamsted Av. HA9: Wemb ... 37Qa 67
Flamsteed Rd. SE7 ... 50Nc 94
Flanaghan Apartments E3 ... 42Bc 92
(off Portia Way)
Flanchford Ho. RH2: Reig ... 5J 207
(off Somers Cl.)
Flanchford Rd. RH2: Leigh, Reig ... 10E 206
W12 ... 48Va 88
Flanders Ct. DA1: Dart ... 57Md 119
E17 ... 31Ac 72
TW20: Egh ... 64E 126
Flanders Cres. SW17 ... 66Hb 133
Flanders Mans. W4 ... 49Va 88
Flanders Rd. E6 ... 40Pc 74
W4 ... 49Ua 88
Flanders Way E9 ... 37Zb 72
Flandrian Cl. EN3: Enf L ... 10Dc 20
Flank St. E1 ... 45Wb 91
Flannery Ct. SE16 ... 48Xb 91
Flansham Ho. E14 ... 44Bc 92
(off Clemence St.)
Flash La. EN2: Enf ... 9Rb 19
Flask Wlk. NW3 ... 35Eb 69
Flatfield Rd. HP3: Hem H ... 4A 4
Flatford Ho. SE6 ... 63Ec 136
Flather Cl. SW16 ... 64Lb 134
Flat Iron Sq. SE1 ... 7E 224
Flatiron Yd. SE1 ... 7E 224
Flats, The DA9: Ghithe ... 57Yd 120
HP8: Chal G ... 15A 24
FLAUNDEN ... 4D 10
Flaunden Bottom HP5: Lat ... 9A 10
Flaunden Hill HP3: Flau ... 5B 10
Flaunden Ho. WD18: Wat ... 16U 26
Flaunden La. HP3: Bov, Flau, Hem H ... 4D 10
WD3: Sarr ... 5G 10
Flaunden Pk. HP3: Flau ... 3C 10
Flavell M. SE10 ... 50Gc 93
Flavian Cl. AL3: St A ... 4M 5
Flaxen Cl. E4 ... 20Dc 34
Flaxen Rd. E4 ... 20Dc 34
Flaxley Ho. SW1 ... 7K 227
Flaxley Rd. SM4: Mord ... 73Db 155
Flaxman Ct. DA17: Belv ... 50Cd 96
(off Hoddesdon Rd.)
W1 ... 3D 222 (44Mb 90)
WC1 ... 4E 216
Flaxman Ho. SE1 ... 3B 230
W4 ... 50Ua 88
(off Devonshire St.)
Flaxman Rd. SE5 ... 55Rb 113
Flaxman Sports Cen. ... 55Sb 113
Flaxman Ter. WC1 ... 4E 216 (41Mb 90)
Flaxton Rd. SE18 ... 53Tc 116
Flecker Cl. HA7: Stan ... 22Ha 46
Flecker Ho. SE5 ... 52Tb 113
(off Lomond Gro.)
Fleece Dr. N9 ... 21Wb 51
Fleece Rd. KT6: Surb ... 74La 152
Fleece Wlk. N7 ... 37Nb 70
Fleeming Cl. E17 ... 26Bc 52
Fleeming Rd. E17 ... 26Bc 52
Fleet Av. DA2: Dart ... 60Sd 120
RM14: Upm ... 30Td 58
Fleetbank Ho. EC4 ... 3A 224
Fleetbrook Ho. SL3: Dat ... 3P 103
Fleet Cl. HA4: Ruis ... 30S 44
KT8: W Mole ... 71Ba 151
RM14: Upm ... 30Td 58
Fleetdale Pde. DA2: Dart ... 60Sd 120
FLEET DOWNS ... 60Sd 120
Fleetfield WC1 ... 3G 217
Fleethall Gro. RM16: Grays ... 46Ce 99
Fleet Ho. E14 ... 45Ac 92
(off Victory Pl.)
Fleet Ho's. DA13: Sflt ... 65De 143
Fleet La. KT8: W Mole ... 72Ba 151
Fleet Pl. EC4 ... 2B 224 (44Rb 91)
Fleet Rd. DA2: Dart ... 60Rd 119
DA11: Nflt ... 62Ee 143
IG11: Bark ... 39Rc 74
NW3 ... 36Gb 69
Fleetside KT8: W Mole ... 71Ba 151
Fleet Sq. WC1 ... 4J 217 (41Pb 90)
Fleet St. EC4 ... 3K 223 (44Qb 90)
Fleet Ter. DA11: Nflt ... 60Fe 121
FLEETVILLE ... 2F 6
Fleetway TW20: Thorpe ... 69E 126
WC1 ... 3G 217
Fleetway W. UB6: G'frd ... 40Ka 66
Fleetwood Cl. CR0: C'don ... 76Vb 157
E16 ... 43Mc 93
KT9: Chess ... 80Ma 153
KT20: Tad ... 92Za 194
Fleetwood Ct. E6 ... 43Pc 94
(off Evelyn Dennington Rd.)
KT14: W Byf ... 85J 169
TW19: Stanw ... 58M 105
(off Douglas Rd.)
Fleetwood Rd. KT1: King T ... 69Ra 131
NW10 ... 36Wa 68
SL2: Slou ... 6K 81
Fleetwood Sq. KT1: King T ... 69Ra 131
Fleetwood St. N16 ... 33Ub 71
Fleetwood Way WD19: Wat ... 21Y 45
Fleming N8 ... 27Nb 50
(off Boyton Cl.)
Fleming Cl. SW10 ... 51Eb 111
(off Winterton Pl.)
W9 ... 42Cb 89
Fleming Collection, The ... 45Kb 90
(off Berkeley St.)
Fleming Ct. CR0: Wadd ... 78Qb 156
DA11: Nflt ... 60Ee 121
W2 ... 7B 214
Fleming Dr. N21 ... 15Pb 32
Fleming Gdns. RM3: Hrld W ... 26Md 57
RM18: Tilb ... 3E 122
Fleming Ho. HA9: Wemb ... 34Sa 67
(off Barnhill Rd.)
N4 ... 32Sb 71
SE16 ... 47Wb 91
(off George Row)
SW17 ... 62Fb 133
Fleming Lodge W9 ... 43Cb 89
(off Admiral Wlk.)
Fleming Mead CR4: Mitc ... 66Gb 133
Fleming Rd. EN9: Walt A ... 7Dc 20
RM16: Chaf H ... 49Yd 98
SE17 ... 51Rb 113
UB1: S'hall ... 44Da 85
Flemings CM13: Gt War ... 23Yd 58
Fleming Wlk. NW9 ... 27Ua 48
Fleming Way SE28 ... 45Zc 95
TW7: Isle ... 56Ha 108
Flemish Flds. KT16: Chert ... 73J 149
Flemming Av. HA4: Ruis ... 32X 65

Flempton Rd.—Fosbury M.

Flempton Rd. E10 .32Ac 72
Fletcher Bldgs. WC2 .3G 223
Fletcher Cl. E6 .44Rc 94
GU21: Wok .10K 167
(off Robin Hood Rd.)
KT16: Ott .79G 148
Fletcher Ct. NW9 .27Ua 48
Fletcher Ho. N1 .1J 219
SE15 .52Yb 114
(off Clifton Way)
Fletcher La. E10 .31Ec 72
Fletcher Path SE8 .52Cc 114
Fletcher Rd. IG7: Chig .22Vc 55
KT16: Ott .79F 148
W4 .48Sa 87
Fletchers Cl. BR2: Brom .70Kc 137
Fletcher St. E1 .45Wb 91
Fletcher Way HP2: Hem H .1L 3
Fletching Rd. E5 .34Yb 72
SE7 .51Lc 115
Flete Ho. WD18: Wat .16U 26
Fletton Rd. N11 .24Nb 50
Fleur de Lis St. E1 .6J 219 (42Vb 91)
Fleur Gates SW19 .59Za 110
Flexlands La. GU24: Chob .2F 166
Flexmere Gdns. N17 .25Tb 51
Flexmere Rd. N17 .25Tb 51
Flight App. NW9 .26Va 48
Flight Ho. N1 .1H 219
Flimwell Cl. BR1: Brom .64Gc 137
Flinders Cl. AL1: St A .4E 6
Flinders Ho. E1 .46Xb 91
(off Green Bank)
Flint Cl. BR6: Chels .79Vc 161
CR0: C'don .72Pb 156
E15 .38Hc 73
KT23: Bookh .98Ea 192
RH1: Redh .5P 207
SM7: Bans .86Db 175
Flint Cotts. KT22: Lea .93Ka 192
(off Gravel Hill)
Flint Down Cl. BR5: St P .67Wc 139
Flintlock Cl. TW19: Stanw M .56J 105
Flintlock St. E1 .44Xb 91
Flintmill Cres. SE3 .54Nc 116
Flinton St. SE17 .7J 231 (50Ub 91)
Flint St. RM20: W Thur .51Xd 120
SE17 .6G 231 (49Tb 91)
Flitcroft St. WC2 .2E 222 (44Mb 90)
Flitton Ho. N1 .38Rb 71
(off The Sutton Est.)
Floathaven Cl. SE28 .46Wc 95
Floats, The TN13: Riv .93Gd 202
Flock Mill Pl. SW18 .60Db 111
Flockton Ho. KT13: Weyb .75Q 150
Flockton St. SE16 .47Wb 91
Flodden Rd. SE5 .53Sb 113
Flood La. TW1: Twick .60Ja 108
Flood Pas. SE18 .48Nc 94
Flood St. SW3 .7E 226 (50Gb 89)
Flood Wlk. SW3 .51Gb 111
Flora Cl. E14 .44Dc 92
HA7: Stan .20Na 29
Flora Gdns. CR0: New Ad .83Ec 178
RM6: Chad H .30Yc 55
W6 .49Xa 88
(off Albion Gdns.)
Flora Gro. AL1: St A .3D 6
Flora Ho. E3 .39Cc 72
(off Garrison Rd.)
Floral Ct. KT21: Asht .90La 172
Floral Dr. AL2: Lon C .8H 7
Floral Ho. KT16: Chert .74H 149
(off Fox La. Sth.)
Floral Pl. N1 .36Tb 71
Floral St. WC2 .4F 223 (45Nb 90)
Flora Rd. WD23: Bush .13Z 27
Flora St. DA17: Belv .50Bd 95
Florence Av. EN2: Enf .13Sb 33
KT15: New H .83J 169
SM4: Mord .71Eb 155
Florence Cantwell Wlk. N19 .31Nb 70
(off Jessie Blythe La.)
Florence Cl. KT2: King T .64Pa 131
KT12: Walt T .73X 151
RM12: Horn .33Nd 77
RM20: Grays .51Ae 121
WD25: Wat .7W 12
Florence Ct. AL1: St A .2C 6
(off Alma Rd.)
E11 .28Kc 53
GU21: Knap .10G 166
N1 .38Rb 71
(off Florence St.)
SW19 .65Ab 132
W9 .4A 214
Florence Dr. EN2: Enf .13Sb 33
Florence Elson Cl. E12 .35Qc 74
Florence Farm Mobile Home Pk.
TN15: W King .79Td 164
Florence Gdns. RM6: Chad H .31Yc 75
TW18: Staines .66K 127
W4 .51Sa 109
Florence Ho. KT2: King T .66Pa 131
(off Florence Rd)
SE16 .50Xb 91
(off Rotherhithe New Rd.)
W11 .45Za 88
(off St Ann's Rd.)
WD18: Wat .14U 26
Florence Longman Ho.
HP3: Hem H .6M 3
(off Weymouth St.)
Florence Mans. NW4 .29Xa 48
(off Vivian Av.)
SW6 .53Bb 111
(off Rostrevor Rd.)
Florence M. SL3: L'ly .10N 81
Florence Nightingale Mus.
.2H 229 (47Pb 90)
Florence Rd. BR1: Brom .67Jc 137
BR3: Beck .68Ac 136
CR2: Sande .81Tb 177
E6 .39Lc 73
E13 .40Jc 73
KT2: King T .66Pa 131
KT12: Walt T .73X 151
N4 .31Pb 70
(not continuous)
SE2 .49Yc 95
SE14 .53Bc 114
SW19 .65Db 133
TW13: Felt .60X 107
UB2: S'hall .49Z 85
W4 .48Ta 87
W5 .45Na 87
Florence Root Ho. IG4: Ilf .29Nc 54
Florence Sq. E3 .42Dc 92
Florence St. E16 .42Hc 93
N1 .38Rb 71
NW4 .28Ya 48
Florence Ter. SE14 .53Bc 114
SW15 .62Ua 132
Florence Way GU21: Knap .10G 166
SW12 .60Hb 111
UB8: Uxb .38L 63
Florey Lodge W9 .43Cb 89
(off Admiral Wlk.)
Florey Sq. N21 .15Pb 32
Florfield Pas. E8 .37Xb 71
(off Reading La.)
Florfield Rd. E8 .37Xb 71
Florian SE5 .53Ub 113
Florian Av. SM1: Sutt .77Fb 155
Florian Ct. E16 .43Jc 93
(off Hastings Rd.)
Florian Rd. SW15 .56Ab 110
Florida Cl. WD23: B Hea .19Fa 28
Florida Ct. BR2: Brom .70Hc 137
(off Westmoreland Rd.)
TW18: Staines .63J 127
Florida Rd. CR7: Thor H .67Rb 135
Florida St. E2 .41Wb 91
Florin Ct. EC1 .7D 218
N18 .21Ub 51
SE1 .2K 231
Floris Pl. SW4 .55Lb 112
Floriston Av. UB10: Hil .38S 64
Floriston Cl. HA7: Stan .25Ka 46
Floriston Ct. UB5: N'olt .36Da 65
Floriston Gdns. HA7: Stan .25Ka 46
Florys Ct. SW19 .60Ab 110
Floss St. SW15 .54Ya 110
Flotilla Ho. SW18 .55Eb 111
Flounder Ho. SE8 .52Dc 114
(off Creative Rd.)
Flower & Dean Wlk. E1 .1K 225 (43Vb 91)
Flower Cres. KT16: Ott .79D 148
Flowerdown Ct. HA4: Eastc .30W 44
(off Lidgould Gro.)
Flowerfield TN14: Otf .89Hd 182
Flowerhill Way DA13: Ist R .6A 144
Flower La. NW7 .22Va 48
RH9: G'stone .2B 210
Flower M. NW11 .30Ab 48
Flower Pot Cl. N15 .30Vb 51
Flowers Av.
HA4: Eastc, Ruis .30W 44
Flowers Cl. NW2 .34Wa 68
Flowersmead SW17 .61Jb 134
Flowers M. N19 .33Lb 70
Flower Wlk., The SW7 .2A 226 (47Eb 89)
Floyd Rd. SE7 .50Lc 93
Floyd's La. GU22: Pyr .88J 169
Floyer Cl. TW10: Rich .57Pa 109
Fludyer St. SE13 .56Gc 115
Flutemakers M. SW4 .57Mb 112
Flux's La. CM16: Epp .5Wc 23
Flyers Way, The TN16: Westrm .98Tc 200
Flying Angel Ho. E16 .45Kc 93
(off Victoria Dock Rd.)
Flynn Ct. E14 .45Cc 92
(off Garford St.)
Fogerty Cl. EN3: Enf L .9Dc 20
Foley Ct. DA1: Dart .60Rd 119
(off Churchill Cl.)
Foley Ho. E1 .44Yb 92
(off Tarling St.)
Foley M. KT10: Clay .79Ga 152
Foley Rd. KT10: Clay .80Ga 152
TN16: Big H .90Mc 179
Foley St. W1 .1B 222 (43Lb 90)
Foley Wood KT10: Clay .80Ha 152
Folgate St. E1 .7J 219 (43Ub 91)
(not continuous)
Foliot Ho. N1 .1H 217
Foliot St. W12 .44Va 88
Folkes La. RM14: Upm .29Vd 58
Folkestone Ct. SL3: L'ly .50C 82
UB5: N'olt .36Da 65
(off Newmarket Av.)
Folkestone Ho. SE17 .7J 231
Folkestone Rd. E6 .40Qc 74
E17 .28Dc 52
N18 .21Wb 51
Folkingham La. NW9 .25Ta 47
Folkington Cnr. N12 .22Bb 49
Folland NW9 .26Va 48
(off Hundred Acre)
Follett Cl. SL4: Old Win .8M 103
Follett Dr. WD5: Ab L .3V 12
Follett Ho. SW10 .52Fb 111
(off Worlds End Est.)
Follett St. E14 .44Ec 92
Follingham Ct. N1 .3J 219
Folly, The GU18: Light .4A 166
Folly Av. AL3: St A .1A 6
Folly Brook & Darland's Lake Nature Reserve
.20Ab 30
Folly Cl. WD7: R'lett .8Ha 14
Folly Ct. AL3: St A .1B 6
(off Folly Av.)
Follyfield Rd. SM7: Bans .86Cb 175
Folly La. AL3: St A .1P 5
E4 .23Bc 52
E17 .25Ac 52
Folly M. W11 .44Bb 89
Folly Pathway WD7: R'lett .7Ha 14
Folly Wall E14 .47Ec 92
Fonda Ct. E14 .45Cc 92
(off Premiere Pl.)
Fondant Ct. E3 .40Dc 72
(off Taylor Pl.)
Fontaine Ho. E17 .28Cc 52
(off Hoe St.)
Fontaine Rd. SW16 .66Pb 134
Fontarabia Rd. SW11 .56Jb 112
Fontayne Av. IG7: Chig .21Sc 54
RM1: Rom .26Gd 56
RM13: Rain .38Gd 76
Fontenelle SE5 .53Ub 113
Fontenoy Ho. SE11 .6B 230
Fontenoy Rd. SW12 .61Kb 134
Fonteyne Gdns. IG8: Wfd G .26Mc 53
Fonthill Cl. SE20 .68Wb 135
Fonthill Gdns. DA1: Dart .55Qd 119
(off Halcrow Av.)
Fonthill Ho. SW1 .7A 228
W14 .48Ab 88
(off Russell Rd.)
Fonthill M. N4 .33Pb 70
Fonthill Rd. N4 .32Pb 70
Font Hills N2 .26Eb 49
Fontley Way SW15 .59Wa 110
Fontmell Cl. TW15: Ashf .64Q 128
Fontmell Pk. TW15: Ashf .64P 127
Fontwell Cl. HA3: Hrw W .24Ga 46
UB5: N'olt .37Ca 65
Fontwell Dr. BR2: Brom .71Qc 160
Fontwell Pk. Gdns. RM12: Horn .35Nd 77
Foord Cl. DA2: Dart .61Ud 142
Football La. HA1: Harr .32Ha 66
Footbury Hill Rd. BR6: St M Cry .72Wc 161
Footpath, The SW15 .58Wa 110
FOOTS CRAY .65Yc 139
Foots Cray High St. DA14: Sidc .65Yc 139
Foots Cray La. DA14: Sidc .60Yc 117
Foots Cray Meadows (Nature Reserve)
.63Zc 139
Footscray Rd. SE9 .58Qc 116
Forbench Cl. GU23: Rip .94K 189
Forber Ho. E2 .41Yb 92
(off Cornwall Av.)
Forbes Av. EN6: Pot B .5Fb 17
Forbes Cl. NW2 .34Wa 68
RM11: Horn .32Kd 77
Forbes Ho. E7 .36Lc 73
(off Romford Rd.)
W4 .50Qa 87
(off Stonehill Rd.)
Forbes St. E1 .44Wb 91
Forbes Way HA4: Ruis .33X 65
Forburg Rd. N16 .32Wb 71
FORCE GREEN .96Tc 200
Force Grn. La. TN16: Westrm .96Tc 200
Fordbridge Cl. KT16: Chert .74K 149
Fordbridge Ct. TW15: Ashf .65N 127
Fordbridge Pk. TW16: Sun .72V 150
Fordbridge Rd. TW15: Ashf .65N 127
TW16: Sun .72U 150
TW17: Shep .72U 150
FORDBRIDGE RDBT. .65N 127
Ford Cl. CR7: Thor H .71Rb 157
E3 .40Ac 72
HA1: Harr .31Fa 66
RM13: Rain .38Hd 76
TW15: Ashf .65N 127
TW17: Shep .70Q 128
WD23: Bush .14Ea 28
Fordcroft Rd. BR5: St M Cry .71Xc 161
Forde Av. BR1: Brom .69Lc 137
Fordel Rd. SE6 .60Ec 114
Ford End IG8: Wfd G .23Kc 53
UB9: Den .33H 63
Fordgate Bus. Pk. DA17: Belv .47Ed 96
Fordham KT1: King T .68Qa 131
(off Excelsior Cl.)
Fordham Cl. EN4: Cockf .13Gb 31
KT4: Wor Pk .74Xa 154
RM11: Horn .31Qd 77
Fordham Ho. SE14 .52Ac 114
(off Angus St.)
Fordham Rd. EN4: Cockf .13Fb 31
Fordhams Row RM16: Ors .3D 100
Fordham St. E1 .44Wb 91
Fordhook Av. W5 .46Pa 87
Ford Ho. EN5: New Bar .15Db 31
Fordie Ho. SW1 .4G 227
Ford Ind. Pk. RM9: Dag .42Dd 96
Fordingley Rd. W9 .41Bb 89
Fordington Ho. SE26 .62Wb 135
Fordington Rd. N6 .29Hb 49
Ford La. RM13: Rain .38Hd 76
SL0: Iver .44J 83
Ford Lodge RM7: Rom .28Fd 56
Fordmill Rd. SE6 .61Cc 136
Ford Pl. RM15: S Ock .45Zd 99
Ford Rd. DA11: Nflt .57De 121
E3 .40Bc 72
GU22: Wok .92D 188
GU24: Bisl, W End .6C 166
GU24: Chob .2G 166
KT16: Chert .74K 149
RM9: Dag .38Bd 75
RM10: Dag .38Bd 75
TW15: Ashf .63P 127
Fords Gro. N21 .18Sb 33
Fords Pk. Rd. E16 .43Jc 93
Fords Pl. HA6: Nwood .26W 44
Ford Sq. E1 .43Xb 91
Ford St. E3 .39Ac 72
E16 .44Hc 93
Fordview Ind. Est. RM13: Rain .41Fd 96
Fordwater Rd. KT16: Chert .74K 149
Fordwater Trad. Est. KT16: Chert .74L 149
Fordwich Cl. BR6: Orp .73Vc 161
Fordwych Rd. NW2 .35Ab 68
Fordyce Cl. RM11: Horn .31Pd 77
Fordyce Ho. SW16 .63Mb 134
Fordyce Rd. SE13 .58Ec 114
Fordyke Rd. RM8: Dag .33Bd 75
Forefield AL2: Chis G .9N 5
Foreign St. SE5 .54Rb 113
Foreland Ct. NW4 .25Za 48
Foreland Ho. W11 .45Ab 88
(off Walmer Rd.)
Foreland St. SE18 .49Tc 94
Forelle Way SM5: Cars .81Hb 175
Foreman Ct. TW1: Twick .60Ha 108
Foreman Ho. SE4 .56Zb 114
(off Billingford Cl.)
Foremark Cl. IG6: Ilf .22Vc 55
Foreshore SE8 .49Bc 92
Forest, The E11 .28Gc 53
Forest App. E4 .17Gc 35
IG8: Wfd G .24Jc 53
Forest Av. E4 .17Gc 35
HP3: Hem H .4M 3
IG7: Chig .22Qc 54
Forest Bus. Pk. E10 .31Zb 72
Forest Cl. BR7: Chst .67Qc 138
E11 .29Jc 53
EN9: Walt A .9Kc 21
GU22: Pyr .87F 168
IG8: Wfd G .20Kc 35
KT24: E Hor .97V 190
N10 .25Kb 50
NW6 .38Ab 68
SL2: Wex .3M 81
Forest Ct. E4 .18Hc 35
E11 .28Gc 53
N12 .22Db 49
Forest Cres. KT21: Asht .88Qa 173
Forest Cft. SE23 .61Xb 135
FORESTDALE .81Bc 178
Forestdale N14 .21Mb 50
Forestdale Cen., The CR0: Sels .80Bc 158
Forest Dene Ct. SM2: Sutt .79Eb 155
Forest Dr. BR2: Kes .77Nc 160
BR3: Beck .73Bc 158
CM16: They B .8Uc 22
E12 .34Mc 73
IG8: Wfd G .24Fc 53
KT20: Kgswd .93Bb 195
TW16: Sun .66V 128
Forest Dr. E. E11 .31Fc 73
Forest Dr. W. E11 .31Ec 72
Forest Edge IG9: Buck H .21Lc 53
Forester Ho. E14 .45Ac 92
(off Victory Pl.)
Forester Rd. SE15 .55Xb 113
Foresters Cl. GU21: Wok .10K 167
SM6: Wall .80Mb 156
Foresters Ct. IG10: Lough .12Qc 36
Foresters Cres. DA7: Bex .56Dd 118
Foresters Dr. E17 .28Fc 53
SM6: Wall .80Mb 156
Forest Gdns. N17 .26Vb 51
FOREST GATE .36Jc 73
Forest Ga. KT24: E Hor .96V 190
NW9 .28Ua 48
Forest Ga. Retreat E7 .36Jc 73
(off Odessa Rd.)
Forest Glade E4 .21Gc 53
E11 .30Gc 53
Forest Gro. E8 .37Vb 71
Forest Hgts. IG9: Buck H .19Jc 35
FOREST HILL .61Yb 136
Forest Hill Bus. Cen. SE23 .61Yb 136
(off Clyde Va.)
Forest Hill Ind. Est. SE23 .61Yb 136
Forest Hill Pool .61Yb 136
Forest Hill Rd. SE22 .57Xb 113
SE23 .57Xb 113
Forest Hill School Sports Cen. .62Zb 136
Forestholme Cl. SE23 .61Yb 136
Forest Ind. Pk. IG6: Ilf .25Uc 54
Forest La. E7 .36Gc 73
E15 .36Gc 73
IG7: Chig .22Qc 54
KT24: E Hor .96V 190
WD7: Shenl .3La 14
Forest Lodge SE23 .62Yb 136
(off Dartmouth Rd.)
Forest Mt. Rd. IG8: Wfd G .24Fc 53
Forest Nature Reserve, The .96V 190
Forest Pk. Crematorium IG6: Ilf .23Yc 55
Forest Point E7 .36Kc 73
(off Windsor Rd.)
Fore St. EC2 .1E 224 (43Sb 91)
HA5: Eastc .28V 44
N9 .21Wb 51
N18 .21Vb 51
Fore St. Av. EC2 .1F 225 (43Tb 91)
Forest Ridge BR2: Kes .77Nc 160
BR3: Beck .69Cc 136
Forest Ri. E17 .27Fc 53
Forest Rd. CM16: Epp .7Qc 22
DA8: Erith .53Jd 118
E7 .35Jc 73
E8 .37Vb 71
E11 .31Fc 73
E17 .27Dc 52
EN3: Enf W .8Ac 20
EN8: Chesh .1Zb 20
EN9: Epp, Walt A .8Nc 22
GU22: Pyr .87F 168
IG6: Chig, Ilf .26Tc 54
IG8: Wfd G .20Jc 35
IG10: Lough .13Mc 35
(Staple's Rd.)
IG10: Lough .9Qc 22
(The Ditches Ride)
KT24: E Hor, Eff J .99V 190
N9 .18Xb 33
N17 .28Yb 52
RM7: Mawney .27Dd 56
SL4: Wind .4B 102
(Ash La.)
SL4: Wind .10B 102
(Plain Ride)
SM3: Sutt .74Cb 155
TW9: Kew .52Qa 109
TW13: Felt .61Y 129
WD25: Wat .5W 12
Forest Side CM16: Epp .5Tc 22
E4 .17Hc 35
E7 .35Kc 73
EN9: Walt A .8Lc 21
IG9: Buck H .18Lc 35
KT4: Wor Pk .74Va 154
Forest St. E7 .36Jc 73
Forest Ter. IG7: Chig .22Qc 54
Forest Trad. Est. E17 .27Zb 52
Forest Vw. E4 .17Fc 35
E11 .31Hc 73
Forest Vw. Av. E10 .29Fc 53
Forest Vw. Rd. E12 .35Nc 74
E17 .25Ec 52
IG10: Lough .14Mc 35
Forest Wlk. N10 .25Kb 50
WD23: Bush .11Ba 27
Forest Way BR5: St M Cry .71Vc 161
DA15: Sidc .59Tc 116
IG8: Wfd G .21Kc 53
IG10: Lough .13Nc 36
KT21: Asht .89Pa 173
N19 .33Lb 70
Forfar Ho. WD19: Wat .20Y 27
Forfar Rd. N22 .25Rb 51
SW11 .53Jb 112
Forge, The EN6: N'thaw .2Gb 17
Forge Av. CR5: Coul .92Qb 196
Forge Bri. La. CR5: Coul .94Kb 196
Forge Cl. BR2: Hayes .74Jc 159
CM13: Gt War .25Wd 58
UB3: Harl .51T 106
WD4: Chfd .3J 11
Forge Cotts. W5 .46Ma 87
Forge Dr. KT10: Clay .80Ja 152
SL2: Farn C .7G 60
Forge End AL2: Chis G .8N 5
GU21: Wok .89A 168
Forgefield TN16: Big H .88Mc 179
Forge La. DA4: Hort K .70Sd 142
DA12: Grav'nd .1H 145
DA12: Shorne .4N 145
HA6: Nwood .24U 44
SM3: Cheam .80Ab 154
TN15: W King .82Wd 184
TW10: Ham .60Na 109
TW13: Hanw .64Aa 129
TW16: Sun .69W 128
Forge M. CR0: Addtn .78Cc 158
TW16: Sun .69W 128
(off Forge La.)
Forge Pl. DA12: Grav'nd .10H 123
NW1 .37Jb 70
WD6: E'tree .16Ma 29
(off New Rd.)
Forge Sq. E14 .49Dc 92
Forge Steading SM7: Bans .87Db 175
Forge Way TN14: S'ham .83Hd 182
Forlong Path UB5: N'olt .37Aa 65
(off Cowings Mead)
Forman Pl. N16 .35Vb 71
Formation, The E16 .47Rc 94
(off Woolwich Mnr. Way)
Formby Av. HA7: Stan .27La 46
Formby Cl. SL3: L'ly .49E 82
Formby Ct. N7 .36Qb 70
(off Morgan Rd.)
Formosa Ho. E1 .42Ac 92
(off Ernest St.)
Formosa St. W9 .42Db 89
Formunt Cl. E16 .43Hc 93
Forres Gdns. NW11 .30Cb 49
Forres Ho. CM14: W'ley .21Yd 58
Forrester Ho. AL1: St A .2B 6
(off St Peter's St.)
Forrester Path SE26 .63Yb 136
Forresters Apartments IG11: Bark .38Sc 74
(off Linton Rd.)
Forrest Gdns. SW16 .69Pb 134
Forris Av. UB3: Hayes .46V 84
Forset Ct. W2 .2E 220
Forset St. W1 .2E 220 (44Gb 89)
(not continuous)
Forstal Cl. BR2: Brom .69Jc 137
Forster Cl. IG8: Wfd G .24Fc 53
Forster Ho. BR1: Brom .63Fc 137
SW17 .62Fb 133
(off Grosvenor Way)
Forster Rd. BR3: Beck .69Ac 136
E17 .30Ac 52
N17 .27Vb 51
SW2 .59Nb 112
Forsters Cl. RM6: Chad H .30Bd 55
Forsters Way UB4: Yead .44X 85
Forston St. N1 .1E 218 (40Sb 71)
Forsyte Cres. SE19 .67Ub 135
Forsyte Ho. SW3 .7E 226
Forsythe Shades Ct. BR3: Beck .67Ec 136
Forsyth Gdns. SE17 .51Rb 113
Forsyth Ho. E9 .38Yb 72
(off Frampton Pk. Rd.)
SW1 .7C 228
Forsythia Cl. IG1: Ilf .36Rc 74
Forsythia Gdns. SL3: L'ly .48A 82
Forsyth Path GU21: Wok .85F 168
Forsyth Pl. EN1: Enf .15Ub 33
Forsyth Rd. GU21: Wok .87E 168
Forterie Gdns. IG3: Bark, Ilf .34Wc 75
Fortescue Av. E8 .38Xb 71
TW2: Twick .62Ea 130
Fortescue Rd. HA8: Edg .25Ta 47
KT13: Weyb .77P 149
SW19 .66Fb 133
Fortess Gro. NW5 .36Lb 70
Fortess Rd. NW5 .36Kb 70
Fortess Wlk. NW5 .36Kb 70
Fortess Yd. NW5 .35Kb 70
Forthbridge Rd. SW11 .56Jb 112
Forth Ho. E3 .40Bc 72
(off Tredegar Rd.)
Forth Rd. RM14: Upm .30Td 58
Fortin Cl. RM15: S Ock .45Wd 98
Fortin Path RM15: S Ock .45Wd 98
Fortin Way RM15: S Ock .45Wd 98
Fortis Cl. E16 .44Lc 93
Fortis Ct. N10 .27Jb 50
FORTIS GREEN .28Hb 49
Fortis Grn. N2 .28Gb 49
N10 .28Gb 49
Fortis Grn. Av. N2 .27Hb 49
Fortis Grn. Rd. N10 .27Jb 50
Fortismere Av. N10 .27Jb 50
Fortius Apartments E3 .40Cc 72
(off Tredegar La.)
Fortius Wlk. E20 .37Ec 72
Fort La. RH2: Reig .2K 207
Fortnam Rd. N19 .33Mb 70
Fortnum's Acre HA7: Stan .23Ha 46
Fortress Distribution Pk.
RM18: Tilb .6C 122
Fort Rd. RM18: Tilb, W Til .6C 122
SE1 .49Vb 91
TN14: Hals .87Ed 182
UB5: N'olt .38Ca 65
Fortrose Cl. E14 .44Fc 93
Fortrose Gdns. SW2 .60Nb 112
(not continuous)
Fortrye Cl. DA11: Nflt .1A 144
Fort St. E1 .1J 225 (43Ub 91)
E16 .46Kc 93
Fortuna Cl. DA3: Hartl .70Be 143
N7 .37Pb 70
Fortuna Ho. E20 .36Dc 72
(off Scarlet Cl.)
Fortune Av. HA8: Edg .25Ra 47
Fortune Ct. E8 .38Vb 71
(off Queensbridge Rd.)
IG11: Bark .40Yc 75
Fortunegate Rd. NW10 .39Ua 68
FORTUNE GREEN .36Cb 69
Fortune Grn. Rd. NW6 .35Cb 69
Fortune Ho. EC1 .6E 218
SE11 .6K 229
Fortune La. WD6: E'tree .16Ma 29
Fortune Pl. SE1 .50Vb 91
Fortunes Mead UB5: N'olt .37Aa 65
Fortune St. EC1 .6E 218 (42Sb 91)
Fortunes Wlk. E20 .36Ec 72
Fortune Theatre .3G 223
Fortune Wlk. SE28 .48Tc 94
(off Broadwater Rd.)
Fortune Way NW10 .41Wa 88
Forty Acre La. E16 .43Jc 93
Forty Av. HA9: Wemb .34Pa 67
Forty Cl. HA9: Wemb .34Pa 67
Forty Footpath SW14 .55Sa 109
Fortyfoot Rd. KT22: Lea .93La 192
Forty Foot Way SE9 .59Sc 116
Forty Hall .9Vb 19
FORTY HILL .10Ub 19
Forty Hill EN2: Enf .10Ub 19
Forty Hill Country Pk. .9Vb 19
Forty La. HA9: Wemb .33Ra 67
Forum, The KT8: W Mole .70Da 129
KT16: Chert .74H 149
Forum Cl. E3 .39Cc 72
Forum Ho. HA9: Wemb .35Qa 67
Forum Magnum Sq. SE1 .1H 229
Forumside HA8: Edg .23Qa 47
Forum Way HA8: Edg .23Qa 47
Forval Cl. CR4: Mitc .71Hb 155
Forward Bus. Cen., The E16 .42Fc 93
Forward Dr. HA3: W'stone .28Ha 46
Fosbrooke Ho. SW8 .52Nb 112
(off Davidson Gdns.)
Fosbury M. W2 .45Db 89

Foscote Ct.—Freightliners City Farm

Foscote Ct. *W9* 42Cb 89
(off Amberley Rd.)
Foscote M. W9 42Cb 89
Foscote Rd. NW4 30Xa 48
Foskett Ho. *N2* 26Fb 49
(off The Grange)
Foskett M. E8 36Vb 71
Foskett Rd. SW6 54Bb 111
Foss Av. CR0: Wadd 78Qb 156
Fossdene Rd. SE7 50Kc 93
Fossdyke Cl. UB4: Yead 43Aa 85
Fosse Ho. AL3: St A 3N 5
Fosset Lodge DA7: Bex 53Ed 118
Fosse Way KT14: W Byf 85H 169
W13 43Ja 86
Foss Ho. *NW8* 40Db 69
(off Carlton Hill)
Fossil Ct. *SE1* 3H 231
(off Long La.)
Fossil Rd. SE13 55Cc 114
Fossington Rd. DA17: Belv 49Zc 95
Foss Rd. SW17 63Fb 133
Fossway RM8: Dag 33Yc 75
Foster Av. SL4: Wind 5C 102
Foster Cl. EN8: Chesh 2Ac 20
Foster Ct. *E16* 45Hc 93
(off Tarling Rd.)
NW1 38Lb 70
(off Royal College St.)
NW4 28Ya 48
Fosterdown RH9: G'stone 1P 209
Foster Dr. DA1: Dart 57Pd 119
Foster Ho. SE14 53Bc 114
WD6: Bore 13Sa 29
Foster La. EC2 2D 224 (44Sb 91)
Foster Rd. E13 42Jc 93
HP1: Hem H 4K 3
W3 45Ua 88
W4 50Ta 87
Fosters Cl. BR7: Chst 64Pc 138
E18 25Kc 53
Fosters Gro. GU20: W'sham 7A 146
Fosters La. GU21: Knap 9G 166
Fosters M. DA3: Lfield 68Ae 143
Fosters Path SL2: Slou 2D 80
Foster St. NW4 28Ya 48
Foster's Way SW18 60Db 111
Foster Wlk. NW4 28Ya 48
Fothergill Cl. E13 40Jc 73
Fothergill Dr. N21 15Nb 32
Fotheringay Gdns. SL1: Slou 5E 80
Fotheringham Rd. EN1: Enf 14Vb 33
(not continuous)
Fotherley Rd. WD3: Rick 19H 25
Foubert's Pl. W1 3B 222 (44Lb 90)
Foulden Rd. N16 35Vb 71
Foulden Ter. N16 35Vb 71
Foulis Ter. SW7 7C 226 (50Fb 89)
Foulser Rd. SW17 62Hb 133
Foulsham Rd. CR7: Thor H 69Sb 135
Foundary Bldg. E14 44Gc 93
Foundation Pl. *SE9* 57Qc 116
(off Archery Rd.)
Founder Cl. E6 44Rc 94
Founders Cl. UB5: N'olt 41Ba 85
Founders Ct. EC2 2F 225
Founders Gdns. SE19 66Sb 135
Founders Ho. SW1 7D 228
Foundling Ct. WC1 5F 217
Foundling Mus., The 5G 217
Foundry, The EC2 4J 219
Foundry Cl. SE16 46Ac 92
Foundry Ct. KT16: Chert 73J 149
SL2: Slou 6K 81
Foundry Ga. EN8: Walt C 5Ac 20
Foundry Ho. *E14* 43Dc 92
(off Morris Rd.)
SW8 53Kb 112
(off Lockington Rd.)
Foundry La. SL3: Hort 55D 104
Foundry M. E17 27Ec 52
KT16: Chert 73J 149
(off Gogmore La.)
NW1 5C 216 (42Lb 90)
TW3: Houn 56Da 107
Foundry Pl. *E1* 43Yb 92
(off Jubilee St.)
SW18 59Db 111
Founes Dr. RM16: Chaf H 48Ae 99
Fountain Cl. SE18 50Rc 94
UB8: Hil 43S 84
Fountain Ct. DA4: Eyns 75Nd 163
DA15: Sidc 58Xc 117
EC4 4K 223 (45Qb 90)
EN8: Chesh 2Zb 20
(off Westbury)
SE23 61Zb 136
SW1 6K 227
W11 47Za 88
(off Clearwater Ter.)
WD6: Bore 12Qa 29
Fountain Dr. SE19 63Vb 135
SM5: Cars 81Hb 175
Fountain Gdns. SL4: Wind 5H 103
Fountain Grn. Sq. SE16 47Wb 91
Fountain Ho. CR4: Mitc 68Hb 133
E2 5K 219
NW6 38Ab 68
SE16 47Wb 91
(off Bermondsey Wall E.)
SW6 54Eb 111
W1 5H 221
Fountain M. *N5* 35Sb 71
(off Highbury Grange)
NW3 37Hb 69
Fountain Pl. EN9: Walt A 6Ec 20
SW9 53Qb 112
Fountain Rd. CR7: Thor H 69Sb 135
RH1: Redh 8N 207
SW17 64Fb 133
FOUNTAIN RDBT. 70Ua 132
Fountains, The IG10: Lough 17Mc 35
N3 24Db 49
(off Ballards La.)
Fountains Av. TW13: Hanw 62Ba 129
Fountains Cl. TW13: Hanw 61Ba 129
(not continuous)
Fountains Cres. N14 17Nb 32
Fountain Sq. SW1 5K 227 (49Kb 90)
Fountain Wlk. DA11: Nflt 8A 122
Fountayne Bus. Cen. N15 28Wb 51
Fountayne Rd. N15 28Wb 51
N16 33Wb 71
Fount St. SW8 52Mb 112
Fouracre Path SE25 72Ub 157
Four Acres KT11: Cobh 85Aa 171
N12 20Db 31
Fouracres EN3: Enf H 11Ac 34
Fouracres Dr. HP3: Hem H 4P 3
Fouracres Wlk. HP3: Hem H 4P 3
Four Dials *E20* 37Ec 72
(within Westfield Stratford City Shop. Cen.)
Fourdrinier Way HP3: Hem H 5M 3
Fourfield Cl. KT18: Head 94Sa 193
Fourland Wlk. HA8: Edg 23Sa 47
Fournier St. E1 7K 219 (43Vb 91)
Four Oaks CM15: B'wood 20Ae 41
Fourscore Mans. *E8* 38Wb 71
(off Shrubland Rd.)
Four Seasons Cl. E3 40Cc 72
Four Seasons Cres. SM3: Sutt 75Bb 155
Four Seasons Ter. UB7: W Dray 47Q 84
Four Sq. Ct. TW3: Houn 58Ca 107
Fourteenth Av. KT20: Lwr K 98Ab 194
Fourth Av. DA11: Nflt 10A 122
E12 35Pc 74
KT20: Lwr K 97Ab 194
RM7: Rush G 32Fd 76
RM20: W Thur 51Wd 120
UB3: Hayes 46V 84
W10 42Ab 88
WD25: Wat 7Z 13
Fourth Cross Rd. TW2: Twick 61Fa 130
Fourth Dr. CR5: Coul 88Lb 176
Fourth Way HA9: Wemb 35Ra 67
Four Trees AL2: Chis G 7P 5
Four Tubs, The WD23: Bush 17Fa 28
Fourways Mkt. *AL9: Wel G* 6E 8
(off Dixons Hill Rd.)
Four Wents KT11: Cobh 86Y 171
Four Wents, The E4 18Fc 35
Four Wents Cl. TN15: Bor G 92Be 205
Fovant Cl. SW8 54Lb 112
Fowey Av. IG4: Ilf 29Mc 53
Fowey Cl. E1 46Xb 91
Fowey Ho. SE11 7A 230
Fowler Cl. SW11 55Fb 111
Fowler Ho. *N15* 29Tb 51
(off South Gro.)
Fowler Rd. CR4: Mitc 68Jb 134
E7 35Jc 73
IG6: Ilf 23Xc 55
N1 39Rb 71
Fowlers Cl. DA14: Sidc 64Ad 139
Fowlers Mead GU24: Chob 1J 167
Fowlers M. *N19* 33Lb 70
(off Holloway Rd.)
Fowler's Wlk. W5 42Ma 87
Fowler Way UB10: Uxb 40N 63
Fowley Cl. EN8: Walt C 6Bc 20
Fowley Mead Pk. EN8: Walt C 6Cc 20
Fownes St. SW11 55Gb 111
Foxacre CR3: Cat'm 94Ub 197
Fox All. WD18: Wat 15Y 27
Fox & Knot St. EC1 7C 218
Foxberry Rd. SE4 55Ac 114
Foxberry Wlk. *DA11: Nflt* 62Fe 143
(off Ashmore Gdns.)
Foxboro Rd. RH1: Redh 4B 208
Foxborough Cl. SL3: L'ly 50C 82
Foxborough Gdns. SE4 57Cc 114
Foxbourne Rd. SW17 61Jb 134
Fox Burrow Rd. IG7: Chig 21Zc 55
Foxburrows Rare Breeds Farm & Zoo 21Zc 55
Foxbury DA3: Nw A G 76Ae 165
TN15: Plat 92De 205
Foxbury Av. BR7: Chst 65Tc 138
Foxbury Cl. BR1: Brom 65Kc 137
BR6: Chels 78Wc 161
Foxbury Dr. BR6: Chels 79Wc 161
Foxbury Rd. BR1: Brom 65Jc 137
Fox Cl. BR6: Chels 78Wc 161
E1 42Yb 92
E16 43Jc 93
GU22: Pyr 87F 168
KT13: Weyb 78T 150
RM5: Col R 22Dd 56
WD6: E'tree 16Ma 29
WD23: Bush 14Da 27
Foxcombe CR0: New Ad 79Dc 158
(not continuous)
Foxcombe Cl. E6 40Mc 73
Foxcombe Rd. SW15 60Wa 110
FOX CORNER 7G 186
Fox Corner Community Wildlife Area 7G 186
Foxcote SE5 50Ub 91
Fox Covert KT22: Fet 96Fa 192
Fox Covert Cl. SL5: S'hill 1A 146
Foxcroft AL1: St A 4E 6
WC1 2J 217
Foxcroft Rd. SE18 53Rc 116
Foxdell HA6: Nwood 23T 44
Foxdell Way SL9: Chal P 22A 42
Foxdene Cl. E18 27Kc 53
Foxearth Cl. TN16: Big H 90Nc 180
Foxearth Rd. CR2: Sels 82Yb 178
Foxearth Spur CR2: Sels 81Yb 178
Foxes Dale BR2: Brom 69Fc 137
SE3 55Jc 115
Foxes Dr. EN7: Chesh 1Wb 19
Foxes Grn. RM16: Ors 7C 100
Foxes La. AL9: Wel G 5F 8
Foxes Pde. *EN9: Walt A* 6Ec 20
(off Stewardstone Rd.)
Foxes Path GU4: Sut G 98B 188
Foxfield NW1 1B 216
Fox Fld. Cl. RM20: W Thur 51Wd 120
Foxfield Cl. HA6: Nwood 23V 44
Foxfield Rd. BR6: Orp 75Tc 160
Foxglove Cl. AL10: Hat 1D 8
DA15: Sidc 58Wc 117
KT16: Chert 74L 149
N9 18Yb 34
TW19: Stanw 60M 105
UB1: S'hall 45Aa 85
Foxglove Ct. *E3* 40Cc 72
(off Four Seasons Cl.)
HA0: Wemb 37Ma 67
Foxglove Gdns. CR8: Purl 83Nb 176
E11 28Lc 53
Foxglove La. KT9: Chess 77Qa 153
Foxglove Path *SE28* 46Uc 94
(off Martins Pl.)
Foxglove Pl. RM3: Rom 23Ld 57
Foxglove Rd. RM7: Rush G 33Gd 76
RM15: S Ock 44Yd 98
Foxgloves, The HP1: Hem H 3G 2
Foxglove St. W12 45Va 88
Foxglove Way SM6: Wall 74Kb 156
Fox Gro. KT12: Walt T 73X 151
Foxgrove N14 20Nb 32
Foxgrove Av. BR3: Beck 66Dc 136
Foxgrove Dr. GU21: Wok 87C 168
Foxgrove Path WD19: Wat 22Z 45
Foxgrove Rd. BR3: Beck 66Dc 136
Foxhall Rd. RM14: Upm 36Sd 78
Foxham Rd. N19 34Mb 70
Foxhanger Gdns.
GU22: Wok 88C 168
FOX HATCH 11Ud 40
Foxherne SL1: Slou 7N 81
SL3: L'ly 7N 81
Fox Hill SE19 66Vb 135
Foxhill WD24: Wat 8W 12
Fox Hill Gdns. SE19 66Vb 135
Foxhills GU21: Wok 9N 167
Foxhills Cl. KT16: Ott 79D 148
Foxhills Golf Course 77B 148
Foxhills M. KT16: Longc 76D 148
Fox Hills Rd. RM16: Grays 46Fe 99
Foxhills Rd. KT16: Ott 77C 148
Foxhole Rd. SE9 57Nc 116
Foxholes KT13: Weyb 78T 150
Fox Hollow Cl. SE18 50Uc 94
Foxhollow Cl. KT12: Walt T 75Z 151
Fox Hollow Dr. DA7: Bex 55Zc 117
Foxhollow Dr. SL2: Farn C 6G 60
Foxhollows AL2: Lon C 8G 6
Foxholt Gdns. NW10 38Sa 67
Foxhome Cl. BR7: Chst 65Qc 138
Foxhounds La. DA13: Sflt 62Ce 143
Fox Ho. *KT16: Chert* 74H 149
(off Fox La. Nth.)
Fox Ho. Rd. DA17: Belv 50Dd 96
(not continuous)
Foxlake Rd. KT14: Byfl 84P 169
Foxlands Cl. WD25: Wat 6W 12
Foxlands Cres. RM10: Dag 36Ed 76
Foxlands La. RM10: Dag 36Fd 76
Foxlands Rd. RM10: Dag 36Ed 76
Fox La. BR2: Kes 78Kc 159
CR3: Cat'm 93Rb 197
KT23: Bookh 96Aa 191
N13 19Pb 32
RH2: Reig 3K 207
W5 42Na 87
Fox La. Nth. KT16: Chert 74H 149
Fox La. Sth. KT16: Chert 74H 149
Fox Lea TN15: Bor G 92Be 205
Foxleas Ct. BR1: Brom 66Gc 137
Foxlees HA0: Wemb 35Ja 66
Foxleigh Grange GU24: Bisl 9F 166
Foxley Cl. E8 36Wb 71
IG10: Lough 12Rc 36
RH1: Redh 10A 208
Foxley Ct. SM2: Sutt 80Eb 155
Foxley Gdns. CR8: Purl 85Rb 177
Foxley Gro. SL1: Burn 1A 80
Foxley Hall CR8: Purl 85Qb 176
Foxley Hill Rd. CR8: Purl 84Qb 176
Foxley Ho. *E3* 41Dc 92
(off Bow Rd.)
Foxley La. CR8: Purl 83Lb 176
Foxley Rd. CR7: Thor H 70Rb 135
CR8: Kenley 86Rb 177
SL2: Slou 2D 80
SW9 52Qb 112
Foxleys WD19: Wat 20Aa 27
Foxley Sq. SW9 52Rb 113
Foxley Wood (Local Nature Reserve) 85Qb 176
Fox Mnr. Way RM20: W Thur 51Xd 120
Foxmead Cl. EN2: Enf 13Pb 32
Foxmoor Ct. UB9: Den 30J 43
Foxmore St. SW11 53Hb 111
Foxon Cl. CR3: Cat'm 93Ub 197
Foxon La. CR3: Cat'm 93Tb 197
Foxon La. Gdns. CR3: Cat'm 93Ub 197
Fox Rd. E16 43Hc 93
SL3: L'ly 9P 81
Fox's Path CR4: Mitc 68Gb 133
Fox's Yd. E2 5K 219
Foxton Gro. CR4: Mitc 68Fb 133
Foxton Ho. *E16* 47Qc 94
(off Albert Rd.)
Foxton M. TW10: Rich 58Na 109
Foxton Rd. RM20: Grays 51Zd 121
Foxtree Ho. WD25: Wat 8Aa 13
Foxwarren KT10: Clay 81Ha 172
Foxwell M. SE4 55Ac 114
Foxwell St. SE4 55Ac 114
Fox Wood KT12: W Vill 80V 150
Foxwood Chase EN9: Walt A 7Ec 20
Foxwood Cl. NW7 21Ua 48
TW13: Felt 62X 129
Foxwood Grn. Cl. EN1: Enf 16Ub 33
Foxwood Gro. BR6: Prat B 82Yc 181
DA11: Nflt 10A 122
Fox Wood Nature Reserve 42Na 87
Foxwood Rd. DA2: Bean 62Xd 142
SE3 56Hc 115
Foxwood Way DA3: Lfield 68Fe 143
Foyle Dr. RM15: S Ock 43Wd 98
Foyle Rd. N17 25Wb 51
SE3 51Hc 115
Frailey Cl. GU22: Wok 88D 168
Frailey Hill GU22: Wok 88D 168
Framewood Rd. SL2: Stoke P, Wex 8N 61
SL3: Stoke P, Wex 8N 61
Framfield Cl. N12 20Cb 31
Framfield Ct. *EN1: Enf* 16Ub 33
(off Queen Anne's Gdns.)
Framfield Rd. CR4: Mitc 66Jb 134
N5 36Rb 71
W7 44Ga 86
Framlingham Cl. E5 33Yb 72
Framlingham Ct. *RM6: Chad H* 29Xc 55
(off Norwich Cres.)
Framlingham Cres. SE9 63Nc 138
Frampton *NW1* 38Mb 70
(off Wrotham Rd.)
Frampton Cl. IG6: Ilf 28Tc 54
SM2: Sutt 80Cb 155
Frampton Ct. UB9: Den 30H 43
W3 47Sa 87
(off Avenue Rd.)
Frampton Ho. NW8 6C 214
Frampton Pk. Est. E9 38Yb 72
Frampton Pk. Rd. E9 37Yb 72
Frampton Rd. CM16: Epp 1Wc 23
EN6: Pot B 2Eb 17
TW4: Houn 57Aa 107
Frampton St. NW8 6C 214 (42Fb 89)
Frampton Ter. SE9 62Rc 138
Francemary Rd. SE4 57Cc 114
Frances Av. RM16: Chaf H 49Yd 98
Frances Ct. E17 30Cc 52
SE25 69Vb 135
Frances Gdns. RM15: S Ock 44Vd 98
Frances Ho. HP3: Hem H 7N 3
Frances M. HP3: Hem H 7A 4
RM3: Rom 23Nd 57
Frances Rd. E4 23Cc 52
SL4: Wind 5G 102
Frances St. SE18 48Pc 94
Frances Wharf E14 44Bc 92
Franche Ct. Rd. SW17 62Eb 133
Francis & Dick James Ct. NW7 24Ab 48
Francis Av. DA7: Bex 54Cd 118
IG1: Ilf 33Tc 74
TW13: Felt 62W 128
Francis Bacon Ct. *SE16* 49Xb 91
(off Galleywall Rd.)
Francis Barber Cl. SW16 64Pb 134
Francis Bentley M. SW4 55Lb 112
Franciscan Rd. SW17 64Hb 133
Francis Chichester Cl. SL5: Asc 10A 124
Francis Chichester Way SW11 53Jb 112
Francis Cl. E14 49Fc 93
KT19: Ewe 77Ta 153
SS17: Horn H 1H 101
TW17: Shep 70Q 128
Francisco Cl. RM16: Chaf H 48Yd 98
Francis Ct. AL1: St A 3C 6
DA8: Erith 50Gd 96
EC1 7B 218
KT5: Surb 70Na 131
(off Cranes Pk. Av.)
NW7 22Va 48
(off Watford Way)
SE14 51Zb 114
(off Myers La.)
Francis Crick Institute 40Mb 70
Francis Greene Ho. *EN9: Walt A* 5Dc 20
(off Grove Ct.)
Francis Gro. SW19 65Bb 133
Francis Harvey Way SE8 53Bc 114
Francis Ho. N1 1H 219
SW10 52Db 111
(off Coleridge Gdns.)
SW18 56Eb 111
(off Eltringham St.)
Francis M. SE12 59Jc 115
Francis Pl. *N6* 31Kb 70
(off Shepherd's Cl.)
Francis Rd. BR5: St P 69Zc 139
CR0: C'don 73Rb 157
CR3: Cat'm 94Tb 197
DA1: Dart 57Md 119
E10 32Ec 72
HA1: Harr 29Ja 46
HA5: Eastc 29Y 45
IG1: Ilf 33Tc 74
N2 28Hb 49
SM6: Wall 79Lb 156
TW4: Houn 54Z 107
UB6: G'frd 40Ka 66
WD18: Wat 14X 27
Francis St. E15 36Gc 73
IG1: Ilf 33Tc 74
SW1 5B 228 (49Lb 90)
Francis Ter. N19 34Lb 70
Francis Ter. M. N19 34Lb 70
Francis Wlk. N1 39Pb 70
Francis Way SL1: Slou 5B 80
Francklyn Gdns. HA8: Edg 20Qa 29
Francombe Gdns. RM1: Rom 30Jd 56
Franconia Rd. SW4 57Mb 112
Frank Bailey Wlk. E12 37Qc 74
Frank Beswick Ho. *SW6* 51Bb 111
(off Clem Attlee Ct.)
Frank Burton Cl. SE7 50Kc 93
Frank Dixon Cl. SE21 59Ub 113
Frank Dixon Way SE21 60Ub 113
Frank Foster Ho. CM16: They B 9Uc 22
Frankfurt Rd. SE24 57Sb 113
Frank Godley Ct. DA14: Sidc 64Xc 139
Frankham Ho. *SE8* 52Cc 114
(off Frankham St.)
Frankham St. SE8 52Cc 114
Frank Ho. *SW8* 52Nb 112
(off Wyvil Rd.)
Frankland Cl. IG8: Wfd G 22Lc 53
SE16 48Xb 91
WD3: Crox G 17Q 26
Frankland Rd. E4 22Cc 52
SW7 4B 226 (48Fb 89)
WD3: Crox G 16R 26
Franklands Dr. KT15: Add 80H 149
Franklin Av. EN7: Chesh 2Wb 19
SL2: Slou 3F 80
WD18: Wat 16W 26
Franklin Bldg. E14 47Cc 92
Franklin Cl. AL4: Col H 4A 8
HP3: Hem H 5N 3
KT1: King T 69Qa 131
N20 17Eb 31
SE13 53Dc 114
SE27 62Rb 135
Franklin Cotts. HA7: Stan 21Ka 46
Franklin Cres. CR4: Mitc 70Lb 134
Franklin Ho. BR2: Brom 69Gc 137
E1 46Xb 91
(off Watts St.)
E14 44Fc 93
(off E. India Dock Rd.)
EN3: Enf L 9Bc 20
NW6 41Cb 89
(off Carlton Va.)
Franklin Ind. Est. *SE20* 67Yb 136
(off Franklin Rd.)
Franklin Pas. SE9 55Nc 116
Franklin Pl. SE13 53Dc 114
Franklin Rd. DA2: Wilm 61Gd 140
DA7: Bex 53Ad 117
DA12: Grav'nd 4F 144
RM12: Horn 37Ld 77
SE20 66Yb 136
WD17: Wat 12X 27
Franklins WD3: Map C 21G 42
Franklins M. HA2: Harr 33Ea 66
Franklin Sq. W14 50Bb 89
Franklin's Row SW3 7G 227 (50Hb 89)
Franklin St. E3 41Dc 92
N15 30Ub 51
Franklin Way CR0: Wadd 73Nb 156
Franklyn Cres. SL4: Wind 5B 102
Franklyn Gdns. IG6: Ilf 23Tc 54
Franklyn Rd. KT12: Walt T 72W 150
NW10 37Va 68
Frank Martin Ct. EN7: Chesh 2Xb 19
Frank M. SE1 49Xb 91
Franks Av. KT3: N Mald 70Sa 131
Franks Cotts. RM14: Upm 32Wd 78
Franks La. DA4: Hort K 71Rd 163
Frank Soskice Ho. *SW6* 51Bb 111
(off Clem Attlee Ct.)
Frank St. E13 42Jc 93
Frank Sutton Way SL1: Slou 5H 81
Franks Wood Av. BR5: Pet W 71Rc 160
Frankswood Av. UB7: Yiew 44P 83
Frank Towell Ct. TW14: Felt 59W 106
Frank Whipple Pl. *E14* 44Ac 92
(off Repton St.)
Frank Whymark Ho. *SE16* 47Yb 92
(off Rupack St.)
Franlaw Cres. N13 21Sb 51
Franmil Rd. RM11: Horn 31Hd 76
RM12: Horn 32Jd 76
Fransfield Gro. SE26 62Xb 135
Frans Hals Ct. E14 48Fc 93
Franshams *WD23: B Hea* 19Ga 28
(off Hartsbourne Rd.)
Frant Cl. SE20 66Yb 136
Franthorne Way SE6 61Dc 136
Frant Rd. CR7: Thor H 71Rb 157
Fraserburgh Ho. *E3* 40Bc 72
(off Vernon Rd.)
Fraser Cl. DA5: Bexl 60Ed 118
E6 44Nc 94
Fraser Ct. *E14* 50Ec 92
(off Ferry St.)
SE1 3E 230
SW11 53Gb 111
(off Surrey La. Est.)
Fraser Ho. TW8: Bford 50Pa 87
Fraser Rd. DA8: Erith 50Fd 96
E17 29Dc 52
N9 20Xb 33
UB6: G'frd 39Ka 66
Fraser St. W4 50Ua 88
Frating Cres. IG8: Wfd G 23Kc 53
Frays Av. UB7: W Dray 47M 83
Frays Cl. UB7: W Dray 48M 83
Frays Island & Mabey's Meadow Nature Reserve 48L 83
Frayslea UB8: Uxb 40L 63
Frays Valley Local Nature Reserve 32M 63
Frays Waye UB8: Uxb 39L 63
Frazer Av. HA4: Ruis 36Y 65
Frazer Cl. RM1: Rom 31Hd 76
Frazier St. SE1 2K 229 (47Qb 90)
Frean St. SE16 48Wb 91
Frearson Ho. WC1 3J 217
Freda Corbett Cl. SE15 52Wb 113
Freda St. SE16 48Wb 91
Frederica Ct. SW2 60Rb 113
Frederica Rd. E4 17Fc 35
Frederica St. N7 38Pb 70
Frederick Andrews Ct.
RM17: Grays 51Fe 121
Frederick Charrington Ho. *E1* 42Yb 92
(off Wickford St.)
Frederick Cl. SM1: Sutt 77Bb 155
W2 4F 221 (45Hb 89)
Frederick Ct. SW3 6G 227
Frederick Cres. EN3: Enf H 12Yb 34
SW9 52Rb 113
Frederick Dobson Ho. *W11* 45Ab 88
(off Cowling Cl.)
Frederick Gdns. CR0: C'don 72Rb 157
SM1: Sutt 78Bb 155
Frederick Ho. *SE18* 49Nc 94
(off Pett St.)
Frederick Pl. AL2: F'mre 9C 6
N8 30Mb 50
(off Crouch Hall Rd.)
SE18 50Rc 94
Frederick Rd. RM13: Rain 40Fd 76
SE17 51Rb 113
SM1: Sutt 78Bb 155
Frederick's Pl. EC2 3F 225 (44Tb 91)
Fredericks Pl. N12 21Eb 49
Frederick Sq. *SE16* 45Ac 92
(off Sovereign Cres.)
Frederick's Row EC1 3B 218 (41Rb 91)
Frederick St. WC1 4H 217 (41Pb 90)
Frederick Ter. E8 38Vb 71
Frederick Vs. *W7* 46Ga 86
(off Lwr. Boston Rd.)
Frederic M. SW1 2G 227
Frederic St. E17 29Ac 52
Fredora Av. UB4: Hayes 42W 84
Fred Styles Ho. SE7 51Lc 115
Fred Tibble Ct. RM9: Dag 35Ad 75
Fred White Wlk. N7 37Nb 70
Freeborne Gdns. RM13: Rain 37Jd 76
Freedom Cl. E17 28Ac 52
Freedom Rd. N17 26Tb 51
Freedom St. SW11 54Hb 111
Freedown La. SM2: Sutt 85Db 175
Freegrove Rd. N7 36Nb 70
(not continuous)
Freehold Ind. Est. TW4: Houn 57Y 107
Freeland Ct. DA15: Sidc 62Wc 139
Freeland Pk. NW4 26Ab 48
Freeland Rd. W5 45Pa 87
Freelands Av. CR2: Sels 81Zb 178
Freelands Gro. BR1: Brom 67Kc 137
Freelands Rd. BR1: Brom 67Kc 137
KT11: Cobh 86X 171
Freeland Way DA8: Erith 53Jd 118
Freeling Ho. *NW8* 39Fb 69
(off Dorman Way)
Freeling St. N1 38Pb 70
(Carnoustie Dr.)
N1 38Nb 70
(Pembroke St.)
Freeman Cl. TW17: Shep 70U 128
UB5: N'olt 38Aa 65
Freeman Ct. N7 34Nb 70
SW16 68Nb 134
Freeman Dr. KT8: W Mole 69Ba 129
Freeman Ho. SE11 5B 230
Freeman Rd. DA12: Grav'nd 2G 144
SM4: Mord 71Fb 155
Freemans Cl. SL2: Stoke P 7K 61
Freemans La. UB3: Hayes 45U 84
Freemantle Av. EN3: Pond E 15Zb 34
Freemantle St. SE17 7H 231 (50Ub 91)
Freeman Wlk. SE9 57Lc 115
Freeman Way RM11: Horn 30Pd 57
Freemasons' Hall 3G 223
Freemasons Pl. *CR0: C'don* 74Ub 157
(off Freemasons Rd.)
Freemasons Rd. CR0: C'don 74Ub 157
E16 43Kc 93
Free Prae Rd. KT16: Chert 74J 149
Freesia Cl. BR6: Chels 78Vc 161
Freesia Dr. GU24: Bisl 8E 166
Freestone Yd. SL3: Coln 52F 104
Freethorpe Cl. SE19 66Tb 135
Free Trade Wharf E1 45Zb 92
Freezeland Way UB10: Hil 37R 64
FREEZY WATER 8Zb 20
Freight La. N1 38Mb 70
Freightliners City Farm 37Qb 70

Freightmaster Est.—Gage M.

Freightmaster Est. RM13: Rain 44Gd 96
Freke Rd. SW11 55Jb 112
Frelford Cl. WD25: Wat 6Y 13
Fremantle Ho. *E1* 42Xb 91
(off Somerford St.)
RM18: Tilb 3B 122
Fremantle Rd. DA17: Belv 49Cd 96
IG6: Ilf 26Rc 54
Fremantle Way GU24: Brkwd 1B 186
UB3: Hayes 45V 84
Fremont St. E9 39Xb 71
(not continuous)
French Apartments, The
CR8: Purl 84Qb 176
Frenchaye KT15: Add 78L 149
Frenches, The RH1: Redh 4A 208
Frenches Ct. RH1: Redh 4A 208
Frenches Rd. RH1: Redh 4A 208
French Gdns. KT11: Cobh 86Y 171
French Horn Yd. WC1 1H 223
Frenchlands Ga. KT24: E Hor 99U 190
French Ordinary Ct. EC3 4J 225
French Pl. E1 5J 219 (41Ub 91)
French Row AL3: St A 2B 6
FRENCH STREET 100Vc 201
French St. TN16: Westrm 100Uc 200
TW16: Sun 68Y 129
French's Wells GU21: Wok 9M 167
Frenchum Gdns. SL1: Slou 5C 80
Frendsbury Rd. SE4 56Ac 114
Frensham Cl. UB1: S'hall 42Ba 85
Frensham Ct. SW19 69Fb 133
Frensham Dr. CR0: New Ad 82Ec 158
SW15 62Va 132
Frensham Rd. CR8: Kenley 86Rb 177
SE9 61Tc 138
Frensham St. SE15 51Wb 113
Frensham Wlk. SL2: Farn C 6G 60
Frensham Way KT17: Eps D 88Ya 174
Frere St. SW11 54Gb 111
Fresham Ho. *BR2: Brom* 69Hc 137
(off Durham Rd.)
Freshfield Av. E8 38Vb 71
Freshfield Cl. SE13 56Fc 115
Freshfield Ct. WD17: Wat 13Y 27
Freshfield Dr. N14 17Kb 32
Freshfield Flats KT20: Lwr K 99Bb 195
Freshfields CR0: C'don 74Bc 158
Freshfields Av. RM14: Upm 36Rd 77
Freshford St. SW18 62Eb 133
Freshill La. UB1: S'hall 42Ca 85
Freshmount Gdns. KT19: Eps 83Ra 173
Freshwater Cl. SW17 65Jb 134
Freshwater Ct. UB1: S'hall 41Ca 85
W1 1E 220
(off Crawford St.)
Freshwater Rd. RM8: Dag 32Zc 75
SW17 65Jb 134
Freshwell Av. RM6: Chad H 28Yc 55
Freshwell Gdns. CM13: W H'dn 30Fe 59
Fresh Wharf Est. IG11: Bark 40Rc 74
Fresh Wharf Rd. IG11: Bark 39Rc 74
Freshwood Cl. BR3: Beck 67Dc 136
Freshwood Way SM6: Wall 81Kb 176
Freston Gdns. EN4: Cockf 15Jb 32
Freston Pk. N3 26Bb 49
Freston Rd. W10 45Za 88
W11 45Za 88
Freswick Ho. *SE8* 49Ac 92
(off Chilton Gro.)
Freta Rd. DA6: Bex 57Bd 117
Freud Mus. 37Eb 69
Frewell Ho. EC1 7K 217
Frewin Rd. SW18 60Fb 111
Friar M. SE27 62Rb 135
Friar Rd. BR5: St M Cry 71Wc 161
UB4: Yead 42Z 85
Friars, The IG7: Chig 21Uc 54
Friars Av. CM15: Shenf 18Ce 41
N20 20Gb 31
SW15 62Va 132
Friar's Cl. CM15: Shenf 17Ce 41
Friars Cl. E4 20Ec 34
IG1: Ilf 32Tc 74
SE1 6C 224
UB5: N'olt 41Z 85
Friars Ct. E17 25Bc 52
RM7: Rush G 30Fd 56
SM6: Wall 77Kb 156
Friars Gdns. W3 44Ta 87
Friarsgate NW10 40Ra 67
Friars Ga. Cl. IG8: Wfd G 21Jc 53
Friars La. TW9: Rich 57Ma 109
Friars Mead E14 48Ec 92
WD4: K Lan 2Q 12
Friars M. SE9 57Qc 116
Friars Orchard KT22: Fet 93Fa 192
Friars Pl. La. W3 45Ta 87
Friars Ri. GU22: Wok 90C 168
Friars Rd. E6 39Mc 73
GU25: Vir W 10P 125
Friars Stile Pl. TW10: Rich 58Na 109
Friars Stile Rd. TW10: Rich 58Na 109
Friar St. EC4 3C 224 (44Rb 91)
Friars Wlk. N14 17Kb 32
SE2 50Zc 95
Friars Way KT16: Chert 72J 149
W3 44Ta 87
WD4: K Lan 2Q 12
WD23: Bush 11Ba 27
Friars Wood CR0: Sels 81Ac 178
Friary, The EN8: Walt C 5Bc 20
SL4: Old Win 8N 103
Friary Cl. N12 22Gb 49
Friary Ct. GU21: Wok 10K 167
SW1 7C 222
Friary Est. SE15 51Wb 113
(not continuous)
FRIARY ISLAND 8N 103
Friary Island TW19: Wray 8N 103
Friary La. IG8: Wfd G 21Jc 53
Friary Pk. W3 44Ta 87
Friary Pk. Ct. W3 44Sa 87
Friary Rd. N12 21Fb 49
N20 21Fb 49
SE15 52Wb 113
TW19: Wray 9N 103
W3 44Sa 87
Friary Way N12 21Gb 49
FRIDAY HILL 19Gc 35
Friday Hill E4 19Gc 35
Friday Hill E. E4 20Gc 35
Friday Hill W. E4 19Gc 35
Friday Rd. CR4: Mitc 66Hb 133
DA8: Erith 50Fd 96
Friday St. EC4 4D 224 (45Sb 91)
Frideswide Pl. NW5 36Lb 70
Friendly Pl. SE13 53Dc 114
Friendly St. SE8 54Cc 114
Friendly St. M. SE8 54Cc 114
Friends Av. EN8: Chesh 4Zb 20
Friendship Ho. SE1 2C 230
Friendship Wlk. UB5: N'olt 41Z 85
Friendship Way E15 39Ec 72
Friends Rd. CR0: C'don 76Tb 157
CR8: Purl 84Rb 177
Friend St. EC1 3B 218 (41Rb 91)
Friends Wlk. TW18: Staines 64H 127
UB8: Uxb 38M 63
FRIERN BARNET 22Hb 49
Friern Barnet La. N11 19Fb 31
N20 19Fb 31
Friern Barnet Rd. N11 22Hb 49
Friern Bri. Retail Pk. N11 23Kb 50
Friern Ct. N20 20Fb 31
Friern Mt. Dr. N20 17Eb 31
Friern Pk. N12 22Eb 49
Friern Rd. SE22 59Wb 113
(not continuous)
Friern Watch Av. N12 21Eb 49
Frigate Ho. *E14* 49Ec 92
(off Stebondale St.)
Frigate M. SE8 51Cc 114
Frimley Av. RM11: Horn 32Qd 77
SM6: Wall 78Nb 156
Frimley Cl. CR0: New Ad 80Ec 158
SW19 61Ab 132
Frimley Ct. DA14: Sidc 64Yc 139
Frimley Cres. CR0: New Ad 80Ec 158
Frimley Dr. SL1: Slou 7D 80
Frimley Gdns. CR4: Mitc 69Gb 133
Frimley Rd. HP1: Hem H 1G 2
IG3: Ilf 34Uc 74
KT9: Chess 78Ma 153
Frimley St. *E1* 42Zb 92
(off Frimley Way)
Frimley Way E1 42Zb 92
Fringewood Cl. HA6: Nwood 25R 44
Frinstead Gro. BR5: St M Cry 70Zc 139
Frinstead Ho. *W10* 45Za 88
(off Freston Rd.)
Frinsted Rd. DA8: Erith 52Fd 118
Frinton Cl. WD19: Wat 19X 27
Frinton Ct. *W13* 43Ka 86
(off Hardwick Grn.)
Frinton Dr. IG8: Wfd G 24Fc 53
Frinton M. IG2: Ilf 30Qc 54
Frinton Rd. DA14: Sidc 61Ad 139
E6 41Mc 93
N15 30Ub 51
RM5: Col R 24Bd 55
SW17 65Jb 134
Friston Path IG7: Chig 22Uc 54
Friston St. SW6 54Db 111
Friswell Pl. DA6: Bex 56Cd 118
Fritham Cl. KT3: N Mald 72Ua 154
Frith Ct. NW7 24Ab 48
Frithe, The SL2: Slou 4M 81
Frith Ho. NW8 6C 214
Frith Knowle KT12: Hers 78X 151
Frith La. NW7 24Ab 48
Frith Rd. CR0: C'don 75Sb 157
E11 35Ec 72
Friths Dr. RH2: Reig 3K 207
Frith St. W1 3D 222 (44Mb 90)
Frithville Ct. *W12* 46Ya 88
(off Frithville Gdns.)
Frithville Gdns. W12 46Ya 88
Frithwald Rd. KT16: Chert 73H 149
Frithwood Av. HA6: Nwood 23U 44
Frizlands La. RM10: Dag 33Dd 76
Frobisher Cl. CR8: Kenley 89Sb 177
HA5: Pinn 31Z 65
WD23: Bush 16Ca 27
Frobisher Ct. NW9 26Ua 48
SE8 50Ac 92
(off Evelyn St.)
SE10 51Fc 115
(off Old Woolwich Rd.)
SE23 61Xb 135
SM3: Cheam 80Ab 154
W12 47Ya 88
(off Lime Gro.)
Frobisher Cres. EC2 7E 218
TW19: Stanw 59N 105
Frobisher Gdns. E10 31Dc 72
RM16: Chaf H 48Ae 99
TW19: Stanw 59N 105
Frobisher Ho. *E1* 46Xb 91
(off Watts St.)
SW1 51Mb 112
(off Dolphin Sq.)
Frobisher M. EN2: Enf 14Tb 33
Frobisher Pas. E14 46Cc 92
Frobisher Pl. SE15 53Yb 114
Frobisher Rd. AL1: St A 4G 6
DA8: Erith 52Hd 118
E6 44Pc 94
N8 28Qb 50
Frobisher St. SE10 51Gc 115
Frobisher Way DA9: Ghithe 56Xd 120
DA12: Grav'nd 4G 144
Froggy La. UB9: Den 34F 62
Froghall La. IG7: Chig 21Tc 54
Frog La. GU4: Sut G 97A 188
RM13: Rain 44Fd 96
Frogley Rd. SE22 56Vb 113
Frogmoor Ct. WD3: Rick 19M 25
Frogmoor La. WD3: Rick 19M 25
FROGMORE
AL2 10C 6
SL4 4J 103
Frogmore AL2: F'mre 9B 6
SW18 57Cb 111
Frogmore Av. UB4: Hayes 42U 84
Frogmore Border SL4: Wind 5J 103
Frogmore Bus. Pk. AL2: F'mre 10C 6
Frogmore Cl. SL1: Slou 7E 80
SM3: Cheam 76Za 154
Frogmore Cotts. WD17: Wat 15Z 27
Frogmore Ct. UB2: S'hall 49Ba 85
Frogmore Dr. SL4: Wind 3J 103
FROGMORE END 5M 3
Frogmore Gdns. SM3: Cheam 77Ab 154
UB4: Hayes 42U 84
Frogmore Home Pk. AL2: F'mre 9B 6
Frogmore House 4K 103
Frogmore Ind. Est. N5 36Sb 71
NW10 41Sa 87
UB3: Hayes 47U 84
Frogmore Ind. Pk.
RM20: W Thur 50Wd 98
Frogmore Paper Mill, The & Visitor Cen.
5M 3
Frogmore Rd. HP3: Hem H 5M 3
Frogmore Rd. Ind. Est. HP3: Hem H 6M 3
Frognal NW3 35Eb 69
Frognal Av. DA14: Sidc 65Wc 139
HA1: Harr 28Ha 46
Frognal Cl. NW3 36Eb 69
FROGNAL CORNER 65Vc 139
Frognal Ct. NW3 37Eb 69
Frognal Gdns. NW3 35Eb 69
Frognal La. NW3 36Db 69
Frognal Pde. NW3 37Eb 69
Frognal Pl. DA14: Sidc 65Wc 139
Frognal Ri. NW3 34Eb 69
Frognal Way NW3 35Eb 69
Frog St. CM15: Dodd, Kel H 11Ud 40
Frogwell Cl. N15 30Tb 51
Froissart Rd. SE9 57Mc 115
Frome RM18: E Til 9L 101
Frome Ho. SE15 56Xb 113
Frome Rd. N22 27Rb 51
Frome St. N1 1D 218 (40Sb 71)
Fromondes Rd. SM3: Cheam 78Ab 154
Fromow Gdns. GU20: W'sham 9B 146
Frontenac NW10 38Xa 68
Frontier Works N17 23Ub 51
Front La. RM14: Upm 33Ud 78
Frost Ct. *NW9* 26Ua 48
(off Salk Cl.)
Frostic Wlk. E1 43Wb 91
Froude St. SW8 54Kb 112
Frowick Cl. AL9: Wel G 5D 8
Frowyke Cres. EN6: S Mim 4Wa 16
Fruen Rd. TW14: Felt 59V 106
Fruiterers Pas. *EC4* 5E 224
(off Queen St. Pl.)
Fryatt Rd. N17 24Tb 51
(not continuous)
Fry Cl. RM5: Col R 22Cd 56
Fryday Gro. M. *SW12* 59Lb 112
(off Weir Rd.)
Frye Ct. *E3* 41Bc 92
(off Benworth St.)
Frye Ho. *E20* 37Ec 72
(off Penny Brookes St.)
Fryent Cl. NW9 30Qa 47
Fryent Country Pk. (Local Nature Reserve)
31Qa 67
Fryent Cres. NW9 30Ua 48
Fryent Flds. NW9 30Ua 48
Fryent Gro. NW9 30Ua 48
Fryent Way NW9 29Qa 47
Fryern Wood CR3: Cat'm 96Sb 197
Fryers Vw. *SE4* 56Zb 114
(off Frendsbury Rd.)
Fry Ho. E6 38Lc 73
Frying Pan Alley E1 1K 225
Frylands Ct. CR0: New Ad 83Ec 178
Frymley Vw. SL4: Wind 3B 102
Fry Rd. E6 38Mc 73
NW10 39Va 68
Frys Ct. *SE10* 51Ec 114
(off Durnford St.)
Fryston Av. CR0: C'don 75Wb 157
CR5: Coul 86Kb 176
Fryth Mead AL3: St A 1P 5
Fuchsia Cl. RM7: Rush G 33Gd 76
Fuchsia St. SE2 50Xc 95
Fuchsia Way GU24: W End 5C 166
Fulbeck Dr. NW9 25Ua 48
Fulbeck Ho. *N7* 37Pb 70
(off Sutterton St.)
Fulbeck Rd. N19 35Lb 70
Fulbeck Wlk. HA8: Edg 19Ra 29
Fulbeck Way HA2: Harr 26Ea 46
Fulbourn *KT1: King T* 68Qa 131
(off Eureka Rd.)
Fulbourne Cl. RH1: Redh 4N 207
Fulbourne Rd. E17 25Ec 52
Fulbourne St. E1 43Xb 91
Fulbrook Av. KT15: New H 83J 169
Fulbrook La. RM15: S Ock 45Vd 98
Fulbrook M. N19 35Lb 70
Fulcher Ho. *N1* 39Ub 71
(off Colville Est.)
SE8 50Bc 92
Fulford Gro. WD19: Wat 19X 27
Fulford Ho. KT19: Ewe 80Ta 153
Fulford Rd. CR3: Cat'm 93Tb 197
KT19: Ewe 80Ta 153
Fulford St. SE16 47Xb 91
FULHAM 54Ab 110
FULHAM BROADWAY 52Cb 111
Fulham B'way. SW6 52Cb 111
Fulham Bus. Exchange *SW6* 53Eb 111
(off The Boulevard)
Fulham B'way Shop. Cen. SW6 52Cb 111
Fulham Cl. UB10: Hil 42S 84
Fulham Ct. SW6 53Cb 111
Fulham FC 53Za 110
Fulham High St. SW6 54Ab 110
Fulham Island *SW6* 52Cb 111
(off Fulham Rd.)
Fulham Palace 54Ab 110
Fulham Pal. Rd. SW6 50Ya 88
W6 50Ya 88
Fulham Pk. Gdns. SW6 54Bb 111
Fulham Pk. Rd. SW6 54Bb 111
Fulham Pools
Virgin Active 51Ab 110
Fulham Rd. SW3 7B 226 (52Db 111)
SW6 54Ab 110
(not continuous)
SW10 7B 226 (52Db 111)
Fullarton Cres. RM15: S Ock 44Vd 98
Fullbrooks Av. KT4: Wor Pk 74Va 154
Fullbrook School Sports Cen. 84J 169
Fuller Cl. BR6: Chels 78Vc 161
E2 42Wb 91
(off Cheshire St.)
WD23: Bush 17Fa 28
Fuller Ct. N8 29Mb 50
Fuller Gdns. WD24: Wat 9X 13
Fullerian Cres. WD18: Wat 14V 26
Fuller Rd. RM8: Dag 34Xc 75
WD24: Wat 9X 13
Fullers Av. IG8: Wfd G 24Hc 53
KT6: Surb 75Pa 153
Fullers Cl. EN9: Walt A 5Jc 21
RM5: Col R 24Ed 56
Fuller's Griffin Brewery & Vis. Cen.
51Va 110
FULLERS HILL 93Sd 204
Fullers Hill TN16: Westrm 98Tc 200
Fullers La. RM5: Col R 24Ed 56
Fullers Rd. E18 24Hc 53
Fuller St. NW4 28Ya 48
TN15: Seal 92Rd 203
Fullers Way Nth. KT6: Surb 76Pa 153
Fullers Way Sth. KT9: Chess 77Na 153
Fuller's Wood CR0: C'don 78Cc 158
Fullers Wood La.
RH1: S Nut 7C 208
Fullerton Cl. KT14: Byfl 86P 169
Fullerton Ct. TW11: Tedd 65Ja 130
Fullerton Dr. KT14: Byfl 86N 169
Fullerton Rd. CR0: C'don 73Vb 157
KT14: Byfl 86N 169
SM5: Cars 81Gb 175
SW18 57Db 111
Fullerton Way KT14: Byfl 86N 169
Fuller Way UB3: Harl 50V 84
WD3: Crox G 15Q 26
Fullmer Way KT15: Wdhm 82H 169
Fullwell Av. IG5: Ilf 25Pc 54
IG6: Ilf 25Rc 54
FULLWELL CROSS 26Sc 54
Fullwell Cross IG6: Ilf 26Tc 54
Fullwell Cross Leisure Cen. 26Sc 54
Fullwell Pde. IG5: Ilf 25Qc 54
Fullwood's M. N1 3G 219 (41Tb 91)
Fulmar Cl. KT5: Surb 72Pa 153
Fulmar Cres.
HP1: Hem H 2J 3
Fulmar Ho. *SE16* 49Zb 92
(off Tawny Way)
Fulmar Rd. RM12: Horn 38Jd 76
Fulmead St. SW6 53Db 111
FULMER 5P 61
Fulmer Cl. TW12: Hamp 64Aa 129
Fulmer Comn. Rd. SL0: Iver H 6P 61
SL3: Ful 6P 61
Fulmer Cnr. SL9: Ger X 32D 62
Fulmer Dr. SL9: Ger X 3P 61
Fulmer Ho. NW8 6E 214
UB8: Uxb 37N 63
Fulmer La. SL3: Ful 34B 62
SL9: Ger X 34B 62
Fulmer Pl. SL3: Ful 35A 62
Fulmer Ri. SL3: Ful 37B 62
Fulmer Rd. E16 43Mc 93
SL3: Ful 5P 61
SL9: Ger X 31A 62
Fulmer Way SL9: Ger X 30A 42
W13 48Ka 86
Fulneck Pl. E1 42Yb 92
Fulready Rd. E10 29Fc 53
Fulstone Cl. TW4: Houn 56Ba 107
Fulthorp Rd. SE3 54Hc 115
Fulton Ct. *WD6: Bore* 10Pa 15
(off Aycliffe Rd.)
Fulton Dr. GU24: Bisl 9E 166
Fulton M. W2 45Eb 89
Fulton Rd. HA9: Wemb 34Qa 67
FULWELL 63Fa 130
Fulwell Ct. IG5: Ilf 25Qc 54
UB1: S'hall 45Ea 86
(off Baird Av.)
Fulwell Golf Course 63Fa 130
Fulwell Pk. Av. TW2: Twick 61Da 129
Fulwell Rd. TW11: Tedd 63Fa 130
Fulwich Rd. DA1: Dart 58Pd 119
Fulwood Av. HA0: Wemb 40Pa 67
Fulwood Cl. UB3: Hayes 44V 84
Fulwood Ct. HA3: Kenton 30Ja 46
Fulwood Gdns. TW1: Twick 58Ha 108
Fulwood Pl. WC1 1J 223 (43Pb 90)
Fulwood Wlk. SW19 60Ab 110
Funky Footprints Nature Reserve 72Q 150
Furber St. W6 48Xa 88
Furham Fld. HA5: Hat E 24Ca 45
Furley Ho. *SE15* 52Wb 113
(off Peckham Pk. Rd.)
Furley Rd. SE15 52Wb 113
Furlong Av. CR4: Mitc 69Gb 133
Furlong Cl. SM6: Wall 74Kb 156
Furlong Rd. N7 37Qb 70
Furlongs HP1: Hem H 1J 3
Furlongs, The KT10: Esh 76Da 151
Furlough, The GU22: Wok 88C 168
Furmage St. SW18 59Db 111
Furneaux Av. SE27 64Rb 135
Furner Cl. DA1: Cray 55Hd 118
Furness SL4: Wind 4A 102
Furness Cl. RM16: Grays 10D 100
(not continuous)
Furness Ho. SW1 7A 228
Furness Pl. *SL4: Wind* 4A 102
(off Furness)
Furness Rd. HA2: Harr 31Da 65
NW10 40Wa 68
SM4: Mord 72Db 155
SW6 54Db 111
Furness Row SL4: Wind 4A 102
Furness Sq. SL4: Wind 4A 102
Furness Wlk. SL4: Wind 4A 102
Furness Way RM12: Horn 36Jd 76
SL4: Wind 4A 102
Furnival Av. SL2: Slou 3F 80
Furnival Cl. GU25: Vir W 2P 147
Furnival Ct. *E3* 40Cc 72
(off Four Seasons Cl.)
Furnival Mans. W1 1B 222
Furnival St. EC4 2K 223 (44Qb 90)
Furrow La. E9 36Yb 72
Furrows, The KT12: Walt T 75Y 151
UB9: Hare 29L 43
Furrows Pl. CR3: Cat'm 95Vb 197
Fursby Av. N3 23Cb 49
Fursecroft W1 2F 221
Furtherfield WD5: Ab L 4U 12
Furtherfield Cl. CR0: C'don 72Qb 156
Further Grn. Rd. SE6 59Gc 115
Furtherground HP2: Hem H 3N 3
Furzebank SL5: S'hill 10B 124
Furzebushes La. AL2: Chis G 7L 5
Furze Cl. RH1: Redh 5P 207
WD19: Wat 22Y 45
FURZEDOWN 64Kb 134
Furzedown Cl. TW20: Egh 65A 126
Furzedown Dr. SW17 64Kb 134
Furzedown Recreation Cen. 64Kb 134
Furzedown Rd. SM2: Sutt 83Eb 175
SW17 64Kb 134
Furze Farm Cl. RM6: Chad H 26Ad 55
Furze Fld. KT22: Oxs 85Fa 172
Furzefield EN8: Chesh 1Xb 19
Furzefield Cen. 3Za 16
Furzefield Cl. BR7: Chst 65Rc 138
Furze Fld. Ct. WD19: Wat 20W 26
Furzefield Ct. EN6: Pot B 3Ab 16
Furzefield Cres. RH2: Reig 8L 207
Furzefield Rd. RH2: Reig 8L 207
SE3 51Kc 115
Furzeground Way UB11: Stock P 46S 84
Furze Gro. KT20: Kgswd 93Bb 195
Furze Hall KT20: Kgswd 93Bb 195
Furzeham Rd. UB7: W Dray 47N 83
FURZE HILL 93Bb 195
Furze Hill CR8: Purl 83Nb 176
KT20: Kgswd 92Bb 195
RH1: Redh 5N 207
Furzehill Cotts. GU24: Pirb 4A 186
Furzehill Pde. WD6: Bore 13Qa 29
Furzehill Rd. WD6: Bore 14Qa 29
(not continuous)
Furzehill Sq. BR5: St M Cry 70Xc 139
Furze La. CR8: Purl 83Nb 176
Furzen Cl. SL2: Slou 1E 80
Furzen Cres. AL10: Hat 3B 8
Furze Pl. RH1: Redh 5P 207
Furze Rd. CR7: Thor H 69Sb 135
HP1: Hem H 3G 2
KT15: Add 79H 149
Furze St. E3 43Cc 92
Furze Vw. WD3: Chor 16E 24
Furzewood TW16: Sun 67W 128
Fusedale Way RM15: S Ock 45Vd 98
Fusiliers Way TW4: Houn 55Y 107
(not continuous)
Fusion RH1: Redh 5P 207
Fuzzens Wlk. SL4: Wind 4C 102
Fydler's Cl. SL4: Wink 5A 124
Fye Foot La. EC4 4D 224
Fyfe Apartments N8 27Pb 50
Fyfe Way BR1: Brom 68Jc 137
Fyfield *N4* 33Qb 70
(off Six Acres Est.)
Fyfield Cl. BR2: Brom 70Fc 137
CM13: W H'dn 30Fe 59
KT17: Eps 86Va 174
Fyfield Ct. E7 37Jc 73
Fyfield Dr. RM15: S Ock 45Vd 98
Fyfield Ho. *E6* 39Nc 74
(off Ron Leighton Way)
Fyfield Rd. E17 27Fc 53
EN1: Enf 13Ub 33
IG8: Wfd G 24Lc 53
RM13: Rain 39Hd 76
SW9 55Qb 112
Fynes St. SW1 5D 228 (49Mb 90)

G

Gabion Av. RM19: Purf 49Td 98
Gable Cl. DA1: Cray 57Jd 118
HA5: Hat E 24Ca 45
WD5: Ab L 4U 12
Gable Ct. *RH1: Redh* 5A 208
(off St Anne's Mt.)
SE26 63Xb 135
Gable M. BR2: Brom 75Nc 160
SL1: Burn 2A 80
Gables, The BR1: Brom 66Kc 137
CM13: Gt War 23Yd 58
DA3: Lfield 68Ee 143
HA9: Wemb 34Qa 67
HP2: Hem H 1M 3
IG11: Bark 37Sc 74
KT13: Weyb 78S 150
KT22: Oxs 84Ea 172
N10 27Jb 50
(off Fortis Grn.)
RM17: Grays 49Be 99
SM7: Bans 89Bb 175
WD19: Wat 17Y 27
WD25: Wat 5Z 13
Gables Av. TW15: Ashf 64P 127
WD6: Bore 13Pa 29
Gables Cl. GU22: Wok 92B 188
SE5 53Ub 113
SE12 60Jc 115
SL3: Dat 1L 103
SL9: Chal P 21A 42
Gables Ct. CR8: Purl 84Rb 177
GU22: Wok 92B 188
Gables Lodge EN4: Had W 10Eb 17
Gables Way SM7: Bans 89Bb 175
Gabriel Cl. RM5: Col R 24Ed 56
RM16: Chaf H 48Yd 98
TW13: Hanw 63Aa 129
Gabriel Gdns. DA12: Grav'nd 4G 144
Gabriel Ho. N1 1B 218
SE11 5H 229 (49Pb 90)
SE16 48Bc 92
(off Odessa St.)
Gabrielle Cl. HA9: Wemb 34Pa 67
Gabrielle Ct. NW3 37Fb 69
Gabriel M. NW2 33Bb 69
Gabriel's M. BR3: Beck 67Zb 136
Gabriel Spring Rd. DA3: Fawk 75Td 164
Gabriel Spring Rd. E.
DA3: Fawk, Hort K 75Ud 164
Gabriel Sq. AL1: St A 3C 6
Gabriel St. SE23 59Zb 114
Gabriels Wharf SE1 6A 224 (46Qb 90)
Gadbrook Rd. RH3: Bet 10A 206
Gad Cl. E13 41Kc 93
Gaddesden Av. HA9: Wemb 37Pa 67
Gaddesden Cres. WD25: Wat 6Z 13
Gaddesden Ho. EC1 4G 219
Gade Av. WD18: Wat 14U 26
Gade Bank WD3: Crox G 14T 26
GADEBRIDGE 1K 3
Gadebridge Ct. HP1: Hem H 1L 3
Gadebridge Ho. *SW3* 7D 226
(off Cale St.)
Gadebridge La. HP1: Hem H 1J 3
(not continuous)
Gadebridge Point *HP1: Hem H* 4L 3
(off Cotterells)
Gadebridge Rd. HP1: Hem H 1J 3
Gade Cl. UB3: Hayes 46X 85
WD18: Wat 14U 26
Gade Pl. *HP1: Hem H* 4L 3
(off Cotterells)
Gadesden Rd. KT19: Ewe 79Sa 153
Gade Side WD25: Wat 7U 12
(not continuous)
Gade Twr. HP3: Hem H 7A 4
Gade Valley Cl. WD4: K Lan 10A 4
Gadeview HP1: Hem H 2L 3
Gade Vw. Gdns. WD4: Hunt C 4S 12
Gadeview Rd. HP3: Hem H 6L 3
Gadsbury Cl. NW9 30Va 48
Gadsden Cl. RM14: Upm 30Ud 58
Gadsden Ho. *W10* 42Ab 88
(off Hazlewood Cres.)
Gadswell Cl. WD25: Wat 8Z 13
Gadwall Cl. E16 44Kc 93
Gadwall Ho. *NW9* 30Wa 48
(off Perryfield Way)
Gadwall Way SE28 47Tc 94
Gage Brown Ho. *W10* 44Za 88
(off Bridge Cl.)
Gage M. CR2: S Croy 78Rb 157

Gage Rd.—Gateacre Ct.

Gage Rd. E16 43Gc 93
Gage St. WC1 7G 217 (43Nb 90)
Gainford Ho. E2 41Xb 91
(off Ellsworth St.)
Gainford St. N1 39Qb 70
Gainsboro Gdns. UB6: G'frd 36Ga 66
Gainsborough Av. AL1: St A 1D 6
DA1: Dart 57Ld 119
E12 36Qc 74
RM18: Tilb 3C 122
Gainsborough Cl. BR3: Beck 66Cc 136
KT10: Esh 74Ga 152
Gainsborough Ct. BR2: Brom 70Lc 137
CM14: W'ley 21Yd 58
(off Gt. Eastern Rd.)
KT12: Walt T 77W 150
KT19: Ewe 79Va 154
N12 22Db 49
SE16 50Xb 91
(off Stubbs Dr.)
SE21 61Ub 135
W4 50Ra 87
(off Chaseley Dr.)
W12 47Ya 88
Gainsborough Dr. CR2: Sande 85Wb 177
DA11: Nflt 62Fe 143
Gainsborough Gdns. HA8: Edg 26Pa 47
NW3 34Fb 69
NW11 31Bb 69
TW7: Isle 57Fa 108
Gainsborough Ho. E14 47Cc 92
(off Cassilis Rd.)
E14 45Ac 92
(off Victory Pl.)
EN1: Enf 15Wb 33
RM8: Dag 35Xc 75
(off Longbridge Rd.)
SW1 6E 228
Gainsborough Lodge HA1: Harr 29Ha 46
(off Hindes Rd.)
Gainsborough Mans. W14 51Ab 110
(off Queen's Club Gdns.)
Gainsborough M. SE26 62Xb 135
Gainsborough Pl. CM13: Hut 18Fe 41
IG7: Chig 20Vc 37
KT11: Cobh 87Aa 171
Gainsborough Rd. E11 31Gc 73
E15 41Gc 93
IG8: Wfd G 23Nc 54
KT3: N Mald 72Ta 153
KT19: Eps 82Sa 173
N12 22Db 49
RM8: Dag 35Xc 75
RM13: Rain 39Jd 76
TW9: Rich 54Pa 109
UB4: Hayes 40S 64
W4 49Va 88
Gainsborough Sq. DA6: Bex 55Zc 117
Gainsborough St. E9 37Bc 72
Gainsborough Studios E. N1 1F 219
Gainsborough Studios Nth. N1 1F 219
Gainsborough Studios Sth. N1 1F 219
Gainsborough Studios W. N1 1F 219
Gainsborough Ter. SM2: Sutt 80Bb 155
(off Belmont Ri.)
Gainsborough Twr. UB5: N'olt 40Z 65
(off Academy Gdns.)
Gainsfield Ct. E11 34Gc 73
Gainsford Pl. RH8: C'rst 10G 210
Gainsford Rd. E17 28Bc 52
Gainsford St. SE1 7K 225 (47Vb 91)
Gairloch Ho. NW1 38Mb 70
(off Stratford Vs.)
Gairloch Rd. SE5 54Ub 113
Gaisford St. NW5 37Lb 70
Gaist Av. CR3: Cat'm 94Xb 197
Gaitskell Ct. SW11 54Gb 111
Gaitskell Ho. E6 39Mc 73
E17 27Dc 52
RM16: Grays 46De 99
(off Grammavill St.)
SE17 51Ub 113
(off Villa St.)
WD6: Bore 14Ta 29
(off Howard Dr.)
Gaitskell Rd. SE9 60Sc 116
Gaitskell Way SE1 1D 230
Gala Bingo
Acton 46Ta 87
(off High St.)
Bexleyheath 56Dd 118
Borehamwood 13Qa 29
(within The Point)
Camberwell 52Sb 113
Dartford 58Md 119
East Ham 39Nc 74
Enfield 14Wb 33
Feltham 61X 129
Harrow 29Ha 46
Hounslow 56Ca 107
Leyton 32Bc 72
Slough 6J 81
Stratford 39Fc 73
Surrey Quays 48Zb 92
Tooting 64Gb 133
Waltham Cross 6Ac 20
Woking 89B 168
(within The Big Apple)
Gala Ct. CR7: Thor H 71Qb 156
Galahad Cl. SL1: Slou 7E 80
Galahad M. E3 40Bc 72
Galahad Rd. BR1: Brom 63Jc 137
N9 20Wb 33
Galata Rd. SW13 52Wa 110
Galatea Sq. SE15 55Xb 113
Galaxy Bldg. E14 49Cc 92
(off Crews St.)
Galaxy Ho. EC2 5G 219
Galba Ct. TW8: Bford 52Ma 109
Galbraith St. E14 48Ec 92
Galdana Av. EN5: New Bar 13Eb 31
Galeborough Av. IG8: Wfd G 24Fc 53
Gale Cl. CR4: Mitc 69Fb 133
TW12: Hamp 65Aa 129
Gale Cres. SM7: Bans 89Cb 175
Galena Arches W6 49Xa 88
(off Galena Rd.)
Galena Hgts. E20 37Ec 72
(off Mirabelle Gdns.)
Galena Ho. SE18 50Vc 95
(off Grosmont Rd.)
Galena Rd. W6 49Xa 88
Galen Cl. KT19: Eps 83Qa 173
Galen Pl. WC1 1G 223 (43Nb 90)
Galesbury Rd. SW18 58Eb 111
Gales Gdns. E2 41Xb 91
Gale St. E3 43Cc 92
RM9: Dag 36Yc 75
Gales Way IG8: Wfd G 24Nc 54
Galey Grn. RM15: S Ock 43Xd 98
Galgate Cl. SW19 60Za 110
Gallants Farm Rd. EN4: E Barn 17Gb 31
Galleon Blvd. DA2: Dart 56Td 120
Galleon Cl. DA8: Erith 49Fd 96
SE16 47Zb 92
Galleon Ho. E14 49Ec 92
(off Glengarnock Av.)
Galleon M. DA11: Nflt 9A 122
Galleon Rd. RM16: Chaf H 49Yd 98
Galleons Dr. IG11: Bark 41Wc 95
Galleons La. SL3: Wex 2N 81
(not continuous)
Galleons Vw. E14 47Ec 92
Galleria Ct. SE15 51Vb 113
Galleria Shop. Mall, The E18 26Jc 53
Galleries, The CM14: W'ley 22Xd 58
NW8 2A 214
Gallery, The 39Sc 74
(off Clockhouse Av.)
Gallery, The E20 37Ec 72
(within Westfield Stratford City Shop. Cen.)
SE14 52Bc 114
(off New Cross Rd.)
Gallery Apartments E1 44Yb 92
(off Commercial Rd.)
SE1 2H 231
Gallery at London Glassblowing, The 1H 231
Gallery Ct. E17 26Ec 52
(off Fulbourne Rd.)
SE1 2F 231
SW10 51Eb 111
(off Gunter Gro.)
Gallery Gdns. UB5: N'olt 40Z 65
Gallery Ho. E8 37Xb 71
(off Hackney Gro.)
Gallery Rd. SE21 60Tb 113
Galley, The E16 45Rc 94
GALLEY HILL 3Hc 21
Galley Hill HP1: Hem H 1H 3
Galley Hill Ind. Est.
DA10: Swans 57Ae 121
Galley Hill Rd. DA10: Swans 57Be 121
DA11: Nflt 57Be 121
Galleyhill Rd. EN9: Walt A 5Gc 21
(not continuous)
Galley La. EN5: Barn 10Wa 16
Galleymead Rd. SL3: Poyle 53H 105
Galleywall Rd. SE16 49Xb 91
Galleywall Rd. Trad. Est. SE16 49Xb 91
Galleywood Cres. RM5: Col R 23Fd 56
Galleywood Ho. W10 43Ya 88
(off Sutton Way)
Gallian Cl. SL0: Iver 44G 82
Galliard Cl. N9 16Yb 34
Galliard Ct. N9 16Wb 33
Galliard Rd. N9 18Wb 33
Gallia Rd. N5 36Rb 71
Gallica Ct. SM1: Sutt 74Db 155
Gallions Cl. IG11: Bark 41Wc 95
Gallions Entrance E16 46Sc 94
Gallions Reach Shop. Pk. E6 43Sc 94
Gallions Rd. E16 45Rc 94
SE7 49Kc 93
(not continuous)
GALLIONS RDBT. 45Rc 94
Gallions Vw. Rd. SE28 47Uc 94
Gallipoli Pl. RM9: Dag 39Xc 75
Gallon Cl. SE7 49Lc 93
Gallop, The CR2: Sels 80Xb 157
SL4: Wind 9G 102
SM2: Sutt 81Fb 175
Gallops, The KT10: Esh 76Da 151
Gallosson Rd. SE18 49Uc 94
Galloway Chase SL2: Slou 5L 81
Galloway Dr. DA1: Cray 59Gd 118
Galloway Path CR0: C'don 77Tb 157
Galloway Rd. W12 46Wa 88
GALLOWS CORNER 26Ld 57
GALLOWS CORNER 25Ld 57
Gallows Hill WD4: Hunt C 4S 12
Gallows Hill La. WD5: Ab L 4S 12
Gallows Wood DA3: Fawk 77Wd 164
Gallus Cl. N21 16Pb 32
Gallus Sq. SE3 55Kc 115
Gallys Rd. SL4: Wind 4B 102
Galpins Rd. CR7: Thor H 71Nb 156
Galsworthy Av. E14 44Ac 92
RM6: Chad H 31Xc 75
Galsworthy Cl. NW2 35Ab 68
SE28 46Xc 95
Galsworthy Ct. W3 48Ra 87
(off Bollo Bri. Rd.)
Galsworthy Cres. SE3 52Lc 115
Galsworthy Ho. W11 44Ab 88
(off Elgin Cres.)
Galsworthy Rd. KT2: King T 66Ra 131
KT16: Chert 73J 149
NW2 35Ab 68
RM18: Tilb 3E 122
Galsworthy Ter. N16 34Tb 71
Galton Ct. NW9 27Ua 48
(off Joslin Av.)
Galton Rd. SL5: S'dale 2D 146
Galton St. W10 41Ab 88
Galva Cl. EN4: Cockf 14Jb 32
Galvani Way CR0: Wadd 74Pb 156
Galveston Ho. E1 42Ac 92
(off Harford St.)
Galveston Rd. SW15 57Bb 111
Galvin Rd. SL1: Slou 6G 80
Galway Cl. SE16 50Xb 91
(off Masters Dr.)
Galway Ho. E1 43Zb 92
(off White Horse La.)
EC1 4E 218
Galway St. EC1 4E 218 (41Sb 91)
Gambado
Beckenham 65Cc 136
Chelsea 53Eb 111
(off Station Ct.)
Watford 6X 13
Gambetta St. SW8 54Kb 112
Gambia St. SE1 7C 224 (46Rb 91)
Gambier Ho. EC1 4E 218
Gambles La. GU23: Rip 96L 189
Gambole Rd. SW17 63Gb 133
Games Rd. EN4: Cockf 13Gb 31
Gamlen Rd. SW15 56Za 110
Gamma Ct. CR0: C'don 74Tb 157
(off Sydenham Rd.)
Gammon Cl. HP3: Hem H 3A 4
Gammon Fld. RM16: Grays 5A 100
Gammons Farm Cl. WD24: Wat 8U 12
Gammons La. WD24: Wat 8U 12
(not continuous)
Gamuel Cl. E17 30Cc 52
Gander Grn. Cres.
TW12: Hamp 67Ca 129
Gander Grn. La. SM1: Sutt 76Bb 155
SM3: Cheam 75Ab 154
Ganders Ash WD25: Wat 5W 12
Gandhi Cl. E17 30Cc 52
Gandhi Ct. WD24: Wat 12Z 27
Gandolfi St. SE15 51Ub 113
Gangers Hill CR3: Wold 100Ac 198
RH9: G'stone 100Ac 198
Ganley Ct. SW11 55Fb 111
(off Winstanley Est.)
Gant Ct. EN9: Walt A 6Hc 21
Ganton St. W1 4B 222 (45Lb 90)
Ganton Wlk. WD19: Wat 21Z 45
GANTS HILL 30Qc 54
GANTS HILL 30Qc 54
Gants Hill IG2: Ilf 30Qc 54
Gantshill Cres. IG2: Ilf 29Qc 54
GANWICK 8Cb 17
GANWICK CORNER 7Cb 17
Gapemouth Rd.
GU24: Pirb 4A 186
Gapp Cl. TN15: W King 80Ud 164
Gap Rd. SW19 64Cb 133
Garage Rd. W3 44Qa 87
Garand Ct. N7 36Pb 70
Garbett Ho. SE17 51Rb 113
(off Doddington Gro.)
Garbrand Wlk. KT17: Ewe 81Va 174
Garbutt Pl. W1 7J 215 (43Jb 90)
Garbutt Rd. RM14: Upm 33Sd 78
Garda Ho. SE10 49Gc 93
(off Cable Wlk.)
Garden Av. AL10: Hat 4C 8
CR4: Mitc 66Kb 134
DA7: Bex 55Bd 117
Garden City HA8: Edg 23Qa 47
Garden Cl. AL1: St A 1F 6
E4 22Cc 52
EN5: Ark 14Ya 30
HA4: Ruis 33U 64
KT3: N Mald 70Ua 132
KT15: Add 77M 149
KT22: Lea 96La 192
SE12 62Kc 137
SM6: Wall 78Nb 156
SM7: Bans 87Cb 175
SW15 59Ya 110
TW12: Hamp 64Ba 129
TW15: Ashf 65S 128
UB5: N'olt 39Aa 65
WD17: Wat 12V 26
Garden Cotts. AL2: F'mre 9B 6
BR5: St P 68Yc 139
Garden Ct. CR0: C'don 75Vb 157
EC4 4K 223
HA7: Stan 22La 46
N12 22Db 49
NW8 3B 214
TN13: S'oaks 94Md 203
(off Garden Rd.)
TW9: Kew 53Pa 109
TW12: Hamp 64Ba 129
W4 48Sa 87
W11 45Ab 88
(off Clarendon Rd.)
Gardener Gro. TW13: Hanw 61Ba 129
Gardeners Cl. N11 19Jb 32
SE9 62Nc 138
Gardeners Cotts. TN14: Hals 83Ad 181
Gardeners Rd. CR0: C'don 74Rb 157
Gardener's Wlk. KT23: Bookh 98Da 191
Garden Farm Cl. KT20: Kgswd 92Ab 194
Garden Fld. La. HP4: Berk 3B 2
Gardenfields KT20: Tad 91Ab 194
Garden Ho. N2 26Fb 49
(off The Grange)
NW6 40Db 69
(off Oxford Rd.)
SW7 48Db 89
(off Cornwall Gdns.)
Garden Ho's., The W6 51Za 110
(off Bothwell St.)
Gardenia Dr. GU24: W End 5D 166
Gardenia Rd. BR1: Brom 69Qc 138
EN1: Enf 16Ub 33
Gardenia Way IG8: Wfd G 23Jc 53
Garden La. BR1: Brom 65Kc 137
SW2 60Pb 112
Garden M. SL1: Slou 6K 81
W2 45Cb 89
Garden Mus., The 4H 229 (48Pb 90)
Garden Pl. DA2: Wilm 62Md 141
E8 39Vb 71
Garden Reach HP8: Chal G 13A 24
Garden Rd. BR1: Brom 66Kc 137
KT12: Walt T 72X 151
NW8 3A 214 (41Eb 89)
SE20 67Yb 136
TN13: S'oaks 94Md 203
TW9: Rich 55Qa 109
WD5: Ab L 3U 12
Garden Row DA11: Nflt 2B 144
SE1 4B 230 (48Rb 91)
Garden Royal SW15 58Za 110
Gardens, The AL9: Brk P 9G 8
BR3: Beck 67Ec 136
E5 31Vb 71
GU24: Pirb 4D 186
HA1: Harr 30Ea 46
HA5: Pinn 30Ba 45
KT10: Esh 77Ca 151
KT11: Cobh 91S 190
N8 28Nb 50
(not continuous)
SE22 56Wb 113
TW14: Felt 57T 106
WD17: Wat 12V 26
Gardens of the Rose, The 8M 5
Garden Sq. SW1 7J 227 (50Jb 90)
Garden St. E1 43Zb 92
Garden Ter. SW1 7D 228 (50Mb 90)
SW7 2E 226
TN15: Seal 93Qd 203
Garden Wlk. BR3: Beck 67Bc 136
CR5: Coul 95Kb 196
EC2 5H 219 (41Ub 91)
Garden Way IG10: Lough 10Qc 22
NW10 37Sa 67
Gardiner Av. NW2 36Ya 68
Gardiner Cl. BR5: St P 68Yc 139
EN3: Pond E 16Zb 34
RM8: Dag 35Zc 75
Gardiner Ct. CR2: S Croy 79Tb 157
Gardiner Ho. SW11 53Gb 111
Gardner Cl. E11 30Kc 53
Gardner Ct. EC1 5B 218
N5 35Sb 71
WD25: Wat 7Y 13
Gardner Ho. TW13: Hanw 61Ba 129
UB1: S'hall 45Z 85
(off The Broadway)
Gardner Ind. Est. BR3: Beck 64Bc 136
Gardner Pl. TW14: Felt 58X 107
Gardner Rd. E13 42Kc 93
Gardners La. EC4 4D 224 (45Sb 91)
Gardner's Way RM20: W Thur 52Wd 120
Gardnor Rd. NW3 35Fb 69
Gard St. EC1 3C 218 (41Rb 91)
Garendon Gdns. SM4: Mord 73Db 155
Garendon Rd. SM4: Mord 73Db 155
Garenne Ct. E4 18Ec 34
Gareth Cl. KT4: Wor Pk 75Za 154
Gareth Ct. SW16 62Mb 134
WD6: Bore 10Pa 15
(off Aycliffe Rd.)
Gareth Dr. N9 19Wb 33
Gareth Gro. BR1: Brom 63Jc 137
Garfield EN2: Enf 15Tb 33
(off London Rd.)
Garfield Ct. NW6 38Ab 68
(off Willesden La.)
Garfield M. SW11 55Jb 112
Garfield Pl. SL4: Wind 4H 103
Garfield Rd. E4 18Fc 35
E13 42Hc 93
EN3: Pond E 14Yb 34
KT15: Add 78L 149
SW11 55Jb 112
SW19 64Eb 133
TW1: Twick 60Ja 108
Garfield St. WD24: Wat 10X 13
Garford St. E14 45Cc 92
Garganey Ct. NW10 37Ta 67
(off Elgar Av.)
Garganey Wlk. SE28 45Yc 95
Gargery Cl. DA12: Grav'nd 10J 123
Garibaldi Rd. RH1: Redh 7P 207
Garibaldi St. SE18 49Uc 94
Garland Cl. EN8: Chesh 3Ac 20
HP2: Hem H 1M 3
SE1 4E 230 (48Sb 91)
Garland Ct. AL1: St A 2C 6
(off Victoria St.)
E14 45Cc 92
(off Premiere Pl.)
SE17 6E 230
Garland Dr. TW3: Houn 54Ea 108
Garland Ho. KT2: King T 67Na 131
(off Skerne Rd.)
UB7: W Dray 47P 83
Garland Rd. HA7: Stan 25Na 47
SE18 52Tc 116
Garlands Ct. CR0: C'don 77Tb 157
(off Chatsworth Rd.)
Garlands Ho. NW8 40Eb 69
(off Carlton Hill)
Garlands La. HA1: Harr 32Ha 66
Garlands Rd. KT22: Lea 93Ka 192
RH1: Redh 7P 207
Garland Way CR3: Cat'm 94Tb 197
RM11: Horn 28Nd 57
Garlichill Rd. KT18: Tatt C 89Xa 174
Garlick Hill EC4 4E 224 (45Sb 91)
Garlies Rd. SE23 62Ac 136
Garlinge Ho. SW9 53Qb 112
(off Gosling Way)
Garlinge Rd. NW2 37Bb 69
Garman Cl. N18 22Tb 51
Garman Rd. N17 24Xb 51
(not continuous)
Garnault M. EC1 4A 218
Garnault Pl. EC1 4A 218 (41Qb 90)
Garnault Rd. EN1: Enf 10Vb 19
Garner Cl. RM8: Dag 32Zc 75
Garner Ct. TW19: Stanw 58M 105
(off Douglas Rd.)
Garner Rd. E17 25Ec 52
Garners Cl. SL9: Chal P 23B 42
Garners End SL9: Chal P 23A 42
Garners Rd. SL9: Chal P 23A 42
Garner St. E2 40Wb 71
Garnet Cl. SL1: Slou 7E 80
Garnet Ho. E1 46Yb 92
(off Garnet St.)
Garnet Rd. CR7: Thor H 70Sb 135
NW10 37Ua 68
Garnet St. E1 45Yb 92
Garnett Cl. SE9 55Pc 116
WD24: Wat 9Z 13
Garnett Dr. AL2: Brick W 1Ba 13
Garnett Rd. NW3 36Hb 69
Garnett Way E17 25Ac 52
(off McEntee Av.)
Garnet Wlk. E6 43Nc 94
Garnham Cl. N16 33Vb 71
Garnham St. N16 33Vb 71
Garnies Cl. SE15 52Vb 113
Garnon Mead CM16: Coop 1Zc 23
Garrad's Rd. SW16 62Mb 134
Garrard Cl. BR7: Chst 64Rc 138
DA7: Bex 55Cd 118
Garrard Rd. SL2: Slou 2C 80
SM7: Bans 88Cb 175
Garrard Wlk. NW10 37Ua 68
Garratt Cl. CR0: Bedd 77Nb 156
Garratt Ct. SW18 59Db 111
Garratt La. SW17 58Db 111
SW18 58Db 111
Garratt Rd. HA8: Edg 24Qa 47
Garratts La. SM7: Bans 88Bb 175
Garratts Rd. WD23: Bush 17Ea 28
Garratt Ter. SW17 63Gb 133
Garraway Ct. SW13 52Ya 110
(off Wyatt Dr.)
Garrett Cl. W3 43Ta 87
Garrett Ho. SE1 1B 230
Garrett St. EC1 5E 218 (42Sb 91)
Garrick Av. NW11 30Ab 48
Garrick Cl. KT12: Hers 77X 151
SW18 56Eb 111
TW9: Rich 57Ma 109
TW18: Staines 66J 127
W5 42Na 87
Garrick Ct. E8 38Vb 71
(off Jacaranda Gro.)
Garrick Cres. CR0: C'don 75Ub 157
Garrick Dr. NW4 26Ya 48
SE28 48Tc 94
Garrick Gdns. KT8: W Mole 69Ca 129
Garrick Ho. KT1: King T 70Na 131
(off Surbiton Rd.)
W1 7K 221
W4 51Ua 110
Garrick Ind. Cen. NW9 29Va 48
Garrick Pk. NW4 26Za 48
Garrick Rd. NW9 30Va 48
TW9: Rich 54Qa 109
UB6: G'frd 42Da 85
Garricks Ho. KT1: King T 68Ma 131
(off Wadbrook St.)
Garrick St. DA11: Grav'nd 8D 122
WC2 4F 223 (45Nb 90)
Garrick Theatre 5F 223
Garrick Way NW4 28Za 48
Garrick Yd. WC2 4F 223
Garrison Cl. SE18 52Qc 116
TW4: Houn 57Ba 107
Garrison La. KT9: Chess 80Ma 153
Garrison Pde. RM19: Purf 49Qd 97
Garrison Rd. E3 39Cc 72
Garrison Sq. SW1 7J 227 (50Jb 90)
Garrolds Cl. BR8: Swan 68Fd 140
Garron La. RM15: S Ock 44Vd 98
Garrow DA3: Lfield 69De 143
Garrowsfield EN5: Barn 16Bb 31
Garry Cl. RM1: Rom 24Gd 56
Garry Way RM1: Rom 24Gd 56
Garsdale Cl. N11 23Jb 50
Garsdale Ter. W14 50Bb 89
(off Aisgill Av.)
Garside Cl. SE28 48Tc 94
TW12: Hamp 65Da 129
Garside Ct. TW11: Hamp W 67La 130
Garsington M. SE4 55Bc 114
Garsmouth Way WD25: Wat 8Z 13
Garson Cl. KT10: Esh 78Ba 151
Garson Ct. WD6: Bore 12Sa 29
Garson Ho. W2 4B 220
Garson La. TW19: Wray 9P 103
Garson Rd. KT10: Esh 79Ba 151
GARSTON 7Y 13
Garston Cres. WD25: Wat 6Y 13
Garston Dr. WD25: Wat 6Y 13
Garston Gdns. CR8: Kenley 87Tb 177
Garston Ho. N1 38Rb 71
(off The Sutton Est.)
Garston La. CR8: Kenley 86Tb 177
WD25: Wat 6Z 13
Garston Pk. Pde. WD25: Wat 6Z 13
Garstons, The KT23: Bookh 97Ca 191
Garter Way SE16 47Zb 92
Garth, The HA3: Kenton 30Pa 47
KT11: Cobh 85Aa 171
TW12: Hamp H 65Da 129
WD5: Ab L 5T 12
Garth Cl. HA4: Ruis 32Z 65
KT2: King T 64Pa 131
SM4: Mord 73Za 154
Garth Ct. HA1: Harr 30Ha 46
(off Northwick Pk. Rd.)
W4 50Ta 87
Garth Ho. NW2 33Bb 69
Garthland Dr. EN5: Barn 15Xa 30
Garth M. W5 42Na 87
Garthorne Rd. SE23 59Zb 114
Garthorne Road Nature Reserve 59Zb 114
Garth Rd. KT2: King T 64Pa 131
NW2 33Bb 69
RM15: S Ock 42Yd 98
SM4: Mord 72Ya 154
TN13: S'oaks 100Ld 203
W4 50Ta 87
Garth Rd. Ind. Cen., The
SM4: Mord 74Za 154
Garthside TW10: Ham 64Na 131
Garthway N12 23Gb 49
Gartlet Rd. WD17: Wat 13Y 27
Gartmoor Gdns. SW19 60Bb 111
Gartmore Rd. IG3: Ilf 33Vc 75
Garton Bank SM7: Bans 89Cb 175
Garton La. RM15: S Ock 44Vd 98
Garton Pl. SW18 58Eb 111
Gartons Cl. EN3: Pond E 14Yb 34
Gartons Way SW11 55Eb 111
Garvary Rd. E16 44Kc 93
Garvock Dr. TN13: S'oaks 98Jd 202
Garway Ct. E3 40Cc 72
(off Matilda Gdns.)
Garway Rd. W2 44Db 89
Garwood Cl. N17 25Xb 51
Gascoigne Cl. N17 25Vb 51
Gascoigne Gdns. IG8: Wfd G 24Gc 53
Gascoigne Pl. E2 3K 219 (41Vb 91)
(not continuous)
Gascoigne Rd. CR0: New Ad 82Ec 178
IG11: Bark 39Sc 74
KT13: Weyb 76R 150
Gascon's Gro. SL2: Slou 2E 80
Gascony Av. NW6 38Cb 69
Gascony Pl. W12 46Za 88
Gascoyne Cl. EN6: S Mim 4Wa 16
RM3: Rom 24Md 57
Gascoyne Dr. DA1: Cray 55Hd 118
Gascoyne Ho. E9 38Ac 72
Gascoyne Rd. E9 38Zb 72
Gaselee St. E14 46Ec 92
(off Baffin Way)
Gasholder Pk. 1E 216 (39Mb 70)
Gaskarth Rd. HA8: Edg 25Sa 47
SW12 58Kb 112
Gaskell Ct. SE20 66Zb 136
Gaskell Rd. N6 30Hb 49
Gaskell St. SW4 54Nb 112
Gaskin St. N1 39Rb 71
Gasoline All. TN15: Wro 89Fe 185
Gaspar Cl. SW5 49Db 89
Gaspar M. SW5 49Db 89
Gassiot Rd. SW17 63Hb 133
Gassiot Way SM1: Sutt 76Fb 155
Gasson Ho. SE14 51Zb 114
(off John Williams Cl.)
Gasson Rd. DA10: Swans 58Ae 121
Gastein Rd. W6 51Za 110
Gastigny Ho. EC1 4E 218
Gaston Bell Cl. TW9: Rich 55Pa 109
Gaston Bri. Rd. TW17: Shep 72T 150
Gaston Rd. CR4: Mitc 69Jb 134
Gaston Way TW17: Shep 71T 150
Gataker Ho. SE16 48Xb 91
(off Slippers Pl.)
Gataker St. SE16 48Xb 91
Gatcombe Ct. AL1: St A 3E 6
(off Dexter Cl.)
BR3: Beck 66Cc 136
Gatcombe Ho. SE22 55Ub 113
Gatcombe M. W5 45Pa 87
Gatcombe Rd. E16 46Jc 93
N19 34Mb 70
Gatcombe Way EN4: Cockf 13Hb 31
Gateacre Ct. DA14: Sidc 63Xc 139

Gate Cen., The—Gillham Ter.

Gate Cen., The TW8: Bford 52Ja 108
Gate Cinema 46Cb 89
(off Notting Hill Ga.)
Gate Cl. WD6: Bore 11Sa 29
Gate Cotts. WD3: Chor 14F 24
Gatecroft HP3: Hem H 4P 3
(not continuous)
Gate End HA6: Nwood 24W 44
Gateforth St. NW8 6D 214 (42Gb 89)
Gate Hill Ct. W11 46Bb 89
(off Ladbroke Ter.)
Gatehill Rd. HA6: Nwood 24V 44
Gatehope Dr. RM15: S Ock 44Vd 98
Gate Ho. E3 39Ac 72
(off Gunmakers La.)
N1 38Tb 71
(off Ufton Rd.)
NW6 40Db 69
(off Oxford Rd.)
Gatehouse Cl. KT2: King T 66Sa 131
SL4: Wind 6F 102
Gate Ho. Pl. WD18: Wat 13W 26
Gatehouse Sq. SE1 6E 224
Gateley Ho. SE4 56Zb 114
(off Coston Wlk.)
Gateley Rd. SW9 55Pb 112
Gate Lodge W9 43Cb 89
(off Admiral Wlk.)
Gately Ct. SE15 52Vb 113
Gate M. SW7 2E 226
Gater Dr. EN2: Enf 11Tb 33
Gatesborough St. EC2 5H 219 (42Ub 91)
Gates Ct. SE17 7D 230 (50Sb 91)
Gatesden WC1 4G 217 (41Nb 90)
Gatesden Cl. KT22: Fet 95Ea 192
Gatesden Rd. KT22: Fet 94Ea 192
Gates Grn. Rd. BR2: Kes 76Hc 159
BR4: W W'ck 76Hc 159
Gateshead Rd. WD6: Bore 11Pa 29
Gateside Rd. SW17 62Hb 133
Gatestone Ct. SE19 65Ub 135
(off Central Hill)
Gatestone Rd. SE19 65Ub 135
Gate St. WC2 2H 223 (44Pb 90)
Gate Theatre, The
London 46Cb 89
(off Pembridge Rd.)
Gateway KT13: Weyb 76R 150
SE17 51Sb 113
Gateway, The GU21: Wok 86D 168
WD18: Wat 15U 26
Gateway Arc. N1 1B 218
Gateway Bus. Cen. SE26 65Ac 136
SE28 48Tc 94
Gateway Bus. Pk. CR5: Coul 87Mb 176
Gateway Cl. HA6: Nwood 23S 44
Gateway Ct. AL2: Brick W 2Aa 13
(off The Uplands)
IG2: Ilf 30Qc 54
(off Parham Dr.)
Gateway Ho. IG11: Bark 39Sc 74
Gateway Ind. Est. NW10 41Va 88
Gateway M. E8 36Vb 71
N11 23Lb 50
Gateway Pde. DA12: Grav'nd 3H 145
Gateway Retail Pk. E6 42Rc 94
Gateway Rd. E10 34Dc 72
Gateways KT6: Surb 71Na 153
(off Surbiton Hill Rd.)
Gateways, The EN7: G Oak 1Tb 19
SW3 6E 226 (49Gb 89)
TW9: Rich 56Ma 109
(off Park La.)
Gateways Ct. SM6: Wall 78Kb 156
Gatewick Cl. SL1: Slou 6J 81
Gatfield Gro. TW13: Hanw 61Ca 129
Gatfield Ho. TW13: Hanw 61Ba 129
Gathorne Rd. N22 26Qb 50
Gathorne St. E2 40Zb 72
Gatley Av. KT19: Ewe 78Ra 153
Gatliff Cl. SW1 7K 227
Gatliff Rd. SW1 7K 227 (50Kb 90)
Gatling Rd. SE2 50Wc 95
Gatonby St. SE15 53Vb 113
Gatting Cl. HA8: Edg 24Sa 47
Gatting Way UB8: Uxb 37N 63
Gattis Wharf N1 1G 217
GATTON 100Hb 195
GATTON BOTTOM 98Kb 196
Gatton Bottom RH1: Mers 1L 207
RH2: Reig 1L 207
Gatton Cl. RH2: Reig 3L 207
SM2: Sutt 81Db 175
Gatton Pk. Bus. Cen. RH1: Mers 1B 208
Gatton Pk. Ct. RH1: Redh 2P 207
Gatton Pk. Rd. RH1: Redh 4M 207
RH2: Reig 4M 207
Gatton Pl. RH1: Redh 3A 208
Gatton Rd. RH2: Reig 4L 207
SW17 63Gb 133
Gattons Way DA14: Sidc 63Bd 139
Gatward Cl. N21 16Rb 33
Gatward Grn. N9 19Vb 33
Gatward Pl. IG11: Bark 41Vc 95
Gatwick Ho. E14 44Bc 92
(off Clemence St.)
Gatwick Rd. DA12: Grav'nd 2D 144
SW18 59Bb 111
Gatwick Way RM12: Horn 34Pd 77
Gauden Cl. SW4 55Mb 112
Gauden Rd. SW4 54Mb 112
Gaudi Apartments N8 27Pb 50
(off Gt. Amwell La.)
Gaugin Ct. SE16 50Xb 91
(off Stubbs Dr.)
Gaumont App. WD17: Wat 13X 27
Gaumont Ter. W12 47Ya 88
(off Lime Gro.)
Gaumont Twr. E8 37Vb 71
(off Dalston Sq.)
Gauntlet NW9 26Va 48
(off Five Acre)
Gauntlet Cl. UB5: N'olt 38Aa 65
Gauntlett Ct. HA0: Wemb 36Ka 66
Gauntlett Rd. SM1: Sutt 78Fb 155
Gaunt St. SE1 3D 230 (48Sb 91)
Gautrey Rd. SE15 54Yb 114
Gautrey Sq. E6 44Pc 94
Gavell Rd. KT11: Cobh 85W 170
Gavel St. SE17 5G 231 (49Tb 91)
Gavenny Path RM15: S Ock 44Vd 98
Gaverick M. E14 49Cc 92
Gaveston Cl. KT14: Byfl 85P 169
Gavestone Cres. SE12 59Lc 115
Gavestone Rd. SE12 59Kc 115
Gaveston Rd. KT22: Lea 92Ja 192
SL2: Slou 1D 80
Gaviller Pl. E5 35Xb 71
Gavina Cl. SM4: Mord 71Gb 155
Gavin Ho. SE18 49Uc 94
Gaviots Cl. SL9: Ger X 32B 62
Gaviots Grn. SL9: Ger X 31A 62
(not continuous)
Gaviots Way SL9: Ger X 31A 62
Gawain Wlk. N9 20Wb 33
Gawber St. E2 41Yb 92
Gawsworth Cl. E15 36Hc 73
Gawthorne Ct. E3 40Cc 72
Gawton Cres. CR5: Coul 94Lb 196
Gay Cl. NW2 36Xa 68
Gaydon Ho. W2 43Db 89
(off Bourne Ter.)
Gaydon La. NW9 25Ua 48
Gayfere Pl. SE25 68Ub 135
(off Grange Hill)
Gayfere Rd. IG5: Ilf 27Pc 54
KT17: Ewe 78Wa 154
Gayfere St. SW1 4F 229 (48Nb 90)
Gayford Rd. W12 47Va 88
Gay Gdns. RM10: Dag 35Ed 76
Gay Ho. N16 36Ub 71
Gayhurst SE17 51Tb 113
(off Hopwood Rd.)
Gayhurst Ct. UB5: N'olt 41Y 85
Gayhurst Ho. NW8 5D 214
Gayhurst Rd. E8 38Wb 71
Gayler Cl. RH1: Blet 5M 209
Gaylor Rd. RM18: Tilb 3B 122
UB5: N'olt 36Ba 65
Gaymead NW8 39Db 69
(off Abbey Rd.)
Gaynes Ct. RM14: Upm 35Rd 77
Gaynesford Rd. SE23 61Zb 136
SM5: Cars 80Hb 155
Gaynes Hill Rd. IG8: Wfd G 23Nc 54
Gaynes Pk. Est. CM16: Coop 3Ad 23
Gaynes Pk. Rd. RM14: Upm 35Qd 77
Gaynes Rd. RM14: Upm 33Rd 77
Gay Rd. E15 40Fc 73
Gaysham Av. IG2: Ilf 29Qc 54
Gaysham Hall IG5: Ilf 27Rc 54
Gaysley Ho. SE11 6K 229
Gay St. SW15 55Za 110
Gayton HA1: Harr 31Ga 66
(off Grove Hill)
Gayton Cl. KT21: Asht 90Na 173
Gayton Ct. HA1: Harr 30Ha 46
RH2: Reig 5J 207
Gayton Cres. NW3 35Fb 69
Gayton Ho. E3 42Cc 92
(off Chiltern Rd.)
Gayton Rd. HA1: Harr 30Ha 46
NW3 35Fb 69
SE2 48Yc 95
Gayville Rd. SW11 58Hb 111
Gaywood Av. EN8: Chesh 2Zb 20
Gaywood Cl. SW2 60Pb 112
Gaywood Rd. E17 27Cc 52
KT21: Asht 90Pa 173
Gaywood St. SE1 4B 230 (48Rb 91)
Gaza St. SE17 7B 230 (50Rb 91)
Gaze Ho. E14 44Fc 93
(off Blair St.)
Gazelle Glade DA12: Grav'nd 4H 145
Gazelle Ho. E15 37Gc 73
Gean Ct. E11 35Fc 73
N11 23Lb 50
(off Cline Rd.)
Gean Wlk. AL10: Hat 3C 8
Geariesville Gdns. IG6: Ilf 28Rc 54
Gearing Cl. SW17 63Jb 134
Geary Ct. CM14: B'wood 18Yd 40
Geary Dr. CM14: B'wood 18Yd 40
CM15: B'wood 18Yd 40
Geary Rd. NW10 36Wa 68
Geary St. N7 36Pb 70
Geddes Pl. DA6: Bex 56Cd 118
(off Arnsberg Way)
Geddes Rd. WD23: Bush 14Ea 28
Geddington Ct. EN8: Walt C 6Cc 20
Geddy Ct. RM2: Rom 27Kd 57
Gedeney Rd. N17 25Sb 51
Gedling Ct. SE1 2K 231
Gedling Pl. SE1 3K 231 (48Vb 91)
Geere Rd. E15 39Hc 73
Geerings, The SS17: Stan H 1P 101
Gees Ct. W1 3J 221 (44Jb 90)
Gee St. EC1 5D 218 (42Sb 91)
Geffery's Ct. SE9 62Nc 138
Geffrye Ct. N1 2J 219 (40Ub 71)
Geffrye Est. N1 2J 219 (40Ub 71)
Geffrye Mus. 2K 219 (40Vb 71)
Geffrye St. E2 1K 219 (40Vb 71)
Geisthorp Ct. EN9: Walt A 5Jc 21
Geldart Rd. SE15 52Xb 113
Geldeston Rd. E5 33Wb 71
Gellatly Rd. SE14 54Yb 114
Gell Cl. UB10: Ick 34P 63
Gelsthorpe Rd. RM5: Col R 24Dd 56
Gem Ct. SE10 52Dc 114
(off Merryweather Pl.)
Gemini Apartments E1 5K 219
Gemini Bus. Cen. E16 42Fc 93
Gemini Bus. Est. SE14 50Zb 92
Gemini Bus. Pk. E6 43Tc 94
Gemini Ct. E1 45Wb 91
(off Vaughan Way)
Gemini Gro. UB5: N'olt 41Aa 85
Gemini Ho. E3 39Cc 72
(off Garrison Rd.)
Gemini Pl. TW15: Ashf 65U 128
Gemmell Cl. CR8: Purl 86Pb 176
Genas Cl. IG6: Ilf 25Rc 54
General Gordon Pl. SE18 49Rc 94
General Gordon Sq. SE18 49Rc 94
(off Woolwich New Rd.)
General's Wlk., The EN3: Enf W 9Ac 20
General Wolfe Rd. SE10 53Fc 115
Genesis Bus. Pk. GU21: Wok 87E 168
NW10 40Ra 67
Genesis Cl. TW19: Stanw 60P 105
Genesta Glade DA12: Grav'nd 4J 145
Genesta Rd. SE18 51Rc 116
Geneva Cl. TW17: Shep 68U 128
Geneva Ct. NW9 29Va 48
Geneva Dr. SW9 56Qb 112
Geneva Gdns. RM6: Chad H 29Ad 55
Geneva Rd. CR7: Thor H 71Sb 157
KT1: King T 70Na 131
Genever Cl. E4 22Cc 52
Genista Rd. N18 22Xb 51
Genoa Av. SW15 57Ya 110
Genoa Ho. E1 42Zb 92
(off Ernest St.)
SW18 55Eb 111
Genoa Rd. SE20 67Yb 136
Genotin M. RM12: Horn 36Ld 77
Genotin Rd. EN1: Enf 13Tb 33
Genotin Ter. EN1: Enf 13Tb 33
Gentian Row SE10 53Ec 114
Gentlemans Row EN2: Enf 13Sb 33
Gentry Cl. SS17: Stan H 1L 101
Gentry Gdns. E13 42Jc 93
Geoff Cade Way E3 43Bc 92
Geoffrey Av. RM3: Hrld W 23Qd 57
Geoffrey Chaucer Way E3 43Bc 92
Geoffrey Cl. SE5 54Sb 113
Geoffrey Ct. SE4 54Bc 114
Geoffrey Gdns. E6 40Nc 74
Geoffrey Ho. SE1 3G 231
Geoffrey Jones Ct. NW10 39Wa 68
Geoffrey Rd. SE4 55Bc 114
Geoffrey Whitworth Theatre 56Jd 118
Geographers' A-Z Map Co. Ltd. 88Ed 182
George V Av. HA5: Pinn 26Ba 45
George V Cl. HA5: Pinn 27Ca 45
WD18: Wat 14V 26
George V Way UB6: G'frd 39Ka 66
WD3: Sarr 8K 11
George Beard Rd. SE8 49Bc 92
George Belt Ho. E2 41Zb 92
(off Smart St.)
George Comberton Wlk. E12 36Qc 74
George Ct. TW15: Ashf 63P 127
(off Church Rd.)
UB3: Hayes 43V 84
WC2 5G 223
George Cres. N10 24Jb 50
George Crooks Ho.
RM17: Grays 51De 121
(off New Rd.)
George Davies Lodge IG6: Ilf 29Sc 54
(off Veronique Gdns.)
George Downing Est. N16 33Vb 71
George Eliot Ho. SE17 7D 230
SW1 6C 228
George Elliston Ho. SE1 50Wb 91
(off Old Kent Rd.)
George Eyre Ho. NW8 2C 214
George Fld. Ho. WD3: Rick 17M 25
(off Northway)
George Furness Ho. NW10 37Xa 68
(off Grange Rd.)
George Gange Way HA3: W'stone 27Ga 46
George Gillett Ct. EC1 5E 218
GEORGE GREEN 44A 82
George Grn. Dr. SL3: Geor G 44A 82
George Grn. Rd. SL3: Geor G 4P 81
George Groves Rd. SE20 67Wb 135
George Hilsdon Ct. E14 44Ac 92
(off Repton St.)
George Ho. NW6 40Bb 69
(off Albert Rd.)
George Hudson Twr. E15 40Dc 72
(off High St.)
George Inn Yd. SE1 7F 225 (46Tb 91)
Georgelands GU23: Rip 93K 189
George La. BR2: Hayes 74Kc 159
E18 26Jc 53
SE6 58Dc 114
SE13 58Dc 114
George Lansbury Ho. E3 41Bc 92
(off Bow Rd.)
N22 25Qb 50
(off Progress Way)
NW10 38Ua 68
George Leybourne Ho. E1 45Wb 91
(off Fletcher St.)
George Lindgren Ho. SW6 52Bb 111
(off Clem Attlee Ct.)
George Livings Cl. IG7: Chig 21Xc 55
George Loveless Ho. E2 3K 219
George Lovell Dr. EN3: Enf L 9Cc 20
George Lowe Ct. W2 43Db 89
(off Bourne Ter.)
George Mathers Rd.
SE11 5B 230 (49Rb 91)
George M. EN2: Enf 13Tb 33
NW1 4B 216
SW9 54Qb 112
George Padmore Ho. E8 39Wb 71
(off Brougham Rd.)
George Peabody Ct. NW1 7D 214
George Peabody St. E13 40Lc 73
George Pl. N17 27Ub 51
George Potter Ho. SW11 54Fb 111
(off George Potter Way)
George Potter Way SW11 54Fb 111
George Rd. E4 23Cc 52
KT2: King T 66Ra 131
KT3: N Mald 70Va 132
George Row SE16 47Wb 91
Georges Cl. BR5: St P 69Yc 139
George Scott Ho. E1 44Zb 92
(off W. Arbour St.)
Georges Dr. CM15: Pil H 15Vd 40
Georges Mead WD6: E'tree 16Na 29
George Sq. SW19 69Cb 133
George's Rd. N7 36Pb 70
TN16: Tats 92Mc 199
George's Sq. SW6 51Bb 111
(off North End Rd.)
Georges Ter. CR3: Cat'm 94Tb 197
George St. AL3: St A 2B 6
CR0: C'don 75Sb 157
E16 44Hc 93
HP2: Hem H 1M 3
HP4: Berk 1A 2
IG11: Bark 38Sc 74
RM1: Rom 30Hd 56
RM17: Grays 51Ce 121
TW3: Houn 54Ba 107
TW9: Rich 57Ma 109
TW18: Staines 63H 127
UB2: S'hall 49Aa 85
UB8: Uxb 38M 63
W1 2F 221 (44Hb 89)
W7 46Ga 86
WD18: Wat 14Y 27
Georges Wood Rd. AL9: Brk P 8J 9
George Tilbury Ho. RM16: Grays 7D 100
Georgetown Cl. SE19 64Ub 135
Georgette Pl. SE10 52Ec 114
George Vale Ho. E2 40Wb 71
(off Mansford St.)
George Vw. Ho. SW18 60Db 111
(off Knaresborough Dr.)
Georgeville Gdns. IG6: Ilf 28Rc 54
George Walter Ct. SE16 49Yb 92
(off Millender Wlk.)
Georgewood Rd. HP3: Hem H 7P 3
George Wyver Cl. SW19 59Ab 110
George Yd. EC3 3G 225 (44Tb 91)
W1 4J 221 (45Jb 90)
Georgia Ct. SE16 48Wb 91
(off Priter Rd.)
Georgiana St. NW1 39Lb 70
Georgian Cl. BR2: Hayes 74Kc 159
HA7: Stan 24Ja 46
TW18: Staines 63K 127
UB10: Ick 35N 63
Georgian Ct. CR0: C'don 74Tb 157
(off Cross Rd.)
E9 39Yb 72
EN5: New Bar 14Eb 31
HA9: Wemb 37Qa 67
N3 25Bb 49
NW4 29Xa 48
SW16 63Nb 134
Georgian Ho. E16 46Jc 93
(off Capulet M.)
N1 39Ub 71
(off Hertford Rd.)
Georgian Way HA1: Harr 33Fa 66
Georgia Rd. CR7: Thor H 67Rb 135
KT3: N Mald 70Sa 131
Georgina Gdns. E2 3K 219 (41Vb 91)
Geraint Rd. BR1: Brom 63Jc 137
Geraldine Rd. SW18 57Eb 111
W4 51Qa 109
Geraldine St. SE11 4B 230 (48Rb 91)
Gerald M. SW1 5J 227
Gerald Pl. E8 37Vb 71
(off Dalston Sq.)
Gerald Rd. DA12: Grav'nd 9G 122
E16 42Hc 93
RM8: Dag 32Bd 75
SW1 5J 227 (49Jb 90)
Gerald's Gro. SM7: Bans 86Za 174
Gerard Av. TW4: Houn 59Ca 107
Gerard Gdns. RM13: Rain 40Gd 76
Gerard Pl. E9 38Zb 72
Gerard Rd. HA1: Harr 30Ja 46
SW13 53Va 110
Gerards Cl. SE16 50Yb 92
Gerards Pl. SW4 56Mb 112
Gerda Rd. SE9 61Sc 138
Gerdview Dr. DA2: Wilm 63Ld 141
Germander Dr. GU24: Bisl 7E 166
Germander Way E15 41Gc 93
Gernigan Ho. SW18 58Fb 111
Gernon Bushes Nature Reserve 1Ad 23
Gernon Cl. RM13: Rain 40Md 77
Gernon Rd. E3 40Ac 72
Geron Way NW2 32Xa 68
Gerpins La. RM14: Upm 40Pd 77
Gerrard Cres. CM14: B'wood 20Yd 40
Gerrard Gdns. HA5: Eastc 29W 44
Gerrard Ho. SE14 52Yb 114
(off Briant St.)
Gerrard Pl. W1 4E 222 (45Mb 90)
Gerrard Rd. N1 1B 218 (40Rb 71)
Gerrards Cl. N14 15Lb 32
Gerrards Ct. W5 48Ma 87
GERRARDS CROSS 29A 42
Gerrards Cross Golf Course 27B 42
Gerrards Cross Rd. SL2: Stoke P 7L 61
Gerrards Mead SM7: Bans 88Bb 175
Gerrard St. W1 4D 222 (45Mb 90)
Gerrard Way SE3 56Lc 115
Gerridge Ct. SE1 3A 230
(off Gerridge St.)
Gerridge St. SE1 3A 230 (48Qb 90)
Gerry Raffles Sq. E15 37Fc 73
Gertrude Rd. DA17: Belv 49Cd 96
Gertrude St. SW10 51Eb 111
Gervaise Cl. SL1: Slou 6D 80
Gervase Cl. HA9: Wemb 34Sa 67
Gervase Rd. HA8: Edg 25Sa 47
Gervase St. SE15 52Xb 113
Gervis Ct. TW7: Isle 52Ea 108
Gews Cnr. EN8: Chesh 1Zb 20
Ghent St. SE6 61Cc 136
Ghent Way E8 37Vb 71
Gherkin, The 2J 225
Giant Arches Rd. SE24 59Sb 113
Giant Tree Hill WD23: B Hea 18Fa 28
Gibbfield Cl. RM6: Chad H 27Ad 55
Gibbings Ho. SE1 2C 230
Gibbins Rd. E15 38Ec 72
Gibbon Ho. NW8 6C 214
Gibbon Rd. KT2: King T 67Na 131
SE15 54Yb 114
W3 45Ua 88
Gibbons Cl. WD6: Bore 11Na 29
Gibbons La. DA1: Dart 58Md 119
Gibbons M. NW11 29Bb 49
Gibbon's Rents SE1 7H 225
Gibbons Rd. NW10 37Ua 68
Gibbon Wlk. SW15 56Wa 110
Gibb's Acre GU24: Pirb 5D 186
Gibbs Av. SE19 64Tb 135
Gibbs Brook La. RH8: Oxt 8H 211
Gibbs Cl. EN8: Chesh 1Zb 20
SE19 65Tb 135
Gibbs Couch WD19: Wat 20Z 27
Gibbs Grn. HA8: Edg 21Sa 47
W14 50Bb 89
(not continuous)
Gibbs Ho. BR1: Brom 67Hc 137
(off Longfield)
Gibb's Rd. N18 21Yb 52
Gibbs Sq. SE19 64Tb 135
Gibney Ter. BR1: Brom 63Hc 137
Gibraltar Cl. CM13: Gt War 23Yd 58
Gibraltar Cres. KT19: Ewe 82Ua 174
Gibraltar Wlk. E2 41Vb 91
(off Shackwell St.)
Gibson Cl. DA11: Nflt 2B 144
E1 42Yb 92
KT9: Chess 78La 152
N21 16Qb 32
TW7: Isle 55Ga 108
Gibson Ct. KT10: Hin W 75Ha 152
RM1: Rom 30Gd 56
SE9 57Lc 115
SL3: L'ly 50B 82
Gibson Gdns. N16 33Vb 71
Gibson Ho. SM1: Sutt 77Cb 155
Gibson M. TW1: Twick 58La 108
Gibson Pl. TW19: Stanw 58L 105
Gibson Rd. RM8: Dag 32Yc 75
SE11 6J 229 (49Pb 90)
SM1: Sutt 78Db 155
UB10: Ick 35P 63
Gibsons Hill SW16 66Qb 134
(not continuous)
Gibsons Pl. DA4: Eyns 75Nd 163
Gibson Sq. N1 39Qb 70
Gibson Sq. Gdns. N1 39Qb 70
(off Gibson Sq.)
Gibson St. SE10 50Gc 93
Gibson Way CR3: Cat'm 95Tb 197
Gidd Hill CR5: Coul 88Jb 176
Gidea Av. RM2: Rom 27Jd 56
Gidea Cl. RM2: Rom 27Jd 56
RM15: S Ock 41Yd 98
(off Benyon Path)
Gidea Lodge RM2: Rom 27Kd 57
GIDEA PARK 27Kd 57
Gideon Cl. DA17: Belv 49Dd 96
HA8: Edg 23Qa 47
Gideon M. W5 47Ma 87
Gideon Rd. SW11 55Jb 112
Gidian Ct. AL2: Park 9B 6
Gielgud Theatre 4D 222
Giesbach Rd. N19 33Mb 70
Giffard Rd. N18 23Ub 51
Giffin Sq. Mkt. SE8 52Cc 114
(off Giffin St.)
Giffin St. SE8 52Cc 114
Gifford Gdns. W7 43Fa 86
Gifford Ho. SE10 50Fc 93
(off Eastney St.)
SW1 7B 228
Gifford Pl. CM14: W'ley 22Zd 59
Gifford Rd. NW10 38Ua 68
Giffords Cross Rd. SS17: Corr 1P 101
Giffordside RM16: Grays 10D 100
Gifford St. N1 38Nb 70
Gift La. E15 39Gc 73
GIGGSHILL 73Ja 152
Giggs Hill BR5: St P 68Wc 139
Giggs Hill Gdns. KT7: T Ditt 74Ja 152
Giggs Hill Rd. KT7: T Ditt 73Ja 152
Gilbert Bri. EC2 1E 224
(off Wood St.)
Gilbert Burnet Ho. HP3: Hem H 4P 3
Gilbert Cl. DA10: Swans 58Zd 121
SE18 53Pc 116
SW19 67Db 133
(off Morden Rd.)
Gilbert Ct. W5 44Pa 87
(off Green Va.)
Gilbert Gro. HA8: Edg 25Ta 47
Gilbert Ho. E2 41Zb 92
(off Usk St.)
E17 27Ec 52
EC2 1E 224
SE8 51Cc 114
SW1 50Kb 90
(off Churchill Gdns.)
SW8 52Nb 112
(off Wyvil Rd.)
SW13 52Xa 110
(off Trinity Chu. Rd.)
Gilbert Pl. WC1 1F 223 (43Nb 90)
Gilbert Rd. BR1: Brom 66Jc 137
DA17: Belv 48Cd 96
HA5: Pinn 28Z 45
RM1: Rom 28Hd 56
RM16: Chaf H 48Yd 98
SE11 6A 230 (49Qb 90)
SW19 66Eb 133
UB9: Hare 26M 43
Gilbert Row DA11: Nflt 1B 144
Gilbert Scott Bldg. SW15 58Ab 110
Gilbert Scott Cl. HA0: Wemb 36Ma 67
Gilbert Sheldon Ho. W2 7C 214
Gilberts Lodge KT17: Eps 84Ua 174
Gilbertson Ho. E14 48Cc 92
(off Mellish St.)
Gilbert St. E15 35Gc 73
EN3: Enf W 9Yb 20
TW3: Houn 55Ea 108
W1 3J 221 (44Jb 90)
Gilbert Way CR0: Wadd 75Pb 156
SL3: L'ly 50B 82
Gilbert White Cl. UB6: G'frd 39Ja 66
Gilbey Cl. UB10: Ick 35R 64
Gilbey Ho. NW1 38Kb 70
Gilbey Rd. SW17 63Gb 133
Gilbeys Yd. NW1 38Jb 70
Gilbourne Rd. SE18 51Vc 117
Gilby Ho. E9 37Zb 72
Gilda Av. EN3: Pond E 15Ac 34
Gilda Ct. NW7 25Wa 48
Gilda Cres. N16 32Wb 71
Gildea Cl. HA5: Hat E 24Ca 45
Gildea St. W1 1A 222 (43Kb 90)
Gilden Cres. NW5 36Jb 70
Gildenhill Rd. BR8: Swan 66Ld 141
Gildersome St. SE18 51Qc 116
Gilders Rd. KT9: Chess 80Pa 153
Giles Cl. RM13: Rain 40Md 77
Giles Coppice SE19 63Vb 135
Giles Cres. UB10: Uxb 39P 63
(off St Andrews Rd.)
Giles Fld. DA12: Grav'nd 10H 123
Gilesfield Cl. RM13: Rain 39Gd 76
Giles Ho. SL2: Stoke P 8L 61
(off Bells Hill Grn.)
W11 44Cb 89
(off Westbourne Gro.)
Gilesmead KT18: Eps 86Ua 174
(off Downside)
SE5 53Tb 113
Giles Travers Cl. TW20: Thorpe 69E 126
Gilford Ho. IG1: Ilf 33Rc 74
(off Clements Rd.)
Gilfrid Cl. UB8: Hil 44R 84
Gilhams Av. SM7: Bans 84Za 174
Gilkes Cres. SE21 58Ub 113
Gilkes Pl. SE21 58Ub 113
Gillam Way RM13: Rain 37Jd 76
Gillan Ct. SE12 62Kc 137
Gillan Grn. WD23: B Hea 19Ea 28
Gillards M. E17 28Cc 52
Gillards Way E17 28Cc 52
Gill Av. E16 44Jc 93
Gill Cl. WD18: Wat 16S 26
Gill Cres. DA11: Nflt 2B 144
Gillender St. E3 42Ec 92
E14 42Ec 92
Gillespie Ho. GU25: Vir W 70A 126
(off Holloway Dr.)
Gillespie Pk. Local Nature Reserve 34Qb 70
Gillespie Rd. N5 34Qb 70
Gillett Av. E6 40Nc 74
GILLETTE CORNER 52Ja 108
Gillett Ho. N8 27Nb 50
(off Campsfield Rd.)
Gillett Pl. N16 36Ub 71
Gillett Rd. CR7: Thor H 70Tb 135
Gillett Sq. N16 36Ub 71
(off Gillett St.)
Gillett St. N16 36Ub 71
Gillfoot NW1 2B 216
Gillham Ter. N17 23Wb 51

Gilliam Gro.—Glenwood Rd.

Gilliam Gro. CR8: Purl 82Qb 176
Gillian Av. AL1: St A 6A 6
Gillian Cres. RM2: Rom 26Ld 57
Gillian Ho. HA3: Hrw W 23Ga 46
Gillian Pk. Rd.
SM3: Sutt 74Bb 155
Gillian St. SE13 57Dc 114
Gilliat Rd. SL1: Slou 5J 81
Gilliats Grn. WD3: Chor 14F 24
Gillies Ho. *NW6* 38Fb 69
(off Hilgrove Rd.)
Gillies Rd. TN15: W King 78Ud 164
Gillies St. NW5 36Jb 70
Gilling Ct. NW3 37Gb 69
Gillingham Ho. *RM3: Rom* 22Nd 57
(off Lindfield Rd.)
Gillingham M. SW1 5B 228 (49Lb 90)
Gillingham Rd. NW2 34Ab 68
Gillingham Row
SW1 5B 228 (49Lb 90)
Gillingham St. SW1 5A 228 (49Lb 90)
Gillings Ct. *EN5: Barn* 14Ab 30
(off Wood St.)
Gillison Wlk. SE16 48Xb 91
Gillis Sq. SW15 58Wa 110
Gillman Dr. E15 39Hc 73
Gillman Ho. *E2* 40Wb 71
(off Pritchard's Rd.)
Gillmans Rd. BR5: Orp 74Xc 161
Gillray Ho. *SW10* 51Fb 111
(off Ann La.)
Gills Hill WD7: R'lett 7Ha 14
Gills Hill La. WD7: R'lett 8Ha 14
Gills Hollow WD7: R'lett 8Ha 14
Gills Rd. DA2: G St G 67Ud 142
DA4: S Dar 67Ud 142
Gill St. E14 44Bc 92
Gillum Cl. EN4: E Barn 18Hb 31
Gilmais KT23: Bookh 97Ea 192
Gilman Cres. SL4: Wind 5B 102
Gilman Ho. *N1* 38Qb 70
(off Drummond Way)
Gilmore Cl. SL3: L'ly 7N 81
UB10: Ick 34Q 64
Gilmore Ct. N11 22Hb 49
Gilmore Cres. TW15: Ashf 64Q 128
Gilmore Rd. SE13 56Fc 115
Gilmour Cl.
EN2: Enf, Walt C 7Wb 19
Gilmour Ho. NW9 26Wa 48
Gilpin Av. SW14 56Ta 109
Gilpin Cl. CR4: Mitc 68Gb 133
W2 7B 214
Gilpin Cres. N18 22Vb 51
TW2: Whitt 59Da 107
Gilpin Rd. E5 35Ac 72
Gilpin's Ride HP4: Berk 1A 2
Gilpin Way UB3: Harl 52T 106
Gilray Ho. W2 4B 220
Gilroy Cl. RM13: Rain 37Hd 76
Gilroy Rd. HP2: Hem H 1M 3
Gilroy Way BR5: Orp 73Xc 161
Gilsland EN9: Walt A 7Gc 21
Gilsland Pl. CR7: Thor H 70Tb 135
Gilsland Rd. CR7: Thor H 70Tb 135
Gilson Pl. N10 24Hb 49
Gilstead Rd. SW6 54Db 111
Gilston Rd. SW10 7A 226 (50Eb 89)
Gilton Rd. SE6 62Gc 137
Giltspur St. EC1 2C 224 (44Rb 91)
Gilwell Cl. E4 14Dc 34
Gilwell La. E4 14Ec 34
(not continuous)
GILWELL PARK 14Fc 35
Gilwell Pk. E4 13Fc 35
Ginger Apartments SE1 1K 231
Ginsburg Yd. NW3 35Eb 69
Gippeswyck Cl. HA5: Pinn 25Z 45
Gipsy Hill SE19 63Ub 135
Gipsy La. RM17: Grays 51Ee 121
SW15 55Xa 110
Gipsy Rd. DA16: Well 52Zc 117
SE27 63Sb 135
Gipsy Rd. Gdns. SE27 63Sb 135
Giralda Cl. E16 43Mc 93
Giraud St. E14 44Dc 92
Girdler's Rd. W14 49Za 88
Girdlestone Wlk. N19 33Lb 70
Girdwood Rd. SW18 59Ab 110
Girling Ho. *N1* 39Ub 71
(off Colville Est.)
Girling Way TW14: Felt 55W 106
Girona Cl. RM16: Chaf H 48Yd 98
Gironde Rd. SW6 52Bb 111
Girtin Ho. *UB5: N'olt* 40Z 65
(off Academy Gdns.)
Girton Av. NW9 27Qa 47
Girton Cl. UB5: N'olt 37Ea 66
Girton Ct. EN8: Chesh 2Ac 20
Girton Gdns. CR0: C'don 76Cc 158
Girton Rd. SE26 64Zb 136
UB5: N'olt 37Ea 66
Girton Vs. W10 44Za 88
Girton Way WD3: Crox G 15S 26
Gisborne Gdns. RM13: Rain 41Hd 96
Gisbourne Cl. SM6: Bedd 76Mb 156
Gisburne Way WD24: Wat 9W 12
Gisburn Ho. *SE15* 51Wb 113
(off Friary Est.)
Gisburn Rd. N8 28Pb 50
Gissing Wlk. N1 38Qb 70
Gittens Cl. BR1: Brom 63Hc 137
Given Wilson Wlk. E13 40Hc 73
Giverny Ho. *SE16* 47Zb 92
(off Water Gdns. Sq.)
GIVONS GROVE 98La 192
Givons Gro. KT22: Lea 97Ka 192
GIVONS GROVE RDBT. 96Ka 192
Glacier Way HA0: Wemb 40Ma 67
Gladbeck Way EN2: Enf 14Rb 33
Gladding Rd. E12 35Mc 73
Glade, The BR1: Brom 68Mc 137
BR4: W W'ck 76Dc 158
CM13: Hut 18Ce 41
CR0: C'don 71Zb 158
CR5: Coul 91Db 196
E8 37Wb 71
EN2: Enf 13Qb 32
IG5: Ilf 25Pc 54
IG8: Wfd G 20Kc 35
KT14: W Byf 85G 168
KT17: Ewe 79Wa 154
KT20: Kgswd 93Cb 195
KT22: Fet 94Ca 191
N12 20Fb 31
N21 16Pb 32
RM14: Upm 36Sd 78
SE7 52Lc 115
Glade, The SL5: S'hill 1A 146
SL9: Ger X 2P 61
SM2: Cheam 81Ab 174
TN13: S'oaks 95Kd 203
TW18: Staines 65K 127
W12 47Xa 88
(off Coningham Rd.)
Glade Apartments *E14* 49Ec 92
(off Stebondale St.)
Glade Bus. Cen., The
RM20: W Thur 50Vd 98
Glade Cl. KT6: Surb 75Ma 153
Glade Ct. IG5: Ilf 25Pc 54
UB8: Uxb 37L 63
Glade Gdns. CR0: C'don 73Ac 158
Glade La. UB2: S'hall 47Da 85
Glades, The BR1: Brom 68Jc 137
DA12: Grav'nd 5F 144
HP1: Hem H 1G 2
KT6: Surb 73Na 153
Glades Cl. RM1: Rom 29Kd 57
Gladeside CR0: C'don 72Zb 158
N21 16Pb 32
Gladeside Cl. KT9: Chess 80Ma 153
Gladeside Ct. CR6: W'ham 92Xb 197
Gladesmere Ct. WD24: Wat 8X 13
Gladesmore Community School &
Sports Cen. 29Wb 51
Gladesmore Rd. N15 30Vb 51
Glades Pl. BR1: Brom 68Jc 137
Glade Spur KT20: Kgswd 93Db 195
Gladeswood Rd. DA17: Belv 49Dd 96
Glade Wlk. E20 37Dc 72
Gladeway, The EN9: Walt A 5Fc 21
Gladiator St. SE23 59Ac 114
Glading Ter. N16 34Vb 71
Gladioli Cl. TW12: Hamp 65Ca 129
Gladsdale Dr. HA5: Eastc 28W 44
Gladsmuir Cl. KT12: Walt T 75Y 151
Gladsmuir Rd. EN5: Barn 12Ab 30
N19 32Lb 70
Gladstone Av. E12 38Nc 74
N22 26Qb 50
TW2: Twick 60Fa 108
TW14: Felt 58W 106
Gladstone Ct. *NW6* 38Eb 69
(off Fairfax Rd.)
SW1 6E 228
Gladstone Ct. Bus. Cen. *SW8* 53Kb 112
(off Pagden St.)
Gladstone Gdns. TW3: Houn 53Ea 108
Gladstone Ho. CR4: Mitc 68Hb 133
E14 44Cc 92
(off E. India Dock Rd.)
Gladstone M. N22 26Qb 50
NW6 38Bb 69
(off Cavendish Rd.)
SE20 66Yb 136
Gladstone Pde. NW2 33Ya 68
Gladstone Pk. Gdns. NW2 35Xa 68
Gladstone Pl. E3 40Bc 72
EN5: Barn 14Za 30
KT8: E Mos 71Ga 152
RM13: Rain 41Ld 97
Gladstone Rd. BR6: Farnb 78Sc 160
CR0: C'don 73Tb 157
DA1: Dart 58Pd 119
IG9: Buck H 18Lc 35
KT1: King T 69Qa 131
KT6: Surb 75Ma 153
KT21: Asht 90Ma 173
SW19 66Cb 133
UB2: S'hall 47Aa 85
W4 48Ta 87
WD17: Wat 13Y 27
Gladstone St. SE1 4B 230 (48Rb 91)
Gladstone Ter. *SE27* 64Sb 135
(off Bentons La.)
SW8 53Kb 112
Gladstone Way HA3: W'stone 27Ga 46
SL1: Slou 6E 80
Gladwell Rd. BR1: Brom 65Jc 137
N8 30Pb 50
Gladwin Ho. NW1 2C 216
Gladwyn Rd. SW15 55Za 110
Gladys Dimson Ho. E7 36Hc 73
Gladys Rd. NW6 38Cb 69
Glaisher St. SE8 51Cc 114
Glaisyer Way SL0: Iver H 40E 62
Glamis Cl. EN7: Chesh 1Wb 19
Glamis Ct. W3 47Ra 87
Glamis Cres. UB3: Harl 48S 84
Glamis Dr. RM11: Horn 32Nd 77
Glamis Pl. E1 45Yb 92
HP2: Hem H 1N 3
Glamis Rd. E1 45Yb 92
Glamis Way UB5: N'olt 37Ea 66
Glamorgan Cl. CR4: Mitc 69Nb 134
Glamorgan Ct. *W7* 43Ha 86
(off Copley Cl.)
Glamorgan Rd. KT1: Hamp W 66La 130
Glandford Way RM6: Chad H 29Xc 55
Glanfield Rd. BR3: Beck 70Bc 136
Glanleam Rd. HA7: Stan 21Ma 47
Glanmead CM15: Shenf 18Ae 41
Glanmor Rd. SL2: Slou 5M 81
Glanthams Cl. CM15: Shenf 19Be 41
Glanthams Rd. CM15: Shenf 19Be 41
GLANTY 63E 126
Glanty, The TW20: Egh 63D 126
Glanville Dr. RM11: Horn 32Pd 77
Glanville M. HA7: Stan 22Ja 46
Glanville Rd. BR2: Brom 69Kc 137
SW2 57Nb 112
Glanville Way KT19: Eps 84Na 173
Glasbrook Av. TW2: Whitt 60Ba 107
Glasbrook Rd. SE9 59Mc 115
Glaserton Rd. N16 31Ub 71
Glasford St. SW17 65Hb 133
Glasfryn Ct. *HA2: Harr* 33Fa 66
(off Roxeth Hill)
Glasfryn Ho. *HA2: Harr* 33Fa 66
(off Roxeth Hill)
Glasgow Ho. *W9* 40Db 69
(off Maida Vale)
Glasgow Rd. E13 40Kc 73
N18 22Xb 51
Glasgow Ter. SW1 7B 228 (50Lb 90)
Glasier Ct. E15 38Gc 73
Glaskin M. E9 37Ac 72
Glass Bldg., The *NW1* 39Kb 70
(off Jamestown Rd.)
Glass Cl. W13 45Ja 86
Glass Foundry Yd. *E13* 43Kc 93
(off Denmark St.)
Glasshill St. SE1 1C 230 (47Rb 91)
Glass Ho. WC2 3F 223
Glass Ho., The SE1 2H 231
Glasshouse Cl. UB8: Hil 43R 84
Glasshouse Flds. E1 45Zb 92
(not continuous)
Glasshouse St. W1 5C 222 (45Lb 90)
Glasshouse Wlk. SE11 7G 229 (50Nb 90)
Glasshouse Yd. EC1 6D 218 (42Sb 91)
Glasslyn Rd. N8 29Mb 50
Glassmill Ho. *HP4: Berk* 1A 2
(off Robertson Rd.)
Glassmill La. BR2: Brom 68Hc 137
Glass Mill Leisure Cen. 55Ec 114
Glass St. E2 42Xb 91
Glassworks Studios E2 3J 219
Glass Yd. SE18 48Qc 94
Glastonbury Av. IG8: Wfd G 24Mc 53
Glastonbury Cl. BR5: Orp 74Yc 161
Glastonbury Ct. *SE14* 52Yb 114
(off Farrow La.)
W13 46Ja 86
(off Talbot Rd.)
Glastonbury Ho. *SE12* 57Hc 115
(off Wantage Rd.)
SW1 7K 227
Glastonbury Pl. E1 44Yb 92
Glastonbury Rd. N9 18Wb 33
SM4: Mord 73Cb 155
Glastonbury St. NW6 36Bb 69
Glaston Ct. *W5* 46Ma 87
(off Grange Rd.)
Glaucus St. E3 43Dc 92
Glazbury Rd. W14 49Ab 88
Glazebrook Cl. SE21 61Tb 135
Glazebrook Rd. TW11: Tedd 66Ha 130
Gleave Cl. AL1: St A 1F 6
Glebe, The BR7: Chst 67Sc 138
KT4: Wor Pk 74Va 154
SE3 55Gc 115
SW16 63Mb 134
UB7: W Dray 49P 83
WD4: K Lan 1Q 12
WD25: Wat 5Z 13
Glebe Av. CR4: Mitc 68Gb 133
EN2: Enf 13Rb 33
HA3: Kenton 28Na 47
HA4: Ruis 37X 65
IG8: Wfd G 23Jc 53
UB10: Ick 34S 64
Glebe Cl. CR2: Sande 83Vb 177
GU18: Light 2A 166
HP3: Hem H 5N 3
KT23: Bookh 98Ca 191
UB10: Ick 35S 64
W4 50Ua 88
Glebe Cotts. *TW13: Hanw* 62Ca 129
(off Twickenham Rd.)
Glebe Ct. CR4: Mitc 69Hb 133
E3 41Dc 92
(off Rainhill Way)
EN8: Chesh 1Zb 20
HA7: Stan 22La 46
N13 20Qb 32
SE3 55Gc 115
TN13: S'oaks 98Kd 203
W5 46Ma 87
W7 45Fa 86
WD25: Wat 5Z 13
Glebe Cres. HA3: Kenton 27Na 47
NW4 28Ya 48
Glebe Farm Bus. Pk. BR2: Kes 81Mc 179
Glebefield, The TN13: Riv 95Hd 202
Glebe Gdns. CM13: Heron 24Fe 59
KT3: N Mald 73Ua 154
KT14: Byfl 86M 169
Glebe Ho. *SE16* 48Xb 91
(off Slippers Pl.)
Glebe Ho. Dr. BR2: Hayes 74Kc 159
Glebe Hyrst CR2: Sande 84Vb 177
SE19 63Ub 135
Glebe Knoll BR2: Brom 68Hc 137
Glebeland Gdns. TW17: Shep 72S 150
Glebelands DA1: Cray 56Hd 118
E10 33Dc 72
IG7: Chig 20Xc 37
KT8: W Mole 71Da 151
KT10: Clay 81Ha 172
Glebelands Av. E18 26Jc 53
IG2: Ilf 31Tc 74
Glebelands Cl. N12 25Fb 49
SE5 55Ub 113
Glebelands Rd. TW14: Felt 60W 106
Glebe La. EN5: Ark 15Wa 30
HA3: Kenton 28Na 47
TN13: S'oaks 99Kd 203
Glebe M. DA15: Sidc 58Vc 117
Glebe Path CR4: Mitc 69Hb 133
Glebe Pl. DA4: Hort K 70Sd 142
SW3 51Gb 111
Glebe Rd. BR1: Brom 67Jc 137
CR6: W'ham 89Zb 178
DA11: Grav'nd 10B 122
E8 38Vb 71
HA7: Stan 22La 46
KT21: Asht 90Ma 173
N3 25Eb 49
N8 28Pb 50
NW10 37Wa 68
RH1: Mers 96Kb 196
RM10: Dag 37Dd 76
RM13: Rain 41Ld 97
SL4: Old Win 7M 103
SM2: Cheam 81Ab 174
SM5: Cars 79Hb 155
SW13 54Wa 110
TW18: Staines 64K 127
TW20: Egh 65D 126
UB3: Hayes 46V 84
UB8: Uxb 40L 63
Glebe Side TW1: Twick 58Ha 108
Glebe Sq. CR4: Mitc 69Hb 133
Glebe St. W4 50Ua 88
Glebe Ter. W4 50Ua 88
Glebe Way BR4: W W'ck 75Ec 158
CR2: Sande 83Vb 177
DA8: Erith 51Gd 118
IG8: Wfd G 22Lc 53
RM11: Horn 31Nd 77
TW13: Hanw 62Ca 129
Gledhow Gdns. SW5 6A 226 (49Eb 89)
Gledhow Wood KT20: Kgswd 93Db 195
Gledstanes Rd. W14 50Ab 88
Gledwood Av. UB4: Hayes 43V 84
Gledwood Cl. UB4: Hayes 43V 84
Gledwood Cres. UB4: Hayes 43V 84
Gledwood Dr. UB4: Hayes 43V 84
Gledwood Gdns. UB4: Hayes 43V 84
Gleed Av. WD23: B Hea 19Fa 28
Gleeson Dr. BR6: Chels 78Vc 161
Gleeson M. KT15: Add 77L 149
Glegg Pl. SW15 56Za 110
Glen, The BR2: Brom 68Gc 137
BR6: Farnb 76Pc 160
CR0: C'don 76Zb 158
EN2: Enf 14Rb 33
HA5: Eastc 29X 45
HA5: Pinn 31Aa 65
HA6: Nwood 24T 44
HA9: Wemb 35Na 67
KT15: Add 78H 149
RH1: Redh 8P 207
RM13: Rain 42Ld 97
SL3: L'ly 9N 81
SL5: S'hill 10B 124
SS17: Stan H 1P 101
UB2: S'hall 50Ba 85
Glenaffric Av. E14 49Ec 92
Glen Albyn Rd. SW19 61Za 132
Glenallan Ho. *W14* 49Bb 89
(off North End Cres.)
Glenalla Rd. HA4: Ruis 31V 64
Glenalmond Ho. TW15: Ashf 62N 127
Glenalmond Rd. HA3: Kenton 28Na 47
Glenalvon Way SE18 49Nc 94
Glena Mt. SM1: Sutt 77Eb 155
Glenarm Rd. E5 35Yb 72
Glen Av. TW15: Ashf 63Q 128
Glenavon Cl. KT10: Clay 79Ja 152
Glenavon Ct. KT4: Wor Pk 75Xa 154
Glenavon Gdns. SL3: L'ly 9N 81
Glenavon Lodge BR3: Beck 66Cc 136
Glenavon Rd. E15 38Gc 73
Glenbarr Cl. SE9 55Rc 116
Glenbower Ct. AL4: St A 2H 7
Glenbow Rd. BR1: Brom 65Gc 137
Glenbrook Nth. EN2: Enf 14Pb 32
Glenbrook Rd. NW6 36Cb 69
Glenbrook Sth. EN2: Enf 14Pb 32
Glenbuck Ct. KT6: Surb 72Na 153
Glenbuck Rd. KT6: Surb 72Ma 153
Glenburnie Rd. SW17 62Hb 133
Glencairn Dr. W5 42La 86
Glencairne Cl. E16 43Mc 93
Glencairn Rd. SW16 67Nb 134
Glencar Ct. SE19 65Rb 135
Glen Chess WD3: Loud 14L 25
Glen Cl. KT20: Kgswd 95Ab 194
TW17: Shep 70Q 128
Glencoe Av. IG2: Ilf 31Tc 74
Glencoe Dr. RM10: Dag 35Cd 76
Glencoe Mans. *SW9* 52Qb 112
(off Mowll St.)
Glencoe Rd. KT13: Weyb 76Q 150
UB4: Yead 43Z 85
WD23: Bush 16Ca 27
Glencorse Grn. WD19: Wat 21Z 45
Glen Ct. *BR1: Brom* 66Hc 137
(off Bromley Av.)
DA15: Sidc 63Wc 139
GU21: Wok 1L 187
KT14: Byfl 83M 169
KT15: Add 78H 149
TW18: Staines 66H 127
(off Riverside Rd.)
Glen Cres. IG8: Wfd G 23Kc 53
Glendale BR8: Swan 70Hd 140
HP1: Hem H 2K 3
Glendale Av. HA8: Edg 21Pa 47
N22 24Qb 50
RM6: Chad H 31Yc 75
Glendale Cl. CM15: Shenf 18Ae 41
GU21: Wok 10N 167
SE9 55Qc 116
Glendale Dr. SW19 64Bb 133
Glendale Gdns. HA9: Wemb 32Ma 67
Glendale M. BR3: Beck 67Dc 136
Glendale Ri. CR8: Kenley 87Rb 177
Glendale Rd. DA8: Erith 49Ed 96
DA11: Nflt 3A 144
Glendale Wlk. EN8: Chesh 2Ac 20
Glendale Way SE28 45Yc 95
Glendall St. SW9 56Pb 112
Glendarvon St. SW15 55Za 110
Glendean Ct. EN3: Enf L 8Ac 20
Glendene Av. KT24: E Hor 98U 190
Glendevon Cl. HA8: Edg 20Ra 29
Glendish Rd. N17 25Xb 51
Glendor Gdns. NW7 21Ta 47
Glendower Cres. BR6: St M Cry 72Wc 161
Glendower Gdns. SW14 55Ta 109
Glendower Pl. SW7 5B 226 (49Fb 89)
Glendower Rd. E4 18Fc 35
SW14 55Ta 109
Glendown Ho. E8 36Wb 71
Glendown Rd. SE2 50Wc 95
Glendun Ct. W3 45Ua 88
Glen Dunlop Ho., The
TN13: S'oaks 94Kd 203
Glendun Rd. W3 45Ua 88
Gleneagle M. SW16 64Mb 134
Gleneagle Rd. SW16 64Mb 134
Gleneagles HA7: Stan 24Ka 46
W13 43Ka 86
(off Malvern Way)
Gleneagles Cl. BR6: Orp 74Tc 160
RM3: Hrld W 24Pd 57
SE16 50Xb 91
TW19: Stanw 58L 105
WD19: Wat 21Z 45
Gleneagles Grn. BR6: Orp 74Tc 160
Gleneagles Twr. *UB1: S'hall* 44Ea 86
(off Fleming Rd.)
Gleneldon M. SW16 63Nb 134
Gleneldon Rd. SW16 63Nb 134
Glenelg Rd. SW2 57Nb 112
Glenesk Rd. SE9 55Qc 116
Glenfarg Rd. SE6 60Ec 114
Glenferrie Rd. AL1: St A 2E 6
Glenfield Cres. HA4: Ruis 31T 64
Glenfield Rd. SM7: Bans 87Db 175
SW12 60Lb 112
TW15: Ashf 65R 128
W13 47Ka 86
Glenfields SL2: Stoke P 9K 61
Glenfield Ter. W13 47Ka 86
Glenfinlas Way SE5 52Rb 113
Glenforth St. SE10 50Hc 93
Glengall Bus. Cen. SE15 51Vb 113
Glengall Gro. E14 48Dc 92
Glengall Pas. *NW6* 39Cb 69
(off Priory Pk. Rd.)
Glengall Pl. AL1: St A 5C 6
Glengall Rd. DA7: Bex 55Ad 117
HA8: Edg 20Ra 29
IG8: Wfd G 23Jc 53
NW6 39Bb 69
SE15 50Vb 91
Glengall Ter. SE15 51Vb 113
Glen Gdns. CR0: Wadd 76Qb 156
Glengariff Mans. *SW9* 52Qb 112
(off Sth. Island Pl.)
Glengarnock Av. E14 49Ec 92
Glengarry Rd. SE22 57Ub 113
Glenham Dr. IG2: Ilf 29Rc 54
Glenhaven Av. WD6: Bore 13Qa 29
Glenhaven Dr. TW19: Stanw M 5J 105
Glenhead Cl. SE9 55Rc 116
Glenheadon Cl. KT22: Lea 95Ma 193
Glenheadon Ri. KT22: Lea 95Ma 193
Glenhill Cl. N3 26Cb 49
Glen Ho. *E16* 46Qc 94
(off Storey St.)
Glenhouse Rd. SE9 57Qc 116
Glenhurst BR3: Beck 67Ec 136
Glenhurst Av. DA5: Bexl 60Bd 117
HA4: Ruis 31S 64
NW5 35Jb 70
Glenhurst Ct. SE19 64Vb 135
Glenhurst Ri. SE19 66Sb 135
Glenhurst Rd. N12 22Fb 49
TW8: Bford 51La 108
Glenilla Rd. NW3 37Gb 69
Glenister Gdns. UB3: Hayes 47X 85
Glenister Ho. *UB3: Hayes* 46X 85
(off Avondale Dr.)
Glenister Pk. Rd. SW16 66Mb 134
Glenister Rd. SE10 50Hc 93
Glenister St. E16 46Qc 93
Glenkerry Ho. *E14* 44Ec 92
(off Burcham St.)
Glenlea Rd. SE9 57Pc 116
Glenlee GU22: Wok 1N 187
Glenloch Rd. EN3: Enf H 12Yb 34
NW3 37Gb 69
Glen Luce EN8: Chesh 3Zb 20
Glenluce Rd. SE3 51Jc 115
Glenlyn Av. AL1: St A 3F 6
Glenlyon Rd. SE9 57Qc 116
Glenmead IG9: Buck H 18Lc 35
Glenmere Av. NW7 24Wa 48
Glenmere Row SE12 58Jc 115
Glen M. E17 29Bc 52
Glenmill TW12: Hamp 64Ba 129
Glenmore Cl. KT15: Add 76K 149
Glenmore Gdns. WD5: Ab L 4W 12
Glenmore Lawns W13 44Ja 86
Glenmore Lodge BR3: Beck 67Dc 136
Glenmore Pde. HA0: Wemb 39Na 67
Glenmore Rd. DA16: Well 52Vc 117
NW3 37Gb 69
Glenmore Way IG11: Bark 40Wc 75
Glenmount Path SE18 50Sc 94
Glenn Av. CR8: Purl 83Rb 177
Glennie Ct. SE22 60Wb 113
Glennie Rd. SE27 62Qb 134
Glenny Rd. IG11: Bark 37Sc 74
Glenorchy Cl. UB4: Yead 43Aa 85
Glenpark Ct. W13 45Ja 86
Glenparke Rd. E7 37Kc 73
Glenridding NW1 2C 216
Glen Ri. IG8: Wfd G 23Kc 53
Glen Rd. E13 42Lc 93
E17 29Bc 52
KT9: Chess 77Pa 153
Glen Rd. End SM6: Wall 81Kb 176
Glenrosa Gdns. DA12: Grav'nd 4H 145
Glenrosa St. SW6 54Eb 111
Glenrose Cl. SL2: Slou 4N 81
Glenrose Ct. DA14: Sidc 64Xc 139
SE1 3H 231
(off Long La.)
Glenroy St. W12 44Ya 88
Glensdale Rd. SE4 55Bc 114
Glenshaw Mans. *SW9* 52Qb 112
(off Brixton Rd.)
Glenshee Cl. HA6: Nwood 23S 44
Glenshiel Rd. SE9 57Qc 116
Glenside IG7: Chig 23Rc 54
Glenside Cl. CR8: Kenley 87Tb 177
Glentanner Way SW17 62Fb 133
Glen Ter. *E14* 47Ec 92
(off Manchester Rd.)
Glentham Gdns. SW13 51Xa 110
Glentham Rd. SW13 51Wa 110
Glenthorne Av. CR0: C'don 74Xb 157
Glenthorne Cl. SM3: Sutt 74Cb 155
UB10: Hil 41Q 84
Glenthorne Gdns. IG6: Ilf 27Qc 54
SM3: Sutt 74Cb 155
Glenthorne M. W6 49Xa 88
Glenthorne Rd. E17 29Ac 52
KT1: King T 70Pa 131
N11 22Hb 49
W6 49Xa 88
Glenthorpe Av. SW15 56Wa 110
Glenthorpe Gdns. HA7: Stan 20Ha 28
Glenthorpe Rd. SM4: Mord 71Za 154
Glenton Cl. RM1: Rom 24Gd 56
Glenton M. SE15 54Yb 114
Glenton Rd. SE13 56Gc 115
Glenton Way RM1: Rom 24Gd 56
Glentrammon Av. BR6: Chels 79Vc 161
Glentrammon Cl. BR6: Chels 78Vc 161
Glentrammon Gdns. BR6: Chels 79Vc 161
Glentrammon Rd. BR6: Chels 79Vc 161
Glentworth Pl. SL1: Slou 6G 80
Glentworth St. NW1 6G 215 (42Hb 89)
Glenure Rd. SE9 57Qc 116
Glenvern Ct. *TW7: Isle* 54Ja 108
(off White Lodge Cl.)
Glen Vw. DA12: Grav'nd 10E 122
Glenview SE2 51Zc 117
Glenview Gdns. HP1: Hem H 2K 3
Glenview Rd. BR1: Brom 68Mc 137
HP1: Hem H 2K 3
Glenville Av. EN2: Enf 10Sb 19
Glenville Gro. SE8 52Bc 114
Glenville M. SW18 59Db 111
Glenville M. Ind. Est. SW18 59Cb 111
Glenville Rd. KT2: King T 67Qa 131
Glen Wlk. TW7: Isle 57Fa 108
(not continuous)
Glen Way WD17: Wat 10U 12
Glenwood Av. NW9 32Ua 68
RM13: Rain 42Jd 96
Glenwood Cl. HA1: Harr 29Ha 46
Glenwood Ct. DA14: Sidc 63Wc 139
E18 27Jc 53
Glenwood Dr. RM2: Rom 29Jd 56
Glenwood Gdns. IG2: Ilf 29Qc 54
Glenwood Gro. NW9 32Sa 67
Glenwood Rd. KT17: Ewe 79Wa 154
N15 29Rb 51
NW7 20Ua 30
SE6 60Bc 114
TW3: Houn 55Fa 108

Glenwood Way
CR0: C'don 72Zb 158
Glenworth Av. E14 . . . . .49Fc 93
Glevum Cl. AL3: St A 4M 5
Gliddon Dr. E5 . . . . .35Xb 71
Gliddon Rd. W14 . . . . .49Ab 88
Glimpsing Grn. DA18: Erith 48Ad 95
Glisson Rd. UB10: Hil 40Q 64
Gload Cres. BR5: Orp 75Zc 161
Global App. E3 . . . . .40Ec 72
Globe Apartments SE8 . . . . .51Bc 114
(off Evelyn St.)
Globe Ho. WD3: Chor 14E 24
Globe Ind. Est.
RM17: Grays 50Ee 99
Globe Pond Rd. SE16 . . . . .46Ac 92
Globe Rd. E1 . . . . .41Yb 92
E2 . . . . .41Yb 92
E15 . . . . .36Hc 73
IG8: Wfd G 23Lc 53
RM11: Horn 30Jd 56
Globe Rope Wlk. E14 . . . . .49Dc 92
(off E. Ferry Rd.)
Globe St. SE1 . . . . .3F 231 (48Tb 91)
Globe Ter. E2 . . . . .41Yb 92
GLOBE TOWN 41Zb 92
Globe Town Mkt. E2 . . . . .41Zb 92
Globe Vw. EC4 . . . . .4D 224
Globe Wharf SE16 . . . . .45Zb 92
Globe Yd. W1 . . . . .3K 221
Gloria Gdns. RM13: Rain 39Jd 76
Glossop Ho. RM3: Rom 22Nd 57
(off Lindfield Rd.)
Glossop Rd. CR2: Sande 81Tb 177
Gloster Ct. GU21: Wok 88B 168
(off Walton Rd.)
Gloster Ridley Ct. E14 . . . . .44Bc 92
(off St Anne's Row)
Gloster Rd. GU22: Wok 92C 188
KT3: N Mald 70Ua 132
Gloucester W14 . . . . .49Bb 89
(off Kensington Village)
Gloucester Arc.
SW7 . . . . .5A 226 (49Eb 89)
Gloucester Av. DA15: Sidc 61Uc 138
DA16: Well 56Vc 117
EN8: Walt C 5Ac 20
NW1 . . . . .38Jb 70
RM11: Horn 28Qd 57
RM16: Grays 47Ee 99
RM18: E Til 10L 101
SL1: Slou 3G 80
Gloucester Cir. SE10 . . . . .52Ec 114
Gloucester Cl. GU21: Brkwd 1E 186
KT7: T Ditt 74Ja 152
NW10 . . . . .38Ta 67
Gloucester Ct. CR4: Mitc 71Nb 156
EC3 . . . . .5J 225 (45Ub 91)
HA1: Harr 27Ga 46
NW11 . . . . .31Bb 69
(off Golders Grn. Rd.)
RH1: Redh 5P 207
(off Gloucester Rd.)
RM18: Tilb 4B 122
SE1 . . . . .7K 231
(Rolls Rd.)
SE1 . . . . .3E 230
(Swan St.)
SE22 .60Wb 113
TW9: Kew 52Qa 109
UB9: Den 31J 63
W7 . . . . .43Ha 86
(off Copley Cl.)
WD3: Crox G 14R 26
WD18: Wat 14V 26
Gloucester Cres. NW1 . . . . .39Kb 70
TW18: Staines 65M 127
Gloucester Dr. N4 . . . . .33Rb 71
NW11 . . . . .28Cb 49
TW18: Staines 62E 126
Gloucester Gdns. EN4: Cockf 14Jb 32
IG1: Ilf 31Nc 74
NW11 . . . . .31Bb 69
SM1: Sutt 75Db 155
W2 . . . . .44Eb 89
Gloucester Ga. NW1 . . . . . .1K 215 (40Kb 70)
(not continuous)
Gloucester Ga. Bri. NW1 . . . . .1K 215
Gloucester Ga. M. NW1 . . .1K 215 (40Kb 70)
Gloucester Gro. HA8: Edg 25Ta 47
Gloucester Ho. E16 . . . . .46Jc 93
(off Gatcombe Rd.)
NW6 . . . . .40Cb 69
(off Cambridge Rd.)
SW9 . . . . .52Qb 112
TW10: Rich 57Qa 109
WD6: Bore 12Qa 29
Gloucester M. E10 . . . . .31Cc 72
W2 . . . . .3A 220 (44Eb 89)
Gloucester M. W. W2 . . . .3A 220 (44Eb 89)
Gloucester Pde. DA15: Sidc 57Wc 117
UB3: Harl 48S 84
Gloucester Pk. Apartments SW7 . . . . . .5A 226
Gloucester Pl. NW1 . . . . .5F 215 (42Hb 89)
SL4: Wind 4H 103
W1 . . . . .7G 215 (42Hb 89)
Gloucester Pl. M. W1 . . . . .1G 221 (43Hb 89)
Gloucester Rd. CM15: Pil H 15Xd 40
CR0: C'don 74Tb 157
DA1: Dart 59Kd 119
DA12: Grav'nd 3E 144
DA17: Belv 50Bd 95
E10 . . . . .31Cc 72
E11 . . . . .29Kc 53
E12 . . . . .34Pc 74
E17 . . . . .26Zb 52
EN2: Enf 10Sb 19
EN5: New Bar 15Db 31
HA1: Harr 29Da 45
KT1: King T 68Qa 131
N17 . . . . .26Tb 51
N18 . . . . .22Vb 51
RH1: Redh 5P 207
RM1: Rom 30Gd 56
SW7 . . . . .3A 226 (48Eb 89)
TW2: Twick 60Ea 108
TW4: Houn 56Aa 107
TW9: Kew 52Qa 109
TW11: Tedd 64Ga 130
TW12: Hamp 66Da 129
TW13: Felt 60Y 107
W3 . . . . .47Sa 87
W5 . . . . .47La 86
Gloucester Sq. E2 . . . . .39Wb 71
GU21: Wok 89A 168
W2 . . . . .3C 220 (44Fb 89)
(not continuous)
Gloucester St. SW1 . . . . . . .7B 228 (50Lb 90)
Gloucester Ter. KT13: Weyb 78S 150
N14 . . . . .18Mb 32
(off Crown La.)
W2 . . . . .2A 220 (44Db 89)
Gloucester Wlk. GU21: Wok 89A 168
W8 . . . . .47Cb 89
Gloucester Way EC1 . . . . .4A 218 (41Qb 90)
Glover Cl. SE2 . . . . .49Yc 95
Glover Dr. N18 . . . . .23Yb 52
Glover Ho. NW6 . . . . .38Eb 69
(off Harben Rd.)
SE15 .56Xb 113
Glover Rd. HA5: Pinn 30Z 45
Glovers Cl. TN16: Big H 88Kc 179
Glovers Gro. HA4: Ruis 31R 64
Glover's Rd. RH2: Reig 7K 207
Gloxinia Rd. DA13: Sflt 65De 143
Gloxinia Wlk. TW12: Hamp 65Ca 129
Glycena Rd. SW11 . . . . .55Hb 111
Glyn Av. EN4: E Barn 14Fb 31
Glyn Cl. KT17: Ewe 81Wa 174
SE25 . . . . .68Ub 135
Glyn Ct. HA7: Stan 23Ka 46
SW16 .62Qb 134
Glyncroft SL1: Slou 7D 80
Glyndale Grange SM2: Sutt 79Db 155
Glyn Davies Cl. TN13: Dun G 92Gd 202
Glyndebourne Ct. UB5: N'olt 41Y 85
(off Canberra Dr.)
Glyndebourne Pk. BR6: Farnb 75Rc 160
Glynde M. SW3 . . . . .4E 226
Glynde Reach WC1 . . . . .4G 217
Glynde Rd. DA7: Bex 55Zc 117
Glynde St. SE4 . . . . .58Bc 114
Glyndon Rd. SE18 . . . . .49Sc 94
(not continuous)
Glyn Dr. DA14: Sidc 63Xc 139
Glynfield Rd. NW10 . . . . .38Ua 68
Glyn Mans. W14 . . . . .49Ab 88
(off Hammersmith Rd.)
Glynne Rd. N22 . . . . .26Qb 50
Glyn Rd. E5 . . . . .34Zb 72
EN3: Pond E 14Yb 34
KT4: Wor Pk 75Za 154
Glyn St. SE11 . . . . .50Pb 90
Glynswood SL9: Chal P 24B 42
Glynswood Pl. HA6: Nwood 24R 44
Glynwood Ct. SE23 . . . . .61Yb 136
Goals Soccer Cen.
Bexleyheath 55Bd 117
Chingford 23Cc 52
Dagenham 39Zc 75
Dartford 60Qd 119
Eltham .58Lc 115
Gillette Corner 51Ha 108
Hayes 46Y 85
Heathrow 49S 84
Ruislip 36Z 65
Sutton 76Za 154
Tolworth 75Sa 153
Wimbledon 69Wa 132
Go Ape
Black Park 40B 62
Trent Park 13Jb 32
Goater's All. SW6 . . . . .52Bb 111
(off Dawes Rd.)
Goat Ho. Bri. SE25 . . . . .69Wb 135
Goat La. EN1: Enf 10Vb 19
Goat Rd. CR4: Cars, Mitc 73Hb 155
Goatsfield Rd. TN16: Tats 92Lc 199
Goatswood La.
RM4: N'side, Noak H 17Kd 39
Goat Wharf TW8: Bford 51Na 109
Gobions Av. RM5: Col R 24Fd 56
Gobions Way EN6: Pot B 10K 9
Goby Ho. SE8 . . . . .52Dc 114
(off Creative Rd.)
Godalming Av. SM6: Wall 78Nb 156
Godalming Rd. E14 . . . . .43Dc 92
Godbold Rd. E15 . . . . .42Gc 93
Goddard Cl. TW17: Shep 69P 127
Goddard Ct. HA3: Kenton 26Ja 46
Goddard Dr. WD23: Bush 15Ea 28
Goddard Ho. SE11 . . . . .6B 230
Goddard Pl. N19 . . . . .34Lb 70
Goddard Rd. BR3: Beck 70Zb 136
RM16: Grays 46Ce 99
Goddards Way IG1: Ilf 32Tc 74
Goddarts Ho. E17 . . . . .27Cc 52
GODDEN GREEN 96Qd 203
GODDINGTON 76Yc 161
Goddington Chase BR6: Chels 77Xc 161
Goddington La. BR6: Chels 76Wc 161
Godfree Ct. SE1 . . . . .1F 231
Godfrey Av. TW2: Whitt 59Fa 108
UB5: N'olt 39Aa 65
Godfrey Hill SE18 . . . . .49Nc 94
Godfrey Ho. EC1 . . . . .4F 219
Godfrey Pl. E2 . . . . .4K 219
Godfrey Rd. SE18 . . . . .49Pc 94
Godfrey St. E15 . . . . .40Ec 72
SW3 . . . . .7E 226 (50Gb 89)
Godfrey Way
TW4: Houn 59Aa 107
Goding St. SE11 . . . . .7G 229 (50Pb 90)
Godley Cl. SE14 . . . . .53Yb 114
Godley Rd. KT14: Byfl 86P 169
SW18 . . . . .60Fb 111
Godliman St. EC4 . . . . . . .3D 224 (44Rb 91)
Godman Rd. RM16: Grays 8D 100
SE15 . . . . .54Xb 113
Godolphin Cl. N13 . . . . .23Rb 51
SM2: Cheam 83Bb 175
Godolphin Ho. NW3 . . . . .38Gb 69
(off Fellows Rd.)
SL4: Eton 1H 103
(off Common La.)
Godolphin Pl. W3 . . . . .45Ta 87
Godolphin Rd. KT13: Weyb 79T 150
SL1: Slou .5H 81
W12 . . . . .46Xa 88
(not continuous)
Godric Cres.
CR0: New Ad 82Fc 179
Godson Rd. CR0: Wadd 76Qb 156
Godson St. N1 . . . . .1K 217 (40Qb 70)
Godson Yd. NW6 . . . . .41Cb 89
(off Kilburn Pk. Rd.)
GODSTONE .3A 210
Godstone By-Pass
RH9: G'stone 1A 210
Godstone Farm & Playbarn 4A 210
Godstone Golf Course 2C 210
Godstone Grn. RH9: G'stone 3P 209
Godstone Hill RH9: G'stone 99Xb 197
Godstone Ho. SE1 . . . . .3G 231
GODSTONE INTERCHANGE 1A 210
Godstone Mt. CR8: Purl 84Rb 177
Godstone Rd. CR3: Cat'm 96Wb 197
CR3: W'ham, Whyt 90Vb 177
CR8: Purl, Kenley 84Rb 177
RH1: Blet 5K 209
RH8: Oxt 3E 210
SM1: Sutt 77Eb 155
TW1: Twick 58Ka 108
Godstone Vineyards 100Yb 198
Godstow Rd. SE2 . . . . .47Xc 95
Godward Sq. E1 . . . . .42Zb 92
Godwin Cl. E4 . . . . .10Ec 20
KT19: Ewe 79Sa 153
N1 . . . . .1E 218 (40Sb 71)
Godwin Ct. NW1 . . . . .1C 216
Godwin Ho. E2 . . . . .1K 219
NW6 . . . . .40Db 69
(off Tollgate Gdns.)
SE1 . . . . .7K 225
Godwin Rd. BR2: Brom 69Lc 137
E7 . . . . .35Kc 73
Godwin Ter. RM3: Hrld W 25Nd 57
Goffers Rd. SE3 . . . . .53Gc 115
Goffs Cres. EN7: G Oak 1Sb 19
Goff's La. EN7: G Oak 1Sb 19
GOFF'S OAK 1Sb 19
Goffs Oak Av. EN7: G Oak 1Rb 19
Goffs Rd. TW15: Ashf 65T 128
Goff's Sports & Arts Cen. 1Wb 19
Gogmore Farm Cl. KT16: Chert 73H 149
Gogmore La. KT16: Chert 73J 149
Goidel Cl. SM6: Bedd 77Mb 156
Golborne Gdns. W10 . . . . .42Ab 88
(not continuous)
Golborne M. W10 . . . . .43Ab 88
Golborne Rd. W10 . . . . .43Ab 88
Goldace RM17: Grays 51Be 121
Golda Cl. EN5: Barn 16Za 30
Golda Ct. N3 . . . . .26Bb 49
Goldbeaters Gro. HA8: Edg 23Ua 48
Goldbeaters Ho. W1 . . . . .3E 222
(off Manette St.)
Goldcliff Cl. SM4: Mord 73Cb 155
Goldcrest Cl. E16 . . . . .43Mc 93
SE28 . . . . .45Yc 95
Goldcrest M. N16 . . . . .34Wb 71
W5 . . . . .43Ma 87
Goldcrest Way CR0: New Ad 81Fc 179
CR8: Purl 82Mb 176
RM3: Hrld W 26Nd 57
WD23: Bush 18Ea 28
Goldcroft HP3: Hem H 4A 4
Golden Bus. Pk. E10 . . . . .32Ac 72
Golden Ct. EN4: E Barn 14Gb 31
TW7: Isle 54Fa 108
TW9: Rich 57Ma 109
Golden Cres. UB3: Hayes 46V 84
Golden Cross M. W11 . . . . .44Bb 89
(off Portobello Rd.)
Golden Hinde 6F 225 (46Tb 91)
Golden Hind Pl. SE8 . . . . .49Bc 92
(off Grove St.)
Golden Jubilee Bridges 7H 223
Golden La. BR4: W W'ck 76Ec 158
EC1 . . . . .5D 218 (42Sb 91)
Golden La. Campus EC1 . . . . .6E 218
Golden La. Est. EC1 . . . . . .6D 218 (42Sb 91)
Golden Lane Leisure Cen. 6D 218
Golden Mnr. W7 . . . . .45Ga 86
Golden M. SE20 . . . . .67Yb 136
Golden Mile Ho. TW8: Bford 50Na 87
(off Clayponds La.)
Golden Oak Cl. SL2: Farn C 7G 60
Golden Pde. E17 . . . . .27Ec 52
(off Wood St.)
Golden Plover Cl. E16 . . . . .44Jc 93
Golden Sq. W1 . . . . .4C 222 (45Lb 90)
Golden Yd. NW3 . . . . .35Eb 69
(off Holly Mt.)
Golders Cl. HA8: Edg 22Ra 47
Golders Ct. NW11 . . . . .31Bb 69
Golders Gdns. NW11 . . . . .31Ab 68
GOLDERS GREEN 30Ab 48
Golders Grn. Crematorium
NW11 . . . . .31Cb 69
Golders Grn. Cres. NW11 . . . . .31Bb 69
Golders Grn. Rd. NW11 . . . . .30Ab 48
Goldersiea NW11 . . . . .32Db 69
Golders Mnr. Dr. NW11 . . . . .30Za 48
Golders Pk. Cl. NW11 . . . . .32Cb 69
Golders Ri. NW4 . . . . .29Za 48
Golders Way NW11 . . . . .31Bb 69
Golderton NW4 . . . . .28Xa 48
(off Prince of Wales Cl.)
Goldfinch Cl. BR6: Chels 78Wc 161
Goldfinch Ct. E3 . . . . .40Cc 72
(off Four Seasons Cl.)
Goldfinch Rd. CR2: Sels 82Ac 178
SE28 . . . . .48Tc 94
Goldfinch Way WD6: Bore 14Qa 29
Goldfort Wlk. GU21: Knap 8J 167
Goldhawk Ho. NW9 . . . . .27Ta 48
(off Caversham Rd.)
Goldhawk Ind. Est. W6 . . . . .48Xa 88
Goldhawk M. W12 . . . . .47Xa 88
Goldhawk Rd. W6 . . . . .49Va 88
W12 . . . . .49Va 88
Goldhaze Cl. IG8: Wfd G 24Lc 53
Gold Hill HA8: Edg 23Ta 47
Gold Hill E. SL9: Chal P 25A 42
Goldhurst Ho. W6 . . . . .51Ya 110
Goldhurst Mans. NW6 . . . . .37Eb 69
(off Goldhurst Ter.)
Goldhurst Ter. NW6 . . . . .38Db 69
Goldie Ho. N19 . . . . .31Mb 70
Goldie Leigh Hospital SE2 . . . . .52Xc 117
Golding Cl. KT9: Chess 79La 152
N18 . . . . .23Tb 51
Golding Ct. IG1: Ilf 34Qc 74
Goldingham Av. IG10: Lough 12Sc 36
Golding Rd. TN13: S'oaks 94Ld 203
Goldings, The GU21: Wok 8K 167
Goldings Hill IG10: Lough 8Pc 22
Goldings Ri. IG10: Lough 11Qc 36
Goldings Rd. IG10: Lough 11Qc 36
Golding St. E1 . . . . .44Wb 91
(not continuous)
Golding Ter. E1 . . . . .44Wb 91
(off Rope Wlk. Gdns.)
SW11 . . . . .54Jb 112
Goldington Bldgs. NW1 . . . . .1D 216
Goldington Cres. NW1 . . . .1D 216 (40Mb 70)
Goldington St. NW1 . . . . .1D 216 (40Mb 70)
Gold La. HA8: Edg 23Ta 47
Goldman Cl. E2 . . . . .42Wb 91
Goldney Rd. W9 . . . . .42Cb 89
Goldrill Dr. N11 . . . . .19Jb 32
Goldrings Rd. KT22: Oxs 85Da 171
Goldring Way AL2: Lon C 9F 6
Goldsboro' Rd. SW8 . . . . .53Mb 112
Goldsborough Cres. E4 . . . . .19Dc 34
Goldsborough Ho. E14 . . . . .50Dc 92
(off St Davids Sq.)
Goldsdown Cl. EN3: Enf H 12Ac 34
Goldsdown Rd. EN3: Enf H 12Zb 34
Goldsel Rd. BR8: Crock, Swan 71Fd 162
Goldsmere Ct. RM11: Horn 32Nd 77
Goldsmid St. SE18 . . . . .50Uc 94
Goldsmith Av. E12 . . . . .37Nc 74
NW9 . . . . .29Ua 48
RM7: Rush G 31Cd 76
W3 . . . . .45Ta 87
Goldsmith Cl. HA2: Harr 32Ca 65
TN16: Big H 89Nc 180
Goldsmith Ct. WC2 . . . . .2G 223
Goldsmith Est. SE15 . . . . .53Wb 113
Goldsmith La. NW9 . . . . .28Ra 47
Goldsmith Rd. E10 . . . . .32Cc 72
E17 . . . . .26Zb 52
N11 . . . . .22Hb 49
SE15 . . . . .53Wb 113
W3 . . . . .46Ta 87
Goldsmiths RM17: Grays 51Be 121
Goldsmiths Av. SS17: Corr, Stan H . . .1P 101
Goldsmith's Bldgs. W3 . . . . .46Ta 87
Goldsmiths Cl. GU21: Wok 10N 167
W3 . . . . .46Ta 87
Goldsmiths College 53Ac 114
Goldsmith's Pl. NW6 . . . . .39Db 69
(off Springfield La.)
Goldsmith's Row E2 . . . . .40Wb 71
Goldsmith's Sq. E2 . . . . .40Wb 71
Goldsmith St. EC2 . . . . . . .2E 224 (44Sb 91)
Goldsmith Way AL3: St A 1A 6
Goldstone Farm Vw.
KT23: Bookh 99Ca 191
GOLD STREET 10G 144
Gold St. DA12: Sole S 10F 144
GOLDSWORTH 10P 167
Goldsworth Orchard GU21: Wok 10L 167
GOLDSWORTH PARK 9L 167
Goldsworth Pk. Cen., The
GU21: Wok 9L 167
Goldsworth Pk. Trad. Est.
GU21: Wok 8L 167
Goldsworth Rd. GU21: Wok 10N 167
Goldsworth Rd. Ind. Est.
GU21: Wok 9P 167
Goldsworthy Gdns. SE16 . . . . .50Yb 92
Goldsworthy Way SL1: Slou 4A 80
Goldthorpe NW1 . . . . .39Lb 70
(off Camden St.)
Goldvale Ho. GU21: Wok 89A 168
(off Church St. W.)
Goldwell Ho. SE22 . . . . .55Ub 113
(off Quorn Rd.)
Goldwell Rd. CR7: Thor H 70Pb 134
Goldwin Cl. SE14 . . . . .53Yb 114
Golding Cl. E16 . . . . .44Jc 93
Gole Rd. GU24: Pirb 3A 186
Golf Cl. CR7: Thor H 67Qb 134
GU22: Pyr 86G 168
HA7: Stan 24La 46
WD23: Bush 13Z 27
Golf Club Cotts. SL5: S'dale 4G 146
Golf Club Dr. KT2: King T 66Ta 131
Golf Club Rd. AL9: Brk P 8J 9
GU22: Wok 2L 187
KT13: Weyb 81R 170
Golfe Rd. IG1: Ilf 34Tc 74
Golf Ho. Rd. RH8: Limp 1N 211
Golf Kingdom
Barking .29Bd 55
Golf Links Av. DA11: Grav'nd 4D 144
Golf Ride EN2: Crew H 7Qb 18
Golf Rd. BR1: Brom 69Qc 138
CR8: Kenley 90Tb 177
W5 . . . . .44Pa 87
Golf Side SM2: Cheam 83Ab 174
TW2: Twick 62Fa 130
Golfside Cl. KT3: N Mald 68Ua 132
N20 . . . . .20Gb 31
Gollogly Ter. SE7 . . . . .50Lc 93
Gombards AL3: St A 1B 6
Gombard's All. AL3: St A 2B 6
Gomer Gdns. TW11: Tedd 65Ja 130
Gomer Pl. TW11: Tedd 65Ja 130
Gomm Rd. SE16 . . . . .48Yb 92
Gomshall Av. SM6: Wall 78Nb 156
Gomshall Gdns. CR8: Kenley 87Ub 177
Gomshall Rd. SM2: Cheam 82Ya 174
Gondar Gdns. NW6 . . . . .36Bb 69
Gonnerston AL3: St A 1P 5
Gonson St. SE8 . . . . .51Dc 114
Gonston Cl. SW19 . . . . .61Ab 132
Gonville Av. WD3: Crox G 16R 26
Gonville Cres. UB5: N'olt 37Da 65
Gonville Rd. CR7: Thor H 71Pb 156
Gonville St. SW6 . . . . .55Ab 110
Gooch Ho. E5 . . . . .34Xb 71
EC1 . . . . .7K 217
Goodacre Cl. EN6: Pot B 4Db 17
KT13: Weyb 78S 150
Goodacre Ct. EN6: Pot B 4Db 17
Goodall Ho. SE4 . . . . .56Zb 114
Goodall Rd. E11 . . . . .34Ec 72
Goodbury Rd. TN15: Knat 85Rd 183
Goodchild Rd. N4 . . . . .32Sb 71
Gooden Ct. HA1: Harr 34Ga 66
Goodenough Cl. CR5: Coul 92Qb 196
Goodenough Rd. SW19 . . . . .66Bb 133
Goodenough Way CR5: Coul 92Pb 196
Gooderham Ho. RM16: Grays 7D 100
Goodey Rd. IG11: Bark 38Vc 75
Goodfaith Ho. E14 . . . . .45Dc 92
(off Simpson's Rd.)
Goodge Pl. W1 . . . . .1C 222 (43Lb 90)
Goodge St. W1 . . . . .1C 222 (43Lb 90)
Goodhall Cl. HA7: Stan 23Ja 46
Goodhall St. NW10 . . . . .41Va 88
(not continuous)
Goodhart Ho. SM7: Bans 90Eb 175
Goodhart Pl. E14 . . . . .45Ac 92
Goodhart Way BR4: W W'ck 73Gc 159
Goodhew Rd. CR0: C'don 72Wb 157
Goodhope Ho. E14 . . . . .45Dc 92
(off Poplar High St.)
Gooding Cl. KT3: N Mald 70Sa 131
Goodinge Cl. N7 . . . . .37Nb 70
Gooding Ho. SE7 . . . . .50Lc 93
Goodison Cl. WD23: Bush 15Ea 28
Goodlake Ct. UB9: Den 31H 63
Goodley Stock Rd.
TN16: Westrm 100Rc 200
Goodman Cres. CR0: C'don 72Rb 157
SW2 . . . . .61Nb 134
Goodman Pk. SL2: Slou 6N 81
Goodman Pl. TW18: Staines 63H 127
Goodman Rd. E10 . . . . .31Ec 72
Goodman's Ct. E1 . . . . .4K 225 (45Vb 91)
Goodmans Ct. HA0: Wemb 35Ma 67
Goodman's Stile E1 . . . . .44Wb 91
Goodmans Yd. E1 . . . . .4K 225 (45Vb 91)
GOODMAYES 33Wc 75
Goodmayes Av. IG3: Ilf 32Wc 75
Goodmayes La. IG3: Ilf 35Wc 75
Goodmayes Lodge RM8: Dag 35Wc 75
Goodmayes Retail Pk.
RM6: Chad H 32Xc 75
Goodmayes Rd. IG3: Ilf 32Wc 75
Goodmead Rd.
BR6: Orp, St M Cry 73Wc 161
Goodrich Cl. WD25: Wat 7W 12
Goodrich Ct. W10 . . . . .44Za 88
Goodrich Ho. E2 . . . . .40Yb 72
(off Sewardstone Rd.)
Goodrich Rd. SE22 . . . . .58Vb 113
Goodridge Ho. E4 . . . . .24Ec 52
Goodson Ho. SM4: Mord 73Eb 155
(off Green La.)
Goodson Rd. NW10 . . . . .38Ua 68
Goodspeed Ho. E14 . . . . .45Dc 92
(off Simpson's Rd.)
Goods Way N1 . . . . .1F 217 (40Nb 70)
Goodway Gdns. E14 . . . . .44Fc 93
Goodwill Dr. HA2: Harr 32Ca 65
Goodwill Ho. E14 . . . . .45Dc 92
(off Simpson's Rd.)
Goodwin Cl. CR4: Mitc 69Fb 133
SE16 . . . . .48Vb 91
Goodwin Ct. EN4: E Barn 16Gb 31
N8 . . . . .27Nb 50
(off Campsbourne Rd.)
SW19 . . . . .66Gb 133
Goodwin Dr. DA14: Sidc 62Zc 139
Goodwin Gdns. CR0: Wadd 79Rb 157
Goodwin Ho. N9 . . . . .18Yb 34
WD18: Wat 16U 26
Goodwin Rd. CR0: Wadd 78Rb 157
N9 . . . . .18Zb 34
SL2: Slou .1D 80
W12 . . . . .47Wa 88
Goodwins Ct. WC2 . . . . . . .4F 223 (45Nb 90)
Goodwin St. N4 . . . . .33Qb 70
Goodwin Way RM3: Rom 22Md 57
Goodwood Apartments E4 . . . . .24Dc 52
Goodwood Av. EN3: Enf W 9Yb 20
RM12: Horn 35Nd 77
WD24: Wat 7U 12
Goodwood Cl. HA7: Stan 22La 46
SM4: Mord 70Cb 133
Goodwood Ct. W1 . . . . .7A 216
Goodwood Cres. DA12: Grav'nd 4E 144
Goodwood Dr. UB5: N'olt 37Ca 65
Goodwood Ho. SE14 . . . . .52Ac 114
(off Goodwood Rd.)
SL4: Wind 3D 102
(off Paddock Cl.)
Goodwood Pde. BR3: Beck 70Ac 136
WD24: Wat 8U 12
Goodwood Path WD6: Bore 12Qa 29
Goodwood Rd. RH1: Redh 4P 207
SE14 . . . . .52Ac 114
Goodworth Rd. RH1: Redh 4B 208
TN15: Wro 88Be 185
Goodwyn Av. NW7 . . . . .22Ua 48
Goodwyns Va. N10 . . . . .25Jb 50
Goodyear Ho. N2 . . . . .26Fb 49
(off The Grange)
Goodyear Pl. SE5 . . . . .51Sb 113
Goodyer Ho. SW1 . . . . .7D 228
Goodyers Av. WD7: R'lett 5Ha 14
Goodyers Gdns. NW4 . . . . .29Za 48
Goosander Way SE28 . . . . .48Tc 94
Gooseacre La. HA3: Kenton 29Ma 47
Goosecroft HP1: Hem H 1H 3
Goosefields WD3: Rick 16L 25
Goose Grn. KT11: D'side 91W 190
SL2: Farn R 10F 60
Goose Grn. Cl. BR5: St P 68Wc 139
Goose Grn. Trad. Est. SE22 . . . . . . .56Vb 113
Goose La. GU22: Wok 4M 187
Gooseley La. E6 . . . . .42Rc 94
(Claps Ga. La.)
E6 . . . . .41Qc 94
(Folkestone Rd.)
Goosens Cl. SM1: Sutt 78Eb 155
Goosepool KT16: Chert 73H 149
Goose Rye Rd. GU3: Worp 8H 187
Goose Sq. E6 . . . . .44Pc 94
Gooshays Dr. RM3: Rom 22Nd 57
Gooshays Gdns. RM3: Rom 23Md 57
Gophir La. EC4 . . . . .4F 225 (45Tb 91)
Gopsall St. N1 . . . . .1G 219 (39Tb 71)
Goral Mead WD3: Rick 18M 25
Gordon Av. CR2: Sande 82Sb 177
E4 . . . . .23Gc 53
HA7: Stan 24Ha 46
RM12: Horn 33Hd 76
SW14 . . . . .56Ua 110
TW1: Twick 57Ja 108
Gordonbrock Rd. SE4 . . . . .57Cc 114
Gordon Cl. AL1: St A 3F 6
E17 . . . . .30Cc 52
KT16: Chert 76G 148
N19 . . . . .32Lb 70
RM18: E Til 2M 123
TW18: Staines 64K 127
Gordon Cotts. W8 . . . . .47Db 89
(off Dukes La.)
Gordon Ct. HA8: Edg 22Pa 47
RH1: Redh 8P 207
(off St John's Ter. Rd.)
Gordon Cres. CR0: C'don 74Ub 157
UB3: Hayes 49W 84
Gordondale Rd. SW19 . . . . .61Cb 133
Gordon Dr. KT16: Chert 76G 148
TW17: Shep 73T 150
Gordon Gdns. HA8: Edg 26Ra 47
Gordon Gro. SE5 . . . . .54Rb 113
Gordon Hill EN2: Enf 11Sb 33
Gordon Ho. AL1: St A 3F 6
E1 . . . . .45Yb 92
(off Glamis Rd.)
SW1 . . . . .4C 228
W5 . . . . .41Na 87
Gordon Ho. Rd. NW5 . . . . .35Jb 70
Gordon Mans. W14 . . . . .48Za 88
(off Addison Gdns.)
WC1 . . . . .6D 216
Gordon Pl. DA12: Grav'nd 8E 122
W8 . . . . .47Cb 89
Gordon Prom. DA12: Grav'nd 8E 122
Gordon Prom. E.
DA12: Grav'nd 8E 122

Gordon Rd. BR3: Beck 69Bc 136
CM15: Shenf 18Ce 41
CR3: Cat'm 93Tb 197
DA1: Dart 59Md 119
DA11: Nflt 9A 122
DA15: Sidc 57Uc 116
DA17: Belv 49Ed 96
E4 17Gc 35
E11 30Jc 53
E15 35Ec 72
E18 25Kc 53
EN2: Enf 11Sb 33
EN9: Walt A 6Cc 20
HA3: W'stone 27Ga 46
IG1: Ilf 34Tc 74
IG11: Bark 39Uc 74
KT2: King T 67Pa 131
KT5: Surb 73Pa 153
KT10: Clay 80Ga 152
N3 24Bb 49
N9 19Xb 33
N11 24Mb 50
RH1: Redh 3A 208
RM6: Chad H 30Bd 55
RM16: Grays 7A 100
SE15 54Xb 113
SL4: Wind 4D 102
SM5: Cars 79Hb 155
SS17: Horn H 1H 101
TN13: S'oaks 97Kd 203
TW3: Houn 56Ea 108
TW9: Rich 54Pa 109
TW15: Ashf 62N 127
TW17: Shep 72T 150
TW18: Staines 63E 126
UB2: S'hall 49Aa 85
UB7: Yiew 45N 83
W4 51Ra 109
W5 45Ka 86
W13 45Ka 86
Gordon Sq. WC1 5D 216 (42Mb 90)
Gordon St. E13 41Jc 93
WC1 5D 216 (42Mb 90)
Gordons Way RH8: Oxt 100Fc 199
Gordon Way BR1: Brom 67Jc 137
EN5: Barn 14Bb 31
Gore Cl. UB9: Hare 28K 43
Gore Cotts. DA2: Daren 62Sd 142
Gore Ct. NW9 29Qa 47
Gorefield Ho. NW6 40Cb 69
(off Gorefield Pl.)
Gorefield Pl. NW6 40Cb 69
Gore Ho. N1 38Qb 70
(off Drummond Way)
Gorelands La. HP8: Chal G 18A 24
Gore Rd. DA2: Dart 61Sd 142
E9 39Yb 72
SL1: Burn 1A 80
SW20 68Ya 132
GORESBROOK INTERCHANGE 40Bd 75
Goresbrook Rd. RM9: Dag 39Xc 75
Gore St. SW7 3A 226 (48Eb 89)
Gorhambury House 1J 5
Gorham Dr. AL1: St A 5C 6
Gorham Ho. SE16 47Zb 92
(off Wolfe Cres.)
Gorham Pl. W11 45Ab 88
Goring Cl. RM5: Col R 25Ed 56
Goring Gdns. RM8: Dag 35Yc 75
Goring Mdw. TN15: Wro 88Be 185
Goring Pl. TN15: Wro 88Ce 185
Goring Rd. N11 23Nb 50
RM10: Dag 37Fd 76
TW18: Staines 64F 126
Gorings Sq. TW18: Staines 63G 126
Goring St. EC3 2J 225
Goring Way UB6: G'frd 40Ea 66
Gorle Cl. WD25: Wat 7W 12
Gorleston Rd. N15 29Tb 51
Gorleston St. W14 49Bb 88
(not continuous)
Gorman Rd. SE18 49Pc 94
Gorringe Av. DA4: S Dar 68Td 142
Gorringe Pk. Av. CR4: Mitc 66Hb 133
Gorse Cl. AL10: Hat 3B 8
E16 44Jc 93
KT20: Tad 92Xa 194
Gorsefield Ho. E14 45Cc 92
(off E. India Dock Rd.)
Gorse Hill DA4: Farni 73Qd 163
GU22: Wok 3K 187
Gorse Hill La. GU25: Vir W 10P 125
Gorse Hill Rd. GU25: Vir W 10P 125
Gorselands Cl. KT14: W Byf 83L 169
Gorse La. GU24: Chob 10J 147
Gorse Meade SL1: Slou 6F 80
Gorse Ri. SW17 64Jb 134
Gorse Rd. BR5: St M Cry 75Cd 162
CR0: C'don 77Cc 158
Gorse Wlk. UB7: Yiew 44N 83
Gorse Way DA3: Hartl 71Be 165
Gorseway RM7: Rush G 32Gd 76
Gorsewood Rd.
DA3: Hartl, Lfield 71Be 165
(not continuous)
GU21: Wok 1H 187
Gorst Rd. NW10 42Sa 87
SW11 58Hb 111
Gorsuch Pl. E2 3K 219 (41Vb 91)
Gorsuch St. E2 3K 219 (40Vb 71)
Gosberton Rd. SW12 60Hb 111
Gosbury Hill KT9: Chess 77Na 153
Gosden Rd. GU24: W End 5D 166
Gosfield Rd. KT19: Eps 84Ta 173
RM8: Dag 33Cd 76
Gosfield St. W1 7B 216 (43Lb 90)
Gosford Gdns. IG4: Ilf 29Pc 54
Gosford Ho. E3 40Bc 72
(off Tredegar Rd.)
WD18: Wat 16U 26
Gosforth La. WD19: Wat 20W 26
Gosforth Path WD19: Wat 20W 26
Gosforth Pl. SL1: Slou 5D 80
Goshawk Ct. NW9 31Va 68
Goshawk Gdns. UB4: Hayes 41U 84
Goslar Way SL4: Wind 4F 102
Goslett Ct. WD23: Bush 15Ca 27
Goslett Yd. WC2 3E 222 (44Mb 90)
Gosling Cl. UB6: G'frd 41Ca 85
Gosling Grn. SL3: L'ly 48A 82
Gosling Ho. E1 45Yb 92
(off Sutton St.)
Gosling Rd. SL3: L'ly 48A 82
Gosling Way SW9 53Qb 112
Gospatrick Rd. N17 24Sb 51
GOSPEL OAK 35Jb 70
Gosport Dr. RM12: Horn 37Ld 77
Gosport Rd. E17 29Bc 52
Gosport Wlk. N17 28Xb 51
Gossage Rd. SE18 50Tc 94
UB10: Uxb 38P 63
Gossamers, The WD25: Wat 6Aa 13
Gosse Ct. N1 39Ub 71
(off Downham Rd.)
W13 44Ja 86
Gosset St. E2 3K 219 (41Vb 91)
Goss Hill BR8: Swan 65Ld 141
Gosshill Rd. BR7: Chst 68Qc 138
Gossington Cl. BR7: Chst 63Rc 138
Gosterwood St. SE8 51Ac 114
Gostling Rd. TW2: Whitt 60Ca 107
Goston Gdns.
CR7: Thor H 69Qb 134
Goston Ga. SW8 53Pb 112
(off Hampson Way)
Goswell Hill SL4: Wind 3H 103
Goswell Pl. EC1 4C 218
Goswell Rd. EC1 2B 218 (40Rb 71)
SL4: Wind 3H 103
Gothic Cl. DA1: Dart 62Md 141
Gothic Cotts. EN2: Enf 12Sb 33
(off Chase Grn. Av.)
Gothic Ct. SE5 52Sb 113
(off Wyndham Rd.)
UB3: Harl 51T 106
Gothic Rd. TW2: Twick 61Fa 130
Gottfried M. NW5 35Lb 70
Goudhurst Rd. BR1: Brom 64Gc 137
Gouge Av. DA11: Nflt 10A 122
Gough Ho. KT1: King T 68Na 131
(off Eden St.)
N1 39Rb 71
(off Windsor St.)
Gough Rd. E15 35Hc 73
EN1: Enf 12Xb 33
Gough Sq. EC4 2A 224 (44Qb 90)
Gough St. WC1 5J 217 (42Pb 90)
Gough Wlk. E14 44Cc 92
Gould Cl. AL9: Wel G 6D 8
Goulden Ho. SW11 54Gb 111
Goulden Ho. App. SW11 54Gb 111
Goulding Gdns.
CR7: Thor H 68Sb 135
Gouldman Ho. E1 42Yb 92
(off Wyllen Cl.)
Gould Rd. TW2: Twick 60Ga 108
TW14: Felt 59U 106
Goulds Cotts. RM4: Abr 13Xc 37
GOULDS GREEN 43R 84
Gould's Grn. UB8: Hil 45R 84
Gould Ter. E8 36Xb 71
Gould Way HA8: Edg 24Ra 47
Goulston St. E1 2K 225 (44Vb 91)
Goulton Rd. E5 35Xb 71
Gourley Pl. N15 29Ub 51
Gourley St. N15 29Ub 51
Gourney Gro. RM16: Grays 45De 99
Gourock Rd. SE9 57Qc 116
Govan St. E2 39Wb 71
Gover Ct. SW4 54Nb 112
GOVER HILL 100Fe 205
Gover Hill TN11: Roug 100Fe 205
Government Row EN3: Enf L 10Cc 20
Govett Av. TW17: Shep 71S 150
Govett Gro. GU20: W'sham 8B 146
Govier Cl. E15 38Gc 73
Gowan Av. SW6 53Ab 110
Gowan Ho. E2 4K 219
Gowan Rd. NW10 37Xa 68
Gowar Fld. EN6: S Mim 4Wa 16
Gower, The TW20: Thorpe 69D 126
Gower Cl. SW4 58Lb 112
Gower Ct. WC1 5C 216 (42Mb 90)
Gower Ho. E17 27Dc 52
KT13: Weyb 79T 150
SE17 7E 230
TW7: Isle 54Ha 108
Gower Lodge KT13: Weyb 79T 150
(off St George's Rd.)
Gower M. WC1 1E 222 (43Mb 90)
Gower M. Mans. WC1 7E 216
Gower Pl. RM16: Chaf H 48Xd 98
WC1 5C 216 (42Mb 90)
Gower Rd. E7 37Jc 73
KT13: Weyb 79T 150
TW7: Isle 51Ha 108
Gowers La. RM16: Ors 7B 100
Gower St. WC1 5C 216 (42Lb 90)
Gower's Wlk. E1 44Wb 91
Gowings Grn. SL1: Slou 7C 80
Gowland Pl. BR3: Beck 68Bc 136
Gowlett Rd. SE15 55Wb 113
Gowlland Cl. CR0: C'don 73Wb 157
Gowrie Pl. CR3: Cat'm 94Sb 197
Gowrie Rd. SW11 55Jb 112
Grabex Bus. Cen. BR5: St P 69Xc 139
Graburn Way KT8: E Mos 69Fa 130
Grace Av. DA7: Bex 54Bd 117
WD7: Shenl 5Ma 15
Grace Bus. Cen. CR4: Mitc 72Hb 155
Gracechurch St. EC3 4G 225 (45Tb 91)
Grace Cl. HA8: Edg 24Sa 47
IG6: Ilf 23Vc 55
SE9 62Mc 137
WD6: Bore 11Ta 29
Grace Ct. CR0: C'don 76Rb 157
(off Waddon Rd.)
SL1: Burn 2A 80
SL1: Slou 6G 80
SM2: Sutt 81Db 175
Gracedale Rd. SW16 64Kb 134
Gracefield Gdns. SW16 62Nb 134
Gracehill E1 43Yb 92
(off Hannibal Rd.)
Grace Ho. SE11 51Pb 112
(off Vauxhall St.)
Grace Jones Cl. E8 37Wb 71
Grace M. BR3: Beck 65Cc 136
SE20 68Yb 136
(off Marlow Rd.)
Grace Path SE26 63Yb 136
Grace Pl. E3 41Dc 92
Grace Rd. CR0: C'don 72Sb 157
Graces All. E1 45Wb 91
Grace's M. SE5 54Tb 113
Graces M. NW8 2A 214 (40Eb 69)
Grace's Rd. SE5 54Ub 113
Grace St. E3 41Dc 92
Gracious Pond Rd.
GU24: Chob 10L 147
Gradient, The SE26 63Wb 135
Grade Cl. WD6: E'tree 14Qa 29
Graduate Pl. SE1 3H 231
Graeme Rd. EN1: Enf 12Tb 33
Graemesdyke Av. SW14 55Ra 109
Graftonbury M.
EN2: Crew H 6Rb 19
Grafton Chambers NW1 4E 216
Grafton Cl. AL4: St A 3H 7
KT4: Wor Pk 76Ua 154
KT14: W Byf 85H 169
SL3: Geor G 44A 82
TW4: Houn 60Aa 107
W13 44Ja 86
Grafton Ct. TW14: Bedf 60T 106
Grafton Cres. NW1 37Kb 70
Grafton Gdns. N4 30Sb 51
RM8: Dag 33Ad 75
Grafton Ho. E3 41Cc 92
(off Wellington Way)
SE8 50Bc 92
Grafton M. W1 6B 216 (42Lb 90)
Grafton Pk. Rd. KT4: Wor Pk 75Ua 154
Grafton Pl. NW1 4D 216 (41Mb 90)
Grafton Rd. CR0: C'don 74Qb 156
EN2: Enf 13Pb 32
HA1: Harr 29Ea 46
KT3: N Mald 69Ua 132
KT4: Wor Pk 76Ta 153
NW5 36Jb 70
RM8: Dag 33Ad 75
W3 45Sa 87
Graftons, The NW2 34Cb 69
Grafton Sq. SW4 55Lb 112
Grafton St. W1 5A 222 (45Kb 90)
Grafton Ter. NW5 36Hb 69
Grafton Way KT8: W Mole 70Ba 129
W1 6B 216 (42Lb 90)
(not continuous)
WC1 6B 216 (42Lb 90)
Grafton Yd. NW5 37Kb 70
Graham Av. CR4: Mitc 67Jb 134
W13 47Ka 86
Graham Cl. AL1: St A 4B 6
CM13: Hut 15Ee 41
CR0: C'don 75Cc 158
Graham Ct. AL3: St A 1B 6
(off Grange St.)
SE14 51Zb 114
(off Myers La.)
UB5: N'olt 36Aa 65
Grahame Ho. RH1: Redh 4N 207
GRAHAME PARK 25Ua 48
Grahame Pk. Way NW7 24Va 48
NW9 26Va 48
Grahame Twr. W3 48Ra 87
(off Hanbury Rd.)
Grahame White Ho. HA3: Kenton 27Ma 47
Graham Gdns. KT6: Surb 74Na 153
Graham Ho. KT23: Bookh 96Ba 191
N9 18Yb 34
(off Cumberland Rd.)
Graham Lodge NW4 30Xa 48
Graham Mans. IG11: Bark 38Wc 75
(off Lansbury Av.)
Graham Rd. CR4: Mitc 67Jb 134
CR8: Purl 85Qb 176
DA6: Bex 56Bd 117
E8 37Wb 71
E13 42Jc 93
GU20: W'sham 9A 146
HA3: W'stone 27Ga 46
N15 27Rb 51
NW4 30Xa 48
SW19 66Bb 133
TW12: Hamp H 63Ca 129
W4 48Ta 87
Graham St. N1 2C 218 (40Rb 71)
Graham Ter. DA15: Sidc 58Xc 117
(off Westerham Dr.)
SW1 6H 227 (49Jb 90)
Grainger Cl. UB5: N'olt 36Da 65
Grainger Ct. SE5 52Sb 113
Grainger Rd. N22 25Sb 51
TW7: Isle 54Ha 108
Graingers Yd. UB8: Uxb 38L 63
Grainstore, The E16 45Jc 93
Gramer Cl. E11 33Fc 73
Grampian Cl. BR6: St M Cry 72Vc 161
SM2: Sutt 80Eb 155
UB3: Harl 52T 106
Grampian Gdns. NW2 32Ab 68
Grampians, The W6 47Za 88
(off Shepherd's Bush Rd.)
Grampian Way SL3: L'ly 50C 82
Gramsci Way SE6 62Dc 136
Granada St. SW17 64Hb 133
Granard Av. SW15 57Xa 110
Granard Bus. Cen. NW7 23Ua 48
Granard Ho. E9 37Zb 72
Granard Rd. SW12 59Hb 111
Granaries, The EN9: Walt A 6Gc 21
Granary Cl. N9 17Yb 34
Granary Ct. E15 37Fc 73
(off Millstone Cl.)
Granary Mans. SE28 47Sc 94
Granary Rd. E1 42Xb 91
Granary Sq. N1 1F 217 (39Nb 70)
Granary St. NW1 1E 216 (39Mb 70)
Granby Pk. Rd. EN7: Chesh 1Vb 19
Granby Pl. SE1 2K 229
Granby Rd. DA11: Nflt 58Ee 121
SE9 54Pc 116
Granby St. E2 42Wb 91
(not continuous)
Granby Ter. NW1 2B 216 (40Lb 70)
Grand Arc. N12 22Eb 49
Grand Av. EC1 7C 218 (43Rb 91)
(not continuous)
HA9: Wemb 36Qa 67
KT5: Surb 71Ra 153
N10 28Jb 50
Grand Av. E. HA9: Wemb 36Ra 67
Grand Canal Apartments N1 39Ub 71
(off De Beauvoir Cres.)
Grand Canal Av. SE16 49Ac 92
Grand Connaught Rooms 2H 223
Grand Courts RM8: Dag 34Ad 75
Grand Depot Rd. SE18 50Qc 94
Grand Dr. SW20 68Ya 132
UB2: S'hall 47Ea 86
Granden Rd. SW16 68Nb 134
Grandfield Av. WD17: Wat 11V 26
Grandfield Ct. W4 51Ta 109
Grandis Cotts. GU23: Rip 94K 189
Grandison Rd. KT4: Wor Pk 75Ya 154
SW11 57Hb 111
Grand Junc. Pl. UB8: Uxb 40K 63
Grand Junc. Wharf E2 41Zb 92
N1 2D 218 (40Sb 71)
Grand Pde. HA9: Wemb 33Qa 67
KT6: Surb 74Qa 153
N4 29Rb 51
SW14 56Sa 109
(off Up. Richmond Rd. W.)
Grand Pde. M. SW15 57Ab 110
Grand Regent Twr. E2 41Zb 92
(off Palmer's Rd.)
Grandstand Rd. KT17: Eps D 89Va 174
Grandstand Way UB5: N'olt 36Ba 65
Grand Twr. SW15 57Ab 110
(off Plaza Gdns.)
Grand Union Canal Wlk. W10 42Ya 88
(off Canal Way)
Grand Union Cen. W10 42Za 88
(off West Row)
Grand Union Cl. W9 43Bb 89
Grand Union Cres. E8 39Wb 71
Grand Union Ent. Pk.
UB2: S'hall 48Ca 85
Grand Union Hgts. HA0: Wemb 39Ma 67
Grand Union Ho. N1 39Ub 71
(off Hertford Rd.)
Grand Union Ind. Est. NW10 40Ra 67
Grand Union Office Pk., The
UB8: Cowl 44L 83
Grand Union Village UB5: N'olt 41Ba 85
Grand Union Wlk. NW1 38Kb 70
(off Kentish Town Rd.)
Grand Union Way UB2: S'hall 47Ca 85
WD4: K Lan 1R 12
Grand Vw. Av. TN16: Big H 89Lc 179
Grand Vitesse Ind. Cen. SE1 7C 224
Grand Wlk. E1 42Ac 92
Granfield St. SW11 53Fb 111
Grange, The AL4: Col H 5P 7
CR0: C'don 75Bc 158
DA4: S Dar 67Td 142
E17 29Ac 52
(off Lynmouth Rd.)
EN9: Walt A 9Fc 21
GU24: Chob 2J 167
GU25: Vir W 70A 126
(off Holloway Dr.)
HA0: Wemb 38Qa 67
KT3: N Mald 71Va 154
KT4: Wor Pk 77Ta 153
KT12: Walt T 75X 151
N2 26Fb 49
N20 18Eb 31
(Grangeview Rd.)
N20 18Fb 31
(Oxford Gdns.)
SE1 3K 231 (48Vb 91)
SL1: Burn 1A 80
(off Green La.)
SL4: Old Win 7M 103
SW19 65Za 132
TN15: W King 81Vd 184
W3 47Ra 87
W4 50Ra 87
W13 43La 86
W14 49Bb 89
WD3: Rick 17M 25
WD5: Ab L 3U 12
Grange Av. EN4: E Barn 18Gb 31
HA7: Stan 26Ka 46
IG8: Wfd G 23Jc 53
N12 22Eb 49
N20 17Ab 30
SE25 68Ub 135
TW2: Twick 61Ga 130
Grangecliffe Gdns. SE25 68Ub 135
Grange Cl. CM13: Ingve 22Ee 59
CR5: Chip 92Hb 195
DA15: Sidc 62Wc 139
HA8: Edg 22Sa 47
HP2: Hem H 3A 4
IG8: Wfd G 24Jc 53
KT8: W Mole 70Da 129
KT22: Lea 92Ma 193
RH1: Blet 5K 209
RH1: Mers 100Kb 196
SL9: Chal P 25A 42
TN16: Westrm 98Sc 200
TW5: Hest 51Ba 107
TW19: Wray 58A 104
UB3: Hayes 43U 84
WD17: Wat 11W 26
Grange Ct. AL3: St A 1B 6
(not continuous)
EN9: Walt A 6Ec 20
HA1: Harr 35Ha 66
HA5: Pinn 27Aa 45
IG10: Lough 15Mc 35
KT12: Walt T 75W 150
NW10 34Ua 68
(off Neasden La.)
RH1: Mers 100Kb 196
RH9: S God 10C 210
SM2: Sutt 80Db 155
SM6: Wall 76Kb 156
TW17: Shep 70Q 128
TW18: Staines 64J 127
TW20: Egh 64B 126
UB5: N'olt 40Y 65
WC2 3J 223 (44Pb 90)
Grangecourt Rd. N16 32Ub 71
Grange Cres. DA2: Dart 58Rd 119
IG7: Chig 22Tc 54
SE28 44Yc 95
Grangedale Cl. HA6: Nwood 25U 44
Grange Dr. BR6: Prat B 81Yc 181
BR7: Chst 65Nc 138
GU21: Wok 87A 168
RH1: Mers 100Kb 196
Grange Farm Cl. HA2: Harr 33Ea 66
Grangefield NW1 38Mb 70
(off Marquis Rd.)
Grange Flds. SL9: Chal P 25A 42
Grangefields Rd. GU4: Jac W 10P 187
Grange Gdns. HA5: Pinn 27Aa 45
N14 18Mb 32
NW3 34Db 69
SE25 68Ub 135
SL2: Farn C 6H 61
SM7: Bans 85Db 175
Grange Gro. N1 37Sb 71
GRANGE HILL 23Tc 54
Grange Hill HA8: Edg 22Sa 47
SE25 68Ub 135
TN15: Plax 99Ae 205
Grangehill Pl. SE9 55Pc 116
Grangehill Rd. SE9 56Pc 116
Grange Ho. DA8: Erith 54Jd 118
DA11: Grav'nd 9C 122
NW10 38Xa 68
SE1 4K 231 (48Vb 91)
Grange La. DA3: Hartl 73Ce 165
SE21 61Vb 135
WD25: Let H 11Fa 28
Grange Lodge SW19 65Za 132
Grange Mans. KT17: Ewe 80Va 154
Grange Mdw. SM7: Bans 85Db 175
Grange M. N21 16Rb 33
TW13: Felt 63W 128
Grangemill Rd. SE6 62Cc 136
Grangemill Way SE6 61Cc 136
Grangemount KT22: Lea 92Ma 193
GRANGE PARK 16Rb 33
Grange Pk. GU21: Wok 87A 168
W5 46Na 87
Grange Pk. Av. N21 16Sb 33
Grange Pk. Pl. SW20 66Xa 132
Grange Pk. Rd. CR7: Thor H 70Tb 135
E10 32Dc 72
Grange Pl. KT12: Walt T 75W 150
NW6 38Cb 69
TW18: Lale 68L 127
Granger Ct. WD6: Bore 14Qa 29
(off Whitehall Cl.)
Grange Rd. BR6: Orp 75Tc 160
CR2: S Croy 82Sb 177
CR3: Cat'm 97Wb 197
CR7: Thor H 70Tb 135
DA11: Grav'nd 9C 122
E10 32Cc 72
E13 41Hc 93
E17 29Ac 52
(not continuous)
GU2: Guild 10M 187
GU21: Wok 86A 168
GU24: Pirb 4A 186
HA1: Harr 29Ja 46
HA2: Harr 33Fa 66
HA8: Edg 23Ta 47
IG1: Ilf 35Rc 74
KT1: King T 69Na 131
KT8: W Mole 70Da 129
KT9: Chess 77Na 153
KT12: Hers 77Aa 151
KT15: New H 82J 169
KT22: Lea 92Ma 193
N6 30Jb 50
N17 23Wb 51
N18 23Wb 51
NW10 37Xa 68
RM3: Rom 23Kd 57
RM15: Avel 46Sd 98
RM17: Grays 51De 121
SE1 4J 231 (48Ub 91)
SE19 70Tb 135
SE25 70Tb 135
SL9: Chal P 25A 42
SM2: Sutt 80Cb 155
SW13 53Wa 110
TN13: S'oaks 99Jd 202
TN15: Plat 92Ee 205
TW20: Egh 64B 126
UB1: S'hall 47Aa 85
UB3: Hayes 44U 84
W4 50Ra 87
W5 46Ma 87
WD6: E'tree 15Pa 29
WD23: Bush 15Aa 27
Granger Way RM1: Rom 30Jd 56
Grange St. AL3: St A 1B 6
N1 1G 219 (39Tb 71)
Grange St. M. AL3: St A 1B 6
Grange Va. SM2: Sutt 80Db 155
Grange Vw. Rd. N20 18Eb 31
Grange Wlk. SE1 3J 231 (48Ub 91)
Grange Wlk. M. SE1 4J 231
Grangewaters Outdoor Education Cen.
43Be 99
Grange Way DA3: Hartl 72Be 165
DA8: Erith 52Kd 119
NW6 38Cb 69
SL0: Iver 44H 83
Grangeway IG8: Wfd G 21Lc 53
N12 21Db 49
Grangeway, The N21 16Rb 33
Grangeway Gdns. IG4: Ilf 29Nc 54
Grangeways Cl. DA11: Nflt 3B 144
Grangewick Rd. RM16: Grays 8A 100
Grangewood DA5: Bexl 60Bd 117
EN6: Pot B 2Db 17
SL3: Wex 3N 81
Grangewood Av. RM13: Rain 42Ld 97
RM16: Grays 8A 100
Grangewood Cl. CM13: B'wood 20Be 41
HA5: Eastc 29W 44
Grangewood Dr. TW16: Sun 66V 128
Grangewood La. BR3: Beck 65Bc 136
Grangewood St. E6 39Mc 73
Grangewood Ter. SE25 68Tb 135
Grange Yd. SE1 4K 231 (48Vb 91)
Granham Gdns. N9 19Vb 33
Granite Apartments E15 37Gc 73
SE10 50Gc 93
Granite St. SE18 50Vc 95
Granleigh Rd. E11 33Gc 73
Gransden Av. E8 38Xb 71
Gransden Ho. SE8 50Bc 92
Gransden Rd. W12 47Va 88
Grant Av. SL1: Slou 4J 81
Grantbridge St. N1 1C 218 (40Rb 71)
Grantchester KT1: King T 68Qa 131
(off St Peters Rd.)
Grantchester Cl. HA1: Harr 34Ha 66
Grant Cl. DA17: Belv 50Bd 95
N14 17Lb 32
N17 26Ub 51
TW17: Shep 72R 150
Grant Ct. E4 18Ec 34
(off The Ridgeway)
NW9 26Va 48
(off Hazel Cl.)
Grantham Cl. HA8: Edg 20Na 29
Grantham Ct. KT2: King T 64Ma 131
RM6: Chad H 31Bd 75
SE16 47Zb 92
(off Eleanor Cl.)
Grantham Gdns. RM6: Chad H 30Bd 55
Grantham Grn. WD6: Bore 15Sa 29
Grantham Ho. SE15 51Wb 113
(off Friary Est.)
TW16: Sun 66U 128
UB5: N'olt 41Ba 85
(off Taywood Rd.)
Grantham M. HP4: Berk 1A 2
Grantham Pl. W1 7K 221 (46Kb 90)
Grantham Rd. E12 35Qc 74
SW9 54Nb 112
W4 52Ua 110
Grantham Way RM16: Grays 46Ce 99
Grant Ho. E17 28Cc 52
(off High St.)
SW9 53Pb 112
(off Liberty St.)
Grantley Ho. SE14 51Zb 114
(off Myers La.)

Grantley Pl.—Greenford Rd.

Grantley Pl. KT10: Esh 78Ea 152
Grantley Rd. TW4: Cran 54Y 107
Grantley St. E1 .... 41Zb 92
Grant Mus. of Zoology 6D 216
Grantock Rd. E17 .... 25Fc 53
Granton Av. RM14: Upm 34Pd 77
Granton Rd. DA14: Sidc 65Yc 139
IG3: Ilf 32Wc 75
SW16 .... 67Lb 134
Grant Pl. CR0: C'don 74Vb 157
Grant Rd. CR0: C'don 74Vb 157
HA3: W'stone 27Ha 46
SW11 .... 56Fb 111
Grants Cl. NW7 .... 24Ya 48
Grants La. RH8: Limp 4N 211
TN8: Eden, Limp 8N 211
Grants Quay Wharf EC3 ... 5G 225 (45Tb 91)
Grant St. E13 .... 41Jc 93
N1 .... 1K 217 (40Qb 70)
Grant Ter. N16 .... 31Wb 71
(off Castlewood Rd.)
Grantully Rd. W9 .... 41Db 89
Grant Wlk. SL5: S'dale 4C 146
Grant Way TW7: Isle 51Ja 108
Grantwood Cl. RH1: Redh 10A 208
Granville Arc. SW9 .... 56Qb 112
Granville Av. N9 .... 20Yb 34
SL2: Slou 3H 81
TW3: Houn 57Ca 107
TW13: Felt 61W 128
Granville Cl. CR0: C'don 75Ub 157
KT13: Weyb 79S 150
KT14: Byfl 85P 169
Granville Ct. AL1: St A 2D 6
(off Granville Rd.)
N1 .... 39Ub 71
N4 .... 32Pb 50
SE14 .... 52Ac 114
(off Nynehead St.)
Granville Dene HP3: Bov 9C 2
Granville Gdns. SW16 .... 67Pb 134
W5 .... 46Pa 87
Granville Gro. SE13 .... 55Ec 114
Granville Ho. E14 .... 44Cc 92
(off E. India Dock Rd.)
Granville Mans. W12 .... 47Ya 88
(off Shepherd's Bush Grn.)
Granville M. DA14: Sidc 63Wc 139
Granville Pk. SE13 .... 55Ec 114
Granville Pl. HA5: Pinn 27Z 45
N12 .... 24Eb 49
SW6 .... 52Db 111
W1 .... 3H 221 (44Jb 90)
Granville Point NW2 .... 33Bb 69
Granville Rd. AL1: St A 2D 6
CM16: Epp 1Xc 23
DA11: Grav'nd 9B 122
DA14: Sidc 63Wc 139
DA16: Well 55Yc 117
E17 .... 30Dc 52
E18 .... 26Kc 53
EN5: Barn 14Ya 30
GU22: Wok 92B 188
IG1: Ilf 32Rc 74
KT13: Weyb 80S 150
N4 .... 30Pb 50
N12 .... 24Eb 49
N13 .... 23Pb 50
N22 .... 25Rb 51
NW2 .... 33Bb 69
NW6 .... 40Cb 69
(not continuous)
RH8: Oxt 1K 211
SW18 .... 59Bb 111
SW19 .... 66Cb 133
TN13: S'oaks 96Jd 202
TN16: Westrm 98Sc 200
UB3: Harl 49V 84
UB10: Hil 37R 64
WD18: Wat 14Y 27
Granville Sq. SE15 .... 52Ub 113
WC1 .... 4J 217 (41Pb 90)
Granville St. WC1 .... 4J 217 (41Pb 90)
Granwood Ct. TW7: Isle 53Ga 108
Grape St. WC2 .... 2F 223 (44Nb 90)
Graphic Ho. WD24: Wat 10W 12
Graphite Apartments, The N1 .... 2F 219
Graphite Point E2 .... 41Zb 92
(off Palmer's Rd.)
Graphite Sq. SE11 .... 7H 229 (50Pb 90)
Grapsome Cl. KT9: Chess 80La 152
Grasdene Rd. SE18 .... 52Wc 117
Grasgarth Cl. W3 .... 45Sa 87
Grasholm Way SL3: L'ly 49E 82
Grasmere NW1 .... 4A 216
SL4: Wind 2C 102
Grasmere Av. BR6: Farnb 76Rc 160
HA4: Ruis 31S 64
HA9: Wemb 31La 66
SL2: Slou 5L 81
SW15 .... 63Ta 131
SW19 .... 69Cb 133
TW3: Houn 58Da 107
W3 .... 45Ta 87
Grasmere Cl. HP3: Hem H 4B 4
IG10: Lough 12Pc 36
TW14: Felt 60V 106
TW20: Egh 66D 126
WD25: Wat 4X 13
Grasmere Ct. N22 .... 23Pb 50
SE26 .... 64Wb 135
SM2: Sutt 79Eb 155
SW13 .... 51Wa 110
(off Verdun Rd.)
Grasmere Gdns. BR6: Farnb 76Rc 160
HA3: W'stone 26Ja 46
IG4: Ilf 29Pc 54
Grasmere Pde. SL2: Slou 5M 81
Grasmere Point SE15 .... 52Yb 114
(off Old Kent Rd.)
Grasmere Rd. AL1: St A 4F 6
BR1: Brom 67Hc 137
BR6: Farnb 76Rc 160
CR8: Purl 83Rb 177
DA7: Bex 54Ed 118
E13 .... 40Jc 73
GU18: Light 2A 166
N10 .... 25Kb 50
N17 .... 23Wb 51
SE25 .... 72Xb 157
SW16 .... 64Nb 134
Grasmere Way KT14: Byfl 84P 169
Graspan Royal Marines Memorial 6E 222
Grassbanks DA1: Dart 60Pd 119
Grassfield Cl. CR5: Coul 91Kb 196
Grasshaven Way SE28 .... 46Vc 95
(not continuous)
Grassingham End SL9: Chal P 24A 42
Grassingham Rd. SL9: Chal P 24A 42
Grassington Cl. AL2: Brick W 2Ca 13
N11 .... 23Jb 50
Grassington Rd. DA14: Sidc 63Wc 139
Grassmere Rd. RM11: Horn 28Pd 57
Grassmount CR8: Purl 82Lb 176
SE23 .... 61Xb 135
Grass Pk. N3 .... 25Bb 49
Grass Rd. RM18: E Til 1K 123
Grassway SM6: Wall 77Lb 156
Grassy Cl. HP1: Hem H 1J 3
Grassy La. TN13: S'oaks 98Kd 203
Grasvenor Av. EN5: Barn 15Cb 31
Gratton Dr. SL4: Wind 6C 102
Gratton Rd. W14 .... 48Ab 88
Gratton Ter. NW2 .... 34Za 68
Gravel Cl. IG7: Chig 19Wc 37
Graveley Av. WD6: Bore 14Sa 29
GRAVEL HILL 23B 42
Gravel Hill CR0: Addtn 79Zb 158
DA6: Bex 56Dd 118
HP1: Hem H 2J 3
IG10: H Beech 10Jc 21
KT22: Lea 93Ka 192
N3 .... 26Bb 49
SL9: Chal P 23A 42
UB8: Uxb 36M 63
Gravel Hill Cl. DA6: Bex 57Dd 118
Gravelhill Ter. HP1: Hem H 3J 3
Gravel La. E1 .... 2K 225 (44Vb 91)
HP1: Hem H 2J 3
IG7: Chig 15Vc 37
Gravelly Hill CR3: Cat'm 100Ub 197
Gravel Path HP1: Hem H 2J 3
HP4: Berk 1A 2
Gravel Pit La. SE9 .... 57Rc 116
Gravel Pit Way BR6: Orp 75Wc 161
Gravel Rd. BR2: Brom 76Nc 160
DA4: Sut H 66Rd 141
TW2: Twick 60Ga 108
Gravelwood Cl. BR7: Chst 62Sc 138
Gravely Ct. HP2: Hem H 3C 4
Gravely Ho. SE8 .... 49Ac 92
(off Chilton Gro.)
Gravenel Gdns. SW17 .... 64Gb 133
(off Nutwell St.)
Graveney Gro. SE20 .... 66Yb 136
Graveney Rd. SW17 .... 63Gb 133
GRAVESEND 8D 122
Gravesend Golf Centre 3J 145
Gravesend Rd. DA12: Shorne 2M 145
ME3: High'm 2M 145
TN15: Stans, Wro 87De 185
W12 .... 45Wa 88
Gravesend Sailing Club 8F 122
Gravesend Vis. Cen. 8D 122
Gravesham Ct. DA12: Grav'nd 9D 122
Gravesham Way BR3: Beck 73Bc 158
Gray Av. RM8: Dag 32Bd 75
Gray Cl. KT15: Add 78K 149
Gray Ct. E1 .... 43Ac 92
HA5: Pinn 28Aa 45
SL4: Wind 4E 102
Gray Gdns. RM13: Rain 37Jd 76
Grayham Cres. KT3: N Mald 70Ta 131
Grayham Rd. KT3: N Mald 70Ta 131
Gray Ho. SE17 .... 7E 230
SL2: Stoke P 8L 61
(off Bells Hill Grn.)
Grayland Cl. BR1: Brom 67Mc 137
Graylands CM16: They B 9Tc 22
GU21: Wok 88A 168
RM17: Grays 51Ae 121
Graylands Cl. GU21: Wok 88A 168
SL1: Slou 6D 80
Grayling KT16: Chert 74L 149
Grayling Cl. E16 .... 42Gc 93
Grayling Ct. W5 .... 46Ma 87
(off Grange Rd.)
Grayling Rd. N16 .... 33Tb 71
Graylings, The WD5: Ab L 5T 12
Grayling Sq. E2 .... 41Wb 91
(off Nelson Gdns.)
Gray Pl. KT16: Ott 79F 148
GRAYS 49De 99
Grays Athletic FC 45Sd 98
Grayscroft Rd. SW16 .... 66Mb 134
Gray's End Cl. RM17: Grays 48Ce 99
Grays Farm Rd. BR5: St P 67Xc 139
Grayshott Rd. SW11 .... 54Jb 112
Gray's Inn 7J 217 (43Pb 90)
Gray's Inn Bldgs. EC1 .... 6K 217
(off Rosebery Av.)
Gray's Inn Pl. WC1 .... 1J 223 (43Pb 90)
Gray's Inn Rd. WC1 .... 3G 217 (41Nb 90)
Gray's Inn Sq. WC1 .... 7K 217 (43Pb 90)
Gray's La. KT18: Eps D 92Qa 193
KT21: Asht 91Pa 193
Grays La. TW15: Ashf 63R 128
Grayson Ho. EC1 .... 4E 218
Grays Pk. Rd. SL2: Stoke P 6K 81
Grays Pl. SL2: Slou 6K 81
Gray's Rd. SL1: Slou 6K 81
Grays Rd. TN16: Westrm 93Rc 200
UB10: Uxb 38N 63
Grays Shop. Cen. RM17: Grays 51Ce 121
Grays Ter. E7 .... 37Lc 73
Grayston Ho. SE3 .... 56Lc 115
Gray St. SE1 .... 2A 230 (47Qb 90)
Grays Wlk. CM13: Hut 17Fe 41
Grayswood Gdns. SW20 .... 68Xa 132
Grayswood Point SW15 .... 60Wa 110
Gray's Yd. W1 .... 3J 221
Graywood Ct. N12 .... 24Eb 49
Grazebrook Rd. N16 .... 33Tb 71
Grazeley Cl. DA6: Bex 57Ed 118
Grazeley Ct. SE19 .... 64Ub 135
Grazings, The HP2: Hem H 1P 3
Gt. Acre Ct. SW4 .... 56Mb 112
Gt. Amwell La. N8 .... 27Pb 50
Gt. Arthur Ho. EC1 .... 6D 218
Gt. Bell All. EC2 .... 2F 225 (44Tb 91)
Great Benty UB7: W Dray 49N 83
GREAT BOOKHAM 98Da 191
Great Bookham Common 93Ba 191
Great Brownings SE21 .... 63Vb 135
GREAT BURGH 89Ya 174
Gt. Bushey Dr. N20 .... 18Db 31
Gt. Cambridge Ind. Est. EN1: Enf 15Xb 33
GREAT CAMBRIDGE JUNC. 21Tb 51
Gt. Cambridge Rd. EN1: Enf 16Wb 33
EN8: Chesh, Walt C 6Yb 20
N9 .... 21Tb 51
N17 .... 22Tb 51
N18 .... 21Tb 51
Gt. Castle St. W1 .... 2A 222 (44Kb 90)
Gt. Central Av. HA4: Ruis 36Y 65
Gt. Central St. NW1 .... 7F 215 (43Hb 89)
Gt. Central Way HA9: Wemb 35Sa 67
NW10 .... 36Ua 68
Gt. Chapel St. W1 .... 2D 222 (44Mb 90)
Gt. Charter Cl. RM12: Horn 36Jd 76
Gt. Chart St. SW11 .... 56Fb 111
Gt. Chertsey Rd. TW2: Twick 62Ba 129
TW13: Hanw, Twick 62Ba 129
W4 .... 53Sa 109
(not continuous)
Gt. Church La. W6 .... 49Za 88
Great Cockcrow Railway 74F 148
Gt. College St. SW1 .... 3F 229 (48Nb 90)
Great Comp Garden 93Fe 205
Great Cft. WC1 .... 4G 217
Gt. Cross Av. SE10 .... 52Fc 115
Great Cullings RM7: Rush G 33Gd 76
Gt. Cumberland M. W1 .... 3F 221 (44Hb 89)
Gt. Cumberland Pl. W1 .... 2F 221 (44Hb 89)
Gt. Dover St. SE1 .... 2E 230 (47Sb 91)
Greatdown Rd. W7 .... 42Ha 86
Gt. Eastern Ent. Cen. E14 .... 47Dc 92
Gt. Eastern Market E20 .... 37Ec 72
(within Westfield Stratford City Shop. Cen.)
Gt. Eastern Rd. CM14: W'ley 21Yd 58
E15 .... 38Fc 73
EN8: Walt C 6Yb 20
Gt. Eastern St. EC2 .... 4H 219 (41Ub 91)
Gt. Eastern Wlk. EC2 .... 1J 225
Gt. Eastern Wharf SW11 .... 52Gb 111
Great Ellshams SM7: Bans 88Cb 175
Gt. Elms Rd. BR2: Brom 70Lc 137
HP3: Hem H 6P 3
Greater London Ho. NW1 .... 1B 216
Great Fld. NW9 .... 25Ua 48
Greatfield NW5 .... 36Lb 70
Greatfield Av. E6 .... 42Pc 94
Greatfield Cl. N19 .... 35Lb 70
SE4 .... 56Cc 114
Greatfields Dr. UB8: Hil 43Q 84
Greatfields Rd. IG11: Bark 39Tc 74
Gt. Fleete Way IG11: Bark 40Yc 75
Gt. Galley Cl. IG11: Bark 41Xc 95
Great Gdns. Rd. RM11: Horn 30Kd 57
Gt. Gatton Cl. CR0: C'don 73Ac 158
Gt. George St. SW1 .... 2E 228 (47Mb 90)
Gt. Gregories La. CM16: Epp 5Uc 22
Great Gro. WD23: Bush 14Da 27
Gt. Guildford Bus. Sq.
SE1 .... 7D 224 (46Sb 91)
Gt. Guildford St. SE1 .... 6D 224 (46Sb 91)
Great Hall 50Hb 89
Great Hall SW11 .... 53Jb 112
(off Battersea Pk. Rd.)
Greatham Rd. WD23: Bush 13Z 27
Greatham Rd. Ind. Est.
WD23: Bush 13Z 27
Greatham Wlk. SW15 .... 60Wa 110
Gt. Harry Dr. SE9 .... 62Qc 138
Great Heart HP2: Hem H 1N 3
Greathurst End KT23: Bookh 96Ba 191
Gt. James St. WC1 .... 7H 217 (43Pb 90)
Gt. Leys Ct. AL2: Lon C 9E 6
Gt. Marlborough St. W1 .... 3B 222 (44Lb 90)
Gt. Maze Pond SE1 .... 1G 231 (47Tb 91)
Gt. Minster Ho. SW1 .... 5E 228
Gt. Nelmes Chase RM11: Horn 29Pd 57
GREATNESS 92Ld 203
Greatness La. TN14: S'oaks 93Ld 203
Greatness Rd. TN14: S'oaks 93Ld 203
Gt. Newport St. WC2 .... 4F 223 (45Nb 90)
Gt. New St. EC4 .... 2A 224
Gt. Norman St. TN14: Ide H 100Bd 201
Great Nth. Leisure Pk. N12 .... 24Fb 49
Great Nth. Rd. AL9: Brk P, Hat, Wel G 2D 8
EN5: Barn 12Bb 31
EN5: New Bar 15Cb 31
EN6: Pot B 5G 8
N2 .... 28Gb 49
N6 .... 28Gb 49
Great Nth. Way NW4 .... 26Xa 48
Great Oaks CM13: Hut 16De 41
IG7: Chig 21Sc 54
Greatorex Ho. E1 .... 43Wb 91
(off Greatorex St.)
Greatorex St. E1 .... 43Wb 91
Gt. Ormond St. WC1 .... 7G 217 (43Nb 90)
Gt. Owl Rd. IG7: Chig 20Qc 36
Great Pk. WD4: K Lan 2P 11
Great Pk. Cl. UB10: Hil 38Q 64
Gt. Percy St. WC1 .... 3J 217 (41Pb 90)
Gt. Peter St. SW1 .... 4D 228 (48Mb 90)
Gt. Portland St. W1 .... 6A 216 (42Kb 90)
Gt. Pulteney St. W1 .... 4C 222 (45Lb 90)
Gt. Queen St. DA1: Dart 59Pd 119
WC2 .... 3G 223 (44Nb 90)
Great Rd. HP2: Hem H 1P 3
Gt. Ropers La. CM13: Gt War 23Wd 58
Gt. Russell Mans. WC1 .... 1F 223
Gt. Russell St. WC1 .... 2E 222 (44Mb 90)
Gt. St Helen's EC3 .... 2H 225 (44Ub 91)
Gt. St Thomas Apostle
EC4 .... 4E 224 (45Sb 91)
Gt. Scotland Yd. SW1 .... 7F 223 (46Nb 90)
Great Slades EN6: Pot B 5Bb 17
Gt. Smith St. SW1 .... 3E 228 (48Mb 90)
Great Sth. W. Rd. TW4: Houn 56V 106
TW14: Bedf, Felt 59S 106
Great Spilmans SE22 .... 57Ub 113
Great Strand NW9 .... 25Va 48
Gt. Sturgess Rd. HP1: Hem H 2H 3
Gt. Suffolk St. SE1 .... 7C 224 (46Rb 91)
Gt. Sutton St. EC1 .... 6C 218 (42Rb 91)
Gt. Swan All. EC2 .... 2F 225 (44Tb 91)
Great Tattenhams KT18: Tatt C 90Xa 174
Great Thrift BR5: Pet W 70Sc 138
Great Till Cl. TN14: Otf 88Gd 182
Gt. Titchfield St. W1 .... 6A 216 (42Kb 90)
Gt. Tower St. EC3 .... 4H 225 (45Ub 91)
Gt. Trinity La. EC4 .... 4E 224 (45Sb 91)
Gt. Turnstile WC1 .... 1J 223 (43Pb 90)
Gt. Turnstile Ho. WC1 .... 1J 223
GREAT WARLEY 25Wd 58
Gt. Warley St. CM13: Gt War 25Wd 58
Gt. Western Ind. Pk. UB2: S'hall 47Da 85
Gt. Western Rd. W9 .... 43Bb 89
W11 .... 43Bb 89
Gt. West Rd. TW5: Hest 54Z 107
TW7: Bford, Isle 52Ga 108
TW8: Bford 52Ga 108
W4 .... 50Ra 87
(Cedars Rd.)
W4 .... 51Va 110
(Dorchester Gro.)
W6 .... 51Va 110
Great W. Trad. Est. TW8: Bford 51Ka 108
Gt. Whites Rd. HP3: Hem H 4P 3
Gt. Winchester St. EC2 .... 2G 225 (44Tb 91)
Gt. Windmill St. W1 .... 4D 222 (45Mb 90)
Greatwood BR7: Chst 66Qc 138
Greatwood Cl. KT16: Ott 81E 168
Gt. Woodcote Dr. CR8: Purl 82Mb 176
Gt. Woodcote Pk. CR8: Purl 82Mb 176
Great Wood Country Pk. 8P 9
Great Wood Vis. Cen. 8P 9
Great Yd. SE1 .... 1J 231
Greaves Cl. IG11: Bark 38Tc 74
Greaves Cotts. E14 .... 43Ac 92
(off Maroon St.)
Greaves Pl. SW17 .... 63Gb 133
Greaves Twr. SW10 .... 52Eb 111
(off Worlds End Est.)
Grebe Av. UB4: Yead 44Z 85
Grebe Cl. E7 .... 36Hc 73
E17 .... 24Ac 52
IG11: Bark 42Wc 95
Grebe Ct. E14 .... 47Ec 92
(off River Barge Cl.)
SE8 .... 51Bc 114
(off Dorking Cl.)
SM1: Sutt 78Bb 155
Grebe Crest RM20: W Thur 49Wd 98
Grebe Ter. KT1: King T 69Na 131
Grecian Cres. SE19 .... 65Rb 135
Greding Wlk. CM13: Hut 19De 41
Greek Ct. W1 .... 3E 222 (44Mb 90)
Greek St. W1 .... 3E 222 (44Mb 90)
Green, The AL2: Lon C 9H 7
AL3: St A 4P 5
BR1: Brom 62Jc 137
(not continuous)
BR2: Hayes 73Jc 159
BR5: St P 66Xc 139
BR6: Prat B 82Yc 181
CM16: They B 8Uc 22
(not continuous)
CR0: Sels 81Bc 178
CR3: Wold 95Cc 198
CR6: W'ham 89Zb 178
DA2: Dart 61Td 142
DA7: Bex 53Cd 118
DA14: Sidc 63Wc 139
DA16: Well 56Uc 116
E4 .... 18Ec 34
E11 .... 30Kc 53
E15 .... 37Gc 73
EN8: Chesh 1Yb 20
EN9: Walt A 6Ec 20
GU23: Rip 93L 189
HA0: Wemb 33Ja 66
IG8: Wfd G 22Jc 53
IG9: Buck H 18Kc 35
KT3: N Mald 69Ta 131
KT10: Clay 79Ha 152
KT12: Hers 78Z 151
KT12: W Vill 82U 170
KT17: Ewe 83Wa 174
KT20: Tad 91Ab 194
(Oatlands Rd.)
KT20: Tad 95Za 194
(Stokes Riding)
KT22: Fet 96Fa 192
N9 .... 19Wb 33
N14 .... 19Mb 32
N17 .... 23Sb 51
N21 .... 17Qb 32
RH3: Bkld 5C 206
RH9: G'stone 4P 209
RM3: Rom 19Ld 39
RM4: Have B 20Gd 38
RM13: Wenn 45Nd 97
RM15: S Ock 41Zd 99
RM16: Ors 3C 100
RM18: W Til 1G 122
SL1: Burn 3A 80
SL1: Slou 7H 81
SL3: Dat 2M 103
SM1: Sutt 76Db 155
SM4: Mord 70Ab 132
SM5: Cars 77Jb 156
SM6: Wall 75Jb 156
SS17: Stan H 2M 101
SW14 .... 55Sa 109
SW19 .... 64Za 132
TN13: S'oaks 94Md 203
TN14: Otf 88Kd 183
TN15: Seal 93Pd 203
(off Church Rd.)
TN16: Westrm 98Tc 200
TW2: Twick 60Ga 108
TW5: Hest 51Ca 107
TW9: Rich 57Ma 109
TW13: Felt 61X 129
TW15: Ashf 64M 127
TW17: Shep 70U 128
TW19: Wray 58A 104
TW20: Eng G 3N 125
UB2: S'hall 48Aa 85
UB7: W Dray 48M 83
UB9: Hare 25L 43
UB10: Ick 33S 64
W3 .... 44Ua 88
W5 .... 46Ma 87
WD3: Crox G 16P 25
WD3: Sarr 7J 11
WD25: Let H 11Ga 28
Greenacre DA1: Dart 61Md 141
GU21: Knap 8J 167
SL4: Wind 5D 102
Greenacre Cl. BR8: Swan 70Gd 140
EN5: Barn 10Bb 17
UB5: N'olt 36Ba 65
Greenacre Ct. TW20: Eng G 5N 125
Greenacre Gdns. E17 .... 28Ec 52
Greenacre Pl. SM6: Wall 75Kb 156
Green Acres CR0: C'don 76Vb 157
DA14: Sidc 63Wc 139
Greenacres CM16: Epp 1Vc 23
HP2: Hem H 4M 3
KT20: Lwr K 100Bb 195
KT23: Bookh 96Da 191
N3 .... 26Bb 49
RH8: Oxt 99Gc 199
SE9 .... 58Qc 116
WD23: B Hea 19Fa 28
Greenacres Av. UB10: Ick 34P 63
Greenacres Cl. BR6: Farnb 77Sc 160
RM13: Rain 41Nd 97
Greenacres Dr. HA7: Stan 23Ka 46
Greenacres Ho. SW18 .... 60Db 111
(off Knaresborough Dr.)
Greenacre Sq. SE16 .... 47Zb 92
Greenacre Wlk. N14 .... 20Mb 32
Greenall Cl. EN8: Chesh 2Ac 20
Greenan Ct. E2 .... 41Zb 92
(off Meath Cres.)
Grn. Arbour Ct. EC1 .... 2B 224
Green Av. NW7 .... 21Ta 47
W13 .... 48Ka 86
Greenaway Av. N18 .... 23Zb 52
Greenaway Gdns. NW3 .... 35Db 69
Greenaway Ho. NW8 .... 39Eb 69
(off Boundary Rd.)
WC1 .... 4K 217
Greenaway Ter. TW19: Stanw 60N 105
(off Victory Cl.)
Green Bank E1 .... 46Xb 91
N12 .... 21Db 49
Greenbank Av. HA0: Wemb 36Ja 66
Greenbank Cl. E4 .... 19Ec 34
RM3: Rom 20Md 39
Greenbank Ct. TW7: Isle 54Ha 108
(off Lanadron Cl.)
Greenbank Cres. NW4 .... 28Ab 48
Greenbank Lodge BR7: Chst 68Qc 138
(off Forest Cl.)
Greenbank Rd. WD17: Wat 8T 12
Greenbanks AL1: St A 4D 6
DA1: Dart 61Nd 141
HA1: Harr 35Ga 66
RM14: Upm 33Td 78
Greenbanks Cl. SE13 .... 55Dc 114
Greenbay Rd. SE7 .... 52Mc 115
Greenberry St. NW8 .... 2D 214 (40Gb 69)
Greenbrook Av. EN4: Had W 11Eb 31
Greenbury Cl. WD3: Chor 14E 24
Green Bus. Cen., The
TW18: Staines 63E 126
Green Cl. AL9: Brk P 8G 8
BR2: Brom 69Gc 137
EN8: Chesh 3Ac 20
NW9 .... 30Sa 47
NW11 .... 31Eb 69
SM5: Cars 75Hb 155
TW13: Hanw 64Aa 129
Greencoat Mans. SW1 .... 4C 228
Greencoat Pl. SW1 .... 5C 228 (49Lb 90)
Greencoat Row SW1 .... 4C 228 (48Lb 90)
Green Ct. TW16: Sun 65V 128
Greencourt Av. CR0: C'don 75Xb 157
HA8: Edg 25Ra 47
Greencourt Gdns. CR0: C'don 74Xb 157
Greencourt Ho. E1 .... 42Zb 92
(off Mile End Rd.)
Green Ct. Rd. BR8: Crock 71Fd 162
Greencourt Rd. BR5: Pet W 71Tc 160
Greencrest Pl. NW2 .... 34Wa 68
Greencroft HA8: Edg 22Sa 47
Greencroft Av. HA4: Ruis 33Y 65
Greencroft Cl. E6 .... 43Mc 93
Greencroft Gdns. EN1: Enf 13Ub 33
NW6 .... 38Db 69
Greencroft Rd. TW5: Hest 53Ba 107
Green Curve SM7: Bans 86Bb 175
Green Dale SE5 .... 56Tb 113
SE22 .... 57Ub 113
Greendale NW7 .... 21Ua 48
Grn. Dale Cl. SE22 .... 57Ub 113
Greendale M. SL2: Slou 5L 81
Greendale Wlk. DA11: Nflt 2A 144
Grn. Dell Way HP3: Hem H 3C 4
Grn. Dragon Ct. SE1 .... 7F 225
Grn. Dragon Ho. WC2 .... 2G 223
Grn. Dragon La. N21 .... 16Qb 32
TW8: Bford 50Na 87
Green Dragons Airsports 92Dc 198
Grn. Dragon Yd. E1 .... 43Wb 91
Green Dr. GU23: Rip 95H 189
SL3: L'ly 49A 82
(not continuous)
UB1: S'hall 46Ca 85
Greene Ct. SE14 .... 51Zb 114
(off Samuel Cl.)
Green Edge WD25: Wat 7W 12
Greene Fielde End
TW18: Staines 66M 127
Greene Ho. SE1 .... 3F 231
SL9: Chal P 21A 42
GREEN END 3J 3
Green End KT9: Chess 77Na 153
N21 .... 19Rb 33
Green End Bus. Cen. WD3: Sarr 9J 11
Green End Gdns. HP1: Hem H 3J 3
Grn. End La. HP1: Hem H 2H 3
Grn. End Rd. HP1: Hem H 2J 3
(not continuous)
Greenend Rd. W4 .... 47Ua 88
Greener Ct. CR0: C'don 72Sb 157
(off Goodman Cres.)
Greener Ho. SW4 .... 55Mb 112
Greene Wlk. HP4: Berk 2A 2
Grn. Farm Cl. BR6: Chels 78Vc 161
Grn. Farm La. DA12: Shorne 1N 145
Greenfell Mans. SE8 .... 51Dc 114
Greenfern Av. SL1: Slou 4A 80
Grn. Ferry Way E17 .... 28Zb 52
(off Forest Rd.)
Greenfield Av. KT5: Surb 73Ra 153
WD19: Wat 19Z 27
Greenfield Dr. BR1: Brom 68Lc 137
N2 .... 28Hb 49
Greenfield End SL9: Chal P 24B 42
Greenfield Gdns. BR5: Pet W 73Tc 160
NW2 .... 33Ab 68
RM9: Dag 39Zc 75
Greenfield Ho. SW19 .... 60Za 110
TW20: Eng G 5M 125
(off Kings La.)
Greenfield Link CR5: Coul 87Nb 176
Greenfield Pl. UB3: Hayes 45V 84
Greenfield Rd. DA2: Wilm 64Fd 140
E1 .... 43Wb 91
N15 .... 29Ub 51
RM9: Dag 40Zc 75
Greenfields EN6: Cuff 2Nb 18
IG10: Lough 14Qc 36
UB1: S'hall 44Ca 85
Greenfields Cl. CM13: Gt War 23Yd 58
IG10: Lough 14Qc 36
Greenfield St. EN9: Walt A 6Ec 20
Greenfield Way HA2: Harr 27Da 45
Greenfinches DA3: Lfield 69De 143
GREENFORD 41Ca 85
Greenford Av. UB1: S'hall 45Ba 85
W7 .... 42Ga 86
Greenford Bus. Cen. UB6: G'frd 38Fa 66
Greenford Gdns. UB6: G'frd 41Da 85
GREENFORD GREEN 37Ga 66
Greenford Ind. Est. UB6: G'frd 38Da 65
Greenford Pk. UB6: G'frd 38Fa 66
Greenford Rd. HA1: Harr 39Fa 66
SM1: Sutt 77Db 155
(not continuous)
UB1: S'hall 46Ea 86
UB6: G'frd 39Fa 66

Greenford Rdbt.—Greystoke Pk. Ter.

GREENFORD RDBT. ... 40Fa 66
Greenford Sports Cen. ... 41Ca 85
Green Gdns. BR6: Farnb ... 78Sc 160
Greengate UB6: G'frd ... 37Ka 66
Greengate Lodge E13 ... 40Kc 73
(off Hollybush St.)
Greengate Pde. IG2: Ilf ... 30Tc 54
Greengate St. E13 ... 40Kc 73
Green Glade CM16: They B ... 9Uc 22
Green Glades RM11: Horn ... 30Pd 57
Greenhalgh Wlk. N2 ... 28Eb 49
Greenham Cl. SE1 ... 2K 229 (47Qb 90)
Greenham Cres. E4 ... 23Bc 52
Greenham Ho. E9 ... 39Yb 72
(off Templecombe Rd.)
TW7: Isle ... 55Fa 108
Greenham Rd. N10 ... 26Jb 50
Greenham Wlk. GU21: Wok ... 10N 167
Greenhaven Dr. SE28 ... 44Xc 95
Greenhayes Av. SM7: Bans ... 86Cb 175
Greenhayes Cl. RH2: Reig ... 6L 207
Greenhayes Gdns.
SM7: Bans ... 87Cb 175
Green Hedges TW1: Twick ... 57La 108
Greenheys Cl. HA6: Nwood ... 25U 44
Greenheys Dr. E18 ... 27Hc 53
Greenheys Pl. GU22: Wok ... 90B 168
GREENHILL ... 29Ga 46
Green Hill BR6: Downe ... 84Pc 180
SE18 ... 50Pc 94
Greenhill HA9: Wemb ... 33Ra 67
IG9: Buck H ... 18Lc 35
NW3 ... 35Fb 69
SM1: Sutt ... 75Eb 155
Greenhill Av. CR3: Cat'm ... 93Xb 197
Greenhill Ct. EN5: New Bar ... 15Db 31
HP1: Hem H ... 3K 3
SE18 ... 50Pc 94
Greenhill Cres. WD18: Wat ... 16U 26
Greenhill Gdns. UB5: N'olt ... 40Ba 65
Greenhill Gro. E12 ... 35Nc 74
Grn. Hill La. CR6: W'ham ... 89Ac 178
Greenhill Pde.
EN5: New Bar ... 15Db 31
Greenhill Pk. EN5: New Bar ... 15Db 31
NW10 ... 39Ua 68
Greenhill Rd. DA11: Nflt ... 1B 144
HA1: Harr ... 30Ga 46
NW10 ... 39Ua 68
TN14: Otf ... 87Ld 183
Greenhills Cl. WD3: Rick ... 15K 25
Greenhill's Rents EC1 ... 7B 218 (43Rb 91)
Greenhills Ter. N1 ... 37Tb 71
Greenhill Ter. SE18 ... 50Pc 94
UB5: N'olt ... 40Ba 65
Greenhill Way HA1: Harr ... 30Ga 46
HA9: Wemb ... 33Ra 67
GREENHITHE ... 57Xd 120
Greenhithe Cl. DA15: Sidc ... 59Uc 116
Greenholm Rd. SE9 ... 57Rc 116
Green Hundred Rd. SE15 ... 51Wb 113
Greenhurst La. RH8: Oxt ... 4K 211
Greenhurst Rd. SE27 ... 64Qb 134
Greening St. SE2 ... 49Yc 95
Grn. Lake Gro. RM3: Rom ... 21Md 57
Greenlake Ter. TW18: Staines ... 66J 127
Greenland Cres. UB2: S'hall ... 48Y 85
Greenland Ho. E1 ... 42Ac 92
(off Ernest St.)
Greenland M. SE8 ... 50Zb 92
Greenland Pl. NW1 ... 39Kb 70
Greenland Quay SE16 ... 49Zb 92
Greenland Rd. EN5: Barn ... 16Ya 30
NW1 ... 39Lb 70
Greenlands KT16: Chert ... 76E 148
KT19: Ewe ... 78Ra 153
TN15: Plat ... 92De 205
Greenlands La. NW4 ... 25Xa 48
Greenlands Rd. KT13: Weyb ... 76R 150
TN15: Kems'g ... 91Rd 203
TW18: Staines ... 63J 127
Greenland St. NW1 ... 39Kb 70
Greenland Way CR0: Bedd ... 73Mb 156
Green La. AL1: St A ... 6E 6
BR7: Chst ... 61Rc 138
CM14: B'wood ... 18Wd 40
CM14: Gt War ... 24Wd 58
CM14: Kel H ... 12Sd 40
CM15: Pil H ... 15Yd 40
CR3: Cat'm ... 94Sb 197
CR5: Coul ... 98Bb 195
CR6: W'ham ... 88Ac 178
CR7: Thor H ... 66Pb 134
CR8: Purl ... 83Lb 176
DA12: Shorne ... 5M 145
E4 ... 11Gc 35
EN9: Walt A ... 6Lc 21
GU4: W Cla ... 99J 189
GU22: Wok ... 3M 187
GU23: Ock ... 96R 190
GU24: Chob ... 2K 167
HA1: Harr ... 34Ga 66
HA6: Nwood ... 23T 44
HA7: Stan ... 21Ka 46
HA8: Edg ... 21Pa 47
(not continuous)
HP2: Hem H ... 3C 4
HP3: Bov ... 10B 2
IG1: Ilf ... 33Tc 74
IG3: Ilf ... 32Xc 75
IG7: Chig ... 18Sc 36
KT3: N Mald ... 71Sa 153
KT4: Wor Pk ... 74Wa 154
KT8: W Mole ... 71Da 151
KT9: Chess ... 81Ma 173
KT11: Cobh ... 84Aa 171
KT12: Hers ... 79X 151
KT14: Byfl ... 84P 169
KT15: Add ... 75G 148
KT16: Chert ... 75G 148
KT20: Lwr K ... 98Bb 195
KT21: Asht ... 89La 172
KT22: Lea ... 93Ma 193
(not continuous)
NW4 ... 28Za 48
RH1: Blet ... 3L 209
RH1: Redh ... 4N 207
RH2: Reig ... 6H 207
RM8: Dag ... 32Xc 75
RM14: Avel, Upm ... 39Td 78
RM16: N Stif, Ors ... 43Ee 99
SE9 ... 60Rc 116
SE20 ... 66Zb 136
SL1: Burn ... 1A 80
SL2: Farn C ... 7F 60
SL3: Dat ... 3M 103
SL4: Wind ... 4E 102
SL5: Asc ... 7C 124
Green La. SM4: Mord ... 72Cb 155
(Central Rd.)
SM4: Mord ... 73Ya 154
(Lwr. Morden La.)
SW16 ... 66Pb 134
TW4: Houn ... 55X 107
TW13: Hanw ... 64Aa 129
TW16: Sun ... 66V 128
TW17: Shep ... 72S 150
TW18: Staines ... 67G 126
TW20: Egh ... 63D 126
(The Avenue)
TW20: Egh ... 64D 126
(Vicarage Cres.)
TW20: Thorpe ... 68E 126
UB8: Hil ... 43S 84
W7 ... 47Ga 86
WD3: Crox G ... 15P 25
WD19: Wat ... 17Y 27
Green La. Av. KT12: Hers ... 78Y 151
Green La. Bus. Pk. SE9 ... 61Qc 138
Green La. Cl. KT14: Byfl ... 84P 169
KT16: Chert ... 75G 148
Green La. Cotts. HA7: Stan ... 21Ka 46
Green La. Ct. SL1: Burn ... 1A 80
Green La. Gdns. CR7: Thor H ... 68Sb 135
Green Lanes KT19: Ewe ... 81Ua 174
N4 ... 27Rb 51
N8 ... 27Rb 51
N13 ... 23Pb 50
N15 ... 27Rb 51
N16 ... 27Rb 51
N21 ... 23Pb 50
Grn. Lanes Wlk. N4 ... 32Sb 71
Green La. W. KT24: W Hor ... 97Q 190
Greenlaw Ct. W5 ... 44Ma 87
(off Mount Pk. Rd.)
Greenlaw Gdns. KT3: N Mald ... 73Va 154
Greenlawn La. TW8: Bford ... 49Ma 87
Green Lawns HA4: Ruis ... 32Y 65
Greenlawns N12 ... 23Db 49
Greenlawns, The SE18 ... 49Rc 94
(off Vincent Rd.)
Greenlaw St. SE18 ... 48Qc 94
Green Leaf Av. SM6: Bedd ... 77Mb 156
Greenleaf Cl. SW2 ... 59Qb 112
Greenleafe Dr. IG6: Ilf ... 27Rc 54
Greenleaf Rd. Bus. Cen.
EN6: Pot B ... 4Cb 17
Greenleaf Rd. E6 ... 39Lc 73
E17 ... 27Bc 52
Greenleaf Way HA3: W'stone ... 27Ha 46
Greenlea Pk. SW19 ... 66Fb 133
Green Leas KT1: King T ... 69Na 131
(off Mill St.)
TW16: Sun ... 65V 128
Greenleas EN9: Walt A ... 6Gc 21
Green Leas Cl. TW16: Sun ... 65V 128
Greenleaves Ct. TW15: Ashf ... 65R 128
Greenleigh Av. BR5: St P ... 70Xc 139
Greenlink Wlk. TW9: Kew ... 53Ra 109
Green Man Gdns. W13 ... 45Ja 86
Green Man La. TW14: Felt ... 56W 106
(not continuous)
W13 ... 45Ja 86
Green Mnr. Way DA11: Nflt ... 56Be 121
Green Man Pas. W13 ... 45Ka 86
(not continuous)
GREEN MAN RDBT. ... 31Hc 73
Greenman St. N1 ... 38Sb 71
Green Mead KT10: Esh ... 79Ba 151
Greenmead DA18: Erith ... 48Ad 95
Greenmead Cl. SE25 ... 71Wb 157
Green Mdw. EN6: Pot B ... 2Db 17
Greenmeads GU22: Wok ... 94A 188
Green M. N1 ... 3G 219 (41Tb 91)
Green Moor Link N21 ... 17Rb 33
Greenmoor Rd. EN3: Enf H ... 12Yb 34
Greenoak Pl. EN4: Cockf ... 12Hb 31
Greenoak Ri. TN16: Big H ... 90Lc 179
Green Oaks UB2: S'hall ... 49Z 85
Greenoak Way SW19 ... 63Za 132
Greenock Rd. SL1: Slou ... 4E 80
SW16 ... 67Mb 134
W3 ... 48Ra 87
Greenock Way RM1: Rom ... 24Gd 56
Greeno Cres. TW17: Shep ... 71Q 150
Green Pde. TW3: Houn ... 57Da 107
Green Pk.
London ... 7A 222 (47Kb 90)
Green Pk. TW18: Staines ... 62G 126
Greenpark Ct. HA0: Wemb ... 38La 66
Green Pk. Way UB6: G'frd ... 38Ga 66
Green Pl. DA1: Cray ... 57Gd 118
SE10 ... 47Gc 93
Green Point E15 ... 37Gc 73
Grn. Pond Cl. E17 ... 27Bc 52
Grn. Pond Rd. E17 ... 27Ac 52
Green Ride CM16: Epp ... 7Rc 22
IG10: Lough ... 14Lc 35
(not continuous)
Green Rd. GU23: Ock ... 96S 190
N14 ... 16Kb 32
N20 ... 20Eb 31
TW20: Thorpe ... 70C 126
Green Rd. Nth. EN3: Pond E ... 14Ac 34
Greenrod Pl. TW8: Bford ... 50Na 87
(off Clayponds La.)
Greenroof Way SE10 ... 48Hc 93
Greensand Cl. RH1: Mers ... 100Mb 196
Green Sand Rd. RH1: Redh ... 5A 208
Greens Cl., The IG10: Lough ... 12Qc 36
Green's Ct. W1 ... 4D 222
W11 ... 46Bb 89
(off Lansdowne M.)
Green's End SE18 ... 49Rc 94
Greenshank Cl. E17 ... 24Ac 52
Greenshank Ho. NW9 ... 30Va 48
Greenshaw CM14: B'wood ... 18Xd 40
Greenshields Ind. Est. E16 ... 47Jc 93
Greenside BR8: Swan ... 68Fd 140
DA5: Bexl ... 60Ad 117
RM8: Dag ... 32Yc 75
SL2: Slou ... 3E 80
WD6: Bore ... 10Qa 15
Greenside Cl. IG6: Ilf ... 23Sc 54
N20 ... 19Fb 31
SE6 ... 61Fc 137
Greenside Cotts. GU23: Rip ... 93L 189
Greenside Dr. KT21: Asht ... 90Ka 172
Greenside Rd. CR0: C'don ... 73Qb 156
W12 ... 48Wa 88
Greenside Wlk. TN16: Big H ... 90Kc 179
Greenslade Av. KT21: Asht ... 91Ra 193
Greenslade Rd. IG11: Bark ... 38Tc 74
Greensleeves Cl. AL4: St A ... 3G 6
Greensleeves Dr. CM14: W'ley ... 22Xd 58
Greenstead Av. IG8: Wfd G ... 24Lc 53
Greenstead Cl. IG8: Wfd G ... 23Lc 53
Greenstead Gdns. IG8: Wfd G ... 23Lc 53
SW15 ... 57Xa 110
Greensted Ct. CR3: Whyt ... 91Wb 197
(off Godstone Rd.)
Greensted Rd. IG10: Lough ... 17Nc 36
Greenstone M. E11 ... 30Jc 53
Green St. AL9: Hat ... 2J 9
E7 ... 37Kc 73
E13 ... 37Kc 73
EN3: Brim, Enf H ... 12Yb 34
TW16: Sun ... 67W 128
W1 ... 4G 221 (45Jb 90)
WD3: Chen, Chor ... 11E 24
WD6: Bore ... 7Qa 15
WD7: Shenl ... 7Qa 15
GREEN STREET GREEN
BR6 ... 79Vc 161
DA2 ... 65Wd 142
Green St. Green Rd. DA1: Dart ... 60Rd 119
DA2: Daren, Dart, G St G ... 62Sd 142
Greenstreet Hill SE14 ... 54Zb 114
Greensward WD23: Bush ... 16Da 27
Green Ter. EC1 ... 4A 218 (41Qb 90)
Green Tiles UB9: Den ... 31H 63
Green Tiles La. UB9: Den ... 30H 43
Green Trees CM16: Epp ... 3Wc 23
Green Va. DA6: Bex ... 57Zc 117
W5 ... 44Pa 87
Greenvale Rd. GU21: Knap ... 10H 167
SE9 ... 56Pc 116
Green Verges HA7: Stan ... 24Ma 47
Green Vw. KT9: Chess ... 80Pa 153
RH9: G'stone ... 3P 209
Greenview Av. BR3: Beck ... 72Ac 158
CR0: C'don ... 72Ac 158
Green Vw. Cl. HP3: Bov ... 1C 10
Greenview Cl. W3 ... 46Ua 88
Green Vw. Ct. WD5: Ab L ... 4T 12
Greenview Ct. TW15: Ashf ... 63P 127
Greenview Dr. SW20 ... 69Xa 132
Green Vw. Ho. DA11: Grav'nd ... 4E 144
(off Southfields Grn.)
Green Wlk. DA1: Cray ... 57Hd 118
HA4: Ruis ... 32V 64
IG8: Wfd G ... 23Nc 54
IG10: Lough ... 17Nc 36
NW4 ... 29Za 48
SE1 ... 4H 231 (48Ub 91)
TW12: Hamp ... 65Ba 129
UB2: S'hall ... 50Ca 85
Green Wlk., The E4 ... 18Fc 35
Greenwatt Way SL1: Slou ... 8H 81
Green Way BR2: Brom ... 72Nc 160
DA3: Hartl ... 71Ae 165
KT23: Bookh ... 95Da 191
RH1: Redh ... 4N 207
SE9 ... 57Mc 115
TW16: Sun ... 70W 128
Greenway BR7: Chst ... 64Qc 138
CM13: Hut ... 17Ce 41
E6 ... 42Qc 94
E15 ... 40Fc 73
E20 ... 39Dc 72
HA3: Kenton ... 29Na 47
HA5: Pinn ... 26X 45
HP2: Hem H ... 2B 4
IG8: Wfd G ... 22Lc 53
N14 ... 19Nb 32
N20 ... 19Cb 31
RM3: Hrld W ... 23Rd 57
RM8: Dag ... 33Yc 75
SL1: Burn ... 10A 60
SM6: Wall ... 77Lb 156
SW20 ... 70Ya 132
TN16: Tats ... 92Lc 199
UB4: Yead ... 41W 84
Greenway, The BR5: St M Cry ... 72Xc 161
EN3: Enf W ... 7Zb 20
EN6: Pot B ... 5Cb 17
HA3: W'stone ... 25Ga 46
HA5: Pinn ... 30Ba 45
KT18: Eps ... 86Qa 173
NW9 ... 26Ta 47
RH8: Oxt ... 5M 211
SL1: Slou ... 6B 80
SL9: Chal P ... 27A 42
TW4: Houn ... 56Ba 107
UB8: Uxb ... 40L 63
UB10: Ick ... 33R 64
WD3: Rick ... 17J 25
Greenway Av. E17 ... 28Fc 53
Greenway Cl. KT14: W Byf ... 85J 169
N4 ... 33Sb 71
N11 ... 23Jb 50
N15 ... 28Vb 51
N20 ... 19Cb 31
NW9 ... 26Ta 47
Greenway Ct. IG1: Ilf ... 32Qc 74
Greenway Dr. TW18: Staines ... 67M 127
Greenway Gdns. CR0: C'don ... 76Bc 158
HA3: W'stone ... 26Ga 46
NW9 ... 26Ta 47
UB6: G'frd ... 41Ca 85
Greenways BR3: Beck ... 69Cc 136
DA3: Lfield ... 69Fe 143
EN7: G Oak ... 1Rb 19
KT10: Hin W ... 77Ga 152
KT20: Walt H ... 97Xa 194
TW20: Egh ... 64A 126
WD5: Ab L ... 4U 12
Greenways, The TW1: Twick ... 58Ja 108
Greenways Ct. RM11: Horn ... 30Md 57
Greenways Dr. SL5: S'dale ... 4C 146
TW4: Houn ... 56Aa 107
Greenwell Cl. RH9: G'stone ... 2P 209
Greenwell St. W1 ... 6A 216 (42Kb 90)
GREENWICH ... 52Ec 114
Greenwich Av. CM14: B'wood ... 18Xd 40
Greenwich Bus. Pk. SE10 ... 52Dc 114
Greenwich Cen., The SE10 ... 50Hc 93
(off Lambarde Sq.)
Greenwich Chu. St. SE10 ... 51Ec 114
Greenwich Ct. AL1: St A ... 3E 6
E1 ... 44Xb 91
(off Cavell St.)
EN8: Walt C ... 6Ac 20
Greenwich Cres. E6 ... 43Nc 94
Greenwich Foot Tunnel SE10 ... 50Ec 92
Greenwich Hgts. SE18 ... 52Nc 116
Greenwich Heritage Cen. ... 48Rc 94
Greenwich High Rd. SE10 ... 53Dc 114
Greenwich Ho. SE13 ... 58Fc 115
Greenwich Mkt. SE10 ... 51Ec 114
GREENWICH MILLENNIUM VILLAGE
... 48Hc 93
Greenwich Pk. ... 52Fc 115
Greenwich Pk. St. SE10 ... 51Fc 115
Greenwich Peninsula Ecology Pk.
... 48Jc 93
Greenwich Peninsula Golf Driving Range
... 47Fc 93
Greenwich Picturehouse ... 52Ec 114
Greenwich Quay SE8 ... 51Dc 114
Greenwich Shop. Pk. SE7 ... 49Kc 93
Greenwich Sth. St. SE10 ... 53Dc 114
Greenwich Theatre ... 52Ec 114
Greenwich Vw. Pl. E14 ... 48Dc 92
Greenwich Way EN9: Walt A ... 8Ec 20
Greenwich Yacht Club ... 48Jc 93
Greenwood NW5 ... 36Lb 70
(off Osney Cres.)
Greenwood Av. EN3: Enf H ... 12Ac 34
EN7: Chesh ... 3Xb 19
RM10: Dag ... 35Dd 76
Greenwood Bus. Cen.
CR0: C'don ... 73Vb 157
Greenwood Cl. BR5: Pet W ... 72Uc 160
DA15: Sidc ... 61Wc 139
EN7: Chesh ... 3Xb 19
KT7: T Ditt ... 74Ja 152
KT15: Wdhm ... 83H 169
SM4: Mord ... 70Ab 132
UB3: Hayes ... 46W 84
WD23: B Hea ... 17Ga 28
Greenwood Cotts. SL5: S'dale ... 2G 146
Greenwood Ct. E4 ... 22Fc 53
WD25: Wat ... 6X 13
Greenwood Gdns. CR3: Cat'm ... 97Wb 197
IG6: Ilf ... 24Sc 54
N13 ... 20Rb 33
RH8: Oxt ... 6L 211
WD7: Shenl ... 5Na 15
Greenwood Ho. EC1 ... 4K 217
N22 ... 25Pb 50
RM17: Grays ... 51De 121
(off Argent St.)
SE4 ... 56Zb 114
Greenwood La. TW12: Hamp H ... 64Da 129
Greenwood Mans. IG11: Bark ... 38Wc 75
(off Lansbury Av.)
Greenwood Pk. KT2: King T ... 66Ua 132
Greenwood Pk. Leisure Cen. ... 7P 5
Greenwood Pl. KT12: Hers ... 76Aa 151
NW5 ... 36Kb 70
TN15: Wro ... 89Ce 185
Greenwood Rd. CR0: C'don ... 73Rb 157
CR4: Mitc ... 69Mb 134
DA5: Bexl ... 63Fd 140
E8 ... 37Wb 71
E13 ... 40Hc 73
GU21: Wok ... 2J 187
GU24: Brkwd ... 3A 186
IG7: Chig ... 21Xc 55
KT7: T Ditt ... 74Ja 152
TW7: Isle ... 55Ha 108
Greenwoods, The HA2: Harr ... 34Ea 66
Greenwood Ter. NW10 ... 39Ta 67
Greenwood Theatre ... 1G 231 (47Tb 91)
Greenwood Way TN13: S'oaks ... 97Hd 202
Grn. Wrythe Cres. SM5: Cars ... 74Gb 155
Grn. Wrythe La. SM5: Cars ... 72Fb 155
Green Yd. WC1 ... 5J 217 (42Pb 90)
Green Yd., The EC3 ... 3H 225
Greenyard EN9: Walt A ... 5Ec 20
Greer Rd. HA3: Hrw W ... 25Ea 46
Greet Ho. SE1 ... 2A 230
Greet St. SE1 ... 7A 224 (46Qb 90)
Greg Cl. E10 ... 30Ec 52
Gregor M. SE3 ... 52Jc 115
Gregory Av. EN6: Pot B ... 5Eb 17
Gregory Cl. BR2: Brom ... 70Gc 137
GU21: Wok ... 9N 167
TN14: S'ham ... 83Hd 182
Gregory Cres. SE9 ... 59Mc 115
Gregory Dr. SL4: Old Win ... 8M 103
Gregory M. EN9: Walt A ... 5Ec 20
Gregory Pl. KT15: Add ... 80L 149
W8 ... 47Db 89
Gregory Rd. RM6: Chad H ... 28Zc 55
SL2: Hedg ... 3H 61
UB2: S'hall ... 48Ca 85
Gregson Cl. WD6: Bore ... 11Sa 29
Gregson's Ride IG10: Lough ... 10Qc 22
Greig Cl. N8 ... 29Nb 50
Greig Ter. SE17 ... 51Rb 113
Grenaby Av. CR0: C'don ... 73Tb 157
Grenaby Rd. CR0: C'don ... 73Tb 157
Grenada Ho. E14 ... 45Bc 92
(off Limehouse C'way.)
Grenada Rd. SE7 ... 52Lc 115
Grenade St. E14 ... 45Bc 92
Grenadier Cl. AL4: St A ... 3G 6
Grenadier Pl. CR3: Cat'm ... 94Sb 197
Grenadier St. E16 ... 46Qc 94
Grena Gdns. TW9: Rich ... 56Pa 109
Grenard Cl. SE15 ... 52Wb 113
Grena Rd. TW9: Rich ... 56Pa 109
Grendon Gdns. HA9: Wemb ... 33Qa 67
Grendon Ho. E9 ... 38Yb 72
(off Shore Pl.)
N1 ... 2H 217
Grendon Lodge HA8: Edg ... 19Sa 29
Grendon St. NW8 ... 5D 214 (42Gb 89)
Grenfell Av. RM12: Horn ... 32Hd 76
Grenfell Cl. WD6: Bore ... 11Sa 29
Grenfell Ct. E3 ... 42Dc 92
(off Barry Blandford Way)
NW7 ... 23Xa 48
Grenfell Gdns. HA3: Kenton ... 31Na 67
IG3: Ilf ... 29Vc 55
Grenfell Ho. SE5 ... 52Sb 113
Grenfell Rd. CR4: Mitc ... 65Hb 133
W11 ... 45Za 88
Grenfell Twr. W11 ... 45Za 88
Grenfell Wlk. W11 ... 45Za 88
Grenier Apartments SE15 ... 52Xb 113
Grennan Cl. CM13: Ingve ... 23Fe 59
Grennell Cl. SM1: Sutt ... 75Fb 155
Grennell Rd. SM1: Sutt ... 75Eb 155
Grenoble Gdns. N13 ... 23Qb 50
Grenside Rd. KT13: Weyb ... 76R 150
Grenville Cl. EN8: Walt C ... 6Zb 20
KT5: Surb ... 74Sa 153
KT11: Cobh ... 85Z 171
N3 ... 25Ab 48
SL1: Burn ... 10A 60
Grenville Ct. W13 ... 43Ka 86
WD3: Chor ... 14E 24
Grenville Gdns. IG8: Wfd G ... 24Lc 53
Grenville Ho. E3 ... 40Ac 72
(off Arbery Rd.)
SE8 ... 51Cc 114
(off New King St.)
SW1 ... 51Mb 112
(off Dolphin Sq.)
Grenville M. N19 ... 32Nb 70
SW7 ... 5A 226 (49Eb 89)
TW12: Hamp H ... 64Da 129
Grenville Pl. NW7 ... 22Ta 47
SW7 ... 4A 226 (48Eb 89)
Grenville Rd. CR0: New Ad ... 81Ec 178
N19 ... 32Nb 70
RM16: Chaf H ... 49Xd 98
Grenville St. WC1 ... 6G 217 (42Nb 90)
Gresford Cl. AL4: St A ... 2H 7
Gresham Av. CR6: W'ham ... 90Ac 178
DA3: Hartl ... 70Be 143
N20 ... 21Hb 49
Gresham Cl. CM14: B'wood ... 20Yd 40
DA5: Bexl ... 58Ad 117
EN2: Enf ... 13Sb 33
RH8: Oxt ... 1K 211
TN16: Tats ... 93Lc 199
Gresham Ct. CM14: B'wood ... 20Yd 40
CR8: Purl ... 83Qb 176
TW18: Staines ... 64J 127
Gresham Dr. RM6: Chad H ... 29Xc 55
Gresham Gdns. NW11 ... 32Ab 68
Gresham Ho. GU22: Wok ... 94C 188
Gresham Lodge E17 ... 29Dc 52
Gresham Pk. Rd. GU22: Wok ... 93D 188
Gresham Pl. N19 ... 33Mb 70
RH8: Oxt ... 1K 211
Gresham Rd. BR3: Beck ... 68Ac 136
CM14: B'wood ... 20Yd 40
E6 ... 40Pc 74
E16 ... 44Kc 93
HA8: Edg ... 23Pa 47
NW10 ... 36Ta 67
RH8: Oxt ... 100Hc 199
SE25 ... 70Wb 135
SL1: Slou ... 4E 80
SW9 ... 55Qb 112
TW3: Houn ... 53Ea 108
TW12: Hamp ... 65Ca 129
TW18: Staines ... 64H 127
UB10: Hil ... 40Q 64
Gresham St. EC2 ... 2D 224 (43Sb 91)
Gresham Way SW19 ... 62Db 133
Gresham Way Ind. Est. SW19 ... 62Db 133
(off Gresham Way)
Gresley Cl. E17 ... 30Ac 52
N15 ... 28Tb 51
Gresley Ct. EN1: Enf ... 7Yb 20
EN6: Pot B ... 2Eb 17
Gresley Rd. N19 ... 32Lb 70
Gressenhall Rd. SW18 ... 58Bb 111
Gresse St. W1 ... 1D 222 (44Mb 90)
Gresswell Cl. DA14: Sidc ... 62Wc 139
Greswell St. SW6 ... 53Za 110
Greta Bank KT24: W Hor ... 98S 190
Gretton Ho. E2 ... 41Yb 92
(off Globe Rd.)
Gretton Rd. N17 ... 24Vb 51
Greville Av. CR2: Sels ... 82Zb 178
Greville Cl. AL9: Wel G ... 6E 8
KT21: Asht ... 91Na 193
TW1: Twick ... 59Ka 108
Greville Ct. E5 ... 34Xb 71
(off Napoleon Rd.)
HA1: Harr ... 35Ga 66
KT21: Asht ... 90Na 173
(off Greville Pk. Rd.)
KT23: Bookh ... 97Da 191
Greville Hall NW6 ... 40Db 69
Greville Ho. SW1 ... 3G 227
Greville Lodge E13 ... 39Kc 73
HA8: Edg ... 21Ra 47
(off Broadhurst Av.)
N12 ... 22Db 49
Greville M. NW6 ... 39Db 69
(off Greville Rd.)
Greville Pk. Av. KT21: Asht ... 90Na 173
Greville Pk. Rd. KT21: Asht ... 90Na 173
Greville Pl. NW6 ... 40Db 69
Greville Rd. E17 ... 28Ec 52
NW6 ... 40Db 69
TW10: Rich ... 58Pa 109
Greville St. EC1 ... 1K 223 (43Qb 90)
(not continuous)
Grey Alders SM7: Bans ... 86Ya 174
Greycaine Rd. WD24: Wat ... 9Z 13
Greycaine Trad. Est. WD24: Wat ... 9Z 13
Grey Cl. NW11 ... 30Eb 49
Greycoat Gdns. SW1 ... 4D 228
Greycoat Pl. SW1 ... 4D 228 (48Mb 90)
Greycoat St. SW1 ... 4D 228 (48Mb 90)
Greycot Rd. BR3: Beck ... 64Cc 136
Grey Eagle St. E1 ... 7K 219 (42Vb 91)
Greyfell Cl. HA7: Stan ... 22Ka 46
Greyfields Cl. CR8: Purl ... 85Rb 177
Greyford Cl. KT22: Lea ... 95La 192
Greyfriars CM13: Hut ... 17De 41
SE26 ... 62Wb 135
(off Wells Pk. Rd.)
Greyfriars Dr. GU24: Bisl ... 7E 166
SL5: Asc ... 1A 146
Greyfriars Ho. RM11: Horn ... 30Md 57
Greyfriars Pas. EC1 ... 2C 224 (44Rb 91)
Greyfriars Rd. GU23: Rip ... 96J 189
Greyhound Commercial Cen., The
DA1: Cray ... 57Gd 118
Greyhound Ct. WC2 ... 4J 223 (45Pb 90)
Greyhound Hill NW4 ... 27Wa 48
Greyhound La. EN6: S Mim ... 5Wa 16
RM16: Ors ... 7C 100
SW16 ... 65Mb 134
Greyhound Mans. W6 ... 51Ab 110
(off Greyhound Rd.)
Greyhound Rd. N17 ... 27Ub 51
NW10 ... 41Xa 88
SM1: Sutt ... 78Eb 155
W6 ... 51Za 110
W14 ... 51Za 110
Greyhound Ter. SW16 ... 67Lb 134
Greyhound Way DA1: Cray ... 57Gd 118
Grey Ho. W12 ... 45Xa 88
(off White City Est.)
Grey Ho., The WD17: Wat ... 12W 26
Greyladies Gdns. SE10 ... 54Ec 114
Greys Pk. Cl. BR2: Kes ... 78Mc 159
Greystead Rd. SE23 ... 59Yb 114
Greystoke Av. HA5: Pinn ... 27Ca 45
Greystoke Ct. W5 ... 42Na 87
Greystoke Dr. HA4: Ruis ... 30R 44
Greystoke Gdns. EN2: Enf ... 14Mb 32
W5 ... 42Na 87
Greystoke Ho. SE15 ... 51Wb 113
(off Peckham Pk. Rd.)
W5 ... 42Na 87
Greystoke Lodge W5 ... 42Pa 87
(off Hanger La.)
Greystoke Pk. Ter. W5 ... 41Ma 87

Greystoke Pl.—Gun M.

Greystoke Pl. EC4 . . . . .2K 223 (44Qb 90)
Greystoke Rd. SL2: Slou 3D 80
Greystone Cl. CR2: Sels 83Yb 178
Greystone Gdns. HA3: Kenton 30La 46
IG6: Ilf 26Sc 54
Greystone Pk. TN14: Sund 97Ad 201
Greystones Cl. RH1: Redh 8M 207
TN15: Kems'g 89Nd 183
Greystones Dr. RH2: Reig 4L 207
Greyswood Av. N18 . . . . .23Zb 52
Greyswood St. SW16 . . . . .65Kb 134
Greythorne Rd. GU21: Wok 10L 167
Grey Towers Av. RM11: Horn 31Md 77
Grey Towers Gdns. RM11: Horn 31Ld 77
Grey Turner Ho. W12 . . . . .44Wa 88
Grice Av. TN16: Big H 85Kc 179
Gridiron Pl. RM14: Upm 34Rd 77
Grierson Ho. SW16 . . . . .63Lb 134
Grierson Rd. SE23 . . . . .59Zb 114
Grieves Rd. DA11: Nflt 2B 144
Griffen Ct. BR3: Beck 67Dc 136
Griffin Av. RM14: Upm 30Ud 58
Griffin Cen. TW14: Felt 57X 107
Griffin Cen., The KT1: King T 68Ma 131
(off Market Pl.)
Griffin Cl. NW10 . . . . .36Xa 68
SL1: Slou .7G 80
Griffin Ct. DA11: Nflt 57Ce 121
KT21: Asht 91Pa 193
KT23: Bookh 98Da 191
TW8: Bford 51Na 109
W4 . . . . .50Va 88
Griffin Ho. CR0: C'don 73Rb 157
E14 . . . . .44Dc 92
(off Ricardo St.)
N1 . . . . .39Ub 71
(off Halcomb St.)
W6 . . . . .49Za 88
(off Hammersmith Rd.)
Griffin Mnr. Way SE28 . . . . .48Tc 94
Griffin M. SW12 . . . . .60Lb 112
Griffin Pk. 51Ma 109
Griffin Rd. N17 . . . . .26Ub 51
SE18 . . . . .50Tc 94
Griffins, The RM16: Grays 47De 99
Griffins Cl. N21 . . . . .17Tb 33
Griffin's Wood Cotts. CM16: Epp 4Tc 22
Griffin Wlk. DA9: Ghithe 57Vd 120
Griffin Way KT23: Bookh 98Ca 191
TW16: Sun 68W 128
Griffith Cl. E17 . . . . .25Fc 53
RM8: Dag 31Yc 75
Griffiths Cl. KT4: Wor Pk 75Xa 154
Griffiths Rd. RM19: Purf 49Sd 98
SW19 . . . . .66Cb 133
Griffiths Way AL1: St A 4A 6
Griffon Way WD25: Wat 6V 12
Grifon Cl. RM16: Chaf H 48Yd 98
Grifon Rd. RM16: Chaf H 49Yd 98
Griggs App. IG1: Ilf 33Sc 74
Griggs Cl. IG3: Ilf 35Uc 74
Griggs Ct. SE1 . . . . .4J 231
Griggs Gdns. RM12: Horn 36Ld 77
Grigg's Pl. SE1 . . . . .3J 231 (48Ub 91)
Griggs Rd. E10 . . . . .30Ec 52
Griggs Way TN15: Bor G 92Ce 205
Grilse Cl. N9 . . . . .21Xb 51
Grimaldi Ho. N1 . . . . .1H 217
Grimsby Gro. E16 . . . . .47Rc 94
Grimsby Rd. SL1: Slou 7D 80
Grimsby St. E2 . . . . .42Vb 91
Grimsdyke Cres. EN5: Barn 13Ya 30
Grim's Dyke Golf Course 22Ca 45
Grimsdyke Lodge AL1: St A 2E 6
Grimsdyke Rd. HA5: Hat E 24Aa 45
Grimsel Path SE5 . . . . .52Rb 113
Grimshaw Cl. N6 . . . . .31Jb 70
Grimshaw Way RM1: Rom 29Hd 56
Grimstone Cl. RM5: Col R 23Dd 56
Grimston Rd. AL1: St A 3D 6
SW6 . . . . .54Bb 111
Grimthorpe Ho. EC1 . . . . .5B 218
Grimwade Av. CR0: C'don 76Wb 157
Grimwade Cl. SE15 . . . . .55Yb 114
Grimwood Rd. TW1: Twick 59Ha 108
Grindall Cl. CR0: Wadd 77Rb 157
Grindall Ho. E1 . . . . .42Xb 91
(off Darling Row)
Grindal St. SE1 . . . . .2K 229 (47Qb 90)
Grindcobbe AL1: St A 5B 6
Grindleford Av. N11 . . . . .19Jb 32
Grindley Gdns. CR0: C'don 72Vb 157
Grindley Ho. E3 . . . . .43Bc 92
(off Leopold St.)
Grindstone Cres. GU21: Knap 10F 166
GRINDSTONE HANDLE CORNER 10F 166
Grinling Pl. SE8 . . . . .51Cc 114
Grinstead Rd. SE8 . . . . .50Ac 92
Grisedale NW1 . . . . .3B 216
Grisedale Cl. CR8: Purl 86Ub 177
Grisedale Gdns. CR8: Purl 86Ub 177
Grittleton Av. HA9: Wemb 37Ra 67
Grittleton Rd. W9 . . . . .42Cb 89
Grizedale Ter. SE23 . . . . .61Xb 135
Grobars Av. GU21: Wok 7N 167
Grocer's Hall Ct. EC2 . . . . . .3F 225 (44Tb 91)
Grocer's Hall Gdns. EC2 . . . . .3F 225
Grogan Cl. TW12: Hamp 65Ba 129
Groombridge Cl. DA16: Well 57Wc 117
KT12: Hers 78X 151
Groombridge Ho. SE17 . . . . .7J 231
Groombridge Rd. E9 . . . . .38Zb 72
Groom Cl. BR2: Brom 70Kc 137
Groom Cres. SW18 . . . . .59Fb 111
Groome Ho. SE11 . . . . .6J 229 (49Pb 90)
Groomfield Cl. SW17 . . . . .63Jb 134
Groom Pl. SW1 . . . . .3J 227 (48Jb 90)
Grooms Dr. HA5: Eastc 29W 44
Grosmont Rd. SE18 . . . . .50Vc 95
Grosse Way SW15 . . . . .58Xa 110
Grosvenor Av. HA2: Harr 30Da 45
N5 . . . . .36Sb 71
SM5: Cars 79Hb 155
SW14 . . . . .55Ua 110
TW10: Rich 57Na 109
UB4: Hayes 40V 64
WD4: K Lan 10C 4
Grosvenor Cl. IG10: Lough 11Rc 36
SL0: Iver H 41F 82
Grosvenor Cotts. SW1 . . . . .5H 227 (49Jb 90)
Grosvenor Ct. E10 . . . . .32Dc 72
E14 . . . . .44Bc 92
(off Wharf La.)
N14 . . . . .17Lb 32
NW6 . . . . .39Za 68
NW7 . . . . .22Ta 47
(off Hale La.)
SE5 . . . . .51Sb 113
Grosvenor Ct. SL1: Slou 4J 81
SL9: Ger X 28A 42
SM2: Sutt 79Db 155
SM4: Mord 70Cb 133
TW11: Tedd 65Ja 130
W3 . . . . .46Qa 87
W5 . . . . .45Na 87
(off The Grove)
W14 . . . . .48Za 88
(off Irving Rd.)
WD3: Crox G 15T 26
Grosvenor Ct. Mans. W2 . . . . .3F 221
Grosvenor Cres. DA1: Dart 57Md 119
NW9 . . . . .28Qa 47
SW1 . . . . .2J 227 (47Jb 90)
UB10: Hil 38R 64
Grosvenor Cres. M.
SW1 . . . . .2H 227 (47Jb 90)
Grosvenor Dr. IG10: Lough 12Rc 36
RM11: Horn 32Ld 77
Grosvenor Est. SW1 . . . . . .5E 228 (49Mb 90)
Grosvenor Gdns. E6 . . . . .41Mc 93
IG8: Wfd G 23Jc 53
KT2: King T 65Ma 131
N10 . . . . .27Lb 50
N14 . . . . .14Mb 32
NW2 . . . . .37Ya 68
NW11 . . . . .30Bb 49
RM14: Upm 32Td 78
SM6: Wall 80Lb 156
SW1 . . . . .3K 227 (48Kb 90)
SW14 . . . . .55Ua 110
Grosvenor Gdns. M. E. SW1 . . . . .3A 228
Grosvenor Gdns. M. Nth. SW1 . . . . . .4K 227
Grosvenor Gdns. M. Sth. SW1 . . . . . .4A 228
Grosvenor Ga. W1 . . . . .5H 221 (45Jb 90)
Grosvenor Hgts. E4 . . . . .17Gc 35
Grosvenor Hill SW19 . . . . .65Ab 132
W1 . . . . .4K 221 (45Kb 90)
Grosvenor Hill Ct. W1 . . . . .4K 221
Grosvenor Ho. SM1: Sutt 78Db 155
(off West St.)
Grosvenor M. KT18: Eps D 91Ta 193
RH2: Reig 9K 207
Grosvenor Pde. W5 . . . . .46Qa 87
(off Uxbridge Rd.)
Grosvenor Pk. SE5 . . . . .52Sb 113
Grosvenor Pk. Rd. E17 . . . . .29Cc 52
Grosvenor Path IG10: Lough 11Rc 36
Grosvenor Pl. GU21: Wok 89B 168
(off Stanley Rd.)
KT13: Weyb 76T 150
SW1 . . . . .1J 227 (47Jb 90)
Grosvenor Ri. E. E17 . . . . .29Dc 52
Grosvenor Rd. AL1: St A 3C 6
BR4: W W'ck 74Dc 158
BR5: St M Cry 72Uc 160
DA6: Bex 57Zc 117
DA17: Belv 51Cd 118
E6 . . . . .39Mc 73
E7 . . . . .37Kc 73
E10 . . . . .32Ec 72
E11 . . . . .29Kc 53
GU24: Chob 5H 167
HA6: Nwood 22V 44
IG1: Ilf 34Sc 74
KT18: Eps D 91Ta 193
N3 . . . . .24Bb 49
N9 . . . . .18Xb 33
N10 . . . . .25Kb 50
RM7: Rush G 31Fd 76
RM8: Dag 32Bd 75
RM16: Ors 4F 100
SE25 . . . . .70Vb 135
SM6: Wall 79Kb 156
SW1 . . . . .7E 228 (51Kb 112)
TW1: Twick 60Ja 108
TW3: Houn 55Ba 107
TW8: Bford 51Ma 109
TW10: Rich 57Na 109
TW18: Staines 66J 127
UB2: S'hall 48Ba 85
W4 . . . . .50Ra 87
W7 . . . . .46Ja 86
WD6: Bore 13Qa 29
WD17: Wat 14Y 27
Grosvenor Sq. DA3: Lfield 69Ae 143
(off Park Dr.)
W1 . . . . .4J 221 (45Jb 90)
WD4: K Lan 10C 4
Grosvenor St. W1 . . . . .4K 221 (45Kb 90)
Grosvenor Studios SW1 . . . . .5H 227
Grosvenor Ter. HP1: Hem H 3J 3
SE5 . . . . .52Sb 113
Grosvenor Va. HA4: Ruis 33V 64
Grosvenor Way E5 . . . . .33Yb 72
SW17 . . . . .62Hb 133
Grosvenor Wharf Rd. E14 . . . . .49Fc 93
Grotes Bldgs. SE3 . . . . .54Gc 115
Grote's Pl. SE3 . . . . .54Gc 115
Groton Rd. SW18 . . . . .61Db 133
Grotto Ct. SE1 . . . . .1D 230 (47Rb 91)
Grotto Pas. W1 . . . . .7J 215 (43Jb 90)
Grotto Rd. KT13: Weyb 76R 150
TW1: Twick 61Ha 130
Groundsel Wlk. HP2: Hem H 2D 4
GROVE, THE 60Wb 113
Grove, The AL9: Brk P 8J 9
BR4: W W'ck 76Dc 158
BR8: Swan 69Hd 140
CM14: B'wood 21Vd 58
CR3: Cat'm 93Rb 197
CR5: Coul 87Mb 176
DA6: Bex 56Zc 117
DA10: Swans 57Be 121
DA12: Grav'nd 9D 122
DA14: Sidc 64Ad 139
E15 . . . . .37Gc 73
EN2: Enf 12Qb 32
EN6: Pot B 4Eb 17
GU21: Wok 88B 168
HA1: Harr 31Ga 66
HA7: Stan 19Ja 28
HA8: Edg 21Ra 47
HP5: Lat 8A 10
KT12: Walt T 73X 151
KT15: Add 78K 149
KT17: Eps 85Ua 174
KT17: Ewe 82Va 174
KT24: Eff 100Z 191
N3 . . . . .25Cb 49
N4 . . . . .31Pb 70
N6 . . . . .32Jb 70
N8 . . . . .29Mb 50
N13 . . . . .21Qb 50
(not continuous)
N14 . . . . .15Lb 32
NW9 . . . . .29Ta 47
Grove, The NW11 . . . . .31Ab 68
RM14: Upm 35Rd 77
SL1: Slou .7L 81
SS17: Stan H 3M 101
TN15: W King 82Vd 184
TN16: Big H 90Mc 179
TW1: Twick 58Ka 108
TW7: Isle 53Ga 108
TW11: Tedd 63Ja 130
TW20: Egh 64C 126
UB6: G'frd 44Ea 86
UB10: Ick 36Q 64
W5 . . . . .46Ma 87
WD3: Crox G 14Q 26
(off Dugdales)
WD4: K Lan 2L 11
WD7: R'lett 6Ja 14
Grove Av. HA5: Pinn 28Aa 45
KT17: Eps 85Ua 174
N3 . . . . .24Cb 49
N10 . . . . .26Lb 50
SM1: Sutt 79Cb 155
TW1: Twick 60Ha 108
W7 . . . . .45Ga 86
Grove Bank WD19: Wat 18Z 27
Grovebarns TW18: Staines 65J 127
Grovebury Cl. DA8: Erith 51Fd 118
Grovebury Ct. DA6: Bex 57Dd 118
N14 . . . . .17Mb 32
Grovebury Gdns. AL2: Park 9A 6
Grovebury Rd. SE2 . . . . .47Xc 95
Grove Cl. BR2: Hayes 75Jc 159
KT1: King T 70Pa 131
KT19: Eps 82Qa 173
N14 . . . . .17Lb 32
SE23 . . . . .60Ac 114
SL1: Slou .8L 81
SL4: Old Win 9M 103
TW13: Hanw 63Aa 129
UB10: Ick 36Q 64
Grove Cnr. KT23: Bookh 98Db 191
Grove Cotts. SW3 . . . . .51Gb 111
(off Chelsea Mnr. St.)
W4 . . . . .51Ua 110
WD23: Bush 16Ca 27
(off Falconer Rd.)
Grove Ct. EN5: Barn 13Bb 31
(off Hadley Ridge)
EN9: Walt A 5Dc 20
KT1: King T 69Na 131
(off Grove Cres.)
KT8: E Mos 71Fa 152
NW8 . . . . .3B 214
RH1: Redh 4B 208
(off Gumbrell M.)
RM14: Upm 35Qd 77
SE15 . . . . .52Ub 113
(off Peckham Rd.)
SW10 . . . . .7A 226
TW3: Houn 56Ca 107
TW20: Egh 64C 126
W5 . . . . .46Na 87
Grove Craft Workshops, The
DA3: Fawk 73Wd 164
Grove Cres. E18 . . . . .26Hc 53
KT1: King T 69Na 131
KT12: Walt T 73X 151
NW9 . . . . .28Sa 47
TW13: Hanw 63Aa 129
WD3: Crox G 14Q 26
Grove Cres. Rd. E15 . . . . .37Fc 73
Grovedale Cl. EN7: Chesh 2Vb 19
Grovedale Rd. N19 . . . . .33Mb 70
Grove Dwellings E1 . . . . .43Yb 92
Grove End E18 . . . . .26Hc 53
NW5 . . . . .35Kb 70
Grove End Gdns. NW8 . . . . .2B 214 (40Fb 69)
Grove End Ho. NW8 . . . . .4B 214
Grove End La. KT10: Esh 74Fa 152
Grove End Rd. NW8 . . . . . .2B 214 (40Fb 69)
Grove Farm Pk. HA6: Nwood 22T 44
Grove Farm Retail Pk.
RM6: Chad H 31Yc 75
Grovefield N11 . . . . .21Kb 50
(off Coppies Gro.)
Grove Footpath KT5: Surb 70Na 131
Grove Gdns. EN3: Enf W 10Zb 20
NW4 . . . . .29Wa 48
NW8 . . . . .4E 214 (41Gb 89)
RM10: Dag 34Ed 76
TW10: Rich 58Pa 109
TW11: Tedd 63Ja 130
Grove Golf Course, The 9S 12
Grove Grn. HA6: Nwood 22T 44
Grove Grn. Rd. E11 . . . . .34Ec 72
Grove Hall Ct. E3 . . . . .40Cc 72
(off Jebb St.)
NW8 . . . . .3A 214 (41Eb 89)
Grove Hall Rd. WD23: Bush 14Aa 27
GROVE HEATH 95K 189
Gro. Heath Ct. GU23: Rip 96L 189
Gro. Heath Nth. GU23: Rip 94K 189
Gro. Heath Rd. GU23: Rip 95K 189
Groveherst Rd. DA1: Dart 55Pd 119
Grove Hill E18 . . . . .26Hc 53
HA1: Harr 31Ga 66
Grovehill Ct. BR1: Brom 65Hc 137
Grove Hill Rd. HA1: Harr 31Ha 66
SE5 . . . . .55Ub 113
Grovehill Rd. RH1: Redh 6P 207
Grove Ho. CM14: W'ley 21Xd 58
EN8: Chesh 2Xb 19
KT17: Eps 85Ua 174
(off The Grove)
N3 . . . . .27Za 48
RH1: Redh 6P 207
(off Huntingdon Rd.)
SW3 . . . . .51Gb 111
(off Chelsea Mnr. St.)
WD23: Bush 16Ba 27
Grove Ho. Rd. N8 . . . . .28Nb 50
Groveland Av. SW16 . . . . .66Pb 134
Groveland Ct. EC4 . . . . .3E 224
Groveland Rd. BR3: Beck 69Bc 136
Grovelands AL2: Park 9P 5
KT1: King T 70Ma 131
(off Palace Rd.)
KT8: W Mole 70Ca 129
Grovelands Cl. HA2: Harr 34Da 65
SE5 . . . . .54Ub 113
Grovelands Ct. N14 . . . . .17Mb 32
Grovelands Rd. BR5: St P 66Wc 139
CR8: Purl 84Nb 176
N13 . . . . .21Pb 50
N15 . . . . .30Wb 51
Grovelands Way
RM17: Grays 50Be 99
Groveland Way KT3: N Mald 71Sa 153
Grove La. CM16: Epp 2Wc 23
CR5: Bans, Coul 84Hb 175
HP5: Whel H 8A 2
IG7: Chig 20Vc 37
KT1: King T 70Na 131
SE5 . . . . .53Tb 113
UB8: Hil 42P 83
Grove La. Ter. SE5 . . . . .54Tb 113
Grove Lea AL10: Hat 3C 8
Groveley Rd. TW13: Felt 64V 128
TW16: Sun 64U 128
Grove Mans. W6 . . . . .47Ya 88
(off Hammersmith Gro.)
Grove Mkt. Pl. SE9 . . . . .58Pc 116
Grove Mead AL10: Hat 1B 8
Grove M. W6 . . . . .48Ya 88
Grove Mill La. WD17: Wat 9R 12
Grove Mill Pl. SM5: Cars 76Jb 156
Grove Nature Reserve, The 42P 83
Grove Pde. SL1: Slou 7L 81
GROVE PARK
SE12 . . . . .62Kc 137
W4 . . . . .53Sa 109
Grove Pk. E11 . . . . .30Kc 53
NW9 . . . . .28Sa 47
SE5 . . . . .54Ub 113
Grove Pk. Av. E4 . . . . .24Dc 52
Grove Pk. Bri. W4 . . . . .52Sa 109
Grove Pk. Gdns. W4 . . . . .52Ra 109
Grove Pk. Ind. Est. NW9 . . . . .27Ta 47
Grove Pk. M. W4 . . . . .52Sa 109
Grove Pk. Nature Reserve 60Hc 115
Grove Pk. Rd. N15 . . . . .28Ub 51
RM13: Rain 39Jd 76
SE9 . . . . .62Lc 137
W4 . . . . .52Ra 109
Grove Pk. Ter. W4 . . . . .52Ra 109
Grove Pas. E2 . . . . .40Xb 71
Grove Path EN7: Chesh 3Wb 19
Grove Pl. AL9: Wel G 6E 8
IG11: Bark 38Sc 74
KT13: Weyb 78S 150
NW3 . . . . .34Fb 69
SW12 . . . . .59Kb 112
W3 . . . . .46Sa 87
WD25: A'ham 11Da 27
Grover Cl. HP2: Hem H 1M 3
Grover Ct. SE13 . . . . .54Dc 114
Grover Ho. SE11 . . . . .7J 229 (50Pb 90)
Grove Rd. AL1: St A 3B 6
CR4: Mitc 69Jb 134
(not continuous)
CR7: Thor H 70Qb 134
DA7: Bex 56Ed 118
DA11: Nflt 57De 121
DA17: Belv 51Bd 117
E3 . . . . .39Zb 72
E4 . . . . .21Ec 52
E11 . . . . .31Hc 73
E17 . . . . .30Dc 52
E18 . . . . .26Hc 53
EN4: Cockf 13Gb 31
GU21: Wok 88B 168
HA5: Pinn 29Ba 45
HA6: Nwood 22T 44
HA8: Edg 23Qa 47
HP1: Hem H 4J 3
KT6: Surb 71Ma 153
KT8: E Mos 70Fa 130
KT16: Chert 72H 149
KT17: Eps 85Ua 174
KT21: Asht 90Pa 173
N11 . . . . .22Kb 50
N12 . . . . .22Fb 49
N15 . . . . .29Ub 51
NW2 . . . . .37Ya 68
RH1: Redh 6P 207
RH8: Tand 5G 210
RM6: Chad H 31Xc 75
RM17: Grays 51De 121
SL1: Burn .1B 80
SL4: Wind 4G 102
SM1: Sutt 79Cb 155
SS17: Stan H 3M 101
SW13 . . . . .54Va 110
SW19 . . . . .66Eb 133
TN14: S'oaks 93Ld 203
TN15: Seal 93Qd 203
TN16: Tats 92Lc 199
TW2: Twick 62Fa 130
TW3: Houn 56Ca 107
TW7: Isle 53Ga 108
TW8: Bford 50La 86
TW10: Rich 58Pa 109
TW17: Shep 72S 150
UB8: Uxb 38M 63
W3 . . . . .46Sa 87
W5 . . . . .45Ma 87
WD3: Rick 19J 25
WD6: Bore 11Qa 29
Grove Rd. W. EN3: Enf W 9Yb 20
Grover Rd. WD19: Wat 17Z 27
Grovers Farm Cotts. KT15: Wdhm . . .83G 168
Groves Cl. RM15: S Ock 45Vd 98
Grove Shaw KT20: Kgswd 96Ab 194
Groveside KT23: Bookh 98Ca 191
Groveside Cl. KT23: Bookh 99Ca 191
SM5: Cars 75Gb 155
W3 . . . . .43Qa 87
Groveside Ct. SW11 . . . . .54Fb 111
Groveside Rd. E4 . . . . .19Gc 35
Grovestile Waye TW14: Bedf 59T 106
Grove St. N18 . . . . .22Vb 51
SE8 . . . . .49Bc 92
Grove Ter. NW5 . . . . .34Kb 70
TW11: Tedd 63Ja 130
UB1: S'hall 45Ca 85
Grove Ter. M. NW5 . . . . .34Kb 70
Grove Va. BR7: Chst 65Qc 138
SE22 . . . . .56Vb 113
Grove Vs. E14 . . . . .45Dc 92
Grove Way HA9: Wemb 36Ra 67
KT10: Esh 73Ea 152
UB8: Uxb 38M 63
WD3: Chor 15D 24
Groveway RM8: Dag 34Zc 75
SW9 . . . . .53Pb 112
Grovewood TW9: Kew 53Qa 109
Grove Wood Cl. BR1: Brom 69Qc 138
Grovewood Cl. WD3: Chor 15D 24
Grove Wood Hill CR5: Coul 86Lb 176
Grovewood Pl. IG8: Wfd G 23Pc 54
Grubbs La. AL9: Hat 4J 9
GRUBB STREET 67Xd 142
Grub St. RH8: Limp 100Lc 199
Grummant Rd. SE15 . . . . .53Vb 113
Grundy Pk. Leisure Cen. 2Ac 20
Grundy St. E14 . . . . .44Dc 92
Gruneisen Rd. N3 . . . . .24Db 49
Grunwick Cl. NW2 . . . . .36Wa 68
Gtec Ho. E15 . . . . .40Fc 73
(off Canning Rd.)
Guardhouse Way NW7 . . . . .22Za 48
Guardian Av. RM16: N Stif 47Zd 99
Guardian Bus. Cen.
RM3: Rom 24Md 57
Guardian Cl. RM11: Horn 33Kd 77
Guardian Ct. SE12 . . . . .57Gc 115
Guards Av. CR3: Cat'm 94Sb 197
Guards Ct. SL5: S'dale 3F 146
Guardsman Cl. CM14: W'ley 22Zd 59
Guards Memorial 7E 222 (46Mb 90)
Guards' Mus., The 2C 228 (47Lb 90)
Guards Polo Club 7J 125
Guards Rd. SL4: Wind 4A 102
Guards Wlk. SL4: Wind 4A 102
Guards Way CR3: Cat'm 94Sb 197
Gubbins La. RM3: Hrld W 24Pd 57
Gubyon Av. SE24 . . . . .57Rb 113
Guerin Sq. E3 . . . . .41Bc 92
Guernsey Cl. TW5: Hest 52Ca 107
Guernsey Farm Dr.
GU21: Wok 7P 167
Guernsey Gro. SE24 . . . . .59Sb 113
Guernsey Ho. EN3: Enf W 10Zb 20
(off Eastfield Rd.)
N1 . . . . .37Sb 71
(off Channel Island Est.)
WD18: Wat 16W 26
Guernsey Rd. E11 . . . . .32Fc 73
Guglielmo Marconi M. E3 . . . . .40Bc 72
Guibal Rd. SE12 . . . . .59Kc 115
Guildable Mnr. Wlk. SE1 . . . . .6G 225
Guildersfield Rd. SW16 . . . . .66Nb 134
Guildford Av. TW13: Felt 61V 128
Guildford Ct. SW8 . . . . .52Nb 112
(off Guildford Rd.)
Guildford Gdns. RM3: Rom 23Nd 57
Guildford Gro. SE10 . . . . .53Dc 114
Guildford La.
GU22: Wok 1P 187
Guildford Rd. AL1: St A 3F 6
CR0: C'don 72Tb 157
E6 . . . . .44Pc 94
E17 . . . . .25Ec 52
GU3: Worp 6D 186
GU4: Sut G 8P 187
GU18: Light 2A 166
GU21: Knap 6D 166
GU21: Wok 83D 168
GU22: Wok 4P 187
(Bourne Way)
GU22: Wok 91A 188
(Wych Hill La.)
GU24: Bisl, W End 4C 166
GU24: Chob 6H 167
GU24: Pirb 5D 186
IG3: Ilf 33Uc 74
KT16: Ott, Chert 78E 148
KT22: Fet 97Fa 192
KT23: Bookh 100Y 191
KT24: E Hor, Eff 100Y 191
RM3: Rom 23Nd 57
SW8 . . . . .53Nb 112
Guildford St. KT16: Chert 73H 149
TW18: Staines 65J 127
Guildford Way SM6: Wall 78Nb 156
Guildhall
City 2E 224
Guildhall Art Gallery 2F 225
Guildhall Bldgs. EC2 . . . . .2F 225
Guildhall Library 2E 224
Guildhall Offices EC2 . . . . .2E 224
Guildhall Yd. EC2 . . . . .2E 224 (44Sb 91)
Guildhouse, The WD3: Crox G 15Q 26
Guildhouse St. SW1 . . . . . .5B 228 (49Lb 90)
Guildown Av. N12 . . . . .21Db 49
Guild Rd. DA8: Erith 52Hd 118
SE7 . . . . .51Mc 115
Guildsway Rd. RM3: Hrld W 26Nd 57
Guildsway E17 . . . . .25Bc 52
Guileshill La. GU23: Ock 95N 189
Guilford Av. KT5: Surb 71Pa 153
Guilford Pl. WC1 . . . . .6H 217 (42Pb 90)
Guilford St. WC1 . . . . .6F 217 (42Nb 90)
Guilfoyle NW9 . . . . .26Va 48
Guillemot Ct. SE8 . . . . .51Bc 114
(off Alexandra Cl.)
Guillemot Pl. N22 . . . . .26Pb 50
Guinea Ct. E1 . . . . .45Wb 91
(off Royal Mint St.)
Guinea Point E14 . . . . .44Ac 92
(off Repton St.)
Guinery Gro. HP3: Hem H 6P 3
Guinevere Gdns. EN8: Chesh 3Ac 20
Guinness Cl. E9 . . . . .38Ac 72
UB3: Harl 48T 84
Guinness Ct. CR0: C'don 75Vb 157
E1 . . . . .3K 225
EC1 . . . . .4E 218
GU21: Wok 10K 167
SE1 . . . . .1H 231
SW3 . . . . .6F 227 (49Hb 89)
Guinness Sq. SE1 . . . . .4H 231 (49Ub 91)
Guinness Trust SW3 . . . . .6F 227
Guinness Trust Bldgs.
SE11 . . . . .7B 230 (50Rb 91)
W6 . . . . .50Za 88
(off Fulham Pal. Rd.)
Guinness Trust Est., The N16 . . . . . . .32Ub 71
Guion Rd. SW6 . . . . .54Bb 111
Gulland Wlk. N1 . . . . .37Sb 71
(off Church Rd.)
Gullane Ho. E3 . . . . .40Bc 72
(off Shetland Rd.)
Gullbrook HP1: Hem H 2J 3
Gullet Wood Rd. WD25: Wat 7W 12
Gulliver Cl. UB5: N'olt 39Ba 65
Gulliver Rd. DA15: Sidc 61Tc 138
Gulliver's Ho. EC1 . . . . .6D 218
Gulliver St. SE16 . . . . .48Ac 92
Gull Wlk. RM12: Horn 38Kd 77
Gulston Wlk. SW3 . . . . .6G 227
Gumbrell M. RH1: Redh 4B 208
Gumleigh Rd. W5 . . . . .49La 86
Gumley Cl. RM20: Grays 51Zd 121
Gumley Gdns. TW7: Isle 55Ja 108
Gumley Rd. RM20: Grays 51Zd 121
Gumping Rd. BR5: Farnb 75Sc 160
Gundulph Rd. BR2: Brom 69Lc 137
Gunfleet Cl. DA12: Grav'nd 9G 122
Gun Hill RM18: W Til 1F 122
Gun Ho. E1 . . . . .46Xb 91
(off Wapping High St.)
Gunmakers La. E3 . . . . .39Ac 72
Gun M. IG9: Buck H 21Mc 53

Gunnell Cl.—Hambalt Rd.

Gunnell Cl. CR0: C'don ... 72Wb 157
SE25 ... 72Wb 157
(off Backley Gdns.)
SE26 ... 63Wb 135
Gunner Dr. EN3: Enf L ... 9Cc 20
Gunner La. SE18 ... 50Qc 94
GUNNERSBURY ... 50Ra 87
Gunnersbury Av. W3 ... 46Pa 87
W4 ... 46Pa 87
W5 ... 46Pa 87
Gunnersbury Cl. W4 ... 50Ra 87
Gunnersbury Ct. W3 ... 47Ra 87
Gunnersbury Cres. W3 ... 47Qa 87
Gunnersbury Dr. W5 ... 47Pa 87
Gunnersbury Gdns. W3 ... 47Qa 87
Gunnersbury La. W3 ... 48Qa 87
Gunnersbury Mnr. W5 ... 46Pa 87
Gunnersbury M. W4 ... 50Ra 87
GUNNERSBURY PARK ... 48Qa 87
Gunnersbury Pk. Mus. ... 48Qa 87
Gunnersbury Triangle Nature Reserve ... 49Sa 87
Gunners Gro. E4 ... 20Ec 34
Gunners Rd. SW18 ... 61Fb 133
Gunnery Ter. SE18 ... 48Sc 94
Gunning Pl. DA8: Erith ... 52Hd 118
Gunning Rd. RM17: Grays ... 50Fe 99
Gunning St. SE18 ... 49Uc 94
Gunn Rd. DA10: Swans ... 58Ae 121
Gunpowder Sq. EC4 ... 2A 224
(not continuous)
Gunstor Rd. N16 ... 35Ub 71
Gun St. E1 ... 1K 225 (43Vb 91)
Gunter Gro. HA8: Edg ... 25Ta 47
SW10 ... 51Eb 111
Gunter Hall Studios SW10 ... 51Eb 111
(off Gunter Gro.)
Gunters Mead KT10: Esh ... 83Ea 172
(not continuous)
KT22: Oxs ... 83Ea 172
Gunterstone Rd. W14 ... 49Ab 88
Gunthorpe St. E1 ... 1K 225 (43Vb 91)
Gunton M. SE13 ... 57Fc 115
Gunton Rd. E5 ... 34Xb 71
SW17 ... 65Jb 134
Gunwhale Cl. SE16 ... 46Zb 92
Gun Wharf E1 ... 46Yb 92
(off Wapping High St.)
Gunyard M. SE18 ... 52Nc 116
Gurdon Ho. E14 ... 44Cc 92
(off Dod St.)
Gurdon Rd. SE7 ... 50Jc 93
Gurnard Cl. UB7: Yiew ... 45M 83
Gurnell Gro. W13 ... 42Ha 86
Gurnell Leisure Cen. ... 41Ha 86
Gurney Cl. E15 ... 36Gc 73
E17 ... 25Zb 52
IG11: Bark ... 37Rc 74
Gurney Ct. Rd. AL1: St A ... 1D 6
Gurney Cres. CR0: C'don ... 74Pb 156
Gurney Dr. N2 ... 28Eb 49
Gurney Ho. E2 ... 40Wb 71
(off Goldsmiths Row)
UB3: Harl ... 50U 84
Gurney Rd. E15 ... 36Gc 73
SM5: Cars ... 77Jb 156
SW6 ... 55Eb 111
UB5: N'olt ... 41X 85
Gurney's Cl. RH1: Redh ... 7P 207
Guru Nanak Marg DA12: Grav'nd ... 9E 122
Gutenberg Ct. SE1 ... 4J 231
Guthrie Ct. SE1 ... 2A 230
Guthrie St. SW3 ... 7D 226 (50Fb 89)
Gutteridge La. RM4: Stap A ... 16Ed 38
Gutter La. EC2 ... 2D 224 (44Sb 91)
Guyatt Gdns. CR4: Mitc ... 68Jb 134
Guy Barnett Gro. SE3 ... 55Jc 115
Guy Rd. SM6: Bedd ... 76Mb 156
Guyscliff Rd. SE13 ... 57Ec 114
Guysfield Cl. RM13: Rain ... 39Jd 76
Guysfield Dr. RM13: Rain ... 39Jd 76
Guys Retreat IG9: Buck H ... 17Lc 35
Guy St. SE1 ... 1G 231 (47Tb 91)
Guy Townsley Sq. E3 ... 43Dc 92
Gwalior Ho. N14 ... 16Lb 32
Gwalior Rd. SW15 ... 56Za 110
Gwendolen Av. SW15 ... 56Za 110
Gwendolen Cl. SW15 ... 57Za 110
Gwendolen Ho. TW19: Stanw ... 60N 105
(off Yeoman Dr.)
Gwendoline Av. E13 ... 39Kc 73
Gwendoline Ct. EN8: Walt C ... 6Bc 20
Gwendwr Rd. W14 ... 50Ab 88
Gweneth Cotts. HA8: Edg ... 23Qa 47
Gwen Morris Ho. SE5 ... 52Sb 113
Gwennap Pl. KT21: Asht ... 91Na 193
Gwent Cl. WD25: Wat ... 6Z 13
Gwent Ct. SE16 ... 46Zb 92
(off Rotherhithe St.)
Gwillim Cl. DA15: Sidc ... 57Wc 117
Gwilym Maries Ho. E2 ... 41Xb 91
(off Blythe St.)
Gwydor Rd. BR3: Beck ... 69Zb 136
Gwydyr Rd. BR2: Brom ... 69Hc 137
Gwyn Cl. SW6 ... 52Eb 111
Gwynedd Cl. TN16: Tats ... 94Mc 199
Gwynne Av. CR0: C'don ... 73Zb 158
Gwynne Cl. SL4: Wind ... 3C 102
W4 ... 51Va 110
Gwynne Ho. E1 ... 43Xb 91
(off Turner St.)
SW1 ... 7H 227
WC1 ... 4K 217
Gwynne Pk. Av. IG8: Wfd G ... 23Pc 54
Gwynne Pl. WC1 ... 4J 217 (41Pb 90)
Gwynne Rd. CR3: Cat'm ... 95Tb 197
SW11 ... 54Fb 111
Gwynn Rd. DA11: Nflt ... 61Ee 143
Gyfford Wlk. EN7: Chesh ... 3Xb 19
Gylcote Cl. SE5 ... 56Tb 113
Gyles Pk. HA7: Stan ... 25La 46
Gyllyngdune Gdns. IG3: Ilf ... 33Vc 75
Gym, The
Hounslow ... 55Da 107
Gymnasium, The N1 ... 40Nb 70
GYPSY CORNER ... 43Ta 87
Gypsy La. SL2: Stoke P ... 5J 61
WD4: Hunt C ... 7T 12

H

Haarlem Rd. W14 ... 48Za 88
Haberdasher Est. N1 ... 3G 219 (41Tb 91)
Haberdasher Pl. N1 ... 3G 219 (41Tb 91)
Haberdashers Ct. SE14 ... 55Zb 114
Haberdasher St. N1 ... 3G 219 (41Tb 91)
Habgood Rd. IG10: Lough ... 13Nc 36
Habitat Cl. SE15 ... 54Xb 113
Habitat Sq. SE10 ... 48Hc 93
(off Teal St.)
Haccombe Rd. SW19 ... 65Eb 133
HACKBRIDGE ... 74Jb 156
Hackbridge Pk. Gdns.
SM5: Cars ... 75Hb 155
Hackbridge Rd. SM6: Wall ... 75Jb 156
Hacketts La. GU22: Pyr ... 86H 169
Hackford Rd. SW9 ... 53Pb 112
Hackford Wlk. SW9 ... 53Pb 112
Hackforth Cl. EN5: Barn ... 15Xa 30
Hackington Cres.
BR3: Beck ... 65Cc 136
HACKNEY ... 37Xb 71
Hackney City Farm ... 40Wb 71
Hackney Cl. WD6: Bore ... 15Ta 29
Hackney Empire Theatre ... 37Xb 71
Hackney Fashion Hub E9 ... 37Yb 72
Hackney Gro. E8 ... 37Xb 71
Hackney Mus. ... 37Xb 71
Hackney Picturehouse ... 37Xb 71
(off Mare St.)
Hackney Rd. E2 ... 4J 219 (41Vb 91)
HACKNEY WICK ... 37Bc 72
HACKNEY WICK ... 37Ac 72
Hackworth Point E3 ... 41Dc 92
(off Rainhill Way)
Hacon Sq. E8 ... 38Xb 71
(off Mare St.)
HACTON ... 36Pd 77
Hacton Dr. RM12: Horn ... 35Md 77
Hacton La. RM12: Horn, Upm ... 33Pd 77
RM14: Upm ... 36Pd 77
Hacton Pde. RM12: Horn ... 34Pd 77
Hadar Cl. N20 ... 18Cb 31
Haddenham Ct. WD19: Wat ... 20Z 27
Hadden Rd. SE28 ... 48Uc 94
Hadden Way UB6: G'frd ... 37Fa 66
Haddington Rd. BR1: Brom ... 62Fc 137
Haddo Ho. SE10 ... 51Dc 114
(off Haddo St.)
Haddon Cl. EN1: Enf ... 16Wb 33
HP3: Hem H ... 3A 4
KT3: N Mald ... 71Va 154
KT13: Weyb ... 76U 150
WD6: Bore ... 12Qa 29
Haddon Ct. NW4 ... 27Ya 48
W3 ... 45Va 88
Haddonfield SE8 ... 49Zb 92
Haddon Gro. DA15: Sidc ... 59Vc 117
Haddon Hall St. SE1 ... 4G 231
Haddon Rd. BR5: St M Cry ... 71Yc 161
SM1: Sutt ... 77Db 155
(not continuous)
WD3: Chor ... 15E 24
Haddo St. SE10 ... 51Dc 114
Haden Ct. N4 ... 33Qb 70
Haden La. N11 ... 21Lb 50
Hadfield Cl. UB1: S'hall ... 41Ba 85
Hadfield Ho. E1 ... 44Wb 91
(off Ellen St.)
Hadfield Rd. SS17: Stan H ... 2M 101
TW19: Stanw ... 58M 105
Hadland Cl. HP3: Bov ... 8C 2
Hadleigh Cl. E1 ... 42Yb 92
HA2: Harr ... 35Ca 65
SW20 ... 68Bb 133
WD7: Shenl ... 2Ma 15
Hadleigh Ct. CM14: B'wood ... 20Wd 40
E4 ... 17Gc 35
NW2 ... 37Ya 68
Hadleigh Dr. SM2: Sutt ... 81Cb 175
Hadleigh Gro. CR5: Coul ... 88Mb 176
Hadleigh Ho. E1 ... 42Yb 92
(off Hadleigh Cl.)
Hadleigh Lodge IG8: Wfd G ... 23Jc 53
(off Snakes La. W.)
Hadleigh Rd. N9 ... 17Xb 33
Hadleigh St. E2 ... 41Yb 92
Hadleigh Wlk. E6 ... 44Nc 94
HADLEY ... 13Bb 31
Hadley Cl. N21 ... 15Qb 32
WD6: E'tree ... 16Pa 29
Hadley Comn.
EN5: Barn, New Bar ... 12Cb 31
Hadley Ct. EN5: New Bar ... 13Db 31
N16 ... 32Wb 71
SL3: Poyle ... 53G 104
(off Coleridge Cres.)
Hadley Gdns. UB2: S'hall ... 50Ba 85
W4 ... 50Ta 87
Hadley Grn. EN5: Barn ... 12Bb 31
Hadley Grn. Rd. EN5: Barn ... 12Bb 31
Hadley Grn. W. EN5: Barn ... 12Bb 31
Hadley Gro. EN5: Barn ... 12Ab 30
Hadley Highstone EN5: Barn ... 11Bb 31
Hadley M. EN5: Barn ... 13Bb 31
Hadley Pde. EN5: Barn ... 13Ab 30
(off High St.)
Hadley Pl. KT13: Weyb ... 80Q 150
Hadley Ridge EN5: Barn ... 13Bb 31
Hadley Rd. CR4: Mitc ... 70Mb 134
DA17: Belv ... 49Bd 95
EN2: Enf ... 10Jb 18
EN4: Had W ... 10Jb 18
EN5: New Bar ... 12Db 31
Hadleys Ct. HP2: Hem H ... 3M 3
(off Selden Hill)
Hadley St. NW1 ... 37Kb 70
(not continuous)
Hadley Way N21 ... 16Qb 32
HADLEY WOOD ... 10Eb 17
Hadley Wood Golf Course ... 11Gb 31
Hadley Wood Lawn Tennis Club ... 10Eb 17
Hadley Wood Nature Reserve ... 12Eb 31
Hadley Wood Ri. CR8: Kenley ... 86Rb 177
Hadley Wood Rd. EN4: Cockf ... 12Eb 31
EN5: Cockf, New Bar ... 12Eb 31
Hadlow Ct. SL1: Slou ... 6G 80
Hadlow Ho. SE17 ... 7J 231
Hadlow Pl. SE19 ... 66Wb 135
Hadlow Rd. DA14: Sidc ... 63Wc 139
DA16: Well ... 52Yc 117
Hadlow Way DA13: Ist R ... 6A 144
Hadrian Cl. AL3: St A ... 4M 5
E3 ... 39Cc 72
(off Garrison Rd.)
TW19: Stanw ... 59N 105
Hadrian Ct. SM2: Sutt ... 80Db 155
Hadrian Est. E2 ... 40Wb 71
Hadrian M. CR4: Mitc ... 69Kb 134
N7 ... 38Pb 70
Hadrians Ride EN1: Enf ... 15Vb 33
Hadrian St. SE10 ... 50Gc 93
Hadrian Way TW19: Stanw ... 59M 105
(not continuous)
Hadstock Ho. NW1 ... 3E 216
Hadyn Pk. Ct. W12 ... 47Wa 88
(off Curwen Rd.)
Hadyn Pk. Rd. W12 ... 47Wa 88
Hafer Rd. SW11 ... 56Hb 111
Hafton Rd. SE6 ... 60Gc 115
Hagden La. WD18: Wat ... 14V 26
Haggard Rd. TW1: Twick ... 59Ka 108
Hagger Ct. E17 ... 27Fc 53
HAGGERSTON ... 1K 219 (38Vb 71)
Haggerston Rd. E8 ... 1K 219 (38Vb 71)
WD6: Bore ... 10Na 15
Haggerston Studios E8 ... 39Vb 71
(off Kingsland Rd.)
Hague St. E2 ... 41Wb 91
Ha Ha Rd. SE18 ... 51Pc 116
Haig Cl. AL1: St A ... 3F 6
Haig Dr. SL1: Slou ... 7F 80
Haig Gdns. DA12: Grav'nd ... 9E 122
Haigh Cres. RH1: Redh ... 8B 208
Haig Ho. AL1: St A ... 3F 6
E2 ... 40Wb 71
(off Shipton St.)
Haig Pl. SM4: Mord ... 72Cb 155
Haig Rd. HA7: Stan ... 22La 46
RM16: Grays ... 8C 100
TN16: Big H ... 89Nc 180
UB8: Hil ... 43R 84
Haig Rd. E. E13 ... 41Lc 93
Haig Rd. W. E13 ... 41Lc 93
Haigville Gdns. IG6: Ilf ... 28Rc 54
Hailes Cl. CR0: Bedd ... 75Mb 156
SW19 ... 65Eb 133
Haileybury Av. EN1: Enf ... 16Vb 33
Haileybury Rd. BR6: Chels ... 77Wc 161
Hailey Rd. DA18: Erith ... 47Cd 96
Hailey Rd. Bus. Pk. DA18: Erith ... 47Cd 96
Hailing M. BR2: Brom ... 69Kc 137
(off Wendover Rd.)
Hailsham Av. SW2 ... 61Pb 134
Hailsham Cl. KT6: Surb ... 73Ma 153
RM3: Rom ... 22Ld 57
Hailsham Dr. HA1: Harr ... 27Fa 46
Hailsham Gdns. RM3: Rom ... 22Ld 57
Hailsham Ho. NW8 ... 6D 214
Hailsham Rd. RM3: Rom ... 22Ld 57
SW17 ... 65Jb 134
Hailsham Ter. N18 ... 22Tb 51
Haimo Rd. SE9 ... 57Mc 115
HAINAULT ... 22Wc 55
Hainault Bri. Pde. IG1: Ilf ... 33Rc 74
(off Hainault St.)
Hainault Bus. Pk. IG6: Ilf ... 22Yc 55
(not continuous)
Hainault Ct. E17 ... 28Fc 53
(off Forest Ri.)
Hainault Forest Country Pk. ... 20Zc 37
Hainault Forest Country Pk. Vis. Cen. ... 21Ad 55
Hainault Forest Golf Course ... 23Zc 55
Hainault Gore RM6: Chad H ... 29Ad 55
Hainault Gro. IG7: Chig ... 21Sc 54
Hainault Lodge Local Nature Reserve ... 23Yc 55
Hainault Rd. E11 ... 32Ec 72
IG7: Chig ... 20Rc 36
RM5: Col R, Rom ... 26Ed 56
RM6: Chad H ... 24Xc 55
(Forest Ri.)
RM6: Chad H ... 30Bd 55
(Sylvan Av.)
Hainault St. IG1: Ilf ... 33Sc 74
SE9 ... 60Rc 116
Haines Cl. N1 ... 38Ub 71
Haines Ct. KT13: Weyb ... 78T 150
Haines St. SW8 ... 52Lb 112
Haines Wlk. SM4: Mord ... 73Db 155
Haines Way WD25: Wat ... 6W 12
Hainford Cl. SE4 ... 56Zb 114
Haining Cl. W4 ... 50Qa 87
Hainthorpe Rd. SE27 ... 62Rb 135
Hainton Cl. E1 ... 44Xb 91
Halberd M. E5 ... 33Xb 71
Halbutt Gdns. RM9: Dag ... 34Bd 75
Halbutt St. RM9: Dag ... 35Bd 75
Halcomb St. N1 ... 1H 219 (39Ub 71)
Halcot Av. DA6: Bex ... 57Dd 118
Halcrow Av. DA1: Dart ... 55Qd 119
Halcrow St. E1 ... 43Xb 91
Halcyon EN1: Enf ... 15Ub 33
(off Private Rd.)
Halcyon Cl. KT22: Oxs ... 87Fa 172
SW13 ... 55Wa 110
Halcyon Way RM11: Horn ... 32Pd 77
Halcyon Wharf E1 ... 46Wb 91
(off Hermitage Wall)
Haldane Cl. EN3: Enf L ... 10Dc 20
N10 ... 24Kb 50
Haldane Gdns. DA11: Nflt ... 60Ee 121
Haldane Pl. SW18 ... 60Db 111
Haldane Rd. E6 ... 41Mc 93
SE28 ... 45Zc 95
SW6 ... 52Bb 111
UB1: S'hall ... 45Ea 86
Haldan Rd. E4 ... 23Ec 52
Haldon Cl. IG7: Chig ... 22Uc 54
Haldon Rd. SW18 ... 58Bb 111
HALE, THE ... 22Ta 47
Hale SL4: Wind ... 3C 102
Hale, The E4 ... 24Fc 53
N17 ... 27Wb 51
Halebourne La.
GU24: Chob, W End ... 10E 146
Hale Cl. BR6: Farnb ... 77Sc 160
E4 ... 20Ec 34
HA8: Edg ... 22Sa 47
Hale Ct. HA8: Edg ... 22Sa 47
Hale Dr. NW7 ... 23Sa 47
HALE END ... 23Gc 53
Hale End RM3: Rom ... 23Kd 57
Hale End Cl. HA4: Ruis ... 30W 44
Hale End Rd. E4 ... 23Fc 53
E17 ... 25Ec 52
IG8: Wfd G ... 24Fc 53
Hale Ends GU22: Wok ... 3M 187
Halefield Rd. N17 ... 25Xb 51
Hale Gdns. N17 ... 28Wb 51
W3 ... 46Qa 87
Hale Gro. Gdns. NW7 ... 22Ua 48
Hale Ho. RM11: Horn ... 30Jd 56
(off Benjamin Cl.)
SW1 ... 7E 228
Hale La. HA8: Edg ... 22Ra 47
NW7 ... 22Ta 47
TN14: Otf ... 89Hd 182
Hale Path SE27 ... 63Rb 135
Hale Pit Rd. KT23: Bookh ... 98Ea 192
Hale Rd. E6 ... 42Nc 94
N17 ... 27Wb 51
Hales Ct. WD25: Wat ... 8Y 13
Hales Oak KT23: Bookh ... 98Ea 192
Halesowen Rd. SM4: Mord ... 73Db 155
Hales Pk. HP2: Hem H ... 1C 4
Hales Pk. Cl. HP2: Hem H ... 1C 4
Hales Prior N1 ... 2H 217
Hales St. SE8 ... 52Cc 114
Hale St. E14 ... 45Dc 92
TW18: Staines ... 63G 126
Haleswood KT11: Cobh ... 86X 171
Haleswood Rd. HP2: Hem H ... 1B 4
Halesworth Cl. E5 ... 33Yb 72
RM3: Rom ... 24Nd 57
Halesworth Rd. RM3: Rom ... 23Nd 57
SE13 ... 55Dc 114
Hale Wlk. W7 ... 43Ga 86
Haley Rd. NW4 ... 30Ya 48
Half Acre HA7: Stan ... 22La 46
TW8: Bford ... 51Ma 109
Halfacre Hill SL9: Chal P ... 25B 42
Half Acre Rd. W7 ... 46Ga 86
Halfhides EN9: Walt A ... 5Fc 21
Half Moon CM16: Epp ... 3Vc 23
Half Moon Cotts. GU23: Rip ... 93L 189
Half Moon Ct. CR0: C'don ... 73Rb 157
EC1 ... 1D 224
Half Moon Cres. N1 ... 1J 217 (40Pb 70)
(not continuous)
Half Moon La. SE24 ... 58Sb 113
Half Moon M. AL1: St A ... 2B 6
Half Moon Pas. E1 ... 3K 225 (44Vb 91)
(not continuous)
Half Moon St. W1 ... 6A 222 (46Kb 90)
Halford Cl. HA8: Edg ... 26Ra 47
Halford Pl. W7 ... 46Ha 86
Halford Rd. E10 ... 29Fc 53
SW6 ... 51Cb 111
TW10: Rich ... 57Na 109
UB10: Ick ... 35Q 64
Halfpence La. DA12: Cobh ... 10J 145
Halfpenny La. SL5: S'dale ... 3E 146
Halfway Ct. RM19: Purf ... 49Qd 97
Halfway Grn. KT12: Walt T ... 76X 151
Halfway St. DA15: Sidc ... 59Tc 116
Haliburton Rd. TW1: Twick ... 57Ja 108
Haliday Ho. N1 ... 37Tb 71
(off Mildmay St.)
Haliday Wlk. N1 ... 37Tb 71
Halidon Cl. E9 ... 36Yb 72
Halidon Ri. RM3: Hrld W ... 23Rd 57
Halifax NW9 ... 26Va 48
Halifax Cl. AL2: Brick W ... 3Ba 13
TW11: Tedd ... 65Ga 130
WD25: Wat ... 6V 12
Halifax Ho. RM3: Rom ... 22Nd 57
(off Lindfield Rd.)
Halifax Rd. EN2: Enf ... 12Sb 33
UB6: G'frd ... 39Da 65
WD3: Herons ... 17E 24
Halifax St. SE26 ... 62Xb 135
Halifield Dr. DA17: Belv ... 48Ad 95
Haling Down Pas. CR2: S Croy ... 81Sb 177
CR8: Purl ... 82Rb 177
(not continuous)
Haling Gro. CR2: S Croy ... 80Sb 157
Haling Pk. Gdns. CR2: S Croy ... 79Rb 157
Haling Pk. Rd. CR2: S Croy ... 78Rb 157
Haling Rd. CR2: S Croy ... 79Tb 157
Halings La. UB9: Den ... 28F 42
Haliwell Ho. NW6 ... 39Db 69
(off Mortimer Cres.)
Halkett Ho. E2 ... 39Yb 72
(off Waterloo Gdns.)
Halkin Arc. SW1 ... 3G 227 (48Hb 89)
Halkingcroft SL3: L'ly ... 7N 81
Halkin M. SW1 ... 3H 227 (48Jb 90)
Halkin Pl. SW1 ... 3H 227 (48Jb 90)
Halkin St. SW1 ... 2J 227 (47Jb 90)
Hall, The SE3 ... 55Jc 115
Hallam Cl. BR7: Chst ... 64Pc 138
WD24: Wat ... 12Y 27
Hallam Ct. W1 ... 7A 216
Hallam Gdns. HA5: Hat E ... 24Aa 45
Hallam Ho. SW1 ... 50Lb 90
(off Churchill Gdns.)
Hallam M. W1 ... 7A 216 (43Kb 90)
Hallam Rd. N15 ... 28Rb 51
SW13 ... 55Xa 110
Hallam St. W1 ... 6A 216 (43Kb 90)
Halland Way HA6: Nwood ... 23T 44
Hallane Ho. SE27 ... 64Sb 135
Hall Apartments E3 ... 43Bc 92
(off Geoff Cade Way)
Hall Av. RM15: Avel ... 46Sd 98
Hall Barns, The CM16: Epp ... 3Pc 22
Hall Cl. W5 ... 43Na 87
WD3: Rick ... 18J 25
Hall Ct. SL3: Dat ... 2M 103
TW11: Tedd ... 64Ha 130
Hall Cres. RM15: Avel ... 47Sd 98
Hall Dr. SE26 ... 64Yb 136
UB9: Hare ... 25L 43
W7 ... 44Ga 86
Halley Gdns. SE13 ... 56Fc 115
Halley Ho. E2 ... 40Wb 71
(off Pritchards Rd.)
SE10 ... 50Hc 93
(off Armitage Rd.)
Halley Rd. E7 ... 37Lc 73
E12 ... 37Lc 73
EN9: Walt A ... 8Dc 20
Halley's App. GU21: Wok ... 9L 167
Halley's Ct. GU21: Wok ... 10L 167
Halley St. E14 ... 43Ac 92
Halley's Wlk. KT15: Add ... 80L 149
Hall Farm Cl. HA7: Stan ... 21Ka 46
Hall Farm Dr. TW2: Whitt ... 59Fa 108
Hallfield Est. W2 ... 2A 220 (44Eb 89)
(not continuous)
Hallford Way DA1: Dart ... 58Ld 119
Hall Gdns. AL4: Col H ... 5P 7
E4 ... 21Bc 52
Hall Ga. NW8 ... 3A 214 (41Fb 89)
Hall Grn. La. CM13: Hut ... 17Ee 41
Hall Heath Cl. AL1: St A ... 1F 6
Hall Hill RH8: Oxt ... 3H 211
TN15: Seal ... 95Rd 203
Halliards, The KT12: Walt T ... 72W 150
Halliday Cl. KT17: Ewe ... 82Wa 174
WD7: Shenl ... 4Na 15
Halliday Ho. E1 ... 44Wb 91
(off Christian St.)
Halliday Sq. UB2: S'hall ... 46Fa 86
Halliford Cl. TW17: Shep ... 70T 128
Halliford Rd. TW16: Sun ... 71U 150
TW17: Shep ... 71U 150
Halliford St. N1 ... 38Sb 71
Halliloo Valley Rd. CR3: Wold ... 92Zb 198
Hallingbury Ct. E17 ... 27Dc 52
Halling Ho. SE1 ... 2G 231
Hallings Wharf Studios E15 ... 39Ec 72
Hallington Cl. GU21: Wok ... 9M 167
Halliwell Ct. SE22 ... 57Wb 113
Halliwell Rd. SW2 ... 58Pb 112
Halliwick Ct. Pde. N12 ... 23Hb 49
(off Woodhouse Rd.)
Halliwick Rd. N10 ... 25Jb 50
HALL LANE ... 22Zb 52
Hall La. CM15: Shenf ... 13Ae 41
E4 ... 22Ac 52
NW4 ... 25Wa 48
RM14: Upm ... 26Sd 58
RM15: S Ock ... 40Zd 79
UB3: Harl ... 52T 106
Hallmark Ho. E14 ... 43Cc 92
(off Ursula Gould Way)
Hallmark Trad. Est. HA9: Wemb ... 35Sa 67
Hall Mdw. SL1: Burn ... 10A 60
Hallmead Rd. SM1: Sutt ... 76Db 155
Hall Oak Wlk. NW6 ... 37Bb 69
Hallowell Av. CR0: Bedd ... 77Nb 156
Hallowell Cl. CR4: Mitc ... 69Jb 134
Hallowell Gdns. CR7: Thor H ... 68Sb 135
Hallowell Rd. HA6: Nwood ... 24U 44
Hallowes Cres. WD19: Wat ... 20W 26
Hallowfield Way CR4: Mitc ... 69Fb 133
Hallows Gro. TW16: Sun ... 64V 128
Hall Pk. HP4: Berk ... 2A 2
Hall Pk. Ga. HP4: Berk ... 3A 2
Hall Pk. Hill HP4: Berk ... 3A 2
Hall Pk. Rd. RM14: Upm ... 36Sd 78
Hall Pl. AL1: St A ... 1C 6
(off St Peters St.)
GU21: Wok ... 88C 168
W2 ... 6B 214 (42Fb 89)
(not continuous)
Hall Place & Gdns. ... 58Ed 118
Hall Pl. Cl. AL1: St A ... 1C 6
Hall Pl. Cres. DA5: Bexl ... 57Ed 118
Hall Pl. Dr. KT13: Weyb ... 78U 150
Hall Pl. Gdns. AL1: St A ... 1C 6
Hall Place Sports Pavilion ... 58Ed 118
Hall Rd. DA1: Dart ... 56Pd 119
DA11: Nflt ... 62Ee 143
E6 ... 39Pc 74
E15 ... 35Fc 73
NW8 ... 4A 214 (41Eb 89)
RM2: Rom ... 27Kd 57
RM6: Chad H ... 30Yc 55
RM15: Avel ... 47Sd 98
SM6: Wall ... 81Kb 176
TW7: Isle ... 57Fa 108
Halls Farm Cl. GU21: Knap ... 9H 167
Hallside Rd. EN1: Enf ... 10Vb 19
Hallsland Way RH8: Oxt ... 5K 211
Halls Ter. UB10: Hil ... 42R 84
Hall St. EC1 ... 3C 218 (41Rb 91)
N12 ... 22Eb 49
Hallsville Rd. E16 ... 44Hc 93
Hallswelle Pde. NW11 ... 29Bb 49
Hallswelle Rd. NW11 ... 29Bb 49
Hall Ter. RM3: Hrld W ... 24Qd 57
RM15: Avel ... 47Td 98
Hall Twr. W2 ... 7C 214
Hall Vw. SE9 ... 61Mc 137
Hall Wlk., The HP4: Berk ... 1A 2
(off Little Bri. Rd.)
Hall Way CR8: Purl ... 85Rb 177
Hallwood Cres. CM15: Shenf ... 17Ae 41
Hallywell Cres. E6 ... 43Pc 94
Halo E15 ... 39Ec 72
Halons Rd. SE9 ... 59Qc 116
Halpin Pl. SE17 ... 6G 231 (49Tb 91)
Halsbrook Rd. SE3 ... 55Lc 115
Halsbury Cl. HA7: Stan ... 21Ka 46
Halsbury Ct. HA7: Stan ... 22Ka 46
Halsbury Ho. N7 ... 35Pb 70
(off Biddestone Rd.)
Halsbury Rd. W12 ... 46Xa 88
Halsbury Rd. E. UB5: N'olt ... 35Ea 66
Halsbury Rd. W. UB5: N'olt ... 35Da 65
Halse Dr. SL2: Farn C ... 5C 60
Halsend UB3: Hayes ... 46X 85
Halsey Ho. WC1 ... 1H 223
Halsey M. SW3 ... 5F 227 (49Hb 89)
Halsey Pk. AL2: Lon C ... 10K 7
Halsey Pl. WD24: Wat ... 10X 13
Halsey Rd. WD18: Wat ... 13X 27
Halsey St. SW3 ... 5F 227 (49Hb 89)
Halsham Cres. IG11: Bark ... 36Vc 75
Halsmere Rd. SE5 ... 53Rb 113
HALSTEAD ... 84Bd 181
Halstead Cl. CR0: C'don ... 76Sb 157
Halstead Ct. E17 ... 31Bc 72
N1 ... 2G 219
Halstead Gdns. N21 ... 18Tb 33
Halstead Hill EN7: G Oak ... 1Ub 19
Halstead Ho. RM3: Rom ... 23Md 57
(off Dartfields)
Halstead La.
TN14: Knock, Hals ... 87Ad 181
Halstead Pl. TN14: Hals ... 84Ad 181
Halstead Rd. DA8: Erith ... 53Gd 118
E11 ... 29Jc 53
EN1: Enf ... 14Ub 33
N21 ... 18Sb 33
Halstead Way CM13: Hut ... 16Ee 41
Halston Cl. SW11 ... 58Hb 111
Halstow Rd. NW10 ... 41Za 88
SE10 ... 50Jc 93
Halsway UB3: Hayes ... 46W 84
Halt Dr. SS17: Linf ... 9J 101
Halter Cl. WD6: Bore ... 15Ta 29
Halton Cl. AL2: Park ... 10A 6
N11 ... 23Hb 49
Halton Ct. SE3 ... 55Kc 115
Halton Cross St. N1 ... 39Rb 71
Halton Ho. N1 ... 38Rb 71
(off Halton Rd.)
Halton Mans. N1 ... 38Rb 71
Halton Pl. N1 ... 39Sb 71
Halton Rd. CR8: Kenley ... 92Ub 197
N1 ... 38Rb 71
RM16: Grays ... 8E 100
Halt Robin La. DA17: Belv ... 49Dd 96
Halt Robin Rd. DA17: Belv ... 49Cd 96
(not continuous)
Haltside AL10: Hat ... 1A 8
Halwick Ct. HP1: Hem H ... 4K 3
Halyard Ho. E14 ... 48Ec 92
(off Manchester Rd.)
Halyard St. RM9: Dag ... 42Ad 95
HAM ... 62La 130
Ham, The TW8: Bford ... 52La 108
Hamara Ghar E13 ... 39Lc 73
Hambalt Rd. SW4 ... 57Lb 112

Hamble Cl.—Harborough Rd.

Hamble Cl. GU21: Wok 9L 167
HA4: Ruis 33U 64
Hamble Ct. WD18: Wat 14W 26
Hambleden Pl. WD7: R'lett 7Ha 14
Hambledon SE17 ....51Tb 113
(off Villa St.)
Hambledon Cl. UB8: Hil 42R 84
Hambledon Ct. SE22 ....56Ub 113
W5 ....45Na 87
Hambledon Gdns. SE25 ....69Vb 135
Hambledon Hill KT18: Eps 88Sa 173
Hambledon Pl.
KT23: Bookh 95Ca 191
SE21 ....60Ub 113
Hambledon Rd. CR3: Cat'm 95Tb 197
SW18 ....59Bb 111
Hambledon Va. KT18: Eps 88Sa 173
Hambledown Rd.
DA15: Sidc 59Tc 116
Hamble Dr. UB3: Hayes 45V 84
Hamblehyrst BR3: Beck 68Dc 136
Hamble La. RM15: S Ock 43Vd 98
Hamble St. SW6 ....55Db 111
Hambleton SL4: Old Win 10N 103
(off Burfield Rd.)
Hambleton Cl. KT4: Wor Pk 75Ya 154
UB9: Hare 26L 43
Hamble Wlk. GU21: Wok 10L 167
UB5: N'olt 40Ca 65
(off Brabazon Rd.)
Hambley Ho. SE16 ....49Xb 91
(off Camilla Rd.)
Hamblings Cl. WD7: Shenl 5Ma 15
Hamblin Ho. UB1: S'hall 45Aa 85
(off The Broadway)
Hambridge Way SW2 ....59Qb 112
Hambro Av. BR2: Hayes 74Jc 159
Hambrook Rd. SE25 ....69Xb 135
Hambro Rd. SW16 ....65Mb 134
Hambrough Ho. UB4: Yead 43Y 85
Hambrough Rd.
UB1: S'hall 46Aa 85
Ham Cl. TW10: Ham 62La 130
(not continuous)
Ham Comn. TW10: Ham 62Ma 131
Ham Common (Nature Reserve)
....63Na 131
Ham Ct. NW9 ....26Ua 48
RM2: Rom 28Ld 57
Ham Cft. Cl. TW13: Felt 62W 128
Hamden Cres.
RM10: Dag 34Dd 76
Hamel Cl. HA3: Kenton 28Ma 47
Hamella Ho. E9 ....36Ac 72
(off Sadler Pl.)
Hamer Cl. HP3: Bov 10C 2
Hamerton Rd. DA11: Nflt 57De 121
Hameway E6 ....41Qc 94
Ham Farm Rd.
TW10: Ham 63Ma 131
Hamfield Cl. RH8: Oxt 99Ec 198
Ham Flds. TW10: Ham 62Ka 130
Hamfrith Rd. E15 ....37Hc 73
Ham Ga. Av. TW10: Ham 62Ma 131
Hamhaugh Island
TW17: Shep 75Q 150
Ham House & Garden 60La 108
Hamilton Av. GU22: Pyr 87G 168
IG6: Ilf 28Rc 54
KT6: Surb 75Qa 153
KT11: Cobh 85W 170
N9 ....17Wb 33
RM1: Rom 26Fd 56
SM3: Cheam 75Ab 154
Hamilton Cl. AL2: Brick W 3Ca 13
CR8: Purl 84Rb 177
EN4: Cockf 14Gb 31
EN6: S Mim 5Wa 16
HA7: Stan 19Ga 28
KT16: Chert 74H 149
KT19: Eps 84Sa 173
N17 ....27Vb 51
NW8 ....4B 214 (41Fb 89)
SE16 ....47Ac 92
TW11: Tedd 65Ka 130
TW13: Felt 64V 128
Hamilton Ct. AL10: Hat 2D 8
CR0: C'don 74Wb 157
DA8: Erith 52Hd 118
(off Frobisher Rd.)
KT11: Cobh 85W 170
KT16: Chert 73J 149
KT23: Bookh 97Da 191
SE6 ....60Hc 115
SW15 ....55Ab 110
TW3: Houn 56Da 107
(off Hanworth Rd.)
W5 ....45Na 87
W9 ....41Eb 89
(off Maida Vale)
Hamilton Cres. CM14: W'ley 21Yd 58
HA2: Harr 34Ba 65
N13 ....21Qb 50
TW3: Houn 57Da 107
Hamilton Dr. RM3: Hrld W 26Nd 57
SL5: S'dale 3C 146
Hamilton Gdns. NW8 ....3A 214 (41Eb 89)
WD23: Bush 14Ba 27
Hamilton Hall NW8 ....40Eb 69
(off Hamilton Ter.)
Hamilton Ho. E3 ....41Bc 92
(off British St.)
E14 ....50Dc 92
(off St Davids Sq.)
E14 ....45Bc 92
(off Victory Pl.)
NW8 ....3B 214
W4 ....51Ua 110
W8 ....47Db 89
(off Vicarage Ga.)
Hamilton La. N5 ....35Rb 71
Hamilton Lodge E1 ....42Yb 92
(off Cleveland Gro.)
Hamilton Mead HP3: Bov 9C 2
Hamilton M. KT13: Weyb 77Q 150
(off Holstein Av.)
SW18 ....60Cb 111
SW19 ....66Cb 133
W1 ....1K 227 (47Kb 90)
Hamilton Pde. TW13: Felt 63V 128
Hamilton Pk. N5 ....35Rb 71
Hamilton Pk. W. N5 ....35Rb 71
Hamilton Pl. KT14: W Byf 85H 169
KT20: Kgswd 94Bb 195
N19 ....34Mb 70
SL9: Ger X 29A 42
TW16: Sun 66X 129
W1 ....7J 221 (46Jb 90)
Hamilton Rd. AL1: St A 1E 6
CR7: Thor H 69Tb 135
DA7: Bex 54Ad 117
DA15: Sidc 63Wc 139
E15 ....41Gc 93
E17 ....26Ac 52
EN4: Cockf 14Gb 31
HA1: Harr 29Ga 46
IG1: Ilf 35Rc 74
N2 ....27Eb 49
N9 ....17Wb 33
NW10 ....36Wa 68
NW11 ....31Za 68
RM2: Rom 29Kd 57
SE27 ....63Tb 135
SL1: Slou 4E 80
SW19 ....66Db 133
TW2: Twick 60Ga 108
TW8: Bford 51Ma 109
TW13: Felt 63V 128
UB1: S'hall 46Ba 85
UB3: Hayes 45X 85
UB8: Cowl 42M 83
W4 ....47Ua 88
W5 ....45Na 87
WD4: Hunt C 5S 12
WD19: Wat 20X 27
Hamilton Rd. Ind. Est. SE27 ....63Tb 135
Hamilton Rd. M. SW19 ....66Db 133
Hamilton Sq. N12 ....23Fb 49
SE1 ....1G 231 (47Tb 91)
Hamilton St. SE8 ....51Cc 114
WD18: Wat 15Y 27
Hamilton Ter. NW8 ....2A 214 (40Db 69)
Hamilton Wlk. DA8: Erith 52Hd 118
Hamilton Way N3 ....23Cb 49
N13 ....21Rb 51
SL2: Farn C 6G 60
SM6: Wall 81Mb 176
HAM ISLAND 6N 103
Ham Lands Nature Reserve 61Ja 130
Ham La. SL4: Old Win 7N 103
TW20: Eng G 3M 125
Hamlea Cl. SE12 ....57Jc 115
Hamlet, The SE5 ....55Tb 113
Hamlet Cl. AL2: Brick W 2Ba 13
RM5: Col R 24Cd 56
SE6 ....59Dc 114
SE13 ....56Gc 115
Hamlet Ct. E3 ....41Cc 92
(off Tomlin's Gro.)
EN1: Enf 15Ub 33
SE11 ....7B 230
W6 ....49Wa 88
Hamlet Gdns. W6 ....49Wa 88
Hamlet Ind. Est. E9 ....38Cc 72
Hamlet Intl. Ind. Est. DA8: Erith 50Fd 96
Hamlet Lodge UB10: Hil 37R 64
Hamlet M. SE21 ....60Tb 113
Hamleton Ter. RM9: Dag 38Yc 75
(off Flamstead Rd.)
Hamlet Rd. RM5: Col R 24Cd 56
SE19 ....66Vb 135
Hamlet Sq. NW2 ....34Ab 68
Hamlets Way E3 ....42Bc 92
Hamlet Way SE1 ....1G 231 (47Tb 91)
Hamlin Cres. HA5: Eastc 29Y 45
Hamlin Rd. TN13: Riv 94Gd 202
Hamlyn Cl. HA8: Edg 20Na 29
Hamlyn Ct. TN13: Dun G 93Gd 202
Hamlyn Gdns. SE19 ....66Ub 135
Hamlyn Ho. TW13: Felt 60X 107
Hamm Ct. KT13: Weyb 75N 149
Hammelton Ct. BR1: Brom 67Hc 137
(off London Rd.)
Hammelton Rd. BR1: Brom 67Hc 137
HAMMERFIELD 2K 3
Hammerfield Ho. SW3 ....7E 226
Hammer La. HP2: Hem H 1P 3
Hammer Pde. WD25: Wat 5W 12
Hammers Ga. AL2: Chis G 8N 5
Hammers La. NW7 ....22Wa 48
Hammersley Ho. SE14 ....52Yb 114
(off Pomeroy St.)
Hammersley Rd. E16 ....43Jc 93
HAMMERSMITH 49Ya 88
Hammersmith Apollo
The Eventim Apollo 50Ya 88
Hammersmith Bri. SW13 ....51Xa 110
Hammersmith Bri. Rd. W6 ....50Ya 88
HAMMERSMITH BROADWAY 49Ya 88
Hammersmith B'way. W6 ....49Ya 88
Hammersmith Emb. W6 ....51Ya 110
Hammersmith Fitness & Squash Cen.
....49Za 88
(off Chalk Hill Rd.)
HAMMERSMITH FLYOVER 50Ya 88
Hammersmith Flyover W6 ....50Ya 88
Hammersmith Gro. W6 ....47Ya 88
Hammersmith Rd. W6 ....49Za 88
W14 ....49Za 88
Hammersmith Ter. W6 ....50Wa 88
Hammerton Cl. DA5: Bexl 62Gd 140
Hammet Cl. UB4: Yead 43Z 85
Hammett St. EC3 ....4K 225 (45Vb 91)
Hamm Moor La. KT15: Add 78N 149
Hammond Av. CR4: Mitc 68Kb 134
Hammond Cl. EN5: Barn 15Ab 30
GU21: Wok 7N 167
TW12: Hamp 67Ca 129
UB6: G'frd 36Fa 66
Hammond Ct. E10 ....33Dc 72
(off Leyton Grange Est.)
E17 ....29Ac 52
(off Maude Rd.)
RM12: Horn 32Hd 76
SE11 ....7K 229
Hammond End SL2: Farn C 5F 60
Hammond Ho. E14 ....48Cc 92
(off Tiller Rd.)
SE14 ....52Yb 114
(off Lubbock St.)
Hammond Lodge W9 ....43Cb 89
(off Admiral Wlk.)
Hammond Rd. EN1: Enf 12Xb 33
GU21: Wok 7N 167
UB2: S'hall 48Aa 85
Hammonds Cl. RM8: Dag 34Yc 75
Hammonds La. CM13: Gt War 23Xd 58
Hammond St. NW5 ....37Lb 70
Hammond Way SE28 ....45Xc 95
HAM MOOR 77N 149
Hamond Cl. CR2: S Croy 81Rb 177
Hamonde Cl. HA8: Edg 19Ra 29
Hamond Sq. N1 ....1H 219 (40Ub 71)
Ham Pk. Rd. E7 ....38Hc 73
E15 ....38Hc 73
Hampden Av. BR3: Beck 68Ac 136
Hampden Cl. NW1 ....2E 216 (40Mb 70)
SL2: Stoke P 1L 81
Hampden Ct. N10 ....24Jb 50
Hampden Cres. CM14: W'ley 21Yd 58
EN7: Chesh 3Xb 19
Hampden Gurney St.
W1 ....3F 221 (44Hb 89)
Hampden Ho. SW9 ....54Qb 112
(off Overton Rd.)
Hampden La. N17 ....25Vb 51
Hampden Pl. AL2: F'mre 1Ga 14
Hampden Rd. BR3: Beck 68Ac 136
HA3: Hrw W 25Ea 46
KT1: King T 69Qa 131
N8 ....28Qb 50
N10 ....24Jb 50
N17 ....25Wb 51
N19 ....33Mb 70
RM5: Col R 24Dd 56
RM17: Grays 50De 99
SL3: L'ly 48B 82
SL9: Chal P 25A 42
Hampden Sq. N14 ....18Kb 32
Hampden Way N14 ....18Kb 32
WD17: Wat 8U 12
Hampermill La. WD19: Wat 19V 26
Hampshire Av. SL1: Slou 3G 80
Hampshire Cl. N18 ....22Xb 51
Hampshire Ct. KT15: Add 78L 149
Hampshire Gdns. SS17: Linf 7J 101
Hampshire Hog La. W6 ....50Xa 88
Hampshire Ho. SL9: Chal P 22A 42
Hampshire Rd. N22 ....24Pb 50
RM11: Horn 28Qd 57
Hampshire St. NW5 ....37Mb 70
Hampson Way SW8 ....53Pb 112
HAMPSTEAD 35Fb 69
Hampstead Av. IG8: Wfd G 24Qc 54
Hampstead Cl. AL2: Brick W 3Ba 13
SE28 ....46Xc 95
Hampstead Gdns. NW11 ....30Cb 49
RM6: Chad H 29Xc 55
HAMPSTEAD GARDEN SUBURB 29Eb 49
Hampstead Ga. NW3 ....36Eb 69
Hampstead Golf Course 31Fb 69
Hampstead Grn. NW3 ....36Gb 69
Hampstead Gro. NW3 ....34Eb 69
Hampstead Heath 33Fb 69
Hampstead Hgts. N2 ....27Eb 49
Hampstead High St. NW3 ....35Fb 69
Hampstead Hill Gdns. NW3 ....35Fb 69
Hampstead Ho. NW1 ....4B 216
Hampstead La. N6 ....32Fb 69
NW3 ....32Fb 69
Hampstead Lodge NW1 ....7D 214
Hampstead M. BR3: Beck 70Dc 136
Hampstead Mus. 35Fb 69
(off New End Sq.)
Hampstead Rd. NW1 ....1B 216 (40Lb 70)
Hampstead Sq. NW3 ....34Eb 69
Hampstead Theatre 38Fb 69
Hampstead Wlk. E3 ....39Bc 72
Hampstead Way NW11 ....29Bb 49
Hampstead W. NW6 ....37Cb 69
HAMPTON 67Da 129
Hampton & Richmond Borough FC
....67Da 129
Hampton Bus. Pk. TW13: Hanw 62Aa 129
Hampton Cl. GU21: Knap 1G 186
N11 ....22Kb 50
NW6 ....41Cb 89
RM16: Chaf H 48Yd 98
SW20 ....66Ya 132
WD6: Bore 15Sa 29
HAMPTON COURT 70Ga 130
HAMPTON COURT 69Ga 130
Hampton Ct. N1 ....37Rb 71
N22 ....25Lb 50
SE14 ....52Ac 114
(off Batavia Rd.)
SE16 ....45Zb 92
(off King & Queen Wharf)
Hampton Ct. Av. KT8: E Mos 72Fa 152
Hampton Ct. Bri. KT8: E Mos 70Ga 130
Hampton Ct. Cres. KT8: E Mos 69Fa 130
Hampton Ct. Est. KT7: T Ditt 70Ga 130
Hampton Ct. M. KT8: E Mos 70Ga 130
(off Feltham Av.)
Hampton Court Palace 70Ha 130
Hampton Court Palace Golf Course
....71La 152
Hampton Ct. Pde. KT8: E Mos 70Ga 130
Hampton Ct. Rd. KT1: Hamp W 69Ha 130
KT8: E Mos 69Ha 130
TW12: E Mos, Hamp 68Ea 130
Hampton Ct. Way KT7: T Ditt 75Ga 152
KT8: E Mos 70Ga 130
KT10: T Ditt 75Ga 152
Hampton Cres. DA12: Grav'nd 1G 144
Hampton Golf Course 62Ca 129
Hampton Grange BR1: Brom 66Lc 137
Hampton Gro. KT17: Ewe 83Va 174
HAMPTON HILL 64Ea 130
Hampton Hill Bus. Pk.
TW12: Hamp H 64Ea 130
(off High St.)
Hampton Hill Playhouse Theatre
....64Ea 130
Hampton Ho. DA7: Bex 54Dd 118
(off Erith Rd.)
SW8 ....52Lb 112
(off Ascalon St.)
Hampton La. TW13: Hanw 63Aa 129
Hampton Mead IG10: Lough 13Rc 36
Hampton M. EN3: Enf H 13Yb 34
NW10 ....41Ta 87
WD23: B Hea 18Ea 28
Hampton Open Air Pool 66Ea 130
Hampton Ri. HA3: Kenton 30Na 47
Hampton Rd. CR0: C'don 72Sb 157
E4 ....22Bc 52
E7 ....36Kc 73
E11 ....32Fc 73
HA7: Stan 20Ga 28
IG1: Ilf 35Sc 74
KT4: Wor Pk 75Wa 154
RH1: Redh 10P 207
TW2: Twick 62Fa 130
TW11: Tedd 64Fa 130
TW12: Hamp H 64Fa 130
Hampton Rd. E. TW13: Hanw 63Ba 129
Hampton Rd. Ind. Pk.
CR0: C'don 72Sb 157
Hampton Rd. W. TW13: Hanw 62Aa 129
Hampton Sports & Fitness Cen. 64Ca 129
Hampton St. SE1 ....6C 230 (49Rb 91)
SE17 ....6C 230 (49Rb 91)
HAMPTON WICK 67La 130
Hampton Youth Project (Sports Hall)
....65Ba 129
Ham Ridings TW10: Ham 64Pa 131
HAMSEY GREEN 88Yb 178
Hamsey Grn. Gdns.
CR6: W'ham 88Xb 177
Hamsey Way CR2: Sande 87Xb 177
Hamshades Cl. DA15: Sidc 62Vc 139
Hamston Ho. W8 ....48Db 89
(off Kensington Ct. Pl.)
Ham St. TW10: Ham 60Ka 108
Ham Vw. CR0: C'don 72Ac 158
Ham Yd. W1 ....4D 222 (45Mb 90)
Hanah Ct. SW19 ....66Za 132
Hanameel St. E16 ....46Kc 93
Hana M. E5 ....35Xb 71
Hanbury Cl. EN8: Chesh 1Ac 20
NW4 ....27Ya 48
Hanbury Ct. HA1: Harr 30Ha 46
Hanbury Dr. E11 ....31Hc 73
N21 ....15Pb 32
TN16: Big H 85Kc 179
Hanbury Ho. E1 ....43Wb 91
(off Hanbury St.)
SW8 ....52Nb 112
(off Regent's Bri. Gdns.)
Hanbury M. N1 ....1E 218 (39Sb 71)
Hanbury Path
GU21: Wok 86F 168
Hanbury Rd. N17 ....26Xb 51
W3 ....47Ra 87
Hanbury St. E1 ....7K 219 (43Vb 91)
Hanbury Wlk. DA5: Bexl 62Gd 140
Hancock Ct. WD6: Bore 11Sa 29
Hancock Nunn Ho. NW3 ....37Hb 69
(off Fellows Rd.)
Hancock Rd. E3 ....41Ec 92
SE19 ....65Tb 135
Hancocks Mt. SL5: S'hill 2B 146
Hancroft Rd. HP3: Hem H 4P 3
Hancross Cl.
AL2: Brick W 2Aa 13
Handa Cl. HP3: Hem H 5B 4
Handa Wlk. N1 ....37Tb 71
Hand Ct. WC1 ....1J 223 (43Pb 90)
Handcroft Rd. CR0: C'don 73Rb 157
Handel Bus. Cen. SW8 ....51Nb 112
Handel Cl. HA8: Edg 23Pa 47
Handel Cres. RM18: Tilb 2C 122
Handel House Mus. 4K 221
Handel Mans. SW13 ....52Ya 110
WC1 ....5G 217
Handel Pde. HA8: Edg 24Qa 47
(off Whitchurch La.)
Handel Pl. NW10 ....37Ta 67
Handel St. WC1 ....5F 217 (42Nb 90)
Handel Way HA8: Edg 24Qa 47
Handen Rd. SE12 ....57Gc 115
Handford Ct. WD25: Wat 6Z 13
Handforth Rd. IG1: Ilf 34Rc 74
SW9 ....52Qb 112
Handley Dr. SE3 ....55Kc 115
Handley Ga. AL2: Brick W 1Ba 13
Handley Gro. NW2 ....34Za 68
Handley Page Rd. SM6: Wall 80Pb 156
Handley Page Way
AL2: Col S 2Ha 14
Handley Rd. E9 ....38Yb 72
Handowe Cl. NW4 ....28Wa 48
Handpost Lodge Gdns.
HP2: Hem H 3D 4
Handside Cl. KT4: Wor Pk 74Za 154
Hands Wlk. E16 ....44Jc 93
Handsworth Av. E4 ....23Fc 53
Handsworth Rd. N17 ....27Tb 51
Handsworth Way WD19: Wat 20W 26
Handtrough Way IG11: Bark 40Rc 74
Handyside St. N1 ....39Mb 70
Hanford Cl. SW18 ....60Cb 111
Hanford Rd. RM15: Avel 46Sd 98
Hanford Row SW19 ....65Ya 132
Hangar Ruding WD19: Wat 20Ba 27
Hangboy Slade IG10: Lough 9Pc 22
Hanger Cl. HP1: Hem H 3K 3
Hanger Ct. GU21: Knap 9J 167
W5 ....42Pa 87
Hanger Grn. W5 ....42Qa 87
HANGER HILL 42Pa 87
Hanger Hill KT13: Weyb 79R 150
HANGER LANE 41Na 87
Hanger La. W5 ....40Na 67
Hanger Va. La. W5 ....44Pa 87
(not continuous)
Hanger Vw. Way W3 ....44Qa 87
Hanging Hill La.
CM13: B'wood, Hut 20De 41
Hanging Sword All. EC4 ....3A 224
Hangrove Hill BR6: Downe 85Rc 180
Hankey Ho. SE1 ....2G 231
Hankey Pl. SE1 ....2G 231 (47Tb 91)
Hankins Ho. SE10 ....48Jc 93
Hankins La. NW7 ....19Ua 30
Hanley Cl. SL4: Wind 3B 102
Hanley Gdns. N4 ....32Pb 70
Hanley Pl. BR3: Beck 66Cc 136
Hanley Rd. N4 ....32Nb 70
Hanmer Wlk. N7 ....33Pb 70
Hannaford Wlk. E3 ....42Dc 92
Hannah Barlow Ho. SW8 ....53Pb 112
Hannah Bldg. E1 ....44Xb 91
(off Watney St.)
Hannah Cl. BR3: Beck 69Ec 136
NW10 ....35Sa 67
Hannah Ct. E15 ....40Hc 73
Hannah Mary Way SE1 ....49Wb 91
Hannah M. SM6: Wall 80Lb 156
Hannards Way IG6: Ilf 22Xc 55
Hannay Ho. SW15 ....58Ab 110
Hannay La. N8 ....31Mb 70
Hannay Wlk. SW16 ....61Mb 134
Hannell Rd. SW6 ....52Ab 110
Hannen Rd. SE27 ....62Rb 135
Hannibal Rd. E1 ....43Yb 92
TW19: Stanw 59M 105
Hannibal Way CR0: Wadd 78Pb 156
Hannington Rd. SW4 ....55Kb 112
Hanno Cl. SM6: Wall 80Mb 156
Hannover Pl. RM1: Rom 29Hd 56
Hanover Av. E16 ....46Jc 93
TW13: Felt 60W 106
Hanover Circ. UB3: Hayes 44S 84
Hanover Cl. RH1: Mers 100Lb 196
SL1: Slou 8L 81
SL4: Wind 3D 102
SM3: Cheam 77Ab 154
TW9: Kew 52Qa 109
TW15: Ashf 63N 127
TW20: Eng G 5M 125
Hanover Ct. E8 ....39Vb 71
(off Stean St.)
EN9: Walt A 5Ec 20
(off Quakers La.)
GU22: Wok 91A 188
HA4: Ruis 34W 64
NW9 ....27Ua 48
SE19 ....66Wb 135
(off Anerley Rd.)
SW15 ....56Va 110
W12 ....46Wa 88
(off Uxbridge Rd.)
WD3: Crox G 15Q 26
Hanover Dr. BR7: Chst 63Sc 138
Hanover Flats W1 ....4J 221
Hanover Gdns. IG6: Ilf 24Sc 54
SE11 ....51Qb 112
WD5: Ab L 2V 12
Hanover Ga. NW1 ....4E 214 (41Gb 89)
SL1: Slou 6E 80
Hanover Ga. Mans.
NW1 ....5E 214 (42Gb 89)
Hanover Grn. HP1: Hem H 4J 3
Hanover Ho. E14 ....46Bc 92
(off Westferry Cir.)
NW8 ....2D 214
SE16 ....47Zb 92
(off Dominion Dr.)
SW9 ....55Qb 112
Hanover Mans. SW2 ....57Qb 112
(off Barnwell Rd.)
Hanover Mead NW11 ....29Ab 48
Hanover Pk. SE15 ....53Wb 113
Hanover Pl. CM14: W'ley 22Xd 58
DA3: Nw A G 75Be 165
E3 ....41Bc 92
WC2 ....3G 223 (44Nb 90)
Hanover Rd. N15 ....28Vb 51
NW10 ....38Ya 68
SW19 ....66Eb 133
Hanover Sq. W1 ....3A 222 (44Kb 90)
Hanover Steps W2 ....3E 220
Hanover St. CR0: C'don 76Rb 157
W1 ....3A 222 (44Kb 90)
Hanover Ter. NW1 ....4F 215 (41Hb 89)
TW7: Isle 53Ja 108
Hanover Ter. M. NW1 ....4E 214 (41Gb 89)
Hanover Trad. Est. N7 ....36Nb 70
Hanover Wlk. AL10: Hat 3B 8
KT13: Weyb 76T 150
Hanover Way DA6: Bex 55Zc 117
SL4: Wind 4D 102
Hanover W. Ind. Est. NW10 ....41Ta 87
Hanover Yd. N1 ....1C 218
Hansa Cl. UB2: S'hall 48Y 85
Hansard M. W14 ....47Za 88
Hansart Way EN2: Enf 11Qb 32
Hanscomb M. SW4 ....56Lb 112
Hans Ct. SW3 ....3F 227
Hans Cres. SW1 ....3F 227 (48Hb 89)
Hanseatic Wlk. EC4 ....5F 225
Hanselin Cl. HA7: Stan 22Ha 46
Hansel Rd. NW6 ....41Cb 89
Hansen Dr. N21 ....15Pb 32
Hanshaw Dr. HA8: Edg 25Ta 47
Hansler Ct. SW19 ....60Ab 110
(off Princes Way)
Hansler Gro. KT8: E Mos 70Fa 130
Hansler Rd. SE22 ....57Vb 113
Hansol Rd. DA6: Bex 57Ad 117
Hansom M. SE11 ....7J 229 (50Pb 90)
Hansom Ter. BR1: Brom 67Kc 137
(off Freelands Gro.)
Hanson Cl. BR3: Beck 65Dc 136
IG10: Lough 12Sc 36
SW12 ....59Kb 112
SW14 ....55Sa 109
UB7: W Dray 48P 83
Hanson Ct. E17 ....30Dc 52
Hanson Dr. IG10: Lough 12Sc 36
Hanson Gdns. UB1: S'hall 47Aa 85
Hanson Grn. IG10: Lough 12Sc 36
Hanson Ho. E1 ....45Wb 91
(off Pinchin St.)
Hanson St. W1 ....7B 216 (43Lb 90)
Hans Pl. SW1 ....3F 227 (48Hb 89)
Hans Rd. SW3 ....3F 227 (48Hb 89)
Hans St. SW1 ....4G 227 (48Hb 89)
Hanway Pl. W1 ....2D 222 (44Mb 90)
Hanway Rd. W7 ....44Fa 86
Hanway St. W1 ....2D 222 (44Mb 90)
HANWELL 46Ha 86
Hanwell Ho. W2 ....43Cb 89
(off Gt. Western Rd.)
HANWORTH 63Z 129
Hanworth Air Pk. Leisure Cen. 61Z 129
Hanworth Ho. SE5 ....52Rb 113
Hanworth La. KT16: Chert 74H 149
Hanworth Rd. RH1: Redh 10P 207
TW3: Houn 60Ba 107
TW4: Houn 60Ba 107
TW12: Hamp 63Ba 129
TW13: Felt 60X 107
TW16: Sun 66W 128
(not continuous)
Hanworth Ter. TW3: Houn 56Da 107
Hanworth Trad. Est. KT16: Chert 74H 149
TW13: Hanw 62Aa 129
Hapgood Cl. UB6: G'frd 36Fa 66
Happy Valley Ind. Est. WD4: K Lan 10B 4
Harad's Pl. E1 ....45Wb 91
Harbans Ct. SL3: Poyle 53G 104
Harben Pde. NW3 ....38Eb 69
(off Finchley Rd.)
Harben Rd. NW6 ....38Eb 69
Harberson Rd. E15 ....39Hc 73
SW12 ....60Kb 112
Harbert Gdns. AL2: Park 10a 13
Harberton Rd. N19 ....32Lb 70
Harbet Rd. E4 ....22Ac 52
N18 ....22Ac 52
W2 ....1C 220 (43Fb 89)
Harbex Cl. DA5: Bexl 59Dd 118
Harbinger Rd. E14 ....49Dc 92
Harbledown Ho. SE1 ....2F 231
Harbledown Pl. BR5: St M Cry 70Yc 139
Harbledown Rd. CR2: Sande 83Wb 177
SW6 ....53Cb 111
Harbord Cl. SE5 ....54Tb 113
Harbord Ho. SE16 ....49Zb 92
(off Cope St.)
Harbord St. SW6 ....53Za 110
Harborne Cl. WD19: Wat 22Y 45
Harborough Av. DA15: Sidc 59Uc 116
Harborough Cl. SL1: Slou 6B 80
Harborough Ho. UB5: N'olt 41Ba 85
(off Taywood Rd.)
Harborough Rd. SW16 ....63Pb 134

Harbour Av.—Harthall La.

Harbour Av. SW10 .53Eb 111
Harbour Cl. CR4: Mitc .67Jb 134
Harbour Club, The
Chelsea .54Eb 111
Harbour Club Notting Hill .43Cb 89
Harbour Ct. WD23: Bush .15Da 27
Harbourer Cl. IG6: Ilf .22Xc 55
Harbourer Rd. IG6: Ilf .22Xc 55
Harbour Exchange Sq. E14 .47Dc 92
Harbourfield Rd.
SM7: Bans .87Db 175
Harbour Quay E14 .46Ec 92
Harbour Reach SW6 .53Eb 111
Harbour Rd. SE5 .55Sb 113
Harbour Vw. DA11: Nflt .57De 121
Harbour Yd. SW10 .53Eb 111
Harbridge Av. SW15 .59Va 110
Harbury Rd. SM5: Cars .81Gb 175
Harbut Rd. SW11 .56Fb 111
Harcombe Rd. N16 .34Ub 71
Harcourt TW19: Wray .58A 104
Harcourt Av. DA15: Sidc .58Yc 117
E12 .35Pc 74
HA8: Edg .20Sa 29
SM6: Wall .77Kb 156
Harcourt Bldgs. EC4 .4K 223
Harcourt Cl. TW7: Isle .55Ja 108
TW20: Egh .65E 126
Harcourt Fld. SM6: Wall .77Kb 156
Harcourt Ho. W1 .2K 221
Harcourt Lodge SM6: Wall .77Kb 156
Harcourt M. RM2: Rom .29Hd 56
Harcourt Rd. CR7: Thor H .72Pb 156
DA6: Bex .56Ad 117
E15 .40Hc 73
N22 .25Mb 50
SE4 .55Bc 114
SL4: Wind .3C 102
SM6: Wall .77Kb 156
SW19 .66Cb 133
WD23: Bush .15Da 27
Harcourt St. W1 .1E 220 (43Gb 89)
Harcourt Ter. SW10 .50Db 89
Harcourt Way RH9: S God .9C 210
Hardcastle Cl. CR0: C'don .72Wb 157
Hardcastle Ho. SE14 .53Ac 114
(off Loring Rd.)
Hardcourts Cl. BR4: W W'ck .76Dc 158
Hardegray Cl. SM2: Sutt .81Cb 175
Hardell Cl. TW20: Egh .64C 126
Hardel Ri. SW2 .60Rb 113
Hardel Wlk. SW2 .59Qb 112
Harden Ct. SE7 .49Nc 94
Harden Farm Cl. CR5: Coul .93Lb 196
Harden Ho. SE5 .54Ub 113
Harden Rd. DA11: Nflt .2B 144
Harden's Manorway SE7 .48Mc 93
(not continuous)
Harders Rd. SE15 .54Xb 113
Hardess St. SE24 .55Sb 113
Hardie Cl. NW10 .36Ta 67
Hardie Rd. RM10: Dag .34Ed 76
SS17: Stan H .1M 101
Harding Cl. CR0: C'don .76Vb 157
SE17 .51Sb 113
WD25: Wat .5Y 13
Harding Dr. RM8: Dag .32Ad 75
Hardinge Cl. UB8: Hil .43R 84
Hardinge Cres. SE18 .48Sc 94
Hardinge La. E1 .44Yb 92
(not continuous)
Hardinge Rd. N18 .23Ub 51
NW10 .39Xa 68
Hardinge St. E1 .45Yb 92
(Johnson St.)
E1 .44Yb 92
(Steel's La.)
Harding Ho. SW13 .51Xa 110
(off Wyatt Dr.)
UB3: Hayes .44X 85
Harding Rd. DA7: Bex .54Bd 117
KT18: Eps D .91Ua 194
RM16: Grays .8C 100
Harding's Cl. KT2: King T .67Pa 131
Hardings Cl. HP3: Hem H .5K 3
SL0: Iver H .41E 82
Hardings La. SE20 .65Zb 136
Harding Spur SL3: L'ly .51B 104
Hardings Row SL0: Iver H .41E 82
Hardingstone Ct. EN8: Walt C .6Bc 20
Hardington NW1 .38Jb 70
(off Belmont St.)
Hardley Cres. RM11: Horn .28Md 57
Hardman Rd. KT2: King T .68Na 131
SE7 .50Kc 93
Hardres Ter. BR5: Orp .74Zc 161
Hardwick Cl. HA7: Stan .22La 46
KT22: Oxs .87Ea 172
Hardwick Ct. DA8: Erith .51Fd 118
Hardwick Cres. DA2: Dart .58Rd 119
Hardwicke Av. TW5: Hest .53Ca 107
Hardwicke M. WC1 .4J 217
Hardwicke Pl. AL2: Lon C .9H 7
Hardwicke Rd. N13 .23Nb 50
RH2: Reig .5J 207
TW10: Ham .63La 130
W4 .49Ta 87
Hardwicke St. IG11: Bark .39Sc 74
Hardwick Grn. W13 .43Ka 86
Hardwick Ho. DA2: Dart .58Sd 120
(off Stone Ho. La.)
NW8 .5E 214
Hardwick La. KT16: Lyne .73E 148
Hardwick Pl. SW16 .66Lb 134
Hardwick Rd. RH1: Redh .8M 207
Hardwicks Sq. SW18 .57Cb 111
Hardwick St. EC1 .4A 218 (41Qb 90)
Hardwidge St. SE1 .1H 231 (47Ub 91)
Hardy Av. DA1: Dart .59Ld 119
DA11: Nflt .1A 144
E16 .46Jc 93
HA4: Ruis .36X 65
Hardy Cl. EN5: Barn .16Ab 30
HA5: Pinn .31Z 65
SE16 .47Zb 92
SL1: Slou .6E 80
Hardy Cotts. SE10 .51Fc 115
Hardy Ct. DA8: Erith .52Hd 118
SW17 .62Fb 133
(off Grosvenor Way)
W3 .48Sa 87
(off Bollo Bri. Rd.)
Hardy Gro. DA1: Dart .56Qd 119
Hardy Ho. SW4 .59Lb 112
SW18 .59Db 111
Hardying Ho. E17 .28Ac 52
Hardy M. UB8: Uxb .39L 63
Hardy Pas. N22 .25Pb 50
Hardy Rd. E4 .23Bc 52
HP2: Hem H .1P 3
SE3 .52Hc 115
SW19 .66Db 133
Hardy's M. KT8: E Mos .70Ga 130
Hardy's Yd. TN13: Dun G .93Gd 202
Hardy Way EN2: Enf .11Qb 32
Hare & Billet Rd. SE3 .53Fc 115
Harebell Dr. E6 .43Qc 94
Harebell Hill KT11: Cobh .86Z 171
Harebell Way RM3: Rom .24Md 57
Harebreaks, The
WD24: Wat .8W 12
Harecastle Cl. UB4: Yead .42Aa 85
Hare Ct. EC4 .3K 223
Harecourt Rd. N1 .37Sb 71
Hare Cres. WD25: Wat .4W 12
Harecroft KT22: Fet .96Da 191
Harecroft La. UB10: Ick .34S 64
Haredale Ho. SE16 .47Wb 91
(off East La.)
Haredale Rd. SE24 .56Sb 113
Haredon Cl. SE23 .59Zb 114
HAREFIELD .25L 43
Harefield KT10: Hin W .76Ga 152
Harefield Av. SM2: Cheam .81Ab 174
Harefield Cl. EN2: Enf .11Qb 32
Harefield Grn. NW7 .23Ya 48
Harefield M. SE4 .55Bc 114
Harefield Rd. DA14: Sidc .62Zc 139
N8 .29Mb 50
SE4 .55Bc 114
SW16 .66Pb 134
UB8: Uxb .38L 63
WD3: Rick .19M 25
Hare Hall La. RM2: Rom .28Kd 57
Harehatch La. SL1: Burn .2C 60
SL2: Burn, Farn C .2C 60
Hare Hill KT15: Add .79G 148
Hare Hill Cl. GU22: Pyr .87J 169
Harelands Cl. GU21: Wok .9N 167
Harelands La. GU21: Wok .10N 167
(not continuous)
Hare La. AL10: Hat .2D 8
KT10: Clay .78Fa 152
Hare Marsh E2 .42Wb 91
Harendon KT20: Tad .93Ya 194
Harepark Cl. HP1: Hem H .1H 3
Harepit Cl. CR2: S Croy .80Rb 157
Hare Pl. EC4 .3A 224
Hare Row E2 .40Xb 71
Hares Bank CR0: New Ad .82Fc 179
Haresfield Rd. RM10: Dag .37Cd 76
Harestone Dr. CR3: Cat'm .96Vb 197
Harestone Hill CR3: Cat'm .98Vb 197
Harestone La. CR3: Cat'm .97Ub 197
Harestone Valley Rd.
CR3: Cat'm .98Ub 197
Hare St. SE18 .48Qc 94
Hare Ter. RM20: Grays .50Zd 99
Hare Wlk. N1 .2J 219 (40Ub 71)
(not continuous)
Harewood WD3: Rick .14K 25
(not continuous)
Harewood Av. NW1 .6E 214 (42Gb 89)
UB5: N'olt .38Ba 65
Harewood Cl. RH2: Reig .3L 207
UB5: N'olt .38Ba 65
Harewood Ct. CR6: W'ham .90Ac 178
Harewood Dr. IG5: Ilf .26Pc 54
Harewood Gdns. CR2: Sande .87Xb 177
Harewood Hill CM16: They B .7Uc 22
Harewood Pl. SL1: Slou .8L 81
W1 .3A 222 (44Kb 90)
Harewood Rd. CM15: Pil H .16Xd 40
CR2: S Croy .79Ub 157
SW19 .65Gb 133
TW7: Isle .52Ha 108
WD19: Wat .20X 27
Harewood Row NW1 .7E 214 (43Gb 89)
Harewood Ter. UB2: S'hall .49Ba 85
Harfield Gdns. SE5 .55Ub 113
Harfield Rd. TW16: Sun .68Z 129
Harfleur Ct. SE11 .6B 230
Harford Cl. E4 .17Dc 34
Harford Dr. WD17: Wat .10U 12
Harford Ho. SE5 .51Sb 113
(off Bethwin Rd.)
W11 .43Bb 89
Harford M. N19 .34Mb 70
Harford Rd. E4 .17Dc 34
Harford St. E1 .42Ac 92
Harford Wlk. N2 .28Fb 49
Harfst Way BR8: Swan .67Ed 140
Hargood Cl. HA3: Kenton .30Na 47
Hargood Rd. SE3 .53Lc 115
Hargrave Mans. N19 .33Mb 70
Hargrave Pk. N19 .33Lb 70
Hargrave Pl. N7 .36Mb 70
Hargrave Rd. N19 .33Lb 70
Hargraves Ho. W12 .45Xa 88
(off White City Est.)
Hargreaves Av. EN7: Chesh .3Xb 19
Hargreaves Cl. EN7: Chesh .3Xb 19
Hargwyne St. SW9 .55Pb 112
Hari Cl. UB5: N'olt .36Da 65
Haringey Independent Cinema .28Sb 51
Haringey Pk. N8 .30Nb 50
Haringey Pas. N8 .28Qb 50
Haringey Rd. N8 .28Nb 50
Harington Ter. N9 .20Tb 33
N18 .20Tb 33
Harkett Cl. HA3: W'stone .26Ha 46
Harkett Ct. HA3: W'stone .26Ha 46
Harkness EN7: Chesh .1Xb 19
Harkness Cl. KT17: Eps D .88Ya 174
RM3: Rom .22Pd 57
Harkness Ct. SM1: Sutt .74Db 155
(off Cleeve Way)
Harkness Ho. E1 .44Wb 91
(off Christian St.)
Harkness Rd. HP2: Hem H .1M 3
Harland Av. CR0: C'don .76Vb 157
DA15: Sidc .62Tc 138
Harland Cl. SW19 .69Db 133
Harland Rd. SE12 .60Jc 115
Harlands Gro. BR6: Farnb .77Rc 160
Harlech Gdns. HA5: Pinn .31Z 65
TW5: Hest .51Y 107
Harlech Rd. N14 .20Nb 32
Harlech Rd. WD5: Ab L .3W 12
Harlech Twr. W3 .47Sa 87
Harlequin, The WD17: Wat .14Y 27
(not continuous)
Harlequin Av. TW8: Bford .51Ja 108
Harlequin Cl. IG11: Bark .42Wc 95
TW7: Isle .57Ga 108
UB4: Yead .43Z 85
Harlequin Ct. E1 .45Wb 91
(off Thomas More St.)
NW10 .37Ta 67
(off Mitchellbrook Way)
W5 .45La 86
Harlequin Ho. DA18: Erith .48Ad 95
(off Kale Rd.)
Harlequin Rd. TW11: Tedd .66Ka 130
Harlequins RUFC .59Ga 108
Harlequin Theatre & Cinema .5P 207
Harlescott Rd. SE15 .56Zb 114
HARLESDEN .40Va 68
Harlesden Cl. RM3: Rom .23Pd 57
Harlesden Gdns. NW10 .39Va 68
Harlesden La. NW10 .39Wa 68
Harlesden Plaza NW10 .40Va 68
Harlesden Rd. AL1: St A .2E 6
NW10 .39Wa 68
RM3: Rom .23Pd 57
Harlesden Wlk. RM3: Rom .24Pd 57
Harleston Cl. E5 .33Yb 72
Harle Way RM13: Rain .42Ld 97
Harley Cl. HA0: Wemb .37Ma 67
Harley Ct. E11 .31Jc 73
HA1: Harr .28Fa 46
N20 .20Eb 31
Harley Cres. HA1: Harr .28Fa 46
Harleyford BR1: Brom .67Kc 137
Harleyford Ct. SE11 .51Pb 112
(off Harleyford Rd.)
Harleyford Mnr. W3 .46Sa 87
(off Edgecote Cl.)
Harleyford Rd. SE11 .51Pb 112
Harleyford St. SE11 .51Qb 112
Harley Gdns. BR6: Orp .77Uc 160
SW10 .7A 226 (50Eb 89)
Harley Gro. E3 .41Bc 92
Harley Ho. E11 .31Fc 73
E14 .44Bc 92
(off Frances Wharf)
NW1 .6J 215
WD6: Bore .12Ra 29
(off Brook Cl.)
Harley Pl. W1 .1K 221 (43Kb 90)
Harley Rd. HA1: Harr .28Fa 46
NW3 .38Fb 69
NW10 .40Ua 68
Harley St. W1 .6K 215 (42Kb 90)
Harley Vs. NW10 .40Ua 68
Harlie Ct. SE6 .58Cc 114
Harling Ct. SW11 .54Hb 111
Harlinger St. SE18 .48Nc 94
HARLINGTON .51T 106
Harlington Cl. UB3: Harl .52S 106
HARLINGTON CORNER .53T 106
Harlington Rd. DA7: Bex .55Ad 117
UB8: Hil .41Q 84
Harlington Rd. E. TW13: Felt .59X 107
TW14: Felt .59X 107
Harlington Rd. W. TW14: Felt .58X 107
Harlington Sports Cen., The .49T 84
(off Pinkwell La.)
Harlow Ct. RH2: Reig .6M 207
(off Wray Comn. Rd.)
Harlow Gdns. RM5: Col R .23Ed 56
Harlow Mans. IG11: Bark .38Rc 74
(off Whiting Av.)
Harlow Rd. N13 .20Tb 33
RM13: Rain .39Hd 76
Harlton Ct. EN9: Walt A .6Hc 21
Harlyn Dr. HA5: Eastc .27X 45
Harlynwood SE5 .52Sb 113
(off Wyndham Rd.)
Harman Av. DA11: Grav'nd .4D 144
IG8: Wfd G .23Hc 53
Harman Cl. E4 .21Fc 53
NW2 .34Ab 68
SE1 .50Wb 91
Harman Dr. DA15: Sidc .58Vc 117
NW2 .34Ab 68
Harman Pl. CR8: Purl .83Rb 177
Harman Ri. IG3: Ilf .35Uc 74
Harman Rd. EN1: Enf .15Vb 33
Harmer Rd. DA10: Swans .58Be 121
Harmer St. DA12: Grav'nd .8E 122
HARMONDSWORTH .51M 105
Harmondsworth La.
UB7: Harm, Sip .51N 105
Harmondsworth Moor Waterside .51K 105
Harmondsworth Moor Waterside Vis. Cen.
.51K 105
Harmondsworth Rd. UB7: W Dray .50N 83
Harmon Ho. SE8 .49Bc 92
Harmonia Ct. WD17: Wat .10W 12
Harmont Ho. W1 .1K 221
Harmony Apartments BR1: Brom .68Jc 137
(off High St.)
Harmony Cl. NW11 .29Ab 48
(not continuous)
SM6: Wall .81Nb 176
Harmony Pl. SE1 .50Vb 91
SE8 .51Dc 114
(off Dancers Way)
Harmony Ter. HA2: Harr .32Da 65
Harmony Way BR1: Brom .68Jc 137
NW4 .28Ya 48
Harmood Gro. NW1 .38Kb 70
Harmood Ho. NW1 .38Kb 70
(off Harmood St.)
Harmood Pl. NW1 .38Kb 70
Harmood St. NW1 .37Kb 70
Harmsworth M. SE11 .4B 230 (48Qb 90)
Harmsworth St. SE17 .50Rb 91
Harmsworth Way N20 .18Ab 30
Harnetts Cl. BR8: Crock .73Fd 162
Harold Av. DA17: Belv .50Bd 95
UB3: Hayes .48V 84
Harold Campbell Ct. DA1: Dart .59Md 119
(off North St.)
Harold Ct. EN8: Walt C .6Bc 20
(off Holdbrook Sth.)
RM3: Hrld W .24Rd 57
SE16 .47Zb 92
(off Christopher Cl.)
Harold Ct. Rd. RM3: Hrld W .23Rd 57
Harold Cres. EN9: Walt A .4Ec 20
Harold Est. SE1 .4J 231 (48Ub 91)
Harold Gibbons Ct. SE7 .51Lc 115
HAROLD HILL .23Pd 57
Harold Hill Ind. Est. RM3: Rom .24Md 57
Harold Ho. E2 .40Zb 72
(off Mace St.)
Harold Laski Ho. EC1 .4C 218
Harold Maddison Ho. SE17 .7C 230
Harold Mugford Ter. E6 .44Qc 94
(off Pearl Cl.)
HAROLD PARK .23Rd 57
Harold Pinter Theatre .5D 222
Harold Pl. SE11 .50Qb 90
Harold Rd. DA2: Hawl .63Pd 141
E4 .21Ec 52
E11 .32Gc 73
E13 .39Kc 73
IG8: Wfd G .25Jc 53
N8 .29Pb 50
N15 .29Vb 51
NW10 .41Ta 87
SE19 .66Tb 135
SM1: Sutt .77Fb 155
Harold's Bridge .5Ec 20
Haroldstone Rd. E17 .29Zb 52
Harold Vw. RM3: Hrld W .26Pd 57
Harold Wilson Ho. SE28 .46Xc 95
SW6 .51Bb 111
(off Clem Attlee Ct.)
HAROLD WOOD .25Pd 57
Harold Wood Hall RM3: Rom .25Md 57
(off Neave Cres.)
Harp All. EC4 .2B 224 (44Rb 91)
Harp Bus. Cen., The NW2 .33Wa 68
Harpenden Rd. AL3: St A .1C 6
E12 .33Lc 73
SE27 .62Rb 135
Harpenmead Point NW2 .33Bb 69
Harper Cl. N14 .15Lb 32
RM16: Chaf H .50Yd 98
Harper Ho. SW9 .55Rb 113
Harper La. WD7: R'lett, Shenl .4Ha 14
Harper M. SW17 .62Eb 133
Harper Rd. E6 .44Pc 94
SE1 .3D 230 (48Sb 91)
Harpers Gym .8H 7
Harper's Yd. N17 .25Vb 51
Harpers Yd. TW7: Isle .54Ga 108
(off Rennels Way)
Harpesford Av. GU25: Vir W .1M 147
Harp Island Cl. NW10 .33Ta 67
Harp La. EC3 .5H 225 (45Ub 91)
Harpley Sq. E1 .42Zb 92
Harpour Rd. IG11: Bark .37Sc 74
Harp Rd. W7 .42Ha 86
Harpsden St. SW11 .53Jb 112
Harps Oak La. RH1: Mers .97Hb 195
Harpswood Cl. CR5: Coul .94Lb 196
Harpur M. WC1 .7H 217 (43Pb 90)
Harpurs KT20: Tad .93Ya 194
Harpur St. WC1 .7H 217 (43Pb 90)
Harraden Rd. SE3 .53Lc 115
Harrap Chase RM17: Grays .50Be 99
Harrap St. E14 .45Ec 92
Harrier Av. E11 .30Kc 53
Harrier Cen., The .79Ta 153
Harrier Cl. HP3: Hem H .7M 3
RM12: Horn .37Kd 77
Harrier Ct. TW4: Houn .55Aa 107
Harrier M. SE28 .47Tc 94
Harrier Rd. NW9 .26Ua 48
Harriers Cl. W5 .45Na 87
Harrier Way E6 .43Pc 94
EN9: Walt A .6Jc 21
Harriescourt EN9: Walt A .4Jc 21
Harries Rd. UB4: Yead .42Y 85
Harriet Cl. E8 .39Wb 71
Harriet Gdns. CR0: C'don .75Wb 157
Harriet Ho. HP3: Hem H .7N 3
SW6 .52Db 111
(off Wandon Rd.)
Harriet M. DA16: Well .54Xc 117
Harriet St. SW1 .2G 227 (47Hb 89)
Harriet Tubman Cl. SW2 .59Pb 112
Harriet Wlk. SW1 .2G 227 (47Hb 89)
Harriet Walker Way WD3: Rick .17H 25
Harriet Way WD23: Bush .17Fa 28
HARRINGAY .29Rb 51
Harringay Gdns. N8 .28Rb 51
Harringay Rd. N15 .29Rb 51
(not continuous)
Harrington Cl. CR0: Bedd .75Nb 156
NW10 .34Ta 67
SL4: Wind .6D 102
Harrington Ct. CR0: C'don .75Tb 157
SW7 .5C 226
W10 .41Bb 89
Harrington Cres. RM16: N Stif .46Zd 99
Harrington Gdns. SW7 .6A 226 (49Db 89)
Harrington Hill E5 .32Xb 71
Harrington Ho. NW1 .3B 216
UB10: Ick .35R 64
Harrington Rd. E11 .32Gc 73
SE25 .70Wb 135
SW7 .5B 226 (49Fb 89)
Harrington Sq. NW1 .1B 216 (40Lb 70)
Harrington St. NW1 .2B 216 (40Lb 70)
(not continuous)
Harrington Way SE18 .48Mc 93
Harriott Cl. SE10 .49Hc 93
Harriott Ho. E1 .43Yb 92
(off Jamaica St.)
Harriott's Cl. KT21: Asht .92La 192
Harriott's La. KT21: Asht .91La 192
Harris Bldgs. E1 .44Wb 91
(off Burslem St.)
Harris Cl. DA11: Nflt .2B 144
EN2: Enf .11Rb 33
N11 .22Hb 49
RM3: Rom .24Nd 57
TW3: Houn .53Ca 107
Harris Ct. HA9: Wemb .34Pa 67
Harris Gdns. SL1: Slou .7G 80
Harris Ho. E3 .41Cc 92
(off Alfred St.)
E11 .32Gc 73
SW9 .55Qb 112
(off St James's Cres.)
Harris La. WD7: Shenl .6Qa 15
Harris Lodge SE6 .60Ec 114
Harrison Av. DA3: Lfield .69Be 143
Harrison Cl. CM13: Hut .15Fe 41
HA6: Nwood .23S 44
N20 .18Gb 31
RH2: Reig .7K 207
RM7: Mawney .27Cd 56
Harrison Ct. E18 .25Jc 53
(off Queen Mary Av.)
Harrison Dr. BR1: Brom .70Qc 138
Harrison Ho. E1 .44Xb 91
SE17 .7F 231
Harrison Rd. EN9: Walt A .7Ec 20
NW10 .39Ta 67
RM10: Dag .37Dd 76
TN15: Bor G .92Be 205
Harrisons Ct. SE14 .51Zb 114
(off Myers La.)
Harrison's Ri. CR0: Wadd .76Rb 157
Harrison St. WC1 .4G 217 (41Nb 90)
Harrisons Wharf RM19: Purf .50Qd 97
Harrison Wlk. EN8: Chesh .2Zb 20
Harrison Way SL1: Slou .6B 80
TN13: S'oaks .94Jd 202
TW17: Shep .71R 150
Harris Rd. DA7: Bex .53Ad 117
RM9: Dag .36Bd 75
WD25: Wat .7W 12
Harris Sports Cen. .57Yb 114
Harris St. E17 .31Bc 72
SE5 .52Tb 113
Harris Way TW16: Sun .67U 128
Harrod Ct. NW9 .28Sa 47
Harrods .3F 227 (48Hb 89)
Harrogate Ct. N11 .23Jb 50
SE12 .59Jc 115
SE26 .62Wb 135
(off Droitwich Cl.)
SL3: L'ly .50C 82
Harrogate Rd. WD19: Wat .20Y 27
Harrold Ho. NW3 .38Fb 69
Harrold Rd. RM8: Dag .36Xc 75
Harrovian Bus. Village HA1: Harr .31Ga 66
HARROW .30Ga 46
Harrow Arts Cen. .24Ca 45
Harrow Av. EN1: Enf .16Vb 33
Harroway Mnr. KT22: Fet .94Ha 192
Harroway Rd. SW11 .54Fb 111
Harrow Borough FC .35Ba 65
Harrow Bottom Rd. GU25: Vir W .72B 148
Harrowby Gdns. DA11: Nflt .1A 144
Harrowby Ho. W1 .2F 221
Harrowby St. W1 .2E 220 (44Gb 89)
Harrow Cl. KT9: Chess .80Ma 153
KT15: Add .75K 149
RM11: Horn .32Kd 77
Harrow Club W10 .45Za 88
Harrow Cres. RM3: Rom .24Kd 57
Harrowdene Cl. HA0: Wemb .35Ma 67
Harrowdene Gdns. TW11: Tedd .65Ja 130
Harrowdene Rd. HA0: Wemb .34Ma 67
Harrow Dr. N9 .18Vb 33
RM11: Horn .30Kd 57
Harrowes Meade HA8: Edg .20Qa 29
Harrow Flds. Gdns. HA1: Harr .34Ga 66
Harrow Gdns. BR6: Chels .77Xc 161
CR6: W'ham .88Bc 178
KT8: E Mos .69Fa 130
Harrowgate Ho. E9 .37Zb 72
Harrowgate Rd. E9 .37Ac 72
Harrow Grn. E11 .34Gc 73
Harrow Hill Golf Course .31Ha 66
Harrow Ho. RH1: Redh .4A 208
(off Old School Cl.)
Harrow La. E14 .45Dc 92
RM14: Bulp .36Ee 79
Harrow Leisure Cen. .27Ha 46
Harrow Lodge NW8 .5B 214
Harrow Mnr. Way SE2 .46Yc 95
SE28 .45Yc 95
Harrow Mkt. SL3: L'ly .48C 82
Harrow Mus. .27Ea 46
HARROW ON THE HILL .32Ga 66
Harrow Pk. HA1: Harr .33Ga 66
Harrow Pl. E1 .2J 225 (44Ub 91)
HARROW ROAD .38Ra 67
Harrow Rd. CR6: W'ham .87Bc 178
E6 .39Nc 74
E11 .34Gc 73
HA0: Wemb .35Ha 66
HA9: Wemb .36Qa 67
IG1: Ilf .35Sc 74
IG11: Bark .39Uc 74
NW10 .41Xa 88
SL3: L'ly .48B 82
SM5: Cars .79Gb 155
TN14: Knock .87Ad 181
TW14: Bedf .60Q 106
W2 .1A 220 (43Eb 89)
(not continuous)
W9 .42Ab 88
W10 .42Ab 88
Harrow Rd. Bri. W2 .7A 214 (43Eb 89)
Harrow Safari Cinema .29Ha 46
Harrow School Golf Course .33Ha 66
Harrow Sports Hall .31Ja 66
Harrow St. NW1 .7E 214
Harrow Vw. HA1: Harr .26Ea 46
HA2: Harr .26Ea 46
UB3: Hayes .44W 84
UB10: Hil .41S 84
Harrow Vw. Rd. W5 .42Ka 86
Harrow Way TW17: Shep .68S 128
WD19: Wat .20Aa 27
HARROW WEALD .25Ga 46
Harrow Weald Lawn Tennis Club .25Ga 46
Harrow Weald Pk. HA3: Hrw W .23Fa 46
Harry Cl. CR0: C'don .72Sb 157
Harry Day M. SE27 .62Sb 135
Harry Hinkins Ho. SE17 .7E 230
Harry Lambourn Ho. SE15 .52Xb 113
(off Gervase St.)
Harrys Pl. RM15: S Ock .43Zd 99
Harry Zeital Way E5 .33Yb 72
Harston Dr. EN3: Enf L .10Cc 20
Harston Wlk. E3 .42Dc 92
Hartcliff Ct. W7 .47Ha 86
Hart Cl. CR0: C'don .76Rb 157
RH1: Blet .5L 209
Hart Cnr. RM20: Grays .50Zd 99
Hart Ct. E6 .38Qc 74
Hart Cres. IG7: Chig .22Vc 55
Hartcroft Cl. HP3: Hem H .3B 4
Hart Dyke Cres. BR8: Swan .69Fd 140
Hart Dyke Rd. BR5: Orp .75Zc 161
BR8: Swan .69Fd 140
Harte Rd. TW3: Houn .54Ba 107
Hartfield Av. UB5: N'olt .40X 65
WD6: E'tree .14Qa 29
Hartfield Cl. WD6: E'tree .15Qa 29
Hartfield Cres.
BR4: W W'ck .76Jc 159
SW19 .66Bb 133
Hartfield Gro. SE20 .67Yb 136
Hartfield Ho. UB5: N'olt .40X 65
(off Hartfield Av.)
Hartfield Pl. DA11: Nflt .59Fe 121
Hartfield Rd. BR4: W W'ck .77Jc 159
KT9: Chess .78Ma 153
SW19 .66Bb 133
Hartfield Ter. E3 .40Cc 72
Hartford Av. HA3: Kenton .27Ja 46
Hartforde Rd. WD6: Bore .12Qa 29
Hartford Rd. DA5: Bexl .58Cd 118
KT19: Ewe .79Ra 153
Hart Gro. UB1: S'hall .43Ca 85
W5 .46Qa 87
Hart Gro. Ct. W5 .46Qa 87
Harthall La. HP3: Hem H .9D 4
WD4: K Lan .10B 4

Hartham Cl.—Hawkshill Cl.

Hartham Cl. N7 ... 36Nb 70
TW7: Isle ... 53Ja 108
Hartham Rd. N7 ... 36Nb 70
N17 ... 26Vb 51
TW7: Isle ... 53Ha 108
Harting Rd. SE9 ... 62Nc 138
Hartington Cl. BR6: Farnb ... 78Sc 160
HA1: Harr ... 35Ga 66
RH2: Reig ... 4J 207
Hartington Ct. SW8 ... 53Nb 112
W4 ... 52Ra 109
Hartington Ho. SW1 ... 7E 228
Hartington Rd. E16 ... 44Kc 93
E17 ... 30Ac 52
SW8 ... 53Nb 112
TW1: Twick ... 59Ka 108
UB2: S'hall ... 48Aa 85
W4 ... 52Ra 109
W13 ... 45Ka 86
Hartismere Rd. SW6 ... 52Bb 111
Hartlake Rd. E9 ... 37Zb 72
Hartland NW1 ... 1C 216
Hartland Cl. HA8: Edg ... 19Qa 29
KT15: New H ... 82L 169
N21 ... 16Sb 33
SL1: Slou ... 6H 81
Hartland Ct. *N11* ... *22Hb 49*
(off Hartland Rd.)
Hartland Dr. HA4: Ruis ... 34X 65
HA8: Edg ... 19Qa 29
Hartland Rd. CM16: Epp ... 3Wc 23
E15 ... 38Hc 73
EN8: Chesh ... 2Zb 20
KT15: Add ... 80J 149
N11 ... 22Hb 49
NW1 ... 38Kb 70
NW6 ... 40Bb 69
RM12: Horn ... 33Jd 76
SM4: Mord ... 73Cb 155
TW7: Isle ... 55Ja 108
TW12: Hamp H ... 63Da 129
Hartlands, The TW5: Cran ... 51X 107
Hartlands Cl. DA5: Bexl ... 58Bd 117
Hartland Way CR0: C'don ... 76Ac 158
SM4: Mord ... 73Bb 155
Hartlepool Ct. E16 ... 46Rc 94
HARTLEY ... 71Ae 165
Hartley Av. E6 ... 39Nc 74
NW7 ... 22Va 48
Hartley Bottom Rd.
DA3: Hartl, Lfield ... 70Ee 143
DA3: Nw A G ... 79Ce 165
TN15: Ash ... 79Ce 165
Hartley Cl. BR1: Brom ... 68Pc 138
NW7 ... 22Va 48
SL3: Stoke P ... 9N 61
Hartley Copse SL4: Old Win ... 8L 103
Hartley Down CR8: Purl ... 87Pb 176
Hartley Farm CR8: Purl ... 87Pb 176
HARTLEY GREEN ... 71Ae 165
HARTLEY HILL ... 74Ce 165
Hartley Hill CR8: Purl ... 87Pb 176
DA3: Hartl ... 74Ce 165
Hartley Ho. SE1 ... 5K 231
Hartley Old Rd. CR8: Purl ... 87Pb 176
Hartley Rd. CR0: C'don ... 73Sb 157
DA3: Lfield ... 68Ae 143
DA16: Well ... 52Yc 117
E11 ... 32Hc 73
TN16: Westrm ... 97Tc 200
Hartley St. E2 ... 41Yb 92
(not continuous)
Hartley Way CR8: Purl ... 87Pb 176
Hart Lodge EN5: Barn ... 13Ab 30
Hartmann Rd. E16 ... 46Mc 93
Hartmoor M. EN3: Enf W ... 9Zb 20
Hartnoll St. N7 ... 36Pb 70
Harton Cl. BR1: Brom ... 67Mc 137
Harton Lodge *SE8* ... *53Cc 114*
(off Harton St.)
Harton Rd. N9 ... 19Xb 33
Harton St. SE8 ... 53Cc 114
Hartop Point *SW6* ... *52Ab 110*
(off Pellant Rd.)
Hart Rd. AL1: St A ... 3B 6
KT14: Byfl ... 85N 169
Hartsbourne Av. WD23: B Hea ... 19Ea 28
Hartsbourne Cl. WD23: B Hea ... 19Fa 28
Hartsbourne Country Club & Golf Course ... 19Ea 28
Hartsbourne Ct. *UB1: S'hall* ... *44Ea 86*
(off Fleming Rd.)
Hartsbourne Pk. WD23: B Hea ... 19Ga 28
Hartsbourne Rd. WD23: B Hea ... 19Fa 28
Hartsbourne Way HP2: Hem H ... 3C 4
Harts Cl. WD23: Bush ... 12Ca 27
Hartscroft CR0: Sels ... 81Ac 178
Harts Gro. IG8: Wfd G ... 22Jc 53
Hartshaw DA3: Lfield ... 68De 143
Hartshill Cl. UB10: Hil ... 38R 64
Hartshill Rd. DA11: Nflt ... 1B 144
Hartshill Wlk. GU21: Wok ... 8M 167
Hartshorn All. EC3 ... 3J 225
Hartshorn Gdns. E6 ... 42Qc 94
Hartslands Rd. TN13: S'oaks ... 95Ld 203
Hart's La. RH9: S God ... 8B 210
SE14 ... 53Ac 114
Harts La. IG11: Bark ... 37Rc 74
Hartslock Dr. SE2 ... 47Zc 95
Hartsmead Rd. SE9 ... 61Pc 138
Hartspiece Rd. RH1: Redh ... 8A 208
Hartspring La. WD23: Bush ... 12Ca 27
WD25: A'ham ... 12Ca 27
Hart Sq. SM4: Mord ... 72Cb 155
Hart St. CM14: B'wood ... 19Yd 40
EC3 ... 4J 225 (45Ub 91)
Hartsway EN3: Pond E ... 14Yb 34
Hartswood Av. RH2: Reig ... 10J 207
Hartswood Cl. CM14: W'ley ... 21Ae 59
WD23: Bush ... 12Ca 27
Hartswood Gdns. W12 ... 48Va 88
Hartswood Grn. WD23: B Hea ... 19Fa 28
Hartswood Rd.
CM13: Gt War, W'ley ... 21Ae 59
CM14: W'ley ... 21Ae 59
W12 ... 47Va 88
Hartsworth Cl. E13 ... 40Hc 73
Hartville Rd. SE18 ... 49Uc 94
Hartwell Cl. SW2 ... 60Pb 112
Hartwell Dr. E4 ... 23Ec 52
Hartwell Ho. *SE7* ... *50Kc 93*
(off Troughton Rd.)
Hartwell St. E8 ... 37Vb 71
Harty Cl. RM16: Grays ... 46De 99
Harvard Ct. NW6 ... 36Db 69
Harvard Hill W4 ... 51Ra 109
Harvard Ho. *SE17* ... *51Rb 113*
(off Doddington Gro.)
Harvard La. W4 ... 50Sa 87
Harvard Rd. SE13 ... 57Ec 114
TW7: Isle ... 53Ga 108
W4 ... 50Ra 87
Harvard Wlk. RM12: Horn ... 35Jd 76
Harvel Cl. BR5: St P ... 69Wc 139
Harvel Cres. SE2 ... 50Zc 95
Harvel Rd. TN15: Fair ... 84Fe 185
Harvest Bank Rd. BR4: W W'ck ... 76Hc 159
Harvest Ct. KT10: Esh ... 75Ca 151
RM13: Rain ... *41Fd 76*
(off Broadis Way)
TW17: Shep ... 70Q 128
Harvest End WD25: Wat ... 8Z 13
Harvester Rd. KT19: Eps ... 82Ta 173
Harvesters Cl. TW7: Isle ... 57Fa 108
Harvest La. IG10: Lough ... 17Mc 35
KT7: T Ditt ... 72Ja 152
Harvest Rd. TW13: Felt ... 63W 128
TW20: Eng G ... 4P 125
WD23: Bush ... 14Da 27
Harvest Way BR8: Crock ... 73Fd 162
Harvey RM16: Grays ... 47De 99
Harvey Cl. NW9 ... 26Ua 48
Harvey Ct. E17 ... 29Cc 52
KT19: Eps ... 81Ra 173
Harvey Dr. TW12: Hamp ... 67Da 129
Harveyfields EN9: Walt A ... 6Ec 20
Harvey Gdns. E11 ... 32Hc 73
IG10: Lough ... 13Rc 36
SE7 ... 50Lc 93
Harvey Ho. *E1* ... *42Xb 91*
(off Brady St.)
EN3: Enf L ... 9Bc 20
N1 ... *39Tb 71*
(off Colville Est.)
RM6: Chad H ... 28Zc 55
SW1 ... *50Mb 90*
(off Aylesford St.)
TW8: Bford ... 50Na 87
Harvey Lodge *W9* ... *43Cb 89*
(off Admiral Wlk.)
Harvey M. *N8* ... *29Pb 50*
(off Harvey Rd.)
Harvey Rd. AL2: Lon C ... 8G 6
E11 ... 32Gc 73
IG1: Ilf ... 36Rc 74
KT12: Walt T ... 73V 150
N8 ... 29Pb 50
SE5 ... 53Tb 113
(not continuous)
SL3: L'ly ... 48D 82
TW4: Houn ... 59Ba 107
UB5: N'olt ... 38Y 65
UB10: Hil ... 40Q 64
WD3: Crox G ... 16Q 26
Harvey's Bldgs. WC2 ... 5G 223 (45Nb 90)
Harveys La. RM7: Rush G ... 33Fd 76
Harvey St. N1 ... 39Tb 71
Harvil Ct. *NW9* ... *27Ua 48*
(off Mornington Cl.)
Harvill Rd. DA14: Sidc ... 64Ad 139
Harvil Rd. UB9: Hare ... 28L 43
UB10: Ick ... 28L 43
Harvington Wlk. E8 ... 38Wb 71
Harvingwell Pl. HP2: Hem H ... 1B 4
Harvist Est. N7 ... 35Qb 70
Harvist Rd. NW6 ... 40Za 68
Harwater Dr. IG10: Lough ... 12Pc 36
Harwell Cl. HA4: Ruis ... 32T 64
Harwell Pas. N2 ... 28Hb 49
Harwich Rd. SL1: Slou ... 4E 80
Harwicke Ho. *E3* ... *41Dc 92*
(off Bow Rd.)
Harwood Av. BR1: Brom ... 68Kc 137
CR4: Mitc ... 69Gb 133
RM11: Horn ... 27Nd 57
Harwood Cl. HA0: Wemb ... 35Ma 67
N12 ... 23Gb 49
Harwood Ct. *N1* ... *39Tb 71*
(off Colville Est.)
SW15 ... 56Ya 110
Harwood Dr. UB10: Hil ... 39P 63
Harwood Gdns. SL4: Old Win ... 9M 103
Harwood Hall La. RM14: Upm ... 37Rd 77
Harwood M. SW6 ... 52Cb 111
Harwood Point SE16 ... 47Bc 92
Harwood Rd. SW6 ... 52Cb 111
Harwoods Rd. WD18: Wat ... 14W 26
Harwoods Yd. N21 ... 17Qb 32
Harwood Ter. SW6 ... 53Db 111
Hascombe Ter. *SE5* ... *54Tb 113*
(off Love Wlk.)
Hasedines Rd. HP1: Hem H ... 1J 3
Haselbury Rd. N9 ... 21Ub 51
N18 ... 21Ub 51
Haseldine Mdws. AL10: Hat ... 1B 8
Haseldine Rd. AL2: Lon C ... 8H 7
Haseley End SE23 ... 59Yb 114
Haselrigge Rd. SW4 ... 56Mb 112
Haseltine Rd. SE26 ... 63Bc 136
Haselwood Dr. EN2: Enf ... 14Rb 33
Haskard Rd. RM9: Dag ... 35Zc 75
Hasker St. SW3 ... 5E 226 (49Gb 89)
Haskins SS17: Stan H ... 1P 101
Haslam Av. SM3: Sutt ... 74Ab 154
Haslam Cl. N1 ... 38Qb 70
UB10: Ick ... 33S 64
Haslam Ct. N11 ... 21Kb 50
Haslam Ho. *N1* ... *38Sb 71*
(off Canonbury Rd.)
Haslam St. SE15 ... 52Vb 113
Haslemere Av. CR4: Mitc ... 68Fb 133
EN4: E Barn ... 18Hb 31
NW4 ... 30Za 48
SW18 ... 61Db 133
TW5: Cran ... 54Y 107
W7 ... 48Ja 86
W13 ... 48Ja 86
Haslemere Bus. Cen. EN1: Enf ... 14Xb 33
Haslemere Cl. SM6: Wall ... 78Nb 156
TW12: Hamp ... 64Ba 129
Haslemere Gdns. N3 ... 27Bb 49
Haslemere Heathrow Est., The
TW4: Cran ... 54X 107
Haslemere Ind. Est. SW18 ... 61Db 133
Haslemere Rd. CR7: Thor H ... 71Rb 157
DA7: Bex ... 54Bd 117
IG3: Ilf ... 33Vc 75
N8 ... 31Mb 70
N21 ... 19Rb 33
SL4: Wind ... 3E 102
Hasler Cl. SE28 ... 45Xc 95
Haslers Wharf *E3* ... *39Ac 72*
(off Old Ford Rd.)
Haslett Rd. TW17: Shep ... 68U 128
Haslingden Ho. *RM3: Rom* ... *22Nd 57*
(off Dagnam Pk. Dr.)
Hasluck Gdns. EN5: New Bar ... 16Db 31
Hassall Ct. GU22: Wok ... 93C 188
Hassard St. E2 ... 2K 219 (40Vb 71)
Hassenbrook Rd. SS17: Stan H ... 1N 101
Hassendean Rd. SE3 ... 52Kc 115
Hassett Rd. E9 ... 37Zb 72
Hassocks Cl. SE26 ... 62Xb 135
Hassocks Rd. SW16 ... 67Mb 134
Hassock Wood BR2: Kes ... 77Mc 159
Hassop Rd. NW2 ... 35Za 68
Hassop Wlk. SE9 ... 63Nc 138
Hasted Cl. DA9: Ghithe ... 58Yd 120
Hasted Rd.
ME2: High'm, Strood ... 7P 145
SE7 ... 50Mc 93
Haste Hill Golf Course ... 26U 44
Hastings Av. EN7: Chesh ... 1Vb 19
IG6: Ilf ... 28Sc 54
Hastings Cl. EN5: New Bar ... 14Eb 31
HA0: Wemb ... 35La 66
RM17: Grays ... 51Ae 121
SE15 ... 52Wb 113
Hastings Ct. TW11: Tedd ... 64Fa 130
Hastings Dr. KT6: Surb ... 72La 152
Hastings Ho. EN3: Enf H ... 12Yb 34
SE18 ... *49Pc 94*
(off Mulgrave Rd.)
W12 ... *45Xa 88*
(off White City Est.)
W13 ... 45Ka 86
WC1 ... 4F 217
Hastings Mdw. SL2: Stoke P ... 9K 61
Hastings Pl. *CR0: C'don* ... *74Vb 157*
(off Hastings Rd.)
Hastings Rd. BR2: Brom ... 74Nc 160
CR0: C'don ... 74Vb 157
E16 ... 43Jc 93
N11 ... 22Lb 50
N17 ... 27Tb 51
RM2: Rom ... 29Kd 57
W13 ... 45Ka 86
Hastings St. SE18 ... 48Sc 94
WC1 ... 4F 217 (41Nb 90)
Hastings Way WD3: Crox G ... 14S 26
WD23: Bush ... 14Aa 27
Hastingwood Ct. E17 ... 29Dc 52
Hastingwood Trad. Est. N18 ... 23Zb 52
Hastoe Cl. UB4: Yead ... 42Aa 85
Hasty Cl. CR4: Mitc ... 67Kb 134
Haswell Cres. SL1: Slou ... 7D 80
Hat & Mitre Ct. EC1 ... 6C 218
Hatch, The EN3: Enf H ... 11Zb 34
SL4: Wind ... 2A 102
Hatcham Mews Bus. Cen.
SE14 ... *53Zb 114*
(off Hatcham Pk. Rd.)
Hatcham Pk. M. SE14 ... 53Zb 114
Hatcham Pk. Rd. SE14 ... 53Zb 114
Hatcham Rd. SE15 ... 51Yb 114
Hatchard Rd. N19 ... 33Mb 70
Hatch Cl. KT15: Add ... 76K 149
Hatchcroft NW4 ... 27Xa 48
HATCH END ... 24Ba 45
Hatch End GU20: W'sham ... 9A 146
Hatch End Lawn Tennis Club ... 23Ca 45
Hatch End Swimming Pool ... 24Ca 45
Hatchers M. SE1 ... 2J 231
Hatchet La. SL4: Wink ... 2A 124
Hatchett Rd. TW14: Bedf ... 60S 106
Hatch Farm M. KT15: Add ... 76L 149
Hatchfield Ho. *N15* ... *30Ub 51*
(off Albert Rd.)
HATCHFORD ... 91U 190
HATCHFORD END ... 91S 190
Hatchford Mnr. KT11: Cobh ... 90U 170
Hatch Gdns. KT20: Tad ... 92Za 194
Hatchgate Gdns. SL1: Burn ... 1B 80
Hatch Gro. RM6: Chad H ... 28Ad 55
Hatchingtan, The GU3: Worp ... 8N 187
Hatchlands Rd. RH1: Redh ... 6N 207
Hatch La. CR5: Bans, Coul ... 87Hb 175
E4 ... 21Fc 53
GU23: Ock ... 92R 190
KT11: Cobh ... 90R 170
SL4: Wind ... 5E 102
UB7: Harm ... 52M 105
Hatch Pl. KT2: King T ... 64Pa 131
Hatch Rd. CM15: Pil H ... 15Wd 40
SW16 ... 68Nb 134
Hatch Side IG7: Chig ... 22Qc 54
Hatchwood Cl. IG8: Wfd G ... 21Hc 53
Hatcliffe Almshouses *SE10* ... *50Gc 93*
(off Tuskar St.)
Hatcliffe Cl. SE3 ... 55Hc 115
Hatcliffe St. SE10 ... 50Hc 93
Hatfeild Cl. CR4: Mitc ... 70Fb 133
Hatfeild Mead SM4: Mord ... 71Cb 155
HATFIELD ... 1C 8
Hatfield Cl. CM13: Hut ... 17Fe 41
IG6: Ilf ... 27Rc 54
KT14: W Byf ... 84K 169
RM12: Horn ... 36Md 77
SE14 ... 52Zb 114
SM2: Sutt ... 81Db 175
Hatfield Ct. SE3 ... 52Jc 115
UB5: N'olt ... *41Y 85*
(off Canberra Dr.)
Hatfield Ho. EC1 ... 6D 218
SE10 ... 52Dc 114
Hatfield Leisure Cen. ... 2D 8
Hatfield M. RM9: Dag ... 38Ad 75
Hatfield Pk. ... 1F 8
Hatfield Rd. AL1: St A ... 2C 6
AL4: S'ford, St A ... 2H 7
E15 ... 36Gc 73
EN6: Pot B ... 2Eb 17
KT21: Asht ... 91Pa 193
RM9: Dag ... 37Ad 75
RM16: Chaf H ... 50Zd 99
SL1: Slou ... 7L 81
W4 ... 47Ta 87
W13 ... 46Ja 86
WD24: Wat ... 11X 27
Hatfields IG10: Lough ... 13Rc 36
SE1 ... 6A 224 (46Qb 90)
Hatham Grn. La. TN15: Stans ... 82Zd 185
Hathaway Cl. BR2: Brom ... 74Pc 160
HA4: Ruis ... 35V 64
HA7: Stan ... 22Ja 46
IG6: Ilf ... 23Rc 54
Hathaway Ct. AL4: St A ... 2J 7
RH1: Redh ... *5A 208*
(off St Anne's Ri.)
Hathaway Cres. E12 ... 37Pc 74
Hathaway Gdns. RM6: Chad H ... 29Zc 55
RM17: Grays ... 48Ce 99
W13 ... 43Ja 86
Hathaway Ho. N1 ... 3H 219 (40Ub 71)
Hathaway Rd. CR0: C'don ... 73Rb 157
RM17: Grays ... 48De 99
Hatherleigh Cl. KT9: Chess ... 78Ma 153
NW7 ... 23Za 48
SM4: Mord ... 70Cb 133
Hatherleigh Gdns. EN6: Pot B ... 4Fb 17
Hatherleigh Rd. HA4: Ruis ... 33W 64
Hatherleigh Way RM3: Rom ... 25Md 57
Hatherley Ct. *W2* ... *44Db 89*
(off Hatherley Gro.)
Hatherley Cres. DA14: Sidc ... 61Wc 139
Hatherley Gdns. E6 ... 41Mc 93
N8 ... 30Nb 50
Hatherley Gro. W2 ... 44Db 89
Hatherley Ho. E17 ... 28Cc 52
Hatherley M. E17 ... 28Cc 52
Hatherley Rd. DA14: Sidc ... 63Wc 139
E17 ... 28Bc 52
TW9: Kew ... 53Pa 109
Hatherley St. SW1 ... 6C 228 (49Lb 90)
Hathern Gdns. SE9 ... 63Qc 138
Hatherop Rd. TW12: Hamp ... 66Ba 129
Hathersage Ct. N1 ... 36Tb 71
Hatherwood KT22: Lea ... 93Ma 193
Hathorne Cl. SE15 ... 54Xb 113
Hathway St. SE14 ... 54Zb 114
Hathway Ter. *SE14* ... *54Zb 114*
(off Hathway St.)
Hatley Av. IG6: Ilf ... 28Sc 54
Hatley Cl. N11 ... 22Hb 49
Hatley Rd. N4 ... 33Pb 70
Hatteraick St. SE16 ... 47Yb 92
Hattersfield Cl. DA17: Belv ... 49Bd 95
Hatters La. WD18: Wat ... 16T 26
HATTON ... 56V 106
Hatton Av. SL2: Slou ... 2H 81
Hatton Cl. DA11: Nflt ... 2A 144
RM16: Chaf H ... 48Zd 99
SE18 ... 52Tc 116
Hatton Ct. SL4: Wind ... 4G 102
HATTON CROSS ... 56V 106
Hatton Cross Cen. TW6: H'row A ... 55V 106
Hatton Gdn. EC1 ... 7A 218 (43Qb 90)
Hatton Gdns. CR4: Mitc ... 71Hb 155
Hatton Grn. TW14: Felt ... 56W 106
Hatton Gro. UB7: W Dray ... 47M 83
HATTON HILL ... 8A 146
Hatton Hill GU20: W'sham ... 7A 146
Hatton Ho. *E1* ... *45Wb 91*
(off Hindmarsh Cl.)
EN8: Chesh ... *1Zb 20*
(off Church La.)
KT1: King T ... *68Pa 131*
(off Victoria Rd.)
Hatton M. DA9: Ghithe ... 56Yd 120
Hatton Pl. EC1 ... 7A 218 (43Qb 90)
Hatton Rd. CR0: C'don ... 74Qb 156
EN8: Chesh ... 1Zb 20
HA0: Wemb ... 39Na 67
TW14: Bedf, Felt ... 59S 106
Hatton Rd. Sth. TW14: Felt ... 56V 106
Hatton Row NW8 ... 6C 214
Hatton St. NW8 ... 6C 214 (42Fb 89)
Hatton Wlk. *EN2: Enf* ... *14Tb 33*
(off London Rd.)
Hatton Wall EC1 ... 7A 218 (43Qb 90)
Haughmond N12 ... 21Db 49
Haunch of Venison Yd.
W1 ... 3K 221 (44Kb 90)
Hauteville Ct. Gdns. *W6* ... *48Va 88*
(off South Side)
Havana Cl. RM1: Rom ... 29Gd 56
Havana Rd. SW19 ... 61Cb 133
Havanna Dr. NW11 ... 29Ab 48
Havannah St. E14 ... 47Cc 92
Havant Ho. *RM3: Rom* ... *24Nd 57*
(off Kingsbridge Cir.)
Havant Rd. E17 ... 27Ec 52
Havelock Cl. W12 ... 45Xa 88
Havelock Ct. *UB2: S'hall* ... *48Ba 85*
(off Havelock Rd.)
Havelock Ho. SE1 ... 6K 231
SE23 ... 60Yb 114
Havelock Pl. HA1: Harr ... 30Ga 46
Havelock Rd. BR2: Brom ... 70Lc 137
CR0: C'don ... 75Vb 157
DA1: Dart ... 59Kd 119
DA11: Grav'nd ... 10B 122
DA17: Belv ... 49Bd 95
HA3: W'stone ... 27Ga 46
N17 ... 26Wb 51
SW19 ... 64Eb 133
UB2: S'hall ... 48Aa 85
WD4: K Lan ... 10P 3
Havelock St. IG1: Ilf ... 33Rc 74
N1 ... 39Nb 70
Havelock Ter. SW8 ... 53Kb 112
Havelock Ter. Arches *SW8* ... *53Kb 112*
(off Havelock Ter.)
Havelock Wlk. SE23 ... 60Yb 114
Haven, The RM16: Grays ... 10C 100
TW9: Rich ... 55Qa 109
TW16: Sun ... 66W 128
Haven Cl. BR8: Swan ... 68Hd 140
DA13: Ist R ... 7B 144
DA14: Sidc ... 65Yc 139
KT10: Esh ... 75Ga 152
SE9 ... 62Pc 138
SW19 ... 62Za 132
UB4: Hayes ... 42U 84
Haven Cl. App. IG7: Chig ... 20Xc 37
Haven Ct. BR3: Beck ... 68Ec 136
KT5: Surb ... 72Pa 153
KT10: Esh ... 75Ga 152
RH1: Redh ... 4B 208
Haven Dr. KT19: Eps ... 82Ra 173
Havengore Av. DA12: Grav'nd ... 9G 122
Haven Grn. W5 ... 44Ma 87
Haven Grn. Ct. W5 ... 44Ma 87
Haven Hill TN15: Ash ... 79Ce 165
Havenhurst Ri. EN2: Enf ... 12Qb 32
Haven La. W5 ... 44Na 87
Haven Lodge *EN1: Enf* ... *16Ub 33*
(off Village Rd.)
SE18 ... *49Rc 94*
(off Vincent Rd.)
Haven M. E3 ... 43Bc 92
N1 ... 38Qb 70
Haven Pl. KT10: Esh ... 75Ga 152
RM16: Grays ... 47Ee 99
W5 ... 45Ma 87
Havenpool *NW8* ... *39Db 69*
(off Abbey Rd.)
Haven Rd. TW15: Ashf ... 63R 128
Havensfield WD4: Chfd ... 3K 11
Haven St. NW1 ... 38Kb 70
Haven Way KT19: Eps ... 83Ra 173
SE1 ... 3K 231 (48Vb 91)
Havenwood HA9: Wemb ... 34Ra 67
Havenwood Cl. CM13: Gt War ... 23Yd 58
Havercroft Cl. AL3: St A ... 4P 5
Haverfield Gdns. TW9: Kew ... 52Qa 109
Haverfield Rd. E3 ... 41Ac 92
Haverford Way HA8: Edg ... 25Pa 47
Haverhill Rd. E4 ... 18Ec 34
SW12 ... 60Lb 112
Havering *NW1* ... *38Kb 70*
(off Castlehaven Rd.)
HAVERING-ATTE-BOWER ... 20Gd 38
Havering Country Pk. ... 21Ed 56
Havering Dr. RM1: Rom ... 28Gd 56
Havering Gdns. RM6: Chad H ... 29Yc 55
Havering Mus. ... 29Gd 56
HAVERING PARK ... 22Dd 56
Havering Rd. RM1: Have B, Rom ... 22Fd 56
Havering St. E1 ... 44Zb 92
Havering Way IG11: Bark ... 41Xc 95
Havers Av. KT12: Hers ... 78Z 151
Haversham Cl. TW1: Twick ... 58Ma 109
Haversham Ct. UB6: G'frd ... 37Ha 66
Haversham Pl. N6 ... 33Hb 69
Haverstock Cl. HA1: Harr ... 31Ea 66
Haverstock Ct. BR5: St P ... 68Xc 139
Haverstock Hill NW3 ... 36Gb 69
Haverstock Pl. N1 ... 2C 218
Haverstock Rd. NW5 ... 36Jb 70
Haverstock St. N1 ... 2C 218 (40Rb 71)
Haverthwaite Rd. BR6: Orp ... 75Tc 160
Havilland Ct. HA8: Edg ... 21Pa 47
Havilland M. W12 ... 47Xa 88
Havil St. SE5 ... 52Ub 113
Havisham Apartments *E15* ... *37Fc 73*
(off Grove Cres. Rd.)
Havisham Ho. SE16 ... 47Wb 91
Havisham Pl. SE19 ... 66Rb 135
Havisham Rd. DA12: Grav'nd ... 10J 123
Hawarden Gro. SE24 ... 59Sb 113
Hawarden Hill NW2 ... 34Wa 68
Hawarden Rd. CR3: Cat'm ... 93Sb 197
E17 ... 28Zb 52
Hawbridge Rd. E11 ... 32Fc 73
Hawbush Ct. RM6: Ilf ... 28Xc 55
Hawes Cl. HA6: Nwood ... 24V 44
Hawes Ho. E17 ... 28Zb 52
Hawes La. BR4: W W'ck ... 74Ec 158
E4 ... 10Ec 20
Hawes Rd. BR1: Brom ... 67Kc 137
(not continuous)
KT20: Tad ... 92Za 194
N18 ... 23Xb 51
Hawes St. N1 ... 38Rb 71
Haweswater Dr. WD25: Wat ... 6Y 13
Haweswater Ho. TW7: Isle ... 57Ha 108
Hawfield Bank BR6: Chels ... 76Zc 161
Hawfield Gdns. AL2: Park ... 8B 6
Hawfinch Gdns. RM3: Hrld W ... 26Nd 57
Hawfinch Ho. NW9 ... 31Va 68
Hawgood St. E3 ... 43Cc 92
Hawk Cl. EN9: Walt A ... 6Jc 21
Hawk Cnr. RM20: Grays ... 50Zd 99
Hawkdene E4 ... 16Dc 34
Hawke Ct. *UB4: Yead* ... *42Y 85*
(off Perth Av.)
Hawke Ho. *E1* ... *42Zb 92*
(off Ernest St.)
Hawke Pk. Rd. N22 ... 27Rb 51
Hawke Pl. SE16 ... 47Zb 92
Hawker *NW9* ... *25Va 48*
(off Everglade Strand)
Hawker Cl. TN16: Big H ... 88Nc 180
Hawker Ct. *KT1: King T* ... *68Pa 131*
(off Church Rd.)
SL3: L'ly ... 48C 82
Hawker Dr. KT15: Add ... 76M 149
Hawke Rd. SE19 ... 65Tb 135
Hawker Pl. E17 ... 26Ec 52
Hawker Rd. CR0: Wadd ... 79Qb 156
Hawkesbury Cl. IG6: Ilf ... 21Xc 55
Hawkesbury Rd. SW15 ... 57Xa 110
Hawkes Cl. SL3: L'ly ... 48D 82
Hawkesfield Rd. SE23 ... 61Ac 136
Hawkes Leap GU20: W'sham ... 7A 146
Hawkesley Cl. TW1: Twick ... 63Ja 130
Hawkesley Ct. WD7: R'lett ... 7Ha 14
Hawkes Pl. TN13: S'oaks ... 99Jd 202
Hawkes Rd. CR4: Mitc ... 67Hb 133
TW14: Felt ... 59W 106
Hawkesworth Cl. HA6: Nwood ... 24U 44
Hawkes Yd. KT7: T Ditt ... 72Ha 152
Hawke Twr. SE14 ... 51Ac 114
Hawkewood Rd. TW16: Sun ... 69W 128
Hawkfield Ct. TW7: Isle ... 54Ga 108
Hawkhirst Rd. CR3: Kenley ... 88Ub 177
CR8: Kenley ... 87Tb 177
Hawkhurst KT11: Cobh ... 86Ca 171
Hawkhurst Gdns. KT9: Chess ... 77Na 153
RM5: Col R ... 23Fd 56
Hawkhurst Rd. SW16 ... 67Mb 134
Hawkhurst Way BR4: W W'ck ... 75Dc 158
KT3: N Mald ... 71Ta 153
Hawkinge *N17* ... *26Tb 51*
(off Gloucester Rd.)
Hawkinge Wlk. BR5: St P ... 69Xc 139
Hawkinge Way RM12: Horn ... 37Ld 77
Hawkins Av. DA12: Grav'nd ... 3E 144
Hawkins Cl. HA1: Harr ... 31Fa 66
NW7 ... 22Ta 47
WD6: Bore ... 12Sa 29
Hawkins Ct. SE18 ... 49Nc 94
Hawkins Dr. RM16: Chaf H ... 47Zd 99
Hawkins Ho. *SE8* ... *51Cc 114*
(off New King St.)
SW1 ... *51Lb 112*
(off Dolphin Sq.)
Hawkins Rd. NW10 ... 38Ua 68
TW11: Tedd ... 65Ka 130
Hawkins Ter. SE7 ... 50Nc 94
Hawkins Way HP3: Bov ... 8C 2
SE6 ... 64Cc 136
Hawkley Gdns. SE27 ... 61Rb 135
Hawkridge Cl. RM6: Chad H ... 30Yc 55
Hawkridge Dr. RM17: Grays ... 50Fe 99
Hawksbrook La. BR3: Beck ... 72Dc 158
Hawkshaw Cl. SW2 ... 59Nb 112
Hawkshead NW1 ... 3B 216
Hawkshead Cl. BR1: Brom ... 66Gc 137
Hawkshead Ct. *EN8: Walt C* ... *6Bc 20*
(off Eleanor Way)
Hawkshead La. AL9: Brk P, N Mym ... 10E 8
Hawkshead Rd. EN6: Pot B ... 10H 9
NW10 ... 38Va 68
W4 ... 47Ua 88
Hawk's Hill KT22: Fet ... 95Ha 192
Hawkshill AL1: St A ... 3E 6
Hawks Hill Cl. KT22: Fet ... 95Ha 192
Hawkshill Cl. KT10: Esh ... 79Ca 151

Hawk's Hill Ct.—Heatherbank Cl.

Hawk's Hill Ct. KT22: Fet 95Ha 192
Hawkshill Dr. HP3: Hem H 5H 3
Hawk's Hill Ho. KT22: Fet 96Ha 192
Hawkshill Pl. KT10: Esh 79Ca 151
Hawkshill Rd. SL2: Slou 1E 80
Hawkshill Way KT10: Esh 79Ba 151
Hawkslade Rd. SE15 ....57Zb 114
Hawksley Rd. N16 ....34Ub 71
Hawksmead Cl. EN3: Enf W 8Zb 20
Hawks M. SE10 ....52Ec 114
Hawksmoor WD7: Shenl 5Qa 15
Hawksmoor Cl. E6 ....44Nc 94
SE18 ....50Uc 94
Hawksmoor Grn. CM13: Hut 15Fe 41
(not continuous)
Hawksmoor Gro. BR2: Brom 72Mc 159
Hawksmoor M. E1 ....45Xb 91
Hawksmoor Pl. *E2* *42Wb 91*
(off Cheshire St.)
Hawksmoor St. W6 ....51Za 110
Hawksmouth E4 ....17Ec 34
Hawks Pas. *KT1: King T* *68Pa 131*
(off Minerva Rd.)
Hawks Rd. KT1: King T 68Pa 131
Hawkstone Rd. SE16 ....49Yb 92
Hawksview KT11: Cobh 85Ba 171
Hawksway TW18: Staines 62H 127
Hawkswell Cl. GU21: Wok 9K 167
Hawkswell Wlk. GU21: Wok 9K 167
Hawkswood Gro. SL3: Ful 37B 62
Hawkswood La. SL3: Ful 36B 62
SL9: Ger X 36B 62
Hawksworth Ho. BR1: Brom 68Jc 137
Hawkwell Ct. E4 ....20Ec 34
Hawkwell Ho. RM8: Dag 32Cd 76
Hawkwell Wlk. *N1* *39Sb 71*
(off Maldon Cl.)
Hawkwood Cres. E4 ....16Dc 34
Hawkwood Dell KT23: Bookh 98Ca 191
Hawkwood La. BR7: Chst 67Sc 138
Hawkwood Mt. E5 ....32Xb 71
Hawkwood Ri. KT23: Bookh 98Ca 191
Hawlands Dr. HA5: Pinn 31Aa 65
HAWLEY 64Qd 141
Hawley Cl. TW12: Hamp 65Ba 129
Hawley Cres. NW1 ....38Kb 70
Hawley M. NW1 ....38Kb 70
Hawley Rd. DA1: Dart 61Nd 141
DA2: Hawl 61Nd 141
N18 ....22Zb 52
NW1 ....38Kb 70
(not continuous)
HAWLEY'S CORNER 93Rc 200
Hawley St. NW1 ....38Kb 70
Hawley Ter. DA2: Hawl 64Qd 141
Hawley Va. DA2: Hawl 64Qd 141
Hawley Way TW15: Ashf 64Q 128
Haws La. TW19: Stanw M 58J 105
Hawstead La.
BR6: Chels, Well H 78Bd 161
Hawstead Rd. SE6 ....58Dc 114
Hawsted IG9: Buck H 17Kc 35
Hawthorn Av. CM13: B'wood 20Be 41
CR7: Thor H 67Rb 135
E3 ....39Bc 72
N13 ....22Nb 50
RM13: Rain 42Kd 97
Hawthorn Cen., The HA1: Harr 29Ha 46
Hawthorn Cl. BR5: Pet W 72Tc 160
CR6: W'ham 90Ac 178
GU22: Wok 92A 188
RH1: Redh 10A 208
SL0: Iver H 40E 62
SM7: Bans 86Ab 174
TW5: Cran 52X 107
TW12: Hamp 64Ca 129
WD5: Ab L 4W 12
WD17: Wat 10V 12
Hawthorn Cotts. *DA16: Well* *55Wc 117*
(off Hook La.)
Hawthorn Ct. *HA5: Pinn* *26Y 45*
(off Rickmansworth Rd.)
TW9: Kew 53Ra 109
TW15: Ashf 66S 128
Hawthorn Cres. CR2: Sels 83Yb 178
SW17 ....64Jb 134
Hawthornden Cl. N12 ....23Gb 49
Hawthorndene Cl. BR2: Hayes 75Hc 159
Hawthorndene Rd. BR2: Hayes 75Hc 159
Hawthorn Dr. BR4: W W'ck 77Gc 159
HA2: Harr 30Ca 45
UB9: Den 37L 63
Hawthorne Av. CR4: Mitc 68Fb 133
EN7: Chesh 3Xb 19
HA3: Kenton 30Ja 46
HA4: Ruis 30X 45
SM5: Cars 80Jb 156
TN16: Big H 87Mc 179
Hawthorne Cl. BR1: Brom 69Pc 138
DA12: Grav'nd 3D 144
EN7: Chesh 3Xb 19
N1 ....37Ub 71
SM1: Sutt 75Eb 155
Hawthorne Ct. HA6: Nwood 26W 44
KT12: Walt T 74Z 151
TW19: Stanw *59M 105*
(off Hawthorne Way)
W5 ....46Na 87
Hawthorne Cres. SE10 ....50Hc 93
SL1: Slou 4J 81
UB7: W Dray 47P 83
Hawthorne Dr. SL4: Wink 1A 124
Hawthorne Gdns. CR3: Cat'm 93Ub 197
Hawthorne Gro. NW9 ....31Sa 67
Hawthorne Ho. N15 ....29Wb 51
SW1 ....*50Lb 90*
(off Churchill Gdns.)
Hawthorne La. HP1: Hem H 1H 3
Hawthorne M. UB6: G'frd 44Ea 86
Hawthorne Pl. KT17: Eps 84Ua 174
UB3: Hayes 45V 84
Hawthorne Rd. BR1: Brom 69Nc 138
E17 ....27Cc 52
TW18: Staines 64E 126
WD7: R'lett 6Ja 14
Hawthornes AL10: Hat 2B 8
Hawthorne Way N9 ....19Vb 33
TW19: Stanw 59M 105
Hawthorn Farm Av. UB5: N'olt 39Aa 65
Hawthorn Gdns. W5 ....48Ma 87
Hawthorn Gro. EN2: Enf 10Tb 19
EN5: Ark 16Va 30
SE20 ....66Xb 135
Hawthorn Hatch TW8: Bford 52Ka 108
Hawthorn Ho. *SE16* *47Ac 92*
(off Blondin Way)
WD23: Bush *15Z 27*
(off Plantation Cl.)
Hawthorn La. SL2: Farn C 8D 60
TN13: S'oaks 94Hd 202
Hawthorn M. NW7 ....25Ab 48
Hawthorn Pk. BR8: Swan 68Jd 140
Hawthorn Rd. DA1: Dart 61Md 141
DA6: Bex 56Bd 117
GU22: Wok 2P 187
GU23: Rip 96J 189
IG9: Buck H 21Mc 53
N8 ....27Mb 50
N18 ....23Vb 51
NW10 ....38Wa 68
SM1: Sutt 79Gb 155
SM6: Wall 80Kb 156
TW8: Bford 52Ka 108
TW13: Felt 60W 106
Hawthorn Row KT22: Lea 89Ja 172
Hawthorns *CR2: S Croy* *77Sb 157*
(off Bramley Hill)
DA3: Hartl 70Be 143
IG8: Wfd G 20Jc 35
Hawthorns, The EN6: Ridge 5Ua 16
HP3: Hem H 6H 3
IG10: Lough 14Qc 36
KT17: Ewe 80Va 154
RH8: Oxt 5L 211
SL3: Poyle 53H 105
WD3: Map C 22F 42
Hawthorns School Sports Cen., The 3H 209
Hawthorn Ter. DA15: Sidc 57Vc 117
N19 ....*32Mb 70*
(off Calverley Gro.)
Hawthorn Wlk. W10 ....42Ab 88
Hawthorn Way AL2: Chis G 6N 5
GU24: Bisl 8E 166
IG7: Chig 21Tc 54
KT15: New H 82L 169
RH1: Redh 8B 208
TW17: Shep 70T 128
Hawtrees WD7: R'lett 7Ha 14
Hawtrey Av. UB5: N'olt 40Z 65
Hawtrey Cl. SL1: Slou 7M 81
Hawtrey Dr. HA4: Ruis 31W 64
Hawtrey Ho. *SL4: Eton* *1H 103*
(off Slough Rd.)
Hawtrey Rd. NW3 ....38Gb 69
SL4: Wind 4G 102
Haxted Rd. BR1: Brom 67Kc 137
Haybourn Mead HP1: Hem H 3K 3
Hayburn Way RM12: Horn 32Hd 76
Hay Cl. E15 ....38Gc 73
WD6: Bore 12Sa 29
Haycroft Cl. CR5: Coul 90Rb 177
Haycroft Gdns. NW10 ....39Wa 68
Haycroft Rd. KT6: Surb 75Ma 153
SW2 ....57Nb 112
Hay Currie St. E14 ....44Dc 92
Hayday Rd. E16 ....43Jc 93
(not continuous)
Hayden Ct. KT15: New H 83K 169
TW13: Felt 63U 128
Hayden Piper Ho. *SW3* *51Hb 111*
(off Caversham St.)
Hayden Rd. EN9: Walt A 7Ec 20
Haydens Cl. BR5: Orp 72Yc 161
Haydens M. W3 ....44Sa 87
Hayden's Pl. W11 ....44Bb 89
Hayden Way RM5: Col R 26Ed 56
Haydn Av. CR8: Purl 86Qb 176
Haydock Av. UB5: N'olt 37Ca 65
Haydock Cl. RM12: Horn 35Pd 77
Haydock Grn. UB5: N'olt 37Ca 65
Haydock Grn. Flats *UB5: N'olt* *37Ca 65*
(off Haydock Grn.)
Haydon Cl. EN1: Enf 16Ub 33
NW9 ....28Sa 47
RM3: Rom 24Kd 57
Haydon Ct. NW9 ....28Sa 47
Haydon Dell WD23: Bush 16Ba 27
Haydon Dr. HA5: Eastc 28W 44
Haydon Hill Ho. WD23: Bush 17Ba 27
Haydon Pk. Rd. SW19 ....64Cb 133
Haydon Rd. RM8: Dag 33Yc 75
WD19: Wat 16Aa 27
Haydons Rd. SW19 ....64Db 133
Haydon St. E1 ....4K 225
EC3 ....4K 225
Haydon Way SW11 ....56Fb 111
Hay Dr. CR4: Mitc 68Gb 133
HAYES
BR2 ....74Jc 159
UB3 ....44U 84
Hayes, The KT18: Eps D 91Ua 194
Hayes & Yeading United FC 46Y 85
Hayes Barton GU22: Pyr 88F 168
Hayes Bri. Retail Pk. UB4: Yead 45Y 85
Hayes Chase BR4: W W'ck 72Fc 159
Hayes Cl. BR2: Hayes 75Jc 159
RM20: Grays 51Yd 120
Hayes Ct. BR2: Hayes 76Jc 159
HA0: Wemb 39Na 67
SE5 ....*52Sb 113*
(off Camberwell New Rd.)
SW2 ....60Nb 112
Hayes Cres. NW11 ....29Bb 49
SM3: Cheam 77Za 154
Hayes Dr. RM13: Rain 38Kd 77
HAYES END 42T 84
Hayes End Cl. UB4: Hayes 42T 84
Hayes End Dr. UB4: Hayes 42T 84
Hayes End Rd. UB4: Hayes 42T 84
Hayesens Ho. SW17 ....63Eb 133
Hayesford Pk. Dr. BR2: Brom 71Hc 159
Hayes Gdn. BR2: Hayes 74Jc 159
Hayes Gro. SE22 ....55Vb 113
Hayes Hill BR2: Hayes 74Gc 159
Hayes Hill Rd. BR2: Hayes 74Hc 159
Hayes La. BR2: Brom, Hayes 71Kc 159
BR3: Beck 69Ec 136
CR8: Kenley 88Rb 177
Hayes Mead Rd. BR2: Hayes 74Gc 159
Hayes Metro Cen. UB4: Yead 45Y 85
Hayes Pk. Lodge UB4: Hayes 42T 84
Hayes Pl. NW1 ....6E 214 (42Gb 89)
Hayes Rd. BR2: Brom 70Jc 137
DA9: Ghithe 59Ud 120
UB2: S'hall 49X 85
Hayes St. BR2: Hayes 74Kc 159
Hayes Swimming Pool 46V 84
Hayes Ter. DA12: Shorne 4N 145
HAYES TOWN 47V 84
Hayes Wlk. EN6: Pot B 5Db 17
Hayes Way BR3: Beck 70Ec 136
Hayes Wood Av. BR2: Hayes 74Kc 159
Hayfield Cl. WD23: Bush 14Da 27
Hayfield Pas. E1 ....42Yb 92
Hayfield Rd. BR5: St M Cry 71Wc 161
Hayfield Yd. E1 ....42Yb 92
Haygarth Pl. SW19 ....64Za 132
Hay Grn. RM11: Horn 30Qd 57
Haygreen Cl. KT2: King T 65Ra 131
Hay Hill W1 ....5A 222 (45Kb 90)
Hayhurst Ct. *N1* *39Rb 71*
(off Dibden St.)
Hayhurst Gro. GU24: Bisl 9E 166
Hayland Cl. NW9 ....28Ta 47
Haylands Ct. TW8: Bford 51La 108
Hay La. NW9 ....28Sa 47
SL3: Ful 5P 61
Hayle RM18: E Til 8L 101
Hayles Bldgs. SE11 ....5C 230
Hayles St. SE11 ....5B 230 (49Rb 91)
Haylett Gdns. KT1: King T 70Ma 131
Hayley Cl. RM16: Chaf H 48Yd 98
Hayling Av. TW13: Felt 62W 128
Hayling Cl. N16 ....36Ub 71
SL1: Slou 6F 80
Hayling Ct. SM3: Cheam 77Ya 154
Hayling Rd. WD19: Wat 20W 26
Hayling Way HA8: Edg 21Pa 47
Haymaker Cl. UB10: Uxb 38P 63
Hayman Cres. UB4: Hayes 40T 64
Haymans Point SE11 ....7H 229 (49Pb 90)
Hayman St. N1 ....38Rb 71
Haymarket SW1 ....5D 222 (45Mb 90)
Haymarket Arc. SW1 ....5D 222
Haymarket Ct. *E8* *38Vb 71*
(off Jacaranda Gro.)
Haymarket Theatre Royal 5E 222
Haymeads Dr. KT10: Esh 79Ea 152
Haymer Gdns. KT4: Wor Pk 76Wa 154
Haymerle Ho. *SE15* *51Wb 113*
(off Haymerle Rd.)
Haymerle Rd. SE15 ....51Wb 113
Hay M. NW3 ....37Hb 69
Haymill Cl. UB6: G'frd 41Ha 86
Haymill Rd. SL1: Slou 2B 80
SL2: Slou 2B 80
Hayne Ho. *W11* *46Ab 88*
(off Penzance Pl.)
Hayne Rd. BR3: Beck 68Bc 136
Haynes Cl. GU23: Rip 94K 189
N11 ....20Jb 32
N17 ....24Xb 51
SE3 ....55Gc 115
SL3: L'ly 50B 82
Haynes Dr. N9 ....20Xb 33
Haynes La. SE19 ....65Ub 135
Haynes Pk. Ct. RM11: Horn 29Ld 57
Haynes Rd. DA11: Nflt 2B 144
HA0: Wemb 38Na 67
RM11: Horn 28Md 57
Hayne St. EC1 ....7C 218 (43Rb 91)
Haynt Wlk. SW20 ....69Ab 132
Hayre Dr. UB2: S'hall 50Aa 85
Hay's Ct. *SE16* *47Yb 92*
(off Rotherhithe St.)
Hayse Hill SL4: Wind 3B 102
Hay's Galleria SE1 ....6H 225 (46Ub 91)
Hays La. SE1 ....6H 225 (46Ub 91)
Haysleigh Gdns. SE20 ....68Wb 135
Hay's M. W1 ....5K 221 (46Kb 90)
Haysoms Cl. RM1: Rom 28Gd 56
Haystall Cl. UB4: Hayes 40U 64
Hay St. E2 ....39Wb 71
Hays Wlk. SM2: Cheam 82Za 174
Hayter Ct. E11 ....33Kc 73
Hayter Rd. SW2 ....57Nb 112
Hayton Cl. E8 ....37Vb 71
Haywain RH8: Oxt 2H 211
Hayward Cl. DA1: Cray 57Fd 118
SW19 ....66Db 133
Hayward Copse WD3: Loud 14M 25
Hayward Ct. *SW9* *54Nb 112*
(off Studley Rd.)
Hayward Dr. DA1: Dart 62Pd 141
Hayward Gallery 6J 223 (46Pb 90)
Hayward Gdns. SW15 ....58Ya 110
Hayward Ho. N1 ....1K 217
Hayward M. SE4 ....57Bc 114
Hayward Rd. KT7: T Ditt 74Ha 152
N20 ....19Eb 31
Haywards Cl. RM6: Chad H 29Xc 55
Haywards Mead SL4: Eton W 10D 80
Hayward's Pl. EC1 ....6B 218 (42Rb 91)
Haywood Cl. HA5: Pinn 26Z 45
Haywood Ct. EN9: Walt A 6Hc 21
Haywood Cres. WD17: Wat 10W 12
Haywood Dr. HP3: Hem H 5H 3
WD3: Chor 15H 25
Haywood Lodge *N11* *23Nb 50*
(off York Rd.)
Haywood M. RM3: Rom 23Nd 57
Haywood Pk. WD3: Chor 15H 25
Haywood Pl. RM16: Grays 7E 100
Haywood Ri. BR6: Orp 78Uc 160
Haywood Rd. BR2: Brom 70Mc 137
Hazel Av. UB7: W Dray 48Q 84
Hazel Bank SE25 ....68Ub 135
Hazelbank KT5: Surb 74Sa 153
WD3: Crox G 16S 26
Hazelbank Ct. KT16: Chert 74L 149
Hazelbank Rd. KT16: Chert 74L 149
SE6 ....61Fc 137
Hazelbourne Av. TN15: Bor G 93Ae 205
Hazelbourne Rd. SW12 ....58Kb 112
Hazelbrouck Gdns. IG6: Ilf 24Tc 54
Hazelbury Av. WD5: Ab L 4S 12
Hazelbury Cl. SW19 ....68Db 133
Hazelbury Grn. N9 ....20Ub 33
Hazelbury La. N9 ....20Ub 33
Hazel Cl. CR0: C'don 73Zb 158
CR4: Mitc 70Mb 134
KT19: Eps 82Ta 173
N13 ....20Tb 33
N19 ....33Lb 70
NW9 ....26Ua 48
RH2: Reig 8L 207
RM12: Horn 34Kd 77
SE15 ....*54Wb 113*
(off Bournemouth Cl.)
TW2: Whitt 59Ea 108
TW8: Bford 52Ka 108
TW20: Eng G 5M 125
Hazel Cotts. TN14: Hals 85Bd 181
Hazel Ct. CR6: W'ham 89Ac 178
IG10: Lough 13Pc 36
KT11: Cobh 85W 170
W5 ....45Na 87
WD7: Shenl 5Pa 15
Hazelcroft HA5: Hat E 23Da 45
Hazelcroft Cl. UB10: Hil 38P 63
Hazeldean Rd. NW10 ....38Ta 67
Hazeldell Link HP1: Hem H 3G 2
Hazeldell Rd. HP1: Hem H 3G 2
Hazelden Cl. TN15: W King 81Wd 184
Hazeldene EN8: Walt C 4Ac 20
KT15: Add 78L 149
Hazeldene Ct. CR8: Kenley 87Tb 177
Hazeldene Dr. HA5: Pinn 27Y 45
Hazeldene Gdns. UB10: Hil 39S 64
Hazeldene Rd. DA16: Well 54Yc 117
IG3: Ilf 33Xc 75
Hazeldon Rd. SE4 ....57Ac 114
Hazel Dr. DA8: Erith 53Jd 118
GU23: Rip 97H 189
RM15: S Ock 41Zd 99
Hazeleigh CM13: B'wood 20De 41
Hazeleigh Gdns. IG8: Wfd G 22Nc 54
Hazel End BR8: Swan 71Gd 162
Hazel Gdns. HA8: Edg 21Ra 47
RM16: Grays 8A 100
Hazelgreen Cl. N21 ....18Rb 33
Hazel Gro. AL10: Hat 3B 8
BR6: Farnb 75Rc 160
EN1: Enf 16Wb 33
HA0: Wemb 39Na 67
RM6: Chad H 27Ad 55
SE26 ....63Zb 136
TW13: Felt 60W 106
TW18: Staines 65K 127
WD25: Wat 7X 13
Hazel Gro. Ho. AL10: Hat 2B 8
Hazel Ho. *E3* *39Bc 72*
(off Barge La.)
Hazelhurst BR3: Beck 67Fc 137
Hazelhurst Ct. *SE6* *64Ec 136*
(off Beckenham Hill Rd.)
Hazelhurst Rd. SL1: Burn 10A 60
SW17 ....63Eb 133
Hazel La. IG6: Ilf 23Rc 54
SE10 ....50Hc 93
TW10: Ham 61Na 131
Hazell Cres. RM5: Col R 25Dd 56
Hazellville Rd. N19 ....31Mb 70
Hazell Way SL2: Stoke P 8K 61
Hazel Mead EN5: Ark 15Xa 30
KT17: Ewe 82Wa 174
Hazelmere Cl. KT22: Lea 91Ka 192
TW14: Felt 58U 106
UB5: N'olt 40Ba 65
Hazelmere Ct. SW2 ....60Pb 112
Hazelmere Dr. UB5: N'olt 40Ba 65
Hazelmere Gdns. RM11: Horn 29Ld 57
Hazelmere Rd. BR5: Pet W 70Sc 138
NW6 ....39Bb 69
UB5: N'olt 40Ba 65
Hazelmere Wlk. UB5: N'olt 40Ba 65
(not continuous)
Hazelmere Way BR2: Hayes 72Jc 159
Hazel M. DA10: Swans 59Be 121
N22 ....*27Qb 50*
(off High Rd.)
Hazelnut Ct. *RM3: Hrld W* *26Nd 57*
(off Firwood La.)
Hazelnut Ho. *BR8: Swan* *69Hd 140*
(off Squirrels Cl.)
Hazel Pde. KT22: Fet 94Ea 192
Hazel Ri. RM11: Horn 30Ld 57
Hazel Rd. AL2: Park 10P 5
DA1: Dart 61Md 141
DA8: Erith 53Jd 118
E15 ....36Gc 73
KT14: W Byf 86J 169
NW10 ....41Xa 88
(not continuous)
RH2: Reig 8L 207
Hazeltree La. UB5: N'olt 41Aa 85
Hazel Tree Rd. WD24: Wat 9X 13
Hazel Wlk. BR2: Brom 72Qc 160
Hazel Way CR5: Chip 91Hb 195
E4 ....23Bc 52
KT22: Fet 94Ea 192
SE1 ....5K 231 (49Vb 91)
Hazelway Cl. KT22: Fet 95Ea 192
HAZELWOOD 83Tc 180
Hazelwood IG10: Lough 15Mc 35
SS17: Linf 9J 101
Hazelwood Av. SM4: Mord 70Db 133
Hazelwood Cl. HA2: Harr 28Da 45
W5 ....47Na 87
Hazelwood Ct. KT6: Surb 72Na 153
N13 ....*21Qb 50*
(off Hazelwood La.)
NW10 ....34Ua 68
Hazelwood Cres. N13 ....21Qb 50
Hazelwood Dr. AL4: St A 1G 6
HA5: Pinn 26X 45
TW16: Sun 69W 128
Hazelwood Gdns. CM15: Pil H 16Wd 40
Hazelwood Gro. CR2: Sande 85Xb 177
Hazelwood Hgts. RH8: Oxt 7L 211
Hazelwood Ho. SE8 ....49Ac 92
TW16: Sun 67W 128
Hazelwood Ho's. BR2: Brom 69Gc 137
Hazelwood La. CR5: Chip 90Gb 175
N13 ....21Qb 50
WD5: Ab L 4S 12
Hazelwood Pk. Cl. IG7: Chig 22Uc 54
Hazelwood Rd. E17 ....29Ac 52
EN1: Enf 16Vb 33
GU21: Knap 10J 167
RH8: Oxt 4M 211
TN14: Cud 84Tc 180
WD3: Crox G 16S 26
Hazelwood Sports Club 17Sb 33
Hazlebury Rd. SW6 ....54Db 111
Hazledean Rd. CR0: C'don 75Tb 157
Hazledene Rd. W4 ....51Sa 109
Hazlemere Gdns. KT4: Wor Pk 74Wa 154
Hazlemere Rd. SL2: Slou 6M 81
Hazle's Pottery Barn 29Xd 58
Hazlewell Rd. SW15 ....57Ya 110
Hazlewood Cl. E5 ....34Ac 72
Hazlewood Cres. W10 ....42Ab 88
Hazlewood M. SW9 ....55Nb 112
Hazlewood Twr. *W10* *42Ab 88*
(off Golborne Gdns.)
Hazlitt Cl. TW13: Hanw 63Aa 129
Hazlitt M. W14 ....48Ab 88
Hazlitt Rd. W14 ....48Ab 88
Hazon Way KT19: Eps 84Sa 173
Heacham Av. UB10: Ick 34S 64
Headbourne Ho. *E17* *27Ac 52*
(off Sutherland Rd.)
SE1 ....3G 231 (48Tb 91)
Headcorn Pl. CR7: Thor H 70Pb 134
Headcorn Rd. BR1: Brom 64Hc 137
CR7: Thor H 70Pb 134
N17 ....24Vb 51
Headfort Pl. SW1 ....2J 227 (47Jb 90)
Headingley Cl. IG6: Ilf 23Vc 55
WD7: Shenl 4Na 15
Headingley Dr. BR3: Beck 65Cc 136
Headington Ct. *CR0: C'don* *77Sb 157*
(off Tanfield Rd.)
Headington Pl. *SL2: Slou* *6K 81*
(off Mill St.)
Headington Rd. SW18 ....61Eb 133
Headlam Rd. SW4 ....58Mb 112
(not continuous)
Headlam St. E1 ....42Xb 91
HEADLEY 98Ta 193
Headley App. IG2: Ilf 29Rc 54
Headley Av. SM6: Wall 78Pb 156
Headley Chase CM14: W'ley 21Yd 58
Headley Cl. KT19: Ewe 79Qa 153
Headley Comn. CM13: Gt War 24Xd 58
Headley Comn. Rd.
KT18: Head, Walt H 99Ta 193
Headley Ct. KT18: Head 95Ra 193
SE26 ....64Yb 136
Headley Dr. CR0: New Ad 80Dc 158
IG2: Ilf 30Rc 54
KT18: Tatt C 91Xa 194
Headley Gro. KT20: Tad 92Ya 194
Headley Heath 100Ra 193
Headley La. RH5: Mick 100La 192
Headley Rd. KT18: Eps D 92Sa 193
KT18: Eps D, Head 94Qa 193
KT18: Eps, Eps D 90Ra 173
KT22: Lea 94La 192
Head's M. W11 ....44Cb 89
HEADSTONE 28Ea 46
Headstone Dr. HA1: Harr 27Fa 46
HA3: W'stone 27Ga 46
Headstone Gdns. HA2: Harr 28Ea 46
Headstone La. HA2: Harr 28Ca 45
HA3: Hrw W 24Da 45
Headstone Manor 27Ea 46
Headstone Pde. HA1: Harr 28Fa 46
Headstone Rd. HA1: Harr 29Ga 46
Head St. E1 ....44Zb 92
(not continuous)
Headway, The KT17: Ewe 81Va 174
Headway Cl. TW10: Ham 63La 130
Headway Gdns. E17 ....25Cc 52
Heald St. SE14 ....53Cc 114
Healey Ho. *E3* *42Cc 92*
(off Wellington Way)
SW9 ....52Qb 112
Healey Rd. WD18: Wat 16V 26
Healey St. NW1 ....37Kb 70
Healy Ct. EN5: Barn 16Za 30
Healy Dr. BR6: Orp 77Vc 161
Heards La. CM15: Shenf 13Be 41
Hearne Rd. W4 ....51Qa 109
Hearn Ri. UB5: N'olt 39Z 65
Hearn Rd. RM1: Rom 30Hd 56
Hearn's Bldgs. SE17 ....6G 231 (49Tb 91)
Hearnshaw St. E14 ....44Ac 92
Hearn's Rd. BR5: St P 70Yc 139
Hearn St. EC2 ....6J 219 (42Ub 91)
Hearnville Rd. SW12 ....60Jb 112
Hearsall Av. SS17: Stan H 1N 101
Heart, The KT12: Walt T 74W 150
HEATH, THE 79R 150
Heath, The CR3: Cat'm 96Sb 197
W7 ....46Ga 86
WD7: R'lett 5Ja 14
Heathacre SL3: Coln 53G 104
Heatham Pk. TW2: Twick 59Ha 108
Heath Av. AL3: St A 1B 6
DA7: Bex 51Zc 117
Heathbourne Rd. HA7: Stan 19Ga 28
WD23: B Hea 18Ga 28
Heathbridge KT13: Weyb 80Q 150
Heathbridge App. KT13: Weyb 79Q 150
Heath Brow HP1: Hem H 4L 3
NW3 ....34Eb 69
Heath Bus. Cen. TW3: Houn 56Ea 108
Heath Cl. BR5: Orp 73Yc 161
BR8: Swan 68Gd 140
CR2: S Croy 79Rb 157
EN6: Pot B 2Db 17
GU25: Vir W 10P 125
HP1: Hem H 3L 3
NW11 ....31Db 69
RM2: Rom 27Jd 56
SM7: Bans 86Db 175
TW19: Stanw 58L 105
UB3: Harl 52T 106
W5 ....42Pa 87
Heathclose Av. DA1: Dart 59Kd 119
Heathclose Rd. DA1: Dart 60Jd 118
Heathcock Ct. *WC2* *5G 223*
(off Exchange Ct.)
Heathcote KT20: Tad 93Za 194
Heathcote Av. IG5: Ilf 26Pc 54
Heathcote Ct. IG5: Ilf 25Pc 54
(not continuous)
SL4: Wind *5H 103*
(off Osbourne Rd.)
Heathcote Ga. SW6 ....55Cb 111
Heathcote Gro. E4 ....20Ec 34
Heathcote Rd. KT18: Eps 86Ta 173
TW1: Twick 58Ka 108
Heathcote St. WC1 ....5H 217 (42Pb 90)
Heathcote Way UB7: Yiew 46M 83
Heath Ct. *CR0: C'don* *77Tb 157*
(off Heathfield Rd.)
SE9 ....60Sc 116
TW4: Houn 56Ba 107
UB8: Uxb 38M 63
Heath Cft. NW11 ....32Db 69
Heathcroft W5 ....42Pa 87
Heathcroft Av. TW16: Sun 66V 128
Heathcroft Gdns. E17 ....25Fc 53
Heathdale Av. TW4: Houn 55Aa 107
Heathdene KT20: Tad 90Ab 174
Heathdene Dr. DA17: Belv 49Dd 96
Heathdene Mnr. WD17: Wat 11V 26
Heathdene Rd. SM6: Wall 80Kb 156
SW16 ....66Pb 134
Heathdown Rd. GU22: Pyr 87F 168
Heath Dr. CM16: They B 8Uc 22
EN6: Pot B 2Cb 17
GU23: Send 94D 188
GU24: Brkwd 2E 186
KT20: Walt H 97Wa 194
NW3 ....35Db 69
RM2: Rom 25Jd 56
SM2: Sutt 81Eb 175
SW20 ....70Ya 132
Heathedge SE26 ....61Xb 135
Heath End Rd. DA5: Bexl 60Gd 118
Heather Av. RM1: Rom 26Fd 56
Heatherbank BR7: Chst 68Qc 138
SE9 ....54Pc 116
Heatherbank Cl. DA1: Cray 58Gd 118
KT11: Cobh 83Z 171

Heather Cl.—Henry Moore Ct.

Heather Cl. CM15: Pil H ... 15Xd 40
E6 ... 44Qc 94
GU21: Wok ... 7N 167
KT15: New H ... 82K 169
KT20: Kgswd ... 94Ab 194
N7 ... 34Pb 70
RH1: Redh ... 3B 208
RM1: Rom ... 25Fd 56
SE13 ... 59Fc 115
SW8 ... 55Kb 112
TW7: Isle ... 57Fa 108
TW12: Hamp ... 67Ba 129
UB8: Hil ... 43P 83
WD5: Ab L ... 4W 12
Heather Ct. AL2: Lon C ... 9H 7
DA14: Sidc ... 65Zc 139
Heatherdale Cl. KT2: King T ... 65Qa 131
Heatherdene KT24: W Hor ... 97T 190
Heatherdene Cl. CR4: Mitc ... 70Fb 133
N12 ... 24Eb 49
Heatherden Grn. SL0: Iver H ... 39E 62
Heatherden Ho. SL0: Iver H ... 38D 62
Heather Dr. DA1: Dart ... 59Jd 118
EN2: Enf ... 12Rb 33
RM1: Rom ... 26Fd 56
SL5: S'dale ... 3F 146
Heather End BR8: Swan ... 70Fd 140
Heatherfield La. KT13: Weyb ... 78U 150
Heatherfields KT15: New H ... 82K 169
Heatherfold Way HA5: Eastc ... 27V 44
Heather Gdns. EN9: Walt A ... 8Ec 20
NW11 ... 30Ab 48
RM1: Rom ... 26Fd 56
SM2: Sutt ... 79Cb 155
Heather Glen RM1: Rom ... 26Fd 56
Heather Ho. *E14* ... *44Ec 92*
(off Dee St.)
Heatherlands TW16: Sun ... 65W 128
Heather La. UB7: Yiew ... 44N 83
WD24: Wat ... 7V 12
Heatherlea Gro. KT4: Wor Pk ... 74Xa 154
Heatherley Ct. E5 ... 34Wb 71
Heatherley Dr. IG5: Ilf ... 27Nc 54
Heather Pk. Dr. HA0: Wemb ... 38Qa 67
Heather Pk. Pde. *HA0: Wemb* ... *38Pa 67*
(off Heather Pk. Dr.)
Heather Pl. KT10: Esh ... 77Da 151
Heather Ri. WD23: Bush ... 12Ba 27
Heather Rd. E4 ... 23Bc 52
NW2 ... 33Va 68
SE12 ... 61Jc 137
Heathers, The TW19: Stanw ... 59P 105
Heatherset Cl. KT10: Esh ... 78Ea 152
Heatherset Gdns. SW16 ... 66Pb 134
Heatherside Cl. KT23: Bookh ... 97Ba 191
Heatherside Dr. GU25: Vir W ... 2L 147
Heatherside Gdns. SL2: Farn C ... 4H 61
Heatherside Rd. DA14: Sidc ... 62Yc 139
KT19: Ewe ... 80Ta 153
Heatherton Ter. N3 ... 26Db 49
Heathervale Cvn. Pk.
KT15: New H ... 82L 169
Heathervale Rd. KT15: New H ... 82K 169
Heathervale Way KT15: New H ... 82L 169
Heather Wlk. GU24: Brkwd ... 3B 186
HA8: Edg ... 22Ra 47
KT12: W Vill ... 82U 170
TW2: Whitt ... *59Ca 107*
(off Stephenson Rd.)
W10 ... 42Ab 88
Heather Way CR2: Sels ... 81Zb 178
EN6: Pot B ... 4Bb 17
GU24: Chob ... 10J 147
HA7: Stan ... 23Ha 46
HP2: Hem H ... 1M 3
RM1: Rom ... 26Fd 56
Heatherwood Cl. E12 ... 33Lc 73
Heatherwood Dr. UB4: Hayes ... 40T 64
Heath Farm Ct. WD17: Wat ... 9T 12
Heath Farm La. AL3: St A ... 1C 6
Heathfield BR7: Chst ... 65Sc 138
E4 ... 20Ec 34
HA1: Harr ... 31Ha 66
KT11: Cobh ... 86Ca 171
Heathfield Av. SL5: S'dale ... 1C 146
SW18 ... 59Fb 111
Heathfield Cl. BR2: Kes ... 78Lc 159
E16 ... 43Mc 93
EN6: Pot B ... 2Db 17
GU22: Wok ... 90C 168
WD19: Wat ... 17Y 27
Heathfield Ct. *AL1: St A* ... *1C 6*
(off Avenue Rd.)
E3 ... *40Cc 72*
(off Tredegar Rd.)
SE14 ... 52Yb 114
SE20 ... 66Yb 136
TW15: Ashf ... 62N 127
W4 ... 50Ta 87
Heathfield Dr. CR4: Mitc ... 67Gb 133
RH1: Redh ... 10N 207
Heathfield Gdns. CR0: C'don ... 77Tb 157
NW11 ... 30Za 48
SE3 ... *54Gc 115*
(off Baizdon Rd.)
SW18 ... 58Fb 111
W4 ... 50Sa 87
Heathfield Ho. SE3 ... 54Gc 115
Heathfield La. BR7: Chst ... 65Sc 138
Heathfield Nth. TW2: Twick ... 59Ga 108
Heathfield Pk. NW2 ... 37Ya 68
Heathfield Pk. Dr. RM6: Chad H ... 29Xc 55
Heathfield Ri. HA4: Ruis ... 31S 64
Heathfield Rd. BR1: Brom ... 66Hc 137
BR2: Kes ... 78Lc 159
CR0: C'don ... 77Tb 157
DA6: Bex ... 56Bd 117
GU22: Wok ... 90C 168
KT12: Hers ... 77Aa 151
SW18 ... 58Eb 111
TN13: S'oaks ... 94Hd 202
W3 ... 47Ra 87
WD23: Bush ... 14Aa 27
Heathfields Cl. KT21: Asht ... 90La 172
Heathfields Ct. TW4: Houn ... 57Aa 107
Heathfield Sth. TW2: Twick ... 59Ha 108
Heathfield Sq. SW18 ... 59Fb 111
Heathfield Ter. BR8: Swan ... 68Fd 140
SE18 ... 51Uc 116
W4 ... 50Sa 87
Heathfield Va. CR2: Sels ... 81Zb 178
Heath Gdns. DA1: Dart ... 60Ld 119
TW1: Twick ... 60Ha 108
Heathgate NW11 ... 30Db 49
Heathgate Pl. NW3 ... 36Hb 69
Heath Gro. SE20 ... 66Yb 136
TW16: Sun ... 66V 128
Heath Ho. DA15: Sidc ... 63Vc 139
Heath Ho. Rd. GU22: Wok ... 4G 186
Heath Hurst Rd. NW3 ... 35Gb 69
Heathhurst Rd. CR2: Sande ... 81Tb 177
Heathland M. KT18: Tatt C ... 91Za 194
Heathland Rd. N16 ... 32Ub 71
Heathlands KT20: Tad ... 94Za 194
Heathlands Cl. GU21: Wok ... 86A 168
TW1: Twick ... 61Ha 130
TW16: Sun ... 68W 128
Heathlands Ri. DA1: Dart ... 58Kd 119
Heathlands Way TW4: Houn ... 57Aa 107
Heathland Way RM16: Grays ... 8A 100
Heath La. HP1: Hem H ... 4L 3
SE3 ... 54Fc 115
(not continuous)
Heath La. (Lwr.) DA1: Dart ... 60Ld 119
Heath La. (Up.) DA1: Dart ... 61Jd 140
Heathlee Rd. DA1: Cray ... 58Gd 118
SE3 ... 56Hc 115
Heathley End BR7: Chst ... 65Sc 138
Heath Lodge WD23: B Hea ... 18Ga 28
Heathmans Rd. SW6 ... 53Bb 111
Heath Mead SW19 ... 62Za 132
Heath M. GU23: Rip ... 95K 189
Heath Mill La. GU3: Worp ... 7F 186
HEATH PARK ... 30Jd 56
Heath Pk. Ct. RM2: Rom ... 29Jd 56
Heath Pk. Dr. BR1: Brom ... 69Nc 138
Heathpark Dr. GU20: W'sham ... 9C 146
Heathpark Golf Course ... 48Q 84
Heath Pk. Ho. HP1: Hem H ... 4L 3
Heath Pk. Rd. RM1: Rom ... 29Jd 56
RM2: Rom ... 29Jd 56
Heath Pas. NW3 ... 33Db 69
Heath Pl. E3 ... 42Bc 92
Heathpool Ct. E1 ... 42Xb 91
Heath Ridge Grn. KT11: Cobh ... 85Ca 171
Heath Ri. BR2: Hayes ... 72Hc 159
GU23: Rip ... 95K 189
GU25: Vir W ... 10P 125
SW15 ... 58Za 110
Heath Rd. AL1: St A ... 1C 6
CR3: Cat'm ... 95Tb 197
CR7: Thor H ... 69Sb 135
DA1: Cray ... 58Hd 118
DA5: Bexl ... 60Ed 118
EN6: Pot B ... 2Cb 17
GU21: Wok ... 87B 168
HA1: Harr ... 31Ea 66
KT13: Weyb ... 77Q 150
KT22: Oxs ... 84Ea 172
RM6: Chad H ... 31Zc 75
RM16: Ors, Grays ... 6B 100
SW8 ... 54Kb 112
TW1: Twick ... 60Ha 108
TW2: Twick ... 60Ha 108
TW3: Houn, Isle ... 56Da 107
TW7: Isle ... 56Da 107
UB10: Hil ... 42S 84
WD19: Wat ... 17Z 27
Heathrow Academy ... 53S 106
HEATHROW AIRPORT
Terminals 1, 2, 3 ... 55Q 106
Terminal 4 ... 57R 106
Terminal 5 ... 55L 105
Heathrow Blvd. UB7: Sip ... 52P 105
(not continuous)
Heathrow Causeway Cen.
TW4: Houn ... 55X 107
Heathrow Cl. UB7: Lford ... 53K 105
Heathrow Gateway TW4: Houn ... 59Aa 107
Heathrow Interchange UB4: Yead ... 46Y 85
Heathrow Intl. Trad. Est.
TW4: Houn ... 55X 107
Heathrow Prologis Pk. UB3: Harl ... 48R 84
Heath Royal SW15 ... 58Za 110
Heaths Cl. EN1: Enf ... 12Ub 33
HEATH SIDE ... 62Hd 140
Heath Side BR5: Pet W ... 74Sc 160
NW3 ... 35Fb 69
Heathside AL4: Col H ... 5M 7
KT10: Hin W ... 76Ga 152
KT13: Weyb ... 78R 150
NW11 ... 32Cb 69
SE13 ... 54Ec 114
TW4: Houn ... 59Ba 107
Heathside Av. DA7: Bex ... 53Ad 117
Heathside Cl. HA6: Nwood ... 22T 44
IG2: Ilf ... 29Tc 54
KT10: Hin W ... 76Ga 152
Heathside Ct. KT20: Tad ... 95Xa 194
Heathside Cres. GU22: Wok ... 89B 168
Heathside Gdns. GU22: Wok ... 89C 168
Heathside Pk. Rd. GU22: Wok ... 90B 168
Heathside Pl. KT18: Tatt C ... 90Za 174
Heathside Rd. GU22: Wok ... 90B 168
HA6: Nwood ... 21T 44
Heathstan Rd. W12 ... 44Wa 88
Heath St. DA1: Dart ... 59Md 119
NW3 ... 34Eb 69
Heath Ter. RM6: Chad H ... 31Zc 75
Heath Vw. KT24: E Hor ... 97V 190
N2 ... 28Eb 49
Heathview NW5 ... 35Jb 70
Heathview Av. DA1: Cray ... 58Gd 118
Heath Vw. Cl. N2 ... 28Eb 49
Heathview Cres. DA1: Dart ... 60Jd 118
Heathview Dr. SE2 ... 51Zc 117
Heathview Gdns. RM16: Grays ... 48Ee 99
SW15 ... 59Ya 110
Heathview Rd. CR7: Thor H ... 70Qb 134
RM16: Grays ... 47Ee 99
Heath Vs. NW3 ... 34Fb 69
SE18 ... 50Vc 95
Heathville Rd. N19 ... 31Nb 70
Heathwall St. SW11 ... 55Hb 111
HEATHWAY ... 39Cd 76
Heath Way DA8: Erith ... 53Ed 118
WD7: Shenl ... 2La 14
Heathway CR0: C'don ... 76Bc 158
CR3: Cat'm ... 97Sb 197
IG8: Wfd G ... 22Lc 53
KT24: E Hor ... 96V 190
RM9: Dag ... 34Bd 75
RM10: Dag ... 34Bd 75
SE3 ... 52Jc 115
SL0: Iver H ... 40F 62
UB2: S'hall ... 49Z 85
Heathway Ct. NW3 ... 33Cb 69
Heathway Ind. Est. RM10: Dag ... 35Dd 76
Heathwood Gdns. BR8: Swan ... 68Ed 140
SE7 ... 49Nc 94
Heathwood Pde. BR8: Swan ... 68Ed 140
Heathwood Point SE23 ... 62Zb 136
Heathwood Wlk. DA5: Bexl ... 60Gd 118
Heaton Av. RM3: Rom ... 24Kd 57
Heaton Cl. E4 ... 20Ec 34
RM3: Rom ... 24Ld 57
Heaton Ct. EN8: Chesh ... 1Zb 20
WD17: Wat ... 10W 12
Heaton Grange Rd. RM2: Rom ... 26Hd 56
Heaton Ho. *SW10* ... *51Eb 111*
(off Fulham Rd.)
Heaton Rd. CR4: Mitc ... 66Jb 134
SE15 ... 54Xb 113
Heaton Way RM3: Rom ... 24Ld 57
Heaven Tree Cl. N1 ... 37Sb 71
Heaver Ct. DA3: Lfield ... 69Ce 143
HEAVERHAM ... 89Ud 184
Heaverham Rd.
TN15: Kems'g ... 89Rd 183
Heaver Rd. SW11 ... 55Fb 111
Heaver Trad. Est. TN15: Ash ... 77Zd 165
Heavitree Cl. SE18 ... 50Tc 94
Heavitree Rd. SE18 ... 50Tc 94
(not continuous)
Hebden Ter. N17 ... 23Ub 51
Hebdon Rd. SW17 ... 62Gb 133
Heberden Ct. *RM19: Purf* ... *50Rd 97*
(off Wingrove Dr.)
Heber Mans. *W14* ... *51Ab 110*
(off Queen's Club Gdns.)
Heber Rd. NW2 ... 36Za 68
SE22 ... 58Vb 113
Hebrides Ct. *E1* ... *43Ac 92*
(off Ocean Est.)
Hebron Rd. W6 ... 48Ya 88
Hecham Cl. E17 ... 26Ac 52
Heckets Ct. KT10: Esh ... 82Ea 172
Heckfield Pl. SW6 ... 52Cb 111
Heckford Cl. WD18: Wat ... 16S 26
Heckford Ho. *E14* ... *44Dc 92*
(off Grundy St.)
Heckford St. E1 ... 45Zb 92
Heckford St. Bus. Cen. *E1* ... *45Zb 92*
(off Heckford St.)
Hector *NW9* ... *25Va 48*
(off Five Acre)
Hector Cl. N9 ... 19Wb 33
Hector Ct. *SW9* ... *52Qb 112*
(off Caldwell St.)
Hector Ho. *E2* ... *40Xb 71*
(off Old Bethnal Grn. Rd.)
Hector St. SE18 ... 49Uc 94
Heddington Gro. N7 ... 36Pb 70
Heddon Cl. TW7: Isle ... 56Ja 108
Heddon Ct. Av. EN4: Cockf ... 15Hb 31
Heddon Ct. Pde. EN4: Cockf ... 15Jb 32
Heddon Rd. EN4: Cockf ... 15Hb 31
Heddon St. W1 ... 4B 222 (45Lb 90)
Hedera Pl. TW4: Houn ... 56Ba 107
Hedgecroft Cotts. GU23: Rip ... 93K 189
Hedgegate Ct. *W11* ... *44Bb 89*
(off Powis Ter.)
Hedge Hill EN2: Enf ... 11Rb 33
Hedge La. N13 ... 20Rb 33
Hedgeley IG4: Ilf ... 28Pc 54
Hedgemans Rd. RM9: Dag ... 38Zc 75
Hedgemans Way RM9: Dag ... 37Ad 75
Hedge Pl. Rd. DA9: Ghithe ... 58Vd 120
HEDGERLEY ... 2H 61
Hedgerley Ct. GU21: Wok ... 9N 167
Hedgerley Gdns. UB6: G'frd ... 40Ea 66
HEDGERLEY GREEN ... 1J 61
HEDGERLEY HILL ... 3H 61
Hedgerley Hill SL2: Hedg ... 4H 61
Hedgerley La. SL2: Ger X, Hedg ... 1J 61
SL9: Ger X ... 2N 61
Hedge Row HP1: Hem H ... 1J 3
Hedgerow SL9: Chal P ... 23A 42
Hedgerow Ct. *E6* ... *39Pc 74*
(off Nelson St.)
Hedgerow La. EN5: Ark ... 15Xa 30
Hedgerows, The DA11: Nflt ... 1A 144
Hedgerow Wlk. EN8: Chesh ... 2Zb 20
Hedgers Cl. IG10: Lough ... 14Qc 36
Hedgers Gro. E9 ... 37Ac 72
Hedger St. SE11 ... 5B 230 (49Rb 91)
Hedges Cl. TW14: Felt ... 58X 107
Hedgeside Rd. HA6: Nwood ... 22S 44
Hedges Way WD3: Crox G ... 17P 25
Hedge Wlk. SE6 ... 64Dc 136
Hedgewood Gdns. IG5: Ilf ... 29Qc 54
Hedgley M. SE12 ... 57Hc 115
Hedgley St. SE12 ... 57Hc 115
Hedingham Cl. N1 ... 38Sb 71
Hedingham Ho. *KT2: King T* ... *67Na 131*
(off Royal Quarter)
Hedingham Rd. RM8: Dag ... 36Xc 75
RM11: Horn ... 32Qd 77
RM16: Chaf H ... 50Yd 98
Hedley Av. RM20: Grays ... 52Yd 120
Hedley Cl. RM1: Rom ... 29Gd 56
Hedley Ho. *E14* ... *48Ec 92*
(off Stewart St.)
Hedley Rd. AL1: St A ... 2F 6
TW2: Whitt ... 59Ca 107
Hedley Row N5 ... 36Tb 71
Hedley Vs. AL1: St A ... 2F 6
Hedsor Ho. E2 ... 5K 219
Hedworth Av. EN8: Walt C ... 5Zb 20
Heenan Cl. IG11: Bark ... 37Sc 74
Heene Rd. EN2: Enf ... 11Tb 33
Heer M. *E2* ... *40Wb 71*
(off Hackney Rd.)
Hega Ho. *E14* ... *43Ec 92*
(off Ullin St.)
Heideck Gdns. CM13: Hut ... 19De 41
Heidegger Cres. SW13 ... 52Xa 110
Heigham Rd. E6 ... 38Nc 74
Heighton Gdns. CR0: Wadd ... 78Rb 157
Heights, The BR3: Beck ... 66Ec 136
(not continuous)
IG10: Lough ... 12Pc 36
KT13: Weyb ... 82Q 170
SE7 ... 50Lc 93
UB5: N'olt ... 36Ba 65
Heights Cl. SM7: Bans ... 88Ab 174
SW20 ... 66Xa 132
Heiron St. SE17 ... 51Rb 113
Helby Rd. SW4 ... 58Mb 112
Heldar Ct. SE1 ... 2G 231 (47Tb 91)
Helder Gro. SE12 ... 59Hc 115
Helder St. CR2: S Croy ... 79Tb 157
Heldmann Cl. TW3: Houn ... 56Fa 108
Helegan Cl. BR6: Chels ... 77Vc 161
Helena Cl. EN4: Had W ... 10Fb 17
Helena Ct. *NW6* ... *38Db 69*
(off Compayne Gdns.)
W5 ... 43Ma 87
Helena Pl. E9 ... 39Xb 71
Helena Rd. E13 ... 40Hc 73
E17 ... 29Cc 52
NW10 ... 36Xa 68
SL4: Wind ... 4H 103
W5 ... 43Ma 87
Helena Sq. *SE16* ... *45Ac 92*
(off Sovereign Cres.)
Helen Av. TW14: Felt ... 59X 107
Helen Cl. DA1: Dart ... 59Kd 119
KT8: W Mole ... 70Da 129
N2 ... 27Eb 49
Helen Gladstone Ho. SE1 ... 1B 230
Helen Ho. *E2* ... *40Xb 71*
(off Old Bethnal Grn. Rd.)
Helen Mackay Ho. *E14* ... *44Fc 93*
(off Blair St.)
Helen Peele Cotts. *SE16* ... *48Yb 92*
(off Lower Rd.)
Helen Rd. RM11: Horn ... 27Md 57
Helenslea Av. NW11 ... 32Cb 69
Helen's Pl. E2 ... 41Yb 92
Helen St. SE18 ... 49Rc 94
Helen Taylor Ho. *SE16* ... *48Wb 91*
(off Evelyn Lowe Est.)
Helford Cl. HA4: Ruis ... 33U 64
Helford Ct. RM15: S Ock ... 45Xd 98
Helford Wlk. GU21: Wok ... 10L 167
Helford Way RM14: Upm ... 30Td 58
Helgiford Gdns. TW16: Sun ... 66U 128
Heligan Ho. *SE16* ... *47Zb 92*
(off Water Gdns. Sq.)
Helios, The W12 ... 45Ya 88
Helios Rd. SM6: Wall ... 74Jb 156
Heliport Ind. Est. SW11 ... 54Fb 111
Helix Ct. *W11* ... *46Za 88*
(off Swanscombe Rd.)
Helix Gdns. SW2 ... 58Pb 112
Helix Rd. SW2 ... 58Pb 112
Helix Ter. SW19 ... 61Za 132
Helleborine RM17: Grays ... 50Be 99
Hellen Way WD19: Wat ... 21Z 45
Hellings St. E1 ... 46Wb 91
Helm, The E16 ... 45Rc 94
Helm Cl. KT19: Eps ... 84Qa 173
Helme Cl. SW19 ... 64Bb 133
Helmet Row EC1 ... 4E 218 (42Sb 91)
Helmore Rd. IG11: Bark ... 38Vc 75
Helmsdale GU21: Wok ... 10M 167
Helmsdale Cl. RM1: Rom ... 24Gd 56
UB4: Yead ... 42Aa 85
Helmsdale Ho. *NW6* ... *40Db 69*
(off Carlton Vale)
Helmsdale Rd. RM1: Rom ... 24Gd 56
SW16 ... 67Mb 134
Helmsley Ho. *RM3: Rom* ... *24Nd 57*
(off Leyburn Cres.)
Helmsley Pl. E8 ... 38Xb 71
Helmsley St. E8 ... 38Xb 71
Helperby Rd. NW10 ... 38Ua 68
Helsby Ct. NW8 ... 5B 214
Helsinki Sq. SE16 ... 48Ac 92
Helston NW1 ... 1C 216
Helston Cl. HA5: Hat E ... 24Ba 45
Helston Ct. *N15* ... *29Ub 51*
(off Culvert Rd.)
Helston Ho. SE11 ... 7A 230
Helston La. SL4: Wind ... 3F 102
Helston Pl. WD5: Ab L ... 4V 12
Helvellyn Cl. TW20: Egh ... 66D 126
Helvetia St. SE6 ... 61Bc 136
Helwys Ct. E4 ... 23Dc 52
Hemans St. SW8 ... 52Mb 112
Hemans St. Est. SW8 ... 52Nb 112
Hemberton Rd. SW9 ... 55Nb 112
HEMEL HEMPSTEAD ... 1M 3
Hemel Hempstead Ind. Est.
HP2: Hem H ... 1B 4
Hemel Hempstead Rd. AL3: St A ... 3L 5
HP3: Hem H ... 4D 4
Hemel Hempstead Town FC ... 2A 4
Hemery Rd. UB6: G'frd ... 36Fa 66
Hemingford Cl. N12 ... 22Fb 49
Hemingford Ct. WD17: Wat ... 13Y 27
Hemingford Rd. N1 ... 39Pb 70
SM3: Cheam ... 77Ya 154
WD17: Wat ... 8U 12
Heming Rd. HA8: Edg ... 24Ra 47
Hemington Av. N11 ... 22Hb 49
Hemingway Cl. NW5 ... 35Jb 70
Hemley Rd. RM16: Ors ... 4F 100
Hemlock Cl. KT20: Kgswd ... 95Ab 194
SW16 ... 68Lb 134
Hemlock Rd. W12 ... 45Va 88
(not continuous)
Hemmen La. UB3: Hayes ... 44V 84
Hemming Cl. TW12: Hamp ... 67Ca 129
Hemmings Cl. DA14: Sidc ... 61Xc 139
Hemmings Mead KT19: Ewe ... 79Sa 153
Hemming St. E1 ... 42Wb 91
Hemming Way SL2: Slou ... 1F 80
WD25: Wat ... 7W 12
Hemnall M. *CM16: Epp* ... *2Wc 23*
(off Hemnall St.)
Hemnall St. CM16: Epp ... 3Vc 23
Hempshaw Av. SM7: Bans ... 88Hb 175
Hempson Av. SL3: L'ly ... 8N 81
Hempstead Cl. IG9: Buck H ... 19Jc 35
Hempstead Rd. E17 ... 27Fc 53
HP3: Bov ... 9C 2
WD4: K Lan ... 8P 3
WD17: Wat ... 8T 12
(not continuous)
Hemp Wlk. SE17 ... 5G 231 (49Tb 91)
Hemsby Rd. KT9: Chess ... 79Pa 153
Hemsley Rd. WD4: K Lan ... 1R 12
Hemstal Rd. NW6 ... 38Cb 69
Hemsted Rd. DA8: Erith ... 52Gd 118
Hemswell Dr. NW9 ... 25Ua 48
Hemsworth Ct. N1 ... 1H 219 (40Ub 71)
Hemsworth St. N1 ... 1H 219 (40Ub 71)
Hemus Pl. SW3 ... 7E 226 (50Gb 89)
Hemwood Rd. SL4: Wind ... 5B 102
Henage La. GU22: Wok ... 92E 188
Hen & Chicken Ct. EC4 ... 3K 223
Hen & Chickens Theatre ... *37Rb 71*
(off St Paul's Rd.)
Henbane Path RM3: Rom ... 24Md 57
Henbit Cl. KT20: Tad ... 91Xa 194
Henbury Way WD19: Wat ... 20Z 27
Henchman St. W12 ... 44Va 88
Hencroft St. Nth. SL1: Slou ... 7K 81
Hencroft St. Sth. SL1: Slou ... 8K 81
Hendale Av. NW4 ... 27Xa 48
Henderson Cl. NW10 ... 37Sa 67
RM11: Horn ... 33Kd 77
Henderson Ct. N12 ... 21Db 49
NW3 ... *36Fb 69*
(off Fitzjohn's Av.)
SE14 ... *51Zb 114*
(off Myers La.)
Henderson Dr. DA1: Dart ... 56Pd 119
NW8 ... 5B 214 (42Fb 89)
Henderson Gro. TN16: Big H ... 84Lc 179
Henderson Ho. *RM10: Dag* ... *34Cd 76*
(off Kershaw Rd.)
Henderson Pl. WD5: Bedm ... 9F 4
Henderson Rd. CR0: C'don ... 72Tb 157
E7 ... 37Lc 73
N9 ... 18Xb 33
SW18 ... 59Gb 111
UB4: Yead ... 41W 84
Hendfield Ct. SM6: Wall ... 79Kb 156
Hendham Rd. SW17 ... 61Gb 133
HENDON ... 28Ya 48
Hendon Av. N3 ... 25Ab 48
Hendon Crematorium NW7 ... 25Za 48
Hendon FC ... 35Ba 65
Hendon Gdns. RM5: Col R ... 23Ed 56
Hendon Golf Course ... 24Ya 48
Hendon Gro. KT19: Eps ... 81Qa 173
Hendon Hall Ct. NW4 ... 27Za 48
Hendon Ho. NW4 ... 29Za 48
Hendon La. N3 ... 27Ab 48
Hendon Leisure Cen. ... 31Za 68
Hendon Lodge NW4 ... 27Xa 48
Hendon Pk. Mans. NW4 ... 29Ya 48
Hendon Pk. Row NW11 ... 30Bb 49
Hendon Rd. N9 ... 19Wb 33
Hendon Ter. TW15: Ashf ... 65T 128
Hendon Way NW2 ... 31Za 68
NW4 ... 30Xa 48
TW19: Stanw ... 58M 105
Hendon Wood La. NW7 ... 16Va 30
Hendre Ho. SE1 ... 6J 231
Hendren Cl. UB6: G'frd ... 36Fa 66
Hendre Rd. SE1 ... 6J 231 (49Ub 91)
Hendrick Av. SW12 ... 59Hb 111
Heneage Cres.
CR0: New Ad ... 82Ec 178
Heneage La. EC3 ... 3J 225 (44Ub 91)
Heneage Pl. EC3 ... 3J 225 (44Ub 91)
Heneage St. E1 ... 1K 225 (43Vb 91)
Henera's Ct. *BR1: Brom* ... *69Qc 138*
(off Brady Dr.)
Henfield Cl. DA5: Bexl ... 58Cd 118
N19 ... 32Lb 70
Henfield Rd. SW19 ... 67Bb 133
Hengelo Gdns. CR4: Mitc ... 70Fb 133
Hengest Av. KT10: Surb ... 76Ja 152
Hengist Rd. DA8: Erith ... 52Dd 118
SE12 ... 59Kc 115
Hengist Way BR2: Brom ... 70Gc 137
SM6: Wall ... 80Mb 156
Hengrave Rd. SE23 ... 58Yb 114
Hengrove Ct. DA5: Bexl ... 60Ad 117
Hengrove Cres. TW15: Ashf ... 62M 127
Henham Ct. RM5: Col R ... 25Ed 56
HENHURST ... 7G 144
Henhurst Rd. DA12: Cobh ... 6F 144
Henley Av. SM3: Cheam ... 76Ab 154
Henley Bus. Pk. GU3: Norm ... 10A 186
Henley Cl. *SE16* ... *47Yb 92*
(off St Marychurch St.)
TW7: Isle ... 53Ha 108
UB6: G'frd ... 40Ea 66
Henley Ct. GU22: Wok ... 92D 188
N14 ... 17Lb 32
NW2 ... 37Za 68
TW20: Egh ... 63C 126
Henley Deane DA11: Nflt ... 3A 144
Henley Dr. KT2: King T ... 66Va 132
SE1 ... 5K 231 (49Vb 91)
Henley Gdns. HA5: Eastc ... 27X 45
RM6: Chad H ... 29Ad 55
Henley Ga. GU3: Norm ... 9A 186
GU24: Pirb ... 9A 186
Henley Hgts. *N1* ... *38Pb 70*
(off Caledonian Rd.)
Henley Ho. *AL1: St A* ... *3C 6*
(off Lattimore Rd.)
E2 ... 5K 219
Henley Prior N1 ... 2H 217
Henley Rd. E16 ... 47Pc 94
IG1: Ilf ... 35Sc 74
N18 ... 21Ub 51
NW10 ... 39Ya 68
SL1: Slou ... 4C 80
Henley St. SW11 ... 54Jb 112
Henley Way TW13: Hanw ... 64Z 129
Henlow Pl. TW10: Ham ... 61Ma 131
HENLYS CORNER ... 28Bb 49
HENLYS RDBT. ... 54Y 107
Henman Way CM14: B'wood ... 18Xd 40
Henneker Cl. RM5: Col R ... 23Ed 56
Hennel Cl. SE23 ... 62Yb 136
Hennesse M. RM8: Dag ... 32Ad 75
Hennessy Ct. E10 ... 30Ec 52
GU21: Wok ... 85E 168
Hennessy Rd. N9 ... 19Yb 34
Henniker Gdns. E6 ... 41Mc 93
Henniker M. SW3 ... 51Fb 111
Henniker Point *E15* ... *36Gc 73*
(off Leytonstone Rd.)
Henniker Rd. E15 ... 36Fc 73
Henningham Rd. N17 ... 25Tb 51
Henning St. SW11 ... 53Gb 111
Henrietta Barnet Wlk. NW11 ... 30Cb 49
Henrietta Cl. KT15: Add ... 80J 149
SE8 ... 51Cc 114
Henrietta Ct. *TW1: Twick* ... *59La 108*
(off Richmond Rd.)
Henrietta Gdns. N21 ... 18Qb 32
Henrietta Ho. *N15* ... *30Ub 51*
(off St Ann's Rd.)
W6 ... *50Ya 88*
(off Queen Caroline St.)
Henrietta M. WC1 ... 5G 217 (42Nb 90)
Henrietta Pl. W1 ... 3K 221 (44Kb 90)
Henrietta St. WC2 ... 4G 223 (45Nb 90)
Henriques St. E1 ... 44Wb 91
Henry Addlington Cl. E6 ... 43Rc 94
Henry Chester Bldg. SW15 ... 54Ya 110
Henry Cl. EN2: Enf ... 10Ub 19
Henry Cooper Way SE9 ... 62Mc 137
Henry Ct. HA7: Stan ... 24Ma 47
Henry Darlot Dr. NW7 ... 23Za 48
Henry De Grey Cl. RM17: Grays ... 49Be 99
Henry Dent Cl. SE5 ... 55Tb 113
Henry Dickens Ct. W11 ... 45Za 88
Henry Doulton Dr. SW17 ... 63Jb 134
Henry Gdns. DA11: Nflt ... 1B 144
Henry Hatch Ct. SM2: Sutt ... 80Eb 155
Henry Ho. SE1 ... 7A 224 (46Qb 90)
SW8 ... *52Nb 112*
(off Wyvil Rd.)
Henry Hudson Apartments *SE10* ... *50Gc 93*
(off Banning St.)
Henry Jackson Rd. SW15 ... 55Za 110
Henry Lodge KT12: Hers ... 79Y 151
Henry Macaulay Av. KT2: King T ... 67Ma 131
Henry Moore Ct. SW3 ... 7D 226 (50Gb 89)

Henry Peters Dr.—Highbridge Rd.

Henry Peters Dr.
TW11: Tedd 64Ga 130
(off Somerset Gdns.)
Henry Purcell Ho. E16 46Kc 93
(off Evelyn Rd.)
Henry Rd. E6 40Nc 74
EN4: E Barn 15Fb 31
N4 32Sb 71
SL1: Slou 7H 81
SW9 53Qb 112
Henrys Av. IG8: Wfd G 22Hc 53
Henrys Grant AL1: St A 3C 6
Henryson Rd. SE4 57Cc 114
Henry St. BR1: Brom 67Kc 137
HP3: Hem H 6M 3
RM17: Grays 51Ee 121
Henry's Wlk. IG6: Ilf 24Tc 54
Henry Tate M. SW16 64Pb 134
Henry Tudor Ct. SE9 59Sc 116
Henry Wise Ho. SW1 6C 228
Hensby M. WD19: Wat 16Aa 27
Hensford Gdns. SE26 63Xb 135
Henshall Point E3 41Dc 92
(off Bromley High St.)
Henshall St. N1 37Tb 71
Henshawe Rd. RM8: Dag 34Zc 75
Henshaw St. SE17 5F 231 (49Tb 91)
Henslowe Rd. SE22 57Wb 113
Henslow Ho. SE15 52Wb 113
(off Peckham Pk. Rd.)
Henslow Way GU21: Wok 86F 168
Henson Av. NW2 36Ya 68
Henson Cl. BR6: Farnb 75Rc 160
Henson Path HA3: Kenton 27Ma 47
Henson Pl. UB5: N'olt 39Y 65
Henstridge Pl. NW8 1D 214 (39Gb 69)
Hensworth Rd.
TW15: Ashf 64M 127
Henty Cl. SW11 52Gb 111
Henty Wlk. SW15 57Xa 110
Henville Rd. BR1: Brom 67Kc 137
Henwick Rd. SE9 55Mc 115
Henwood Side IG8: Wfd G 23Pc 54
Hepburn Cl. RM16: Chaf H 49Zd 99
Hepburn Ct. EN6: S Mim 4Wa 16
WD6: Bore 14Qa 29
(off Whitehall Cl.)
Hepburn Gdns.
BR2: Hayes 74Gc 159
Hepburn M. SW11 57Hb 111
Hepburn Pl. W3 45Ra 87
Hepdon M. SW17 64Fb 133
Hepple Cl. TW7: Isle 54Ka 108
Hepplestone Cl. SW15 58Xa 110
Hepscott Rd. E9 37Cc 72
Hepworth Ct. N1 39Rb 71
(off Gaskin St.)
NW3 36Gb 69
SM3: Sutt 74Cb 155
SW1 7K 227 (50Kb 90)
Hepworth Gdns. IG11: Bark 36Wc 75
Hepworth Rd. SW16 66Nb 134
Hepworth Way KT12: Walt T 74V 150
Hera Av. EN5: Barn 15Bb 31
Heracles NW9 25Va 48
(off Five Acre)
Heracles Cl. AL2: Park 10A 6
Hera Ct. E14 49Cc 92
(off Homer Dr.)
Herald Gdns. SM6: Wall 75Kb 156
Herald's Pl. SE11 5B 230 (49Rb 91)
Herald St. E2 42Xb 91
Herald Wlk. DA1: Dart 57Pd 119
Herbal Hill EC1 6A 218 (42Qb 90)
Herbal Hill Gdns. EC1 6A 218
Herbal Pl. EC1 6A 218
Herbert Cres. GU21: Knap 10J 167
SW1 3G 227 (48Hb 89)
Herbert Gdns. NW10 40Xa 68
RM6: Chad H 31Zc 75
W4 51Ra 109
Herbert Ho. E1 2K 225
Herbert M. SW2 58Qb 112
Herbert Morrison Ho.
SW6 51Bb 111
(off Clem Attlee Ct.)
Herbert Pl. SE18 51Rc 116
TW7: Isle 54Fa 108
Herbert Rd. BR2: Brom 71Mc 159
BR8: Hext 65Kd 141
DA7: Bex 54Ad 117
DA10: Swans 58Be 121
E12 35Nc 74
E17 31Bc 72
IG3: Ilf 33Uc 74
KT1: King T 69Pa 131
N11 24Nb 50
N15 29Vb 51
NW9 30Wa 48
RM11: Horn 31Nd 77
SE18 52Qc 116
(not continuous)
SW19 66Bb 133
(not continuous)
UB1: S'hall 46Ba 85
Herbert St. E13 40Jc 73
HP2: Hem H 1M 3
NW5 37Jb 70
Herbrand Est. WC1 5F 217 (42Nb 90)
Herbrand St.
WC1 5F 217 (42Nb 90)
Hercies Rd. UB10: Hil 38P 63
Hercules Ct. SE14 51Ac 114
Hercules Pl. N7 34Nb 70
(not continuous)
Hercules Rd. SE1 4J 229 (48Pb 90)
Hercules St. N7 34Nb 70
Hercules Way WD25: Wat 6V 12
Hercules Wharf E14 45Gc 93
(off Orchard Pl.)
Hercules Yd. N7 34Nb 70
Here East E20 36Cc 72
Hereford Av. EN4: E Barn 18Hb 31
Hereford Bldgs. SW3 51Fb 111
(off Old Church St.)
Hereford Cl. GU21: Knap 1E 186
KT18: Eps 85Ta 173
TW18: Staines 67K 127
Hereford Copse
GU22: Wok 1M 187
Hereford Ct. HA1: Harr 28Ga 46
SM2: Sutt 80Cb 155
W7 43Ha 86
(off Copley Cl.)
Hereford Gdns. HA5: Pinn 29Aa 45
IG1: Ilf 31Nc 74
SE13 57Gc 115
TW2: Twick 60Ea 108
Hereford Ho. N18 22Xb 51
(off Cameron Cl.)
NW6 40Cb 69
(off Carlton Vale)
SW3 3E 226
SW10 52Db 111
(off Fulham Rd.)
Hereford Mans. W2 44Cb 89
(off Hereford Rd.)
Hereford M. W2 44Cb 89
Hereford Pl. SE14 52Bc 114
Hereford Retreat SE15 52Wb 113
Hereford Rd. E3 40Bc 72
E11 29Kc 53
TW13: Felt 60Y 107
W2 44Cb 89
W3 45Ra 87
W5 48La 86
Hereford Sq. SW7 6A 226 (49Eb 89)
Hereford St. E2 42Wb 91
Hereford Way KT9: Chess 78La 152
Herent Dr. IG5: Ilf 28Nc 54
Herent Gdns. IG5: Ilf 28Pc 54
Hereward Av. CR8: Purl 83Qb 176
Hereward Cl. EN9: Walt A 4Fc 21
Hereward Gdns. N13 22Qb 50
Hereward Grn. IG10: Lough 11Sc 36
Hereward Lincoln Ho. DA11: Nflt 58Fe 121
(off London Rd.)
Hereward Rd. SW17 63Hb 133
Herga Ct. HA1: Harr 34Ga 66
WD17: Wat 12W 26
Herga Hyll RM16: Ors 3C 100
Herga Rd. HA3: W'stone 28Ha 46
Herington Gro. CM13: Hut 17Ce 41
Heriot Av. E4 19Cc 34
Heriot Cl. KT16: Chert 73H 149
Heriot Rd. KT16: Chert 73J 149
NW4 29Ya 48
Heriots Cl. HA7: Stan 21Ja 46
Heritage Av. NW9 27Va 48
Heritage Cl. AL3: St A 2B 6
SW9 55Rb 113
TW16: Sun 67W 128
UB8: Cowl 42L 83
Heritage Ct. SE8 50Zb 92
TW20: Egh 64C 126
(off Station Rd.)
Heritage Ga. SL9: Ger X 27A 42
Heritage Hill BR2: Kes 78Lc 159
Heritage La. NW6 37Cb 69
Heritage Pl. SW18 60Eb 111
Heritage Quay DA12: Grav'nd 8E 122
Heritage Vw. HA1: Harr 34Ha 66
Heritage Wlk. WD3: Chor 13G 24
Herkomer Cl. WD23: Bush 16Da 27
Herkomer Rd. WD23: Bush 15Ca 27
Herlwyn Av. HA4: Ruis 33U 64
Herlwyn Gdns. SW17 63Hb 133
Her Majesty's Theatre 6D 222
Herm Cl. TW7: Isle 52Ea 108
Hermes Cl. W9 42Cb 89
Hermes Ct. SW2 58Pb 112
SW9 53Qb 112
(off Southey Rd.)
Hermes St. N1 2K 217 (40Qb 70)
Hermes Wlk. UB5: N'olt 40Ca 65
Herm Ho. EN3: Enf W 10Zb 20
N1 37Sb 71
(off Clifton Rd.)
Hermiston Av. N8 29Nb 50
Hermitage, The KT1: King T 70Ma 131
SE13 54Ec 114
SE23 60Yb 114
SW13 53Va 110
TW10: Rich 57Na 109
TW13: Felt 62V 128
UB8: Uxb 37M 63
Hermitage Bri. GU21: Wok 2H 187
Hermitage Bri. Cotts. GU21: Wok 1H 187
Hermitage Cl. E18 28Hc 53
EN2: Enf 12Rb 33
KT10: Clay 79Ja 152
SE2 48Yc 95
SL3: L'ly 8N 81
TW17: Shep 70Q 128
Hermitage Ct. E1 46Wb 91
(off Knighten St.)
E18 28Jc 53
EN6: Pot B 5Eb 17
NW2 34Cb 69
TW18: Staines 64H 127
Hermitage Gdns. NW2 34Cb 69
SE19 66Sb 135
Hermitage Grn. SW16 67Nb 134
Hermitage Ho. N1 1B 218
Hermitage La. CR0: C'don 73Wb 157
N18 22Tb 51
NW2 34Cb 69
SE25 72Wb 157
SL4: Wind 6E 102
SW16 66Pb 134
Hermitage Moorings E1 46Wb 91
Hermitage Path SW16 67Nb 134
Hermitage Rd. CR8: Kenley 87Sb 177
GU21: Wok 1H 187
N4 31Rb 71
N15 31Rb 71
SE19 66Sb 135
Hermitage Row E8 36Wb 71
Hermitage St. W2 1B 220 (43Fb 89)
Hermitage Vs. SW6 51Cb 111
(off Lillie Rd.)
Hermitage Wlk. E18 28Hc 53
Hermitage Wall E1 46Wb 91
Hermitage Waterside E1 46Wb 91
(off Thomas More St.)
Hermitage Way HA7: Stan 25Ja 46
Hermitage Woods Cres.
GU21: Wok 1J 187
Hermitage Woods Est. GU21: Wok 1J 187
Hermit Pl. NW6 39Db 69
Hermit Rd. E16 43Hc 93
Hermit St. EC1 3B 218 (41Rb 91)
Hermon Gro. UB3: Hayes 46W 84
Hermon Hill E11 29Jc 53
E18 29Jc 53
Hern, The TN15: Crou 94Ee 205
Herndon Cl. TW20: Egh 63C 126
Herndon Rd. SW18 57Eb 111
Herne Cl. NW10 36Ta 67
UB3: Hayes 44V 84
Herne Ct. WD23: Bush 17Ea 28
HERNE HILL 57Sb 113
Herne Hill SE24 58Sb 113
Herne Hill Ho. SE24 58Rb 113
(off Railton Rd.)
Herne Hill Rd. SE24 55Sb 113
Herne Hill Stadium 58Tb 113
Herne M. N18 21Wb 51
Herne Pl. SE24 57Rb 113
Herne Rd. KT6: Surb 75Ma 153
WD23: Bush 16Da 27
Hernes Cl. TW18: Staines 67K 127
Herneshaw AL10: Hat 2B 8
Hernshaw CM13: Heron 24Fe 59
Herold Cl. RM13: Rain 39Jd 76
Heron Chase CM13: Heron 24Fe 59
Heron Cl. E17 26Bc 52
HP3: Hem H 7P 3
IG9: Buck H 18Jc 35
NW10 37Ua 68
SM1: Sutt 78Bb 155
UB8: Uxb 37M 63
WD3: Rick 19M 25
Heron Ct. BR2: Brom 70Lc 137
CM13: Heron 25Fe 59
E14 48Ec 92
(off New Union Cl.)
HA4: Ruis 33T 64
KT1: King T 69Na 131
KT17: Eps 86Wa 174
NW9 26Ua 48
TW19: Stanw 60N 105
Heron Cres. DA14: Sidc 62Uc 138
Heron Dale KT15: Add 78M 149
Herondale CR2: Sels 81Zb 178
Herondale Av. SW18 60Fb 111
Heron Dr. N4 33Sb 71
SL3: L'ly 49D 82
Heronfield EN6: Pot B 2Eb 17
TW20: Eng G 5N 125
Heron Flight Av.
RM12: Horn 38Jd 76
HERONGATE 24Fe 59
Herongate N1 39Sb 71
(off Ridgewell Cl.)
Herongate Rd. BR8: Hext 65Gd 140
E12 33Lc 73
Heron Hill DA17: Belv 50Bd 95
Heron Ho. DA14: Sidc 62Xc 139
E3 39Bc 72
(off Sycamore Av.)
E6 38Nc 74
NW8 2D 214
SW11 52Gb 111
(off Searles Cl.)
UB7: Yiew 45M 83
(off Wraysbury Dr.)
W13 42Ja 86
Heron Mead EN3: Enf L 10Cc 20
Heron M. IG1: Ilf 33Rc 74
Heron Pl. E16 46Lc 93
(off Bramwell Way)
SE16 46Ac 92
UB9: Hare 23J 43
W1 3J 221
Heron Quay E14 46Cc 92
Heron Rd. CR0: C'don 75Ub 157
SE24 56Sb 113
TW1: Twick 56Ja 108
Heronry, The KT12: Hers 79W 150
Herons, The E11 30Hc 53
RM12: Horn 32Md 77
Heronsbrook SL5: Asc 8C 124
Heronscourt GU18: Light 3A 166
Herons Cft. KT13: Weyb 79S 150
Heronsforde W13 44La 86
HERONSGATE 17E 24
Heronsgate HA8: Edg 22Qa 47
Heronsgate Rd. WD3: Chor 16D 24
Heron's Lea N6 30Hb 49
Heronslea WD25: Wat 8Y 13
Heronslea Dr. HA7: Stan 22Na 47
Heron's Pl. TW7: Isle 55Ka 108
Heron Sq. TW9: Rich 57Ma 109
Herons Ri. EN4: E Barn 14Gb 31
Herons Way AL1: St A 6E 6
(not continuous)
GU24: Brkwd 3B 186
Heronswood EN9: Walt A 6Gc 21
Heron Tower 2H 225
Heron Trad. Est. W3 43Ra 87
Heron Vw. TW8: Bford 52La 108
(off Commerce Rd.)
Heron Wlk. GU21: Wok 86E 168
HA6: Nwood 21U 44
Heron Way AL10: Hat 2C 8
RM14: Upm 32Ud 78
RM20: W Thur 50Xd 98
SM6: Wall 80Mb 156
TW14: Felt 56W 106
Heronway CM13: Hut 18De 41
IG8: Wfd G 21Lc 53
Herrick Ct. W3 48Sa 87
(off Bollo Bri. Rd.)
Herrick Ho. N16 35Tb 71
(off Howard Rd.)
SE5 52Tb 113
(off Elmington Est.)
Herrick Rd. N5 34Sb 71
Herrick St. SW1 6E 228 (49Mb 90)
Herries St. W10 40Ab 68
Herringham Rd. SE7 48Lc 93
Herrings La. GU20: W'sham 8B 146
KT16: Chert 72J 149
Herron Ct. BR2: Brom 70Hc 137
Herrongate Cl. EN1: Enf 12Vb 33
Hersant Cl. NW10 39Wa 68
Herschell M. SE5 55Sb 113
Herschell Rd. SE23 59Ac 114
Herschel Pk. Dr. SL1: Slou 7K 81
Herschel Sports 5H 81
Herschel St. SL1: Slou 7K 81
HERSHAM 78Z 151
Hersham By-Pass KT12: Hers 78X 151
Hersham Cl. SW15 59Wa 110
Hersham Gdns. KT12: Hers 77X 151
Hersham Golf Course 76Aa 151
HERSHAM GREEN 78Z 151
Hersham Grn. Shop. Cen.
KT12: Hers 78Z 151
Hersham Pl. KT12: Hers 78Z 151
Hersham Rd. KT12: Hers, Walt T 75X 151
Hersham Trad. Est. KT12: Walt T 75Aa 151
Hershell Ct. SW14 56Ra 109
Hertford Av. SW14 57Ta 109
Hertford Cl. EN4: Cockf 13Fb 31
WD3: Crox G 14R 26
Hertford Ct. E6 41Pc 94
N13 20Qb 32
Hertford End Ct. HA6: Nwood 22U 44
Hertford Ho. UB5: N'olt 42Ba 85
Hertford Lock Ho. E3 39Bc 72
(off Parnell Rd.)
Hertford M. EN6: Pot B 3Eb 17
Hertford Pl. W1 6C 216 (42Lb 90)
WD3: Map C 21H 43
Hertford Rd. EN3: Enf H, Enf W 13Yb 34
EN4: Cockf 13Eb 31
EN8: Walt C 13Yb 34
IG2: Ilf 30Uc 54
IG11: Bark 38Qc 74
N1 39Ub 71
(not continuous)
N2 27Gb 49
N9 19Xb 33
Hertford St. W1 7K 221 (46Kb 90)
Hertford Wlk. DA17: Belv 50Cd 96
Hertford Way CR4: Mitc 70Nb 134
Hertford Wharf N1 39Ub 71
(off Hertford Rd.)
Herts Bus. Cen. AL2: Lon C 8H 7
Hertslet Rd. N7 34Pb 70
Hertsmere Ho. E14 45Cc 92
(off Hertsmere Rd.)
Hertsmere Ind. Pk.
WD6: Bore 13Ta 29
Hertsmere Rd. E14 46Cc 92
Hertswood Cen. 11Sa 29
Hertswood Ct. EN5: Barn 14Ab 30
Herts Young Mariners Base 2Bc 20
Hervey Cl. N3 25Cb 49
Hervey Pk. Rd. E17 28Ac 52
Hervey Rd. SE3 53Kc 115
Hervey Way N3 25Cb 49
Hesa Rd. UB3: Hayes 44W 84
Hesewall Cl. SW4 54Lb 112
Hesiers Hill CR6: W'ham 89Gc 179
Hesiers Rd. CR6: W'ham 88Gc 179
Hesketh Av. DA2: Dart 60Rd 119
Hesketh Pl. W11 45Ab 88
Hesketh Rd. E7 34Jc 73
Heslop Rd. SW12 60Hb 111
Hesper M. SW5 49Db 89
Hesperus Cres. E14 49Dc 92
Hessel Rd. W13 47Ja 86
Hessel St. E1 44Xb 91
Hesselyn Dr. RM13: Rain 38Kd 77
Hessle Gro. KT17: Ewe 83Va 174
Hestercombe Av. SW6 54Ab 110
Hesterman Way CR0: Wadd 74Pb 156
Hester Rd. N18 22Wb 51
SW11 52Gb 111
Hester Ter. TW9: Rich 55Qa 109
Hestia Ho. SE1 2H 231
HESTON 52Ca 107
Heston Av. TW5: Hest 51Aa 107
Heston Cen., The TW5: Cran 50Y 85
Heston Community Sports Hall 52Ca 107
Heston Grange TW5: Hest 51Ba 107
Heston Grange La. TW5: Hest 51Ba 107
Heston Ho. SE8 53Cc 114
Heston Ind. Mall TW5: Hest 52Ba 107
Heston Phoenix Distribution Pk.
TW5: Hest 51Y 107
Heston Pool 51Ba 107
Heston Rd. RH1: Redh 10P 207
TW5: Hest 51Ca 107
HESTON SERVICE AREA 51Z 107
Heston St. SE14 53Cc 114
Heston Wlk. RH1: Redh 10P 207
Heswell Grn. WD19: Wat 20W 26
Hetherington Cl. SL2: Slou 1D 80
Hetherington Rd. SW4 56Nb 112
TW17: Shep 68S 128
Hetherington Way UB10: Ick 35N 63
Hethersett Cl. RH2: Reig 3L 207
Hethpool Ho. W2 6B 214
Hetley Gdns. SE19 66Vb 135
Hetley Rd. W12 46Xa 88
Heton Gdns. NW4 28Xa 48
Heusden Way SL9: Ger X 32B 62
Hevelius Cl. SE10 50Hc 93
Hever Av. TN15: W King 78Ud 164
Hever Cotts. DA12: Sole S 10G 144
Hever Ct. Rd. DA12: Grav'nd 5E 144
Hever Cft. SE9 63Qc 138
Hever Gdns. BR1: Brom 68Qc 138
Heverham Rd. SE18 49Uc 94
Hever Ho. SE15 51Zb 114
(off Lovelinch Cl.)
Hever Pl. KT8: E Mos 69Ea 130
Hever Rd. TN15: W King 79Ud 164
Heversham Ho. SE15 51Yb 114
Heversham Rd. DA7: Bex 54Cd 118
Hever Wood Rd. TN15: W King 80Ud 164
Hevingham Dr. RM6: Chad H 29Yc 55
Hewens Rd. UB4: Hil 42S 84
UB10: Hil 42S 84
Hewer St. W10 43Za 88
Hewers Way KT20: Tad 92Xa 194
Hewett Cl. HA7: Stan 21Ka 46
Hewett Pl. BR8: Swan 70Fd 140
Hewett Rd. RM8: Dag 36Zc 75
Hewetts Quay IG11: Bark 39Rc 74
Hewett St. EC2 6J 219 (42Ub 91)
Hewins Cl. EN9: Walt A 4Gc 21
Hewish Rd. N18 21Ub 51
Hewison St. E3 40Bc 72
Hewitt Av. N22 26Rb 51
Hewitt Cl. CR0: C'don 76Cc 158
Hewitt Rd. N8 29Qb 50
Hewitts Rd. BR6: Well H 80Bd 161
HEWITTS RDBT. 81Bd 181
Hewlett Cl. KT15: Add 76M 149
Hewlett Ho. SW8 52Kb 112
(off Havelock Ter.)
Hewlett Rd. E3 40Ac 72
Hew Watt Cl. RM16: Ors 3C 100
Hexagon, The N6 32Hb 69
Hexagon Bus. Cen. UB4: Yead 45Y 85
Hexagon Ho. RM1: Rom 29Fd 56
(off Mercury Gdns.)
Hexal Rd. SE6 62Gc 137
Hexham Gdns. TW7: Isle 52Ja 108
UB5: N'olt 36Ba 65
Hexham Rd. EN5: New Bar 14Db 31
SE27 61Sb 135
SM4: Mord 74Db 155
HEXTABLE 66Hd 140
Hextable Heritage Cen. & Gdns.
66Gd 140
Hextalls La. CR3: Blet, Cat'm 100Ub 197
RH1: Blet 100Tb 197
Heybourne Cres. NW9 25Ua 48
Heybourne Rd. N17 24Xb 51
Heybridge NW1 37Kb 70
(off Lewis St.)
Heybridge Av. SW16 66Nb 134
Heybridge Dr. IG6: Ilf 26Tc 54
Heybridge Way E10 31Ac 72
Heydon Ct. BR4: W W'ck 75Gc 159
(off Deer Pk. Way)
Heydon Ho. SE14 53Yb 114
(off Kender St.)
Heyford Av. SW8 52Nb 112
SW20 69Bb 133
Heyford End AL2: Park 10A 6
Heyford Rd. CR4: Mitc 68Gb 133
WD7: R'lett 9Ha 14
Heyford Ter. SW8 52Nb 112
Heygate St. SE17 6D 230 (49Sb 91)
Heylyn Sq. E3 41Bc 92
Heymede KT22: Lea 95La 192
Heynes Rd. RM8: Dag 35Yc 75
Heysham Dr. WD19: Wat 22Y 45
Heysham La. NW3 34Db 69
Heysham Rd. N15 30Tb 51
Heythorp Cl. GU21: Wok 9K 167
Heythorp St. SW18 60Bb 111
Heythrop Dr. UB10: Ick 35P 63
Heywood Av. NW9 25Ua 48
Heywood Ct. HA7: Stan 22La 46
Heywood Ho. SE14 51Zb 114
(off Myers La.)
Heyworth Rd. E5 35Xb 71
E15 36Hc 73
Hibbert Av. WD24: Wat 10Z 13
Hibbert Ho. E14 48Cc 92
(off Tiller Rd.)
Hibbert Lodge SL9: Chal P 26A 42
Hibbert Rd. E17 31Bc 72
HA3: W'stone 26Ha 46
Hibbert's All. SL4: Wind 3H 103
Hibbert St. SW11 55Fb 111
Hibbets Way SL9: Ger X 27A 42
Hibbs Cl. BR8: Swan 68Fd 140
Hibernia Cl. DA9: Ghithe 56Wd 120
Hibernia Dr. DA12: Grav'nd 2H 145
Hibernia Gdns. TW3: Houn 56Ca 107
Hibernia Point SE2 47Zc 95
(off Wolvercote Rd.)
Hibernia Rd. TW3: Houn 56Ca 107
Hibiscus Cl. HA8: Edg 21Sa 47
Hibiscus Ho. E17 27Dc 52
TW13: Felt 60W 106
Hibiscus Lodge E15 38Gc 73
(off Glenavon Rd.)
Hichisson Rd. SE15 57Yb 114
Hicken Rd. SW2 57Pb 112
Hickes Ho. NW6 38Fb 69
Hickey's Almshouses TW9: Rich 56Pa 109
Hickin Cl. SE7 49Mc 93
Hickin St. E14 48Ec 92
Hickleton NW1 1C 216
Hickling Ho. SE16 48Xb 91
(off Slippers Pl.)
Hickling Rd. IG1: Ilf 36Rc 74
Hickman Av. E4 23Ec 52
Hickman Cl. E16 43Mc 93
Hickman Rd. RM6: Chad H 31Yc 75
Hickmans Cl. RH9: G'stone 4A 210
Hickmore Wlk. SW4 55Mb 112
Hickory Cl. N9 17Wb 33
Hicks Av. UB6: G'frd 41Fa 86
Hicks Bolton Ho. NW6 40Bb 69
(off Denmark Ho.)
Hicks Cl. SW11 55Gb 111
Hicks Ct. RM10: Dag 34Dd 76
Hicks Gallery 64Cb 133
Hicks Ho. SE16 48Wb 91
(off Spa Rd.)
Hicks St. SE8 50Ac 92
Hidcote Apartments SW11 56Gb 111
(off Danvers Av.)
Hidcote Cl. GU22: Wok 88D 168
Hidcote Gdns. SW20 69Xa 132
Hidden Cl. KT8: W Mole 70Ea 130
Hide E6 44Qc 94
Hideaway, The WD5: Ab L 3V 12
Hide Pl. SW1 6D 228 (49Mb 90)
Hider Ct. SE3 52Lc 115
Hide Rd. HA1: Harr 28Ea 46
Hides St. N7 37Pb 70
Hide Twr. SW1 6D 228
Hierro Ct. E1 43Ac 92
(off Ocean Est.)
Higgins Ho. N1 39Ub 71
(off Colville Est.)
Higginson Ho. NW3 38Hb 69
(off Fellows Rd.)
Higgins Wlk. TW12: Hamp 65Aa 129
(off Abbott Cl.)
Higgs Ind. Est. SE24 55Rb 113
High Acres EN2: Enf 13Rb 33
WD5: Ab L 4T 12
HIGHAM HILL 26Ac 52
Higham Hill Rd. E17 25Ac 52
Higham M. UB5: N'olt 42Ba 85
Higham Path E17 27Ac 52
Higham Pl. E17 27Ac 52
Higham Rd. IG8: Wfd G 23Jc 53
N17 27Tb 51
Highams, The E17 25Ec 52
Highams Ct. E4 20Ec 34
Highams Hill CR6: W'ham 84Zc 179
Highams La. GU24: Chob 9E 146
Highams Lodge Bus. Cen. E17 27Zb 52
HIGHAMS PARK 23Fc 53
Higham Sta. Av. E4 23Cc 52
Higham St. E17 27Ac 52
High Ash Cl. SS17: Linf 8J 101
High Ashton KT2: King T 66Ra 131
Highbanks Cl. DA16: Well 52Xc 117
Highbanks Rd. HA5: Hat E 23Da 45
Highbank Way N8 30Qb 50
HIGH BARNET 12Za 30
High Barn Rd. KT24: Eff, Ran C 100Z 191
Highbarns HP3: Hem H 7A 4
Highbarrow Cl. CR8: Purl 82Pb 176
Highbarrow Rd. CR0: C'don 74Wb 157
HIGH BEECH 10Kc 21
High Beech CR2: S Croy 80Ub 157
N21 16Pb 32
High Beeches BR6: Chels 79Wc 161
DA14: Sidc 64Ad 139
KT13: Weyb 79U 150
SL9: Ger X 2P 61
SM7: Bans 86Ya 174
High Beeches Cl. CR8: Purl 82Mb 176
High Beech Golf Course 10Kc 21
High Beech Rd. IG10: Lough 14Nc 36
High Birch Ct. EN4: E Barn 14Gb 31
(off Park Rd.)
High Bri. SE10 50Fc 93
Highbridge Cl. WD7: R'lett 5Ja 14
Highbridge Ct. SE14 52Yb 114
(off Farrow La.)
Highbridge Ind. Est. UB8: Uxb 38L 63
Highbridge Retail Pk. EN9: Walt A 6Dc 20
Highbridge Rd. IG11: Bark 39Rc 74

Highbridge St.—Hillary Cres.

Highbridge St. EN9: Walt A 5Dc 20
(not continuous)
High Bri. Wharf *SE10* 50Fc 93
(off High Bri.)
Highbrook Rd. SE3 55Mc 115
High Broom Cres. BR4: W W'ck 73Dc 158
HIGHBURY 35Rb 71
Highbury Av. CR7: Thor H 68Qb 134
Highbury Cl. BR4: W W'ck 75Dc 158
KT3: N Mald 70Sa 131
HIGHBURY CORNER 37Rb 71
Highbury Cres. N5 36Rb 71
Highbury Dr. KT22: Lea 93Ja 192
Highbury Est. N5 36Sb 71
Highbury Gdns. IG3: Ilf 33Uc 74
N7 36Qb 70
Highbury Grange N5 35Sb 71
Highbury Gro. N5 36Rb 71
Highbury Gro. Ct. N5 37Sb 71
Highbury Hill N5 34Qb 70
Highbury Mans. *N1* 38Rb 71
(off Upper St.)
Highbury New Pk. N5 36Sb 71
Highbury Pk. N5 34Rb 71
Highbury Pl. N5 37Rb 71
Highbury Pool 37Rb 71
Highbury Quad. N5 34Sb 71
Highbury Rd. SW19 64Ab 132
Highbury Sq. N14 18Lb 32
Highbury Stadium Sq. N5 34Rb 71
Highbury Sta. Rd. N1 37Qb 70
Highbury Ter. N5 36Rb 71
Highbury Ter. M. N5 36Rb 71
High Canons WD6: Bore 9Sa 15
High Cedar Dr. SW20 66Ya 132
Highclere SL5: S'hill 1B 146
Highclere Cl. CR8: Kenley 87Sb 177
Highclere Ct. *AL1: St A* 1C 6
(off Avenue Rd.)
GU21: Knap 9G 166
Highclere Dr. HP3: Hem H 6A 4
Highclere Gdns. GU21: Knap 9G 166
Highclere Rd. GU21: Knap 9G 166
KT3: N Mald 69Ta 131
Highclere St. SE26 63Ac 136
Highcliffe *W13* 43Ka 86
(off Clivedon Ct.)
Highcliffe Dr. SW15 58Va 110
Highcliffe Gdns. IG4: Ilf 29Nc 54
High Cl. WD3: Rick 15L 25
Highcombe SE7 51Kc 115
Highcombe Cl. SE9 60Mc 115
High Coombe Pl. KT2: King T 65Ta 131
Highcotts La. GU4: W Cla 98H 189
Highcroft NW9 29Ua 48
Highcroft Av. HA0: Wemb 38Qa 67
High Cft. Cotts. BR8: Swan 70Jd 140
Highcroft Ct. KT23: Bookh 95Ca 191
Highcroft Est. N19 31Nb 70
Highcroft Gdns. NW11 30Bb 49
Highcroft Rd. HP3: Hem H 6J 3
N19 31Nb 70
Highcroft Trailer Gdns. HP3: Bov 8D 2
HIGH CROSS 9Fa 14
High Cross WD25: A'ham 9Fa 14
High Cross Cen., The N15 28Wb 51
Highcross Pl KT16: Chert 74H 149
High Cross Rd. N17 27Wb 51
TN15: Ivy H 98Xd 204
Highcross Rd. DA13: Sflt 64Zd 143
Highcross Way SW15 60Wa 110
Highdaun Dr. SW16 70Pb 134
High Dells AL10: Hat 1B 8
Highdene *GU22: Wok* 90B 168
(off Fairview Av.)
Highdown KT4: Wor Pk 75Ua 154
Highdown Cl. SM7: Bans 88Bb 175
Highdown La. SM2: Sutt 83Db 175
Highdown Rd. SW15 58Xa 110
High Dr. CR3: Wold 94Bc 198
KT3: N Mald 67Sa 131
KT22: Oxs 86Fa 172
High Elms IG7: Chig 21Uc 54
IG8: Wfd G 22Jc 53
RM14: Upm 32Ud 78
High Elms Cl. HA6: Nwood 23S 44
High Elms Country Pk.
(Local Nature Reserve) 80Tc 160
High Elms Golf Course 80Sc 160
High Elms La. WD25: Wat 3X 13
High Elms Rd. BR6: Downe 83Qc 180
HIGHER DENHAM 31E 62
Higher Dr. CR8: Purl 85Qb 176
KT24: E Hor 99U 190
SM7: Bans 84Za 174
Higher Grn. KT17: Eps 85Wa 174
HIGHFIELD 1N 3
Highfield HP8: Chal G 19A 24
SM7: Bans 89Gb 175
WD4: K Lan 10N 3
WD19: Wat 20Ba 27
WD23: B Hea 19Ga 28
WD25: Wat 6V 12
Highfield Av. BR6: Chels 78Vc 161
DA8: Erith 51Dd 118
HA5: Pinn 29Ba 45
HA9: Wemb 34Pa 67
NW9 29Sa 47
NW11 31Za 68
UB6: G'frd 36Ga 66
Highfield Cl. HA6: Nwood 25U 44
KT6: Surb 74La 152
KT14: W Byf 85J 169
KT22: Oxs 83Fa 172
N22 25Qb 50
NW9 29Sa 47
RM5: Col R 23Ed 56
SE13 58Fc 115
TW20: Eng G 5N 125
Highfield Cotts. DA2: Wilm 65Kd 141
Highfield Ct. N14 16Lb 32
NW11 30Ab 48
SL2: Farn R 9F 60
SL9: Chal P 22B 42
TW20: Eng G 5P 125
(off Highfield Rd.)
Highfield Cres. HA6: Nwood 25U 44
RM12: Horn 33Pd 77
Highfield Dr. BR2: Brom 70Gc 137
BR4: W W'ck 75Dc 158
CR3: Cat'm 94Wb 197
KT19: Ewe 79Va 154
UB10: Ick 35N 63
Highfield Gdns. NW11 30Ab 48
RM16: Grays 47Fe 99
Highfield Grn. CM16: Epp 3Uc 22
Highfield Hall AL4: St A 6J 7
Highfield Hill SE19 66Tb 135
Highfield La. AL4: St A 4G 6
HP2: Hem H 1P 3
Highfield Link RM5: Col R 23Ed 56
Highfield Mnr. AL4: St A 6J 7
Highfield M. *NW6* 38Db 69
(off Compayne Gdns.)
Highfield Pk. KT15: Add 79J 149
Highfield Pk. Cen. 3G 6
Highfield Pk. Dr. AL4: St A 5F 6
Highfield Pl. CM16: Epp 3Uc 22
Highfield Rd. BR1: Brom 70Pc 138
BR7: Chst 69Vc 139
CR3: Cat'm 94Wb 197
CR8: Purl 82Pb 176
DA1: Dart 59Md 119
DA6: Bex 57Bd 117
HA6: Nwood 25U 44
IG8: Wfd G 24Nc 54
KT5: Surb 73Sa 153
KT12: Walt T 74W 150
KT14: W Byf 85J 169
KT16: Chert 74J 149
N21 19Rb 33
NW11 30Ab 48
RM5: Col R 24Ed 56
RM12: Horn 33Pd 77
SL4: Wind 5D 102
SM1: Sutt 78Gb 155
TN15: Kems'g 88Nd 183
TN16: Big H 89Lc 179
TW7: Isle 53Ha 108
TW13: Felt 61W 128
TW16: Sun 71V 150
TW20: Eng G 5N 125
W3 43Ra 87
WD23: Bush 15Aa 27
Highfield Rd. Nth. DA1: Dart 58Md 119
Highfield Rd. Sth. DA1: Dart 59Md 119
High Flds. SL5: S'dale 1D 146
Highfields KT21: Asht 91Ma 193
KT22: Fet 96Fa 192
KT24: E Hor 100V 190
SM1: Sutt 75Cb 155
WD7: R'lett 7Ha 14
Highfields Gro. N6 32Hb 69
Highfield Towers RM5: Col R 22Fd 56
Highfield Way EN6: Pot B 4Db 17
RM12: Horn 33Pd 77
WD3: Rick 16J 25
High Firs BR8: Swan 70Gd 140
WD7: R'lett 7Ha 14
High Foleys KT10: Clay 80Ka 152
High Gables BR2: Brom 68Gc 137
IG10: Lough 15Mc 35
High Gdns. GU22: Wok 1M 187
High Garth KT10: Esh 79Ea 152
HIGHGATE 30Jb 50
Highgate Av. N6 31Kb 70
Highgate Cemetery N6 32Jb 70
Highgate Cl. N6 31Jb 70
Highgate Edge N2 29Gb 49
Highgate Golf Course 30Gb 49
Highgate Hgts. N6 30Lb 50
Highgate High St. N6 32Jb 70
Highgate Hill N6 32Kb 70
N19 32Kb 70
Highgate Ho. SE26 62Wb 135
Highgate Rd. NW5 34Jb 70
Highgate Spinney N8 30Mb 50
Highgate Wlk. SE23 61Yb 136
Highgate West Hill N6 32Jb 70
High Gro. BR1: Brom 67Mc 137
SE18 52Tc 116
Highgrove CM15: Pil H 16Xd 40
Highgrove Cl. BR7: Chst 67Nc 138
N11 22Jb 50
Highgrove Ct. BR3: Beck 66Cc 136
EN8: Walt C 6Yb 20
SM1: Sutt 79Cb 155
Highgrove Ho. *CM14: B'wood* 19Yd 40
(off Regency Ct.)
HA4: Ruis 30W 44
Highgrove M. RM17: Grays 50Ee 99
SM5: Cars 76Hb 155
Highgrove Rd. RM8: Dag 36Yc 75
Highgrove Swimming Pool 30W 44
Highgrove Ter. E4 19Fc 35
Highgrove Way HA4: Ruis 30W 44
High Hill Est. E5 32Xb 71
High Hill Ferry E5 32Xb 71
High Hill Rd. CR6: W'ham 87Ec 178
High Holborn WC1 2F 223 (44Nb 90)
High Ho. La. RM18: W Til 8F 100
High Ho. Production Pk.
RM19: Purf 50Td 98
Highland Av. CM15: B'wood 18Yd 40
IG10: Lough 16Nc 36
RM10: Dag 34Ed 76
W7 44Ga 86
Highland Cotts. SM6: Wall 77Lb 156
Highland Ct. BR1: Brom 67Hc 137
E18 25Kc 53
Highland Cft. BR3: Beck 64Dc 136
Highland Dr. HP3: Hem H 2B 4
WD23: Bush 17Da 27
Highland Pk. TW13: Felt 63V 128
Highland Rd. BR1: Brom 67Hc 137
BR2: Brom 67Hc 137
CR8: Purl 86Qb 176
DA6: Bex 57Cd 118
HA6: Nwood 26V 44
SE19 65Ub 135
TN14: Bad M 82Dd 182
Highlands KT21: Asht 91La 192
N20 19Fb 31
SL2: Farn C 6G 60
WD19: Wat 18Y 27
Highlands, The EN5: New Bar 14Cb 31
EN6: Pot B 2Eb 17
HA8: Edg 26Ra 47
KT24: E Hor 97U 190
WD3: Rick 17K 25
Highlands Av. KT22: Lea 94La 192
N21 15Pb 32
W3 45Sa 87
Highlands Cl. KT22: Lea 94Ka 192
N4 31Nb 70
SL9: Chal P 24B 42
TW3: Houn 53Da 107
Highlands Ct. SE19 65Ub 135
Highlands End SL9: Chal P 24B 42
Highlands Farm Bus. Pk.
BR8: Swan 67Jd 140
Highlands Gdns. IG1: Ilf 32Pc 74
Highlands Heath SW15 59Xa 110
Highlands Hill BR8: Swan 67Jd 140
Highlands La. GU22: Wok 93A 188
SL9: Chal P 24B 42
Highlands Pk. KT22: Lea 95Ma 193
TN15: Seal 93Nd 203
Highlands Rd. BR5: Orp 73Xc 161
EN5: New Bar 15Cb 31
KT22: Lea 94Ka 192
RH2: Reig 5M 207
HIGHLANDS VILLAGE 15Pb 32
Highland Ter. *SE13* 55Dc 114
(off Algernon Rd.)
Highland Vw. Pk. Homes
UB7: W Dray 49L 83
High La. CR3: Wold 91Bc 198
CR6: W'ham, Wold 90Bc 178
W7 43Fa 86
Highlawn Hall HA1: Harr 34Ga 66
Highlea Cl. NW9 24Ua 48
High Level Dr. SE26 63Wb 135
Highlever Rd. W10 43Ya 88
High Mead BR4: W W'ck 75Fc 159
HA1: Harr 29Ga 46
IG7: Chig 19Sc 36
Highmead SE18 52Vc 117
Highmead Ct. CM15: B'wood 18Zd 41
Highmead Cres. HA0: Wemb 38Pa 67
High Mdw. Cl. HA5: Eastc 28Y 45
Highmeadow Cres. NW9 29Ta 47
High Mdw. Pl. KT16: Chert 72H 149
High Mdws. IG7: Chig 22Tc 54
High Meads Rd. E16 44Mc 93
Highmore Rd. SE3 52Gc 115
High Mt. NW4 30Wa 48
High Oaks EN2: Enf 10Pb 18
HA6: Nwood 22V 44
High Oaks Cl. CR5: Coul 91Kb 196
High Pde., The SW16 62Nb 134
High Pk. Av. KT24: E Hor 98V 190
TW9: Kew 53Qa 109
High Pk. Rd. TW9: Kew 53Qa 109
High Path SW19 67Db 133
High Pine Cl. KT13: Weyb 78S 150
High Pines CR6: W'ham 91Yb 198
High Point N6 31Jb 70
SE9 62Rc 138
Highpoint KT13: Weyb 78Q 150
High Ridge N10 25Kb 50
High Ridge Cl. HP3: Hem H 7M 3
Highridge Cl. KT18: Eps 86Ua 174
Highridge Pl. *EN2: Enf* 10Pb 18
(off Oak Av.)
High Ridge Rd. HP3: Hem H 7M 3
High Rd. AL9: Ess 3N 9
CM16: Epp 5Rc 22
CR5: Chip, Coul 97Gb 195
DA2: Wilm 62Ld 141
E18 25Jc 53
HA0: Wemb 36Ma 67
HA3: Hrw W 24Ga 46
HA5: Eastc 30W 44
HA9: Wemb 36Ma 67
IG1: Ilf 34Rc 74
(not continuous)
IG3: Ilf 32Vc 75
IG7: Chig 22Qc 54
IG9: Buck H 19Kc 35
IG10: Lough 16Lc 35
KT14: Byfl 84M 169
N11 22Kb 50
N15 28Vb 51
N17 26Vb 51
N22 25Pb 50
NW10 37Ua 68
RH2: Reig 99Eb 195
RM6: Chad H 31Zc 75
RM16: N Stif 46Zd 99
RM16: Ors 4A 100
SS17: Corr, Stan H 2P 101
(not continuous)
UB4: Hayes 43U 84
UB8: Cowl 43L 83
UB10: Ick 34R 64
WD23: B Hea 18Fa 28
WD25: Wat 7V 12
High Rd. E. Finchley N2 25Fb 49
High Rd. Leyton E10 30Dc 52
E15 33Dc 72
High Rd. Leytonstone E11 34Gc 73
E15 35Gc 73
High Rd. Nth. Finchley N12 20Eb 31
(not continuous)
High Rd. Whetstone N20 17Eb 31
High Rd. Woodford Grn. E18 24Hc 53
IG8: Wfd G 23Hc 53
High Sheldon N6 30Hb 49
Highshore Rd. SE15 54Vb 113
(not continuous)
High Silver IG10: Lough 14Mc 35
High Standing CR3: Cat'm 97Sb 197
Highstead Cres. DA8: Erith 53Gd 118
Highstone Av. E11 30Jc 53
Highstone Ct. *E11* 30Hc 53
(off New Wanstead)
Highstone Mans. *NW1* 38Lb 70
(off Camden Rd.)
High St. AL2: Lon C 7G 6
AL3: St A 2B 6
AL4: Col H 4M 7
BR1: Brom 68Jc 137
(not continuous)
BR3: Beck 68Cc 136
BR4: W W'ck 74Dc 158
BR5: St M Cry 72Yc 161
(not continuous)
BR6: Chels 80Vc 161
BR6: Downe 83Qc 180
BR6: Farnb 78Rc 160
BR6: Orp 75Wc 161
BR7: Chst 65Rc 138
BR8: Swan 69Hd 140
CM14: B'wood 19Yd 40
CM16: Epp 3Vc 23
CR0: C'don 76Sb 157
CR3: Cat'm 95Ub 197
CR7: Thor H 70Sb 135
CR8: Purl 83Qb 176
DA1: Dart 58Nd 119
DA2: Bean 62Xd 142
DA4: Eyns 75Nd 163
DA4: Farni 72Pd 163
DA9: Ghithe 56Xd 120
DA10: Swans 57Be 121
DA11: Grav'nd 8D 122
DA11: Nflt 58De 121
E11 29Jc 53
E13 40Jc 73
E15 40Ec 72
E17 29Ac 52
EN3: Pond E 16Yb 34
EN5: Barn 13Ab 30
High St. EN6: Pot B 5Db 17
EN8: Chesh 1Zb 20
EN8: Walt C 5Ac 20
GU21: Knap 9G 166
GU21: Wok 89B 168
(Commercial Way)
GU21: Wok 7M 167
(Horsell Birch)
GU22: Wok 93C 188
GU23: Rip 93L 189
GU24: Chob 3J 167
GU24: W End 4D 166
HA1: Harr 32Ga 66
HA3: Hrw W, W'stone 26Ga 46
HA4: Ruis 31U 64
HA5: Pinn 27Aa 45
HA6: Nwood 25V 44
HA8: Edg 23Qa 47
HA9: Wemb 35Pa 67
HP1: Hem H 1L 3
HP3: Bov 9C 2
HP4: Berk 1A 2
IG6: Ilf 27Sc 54
KT1: Hamp W 67La 130
KT1: King T 69Ma 131
KT3: N Mald 70Ua 132
KT7: T Ditt 72Ja 152
KT8: W Mole 70Ca 129
KT10: Clay 79Ha 152
KT10: Esh 77Da 151
KT11: Cobh 86X 171
KT12: Walt T 74W 150
KT13: Weyb 77Q 150
KT15: Add 77K 149
KT17: Eps 85Ta 173
KT17: Ewe 81Va 174
KT19: Eps 85Ta 173
KT20: Tad 95Ya 194
KT22: Lea 94Ka 192
KT22: Oxs 85Fa 172
KT23: Bookh 97Da 191
N8 28Nb 50
N14 18Mb 32
NW7 22Xa 48
RH1: Blet 5J 209
RH1: Mers 100Kb 196
RH1: Nutf 5F 208
RH1: Redh 6P 207
RH2: Reig 6J 207
RH8: Limp 100Jc 199
RH8: Oxt 2H 211
RH9: G'stone 2A 210
RM1: Rom 29Gd 56
RM11: Horn 32Md 77
RM12: Horn 32Md 77
RM15: Avel 46Sd 98
RM17: Grays 51Ce 121
(not continuous)
RM19: Purf 50Qd 97
SE20 65Yb 136
SE25 70Vb 135
SL0: Iver 44G 82
SL1: Burn 1A 80
SL1: Slou 8G 80
(Brammas Cl.)
SL1: Slou 6J 81
(Wellington St.)
SL1: Slou 7K 81
(William St., not continuous)
SL3: Coln 52E 104
SL3: Dat 3M 103
SL3: L'ly 50B 82
SL4: Eton 1H 103
SL4: Wind 3H 103
SL5: S'dale 1E 146
SL5: S'hill 1B 146
SL9: Chal P 25A 42
SM1: Sutt 77Db 155
SM3: Cheam 79Ab 154
SM5: Cars 78Jb 156
SM7: Bans 87Cb 175
SS17: Stan H 2L 101
SW19 64Za 132
TN13: Chip 94Ed 202
TN13: S'oaks 97Jd 203
TN14: Otf 88Jd 182
TN14: S'ham 82Hd 182
TN15: Bor G 92Be 205
TN15: Kems'g 89Rd 183
TN15: Seal 93Pd 203
TN15: Wro 88Ce 185
TN16: Bras 96Xc 201
TN16: Westrm 99Sc 200
TW2: Whitt 59Ea 108
TW3: Houn 55Da 107
TW5: Cran 53W 106
TW8: Bford 52La 108
TW11: Tedd 64Ha 130
TW12: Hamp, Hamp H 67Ea 130
TW13: Felt 62V 128
TW17: Shep 72R 150
TW18: Staines 63G 126
(not continuous)
TW19: Stanw 58M 105
TW19: Wray 58A 104
TW20: Egh 64B 126
UB1: S'hall 46Ba 85
UB3: Harl 51T 106
UB7: Harm 51M 105
UB7: Yiew 45M 83
UB8: Cowl 42L 83
UB8: Uxb 38L 63
UB9: Hare 26L 43
W3 46Ra 87
W5 46Ma 87
WD3: Rick 18M 25
WD4: K Lan 1Q 12
WD5: Ab L 3U 12
WD5: Bedm 9F 4
WD6: E'tree 16Ma 29
WD17: Wat 13X 27
WD23: Bush 16Ca 27
High St. Colliers Wood
SW19 66Fb 133
High St. Grn. HP2: Hem H 1A 4
High St. Harlesden
NW10 40Va 68
High St. M. SW19 64Ab 132
High St. Nth. E6 39Nc 74
E12 36Nc 74
High St. Sth. E6 40Pc 74
High St. W. SL1: Slou 7J 81
High Timber St.
EC4 4D 224 (45Sb 91)
High Tor Cl. BR1: Brom 66Kc 137
High Tor Vw. SE28 46Uc 94
High Tree Cl. CR8: Purl 82Pb 176
KT15: Add 78J 149
High Trees CR0: C'don 74Ac 158
DA2: Dart 58Rd 119
EN4: E Barn 15Gb 31
HP2: Hem H 2M 3
N20 20Eb 31
SW2 60Qb 112
High Trees Cl. CR3: Cat'm 94Vb 197
High Trees Ct. CR3: Cat'm 95Vb 197
Hightrees Ct. CM14: W'ley 21Sa 47
W7 45Ga 86
Hightrees Ho. SW12 58Jb 112
High Trees Rd. RH2: Reig 7L 207
High Vw. AL10: Hat 2B 8
HA5: Pinn 28Y 45
HP8: Chal G 19A 24
SM2: Cheam 83Bb 175
WD3: Chor 14J 25
WD18: Wat 16V 26
Highview CR3: Cat'm 96Ub 197
GU21: Knap 9J 167
N6 30Lb 50
NW7 20Ta 29
UB5: N'olt 41Aa 85
High Vw. Av. RM17: Grays 50Ee 99
Highview Av. HA8: Edg 21Sa 47
SM6: Wall 78Pb 156
High Vw. Cl. IG10: Lough 15Lc 35
SE19 68Vb 135
Highview Cl. EN6: Pot B 5Eb 17
KT20: Tad 93Wa 194
High Vw. Ct. HA3: Hrw W 24Ga 46
Highview Ct. *IG10: Lough* 15Mc 35
(off High Rd.)
RH2: Reig 6M 207
(off Wray Comn. Rd.)
Highview Cres. CM13: Hut 16Ee 41
High Vw. Gdns. RM17: Grays 50Ee 99
Highview Gdns. EN6: Pot B 5Eb 17
HA8: Edg 21Sa 47
N3 27Ab 48
N11 22Lb 50
RM14: Upm 33Rd 77
Highview Ho. RM6: Chad H 28Ad 55
Highview Lodge *EN2: Enf* 13Rb 33
(off The Ridgeway)
High Vw. Pde. IG4: Ilf 29Pc 54
High Vw. Pk. WD4: K Lan 10D 4
Highview Path SM7: Bans 87Cb 175
High Vw. Rd. BR6: Downe 82Qc 180
E18 26Hc 53
SE19 65Tb 135
Highview Rd. DA14: Sidc 63Xc 139
W13 43Ja 86
Highway, The BR6: Chels 78Xc 161
E1 45Wb 91
HA7: Stan 25Ha 46
SM2: Sutt 81Eb 175
Highwayman's Ridge
GU20: W'sham 7A 146
Highway Trad. Cen., The *E1* 45Zb 92
(off Heckford St.)
Highwold CR5: Chip 90Jb 176
Highwood BR2: Brom 69Fc 137
Highwood Av. N12 21Eb 49
WD23: Bush 11Ba 27
Highwood Cl. BR6: Farnb 75Sc 160
CM14: B'wood 17Xd 40
CR8: Kenley 89Sb 177
SE22 60Wb 113
Highwood Ct. EN5: New Bar 15Cb 31
N12 20Eb 31
Highwood Dr. BR6: Farnb 75Sc 160
Highwood Gdns. IG5: Ilf 29Pc 54
Highwood Gro. NW7 22Ta 47
Highwoodhall La. HP3: Hem H 7A 4
HIGHWOOD HILL 20Va 30
Highwood Hill NW7 19Va 30
Highwood La. IG10: Lough 15Qc 36
Highwood Rd. N19 34Nb 70
Highwoods CR3: Cat'm 97Ub 197
KT22: Lea 93La 192
High Worple HA2: Harr 31Ba 65
Highworth Rd. N11 23Mb 50
Highworth St. NW1 7E 214
Hi-Gloss Cen. SE8 50Ac 92
Hilary Av. CR4: Mitc 69Jb 134
Hilary Cl. DA8: Erith 53Dd 118
RM12: Horn 36Md 77
SW6 52Db 111
Hilary Dennis Ct. E11 28Jc 53
Hilary Rd. W12 44Va 88
(not continuous)
Hilberry Ct. WD23: Bush 17Da 27
Hilbert Rd. SM3: Cheam 76Za 154
Hilborough Cl. SW19 66Eb 133
Hilborough Ct. E8 38Vb 71
Hilborough Way BR6: Farnb 78Tc 160
Hilbury AL10: Hat 1B 8
Hilda Ct. KT6: Surb 73Ma 153
Hilda Lockert Wlk. *SW9* 54Rb 113
(off Loughborough Rd.)
Hilda May Av. BR8: Swan 68Gd 140
Hilda Rd. E6 38Mc 73
E16 42Gc 93
Hilda Ter. SW9 54Qb 112
Hilda Va. Cl. BR6: Farnb 77Rc 160
Hilda Va. Rd. BR6: Farnb 77Qc 160
Hildenborough Gdns.
BR1: Brom 65Gc 137
Hildenborough Ho. *BR3: Beck* 66Bc 136
(off Bethersden Cl.)
Hilden Dr. DA8: Erith 52Kd 119
Hildenlea Pl. BR2: Brom 68Fc 137
Hildenley Cl. RH1: Mers 100Mb 196
Hilderley Ho. *KT1: King T* 69Pa 131
(off Winery La.)
Hilders, The KT21: Asht 89Ra 173
Hildreth St. SW12 60Kb 112
Hildreth St. M. SW12 60Kb 112
Hildyard Rd. SW6 51Cb 111
Hiley Rd. NW10 41Ya 88
Hilfield La. WD25: A'ham 11Da 27
Hilfield La. Sth. WD23: Bush 16Ha 28
Hilgrove Rd. NW6 38Eb 69
Hiliary Gdns. HA7: Stan 26La 46
Hiljon Cres. SL9: Chal P 25A 42
Hill, The CR3: Cat'm 96Vb 197
DA11: Nflt 58Ee 121
Hillacre CR3: Cat'm 97Ub 197
Hillars Heath Rd. CR5: Coul 87Nb 176
Hillary *N8* 27Nb 50
(off Boyton Cl.)
Hillary Av. DA11: Nflt 2A 144
Hillary Ct. *TW19: Stanw* 60N 105
(off Explorer Av.)
W12 47Ya 88
(off Titmuss St.)
Hillary Cres. KT12: Walt T 74Y 151

Hillary Dr.—Hobbs Pl. Est.

Hillary Dr. TW7: Isle 57Ha 108
Hillary Ho. *WD6: Bore 13Ra 29*
(off Eldon Av.)
Hillary M. E14 43Dc 92
Hillary Ri. EN5: New Bar 14Cb 31
Hillary Rd. HP2: Hem H 1A 4
SL3: L'ly 47A 82
UB2: S'hall 48Ca 85
Hill Barn CR2: Sande 83Ub 177
Hillbeck Cl. SE15 52Yb 114
(not continuous)
Hillbeck Way UB6: G'frd 39Fa 66
Hillborne Cl. UB3: Harl 50W 84
Hillboro Ct. E11 31Fc 73
Hillborough Av.
TN13: S'oaks 94Md 203
Hillbrook Gdns. KT13: Weyb 80Q 150
Hillbrook Rd. SW17 62Hb 133
Hill Brow BR1: Brom 67Mc 137
DA1: Cray 58Hd 118
Hillbrow KT3: N Mald 69Va 132
RH2: Reig 6L 207
Hillbrow Cl. DA5: Bexl 63Fd 140
Hillbrow Cotts.
RH9: G'stone 4A 210
Hillbrow Ct. RH9: G'stone 4A 210
Hillbrow Rd. BR1: Brom 66Gc 137
KT10: Esh 77Ea 152
Hillbury Av. HA3: Kenton 29Ka 46
Hillbury Cl. CR6: W'ham 90Yb 178
Hillbury Cres. CR6: W'ham 90Yb 178
Hillbury Gdns. CR6: W'ham 90Yb 178
Hillbury Rd. CR3: Whyt 89Wb 177
CR6: W'ham 89Wb 177
SW17 62Kb 134
Hill Cl. BR7: Chst 64Rc 138
CR8: Purl 85Sb 177
DA13: Ist R 6A 144
EN5: Barn 15Ya 30
GU21: Wok 8P 167
HA1: Harr 34Ga 66
HA7: Stan 21Ka 46
KT11: Cobh 84Ca 171
NW2 34Xa 68
NW11 30Cb 49
Hill Comn. HP3: Hem H 6A 4
Hillcote Av. SW16 66Qb 134
Hill Ct. EN4: E Barn 14Gb 31
EN6: Pot B 6Eb 17
RM1: Rom 28Hd 56
UB5: N'olt 36Ca 65
W5 42Pa 87
Hillcourt Av. N12 23Db 49
Hillcourt Est. N16 32Tb 71
Hillcourt Rd. SE22 58Xb 113
Hill Cres. DA5: Bexl 60Ed 118
HA1: Harr 29Ja 46
KT4: Wor Pk 75Ya 154
KT5: Surb 71Pa 153
N20 19Db 31
RM11: Horn 30Ld 57
Hill Crest DA15: Sidc 59Wc 117
EN6: Pot B 6Eb 17
KT6: Surb 73Na 153
TN13: S'oaks 94Jd 202
Hillcrest AL3: St A 4P 5
AL10: Hat 1C 8
KT13: Weyb 77R 150
N6 31Jb 70
N21 17Qb 32
SE24 56Tb 113
W11 45Bb 89
(off St John's Gdns.)
Hillcrest Av. HA5: Pinn 28Z 45
HA8: Edg 21Ra 47
KT16: Chert 76G 148
NW11 29Bb 49
RM20: W Thur 51Wd 120
Hillcrest Cl. BR3: Beck 72Bc 158
EN7: G Oak 1Sb 19
KT18: Eps 87Va 174
SE26 63Wb 135
Hillcrest Ct. KT13: Weyb 77R 150
RM5: Col R 25Fd 56
SM2: Sutt 79Fb 155
(off Eaton Rd.)
Hillcrest Dr. DA9: Ghithe 57Wd 120
Hillcrest Gdns. KT10: Hin W 76Ha 152
N3 28Ab 48
NW2 34Wa 68
Hillcrest Pde. CR5: Coul 86Kb 176
Hillcrest Rd. BR1: Brom 64Jc 137
BR6: Chels 75Wc 161
CR3: Whyt 89Vb 177
CR8: Purl 82Pb 176
DA1: Dart 59Gd 118
E17 26Fc 53
E18 26Hc 53
IG10: Lough 16Mc 35
RM11: Horn 31Jd 76
TN16: Big H 88Mc 179
W3 46Ra 87
W5 43Na 87
WD7: Shenl 5Qa 15
Hillcrest Vw. BR3: Beck 72Bc 158
Hillcrest Way CM16: Epp 3Wc 23
Hillcrest Waye SL9: Ger X 31B 62
Hill Cft. WD7: R'lett 5Ja 14
Hillcroft IG10: Lough 12Qc 36
Hillcroft Av. CR8: Purl 85Lb 176
HA5: Pinn 30Ba 45
Hillcroft Ct. CR3: Cat'm 95Ub 197
Hillcroft Cres. HA4: Ruis 34Z 65
HA9: Wemb 35Pa 67
W5 44Ma 87
WD19: Wat 18X 27
Hillcroft Rd. E6 43Rc 94
Hillcroome Rd. SM2: Sutt 79Fb 155
Hillcross Av. SM4: Mord 72Za 154
Hilldale Rd. SM1: Sutt 77Bb 155
Hilldeane Rd. CR8: Purl 81Qb 176
Hilldene Av. RM3: Rom 23Ld 57
Hilldene Cl. RM3: Rom 22Md 57
Hilldown Ct. SW16 66Nb 134
Hilldown Rd. BR2: Hayes 74Gc 159
SW16 66Nb 134
Hill Dr. NW9 32Sa 67
SW16 69Pb 134
Hilldrop Cres. N7 36Mb 70
Hilldrop Est. N7 36Mb 70
(not continuous)
Hilldrop La. N7 36Mb 70
Hilldrop Rd. BR1: Brom 65Kc 137
N7 36Mb 70
Hille Bus. Cen. WD24: Wat 11X 27
HILL END 23K 43
Hill End BR6: Orp 75Vc 161
Hillend SE18 53Qc 116
Hill End La. AL4: St A 5F 6
Hill End Rd. UB9: Hare 24L 43
Hillersden Ho. SW1 7K 227
Hillersdon SL2: Slou 3M 81
Hillersdon Av. HA8: Edg 22Pa 47
SW13 54Wa 110
Hillery Cl. SE17 6G 231 (49Tb 91)
Hilley Fld. La. KT22: Fet 94Ea 192
Hill Farm Av. WD25: Wat 5W 12
(not continuous)
Hill Farm Cl. WD25: Wat 5W 12
Hill Farm Cotts. HA4: Ruis 31S 64
Hill Farm Ind. Est.
WD25: Wat 5W 12
Hill Farm Rd. SL9: Chal P 24A 42
UB10: Ick 35T 64
W10 43Ya 88
Hillfield Av. HA0: Wemb 38Na 67
N8 29Nb 50
NW9 29Ua 48
SM4: Mord 72Gb 155
Hillfield Cl. HA2: Harr 28Ea 46
RH1: Redh 6A 208
Hillfield Ct. HP2: Hem H 2N 3
KT10: Esh 78Da 151
NW3 36Gb 69
Hillfield Ho. N5 36Sb 71
Hillfield M. N8 28Pb 50
Hillfield Pde. SM4: Mord 72Fb 155
Hillfield Pk. N10 28Kb 50
N21 19Qb 32
Hillfield Pk. M. N10 28Kb 50
Hillfield Pl. TN13: Dun G 92Gd 202
Hill Fld. Rd. TW12: Hamp 66Ba 129
Hillfield Rd. HP2: Hem H 2M 3
NW6 36Bb 69
RH1: Redh 6A 208
SL9: Chal P 24A 42
TN13: Dun G 92Gd 202
Hillfield Sq. SL9: Chal P 24A 42
Hillfoot Av. RM5: Col R 25Ed 56
Hillfoot Rd. RM5: Col R 25Ed 56
Hillgate Pl. SW12 59Kb 112
W8 46Cb 89
Hillgate St. W8 46Cb 89
Hill Ga. Wlk. N6 30Lb 50
Hillground Gdns.
CR2: S Croy 82Rb 177
Hill Gro. RM1: Rom 27Gd 56
TW13: Hanw 61Ba 129
Hillgrove SL9: Chal P 25A 42
Hill Hall 8Bd 23
Hillhampton Pl. SL5: S'dale 3D 146
Hill Ho. BR2: Brom 68Hc 137
E5 32Xb 71
(off Harrington Hill)
N19 33Lb 70
(off Highgate Hill)
SE28 46Tc 94
Hillhouse EN9: Walt A 5Hc 21
Hill Ho. Apartments N1 2J 217
Hill Ho. Av. HA7: Stan 24Ha 46
Hill Ho. Cl. N21 17Qb 32
SL9: Chal P 24A 42
Hill Ho. Dr. KT13: Weyb 83Q 170
RH2: Reig 8K 207
RM16: Grays 10E 100
TW12: Hamp 67Ca 129
Hill Ho. M. BR2: Brom 68Hc 137
Hill Ho. Rd. DA2: Dart 59Sd 120
SW16 64Pb 134
Hillhurst Gdns. CR3: Cat'm 92Ub 197
Hilliard Ho. *E1 46Xb 91*
(off Prusom St.)
Hilliard Rd. HA6: Nwood 25V 44
Hilliards Ct. E1 46Yb 92
Hilliards Rd. UB8: Cowl 44M 83
Hillier Cl. EN5: New Bar 16Db 31
Hillier Gdns. CR0: Wadd 78Qb 156
Hillier Ho. *NW1 38Mb 70*
(off Camden Sq.)
Hillier Lodge TW11: Tedd 64Fa 130
Hillier Pl. KT9: Chess 79Ma 153
Hillier Rd. SW11 58Hb 111
Hilliers Av. UB8: Hil 41Q 84
Hilliers La. CR0: Bedd 76Nb 156
Hillier Way SL3: L'ly 49C 82
Hillingdale TN16: Big H 90Kc 179
HILLINGDON 41Q 84
Hillingdon Athletic Club 29T 44
Hillingdon Athletics Stadium 37N 63
Hillingdon Av. TN13: S'oaks 93Ld 203
TW19: Stanw 60N 105
HILLINGDON CIRCUS 37R 64
Hillingdon Ct. HA3: Kenton 28Ma 47
Hillingdon Cycling Circuit 46Y 85
Hillingdon Golf Course 40P 63
HILLINGDON HEATH 42R 84
Hillingdon Hill UB10: Hil 40N 63
Hillingdon Outdoor Activities Cen. 31T 63
Hillingdon Pde. *UB10: Hil 42R 84*
(off Uxbridge Rd.)
Hillingdon Ri. TN13: S'oaks 94Md 203
Hillingdon Rd. DA7: Bex 54Ed 118
DA11: Grav'nd 1D 144
UB8: Uxb 39M 63
UB10: Uxb 39N 63
WD25: Wat 6W 12
Hillingdon Sports & Leisure Complex
37N 63
Hillingdon St. SE17 51Rb 113
Hillington Gdns. IG8: Wfd G 26Mc 53
Hill La. HA4: Ruis 32S 64
KT20: Kgswd 93Ab 194
Hill Ley AL10: Hat 1B 8
Hillman Cl. RM11: Horn 27Md 57
UB8: Uxb 36N 63
Hillman Dr. W10 42Ya 88
Hillman St. E8 37Xb 71
Hillmarton Rd. N7 36Nb 70
Hillmarton Ter. *N7 36Nb 70*
(off Hillmarton Rd.)
Hillmead Dr. SW9 56Rb 113
Hillmont Rd. KT10: Hin W 76Ga 152
Hillmore Ct. *SE13 55Fc 115*
(off Belmont Hill)
Hillmore Gro. SE26 64Ac 136
Hillmount *GU22: Wok 90A 168*
(off Constitution Hill)
HILL PARK 95Rc 200
Hill Pk. Ct. KT22: Lea 91Ha 192
Hill Pk. Dr. KT22: Lea 91Ha 192
Hill Pk. (Local Nature Reserve) 94Nc 200
Hill Pk. Sth. KT22: Lea 92Ha 192
Hill Path SW16 64Pb 134
Hill Pl. SL2: Farn C 8F 60
Hillpoint WD3: Loud 15L 25
Hillreach SE18 50Pc 94
Hill Ri. DA2: Daren 64Td 142
EN6: Cuff 1Nb 18
EN6: Pot B 6Eb 17
HA4: Ruis 32S 64
KT10: Hin W 75Ka 152
N9 16Xb 33
NW11 28Db 49
RM14: Upm 33Qd 77
SE23 60Xb 113
SL9: Chal P 26A 42
TW10: Rich 57Ma 109
UB6: G'frd 38Ea 66
WD3: Rick 16K 25
Hillrise KT12: Walt T 73V 150
SL3: L'ly 51C 104
Hillrise Av. WD24: Wat 10Z 13
Hill Rise Ct. *KT22: Lea 93Ka 192*
(off Park Rise)
Hill Rise Cres.
SL9: Chal P 26A 42
Hillrise Mans. *N19 31Nb 70*
(off Warltersville Rd.)
Hillrise Rd. N19 31Nb 70
RM5: Col R 23Ed 56
Hill Rd. CM14: B'wood 20Wd 40
CM16: They B 10Uc 22
CR4: Mitc 67Kb 134
CR8: Purl 84Pb 176
DA2: Wilm 61Nd 141
HA0: Wemb 34Ka 66
HA1: Harr 29Ja 46
HA5: Pinn 29Aa 45
HA6: Nwood 23T 44
KT22: Fet 94Da 191
N10 25Hb 49
NW8 3A 214 (40Eb 69)
SM1: Sutt 78Db 155
SM5: Cars 79Gb 155
Hillsboro' Rd. SE22 57Ub 113
Hillsborough Ct. *NW6 39Db 69*
(off Mortimer Cres.)
Hillsborough Grn.
WD19: Wat 20W 26
Hill's Chace CM14: W'ley 21Yd 58
Hillsgrove Cl.
DA16: Well 52Yc 117
HILLSIDE 49Ed 96
Hillside AL10: Hat 1C 8
DA2: Daren 64Ud 142
DA4: Farni 73Pd 163
DA8: Erith 49Ed 96
EN5: New Bar 15Eb 31
GU22: Wok 2P 187
GU25: Vir W 2N 147
KT10: Esh 78Da 151
N8 30Mb 50
NW5 34Jb 70
NW9 28Ta 47
NW10 38Sa 67
RM3: Rom 21Md 57
RM17: Grays 49Fe 99
SE10 52Fc 115
(off Croom's Hill)
SL1: Slou 7J 81
SL5: S'hill 1A 146
SM7: Bans 87Ab 174
SW19 65Za 132
UB9: Hare 29L 43
Hillside, The
BR6: Prat B 81Xc 181
Hillside Av. CR8: Purl 85Rb 177
DA12: Grav'nd 1F 144
EN8: Chesh 3Zb 20
HA9: Wemb 35Pa 67
IG8: Wfd G 23Lc 53
N11 23Hb 49
WD6: Bore 14Ra 29
Hillside Cl. GU21: Knap 9H 167
IG8: Wfd G 22Lc 53
NW8 40Db 69
SL9: Chal P 23A 42
SM4: Mord 70Ab 132
SM7: Bans 88Ab 174
WD5: Ab L 4U 12
Hillside Cotts. HP3: Hem H 3C 4
Hillside Ct. *AL1: St A 1C 6*
(off Hillside Rd.)
BR8: Swan 70Jd 140
EN8: Chesh 3Zb 20
Hillside Cres. EN2: Enf 10Tb 19
EN8: Chesh 3Zb 20
HA2: Harr 32Ea 66
HA6: Nwood 25W 44
WD19: Wat 16Aa 27
Hillside Dr.
DA12: Grav'nd 1F 144
HA8: Edg 23Qa 47
Hillside Gdns. E17 27Fc 53
EN5: Barn 14Ab 30
HA3: Kenton 31Na 67
HA6: Nwood 24W 44
HA8: Edg 21Pa 47
HP4: Berk 2A 2
KT15: Add 78H 149
N6 30Kb 50
N11 23Lb 50
SM6: Wall 80Lb 156
SW2 61Qb 134
Hillside Ga. *AL1: St A 1C 6*
(off Hillside Rd.)
Hillside Gro. N14 17Mb 32
NW7 24Wa 48
Hillside Ho. *CR0: Wadd 77Rb 157*
(off Duppas Av.)
Hillside La. BR2: Hayes 75Hc 159
(not continuous)
Hillside Mans. EN5: Barn 14Bb 31
WD23: Bush 18Ca 27
Hillside Pk. SL5: S'dale 4D 146
Hillside Pas. SW2 61Pb 134
Hillside Path CR5: Coul 90Nb 176
Hillside Ri.
HA6: Nwood 24W 44
Hillside Rd. AL1: St A 1C 6
BR2: Brom 69Hc 137
CR0: Wadd 78Rb 157
CR3: Whyt 90Wb 177
CR5: Coul 90Nb 176
DA1: Cray 58Jd 118
HA5: Pinn 24X 45
HA6: Nwood 24W 44
KT5: Surb 70Pa 131
KT17: Ewe 82Ya 174
KT21: Asht 89Pa 173
N15 31Ub 71
SM2: Sutt 80Bb 155
SW2 61Pb 134
TN13: S'oaks 95Md 203
Hillside Rd. TN15: Kems'g 89Pd 183
TN16: Tats 91Nc 200
UB1: S'hall 42Ca 85
W5 43Na 87
WD3: Chor 15E 24
WD7: R'lett 7Ka 14
WD23: Bush 15Aa 27
Hillside Wlk. CM14: B'wood 20Vd 40
Hills La. HA6: Nwood 25U 44
TN15: Knat 85Rd 183
Hillsleigh Rd. W8 46Bb 89
Hillsmead Way CR2: Sande 85Wb 177
Hills M. W5 45Na 87
Hills Pl. W1 3B 222 (44Lb 90)
Hills Rd. IG9: Buck H 18Kc 35
Hillstone Ct. *E3 42Dc 92*
(off Empson St.)
Hillstowe St. E5 34Yb 72
Hill St. AL3: St A 2A 6
TW9: Rich 57Ma 109
W1 6J 221 (46Jb 90)
Hillswood Dr. KT16: Chert 77D 148
Hillthorpe Cl. CR8: Purl 82Pb 176
Hill Top IG10: Lough 12Qc 36
NW11 28Db 49
SM3: Sutt 73Bb 155
SM4: Mord 72Cb 155
Hilltop E17 27Dc 52
Hilltop Av. NW10 38Sa 67
(not continuous)
Hill Top Cl. IG10: Lough 13Qc 36
Hilltop Cl. KT22: Lea 95La 192
SL5: Asc 8C 124
Hill Top Ct. IG8: Wfd G 23Pc 54
Hilltop Ct. *NW8 38Eb 69*
(off Alexandra Rd.)
Hilltop Farm WD4: K Lan 9D 4
Hilltop Gdns. BR6: Orp 75Uc 160
DA1: Dart 57Pd 119
NW4 26Xa 48
Hilltop Ho. N6 31Mb 70
Hilltop La. CR3: Cat'm 98Qb 196
RH1: Mers 98Qb 196
Hill Top Pl. IG10: Lough 13Qc 36
Hilltop Ri. KT23: Bookh 98Ea 192
Hilltop Rd. CR3: Whyt 89Ub 177
NW6 38Cb 69
RH2: Reig 8K 207
RM20: W Thur 51Xd 120
WD4: K Lan 9D 4
Hill Top Vw. IG8: Wfd G 23Pc 54
Hilltop Wlk. CR3: Wold 92Ac 198
Hilltop Way HA7: Stan 20Ja 28
Hill Vw. CR3: Whyt 89Vb 177
GU24: Chob 7G 146
NW3 39Hb 69
(off Ainger Rd.)
SL2: Hedg 2H 61
TN15: Bor G 92Ce 205
Hillview SW20 66Xa 132
TN15: Bor G 95Be 205
Hillview Av. HA3: Kenton 29Na 47
RM11: Horn 30Ld 57
Hill Vw. Cl. KT20: Tad 93Ya 194
TN15: Bor G 92Ce 205
Hillview Cl. CR8: Purl 83Rb 177
HA5: Hat E 23Ba 45
HA9: Wemb 33Pa 67
Hill Vw. Ct. GU22: Wok 90B 168
Hill Vw. Cres. IG1: Ilf 30Pc 54
Hillview Cres. BR6: Orp 74Uc 160
Hill Vw. Dr. DA16: Well 54Uc 116
SE28 46Uc 94
Hillview Dr. RH1: Redh 7A 208
Hill Vw. Gdns. NW9 29Ta 47
Hillview Gdns. HA2: Harr 27Ca 45
NW4 28Za 48
Hillview Ho. DA12: Grav'nd 10E 122
Hill Vw. Pl. KT11: Cobh 85Ba 171
Hill Vw. Rd. DA3: Lfield 69De 143
GU22: Wok 90B 168
KT10: Clay 80Ja 152
TW1: Twick 58Ja 108
TW19: Wray 8P 103
Hillview Rd. BR6: Orp 74Vc 161
BR7: Chst 64Qc 138
HA5: Hat E 24Ba 45
NW7 22Ab 48
SM1: Sutt 76Eb 155
Hillway N6 33Jb 70
NW9 32Ua 68
Hillway, The CM15: Mount 11Fe 41
Hill Waye SL9: Ger X 30B 42
Hillwood Cl. CM13: Hut 18De 41
Hillwood Gro. CM13: Hut 18De 41
Hill-Wood Ho. NW1 2C 216
Hillworth BR3: Beck 68Dc 136
Hillworth Rd. SW2 59Qb 112
Hillyard Ho. SW9 53Qb 112
Hillyard Rd. W7 43Ga 86
Hillyard St. SW9 53Qb 112
Hillydeal Rd. TN14: Otf 87Ld 183
Hillyfield E17 26Ac 52
Hillyfield Cl. E9 36Ac 72
Hillyfields IG10: Lough 12Qc 36
Hilly Flds. Cres. SE4 55Cc 114
SE13 55Cc 114
Hilmay Dr. HP1: Hem H 3K 3
Hilperton Rd. SL1: Slou 7J 81
Hilsea Point SW15 60Xa 110
Hilsea St. E5 35Yb 72
Hilton W13 44La 86
Hilton Av. N12 22Fb 49
Hilton Cl. UB8: Uxb 40K 63
Hilton Ho. SE4 56Zb 114
Hilton's Wharf *SE10 51Dc 114*
(off Norman Rd.)
Hilton Way CR2: Sande 87Xb 177
Hilversum Cres. SE22 57Ub 113
Himalayan Way WD18: Wat 16V 26
Himalaya Palace Cinema 46Ba 85
Himley Rd. SW17 64Gb 133
Hinchinbrook Ho. *NW6 39Db 69*
(off Mortimer Cres.)
Hinchley Cl. KT10: Hin W 77Ha 152
Hinchley Dr. KT10: Hin W 76Ha 152
Hinchley Mnr. KT10: Hin W 76Ha 152
Hinchley Way KT10: Hin W 76Ja 152
HINCHLEY WOOD 76Ha 152
Hinckley Rd. SE15 56Wb 113
Hind Cl. IG7: Chig 22Vc 55
Hind Ct. EC4 3A 224 (44Qb 90)
Hind Cres. DA8: Erith 51Fd 118
Hinde Ho. W1 2J 221
Hinde M. W1 2J 221
Hindes Rd. HA1: Harr 29Fa 46
Hinde St. W1 2J 221 (44Jb 90)
Hind Gro. E14 44Cc 92
Hindhead Cl. N16 32Ub 71
UB8: Hil 43R 84
Hindhead Gdns. UB5: N'olt 39Aa 65
Hindhead Grn. WD19: Wat 22Y 45
Hindhead Point SW15 60Xa 110
Hindhead Way SM6: Wall 78Nb 156
Hind Ho. N7 35Qb 70
SE14 51Zb 114
(off Myers La.)
Hindle Ho. E8 36Vb 71
Hindlip Ho. SW8 53Mb 112
Hindmans Rd. SE22 57Wb 113
Hindmans Way RM9: Dag 42Bd 95
Hindmarsh Cl. E1 45Wb 91
Hindmarsh Cres. DA11: Nflt 61Ee 143
Hindon Ct. SW1 5B 228
Hindrey Rd. E5 36Xb 71
Hindsley's Pl. SE23 61Yb 136
Hind Ter. RM20: Grays 50Zd 99
Hine Cl. CR5: Coul 94Lb 196
KT19: Eps 83Ra 173
Hine Ho. AL4: St A 3H 7
Hinkler Rd. HA3: Kenton 27Ma 47
Hinkley Cl. UB9: Hare 28L 43
Hinksey Cl. SL3: L'ly 48D 82
Hinksey Path SE2 47Zc 95
Hinstock *NW6 39Db 69*
(off Belsize Rd.)
Hinstock Rd. SE18 51Sc 116
Hinton Av. TW4: Houn 56Z 107
Hinton Cl. SE9 60Nc 116
Hinton Ct. *E10 33Dc 72*
(off Leyton Grange Est.)
Hinton Rd. N18 21Ub 51
SE24 55Sb 113
SL1: Slou 5C 80
SM6: Wall 79Lb 156
SW9 55Rb 113
UB8: Uxb 39L 63
Hipley St. GU22: Wok 92D 188
Hippisley Ct. TW7: Isle 55Ha 108
Hippodrome M. W11 45Ab 88
Hippodrome Pl. W11 45Ab 88
Hiroshima Prom. SE7 48Lc 93
Hirst Ct. SW1 51Kb 112
Hirst Cres. HA9: Wemb 34Na 67
Hispano M. EN3: Enf L 9Cc 20
Hitcham Rd. E17 31Bc 72
Hitchcock Cl. TW17: Shep 69P 127
Hitchcock Ct. WD6: Bore 12Sa 29
Hitchcock La. E20 37Ec 72
Hitchen Hatch La. TN13: S'oaks 96Jd 202
Hitchen Hatch Pl. TN13: S'oaks 95Kd 203
Hitchens Cl. HP1: Hem H 1H 3
Hitchin Cl. RM3: Rom 21Ld 57
Hitchings Way RH2: Reig 10J 207
Hitchin La. HA7: Stan 24Ma 47
Hitchin Rd. HA7: Stan 24Na 47
Hitchin Sq. E3 40Ac 72
Hitch St. RM9: Dag 41Ad 95
Hithe Gro. SE16 48Yb 92
Hitherbroom Rd. UB3: Hayes 46W 84
Hither Farm Rd. SE3 55Lc 115
Hitherfield Rd. RM8: Dag 33Ad 75
SW16 61Pb 134
Hither Flds. DA11: Grav'nd 4E 144
HITHER GREEN 58Fc 115
Hither Green Crematorium SE6 61Hc 137
Hither Grn. La. SE13 57Ec 114
Hither Mdw. SL9: Chal P 25A 42
Hithermoor Rd. TW19: Stanw M 58H 105
Hitherwell Dr. HA3: Hrw W 25Fa 46
Hitherwood Cl. RH2: Reig 4M 207
RM12: Horn 35Md 77
Hitherwood Ct. *NW9 26Ua 48*
(off Charcot Rd.)
Hitherwood Dr. SE19 63Vb 135
Hittard Ct. *SE17 51Tb 113*
(off Red Lion Row)
Hive, The 25Na 47
Hive, The DA11: Nflt 58De 121
Hive Cl. CM14: B'wood 19Wd 40
WD23: B Hea 19Fa 28
Hive Football & Fitness Cen., The
25Na 47
Hive La. DA11: Nflt 58De 121
Hive Rd. WD23: B Hea 19Fa 28
Hixberry La. AL4: St A 3H 7
HMP Belmarsh SE28 47Uc 94
HMP Brixton SW2 58Nb 112
HMP Bronzefield TW15: Ashf 63L 127
HMP Coldingley GU24: Bisl 9D 166
HMP Downview SM2: Sutt 84Eb 175
HMP High Down SM2: Sutt 84Eb 175
HMP Isis SE28 47Vc 95
HMP Pentonville N7 37Pb 70
HMP Send GU23: Send 99L 189
HMP Thameside SE28 48Uc 94
HMP The Mount HP3: Bov 8C 2
HMP Wandsworth SW18 59Fb 111
HMP Wormwood Scrubs W12 44Wa 88
HMS Belfast 6J 225 (46Ub 91)
HMYOI Feltham TW13: Felt 62T 128
Hoad Cres. GU22: Wok 94B 188
Hoadly Ho. SE1 7D 224
Hoadly Rd. SW16 62Mb 134
Hobart Cl. N20 19Gb 31
UB4: Yead 42Z 85
Hobart Ct. *CR2: S Croy 78Tb 157*
(off South Pk. Hill Rd.)
IG8: Wfd G 21Hc 53
Hobart Dr. UB4: Yead 42Z 85
Hobart Gdns. CR7: Thor H 69Tb 135
Hobart La. UB4: Yead 42Z 85
Hobart Pl. SW1 3K 227 (48Kb 90)
TW10: Rich 59Pa 109
Hobart Rd. IG6: Ilf 26Sc 54
KT4: Wor Pk 76Xa 154
RM9: Dag 35Zc 75
RM18: Tilb 3C 122
UB4: Yead 42Z 85
Hobbayne Rd. W7 44Fa 86
Hobbes Wlk. SW15 57Xa 110
Hobbs Cl. AL4: St A 3J 7
EN8: Chesh 1Zb 20
KT14: W Byf 85K 169
Hobbs Ct. *SE1 47Vb 91*
(off Mill St.)
HOBBS CROSS 8Zc 23
Hobbs Cross Golf Course 6Zc 23
Hobbs Cross Rd.
CM16: Epp, Fidd H, They G 6Yc 23
Hobbs Grn. N2 27Eb 49
Hobbs Hill Rd. HP3: Hem H 6N 3
Hobbs La. EN8: Chesh 1Zb 20
Hobbs M. IG3: Ilf 33Vc 75
Hobbs Pl. N1 1H 219 (39Ub 71)
Hobbs Pl. Est. N1 1H 219

Hobbs Rd.—Holmes Pl.

Hobbs Rd. SE27 . . . . .63Sb 135
Hobby Ho. SE1 . . . . .49Xb 91
Hobby St. EN3: Pond E 15Zb 34
Hobday St. E14 . . . . .44Dc 92
Hobhouse Ct. *SW1* *5E 222*
(off Suffolk St.)
Hobill Wlk. KT5: Surb 72Pa 153
Hoblands End BR7: Chst 65Uc 138
Hobletts Rd. HP2: Hem H 1P 3
Hobson's Pl. E1 . . . . .43Wb 91
Hobury St. SW10 . . . . .51Eb 111
HOCKENDEN 69Cd 140
Hockenden La. BR8: Swan 69Cd 140
Hockering Est. GU22: Wok 90D 168
Hockering Gdns. GU22: Wok 90C 168
Hockering Rd. GU22: Wok 90C 168
Hocker St. E2 . . . . .4K 219 (41Vb 91)
Hockett Cl. SE8 . . . . .49Ac 92
Hockford Cl. GU24: Pirb 8F 186
Hockington Ct. EN5: New Bar 14Db 31
Hockley Av. E6 . . . . .40Nc 74
Hockley Ct. E18 . . . . .25Jc 53
Hockley Dr. RM2: Rom 26Kd 57
HOCKLEY HOLE 9M 61
Hockley La. SL2: Stoke P 8M 61
Hockley M. IG11: Bark 41Uc 94
Hockliffe Ho. *W10* *43Ya 88*
(off Sutton Way)
Hockney Ct. *SE16* *50Xb 91*
(off Rossetti Rd.)
Hocroft Av. NW2 . . . . .34Bb 69
Hocroft Ct. NW2 . . . . .34Bb 69
Hocroft Rd. NW2 . . . . .35Bb 69
Hocroft Wlk. NW2 . . . . .34Bb 69
Hodder Dr. UB6: G'frd 40Ha 66
Hoddesdon Rd. DA17: Belv 50Cd 96
Hodes Row NW3 . . . . .35Jb 70
Hodford Rd. NW11 . . . . .32Bb 69
Hodges Cl. RM16: Chaf H 50Zd 99
Hodges Way WD18: Wat 16W 26
Hodgkin Cl. SE28 . . . . .45Zc 95
Hodgkin Ct. *SE5* *52Tb 113*
(off Dobson Wlk.)
Hodgkins M. HA7: Stan 22Ka 46
Hodister Cl. SE5 . . . . .52Sb 113
Hodnet Gro. SE16 . . . . .49Zb 92
Hodsoll Ct. BR5: St M Cry 71Zc 161
HODSOLL STREET 81Fe 185
Hodsoll St. TN15: Hod S 81Fe 185
Hodson Cl. HA2: Harr 34Ba 65
Hodson Cres. BR5: St M Cry 71Zc 161
Hodson Pl. EN3: Enf L 10Cc 20
Hoe, The WD19: Wat 19Z 27
Hoebridge Golf Course 91E 188
Hoebrook Cl. GU22: Wok 3P 187
Hoe Ct. GU22: Wok 91A 188
Hoecroft Ct. *EN3: Enf W* *10Yb 20*
(off Hoe La.)
Hoe La. EN1: Enf 10Wb 19
EN3: Enf W 10Xb 19
RM4: Abr 13Xc 37
Hoe St. E17 . . . . .28Cc 52
Hoever Ho. SE6 . . . . .63Ec 136
Hoey Ct. *E3* *42Dc 92*
(off Barry Blandford Way)
Hoffmann Gdns. CR2: Sels 80Xb 157
Hoffman Sq. N1 . . . . .3G 219
Hoffmans Rd. E17 . . . . .27Zb 52
Hofland Rd. W14 . . . . .48Ab 88
Hoford Rd. RM18: W Til 9F 100
SS17: Linf 6H 101
Hogan Bus. Cen. GU21: Wok 89A 168
Hogan M. W2 . . . . .7B 214 (43Eb 89)
Hogan Way E5 . . . . .33Wb 71
Hogarth Av. CM15: B'wood 20Ae 41
TW15: Ashf 65S 128
Hogarth Bus. Pk. W4 . . . . .51Ua 110
Hogarth Cl. E16 . . . . .43Mc 93
SL1: Slou 5C 80
UB8: Uxb 41L 83
W5 . . . . .43Na 87
Hogarth Ct. *E1* *44Wb 91*
(off Batty St.)
EC3 . . . . .3J 225 (44Ub 91)
NW1 . . . . .*38Lb 70*
(off St Pancras Way)
SE19 . . . . .63Vb 135
TW5: Hest 52Aa 107
WD23: Bush 17Da 27
Hogarth Cres. CR0: C'don 73Sb 157
SW19 . . . . .67Fb 133
Hogarth Gdns. TW5: Hest 52Ca 107
Hogarth Health Club, The 49Va 88
Hogarth Hill NW11 . . . . .28Bb 49
Hogarth Ho. *EC1* *1C 224*
(off Bartholomew Cl.)
SW1 . . . . .6E 228
UB5: N'olt *40Z 65*
(off Gallery Gdns.)
Hogarth Ind. Est. NW10 . . . . .42Wa 88
Hogarth La. W4 . . . . .51Ua 110
Hogarth Pl. *SW5* *49Db 89*
(off Hogarth Rd.)
Hogarth Reach IG10: Lough 15Pc 36
Hogarth Rd. HA8: Edg 26Qa 47
RM8: Dag 36Xc 75
RM16: Grays 46Ce 99
SW5 . . . . .49Db 89
HOGARTH RDBT. 51Ua 110
Hogarth's House *51Ua 110*
(off Hogarth La.)
Hogarth Ter. W4 . . . . .51Ua 110
Hogarth Way TW12: Hamp 67Ea 130
Hogden Cl. KT20: Kgswd 97Bb 195
Hogfair La. SL1: Burn 1A 80
Hogg La. RM16: Grays 48Ce 99
RM17: Grays 47Ce 99
(not continuous)
WD6: E'tree 14Ja 28
Hog Hill Rd. RM5: Col R 24Bd 55
Hognore La. TN15: Wro 86Fe 185
HOGPITS BOTTOM 4D 10
Hogscross La. CR5: Coul 95Hb 195
Hogshead Pas. *E1* *45Xb 91*
(off Tobacco Dock)
Hogshill La. KT11: Cobh 86X 171
(not continuous)
Hogs La. DA11: Nflt 62Fe 143
Hogsmill Ho. *KT1: King T* *69Pa 131*
(off Vineyard Cl.)
Hogsmill La. KT1: King T 69Pa 131
Hogsmill Local Nature Reserve 78Ra 153
Hogsmill Wlk. *KT1: King T* *69Na 131*
(off Penrhyn Rd.)
Hogsmill Way KT19: Ewe 78Sa 153
Hogs Orchard BR8: Swan 67Kd 141
Hogtrough Hill
TN16: Bras, S'oaks 92Vc 201
Hogtrough La. RH1: S Nut 7C 208
RH8: Oxt 100Dc 198
RH9: G'stone 99Cc 198
Holbeach Cl. NW9 . . . . .25Ua 48
Holbeach Gdns. DA15: Sidc 58Uc 116
Holbeach M. SW12 . . . . .60Kb 112
Holbeach Rd. SE6 . . . . .59Cc 114
Holbeck Row SE15 . . . . .52Wb 113
Holbein Ga. HA6: Nwood 22U 44
Holbein Ho. SW1 . . . . .7H 227
Holbein M. SW1 . . . . .7H 227 (50Jb 90)
Holbein Pl. SW1 . . . . .6H 227 (49Jb 90)
Holbein Ter. *RM8: Dag* *35Yc 75*
(off Marlborough Rd.)
Holberton Gdns. NW10 . . . . .41Xa 88
HOLBORN 1H 223 (44Nb 90)
Holborn EC1 . . . . .1K 223 (43Qb 90)
Holborn Bars EC1 . . . . .1K 223
Holborn Cir. EC1 . . . . .1A 224 (43Qb 90)
Holborn Cl. NW7 . . . . .21Va 48
Holborn Ho. W12 . . . . .44Xa 88
Holborn Pl. WC1 . . . . .1H 223 (43Pb 90)
Holborn Rd. E13 . . . . .42Kc 93
Holborn Viaduct EC1 . . . . .1A 224 (43Rb 91)
Holborn Way CR4: Mitc 68Hb 133
Holbreck Pl. GU22: Wok 90B 168
Holbrook Cl. EN1: Enf 11Vb 33
N19 . . . . .32Kb 70
Holbrook Ct. TW20: Egh 64E 126
Holbrooke Ct. N7 . . . . .35Nb 70
Holbrooke Pl. TW10: Rich 57Ma 109
Holbrook Gdns. WD25: A'ham 8Da 13
Holbrook Ho. BR7: Chst 67Tc 138
Holbrook La. BR7: Chst 66Tc 138
Holbrook Mdw. TW20: Egh 65E 126
Holbrook Rd. E15 . . . . .40Hc 73
Holbrook Way BR2: Brom 72Pc 160
Holburne Cl. SE3 . . . . .53Lc 115
Holburne Gdns. SE3 . . . . .53Mc 115
Holburne Rd. SE3 . . . . .53Lc 115
Holcombe Cl. TN16: Westrm 98Tc 200
Holcombe Hill NW7 . . . . .20Wa 30
Holcombe Ho. *SW9* *55Nb 112*
(off Landor Rd.)
Holcombe Pl. *SE4* *55Ac 114*
(off St Asaph Rd.)
Holcombe Rd. IG1: Ilf 31Qc 74
N17 . . . . .27Vb 51
Holcombe St. W6 . . . . .49Xa 88
Holcon Ct. RH1: Redh 3A 208
Holcote Cl. DA17: Belv 48Ad 95
Holcroft Ct. W1 . . . . .7B 216
Holcroft Ho. SW11 . . . . .55Fb 111
Holcroft Rd. E9 . . . . .38Yb 72
HOLDBROOK 6Bc 20
Holdbrook Nth. EN8: Walt C 5Bc 20
Holdbrook Sth. EN8: Walt C 6Bc 20
Holdbrook Way RM3: Hrld W 26Pd 57
Holden Av. N12 . . . . .22Db 49
NW9 . . . . .32Sa 67
Holdenby Rd. SE4 . . . . .57Ac 114
Holden Cl. RM8: Dag 34Xc 75
Holden Ct. KT13: Weyb 80Q 150
Holden Gdns. CM14: W'ley 22Zd 59
Holden Ho. *N1* *39Sb 71*
(off Prebend St.)
SE8 . . . . .52Cc 114
Holdenhurst Av. N12 . . . . .24Eb 49
Holden Pl. KT11: Cobh 86X 171
Holden Point *E15* *37Fc 73*
(off Waddington St.)
Holden Rd. N12 . . . . .22Db 49
Holden St. SW11 . . . . .54Jb 112
Holden Way RM14: Upm 32Td 78
Holder Cl. N3 . . . . .24Db 49
Holdernesse Cl. TW7: Isle 53Ja 108
Holdernesse Rd. SW17 . . . . .62Hb 133
Holderness Ho. SE5 . . . . .55Ub 113
Holderness Way SE27 . . . . .64Rb 135
HOLDERS HILL 26Za 48
Holder's Hill Av. NW4 . . . . .26Za 48
Holders Hill Cir. NW7 . . . . .24Ab 48
Holders Hill Cres. NW4 . . . . .26Za 48
Holders Hill Dr. NW4 . . . . .27Za 48
Holder's Hill Gdns. NW4 . . . . .26Ab 48
Holders Hill Pde. NW7 . . . . .25Ab 48
Holders Hill Rd. NW4 . . . . .26Za 48
NW7 . . . . .26Za 48
Holecroft EN9: Walt A 6Gc 21
Hole Farm La. CM13: Gt War 27Xd 58
Hole in the Wall All.
DA11: Grav'nd *8D 122*
(off High St.)
Holford Ho. *SE16* *49Xb 91*
(off Camilla Rd.)
WC1 . . . . .3J 217
Holford M. WC1 . . . . .3K 217
Holford Pl. WC1 . . . . .3J 217 (41Pb 90)
Holford Rd. NW3 . . . . .34Eb 69
Holford St. WC1 . . . . .3K 217 (41Pb 90)
Holford Way SW15 . . . . .58Wa 110
Holford Yd. WC1 . . . . .2J 217
Holgate Av. SW11 . . . . .55Fb 111
Holgate Ct. *RM1: Rom* *29Gd 56*
(off Western Rd.)
Holgate Gdns. RM10: Dag 37Cd 76
Holgate Rd. RM10: Dag 36Cd 76
Holgate St. SE7 . . . . .48Mc 93
Holinser Ter. W5 . . . . .46Ma 87
Hollam Ho. N8 . . . . .28Pb 50
HOLLAND 5L 211
Holland Av. SM2: Sutt 80Cb 155
SW20 . . . . .67Va 132
Holland Cl. BR2: Hayes 75Hc 159
EN5: New Bar 17Fb 31
HA7: Stan 22Ka 46
KT19: Eps 83Sa 173
RH1: Redh 6P 207
RM7: Rom 29Ed 56
Holland Ct. *E17* *28Ec 52*
(off Evelyn Rd.)
KT6: Surb 73Ma 153
NW7 . . . . .23Wa 48
Holland Cres. RH8: Oxt 5L 211
Holland Dr. SE23 . . . . .62Ac 136
Holland Dwellings WC2 . . . . .2G 223
Holland Gdns. TW8: Bford 51Na 109
TW20: Thorpe 68H 127
W14 . . . . .48Ab 88
WD25: Wat 7Y 13
Holland Grn. Pl. W8 . . . . .48Cb 89
Holland Gro. SW9 . . . . .52Qb 112
Holland Ho. E4 . . . . .21Ec 52
NW10 . . . . .*40Xa 68*
(off Holland Rd.)
SL4: Eton *10H 81*
(off Common La.)
Holland La. RH8: Oxt 5L 211
HOLLAND PARK 46Bb 89
Holland Pk. 47Bb 89
Holland Pk. CR3: Cat'm 95Tb 197
W11 . . . . .46Ab 88
Holland Pk. Av. IG3: Ilf 30Uc 54
W11 . . . . .47Ab 88
Holland Pk. Ct. *W14* *47Ab 88*
(off Holland Pk. Gdns.)
Holland Pk. Gdns. W14 . . . . .47Ab 88
Holland Pk. Mans. *W14* *46Ab 88*
(off Holland Pk. Gdns.)
Holland Pk. M. W11 . . . . .46Ab 88
Holland Pk. Rd. W14 . . . . .48Bb 89
HOLLAND PARK RDBT. 47Za 88
Holland Pk. Ter. *W11* *46Ab 88*
(off Portland Rd.)
Holland Pk. Theatre (Open Air) 47Bb 89
Holland Pas. *N1* *39Sb 71*
(off Basire St.)
Holland Pl. *W8* *47Db 89*
(off Kensington Chu. St.)
Holland Pl. Chambers *W8* *47Db 89*
(off Holland Pl.)
Holland Ri. Ho. *SW9* *52Pb 112*
(off Clapham Rd.)
Holland Rd. E6 . . . . .39Pc 74
E15 . . . . .41Gc 93
HA0: Wemb 37Ma 67
NW10 . . . . .39Wa 68
RH8: Oxt 5L 211
SE25 . . . . .71Wb 157
W14 . . . . .47Za 88
Hollands, The GU22: Wok 90A 168
KT4: Wor Pk 74Va 154
TW13: Hanw 63Z 129
Hollands Cl. DA12: Shorne 4N 145
Holland St. SE1 . . . . .6C 224 (46Rb 91)
W8 . . . . .47Cb 89
Holland Vs. Rd. W14 . . . . .47Ab 88
Holland Wlk. HA7: Stan 22Ja 46
N19 . . . . .32Mb 70
W8 . . . . .46Bb 89
Holland Way BR2: Hayes 75Hc 159
Hollar Rd. N16 . . . . .34Vb 71
Hollen St. W1 . . . . .2D 222 (44Mb 90)
Holles Cl. TW12: Hamp 65Ca 129
Holles Ho. SW9 . . . . .54Qb 112
Holles St. W1 . . . . .2A 222 (44Kb 90)
Holley Rd. W3 . . . . .47Ua 88
Hollickwood Av. N12 . . . . .23Hb 49
Holliday Sq. *SW11* *55Fb 111*
(off Fowler Cl.)
Hollidge Way RM10: Dag 38Dd 76
Holliers Way AL10: Hat 1C 8
Hollies, The *AL3: St A* *1C 6*
(off Carlisle Av.)
DA3: Lfield 69Ee 143
DA12: Grav'nd 5F 144
E11 . . . . .*29Jc 53*
(off New Wanstead)
EN9: Walt A *7Lc 21*
(within Woodbine Cl. Caravan Pk.)
HA3: W'stone 28Ja 46
HP3: Bov 1C 10
KT15: Add *78L 149*
(off Bourne Way)
KT23: Bookh 96Ea 192
N20 . . . . .18Fb 31
RH8: Oxt 5M 211
SS17: Stan H 2L 101
WD18: Wat 14V 26
Hollies Av. DA15: Sidc 61Vc 139
KT14: W Byf 85H 169
Hollies Cl. SW16 . . . . .65Qb 134
TW1: Twick 61Ha 130
Hollies Ct. KT15: Add 78L 149
Hollies End NW7 . . . . .22Xa 48
Hollies Rd. W5 . . . . .49La 86
Hollies Way EN6: Pot B 3Eb 17
SW12 . . . . .59Jb 112
Holligrave Rd. BR1: Brom 67Jc 137
Hollingbourne Av. DA7: Bex 53Bd 117
Hollingbourne Gdns. W13 . . . . .43Ka 86
Hollingbourne Rd. SE24 . . . . .57Sb 113
Hollingsworth Ct. KT6: Surb 73Ma 153
Hollingsworth M. WD25: Wat 6W 12
Hollingsworth Rd. CR0: C'don 79Xb 157
Hollington Ct. BR7: Chst 65Rc 138
Hollington Cres. KT3: N Mald 72Va 154
Hollington Rd. E6 . . . . .41Pc 94
N17 . . . . .26Wb 51
Hollingworth Cl. KT8: W Mole 70Ba 129
Hollingworth Rd. BR5: Pet W 72Rc 160
Hollingworth Way TN16: Westrm 98Tc 200
Hollins Ho. N7 . . . . .35Nb 70
Hollisfield WC1 . . . . .4G 217
Hollis Pl. RM17: Grays 49Ce 99
Hollis Row RH1: Redh 8P 207
Hollister Ho. *NW6* *41Cb 89*
(off Kilburn Pk. Rd.)
Hollman Gdns. SW16 . . . . .65Rb 135
Hollow, The IG8: Wfd G 21Hc 53
HOLLOWAY 34Nb 70
Holloway Cl. UB7: Harm 50N 83
Holloway Dr. GU25: Vir W 70A 126
Holloway Hill KT16: Chert, Lyne 76E 148
Holloway Ho. *NW2* *34Ya 68*
(off Stoll Cl.)
TW20: Egh *64B 126*
(off Stoneylands Rd.)
Holloway La. UB7: Harm, W Dray 51M 105
WD3: Chen, Sarr 10D 10
Holloway M. TW20: Eng G 5N 125
Holloway Rd. E6 . . . . .41Pc 94
E11 . . . . .34Fc 73
N7 . . . . .35Pb 70
N19 . . . . .33Mb 70
Holloways La. AL9: Wel G 5F 8
Holloway St. TW3: Houn 55Da 107
Hollow Cotts. RM19: Purf 50Qd 97
Hollowfield Av. RM17: Grays 49Fe 99
Hollowfield Wlk. UB5: N'olt 37Aa 65
Hollow Hill La. SL0: Iver 45D 82
Hollow La. GU25: Vir W 9N 125
Hollows, The TW8: Bford 51Pa 109
Hollowtree M. WD3: Crox G 15Q 26
Holly Av. HA7: Stan 26Na 47
KT12: Walt T 74Z 151
KT15: New H 82J 169
Hollybank GU24: W End 5D 166
HP3: Hem H 7N 3
Hollybank Cl. TW12: Hamp 64Ca 129
Holly Bank Rd. GU22: Wok 3M 187
Hollybank Rd.
KT14: W Byf 86J 169
Hollyberry La. NW3 . . . . .35Eb 69
Hollybrake Cl. BR7: Chst 66Tc 138
Hollybush Av. AL2: Chis G 6N 5
Hollybush Cl. E11 . . . . .29Jc 53
HA3: Hrw W 25Ga 46
RM5: Col R 22Ed 56
TN13: S'oaks 96Ld 203
WD19: Wat 17Y 27
Hollybush Ct. TN13: S'oaks 96Ld 203
Hollybush Gdns. E2 . . . . .41Xb 91
Holly Bush Hill NW3 . . . . .35Eb 69
Hollybush Hill E11 . . . . .30Hc 53
SL2: Stoke P 8L 61
Hollybush Ho. E2 . . . . .41Xb 91
Holly Bush La. TN13: S'oaks 96Ld 203
TW12: Hamp 66Ba 129
Hollybush La. BR6: Well H 79Cd 162
GU23: Rip 91M 189
HP1: Hem H 1H 3
SL0: Iver 44D 82
UB9: Den 33E 62
Hollybush Pl. E2 . . . . .41Xb 91
Hollybush Rd. DA12: Grav'nd 1E 144
KT2: King T 64Na 131
Hollybush Sports Complex 95Md 203
Holly Bush Steps *NW3* *35Eb 69*
(off Holly Mt.)
Hollybush St. E13 . . . . .41Kc 93
Holly Bush Va. NW3 . . . . .35Eb 69
Hollybush Wlk. SW9 . . . . .56Rb 113
Hollybush Way EN7: Chesh 1Wb 19
Holly Cl. AL10: Hat 1B 8
BR3: Beck 70Ec 136
GU21: Wok 1M 187
IG9: Buck H 20Mc 35
KT16: Longc 6L 147
KT19: Eps 81Ta 173
SL2: Farn C 5G 60
SM6: Wall 80Kb 156
TW13: Hanw 64Aa 129
TW16: Sun 69X 129
TW20: Eng G 5M 125
Hollycombe TW20: Eng G 3N 125
Holly Cott. M. UB8: Hil 43Q 84
Holly Ct. DA11: Nflt 57De 121
DA14: Sidc *63Xc 139*
(off Sidcup Hill)
KT16: Chert *74H 149*
(off King St.)
KT22: Lea *94Ja 192*
(off Belmont Rd.)
N15 . . . . .28Ub 51
RM1: Rom *28Hd 56*
(off Dolphin App.)
SE10 . . . . .48Hc 93
SM2: Sutt 80Cb 155
Holly Cres. BR3: Beck 71Bc 158
IG8: Wfd G 24Fc 53
SL4: Wind 4B 102
Hollycroft Av. HA9: Wemb 33Pa 67
NW3 . . . . .34Cb 69
Hollycroft Cl. CR2: S Croy 78Ub 157
UB7: Sip 51Q 106
Hollycroft Gdns. UB7: Sip 51Q 106
Hollydale Cl. UB5: N'olt 35Da 65
Hollydale Dr. BR2: Brom 76Pc 160
Hollydale Rd. SE15 . . . . .53Yb 114
Hollydene *BR2: Brom* *67Hc 137*
(off Beckenham La.)
SE13 . . . . .58Fc 115
SE15 . . . . .53Xb 113
Hollydown Way E11 . . . . .34Fc 73
Holly Dr. E4 . . . . .17Dc 34
EN6: Pot B 5Db 17
HP4: Berk 2A 2
RM15: S Ock 41Zd 99
SL4: Old Win 8J 103
Holly Farm Rd. UB2: S'hall 50Aa 85
Hollyfield AL10: Hat 3C 8
Hollyfield Av. N11 . . . . .22Hb 49
Hollyfield Rd. KT5: Surb 73Pa 153
Holly Gdns. DA7: Bex 56Ed 118
UB7: W Dray 47P 83
Holly Ga. KT15: Add 77K 149
Holly Grn. KT13: Weyb 77T 150
Holly Gro. HA5: Pinn 25Aa 45
NW9 . . . . .31Sa 67
SE15 . . . . .54Vb 113
Hollygrove WD23: Bush 17Fa 28
Hollygrove Cl. TW3: Houn 56Ba 107
Hollyhedge Rd. KT11: Cobh 86X 171
Holly Hedges La. HP3: Bov 2E 10
Holly Hedge Ter. SE13 . . . . .57Fc 115
Holly Hill N21 . . . . .16Pb 32
NW3 . . . . .35Eb 69
Holly Hill Dr. SM7: Bans 88Cb 175
Holly Hill Pk. SM7: Bans 89Cb 175
Holly Hill Rd. DA8: Erith 50Dd 96
DA17: Belv, Erith 50Dd 96
Hollyhock Cl. HP1: Hem H 1G 2
Hollyhock Dr. GU24: Bisl 7E 166
Holly Ho. CM15: B'wood 18Zd 41
TW8: Bford 51La 108
W10 . . . . .*42Ab 88*
(off Hawthorn Wlk.)
Holly Ind. Pk. WD24: Wat 11Y 27
Holly La. GU3: Worp 10G 186
IG3: Ilf 33Wc 75
SM7: Bans 88Cb 175
Holly La. E. SM7: Bans 88Cb 175
Holly La. W. SM7: Bans 89Cb 175
Holly Lea GU4: Jac W 10P 187
Holly Lodge *GU22: Wok* *89B 168*
(off Heathside Cres.)
HA1: Harr 29Fa 46
KT20: Lwr K 98Ab 194
SL1: Burn 2A 80
W8 . . . . .*47Cb 89*
(off Thornwood Gdns.)
Holly Lodge Gdns. N6 . . . . .33Jb 70
Holly Lodge Mans. N6 . . . . .33Jb 70
Hollymead SM5: Cars 76Hb 155
Hollymead Rd. CR5: Chip 90Jb 176
Hollymeoak Rd. CR5: Coul 91Kb 196
Holly M. SW10 . . . . .7A 226 (50Eb 89)
Hollymoor La. KT19: Ewe 82Ta 173
Holly Mt. NW3 . . . . .35Eb 69
Hollymount Cl. SE10 . . . . .53Ec 114
Holly Pde. *KT11: Cobh* *86X 171*
(off High St.)
TW13: Felt *62V 128*
(off High St.)
Holly Pk. N3 . . . . .27Bb 49
N4 . . . . .31Nb 70
(not continuous)
Holly Pk. Est. N4 . . . . .31Pb 70
Holly Pk. Gdns. N3 . . . . .27Cb 49
Holly Pk. Rd. N11 . . . . .22Jb 50
W7 . . . . .46Ha 86
Holly Pl. *NW3* *35Eb 69*
(off Holly Berry La.)
Holly Rd. BR6: Chels 80Wc 161
DA1: Dart 60Md 119
E11 . . . . .31Hc 73
EN3: Enf W 8Zb 20
RH2: Reig 8K 207
TW1: Twick 60Ha 108
TW3: Houn 56Da 107
TW12: Hamp H 65Ea 130
W4 . . . . .49Ta 87
Holly St. E8 . . . . .38Vb 71
Holly Ter. N6 . . . . .32Jb 70
N20 . . . . .19Eb 31
Hollytree Av. BR8: Swan 68Gd 140
Holly Tree Cl. SW19 . . . . .60Za 110
Hollytree Cl. SL9: Chal P 22A 42
Holly Tree Ct. HP2: Hem H 2B 4
Holly Tree Ho. *SE4* *55Bc 114*
(off Brockley Rd.)
Hollytree Ho. WD24: Wat 8U 12
Hollytree Pde. *DA14: Sidc* *65Yc 139*
(off Sidcup Hill)
Holly Tree Rd. CR3: Cat'm 94Ub 197
Hollyview Cl. NW4 . . . . .30Wa 48
Holly Village N6 . . . . .33Kb 70
Holly Vs. *W6* *48Xa 88*
(off Wellesley Av.)
Holly Wlk. EN2: Enf 13Sb 33
NW3 . . . . .35Eb 69
SL4: Wind 3C 124
Holly Way CR4: Mitc 70Mb 134
Hollywell Gro. RM12: Horn 32Hd 76
Hollywood Bowl
Finchley 24Fb 49
Surrey Quays 48Zb 92
Tolworth 75Ra 153
Watford 5Y 13
Hollywood Ct. *SW10* *51Eb 111*
(off Hollywood Rd.)
W5 . . . . .45Pa 87
WD6: E'tree 14Qa 29
Hollywood Gdns. UB4: Yead 44X 85
Hollywood La. TN15: W King 83Vd 184
Hollywood M. SW10 . . . . .51Eb 111
Hollywood Rd. E4 . . . . .22Ac 52
SW10 . . . . .51Eb 111
Hollywoods CR0: Sels 81Bc 178
Hollywood Way DA8: Erith 52Kd 119
IG8: Wfd G 24Fc 53
Holman Ct. KT17: Ewe 81Wa 174
Holman Ho. *E2* *41Zb 92*
(off Roman Rd.)
Holman Hunt Ho. *W6* *50Ab 88*
(off Field Rd.)
Holman Rd. KT19: Ewe 78Sa 153
SW11 . . . . .54Fb 111
Holmbank Dr. TW17: Shep 70U 128
Holmbridge Gdns. EN3: Pond E 14Zb 34
Holmbrook NW1 . . . . .2C 216
Holmbrook Dr. NW4 . . . . .29Za 48
Holmbury Ct. CR2: S Croy 78Ub 157
SW17 . . . . .62Hb 133
SW19 . . . . .66Gb 133
Holmbury Gdns. UB3: Hayes 46V 84
Holmbury Gro. CR0: Sels 80Bc 158
Holmbury Ho. SE24 . . . . .57Rb 113
Holmbury Mnr. DA14: Sidc 63Wc 139
Holmbury Pk. BR1: Brom 66Nc 138
Holmbury Vw. E5 . . . . .32Xb 71
Holmbush Rd. SW15 . . . . .58Ab 110
Holm Cl. KT15: Wdhm 84G 168
Holmcote Gdns. N5 . . . . .36Sb 71
Holm Ct. SE12 . . . . .62Kc 137
Holmcroft KT20: Walt H 97Xa 194
Holmcroft Ho. E17 . . . . .28Dc 52
Holmcroft Way BR2: Brom 71Pc 160
Holmdale Cl. WD6: Bore 12Pa 29
Holmdale Gdns. NW4 . . . . .29Za 48
Holmdale Rd. BR7: Chst 64Sc 138
NW6 . . . . .36Cb 69
Holmdale Ter. N15 . . . . .30Ub 51
Holmdene N12 . . . . .22Db 49
Holmdene Av. HA2: Harr 27Da 45
NW7 . . . . .23Wa 48
SE24 . . . . .57Sb 113
Holmdene Cl. BR3: Beck 68Ec 136
Holmdene Ct. BR1: Brom 69Nc 138
Holmead Rd. SW6 . . . . .52Db 111
Holmebury Cl. WD23: B Hea 19Ga 28
Holme Chase KT13: Weyb 79S 150
Holme Cl. EN8: Chesh 3Ac 20
Holme Ct. TW7: Isle 55Ja 108
Holmedale SL2: Slou 5N 81
Holmefield Ho. *W10* *42Ab 88*
(off Hazlewood Cres.)
Holmefield Pl. KT15: New H 82K 169
Holme Ho. *SE15* *52Xb 113*
(off Studholme St.)
Holme Lacey Rd. SE12 . . . . .58Hc 115
Holme Lea WD25: Wat 6Y 13
Holmeoak Av. RM13: Rain 40Fd 76
Holme Pk. WD6: Bore 12Pa 29
Holme Pl. HP2: Hem H 1C 4
Holme Rd. E6 . . . . .39Nc 74
RM11: Horn 32Qd 77
Holmes Av. E17 . . . . .27Bc 52
Holmes Cl. CR8: Purl 85Pb 176
GU22: Wok 93B 188
SE22 . . . . .56Wb 113
SL5: S'hill 2A 146
Holmes Ct. *AL3: St A* *1C 6*
(off Carlisle Av.)
DA12: Grav'nd 10H 123
Holmesdale EN8: Walt C 7Yb 20
KT13: Weyb *79T 150*
(off Bridgewater Rd.)
Holmesdale Av. RH1: Mers 3C 208
SW14 . . . . .55Ra 109
Holmesdale Cl. SE25 . . . . .69Vb 135
Holmesdale Hill DA4: S Dar 67Sd 142
Holmesdale Ho. *NW6* *39Cb 69*
(off Kilburn Vale)
Holmesdale Mnr. RH1: Redh 4A 208
Holmesdale Natural History Mus. 6K 207
Holmesdale Pk. RH1: Nutf 6F 208
Holmesdale Rd. CR0: C'don 71Tb 157
DA4: S Dar 67Sd 142
DA7: Bex 54Zc 117
N6 . . . . .31Kb 70
RH1: S Nut 8F 208
RH2: Reig 5J 207
SE25 . . . . .71Tb 157
TN13: S'oaks 95Ld 203
TW9: Kew 53Pa 109
TW11: Tedd 66La 130
Holmesdale Tunnel EN8: Walt C 6Zb 20
Holmesley Rd. SE23 . . . . .58Ac 114
Holmes Mead GU22: Pyr 87H 169
Holmes Pl. SW10 . . . . .51Eb 111

Holmes Rd.—Horn Park

Holmes Rd. NW5 36Kb 70
SW19 66Eb 133
TW1: Twick 61Ha 130
Holmes Ter. SE1 1K 229
Holmeswood SM2: Sutt 79Db 155
Holmeswood Ct. N22 26Qb 50
HOLMETHORPE 3B 208
Holmethorpe Av. RH1: Redh 3B 208
Holmethorpe Ind. Est. RH1: Redh 3B 208
Holmethorpe Lagoons Nature Reserve 3C 208
Holme Way HA7: Stan 23Ha 46
Holmewood Gdns. SW2 59Pb 112
Holmewood Rd. SE25 69Ub 135
SW2 59Pb 112
Holmfield Av. NW4 29Za 48
Holmfield Ct. NW3 36Gb 69
Holm Gro. UB10: Hil 38Q 64
Holmgrove Ho. CR8: Purl 84Qb 176
Holmhurst SE13 58Fc 115
Holmhurst Rd. DA17: Belv 50Dd 96
Holmlea Ct. CR0: C'don 77Tb 157
(off Chatsworth Rd.)
Holmlea Rd. SL3: Dat 3P 103
Holmlea Wlk. SL3: Dat 3N 103
Holmleigh Av. DA1: Dart 57Md 119
Holmleigh Ct. EN3: Pond E 14Yb 34
Holmleigh Rd. N16 32Ub 71
Holmleigh Rd. Est. N16 32Ub 71
Holm Oak Cl. SW15 58Bb 111
Holmoak Cl. CR8: Purl 82Pb 176
Holm Oak M. SW4 57Nb 112
Holm Oak Pk. WD18: Wat 15V 26
Holmoaks Ho. BR3: Beck 68Ec 136
Holmsdale Cl. SL0: Iver 44H 83
Holmsdale Gro. DA7: Bex 54Gd 118
Holmsdale Ho. E14 45Dc 92
(off Poplar High St.)
N11 21Kb 50
(off Coppies Gro.)
Holmshaw Cl. SE26 63Ac 136
Holmshill La. WD6: Bore 8Ua 16
Holmside Ri. WD19: Wat 20X 27
Holmside Rd. SW12 58Jb 112
Holmsley Cl. KT3: N Mald 72Va 154
Holmsley Ho. SW15 59Va 110
(off Tangley Gro.)
Holmstall Av. HA8: Edg 27Sa 47
Holmstall Pde. HA8: Edg 26Sa 47
Holmstead Ct. CR2: S Croy 78Tb 157
Holm Wlk. SE3 54Jc 115
Holmwood Av. CM15: Shenf 16Ce 41
CR2: Sande 85Vb 177
Holmwood Cl. HA2: Harr 27Ea 46
KT15: Add 78J 149
KT24: E Hor 100U 190
SM2: Cheam 81Za 174
UB5: N'olt 37Da 65
Holmwood Gdns. N3 26Cb 49
SM6: Wall 79Kb 156
Holmwood Gro. NW7 22Ta 47
Holmwood Rd. EN3: Enf W 8Zb 20
IG3: Ilf 33Uc 74
KT9: Chess 78Ma 153
SM2: Cheam 81Ya 174
Holmwood Vs. SE7 50Jc 93
Holne Chase N2 30Eb 49
SM4: Mord 72Bb 155
Holness Rd. E15 37Hc 73
Holocaust Memorial 1G 227 (47Hb 89)
Holocaust Memorial Garden, The 1G 227
Holroyd Cl. KT10: Clay 81Ha 172
Holroyd Rd. KT10: Clay 81Ha 172
SW15 56Ya 110
Holsart Cl. KT20: Tad 94Xa 194
Holsgrove Ho. W3 46Ua 88
Holst Ct. SE1 3K 229
Holstein Av. KT13: Weyb 77Q 150
Holstein Way DA18: Erith 48Zc 95
Holst Ho. W12 44Xa 88
(off Du Cane Rd.)
Holst Mans. SW13 51Ya 110
Holstock Rd. IG1: Ilf 33Sc 74
Holsworth Cl. HA2: Harr 29Ea 46
Holsworthy Ho. E3 41Dc 92
(off Talwin St.)
RM3: Rom 25Ld 57
Holsworthy Sq. WC1 6J 217
Holsworthy Way KT9: Chess 78La 152
Holt, The HP2: Hem H 3N 3
IG6: Ilf 23Sc 54
SM4: Mord 70Cb 133
SM6: Wall 77Lb 156
Holt Cl. BR7: Chst 64Pc 138
DA14: Sidc 63Ad 139
IG7: Chig 22Vc 55
N10 28Jb 50
SE28 45Xc 95
WD6: E'tree 14Pa 29
Holt Ct. SE10 51Ec 114
(off Horseferry Pl.)
Holt Ho. EN8: Chesh 1Xb 19
SW2 58Qb 112
Holton St. E1 42Zb 92
Holt Rd. E16 46Nc 94
HA0: Wemb 34Ka 66
RM3: Rom 24Nd 57
Holtsmere Cl. WD25: Wat 7Y 13
Holt Way IG7: Chig 22Vc 55
Holtwhite Av. EN2: Enf 12Sb 33
Holtwhite's Hill EN2: Enf 11Rb 33
Holt Wood CR6: W'ham 88Cc 178
Holtwood Rd. KT22: Oxs 85Ea 172
Holwell Pl. HA5: Pinn 28Aa 45
Holwood Cl. KT12: Walt T 75Y 151
Holwood Est. BR2: Kes 79Nc 160
Holwood Pk. Av. BR6: Farnb 77Pc 160
Holwood Pl. SW4 56Mb 112
Holybourne Av. SW15 59Wa 110
Holycross Cl. SM4: Mord 73Cb 155
HOLYFIELD 1Fc 21
Holyfield Rd. EN9: Walt A 1Ec 20
Holyhead Cl. E6 43Pc 94
Holyhead Ct. KT1: King T 70Ma 131
(off Anglesea Rd.)
Holyhead M. SL1: Slou 4B 80
(off Kelpatrick Rd.)
Holyoake Av. GU21: Wok 9N 167
Holyoake Ct. SE16 47Bc 92
Holyoake Cres. GU21: Wok 9N 167
Holyoake Ho. W5 42La 86
Holyoake Mt. DA12: Grav'nd 10F 122
Holyoake Ter. TN13: S'oaks 96Jd 202
Holyoake Wlk. N2 27Eb 49
W5 42La 86
Holyoak Rd. SE11 6B 230 (49Rb 91)
Holyport Rd. SW6 52Za 110
Holyrood Av. HA2: Harr 35Aa 65
Holyrood Ct. NW1 1K 215
WD18: Wat 14X 27
(off Marlborough Rd.)
Holyrood Cres. AL1: St A 5C 6
Holyrood Gdns. HA8: Edg 27Ra 47
RM16: Grays 9E 100
Holyrood M. E16 46Jc 93
Holyrood Rd. EN5: New Bar 16Eb 31
Holyrood St. SE1 7H 225 (46Ub 91)
HOLYWELL 16V 26
Holywell Cl. BR6: Chels 77Wc 161
SE3 51Jc 115
SE16 50Xb 91
TW19: Stanw 60N 105
Holywell Hill AL1: St A 3B 6
Holywell La. EC2 5J 219 (42Ub 91)
Holywell M. AL1: St A 2B 6
(off Holywell Hill)
Holywell Rd. WD18: Wat 15W 26
Holywell Row EC2 6H 219 (42Ub 91)
Holywell Way TW19: Stanw 60N 105
Homan Ct. N12 21Fb 49
Homebeech Ho. GU22: Wok 90A 168
(off Mt. Hermon Rd.)
Homebush Ho. E4 17Dc 34
Homecedars Ho. WD23: B Hea 18Fa 28
Home Cl. GU25: Vir W 2P 147
KT22: Fet 93Fa 192
SM5: Cars 75Hb 155
UB5: N'olt 41Ba 85
Home Ct. KT6: Surb 71Ma 153
Homecroft Gdns. IG10: Lough 14Rc 36
Homecroft Rd. N22 25Sb 51
SE26 64Yb 136
Homedean Rd. TN13: Chip 94Ed 202
Home Farm BR6: Chels 78Cd 162
Home Farm Cl. KT7: T Ditt 73Ha 152
KT10: Esh 79Da 151
KT16: Ott 80C 148
KT20: Tad 89Za 174
RH3: Bet 7A 206
TW17: Shep 70U 128
Home Farm Ct. HP3: Bov 2A 10
Home Farm Gdns. KT12: Walt T 75Y 151
Home Farm Pl. RH1: Mers 100Kb 196
Home Farm Rd. AL9: N Mym 8D 8
CM13: B'wood, L War 25Ae 59
WD3: Rick 21Q 44
Homefarm Rd. W7 44Ga 86
Home Farm Way SL3: Stoke P 9N 61
Home Fld. EN5: Barn 15Bb 31
Homefield EN9: Walt A 4Jc 21
HP3: Bov 10D 2
SM4: Mord 70Cb 133
Homefield Av. IG2: Ilf 29Uc 54
KT12: Hers 77Z 151
Homefield Cl. BR5: St P 70Xc 139
BR8: Swan 69Hd 140
CM16: Epp 2Wc 23
KT15: Wdhm 84G 168
KT22: Lea 93La 192
NW10 37Sa 67
UB4: Yead 42Z 85
Homefield Farm Rd.
DA4: S Dar, Sut H 67Qd 141
Homefield Gdns. CR4: Mitc 68Eb 133
KT20: Tad 92Ya 194
N2 27Fb 49
Homefield Ho. SE23 62Yb 136
Homefield M. BR3: Beck 67Cc 136
Homefield Pk. SM1: Sutt 79Db 155
Homefield Pl. CR0: C'don 75Vb 157
Homefield Ri. BR6: Orp 74Wc 161
Homefield Rd. BR1: Brom 67Lc 137
CR3: Coul 91Rb 197
CR5: Coul 91Rb 197
CR6: W'ham 91Yb 198
HA0: Wemb 35Ja 66
HA8: Edg 23Ta 47
HP2: Hem H 2A 4
KT12: Walt T 73Aa 151
SW19 65Za 132
TN13: Riv 94Gd 202
W4 50Va 88
WD3: Chor 14E 24
WD7: R'lett 9Ha 14
WD23: Bush 14Ca 27
Homefield St. N1 2H 219 (40Ub 71)
Homefirs Ho. HA9: Wemb 34Pa 67
Home Gdns. DA1: Dart 58Nd 119
RM10: Dag 34Ed 76
Homeheather Ho. IG4: Ilf 29Pc 54
Home Hill BR8: Hext 66Hd 140
Homehurst Ho. CM15: B'wood 18Zd 41
Homeland Dr. SM2: Sutt 81Db 175
Homelands KT22: Lea 93La 192
SL4: Wink 1A 124
Homelands Dr. SE19 66Ub 135
Homelands Pl. TN16: Big H 89Nc 180
Home Lea BR6: Chels 78Vc 161
Homeleigh Ct. EN8: Chesh 1Xb 19
SW16 62Nb 134
Homeleigh Rd. SE15 57Zb 114
Homeleigh St. EN8: Chesh 2Xb 19
Homeleigh Ter. SL2: Slou 4L 81
Homemanor Ho. WD18: Wat 13X 27
(off Cassio Rd.)
Home Mead HA7: Stan 25La 46
Homemead DA9: Ghithe 58Xd 120
DA12: Grav'nd 9D 122
Homemead Cl. DA12: Grav'nd 9D 122
Home Mead Local Nature Reserve 11Rc 36
Home Mdw. SL2: Farn R 10G 60
SM7: Bans 88Cb 175
Home Mdw. M. SE22 57Wb 113
Homemead Rd. BR2: Brom 71Pc 160
CR0: C'don 72Lb 156
Home Orchard DA1: Dart 58Nd 119
Home Pk. RH8: Oxt 3L 211
WD4: K Lan 2R 12
Home Pk. Cotts. WD4: K Lan 2R 12
Home Pk. Ct. KT1: King T 70Ma 131
(off Palace Rd.)
Home Pk. Ind. Est. WD4: K Lan 2R 12
Home Pk. Pde. KT1: Hamp W 68Ma 131
(off High St.)
Home Pk. Rd. SW19 63Bb 133
Home Pk. Ter. KT1: Hamp W 68Ma 131
(off Hampton Ct. Rd.)
Home Pk. Wlk. KT1: King T 70Ma 131
Homer Cl. DA7: Bex 53Ed 118
Homer Dr. E14 49Cc 92
Home Rd. SW11 54Gb 111
Homer Rd. CR0: C'don 72Zb 158
E9 37Ac 72
Homer Row W1 1E 220 (43Gb 89)
Homersham Rd. KT1: King T 68Qa 131
Homers Rd. SL4: Wind 3B 102
Homer St. W1 1E 220 (43Gb 89)
HOMERTON 36Zb 72
Homerton Gro. E9 36Zb 72
Homerton High St. E9 36Zb 72
Homerton Rd. E9 36Ac 72
Homerton Row E9 36Yb 72
Homerton Ter. E9 37Yb 72
(not continuous)
Homesdale Cl. E11 29Jc 53
Homesdale Rd. BR1: Brom 70Lc 137
BR2: Brom 70Lc 137
BR5: Pet W 73Uc 160
CR3: Cat'm 95Tb 197
Homesfield NW11 29Cb 49
Homestall Rd. SE22 57Yb 114
Homestead, The DA1: Cray 57Gd 118
(off Crayford High St.)
DA1: Dart 58Ld 119
Homestead Cl. AL2: Park 9A 6
Homestead Ct. EN5: New Bar 15Cb 31
Homestead Gdns. KT10: Clay 78Ga 152
Homestead Paddock N14 15Kb 32
Homestead Pk. NW2 34Va 68
Homestead Rd. BR6: Chels 80Xc 161
CR3: Cat'm 95Tb 197
RM8: Dag 33Bd 75
SW6 52Bb 111
TW18: Staines 65K 127
WD3: Rick 17M 25
Homesteads, The N11 21Kb 50
Homestead Way CR0: New Ad 83Ec 178
Homevale Cl. BR2: Hayes 73Hc 159
Homewalk Ho. SE26 63Xb 135
Homewater Ho. KT17: Eps 85Ua 174
Homewaters Av. TW16: Sun 67V 128
Home Way WD3: Rick 18H 25
Homeway RM3: Hrld W 23Rd 57
Homewillow Cl. N21 16Rb 33
Homewood SL3: Geor G 4P 81
Homewood Cl. TW12: Hamp 65Ba 129
Homewood Ct. WD3: Chor 14H 25
Homewood Cres. BR7: Chst 65Uc 138
Homewood Rd. AL1: St A 1F 6
Homewoods SW12 59Lb 112
Homeworth Ho. GU22: Wok 90A 168
(off Ashdown Cl.)
Homildon Ho. SE26 62Wb 135
Homlesdale Bus. Cen.
TN15: Plat 91Ee 205
Honduras St. EC1 5D 218 (42Sb 91)
Honeybourne Rd. NW6 36Db 69
Honeybourne Way BR5: Pet W 74Tc 160
Honey Brook EN9: Walt A 5Gc 21
Honeybrook Rd. SW12 59Lb 112
Honey Cl. RM10: Dag 37Dd 76
Honeycroft IG10: Lough 14Rc 36
Honeycroft Dr. AL4: St A 5G 6
Honeycroft Hill UB10: Uxb 38N 63
Honeycross Rd. HP1: Hem H 3G 2
Honeyden Rd. DA14: Sidc 65Ad 139
Honeyfield M. SE23 62Zb 136
Honey Hill UB10: Uxb 38P 63
Honey La. EC2 3E 224
EN9: Walt A 5Gc 21
Honey La. Ho. EN9: Walt A 6Jc 21
SW10 51Db 111
(off Finborough Rd.)
Honeyman Cl. NW6 38Za 68
Honeymead N8 27Nb 50
(off Campsfield Rd.)
Honey M. RM7: Rom 29Ed 56
SE27 63Sb 135
(off Norwood High St.)
Honeypot Bus. Cen. HA7: Stan 25Na 47
Honeypot Cl. HP2: Hem H 1M 3
NW9 28Pa 47
Honey Pot La. TN15: Kems'g 91Rd 203
Honeypot La. CM14: B'wood 20Wd 40
EN9: Walt A 6Lc 21
HA7: Stan 24Ma 47
NW9 24Ma 47
TN15: Hod S 81Ee 185
Honeypots Rd. GU22: Wok 4P 187
Honeysett Rd. N17 26Vb 51
Honeysuckle Cl. CM15: Pil H 15Xd 40
RM3: Rom 23Ld 57
SL0: Iver 44E 82
UB1: S'hall 45Aa 85
Honeysuckle Ct. IG1: Ilf 37Rc 74
IG9: Buck H 20Mc 35
Honeysuckle Gdns. AL10: Hat 1D 8
CR0: C'don 73Zb 158
E17 27Cc 52
Honeysuckle La. N22 26Sb 51
Honeysuckle Pl. KT17: Eps D 88Xa 174
Honeytree Ct. IG10: Lough 12Rc 36
Honeywell Rd. SW11 58Hb 111
Honeywood Cl. EN6: Pot B 5Fb 17
Honeywood Ho. SE15 53Wb 113
(off Goldsmith Rd.)
Honeywood Mus. 78Hb 155
Honeywood Rd. NW10 40Va 68
TW7: Isle 56Ja 108
Honeywood Wlk. SM5: Cars 77Hb 155
Honister Cl. HA7: Stan 25Ka 46
Honister Gdns. HA7: Stan 24Ka 46
Honister Hgts. CR8: Purl 86Tb 177
Honister Pl. HA7: Stan 25Ka 46
Honiton Gdns. NW7 24Za 48
SE15 54Yb 114
(off Gibbon Rd.)
Honiton Ho. EN3: Pond E 13Zb 34
Honiton Rd. DA16: Well 54Vc 117
NW6 40Bb 69
RM7: Rom 30Fd 56
Honley Rd. SE6 59Dc 114
Honnor Gdns. TW7: Isle 54Fa 108
Honnor Rd. TW18: Staines 66M 127
HONOR OAK 58Yb 114
Honor Oak Crematorium SE23 57Zb 114
HONOR OAK PARK 59Ac 114
Honor Oak Pk. SE23 58Yb 114
Honor Oak Ri. SE23 58Yb 114
Honor Oak Rd. SE23 60Yb 114
Honour Gdns. RM8: Dag 35Wc 75
Honour Lea Av. E20 36Dc 72
Honours Mead HP3: Bov 9C 2
Hood Av. BR5: St M Cry 71Xc 161
N14 16Kb 32
SW14 57Sa 109
Hood Cl. CR0: C'don 74Rb 157
Hoodcote Gdns. N21 17Rb 33
Hood Ct. EC4 3A 224
Hood Ho. SE5 52Tb 113
(off Elmington Est.)
SW1 50Mb 90
(off Dolphin Sq.)
Hood Point SE16 47Bc 92
(off Rotherhithe St.)
Hood Rd. RM13: Rain 40Gd 76
SW20 66Va 132
Hood Wlk. RM7: Mawney 25Dd 56
HOOK 77Ma 153
Hook, The EN5: New Bar 16Fb 31
Hooke Ct. SE10 53Ec 114
(off Winforton St.)
Hooke Ho. E3 40Ac 72
(off Gernon Rd.)
Hooke Rd. KT24: E Hor 97V 190
Hookers Rd. E17 27Zb 52
Hook Farm Rd. BR2: Brom 71Mc 159
Hookfield KT19: Eps 85Sa 173
Hookfield M. KT19: Eps 85Sa 173
Hookfields DA11: Nflt 2A 144
Hook Ga. EN1: Enf 8Xb 19
HOOK GREEN
DA2 63Jd 140
DA13 65Ce 143
Hook Grn. La. DA2: Wilm 62Hd 140
Hook Grn. Rd. DA13: Sflt 66Ae 143
Hookham Ct. SW8 53Mb 112
HOOK HEATH 2M 187
Hook Heath Av. GU22: Wok 1M 187
Hook Heath Gdns. GU22: Wok 3K 187
Hook Heath Rd. GU22: Wok 3J 187
Hook Hill CR2: Sande 82Ub 177
Hook Hill La. GU22: Wok 3M 187
Hook Hill Pk. GU22: Wok 3M 187
Hooking Grn. HA2: Harr 29Da 45
HOOK JUNC. 76Na 153
Hook La. DA16: Well 56Vc 117
EN6: N'thaw 4Hb 17
GU24: W End 5A 166
RM4: Abr, Stap A 16Bd 37
Hook Mill La. GU18: Light 1B 166
Hook Ri. Nth. KT6: Surb 76Na 153
Hook Ri. Sth. KT6: Surb 76Na 153
Hook Ri. Sth. Ind. Pk. KT6: Surb 76Pa 153
Hook Rd. KT6: Surb 75Na 153
KT9: Chess 78Ma 153
KT19: Eps, Ewe 81Sa 173
Hooks Cl. SE15 53Xb 113
Hooks Hall Dr. RM10: Dag 34Ed 76
Hookstone La. GU24: W End 3D 166
Hookstone Way IG8: Wfd G 24Mc 53
Hook Wlk. HA8: Edg 23Sa 47
Hookwood Cnr. RH8: Limp 100Kc 199
Hookwood Cotts. BR6: Prat B 83Yc 181
KT18: Head 96Sa 193
HOOKWOOD PARK 100Kc 199
Hookwood Pk. RH8: Limp 1M 211
Hookwood Rd. BR6: Prat B 83Yc 181
Hool Cl. NW9 29Sa 47
HOOLEY 93Kb 196
Hooley La. RH1: Redh 7P 207
Hooper Dr. UB8: Hil 43R 84
Hooper Ho. TW15: Ashf 62N 127
Hooper Rd. E16 44Jc 93
Hooper's Ct. SW3 2F 227 (47Hb 89)
Hooper's M. W3 46Sa 87
Hoopers M. WD23: Bush 18Da 27
Hooper Sq. E1 44Wb 91
(off Hooper St.)
Hooper St. E1 44Wb 91
Hoopers Yd. E1 44Wb 91
(off Hooper St.)
NW6 39Bb 69
(off Kimberley Rd.)
TN13: S'oaks 98Ld 203
Hoop La. NW11 31Bb 69
Hop Ct. HA0: Wemb 36Ja 66
(off Brewery Cl.)
Hope Cl. CM15: Mount 11Fe 41
IG8: Wfd G 23Lc 53
N1 37Sb 71
RM6: Chad H 28Zc 55
SE12 62Kc 137
SM1: Sutt 78Eb 155
TW8: Bford 50Na 87
Hope Ct. NW10 41Za 88
(off Chamberlayne Rd.)
SE1 50Wb 91
(off Avocet Cl.)
Hopedale Rd. SE7 51Kc 115
Hopefield Animal Sanctuary 16Yd 40
Hopefield Av. NW6 40Ab 68
Hope Gdns. W3 47Ra 87
Hope Grn. WD25: Wat 5W 12
Hope Ho. CR0: C'don 77Ub 157
(off Steep Hill)
Hope La. SE9 61Rc 138
Hope Pk. BR1: Brom 66Hc 137
Hope Rd. DA10: Swans 58Be 121
SS17: Stan H 3M 101
Hopes Cl. TW5: Hest 51Ca 107
Hope Sq. EC2 1H 225
Hope St. SW11 55Fb 111
Hope Taylor Wlk. KT20: Tad 92Ya 194
Hope Ter. RM20: Grays 50Zd 99
Hopetown St. E1 43Vb 91
Hopewell Cl. RM16: Chaf H 50Zd 99
Hopewell Dr. DA12: Grav'nd 4H 145
Hopewell St. SE5 52Tb 113
Hopewell Yd. SE5 52Tb 113
(off Hopewell St.)
Hope Wharf SE16 47Yb 92
Hopfield GU21: Wok 88A 168
Hopfield Av. KT14: Byfl 84N 169
Hopfield Cl. TN14: Otf 88Ld 183
Hopgarden, The SL4: Eton 10H 81
(off Common La.)
Hopgarden La. TN13: S'oaks 100Jd 202
Hop Gdns. WC2 5F 223 (45Nb 90)
Hop Gdn. Way WD25: Wat 3Y 13
Hopgood St. W12 46Ya 88
Hopground Cl. AL1: St A 4E 6
Hopground Ho. E20 37Ec 72
(off De Coubertin St.)
Hopkins Cl. N10 24Jb 50
RM2: Rom 27Ld 57
Hopkins Ho. E14 44Cc 92
(off Canton St.)
Hopkins M. E15 39Hc 73
Hopkinsons Pl. NW1 39Jb 70
Hopkins Rd. E10 31Dc 72
Hopkins St. W1 3C 222 (44Lb 90)
Hopkins Yd. AL1: St A 3C 6
Hoppers Rd. N13 19Qb 32
N21 19Qb 32
Hoppett Rd. E4 19Gc 35
Hoppety, The KT20: Tad 94Za 194
Hopping La. N1 37Rb 71
Hoppingwood Av. KT3: N Mald 69Ua 132
Hoppner Rd. UB4: Hayes 40T 64
Hop St. SE10 49Hc 93
Hopton Ct. BR2: Hayes 74Kc 159
Hopton Gdns. KT3: N Mald 72Wa 154
Hopton Rd. SE18 48Rc 94
SW16 64Nb 134
Hopton's Gdns. SE1 6C 224
Hopton St. SE1 5B 224 (45Rb 91)
Hoptree Cl. N12 22Db 49
Hopwood Cl. SW17 62Eb 133
WD17: Wat 8U 12
Hopwood Rd. SE17 51Tb 113
Hopwood Wlk. E8 38Wb 71
Horace Av. RM7: Rush G 32Ed 76
Horace Bldg. SW8 52Kb 112
Horace Jones Ho. SE1 7K 225
Horace Rd. E7 35Kc 73
IG6: Ilf 27Sc 54
KT1: King T 69Pa 131
Horatio Ct. SE16 46Yb 92
(off Rotherhithe St.)
Horatio Ho. E2 40Vb 71
(off Horatio St.)
W6 50Za 88
(off Fulham Pal. Rd.)
Horatio Pl. E14 46Ec 92
(off Managers St.)
SW19 67Cb 133
Horatio St. E2 40Vb 71
Horatius Way CR0: Wadd 78Pb 156
Horbury Cres. W11 45Cb 89
Horbury M. W11 45Bb 89
Horder Rd. SW6 53Ab 110
Hordle Gdns. AL1: St A 4D 6
Hordle Prom. E. SE15 52Vb 113
Hordle Prom. Sth. SE15 52Vb 113
(off Quarley Way)
Horizon Bldg. E14 45Cc 92
(off Hertsmere Rd.)
Horizon Bus. Cen. N9 19Zb 34
(off Goodwin Rd.)
Horizon Bus. Village KT13: Weyb 84Q 170
Horizon Cl. TN16: Westrm 97Wc 201
Horizon Ct. SM2: Cheam 80Ab 154
(off Up. Mulgrave Rd.)
Horizon Ho. BR8: Swan 70Gd 140
KT17: Eps 85Ua 174
SW18 55Eb 111
(off Juniper Dr.)
Horizon Ind. Est. SE15 51Wb 113
Horksley Gdns. CM13: Hut 16Ee 41
Horle Wlk. SE5 54Rb 113
Horley Cl. DA6: Bex 57Cd 118
Horley Rd. RH1: Redh 8P 207
SE9 63Nc 138
Hormead Rd. W9 42Bb 89
Hornbeam Av. RM14: Upm 35Qd 77
Hornbeam Chase RM15: S Ock 41Zd 99
Hornbeam Cl. CM13: B'wood 20De 41
CM16: They B 9Tc 22
IG1: Ilf 36Tc 74
IG9: Buck H 20Mc 35
IG11: Bark 41Wc 95
NW7 20Va 30
SE11 5K 229 (49Qb 90)
UB5: N'olt 36Ba 65
WD6: Bore 11Qa 29
Hornbeam Cres. TW8: Bford 52Ka 108
Hornbeam Gdns. KT3: N Mald 72Wa 154
SL1: Slou 8L 81
Hornbeam Gro. E4 20Gc 35
Hornbeam Ho. IG9: Buck H 20Mc 35
Hornbeam La. AL9: Ess 3N 9
DA7: Bex 54Ed 118
E4 15Gc 35
Hornbeam Rd. CM16: They B 9Tc 22
IG9: Buck H 20Mc 35
RH2: Reig 9K 207
UB4: Yead 43Y 85
Hornbeams AL2: Brick W 2Ba 13
Hornbeams Av. EN1: Enf 7Yb 20
Hornbeam Sq. E3 39Bc 72
Hornbeams Ri. N11 23Jb 50
Hornbeam Ter. SM5: Cars 74Gb 155
Hornbeam Wlk. KT12: W Vill 81V 170
TW10: Rich 61Pa 131
Hornbeam Way BR2: Brom 72Qc 160
EN7: Chesh 1Vb 19
Hornbean Ho. E15 41Gc 93
(off Manor Rd.)
Hornbill Cl. UB8: Cowl 44M 83
Hornblower Cl. SE16 48Ac 92
Hornbuckle Cl. HA2: Harr 33Fa 66
Hornby Cl. NW3 38Fb 69
Hornby Ct. NW10 37Va 68
Hornby Ho. SE11 51Qb 112
(off Clayton St.)
Horncastle Cl. SE12 59Jc 115
Horncastle Rd. SE12 59Jc 115
HORNCHURCH 32Md 77
Hornchurch N17 26Tb 51
(off Gloucester Rd.)
Hornchurch Cl. KT2: King T 63Ma 131
Hornchurch Country Pk. 38Ld 77
Hornchurch Hill CR3: Whyt 90Vb 177
Hornchurch Rd. RM11: Horn 32Jd 76
RM12: Horn 32Jd 76
Hornchurch Sports Cen. 33Ld 77
Horndean Cl. SW15 60Wa 110
Horndon Cl. RM5: Col R 25Ed 56
Horndon Grn. RM5: Col R 25Ed 56
Horndon Ind. Pk. CM13: W H'dn 30Ee 59
HORNDON ON THE HILL 1H 101
Horndon Rd. RM5: Col R 25Ed 56
SS17: Horn H 2J 101
Horner Ho. N1 1J 219
Horner La. CR4: Mitc 68Fb 133
Horne Rd. TW17: Shep 70Q 128
Horner Sq. E1 7K 219
Hornet Bus. Est. TN15: Bor G 93Ae 205
Hornets, The WD18: Wat 14X 27
Hornet Way E6 43Tc 94
Horne Way SW15 54Ya 110
Hornfair Rd. SE7 51Lc 115
Hornford Way RM7: Rush G 31Gd 76
HORN HILL 21D 42
Horn Hill La. SL9: Chal P 22B 42
Hornhill Rd. WD3: Map C 22D 42
Horniman Dr. SE23 60Xb 113
Horniman Gdns. 60Xb 113
Horniman Mus. 60Xb 113
Horning Cl. SE9 63Nc 138
Horn La. IG8: Wfd G 23Jc 53
SE10 50Jc 93
(not continuous)
W3 45Sa 87
(not continuous)
Horn Link Way SE10 49Jc 93
Hornminster Glen RM11: Horn 33Qd 77
HORN PARK 57Kc 115

Horn Pk. Cl.—Huntingdon Dr.

Horn Pk. Cl. SE12 57Kc 115
Horn Pk. La. SE12 57Kc 115
Hornsby La. RM16: Ors 5C 100
Hornscroft Cl. IG11: Bark 38Uc 74
HORNS CROSS 58Ud 120
Horns End Pl. HA5: Eastc 28Y 45
HORNSEY 28Nb 50
Hornsey N8 28Nb 50
Hornsey Cricket Club 29Mb 50
Hornsey La. N6 32Kb 70
Hornsey La. Est. N19 31Mb 70
Hornsey La. Gdns. N6 31Lb 70
Hornsey Pk. Rd. N8 27Pb 50
Hornsey Ri. N19 31Mb 70
Hornsey Ri. Gdns. N19 31Mb 70
Hornsey Rd. N7 32Nb 70
N19 32Nb 70
Hornsey St. N7 36Pb 70
HORNSEY VALE 29Pb 50
HORNS GREEN 89Uc 180
Hornshay St. SE15 51Yb 114
Horns Lodge Rd. TN15: Stans 82Ce 185
Horns Rd. IG2: Ilf 29Sc 54
IG6: Ilf 28Tc 54
Hornton Ct. *W8* 47Cb 89
(off Kensington High St.)
Hornton Pl. W8 47Db 89
Hornton St. W8 47Cb 89
Horsa Rd. DA8: Erith 52Dd 118
SE12 59Lc 115
Horse & Dolphin Yd. W1 4E 222
Horsebridges Cl. RM9: Dag 39Ad 75
Horsecroft SM7: Bans 89Bb 175
Horsecroft Cl. BR6: Orp 74Xc 161
Horsecroft Mdws.
SM7: Bans 88Bb 175
Horsecroft Rd. HA8: Edg 24Ta 47
HP1: Hem H 4J 3
Horse Fair KT1: King T 68Ma 131
Horseferry Pl. SE10 51Ec 114
Horseferry Rd. E14 45Ac 92
SW1 4D 228 (48Mb 90)
Horseferry Rd. Est. SW1 4D 228
Horse Guards Av. SW1 7F 223 (46Nb 90)
Horse Guards Parade 7E 222 (46Mb 90)
Horse Guards Rd.
SW1 7E 222 (46Mb 90)
Horse Hill HP5: Ley H 4A 10
Horse Leaze E6 44Qc 94
Horselers HP3: Hem H 5A 4
Horseley Ct. E1 43Ac 92
HORSELL 8N 167
Horsell Birch GU21: Wok 7L 167
HORSELL COMMON 5P 167
Horsell Comn. Rd. GU21: Wok 6N 167
Horsell Ct. KT16: Chert 73K 149
Horsell Moor GU21: Wok 9P 167
Horsell Pk. GU21: Wok 8P 167
Horsell Pk. Cl. GU21: Wok 8P 167
Horsell Ri. GU21: Wok 7P 167
Horsell Ri. Cl. GU21: Wok 7P 167
Horsell Rd. BR5: St P 67Xc 139
N5 36Qb 70
(not continuous)
Horsell Va. GU21: Wok 88A 168
Horsell Way GU21: Wok 8N 167
Horselydown La. SE1 1K 231 (47Vb 91)
Horselydown Mans. SE1 1K 231
HORSEMAN SIDE 14Nd 39
Horseman Side CM14: N'side 15Md 39
RM4: N'side, Stap A 17Kd 39
Horsemans Ride AL2: Chis G 8N 5
Horsemongers M. SE1 2E 230
Horsemoor Cl. SL3: L'ly 49C 82
Horsenden Av. UB6: G'frd 36Ha 66
Horsenden Cres. UB6: G'frd 36Ha 66
Horsenden Hill Golf Course 38Ja 66
Horsenden La. Nth. UB6: G'frd 37Ga 66
Horsenden La. Sth. UB6: G'frd 39Ja 66
Horse Ride CM16: Epp, They B 7Rc 22
SM5: Cars 82Gb 175
SM7: Bans 84Hb 175
SW1 1C 228 (46Lb 90)
Horseshoe, The CR5: Coul 85Mb 176
HP3: Hem H 4C 4
SM7: Bans 87Bb 175
Horseshoe Bus. Pk. AL2: Brick W 2Da 13
Horseshoe Cl. E14 50Ec 92
EN9: Walt A 6Jc 21
NW2 33Xa 68
Horseshoe Ct. EC1 5C 218
Horse Shoe Cres. UB5: N'olt 40Ca 65
Horseshoe Dr. UB8: Hil 44Q 84
Horse Shoe Grn. SM1: Sutt 75Db 155
Horseshoe Hill EN9: Walt A 5Lc 21
SL1: Burn 5A 60
Horseshoe La. EN2: Enf 13Sb 33
N20 18Za 30
WD25: Wat 4X 13
Horseshoe M. SW2 56Nb 112
Horseshoe Wharf SE1 6F 225
Horses Ride IG10: Lough 9Pc 22
Horse Yd. *N1* 39Rb 71
(off Essex Rd.)
Horsfeld Gdns. SE9 57Nc 116
Horsfeld Rd. SE9 57Mc 115
Horsfield Cl. DA2: Dart 59Sd 120
Horsfield Ho. *N1* 38Sb 71
(off Northampton St.)
Horsford Rd. SW2 57Pb 112
Horsham Av. N12 22Gb 49
Horsham Cl. *N17* 25Wb 51
(off Lansdowne Rd.)
Horsham Rd. DA6: Bex 57Cd 118
TW14: Bedf 58S 106
Horsley Camping & Caravanning Club Site
KT24: W Hor 96S 190
Horsley Cl. KT19: Eps 85Ta 173
Horsley Ct. KT24: E Hor 98U 190
SW1 6E 228
Horsley Dr. CR0: New Ad 80Ec 158
KT2: King T 64Ma 131
Horsley Rd. BR1: Brom 67Kc 137
E4 19Ec 34
KT11: D'side 94W 190
Horsleys WD3: Map C 22F 42
Horsley St. SE17 51Tb 113
Horsman Ho. *SE5* 51Sb 113
(off Bethwin Rd.)
Horsmans Pl. *DA1: Dart* 59Md 119
(off Instone Rd.)
Horsman St. SE5 51Sb 113
Horsmonden Cl. BR6: Orp 73Vc 161
Horsmonden Rd. SE4 57Bc 114
Hortensia Ho. *SW10* 52Eb 111
(off Gunter Gro.)
Hortensia Rd. SW10 52Eb 111
Horticultural Pl. W4 50Ta 87
HORTON
KT19 83Sa 173
SL3 55C 104
Horton Av. NW2 35Ab 68
Horton Bri. Rd. UB7: Yiew 46P 83
Horton Cl. UB7: Yiew 46Q 84
Horton Country Pk. 82Pa 173
Horton Country Pk. Local Nature Reserve
81Pa 173
Horton Cres. KT19: Eps 83Qa 173
Horton Footpath KT19: Eps 83Sa 173
Horton Gdns. KT19: Eps 83Sa 173
SL3: Hort 55B 104
Horton Halls SW17 62Fb 133
Horton Hill KT19: Eps 83Sa 173
Horton Ho. SE15 51Yb 114
SW8 52Pb 112
W6 50Ab 88
(off Field Rd.)
Horton Ind. Pk. UB7: Yiew 46P 83
HORTON KIRBY 70Sd 142
Horton Kirby Trad. Est.
DA4: S Dar 68Sd 142
Horton La. KT19: Eps 84Qa 173
Horton Pde. UB7: Yiew 46N 83
Horton Pk. Children's Farm 82Qa 173
Horton Pk. Golf Course 80Sa 153
Horton Pl. TN16: Westrm 98Tc 200
Horton Rd.
DA4: Hort K, S Dar 70Sd 142
E8 37Xb 71
SL3: Coln, Hort 54C 104
SL3: Dat, Hort 2M 103
SL3: Poyle 55G 104
TW19: Stanw M 56H 105
UB7: Yiew 46N 83
UB11: Stock P 46N 83
Horton Rd. Ind. Est. UB7: Yiew 46P 83
Hortons Way TN16: Westrm 98Tc 200
Horton Trad. Est. SL3: Hort 55E 104
Horton Way CR0: C'don 71Zb 158
DA4: Farni 73Pd 163
Hortus Rd. E4 19Ec 34
UB2: S'hall 47Ba 85
Horvath Cl. KT13: Weyb 77T 150
Horwood Cl. WD3: Rick 17J 25
Horwood Ct. WD24: Wat 9Z 13
Horwood Ho. *E2* 41Xb 91
(off Pott St.)
NW8 5E 214
Hosack Rd. SW17 61Jb 134
Hoselands Vw. DA3: Hartl 70Ae 143
Hoser Av. SE12 61Jc 137
Hosey Comn. Rd.
TN16: Westrm 100Uc 200
HOSEY HILL 100Uc 200
Hosey Hill TN16: Westrm 99Uc 200
Hosier La. EC1 1B 224 (43Rb 91)
Hoskins, The *RH8: Oxt* 1J 211
(off Station Rd. W.)
Hoskins Cl. E16 44Lc 93
UB3: Harl 50V 84
Hoskins Rd. RH8: Oxt 1J 211
(not continuous)
Hoskins St. SE10 50Fc 93
Hoskins Wlk. *RH8: Oxt* 1J 211
(off Station Rd. W.)
Hospital Bri. Rd.
TW2: Twick, Whitt 59Da 107
HOSPITAL BRIDGE RDBT. 61Da 129
Hospital Rd. E9 36Zb 72
E11 29Fc 53
TN13: S'oaks 93Ld 203
TW3: Houn 55Ca 107
Hospital Way SE13 59Fc 115
Hotham Cl. BR8: Swan 67Kd 141
DA4: Sut H 66Rd 141
KT8: W Mole 69Ca 129
Hotham Rd. SW15 55Ya 110
SW19 66Eb 133
Hotham Rd. M. SW19 66Eb 133
Hotham St. E15 39Gc 73
Hothfield Pl. SE16 48Yb 92
Hotshots Tenpin Bowl
Hemel Hempstead 4P 3
Hotspur Ind. Est. N17 23Xb 51
Hotspur Rd. UB5: N'olt 40Ca 65
Hotspur St. SE11 7K 229 (49Qb 90)
Hotspur Way EN2: Enf 7Vb 19
Hottsfield DA3: Hartl 69Ae 143
Houblon Rd. TW10: Rich 57Na 109
Houblons Hill CM16: Coop 3Yc 23
Houghton Cl. E8 37Vb 71
TW12: Hamp 65Aa 129
Houghton Ct. EC1 6D 218
Houghton Rd. N15 28Vb 51
Houghton Sq. *SW9* 54Nb 112
(off Clapham Rd.)
Houghton St. WC2 3J 223 (44Pb 90)
(not continuous)
Houlder Cres. CR0: Wadd 79Rb 157
Houlton Ho. SW3 7F 227
Houlton Pl. *E3* 42Bc 92
(off Hamlets Way)
Houndsden Rd. N21 16Pb 32
Houndsditch EC3 2J 225 (44Ub 91)
Houndsfield Rd. N9 17Xb 33
HOUNSLOW 55Da 107
Hounslow and District Indoor Bowls Club
54Ba 107
Hounslow Av. TW3: Houn 57Da 107
Hounslow Bus. Pk. TW3: Houn 56Ca 107
Hounslow Cen. TW3: Houn 55Da 107
Hounslow Gdns. TW3: Houn 57Da 107
Hounslow Heath Golf Course 57Y 107
Hounslow Heath Nature Reserve
58Aa 107
Hounslow Rd. TW2: Whitt 58Da 107
TW13: Hanw 63Z 129
TW14: Felt 60X 107
Hounslow Urban Farm 57W 106
HOUNSLOW WEST 55Aa 107
Housefield Way AL4: St A 5G 6
Household Cavalry Mus., The
Whitehall 7E 222 (46Mb 90)
Houseman Way SE5 52Tb 113
House Mill, The 41Ec 92
Houses of Parliament 3G 229 (48Nb 90)
Houston Bus. Pk. UB4: Yead 46Y 85
Houston Pl. KT10: Esh 74Ga 152
Houston Rd. KT6: Surb 72Ka 152
SE23 61Ac 136
Houstoun Ct. TW5: Hest 52Ba 107
Hove Av. E17 29Bc 52
Hove Cl. CM13: Hut 19Ee 41
RM17: Grays 51Ce 121
Hoveden Rd. NW2 36Ab 68
Hove Gdns. SM1: Sutt 74Db 155
Hove St. *SE15* 52Yb 114
(off Culmore Rd.)
Hoveton Rd. SE28 44Yc 95
Hoveton Way IG6: Ilf 24Rc 54
Howard Agne Cl. HP3: Bov 9C 2
Howard Av. DA5: Bexl 60Yc 117
KT17: Ewe 82Wa 174
SL2: Slou 3H 81
Howard Bldg. SW8 51Kb 112
Howard Bus. Pk. EN9: Walt A 6Fc 21
Howard Cl. AL1: St A 4G 6
EN9: Walt A 5Fc 21
IG10: Lough 16Nc 36
KT20: Walt H 97Va 194
KT21: Asht 90Pa 173
KT22: Lea 95La 192
KT24: W Hor 97T 190
N11 19Jb 32
NW2 35Ab 68
TW12: Hamp 66Ea 130
TW16: Sun 65V 128
W3 44Ra 87
WD23: B Hea 17Ga 28
WD24: Wat 9W 12
Howard Ct. *AL1: St A* 4B 6
(off Cottonmill La.)
GU21: Knap 1G 186
(off Tudor Way)
IG11: Bark 39Tc 74
RH2: Reig 5L 207
Howard Dr. WD6: Bore 14Ta 29
Howard Ho. *E16* 46Kc 93
(off Wesley Av.)
SE8 51Bc 114
(off Evelyn St.)
SW1 50Lb 90
(off Dolphin Sq.)
SW9 55Rb 113
(off Barrington Rd.)
W1 6A 216
Howard M. N5 35Rb 71
Howard Pl. RH2: Reig 4J 207
Howard Rd. BR1: Brom 66Jc 137
CR5: Coul 87Lb 176
DA1: Dart 58Qd 119
E6 40Pc 74
E11 34Gc 73
E17 27Cc 52
HA7: Stan 25Ma 47
IG1: Ilf 35Rc 74
IG11: Bark 39Tc 74
KT3: N Mald 69Ua 132
KT5: Surb 72Pa 153
KT23: Bookh 99Da 191
KT24: Eff J 95W 190
N15 30Ub 51
N16 35Tb 71
NW2 35Za 68
RH2: Reig 7K 207
RM14: Upm 33Sd 78
RM16: Chaf H 48Yd 98
SE20 67Yb 136
SE25 71Wb 157
TW7: Isle 55Ha 108
UB1: S'hall 44Da 85
Howards Cl. GU22: Wok 92C 188
HA5: Pinn 26X 45
Howards Crest Cl. BR3: Beck 68Ec 136
Howards Ga. SL2: Farn R 1F 80
Howards Ho. RH2: Reig 5K 207
Howard's La. SW15 56Xa 110
Howards La. KT15: Add 79H 149
Howards Rd. E13 41Jc 93
GU22: Wok 92B 188
Howards Thicket SL9: Ger X 3N 61
Howard St. KT7: T Ditt 73Ka 152
Howards Wood Dr. SL9: Ger X 3P 61
Howard Wlk. N2 28Eb 49
Howard Way EN5: Barn 15Za 30
Howarth Rd. SE2 50Wc 95
Howberry Cl. HA8: Edg 23Ma 47
Howberry Rd. CR7: Thor H 67Tb 135
HA7: Stan 23Ma 47
HA8: Edg 23Ma 47
Howburgh Ct. *RM19: Purf* 50Rd 97
(off Wingrove Dr.)
Howbury La. DA8: Erith 54Jd 118
Howbury Rd. SE15 55Yb 114
Howcroft Cres. N3 24Cb 49
Howcroft Ho. *E3* 41Bc 92
(off Benworth St.)
Howcroft La. UB6: G'frd 41Fa 86
Howden Cl. SE28 45Zc 95
Howden Dr. KT15: Add 80J 149
Howden Rd. SE25 68Vb 135
Howden St. SE15 55Wb 113
Howe Cl. RM7: Mawney 25Cd 56
WD7: Shenl 4Na 15
Howe Dr. CR3: Cat'm 94Tb 197
Howell Cl. RM6: Chad H 29Zc 55
Howell Ct. E10 31Dc 72
Howell Hill SM2: Cheam 82Ya 174
Howell Hill Cl. KT17: Ewe 83Ya 174
Howell Hill Gro. KT17: Ewe 83Ya 174
Howell Hill Nature Reserve 83Za 174
Howells Cl. TN15: W King 79Ud 164
Howell Wlk. SE1 6C 230 (49Rb 91)
Howerd Way SE18 53Nc 116
(not continuous)
Howe Rd. HP3: Hem H 4A 4
Howes Cl. N3 27Cb 49
Howeth Ct. *N11* 23Hb 49
(off Ribblesdale Av.)
Howfield Pl. N17 27Vb 51
Howgate Rd. SW14 55Ta 109
Howick Pl. SW1 4C 228 (48Lb 90)
Howie St. SW11 52Gb 111
Howitt Cl. N16 35Ub 71
NW3 37Gb 69
Howitt Rd. NW3 37Gb 69
Howitts Cl. KT10: Esh 79Ca 151
Howland Ct. HA5: Hat E 23Ca 45
Howland Est. SE16 48Yb 92
Howland Gth. AL1: St A 6A 6
Howland Ho. SW16 62Nb 134
Howland M. E. W1 7C 216 (43Lb 90)
Howlands TN15: Wro 87Be 185
Howlands Ct. *TN15: Wro* 87Be 185
(off Howlands)
Howland St. W1 7B 216 (43Lb 90)
Howland Way SE16 47Ac 92
How La. CR5: Chip 89Jb 176
Howlett Apartments *N1* 38Nb 70
(off Caledonian Rd.)
Howletts La. HA4: Ruis 29S 44
Howlett's Rd. SE24 58Sb 113
Howley Pl. W2 7A 214 (43Eb 89)
Howley Rd. CR0: C'don 76Rb 157
Hows Cl. UB8: Uxb 39L 63
Howse Rd. EN9: Walt A 7Dc 20
Howsman Rd. SW13 51Wa 110
Howson Rd. SE4 56Ac 114
Howson Ter. TW10: Rich 58Na 109
Hows Rd. UB8: Uxb 39L 63
How's St. E2 1K 219 (40Vb 71)
Howton Pl. WD23: B Hea 18Fa 28
HOW WOOD 6M 5
How Wood AL2: Park 10P 5
HOXTON 2G 219 (40Ub 71)
Hoxton Hall Theatre 2J 219
Hoxton Mkt. N1 4H 219
Hoxton Sq. N1 4H 219 (41Ub 91)
Hoxton St. N1 1H 219 (39Ub 71)
Hoylake Cl. SL1: Slou 7C 80
Hoylake Cres. UB10: Ick 33Q 64
Hoylake Gdns. CR4: Mitc 69Lb 134
HA4: Ruis 32X 65
RM3: Hrld W 24Qd 57
WD19: Wat 21Z 45
Hoylake Rd. W3 44Ua 88
Hoyland Cl. SE15 52Xb 113
Hoyle Rd. SW17 64Gb 133
Hoy St. E16 44Hc 93
Hoy Ter. RM20: Grays 50Zd 99
HQS Wellington 5K 223
Hub, The
Westminster 2G 215 (40Hb 69)
Hub, The TW20: Egh 64B 126
Hubbard Ct. IG10: Lough 17Nc 36
Hubbard Dr. KT9: Chess 79Ma 153
Hubbard Ho. *SW10* 52Fb 111
(off World's End Pas.)
Hubbard Rd. SE27 63Sb 135
Hubbards Chase RM11: Horn 29Qd 57
Hubbards Cl. RM11: Horn 29Qd 57
UB8: Hil 44R 84
Hubbards Rd. WD3: Chor 15F 24
Hubbard St. E15 39Gc 73
Hubbinet Ind. Est. RM7: Mawney 27Ed 56
Huberd Ho. SE1 3G 231
Hubert Gro. SW9 55Nb 112
Hubert Ho. NW8 6D 214
Hubert Rd. CM14: B'wood 20Xd 40
E6 41Mc 93
RM13: Rain 41Hd 96
SL3: L'ly 8P 81
Hucknall Ct. RM3: Rom 23Pd 57
Hucknall Ct. NW8 5B 214
Huddart St. E3 43Bc 92
(not continuous)
Huddleston Cl. E2 40Yb 72
Huddleston Cres. RH1: Mers 100Mb 196
Huddlestone Rd. E7 35Hc 73
NW2 37Xa 68
Huddleston Rd. N7 34Lb 70
Hudson *NW9* 25Va 48
(off Five Acre)
Hudson Apartments N8 27Pb 50
Hudson Bldg. *E1* 43Wb 91
(off Chicksand St.)
Hudson Cl. AL1: St A 5B 6
DA12: Grav'nd 3E 144
E15 39Jc 73
W12 45Xa 88
WD24: Wat 8V 12
Hudson Ct. *E14* 50Cc 92
(off Maritime Quay)
Hudson Gdns. BR6: Chels 79Vc 161
Hudson Ho. KT19: Eps 85Ta 173
SW10 52Eb 111
(off Hortensia Rd.)
W11 44Ab 88
(off Ladbroke Gro.)
Hudson Pl. SE18 50Sc 94
SL3: L'ly 50B 82
Hudson Rd. DA7: Bex 54Bd 117
UB3: Harl 51T 106
Hudsons KT20: Tad 93Za 194
Hudsons Cl. SS17: Stan H 1M 101
Hudsons Ct. EN6: Pot B 3Cb 17
Hudson's Pl. SW1 5B 228 (49Kb 90)
Hudson Way N9 20Yb 34
NW2 34Za 68
Huggens College DA11: Nflt 57De 121
Huggin Ct. EC4 4E 224
Huggin Hill EC4 4E 224 (45Sb 91)
Huggins Ho. *E3* 41Cc 92
(off Alfred St.)
Huggins La. AL9: Wel G 5E 8
Huggins Pl. SW2 60Pb 112
Hughan Rd. E15 36Fc 73
Hugh Astor Ct. SE1 3C 230
Hugh Clark Ho. *W13* 46Ja 86
(off Singapore Rd.)
Hugh Cubitt Ho. N1 2J 217
Hugh Dalton Av. SW6 51Bb 111
Hughenden Av. HA3: Kenton 29Ka 46
Hughenden Gdns. UB5: N'olt 41Y 85
(not continuous)
Hughenden Ho. NW8 5D 214
Hughenden Rd. KT4: Wor Pk 73Wa 154
SL1: Slou 4H 81
Hughendon EN5: New Bar 14Db 31
Hughendon Ct. *UB3: Hayes* 45V 84
(off Chamberlain Cl.)
Hughendon Ter. E15 35Ec 72
Hughes Cl. N12 22Eb 49
Hughes Ct. N7 36Mb 70
Hughes Ho. *E2* 41Yb 92
(off Sceptre Ho.)
E3 41Cc 92
(off Trevithick Way)
SE5 53Sb 113
(off Flodden Rd.)
SE8 51Cc 114
(off Benbow St.)
SE17 6C 230
Hughes Mans. E1 42Wb 91
Hughes Rd. RM16: Grays 8C 100
TW15: Ashf 66S 128
UB3: Hayes 47X 85
Hughes Ter. *SW9* 55Rb 113
(off Styles Gdns.)
Hughes Wlk. CR0: C'don 73Sb 157
Hugh Gaitskell Cl. SW6 51Bb 111
Hugh Gaitskell Ho. N16 33Vb 71
Hugh Herland Ho. KT1: King T 69Na 131
Hugh M. SW1 6A 228 (49Kb 90)
Hugh Platt Ho. *E2* 40Xb 71
(off Patriot Sq.)
Hugh St. SW1 6A 228 (49Kb 90)
Hugo Cl. WD18: Wat 14U 26
Hugo Gdns. RM13: Rain 37Jd 76
Hugo Gryn Way WD7: Shenl 3Na 15
Hugo Ho. SW1 3G 227
Hugon Rd. SW6 55Db 111
Hugo Rd. N19 35Lb 70
Huguenot Pl. E1 43Vb 91
SW18 57Eb 111
Huguenot Sq. SE15 55Xb 113
HULBERRY 75Jd 162
Hullbridge M. N1 39Tb 71
Hull Cl. SE16 47Zb 92
SL1: Slou 7G 80
Hullett's La. CM15: Pil H 13Ud 40
Hull Pl. E16 46Sc 94
Hull St. EC1 4D 218 (41Sb 91)
Hulme Pl. SE1 2E 230 (47Sb 91)
Hulse Av. IG11: Bark 37Tc 74
RM7: Mawney 25Dd 56
Hulsewood Cl. DA2: Wilm 62Kd 141
Hult International Studios 44Wb 91
(off Alder St.)
Hulton Cl. KT22: Lea 95La 192
Hult Twr. *E1* 44Wb 91
(off Alder St.)
Hulverston Cl. SM2: Sutt 82Db 175
Humber Av. RM15: S Ock 44Vd 98
Humber Cl. UB7: W Dray 46M 83
Humber Ct. *W7* 44Fa 86
(off Hobbayne Rd.)
Humber Dr. RM14: Upm 30Td 58
W10 42Za 88
Humber Rd. DA1: Dart 57Md 119
NW2 33Xa 68
SE3 51Hc 115
Humberstone Rd. E13 41Lc 93
Humberton Cl. E9 36Ac 72
Humber Trad. Est. NW2 33Xa 68
Humber Way SL3: L'ly 49C 82
Humbleward Pl. RM3: Rom 22Nd 57
Humbolt Rd. W6 51Ab 110
Hume Av. RM18: Tilb 5D 122
Hume Cl. RM18: Tilb 5C 122
Hume Ct. *N1* 38Rb 71
(off Hawes St.)
Hume Ho. *W11* 46Za 88
(off Queensdale Cres.)
Hume M. RM18: Tilb 4D 122
Humes Av. W7 48Ga 86
Hume Ter. E16 43Kc 93
Hume Way HA4: Ruis 30W 44
Hummer Rd. TW20: Egh 63C 126
Humphrey Cl. IG5: Ilf 25Pc 54
KT22: Fet 94Ea 192
Humphrey St. SE1 7K 231 (50Vb 91)
Humphries Cl. RM9: Dag 35Bd 75
Hundred Acre NW9 26Va 48
Hundred Acres EN8: Walt C 6Cc 20
Hungerdown E4 18Ec 34
Hungerford Av. SL2: Slou 3J 81
Hungerford Ho. *SW1* 51Lb 112
(off Churchill Gdns.)
Hungerford La. WC2 6F 223
(not continuous)
Hungerford Rd. N7 37Mb 70
Hungerford Sq. KT13: Weyb 77T 150
Hungerford St. E1 44Xb 91
Hungry Hill La. GU23: Rip, Send 98L 189
Hunsdon Cl. RM9: Dag 37Ad 75
Hunsdon Dr. TN13: S'oaks 95Kd 203
Hunsdon Rd. SE14 52Zb 114
Hunslett St. E2 41Yb 92
Hunstanton Cl. SL3: Coln 52E 104
Hunston Rd. NW1 7E 214
Hunston Rd. SM4: Mord 74Db 155
Hunt Cl. W11 46Za 88
Hunt Ct. N14 17Kb 32
RM7: Rush G 30Gd 56
(off Union Rd.)
UB5: N'olt 40Z 65
(off Gallery Gdns.)
Hunter Av. CM15: Shenf 16Ce 41
Hunter Cl. EN6: Pot B 5Db 17
SE1 4G 231 (48Tb 91)
SM6: Wall 80Nb 156
SW12 60Jb 112
WD6: Bore 15Sa 29
Huntercombe Cl. SL6: Tap 4A 80
Huntercombe La. Nth.
SL1: Burn, Slou 3A 80
SL6: Tap 3A 80
Huntercombe La. Sth. SL6: Tap 6A 80
Hunter Ct. KT19: Eps 82Qa 173
SL1: Slou 3A 80
Huntercrombe Gdns. WD19: Wat 21Y 45
Hunter Dr. RM12: Horn 35Ld 77
Hunter Ho. SE1 2C 230
SW5 50Cb 89
(off Old Brompton Rd.)
SW8 52Mb 112
(off Fount St.)
TW13: Felt 60W 106
(off Hazel Gro.)
WC1 5F 217
Hunterian Mus., The 3J 223
Hunter Lodge *W9* 43Cb 89
(off Admiral Wlk.)
Hunter Rd. CR7: Thor H 69Tb 135
IG1: Ilf 36Rc 74
SW20 67Ya 132
Hunters Chase RH9: S God 9D 210
Hunters Cl. DA5: Bexl 62Gd 140
HP3: Bov 1C 10
KT19: Eps 85Sa 173
Hunters Ct. TW9: Rich 57Ma 109
Huntersfield Cl. RH2: Reig 3K 207
Hunters Ga. RH1: Nutf 5F 208
WD25: Wat 5W 12
Hunters Gro. BR6: Farnb 77Sc 160
HA3: Kenton 28La 46
RM5: Col R 22Dd 56
UB3: Hayes 46W 84
Hunters Hall Rd.
RM10: Dag 35Cd 76
Hunters Hill HA4: Ruis 34Y 65
Hunter's La. WD25: Wat 5V 12
Hunters Mdw. SE19 63Ub 135
Hunters M. SL4: Wind 3G 102
Hunters Reach EN7: Chesh 1Vb 19
Hunters Ride AL2: Brick W 3Ca 13
Hunter's Rd. KT9: Chess 76Na 153
Hunters Sq. RM10: Dag 35Cd 76
Hunter St. WC1 5G 217 (42Nb 90)
Hunters Wlk. TN14: Knock 86Ad 181
Hunters Way CR0: C'don 77Ub 157
Hunters Way EN2: Enf 11Qb 32
SL1: Slou 6C 80
Hunter Wlk. E13 40Jc 73
WD6: Bore 15Ta 29
Hunting Cl. KT10: Esh 77Ca 151
Huntingdon Cl. CR4: Mitc 69Nb 134
UB5: N'olt 37Ca 65
Huntingdon Dr. RM3: Hrld W 25Nd 57

Huntingdon Gdns. KT4: Wor Pk 76Ya 154
W4 52Sa 109
Huntingdon Rd. GU21: Wok 9K 167
N2 27Gb 49
N9 19Yb 34
RH1: Redh 6P 207
Huntingdon St. E16 44Hc 93
N1 38Pb 70
Huntingfield CR0: Sels 80Bc 158
Huntingfield Rd. SW15 56Wa 110
Huntingfield Way TW20: Egh 66F 126
Hunting Ga. Cl. EN2: Enf 13Qb 32
Hunting Ga. Dr. KT9: Chess 80Na 153
Hunting Ga. M. SM1: Sutt 76Db 155
TW2: Twick 60Ga 108
Hunting Pl. TW5: Hest 51Ba 107
Huntings Farm IG1: Ilf 33Uc 74
Huntings Rd. RM10: Dag 37Cd 76
Huntington Cl. DA5: Bexl 60Dd 118
Huntington Pl. SL3: L'ly 48D 82
Huntland Cl. RM13: Rain 43Kd 97
Huntley Av. DA11: Nflt 58De 121
Huntley Cl. TW19: Stanw 59N 105
Huntley Ho. KT12: W Vill 81V 170
Huntley St. WC1 6C 216 (42Lb 90)
Huntley Way SW20 68Wa 132
Huntloe Ho. *SE14* 53Yb 114
(off Kender St.)
Huntly Dr. N3 23Cb 49
Huntly Rd. SE25 70Ub 135
HUNTON BRIDGE 5S 12
HUNTON BRIDGE 7T 12
Hunton Bri. Hill WD4: Hunt C 5S 12
Hunton Cl. WD4: Hunt C 5S 12
Hunton St. E1 43Wb 91
Hunt Rd. DA11: Nflt 2A 144
UB2: S'hall 48Ca 85
Hunt's Cl. SE3 54Jc 115
Hunt's Ct. WC2 5E 222 (45Mb 90)
Hunts Farm Cl. TN15: Bor G 92Ce 205
Huntshaw Ho. *E3* 41Dc 92
(off Devons Rd.)
Hunts La. E15 40Ec 72
Huntsman La. TN15: Wro H 90Fe 185
Huntsman Rd. IG6: Ilf 22Xc 55
Huntsmans Cl. CR6: W'ham 91Yb 198
KT22: Fet 96Fa 192
TW13: Felt 63X 129
Huntsmans Ct. *CR3: Cat'm* 93Sb 197
(off Coulsdon Rd.)
Huntsmans Dr. RM14: Upm 36Sd 78
Huntsman St. SE17 6H 231 (49Ub 91)
Hunts Mead EN3: Enf H 13Zb 34
Hunts Mead Cl. BR7: Chst 66Pc 138
Huntsmill Rd. HP1: Hem H 3G 2
Huntsmoor Rd. KT19: Ewe 78Ta 153
Huntspill St. SW17 62Eb 133
Hunts Slip Rd. SE21 62Ub 135
Huntsworth M. NW1 5F 215 (42Hb 89)
Hurdwick Ho. NW1 1B 216
Hurdwick Pl. *NW1* 1B 216
(off Hampstead Rd.)
Hurleston Ho. SE8 50Bc 92
Hurley Cl. KT12: Walt T 75X 151
SM7: Bans 88Bb 175
Hurley Ct. *SW17* 65Jb 134
(off Mitcham Rd.)
W5 44La 86
Hurley Cres. SE16 47Ac 92
Hurley Ho. SE11 6A 230 (49Rb 91)
UB7: W Dray 47P 83
(off Park Lodge Av.)
Hurley Rd. UB6: G'frd 44Da 85
Hurlfield DA2: Wilm 62Ld 141
Hurlford GU21: Wok 9L 167
HURLINGHAM 55Db 111
Hurlingham Bus. Pk. SW6 55Cb 111
Hurlingham Club, The 55Cb 111
Hurlingham Ct. SW6 55Bb 111
Hurlingham Gdns. SW6 55Bb 111
Hurlingham Pk. 54Bb 111
Hurlingham Retail Pk. SW6 55Db 111
Hurlingham Rd. DA7: Bex 52Bd 117
SW6 54Bb 111
Hurlingham Sq. SW6 55Cb 111
Hurlingham Yacht Club 55Ab 110
Hurlock St. N5 34Rb 71
Hurlstone Rd. SE25 71Ub 157
Hurn Ct. TW4: Houn 54Z 107
Hurn Ct. Rd. TW4: Houn 54Z 107
Hurnford Cl. CR2: Sande 82Ub 177
Huron Cl. BR6: Chels 79Uc 160
Huron Rd. SW17 61Jb 134
Hurren Cl. SE3 55Gc 115
Hurricane Rd. SM6: Wall 80Nb 156
Hurricane Trad. Cen. NW9 25Wa 48
Hurricane Way SL3: L'ly 50D 82
WD5: Ab L 4W 12
Hurry Cl. E15 38Gc 73
Hursley Rd. IG7: Chig 22Vc 55
Hurst, The TN11: Roug 99Fe 205
TN15: Crou 97Ee 205
Hurst Av. E4 21Cc 52
N6 30Lb 50
Hurstbourne KT10: Clay 79Ha 152
Hurstbourne Gdns. IG11: Bark 37Uc 74
Hurstbourne Ho. *SW15* 58Va 110
(off Tangley Gro.)
Hurstbourne Rd. SE23 60Ac 114
Hurst Cl. BR2: Hayes 74Hc 159
E4 20Cc 34
GU22: Wok 2N 187
KT9: Chess 78Qa 153
KT18: Head 96Sa 193
NW11 30Db 49
UB5: N'olt 37Ba 65
Hurstcombe IG9: Buck H 19Jc 35
Hurst Ct. DA15: Sidc 61Wc 139
E6 43Mc 93
(off Tollgate Rd.)
IG8: Wfd G 23Kc 53
(off Snakes La. W.)
WD17: Wat 10W 12
Hurstcourt Rd. SM1: Sutt 75Db 155
Hurstdene Av. BR2: Hayes 74Hc 159
TW18: Staines 65K 127
Hurstdene Gdns. N15 31Ub 71
Hurst Dr. EN8: Walt C 6Zb 20
KT20: Walt H 98Wa 194
Hurstfield BR2: Brom 71Jc 159
Hurstfield Cres. UB4: Hayes 42U 84
Hurstfield Dr. SL6: Tap 4A 80
Hurstfield Rd. KT8: W Mole 69Ca 129
HURST GREEN 4L 211
Hurst Grn. Cl. RH8: Oxt 4L 211
Hurst Grn. Rd. RH8: Oxt 4K 211
Hurst Gro. KT12: Walt T 74V 150
Hurst Ho. WC1 2J 217

Hurstlands RH8: Oxt 4L 211
Hurstlands Cl. RM11: Horn 31Ld 77
Hurstlands Dr. BR6: Chels 76Yc 161
Hurst La. KT8: E Mos 70Ea 130
KT18: Head 96Sa 193
SE2 50Zc 95
TW20: Egh 68C 126
Hurst La. Est. SE2 50Zc 95
Hurstleigh WD3: Chor 15E 24
Hurstleigh Cl. RH1: Redh 4P 207
Hurstleigh Dr. RH1: Redh 4P 207
Hurstleigh Gdns. IG5: Ilf 25Pc 54
Hurst Lodge *KT13: Weyb* 79T 150
(off Gower Rd.)
Hurstmead Ct. HA8: Edg 21Ra 47
HURST PARK 68Ea 130
Hurst Pk. Av. RM12: Horn 35Nd 77
Hurst Pl. DA1: Dart 58Ld 119
HA6: Nwood 25R 44
Hurst Pool 69Da 129
Hurst Ri. EN5: New Bar 13Cb 31
Hurst Rd. CR0: C'don 78Tb 157
DA5: Bexl 60Zc 117
DA8: Erith 53Ed 118
DA15: Bexl, Sidc 61Wc 139
E17 27Dc 52
IG9: Buck H 18Mc 35
KT8: W Mole, E Mos 71Y 151
KT12: Walt T 71Y 151
KT18: Head 95Ta 193
KT19: Eps 83Ta 173
KT20: Walt H 95Ta 193
N21 18Qb 32
SL1: Slou 3B 80
Hurst Springs DA5: Bexl 60Ad 117
Hurst St. SE24 58Rb 113
Hurstview Grange
CR2: S Croy 80Rb 157
Hurst Vw. Rd. CR2: S Croy 80Ub 157
Hurst Way CR2: S Croy 79Ub 157
GU22: Pyr 86G 168
TN13: S'oaks 99Ld 203
Hurstway Rd. *W11* 45Za 88
(off Hurstway Wlk.)
Hurstway Wlk. W11 45Za 88
Hurstwood Av. CM15: Pil H 17Xd 40
DA5: Bexl 60Ad 117
DA7: Bex 53Gd 118
DA8: Erith 53Gd 118
E18 28Kc 53
Hurstwood Ct. N12 23Gb 49
NW11 28Bb 49
(off Finchley Rd.)
RM14: Upm 32Sd 78
Hurstwood Dr. BR1: Brom 69Pc 138
Hurstwood Rd. NW11 28Ab 48
Hurtwood Rd. KT12: Walt T 73Ba 151
Hurworth Av. SL3: L'ly 8N 81
Husborne Ho. *SE8* 49Ac 92
(off Chilton Gro.)
Huskards RM14: Upm 33Rd 77
Huson Cl. NW3 38Gb 69
Hussain Cl. HA1: Harr 35Ha 66
Hussars Cl. TW4: Houn 55Aa 107
Husseywell Cres. BR2: Hayes 74Jc 159
Hutchings Lodge WD3: Rick 18N 25
Hutchingsons Rd.
CR0: New Ad 83Ec 178
Hutchings St. E14 47Cc 92
Hutchings Wlk. NW11 28Db 49
Hutchings Wharf *E14* 47Cc 92
(off Hutchings St.)
Hutchins Cl. E15 38Ec 72
RM12: Horn 34Nd 77
Hutchinson Ct. RM6: Chad H 28Zc 55
Hutchinson Ho. NW3 38Hb 69
SE14 52Yb 114
Hutchinson's Bank Nature Reserve
84Ec 178
Hutchinson Ter. HA9: Wemb 34Ma 67
Hutchins Rd. SE28 45Wc 95
Hutson Ter. RM19: Purf 51Td 120
HUTTON 15Ee 41
Hutton Cl. GU20: W'sham 10B 146
IG8: Wfd G 23Kc 53
KT12: Hers 78X 151
UB6: G'frd 36Fa 66
Hutton Ct. *N4* 32Pb 70
(off Victoria Rd.)
N9 17Yb 34
(off Tramway Av.)
W5 43Ka 86
Hutton Dr. CM13: Hut 17Ee 41
Hutton Gdns. HA3: Hrw W 24Ea 46
Hutton Ga. CM13: Hut 17De 41
Hutton Gro. N12 22Db 49
Hutton La. HA3: Hrw W 24Ea 46
Hutton M. SW15 57Xa 110
HUTTON MOUNT 18De 41
Hutton Pl. CM13: Hut 16Fe 41
(Cedar Rd.)
CM13: Hut 16De 41
(Yew Tree Cl.)
Hutton Rd. CM15: Shenf 17Be 41
Hutton Row HA8: Edg 24Sa 47
Hutton St. EC4 3B 224 (44Rb 91)
Hutton Village CM13: Hut 17Fe 41
Hutton Wlk. HA3: Hrw W 24Ea 46
Huxbear St. SE4 57Bc 114
Huxley Cl. EN7: Chesh 1Vb 19
SL3: Wex 2M 81
UB5: N'olt 40Aa 65
UB8: Cowl 42M 83
Huxley Dr. RM6: Chad H 31Xc 75
Huxley Gdns. NW10 41Pa 87
Huxley Ho. NW8 6C 214
Huxley Pde. N18 22Tb 51
Huxley Pl. N13 20Rb 33
Huxley Rd. DA16: Well 55Vc 117
E10 33Ec 72
N18 21Tb 51
Huxley Sayze N18 22Tb 51
Huxley Sth. N18 22Tb 51
Huxley St. W10 41Ab 88
Hyacinth Cl. IG1: Ilf 37Rc 74
TW12: Hamp 65Ca 129
Hyacinth Ct. UB10: Uxb 38N 63
Hyacinth Ho. *E17* 27Dc 52
(off Vine St.)
Hyacinth Rd. SW15 60Wa 110
Hybrid Ho. W3 46Ua 88
Hyburn Cl. AL2: Brick W 2Ba 13
HP3: Hem H 3B 4
Hycliffe Gdns. IG7: Chig 21Sc 54
HYDE, THE 29Va 48
Hyde, The NW9 28Ua 48
(not continuous)
Hyde Av. EN6: Pot B 5Db 17

Hyde Cl. E13 40Jc 73
EN5: Barn 13Bb 31
RM1: Rom 23Fd 56
RM16: Chaf H 48Zd 99
TW15: Ashf 65U 128
Hyde Ct. AL2: Lon C 9F 6
EN8: Walt C 6Ac 20
N20 20Fb 31
Hyde Cres. NW9 29Ua 48
Hyde Dr. BR5: St P 70Xc 139
Hyde Est. Rd. NW9 29Va 48
Hyde Farm M. SW12 60Mb 112
Hydefield Cl. N21 18Tb 33
Hydefield Ct. N9 19Ub 33
Hyde Gro. DA1: Dart 54Pd 119
Hyde Ho. *E3* 43Cc 92
(off Furze St.)
TW3: Houn 55Ea 108
UB8: Uxb 37N 63
W13 46Ja 86
(off Singapore Rd.)
Hyde Ind. Est., The NW9 29Va 48
Hyde La. AL2: F'mre, Park 10A 6
(not continuous)
GU23: Ock 92R 190
HP3: Bov 9B 2
HP3: Hem H 9A 4
SW11 53Gb 111
Hyde Mdws. HP3: Bov 10C 2
Hyde M. RM1: Rom 23Fd 56
Hyde Pk. 5E 220 (46Hb 89)
Hyde Pk. Av. N21 19Sb 33
HYDE PARK CORNER 1J 227 (47Kb 90)
Hyde Pk. Cnr. W1 1J 227 (47Jb 90)
Hyde Pk. Cres. W2 3D 220 (44Gb 89)
Hyde Pk. Gdns. N21 18Sb 33
W2 4C 220 (45Fb 89)
(not continuous)
Hyde Pk. Gdns. M.
W2 4C 220 (45Fb 89)
Hyde Pk. Ga. SW7 47Eb 89
(not continuous)
Hyde Pk. Ga. M.
SW7 2A 226 (47Eb 89)
Hyde Pk. Mans. NW1 1D 220
(not continuous)
Hyde Pk. Pl. W2 4E 220 (45Gb 89)
Hyde Pk. Sq. W2 3D 220 (44Gb 89)
Hyde Pk. Sq. M. W2 3D 220
Hyde Pk. St. W2 3D 220 (44Gb 89)
Hyde Pk. Towers W2 5A 220 (45Eb 89)
Hyderabad Way E15 38Gc 73
Hyde Rd. CR2: Sande 85Ub 177
DA7: Bex 54Bd 117
N1 1H 219 (39Ub 71)
TW10: Rich 57Pa 109
WD17: Wat 12W 26
Hyder Rd. RM16: Grays 8E 100
Hyders Forge TN15: Plax 99Ce 205
(not continuous)
Hydeside Gdns. N9 19Vb 33
Hyde's Pl. N1 38Rb 71
Hyde St. SE8 51Cc 114
Hyde Ter. HP3: Hem H 6E 4
TW15: Ashf 65U 128
Hydethorpe Av. N9 19Vb 33
Hydethorpe Rd. SW12 60Lb 112
Hyde Va. SE10 52Ec 114
Hyde Wlk. SM4: Mord 73Cb 155
Hyde Way N9 19Vb 33
UB3: Harl 49V 84
Hydon Ct. N11 22Hb 49
Hydra Bldg., The EC1 4A 218
Hydro Ho. KT16: Chert 74L 149
Hyland Cl. RM11: Horn 31Kd 77
Hylands Cl. KT18: Eps 87Sa 173
Hylands M. KT18: Eps 87Sa 173
Hylands Rd. E17 26Fc 53
KT18: Eps 87Sa 173
Hyland Way RM11: Horn 31Kd 77
Hylle Cl. SL4: Wind 3C 102
Hylton Pl. RH1: Mers 3C 208
Hylton St. SE18 49Vc 95
Hyndewood SE23 62Zb 136
Hyndford Cres. *DA9: Ghithe* 57Yd 120
(off Calcroft Av.)
Hyndman Ho. *RM10: Dag* 34Cd 76
(off Kershaw Rd.)
Hyndman St. SE15 51Xb 113
Hynton Rd. RM8: Dag 33Yc 75
Hyperion Ct. *E16* 43Jc 93
(off Robertson Rd.)
Hyperion Ho. *E3* 40Ac 72
(off Arbery Rd.)
SW2 58Pb 112
Hyperion Pl. KT19: Ewe 81Ta 173
Hyrstdene CR2: S Croy 77Rb 157
Hyson Rd. SE16 50Xb 91
Hythe, The TW18: Staines 64G 126
Hythe Av. DA7: Bex 52Ad 117
Hythe Cl. BR5: St M Cry 70Yc 139
N18 21Wb 51
HYTHE END 61D 126
Hythe End Rd. TW19: Wray 61B 126
Hythe Fld. Av. TW20: Egh 65F 126
Hythe Ho. *SE16* 47Yb 92
(off Swan Rd.)
W6 49Ya 88
(off Shepherd's Bush Rd.)
Hythe Pk. Rd. TW20: Egh 64E 126
Hythe Rd. CR7: Thor H 68Tb 135
KT6: Surb 72Na 153
NW10 41Va 88
TW18: Staines 64F 126
Hythe Rd. Ind. Est. NW10 41Wa 88
Hythe St. DA1: Dart 58Nd 119
Hythe St. (Lower) DA1: Dart 57Nd 119
Hyver Hill NW7 16Ta 29

I

Ian Bowater Ct. N1 3G 219
Ian Ct. SE23 61Yb 136
Ian Sq. EN3: Enf H 11Zb 34
Ibberton Ho. *SW8* 52Pb 112
(off Meadow Rd.)
W14 48Ab 88
(off Russell Rd.)
Ibbetson Path
IG10: Lough 13Rc 36
Ibbotson Av. E16 44Hc 93
Ibbotson Ct. SL3: Poyle 53G 104
Ibbott St. E1 42Yb 92
Iberia Ho. N19 31Mb 70
Iberian Av. SM6: Bedd 77Mb 156
Ibex Ho. *E15* 36Gc 73
(off Forest La.)

Ibis Ct. *BR3: Beck* 67Fc 137
(off Albemarle Rd.)
SE8 51Bc 114
(off Edward Pl.)
Ibis La. W4 53Sa 109
Ibis Way UB4: Yead 44Z 85
Ibrox Ct. IG9: Buck H 19Lc 35
Ibscott Cl. RM10: Dag 37Ed 76
Ibsley Gdns. SW15 60Wa 110
Ibsley Way EN4: Cockf 15Gb 31
ICA Cinema 7E 222
Icarus Ho. *E3* 41Bc 92
(off British St.)
ICA Theatre 7E 222
Icehouse Wood RH8: Oxt 3J 211
Iceland Rd. E3 39Cc 72
Iceland Wharf SE16 49Ac 92
Iceni Ct. *E3* 39Bc 72
(off Parnell Rd.)
IG9: Buck H 18Kc 35
Ice Wharf N1 1H 217 (40Nb 70)
Ice Wharf Marina N1 1G 217
Ice Works, The *NW1* 38Kb 70
(off Jamestown Rd.)
Ickburgh Est. E5 33Xb 71
Ickburgh Rd. E5 34Xb 71
ICKENHAM 34R 64
Ickenham Cl. HA4: Ruis 33T 64
Ickenham Grn. UB10: Ick 32R 64
Ickenham Rd. HA4: Ruis 33S 64
Ickleton Rd. SE9 63Nc 138
Icklingham Ga. KT11: Cobh 84Y 171
Icklingham Rd. KT11: Cobh 84Y 171
Icknield Cl. AL3: St A 4M 5
Icknield Dr. IG2: Ilf 29Rc 54
Icknield Ho. SW3 7E 226
Ickworth Pk. Rd. E17 28Ac 52
Icon Apartments SE1 3H 231
Icona Point *E15* 39Ec 72
(off Warton Rd.)
Iconia Ho. BR2: Brom 70Lc 137
Idaho Bldg. *SE13* 53Dc 114
(off Deal's Gateway)
Ida Rd. N15 28Tb 51
Ida St. E14 44Ec 92
(not continuous)
Ide Mans. *E1* 45Zb 92
(off Cable St.)
Iden Cl. BR2: Brom 69Gc 137
Idlecombe Rd. SW17 65Jb 134
Idleigh Ct. Rd. DA13: Meop 75De 165
Idmiston Rd. E15 35Hc 73
KT4: Wor Pk 73Va 154
SE27 62Sb 135
Idmiston Sq. KT4: Wor Pk 73Va 154
Idol La. EC3 5H 225 (45Ub 91)
Idonia St. SE8 52Cc 114
Iffley Cl. UB8: Uxb 38M 63
Iffley Ct. TW18: Staines 64H 127
Iffley Rd. W6 48Xa 88
IFIELD 6E 144
Ifield Cl. RH1: Redh 8N 207
Ifield Ho. SE17 7J 231
Ifield Rd. DA13: Meop 78Fe 165
SW10 51Db 111
Ifield Way DA12: Grav'nd 5F 144
Ifold Rd. RH1: Redh 8A 208
Ifor Evans Pl. E1 42Zb 92
IGHTHAM 93Zd 205
Ightham By-Pass TN15: Igh 93Yd 204
Ightham Cl. DA3: Lfield 69Ae 143
IGHTHAM COMMON 95Xd 204
Ightham Ho. *BR3: Beck* 66Bc 136
(off Bethersden Cl.)
SE17 6H 231
Ightham Mote 99Wd 204
Ightham Rd. DA8: Erith 52Cd 118
TN11: S'brne 100Yd 204
TN15: S'brne 100Yd 204
Ikona Ct. KT13: Weyb 78S 150
Ikon Ho. *E1* 45Yb 92
(off Devonport St.)
Ilbert St. W10 41Za 88
Ilchester Gdns. W2 45Db 89
Ilchester Mans. *W8* 48Cb 89
(off Abingdon Rd.)
Ilchester Pl. W14 48Bb 89
Ilchester Rd. RM8: Dag 36Xc 75
Ildersly Gro. SE21 61Tb 135
Ilderton Rd. SE15 50Xb 91
SE16 50Xb 91
Ilderton Wharf *SE15* 51Yb 114
(off Rollins St.)
Ilex Cl. TW16: Sun 68Y 129
TW20: Eng G 6M 125
Ilex Ho. KT15: New H 82J 169
Ilex Rd. NW10 37Va 68
Ilex Way SW16 64Qb 134
ILFORD 34Rc 74
Ilford Bldg. IG1: Ilf 34Qc 74
Ilford Golf Course 32Pc 74
Ilford Hill IG1: Ilf 34Qc 74
Ilford Ho. *N1* 37Tb 71
(off Dove Rd.)
Ilford La. IG1: Ilf 34Rc 74
Ilford Sports Club 33Uc 74
Ilfracombe Cres. RM12: Horn 35Ld 77
Ilfracombe Flats *SE1* 1E 230
(off Marshalsea Rd.)
Ilfracombe Gdns. RM6: Chad H 31Xc 75
Ilfracombe Rd. BR1: Brom 62Hc 137
Iliffe St. SE17 7C 230 (50Rb 91)
Iliffe Yd. SE17 7C 230
Ilkeston Ct. *E5* 35Zb 72
(off Overbury St.)
Ilkley Cl. SE19 65Tb 135
Ilkley Rd. E16 43Lc 93
WD19: Wat 22Z 45
Illingworth SL4: Wind 5C 102
Illingworth Cl. CR4: Mitc 69Fb 133
Illingworth Way EN1: Enf 15Ub 33
Illumina Ho. *SW18* 57Cb 111
(off Broomhill Rd.)
Ilmington Rd. HA3: Kenton 30Ma 47
Ilminster Gdns. SW11 56Gb 111
Ilsley Ct. SW8 54Lb 112
Images IG2: Ilf 30Qc 54
Imani Mans. SW11 54Fb 111
IMAX (BFI) 7K 223 (46Qb 90)
Imber Cl. KT10: Esh 74Fa 152
N14 17Lb 32
Imber Court 73Fa 152
Imber Ct. Trad. Est. KT8: E Mos 72Fa 152
Imber Cross KT7: T Ditt 72Ha 152
Imber Gro. KT10: Esh 73Fa 152
Imber Pk. Rd. KT10: Esh 74Fa 152
Imber St. N1 1F 219 (39Tb 71)
Impact Bus. Pk. UB6: G'frd 40Ka 66

Impact Ct. SE20 68Xb 135
Imperial Av. N16 35Ub 71
Imperial Bus. Est. DA11: Nflt 8B 122
Imperial Cancer Research Cen. 6Va 16
Imperial Cl. HA2: Harr 30Ca 45
NW2 36Xa 68
Imperial College London
Chelsea & Westminster Campus
51Eb 111
(within Chelsea & Westminster Hospital)
Royal Brompton Campus 50Gb 89
(off Manresa Rd.)
St Mary's 2C 220
Silwood Pk. Campus 9C 124
Sth. Kensington Campus
3B 226 (48Fb 89)
Imperial Coll. Rd. SW7 4A 226 (48Fb 89)
Imperial Ct. HA2: Harr 31Ca 65
N6 30Lb 50
N20 20Eb 31
NW8 1E 214
SE11 7K 229 (50Qb 90)
SL4: Wind 5E 102
Imperial Cres. SW6 54Eb 111
Imperial Dr. DA12: Grav'nd 4H 145
HA2: Harr 31Ca 65
Imperial Gdns. CR4: Mitc 69Kb 134
Imperial Gro. EN4: Had W 11Db 31
Imperial Hgts. *E18* 25Jc 53
(off Queen Mary Av.)
Imperial Ho. *E3* 41Ac 92
(off Grove Rd.)
E14 45Bc 92
(off Victory Pl.)
Imperial M. E6 40Mc 73
SW9 56Pb 112
(off Brighton Ter.)
Imperial Pk. KT22: Lea 92Ja 192
WD24: Wat 11Y 27
Imperial Pl. BR7: Chst 67Qc 138
WD6: Bore 13Ra 29
Imperial Retail Pk. DA11: Grav'nd 8C 122
Imperial Rd. N22 24Nb 50
SL4: Wind 5E 102
SW6 53Db 111
TW14: Felt 59U 106
Imperial Sq. SW6 53Db 111
Imperial St. E3 41Ec 92
Imperial Trad. Est. RM13: Rain 42Ld 97
Imperial War Mus.
All Saints Annexe 4A 230
Lambeth Rd. 4A 230 (48Qb 90)
Imperial Way BR7: Chst 62Sc 138
CR0: Wadd 79Pb 156
HA3: Kenton 30Na 47
HP3: Hem H 6N 3
WD3: Crox G 17R 26
WD24: Wat 11Y 27
Imperial Wharf *E2* 40Xb 71
(off Darwen Pl.)
SW6 54Eb 111
Imperium Ho. *E1* 44Xb 91
(off Cannon St. Rd.)
Imprimo Pk. IG10: Lough 14Sc 36
Impulse Leisure
Belhus Pk. 44Ud 98
Blackshots 47Fe 99
Imre Cl. W12 46Xa 88
Inca Dr. SE9 59Rc 116
Inca Ter. N15 27Rb 51
Ince Rd. KT12: Hers 79U 150
Inchmery Rd. SE6 61Dc 136
Inchwood BR4: Addtn 77Dc 158
Indells AL10: Hat 1B 8
Independence Ho. *SW19* 67Fb 133
(off Chapter Way)
Independent Ind. Est. UB7: Yiew 46N 83
Independent Pl. E8 36Vb 71
Independents Rd. SE3 55Hc 115
Inderwick Rd. N8 29Pb 50
Indescon Cl. E14 47Dc 92
Indescon Sq. E14 47Cc 92
Index Apartments *RM1: Rom* 28Hd 56
(off Mercury Gdns.)
India Gdns. UB5: N'olt 38Y 65
India Ho. WC2 4H 223
Indiana Bldg. *SE13* 53Cc 114
(off Deal's Gateway)
India Pl. WC2 4H 223
India Rd. SL1: Slou 7M 81
India St. EC3 3K 225 (44Vb 91)
India Way SW15 58Wa 110
W12 45Xa 88
IndigO2 46Gc 93
Indigo M. E14 45Ec 92
N16 34Tb 71
Indigo Wlk. N6 28Hb 49
Indus Ct. *SE15* 52Vb 113
(off Amstel Ct.)
Indus Rd. SE7 52Lc 115
Infirmary Ct. *SW3* 51Hb 111
(off West Rd.)
Inforum M. SE15 52Wb 113
Ingal Rd. E13 42Jc 93
Ingate Pl. SW8 53Kb 112
Ingatestone Rd. E12 32Lc 73
IG8: Wfd G 24Kc 53
SE25 70Xb 135
Ingelow Ho. *W8* 47Db 89
(off Holland St.)
Ingelow Rd. SW8 54Kb 112
Ingels Mead CM16: Epp 1Vc 23
Ingersoll Rd. EN3: Enf W 10Yb 20
W12 46Xa 88
Ingestre Pl. W1 3C 222 (44Lb 90)
Ingestre Rd. E7 35Jc 73
NW5 35Kb 70
Ingham Cl. CR2: Sels 81Zb 178
Ingham Rd. CR2: Sels 81Yb 178
NW6 35Cb 69
Inglebert St. EC1 3K 217 (41Qb 90)
Ingleboro Dr. CR8: Purl 85Tb 177
Ingleborough La.
TN15: Plat 91Fe 205
Ingleborough St. SW9 54Qb 112
Ingleby Dr. HA1: Harr 34Fa 66
Ingleby Gdns. IG7: Chig 20Xc 37
Ingleby Rd. IG1: Ilf 32Rc 74
N7 34Nb 70
RM10: Dag 37Dd 76
RM16: Grays 8D 100
Ingleby Way BR7: Chst 64Qc 138
SM6: Wall 81Mb 176
Ingle Cl. HA5: Pinn 27Aa 45
Ingledew Rd. SE18 50Tc 94
Inglefield EN6: Pot B 2Cb 17
Inglefield Sq. *E1* 46Xb 91
(off Prusom St.)

Ingleglen—James Clavell Sq.

Ingleglen RM11: Horn ... 31Qd 77
SL2: Farn C ... 6F 60
Inglehurst KT15: New H ... 82K 169
Inglehurst Gdns. IG4: Ilf ... 29Pc 54
Inglemere Rd. CR4: Mitc ... 66Hb 133
SE23 ... 62Zb 136
Ingle M. EC1 ... 3K 217 (41Qb 90)
Inglenorth Ct. BR8: Crock ... 72Ed 162
Inglesham Wlk. E9 ... 37Bc 72
Ingleside SL3: Poyle ... 53G 104
Ingleside Cl. BR3: Beck ... 66Cc 136
Ingleside Gro. SE3 ... 51Hc 115
Inglethorpe St. SW6 ... 53Za 110
Ingleton Av. DA16: Well ... 57Wc 117
Ingleton Rd. N18 ... 23Wb 51
SM5: Cars ... 81Gb 175
Ingleton St. SW9 ... 54Qb 112
Ingleway N12 ... 23Fb 49
Inglewood BR7: Chst ... 65Tc 138
BR8: Swan ... 68Gd 140
CR0: Sels ... 81Ac 178
GU21: Wok ... 10M 167
KT16: Chert ... 76H 149
Inglewood Cl. E14 ... 49Cc 92
IG6: Ilf ... 23Vc 55
RM12: Horn ... 35Md 77
Inglewood Copse
BR1: Brom ... 68Nc 138
Inglewood Ct. BR1: Brom ... 66Gc 137
Inglewood Gdns. AL2: St A ... 7C 6
Inglewood M. KT6: Surb ... 74Qa 153
SE27 ... 64Sb 135
(off Elder Rd.)
Inglewood Rd. DA7: Bex ... 56Fd 118
NW6 ... 36Cb 69
Inglis Barracks NW7 ... 23Za 48
Inglis Rd. CR0: C'don ... 74Vb 157
W5 ... 45Pa 87
Inglis St. SE5 ... 53Rb 113
Inglis Way NW7 ... 23Za 48
Ingoldisthorpe Gro. SE15 ... 51Vb 113
Ingoldsby Rd.
DA12: Grav'nd ... 10G 122
Ingot Twr. *E14 ... 43Cc 92*
(off Ursula Gould Way)
Ingram Av. NW11 ... 31Eb 69
Ingram Cl. HA7: Stan ... 22La 46
SE11 ... 5J 229 (49Pb 90)
Ingram Ct. CR0: C'don ... 74Rb 157
Ingram Ho. E3 ... 39Ac 72
Ingram Rd. CR7: Thor H ... 67Sb 135
DA1: Dart ... 60Nd 119
N2 ... 28Gb 49
RM17: Grays ... 49Ee 99
Ingrams Cl. KT12: Hers ... 78Y 151
Ingram Way UB6: G'frd ... 39Fa 66
INGRAVE ... 22Ee 59
INGRAVE COMMON ... 21Ce 59
Ingrave Rd. CM13: B'wood ... 19Zd 41
CM15: B'wood ... 19Zd 41
RM1: Rom ... 28Gd 56
Ingrave St. SW11 ... 55Fb 111
Ingrebourne Apartments SW6 ... 55Db 111
Ingrebourne Av. RM3: Rom ... 21Md 57
Ingrebourne Ct. E4 ... 20Dc 34
Ingrebourne Gdns. RM14: Upm ... 32Sd 78
Ingrebourne Hill ... 40Jd 76
Ingrebourne Ho. *BR1: Brom ... 64Fc 137*
(off Brangbourne Rd.)
NW8 ... 7C 214
Ingrebourne Rd. RM13: Rain ... 42Kd 97
Ingress Gdns. DA9: Ghithe ... 57Zd 121
INGRESS PARK ... 56Yd 120
Ingress Pk. Av. DA9: Ghithe ... 56Yd 120
Ingress St. W4 ... 50Ua 88
Ingress Ter. DA13: Sflt ... 63Ae 143
Ingreway RM3: Hrld W ... 23Rd 57
Inigo Jones Rd. SE7 ... 52Nc 116
Inigo Pl. WC2 ... 4F 223
Ink Bldg. W10 ... 43Za 88
Inkerman Rd. AL1: St A ... 3C 6
GU21: Knap ... 10J 167
NW5 ... 37Kb 70
SL4: Eton W ... 9D 80
Inkerman Ter. *W8 ... 48Cb 89*
(off Allen St.)
Inkerman Way GU21: Wok ... 10J 167
Inks Grn. E4 ... 22Ec 52
Inkster Ho. SW11 ... 55Gb 111
Inkwell Cl. N12 ... 20Eb 31
Ink Works Ct. SE1 ... 2J 231
Inman Rd. NW10 ... 39Ua 68
SW18 ... 59Eb 111
Inmans Row IG8: Wfd G ... 21Jc 53
Inner Circ. NW1 ... 4H 215 (41Jb 90)
Inner Ct. SW3 ... 51Gb 111
Innerd Ct. *CR0: C'don ... 72Sb 157*
(off Harry Cl.)
Inner Pk. Rd. SW19 ... 60Za 110
Inner Ring E. TW6: H'row A ... 55R 106
Inner Ring W. TW6: H'row A ... 55Q 106
Inner Temple La. EC4 ... 3K 223
Innes Cl. SW20 ... 68Ab 132
Innes Ct. HP3: Hem H ... 5M 3
Innes Gdns. SW15 ... 58Xa 110
Innes St. SE15 ... 52Ub 113
Innes Yd. CR0: C'don ... 76Sb 157
Innis Ho. SE17 ... 7H 231
Inniskilling Rd. E13 ... 40Lc 73
Innova Bus. Pk. EN3: Enf L ... 8Bc 20
Innova Ct. CR0: C'don ... 74Ub 157
Innova Pas. E1 ... 5K 219
Innovation Cen., The *E14 ... 47Ec 92*
(off Marsh Wall)
Innovation Cl. HA0: Wemb ... 39Na 67
Innova Way EN3: Enf L ... 8Bc 20
Inns of Court & City Yeomanry Mus.
... 1J 223 (43Pb 90)
Inskip Cl. E10 ... 33Dc 72
Inskip Dr. RM11: Horn ... 32Nd 77
Inskip Rd. RM8: Dag ... 32Zc 75
Insley Ho. *E3 ... 41Dc 92*
(off Bow Rd.)
Inspirations Way BR6: Orp ... 73Wc 161
Institute of Archaeology Collections
... 5D 216 (42Mb 90)
Institute of Contemporary Arts ... 7E 222
Institute Pl. E8 ... 36Xb 71
Institute Rd. CM16: Coop ... 1Zc 23
Instone Rd. DA1: Dart ... 59Md 119
Integer Gdns. E11 ... 31Fc 73
Interchange, The BR8: Swan ... 72Jd 162
NW1 ... 38Kb 70
(off Camden Lock Pl.)
Interface Ho. *TW3: Houn ... 55Ca 107*
(off Staines Rd.)
International Av. TW5: Cran ... 50Y 85
International Bus. Pk. E15 ... 39Fc 73
International Ho. E1 ... 5K 225
TW8: Bford ... 50Na 87
(off Gt. West Rd.)
INTERNATIONAL QUARTER, THE ... 37Ec 72
International Sq. *E20 ... 37Ec 72*
(within Westfield Stratford City Shop. Cen.)
International Trad. Est. UB2: S'hall ... 48X 85
International Way DA10: Ebbs ... 59Ce 121
E20 ... 37Ec 72
TW16: Sun ... 67U 128
INTU Bromley BR1: Brom ... 68Jc 137
Intu Lakeside (Thurrock Lakeside)
RM20: W Thur ... 48Xd 98
Inverary Pl. SE18 ... 51Tc 116
Inver Cl. E5 ... 33Yb 72
Inverclyde Gdns. RM6: Chad H ... 28Yc 55
(not continuous)
Inver Ct. W2 ... 44Db 89
W6 ... 48Wa 88
Inveresk Gdns. KT4: Wor Pk ... 76Wa 154
Inverforth Cl. NW3 ... 33Eb 69
Inverforth Rd. N11 ... 22Kb 50
Invergarry Ho. *NW6 ... 40Db 69*
(off Carlton Vale)
Inverine Rd. SE7 ... 50Kc 93
Invermead Cl. W6 ... 48Wa 88
Invermore Pl. SE18 ... 49Sc 94
Inverness Av. EN1: Enf ... 11Ub 33
Inverness Ct. SE6 ... 60Hc 115
Inverness Dr. IG6: Ilf ... 23Uc 54
Inverness Gdns. W8 ... 46Db 89
Inverness M. E16 ... 46Sc 94
W2 ... 45Db 89
Inverness Pl. W2 ... 45Db 89
Inverness Rd. KT4: Wor Pk ... 74Za 154
N18 ... 22Xb 51
TW3: Houn ... 56Ba 107
UB2: S'hall ... 49Aa 85
Inverness St. NW1 ... 39Kb 70
Inverness Ter. W2 ... 44Db 89
Inverton Rd. SE15 ... 56Zb 114
Invicta Bus. Pk. TN15: Wro ... 89Ee 185
Invicta Cen., The IG11: Bark ... 39Wc 75
Invicta Cl. BR7: Chst ... 64Qc 138
E3 ... 43Cc 92
TW14: Felt ... 60V 106
Invicta Gro. UB5: N'olt ... 41Ba 85
Invicta Pde. DA14: Sidc ... 63Xc 139
Invicta Pk. DA1: Dart ... 56Ld 119
Invicta Plaza SE1 ... 6B 224 (46Rb 91)
Invicta Rd. DA2: Dart ... 58Rd 119
SE3 ... 52Jc 115
In Vw. Ct. KT12: Hers ... 77W 150
Inville Rd. SE17 ... 7G 231 (50Tb 91)
(not continuous)
Inville Wlk. SE17 ... 7G 231 (50Tb 91)
Invito IG2: Ilf ... 30Qc 54
Inwen Ct. SE8 ... 50Ac 92
(not continuous)
Inwood Av. CR5: Coul ... 92Qb 196
TW3: Houn ... 55Ea 108
Inwood Bus. Pk. TW3: Houn ... 56Da 107
Inwood Cl. CR0: C'don ... 75Ac 158
GU22: Wok ... 94B 188
Inwood Ct. KT12: Walt T ... 75Y 151
NW1 ... 38Lb 70
(off Rochester Sq.)
Inwood Ho. *N1 ... 39Rb 71*
(off Elliott's Pl.)
Inwood Rd. TW3: Houn ... 56Da 107
Inworth St. SW11 ... 54Gb 111
Inworth Wlk. *N1 ... 39Sb 71*
(off Popham St.)
IO Centre EN9: Walt A ... 7Cc 20
SE18 ... 48Sc 94
(not continuous)
Iona Cl. SE6 ... 59Cc 114
SM4: Mord ... 73Db 155
Iona Cres. SL1: Slou ... 4C 80
Ion Ct. E2 ... 40Wb 71
Ionian Bldg. *E14 ... 45Ac 92*
(off Narrow St.)
Ionian Ho. *E1 ... 42Zb 92*
(off Duckett St.)
Ionia Wlk. DA12: Grav'nd ... 2H 145
Ion Sq. E2 ... 40Wb 71
IO Trade Cen. CR0: Bedd ... 77Pb 156
Ipsden Bldgs. SE1 ... 1A 230
Ipswich Rd. SL1: Slou ... 4D 80
SW17 ... 65Jb 134
Ira Ct. SE27 ... 61Rb 135
Ireland Cl. E6 ... 43Pc 94
Ireland Pl. N22 ... 24Nb 50
Ireland Yd. EC4 ... 3C 224 (44Rb 91)
Irene M. *W7 ... 46Ha 86*
(off Uxbridge Rd.)
Irene Rd. BR6: Orp ... 73Vc 161
KT11: Stoke D ... 86Da 171
SW6 ... 53Cb 111
Irene Stebbings Ho. AL4: St A ... 1G 6
Ireton Av. KT12: Walt T ... 75U 150
Ireton Cl. N10 ... 24Jb 50
Ireton Ho. *SW15 ... 57Ab 110*
(off Stamford Sq.)
Ireton Pl. RM17: Grays ... 49Ce 99
Ireton St. E3 ... 42Cc 92
Iris Av. DA5: Bexl ... 57Ad 117
Iris Cl. BR5: St M Cry ... 71Yc 161
CM15: Pil H ... 15Xd 40
CR0: C'don ... 74Zb 158
E6 ... 43Nc 94
KT6: Surb ... 73Pa 153
N14 ... 17Mb 32
Iris Ct. *SE14 ... 53Yb 114*
(off Briant St.)
Iris Cres. DA7: Bex ... 51Bd 117
Iris Dr. GU24: Bisl ... 7E 166
Iris Gdns. KT7: T Ditt ... 73Ga 152
Iris M. TW4: Houn ... 58Ca 107
Iris Path RM3: Rom ... 24Ld 57
Iris Rd. GU24: Bisl ... 7E 166
KT19: Ewe ... 78Ra 153
Iris Wlk. HA8: Edg ... 21Sa 47
Iris Way E4 ... 23Bc 52
Irkdale Av. EN1: Enf ... 11Vb 33
Iron Bri. Cl. NW10 ... 36Ua 68
Ironbridge Cl. UB2: S'hall ... 46Ea 86
Iron Bri. Ho. NW1 ... 38Hb 69
Iron Bri. Rd. Nth.
UB11: Stock P ... 47Q 84
Iron Bri. Rd. Sth. UB7: W Dray ... 47Q 84
Iron Mill La. DA1: Cray ... 56Gd 118
Iron Mill Pl. DA1: Cray ... 56Hd 118
SW18 ... 58Db 111
Iron Mill Rd. SW18 ... 58Db 111
Ironmonger La. EC2 ... 3E 224 (44Sb 91)
Ironmonger Pas. EC1 ... 4E 218
Ironmonger Row EC1 ... 4E 218 (41Sb 91)
Ironmonger Row Baths ... 4D 218
Ironmongers Pl. E14 ... 49Cc 92
Ironside Cl. SE16 ... 47Zb 92
Ironside Ct. CR2: S Croy ... 79Tb 157
TW11: Hamp W ... 67La 130
Ironside Ho. E9 ... 35Ac 72
Irons Way RM5: Col R ... 24Ed 56
Iron Works E3 ... 39Cc 72
Ironworks, The N1 ... 2G 217
Irvine Av. HA3: Kenton ... 27Ja 46
Irvine Cl. E14 ... 43Dc 92
N20 ... 19Gb 31
Irvine Ct. W1 ... 6C 216
Irvine Gdns. RM15: S Ock ... 44Vd 98
Irvine Ho. *N7 ... 37Pb 70*
(off Caledonian Rd.)
Irvine Pl. GU25: Vir W ... 71A 148
Irvine Way BR6: Orp ... 73Vc 161
Irving Av. UB5: N'olt ... 39Z 65
Irving Gro. SW9 ... 54Pb 112
Irving Ho. *SE17 ... 50Rb 91*
(off Doddington Gro.)
Irving Mans. *W14 ... 51Ab 110*
(off Queen's Club Gdns.)
Irving M. N1 ... 37Sb 71
Irving Rd. W14 ... 48Za 88
Irving St. WC2 ... 5E 222 (45Mb 90)
Irving Wlk. DA10: Swans ... 59Ae 121
Irving Way BR8: Swan ... 68Fd 140
NW9 ... 29Wa 48
Irwell Ct. *W7 ... 44Fa 86*
(off Hobbayne Rd.)
Irwell Est. SE16 ... 48Yb 92
Irwin Av. SE18 ... 52Uc 116
Irwin Cl. UB10: Ick ... 34Q 64
Irwin Gdns. NW10 ... 39Xa 68
Isaac Way SE1 ... 1E 230
Isabel Hill Cl.
TW12: Hamp ... 67Da 129
Isabella Cl. N14 ... 17Lb 32
Isabella Ct. *TW10: Rich ... 58Pa 109*
(off Kingsmead)
Isabella Dr. BR6: Farnb ... 77Sc 160
Isabella Ho. SE11 ... 7B 230
W6 ... 50Ya 88
(off Queen Caroline St.)
Isabella Pl. KT2: King T ... 64Pa 131
Isabella Plantation Garden ... 62Ra 131
Isabella Rd. E9 ... 36Yb 72
Isabella St. SE1 ... 7B 224 (46Rb 91)
Isabel St. SW9 ... 53Pb 112
Isambard Cl. UB8: Cowl ... 42M 83
Isambard M. E14 ... 48Ec 92
Isambard Pl. SE16 ... 46Yb 92
Isbell Gdns. RM1: Rom ... 24Gd 56
Isbells Dr. RH2: Reig ... 7K 207
Isel Way SE22 ... 57Ub 113
Isham Rd. SW16 ... 68Nb 134
Isis Cl. HA4: Ruis ... 30S 44
SW15 ... 56Ya 110
Isis Ct. W4 ... 52Ra 109
Isis Dr. RM14: Upm ... 30Ud 58
Isis Ho. KT16: Chert ... 73L 149
N18 ... 23Vb 51
NW8 ... 6C 214
SE20 ... 66Wb 135
Isis St. SW18 ... 61Eb 133
Island, The KT7: T Ditt ... 72Ja 152
KT11: D'side ... 90X 171
KT13: Weyb ... 79N 149
TW19: Wray ... 62C 126
UB7: Lford ... 52L 105
Island Apartments N1 ... 39Sb 71
Island Barn Reservoir Sailing Club
... 72Da 151
Island Cen. Way EN3: Enf L ... 9Cc 20
Island Cl. TW18: Staines ... 63G 126
Island Farm Av. KT8: W Mole ... 71Ba 151
Island Farm Rd. KT8: W Mole ... 71Ba 151
Island Ho. E3 ... 41Ec 92
Island Rd. CR4: Mitc ... 66Hb 133
SE16 ... 49Zb 92
Island Row E14 ... 44Bc 92
Isla Rd. SE18 ... 51Sc 116
Islay Gdns. TW4: Houn ... 57Z 107
Islay Ho. WD18: Wat ... 16V 26
Islay Wlk. *N1 ... 37Sb 71*
(off Douglas Rd. Sth.)
Isleden Ho. *N1 ... 39Sb 71*
(off Prebend St.)
Isledon Rd. N7 ... 34Qb 70
ISLEDON VILLAGE ... 34Qb 70
Islehurst Cl. BR7: Chst ... 67Qc 138
ISLE OF DOGS ... 47Dc 92
Isles Quarry Rd. TN15: Bor G ... 93Ae 205
ISLEWORTH ... 55Ja 108
Isleworth Ait Nature Reserve ... 55Ka 108
Isleworth Bus. Complex
TW7: Isle ... 54Ha 108
Isleworth Prom.
TW1: Twick ... 56Ka 108
Isleworth Recreation Cen. ... 56Ha 108
Isley Ct. SW8 ... 54Lb 112
ISLINGTON ... 1B 218 (38Rb 71)
Islington Bus. Cen. *N1 ... 39Sb 71*
(off Coleman Flds.)
Islington Crematorium N2 ... 25Hb 49
Islington Ecology Cen., The ... 34Qb 70
Islington Grn. N1 ... 1B 218 (39Rb 71)
(not continuous)
Islington High St. N1 ... 2A 218 (40Qb 70)
(not continuous)
Islington Mus. ... 4B 218 (41Rb 91)
Islington Pk. M. N1 ... 38Rb 71
Islington Pk. St. N1 ... 38Qb 70
Islington Pl. N1 ... 1K 217 (39Qb 70)
Islington Sq. N1 ... 39Rb 71
Islington Tennis Cen. ... 37Nb 70
Islip Gdns. HA8: Edg ... 24Ta 47
UB5: N'olt ... 38Aa 65
Islip Mnr. Rd. UB5: N'olt ... 38Aa 65
Islip St. NW5 ... 36Lb 70
Ismailia Rd. E7 ... 38Kc 73
Ismay Ct. SL2: Slou ... 4J 81
Ismays Rd. TN15: Igh, Ivy H ... 97Xd 204
Isobel Ho. HA1: Harr ... 29Ha 46
Isobel Pl. N15 ... 28Vb 51
Isola Ct. *N1 ... 39Sb 71*
(off Popham Rd.)
Isom Cl. E13 ... 41Kc 93
Isopad Ho. *WD6: Bore ... 13Ra 29*
(off Shenley Rd.)
Issa Rd. TW3: Houn ... 56Ba 107
Issigonis Ho. *W3 ... 46Va 88*
(off Cowley Rd.)
ISTEAD RISE ... 6B 144
Istead Ri. DA13: Ist R ... 6B 144
Istra Ho. *E20 ... 36Ec 72*
(off Logan Cl.)
Italia Conti Academy of Theatre Arts
Avondale ... 55Nb 112
(off Landor Rd.)
Itaska Cotts. WD23: B Hea ... 18Ga 28
ITCHINGWOOD COMMON ... 5N 211
Itchingwood Comn. Rd.
RH8: Limp ... 5N 211
Ithell Ct. HA0: Wemb ... 36Ma 67
Ivanhoe Cl. UB8: Cowl ... 43M 83
Ivanhoe Dr. HA3: Kenton ... 27Ja 46
Ivanhoe Ho. *E3 ... 40Ac 72*
(off Grove Rd.)
Ivanhoe Rd. SE5 ... 55Vb 113
TW4: Houn ... 55Z 107
Ivaro Cl. RM5: Col R ... 25Ed 56
Ivatt Pl. W14 ... 50Bb 89
Ivatt Way N17 ... 27Rb 51
Iveagh Av. NW10 ... 40Qa 67
Iveagh Cl. E9 ... 39Zb 72
HA6: Nwood ... 25R 44
NW10 ... 40Qa 67
Iveagh Ct. BR3: Beck ... 69Ec 136
E1 ... 3K 225
HP2: Hem H ... 1M 3
Iveagh Ho. SW9 ... 54Rb 113
SW10 ... 52Eb 111
(off King's Rd.)
Iveagh Ter. *NW10 ... 40Qa 67*
(off Iveagh Av.)
Ivedon Rd. DA16: Well ... 54Yc 117
Ive Farm Cl. E10 ... 33Cc 72
Ive Farm La. E10 ... 33Cc 72
Iveley Rd. SW4 ... 54Lb 112
IVER ... 44G 82
Iver Ct. SL0: Iver ... 44H 83
Iverdale Cl. SL0: Iver ... 45E 82
Ivere Dr. EN5: New Bar ... 16Db 31
Iver Golf Course ... 46D 82
IVER HEATH ... 40F 62
Iver Ho. *N1 ... 1H 219*
(off Halcomb St.)
Iverhurst Cl. DA6: Bex ... 57Zc 117
Iver La. SL0: Iver ... 44J 83
UB8: Cowl ... 44J 83
Iver Lodge SL0: Iver ... 43H 83
Iverna Ct. W8 ... 48Cb 89
Iverna Gdns. TW14: Felt ... 57T 106
W8 ... 48Cb 89
Iver Rd. CM15: Pil H ... 16Xd 40
Iverson Rd. NW6 ... 37Bb 69
Ivers Way
CR0: New Ad ... 80Dc 158
Ives Gdns. RM1: Rom ... 28Hd 56
Ives Rd. E16 ... 43Gc 93
SL3: L'ly ... 48B 82
Ives St. SW3 ... 5E 226 (49Gb 89)
Ivestor Ter. SE23 ... 59Yb 114
Ivimey St. E2 ... 41Wb 91
Ivinghoe Cl. EN1: Enf ... 11Ub 33
WD25: Wat ... 7Z 13
Ivinghoe Ho. N7 ... 36Mb 70
Ivinghoe Rd. RM8: Dag ... 36Xc 75
WD3: Rick ... 17J 25
WD23: Bush ... 17Fa 28
Ivo Pl. N19 ... 34Mb 70
Ivor Ct. N8 ... 30Nb 50
NW1 ... 5F 215
Ivor Gro. SE9 ... 60Rc 116
Ivories, The *N1 ... 38Sb 71*
(off Northampton St.)
Ivor Pl. NW1 ... 6F 215 (42Hb 89)
Ivor St. NW1 ... 38Lb 70
Ivory Cl. AL4: St A ... 4G 6
Ivory Ct. E18 ... 25Jc 53
HP3: Hem H ... 5N 3
TW13: Felt ... 60W 106
Ivorydown BR1: Brom ... 63Jc 137
Ivory Ho. E1 ... 6K 225 (46Vb 91)
Ivory Pl. *W11 ... 45Ab 88*
(off Treadgold St.)
Ivory Sq. SW11 ... 55Eb 111
Ivy Bower Cl.
DA9: Ghithe ... 57Xd 120
Ivybridge Cl. TW1: Twick ... 59Ja 108
UB8: Uxb ... 41N 83
Ivybridge Ct. *BR7: Chst ... 67Qc 138*
(off Old Hill)
NW1 ... 38Kb 70
(off Lewis St.)
Ivybridge La. WC2 ... 5G 223 (45Nb 90)
Ivy Bri. Retail Pk. TW7: Isle ... 57Ha 108
IVY CHIMNEYS ... 5Wc 23
Ivy Chimneys Rd.
CM16: Epp ... 4Uc 22
Ivychurch Cl. SE20 ... 66Yb 136
Ivychurch La. SE17 ... 7K 231 (50Vb 91)
Ivy Cl. DA1: Dart ... 58Qd 119
DA12: Grav'nd ... 3E 144
HA2: Harr ... 35Ba 65
HA5: Eastc ... 31Y 65
TW16: Sun ... 68Y 129
WD25: Wat ... 5V 12
Ivy Cotts. E14 ... 45Ec 92
UB10: Hil ... 41Q 84
Ivy Ct. *SE16 ... 50Wb 91*
(off Argyle Way)
Ivy Cres. SL1: Slou ... 5D 80
W4 ... 49Sa 87
Ivydale Rd. SE15 ... 55Zb 114
SM5: Cars ... 75Hb 155
Ivyday Gro. SW16 ... 62Pb 134
Ivydene GU21: Knap ... 10F 166
KT8: W Mole ... 71Ba 151
Ivydene Cl. SM1: Sutt ... 77Eb 155
Ivydene Ct. *IG9: Buck H ... 19Lc 35*
(off Queen's Rd.)
Ivy Gdns. CR4: Mitc ... 69Mb 134
N8 ... 30Nb 50
IVY HATCH ... 98Xd 204
Ivy Ho. WD19: Wat ... 16Z 27
Ivy Ho. La. HP4: Berk ... 1A 2
TN13: Dun G, Otf ... 90Fd 182
TN14: Otf ... 90Fd 182
Ivy Ho. Rd. UB10: Ick ... 34R 64
Ivyhouse Rd. RM9: Dag ... 37Zc 75
Ivy La. GU22: Wok ... 89D 168
TN14: Knock ... 88Ad 181
TW4: Houn ... 56Ba 107
Ivy Lea WD3: Rick ... 18J 25
Ivy Lodge *W11 ... 46Cb 89*
(off Notting Hill Ga.)
Ivy Lodge La.
RM3: Hrld W ... 25Rd 57
Ivy Mill Cl. RH9: G'stone ... 4P 209
Ivy Mill La. RH9: G'stone ... 4N 209
Ivymount Rd. SE27 ... 62Qb 134
Ivy Rd. E16 ... 44Jc 93
E17 ... 30Cc 52
KT6: Surb ... 74Qa 153
N14 ... 17Lb 32
NW2 ... 35Ya 68
SE4 ... 56Bc 114
SW17 ... 64Gb 133
TW3: Houn ... 56Da 107
Ivy St. N1 ... 1H 219 (40Ub 71)
Ivy Vs. DA9: Ghithe ... 57Wd 120
Ivy Wlk. HA6: Nwood ... 25U 44
RM9: Dag ... 37Ad 75
Ixworth Pl. SW3 ... 7D 226 (50Gb 89)
Izane Rd. DA6: Bex ... 56Bd 117

J

Jacana Ct. *E1 ... 45Vb 91*
(off Star Pl.)
Jacaranda Cl. KT3: N Mald ... 69Ua 132
Jacaranda Gro. E8 ... 38Vb 71
Jacaranda Ho. KT15: Add ... 75M 149
Jackass La. BR2: Kes ... 78Kc 159
RH8: G'stone, Tand ... 3D 210
Jack Barnett Way N22 ... 26Pb 50
Jack Clow Rd. E15 ... 40Gc 73
Jack Cook Ho. IG11: Bark ... 38Rc 74
Jack Cornwell St. E12 ... 35Qc 74
Jack Dash Way E6 ... 42Nc 94
Jack Dimmer Cl. SW16 ... 68Lb 134
Jackets La. HA6: Nwood ... 25R 44
UB9: Hare ... 24Q 44
Jacketts Fld. WD5: Ab L ... 3V 12
Jack Evans Ct. RM15: S Ock ... 44Wd 98
Jack Goodchild Way KT1: King T ... 69Ra 131
Jack Jones Way RM9: Dag ... 39Bd 75
Jacklin Grn. IG8: Wfd G ... 21Jc 53
Jackman Ho. *E1 ... 46Xb 91*
(off Watts St.)
Jackman M. NW2 ... 34Ua 68
Jackmans La. GU21: Wok ... 1L 187
Jackman St. E8 ... 39Xb 71
Jacks Farm Way E4 ... 23Ec 52
Jacks La. UB9: Hare ... 25J 43
Jackson & Joseph Bldg. E1 ... 7K 219
Jackson Cl. DA9: Ghithe ... 57Vd 120
E9 ... 38Yb 72
KT18: Eps ... 86Ta 173
RM11: Horn ... 28Pd 57
SL3: L'ly ... 48A 82
UB10: Uxb ... 38N 63
Jackson Ct. E7 ... 37Kc 73
Jackson Ho. N11 ... 22Lb 50
Jackson Rd. BR2: Brom ... 75Pc 160
EN4: E Barn ... 16Gb 31
IG11: Bark ... 39Tc 74
N7 ... 35Pb 70
UB10: Uxb ... 38N 63
Jacksons La. N6 ... 31Jb 70
Jacksons Lane Theatre ... *30Kb 50*
(off Archway Rd.)
Jacksons Pl. CR0: C'don ... 74Tb 157
Jackson St. SE18 ... 51Qc 116
Jackson's Way CR0: C'don ... 76Cc 158
Jackson Way KT19: Eps ... 81Qa 173
UB2: S'hall ... 47Da 85
Jacks Pl. E1 ... 7K 219
Jack the Ripper Mus. ... 45Wb 91
Jack Walker Ct. N5 ... 35Rb 71
Jacob Cl. SL4: Wind ... 3C 102
Jacob Ct. AL4: St A ... 4G 6
Jacob Ho. *DA18: Erith ... 47Zc 95*
(off Kale Rd.)
Jacobin Lodge N7 ... 36Nb 70
Jacob Mans. *E1 ... 44Xb 91*
(off Commercial Rd.)
Jacob M. HA7: Stan ... 19Ja 28
Jacobs Av. RM3: Hrld W ... 26Nd 57
Jacobs Cl. RM10: Dag ... 35Dd 76
Jacobs Ct. *E1 ... 44Wb 91*
(off Plumber's Row)
Jacobs Ho. *E13 ... 41Lc 93*
(off New City Rd.)
Jacobs Island Ho. *SE16 ... 48Vb 91*
(off Spa Rd.)
Jacobs Island Pier *SE16 ... 47Wb 91*
(off Bermondsey Wall W.)
Jacob's Ladder CR6: W'ham ... 91Wb 197
Jacobs La. DA4: Hort K ... 69Sd 142
Jacobs M. SW15 ... 56Ab 110
Jacob St. SE1 ... 47Wb 91
JACOBS WELL ... 10P 187
Jacob's Well M. W1 ... 2J 221 (43Jb 90)
Jacob's Well Rd. GU4: Jac W ... 10P 187
Jacotts Ho. *W10 ... 42Ya 88*
(off Sutton Way)
Jacqueline Cl. UB5: N'olt ... 39Aa 65
Jacqueline Creft Ter. *N6 ... 30Jb 50*
(off Grange Rd.)
Jacqueline Ho. *NW1 ... 39Hb 69*
(off Regent's Pk. Rd.)
Jacqueline Vs. *E17 ... 29Ec 52*
(off Shernhall St.)
Jade Cl. E16 ... 44Mc 93
NW2 ... 31Za 68
RM8: Dag ... 32Yc 75
Jade Ter. NW6 ... 38Eb 69
Jaffe Rd. IG1: Ilf ... 32Tc 74
Jaffray Pl. SE27 ... 63Rb 135
Jaffray Rd. BR2: Brom ... 70Mc 137
Jaggard Way SW12 ... 59Hb 111
Jagger Cl. DA2: Dart ... 59Sd 120
Jagger Ho. *SW11 ... 53Hb 111*
(off Rosenau Rd.)
Jago Cl. SE18 ... 51Sc 116
Jago Wlk. SE5 ... 52Tb 113
Jail La. TN16: Big H ... 87Mc 179
Jake Russell Wlk. E16 ... 45Lc 93
Jakes Vw. AL2: Park ... 9A 6
Jamaica Rd. CR7: Thor H ... 72Rb 157
SE1 ... 2K 231 (47Vb 91)
SE16 ... 47Vb 91
Jamaica St. E1 ... 44Yb 92
James Allens School Swimming Pool
... 57Ub 113
James Anderson Ct. E2 ... 1J 219
James Av. NW2 ... 36Ya 68
RM8: Dag ... 32Bd 75
TN15: W King ... 80Ud 164
(off London Rd.)
James Bedford Cl. HA5: Pinn ... 26Y 45
James Boswell Cl. SW16 ... 63Pb 134
James Brine Ho. E2 ... 3K 219
James Campbell Ho. *E2 ... 40Yb 72*
(off Old Ford Rd.)
James Clavell Sq. *SE18 ... 48Rc 94*
(off No 1 St.)

James Cl. E13 40Jc 73
NW11 30Ab 48
RM2: Rom 29Jd 56
WD23: Bush 15Aa 27
James Collins Cl. W9 42Bb 89
James Ct. AL2: Lon C 9F 6
HA6: Nwood 25V 44
N1 39Sb 71
(off Raynor Pl.)
NW9 26Ua 48
UB5: N'olt 40Aa 65
(off Church Rd.)
James Docherty Ho. *E2* 40Xb 71
(off Patriot Sq.)
James Dudson Ct. NW10 38Sa 67
James Est. CR4: Mitc 68Hb 133
James Gdns. N22 24Rb 51
James Hammett Ho. E2 3K 219
James Hill Ho. *W10* 42Ab 88
(off Kensal Rd.)
James Ho. *E1* 42Ac 92
(off Solebay St.)
SE16 47Zb 92
(off Wolfe Cres.)
SW8 52Nb 112
(off Wyvil Rd.)
W10 42Ab 88
James Joyce Wlk. SE24 56Rb 113
James La. E10 31Ec 72
E11 31Fc 73
James Leal Cen.
Woodford 22Mc 53
James Lee Sq. EN3: Enf L 10Cc 20
James Lighthill Ho. WC1 2J 217
James Lind Ho. *SE8* 49Bc 92
(off Grove St.)
James Martin Cl. UB9: Den 30J 43
James Mdw. SL3: L'ly 51B 104
James Middleton Ho. *E2* 41Xb 91
(off Middleton St.)
James Morgan M.
N1 1E 218 (39Sb 71)
James Newman Ct. SE9 62Qc 138
Jameson Cl. W3 47Sa 87
Jameson Ct. *AL1: St A* 1D 6
(off Avenue Rd.)
E2 40Yb 72
(off Russia La.)
Jameson Ho. SE11 7H 229
Jameson Lodge N6 30Lb 50
Jameson St. W8 46Cb 89
James Pl. N17 25Vb 51
James Riley Point *E15* 39Ec 72
(off Carpenters Rd.)
James Rd. DA1: Dart 59Jd 118
James's Cotts. TW9: Kew 52Qa 109
James Stewart Ho. NW6 38Bb 69
James St. CM16: Epp 1Wc 23
EN1: Enf 15Vb 33
IG11: Bark 38Sc 74
SL4: Wind 3H 103
TW3: Houn 55Fa 108
W1 2J 221 (44Jb 90)
WC2 3G 223 (45Nb 90)
James Stroud Ho. SE17 7E 230
James Ter. *SW14* 55Ta 109
(off Church Path)
Jameston Lodge HA4: Ruis 32V 64
Jamestown Rd. NW1 39Kb 70
Jamestown Way E14 45Fc 93
James Voller Way E1 44Yb 92
James Watt Way DA8: Erith 51Hd 118
James Way WD19: Wat 21Z 45
James Yd. E4 23Fc 53
Jam Factory, The SE1 4H 231
Jamieson Ho. TW4: Houn 58Ba 107
Jamilah Ho. *E16* 45Qc 94
(off University Way)
Jamnagar Cl. TW18: Staines 65H 127
Jamuna Cl. E14 43Ac 92
Jane Austen Hall *E16* 46Kc 93
(off Wesley Av.)
Jane Austen Ho. *SW1* 50Lb 90
(off Churchill Gdns.)
Jane Seymour Ct. SE9 59Tc 116
Jane St. E1 44Xb 91
Janet Adegoke Swimming Pool 45Wa 88
Janet St. E14 48Cc 92
Janeway Pl. SE16 47Xb 91
Janeway St. SE16 47Wb 91
Janice M. IG1: Ilf 33Rc 74
Janmead CM13: Hut 17De 41
Janoway Hill La. GU21: Wok 1N 187
Jansen Wlk. SW11 55Fb 111
Janson Cl. E15 36Gc 73
NW10 34Ua 68
Janson Rd. E15 36Gc 73
Jansons Rd. N15 27Ub 51
Japan Cres. N4 31Pb 70
Japan Rd. RM6: Chad H 30Zc 55
Japonica Cl. GU21: Wok 10N 167
Japonica Ho. KT15: Add 75M 149
Jaquard Ct. *E2* 40Yb 72
(off Bishop's Way)
Jardine Rd. E1 45Zb 92
Jarman Cl. HP3: Hem H 4N 3
Jarman Ho. *E1* 43Yb 92
(off Jubilee St.)
SE16 49Zb 92
(off Hawkstone Rd.)
Jarman Pk. HP2: Hem H 3P 3
Jarman Way HP2: Hem H 3P 3
Jarrah Cotts. RM19: Purf 51Td 120
Jarratt Ho. *SL4: Wind* 5F 102
(off St Leonard's Rd.)
Jarret Ho. *E3* 41Cc 92
(off Bow Rd.)
Jarrett Cl. SW2 60Rb 113
Jarrow Cl. SM4: Mord 71Db 155
Jarrow Rd. N17 28Xb 51
RM6: Chad H 30Yc 55
SE16 49Yb 92
Jarrow Way E9 35Bc 72
Jarvis Cl. EN5: Barn 15Za 30
IG11: Bark 39Tc 74
Jarvis Ho. *SE15* 53Wb 113
(off Goldsmith Rd.)
Jarvis Rd. CR2: S Croy 79Tb 157
SE22 56Ub 113
Jarvis Way RM3: Hrld W 26Nd 57
Jashoda Ho. *SE18* 50Qc 94
(off Connaught M.)
Jasmin Cl. HA6: Nwood 25V 44
Jasmin Ct. SE12 58Jc 115
Jasmine Cl. BR6: Farnb 75Rc 160
GU21: Wok 8K 167
IG1: Ilf 36Rc 74
UB1: S'hall 45Aa 85
Jasmine Ct. SW19 64Cb 133
TN15: W King 80Ud 164
Jasmine Gdns. CR0: C'don 76Dc 158
HA2: Harr 33Ca 65
Jasmine Gro. SE20 67Xb 135
Jasmine Ho. SW18 55Eb 111
Jasmine Rd. RM7: Rush G 33Gd 76
Jasmine Sq. *E3* 39Bc 72
(off Hawthorn Av.)
Jasmine Ter. CM15: Pil H 15Vd 40
UB7: W Dray 47Q 84
Jasmine Way KT8: E Mos 70Ga 130
Jasmin Ho. KT15: Add 75M 149
Jasmin Lodge *SE16* 50Xb 91
(off Sherwood Gdns.)
Jasmin Rd. KT19: Ewe 78Ra 153
Jasmin Way HP1: Hem H 1G 2
Jason Cl. CM14: B'wood 21Vd 58
KT13: Weyb 78S 150
RH1: Redh 10N 207
RM16: Ors 4G 100
Jason Ct. *SW9* 53Qb 112
(off Southey Rd.)
W1 2J 221
Jason Wlk. SE9 63Qc 138
Jasper Av. W7 47Ha 86
Jasper Cl. EN3: Enf W 10Yb 20
Jasper Pas. SE19 65Vb 135
Jasper Rd. E16 44Mc 93
SE19 64Vb 135
Jasper Wlk. N1 3F 219 (41Tb 91)
Java Wharf SE1 1K 231
Javelin Ct. *HA7: Stan* 22Ka 46
(off William Dr.)
Javelin Way UB5: N'olt 41Z 85
Jay Av. KT15: Add 76N 149
Jaycroft EN2: Enf 11Qb 32
Jay Gdns. BR7: Chst 63Pc 138
Jay Ho. *E3* 39Bc 72
(off Hawthorn Av.)
Jay M. SW7 2A 226 (47Eb 89)
Jays Cl. AL2: Brick W 3Ca 13
Jays St. N1 1J 217 (39Pb 70)
Jazzfern Ter. HA0: Wemb 36Ja 66
Jeal Oakwood Ct. KT18: Eps 86Ua 174
Jean Batten Cl. SM6: Wall 80Pb 156
Jean Brown Indoor Arena, The 25Tc 54
Jean Darling Ho. *SW10* 51Fb 111
(off Milman's St.)
Jean Ho. SW17 64Gb 133
Jean Pardies Ho. *E1* 43Yb 92
(off Jubilee St.)
Jebb Av. SW2 58Nb 112
(not continuous)
Jebb Cl. SL4: Wind 4B 102
Jebb St. E3 40Cc 72
Jedburgh Rd. E13 41Lc 93
Jedburgh St. SW11 56Jb 112
Jeddo M. W12 47Va 88
Jeddo Rd. W12 47Va 88
Jeeyas Apartments E16 43Hc 93
Jefferies Way SS17: Stan H 1P 101
Jefferson Bldg. E14 47Cc 92
Jefferson Cl. IG2: Ilf 29Rc 54
SL3: L'ly 49C 82
W13 48Ka 86
Jefferson Ho. TW8: Bford 51Na 109
UB7: W Dray 47P 83
(off Park Lodge Av.)
Jefferson Pl. BR2: Brom 72Mc 159
Jefferson Plaza *E3* 42Ec 92
(off Hannaford Wlk.)
Jefferson Rd. GU24: Brkwd 2A 186
Jefferson Wlk. SE18 51Qc 116
Jeffery Harrison Vis. Cen. 93Hd 202
Jeffrey Row SE12 57Kc 115
Jeffrey's Pl. NW1 38Lb 70
Jeffreys Rd. EN3: Brim 14Ac 34
SW4 54Nb 112
Jeffrey's St. NW1 38Lb 70
Jeffreys Wlk. SW4 54Nb 112
Jeffs Cl. TW12: Hamp 65Da 129
Jeffs Rd. SM1: Sutt 77Bb 155
Jeger Av. E2 1K 219 (39Vb 71)
Jeken Rd. SE9 56Lc 115
Jelf Rd. SW2 57Qb 112
Jelico Point *SE16* 47Bc 92
(off Rotherhithe St.)
Jelley Way GU22: Wok 94B 188
Jellicoe Av. DA12: Grav'nd 2E 144
Jellicoe Av. W. DA12: Grav'nd 2E 144
Jellicoe Cl. SL1: Slou 7F 80
Jellicoe Gdns. HA7: Stan 23Ha 46
Jellicoe Ho. *E2* 40Wb 71
(off Ropley St.)
Jellicoe Rd. E13 42Jc 93
N17 24Tb 51
WD18: Wat 16W 26
Jemma Knowles Cl. *SW2* 60Qb 112
(off Tulse Hill)
Jemmett Cl. KT2: King T 67Ra 131
Jemotts Ct. *SE14* 51Zb 114
(off Myers La.)
Jem Paterson Ct. HA1: Harr 35Ga 66
Jengar Cl. SM1: Sutt 77Db 155
Jenkins Av. AL2: Brick W 2Aa 13
Jenkins Cl. DA11: Nflt 2B 144
Jenkins La. IG11: Bark 40Sc 74
Jenkinson Ho. *E2* 41Zb 92
(off Usk St.)
Jenkins Rd. E13 42Kc 93
Jenner Av. W3 43Ta 87
Jenner Cl. DA14: Sidc 63Wc 139
Jenner Ct. *N21* 15Nb 32
(off Pennington Dr.)
Jenner Dr. GU24: W End 5E 166
Jenner Ho. WC1 5G 217
Jenner Pl. SW13 51Xa 110
Jenner Rd. N16 34Vb 71
Jenner Way KT19: Eps 81Qa 173
Jennery La. SL1: Burn 1A 80
Jennett Rd. CR0: Wadd 76Qb 156
Jennifer Ho. E14 44Ec 92
SE11 6A 230
Jennifer Rd. BR1: Brom 62Hc 137
Jenningham Dr. RM16: Grays 46Ce 99
Jenningsbury Ho. *SW3* 7E 226
(off Cale St.)
Jennings Cl. KT6: Surb 73La 152
KT15: New H 81L 169
RM8: Dag 32Ad 75
Jennings Ho. *SE10* 50Fc 93
(off Old Woolwich Rd.)
Jennings Rd. AL1: St A 1D 6
SE22 58Vb 113
Jennings Way EN5: Barn 13Ya 30
HP3: Hem H 4N 3
Jenningtree Rd. DA8: Erith 52Kd 119
Jenningtree Way DA17: Belv 47Ed 96
Jenny Hammond Cl. E11 34Hc 73
Jenny Path RM3: Rom 24Md 57
Jennys Way CR5: Coul 94Lb 196
Jensen Ho. *E3* 42Cc 92
(off Wellington Way)
Jenson Hgts. *N1* 38Pb 70
(off Caledonian Rd.)
Jenson Way SE19 66Vb 135
Jenton Av. DA7: Bex 53Ad 117
Jephson Ct. SW4 54Nb 112
Jephson Ho. *SE17* 51Rb 113
(off Doddington Gro.)
Jephson Rd. E7 38Lc 73
Jephson St. SE5 53Tb 113
Jephtha Rd. SW18 58Cb 111
Jeppos La. CR4: Mitc 70Hb 133
Jepson Dr. DA2: Dart 58Sd 120
Jepson Ho. *SW6* 53Db 111
(off Pearscroft Rd.)
Jerdan Ho. *SW6* 52Cb 111
(off North End Rd.)
Jerdan Pl. SW6 52Cb 111
Jeremiah Ct. RH1: Mers 3C 208
Jeremiah St. E14 44Dc 92
Jeremy Bentham Ho. *E2* 41Wb 91
(off Mansford St.)
Jeremy's Grn. N18 21Xb 51
Jermyn St. SW1 6B 222 (46Lb 90)
Jermyn Street Theatre 5D 222
Jerningham Av. IG5: Ilf 26Rc 54
Jerningham Ct. SE14 53Ac 114
Jerningham Rd. SE14 54Ac 114
Jerome Cres. NW8 5D 214 (42Gb 89)
Jerome Dr. AL3: St A 4N 5
Jerome Ho. *KT1: Hamp W* 68Ma 131
(off Old Bridge St.)
NW1 7E 214
SW7 5B 226
Jerome Pl. *KT1: King T* 68Ma 131
(off Wadbrook St.)
Jerome St. E1 7K 219 (42Vb 91)
Jerome Twr. W3 47Ra 87
Jerrard St. SE13 55Dc 114
Jerrold St. N1 2J 219 (40Vb 71)
Jersey Av. HA7: Stan 26Ka 46
Jersey Cl. KT16: Chert 76H 149
Jersey Dr. BR5: Pet W 72Tc 160
Jersey Ho. *EN3: Enf W* 10Zb 20
(off Eastfield Rd.)
N1 37Sb 71
(off Jersey Rd.)
WD18: Wat 16V 26
Jersey Pl. SL5: S'hill 2B 146
Jersey Rd. E11 32Fc 73
E16 44Lc 93
IG1: Ilf 35Rc 74
N1 37Sb 71
RM13: Rain 38Jd 76
SW17 65Kb 134
TW3: Houn 53Da 107
TW5: Hest, Isle 53Da 107
TW7: Isle 52Fa 108
W7 47Ja 86
Jersey St. E2 41Xb 91
Jerusalem Pas. EC1 6B 218 (42Rb 91)
Jervis Av. EN3: Enf W 7Ac 20
Jervis Bay Ho. *E14* 44Fc 93
(off Blair St.)
Jervis Ct. RM10: Dag 37Dd 76
SE10 53Ec 114
(off Blissett St.)
W1 3A 222
Jervis Rd. SW6 51Bb 111
Jerviston Gdns. SW16 65Qb 134
Jerwood Space Art Gallery 1C 230
Jeskyns 8G 144
Jeskyns Rd. DA12: Cobh 9E 144
DA13: Sole S, Cobh 9E 144
Jesmond Av. HA9: Wemb 37Pa 67
Jesmond Cl. CR4: Mitc 69Kb 134
Jesmond Dene CM16: They B 8Tc 22
NW3 37Eb 69
Jesmond Rd. CR0: C'don 73Vb 157
RM16: Grays 46Fe 99
Jesmond Way HA7: Stan 22Na 47
Jessam Av. E5 32Xb 71
Jessamine Pl. DA2: Dart 59Sd 120
Jessamine Rd. W7 46Ha 86
Jessamine Ter. BR8: Swan 67Ed 140
Jessamy Rd. KT13: Weyb 75Q 150
Jessel Dr. IG10: Lough 11Sc 36
Jessel Ho. SW1 5E 228
WC1 4F 217
Jessel Mans. *W14* 51Ab 110
(off Queen's Club Gdns.)
Jesse Rd. E10 32Ec 72
Jessett Cl. DA8: Erith 49Fd 96
Jessica Rd. SW18 58Eb 111
Jessie Blythe La. N19 31Nb 70
Jessie Duffett Ho. *SE5* 52Sb 113
(off Pitman St.)
Jessie Wood Ct. *SW9* 52Qb 112
(off Caldwell St.)
Jessiman Ter. TW17: Shep 71Q 150
Jesson Ho. SE17 6F 231
Jessop Av. UB2: S'hall 49Ba 85
Jessop Ct. N1 2C 218 (40Rb 71)
Jessop Ho. *W4* 49Ta 87
(off Kirton Cl.)
Jessopp Ct. EN9: Walt A 6Hc 21
Jessop Pl. W7 48Ga 86
Jessop Rd. SE24 56Rb 113
Jessop Sq. E14 46Cc 92
Jessops Way CR0: Bedd, Mitc 72Lb 156
Jessup Cl. SE18 49Sc 94
Jetstar Way UB5: N'olt 41Aa 85
Jetty Ho. KT16: Chert 73L 149
Jetty Wlk. RM17: Grays 51Ce 121
Jevington Way SE12 60Kc 115
Jevons Ho. *NW8* 38Fb 69
(off Hilgrove Rd.)
Jewell Ct. WD25: Wat 6Z 13
Jewel Rd. E17 27Cc 52
Jewels Hill TN16: Big H 84Jc 179
Jewel Tower 3F 229
Jewish Military Mus. 28Ya 48
(off Harmony Way)
Jewish Mus.
Camden Town 39Kb 70
Jewry St. EC3 3K 225 (44Vb 91)
Jew's Row SW18 56Db 111
Jews' Wlk. SE26 63Xb 135
Jeymer Av. NW2 36Xa 68
Jeymer Dr. UB6: G'frd 39Da 65
(not continuous)
Jeypore Rd. SW18 59Eb 111
Jeypore Rd. Pas. SW18 58Eb 111
JFK Ho. WD23: Bush 14Ba 27
Jhumat Pl. *IG1: Ilf* 34Qc 74
(off Roden St.)
Jigger Mast Ho. SE18 48Qc 94
Jillian Cl. TW12: Hamp 66Ca 129
Jim Bradley Cl. SE18 49Qc 94
Jim Griffiths Ho. *SW6* 51Bb 111
(off Clem Attlee Ct.)
Jim Veal Dr. N7 37Nb 70
JJ's Clay Shooting Club 62Vd 142
Joan Cres. SE9 59Mc 115
Joan Gdns. RM8: Dag 33Ad 75
Joanna Ho. *W6* 50Ya 88
(off Queen Caroline St.)
Joan Rd. RM8: Dag 33Ad 75
Joan St. SE1 7B 224 (46Rb 91)
Job Drain Pl. IG11: Bark 40Wc 75
Jocelin Ho. N1 1J 217
Jocelyn Rd. TW9: Rich 55Na 109
Jocelyn St. SE15 53Wb 113
Jocketts Hill HP1: Hem H 2H 3
Jocketts Rd. HP1: Hem H 3H 3
Jockey's Flds. WC1 7J 217 (43Pb 90)
Jodane St. SE8 49Bc 92
Jodrell Cl. TW7: Isle 53Ja 108
Jodrell Rd. E3 39Bc 72
Jodrell Way RM20: W Thur 50Vd 98
Joe Hunte Ct. SE27 64Rb 135
Joel St. HA5: Eastc 27W 44
HA6: Nwood 26W 44
Johanna St. SE1 2K 229 (47Qb 90)
John Adams Ct. N9 19Vb 33
John Adam St. WC2 5G 223 (45Nb 90)
John Aird Ct. W2 7A 214
(not continuous)
John Archer Way SW18 58Fb 111
John Ashby Cl. SW2 58Nb 112
John Austin Cl. KT2: King T 67Pa 131
John Baird Ct. SE26 63Yb 136
John Barker Ct. NW6 38Ab 68
John Barnes Wlk. E15 37Hc 73
John Battleday Water Ski Cen. 70F 126
John Bell Twr. E. *E3* 40Cc 72
(off Pancras Way)
John Bell Twr. W. *E3* 40Cc 72
(off Pancras Way)
John Betts' Ho. W12 48Va 88
John Bond Ho. *E3* 40Bc 72
(off Wright's Rd.)
John Bowles Ct. *E1* 45Zb 92
(off Schoolhouse La.)
John Bradshaw Rd. N14 18Mb 32
John Brent Ho. *SE8* 49Zb 92
(off Haddonfield)
John Buck Ho. NW10 39Va 68
John Bull Pl. W4 49Ra 87
John Bunn Mill *KT15: Add* 78N 149
(off Bourneside Rd.)
John Burns Dr. IG11: Bark 38Uc 74
Johnby Cl. EN3: Enf W 9Ac 20
John Campbell Rd. N16 36Ub 71
John Carpenter St. EC4 4B 224 (45Rb 91)
John Cartwright Ho. *E2* 41Xb 91
(off Old Bethnal Grn. Rd.)
John Clay Gdns. RM16: Grays 46De 99
John Cobb Rd. KT13: Weyb 80Q 150
John Crane St. SE17 51Tb 113
John Donne Way *SE10* 52Dc 114
(off Norman Rd.)
John Drinkwater Cl. E11 31Hc 73
John Fearon Wlk. *W10* 41Ab 88
(off Dart St.)
John Felton Rd. SE16 47Wb 91
John Fielden Ho. *E2* 41Xb 91
(off Canrobert St.)
John Fisher St. E1 45Wb 91
John F Kennedy Memorial 1N 125
John Gale Ct. *KT17: Ewe* 81Va 174
(off West St.)
John Goddard Way TW13: Felt 61X 129
John Gooch Dr. EN2: Enf 11Rb 33
John Harrison Way SE10 48Hc 93
John Horner M. N1 1D 218 (40Sb 71)
John Islip St. SW1 7E 228 (49Mb 90)
John Kaye Ct. TW17: Shep 71Q 150
John Keats Ho. N22 24Pb 50
John Keats Lodge EN2: Enf 11Tb 33
John Kennedy Ct. *N1* 37Tb 71
(off Newington Grn. Rd.)
John Kennedy Ho. *SE16* 49Zb 92
(off Rotherhithe Old Rd.)
John Knight Lodge SW6 52Cb 111
John Lamb Ct. HA3: W'stone 25Ga 46
John McDonald Ho. *E14* 48Cc 92
(off Glengall Gro.)
John McKenna Wlk. SE16 48Wb 91
John Masefield Ho. *N15* 30Tb 51
(off Fladbury Rd.)
John Maurice Cl. SE17 5F 231 (49Tb 91)
John Mills Ct. *UB9: Den* 30H 43
(off Stewarts Cl.)
John Milton Pas. EC4 3E 224
John Nash M. *E14* 44Ac 92
(off Commercial Rd.)
John Newton Ct. DA16: Well 55Xc 117
John Norman Gro. GU18: Light 2A 166
Johnny Andrews Ho. *E1* 44Zb 92
(off Boulcott St.)
John Orwell Sports Cen. 46Xb 91
John Parker Cl. RM10: Dag 38Dd 76
John Parker Sq. SW11 55Fb 111
John Parry Ct. N1 1J 219
John Penn Ho. *SE14* 52Bc 114
(off Amersham Va.)
John Penn St. SE13 53Dc 114
John Penry Ho. *SE1* 50Wb 91
(off Marlborough Gro.)
John Perrin Pl. HA3: Kenton 31Na 67
John Prince's St. W1 2A 222 (44Kb 90)
John Pritchard Ho. *E1* 42Wb 91
(off Buxton St.)
John Ratcliffe Ho. *NW6* 41Cb 89
(off Chippenham Gdns.)
John Rennie Wlk. E1 45Xb 91
John Riley Ho. *E3* 43Bc 92
(off Geoffrey Chaucer Way)
John Roll Way SE16 48Wb 91
John Ruskin St. SE5 52Rb 113
John's Av. NW4 28Ya 48
John Sayer Cl. IG11: Bark 41Vc 95
John's Cl. TW15: Ashf 63S 128
Johns Cl. DA3: Hartl 71Be 165
John Scurr Ho. *E14* 44Ac 92
(off Ratcliffe La.)
Johnsdale RH8: Oxt 1K 211
JOHN'S HOLE 59Sd 120
John Silkin La. SE8 50Zb 92
John's La. SM4: Mord 71Eb 155
John's M. WC1 6J 217 (42Pb 90)
John Smith Av. SW6 52Bb 111
John Smith M. E14 45Fc 93
Johnson Cl. DA11: Nflt 62Fe 143
E8 39Wb 71
Johnson Ct. HP3: Hem H 4N 3
SE9 56Lc 115
Johnson Ho. *E2* 41Wb 91
(off Roberta St.)
NW1 2C 216
NW3 38Hb 69
(off Adelaide Rd.)
SW1 6J 227
SW8 52Mb 112
(off Wandsworth Rd.)
W8 47Cb 89
(off Campden Hill)
Johnson Lock Ct. E1 43Ac 92
Johnson Lodge *W9* 43Cb 89
(off Admiral Wlk.)
Johnson Mans. *W14* 51Ab 110
(off Queen's Club Gdns.)
Johnson Rd. BR2: Brom 71Mc 159
CR0: C'don 73Tb 157
NW10 39Ta 67
TW5: Hest 52Y 107
Johnson's Av. TN14: Bad M 82Dd 182
Johnsons Cl. SM5: Cars 75Hb 155
Johnson's Ct. EC4 3A 224 (44Qb 90)
Johnsons Ct. TN15: Seal 93Pd 203
Johnsons Dr. TW12: Hamp 67Ea 130
Johnsons Ind. Est. UB3: Hayes 47V 84
Johnson's Pl. SW1 7B 228 (50Lb 90)
Johnson St. E1 45Yb 92
UB2: S'hall 48X 85
Johnson's Way DA9: Ghithe 58Yd 120
Johnsons Way NW10 42Ra 87
Johnson's Yd. UB8: Uxb 38L 63
John Spencer Sq. N1 37Rb 71
John's Pl. E1 44Xb 91
John's Rd. DA13: Meop 10B 144
TN16: Tats 92Mc 199
John's Ter. CR0: C'don 74Ub 157
RM3: Hrld W 23Rd 57
Johnston Cl. SW9 53Pb 112
Johnston Ct. E10 34Dc 72
Johnstone Cl. WD19: Wat 20Z 27
Johnstone Ho. *SE13* 55Fc 115
(off Belmont Hill)
Johnstone Rd. E6 41Pc 94
Johnston Rd. IG8: Wfd G 23Jc 53
Johnston Ter. NW2 34Za 68
John Strachey Ho. *SW6* 51Bb 111
(off Clem Attlee Ct.)
John St. E15 39Hc 73
EN1: Enf 15Vb 33
RM17: Grays 51Ee 121
SE25 70Wb 135
TW3: Houn 54Aa 107
WC1 6J 217 (42Pb 90)
John Strype Ct. E10 32Dc 72
Johns Wlk. CR3: W'ham 91Wb 197
John's Way RM15: S Ock 44Zd 99
John Trundle Ct. EC2 7D 218
John Trundle Highwalk EC2 7D 218
John Tucker Ho. *E14* 48Cc 92
(off Mellish St.)
John Watkin Cl. KT19: Eps 81Ra 173
John Wesley Cl. E6 41Pc 94
John Wesley Ct. TW1: Twick 60Ja 108
John Wesley Highwalk EC2 1D 224
John Wetherby Ct. *E15* 40Dc 72
(off High St.)
John Wetherby Ct. E. *E15* 40Dc 72
(off High St.)
John Wetherby Ct. W. *E15* 40Dc 72
(off High St.)
John Wheatley Ho. *SW6* 51Bb 111
(off Clem Attlee Ct.)
John William Cl. RM16: Chaf H 50Zd 99
John Williams Cl. KT2: King T 67Ma 131
SE14 51Zb 114
John Wilson St. SE18 48Qc 94
John Woolley Cl. SE13 56Gc 115
Joiners Arms Yd. SE5 53Tb 113
Joiners Cl. SL9: Chal P 2B 42
Joiner's La. SL9: Chal P 25A 42
Joiners Pl. N5 35Tb 71
Joiner St. SE1 7G 225 (46Tb 91)
Joiners Way SL9: Chal P 24A 42
Joiners Yd. N1 2G 217
Joinville Pl. KT15: Add 77M 149
Jolles Ho. *E3* 41Dc 92
(off Bromley High St.)
Jolliffe Rd. RH1: Mers 98Lb 196
Jolly M. SW16 68Lb 134
Jollys La. HA2: Harr 32Fa 66
UB4: Yead 43Z 85
Jonathans *RM11: Horn* 32Nd 77
(off High St.)
Jonathan St. SE11 7H 229 (50Pb 90)
Jones Cotts. EN5: Ark 15Wa 30
Jones Ho. *E14* 44Fc 93
(off Blair St.)
Jones M. SW15 56Ab 110
Jones Rd. E13 42Kc 93
EN7: G Oak 2Rb 19
Jones St. W1 5K 221 (45Kb 90)
Jones Wlk. TW10: Rich 58Pa 109
Jones Way SL2: Hedg 3H 61
Jonquil Gdns. TW12: Hamp 65Ca 129
Jonson Cl. CR4: Mitc 70Kb 134
UB4: Hayes 43W 84
Jonson Ho. SE1 4G 231
Jonzen Wlk. E14 44Cc 92
Jopling Rd. GU24: Bisl 9E 166
Jordan Cl. CR2: Sande 83Vb 177
HA2: Harr 34Ba 65
WD25: Wat 7V 12
Jordan Ct. SW15 56Za 110
Jordan Ho. *N1* 39Tb 71
(off Colville Est.)
SE4 56Zb 114
(off St Norbert Rd.)
Jordan Rd. UB6: G'frd 39Ka 66
Jordans Cl. RM10: Dag 35Dd 76
TW7: Isle 53Ga 108
TW19: Stanw 59L 105
Jordans Ho. NW8 5C 214
Jordans M. TW2: Twick 61Ga 130
Jordans Rd. WD3: Rick 17J 25
Jordan's Way AL2: Brick W 2Aa 13
Jordans Way RM13: Rain 40Md 77
Joscoyne Ho. *E1* 44Xb 91
(off Philpot St.)
Joseph Av. W3 44Ta 87
Joseph Cl. N4 33Rb 71
Joseph Conrad Ho. SW1 6C 228

Joseph Ct.—Kemmel Rd.

Joseph Ct. AL1: St A 3F 6
(off Cambridge Rd.)
CM14: W'ley 22Xd 58
N16 30Ub 51
(off Amhurst Pk.)
Joseph Hardcastle Cl. SE14 52Zb 114
Josephine Av. KT20: Lwr K 98Bb 195
SW2 57Pb 112
Josephine Cl. KT20: Lwr K 99Bb 195
Joseph Irwin Ho. E14 45Bc 92
(off Gill St.)
Joseph Lister Ct. E7 38Jc 73
Joseph Locke Way KT10: Esh 75Ca 151
Joseph M. N7 37Qb 70
(off Westbourne Rd.)
SE15 57Zb 114
Joseph Powell Cl. SW12 58Lb 112
Joseph Priestley Ho. E2 41Xb 91
(off Canrobert St.)
Joseph Ray Rd. E11 33Gc 73
Joseph St. E3 42Bc 92
Joseph Trotter Cl. EC1 4A 218
Joshua Cl. CR2: S Croy 80Rb 157
N10 24Kb 50
Joshua Pedley M. E3 40Cc 72
(off Douro St.)
Joshua St. E14 44Ec 92
Joshua Wlk. EN8: Walt C 6Cc 20
Josiah Dr. UB10: Ick 33S 64
Joslin Av. NW9 27Ua 48
Josling Cl. RM17: Grays 51Be 121
Joslings Cl. W12 45Wa 88
Joslin Rd. RM19: Purf 50Sd 98
Joslyn Cl. EN3: Enf L 10Cc 20
Jossiline Ct. E3 40Ac 72
(off Ford St.)
Joubert Mans. SW3 7E 226
Joubert St. SW11 54Hb 111
Jourdelay's SL4: Eton 1H 103
(off Jourdelay's Pas.)
Jourdelay's Pas. SL4: Eton 1H 103
Journeys End SL2: Stoke P 3J 81
Jowett St. SE15 52Vb 113
Jowitt Ho. E2 41Zb 92
(off Morpeth St.)
Joyce Av. N18 22Vb 51
Joyce Butler Ho. N22 25Pb 50
Joyce Ct. EN9: Walt A 6Fc 21
Joyce Dawson Way SE28 45Wc 95
JOYCE GREEN 56Pd 119
Joyce Grn. La. DA1: Dart 53Md 119
(not continuous)
Joyce Grn. Wlk. DA1: Dart 56Pd 119
Joyce Latimore Ct. N9 20Xb 33
(off Colthurst Dr.)
Joyce Page Cl. SE7 51Mc 115
Joyce Wlk. SW2 58Qb 112
JOYDENS WOOD 63Fd 140
Joydens Wood 63Dd 140
Joydens Wood Rd. DA5: Bexl 63Fd 140
Joydon Dr. RM6: Chad H 30Xc 55
Joyes Cl. RM3: Rom 21Md 57
Joyners Cl. RM9: Dag 35Bd 75
Joy of Life Fountain 6H 221 (46Hb 89)
Joy Rd. DA12: Grav'nd 10E 122
Joystone Ct. EN4: E Barn 14Gb 31
(off Park Rd.)
Jubb Powell Ho. N15 30Ub 51
Jubilee, The SE10 52Dc 114
Jubilee Arch SL4: Wind 3H 103
Jubilee Av. AL2: Lon C 8H 7
E4 23Ec 52
RM7: Rom 29Dd 56
TW2: Whitt 60Ea 108
Jubilee Bldgs. NW8 1B 214 (39Fb 69)
Jubilee Cl. DA9: Ghithe 58Yd 120
HA5: Pinn 26Y 45
KT1: Hamp W 67La 130
NW9 30Ta 47
NW10 40Ua 68
RM7: Rom 29Dd 56
TW19: Stanw 59L 105
Jubilee Cotts. HP5: Whel H 8A 2
SL3: L'ly 50E 82
TN14: S'oaks 92Kd 203
Jubilee Country Pk. 70Rc 138
Jubilee Country Pk. Local Nature Reserve
71Qc 160
Jubilee Ct. BR4: W W'ck 74Ec 158
DA1: Dart 59Md 119
(off Spring Vale Sth.)
E16 43Hc 93
(off Rathbone St.)
E18 25Jc 53
EN9: Walt A 5Hc 21
HA3: Kenton 31Na 67
N10 27Jb 50
SE10 51Dc 114
(off Dowells St.)
TW3: Houn 55Da 107
(off Bristow Rd.)
TW18: Staines 64J 127
Jubilee Cres. DA12: Grav'nd 1G 144
E14 48Ec 92
KT15: Add 78M 149
N9 18Wb 33
TN15: Igh 93Yd 204
Jubilee Dr. HA4: Ruis 35Z 65
Jubilee Gdns. UB1: S'hall 43Ca 85
Jubilee Hall Gym 4G 223
Jubilee Hgts. SE10 53Ec 114
(off Parkside Av.)
Jubilee Ho. HA7: Stan 22Ma 47
SE11 6A 230
WC1 5H 217
Jubilee La. W5 44Na 87
Jubilee Lodge IG7: Chig 17Rc 36
Jubilee Mans. E1 44Yb 92
(off Jubilee St.)
Jubilee Mkt. IG8: Wfd G 23Lc 53
WC2 4G 223
(off Covent Gdn.)
Jubilee Pde. IG8: Wfd G 23Lc 53
Jubilee Pl. SW3 7E 226 (50Gb 89)
Jubilee Pl. Shop. Mall E14 46Dc 92
(off Bank St.)
Jubilee Ri. TN15: Seal 93Pd 203
Jubilee Rd. BR6: Well H 79Cd 162
RM20: W Thur 51Xd 120
SM3: Cheam 80Za 154
UB6: G'frd 39Ka 66
WD24: Wat 10W 12
Jubilee Sports Cen.
London 41Bb 89
Jubilee Sq. GU21: Wok 89B 168
(off Church St. E.)
Jubilee Statue 3E 124
Jubilee St. E1 44Yb 92
Jubilee Vs. KT10: Esh 74Fa 152
Jubilee Wlk. WD4: K Lan 2Q 12
WD6: E'tree 16Ma 29
(off High St.)
WD19: Wat 21X 45
Jubilee Walkway SE1 5C 224 (45Rb 91)
Jubilee Way CR5: Coul 90Pb 176
DA14: Sidc 61Wc 139
KT9: Chess 77Qa 153
SL3: Dat 2N 103
SW19 67Db 133
TW14: Felt 60W 106
Jubilee Way Training Track 76Ra 153
Jubilee Yd. SE1 1K 231
Judd Apartments N8 27Pb 50
(off Gt. Amwell La.)
Judd St. WC1 3F 217 (41Nb 90)
Jude St. E16 44Hc 93
Judeth Gdns. DA12: Grav'nd 4G 144
Judge Heath La. UB3: Hayes 44S 84
UB8: Hil 44S 84
Judge's Hill EN6: N'thaw 1Gb 17
Judge St. WD24: Wat 10X 13
Judges Wlk. NW3 34Eb 69
Judge Wlk. KT10: Clay 79Ga 152
Judith Anne Ct. RM14: Upm 33Ud 78
Judith Av. RM5: Col R 23Dd 56
Judy's Pas. SL4: Eton 10G 80
Juer St. SW11 52Gb 111
Jug Hill TN16: Big H 88Mc 179
Juglans Rd. BR6: Orp 74Wc 161
Jules Thorn Av. EN1: Enf 14Wb 33
Julia Ct. E17 29Dc 52
Julia Gdns. IG11: Bark 40Zc 75
Julia Garfield M. E16 46Kc 93
(not continuous)
Juliana Cl. N2 26Eb 49
Julian Av. W3 45Ra 87
Julian Cl. EN5: New Bar 13Db 31
GU21: Wok 10N 167
Julian Ct. NW1 38Lb 70
(off Rochester Sq.)
Julian Hill HA1: Harr 33Ga 66
KT13: Weyb 80Q 150
Julian Ho. SE21 63Ub 135
Julian Pl. E14 50Dc 92
Julian Rd. BR6: Chels 79Wc 161
Julians Cl. TN13: S'oaks 99Jd 202
Julians Way TN13: S'oaks 99Jd 202
Julian Taylor Path SE23 61Xb 135
Julia St. NW5 35Jb 70
Julien Rd. CR5: Coul 87Mb 176
W5 48La 86
Juliet Ho. N1 2H 219
Juliette Cl. RM15: Avel 47Pd 97
Juliette M. RM1: Rom 29Hd 56
Juliette Rd. E13 40Jc 73
Juliet Way RM15: Avel 47Pd 97
Julius Caesar Way HA7: Stan 20Ma 29
Julius Ho. E14 44Fc 93
(off E. India Dock Rd.)
Julius Nyerere Cl. N1 1H 217
Jump Giants 50Wd 98
Junction App. SE13 55Ec 114
SW11 55Gb 111
Junction M. W2 2D 220 (44Gb 89)
Junction Pl. W2 2C 220
Junction Rd. CM14: W'ley 21Yd 58
CR2: S Croy 78Tb 157
DA1: Dart 58Md 119
E13 40Kc 73
GU18: Light 2A 166
HA1: Harr 30Fa 46
(not continuous)
N9 18Wb 33
N17 27Wb 51
N19 35Lb 70
RM1: Rom 28Hd 56
TW8: Bford 49La 86
TW15: Ashf 64S 128
W5 49La 86
Junction Rd. E. RM6: Chad H 31Ad 75
Junction Rd. W. RM6: Chad H 31Ad 75
Junction Shop. Cen., The
SW11 56Gb 111
June Cl. CR5: Coul 86Kb 176
Junewood Cl. KT15: Wdhm 83H 169
Juniper Av. AL2: Brick W 3Ca 13
Juniper Cl. EN5: Barn 15Za 30
HA2: Harr 33Da 65
HA9: Wemb 36Qa 67
KT9: Chess 78Pa 153
KT19: Eps 81Ta 173
RH2: Reig 8L 207
RH8: Oxt 5M 211
TN16: Big H 89Nc 180
TW13: Felt 62X 129
WD3: Rick 20M 25
Juniper Ct. CM13: B'wood 20Be 41
(off The Limes)
HA3: Hrw W 25Ha 46
HA6: Nwood 25W 44
KT8: W Mole 70Da 129
RM6: Chad H 30Xc 55
SL1: Slou 7L 81
TW3: Houn 56Da 107
(off Grove Rd.)
W8 48Db 89
(off St Mary's Pl.)
WD3: Chor 16E 24
Juniper Cres. NW1 38Jb 70
Juniper Dr. GU24: Bisl 7E 166
RM15: S Ock 41Ae 99
SW18 56Eb 111
Juniper Gdns. SW16 67Lb 134
TW16: Sun 65V 128
WD7: Shenl 5Na 15
Juniper Ga. WD3: Rick 20M 25
Juniper Grn. HP1: Hem H 2G 2
Juniper Gro. WD17: Wat 10W 12
Juniper Ho. SE14 52Yb 114
TW9: Kew 53Ra 109
W10 42Ab 88
(off Fourth Av.)
Juniper La. E6 43Nc 94
Juniper Pl. KT17: Bans 87Ya 174
Juniper Rd. IG1: Ilf 34Qc 74
RH2: Reig 8L 207
Juniper St. E1 45Yb 92
Juniper Wlk. BR8: Swan 68Fd 140
Juniper Way RM3: Hrld W 25Nd 57
UB3: Hayes 45T 84
Juno Ct. AL3: St A 4N 5
SW9 52Qb 112
(off Caldwell St.)
Juno Ent. Cen. SE14 51Zb 114
Juno Ho. E3 39Cc 72
(off Garrison Rd.)
Juno Way SE14 51Zb 114
Juno Way Ind. Est. SE14 51Zb 114
Jupiter Ct. AL3: St A 4N 5
E3 40Cc 72
(off Four Seasons Cl.)
SL1: Slou 5C 80
SW9 52Qb 112
(off Caldwell St.)
UB5: N'olt 41Z 85
(off Seasprite Cl.)
Jupiter Dr. HP2: Hem H 1P 3
Jupiter Hgts. UB10: Uxb 39P 63
Jupiter Ho. E14 50Dc 92
(off St Davids Sq.)
E16 44Hc 93
(off Turner St.)
HA2: Harr 32Ca 65
Jupiter Way N7 37Pb 70
Jupp Rd. E15 38Fc 73
Jupp Rd. W. E15 39Fc 73
Jura Ho. SE16 49Zb 92
(off Plough Way)
Jurassic Encounter 69Wa 132
Jurgens Rd. RM19: Purf 51Td 120
Jurston Ct. SE1 2A 230
Jury St. DA11: Grav'nd 8D 122
Justice Apartments E1 44Zb 92
(off Aylward St.)
Justice Wlk. SW3 51Gb 111
Justin Cl. TW8: Bford 52Ma 109
Justines Pl. E2 41Zb 92
Justin Pl. N22 24Pb 50
Justin Plaza CR4: Mitc 70Gb 133
Justin Rd. E4 23Bc 52
Jute La. EN3: Brim 12Ac 34
Jutland Cl. N19 32Nb 70
Jutland Gdns. CR5: Coul 92Pb 196
Jutland Ho. SE5 54Sb 113
SE18 49Nc 94
(off Prospect Va.)
SL4: Wind 4D 102
Jutland Pl. TW20: Egh 64E 126
Jutland Rd. E13 42Jc 93
SE6 59Ec 114
Jutsums Av. RM7: Rom 30Dd 56
Jutsums Ct. RM7: Rom 30Dd 56
Jutsums La. RM7: Rom, Rush G 30Dd 56
Juxon Cl. HA3: Hrw W 25Da 45
Juxon Ho. EC4 3C 224
Juxon St. SE11 5J 229 (49Pb 90)
JVC Bus. Pk. NW2 32Wa 68

K

Kaduna Cl. HA5: Eastc 29W 44
Kaine Pl. CR0: C'don 73Ac 158
Kaleidoscope 97Ld 203
Kaleidoscope Ho. E20 36Ec 72
(off Mirabelle Gdns.)
Kale Rd. DA18: Erith 47Zc 95
Kalima Cvn. Site GU24: Chob 2M 167
Kambala Rd. SW11 55Fb 111
Kamen Ho. SE1 7H 225
Kamrans Pl. HA8: Edg 26Pa 47
Kandlewood CM13: Hut 17De 41
Kangley Bri. Rd. SE26 65Bc 136
Kangley Bus. Cen. SE26 64Bc 136
Kaplan Dr. N21 15Pb 32
Kapuvar Cl. SE15 54Wb 113
Karachi Ho. E15 37Gc 73
(off Well St.)
Karanjia Ct. NW2 37Ya 68
Kara Way NW2 35Za 68
Kareena Ct. RM12: Horn 32Nd 77
Karen Cl. CM15: B'wood 17Yd 40
RM13: Rain 40Gd 76
SS17: Stan H 1L 101
Karen Ct. BR1: Brom 67Hc 137
Karen Ter. E11 33Hc 73
Karenza Ct. HA9: Wemb 31La 66
Kariba Cl. N9 20Yb 34
Karim M. E17 28Ac 52
Karina Cl. IG7: Chig 22Uc 54
Karma Way HA2: Harr 32Ca 65
Karner Ho. E20 36Dc 72
(off Logan Cl.)
Karoline Gdns. UB6: G'frd 40Fa 66
Kashgar Rd. SE18 49Vc 95
Kashmir Cl. KT15: New H 81M 169
Kashmir Rd. SE7 52Mc 115
Kassala Rd. SW11 53Hb 111
Katana GU22: Wok 91A 188
(off Brooklyn Rd.)
Katella Trad. Est. IG11: Bark 41Uc 94
Kates Cl. EN5: Ark 15Wa 30
Katharine Ho. CR0: C'don 76Sb 157
(off Katharine St.)
Katharine St. CR0: C'don 76Sb 157
Katherine Bell Twr. E3 40Cc 72
(off Pancras Way)
Katherine Cl. HP3: Hem H 5N 3
KT15: Add 79J 149
N4 31Sb 71
NW7 24Ya 48
SE16 46Zb 92
Katherine Ct. GU21: Knap 1G 186
(off Tudor Way)
SE23 60Xb 113
Katherine Gdns. IG6: Ilf 24Sc 54
SE9 56Mc 115
Katherine Ho. W10 42Ab 88
(off Portobello Rd.)
Katherine M. CR3: Whyt 89Vb 177
Katherine Pl. WD5: Ab L 4W 12
Katherine Rd. E6 36Lc 73
E7 36Lc 73
TW1: Twick 60Ja 108
Katherine Sq. W11 46Ab 88
Kathleen Av. HA0: Wemb 38Na 67
W3 43Sa 87
Kathleen Godfree Ct. SW19 65Cb 133
Kathleen Rd. SW11 55Hb 111
Kavanagh Ct. CM14: W'ley 22Xd 58
KT18: Eps 86Ua 174
(off Martin's Av.)
Kavanaghs Rd. CM14: B'wood 20Wd 40
Kavanaghs Ter. CM14: B'wood 20Xd 40
Kavan Gdns. TW5: Cran 52W 106
Kavsan Pl. TW5: Cran 52W 106
Kayani Av. N4 32Sb 71
Kayani Ho. E16 44Kc 93
(off Burrard Rd.)
Kay Av. KT15: Add 76N 149
Kaye Don Way KT13: Weyb 82Q 170
Kayemoor Rd. SM2: Sutt 79Fb 155
Kay Rd. SW9 54Nb 112
Kaysland Pk. TN15: W King 80Ud 164
Kays Ter. E18 25Hc 53
Kay St. DA16: Well 53Xc 117
E2 40Wb 71
E15 38Fc 73
(off New Mount St.)
Kay Wlk. AL4: St A 2H 7
Kaywood Cl. SL3: L'ly 8N 81
K D Plaza HP1: Hem H 4L 3
KD Tower HP1: Hem H 4L 3
(off Cotterells)
Kean Cres. RM8: Dag 32Ad 75
Kean Ho. SE17 51Rb 113
TW1: Twick 58Ma 109
(off Arosa Rd.)
Kean St. WC2 3H 223 (44Pb 90)
Kearton Cl. CR8: Kenley 89Sb 177
Kearton Pl. CR3: Cat'm 94Wb 197
Keary Rd. DA10: Swans 59Ae 121
Keate Ho. SL4: Eton 1H 103
(off Keates La.)
Keates La. SL4: Eton 1G 102
Keatley Grn. E4 23Bc 52
Keats CR0: C'don 74Sb 157
(off Saffron Central Sq.)
Keats Apartments E3 42Bc 92
(off Wraxall Rd.)
Keats Av. E16 46Kc 93
RH1: Redh 4A 208
RM3: Rom 24Kd 57
Keats Cl. E11 29Kc 53
EN3: Pond E 15Zb 34
IG7: Chig 23Sc 54
NW3 35Gb 69
SE1 6K 231 (49Vb 91)
SE7 52Lc 115
SW19 65Fb 133
UB4: Hayes 43W 84
WD6: Bore 14Qa 29
Keats Est. N16 33Vb 71
(off Kyverdale Rd.)
Keats Gdns. RM18: Tilb 4D 122
Keats Gro. NW3 35Gb 69
Keats House 35Gb 69
Keats Ho. DA1: Cray 57Gd 118
E2 41Yb 92
(off Roman Rd.)
HA2: Harr 33Ga 66
SE5 52Sb 113
(off Elmington Est.)
SW1 51Lb 112
(off Churchill Gdns.)
Keats Pde. N9 19Wb 33
(off Church St.)
Keats Pl. EC2 1F 225
Keats Rd. DA16: Well 53Uc 116
DA17: Belv 48Ed 96
E10 31Dc 72
Keats Wlk. CM13: Hut 17Fe 41
Keats Way CR0: C'don 72Yb 158
CR5: Coul 89Lb 176
UB6: G'frd 43Da 85
UB7: W Dray 49P 83
Kebbell Ter. E7 36Kc 73
(off Claremont Rd.)
Keble Cl. KT4: Wor Pk 74Va 154
UB5: N'olt 36Ea 66
Keble Ct. AL1: St A 2C 6
(off Newsom Pl.)
WD6: Bore 11Pa 29
(off Gateshead Rd.)
Keble Pl. SW13 51Xa 110
Keble St. SW17 63Eb 133
Keble Ter. WD5: Ab L 4V 12
Kebony Cl. UB7: W Dray 47Q 84
Kechill Gdns. BR2: Hayes 73Jc 159
Kedeston Ct. SM1: Sutt 74Db 155
Kedge Ho. E14 48Cc 92
(off Tiller Rd.)
Kedleston Dr. BR5: St M Cry 71Vc 161
Kedleston Wlk. E2 41Xb 91
Kedyngton Ho. HA8: Edg 26Sa 47
(off Burnt Oak B'way.)
Keeble Cl. SE18 51Rc 116
Keedonwood Rd. BR1: Brom 64Gc 137
Keel KT16: Chert 74L 149
Keel Cl. IG11: Bark 40Yc 75
N18 23Ub 51
SE16 46Zb 92
Keel Ct. E14 45Fc 93
(off Newport Av.)
Keel Dr. SL1: Slou 7F 80
Keele Cl. WD24: Wat 12Y 27
Keele Ho. RM8: Dag 35Wc 75
Keeler Cl. SL4: Wind 5C 102
Keeley Rd. CR0: C'don 75Sb 157
Keeley St. WC2 3H 223 (44Pb 90)
Keeling Ho. E2 40Xb 71
(off Claredale St.)
Keeling Rd. SE9 57Mc 115
Keelson Ho. E14 48Cc 92
(off Mellish St.)
Keely Cl. EN4: E Barn 15Gb 31
Keemor Cl. SE18 52Qc 116
Keen's Acre SL2: Stoke P 9L 61
Keensacre SL0: Iver H 40F 62
Keens Cl. SW16 64Mb 134
Keens Rd. CR0: C'don 77Sb 157
Keen's Yd. N1 37Rb 71
Keep, The KT2: King T 65Pa 131
SE3 54Jc 115
Keepers Ct. CR2: S Croy 78Sb 157
(off Warham Rd.)
Keepers Farm Cl. SL4: Wind 4C 102
(not continuous)
Keepers M. TW11: Tedd 65La 130
Keepers Wlk. GU25: Vir W 1P 147
Keepier Wharf E14 45Zb 92
(off Narrow St.)
Keeping Ct. BR2: Brom 69Jc 137
(off St Mark's Sq.)
Keeton's Rd. SE16 48Xb 91
(not continuous)
Keevil Dr. SW19 59Za 110
Keighley Cl. N7 36Nb 70
Keighley Rd. RM3: Rom 24Nd 57
Keightley Dr. SE9 60Sc 116
Keilder Cl. UB10: Hil 40Q 64
Keildon Rd. SW11 56Hb 111
Keiller Ho. E16 46Pc 94
(off Kennard St.)
Keir, The SW19 64Ya 132
Keir Hardie Est. E5 32Xb 71
Keir Hardie Ho. N19 31Mb 70
NW10 38Va 68
W6 51Za 110
(off Fulham Pal. Rd.)
Keir Hardie Way IG11: Bark 38Wc 75
UB4: Yead 41W 84
Keirin Rd. E20 36Dc 72
Keith Av. DA4: Sut H 65Rd 141
Keith Connor Cl. SW8 55Kb 112
Keith Gro. W12 47Wa 88
Keith Ho. NW6 40Db 69
(off Carlton Vale)
SW8 52Nb 112
(off Wheatsheaf La.)
Keith Pk. Cres. TN16: Big H 85Kc 179
Keith Pk. Rd. UB10: Uxb 38P 63
Keith Rd. E17 25Bc 52
IG11: Bark 40Tc 74
UB3: Hayes 48U 84
Keiths Rd. HP3: Hem H 3A 4
Keith Way RM11: Horn 31Nd 77
Kelbrook Rd. SE3 54Nc 116
Kelburn Way RM13: Rain 41Jd 96
Kelby Ho. N7 37Pb 70
(off Sutterton St.)
Kelby Path SE9 62Rc 138
Kelceda Cl. NW2 33Wa 68
Kelday Hgts. E1 44Xb 91
(off Spencer Way)
Kelf Gro. UB3: Hayes 44V 84
Kelfield Ct. W10 44Za 88
Kelfield Gdns. W10 44Ya 88
Kelfield M. W10 44Za 88
Kelland Cl. N8 29Mb 50
Kelland Rd. E13 42Jc 93
Kellaway Rd. SE3 54Mc 115
Keller Cres. E12 35Mc 73
Kellerton Rd. SE13 57Gc 115
Kellet Ho's. WC1 4G 217
(off Tankerton St.)
Kellett Ho. N1 39Ub 71
(off Colville Est.)
Kellett Rd. SW2 56Qb 112
Kelling Gdns. CR0: C'don 73Rb 157
Kellino St. SW17 63Hb 133
Kellner Rd. SE28 48Vc 95
Kellogg Twr. UB6: G'frd 36Ga 66
Kellow Ho. SE1 1F 231
Kell St. SE1 3C 230 (48Rb 91)
Kelly Av. SE15 52Vb 113
Kelly Cl. NW10 34Ta 67
TW17: Shep 68U 128
Kelly Ct. E14 45Cc 92
(off Garford St.)
WD6: Bore 12Ta 29
Kelly M. W9 42Bb 89
Kelly St. NW1 37Kb 70
Kelly Ter. E17 28Cc 52
Kelly Way RM6: Chad H 29Ad 55
Kelman Cl. EN8: Chesh 3Zb 20
SW4 54Mb 112
Kelmore Gro. SE22 56Wb 113
Kelmscott Cl. E17 25Bc 52
WD18: Wat 15W 26
Kelmscott Cres. WD18: Wat 15W 26
Kelmscott Gdns. W12 48Wa 88
Kelmscott House 50Xa 88
Kelmscott Pl. KT21: Asht 89La 172
Kelmscott Rd. SW11 57Gb 111
Kelpatrick Rd. SL1: Slou 4B 80
Kelross Pas. N5 35Sb 71
Kelross Rd. N5 35Sb 71
Kelsall Cl. SE3 54Kc 115
Kelsall M. TW9: Kew 53Ra 109
Kelsall Pl. SL5: Asc 3A 146
Kelsey Cl. KT9: Chess 80Ma 153
Kelsey Ga. BR3: Beck 68Dc 136
Kelsey La. BR3: Beck 68Cc 136
Kelsey Pk. Av. BR3: Beck 68Dc 136
Kelsey Pk. Rd. BR3: Beck 68Cc 136
Kelsey Rd. BR5: St P 68Xc 139
Kelsey Sq. BR3: Beck 68Cc 136
Kelsey St. E2 42Wb 91
Kelsey Way BR3: Beck 69Cc 136
Kelshall WD25: Wat 8Aa 13
Kelsie Way IG6: Ilf 23Uc 54
Kelso Dr. DA12: Grav'nd 3H 145
Kelson Ho. E14 48Ec 92
Kelso Pl. W8 48Db 89
Kelso Rd. SM5: Cars 73Eb 155
Kelston Rd. IG6: Ilf 26Rc 54
Kelvedon Av. KT12: Hers 80U 150
Kelvedon Cl. CM13: Hut 16Fe 41
KT2: King T 65Qa 131
KELVEDON COMMON 11Td 40
Kelvedon Ho. SW8 53Nb 112
Kelvedon Rd. SW6 52Bb 111
Kelvedon Wlk. RM13: Rain 39Hd 76
Kelvedon Way IG8: Wfd G 23Pc 54
Kelvin Av. KT22: Lea 91Ha 192
N13 23Pb 50
TW11: Tedd 65Ga 130
Kelvinbrook KT8: W Mole 69Da 129
Kelvin Cl. KT19: Ewe 79Qa 153
Kelvin Ct. SE20 67Xb 135
TW7: Isle 54Ga 108
W11 45Cb 89
(off Kensington Pk. Rd.)
Kelvin Cres. HA3: Hrw W 24Ga 46
Kelvin Dr. TW1: Twick 58Ka 108
Kelvin Gdns. CR0: Wadd 73Nb 156
UB1: S'hall 44Ca 85
Kelvin Gro. KT9: Chess 76Ma 153
SE26 62Xb 135
Kelvington Cl. CR0: C'don 73Ac 158
Kelvington Rd. SE15 57Zb 114
Kelvin Ho. SE26 63Bc 136
(off Worsley Bri. Rd.)
Kelvin Ind. Est. UB6: G'frd 38Da 65
Kelvin Pde. BR6: Orp 74Uc 160
Kelvin Rd. DA16: Well 55Wc 117
N5 35Sb 71
RM18: Tilb 4C 122
Kelway Ho. W14 50Bb 89
Kember St. N1 38Pb 70
Kemble Av. KT15: Add 80H 149
Kemble Cl. EN6: Pot B 5Fb 17
KT13: Weyb 77T 150
Kemble Cotts. KT15: Add 77J 149
Kemble Dr. BR2: Brom 76Nc 160
Kemble Ho. SW9 55Rb 113
(off Barrington Rd.)
Kemble Pde. EN6: Pot B 4Eb 17
Kemble Rd. CR0: Wadd 76Rb 157
N17 25Wb 51
SE23 60Zb 114
Kembleside Rd. TN16: Big H 90Lc 179
Kemble St. WC2 3H 223 (44Pb 90)
Kemerton Rd. BR3: Beck 68Dc 136
CR0: C'don 73Vb 157
SE5 55Sb 113
Kemey's St. E9 36Ac 72
Kemishford GU22: Wok 5L 187
Kemmel Rd. RM9: Dag 39Xc 75

Kemnal Rd. BR7: Chst 63Tc 138
Kemp *NW9* *25Va 48*
(off Quakers Course)
Kemp Ct. *SW8* *52Nb 112*
(off Hartington Rd.)
Kempe Cl. AL1: St A 6A 6
SL3: L'ly 49E 82
Kempe Ho. SE1 4G 231
Kempe Rd. EN1: Enf 8Xb 19
NW6 40Za 68
Kemp Gdns. CR0: C'don 72Sb 157
Kemp Ho. *E2* *40Zb 72*
(off Sewardstone Rd.)
E6 37Qc 74
W1 4D 222
Kempis Way SE22 57Ub 113
Kemplay Rd. NW3 35Fb 69
Kempley Ct. RM17: Grays 51Fe 121
Kemp Pl. WD23: Bush 16Ca 27
Kemp Rd. RM8: Dag 32Zc 75
KEMPROW 8Fa 14
Kemprow WD25: A'ham 8Fa 14
Kemps Ct. W1 3D 222
Kemps Dr. E14 45Cc 92
HA6: Nwood 24V 44
Kempsford Gdns. SW5 50Cb 89
Kempsford Rd. SE11 6A 230 (49Qb 90)
(not continuous)
Kemps Gdns. SE13 57Ec 114
Kempshott Rd. SW16 66Mb 134
Kempson Rd. SW6 53Cb 111
Kempthorne Rd. SE8 49Bc 92
Kempthorne St. DA11: Grav'nd 8D 122
Kempton Av. RM12: Horn 35Pd 77
TW16: Sun 67X 129
UB5: N'olt 37Ca 65
Kempton Cl. DA8: Erith 51Ed 118
UB10: Ick 35S 64
Kempton Ct. E1 43Xb 91
TW16: Sun 67X 129
Kempton Ga. TW12: Hamp 67Ba 129
Kempton Ho. N1 1H 219
SL4: Wind *3D 102*
(off Paddock Cl.)
Kempton Nature Reserve 65Z 129
Kempton Pk. Racecourse 66Y 129
Kempton Rd. E6 39Pc 74
Kemptons, The TW15: Ashf 61Q 128
Kempton Wlk. CR0: C'don 72Ac 158
Kempt St. SE18 51Qc 116
KEMSING 89Rd 183
Kemsing Cl. BR2: Hayes 75Hc 159
CR7: Thor H 70Sb 135
DA5: Bexl 59Ad 117
Kemsing Down Nature Reserve 88Pd 183
Kemsing Heritage Cen. 89Rd 183
Kemsing Ho. SE1 2G 231
Kemsing Rd. SE10 50Jc 93
TN15: Kems'g, Wro 88Vd 184
Kemsley SE13 57Dc 114
Kemsley Chase SL2: Farn R 9G 60
Kemsley Cl. DA9: Ghithe 58Xd 120
DA11: Nflt 3B 144
Kemsley Ct. W13 46La 86
Kemsley Rd. TN16: Tats 91Mc 199
Kenbrook Ho. NW5 36Lb 70
W14 48Bb 89
Kenbury Cl. UB10: Ick 34Q 64
Kenbury Dr. SL1: Slou 7D 80
Kenbury Gdns. SE5 54Sb 113
Kenbury Mans. *SE5* *54Sb 113*
(off Kenbury St.)
Kenbury St. SE5 54Sb 113
Kenchester Cl. SW8 52Nb 112
Kencot Way DA18: Erith 47Bd 95
Kendal NW1 3A 216
RM19: Purf 50Sd 98
Kendal Av. CM16: Epp 2Wc 23
IG11: Bark 39Uc 74
N18 21Tb 51
W3 42Qa 87
Kendal Cl. IG8: Wfd G 19Hc 35
N20 19Gb 31
RH2: Reig 5M 207
SL2: Slou 5L 81
SW9 52Rb 113
TW14: Felt 60V 106
UB4: Hayes 40U 64
Kendal Ct. W3 43Qa 87
Kendal Cft. RM12: Horn 36Jd 76
Kendal Dr. SL2: Slou 5L 81
Kendale HP3: Hem H 3B 4
RM16: Grays 8D 100
Kendale Rd. BR1: Brom 64Gc 137
Kendal Gdns. N18 21Tb 51
SM1: Sutt 75Eb 155
Kendal Ho. E9 39Yb 72
N1 2J 217
SE20 *68Wb 135*
(off Derwent Rd.)
Kendall Av. BR3: Beck 68Ac 136
CR2: Sande 81Tb 177
Kendall Av. Sth. CR2: Sande 82Sb 177
Kendall Ct. CM14: W'ley 22Xd 58
DA15: Sidc 62Wc 139
SW19 65Fb 133
WD6: Bore 12Sa 29
Kendall Gdns. DA11: Grav'nd 9B 122
Kendall Lodge *BR1: Brom* *67Kc 137*
(off Willow Tree Wlk.)
CM16: Epp 2Wc 23
Kendall Mnr. HA6: Nwood 24R 44
Kendall Pl. W1 1H 221 (43Jb 90)
Kendall Rd. BR3: Beck 68Ac 136
SE18 53Nc 116
TW7: Isle 54Ja 108
Kendalmere Cl. N10 25Kb 50
Kendal Pde. N18 21Tb 51
Kendal Pl. SW15 57Bb 111
Kendal Rd. EN9: Walt A 7Ec 20
NW10 35Wa 68
Kendals Cl. WD7: R'lett 8Ga 14
Kendal Steps W2 3E 220
Kendal St. W2 3E 220 (44Gb 89)
Kender Est. *SE14* *53Yb 114*
(off Queen's Rd.)
Kender St. SE14 52Yb 114
Kendoa Rd. SW4 56Mb 112
Kendon Cl. E11 29Kc 53
Kendon Ho. *E15* *38Fc 73*
(off Bryant St.)
Kendor Av. KT19: Eps 83Sa 173
Kendra Hall Rd. CR2: S Croy 80Rb 157
Kendrey Gdns. TW2: Whitt 59Ga 108
Kendrick Ct. *SE15* *53Xb 113*
(off Colmore M.)
Kendrick M. SW7 5B 226 (49Fb 89)
Kendrick Pl. SW7 6B 226 (49Fb 89)
Kendrick Rd. SL3: Slou 8M 81
Kenelm Cl. HA1: Harr 34Ja 66
Kenerne Dr. EN5: Barn 15Ab 30
Kenford Cl. WD25: Wat 4X 13
Ken Friar Bri. N7 35Qb 70
Kenia Wlk. DA12: Grav'nd 2H 145
Kenilford Rd. SW12 59Kb 112
Kenilworth Av. E17 26Cc 52
HA2: Harr 35Ba 65
KT11: Stoke D 86Da 171
RM3: Rom 23Rd 57
SW19 64Cb 133
Kenilworth Cl. HP2: Hem H 3N 3
SL1: Slou 8K 81
SM7: Bans 88Db 175
WD6: Bore 13Sa 29
Kenilworth Ct. *DA2: Dart* *58Rd 119*
(off Osbourne Rd.)
SW15 *55Ab 110*
(off Lwr. Richmond Rd.)
WD17: Wat 11W 26
Kenilworth Cres. EN1: Enf 11Ub 33
Kenilworth Dr. KT12: Walt T 76Z 151
WD3: Crox G 14R 26
WD6: Bore 13Sa 29
Kenilworth Gdns. IG3: Ilf 33Vc 75
IG10: Lough 16Pc 36
RM12: Horn 34Ld 77
SE18 54Rc 116
TW18: Staines 64L 127
UB1: S'hall 41Ba 85
UB4: Hayes 43V 84
WD19: Wat 22Y 45
Kenilworth Rd. BR5: Pet W 72Sc 160
E3 40Ac 72
HA8: Edg 20Sa 29
KT17: Ewe 78Wa 154
NW6 39Bb 69
SE20 67Zb 136
TW15: Ashf 62M 127
W5 46Na 87
KENLEY 86Sb 177
Kenley *N17* *26Tb 51*
(off Gloucester Rd.)
KENLEY AERODROME 91Tb 197
Kenley Av. NW9 25Ua 48
Kenley Cl. BR7: Chst 69Uc 138
DA5: Bexl 59Cd 118
EN4: E Barn 14Gb 31
Kenley Gdns. CR7: Thor H 70Rb 135
RM12: Horn 33Pd 77
Kenley La. CR8: Kenley 86Sb 177
Kenley Rd. KT1: King T 68Ra 131
SW19 68Cb 133
TW1: Twick 58Ka 108
Kenley Wlk. SM3: Cheam 77Za 154
W11 45Ab 88
Kenlor Rd. SW17 64Fb 133
Kenmare Cl. UB10: Ick 33T 64
Kenmare Dr. CR4: Mitc 66Hb 133
N17 26Vb 51
Kenmare Gdns. N13 21Sb 51
Kenmare Rd. CR7: Thor H 72Qb 156
Kenmere Gdns. HA0: Wemb 39Qa 67
Kenmere Rd. DA16: Well 54Yc 117
Kenmont Gdns. NW10 41Xa 88
(not continuous)
Kenmore Av.
HA3: Kenton, W'stone 28Ja 46
Kenmore Cl. TW9: Kew 52Qa 109
Kenmore Ct. *NW6* *38Db 69*
(off Acol Rd.)
Kenmore Cres. UB4: Hayes 41V 84
Kenmore Gdns. HA8: Edg 26Ra 47
Kenmore Rd. CR8: Kenley 86Rb 177
HA3: Kenton 27Ma 47
Kenmure Rd. E8 36Xb 71
Kenmure Yd. E8 36Xb 71
Kennacraig Cl. E16 46Jc 93
Kennard Ho. SW11 54Jb 112
Kennard Rd. E15 38Fc 73
N11 22Hb 49
Kennard St. E16 46Pc 94
SW11 53Jb 112
Kenneally SL4: Wind 4A 102
Kenneally Cl. *SL4: Wind* *4A 102*
(off Kenneally)
Kenneally Pl. *SL4: Wind* *4A 102*
(off Kenneally)
Kenneally Row *SL4: Wind* *4A 102*
(off Kenneally)
Kenneally Wlk. SL4: Wind 4A 102
Kennedy Av. EN3: Pond E 16Yb 34
Kennedy Cl. AL2: Lon C 8H 7
BR5: Pet W 74Tc 160
CR4: Mitc 67Jb 134
E13 40Jc 73
HA5: Hat E 23Ba 45
SL2: Farn C 7G 60
Kennedy Ct. TW15: Ashf 64S 128
WD23: B Hea 19Fa 28
Kennedy Cox Ho. *E16* *43Hc 93*
(off Burke St.)
Kennedy Gdns. TN13: S'oaks 95Ld 203
Kennedy Ho. DA11: Nflt 2A 144
SE11 7H 229
SL1: Slou *6B 80*
(off Harrison Way)
Kennedy Path W7 42Ha 86
Kennedy Rd. IG11: Bark 39Uc 74
W7 43Ga 86
Kennedy Wlk. SE17 6G 231
Kennel Cl. KT22: Fet 96Ea 192
Kennel Cotts. HP3: Hem H 7M 3
Kennel La. CM15: Dodd, Kel H 11Ud 40
GU20: W'sham 8A 146
KT22: Fet 94Da 191
Kennelwood Cres. CR0: New Ad 83Fc 179
Kennet Cl. RM14: Upm 30Ud 58
SW11 56Fb 111
Kennet Ct. *W9* *43Cb 89*
(off Elmfield Way)
Kennet Grn. RM15: S Ock 45Xd 98
Kenneth Av. IG1: Ilf 35Rc 74
Kenneth Campbell Ho. NW8 5C 214
Kenneth Chambers Ct.
IG8: Wfd G 23Nc 54
Kenneth Ct. SE11 5A 230 (49Qb 90)
Kenneth Cres. NW2 36Xa 68
Kenneth Gdns. HA7: Stan 23Ja 46
Kenneth Moore Rd. IG1: Ilf 34Rc 74
Kenneth More Theatre 34Rc 74
Kennet Ho. NW8 6C 214
SW18 *56Cb 111*
(off Enterprise Way)
Kenneth Rd. RM6: Chad H 31Zc 75
SM7: Bans 87Fb 175
Kenneth Robbins Ho. N17 24Xb 51
Kenneth Younger Ho. *SW6* *51Bb 111*
(off Clem Attlee Ct.)
Kennet Rd. DA1: Cray 55Jd 118
TW7: Isle 55Ha 108
W9 42Bb 89
Kennet Sq. CR4: Mitc 67Gb 133
Kennet St. E1 46Wb 91
Kennett Ct. *BR8: Swan* *69Gd 140*
(off Oakleigh Cl.)
W4 52Ra 109
WD18: Wat *14X 27*
(off Whippendell Rd.)
Kennett Dr. UB4: Yead 43Aa 85
Kennett Rd. SL3: L'ly 48D 82
Kennett Wharf La.
EC4 4E 224 (45Sb 91)
KENNINGHALL 22Yb 52
Kenninghall Rd. E5 34Wb 71
N18 22Yb 52
Kenning Ho. *N1* *39Ub 71*
(off Colville Est.)
Kenning St. SE16 47Yb 92
Kennings Way SE11 7A 230 (50Qb 90)
KENNINGTON 7A 230 (51Qb 112)
Kennington Grn. SE11 50Qb 90
Kennington La. SE11 7J 229 (50Pb 90)
KENNINGTON OVAL 51Qb 112
Kennington Oval SE11 51Pb 112
Kennington Pal. Ct. SE11 7K 229
Kennington Pk. Gdns.
SE11 51Rb 113
Kennington Pk. Ho. *SE11* *50Qb 90*
(off Kennington Pk. Pl.)
Kennington Pk. Pl. SE11 51Qb 112
Kennington Pk. Rd.
SE11 7B 230 (51Qb 112)
Kennington Rd. SE1 3K 229 (48Qb 90)
SE11 7K 229 (48Qb 90)
Kennistoun Ho. NW5 36Lb 70
Kennoldes *SE21* *61Tb 135*
(off Croxted Rd.)
Kenny Dr. SM5: Cars 81Jb 176
Kennyland Ct. *NW4* *30Xa 48*
(off Hendon Way)
Kennylands Rd. IG6: Ilf 24Wc 55
Kenrick Pl. W1 7H 215 (43Jb 90)
Kenrick Sq. RH1: Blet 5L 209
KENSAL GREEN 41Ya 88
Kensal Ho. *W10* *42Za 88*
(off Ladbroke Gro.)
KENSAL RISE 40Za 68
Kensal Rd. W10 42Ab 88
KENSAL TOWN 42Ab 88
Kensal Wharf W10 42Za 88
KENSINGTON 48Cb 89
Kensington Arc. *W8* *47Db 89*
(off Kensington High St.)
Kensington Av. CR7: Thor H 67Qb 134
E12 37Nc 74
WD18: Wat 14V 26
Kensington Cen. W14 49Ab 88
(not continuous)
Kensington Chu. Ct. W8 47Db 89
Kensington Chu. St. W8 46Cb 89
Kensington Chu. Wlk. W8 47Db 89
(not continuous)
Kensington Cl. AL1: St A 4E 6
N11 23Jb 50
Kensington Ct. RM17: Grays 51Ee 121
SE16 *46Zb 92*
(off King & Queen Wharf)
W8 47Db 89
Kensington Ct. Gdns. *W8* *48Db 89*
(off Kensington Ct. Pl.)
Kensington Ct. Mans. *W8* *47Db 89*
(off Kensington Ct.)
Kensington Ct. M. *W8* *48Db 89*
(off Kensington Ct. Pl.)
Kensington Ct. Pl. W8 48Db 89
Kensington Dr. IG8: Wfd G 26Mc 53
Kensington Gdns. 6A 220 (46Eb 89)
Kensington Gdns. IG1: Ilf 32Pc 74
KT1: King T 69Ma 131
RM18: E Til *9L 101*
(off Queen Mary Av.)
Kensington Gdns. Sq. W2 44Db 89
Kensington Ga. W8 3A 226 (48Eb 89)
Kensington Gore SW7 2A 226 (47Eb 89)
Kensington Hall Gdns. W14 50Bb 89
Kensington Hgts. *HA1: Harr* *30Ha 46*
(off Sheepcote Rd.)
W8 46Cb 89
Kensington High St. W8 48Bb 89
W14 48Bb 89
Kensington Ho. IG8: Wfd G 24Qc 54
UB7: W Dray *47P 83*
(off Park Lodge Av.)
W8 *47Db 89*
(off Kensington Ct.)
W14 47Za 88
Kensington Leisure Cen. 45Ab 88
Kensington Mall W8 46Cb 89
Kensington Mans. *SW5* *50Cb 89*
(off Trebovir Rd.)
Kensington M. SL4: Wind 5G 102
Kensington Palace 46Db 89
Kensington Pal. Gdns. W8 46Db 89
Kensington Pk. RM4: Stap A 17Gd 38
Kensington Pk. Gdns. W11 45Bb 89
Kensington Pk. M. W11 44Bb 89
Kensington Pk. Rd. W11 44Bb 89
Kensington Path *E10* *33Dc 72*
(off Osborne Rd.)
Kensington Pl. W8 46Cb 89
Kensington Rd. CM15: Pil H 16Wd 40
RM7: Rom 30Ed 56
SW7 2C 226 (47Db 89)
UB5: N'olt 41Ca 85
W8 2A 226 (47Db 89)
Kensington Sq. W8 48Db 89
Kensington Ter. CR2: S Croy 80Tb 157
Kensington Village W14 49Bb 89
Kensington Way CM14: B'wood 18Yd 40
WD6: Bore 13Ta 29
Kensington W. W14 49Ab 88
Kensworth Ho. EC1 4G 219
Kent Av. DA16: Well 57Vc 117
RM9: Dag 42Cd 96
SL1: Slou 3G 80
W13 43Ka 86
Kent Cl. BR6: Chels 79Uc 160
CR4: Mitc 70Nb 134
TN15: W King 80Ud 164
TW18: Staines 65M 127
UB8: Uxb 37L 63
WD6: Bore 10Ta 15
Kent Ct. E2 40Vb 71
NW9 26Ua 48
Kent Dr. EN4: Cockf 14Jb 32
RM12: Horn 35Md 77
TW11: Tedd 64Ga 130
Kent Firefighting Mus. 83Yd 184
Kentford Way UB5: N'olt 39Aa 65
Kent Gdns. HA4: Ruis 30W 44
W13 43Ka 86
Kent Ga. Way CR0: Addtn 79Bc 158
Kent Hatch Rd. RH8: Limp 1N 211
Kent Ho. SE1 7K 231 (50Vb 91)
SL9: Chal P 22A 42
SW1 7D 228
W4 *50Ua 88*
(off Devonshire St.)
W8 *47Db 89*
(off Kensington Ct.)
W11 *46Bb 89*
(off Boyne Ter. M.)
WD23: Bush 14Ba 27
Kent Ho. App. Rd. BR3: Beck 67Ac 136
Kent Ho. La. BR3: Beck 65Ac 136
Kent Ho. Rd. BR3: Beck 67Zb 136
SE26 64Ac 136
Kentish Bldgs. SE1 7F 225 (47Tb 91)
Kentish La. AL9: Brk P, Hat 8L 9
Kentish Pl. SE2 48Wc 95
Kentish Rd. DA17: Belv 49Cd 96
KENTISH TOWN 36Kb 70
Kentish Town Ind. Est. NW5 36Kb 70
Kentish Town Rd. NW1 38Kb 70
NW5 38Kb 70
Kentish Town Sports Cen. 37Kb 70
Kentish Way BR1: Brom 68Kc 137
BR2: Brom 68Kc 137
Kent Kraft Ind. Est. DA11: Nflt 57Be 121
Kentlea Rd. SE28 47Uc 94
Kentmere Ho. SE15 51Yb 114
Kentmere Mans. W5 42Ka 86
Kentmere Rd. SE18 49Uc 94
KENTON 29La 46
Kenton Av. HA1: Harr 31Ha 66
TW16: Sun 68Z 129
UB1: S'hall 45Ca 85
Kenton Ct. HA3: Kenton 30Ka 46
SE26 *63Ac 136*
(off Adamsrill Rd.)
TW1: Twick 58Ma 109
W14 48Bb 89
Kentone Ct. SE25 70Xb 135
Kenton Gdns. AL1: St A 3D 6
HA3: Kenton 29La 46
Kenton Ho. *E1* *42Yb 92*
(off Mantus Cl.)
Kentonian Cl. HA3: Kenton 29Ka 46
Kenton La.
HA3: Hrw W, Kenton, W'stone
23Ha 46
Kenton Pk. Av. HA3: Kenton 29Ma 47
Kenton Pk. Cl. HA3: Kenton 28La 46
Kenton Pk. Cres. HA3: Kenton 28Ma 47
Kenton Pk. Mans. *HA3: Kenton* *29La 46*
(off Kenton Rd.)
Kenton Pk. Pde. HA3: Kenton 29La 46
Kenton Pk. Rd. HA3: Kenton 28La 46
Kenton Rd. E9 37Zb 72
HA1: Harr 31Ha 66
HA3: Kenton 30Ja 46
Kentons La. SL4: Wind 4C 102
Kenton St. WC1 5F 217 (42Nb 90)
Kenton Way GU21: Wok 9K 167
UB4: Hayes 41U 84
Kent Pk. Ind. Est. SE15 51Xb 113
Kent Pas. NW1 5F 215 (42Hb 89)
Kent Rd. BR4: W W'ck 74Dc 158
BR5: St M Cry 72Xc 161
DA1: Dart 58Md 119
DA3: Lfield 68Zd 143
DA11: Grav'nd 10C 122
GU20: W'sham 8B 146
GU22: Wok 88D 168
KT1: King T 69Ma 131
KT8: E Mos 70Ea 130
N21 18Tb 33
RM10: Dag 36Dd 76
RM17: Grays 51Ee 121
TW9: Kew 52Qa 109
W4 48Sa 87
Kents Av. HP3: Hem H 6M 3
Kent's Pas. TW12: Hamp 67Ba 129
Kent St. E2 1K 219 (40Vb 71)
E13 41Lc 93
Kent Ter. NW1 4E 214 (41Gb 89)
Kent Vw. RM13: Wenn 45Md 97
RM15: Avel 47Sd 98
Kent Vw. Gdns. IG3: Ilf 33Uc 74
Kent Wlk. SW9 56Rb 113
Kent Way KT6: Surb 76Na 153
Kentwell Cl. SE4 56Ac 114
Kent Wharf *SE8* *52Dc 114*
(off Creekside)
Kentwode Grn. SW13 52Wa 110
Kentwyns Ri. RH1: S Nut 7F 208
Kent Yd. SW7 2E 226 (47Gb 89)
Kenver Av. N12 23Fb 49
Kenward Rd. SE9 57Lc 115
Kenward Way SW11 54Jb 112
Ken Way HA9: Wemb 34Sa 67
Kenway RM5: Col R 26Ed 56
RM13: Rain 41Md 97
Kenway Cl. RM13: Rain 41Ld 97
Kenway Rd. SW5 49Db 89
Kenway Wlk. RM13: Rain 41Md 97
Ken Wilson Ho. *E2* *40Wb 71*
(off Pritchards Rd.)
Kenwood Av. DA3: Lfield 69Ee 143
N14 15Mb 32
Kenwood Cl. NW3 32Fb 69
UB7: Sip 51Q 106
Kenwood Ct. *NW9* *28Sa 47*
(off Elmwood Cres.)
Kenwood Dr. BR3: Beck 69Ec 136
KT12: Hers 79X 151
WD3: Rick 19H 25
Kenwood Gdns. E18 27Kc 53
IG2: Ilf 29Qc 54
IG5: Ilf 28Qc 54
Kenwood House 32Gb 69
Kenwood Ho. SW9 56Rb 113
WD18: Wat 17T 26
Kenwood Pk. KT13: Weyb 79T 150
Kenwood Pl. N6 32Hb 69
Kenwood Ridge CR8: Kenley 89Rb 177
Kenwood Rd. N6 30Hb 49
N9 18Wb 33
Kenworth Cl. EN8: Walt C 5Zb 20
Kenworthy Rd. E9 36Ac 72
Kenwrick Ho. N1 1J 217
Kenwyn Dr. NW2 33Ua 68
Kenwyn Lodge N2 28Hb 49
Kenwyn Rd. DA1: Dart 57Md 119
SW4 56Mb 112
SW20 67Ya 132
Kenya Rd. SE7 52Mc 115
Kenyngton Ct. TW16: Sun 64W 128
Kenyngton Dr. TW16: Sun 64W 128
Kenyngton Pl. HA3: Kenton 29La 46
Kenyon Ho. *SE5* *52Sb 113*
(off Camberwell Rd.)
Kenyon Mans. *W14* *51Ab 110*
(off Queen's Club Gdns.)
Kenyons KT24: W Hor 100R 190
Kenyon St. SW6 53Za 110
Keogh Rd. E15 37Gc 73
Kepler Ho. *SE10* *50Hc 93*
(off Armitage Rd.)
Kepler Rd. SW4 56Nb 112
Keppel Cl. DA9: Ghithe 56Xd 120
Keppel Ho. SE8 50Bc 92
SW3 6D 226
Keppel Rd. E6 38Pc 74
RM9: Dag 35Ad 75
Keppel Row SE1 7D 224 (46Sb 91)
Keppel Spur SL4: Old Win 9M 103
Keppel St. WC1 7E 216 (43Mb 90)
Kepplestone M. BR3: Beck 68Ec 136
Kepple St. SL4: Wind 4H 103
Kerbela St. E2 42Wb 91
Kerbey St. E14 44Dc 92
Kerdistone Cl. EN6: Pot B 2Db 17
Kerfield Cres. SE5 53Tb 113
Kerfield Pl. SE5 53Tb 113
Kerlin Vw. SW16 68Lb 134
Kernow Cl. RM12: Horn 33Nd 77
Kerr Cl. CR2: Sels 80Ac 158
Kerria Way GU24: W End 5C 166
Kerri Cl. EN5: Ark 14Ya 30
Kerridge Ct. *N1* *37Ub 71*
(off Balls Pond Rd.)
Kerrier Ho. *SW10* *52Eb 111*
(off Stadium St.)
Kerrill Av. CR5: Coul 91Qb 196
Kerrington Ct. *W10* *42Ab 88*
(off Wornington Rd.)
W12 *47Ya 88*
(off Uxbridge Rd.)
Kerris Ho. SE11 7A 230
Kerrison Pl. W5 46Ma 87
Kerrison Rd. E15 39Fc 73
SW11 55Gb 111
W5 46Ma 87
Kerrison Vs. W5 46Ma 87
Kerry Av. HA7: Stan 21La 46
RM15: Avel 47Pd 97
Kerry Cl. E16 44Kc 93
N13 19Pb 32
RM14: Upm 31Vd 78
Kerry Ct. HA7: Stan 21Ma 47
Kerry Dr. RM14: Upm 31Vd 78
Kerry Ho. *E1* *44Yb 92*
(off Sidney St.)
Kerry Path SE14 51Bc 114
Kerry Rd. RM16: Grays 46Fe 99
SE14 51Bc 114
Kerry Ter. GU21: Wok 88D 168
Kerscott Ho. *E3* *41Dc 92*
(off Rainhill Way)
Kersey Dr. CR2: Sels 84Yb 178
Kersey Gdns.
RM3: Hrld W 24Nd 57
SE9 63Nc 138
Kersfield Ho. SW15 58Za 110
Kersfield Rd. SW15 58Za 110
Kershaw Cl. RM11: Horn 31Nd 77
RM16: Chaf H 49Yd 98
SW18 58Fb 111
Kershaw Rd. RM10: Dag 34Cd 76
Kerslake Ho.
SL9: Chal P 22A 42
Kersley M. SW11 53Hb 111
Kersley Rd. N16 33Ub 71
Kersley St. SW11 54Hb 111
Kerstin Cl. UB3: Hayes 45V 84
Kerswell Cl. N15 29Ub 51
SL2: Slou 2D 80
Kerwick Cl. N7 38Nb 70
Keslake Mans. *NW10* *40Za 68*
(off Station Ter.)
Keslake Rd. NW6 40Za 68
Kessock Cl. N17 29Xb 51
Kesteven Cl. IG6: Ilf 23Vc 55
Kestlake Rd. DA5: Bexl 58Yc 117
KESTON 78Lc 159
Keston Av. BR2: Kes 78Lc 159
CR5: Coul 91Qb 196
KT15: New H 83J 169
Keston Cl. DA16: Well 52Yc 117
N18 20Tb 33
Keston Ct. DA5: Bexl 59Bd 117
KT5: Surb *71Pa 153*
(off Cranes Pk.)
Keston Gdns. BR2: Kes 77Lc 159
Keston Ho. SE17 7J 231
KESTON MARK 77Nc 160
KESTON MARK 76Nc 160
Keston M. WD17: Wat 12X 27
Keston Pk. Cl. BR2: Kes 76Pc 160
Keston Rd. CR7: Thor H 72Qb 156
N17 27Tb 51
SE15 55Wb 113
Kestrel Av. E6 43Nc 94
SE24 57Rb 113
TW18: Staines 62H 127
Kestrel Cl. IG6: Ilf 21Xc 55
KT2: King T 63Ma 131
KT19: Eps 84Qa 173
NW9 26Ua 48
NW10 36Ta 67
RM12: Horn 38Kd 77
WD25: Wat 6Aa 13
Kestrel Ct. CR2: S Croy 79Sb 157
E3 *40Cc 72*
(off Four Seasons Cl.)
E17 26Zb 52
HA4: Ruis 33U 64
SM6: Wall 78Lb 156
Kestrel Grn. AL10: Hat 1C 8
Kestrel Ho. EC1 3D 218
EN3: Pond E 15Ac 34
SE10 *53Ec 114*
(off Parkside Av.)
Kestrel Pk. CM13: Hut 15Fe 41
Kestrel Path SL2: Slou 2C 80
Kestrel Pl. *DA9: Ghithe* *58Wd 120*
(off Woodpecker Dr.)
SE14 51Ac 114
Kestrel Rd. EN9: Walt A 6Jc 21

Kestrels, The—Kingscote St.

Kestrels, The AL2: Brick W 3Ba 13
UB9: Den 29H 43
(off Patrons Way E.)
Kestrel Way CR0: New Ad 81Fc 179
GU21: Wok 7M 167
UB3: Hayes 47T 84
Keswick Av. RM11: Horn 32Md 77
SW15 .64Ua 132
SW19 .68Cb 133
TW17: Shep 69U 128
Keswick B'way. SW15 . . . . .57Bb 111
(off Up. Richmond Rd.)
Keswick Cl. AL1: St A 3F 6
SM1: Sutt 77Eb 155
Keswick Ct. BR2: Brom 70Hc 137
SE6 . . . . .60Hc 115
SE13 .57Dc 114
SL2: Slou 5K 81
Keswick Dr. EN3: Enf W 8Yb 20
GU18: Light 3A 166
Keswick Gdns. HA4: Ruis 30T 44
HA9: Wemb 35Na 67
IG4: Ilf .28Nc 54
RM19: Purf 51Sd 120
Keswick Ho. RM3: Rom 23Md 57
(off Dartfields)
SE5 . . . . .54Sb 113
Keswick M. W5 . . . . .46Na 87
Keswick Rd. BR4: W W'ck 75Gc 159
BR6: Orp 74Vc 161
DA7: Bex 53Cd 118
KT22: Fet 96Ea 192
KT23: Bookh 97Da 191
SW15 .57Ab 110
TW2: Whitt 58Ea 108
TW20: Egh 66D 126
Kettering Ct. CR7: Thor H 70Sb 135
Kettering Rd. EN3: Enf W 9Zb 20
RM3: Rom 24Nd 57
Kettering St. SW16 . . . . .65Lb 134
Kett Gdns. SW2 . . . . .57Pb 112
Kettlebaston Rd. E10 . . . . .32Bc 72
Kettleby Ho. SW9 . . . . .55Rb 113
(off Barrington Rd.)
Kettlewell Cl. GU21: Wok 6P 167
N11 . . . . .23Jb 50
Kettlewell Ct.
BR8: Swan 68Hd 140
Kettlewell Dr. GU21: Wok 86A 168
Kettlewell Hill GU21: Wok 86A 168
Ketton Grn. RH1: Mers 100Mb 196
Ketton Ho. W10 . . . . .42Ya 88
(off Sutton Way)
Kevan Ct. E17 . . . . .28Cc 52
Kevan Dr. GU23: Send 96G 188
Kevan Ho. SE5 . . . . .52Sb 113
Kevelioc Rd. N17 . . . . .25Sb 51
Kevere Ct. HA6: Nwood 22R 44
Kevin Cl. TW4: Houn 54Z 107
KEVINGTON 72Ad 161
Kevington Cl. BR5: St P 70Vc 139
Kevington Dr. BR5: St P 70Vc 139
BR7: Chst 70Vc 139
KEW 53Qa 109
KEW BRIDGE 50Pa 87
Kew Bri. TW8: Bford 51Qa 109
Kew Bri. Arches TW9: Kew 51Qa 109
Kew Bri. Ct. W4 . . . . .50Qa 87
Kew Bri. Distribution Cen.
TW8: Bford 50Pa 87
Kew Bri. Rd. TW8: Bford 51Pa 109
Kew Cl. RM1: Rom 23Gd 56
UB8: Uxb .40M 63
Kew Ct. KT2: King T 67Na 131
Kew Cres. SM3: Cheam 76Ab 154
Kewferry Dr. HA6: Nwood 22R 44
Kewferry Rd. HA6: Nwood 23S 44
Kew Foot Rd. TW9: Rich 56Na 109
Kew Gdns. 52Na 109
Kew Gdns. Rd. TW9: Kew 52Pa 109
KEW GREEN 52Qa 109
Kew Grn. TW9: Kew 51Pa 109
Kew Mdw. Path TW9: Kew 54Sa 109
(Clifford Av.)
TW9: Kew 53Ra 109
(Magnolia Ct.)
Kew Retail Pk. TW9: Kew 53Ra 109
Kew Riverside Pk. TW9: Kew 52Ra 109
Kew Rd. TW9: Kew, Rich 51Qa 109
Keybridge Ho. SW8 . . . . .51Nb 112
(off Miles St.)
Key Cl. E1 .42Yb 92
Keyes Ho. SW1 . . . . .7D 228
Keyes Rd. DA1: Dart 56Pd 119
NW2 . . . . .36Za 68
Keyfield Ter. AL1: St A 3B 6
(not continuous)
Keyham Ho. W2 . . . . .43Cb 89
(off Westbourne Pk. Rd.)
Key Ho. SE11 . . . . .51Qb 112
Keymer Cl. TN16: Big H 88Lc 179
Keymer Rd. SW2 . . . . .61Pb 134
Keynes Cl. N2 . . . . .28Hb 49
Keynes Ct. SE28 . . . . .45Xc 95
(off Attlee Rd.)
Keynsham Av. IG8: Wfd G 21Gc 53
Keynsham Gdns. SE9 . . . . .57Nc 116
Keynsham Rd. SE9 . . . . .57Mc 115
SM4: Mord 74Db 155
Keynsham Wlk. SM4: Mord 74Db 155
Keys Ct. CR0: C'don 76Tb 157
(off Beech Ho. Rd.)
Keyse Rd. SE1 . . . . .4K 231 (48Vb 91)
Keyser Pl. WD23: Bush 15Aa 27
Keysham Av. TW5: Cran 53W 106
Keystone Cres. N1 . . . . . . .2G 217 (40Nb 70)
Key W. Ct. IG7: Chig 21Rc 54
Keywood Dr. TW16: Sun 65W 128
Keyworth Cl. E5 . . . . .35Ac 72
Keyworth Pl. SE1 . . . . .3C 230
Keyworth St. SE1 . . . . .3C 230 (48Rb 91)
Kezia M. SE8 . . . . .50Ac 92
Kezia St. SE8 . . . . .50Ac 92
Khalsa Av. DA12: Grav'nd 9E 122
Khalsa Ct. N22 . . . . .25Rb 51
Khama Rd. SW17 . . . . .63Gb 133
Khartoum Pl. DA12: Grav'nd 8E 122
Khartoum Rd. E13 . . . . .41Kc 93
IG1: Ilf 36Rc 74
SW17 . . . . .63Fb 133
Khyber Rd. SW11 . . . . .54Gb 111
Kia Oval 51Pb 112
Kibble Cl. RM6: Chad H 31Yc 75
Kibworth St. SW8 . . . . .52Pb 112
Kidborough Down KT23: Bookh 99Ca 191
KIDBROOKE 54Kc 115
Kidbrooke Est. SE3 . . . . .55Lc 115
Kidbrooke Gdns. SE3 . . . . .54Jc 115
Kidbrooke Green Nature Reserve
. . . . .55Lc 115
Kidbrooke Gro. SE3 . . . . .53Jc 115
Kidbrooke La. SE9 . . . . .56Nc 116
Kidbrooke Pk. Cl. SE3 . . . . .53Kc 115
Kidbrooke Pk. Rd. SE3 . . . . .53Kc 115
Kidbrooke Way SE3 . . . . .54Kc 115
Kidderminster Pl. CR0: C'don 74Rb 157
Kidderminster Rd. CR0: C'don 74Rb 157
SL2: Slou .1E 80
Kidderpore Av. NW3 . . . . .35Cb 69
Kidderpore Gdns. NW3 . . . . .35Cb 69
Kidd Pl. SE7 . . . . .50Nc 94
Kidman Cl. RM2: Rom 27Ld 57
Kidspace
Croydon 79Qb 156
Kielder Cl. IG6: Ilf 23Vc 55
Kierbeck Bus. Complex E16 . . . . .47Kc 93
(not continuous)
Kier Hardie Ho. RM16: Grays 6A 100
Kier Pk. SL5: Asc 9A 124
Kiffen St. EC2 . . . . .5G 219 (42Tb 91)
Kilberry Cl. TW7: Isle 53Fa 108
Kilbrennan Ho. E14 . . . . .44Ec 92
(off Findhorn St.)
KILBURN 40Bb 69
Kilburn Bri. NW6 . . . . .39Cb 69
Kilburn Ga. NW6 . . . . .40Db 69
Kilburn High Rd. NW6 . . . . .38Bb 69
Kilburn Ho. NW6 . . . . .40Bb 69
(off Malvern Pl.)
Kilburn La. W9 . . . . .41Za 88
W10 . . . . .41Za 88
Kilburn Pk. Rd. NW6 . . . . .41Cb 89
Kilburn Pl. NW6 . . . . .39Cb 69
Kilburn Priory NW6 . . . . .39Db 69
Kilburn Sq. NW6 . . . . .39Cb 69
Kilburn Va. NW6 . . . . .39Db 69
Kilburn Va. Est. NW6 . . . . .39Db 69
(off Kilburn Vale)
Kilby Cl. WD25: Wat 7Z 13
Kilby Ct. SE10 . . . . .48Hc 93
(off Greenroof Way)
Kilcorral Cl. KT17: Eps 86Wa 174
Kildare Cl. HA4: Ruis 32Y 65
Kildare Ct. W2 . . . . .44Cb 89
(off Kildare Ter.)
Kildare Gdns. W2 . . . . .44Cb 89
Kildare Rd. E16 . . . . .43Jc 93
Kildare Ter. W2 . . . . .44Cb 89
Kildare Wlk. E14 . . . . .44Cc 92
Kildonan Cl. WD17: Wat 11V 26
Kildoran Rd. SW2 . . . . .57Nb 112
Kildowan Rd. IG3: Ilf 32Wc 75
Kilgour Rd. SE23 . . . . .58Ac 114
Kilkie St. SW6 . . . . .54Eb 111
Killarney Rd. SW18 . . . . .58Eb 111
Killasser Ct. KT20: Tad 95Ya 194
Killburns Mill Cl. SM6: Wall 75Kb 156
Killearn Rd. SE6 . . . . .60Fc 115
Killester Gdns. KT4: Wor Pk 77Xa 154
Killewarren Way BR5: Orp 72Yc 161
Killick Cl. TN13: Dun G 93Gd 202
Killick Ho. SM1: Sutt 77Db 155
Killick M. SM3: Cheam 79Ab 154
Killick St. N1 . . . . .1H 217 (40Pb 70)
Killick Way E1 . . . . .43Zb 92
Killieser Av. SW2 . . . . .61Nb 134
Killigarth Ct. DA14: Sidc 63Wc 139
Killigrew Ho. TW16: Sun 66U 128
Killip Cl. E16 . . . . .44Hc 93
Killoran Ho. E14 . . . . .48Ec 92
(off Galbraith St.)
Killowen Av. UB5: N'olt 36Ea 66
Killowen Cl. KT20: Tad 94Za 194
Killowen Rd. E9 . . . . .37Zb 72
Killy Hill GU24: Chob 10J 147
Killyon Rd. SW8 . . . . .54Lb 112
Killyon Ter. SW8 . . . . .54Lb 112
Kilmaine Rd. SW6 . . . . .52Ab 110
Kilmarnock Gdns. RM8: Dag 34Yc 75
Kilmarnock Pk. RH2: Reig 5K 207
Kilmarnock Rd. WD19: Wat 21Z 45
Kilmarsh Rd. W6 . . . . .49Ya 88
Kilmartin Av. SW16 . . . . .69Qb 134
Kilmartin Rd. IG3: Ilf 33Wc 75
Kilmartin Way RM12: Horn 36Kd 77
Kilmington Cl. CM13: Hut 19De 41
Kilmington Rd. SW13 . . . . .51Wa 110
Kilmiston Av. TW17: Shep 72S 150
Kilmiston Ho. TW17: Shep 72S 150
Kilmore Ho. E14 . . . . .44Dc 92
(off Vesey Path)
Kilmorey Gdns. TW1: Twick 57Ka 108
Kilmorey Rd. TW1: Twick 56Ka 108
Kilmorie Rd. SE23 . . . . .60Ac 114
Kilmuir Ho. KT17: Eps 85Ua 174
(off Depot Rd.)
SW1 . . . . .6J 227
Kiln Ct. UB3: Harl 51T 106
Kiln Cotts. HP2: Hem H 1B 4
Kiln Ct. E14 . . . . .45Bc 92
(off Newell St.)
Kilncroft HP3: Hem H 4B 4
Kilndown DA12: Grav'nd 5F 144
Kilner Ho. E16 . . . . .43Kc 93
(off Freemasons Rd.)
SE11 . . . . .51Qb 112
(off Clayton St.)
Kilner St. E14 . . . . .43Cc 92
Kilnfields BR6: Well H 79Cd 162
Kiln Ground HP3: Hem H 4A 4
Kiln Ho. E1 . . . . .43Zb 92
(off Duckett St.)
UB7: Yiew 45M 83
Kiln La. GU23: Rip 96J 189
GU24: Bisl 9F 166
KT17: Eps 83Ua 174
SL2: Hedg .2G 60
SL4: Wink 5A 124
SL5: S'dale 1E 146
Kiln M. SW17 . . . . .64Fb 133
Kiln Pl. NW5 . . . . .36Jb 70
Kilns, The RH1: Mers, Redh 3B 208
Kilnside KT10: Clay 80Ja 152
Kiln Wlk. RH1: Redh 10A 208
Kiln Way HA6: Nwood 23U 44
RM17: Grays 50Be 99
Kilnwood TN14: Hals 85Bd 181
Kiln Wood La. RM4: Have B 22Fd 56
Kilpatrick Way UB4: Yead 43Aa 85
Kilravock St. W10 . . . . .41Ab 88
Kilronan W3 . . . . .44Ta 87
Kilross Rd. TW14: Bedf 60T 106
Kilrue La. KT12: Hers 77V 150
Kilrush Ter. GU21: Wok 88C 168
Kilsby Wlk. RM9: Dag 37Xc 75
Kilsha Rd. KT12: Walt T 72Y 151
Kilsmore La. EN8: Chesh 1Zb 20
Kilvinton Dr. EN2: Enf 10Tb 19
Kilworth Av. CM15: Shenf 16Ce 41
Kimbell Gdns. SW6 . . . . .53Ab 110
Kimbell Pl. SE3 . . . . .56Lc 115
Kimber Cl. SL4: Wind 5E 102
Kimber Ct. SE1 . . . . .3H 231
(off Long La.)
Kimberley Av. E6 . . . . .40Nc 74
IG2: Ilf 31Tc 74
RM7: Rom 30Ed 56
SE15 . . . . .54Xb 113
Kimberley Bus. Pk. BR2: Kes 81Lc 179
Kimberley Cl. SL3: L'ly 49B 82
Kimberley Ct. NW6 . . . . .39Ab 68
(off Kimberley Rd.)
Kimberley Dr. DA14: Sidc 61Zc 139
Kimberley Gdns. EN1: Enf 13Vb 33
N4 . . . . .29Rb 51
Kimberley Ga. BR1: Brom 66Gc 137
Kimberley Ho. E14 . . . . .48Ec 92
(off Galbraith St.)
Kimberley Pl. CR8: Purl 83Qb 176
Kimberley Ride KT11: Cobh 85Da 171
Kimberley Rd. AL3: St A 1A 6
BR3: Beck 68Zb 136
CR0: C'don 72Rb 157
E4 . . . . .18Gc 35
E11 . . . . .33Fc 73
E16 . . . . .42Hc 93
E17 . . . . .25Ac 52
N17 . . . . .26Wb 51
N18 . . . . .23Xb 51
NW6 . . . . .39Ab 68
SW9 . . . . .54Nb 112
Kimberley Wlk. KT12: Walt T 73X 151
Kimberley Way E4 . . . . .18Gc 35
Kimber Pl. TW4: Houn 59Ba 107
(Conway Rd.)
TW4: Houn 56Ba 107
(Marryat Cl.)
Kimber Rd. SW18 . . . . .59Cb 111
Kimbers Dr. SL1: Burn 1B 80
Kimble Cl. WD18: Wat 17U 26
Kimble Cres. WD23: Bush 17Ea 28
Kimble Ho. NW8 . . . . .5E 214
(off Lilestone St.)
Kimble Rd. SW19 . . . . .65Fb 133
Kimblewick WD19: Wat 18Aa 27
Kimbolton Cl. SE12 . . . . .58Hc 115
Kimbolton Ct. SW3 . . . . .6D 226
Kimbolton Grn. WD6: Bore 14Sa 29
Kimbolton Row SW3 . . . . .6D 226
Kimmeridge Gdns. SE9 . . . . .63Nc 138
Kimmeridge Rd. SE9 . . . . .63Nc 138
Kimmins Ct. SE16 . . . . .48Wb 91
(off Old Jamaica Rd.)
Kimps Way HP3: Hem H 5A 4
Kimpton Av. CM15: B'wood 17Xd 40
Kimpton Ho. SW15 . . . . .59Wa 110
Kimpton Ind. Est. SM3: Sutt 75Bb 155
Kimpton Link Bus. Cen.
SM3: Sutt 75Bb 155
Kimpton Pk. Way SM1: Sutt 75Ab 154
SM3: Sutt 75Ab 154
Kimpton Pl. WD25: Wat 6Z 13
Kimpton Rd. SE5 . . . . .53Tb 113
SM3: Sutt 75Bb 155
Kimptons Cl. EN6: Pot B 4Za 16
Kimptons Mead EN6: Pot B 5Za 16
Kimpton Trade & Bus. Cen.
SM3: Sutt 75Bb 155
Kinburn Dr. TW20: Egh 64A 126
Kinburn St. SE16 . . . . .47Zb 92
Kincaid Rd. SE15 . . . . .52Xb 113
Kincardine Gdns. W9 . . . . .42Bb 89
(off Harrow Rd.)
Kincha Lodge KT2: King T 67Pa 131
(off Elm Rd.)
Kinch Gro. HA9: Wemb 31Pa 67
Kincraig Dr. TN13: S'oaks 96Jd 202
Kinder Cl. SE28 . . . . .45Zc 95
Kinder Ho. N1 . . . . .1G 219
Kinderscout HP3: Hem H 4A 4
Kindersley Ho. E1 . . . . .44Wb 91
(off Pinchin St.)
Kindersley Way WD5: Ab L 3S 12
Kinder St. E1 . . . . .44Xb 91
Kinderton Cl. N14 . . . . .18Lb 32
Kinefold Ho. N7 . . . . .37Nb 70
(off York Way Est.)
Kinesis Gym & Fitness Cen 56Nc 116
(off Well Hall Rd.)
Kinetic Bus. Cen. WD6: Bore 13Qa 29
Kinetic Cres. EN3: Enf L 8Bc 20
Kinfauns Av. RM11: Horn 30Ld 57
Kinfauns Rd. IG3: Ilf 32Wc 75
SW2 . . . . .61Qb 134
Kingaby Gdns. RM13: Rain 38Jd 76
King Acre Ct. TW18: Staines 62G 126
King Alfred Av. SE6 . . . . .63Cc 136
(not continuous)
King Alfred Rd. RM3: Hrld W 26Pd 57
King & Queen Cl. SE9 . . . . .63Nc 138
King & Queen St. SE17 . . . .6E 230 (50Sb 91)
King & Queen Wharf SE16 . . . . .45Zb 92
King Arthur Cl. SE15 . . . . .52Yb 114
King Arthur Ct. EN8: Chesh 3Ac 20
KING CHARLES I ISLAND 6F 223
King Charles Ct. SE17 . . . . .51Rb 113
(off Royal Rd.)
King Charles Cres. KT5: Surb 73Pa 153
King Charles Ho. SW6 . . . . .52Db 111
(off Wandon Rd.)
King Charles Rd. KT5: Surb 71Pa 153
WD7: Shenl 4Na 15
King Charles's Ct. SE10 . . . . .51Ec 114
(off Park Row)
King Charles St. SW1 . . . .1E 228 (47Mb 90)
King Charles Ter. E1 . . . . .45Xb 91
(off Sovereign Cl.)
King Charles Wlk. SW19 . . . . .60Ab 110
King Ct. E10 . . . . .31Dc 72
Kingcup Av. HP2: Hem H 2D 4
Kingcup Cl. CR0: C'don 73Zb 158
Kingcup Dr. GU24: Bisl 7E 166
King David La. E1 . . . . .45Yb 92
Kingdom St. W2 . . . . .1A 220 (43Eb 89)
Kingdom Way UB8: Cowl 43M 83
Kingdon Ho. E14 . . . . .48Ec 92
(off Galbraith St.)
Kingdon Rd. NW6 . . . . .37Cb 69
King Edward III M. SE16 . . . . .47Xb 91
King Edward VII Av. SL4: Wind 2J 103
King Edward Av. DA1: Dart 58Md 119
RM13: Rain 40Md 77
King Edward Bldg. EC1 . . . . .2C 224
King Edward Ct. HA9: Wemb 36Na 67
(off Elm Rd.)
King Edward Ct. Shop. Cen.
SL4: Wind 3H 103
King Edward Dr. KT9: Chess 76Na 153
RM16: Grays 7A 100
King Edward Ho. WD23: Bush 14Ba 27
King Edward Mans. E8 . . . . .39Xb 71
(off Mare St.)
King Edward M. SW13 . . . . .53Wa 110
King Edward Pl. WD23: Bush 14Ba 27
King Edward Rd. CM14: B'wood 20Yd 40
DA9: Ghithe 57Wd 120
(not continuous)
E10 . . . . .32Ec 72
E17 . . . . .27Ac 52
EN5: New Bar 14Cb 31
EN8: Walt C 5Ac 20
RM1: Rom 30Hd 56
SS17: Stan H 3M 101
WD7: Shenl 5Pa 15
WD19: Wat 16Aa 27
King Edward's Gdns. W3 . . . . .46Qa 87
King Edwards Gro. TW11: Tedd 65Ka 130
King Edwards Mans. SW6 . . . . .52Cb 111
(off Fulham Rd.)
King Edward's Pl. W3 . . . . .46Qa 87
King Edward's Rd. E9 . . . . .39Xb 71
EN3: Pond E 14Zb 34
HA4: Ruis .32T 64
N9 . . . . .17Xb 33
King Edwards Rd. IG11: Bark 39Tc 74
King Edward St. EC1 . . . . . .2D 224 (44Sb 91)
HP3: Hem H .6L 3
SL1: Slou 7H 81
King Edward Wlk. SE1 . . . .3A 230 (48Qb 90)
KINGFIELD .92C 188
Kingfield Cl. GU22: Wok 92B 188
Kingfield Dr. GU22: Wok 92B 188
Kingfield Gdns. GU22: Wok 92B 188
KINGFIELD GREEN 92B 188
Kingfield Grn. GU22: Wok 92B 188
Kingfield Rd. GU22: Wok 92A 188
W5 . . . . .42Ma 87
Kingfield Stadium 92B 188
Kingfield St. E14 . . . . .49Ec 92
Kingfisher Av. E11 . . . . .30Kc 53
Kingfisher Cl. BR5: St P 70Zc 139
CM13: Hut 17Ce 41
HA3: Hrw W 24Ha 46
HA6: Nwood 25R 44
KT12: Hers 78Aa 151
KT16: Chert 74L 149
KT22: Lea 92La 192
SE28 . . . . .45Yc 95
Kingfisher Ct. CR0: C'don 76Sb 157
(off Wandle Rd.)
E14 . . . . .47Ec 92
(off River Barge Cl.)
EN2: Enf .10Pb 18
GU21: Wok 89A 168
(off Vale Farm Rd.)
GU21: Wok 86E 168
(Woodlands Pk.)
KT8: E Mos 70Ga 130
SE1 . . . . .2E 230
SL2: Slou 2F 80
SM1: Sutt 78Bb 155
SW19 . . . . .61Za 132
TN15: W King 80Ud 164
TW3: Houn 57Da 107
TW7: Isle .54Fa 108
Kingfisher Dr. DA9: Ghithe 57Wd 120
HP3: Hem H .7P 3
RH1: Redh .3A 208
TW10: Ham 63Ka 130
TW18: Staines 63H 127
Kingfisher Gdns. CR2: Sels 83Zb 178
Kingfisher Hgts. E16 . . . . .46Lc 93
(off Bramwell Way)
N17 . . . . .27Xb 51
(off Waterside Way)
RM17: Grays 50Ce 99
Kingfisher Ho. SW18 . . . . .55Eb 111
W14 . . . . .48Bb 89
(off Melbury Rd.)
Kingfisher Leisure Cen.
Kingston upon Thames 68Na 131
Kingfisher Lure WD3: Loud 14K 25
WD4: K Lan 1R 12
Kingfisher M. SE13 . . . . .56Cc 114
Kingfisher Pl. DA4: S Dar 68Sd 142
N22 . . . . .26Pb 50
Kingfisher Rd. RM14: Upm 32Vd 78
Kingfishers, The UB9: Den 30J 43
(off Patrons Way E.)
Kingfisher Sq. SE8 . . . . .51Bc 114
(off Clyde St.)
Kingfisher St. E6 . . . . .43Nc 94
Kingfisher Wlk. NW9 . . . . .26Ua 48
Kingfisher Way BR3: Beck 71Zb 158
NW10 . . . . .37Ta 67
King Frederick IX Twr. SE16 . . . . . . .48Bc 92
King Gdns. CR0: Wadd 78Rb 157
King George IV Ct. SE17 . . . . .7F 231
(off Dawes St.)
King George VI Av. CR4: Mitc 70Hb 133
RM18: E Til 9K 101
TN16: Big H 88Mc 179
King George VI Memorial 7D 222
King George Av. E16 . . . . .44Lc 93
IG2: Ilf 29Tc 54
KT12: Walt T 74Z 151
WD23: Bush 16Da 27
King George Cl. RM7: Mawney 27Ed 56
TW16: Sun 64U 128
King George Cres. HA0: Wemb 36Ma 67
King George M. SW17 . . . . .64Hb 133
King George Rd. EN9: Walt A 6Ec 20
King George's Av. WD18: Wat 15U 26
King George's Dr. KT15: New H 82J 169
UB1: S'hall 43Ba 85
King George Sq. TW10: Rich 58Pa 109
King Georges Rd. CM15: Pil H 16Xd 40
King George's Sailing Club 16Cc 34
King George's Trad. Est.
KT9: Chess 77Qa 153
King George St. SE10 . . . . .52Ec 114
King Georges Wlk. KT10: Esh 77Ea 152
King George Way E4 . . . . .14Dc 34
Kingham Cl. SW18 . . . . .59Eb 111
W11 . . . . .47Ab 88
King Harold Ct. EN9: Walt A 5Ec 20
(off Sun St.)
King Harold Lodge EN9: Walt A 5Fc 21
King Harolds Way DA7: Belv, Bex . . .52Zc 117
DA17: Belv 52Zc 117
King Harry La. AL3: St A 3N 5
King Harry St HP2: Hem H 3M 3
King Harry St. HP1: Hem H 3M 3
King Henry Ct. EN9: Walt A 8Ec 20
King Henry Lodge E4 . . . . .21Cc 52
King Henry M. BR6: Chels 78Vc 161
HA2: Harr .32Ga 66
King Henry's Dr. CR0: New Ad 81Dc 178
King Henry's M. EN3: Enf L 9Cc 20
(off Shepley M.)
King Henry's Reach W6 . . . . .51Ya 110
King Henry's Rd. KT1: King T 69Ra 131
NW3 . . . . .38Gb 69
King Henry's Stairs E1 . . . . .46Xb 91
King Henry St. N16 . . . . .36Ub 71
King Henry's Wlk. N1 . . . . .37Ub 71
King Henrys Wlk. CM16: Epp 1Xc 23
(off Boleyn Row)
King Henry Ter. E1 . . . . .45Xb 91
(off Sovereign Cl.)
Kinghorn St. EC1 . . . . .7C 218 (43Sb 91)
King Ho. W12 . . . . .44Xa 88
Kingisholt Ct. NW10 . . . . .41Za 88
(off Wellington Rd.)
King James' Av. EN6: Cuff 1Nb 18
King James Ct. SE1 . . . . .2C 230
King James St. SE1 . . . . . .2C 230 (47Rb 91)
King John Ct. EC2 . . . . .5J 219 (42Ub 91)
King John La. TW19: Wray 7P 103
King John's Cl. TW19: Wray 7P 103
King Johns Pl. TW20: Egh 64A 126
King John St. E1 . . . . .43Zb 92
King John's Wlk. SE9 . . . . .59Nc 116
Kinglake Ct. GU21: Wok 10J 167
Kinglake Est. SE17 . . . . . . .7J 231 (50Ub 91)
Kinglake St. SE17 . . . . .7H 231 (50Ub 91)
(not continuous)
Kinglet Cl. E7 . . . . .37Jc 73
Kingley Pk. WD4: K Lan 1R 12
Kingly Ct. W1 . . . . .4C 222
Kingly St. W1 . . . . .3B 222 (44Lb 90)
Kings Acre RH1: S Nut 9F 208
Kingsand Rd. SE12 . . . . .61Jc 137
Kings Arbour UB2: S'hall 50Aa 85
King's Arms All. TW8: Bford 51Ma 109
Kings Arms Ct. E1 . . . . .43Wb 91
Kings Arms Yd. SW18 . . . . .57Db 111
Kings Arms Yd. EC2 . . . . . . .2F 225 (44Tb 91)
RM1: Rom .29Gd 56
Kingsash Dr. UB4: Yead 42Aa 85
King's Av. GU24: Brkwd 1B 186
IG8: Wfd G 23Kc 53
IG9: Buck H 19Mc 35
(Langfords)
IG9: Buck H 23Kc 53
(The Broadway)
N10 . . . . .27Jb 50
SM5: Cars 80Gb 155
TW16: Sun 64V 128
UB6: G'frd 43Da 85
WD18: Wat 14V 26
Kings Av. BR1: Brom 65Hc 137
HP3: Hem H .6P 3
KT3: N Mald 70Ua 132
KT14: Byfl 84M 169
N21 . . . . .18Rb 33
RH1: Redh .8N 207
RM6: Chad H 30Bd 55
SW4 . . . . .60Mb 112
SW12 . . . . .60Mb 112
TW3: Houn 53Da 107
W5 . . . . .44Ma 87
King's Bench St. SE1 . . . . . .1C 230 (47Rb 91)
King's Bench Wlk. EC4 . . . .3A 224 (44Qb 90)
King's Blvd. N1 . . . . .2F 217 (40Nb 70)
Kingsbridge Av. W3 . . . . .47Pa 87
Kingsbridge Cir. RM3: Rom 23Nd 57
Kingsbridge Cl. RM3: Rom 23Nd 57
Kingsbridge Ct. E14 . . . . .48Cc 92
(off Dockers Tanner Rd.)
NW1 . . . . .38Kb 70
(off Castlehaven Rd.)
Kingsbridge Cres. UB1: S'hall 43Ba 85
Kingsbridge Dr. NW7 . . . . .24Za 48
Kingsbridge Rd. IG11: Bark 40Tc 74
KT12: Walt T 73X 151
RM3: Rom 23Nd 57
SM4: Mord 72Za 154
UB2: S'hall 49Ba 85
W10 . . . . .44Ya 88
Kingsbridge Way UB4: Hayes 41U 84
Kingsbridge Wharf IG11: Bark 41Uc 94
Kingsbrook KT22: Lea 90Ja 172
KINGSBURY 29Ra 47
Kingsbury Av. AL3: St A 1A 6
Kingsbury Circ. NW9 . . . . .29Qa 47
Kingsbury Cl. TW18: Staines 63F 126
Kingsbury Dr. SL4: Old Win 9L 103
KINGSBURY GREEN 30Ta 47
Kingsbury M. AL3: St A 1P 5
Kingsbury Rd. N1 . . . . .37Ub 71
NW9 . . . . .29Qa 47
Kingsbury Ter. N1 . . . . .37Ub 71
Kingsbury Trad. Est. NW9 . . . . .30Ta 47
Kingsbury Watermill Mus. 1P 5
Kings Chase CM14: B'wood 20Yd 40
KT8: E Mos 69Ea 130
Kings Chase Vw. EN2: Enf 12Qb 32
Kingsclere Cl. SW15 . . . . .59Wa 110
Kingsclere Ct. N12 . . . . .22Gb 49
Kingsclere Pl. EN2: Enf 12Sb 33
Kingscliffe Gdns. SW19 . . . . .60Bb 111
King's Cl. DA1: Cray 56Gd 118
NW4 . . . . .28Za 48
WD4: Chfd .3K 11
WD18: Wat 14X 27
Kings Cl. E10 . . . . .31Dc 72
HA6: Nwood 23V 44
HP8: Chal G 19A 24
KT7: T Ditt 72Ja 152
KT12: Walt T 74X 151
TW18: Staines 66M 127
King's Club, The 65Ya 132
Kings Coll. Ct. NW3 . . . . .38Gb 69
King's College London
Denmark Hill Campus 54Tb 113
Guy's Campus 46Tb 91
Maughan Library 2K 223
St Thomas' Campus -
Lambeth Pal. Rd. 4G 229
St Thomas' House 3H 229
Strand Campus 4J 223 (45Pb 90)
Waterloo Campus 7K 223 (46Qb 90)
King's Coll. Rd. NW3 . . . . .38Gb 69
Kings Coll. Rd. HA4: Ruis 30V 44
King's College School of
Medicine & Dentistry 54Sb 113
Kingscote Rd. CR0: C'don 73Xb 157
KT3: N Mald 69Ta 131
W4 . . . . .48Ta 87
Kingscote St. EC4 . . . . .4B 224 (45Rb 91)

King's Ct.—Kinveachy Gdns.

King's Ct. E13 39Kc 73
KT20: Tad 94Xa 194
SE1 1C 230 (47Rb 91)
Kings Ct. HA9: Wemb 33Ra 67
IG9: Buck H 19Mc 35
KT12: Walt T 76X 151
KT14: Byfl 83M 169
N7 38Pb 70
(off Caledonian Rd.)
NW8 1F 215
W6 49Wa 88
WD6: Bore 11Pa 29
(off Bennington Dr.)
Kings Ct. Mans. *SW6* 53Bb 111
(off Fulham Rd.)
Kings Ct. M. KT8: E Mos 71Fa 152
Kings Ct. Nth. SW3 50Gb 89
Kingscourt Rd. SW16 62Mb 134
Kings Ct. Sth. *SW3* 50Gb 89
(off Chelsea Mnr. Gdns.)
King's Cres. N4 34Sb 71
Kings Cres. Est. N4 33Sb 71
Kingscroft SW4 58Nb 112
Kingscroft Rd. KT22: Lea 92Ka 192
NW2 37Bb 69
SM7: Bans 87Fb 175
KING'S CROSS 1F 217 (40Nb 70)
King's Cross Bri. N1 3G 217
Kings Cross La. RH1: S Nut 8D 208
King's Cross Rd. WC1 3H 217 (41Pb 90)
King's Cross Sq. N1 3F 217
Kingsdale Ct. DA10: Swans 58Ae 121
EN9: Walt A 6Jc 21
(off Lamplighters Cl.)
Kingsdale Gdns. W11 46Za 88
Kingsdale Rd. SE18 52Vc 117
SE20 66Zb 136
Kingsdene KT20: Tad 93Xa 194
Kingsdown Av.
CR2: S Croy 82Rb 177
W3 45Ua 88
W13 47Ka 86
Kingsdown Cl. DA12: Grav'nd 10H 123
SE16 50Xb 91
(off Masters Dr.)
W10 44Za 88
Kingsdowne Rd. KT6: Surb 73Na 153
Kingsdown Ho. E8 36Wb 71
Kingsdown Point SW2 61Qb 134
Kingsdown Rd. E11 34Gc 73
KT17: Eps 85Wa 174
N19 33Nb 70
SM3: Cheam 78Ab 154
Kingsdown Way BR2: Hayes 73Jc 159
King's Dr. HA8: Edg 21Pa 47
Kings Dr. DA12: Grav'nd 2D 144
HA9: Wemb 33Ra 67
KT5: Surb 73Qa 153
KT7: T Ditt 73Ka 152
KT12: W Vill 81V 170
TW11: Tedd 64Fa 130
Kingsend HA4: Ruis 32T 64
Kingsend Ct. HA4: Ruis 32U 64
KINGS FARM 2E 144
Kings Farm E17 25Dc 52
Kings Farm Av. TW10: Rich 56Qa 109
Kings Farm Rd. WD3: Chor 16F 24
Kingsfield SL4: Wind 3B 102
Kingsfield Av. HA2: Harr 28Da 45
Kingsfield Bus. Cen. RH1: Redh 7A 208
Kingsfield Ct. WD19: Wat 17Z 27
Kingsfield Dr. EN3: Enf W 7Zb 20
Kingsfield Ho. SE9 62Mc 137
Kingsfield Rd. HA1: Harr 31Fa 66
WD19: Wat 17Z 27
Kingsfield Ter. DA1: Dart 57Md 119
HA1: Harr 32Fa 66
Kingsfield Way EN3: Enf W 7Zb 20
RH1: Redh 7A 208
Kingsford St. NW5 36Hb 69
Kingsford Way E6 43Pc 94
King's Gdns. NW6 38Cb 69
Kings Gdns. IG1: Ilf 32Tc 74
KT12: Walt T 74X 151
RM14: Upm 31Ud 78
Kings Gth. M. SE23 61Yb 136
Kings Ga. KT15: Add 77K 149
Kingsgate AL3: St A 4P 5
HA9: Wemb 34Sa 67
Kingsgate Av. N3 27Cb 49
Kingsgate Bus. Cen. *KT2: King T* 67Na 131
(off Kingsgate Rd.)
Kingsgate Cl. BR5: St P 68Yc 139
DA7: Bex 53Ad 117
Kingsgate Est. N1 37Ub 71
Kingsgate Ho. SW9 53Qb 112
Kingsgate Mans. WC1 7H 217
Kings Ga. M. *N8* 29Pb 50
(off Spencer Rd.)
Kingsgate Pde. SW1 4C 228
Kingsgate Pl. NW6 38Cb 69
Kingsgate Rd. KT1: King T 67Na 131
KT2: King T 67Na 131
NW6 38Cb 69
Kings Ga. Wlk. SW1 3C 228
Kings Grange HA4: Ruis 32V 64
Kings Grn. IG10: Lough 13Nc 36
Kingsground SE9 59Mc 115
King's Gro. SE15 52Xb 113
(not continuous)
Kings Gro. RM1: Rom 29Jd 56
Kingsgrove Cl. DA14: Sidc 63Vc 139
Kings Hall Leisure Cen. 36Yb 72
Kings Hall M. SE13 55Ec 114
Kings Hall Rd. BR3: Beck 66Ac 136
Kings Head Hill E4 17Dc 34
Kingshead Ho. NW7 21Xa 48
Kings Head La. KT14: Byfl 83M 169
Kings Head Pas. *SW4* 56Mb 112
(off Clapham Pk. Rd.)
Kings Head Theatre 39Rb 71
(off Upper St.)
King's Head Yd. SE1 7F 225 (46Tb 91)
King's Highway SE18 51Uc 116
King's Hill IG10: Lough 12Nc 36
Kingshill Av. HA3: Kenton 28Ka 46
KT4: Wor Pk 73Wa 154
RM5: Col R 23Ed 56
UB4: Hayes, Yead 41U 84
UB5: N'olt 41W 84
Kingshill Cl. UB4: Hayes 41W 84
WD23: Bush 16Ea 28
Kingshill Ct. EN5: Barn 14Ab 30
Kingshill Dr. HA3: Kenton 26Ka 46
Kingshold Rd. E9 38Yb 72
Kingsholm Gdns. SE9 56Mc 115
King's Ho. *SW10* 51Fb 111
(off King's Rd.)
Kings Ho. *SW8* 52Nb 112
(off Sth. Lambeth Rd.)
King's Ho. Studios *SW10* 51Fb 111
(off Lamont Rd. Pas.)
Kingshurst Rd. SE12 59Jc 115
Kingside SE18 48Nc 94
Kingsingfield Cl. TN15: W King 80Ud 164
Kingsingfield Rd. TN15: W King 81Ud 184
Kings Keep BR2: Brom 68Gc 137
KT1: King T 70Na 131
SW15 57Za 110
KINGSLAND 37Ub 71
Kingsland EN6: Pot B 5Bb 17
NW8 1E 214 (39Gb 69)
Kingsland Grn. E8 37Ub 71
Kingsland High St. E8 37Vb 71
Kingsland Pas. E8 37Ub 71
Kingsland Rd. E2 3J 219 (41Ub 91)
E8 41Ub 91
E13 41Lc 93
HP1: Hem H 4J 3
Kingsland Shop. Cen. E8 37Vb 71
King's La. WD4: Chfd 3J 11
Kings La. GU20: W'sham 8C 146
SM1: Sutt 79Fb 155
TW20: Eng G 4L 125
KINGS LANGLEY 1Q 12
Kings Langley By-Pass HP1: Hem H 4G 2
HP3: Hem H 4G 2
WD4: K Lan 7L 3
Kingslawn Cl. SW15 57Xa 110
Kingslea KT22: Lea 92Ja 192
Kingslee Ct. SM2: Sutt 80Db 155
Kingsleigh Cl. TW8: Bford 51Ma 109
Kingsleigh Pl. CR4: Mitc 69Hb 133
Kingsleigh Wlk. BR2: Brom 70Hc 137
Kingsley Av. DA1: Dart 57Qd 119
EN8: Chesh 1Xb 19
SM1: Sutt 77Fb 155
SM7: Bans 87Cb 175
TW3: Houn 54Ea 108
TW20: Eng G 5M 125
UB1: S'hall 45Ca 85
W13 43Ja 86
WD6: Bore 12Pa 29
Kingsley Cl. N2 29Eb 49
RM10: Dag 35Dd 76
Kingsley Ct. DA6: Bex 56Cd 118
HA8: Edg 20Ra 29
KT4: Wor Pk 75Va 154
(off The Avenue)
KT12: Walt T 76W 150
(off Ashley Pk. Rd.)
NW2 37Xa 68
RM2: Rom 30Kd 57
Kingsley Dr. KT4: Wor Pk 75Va 154
Kingsley Flats SE1 5H 231
Kingsley Gdns. E4 22Cc 52
KT16: Ott 79F 148
RM11: Horn 28Md 57
Kingsley Gro. RH2: Reig 9J 207
Kingsley Ho. *SW3* 51Fb 111
(off Beaufort St.)
W14 49Ab 88
(off Avonmore Pl.)
Kingsley Mans. *W14* 51Ab 110
(off Greyhound Rd.)
Kingsley M. BR7: Chst 65Rc 138
E1 45Xb 91
W8 48Db 89
Kingsley Path SL2: Slou 2B 80
Kingsley Pl. N6 31Jb 70
Kingsley Rd. BR6: Chels 80Vc 161
CM13: Hut 17Fe 41
CR0: C'don 74Qb 156
E7 38Jc 73
E17 26Ec 52
HA2: Harr 35Ea 66
HA5: Pinn 28Ba 45
IG6: Ilf 25Sc 54
IG10: Lough 13Tc 36
N13 21Qb 50
NW6 39Bb 69
SW19 64Db 133
TW3: Houn 53Da 107
Kingsley St. SW11 55Hb 111
Kingsley Wlk. RM16: Grays 9C 100
Kingsley Way N2 29Eb 49
Kingsley Wood Dr. SE9 62Pc 138
Kings Lodge *HA4: Ruis* 32U 64
(off Pembroke Rd.)
N12 23Eb 49
Kingslyn Cres. SE19 67Ub 135
Kings Lynn Cl. RM3: Rom 23Md 57
Kings Lynn Dr. RM3: Rom 23Md 57
Kings Lynn Path RM3: Rom 23Md 57
Kings Mall W6 49Ya 88
Kingsman Dr. RM16: Grays 45De 99
Kingsman Pde. SE18 48Pc 94
Kingsman Rd. SS17: Stan H 2K 101
Kings Mans. *SW3* 51Gb 111
(off Lawrence St.)
Kingsman St. SE18 48Pc 94
Kings Mead RH1: S Nut 8E 208
Kingsmead EN5: New Bar 14Cb 31
EN6: Cuff 1Nb 18
EN8: Chesh 1Zb 20
GU21: Wok 88C 168
KT13: Weyb 79T 150
TN16: Big H 88Mc 179
TW10: Rich 58Pa 109
Kingsmead Av. CR4: Mitc 69Lb 134
KT4: Wor Pk 75Xa 154
KT6: Surb 75Qa 153
N9 18Xb 33
NW9 31Ta 67
RM1: Rom 30Gd 56
TW16: Sun 68Y 129
Kingsmead Cl. DA15: Sidc 61Wc 139
KT19: Ewe 80Ta 153
TW11: Tedd 65Ka 130
Kingsmead Cotts. BR2: Brom 74Nc 160
Kingsmead Ct. N6 31Mb 70
Kingsmead Dr. UB5: N'olt 38Ba 65
Kingsmead Ho. E9 35Ac 72
SL1: Slou 6G 80
Kingsmead Lodge SM2: Sutt 79Fb 155
Kingsmead Mans. *RM1: Rom* 30Hd 56
(off Kingsmead Av.)
Kingsmeadow 69Qa 131
Kings Mdw. WD4: K Lan 10A 4
Kingsmeadow Athletics Cen. 69Qa 131
Kings Mdw. Ct. *EN9: Walt A* 6Jc 21
(off Horseshoe Cl.)
Kings Mead Pk. KT10: Clay 80Ga 152
Kingsmead Rd. SW2 61Qb 134
Kingsmead Way E9 35Ac 72
Kingsmere Cl. SW15 55Za 110
Kingsmere Pk. NW9 32Ra 67
Kingsmere Pl. N16 32Tb 71
Kingsmere Rd. SW19 61Za 132
King's M. SW4 57Nb 112
WC1 6J 217 (42Pb 90)
Kings M. *HP2: Hem H* 1M 3
(off George St.)
IG7: Chig 19Sc 36
Kingsmill NW8 1C 214
Kingsmill Bus. Pk. KT1: King T 69Pa 131
Kingsmill Ct. AL10: Hat 2D 8
Kingsmill Gdns. RM9: Dag 36Bd 75
Kingsmill Ho. *SW3* 7E 226
(off Cale St.)
Kings Mill La. RH1: Redh, S Nut 10C 208
Kingsmill Rd. RM9: Dag 36Bd 75
Kingsmill Ter. NW8 1C 214 (40Fb 69)
Kings Mill Way UB9: Den 37L 63
Kingsmoor Pk. GU22: Wok 94B 188
Kingsnorth Ho. W10 44Za 88
Kingsnympton Pk. KT2: King T 66Ra 131
King's Oak WD3: Crox G 14Q 26
Kings Oak RM7: Mawney 27Cd 56
Kingsoak Ho. GU21: Wok 88C 168
King's Orchard SE9 58Nc 116
King's Paddock TW12: Hamp 67Ea 130
King's Pde. *HA8: Edg* 22Qa 47
(off Edgwarebury La.)
SM5: Cars 76Hb 155
(off Wrythe La.)
Kings Pde. N17 27Vb 51
NW10 39Ya 68
SS17: Stan H 2L 101
(off King St.)
W12 48Wa 88
WD18: Wat 15X 27
(off Vicarage Rd.)
Kings Pk. SL3: Coln 52F 104
Kingspark Bus. Cen.
KT3: N Mald 70Sa 131
Kingspark Ct. E18 27Jc 53
Kings Pk. Ind. Est. WD4: K Lan 1R 12
King's Pas. KT2: King T 67Ma 131
Kings Pas. E11 31Gc 73
KT1: King T 68Ma 131
Kings Place 1G 217 (40Nb 70)
King's Pl. SE1 2D 230 (47Sb 91)
W4 50Sa 87
Kings Pl. IG9: Buck H 19Lc 35
IG10: Lough 17Mc 35
King Sq. EC1 4D 218 (41Sb 91)
Kings Quarter Apartments *N1* 39Pb 70
(off Copenhagen St.)
King's Quay *SW10* 53Eb 111
(off Chelsea Harbour Dr.)
Kings Reach SL3: L'ly 9N 81
Kings Reach Twr. SE1 6A 224
Kings Ride Ga. TW10: Rich 56Qa 109
Kingsridge SW19 61Ab 132
Kingsridge Gdns. DA1: Dart 58Md 119
King's Rd. AL2: Lon C 8G 6
AL3: St A 2P 5
BR6: Orp 77Vc 161
CM14: B'wood, W'ley 19Yd 40
E6 39Lc 73
KT2: King T 66Na 131
KT6: Surb 74La 152
N17 25Vb 51
RM1: Rom 29Jd 56
SL1: Slou 8J 81
SL4: Wind 4H 103
SL5: S'dale, S'hill 1B 146
SM2: Sutt 82Cb 175
SW3 7E 226 (52Db 111)
SW6 52Db 111
SW10 52Db 111
SW19 65Cb 133
TW11: Tedd 64Fa 130
UB7: W Dray 47P 83
UB8: Uxb 40M 63
Kings Rd. CR4: Mitc 69Jb 134
E4 18Fc 35
E11 31Gc 73
EN5: Barn 13Ya 30
EN8: Walt C 5Ac 20
GU21: Wok 88C 168
GU24: W End 6E 166
HA2: Harr 33Ba 65
HP8: Chal G 19A 24
IG11: Bark 38Sc 74
KT12: Walt T 75X 151
KT15: New H 82K 169
N18 22Wb 51
N22 25Pb 50
NW10 38Xa 68
SE25 69Wb 135
SW14 55Ta 109
TN16: Big H 88Lc 179
TW1: Twick 58Ka 108
TW10: Rich 58Pa 109
TW13: Felt 60Y 107
TW20: Egh 63C 126
W5 43Ma 87
King's Scholars' Pas. SW1 4B 228
King's Shade Wlk. KT19: Eps 85Ta 173
King Stable St. SL4: Eton 2H 103
King Stairs Cl. SE16 47Xb 91
King's Ter. NW1 1B 216 (39Lb 70)
TW7: Isle 56Ja 108
Kings Ter. SL3: L'ly 51D 104
Kingsthorpe Rd. SE26 63Zb 136
Kingston Av. KT22: Lea 93Ka 192
KT24: E Hor 98U 190
SM3: Cheam 76Ab 154
TW14: Felt 58U 106
UB7: Yiew 45P 83
(Ash Gro.)
UB7: Yiew 46P 83
(Whitethorn Av.)
Kingston Bri. KT1: King T 68Ma 131
Kingston Bus. Cen. KT9: Chess 76Na 153
Kingston By-Pass KT3: N Mald 71Ua 154
KT6: Surb 76Ma 153
SW15 63Ua 132
SW20 68Wa 132
Kingston By-Pass Rd. KT6: Surb 75Ga 152
KT10: Hin W, Surb 75Ga 152
Kingston Cl. RM6: Chad H 27Ad 55
(not continuous)
TW11: Tedd 65Ka 130
UB5: N'olt 39Ba 65
Kingston Ct. DA11: Nflt 57De 121
Kingston Crematorium
KT1: King T 69Qa 131
Kingston Cres. BR3: Beck 67Bc 136
TW15: Ashf 64L 127
Kingston Gdns. CR0: Bedd 76Nb 156
Kingston Hall Rd. KT1: King T 69Ma 131
Kingston Hill KT2: King T 67Qa 131
Kingston Hill Av.
RM6: Chad H 27Ad 55
Kingston Hill Pl. KT2: King T 63Sa 131
Kingston Ho. *KT1: King T* 70Ma 131
(off Surbiton Rd.)
NW1 1C 216
(off Camden St.)
NW6 38Ab 68
Kingston Ho. E. SW7 2D 226
Kingston Ho. Est. KT6: Surb 72Ka 152
Kingston Ho. Gdns.
KT22: Lea 93Ka 192
Kingston Ho. Nth. SW7 2D 226
Kingston Ho. Sth. SW7 2D 226
Kingstonian FC 69Qa 131
Kingston La. KT24: W Hor 99Q 190
TW11: Tedd 64Ja 130
UB7: W Dray 47P 83
UB8: Hil 41N 83
Kingston Lodge
KT3: N Mald 70Ua 132
Kingston Mans. *SW9* 53Pb 112
(off Clapham Rd.)
Kingston Pl. HA3: Hrw W 24Ha 46
Kingston Ri. KT15: New H 82J 169
Kingston Rd. EN4: E Barn 15Fb 31
IG1: Ilf 35Rc 74
KT1: King T 69Ra 131
KT3: N Mald 69Ra 131
KT4: Wor Pk 75Ra 153
KT5: Surb 75Ra 153
KT17: Ewe 81Va 174
KT19: Ewe 75Ra 153
KT22: Lea 90Ja 172
(not continuous)
N9 19Wb 33
RM1: Rom 28Hd 56
SW15 61Wa 132
SW19 61Wa 132
(Norstead Pl.)
SW19 68Bb 133
(Rothesay Av.)
SW20 68Za 132
TW11: Tedd 64Ka 130
TW15: Ashf 65N 127
TW18: Staines 63H 127
UB2: S'hall 47Ba 85
Kingston Sq. *KT22: Lea* 91Ja 192
(off Buffers La.)
SE19 64Tb 135
Kingston University
Kingston Hill Campus 64Ta 131
Knights Pk. Campus 69Na 131
Penrhyn Road Campus 70Na 131
Roehampton Vale Cen. 62Va 132
KINGSTON UPON THAMES 68Ma 131
Kingston upon Thames Art Gallery & Mus.
68Na 131
KINGSTON VALE 63Ua 132
Kingston Va. SW15 63Ta 131
Kingstown St. NW1 39Jb 70
(not continuous)
King St. DA12: Grav'nd 8D 122
E13 42Jc 93
EC2 3E 224 (44Sb 91)
KT16: Chert 74J 149
N2 27Fb 49
N17 25Vb 51
SS17: Stan H 2L 101
SW1 7C 222 (46Lb 90)
TW1: Twick 60Ja 108
TW9: Rich 57Ma 109
UB2: S'hall 48Aa 85
W3 46Sa 87
W6 49Wa 88
WC2 4F 223 (45Nb 90)
WD18: Wat 14Y 27
King St. Cloisters *W6* 49Xa 88
(off King St.)
King St. M. N2 27Fb 49
King St. Pde. *TW1: Twick* 60Ja 108
(off King St.)
Kingsville Ct. UB7: Yiew 45M 83
Kings Wlk. CR2: Sande 86Xb 177
RM17: Grays 51Ce 121
Kings Wlk. Shop. Cen.
SW3 7F 227 (50Hb 89)
Kings Warren KT22: Oxs 83Ea 172
Kingswater Pl. SW11 52Gb 111
King's Way CR0: Wadd 78Pb 156
Kings Way HA1: Harr 28Ga 46
Kingsway BR4: W W'ck 76Gc 159
BR5: Pet W 71Tc 160
EN3: Pond E 15Xb 33
EN6: Cuff 2Nb 18
GU21: Wok 10P 167
HA9: Wemb 35Na 67
IG8: Wfd G 22Lc 53
KT3: N Mald 70Ya 132
N12 23Eb 49
SL0: Iver 44G 82
SL2: Farn C 7F 60
SL9: Chal P 27A 42
SW14 55Ra 109
TW19: Stanw 60M 105
UB3: Hayes 43S 84
WC2 2H 223 (44Pb 90)
Kingsway, The KT17: Ewe 83Ua 174
Kingsway Av. CR2: Sels 81Yb 178
GU21: Wok 10P 167
Kingsway Bus. Pk. TW12: Hamp 67Ba 129
Kingsway Cres. HA2: Harr 28Ea 46
Kingsway Est. N18 23Zb 52
Kingsway Mans. WC1 7H 217
Kingsway Pl. SL2: Farn C 7F 60
Kingsway Nth. Orbital Rd.
WD25: Wat 7V 12
Kingsway Pde. *N16* 34Tb 71
(off Albion Rd.)
Kingsway Pl. EC1 5A 218
Kingsway Rd. SM3: Cheam 80Ab 154
Kingsway Ter. KT13: Weyb 81Q 170
Kingswear Rd. HA4: Ruis 33W 64
NW5 34Kb 70
Kingswell Ride EN6: Cuff 2Nb 18
Kingswey Bus. Pk. GU21: Wok 86E 168
King's Wharf *SE10* 51Dc 114
(off Wood Wharf)
Kings Wharf *E8* 39Ub 71
(off Kingsland Rd.)
Kingswick Cl. SL5: S'hill 10C 124
Kingswick Dr. SL5: S'hill 10B 124
KINGSWOOD
KT20 96Ab 194
WD25 6X 13
Kingswood *E2* 40Yb 72
(off Cyprus St.)
Kingswood Av. BR2: Brom 69Gc 137
BR8: Swan 70Hd 140
CR2: Sande 87Xb 177
CR7: Thor H 71Qb 156
DA17: Belv 49Bd 95
NW6 39Ab 68
TW3: Houn 53Ba 107
TW12: Hamp 65Da 129
Kingswood Cl. BR6: Orp 73Uc 160
DA1: Dart 58Ld 119
EN1: Enf 15Ub 33
KT3: N Mald 72Va 154
KT6: Surb 73Na 153
KT13: Weyb 80R 150
N20 17Eb 31
SW8 52Nb 112
TW15: Ashf 64T 128
TW20: Eng G 3P 125
Kings Wood Ct. TW10: Rich 57Pa 109
Kingswood Ct. E4 22Cc 52
GU21: Wok 88A 168
KT20: Kgswd 96Ab 194
NW6 38Cb 69
(off West End La.)
SE13 58Fc 115
TN15: W King 80Ud 164
Kingswood Creek TW19: Wray 7P 103
Kingswood Dr. SE19 63Ub 135
SM2: Sutt 81Db 175
SM5: Cars 74Hb 155
Kingswood Est. SE21 63Ub 135
Kingswood Flds. Bus. Pk.
KT20: Kgswd 97Cb 195
Kingswood Golf Course 96Cb 195
Kingswood Grange
KT20: Lwr K 100Cb 195
Kingswood Hgts. *E18* 25Jc 53
(off Queen Mary Av.)
Kingswood Ho. KT20: Kgswd 92Bb 195
SL2: Slou 3G 80
Kingswood La. CR2: Sande 86Zb 178
CR6: W'ham 87Yb 178
Kingswood M. N15 28Rb 51
Kings Wood Pk. CM16: Epp 1Xc 23
Kingswood Pk. CM16: Epp 1Xc 23
KT20: Kgswd 93Ab 194
N3 26Bb 49
Kingswood Pl. CR3: Cat'm 95Vb 197
SE13 56Gc 115
UB3: Hayes 43U 84
Kingswood Ri. TW20: Eng G 4P 125
Kingswood Rd. BR2: Brom 70Fc 137
E11 31Gc 73
HA9: Wemb 34Qa 67
IG3: Ilf 32Wc 75
KT20: Tad 93Xa 194
SE20 65Yb 136
SW2 58Nb 112
SW19 66Bb 133
TN13: Dun G 92Gd 202
W4 48Sa 87
WD25: Wat 6X 13
Kingswood Ter. W4 48Sa 87
Kingswood Way
CR2: Sande, Sels 85Yb 178
(not continuous)
SM6: Wall 78Nb 156
Kingsworth Cl. BR3: Beck 71Ac 158
Kingsworthy Cl. KT1: King T 69Pa 131
Kings Yd. *SW15* 55Ya 110
(off Lwr. Richmond Rd.)
Kingthorpe Rd. NW10 38Ta 67
Kingthorpe Ter. NW10 37Ta 67
Kington Ho. *NW6* 39Db 69
(off Mortimer Cres.)
Kingward Ho. *E1* 43Wb 91
(off Hanbury St.)
King Wardrobe Apartments *EC4* 3C 224
(off Carter La.)
Kingwell Rd. EN4: Had W 10Fb 17
Kingweston Cl. NW2 34Ab 68
King William IV Gdns. SE20 65Yb 136
King William Ct. *EN9: Walt A* 7Ec 20
(off Kendal Rd.)
King William La. SE10 50Gc 93
King William's Ct. *SE10* 51Fc 115
(off Park Row)
King William St. EC4 3G 225 (44Tb 91)
King William Wlk. SE10 51Ec 114
(not continuous)
Kingwood Gdns. *E1* 44Wb 91
(off Piazza Wlk.)
Kingwood Rd. SW6 53Ab 110
Kinlet Rd. SE18 53Sc 116
Kinloch Dr. NW9 31Ta 67
Kinloch St. N7 34Pb 70
Kinloss Ct. N3 28Bb 49
Kinloss Gdns. N3 27Bb 49
Kinloss Rd. SM5: Cars 73Eb 155
Kinnaird Av. BR1: Brom 65Hc 137
W4 52Sa 109
Kinnaird Cl. BR1: Brom 65Hc 137
SL1: Slou 4A 80
Kinnaird Ho. SE17 5G 231 (49Tb 91)
Kinnaird Way IG8: Wfd G 23Pc 54
Kinnear Apartments N8 27Pb 50
Kinnear Rd. W12 47Va 88
Kinnersley Wlk. RH2: Reig 10J 207
Kinnerton Pl. Nth. SW1 2G 227
Kinnerton Pl. Sth. SW1 2G 227
Kinnerton St. SW1 2H 227 (47Jb 90)
Kinnerton Yd. SW1 2G 227
Kinnoul Rd. W6 51Ab 110
Kinross Av. KT4: Wor Pk 75Wa 154
Kinross Cl. HA3: Kenton 29Pa 47
HA8: Edg 19Ra 29
TW16: Sun 64V 128
Kinross Ct. *BR1: Brom* 67Hc 137
(off Highland Rd.)
SE6 60Hc 115
Kinross Dr. TW16: Sun 64V 128
Kinross Ho. *N1* 39Pb 70
(off Bemerton Est.)
Kinross Ter. E17 26Bc 52
Kinsale Cl. NW7 23Za 48
Kinsale Rd. SE15 55Wb 113
Kinsella Gdns. SW19 64Xa 132
Kinsham Ho. *E2* 42Wb 91
(off Ramsey St.)
Kinsheron Pl. KT8: E Mos 70Ea 130
Kintore Way SE1 5K 231 (49Vb 91)
Kintyre Cl. SW16 68Pb 134
Kintyre Ct. SW2 59Nb 112
Kintyre Ho. *E14* 46Ec 92
(off Coldharbour)
Kintyre Pl. *WD18: Wat* 16V 26
(off Explorer Dr.)
Kinveachy Gdns. SE7 50Nc 94

Kinver Ho.—Lagonier Ho.

Kinver Ho. N19 33Mb 70
Kinver Rd. SE26 63Yb 136
Kipings KT20: Tad 93Za 194
Kipling Av. RM18: Tilb 3D 122
Kipling Cl. CM14: W'ley 22Xd 58
Kipling Ct. SL4: Wind 4F 102
W7 45Ha 86
Kipling Dr. SW19 65Fb 133
Kipling Est. SE1 2G 231 (47Tb 91)
Kipling Ho. N19 32Nb 70
(off Charles St.)
SE5 52Tb 113
(off Elmington Est.)
Kipling Pl. HA7: Stan 23Ha 46
Kipling Rd. DA1: Dart 57Rd 119
DA7: Bex 53Ad 117
Kipling St. SE1 2G 231 (47Tb 91)
Kipling Ter. N9 20Tb 33
Kipling Twr. W3 48Sa 87
(off Palmerston Rd.)
Kipling Towers RM3: Rom 24Kd 57
KIPPINGTON 98Jd 202
Kippington Cl. TN13: S'oaks 96Hd 202
Kippington Dr. SE9 60Mc 115
Kippington Rd. TN13: S'oaks 96Jd 202
Kira Bldg. E3 41Bc 92
Kiran Apartments E1 43Vb 91
(off Chicksand St.)
Kirby Cl. HA6: Nwood 23V 44
IG6: Ilf 23Uc 54
IG10: Lough 17Nc 36
KT19: Ewe 78Va 154
RM3: Rom 22Qd 57
Kirby Est. SE16 48Xb 91
UB7: Yiew 45M 83
Kirby Gro. SE1 1H 231 (47Ub 91)
Kirby Rd. DA2: Dart 59Td 120
GU21: Wok 9N 167
Kirby St. EC1 7A 218 (43Qb 90)
Kirby Way KT12: Walt T 72Y 151
UB8: Hil 42P 83
Kirchen Rd. W13 45Ka 86
Kirkby Apartments E3 43Bc 92
(off St Paul's Way)
Kirkby Cl. N11 23Jb 50
Kirkcaldy Grn. WD19: Wat 20Y 27
Kirkcourt TN13: S'oaks 95Jd 202
Kirkdale SE26 61Xb 135
Kirkdale Cnr. SE26 63Yb 136
Kirkdale Rd. E11 32Gc 73
Kirkeby Ho. EC1 7K 217
Kirkfield Cl. W13 46Ka 86
Kirkgate, The KT17: Eps 85Ua 174
Kirkham Apartments IG11: Bark 38Sc 74
(off Linton Rd.)
Kirkham Ho. RM3: Rom 22Md 57
(off Montgomery Cres.)
Kirkham Rd. E6 44Nc 94
Kirkham St. SE18 51Uc 116
Kirk Ho. HA9: Wemb 34Na 67
Kirkland Av. GU21: Wok 8J 167
IG5: Ilf 26Qc 54
Kirkland Cl. DA15: Sidc 58Uc 116
Kirkland Dr. EN2: Enf 11Sb 33
Kirkland Ho. E14 50Dc 92
(off St Davids Sq.)
E14 50Dc 92
(off Westferry Rd.)
Kirkland Ter. BR3: Beck 65Cc 136
Kirkland Wlk. E8 37Vb 71
Kirk La. SE18 51Sc 116
Kirkleas Rd. KT6: Surb 74Na 153
Kirklees Rd. CR7: Thor H 71Qb 156
RM8: Dag 36Yc 75
Kirkley Rd. SW19 67Cb 133
Kirkly Cl. CR2: Sande 81Ub 177
Kirkman Pl. W1 1D 222
Kirkmichael Rd. E14 44Ec 92
Kirk Ri. SM1: Sutt 76Db 155
Kirk Rd. E17 30Bc 52
Kirkside Rd. SE3 51Jc 115
Kirk's Place 43Bc 92
Kirkstall Av. N17 28Tb 51
Kirkstall Gdns. SW2 60Nb 112
Kirkstall Ho. SW1 7K 227
Kirkstall Rd. SW2 60Mb 112
Kirkstead Ct. E5 35Zb 72
Kirksted Rd. SM4: Mord 74Db 155
Kirkstone NW1 3B 216
Kirkstone Way BR1: Brom 66Gc 137
Kirk St. WC1 6J 217
Kirkton Rd. N15 28Ub 51
Kirkwall Pl. E2 41Yb 92
Kirkwall Spur SL1: Slou 3J 81
Kirkwood Pl. NW1 38Jb 70
Kirkwood Rd. SE15 54Xb 113
Kirn Rd. W13 45Ka 86
Kirrane Cl. KT3: N Mald 71Va 154
Kirtley Ho. SW8 53Lb 112
Kirtley Rd. SE26 63Ac 136
Kirtling St. SW8 52Lb 112
Kirton Cl. RM12: Horn 37Ld 77
W4 49Ta 87
Kirton Gdns. E2 4K 219 (41Vb 91)
(not continuous)
Kirton Lodge SW18 58Db 111
Kirton Rd. E13 40Lc 73
Kirton Wlk. HA8: Edg 24Sa 47
Kirwyn Way SE5 52Rb 113
Kitcat Ter. E3 41Cc 92
Kitchen Ct. E10 33Dc 72
Kitchener Av. DA12: Grav'nd 3E 144
Kitchener Cl. AL1: St A 3F 6
Kitchener Ho. SE18 52Qc 116
SL9: Chal P 21A 42
Kitchener Rd. CR7: Thor H 69Tb 135
E7 37Kc 73
E17 25Dc 52
N2 27Gb 49
N17 27Ub 51
RM10: Dag 37Dd 76
Kite Ho. SE1 49Xb 91
SE3 56Kc 115
Kite Pl. E2 41Wb 91
(off Warner Pl.)
Kite Yd. SW11 53Hb 111
(off Cambridge Rd.)
Kitley Gdns. SE19 67Vb 135
Kitsmead La. KT16: Longc, Vir W 4N 147
Kitson Rd. SE5 52Tb 113
SW13 53Wa 110
Kitswell Way WD7: R'lett 5Ha 14
Kitters Grn. WD5: Ab L 3U 12
Kittiwake Cl. CR2: Sels 82Ac 178
Kittiwake Ct. SE1 2E 230
(off Gt. Dover St.)
SE8 51Bc 114
(off Abinger Gro.)
Kittiwake Ho. SL1: Slou 6J 81
Kittiwake Pl. SM1: Sutt 78Bb 155
Kittiwake Rd. UB5: N'olt 41Z 85
Kittiwake Way UB4: Yead 43Z 85
Kitto Rd. SE14 54Zb 114
KITT'S END 9Ab 16
Kitts End Rd. EN5: Barn 8Za 16
Kiver Rd. N19 33Mb 70
Klea Av. SW4 58Lb 112
Kleine Wharf N1 39Ub 71
Klein's Wharf E14 48Cc 92
(off Westferry Rd.)
Knapdale Cl. SE23 61Xb 135
KNAPHILL 9H 167
Knapmill Rd. SE6 61Cc 136
Knapmill Way SE6 61Dc 136
Knapp Cl. NW10 37Ua 68
Knapp Rd. E3 42Cc 92
TW15: Ashf 63P 127
Knapton M. SW17 65Jb 134
Knaresborough Dr. SW18 60Db 111
Knaresborough Pl. SW5 49Db 89
Knatchbull Rd. NW10 39Ta 67
SE5 54Rb 113
Knatts La. TN15: Knat, W King 83Td 184
KNATTS VALLEY 83Td 184
Knatts Valley Cvn. Pk.
TN15: Knat 82Ud 184
Knatts Valley Rd. TN15: Knat 79Sd 164
Knave Wood Rd. TN15: Kems'g 89Nd 183
Knebworth Av. E17 25Cc 52
Knebworth Cl. EN5: New Bar 14Db 31
Knebworth Ho. SW8 54Mb 112
Knebworth Path WD6: Bore 14Ta 29
Knebworth Rd. N16 35Ub 71
Knee Hill SE2 49Xc 95
Knee Hill Cres. SE2 49Xc 95
Kneller Gdns. TW7: Isle 58Fa 108
Kneller Ho. UB5: N'olt 40Z 65
(off Academy Gdns.)
Kneller Rd. KT3: N Mald 73Ua 154
SE4 56Ac 114
TW2: Whitt 58Ea 108
Knevett Ter. TW3: Houn 56Ca 107
Knifton Ct. EN6: Pot B 3Za 16
Knight Cl. RM8: Dag 33Yc 75
Knight Ct. E4 18Ec 34
(off The Ridgeway)
N15 29Ub 51
Knighten St. E1 46Xb 91
Knighthead Point E14 47Cc 92
Knight Ho. SE17 6H 231
Knightland Rd. E5 33Xb 71
Knightleas Ct. NW2 37Ya 68
Knightleys Ct. E10 32Ac 72
(off Wellington Rd.)
Knightley Wlk. SW18 56Cb 111
Knighton Cl. CR2: S Croy 81Rb 177
IG8: Wfd G 21Kc 53
RM7: Rom 30Fd 56
Knighton Dr. IG8: Wfd G 21Kc 53
Knighton Grn. IG9: Buck H 19Kc 35
Knighton La. IG9: Buck H 19Kc 35
Knighton Pk. Rd. SE26 64Zb 136
Knighton Pl. IG9: Buck H 19Kc 35
(off Knighton La.)
KT11: Cobh 88Aa 171
Knighton Rd. E7 34Jc 73
RH1: Redh 8A 208
RM7: Rom 30Ed 56
TN14: Otf 88Hd 182
Knighton Way La. UB9: Den 37K 63
Knightrider Ct. EC4 4D 224
Knightrider St. EC4 4C 224 (44Rb 91)
Knights Arc. SW1 2F 227
Knights Av. W5 47Na 87
KNIGHTSBRIDGE 2E 226 (47Gb 89)
Knightsbridge SW1 2E 226 (47Hb 89)
SW7 2E 226 (47Hb 89)
Knightsbridge Apartments, The
SW7 2F 227
Knightsbridge Ct. BR2: Brom 72Nc 160
(off Wells Vw. Dr.)
SL3: L'ly 49C 82
(off High St.)
SW1 2G 227
WD18: Wat 14U 26
Knightsbridge Cres.
TW18: Staines 65K 127
Knightsbridge Gdns. RM7: Rom 29Fd 56
Knightsbridge Grn. SW1 2F 227 (47Hb 89)
(not continuous)
Knightsbridge Way HP2: Hem H 1N 3
Knights Cl. E9 36Yb 72
KT8: W Mole 71Ba 151
SL4: Wind 3B 102
TW20: Egh 65F 126
Knightscote Cl. UB9: Hare 26M 43
Knights Ct. BR1: Brom 62Hc 137
KT1: King T 69Na 131
RM6: Chad H 30Ad 55
(off High Rd.)
WD23: B Hea 18Fa 28
Knights Cft. DA3: Nw A G 76Be 165
(not continuous)
Knights Fld. DA4: Eyns 76Nd 163
Knights Grn. WD3: Chor 13G 24
Knights Hill SE27 64Rb 135
Knights Hill Sq. SE27 63Rb 135
Knight's Ho. SW10 52Eb 111
(off Hortensia Rd.)
W14 50Bb 89
(off Baron's Ct. Rd.)
Knights Ho. SW8 52Nb 112
(off Sth. Lambeth Rd.)
Knights Mnr. Way DA1: Dart 57Pd 119
Knights Mead KT16: Chert 73K 149
Knight's Orchard AL3: St A 2A 6
Knight's Pk. KT1: King T 69Na 131
Knight's Pl. TW2: Twick 60Ga 108
Knights Pl. RH1: Redh 5A 208
SL4: Wind 4G 102
Knightsplace Farm Equestrian Cen.
9P 145
Knights Ridge BR6: Chels 78Xc 161
Knight's Rd. E16 47Jc 93
Knights Rd. HA7: Stan 21La 46
Knights Twr. SE8 51Cc 114
Knight's Wlk. SE11 6B 230 (49Rb 91)
(not continuous)
Knights Wlk. RM4: Abr 13Xc 37
Knights Way CM13: B'wood 20Ce 41
IG6: Ilf 23Sc 54
Knightswood GU21: Wok 10K 167
Knightswood Cl. HA8: Edg 19Sa 29
Knightswood Ct. N6 31Mb 70
Knightswood Ho. N12 23Eb 49
Knightswood Rd. RM13: Rain 40Jd 76
Knightwood Cl. RH2: Reig 8J 207
Knightwood Cres. KT3: N Mald 72Ua 154
Knipp Hill KT11: Cobh 85Ba 171
Knivet Rd. SW6 51Cb 111
KNOCKHALL 57Yd 120
Knockhall Chase
DA9: Ghithe 57Xd 120
Knockhall Rd. DA9: Ghithe 58Yd 120
KNOCKHOLT 89Xc 181
Knockholt Cl. SM2: Sutt 82Db 175
Knockholt Main Rd.
TN14: Knock 91Vc 201
KNOCKHOLT POUND 87Ad 181
Knockholt Rd. SE9 57Mc 115
TN14: Hals 86Bd 181
KNOCKMILL 84Vd 184
Knock Mill La. TN15: W King 85Wd 184
Knole 98Nd 203
Knole, The DA13: Ist R 6A 144
SE9 63Qc 138
Knole Academy Sports & Leisure Cen.
93Jd 202
Knole Cl. CR0: C'don 72Yb 158
Knole Ct. UB5: N'olt 41Y 85
(off Broomcroft Av.)
Knole Ga. DA15: Sidc 62Uc 138
Knole La. TN13: S'oaks 98Ld 203
Knole Pk. 97Md 203
Knole Pk. Golf Course 96Md 203
Knole Rd. DA1: Dart 59Jd 118
TN13: S'oaks 95Md 203
Knole Way TN13: S'oaks 97Ld 203
Knole Wood SL5: S'dale 4C 146
Knoll, The BR2: Hayes 75Jc 159
BR3: Beck 67Dc 136
HA1: Harr 32Ha 66
KT11: Cobh 85Ca 171
KT16: Chert 74H 149
KT22: Lea 93La 192
W13 43La 86
Knoll Ct. SE19 64Vb 135
(off Farquhar Rd.)
Knoll Cres. HA6: Nwood 26U 44
(not continuous)
Knoll Dr. N14 17Jb 32
Knolles Cres. AL9: Wel G 5D 8
Knoll Ho. NW8 40Eb 69
(off Carlton Hill)
Knollmead KT5: Surb 74Sa 153
Knoll Pk. Rd. KT16: Chert 74H 149
Knoll Ri. BR6: Orp 74Vc 161
Knoll Rd. DA5: Bexl 59Cd 118
DA14: Sidc 64Xc 139
SW18 57Eb 111
KNOLL RDBT. 93La 192
Knolls, The KT17: Eps D 88Ya 174
Knolls Cl. KT4: Wor Pk 76Xa 154
Knollys Cl. SW16 62Qb 134
Knolly's Ho. WC1 5F 217
Knollys Rd. SW16 62Pb 134
Knolton Way SL2: Slou 4M 81
Knot Ho. SE1 7K 225
Knotley Way BR4: W W'ck 75Dc 158
Knottisford St. E2 41Yb 92
Knotts Grn. M. E10 30Dc 52
Knotts Grn. Rd. E10 30Dc 52
Knotts Pl. TN13: S'oaks 96Jd 202
Knowlden Ho. E1 45Yb 92
(off Cable St.)
Knowle, The KT20: Tad 93Ya 194
Knowle Av. DA7: Bex 52Ad 117
Knowle Cl. SW9 55Qb 112
Knowledge Ct. SW16 69Pb 134
Knowle Gdns. KT14: W Byf 85H 169
KNOWLE GREEN 64K 127
Knowle Grn. TW18: Staines 64J 127
Knowle Gro. GU25: Vir W 3N 147
Knowle Gro. Cl. GU25: Vir W 3N 147
KNOWLE HILL 3N 147
Knowle Hill GU25: Vir W 3M 147
Knowle Lodge CR3: Cat'm 95Wb 197
Knowle Pk. KT11: Cobh 88Aa 171
Knowle Pk. Av. TW18: Staines 65K 127
Knowle Rd. BR2: Brom 75Pc 160
TW2: Twick 60Ga 108
Knowles Cl. UB7: Yiew 46N 83
Knowles Ct. HA1: Harr 30Ha 46
Knowles Hill Cres. SE13 57Fc 115
Knowles Ho. SW18 58Db 111
(off Neville Gill Cl.)
Knowles Wlk. SW4 55Lb 112
Knowles Wharf NW1 39Lb 70
(off St Pancras Way)
Knowl Hill GU22: Wok 91D 188
Knowl Pk. WD6: E'tree 15Na 29
Knowlton Cotts. RM15: S Ock 43Yd 98
Knowlton Grn. BR2: Brom 71Hc 159
Knowlton Ho. SW9 53Qb 112
(off Cowley Rd.)
Knowl Way WD6: E'tree 15Pa 29
Knowl Wood La. BR6: Farnb 75Qc 160
Knowsley Av. UB1: S'hall 46Da 85
Knowsley Rd. SW11 54Hb 111
Knox Ct. SW4 54Nb 112
Knox Rd. E7 37Hc 73
Knox St. W1 7F 215 (43Hb 89)
Knoyle Ho. W14 48Ab 88
(off Russell Rd.)
Knoyle St. SE14 51Ac 114
Knutsford Av. WD24: Wat 10Z 13
Koblenz Ho. N8 27Nb 50
(off Newland Rd.)
Kohat Rd. SW19 64Db 133
Koh-I-Noor Av. WD23: Bush 16Ca 27
Kola Ct. SL2: Slou 4M 81
Koonowla Cl. TN16: Big H 87Mc 179
Koops Mill M. SE1 48Vb 91
Kooringa CR6: W'ham 91Xb 197
Korda Cl. TW17: Shep 69P 127
WD6: Bore 12Sa 29
Korea Cotts. KT11: Cobh 88Z 171
Kossuth St. SE10 50Gc 93
Kotan Dr. TW18: Staines 63E 126
Kotata Ho. E20 37Ec 72
(off Ravens Wlk.)
Kotree Way SE1 49Wb 91
Kramer M. SW5 50Cb 89
Kreedman Wlk. E8 36Wb 71
Kreisel Wlk. TW9: Kew 51Pa 109
Kristina Ct. SM2: Sutt 79Cb 155
(off Overton Rd.)
Krithia Rd. RM9: Dag 39Xc 75
Krupnik Pl. EC2 5J 219
Kuala Gdns. SW16 67Pb 134
Kubrick Bus. Est. E7 35Kc 73
(off Station App.)
Kuhn Way E7 36Jc 73
Kurdish Mus. 49Wa 88
Kwame Ho. E16 45Rc 94
(off University Way)
Kwesi M. SE27 64Qb 134
Kydbrook Cl. BR5: Pet W 73Sc 160
Kyle Ho. NW6 39Cb 69
Kylemore Cl. E6 40Mc 73
Kylemore Rd. NW6 38Cb 69
Kylestrome Ho. SW1 6J 227
Kymberley Rd. HA1: Harr 30Ga 46
Kyme Rd. RM11: Horn 30Hd 56
Kymes Ct. HA2: Harr 33Fa 66
Kynance Cl. RM3: Rom 21Ld 57
Kynance Gdns. HA7: Stan 25La 46
Kynance M. SW7 4A 226 (48Db 89)
Kynance Pl. SW7 4A 226 (48Eb 89)
Kynaston Av. CR7: Thor H 71Sb 157
N16 34Vb 71
Kynaston Cl. HA3: Hrw W 24Fa 46
Kynaston Ct. CR3: Cat'm 97Ub 197
Kynaston Cres. CR7: Thor H 71Sb 157
Kynaston Rd. BR1: Brom 64Jc 137
BR5: Orp 73Xc 161
CR7: Thor H 71Sb 157
EN2: Enf 11Tb 33
N16 34Ub 71
Kynaston Wood HA3: Hrw W 24Fa 46
Kynersley Cl. SM5: Cars 76Hb 155
Kynoch Ct. SS17: Stan H 2N 101
Kynoch Rd. N18 21Yb 52
Kyrkly Ct. RM19: Purf 50Rd 97
(off Linnet Way)
Kyrle Rd. SW11 58Jb 112
Kytes Dr. WD25: Wat 5Z 13
Kytes Est. WD25: Wat 5Z 13
Kyverdale Rd. N16 31Vb 71

L

Laban Cen. 51Dc 114
Laban Wlk. SE8 51Dc 114
(off Copperas St.)
Laboratory Spa and Health Club, The
27Lb 50
Labour in Vain Rd.
TN15: Stans, Wro 85Zd 185
Labrun Sq. SE3 55Kc 115
Laburnham Ct. EN5: Barn 13Bb 31
RM14: Upm 31Wd 78
Laburnham Gdns. RM14: Upm 31Vd 78
Laburnham La. E2 1K 219 (40Vb 71)
Laburnum Av. BR8: Swan 69Ed 140
DA1: Dart 60Ld 119
N9 19Vb 33
N17 24Tb 51
RM12: Horn 33Jd 76
SM1: Sutt 76Gb 155
UB7: Yiew 45P 83
Laburnum Cl. E4 23Bc 52
EN8: Chesh 3Zb 20
HA0: Wemb 39Qa 67
N11 23Jb 50
SE15 52Yb 114
Laburnum Ct. E2 1K 219 (39Vb 71)
HA1: Harr 29Da 45
HA7: Stan 21La 46
SE16 47Yb 92
(off Albion St.)
UB8: Uxb 37L 63
(off Harefield Rd.)
Laburnum Cres. TW16: Sun 67X 129
Laburnum Gdns. CR0: C'don 73Zb 158
N21 19Sb 33
Laburnum Gro. AL2: Chis G 7P 5
DA11: Nflt 59Fe 121
HA4: Ruis 30T 44
KT3: N Mald 68Ta 131
N21 19Sb 33
NW9 31Sa 67
RM15: S Ock 41Yd 98
SL3: L'ly 51D 104
TW3: Houn 56Ba 107
UB1: S'hall 42Ba 85
Laburnum Ho. BR2: Brom 67Fc 137
RM10: Dag 33Cd 76
Laburnum Lodge N3 26Bb 49
Laburnum Pl. SE9 57Qc 116
TW20: Eng G 5M 125
Laburnum Rd. CM16: Coop 1Yc 23
CR4: Mitc 68Jb 134
GU22: Wok 2P 187
KT16: Chert 74J 149
KT18: Eps 85Ua 174
SW19 66Eb 133
UB3: Harl 49V 84
Laburnums, The E6 42Nc 94
Laburnum St. E2 1K 219 (39Vb 71)
Laburnum Wlk. RM12: Horn 36Ld 77
Laburnum Way BR2: Brom 73Qc 160
TW19: Stanw 60P 105
Labyrinth Twr. E8 37Vb 71
(off Dalston Sq.)
Lacebark Cl. DA15: Sidc 59Vc 117
Lace Ct. E1 43Zb 92
(off Master's St.)
Laceman M. RM5: Col R 23Ed 56
Lacewing Cl. E13 41Jc 93
Lacey Av. CR5: Coul 92Qb 196
Lacey Cl. N9 19Wb 33
TW20: Egh 66F 126
Lacey Dr. CR5: Coul 92Rb 197
HA8: Edg 21Na 47
RM8: Dag 34Yc 75
TW12: Hamp 67Ba 129
Lacey Grn. CR5: Coul 92Qb 196
Lacey Gro. UB10: Uxb 40N 63
Lacey M. E3 40Cc 72
Lacine Ct. SE16 47Zb 92
(off Christopher Cl.)
Lackford Rd. CR5: Chip 90Hb 175
Lackington St. EC2 7G 219 (43Tb 91)
Lackland Ho. SE1 7K 231
Lackmore Rd. EN1: Enf 7Yb 20
Lacland Ho. SW10 52Fb 111
(off Worlds End Est.)
Lacock Cl. SW19 65Eb 133
Lacock Ct. W13 46Ja 86
Lacon Ho. WC1 7H 217
Lacon Rd. SE22 56Wb 113
Lacrosse Way SW16 67Mb 134
Lacy Rd. SW15 56Za 110
Ladas Rd. SE27 63Sb 135
Ladbroke Cotts. RH1: Redh 5A 208
(off Ladbroke Rd.)
Ladbroke Ct. E1 1K 225 (44Vb 91)
RH1: Redh 4A 208
Ladbroke Cres. W11 44Ab 88
Ladbroke Gdns. W11 45Bb 89
Ladbroke Gro. RH1: Redh 5A 208
W10 42Za 88
W11 42Za 88
Ladbroke Gro. Ho. W11 45Bb 89
(off Ladbroke Gro.)
Ladbroke Grove Memorial 42Za 88
(off Canal Way)
Ladbroke M. W11 46Ab 88
Ladbroke Rd. EN1: Enf 16Vb 33
KT18: Eps 86Ta 173
RH1: Redh 5A 208
W11 46Bb 89
Ladbroke Sq. W11 45Bb 89
Ladbroke Ter. W11 45Bb 89
Ladbroke Wlk. W11 46Bb 89
Ladbrook Cl. BR1: Brom 65Gc 137
HA5: Pinn 29Ba 45
Ladbrooke Cl. EN6: Pot B 4Cb 17
Ladbrooke Cres. DA14: Sidc 62Zc 139
Ladbrooke Dr. EN6: Pot B 4Cb 17
Ladbrooke Rd. SL1: Slou 8G 80
Ladbrook Rd. SE25 70Tb 135
Ladderstile Ride KT2: King T 64Ra 131
Ladderswood Way N11 22Lb 50
Ladds Way BR8: Swan 70Fd 140
Ladies Gro. AL3: St A 1P 5
(not continuous)
Ladlands SE22 59Wb 113
Lady Anne Ct. E18 25Jc 53
(off Queen Mary Av.)
Lady Astor Ct. SL1: Slou 7J 81
Lady Aylesford Av. HA7: Stan 22Ja 46
Lady Booth Rd. KT1: King T 68Na 131
Lady Craig Ct. UB8: Hil 43R 84
Ladycroft Gdns. BR6: Farnb 78Sc 160
Ladycroft Rd. SE13 55Dc 114
Ladycroft Wlk. HA7: Stan 25Ma 47
Ladycroft Way BR6: Farnb 78Sc 160
Ladyday Pl. SL1: Slou 6G 80
Lady Dock Path SE16 47Ac 92
Lady Elizabeth Ho. SW14 55Sa 109
Ladyfern Ho. E3 43Cc 92
(off Gail St.)
Ladyfields DA11: Nflt 3B 144
IG10: Lough 14Sc 36
Ladyfields Cl. IG10: Lough 14Sc 36
Lady Florence Courtyard SE8 52Cc 114
(off Reginald Sq.)
Lady Forsdyke Way KT19: Eps 81Qa 173
Ladygate La. HA4: Ruis 30R 44
Ladygrove CR0: Sels 81Ac 178
Lady Harewood Way KT19: Eps 81Qa 173
Lady Hay KT4: Wor Pk 75Va 154
Lady Jane Ct. KT2: King T 68Pa 131
(off Cambridge Rd.)
Lady Jane Pl. DA1: Dart 54Pd 119
Lady Margaret Ho. SE17 51Tb 113
(off Queen's Row)
Lady Margaret Rd. N19 35Lb 70
NW5 36Lb 70
SL5: S'dale 4D 146
UB1: S'hall 45Ba 85
Lady May Ho. SE5 52Sb 113
(off Pitman St.)
Lady Mdw. WD4: K Lan 9M 3
Lady Micos Almshouses E1 44Yb 92
(off Aylward St.)
Lady Sarah Cohen Ho. N11 23Hb 49
(off Asher Loftus Way)
Lady's Cl. WD18: Wat 14Y 27
Lady Shaw Ct. N13 19Pb 32
Ladyship Ter. SE22 59Wb 113
Ladysmith Av. E6 40Nc 74
IG2: Ilf 31Uc 74
Ladysmith Cl. NW7 24Wa 48
Ladysmith Rd. AL3: St A 1B 6
E16 41Hc 93
EN1: Enf 13Ub 33
(not continuous)
HA3: W'stone 26Ga 46
N17 26Wb 51
N18 22Xb 51
SE9 58Qc 116
Lady Somerset Rd. NW5 35Kb 70
Lady Spencer's Gro. AL1: St A 3A 6
AL3: St A 3A 6
Lady's Wlk. TN15: Igh, Ivy H 96Wd 204
Ladythorpe Cl. KT15: Add 77K 149
Ladywalk WD3: Map C 22G 42
LADYWELL 57Dc 114
Ladywell Arena (Running Track)
58Cc 114
Ladywell Cl. SE4 57Cc 114
Ladywell Hgts. SE4 58Bc 114
Ladywell Rd. SE13 57Cc 114
Ladywell St. E15 39Hc 73
Ladywood Av. BR5: Pet W 71Uc 160
Ladywood Cl. WD3: Loud 13K 25
Ladywood Rd. DA2: Daren 64Ud 142
KT6: Surb 75Qa 153
Lady Yorke Pk. SL0: Iver H 37F 62
Laelia Ho's. AL1: St A 3E 6
LA Fitness
Brentwood 22Yd 58
Burnham 4C 80
Croydon 80Qb 156
Edgware 23Qa 47
Epsom 77Ta 153
Ewell 84Ya 174
Finchley 27Db 49
Golders Green 31Bb 69
Goldsworth 9P 167
Isleworth 55Ka 108
(off Swan St.)
London Wall 1F 225
Muswell Hill 28Kb 50
(off Hillfield Pk.)
New Barnet 14Fb 31
Northolt 39Ca 65
Northwood 26V 44
Orpington 67Zc 139
Purley 82Sb 177
South Kensington 5D 226 (49Gb 89)
Southgate 18Mb 32
St Pauls 1D 224
Sydenham 63Yb 136
Lafone Av. TW13: Felt 61Y 129
Lafone St. SE1 1K 231 (47Vb 91)
Lagado M. SE16 46Zb 92
Lagare Apartments SE1 1C 230
Lagham Pk. RH9: S God 9C 210
Lagham Rd. RH9: S God 10C 210
Laglands Cl. RH2: Reig 4L 207
Lagonda Av. IG6: Ilf 23Vc 55
Lagonda Ho. E3 42Cc 92
(off Tidworth Rd.)
Lagonda Way DA1: Dart 56Ld 119
Lagonier Ho. EC1 4E 218

Lagoon Rd.—Langholm Cl.

Lagoon Rd. BR5: St M Cry 71Yc 161
Laguna Ct. *AL1: St A* *2C 6*
(off Beaconsfield Rd.)
Laharna Trad. Est. WD24: Wat 10Y 13
Laidlaw Dr. N21 ....15Pb 32
Laing Cl. IG6: Ilf 23Tc 54
Laing Dean UB5: N'olt 39Y 65
Laing Ho. SE5 ....52Sb 113
Laings Av. CR4: Mitc 68Hb 133
Lainlock Pl. TW3: Houn 53Da 107
Lainson St. SW18 ....59Cb 111
Lairdale Cl. SE21 ....60Sb 113
Laird Av. RM16: Grays 47Fe 99
Laird Ho. *SE5* *52Sb 113*
(off Redcar St.)
Lairs Cl. N7 ....36Nb 70
Lait Ho. BR3: Beck 67Dc 136
Laitwood Rd. SW12 ....60Kb 112
Lakanal *SE5* *53Ub 113*
(off Sceaux Gdns.)
Lake, The WD23: B Hea 18Fa 28
Lake Av. BR1: Brom 65Jc 137
RM13: Rain 40Md 77
SL1: Slou 5H 81
Lake Bus. Cen. N17 ....24Wb 51
Lake Cl. KT14: Byfl 84M 169
RM8: Dag 34Zc 75
SW19 ....64Bb 133
Lakedale Ct. IG11: Bark 42Xc 95
Lakedale Rd. SE18 ....51Uc 116
Lake Dr. WD23: B Hea 19Fa 28
LAKE END 7A 80
Lake End Rd. SL4: Dor 5A 80
SL6: Dor R, Tap 5A 80
Lake Farm Country Pk. 46U 84
Lakefield Cl. SE20 ....66Xb 135
Lakefield Rd. N22 ....26Rb 51
Lakefields Cl. RM13: Rain 40Md 77
Lake Gdns. RM10: Dag 36Cd 76
SM6: Wall 76Kb 156
TW10: Ham 61Ka 130
Lakehall Gdns. CR7: Thor H 71Rb 157
Lakehall Rd. CR7: Thor H 71Rb 157
Lake Ho. SE1 ....2D 230
Lake Ho. Rd. E11 ....34Jc 73
Lakehurst Rd. KT19: Ewe 78Ua 154
Lakeland Cl. HA3: Hrw W 23Fa 46
IG7: Chig 21Xc 55
Lakeman Ho. SL9: Chal P 22B 42
Lakenham Pl. E3 ....42Bc 92
Lakenheath N14 ....15Lb 32
Laker Ct. SW4 ....53Nb 112
Laker Ind. Est. BR3: Beck 64Ac 136
Lake Ri. RM1: Rom 26Hd 56
Lake Rd. CR0: C'don 75Bc 158
E10 ....31Dc 72
GU25: Vir W 1M 147
RM6: Chad H 28Zc 55
RM9: Dag 41Dd 96
SW19 ....64Bb 133
Laker Pl. SW15 ....58Ab 110
Lakers Ri. SM7: Bans 88Gb 175
Lakeside BR3: Beck 69Dc 136
EN2: Enf 14Mb 32
GU21: Wok 1J 187
KT2: King T 66Ra 131
KT13: Weyb 75U 150
KT19: Ewe 79Ua 154
N3 ....26Db 49
RH1: Redh 4A 208
RM13: Rain 40Nd 77
SM6: Wall 77Kb 156
W13 ....44La 86
Lakeside Av. IG4: Ilf 28Mc 53
SE28 ....46Wc 95
Lakeside Bus. Village
RM16: Chaf H *49Xd 98*
(off Fleming Rd.)
Lakeside Cl. DA15: Sidc 57Yc 117
GU21: Wok 1J 187
HA4: Ruis 28T 44
IG7: Chig 21Vc 55
SE25 ....68Wb 135
Lakeside Ct. N4 ....33Sb 71
WD6: E'tree 15Qa 29
Lakeside Cres. CM14: B'wood 20Zd 41
EN4: E Barn 15Hb 31
Lakeside Dr. BR2: Brom 76Nc 160
GU24: Chob 5J 167
KT10: Esh 79Ea 152
NW10 ....41Pa 87
SL2: Stoke P 9J 61
Lakeside Grange KT13: Weyb 76S 150
Lakeside Ind. Est. SL3: Coln 51J 105
Lakeside Karting 47Xd 98
Lakeside Leisure Pk.
RM20: W Thur 49Wd 98
Lakeside Pk. KT16: Chert 74K 149
Lakeside Pl. AL2: Lon C 9H 7
Lakeside Retail Pk.
RM20: W Thur 49Wd 98
Lakeside Rd. N13 ....21Pb 50
SL0: Rich P 52H 105
SL3: Coln, Rich P 52H 105
W14 ....48Za 88
Lakeside Ter. EC2 ....7E 218
Lakeside Way HA9: Wemb 35Qa 67
Lakes Rd. BR2: Kes 78Lc 159
Lakestreet Grn. RH8: Limp 1P 211
Lakeswood Rd. BR5: Pet W 72Rc 160
Lake Vw. EN6: Pot B 5Eb 17
(not continuous)
HA8: Edg 22Pa 47
WD4: K Lan 10B 4
Lakeview Ct. SE28 ....45Xc 95
Lake Vw. Est. E3 ....40Ac 72
Lakeview Pk. RM3: Rom 20Ld 39
Lake Vw. Rd. TN13: S'oaks 95Jd 202
Lakeview Rd. DA16: Well 56Xc 117
SE27 ....64Qb 134
Lake Vw. Ter. *N18* *21Vb 51*
(off Sweet Briar Wlk.)
Lakewood KT10: Esh 83Ba 171
Lakin Cl. SM5: Cars 77Jb 156
Lakis Cl. NW3 ....35Eb 69
LALEHAM 69L 127
Laleham Abbey TW18: Lale 70L 127
Laleham Av. NW7 ....20Ta 29
Laleham Camping Site
TW18: Lale 71L 149
Laleham Cl. TW18: Staines 67K 127
Laleham Ct. GU21: Wok 88A 168
SM1: Sutt 78Eb 155
Laleham Golf Course 70K 127
Laleham Ho. E2 ....5K 219
Laleham Pk. 70L 127
LALEHAM REACH 69J 127
Laleham Reach KT16: Chert 69J 127
Laleham Rd. SE6 ....59Ec 114
TW17: Shep 70P 127
TW18: Staines 64H 127
Lalor St. SW6 ....54Ab 110
Lalsham Ho. WD19: Wat 20Y 27
Lamb All. *AL1: St A* *2B 6*
(off Chequer St.)
Lambarde Av. SE9 ....63Qc 138
Lambarde Dr. TN13: S'oaks 95Jd 202
Lambarde Rd. TN13: S'oaks 94Jd 202
Lambardes DA3: Nw A G 76Be 165
Lambardes Cl. BR6: Prat B 83Yc 181
Lambarde Sq. SE10 ....50Hc 93
Lambard Ho. *SE10* *52Ec 114*
(off Langdale Rd.)
Lamb Cl. AL10: Hat 1D 8
RM18: Tilb 4E 122
UB5: N'olt 41Aa 85
WD25: Wat 6Y 13
Lamb Ct. *E14* *45Ac 92*
(off Narrow St.)
Lamberhurst Cl. BR5: Orp 74Zc 161
Lamberhurst Ho. SE15 ....51Yb 114
Lamberhurst Rd. RM8: Dag 32Bd 75
SE27 ....63Qb 134
Lambert Av. SL3: L'ly 48A 82
TW9: Rich 55Qa 109
Lambert Cl. TN16: Big H 88Mc 179
Lambert Cotts. RH1: Blet 5L 209
Lambert Ct. *DA8: Erith* *51Ed 118*
(off Park Cres.)
KT13: Weyb 80P 149
WD23: Bush 14Z 27
Lambert Jones M. EC2 ....7D 218
Lambert Lodge *TW8: Bford* *50Ma 87*
(off Layton Rd.)
Lambert M. DA13: Sflt 65Ce 143
Lamberton Ct. *WD6: Bore* *11Qa 29*
(off Gateshead Rd.)
Lambert Rd. E16 ....44Kc 93
N12 ....22Fb 49
SM7: Bans 86Cb 175
SW2 ....57Nb 112
Lambert's Pl. CR0: C'don 74Tb 157
Lamberts Rd. KT5: Surb 71Na 153
Lambert St. N1 ....38Qb 70
Lambert Wlk. HA9: Wemb 34Na 67
Lambert Way N12 ....22Eb 49
LAMBETH 4H 229 (48Pb 90)
Lambeth Bri. SW1 ....5G 229 (49Nb 90)
Lambeth Crematorium SW17 ....63Eb 133
Lambeth High St. SE1 ......6H 229 (49Pb 90)
Lambeth Hill EC4 ....4D 224 (45Sb 91)
Lambeth Palace 4H 229 (48Pb 90)
Lambeth Pal. Rd. SE1 ......4H 229 (48Pb 90)
Lambeth Rd. CR0: C'don 73Qb 156
SE1 ....5H 229 (49Pb 90)
SE11 ....5H 229 (49Pb 90)
Lambeth Towers SE11 ....4K 229
Lambeth Wlk. SE11 ....4K 229 (49Pb 90)
(not continuous)
Lambfold Ho. *N7* *37Nb 70*
(off North Rd.)
Lamb Ho. *SE5* *52Sb 113*
(off Elmington Est.)
SE10 ....*51Ec 114*
(off Haddo St.)
Lambkins M. E17 ....28Ec 52
Lamb La. E8 ....38Xb 71
Lamble St. NW5 ....36Jb 70
Lambley Rd. RM9: Dag 37Xc 75
Lambly Hill GU25: Vir W 69A 126
Lambolle Pl. NW3 ....37Gb 69
Lambolle Rd. NW3 ....37Gb 69
Lambourn Chase WD7: R'lett 8Ha 14
Lambourn Cl. CR2: S Croy 81Rb 177
NW5 ....35Lb 70
W7 ....47Ha 86
LAMBOURNE 14Zc 37
Lambourne RM18: E Til 9L 101
Lambourne Av. SW19 ....63Bb 133
Lambourne Cl. IG7: Chig 20Xc 37
SL1: Burn 10A 60
Lambourne Ct. IG8: Wfd G 24Lc 53
UB8: Uxb 39K 63
Lambourne Cres. GU21: Wok 85F 168
IG7: Chig 19Xc 37
Lambourne Dr. CM13: Hut 17Fe 41
KT11: Cobh 87Z 171
LAMBOURNE END 17Ad 37
Lambourne End Outdoor Cen. 17Ad 37
Lambourne Gdns. E4 ....19Cc 34
EN1: Enf 12Vb 33
IG11: Bark 38Vc 75
RM12: Horn 33Md 77
Lambourne Golf Course, The 7A 60
Lambourne Gro. SE16 ....50Zb 92
Lambourne Ho. NW8 ....7C 214
Lambourne Pl. SE3 ....53Kc 115
Lambourne Rd. E11 ....31Ec 72
IG3: Ilf 33Uc 74
IG7: Chig 21Vc 55
IG11: Bark 38Uc 74
Lambourne Sq. RM4: Abr 18Yc 37
Lambourn Gro. KT1: King T 68Ra 131
Lambourn Rd. SW4 ....55Kb 112
Lambrook Ho. SE15 ....53Wb 113
Lambrook Ter. SW6 ....53Ab 110
Lamb's Bldgs. EC1 ....6F 219 (42Tb 91)
Lambs Bus. Pk. RH9: S God 10P 209
Lamb's Cl. N9 ....19Wb 33
Lambs Cl. EN6: Cuff 1Pb 18
Lamb's Conduit Pas.
WC1 ....7H 217 (43Pb 90)
Lamb's Conduit St.
WC1 ....6H 217 (42Pb 90)
(not continuous)
Lambscroft Av. SE9 ....62Lc 137
Lambscroft Way SL9: Chal P 26A 42
Lamb's La. Nth. RM13: Rain 42Md 97
Lamb's La. Sth. RM13: Rain 43Kd 97
Lambs Mdw. IG8: Wfd G 26Mc 53
Lamb's M. N1 ....1B 218 (39Rb 71)
Lambs Pas. EC1 ....7F 219 (42Tb 91)
Lambs Ter. N9 ....19Tb 33
Lamb St. E1 ....7K 219 (43Vb 91)
Lamb's Wlk. EN2: Enf 12Sb 33
Lambton Av. EN8: Walt C 5Zb 20
Lambton Ho. SL4: Wind 5E 102
Lambton M. *N19* *32Nb 70*
(off Lambton Rd.)
Lambton Pl. W11 ....45Bb 89
Lambton Rd. N19 ....32Nb 70
SW20 ....67Ya 132
Lamb Wlk. SE1 ....2H 231 (47Ub 91)
LAMDA 50Za 88
Lamerock Rd. BR1: Brom 63Hc 137
Lamerton Rd. IG6: Ilf 26Rc 54
Lamerton St. SE8 ....51Cc 114
Lamford Cl. N17 ....24Tb 51
Lamington St. W6 ....49Xa 88
Lamlash St. SE11 ....5B 230 (49Rb 91)
Lamley Ho. *SE10* *52Dc 114*
(off Ashburnham Pl.)
Lammas Av. CR4: Mitc 68Jb 134
SL4: Wind 4G 102
Lammas Cl. TW18: Staines 62G 126
Lammas Ct. SL4: Wind 4G 102
TW19: Staines 61F 126
Lammas Dr. TW18: Staines 63F 126
Lammas Grn. SE26 ....62Xb 135
Lammas Hill KT10: Esh 77Da 151
Lammas La.
KT10: Esh, Hers 77Ba 151
Lammas Pk. Gdns. W5 ....46La 86
Lammas Pk. Rd. W5 ....47Ma 87
Lammas Rd. E9 ....38Zb 72
E10 ....33Ac 72
SL1: Slou 3B 80
TW10: Ham 63La 130
WD18: Wat 15Y 27
Lammermoor Rd. SW12 ....59Kb 112
Lamont Rd. SW10 ....51Fb 111
Lamont Rd. Pas. *SW10* *51Fb 111*
(off Lamont Rd.)
LAMORBEY 60Vc 117
Lamorbey Cl. DA15: Sidc 60Vc 117
Lamorbey Pk. 60Xc 117
Lamorna Av.
DA12: Grav'nd 1F 144
Lamorna Cl. BR6: Orp 73Wc 161
E17 ....26Ec 52
WD7: R'lett 6Ka 14
Lamorna Gro. HA7: Stan 25Ma 47
Lampard Gro. N16 ....32Vb 71
Lampern Sq. E2 ....41Wb 91
Lampeter Cl. GU22: Wok 90A 168
NW9 ....30Ua 48
Lampeter Ho. *RM3: Rom* *24Nd 57*
(off Kingsbridge Cir.)
Lampeter Sq. W6 ....51Ab 110
Lamplighter Cl. E1 ....42Yb 92
Lamplighters Cl. DA1: Dart 58Pd 119
EN9: Walt A 6Jc 21
Lampmead Rd. SE12 ....57Hc 115
Lamp Office Ct. WC1 ....6H 217
Lamport Cl. SE18 ....49Pc 94
LAMPTON 53Da 107
Lampton Av. TW3: Houn 53Da 107
Lampton Ct. TW3: Houn 53Da 107
Lampton Ho. Cl. SW19 ....63Za 132
Lampton Pk. Rd. TW3: Houn 54Da 107
Lampton Rd. TW3: Houn 54Ca 107
Lampton Sports Cen. 54Ca 107
Lamsey Rd. HP3: Hem H 4M 3
Lamson Rd. RM13: Rain 42Hd 96
(not continuous)
Lanacre Av. NW9 ....25Ta 47
Lanadron Cl. TW7: Isle 54Ha 108
Lanain Ct. SE12 ....59Hc 115
Lanark Cl. W5 ....43La 86
Lanark Ct. *UB5: N'olt* *36Ca 65*
(off Newmarket Av.)
Lanark Ho. *SE1* *50Wb 91*
(off Old Kent Rd.)
Lanark Mans. W9 ....5A 214
W12 ....*47Ya 88*
(off Pennard Rd.)
Lanark M. W9 ....4A 214 (41Eb 89)
Lanark Pl. W9 ....5A 214 (42Eb 89)
Lanark Rd. W9 ....4A 214 (40Db 69)
Lanark Sq. E14 ....48Dc 92
Lanata Wlk. *UB4: Yead* *42Z 85*
(off Alba Cl.)
Lanbury Rd. SE15 ....56Zb 114
Lancashire Ct. W1 ....4K 221 (45Kb 90)
Lancaster Av. CR4: Mitc 71Nb 156
E18 ....28Kc 53
EN4: Had W 10Eb 17
IG11: Bark 38Uc 74
SE27 ....61Rb 135
SL2: Slou 2G 80
SW19 ....64Za 132
Lancaster Cl. BR2: Brom 70Hc 137
CM15: Pil H 15Wd 40
GU21: Wok 88C 168
KT2: King T 64Ma 131
N1 ....38Ub 71
N17 ....24Wb 51
NW9 ....24Va 48
TW15: Ashf 63N 127
TW19: Stanw 58N 105
TW20: Eng G 4P 125
W2 ....*45Db 89*
(off St Petersburgh Pl.)
Lancaster Cotts. TW10: Rich 58Na 109
Lancaster Ct. DA12: Grav'nd 2E 144
KT12: Walt T 73W 150
KT19: Ewe 82Ta 173
SE27 ....61Rb 135
SM2: Sutt *80Cb 155*
(off Mulgrave Rd.)
SM7: Bans 86Bb 175
SW6 ....52Bb 111
TW19: Stanw 60N 105
W2 ....4A 220
Lancaster Dr. E14 ....46Ec 92
HP3: Bov 9B 2
IG10: Lough 16Nc 36
NW3 ....37Gb 69
RM12: Horn 36Kd 77
Lancaster Gdns. BR1: Brom 71Nc 160
KT2: King T 64Ma 131
SW19 ....64Ab 132
W13 ....47Ka 86
Lancaster Ga. W2 ....5A 220 (45Eb 89)
Lancaster Gro. NW3 ....37Fb 69
Lancaster Hall *E16* *46Jc 93*
(off Wesley Av.)
Lancaster House 1C 228
Lancaster Ho. E11 ....33Hc 73
EN2: Enf 11Tb 33
RH1: Redh 9N 207
RM8: Dag 35Xc 75
TW7: Isle 52Ha 108
Lancaster Lodge *W11* *44Ab 88*
(off Lancaster Rd.)
Lancaster M. SW18 ....57Db 111
TW10: Rich 58Na 109
W2 ....4A 220 (45Eb 89)
Lancaster Pk. TW10: Rich 57Na 109
Lancaster Pl. IG1: Ilf 36Sc 74
SW19 ....64Za 132
TW1: Twick 58Ja 108
TW4: Houn 54Y 107
WC2 ....4H 223 (45Pb 90)
Lancaster Rd. AL1: St A 1D 6
E7 ....38Jc 73
E11 ....33Gc 73
E17 ....26Zb 52
EN2: Enf 11Tb 33
EN4: E Barn 15Fb 31
HA2: Harr 29Ca 45
N4 ....31Pb 70
N11 ....23Mb 50
N18 ....22Vb 51
NW10 ....36Wa 68
RM16: Chaf H 50Zd 99
SE25 ....68Vb 135
SW19 ....64Za 132
UB1: S'hall 45Aa 85
UB5: N'olt 37Ea 66
UB8: Uxb 37M 63
W11 ....44Ab 88
Lancaster Rd. Ind. Est.
EN4: E Barn 15Fb 31
Lancaster Stables NW3 ....37Gb 69
Lancaster St. SE1 ....2B 230 (47Rb 91)
Lancaster Ter. W2 ....4B 220 (45Fb 89)
Lancaster Wlk. UB3: Hayes 44S 84
W2 ....5A 220 (46Eb 89)
Lancaster Way KT4: Wor Pk 73Xa 154
WD5: Ab L 3V 12
Lancastrian Rd. SM6: Wall 80Nb 156
Lance Cft. DA3: Nw A G 75Be 165
Lancefield Ho. SE15 ....56Xb 113
Lancefield St. W10 ....41Bb 89
Lancell St. N16 ....33Vb 71
Lancelot Av. HA0: Wemb 35Ma 67
Lancelot Cl. SL1: Slou 7E 80
Lancelot Ct. BR6: Orp 75Xc 161
Lancelot Cres. HA0: Wemb 35Ma 67
Lancelot Gdns. EN4: E Barn 17Jb 32
Lancelot Pl. SW7 ....2F 227 (47Hb 89)
Lancelot Rd. DA16: Well 56Wc 117
HA0: Wemb 35Ma 67
IG6: Ilf 23Uc 54
Lance Rd. HA1: Harr 31Ea 66
Lancer Sq. *W8* *47Db 89*
(off Kensington Chu. St.)
Lancey Cl. SE7 ....49Nc 94
Lanchester Ct. W2 ....3F 221
Lanchester Rd. N6 ....29Hb 49
Lanchester Way SE14 ....53Yb 114
Lancing Gdns. N9 ....18Vb 33
Lancing Ho. *CR0: C'don* *77Tb 157*
(off Coombe Rd.)
WD24: Wat *12Y 27*
(off Hallam Cl.)
Lancing Rd. BR6: Orp 75Wc 161
CR0: C'don 73Pb 156
IG2: Ilf 30Tc 54
RM3: Rom 24Nd 57
TW13: Felt 61V 128
W13 ....45Ka 86
Lancing St. NW1 ....4D 216 (41Mb 90)
Lancing Way WD3: Crox G 15R 26
Lancresse Cl. UB8: Uxb 37M 63
Lancresse Ct. *N1* *39Ub 71*
(off De Beauvoir Est.)
Landale Gdns. DA1: Dart 59Ld 119
Landale Ho. *SE16* *48Yb 92*
(off Lower Rd.)
Landau Apartments SW6 ....51Cb 111
Landau Ct. *CR2: S Croy* *78Sb 157*
(off Warham Rd.)
Landau Way DA8: Erith 50Md 97
Landcroft Rd. SE22 ....57Vb 113
Landells Rd. SE22 ....58Vb 113
Lander Cl. DA12: Grav'nd 3F 144
Lander Rd. RM17: Grays 50Fe 99
Landford Cl. WD3: Rick 19N 25
Landford Rd. SW15 ....55Ya 110
Landgrove Rd. SW19 ....64Cb 133
Landin Ho. *E14* *44Cc 92*
(off Thomas Rd.)
Landleys Fld. *N7* *36Mb 70*
(off Long Mdw.)
Landmann Ho. *SE16* *49Xb 91*
(off Rennie Est.)
Landmann Point SE10 ....48Jc 93
Landmann Way SE14 ....50Zb 92
Landmark Arts Cen. 64Ka 130
Landmark Commercial Cen.
N18 ....23Ub 51
Landmark East Twr. *E14* *47Cc 92*
(off Marsh Wall)
Landmark Hgts. E5 ....35Ac 72
Landmark Ho. IG10: Lough 14Sc 36
W6 ....*50Ya 88*
(off Hammersmith Bri. Rd.)
Landmark Pl. UB10: Hil 40R 64
Landmark Row SL3: L'ly 51D 104
Landmark Sq. E14 ....47Cc 92
Landmark West Twr. *E14* *47Cc 92*
(off Marsh Wall)
Landmead Rd. EN8: Chesh 1Ac 20
Landon Pl. SW1 ....3F 227 (48Hb 89)
Landon's Cl. E14 ....46Ec 92
Landon Wlk. E14 ....45Dc 92
Landon Way TW15: Ashf 65R 128
Landor Ho. *SE5* *52Tb 113*
(off Elmington Est.)
W2 ....*43Cb 89*
(off Westbourne Pk. Rd.)
Landor Rd. SW9 ....55Nb 112
Landor Theatre 55Nb 112
Landor Wlk. W12 ....47Wa 88
Landra Gdns. N21 ....16Rb 33
Landrake NW1 ....1C 216
Landridge Dr. EN1: Enf 10Xb 19
Landridge Rd. SW6 ....54Bb 111
Landrock Rd. N8 ....30Nb 50
Landscape Rd. CR6: W'ham 91Xb 197
IG8: Wfd G 24Kc 53
Landsdown Cl. EN5: New Bar 14Eb 31
Landsdowne Ct. *N19* *32Nb 70*
(off Fairbridge Rd.)
Landseer Av. DA11: Nflt 62Fe 143
E12 ....36Qc 74
Landseer Cl. HA8: Edg 26Qa 47
RM11: Horn 32Kd 77
SW19 ....67Eb 133
Landseer Ct. UB4: Hayes 40T 64
Landseer Ho. NW8 ....5C 214
SW1 ....6E 228
SW11 ....53Jb 112
UB5: N'olt *40Z 65*
(off Parkfield Dr.)
Landseer Rd. EN1: Enf 15Wb 33
KT3: N Mald 73Ta 153
N19 ....34Nb 70
(not continuous)
SM1: Sutt 79Cb 155
Lands End WD6: E'tree 16Ma 29
Landstead Rd. SE18 ....52Tc 116
Landulph Ho. SE11 ....7A 230
Landward Ct. W1 ....2E 220
Landway TN15: Seal 92Pd 203
Landway, The BR5: St P 69Yc 139
TN15: Bor G 92Be 205
TN15: Kems'g 89Qd 183
Lane, The GU25: Vir W 69A 126
KT16: Chert 69J 127
NW8 ....2A 214 (40Eb 69)
SE3 ....55Jc 115
Lane Av. DA9: Ghithe 58Yd 120
Lane Cl. KT15: Add 78K 149
NW2 ....34Xa 68
LANE END 63Td 142
Lane End AL10: Hat 3B 8
DA7: Bex 55Dd 118
KT18: Eps 86Ra 173
SW15 ....58Za 110
Lane End Dr. GU21: Knap 9G 166
Lane Gdns. KT10: Clay 80Ha 152
WD23: B Hea 17Ga 28
Lane M. E12 ....34Pc 74
Lanercost Cl. SW2 ....61Qb 134
Lanercost Gdns. N14 ....17Nb 32
Lanercost Rd. SW2 ....61Qb 134
Lanes Av. DA11: Nflt 2B 144
Lanesborough Ct. N1 ....3H 219
Lanesborough Pl. SW1 ....1J 227
Lanesborough Way SW17 ....62Fb 133
Laneside BR7: Chst 64Rc 138
HA8: Edg 22Sa 47
Laneside Av. RM8: Dag 31Bd 75
Laneway SW15 ....57Xa 110
Laney Ho. EC1 ....7K 217
Lanfranc Ct. HA1: Harr 34Ha 66
Lanfranc Rd. E3 ....40Ac 72
Lanfrey Pl. W14 ....50Bb 89
Langafel Cl. DA3: Lfield 68Ae 143
Langaller La. KT22: Fet 94Da 191
Langbourne Av. N6 ....33Jb 70
Langbourne Ct. E17 ....30Ac 52
Langbourne Mans. N6 ....33Jb 70
Langbourne Pl. E14 ....50Dc 92
Langbourne Way KT10: Clay 79Ja 152
Langbrook Rd. SE3 ....55Mc 115
Lang Cl. KT22: Fet 95Da 191
Langcroft Cl. SM5: Cars 76Hb 155
Langdale NW1 ....3B 216
Langdale Av. CR4: Mitc 69Hb 133
Langdale Cl. BR6: Farnb 76Rc 160
GU21: Wok 8N 167
RM8: Dag 32Yc 75
SE17 ....51Sb 113
SW14 ....56Ra 109
Langdale Cres. DA7: Bex 52Cd 118
Langdale Dr. UB4: Hayes 40U 64
Langdale Gdns. EN8: Walt C 7Zb 20
RM12: Horn 36Jd 76
UB6: G'frd 41Ka 86
Langdale Ho. *SW1* *50Lb 90*
(off Churchill Gdns.)
Langdale Lodge *WD3: Rick* *17M 25*
(off Parsonage Rd.)
Langdale Pde. CR4: Mitc 69Hb 133
Langdale Rd. CR7: Thor H 70Qb 134
SE10 ....52Ec 114
Langdale St. E1 ....44Xb 91
Langdale Ter. WD6: Bore 13Sa 29
Langdale Wlk. *DA11: Nflt* *2A 144*
(off Landseer Av.)
Langdon Ct. EC1 ....2C 218
NW10 ....39Ua 68
Langdon Cres. E6 ....40Qc 74
Langdon Dr. NW9 ....32Sa 67
Langdon Ho. *E14* *44Ec 92*
(off Ida St.)
Langdon Pk. TW11: Tedd 66La 130
Langdon Pk. Rd. N6 ....31Lb 70
Langdon Pl. SW14 ....55Sa 109
Langdon Rd. BR2: Brom 69Kc 137
E6 ....39Qc 74
SM4: Mord 71Eb 155
Langdons Ct. UB2: S'hall 48Ca 85
Langdon Shaw DA14: Sidc 64Vc 139
Langdon Wlk. SM4: Mord 71Eb 155
Langdon Way SE1 ....49Wb 91
Langford Cl. AL4: St A 1G 6
E8 ....36Wb 71
NW8 ....1A 214 (40Eb 69)
W3 ....47Ra 87
Langford Ct. NW8 ....2A 214
Langford Cres. EN4: Cockf 14Hb 31
Langford Grn. CM13: Hut 15Ee 41
SE5 ....55Ub 113
Langford Ho. SE8 ....51Cc 114
Langford M. N1 ....38Qb 70
SW11 ....*56Fb 111*
(off St John's Hill)
Langford Pl. DA14: Sidc 62Wc 139
NW8 ....1A 214 (40Eb 69)
Langford Rd. EN4: Cockf 14Hb 31
IG8: Wfd G 23Lc 53
SW6 ....54Db 111
Langfords IG9: Buck H 19Nc 36
Langham Cl. BR2: Brom 75Nc 160
N15 ....*27Rb 51*
(off Langham Rd.)
Langham Ct. HA4: Ruis 36X 65
NW4 ....29Za 48
RH9: S God 10C 210
RM11: Horn 31Md 77
SW20 ....68Ya 132
Langham Dene CR8: Kenley 87Rb 177
Langham Dr. RM6: Chad H 30Xc 55
Langham Gdns. HA0: Wemb 33La 66
HA8: Edg 24Sa 47
N21 ....15Qb 32
TW10: Ham 63La 130
W13 ....45Ka 86
Langham Ho. Cl. TW10: Ham 63Ma 131
Langham Mans. *SW5* *50Db 89*
(off Earl's Ct. Sq.)
Langham Pk. Pl. BR2: Brom 70Hc 137
Langham Pl. N15 ....27Rb 51
TW20: Egh 64B 126
W1 ....1A 222 (43Kb 90)
W4 ....51Ua 110
Langham Rd. HA8: Edg 23Sa 47
N15 ....27Rb 51
SW20 ....67Ya 132
TW11: Tedd 64Ka 130
Langham St. W1 ....1A 222 (43Kb 90)
Langhedge Cl. N18 ....23Vb 51
Langhedge La. N18 ....23Vb 51
Langhedge La. Ind. Est. N18 ....23Vb 51
Langholm Cl. SW12 ....59Mb 112

Langholme WD23: Bush 18Ea 28
Langhorn Dr. TW2: Twick 59Ga 108
Langhorne Ct. *NW8* 38Fb 69
(off Dorman Way)
Langhorne Rd. RM10: Dag 38Cd 76
Langhorne St. SE18 52Pc 116
Lang Ho. *SW8* 52Nb 112
(off Hartington Rd.)
TW19: Stanw 60N 105
Langland Ct. HA6: Nwood 24S 44
Langland Cres. HA7: Stan 26Ma 47
Langland Dr. HA5: Pinn 24Aa 45
Langland Gdns. CR0: C'don 75Bc 158
NW3 36Db 69
Langland Ho. *SE5* 52Tb 113
(off Edmund St.)
Langlands Dr. DA2: Daren 64Ud 142
Langlands Ri. KT19: Eps 85Sa 173
Langler Rd. NW10 40Ya 68
LANGLEY 48C 82
Langley Av. HA4: Ruis 33X 65
HP3: Hem H 5N 3
KT4: Wor Pk 74Za 154
KT6: Surb 74Ma 153
LANGLEY BOTTOM 91Ta 193
Langley Broom SL3: L'ly 50B 82
LANGLEYBURY 6R 12
Langleybury Flds. WD4: Lang 6P 11
Langleybury La. WD4: Lang 9R 12
WD17: Wat 9R 12
Langley Bus. Cen. SL3: L'ly 47C 82
Langley Bus. Pk. SL3: L'ly 47C 82
Langley Cl. KT18: Eps D 91Ta 193
RM3: Rom 24Md 57
Langley Ct. EN7: G Oak 1Sb 19
RH2: Reig 5K 207
WC2 4F 223 (45Nb 90)
Langley Cres. E11 31Lc 73
HA8: Edg 20Sa 29
RM9: Dag 38Yc 75
UB3: Harl 52V 106
WD4: K Lan 2Q 12
Langley Dr. CM14: B'wood 20Wd 40
E11 31Kc 73
W3 47Ra 87
Langley Gdns. BR2: Brom 70Lc 137
BR5: Pet W 72Rc 160
RM9: Dag 38Zc 75
Langley Gro. KT3: N Mald 68Ua 132
Langley Hill WD4: K Lan 1P 11
Langley Hill Cl. WD4: K Lan 1Q 12
Langley Ho. *W2* 43Cb 89
(off Alfred Rd.)
Langley La. KT18: Head 97Ra 193
SW8 51Pb 112
WD5: Ab L 3V 12
WD25: Wat 3V 12
Langley Leisure Cen. 49D 82
Langley Lodge La. WD4: K Lan 3N 11
Langley Mans. *SW8* 51Pb 112
(off Langley La.)
Langley Mdw. IG10: Lough 12Tc 36
Langley M. RM9: Dag 38Zc 75
Langley Oaks Av. CR2: Sande 82Wb 177
Langley Pk. NW7 23Ua 48
SL3: L'ly 47B 82
Langley Pk. Country Pk. 42A 82
Langley Pk. Golf Course 72Fc 159
Langley Pk. La. SL0: Iver 45D 82
Langley Pk. Rd. SL0: Iver 47C 82
SL3: L'ly 47C 82
SM1: Sutt 78Eb 155
SM2: Sutt 78Eb 155
Langley Pk. Sports Cen. 72Ec 158
Langley Quay SL3: L'ly 47C 82
Langley Rd. BR3: Beck 70Ac 136
CR2: Sels 81Zb 178
DA16: Well 51Yc 117
KT6: Surb 73Na 153
SL3: L'ly 7N 81
SW19 67Bb 133
TW7: Isle 54Ha 108
TW18: Staines 65H 127
WD4: Chfd 2K 11
WD5: Ab L 3U 12
WD17: Wat 11V 26
LANGLEY RDBT. 50C 82
Langley Row EN5: Barn 11Bb 31
Langley St. WC2 3F 223 (44Nb 90)
Langley Tennis Club 7B 4
LANGLEY VALE 91Ua 194
Langley Va. Rd. KT18: Eps D 92Sa 193
Langley Wlk. GU22: Wok 91A 188
Langley Way BR4: W W'ck 74Fc 159
WD17: Wat 12U 26
Langley Wharf WD4: K Lan 9A 4
Langmans La. GU21: Wok 10M 167
Langmans Way GU21: Wok 8J 167
Langmead Dr. WD23: B Hea 18Ga 28
Langmead Ho. *E3* 41Dc 92
(off Bruce Rd.)
Langmead St. SE27 63Rb 135
Langmore Ct. DA6: Bex 55Zc 117
Langmore Ho. *E1* 44Wb 91
(off Stutfield St.)
Langport Ct. KT12: Walt T 74Y 151
Langport Ho. *RM3: Rom* 24Nd 57
(off Leyburn Rd.)
SW9 54Rb 113
Langridge M. TW12: Hamp 65Ba 129
Langroyd Rd. SW17 61Hb 133
Langshott Cl. KT15: Wdhm 83G 168
Langside Av. SW15 56Wa 110
Langside Cres. N14 20Mb 32
Langstone Way NW7 24Za 48
Langston Hughes Cl. SE24 56Rb 113
Langston Rd. IG10: Lough 15Sc 36
Lang St. E1 42Yb 92
Langthorn Ct. EC2 2G 225 (44Tb 91)
Langthorne Ct. BR1: Brom 63Ec 136
Langthorne Cres. RM17: Grays 49Ee 99
Langthorne Ho. *E3* 41Bc 92
(off Merchant St.)
UB3: Harl 49U 84
Langthorne Rd. E11 34Ec 72
(not continuous)
Langthorne St. SW6 52Za 110
Langton Av. E6 41Qc 94
KT17: Ewe 83Va 174
N20 17Eb 31
Langton Cl. GU21: Wok 9K 167
KT15: Add 76K 149
SL1: Slou 6B 80
WC1 5J 217 (42Pb 90)
Langton Gro. HA6: Nwood 22S 44
Langton Ho. SE11 5J 229
Langton Pl. SW18 60Cb 111
Langton Ri. SE23 59Xb 113
Langton Rd. HA3: Hrw W 24Ea 46
KT8: W Mole 70Ea 130
NW2 34Ya 68
SW9 52Rb 113
Langton's Mdw. SL2: Farn C 7G 60
Langton St. SW10 51Eb 111
Langton Way CR0: C'don 76Ub 157
RM16: Grays 9E 100
SE3 53Hc 115
TW20: Egh 65E 126
Langtree Av. SL1: Slou 7D 80
Langtry Ct. TW7: Isle 54Ha 108
Langtry Ho. *KT2: King T* 67Qa 131
(off London Rd.)
Langtry Pl. SW6 51Cb 111
Langtry Rd. NW8 39Db 69
UB5: N'olt 40Z 65
Langtry Wlk. NW8 39Db 69
Langwood WD17: Wat 11W 26
Langwood Chase
TW11: Tedd 65La 130
Langwood Cl. KT21: Asht 89Qa 173
Langwood Gdns. WD17: Wat 11W 26
Langworth Cl. DA2: Wilm 62Md 141
Langworth Dr. UB4: Yead 44X 85
Langworthy HA5: Hat E 23Ca 45
Lanhill Rd. W9 42Cb 89
Lanier Rd. SE13 58Fc 115
Lanigan Dr. TW3: Houn 57Da 107
Lankaster Gdns. N2 25Fb 49
Lankers Dr. HA2: Harr 30Ba 45
Lankester Sq. RH8: Oxt 100Fc 199
Lankton Cl. BR3: Beck 67Ec 136
Lannock Rd. UB3: Hayes 46V 84
Lannoy Point *SW6* 52Ab 110
(off Pellant Rd.)
Lannoy Rd. SE9 60Sc 116
Lanrick Rd. E14 44Fc 93
Lanridge Rd. SE2 48Zc 95
Lansbury Av. IG11: Bark 38Wc 75
N18 22Tb 51
RM6: Chad H 29Ad 55
TW14: Felt 58X 107
Lansbury Cl. NW10 36Sa 67
Lansbury Ct. *SE28* 45Xc 95
(off Saunders Way)
Lansbury Cres. DA1: Dart 57Qd 119
Lansbury Dr. UB4: Hayes 40U 64
Lansbury Est. E14 44Dc 92
GU21: Knap 10H 167
Lansbury Gdns. E14 44Fc 93
RM18: Tilb 3C 122
Lansbury Rd. EN3: Enf H 11Zb 34
Lansbury Way N18 22Ub 51
Lanscombe Wlk. SW8 53Nb 112
Lansdell Ho. SW2 58Qb 112
Lansdell Rd. CR4: Mitc 68Jb 134
Lansdown Cl. GU21: Wok 1K 187
KT12: Walt T 74Y 151
Lansdowne Av. BR6: Farnb 74Rc 160
DA7: Bex 52Zc 117
SL1: Slou 6J 81
Lansdowne Cl. KT6: Surb 75Ra 153
SW20 66Za 132
TW1: Twick 60Ha 108
WD25: Wat 7Z 13
Lansdowne Ct. CR8: Purl 82Rb 177
IG5: Ilf 27Nc 54
KT4: Wor Pk 75Wa 154
SL1: Slou 6J 81
W11 45Ab 88
(off Lansdowne Ri.)
Lansdowne Cres. W11 45Ab 88
Lansdowne Dr. E8 37Wb 71
Lansdowne Gdns. SW8 53Nb 112
Lansdowne Grn. SW8 53Nb 112
Lansdowne Gro. NW10 35Ua 68
Lansdowne Hill SE27 62Rb 135
Lansdowne Ho. *KT18: Eps* 86Sa 173
(off Dalmeny Way)
W11 46Bb 89
(off Ladbroke Rd.)
Lansdowne La. SE7 51Mc 115
Lansdowne M. SE7 50Mc 93
W11 46Bb 89
Lansdowne Pl. SE1 3G 231 (48Tb 91)
SE19 66Vb 135
Lansdowne Ri. W11 45Ab 88
Lansdowne Rd. BR1: Brom 66Jc 137
CR0: C'don 75Tb 157
CR8: Purl 84Qb 176
E4 19Cc 34
E11 33Hc 73
E17 30Cc 52
E18 27Jc 53
HA1: Harr 31Ga 66
HA7: Stan 23La 46
IG3: Ilf 32Vc 75
KT19: Ewe 80Sa 153
N3 24Cb 49
N10 26Lb 50
N17 25Vb 51
RM18: Tilb 4B 122
SW20 66Ya 132
TN13: S'oaks 94Md 203
TW3: Houn 55Da 107
TW18: Staines 66K 127
UB8: Hil 44S 84
W11 45Ab 88
Lansdowne Row W1 6A 222 (46Kb 90)
Lansdowne Sq. DA11: Nflt 8B 122
Lansdowne Ter. WC1 6G 217 (42Nb 90)
Lansdowne Wlk. W11 46Bb 89
Lansdowne Way SW8 53Mb 112
Lansdowne Wood Cl. SE27 62Rb 135
Lansdowne Workshops SE7 50Lc 93
Lansdown Pl. DA11: Nflt 10B 122
Lansdown Rd. DA11: Nflt 10B 122
DA14: Sidc 62Xc 139
E7 38Lc 73
Lansfield Av. N18 21Wb 51
Lanson Apartments SW8 52Kb 112
Lantern SE1 1D 230
Lantern Cl. BR6: Farnb 77Rc 160
HA0: Wemb 36Ma 67
SW15 56Wa 110
Lantern Ho. *UB3: Harl* 48S 84
(off Nine Acres Cl.)
Lanterns Way E14 47Cc 92
Lantern Way UB7: W Dray 47N 83
Lant Ho. SE1 2D 230
Lantry Ct. W3 46Ra 87
Lant St. SE1 1D 230 (47Sb 91)
Lanvanor Rd. SE15 54Yb 114
Lanward Apartments *N1* 38Pb 70
(off Caledonian Rd.)
Lanyard Ho. SE8 49Bc 92
Lapford Cl. W9 42Bb 89
Lapis Cl. DA12: Grav'nd 10K 123
NW10 41Qa 87
Lapis M. E15 39Ec 72
La Plata Gro. CM14: B'wood 20Xd 40
Lapponum Wlk. UB4: Yead 42Z 85
Lapse Wood Wlk. SE23 60Xb 113
Lapstone Gdns. HA3: Kenton 30La 46
Lapwing Cl. CR2: Sels 82Ac 178
DA8: Erith 52Kd 119
RM18: E Til 9K 101
Lapwing Ct. KT6: Surb 76Qa 153
SE1 2E 230
(off Swan St.)
Lapwing Pl. WD25: Wat 4Y 13
Lapwings DA3: Lfield 69De 143
Lapwings, The DA12: Grav'nd 1F 144
Lapwing Ter. E7 36Mc 73
Lapwing Twr. *SE8* 51Bc 114
(off Taylor Cl.)
Lapwing Way UB4: Yead 44Z 85
WD5: Ab L 3W 12
Lapworth *N11* 21Kb 50
(off Coppies Gro.)
Lapworth Cl. BR6: Chels 75Yc 161
Lapworth Ct. *W2* 43Db 89
(off Delamere Ter.)
Lara Cl. KT9: Chess 80Na 153
SE13 58Ec 114
Larbert Rd. SW16 66Lb 134
Larby Pl. KT17: Ewe 82Ua 174
Larch Av. AL2: Brick W 2Aa 13
SL5: S'dale 1C 146
W3 46Ua 88
Larch Cl. CR6: W'ham 91Ac 198
E13 42Kc 93
KT20: Kgswd 93Eb 195
N11 24Jb 50
N19 33Lb 70
RH1: Redh 8L 207
SE8 51Bc 114
SL2: Slou 3F 80
SW12 61Kb 134
Larch Ct. SE1 2H 231
W9 43Cb 89
(off Admiral Wlk.)
Larch Cres. KT19: Ewe 79Ra 153
UB4: Yead 42Y 85
Larch Dene BR6: Farnb 75Qc 160
Larch Dr. W4 50Qa 87
Larches, The GU21: Wok 88A 168
HA6: Nwood 23S 44
N13 20Sb 33
UB10: Hil 41R 84
WD23: Bush 15Aa 27
Larches Av. EN1: Enf 7Yb 20
SW14 56Ta 109
Larchfield Cl. KT13: Weyb 76V 150
Larch Grn. NW9 25Ua 48
Larch Gro. DA15: Sidc 60Vc 117
Larch Ho. BR2: Brom 67Gc 137
SE16 47Yb 92
(off Ainsty Est.)
UB4: Yead 43Y 85
W10 42Ab 88
(off Rowan Wlk.)
Larchmoor Pk. SL2: Stoke P 6L 61
Larch Pl. RM3: Hrld W 26Nd 57
Larch Rd. DA1: Dart 59Md 119
E10 33Cc 72
NW2 35Ya 68
Larch Tree Way CR0: C'don 76Cc 158
Larchvale Ct. SM2: Sutt 80Db 155
Larch Vw. HP1: Hem H 3K 3
Larch Wlk. BR8: Swan 68Fd 140
Larch Way BR2: Brom 73Qc 160
Larchwood Av. RM5: Col R 23Dd 56
Larchwood Cl. RM5: Col R 23Ed 56
SM7: Bans 87Ab 174
Larchwood Dr. TW20: Eng G 5M 125
Larchwood Gdns. CM15: Pil H 16Wd 40
Larchwood Ho. *UB7: W Dray* 47P 83
(off Park Lodge Av.)
Larchwood Rd. GU21: Wok 2H 187
SE9 61Rc 138
Larcombe Cl. CR0: C'don 77Vb 157
Larcombe Ct. *SM2: Sutt* 80Db 155
(off Worcester Rd.)
Larcom St. SE17 6D 230 (49Sb 91)
Larden Rd. W3 46Ua 88
Largewood Av. KT6: Surb 75Qa 153
Largo Wlk. DA8: Erith 53Gd 118
Larissa St. SE17 7G 231 (50Tb 91)
Lark Av. TW18: Staines 62H 127
Larkbere Rd. SE26 63Ac 136
Lark Cl. CM14: W'ley 21Xd 58
Lark Ct. *NW9* 25Ua 48
(off Lanacre Av.)
Larken Cl. WD23: Bush 18Ea 28
Larken Dr. WD23: Bush 18Ea 28
Larkfield KT11: Cobh 85W 170
Larkfield Av. HA3: Kenton 27Ka 46
Larkfield Cl. BR2: Hayes 75Hc 159
Larkfield Rd. DA14: Sidc 62Vc 139
TN13: Bes G 95Ed 202
TW9: Rich 56Na 109
Larkfields DA11: Nflt 2A 144
Larkhall Cl. KT12: Hers 79Y 151
Larkhall La. SW4 54Mb 112
Larkhall Ri. SW4 55Lb 112
(not continuous)
Larkham Cl. TW13: Felt 62U 128
Lark Hill Ter. *SE18* 52Qc 116
(off Prince Imperial Rd.)
Larkin Cl. CM13: Hut 17Ee 41
CR5: Coul 89Pb 176
Larkings La. SL2: Stoke P 9M 61
Lark Ri. AL10: Hat 2C 8
Lark Row E2 39Yb 72
Larks Fld. DA3: Hartl 70Be 143
Larksfield TW20: Eng G 6M 125
Larksfield Gro. EN1: Enf 11Xb 33
Larks Gro. IG11: Bark 38Uc 74
Larkshall Cres. RM7: Mawney 26Ed 56
Larkshall Cres. E4 21Ec 52
Larkshall Rd. E4 22Ec 52
Larkspur Cl. BR6: Chels 75Yc 161
E6 43Nc 94
HA4: Ruis 31S 64
HP1: Hem H 1G 2
N17 24Tb 51
NW9 29Ra 47
RM15: S Ock 41Yd 98
Larkspur Gro. HA8: Edg 21Sa 47
Larkspur Lodge DA14: Sidc 62Xc 139
Larkspur Way KT19: Ewe 78Sa 153
Larks Ridge AL2: Chis G 9N 5
Larks Way GU21: Knap 8G 166
Larkswood Cl. DA8: Erith 53Jd 118
Larkswood Ct. E4 22Fc 53
Larkswood Ri. HA5: Eastc 28Y 45
Larkswood Rd. E4 21Cc 52
Lark Way SM5: Cars 73Gb 155
Larkway Cl. NW9 28Ta 47
Larkwell La. DA3: Hartl 70Be 143
Larmans Rd. EN3: Enf W 8Yb 20
Larnach Rd. W6 51Za 110
Larne Rd. HA4: Ruis 31V 64
Larner Rd. DA8: Erith 52Gd 118
La Roche Cl. SL3: L'ly 8N 81
Larpent Av. SW15 57Ya 110
Larsen Dr. EN9: Walt A 6Fc 21
Larson Wlk. E14 48Cc 92
Larwood Cl. UB6: G'frd 36Fa 66
Lascar Cl. TW3: Houn 55Ba 107
Lascar Wharf Bldg. *E14* 44Ac 92
(off Parnham St.)
Lascelles Av. HA1: Harr 31Fa 66
Lascelles Cl. CM15: Pil H 15Wd 40
E11 33Fc 73
Lascelles Ho. NW1 6E 214
Lascelles Rd. SL3: Slou 8M 81
Lascotts Rd. N22 23Pb 50
Laseron Ho. *N15* 28Vb 51
(off Tottenham Grn. E.)
Laserquest
Woking 89B 168
(within The Big Apple)
Las Palmas Est. TW17: Shep 73S 150
Lassa Rd. SE9 57Nc 116
Lassell St. SE10 50Fc 93
Lasseter Pl. SE3 51Hc 115
Lasswade Ct. KT16: Chert 73G 148
Lasswade Rd. KT16: Chert 73G 148
Lastingham Ct. TW18: Staines 65J 127
Latchett Rd. E18 25Kc 53
Latchford Pl. HP1: Hem H 3J 3
IG7: Chig 21Xc 55
Latching Cl. RM3: Rom 21Md 57
Latchingdon Ct. E17 28Zb 52
Latchingdon Gdns.
IG8: Wfd G 23Nc 54
Latchmere Cl. TW10: Ham 64Na 131
Latchmere La. KT2: King T 65Pa 131
TW10: Ham 65Pa 131
Latchmere Leisure Cen. 54Hb 111
Latchmere Pas. SW11 54Gb 111
Latchmere Pl. TW15: Ashf 61N 127
Latchmere Rd. KT2: King T 66Na 131
SW11 54Hb 111
Latchmere St. SW11 54Hb 111
Latchmoor Av. SL9: Chal P 28A 42
Latchmoor Gro. SL9: Chal P 28A 42
Latchmoor Way SL9: Chal P 28A 42
Lateward Rd. TW8: Bford 51Ma 109
Latham Cl. DA2: Dart 61Ud 142
E6 43Nc 94
TN16: Big H 88Lc 179
TW1: Twick 59Ja 108
Latham Ct. *N11* 23Nb 50
(off Brownlow Rd.)
SW5 49Cb 89
(off W. Cromwell Rd.)
UB5: N'olt 41Z 85
(off Delta Gro.)
Latham Ho. *E1* 44Zb 92
(off Chudleigh St.)
Latham Pl. RM14: Upm 32Sd 78
Latham Rd. DA6: Bex 57Cd 118
TW1: Twick 59Ha 108
Latham's Way CR0: Wadd 74Pb 156
Lathkill Cl. EN1: Enf 17Wb 33
Lathkill Ct. BR3: Beck 67Bc 136
Lathom Rd. E6 38Nc 74
LATIMER 9A 10
Latimer Av. E6 39Pc 74
Latimer Chase WD3: Chen 12E 24
Latimer Cl. GU22: Wok 88D 168
HA5: Pinn 25Y 45
KT4: Wor Pk 77Xa 154
WD18: Wat 17U 26
Latimer Ct. *BR2: Brom* 70Hc 137
(off Durham Rd.)
EN8: Walt C 6Bc 20
RH1: Redh 8P 207
Latimer Dr. RM12: Horn 34Md 77
Latimer Gdns. HA5: Pinn 25Y 45
Latimer Ho. E9 37Zb 72
W11 45Bb 89
(off Kensington Pk. Rd.)
Latimer Ind. Est. W10 44Ya 88
Latimer Pl. W10 44Ya 88
Latimer Rd. CR0: C'don 76Rb 157
E7 35Kc 73
EN5: New Bar 13Db 31
HP5: Lat 9A 10
N15 30Ub 51
SW19 65Db 133
TW11: Tedd 64Ha 130
W10 43Ya 88
(not continuous)
WD3: Chen 9A 10
Latitude *KT16: Chert* 74L 149
(off Bridge Wharf)
Latitude Apartments *CR0: C'don* 76Tb 157
(off Fairfield Rd.)
Latitude Ct. E16 45Sc 94
Latitude Ho. *NW1* 39Kb 70
(off Oval Rd.)
Latium Cl. AL1: St A 3B 6
Latona Ct. *SW9* 52Qb 112
(off Caldwell St.)
Latona Dr. DA12: Grav'nd 4H 145
Latona Rd. SE15 51Wb 113
La Tourne Gdns. BR6: Farnb 76Sc 160
Lattimer Pl. W4 52Ua 110
Lattimore Ho. *AL1: St A* 2C 6
(off Lattimore Rd.)
Lattimore Rd. AL1: St A 3C 6
Latton Cl. KT10: Esh 77Da 151
KT12: Walt T 73Aa 151
Latvia Ct. *SE17* 50Sb 91
(off Macleod St.)
Latymer Cl. KT13: Weyb 77S 150
Latymer Ct. W6 49Za 88
Latymer Gdns. N3 26Ab 48
Latymer Rd. N9 18Vb 33
Latymer Way N9 19Ub 33
Laubin Cl. TW1: Twick 56Ka 108
Lauder Cl. UB5: N'olt 40Z 65
Lauder Ct. N14 17Nb 32
Lauderdale Dr. TW10: Ham 62Ma 131
Lauderdale House 32Kb 70
Lauderdale Ho. *SW9* 53Qb 112
(off Gosling Way)
TW18: Staines 64H 127
(off Gresham Rd.)
Lauderdale House Community Arts Cen.
32Kb 70
Lauderdale Mans. *W9* 41Db 89
(off Lauderdale Rd.)
Lauderdale Pde. W9 42Db 89
Lauderdale Pl. EC2 7D 218
Lauderdale Rd. W9 41Db 89
WD4: Hunt C 5S 12
Lauderdale Twr. EC2 7D 218
Laud St. CR0: C'don 76Sb 157
SE11 7H 229 (50Pb 90)
Laugan Wlk. SE17 7E 230 (50Sb 91)
Laughton Ct. WD6: Bore 12Sa 29
Laughton Rd. UB5: N'olt 39Z 65
Launcelot Rd. BR1: Brom 63Jc 137
Launcelot St. SE1 2K 229 (47Qb 90)
Launceston WD3: Chor 16D 24
Launceston Cl. RM3: Rom 25Ld 57
Launceston Gdns. UB6: G'frd 39Ja 66
Launceston Pl. W8 4A 226 (48Eb 89)
Launceston Rd. UB6: G'frd 39La 66
Launch St. E14 48Ec 92
Launders Ga. W3 47Ra 87
Launder's La. RM13: Rain, Wenn 41Pd 97
Laundress La. N16 34Wb 71
Laundry La. CM15: Mount 11Fe 41
N1 39Sb 71
Laundry M. SE23 59Ac 114
Laundry Rd. W6 51Ab 110
Launton Dr. DA6: Bex 56Zc 117
Laura Cl. E11 29Lc 53
EN1: Enf 15Ub 33
Lauradale Rd. N2 28Hb 49
Laura Dr. BR8: Hext 66Jd 140
Laura Pl. E5 35Yb 72
Laura Ter. N4 33Rb 71
Laureate Way HP1: Hem H 1K 3
Laurel Apartments SE17 5H 231
Laurel Av. DA12: Grav'nd 1E 144
EN6: Pot B 4Bb 17
SL3: L'ly 47A 82
TW1: Twick 60Ha 108
TW20: Eng G 4M 125
Laurel Bank *GU24: Chob* 3J 167
(off Bagshot Rd.)
HP3: Hem H 5H 3
N12 21Eb 49
Laurel Bank Cl. TN16: Big H 88Lc 179
Laurel Bank Gdns. SW6 54Bb 111
Laurel Bank Rd. EN2: Enf 11Sb 33
Laurel Bank Vs. *W7* 47Ga 86
(off Lwr. Boston Rd.)
Laurel Cl. CM13: Hut 15De 41
DA1: Dart 60Ld 119
DA14: Sidc 62Wc 139
HP2: Hem H 1P 3
IG6: Ilf 23Sc 54
N19 33Lb 70
SL3: Poyle 52G 104
SW17 64Gb 133
WD19: Wat 17Z 27
Laurel Ct. *CM13: Hut* 16Ee 41
(off The Spinney)
CM16: Epp 3Wc 23
CR2: S Croy 77Ub 157
(off South Pk. Hill Rd.)
EN6: Cuff 1Pb 18
HA0: Wemb 40Na 67
RM13: Rain 42Ld 97
SE1 4F 231
SL0: Iver H 38F 62
Laurel Cres. CR0: C'don 76Cc 158
GU21: Wok 85E 168
RM7: Rush G 32Gd 76
Laurel Dr. N21 17Qb 32
RH8: Oxt 3K 211
RM15: S Ock 42Zd 99
Laurel Edge *AL1: St A* 1D 6
(off Avenue Rd.)
Laurel Flds. EN6: Pot B 3Bb 17
Laurel Gdns. BR1: Brom 70Nc 138
E4 17Dc 34
KT15: New H 82K 169
NW7 20Ta 29
TW4: Houn 56Aa 107
TW15: Ashf 64S 128
W7 46Ga 86
Laurel Gro. SE20 66Yb 136
SE26 63Zb 136
Laurel Ho. BR2: Brom 67Gc 137
E3 39Bc 72
(off Hornbeam Sq.)
SE8 51Bc 114
Laurel La. RM12: Horn 33Nd 77
UB7: W Dray 49N 83
Laurel Lodge La. EN5: Barn 8Ya 16
Laurells, The KT22: Fet 96Fa 192
Laurel Mnr. SM2: Sutt 80Eb 155
Laurel M. *SE5* 55Sb 113
(off Harbour Rd.)
Laurel Pk. HA3: Hrw W 24Ha 46
Laurel Rd. AL1: St A 2D 6
SL9: Chal P 25A 42
SW13 54Wa 110
SW20 67Xa 132
TW12: Hamp H 64Fa 130
Laurels, The AL2: Brick W 10N 5
BR1: Brom 67Kc 137
BR2: Brom 70Jc 137
DA2: Wilm 62Ld 141
DA3: Lfield 69Ee 143
IG9: Buck H 18Lc 35
KT11: Cobh 87Aa 171
KT13: Weyb 76T 150
NW10 39Xa 68
SM7: Bans 89Bb 175
SW9 52Rb 113
(off Langton Rd.)
WD6: Bore 11Qa 29
WD23: B Hea 19Ga 28
Laurelsfield AL3: St A 5P 5
Laurels Rd. SL0: Iver H 40F 62
Laurel St. E8 37Vb 71
Laurel Vw. N12 20Db 31
Laurel Way E18 28Hc 53
N20 20Cb 31
Laurence Calvert Cl. IG11: Bark 40Uc 74
Laurence Ct. E10 31Dc 72
W11 45Ab 88
(off Lansdowne Rd.)
Laurence M. W12 47Wa 88
Laurence Pountney Hill
EC4 4F 225 (45Tb 91)
Laurence Pountney La.
EC4 4F 225 (45Tb 91)
Laurence Ri. DA2: Dart 58Sd 120
Laurence Rd. TW3: Houn 55Ea 108
Laurie Cl. TN14: S'oaks 92Kd 203

Laurie Gro.—Legatt Rd.

Laurie Gro. SE14 .53Ac 114
Laurie Ho. SE1 .4C 230
W8 .46Cb 89
(off Airlie Gdns.)
Laurie Rd. W7 .43Ga 86
Laurier Rd. CR0: C'don .73Vb 157
NW5 .34Kb 70
Lauries Cl. HP1: Hem H .4E 2
Laurie Wlk. RM1: Rom .29Gd 56
Laurimel Cl. HA7: Stan .23Ka 46
Laurino Pl. WD23: B Hea .19Ea 28
Lauriston Cl. GU21: Knap .9H 167
Lauriston Ho. *E9* .38Yb 72
(off Lauriston Rd.)
Lauriston Rd. E9 .38Yb 72
SW19 .65Za 132
Lausanne Rd. N8 .28Qb 50
SE15 .53Yb 114
Lauser Rd. TW19: Stanw .59L 105
Laval Ho. *TW8: Bford* .50Na 87
(off Ealing Rd.)
Lavell St. N16 .35Tb 71
Lavender Av. CM15: Pil H .15Xd 40
CR4: Mitc .67Gb 133
KT4: Wor Pk .76Ya 154
NW9 .32Sa 67
Lavender Cl. BR2: Brom .72Nc 160
CR3: Cat'm .97Sb 197
CR5: Coul .91Lb 196
E4 .21Cc 52
KT22: Lea .94La 192
RM3: Rom .24Md 57
RM15: S Ock .42Ae 99
SM5: Cars .77Kb 156
SW3 .51Fb 111
Lavender Ct. KT8: W Mole .69Da 129
KT22: Lea .94La 192
SM2: Sutt .80Eb 155
TW14: Felt .58X 107
Lavender Gdns. EN2: Enf .11Rb 33
HA3: Hrw W .23Ga 46
SW11 .56Hb 111
Lavender Ga. KT22: Oxs .86Da 171
Lavender Gro. CR4: Mitc .67Gb 133
E8 .38Wb 71
Lavender Hill BR8: Swan .69Fd 140
EN2: Enf .11Qb 32
SW11 .56Gb 111
Lavender Ho. *SE16* .46Zb 92
(off Rotherhithe St.)
TW9: Kew .53Ra 109
Lavender M. SS17: Stan H .1N 101
Lavender Pk. Rd. KT14: W Byf .84J 169
Lavender Pl. IG1: Ilf .36Rc 74
Lavender Pond Nature Pk. .46Ac 92
Lavender Ri. UB7: W Dray .47Q 84
Lavender Rd. CR0: C'don .72Pb 156
EN2: Enf .11Tb 33
GU22: Wok .88D 168
KT19: Ewe .78Ra 153
SE16 .46Ac 92
SM1: Sutt .77Fb 155
SM5: Cars .77Jb 156
SW11 .55Fb 111
UB8: Hil .43P 83
Lavender Sq. *SW9* .53Pb 112
(off Printers Rd.)
Lavender St. E15 .37Gc 73
Lavender Sweep SW11 .56Hb 111
Lavender Ter. SW11 .55Gb 111
Lavender Va. SM6: Wall .79Mb 156
Lavender Wlk. CR4: Mitc .69Jb 134
HP2: Hem H .1M 3
SW11 .56Hb 111
Lavender Way CR0: C'don .72Zb 158
Lavendon Ho. NW8 .5E 214
Lavengro Rd. SE27 .61Sb 135
Lavenha Ct. CM15: B'wood .18Zd 41
Lavenham Rd. SW18 .61Bb 133
Lavernock Rd. DA7: Bex .54Cd 118
Lavers Rd. N16 .34Ub 71
Laverstoke Gdns. SW15 .59Va 110
Laverton M. SW5 .49Db 89
Laverton Pl. SW5 .49Db 89
Lavette Ho. *E3* .41Cc 92
(off Rainhill Way)
Lavidge Rd. SE9 .61Nc 138
Lavina Gro. N1 .1H 217 (40Pb 70)
Lavington Cl. E9 .37Bc 72
Lavington Rd. CR0: Bedd .76Pb 156
W13 .46Ka 86
Lavington St. SE1 .7C 224 (46Rb 91)
Lavinia Av. WD25: Wat .6Z 13
Lavinia Rd. DA1: Dart .58Pd 119
Lavisham Ho. BR1: Brom .64Kc 137
Lavrock La. WD3: Crox G .17P 25
Lawdons Gdns. CR0: Wadd .77Rb 157
Lawes Ho. *W10* .41Bb 89
(off Lancefield St.)
Lawes Way IG11: Bark .41Vc 95
Lawford Av. WD3: Chor .16E 24
Lawford Cl. RM12: Horn .35Ld 77
WD3: Chor .16E 24
Lawford Gdns. CR8: Kenley .88Sb 177
DA1: Dart .57Ld 119
Lawford Rd. N1 .38Ub 71
NW5 .37Lb 70
W4 .52Sa 109
Lawford's Hill Cl. GU3: Worp .6G 186
Lawford's Hill Rd. GU3: Worp .6G 186
Lawfords Wharf *NW1* .38Lb 70
(off Lyme St.)
Law Ho. IG11: Bark .40Wc 75
Lawkland SL2: Farn R .1G 80
Lawless Ho. *E14* .45Ec 92
(off Bazely St.)
Lawless St. E14 .45Dc 92
Lawley Ho. TW1: Twick .58Ma 109
Lawley Rd. N14 .17Kb 32
Lawley St. E5 .35Yb 72
Lawlor Cl. TW16: Sun .67X 129
Lawn, The SL3: Dat .3N 103
UB2: S'hall .50Ca 85
Lawn Av. UB7: W Dray .47L 83
Lawn Cl. BR1: Brom .65Kc 137
BR8: Swan .68Ed 140
HA4: Ruis .34V 64
KT3: N Mald .68Ua 132
N9 .17Vb 33
SL3: Dat .2N 103
Lawn Cres. TW9: Kew .54Qa 109
Lawn Farm Gro. RM6: Chad H .28Ad 55
Lawnfield Ct. *NW6* .38Za 68
(off Coverdale Rd.)
Lawn Gdns. W7 .46Ga 86
Lawn Ho. Cl. E14 .47Ec 92
Lawn La. HP3: Hem H .4M 3
SW8 .51Pb 112
Lawn Pk. TN13: S'oaks .99Kd 203
Lawn Rd. BR3: Beck .66Bc 136
DA11: Nflt .58Ee 121
NW3 .36Hb 69
UB8: Uxb .38L 63
Lawns, The AL3: St A .1A 6
CM14: W'ley .22Ae 59
(off Uplands Rd.)
DA14: Sidc .63Xc 139
E4 .22Cc 52
HA5: Hat E .24Da 45
HP1: Hem H .1G 2
SE3 .55Hc 115
SE19 .67Tb 135
SL3: Poyle .53G 104
SM2: Cheam .80Ab 154
SW19 .64Bb 133
WD7: Shenl .5Na 15
Lawns Ct. HA9: Wemb .33Pa 67
Lawns Cres. RM17: Grays .51Fe 121
Lawnside SE3 .56Hc 115
Lawns Pl. RM17: Grays .51Fe 121
Lawns Way RM5: Col R .24Ed 56
Lawnswood EN5: Barn .15Ab 30
Lawn Ter. SE3 .55Gc 115
Lawn Va. HA5: Pinn .26Aa 45
Lawrance Gdns.
EN8: Chesh .1Zb 20
Lawrance Sq. DA11: Nflt .2B 144
Lawrence Av. E12 .35Qc 74
E17 .25Zb 52
KT3: N Mald .72Ta 153
N13 .21Rb 51
NW7 .21Ua 48
NW10 .39Ta 67
Lawrence Bldgs. N16 .34Vb 71
Lawrence Campe Cl. N20 .20Fb 31
Lawrence Cl. E3 .41Cc 92
N15 .28Ub 51
W12 .45Xa 88
Lawrence Ct. N10 .27Lb 50
N16 .34Vb 71
(off Smalley Rd. Est.)
NW7 .22Ua 48
SE6 .58Cc 114
SL4: Wind .4G 102
W3 .48Sa 87
(off Stanley Rd.)
WD19: Wat .20Z 27
Lawrence Cres. GU20: W'sham .9B 146
HA8: Edg .26Qa 47
RM10: Dag .34Dd 76
Lawrence Dr. DA12: Cobh .10J 145
UB10: Ick .35S 64
Lawrence Est. TW4: Houn .56Y 107
Lawrence Gdns. NW7 .20Va 30
RM18: Tilb .2D 122
Lawrence Gro. UB10: Uxb .40N 63
Lawrence Hill E4 .19Cc 34
Lawrence Hill Gdns. DA1: Dart .58Ld 119
Lawrence Hill Rd. DA1: Dart .58Ld 119
Lawrence Ho. *NW1* .38Kb 70
(off Hawley Cres.)
SW1 .6E 228
Lawrence La. EC2 .3E 224 (44Sb 91)
RH3: Bkld .4D 206
Lawrence Mans. *SW3* .51Gb 111
(off Lordship Pl.)
Lawrence M. SW15 .56Ya 110
Lawrence Pde. *TW7: Isle* .55Ka 108
(off Lower Sq.)
Lawrence Pl. *N1* .39Nb 70
(off Brydon Wlk.)
Lawrence Rd. BR4: W W'ck .77Jc 159
DA8: Erith .52Dd 118
E6 .39Nc 74
E13 .39Kc 73
HA5: Pinn .30Z 45
N15 .28Ub 51
N18 .21Xb 51
(not continuous)
RM2: Rom .29Kd 57
SE25 .70Vb 135
TW4: Houn .56Y 107
TW10: Ham .63La 130
TW12: Hamp .66Ba 129
UB4: Hayes .40S 64
W5 .49Ma 87
Lawrence St. E16 .43Hc 93
NW7 .22Va 48
SW3 .51Gb 111
Lawrence Trad. Est. RM17: Grays .50Ae 99
SE10 .49Gc 93
Lawrence Way NW10 .34Sa 67
SL1: Slou .3A 80
Lawrence Weaver Cl.
SM4: Mord .72Cb 155
Lawrence Yd. N15 .28Ub 51
Lawrie Ho. *SW19* .64Db 133
(off Durnsford Rd.)
Lawrie Pk. Av. SE26 .64Xb 135
Lawrie Pk. Cres. SE26 .64Xb 135
Lawrie Pk. Gdns. SE26 .63Xb 135
Lawrie Pk. Rd. SE26 .65Xb 135
Laws Cl. SE25 .70Tb 135
Lawson Cl. E16 .43Lc 93
IG1: Ilf .36Tc 74
SW19 .62Za 132
Lawson Ct. KT6: Surb .73Ma 153
N4 .32Pb 70
(off Lorne Rd.)
N11 .23Lb 50
(off Ring Way)
Lawson Gdns. DA1: Dart .57Md 119
HA5: Eastc .27X 45
Lawson Ho. *SE18* .51Qc 116
(off Nightingale Pl.)
W12 .45Xa 88
(off White City Est.)
Lawson Rd. DA1: Dart .56Md 119
EN3: Enf H .11Yb 34
UB1: S'hall .42Ca 85
Lawson Ter. SE15 .56Yb 114
Lawson Wlk. SM5: Cars .81Jb 176
Lawson Way SL5: S'dale .2F 146
Law St. SE1 .3G 231 (48Tb 91)
Lawton Rd. E3 .41Ac 92
(not continuous)
E10 .32Ec 72
EN4: Cockf .13Fb 31
IG10: Lough .12Rc 36
Laxcon Cl. NW10 .36Ta 67
Laxey Rd. BR6: Chels .79Vc 161
Laxfield Ct. *E8* .39Wb 71
(off Pownall Rd.)
Laxford Ho. SW1 .6J 227
Laxley Cl. SE5 .52Rb 113
Laxton Ct. CR7: Thor H .70Sb 135
Laxton Gdns. RH1: Mers .100Mb 196
WD7: Shenl .4Na 15
Laxton Pl. NW1 .5A 216 (42Kb 90)
Layard Rd. CR7: Thor H .68Tb 135
EN1: Enf .11Vb 33
SE16 .49Xb 91
Layard Sq. SE16 .49Xb 91
Layborne Av. RM3: Rom .19Ld 39
Laybourne Ho. *E14* .47Cc 92
(off Admirals Way)
Laybrook Lodge E18 .28Hc 53
Layburn Cres. SL3: L'ly .51D 104
Laycock St. N1 .37Qb 70
Layer Gdns. W3 .45Qa 87
Layfield Cl. NW4 .31Xa 68
Layfield Cres. NW4 .31Xa 68
Layfield Ho. *SE10* .50Jc 93
(off Kemsing Rd.)
Layfield Rd. NW4 .31Xa 68
Layhams Rd. BR2: Kes .77Gc 159
BR4: W W'ck .77Gc 159
CR6: W'ham .84Hc 179
Laymarsh Cl. DA17: Belv .48Bd 95
Laymead Cl. UB5: N'olt .37Aa 65
Laystall Ct. WC1 .6K 217
Laystall St. EC1 .6K 217 (42Qb 90)
Layters Way SL9: Ger X .29A 42
Layton Ct. KT13: Weyb .77R 150
TW8: Bford .50Ma 87
Layton Cres. CR0: Wadd .78Qb 156
Layton Pl. TW9: Kew .53Qa 109
Layton Rd. TW3: Houn .56Da 107
TW8: Bford .50Ma 87
Layton's La. TW16: Sun .68V 128
Layzell Wlk. SE9 .60Mc 115
Lazare Ct. *TW18: Staines* .64H 127
(off Gresham Rd.)
Lazar Wlk. N7 .33Pb 70
Lazenby Ct. WC2 .4F 223
Lea, The TW20: Egh .66E 126
Leabank Cl. HA1: Harr .34Ga 66
Leabank Sq. E9 .37Cc 72
Leabank Vw. N15 .30Wb 51
Lea Bon Ct. *E15* .39Hc 73
(off Plaistow Gro.)
Leabourne Rd. N16 .31Wb 71
LEA BRIDGE .34Zb 72
Lea Bri. Ind. Cen. E10 .32Ac 72
Lea Bri. Rd. E5 .34Yb 72
E10 .31Cc 72
E17 .27Fc 53
Lea Bushes WD25: Wat .7Aa 13
Leach Gro. KT22: Lea .94La 192
Lea Cl. TW2: Whitt .59Ba 107
WD23: Bush .15Da 27
Lea Ct. E4 .19Ec 34
E13 .41Jc 93
N15 .28Wb 51
Lea Cres. HA4: Ruis .35V 64
Leacroft SL1: Slou .7D 80
SL5: S'dale .1E 146
TW18: Staines .64J 127
Leacroft Av. SW12 .59Hb 111
Leacroft Cl. CR8: Kenley .88Sb 177
N21 .19Rb 33
TW18: Staines .63K 127
UB7: Yiew .44N 83
Leacroft Rd. SL0: Iver .44G 82
Leadale Av. E4 .19Cc 34
Leadale Rd. N15 .30Wb 51
N16 .30Wb 51
Leadbeaters Cl. N11 .22Hb 49
Leadbetter Ct. *NW10* .38Ta 67
(off Melville Rd.)
Leaden Cl. IG10: Lough .13Rc 36
Leadenhall Mkt. EC3 .3H 225 (44Ub 91)
Leadenhall Pl. EC3 .3H 225 (44Ub 91)
Leadenhall St. EC3 .3H 225 (44Ub 91)
Leadenham Ct. E3 .42Cc 92
Leaden Hill CR5: Coul .87Mb 176
Leader Av. E12 .36Qc 74
Leadings, The HA9: Wemb .34Sa 67
Leadmill La. E20 .35Dc 72
Leaf Cl. HA6: Nwood .24T 44
KT7: T Ditt .71Ga 152
Leaf Gro. SE27 .64Qb 134
Leaf Hill Dr. RM3: Rom .21Ld 57
Leaf Ho. *HA1: Harr* .29Ha 46
(off Catherine Pl.)
Leafield Cl. GU21: Wok .10N 167
SW16 .65Rb 135
Leafield La. DA14: Sidc .62Bd 139
Leafield Rd. SM1: Sutt .75Cb 155
SW20 .69Bb 133
Leaford Ct. WD24: Wat .8V 12
Leaford Cres. WD24: Wat .9V 12
Leaf Wlk. N7 .35Mb 70
Leaf Way AL1: St A .5B 6
Leafy Gro. BR2: Kes .78Lc 159
Leafy Oak Rd. SE12 .63Lc 137
Leafy Way CM13: Hut .18Fe 41
CR0: C'don .75Vb 157
Lea Gdns. HA9: Wemb .35Pa 67
Leagrave St. E5 .34Yb 72
Lea Hall Gdns. E10 .32Cc 72
Lea Hall Rd. E10 .32Cc 72
Leaholme Gdns. SL1: Slou .3A 80
Leaholme Way HA4: Ruis .30S 44
Lea Ho. NW8 .6D 214
Leahurst Rd. SE13 .57Fc 115
LEA INTERCHANGE .36Cc 72
Leake Ct. SE1 .2J 229 (47Pb 90)
Leake St. SE1 .1J 229 (47Pb 90)
(not continuous)
Lealand Rd. N15 .30Vb 51
Leamington Av. BR1: Brom .64Lc 137
BR6: Orp .77Uc 160
E17 .29Cc 52
SM4: Mord .70Ab 132
Leamington Cl. BR1: Brom .63Lc 137
E12 .36Nc 74
RM3: Rom .23Qd 57
TW3: Houn .57Ea 108
Leamington Ct. SE3 .51Gc 115
Leamington Cres. HA2: Harr .34Aa 65
Leamington Gdns. IG3: Ilf .33Vc 75
Leamington Ho. HA8: Edg .22Pa 47
W11 .43Bb 89
(off Tavistock Rd.)
Leamington Pk. W3 .43Ta 87
Leamington Pl. UB4: Hayes .42V 84
Leamington Rd. RM3: Rom .22Qd 57
UB2: S'hall .49Z 85
Leamington Rd. Vs. W11 .43Bb 89
Leamore Ct. E2 .41Zb 92
Leamore St. W6 .49Ya 88
Lea Mt. EN7: G Oak .1Ub 19
LEAMOUTH .45Gc 93
Leamouth Rd. E6 .43Nc 94
E14 .44Fc 93
Leander Ct. *E9* .38Zb 72
(off Lauriston Rd.)
KT6: Surb .73Ma 153
NW9 .25Ua 48
SE8 .53Cc 114
Leander Dr. DA12: Grav'nd .3H 145
Leander Gdns. WD25: Wat .9Aa 13
Leander Rd. CR7: Thor H .70Pb 134
SW2 .58Pb 112
UB5: N'olt .40Ca 65
Lea Pk. Trad. Est. E10 .31Bc 72
Learner Dr. HA2: Harr .33Ca 65
Lea Rd. BR3: Beck .68Cc 136
EN2: Enf .11Tb 33
EN9: Walt A .6Cc 20
RM16: Grays .10C 100
TN13: S'oaks .99Ld 203
UB2: S'hall .49Aa 85
WD24: Wat .10X 13
Lea Rd. Ind. Pk. EN9: Walt A .6Cc 20
Lea Rd. Trad. Est. EN9: Walt A .6Cc 20
Learoyd Gdns. E6 .45Qc 94
Leary Ho. SE11 .7J 229 (50Pb 90)
Leas, The HP3: Hem H .6A 4
RM14: Upm .31Td 78
TW18: Staines .63J 127
WD23: Bush .11Ba 27
Leas Cl. KT9: Chess .80Pa 153
Leas Dale SE9 .62Qc 138
Leas Dr. SL0: Iver .44G 82
Leas Grn. BR7: Chst .65Vc 139
Leaside HP2: Hem H .3C 4
KT23: Bookh .95Ca 191
Leaside Av. N10 .27Jb 50
Leaside Bus. Cen. EN3: Brim .12Bc 34
Leaside Ct. UB10: Hil .41R 84
Leaside Mans. *N10* .27Jb 50
(off Fortis Grn.)
Leaside Rd. E5 .32Yb 72
Leas La. CR6: W'ham .90Zb 178
Leasowes Rd. E10 .32Cc 72
Lea Sq. E3 .39Bc 72
Leas Rd. CR6: W'ham .90Zb 178
Leasway CM14: B'wood .20Zd 41
RM14: Upm .35Sd 78
RM16: Grays .46Ee 99
Leathart Cl. RM12: Horn .38Kd 77
Leatherbottle Grn. DA18: Erith .48Bd 95
Leather Bottle La. DA17: Belv .49Ad 95
Leather Cl. CR4: Mitc .68Jb 134
Leatherdale St. E1 .41Zb 92
Leather Gdns. E15 .39Gc 73
LEATHERHEAD .94Ka 192
Leatherhead Bus. Pk. KT22: Lea .91Ha 192
Leatherhead Cl. N16 .32Vb 71
LEATHERHEAD COMMON .91Ja 192
Leatherhead Fitness & Wellbeing Cen.
.94Ka 192
(off The Crescent)
Leatherhead Golf Course .88Ja 172
Leatherhead Leisure Cen. .95Ja 192
Leatherhead Mus. of Local History
.94Ka 192
Leatherhead Rd. KT9: Chess .86Ka 172
KT21: Asht .93Ma 193
KT22: Lea .93Ma 193
KT22: Oxs .86Fa 172
KT23: Bookh .98Da 191
Leatherhead Theatre .94Ka 192
Leatherhead Trade Pk.
KT22: Lea .93Ja 192
Leather La. EC1 .7K 217 (43Qb 90)
(not continuous)
RM11: Horn .32Md 77
Leathermarket, The SE1 .2H 231
Leathermarket Ct. SE1 .2H 231 (47Ub 91)
Leathermarket St. SE1 .2H 231 (47Ub 91)
Leather Rd. SE16 .49Zb 92
Leathersellers Cl. *EN5: Barn* .13Ab 30
(off The Avenue)
Leather St. E1 .45Zb 92
Leathsail Rd. HA2: Harr .34Da 65
Leathwaite Rd. SW11 .56Hb 111
Leathwell Rd. SE8 .54Dc 114
Lea Va. DA1: Cray .56Fd 118
Lea Valley Bus. Pk. E10 .33Ac 72
Lea Valley Rd. E4 .15Ac 34
EN3: Pond E .15Ac 34
Lea Valley Trad. Est. N18 .23Zb 52
Lea Valley Viaduct E4 .22Zb 52
N18 .22Zb 52
Leaveland Cl. BR3: Beck .70Cc 136
Leaver Gdns. UB6: G'frd .40Fa 66
LEAVESDEN .4V 12
Leavesden Country Pk. .4W 12
Leavesden Ct. WD5: Ab L .3W 12
Leavesden Film Studios
WD25: Hunt C .5U 12
LEAVESDEN GREEN .5W 12
LEAVESDEN GREEN .7U 12
Leavesden Pk. WD25: Wat .5V 12
Leavesden Rd. HA7: Stan .23Ja 46
KT13: Weyb .78R 150
WD24: Wat .10X 13
LEAVES GREEN .83Mc 179
Leaves Grn. Cres. BR2: Kes .83Lc 179
Leaves Grn. Rd. BR2: Kes .83Mc 179
Lea Vw. EN9: Walt A .5Dc 20
Lea Vw. Ho. E5 .32Xb 71
Leaway E10 .32Zb 72
Leazes Av. CR3: Cat'm .95Qb 196
Lebanon Av. TW13: Hanw .64Z 129
Lebanon Cl. WD17: Wat .8T 12
Lebanon Ct. TW1: Twick .59Ka 108
Lebanon Dr. KT11: Cobh .85Ca 171
Lebanon Gdns. SW18 .58Cb 111
TN16: Big H .89Mc 179
Lebanon Pk. TW1: Twick .59Ka 108
Lebanon Rd. CR0: C'don .74Ub 157
SW18 .57Cb 111
Lebus Ho. NW8 .2D 214
Lebus St. N17 .27Xb 51
Le Chateau *CR0: C'don* .76Tb 157
(off Chatsworth Rd.)
Lechmere App. IG8: Wfd G .26Lc 53
Lechmere Av. IG7: Chig .21Sc 54
IG8: Wfd G .26Mc 53
Lechmere Rd. NW2 .37Xa 68
Leckford Rd. SW18 .61Eb 133
Leckhampton Pl. SW2 .59Qb 112
Leckwith Av. DA7: Bex .51Ad 117
Lecky St. SW7 .7B 226 (50Fb 89)
Leconfield Av. SW13 .55Va 110
Leconfield Ho. SE5 .56Ub 113
Leconfield Rd. N5 .35Tb 71
Leconfield Wlk. RM12: Horn .37Ld 77
Le Cordon Bleu
London .1G 223
London Culinary Arts Institute *.1J 221*
(off Marylebone La.)
Le Corte Cl. WD4: K Lan .1P 11
Lectern La. AL1: St A .6C 6
Leda Av. EN3: Enf W .10Zb 20
Leda Ct. *SW9* .52Qb 112
(off Caldwell St.)
Leda M. HP2: Hem H .1P 3
Ledam Ho. EC1 .7K 217
Leda Rd. SE18 .48Pc 94
Ledbury Ho. SE22 .55Ub 113
W11 .44Bb 89
(off Colville Rd.)
Ledbury M. Nth. W11 .45Cb 89
Ledbury M. W. W11 .45Cb 89
Ledbury Pl. CR0: C'don .77Sb 157
Ledbury Rd. CR0: C'don .77Tb 157
RH2: Reig .6J 207
W11 .44Bb 89
Ledbury St. SE15 .52Wb 113
Ledger Dr. KT15: Add .78H 149
Ledger M. E17 .30Cc 52
Ledgers La. CR6: W'ham .89Dc 178
Ledgers Rd. CR6: W'ham .88Cc 178
SL1: Slou .7H 81
Ledrington Rd. SE19 .65Wb 135
Ledway Dr. HA9: Wemb .31Pa 67
LEE .58Jc 115
Lee, The HA6: Nwood .22V 44
Lee Av. RM6: Chad H .30Ad 55
Lee Bri. SE13 .55Ec 114
Leechcroft Av. BR8: Swan .69Hd 140
DA15: Sidc .57Vc 117
Leechcroft Rd. SM6: Wall .76Jb 156
Leech La. KT18: Head .98Ra 193
Lee Chu. St. SE13 .56Gc 115
Lee Cl. E17 .25Zb 52
EN5: New Bar .14Eb 31
Lee Conservancy Rd. E9 .36Bc 72
Lee Ct. *E3* .42Ec 92
(off Navigation Rd.)
SE13 .56Fc 115
(off Lee High Rd.)
Leecroft Rd. EN5: Barn .15Ab 30
Leeds Ct. BR6: Chels .75Zc 161
Leeds Ct. EC1 .5B 218
Leeds Pl. N4 .32Pb 70
Leeds Rd. IG1: Ilf .32Tc 74
SL1: Slou .5J 81
Leeds St. N18 .22Wb 51
Leefern Rd. W12 .47Wa 88
Leefe Way EN6: Cuff .1Mb 18
Lee Gdns. Av. RM11: Horn .32Qd 77
Leegate SE12 .57Hc 115
Leegate Cl. GU21: Wok .8M 167
LEE GREEN .57Hc 115
Lee Grn. BR5: St M Cry .71Wc 161
Lee Grn. La. KT18: Head .96Ra 193
Lee Gro. IG7: Chig .19Rc 36
Lee High Rd. SE12 .55Ec 114
SE13 .55Ec 114
Leeke St. WC1 .3H 217 (41Pb 90)
Leeland Rd. W13 .46Ja 86
Leeland Ter. W13 .46Ja 86
Leeland Way NW10 .35Va 68
Lee M. BR3: Beck .69Ac 136
Leeming Rd. WD6: Bore .11Pa 29
Leemount Ho. NW4 .28Za 48
Lee Pk. SE3 .56Hc 115
Lee Pk. Way N9 .21Zb 52
N18 .21Zb 52
Leerdam Dr. E14 .48Ec 92
Lee Rd. EN1: Enf .16Wb 33
NW7 .24Za 48
SE3 .55Hc 115
SW19 .67Db 133
UB6: G'frd .39La 66
Lees, The CR0: C'don .75Bc 158
Lees Av. HA6: Nwood .25V 44
Lees Ct. W1 .4H 221
Lees Ho. SE17 .7G 231
Leeside EN5: Barn .15Ab 30
EN6: Pot B .4Fb 17
Leeside Ct. *SE16* .46Zb 92
(off Rotherhithe St.)
Leeside Cres. NW11 .30Ab 48
Leeside Ind. Est. N17 .24Yb 52
Leeside Rd. N17 .23Xb 51
Leeside Works N17 .24Yb 52
Leeson Gdns. SL4: Eton W .9C 80
Leeson Ho. TW1: Twick .59Ka 108
Leeson Rd. SE24 .56Qb 112
Leesons Hill BR5: St P .69Uc 138
BR7: Chst .69Uc 138
Leeson's Way BR5: St P .68Vc 139
Lees Pde. UB10: Hil .42R 84
Lees Pl. W1 .4H 221 (45Jb 90)
Lees Rd. UB8: Hil .42R 84
Lee St. E8 .39Vb 71
Lee Ter. SE3 .55Gc 115
SE13 .55Gc 115
Lee Valley Athletics Cen. .18Ac 34
Lee Valley Golf Course .17Ac 34
Lee Valley Hockey & Tennis Cen.
.35Dc 72
Lee Valley Ice Cen. .33Zb 72
Lee Valley Pk. .24Zb 52
Lee Valley Pk. Info. Cen. .8Wb 19
Lee Valley Regional Pk. .3Cc 20
Lee Valley Technopark N17 .27Wb 51
Lee Valley VeloPark .36Dc 72
Lee Valley White Water Cen. .5Cc 20
Leeve Ho. *W10* .41Bb 89
(off Lancefield St.)
Lee Vw. EN2: Enf .11Rb 33
Leeward Ct. E1 .45Wb 91
SE8 .49Ac 92
(off Yeoman St.)
Leeward Gdns. SW19 .64Ab 132
Leeward Ho. *N1* .39Ub 71
(off Halcomb St.)
Leeway SE8 .50Bc 92
Leeway Cl. HA5: Hat E .24Ba 45
Leeways, The SM3: Cheam .79Ab 154
Leewood Cl. SE12 .58Jc 115
Leewood Pl. BR8: Swan .70Fd 140
Leewood Way KT24: Eff .99Y 191
Lefa Bus. & Ind. Pk. DA14: Sidc .65Zc 139
Lefevre Wlk. E3 .40Cc 72
Leff Ho. NW6 .39Ab 68
Lefroy Ho. SE1 .2D 230
Lefroy Rd. W12 .47Va 88
Left Side *N14* .18Mb 32
(off Statione Pde.)
Legard Rd. N5 .34Rb 71
Legatt Rd. SE9 .57Mc 115

Leggatt Rd.—Lichfield Way

Leggatt Rd. E15 40Ec 72
Leggatts Cl. WD24: Wat 8V 12
Leggatts Ri. WD25: Wat 7W 12
Leggatts Way WD24: Wat 8V 12
Leggatts Wood Av.
WD24: Wat 8X 13
Legge St. SE13 57Ec 114
Leggfield Ter. HP1: Hem H 2H 3
Leghorn Rd. NW10 40Va 68
SE18 50Tc 94
Legion Cl. N1 38Qb 70
Legion Ct. SM4: Mord 72Cb 155
Legion Rd. UB6: G'frd 39Ea 66
Legion Ter. E3 39Bc 72
Legion Way N12 24Gb 49
Legoland 7B 102
Leg O'Mutton Local Nature Reserve
52Va 110
Legon Av. RM7: Rush G 32Ed 76
Legrace Av. TW4: Houn 54Z 107
Leicester Av. CR4: Mitc 70Nb 134
Leicester Cl. KT4: Wor Pk 77Ya 154
Leicester Ct. TW1: Twick 58Ma 109
(off Clevedon Rd.)
W9 43Cb 89
(off Elmfield Way)
WC2 4E 222
Leicester Flds. WC2 5E 222
Leicester Gdns. IG3: Ilf 31Uc 74
Leicester Ho. N18 22Xb 51
(off Cavendish Cl.)
SW9 55Rb 113
(off Loughborough Rd.)
Leicester M. N2 27Gb 49
Leicester Pl. WC2 4E 222 (45Mb 90)
Leicester Rd.
CR0: C'don 73Ub 157
E11 29Kc 53
EN5: New Bar 15Db 31
N2 27Gb 49
NW10 38Ta 67
RM18: Tilb 3B 122
Leicester Sq. WC2 5E 222 (45Mb 90)
Leicester Square Theatre 4E 222
Leicester St. WC2 4E 222 (45Mb 90)
Leigh, The KT2: King T 66Ua 132
Leigham Av. SW16 62Nb 134
Leigham Cl. SW16 62Pb 134
Leigham Ct. SM6: Wall 79Lb 156
Leigham Ct. Rd. SW16 61Nb 134
Leigham Dr. TW7: Isle 52Ga 108
Leigham Hall Pde. SW16 62Nb 134
(off Streatham High Rd.)
Leigham Va. SW2 62Pb 134
SW16 62Pb 134
Leigh Av. IG4: Ilf 28Mc 53
Leigh Cl. KT3: N Mald 70Sa 131
KT15: Add 80H 149
Leigh Cl. Ind. Est. KT3: N Mald 70Ta 131
Leigh Cnr. KT11: Cobh 87Y 171
Leigh Ct. HA2: Harr 32Ga 66
KT11: Cobh 86Z 171
W14 49Bb 89
(off Avonmore Pl.)
WD6: Bore 12Ta 29
Leigh Ct. Cl. KT11: Cobh 86Y 171
Leigh Cres. CR0: New Ad 80Dc 158
Leigh Dr. RM3: Rom 21Md 57
Leigh Gdns. NW10 40Ya 68
Leigh Hill Rd. KT11: Cobh 87Y 171
Leigh Hunt Dr. N14 18Mb 32
Leigh Orchard Cl. SW16 62Pb 134
Leigh Pk. SL3: Dat 2M 103
Leigh Pl. DA2: Hawl 63Qd 141
DA16: Well 54Wc 117
EC1 7K 217 (43Qb 90)
KT11: Cobh 87Y 171
TW13: Felt 60Y 107
Leigh Pl. La. RH9: G'stone 4B 210
Leigh Rd. DA11: Grav'nd 1D 144
E6 37Qc 74
E10 31Ec 72
KT11: Cobh 86X 171
N5 35Rb 71
SL1: Slou 5F 80
TW3: Houn 56Fa 108
Leigh Rodd WD19: Wat 20Ba 27
Leigh Sq. SL4: Wind 4B 102
Leigh St. WC1 5F 217 (41Nb 90)
Leigh Ter. BR5: St P 69Xc 139
Leighton Av. E12 36Qc 74
HA5: Pinn 27Aa 45
Leighton Buzzard Rd. HP1: Hem H 1L 3
Leighton Cl. HA8: Edg 26Qa 47
Leighton Ct. EN8: Chesh 1Zb 20
Leighton Cres. NW5 36Lb 70
Leighton Gdns. CR0: C'don 74Rb 157
CR2: Sande 85Xb 177
NW10 40Xa 68
RM18: Tilb 2C 122
Leighton Gro. NW5 36Lb 70
Leighton Ho. EN6: Pot B 4Cb 17
SW1 6E 228
Leighton House Mus. 48Bb 89
Leighton Mans. W14 51Ab 110
(off Greyhound Rd.)
Leighton Pl. NW5 36Lb 70
Leighton Rd. EN1: Enf 15Vb 33
HA3: Hrw W 26Fa 46
NW5 36Lb 70
W13 47Ja 86
Leighton St. CR0: C'don 74Rb 157
Leighton Way KT18: Eps 86Ta 173
Leila Parnell Pl. SE7 51Lc 115
Leinster Av. SW14 55Sa 109
Leinster Gdns. W2 3A 220 (44Eb 89)
Leinster M. EN5: Barn 13Ab 30
W2 4A 220 (45Eb 89)
Leinster Pl. W2 3A 220 (44Eb 89)
Leinster Rd. N10 28Kb 50
Leinster Sq. W2 44Cb 89
(not continuous)
Leinster Ter. W2 4A 220 (45Eb 89)
Leirum St. N1 1J 217 (39Pb 70)
Leiston Spur SL1: Slou 4J 81
Leisure La. KT14: W Byf 84K 169
Leisure Way N12 24Fb 49
Leisure W. TW13: Felt 61X 129
Leisure World
Hemel Hempstead 3P 3
Leitch Ho. NW8 38Fb 69
(off Hilgrove Rd.)
Leith Cl. NW9 32Ta 67
SL1: Slou 6L 81
Leithcote Gdns. SW16 63Pb 134
Leithcote Path SW16 62Pb 134
Leith Hill BR5: St P 67Wc 139
Leith Hill Grn. BR5: St P 67Wc 139
Leith Mans. W9 41Db 89
(off Grantully Rd.)
Leith Pk. Rd. DA12: Grav'nd 10D 122
Leith Rd. KT17: Eps 84Ua 174
N22 25Rb 51
Leith Towers SM2: Sutt 80Db 155
Leith Yd. NW6 39Cb 69
(off Quex Rd.)
Lela Av. TW4: Houn 54Y 107
Lelitia Cl. E8 39Wb 71
Lely Ho. UB5: N'olt 40Z 65
(off Academy Gdns.)
Leman Pas. E1 44Wb 91
(off Leman St.)
Leman St. E1 2K 225 (44Vb 91)
Lemark Cl. HA7: Stan 23La 46
Le May Av. SE12 62Kc 137
Lemmon Rd. SE10 51Gc 115
Lemna Rd. E11 31Hc 73
Le Moal Ho. E1 43Yb 92
(off Stepney Way)
Lemonade Bldg. IG11: Bark 38Sc 74
(off Ripple Rd.)
Lemonfield Dr. WD25: Wat 4Aa 13
Lemon Gro. TW13: Felt 60W 106
Lemon Tree Ho. E3 41Bc 92
(off Bow Rd.)
Lemonwell Dr. SE9 57Sc 116
Lemsford Cl. N15 30Wb 51
Lemsford Ct. N4 33Sb 71
WD6: Bore 14Sa 29
Lemsford Rd. AL1: St A 2D 6
Lemuel St. SW18 58Eb 111
Lena Cres. N9 19Yb 34
Lena Gdns. W6 48Ya 88
Lena Kennedy Cl. E4 23Ec 52
Lenanton Steps E14 47Cc 92
(off Manilla St.)
Len Bishop Ct. E1 45Zb 92
(off Schoolhouse La.)
Len Clifton Ho. SE18 49Pc 94
(off Cambridge Barracks Rd.)
Lendal Ter. SW4 55Mb 112
Lenderyou Ct. DA1: Dart 59Md 119
(off Phoenix Pl.)
Lendon Rd. TN15: Bor G 93Be 205
Lendy Pl. TW16: Sun 70W 128
Lenelby Rd. KT6: Surb 74Qa 153
Len Freeman Pl. SW6 51Bb 111
W6 49Va 88
(off Goldhawk Rd.)
Lenham Ho. SE1 3G 231
Lenham Rd. CR7: Thor H 68Tb 135
DA7: Bex 51Bd 117
SE12 56Hc 115
SM1: Sutt 77Db 155
Lenmore Av. RM17: Grays 48Ee 99
Lennard Av. BR4: W W'ck 75Gc 159
Lennard Cl. BR4: W W'ck 75Gc 159
Lennard Rd. BR2: Brom 74Pc 160
BR3: Beck 65Zb 136
CR0: C'don 74Sb 157
SE20 65Zb 136
TN13: Dun G 92Gd 202
Lennard Row RM15: Avel 46Td 98
Lennon Rd. NW2 36Ya 68
Lennox Av. DA11: Grav'nd 8B 122
Lennox Cl. RM1: Rom 30Hd 56
RM16: Chaf H 49Yd 98
Lennox Ct. RH1: Redh 5A 208
(off St Anne's Ri.)
Lennox Gdns. CR0: Wadd 77Rb 157
IG1: Ilf 32Pc 74
NW10 35Va 68
SW1 4F 227 (48Hb 89)
Lennox Gdns. M. SW1 4F 227 (48Hb 89)
Lennox Ho. DA17: Belv 48Cd 96
(off Ambrooke Rd.)
TW1: Twick 58Ma 109
(off Clevedon Rd.)
Lennox Rd. DA11: Grav'nd 8B 122
E17 30Bc 52
N4 33Pb 70
SW9 53Rb 113
Lennox Rd. E. DA11: Grav'nd 9C 122
Le Noke Av. RM3: Rom 22Ld 57
Lenor Cl. DA6: Bex 56Ad 117
Lensbury Av. SW6 54Eb 111
Lensbury Cl. EN8: Chesh 1Ac 20
Lensbury Way SE2 48Yc 95
Lens Rd. E7 38Lc 73
LENT 2A 80
Len Taylor Cl. UB4: Hayes 42U 84
Lent Grn. La. SL1: Burn 2A 80
Lenthall Av. RM17: Grays 47Ce 99
Lenthall Ho. SW1 50Lb 90
(off Churchill Gdns.)
Lenthall Rd. E8 38Wb 71
IG10: Lough 14Tc 36
Lenthorp Rd. SE10 49Hc 93
Lentmead Rd. BR1: Brom 62Hc 137
Lenton Path SE18 51Tc 116
Lenton Ri. TW9: Rich 55Na 109
Lenton St. SE18 49Tc 94
Lenton Ter. N4 33Qb 70
LENT RISE 4A 80
Len Williams Ct. NW6 40Cb 69
Leo Ct. TW8: Bford 52Ma 109
Leof Cres. SE6 64Dc 136
Leominster Rd. SM4: Mord 72Eb 155
Leominster Wlk. SM4: Mord 72Eb 155
Leonard Av. DA10: Swans 59Ae 121
RM7: Rush G 32Fd 76
SM4: Mord 71Eb 155
TN14: Otf 88Hd 183
(not continuous)
Leonard Ct. HA3: Hrw W 25Ga 46
W8 48Cb 89
WC1 5E 216 (42Mb 90)
Leonard Pl. N16 35Ub 71
Leonard Rd. E4 23Cc 52
E7 35Jc 73
N9 20Wb 33
SW16 67Lb 134
UB2: S'hall 48Z 85
Leonard Robbins Path SE28 45Xc 95
(off Tawney Rd.)
Leonard St. E16 46Nc 94
EC2 5G 219 (42Tb 91)
Leonard Way CM14: B'wood 21Ud 58
Leonora Ho. W9 5A 214
Leonora Tyson M. SE21 61Tb 135
Leontine Cl. SE15 52Wb 113
Leopards Ct. EC1 7K 217
Leopold Av. SW19 64Bb 133
Leopold Bldgs. E2 3K 219
Leopold Ct. KT10: Esh 79Ea 152
(off Princess Sq.)
Leopold M. E9 39Yb 72
Leopold Rd. E17 29Cc 52
N2 27Fb 49
N18 22Xb 51
NW10 38Ua 68
SW19 63Bb 133
W5 46Pa 87
Leopold St. E3 43Bc 92
Leopold Ter. SW19 64Bb 133
Leopold Wlk. SE11 7H 229
Leo St. SE15 52Xb 113
Leo Yd. EC1 6C 218
Le Personne Homes CR3: Cat'm 94Tb 197
(off Banstead Rd.)
Le Personne Rd. CR3: Cat'm 94Tb 197
Leppoc Rd. SW4 57Mb 112
Leret Way KT22: Lea 93Ka 192
Leroy St. SE1 4H 231 (49Ub 91)
Lerry Cl. W14 51Bb 111
Lerwick Ct. EN1: Enf 15Ub 33
Lerwick Dr. SL1: Slou 3J 81
Lesbourne Rd. RH2: Reig 7K 207
Lescombe Cl. SE23 62Ac 136
Lescombe Rd. SE23 62Ac 136
Lescot Pl. BR2: Brom 72Nc 160
Lesley Cl. BR8: Swan 69Fd 140
DA5: Bexl 59Dd 118
DA13: Ist R 7B 144
Lesley Ct. SW1 4D 228
Leslie Dunne Ho. SL4: Wind 4C 102
Leslie Foster Cl. IG11: Bark 40Vc 75
Leslie Gdns. SM2: Sutt 79Cb 155
Leslie Gro. CR0: C'don 74Ub 157
Leslie Gro. Pl. CR0: C'don 74Ub 157
Leslie Ho. SW8 52Nb 112
(off Wheatsheaf La.)
Leslie Pk. Rd. CR0: C'don 74Ub 157
Leslie Prince Ct. SE5 52Tb 113
Leslie Rd. E11 35Ec 72
E16 44Kc 93
GU24: Chob 2J 167
N2 27Fb 49
Leslie Smith Sq. SE18 51Qc 116
Lesnes Abbey 49Zc 95
Lesnes Abbey Woods (Nature Reserve)
49Zc 95
Lesney Av. E20 36Cc 72
Lesney Farm Est. DA8: Erith 52Fd 118
Lesney Pk. DA8: Erith 51Fd 118
Lesney Pk. Rd. DA8: Erith 51Fd 118
Lessar Av. SW4 58Lb 112
Lessingham Av. IG5: Ilf 27Qc 54
SW17 63Hb 133
Lessing St. SE23 59Ac 114
Lessington Av. RM7: Rom 30Ed 56
Lessness Av. DA7: Bex 52Zc 117
LESSNESS HEATH 50Cd 96
Lessness Pk. DA17: Belv 50Bd 95
Lessness Rd. DA17: Belv 51Cd 118
SM4: Mord 72Eb 155
Lester Av. E15 42Gc 93
Lester Ct. E3 41Dc 92
(off Bruce Rd.)
WD24: Wat 9Y 13
Lestock Cl. SE25 69Wb 135
(off Manor Rd.)
Leston Cl. RM13: Rain 41Kd 97
Leswin Pl. N16 34Vb 71
Leswin Rd. N16 34Vb 71
Letchford Gdns. NW10 41Wa 88
Letchford Ho. E3 40Cc 72
(off Thomas Fyre Dr.)
Letchford M. NW10 41Wa 88
Letchford Ter. HA3: Hrw W 25Da 45
LETCHMORE HEATH 11Ga 28
Letchmore Ho. W10 42Ya 88
(off Sutton Way)
Letchmore Rd. WD7: R'lett 8Ja 14
Letchworth Av. TW14: Felt 59V 106
Letchworth Cl. BR2: Brom 71Jc 159
WD19: Wat 22Z 45
Letchworth Dr. BR2: Brom 71Jc 159
Letchworth Rd. HA7: Stan 24Na 47
Letchworth St. SW17 63Hb 133
Lethbridge Cl. SE10 53Ec 114
Letter Box La. TN13: S'oaks 100Ld 203
Letterstone Rd. SW6 52Bb 111
Lettice St. SW6 53Bb 111
Lett Rd. E15 38Fc 73
SW9 53Pb 112
LETT'S GREEN 88Vc 181
Lettsom St. SE5 54Ub 113
Lettsom Wlk. E13 40Jc 73
Leucha Rd. E17 29Ac 52
Levana Cl. SW19 60Ab 110
Levant Ho. E1 42Zb 92
(off Ernest St.)
Levehurst Ho. SE27 64Sb 135
Leven Cl. EN8: Walt C 5Zb 20
WD19: Wat 22Z 45
Levendale Rd. SE23 61Ac 136
Leven Dr. EN8: Walt C 5Zb 20
Levenhurst Way SW4 54Nb 112
Leven Rd. E14 43Ec 92
Leven Way UB3: Hayes 44U 84
Leveret Cl. CR0: New Ad 83Fc 179
WD25: Wat 6W 12
Leverett St. SW3 5E 226 (49Gb 89)
Leverholme Gdns. SE9 63Qc 138
Leverington Pl. N1 4H 219 (41Tb 91)
Leverson St. SW16 65Lb 134
Lever Sq. RM16: Grays 9B 100
LEVERSTOCK GREEN 3C 4
Leverstock Grn. Rd. HP2: Hem H 1A 4
HP3: Hem H 2B 4
(not continuous)
Leverstock Grn. Way HP3: Hem H 2C 4
Leverstock Ho. SW3 7E 226
Lever St. EC1 4C 218 (41Rb 91)
Leverton Cl. N22 25Pb 50
Leverton Pl. NW5 36Lb 70
Leverton St. NW5 36Lb 70
Leverton Way EN9: Walt A 5Ec 20
Leveson Rd. RM16: Grays 8D 100
Levett Gdns. IG3: Ilf 35Vc 75
Levett Rd. IG11: Bark 37Uc 74
KT22: Lea 92Ka 192
SS17: Stan H 1N 101
Levine Gdns. IG11: Bark 40Zc 75
Levison Way N19 32Mb 70
Levita Ho. NW1 3E 216
(not continuous)
Levyne Ct. EC1 5K 217
Lewen Cl. CR0: C'don 74Tb 157
Lewes Cl. RM17: Grays 51Ce 121
UB5: N'olt 37Ca 65
Lewes Ct. CR4: Mitc 69Hb 133
(off Chatsworth Pl.)
SL1: Slou 8G 80
Lewesdon Cl. SW19 60Za 110
Lewes Ho. SE1 1J 231
SE15 51Wb 113
(off Friary Est.)
Lewes Rd. BR1: Brom 68Mc 137
N12 22Gb 49
RM3: Rom 21Md 57
Leweston Pl. N16 31Vb 71
Lewes Way WD3: Crox G 14S 26
Lew Evans Ho. SE22 57Wb 113
Lewey Ho. E3 42Bc 92
(off Joseph St.)
Lewgars Av. NW9 30Sa 47
Lewing Cl. BR6: Orp 74Uc 160
Lewington Apartments SE16 49Yb 92
(off Alpine Rd.)
Lewington Cen. SE16 49Yb 92
(off Alpine Rd.)
Lewington Ct. EN3: Enf W 9Zb 20
Lewin Rd. DA6: Bex 56Ad 117
SW14 55Ta 109
SW16 65Mb 134
Lewins Farm Ct. SL1: Slou 5D 80
Lewins Rd. KT18: Eps 86Ra 173
SL9: Chal P 27A 42
Lewins Way SL1: Slou 5D 80
Lewin Ter. TW14: Bedf 59T 106
Lewis Av. E17 25Cc 52
Lewis Cl. CM15: Shenf 17Be 41
KT15: Add 77L 149
N14 17Lb 32
UB9: Hare 26L 43
Lewis Ct. DA11: Nflt 1B 144
KT22: Lea 93Ja 192
(off Highbury Dr.)
SE16 50Xb 91
(off Stubbs Dr.)
Lewis Cres. NW10 36Ta 67
Lewis Cubitt Pk. 39Nb 70
Lewis Cubitt Sq. N1 39Nb 70
Lewis Gdns. N2 26Fb 49
N16 30Vb 51
Lewis Gro. SE13 55Ec 114
LEWISHAM 55Ec 114
Lewisham Cen. SE13 56Ec 114
Lewisham Hgts. SE23 60Yb 114
Lewisham High St. SE13 55Ec 114
(not continuous)
Lewisham Hill SE13 54Ec 114
Lewisham Indoor Bowls Cen. 64Bc 136
Lewisham Lions Cen. 50Yb 92
Lewisham Model Mkt. SE13 56Ec 114
(off Lewisham High St.)
Lewisham Pk. SE13 57Ec 114
Lewisham Rd. SE13 53Dc 114
Lewisham St. SW1 2E 228 (47Mb 90)
Lewisham Way SE4 53Bc 114
SE14 53Bc 114
Lewis Ho. E14 46Ec 92
(off Coldharbour)
N1 37Rb 71
(off Canonbury Rd.)
WD18: Wat 16V 26
Lewis La. SL9: Chal P 25A 42
Lewis M. BR7: Chst 64Pc 138
Lewis Pl. E8 36Wb 71
Lewis Rd. CR4: Mitc 68Fb 133
DA10: Swans 58Ae 121
DA13: Ist R 7B 144
DA14: Sidc 62Yc 139
DA16: Well 55Yc 117
RM11: Horn 30Ld 57
SM1: Sutt 77Db 155
TW10: Rich 57Ma 109
UB1: S'hall 47Aa 85
Lewis Silkin Ho. SE15 51Yb 114
(off Lovelinch Cl.)
Lewis Sports and Leisure Cen. 67Vb 135
Lewis St. NW1 37Kb 70
(not continuous)
Lewiston Cl. KT4: Wor Pk 73Xa 154
Lewis Way RM10: Dag 37Dd 76
Leworth Pl. SL4: Wind 3H 103
Lexden Dr. RM6: Chad H 30Xc 55
Lexden Rd. CR4: Mitc 70Mb 134
W3 45Ra 87
Lexden Ter. EN9: Walt A 6Ec 20
(off Sewardstone Rd.)
Lexham Gdns. W8 49Cb 89
Lexham Gdns. M. W8 48Db 89
Lexham Ho. W8 49Db 89
(off Lexham Gdns.)
Lexham M. W8 49Cb 89
Lexham Wlk. W8 48Db 89
Lexicon Apartments RM1: Rom 28Hd 56
(off Mercury Gdns.)
Lexington Apartments
EC1 5F 219 (42Tb 91)
Lexington Bldg. E3 40Cc 72
Lexington Cl. WD6: Bore 13Pa 29
Lexington Ct. CR8: Purl 82Sb 177
EN6: Pot B 3Za 16
(off Mimms Hall Rd.)
Lexington Ho. UB7: W Dray 47P 83
(off Park Lodge Av.)
Lexington Pl. KT1: Hamp W 66Ma 131
Lexington St. W1 3C 222 (45Lb 90)
Lexington Way EN5: Barn 14Za 30
RM14: Upm 30Vd 58
Lexton Gdns. SW12 60Mb 112
Leyborne Av. W13 47Ka 86
Leyborne Pk. TW9: Kew 53Qa 109
Leybourne Av. KT14: Byfl 85P 169
Leybourne Cl. BR2: Brom 72Jc 159
KT14: Byfl 85P 169
Leybourne Ho. E14 44Bc 92
(off Dod St.)
SE15 51Yb 114
Leybourne Rd. E11 32Hc 73
NW1 38Kb 70
NW9 29Qa 47
UB10: Hil 39S 64
Leybourne St. NW1 38Kb 70
Leybridge Ct. SE12 57Jc 115
Leyburn Cl. E17 28Dc 52
Leyburn Cres. RM3: Rom 24Nd 57
Leyburn Gdns. CR0: C'don 75Ub 157
Leyburn Gro. N18 23Wb 51
Leyburn Rd. N18 23Wb 51
RM3: Rom 24Nd 57
Leycester Cl. GU20: W'sham 7A 146
Leycroft Cl. IG10: Lough 15Qc 36
Leycroft Gdns. DA8: Erith 53Kd 119
Leydenhatch La. BR8: Swan 67Ed 140
Leyden Mans. N19 31Nb 70
Leyden St. E1 1K 225 (43Vb 91)
Leydon Cl. SE16 46Zb 92
Leyes Rd. E16 44Mc 93
Ley Farm Cl. WD25: Wat 8Y 13
Leyfield KT4: Wor Pk 74Ua 154
Leyhill Cl. BR8: Swan 70Gd 140
Ley Hill Rd. HP3: Bov 1A 10
Ley Ho. SE1 2D 230
Leyland Av. AL1: St A 4B 6
EN3: Enf H 12Ac 34
Leyland Cl. EN8: Chesh 1Yb 20
Leyland Gdns. IG8: Wfd G 22Lc 53
Leyland Ho. E14 45Dc 92
(off Hale St.)
Leyland Rd. SE12 57Jc 115
Leylands SW18 58Bb 111
Leylands La. TW19: Stanw M 56H 105
(not continuous)
Leylang Rd. SE14 52Zb 114
Leys, The HA3: Kenton 30Pa 47
KT12: Hers 77Ba 151
N2 28Eb 49
WD7: R'lett 9Ja 14
Leys Av. RM10: Dag 39Ed 76
Leys Cl. HA1: Harr 29Fa 46
RM10: Dag 38Ed 76
UB9: Hare 25M 43
Leys Ct. SW9 54Qb 112
Leysdown Av. DA7: Bex 56Ed 118
Leysdown Ho. SE17 7J 231
Leysdown Rd. SE9 61Nc 138
Leysfield Rd. W12 48Wa 88
Leys Gdns. EN4: Cockf 15Jb 32
Leyspring Rd. E11 32Hc 73
Leys Rd. HP3: Hem H 4N 3
KT22: Oxs 84Fa 172
Leys Rd. E. EN3: Enf H 11Ac 34
Leys Rd. W. EN3: Enf H 11Ac 34
Leys Sq. N3 25Db 49
Ley St. IG1: Ilf 33Rc 74
IG2: Ilf 33Sc 74
Leyswood Dr. IG2: Ilf 29Uc 54
Leythe Rd. W3 47Sa 87
LEYTON 33Ec 72
Leyton Bus. Cen. E10 33Cc 72
Leyton Ct. SE23 60Yb 114
LEYTON CROSS 61Jd 140
Leyton Cross Rd. DA2: Wilm 62Hd 140
Leyton Grange E10 32Cc 72
Leyton Grn. Rd. E10 30Ec 52
Leyton Grn. Twr. E10 30Ec 52
(off Leyton Grn. Rd.)
Leyton Ho. E2 4K 219
(off Calvert Av.)
Leyton Ind. Village E10 31Zb 72
Leyton Leisure Cen. 31Ec 72
Leyton Link Est. E10 31Ac 72
Leyton Mills E10 34Ec 72
Leyton Orient FC
Brisbane Road Stadium 34Dc 72
Leyton Pk. Rd. E10 34Fc 72
Leyton Rd. E15 36Ec 72
SW19 66Eb 133
LEYTONSTONE 32Gc 73
Leytonstone Ho. E11 31Hc 73
(off Hanbury Dr.)
Leytonstone Leisure Cen. 33Gc 73
Leytonstone Rd. E15 37Gc 73
Leyton Way E11 31Gc 73
Leywick St. E15 40Gc 73
Lezayre Rd. BR6: Chels 79Vc 161
Lianne Gro. SE9 62Lc 137
Liardet St. SE14 51Ac 114
Libari Mans. E20 36Ec 72
(off Victory Pde.)
Liberia Rd. N5 37Rb 71
Liberty, The RM1: Rom 29Gd 56
Liberty Av. SW19 67Fb 133
Liberty Bri. Rd. E15 36Ec 72
E20 36Ec 72
Liberty Cen. HA0: Wemb 39Pa 67
Liberty Cl. KT4: Wor Pk 74Ya 154
N18 21Vb 51
Liberty Ct. BR1: Brom 69Mc 137
CR8: Purl 84Qb 176
IG11: Bark 40Xc 75
Liberty Hall Rd. KT15: Add 78J 149
Liberty Ho. CR7: Thor H 71Qb 156
(off Thornton Rd.)
E1 45Wb 91
(off Ensign St.)
E13 40Jc 73
KT16: Chert 74H 149
(off Guildford St.)
Liberty La. KT15: Add 78J 149
Liberty M. N22 25Rb 51
SW12 58Kb 112
Liberty Point CR0: C'don 73Wb 157
(off Blackhorse La.)
Liberty Ri. KT15: Add 79J 149
Liberty St. SW9 53Pb 112
Liberty Wlk. AL1: St A 3G 6
Libra Mans. E3 40Bc 72
(off Libra Rd.)
Libra Rd. E3 39Bc 72
E13 40Jc 73
Library Ct. N17 27Vb 51
Library Hill CM14: B'wood 19Zd 41
Library Mans. W12 47Ya 88
(off Pennard Rd.)
Library M. TW12: Hamp H 65Ea 130
Library Pde. NW10 39Ua 68
(off Craven Pk. Rd.)
Library Pl. E1 45Xb 91
Library Sq. E1 42Ac 92
Library St. SE1 3B 230 (47Rb 91)
Library Way TW2: Whitt 59Ea 108
Libro Ct. E4 21Cc 52
Lichfield Cl. EN4: Cockf 13Hb 31
Lichfield Ct. KT6: Surb 71Na 153
(off Claremont Rd.)
TW9: Rich 57Na 109
Lichfield Gdns. TW9: Rich 56Na 109
Lichfield Gro. N3 25Cb 49
Lichfield Ho. WD6: Bore 12Qa 29
(off Stratfield Rd.)
Lichfield La. TW2: Whitt 60Ea 108
Lichfield Pl. AL1: St A 1D 6
Lichfield Rd. E3 41Ac 92
E6 41Mc 93
HA6: Nwood 27W 44
IG8: Wfd G 21Gc 53
N9 19Wb 33
NW2 35Ab 68
RM8: Dag 35Xc 75
TW4: Houn 55Y 107
TW9: Kew 53Pa 109
Lichfield Ter. RM14: Upm 33Ud 78
TW9: Rich 57Na 109
(off Sheen Rd.)
Lichfield Way CR2: Sels 82Zb 178

Lichlade Cl.—Link Rd.

Lichlade Cl. BR6: Orp 77Vc 161
Lickey Ho. W14 51Bb 111
(off North End Rd.)
Lidcote Gdns. SW9 54Pb 112
Liddall Way UB7: Yiew 46P 83
Liddell SL4: Wind 5A 102
Liddell Cl. HA3: Kenton 27Ma 47
Liddell Gdns. NW10 40Ya 68
Liddell Pl. SL4: Wind 4A 102
Liddell Rd. NW6 37Cb 69
Liddell Sq. SL4: Wind 4A 102
Liddell Way SL4: Wind 5A 102
Liddiard Ho. W11 45Ab 88
(off Lansdowne Rd.)
Lidding Rd. HA3: Kenton 29Ma 47
Liddington Rd. E15 39Hc 73
Liddon Rd. BR1: Brom 69Lc 137
E13 41Kc 93
Liden Cl. E17 31Bc 72
Lidfield Rd. N16 35Tb 71
Lidgate Rd. SE15 52Vb 113
Lidgould Gro. HA4: Ruis 30W 44
Lidiard Rd. SW18 61Eb 133
Lidlington Pl. NW1 2C 216 (40Lb 70)
Lido Sq. N17 26Tb 51
Lidstone Cl. GU21: Wok 9M 167
Lidstone Ct. SL3: Geor G 4P 81
Lidyard Rd. N19 32Lb 70
Lieutenant Ellis Way
EN7: Chesh, G Oak 2Vb 19
EN8: Chesh, Walt C 3Vb 19
Lifestyle Club @ Charlton, The 52Mc 115
Liffler Rd. SE18 50Uc 94
Liffords Pl. SW13 54Va 110
Lifford St. SW15 56Za 110
Lightbox Mus., The 88A 168
Lightcliffe Rd. N13 21Qb 50
Lighterage Ct. TW8: Bford 51Na 109
Lighter Cl. SE16 49Ac 92
Lighterman Ho. E14 45Ec 92
Lighterman M. E1 44Zb 92
Lighterman Point E14 44Fc 93
(off New Village Av.)
Lighterman Rd. RM13: Rain 38Gd 76
(off Ongar Way)
Lighterman's M. DA11: Nflt 9A 122
Lightermans Rd. E14 47Cc 92
Lightermans Wlk. SW18 56Cb 111
Lightermans Way DA9: Ghithe 56Yd 120
Lightfoot Rd. N8 29Nb 50
Lightfoot Vs. N1 38Qb 70
(off Augustas La.)
Light Horse Ct. SW3 7H 227
Lighthouse Apartments E1 44Yb 92
(off Commercial Rd.)
Lighthouse Bldg. E14 44Gc 93
Lightley Cl. HA0: Wemb 39Na 67
LIGHTWATER 2A 166
Lightwater By-Pass GU18: Light 2A 166
Lightwater Mdw. GU18: Light 3A 166
Lightwater Rd. GU18: Light 3A 166
Ligonier St. E2 5K 219 (42Vb 91)
Lilac Av. EN1: Enf 8Yb 20
GU22: Wok 2P 187
Lilac Cl. CM15: Pil H 15Xd 40
E4 23Bc 52
EN7: Chesh 3Xb 19
Lilac Ct. E13 39Lc 73
SL2: Slou 1D 80
TW11: Tedd 63Ha 130
Lilac Gdns. BR8: Swan 69Fd 140
CR0: C'don 76Cc 158
RM7: Rush G 32Gd 76
UB3: Hayes 44U 84
W5 48Ma 87
Lilac Ho. SE4 55Cc 114
Lilac M. N22 27Qb 50
(off High Rd.)
Lilac Pl. SE11 6H 229 (49Pb 90)
UB7: Yiew 45P 83
Lilac St. W12 45Wa 88
Lilah M. BR2: Brom 68Gc 137
Lila Pl. BR8: Swan 70Gd 140
Lilburne Gdns. SE9 57Nc 116
Lilburne Rd. SE9 57Nc 116
Lilburne Wlk. NW10 37Sa 67
Lile Cres. W7 43Ga 86
Lilestone Ho. NW8 5C 214
Lilestone St. NW8 5D 214 (42Gb 89)
Lilford Ho. SE5 54Sb 113
Lilford Rd. SE5 54Rb 113
Lilian Barker Cl. SE12 57Jc 115
Lilian Board Way UB6: G'frd 36Fa 66
Lilian Cl. N16 34Ub 71
Lilian Cres. CM13: Hut 19Ee 41
Lilian Gdns. IG8: Wfd G 25Kc 53
Lilian Knowles Ho. E1 1K 225
Lilian Rd. SW16 67Lb 134
Lilium M. E10 31Cc 72
Lillechurch Rd. RM8: Dag 37Xc 75
Lilleshall Rd. SM4: Mord 72Fb 155
Lilley Cl. CM14: B'wood 21Vd 58
E1 46Wb 91
Lilley Dr. KT20: Kgswd 94Db 195
Lilley La. NW7 22Ta 47
Lilley Mead RH1: Mers 3C 208
Lilley Way SL1: Slou 6C 80
Lillian Av. W3 47Qa 87
Lillian Rd. SW13 51Wa 110
Lillie Bri. Dpt. W14 50Bb 89
(off Aisgill Av.)
Lillie Mans. SW6 51Ab 110
(off Lillie Rd.)
Lillie Rd. SW6 51Ab 110
TN16: Big H 90Mc 179
Lillie Road Fitness Cen. 52Za 110
Lillieshall Rd. SW4 55Kb 112
Lillie Sq. SW6 51Cb 111
Lillie Yd. SW6 51Cb 111
Lillingston Ho. N7 35Qb 70
Lillington Gdns. Est. SW1 6C 228
Lilliot's La. KT22: Lea 91Ja 192
Lilliput Av. UB5: N'olt 39Aa 65
Lilliput Ct. SE12 57Kc 115
Lilliput Rd. E15 39Gc 73
RM7: Rush G 31Fd 76
Lily Cl. HA5: Pinn 26Y 45
RM13: Rain 42Ld 97
W14 49Za 88
Lily Dr. UB7: W Dray 49M 83
Lily Gdns. HA0: Wemb 40La 66
Lily M. SE11 5B 230 (49Rb 91)
Lily Nichols Ho. E16 46Mc 93
(off Connaught Rd.)
Lily Pl. EC1 7A 218 (43Qb 90)
Lily Rd. E17 30Cc 52
Lilyville Rd. SW6 53Bb 111
Limasol St. SE16 3K 231 (48Vb 91)
Limborough Ho. E14 43Cc 92
(off Thomas Rd.)
Limbourne Av. RM8: Dag 31Bd 75
Limburg Rd. SW11 56Gb 111
Lime Av. CM13: B'wood 20Be 41
DA11: Nflt 59Fe 121
RM14: Upm 35Qd 77
SL4: Wind 3K 103
(Adelaide Rd.)
SL4: Wind 2D 124
(Holly Wlk.)
UB7: Yiew 45P 83
Limeburner La. EC4 3B 224 (44Rb 91)
Limebush Cl. KT15: New H 81L 169
Lime Cl. BR1: Brom 70Nc 138
E1 46Wb 91
GU4: W Cla 100K 189
HA3: W'stone 26Ja 46
HA5: Eastc 27V 44
IG9: Buck H 19Mc 35
RH2: Reig 9K 207
RM7: Rom 28Ed 56
RM15: S Ock 41Yd 98
SM5: Cars 75Hb 155
WD19: Wat 17Z 27
Lime Ct. CR4: Mitc 68Fb 133
E11 33Gc 73
(off Trinity Cl.)
E17 29Ec 52
HA1: Harr 30Ha 46
(off Gayton Rd.)
HA4: Ruis 31X 65
SE9 61Rc 138
Lime Cres. TW16: Sun 66Y 129
Limecroft Cl. KT19: Ewe 80Ta 153
Limecroft Rd. GU21: Knap 9F 166
Limedene Cl. HA5: Pinn 25Z 45
Lime Gro. BR6: Farnb 75Rc 160
CR6: W'ham 90Ac 178
DA15: Sidc 58Vc 117
E4 23Bc 52
GU4: W Cla 100J 189
GU22: Wok 93A 188
HA4: Ruis 30X 45
IG6: Ilf 23Vc 55
KT3: N Mald 69Ta 131
KT15: Add 77J 149
N20 18Bb 31
TW1: Twick 58Ha 108
UB3: Hayes 45T 84
W12 47Ya 88
Limeharbour E14 48Dc 92
LIMEHOUSE 44Bc 92
Lime Ho. TW9: Kew 53Ra 109
Limehouse C'way. E14 45Bc 92
Lime Ho. Ct. E14 44Bc 92
(off Wharf La.)
Limehouse Ct. E14 44Cc 92
Limehouse Cut E14 43Dc 92
(off Morris Rd.)
Limehouse Flds. Est. E14 43Ac 92
Limehouse Link E14 44Ac 92
Limehouse Lodge E5 33Yb 72
(off Harry Zeital Way)
Lime Kiln Dr. SE7 51Kc 115
Limekiln Pl. SE19 66Vb 135
Limekiln Wharf E14 45Bc 92
Limelight Ho. SE11 6B 230
Lime Lodge TW16: Sun 66V 128
(off Forest Dr.)
Lime Mdw. Av. CR2: Sande 85Wb 177
Lime Pit La. TN13: Dun G 89Ed 182
Lime Quay E14 42Ec 92
Limerick Cl. SW12 59Lb 112
Limerick Gdns. RM14: Upm 31Vd 78
Limerick M. N2 27Gb 49
Lime Rd. BR8: Swan 69Fd 140
TW9: Rich 56Pa 109
Lime Row DA18: Erith 48Bd 95
Limerston St. SW10 51Eb 111
Limes, The AL1: St A 1C 6
BR2: Brom 75Nc 160
CM13: B'wood 20Be 41
DA1: Dart 59Pd 119
GU21: Wok 88C 168
(off Maybury Rd.)
GU21: Wok 7P 167
(Ridgeway)
HP3: Hem H 5M 3
KT8: W Mole 70Da 129
KT19: Eps 82Ra 173
KT22: Lea 95Ka 192
RM11: Horn 27Md 57
RM19: Purf 50Qd 97
SL4: Wind 4A 102
SW18 58Cb 111
W2 45Cb 89
WD3: Rick 18L 25
WD4: Hunt C 5S 12
(off Bridge Rd.)
Limes Av. CR0: Wadd 76Qb 156
E11 28Kc 53
IG7: Chig 22Sc 54
N12 21Eb 49
NW7 23Ua 48
NW11 31Ab 68
SE20 66Xb 135
SM5: Cars 74Hb 155
SW13 54Va 110
Limes Av., The N11 22Kb 50
Limes Cl. KT22: Lea 93La 192
N11 22Lb 50
RH1: Redh 10P 207
TW15: Ashf 64Q 128
Limes Ct. BR3: Beck 68Dc 136
CM15: B'wood 18Zd 41
NW6 38Ab 68
(off Brondesbury Pk.)
Limesdale Gdns. HA8: Edg 26Sa 47
Limes Fld. Rd. SW13 55Ua 110
Limesford Rd. SE15 56Zb 114
Limes Gdns. SW18 58Cb 111
Limes Gro. SE13 56Ec 114
Limes M. TW20: Egh 64B 126
Limes Pl. CR0: C'don 73Tb 157
Limes Rd. BR3: Beck 68Dc 136
CR0: C'don 73Tb 157
EN8: Chesh 4Ac 20
KT13: Weyb 77Q 150
TW20: Egh 64B 126
Limes Row BR6: Farnb 78Rc 160
Limestone Wlk. DA18: Erith 47Zc 95
Lime St. E17 28Ac 52
EC3 4H 225 (45Ub 91)
Lime St. Pas. EC3 3H 225 (44Ub 91)
Limes Wlk. SE15 56Yb 114
W5 47Ma 87
Lime Ter. W7 45Ga 86
Lime Tree Av. CR5: Coul 89Lb 176
DA9: Bluew 59Wd 120
KT7: T Ditt 74Fa 152
KT10: Esh 74Fa 152
Lime Tree Cl. E18 28Lc 53
KT23: Bookh 96Ca 191
WD23: Bush 16Ea 28
Limetree Cl. SW2 60Pb 112
Lime Tree Ct. AL2: Lon C 8F 6
CR2: S Croy 79Sb 157
E3 43Cc 92
(off Whitehorn St.)
HA5: Hat E 24Ca 45
(off The Avenue)
KT21: Asht 90Na 173
SE17 7E 230
Lime Tree Gro. CR0: C'don 76Bc 158
Lime Tree Ho. DA4: Farni 72Nd 163
Lime Tree Pl. AL1: St A 3D 6
BR5: St M Cry 73Ad 161
CR4: Mitc 67Kb 134
Lime Tree Rd. TW5: Hest 53Da 107
Lime Trees Pk. Golf Course 39Y 65
Limetree Ter. DA16: Well 55Wc 117
SE6 60Bc 114
Lime Tree Wlk.
BR4: W W'ck 77Hc 159
EN2: Enf 10Sb 19
GU21: Wok 8P 167
GU25: Vir W 70A 126
TN13: S'oaks 97Kd 203
WD3: Rick 15K 25
WD23: B Hea 18Ga 28
Limetree Wlk. SW17 64Jb 134
Lime View Apartments E14 44Ac 92
(off Commerical Rd.)
Lime Wlk. E15 39Gc 73
HP3: Hem H 4P 3
KT8: E Mos 70Ha 130
UB9: Den 36L 63
Lime Way WD7: Shenl 3La 14
Limewood Cl. BR3: Beck 71Ec 158
E17 28Bc 52
GU21: Wok 2H 187
W13 44Ka 86
Limewood Ct. IG4: Ilf 29Pc 54
Limewood Ho. KT19: Eps 81Ta 173
Limewood M. SE20 66Wb 135
(off Lullington Rd.)
Limewood Rd. DA8: Erith 52Ed 118
Lime Works Rd.
RH1: Mers 98Lb 196
LIMPSFIELD 1M 211
Limpsfield Av. CR7: Thor H 71Pb 156
SW19 61Za 132
LIMPSFIELD CHART 2P 211
Limpsfield Chart Golf Course 1N 211
Limpsfield Rd. CR2: Sande 84Wb 177
CR6: W'ham 84Wb 177
Limscott Ho. E3 41Dc 92
(off Bruce Rd.)
Linacre Cl. SE15 55Xb 113
Linacre Ct. W6 50Za 88
Linacre Rd. NW2 37Xa 68
Linale Ho. N1 2F 219
Linberry Wlk. SE8 49Bc 92
Linchfield Rd. SL3: Dat 3N 103
Linchmere Rd. SE12 59Hc 115
Lincoln Av. N14 20Lb 32
RM7: Rush G 33Fd 76
SW19 62Za 132
TW2: Twick 61Ea 130
Lincoln Cl. DA8: Erith 54Hd 118
HA2: Harr 29Ba 45
RM11: Horn 29Qd 57
SE25 72Wb 157
UB6: G'frd 39Ea 66
Lincoln Ct. CR2: S Croy 78Sb 157
(off Warham Rd.)
IG2: Ilf 30Sc 54
KT13: Weyb 79T 150
(off Old Av.)
N16 31Tb 71
SE12 62Kc 137
SL1: Slou 8J 81
UB9: Den 30H 43
WD6: Bore 15Ta 29
WD25: Wat 5X 13
Lincoln Cres. EN1: Enf 15Ub 33
Lincoln Dr. GU22: Pyr 87G 168
WD3: Crox G 14R 26
WD19: Wat 20Y 27
Lincoln Fld. WD23: Bush 13Ba 27
Lincoln Gdns. IG1: Ilf 31Nc 74
Lincoln Grn. Rd. BR5: St M Cry 71Vc 161
Lincoln Gro. KT13: Weyb 76R 150
Lincoln Hatch La. SL1: Burn 2A 80
Lincoln Ho. SE5 52Qb 112
SW3 2F 227 (47Hb 89)
TW8: Bford 50Ma 87
(off Ealing Rd.)
Lincoln M. AL3: St A 3A 6
N15 28Sb 51
NW6 39Bb 69
SE21 61Tb 135
Lincoln Pde. HA9: Wemb 32Na 67
N2 27Gb 49
(off Lincoln Rd.)
Lincoln Plaza E14 47Dc 92
(off Lightermans Rd.)
Lincoln Rd. CR4: Mitc 71Nb 156
DA8: Erith 54Hd 118
DA14: Sidc 64Xc 139
E7 37Mc 73
E13 42Kc 93
E18 25Jc 53
EN1: Enf 14Ub 33
EN3: Pond E 15Wb 33
HA0: Wemb 37Ma 67
HA2: Harr 29Ba 45
HA6: Nwood 27V 44
KT3: N Mald 69Sa 131
KT4: Wor Pk 74Xa 154
N2 27Gb 49
SE25 69Xb 135
SL9: Chal P 25A 42
TW13: Hanw 62Ba 129
Lincolns, The NW7 20Va 30
Lincolns Fld. CM16: Epp 2Vc 23
Lincolnshire Ter. DA2: Daren 63Td 142
Lincoln's Inn Flds. WC2 2H 223 (44Pb 90)
Lincoln's Inn Hall 2J 223 (44Pb 90)
Lincolns La.
CM14: Pil H, S Weald 15Sd 40
Lincoln St. E11 33Gc 73
SW3 6F 227 (49Hb 89)
Lincoln Ter. SM2: Sutt 80Cb 155
Lincoln Wlk. KT19: Ewe 82Ta 173
Lincoln Way EN1: Enf 15Xb 33
SL1: Slou 5B 80
TW16: Sun 67U 128
WD3: Crox G 14R 26
Lincombe Ct. KT15: Add 78K 149
Lincombe Rd. BR1: Brom 62Hc 137
Lindal Ct. E18 25Hc 53
Lindal Cres. EN2: Enf 14Nb 32
Lindale Cl. GU25: Vir W 10K 125
IG4: Ilf 29Pc 54
Lindales, The N17 23Wb 51
(off Grasmere Rd.)
Lindal Rd. SE4 57Bc 114
Lindbergh Rd. SM6: Wall 80Nb 156
Linden SL3: L'ly 50D 82
Linden Av. CR5: Coul 88Kb 176
CR7: Thor H 70Rb 135
DA1: Dart 60Ld 119
EN1: Enf 11Wb 33
HA4: Ruis 32W 64
HA9: Wemb 36Pa 67
NW10 40Za 68
TW3: Houn 57Da 107
WD18: Wat 14U 26
Linden Chase
TN13: S'oaks 94Kd 203
Linden Cl. BR6: Chels 78Wc 161
EN7: Chesh 2Xb 19
HA4: Ruis 32W 64
HA7: Stan 22Ka 46
KT7: T Ditt 73Ha 152
KT15: New H 83J 169
KT20: Tad 92Za 194
N14 16Lb 32
RM19: Purf 51Sd 120
SL0: Iver H 40F 62
Linden Ct. DA14: Sidc 63Uc 138
KT22: Lea 93Ka 192
SE20 66Xb 135
(off Anerley Pk.)
TW20: Eng G 5M 125
W12 46Ya 88
Linden Cres. AL1: St A 2G 6
IG8: Wfd G 23Kc 53
KT1: King T 68Pa 131
UB6: G'frd 37Ha 66
Linden Dr. CR3: Cat'm 96Sb 197
SL2: Farn R 9G 60
SL9: Chal P 25A 42
Lindenfield BR7: Chst 68Rc 138
Linden Gdns. EN1: Enf 11Wb 33
KT22: Lea 93La 192
W2 45Cb 89
W4 50Ua 88
Linden Glade HP1: Hem H 3K 3
Linden Gro. CR6: W'ham 90Ac 178
KT3: N Mald 69Ua 132
KT12: Walt T 75V 150
SE15 55Xb 113
SE26 65Yb 136
TW11: Tedd 64Ha 130
Linden Ho. CM16: Epp 3Wc 23
SE8 51Bc 114
(off Abinger Gro.)
TW12: Hamp 65Ca 129
Linden Lawns HA9: Wemb 35Pa 67
Linden Lea HA5: Hat E 24Ba 45
N2 29Eb 49
WD25: Wat 5W 12
Linden Leas BR4: W W'ck 75Fc 159
Linden Mans. N6 32Kb 70
(off Hornsey La.)
Linden M. N1 36Tb 71
W2 45Cb 89
Linden Pit Path KT22: Lea 92La 192
(Kingfisher Cl.)
KT22: Lea 93Ka 192
(Linden Rd.)
Linden Pl. CR4: Mitc 70Gb 133
KT17: Eps 84Ua 174
KT24: E Hor 98U 190
TW18: Staines 63J 127
Linden Ri. CM14: W'ley 22Zd 59
Linden Rd. KT13: Weyb 81S 170
KT22: Lea 93Ka 192
N10 28Kb 50
N11 19Hb 31
N15 28Sb 51
TW12: Hamp 66Ca 129
Lindens, The CR0: New Ad 79Ec 158
E17 28Dc 52
(off Prospect Hill)
EN9: Walt A 7Lc 21
(within Woodbine Cl. Caravan Pk.)
HP3: Hem H 5H 3
IG10: Lough 15Pc 36
N12 22Fb 49
W4 53Sa 109
Lindens Cl. KT24: Eff 100Aa 191
Linden Sq. TN13: Riv 94Gd 202
UB9: Hare 23J 43
Linden St. RM7: Rom 28Fd 56
Linden Wlk. N19 33Lb 70
Linden Way CR8: Purl 82Lb 176
GU22: Wok 93B 188
GU23: Rip 97H 189
N14 16Lb 32
TW17: Shep 71S 150
Linder's Field Local Nature Reserve
17Mc 35
Lindeth Cl. HA7: Stan 23Ka 46
Lindfield Gdns. NW3 36Db 69
Lindfield Rd. CR0: C'don 72Vb 157
RM3: Rom 22Nd 57
W5 42La 86
Lindfield St. E14 44Cc 92
Lindhill Cl. EN3: Enf H 12Zb 34
Lindholme Ct. NW9 25Ua 48
(off Pageant Av.)
Lindie Gdns. UB8: Uxb 38N 63
Lindisfarne Cl. DA12: Grav'nd 1G 144
Lindisfarne Ct. HA8: Edg 21Pa 47
Lindisfarne Rd. RM8: Dag 34Yc 75
SW20 66Wa 132
Lindisfarne Way E9 35Ac 72
Lindiswara Ct. WD3: Crox G 16Q 26
Lindley Ct. KT1: Hamp W 67La 130
Lindley Est. SE15 52Wb 113
Lindley Ho. E1 43Yb 92
(off Lindley St.)
SE15 52Wb 113
(off Peckham Pk. Rd.)
Lindley Pl. TW9: Kew 53Qa 109
Lindley Rd. E10 33Ec 72
KT12: Walt T 76Z 151
RH9: G'stone 2A 210
Lindley St. E1 43Yb 92
Lindlings HP1: Hem H 3G 2
Lindop Ho. E1 42Ac 92
(off Mile End Rd.)
Lindore Rd. SW11 56Hb 111
Lindores Rd. SM5: Cars 73Eb 155
Lindo St. SE15 54Yb 114
Lindrick Ho. WD19: Wat 20Y 27
Lind Rd. SM1: Sutt 78Eb 155
Lindrop St. SW6 54Eb 111
Lindsay Cl. KT9: Chess 80Na 153
KT19: Eps 85Sa 173
TW19: Stanw 57M 105
Lindsay Ct. AL3: St A 2A 6
(off Verulam Rd.)
CR0: C'don 77Tb 157
(off Eden Rd.)
SE13 55Dc 114
(off Loampit Va.)
SW11 53Fb 111
(off Battersea High St.)
Lindsay Dr. HA3: Kenton 30Na 47
TW17: Shep 72T 150
Lindsay Ho. SW7 3A 226
Lindsay Pl. EN7: Chesh 2Xb 19
Lindsay Rd. KT4: Wor Pk 75Xa 154
KT15: New H 82J 169
TW12: Hamp H 63Da 129
Lindsay Sq. SW1 7E 228 (50Mb 90)
Lindsell St. SE10 53Ec 114
Lindsey Cl. BR1: Brom 69Mc 137
CM14: B'wood 21Wd 58
CR4: Mitc 70Nb 134
Lindsey Ct. N13 20Qb 32
(off Green Lanes)
Lindsey Gdns. TW14: Bedf 59T 106
Lindsey Ho. W5 49Ma 87
Lindsey M. N1 38Sb 71
Lindsey Rd. RM8: Dag 35Yc 75
UB9: Den 34J 63
Lindsey St. CM16: Epp 1Vc 23
EC1 7C 218 (43Rb 91)
Lindsey Way RM11: Horn 29Ld 57
Lind St. SE8 54Cc 114
Lindum Pl. AL3: St A 4M 5
Lindum Rd. TW11: Tedd 66La 130
Lindvale GU21: Wok 87A 168
Lindway SE27 64Rb 135
Lindwood Cl. E6 44Pc 94
Linen Ho., The W10 40Ab 68
Linfield WC1 4H 217
Linfield Cl. KT12: Hers 78X 151
NW4 27Ya 48
LINFORD 7J 101
Linford Christie Stadium 43Wa 88
Linford Ho. E2 39Wb 71
(off Whiston Rd.)
E16 43Jc 93
(off Hammersley Rd.)
Linford Rd. E17 27Ec 52
RM16: Grays, W Til 9D 100
Linford St. SW8 53Lb 112
Linford St. Bus. Est. SW8 53Lb 112
(off Linford St.)
Linford Wood Local Nature Reserve
7J 101
Lingard Av. NW9 26Ua 48
Lingard Ho. E14 48Ec 92
(off Marshfield St.)
Lingards Rd. SE13 56Ec 114
Lingey Cl. DA15: Sidc 61Vc 139
Lingfield Apartments E4 24Dc 52
Lingfield Av. DA2: Dart 59Rd 119
KT1: King T 70Na 131
RM14: Upm 34Pd 77
Lingfield Cl. EN1: Enf 16Ub 33
HA6: Nwood 24U 44
Lingfield Ct. UB5: N'olt 40Ca 65
Lingfield Cres. SE9 56Tc 116
Lingfield Gdns. CR5: Coul 91Rb 197
N9 17Xb 33
Lingfield Ho. SE1 2C 230
Lingfield Rd. DA12: Grav'nd 1D 144
KT4: Wor Pk 76Ya 154
SW19 64Za 132
TN15: Bor G 92De 205
Lingfield Way WD17: Wat 10V 12
Lingham Ct. SW9 54Nb 112
Lingham St. SW9 54Nb 112
Lingholm Way EN5: Barn 15Za 30
Lingmere Cl. IG7: Chig 19Sc 36
Lingmoor Dr. WD25: Wat 5Y 13
Ling Rd. DA8: Erith 51Ed 118
E16 43Jc 93
Lingrove Gdns. IG9: Buck H 19Kc 35
Lings Coppice SE21 61Tb 135
Lingwell Rd. SW17 62Gb 133
Lingwood DA7: Bex 54Dd 118
Lingwood Ct. N2 27Gb 49
(off Norfolk Cl.)
Lingwood Gdns. TW7: Isle 52Ga 108
Lingwood Rd. E5 31Wb 71
Linhope St. NW1 5F 215 (42Hb 89)
Link, The DA3: Nw A G 75Be 165
EN3: Enf H 11Ac 34
HA0: Wemb 32La 66
HA5: Eastc 31Y 65
NW2 32Wa 68
SE9 62Qc 138
(off William Barefoot Dr.)
SL2: Slou 4M 81
UB5: N'olt 36Ba 65
W3 44Ra 87
Link Av. GU22: Pyr 87F 168
Linkenholt Mans. W6 49Va 88
(off Stamford Brook Av.)
Linkfield BR2: Hayes 72Jc 159
KT8: W Mole 69Da 129
Linkfield Cnr. RH1: Redh 5N 207
Linkfield Gdns. RH1: Redh 6N 207
Linkfield La. RH1: Redh 5N 207
Linkfield Lodge
RH1: Redh 5N 207
Linkfield Rd. TW7: Isle 54Ha 108
Linkfield St. RH1: Redh 6N 207
Link Ho. E3 40Dc 72
W10 44Za 88
(off Kingsdown Cl.)
Link La. SM6: Wall 79Mb 156
Linklea Cl. NW9 24Ua 48
Link Pl. IG6: Ilf 23Vc 55
Link Rd. E1 45Wb 91
KT15: Add 77N 149
N11 21Jb 50
RM9: Dag 40Dd 76
SL3: Dat 3N 103
SM6: Wall 74Jb 156
TW14: Felt 59V 106
WD23: Bush 12Z 27
WD24: Bush, Wat 12Z 27

344

Lockton St.—Longridge La.

Lockton St. W10 ... 45Za 88
(off Bramley Rd.)
Lock Vw. Ct. E14 ... 45Ac 92
(off Narrow St.)
Lockview Ct. HP3: Hem H ... 6N 3
Lockwell Rd. RM10: Dag ... 34Cd 76
Lockwood Cl. SE26 ... 63Zb 136
Lockwood Ct. WD6: Bore ... 12Sa 29
Lockwood Ho. E5 ... 33Yb 72
SE11 ... 51Qb 112
Lockwood Ind. Pk. N17 ... 27Xb 51
Lockwood Path GU21: Wok ... 85F 168
Lockwood Pl. DA1: Dart ... 55Qd 119
E4 ... 23Cc 52
Lockwood Sq. SE16 ... 48Xb 91
Lockwood Wlk. RM1: Rom ... 29Gd 56
Lockwood Way E17 ... 26Zb 52
KT9: Chess ... 78Qa 153
Lockyer Est. SE1 ... 1G 231
(not continuous)
Lockyer Ho. SE10 ... 50Hc 93
(off Armitage Rd.)
SW8 ... 52Mb 112
(off Wandsworth Rd.)
SW15 ... 55Za 110
Lockyer M. EN3: Enf L ... 10Dc 20
Lockyer Rd. RM19: Purf ... 51Sd 120
Lockyer St. SE1 ... 2G 231 (47Tb 91)
Locomotive Dr.
TW14: Felt ... 60W 106
Locton Grn. E3 ... 39Bc 72
Loddiges Ho. E9 ... 38Yb 72
Loddiges Rd. E9 ... 38Yb 72
Loddon Ho. NW8 ... 6C 214
Loddon Spur SL1: Slou ... 5J 81
Loder Cl. GU21: Wok ... 85F 168
Loder St. SE15 ... 52Yb 114
Lodge, The CM16: Epp ... 1Yc 23
SM7: Bans ... 89Eb 175
W12 ... 47Za 88
(off Richmond Way)
WD24: Wat ... 12Y 27
Lodge Av. CR0: Wadd ... 76Qb 156
DA1: Dart ... 58Ld 119
HA3: Kenton ... 28Na 47
RM2: Rom ... 28Jd 56
RM8: Dag ... 37Xc 75
RM9: Dag ... 39Wc 75
SW14 ... 55Ua 110
WD6: E'tree ... 15Pa 29
LODGE AVENUE FLYOVER JUNC. ... 39Wc 75
Lodgebottom Rd. KT18: Head ... 99Qa 193
RH5: Mick ... 99Qa 193
Lodge Cl. BR6: Orp ... 74Xc 161
HA8: Edg ... 23Pa 47
IG7: Chig ... 20Wc 37
KT11: Stoke D ... 88Ba 171
KT17: Ewe ... 82Ya 174
KT22: Fet ... 94Fa 192
N18 ... 22Sb 51
SL1: Slou ... 7G 80
SL5: Asc ... 8A 124
SM6: Wall ... 74Jb 156
TW7: Isle ... 53Ka 108
TW20: Eng G ... 4P 125
UB8: Cowl ... 4L 83
WD25: Wat ... 4Aa 13
Lodge Ct. HA0: Wemb ... 36Na 67
(off Station Gro.)
RM12: Horn ... 33Nd 77
Lodge Cres. BR6: Orp ... 74Xc 161
EN8: Walt C ... 6Zb 20
Lodge Dr. N13 ... 21Qb 50
WD3: Loud ... 14L 25
Lodge End WD3: Crox G ... 14T 26
WD7: R'lett ... 6Ka 14
Lodge Gdns. BR3: Beck ... 71Bc 158
Lodge Hill CR8: Purl ... 87Qb 176
DA16: Well ... 52Xc 117
IG4: Ilf ... 28Nc 54
SE2 ... 52Xc 117
Lodgehill Pk. Cl. HA2: Harr ... 33Da 65
Lodge La. CR0: New Ad ... 79Cc 158
DA5: Bexl ... 58Zc 117
DA12: Cobh ... 10J 145
EN9: Walt A ... 7Fc 21
HP8: Chal G ... 11A 24
N12 ... 22Eb 49
RM5: Col R ... 24Cd 56
RM16: Grays ... 47Ce 99
RM17: Grays ... 47Ce 99
TN16: Westrm ... 99Sc 200
Lodge Pl. SM1: Sutt ... 78Db 155
Lodge Rd. BR1: Brom ... 66Lc 137
CM16: Epp, Walt A ... 6Qc 22
CR0: C'don ... 72Rb 157
KT22: Fet ... 94Ea 192
NW4 ... 28Ya 48
NW8 ... 4C 214 (41Fb 89)
SM6: Wall ... 78Kb 156
Lodge Vs. IG8: Wfd G ... 23Hc 53
Lodge Wlk. CR6: W'ham ... 88Cc 178
Lodge Way SL4: Wind ... 5C 102
TW15: Ashf ... 61N 127
TW17: Shep ... 68S 128
Lodore Gdns. NW9 ... 29Ua 48
Lodore Grn. UB10: Ick ... 34N 63
Lodore St. E14 ... 44Ec 92
Lodysons Cl. RM16: Ors ... 3C 100
Loewen Rd. RM16: Grays ... 8C 100
Loft, The W12 ... 46Za 88
Loft Ho. E1 ... 2K 225
Lofthouse Pl. KT9: Chess ... 79La 152
Loftie St. SE16 ... 47Wb 91
Lofting Ho. N1 ... 38Qb 70
(off Liverpool Rd.)
Lofting Rd. N1 ... 38Pb 70
Lofts on the Park E9 ... 37Zb 72
(off Cassland Rd.)
Loftus Road ... 46Xa 88
Loftus Rd. IG11: Bark ... 37Sc 74
W12 ... 46Xa 88
Loftus Vs. W12 ... 46Xa 88
(off Loftus Rd.)
Logan Cl. E20 ... 36Ec 72
EN3: Enf H ... 11Zb 34
TW4: Houn ... 55Ba 107
Logan Ct. AL2: Lon C ... 9F 6
RM1: Rom ... 29Gd 56
Logan M. RM1: Rom ... 29Gd 56
W8 ... 49Cb 89
Logan Pl. W8 ... 49Cb 89
Logan Rd. HA9: Wemb ... 33Ma 67
N9 ... 19Xb 33
Loggetts SE21 ... 61Ub 135
Logs Hill BR1: Brom ... 66Nc 138
BR7: Chst ... 66Nc 138
Logs Hill Cl. BR7: Chst ... 67Nc 138
Lohmann Ho. SE11 ... 51Qb 112
(off Kennington Oval)
Lois Dr. TW17: Shep ... 71R 150
Lolesworth Cl. E1 ... 1K 225 (43Vb 91)
Lolland Ho. SE7 ... 49Nc 94
Lollard St. SE11 ... 5J 229 (49Pb 90)
(not continuous)
Lollesworth La. KT24: W Hor ... 98S 190
Loman Path RM15: S Ock ... 44Vd 98
Loman St. SE1 ... 1C 230 (47Rb 91)
Lomas Cl. CR0: New Ad ... 80Ec 158
Lomas Dr. E8 ... 38Vb 71
Lomas St. E1 ... 43Wb 91
Lombard Av. EN3: Enf H ... 11Yb 34
IG3: Ilf ... 32Uc 74
Lombard Bus. Pk.
CR0: C'don ... 73Pb 156
SW19 ... 68Db 133
Lombard Ct. EC3 ... 4G 225 (45Tb 91)
RM7: Rom ... 28Ed 56
W3 ... 46Ra 87
Lombard La. EC4 ... 3A 224 (44Qb 90)
Lombard Pl. E3 ... 40Ac 72
Lombard Rd. N11 ... 22Kb 50
SW11 ... 54Fb 111
SW19 ... 68Db 133
LOMBARD RDBT. ... 73Pb 156
Lombards, The RM11: Horn ... 31Pd 77
Lombards Chase CM13: W H'dn ... 30Fe 59
Lombard St. DA4: Hort K ... 71Sd 164
EC3 ... 3G 225 (44Tb 91)
Lombard Trad. Est. SE7 ... 49Kc 93
Lombard Wall SE7 ... 48Kc 93
Lombard Wharf SW11 ... 54Fb 111
Lombardy Cl. GU21: Wok ... 9K 167
HP2: Hem H ... 3D 4
IG6: Ilf ... 24Rc 54
Lombardy Dr. HP4: Berk ... 2A 2
Lombardy Pl. W2 ... 45Db 89
Lombardy Retail Pk. UB3: Hayes ... 45X 85
Lombardy Way WD6: Bore ... 11Na 29
Lomond Cl. HA0: Wemb ... 38Pa 67
N15 ... 29Ub 51
Lomond Gdns. CR2: Sels ... 80Ac 158
Lomond Gro. SE5 ... 52Tb 113
Lomond Ho. SE5 ... 52Tb 113
Loncin Mead Av. KT15: New H ... 81L 169
Loncroft Rd. SE5 ... 51Vb 113
Londesborough Rd. N16 ... 35Ub 71
Londinium Twr. E1 ... 4K 225
LONDON ... 6F 223 (46Nb 90)
London Ambulance Service Mus. ... 29Vc 55
London Aquatics Cen.
Queen Elizabeth Olympic Pk.
... 38Ec 72
LONDON BIGGIN HILL AIRPORT
... 84Mc 179
London Bri. SE1 ... 6G 225 (46Tb 91)
London Bridge Experience ... 6G 225
(off Tooley St.)
London Bri. St. SE1 ... 7G 225 (46Tb 91)
London Bri. Wlk. SE1 ... 6G 225
London Broncos RLFC ... 25Na 47
London Business School
... 5F 215 (42Hb 89)
London Bus Mus., The ... 81Q 170
London Canal Mus. ... 1G 217 (40Nb 70)
LONDON CITY AIRPORT ... 46Nc 94
London City College ... 7K 223
(off Waterloo Rd.)
London Coliseum ... 5F 223
(off St Martin's La.)
London College of Fashion, The
Hackney ... 38Yb 72
LONDON COLNEY ... 8H 7
London Colney By-Pass AL2: Lon C ... 7H 7
London Ct. CM14: W'ley ... 22Xd 58
Londonderry Pde. DA8: Erith ... 52Fd 118
London Designer Outlet
HA9: Wemb ... 35Qa 67
London Distribution Pk.
RM18: Tilb ... 3A 122
London Dungeon ... 1H 229 (47Pb 90)
London Eye ... 1H 229 (47Pb 90)
London Flds. East Side E8 ... 38Xb 71
London Fields Lido ... 38Xb 71
London Flds. West Side E8 ... 38Wb 71
London Film Mus. ... 4G 223
London Fire Brigade Mus.
... 1D 230 (47Sb 91)
London Fruit Exchange E1 ... 1K 225
LONDON GATEWAY SERVICE AREA
... 18Sa 29
London Golf Course, The ... 80Yd 164
London Group Bus. Pk. NW2 ... 32Va 68
LONDON HEATHROW AIRPORT
Terminals 1, 2, 3 ... 55Q 106
Terminal 4 ... 57R 106
Terminal 5 ... 55L 105
London Heliport, The ... 54Eb 111
London Ho. EC1 ... 1D 224
NW8 ... 1E 214
WC1 ... 5H 217 (42Pb 90)
London Ind. Pk., The E6 ... 43Rc 94
(not continuous)
London Intl. Cruise Terminal
RM18: Tilb ... 6C 122
London Irish RFC (Hazelwood)
... 69V 128
London La. BR1: Brom ... 66Hc 137
E8 ... 38Xb 71
London Master Bakers Almshouses
E10 ... 30Dc 52
London Mercantile Court
... 2K 223 (44Qb 90)
London Metropolitan Archives ... 5A 218
London Metropolitan University
London City Campus -
Calcutta House & Goulston St.
... 2K 225 (44Vb 91)
Central House ... 44Wb 91
(off Whitechapel High St.)
Commercial Road ... 44Wb 91
Jewry St. ... 3K 225
Moorgate ... 1G 225
Tower Hill ... 4K 225
North London Campus -
Eden Grove ... 36Pb 70
Stapleton House ... 36Pb 70
Tower Building & Graduate Cen.
... 36Qb 70
London M. W2 ... 3C 220 (44Fb 89)
London Mill Apartments E2 ... 1K 219
London Motorcycle Mus.
(Ravenor Farm) ... 41Ea 86
London Motor Mus. ... 48V 84
London Palladium ... 3B 222
London Pavilion ... 5D 222
London Plane Ho. E15 ... 41Gc 93
(off Teasel Way)
London Regatta Cen. ... 45Mc 93
London Rd. AL1: St A ... 3C 6
BR1: Brom ... 66Hc 137
BR8: Swan ... 67Ed 140
(Birchwood Rd., not continuous)
BR8: Swan ... 70Hd 140
(High St.)
CM14: B'wood ... 21Vd 58
CR0: C'don ... 73Rb 157
CR3: Cat'm ... 95Tb 197
CR4: Mitc ... 71Gb 155
(Brookfields Av.)
CR4: Mitc ... 73Jb 156
(Mill Grn. Rd.)
CR7: Thor H ... 71Qb 156
DA1: Bexl, Cray ... 57Fd 118
DA2: Dart ... 59Rd 119
DA4: Farni ... 72Nd 163
DA9: Ghithe ... 57Xd 120
DA10: Swans ... 57Xd 120
DA11: Nflt ... 58Fe 121
E13 ... 40Jc 73
EN2: Enf ... 13Tb 33
GU4: Burp ... 100E 188
GU20: W'sham ... 6A 146
GU23: Send ... 100E 188
GU25: Vir W ... 10J 125
HA1: Harr ... 33Ga 66
HA7: Stan ... 22La 46
HA9: Wemb ... 36Na 67
HP1: Hem H ... 4G 2
HP3: Hem H ... 5K 3
HP4: Berk ... 2A 2
IG11: Bark ... 38Rc 74
KT2: King T ... 68Pa 131
KT17: Ewe ... 81Va 174
RH1: Redh ... 5P 207
RH2: Reig ... 6J 207
RM4: Abr ... 14Vc 37
RM4: Stap T ... 11Ed 38
RM6: Chad H ... 30Cd 56
RM7: Chad H, Rom ... 30Cd 56
RM15: Avel, Purf ... 46Pd 97
RM17: Grays ... 51Ae 121
RM18: Tilb ... 4D 122
RM19: Purf ... 46Pd 97
(Juliette Way)
RM19: Purf ... 50Qd 97
(Tank Hill Rd.)
RM20: Grays, W Thur ... 51Ud 120
SE1 ... 3B 230 (48Rb 91)
SE23 ... 60Xb 113
SL3: L'ly ... 8N 81
SL3: Dat ... 2M 103
(not continuous)
SL5: Asc, S'hill ... 9A 124
SL5: S'dale ... 3E 146
SM3: Cheam ... 76Za 154
SM4: Mord ... 71Cb 155
SM6: Wall ... 77Kb 156
SS17: Stan H ... 2K 101
SW16 ... 67Pb 134
SW17 ... 66Hb 133
TN13: Dun G, Riv ... 89Fd 182
(not continuous)
TN13: S'oaks ... 95Hd 202
TN14: Hals ... 81Bd 181
(Old London Rd.)
TN14: Hals ... 84Dd 182
(Shacklands Rd.)
TN15: Bor G, W King, Wro, Wro H
... 78Td 164
TN16: Westrm ... 95Sc 200
TW1: Twick ... 59Ja 108
TW3: Houn ... 55Ea 108
TW7: Bford, Isle ... 54Ha 108
TW7: Isle, Twick ... 57Ja 108
TW8: Bford ... 54Ha 108
TW14: Bedf ... 62K 127
TW15: Ashf ... 62K 127
TW18: Staines ... 63J 127
TW20: Eng G ... 8L 125
WD3: Rick ... 19N 25
WD6: Bore ... 6Qa 15
WD7: Shenl ... 5Pa 15
WD23: Bush ... 16Aa 27
LONDON ROAD MOOR LANE RDBT.
... 19N 25
London Rd. Nth. RH1: Mers ... 98Kb 196
London Rd. Retail Pk. HP3: Hem H ... 5L 3
LONDON ROAD RDBT. ... 58Ja 108
London Rd. Sth. RH1: Mers, Redh ... 2A 208
London School of Economics &
Political Science, The
... 3J 223 (44Pb 90)
Londons Cl. RM14: Upm ... 36Sd 78
London Scottish & Richmond
Rugby Football Ground ... 55Ma 109
London Scottish Golf Course ... 62Xa 132
London's Death Trap ... 2H 229
London Shootfighters Gym ... 42Qa 87
London South Bank University
Havering ... 26Nd 57
Keyworth St. ... 3C 230 (48Rb 91)
Southwark Campus
... 3C 230 (48Rb 91)
Sports Cen. ... 3C 230
Technopark ... 3C 230
London's Roman Amphitheatre ... 2F 225
London Stadium
Queen Elizabeth Olympic Pk.
... 38Dc 72
London Stile W4 ... 50Qa 87
London Stock Exchange ... 2C 224
London St. EC3 ... 4J 225 (45Ub 91)
KT16: Chert ... 73J 149
W2 ... 2B 220 (44Fb 89)
London Telecom Tower, The ... 7B 216
London Television Cen., The
... 6K 223 (45Qb 90)
London Ter. E2 ... 40Wb 71
London Transport Mus. ... 4G 223 (45Nb 90)
London Transport Mus. Depot ... 47Qa 87
London Trocadero ... 5D 222 (45Mb 90)
London Underwriting Cen. ... 4J 225
London Wall EC2 ... 1E 224 (43Sb 91)
London Wall Bldgs. EC2 ... 1G 225
London Wall Pl. EC2 ... 1E 224
London Wetland Cen. ... 53Xa 110
London Wetland Cen. Vis. Cen. ... 53Xa 110
London Wharf E2 ... 39Xb 71
(off Wharf Pl.)
London Zoo ... 1H 215 (40Jb 70)
Londrina Ct. HP4: Berk ... 1A 2
(off Londrina Ter.)
Londrina Ter. HP4: Berk ... 1A 2
Loneacre GU20: W'sham ... 9C 146
LONESOME ... 67Lb 134
Lonesome Cvn. Site SW16 ... 67Kb 134
Lonesome La. RH2: Reig ... 10K 207
Lonesome Way SW16 ... 67Kb 134
Long Acre BR6: Orp ... 75Zc 161
WC2 ... 4F 223 (45Nb 90)
Long Acre Ct. W13 ... 43Ja 86
Longacre Pl. SM5: Cars ... 79Jb 156
Longacre Rd. E17 ... 25Fc 53
Longacres AL4: St A ... 2H 7
(not continuous)
Longaford Way CM13: Hut ... 18Ee 41
Long Arrotts HP1: Hem H ... 1K 3
Long Barn Cl. WD25: Wat ... 4W 12
Longbeach Rd. SW11 ... 55Hb 111
Longberrys NW2 ... 34Bb 69
Longboat Row UB1: S'hall ... 44Ba 85
Longbourn SL4: Wind ... 5E 102
Longbourne Way KT16: Chert ... 72H 149
Longbow Ho. EC1 ... 7F 219
Longboyds KT11: Cobh ... 87X 171
Longbridge Ho. E16 ... 45Rc 94
(off University Way)
RM8: Dag ... 35Xc 75
(off Longbridge Rd.)
Longbridge Rd. IG11: Bark ... 37Tc 74
RM8: Dag ... 35Wc 75
Longbridge Way SE13 ... 57Ec 114
UB8: Uxb ... 40K 63
Longbury Cl. BR5: St P ... 69Xc 139
Longbury Dr. BR5: St P ... 69Xc 139
Long Chaulden HP1: Hem H ... 2G 2
Longcliffe Path WD19: Wat ... 20W 26
Long Cl. SL2: Farn C ... 8F 60
Long Copse Cl. KT23: Bookh ... 95Da 191
Long Ct. RM19: Purf ... 49Qd 97
Longcourt M. E11 ... 28Lc 53
Longcroft SE9 ... 62Pc 138
WD19: Wat ... 17X 27
Longcroft Av. SM7: Bans ... 86Eb 175
Longcroft Dr. EN8: Walt C ... 6Bc 20
Longcrofte Rd. HA8: Edg ... 24Ma 47
Longcroft La. HP3: Bov, Hem H ... 10E 2
Longcroft Ri. IG10: Lough ... 15Qc 36
Longcroft Rd. WD3: Map C ... 22F 42
Longcrofts EN9: Walt A ... 6Gc 21
LONGCROSS ... 6L 147
Longcross Grange KT16: Vir W ... 5L 147
Longcross Rd. KT16: Longc ... 6K 147
Long Deacon Rd. E4 ... 18Gc 35
Longdean Pk. HP3: Hem H ... 6A 4
Long Deans Nature Reserve ... 7B 4
Longden Av. KT15: Add ... 80H 149
LONG DITTON ... 74La 152
Longdon Ct. RM1: Rom ... 29Hd 56
Longdon Wood BR2: Kes ... 77Nc 160
Longdown La. Nth. KT17: Eps ... 86Wa 174
Longdown La. Sth.
KT17: Eps, Eps D ... 86Wa 174
Longdown Rd. KT17: Eps ... 86Wa 174
SE6 ... 63Cc 136
Long Dr. HA4: Ruis ... 36Y 65
SL1: Burn ... 1A 80
UB6: G'frd ... 39Da 65
UB7: W Dray ... 47N 83
W3 ... 44Ua 88
Long Elmes HA3: Hrw W ... 25Da 45
Long Elms WD5: Ab L ... 5T 12
Long Elms Cl. WD5: Ab L ... 5T 12
Long Fallow AL2: Chis G ... 9N 5
Longfellow Dr. CM13: Hut ... 17Ee 41
Longfellow Rd. E17 ... 30Bc 52
KT4: Wor Pk ... 75Wa 154
Longfellow Way SE1 ... 6K 231 (49Vb 91)
LONGFIELD ... 68Ae 143
Long Fld. NW9 ... 24Ua 48
Longfield BR1: Brom ... 67Hc 137
HP3: Hem H ... 4B 4
IG10: Lough ... 15Mc 35
SL2: Hedg ... 4H 61
Longfield Av. DA3: Lfield ... 68Ee 143
DA13: Meop ... 68Ee 143
E17 ... 28Ac 52
EN3: Enf W ... 9Yb 20
HA9: Wemb ... 32Na 67
NW7 ... 24Wa 48
RM11: Horn ... 31Hd 76
SM6: Wall ... 74Jb 156
W5 ... 45La 86
Longfield Chalk Bank Local Nature Reserve
... 68Yd 142
Longfield Cres. KT20: Tad ... 92Ya 194
SE26 ... 62Yb 136
Longfield Dr. CR4: Mitc ... 67Gb 133
SW14 ... 57Ra 109
Longfield Est. SE1 ... 5K 231 (49Vb 91)
LONGFIELD HILL ... 70Fe 143
Longfield Ho. E17 ... 29Bc 52
W5 ... 45La 86
Longfield Rd. DA3: Long H ... 71Fe 165
W5 ... 44La 86
Longfield St. SW18 ... 59Cb 111
Longfield Wlk. W5 ... 44La 86
LONGFORD
TN13 ... 92Gd 202
UB7 ... 53K 105
Longford Av. TW14: Felt ... 58U 106
TW19: Stanw ... 60N 105
UB1: S'hall ... 45Da 85
Longford Cir. UB7: Lford ... 53K 105
Longford Cl. TW12: Hamp H ... 63Ca 129
TW13: Hanw ... 62Aa 129
UB4: Yead ... 45Z 85
Longford Ct. E5 ... 35Zb 72
(off Pedro St.)
KT19: Ewe ... 77Sa 153
NW4 ... 28Za 48
TN13: Dun G ... 92Gd 202
TW12: Hamp H ... 65Da 129
UB1: S'hall ... 46Ca 85
(off Uxbridge Rd.)
Longford Gdns. SM1: Sutt ... 76Eb 155
UB4: Yead ... 45Z 85
Longford Ho. BR1: Brom ... 64Fc 137
(off Brangbourne Rd.)
E1 ... 44Yb 92
(off Jubilee St.)
TW12: Hamp H ... 63Ca 129
Longford Ind. Est. TW12: Hamp ... 65Da 129
LONGFORDMOOR ... 53J 105
Longford Rd. TW2: Whitt ... 60Ca 107
Longford St. NW1 ... 5A 216 (42Kb 90)
Longford Wlk. SW2 ... 59Qb 112
Longford Way TW19: Stanw ... 60N 105
Long Furlong Dr. SL2: Slou ... 2B 80
Long Gables SL9: Ger X ... 29B 42
Long Grn. IG7: Chig ... 21Uc 54
Long Gro. RM3: Hrld W ... 26Nd 57
Long Gro. Rd. KT19: Eps ... 83Sa 173
Longhayes Av. RM6: Chad H ... 28Zc 55
Longhayes Ct. RM6: Chad H ... 28Zc 55
Long Heath Dr. KT23: Bookh ... 96Aa 191
Longheath Gdns. CR0: C'don ... 71Yb 158
Longhedge Ho. SE26 ... 63Wb 135
(off High Level Dr.)
Long Hedges TW3: Houn ... 54Ca 107
Longhedge St. SW11 ... 54Jb 112
Long Hill CR3: Wold ... 93Zb 198
Longhill Rd. SE6 ... 61Fc 137
Longhook Gdns. UB5: N'olt ... 40W 64
Longhope Cl. SE15 ... 51Ub 113
Longhouse Rd. RM16: Grays ... 8D 100
Long Ho's. GU24: Pirb ... 6B 186
Longhurst Ho. W10 ... 41Bb 89
(off Lancefield St.)
Longhurst Rd. CR0: C'don ... 72Xb 157
SE13 ... 57Fc 115
Longitude Apartments
CR0: C'don ... 75Tb 157
(off Addiscombe Gro.)
Long John HP3: Hem H ... 4P 3
Longland Ct. E9 ... 36Ac 72
(off Mabley St.)
SE1 ... 50Wb 91
Longland Dr. N20 ... 20Db 31
Longland Pl. KT19: Eps ... 84Na 173
LONGLANDS ... 62Sc 138
Longlands HP2: Hem H ... 2P 3
Longlands Av. CR5: Coul ... 86Jb 176
Longlands Cl. EN8: Chesh ... 4Zb 20
Longlands Ct. CR4: Mitc ... 67Jb 134
DA15: Sidc ... 61Vc 139
W11 ... 45Bb 89
Longlands Pk. Cres. DA15: Sidc ... 62Uc 138
Longlands Rd. DA15: Sidc ... 62Uc 138
Long La. CR0: C'don ... 72Xb 157
DA7: Bex ... 52Zc 117
EC1 ... 1C 224 (43Rb 91)
HP3: Bov, Flau ... 3B 10
N2 ... 25Db 49
N3 ... 25Db 49
RM16: Grays ... 47Ce 99
SE1 ... 2F 231 (47Tb 91)
TW19: Stanw ... 61P 127
UB10: Hil, Ick ... 40Q 64
WD3: Herons ... 16E 24
WD3: Rick ... 18G 24
Longleat Ho. SW1 ... 7D 228
Longleat M. BR5: St M Cry ... 70Yc 139
Longleat Rd. EN1: Enf ... 15Ub 33
Longleat Way TW14: Bedf ... 59T 106
Longlees WD3: Map C ... 22F 42
Longleigh Ho. SE5 ... 53Ub 113
(off Peckham Rd.)
Longleigh La. DA7: Bex ... 51Yc 117
SE2 ... 51Yc 117
Long Lents Ho. NW10 ... 39Ta 67
(off Shrewsbury Rd.)
Longley Av. HA0: Wemb ... 39Pa 67
Longley Ct. SW8 ... 53Nb 112
Longley M. RM16: Ors ... 7B 100
Longley Rd. CR0: C'don ... 73Rb 157
HA1: Harr ... 29Ea 46
SW17 ... 65Gb 133
Long Leys E4 ... 23Dc 52
Longley St. SE1 ... 49Wb 91
Longley Way NW2 ... 34Ya 68
Long Lodge Dr. KT12: Walt T ... 76Y 151
Longman Ct. HP3: Hem H ... 7N 3
Longman Ho. E2 ... 40Zb 72
(off Mace St.)
E8 ... 39Vb 71
(off Haggerston Rd.)
Longmans Cl. WD18: Wat ... 16S 26
Long Mark Rd. E16 ... 43Mc 93
Longmarsh La. SE28 ... 46Uc 94
Longmarsh Vw. DA4: Sut H ... 67Rd 141
Long Mead NW9 ... 25Va 48
Longmead BR7: Chst ... 68Qc 138
SL4: Wind ... 3C 102
Longmead Bus. Cen. KT19: Eps ... 83Ta 173
Longmead Cl. CM15: Shenf ... 18Ae 41
CR3: Cat'm ... 94Ub 197
Longmead Dr. DA14: Sidc ... 61Zc 139
Longmeade DA12: Grav'nd ... 10H 123
Longmead Ho. SE27 ... 64Sb 135
Longmead La. SL1: Burn ... 8B 60
Long Mdw. CM13: Hut ... 19Ee 41
NW5 ... 36Mb 70
RM3: Norm ... 19Ld 39
TN13: Riv ... 93Fd 202
Longmeadow KT23: Bookh ... 97Ba 191
Long Mdw. Cl. BR4: W W'ck ... 73Ec 158
Longmeadow Rd. DA15: Sidc ... 60Uc 116
Longmead Rd. KT7: T Ditt ... 73Ga 152
KT19: Eps, Ewe ... 83Ta 173
SW17 ... 64Hb 133
UB3: Hayes ... 45V 84
Longmere Gdns. KT20: Tad ... 91Za 194
Long Mill SE10 ... 53Dc 114
(off Greenwich High Rd.)
Long Mill La. TN11: Dun G ... 99Ce 205
TN15: Crou, Plat, Plax ... 92De 205
Long Mill La. Crouch
TN15: Crou ... 94Ee 205
Long Mimms HP2: Hem H ... 1N 3
Long Moor EN8: Chesh ... 1Ac 20
Longmoore St. SW1 ... 6B 228 (49Lb 90)
Longmoor Point SW15 ... 60Xa 110
(off Norley Va.)
Longmore Av. EN4: E Barn ... 16Eb 31
EN5: New Bar ... 16Eb 31
Longmore Cl. WD3: Map C ... 21H 43
Longmore Gdns. Est. SW1 ... 6C 228
Longmore Rd. KT12: Hers ... 77Aa 151
Longnor Est. E1 ... 41Zb 92
Longnor Rd. E1 ... 41Zb 92
Long Orchards
KT20: Kgswd ... 92Ab 194
Long Pightle Mobile Home Pk.
WD3: Chan C ... 9P 11
Long Pond Rd. SE3 ... 53Gc 115
Longport Cl. IG6: Ilf ... 23Wc 55
Long Reach GU23: Ock ... 95Q 190
KT24: W Hor ... 95Q 190
Longreach DA1: Dart ... 55Qd 119
(off Vickers La.)
Longreach Ct. IG11: Bark ... 40Tc 74
Long Reach Rd. IG11: Bark ... 42Vc 95
Longreach Rd. DA8: Erith ... 52Kd 119
Long Readings La. SL2: Slou ... 1F 80
Longridge WD7: R'lett ... 6Ka 14
Longridge Gro. GU22: Pyr ... 86H 169
Longridge Ho. SE1 ... 4E 230 (48Sb 91)
Longridge La. UB1: S'hall ... 44Da 85

Longridge Rd.—Lucas Ho.

Longridge Rd. IG11: Bark 38Sc 74
SW5 49Cb 89
Long Ridges N2 27Jb 50
(off Fortis Grn.)
Longridge Vw. CR5: Chip 92Hb 195
Long Ridings Av. CM13: Hut 15De 41
Long Rd. SW4 56Kb 112
Long Room, The UB9: Hare 24J 43
Longroyd KT24: E Hor 98U 190
(off Cobham Way)
Longs Cl. GU22: Pyr 88J 169
Long's Ct. WC2 5E 222
Longs Ct. TW9: Rich 56Pa 109
Longsdon Way CR3: Cat'm 96Wb 197
Longshaw KT22: Lea 92Ja 192
Longshaw Rd. E4 20Fc 35
Longshore SE8 49Bc 92
Longshott Ct. SW5 49Cb 89
(off W. Cromwell Rd.)
Longside Cl. TW20: Egh 67E 126
Longspring WD24: Wat 9X 13
Longspring Wood Nature Reserve 10E 4
Longstaff Cres. SW18 58Cb 111
Longstaff Rd. SW18 58Cb 111
Longstone Av. NW10 38Va 68
Longstone Ct. SE1 2F 231
Longstone Rd. SL0: Iver H 40E 62
SW17 64Kb 134
Long St. E2 3K 219 (41Vb 91)
EN9: Walt A 2Mc 21
Longthornton Rd. SW16 68Lb 134
Longthorpe Ct. W6 49Wa 88
Longton Av. SE26 63Wb 135
Longton Gro. SE26 63Xb 135
Longtown Cl. RM3: Rom 22Ld 57
Longtown Ct. DA2: Dart 58Rd 119
(off Osbourne Rd.)
Longtown Rd. RM3: Rom 22Ld 57
Longview Vs. RM5: Col R 25Bd 55
Longview Way RM5: Col R 25Fd 56
Longville Rd. SE11 5B 230 (49Rb 91)
Long Wlk. DA13: Ist R 7A 144
EN9: Walt A 2Cc 20
GU4: E Clan 100P 189
HP8: Chal G 13A 24
KT3: N Mald 69Sa 131
KT14: W Byf 86L 169
KT18: Tatt C 91Ya 194
SE1 3J 231 (48Ub 91)
SE18 51Rc 116
SL4: Wind 6H 103
SW13 54Ua 110
Long Walk, The SL4: Wind 10H 103
Longwalk Rd. UB11: Stock P 46R 84
Long Wall E15 41Fc 93
Longwater Ho. KT1: King T 69Ma 131
(off Portsmouth Rd.)
Longwood Av. SL3: L'ly 50D 82
Longwood Bus. Pk. TW16: Sun 71V 150
Longwood Cl. RM14: Upm 36Sd 78
Longwood Ct. RM14: Upm 36Sd 78
(off Corbets Tey Rd.)
Longwood Dr. SW15 58Wa 110
Longwood Gdns. IG5: Ilf 28Pc 54
IG6: Ilf 28Pc 54
Longwood Rd. CR8: Kenley 88Tb 177
Longworth Cl. SE28 44Zc 95
Long Yd. WC1 6H 217 (42Pb 90)
Loning, The EN3: Enf W 10Yb 20
NW9 28Ua 48
Lonsdale Av. CM13: Hut 16Fe 41
E6 42Mc 93
HA9: Wemb 36Na 67
RM7: Rom 30Ed 56
Lonsdale Cl. E6 42Nc 94
HA5: Hat E 24Aa 45
HA8: Edg 22Pa 47
SE9 62Mc 137
UB8: Hil 43S 84
Lonsdale Ct. KT6: Surb 73Ma 153
Lonsdale Cres. DA2: Dart 60Sd 120
IG2: Ilf 30Rc 54
Lonsdale Dr. EN2: Enf 14Mb 32
Lonsdale Dr. Nth. EN2: Enf 15Nb 32
Lonsdale Gdns. CR7: Thor H 70Pb 134
Lonsdale Ho. W11 44Bb 89
(off Lonsdale Rd.)
Lonsdale M. TW9: Kew 53Qa 109
W11 44Bb 89
(off Colville M.)
Lonsdale Pl. N1 38Qb 70
Lonsdale Rd. DA7: Bex 54Bd 117
E11 30Hc 53
KT13: Weyb 80Q 150
NW6 40Bb 69
SE25 70Xb 135
SW13 53Va 110
UB2: S'hall 48Z 85
W4 49Va 88
W11 44Bb 89
Lonsdale Sq. N1 38Qb 70
Lonsdale Yd. W11 45Cb 89
Loobert Rd. N15 27Ub 51
Looe Gdns. IG6: Ilf 27Rc 54
Look Ahead SL1: Slou 7J 81
Lookout Education Cen., The
6F 221 (46Hb 89)
Loom Gro. RM1: Rom 29Jd 56
Loom La. WD7: R'lett 9Ha 14
Loom Pl. WD7: R'lett 8Ja 14
Loop Ct. SE10 49Gc 93
(off Telegraph Av.)
Loop Rd. BR7: Chst 65Sc 138
GU22: Wok 92B 188
KT18: Eps 88Sa 173
Lopen Rd. N18 21Ub 51
Lopez Ho. SW9 55Nb 112
Lorac Ct. SM2: Sutt 80Cb 155
Loraine Cl. EN3: Pond E 15Yb 34
Loraine Cotts. N7 35Pb 70
Loraine Ct. BR7: Chst 64Rc 138
Loraine Gdns. KT21: Asht 89Na 173
Loraine Ho. SM6: Wall 77Kb 156
Loraine Rd. N7 35Pb 70
W4 51Ra 109
Lorane Ct. WD17: Wat 10V 13
Lord Admiral's Vw. SE18 49Pc 94
(off Frances St.)
Lord Alexander Ho. HP1: Hem H 3L 3
Lord Amory Way E14 47Ec 92
Lord Av. IG5: Ilf 28Pc 54
Lord Chancellor Wlk.
KT2: King T 67Sa 131
Lord Ct. IG5: Ilf 28Pc 54
Lord Darby M. TN14: Cud 87Tc 180
Lordell Pl. SW19 65Ya 132
Lorden Wlk. E2 41Wb 91
Lord Gdns. IG5: Ilf 28Pc 54
Lord Graham M. N18 22Wb 51
Lord Hills Bri. W2 43Db 89
Lord Hills Rd. W2 43Db 89
Lord Holland La. SW9 54Qb 112
Lord Kensington Ho. W14 49Bb 89
(off Radnor Ter.)
Lord Knyvett Cl. TW19: Stanw 58M 105
Lord Knyvetts Ct. TW19: Stanw 58M 105
Lord Mayor's Dr. SL2: Farn C 7D 60
Lord Napier Pl. W6 50Wa 88
Lord Nth. St. SW1 4F 229 (48Nb 90)
Lord Raglan Ho. SL4: Wind 5G 102
Lord Roberts M. SW6 52Db 111
Lord Robert's Ter. SE18 50Qc 94
Lord Rosebery Lodge KT18: Eps 86Sa 173
Lord's 4C 214 (41Fb 89)
(off Avenue Rd.)
Lordsbury Fld. SM6: Wall 82Lb 176
Lords Cl. SE21 61Sb 135
TW13: Hanw 61Aa 129
WD7: Shenl 4Na 15
Lordsgrove Cl. KT20: Tad 92Xa 194
Lordship Cl. CM13: Hut 17Fe 41
Lordship Gro. N16 33Tb 71
Lordship La. N17 25Tb 51
N22 26Qb 50
SE22 56Vb 113
Lordship La. Est. SE21 59Wb 113
Lordship Pk. N16 33Sb 71
Lordship Pk. M. N16 33Sb 71
Lordship Pl. SW3 51Gb 111
Lordship Rd. EN7: Chesh 2Xb 19
N16 32Tb 71
UB5: N'olt 38Aa 65
Lordship Ter. N16 33Tb 71
Lordsmead Rd. N17 25Ub 51
Lord St. DA12: Grav'nd 9D 122
E16 46Nc 94
WD17: Wat 13Y 27
Lords Vw. NW8 4D 214 (41Fb 89)
(not continuous)
Lordswood Cl. DA2: Daren 63Ud 142
DA6: Bex 57Ad 117
Lords Wood Ho. CR5: Coul 94Mb 196
Lord Warwick St. SE18 48Pc 94
Loreburn Ho. N7 35Pb 70
Lorenzo Ho. IG3: Ilf 30Wc 55
Lorenzo St. WC1 3H 217 (41Pb 90)
Loretto Gdns. HA3: Kenton 28Na 47
Lorian Cl. N12 21Db 49
Lorian Dr. RH2: Reig 5L 207
Lorimer Row BR2: Brom 72Mc 159
Loriners Cl. KT11: Cobh 86W 170
Loriners Link HP2: Hem H 1N 3
Loring Rd. N20 19Gb 31
SE14 53Ac 114
SL4: Wind 3D 102
TW7: Isle 54Ha 108
Loris Rd. W6 48Ya 88
Lorn Ct. SW9 54Qb 112
Lorne, The KT23: Bookh 98Ca 191
Lorne Av. CR0: C'don 73Zb 158
Lorne Cl. NW8 4E 214 (41Gb 89)
SL1: Slou 8F 80
Lorne Ct. SL1: Slou 8F 80
Lorne Gdns. CR0: C'don 73Zb 158
E11 28Lc 53
GU21: Knap 1H 187
W11 47Za 88
Lorne Ho. E1 43Ac 92
(off Ben Jonson Rd.)
Lorne Rd. CM14: W'ley 21Yd 58
E7 35Kc 73
E17 29Cc 52
HA3: W'stone 26Ha 46
N4 32Pb 70
TW10: Rich 57Pa 109
Lorne Ter. N3 26Bb 49
Lorn Rd. SW9 54Pb 112
Lorraine Ct. NW1 38Kb 70
Lorraine Pk. HA3: Hrw W 24Ga 46
Lorrimore Rd. SE17 51Rb 113
Lorrimore Sq. SE17 51Rb 113
Lorton Cl. DA12: Grav'nd 1G 144
Lorton Ho. NW6 39Cb 69
(off Kilburn Vale)
Loseberry Rd. KT10: Clay 78Fa 152
Losfield Rd. SL4: Wind 3C 102
Lossie Dr. SL0: Iver 45D 82
Lost Theatre 53Mb 112
Lothair Rd. W5 47Ma 87
Lothair Rd. Nth. N4 30Rb 51
Lothair Rd. Sth. N4 31Qb 70
Lothair St. SW11 55Gb 111
Lothbury EC2 2F 225 (44Tb 91)
Lothian Av. UB4: Yead 43X 85
Lothian Cl. HA0: Wemb 34Ja 66
Lothian Rd. SW9 53Rb 113
Lothian Wood KT20: Tad 94Xa 194
Lothrop St. W10 41Ab 88
Lots Rd. SW10 52Eb 111
Lotus Cl. SE21 62Tb 135
Lotus M. N19 33Nb 70
Lotus Pk. TW18: Staines 63F 126
Lotus Rd. TN16: Big H 90Pc 180
Lotus St. SW17 65Hb 133
Loudhams Wood La. HP8: Chal G 12A 24
Loudoun Av. IG6: Ilf 29Rc 54
Loudoun Rd. NW8 1A 214 (39Eb 69)
LOUDWATER 13L 25
Loudwater Cl. TW16: Sun 70W 128
Loudwater Dr. WD3: Loud 14L 25
Loudwater Hgts. WD3: Loud 13K 25
Loudwater Ho. WD3: Loud 14L 25
Loudwater La. WD3: Crox G, Loud 15L 25
Loudwater Ridge WD3: Loud 14L 25
Loudwater Rd. TW16: Sun 70W 128
Loughborough Est. SW9 55Rb 113
Loughborough Ho. RM8: Dag 35Wc 75
(off Academy Way)
Loughborough Pk. SW9 56Rb 113
Loughborough Rd. SW9 54Qb 112
Loughborough St. SE11 7J 229 (50Pb 90)
Lough Rd. N7 36Pb 70
LOUGHTON 14Nc 36
Loughton Bus. Cen. IG10: Lough 14Sc 36
Loughton Ct. EN9: Walt A 5Kc 21
Loughton Golf Course 11Rc 36
Loughton La. CM16: They B 10Tc 22
Loughton Leisure Cen. 14Nc 36
Loughton Seedbed Cen.
IG10: Lough 14Tc 36
Loughton Way IG9: Buck H 18Mc 35
Louisa Cl. E9 39Zb 72
Louisa Ct. TW2: Twick 61Ga 130
Louisa Gdns. E1 42Zb 92
Louisa Ho. IG3: Ilf 30Wc 55
Louisa Oakes Cl. E4 21Bc 52
Louisa St. E1 42Zb 92
Louise Aumonier Wlk. N19 31Nb 70
(off Jessie Blythe La.)
Louise Bennett Cl. SE24 56Rb 113
Louise Ct. E11 29Kc 53
N22 25Qb 50
Louise De Marillac Ho. E1 43Yb 92
(off Smithy St.)
Louise Gdns. RM13: Rain 41Gd 96
Louise Rd. E15 37Gc 73
Louise Wlk. HP3: Bov 10C 2
Louise White Ho. N19 32Mb 70
Louis Gdns. BR7: Chst 63Pc 138
Louis M. N10 25Kb 50
Louisville Rd. SW17 62Jb 134
Lousada Lodge N14 16Lb 32
(off Avenue Rd.)
Louvaine Rd. SW11 56Fb 111
Louvain Rd. DA9: Ghithe 59Ud 120
Louvain Way WD25: Wat 4X 13
Lovage App. E6 43Nc 94
Loval Cl. E14 44Bc 92
NW2 34Ya 68
Lovat La. EC3 4H 225 (45Ub 91)
Lovatt Cl. HA8: Edg 23Ra 47
Lovatt Ct. SW12 60Kb 112
Lovatt Dr. HA4: Ruis 29W 44
Lovatts WD3: Crox G 14Q 26
Lovatts Cotts. AL2: Park 9B 6
Lovat Wlk. TW5: Hest 52Aa 107
Loveday Rd. W13 47Ka 86
Love Grn. La. SL0: Iver 43F 82
Lovegrove Cl. CR2: Sande 82Tb 177
Lovegrove Dr. SL2: Slou 2D 80
Lovegrove St. SE1 50Wb 91
Lovegrove Wlk. E14 46Ec 92
Love Hill La. SL3: L'ly 45C 82
Lovejoy La. SL4: Wind 4B 102
Lovekyn Cl. KT2: King T 68Na 131
Lovelace Av. BR2: Brom 72Qc 160
Lovelace Cl. KT24: Eff J 95W 190
TN15: W King 79Ud 164
Lovelace Dr. GU22: Pyr 88G 168
Lovelace Gdns. IG11: Bark 35Wc 75
KT6: Surb 73Ma 153
KT12: Hers 78Y 151
Lovelace Grn. SE9 55Pc 116
Lovelace Ho. W13 45Ka 86
Lovelace Rd. EN4: E Barn 17Gb 31
KT6: Surb 73La 152
SE21 61Sb 135
Lovelace St. E8 39Vb 71
Lovelace Vs. KT7: T Ditt 73Ka 152
(off Portsmouth Rd.)
Loveland Ct. SE1 47Vb 91
(off Jamaica Rd.)
Loveland Mans. IG11: Bark 38Vc 75
(off Upney La.)
Lovelands La. GU24: Chob 5G 166
Love La. AL9: N Mym 10D 8
BR1: Brom 69Kc 137
CR4: Mitc 69Gb 133
(not continuous)
DA5: Bexl 58Bd 117
DA12: Grav'nd 9E 122
EC2 2E 224 (44Sb 91)
HA5: Pinn 26Z 45
IG8: Wfd G 23Pc 54
KT6: Surb 75La 152
KT20: Walt H 99Va 194
N17 24Vb 51
RH9: G'stone 4A 210
RM15: Avel 47Sd 98
RM18: E Til 1K 123
SE18 49Rc 94
SE25 69Xb 135
SL0: Iver 44F 82
SM1: Sutt 79Bb 155
SM3: Cheam, Sutt 79Ab 154
SM4: Mord 73Cb 155
WD4: K Lan 10N 3
WD5: Ab L 2V 12
Lovel Av. DA16: Well 54Wc 117
Lovel Cl. HP1: Hem H 2J 3
Lovelinch Cl. SE15 51Yb 114
Lovel La. SL4: Wink 4A 124
Lovell Ho. E8 39Wb 71
(off Shrubland Rd.)
Lovell Pl. SE16 48Ac 92
Lovell Rd. EN1: Enf 7Xb 19
TW10: Ham 62La 130
UB1: S'hall 44Da 85
Lovells Cl. GU18: Light 2A 166
Lovell Wlk. RM13: Rain 37Jd 76
Lovelock Cl. CR8: Kenley 89Sb 177
Loveridge M. NW6 37Bb 69
Loveridge Rd. NW6 37Bb 69
Lovers La. DA9: Ghithe 56Zd 121
Lovers Wlk. N3 24Cb 49
(not continuous)
NW7 23Bb 49
RM5: Col R 22Fd 56
SE10 51Fc 115
Lovers' Wlk. W1 6H 221 (46Jb 90)
Lovett Dr. SM5: Cars 73Eb 155
Lovett Rd. AL2: Lon C 8E 6
TW18: Staines 63D 126
UB9: Hare 27L 43
Lovett's Pl. SW18 56Db 111
Lovett Way NW10 36Sa 67
Love Wlk. SE5 54Tb 113
Lovibond La. SE10 52Dc 114
(off Norman Rd.)
Lovibonds Av. BR6: Farnb 77Rc 160
UB7: Yiew 44P 83
Lowbell La. AL2: Lon C 9J 7
Lowbrook Rd. IG1: Ilf 35Rc 74
Low Cl. DA9: Ghithe 57Wd 120
Low Cross Wood La. SE21 62Vb 135
Lowdell Cl. UB7: Yiew 44N 83
Lowden Rd. N9 18Xb 33
SE24 56Rb 113
UB1: S'hall 45Aa 85
Lowder Ho. E1 46Xb 91
(off Wapping La.)
Lowe, The IG7: Chig 21Wc 55
Lowe Av. E16 43Jc 93
Lowe Cl. IG7: Chig 22Wc 55
Lowell Ho. SE5 52Sb 113
(off Wyndham Est.)
Lowell St. E14 44Ac 92
Lowen Rd. RM13: Rain 40Fd 76
Lwr. Addiscombe Rd.
CR0: C'don 74Ub 157
Lwr. Addison Gdns. W14 47Ab 88
Lwr. Adeyfield Rd. HP2: Hem H 1M 3
Lwr. Alderton Hall La.
IG10: Lough 15Qc 36
Lwr. Ash Est. TW17: Shep 72V 150
LOWER ASHTEAD 91Ma 193
Lower Barn HP3: Hem H 5P 3
Lwr. Barn Rd. CR8: Purl 84Sb 177
Lwr. Bedfords Rd.
RM1: Have B, Rom 23Gd 56
Lwr. Belgrave St. SW1 4K 227 (48Kb 90)
LOWER BITCHET 98Sd 204
Lwr. Boston Rd. W7 46Ga 86
Lwr. Bridge Rd. RH1: Redh 6P 207
Lwr. Britwell Rd. SL2: Slou 2B 80
(not continuous)
Lwr. Broad St. RM10: Dag 39Cd 76
Lwr. Bury La. CM16: Epp 3Uc 22
Lower Camden BR7: Chst 66Pc 138
Lwr. Church Hill DA9: Ghithe 57Ud 120
Lwr. Church St. CR0: C'don 75Rb 157
Lwr. Cippenham La.
SL1: Slou 6C 80
LOWER CLAPTON 35Xb 71
Lwr. Clapton Rd. E5 34Xb 71
Lwr. Clarendon Wlk. W11 44Ab 88
(off Clarendon Rd.)
Lwr. Common Sth. SW15 55Xa 110
Lwr. Coombe St. CR0: C'don 77Sb 157
Lower Ct. Rd. KT19: Eps 83Sa 173
Lower Cres. SS17: Linf 8J 101
Lower Cft. BR8: Swan 70Hd 140
Lwr. Dagnall St. AL3: St A 2A 6
Lwr. Derby Rd. WD17: Wat 14Y 27
Lwr. Downs Rd. SW20 67Za 132
Lwr. Drayton Pl. CR0: C'don 75Rb 157
Lower Dunnymans SM7: Bans 86Bb 175
LOWER EDMONTON 19Wb 33
Lwr. Farm Rd. KT24: Eff 96X 191
LOWER FELTHAM 62W 128
Lower Fosters NW4 29Ya 48
(off New Brent St.)
Lwr. George St. TW9: Rich 57Ma 109
Lwr. Gravel Rd. BR2: Brom 74Nc 160
LOWER GREEN 75Da 151
Lower Grn. Gdns. KT4: Wor Pk 74Wa 154
Lower Grn. Rd. KT10: Esh 75Da 151
Lower Grn. W. CR4: Mitc 69Gb 133
Lwr. Grosvenor Pl. SW1 3A 228 (48Kb 90)
Lower Gro. Rd. TW10: Rich 58Pa 109
Lwr. Guildford Rd. GU21: Knap 9H 167
Lwr. Guild Hall DA9: Bluew 59Vd 120
LOWER HALLIFORD 73T 150
Lwr. Hall La. E4 22Ac 52
(not continuous)
Lwr. Hampton Rd. TW16: Sun 69Y 129
Lwr. Ham Rd. KT2: King T 64Ma 131
Lwr. Higham Rd.
DA12: Grav'nd, Shorne 10H 123
Lwr. High St. WD17: Wat 14Y 27
Lwr. Hill Rd. KT19: Eps 84Ra 173
LOWER HOLLOWAY 36Pb 70
Lwr. Hook Bus. Pk. BR6: Downe 80Pc 160
Lwr. James St. W1 4C 222 (45Lb 90)
Lwr. John St. W1 4C 222 (45Lb 90)
Lwr. Kenwood Av. EN2: Enf 15Nb 32
Lwr. King's Rd. KT2: King T 67Na 131
LOWER KINGSWOOD 99Bb 195
Lwr. Lea Crossing E14 45Gc 93
E16 45Gc 93
Lwr. Lees Rd. SL2: Slou 1E 80
Lwr. Maidstone Rd. N11 23Lb 50
Lower Mall W6 50Xa 88
Lwr. Mardyke Av. RM13: Rain 40Ed 76
Lower Marsh SE1 2K 229 (47Qb 90)
Lwr. Marsh La. KT1: King T 70Pa 131
Lower Mead RH1: Redh 4P 207
SL0: Iver H 41F 82
Lwr. Merton Ri. NW3 38Gb 69
Lower Mill KT17: Ewe 80Va 154
Lwr. Morden La. SM4: Mord 72Ya 154
Lwr. Mortlake Rd. TW9: Rich 56Na 109
Lwr. New Change Pas. EC4 3E 224
(off One New Change)
Lwr. Noke Cl.
CM14: Rom, S Weald 19Nd 39
Lower Northfield SM7: Bans 86Bb 175
Lower Nursery SL5: S'dale 1E 146
Lwr. Paddock Rd. WD19: Wat 16Aa 27
Lower Pk. Rd. CR5: Chip 90Gb 175
DA17: Belv 49Cd 96
IG10: Lough 15Mc 35
N11 22Lb 50
Lwr. Park Trad. Est. NW10 42Sa 87
Lwr. Paxton Rd. AL1: St A 3C 6
Lower Peryers KT24: E Hor 100U 190
Lwr. Pillory Down CR5: Coul 85Kb 176
SM6: Wall 85Kb 176
LOWER PLACE 40Sa 67
Lower Pl. Bus. Cen. NW10 40Ta 67
(off Steele Rd.)
Lower Plantation WD3: Loud 13L 25
Lwr. Pyrford Rd. GU22: Pyr 88K 169
Lwr. Queen's Rd. IG9: Buck H 19Mc 35
Lwr. Range Rd. DA12: Grav'nd 9G 122
Lwr. Richmond Rd. SW14 55Qa 109
SW15 55Xa 110
TW9: Rich 55Qa 109
Lower Rd. BR5: St M Cry 72Xc 161
BR8: Hext, Swan 66Jd 140
CM15: Mount 12Fe 41
CR8: Kenley 85Rb 177
DA8: Erith 48Dd 96
DA11: Nflt 56Ce 121
DA12: High'm, Shorne 1N 145
DA17: Belv 48Dd 96
HA2: Harr 32Fa 66
HP3: Hem H 8A 4
IG10: Lough 11Qc 36
KT22: Fet 96Fa 192
KT23: Bookh 97Ca 191
KT24: Eff 99Z 191
RH1: Redh 8M 207
SE1 1K 229 (47Qb 90)
SE8 49Zb 92
SE16 47Yb 92
(not continuous)
SL9: Chal P, Ger X 25A 42
(not continuous)
SM1: Sutt 77Eb 155
UB9: Den 31E 62
WD3: Chor 14E 24
Lwr. Robert St. WC2 5G 223
Lwr. Rose Gallery DA9: Bluew 59Vd 120
Lower Sales HP1: Hem H 3H 3
Lower Sandfields GU23: Send 96F 188
Lwr. Sand Hills KT6: Surb 73La 152
Lwr. Sawley Wood SM7: Bans 86Bb 175
LOWER SHORNE 3N 145
Lower Shott KT23: Bookh 98Ca 191
Lwr. Sloane St. SW1 6H 227 (49Jb 90)
Lower Sq. TW7: Isle 55Ka 108
Lower Sq., The SM1: Sutt 78Db 155
(off St Nicholas Way)
Lwr. Station Rd. DA1: Cray 58Gd 118
Lower Strand NW9 26Va 48
Lwr. Sunbury Rd. TW12: Hamp 68Ba 129
Lower Swaines CM16: Epp 2Uc 22
LOWER SYDENHAM 63Zb 136
Lwr. Sydenham Ind. Est. SE26 64Bc 136
Lower Tail WD19: Wat 20Aa 27
Lwr. Teddington Rd.
KT1: Hamp W 67Ma 131
Lower Ter. NW3 34Eb 69
SE27 64Rb 135
(off Woodcote Pl.)
Lwr. Thames St. EC3 5G 225 (45Tb 91)
Lwr. Thames Wlk. DA9: Bluew 60Vd 120
Lower Tub WD23: Bush 17Fa 28
Lwr. Village Rd. SL5: S'hill 1A 146
Lowerwood Ct. W11 44Ab 88
(off Westbourne Pk. Rd.)
Lwr. Wood Rd. KT10: Clay 79Ka 152
LOWER WOODSIDE 4H 9
Lower Yott HP2: Hem H 3P 3
Lowestoft Cl. E5 33Yb 72
(off Theydon Rd.)
Lowestoft Dr. SL1: Slou 4B 80
Lowestoft M. E16 47Rc 94
Lowestoft Rd. WD24: Wat 11X 27
Loweswater Cl. HA9: Wemb 33Ma 67
WD25: Wat 5Y 13
Loweswater Ho. E3 42Bc 92
Loweswood Rd. RM3: Rom 22Ld 57
Lowfield Rd. NW6 38Cb 69
W3 44Ra 87
Lowfield St. DA1: Dart 59Nd 119
Low Hall Cl. E4 17Dc 34
Low Hall La. E17 30Ac 52
Low Hall Mnr. Bus. Cen. E17 30Ac 52
Lowick Rd. HA1: Harr 28Ga 46
Lowlands Dr. TW19: Stanw 57M 105
Lowlands Gdns. RM7: Rom 30Dd 56
Lowlands Rd. HA1: Harr 30Ga 46
HA5: Eastc 31Y 65
RM15: Avel 46Sd 98
Lowman Rd. N7 35Pb 70
Lownde M. SW16 61Nb 134
Lowndes Cl. SW1 4J 227 (48Jb 90)
Lowndes Ct. SW1 3G 227 (48Hb 89)
W1 3B 222
Lowndes Lodge SW1 3G 227
Lowndes M. SW16 61Nb 134
Lowndes Pl. SW1 4H 227 (48Jb 90)
Lowndes Sq. SW1 2G 227 (47Hb 89)
Lowndes St. SW1 3G 227 (48Jb 90)
Lowndes Ct. BR1: Brom 68Jc 137
Lowood Ct. SE19 64Vb 135
(off Farquhar Rd.)
Lowood Ho. E1 45Yb 92
(off Bewley St.)
Lowood St. E1 45Xb 91
Lowry Cl. DA8: Erith 49Fd 96
Lowry Ct. SE16 50Xb 91
(off Stubbs Dr.)
Lowry Cres. CR4: Mitc 68Gb 133
Lowry Ho. E14 47Cc 92
(off Cassilis Rd.)
N17 25Vb 51
(off Pembury Rd.)
W3 48Sa 87
(off Palmerston Rd.)
Lowry Rd. RM8: Dag 36Xc 75
Lowshoe La. RM5: Col R 25Cd 56
Lowson Gro. WD19: Wat 17Aa 27
LOW STREET 1H 123
Low St. La. RM18: W Til 9H 101
Lowswood Cl. HA6: Nwood 25S 44
Lowther Cl. KT16: Chert 76G 148
WD6: E'tree 15Pa 29
Lowther Dr. EN2: Enf 14Nb 32
Lowther Hill SE23 59Ac 114
Lowther Ho. SW1 50Lb 90
(off Churchill Gdns.)
Lowther Rd. E17 26Ac 52
HA7: Stan 27Pa 47
KT2: King T 67Pa 131
N7 36Qb 70
SW13 53Va 110
Lowthorpe GU21: Wok 10L 167
Lowth Rd. SE5 53Sb 113
LOXFORD 36Sc 74
Loxford Av. E6 40Mc 73
Loxford Cl. CR3: Cat'm 97Vb 197
Loxford Gdns. N5 35Rb 71
Loxford Ho. KT17: Eps 84Ua 174
Loxford La. IG1: Ilf 36Sc 74
IG3: Ilf 36Sc 74
Loxford Rd. CR3: Cat'm 97Vb 197
IG11: Bark 37Rc 74
Loxford Ter. IG11: Bark 37Sc 74
Loxford Way CR3: Cat'm 97Vb 197
Loxham Rd. E4 24Dc 52
Loxham St. WC1 4G 217 (41Nb 90)
Loxley Cl. KT14: Byfl 86N 169
SE26 64Zb 136
Loxley Ho. HA9: Wemb 34Na 67
Loxley Rd. SW18 60Fb 111
TW12: Hamp 63Ba 129
Loxton Rd. SE23 60Zb 114
Loxwood KT13: Weyb 76U 150
Loxwood Cl. BR5: Orp 75Zc 161
HP3: Hem H 5H 3
TW14: Bedf 60T 106
Loxwood Rd. N17 27Ub 51
Loyd Ct. AL4: St A 4G 6
LSO St Lukes 5E 218
Lubbock Ho. E14 45Dc 92
(off Poplar High St.)
Lubbock Rd. BR7: Chst 66Pc 138
Lubbock St. SE14 52Yb 114
Lucan Dr. TW18: Staines 66M 127
Lucan Ho. N1 39Tb 71
(off Colville Est.)
Lucan Pl. SW3 6D 226 (49Gb 89)
Lucan Rd. EN5: Barn 13Ab 30
Lucas Av. E13 39Kc 73
HA2: Harr 33Ca 65
Lucas Cl. NW10 38Wa 68
Lucas Ct. EN9: Walt A 5Hc 21
SE26 64Ac 136
SW11 53Jb 112
Lucas Cres. DA9: Ghithe 56Yd 120
(off Ingress Pk. Av.)
Lucas Gdns. N2 26Eb 49
LUCAS GREEN 7B 166
Lucas Grn. Rd. GU24: W End 7B 166
Lucas Ho. SW10 52Db 111
(off Coleridge Gdns.)
WC1 4G 217

Lucas Pk. Dr.—Macauley Ho.

Lucas Pk. Dr. KT20: Walt H 95Wa 194
Lucas Rd. RM17: Grays 48Ce 99
SE20 65Yb 136
Lucas Sq. NW11 30Cb 49
Lucas St. SE8 53Cc 114
Lucent Ho. *SW18* 57Cb 111
(off Hardwicks Sq.)
Lucerna Ct. *DA3: Lfield* 69Be 143
(off Harrison Av.)
Lucerne Cl. GU22: Wok 91A 188
N13 20Nb 32
Lucerne Ct. DA18: Erith 48Ad 95
Lucerne Gro. E17 28Fc 53
Lucerne M. W8 46Cb 89
Lucerne Rd. BR6: Orp 74Vc 161
CR7: Thor H 71Rb 157
N5 35Rb 71
Lucerne Way RM3: Rom 23Md 57
Lucey Rd. SE16 48Wb 91
Lucey Way SE16 48Wb 91
Lucia Hgts. *E20* 36Ec 72
(off Logan Cl.)
Lucida Ct. *WD18: Wat* 15U 26
(off Whippendell Rd.)
Lucie Av. TW15: Ashf 65R 128
Lucien Rd. SW17 63Jb 134
SW19 61Db 133
Lucinda Ct. E17 26Zb 52
EN1: Enf 14Ub 33
Lucknow St. SE18 52Uc 116
Lucks Hill HP1: Hem H 2G 2
Lucorn Cl. SE12 58Hc 115
Lucton M. IG10: Lough 14Rc 36
Luctons Av. IG9: Buck H 18Lc 35
Lucy Brown Ho. SE1 7E 224
Lucy Cres. W3 43Sa 87
Lucy Gdns. RM8: Dag 34Bd 75
Luddesdon Rd. DA8: Erith 52Cd 118
Luddington Av. GU25: Vir W 68B 126
Ludford Cl. CR0: Wadd 76Rb 157
Ludgate B'way. EC4 3B 224 (44Rb 91)
Ludgate Cir. EC4 3B 224 (44Rb 91)
Ludgate Hill EC4 3B 224 (44Rb 91)
Ludgate Sq. EC4 3C 224 (44Rb 91)
Ludham NW5 36Hb 69
Ludham Cl. IG6: Ilf 25Sc 54
SE28 44Yc 95
Ludlow Cl. BR2: Brom 69Jc 137
HA2: Harr 35Ba 65
Ludlow Ct. W3 47Sa 87
Ludlow Mead WD19: Wat 20X 27
Ludlow Pl. RM17: Grays 48De 99
Ludlow Rd. TW13: Felt 63W 128
W5 42La 86
Ludlow St. EC1 5D 218 (42Sb 91)
Ludlow Way N2 28Eb 49
WD3: Crox G 14S 26
Ludovick Wlk. SW15 56Ua 110
Ludwell Ho. *W14* 48Ab 88
(off Russell Rd.)
Ludwick M. SE14 52Ac 114
Luff Cl. SL4: Wind 5C 102
Luffenham Ho. WD19: Wat 20Z 27
Luffield Rd. SE2 48Xc 95
Luffman Rd. SE12 62Kc 137
Lugard Ho. *W12* 46Xa 88
(off Bloemfontein Rd.)
Lugard Rd. SE15 54Xb 113
Lugg App. E12 34Qc 74
Luke Allsopp Sq. RM10: Dag 34Dd 76
Luke Ho. *E1* 44Xb 91
(off Tillman St.)
Lukes Cl. NW2 33Wa 68
Luke St. EC2 5H 219 (42Ub 91)
Lukin Cres. E4 20Fc 35
Lukin St. E1 44Yb 92
Lukintone Cl. IG10: Lough 16Nc 36
Luli Ct. SE14 51Bc 114
Lullarook Cl. TN16: Big H 88Lc 179
LULLINGSTONE 78Ld 163
Lullingstone Av. BR8: Swan 69Hd 140
Lullingstone Castle 78Ld 163
Lullingstone Cl. BR5: St P 66Xc 139
Lullingstone Country Pk. 78Gd 162
Lullingstone Country Pk. Vis. Cen. 79Kd 163
Lullingstone Cres. BR5: St P 66Wc 139
Lullingstone Ho. *SE15* 51Yb 114
(off Lovelinch Cl.)
Lullingstone La. DA4: Eyns 76Ld 163
SE13 58Fc 115
Lullingstone Pk. Golf Course 77Fd 162
Lullingstone Rd. DA17: Belv 51Bd 117
Lullingstone Roman Villa 76Kd 163
Lullington Gth. BR1: Brom 66Gc 137
N12 22Bb 49
WD6: Bore 15Ra 29
Lullington Rd. RM9: Dag 38Ad 75
SE20 66Wb 135
Lulot Gdns. N19 33Kb 70
Lulsgate M. E3 42Bc 92
Lulworth *NW1* 38Mb 70
(off Wrotham Rd.)
SE17 7F 231
Lulworth Av. EN7: G Oak 1Rb 19
HA9: Wemb 31La 66
TW5: Hest 53Da 107
Lulworth Cl. HA2: Harr 34Ba 65
SS17: Stan H 3K 101
Lulworth Ct. *N1* 38Ub 71
(off St Peter's Way)
Lulworth Cres. CR4: Mitc 68Gb 133
Lulworth Dr. HA5: Pinn 30Z 45
RM5: Col R 22Dd 56
Lulworth Gdns. HA2: Harr 33Aa 65
Lulworth Ho. SW8 52Pb 112
Lulworth Pl. KT19: Eps 84Na 173
Lulworth Rd. DA16: Well 54Vc 117
SE9 61Nc 138
SE15 54Xb 113
Lulworth Waye UB4: Yead 44X 85
Lumen Rd. HA9: Wemb 33Ma 67
Lumiere Apartments SW11 56Fb 111
Lumiere Bldg., The *E7* 36Mc 73
(off Romford Rd.)
Lumiere Ct. SW17 61Jb 134
Lumina Bldgs. *E14* 46Ec 92
(off Prestons Rd.)
Lumina Bus. Pk. EN1: Enf 15Wb 33
Lumina Loft Apartments SE1 2J 231
Lumina Way EN1: Enf 15Wb 33
Luminosity Ct. W13 45Ka 86
Lumley Cl. DA17: Belv 50Cd 96
Lumley Ct. WC2 5G 223 (45Nb 90)
Lumley Flats SW1 7H 227
Lumley Gdns. SM3: Cheam 78Ab 154
Lumley Rd. SM3: Cheam 78Ab 154
Lumley St. W1 3J 221 (44Jb 90)
Lumsdon *NW8* 39Db 69
(off Abbey Rd.)
Luna Ho. SE16 47Wb 91
Lunan Ho. *E3* 40Bc 72
(off Shetland Rd.)
Luna Pl. AL1: St A 2E 6
Lunar Cl. TN16: Big H 88Mc 179
Lunaria Ho. *E20* 36Ec 72
(off Elis Way)
Luna Rd. CR7: Thor H 69Sb 135
Lundin Wlk. WD19: Wat 21Z 45
Lund Point E15 39Ec 72
Lundy Ct. SL1: Slou 5C 80
Lundy Dr. UB3: Harl 49U 84
Lundy Ho. WD18: Wat 15V 26
Lundy Wlk. N1 37Sb 71
Lunedale Rd. DA2: Dart 60Sd 120
Lunghurst Rd. CR3: Wold 92Bc 198
Lunham Rd. SE19 65Ub 135
Luntley Pl. *E1* 43Wb 91
(off Chicksand St.)
Lupin Cl. CR0: C'don 74Zb 158
RM7: Rush G 33Fd 76
SW2 61Rb 135
UB7: W Dray 50M 83
Lupin Cres. IG1: Ilf 37Rc 74
Lupin M. E17 27Ec 52
Lupino Ct. SE11 5J 229 (49Pb 90)
Lupin Point *SE1* 47Vb 91
(off Abbey St.)
Luppit Cl. CM13: Hut 18Ce 41
Lupton Cl. SE12 62Kc 137
Lupton St. NW5 35Lb 70
(not continuous)
Lupus St. SW1 7A 228 (50Kb 90)
Luralda Wharf E14 50Fc 93
Lurgan Av. W6 51Za 110
Lurline Gdns. SW11 53Jb 112
Luscombe Ct. BR2: Brom 68Gc 137
Luscombe Way SW8 52Nb 112
Lushes Ct. IG10: Lough 15Rc 36
Lushes Rd. IG10: Lough 15Rc 36
Lushington Dr. KT11: Cobh 86X 171
Lushington Ho. KT12: Walt T 72Y 151
Lushington Rd. NW10 40Xa 68
SE6 63Dc 136
Lushington Ter. E8 36Wb 71
Lusted Hall La.
TN16: Tats, Big H 92Kc 199
Lusted Rd. TN13: Dun G 92Gd 202
Lutea Ho. *SM2: Sutt* 80Eb 155
(off Walnut M.)
Luther Cl. HA8: Edg 19Sa 29
Luther King Cl. E17 30Bc 52
Luther M. TW11: Tedd 64Ha 130
Luther Rd. TW11: Tedd 64Ha 130
Luton Ho. *E13* 42Jc 93
(off Luton Rd.)
RM3: Rom 22Nd 57
(off Lindfield Rd.)
Luton Pl. SE10 52Ec 114
Luton Rd. DA14: Sidc 62Yc 139
E13 42Jc 93
E17 27Bc 52
Luton St. NW8 6C 214 (42Fb 89)
Lutton Ter. *NW3* 35Eb 69
(off Lakis Cl.)
Luttrell Av. SW15 57Xa 110
Lutwyche M. SE6 61Bc 136
Lutwyche Rd. SE6 61Bc 136
Lutyens Cl. KT24: Eff 99Z 191
Lutyens Ho. *SW1* 50Lb 90
(off Churchill Gdns.)
Lux Apartments *SW18* 57Cb 111
(off Broomhill Rd.)
Luxborough Ho. W1 7H 215
Luxborough La. IG7: Chig 20Nc 36
Luxborough St. W1 6H 215 (43Jb 90)
Luxborough Twr. W1 7H 215
Luxembourg M. E15 36Gc 73
Luxemburg Gdns. W6 49Za 88
Luxfield Rd. SE9 60Nc 116
Luxford St. SE16 49Zb 92
Luxmore St. SE4 53Bc 114
Luxor St. SE5 55Sb 113
LUXTED 86Qc 180
Luxted Rd. BR6: Downe 84Qc 180
Lyall Av. SE21 63Ub 135
Lyall M. SW1 4H 227 (48Jb 90)
Lyall M. W. SW1 4H 227 (48Jb 90)
Lyall St. SW1 4H 227 (48Jb 90)
Lyal Rd. E3 40Ac 72
Lycaste Cl. AL1: St A 3D 6
Lycett Pl. W12 47Wa 88
Lyceum Theatre
Covent Garden 4H 223
Lych Ga. WD25: Wat 5Z 13
Lychgate Mnr. HA1: Harr 31Ga 66
Lych Ga. Rd. BR6: Orp 74Wc 161
Lych Ga. Wlk. UB3: Hayes 45V 84
(not continuous)
Lych Way GU21: Wok 8P 167
Lyconby Gdns. CR0: C'don 73Ac 158
Lydd Cl. DA14: Sidc 62Uc 138
Lydden Ct. SE9 58Uc 116
Lydden Gro. SW18 59Db 111
Lydden Rd. SW18 59Db 111
Lydd Rd. DA7: Bex 52Bd 117
Lydeard Rd. E6 38Pc 74
Lydele Cl. GU21: Wok 87B 168
Lydford NW1 1C 216
Lydford Av. SL2: Slou 3H 81
Lydford Cl. *N16* 36Ub 71
(off Pellerin Rd.)
Lydford Ct. *DA2: Dart* 58Rd 119
(off Osbourne Rd.)
Lydford Rd. N15 29Tb 51
NW2 37Ya 68
W9 42Bb 89
Lydger Cl. GU22: Wok 92D 188
Lydhurst Av. SW2 61Pb 134
Lydia Cotts. DA11: Grav'nd 9D 122
Lydia Ct. AL9: Wel G 6E 8
KT1: King T 69Na 131
(off Grove Cres.)
N12 23Eb 49
Lydia M. AL9: Wel G 6E 8
Lydia Rd. DA8: Erith 51Hd 118
Lydney Cl. SW19 61Ab 132
Lydon Rd. SW4 55Lb 112
Lydsey Cl. SL2: Slou 1E 80
Lydstep Rd. BR7: Chst 63Qc 138
Lye, The KT20: Tad 94Ya 194
Lye La. AL2: Brick W 10N 5
Lyell Pl. E. SL4: Wind 5A 102
Lyell Pl. W. SL4: Wind 5A 102
Lyell Rd. SL4: Wind 5A 102
Lyell Wlk. E. SL4: Wind 5A 102
Lyell Wlk. W. SL4: Wind 5A 102
Lyfield KT22: Oxs 86Da 171
Lyfield Ct. KT23: Bookh 97Ca 191
Lyford Rd. SW18 59Fb 111
Lyford St. SE7 49Nc 94
Lygon Ho. *E2* 41Vb 91
(off Gosset St.)
SW6 53Ab 110
(off Fulham Pal. Rd.)
Lygon Pl. SW1 4K 227 (48Kb 90)
Lyham Cl. SW2 58Nb 112
Lyham Rd. SW2 57Nb 112
Lyle Cl. CR4: Mitc 73Jb 156
Lyle Ct. SM4: Mord 72Fb 155
Lyle Pk. TN13: S'oaks 95Kd 203
Lyly Ho. SE1 4G 231
Lymbourne Cl. SM2: Sutt 82Cb 175
Lymden Gdns. RH2: Reig 7K 207
Lyme Farm Rd. SE12 56Jc 115
Lyme Gro. E9 38Yb 72
Lyme Gro. Ho. *E9* 38Yb 72
(off Lyme Gro.)
Lymer Av. SE19 64Vb 135
Lyme Regis Rd. SM7: Bans 89Bb 175
Lyme Rd. DA16: Well 53Xc 117
Lymescote Gdns. SM1: Sutt 75Cb 155
Lyme St. NW1 38Lb 70
Lyme Ter. NW1 38Lb 70
Lyminge Cl. DA14: Sidc 63Vc 139
Lyminge Gdns. SW18 60Gb 111
Lymington Av. N22 26Qb 50
Lymington Cl. E6 43Pc 94
SW16 68Mb 134
Lymington Ct. SM1: Sutt 76Db 155
WD25: Wat 6W 12
Lymington Dr. HA4: Ruis 33T 64
Lymington Gdns. KT19: Ewe 78Va 154
Lymington Lodge *E14* 48Fc 93
(off Schooner Cl.)
Lymington Rd. NW6 37Db 69
RM8: Dag 32Zc 75
Lyminster Cl. UB4: Yead 43Aa 85
Lympne *N17* 26Tb 51
(off Gloucester Rd.)
Lympstone Gdns. SE15 52Wb 113
Lynbridge Gdns. N13 21Rb 51
Lynbrook Cl. RM13: Rain 40Fd 76
Lynbrook Gro. SE15 52Ub 113
Lynbury Ct. WD18: Wat 13W 26
Lynceley Grange CM16: Epp 1Wc 23
Lynch, The UB8: Uxb 38L 63
Lynch Cl. SE3 54Hc 115
UB8: Uxb 38L 63
Lynch Ct. AL4: St A 3G 6
Lynchen Cl. TW5: Cran 53X 107
LYNCH HILL 1C 80
Lynch Hill La. SL2: Slou 2C 80
Lynch Wlk. *SE8* 51Bc 114
(off Prince St.)
Lyncott Cres. SW4 56Kb 112
Lyncourt SE3 54Fc 115
Lyncroft Av. HA5: Pinn 29Aa 45
Lyncroft Gdns. KT17: Ewe 81Va 174
NW6 36Cb 69
TW3: Houn 57Ea 108
W13 47La 86
Lyncroft Mans. NW6 36Cb 69
Lyndale KT7: T Ditt 73Ga 152
NW2 35Bb 69
Lyndale Av. NW2 34Bb 69
Lyndale Cl. SE3 51Hc 115
Lyndale Ct. KT14: W Byf 85J 169
RH1: Redh 3A 208
Lyndale Est. RM20: W Thur 51Xd 120
Lyndale Rd. RH1: Redh 3P 207
Lyndean Ind. Est. SE2 48Yc 95
Lynde Ho. KT12: Walt T 72Y 151
SW4 55Mb 112
Lynden Ho. *E1* 41Zb 92
(off Westfield Way)
Lynden Hyrst CR0: C'don 75Vb 157
Lynden Way BR8: Swan 69Ed 140
Lyndhurst Av. HA5: Pinn 25X 45
KT5: Surb 74Ra 153
N12 23Hb 49
NW7 23Ua 48
SW16 68Mb 134
TW2: Whitt 60Ba 107
TW16: Sun 69W 128
UB1: S'hall 46Da 85
Lyndhurst Cl. BR6: Farnb 77Rc 160
CR0: C'don 76Vb 157
DA7: Bex 55Dd 118
GU21: Wok 7P 167
NW10 34Ta 67
Lyndhurst Ct. E18 25Jc 53
NW8 1B 214
SM2: Sutt 80Cb 155
(off Grange Rd.)
Lyndhurst Dr. E10 31Ec 72
KT3: N Mald 73Ua 154
RM11: Horn 32Ld 77
TN13: S'oaks 96Gd 202
Lyndhurst Gdns. EN1: Enf 14Ub 33
HA5: Pinn 25X 45
IG2: Ilf 30Tc 54
IG11: Bark 37Uc 74
N3 25Ab 48
NW3 36Fb 69
Lyndhurst Gro. SE15 54Ub 113
Lyndhurst Lodge *E14* 49Fc 93
(off Millennium Dr.)
Lyndhurst Ri. IG7: Chig 21Qc 54
Lyndhurst Rd. CR5: Coul 88Jb 176
CR7: Thor H 70Qb 134
DA7: Bex 55Dd 118
E4 24Ec 52
N18 21Wb 51
N22 23Qb 50
NW3 36Fb 69
RH2: Reig 9J 207
UB6: G'frd 42Da 85
Lyndhurst Sq. SE15 53Vb 113
Lyndhurst Ter. NW3 36Fb 69
Lyndhurst Vs. RH1: Redh 3P 207
Lyndhurst Wlk. WD6: Bore 11Pa 29
Lyndhurst Way CM13: Hut 17Ee 41
DA13: Ist R 7A 144
KT16: Chert 76G 148
SE15 53Vb 113
SM2: Sutt 81Cb 175
Lyndon Av. DA15: Sidc 57Vc 117
HA5: Hat E 23Aa 45
SM6: Wall 76Jb 156
Lyndon Ho. *E18* 25Jc 53
(off Queen Mary Av.)
Lyndon Rd. DA17: Belv 49Cd 96
Lyndon Yd. SW17 63Eb 133
Lyndwood Dr. SL4: Old Win 8L 103
Lyndwood Pde. *SL4: Old Win* 8L 103
(off St Luke's Rd.)
LYNE 74C 148
Lyne Cl. GU25: Vir W 72B 148
Lyne Cres. E17 25Bc 52
Lyne Crossing Rd. KT16: Lyne 72C 148
Lyne Gdns. TN16: Big H 90Nc 180
Lynegrove Av. TW15: Ashf 64S 128
Lyneham Dr. NW9 25Ua 48
Lyneham Wlk. E5 36Ac 72
HA5: Eastc 27V 44
Lyne La. GU25: Vir W 72C 148
KT16: Lyne 72C 148
TW20: Thorpe 72C 148
Lyne Rd. GU25: Vir W 2P 147
Lynette Av. SW4 58Kb 112
Lyne Way HP1: Hem H 1H 3
Lynford Cl. EN5: Ark 15Va 30
HA8: Edg 25Sa 47
Lynford Ct. *CR2: S Croy* 77Ub 157
(off Coombe Rd.)
Lynford French Ho. SE17 7D 230
Lynford Gdns. HA8: Edg 20Ra 29
IG3: Ilf 33Vc 75
Lynford Ter. N9 18Vb 33
Lyngarth Cl. KT23: Fet 97Fa 192
Lynhurst KT13: Weyb 79R 150
Lynhurst Cres. UB10: Hil 38S 64
Lynhurst Rd. UB10: Hil 38S 64
Lynmere Rd. DA16: Well 54Xc 117
Lyn M. E3 41Bc 92
N16 35Ub 71
Lynmouth Av. EN1: Enf 16Vb 33
SM4: Mord 72Za 154
Lynmouth Dr. HA4: Ruis 33X 65
Lynmouth Gdns. TW5: Hest 52Z 107
UB6: G'frd 39Ka 66
Lynmouth Ho. *RM3: Rom* 22Nd 57
(off Dagnam Pk. Dr.)
Lynmouth Ri. BR5: St M Cry 70Xc 139
Lynmouth Rd. E17 30Ac 52
N2 27Hb 49
N16 32Vb 71
UB6: G'frd 39Ka 66
Lynn Cl. HA3: Hrw W 26Fa 46
TW15: Ashf 64T 128
Lynn Ct. CR3: Whyt 90Vb 177
Lynne Cl. BR6: Chels 79Vc 161
CR2: Sels 83Yb 178
SE23 59Bc 114
Lynne Ct. *CR2: S Croy* 77Ub 157
(off Birdhurst Rd.)
NW6 38Db 69
(off Priory Rd.)
Lynnett Ct. *E9* 37Ac 72
(off Annis Rd.)
Lynnett Rd. RM8: Dag 33Zc 75
Lynne Wlk. KT10: Esh 78Ea 152
Lynne Way UB5: N'olt 40Z 65
Lynn Ho. *SE15* 51Xb 113
(off Friary Est.)
Lynn M. E11 33Gc 73
Lynn Rd. E11 33Gc 73
IG2: Ilf 31Tc 74
SW12 59Kb 112
Lynn St. EN2: Enf 11Tb 33
Lynn Wlk. RH2: Reig 9K 207
Lynross Cl. RM3: Hrld W 26Pd 57
Lynscott Way CR2: S Croy 81Rb 177
Lynstead Ct. BR3: Beck 68Ac 136
Lynsted Cl. BR1: Brom 68Lc 137
DA6: Bex 57Dd 118
Lynsted Gdns. SE9 56Mc 115
Lynton Av. AL1: St A 3G 6
BR5: St M Cry 70Xc 139
N12 21Fb 49
NW9 28Va 48
RM7: Mawney 25Cd 56
W13 44Ja 86
Lynton Cl. KT9: Chess 77Na 153
NW10 36Ua 68
TW7: Isle 56Ha 108
Lynton Ct. KT17: Ewe 83Va 174
Lynton Cres. IG2: Ilf 30Rc 54
Lynton Crest EN6: Pot B 4Cb 17
Lynton Est. SE1 49Wb 91
Lynton Gdns. EN1: Enf 17Ub 33
N11 23Mb 50
Lynton Grange N2 27Hb 49
Lynton Ho. *GU22: Wok* 90A 168
(off Station App.)
IG1: Ilf 33Sc 74
(off High Rd.)
W2 44Eb 89
(off Hallfield Est.)
Lynton Mans. SE1 3K 229
Lynton Mead N20 20Cb 31
Lynton Pde. EN8: Chesh 2Ac 20
Lynton Rd. CR0: C'don 72Qb 156
DA11: Grav'nd 10C 122
E4 22Dc 52
HA2: Harr 33Aa 65
KT3: N Mald 71Ta 153
N8 29Mb 50
(not continuous)
NW6 40Bb 69
SE1 6K 231 (49Vb 91)
W3 45Qa 87
Lynton Rd. Sth. DA11: Grav'nd 10C 122
Lynton Ter. W3 44Sa 87
Lynton Wlk. UB4: Hayes 41U 84
Lynwood Av. CR5: Coul 87Kb 176
KT17: Eps 86Va 174
SL3: L'ly 8P 81
TW20: Egh 65A 126
Lynwood Cl. E18 25Lc 53
GU21: Wok 85F 168
HA2: Harr 34Aa 65
RM5: Col R 23Dd 56
Lynwood Ct. KT1: King T 68Ra 131
KT17: Eps 85Va 174
Lynwood Cres. SL5: S'dale 2C 146
Lynwood Dr. HA6: Nwood 25V 44
KT4: Wor Pk 75Wa 154
RM5: Col R 23Dd 56
Lynwood Gdns. CR0: Wadd 77Pb 156
UB1: S'hall 44Ba 85
Lynwood Gro. BR6: Orp 73Uc 160
N21 18Qb 32
Lynwood Hgts. WD3: Rick 15K 25
Lynwood Rd. KT7: T Ditt 75Ha 152
KT17: Eps 86Va 174
RH1: Redh 4A 208
SW17 62Hb 133
W5 41Ma 87
Lynx Hill KT24: E Hor 100V 190
Lynx Way E16 45Mc 93
Lyon Bus. Pk. IG11: Bark 40Uc 74
Lyon Ct. HA4: Ruis 32V 64
KT12: Walt T 75Aa 151
Lyon Ho. NW8 6D 214
Lyon Ind. Est. NW2 33Xa 68
Lyon Meade HA7: Stan 25La 46
Lyon Pk. Av. HA0: Wemb 37Na 67
(not continuous)
Lyon Rd. HA1: Harr 30Ha 46
KT12: Walt T 75Aa 151
RM1: Rom 31Hd 76
SW19 67Eb 133
Lyonsdene KT20: Lwr K 99Bb 195
LYONSDOWN 15Eb 31
Lyonsdown Av. EN5: New Bar 16Eb 31
Lyonsdown Rd. EN5: New Bar 16Eb 31
Lyons Dr. GU2: Guild 10L 187
Lyons Ind. Est. UB8: Cowl 45M 83
Lyons Pl. HA7: Stan 20Ga 28
NW8 6B 214 (42Fb 89)
Lyon St. N1 38Pb 70
Lyons Wlk. W14 49Ab 88
Lyon Way AL4: St A 2L 7
UB6: G'frd 39Ga 66
Lyoth Rd. BR5: Farnb 75Sc 160
Lyrical Way HP1: Hem H 1K 3
Lyric Ct. *E8* 38Vb 71
(off Holly St.)
Lyric Dr. UB6: G'frd 42Da 85
Lyric M. SE26 63Yb 136
Lyric Rd. SW13 53Va 110
Lyric Sq. *W6* 49Ya 88
(off King St.)
Lyric Theatre
Hammersmith 49Ya 88
Westminster 4D 222
Lysander NW9 25Va 48
Lysander Cl. HP3: Bov 9B 2
Lysander Gdns. KT6: Surb 72Pa 153
Lysander Gro. N19 32Mb 70
Lysander Ho. *E2* 40Xb 71
(off Temple St.)
Lysander M. N19 32Lb 70
Lysander Rd. CR0: Wadd 79Pb 156
HA4: Ruis 33T 64
Lysander Way BR6: Farnb 76Sc 160
WD5: Ab L 4W 12
Lysia Ct. *SW6* 52Za 110
(off Lysia St.)
Lysias Rd. SW12 58Kb 112
Lysia St. SW6 52Za 110
Lysley Pl. AL9: Brk P 9L 9
Lysons Wlk. SW15 56Wa 110
Lyster M. KT11: Cobh 85Y 171
Lytchet Rd. BR1: Brom 66Jc 137
Lytchet Way EN3: Enf H 11Yb 34
Lytchgate Cl. CR2: S Croy 80Ub 157
Lytcott Dr. KT8: W Mole 69Ba 129
Lytcott Gro. SE22 57Ub 113
Lytham Av. WD19: Wat 22Z 45
Lytham Cl. SE28 44Ad 95
Lytham Ct. SL5: S'hill 1A 146
Lytham Gro. W5 41Pa 87
Lytham St. SE17 50Tb 91
Lyttelton Cl. NW3 38Gb 69
Lyttelton Ct. N2 29Eb 49
Lyttelton Ho. *E9* 38Yb 72
(off Well St.)
Lyttelton Rd. E10 34Dc 72
N2 29Eb 49
Lyttelton Theatre *6K 223*
(within National Theatre)
Lyttleton Ct. *UB4: Yead* 42Y 85
(off Dunedin Way)
Lyttleton Rd. N8 27Qb 50
Lytton Av. EN3: Enf L 10Ac 20
N13 19Qb 32
Lytton Cl. IG10: Lough 13Tc 36
N2 30Fb 49
UB5: N'olt 38Ba 65
Lytton Ct. WC1 1G 223
Lytton Gdns. SM6: Bedd 77Mb 156
Lytton Gro. SW15 57Za 110
Lytton Pk. KT11: Cobh 84Ba 171
Lytton Rd. E11 31Gc 73
EN5: New Bar 14Eb 31
GU22: Wok 88D 168
HA5: Pinn 24Aa 45
RM2: Rom 29Kd 57
RM16: Grays 9C 100
Lytton Strachey Path SE28 45Xc 95
Lytton Ter. E12 37Pc 74
Lyveden Rd. SE3 52Kc 115
SW17 65Hb 133
Lywood Cl. KT20: Tad 94Ya 194

M

Mabbett Ho. *SE18* 51Qc 116
(off Nightingale Pl.)
Mabbotts KT20: Tad 93Za 194
Mabbutt Cl. AL2: Brick W 2Aa 13
Mabel Evetts Ct. UB3: Hayes 45X 85
Mabel Rd. BR8: Hext 65Jd 140
Mabel St. GU21: Wok 10P 167
Maberley Cres. SE19 66Wb 135
Maberley Rd. BR3: Beck 69Zb 136
SE19 67Vb 135
Mabledon Pl. WC1 4E 216 (41Mb 90)
Mablethorpe Rd. SW6 52Ab 110
Mabley St. E9 36Ac 72
Mablin Lodge IG9: Buck H 18Lc 35
McAdam Dr. EN2: Enf 12Rb 33
McAllister Gro. IG11: Bark 41Wc 95
McArdle Way SL3: Coln 52F 104
Macaret Cl. N20 17Db 31
Macarthur Cl. DA8: Erith 50Gd 96
E7 37Jc 73
HA9: Wemb 37Ra 67
Macarthur Ter. SE7 51Mc 115
Macartney Ho. *SE10* 52Fc 115
(off Chesterfield Wlk.)
SW9 53Qb 112
(off Gosling Way)
Macaulay Av. KT10: Hin W 75Ha 152
Macaulay Ct. SW4 55Kb 112
Macaulay Rd. CR3: Cat'm 94Ub 197
E6 40Mc 73
SW4 55Kb 112
Macaulay Sq. SW4 56Kb 112
Macaulay Wlk. *SW9* 53Pb 112
(off Lett Rd.)
Macaulay Way SE28 46Xc 95
McAuley Cl. SE1 3K 229 (48Qb 90)
SE9 57Rc 116
Macauley Ho. *W10* 43Ab 88
(off Portobello Rd.)

Macauley M. SE13 54Ec 114
McAuliffe Dr. SL2: Farn C 5D 60
McAusland Ho. E3 40Bc 72
(off Wright's Rd.)
Macbean St. SE18 48Rc 94
Macbeth Ho. N1 1H 219 (40Ub 71)
Macbeth St. W6 50Xa 88
McBride Ho. E3 40Bc 72
(off Libra Rd.)
McCabe Ct. E16 43Hc 93
(off Barking Rd.)
McCall Cl. SW4 54Nb 112
McCall Cres. SE7 50Nc 94
McCall Ho. N7 35Nb 70
McCarthy Rd. TW13: Hanw 64Z 129
McClaren Technology Cen.
GU21: Wok 83C 168
Macclesfield Apartments N1 39Tb 71
(off Branch Pl.)
Macclesfield Ho. EC1 4D 218
RM3: Rom 22Nd 57
(off Dagnam Pk. Dr.)
Macclesfield Rd. EC1 3D 218 (41Sb 91)
SE25 71Yb 158
Macclesfield St. W1 4E 222 (45Mb 90)
McClintock Pl. EN3: Enf L 10Dc 20
McCoid Way SE1 2D 230 (47Sb 91)
McCrone M. NW3 37Fb 69
McCudden Rd. DA1: Dart 55Pd 119
McCullum Rd. E3 39Bc 72
McDermott Cl. SW11 55Gb 111
McDermott Rd. SE15 55Wb 113
TN15: Bor G 92Be 205
Macdonald Av. RM10: Dag 34Dd 76
RM11: Horn 27Nd 57
McDonald Ct. AL10: Hat 2C 8
(not continuous)
Macdonald Ho. SW11 54Jb 112
(off Dagnall St.)
McDonald Ho. NW6 41Cb 89
(off Malvern Rd.)
Macdonald Rd. E7 35Jc 73
E17 26Ec 52
(not continuous)
N11 22Hb 49
N19 33Lb 70
Macdonald Way RM11: Horn 28Nd 57
Macdonnell Gdns. WD25: Wat 7V 12
McDonough Cl. KT9: Chess 77Na 153
McDougall Ct. TW9: Rich 54Qa 109
McDougall Rd. HP4: Berk 1A 2
McDowall Cl. E16 43Hc 93
McDowall Rd. SE5 53Sb 113
Macduff Rd. SW11 53Jb 112
Mace Cl. E1 46Xb 91
Mace Ct. RM17: Grays 1A 122
Mace Ho. TW7: Isle 53Ka 108
Mace La. TN14: Cud 85Tc 180
McEntee Av. E17 25Ac 52
Mace St. E2 40Zb 72
McEwan Ho. E3 40Bc 72
(off Roman Rd.)
McEwen Way E15 39Fc 73
(off Rokeby St.)
Macey Ho. SW11 53Gb 111
Macey St. SE10 51Ec 114
(off Thames St.)
McFadden Ct. E10 34Dc 72
(off Buckingham Rd.)
Macfarland Gro. SE15 52Ub 113
Macfarlane La. TW7: Isle 51Ha 108
Macfarlane Rd. W12 46Ya 88
Macfarren Pl. NW1 6J 215 (42Jb 90)
Macfarron Ho. W10 41Ab 88
(off Parry Rd.)
McGlashon Ho. E1 42Wb 91
(off Hunton St.)
McGrath Rd. E15 36Hc 73
McGredy EN7: Chesh 1Xb 19
McGregor Ct. N1 3J 219
Macgregor Rd. E16 43Lc 93
McGregor Rd. W11 44Bb 89
Machell Rd. SE15 55Yb 114
McIndoe Ct. N1 39Tb 71
(off Sherborne St.)
McIntosh Cl. RM1: Rom 27Gd 56
SM6: Wall 80Nb 156
Macintosh Ho. W1 7J 215
McIntosh Ho. SE16 49Yb 92
(off Millender Wlk.)
McIntosh Rd. RM1: Rom 27Gd 56
McIntyre Ct. SE18 49Nc 94
(off Prospect Va.)
Mackay Ho. W12 45Xa 88
(off White City Est.)
Mackay Rd. SW4 55Kb 112
McKay Rd. SW20 66Xa 132
McKay Trad. Est. SL3: Poyle 54G 104
McKeever Cl. EN9: Walt A 5Dc 20
McKeever Ho. E16 43Jc 93
(off Hammersley Rd.)
McKellar Cl. WD23: B Hea 19Ea 28
McKenna Ho. E3 40Bc 72
(off Wright's Rd.)
Mackennal St. NW8 2E 214 (40Gb 69)
Mackenzie Cl. W12 45Xa 88
Mackenzie Ho. N8 28Nb 50
(off Pembroke Rd.)
NW2 34Wa 68
Mackenzie Mall SL1: Slou 7K 81
(within Queensmere Shop. Cen.)
Mackenzie Rd. BR3: Beck 68Yb 136
N7 37Pb 70
Mackenzie St. SL1: Slou 7K 81
Mackenzie Wlk. E14 46Cc 92
Mackenzie Way DA12: Grav'nd 5F 144
McKenzie Way KT19: Eps 81Qa 173
McKerrell Rd. SE15 53Wb 113
Mackeson Rd. NW3 35Hb 69
Mackie Rd. SW2 59Qb 112
McKillop Way DA14: Sidc 66Yc 139
Mackintosh Ct. SL9: Ger X 28A 42
Mackintosh La. E9 36Zb 72
Mackintosh St. BR2: Brom 72Mc 159
Macklin St. WC2 2G 223 (44Nb 90)
Mackonochie Ho. EC1 7K 217
Mackrells RH1: Redh 9L 207
Mackrow Wlk. E14 45Ec 92
Mack's Rd. SE16 49Wb 91
Mackworth Ho. NW1 3B 216
Mackworth St. NW1 3B 216 (41Lb 90)
McLaren Ho. SE1 2B 230
Maclaren M. SW15 56Ya 110
Maclean Rd. SE23 58Ac 114
Maclean Ter. DA12: Grav'nd 1H 145
Maclennan Av. RM13: Rain 41Md 97
Macleod Cl. RM17: Grays 49Fe 99
McLeod Ct. SE22 60Wb 113
Macleod Rd. N21 15Nb 32
McLeod Rd. SE2 49Xc 95
McLeod's M. SW7 49Db 89
Macleod St. SE17 50Sb 91
Maclise Ho. SW1 6F 229
Maclise Rd. W14 48Ab 88
Macmahon Cl. GU24: Chob 2J 167
McMillan Cl. DA12: Grav'nd 3E 144
Macmillan Ct. HA2: Harr 32Ca 65
UB6: G'frd 42Fa 86
Macmillan Gdns. DA1: Dart 56Qd 119
Macmillan Ho. NW8 4E 214
SM7: Bans 86Bb 175
(off Basing Rd.)
McMillan Ho. SE4 55Ac 114
(off Arica Rd.)
SE14 53Ac 114
Macmillan Rd. TN14: Dun G 92Hd 202
McMillan St. SE8 51Cc 114
McMillan Student Village SE8 51Cc 114
Macmillan Way SW17 63Kb 134
McNair Rd. UB2: S'hall 48Da 85
Macnamara Ho. SW10 52Fb 111
(off Worlds End Est.)
McNeil Rd. SE5 54Ub 113
McNicol Dr. NW10 40Sa 67
Macoma Rd. SE18 51Tc 116
Macoma Ter. SE18 51Tc 116
Maconochies Rd. E14 50Dc 92
Macon Way RM14: Upm 31Ud 78
MacOwan Theatre 49Cb 89
Macquarie Way E14 49Dc 92
McRae La. CR4: Mitc 73Hb 155
Macready Ho. W1 1E 220
Macready Pl. N7 35Nb 70
(not continuous)
Macrea Ho. E3 41Bc 92
(off Bow Rd.)
Macroom Ho. W9 41Bb 89
(off Macroom Rd.)
Macroom Rd. W9 41Bb 89
Macs Ho. E17 27Dc 52
Mac's Pl. EC4 2A 224
Madame Tussaud's 6H 215 (42Jb 90)
Madan Cl. TN16: Westrm 97Uc 200
Madan Rd. TN16: Westrm 97Tc 200
Madans Wlk. KT18: Eps 87Ta 173
(not continuous)
Mada Rd. BR6: Farnb 76Rc 160
Maddams St. E3 42Dc 92
Madden Cl. DA10: Swans 58Zd 121
Madderfields Ct. N11 25Mb 50
Maddison Cl. N2 26Eb 49
TW11: Tedd 65Ha 130
Maddison Ct. E16 43Jc 93
(off Hastings Rd.)
Maddison Hgts. WD18: Wat 14V 26
(off Chiltern Cl.)
Maddocks Cl. DA14: Sidc 64Ad 139
Maddocks Ho. E1 45Xb 91
(off Cornwall St.)
Maddock Way SE17 51Rb 113
Maddox La. KT23: Bookh 94Aa 191
Maddox Pk. KT23: Bookh 95Aa 191
Maddox Rd. HP2: Hem H 2B 4
Maddox St. W1 4A 222 (45Kb 90)
Madeira Av. BR1: Brom 66Gc 137
Madeira Cl. KT14: W Byf 85J 169
Madeira Cres. KT14: W Byf 85H 169
Madeira Gro. IG8: Wfd G 23Lc 53
Madeira Rd. CR4: Mitc 70Hb 133
E11 32Fc 73
KT14: W Byf 85H 169
N13 21Rb 51
SW16 64Nb 134
Madeira Wlk. CM15: B'wood 20Ae 41
RH2: Reig 5M 207
SL4: Wind 3H 103
Madeleine Cl. RM6: Chad H 30Yc 55
Madeleine Ct. HA7: Stan 24Na 47
(off Letchworth Rd.)
Madeley Rd. W5 44Ma 87
Madeline Gro. IG1: Ilf 36Tc 74
Madeline Rd. SE20 66Wb 135
Madells CM16: Epp 3Vc 23
Madge Gill Way E6 39Nc 74
(off High St. Nth.)
Madge Hill W7 45Ga 86
Madinah Rd. E8 37Wb 71
Madison, The SE1 1F 231
Madison Bldg. SE10 53Dc 114
(off Blackheath Rd.)
Madison Cl. SM2: Sutt 80Fb 155
Madison Ct. RM10: Dag 37Dd 76
Madison Cres. DA7: Bex 52Yc 117
Madison Gdns. BR2: Brom 69Hc 137
DA7: Bex 52Yc 117
Madison Ho. E14 45Bc 92
(off Victory Pl.)
Madison Wlk. RM16: Chaf H 47Be 99
Madison Way E20 36Dc 72
TN13: S'oaks 95Hd 202
Madoc Cl. NW2 33Cb 69
Madras Pl. N7 37Qb 70
Madras Rd. IG1: Ilf 35Rc 74
Madresfield Ct. WD7: Shenl 4Ma 15
Madrid Rd. SW13 53Wa 110
Madrigal La. SE5 52Rb 113
Madron St. SE17 7J 231 (50Ub 91)
Maesmaur Rd. TN16: Tats 93Mc 199
Mafeking Av. E6 40Nc 74
IG2: Ilf 31Tc 74
TW8: Bford 51Na 109
Mafeking Rd. E16 42Hc 93
EN1: Enf 13Vb 33
N17 26Wb 51
TW19: Wray 61D 126
Magazine Ga. W2 6E 220 (46Gb 89)
Magazine Pl. KT22: Lea 94Ka 192
Magazine Rd. CR3: Cat'm 94Rb 197
Magdala Av. N19 33Lb 70
Magdala Rd. CR2: S Croy 80Tb 157
TW7: Isle 55Ja 108
Magdalen Cl. KT14: Byfl 86N 169
Magdalen Ct. AL1: St A 1C 6
(off Newsom Pl.)
Magdalen Cres. KT14: Byfl 86N 169
Magdalene Cl. SE15 54Xb 113
Magdalene Gdns. E6 42Qc 94
N20 18Hb 31
Magdalene Rd. TW17: Shep 70P 127
Magdalen Gro. BR6: Chels 77Xc 161
Magdalen Ho. E16 46Kc 93
(off Keats Av.)
Magdalen M. NW3 37Eb 69
(off Frognal)
Magdalen Pas. E1 45Vb 91
Magdalen Rd. SW18 60Eb 111
Magdalen St. SE1 7H 225 (46Ub 91)
Magee St. SE11 51Qb 112
Magellan Blvd. E16 45Sc 94
Magellan Ct. NW10 38Ta 67
(off Brentfield Rd.)
Magellan Ho. E1 42Zb 92
(off Ernest St.)
Magellan Pl. E14 49Cc 92
Magisters Lodge WD3: Crox G 16Q 26
Magistrates' Court
Barkingside 27Sc 54
Belmarsh 47Uc 94
Bexley 56Cd 118
Bromley 67Hc 137
Camberwell Green 53Tb 113
City of London 3F 225
Croydon 76Tb 157
Ealing 46Ja 86
(off Green Man La.)
East Berkshire, Slough 7J 81
Hammersmith 50Za 88
Hendon 30Va 48
Highbury Corner 37Qb 70
Lavender Hill 55Hb 111
Redhill 6M 207
Richmond-upon-Thames 56Ma 109
Romford 28Hd 56
St Albans 2B 6
Sevenoaks 95Hd 202
Staines Upon Thames 64J 127
Stratford 38Fc 73
Thames 41Cc 92
Uxbridge 38L 63
Westminster 7E 214 (43Gb 89)
Willesden 37Va 68
Wimbledon 65Cb 133
Magna Carta La. TW19: Wray 10P 103
Magna Carta Memorial 1P 125
Magna Ct. TW18: Staines 64G 126
Magna Rd. TW20: Eng G 5M 125
Magna Sq. SW14 55Sa 109
(off Moore Cl.)
Magnaville Rd. WD23: B Hea 17Ga 28
Magnetic Cres. EN3: Enf L 9Bc 20
Magnet Point Est.
RM20: Grays 51Yd 120
Magnet Rd. HA9: Wemb 33Ma 67
RM20: Grays 51Yd 120
Magnin Cl. E8 39Wb 71
Magnolia Av. WD5: Ab L 4W 12
Magnolia Cl. AL2: Park 8B 6
E10 33Cc 72
KT2: King T 65Ra 131
RM15: S Ock 42Ae 99
Magnolia Ct. HA3: Kenton 31Pa 67
SM2: Sutt 80Cb 155
(off Grange Rd.)
SM6: Wall 78Kb 156
TW9: Kew 53Ra 109
TW13: Felt 60W 106
(off Plum Cl.)
UB5: N'olt 42Aa 85
UB10: Hil 37R 64
Magnolia Cres. CM14: Gt War 23Xd 58
Magnolia Dr. SM7: Bans 88Bb 175
TN16: Big H 88Mc 179
Magnolia Gdns. AL1: St A 4E 6
E10 33Cc 72
HA8: Edg 21Sa 47
SL3: L'ly 8N 81
Magnolia Ho. SE8 51Bc 114
(off Evelyn St.)
TW16: Sun 66V 128
Magnolia Lodge E4 20Dc 34
W8 48Db 89
(off St Mary's Ga.)
Magnolia Pl. HA2: Harr 26Fa 46
SW4 57Nb 112
W5 43Ma 87
Magnolia Rd. W4 51Ra 109
Magnolia St. UB7: W Dray 50M 83
Magnolia Vs. TW18: Staines 66K 127
Magnolia Way CM15: Pil H 15Xd 40
EN8: Chesh 1Yb 20
KT19: Ewe 78Sa 153
Magnolia Wharf W4 51Qa 109
Magnum Cl. RM13: Rain 42Kd 97
Magpie All. EC4 3A 224 (44Qb 90)
Magpie Bottom TN15: Knat 85Md 183
Magpie Cl. CR5: Coul 90Lb 176
E7 36Hc 73
EN1: Enf 10Wb 19
NW9 26Ua 48
Magpie Hall Cl. BR2: Brom 72Nc 160
Magpie Hall La. BR2: Brom 71Pc 160
Magpie Hall Rd. WD23: B Hea 19Ga 28
Magpie Ho. E3 39Bc 72
(off Sycamore Av.)
Magpie La. CM13: L War 26Zd 59
Magpie Pl. SE14 51Ac 114
WD25: Wat 4Y 13
Magpie Wlk. AL10: Hat 2C 8
Magpie Way SL2: Slou 2D 80
Magri Wlk. E1 43Yb 92
Maguire Apartments E3 43Bc 92
(off Geoff Cade Way)
Maguire Dr. TW10: Ham 63La 130
Maguire St. SE1 1K 231 (47Vb 91)
Maha Bldg. E3 41Cc 92
(off Merchant St.)
Mahatma Gandhi Ind. Est.
SE24 56Rb 113
Mahlon Av. HA4: Ruis 36X 65
(not continuous)
Mahogany Cl. SE16 46Ac 92
Mahon Cl. EN1: Enf 11Vb 33
Mahoney Ho. SE14 53Bc 114
(off Heald St.)
Mahonia Cl. GU24: W End 5D 166
Maibeth Gdns. BR3: Beck 70Ac 136
Maida Av. E4 17Dc 34
W2 7A 214 (43Eb 89)
MAIDA HILL 42Bb 89
Maida Rd. DA17: Belv 48Cd 96
MAIDA VALE 3A 214 (42Db 89)
Maida Va. W9 3A 214 (40Db 69)
Maida Va. Rd. DA1: Dart 57Jd 118
Maida Way E4 17Dc 34
Maiden Erlegh Av. DA5: Bexl 60Ad 117
Maidenhead Rd. SL4: Wind 2A 102
Maiden La. DA1: Cray 55Jd 118
NW1 38Mb 70
SE1 7E 224 (46Sb 91)
WC2 5G 223 (45Nb 90)
Maiden Pl. NW5 34Lb 70
Maiden Rd. E15 38Gc 73
Maidenshaw Rd. KT19: Eps 84Ta 173
Maidenstone Hill SE10 53Ec 114
Maids of Honour Row
TW9: Rich 57Ma 109
Maidstone Av. RM5: Col R 26Ed 56
Maidstone Bldgs. M.
SE1 7E 224 (46Sb 91)
Maidstone Ho. E14 44Dc 92
(off Carmen St.)
Maidstone Rd.
DA14: Sidc, Swan 65Zc 139
N11 23Lb 50
RM17: Grays 51Ce 121
TN13: Riv 94Gd 202
TN15: Bor G, Plat, Wro H 92Ce 205
TN15: Seal 93Qd 203
Mailcoach Yd. E2 3J 219 (41Ub 91)
Main Av. EN1: Enf 15Vb 33
HA6: Nwood 20S 26
Main Dr. HA9: Wemb 34Ma 67
SL0: Rich P 49G 82
Main Mill SE10 52Dc 114
(off Greenwich High St.)
Main Pde. WD3: Chor 14E 24
Main Pde. Flats WD3: Chor 14E 24
Mainridge Rd. BR7: Chst 63Qc 138
Main Rd. BR2: Kes 85Lc 179
BR5: St P 67Yc 139
BR8: Crock 72Fd 162
BR8: Hext 66Hd 140
DA3: Lfield, Long H 68Zd 143
DA4: Farni 75Sd 164
(Donkey La.)
DA4: Farni 72Nd 163
(London Rd.)
DA4: Sut H 65Rd 141
DA14: Sidc 62Tc 138
RM1: Rom 28Hd 56
RM2: Rom 28Hd 56
SL4: Wind 2A 102
TN14: Sund 96Zc 201
TN16: Big H, Westrm 85Lc 179
Main Rd. Cotts. BR6: Prat B 81Yc 181
Mainstone Cres. GU24: Brkwd 3B 186
Mainstone Rd. GU24: Bisl 8D 166
Main St. KT15: Add 76N 149
TW13: Hanw 64Z 129
Mainwaring Ct. CR4: Mitc 68Jb 134
Mais Ho. SE26 61Xb 135
Maisie Webster Cl. TW19: Stanw 59M 105
Maismore St. SE15 51Wb 113
Maisonettes, The SM1: Sutt 78Bb 155
Maitland Cl. KT12: Walt T 75Aa 151
KT14: W Byf 85J 169
SE10 52Dc 114
TW4: Houn 55Ba 107
Maitland Ct. W2 4B 220
Maitland Ho. E2 40Yb 72
(off Waterloo Gdns.)
SW1 51Lb 112
(off Churchill Gdns.)
Maitland Pk. Est. NW3 37Hb 69
Maitland Pk. Rd. NW3 37Hb 69
Maitland Pk. Vs. NW3 37Hb 69
Maitland Pl. E5 35Xb 71
Maitland Rd. E15 37Hc 73
SE26 65Zb 136
Maitlands IG10: Lough 13Pc 36
Maitland Yd. W13 46Ja 86
Maize Row E14 45Bc 92
Maizey Ct. CM15: Pil H 15Wd 40
Majendie Rd. SE18 50Tc 94
Majestic Way CR4: Mitc 68Hb 133
Major Cl. SW9 55Rb 113
Major Draper St. SE18 48Rc 94
Major Rd. E15 36Fc 73
SE16 48Wb 91
Majors Farm Rd. SL3: Dat 2P 103
Makepeace Av. N6 33Jb 70
Makepeace Mans. N6 33Jb 70
Makepeace Rd. E11 28Jc 53
UB5: N'olt 40Aa 65
Makinen Ho. IG9: Buck H 18Lc 35
Makins St. SW3 6E 226 (49Gb 89)
Malabar Ct. W12 45Xa 88
(off India Way)
Malabar St. E14 47Cc 92
Malacca Farm GU4: W Cla 99K 189
Malam Ct. SE11 6K 229 (49Qb 90)
Malam Gdns. E14 45Dc 92
Malan Cl. TN16: Big H 89Nc 180
Malan Sq. RM13: Rain 37Kd 77
Malbrook Rd. SW15 56Xa 110
Malcolm Cl. SE20 66Yb 136
Malcolm Ct. E7 37Hc 73
HA7: Stan 22La 46
NW4 30Wa 48
Malcolm Cres. NW4 30Wa 48
Malcolm Dr. KT6: Surb 74Na 153
Malcolm Ho. N1 2H 219
Malcolm Pl. E2 42Yb 92
Malcolm Rd. CR5: Coul 87Mb 176
E1 42Yb 92
SE20 66Yb 136
SE25 72Wb 157
SW19 65Ab 132
UB10: Ick 35P 63
Malcolm Sargent Ho. E16 46Kc 93
(off Evelyn Rd.)
Malcolmson Ho. SW1 7D 228
Malcolms Way N14 15Lb 32
Malcolm Way E11 29Jc 53
Malden Av. SE25 70Xb 135
UB6: G'frd 36Ga 66
Malden Ct. KT3: N Mald 69Xa 132
N4 30Sb 51
Malden Cres. NW1 37Jb 70
Malden Flds. WD23: Bush 15Z 27
Malden Golf Course 68Ua 132
MALDEN GREEN 74Wa 154
Malden Grn. Av. KT4: Wor Pk 74Va 154
Malden Grn. M. KT4: Wor Pk 74Wa 154
Malden Hill KT3: N Mald 69Va 132
Malden Hill Gdns. KT3: N Mald 69Va 132
Malden Ho. WD19: Wat 20Y 27
MALDEN JUNC. 71Va 154
Malden Lodge WD17: Wat 12X 27
Malden Pk. KT3: N Mald 72Va 154
Malden Pl. NW5 36Jb 70
Malden Rd. KT3: N Mald 71Ua 154
KT4: Wor Pk 72Va 154
NW5 36Hb 69
SM3: Cheam 77Za 154
WD6: Bore 13Qa 29
WD17: Wat 12X 27
MALDEN RUSHETT 83La 172
Malden Way KT3: N Mald 72Ta 153
Maldon Cl. E15 36Gc 73
N1 39Sb 71
SE5 55Ub 113
Maldon Ct. E6 39Qc 74
SM6: Wall 78Lb 156
Maldon District Society of
Model Engineers, The 74Ja 152
Maldon Rd. N9 20Vb 33
RM7: Rush G 31Ed 76
SM6: Wall 78Kb 156
W3 45Sa 87
Maldon Wlk. IG8: Wfd G 23Lc 53
Malet Cl. TW20: Egh 65F 126
Malet Pl. WC1 6D 216 (42Mb 90)
Malet St. WC1 6D 216 (42Mb 90)
Maley Av. SE27 61Rb 135
Malford Ct. E18 26Jc 53
Malford Gro. E18 28Hc 53
Malfort Rd. SE5 55Ub 113
Malham Cl. N11 23Jb 50
Malham Rd. SE23 60Zb 114
Malham Rd. Ind. Est. SE23 60Zb 114
Malham Ter. N18 22Xb 51
Malibu Ct. SE26 62Xb 135
Malin Ct. HP3: Hem H 5L 3
Malins Cl. EN5: Barn 15Xa 30
Malkin Way WD18: Wat 14U 26
Mall, The AL2: Park 9A 6
BR1: Brom 69Jc 137
BR8: Swan 69Gd 140
CR0: C'don 75Sb 157
DA6: Bex 56Cd 118
E15 38Fc 73
HA3: Kenton 31Pa 67
KT6: Surb 71Ma 153
KT12: Hers 78Z 151
(off Hersham Grn. Shop. Cen.)
N14 20Nb 32
RM10: Dag 37Cd 76
RM11: Horn 32Kd 77
(not continuous)
RM17: Grays 51Ce 121
(off Grays Shop. Cen.)
SW1 1C 228 (47Lb 90)
SW14 57Sa 109
TW8: Bford 51Ma 109
W5 45Na 87
Mallams M. SW9 55Rb 113
Mallard Cl. DA1: Dart 57Pd 119
E9 37Bc 72
EN5: New Bar 16Fb 31
NW6 40Cb 69
RH1: Redh 3A 208
RM14: Upm 31Vd 78
TW2: Whitt 59Ca 107
W7 47Ga 86
Mallard Ct. E17 27Fc 53
WD3: Rick 17M 25
(off Swan Cl.)
Mallard Dr. SL1: Slou 5D 80
Mallard Ho. NW8 2D 214
SW6 53Eb 111
(off Station Ct.)
Mallard Path SE28 48Tc 94
Mallard Pl. N22 26Pb 50
TW1: Twick 62Ja 130
Mallard Point E3 41Dc 92
(off Rainhill Way)
Mallard Rd. CR2: Sels 82Zb 178
WD5: Ab L 3W 12
Mallards E11 31Jc 73
(off Blake Hall Rd.)
Mallards, The HP3: Hem H 7P 3
TW18: Lale 68K 127
Mallards Ct. WD19: Wat 20Ba 27
(off Hangar Ruding)
Mallards Reach KT13: Weyb 75T 150
Mallards Rd. IG8: Wfd G 24Kc 53
IG11: Bark 42Wc 95
Mallard Wlk. BR3: Beck 71Zb 158
DA14: Sidc 65Yc 139
Mallard Way CM13: Hut 17De 41
HA6: Nwood 24S 44
NW9 31Sa 67
SM6: Wall 81Lb 176
WD25: Wat 9Aa 13
Mall Chambers W8 46Cb 89
(off Kensington Mall)
Mallet Dr. UB5: N'olt 36Ba 65
Mallet Rd. SE13 58Fc 115
Mall Galleries 6E 222
Malling SE13 57Dc 114
Malling Cl. CR0: C'don 72Yb 158
Malling Gdns. SM4: Mord 72Eb 155
Malling Way BR2: Hayes 73Hc 159
Mallinson Cl. RM12: Horn 36Ld 77
Mallinson Rd. CR0: Bedd 76Mb 156
SW11 57Gb 111
Mallinson Sports Cen. 31Hb 69
Mallins Way RM16: Grays 9B 100
Mallion Ct. EN9: Walt A 5Hc 21
Mallon Gdns. E1 1K 225
Mallord St. SW3 51Fb 111
Mallory Bldgs. EC1 6B 218
Mallory Cl. DA12: Grav'nd 3E 144
E14 43Dc 92
SE4 56Ac 114
Mallory Ct. N17 23Vb 51
(off Cannon Rd.)
SE12 59Kc 115
Mallory Gdns. EN4: E Barn 17Jb 32
Mallory St. NW8 5E 214 (42Gb 89)
Mallory Way SE3 56Kc 115
Mallow Cl. CR0: C'don 74Zb 158
DA11: Nflt 3A 144
KT20: Tad 92Xa 194
Mallow Ct. RM17: Grays 51Fe 121
Mallow Mead NW7 24Ab 48
Mallows, The UB10: Ick 34R 64
Mallow St. EC1 5F 219 (42Tb 91)
Mall Rd. W6 50Xa 88
Mall Vs. W6 50Xa 88
(off Mall Rd.)
Mallys Pl. DA4: S Dar 67Sd 142
Malmains Cl. BR3: Beck 70Fc 137
Malmains Way BR3: Beck 70Ec 136
Malm Cl. WD3: Rick 19M 25
Malmesbury E2 40Yb 72
(off Cyprus St.)
Malmesbury Cl. HA5: Eastc 28V 44
Malmesbury Rd. E3 41Bc 92
E16 43Gc 93
E18 25Hc 53
SM4: Mord 73Eb 155
Malmesbury Ter. E16 43Hc 93
Malmes Cft. HP3: Hem H 4C 4
Malmsey Ho. SE11 7J 229 (50Pb 90)
Malmsmead Ho. E9 36Bc 72
(off Homerton Rd.)
Malmstone Av. RH1: Mers 100Lb 196
Malory Cl. BR3: Beck 68Ac 136

Malpas Dr.—Manson M.

Malpas Dr. HA5: Pinn . . . 29Z 45
Malpas Rd. E8 . . . 36Xb 71
RM9: Dag . . . 37Zc 75
RM16: Grays . . . 8E 100
SE4 . . . 54Bc 114
SL2: Slou . . . 5M 81
Malswick Ct. *SE15* . . . *52Ub 113*
(off Tower Mill Rd.)
Malta Rd. E10 . . . 32Cc 72
RM18: Tilb . . . 4B 122
Malta St. EC1 . . . 5C 218 (42Rb 91)
Maltby Cl. BR6: Orp . . . 74Wc 161
Maltby Dr. EN1: Enf . . . 10Xb 19
Maltby Ho. SE1 . . . 3K 231
SE3 . . . 56Lc 115
Maltby Rd. KT9: Chess . . . 79Qa 153
Maltby St. SE1 . . . 2K 231 (47Vb 91)
Malt Hill TW20: Egh . . . 64A 126
Malt Ho. Cl. SL4: Old Win . . . 9M 103
Malthouse Ct. *AL1: St A* . . . *3B 6*
(off Sopwell La.)
GU24: W End . . . 4D 166
TW8: Bford . . . *51Na 109*
(off High St.)
Malthouse Dr. TW13: Hanw . . . 64Z 129
W4 . . . 51Va 110
Malthouse La. DA12: Shorne . . . 4N 145
GU3: Worp . . . 6G 186
GU24: Pirb . . . 5F 186
GU24: W End . . . 5D 166
TW20: Egh . . . 64C 126
Malthouse M. UB9: Hare . . . 26L 43
Malthouse Pas. *SW13* . . . *54Va 110*
(off Clevelands Gdns.)
Malt Ho. Pl. RM1: Rom . . . 29Gd 56
Malthouse Pl. WD7: R'lett . . . 6Ja 14
Malthouse Rd. TN15: Stans, Ash . . . 81Be 185
Malthus Path SE28 . . . 46Yc 95
Malting Ho. *E14* . . . *45Bc 92*
(off Oak La.)
Malting La. RM16: Ors . . . 2C 100
Maltings, The AL1: St A . . . 2B 6
BR6: Orp . . . 74Vc 161
DA11: Grav'nd . . . *8C 122*
(off West St.)
HP2: Hem H . . . 1M 3
KT14: Byfl . . . 85P 169
RH8: Oxt . . . 3K 211
RM1: Rom . . . 31Hd 76
TW18: Staines . . . 63G 126
W4 . . . *50Qa 87*
(off Spring Gro.)
WD4: Hunt C . . . 6S 12
Maltings Arts Theatre . . . 2B 6
Maltings Cl. E3 . . . 41Ec 92
SW13 . . . 54Va 110
Maltings Dr. CM16: Epp . . . 1Wc 23
Maltings Ent. Cen., The
DA12: Grav'nd . . . 10H 123
Maltings La. CM16: Epp . . . 1Wc 23
Maltings Lodge *W4* . . . *51Ua 110*
(off Corney Reach Way)
Maltings M. DA15: Sidc . . . 62Wc 139
Maltings Pl. SE1 . . . 2J 231
SW6 . . . 53Db 111
Malting Way TW7: Isle . . . 55Ha 108
Malt Kiln Pl. DA2: Dart . . . 58Rd 119
Malt La. WD7: R'lett . . . 7Ja 14
Malton Av. SL1: Slou . . . 4F 80
Malton M. SE18 . . . 51Uc 116
W10 . . . 44Ab 88
Malton Rd. W10 . . . 44Ab 88
Malton St. SE18 . . . 51Uc 116
Maltravers St. WC2 . . . 4J 223 (45Pb 90)
Malt Shovel Cotts. DA4: Eyns . . . 76Md 163
Malt St. SE1 . . . 51Wb 113
Malus Cl. HP2: Hem H . . . 1A 4
KT15: Add . . . 80H 149
Malus Dr. KT15: Add . . . 80H 149
Malva Cl. SW18 . . . 57Db 111
Malvern Av. DA7: Bex . . . 52Ad 117
E4 . . . 24Fc 53
HA2: Harr . . . 34Aa 65
Malvern Cl. CR4: Mitc . . . 69Lb 134
KT6: Surb . . . 74Na 153
KT16: Ott . . . 79E 148
SE20 . . . 68Wb 135
UB10: Ick . . . 33Q 64
W10 . . . 43Bb 89
WD23: Bush . . . 16Ea 28
Malvern Ct. KT18: Eps . . . 86Ta 173
SL3: L'ly . . . 51C 104
SM2: Sutt . . . 80Cb 155
SW7 . . . 5C 226
W12 . . . *47Wa 88*
(off Hadyn Pk. Rd.)
Malvern Dr. IG3: Bark, Ilf . . . 35Vc 75
IG8: Wfd G . . . 22Lc 53
TW13: Hanw . . . 64Z 129
Malvern Gdns. HA3: Kenton . . . 28Na 47
IG10: Lough . . . 16Pc 36
NW2 . . . 33Ab 68
Malvern Ho. *CR8: Kenley* . . . *86Rb 177*
(off Foxley Rd.)
DA11: Nflt . . . *58Fe 121*
(off Laburnum Gro.)
N16 . . . 32Vb 71
SE17 . . . 7E 230
WD18: Wat . . . 16T 26
Malvern M. NW6 . . . 41Cb 89
Malvern Pl. NW6 . . . 41Bb 89
Malvern Rd. BR6: Chels . . . 77Xc 161
CR7: Thor H . . . 70Qb 134
E6 . . . 39Nc 74
E8 . . . 38Wb 71
E11 . . . 33Gc 73
EN3: Enf W . . . 9Ac 20
KT6: Surb . . . 75Na 153
N8 . . . 27Qb 50
N17 . . . 27Wb 51
NW6 . . . 40Bb 69
(not continuous)
RM11: Horn . . . 30Jd 56
RM17: Grays . . . 9A 100
TW12: Hamp . . . 66Ca 129
UB3: Harl . . . 52U 106
Malvern Ter. N1 . . . 39Qb 70
N9 . . . 18Vb 33
Malvern Way W13 . . . 43Ka 86
WD3: Crox G . . . 15R 26
Malvina Av. DA12: Grav'nd . . . 1D 144
Malwood Rd. SW12 . . . 58Kb 112
Malyons, The TW17: Shep . . . 72T 150
Malyons Rd. BR8: Hext . . . 66Hd 140
SE13 . . . 58Dc 114
Malyons Ter. SE13 . . . 57Dc 114
Managers St. E14 . . . 46Ec 92
Manan Cl. HP3: Hem H . . . 4C 4
Manatee Pl. SM6: Bedd . . . 76Mb 156
Manaton Cl. SE15 . . . 55Xb 113
Manaton Cres. UB1: S'hall . . . 44Ca 85
Manbey Gro. E15 . . . 37Gc 73
Manbey M. E15 . . . 37Gc 73
Manbey Pk. Rd. E15 . . . 37Gc 73
Manbey Rd. E15 . . . 37Gc 73
Manbey St. E15 . . . 37Gc 73
Manbre Rd. W6 . . . 51Ya 110
Manbrough Av. E6 . . . 41Pc 94
Manchester Ct. *E16* . . . *44Kc 93*
(off Garvary Rd.)
Manchester Dr. W10 . . . 42Ab 88
Manchester Gro. E14 . . . 50Ec 92
Manchester Ho. SE17 . . . 7E 230
Manchester M. W1 . . . 1H 221
Manchester Rd. CR7: Thor H . . . 69Sb 135
E14 . . . 50Ec 92
N15 . . . 30Tb 51
Manchester Sq. W1 . . . 2J 221 (44Jb 90)
Manchester St. W1 . . . 1H 221 (43Jb 90)
Manchester Way RM10: Dag . . . 35Dd 76
Manchuria Rd. SW11 . . . 58Jb 112
Manciple St. SE1 . . . 2F 231 (47Tb 91)
Mancroft Ct. *NW8* . . . *39Fb 69*
(off St John's Wood Pk.)
Mandalay Rd. SW4 . . . 57Lb 112
Mandara Pl. *SE8* . . . *49Ac 92*
(off Yeoman St.)
Mandarin Ct. *NW10* . . . *37Ta 67*
(off Mitchellbrook Way)
SE8 . . . 51Bc 114
Mandarin St. E14 . . . 45Cc 92
Mandarin Way UB4: Yead . . . 44Z 85
Mandarin Wharf *N1* . . . *39Ub 71*
(off De Beauvoir Cres.)
Mandela Cl. NW10 . . . 38Sa 67
W12 . . . 45Xa 88
Mandela Ct. UB8: Cowl . . . 43L 83
Mandela Ho. E2 . . . 3K 219
SE5 . . . 54Rb 113
Mandela Pl. WD24: Wat . . . 12Z 27
Mandela Rd. E16 . . . 44Jc 93
Mandela St. NW1 . . . 39Lb 70
SW9 . . . 52Qb 112
(not continuous)
Mandela Way SE1 . . . 5H 231 (49Ub 91)
Mandel Ho. SW18 . . . 56Cb 111
Manderley *W14* . . . *48Bb 89*
(off Oakwood La.)
Mandeville Cl. SE3 . . . 52Hc 115
SW20 . . . 66Ab 132
WD17: Wat . . . 10V 12
Mandeville Ct. E4 . . . 22Ac 52
TW20: Egh . . . 63C 126
Mandeville Dr. AL1: St A . . . 5B 6
KT6: Surb . . . 74Ma 153
Mandeville Ho. SE1 . . . 7K 231
SW4 . . . 57Lb 112
Mandeville M. SW4 . . . 56Nb 112
Mandeville Pl. W1 . . . 2J 221 (44Jb 90)
Mandeville Rd. EN3: Enf W . . . 8Ac 20
EN6: Pot B . . . 4Eb 17
N14 . . . 19Kb 32
TW7: Isle . . . 54Ja 108
TW17: Shep . . . 71Q 150
UB5: N'olt . . . 38Ca 65
Mandeville St. E5 . . . 34Ac 72
Mandeville Wlk. CM13: Hut . . . 17Fe 41
Mandrake Rd. SW17 . . . 62Hb 133
Mandrake Way E15 . . . 38Gc 73
Mandrell Rd. SW2 . . . 57Nb 112
Manesty Ct. *N14* . . . *17Mb 32*
(off Ivy Rd.)
Manette St. W1 . . . 3E 222 (44Mb 90)
Manfield Cl. SL2: Slou . . . 1E 80
Manford Cl. IG7: Chig . . . 21Wc 55
Manford Ct. *IG7: Chig* . . . *22Vc 55*
(off Manford Way)
Manford Cross IG7: Chig . . . 22Wc 55
Manford Ind. Est. DA8: Erith . . . 51Jd 118
Manford Way IG7: Chig . . . 22Uc 54
Manfred Rd. SW15 . . . 57Bb 111
Manger Rd. N7 . . . 37Nb 70
Mangold Way DA18: Erith . . . 48Zc 95
Manhattan Av. WD18: Wat . . . 14V 26
Manhattan Bldg. E3 . . . 40Cc 72
Manhattan Bus. Pk. W5 . . . 41Na 87
Manhattan Loft Gdns. E20 . . . 37Ec 72
Manilla Ct. *RM6: Chad H* . . . *30Xc 55*
(off Quarles Pk. Rd.)
Manilla St. E14 . . . 47Cc 92
Manilla Wlk. SE10 . . . 49Gc 93
Manister Rd. SE2 . . . 48Wc 95
Manitoba Ct. *SE16* . . . *47Yb 92*
(off Canada Est.)
Manitoba Gdns.
BR6: Chels . . . 79Vc 161
Manley Ct. N16 . . . 34Vb 71
Manley Ho. SE11 . . . 7K 229 (49Qb 90)
Manley Rd. HP2: Hem H . . . 1N 3
Manley St. NW1 . . . 39Jb 70
Manly Dixon Dr. EN3: Enf W . . . 9Ac 20
Manna Ho. *E20* . . . *37Ec 72*
(off Glade Wlk.)
Mannamead KT18: Eps D . . . 91Ua 194
Mannamead Cl. KT18: Eps D . . . 91Ua 194
Mannan Ho. *E3* . . . *40Bc 72*
(off Roman Rd.)
Mann Cl. CR0: C'don . . . 76Sb 157
Manneby Prior N1 . . . 2J 217
Mannequin Ho. E17 . . . 27Zb 52
Manning Ct. *SE28* . . . *46Xc 95*
(off Titmuss Av.)
WD19: Wat . . . 16Z 27
Manningford Cl. EC1 . . . 3B 218 (41Rb 91)
Manning Gdns.
CR0: C'don . . . 73Xb 157
HA3: Kenton . . . 31Ma 67
Manning Ho. *W11* . . . *44Ab 88*
(off Westbourne Pk. Rd.)
Manning Pl. TW10: Rich . . . 58Pa 109
Manning Rd. BR5: St M Cry . . . 71Zc 161
E17 . . . 29Ac 52
RM10: Dag . . . 37Cd 76
Manning St. RM15: Avel . . . 46Sd 98
Manningtree Cl. SW19 . . . 60Ab 110
Manningtree Rd. HA4: Ruis . . . 35X 65
Manningtree St. E1 . . . 44Wb 91
Mannin Rd. RM6: Chad H . . . 31Xc 75
Mannock Cl. NW9 . . . 27Ta 47
Mannock Dr. IG10: Lough . . . 12Sc 36
Mannock M. E18 . . . 25Lc 53
Mannock Rd. DA1: Dart . . . 55Pd 119
N22 . . . 27Rb 51
Mann's Cl. TW7: Isle . . . 57Ha 108
Manns Rd. HA8: Edg . . . 23Qa 47
Manns Ter. SE27 . . . 62Sb 135
Manny Shinwell Ho. *SW6* . . . *51Bb 111*
(off Clem Attlee Ct.)
Manoel Rd. TW2: Twick . . . 61Ea 130
Manor, The IG8: Wfd G . . . 24Qc 54
Manor Av. CR3: Cat'm . . . 96Ub 197
HP3: Hem H . . . 5M 3
RM11: Horn . . . 29Ld 57
SE4 . . . 54Bc 114
TW4: Houn . . . 55Z 107
UB5: N'olt . . . 38Ba 65
Manorbrook SE3 . . . 56Jc 115
Manor Chase KT13: Weyb . . . 78R 150
MANOR CIRCUS . . . **55Qa 109**
Manor Cl. CR6: W'ham . . . 89Ac 178
DA1: Cray . . . 56Fd 118
DA2: Wilm . . . 62Jd 140
DA12: Grav'nd . . . 1K 145
E17 . . . 25Ac 52
EN5: Barn . . . 14Ab 30
GU22: Pyr . . . 89H 169
HA4: Ruis . . . 32V 64
KT4: Wor Pk . . . 74Ua 154
KT24: E Hor . . . 100U 190
NW7 . . . 22Ta 47
NW9 . . . 29Ra 47
RH9: S God . . . 10D 210
RM1: Rom . . . 29Jd 56
RM10: Dag . . . 37Fd 76
RM15: Avel . . . 46Sd 98
SE28 . . . 45Yc 95
Manor Cl. Sth. RM15: Avel . . . 46Sd 98
Manor Cotts. HA6: Nwood . . . 25V 44
N2 . . . *26Eb 49*
(off Manor Cotts. App.)
WD3: Chor . . . 16D 24
Manor Cotts. App. N2 . . . 26Eb 49
Manor Ct. BR4: W W'ck . . . 74Dc 158
DA7: Bex . . . 56Dd 118
DA13: Sole S . . . 10F 144
E4 . . . 18Gc 35
E10 . . . 32Dc 72
EN1: Enf . . . 8Xb 19
EN6: Pot B . . . 4Bb 17
EN8: Chesh . . . 3Zb 20
HA1: Harr . . . 30Ha 46
HA9: Wemb . . . 36Na 67
IG11: Bark . . . 38Vc 75
KT2: King T . . . 67Qa 131
KT8: W Mole . . . 70Ca 129
KT13: Weyb . . . 77R 150
N2 . . . 29Hb 49
N14 . . . 19Mb 32
N20 . . . *20Hb 31*
(off York Way)
SL1: Slou . . . 6D 80
SM5: Cars . . . 76Jb 156
SW2 . . . 57Pb 112
SW3 . . . 7E 226
SW6 . . . 53Db 111
SW16 . . . 62Nb 134
TW2: Twick . . . 61Ea 130
TW18: Staines . . . 64F 126
UB9: Hare . . . 26L 43
W3 . . . 49Qa 87
WD7: R'lett . . . 10Ha 14
Manor Ct. Rd. W7 . . . 45Ga 86
Manor Cres. GU24: Brkwd . . . 2B 186
KT5: Surb . . . 72Qa 153
KT14: Byfl . . . 85P 169
KT19: Eps . . . 84Qa 173
RM11: Horn . . . 29Ld 57
Manorcroft Pde. EN8: Chesh . . . 2Zb 20
Manorcrofts Rd. TW20: Egh . . . 65C 126
Manor Dene SE28 . . . 44Yc 95
Manordene Cl. KT7: T Ditt . . . 74Ja 152
Manordene Rd. SE28 . . . 44Yc 95
Manor Dr. AL2: Chis G . . . 9N 5
DA3: Hartl . . . 72Ce 165
HA9: Wemb . . . 35Pa 67
KT5: Surb . . . 72Pa 153
KT10: Hin W . . . 75Ha 152
KT15: New H . . . 82J 169
KT19: Ewe . . . 79Ua 154
N14 . . . 18Kb 32
N20 . . . 21Hb 49
NW7 . . . 22Ta 47
TW13: Hanw . . . 64Z 129
TW16: Sun . . . 68W 128
Manor Dr., The KT4: Wor Pk . . . 74Ua 154
Manor Dr. Nth. KT3: N Mald . . . 73Ta 153
KT4: Wor Pk . . . 73Ta 153
Manor Est. SE16 . . . 49Xb 91
Manor Farm
Ruislip . . . 31U 64
Manor Farm TW20: Egh . . . 64C 126
Mnr. Farm Av. TW17: Shep . . . 72R 150
Mnr. Farm Cl. KT4: Wor Pk . . . 74Ua 154
SL4: Wind . . . 5D 102
Mnr. Farm Cotts. SL4: Old Win . . . 7L 103
TN15: Igh . . . 93Wd 204
Mnr. Farm Ct. E6 . . . 41Pc 94
TW20: Egh . . . 64C 126
Mnr. Farm Dr. E4 . . . 20Gc 35
MANOR FARM ESTATE . . . 9N 103
Mnr. Farm Ho. SL4: Wind . . . 5D 102
Mnr. Farm La. TW20: Egh . . . 64C 126
Mnr. Farm Rd. EN1: Enf . . . 7Xb 19
HA0: Wemb . . . 40Ma 67
SW16 . . . 68Qb 134
Manor Fld. DA12: Shorne . . . 4N 145
Manorfield Cl. *N19* . . . *35Lb 70*
(off Fulbrook M.)
Manor Flds. SW15 . . . 58Za 110
Manorfields Cl. BR7: Chst . . . 69Vc 139
Manor Forstal
DA3: Nw A G . . . 76Be 165
Manor Gdns. CR2: S Croy . . . 79Vb 157
HA4: Ruis . . . 36Y 65
KT24: Eff . . . 100Z 191
N7 . . . 34Nb 70
SW4 . . . *54Lb 112*
(off Larkhall Ri.)
SW20 . . . 68Bb 133
TW9: Rich . . . 56Pa 109
TW12: Hamp . . . 66Da 129
TW16: Sun . . . 67W 128
W3 . . . 49Qa 87
W4 . . . 50Ua 88
Manor Ga. UB5: N'olt . . . 38Aa 65
Manor Ga. La. DA2: Wilm . . . 62Jd 140
Manorgate Rd.
KT2: King T . . . 67Qa 131
Manor Grn. Rd. KT19: Eps . . . 85Ra 173
Manor Gro. BR3: Beck . . . 68Dc 136
SE15 . . . 51Yb 114
TW9: Rich . . . 56Qa 109
Manor Hall IG7: Chig . . . 22Sc 54
Mnr. Hall Av. NW4 . . . 26Za 48
Mnr. Hall Dr. NW4 . . . 26Za 48
Manorhall Gdns. E10 . . . 32Cc 72
Manor Hill SM7: Bans . . . 87Hb 175
MANOR HOUSE . . . 31Tb 71
MANOR HOUSE . . . **31Sb 71**
Manor Ho. DA3: Nw A G . . . 76Be 165
NW1 . . . 7E 214
SL4: Eton . . . *1H 103*
(off Common La.)
UB2: S'hall . . . 48Aa 85
Manor Ho., The
KT20: Kgswd . . . 95Eb 195
Manor Ho. Ct. KT18: Eps . . . 85Sa 173
TW17: Shep . . . 73R 150
W9 . . . *42Eb 89*
(off Warrington Gdns.)
Manor Ho. Dr. HA6: Nwood . . . 24R 44
KT12: Hers . . . 78V 150
NW6 . . . 38Za 68
Manor Ho. Est. HA7: Stan . . . 23Ka 46
Manor Ho. Gdn. E11 . . . 30Kc 53
Manor Ho. Gdns.
WD5: Ab L . . . 3T 12
Manor Ho. La. KT23: Bookh . . . 98Aa 191
SL3: Dat . . . 3M 103
Manor Ho. Way TW7: Isle . . . 55Ka 108
Manor La. DA3: Fawk . . . 73Yd 164
DA3: Hartl . . . 72Ce 165
KT20: Lwr K . . . 1J 207
SE12 . . . 57Gc 115
SE13 . . . 57Gc 115
SL9: Ger X . . . 1P 61
SM1: Sutt . . . 78Eb 155
TN15: Ash . . . 73Yd 164
TW13: Felt . . . 61W 128
TW16: Sun . . . 68W 128
UB3: Harl . . . 51T 106
Manor La. Ter. SE13 . . . 56Gc 115
Manor Leaze
TW20: Egh . . . 64D 126
Manor Lodge *NW6* . . . *38Za 68*
(off Willesden La.)
Manor M. *NW6* . . . *40Cb 69*
(off Cambridge Av.)
SE4 . . . 54Bc 114
Manor Mt. SE23 . . . 60Yb 114
Manor Pde. HA1: Harr . . . 30Ha 46
N16 . . . 33Vb 71
NW10 . . . *40Va 68*
(off High St. Harlesden)
MANOR PARK
E12 . . . 35Mc 73
SL2 . . . 3H 81
Manor Pk. BR7: Chst . . . 68Tc 138
DA8: Erith . . . 51Jd 118
SE13 . . . 56Fc 115
TW9: Rich . . . 56Pa 109
TW13: Felt . . . 61W 128
TW18: Staines . . . 62F 126
Manor Pk. Cl. BR4: W W'ck . . . 74Dc 158
Manor Pk. Crematorium E7 . . . 35Lc 73
Manor Pk. Cres. HA8: Edg . . . 23Qa 47
Manor Pk. Dr. HA2: Harr . . . 27Da 45
Manor Pk. Gdns. HA8: Edg . . . 22Qa 47
Manor Pk. Pde. *SE13* . . . *56Fc 115*
(off Lee High Rd.)
Manor Pk. Rd. BR4: W W'ck . . . 74Dc 158
BR7: Chst . . . 67Sc 138
E12 . . . 35Mc 73
(not continuous)
N2 . . . 27Eb 49
NW10 . . . 39Va 68
SM1: Sutt . . . 78Eb 155
Manor Pl. BR1: Brom . . . 67Nc 138
BR7: Chst . . . 68Tc 138
CR4: Mitc . . . 69Lb 134
DA1: Dart . . . 60Nd 119
KT12: Walt T . . . 73V 150
(not continuous)
KT20: Kgswd . . . 93Bb 195
KT23: Bookh . . . 98Ca 191
SE17 . . . 7C 230 (50Rb 91)
SM1: Sutt . . . 77Db 155
TW14: Felt . . . 60W 106
TW18: Staines . . . 64K 127
Manor Pl. Ind. Est. WD6: Bore . . . 13Sa 29
Manor Rd. AL1: St A . . . 1C 6
AL2: Lon C . . . 8G 6
BR3: Beck . . . 68Dc 136
BR4: W W'ck . . . 75Dc 158
CR4: Mitc . . . 70Lb 134
DA1: Cray . . . 56Gd 118
DA3: Long H . . . 71Ee 165
DA5: Bexl . . . 60Dd 118
DA8: Erith . . . 51Hd 118
DA10: Swans . . . 58Zd 121
DA12: Grav'nd . . . 8D 122
DA13: Sole S . . . 10E 144
DA15: Sidc . . . 62Vc 139
E10 . . . 31Cc 72
E15 . . . 41Gc 93
E16 . . . 41Gc 93
E17 . . . 26Ac 52
EN2: Enf . . . 12Sb 33
EN5: Barn . . . 14Ab 30
EN6: Pot B . . . 3Bb 17
EN9: Walt A . . . 5Fc 21
GU21: Wok . . . 8N 167
GU23: Rip . . . 95H 189
HA1: Harr . . . 30Ja 46
HA4: Ruis . . . 32T 64
IG7: Chig . . . 22Sc 54
IG8: Wfd G . . . 23Pc 54
IG10: H Beech . . . 11Kc 35
IG10: Lough . . . 16Kc 35
IG11: Bark . . . 37Vc 75
KT8: E Mos . . . 71Fa 130
KT12: Walt T . . . 73V 150
N16 . . . 33Tb 71
N17 . . . 25Wb 51
N22 . . . 23Nb 50
RH1: Mers . . . 1C 208
RH2: Reig . . . 4H 207
RM1: Rom . . . 29Jd 56
RM4: Abr, Stap A . . . 19Yc 37
RM6: Chad H . . . 30Zc 55
RM10: Dag . . . 37Ed 76
RM17: Grays . . . 51Ee 121
RM18: Tilb . . . 4C 122
RM20: W Thur . . . 51Yd 120
SE25 . . . 70Wb 135
SL4: Wind . . . 4C 102
SM2: Cheam . . . 80Bb 155
SM6: Wall . . . 77Kb 156
SS17: Stan H . . . 2M 101
SW20 . . . 68Bb 133
TN14: Sund . . . 96Zc 201
TN15: W King . . . 83Vd 184
Manor Rd. TN16: Tats . . . 92Nc 200
TW2: Twick . . . 61Ea 130
TW9: Rich . . . 56Qa 109
TW11: Tedd . . . 64Ja 130
(not continuous)
TW15: Ashf . . . 64P 127
UB3: Hayes . . . 44W 84
W13 . . . 45Ja 86
WD17: Wat . . . 11X 27
Manor Rd. Ho. HA1: Harr . . . 30Ja 46
Manor Rd. Nth. KT7: T Ditt . . . 76Ha 152
KT10: Hin W, T Ditt . . . 76Ha 152
SM6: Wall . . . 77Kb 156
Manor Rd. Sth. KT10: Hin W . . . 77Fa 152
Manorside EN5: Barn . . . 14Ab 30
Manorside Cl. SE2 . . . 49Yc 95
Manor Sq. RM8: Dag . . . 33Yc 75
Manor Va. TW8: Bford . . . 50La 86
Manor Vw. DA3: Hartl . . . 72Ce 165
N3 . . . 26Db 49
Manorville Rd. HP3: Hem H . . . 6L 3
Manor Wlk. KT13: Weyb . . . 78R 150
Manor Way BR2: Brom . . . 72Nc 160
BR3: Beck . . . 68Cc 136
BR5: Pet W . . . 70Sc 138
CM14: B'wood . . . 20Wd 40
CR2: S Croy . . . 79Ub 157
CR4: Mitc . . . 69Lb 134
CR8: Purl . . . 84Nb 176
DA5: Bexl . . . 60Cd 118
DA7: Bex . . . 55Fd 118
DA10: Nflt, Swans . . . 56Zd 121
DA11: Nflt . . . 56Ce 121
(Botany Rd.)
DA11: Nflt . . . 56Zd 121
(Pilgrims Rd.)
E4 . . . 21Fc 53
EN6: Pot B . . . 2Cb 17
EN8: Chesh . . . 3Ac 20
GU22: Wok . . . 93D 188
HA2: Harr . . . 28Da 45
HA4: Ruis . . . 31U 64
KT4: Wor Pk . . . 74Ua 154
KT22: Oxs . . . 87Ea 172
NW9 . . . 28Ua 48
RM13: Rain . . . 42Gd 96
RM17: Grays . . . 52De 121
SE3 . . . 56Hc 115
SE23 . . . 59Yb 114
SM7: Bans . . . 88Hb 175
SS17: Stan H . . . 1P 101
TW20: Egh . . . 65B 126
UB2: S'hall . . . 49Z 85
WD3: Crox G . . . 14Q 26
WD6: Bore . . . 13Sa 29
Manor Way, The SM6: Wall . . . 77Kb 156
Manorway EN1: Enf . . . 17Ub 33
IG8: Wfd G . . . 22Lc 53
Manorway, The SS17: Corr, Stan H . . . 1L 101
Manor Way Bus. Cen.
RM13: Rain . . . 43Fd 96
Manor Way Bus. Pk. DA10: Nflt . . . 57Be 121
Manor Waye UB8: Uxb . . . 39M 63
Mnr. Wood Rd. CR8: Purl . . . 85Nb 176
Manpreet Ct. E12 . . . 36Pc 74
Manresa Rd. SW3 . . . 7D 226 (50Gb 89)
Mansard Beeches SW17 . . . 64Jb 134
Mansard Cl. HA5: Pinn . . . 27Z 45
RM12: Horn . . . 33Jd 76
Mansards, The AL1: St A . . . 1C 6
Manse Cl. UB3: Harl . . . 51T 106
Mansel Cl. GU2: Guild . . . 10M 187
SL2: Slou . . . 3M 81
Mansel Gro. E17 . . . 25Cc 52
Mansell Cl. SL4: Wind . . . 3C 102
Mansell Rd. UB6: G'frd . . . 43Da 85
W3 . . . 47Ta 87
Mansell St. E1 . . . 3K 225 (44Vb 91)
EC3 . . . 5K 225 (44Vb 91)
Mansell Way CR3: Cat'm . . . 94Tb 197
Mansel Rd. SW19 . . . 65Ab 132
Manse Pde. BR8: Swan . . . 70Jd 140
Manser Ct. RM13: Rain . . . 41Gd 96
Mansergh Cl. SE18 . . . 52Nc 116
Manse Rd. N16 . . . 34Vb 71
Manser Rd. RM13: Rain . . . 41Gd 96
Manse Way BR8: Swan . . . 70Jd 140
Mansfield Av. EN4: E Barn . . . 16Hb 31
HA4: Ruis . . . 32X 65
N15 . . . 28Tb 51
Mansfield Cl. BR5: St M Cry . . . 73Zc 161
N9 . . . 16Wb 33
Mansfield Ct. E2 . . . 1K 219
SE15 . . . *52Vb 113*
(off Sumner Rd.)
Mansfield Dr. RH1: Mers . . . 100Mb 196
UB4: Hayes . . . 42U 84
Mansfield Gdns. RM12: Horn . . . 33Md 77
Mansfield Hgts. N2 . . . 29Gb 49
Mansfield Hill E4 . . . 17Dc 34
Mansfield Ho. *N1* . . . *39Ub 71*
(off Halcomb St.)
Mansfield M. W1 . . . 1K 221 (43Kb 90)
Mansfield Pl. CR2: S Croy . . . 79Tb 157
EN6: Cuff . . . 1M 19
NW3 . . . 35Eb 69
Mansfield Rd. BR8: Hext . . . 65Gd 140
CR2: S Croy . . . 79Tb 157
E11 . . . 30Kc 53
E17 . . . 28Bc 52
IG1: Ilf . . . 33Qc 74
KT9: Chess . . . 78La 152
NW3 . . . 36Hb 69
W3 . . . 42Ra 87
Mansfield St. W1 . . . 1K 221 (43Kb 90)
Mansford St. E2 . . . 40Wb 71
Manship Rd. CR4: Mitc . . . 66Jb 134
Mansion Cvn. Site SL0: Iver . . . 46E 82
Mansion Cl. SW9 . . . 53Qb 112
(not continuous)
Mansion Gdns. NW3 . . . 34Db 69
Mansion House . . . 3F 225 (44Tb 91)
Mansion Ho. Dr. HA7: Stan . . . 19Ga 28
Mansion Ho. Pl. EC4 . . . 3F 225 (44Tb 91)
Mansion Ho. St. EC4 . . . 3F 225
Mansion La. SL0: Iver . . . 46E 82
Mansion Lock Ho. *NW1* . . . *38Kb 70*
(off Hawley Cres.)
Mansion Ri. DA10: Swans . . . 59Be 121
Mansions, The SW5 . . . 50Db 89
(Earl's Ct. Rd.)
SW5 . . . *50Db 89*
(off Old Brompton Rd.)
Mansion Vw. *E15* . . . *39Fc 73*
(off High St.)
Manson Ho. *N1* . . . *38Qb 70*
(off Drummond Way)
Manson M. SW7 . . . 6A 226 (49Fb 89)

Manson Pl.—Marlborough M.

Manson Pl. SW7 . . . 6B 226 (49Fb 89)
Manstead Gdns. RM13: Rain . . . 44Kd 97
Mansted Gdns. RM6: Chad H . . . 31Yc 75
Manston N17 . . . 26Tb 51
(off Adams Rd.)
NW1 . . . 38Lb 70
(off Agar Gro.)
Manston Av. UB2: S'hall . . . 49Ca 85
Manston Cl. EN8: Chesh . . . 2Yb 20
SE20 . . . 67Yb 136
Manston Ct. E17 . . . 25Bc 52
Manstone Rd. NW2 . . . 36Ab 68
Manston Gro. KT2: King T . . . 64Ma 131
Manston Ho. W14 . . . 48Ab 88
(off Russell Rd.)
Manston Way AL4: St A . . . 3H 7
RM12: Horn . . . 37Kd 77
Manthorp Rd. SE18 . . . 50Sc 94
Mantilla Rd. SW17 . . . 63Jb 134
Mantle Cl. SL4: Wind . . . 5B 102
Mantle Ct. SW18 . . . 58Db 111
(off Mapleton Rd.)
Mantle Rd. SE4 . . . 55Ac 114
Mantlet Cl. SW16 . . . 66Lb 134
Mantle Way E15 . . . 38Gc 73
Manton Av. W7 . . . 47Ha 86
Manton Cl. UB3: Hayes . . . 45U 84
Manton Rd. EN3: Enf L . . . 9Cc 20
SE2 . . . 49Wc 95
Manton Way EN3: Enf L . . . 10Dc 20
Mantua St. SW11 . . . 55Fb 111
Mantus Cl. E1 . . . 42Yb 92
Mantus Rd. E1 . . . 42Yb 92
Manuka Cl. W7 . . . 46Ja 86
Manuka Hgts. E20 . . . 36Ec 72
(off Napa Cl.)
Manus Way N20 . . . 19Eb 31
Manville Gdns. SW17 . . . 62Kb 134
Manville Rd. SW17 . . . 61Jb 134
Manwood Rd. SE4 . . . 57Bc 114
Manwood St. E16 . . . 46Pc 94
Manygate La. TW17: Shep . . . 73S 150
Manygate Pk. TW17: Shep . . . 72T 150
(off Mitre Cl.)
Manygates SW12 . . . 61Kb 134
Mapesbury Ct. NW2 . . . 36Ab 68
Mapesbury M. NW4 . . . 30Wa 48
Mapesbury Rd. NW2 . . . 38Ab 68
Mapeshill Pl. NW2 . . . 37Ya 68
Mapes Ho. NW6 . . . 38Ab 68
Mape St. E2 . . . 42Xb 91
(not continuous)
Maple Av. E4 . . . 22Bc 52
HA2: Harr . . . 33Da 65
RM14: Upm . . . 34Rd 77
UB7: Yiew . . . 45N 83
W3 . . . 46Ua 88
Maple Cl. AL10: Hat . . . 1C 8
BR5: Pet W . . . 71Tc 160
BR8: Swan . . . 68Gd 140
CM13: B'wood . . . 20Be 41
CM16: They B . . . 9Tc 22
CR3: Whyt . . . 89Vb 177
CR4: Mitc . . . 67Kb 134
HA4: Ruis . . . 30X 45
IG6: Ilf . . . 22Uc 54
IG9: Buck H . . . 20Mc 35
KT19: Eps . . . 81Ta 173
N3 . . . 23Cb 49
N16 . . . 30Wb 51
RM12: Horn . . . 34Kd 77
SW4 . . . 58Mb 112
TW12: Hamp . . . 65Ba 129
UB4: Yead . . . 41Z 85
WD23: Bush . . . 12Aa 27
Maple Ct. CR0: C'don . . . 77Sb 157
(off Lwr. Coombe St.)
CR0: C'don . . . 77Sb 157
(off The Waldrons)
DA8: Erith . . . 52Hd 118
DA9: Ghithe . . . 59Ud 120
E3 . . . 40Cc 72
(off Four Seasons Cl.)
E6 . . . 43Qc 94
GU21: Wok . . . 8N 167
KT3: N Mald . . . 69Ta 131
KT22: Lea . . . 92Ha 192
SE6 . . . 60Dc 114
SL4: Wind . . . 5G 102
SL9: Ger X . . . 29B 42
TW15: Ashf . . . 66T 128
TW20: Eng G . . . 5M 125
WD6: Bore . . . 14Qa 29
(off Drayton Rd.)
WD25: Wat . . . 8Z 13
Maple Cres. DA15: Sidc . . . 58Wc 117
SL2: Slou . . . 5M 81
Maplecroft Cl. E6 . . . 44Mc 93
MAPLE CROSS . . . 22F 42
Maple Cross Ind. Est. WD3: Map C . . . 21H 43
Mapledale Av. CR0: C'don . . . 75Wb 157
Mapledene BR7: Chst . . . 65Sc 138
Mapledene Est. E8 . . . 38Wb 71
Mapledene Rd. E8 . . . 38Vb 71
Maple Dr. IG7: Chig . . . 21Tc 54
KT23: Bookh . . . 97Da 191
RM15: S Ock . . . 42Zd 99
Maplefield AL2: Park . . . 1Da 13
Maple Gdns. HA8: Edg . . . 24Ua 48
KT17: Eps . . . 85Ua 174
(off Up. High St.)
TW19: Stanw . . . 61N 127
Maple Ga. IG10: Lough . . . 12Qc 36
Maple Grn. HP1: Hem H . . . 1G 2
Maple Gro. GU22: Wok . . . 93A 188
KT23: Bookh . . . 99Ca 191
NW9 . . . 31Sa 67
TW8: Bford . . . 52Ka 108
UB1: S'hall . . . 43Ba 85
W5 . . . 48Ma 87
WD17: Wat . . . 11W 26
Maple Gro. Bus. Cen. TW4: Houn . . . 56Y 107
MAPLE HILL . . . 2A 10
Maple Ho. E17 . . . 27Dc 52
EN6: Pot B . . . 5Db 17
KT1: King T . . . 71Na 153
(off Maple Rd.)
N19 . . . 34Lb 70
RH1: Redh . . . 6P 207
(off Chapel Rd.)
SE8 . . . 52Bc 114
(off Idonia St.)
TW9: Kew . . . 53Ra 109
Maplehurst BR2: Brom . . . 68Gc 137
KT22: Fet . . . 95Fa 192
Maplehurst Cl. DA2: Wilm . . . 61Gd 140
KT1: King T . . . 70Na 131
Maple Ind. Est. TW13: Felt . . . 62W 128
Maple Leaf Cl. TN16: Big H . . . 88Mc 179
WD5: Ab L . . . 4W 12
Mapleleaf Cl. CR2: Sels . . . 83Zb 178
Maple Leaf Dr. DA15: Sidc . . . 60Vc 117
Mapleleafe Gdns. IG6: Ilf . . . 27Rc 54
Maple Leaf Sq. SE16 . . . 47Zb 92
Maple Lodge W8 . . . 48Db 89
(off Abbots Wlk.)
Maple Lodge Cl. WD3: Map C . . . 21G 42
Maple Lodge Nature Reserve . . . 22H 43
Maple M. NW6 . . . 40Db 69
SE16 . . . 47Zb 92
SW16 . . . 64Pb 134
Maple Pl. KT20: Kgswd . . . 96Bb 195
N17 . . . 24Wb 51
SM7: Bans . . . 86Za 174
UB7: Yiew . . . 46N 83
W1 . . . 6C 216 (42Lb 90)
Maple Rd. CR3: Whyt . . . 89Vb 177
DA1: Dart . . . 60Ld 119
DA12: Grav'nd . . . 3E 144
E11 . . . 30Gc 53
GU23: Rip . . . 96J 189
KT6: Surb . . . 72Ma 153
KT21: Asht . . . 91Ma 193
RH1: Redh . . . 10P 207
RM17: Grays . . . 51Ee 121
SE20 . . . 67Xb 135
UB4: Yead . . . 41Y 85
Maples SS17: Stan H . . . 1N 101
Maples, The DA3: Lfield . . . 68De 143
EN7: G Oak . . . 1Ub 19
EN9: Walt A . . . 7Lc 21
KT1: Hamp W . . . 66La 130
KT10: Clay . . . 80Ja 152
KT16: Ott . . . 79D 148
SM7: Bans . . . 86Db 175
WD6: Bore . . . 11Qa 29
MAPLESCOMBE . . . 78Sd 164
Maplescombe La. DA4: Farni . . . 76Qd 163
Maples Pl. E1 . . . 43Xb 91
Maple Springs EN9: Walt A . . . 5Jc 21
Maplestead Rd. RM9: Dag . . . 39Xc 75
SW2 . . . 59Pb 112
Maple St. E2 . . . 40Xb 71
RM7: Rom . . . 28Ed 56
W1 . . . 7B 216 (43Lb 90)
Maplethorpe Rd. CR7: Thor H . . . 70Qb 134
Mapleton Cl. BR2: Brom . . . 72Jc 159
Mapleton Cres. EN3: Enf W . . . 10Yb 20
SW18 . . . 58Db 111
Mapleton Rd. E4 . . . 20Ec 34
EN1: Enf . . . 12Xb 33
SW18 . . . 58Cb 111
(not continuous)
Maple Tree Pl. SE3 . . . 53Nc 116
Maple Wlk. SM2: Sutt . . . 82Db 175
W10 . . . 41Za 88
Maple Way CR5: Coul . . . 93Kb 196
EN9: Walt A . . . 1Kc 21
TW13: Felt . . . 62W 128
Maplewood Apartments N4 . . . 31Sb 71
(off Katherine Cl.)
Maplewood Ct. HA6: Nwood . . . 22V 44
(off Eastbury Av.)
TW15: Ashf . . . 63N 127
Maplin Cl. N21 . . . 16Pb 32
Maplin Ho. SE2 . . . 47Zc 95
(off Wolvercote Rd.)
Maplin Pk. SL3: L'ly . . . 47D 82
Maplin Rd. E16 . . . 44Jc 93
Maplin St. E3 . . . 41Bc 92
Mapperley Cl. E11 . . . 30Hc 53
Mapperley Dr. IG8: Wfd G . . . 24Gc 53
Marabou Cl. E12 . . . 36Nc 74
Mara Ho. E20 . . . 36Dc 72
(off Victory Pde.)
Maran Way DA18: Erith . . . 47Zc 95
Maraschino Apartment
CR0: C'don . . . 74Tb 157
(off Cherry Orchard Rd.)
Marathon Ho. NW1 . . . 7F 215
Marathon Way SE28 . . . 47Vc 95
Marbaix Gdns. TW7: Isle . . . 53Fa 108
Marban Rd. W9 . . . 41Bb 89
Marbeck Cl. SL4: Wind . . . 3B 102
Marble Arch . . . 4G 221
MARBLE ARCH . . . 4F 221 (45Hb 89)
Marble Arch W1 . . . 4F 221 (45Hb 89)
Marble Arch Apartments W1 . . . 2F 221
Marble Cl. W3 . . . 46Ra 87
Marble Dr. NW2 . . . 32Za 68
Marble Hill Cl. TW1: Twick . . . 59Ka 108
Marble Hill Gdns. TW1: Twick . . . 59Ka 108
Marble Hill House . . . 59La 108
Marble Ho. SE18 . . . 50Vc 95
W9 . . . 42Bb 89
Marble Quay E1 . . . 46Wb 91
Marbles Ho. SE5 . . . 51Sb 113
(off Grosvenor Ter.)
Marbles Way KT20: Tad . . . 91Za 194
Marbrook Ct. SE12 . . . 62Lc 137
Marcella Rd. SW9 . . . 54Qb 112
Marcellina Way BR6: Orp . . . 76Uc 160
Marcet Rd. DA1: Dart . . . 57Ld 119
March NW9 . . . 25Va 48
(off Long Mead)
Marchant Cl. NW7 . . . 23Ua 48
Marchant Ho. N1 . . . 1H 219
(off Halcomb St.)
Marchant Rd. E11 . . . 33Fc 73
Marchant St. SE14 . . . 51Ac 114
Marchbank Rd. W14 . . . 51Bb 111
March Ct. SW15 . . . 56Xa 110
Marchmant Cl. RM12: Horn . . . 34Ld 77
Marchmont Gdns. TW10: Rich . . . 57Pa 109
Marchmont Rd. SM6: Wall . . . 80Lb 156
TW10: Rich . . . 57Pa 109
Marchmont St. WC1 . . . 5F 217 (42Nb 90)
March Rd. KT13: Weyb . . . 78Q 150
TW1: Twick . . . 59Ja 108
Marchside Cl. TW5: Hest . . . 53Z 107
Marchwood Cl. SE5 . . . 52Ub 113
Marchwood Cres. W5 . . . 44La 86
Marcia Ct. SE1 . . . 6J 231
SL1: Slou . . . 6D 80
Marcia Rd. SE1 . . . 6J 231 (49Ub 91)
Marcilly Rd. SW18 . . . 57Fb 111
Marco Dr. HA5: Hat E . . . 24Ba 45
Marcon Ct. E8 . . . 36Xb 71
(off Amhurst Rd.)
Marconi Gdns. CM15: Pil H . . . 15Yd 40
Marconi Pl. N11 . . . 21Kb 50
Marconi Rd. DA11: Nflt . . . 62Fe 143
E10 . . . 32Cc 72
Marconi Way AL4: St A . . . 2H 7
UB1: S'hall . . . 44Da 85
Marcon Pl. E8 . . . 37Xb 71
Marco Rd. W6 . . . 48Ya 88
Marcourt Lawns W5 . . . 42Na 87
Marcus Ct. E15 . . . 39Gc 73
GU22: Wok . . . 90B 168
Marcuse Rd. CR3: Cat'm . . . 95Tb 197
Marcus Garvey M. SE22 . . . 58Xb 113
Marcus Garvey Way SE24 . . . 56Qb 112
Marcus Rd. DA1: Dart . . . 59Jd 118
Marcus St. E15 . . . 39Hc 73
SW18 . . . 58Db 111
Marcus Ter. SW18 . . . 58Db 111
Mardale Ct. NW7 . . . 24Wa 48
Mardale Dr. NW9 . . . 29Ta 47
Mardell Rd. CR0: C'don . . . 71Zb 158
Marden Av. BR2: Hayes . . . 72Jc 159
Marden Cl. IG7: Chig . . . 19Xc 37
Marden Cres. CR0: C'don . . . 72Pb 156
DA5: Bexl . . . 57Ed 118
Marden Ho. E8 . . . 36Xb 71
MARDEN PARK . . . 95Ac 198
Marden Rd. CR0: C'don . . . 72Pb 156
N17 . . . 26Ub 51
RM1: Rom . . . 30Gd 56
Marden Sq. SE16 . . . 48Xb 91
Marder Rd. W13 . . . 47Ja 86
Mardon HA5: Hat E . . . 24Ba 45
Mardyke Cl. RM13: Rain . . . 40Ed 76
Mardyke Ho. SE17 . . . 5G 231
Mardyke Valley Golf Course . . . 45Zd 99
Mardyke Vw. RM19: Purf . . . 48Ud 98
Mardyke Wlk. RM16: Grays . . . 46Ce 99
Marechal Niel Av. DA15: Sidc . . . 62Tc 138
Marechal Niel Pde.
DA14: Sidc . . . 62Tc 138
(off Main Rd.)
Maresby Ho. E4 . . . 19Dc 34
Marescroft Rd. SL2: Slou . . . 2C 80
Maresfield CR0: C'don . . . 76Ub 157
Maresfield Gdns. NW3 . . . 36Eb 69
Mare St. E8 . . . 36Xb 71
Marfleet Cl. SM5: Cars . . . 75Gb 155
Margaret Av. CM15: Shenf . . . 17Be 41
E4 . . . 16Dc 34
Margaret Barr Row
DA10: Swans . . . 59Ae 121
Margaret Bondfield Av.
IG11: Bark . . . 38Wc 75
Margaret Bondfield Ho. E3 . . . 40Ac 72
(off Driffield Rd.)
Margaret Cl. CM16: Epp . . . 1Vc 23
E11 . . . 30Gc 53
EN6: Pot B . . . 5Eb 17
EN9: Walt A . . . 5Fc 21
RM2: Rom . . . 29Kd 57
TW18: Staines . . . 65M 127
WD5: Ab L . . . 4V 12
Margaret Ct. EN4: E Barn . . . 14Fb 31
W1 . . . 2B 222
Margaret Dr. RM11: Horn . . . 32Pd 77
Margaret Gardner Dr. SE9 . . . 61Pc 138
Margaret Herbison Ho. SW6 . . . 51Bb 111
(off Clem Attlee Ct.)
Margaret Ho. W6 . . . 50Ya 88
(off Queen Caroline St.)
WD5: Ab L . . . 2U 12
Margaret Ingram Cl. SW6 . . . 51Bb 111
Margaret Lockwood Cl.
KT1: King T . . . 70Pa 131
Margaret McMillan Ho. E16 . . . 44Lc 93
Margaret Rd. CM16: Epp . . . 1Wc 23
DA5: Bexl . . . 58Zc 117
EN4: E Barn . . . 14Fb 31
N16 . . . 32Vb 71
RM2: Rom . . . 29Kd 57
Margaret Rutherford Pl. SW12 . . . 60Lb 112
Margaret St. W1 . . . 2A 222 (44Kb 90)
Margaretta Ter. SW3 . . . 51Gb 111
Margaretting Rd. E12 . . . 32Lc 73
Margaret Way CR5: Coul . . . 91Rb 197
IG4: Ilf . . . 30Nc 54
Margaret White Ho. NW1 . . . 3D 216
Margate Rd. SW2 . . . 57Nb 112
Margeholes WD19: Wat . . . 19Aa 27
MARGERY . . . 1J 207
Margery Fry Ct. N7 . . . 34Nb 70
Margery Gro. KT20: Lwr K . . . 1G 206
Margery La. KT20: Lwr K . . . 1H 207
Margery Pk. Rd. E7 . . . 37Jc 73
Margery Rd. RM8: Dag . . . 34Zc 75
Margery St. WC1 . . . 4K 217 (41Qb 90)
Margery Ter. E7 . . . 37Jc 73
(off Margery Pk. Rd.)
Margery Wood La.
KT20: Lwr K, Reig . . . 1H 207
Margherita Pl. EN9: Walt A . . . 6Hc 21
Margherita Rd. EN9: Walt A . . . 6Jc 21
Margin Dr. SW19 . . . 64Za 132
Margravine Gdns. W6 . . . 50Za 88
Margravine Rd. W6 . . . 50Za 88
Marham Dr. NW9 . . . 25Ua 48
Marham Gdns. SM4: Mord . . . 72Eb 155
SW18 . . . 60Gb 111
Mar Ho. NW9 . . . 27Ta 47
Maria Cl. SE1 . . . 49Xb 91
Maria Ct. SE25 . . . 68Ub 135
Mariam Gdns. RM12: Horn . . . 33Pd 77
Marian Cl. RM16: N Stif . . . 46Ae 99
UB4: Yead . . . 42Z 85
Marian Ct. E9 . . . 36Yb 72
SM1: Sutt . . . 78Db 155
Marian Gdns. BR1: Brom . . . 66Lc 137
WD25: Wat . . . 5X 13
Marian Lawson Ct. IG7: Chig . . . 22Wc 55
Marianne Cl. SE5 . . . 53Ub 113
Marian Pl. E2 . . . 40Xb 71
Marian Rd. SW16 . . . 67Lb 134
Marian St. E2 . . . 40Xb 71
Marian Way NW10 . . . 38Va 68
Maria Ter. E1 . . . 43Zb 92
Maria Theresa Cl. KT3: N Mald . . . 71Ta 153
Maribor SE10 . . . 52Ec 114
(off Burney St.)
Maricas Av. HA3: Hrw W . . . 25Fa 46
Marie Curie SE5 . . . 53Vb 113
Marie Lloyd Gdns. N19 . . . 31Nb 70
Marie Lloyd Ho. N1 . . . 2F 219
Marie Lloyd Wlk. E8 . . . 37Vb 71
Marie Mnr. Way DA2: Dart . . . 56Ud 120
Marien Ct. E4 . . . 22Fc 53
Mariette Way SM6: Wall . . . 81Nb 176
Marigold All. SE1 . . . 5B 224 (45Rb 91)
Marigold Cl. UB1: S'hall . . . 45Aa 85
Marigold Dr. GU24: Bisl . . . 7E 166
Marigold Rd. N17 . . . 24Yb 52
Marigold St. SE16 . . . 47Xb 91
Marigold Way CR0: C'don . . . 74Zb 158
Marina App. UB4: Yead . . . 43Aa 85
Marina Av. KT3: N Mald . . . 71Xa 154
Marina Cl. BR2: Brom . . . 69Jc 137
KT16: Chert . . . 74L 149
Marina Ct. E3 . . . 41Bc 92
(off Alfred St.)
SW6 . . . 54Eb 111
Marina Dr. DA1: Dart . . . 60Qd 119
DA11: Nflt . . . 9B 122
DA16: Well . . . 54Uc 116
Marina Gdns. EN8: Chesh . . . 2Yb 20
RM7: Rom . . . 29Ed 56
Marina One N1 . . . 1G 217
Marina Pde. TW18: Staines . . . 66K 127
Marina Pl. KT1: Hamp W . . . 67Ma 131
Marina Point E14 . . . 48Dc 92
(off Lanark Sq.)
Marina Way SL0: Iver . . . 45J 83
SL1: Slou . . . 5B 80
TW11: Tedd . . . 66Ma 131
Marine Ct. DA8: Erith . . . 52Hd 118
E11 . . . 33Gc 73
RM19: Purf . . . 49Pd 97
Marine Dr. IG11: Bark . . . 42Wc 95
SE18 . . . 49Pc 94
Marinefield Rd. SW6 . . . 54Db 111
Marinel Ho. SE5 . . . 52Sb 113
Mariner Bus. Cen. CR0: Wadd . . . 78Qb 156
Mariner Gdns. TW10: Ham . . . 62La 130
Mariner Rd. RM9: Dag . . . 39Xc 75
Mariner Rd. E12 . . . 35Qc 74
Mariners Cl. EN4: E Barn . . . 15Fb 31
Mariners Ct. DA9: Ghithe . . . 56Xd 120
(off High St.)
Mariners M. E14 . . . 49Fc 93
Mariners Pl. SE16 . . . 49Ac 92
(off Plough Way)
Mariners Wlk. DA8: Erith . . . 51Hd 118
Mariners Way DA11: Nflt . . . 9A 122
Mariner Way HP2: Hem H . . . 3A 4
Marine St. SE16 . . . 48Wb 91
Marine Twr. SE8 . . . 51Bc 114
(off Abinger Gro.)
Marion Av. TW17: Shep . . . 71R 150
Marion Cl. IG6: Ilf . . . 24Tc 54
WD23: Bush . . . 11Ba 27
Marion Cres. BR5: St M Cry . . . 71Wc 161
Marion Gro. IG8: Wfd G . . . 22Gc 53
Marion Ho. NW1 . . . 39Hb 69
(off Regent's Pk. Rd.)
Marion M. SE21 . . . 62Tb 135
Marion Rd. CR7: Thor H . . . 71Sb 157
NW7 . . . 22Wa 48
Marischal Rd. SE13 . . . 55Fc 115
Marisco Cl. RM16: Grays . . . 9D 100
Marish Ct. SL3: L'ly . . . 48C 82
Marish La. UB9: Den . . . 29E 42
Marish Wharf SL3: L'ly . . . 47A 82
Maritime Cl. DA9: Ghithe . . . 57Xd 120
Maritime Ga. DA11: Nflt . . . 9A 122
Maritime Ho. SE18 . . . 49Rc 94
Maritime Quay E14 . . . 50Cc 92
Maritime St. E3 . . . 42Bc 92
Marius Mans. SW17 . . . 61Jb 134
Marius Rd. SW17 . . . 61Jb 134
Marjoram Cl. SS17: Stan H . . . 1M 101
Marjorams Av. IG10: Lough . . . 12Qc 36
Marjorie Fosters Way
GU24: Brkwd . . . 1B 186
Marjorie Gro. SW11 . . . 56Hb 111
Marjorie M. E1 . . . 44Zb 92
Markab Rd. HA6: Nwood . . . 22V 44
Mark Av. E4 . . . 16Dc 34
Mark Cl. DA7: Bex . . . 53Ad 117
UB1: S'hall . . . 45Da 85
Mark Dr. SL9: Chal P . . . 21A 42
Marke Cl. BR2: Kes . . . 77Nc 160
Markedge La. CR5: Coul . . . 96Hb 195
RH1: Mers . . . 96Hb 195
Markeston Grn. WD19: Wat . . . 21Z 45
Market, The SM1: Sutt . . . 74Eb 155
SM5: Cars . . . 74Eb 155
Market All. DA12: Grav'nd . . . 8D 122
Market App. W12 . . . 47Ya 88
Market Chambers EN2: Enf . . . 13Tb 33
(off Church St.)
Market Ct. W1 . . . 2B 222
Market Dr. W4 . . . 52Ua 110
Market Entrance SW8 . . . 52Lb 112
Market Est. N7 . . . 37Nb 70
Marketfield Rd. RH1: Redh . . . 6P 207
Marketfield Way RH1: Redh . . . 6P 207
Market Hall N22 . . . 26Qb 50
Market Hill SE18 . . . 48Qc 94
Market Ho. SL9: Chal P . . . 25A 42
Market La. HA8: Edg . . . 25Sa 47
SL0: Iver . . . 48E 82
SL3: L'ly . . . 48E 82
W12 . . . 47Ya 88
Market Link RM1: Rom . . . 28Gd 56
Market Mdw. BR5: St M Cry . . . 70Yc 139
Market M. W1 . . . 7K 221 (46Kb 90)
Market Oak La. HP3: Hem H . . . 6A 4
Market Pde. BR1: Brom . . . 67Jc 137
(off East St.)
DA14: Sidc . . . 63Xc 139
E10 . . . 30Ec 52
(off High Rd. Leyton)
E17 . . . 27Bc 52
(off Higham Hill Rd.)
KT17: Ewe . . . 81Va 174
(off High St.)
N9 . . . 19Wb 33
(off Winchester Rd.)
N16 . . . 32Wb 71
(off Oldhill St.)
SE25 . . . 70Wb 135
TW13: Hanw . . . 62Aa 129
Market Pav. E10 . . . 34Cc 72
Market Pl. AL3: St A . . . 2B 6
DA1: Dart . . . 59Nd 119
DA6: Bex . . . 56Cd 118
EN2: Enf . . . 13Tb 33
KT1: King T . . . 68Ma 131
N2 . . . 27Fb 49
RM1: Rom . . . 29Gd 56
RM4: Abr . . . 13Xc 37
RM18: Tilb . . . 4C 122
SE16 . . . 49Wb 91
(not continuous)
SL3: Coln . . . 52E 104
SL9: Chal P . . . 25A 42
TW8: Bford . . . 52La 108
UB1: S'hall . . . 46Ba 85
W1 . . . 2B 222 (44Lb 90)
W3 . . . 46Sa 87
Market Pl., The NW11 . . . 28Eb 49
Market Rd. N7 . . . 37Nb 70
TW9: Rich . . . 55Qa 109
Market Row SW9 . . . 56Qb 112
Market Sq. BR1: Brom . . . 68Jc 137
(not continuous)
E14 . . . 44Dc 92
EN9: Walt A . . . 5Ec 20
GU21: Wok . . . 89A 168
KT1: King T . . . 68Ma 131
(off Market Pl.)
TN16: Westrm . . . 98Tc 200
TW18: Staines . . . 64G 126
UB8: Uxb . . . 38L 63
Market Square, The N9 . . . 19Xb 33
(within Edmonton Grn. Shop. Cen.)
Market St. DA1: Dart . . . 59Nd 119
E1 . . . 7K 219 (43Vb 91)
E6 . . . 40Pc 74
SE18 . . . 49Qc 94
SL4: Wind . . . 3H 103
WD18: Wat . . . 14X 27
Market Ter. TW8: Bford . . . 51Na 109
(off Albany Rd.)
Market Trad. Est. UB2: S'hall . . . 49X 85
Market Way E14 . . . 44Dc 92
HA0: Wemb . . . 36Na 67
TN16: Westrm . . . 98Tc 200
Market Yd. SE8 . . . 52Cc 114
Market Yd. M. SE1 . . . 3H 231 (47Ub 91)
Markfield CR0: Sels . . . 82Bc 178
(not continuous)
Markfield Beam Engine & Mus. . . . 29Wb 51
Markfield Gdns. E4 . . . 17Dc 34
Markfield Rd. CR3: Cat'm . . . 98Xb 197
N15 . . . 28Wb 51
Markham Cl. WD6: Bore . . . 12Pa 29
Markham Ho. RM10: Dag . . . 34Cd 76
(off Uvedale Rd.)
Markham Pl. SW3 . . . 7F 227 (50Hb 89)
Markhams SS17: Stan H . . . 1P 101
Markham Sq. SW3 . . . 7F 227 (50Hb 89)
Markham St. SW3 . . . 7E 226 (50Gb 89)
Markhole Cl. TW12: Hamp . . . 66Ba 129
Mark Ho. E2 . . . 40Zb 72
(off Sewardstone Rd.)
Markhouse Av. E17 . . . 30Ac 52
Markhouse Pas. E17 . . . 30Bc 52
(off Downsfield Rd.)
Markhouse Rd. E17 . . . 30Bc 52
Markland Ho. W10 . . . 45Za 88
(off Darfield Way)
Mark La. DA12: Grav'nd . . . 9G 122
(not continuous)
EC3 . . . 4J 225 (45Ub 91)
Mark Lodge EN4: Cockf . . . 14Gb 31
(off Edgeworth Rd.)
Markmanor Av. E17 . . . 31Ac 72
Mark Oak La. KT22: Fet . . . 94Ca 191
Mark Rd. HP2: Hem H . . . 1B 4
N22 . . . 26Rb 51
Marksbury Av. TW9: Rich . . . 55Qa 109
MARKS GATE . . . 25Ad 55
Mark Sq. EC2 . . . 5H 219 (42Ub 91)
Marks Rd. CR6: W'ham . . . 90Ac 178
RM7: Rom . . . 29Ed 56
(not continuous)
Marks Sq. DA11: Nflt . . . 3B 144
Markstone Ho. SE1 . . . 2B 230
Markstone T. BR6: Orp . . . 73Wc 161
Mark St. E15 . . . 38Gc 73
EC2 . . . 5H 219 (42Ub 91)
RH2: Reig . . . 5K 207
Markville Gdns. CR3: Cat'm . . . 97Wb 197
Mark Wade Cl. E12 . . . 32Mc 73
Mark Way BR8: Swan . . . 71Jd 162
Markway TW16: Sun . . . 68Y 129
Markwell Cl. SE26 . . . 63Xb 135
Markyate Ho. W10 . . . 42Ya 88
(off Sutton Way)
Markyate Rd. RM8: Dag . . . 36Xc 75
Marland Ho. SW1 . . . 3G 227
Marlands Rd. IG5: Ilf . . . 27Nc 54
Marlborough SW19 . . . 60Za 110
(off Inner Pk. Rd.)
W9 . . . 3A 214
Marlborough Av. E8 . . . 39Wb 71
(not continuous)
HA4: Ruis . . . 30S 44
HA8: Edg . . . 20Ra 29
N14 . . . 20Lb 32
Marlborough Bldgs. AL1: St A . . . 2C 6
Marlborough Bus. Cen.
KT16: Chert . . . 75H 149
Marlborough Cl. BR6: Orp . . . 72Vc 161
KT12: Hers . . . 76Z 151
N20 . . . 20Hb 31
RM14: Upm . . . 32Ud 78
RM16: Grays . . . 47Ee 99
SE17 . . . 6C 230 (49Sb 91)
SW19 . . . 65Gb 133
Marlborough Ct. CR2: S Croy . . . 77Ub 157
(off Birdhurst Rd.)
EN1: Enf . . . 15Ub 33
HA1: Harr . . . 28Fa 46
HA6: Nwood . . . 24V 44
IG9: Buck H . . . 19Lc 35
N17 . . . 25Wb 51
(off Kemble Rd.)
SM6: Wall . . . 80Lb 156
TN16: Westrm . . . 98Sc 200
(off Croydon Rd.)
W1 . . . 3B 222
W8 . . . 49Cb 89
(off Pembroke Rd.)
Marlborough Cres. TN13: S'oaks . . . 96Gd 202
UB3: Harl . . . 52T 106
W4 . . . 48Ta 87
Marlborough Dr. IG5: Ilf . . . 27Nc 54
KT13: Weyb . . . 76S 150
WD23: Bush . . . 14Ba 27
Marlborough Flats SW3 . . . 5E 226
Marlborough Gdns. KT6: Surb . . . 73Ma 153
N20 . . . 20Hb 31
RM14: Upm . . . 32Td 78
Marlborough Ga. AL1: St A . . . 2C 6
Marlborough Ga. Ho. W2 . . . 4B 220
Marlborough Gro. SE1 . . . 50Wb 91
Marlborough Hill HA1: Harr . . . 28Fa 46
NW8 . . . 1A 214 (40Eb 69)
Marlborough House . . . 7C 222 (46Lb 90)
Marlborough Ho. E16 . . . 46Jc 93
(off Hardy Av.)
UB7: W Dray . . . 47P 83
(off Park Lodge Av.)
WD23: Bush . . . 14Ca 27
Marlborough La. SE7 . . . 51Lc 115
Marlborough Lodge NW8 . . . 2A 214
Marlborough Mans. NW6 . . . 36Db 69
(off Canon Hill)
Marlborough M. SM7: Bans . . . 87Cb 175
SW2 . . . 56Pb 112

Marlborough Pde.—Matheson Rd.

Marlborough Pde. HA8: Edg 20Ra 29
(off Marlborough Av.)
UB10: Hil 42R 84
Marlborough Pk. Av.
DA15: Sidc 59Wc 117
Marlborough Pl. NW8 2A 214 (40Eb 69)
Marlborough Rd. AL1: St A 2C 6
BR2: Brom 70Lc 137
CM15: Pil H 16Wd 40
CR2: S Croy 80Sb 157
DA1: Dart 58Ld 119
DA7: Bex 55Zc 117
E4 23Dc 52
E7 38Lc 73
E15 35Gc 73
E18 26Jc 53
GU21: Wok 88C 168
N9 18Wb 33
N19 33Mb 70
N22 24Nb 50
RM7: Mawney 28Cd 56
RM8: Dag 35Xc 75
SE18 48Rc 94
SE28 48Sc 94
SL3: L'ly 9P 81
SM1: Sutt 76Cb 155
SW1 7C 222 (46Lb 90)
SW19 65Gb 133
TW7: Isle 53Ka 108
TW10: Rich 58Pa 109
TW12: Hamp 65Ca 129
TW13: Felt 61Z 129
TW15: Ashf 64M 127
UB2: S'hall 48Y 85
UB10: Hil 42R 84
W4 50Sa 87
W5 47Ma 87
WD18: Wat 14X 27
Marlborough St. SW3 6D 226 (49Gb 89)
Marlborough Yd. N19 33Mb 70
Marlbury NW8 39Db 69
(off Abbey Rd.)
Marld, The KT21: Asht 90Pa 173
Marle Gdns. EN9: Walt A 4Ec 20
Marler Ho. DA8: Erith 54Hd 118
Marler Rd. SE23 60Ac 114
Marlescroft Way IG10: Lough 15Rc 36
Marley Av. DA7: Bex 51Zc 117
Marley Cl. KT15: Add 79H 149
N15 28Rb 51
UB6: G'frd 41Ca 85
Marley Ho. E16 45Rc 94
(off University Way)
W11 45Za 88
(off St Ann's Rd.)
Marley St. SE16 49Zb 92
Marley Wlk. NW2 36Ya 68
Marl Fld. Cl. KT4: Wor Pk 74Wa 154
Marlin Cl. TW16: Sun 65U 128
Marling Ct. TW12: Hamp 65Ba 129
Marlingdene Cl. TW12: Hamp 65Ca 129
MARLING PARK 66Ba 129
Marlings Cl. BR7: Chst 70Uc 138
CR3: Whyt 89Ub 177
Marlings Pk. Av. BR7: Chst 70Uc 138
Marling Way DA12: Grav'nd 5G 144
Marlin Ho. WD18: Wat 16T 26
Marlin Pk. TW14: Felt 57X 107
Marlins, The HA6: Nwood 22V 44
Marlins Cl. SM1: Sutt 78Eb 155
WD3: Chor 12G 24
Marlins Mdw. WD18: Wat 16T 26
Marlin Sq. WD5: Ab L 3V 12
Marloes Cl. HA0: Wemb 35Ma 67
Marloes Rd. W8 48Db 89
Marlow Av. RM19: Purf 49Qd 97
Marlow Cl. SE20 69Xb 135
Marlow Ct. N14 17Lb 32
NW6 38Za 68
NW9 27Va 48
Marlow Cres. TW1: Twick 58Ha 108
Marlow Dr. SM3: Cheam 75Za 154
Marlowe Cl. BR7: Chst 65Tc 138
DA11: Nflt 61De 143
IG6: Ilf 25Sc 54
Marlowe Ct. SE19 64Vb 135
SW3 6E 226
Marlowe Gdns. RM3: Rom 25Ld 57
SE9 58Qc 116
Marlowe Ho. IG8: Wfd G 24Qc 54
KT1: King T 70Ma 131
(off Portsmouth Rd.)
Marlowe Path SE8 51Cc 114
Marlowe Rd. E17 28Ec 52
Marlowes HP1: Hem H 2M 3
Marlowes, The DA1: Cray 56Fd 118
NW8 39Fb 69
Marlowes Cen., The HP1: Hem H 3M 3
Marlowe Sq. CR4: Mitc 70Lb 134
Marlowe Way CR0: Bedd 75Nb 156
Marlow Gdns. UB3: Harl 48T 84
Marlow Ho. E2 4K 219
KT5: Surb 71Na 153
(off Cranes Pk.)
SE1 3K 231
TW11: Tedd 63Ja 130
W2 44Db 89
(off Hallfield Est.)
Marlow Rd. E6 41Pc 94
SE20 69Xb 135
UB2: S'hall 48Ba 85
Marlow Way SE16 47Zb 92
Marlow Workshops E2 4K 219
Marlpit Av. CR5: Coul 89Nb 176
Marlpit La. CR5: Coul 88Mb 176
Marl Rd. SW18 56Eb 111
Marlston NW1 4A 216
Marlton St. SE10 50Hc 93
Marlu Ct. SE14 53Zb 114
(off Hatcham Pk. M.)
Marlu Ho. SE14 53Zb 114
(off Hatcham Pk. M.)
Marlwood Cl. DA15: Sidc 61Uc 138
Marlyon Rd. IG6: Ilf 22Xc 55
Marmadon Rd. SE18 49Vc 95
Marmara Apartments E16 45Jc 93
(off Western Gateway)
Marmion App. E4 21Cc 52
Marmion Av. E4 21Bc 52
Marmion Cl. E4 21Bc 52
Marmion M. SW11 55Jb 112
Marmion Rd. SW11 56Jb 112
Marmont Rd. SE15 53Wb 113
Marmora Rd. SE22 58Yb 114
Marmot Rd. TW4: Houn 55Z 107
Marncrest Cl. KT12: Hers 78X 151
Marne Av. DA16: Well 55Wc 117
N11 21Kb 50
Marnell Way TW4: Houn 55Z 107
Marner Point E3 42Ec 92
Marne St. W10 41Ab 88
Marney Rd. SW11 56Jb 112
Marneys Cl. KT18: Eps 87Qa 173
Marnfield Cres. SW2 60Qb 112
Marnham Av. NW2 35Ab 68
Marnham Ct. HA0: Wemb 36La 66
Marnham Cres.
UB6: G'frd 41Da 85
Marnham Pl. KT15: Add 77L 149
Marnham Ri. HP1: Hem H 1J 3
Marnock Ho. SE17 7F 231
Marnock Rd. SE4 57Bc 114
Maroon St. E14 43Ac 92
Maroons Way SE6 64Cc 136
Marqueen Ct. W8 47Db 89
(off Kensington Chu. St.)
Marqueen Towers SW16 66Pb 134
Marquess Hgts. E18 25Kc 53
Marquess Rd. N1 37Tb 71
Marquis Cl. HA0: Wemb 38Pa 67
Marquis Ct. IG11: Bark 36Uc 74
KT1: King T 70Ma 131
(off Anglesea Rd.)
KT19: Eps 85Ta 173
N4 32Pb 70
(off Marquis Rd.)
TW19: Stanw 60N 105
Marquis Rd. N4 32Pb 70
N22 23Pb 50
NW1 37Mb 70
Marrabon Cl. DA15: Sidc 60Wc 117
Marram Ct. RM17: Grays 1A 122
Marrick Cl. SW15 56Wa 110
Marrick Ho. NW6 39Db 69
(off Mortimer Cres.)
Marriett Ho. SE6 63Ec 136
Marrilyne Av. EN3: Enf L 10Bc 20
Marriner Ct. UB3: Hayes 45U 84
(off Barra Hall Rd.)
Marriott Cl. TW14: Felt 58T 106
Marriott Ter. WD3: Chor 14H 25
Marriott Lodge Cl.
KT15: Add 77L 149
Marriott Rd. DA1: Dart 59Pd 119
E15 39Gc 73
EN5: Barn 13Za 30
N4 32Pb 70
N10 25Hb 49
Marriotts Cl. NW9 30Va 48
Marriotts Way HP3: Hem H 4M 3
Marriotts Wharf DA11: Grav'nd 7D 122
Mar Rd. RM15: S Ock 42Yd 98
Marrowells KT13: Weyb 76V 150
Marryat Cl. TW4: Houn 56Ba 107
Marryat Ho. SW1 7B 228
Marryat Pl. SW19 63Ab 132
Marryat Rd. EN1: Enf 7Xb 19
SW19 64Za 132
Marryat Sq. SW6 53Ab 110
Marsala Rd. SE13 56Dc 114
Marsalis Ho. E3 41Cc 92
(off Rainhill Way)
Marsden Gdns. DA1: Dart 54Pd 119
Marsden Rd. N9 19Xb 33
SE15 55Vb 113
Marsden St. NW5 37Jb 70
Marsden Way BR6: Orp 77Vc 161
Marshall Bldg. W2 1B 220
Marshall Cl. CR2: Sande 85Wb 177
CR3: Cat'm 96Sb 197
HA1: Harr 31Fa 66
SW18 58Eb 111
TW4: Houn 57Ba 107
Marshall Ct. NW6 38Za 68
(off Coverdale Rd.)
SE20 66Xb 135
(off Anerley Pk.)
Marshall Dr. UB4: Hayes 43V 84
Marshall Est. NW7 21Wa 48
Marshall Ho. N1 1G 219
SE1 4J 231
SE17 7F 231
Marshall Pde. GU22: Pyr 87H 169
Marshall Path SE28 45Xc 95
Marshall Pl. KT15: New H 81L 169
Marshall Rd. E10 34Dc 72
N17 25Tb 51
Marshalls Cl. KT19: Eps 85Sa 173
N11 21Kb 50
Marshalls Ct. AL1: St A 1F 6
Marshalls Dr. RM1: Rom 27Gd 56
Marshalls Gro. SE18 49Nc 94
Marshall's Pl. SE16 4K 231 (48Vb 91)
Marshall's Rd. SM1: Sutt 77Db 155
Marshalls Rd. RM7: Rom 28Fd 56
Marshall St. NW10 38Ta 67
W1 3C 222 (44Lb 90)
Marshall Street Leisure Cen.
3C 222 (44Lb 90)
Marshalsea Rd. SE1 1E 230 (47Sb 91)
Marshalswick La. AL1: St A 1F 6
Marsham Cl. BR7: Chst 64Rc 138
Marsham Ct. SW1 5E 228 (49Mb 90)
Marsham La. SL9: Ger X 30A 42
Marsham Lodge SL9: Ger X 30A 42
Marsham St. SW1 4E 228 (48Mb 90)
Marsham Way SL9: Ger X 29A 42
Marsh Av. CR4: Mitc 68Hb 133
KT19: Ewe 82Ua 174
Marshbrook Cl. SE3 55Mc 115
Marsh Cen., The E1 2K 225
Marsh Cl. EN8: Walt C 5Ac 20
KT15: Add 77K 149
NW7 20Va 30
Marsh Ct. E8 37Wb 71
SW19 67Eb 133
Marshcroft Dr. EN8: Chesh 2Ac 20
Marsh Dr. NW9 30Va 48
Marshe Cl. EN6: Pot B 4Fb 17
Marsh Farm Rd. TW2: Twick 60Ha 108
Marshfield SL3: Dat 3N 103
Marshfield St. E14 48Ec 92
Marshfoot Ct. RM15: Avel 45Td 98
Marshfoot Rd. RM16: Grays 10C 100
RM17: Grays 10A 100
Marshgate Bus. Cen. E15 39Ec 72
Marshgate La. E15 40Ec 72
E20 38Cc 72
Marshgate Path SE28 48Sc 94
Marsh Grn. Rd.
RM10: Dag 39Cd 76
Marsh Hall HA9: Wemb 34Pa 67
Marsh Hill E9 36Ac 72
Marsh Ho. SW1 50Mb 90
(off Aylesford St.)
SW8 53Lb 112
Marsh La. E10 33Bc 72
HA7: Stan 22La 46
KT15: Add 77K 149
N17 24Xb 51
NW7 20Ua 30
MARSHMOOR 4E 8
Marshmoor Cres. AL9: Wel G 4F 8
Marshmoor La. AL9: Wel G 4E 8
Marsh Rd. HA0: Wemb 41Ma 87
HA5: Pinn 28Aa 45
Marshside Cl. N9 18Yb 34
Marsh St. DA1: Dart 55Qd 119
(Bob Dunn Way, not continuous)
DA1: Dart 57Pd 119
(Hilltop Gdns.)
E14 49Dc 92
Marsh St. Nth. DA1: Dart 55Qd 119
Marsh Vw. DA12: Grav'nd 10H 123
Marsh Wall E14 46Cc 92
Marsh Way RM13: Rain 41Fd 96
Marshwood Ho. NW6 39Cb 69
(off Kilburn Vale)
Marshwood Rd. GU18: Light 3B 166
Marsland Cl. SE17 7C 230 (50Rb 91)
Marsom Ho. N1 2F 219
Marston KT19: Eps 83Sa 173
Marston Av. KT9: Chess 79Na 153
RM10: Dag 33Cd 76
Marston Cl. HP3: Hem H 3A 4
NW6 38Eb 69
RM10: Dag 34Cd 76
Marston Ct. DA9: Ghithe 56Wd 120
KT12: Walt T 74X 151
Marston Dr. CR6: W'ham 90Ac 178
Marston Ho. SW9 54Qb 112
Marston Rd. GU21: Wok 9M 167
IG5: Ilf 25Nc 54
TW11: Tedd 64Ka 130
Marston Way SE19 66Rb 135
Marsworth Av. HA5: Pinn 25Z 45
Marsworth Cl. UB4: Yead 43Aa 85
WD18: Wat 16U 26
Marsworth Ho. E2 39Wb 71
(off Whiston Rd.)
HA0: Wemb 39Na 67
Martaban Rd. N16 33Vb 71
Martara M. SE17 7D 230 (50Sb 91)
Marta Rose Ct. SE20 68Xb 135
(off Wadhurst Cl.)
Martello Cl. RM17: Grays 51Fe 121
Martello St. E8 38Xb 71
Martello Ter. E8 38Xb 71
Martell Rd. SE21 62Tb 135
Martel Pl. E8 37Vb 71
Marten Rd. E17 26Cc 52
Martens Av. DA7: Bex 56Dd 118
Martens Cl. DA7: Bex 56Ed 118
Martham Cl. IG6: Ilf 25Rc 54
SE28 45Zc 95
Martha Rd. E15 37Gc 73
Martha's Bldgs. EC1 5F 219 (42Tb 91)
Martha St. E1 44Yb 92
Marthorne Cres. HA3: Hrw W 26Fa 46
Martina Ter. IG7: Chig 22Uc 54
Martin Bowes Rd. SE9 55Pc 116
Martinbridge Trad. Est. EN1: Enf 15Wb 33
Martin Cl. AL10: Hat 2C 8
CR2: Sels 83Zb 178
CR6: W'ham 88Xb 177
N9 18Zb 34
SL4: Wind 3A 102
UB10: Uxb 40N 63
Martin Ct. AL1: St A 2C 6
(off St Peter's St.)
CR2: S Croy 78Ub 157
(off Birdhurst Rd.)
E14 47Ec 92
(off River Barge Cl.)
Martin Cres. CR0: C'don 74Qb 156
Martindale SL0: Iver 42F 82
SW14 57Sa 109
Martindale Av. BR6: Chels 78Wc 161
E16 45Jc 93
Martindale Ho. E14 45Dc 92
(off Poplar High St.)
Martin Dale Ind. Est. EN1: Enf 13Xb 33
Martindale Rd. GU21: Wok 10L 167
HP1: Hem H 1H 3
SW12 59Kb 112
TW4: Houn 55Aa 107
Martin Dene DA6: Bex 57Bd 117
Martin Dr. DA2: Dart 58Sd 120
RM13: Rain 42Kd 97
UB5: N'olt 36Ba 65
Martineau Cl. KT10: Esh 77Fa 152
Martineau Dr. TW1: Twick 56Ka 108
Martineau Est. E1 45Yb 92
Martineau Ho. SL9: Chal P 22A 42
SW1 7B 228
Martineau M. N5 35Rb 71
Martineau Rd. N5 35Rb 71
Martineau Sq. E1 45Wb 91
Martingale Cl. TW16: Sun 70W 128
Martingale Ho. E1 46Xb 91
(off Raine St.)
Martingales Cl. TW10: Ham 62Ma 131
Martin Gdns. RM8: Dag 35Yc 75
Martin Gro. SM4: Mord 69Cb 133
Martin Ho. DA2: Dart 59Sd 120
DA11: Nflt 2C 144
E3 39Bc 72
(off Old Ford Rd.)
SE1 4E 230 (48Sb 91)
SW8 52Nb 112
(off Wyvil Rd.)
Martini Dr. EN3: Enf L 9Cc 20
Martin Kinggett Gdns. RM9: Dag 39Ad 75
Martin La. EC4 4G 225 (45Tb 91)
(not continuous)
Martin Ri. DA6: Bex 57Bd 117
Martin Rd. DA2: Wilm 62Ld 141
RM8: Dag 35Yc 75
RM15: Avel 46Td 98
SL1: Slou 8J 81
Martins, The HA9: Wemb 34Pa 67
SE26 64Xb 135
Martins Cl. BR4: W W'ck 74Fc 159
BR5: St P 69Zc 139
SS17: Stan H 1M 101
WD7: R'lett 8Ga 14
Martins Ct. AL1: St A 5F 6
Martins Dr. EN8: Chesh 1Ac 20
Martinsfield Cl. IG7: Chig 21Uc 54
Martin's Mt. EN5: New Bar 14Cb 31
Martins Pl. SE28 46Uc 94
Martin St. SE28 46Uc 94
Martin's Plain SL2: Stoke P 1K 81
Martin's Rd. BR2: Brom 68Gc 137
Martins Shaw TN13: Chip 94Ed 202
Martinstown Cl. RM11: Horn 30Qd 57
Martin St. SE28 46Uc 94
Martins Wlk. N10 25Jb 50
N22 27Qb 50
SE28 46Uc 94
WD6: Bore 14Qa 29
Martinsyde GU22: Wok 89E 168
Martin Way GU21: Wok 10L 167
SM4: Mord 68Za 132
SW20 68Za 132
Martlands Ind. Est. GU22: Wok 5L 187
Martlesham N17 26Ub 51
(off Adams Rd.)
Martlesham Cl. RM12: Horn 36Ld 77
Martlesham Wlk. NW9 26Ua 48
Martlet Gro. UB5: N'olt 41Z 85
Martlett Ct. WC2 3G 223 (44Nb 90)
Martley Dr. IG2: Ilf 29Rc 54
Martock Cl. HA3: W'stone 28Ja 46
Martock Gdns. N11 22Hb 49
Marton Cl. SE6 62Cc 136
Marton Rd. N16 33Ub 71
Martynside NW9 25Va 48
Martyr Cl. AL1: St A 6B 6
MARTYR'S GREEN 92T 190
Martyr's La. GU21: Wok 84D 168
Martys Yd. NW3 35Fb 69
Marunden Grn. SL2: Slou 1D 80
Marvell Av. UB4: Hayes 43W 84
Marvell Ct. RM6: Chad H 30Xc 55
(off Quarles Pk. Rd.)
Marvell Ho. SE5 52Tb 113
(off Camberwell Rd.)
Marvels Cl. SE12 61Kc 137
Marvels La. SE12 61Kc 137
Marville Rd. SW6 52Bb 111
Marvin St. E8 37Xb 71
Marwell TN16: Westrm 98Rc 200
Marwell Cl. BR4: W W'ck 75Hc 159
RM1: Rom 29Jd 56
Marwood Cl. DA16: Well 55Xc 117
WD4: K Lan 1P 11
Marwood Dr. NW7 24Za 48
Mary Adelaide Cl. SW15 63Ua 132
Mary Ann Gdns. SE8 51Cc 114
Maryatt Av. HA2: Harr 33Da 65
Marybank SE18 49Pc 94
Mary Bayly Ho. W11 46Ab 88
(off Wilsham St.)
Mary Boast Wlk. SE5 54Tb 113
Mary Burrows Gdns.
TN15: Kems'g 89Rd 183
Mary Cl. HA7: Stan 28Pa 47
Mary Datchelor Cl. SE5 53Tb 113
Mary Datchelor Ho. SE5 53Tb 113
(off Grove La.)
Mary Drew Almshouses
TW20: Eng G 5P 125
Maryfield Cl. DA5: Bexl 62Gd 140
Mary Flux Ct. SW5 50Db 89
(off Bramham Gdns.)
Mary Grn. NW8 39Db 69
Maryhill Cl. CR8: Kenley 89Sb 177
Mary Holben Ho. SW16 64Lb 134
Mary Ho. W6 50Ya 88
(off Queen Caroline St.)
Mary Jones Ct. E14 45Cc 92
(off Garford St.)
Maryland AL10: Hat 1B 8
Maryland Ind. Est. E15 36Gc 73
Maryland Pk. E15 36Gc 73
(not continuous)
Maryland Point E15 37Gc 73
(off The Grove)
Maryland Rd. CR7: Thor H 67Rb 135
E15 36Fc 73
N22 23Pb 50
MARYLANDS INTERCHANGE 13Ee 41
Maryland Sq. E15 36Gc 73
Marylands Rd. W9 42Cb 89
(not continuous)
Maryland St. E15 36Fc 73
Maryland Wlk. N1 39Sb 71
(off Popham St.)
Maryland Way TW16: Sun 68W 128
Mary Lawrenson Pl. SE3 52Jc 115
MARYLEBONE 7J 215 (43Jb 90)
Marylebone Cricket Club 3C 214
MARYLEBONE FLYOVER
1D 220 (43Gb 89)
Marylebone Fly-Over
NW1 1C 220 (43Fb 89)
W2 1C 220 (43Fb 89)
Marylebone Gdns. TW9: Rich 56Qa 109
Marylebone High St. W1 7J 215 (43Jb 90)
Marylebone La. W1 1J 221 (43Kb 90)
Marylebone M. W1 1K 221 (43Kb 90)
Marylebone Pas. W1 2C 222 (44Lb 90)
Marylebone Rd. NW1 7E 214 (43Gb 89)
Marylebone St. W1 1J 221 (43Jb 90)
Marylee Way SE11 6J 229 (49Pb 90)
Mary Macarthur Ho. E2 41Zb 92
(off Warley St.)
RM10: Dag 34Cd 76
(off Wythenshawe Rd.)
W6 51Ab 110
Mary Morgan Ct. SL2: Slou 3H 81
Mary Neuner Rd. N8 27Pb 50
N22 27Pb 50
Maryon Gro. SE7 49Nc 94
Maryon Ho. NW6 38Eb 69
(off Goldhurst Ter.)
Maryon M. NW3 35Gb 69
Maryon Rd. SE7 49Nc 94
SE18 49Nc 94
Mary Peters Dr. UB6: G'frd 36Fa 66
Mary Pl. W11 45Ab 88
Mary Rose Cl. RM16: Chaf H 49Yd 98
TW12: Hamp 67Ca 129
Mary Rose Mall E6 43Pc 94
Mary Rose Sq. SE16 49Ac 92
(off Cary Av.)
Maryrose Way N20 18Fb 31
Marys Ct. NW1 5E 214
Mary Seacole Cl. E8 39Vb 71
Mary Seacole Ho. W6 48Wa 88
(off Invermead Cl.)
Maryside SL3: L'ly 47A 82
Mary Smith Ct. SW5 49Cb 89
(off Trebovir Rd.)
Marysmith Ho. SW1 7E 228
Mary's Ter. TW1: Twick 59Ja 108
Mary St. E16 43Hc 93
N1 1E 218 (39Sb 71)
Mary Ter. NW1 1A 216 (39Kb 70)
Maryville DA16: Well 54Vc 117
Mary Wallace Theatre
Twickenham 60Ja 108
Mary Way WD19: Wat 21Y 45
Mary Wharrie Ho. NW3 38Hb 69
(off Fellows Rd.)
Marzell Ho. W14 50Bb 89
(off North End Rd.)
Marzena Ct. TW3: Houn 58Ea 108
Masault Ct. TW9: Rich 56Na 109
(off Kew Foot Rd.)
Masbro' Rd. W14 48Za 88
Mascalls Ct. SE7 51Lc 115
Mascalls Gdns. CM14: B'wood 21Vd 58
Mascalls La. CM13: Gt War 21Vd 58
CM14: B'wood, Gt War 21Vd 58
Mascalls Rd. SE7 51Lc 115
Mascoll Path SL2: Slou 1D 80
Mascotte Rd. SW15 56Za 110
Mascotts Cl. NW2 34Xa 68
Masefield Av. HA7: Stan 22Ha 46
UB1: S'hall 45Ca 85
WD6: Bore 15Ra 29
Masefield Cl. DA8: Erith 53Hd 118
RM3: Rom 25Kd 57
Masefield Ct. CM14: W'ley 21Yd 58
EN5: New Bar 14Eb 31
KT6: Surb 73Ma 153
Masefield Cres. N14 15Lb 32
RM3: Rom 25Ld 57
Masefield Dr. RM14: Upm 31Sd 78
Masefield Gdns. E6 42Qc 94
Masefield Ho. NW6 41Cb 89
(off Stafford Rd.)
Masefield La. UB4: Yead 42X 85
Masefield Rd. DA1: Dart 57Rd 119
DA11: Nflt 62Fe 143
RM16: Grays 7A 100
TW12: Hamp 63Ba 129
Masefield Vw. BR6: Farnb 76Sc 160
Masefield Way TW19: Stanw 60P 105
Masey M. SW2 57Qb 112
Masham Ho. DA18: Erith 47Zc 95
(off Kale Rd.)
Mashie Rd. W3 44Ua 88
Mashiters Hill RM1: Rom 25Fd 56
Mashiters Wlk. RM1: Rom 27Gd 56
Maskall Cl. SW2 60Qb 112
Maskani Wlk. SW16 66Lb 134
Maskell Rd. SW17 62Eb 133
Maskelyne Cl. SW11 53Gb 111
Maslen Rd. AL4: St A 5G 6
Mason Cl. DA7: Bex 55Dd 118
E16 45Jc 93
EN9: Walt A 6Hc 21
SE16 50Wb 91
SW20 67Za 132
TW12: Hamp 67Ba 129
WD6: Bore 12Ta 29
Mason Dr. RM3: Hrld W 26Nd 57
Mason Ho. E9 38Yb 72
(off Frampton Pk. Rd.)
SE1 49Wb 91
(off Simms Rd.)
Masonic Hall Rd. KT16: Chert 72H 149
Mason Rd. IG8: Wfd G 21Gc 53
SM1: Sutt 78Db 155
Masonry Ho. SE14 53Zb 114
(off Fishers Ct.)
Mason's Arms M. W1 3A 222 (44Kb 90)
Mason's Av. CR0: C'don 76Sb 157
EC2 2F 225 (44Tb 91)
Masons Av. HA3: W'stone 28Ha 46
Mason's Bri. Rd. RH1: Redh 10B 208
Masons Ct. SL1: Slou 5C 80
Masons Grn. La. W3 42Qa 87
W5 42Qa 87
Masons Hill BR1: Brom 69Jc 137
BR2: Brom 69Kc 137
SE18 49Rc 94
Mason's Pde. EN7: G Oak 1Sb 19
Masons Pl. CR4: Mitc 67Hb 133
EC1 3C 218 (41Sb 91)
Masons Rd. EN1: Enf 8Xb 19
HP2: Hem H 1B 4
SL1: Slou 5C 80
Mason St. SE17 6G 231 (49Tb 91)
Mason's Yd. SW1 6C 222 (46Lb 90)
SW19 64Za 132
Masons Yd. EC1 3C 218 (41Rb 91)
Mason Way EN9: Walt A 5Gc 21
Massey Cl. N11 22Kb 50
Massey Ct. E6 39Lc 73
(off Florence Rd.)
Massie Rd. E8 37Wb 71
Massingberd Way SW17 63Kb 134
Massinger St. SE17 6H 231 (49Ub 91)
Massingham St. E1 42Zb 92
Masson Av. HA4: Ruis 37Y 65
Masson Ho. TW8: Bford 51Pa 109
Mast, The E16 45Sc 94
Mast Ct. SE16 49Ac 92
(off Boat Lifter Way)
Master Cl. RH8: Oxt 1J 211
Master Gunner Pl. SE18 52Nc 116
Masterman Ho. SE5 52Tb 113
(off Elmington Est.)
Masterman Rd. E6 41Nc 94
Masters Cl. SW16 65Lb 134
Masters Ct. RM2: Rom 29Kd 57
(off Academy Flds. Rd.)
Masters Dr. SE16 50Xb 91
Masters Lodge E1 44Yb 92
(off Johnson St.)
Masters St. E1 43Zb 92
Masthead Cl. DA2: Dart 56Sd 120
Mast Ho. Ter. E14 49Cc 92
(not continuous)
Mastin M. DA12: Grav'nd 8F 122
Mastmaker Ct. E14 47Cc 92
Mastmaker Rd. E14 47Cc 92
Mast Quay SE18 48Pc 94
MASWELL PARK 57Ea 108
Maswell Pk. Cres. TW3: Houn 57Ea 108
Maswell Pk. Rd. TW3: Houn 57Da 107
Matcham Ct. TW1: Twick 58Ma 109
(off Clevedon Rd.)
Matcham Rd. E11 34Gc 73
Match Ct. E3 40Cc 72
(off Blondin St.)
Matching Ct. E3 41Bc 92
(off Merchant St.)
Matchless Dr. SE18 52Qc 116
Matfield Cl. BR2: Brom 71Jc 159
Matfield Rd. DA17: Belv 51Cd 118
Matha Ct. BR1: Brom 67Lc 137
Matham Gro. SE22 56Vb 113
Matham Rd. KT8: E Mos 71Fa 152
Mathecombe Rd. SL1: Slou 7D 80
Matheson Lang Ho. SE1 2K 229
Matheson Rd. W14 49Bb 89

Mathews Av.—Meadow Rd.

Mathews Av. E6 .....40Qc 74
Mathews Pk. Av. E15 .....37Hc 73
Mathews Yd. WC2 .....3F 223 (44Nb 90)
Mathias Cl. KT18: Eps 85Sa 173
Mathieson Ct. SE1 .....2C 230
Mathisen Way SL3: Poyle 53G 104
Mathison Ho. SW10 .....52Eb 111
(off Coleridge Gdns.)
Matilda Cl. SE19 .....66Tb 135
Matilda Gdns. E3 .....40Cc 72
Matilda Ho. E1 .....46Wb 91
(off St Katherine's Way)
Matilda St. N1 .....39Pb 70
Matisse Ct. EC1 .....5F 219
Matisse Rd. TW3: Houn 55Da 107
Matlock Cl. EN5: Barn 15Za 30
SE24 .....56Sb 113
Matlock Ct. NW8 .....1A 214
SE5 .....56Tb 113
W11 .....45Cb 89
(off Kensington Pk. Rd.)
Matlock Cres. SM3: Cheam 77Ab 154
WD19: Wat 20Y 27
Matlock Gdns. RM12: Horn 34Nd 77
SM3: Cheam 77Ab 154
Matlock Pl. SM3: Cheam 77Ab 154
Matlock Rd. CR3: Cat'm 93Ub 197
E10 .....30Ec 52
Matlock St. E14 .....44Ac 92
Matlock Way KT3: N Mald 67Ta 131
Maton Ho. SW6 .....52Bb 111
(off Estcourt Rd.)
Matrimony Pl. SW8 .....54Lb 112
Matson Ct. IG8: Wfd G 24Gc 53
Matson Ho. SE16 .....48Xb 91
Matthew Arnold Cl. KT11: Cobh 86W 170
TW18: Staines 65L 127
Matthew Arnold Sports Cen. 65L 127
Matthew Cl. W10 .....42Za 88
Matthew Ct. CR4: Mitc 71Mb 156
E17 .....27Ec 52
Matthew Parker St.
SW1 .....2E 228 (47Mb 90)
Matthews Cl. HA9: Wemb 34Qa 67
RM3: Hrld W 25Pd 57
Matthews Ct. E17 .....25Cc 52
(off Chingford Rd.)
SL5: S'hill 10B 124
Matthews Gdns. CR0: New Ad 83Fc 179
Matthews Ho. E14 .....43Cc 92
(off Burgess St.)
Matthews La. TW18: Staines 63H 127
Matthews Lodge KT15: Add 77M 149
Matthews Rd. UB6: G'frd 36Fa 66
Matthews St. RH2: Reig 10J 207
SW11 .....54Hb 111
Matthews Yd. CR0: C'don 76Sb 157
(off Surrey St.)
Matthias Apartments N1 .....38Tb 71
(off Northchurch Rd.)
Matthias Ct. TW10: Rich 57Na 109
Matthias Rd. N16 .....36Ub 71
Mattison Rd. N4 .....30Qb 50
Mattock La. W5 .....46Ka 86
W13 .....46Ka 86
Maud Cashmore Way SE18 .....48Pc 94
Maud Chadburn Pl. SW4 .....58Kb 112
Maude Cres. WD24: Wat 9X 13
Maude Ho. E2 .....40Wb 71
(off Ropley St.)
Maude Rd. BR8: Hext 65Jd 140
E17 .....29Ac 52
SE5 .....53Ub 113
Maude Ter. E17 .....29Ac 52
Maud Gdns. E13 .....39Hc 73
IG11: Bark 40Vc 75
Maudlins Grn. E1 .....46Wb 91
Maud Rd. E10 .....34Ec 72
E13 .....40Hc 73
Maudslay Rd. SE9 .....55Pc 116
Maudsley Ho. TW8: Bford 50Na 87
Maud St. E16 .....43Hc 93
Maudsville Cotts. W7 .....46Ga 86
Maud Wilkes Cl. NW5 .....36Lb 70
Maugham Way W3 .....48Sa 87
Mauleverer Rd. SW2 .....57Nb 112
Maundeby Wlk. NW10 .....37Ua 68
Maunder Cl. RM16: Chaf H 49Zd 99
Maunder Rd. W7 .....46Ha 86
Maunsel St. SW1 .....5D 228 (49Mb 90)
Maureen Campbell Ct.
TW17: Shep 71R 150
(off Harrison Way)
Maureen Ct. BR3: Beck 68Yb 136
Maurer Ct. SE10 .....48Hc 93
Mauretania Bldg. E1 .....45Zb 92
(off Jardine Rd.)
Maurice Av. CR3: Cat'm 94Tb 197
N22 .....26Rb 51
Maurice Browne Av. NW7 .....23Za 48
Maurice Ct. E1 .....41Zb 92
N22 .....25Pb 50
TW8: Bford 52Ma 109
Maurice Drummond Ho. SE10 .....53Dc 114
(off Catherine Gro.)
Maurice St. W12 .....44Xa 88
Maurice Wlk. NW11 .....28Eb 49
Maurier Cl. UB5: N'olt 39Y 65
Mauritius Rd. SE10 .....49Gc 93
Maury Rd. N16 .....33Wb 71
Mausoleum
Windsor 5K 103
Mauveine Gdns. TW3: Houn 56Ca 107
Mavelstone Cl. BR1: Brom 67Nc 138
Mavelstone Rd. BR1: Brom 67Mc 137
Maverton Rd. E3 .....39Cc 72
Mavery Ct. BR1: Brom 66Hc 137
(off Bromley Av.)
Mavis Av. KT19: Ewe 78Ua 154
Mavis Cl. KT19: Ewe 78Ua 154
Mavis Gro. RM12: Horn 33Nd 77
Mavis Wlk. E6 .....43Nc 94
(off Greenwich Cres.)
Mavor Ho. N1 .....1J 217
Mawbey Gro. RM3: Rom 22Qd 57
Mawbey Ho. SE1 .....50Wb 91
Mawbey Pl. SE1 .....7K 231 (50Vb 91)
Mawbey Rd. KT16: Ott 79F 148
SE1 .....50Vb 91
Mawbey St. SW8 .....52Nb 112
Mawdley Ho. SE1 .....2A 230
MAWNEY 27Dd 56
Mawney Cl. RM7: Mawney 26Dd 56
Mawney Rd. RM7: Mawney, Rom 26Dd 56
Mawson Cl. SW20 .....68Ab 132
Mawson Ct. N1 .....1G 219
Mawson Ho. EC1 .....7K 217
Mawson La. W4 .....51Va 110
Maxden Ct. SE15 .....55Vb 113
Maxey Gdns. RM9: Dag 35Ad 75
Maxey Rd. RM9: Dag 35Ad 75
SE18 .....49Sc 94
Maxfield Cl. N20 .....17Eb 31
Maxilla Wlk. W10 .....44Za 88
Maxim Apartments BR2: Brom 70Kc 137
(off Tiger La.)
Maximfeldt Rd. DA8: Erith 50Gd 96
Maxim Rd. DA1: Cray 57Gd 118
DA8: Erith 49Gd 96
N21 .....16Qb 32
Maxin Tower RM1: Rom 28Hd 56
(off Mercury Gdns.)
Maxted Cl. HP2: Hem H 1C 4
Maxted Pk. HA1: Harr 31Ga 66
Maxted Rd. SE15 .....55Vb 113
Maxwell Cl. CR0: Wadd 74Nb 156
UB3: Hayes 45W 84
WD3: Rick 19J 25
Maxwell Ct. IG7: Chig 20Xc 37
SE22 .....60Wb 113
SW4 .....57Mb 112
Maxwell Dr. KT14: W Byf 83L 169
Maxwell Gdns. BR6: Orp 76Vc 161
Maxwell Ri. WD19: Wat 17Aa 27
Maxwell Rd. AL1: St A 3F 6
DA16: Well 55Vc 117
HA6: Nwood 24T 44
RM7: Rush G 30Gd 56
SW6 .....52Db 111
TW15: Ashf 65S 128
UB7: W Dray 49P 83
WD6: Bore 13Ra 29
Maxwells West EN8: Chesh 3Yb 20
Maxwelton Av. NW7 .....22Ta 47
Maxwelton Cl. NW7 .....22Ta 47
Maya Angelou Ct. E4 .....21Ec 52
Maya Apartments E20 .....36Ec 72
(off Victory Pde.)
Maya Cl. SE15 .....54Xb 113
Mayall Cl. EN3: Enf L 10Cc 20
Mayall Rd. SE24 .....57Rb 113
Maya Pl. N11 .....24Mb 50
Maya Rd. N2 .....28Eb 49
May Av. BR5: St M Cry 71Xc 161
DA11: Nflt 10B 122
May Av. Ind. Est. DA11: Nflt 10B 122
(off May Av.)
Maybank Av. E18 .....26Kc 53
HA0: Wemb 36Ha 66
RM12: Horn 36Kd 77
Maybank Gdns. HA5: Eastc 29W 44
Maybank Lodge RM12: Horn 36Ld 77
Maybank Rd. E18 .....25Kc 53
May Bate Av. KT2: King T 67Ma 131
Maybells Commercial Est.
IG11: Bark 40Zc 75
Mayberry Ct. BR3: Beck 66Bc 136
(off Copers Cope Rd.)
Mayberry Pl. KT5: Surb 73Pa 153
Maybourne Cl. SE26 .....65Xb 135
Maybourne Ri. GU22: Wok 6P 187
Maybrick Rd. RM11: Horn 30Ld 57
MAYBURY 88E 168
Maybury Av. DA2: Dart 60Sd 120
EN8: Chesh 1Xb 19
Maybury Cl. BR5: Pet W 71Rc 160
EN1: Enf 10Xb 19
IG10: Lough 14Rc 36
KT20: Tad 91Ab 194
SL1: Slou 4B 80
Maybury Ct. CR2: S Croy 78Rb 157
(off Haling Pk. Rd.)
HA1: Harr 30Fa 46
W1 .....1J 221
Maybury Est. GU22: Wok 88E 168
Maybury Gdns. NW10 .....37Xa 68
Maybury Hill GU22: Wok 88D 168
Maybury M. N6 .....31Lb 70
Maybury Rd. E13 .....42Lc 93
GU21: Wok 89B 168
IG11: Bark 40Vc 75
Maybury Rough GU22: Wok 89D 168
Maybury St. SW17 .....64Gb 133
Maybush Rd. RM11: Horn 31Nd 77
Maychurch Cl. HA7: Stan 24Ma 47
May Cl. AL3: St A 1B 6
KT9: Chess 79Pa 153
Maycock Gro. HA6: Nwood 23V 44
May Cotts. WD18: Wat 15Y 27
(off Lammas Rd.)
May Ct. RM17: Grays 1A 122
SW19 .....67Eb 133
(off Pincott Rd.)
Maycroft HA5: Pinn 26X 45
Maycroft Av. RM17: Grays 50Fe 99
Maycroft Gdns. RM17: Grays 50Fe 99
Maycross Av. SM4: Mord 70Bb 133
Mayday Gdns. SE3 .....54Nc 116
Mayday Rd. CR7: Thor H 72Rb 157
Maydeb Ct. RM6: Chad H 30Bd 55
Maydew Ho. SE16 .....49Yb 92
(off Abbeyfield Est.)
Maydwell Ho. E14 .....43Cc 92
(off Thomas Rd.)
Maydwell Lodge WD6: Bore 12Pa 29
Mayell Cl. KT22: Lea 95La 192
Mayerne Rd. SE9 .....57Mc 115
Mayer Rd. EN9: Walt A 8Dc 20
Mayesbrook Pk. Arena 36Wc 75
Mayesbrook Rd. IG3: Ilf 34Wc 75
IG11: Bark 39Vc 75
RM8: Dag 34Wc 75
Mayes Cl. BR8: Swan 70Jd 140
CR0: New Ad 80Fc 159
CR6: W'ham 90Zb 178
Mayesford Rd. RM6: Chad H 31Yc 75
Mayes Rd. N22 .....26Pb 50
Mayeswood Rd. SE12 .....63Lc 137
MAYFAIR 5K 221 (45Kb 90)
Mayfair Av. DA7: Bex 53Zc 117
IG1: Ilf 33Pc 74
KT4: Wor Pk 74Wa 154
RM6: Chad H 30Zc 55
TW2: Whitt 59Ea 108
Mayfair Cl. BR3: Beck 67Dc 136
KT6: Surb 74Na 153
Mayfair Ct. HA8: Edg 22Pa 47
WD18: Wat 14U 26
Mayfair Gdns. IG8: Wfd G 24Jc 53
N17 .....23Sb 51
Mayfair M. NW1 .....38Hb 69
(off Regents Pk. Rd.)
SW12 .....60Kb 112
Mayfair Pl. W1 .....6A 222 (46Kb 90)
Mayfair Rd. DA1: Dart 57Md 119
Mayfair Ter. N14 .....17Mb 32
Mayfare WD3: Crox G 15T 26
Mayfield DA7: Bex 55Bd 117
EN9: Walt A 6Fc 21
KT22: Lea 93La 192
(not continuous)
Mayfield Av. BR6: Orp 74Vc 161
HA3: Kenton 29Ka 46
IG8: Wfd G 23Jc 53
KT15: New H 82K 169
N12 .....21Eb 49
N14 .....19Mb 32
W4 .....49Ua 88
W13 .....48Ka 86
Mayfield Cvn. Pk. UB7: W Dray 48L 83
Mayfield Cl. E8 .....37Vb 71
KT7: T Ditt 74Ka 152
KT12: Hers 77W 150
KT15: New H 82L 169
SE20 .....67Xb 135
SW4 .....57Mb 112
TW15: Ashf 65R 128
UB10: Hil 41R 84
Mayfield Ct. EN9: Walt A 6Jc 21
(off Lamplighters Cl.)
RH1: Redh 10P 207
Mayfield Cres. CR7: Thor H 70Pb 134
N9 .....16Xb 33
Mayfield Dr. HA5: Pinn 28Ba 45
SL4: Wind 5E 102
Mayfield Gdns. CM14: B'wood 18Xd 40
KT12: Hers 77W 150
KT15: New H 82K 169
NW4 .....30Za 48
TW18: Staines 65H 127
W7 .....44Fa 86
Mayfield Grn. KT23: Bookh 99Ca 191
Mayfield Gro. RM13: Rain 41Ld 97
Mayfield Ho. E2 .....40Xb 71
Mayfield Mans. SW15 .....57Bb 111
Mayfield Pl. SL4: Wink 2A 124
Mayfield Rd. BR1: Brom 71Nc 160
CR2: Sande 81Tb 177
CR7: Thor H 70Pb 134
DA11: Grav'nd 9B 122
DA17: Belv 49Ed 96
E4 .....19Ec 34
E8 .....38Vb 71
E13 .....42Hc 93
E17 .....26Ac 52
EN3: Enf H 12Zb 34
KT12: Hers 77W 150
KT13: Weyb 78P 149
N8 .....29Pb 50
RM8: Dag 32Yc 75
SM2: Sutt 79Fb 155
SW19 .....67Bb 133
W3 .....45Ra 87
W12 .....47Ua 88
Mayfield Rd. Flats N8 .....30Pb 50
Mayfields DA10: Swans 58Ae 121
HA9: Wemb 33Qa 67
RM16: Grays 47Ee 99
Mayfields Cl. HA9: Wemb 33Qa 67
Mayfield Vs. DA14: Sidc 65Yc 139
Mayflower Av. HP2: Hem H 2M 3
Mayflower Cl. HA4: Ruis 30S 44
RM15: S Ock 42Yd 98
SE16 .....49Zb 92
Mayflower Ho. CM13: Gt War 23Yd 58
E14 .....47Cc 92
(off Westferry Rd.)
IG11: Bark 39Tc 74
(off Westbury Rd.)
Mayflower Path CM13: Gt War 23Yd 58
Mayflower Rd. AL2: Park 9P 5
RM16: Chaf H 50Yd 98
SW9 .....55Nb 112
Mayflower St. SE16 .....47Yb 92
Mayflower Way SL2: Farn C 6G 60
Mayfly Cl. BR5: St P 70Zc 139
HA5: Eastc 31Y 65
Mayfly Gdns. UB5: N'olt 41Z 85
MAYFORD 4N 187
Mayford NW1 .....1C 216 (40Lb 70)
(not continuous)
Mayford Cl. BR3: Beck 69Zb 136
GU22: Wok 4P 187
SW12 .....59Hb 111
Mayford Grn. GU22: Wok 4N 187
Mayford Meadows Local Nature Reserve
.....4P 187
Mayford Rd. SW12 .....59Hb 111
May Gdns. HA0: Wemb 41La 86
WD6: E'tree 16Ma 29
Maygood Ho. N1 .....1K 217
Maygoods Cl. UB8: Cowl 43M 83
Maygoods Grn. UB8: Cowl 43M 83
Maygoods La. UB8: Cowl 43M 83
Maygood St. N1 .....1K 217 (40Qb 70)
Maygoods Vw. UB8: Cowl 43L 83
Maygreen Cres. RM11: Horn 31Jd 76
Maygrove Rd. NW6 .....37Bb 69
Mayhew Cl. E4 .....20Cc 34
Mayhew Ct. SE5 .....56Tb 113
Mayhill Ct. SE15 .....52Ub 113
(off Tower Mill Rd.)
Mayhill Rd. EN5: Barn 16Ab 30
SE7 .....51Kc 115
May Ho. E3 .....40Cc 72
(off Thomas Fyre Dr.)
Mayhurst Av. GU22: Wok 88E 168
Mayhurst Cl. GU22: Wok 88E 168
Mayhurst Cres. GU22: Wok 88E 168
Mayhurst M. GU22: Wok 88E 168
Mayland Mans. IG11: Bark 38Rc 74
(off Whiting Av.)
Maylands Av. HP2: Hem H 1B 4
RM12: Horn 35Kd 77
Maylands Ct. HP2: Hem H 1B 4
Maylands Dr. DA14: Sidc 62Zc 139
UB8: Uxb 37M 63
Maylands Golf Course 22Rd 57
Maylands Ho. SW3 .....6E 226
Maylands Rd. WD19: Wat 21Y 45
Maylands Way RM3: Hrld W 23Sd 58
May La. HA3: Kenton 31Pa 67
Maylie Ho. SE16 .....47Xb 91
(off Marigold St.)
Maynard Cl. DA8: Erith 52Hd 118
N15 .....29Ub 51
SW6 .....52Db 111
Maynard Ct. EN3: Enf L 10Cc 20
EN9: Walt A 6Hc 21
SL4: Wind 3E 102
TW18: Staines 63J 127
Maynard Dr. AL1: St A 5B 6
Maynard Path E17 .....29Ec 52
Maynard Pl. EN6: Cuff 1Pb 18
Maynard Rd. E17 .....29Ec 52
HP2: Hem H 3M 3
Maynards RM11: Horn 31Nd 77
Maynards Quay E1 .....45Yb 92
Mayne Av. AL3: St A 4M 5
Mayne Ct. SE26 .....64Xb 135
Maynooth Gdns. SM5: Cars 73Hb 155
Mayo Ct. W13 .....48Ka 86
Mayo Gdns. HP1: Hem H 3K 3
Mayo Ho. E1 .....43Yb 92
(off Lindley St.)
Mayola Rd. E5 .....35Yb 72
Mayo Rd. CR0: C'don 71Tb 157
KT12: Walt T 73W 150
NW10 .....37Ua 68
Mayor's & City of London Court, The
.....2F 225
Mayor's La. DA2: Wilm 63Ld 141
Mayow Rd. SE23 .....63Zb 136
SE26 .....63Zb 136
Mayplace Av. DA1: Cray 56Jd 118
Mayplace Cl. DA7: Bex 55Dd 118
Mayplace La. SE18 .....51Rc 116
(not continuous)
Mayplace Rd. E. DA1: Cray 55Ed 118
DA7: Bex 55Dd 118
Mayplace Rd. W. DA7: Bex 56Cd 118
MAYPOLE
BR6 .....79Cd 162
DA5 .....60Gd 118
Maypole Ct. UB2: S'hall 47Ba 85
(off Merrick Rd.)
Maypole Cres. DA8: Erith 51Md 119
IG6: Ilf 24Tc 54
Maypole Dr. IG7: Chig 20Wc 37
Maypole Rd. BR6: Chels, Well H 78Bd 161
DA12: Grav'nd 10H 123
May Rd. DA2: Hawl 63Pd 141
E4 .....23Cc 52
E13 .....40Jc 73
TW2: Twick 60Ga 108
Mayroyd Av. KT6: Surb 75Qa 153
May's Bldgs. M. SE10 .....52Ec 114
Mays Cl. KT13: Weyb 82P 169
May's Ct. SE10 .....52Fc 115
Mays Ct. WC2 .....5F 223 (45Nb 90)
Maysfield Rd. GU23: Send 95F 188
MAY'S GREEN 92U 190
Mays Gro. GU23: Send 95F 188
Mays Hill Rd. BR2: Brom 68Gc 137
Mays La. EN5: Ark, Barn 17Xa 30
Maysoule Rd. SW11 .....56Fb 111
Mays Rd. TW11: Tedd 64Fa 130
Mayston M. SE10 .....50Jc 93
(off Ormiston Rd.)
May St. W14 .....50Bb 89
(Kelway Ho.)
W14 .....50Bb 89
(Orchard Sq.)
Mayswood Gdns. RM10: Dag 37Ed 76
Maythorne Cl. WD18: Wat 14U 26
Maythorne Cotts. SE13 .....57Fc 115
Mayton St. N7 .....34Pb 70
Maytree Cl. HA8: Edg 20Sa 29
RM13: Rain 40Gd 76
Maytree Ct. CR4: Mitc 69Jb 134
UB5: N'olt 41Aa 85
Maytree Cres. WD24: Wat 7V 12
Maytree Gdns. W5 .....47Ma 87
May Tree Ho. SE4 .....55Bc 114
(off Wickham Rd.)
Maytree La. HA7: Stan 24Ja 46
Maytrees GU21: Knap 9G 166
WD7: R'lett 9Ja 14
Maytree Wlk. SW2 .....61Qb 134
Mayville Est. N16 .....36Ub 71
Mayville Rd. E11 .....33Gc 73
(not continuous)
IG1: Ilf 36Rc 74
May Wlk. E13 .....40Kc 73
Mayward Ho. SE5 .....53Ub 113
(off Peckham Rd.)
Maywater Cl. CR2: Sande 83Tb 177
Maywin Dr. RM11: Horn 32Pd 77
Maywood Cl. BR3: Beck 66Dc 136
May Wynne Ho. E16 .....45Kc 93
(off Murray Sq.)
Maze Hill SE3 .....52Hc 115
SE10 .....51Gc 115
Maze Hill Lodge SE10 .....51Fc 115
(off Park Vista)
Mazenod Av. NW6 .....38Cb 69
Maze Rd. TW9: Kew 52Qa 109
MCC Cricket Mus. & Tours
.....4B 214 (41Fb 89)
Mead, The BR3: Beck 67Ec 136
BR4: W W'ck 74Fc 159
DA3: Nw A G 75Ae 165
EN8: Chesh 1Yb 20
KT21: Asht 91Na 193
N2 .....26Eb 49
SM6: Wall 79Mb 156
UB10: Ick 33Q 64
W13 .....43Ka 86
WD19: Wat 20Aa 27
Mead Av. SL3: L'ly 47D 82
Meadbank Studios SW11 .....52Gb 111
(off Parkgate Rd.)
Mead Cl. BR8: Swan 71Jd 162
HA3: Hrw W 25Fa 46
IG10: Lough 12Rc 36
NW1 .....37Jb 70
RH1: Redh 3A 208
RM2: Rom 26Jd 56
RM16: Grays 47De 99
SL3: L'ly 47D 82
TW20: Egh 65D 126
UB9: Den 33J 63
Mead Ct. EN9: Walt A 6Dc 20
GU21: Knap 8J 167
NW9 .....29Sa 47
TW20: Egh 65E 126
Mead Cres. DA1: Dart 60Md 119
E4 .....21Ec 52
KT23: Bookh 97Ca 191
SM1: Sutt 76Gb 155
Meadcroft Rd. SE11 .....51Rb 113
(not continuous)
SE17 .....51Rb 113
Meade Cl. W4 .....51Qa 109
Meade Ct. KT20: Walt H 96Wa 194
Meade M. SW1 .....7E 228
(off Causton St.)
Mead End KT21: Asht 89Pa 173
Meader Ct. SE14 .....52Zb 114
Meades, The KT13: Weyb 79S 150
Meadfarm Cl. RM3: Rom 22Nd 57
Mead Fld. HA2: Harr 34Ba 65
Meadfield HA8: Edg 19Ra 29
(not continuous)
Meadfield Av. SL3: L'ly 47C 82
Meadfield Grn. HA8: Edg 19Ra 29
Meadfield Rd. SL3: L'ly 48C 82
Meadfoot Rd. SW16 .....66Lb 134
Meadgate Av. IG8: Wfd G 22Nc 54
Mead Gro. RM6: Chad H 27Zc 55
Mead Ho. SL0: Iver H 41F 82
W11 .....46Bb 89
(off Ladbroke Rd.)
Mead Ho. La. UB4: Hayes 42T 84
Meadhurst Club 64V 128
Meadhurst Pk. TW16: Sun 65U 128
Meadhurst Rd. KT16: Chert 74K 149
Meadlands Dr. TW10: Ham 61Ma 131
Mead La. KT16: Chert 73K 149
Mead Lodge W4 .....47Ta 87
Meadow, The BR7: Chst 65Sc 138
N10 .....27Jb 50
Meadow Av. CR0: C'don 72Zb 158
WD7: Shenl 3La 14
Meadow Bank KT24: E Hor 99V 190
N21 .....16Pb 32
Meadowbank KT5: Surb 72Pa 153
NW3 .....38Hb 69
SE3 .....55Hc 115
WD4: K Lan 2Q 12
WD19: Wat 17Y 27
Meadow Bank Cl. TN15: W King 81Vd 184
Meadowbank Cl. HP3: Bov 10D 2
SW6 .....52Ya 110
TW7: Isle 53Ga 108
Meadowbank Gdns. TW5: Cran 53W 106
Meadowbank Rd. GU18: Light 2A 166
NW9 .....31Ta 67
Meadowbanks EN5: Ark 15Wa 30
Meadowbridge Ct. CR0: C'don 71Tb 157
(off Princess Rd.)
Meadowbrook RH8: Oxt 2G 210
Meadowbrook Cl. SL3: Poyle 53H 105
Meadowbrook Ct. TW7: Isle 55Ga 108
Meadow Cl. AL2: Brick W 1Ca 13
AL2: Lon C 9H 7
AL9: Wel G 6F 8
BR7: Chst 64Rc 138
CR8: Purl 85Mb 176
DA6: Bex 57Bd 117
E4 .....18Dc 34
E9 .....37Bc 72
EN3: Enf W 10Ac 20
EN5: Barn 16Bb 31
HA4: Ruis 30V 44
IG11: Bark 38Wc 75
KT10: Hin W 76Ha 152
KT12: Hers 77Ba 151
RM3: Rom 20Ld 39
SE6 .....64Cc 136
SL4: Old Win 7M 103
SM1: Sutt 75Eb 155
SS17: Linf 8J 101
SW20 .....70Ya 132
TN13: S'oaks 95Jd 202
TW4: Houn 58Ca 107
TW10: Ham 60Na 109
UB5: N'olt 40Ca 65
WD7: Shenl 2La 14
Meadow Cotts. GU24: W End 4D 166
Meadow Ct. E16 .....46Lc 93
(off Booth Rd.)
KT18: Eps 85Sa 173
N1 .....1H 219 (40Ub 71)
RH1: Mers 2C 208
TW3: Houn 58Da 107
TW18: Staines 62G 126
Meadowcourt Rd. SE3 .....56Hc 115
Meadow Cft. TW18: Staines 65G 126
(off Bowes Rd.)
Meadowcroft AL1: St A 5E 6
BR1: Brom 69Pc 138
SL9: Chal P 26A 42
W4 .....50Qa 87
(off Brooks Rd.)
WD23: Bush 16Da 27
Meadowcroft Cl. E10 .....31Dc 72
N13 .....19Qb 32
Meadowcroft M. E1 .....45Wb 91
(off Cable St.)
SE6 .....58Dc 114
Meadowcroft Rd. N13 .....19Qb 32
Meadow Cross EN9: Walt A 6Gc 21
Meadow Dr. GU23: Rip 95H 189
HP3: Bov 10B 2
N10 .....27Kb 50
NW4 .....26Ya 48
RM15: Avel 45Td 98
Meadowford Cl. SE28 .....45Wc 95
Meadow Gdns. HA8: Edg 23Ra 47
TW18: Staines 64F 126
Meadow Gth. NW10 .....37Sa 67
Meadow Ga. HA2: Harr 34Da 65
KT21: Asht 89Na 173
Meadowgate Cl. NW7 .....22Va 48
Meadow Hill CR5: Coul 86Lb 176
CR8: Purl 86Lb 176
KT3: N Mald 72Ua 154
Meadowlands KT11: Cobh 85W 170
RH8: Oxt 6L 211
RM11: Horn 31Nd 77
TN15: Seal 92Pd 203
Meadowlands Pk. KT15: Add 76N 149
Meadow La. DA3: Nw A G 75Be 165
KT22: Fet 94Ea 192
SE12 .....62Kc 137
SL4: Eton, Eton W 1F 102
Meadowlark Ho. NW9 .....31Va 68
Meadowlea Cl. UB7: Harm 51M 105
Meadow M. SW8 .....51Pb 112
Meadow Pk. 12Ra 29
Meadow Pl. SW8 .....52Nb 112
W4 .....52Ua 110
Meadow Ri. CR5: Coul 85Mb 176
GU21: Knap 9G 166
Meadow Rd. BR2: Brom 68Gc 137
CM16: Epp 1Vc 23
DA11: Grav'nd 1C 144
GU25: Vir W 1J 147
HA5: Pinn 28Z 45
HP3: Hem H 6A 4
IG10: Lough 15Nc 36
IG11: Bark 38Vc 75
KT10: Clay 79Ga 152
KT21: Asht 89Na 173
RM7: Rush G 32Ed 76
RM9: Dag 37Bd 75
RM16: Grays 46Ee 99
SL3: L'ly 48A 82

Meadow Rd.—Mereside Pl.

Meadow Rd. SM1: Sutt ... 77Gb 155
SW8 ... 52Pb 112
SW19 ... 66Eb 133
TW13: Felt ... 61Aa 129
TW15: Ashf ... 64T 128
UB1: S'hall ... 45Ba 85
WD6: Bore ... 12Ra 29
WD23: Bush ... 15Da 27
WD25: Wat ... 6W 12
Meadow Row SE1 ... 4D 230 (48Sb 91)
Meadows, The BR6: Chels ... 79Yc 161
CM13: Ingve ... 23Ee 59
CR6: W'ham ... 89Zb 178
E4 ... 21Fc 53
EN6: S Mim ... 5Wa 16
HP1: Hem H ... 1G 2
TN14: Hals ... 85Bd 181
WD25: Wat ... 8Z 13
Meadows Cl. CM13: Ingve ... 23Ee 59
E10 ... 33Cc 72
Meadows Ct. DA14: Sidc ... 65Xc 139
Meadows End TW16: Sun ... 67W 128
Meadows Ho.
KT12: Walt T ... 74W 150
Meadowside DA1: Dart ... 60Md 119
KT12: Walt T ... 75Y 151
KT23: Bookh ... 95Ca 191
SE3 ... 56Lc 115
SE9 ... 56Lc 115
TW1: Twick ... 59Ma 109
TW18: Staines ... 64J 127
WD25: Wat ... 3X 13
Meadowside Rd.
RM14: Upm ... 36Sd 78
SM2: Cheam ... 81Ab 174
Meadows Leigh Cl.
KT13: Weyb ... 76R 150
Meadow Stile CR0: C'don ... 76Sb 157
Meadows Way SE4 ... 55Ac 114
Meadowsweet Cl. E16 ... 43Mc 93
SW20 ... 70Ya 132
Meadow Vw. BR5: St P ... 69Yc 139
CM16: Epp ... 1Wc 23
DA15: Sidc ... 59Xc 117
GU22: Wok ... 93B 188
(not continuous)
HA1: Harr ... 32Ga 66
KT16: Chert ... 74L 149
SL3: L'ly ... 46B 82
TN13: Dun G ... 90Fd 182
UB8: Cowl ... 43L 83
Meadowview
TW19: Stanw M ... 57H 105
Meadow Vw. Rd.
CR7: Thor H ... 71Rb 157
SW20 ... 70Ya 132
UB4: Hayes ... 42T 84
Meadowview Rd.
DA5: Bexl ... 58Ad 117
KT19: Ewe ... 81Ua 174
SE6 ... 64Bc 136
Meadow Wlk. DA2: Wilm ... 63Ld 141
(not continuous)
E18 ... 28Jc 53
KT17: Ewe ... 80Va 154
KT19: Ewe ... 79Ua 154
KT20: Walt H ... 96Xa 194
RM9: Dag ... 37Bd 75
SM6: Wall ... 76Kb 156
Meadow Walks
EN5: New Bar ... 16Db 31
Meadow Way BR6: Farnb ... 76Qc 160
DA2: Dart ... 59Sd 120
EN6: Pot B ... 6Cb 17
GU24: W End ... 4D 166
HA4: Ruis ... 30X 45
HA9: Wemb ... 35Ma 67
HP3: Hem H ... 5H 3
IG7: Chig ... 20Sc 36
KT9: Chess ... 78Na 153
KT15: Add ... 77K 149
KT20: Tad ... 89Ab 174
KT23: Bookh ... 95Da 191
KT24: W Hor ... 97T 190
NW9 ... 29Ta 47
RH2: Reig ... 10K 207
RM14: Upm ... 34Sd 78
SL4: Old Win ... 8M 103
WD3: Rick ... 17L 25
WD4: K Lan ... 2Q 12
WD5: Bedm ... 9F 4
Meadow Way, The
HA3: Hrw W ... 25Ga 46
Meadow Waye TW5: Hest ... 51Aa 107
Mead Path SW17 ... 63Eb 133
Mead Pl. CR0: C'don ... 74Sb 157
E9 ... 37Yb 72
WD3: Rick ... 18K 25
Mead Plat NW10 ... 37Sa 67
Mead Rd. BR7: Chst ... 65Sc 138
CR3: Cat'm ... 95Vb 197
DA1: Dart ... 60Md 119
DA11: Grav'nd ... 1D 144
HA8: Edg ... 23Qa 47
KT12: Hers ... 77Aa 151
TW10: Ham ... 62La 130
UB8: Uxb ... 38M 63
WD7: Shenl ... 5Qa 15
Mead Row SE1 ... 3K 229 (48Qb 90)
Meads, The AL2: Brick W ... 1Ba 13
HA8: Edg ... 23Ta 47
RM14: Upm ... 33Ud 78
SL4: Wind ... 4E 102
SM3: Cheam ... 76Ab 154
SM4: Mord ... 71Gb 155
UB8: Cowl ... 42N 83
Meads Ct. E15 ... 37Hc 73
Meadside *GU22: Wok* ... *90B 168*
(off Park Dr.)
KT18: Eps ... *86Ta 173*
(off South St.)
Meadside Cl. BR3: Beck ... 67Ac 136
Meads La. IG3: Ilf ... 31Uc 74
Meads Rd. EN3: Enf H ... 11Ac 34
N22 ... 26Rb 51
Meadsway CM13: Gt War ... 23Xd 58
Mead Ter. HA9: Wemb ... 35Ma 67
MEAD VALE ... 8M 207
Meadvale Rd.
CR0: C'don ... 73Vb 157
W5 ... 42Ka 86
Mead Wlk. SL3: L'ly ... 47D 82
Mead Way BR2: Hayes ... 72Hc 159
CR0: C'don ... 75Ac 158
CR5: Coul ... 90Nb 176
HA4: Ruis ... 30T 44
SL1: Slou ... 3B 80
WD23: Bush ... 12Aa 27
Meadway AL4: Col H ... 5P 7
BR3: Beck ... 67Ec 136
CR6: W'ham ... 88Yb 178
EN3: Enf W ... 8Yb 20
EN5: Barn, New Bar ... 14Cb 31
HP4: Berk ... 1A 2
IG3: Bark, Ilf ... 35Uc 74
IG8: Wfd G ... 22Lc 53
KT5: Surb ... 74Sa 153
KT10: Esh ... 81Da 171
KT19: Eps ... 84Sa 173
KT22: Oxs ... 86Ga 172
KT24: Eff ... 100Aa 191
N14 ... 19Mb 32
NW11 ... 30Cb 49
RM2: Rom ... 26Jd 56
RM17: Grays ... 49Fe 99
SW20 ... 70Ya 132
TN14: Hals ... 85Bd 181
TW2: Twick ... 60Fa 108
TW15: Ashf ... 63Q 128
TW18: Staines ... 66J 127
Meadway, The BR6: Chels ... 78Xc 161
EN6: Cuff ... 1Pb 18
IG9: Buck H ... 18Mc 35
IG10: Lough ... 16Pc 36
SE3 ... 54Fc 115
TN13: S'oaks ... 94Hd 202
Meadway Cl. EN5: Barn ... 14Cb 31
HA5: Hat E ... 23Da 45
NW11 ... 30Db 49
TW18: Staines ... 66H 127
Meadway Ct. RM8: Dag ... 33Bd 75
TW11: Tedd ... 64La 130
W5 ... 42Pa 87
Meadway Dr. GU21: Wok ... 8N 167
KT15: Add ... 80L 149
Meadway Gdns. HA4: Ruis ... 30T 44
Meadway Ga. NW11 ... 30Cb 49
Meadway Pk. SL9: Ger X ... 2P 61
Mead Way Path CR5: Coul ... 90Pb 176
Meaford Way SE20 ... 66Xb 135
Meakin Est. SE1 ... 3H 231 (48Ub 91)
Meander Ho. *E20* ... *36Dc 72*
(off Logan Cl.)
Meanley Rd. E12 ... 35Nc 74
Meard St. W1 ... 3D 222 (44Mb 90)
(not continuous)
Meare Cl. KT20: Tad ... 95Ya 194
Mears Cl. *E1* ... *43Wb 91*
(off Settles St.)
Meath Cl. BR5: St M Cry ... 71Xc 161
Meath Cres. E2 ... 41Zb 92
Meath Ho. *SE24* ... *58Rb 113*
(off Dulwich Rd.)
Meath Rd. E15 ... 40Hc 73
IG1: Ilf ... 34Sc 74
Meath St. SW11 ... 53Kb 112
Meautys AL3: St A ... 4M 5
Mecca Bingo
Burnt Oak ... 26Sa 47
Camden ... *39Kb 70*
(off Arlington Rd.)
Catford ... 59Dc 114
Chadwell Heath ... 31Zc 75
Croydon ... 75Sb 157
Dagenham ... 39Ad 75
Grays ... *50Ce 99*
(off Quarry Hill)
Hayes ... 44X 85
Hornchurch ... 32Md 77
Morden ... 73Eb 155
Romford ... *29Hd 56*
(within The Mercury Mall Shop. Cen.)
Wandsworth ... 60Db 111
Wood Green ... *26Qb 50*
(off Lordship La.)
Watford ... 14Y 27
Mecklenburgh Pl. WC1 ... 5H 217 (42Pb 90)
Mecklenburgh Sq. WC1 ... 5H 217 (42Pb 90)
Mecklenburgh St. WC1 ... 5H 217 (42Pb 90)
Medals Way E20 ... 36Ec 72
Medbree Ct. RM16: Ors ... 3C 100
Medburn St. NW1 ... 1D 216 (40Mb 70)
Medbury Rd. DA12: Grav'nd ... 10H 123
Medcalf Rd. EN3: Enf L ... 9Bc 20
Medcroft Gdns. SW14 ... 56Sa 109
Medd Ct. *AL1: St A* ... *2C 6*
(off St Peter's St.)
Medebourne Cl. SE3 ... 55Jc 115
Medebridge Rd.
RM16: N Stif, Ors ... 45Be 99
Mede Cl. TW19: Wray ... 10P 103
Mede Ct. TW18: Staines ... 62G 126
Medefield KT22: Fet ... 96Fa 192
Mede Ho. *BR1: Brom* ... *64Kc 137*
(off Pike Cl.)
Medesenge Way N13 ... 23Rb 51
Medfield St. SW15 ... 59Wa 110
Medhurst Cl. E3 ... 40Ac 72
(not continuous)
GU24: Chob ... 1K 167
Medhurst Cres. DA12: Grav'nd ... 2G 144
Medhurst Dr. BR1: Brom ... 64Gc 137
Medhurst Gdns. DA12: Grav'nd ... 2H 145
Median Rd. E5 ... 36Yb 72
Medici Cl. IG3: Ilf ... 30Wc 55
(not continuous)
Medick Ct. RM17: Grays ... 1A 122
Medina Av. KT10: Hin W ... 76Ga 152
Medina Gro. N7 ... 34Qb 70
Medina Rd. N7 ... 34Qb 70
RM17: Grays ... 50Fe 99
Medina Sq. KT19: Eps ... 81Qa 173
Medlake Pl. TW20: Egh ... 66E 126
Medlake Rd. TW20: Egh ... 65E 126
Medland Cl. SM6: Wall ... 74Jb 156
Medland Ho. E14 ... 45Ac 92
Medlar Cl. UB5: N'olt ... 40Z 65
Medlar Ct. SL2: Slou ... 6N 81
Medlar Dr. RM15: S Ock ... 42Ae 99
Medlar Ho. DA15: Sidc ... 62Wc 139
Medlar Rd. RM17: Grays ... 51Fe 121
Medlar St. SE5 ... 53Sb 113
Medley Rd. NW6 ... 37Cb 69
Medman Cl. UB8: Uxb ... 40L 63
Medora Rd. RM7: Rom ... 28Fd 56
SW2 ... 59Pb 112
Medow Mead WD7: R'lett ... 5Ha 14
Medusa Ct. *DA12: Grav'nd* ... *8F 122*
(off Admirals Way)
Medusa Rd. SE6 ... 58Dc 114
Medway Bldgs. *E3* ... *40Ac 72*
(off Medway Rd.)
Medway Cl. CR0: C'don ... 72Yb 158
IG1: Ilf ... 36Sc 74
RM7: Mawney ... 25Dd 56
WD25: Wat ... 6Y 13
Medway Ct. NW11 ... 30Db 49
WC1 ... 4F 217
Medway Dr. UB6: G'frd ... 40Ha 66
Medway Gdns. HA0: Wemb ... 35Ja 66
Medway Ho. KT2: King T ... 67Ma 131
NW8 ... 6D 214
SE1 ... 2G 231
Medway M. E3 ... 40Ac 72
Medway Pde. UB6: G'frd ... 40Ha 66
Medway Rd. DA1: Cray ... 55Jd 118
E3 ... 40Ac 72
Medway St. SW1 ... 4D 228 (48Mb 90)
Medwin St. SW4 ... 56Pb 112
Meerbrook Rd. SE3 ... 55Lc 115
Meeson Rd. E15 ... 38Hc 73
Meesons La. RM17: Grays ... 49Be 99
Meeson St. E5 ... 35Ac 72
Meeson's Wharf E15 ... 40Ec 72
Meeting Fld. Path E9 ... 37Yb 72
Meeting Ho. All. E1 ... 46Xb 91
Meeting Ho. La. SE15 ... 53Xb 113
Meeting La. WD17: Wat ... 14Y 27
Megelish M. UB1: S'hall ... 41Ca 85
Megg La. WD4: Chfd ... 1K 11
Mehetabel Rd. E9 ... 36Yb 72
Meister Cl. IG1: Ilf ... 32Tc 74
Melancholy Wlk.
TW10: Ham ... 61La 130
Melanda Cl. BR7: Chst ... 64Pc 138
Melanie Cl. DA7: Bex ... 53Ad 117
Melba Gdns. RM18: Tilb ... 2C 122
Melba Way SE13 ... 53Dc 114
Melbourne Av. HA5: Pinn ... 27Da 45
N13 ... 23Pb 50
SL1: Slou ... 4G 80
W13 ... 46Ja 86
Melbourne Cl. BR6: Orp ... 73Uc 160
SE20 ... 66Wb 135
SM6: Wall ... 78Lb 156
UB10: Ick ... 35Q 64
Melbourne Ct. *E5* ... *35Ac 72*
(off Daubeney Rd.)
EN8: Walt C ... *6Bc 20*
(off Holdbrook Sth.)
N10 ... 24Kb 50
W9 ... 5A 214
Melbourne Gdns. RM6: Chad H ... 29Ad 55
Melbourne Gro. SE22 ... 56Ub 113
Melbourne Ho. UB4: Yead ... 42Y 85
W8 ... *46Cb 89*
(off Kensington Pl.)
Melbourne Mans. *W14* ... *51Ab 110*
(off Musard Rd.)
Melbourne M. SE6 ... 59Ec 114
SW9 ... 53Qb 112
Melbourne Pl. WC2 ... 4J 223 (44Pb 90)
Melbourne Quay DA11: Grav'nd ... 8D 122
Melbourne Rd. E6 ... 40Pc 74
E10 ... 31Dc 72
E17 ... 28Ac 52
IG1: Ilf ... 32Rc 74
RM18: Tilb ... 3A 122
SM6: Wall ... 78Kb 156
SW19 ... 67Cb 133
TW11: Tedd ... 65La 130
WD23: Bush ... 15Da 27
Melbourne Sq. SW9 ... 53Qb 112
Melbourne Ter. *SW6* ... *52Db 111*
(off Moore Pk. Rd.)
Melbourne Way EN1: Enf ... 16Vb 33
Melbourne Yd. SE19 ... 65Ub 135
Melbray M. SW6 ... 54Bb 111
Melbreak Ho. SE22 ... 55Ub 113
Melbury Av. UB2: S'hall ... 48Da 85
Melbury Cl. BR7: Chst ... 65Nc 138
KT10: Clay ... 79Ka 152
KT14: W Byf ... 86J 169
KT16: Chert ... 73J 149
Melbury Ct. W8 ... 48Bb 89
Melbury Dr. SE5 ... 52Ub 113
Melbury Gdns. CR2: Sande ... 83Ub 177
SW20 ... 67Xa 132
Melbury Ho. *SW8* ... *52Pb 112*
(off Richborne Ter.)
Melbury Rd. HA3: Kenton ... 29Pa 47
W14 ... 48Bb 89
Melchester *W11* ... *44Bb 89*
(off Ledbury Rd.)
Melchester Ho. *N19* ... *34Mb 70*
(off Wedmore St.)
Melcombe Ct. NW1 ... 7F 215
Melcombe Gdns. HA3: Kenton ... 30Pa 47
Melcombe Ho. *SW8* ... *52Pb 112*
(off Dorset Rd.)
Melcombe Pl. NW1 ... 7F 215 (43Hb 89)
Melcombe Regis Ct. *W1* ... *1J 221*
(off Weymouth St.)
Melcombe St. NW1 ... 6G 215 (42Hb 89)
Meldex Cl. NW7 ... 23Ya 48
Meldon Cl. SW6 ... 53Db 111
Meldone Cl. KT5: Surb ... 73Ra 153
Meldon Vw. DA1: Dart ... 55Qd 119
Meldrum Cl. BR5: Orp ... 72Yc 161
RH8: Oxt ... 4K 211
Meldrum Rd. IG3: Ilf ... 33Wc 75
Melfield Gdns. SE6 ... 63Ec 136
Melford Av. IG11: Bark ... 37Uc 74
Melford Cl. KT9: Chess ... 78Pa 153
Melford Ct. SE1 ... 3J 231
SE22 ... 60Wb 113
(not continuous)
Melford Pas. SE22 ... 59Wb 113
Melford Pl. CM14: B'wood ... 18Yd 40
CM15: B'wood ... 18Yd 40
Melford Rd. E6 ... 42Pc 94
E11 ... 33Gc 73
E17 ... 28Ac 52
IG1: Ilf ... 33Tc 74
SE22 ... 59Wb 113
SL2: Slou ... 2D 80
Melfort Av. CR7: Thor H ... 69Rb 135
Melfort Rd. CR7: Thor H ... 69Rb 135
Melgund Rd. N5 ... 36Qb 70
Melia Cl. WD25: Wat ... 7Y 13
Melina Cl. UB3: Hayes ... 43T 84
Melina Ct. NW8 ... 4B 214
SW15 ... 55Wa 110
Melina Pl. NW8 ... 4B 214 (41Fb 89)
Melina Rd. W12 ... 47Xa 88
Melior Ct. N6 ... 30Lb 50
Melior Pl. SE1 ... 1H 231 (47Ub 91)
Melior St. SE1 ... 1H 231 (47Ub 91)
Meliot Rd. SE6 ... 61Fc 137
Melksham Cl. RM3: Rom ... 24Pd 57
Melksham Dr. RM3: Rom ... 24Pd 57
Melksham Gdns. RM3: Rom ... 24Nd 57
Melksham Grn. RM3: Rom ... 24Pd 57
Meller Cl. CR0: Bedd ... 76Nb 156
Meller Ho. *E20* ... *37Ec 72*
(off Champions Wlk.)
Mellifont Cl. SM5: Cars ... 73Fb 155
Melling Dr. EN1: Enf ... 11Wb 33
Melling St. SE18 ... 51Uc 116
Mellish Cl. IG11: Bark ... 39Vc 75
Mellish Flats E10 ... 31Cc 72
Mellish Gdns. IG8: Wfd G ... 22Jc 53
Mellish Ho. *E1* ... *44Xb 91*
(off Varden St.)
Mellish Ind. Est. SE18 ... 48Mc 93
Mellish St. E14 ... 48Cc 92
Mellish Way RM11: Horn ... 29Ld 57
Mellison Rd. SW17 ... 64Gb 133
Melliss Av. TW9: Kew ... 53Ra 109
Mellitus St. W12 ... 43Va 88
Mellonde Cl. RM3: Rom ... 24Kd 57
Mellor Cl. KT12: Walt T ... 73Ba 151
Mellor Wlk. *SL4: Wind* ... *3H 103*
(off Bachelors Acre)
Mellow Cl. SM7: Bans ... 86Eb 175
Mellowes Rd. RM11: Horn ... 30Jd 56
Mellow La. E. UB4: Hayes ... 41S 84
Mellow La. W. UB10: Hil ... 41S 84
Mellows Rd. IG5: Ilf ... 27Pc 54
SM6: Wall ... 78Mb 156
Mells Cres. SE9 ... 63Pc 138
Mell St. SE10 ... 50Gc 93
Melody La. N5 ... 36Sb 71
Melody Rd. SW18 ... 57Eb 111
TN16: Big H ... 90Lc 179
Melon Pl. W8 ... 47Bb 89
Melon Rd. E11 ... 34Gc 73
SE15 ... 53Wb 113
Melrose Av. CR4: Mitc ... 66Kb 134
DA1: Cray ... 59Gd 118
EN6: Pot B ... 4Cb 17
N22 ... 25Rb 51
NW2 ... 36Xa 68
SW16 ... 69Pb 134
SW19 ... 61Bb 133
TW2: Whitt ... 59Da 107
UB6: G'frd ... 40Da 65
WD6: Bore ... 15Ra 29
Melrose Cl. SE12 ... 60Jc 115
UB4: Hayes ... 43W 84
UB6: G'frd ... 40Da 65
Melrose Ct. EN8: Chesh ... 1Zb 20
W13 ... *46Ja 86*
(off Williams Rd.)
Melrose Cres. BR6: Orp ... 77Tc 160
Melrose Dr. UB1: S'hall ... 46Ca 85
Melrose Gdns. HA8: Edg ... 27Ra 47
KT3: N Mald ... 69Ta 131
KT12: Hers ... 78Y 151
W6 ... 48Ya 88
Melrose Ho. *NW6* ... *41Cb 89*
(off Carlton Vale)
SW1 ... 7K 227
Melrose Pl. WD17: Wat ... 10V 12
Melrose Rd. CR5: Coul ... 87Kb 176
HA5: Pinn ... 28Ba 45
KT13: Weyb ... 78Q 150
SW13 ... 54Va 110
SW18 ... 58Bb 111
SW19 ... 68Cb 133
TN16: Big H ... 88Lc 179
W3 ... 48Sa 87
Melrose Ter. W6 ... 48Ya 88
Melrose Tudor *SM6: Wall* ... *78Nb 156*
(off Plough La.)
Melsa Rd. SM4: Mord ... 72Eb 155
Melsted Rd. HP1: Hem H ... 2K 3
Melstock Av. RM14: Upm ... 35Sd 78
Melthorne Dr. HA4: Ruis ... 34Y 65
Melthorpe Gdns. SE3 ... 53Nc 116
Melton Cl. HA4: Ruis ... 32Y 65
Melton Ct. SM2: Sutt ... 80Eb 155
SW7 ... 6C 226 (49Fb 89)
Melton Flds. KT19: Ewe ... 81Ta 173
Melton Gdns. RM1: Rom ... 31Hd 76
Melton Pl. KT19: Ewe ... 81Ta 173
Melton Rd. RH1: Mers ... 2C 208
Melton St. NW1 ... 4C 216 (41Lb 90)
Melville Av. CR2: S Croy ... 78Vb 157
SW20 ... 66Wa 132
UB6: G'frd ... 36Ha 66
Melville Cl. UB10: Ick ... 33T 64
Melville Ct. RM3: Rom ... 24Nd 57
SE8 ... 49Ac 92
W4 ... *50Qa 87*
(off Haining Cl.)
W12 ... *48Xa 88*
(off Goldhawk Rd.)
Melville Gdns. N13 ... 22Rb 51
Melville Ho. EN5: New Bar ... 15Fb 31
Melville Pl. N1 ... 38Sb 71
Melville Rd. DA14: Sidc ... 61Yc 139
E17 ... 27Bc 52
NW10 ... 38Ta 67
RM5: Col R ... 24Dd 56
RM13: Rain ... 42Jd 96
SW13 ... 53Wa 110
Melville Vs. Rd. W3 ... 46Sa 87
Melvin Rd. SE20 ... 67Yb 136
Melvinshaw KT22: Lea ... 93La 192
Melwood Ho. *E1* ... *44Xb 91*
(off Watney Mkt.)
Melyn Cl. N7 ... 35Lb 70
Memel Ct. EC1 ... 6D 218
Memel St. EC1 ... 6D 218 (42Sb 91)
Memess Path SE18 ... 51Qc 116
Memorial Av. E15 ... 41Gc 93
Memorial Cl. RH8: Oxt ... 99Fc 199
TW5: Hest ... 51Ba 107
Memorial Hgts. IG2: Ilf ... 30Tc 54
Menai Pl. *E3* ... *40Cc 72*
(off Blondin St.)
Menard Ct. EC1 ... 4E 218
Mendez Way SW15 ... 58Wa 110
Mendham Ho. SE1 ... 3H 231
Mendip Cl. KT4: Wor Pk ... 74Ya 154
SE26 ... 63Yb 136
SL3: L'ly ... 50C 82
UB3: Harl ... 52T 106
Mendip Ct. *SE14* ... *51Yb 114*
(off Avonley Rd.)
SW11 ... 55Eb 111
Mendip Dr. NW2 ... 33Ab 68
Mendip Ho. *N9* ... *19Wb 33*
(within Edmonton Grn. Shop. Cen.)
Mendip Ho's. *E2* ... *41Yb 92*
(off Welwyn St.)
Mendip Rd. DA7: Bex ... 53Gd 118
IG2: Ilf ... 29Uc 54
RM11: Horn ... 31Jd 76
SW11 ... 55Eb 111
WD23: Bush ... 16Ea 28
Mendora Rd. SW6 ... 52Ab 110
Mendoza Cl. RM11: Horn ... 29Nd 57
Menelik Rd. NW2 ... 35Ab 68
Menier Chocolate Factory
(Theatre & Art Gallery) ... 7E 224
Menlo Gdns. SE19 ... 66Tb 135
Menlo Lodge *N13* ... *20Pb 32*
(off Crothall Cl.)
Menon Dr. N9 ... 20Xb 33
Menotti St. E2 ... 42Wb 91
Menteath Ho. *E14* ... *44Cc 92*
(off Dod St.)
Menthone Pl. RM11: Horn ... 31Md 77
Mentmore Cl. HA3: Kenton ... 30La 46
Mentmore Ho. *KT18: Eps* ... *86Sa 173*
(off Dalmeny Way)
Mentmore Rd. AL1: St A ... 4B 6
Mentmore Ter. E8 ... 38Xb 71
Mentone Mans. *SW10* ... *52Db 111*
(off Fulham Rd.)
Meon Cl. KT20: Tad ... 94Xa 194
Meon Ct. TW7: Isle ... 54Ga 108
Meon Rd. W3 ... 47Sa 87
Meopham Rd. CR4: Mitc ... 67Lb 134
MEOPHAM STATION ... 10C 144
Mepham Cres. HA3: Hrw W ... 24Ea 46
Mepham Gdns. HA3: Hrw W ... 24Ea 46
Mepham St. SE1 ... 7J 223 (46Qb 90)
Mera Dr. DA7: Bex ... 56Cd 118
Meranti Ho. *E1* ... *44Wb 91*
(off Goodman's Stile)
Merantun Way SW19 ... 67Db 133
Merbury Cl. SE13 ... 57Ec 114
SE28 ... 46Tc 94
Merbury Rd. SE28 ... 46Tc 94
Mercator Pl. E14 ... 50Cc 92
Mercator Rd. SE13 ... 56Fc 115
Mercedes-Benz World ... 81P 169
Mercer Av. DA10: Swans ... 59Be 121
Mercer Bldg. EC2 ... 5J 219
Mercer Cl. KT7: T Ditt ... 73Ha 152
Mercer Ct. E1 ... 43Ac 92
Mercer Ho. SW1 ... 7K 227
Merceron Ho's. *E2* ... *41Yb 92*
(off Globe Rd.)
Merceron St. E1 ... 42Xb 91
Mercer Pl. HA5: Pinn ... 26Y 45
Mercers HP2: Hem H ... 1N 3
Mercers Cl. SE10 ... 49Hc 93
Mercer's Cotts. *E1* ... *44Ac 92*
(off White Horse Rd.)
Mercers Country Pk. ... 3D 208
Mercers M. N19 ... 34Mb 70
Mercers Pl. W6 ... 49Za 88
Mercers Rd. N19 ... 34Mb 70
(not continuous)
Mercers Row AL1: St A ... 4A 6
Mercer St. WC2 ... 3F 223 (44Nb 90)
Mercer Wlk. UB8: Uxb ... 38L 63
Merchant Cl. KT19: Ewe ... 78Ta 153
Merchant Ct. *E1* ... *46Yb 92*
(off Wapping Wall)
Merchant Ho. *E14* ... *48Dc 92*
(off Selsdon Way)
Merchant Ind. Ter. NW10 ... 42Sa 87
Merchant Navy (Tower Hill) Memorial
... 5J 225 (45Vb 91)
Merchants Cl. GU21: Knap ... 9G 166
SE25 ... 70Wb 135
Merchants Ho. *E14* ... *44Fc 93*
(off New Village Av.)
SE10 ... *50Fc 93*
(off Collington St.)
Merchants Lodge *E17* ... *28Cc 52*
(off Westbury Rd.)
Merchant Sq. W2 ... 1C 220
Merchants Row *SE10* ... *50Fc 93*
(off Hoskins St.)
Merchant St. E3 ... 41Bc 92
Merchiston Rd. SE6 ... 61Fc 137
Merchland Rd. SE9 ... 60Sc 116
Mercia Gro. SE13 ... 56Ec 114
Mercia Ho. *SE5* ... *54Sb 113*
(off Denmark Rd.)
TW15: Ashf ... 67S 128
Mercian Way SL1: Slou ... 6B 80
Mercia Wlk. GU21: Wok ... 89B 168
Mercier Rd. SW15 ... 57Ab 110
Mercury *NW9* ... *25Va 48*
(off Quakers Course)
Mercury Cen. TW14: Felt ... 57W 106
Mercury Ct. *E14* ... *49Cc 92*
(off Homer Dr.)
RM1: Rom ... 29Hd 56
SW9 ... *53Qb 112*
(off Southey Rd.)
Mercury Gdns. RM1: Rom ... 29Gd 56
Mercury Ho. *E3* ... *39Cc 72*
(off Garrison Rd.)
E16 ... *44Hc 93*
(off Jude St.)
KT17: Ewe ... *82Wa 174*
(off Cheam Rd.)
TW8: Bford ... *51La 108*
(off Glenhurst Rd.)
W5 ... 42Pa 87
Mercury Mall, The RM1: Rom ... 29Hd 56
Mercury Rd. TW8: Bford ... 51La 108
Mercury Way SE14 ... 51Zb 114
Mercy Ter. SE13 ... 57Dc 114
Merebank Cl. RH9: G'stone ... 2A 210
Merebank La. CR0: Wadd ... 78Pb 156
Mere Cl. BR6: Farnb ... 75Qc 160
SW15 ... 59Za 110
Mereden Ct. *AL1: St A* ... *5A 6*
(off Tavistock Av.)
Meredith Av. NW2 ... 36Ya 68
Meredith Cl. HA5: Pinn ... 24Z 45
Meredith Ct. EN8: Chesh ... 3Zb 20
Meredith Ho. N16 ... 36Ub 71
Meredith M. SE4 ... 56Bc 114
Meredith Rd. RM16: Grays ... 9C 100
Meredith St. E13 ... 41Jc 93
EC1 ... 4B 218 (41Rb 91)
Meredith Twr. *W3* ... *48Ra 87*
(off Hanbury Rd.)
Meredyth Rd. SW13 ... 54Wa 110
Mere End CR0: C'don ... 73Zb 158
Merefield Gdns. KT20: Tad ... 91Za 194
Mere Rd. KT13: Weyb ... 76T 150
KT20: Tad ... 96Xa 194
SE2 ... 47Zc 95
SL1: Slou ... 8K 81
TN14: Dun G ... 93Gd 202
TW17: Shep ... 72R 150
Mereside BR6: Farnb ... 75Qc 160
Mereside Pk. TW15: Ashf ... 63S 128
Mereside Pl. GU25: Vir W ... 4L 147

Meretone Cl.—Mile Ho. Cl.

Meretone Cl. SE4 56Ac 114
Mereton Mans. *SE8* 53Cc 114
(off Brookmill Rd.)
Merevale Cres. SM4: Mord 72Eb 155
Mereway Rd. TW2: Twick 60Fa 108
Merewood Cl. BR1: Brom 68Qc 138
Merewood Gdns. CR0: C'don 73Zb 158
Merewood Rd. DA7: Bex 54Ed 118
Mereworth Cl. BR2: Brom 71Hc 159
Mereworth Dr. SE18 52Rc 116
Mereworth Ho. SE15 51Yb 114
Merganser Ct. *E1* 45Wb 91
(off Star Pl.)
SE8 51Bc 114
(off Edward St.)
Merganser Gdns. SE28 48Tc 94
MERIDEN 8Aa 13
Meriden Cl. BR1: Brom 66Mc 137
IG6: Ilf 25Sc 54
Meriden Ct. SW3 7D 226
Meriden Ho. N1 1J 219
Meriden Way WD25: Wat 7Aa 13
Merideth Ct. KT1: King T 68Pa 131
Meridia Ct. *E15* 39Ec 72
(off Biggerstaff Rd.)
Meridian Bus. Pk. EN3: Pond E 16Ac 34
EN9: Walt A 7Dc 20
Meridian Cen. CR0: New Ad 82Gc 179
Meridian Cl. NW7 21Ta 47
Meridian Ct. RM17: Grays 52De 121
SE15 52Xb 113
(off Gervase St.)
SE16 47Wb 91
(off East La.)
SL5: Asc 4A 146
UB4: Yead 42Y 85
Meridian Ga. E14 47Dc 92
Meridian Ho. *NW1* 38Lb 70
(off Baynes St.)
SE10 49Gc 93
(off Azof St.)
SE10 52Ec 114
(off Royal Hill)
SW18 56Eb 111
(off Juniper Dr.)
MERIDIAN PARK 8Ec 20
Meridian Pl. E14 47Dc 92
Meridian Point SE8 51Dc 114
Meridian Rd. SE7 52Mc 115
Meridian Sq. E15 38Fc 73
Meridian Trad. Est. SE7 49Kc 93
Meridian Wlk. N17 23Ub 51
Meridian Way EN3: Pond E 21Yb 52
EN9: Walt A 6Dc 20
N9 21Yb 52
N18 22Yb 52
Merield Wlk. DA9: Ghithe 56Xd 120
Merifield Rd. SE9 56Lc 115
Merileys Cl. DA3: Lfield 69Ee 143
Merino Cl. E11 28Lc 53
Merino Ct. EC1 4E 218
Merino Pl. DA15: Sidc 58Wc 117
Merioneth Ct. *W7* 43Ha 86
(off Copley Cl.)
Merita Ho. *E1* 46Wb 91
(off Nesham St.)
Merivale Rd. HA1: Harr 31Ea 66
SW15 56Ab 110
Merland Cl. KT20: Tad 92Ya 194
Merland Grn. KT20: Tad 92Ya 194
Merland Ri. KT18: Tatt C 91Ya 194
KT20: Tad 91Ya 194
Merle Av. UB9: Hare 26K 43
MERLE COMMON 8M 211
Merle Comn. Rd. RH8: Oxt 7L 211
Merle Mans. *E20* 37Ec 72
(off Glade Wlk.)
Merlewood TN13: S'oaks 95Kd 203
Merlewood Cl. CR3: Cat'm 92Tb 197
Merlewood Dr. BR7: Chst 67Pc 138
Merley Ct. NW9 32Sa 67
Merlin *NW9* 25Va 48
(off Near Acre)
Merlin Cen., The AL4: St A 2K 7
Merlin Cl. CR0: C'don 77Ub 157
CR4: Mitc 69Gb 133
EN9: Walt A 6Jc 21
IG6: Ilf 22Yc 55
RM5: Col R 23Fd 56
RM16: Chaf H 48Ae 99
SL3: L'ly 51D 104
SM6: Wall 79Pb 156
UB5: N'olt 41Y 85
Merlin Ct. BR2: Brom 69Hc 137
DA9: Ghithe 58Wd 120
(off Waterstone Way)
GU21: Wok 86E 168
HA4: Ruis 33T 64
HA7: Stan 22Ka 46
(off William Dr.)
SE3 56Kc 115
Merlin Cres. HA8: Edg 25Pa 47
Merlin Gdns. BR1: Brom 62Jc 137
RM5: Col R 23Fd 56
Merling Cl. KT9: Chess 78La 152
Merlin Gro. BR3: Beck 70Bc 136
IG6: Ilf 24Rc 54
Merlin Hgts. *N17* 27Xb 51
(off Daneland Wlk.)
Merlin Ho. EN3: Pond E 15Zb 34
Merlin Rd. DA16: Well 56Wc 117
E12 33Mc 73
RM5: Col R 23Fd 56
Merlin Rd. Nth. DA16: Well 56Wc 117
Merlins Av. HA2: Harr 34Ba 65
Merlins Ct. WC1 4K 217
Merlin St. WC1 4K 217 (41Qb 90)
Merlin Way WD25: Wat 6V 12
Mermagen Dr. RM13: Rain 38Kd 77
Mermaid Cl. DA11: Nflt 59Fe 121
Mermaid Ct. *E8* 38Vb 71
(off Celandine Dr.)
SE1 1F 231 (47Tb 91)
SE16 46Bc 92
Mermaid Ho. *E14* 45Ec 92
(off Bazely St.)
Mermaid Twr. *SE8* 51Bc 114
(off Abinger Gro.)
Mermerus Gdns. DA12: Grav'nd 3H 145
Meroe Ct. N16 33Ub 71
Merredene St. SW2 58Pb 112
Merriall Cl. DA10: Swans 59Be 121
Merriam Av. E9 37Bc 72
Merriam Cl. E4 22Ec 52
Merrick Rd. UB2: S'hall 47Ba 85
Merrick Sq. SE1 3F 231 (48Tb 91)
Merridene N21 16Rb 33
Merrielands Cres. RM9: Dag 40Bd 75
Merrielands Retail Pk. RM9: Dag 39Bd 75
Merrilands Rd. KT4: Wor Pk 74Ya 154
Merrilees Rd. DA15: Sidc 59Uc 116
Merrilyn Cl. KT10: Clay 79Ja 152
Merriman Rd. SE3 53Lc 115
Merrington Rd. SW6 51Cb 111
Merrin Hill CR2: Sande 83Ub 177
Merrion Av. HA7: Stan 22Ma 47
Merrion Ct. *HA4: Ruis* 32V 64
(off Pembroke Rd.)
Merrist Wood Golf Course 10F 186
Merritt Gdns. KT9: Chess 79La 152
Merritt Ho. *RM1: Rom* 31Hd 76
(off South St.)
Merritt Rd. SE4 57Bc 114
Merritt Wlk. AL9: Wel G 5D 8
Merrivale N14 16Mb 32
NW1 1C 216
Merrivale Av. IG4: Ilf 28Mc 53
Merrivale Gdns. GU21: Wok 9N 167
Merrivale M. HA8: Edg 25Sa 47
UB7: View 46M 83
Merrow Bldgs. SE1 1C 230
Merrow Ct. CR4: Mitc 68Fb 133
Merrow Dr. HP1: Hem H 1G 2
Merrow La. GU4: Burp, Guild 100E 188
Merrow Rd. SM2: Cheam 81Za 174
Merrows Cl. HA6: Nwood 23S 44
Merrow St. SE17 7G 231 (50Tb 91)
Merrow Wlk. SE17 7G 231 (50Tb 91)
Merrow Way CR0: New Ad 79Ec 158
Merrydown Way BR7: Chst 67Nc 138
Merryfield SE3 54Hc 115
Merryfield Gdns. HA7: Stan 22La 46
Merryfield Ho. *SE9* 62Lc 137
(off Grove Pk. Rd.)
Merryfields AL4: St A 2J 7
UB8: Uxb 40M 63
WD24: Wat 10W 12
Merryfields Cl. DA3: Hartl 70Be 143
Merryfields Way SE6 59Dc 114
MERRY HILL 18Da 27
Merryhill Cl. E4 17Dc 34
Merry Hill Mt. WD23: Bush 18Da 27
Merry Hill Rd. WD23: Bush 16Ba 27
Merryhills Cl. TN16: Big H 88Mc 179
Merryhills Ct. N14 15Lb 32
Merryhills Dr. EN2: Enf 14Mb 32
Merrylands KT16: Chert 76G 148
Merrylands Rd. KT23: Bookh 95Ba 191
Merrymeade Chase
CM15: B'wood 18Zd 41
Merrymeade Country Pk. 16Zd 41
Merrymeet SM7: Bans 86Hb 175
Merryweather Cl. DA1: Dart 58Pd 119
Merryweather Ct. KT3: N Mald 71Ua 154
N19 34Lb 70
Merryweather Pl. SE10 52Dc 114
Merrywood Gro. KT20: Lwr K 2G 206
Merrywood Pk. RH2: Reig 4K 207
Mersea Ho. IG11: Bark 37Rc 74
Mersey Av. RM14: Upm 30Td 58
Mersey Ct. *KT2: King T* 67Ma 131
(off Samuel Gray Gdns.)
Mersey Rd. E17 27Bc 52
Mersey Wlk. UB5: N'olt 40Ca 65
Mersham Dr. NW9 29Qa 47
Mersham Pl. *CR7: Thor H* 68Tb 135
(off Livingstone Rd.)
SE20 67Xb 135
Mersham Rd. CR7: Thor H 69Tb 135
MERSTHAM 100Lb 196
Merstham Rd. RH1: Blet 1G 208
Merten Rd. RM6: Chad H 31Ad 75
Merthyr Ter. SW13 51Xa 110
MERTON 66Eb 133
Merton Abbey Mills SW19 67Eb 133
Merton Av. DA3: Hartl 70Ae 143
(not continuous)
UB5: N'olt 36Ea 66
UB10: Hil 38R 64
W4 49Va 88
Merton Ct. DA16: Well 54Xc 117
IG1: Ilf 30Nc 54
WD6: Bore 11Pa 29
Merton Gdns. BR5: Pet W 71Rc 160
KT20: Tad 91Za 194
Merton Hall Gdns. SW20 67Ab 132
Merton Hall Rd. SW19 66Ab 132
Merton High St. SW19 66Db 133
Merton Ind. Pk. SW19 67Db 133
Merton La. N6 33Hb 69
Merton Lodge EN5: New Bar 15Eb 31
Merton Mans. SW20 68Za 132
MERTON PARK 68Cb 133
Merton Pk. Pde. SW19 67Bb 133
Merton Pl. RM16: Grays 9C 100
SW19 67Eb 133
(off Nelson Gro. Rd.)
Merton Ri. NW3 38Gb 69
Merton Rd. E17 29Ec 52
EN2: Enf 10Tb 19
HA2: Harr 32Ea 66
IG3: Ilf 31Vc 75
IG11: Bark 38Vc 75
SE25 71Vb 157
SL1: Slou 8L 81
SW18 58Cb 111
SW19 66Db 133
WD18: Wat 14X 27
Merton's Intergenerational Cen.
68Kb 134
Merton Wlk. KT22: Lea 90Ja 172
Merton Way KT8: W Mole 70Da 129
KT22: Lea 91Ja 192
UB10: Hil 38R 64
Mertoun Ter. W1 1F 221
Mertins Rd. SE15 57Zb 114
Meru Cl. NW5 35Jb 70
Mervan Rd. SW2 56Qb 112
Mervyn Av. SE9 62Sc 138
Mervyn Rd. TW17: Shep 73S 150
W13 48Ja 86
Merwin Way SL4: Wind 4B 102
Meryfield Cl. WD6: Bore 12Pa 29
Meryton Ho. SL4: Wind 5E 102
Mesne Way TN14: S'ham 84Hd 182
Messaline Av. W3 44Sa 87
Messant Cl. RM3: Hrld W 26Md 57
Messenger Ct. *SE16* 48Wb 91
(off Spa Rd.)
Messent Rd. SE9 57Lc 115
Messeter Pl. SE9 58Qc 116
Messina Av. NW6 38Cb 69
Messina Way RM9: Dag 40Bd 75
Messiter Ho. N1 1J 217
Metcalfe Av. SM5: Cars 82Gb 175
Metcalfe Ct. SE10 48Hc 93
Metcalf Rd. TW15: Ashf 64R 128
Metcalf Wlk. TW13: Hanw 63Aa 129
Meteor St. SW11 56Jb 112
Meteor Way SM6: Wall 80Nb 156
Metford Cres. EN3: Enf L 10Cc 20
Methley St. SE11 7A 230 (50Qb 90)
Methuen Cl. HA8: Edg 24Qa 47
Methuen Pk. N10 27Kb 50
Methuen Rd. DA6: Bex 56Bd 117
DA17: Belv 49Dd 96
HA8: Edg 24Qa 47
Methven Ct. *N9* 20Wb 33
(off The Broadway)
Methwold Rd. W10 43Za 88
Metro Bus. Cen. SE26 65Bc 136
Metro Central Hgts. SE1 4D 230
Metro Cen. BR5: St M Cry 72Xc 161
WD18: Wat 17S 26
Metro Golf Cen. 24Ya 48
Metro Ind. Cen. TW7: Isle 54Ga 108
Metropolis SE11 4C 230
Metropolitan Bus. Cen. *N1* 38Ub 71
(off Enfield Rd.)
Metropolitan Cen., The
UB6: G'frd 39Da 65
Metropolitan Cl. E14 43Cc 92
Metropolitan Ho. TW8: Bford 51Pa 109
Metropolitan M. WD18: Wat 14U 26
Metropolitan Pl. WD18: Wat 14V 26
Metropolitan Police FC 72Fa 152
Metropolitan Sta. App. WD18: Wat 15X 26
Metropolitan Sta. Bldgs. *W6* 49Ya 88
(off Beadon Rd.)
Metropolitan Wharf E1 46Yb 92
Metro Trad. Est. HA9: Wemb 35Ra 67
Meux Cl. EN7: Chesh 3Wb 19
Mews, The AL1: St A 1C 6
DA3: Lfield 69Ae 143
(off Bramblefield Cl.)
DA14: Sidc 63Wc 139
IG4: Ilf 29Mc 53
KT10: Clay 79Ga 152
N1 39Sb 71
N8 27Qb 50
RH2: Reig 5K 207
RM1: Rom 28Gd 56
RM17: Grays 49Ee 99
TN13: S'oaks 95Jd 203
(Hartslands Rd.)
TN13: S'oaks 96Jd 202
(Hitchen Hatch La.)
TW1: Twick 58Ka 108
TW12: Hamp H 65Ea 130
TW20: Eng G 3P 125
WD7: R'lett 8Ka 14
WD18: Wat 14Y 27
(off Smith St.)
WD25: A'ham 10Ea 14
Mews Cotts. CM13: Ingve 23De 59
Mews End TN16: Big H 90Mc 179
Mews Mdw. TN15: W King 81Wd 184
Mews Pl. IG8: Wfd G 21Jc 53
Mews St. E1 46Wb 91
Mexborough NW1 39Lb 70
Mexfield Rd. SW15 57Bb 111
Meyer Grn. EN1: Enf 10Wb 19
Meyer Rd. DA8: Erith 51Fd 118
Meyers Cl. SL1: Slou 7N 81
Meymott St. SE1 7B 224 (46Rb 91)
Meynell Cres. E9 38Zb 72
Meynell Gdns. E9 38Zb 72
Meynell Rd. E9 38Zb 72
RM3: Rom 24Kd 57
Meyrick Cl. GU21: Knap 8J 167
Meyrick Ct. AL1: St A 2F 6
Meyrick Ho. *E14* 43Cc 92
(off Burgess St.)
Meyrick Rd. NW10 37Wa 68
SW11 55Fb 111
Mezen Cl. HA6: Nwood 22T 44
MFA Bowl
Lewisham 55Ec 114
Miah Ter. E1 46Wb 91
Miall Wlk. SE26 63Ac 136
Mia M. N13 22Qb 50
Mica Ho. N1 38Qb 70
Micawber Av. UB8: Hil 42Q 84
Micawber Ct. N1 3E 218
Micawber Ho. *SE16* 47Wb 91
(off Llewellyn St.)
Micawber St. N1 3E 218 (41Sb 91)
Michael Cliffe Ho. EC1 4A 218
Michael Cl. E3 42Bc 92
Michael Edwards Studio Theatre, The
51Ec 114
(within Cutty Sark)
Michael Faraday Ho. SE17 7H 231
Michael Gdns. DA12: Grav'nd 4G 144
RM11: Horn 28Md 57
Michael Gaynor Cl. W7 46Ha 86
Michael Haines Ho. *SW9* 52Qb 112
(off Sth. Island Pl.)
Michael Manley Ind. Est. SW8 53Lb 112
Michaelmas Cl. SW20 69Ya 132
Michael Rd. E11 32Gc 73
SE25 69Ub 135
SW6 53Db 111
Michaels Cl. SE13 56Gc 115
Michaels La. DA3: Fawk 75Xd 164
TN15: Ash 75Xd 164
Michael Stewart Ho. *SW6* 51Bb 111
(off Clem Attlee Ct.)
Michelangelo Ct. *SE16* 50Xb 91
(off Stubbs Dr.)
Micheldever Rd. SE12 58Gc 115
Michelet Cl. GU18: Light 2A 166
Michelham Gdns. KT20: Tad 92Ya 194
TW1: Twick 62Ha 130
Michelle Ct. *BR1: Brom* 67Hc 137
(off Blyth Rd.)
N12 22Eb 49
W3 45Ta 87
Michelsdale Dr. TW9: Rich 56Na 109
Michelson Ho. SE11 6J 229
Michel's Row *TW9: Rich* 56Na 109
(off Michelsdale Dr.)
Michel Wlk. SE18 50Rc 94
Michie Ct. GU24: Bisl 9E 166
Michigan Av. E12 35Pc 74
Michigan Bldg. *E14* 46Fc 93
(off Biscayne Av.)
Michigan Ho. E14 48Cc 92
Michleham Down N12 21Bb 49
Micholls Av. SL9: Chal P 21A 42
Micholls Cotts. *SL9: Chal P* 22B 42
(off Micholls Av.)
Mick Jagger Cen., The 58Ld 119
(off Shepherd's La.)
Mickledore NW1 2C 216
MICKLEFIELD GREEN 10K 11
Micklefield Rd. HP2: Hem H 2C 4
Micklefield Way WD6: Bore 10Na 15
MICKLEHAM 100La 192
Mickleham By-Pass
RH5: Mick 99Ka 192
Mickleham Cl. BR5: St P 68Vc 139
MICKLEHAM DOWNS 98Ma 193
Mickleham Dr. RH5: Mick 98La 192
Mickleham Gdns. SM3: Cheam 79Ab 154
Mickleham Rd. BR5: St P 67Vc 139
Mickleham Way
CR0: New Ad 80Fc 159
Micklem Dr. HP1: Hem H 1H 3
Micklethwaite Rd. SW6 51Cb 111
Mickleton Ho. *W2* 43Cb 89
(off Westbourne Pk. Rd.)
Midas Bus. Cen. RM10: Dag 35Dd 76
Midas Ind. Est. UB8: Uxb 40K 63
Midas Metropolitan Ind. Est.
SM4: Mord 73Ya 154
MID BECKTON 43Pc 94
Midcroft HA4: Ruis 32U 64
SL2: Slou 2F 80
Mid Cross La. SL9: Chal P 22B 42
Middle Boy RM4: Abr 13Yc 37
Middle Cl. CR5: Coul 92Qb 196
KT17: Eps 84Ua 174
Middle Cres. UB9: Den 31F 62
Middle Dartrey Wlk. *SW10* 52Eb 111
(off Dartrey Wlk.)
Middle Dene NW7 20Ta 29
Middle Down WD25: A'ham 8Da 13
Middle Farm Cl. KT24: Eff 99Z 191
Middle Farm Pl. KT24: Eff 99Y 191
Middlefield NW8 39Fb 69
Middlefield Cl. CR5: Chip 91Gb 195
Middlefielde W13 43Ka 86
Middlefield Gdns. IG2: Ilf 30Rc 54
Middlefields CR0: Sels 81Ac 178
Middle Furlong WD23: Bush 14Da 27
MIDDLE GREEN 46A 82
Middle Grn. SL3: L'ly 46A 82
TW18: Staines 66M 127
Middle Grn. Cl. KT5: Surb 72Pa 153
Middlegreen Rd. SL3: L'ly 7P 81
Middleham Ct. *DA2: Dart* 58Rd 119
(off Osbourne Rd.)
Middleham Gdns. N18 23Wb 51
Middleham Rd. N18 23Wb 51
Middle Hill HP1: Hem H 2G 3
TW20: Egh, Eng G 3N 125
Middle La. HP3: Bov 1C 10
KT17: Eps 84Ua 174
N8 29Nb 50
TN15: Seal 93Pd 203
TW11: Tedd 65Ha 130
Middle La. M. N8 29Nb 50
Middlemarch Lodge WD3: Rick 17N 25
Middlemead Cl. KT23: Bookh 97Ca 191
Middlemead Rd. KT23: Bookh 97Ba 191
Middle Mill Halls of Residence
KT1: King T 69Pa 131
Middle New St. EC4 2A 224
Middle Ope WD24: Wat 9X 13
Middle Pk. Av. SE9 58Mc 115
Middle Path HA2: Harr 32Fa 66
Middle Rd. CM13: Ingve 22Ee 59
E13 40Jc 73
EN4: E Barn 16Gb 31
HA2: Harr 33Fa 66
KT22: Lea 93Ka 192
SW16 68Mb 134
UB9: Den 31E 62
Middle Row W10 42Ab 88
Middlesborough Ho. *RM3: Rom* 24Nd 57
(off Kingsbridge Cir.)
Middlesborough Rd. N18 23Wb 51
Middlesex Bldg., The *E1* 1J 225
(off Artillery La.)
Middlesex Bus. Cen. UB2: S'hall 47Ca 85
Middlesex CCC 3C 214 (41Fb 89)
Middlesex Cl. UB1: S'hall 42Da 85
Middlesex Ct. HA1: Harr 29Ha 46
KT15: Add 78L 149
(off Bush Cl.)
TW8: Bford 50La 86
(off Glenhurst Rd.)
W4 49Va 88
Middlesex Filter Beds Nature Reserve
34Zb 72
Middlesex Guildhall 2E 228
Middlesex Ho. HA0: Wemb 39Ma 67
UB8: Uxb 38L 63
(off Mercer Wlk.)
Middlesex Pas. EC1 1C 224
Middlesex Pl. *E9* 37Yb 72
(off Elsdale St.)
Middlesex Rd. CR4: Mitc 71Nb 156
Middlesex St. E1 1J 225 (43Ub 91)
(not continuous)
Middlesex University
Archway Campus 32Lb 70
Hendon Campus 28Xa 48
Middlesex Wharf E5 33Yb 72
Middle St. CR0: C'don 75Sb 157
EC1 7D 218 (43Sb 91)
Middle Temple La. EC4 3K 223 (44Qb 90)
Middleton Av. DA14: Sidc 65Xc 139
E4 21Bc 52
UB6: G'frd 40Fa 66
Middleton Cl. E4 20Bc 34
Middleton Dr. HA5: Eastc 27W 44
SE16 47Zb 92
Middleton Gdns. IG2: Ilf 30Rc 54
Middleton Gro. IG11: Bark 41Wc 95
N7 36Nb 70
Middleton Hall La. CM15: B'wood 19Ae 41
Middleton Ho. E8 38Wb 71
SE1 4F 231
SW1 6E 228
Middleton M. N7 36Nb 70
Middleton Pl. W1 1B 222
Middleton Rd. CM15: Shenf 18Ae 41
E8 38Vb 71
KT11: D'side 91X 191
KT19: Ewe 82Ta 173
NW11 31Cb 69
SM4: Mord 72Db 155
SM5: Cars 72Db 155
UB3: Hayes 43T 84
WD3: Rick 18J 25
Middleton St. E2 41Xb 91
Middleton Way SE13 56Fc 115
Middle Wlk. GU21: Wok 89A 168
SL1: Burn 1A 80
Middle Way DA18: Erith 48Ad 95
SW16 68Mb 134
UB4: Yead 42Y 85
WD24: Wat 9W 12
Middle Way, The HA3: W'stone 26Ha 46
Middleway NW11 29Db 49
Middle Yd. SE1 6H 225 (46Ub 91)
Middlings, The TN13: S'oaks 98Hd 202
Middlings Ri. TN13: S'oaks 97Hd 202
Middlings Wood TN13: S'oaks 97Jd 202
Midfield Av. BR8: Hext 65Jd 140
DA7: Bex 55Ed 118
Midfield Pde. DA7: Bex 55Ed 118
Midfield Way BR5: St P 67Wc 139
Midford Ho. *NW4* 28Ya 48
(off Belle Vue Est.)
Midford Pl. W1 6C 216 (42Lb 90)
Midgarth Cl. KT22: Oxs 86Ea 172
Midholm HA9: Wemb 32Qa 67
NW11 28Db 49
Midholm Cl. NW11 28Db 49
Midholm Rd. CR0: C'don 75Ac 158
Midhope Cl. GU22: Wok 91A 188
Midhope Gdns. GU22: Wok 91A 188
Midhope Ho. WC1 4G 217
Midhope Rd. GU22: Wok 91A 188
Midhope St. WC1 4G 217 (41Nb 90)
Midhurst SE26 65Yb 136
Midhurst Av. CR0: C'don 73Qb 156
N10 27Jb 50
Midhurst Cl. RM12: Horn 35Jd 76
Midhurst Gdns. UB10: Hil 39S 64
Midhurst Hill DA6: Bex 58Cd 118
Midhurst Ho. *E14* 44Bc 92
(off Salmon La.)
Midhurst Pde. *N10* 27Jb 50
(off Fortis Grn.)
Midhurst Rd. W13 47Ja 86
Midhurst Way E5 35Wb 71
Mid Kent Golf Course 2D 144
Midland Goods Shed N1 1G 217
Midland Ho. *AL1: St A* 2C 6
(off Alma Rd.)
Midland Pde. NW6 37Db 69
Midland Pl. E14 50Ec 92
Midland Rd. E10 31Ec 72
HP2: Hem H 2M 3
NW1 2E 216 (40Mb 70)
Midland Ter. NW2 34Za 68
NW10 42Ua 88
Midleton Rd. KT3: N Mald 69Sa 131
Midlothian Rd. *E3* 42Bc 92
(off Burdett Rd.)
Midmoor Rd. SW12 60Lb 112
SW19 67Za 132
Midnight Av. SE5 52Rb 113
Midship Cl. SE16 46Zb 92
Midship Point *E14* 47Cc 92
(off The Quarterdeck)
Midstrath Rd. NW10 35Ua 68
Mid St. RH1: S Nut 9F 208
Midsummer Av. TW4: Houn 56Ba 107
Midsummer Ct. *TW18: Staines* 63J 127
(off Kingston Rd.)
Midsummer Wlk. GU21: Wok 8P 167
Midway AL3: St A 5P 5
KT12: Walt T 75X 151
SM3: Sutt 73Bb 155
Midway Av. KT16: Chert 69J 127
TW20: Thorpe 69D 126
Midway Cl. TW18: Staines 62K 127
(not continuous)
Midway Ho. EC1 3C 218
Midwinter Cl. DA16: Well 55Wc 117
Midwood Cl. NW2 34Xa 68
Miena Way KT21: Asht 89Ma 173
Miers Cl. E6 39Qc 74
Mighell Av. IG4: Ilf 29Mc 53
Mikado Cl. UB9: Hare 26M 43
Mikardo Ct. *E14* 45Ec 92
(off Poplar High St.)
Mike Spring Ct. DA12: Grav'nd 3F 144
Milan Ct. N11 25Mb 50
Milan Ho. AL1: St A 3D 6
Milan Rd. UB1: S'hall 47Ba 85
Milan Wlk. CM14: B'wood 18Xd 40
Milborne Gro. SW10 50Eb 89
Milborne St. E9 37Yb 72
Milborough Cres. SE12 58Gc 115
Milbourne Ct. WD17: Wat 12W 26
Milbourne Ho. *KT1: King T* 67Qa 131
(off Coombe Rd.)
Milbourne La. KT10: Esh 79Ea 152
Milbourne Pl. KT19: Ewe 77Ta 153
Milbrook KT10: Esh 79Ea 152
Milburn Dr. UB7: Yiew 45N 83
Milburn Wlk. KT18: Eps 87Ua 174
Milby Ct. WD6: Bore 11Pa 29
Milcombe Cl. GU21: Wok 10N 167
Milcote St. SE1 2B 230 (47Rb 91)
Mildenhall Ho. *RM3: Rom* 22Qd 57
(off Redcar Rd.)
Mildenhall Rd. E5 35Yb 72
SL1: Slou 4J 81
Mildmay Av. N1 37Tb 71
Mildmay Gro. Nth. N1 36Tb 71
Mildmay Gro. Sth. N1 36Tb 71
Mildmay Pk. N1 36Tb 71
Mildmay Pl. N16 36Ub 71
TN14: S'ham 83Hd 182
Mildmay Rd. IG1: Ilf 34Rc 74
N1 36Tb 71
RM7: Rom 29Ed 56
Mildmay St. N1 37Tb 71
Mildred Av. UB3: Harl 49T 84
UB5: N'olt 36Da 65
WD6: Bore 14Qa 29
(not continuous)
WD18: Wat 14V 26
Mildred Cl. DA1: Dart 58Qd 119
Mildred Ct. CR0: C'don 74Wb 157
Mildred Rd. DA8: Erith 50Gd 96
Mildrose Ct. *NW6* 41Cb 89
(off Malvern M.)
Mildura Ct. N8 28Pb 50
Mile Cl. EN9: Walt A 5Ec 20
MILE END 42Bc 92
Mile End, The E17 25Zb 52
Mile End Climbing Wall 41Ac 92
MILE END GREEN 68Zd 143
Mile End Pk. 40Ac 72
Mile End Pk. Leisure Cen. 43Ac 92
Mile End Pl. E1 42Zb 92
Mile End Rd. E1 43Yb 92
E3 43Yb 92
Mile End Stadium 43Bc 92
Milehams Ind. Est. RM19: Purf 48Qd 97
Mile Ho. Cl. AL1: St A 5E 6

Mile Ho. La.—Mint Rd.

Mile Ho. La. AL1: St A 5E 6
Mile Path GU22: Wok 3K 187
Mile Rd. SM6: Bedd, Wall 74Kb 156
(not continuous)
Miles Bldgs. NW1 7D 214
(not continuous)
Miles Cl. SE28 46Tc 94
Miles Ct. *CR0: C'don 75Rb 157*
(off Cuthbert Rd.)
E1 44Xb 91
(off Tillman St.)
Miles Dr. SE28 46Uc 94
MILES GREEN 9D 166
Miles Ho. *SE10 50Gc 93*
(off Tuskar St.)
Miles La. KT11: Cobh 85Aa 171
RH8: Tand 8D 210
RH9: S God 8D 210
Miles Lodge *E15 36Fc 73*
(off Colegrave Rd.)
HA1: Harr 29Fa 46
Milespit Hill NW7 22Xa 48
Miles Pl. KT5: Surb 70Pa 131
NW8 7C 214
Miles Rd. CR4: Mitc 69Gb 133
KT19: Eps 84Ta 173
N8 27Nb 50
Miles St. SW8 51Nb 112
(not continuous)
Milestone Cl. GU23: Rip 94J 189
N9 19Wb 33
SM2: Sutt 79Fb 155
Milestone Ct. E10 31Dc 72
Milestone Dr. CR8: Purl 86Pb 176
MILESTONE GREEN 56Sa 109
Milestone Ho.
KT1: King T 69Ma 131
(off Surbiton Rd.)
Milestone Rd. DA2: Dart 58Rd 119
SE19 65Vb 135
Miles Way N20 19Gb 31
Milfoil St. W12 45Wa 88
Milford Cl. SE2 51Ad 117
Milford Ct. SL1: Slou 7L 81
UB1: S'hall 46Ca 85
Milford Gdns. CR0: C'don 71Yb 158
HA0: Wemb 35Ma 67
HA8: Edg 24Qa 47
Milford Gro. SM1: Sutt 77Eb 155
Milford La. WC2 4K 223 (45Qb 90)
Milford M. SW16 62Pb 134
Milford Rd. RM16: Grays 46Fe 99
UB1: S'hall 45Ca 85
W13 46Ka 86
Milford Towers SE6 59Dc 114
Milking La. BR2: Kes 83Mc 179
BR6: Downe 84Nc 180
Milk St. BR1: Brom 65Kc 137
E16 46Rc 94
EC2 3E 224 (44Sb 91)
Milkwell Gdns. IG8: Wfd G 24Kc 53
Milkwell Yd. SE5 53Sb 113
Milkwood Rd. SE24 57Rb 113
Milk Yd. E1 45Yb 92
Mill, The KT13: Weyb 75Q 150
Millais Av. E12 36Qc 74
Millais Ct. *UB5: N'olt 40Z 65*
(off Academy Gdns.)
Millais Cres. KT19: Ewe 78Ua 154
Millais Gdns. HA8: Edg 26Qa 47
Millais Ho. SW1 6F 229
Millais Pl. RM18: Tilb 2C 122
Millais Rd. E11 35Ec 72
EN1: Enf 15Vb 33
KT3: N Mald 73Ua 154
Millais Way KT19: Ewe 77Sa 153
Millan Cl. KT15: New H 82K 169
Milland Ct. WD6: Bore 11Ta 29
Millard Cl. N16 36Ub 71
Millard Rd. SE8 50Bc 92
Millard Ter. RM10: Dag 37Cd 76
Mill Av. UB8: Uxb 40L 63
Millbank HP3: Hem H 6M 3
SM6: Wall 78Mb 156
SW1 4F 229 (48Nb 90)
Millbank Ct. SW1 5F 229
Millbank Twr. SW1 6F 229 (49Nb 90)
Millbank Way SE12 57Jc 115
Millbourne Ho. *KT10: Esh 79Ea 152*
(off Princess Sq.)
Millbourne Rd. TW13: Hanw 63Aa 129
Mill Bri. EN5: Barn 16Bb 31
Mill Bri. Pl. UB8: Uxb 40L 63
Millbro BR8: Hext 67Jd 140
Millbroke M. IG8: Wfd G 23Gc 53
Millbrook KT13: Weyb 77U 150
Millbrook Av. DA16: Well 56Tc 116
Millbrooke Ct. *SW15 57Ab 110*
(off Keswick Rd.)
Millbrook Gdns. RM2: Rom 26Gd 56
RM6: Chad H 30Bd 55
Millbrook Ho. *SE15 51Wb 113*
(off Peckham Pk. Rd.)
Millbrook Pas. SW9 55Rb 113
Millbrook Pl. *NW1 1B 216*
(off Hampstead Rd.)
Mill Brook Rd. BR5: St M Cry 70Yc 139
Millbrook Rd. N9 18Xb 33
SW9 55Rb 113
WD23: Bush 11Ba 27
Millbrook Way SL3: Poyle 54G 104
Mill Cleave *KT14: W Byf 84J 169*
(off Claremont Rd.)
Mill Cl. HP3: Hem H 7A 4
KT23: Bookh 96Ca 191
NW7 25Ab 48
SM5: Cars 75Jb 156
UB7: W Dray 48M 83
Mill Cnr. EN5: Barn 11Bb 31
Mill Ct. DA4: S Dar 68Sd 142
E5 33Yb 72
E10 34Ec 72
SE28 45Xc 95
(off Titmuss Av.)
SL2: Slou 6K 81
Millcrest Rd.
EN7: G Oak 1Rb 19
Millcroft Ho. *SE6 63Ec 136*
(off Melfield Gdns.)
Mill Dr. HA4: Ruis 31T 64
Millen Ct. DA4: Hort K 70Sd 142
MILL END 18H 25
Millender Wlk. *SE16 49Yb 92*
(off New Rotherhithe Rd.)
Millennium Arena 52Jb 112
Millennium Bridge 5C 224 (45Sb 91)
Millennium Bri. Ho.
EC4 4D 224
Millennium Bus. Cen.
NW2 33Xa 68
Millennium Cen., The 35Fd 76
Millennium Cl. E16 44Kc 93
UB8: Uxb 40L 63
Millennium Ct. EN8: Chesh 1Xb 19
Millennium Dr. E14 49Fc 93
Millennium Ho. E17 29Zb 52
SW15 57Ab 110
(off Plaza Gdns.)
Millennium Pl. E2 40Xb 71
Millennium Sq. SE1 1K 231 (47Vb 91)
Millennium Wlk.
CM14: B'wood 19Zd 41
(off High St.)
Millennium Way SE10 47Gc 93
Millennium Wharf
WD3: Rick 17N 25
Miller Av. EN3: Enf L 10Cc 20
Miller Cen., The 96Wb 197
Miller Cl. BR1: Brom 64Kc 137
CR4: Mitc 73Hb 155
HA5: Pinn 26Y 45
RM5: Col R 24Cd 56
Miller Ct. DA7: Bex 55Ed 118
Miller Ho. *E1 43Zb 92*
(off Shandy St.)
W10 42Bb 89
(off Harrow Rd.)
Miller Pl. KT19: Eps 84Na 173
SL9: Ger X 29A 42
Miller Rd. CR0: C'don 74Pb 156
DA12: Grav'nd 1J 145
SW19 65Fb 133
Miller's Av. E8 36Vb 71
Millers Cl. DA1: Dart 59Md 119
IG7: Chig 19Xc 37
KT12: Hers 77Y 151
NW7 21Wa 48
TW18: Staines 64K 127
WD3: Chor 13H 25
Millers Copse
KT18: Eps D 91Ta 193
Millers Ct. *HA0: Wemb 40Na 67*
(off Vicars Bri. Cl.)
TW20: Egh 65F 126
Millers Grn. Cl.
EN2: Enf 13Rb 33
Miller's La. IG7: Chig 18Xc 37
SL4: Old Win 8K 103
Millers Mdw. Cl. SE3 56Hc 115
Miller Smith Cl. KT20: Tad 95Ya 194
Millers Ri. AL1: St A 3C 6
Miller's Ter. E8 36Vb 71
Miller St. NW1 1B 216 (40Lb 70)
(not continuous)
Millers Way W6 47Ya 88
Millers Wharf Ho. *E1 46Wb 91*
(off St Katherine's Way)
Millers Yd. N3 25Db 49
Miller Wlk. SE1 7A 224 (46Qb 90)
Milles Sq. SW9 56Qb 112
Millet Rd. UB6: G'frd 40Da 65
Mill Farm Av. TW16: Sun 66U 128
Mill Farm Bus. Pk. TW4: Houn 59Aa 107
Mill Farm Cl. HA5: Pinn 26Y 45
Mill Farm Cres. TW4: Houn 60Aa 107
Mill Field, The 45Sd 98
Millfield DA3: Nw A G 75Ae 165
HP4: Berk 1A 2
KT1: King T 69Pa 131
N4 33Qb 70
TW16: Sun 67T 128
Millfield Av. E17 25Ac 52
Millfield Cl. AL2: Lon C 8H 7
RM11: Horn 31Jd 76
Millfield Dr. DA11: Nflt 1A 144
Millfield Ho. WD18: Wat 16T 26
Millfield La. DA3: Nw A G 75Ae 165
KT20: Kgswd 97Bb 195
N6 32Gb 69
Millfield Pl. N6 33Jb 70
Millfield Rd. HA8: Edg 26Sa 47
TW15: W King 79Td 164
TW4: Houn 60Aa 107
Millfields Cl. BR5: St P 70Xc 139
Millfields Cotts. BR5: St M Cry 70Yc 139
Millfields Rd. E5 35Yb 72
Millfield Theatre 21Tb 51
Millfield Wlk. HP3: Hem H 5M 3
Mill Footpath *RM1: Rom 30Hd 56*
(off Thurloe Gdns.)
Millford GU21: Wok 9M 167
Mill Gdns. SE26 62Xb 135
Mill Grn. CR4: Mitc 73Jb 156
Mill Grn. Bus. Pk. CR4: Mitc 73Jb 156
Mill Grn. Rd. CR4: Mitc 73Hb 155
Millgrove St. SW11 53Jb 112
Millharbour E14 47Dc 92
Millhaven Cl. RM6: Chad H 30Xc 55
Millhedge Cl. KT11: Cobh 88Aa 171
MILL HILL 22Ua 48
Mill Hill CM15: Shenf 17Ae 41
SW13 54Wa 110
MILL HILL CIRCUS 22Va 48
Mill Hill Cir. NW7 22Va 48
Mill Hill Golf Course 19Ua 30
Mill Hill Gro. W3 46Sa 87
Mill Hill Ind. Est. NW7 23Va 48
Mill Hill La. DA12: Shorne 4M 145
Mill Hill Old Railway Nature Reserve
23Sa 47
Mill Hill Rd. SW13 54Wa 110
W3 47Ra 87
Mill Hill School Sports Cen. 21Wa 48
Mill Hill Ter. W3 46Ra 87
Millhoo Ct. EN9: Walt A 6Hc 21
Mill Ho. IG8: Wfd G 22Hc 53
Mill Ho. Cl. DA4: Eyns 74Nd 163
Mill Ho. La. TW20: Thorpe 70D 126
Millhouse La. WD5: Bedm 9F 4
Millhouse Pl. SE27 63Rb 135
Millicent Fawcett Ct. N17 25Vb 51
Millicent Gro. N13 22Rb 51
Millicent Preston Ho. *IG11: Bark 39Tc 74*
(off Ripple Rd.)
Millicent Rd. E10 32Bc 72
Milligan St. E14 45Bc 92
Milliner Ho. *SW10 52Eb 111*
(off Hortensia Rd.)
Milliner's Ct. AL1: St A 2C 6
Millers Ct. IG10: Lough 12Qc 36
Milliners Ho. SE1 2J 231
SW18 56Cb 111
Milling Rd. HA8: Edg 24Ta 47
Millington Ct. SL1: Slou 6D 80
Millington Ho. N16 34Tb 71
Millington Rd. UB3: Harl 48U 84
Mill La. BR6: Downe 82Qc 180
CR0: Wadd 76Pb 156
DA4: Eyns 74Nd 163
E4 13Dc 34
GU23: Rip 91M 189
GU24: Pirb 6B 186
IG8: Wfd G 22Hc 53
KT14: Byfl 85P 169
KT17: Ewe 81Va 174
KT22: Fet 94Ja 192
NW6 36Bb 69
RH1: Mers 3C 208
RH8: Oxt 4K 211
RM4: Nave 11Kd 39
RM6: Chad H 30Ad 55
RM16: Chaf H 49Zd 99
RM16: Ors 3C 100
(not continuous)
RM20: Chaf H, Grays 50Zd 99
SE8 53Cc 114
(off Deptford Bri.)
SE18 50Qc 94
SL3: Hort 55D 104
SL4: Wind 2E 102
SL5: S'hill 8D 124
SL9: Ger X 30B 42
SM5: Cars 77Hb 155
TN14: S'ham 82Hd 182
TN14: S'oaks 93Ld 203
TN15: Bor G, Igh 94Zd 205
TN16: Westrm 99Sc 200
TW20: Thorpe 70E 126
WD3: Crox G 16S 26
WD4: K Lan 1Q 12
Mill La. Trad. Est. CR0: Wadd 76Pb 156
Mill Link Rd. WD4: K Lan 2R 12
Millman Ct. WC1 6H 217
Millman M. WC1 6H 217 (42Pb 90)
Millman Pl. WC1 6H 217
Millman Rd. E16 45Pc 94
Millman St. WC1 6H 217 (42Pb 90)
Millmark Gro. SE14 54Ac 114
Millmarsh La. EN3: Brim 12Ac 34
Mill Mead TW18: Staines 63H 127
Millmead KT10: Esh 75Ca 151
KT14: Byfl 84P 169
Millmead Ind. Cen. N17 26Xb 51
Mill Mead Rd. N17 27Xb 51
MILL MEADS 40Fc 73
Mill Pk. Av. RM12: Horn 33Nd 77
Mill Pl. BR7: Chst 67Qc 138
DA1: Cray 56Jd 118
E14 44Ac 92
KT1: King T 69Pa 131
SL3: Dat 1P 103
Mill Pl. Cvn. Pk. SL3: Dat 4N 103
Mill Plat TW7: Isle 54Ja 108
(not continuous)
Mill Plat Av. TW7: Isle 54Ja 108
Mill Pond Cl. SW8 52Mb 112
TN14: S'oaks 93Md 203
Millpond Ct. KT15: Add 78N 149
Millpond Est. SE16 47Xb 91
Millpond Pl. SM5: Cars 76Jb 156
Mill Pond Rd. DA1: Dart 58Nd 119
GU20: W'sham 7A 146
Mill Ridge HA8: Edg 22Pa 47
Mill River Trad. Est. EN3: Pond E 13Ac 34
Mill Rd. DA2: Hawl 63Pd 141
DA8: Erith 52Ed 118
DA11: Nflt 9A 122
E16 46Kc 93
IG1: Ilf 34Qc 74
KT10: Esh 75Ca 151
KT11: Cobh 87Y 171
KT17: Eps 84Va 174
KT20: Tad 95Za 194
RM15: Avel 45Sd 98
RM19: Purf 51Rd 119
SW19 66Eb 133
TN13: Dun G 92Gd 202
TW2: Twick 61Ea 130
UB7: W Dray 48L 83
Mill Row DA5: Bexl 60Dd 118
N1 1J 219 (39Ub 71)
Mills Cl. UB10: Hil 40Q 64
Mills Ct. EC2 5H 219
WD6: Bore 12Sa 29
Mills Cres. TN15: Seal 91Pd 203
Mills Gro. E14 44Ec 92
NW4 27Za 48
Mill Shaw RH8: Oxt 4K 211
Millshott Cl. SW6 53Ya 110
Mills Ho. *SW8 53Lb 112*
(off Thessaly Rd.)
Millside SM5: Cars 75Hb 155
Millside Ct. KT23: Bookh 97Ca 191
SL0: Thorn 47K 83
Millside Ind. Est. DA1: Dart 56Md 119
Millside Pl. TW7: Isle 54Ka 108
Millsmead Way IG10: Lough 12Pc 36
Millson Cl. N20 19Fb 31
Mills Rd. KT12: Hers 78Y 151
Mills Row W4 49Ta 87
Mills Spur SL4: Old Win 9M 103
Millstead Cl. KT20: Tad 94Xa 194
Millstone Cl. DA4: S Dar 68Sd 142
E15 37Fc 73
Millstone M. DA4: S Dar 67Sd 142
Millstream Cl. N13 22Qb 50
Millstream Ho. *SE16 47Xb 91*
(off Jamaica Rd.)
Millstream La. SL1: Slou 6C 80
Mill Stream Lodge WD3: Rick 19J 25
Millstream Rd. SE1 2K 231 (47Vb 91)
Mill St. *HP3: Hem H 5M 3*
(off Durrants Hill Rd.)
KT1: King T 69Na 131
RH1: Redh 7N 207
SE1 2K 231 (47Vb 91)
SL2: Slou 6K 81
SL3: Coln 52F 104
TN16: Westrm 99Tc 200
W1 4A 222 (45Kb 90)
Mills Way CM13: Hut 18Ee 41
Mills Yd. SW6 55Db 111
Mill Trad. Est., The NW10 41Sa 87
Mill Va. BR2: Brom 68Hc 137
Mill Vw. AL2: Park 9B 6
Mill Vw. Cl. KT17: Ewe 80Va 154
Millview Cl. RH2: Reig 4M 207
Mill Vw. Gdns. CR0: C'don 76Zb 158
Millview Pk. TN15: W King 82Wd 184
MILLWALL 49Dc 92
Millwall Dock Rd. E14 48Cc 92
Millwall FC 50Yb 92
Millwall Pk. 49Ec 92
Millwards AL10: Hat 3D 8
Mill Way KT18: Head, Lea 96Pa 193
KT22: Lea 96Pa 193
TW14: Felt 57X 107
WD3: Rick 18H 25
WD23: Bush 12Aa 27
Millway NW7 21Ua 48
RH2: Reig 6M 207
Millway Gdns. UB5: N'olt 37Ba 65
Millwell Cres. IG7: Chig 22Tc 54
Mill West SL2: Slou 6K 81
Millwood Rd. BR5: St P 69Yc 139
TW3: Houn 57Ea 108
Millwood St. W10 43Ab 88
Millwrights Wlk. *HP3: Hem H 7P 3*
(off Belswains La.)
Mill Yd. E1 45Wb 91
Mill Yd. Ind. Est. HA8: Edg 25Ra 47
Milman Cl. HA5: Pinn 27Z 45
Milman Rd. NW6 40Za 68
Milman's Ho. *SW10 51Fb 111*
(off Milman's St.)
Milman's St. SW10 51Fb 111
Milne Ct. E18 25Jc 53
Milne Feild HA5: Hat E 24Ca 45
Milne Gdns. SE9 57Nc 116
Milne Ho. *SE18 49Pc 94*
(off Ogilby St.)
Milne Pk. E. CR0: New Ad 83Fc 179
Milne Pk. W. CR0: New Ad 83Fc 179
Milner App. CR3: Cat'm 93Wb 197
Milner Cl. CR3: Cat'm 94Vb 197
WD25: Wat 6X 13
Milner Ct. *SE15 52Vb 113*
(off Colegrove Rd.)
WD23: Bush 16Da 27
Milner Dr. KT11: Cobh 84Ba 171
TW2: Whitt 59Fa 108
Milner Pl. N1 39Qb 70
SM5: Cars 77Jb 156
Milner Rd. CR3: Cat'm 94Wb 197
CR7: Thor H 69Tb 135
E15 41Gc 93
KT1: King T 69Ma 131
RM8: Dag 33Yc 75
SM4: Mord 71Fb 155
SW19 67Db 133
Milner Sq. N1 38Rb 71
Milner St. SW3 5F 227 (49Hb 89)
Milner Wlk. SE9 61Tc 138
Milne Way UB9: Hare 25K 43
Milnthorpe Rd. W4 51Ta 109
Milo Gdns. SE22 58Vb 113
Milo Rd. SE22 58Vb 113
Milrood Ho. *E1 43Zb 92*
(off Stepney Grn.)
Milroy Av. DA11: Nflt 1A 144
Milroy Wlk. SE1 6B 224 (46Rb 91)
Milson Rd. W14 48Za 88
Milstead Ho. E5 36Xb 71
Milthorne Cl. WD3: Crox G 15P 25
MILTON 8E 122
Milton Av. CR0: C'don 73Tb 157
DA12: Grav'nd 10E 122
E6 38Mc 73
EN5: Barn 15Bb 31
N6 31Lb 70
NW9 27Sa 47
NW10 39Sa 67
RM12: Horn 33Hd 76
SL9: Chal P 28A 42
SM1: Sutt 76Fb 155
TN14: Bad M 82Dd 182
Milton Cl. N2 29Eb 49
SE1 6K 231 (49Vb 91)
SL3: Hort 55C 104
SM1: Sutt 76Fb 155
UB4: Hayes 44W 84
Milton Ct. DA12: Grav'nd 10E 122
E17 28Cc 52
EC2 7F 219 (43Tb 91)
EN9: Walt A 6Ec 20
RM6: Chad H 31Yc 75
SE14 51Bc 114
(not continuous)
SW18 57Cb 111
TW2: Twick 62Ga 130
UB10: Ick 34R 64
Milton Court Concert Hall 7F 219
Milton Ct. Rd. SE14 51Ac 114
Milton Cres. IG2: Ilf 31Rc 74
Milton Dr. TW17: Shep 70N 127
WD6: Bore 15Ra 29
Milton Gdn. Est. N16 35Tb 71
Milton Gdns. KT18: Eps 86Ua 174
RM18: Tilb 3D 122
TW19: Stanw 60P 105
Milton Gro. N11 22Lb 50
N16 35Tb 71
Milton Hall Rd. DA12: Grav'nd 10F 122
Milton Ho. AL3: St A 4P 5
E2 41Yb 92
(off Roman Rd.)
E17 28Cc 52
SE5 52Tb 113
(off Elmington Est.)
SL9: Chal P 21A 42
SM1: Sutt 76Cb 155
TW20: Egh 64C 126
(off Station Rd.)
Milton Lodge DA14: Sidc 63Wc 139
TW1: Twick 59Ha 108
Milton Mans. *W14 51Ab 110*
(off Queen's Club Gdns.)
Milton Pk. N6 31Lb 70
TW20: Egh 66C 126
Milton Pl. DA12: Grav'nd 8E 122
N7 36Qb 70
(off Eastwood Cl.)
Milton Rd. CM14: W'ley 21Yd 58
CR0: C'don 73Tb 157
CR3: Cat'm 93Tb 197
CR4: Mitc 66Jb 134
DA10: Swans 58Ae 121
DA12: Grav'nd 8D 122
DA16: Well 53Vc 117
DA17: Belv 49Cd 96
E17 28Cc 52
HA1: Harr 28Ga 46
KT12: Walt T 76Z 151
KT15: Add 79J 149
N6 31Lb 70
N15 28Rb 51
NW7 22Wa 48
NW9 31Wa 68
RM1: Rom 30Jd 56
RM17: Grays 50De 99
SE24 57Rb 113
SL2: Slou 2H 81
Milton Rd. SM1: Sutt 76Cb 155
SM6: Wall 79Lb 156
SW14 55Ta 109
SW19 65Eb 133
TN13: Dun G 93Gd 202
TW12: Hamp 66Ca 129
TW20: Egh 64B 126
UB10: Ick 35R 64
W3 46Ta 87
W7 45Ha 86
Milton Rd. Bus. Pk.
DA12: Grav'nd 9E 122
Milton St. DA10: Swans 58Zd 121
EC2 7F 219 (43Tb 91)
EN9: Walt A 6Ec 20
WD24: Wat 10X 13
Milton Way KT22: Fet 97Ea 192
UB7: W Dray 49P 83
Milverton Dr. UB10: Ick 35S 64
Milverton Gdns. IG3: Ilf 33Vc 75
Milverton Ho. SE6 62Ac 136
Milverton Pl. BR1: Brom 64Lc 137
Milverton Rd. NW6 38Ya 68
Milverton St. SE11 7A 230 (50Qb 90)
Milverton Way SE9 63Qc 138
Milward St. E1 43Xb 91
Milward Wlk. SE18 51Qc 116
MIMBRIDGE 5L 167
Mimms Hall Rd. EN6: Pot B 3Za 16
Mimms La. EN6: Ridge 5Qa 15
WD7: Shenl 5Qa 15
Mimosa Cl. BR6: Chels 75Yc 161
CM15: Pil H 15Xd 40
RM3: Rom 24Ld 57
Mimosa Ho. *E20 36Ec 72*
(off Liberty Bri. Rd.)
UB4: Yead 43Y 85
Mimosa Lodge NW10 36Va 68
Mimosa Rd. UB4: Yead 43Y 85
Mimosa St. SW6 53Bb 111
Mina Av. SL3: L'ly 7P 81
Minard Rd. SE6 59Gc 115
Mina Rd. SE17 7J 231 (50Ub 91)
SW19 67Cb 133
Minchenden Ct. N14 19Mb 32
Minchenden Cres. N14 20Lb 32
Minchin Cl. KT22: Lea 94Ja 192
Minchin Ho. *E14 44Cc 92*
(off Dod St.)
Mincing La. EC3 4H 225 (45Ub 91)
GU24: Chob 10K 147
Minden Gdns. IG11: Bark 41Xc 95
Minden Rd. SE20 67Xb 135
SM3: Sutt 75Ab 154
Minehead Ho. *RM3: Rom 22Nd 57*
(off Dagnam Pk. Dr.)
Minehead Rd. HA2: Harr 34Ca 65
SW16 64Pb 134
Mineral Cl. EN5: Barn 16Ya 30
Mineral St. SE18 49Uc 94
Minera M. SW1 5J 227 (49Jb 90)
Minerva Cl. DA14: Sidc 62Uc 138
SW9 52Qb 112
TW19: Stanw M 57J 105
Minerva Ct. EC1 6A 218
Minerva Dr. WD24: Wat 8U 12
Minerva Lodge N7 37Pb 70
Minerva Rd. E4 24Dc 52
KT1: King T 68Pa 131
NW10 42Sa 87
Minerva St. E2 40Xb 71
Minerva Wlk. EC1 2C 224 (44Rb 91)
Minerva Way EN5: Barn 15Bb 31
Minet Av. NW10 40Ua 68
Minet Country Pk. 47Y 85
Minet Dr. UB3: Hayes 46W 84
Minet Gdns. NW10 40Ua 68
UB3: Hayes 46X 85
Minet Rd. SW9 54Rb 113
Minford Gdns. W14 47Za 88
Minford Ho. *W14 47Za 88*
(off Minford Gdns.)
Mingard Wlk. N7 33Pb 70
Ming St. E14 45Cc 92
Minimax Cl. TW14: Felt 58W 106
Minima Yacht Club *69Ma 131*
(off High St.)
Minister Ct. AL2: F'mre 10C 6
Ministry Way SE9 61Pc 138
Miniver Pl. EC4 4E 224
Mink Ct. TW4: Houn 54Y 107
Minley Ct. RH2: Reig 5J 207
Minniecroft Rd. SL1: Burn 1A 80
Minniedale KT5: Surb 71Pa 153
Minnow St. SE17 6J 231 (49Ub 91)
Minnow Wlk. SE17 6J 231 (49Ub 91)
Minoan Dr. HP3: Hem H 6N 3
Minorca Rd. KT13: Weyb 77Q 150
Minories EC3 3K 225 (44Vb 91)
Minshaw Ct. DA14: Sidc 63Vc 139
Minshill St. SW8 53Mb 112
Minshull Pl. BR3: Beck 66Cc 136
Minson Rd. E9 39Zb 72
Minstead Gdns. SW15 59Va 110
Minstead Way KT3: N Mald 72Ua 154
Minster Av. SM1: Sutt 75Cb 155
Minster Cl. AL10: Hat 2C 8
Minster Ct. EC3 4J 225
RM11: Horn 33Qd 77
W5 42Na 87
Minster Dr. CR0: C'don 77Ub 157
Minster Gdns. KT8: W Mole 70Ba 129
Minster Ho. AL10: Hat 2C 8
Minsterley Av. TW17: Shep 70U 128
Minster Pavement EC3 4J 225
Minster Rd. BR1: Brom 66Kc 137
NW2 36Ab 68
Minster Wlk. N8 28Nb 50
Minster Way RM11: Horn 32Pd 77
SL3: L'ly 47B 82
Minstrel Cl. HP1: Hem H 1K 3
Minstrel Gdns. KT5: Surb 70Pa 131
Mint Bus. Pk. E16 43Kc 93
Mint Cl. UB10: Hil 41R 84
Mintern Cl. N13 20Rb 33
Minterne Av. UB2: S'hall 49Ca 85
Minterne Rd. HA3: Kenton 29Pa 47
Minterne Waye UB4: Yead 44Y 85
Mintern St. N1 1G 219 (40Tb 71)
Minter Rd. IG11: Bark 42Wc 95
Minters Orchard
TN15: Plat 92De 205
Mint La. KT20: Lwr K 1J 207
Minton Ho. SE11 5K 229
Minton M. NW6 37Db 69
Minton Ri. SL6: Tap 4B 80
Mint Rd. SM6: Wall 77Kb 156
SM7: Bans 88Eb 175

Mint St.—Monument Bri. Ind. Est. E.

Mint St. E2 42Xb 91
(off Three Colts La.)
SE1 1D 230 (47Sb 91)
Mint Wlk. CR0: C'don 76Sb 157
CR6: W'ham 89Zb 178
GU21: Knap 9J 167
Mintwater Cl. KT17: Ewe 82Wa 174
Mirabelle Gdns. E20 36Ec 72
Mirabel Rd. SW6 52Bb 111
Mirador Cres. SL2: Slou 5M 81
Mira Ho. E20 36Ec 72
(off Prize Wlk.)
Miramar Way RM12: Horn 36Md 77
Miranda Cl. E1 43Yb 92
Miranda Ct. W3 44Pa 87
Miranda Ho. N1 2H 219
Miranda Rd. N19 32Lb 70
Mirfield St. SE7 49Mc 93
Miriam La. AL2: Chis G 8M 5
Miriam Rd. SE18 50Uc 94
Mirravale Trad. Est. RM8: Dag 31Ad 75
Mirren Cl. HA2: Harr 35Ba 65
Mirrie La. UB9: Den 29E 42
Mirror Path SE9 62Lc 137
Misbourne Av. SL9: Chal P 22A 42
Misbourne Cl. SL9: Chal P 22A 42
Misbourne Ct. SL3: L'ly 49C 82
Misbourne Mdws. UB9: Den 32E 62
Misbourne Rd. UB10: Hil 39Q 64
Misbourne Va. SL9: Chal P 22A 42
Miskin Rd. DA1: Dart 59Ld 119
(not continuous)
Miskin Theatre 61Ld 141
Miskin Way DA12: Grav'nd 5F 144
Missden Dr. HP3: Hem H 4C 4
Missenden SE17 7G 231
Missenden Cl. TW14: Felt 60V 106
Missenden Gdns. SL1: Burn 4A 80
SM4: Mord 72Eb 155
Missenden Ho. NW8 5D 214
WD18: Wat 17U 26
(off Chenies Way)
Mission, The E14 44Bc 92
(off Commercial Rd.)
Mission Gro. E17 29Ac 52
Mission Pl. SE15 53Wb 113
Mission Sq. TW8: Bford 51Na 109
Missouri Ct. HA5: Eastc 30Y 45
Mistletoe Cl. CR0: C'don 74Zb 158
Mistley Ct. KT18: Eps 85Ta 173
(off Ashley Rd.)
Mistral SE5 53Ub 113
Mistral Ct. AL1: St A 3E 6
(off Bakers Ct.)
Misty's Fld. KT12: Walt T 74Y 151
Mitali Pas. E1 44Wb 91
MITCHAM 69Hb 133
Mitcham Gdn. Village CR4: Mitc 71Jb 156
Mitcham Golf Course 71Jb 156
Mitcham Ho. SE5 53Sb 113
Mitcham Ind. Est. CR4: Mitc 67Jb 134
Mitcham La. SW16 65Lb 134
Mitcham Pk. CR4: Mitc 70Gb 133
Mitcham Rd. CR0: C'don 72Nb 156
E6 41Nc 94
IG3: Ilf 31Vc 75
SW17 64Hb 133
Mitchell NW9 25Va 48
(off Quakers Course)
Mitchell Av. DA11: Nflt 61Fe 143
Mitchellbrook Way NW10 37Ta 67
Mitchell Cl. AL1: St A 6B 6
DA1: Dart 61Nd 141
DA17: Belv 48Ed 96
HP3: Bov 9B 2
RM13: Rain 40Ld 77
SE2 49Yc 95
SL1: Slou 8E 80
WD5: Ab L 4W 12
Mitchell Ho. N1 38Rb 71
(off College Cross)
W12 45Xa 88
(off White City Est.)
Mitchell Rd. BR6: Orp 77Vc 161
N13 22Sb 51
Mitchell's Pl. SE21 58Ub 113
(off Aysgarth Rd.)
Mitchell St. EC1 5D 218 (42Sb 91)
(not continuous)
Mitchell Wlk. DA10: Swans 59Ae 121
E6 43Nc 94
(off Allhallows Rd.)
E6 43Pc 94
(Elmley Cl.)
Mitchell Way BR1: Brom 67Jc 137
NW10 37Sa 67
Mitchem Cl. TN15: W King 80Ud 164
Mitchener's La. RH1: Blet 6K 209
Mitchison Ct. TW16: Sun 67W 128
(off Downside)
Mitchison Rd. N1 37Tb 71
Mitchley Av. CR2: Sande 85Sb 177
CR8: Purl 85Sb 177
Mitchley Gro. CR2: Sande 85Wb 177
Mitchley Hill CR2: Sande 85Vb 177
Mitchley Rd. N17 27Wb 51
Mitchley Vw. CR2: Sande 85Wb 177
Mitford Bldgs. SW6 52Cb 111
(off Dawes Rd.)
Mitford Cl. KT9: Chess 79La 152
Mitford Rd. N19 33Nb 70
Mitre, The E14 45Bc 92
Mitre Av. E17 27Cc 52
Mitre Bri. Ind. Pk. W10 42Xa 88
(not continuous)
Mitre Cl. BR2: Brom 68Hc 137
SM2: Sutt 80Eb 155
TW17: Shep 72T 150
Mitre Ho. SW3 7F 227
Mitre Pas. EC3 3J 225
SE10 47Gc 93
Mitre Rd. E15 40Gc 73
SE1 1A 230 (47Qb 90)
Mitre Sq. EC3 3J 225 (44Ub 91)
Mitre St. EC3 3J 225 (44Ub 91)
Mitre Way W10 42Xa 88
Mitre Yd. SW3 5E 226 (49Gb 89)
Mitten Ho. SE8 52Dc 114
(off Creative Rd.)
Mixbury Gro. KT13: Weyb 79T 150
Mixnams La. KT16: Chert 69J 127
Mizen Cl. KT11: Cobh 86Z 171
Mizen Ct. E14 47Cc 92
(off Alpha Gro.)
Mizens Railway 8H 167
Mizen Way KT11: Cobh 87Y 171
Mizzen Mast Ho. SE18 48Pc 94
Moat, The KT3: N Mald 67Ua 132
Moat Cl. BR6: Chels 79Vc 161
TN13: Chip 94Ed 202
WD23: Bush 15Da 27
Moat Ct. DA15: Sidc 62Vc 139
KT16: Ott 79E 148
KT21: Asht 89Na 173
SE9 58Pc 116
Moat Cres. N3 27Db 49
Moat Cft. DA16: Well 55Yc 117
Moat Dr. E13 40Lc 73
HA1: Harr 28Ea 46
HA4: Ruis 31U 64
SL2: Slou 3N 81
Moated Farm Dr.
KT15: Add, New H 80L 149
Moat Farm Rd. UB5: N'olt 37Ba 65
Moatfield NW6 38Ab 68
Moatfield Rd. WD23: Bush 15Da 27
Moatlands Ho. WC1 4G 217
Moat La. DA8: Erith 53Jd 118
KT8: E Mos 69Ha 130
Moat Lodge, The HA2: Harr 33Ga 66
Moat Pl. SW9 55Pb 112
UB9: Den 35K 63
W3 44Ra 87
Moat Side EN3: Pond E 14Zb 34
TW13: Hanw 63Y 129
Moat Vw. Ct. WD23: Bush 15Da 27
Moberly Rd. SW4 59Mb 112
Moberly Sports & Education Cen. 41Za 88
(off Chamberlayne Rd.)
Moberly Way CR8: Kenley 92Tb 197
Mobil Ct. WC2 3J 223
(off Clement's Inn)
MOBY DICK 28Ad 55
Mocatta Ho. E1 43Xb 91
(off Brady St.)
Mocatta M. RH1: Mers 3C 208
Mocha Ct. E3 40Dc 72
(off Taylor Pl.)
Mockford M. RH1: Mers 3C 208
MODA
Mus. of Domestic
Design & Architecture 26Va 48
Modbury Gdns. NW5 37Jb 70
Modder Pl. SW15 56Za 110
Model Cotts. GU24: Pirb 3B 186
SW14 56Sa 109
W13 47Ka 86
Model Farm Cl. SE9 62Nc 138
Modena M. WD18: Wat 14U 26
Modern Ct. EC4 2B 224
Modling Ho. E2 40Zb 72
(off Mace St.)
Moelwyn N7 36Mb 70
Moelyn M. HA1: Harr 29Ja 46
Moffat Ct. SW19 64Cb 133
Moffat Ho. SE5 52Sb 113
Moffat Rd. CR7: Thor H 68Sb 135
N13 23Nb 50
SW17 63Hb 133
Moffats Cl. AL9: Brk P 8J 9
Moffats La. AL9: Brk P 9G 8
MOGADOR 100Ab 194
Mogador Rd. KT20: Lwr K 100Ab 194
Mogden La. TW7: Isle 57Ha 108
Mohammedi Pk. UB5: N'olt 39Ca 65
Mohawk Ho. E3 40Ac 72
(off Gernon Rd.)
Mohmmad Khan Rd. E11 32Hc 73
Moineau NW9 25Va 48
(off Long Mead)
Moira Cl. N17 26Ub 51
Moira Ho. SW9 53Qb 112
(off Gosling Way)
Moira Rd. SE9 56Pc 116
Moir Cl. CR2: Sande 81Wb 177
Mokswell Ct. N10 25Jb 50
Molash Rd. BR5: St M Cry 70Zc 139
Molasses Ho. SW11 55Eb 111
(off Clove Hitch Quay)
Molasses Row SW11 55Eb 111
Mole Abbey Gdns. KT8: W Mole 69Da 129
Mole Bus. Pk. KT22: Lea 93Ja 192
Mole Ct. KT19: Ewe 77Sa 153
Mole Ho. NW8 6C 214
Molember Ct. KT8: E Mos 70Ga 130
Molember Rd. KT8: E Mos 71Ga 152
Mole Pl. KT8: W Mole 70Da 129
Mole Rd. KT12: Hers 78Z 151
KT22: Fet 93Fa 192
Molescroft SE9 62Sc 138
Molesey Av. KT8: W Mole 71Ba 151
Molesey Cl. KT12: Hers 77Aa 151
Molesey Dr. SM3: Cheam 75Ab 154
Molesey Heath Local Nature Reserve 72Ca 151
Molesey Pk. Av. KT8: W Mole 71Da 151
Molesey Pk. Cl. KT8: E Mos 71Ea 152
Molesey Pk. Rd.
KT8: W Mole, E Mos 71Da 151
Molesey Road 75Aa 151
Molesey Rd. KT8: W Mole 73Aa 151
KT12: Hers, Walt T 78Z 151
Molesford Rd. SW6 53Cb 111
Molesham Cl. KT8: W Mole 69Da 129
Molesham Way KT8: W Mole 69Da 129
Moles Hill KT22: Oxs 83Fa 172
Molesworth Ho. SE17 51Rb 113
(off Brandon Est.)
Molesworth Rd. KT11: Cobh 85W 170
Molesworth St. SE13 56Ec 114
Mole Valley Pl. KT21: Asht 91Ma 193
Moliner Ct. BR3: Beck 66Cc 136
Mollands Ct. RM15: S Ock 42Ae 99
Mollands La. RM15: S Ock 42Yd 98
Mollis Ho. E3 43Cc 92
(off Gale St.)
Mollison Av.
EN3: Brim, Enf L, Enf W, Pond E 7Ac 20
Mollison Dr. SM6: Wall 80Mb 156
Mollison Ri. DA12: Grav'nd 4G 144
Mollison Sq. SM6: Wall 80Mb 156
(off Mollison Dr.)
Mollison Way HA8: Edg 26Pa 47
Molloy Ct. GU21: Wok 88C 168
Molly Huggins Cl. SW12 59Lb 112
Molteno Rd. WD17: Wat 10W 12
Molton Ho. N1 1J 217
Molyneaux Av. HP3: Bov 9B 2
Molyneux Dr. SW17 63Kb 134
Molyneux Rd. GU20: W'sham 9B 146
KT13: Weyb 78Q 150
Molyneux St. W1 1E 220 (43Gb 89)
Molyns M. SL1: Slou 6C 80
Monaco Works WD4: K Lan 2R 12
Monahan Av. CR8: Purl 84Pb 176
Monarch Cl. BR4: W W'ck 77Hc 159
RM13: Rain 40Jd 76
RM18: Tilb 4D 122
TW14: Felt 59U 106
Monarch Ct. HA7: Stan 24Ma 47
(off Howard Rd.)
N2 29Fb 49
Monarch Dr. E16 43Mc 93
UB3: Hayes 45V 84
Monarch Ho. W8 48Cb 89
(off Kensington High St.)
Monarch M. E17 30Dc 52
SW16 64Qb 134
Monarch Pde. CR4: Mitc 68Hb 133
Monarch Pl. IG9: Buck H 19Lc 35
Monarch Point SW6 54Eb 111
Monarch Rd. DA17: Belv 48Cd 96
Monarch Sq. SW11 56Gb 111
Monarchs Way EN8: Walt C 5Ac 20
HA4: Ruis 32T 64
Monarch Wlk. WD7: Shenl 5Pa 15
Monarch Way IG2: Ilf 30Tc 54
Mona Rd. SE15 54Yb 114
Monastery Cl. AL3: St A 2A 6
Monastery Gdns. EN2: Enf 12Tb 33
SL3: Dat 5M 103
Mona St. E16 43Hc 93
Monaveen Gdns. KT8: W Mole 69Da 129
Monck Ho. SE1 2E 230
Moncks Row SW18 58Bb 111
Monck St. SW1 4E 228 (48Mb 90)
Monckton Ct. W14 48Bb 89
(off Strangways Ter.)
Monckton Rd. TN15: Bor G 92Be 205
Monclar Rd. SE5 56Tb 113
Moncorvo Cl. SW7 2D 226 (47Gb 89)
Moncrieff Cl. E6 44Nc 94
Moncrieff Pl. SE15 54Wb 113
Moncrieff St. SE15 54Wb 113
Monday All. N16 33Vb 71
(off High St.)
Mondial Way UB3: Harl 52S 106
Mondragon Ho. SW8 53Nb 112
(off Guildford Rd.)
Monds Cotts. TN14: Sund 96Ad 201
Monega Rd. E7 37Lc 73
E12 37Lc 73
Monet Ct. SE16 50Xb 91
(off Stubbs Dr.)
Money Av. CR3: Cat'm 94Ub 197
Moneyer Ho. N1 3F 219
MONEYHILL 18L 25
Moneyhill Ct. WD3: Rick 18K 25
Moneyhill Pde. WD3: Rick 18K 25
Money Hill Rd. WD3: Rick 18L 25
Money La. UB7: W Dray 48M 83
Money Rd. CR3: Cat'm 94Tb 197
Mongers Almshouses E9 38Zb 72
(off Church Cres.)
Mongers La. KT17: Ewe 82Va 174
(not continuous)
Monica Cl. WD24: Wat 12Y 27
Monica Ct. EN1: Enf 15Ub 33
Monica James Ho. DA14: Sidc 62Wc 139
Monica Shaw Ct. NW1 2E 216
(not continuous)
Monier Rd. E3 38Cc 72
Monivea Rd. BR3: Beck 66Bc 136
Monkchester Cl. IG10: Lough 11Pc 36
Monk Ct. W12 46Wa 88
Monk Dr. E16 45Jc 93
MONKEN HADLEY 12Bb 31
Monkey Puzzle Way SM5: Cars 81Hb 175
Monkfrith Av. N14 16Kb 32
Monkfrith Cl. N14 17Kb 32
Monkfrith Way N14 17Jb 32
Monkhams EN9: Walt A 2Ec 20
Monkham's Av. IG8: Wfd G 22Kc 53
Monkham's Dr. IG8: Wfd G 22Kc 53
Monkham's La. IG8: Wfd G 22Jc 53
IG9: Buck H 20Kc 35
Monkleigh Rd. SM4: Mord 69Ab 132
Monk Pas. E16 45Jc 93
(off Monk Dr.)
Monks Av. EN5: New Bar 16Eb 31
KT8: W Mole 71Ba 151
Monks Chase CM13: Ingve 22Ee 59
Monks Cl. AL1: St A 4C 6
EN2: Enf 12Sb 33
HA2: Harr 33Da 65
HA4: Ruis 35Z 65
SE2 49Zc 95
SL5: Asc 2A 146
Monks Ct. RH2: Reig 6K 207
Monks Cres. KT12: Walt T 74X 151
KT15: Add 78K 149
Monksdene Gdns. SM1: Sutt 76Db 155
Monks Dr. SL5: Asc 2A 146
W3 43Qa 87
Monksfield Way SL2: Slou 2E 80
Monks Ga. AL1: St A 4C 6
Monks Grn. KT22: Fet 93Ea 192
Monksgrove IG10: Lough 15Qc 36
Monks Haven SS17: Stan H 1N 101
Monks Horton Way AL1: St A 1E 6
Monksmead WD6: Bore 14Sa 29
MONKS ORCHARD 73Ac 158
Monks Orchard DA1: Dart 61Md 141
Monks Orchard Rd. BR3: Beck 74Cc 158
Monks Pk. HA9: Wemb 37Ra 67
Monks Pk. Gdns. HA9: Wemb 38Ra 67
Monks Pl. CR3: Cat'm 94Xb 197
Monks Rd. EN2: Enf 12Rb 33
GU25: Vir W 10P 125
SL4: Wind 4B 102
SM7: Bans 89Cb 175
Monk St. SE18 49Qc 94
Monk's Wlk. KT16: Chert 70G 126
RH2: Reig 6K 207
TW20: Thorpe 69F 126
Monks Wlk. DA13: Sflt 65Ce 143
SL5: Asc 2A 146
Monks Way BR3: Beck 72Cc 158
BR5: Farnb 74Sc 160
NW11 28Bb 49
TW18: Staines 66M 127
UB7: Harm 51N 105
Monks Well DA9: Ghithe 56Yd 120
(off Watermans Way)
Monkswell La. CR5: Coul 96Db 195
Monkswood Av. EN9: Walt A 5Fc 21
Monkswood Gdns. IG5: Ilf 27Qc 54
WD6: Bore 15Ta 29
Monkton Ho. E5 36Xb 71
SE16 47Zb 92
(off Wolfe Cres.)
Monkton Rd. DA16: Well 54Vc 117
Monkton St. SE11 5A 230 (49Qb 90)
Monkville Av. NW11 28Bb 49
Monkville Pde. NW11 28Bb 49
Monkwell Sq. EC2 1E 224 (43Sb 91)
Monkwood Cl. RM1: Rom 29Jd 56
Monmouth Av. E18 27Kc 53
KT1: Hamp W 66La 130
Monmouth Cl. CR4: Mitc 70Nb 134
DA16: Well 56Wc 117
W4 48Sa 87
Monmouth Ct. DA12: Grav'nd 8F 122
(off Romulus Rd.)
W7 43Ha 86
(off Copley Cl.)
Monmouth Gro. TW8: Bford 49Na 87
Monmouth Pl. W2 44Db 89
(off Monmouth Rd.)
Monmouth Rd. E6 41Pc 94
N9 19Xb 33
RM9: Dag 36Bd 75
UB3: Harl 49U 84
W2 44Cb 89
WD17: Wat 13X 27
Monmouth St. WC2 3F 223 (44Nb 90)
Monnery Rd. N19 34Lb 70
Monnow Grn. RM15: Avel 45Sd 98
Monnow Rd. RM15: Avel 45Sd 98
SE1 50Wb 91
Mono La. TW13: Felt 61X 129
Monoux Almshouses E17 28Dc 52
Monoux Gro. E17 25Cc 52
Monro Ct. E16 42Hc 93
Monroe Cres. EN1: Enf 11Xb 33
Monroe Dr. SW14 57Ra 109
Monroe Ho. NW8 4E 214
Monro Gdns. HA3: Hrw W 24Ga 46
Monro Ind. Est. EN8: Walt C 6Ac 20
Monro Pl. KT19: Eps 81Qa 173
Monro Way E5 35Wb 71
Monsell Ct. N4 34Rb 71
Monsell Gdns. TW18: Staines 64G 126
Monsell Rd. N4 34Qb 70
Monsey Pl. E1 42Ac 92
Monson Rd. NW10 40Wa 68
RH1: Redh 3P 207
SE14 52Zb 114
Mons Wlk. TW20: Egh 64E 126
Mons Way BR2: Brom 72Nc 160
Montacute Rd. CR0: New Ad 81Ec 178
SE6 59Bc 114
SM4: Mord 72Fb 155
WD23: B Hea 17Ga 28
Montagu Ct. W1 1G 221
Montagu Cres. N18 21Xb 51
Montague Av. CR2: Sande 84Ub 177
SE4 56Bc 114
W7 46Ha 86
Montague Cl. EN5: Barn 14Bb 31
KT12: Walt T 73X 151
SE1 6F 225 (46Tb 91)
SL2: Farn R 10F 60
Montague Ct. DA15: Sidc 62Wc 139
N7 38Qb 70
(off St Clements St.)
Montague Dr. CR3: Cat'm 94Sb 197
Montague Gdns. W3 45Qa 87
Montague Hall Pl. WD23: Bush 16Ca 27
Montague Ho. E16 46Kc 93
(off Wesley Av.)
IG3: Ilf 32Wc 75
N1 39Ub 71
(off Halcomb St.)
Montague M. E3 41Bc 92
(off Tredegar Ter.)
SE20 65Yb 136
Montague Pas. UB8: Uxb 38M 63
Montague Pl. BR8: Swan 70Hd 140
WC1 7E 216 (43Mb 90)
Montague Rd. CR0: C'don 74Rb 157
E8 36Wb 71
E11 33Hc 73
N8 29Pb 50
N15 28Wb 51
SL1: Slou 5K 81
SW19 66Db 133
TW3: Houn 55Da 107
TW10: Rich 58Na 109
UB2: S'hall 49Aa 85
UB8: Uxb 38M 63
W7 46Ha 86
W13 44Ka 86
Montague Sq. SE15 52Yb 114
Montague St. EC1 1D 224 (43Sb 91)
WC1 7F 217 (43Nb 90)
Montague Ter. BR2: Brom 70Hc 137
Montague Walks HA0: Wemb 39Pa 67
Montague Waye UB2: S'hall 48Aa 85
Montagu Gdns. DA1: Dart 54Pd 119
N18 21Xb 51
SM6: Wall 77Lb 156
Montagu Ind. Est. N18 21Yb 52
Montagu Mans. W1 7G 215 (43Hb 89)
Montagu M. Nth. W1 1G 221 (43Hb 89)
Montagu M. Sth. W1 2G 221 (44Hb 89)
Montagu M. W. W1 2G 221 (44Hb 89)
Montagu Pl. W1 1F 221 (43Hb 89)
Montagu Rd. N9 22Xb 51
N18 22Xb 51
NW4 30Wa 48
SL3: Dat 3M 103
Montagu Row W1 1G 221 (43Hb 89)
Montagu Sq. W1 1G 221 (43Hb 89)
Montagu St. W1 2G 221 (44Hb 89)
Montaigne Cl. SW1 6E 228 (49Mb 90)
Montalt Rd. IG8: Wfd G 21Hc 53
Montana Bldg. SE13 53Dc 114
(off Deal's Gateway)
Montana Cl. CR2: Sande 82Tb 177
Montana Gdns. SE26 64Bc 136
SM1: Sutt 78Eb 155
Montana Rd. SW17 62Jb 134
SW20 67Ya 132
Montanaro Ct. N1 39Sb 71
(off Coleman Flds.)
Montayne Rd. EN8: Chesh 4Zb 20
Montbazon Ct. CM14: B'wood 18Xd 40
Montbelle Rd. SE9 62Rc 138
Montbretia Cl. BR5: St M Cry 70Yc 139
Montcalm Cl. BR2: Hayes 72Jc 159
UB4: Yead 41X 85
Montcalm Ho. E14 49Bc 92
Montcalm Rd. SE7 52Mc 115
Montclare St. E2 4K 219 (42Vb 91)
Monteagle Av. IG11: Bark 37Sc 74
Monteagle Ct. N1 1J 219 (40Ub 71)
Monteagle Way E5 34Wb 71
SE15 55Xb 113
Montefiore Ct. N16 32Vb 71
Montefiore St. SW8 54Kb 112
Montego Cl. SE24 56Qb 112
Montem La. SL1: Slou 6H 81
Montem Leisure Cen. 7H 81
Montem Rd. KT3: N Mald 70Ua 132
SE23 59Bc 114
Montem St. N4 32Pb 70
Montenotte Rd. N8 29Lb 50
Monterey Apartments N15 29Tb 51
Monterey Cl. DA5: Bexl 61Ed 140
NW7 22Ua 48
(off The Broadway)
UB10: Hil 38Q 64
Monterey Studios W10 40Ab 68
Montesole Ct. HA5: Pinn 26Y 45
Montevetro SW11 53Fb 111
Montfichet Rd. E20 38Ec 72
Montford Pl. SE11 50Qb 90
Montford Rd. TW16: Sun 70W 128
Montfort Gdns. IG6: Ilf 23Sc 54
Montfort Ho. E2 41Yb 92
(off Victoria Pk. Sq.)
E14 48Ec 92
(off Galbraith St.)
Montfort Pl. SW19 60Za 110
Montfort Rd. TN15: Kems'g 89Nd 183
Montgolfier Wlk. UB5: N'olt 41Aa 85
Montgomerie M. SE23 59Yb 114
Montgomery Av. HP2: Hem H 1A 4
KT10: Hin W 75Ga 152
Montgomery Cl. CR4: Mitc 70Nb 134
DA12: Grav'nd 3F 144
DA15: Sidc 58Vc 117
RM16: Grays 47Ee 99
Montgomery Ct. CR2: S Croy 78Ub 157
(off Birdhurst Rd.)
KT22: Lea 92Ka 192
(off Levett Rd.)
W4 52Sa 109
Montgomery Cres. RM3: Rom 22Ld 57
Montgomery Gdns. SM2: Sutt 80Fb 155
Montgomery Ho. UB5: N'olt 41Ba 85
(off Taywood Rd.)
W2 1B 220
Montgomery Lodge E1 42Yb 92
(off Cleveland Gro.)
Montgomery Pl. SL2: Slou 4N 81
Montgomery Rd. DA4: S Dar 67Td 142
GU22: Wok 90A 168
HA8: Edg 23Pa 47
W4 49Sa 87
Montgomery Sq. E14 46Dc 92
Montgomery St. E14 46Dc 92
Montgomery Way CR8: Kenley 92Tb 197
Montholme Rd. SW11 58Hb 111
Monthope Rd. E1 43Wb 91
Montolieu Gdns. SW15 57Xa 110
Montpelier Av. DA5: Bexl 59Zc 117
W5 43La 86
Montpelier Cl. UB10: Hil 39Q 64
Montpelier Ct. BR2: Brom 70Hc 137
(off Westmoreland Rd.)
SL4: Wind 4G 102
W5 43Ma 87
Montpelier Gdns. E6 41Mc 93
RM6: Chad H 31Yc 75
Montpelier Gro. NW5 36Lb 70
Montpelier M. SW7 3E 226 (48Gb 89)
Montpelier Pl. E1 44Yb 92
SW7 3E 226 (48Gb 89)
Montpelier Ri. HA9: Wemb 32Ma 67
NW11 31Ab 68
(not continuous)
Montpelier Rd. CR8: Purl 82Rb 177
N3 25Eb 49
SE15 53Xb 113
SM1: Sutt 77Eb 155
W5 43Ma 87
Montpelier Row SE3 54Hc 115
TW1: Twick 59La 108
Montpelier Sq. SW7 2E 226 (47Gb 89)
Montpelier St. SW7 3E 226 (48Gb 89)
Montpelier Ter. SW7 2E 226 (47Gb 89)
Montpelier Va. SE3 54Hc 115
Montpelier Wlk. SW7 2E 226 (48Gb 89)
Montpelier Way NW11 31Ab 68
Montpellier Ct. KT12: Walt T 72W 150
Montpellier Ho. IG7: Chig 22Sc 54
Montrave Rd. SE20 65Yb 136
Montreal Ho. SE16 47Zb 92
(off Maple M.)
UB4: Yead 41X 85
(off Ayles Rd.)
Montreal Pl. WC2 4H 223 (45Pb 90)
Montreal Rd. IG1: Ilf 31Sc 74
RM18: Tilb 5C 122
TN13: Riv 95Gd 202
Montrell Rd. SW2 60Nb 112
Montrose SL1: Slou 4F 80
Montrose Av. DA15: Sidc 59Wc 117
DA16: Well 55Tc 116
HA8: Edg 26Sa 47
NW6 40Ab 68
RM2: Rom 26Ld 57
SL1: Slou 4F 80
(not continuous)
SL3: Dat 2N 103
TW2: Whitt 59Da 107
Montrose Cl. DA16: Well 55Vc 117
IG8: Wfd G 21Jc 53
TW15: Ashf 65S 128
Montrose Ct. HA1: Harr 29Da 45
NW9 26Sa 47
NW11 28Bb 49
SE6 61Hc 137
SW7 2C 226 (47Fb 89)
Montrose Cres. HA0: Wemb 37Na 67
N12 23Eb 49
Montrose Gdns. CR4: Mitc 68Hb 133
KT22: Oxs 84Fa 172
SM1: Sutt 75Db 155
Montrose Ho. E14 48Cc 92
SW1 2J 227
Montrose Pl. SW1 2J 227 (47Jb 90)
Montrose Rd. HA3: W'stone 26Ga 46
TW14: Bedf 58T 106
Montrose Wlk. HA7: Stan 23Ka 46
KT13: Weyb 76R 150
Montrose Way SE23 60Zb 114
SL3: Dat 3P 103
Montrouge Cres. KT17: Eps D 88Ya 174
Montserrat Av. IG8: Wfd G 24Fc 53
Montserrat Cl. SE19 64Tb 135
Montserrat Rd. SW15 56Ab 110
Monument, The 4G 225
Monument Bri. Ind. Est. E.
GU21: Wok 87D 168

Monument Bri. Ind. Est. W.—Mount, The

Monument Bri. Ind. Est. W.
GU21: Wok 87C 168
Monument Bus. Cen. GU21: Wok 87D 168
Monument Gdns. SE13 57Ec 114
Monument Grn. KT13: Weyb 76R 150
Monument Hill KT13: Weyb 77R 150
Monument La. SL9: Chal P 23A 42
Monument Pl. *AL3: St A* *1B 6*
(off Ashwell St.)
Monument Rd. GU21: Wok 86C 168
KT13: Weyb 77R 150
Monument St. EC3 4G 225 (45Tb 91)
Monument Way N17 27Vb 51
Monument Way E. GU21: Wok 87D 168
Monument Way W. GU21: Wok 87C 168
Monza St. E1 45Yb 92
Moodkee St. SE16 48Yb 92
Moody Rd. SE15 53Vb 113
Moody St. E1 41Zb 92
Moon Ct. SE12 56Jc 115
Moon Ho. HA1: Harr 28Ga 46
Moon La. EN5: Barn 13Bb 31
Moonlight Dr. SE23 59Xb 113
Moonraker Point SE1 1C 230
Moon St. N1 39Rb 71
MOOR, THE 61F 126
Moorcroft HA8: Edg 25Ra 47
Moorcroft Gdns. BR2: Brom 71Nc 160
Moorcroft La. UB8: Hil 43Q 84
Moorcroft Rd. SW16 62Nb 134
Moorcroft Way HA5: Pinn 29Aa 45
Moordown SE18 52Rc 116
Moore Av. RM18: Tilb 4D 122
RM20: Grays 50Ae 99
Moore Cl. CR4: Mitc 68Kb 134
DA2: Dart 61Td 142
KT15: Add 78K 149
SL1: Slou 7F 80
SW14 55Sa 109
Moore Ct. HA0: Wemb 37Na 67
HA7: Stan 25Ma 47
N1 *39Rb 71*
(off Gaskin St.)
Moore Cres. RM9: Dag 39Xc 75
Moorefield Rd. N17 26Vb 51
Moore Gro. Cres. TW20: Egh 65B 126
Moore Ho. AL3: St A 4N 5
E1 *45Yb 92*
(off Cable St.)
E2 *41Yb 92*
(off Roman Rd.)
E14 47Cc 92
N8 *28Nb 50*
(off Pembroke Rd.)
RM11: Horn *30Jd 56*
(off Benjamin Cl.)
SE10 *50Hc 93*
(off Armitage Rd.)
SW1 7K 227
Mooreland Rd. BR1: Brom 66Hc 137
Moor End Rd. HP1: Hem H 3L 3
Moore Pk. Rd. SW6 52Db 111
Moore Place Golf Course 78Ca 151
Moore Rd. DA10: Swans 58Ae 121
GU24: Brkwd 3A 186
SE19 65Sb 135
Moores La. SL4: Eton W 9D 80
Moores Pl. CM14: B'wood 19Zd 41
Moore St. SW3 5F 227 (49Hb 89)
Moore Wlk. E7 35Jc 73
Moore Way SM2: Sutt 81Cb 175
Moorey Cl. E15 39Hc 73
Moorfield Av. W5 42Ma 87
Moorfield Rd. BR6: Orp 73Wc 161
EN3: Enf H 11Yb 34
KT9: Chess 78Na 153
UB8: Cowl 44M 83
UB9: Den 31J 63
Moorfields EC2 1F 225 (43Tb 91)
Moorfields Cl. TW18: Staines 67G 126
Moorfields Highwalk EC2 1F 225
(not continuous)
Moor Furlong SL1: Slou 6B 80
Moorgate EC2 2F 225 (44Tb 91)
Moorgate Pl. EC2 2F 225
Moorgreen Ho. EC1 3B 218
Moorhall Rd. UB9: Hare 30K 43
Moorhayes Dr. TW18: Lale 69L 127
Moorhead Way SE3 55Jc 115
Moorhen Cl. DA8: Erith 51Kd 119
Moorhen Dr. NW9 30Va 48
Moorhen Ho. *E3* *39Bc 72*
(off Old Ford Rd.)
Moorhen Wlk. *DA9: Ghithe* *58Wd 120*
(off Sanderling Way)
Moorholme GU22: Wok 91A 188
MOORHOUSE 99Pc 200
Moorhouse NW9 25Va 48
MOORHOUSE BANK 100Qc 200
Moorhouse Rd. HA3: Kenton 27Ma 47
RH8: Limp, Westrm 100Qc 200
TN16: Westrm 100Qc 200
W2 44Cb 89
Moorhurst Av. EN7: G Oak 1Qb 18
Moorings, The *AL1: St A* *1D 6*
(off Althorp Rd.)
E16 *43Lc 93*
(off Prince Regent La.)
KT14: W Byf 84L 169
KT23: Bookh 97Ca 191
SL4: Wind 2A 102
WD23: Bush 14Aa 27
Moorings Ho. TW8: Bford 52La 108
MOOR JUNC. 52K 105
Moorland Cl. RM5: Col R 24Dd 56
TW2: Whitt 59Ca 107
Moorland Rd. HP1: Hem H 4J 3
SW9 56Rb 113
UB7: Harm 51L 105
Moorlands AL2: F'mre 10C 6
KT12: Walt T *76W 150*
(off Ashley Pk. Rd.)
UB5: N'olt 39Aa 65
Moorlands, The GU22: Wok 93B 188
Moorlands Av. NW7 23Xa 48
Moor La. EC2 1F 225 (43Tb 91)
(not continuous)
GU22: Wok 94A 188
KT9: Chess 77Na 153
RM14: Upm 32Ud 78
TW18: Staines 62G 126
TW19: Staines 60F 104
UB7: Harm 51L 105
WD3: Rick 18P 25
WD3: Sarr 8G 10
Moor La. Crossing WD18: Wat 17S 26
Moormead Dr. KT19: Ewe 78Ua 154
Moor Mead Rd. TW1: Twick 58Ja 108
Moormede Cres.
TW18: Staines 63H 127
Moor Mill La. AL2: Col S 1Ga 14
(not continuous)
MOOR PARK 20S 26
Moor Pk.
Rickmansworth 20Q 26
Moor Pk. Gdns. KT2: King T 66Ua 132
Moor Pk. Golf Course 20Q 26
Moor Pk. Ind. Cen. WD18: Wat 17S 26
Moor Pk. Rd. HA6: Nwood 22T 44
Moor Pl. EC2 1F 225 (43Tb 91)
GU20: W'sham 8A 146
Moor Rd. TN14: S'oaks 92Kd 203
Moors, The RH1: Mers 3C 208
Moorside HP3: Hem H 5K 3
Moorside Rd. BR1: Brom 62Gc 137
Moors Nature Reserve, The
Redhill 4B 208
Moorsom Way CR5: Coul 89Mb 176
Moorstown Ct. SL1: Slou 7J 81
Moor St. W1 3E 222 (44Mb 90)
Moortown Rd. WD19: Wat 21Y 45
Moor Vw. WD18: Wat 17W 26
Moorview Ho. *HP2: Hem H* *3M 3*
(off The Spires)
Moot Ct. NW9 29Qa 47
Moran Cl. AL2: Brick W 3Ba 13
Moran Ho. *E1* *46Xb 91*
(off Wapping La.)
Morant Gdns. RM5: Col R 22Dd 56
Morant Pl. N22 25Pb 50
Morant Rd. RM16: Grays 8D 100
Morants Ct. Rd. TN13: Dun G 90Ed 182
TN14: Dun G 90Ed 182
Morant St. E14 45Cc 92
Mora Rd. NW2 35Ya 68
Mora St. EC1 4E 218 (41Sb 91)
Morat St. SW9 53Pb 112
Moravian Cl. SW10 51Fb 111
Moravian Pl. SW10 51Fb 111
Moravian St. E2 40Yb 72
Moray Av. UB3: Hayes 46V 84
Moray Cl. HA8: Edg 19Ra 29
RM1: Rom 24Gd 56
Moray Ct. *CR2: S Croy* *78Sb 157*
(off Warham Rd.)
Moray Dr. SL2: Slou 4L 81
Moray Ho. *E1* *42Ac 92*
(off Harford St.)
Moray M. N7 33Pb 70
Moray Rd. N4 33Pb 70
Moray Way RM1: Rom 24Fd 56
Mordaunt Gdns. RM9: Dag 38Ad 75
Mordaunt Ho. *NW10* *39Ta 67*
(off Stracey Rd.)
Mordaunt Rd. NW10 39Ta 67
Mordaunt St. SW9 55Pb 112
MORDEN 69Db 133
Morden Cl. KT20: Tad 92Za 194
Morden Ct. SM4: Mord 70Db 133
Morden Ct. Pde. SM4: Mord 70Db 133
Morden Gdns. CR4: Mitc 70Fb 133
UB6: G'frd 36Ha 66
Morden Hall Pk. 69Eb 133
Morden Hall Rd. SM4: Mord 69Db 133
Morden Hill SE13 54Ec 114
Morden Ho. SM4: Mord 70Cb 133
Morden La. SE13 54Ec 114
MORDEN PARK 72Ab 154
Morden Pk. Pools 72Bb 155
Morden Rd. CR4: Mitc 70Eb 133
RM6: Chad H 31Ad 75
SE3 54Jc 115
SM4: Mord 70Eb 133
SW19 67Db 133
Morden Rd. M. SE3 54Jc 115
Morden St. SE13 53Dc 114
Morden Way SM3: Sutt 73Cb 155
Morden Wharf *SE10* *48Gc 93*
(off Morden Wharf Rd.)
Morden Wharf Rd. SE10 48Gc 93
Mordern Ho. NW1 6E 214
Mordon Rd. IG3: Ilf 31Vc 75
Mordred Rd. SE6 61Gc 137
Morea M. N5 36Sb 71
Moreau Wlk. SL3: Geor G 44A 82
Morecambe Cl. E1 43Zb 92
RM12: Horn 36Kd 77
Morecambe Gdns. HA7: Stan 21Ma 47
Morecambe Ho. *RM3: Rom* *22Nd 57*
(off Chudleigh Rd.)
Morecambe St. SE17 6E 230 (49Sb 91)
More Cl. CR8: Purl 83Qb 176
E16 44Hc 93
W14 49Za 88
Morecoombe Cl. KT2: King T 66Ra 131
More Copper Ho. *SE1* *7H 225*
(off Magdalen St.)
Moree Way N18 21Wb 51
Moreing Dr. DA9: Ghithe 56Yd 120
Moreland Av. RM16: Grays 47Ee 99
SL3: Coln 52E 104
Moreland Cl. SL3: Coln 52E 104
Moreland Cotts. *E3* *40Cc 72*
(off Fairfield Rd.)
Moreland Ct. NW2 34Cb 69
Moreland Dr. SL9: Ger X 31B 62
Moreland St. EC1 3C 218 (41Rb 91)
Moreland Way E4 20Dc 34
More La. KT10: Esh 75Da 151
Morel Ct. TN13: S'oaks 94Kd 203
Morella Cl. GU25: Vir W 10P 125
Morella Rd. SW12 59Hb 111
Morell Cl. EN5: New Bar 13Eb 31
Morello Av. UB8: Hil 43R 84
Morello Cl. BR8: Swan 70Fd 140
Morello Ct. SL3: L'ly 46B 82
Morello Dr. SL3: L'ly 46B 82
Morel M. RM8: Dag 32Zc 75
More London Pl. SE1 7H 225 (46Ub 91)
(not continuous)
More London Riverside
SE1 7J 225 (46Ub 91)
(not continuous)
Moremead EN9: Walt A 5Fc 21
Moremead Rd. SE6 63Bc 136
Morena St. SE6 59Dc 114
Moresby Av. KT5: Surb 73Ra 153
Moresby Rd. E5 32Xb 71
Moresby Wlk. SW8 54Lb 112
More's Gdn. *SW3* *51Fb 111*
(off Cheyne Wlk.)
Mores La. CM14: Pil H 14Sd 40
Moretaine Rd. TW15: Ashf 62M 127
Moreton Almshouses
TN16: Westrm 98Tc 200
Moreton Av. TW7: Isle 53Ga 108
Moreton Bay Ind. Est. RM2: Rom 26Md 57
Moreton Cl. BR8: Swan 68Gd 140
E5 33Xb 71
N15 30Tb 51
NW7 23Ya 48
SW1 7C 228
Moreton Ct. DA1: Cray 55Hd 118
Moreton Gdns. IG8: Wfd G 22Nc 54
Moreton Ho. SE16 48Xb 91
Moreton Ind. Est. BR8: Swan 70Kd 141
Moreton Pl. SW1 7C 228 (50Lb 90)
Moreton Rd. CR2: S Croy 78Tb 157
KT4: Wor Pk 75Wa 154
N15 30Tb 51
Moretons HA1: Harr 32Ga 66
Moreton St. SW1 7C 228 (50Lb 90)
Moreton Ter. SW1 7C 228
Moreton Ter. M. Nth. SW1 7C 228
Moreton Ter. M. Sth. SW1 7C 228
Moreton Twr. W3 46Ra 87
Moreton Way SL1: Slou 6B 80
Morewood Cl. TN13: S'oaks 95Hd 202
Morewood Cl. Ind. Est.
TN13: S'oaks 95Hd 202
Morford Cl. HA4: Ruis 31X 65
Morford Way HA4: Ruis 31X 65
Morgan Av. E17 28Fc 53
Morgan Cl. HA6: Nwood 23V 44
RM10: Dag 38Cd 76
Morgan Ct. SM5: Cars 77Hb 155
TW15: Ashf 64R 128
Morgan Cres. CM16: They B 8Tc 22
RM8: Dag 32Ad 75
Morgan Dr. DA9: Ghithe 59Ud 120
Morgan Gdns. WD25: A'ham 10Da 13
Morgan Ho. SW1 6C 228
SW8 *53Lb 112*
(off Wadhurst Rd.)
Morgan Mans. *N7* *36Qb 70*
(off Morgan Rd.)
Morgan Rd. BR1: Brom 66Jc 137
N7 36Qb 70
W10 43Bb 89
Morgan's La. UB3: Hayes 43T 84
Morgans La. *SE1* *7H 225*
(off Tooley St.)
Morgan St. E3 41Ac 92
(not continuous)
E16 43Hc 93
Morgan Wlk. BR3: Beck 70Dc 136
Morgan Way IG8: Wfd G 23Nc 54
RM13: Rain 41Ld 97
Moriarty Cl. BR1: Brom 70Qc 138
Moriatry Cl. N7 35Nb 70
Morie St. SW18 57Db 111
Morieux Rd. E10 32Bc 72
Moring Rd. SW17 63Jb 134
Morkyns Wlk. SE21 62Ub 135
Morland Av. CR0: C'don 74Ub 157
DA1: Dart 57Kd 119
Morland Cl. CR4: Mitc 69Gb 133
NW11 32Db 69
TW12: Hamp 64Ba 129
Morland Ct. *W12* *47Xa 88*
(off Coningham Rd.)
Morland Est. E8 38Wb 71
Morland Gdns. NW10 38Ta 67
UB1: S'hall 46Da 85
Morland Ho. NW1 2C 216
NW6 39Cb 69
SW1 5F 229
W11 *44Ab 88*
(off Lancaster Rd.)
Morland M. N1 38Qb 70
Morland Pl. N15 28Ub 51
Morland Rd. CR0: C'don 74Ub 157
E17 29Zb 52
HA3: Kenton 29Na 47
IG1: Ilf 33Rc 74
RM10: Dag 38Cd 76
SE20 65Zb 136
SM1: Sutt 78Eb 155
Morland Way EN8: Chesh 1Ac 20
Morley Av. E4 24Fc 53
N18 21Wb 51
N22 26Qb 50
Morley Cl. BR6: Farnb 75Rc 160
SL3: L'ly 47B 82
Morley Ct. BR2: Brom 70Hc 137
E4 22Bc 52
KT22: Fet 93Fa 192
Morley Cres. HA4: Ruis 33Y 65
HA8: Edg 19Sa 29
Morley Cres. E. HA7: Stan 26La 46
Morley Cres. W. HA7: Stan 27La 46
Morley Hill EN2: Enf 10Tb 19
Morley Ho. *SE15* *52Vb 113*
(off Commercial Way)
Morley Rd. BR7: Chst 67Sc 138
CR2: Sande 82Vb 177
E10 32Ec 72
E15 40Hc 73
IG11: Bark 39Tc 74
RM6: Chad H 29Ad 55
SE13 56Ec 114
SM3: Sutt 74Bb 155
TW1: Twick 58Ma 109
Morley Sq. RM16: Grays 9C 100
Morley St. SE1 3A 230 (48Qb 90)
Morna Rd. SE5 54Sb 113
Morning La. E9 37Yb 72
Morningside Cl. GU25: Vir W 3P 147
Morningside Rd. KT4: Wor Pk 75Ya 154
Mornington Av. BR1: Brom 69Lc 137
IG1: Ilf 31Qc 74
W14 49Bb 89
Mornington Av. Mans. *W14* *49Bb 89*
(off Mornington Av.)
Mornington Cl. IG8: Wfd G 21Jc 53
NW9 27Ua 48
TN16: Big H 89Mc 179
Mornington Ct. DA5: Bexl 60Fd 118
NW1 1B 216
Mornington Cres. NW1 1B 216 (40Lb 70)
TW5: Cran 53X 107
Mornington Gro. E3 41Cc 92
Mornington M. SE5 53Sb 113
Mornington Pl. NW1 1A 216 (40Lb 70)
SE8 *52Bc 114*
(off Mornington Rd.)
Mornington Rd. E4 17Fc 35
E11 31Hc 73
IG8: Wfd G 21Hc 53
IG10: Lough 13Sc 36
SE8 52Bc 114
TW15: Ashf 64S 128
UB6: G'frd 43Da 85
WD7: R'lett 6Ja 14
Mornington St. NW1 1A 216 (40Kb 70)
Mornington Ter. NW1 1A 216 (39Kb 70)
Mornington Wlk. TW10: Ham 63La 130
Moro Apartments *E14* *44Cc 92*
(off New Festival Av.)
Morocco St. SE1 2H 231 (47Ub 91)
Morocco Wharf *E1* *46Xb 91*
(off Wapping High St.)
Morpeth Av. WD6: Bore 10Pa 15
Morpeth Cl. HP2: Hem H 3N 3
Morpeth Gro. E9 39Zb 72
Morpeth Mans. SW1 4B 228
Morpeth Rd. E9 39Zb 72
Morpeth St. E2 41Yb 92
Morpeth Ter. SW1 4B 228 (48Lb 90)
Morpeth Wlk. N17 24Xb 51
Morphou Rd. NW7 23Ab 48
Morrab Gdns. IG3: Ilf 34Vc 75
Morrel Ct. *E2* *40Wb 71*
(off Goldsmiths Row)
Morrells Yd. SE11 7A 230
Morrice Cl. SL3: L'ly 49B 82
Morris Av. E12 36Pc 74
UB8: Uxb 37N 63
Morris Blitz Ct. N16 35Vb 71
Morris Cl. BR6: Orp 76Uc 160
CR0: C'don 71Ac 158
SL9: Chal P 25B 42
Morris Ct. E4 20Dc 34
EN9: Walt A 6Hc 21
SL4: Wind 3C 102
Morris Dr. DA17: Belv 49Ed 96
Morris Gdns. DA1: Dart 57Qd 119
SW18 59Cb 111
Morris Ho. *E2* *41Yb 92*
(off Roman Rd.)
NW8 6D 214
W3 47Va 88
Morrish Rd. SW2 59Nb 112
Morris M. SW19 64Eb 133
Morrison Av. E4 23Cc 52
N17 27Ub 51
Morrison Bldgs. Nth. *E1* *44Wb 91*
(off Commercial Rd.)
Morrison Ct. *EN5: Barn* *14Ab 30*
(off Manor Way)
N12 24Gb 49
SW1 3E 228
Morrison Ho. RM16: Grays 47Fe 99
SW2 *60Qb 112*
(off Tulse Hill)
Morrison Rd. IG11: Bark 40Ad 75
RM9: Bark, Dag 40Ad 75
SW9 54Qb 112
UB4: Yead 41X 85
Morrison St. SW11 55Jb 112
Morris Pl. N4 33Qb 70
Morris Rd. E14 43Dc 92
E15 35Gc 73
RH1: S Nut 8E 208
RM3: Rom 24Kd 57
RM8: Dag 33Bd 75
TW7: Isle 55Ha 108
Morriss Ho. *SE16* *47Xb 91*
(off Cherry Gdn. St.)
Morris St. E1 44Xb 91
Morriston Cl. WD19: Wat 22Y 45
Morris Wlk. DA1: Dart 54Qd 119
Morris Way AL2: Lon C 8H 7
Morritt Ho. *HA0: Wemb* *36Ma 67*
(off Talbot Rd.)
Morse Cl. E13 41Jc 93
UB9: Hare 26L 43
Morshead Mans. *W9* *41Cb 89*
(off Morshead Rd.)
Morshead Rd. W9 41Cb 89
Morson Rd. EN3: Pond E 16Ac 34
Morston Cl. KT20: Tad 92Xa 194
Morston Gdns. SE9 63Pc 138
Mortain Ho. *SE16* *49Xb 91*
(off Roseberry St.)
Morten Cl. SW4 58Mb 112
Morten Gdns. UB9: Den 31J 63
Morteyne Rd. N17 25Tb 51
Mortgramit Sq. SE18 48Qc 94
Mortham St. E15 39Gc 73
Mortimer Cl. NW2 33Bb 69
SW16 61Mb 134
WD23: Bush 16Da 27
Mortimer Ct. NW8 2A 214
Mortimer Cres. AL3: St A 4N 5
KT4: Wor Pk 76Ta 153
NW6 39Db 69
Mortimer Dr. EN1: Enf 15Ub 33
RM3: Rom 22Ld 57
TN16: Big H 84Lc 179
Mortimer Est. *NW6* *39Db 69*
(off Mortimer Pl.)
Mortimer Ho. W11 46Za 88
W14 *49Ab 88*
(off North End Rd.)
Mortimer Mkt. WC1 6C 216 (42Lb 90)
Mortimer Pl. NW6 39Db 69
Mortimer Rd. BR6: Orp 74Wc 161
CR4: Mitc 67Hb 133
DA8: Erith 51Fd 118
E6 41Pc 94
N1 38Ub 71
(not continuous)
NW10 41Ya 88
SL3: L'ly 8P 81
W13 44La 86
Mortimer Sq. W11 45Za 88
Mortimer St. W1 2A 222 (44Lb 90)
Mortimer Ter. NW5 35Kb 70
MORTLAKE 55Ta 109
Mortlake Cl. CR0: Bedd 76Nb 156
Mortlake Crematorium
TW9: Kew 54Ra 109
Mortlake Dr. CR4: Mitc 67Gb 133
Mortlake High St. SW14 55Ta 109
Mortlake Rd. E16 44Kc 93
IG1: Ilf 35Sc 74
TW9: Kew, Rich 52Qa 109
Mortlake Ter. *TW9: Kew* *52Qa 109*
(off Mortlake Rd.)
Mortlock Cl. SE15 53Xb 113
Mortlock Ct. E7 35Mc 73
Morton KT20: Tad 93Za 194
Morton Cl. E1 44Yb 92
GU21: Wok 7N 167
SM6: Wall 80Pb 156
UB8: Hil 42P 83
Morton Ct. UB5: N'olt 36Ea 66
Morton Cres. N14 21Mb 50
Morton Dr. SL2: Farn C 5C 60
Morton Gdns. SM6: Wall 78Lb 156
Morton Ho. SE17 51Rb 113
Morton M. SW5 49Db 89
Morton Pl. SE1 4K 229 (48Qb 90)
Morton Rd. E15 38Hc 73
GU21: Wok 7P 167
N1 38Sb 71
SM4: Mord 71Fb 155
Morton Way N14 20Lb 32
Morvale Cl. DA17: Belv 49Bd 95
Morval Rd. SW2 57Qb 112
Morven Cl. EN6: Pot B 3Eb 17
Morven Rd. SW17 62Hb 133
Morville Ho. *SW18* *58Fb 111*
(off Fitzhugh Gro.)
Morville St. E3 40Cc 72
Morwell St. WC1 1D 222 (43Mb 90)
Mosaic Ho. HP2: Hem H 2M 3
Mosbach Gdns. CM13: Hut 19De 41
Moscow Mans. *SW5* *49Cb 89*
(off Cromwell Rd.)
Moscow Pl. W2 45Db 89
Moscow Rd. W2 45Cb 89
Mosedale NW1 4B 216
Moseley Row SE10 49Hc 93
Moselle Av. N22 26Qb 50
Moselle Cl. N8 27Pb 50
Moselle Ho. *N17* *24Vb 51*
(off William St.)
Moselle Pl. N17 24Vb 51
Moselle Rd. TN16: Big H 90Nc 180
Moselle St. N17 24Vb 51
Mospey Cres. KT17: Eps 87Va 174
Mosque Ter. *E1* *43Wb 91*
(off Whitechapel Rd.)
Mosque Twr. *E1* *43Wb 91*
(off Fieldgate St.)
E3 *40Ac 72*
(off Ford St.)
Mosquito Cl. SM6: Wall 80Nb 156
Moss Bank RM17: Grays 49Be 99
(not continuous)
Mossborough Cl. N12 23Db 49
Mossbury Rd. SW11 55Gb 111
Moss Cl. E1 43Wb 91
HA5: Pinn 26Ba 45
N9 18Wb 33
WD3: Rick 19M 25
Mossdown Cl. DA17: Belv 49Cd 96
Mossendew Cl. UB9: Hare 25M 43
Mossfield KT11: Cobh 85W 170
Mossford Ct. IG6: Ilf 27Rc 54
Mossford Grn. IG6: Ilf 27Rc 54
Mossford La. IG6: Ilf 26Rc 54
Mossford St. E3 42Bc 92
Moss Gdns. CR2: Sels 80Zb 158
TW13: Felt 61W 128
Moss Hall Ct. N12 23Db 49
Moss Hall Cres. N12 23Db 49
Moss Hall Gro. N12 23Db 49
Mossington Gdns. SE16 49Yb 92
Moss La. HA5: Pinn 25Aa 45
RM1: Rom 30Hd 56
Mosslea Rd. BR2: Brom 71Mc 159
BR6: Farnb 76Sc 160
CR3: Whyt 88Vb 177
SE20 65Yb 136
(not continuous)
Mossop St. SW3 5E 226 (49Gb 89)
Moss Rd. RM10: Dag 38Cd 76
RM15: S Ock 43Yd 98
WD25: Wat 6X 13
Moss Side AL2: Brick W 2Ba 13
Mossville Gdns. SM4: Mord 69Bb 133
Moss Way DA2: Daren 63Td 142
Mosswell Ho. N10 25Jb 50
Moston Cl. UB3: Harl 50V 84
Mostyn Av. HA9: Wemb 36Pa 67
Mostyn Gdns. NW10 41Za 88
Mostyn Gro. E3 40Cc 72
Mostyn Rd. HA8: Edg 24Ua 48
SW9 53Qb 112
SW19 67Bb 133
WD23: Bush 15Ea 28
Mostyn Ter. RH1: Redh 7A 208
Mosul Way BR2: Brom 72Nc 160
Mosyer Dr. BR5: Orp 75Zc 161
Motcomb St. SW1 3H 227 (48Jb 90)
Mote, The DA3: Nw A G 75Be 165
Mote Rd. TN11: S'brne 100Wd 204
TN15: S'brne, Ivy H 100Wd 204
Moth Cl. SM6: Wall 80Nb 156
Mothers Sq. E5 35Xb 71
Motherwell Way RM20: W Thur 50Wd 98
Motley Av. EC2 5H 219
MOTSPUR PARK 72Wa 154
Motspur Pk. KT3: N Mald 72Va 154
MOTTINGHAM 61Nc 138
Mottingham Gdns. SE9 60Mc 115
Mottingham La. SE9 60Lc 115
SE12 60Lc 115
Mottingham Rd. N9 16Zb 34
SE9 61Nc 138
Mottisfont Rd. SE2 48Wc 95
Mottistone Gro. SM2: Sutt 81Db 175
Motts Hill La. KT20: Tad, Walt H 95Wa 194
Motts La. RM8: Dag 33Bd 75
Mott St. E4 10Fc 21
IG10: H Beech, Lough 11Gc 35
Mouchotte Cl. TN16: Big H 84Kc 179
Moules Ct. SE5 52Sb 113
Moulins Rd. E9 38Yb 72
Moulsford Ho. N7 36Mb 70
W2 *43Cb 89*
(off Westbourne Pk. Rd.)
Moultain Hill BR8: Swan 70Jd 140
Moulton Av. TW3: Houn 54Aa 107
Moultrie Way RM14: Upm 30Ud 58
Mound, The SE9 62Qc 138
Moundfield Rd. N16 30Wb 51
Moundsfield Way SL1: Slou 7C 80
Mounsey Ho. *W10* *41Ab 88*
(off Third Av.)
Mount, The BR1: Brom 67Nc 138
CM14: B'wood 20Yd 40
CR2: S Croy *78Sb 157*
(off Warham Rd.)
CR5: Coul 87Jb 176
CR6: W'ham 91Wb 197
DA6: Bex 57Dd 118
E5 33Xb 71
(not continuous)
EN6: Pot B 2Db 17
GU21: Knap 1G 186
GU21: Wok 10P 167
(Elm Rd.)
GU21: Wok 1L 187
(St John's Hill)
GU25: Vir W 2P 147
HA9: Wemb 33Ra 67
IG10: Lough 14Nc 36

Myrtle Rd.—New Brent St.

Myrtle Rd. CM14: W'ley 21Yd 58
CR0: C'don 76Cc 158
DA1: Dart 60Md 119
E6 39Pc 74
E17 30Ac 52
IG1: Ilf 33Rc 74
N13 20Sb 33
RM3: Rom 23Ld 57
SM1: Sutt 78Eb 155
TW3: Houn 54Ea 108
TW12: Hamp H 65Ea 130
W3 46Sa 87
Myrtleside Cl. HA6: Nwood 24T 44
Myrtle Wlk. N1 2H 219 (40Ub 71)
Mysore Rd. SW11 55Hb 111
Myton Rd. SE21 62Tb 135
Mytton Ho. SW8 52Pb 112
(off St Stephens Ter.)

N

N1 Shop. Cen. N1 1A 218 (40Qb 70)
Nacton Ct. RM6: Chad H 29Yc 55
(off Hevingham Dr.)
Nadine Ct. SM6: Wall 81Lb 176
Nadine St. SE7 50Lc 93
Nafferton Ri. IG10: Lough 15Mc 35
Nagasaki Wlk. SE7 48Kc 93
Nagle Cl. E17 26Fc 53
NAG'S HEAD 34Nb 70
Nags Head Ct. EC1 6E 218
Nags Head La.
CM14: B'wood, Upm 25Sd 58
DA16: Well 55Xc 117
RM14: Upm 25Sd 58
Nags Head Rd. EN3: Pond E 14Yb 34
Nags Head Shop. Cen. N7 35Pb 70
Nailsworth Cres. RH1: Mers 1D 208
Nailzee Cl. SL9: Ger X 31A 62
Nainby Ho. SE11 6K 229
Nairn Ct. RM18: Tilb 4B 122
Nairne Gro. SE24 57Tb 113
Nairn Grn. WD19: Wat 20W 26
Nairn Ho. CM14: W'ley 21Yd 58
(off Cameron Cl.)
Nairn Rd. HA4: Ruis 37Y 65
Nairn St. E14 43Ec 92
Naldera Gdns. SE3 51Jc 115
Nallhead Rd. TW13: Hanw 64Y 129
Nalton Ho. NW6 38Eb 69
(off Belsize Rd.)
Namba Roy Cl. SW16 63Pb 134
Namco Funscape
Romford 30Gd 56
Namton Dr. CR7: Thor H 70Pb 134
Nan Clark's La. NW7 19Ua 30
Nancy Downs WD19: Wat 17Y 27
Nankin St. E14 44Cc 92
Nanscott Ho. WD19: Wat 20Z 27
Nansen Ho. NW10 38Ta 67
(off Stonebridge Pk.)
Nansen Rd. DA12: Grav'nd 3F 144
SW11 55Jb 112
Nansen Village N12 21Db 49
Nant Ct. NW2 33Bb 69
Nanterre Ct. WD17: Wat 12W 26
Nantes Cl. SW18 56Eb 111
Nantes Pas. E1 7K 219 (43Vb 91)
Nant Rd. NW2 33Bb 69
Nant St. E2 41Xb 91
Nantwich Ho. RM3: Rom 22Nd 57
(off Lindfield Rd.)
Naomi St. SE8 49Ac 92
Naoroji St. WC1 4K 217 (41Qb 90)
Nap, The WD4: K Lan 1Q 12
Napa Cl. E20 36Ec 72
Napier NW9 25Va 48
Napier Av. E14 50Cc 92
SW6 55Bb 111
Napier Cl. AL2: Lon C 7H 7
RM11: Horn 32Kd 77
SE8 52Bc 114
UB7: W Dray 48P 83
W14 48Ab 88
Napier Ct. BR2: Brom 70Kc 137
(off Napier Rd.)
CR3: Cat'm 94Ub 197
GU21: Wok 88A 168
N1 1F 219
SE12 62Kc 137
SW6 55Bb 111
(off Ranelagh Gdns.)
UB4: Yead 42Y 85
(off Dunedin Way)
Napier Dr. WD23: Bush 14Aa 27
Napier Gro. N1 2E 218 (40Sb 71)
Napier Ho. E3 41Cc 92
(off Campbell Rd.)
RM13: Rain 41Hd 96
(off Dunedin Rd.)
SE17 51Rb 113
(off Cooks Rd.)
W3 46Ua 88
Napier Lodge TW15: Ashf 65T 128
Napier Pl. W14 48Bb 89
Napier Rd. BR2: Brom 70Kc 137
CR2: S Croy 80Tb 157
DA11: Nflt 10B 122
DA17: Belv 49Bd 95
E6 39Qc 74
E11 35Gc 73
E15 40Gc 73
(not continuous)
EN3: Pond E 15Zb 34
HA0: Wemb 37Ma 67
N17 27Ub 51
NW10 41Xa 88
SE25 70Xb 135
TW7: Isle 56Ja 108
TW15: Ashf 66T 128
W14 48Bb 89
Napier St. SE8 52Bc 114
(off Napier Cl.)
Napier Ter. N1 38Rb 71
Napier Wlk. TW15: Ashf 66T 128
Napoleon La. SE18 52Pc 116
Napoleon Rd. E5 34Xb 71
TW1: Twick 59Ka 108
NAPSBURY 9G 6
Napsbury Av. AL2: Lon C 8G 6
Napsbury La. AL1: St A 5E 6
Napton Cl. UB4: Yead 42Aa 85
Nara SE13 54Dc 114
Narbonne Av. SW4 57Lb 112
Narboro Ct. RM1: Rom 29Jd 56
Narborough Cl. UB10: Ick 33S 64
Narborough St. SW6 54Db 111

Narcissus Rd. NW6 36Cb 69
Nardini NW9 25Va 48
(off Long Mead)
Nare Rd. RM15: Avel 45Sd 98
Naresby Fold HA7: Stan 23La 46
Nares Cl. TW19: Stanw 60N 105
Narford Rd. E5 34Wb 71
Narrowboat Av. TW8: Bford 52La 108
Narrow Boat Cl. SE28 47Tc 94
Narrow La. CR6: W'ham 91Xb 197
Narrow St. E14 45Ac 92
W3 46Ra 87
Narrow Way BR2: Brom 72Nc 160
Narvic Ho. SE5 54Sb 113
Narwhal Inuit Art Gallery 49Ta 87
Nascot Pl. WD17: Wat 12X 27
Nascot Rd. WD17: Wat 12X 27
Nascot St. W12 44Ya 88
WD17: Wat 12X 27
Nascot Wood Rd. WD17: Wat 9V 12
Naseby Cl. NW6 38Eb 69
TW7: Isle 53Ga 108
Naseby Ct. DA14: Sidc 63Vc 139
KT12: Walt T 75Y 151
Naseby Rd. IG5: Ilf 25Pc 54
RM10: Dag 34Cd 76
SE19 65Tb 135
NASH 79Jc 159
Nash Bank DA13: Meop, Ist R 8B 144
Nash Cl. AL9: Wel G 5F 8
SM1: Sutt 76Fb 155
WD6: E'tree 14Pa 29
Nash Ct. HA3: Kenton 30Ka 46
Nash Cft. DA11: Nflt 3A 144
Nashdom La. SL1: Burn 7A 60
Nash Dr. RH1: Redh 4P 207
Nashe Ho. SE1 4F 231
Nash Gdns. RH1: Redh 4P 207
Nash Grn. BR1: Brom 65Jc 137
HP3: Hem H 7P 3
Nash Ho. E14 47Cc 92
(off Alpha Gro.)
E17 27Dc 52
NW1 1K 215
SW1 7A 228
Nash La. BR2: Kes 80Jc 159
NASH MILLS 8A 4
Nash Mills La. HP3: Hem H 8P 3
Nash Mills Recreation Cen. 8P 3
Nash Pl. E14 46Dc 92
Nash Rd. N9 19Yb 34
RM6: Chad H 28Zc 55
SE4 56Ac 114
SL3: L'ly 49B 82
NASH STREET 8B 144
Nash St. DA13: Meop 8B 144
NW1 3A 216 (41Kb 90)
Nash's Yd. UB8: Uxb 38M 63
Nash Way HA3: Kenton 30Ka 46
Nasmyth St. W6 48Xa 88
Nassau Path SE28 46Yc 95
Nassau Rd. SW13 53Va 110
Nassau St. W1 1B 222 (43Lb 90)
Nassington Rd. NW3 35Hb 69
NAST HYDE 1A 8
Nasturtium Dr. GU24: Bisl 7E 166
Natalie Cl. TW14: Bedf 59T 106
Natalie M. N22 23Nb 50
TW2: Twick 62Fa 130
Natal Rd. CR7: Thor H 69Tb 135
IG1: Ilf 35Rc 74
N11 23Nb 50
SW16 65Mb 134
Natasha Ct. RM3: Rom 24Ld 57
Natasha M. SE15 56Yb 114
Nathan Cl. RM14: Upm 32Ud 78
Nathan Ct. N9 17Yb 34
(off Causeyware Rd.)
Nathan Ho. SE11 6A 230
Nathaniel Ct. E1 1K 225 (43Vb 91)
Nathaniel Ct. E17 31Ac 72
Nathans Rd. HA0: Wemb 32La 66
Nathan Way SE28 49Uc 94
National Archives, The 52Ra 109
National Army Mus. 51Hb 111
National Gallery 5E 222 (45Mb 90)
National Maritime Mus. 51Fc 115
National Portrait Gallery 5E 222
National Rifle Association &
National Shooting Cen. Headquarters
1B 186
(off Queen's Way)
National Rifle Association Mus. 1B 186
National Tennis Cen. 57Ua 110
National Ter. SE16 47Xb 91
(off Bermondsey Wall E.)
National Theatre 6J 223 (46Qb 90)
National Works TW4: Houn 55Ba 107
Nation Way E4 18Ec 34
Natural History Mus.
Eton 1H 103
Knightsbridge 4B 226 (48Fb 89)
Naunton Way RM12: Horn 34Md 77
Nautical Ho. SW18 56Eb 111
(off Juniper Dr.)
Nautilus Building, The EC1 3A 218
Naval Ho. E14 45Fc 93
(off Quixley St.)
SE18 48Rc 94
Naval Row E14 45Ec 92
Naval Wlk. BR1: Brom 68Jc 137
(off Mitre Cl.)
Navarino Gro. E8 37Wb 71
Navarino Mans. E8 37Wb 71
Navarino Rd. E8 37Wb 71
Navarre Ct. WD4: K Lan 10B 4
Navarre Gdns. RM5: Col R 22Dd 56
Navarre Rd. E6 40Nc 74
SW9 53Rb 113
Navarre St. E2 5K 219 (42Vb 91)
Navenby Wlk. E3 42Cc 92
NAVESTOCK 12Md 39
Navestock Cl. E4 20Ec 34
Navestock Cres. IG8: Wfd G 24Lc 53
NAVESTOCK HEATH 12Md 39
NAVESTOCK SIDE 12Sd 40
Navestockside
CM14: Kel C, N'side 12Sd 40
Navigation Ct. E16 45Sc 94
Navigation Dr. EN3: Enf L 10Cc 20
Navigation Ho. KT15: Add 77N 149
SE16 49Ac 92
(off Grand Canal Av.)
Navigation Rd. E3 42Ec 92
Navigator Dr. UB2: S'hall 47Ea 86
Navigator Pk. UB2: S'hall 49Y 85
Navy St. SW4 55Mb 112
Naxos Bldg. E14 47Bc 92

Nayim Pl. E8 36Xb 71
Nayland Ho. SE6 63Ec 136
Naylor Bldg. E. E1 44Wb 91
(off Assam St.)
Naylor Bldg. W. E1 44Wb 91
(off Adler St.)
Naylor Gro. EN3: Pond E 15Zb 34
Naylor Ho. SE17 6G 231
W10 41Ab 88
(off Dart St.)
Naylor Rd. N20 19Eb 31
SE15 52Xb 113
Nazareth Gdns. SE15 54Xb 113
Nazeing Wlk. RM13: Rain 38Hd 76
Nazrul St. E2 3J 219 (41Vb 91)
NCR Bus. Cen. NW10 36Ua 68
Neagle Cl. WD6: Bore 11Sa 29
Neagle Ho. NW2 34Ya 68
(off Stoll Cl.)
Neal Av. UB1: S'hall 42Ba 85
Neal Cl. HA6: Nwood 25W 44
SL9: Ger X 32D 62
Neal Ct. EN9: Walt A 5Hc 21
Nealden St. SW9 55Pb 112
Neale Cl. N2 27Eb 49
Neale Ct. RM9: Dag 37Xc 75
Neal Rd. TN15: W King 79Ud 164
Neal St. WC2 3F 223 (44Nb 90)
WD18: Wat 15Y 27
Neal's Yd. WC2 3F 223 (44Nb 90)
Neap Ct. E3 42Ec 92
(off Navigation Rd.)
Near Acre NW9 25Va 48
NEASDEN 34Ua 68
Neasden Cl. NW10 36Ua 68
NEASDEN JUNC. 35Ua 68
Neasden La. NW10 34Ua 68
Neasden La. Nth. NW10 34Ta 67
Neasham Rd. RM8: Dag 36Xc 75
Neate Ho. SW1 7C 228
Neate St. SE5 51Ub 113
Neath Gdns. SM4: Mord 72Eb 155
Neathouse Pl. SW1 5B 228 (49Lb 90)
Neats Acre HA4: Ruis 31T 64
Neatscourt Rd. E6 43Mc 93
Neave Cres. RM3: Rom 25Ld 57
Neb La. RH8: Oxt 3G 210
Nebraska Bldg. SE13 53Dc 114
(off Deal's Gateway)
Nebraska St. SE1 2F 231 (47Tb 91)
Nebula SW11 54Hb 111
Nebula Ct. E13 40Jc 73
(off Umbriel Pl.)
Neckinger SE16 3K 231 (48Vb 91)
Neckinger Est. SE16 3K 231 (48Vb 91)
Neckinger St. SE1 2K 231 (47Vb 91)
Nectarine Way SE13 54Dc 114
Needham Cl. SL4: Wind 3C 102
Needham Ho. SE11 6K 229
Needham Rd. W11 44Cb 89
Needham Ter. NW2 34Za 68
Needleman Cl. NW9 26Ua 48
Needleman St. SE16 47Zb 92
Needles Bank RH9: G'stone 3P 209
(not continuous)
Needwood Ho. N4 32Sb 71
Neela Cl. UB10: Ick 35R 64
Neeld Cres. HA9: Wemb 36Qa 67
NW4 29Xa 48
Neeld Pde. HA9: Wemb 36Pa 67
Neeld Pl. W9 43Bb 89
Neil Cl. TW15: Ashf 64S 128
Neild Way WD3: Rick 17H 25
Neilson Cl. WD18: Wat 15V 26
Neil Wates Cres. SW2 60Qb 112
Nelgarde Rd. SE6 59Cc 114
Nella Rd. W6 51Za 110
Nelldale Rd. SE16 49Yb 92
Nellgrove Rd. UB10: Hil 42R 84
Nell Gwynn Av. TW17: Shep 72T 150
Nell Gwynn Cl. WD7: Shenl 4Na 15
Nell Gwynne Av. SL5: S'hill 10B 124
Nell Gwynne Cl. KT19: Eps 83Qa 173
SL5: S'hill 10B 124
Nell Gwynn Ho. SW3 6E 226 (49Gb 89)
Nello James Gdns. SE27 63Tb 135
Nelmes Cl. RM11: Horn 29Pd 57
Nelmes Cres. RM11: Horn 29Nd 57
Nelmes Rd. RM11: Horn 31Nd 77
Nelmes Way RM11: Horn 28Md 57
Nelson Arc. SE10 51Ec 114
(off Nelson Rd.)
Nelson Av. AL1: St A 5F 6
Nelson Cl. CM14: W'ley 22Zd 59
CR0: C'don 74Rb 157
KT12: Walt T 74X 151
NW6 41Cb 89
RM7: Mawney 25Dd 56
SL3: L'ly 9P 81
TN16: Big H 89Nc 180
TW14: Felt 60V 106
UB10: Hil 41R 84
Nelson Ct. DA8: Erith 52Hd 118
(off Frobisher Rd.)
KT16: Chert 74J 149
SE16 46Yb 92
(off Brunel Rd.)
Nelson Gdns. E2 41Wb 91
TW3: Houn 58Ca 107
Nelson Gro. Rd. SW19 67Db 133
Nelson Ho. DA9: Ghithe 57Zd 121
RM3: Rom 22Nd 57
(off Lindfield Rd.)
SW1 51Lb 112
(off Dolphin Sq.)
Nelson La. UB10: Hil 41R 84
Nelson Mandela Cl. N10 26Jb 50
Nelson Mandela Ho. N16 33Wb 71
Nelson Mandela Rd. SE3 55Lc 115
Nelson Pas. EC1 3E 218 (41Sb 91)
Nelson Pl. DA14: Sidc 63Wc 139
N1 2C 218 (40Rb 71)
Nelson Rd. BR2: Brom 70Lc 137
CR3: Cat'm 95Tb 197
DA1: Dart 58Ld 119
DA11: Nflt 1B 144
DA14: Sidc 63Wc 139
DA17: Belv 50Bd 95
E4 23Dc 52
E11 28Jc 53
EN3: Pond E 16Zb 34
HA1: Harr 32Fa 66
HA7: Stan 23La 46
KT3: N Mald 71Ta 153
N8 29Pb 50
N9 19Xb 33
N15 28Ub 51
RM13: Rain 40Hd 76

Nelson Rd. RM15: S Ock 40Yd 78
RM16: Ors 4F 100
SE10 51Ec 114
SL4: Wind 5D 102
SW19 66Db 133
TW2: Whitt 59Da 107
TW3: Houn 58Ca 107
TW6: H'row A 57P 105
TW15: Ashf 64N 127
UB10: Hil 41R 84
Nelson Rd. M. SW19 66Db 133
(off Nelson Rd.)
Nelson's Column 6E 222 (46Mb 90)
Nelson Sq. SE1 1B 230 (47Rb 91)
Nelson's Row SW4 56Mb 112
Nelson St. E1 44Xb 91
E6 40Pc 74
(not continuous)
E16 44Hc 93
Nelsons Yd. NW1 1B 216
Nelson Ter. N1 2C 218 (40Rb 71)
Nelson Trad. Est. SW19 67Db 133
Nelson Wlk. E3 42Dc 92
KT19: Eps 81Qa 173
SE16 46Ac 92
Nelwyn Av. RM11: Horn 29Pd 57
Nemoure Rd. W3 45Sa 87
Nemus Apartments SE8 49Zb 92
Nene Gdns. TW13: Hanw 62Ba 129
Nene Rd. TW6: H'row A 53R 106
NENE ROAD RDBT. 53R 106
Neo Apartments SL1: Slou 7L 81
Nepaul Rd. SW11 54Gb 111
Nepean St. SW15 58Wa 110
Nepicar La. TN15: Wro 87Ee 185
Neptune Bus. Pk. RM19: Purf 50Ud 98
Neptune Cl. RM13: Rain 40Hd 76
Neptune Ct. DA8: Erith 52Hd 118
(off Frobisher Rd.)
E14 49Cc 92
(off Homer Dr.)
E16 43Jc 93
(off Hammersley Rd.)
WD6: Bore 13Qa 29
Neptune Dr. HP2: Hem H 1N 3
Neptune Ho. E3 39Cc 72
(off Garrison Rd.)
SE16 48Yb 92
(off Moodkee St.)
Neptune Rd. HA1: Harr 30Fa 46
TW6: H'row A 53T 106
Neptune St. SE16 48Yb 92
Neptune Wlk. DA8: Erith 49Fd 96
Neptune Way SL1: Slou 7C 80
Nero Ct. TW8: Bford 52Ma 109
Nero Ho. AL1: St A 3D 6
E20 37Ec 72
(off Anthems Way)
Nesbit Ct. SE17 51Rb 113
(off Cook's Rd.)
Nesbit Rd. SE9 56Mc 115
Nesbitt Cl. SE3 55Gc 115
Nesbitts All. EN5: Barn 13Bb 31
Nesbitt Sq. SE19 66Ub 135
Nescot Sports Cen. 83Wa 174
Nesham Ho. N1 1H 219
Nesham St. E1 45Wb 91
Ness Rd. DA8: Erith 51Md 119
Ness St. SE16 48Wb 91
Nesta Rd. IG8: Wfd G 23Gc 53
Nestles Av. UB3: Hayes 48V 84
Neston Rd. WD24: Wat 9Y 13
Nestor Av. N21 16Rb 33
Nestor Ho. E2 40Xb 71
(off Old Bethnal Grn. Rd.)
Nethan Dr. RM15: Avel 45Sd 98
Netheravon Rd. W4 49Va 88
W7 46Ha 86
Netheravon Rd. Sth. W4 50Va 88
Netherbury Rd. W5 48Ma 87
Netherby Gdns. EN2: Enf 14Nb 32
Netherby Pk. KT13: Weyb 78U 150
Netherby Rd. SE23 59Yb 114
Nether Cl. N3 24Cb 49
Nethercote Av. GU21: Wok 9K 167
Nethercott Ho. E3 41Dc 92
(off Bruce Rd.)
Nethercourt Av. N3 23Cb 49
Netherene La. CR5: Coul 95Lb 196
Netherfield Gdns. IG11: Bark 37Tc 74
Netherfield Rd. N12 22Db 49
SW17 62Jb 134
Netherford Rd. SW4 54Lb 112
Netherhall Gdns. NW3 37Eb 69
Netherhall Way NW3 36Eb 69
Netherheys Dr. CR2: S Croy 80Rb 157
Netherlands, The CR5: Coul 91Lb 196
Netherlands Rd. EN5: New Bar 16Fb 31
Netherleigh Cl. N6 32Kb 70
Netherleigh Pk. RH1: S Nut 9E 208
Nethern Ct. Rd. CR3: Wold 95Cc 198
Netherne Dr. CR5: Coul 93Kb 196
Netherne La. CR5: Coul 93Lb 196
RH1: Coul 95Lb 196
Netherne Leisure Cen. 94Mb 196
NETHERNE-ON-THE-HILL 94Mb 196
Netherpark Dr. RM2: Rom 26Hd 56
Nether St. N3 24Cb 49
N12 22Eb 49
(not continuous)
Netherton Gro. SW10 51Eb 111
Netherton Rd. N15 30Tb 51
TW1: Twick 57Ja 108
Netherway AL3: St A 5N 5
Netherwood N2 26Fb 49
Netherwood Pl. W14 48Za 88
(off Netherwood Rd.)
Netherwood Rd. W14 48Za 88
Netherwood St. NW6 38Bb 69
Nethewode Ct. DA17: Belv 48Dd 96
(off Lower Pk. Rd.)
Netley SE5 53Ub 113
(off Redbridge Gdns.)
Netley Cl. CR0: New Ad 80Ec 158
SM3: Cheam 78Za 154
Netley Dr. KT12: Walt T 73Ba 151
Netley Gdns. SM4: Mord 73Eb 155
Netley Rd. E17 29Bc 52
IG2: Ilf 29Tc 54
SM4: Mord 73Eb 155
TW8: Bford 51Na 109
Netley St. NW1 4B 216 (41Lb 90)
Nettlecombe NW1 38Mb 70
(off Agar Gro.)
Nettlecombe Cl. SM2: Sutt 81Db 175
Nettlecroft HP1: Hem H 3K 3
Nettleden Av. HA9: Wemb 37Qa 67
Nettleden Ho. SW3 6E 226

Nettlefold Pl. SE27 62Rb 135
TW16: Sun 71W 150
Nettlefold Wlk. KT12: Walt T 74V 150
Nettlestead Cl. BR3: Beck 66Bc 136
Nettleton Ct. EC2 1D 224
Nettleton Rd. SE14 53Zb 114
TW6: H'row A 53R 106
UB10: Ick 35P 63
Nettlewood Rd. SW16 66Mb 134
Neuchatel Rd. SE6 61Bc 136
Neutron Twr. E14 45Fc 93
Nevada Bldg. SE10 53Dc 114
(off Blackheath Rd.)
Nevada Cl. KT3: N Mald 70Sa 131
Nevada St. SE10 51Ec 114
Nevell Rd. RM16: Grays 8D 100
Nevern Mans. SW5 50Cb 89
(off Warwick Rd.)
Nevern Pl. SW5 49Cb 89
Nevern Rd. SW5 49Cb 89
Nevern Sq. SW5 49Cb 89
Nevil Cl. HA6: Nwood 22T 44
Nevil Ho. SW9 54Rb 113
(off Loughborough Est.)
Nevill Ct. SW10 52Eb 111
(off Edith Ter.)
Neville Av. KT3: N Mald 67Ta 131
Neville Cl. DA15: Sidc 63Vc 139
E11 34Hc 73
EN6: Pot B 3Bb 17
KT10: Esh 79Ba 151
NW1 2E 216 (40Mb 70)
NW6 40Bb 69
SE15 53Wb 113
SL2: Stoke P 7K 61
SM7: Bans 86Db 175
TW3: Houn 54Da 107
W3 47Sa 87
Neville Ct. NW8 2B 214
SL1: Burn 1A 80
Neville Dr. N2 30Eb 49
Neville Gdns. RM8: Dag 34Zc 75
Neville Gill Cl. SW18 58Cb 111
Neville Ho. N11 21Jb 50
N22 25Pb 50
(off Neville Pl.)
NW6 40Bb 69
(off Denmark Rd.)
Neville Ho. Yd. KT1: King T 68Na 131
Neville Pl. N22 25Pb 50
Neville Rd. CR0: C'don 73Tb 157
E7 38Jc 73
IG6: Ilf 25Sc 54
KT1: King T 68Qa 131
NW6 40Bb 69
RM8: Dag 34Zc 75
TW10: Ham 62La 130
W5 42Ma 87
Nevilles Ct. NW2 34Wa 68
Neville St. SW7 7B 226 (50Fb 89)
Neville Ter. SW7 7B 226 (50Fb 89)
Neville Wlk. SM5: Cars 73Gb 155
Nevill Gro. WD24: Wat 11X 27
Nevill La. EC4 2A 224
Nevill Rd. N16 35Ub 71
Nevill Way IG10: Lough 16Nc 36
Nevin Dr. E4 18Dc 34
Nevin Ho. UB3: Harl 48S 84
Nevinson Cl. SW18 58Fb 111
Nevis Cl. E13 40Kc 73
RM1: Rom 23Gd 56
Nevis Rd. SW17 61Jb 134
Nevitt Ho. N1 2G 219
New Acres Rd. SE28 47Uc 94
NEW ADDINGTON 82Ec 178
New Addington Leisure Cen. 82Ec 178
Newall Cl. UB10: Uxb 39P 63
Newall Ho. SE1 3E 230
Newall Rd. TW6: H'row A 53S 106
New Arc. UB8: Uxb 39M 63
Newark Cl. GU23: Rip 93J 189
Newark Cotts. GU23: Rip 93J 189
Newark Ct. KT12: Walt T 74Y 151
Newark Cres. NW10 41Ta 87
Newark Grn. WD6: Bore 13Ta 29
Newark Ho. SW9 54Rb 113
Newark Knok E6 44Qc 94
Newark La. GU22: Pyr 91H 189
GU23: Rip 91H 189
Newark Rd. CR2: S Croy 79Tb 157
GU20: W'sham 7A 146
Newark St. E1 43Xb 91
(not continuous)
Newark Way NW4 28Wa 48
New Ash Cl. N2 27Fb 49
NEW ASH GREEN 75Be 165
New Atlas Wharf E14 48Cc 92
(off Arnhem Pl.)
New Baltic Wharf SE8 50Ac 92
(off Evelyn St.)
NEW BARN 69Ee 143
New Barn Cl. SM6: Wall 79Pb 156
New Barnes Av. AL1: St A 5E 6
NEW BARNET 14Fb 31
New Barn La. CR3: Whyt 88Ub 177
TN14: Cud 90Sc 180
TN16: Cud, Westrm 90Sc 180
New Barn Rd. BR8: Swan 67Gd 140
DA3: Ist R, Lfield 69De 143
DA13: Ist R, Lfield, Nflt G, Sflt
62Ee 143
New Barns Av. CR4: Mitc 70Mb 134
New Barn St. E13 42Jc 93
New Barns Way IG7: Chig 20Rc 36
New Battlebridge La. RH1: Mers 2B 208
Newbeach Ho. SL2: Slou 1F 80
Newbeck Ct. BR3: Beck 66Bc 136
NEW BECKENHAM 65Bc 136
New Bell Yd. EC4 3C 224
New Bentham Ct. N1 38Sb 71
(off Ecclesbourne Rd.)
Newberries Av. WD7: R'lett 7Ka 14
Newberry Cres. SL4: Wind 4B 102
New Berry La. KT12: Hers 78Z 151
Newbery Cl. CR3: Cat'm 97Ub 197
Newbery Ho. N1 38Sb 71
(off Northampton St.)
Newbery Rd. DA8: Erith 53Hd 118
Newbery Way SL1: Slou 7H 81
Newbiggin Path WD19: Wat 21Y 45
Newbold Cotts. E1 44Yb 92
Newbolt Av. SM3: Cheam 78Ya 154
Newbolt Ho. SE17 7F 231
Newbolt Rd. HA7: Stan 22Ha 46
New Bond St. W1 3K 221 (44Kb 90)
Newborough Grn.
KT3: N Mald 70Ta 131
New Brent St. NW4 29Ya 48

Newbridge Point—Nicholls

Newbridge Point SE23 .62Zb 136
(off Windrush La.)
New Bri. St. EC4 .3B 224 (44Rb 91)
New Broad St. EC2 .1G 225 (43Ub 91)
New Broadway TW12: Hamp H .64Fa 130
UB10: Hil .41R 84
W5 .45Ma 87
New Broadway Bldgs. W5 .45Ma 87
New Bldgs. SL4: Eton .1H 103
(off Westons Yd.)
Newburgh Rd. RM17: Grays .50Fe 99
W3 .46Sa 87
Newburgh St. W1 .3B 222 (44Lb 90)
New Burlington M. W1 .4B 222 (45Lb 90)
New Burlington Pl. W1 .4B 222 (45Lb 90)
New Burlington St. W1 .4B 222 (45Lb 90)
Newburn Ho. SE11 .7J 229
Newburn St. SE11 .7J 229 (50Pb 90)
Newbury Av. EN3: Enf L .10Bc 20
Newbury Cl. DA2: Dart .59Rd 119
RM3: Rom .23Ld 57
RM10: Dag .33Cd 76
UB5: N'olt .37Ba 65
Newbury Ct. DA14: Sidc .63Vc 139
E5 .36Ac 72
(off Daubeney Rd.)
Newbury Gdns. KT19: Ewe .77Va 154
RM3: Rom .23Md 57
RM14: Upm .34Pd 77
Newbury Ho. N22 .25Nb 50
SW9 .54Rb 113
W2 .44Db 89
(off Hallfield Est.)
Newbury M. NW5 .37Jb 70
NEWBURY PARK .29Tc 54
Newbury Rd. BR2: Brom .69Jc 137
E4 .23Ec 52
IG2: Ilf .30Uc 54
RM3: Rom .22Md 57
TW6: H'row A .53P 105
Newbury St. EC1 .7D 218 (43Sb 91)
Newbury Wlk. RM3: Rom .22Md 57
Newbury Way UB5: N'olt .37Aa 65
New Bus. Cen., The NW10 .41Va 88
New Butt La. SE8 .52Cc 114
New Butt La. Nth. SE8 .52Cc 114
(off Hales St.)
Newby NW1 .4B 216
Newby Cl. EN1: Enf .12Ub 33
Newby Ho. E14 .45Ec 92
(off Newby Pl.)
Newby Pl. E14 .45Ec 92
Newby St. SW8 .55Kb 112
New Caledonian Mkt. SE1 .3J 231
New Caledonian Wharf SE16 .48Bc 92
Newcastle Av. IG6: Ilf .23Wc 55
Newcastle Cl. EC4 .2B 224 (44Rb 91)
Newcastle Ct. EC4 .4E 224
Newcastle Ho. W1 .7H 215
Newcastle Pl. W2 .7C 214 (43Fb 89)
Newcastle Row EC1 .6A 218 (42Qb 90)
New Causeway RH2: Reig .9K 207
New Cavendish St. W1 .1J 221 (43Jb 90)
New Century Ho. E16 .44Hc 93
(off Jude St.)
New Change EC4 .3D 224 (44Sb 91)
New Change Pas. EC4 .3D 224
New Chapel Sq. TW13: Felt .60X 107
New Charles St. EC1 .3C 218 (41Rb 91)
NEW CHARLTON .49Lc 93
New Chiswick Pool .52Ua 110
New Church Rd. SE5 .52Sb 113
(not continuous)
Newchurch Rd. SL2: Slou .3D 80
New City Rd. E13 .41Lc 93
New Claremont Apartments SE1 .5K 231
New Clock Twr. Pl. N7 .37Nb 70
New Cl. SW19 .69Eb 133
TW13: Hanw .64Aa 129
New Colebrooke Ct. SM5: Cars .80Hb 155
New College Ct. NW3 .37Eb 69
(off College Cres.)
New College M. N1 .38Qb 70
New College Pde. NW3 .37Fb 69
(off Finchley Rd.)
Newcombe Gdns. SW16 .63Nb 134
TW4: Houn .56Ba 107
Newcombe Ho. E5 .34Xb 71
Newcombe Pk. HA0: Wemb .39Pa 67
NW7 .22Ua 48
Newcombe Ri. UB7: Yiew .44N 83
Newcombe St. W8 .46Cb 89
Newcomen Rd. E11 .34Hc 73
SW11 .55Fb 111
Newcomen St. SE1 .1F 231 (47Tb 91)
Newcome Path WD7: Shenl .6Qa 15
Newcome Rd. WD7: Shenl .6Qa 15
New Compton St. WC2 .3E 222 (44Mb 90)
New Concordia Wharf SE1 .47Wb 91
New Coppice GU21: Wok .1J 187
New Cotts. GU24: Pirb .4B 186
KT23: Bookh .98Da 191
(off Dorking Rd.)
RM13: Wenn .44Ld 97
New Ct. EC4 .3K 223
KT15: Add .76L 149
UB5: N'olt .36Da 65
Newcourt UB8: Cowl .43L 83
Newcourt Ho. E2 .41Xb 91
(off Pott St.)
Newcourt St. NW8 .2D 214 (40Gb 69)
New Covent Garden Market .52Mb 112
New Crane Pl. E1 .46Yb 92
New Crane Wharf E1 .46Yb 92
(off New Crane Pl.)
New Cres. Yd. NW10 .40Va 68
Newcroft Cl. UB8: Hil .43R 84
Newcroft Ho. CR0: C'don .75Vb 157
(off Homefield Pl.)
NEW CROSS .52Bc 114
NEW CROSS .53Bc 114
NEW CROSS GATE .53Zb 114
NEW CROSS GATE .53Zb 114
New Cross Rd. SE14 .52Yb 114
Newdales Cl. N9 .19Wb 33
Newdene Av. UB5: N'olt .40Z 65
NEW DENHAM .37K 63
Newdigate Grn. UB9: Hare .25M 43
Newdigate Ho. E14 .44Bc 92
(off Norbiton Rd.)
Newdigate Rd. UB9: Hare .25L 43
Newdigate Rd. E. UB9: Hare .25M 43
New Diorama Theatre .5A 216 (42Kb 90)
Newell Ri. HP3: Hem H .5N 3
Newell Rd. HP3: Hem H .5N 3
Newell St. E14 .44Bc 92
NEW ELTHAM .61Sc 138
New End NW3 .34Eb 69
New End Sq. NW3 .35Fb 69
New England Hill GU24: W End .4B 166
New England Ind. Est. IG11: Bark .40Sc 74
New England St. AL3: St A .2A 6
Newenham Rd. KT23: Bookh .98Ca 191
Newent Cl. SE15 .52Ub 113
SM5: Cars .74Hb 155
New Era Est. N1 .1H 219
New Era Ho. N1 .39Ub 71
(off Halcomb St.)
New Farm Av. BR2: Brom .70Jc 137
New Farm Cl. TW18: Staines .67L 127
New Farm Dr. RM4: Abr .13Yc 37
New Farm La. HA6: Nwood .25U 44
New Festival Av. E14 .44Cc 92
New Fetter La. EC4 .2A 224 (44Qb 90)
Newfield Cl. TW12: Hamp .67Ca 129
Newfield La. HP2: Hem H .2N 3
Newfield Ri. NW2 .34Wa 68
Newfield Way AL4: St A .4G 6
Newford Cl. HP2: Hem H .1B 4
New Ford Rd. EN8: Walt C .6Bc 20
New Forest La. IG7: Chig .23Qc 54
Newgale Gdns. HA8: Edg .25Pa 47
New Gdn. Dr. UB7: W Dray .47N 83
Newgate CR0: C'don .74Sb 157
Newgate Cl. TW13: Hanw .61Aa 129
Newgate St. E4 .20Gc 35
(not continuous)
EC1 .2C 224 (44Rb 91)
Newgatestreet Rd. EN7: G Oak .1Sb 19
New Globe Wlk. SE1 .6D 224 (46Sb 91)
New Goulston St. E1 .2K 225 (44Vb 91)
New Grn. Pl. SE19 .65Ub 135
New Gun Wharf E3 .39Ac 72
(off Gunmaker's La.)
New Hall Cl. HP3: Bov .9C 2
Newhall Ct. EN9: Walt A .5Hc 21
N1 .39Sb 71
(off Popham Rd.)
New Hall Dr. RM3: Hrld W .25Nd 57
Newhall Gdns. KT12: Walt T .75Y 151
Newham City Farm .44Mc 93
Newham Dockside E16 .45Nc 94
Newham Leisure Cen. .42Lc 93
Newham's Row SE1 .2J 231 (48Ub 91)
Newham Way E6 .43Hc 93
E16 .43Hc 93
Newhaven Cl. UB3: Harl .49V 84
Newhaven Cres. TW15: Ashf .64T 128
Newhaven Gdns. SE9 .56Mc 115
Newhaven La. E16 .42Hc 93
Newhaven Rd. SE25 .71Tb 157
Newhaven Spur SL2: Slou .2F 80
NEW HAW .81K 169
New Haw Rd. KT15: Add .78L 149
New Heston Rd. TW5: Hest .52Ba 107
Newholme Ct. KT13: Weyb .76U 150
New Hope Ct. NW10 .41Xa 88
New Horizons Ct. TW8: Bford .51Ja 108
NEW HOUSE .1A 144
Newhouse Av. RM6: Chad H .27Zc 55
Newhouse Cl. KT3: N Mald .73Ua 154
Newhouse Cres. WD25: Wat .4X 13
New Ho. La. DA11: Nflt, Grav'nd .2B 144
TN15: Wro .88Ae 185
New Ho. Pk. AL1: St A .5E 6
Newhouse Rd. HP3: Bov .8C 2
Newhouse Wlk. SM4: Mord .73Eb 155
Newick Cl. DA5: Bexl .58Dd 118
Newick Rd. E5 .35Xb 71
Newing Grn. BR1: Brom .66Mc 137
NEWINGTON .4D 230 (48Sb 91)
Newington Barrow Way N7 .34Pb 70
Newington Butts SE1 .6C 230 (49Rb 91)
SE11 .6C 230 (49Rb 91)
Newington C'way. SE1 .4C 230 (48Rb 91)
Newington Ct. N16 .35Sb 71
(off Green Lanes)
Newington Ct. Bus. Cen. SE1 .3D 230
Newington Grn. N1 .36Tb 71
N16 .36Tb 71
Newington Grn. Community Gdns.
N16 .36Tb 71
(off Newington Grn.)
Newington Grn. Mans. N16 .36Tb 71
Newington Grn. Rd. N1 .37Tb 71
Newington Ind. Est.
SE17 .6D 230 (49Rb 91)
New Inn B'way. EC2 .5J 219 (42Ub 91)
New Inn Pas. WC2 .3J 223
New Inn Sq. EC2 .5J 219
New Inn St. EC2 .5J 219 (42Ub 91)
New Inn Yd. EC2 .5J 219 (42Ub 91)
New Jubilee Ct. IG8: Wfd G .24Jc 53
New Jubilee Wharf E1 .46Yb 92
(off Wapping Wall)
New Kelvin Av. TW11: Tedd .65Ga 130
New Kent Rd. AL1: St A .2B 6
SE1 .4D 230 (48Sb 91)
New Kings Rd. SW6 .54Bb 111
New King St. SE8 .51Cc 114
Newland Cl. AL1: St A .5E 6
HA5: Hat E .23Aa 45
Newland Ct. EC1 .5F 219
HA9: Wemb .33Qa 67
Newland Dr. EN1: Enf .11Xb 33
Newland Gdns. W13 .47Ja 86
Newland Ho. N8 .27Nb 50
(off Newland Rd.)
SE14 .51Zb 114
(off John Williams Cl.)
Newland Rd. N8 .27Nb 50
NEWLANDS
HA8 .20Na 29
SE23 .57Zb 114
Newlands HA1: Harr .32Ga 66
NW1 .3B 216
Newlands, The KT7: T Ditt .74Ga 152
SM6: Wall .80Lb 156
Newlands Av. GU22: Wok .93B 188
KT7: T Ditt .74Ga 152
WD7: R'lett .6Ha 14
Newlands Cl. CM13: Hut .17Fe 41
HA0: Wemb .37La 66
HA8: Edg .20Na 29
KT12: Hers .77Aa 151
UB2: S'hall .50Aa 85
Newlands Ct. CR3: Cat'm .93Sb 197
(off Coulsdon Rd.)
KT15: Add .78K 149
(off Church Rd.)
SE9 .58Qc 116
Newlands Dr. SL3: Poyle .55G 104
Newlands Pk. SE26 .65Yb 136
Newlands Pk. Cvn. Site WD5: Bedm .8F 4
Newlands Pl. EN5: Barn .15Za 30
Newlands Quay E1 .45Yb 92
Newlands Rd. HP1: Hem H .1G 2
IG8: Wfd G .19Hc 35
SW16 .68Nb 134
Newland St. E16 .46Nc 94
Newlands Wlk. WD25: Wat .5Z 13
Newlands Way EN6: Pot B .2Db 17
KT9: Chess .78La 152
Newlands Woods
CR0: Sels .81Bc 178
New La. GU4: Sut G .94A 188
Newling Cl. E6 .44Pc 94
New Lodge Dr. RH8: Oxt .100Hc 199
New London Performing Arts Cen.
.28Kb 50
New London St. EC3 .4J 225
New London Theatre .2G 223
New Lydenburg Commercial Est.
SE7 .48Lc 93
New Lydenburg St. SE7 .48Lc 93
Newlyn KT13: Weyb .77V 150
NW1 .1C 216
Newlyn Cl. AL2: Brick W .2Aa 13
BR6: Chels .77Wc 161
UB8: Hil .43Q 84
Newlyn Gdns. HA2: Harr .31Ba 65
Newlyn Ho. HA5: Hat E .24Ba 45
Newlyn Rd. DA16: Well .54Vc 117
EN5: Barn .14Bb 31
N17 .25Vb 51
NEW MALDEN .70Ua 132
New Maltings
RM15: Avel .46Td 98
Newman Cl. NW10 .37Xa 68
RM11: Horn .29Nd 57
SE26 .63Yb 136
Newman Ct. BR1: Brom .67Jc 137
(off North St.)
TW15: Ashf .65R 128
Newman Ho. SE1 .4B 230 (48Rb 91)
Newman Pas. W1 .1C 222 (43Lb 90)
Newman Rd. BR1: Brom .67Jc 137
CR0: C'don .74Pb 156
E13 .41Kc 93
E17 .29Zb 52
UB3: Hayes .45X 85
Newman Rd. Ind. Est.
CR0: C'don .73Pb 156
Newmans Cl. IG10: Lough .13Qc 36
Newman's Ct. EC3 .3G 225
Newmans Dr. CM13: Hut .17Ee 41
Newmans Ga. CM13: Hut .17Ee 41
Newmans La. IG10: Lough .13Qc 36
KT6: Surb .72Ma 153
Newmans Pl. SL5: S'dale .3F 146
Newmans Rd. DA11: Nflt .1B 144
Newman's Row WC2 .1J 223 (43Pb 90)
Newman St. W1 .1C 222 (43Lb 90)
Newman's Way EN4: Had W .11Eb 31
Newman Yd. W1 .2D 222 (44Lb 90)
Newmarket Av. UB5: N'olt .36Ca 65
Newmarket Ct. AL3: St A .1A 6
Newmarket Grn. SE9 .59Mc 115
Newmarket Ho. RM3: Rom .22Nd 57
(off Lindfield Rd.)
Newmarket Way RM12: Horn .35Nd 77
Newmarsh Rd. SE28 .46Vc 95
New Mile Rd. SL5: Asc .8A 124
Newmill Ho. E3 .42Ec 92
New Mill Rd. BR5: St P .67Yc 139
SW8 .51Mb 112
Newminster Rd. SM4: Mord .72Eb 155
New Mossford Way IG6: Ilf .28Sc 54
New Mt. St. E15 .38Fc 73
Newnes Path SW15 .56Xa 110
Newnham Av. HA4: Ruis .32Y 65
Newnham Cl. CR7: Thor H .68Sb 135
IG10: Lough .16Mc 35
SL2: Slou .6K 81
UB5: N'olt .37Ea 66
Newnham Gdns. UB5: N'olt .37Ea 66
Newnham Grn. N22 .25Qb 50
(off Highfield Cl.)
Newnham Ho. IG10: Lough .16Mc 35
Newnham Lodge DA17: Belv .50Cd 96
(off Erith Rd.)
Newnham M. N22 .24Qb 50
Newnham Pde. EN8: Chesh .2Zb 20
Newnham Pl. RM16: Grays .9C 100
Newnham Rd. N22 .25Pb 50
Newnhams Cl. BR1: Brom .69Pc 138
Newnham Ter. SE1 .3K 229 (48Qb 90)
Newnham Way HA3: Kenton .29Na 47
New Nth. Pl. EC2 .5H 219 (42Ub 91)
New Nth. Rd. IG6: Ilf .21Tc 54
N1 .1F 219 (38Sb 71)
RH2: Reig .9H 207
New Nth. Sq. IG6: Ilf .23Tc 54
New Nth. St. WC1 .7H 217 (43Pb 90)
Newnton Cl. N4 .31Tb 71
New Oak Rd. N2 .26Eb 49
New Orleans Wlk. N19 .31Mb 70
New Oxford St. WC1 .2E 222 (44Mb 90)
New Pde. KT23: Bookh .97Ea 192
TW15: Ashf .63P 127
UB7: Yiew .46N 83
WD3: Chor .14E 24
New Pde. Flats WD3: Chor .14E 24
New Paragon Wlk. SE17 .5F 231 (49Tb 91)
New Pk. Av. N13 .20Sb 33
New Pk. Cl. UB5: N'olt .37Aa 65
New Pk. Dr. HP2: Hem H .1B 4
New Pk. Est. N18 .22Yb 52
New Pk. Ho. N13 .21Pb 50
New Pk. Pde. SW2 .59Nb 112
(off New Pk. Rd.)
New Pk. Rd. SW2 .60Mb 112
TW15: Ashf .64S 128
UB9: Hare .25L 43
New Peachey La. UB8: Cowl .44M 83
Newpiece IG10: Lough .13Rc 36
New Pl. CR0: Addtn .79Cc 158
SL5: S'dale .5C 146
New Pl. Gdns. RM14: Upm .33Td 78
New Pl. Sq. SE16 .48Xb 91
New Plaistow Rd. E15 .39Gc 73
New Plymouth Ho. RM13: Rain .41Hd 96
(off Dunedin Rd.)
New Pond Pde. HA4: Ruis .34W 64
Newport Av. E13 .42Kc 93
E14 .45Fc 93
Newport Cl. EN3: Enf W .9Ac 20
Newport Ct. WC2 .4E 222 (45Mb 90)
Newport Ho. E3 .41Ac 92
(off Strahan Rd.)
Newport Lodge EN1: Enf .15Ub 33
(off Village Rd.)
Newport Mead WD19: Wat .21Z 45
Newport Pl. WC2 .4E 222 (45Mb 90)
Newport Rd. E10 .33Ec 72
E17 .28Ac 52
SL2: Slou .2C 80
SW13 .53Wa 110
TW6: H'row A .53Q 106
UB4: Hayes .43T 84
W3 .47Sa 87
Newports BR8: Crock .73Fd 162
Newport St. SE11 .6H 229 (49Pb 90)
Newport Street Gallery .5J 229 (49Pb 90)
New Priory Ct. NW6 .38Cb 69
(off Mazenod Av.)
New Providence Wharf E14 .46Fc 93
New Provident Pl. HP4: Berk .1A 2
Newquay Cres. HA2: Harr .33Aa 65
Newquay Gdns. WD19: Wat .19X 27
Newquay Ho. SE11 .7K 229 (50Qb 90)
Newquay Rd. SE6 .61Dc 136
New Quebec St. W1 .3G 221 (44Hb 89)
New Rathmore Rd.
DA11: Grav'nd .9D 122
New Ride SW1 .2C 226 (47Gb 89)
SW7 .2C 226 (47Gb 89)
New River Av. N8 .27Pb 50
New River Ct. EN7: Chesh .3Xb 19
N5 .35Sb 71
New River Cres. N13 .21Rb 51
New River Head EC1 .3A 218 (41Qb 90)
New River Wlk. N1 .37Sb 71
(not continuous)
New River Way N4 .31Tb 71
New Rd. BR6: Orp .73Wc 161
BR8: Hext .66Hd 140
BR8: Swan .69Hd 140
CM14: B'wood .19Zd 41
CR4: Mitc .74Hb 155
DA4: S Dar .68Sd 142
DA11: Grav'nd .8C 122
DA16: Well .54Xc 117
E1 .43Xb 91
E4 .21Dc 52
EN6: S Mim .5Wa 16
GU20: W'sham .9A 146
HA1: Harr .35Ha 66
HP4: Berk .1A 2
HP8: Chal G .13A 24
IG3: Ilf .33Uc 74
KT2: King T .66Qa 131
KT8: W Mole .70Ca 129
KT10: Esh .76Ea 152
KT13: Weyb .78S 150
KT20: Tad .95Ya 194
KT22: Oxs .83Ha 172
N8 .29Nb 50
N9 .19Xb 33
N17 .25Vb 51
N22 .25Sb 51
NW7 .24Ab 48
(Bittacy Ct.)
NW7 .17Va 30
(Hendon Wood La.)
RH8: Limp .2M 211
RH8: Tand .8E 210
RM4: Abr .16Zc 37
RM9: Dag .40Cd 76
RM10: Dag .40Cd 76
RM13: Rain, Wenn .41Jd 96
RM17: Grays .51Ce 121
(not continuous)
SE2 .49Zc 95
SL3: Dat .3P 103
SL3: L'ly .48C 82
TN14: Sund .96Zc 201
TW3: Houn .56Da 107
TW8: Bford .51Ma 109
TW10: Ham .63La 130
TW13: Hanw .64Aa 129
TW14: Bedf .58T 106
TW14: Felt .60X 107
TW17: Shep .69Q 128
TW18: Staines .64E 126
UB3: Harl .52S 106
UB8: Hil .42S 84
WD3: Crox G .15Q 26
WD3: Sarr .11H 25
WD4: Chfd .2H 11
WD6: E'tree .16Ma 29
WD7: R'lett .8Ga 14
WD7: Shenl .6Qa 15
WD17: Wat .14Y 27
WD25: Let H .11Ga 28
New Rd. Hill BR2: Kes .81Nc 180
BR6: Downe .81Nc 180
New Rochford St. NW5 .36Hb 69
New Row NW2 .34Ya 68
WC2 .4F 223 (45Nb 90)
Newry Rd. TW1: Twick .57La 108
Newsam Av. N15 .29Tb 51
Newsham Rd. GU21: Wok .9K 167
Newsholme Dr. N21 .15Pb 32
New Site KT15: Add .76N 149
Newsom Pl. AL1: St A .1C 6
NEW SOUTHGATE .22Kb 50
New Southgate Crematorium
N11 .20Kb 32
New Southgate Ind. Est. N11 .22Lb 50
New Spitalfields Mkt. E10 .34Cc 72
New Spring Gdns. Wlk.
SE11 .7G 229 (50Nb 90)
New Sq. SL1: Slou .7J 81
TW14: Bedf .60S 106
WC2 .2K 223 (44Qb 90)
New Sq. Pk. TW14: Bedf .60S 106
New Sq. Pas. WC2 .2K 223
Newstead AL10: Hat .3B 8
Newstead Av. BR6: Orp .76Tc 160
Newstead Cl. N12 .23Gb 49
Newstead Ct. UB5: N'olt .41Aa 85
Newstead Ho. CR3: Cat'm .98Xb 197
N1 .1A 218
RM3: Rom .21Md 57
(off Troopers Dr.)
Newstead Ri. CR3: Cat'm .98Xb 197
Newstead Rd. SE12 .59Hc 115
Newstead Wlk. SM5: Cars .73Eb 155
Newstead Way SW19 .63Za 132
NEW STREET .78Fe 165
New St. EC2 .1J 225 (43Ub 91)
HP4: Berk .1A 2
TN16: Westrm .99Sc 200
TW18: Staines .63J 127
WD18: Wat .14Y 27
New St. Hill BR1: Brom .64Kc 137
New St. Rd. DA13: Meop .76Ee 165
TN15: Ash, Nw A G .77Ee 165
New St. Sq. EC4 .2A 224 (44Qb 90)
(not continuous)
New Swan Yd. DA12: Grav'nd .8D 122
New Tank Hill Rd.
RM15: Avel .48Qd 97
RM19: Avel, Purf .48Qd 97
New Tavern Fort .8E 122
(off Commercial Pl.)
Newteswell Dr. EN9: Walt A .4Fc 21
Newton Abbot Rd. DA11: Nflt .1B 144
Newton Av. N10 .25Jb 50
W3 .47Sa 87
Newton Cl. E17 .30Ac 52
HA2: Harr .33Ca 65
SL3: L'ly .47B 82
Newton Ct. E3 .43Cc 92
NW6 .38Eb 69
(off Fairfax Rd.)
SL4: Old Win .8L 103
SW17 .62Fb 133
(off Grosvenor Way)
W8 .47Cb 89
(off Kensington Chu. St.)
Newton Cres. WD6: Bore .14Sa 29
Newton Gro. W4 .49Ua 88
Newton Ho. E1 .45Xb 91
(off Cornwall St.)
E17 .27Dc 52
(off Prospect Hill)
EN3: Enf H .13Zb 34
NW8 .39Db 69
(off Abbey Rd.)
SE20 .66Zb 136
Newton Ind. Est.
RM6: Chad H .28Zc 55
Newton La. SL4: Old Win .8M 103
Newton Lodge SE10 .48Hc 93
(off Teal St.)
Newton Mans. W14 .51Ab 110
(off Queen's Club Gdns.)
Newton Pk. Pl. BR7: Chst .66Pc 138
Newton Pl. E14 .49Cc 92
Newton Rd. CR8: Purl .84Lb 176
DA16: Well .55Wc 117
E15 .36Fc 73
HA0: Wemb .38Pa 67
HA3: Hrw W .26Ga 46
IG7: Chig, Ilf .22Xc 55
N15 .29Wb 51
NW2 .35Ya 68
RM18: Tilb .5C 122
SW19 .66Ab 132
TW7: Isle .54Ha 108
W2 .44Db 89
Newtons Cl. RM13: Rain .38Hd 76
Newtons Ct. DA2: Dart .56Td 120
Newtonside Orchard SL4: Old Win .8L 103
Newton St. WC2 .2G 223 (44Nb 90)
Newton's Yd. SW18 .57Cb 111
Newton Ter. BR2: Brom .72Mc 159
Newton Wlk. HA8: Edg .25Ra 47
Newton Way N18 .22Sb 51
Newton Wood Rd. KT21: Asht .88Pa 173
New Tower Bldgs. E1 .46Xb 91
NEW TOWN .58Pd 119
Newtown Rd. UB9: Den .37K 63
Newtown St. SW11 .53Kb 112
New Trinity Rd. N2 .27Fb 49
New Turnstile WC1 .1H 223
New Union Cl. E14 .48Ec 92
New Union Sq. SW8 .51Mb 112
New Union St. EC2 .1F 225 (43Tb 91)
New Victoria Theatre
Woking .89A 168
New Village Av. E14 .44Fc 93
New Wlk. TN15: Wro .88Be 185
New Wanstead E11 .30Hc 53
New Way Rd. NW9 .28Ua 48
New Wharf Rd. N1 .1G 217 (40Nb 70)
New Wickham La. TW20: Egh .66C 126
New Willow Ho. E13 .40Jc 73
(off Plaistow Rd.)
NEW WINDSOR .5H 103
New Windsor St. UB8: Uxb .39L 63
NEWYEARS GREEN .31P 63
New Years Grn. La. UB9: Hare .30N 43
New Years La. TN14: Knock .88Vc 181
New Zealand Av. KT12: Walt T .74V 150
New Zealand Golf Course .84F 168
New Zealand War Memorial .1J 227
New Zealand Way RM13: Rain .41Hd 96
W12 .45Xa 88
Nexus Apartments BR1: Brom .69Kc 137
(off Elmfield Rd.)
Nexus Cl. TW14: Felt .57W 106
Nexus Ct. AL1: St A .3B 6
E11 .32Gc 73
NW6 .41Cb 89
Niagara Av. W5 .49La 86
Niagara Cl. EN8: Chesh .1Zb 20
N1 .1E 218 (40Sb 71)
Niagra Ct. SE16 .48Yb 92
(off Canada Est.)
Nibthwaite Rd. HA1: Harr .29Ga 46
Nice Bus. Pk. SE15 .51Xb 113
Nicholas Cl. RM15: S Ock .41Yd 98
UB6: G'frd .40Da 65
WD24: Wat .9X 13
Nicholas Ct. E13 .41Kc 93
N7 .36Pb 70
SE12 .60Jc 115
W4 .51Ua 110
(off Corney Reach Way)
Nicholas Gdns. GU22: Pyr .88H 169
SL1: Slou .6C 80
W5 .47Ma 87
Nicholas Ho. AL4: St A .3H 7
Nicholas La. EC4 .4G 225 (45Tb 91)
(not continuous)
Nicholas Lodge
KT10: Esh .75Ca 151
Nicholas M. W4 .51Ua 110
Nicholas Pas. EC4 .4G 225
Nicholas Rd. CR0: Bedd .77Nb 156
E1 .42Yb 92
RM8: Dag .33Bd 75
W11 .45Za 88
WD6: E'tree .16Pa 29
Nicholas Stacey Ho. SE7 .50Kc 93
(off Frank Burton Cl.)
Nicholas Way HA6: Nwood .25S 44
HP2: Hem H .1P 3
Nicholay Rd. N19 .32Mb 70
(not continuous)
Nichol Cl. N14 .18Mb 32
Nicholes Rd.
TW3: Houn .56Ca 107
Nichol La. BR1: Brom .66Jc 137
Nicholl Ho. N4 .32Sb 71
Nicholl Rd. CM16: Epp .3Vc 23
Nicholls SL4: Wind .5A 102

Nicholls Av.—Nth. Cray Rd.

Nicholls Av. UB8: Hil 42Q 84
Nicholls Cl. CR3: Cat'm 94Sb 197
Nichollsfield Wlk. N7 36Pb 70
Nicholls M. SW16 63Nb 134
Nicholls Point E15 39Jc 73
(off Park Gro.)
Nicholl St. E2 39Wb 71
Nichols Wlk. SL4: Wind 5A 102
Nichols Cl. KT9: Chess 79La 152
N4 32Qb 70
(off Osborne Rd.)
Nichols Ct. E2 2K 219 (40Vb 71)
Nichols Grn. W5 43Na 87
Nicholson Ct. E17 28Zb 52
N17 27Vb 51
Nicholson Ho. SE17 7F 231 (50Tb 91)
Nicholson M.
KT1: King T 70Na 131
TW20: Egh 64C 126
(off Station Rd.)
Nicholson Rd. CR0: C'don 74Vb 157
Nicholson St. SE1 7B 224 (46Rb 91)
Nicholson Wlk.
TW20: Egh 64C 126
Nickelby Apartments E15 37Fc 73
(off Grove Cres. Rd.)
Nickelby Cl. SE28 44Yc 95
Nickleby Cl. UB8: Hil 44R 84
Nickleby Ho. SE16 47Wb 91
(off Parkers Row)
W11 46Za 88
(off St Ann's Rd.)
Nickleby Rd.
DA12: Grav'nd 10J 123
Nickols Wlk. SW18 56Db 111
Nicky La. HP2: Hem H 1N 3
Nicola Cl. CR2: S Croy 79Sb 157
HA3: Hrw W 26Fa 46
Nicola M. IG6: Ilf 23Rc 54
Nicolas Wlk.
RM16: Grays 7D 100
Nicola Ter. DA7: Bex 53Ad 117
Nicol Cl. TW1: Twick 58Ka 108
Nicoll Cir. NW7 23Ab 48
Nicoll Ct. N10 24Kb 50
NW10 39Ua 68
Nicoll Pl. NW4 30Xa 48
Nicoll Rd. NW10 39Ua 68
Nicoll Way
WD6: Bore 15Ta 29
Nicolson NW9 25Ua 48
Nicolson Dr. WD23: B Hea 18Ea 28
Nicolson Rd. BR5: Orp 73Zc 161
Nicolson Way TN13: S'oaks 94Md 203
Nicosia Rd. SW18 59Gb 111
Niederwald Rd. SE26 63Ac 136
Nield Rd. UB3: Hayes 47V 84
Nigel Cl. UB5: N'olt 39Aa 65
Nigel Ct. N3 24Db 49
Nigel Fisher Way KT9: Chess 80La 152
Nigel Ho. EC1 7K 217
Nigel M. IG1: Ilf 35Rc 74
Nigel Playfair Av. W6 49Xa 88
Nigel Rd. E7 36Lc 73
SE15 55Wb 113
Nigeria Rd. SE7 52Lc 115
Nighthawk NW9 25Va 48
Nightingale Av. E4 22Gc 53
HA1: Harr 31Ka 66
KT24: W Hor 96T 190
RM14: Upm 32Vd 78
Nightingale Cl. DA11: Nflt 2A 144
E4 21Fc 53
HA5: Eastc 29Y 45
KT11: Cobh 83Z 171
KT19: Eps 84Qa 173
SM5: Cars 75Jb 156
TN16: Big H 87Lc 179
W4 51Sa 109
WD5: Ab L 3W 12
WD7: R'lett 8Ha 14
Nightingale Cnr. BR5: St M Cry 70Zc 139
Nightingale Ct. BR2: Brom 68Gc 137
E14 47Ec 92
(off Ovex Cl.)
GU21: Wok 10J 167
HA1: Harr 30Ha 46
N4 33Pb 70
(off Tollington Pk.)
RH1: Redh 5A 208
(off St Anne's Mt.)
SL1: Slou 8L 81
SM1: Sutt 78Eb 155
SW6 53Db 111
(off Maltings Pl.)
WD3: Rick 17L 25
WD7: R'lett 7Ja 14
Nightingale Cres. KT24: W Hor 97S 190
RM3: Hrld W 26Nd 57
Nightingale Dr. KT19: Ewe 79Ra 153
Nightingale Gro. DA1: Dart 56Qd 119
SE13 57Fc 115
Nightingale Hgts. SE18 51Rc 116
Nightingale Ho. BR8: Swan 69Gd 140
(off London Rd.)
E1 46Wb 91
(off Thomas More St.)
E2 1J 219
KT17: Eps 84Ua 174
(off Winter Cl.)
KT17: Eps 84Ua 174
(East St.)
NW8 6D 214
SE18 50Qc 94
(off Connaught M.)
UB7: W Dray 47P 83
W12 44Ya 88
(off Du Cane Rd.)
Nightingale La. AL1: St A 5G 6
AL4: St A 6G 6
BR1: Brom 68Lc 137
E11 28Kc 53
N8 28Nb 50
SW4 59Hb 111
SW12 59Hb 111
TW10: Rich 59Na 109
Nightingale Lodge W9 43Cb 89
(off Admiral Wlk.)
Nightingale M. E3 40Zb 72
E11 29Jc 53
KT1: King T 69Ma 131
(off South La.)
SE11 5B 230 (49Rb 91)
Nightingale Pk. SL2: Farn C 8D 60
Nightingale Pl. SE18 51Qc 116
SW10 51Eb 111
WD3: Rick 17M 25
Nightingale Ri. KT15: Add 76N 149
Nightingale Rd. BR5: Pet W 72Sc 160
CR2: Sels 83Zb 178
E5 34Xb 71
KT8: W Mole 71Da 151
KT10: Esh 78Ba 151
KT12: Walt T 73Y 151
KT24: E Hor 97V 190
N1 37Sb 71
N9 16Yb 34
N22 25Nb 50
NW10 40Va 68
SM5: Cars 76Hb 155
TN15: Kems'g 89Md 183
TW12: Hamp 64Ca 129
W7 46Ha 86
WD3: Rick 17L 25
WD23: Bush 15Ca 27
Nightingales EN9: Walt A 6Gc 21
Nightingales, The TW19: Stanw 60P 105
Nightingale Shott TW20: Egh 65B 126
Nightingales La. HP8: Chal G 14A 24
Nightingale Sq. SW12 59Jb 112
Nightingale Va. SE18 51Qc 116
Nightingale Wlk. N1 37Sb 71
SL4: Wind 5G 102
SW4 58Kb 112
Nightingale Way BR8: Swan 69Gd 140
E6 43Nc 94
RH1: Blet 6L 209
UB9: Den 31H 63
Nile Cl. N16 34Vb 71
Nile Dr. N9 19Yb 34
Nile Ho. N1 3F 219
Nile Path SE18 51Qc 116
Nile Rd. E13 40Lc 73
Nile St. N1 3E 218 (41Sb 91)
Nile Ter. SE15 7K 231 (50Vb 91)
Nimbus Rd. KT19: Eps 82Ta 173
Nimegen Way SE22 57Ub 113
Nimmo Dr. WD23: B Hea 17Fa 28
Nimrod NW9 25Ua 48
Nimrod Cl. UB5: N'olt 41Z 85
Nimrod Ho. E16 43Kc 93
(off Vanguard Cl.)
Nimrod Pas. N1 37Ub 71
Nimrod Rd. SW16 65Kb 134
Nina Mackay Cl. E15 39Gc 73
Nine Acre La. AL10: Hat 1B 8
Nine Acres SL1: Slou 6D 80
Nine Acres Cl. E12 36Nc 74
UB3: Harl 48S 84
Nineacres Way CR5: Coul 88Nb 176
Ninedells Pl. AL1: St A 2D 6
NINE ELMS 52Lb 112
Nine Elms Av. UB8: Cowl 43M 83
Nine Elms Cl. TW14: Felt 60V 106
UB8: Cowl 44M 83
Nine Elms Gro. DA11: Grav'nd 9C 122
Nine Elms La. SW8 52Lb 112
Ninefields EN9: Walt A 5Hc 21
Ninehams Cl. CR3: Cat'm 92Tb 197
Ninehams Gdns. CR3: Cat'm 92Tb 197
Ninehams Rd. CR3: Cat'm 93Tb 197
TN16: Tats 93Lc 199
Nine Stiles Cl. UB9: Den 37K 63
Nineteenth Rd. CR4: Mitc 70Nb 134
Ninhams Wood BR6: Farnb 77Qc 160
Ninnings Rd. SL9: Chal P 24B 42
Ninnings Way SL9: Chal P 24B 42
Ninth Av. KT20: Lwr K 97Bb 195
UB3: Hayes 45W 84
Nipper All. KT1: King T 68Na 131
(off Clarence St.)
Nipponzan Myohoji Peace Pagoda
51Hb 111
Nisbet Ho. E9 36Zb 72
Nisbett Wlk. DA14: Sidc 63Wc 139
(off Sidcup High St.)
Nita Ct. SE12 60Jc 115
Nita Rd. CM14: W'ley 22Yd 58
Nithdale Rd. SE18 52Rc 116
Nithsdale Gro. UB10: Ick 34S 64
Niton Cl. EN5: Barn 16Za 30
Niton Ct. SS17: Stan H 3L 101
Niton Rd. TW9: Rich 55Qa 109
Niton St. SW6 52Za 110
Niveda Cl. W12 47Wa 88
Niven Cl. WD6: Bore 11Sa 29
Nixey Cl. SL1: Slou 7L 81
No 1 St. SE18 48Rc 94
Noah Cl. EN3: Enf W 10Yb 20
NOAH'S ARK 91Rd 203
Noah's Ark TN15: Kems'g 90Rd 183
Noah's Yd. N1 2G 217 (40Nb 70)
Noakes Ind. Site RM13: Wenn 45Pd 97
NOAK HILL 19Nd 39
Noak Hill Rd. RM3: Rom 22Kd 57
Nobel Cl. NW9 26Ta 47
Nobel Dr. UB3: Harl 53T 106
Nobel Ho. RH1: Redh 5P 207
SE5 54Sb 113
Nobel Rd. N18 21Yb 52
Nobel Vs. EN9: Walt A 6Fc 21
Noble Cnr. TW5: Hest 53Ca 107
Noble Ct. CR4: Mitc 68Fb 133
E1 45Xb 91
SL2: Slou 6K 81
(off Mill St.)
Noblefield Hgts. N2 29Gb 49
Noble M. N16 34Tb 71
(off Albion Rd.)
Noble St. EC2 2D 224 (44Sb 91)
KT12: Walt T 76Y 151
Nobles Way TW20: Egh 65A 126
Noble Yd. N1 1B 218
Nocavia Ho. SW6 54Eb 111
(off Townmead Rd.)
Noel NW9 25Ua 48
Noel Ct. CR0: C'don 73Tb 157
TW4: Houn 55Ba 107
Noel Coward Ho. SW1 6C 228
Noel Coward Theatre 4F 223
Noel Ho. NW6 38Fb 69
(off Harben Rd.)
NOEL PARK 26Rb 51
Noel Pk. Rd. N22 26Qb 50
Noel Rd. E6 42Nc 94
N1 1B 218 (40Rb 71)
W3 45Qa 87
Noel Sq. RM8: Dag 35Yc 75
TW11: Tedd 64Ha 130
Noel St. W1 3C 222 (44Lb 90)
Noel Ter. DA14: Sidc 63Xc 139
SE23 61Yb 136
Noke Dr. RH1: Redh 5A 208
Noke La. AL2: Chis G 8L 5
Noke La. Bus. Cen. AL2: Chis G 9M 5
Noke Side AL2: Chis G 9N 5
Noko W10 41Za 88
Nolands Cl. RM5: Col R 26Ed 56
Nolan Mans. E20 36Dc 72
(off Honour Lea Av.)
Nolan Path WD6: Bore 11Pa 29
(off Bennington Dr.)
Nolan Way E5 35Wb 71
Noll Ho. N7 33Pb 70
(off Tomlins Wlk.)
Nolton Pl. HA8: Edg 25Pa 47
Nomad Theatre 100V 190
Nonsuch Cl. IG6: Ilf 23Rc 54
Nonsuch Ct. Av. KT17: Ewe 82Xa 174
Nonsuch Ho. SW19 67Fb 133
(off Chapter Way)
Nonsuch Ind. Est. KT17: Eps 83Ua 174
Nonsuch Pl. SM3: Cheam 80Za 154
(off Ewell Rd.)
Nonsuch Wlk. SM2: Cheam 82Ya 174
(not continuous)
Nook Apartments E1 44Vb 91
(off Scarborough St.)
Nora Gdns. NW4 28Za 48
Nora Leverton Ct. NW1 38Lb 70
(off Randolph St.)
NORBITON 68Qa 131
Norbiton Av. KT1: King T 67Qa 131
Norbiton Comn. Rd. KT1: King T 69Ra 131
Norbiton Hall KT2: King T 68Pa 131
Norbiton Ho. NW1 1C 216
(off Camden St.)
Norbiton Rd. E14 44Bc 92
Norbreck Gdns. NW10 41Pa 87
Norbreck Pde. NW10 41Na 87
Norbroke St. W12 45Va 88
Norburn St. W10 43Ab 88
NORBURY 67Pb 134
Norbury Av. CR7: Thor H 67Pb 134
SW16 67Pb 134
TW3: Houn 56Fa 108
WD24: Wat 11Y 27
Norbury Cl. SW16 67Qb 134
Norbury Ct. Rd. SW16 69Nb 134
Norbury Cres. SW16 67Pb 134
Norbury Cross SW16 69Nb 134
Norbury Gdns. RM6: Chad H 29Zc 55
Norbury Gro. NW7 20Ua 30
Norbury Hill SW16 66Qb 134
NORBURY PARK 98Ka 192
Norbury Pl. KT22: Fet 94Ga 192
Norbury Ri. SW16 69Nb 134
Norbury Rd. CR7: Thor H 68Sb 135
E4 22Cc 52
RH2: Reig 6H 207
TW13: Felt 62V 128
Norbury Trad. Est. SW16 68Pb 134
Norbury Way KT23: Bookh 97Ea 192
Norcombe Gdns. HA3: Kenton 30La 46
Norcombe Ho. N19 34Mb 70
(off Wedmore St.)
Norcott Cl. UB4: Yead 42Y 85
Norcott Rd. N16 33Wb 71
Norcroft Gdns. SE22 59Wb 113
Norcutt Rd. TW2: Twick 60Ga 108
Nordenfeldt Rd. DA8: Erith 50Fd 96
Norden Ho. E2 41Xb 91
(off Pott St.)
Nordmann Pl. RM15: S Ock 42Zd 99
Nore Hill Pinnacle (Local Nature Reserve)
91Dc 198
Norelands Dr. SL1: Burn 10A 60
Norfield Rd. DA2: Wilm 63Ed 140
Norfolk Apartments E4 24Dc 52
Norfolk Av. CR2: Sande 82Vb 177
N13 23Rb 51
N15 30Vb 51
SL1: Slou 3G 80
WD24: Wat 10Y 13
Norfolk Cl. DA1: Dart 58Qd 119
EN4: Cockf 14Jb 32
N2 27Gb 49
N13 23Rb 51
SL0: Iver 44F 82
TW1: Twick 58Ka 108
Norfolk Cotts. RH1: S Nut 8E 208
Norfolk Ct. EN5: Barn 14Ab 30
RM6: Chad H 29Xc 55
(off Norwich Cres.)
Norfolk Cres. DA15: Sidc 59Uc 116
W2 2D 220 (44Gb 89)
Norfolk Farm Cl. GU22: Pyr 88F 168
Norfolk Farm Rd. GU22: Pyr 87F 168
Norfolk Gdns. DA7: Bex 53Bd 117
WD6: Bore 14Ta 29
Norfolk Ho. BR2: Brom 70Hc 137
(off Westmoreland Rd.)
EC4 4D 224
SE8 53Cc 114
(off Brookmill Rd.)
SE20 67Yb 136
SL2: Farn C 4G 60
SW1 5E 228
Norfolk Ho. Rd. SW16 62Mb 134
Norfolk Mans. SW11 53Hb 111
(off Prince of Wales Dr.)
Norfolk M. W10 43Ab 88
(off Blagrove Rd.)
Norfolk Pl. DA16: Well 54Wc 117
RM16: Chaf H 49Yd 98
W2 2C 220 (44Fb 89)
(not continuous)
Norfolk Rd. CR7: Thor H 69Sb 135
DA12: Grav'nd 8F 122
(not continuous)
E6 39Pc 74
E17 26Zb 52
EN3: Pond E 16Xb 33
EN5: New Bar 13Cb 31
HA1: Harr 29Da 45
IG3: Ilf 32Uc 74
IG11: Bark 38Uc 74
KT10: Clay 78Ga 152
NW8 1C 214 (39Fb 69)
NW10 38Ua 68
RM7: Rom 30Ed 56
RM10: Dag 36Dd 76
RM14: Upm 34Qd 77
SW19 66Gb 133
TW13: Felt 60Y 107
UB8: Uxb 37M 63
WD3: Rick 18N 25
Norfolk Row SE1 5H 229 (49Pb 90)
Norfolk Sq. W2 3C 220 (44Fb 89)
Norfolk Sq. M. W2 3C 220
Norfolk St. E7 36Jc 73
Norfolk Ter. W6 50Ab 88
Norgrove Pk. SL9: Ger X 28A 42
Norgrove St. SW12 59Jb 112
Norham Ct. DA2: Dart 58Rd 119
(off Osbourne Rd.)
Norheads La. CR6: W'ham 91Jc 199
TN16: Big H 91Jc 199
Norhyrst Av. SE25 69Vb 135
NORK 87Za 174
Nork Gdns. SM7: Bans 86Ab 174
Nork Ri. SM7: Bans 88Za 174
Nork Way SM7: Bans 88Ya 174
Norland Ho. W11 46Za 88
(off Queensdale Cres.)
Norland Pl. W11 46Ab 88
Norland Rd. W11 46Za 88
Norlands Cres. BR7: Chst 67Rc 138
Norlands Ga. BR7: Chst 67Rc 138
Norlands La. TW20: Thorpe 69G 126
Norland Sq. W11 46Ab 88
Norland Sq. Mans. W11 46Ab 88
(off Norland Sq.)
Norlem Ct. SE8 49Ac 92
(off Seafarer Way)
Norley Va. SW15 60Wa 110
Norlington Rd. E10 32Ec 72
E11 32Ec 72
Norman Av. CR2: Sande 82Sb 177
KT17: Eps 84Va 174
N22 25Rb 51
TW1: Twick 59La 108
TW13: Hanw 61Aa 129
UB1: S'hall 45Aa 85
Norman Butler Ho. W10 42Ab 88
(off Ladbroke Gro.)
Normanby Cl. SW15 57Bb 111
Normanby Rd. NW10 35Va 68
Norman Cl. AL1: St A 5C 6
BR6: Farnb 76Sc 160
EN9: Walt A 5Fc 21
KT18: Tatt C 91Xa 194
N22 25Sb 51
RM5: Col R 25Dd 56
TN15: Kems'g 89Md 183
Norman Colyer Ct. KT19: Eps 82Ta 173
Norman Ct. EN6: Pot B 2Eb 17
IG2: Ilf 31Tc 74
N3 25Cb 49
(off Nether St.)
N4 31Qb 70
NW10 38Wa 68
W13 46Ka 86
(off Kirkfield Cl.)
Norman Cres. CM13: B'wood 20Ce 41
HA5: Pinn 25Y 45
TW5: Hest 52Z 107
Normand Gdns. W14 51Ab 110
(off Greyhound Rd.)
Normand Mans. W14 51Ab 110
(off Normand M.)
Normand M. W14 51Ab 110
Normand Rd. W14 51Bb 111
Normandy Av. EN5: Barn 15Bb 31
Normandy Bus. Pk. GU3: Norm 10C 186
Normandy Cl. SE26 62Ac 136
Normandy Ct. HP2: Hem H 1M 3
Normandy Dr. UB3: Hayes 44S 84
Normandy Ho. E14 47Ec 92
(off Plevna St.)
EN2: Enf 10Sb 19
Normandy Pl. W12 46Za 88
Normandy Rd. AL3: St A 1B 6
SW9 53Qb 112
Normandy Ter. E16 44Kc 93
Normandy Wlk. TW20: Egh 64E 126
Normandy Way DA8: Erith 53Gd 118
Norman Gro. E3 40Ac 72
Norman Hay Trad. Est., The
UB7: Sip 52P 105
Norman Ho. SE1 3J 231
SW8 52Nb 112
(off Wyvil Rd.)
TW13: Hanw 61Ba 129
(off Watermill Way)
Normanhurst CM13: Hut 16Ee 41
TW15: Ashf 64Q 128
Normanhurst Av. DA7: Bex 53Zc 117
Normanhurst Dr. TW1: Twick 57Ja 108
Normanhurst Rd. BR5: St P 68Xc 139
KT12: Walt T 75Z 151
SW2 61Pb 134
TN15: Bor G 92Ce 205
Norman Leddy Memorial Gdns. 44V 84
Norman Pde. DA14: Sidc 61Zc 139
Norman Pk. Athletics Track 72Kc 159
Norman Rd. CR7: Thor H 71Rb 157
DA1: Dart 60Nd 119
DA17: Belv 48Dd 96
(not continuous)
E6 42Pc 94
E11 33Fc 73
IG1: Ilf 36Rc 74
N15 29Vb 51
RM11: Horn 31Jd 76
SE10 52Dc 114
SM1: Sutt 78Cb 155
SW19 66Eb 133
TW15: Ashf 65T 128
Normans, The SL2: Slou 4M 81
Norman's Cl. DA11: Grav'nd 9C 122
NW10 37Ta 67
Normans Cl. UB8: Hil 43P 83
Normansfield Av. TW11: Tedd 66La 130
Normansfield Cl. WD23: Bush 17Da 27
Normanshire Dr. E4 21Cc 52
Norman's Mead NW10 37Ta 67
Norman St. EC1 4D 218 (41Sb 91)
Norman Ter. NW6 36Bb 69
Normanton Av. SW19 61Cb 133
Normanton Ct. CR2: S Croy 78Ub 157
(off Croham Rd.)
Normanton Pk. E4 19Gc 35
Normanton Rd. CR2: S Croy 78Ub 157
Normanton St. SE23 61Zb 136
Norman Way N14 19Nb 32
W3 43Ra 87
Normington Cl. SW16 64Qb 134
Norrels Dr. KT24: E Hor 98V 190
Norrels Ride KT24: E Hor 97V 190
Norrice Lea N2 29Fb 49
Norris NW9 25Va 48
(off Withers Mead)
Norris Cl. AL2: Lon C 8F 6
KT19: Eps 83Ra 173
Norris Ho. E9 39Yb 72
(off Handley Rd.)
N1 1H 219
SE8 50Bc 92
(off Grove St.)
TW7: Isle 54Ja 108
Norris Rd. TW18: Staines 63H 127
Norris St. SW1 5D 222 (45Mb 90)
Norris Way DA1: Cray 55Hd 118
Norroy Rd. SW15 56Za 110
Norry's Cl. EN4: Cockf 14Hb 31
Norry's Rd. EN4: Cockf 14Hb 31
Norseman Cl. IG3: Ilf 32Xc 75
Norseman Way UB6: G'frd 39Da 65
Norstead Pl. SW15 61Wa 132
Norsted La. BR6: Prat B 84Wc 181
Nth. Access Rd. E17 30Zb 52
North Acre NW9 25Ua 48
SM7: Bans 88Bb 175
NORTH ACTON 42Ta 87
Nth. Acton Bus. Pk. W3 43Ta 87
Nth. Acton Rd. NW10 40Ta 67
Northallerton Way RM3: Rom 22Md 57
Northall Rd. DA7: Bex 54Ed 118
Northampton Av. SL1: Slou 4G 80
Northampton Gro. N1 36Tb 71
Northampton Ho. RM3: Rom 21Nd 57
(off Broseley Rd.)
Northampton Pk. N1 37Sb 71
Northampton Pl. SL1: Slou 4G 80
(off Northampton Av.)
Northampton Rd. CR0: C'don 75Wb 157
EC1 5A 218 (42Qb 90)
EN3: Pond E 14Ac 34
Northampton Row EC1 4A 218
Northampton Sq. EC1 4B 218 (41Rb 91)
Northampton St. N1 38Sb 71
Northanger Rd. SW16 65Nb 134
North App. HA6: Nwood 19S 26
WD25: Wat 7V 12
Nth. Ash Rd. DA3: Nw A G 76Ae 165
Nth. Audley St. W1 3H 221 (45Jb 90)
North Av. HA2: Harr 30Da 45
KT12: W Vill 81U 170
N18 21Wb 51
SM5: Cars 80Jb 156
TW9: Kew 53Qa 109
UB1: S'hall 45Ba 85
UB3: Hayes 45W 84
W13 43Ka 86
WD7: Shenl 4Na 15
NORTHAW 2Hb 17
Northaw Ho. W10 42Ya 88
(off Sutton Way)
NORTHAW PARK 4Hb 17
Northaw Pl. EN6: N'thaw 2Fb 17
Northaw Rd. E. EN6: Cuff 3Mb 18
Northaw Rd. W. EN6: N'thaw 2Hb 17
North Bank NW8 4D 214 (41Gb 89)
Northbank Rd. E17 26Ec 52
NORTH BECKTON 43Pc 94
Nth. Birkbeck Rd. E11 34Fc 73
North Block RM2: Rom 27Md 57
SE1 1J 229
Northborough Rd. SL2: Slou 2E 80
SW16 69Mb 134
Northbourne BR2: Hayes 73Jc 159
Northbourne Rd. SW4 57Mb 112
Northbrook Dr. HA6: Nwood 25U 44
Northbrook Rd. CR0: C'don 71Tb 157
EN5: Barn 16Ab 30
IG1: Ilf 33Qc 74
N22 24Nb 50
SE13 57Gc 115
Northburgh St. EC1 6C 218 (42Rb 91)
Nth. Burnham Cl. SL1: Burn 10A 60
Northbury Cl. IG11: Bark 38Sc 74
Nth. Carriage Dr. W2 4D 220
NORTH CHEAM 76Ya 154
Northchurch SE17 7G 231 (50Tb 91)
(not continuous)
Northchurch Ho. E2 39Wb 71
(off Whiston Rd.)
Northchurch Rd. HA9: Wemb 37Qa 67
N1 38Tb 71
(not continuous)
Northchurch Ter. N1 38Ub 71
Nth. Circular Rd. E4 23Bc 52
E18 26Lc 53
IG1: Ilf 31Nc 74
IG11: Bark 38Qc 74
N3 27Cb 49
N12 27Cb 49
N13 22Qb 50
NW2 36Ua 68
NW4 36Ua 68
NW10 41Pa 87
NW11 36Ua 68
Northcliffe Cl. KT4: Wor Pk 76Ua 154
Northcliffe Dr. N20 18Bb 31
North Cl. AL2: Chis G 7P 5
DA6: Bex 56Zc 117
EN5: Barn 15Ya 30
IG7: Chig 22Wc 55
RM10: Dag 39Cd 76
SL4: Wind 3D 102
SM4: Mord 70Ab 132
TW14: Bedf 58T 106
Nth. Colonnade, The E14 46Cc 92
(not continuous)
North Comn. KT13: Weyb 77S 150
North Comn. Rd. UB8: Uxb 36M 63
W5 45Na 87
Northcote HA5: Pinn 26Y 45
KT15: Add 77M 149
Northcote Av. KT5: Surb 73Ra 153
TW7: Isle 57Ja 108
UB1: S'hall 45Aa 85
W5 45Na 87
Northcote Cl. KT24: W Hor 97S 190
Northcote Cres. KT24: W Hor 97S 190
Northcote Pk. KT22: Oxs 86Ea 172
Northcote Rd. CR0: C'don 72Tb 157
DA11: Grav'nd 10B 122
DA14: Sidc 63Uc 138
E17 28Ac 52
KT3: N Mald 69Sa 131
KT24: W Hor 97S 190
NW10 38Ua 68
SW11 57Gb 111
TW1: Twick 57Ja 108
North Cotts. AL2: Lon C 7E 6
Northcott Av. N22 25Nb 50
Northcotts Long Elms Cl. WD5: Ab L 5T 12
(off Long Elms Cl.)
Nth. Countess Rd. E17 26Bc 52
North Ct. BR1: Brom 67Kc 137
(off Palace Gro.)
SE24 55Rb 113
SW1 4F 229
W1 7C 216 (43Lb 90)
Northcourt WD3: Rick 18J 25
NORTH CRAY 64Ad 139
Nth. Cray Rd. DA5: Bexl 60Dd 118
DA14: Sidc 65Ad 139

North Cray Woods—Nunns Rd.

North Cray Woods 63Zc 139
North Cres. E16 42Fc 93
N3 26Bb 49
WC1 7D 216 (43Mb 90)
Northcroft SL2: Slou 2F 80
Northcroft Cl. TW20: Eng G 4M 125
Northcroft Ct. W12 47Wa 88
Northcroft Gdns. TW20: Eng G 4M 125
Northcroft Rd. KT19: Ewe 80Ta 153
TW20: Eng G 4M 125
W13 47Ka 86
North Crofts SE23 60Xb 113
Northcroft Ter. W13 47Ka 86
Northcroft Vs. TW20: Eng G 4M 125
Nth. Cross Rd. IG6: Ilf 28Sc 54
SE22 57Vb 113
Northdale Ct. SE25 69Vb 135
North Dene IG7: Chig 22Tc 54
NW7 20Ta 29
TW3: Houn 53Da 107
Northdene Gdns. N15 30Vb 51
North Down CR2: Sande 83Ub 177
Northdown Cl. HA4: Ruis 34V 64
Northdown Ct. RH9: G'stone 2A 210
Northdown Gdns. IG2: Ilf 29Uc 54
Northdown Rd. AL10: Hat 3C 8
CR3: Wold 96Zc 198
DA3: Lfield 68Zd 143
DA16: Well 54Xc 117
RM11: Horn 31Kd 77
SL9: Chal P 23A 42
SM2: Sutt 82Cb 175
TN15: Kems'g 89Nd 183
Nth. Downs Bus. Pk.
TN13: Dun G 88Ed 182
Nth. Downs Cres. CR0: New Ad 81Dc 178
North Downs Golf Course 97Cc 198
Nth. Downs Rd. CR0: New Ad 82Dc 178
Northdown St. N1 1G 217 (40Nb 70)
North Dr. AL4: St A 1J 7
BR3: Beck 70Dc 136
BR6: Orp 77Uc 160
GU24: Brkwd 3A 186
GU25: Vir W 2J 147
HA4: Ruis 31U 64
RM2: Rom 27Ld 57
SL2: Stoke P 1J 81
SW16 63Lb 134
TW3: Houn 54Ea 108
Nth. E. Surrey Crematorium
SM4: Mord 72Ya 154
NORTH END
DA8 53Hd 118
NW3 33Eb 69
North End CR0: C'don 75Sb 157
IG9: Buck H 17Lc 35
NW3 33Eb 69
RM3: Rom 19Ld 39
Northend CM14: W'ley 22Yd 58
HP3: Hem H 4B 4
Nth. End Av. NW3 33Eb 69
Nth. End Cres. W14 49Bb 89
Nth. End Ho. W14 49Ab 88
Nth. End La. BR6: Downe 83Qc 180
SL5: S'dale 3F 146
Nth. End Pde. W14 49Ab 88
(off North End Rd.)
Nth. End Rd. HA9: Wemb 34Qa 67
NW11 32Cb 69
SW6 49Ab 88
W14 49Ab 88
Northend Rd. DA1: Erith 52Hd 118
DA8: Erith 52Hd 118
Northend Trad. Est. DA8: Erith 52Gd 118
Nth. End Way NW3 33Eb 69
Northern Av. N9 19Ub 33
Northernhay Wlk. SM4: Mord 70Ab 132
Northern Hgts. N8 31Mb 70
(off Crescent Rd.)
Northern La. E2 40Wb 71
(off Kay St.)
Northern Perimeter Rd.
TW6: H'row A 53R 106
Northern Perimeter Rd. (W.)
TW6: H'row A 53M 105
Northern Pct. RM20: W Thur 49Vd 98
Northern Rd. E13 40Kc 73
SL2: Slou 2H 81
Northesk Ho. E1 42Xb 91
(off Tent St.)
Northey Av. SM2: Cheam 82Za 174
Nth. Eyot Gdns. W6 50Va 88
Northey St. E14 45Ac 92
NORTH FELTHAM 58X 107
Nth. Feltham Trad. Est.
TW14: Felt 57X 107
Northfield DA3: Hartl 69Be 143
GU18: Light 3A 166
IG10: Lough 14Mc 35
Northfield Av. BR5: Orp 72Yc 161
HA5: Pinn 28Z 45
W5 46Ka 86
W13 46Ka 86
Northfield Cl. BR1: Brom 67Nc 138
UB3: Harl 48V 84
Northfield Ct. TW18: Staines 67K 127
Northfield Cres. SM3: Cheam 77Ab 154
Northfield Farm M. KT11: Cobh 85W 170
Northfield Gdns. RM9: Dag 35Bd 75
WD24: Wat 9Y 13
Northfield Ho. SE15 51Wb 113
Northfield Pde. UB3: Harl 48U 84
Northfield Pk. UB3: Harl 48V 84
Northfield Path RM9: Dag 35Bd 75
Northfield Pl. KT13: Weyb 80R 150
Northfield Recreation Grd. W5 49Ka 86
Northfield Rd. E6 38Pc 74
EN3: Pond E 15Xb 33
EN4: Cockf 13Gb 31
EN8: Walt C 4Ac 20
KT11: Cobh 85W 170
N16 31Ub 71
RM9: Dag 35Bd 75
SL4: Eton W 9D 80
TW5: Hest 51Z 107
TW18: Staines 67K 127
W13 47Ka 86
WD6: Bore 11Ra 29
NORTHFIELDS 48Ka 86
Northfields KT17: Eps 83Ua 174
KT21: Asht 90Na 173
(not continuous)
RM17: Grays 49Ee 99
SW18 56Cb 111
Northfields Ind. Est. HA0: Wemb 39Qa 67
Northfields Prospect Bus. Cen.
SW18 56Cb 111
Northfields Rd. W3 43Ra 87
NORTH FINCHLEY 22Eb 49
NORTHFLEET 58De 121
NORTHFLEET GREEN 64Ee 143
Northfleet Grn. Rd. DA13: Nflt G 65Ee 143
Northfleet Ho. SE1 1F 231
Northfleet Ind. Est. DA11: Nflt 56Be 121
(not continuous)
Northfleet Lodge GU22: Wok 91A 188
Northfleet Urban Country Pk. 60Fe 121
Northflock St. SE16 47Wb 91
Nth. Flower Wlk. W2 5A 220
North Gdn. E14 46Bc 92
North Gdns. SW19 66Fb 133
North Ga. NW8 2D 214
Northgate HA6: Nwood 28S 44
Northgate Bus. Cen. EN1: Enf 13Xb 33
Northgate Ct. SW9 55Qb 112
Northgate Dr. NW9 30Ua 48
Northgate Ho. E14 45Cc 92
(off E. India Dock Rd.)
EN8: Chesh 1Ac 20
(off Turner's Hill)
Northgate Ind. Pk. RM5: Col R 25Bd 55
Northgate Path WD6: Bore 10Pa 15
North Gates N12 25Eb 49
(off Bow La.)
Nth. Glade, The DA5: Bexl 59Bd 117
Nth. Gower St. NW1 4B 216 (41Lb 90)
North Grn. NW9 24Ua 48
SL1: Slou 5J 81
North Gro. KT16: Chert 72H 149
N6 31Jb 70
N15 29Tb 51
NORTH HARROW 29Da 45
Nth. Hatton Rd. TW6: H'row A 53T 106
North Hill N6 30Hb 49
WD3: Chor 12G 24
North Hill Av. N6 30Jb 50
North Hill Dr. RM3: Rom 20Md 39
North Hill Grn. RM3: Rom 21Md 57
NORTH HILLINGDON 38S 64
North Ho. SE8 50Bc 92
Nth. Hyde Gdns. UB3: Harl, Hayes 49W 84
Nth. Hyde La. TW5: Hest 52Ba 107
UB2: S'hall 50Z 85
Nth. Hyde Rd. UB3: Harl, Hayes 48U 84
Northiam N12 21Cb 49
(not continuous)
WC1 4G 217
Northiam St. E9 39Xb 71
Northington St. WC1 6J 217 (42Pb 90)
NORTH KENSINGTON 43Ya 88
Nth. Kent Av. DA11: Nflt 58Ee 121
North Kent Indoor Bowls Club 48Dd 96
Northlands EN6: Pot B 3Fb 17
Northlands Av. BR6: Orp 77Uc 160
Northlands St. SE5 54Sb 113
North La. DA11: Grav'nd 4E 144
TW11: Tedd 65Ha 130
North Lawns DA11: Nflt 58Ee 121
(off Lawn Rd.)
Northleigh Ho. E3 41Dc 92
(off Powis Rd.)
North Lodge E16 46Kc 93
(off Wesley Av.)
EN5: New Bar 15Eb 31
Nth. Lodge Cl. SW15 57Za 110
Nth. London Bus. Pk. N11 19Jb 32
NORTH LOOE 85Ya 174
North Mall N9 19Xb 33
(within Edmonton Grn. Shop. Cen.)
RM17: Grays 51De 121
(off Grays Shop. Cen.)
SW18 57Db 111
(off Southside Shop. Cen.)
TW18: Staines 63H 127
(within The Elmsleigh Cen.)
Northmead RH1: Redh 3P 207
Northmead Rd. SL2: Slou 2D 80
North M. WC1 6J 217 (42Pb 90)
North Middlesex Golf Course 20Fb 31
North Mill Apartments E8 39Vb 71
(off Lovelace St.)
Northmoor Hill Wood Nature Reserve
28H 43
North Mt. N20 19Eb 31
(off High Rd.)
NORTH MYMMS 7C 8
NORTH OCKENDON 37Xd 78
Northolm HA8: Edg 21Ta 47
Northolme Cl. RM16: Grays 48Ee 99
Northolme Gdns. HA8: Edg 25Qa 47
Northolme Ri. BR6: Orp 75Uc 160
Northolme Rd. N5 35Sb 71
NORTHOLT 38Ca 65
Northolt N17 26Ub 51
(off Griffin Rd.)
Northolt Av. HA4: Ruis 36X 65
Northolt Gdns. UB6: G'frd 36Ha 66
Northolt Golf Course 40Aa 65
Northolt Leisure Cen. 37Ca 65
Northolt Rd. HA2: Harr 35Da 65
TW6: H'row A 53N 105
(not continuous)
Northolt Trad. Est. UB5: N'olt 38Da 65
Northolt Way RM12: Horn 37Ld 77
Nth. Orbital Commercial Pk.
AL1: St A 6E 6
Nth. Orbital Rd. AL1: St A 6B 6
AL2: Brick W, Chis G 2Z 13
AL2: St A 6B 6
AL4: S'ford, St A 6H 7
UB9: Den 29J 43
WD3: Map C 22G 42
WD3: W Hyd 25G 42
Northover BR1: Brom 62Hc 137
North Pde. HA8: Edg 26Qa 47
KT9: Chess 78Pa 153
UB1: S'hall 44Ca 85
(off North Rd.)
North Pk. SE9 58Pc 116
SL0: Rich P 48E 82
SL9: Chal P, Ger X 27A 42
North Pk. La. RH9: G'stone 1N 209
North Pas. SW18 57Cb 111
North Pl. CR4: Mitc 66Hb 133
EN9: Walt A 5Dc 20
TW11: Tedd 65Ha 130
North Point N8 29Pb 50
Northpoint Cl. SM1: Sutt 76Eb 155
Northpoint Ho. N1 37Tb 71
(off Essex Rd.)
Northpoint Sq. NW1 37Mb 70
Nth. Pole La. BR2: Kes 79Hc 159
Nth. Pole Rd. W10 43Ya 88
Northport St. N1 1G 219 (39Tb 71)
North Quay Pl. E14 45Dc 92
North Ride W2 4D 220 (45Gb 89)
Northridge Rd. DA12: Grav'nd 2E 144
Northridge Way HP1: Hem H 3H 3
North Riding AL2: Brick W 2Ca 13
DA3: Lfield 69Fe 143
North Ri. W2 3E 220 (44Gb 89)
North Rd. BR1: Brom 67Kc 137
BR4: W W'ck 74Dc 158
CM14: B'wood 18Yd 40
DA1: Dart 58Hd 118
DA17: Belv 48Dd 96
EN8: Walt C 5Ac 20
GU21: Wok 88C 168
HA1: Harr 31Ja 66
HA8: Edg 25Ra 47
IG3: Ilf 33Uc 74
KT6: Surb 72Ma 153
KT12: Hers 78Y 151
N6 31Jb 70
N7 37Nb 70
N9 18Xb 33
RH2: Reig 9H 207
RM4: Have B 20Gd 38
RM6: Chad H 29Ad 55
RM15: N Ock, S Ock 38Zd 79
RM19: Purf 49Sd 98
SE18 49Uc 94
SW19 65Eb 133
TW5: Hest 51Y 107
TW8: Bford 51Na 109
TW9: Kew, Rich 55Qa 109
TW14: Bedf 58T 106
UB1: S'hall 44Ca 85
UB3: Hayes 43T 84
UB7: W Dray 48P 83
W5 48Ma 87
WD3: Chor 15F 24
North Rd. Av. CM14: B'wood 18Yd 40
Northrop Rd. TW6: H'row A 53U 106
North Row SL3: Ful 35A 62
W1 4G 221 (45Hb 89)
Nth. Row Bldgs. W1 4H 221
Nth. Service Rd. CM14: B'wood 19Yd 40
North Several SE3 54Fc 115
NORTH SHEEN 55Qa 109
North Side EN9: Walt A 2Kc 21
Northside Rd. BR1: Brom 67Jc 137
Northside Studios E8 39Xb 71
(off Andrew's Rd.)
Nth. Side Wandsworth Comn.
SW18 57Fb 111
Northspur Rd. SM1: Sutt 76Cb 155
North Sq. DA3: Nw A G 75Be 165
N9 19Xb 33
(off New Rd.)
NW11 29Cb 49
North Stand N5 34Rb 71
Nth. Star Blvd. DA9: Ghithe 56Wd 120
(off Evelyn Wlk.)
Nth. Station App. RH1: S Nut 8F 208
Northstead Rd. SW2 61Qb 134
NORTH STIFFORD 46Ae 99
North St. BR1: Brom 67Jc 137
DA1: Dart 59Md 119
DA7: Bex 56Cd 118
DA12: Grav'nd 9D 122
E13 40Kc 73
IG11: Bark 37Rc 74
KT22: Lea 93Ja 192
NW4 29Xa 48
RH1: Redh 5P 207
RM1: Rom 27Fd 56
RM5: Rom 27Fd 56
RM11: Horn 31Md 77
SL4: Wink 10A 102, 1A 124
SM5: Cars 76Hb 155
SW4 55Lb 112
TW7: Isle 55Ja 108
TW20: Egh 64B 126
Nth. St. Pas. E13 40Kc 73
Nth. Tenter St. E1 3K 225 (44Vb 91)
North Ter. SL4: Wind 2H 103
SW3 4D 226 (48Gb 89)
WC2 6E 222
Northumberland All.
EC3 3J 225 (44Ub 91)
(not continuous)
Northumberland Av. DA16: Well 56Tc 116
E12 32Lc 73
EN1: Enf 11Xb 33
RM11: Horn 29Ld 57
TW7: Isle 53Ha 108
WC2 6F 223 (46Nb 90)
Northumberland Cl. DA8: Erith 52Ed 118
TW19: Stanw 58N 105
Northumberland Cres. TW14: Felt 58U 106
Northumberland Gdns.
BR1: Brom 70Qc 138
CR4: Mitc 71Mb 156
N9 20Vb 33
TW7: Isle 52Ja 108
Northumberland Gro. N17 24Xb 51
Northumberland Hall AL9: N Mym 10F 8
NORTHUMBERLAND HEATH 52Ed 118
Northumberland Ho. IG8: Wfd G 24Qc 54
SW1 6F 223
Northumberland Pk. DA8: Erith 52Ed 118
N17 24Vb 51
Northumberland Pk. Ind. Est.
N17 24Xb 51
Northumberland Pk. School Sports Cen.
24Wb 51
Northumberland Pl. TW10: Rich 57Ma 109
W2 44Cb 89
Northumberland Rd. DA13: Ist R 6B 144
E6 44Nc 94
E17 31Cc 72
EN5: New Bar 16Eb 31
HA2: Harr 29Ba 45
SS17: Linf 7J 101
Northumberland St.
WC2 6F 223 (46Nb 90)
Northumberland Wlk. SL0: Rich P 47G 82
Northumberland Way DA8: Erith 53Ed 118
Northumbria St. E14 44Cc 92
Nth. Verbena Gdns. W6 50Wa 88
North Vw. HA5: Eastc 31Y 65
SW19 64Ya 132
W5 42La 86
Northview BR8: Swan 68Gd 140
HP1: Hem H 4F 2
Northview Av. RM18: Tilb 3C 122
Nth. Vw. Cvn. Site IG6: Ilf 24Wc 55
North Vw. Cres. KT18: Tatt C 89Ya 174
Northview Cres. NW10 35Va 68
North Vw. Dr. IG8: Wfd G 26Mc 53
Northview Pde. N7 34Nb 70
North Vw. Rd. N8 28Mb 50
TN14: S'oaks 93Ld 203
North Vs. NW1 37Mb 70
North Wlk. CR0: New Ad 79Dc 158
(not continuous)
W2 5A 220 (45Db 89)
W8 45Db 89
(off The Broad Wlk.)
Northwall Rd. E20 36Cc 72
NORTH WATFORD 9X 13
North Way HA5: Pinn 28Z 45
N9 19Zb 34
N11 23Lb 50
NW9 27Ra 47
UB10: Uxb 38N 63
Northway NW11 29Db 49
SM4: Mord 69Ab 132
SM6: Wall 77Lb 156
WD3: Rick 17M 25
Northway Cir. NW7 21Ta 47
Northway Ct. NW7 21Ua 48
Northway Cres. NW7 21Ta 47
Northway Gdns. NW11 29Db 49
Northway Rd. CR0: C'don 72Vb 157
SE5 55Sb 113
Northways NW3 38Fb 69
(off College Cres.)
Northways Pde. NW3 38Fb 69
(off College Cres.)
Nth. Weald Cl. RM12: Horn 38Kd 77
Northweald La. KT2: King T 64Ma 131
NORTH WEMBLEY 34Ma 67
Nth. Western Av. WD24: Wat 7V 12
WD25: Wat, A'ham 7T 12
(not continuous)
Northwest Pl. N1 1A 218 (40Qb 70)
Nth. Weylands Ind. Est.
KT12: Walt T 75Aa 151
North Wharf E14 46Ec 92
(off Coldharbour)
Nth. Wharf Rd. W2 1B 220 (43Fb 89)
Northwick Av. HA3: Kenton 30Ja 46
Northwick Circ. HA3: Kenton 30La 46
Northwick Cl. HA1: Harr 32Ka 66
NW8 5B 214 (42Fb 89)
Northwick Ho. NW8 5A 214
Northwick Pk. Playgolf 32Ja 66
Northwick Pk. Rd. HA1: Harr 30Ha 46
NORTHWICK PARK RDBT. 31Ja 66
Northwick Rd. HA0: Wemb 39Ma 67
WD19: Wat 21Y 45
Northwick Ter. NW8 5B 214 (42Fb 89)
Northwick Wlk. HA1: Harr 31Ha 66
Northwold Dr. HA5: Pinn 26Y 45
Northwold Rd. E5 33Vb 71
N16 33Vb 71
NORTHWOOD 23U 44
Northwood RM16: Grays 7D 100
Northwood Av. CR8: Purl 84Qb 176
GU21: Knap 10H 167
RM12: Horn 35Jd 76
Nth. Wood Ct. SE25 69Wb 135
Northwood Dr. DA9: Ghithe 58Wd 120
Northwood Est. E5 33Wb 71
Northwood Gdns. IG5: Ilf 28Qc 54
N12 22Fb 49
UB6: G'frd 36Ha 66
Northwood Golf Course 24T 44
Northwood Hall N6 31Lb 70
Northwood Health & Racquets Club
23R 44
NORTHWOOD HILLS 26W 44
Northwood Hills Cir. HA6: Nwood 25W 44
Northwood Ho. KT2: King T 68Qa 131
(off Coombe Rd.)
SE27 63Tb 135
Northwood Pl. DA18: Erith 48Bd 95
Northwood Rd. CR7: Thor H 68Rb 135
N6 31Kb 70
SE23 60Bc 114
SM5: Cars 79Jb 156
TW6: H'row A 53M 105
UB9: Hare 25L 43
Northwood Way HA6: Nwood 24V 44
SE19 65Tb 135
UB9: Hare 25M 43
NORTH WOOLWICH 47Qc 94
Nth. Woolwich Rd. E16 46Hc 93
Nth. Worple Way SW14 55Ta 109
Nortoft Rd. SL9: Chal P 23B 42
Norton Almshouses EN8: Chesh 2Zb 20
(off Turner's Hill)
Norton Av. KT5: Surb 73Ra 153
Norton Cl. E4 22Cc 52
EN1: Enf 12Xb 33
GU3: Worp 9H 187
WD6: Bore 11Qa 29
Norton Ct. BR3: Beck 67Bc 136
Norton Folgate E1 7J 219 (43Ub 91)
Norton Folgate Ho. E1 7K 219
Norton Gdns. SW16 68Nb 134
Norton Ho. E1 44Xb 91
(off Bigland St.)
E2 40Zb 72
(off Mace St.)
SW1 4E 228
SW9 54Pb 112
(off Aytoun Rd.)
Norton La. KT11: Cobh 91V 190
Norton Pk. SL5: S'hill 1A 146
Norton Rd. E10 32Bc 72
HA0: Wemb 37Ma 67
RM10: Dag 37Fd 76
UB8: Uxb 41M 83
Norval Rd. HA0: Wemb 33Ka 66
Norway Dr. SL2: Slou 3M 81
Norway Ga. SE16 48Ac 92
Norway Ho. N1 39Ub 71
(off Hertford Rd.)
Norway Pl. E14 44Bc 92
Norway St. SE10 51Dc 114
Norway Wlk. RM13: Rain 42Ld 97
Norway Wharf E14 44Bc 92
Norwegian War Memorial
7E 220 (46Gb 89)
Norwich Cres. RM6: Chad H 29Xc 55
Norwich Ho. E14 44Dc 92
(off Cordelia St.)
WD6: Bore 12Qa 29
(off Stratfield Rd.)
Norwich M. IG3: Ilf 32Wc 75
Norwich Pl. DA6: Bex 56Cd 118
Norwich Rd. CR7: Thor H 69Sb 135
E7 36Jc 73
HA6: Nwood 27V 44
RM9: Dag 40Cd 76
UB6: G'frd 39Da 65
Norwich St. EC4 2K 223 (44Qb 90)
Norwich Wlk. HA8: Edg 24Sa 47
Norwich Way WD3: Crox G 13R 26
NORWOOD 65Ub 135
Norwood Av. HA0: Wemb 39Pa 67
RM7: Rush G 31Gd 76
Norwood Cl. KT24: Eff 100Aa 191
NW2 34Ab 68
TW2: Twick 61Fa 130
UB2: S'hall 49Ca 85
Norwood Ct. DA1: Dart 57Qd 119
(off Farnol Rd.)
Norwood Dr. HA2: Harr 30Ba 45
Norwood Farm La. KT11: Cobh 83W 170
KT12: Cobh 83W 170
Norwood Gdns. UB2: S'hall 49Ba 85
UB4: Yead 42Y 85
NORWOOD GREEN 49Ba 85
Norwood Grn. Rd. UB2: S'hall 49Ca 85
Norwood High St. SE27 62Rb 135
Norwood Ho. E14 45Dc 92
(off Poplar High St.)
Norwood La. SL0: Iver 42F 82
NORWOOD NEW TOWN 65Sb 135
Norwood Pk. Rd. SE27 64Sb 135
Norwood Rd. EN8: Chesh 2Ac 20
KT24: Eff 100Aa 191
SE24 60Rb 113
SE27 61Rb 135
UB2: S'hall 48Aa 85
Norwood Ter. UB2: S'hall 49Da 85
Nota M. N3 25Cb 49
Notley End TW20: Eng G 6N 125
Notley Pl. SW4 59Nb 112
Notley St. SE5 52Tb 113
Notson Rd. SE25 70Xb 135
Notting Barn Rd. W10 42Za 88
Nottingdale Sq. W11 46Ab 88
Nottingham Av. E16 43Lc 93
Nottingham Cl. GU21: Wok 10K 167
WD25: Wat 5W 12
Nottingham Ct. GU21: Wok 10K 167
(off Nottingham Cl.)
WC2 3F 223 (44Nb 90)
Nottingham Ho. WC2 3F 223
Nottingham Pl. W1 6H 215 (43Jb 90)
Nottingham Rd. CR2: S Croy 77Sb 157
E10 30Ec 52
SW17 60Hb 111
TW7: Isle 54Ha 108
WD3: Herons 17E 24
Nottingham St. W1 7H 215 (43Jb 90)
Nottingham Ter. NW1 6H 215
NOTTING HILL 45Bb 89
Notting Hill Ga. W11 46Cb 89
Nottingwood Ho. W11 45Ab 88
(off Clarendon Rd.)
Nova Bldg. E14 49Cc 92
Nova Ct. E. E14 46Ec 92
(off Yabsley St.)
Nova Ct. W. E14 46Ec 92
(off Yabsley St.)
Nova M. SM3: Sutt 74Ab 154
Novar Cl. BR6: Orp 73Vc 161
Nova Rd. CR0: C'don 74Rb 157
Novar Rd. SE9 60Sc 116
Novello Ct. N1 39Sb 71
(off Dibden St.)
Novello St. SW6 53Cb 111
Novello Theatre
Covent Garden 4H 223
Sunninghill 1B 146
Novello Way WD6: Bore 11Ta 29
Novellus Ct. KT18: Eps 86Ta 173
(off South St.)
Novem Ho. E1 43Wb 91
(off Chicksand St.)
Nowell Rd. SW13 51Wa 110
Nower, The TN14: Knock 91Vc 201
Nower Ct. HA5: Pinn 28Ba 45
Nower Hill HA5: Pinn 28Ba 45
Noyna Rd. SW17 62Hb 133
NRG Gym
Gravesend 8D 122
(off Garrick St.)
Nubia Way BR1: Brom 62Gc 137
Nucleus Bus. & Innovation Cen., The
DA1: Dart 55Qd 119
Nuding Cl. SE13 55Cc 114
Nuffield Ct. TW5: Hest 52Ba 107
Nuffield Health
Battersea 54Hb 111
(within Latchmere Leisure Cen.)
Bloomsbury 5H 217
Bromley 71Kc 159
Cannon Street 4F 225
Cheam 80Ab 154
Covent Garden 3G 223
Croydon 79Qb 156
Fulham 53Za 110
Norbury 68Pb 134
Paddington 1A 220 (43Eb 89)
St Albans 5F 6
Stoke Poges 10M 61
Surbiton 72La 152
Twickenham 59Ga 108
Wandsworth 59Db 111
West Byfleet 86K 169
Willesden Green 38Ya 68
Wimbledon 65Bb 133
Nuffield Lodge N6 30Lb 50
W9 43Cb 89
(off Admiral Wlk.)
Nuffield Rd. BR8: Hext 65Jd 140
Nugent Rd. N19 32Nb 70
SE25 69Vb 135
Nugents Ct. HA5: Pinn 25Aa 45
Nugent Shop. Pk. BR5: St M Cry 70Yc 139
Nugent's Pk. HA5: Hat E 25Aa 45
Nugent Ter. NW8 2A 214 (40Eb 69)
Numa Ct. TW8: Bford 52Ma 109
Number One EC1 6F 219 (42Sb 91)
Numbers Farm WD4: K Lan 1S 12
Nunappleton Way RH8: Oxt 4L 211
Nun Ct. EC2 2F 225
Nuneaton Rd. RM9: Dag 38Ad 75
Nunfield WD4: Chfd 3K 11
NUNHEAD 55Xb 113
Nunhead Cemetery Nature Reserve
56Yb 114
Nunhead Cres. SE15 55Xb 113
Nunhead Est. SE15 56Xb 113
Nunhead Grn. SE15 55Xb 113
Nunhead Gro. SE15 55Xb 113
Nunhead La. SE15 55Xb 113
Nunhead Pas. SE15 55Wb 113
Nunnery Cl. AL1: St A 4C 6
Nunnery Stables AL1: St A 4B 6
Nunnington Cl. SE9 62Nc 138
Nunns Rd. EN2: Enf 12Sb 33

Nunns Way—Oaks, The

Nunns Way RM17: Grays .49Fe 99
Nuns La. AL1: St A .6C 6
Nuns Wlk. GU25: Vir W .1P 147
NUPER'S HATCH .17Gd 38
Nupton Dr. EN5: Barn .16Ya 30
Nuralite Ind. Cen. ME3: High'm .9P 123
Nurse Cl. HA8: Edg .25Sa 47
Nursery, The DA8: Erith .52Hd 118
Nursery App. N12 .23Gb 49
Nursery Av. CR0: C'don .75Zb 158
DA7: Bex .55Bd 117
N3 .26Eb 49
Nursery Cl. BR6: Orp .73Wc 161
BR8: Swan .68Ed 140
CR0: C'don .75Zb 158
DA2: Dart .59Sd 120
EN3: Enf H .11Zb 34
GU21: Wok .8N 167
IG8: Wfd G .22Kc 53
KT15: Wdhm .82H 169
KT17: Ewe .82Ua 174
KT20: Walt H .97Xa 194
RM6: Chad H .30Zc 55
RM15: S Ock .42Yd 98
SE4 .54Bc 114
SW15 .56Za 110
TN13: S'oaks .94Ld 203
TW14: Felt .59X 107
(not continuous)
WD19: Wat .18X 27
Nursery Cotts. AL1: St A .5P 5
Nursery Ct. N17 .24Vb 51
W13 .43Ja 86
Nursery Gdns. BR7: Chst .65Rc 138
EN3: Enf H .11Zb 34
TW4: Houn .57Ba 107
TW12: Hamp .63Ba 129
TW16: Sun .68V 128
TW18: Staines .65K 127
Nursery Gro. DA11: Grav'nd .4D 144
Nursery La. E2 .1K 219 (39Vb 71)
E7 .37Jc 73
SL3: L'ly .6P 81
UB8: Cowl .42M 83
W10 .43Ya 88
Nurserymans Rd. N11 .19Jb 32
Nursery M. DA11: Grav'nd .4E 144
Nursery Pl. SL4: Old Win .8M 103
TN13: Chip .94Fd 202
Nursery Rd. CR4: Mitc .69Gb 133
CR7: Thor H .70Tb 135
DA13: Meop .10C 144
E9 .37Yb 72
EN9: Walt A .3Fc 21
GU21: Knap .9H 167
HA5: Pinn .27Y 45
IG10: Lough .15Lc 35
KT20: Walt H .97Wa 194
N2 .25Fb 49
N14 .17Lb 32
SL6: Tap .4A 80
SM1: Sutt .77Eb 155
SS17: Stan H .1N 101
SW9 .56Pb 112
SW19 .66Ab 132
(Elm Gro.)
SW19 .68Db 133
(Parkleigh Rd.)
TW16: Sun .68U 128
Nursery Row EN5: Barn .13Ab 30
SE17 .6F 231 (49Tb 91)
Nursery St. N17 .24Vb 51
Nursery Wlk. NW4 .27Ya 48
RM7: Rush G .31Fd 76
Nursery Way RH8: Oxt .1J 211
TW19: Wray .8P 103
Nursery Waye UB8: Uxb .39M 63
NURSTEAD .9B 144
Nurstead Av. DA3: Lfield .70Fe 143
Nurstead Chu. La.
DA13: Meop, Sole S .10B 144
Nurstead Hill Farm DA3: Long H .70Fe 143
Nurstead La. DA3: Long H .70Fe 143
DA13: Meop .70Fe 143
Nurstead Rd. DA8: Erith .52Cd 118
Nut Ash La. KT18: Head .98Ta 193
Nutberry Av. RM16: Grays .47Ce 99
Nutberry Cl. RM16: Grays .47Ce 99
Nutbourne Ct. TW18: Staines .66H 127
(off Riverside Rd.)
Nutbourne St. W10 .41Ab 88
Nutbrook St. SE15 .55Wb 113
Nutbrowne Rd. RM9: Dag .39Bd 75
Nutcroft Gro. KT22: Fet .93Ga 192
Nutcroft Rd. SE15 .52Xb 113
NUTFIELD .5F 208
Nutfield Cl. N18 .23Wb 51
SM5: Cars .76Gb 155
Nutfield Ct. BR1: Brom .69Jc 137
RH1: Nutf .4F 208
RH1: Redh .4B 208
(off Goodworth Rd.)
Nutfield Gdns. IG3: Ilf .33Vc 75
UB5: N'olt .40Y 65
Nutfield Marsh Rd. RH1: Nutf .3D 208
NUTFIELD PARK .9G 208
Nutfield Pas. CR7: Thor H .70Rb 135
(off Nutfield Rd.)
Nutfield Rd. CR5: Coul .88Jb 176
CR7: Thor H .70Rb 135
E15 .35Ec 72
NW2 .34Wa 68
RH1: Mers .1C 208
RH1: Redh, Nutf .6B 208
SE22 .56Vb 113
Nutfields TN15: Igh .95Xd 204
Nutfield Way BR6: Farnb .75Rc 160
Nutford Pl. W1 .2E 220 (44Hb 89)
Nuthatch DA3: Lfield .69De 143
Nuthatch Cl. RM3: Rom .21Md 57
TW19: Stanw .60P 105
Nuthatch Gdns.
RH2: Reig .10L 207
SE28 .47Tc 94
(not continuous)
Nuthatch Pl. KT17: Ewe .82Wa 174
Nuthatch Row KT10: Clay .79Ha 152
Nuthurst Av. SW2 .61Pb 134
Nutkin Wlk. UB8: Uxb .38N 63
Nutley Cl. BR8: Hext .67Hd 140
Nutley Ct. RH2: Reig .6H 207
(off Nutley La.)
Nutley Gro. RH2: Reig .6J 207
Nutley La. RH2: Reig .5H 207
Nutley Ter. NW3 .37Eb 69
Nutmead Cl. DA5: Bexl .60Ed 118
Nutmeg Cl. E16 .42Gc 93
Nutmeg La. E14 .44Fc 93
Nuttall St. N1 .1J 219 (40Ub 71)
Nutter La. E11 .30Lc 53
Nuttfield Cl. WD3: Crox G .16S 26
Nutt Gro. HA8: Edg .19Ma 29
Nut Tree Cl. BR6: Chels .76Zc 161
Nutt St. SE15 .52Vb 113
Nutty La. TW17: Shep .69S 128
Nutwell St. SW17 .64Gb 133
Nuxley Rd. DA17: Belv .51Bd 117
Nyall Ct. RM2: Rom .27Jd 57
Nyanza St. SE18 .51Tc 116
Nye Bevan Est. E5 .34Zb 72
Nye Bevan Ho. SW6 .52Bb 111
(off St Thomas's Way)
Nyefield Pk. KT20: Walt H .98Wa 194
Nye Way HP3: Bov .10C 2
Nyland Ct. SE8 .49Ac 92
(off Naomi St.)
Nylands Av. TW9: Kew .53Qa 109
Nymans Gdns. SW20 .69Xa 132
Nynehead St. SE14 .52Ac 114
Nyon Gro. SE6 .61Bc 136
Nyssa Cl. IG8: Wfd G .23Pc 54
Nyth Cl. RM14: Upm .30Td 58
Nyton Cl. N19 .32Nb 70

O

O2, The .46Gc 93
O2 Brixton Academy .55Qb 112
O2 Cen. NW3 .37Eb 69
O2 Forum Kentish Town .36Kb 70
O2 Shepherd's Bush Empire Theatre
.47Ya 88
Oakapple Cl. CR2: Sande .86Xb 177
Oak Apple Ct. SE12 .60Jc 115
Oak Av. AL2: Brick W .2Ca 13
CR0: C'don .74Cc 158
EN2: Enf .10Pb 18
N8 .28Nb 50
N10 .24Kb 50
N17 .24Tb 51
RM14: Upm .34Rd 77
TN13: S'oaks .100Kd 203
TW5: Hest .52Z 107
TW12: Hamp .64Aa 129
TW20: Egh .66E 126
UB7: W Dray .48Q 84
UB10: Ick .33R 64
Oak Avenue Local Nature Reserve
.64Aa 129
Oak Bank CR0: New Ad .79Ec 158
Oakbank CM13: Hut .15Fe 41
GU22: Wok .91A 188
KT22: Fet .95Ea 192
WD7: R'lett .8Ka 14
Oakbank Av. KT12: Walt T .73Ba 151
Oakbank Gro. SE24 .56Sb 113
Oakbark Ho. TW8: Bford .52La 108
(off High St.)
Oakbrook Cl. BR1: Brom .63Kc 137
Oakbury Rd. SW6 .54Db 111
Oak Cl. DA1: Cray .56Hd 118
EN9: Walt A .6Fc 21
HP3: Hem H .6P 3
N14 .17Kb 32
RH8: Oxt .4L 211
SM1: Sutt .75Eb 155
Oakcombe Cl. KT3: N Mald .67Ua 132
Oak Cott. Cl. SE6 .60Hc 115
Oak Cotts. W7 .47Ga 86
Oak Ct. HA6: Nwood .23T 44
RM15: S Ock .40Yd 78
SE15 .52Vb 113
(off Sumner Rd.)
Oak Cres. E16 .43Gc 93
Oakcroft SL2: Slou .1E 80
Oakcroft Bus. Cen. KT9: Chess .77Pa 153
Oakcroft Cl. HA5: Pinn .26X 45
KT14: W Byf .86H 169
Oakcroft Rd. KT9: Chess .77Pa 153
KT14: W Byf .86H 169
SE13 .54Fc 115
Oakcroft Vs. KT9: Chess .77Pa 153
Oakdale N14 .18Kb 32
Oakdale Av. HA3: Kenton .29Na 47
HA6: Nwood .26W 44
Oakdale Cl. WD19: Wat .21Y 45
Oakdale Ct. E4 .22Ec 52
Oakdale Gdns. E4 .22Ec 52
Oakdale Rd. E7 .38Kc 73
E11 .33Fc 73
E18 .26Kc 53
KT13: Weyb .76Q 150
KT19: Ewe .81Ta 173
N4 .30Sb 51
SE15 .55Yb 114
SW16 .64Nb 134
WD19: Wat .20Y 27
Oakdale Way CR4: Mitc .73Jb 156
Oak Dene W13 .43Ka 86
Oakdene EN8: Chesh .2Ac 20
GU24: Chob .2K 167
KT20: Tad .92Ab 194
RM3: Hrld W .26Pd 57
SE15 .53Xb 113
SL5: S'dale .2D 146
Oakdene Av. BR7: Chst .64Qc 138
DA8: Erith .51Ed 118
KT7: T Ditt .74Ja 152
Oakdene Cl. HA5: Hat E .24Ba 45
KT23: Bookh .99Ea 192
RM11: Horn .30Kd 57
Oakdene Ct. KT11: Cobh .86X 171
(off Between Streets)
KT12: Walt T .76X 151
KT13: Weyb .77Q 150
Oakdene Dr. KT5: Surb .73Sa 153
Oakdene M. SM3: Sutt .74Bb 155
Oakdene Pde. KT11: Cobh .86X 171
Oakdene Pk. N3 .24Bb 49
Oakdene Rd.
BR5: St M Cry .71Vc 161
HP3: Hem H .6P 3
KT11: Cobh .86X 171
KT23: Bookh .96Ba 191
RH1: Redh .6P 207
TN13: S'oaks .94Jd 202
UB10: Hil .40R 64
WD24: Wat .8X 13
Oakdene Way AL1: St A .2G 6
Oakden St. SE11 .5A 230 (49Qb 90)
Oak Dr. HP4: Berk .2A 2
Oake Ct. SW15 .57Ab 110
Oakeford Ho. W14 .48Ab 88
(off Russell Rd.)
Oaken Coppice KT21: Asht .91Qa 193
Oak End Dr. SL0: Iver H .40E 62
Oaken Dr. KT10: Clay .79Ha 152
Oak End Way
KT15: Wdhm .84G 168
SL9: Ger X .29B 42
Oakenholt Ho. SE2 .46Zc 95
Oaken La. KT10: Clay .77Ga 152
Oakenshaw Cl.
CR6: W'ham .87Yb 178
KT6: Surb .73Na 153
Oakenwood KT23: Bookh .97Ba 191
Oakes Cl. E6 .44Pc 94
Oakes Cres. DA1: Dart .57Pd 119
Oakeshott Av. N6 .33Jb 70
Oakes M. E14 .43Ec 92
(off Nairn St.)
Oakey La. SE1 .3K 229 (48Qb 90)
Oak Farm WD6: Bore .15Sa 29
Oak Farm La. TN15: Fair .82Fe 185
Oakfield E4 .22Dc 52
GU21: Wok .9J 167
WD3: Rick .17H 25
Oakfield Av. HA3: Kenton .27Ka 46
SL1: Slou .6F 80
Oakfield Cl. EN6: Pot B .3Bb 17
HA4: Ruis .30V 44
KT3: N Mald .71Va 154
KT13: Weyb .77S 150
Oakfield Ct. KT13: Weyb .77S 150
N8 .31Nb 70
NW2 .31Za 68
WD6: Bore .13Ra 29
Oakfield Dr. RH2: Reig .4J 207
Oakfield Gdns. BR3: Beck .71Dc 158
N18 .21Ub 51
SE19 .64Ub 135
(not continuous)
SM5: Cars .74Gb 155
UB6: G'frd .42Fa 86
Oakfield Glade KT13: Weyb .77S 150
Oakfield Ho. E3 .43Cc 92
(off Gale St.)
Oakfield La. BR2: Kes .77Lc 159
DA1: Dart .61Gd 140
DA2: Dart, Wilm .61Kd 141
Oakfield Lodge IG1: Ilf .34Rc 74
(off Albert Rd.)
Oakfield Pk. Rd.
DA1: Dart .61Md 141
Oakfield Pl. DA1: Dart .61Md 141
Oakfield Rd. BR6: Orp .73Wc 161
CR0: C'don .74Sb 157
E6 .39Nc 74
E17 .26Ac 52
IG1: Ilf .34Rc 74
KT11: Cobh .86X 171
KT21: Asht .89Ma 173
N3 .25Db 49
N4 .30Qb 50
N14 .19Nb 32
SE20 .66Xb 135
SW19 .62Za 132
TW15: Ashf .64R 128
Oakfield Rd. Ind. Est. SE20 .66Xb 135
Oakfields IG10: Lough .15Qc 36
KT12: Walt T .74W 150
KT14: W Byf .86K 169
TN13: S'oaks .98Kd 203
Oakfields Rd. NW11 .30Ab 48
Oakfield St. SW10 .51Eb 111
Oakford Rd. NW5 .35Lb 70
Oak Gdns. CR0: C'don .75Cc 158
HA8: Edg .26Sa 47
Oak Glade CM16: Coop .1Zc 23
HA6: Nwood .25R 44
KT19: Eps .84Qa 173
Oak Glen RM11: Horn .27Nd 57
Oak Grange Rd. GU4: W Cla .100K 189
Oak Grn. WD5: Ab L .4U 12
Oak Grn. Way WD5: Ab L .4U 12
Oak Gro. AL10: Hat .1B 8
BR4: W W'ck .74Ec 158
HA4: Ruis .31X 65
NW2 .35Ab 68
TW16: Sun .66X 129
Oakgrove CR3: Cat'm .95Tb 197
Oak Gro. Rd. SE20 .67Yb 136
Oakhall Ct. E11 .30Kc 53
TW16: Sun .64V 128
Oakhall Dr. TW16: Sun .64V 128
Oak Hall Rd. E11 .30Kc 53
Oakham Cl. EN4: Cockf .13Hb 31
SE6 .61Bc 136
Oakham Dr. BR2: Brom .70Hc 137
Oakham Ho. W10 .42Ya 88
(off Sutton Way)
Oakhampton Rd. NW7 .24Za 48
Oak Hill IG8: Wfd G .24Fc 53
KT6: Surb .73Na 153
KT18: Eps .88Ta 173
TN13: S'oaks .96Jd 202
Oakhill KT10: Clay .79Ja 152
Oakhill Av. HA5: Pinn .26Aa 45
NW3 .35Db 69
Oak Hill Cl. IG8: Wfd G .24Fc 53
Oakhill Cl. KT21: Asht .90La 172
WD3: Map C .21G 42
Oak Hill Ct. IG8: Wfd G .24Fc 53
Oakhill Ct. SE23 .58Yb 114
SW19 .66Za 132
Oak Hill Cres. IG8: Wfd G .24Fc 53
KT6: Surb .73Na 153
Oakhill Dr. KT6: Surb .73Na 153
Oak Hill Gdns. IG8: Wfd G .25Gc 53
Oakhill Gdns.
KT13: Weyb .75U 150
Oak Hill Gro. KT6: Surb .72Na 153
Oak Hill Pk. NW3 .35Db 69
Oak Hill Pk. M. NW3 .35Eb 69
Oak Hill Path KT6: Surb .72Na 153
Oakhill Pl. SW15 .57Cb 111
Oak Hill Rd. KT6: Surb .72Na 153
RM4: Stap A .17Fd 38
Oakhill Rd.
BR3: Beck .68Ec 136
BR6: Orp .74Vc 161
KT15: Add .79H 149
KT21: Asht .90La 172
RH2: Reig .7K 207
RM19: Purf .50Rd 97
SM1: Sutt .76Db 155
SW15 .57Bb 111
SW16 .67Nb 134
TN13: S'oaks .96Jd 202
WD3: Map C .21F 42
Oak Hill Way NW3 .35Db 69
(not continuous)
Oak Hill Woods Nature Reserve .16Hb 31
Oak Ho. E14 .47Ec 92
(off Stewart St.)
KT15: Add .77M 149
(off Victory Pk. Rd.)
KT19: Eps .82Sa 173
KT22: Lea .92Ha 192
N2 .26Fb 49
RM7: Rom .29Fd 56
TN13: S'oaks .96Kd 203
TW9: Kew .53Ra 109
W10 .42Ab 88
(off Sycamore Wlk.)
Oakhouse Rd. DA6: Bex .57Cd 118
Oakhurst GU21: Wok .8P 167
GU24: Chob .1J 167
Oakhurst Av. DA7: Bex .52Ad 117
EN4: E Barn .17Gb 31
Oakhurst Cl. BR7: Chst .67Pc 138
E17 .28Gc 53
IG6: Ilf .25Sc 54
KT2: King T .65Pa 131
TW11: Tedd .64Ga 130
Oakhurst Ct. E17 .28Gc 53
(off Woodford New Rd.)
Oakhurst Gdns. DA7: Bex .52Ad 117
E4 .18Hc 35
E17 .28Gc 53
Oakhurst Gro. SE22 .56Wb 113
Oakhurst Pl. WD18: Wat .14V 26
Oakhurst Ri. SM5: Cars .82Gb 175
Oakhurst Rd. EN3: Enf W .8Zb 20
KT19: Ewe .79Sa 153
Oakington Av. HA2: Harr .31Ca 65
HA9: Wemb .34Pa 67
HP6: L Chal .11A 24
UB3: Harl .49T 84
Oakington Cl. TW16: Sun .68Y 129
Oakington Ct. EN2: Enf .12Rb 33
Oakington Dr. TW16: Sun .68Y 129
Oakington Mnr. Dr.
HA9: Wemb .36Qa 67
Oakington Rd. W9 .42Cb 89
Oakington Way N8 .31Nb 70
Oakland Ct. KT15: Add .76K 149
Oakland Gdns. CM13: Hut .15Ee 41
Oakland Pl. IG9: Buck H .19Jc 35
Oakland Quay E14 .48Dc 92
Oakland Rd. E15 .35Fc 73
Oaklands BR3: Beck .67Dc 136
CR8: Kenley .86Sb 177
KT22: Fet .96Fa 192
N21 .19Pb 32
RH9: S God .9C 210
W13 .43Ja 86
Oaklands, The
WD5: Bedm .1V 12
Oaklands Av. AL9: Brk P .9G 8
BR4: W W'ck .76Dc 158
CR7: Thor H .70Qb 134
DA15: Sidc .59Vc 117
KT10: Esh .74Fa 152
N9 .16Xb 33
RM1: Rom .27Gd 56
TW7: Isle .51Ha 108
WD19: Wat .18X 27
Oaklands Cl. BR5: Pet W .72Uc 160
DA6: Bex .57Bd 117
GU22: Wok .94B 188
HA0: Wemb .36Ma 67
KT9: Chess .77La 152
TN15: W King .79Ud 164
Oaklands Ct. HA0: Wemb .36Ma 67
NW10 .39Ua 68
(off Nicoll Rd.)
SE20 .66Yb 136
(off Chestnut Gro.)
WD17: Wat .11W 26
Oaklands Dr. RH1: Redh .8B 208
RM15: S Ock .43Yd 98
TW2: Whitt .59Ea 108
Oaklands Est. SW4 .58Lb 112
Oaklands Gdns. CR8: Kenley .86Sb 177
Oaklands Ga. HA6: Nwood .23U 44
Oaklands Gro. W12 .46Wa 88
Oaklands La. AL4: S'ford .1K 7
EN5: Ark .14Xa 30
TN16: Big H .85Kc 179
Oaklands M. NW2 .35Za 68
(off Oaklands Rd.)
Oaklands Pk. CM13: Hut .18De 41
Oaklands Pk. Av. IG1: Ilf .33Sc 74
Oaklands Pas. NW2 .35Za 68
(off Oaklands Rd.)
Oaklands Pl. SW4 .56Lb 112
Oaklands Rd. BR1: Brom .66Gc 137
DA2: Dart .60Rd 119
DA6: Bex .56Bd 117
DA11: Nflt .3B 144
N20 .17Bb 31
NW2 .35Za 68
SW14 .55Ta 109
W7 .47Ha 86
(not continuous)
W13 .47Ha 86
Oaklands Way KT20: Tad .94Ya 194
SM6: Wall .80Mb 156
Oakland Way KT19: Ewe .79Ua 154
Oak La. E14 .45Bc 92
EN6: Cuff .1Pb 18
GU22: Wok .88D 168
IG8: Wfd G .21Hc 53
N2 .26Fb 49
N11 .23Mb 50
SL4: Wind .3E 102
TN13: S'oaks .100Hd 202
TW1: Twick .59Ja 108
TW7: Isle .56Ga 108
TW20: Eng G .2N 125
Oaklawn Rd. KT22: Lea .90Ga 172
Oak Leaf Cl. KT19: Eps .84Sa 173
Oakleafe Gdns. IG6: Ilf .27Rc 54
Oaklea Lodge IG3: Ilf .34Wc 75
Oaklea Pas. KT1: King T .69Ma 131
Oakleigh GU18: Light .3A 166
KT18: Eps .86Ua 174
RH9: G'stone .2A 210
Oakleigh Av. HA8: Edg .26Ra 47
KT6: Surb .74Qa 153
N20 .19Fb 31
Oakleigh Cl. BR8: Swan .69Gd 140
N20 .20Hb 31
Oakleigh Ct. EN4: E Barn .16Gb 31
HA8: Edg .26Sa 47
N1 .3F 219
RH8: Oxt .1J 211
UB1: S'hall .46Ba 85
Oakleigh Cres. N20 .19Gb 31
Oakleigh Dr. WD3: Crox G .16S 26
Oakleigh Gdns. BR6: Orp .77Uc 160
HA8: Edg .22Pa 47
N20 .18Eb 31
Oakleigh M. N20 .18Eb 31
OAKLEIGH PARK .18Eb 31
Oakleigh Pk. Av. BR7: Chst .67Qc 138
Oakleigh Pk. Nth. N20 .18Fb 31
Oakleigh Pk. Sth. N20 .17Gb 31
Oakleigh Ri. CM16: Epp .4Wc 23
Oakleigh Rd. HA5: Hat E .23Ba 45
UB10: Hil .38S 64
Oakleigh Rd. Nth. N20 .19Fb 31
Oakleigh Rd. Sth. N11 .20Jb 32
Oakleigh Way CR4: Mitc .67Kb 134
KT6: Surb .74Qa 153
Oakley Av. CR0: Bedd .77Pb 156
IG11: Bark .38Vc 75
W5 .45Qa 87
Oakley Cl. E4 .20Ec 34
E6 .44Nc 94
KT15: Add .77M 149
RM20: Grays .51Yd 120
TW7: Isle .53Fa 108
W7 .45Ga 86
Oakley Ct. CR4: Mitc .73Jb 156
IG10: Lough .12Qc 36
RH1: Redh .5A 208
(off St Anne's Ri.)
Oakley Cres. EC1 .2C 218 (40Rb 71)
SL1: Slou .5J 81
Oakley Dr. BR2: Brom .76Nc 160
RM3: Rom .22Qd 57
SE9 .60Tc 116
SE13 .58Fc 115
Oakley Gdns. N8 .29Pb 50
SM7: Bans .87Db 175
SW3 .51Gb 111
Oakley Grange HA1: Harr .33Fa 66
OAKLEY GREEN .4A 102
Oakley Grn. Rd. SL4: Oak G, Wind .4A 102
Oakley Ho. SE11 .6K 229
SW1 .5G 227 (49Hb 89)
W5 .45Qa 87
Oakley Pk. DA5: Bexl .59Yc 117
Oakley Pl. SE1 .7K 231 (50Vb 91)
Oakley Rd. BR2: Brom .76Nc 160
CR6: W'ham .90Wb 177
HA1: Harr .30Ga 46
N1 .38Tb 71
SE25 .71Xb 157
Oakley Sq. NW1 .1C 216 (40Lb 70)
Oakley St. SW3 .51Gb 111
Oakley Studios SW3 .51Gb 111
(off Up. Cheyne Row)
Oakley Wlk. W6 .51Za 110
Oakley Yd. E2 .42Vb 91
Oak Lock M. W4 .50Ua 88
Oak Lodge E11 .30Jc 53
KT11: Cobh .87Y 171
(off Leigh Cnr.)
SM1: Sutt .77Eb 155
TN13: S'oaks .96Jd 202
TW16: Sun .66V 128
(off Forest Dr.)
W8 .48Db 89
(off Chantry Sq.)
Oak Lodge Av. IG7: Chig .22Tc 54
Oak Lodge Cl. HA7: Stan .22La 46
KT12: Hers .78Y 151
Oak Lodge Dr. BR4: W W'ck .73Dc 158
Oak Lodge La. TN16: Westrm .97Tc 200
Oaklodge Way NW7 .22Va 48
Oakman Ho. SW19 .60Za 110
Oakmead Av. BR2: Hayes .72Jc 159
Oakmead Ct. HA7: Stan .21La 46
Oakmeade HA5: Hat E .23Ca 45
Oakmead Gdns. HA8: Edg .21Ta 47
Oakmead Grn. KT18: Eps .87Sa 173
Oakmead Pl. CR4: Mitc .67Gb 133
Oakmead Rd. CR0: C'don .72Mb 156
SW12 .60Jb 112
Oakmede EN5: Barn .14Za 30
OAKMERE .4Eb 17
Oakmere Av. EN6: Pot B .5Eb 17
Oakmere Cl. EN6: Pot B .3Fb 17
Oakmere La. EN6: Pot B .4Eb 17
Oakmere M. EN6: Pot B .4Eb 17
Oakmere Rd. SE2 .51Wc 117
Oakmont Pl. BR6: Orp .74Tc 160
Oakmoor Way IG7: Chig .22Uc 54
Oak Pk. KT14: W Byf .85G 168
Oak Pk. Gdns. SW19 .60Za 110
Oak Pk. M. N16 .34Vb 71
Oak Path WD23: Bush .16Da 27
(off Mortimer Cl.)
Oak Pl. SW18 .57Db 111
Oakridge AL2: Brick W .1Ba 13
GU24: W End .5D 166
Oakridge Av. WD7: R'lett .6Ha 14
Oakridge Dr. N2 .27Fb 49
Oakridge Ho. SL9: Ger X .29A 42
Oakridge La. BR1: Brom .64Fc 137
WD7: R'lett .5Ha 14
WD25: A'ham, R'lett .6Fa 14
Oakridge Pl. SL2: Farn C .5G 60
SL9: Ger X .29A 42
Oakridge Rd. BR1: Brom .63Fc 137
Oak Ri. IG9: Buck H .20Mc 35
Oak Rd. BR6: Chels .80Wc 161
CM16: Epp .2Vc 23
CR3: Cat'm .94Ub 197
DA8: Erith .52Ed 118
(Mill Rd.)
DA8: Erith .54Jd 118
(Moat La.)
DA9: Ghithe .58Ud 120
DA12: Grav'nd .2E 144
KT3: N Mald .68Ta 131
KT11: Cobh .87Z 171
KT22: Lea .90Ja 172
RH2: Reig .5K 207
RM3: Hrld W .25Pd 57
RM17: Grays .51Ee 121
TN16: Westrm .97Tc 200
W5 .45Ma 87
Oak Row SW16 .68Lb 134
Oakroyd Av. EN6: Pot B .5Bb 17
Oakroyd Cl. EN6: Pot B .5Bb 17
Oaks, The BR2: Brom .72Qc 160
BR8: Swan .68Gd 140
DA2: Dart .58Rd 119
EN2: Enf .13Rb 33
EN9: Walt A .1Kc 21
(within Woodbine Cl. Cvn. Pk.)
HA4: Ruis .31T 64
IG8: Wfd G .23Gc 53
KT14: W Byf .86J 169
KT18: Eps .86Va 174

Oaks, The KT20: Tad 95Ya 194
KT22: Fet 95Ea 192
N12 21Db 49
NW6 38Za 68
(off Brondesbury Pk.)
NW10 38Xa 68
SE18 50Sc 94
SM4: Mord 70Ab 132
TW13: Felt 61Z 129
TW18: Staines 63H 127
UB4: Hayes 40S 64
WD6: Bore 11Qa 29
WD19: Wat 18Y 27
Oaks Av. KT4: Wor Pk 76Xa 154
RM5: Col R 26Ed 56
SE19 64Ub 135
TW13: Felt 61Aa 129
Oaks Cvn. Pk., The
KT9: Chess 76La 152
Oaks Cl. KT22: Lea 93Ja 192
WD7: R'lett 7Ha 14
Oaksend Cl.
KT22: Oxs 83Ea 172
Oaksford Av. SE26 62Xb 135
Oaks Gro. E4 19Gc 35
Oakshade Rd.
BR1: Brom 63Fc 137
KT22: Oxs 86Ea 172
Oakshaw RH8: Oxt 99Fc 199
Oakshaw Rd. SW18 59Db 111
Oakshott Ct. NW1 2D 216 (40Mb 70)
(not continuous)
Oakside UB9: Den 36K 63
Oakside Ct. IG6: Ilf 26Tc 54
Oakside Ter. NW10 34Ta 67
Oaks La. CR0: C'don 76Xb 157
IG2: Ilf 29Uc 54
Oaks Pk. 83Hb 175
Oaks Path WD25: Wat 4Ba 13
Oaks Pavilion M. SE19 64Ub 135
Oak Sq. SW9 54Pb 112
TN13: S'oaks 98Ld 203
Oaks Rd. CR0: C'don 78Xb 157
CR8: Kenley 86Rb 177
GU21: Wok 89A 168
RH2: Reig 5M 207
TW19: Stanw 58M 105
Oaks Shop. Cen., The W3 46Sa 87
Oaks Sports Cen. 83Gb 175
Oaks Sports Cen. Golf Course
83Hb 175
Oaks Sq., The KT19: Eps 85Ta 173
(off High St.)
Oaks Track SM5: Cars 83Hb 175
SM6: Wall 83Hb 175
Oak St. HP3: Hem H 6P 3
RM7: Rom 29Ed 56
Oaks Vw. KT23: Bookh 97Ba 191
Oaks Way CR8: Kenley 86Sb 177
GU23: Rip 96J 189
KT6: Surb 74Ma 153
KT18: Tatt C 91Xa 194
SM5: Cars 80Hb 155
Oakthorpe Ct. N13 22Sb 51
Oakthorpe Est. N13 22Sb 51
Oakthorpe Rd. N13 22Qb 50
Oak Tree Av. DA9: Bluew 59Vd 120
Oaktree Av. N13 20Rb 33
Oak Tree Cl. GU4: Jac W 10P 187
GU21: Knap 10F 166
GU25: Vir W 2P 147
HA7: Stan 24La 46
IG10: Lough 11Sc 36
KT19: Ewe 79Ra 153
KT23: Bookh 97Ba 191
TN13: S'oaks 98Ld 203
W5 44La 86
WD5: Ab L 4T 12
Oaktree Cl. CM13: B'wood 20Be 41
Oak Tree Ct. UB5: N'olt 40Y 65
W3 45Ra 87
Oaktree Ct. KT15: Add 78K 149
WD6: E'tree 16Ma 29
Oak Tree Dell NW9 29Sa 47
Oak Tree Dr. N20 18Db 31
SL3: L'ly 50D 82
TW20: Eng G 4N 125
Oak Tree Gdns. BR1: Brom 64Kc 137
Oaktree Gdns. SE9 62Rc 138
Oaktree Gro. IG1: Ilf 36Tc 74
Oak Tree Ho. W9 42Cb 89
(off Shirland Rd.)
Oak Tree M. NW2 37Wa 68
Oak Tree Pl. KT10: Esh 75Da 151
Oak Tree Rd.
GU21: Knap 10F 166
NW8 4C 214 (41Gb 89)
Oaktree Wlk. CR3: Cat'm 94Ub 197
Oak Vw. HP3: Bov 10D 2
TW20: Egh 65E 126
WD18: Wat 13U 26
Oakview Apartments
SM1: Sutt 77Fb 155
Oakview Cl. EN7: Chesh 1Xb 19
WD19: Wat 16Y 27
Oak Vw. Gdns. SL3: L'ly 49B 82
Oakview Gdns. N2 28Fb 49
Oakview Gro.
CR0: C'don 74Ac 158
Oakview Lodge NW11 31Bb 69
(off Beechcroft Av.)
Oakview Rd. SE6 64Dc 136
Oak Village NW5 35Jb 70
Oak Vs. NW11 30Bb 49
(off Hendon Pk. Row)
Oakville Ho. SE16 47Zb 92
(off Dominion Dr.)
Oak Wlk. SM6: Wall 74Jb 156
(off Helios Rd.)
Oak Way CR0: C'don 72Zb 158
KT21: Asht 88Qa 173
N14 17Kb 32
RH2: Reig 7M 207
TW14: Felt 60U 106
W3 46Ua 88
Oakway BR2: Brom 68Fc 137
GU21: Wok 1J 187
RM16: Grays 46De 99
SW20 70Ya 132
Oakway Cl. DA5: Bexl 58Ad 117
Oakway Pl. WD7: R'lett 6Ja 14
Oakways SE9 58Rc 116
Oakwell Dr. EN6: N'thaw 4Kb 18
OAKWOOD 14Mb 32
Oakwood EN9: Walt A 7Gc 21
KT18: Eps 86Ua 174
(off Worple Rd.)
SM6: Wall 81Kb 176
Oakwood Av. BR2: Brom 69Kc 137
BR3: Beck 68Ec 136
CR4: Mitc 68Fb 133
CR8: Purl 84Rb 177
KT19: Eps 81Qa 173
N14 17Mb 32
UB1: S'hall 45Ca 85
WD6: Bore 14Ra 29
Oakwood Bus. Pk. NW10 42Ta 87
Oakwood Chase RM11: Horn 30Pd 57
Oakwood Cl. BR7: Chst 65Pc 138
DA1: Dart 60Rd 119
IG8: Wfd G 23Nc 54
KT24: E Hor 99U 190
N14 16Lb 32
RH1: Redh 6A 208
RH1: S Nut 8F 208
RM3: Rom 23Nd 57
SE13 58Fc 115
Oakwood Ct. BR8: Swan 68Ed 140
(off Lawn Cl.)
E6 39Nc 74
GU24: Bisl 8E 166
HA1: Harr 30Fa 46
SL1: Slou 4J 81
(off Mildenhall Rd.)
W14 48Bb 89
Oakwood Cres. N21 16Nb 32
UB6: G'frd 37Ja 66
Oakwood Dr. AL4: St A 1G 6
DA7: Bex 56Ed 118
HA8: Edg 23Sa 47
KT24: E Hor 99U 190
SE19 65Tb 135
TN13: S'oaks 95Kd 203
Oakwood Farm TN15: Fair 84Ee 185
Oakwood Gdns. BR6: Farnb 75Sc 160
GU21: Knap 10E 166
IG3: Ilf 33Vc 75
SM1: Sutt 75Cb 155
Oakwood Grange KT13: Weyb 76U 150
Oakwood Hall KT20: Kgswd 95Eb 195
Oakwood Hill IG10: Lough 16Pc 36
Oakwood Hill Ind. Est.
IG10: Lough 15Sc 36
Oakwood Ho. E9 37Yb 72
(off Frampton Pk. Rd.)
Oakwood Ind. Est. DA11: Nflt 57Ce 121
Oakwood La. W14 48Bb 89
Oakwood Lodge N14 16Lb 32
(off Avenue Rd.)
Oakwood Mans. W14 48Bb 89
(off Oakwood Ct.)
Oakwood Pde. IG10: Lough 16Pc 36
N14 15Lb 32
Oakwood Pk. Rd. N14 17Mb 32
Oak Wood Pl. SL9: Ger X 33A 62
Oakwood Pl. CR0: C'don 72Qb 156
Oakwood Ri. CR3: Cat'm 97Ub 197
DA3: Lfield 69Ae 143
Oakwood Rd. AL2: Brick W 1Ba 13
BR6: Farnb 75Sc 160
CR0: C'don 72Qb 156
GU20: W'sham 9C 146
GU21: Wok 1J 187
GU25: Vir W 1N 147
HA5: Pinn 26X 45
NW11 28Cb 49
RH1: Mers 1G 208
SW20 67Wa 132
Oakwood Vw. N14 16Mb 32
Oakworth Rd. W10 43Ya 88
Oak Yd. WD17: Wat 13Y 27
Oarsman Pl. KT8: E Mos 70Ga 130
Oasis, The BR1: Brom 68Lc 137
Oasis Academy Sports Hall 10Zb 20
Oasis Sports Cen. 2F 223 (44Nb 90)
Oast Cotts. TN13: S'oaks 94Jd 202
Oast Ct. E14 45Bc 92
(off Newell St.)
Oast Ho. Cl. TW19: Wray 59A 104
Oasthouse Way BR5: St M Cry 70Xc 139
Oast Lodge W4 52Ua 110
(off Corney Reach Way)
Oast Rd. RH8: Oxt 3K 211
Oast Way DA3: Hartl 72Ae 165
Oates Cl. BR2: Brom 69Fc 137
Oates Rd. RM5: Col R 22Dd 56
Oatfield Ho. N15 30Ub 51
(off Perry Ct.)
Oatfield Rd. BR6: Orp 74Vc 161
KT20: Tad 92Xa 194
Oatland Ri. E17 26Ac 52
Oatlands Av. KT13: Weyb 78T 150
Oatlands Chase KT13: Weyb 76U 150
Oatlands Cl. KT13: Weyb 77S 150
Oatlands Dr. KT13: Weyb 77S 150
SL1: Slou 4H 81
Oatlands Grn. KT13: Weyb 76T 150
Oatlands Mere KT13: Weyb 76T 150
OATLANDS PARK 76T 150
Oatlands Rd. EN3: Enf H 11Yb 34
KT20: Tad 91Ab 194
Oat La. EC2 2D 224 (44Sb 91)
Oatridge Gdns. HP2: Hem H 1B 4
Oatwell Ho. SW3 7E 226
(off Cale St.)
Oban Cl. E13 42Lc 93
Oban Ct. SL1: Slou 7H 81
Oban Ho. E14 44Fc 93
(off Oban St.)
IG11: Bark 40Tc 74
Oban Rd. E13 41Lc 93
SE25 70Tb 135
Oban St. E14 44Fc 93
Obelisk Ride TW20: Eng G 5J 125
Oberon Cl. WD6: Bore 11Sa 29
Oberon Ct. E6 38Mc 73
UB9: Den 30H 43
Oberon Ho. N1 1H 219
Oberon Way TW17: Shep 69N 127
Oberstein Rd. SW11 56Fb 111
Oborne Cl. SE24 57Rb 113
O'Brien Ho. E2 41Zb 92
(off Roman Rd.)
Observatory Gdns. W8 47Cb 89
Observatory M. E14 49Fc 93
Observatory Rd. SW7 4B 226 (48Fb 89)
SW14 56Sa 109
Observatory Shop. Cen., The
SL1: Slou 7L 81
Observatory Wlk. RH1: Redh 6P 207
Observer Dr. WD18: Wat 14U 26
Occupation La. SE18 53Rc 116
W5 49Ma 87
Occupation Rd. KT19: Ewe 80Ta 153
SE17 7D 230 (50Sb 91)
W13 47Ka 86
WD18: Wat 15X 27
Ocean Est. E1 43Ac 92
(Ben Jonson Rd.)
E1 42Zb 92
(Ernest St.)
Oceanis Apartments E16 45Jc 93
(off Seagull La.)
Ocean St. E1 43Zb 92
Ocean Wharf E14 47Bc 92
Ockbrook E1 43Yb 92
(off Hannibal Rd.)
Ockenden GU22: Wok 91A 188
(off Constitution Hill)
Ockenden Cl. GU22: Wok 90B 168
Ockenden Gdns. GU22: Wok 90B 168
Ockenden Rd. GU22: Wok 90B 168
Ockendon Leisure Cen. 43Wd 98
Ockendon M. N1 37Tb 71
Ockendon Rd. N1 37Tb 71
RM14: N Ock, Upm 36Sd 78
OCKHAM 93R 190
Ockham Bldg. SE16 3K 231
Ockham Dr. BR5: St P 66Wc 139
KT24: W Hor 96T 190
UB6: G'frd 38Ea 66
Ockham La. GU23: Ock 93Q 190
KT11: Cobh 92U 190
Ockham Rd. Nth. GU23: Ock 92N 189
KT24: E Hor, W Hor 92N 189
Ockham Rd. Sth. KT24: E Hor 98U 190
Ockley Ct. DA14: Sidc 62Uc 138
SM1: Sutt 77Eb 155
Ockley Rd. CR0: C'don 73Pb 156
SW16 63Nb 134
Ockleys Mead RH9: G'stone 1A 210
Octagon, The SW10 52Db 111
(off Coleridge Gdns.)
Octagon Arc. EC2 1H 225 (43Ub 91)
Octagon Ct. SE16 46Zb 92
(off Rotherhithe St.)
Octagon Rd. KT12: W Vill 81U 170
Octavia Cl. CR4: Mitc 71Gb 155
Octavia Ct. WD24: Wat 12Y 27
Octavia Ho. SW1 4D 228
W10 42Bb 89
Octavia M. W9 42Bb 89
Octavia Rd. TW7: Isle 55Ga 108
Octavia St. SW11 53Gb 111
Octavia Way SE28 45Xc 95
TW18: Staines 65J 127
Octavius St. SE8 52Cc 114
October Pl. NW4 27Za 48
Odard Rd. KT8: W Mole 70Ca 129
Oddesey Rd. WD6: Bore 11Ra 29
Oddmark Ho. IG11: Bark 40Tc 74
Odelia Ct. E15 39Ec 72
(off Biggerstaff Rd.)
Odell Cl. IG11: Bark 38Vc 75
Odell Ho. E14 44Cc 92
(off New Festival Av.)
Odell Wlk. SE13 55Ec 114
Odencroft Rd. SL2: Slou 1E 80
Odeon, The IG11: Bark 38Tc 74
Odeon Cinema
Barnet 15Cb 31
Beckenham 68Cc 136
Camden Town 39Kb 70
(off Parkway)
Covent Garden 3E 222
Edmonton 17Zb 34
Epsom 85Ua 174
Esher 77Da 151
Gerrards Cross 29A 42
Greenwich 49Hc 93
Holloway 34Nb 70
IMAX (BFI) 7K 223 (46Qb 90)
Kingston upon Thames 68Na 131
(within The Rotunda Cen.)
Leicester Square 5E 222
Marble Arch 44Hb 89
(off Marble Arch)
Muswell Hill 28Kb 50
Panton Street 5E 222
Putney 55Ab 110
Richmond upon Thames -
Hill Street 57Ma 109
Red Lion Street 57Ma 109
South Woodford 26Jc 53
Streatham 62Nb 134
Surrey Quays 48Zb 92
Swiss Cottage 38Fb 69
Tottenham Court Road 1D 222
Uxbridge 39M 63
Whiteleys 44Db 89
Wimbledon 65Bb 133
Odeon Ct. E16 43Jc 93
NW10 39Ua 68
(off St Albans Rd.)
Odeon Pde. SE9 56Nc 116
(off Well Hall Rd.)
UB6: G'frd 37Ka 66
(off Allendale Rd.)
W3 47Qa 87
(off Allendale Rd.)
Odessa Rd. E7 34Hc 73
NW10 40Wa 68
Odessa St. SE16 47Bc 92
Odessa Wharf SE16 48Bc 92
(off Odessa St.)
Odette Ct. WD6: Bore 14Qa 29
(off Whitehall Cl.)
Odette Duval Ho. E1 43Yb 92
(off Stepney Way)
Odger St. SW11 54Hb 111
Odhams Trad. Est. WD24: Wat 9Y 13
Odhams Wlk. WC2 3G 223 (44Nb 90)
Odiam Hall AL9: N Mym 10F 8
Odin Ho. SE5 54Sb 113
O'Donaghue Ho's. SS17: Stan H 1N 101
O'Donnell Ct. WC1 5G 217 (42Nb 90)
O'Driscoll Ho. W12 44Xa 88
Odyssey Bus. Pk. HA4: Ruis 36X 65
Offa Cl. RM12: Horn 36Hd 76
Offa Rd. AL3: St A 2A 6
Offa's Mead E9 35Bc 72
Offenbach Ho. E2 40Zb 72
(off Mace St.)
Offenham Rd. SE9 63Pc 138
SW9 53Qb 112
Offers Ct. KT1: King T 69Pa 131
Offerton Ho. WD19: Wat 20Y 27
Offerton Rd. SW4 55Lb 112
Offham Ho. SE17 6H 231
Offham Slope N12 22Bb 49
Office Pk., The KT22: Lea 91Ha 192
Offley Pl. TW7: Isle 54Fa 108
Offley Rd. SW9 52Qb 112
Offord Cl. N17 23Wb 51
Offord Gro. WD25: Wat 5V 12
Offord Rd. N1 38Pb 70
Offord St. N1 38Pb 70
Ogden Ho. TW13: Hanw 62Aa 129
Ogilby St. SE18 49Pc 94
Ogilvie Ho. E1 44Zb 92
(off Stepney C'way.)
Oglander Rd. SE15 56Vb 113
Ogle St. W1 7B 216 (43Lb 90)
Oglethorpe Rd. RM10: Dag 34Bd 75
O'Gorman Ho. SW10 52Eb 111
(off King's Rd.)
O'Grady Ho. E17 27Dc 52
Ohio Bldg. SE13 53Dc 114
(off Deal's Gateway)
Ohio Rd. E13 42Hc 93
Oil Mill La. W6 50Wa 88
Okeburn Rd. SW17 64Jb 134
Okehampton Cl. N12 22Fb 49
Okehampton Cres. DA16: Well 53Xc 117
Okehampton Rd. NW10 39Ya 68
RM3: Rom 23Ld 57
Okehampton Sq. RM3: Rom 23Ld 57
Okemore Gdns. BR5: St M Cry 70Yc 139
Olaf Ct. W8 47Cb 89
(off Kensington Chu. St.)
Olaf St. W11 45Za 88
Old Acre GU22: Pyr 86J 169
Oldacre GU24: W End 4D 166
Oldacre M. SW12 59Jb 112
Old Aeroworks, The NW8 6C 214
Old Amersham Rd. SL9: Ger X 32D 62
Old Av. KT13: Weyb 80S 150
KT14: W Byf 85G 168
Old Av. Cl. KT14: W Byf 85G 168
Old Bailey
Central Criminal Court
2C 224 (44Rb 91)
Old Bailey EC4 3C 224 (44Rb 91)
Old Bakery Ct. SL0: Iver 44H 83
Old Barge Ho. All. SE1 5A 224
Old Barn Cl. SM2: Cheam 80Ab 154
TN15: Kems'g 89Qd 183
Old Barn La. CR8: Kenley 88Vb 177
WD3: Crox G 15P 25
Old Barn M. WD3: Crox G 15P 25
Old Barn Rd. KT18: Eps 89Sa 173
Old Barn Way DA7: Bex 55Fd 118
Old Barracks W8 47Db 89
Old Barrack Yd. SW1 2H 227 (47Jb 90)
(not continuous)
Old Barrowfield E15 39Gc 73
Old Beaconsfield Rd. SL2: Farn C 7G 60
Old Bell Ct. HP2: Hem H 1M 3
Old Bellgate Pl. E14 48Cc 92
Oldberry Rd. HA8: Edg 23Ta 47
Old Bethnal Grn. Rd. E2 41Wb 91
OLD BEXLEY 59Dd 118
Old Bexley Bus. Pk. DA5: Bexl 59Dd 118
Old Bexley La. DA1: Dart 60Hd 118
DA5: Bexl, Dart 61Fd 140
Old Billingsgate Mkt. EC3 5H 225
Old Billingsgate Wlk.
EC3 5H 225 (45Ub 91)
Old Bond St. W1 5B 222 (45Lb 90)
Oldborough Rd. HA0: Wemb 34La 66
OLD BRENTFORD 52Ma 109
Old Brewer's Yd. WC2 3F 223 (44Nb 90)
Old Brewery M. NW3 35Fb 69
Old Brickworks Ind. Est., The
RM3: Hrld W 25Qd 57
Old Bri. Cl. UB5: N'olt 40Ca 65
Old Bridge La. KT17: Eps 84Ta 174
Old Bridge St. KT1: Hamp W 68Ma 131
Old Broad St. EC2 3G 225 (44Tb 91)
Old Bromley Rd. BR1: Brom 64Fc 137
Old Brompton Rd. SW5 7A 226 (50Cb 89)
SW7 7A 226 (50Cb 89)
Old Buildings WC2 2K 223
Old Burlington St. W1 4B 222 (45Lb 90)
OLDBURY 94Xd 204
Oldbury Cl. BR5: St M Cry 70Zc 139
TN15: Igh 94Xd 204
Oldbury Cotts. TN15: Igh 93Xd 204
Oldbury Ct. E9 36Ac 72
(off Mabley St.)
Oldbury Hill 93Wd 204
Oldbury Hill Camping & Caravanning Club Site
TN15: Seal 94Vd 204
Oldbury Hillfort 94Wd 204
Oldbury Ho. W2 43Db 89
(off Harrow Rd.)
Oldbury La. TN15: Igh 93Xd 204
Oldbury Pl. W1 6J 215 (43Jb 90)
Oldbury Rd. EN1: Enf 12Wb 33
KT16: Chert 73G 148
Oldbury Vs. TN15: Igh 94Xd 204
Old Canal M. SE15 7K 231
Old Carriageway, The
TN13: Chip 94Ed 202
Old Castle St. E1 1K 225 (44Vb 91)
Old Cavendish St. W1 2K 221 (44Kb 90)
Old Change Ct. EC4 3D 224
Old Chapel Pl. SW9 54Qb 112
Old Chapel Rd. BR8: Crock 73Ed 162
Old Charlton Rd. TW17: Shep 71S 150
Old Chelsea M. SW3 51Gb 111
Old Chertsey Rd. GU24: Chob 2M 167
Old Chestnut Av. KT10: Esh 79Ca 151
Old Chiswick Yd. W4 51Ua 110
(off Pumping Sta. Rd.)
Old Chorleywood Rd. WD3: Rick 16M 25
Old Church Cl. BR6: Orp 74Xc 161
Old Church Ct. N11 22Kb 50
Oldchurch Gdns. RM7: Rush G 31Fd 76
Old Church La. HA7: Stan 22Ka 46
NW9 33Ta 67
UB6: G'frd 41Ja 86
Old Church Path KT10: Esh 77Da 151
Oldchurch Ri. RM7: Rush G 31Gd 76
Old Church Rd. E1 44Zb 92
E4 21Cc 52
Oldchurch Rd. RM7: Rush G 31Fd 76
Old Church St. SW3 7C 226 (50Fb 89)
Old Claygate La. KT10: Clay 79Ja 152
Old Clem Sq. SE18 51Qc 116
(off Woolwich Comn.)
Old Coach Rd. KT16: Chert 71F 148
TN15: Wro 86Ae 185
Old Coal Yd. SE28 49Tc 94
Old Coalyard, The TW20: Egh 65B 126
Old College Ct. DA17: Belv 50Dd 96
OLD COMMON 85X 171
Old Common (Local Nature Reserve)
84X 171
Old Common Rd. KT11: Cobh 84X 171
WD3: Chor 14F 24
Old Compton St. W1 4D 222 (45Mb 90)
Old Copple La. SE19 64Vb 135
Old Cote Dr. TW5: Hest 51Ca 107
Old Cotts. AL2: Lon C 1Na 15
TN15: Igh 94Xd 204
OLD COULSDON 91Qb 196
Old Ct. KT21: Asht 91Na 193
Old Ct. Ho. W8 47Db 89
(off Old Court Pl.)
Old Courthouse, The KT18: Eps 85Ta 173
(off The Parade)
Old Ct. Pl. W8 47Db 89
Old Courtyard, The
BR1: Brom 67Kc 137
Old Crabtree La. HP2: Hem H 3N 3
Old Crown SL1: Slou 7K 81
Old Crown Cl. CM14: Kel H 12Td 40
Old Curiosity Shop 2J 223
Old Dairy N15 30Ub 51
Old Dairy Gro. UB2: S'hall 50Ca 85
Old Dairy M. NW5 37Kb 70
SW4 56Nb 112
(off Tintern St.)
SW12 60Jb 112
Old Dairy Sq. N21 17Qb 32
(off Wade Hill)
Old Dartford Rd. DA4: Farni 72Pd 163
Old Dean HP3: Bov 10C 2
Old Deer Pk. 54La 108
Old Deer Pk. Gdns.
TW9: Rich 55Na 109
Old Devonshire Rd. SW12 59Kb 112
Old Dock Cl. TW9: Kew 51Qa 109
Old Dover Rd. SE3 52Jc 115
Old Downs DA3: Hartl 71Ae 165
Oldegate Ho. E6 38Mc 73
Olden La. CR8: Purl 84Qb 176
Old Esher Cl. KT12: Hers 78Z 151
Old Esher Rd. KT12: Hers 78Z 151
Old Farleigh Rd. CR2: Sels 82Yb 178
CR6: W'ham 85Ac 178
Old Farm Av. DA15: Sidc 60Tc 116
N14 17Lb 32
Old Farm Cl. SW17 61Gb 133
TW4: Houn 56Ba 107
Old Farm Gdns. BR8: Swan 69Hd 140
Old Farmhouse Dr.
KT22: Oxs 87Fa 172
Old Farmhouse M. AL9: Wel G 5E 8
Old Farm La. SW19 64Db 133
Old Farm Pas. TW12: Hamp 67Ea 130
Old Farm Rd. N2 25Fb 49
TW12: Hamp 65Ba 129
UB7: W Dray 47M 83
Old Farm Rd. E. DA15: Sidc 61Wc 139
Old Farm Rd. W. DA15: Sidc 61Vc 139
Old Ferry Dr. TW19: Wray 8N 103
Old Field Cl. HP6: L Chal 11A 24
Oldfield Cl. BR1: Brom 70Pc 138
HA7: Stan 22Ja 46
UB6: G'frd 36Ga 66
Oldfield Ct. AL1: St A 3C 6
KT5: Surb 70Pa 131
(off Cranes Pk. Cres.)
Oldfield Farm Gdns. UB6: G'frd 39Fa 66
Oldfield Gdns. KT21: Asht 91Ma 193
Oldfield Gro. SE16 49Zb 92
Oldfield Ho. W4 50Ua 88
(off Devonshire Rd.)
Oldfield La. Nth. UB6: G'frd 40Fa 66
Oldfield La. Sth. UB6: G'frd 42Ea 86
Oldfield M. N6 31Lb 70
Oldfield Rd. AL2: Lon C 7H 7
BR1: Brom 70Pc 138
DA7: Bex 54Ad 117
HP1: Hem H 3G 2
N16 34Ub 71
NW10 38Va 68
SW19 65Ab 132
TW12: Hamp 67Ba 129
W3 47Va 88
Oldfields CM14: W'ley 21Yd 58
Oldfields Cir. UB5: N'olt 37Ea 66
Oldfields Rd. SM1: Sutt 76Bb 155
Oldfield Wood GU22: Wok 89D 168
Old Fire Station, The SE18 52Rc 116
Old Fishery La. HP1: Hem H 5H 3
(not continuous)
Old Fish St. Hill EC4 4D 224
Old Fives Ct. SL1: Burn 1A 80
Old Fleet La. EC4 2B 224 (44Rb 91)
Old Fold Cl. EN5: Barn 11Bb 31
Old Fold La. EN5: Barn 11Bb 31
Old Fold Manor Golf Course 11Ab 30
Old Fold Vw. EN5: Barn 13Ya 30
OLD FORD 39Bc 72
OLD FORD 39Cc 72
Old Ford Rd. E2 41Yb 92
E3 40Ac 72
Old Ford Trading Cen. E3 39Cc 72
(off Maverton Rd.)
Old Forge Cl. HA7: Stan 21Ja 46
WD25: Wat 5W 12
Old Forge Ct. EN9: Walt A 6Jc 21
(off Lamplighters Cl.)
Old Forge Cres. TW17: Shep 72R 150
Old Forge M. W12 47Xa 88
Old Forge Rd. EN1: Enf 10Vb 19
N19 33Mb 70
Old Forge Way DA14: Sidc 63Xc 139
Old Fox Cl. CR3: Cat'm 93Rb 197
Old Gannon Cl. HA6: Nwood 21S 44
Old Gdn., The TN13: Chip 95Ed 202
Old Garden Ct. AL3: St A 2A 6
Old Gloucester St. WC1 7G 217 (43Nb 90)
Old Goods Yd., The W2 1A 220 (43Eb 89)
Old Gorhambury House (remains of) 1H 5
Old Hall Cl. HA5: Pinn 25Aa 45
Old Hall Dr. HA5: Pinn 25Aa 45
Oldham Ter. W3 46Sa 87
(not continuous)
Old Harrow La. TN16: Westrm 91Sc 200
Old Hatch Mnr. HA4: Ruis 31V 64
Old Hat Factory, The AL1: St A 3C 6
(off Inkerman Rd.)
Old Heath Rd. KT13: Weyb 79Q 150
Old Highwayman Pl. SW15 60Xa 110
Old Hill BR6: Downe 79Tc 160
BR7: Chst 67Qc 138
GU22: Wok 2P 187
Old Hill Est. GU22: Wok 2P 187
Oldhill St. N16 32Wb 71
Old Homesdale Rd. BR2: Brom 70Lc 137
Old Hospital Cl. SW12 60Hb 111
Old Ho. Cl. KT17: Ewe 82Va 174
SW19 64Ab 132
Old House Ct. HP2: Hem H 2P 3
SL3: Wex 3P 81
Old Ho. Gdns. TW1: Twick 58La 108
Old Ho. La. WD4: Bucks, Lang 7N 11

Oldhouse La.—Orchard Grn.

Oldhouse La.
GU20: W'sham 1A 166, 10A 146
(not continuous)
GU24: Bisl 6E 166
Old House Rd. HP2: Hem H 2P 3
Old Howlett's La. HA4: Ruis 30T 44
OLD ISLEWORTH 55Ka 108
Old Jamaica Bus. Est. SE16 . . . . . .48Vb 91
Old Jamaica Rd. SE16 . . . . .48Wb 91
Old James St. SE15 . . . . .55Xb 113
Old Jenkins Cl. SS17: Stan H 2K 101
Old Jewry EC2 . . . . .3F 225 (44Tb 91)
Old Kenton La. NW9 . . . . .29Ra 47
Old Kent Rd. SE1 . . . . .5H 231 (49Ub 91)
SE15 . . . . .49Ub 91
Old Kingston Rd. KT4: Wor Pk 75Sa 153
Old La. KT11: Cobh 89R 170
RH8: Oxt 1K 211
(not continuous)
TN15: Igh 95Xd 204
TN16: Tats 92Mc 199
Old La. Gdns. KT11: Cobh 94W 190
Old Laundry, The BR7: Chst 67Sc 138
Old Leys AL10: Hat 3C 8
Old Library Ct. HA4: Ruis 33W 64
Old Library Ho. E3 . . . . .40Ac 72
(off Roman Rd.)
Old Lodge La. CR8: Purl, Kenley . . .85Pb 176
Old Lodge Pl. TW1: Twick 58Ka 108
Old Lodge Way HA7: Stan 22Ja 46
Old London Rd. AL1: St A 3B 6
DA14: Sidc, Swan 66Cd 140
KT2: King T 68Na 131
KT18: Eps D 91Wa 194
(not continuous)
KT24: E Hor 98W 190
RH5: Mick 99La 192
TN14: Bad M, Hals 81Bd 181
TN14: Knock 87Ad 181
TN15: Wro 87Be 185
Old Lyonian Sports Club 29Ea 46
Old MacDonald's Farm 18Pd 39
Old Maidstone Rd. DA14: Sidc 66Bd 139
OLD MALDEN 74Ua 154
Old Malden La. KT4: Wor Pk 75Ta 153
Old Malt Way GU21: Wok 9P 167
Old Mnr. Ct. NW8 . . . . .1A 214 (40Eb 69)
Old Mnr. Dr. DA12: Grav'nd 10E 122
TW7: Isle 58Ea 108
Old Mnr. Ho. M. TW17: Shep 69Q 128
Old Mnr. Rd. UB2: S'hall 49Z 85
Old Mnr. Way BR7: Chst 64Pc 138
DA7: Bex 54Fd 118
Old Manor Yd. SW5 . . . . .49Db 89
Old Mkt. Ct. SM1: Sutt 77Db 155
Old Mkt. Sq. E2 . . . . .3K 219 (41Vb 91)
Old Marylebone Rd.
NW1 . . . . .1E 220 (43Gb 89)
Old Mead SL9: Chal P 23A 42
Oldmead Cl. RM3: Rom 23Nd 57
Oldmead Ho. RM10: Dag 37Dd 76
Old M. HA1: Harr 29Ga 46
Old Mile Ho. Ct. AL1: St A 5E 6
Old Mill Cl. DA4: Eyns 74Nd 163
UB8: Cowl 43K 83
Old Mill Ct. E18 . . . . .27Lc 53
Old Mill Gdns. HP4: Berk 1A 2
Old Mill La. RH1: Mers 100Kb 196
UB8: Cowl 44K 83
Old Mill Pde. RM1: Rom 29Hd 56
Old Mill Pl. RM7: Rom 30Fd 56
TW19: Wray 58D 104
Old Mill Rd. SE18 . . . . .51Tc 116
UB9: Den .34J 63
WD4: Hunt C 5S 12
Old Mitre Ct. EC4 . . . . .3A 224 (44Qb 90)
Old Moat M. RM3: Rom 22Md 57
Old Montague St. E1 . . . . .43Wb 91
Old Nichol St. E2 . . . . .5K 219 (42Vb 91)
Old North St. WC1 . . . . .7H 217
Old Nurseries La. KT11: Cobh 85X 171
Old Nursery DA13: Ist R 6B 144
Old Nursery Cl. WD7: Shenl 6Qa 15
Old Nursery Ct. E2 . . . . .2K 219
SL2: Hedg 3G 60
Old Nursery Pl. TW15: Ashf 64R 128
Old Oak AL1: St A 5C 6
Old Oak Av. CR5: Chip 91Gb 195
Old Oak Cl. KT9: Chess 77Pa 153
KT11: Cobh 85X 171
OLD OAK COMMON 43Ua 88
Old Oak Comn. La. NW10 . . . . .43Ua 88
W3 . . . . .43Ua 88
Old Oak Gdns. GU21: Wok 7P 167
Old Oak La. NW10 . . . . .41Ua 88
Old Oak Rd. W3 . . . . .45Va 88
Old Oaks EN9: Walt A 4Gc 21
Old Operating Theatre Mus. & Herb Garret
. . . . .7G 225
Old Orchard AL2: Park 8A 6
KT14: Byfl 84P 169
SL0: Iver .44H 83
(off Bangors Rd. Sth.)
TW16: Sun 68Y 129
Old Orchard, The NW3 . . . . .35Hb 69
SL0: Iver .44H 83
Old Orchard Cl. EN4: Had W 10Fb 17
UB8: Hil .44Q 84
Old Otford Rd. TN14: Otf, S'oaks . . .89Kd 183
(not continuous)
OLD OXTED 2H 211
Old Palace La. TW9: Rich 57La 108
Old Palace Rd. CR0: C'don 76Rb 157
KT13: Weyb 76R 150
Old Palace Ter. TW9: Rich 57Ma 109
Old Palace Yd. SW1 . . . . . . .3F 229 (48Nb 90)
TW9: Rich 57La 108
Old Paradise St. SE11 . . . . .5H 229 (49Pb 90)
Old Pk. Av. EN2: Enf 14Sb 33
SW12 . . . . .58Jb 112
Old Parkbury La. AL2: Col S 1Ha 14
Old Pk. Gro. EN2: Enf 14Sb 33
Old Pk. La. W1 . . . . .7J 221 (46Kb 90)
Old Pk. M. TW5: Hest 52Ba 107
Old Park Ride EN7: Walt C 3Rb 19
Old Pk. Ridings N21 . . . . .16Rb 33
Old Pk. Rd. EN2: Enf 13Rb 33
N13 . . . . .21Pb 50
SE2 . . . . .50Wc 95
Old Pk. Rd. Sth. EN2: Enf 14Rb 33
Old Pk. Vw. EN2: Enf 13Qb 32
Old Pk. Wood Nature Reserve 24K 43
Old Parsonage Yd. DA4: Hort K 69Sd 142
Old Parvis Rd. KT14: W Byf 84L 169
Old Pearson St. SE10 . . . . .52Dc 114
Old Perry St. BR7: Chst 65Uc 138
DA11: Nflt 1A 144
Old Polhill TN14: Hals, Otf 86Ed 182
Old Police Station, The SW17 . . . . .61Hb 133
Old Police Station M. SE20 . . . . . . .66Zb 136
Old Post Office La. SE3 . . . . .55Kc 115
Old Post Office M. GU21: Wok 10L 167
Old Post Office Wlk. KT6: Surb 72Ma 153
(off Victoria Rd.)
Old Pottery Cl. RH2: Reig 8K 207
Old Pound Cl. TW7: Isle 53Ja 108
Old Priory UB9: Hare 31R 64
Old Priory Av. BR6: Orp 73Xc 161
Old Priory Pk. AL1: St A 3C 6
(off Old London Rd.)
Old Pye St. SW1 . . . . .3D 228 (48Mb 90)
Old Pye St. Est. SW1 . . . . .4D 228
Old Quebec St. W1 . . . . . . .3G 221 (44Hb 89)
(not continuous)
Old Queen St. SW1 . . . . . .2E 228 (47Mb 90)
Old Railway Wlk. SE16 . . . . .47Yb 92
(off Brunel Rd.)
Old Rectory, The KT23: Bookh 99Ba 191
Old Rectory Cl. KT20: Walt H 96Wa 194
Old Rectory Dr. AL10: Hat 1D 8
Old Rectory Gdns. HA8: Edg 23Qa 47
KT11: Cobh 87X 171
Old Rectory La. KT24: E Hor 98U 190
UB9: Den .31G 62
Old Redding HA3: Hrw W 22Da 45
Old Red Lion Theatre 2A 218
Old Redstone Dr. RH1: Redh 7A 208
Old Reigate Rd. RH3: Bet 6A 206
Oldridge Rd. SW12 . . . . .59Jb 112
Old Rd. CM14: Nave, N'side 14Nd 39
DA1: Cray 57Fd 118
EN3: Enf H 11Yb 34
KT15: Add 80H 149
RH3: Bkld .6A 206
RM4: Nave 12Md 39
SE13 . . . . .56Gc 115
Old Rd. E. DA12: Grav'nd 10D 122
Old Rd. W. DA11: Grav'nd 10B 122
Old Rope Wlk. TW16: Sun 69X 129
Old Royal Free Pl. N1 . . . . .39Qb 70
Old Royal Free Sq. N1 . . . . .39Qb 70
Old Royal Naval College 50Fc 93
Old Ruislip Rd. UB5: N'olt 40Y 65
Old's App. WD18: Wat 18R 26
Old Saw Mill, The TN15: Plat 94Fe 205
Old School, The WC1 . . . . .7J 217
Old School Cl. BR3: Beck 68Zb 136
RH1: Redh .4A 208
SE10 . . . . .48Gc 93
SW19 . . . . .68Cb 133
Old School Cotts. HP5: Whel H 8A 2
Old School Ct. BR8: Swan 68Gd 140
(off Bonney Way)
KT22: Lea 94Ka 192
N17 . . . . .27Vb 51
TN13: S'oaks 94Ld 203
TW19: Wray 59A 104
Old School Cres. E7 . . . . .37Jc 73
Old School Houses TN15: God G 96Qd 203
Old School M. KT13: Weyb 77T 150
TW18: Staines 64F 126
Old School Pl. CR0: Wadd 77Qb 156
GU22: Wok 93A 188
Old School Rd. UB8: Hil 42P 83
Old Schools La. KT17: Ewe 81Va 174
Old School Sq. E14 . . . . .44Cc 92
(off Pelling St.)
KT7: T Ditt 72Ha 152
Old School Ter. SM3: Cheam 80Za 154
Old School Wlk. TN13: S'oaks 97Kd 203
(off London Rd.)
Old School Yd. DA12: Grav'nd 9G 122
RH1: Nutf .5F 208
Old's Cl. WD18: Wat 18R 26
Old Seacoal La. EC4 . . . . . .3B 224 (44Rb 91)
Old Shire La. EN9: Walt A 7Jc 21
WD3: Chor 16C 24
Old Slade La. SL0: Rich P 48G 82
SL3: Coln 50H 83
Old Soar Manor 98De 205
Old Soar Rd. TN15: Plax 99De 205
Old Solesbridge La. WD3: Chor 13J 25
Old Sopwell Gdns. AL1: St A 4C 6
Old Sth. Cl. HA5: Pinn 25Z 45
Old Sth. Lambeth Rd. SW8 . . . . . . .52Nb 112
Old Speech Room Gallery 32Ga 66
Old Spitalfields Market 7K 219 (43Vb 91)
Old Sq. WC2 . . . . .2K 223 (44Pb 90)
Old Stable M. N5 . . . . .34Sb 71
Old Stable Row SE18 . . . . .49Qc 94
(off Woolwich New Rd.)
Old Stables Ct. SE5 . . . . .53Sb 113
(off Camberwell New Rd.)
Old Stable Yd. DA2: Bean 62Zd 143
Old Stable Yd., The BR8: Swan 67Ld 141
Old Station App. KT22: Lea 93Ja 192
Old Station Bus. Cen., The AL1: St A . . .4D 6
Old Station Gdns. TW11: Tedd 65Ja 130
(off Victoria Rd.)
Old Station Ho. SE17 . . . . .7E 230 (50Sb 91)
Old Station La. RM13: Rain 42Jd 96
Old Station Pas. TW9: Rich 56Ma 109
(off Little Green)
Old Station Rd. IG10: Lough 15Nc 36
UB3: Harl .48V 84
Old Station Way SW4 . . . . .55Mb 112
(off Voltaire Rd.)
Old Station Yd., The E17 . . . . .28Ec 52
Oldstead Rd. BR1: Brom 63Ec 136
Old Stede Cl. KT21: Asht 89Pa 173
Old Stockley Rd. UB7: W Dray 47R 84
OLD STREET 4F 219 (42Tb 91)
Old St. E13 .40Kc 73
EC1 . . . . .6D 218 (42Sb 91)
Old St., The KT22: Fet 95Fa 192
Old Studio Cl. CR0: C'don 73Tb 157
Old Sungate Cotts. RM5: Col R 25Bd 55
Old Sun Wharf E14 . . . . .45Ac 92
(off Narrow St.)
Old Surrey M., The RH9: G'stone 2A 210
Old Swan Wharf SW11 . . . . .53Fb 111
Old Swan Yd. SM5: Cars 77Hb 155
Old Terry's Lodge Rd.
TN15: Kems'g 88Vd 184
Old Theatre Ct. SE1 . . . . .6E 224
Old Tilburstow Rd. RH9: S God 6A 210
Old Town CR0: C'don 76Rb 157
SW4 . . . . .55Lb 112
Old Town Hall Apartments
SE16 . . . . .4K 231 (48Vb 91)
Old Town Hall Arts Cen., The 1L 3
Old Tramyard SE18 . . . . .49Uc 94
Old Trowley WD5: Ab L 3V 12
Old Twelve Cl. W7 . . . . .42Ga 86
Old Tye Av. TN16: Big H 88Nc 180
Old Uxbridge Rd.
WD3: Map C, W Hyd 22G 42
Old Vic Theatre, The 1A 230
Old Wlk., The TN14: Otf 89Ld 183
Old Watermen's Walk EC3 . . . . .5G 225
Old Watford Rd. AL2: Brick W 2Aa 13
Old Watling St. DA11: Grav'nd 4C 144
Oldway La. SL1: Slou 5B 80
(not continuous)
Old Westhall Cl. CR6: W'ham 91Yb 198
Old Wharf Way KT13: Weyb 77P 149
Old Willow Cl. E3 . . . . .41Cc 92
OLD WINDSOR 8L 103
Old Windsor Lock SL4: Old Win 7N 103
OLD WOKING 93D 188
Old Woking Rd. GU22: Wok, Pyr 91D 188
KT14: W Byf 85H 169
Old Woolwich Rd. SE10 . . . . .51Fc 115
Old Works, The AL1: St A 3C 6
(off Black Cut)
Old Yd., The RH1: Blet 5J 209
TN16: Bras 96Yc 201
Old Yews, The DA3: Lfield 69De 143
Old York Rd. SW18 . . . . .57Db 111
Oleander Cl. BR6: Farnb 78Tc 160
Oleander Ho. SE15 . . . . .50Vb 91
O'Leary Sq. E1 . . . . .43Yb 92
Olga St. E3 .40Ac 72
Olinda Rd. N16 . . . . .30Vb 51
Oliphant St. E14 . . . . .45Ec 92
(off Bullivant St.)
W10 . . . . .41Za 88
Olive Blythe Ho. W10 . . . . .42Ab 88
(off Ladbroke Gro.)
Olive Cl. AL1: St A 3F 6
Olive Ct. E5 .33Yb 72
(off Woodmill Rd.)
N1 . . . . .1A 218
Olive Gro. N15 . . . . .28Sb 51
Olive Haines Lodge SW15 . . . . .57Bb 111
Olive Ho. EC1 . . . . .5A 218
Oliver Av. SE25 . . . . .69Vb 135
Oliver Bus. Pk. NW10 . . . . .40Sa 67
Oliver Cl. AL2: Park 9B 6
HP3: Hem H 6N 3
KT15: Add 77J 149
RM20: W Thur 52Vd 120
W4 . . . . .51Ra 109
Oliver Cl. Ind. Est.
RM20: W Thur 52Vd 120
Oliver Ct. SE18 . . . . .49Sc 94
WD25: Wat .8Z 13
Oliver Cres. DA4: Farni 73Pd 163
Oliver Gdns. E6 . . . . .43Nc 94
Oliver Goldsmith Est. SE15 . . . . .53Wb 113
Oliver Gro. SE25 . . . . .70Vb 135
Oliver Ho. SE14 . . . . .52Bc 114
(off New Cross Rd.)
SE16 . . . . .47Wb 91
(off George Row)
SW8 . . . . .52Nb 112
(off Wyvil Rd.)
Oliver M. SE15 . . . . .54Wb 113
Olive Rd. DA1: Dart 60Md 119
E13 . . . . .41Lc 93
NW2 . . . . .35Xa 68
SW19 . . . . .66Eb 133
W5 . . . . .48Ma 87
Oliver Ri. HP3: Hem H 6N 3
Oliver Rd. BR8: Swan 69Fd 140
CM15: Shenf 15Ce 41
E10 . . . . .33Dc 72
E17 . . . . .29Ec 52
HP3: Hem H 6N 3
KT3: N Mald 68Sa 131
NW10 . . . . .40Sa 67
RM13: Rain 39Hd 76
RM20: W Thur 52Vd 120
SM1: Sutt 77Fb 155
Olivers Mill DA3: Nw A G 75Ae 165
Olivers Wharf E1 . . . . .46Xb 91
(off Wapping High St.)
Olivers Yd. EC1 . . . . .5G 219 (42Tb 91)
Olive St. RM7: Rom 29Fd 56
Olive Tree Ho. SE15 . . . . .51Yb 114
(off Sharratt St.)
Olivette St. SW15 . . . . .55Za 110
Olive Waite Ho. NW6 . . . . .38Cb 69
Olivia Ct. CR0: C'don 73Sb 157
(off Whitehorse Rd.)
EN2: Enf 11Sb 33
(off Chase Side)
Olivia Dr. SL3: L'ly 50B 82
Olivia Gdns. UB9: Hare 25L 43
Olivia M. HA3: Hrw W 24Ga 46
Olivier Ct. UB9: Den 30H 43
(off Patrons Way E.)
Olivier Theatre 6K 223
(within National Theatre)
Ollard's Ct. IG10: Lough 15Mc 35
Ollard's Gro. IG10: Lough 14Mc 35
Olleberrie La. WD3: Sarr 3F 10
Ollerton Grn. E3 . . . . .39Bc 72
Ollerton Rd. N11 . . . . .22Mb 50
Olley Cl. SM6: Wall 80Nb 156
Ollgar Cl. W12 . . . . .46Va 88
Olliffe St. E14 . . . . .48Ec 92
Olmar St. SE1 . . . . .51Wb 113
Olney Ho. NW8 . . . . .5E 214
Olney Rd. SE17 . . . . .51Rb 113
(not continuous)
Olron Cres. DA6: Bex 57Zc 117
Olven Rd. SE18 . . . . .51Sc 116
Olveston Wlk. SM5: Cars 72Fb 155
Olwen M. HA5: Pinn 26Z 45
Olyffe Av. DA16: Well 53Wc 117
Olyffe Dr. BR3: Beck 67Ec 136
Olympia 48Ab 88
Olympia Ind. Est. N22 . . . . .27Pb 50
Olympia M. W2 . . . . .45Db 89
Olympian Cl. TW19: Stanw 58M 105
Olympian Ct. E3 . . . . .40Cc 72
(off Wick La.)
E14 . . . . .49Cc 92
(off Homer Dr.)
Olympian Way SE10 . . . . .46Gc 93
(not continuous)
Olympia Way W14 . . . . .48Ab 88
Olympic Golf Driving Range, The
. . . . .70Kd 141
Olympic Ho. N16 . . . . .35Vb 71
Olympic M. SW18 . . . . .57Eb 111
Olympic Pk. Av. E20 . . . . .36Dc 72
Olympic Sq. HA9: Wemb 34Qa 67
Olympic Way HA9: Wemb 34Qa 67
UB6: G'frd .39Ea 66
Olympus Gro. N22 . . . . .25Qb 50
Olympus Sq. E5 . . . . .34Wb 71
O'Mahoney Ct. SW17 . . . . .62Eb 133
Oman Av. NW2 . . . . .35Ya 68
O'Meara St. SE1 . . . . .7E 224 (46Sb 91)
Omega Cl. E14 . . . . .48Dc 92
Omega Ct. RM7: Rom 29Fd 56
WD18: Wat 15U 26
Omega Ho. SW10 . . . . .52Eb 111
(off King's Rd.)
Omega Pl. N1 . . . . .2G 217
Omega Rd. GU21: Wok 88C 168
Omega St. SE14 . . . . .53Cc 114
Omega Way TW20: Thorpe 67E 126
Omega Works E3 . . . . .38Cc 72
Ommaney Rd. SE14 . . . . .53Zb 114
Omnibus Bldg. RH2: Reig 7K 207
Omnibus Ho. N22 . . . . .26Qb 50
(off Lordship La.)
Omnibus Way E17 . . . . .26Cc 52
Omnium Ct. WC1 . . . . .7H 217
(off Princeton St.)
Ondine Rd. SE15 . . . . .56Vb 113
Onedin Ct. E1 . . . . .45Wb 91
(off Ensign St.)
Onega Ga. SE16 . . . . .48Ac 92
One Hyde Pk. SW1 . . . . . . .1F 227 (47Hb 89)
O'Neill Ho. NW8 . . . . .2D 214
O'Neill Path SE18 . . . . .51Qc 116
One New Change EC4 . . . . .3E 224 (44Sb 91)
One Owen St. EC1 . . . . .2B 218
One Pin La. SL2: Farn C 5G 60
One Pin Pl. SL2: Farn C 4H 61
One Tree Cl. SE23 . . . . .58Yb 114
One Tree Hill Local Nature Reserve
. . . . .58Yb 114
Ongar Cl. KT15: Add 79H 149
RM6: Chad H 29Yc 55
Ongar Hill KT15: Add 79J 149
Ongar Pde. KT15: Add 79J 149
Ongar Pl. CM14: B'wood 19Zd 41
KT15: Add .79J 149
Ongar Rd.
CM15: B'wood, Kel H, Pil H 13Td 40
KT15: Add .78J 149
RM4: Abr, Stap T 13Xc 37
SW6 . . . . .51Cb 111
Ongar Way RM13: Rain 39Gd 76
Onra Rd. E17 . . . . .31Cc 72
Onslow Av. SM2: Cheam 82Bb 175
TW10: Rich 57Na 109
Onslow Cl. E4 . . . . .19Ec 34
GU22: Wok 89C 168
KT7: T Ditt 74Ga 152
W10 . . . . .41Bb 89
Onslow Ct. SW10 . . . . .7A 226
Onslow Cres. BR7: Chst 67Rc 138
GU22: Wok 89C 168
SW7 . . . . .6C 226 (49Fb 89)
Onslow Dr. DA14: Sidc 61Zc 139
Onslow Gdns. CR2: Sande 84Wb 177
E18 . . . . .27Kc 53
KT7: T Ditt 74Ga 152
N10 . . . . .29Kb 50
N21 . . . . .15Qb 32
SM6: Wall .79Lb 156
SW7 . . . . .6B 226 (49Fb 89)
Onslow Ho. KT2: King T 67Pa 131
(off Acre Rd.)
Onslow M. KT16: Chert 72H 149
Onslow M. E. SW7 . . . . . . .6B 226 (49Fb 89)
Onslow M. W. SW7 . . . . . . .6B 226 (49Fb 89)
Onslow Pde. N14 . . . . .18Kb 32
Onslow Rd. CR0: C'don 73Pb 156
KT3: N Mald 70Wa 132
KT12: Hers 77V 150
SL5: S'dale .3F 146
TW10: Rich 57Na 109
Onslow Sq. SW7 . . . . .5C 226 (49Fb 89)
Onslow St. EC1 . . . . .6A 218 (42Qb 90)
Onslow Way GU22: Pyr 87H 169
KT7: T Ditt 74Ga 152
Ontario Point SE16 . . . . .47Yb 92
(off Surrey Quays Rd.)
Ontario St. SE1 . . . . .4C 230 (48Rb 91)
Ontario Twr. E14 . . . . .45Ec 93
Ontario Way E14 . . . . .45Cc 92
(not continuous)
On the Hill WD19: Wat 19Aa 27
Onyx M. E15 . . . . .37Hc 73
Opal Apartments W2 . . . . .44Cb 89
(off Hereford Rd.)
Opal Cl. E16 . . . . .44Mc 93
Opal Ct. E15 . . . . .39Ec 72
SL3: Wex 2N 81
Opal M. IG1: Ilf 33Rc 74
NW6 . . . . .39Bb 69
Opal St. SE11 . . . . .6B 230 (50Rb 91)
Opeck's Cl. SL2: Stoke P 2M 81
SL2: Wex 2M 81
Open Air Stage 32Gb 69
Opendale Rd. SL1: Burn 3A 80
Openshaw Rd. SE2 . . . . .49Xc 95
Openview SW18 . . . . .60Eb 111
Opera Ct. N19 . . . . .34Mb 70
(off Wedmore St.)
Ophelia Gdns. NW2 . . . . .34Ab 68
Ophelia Ho. W6 . . . . .50Za 88
(off Fulham Pal. Rd.)
Ophir Ter. SE15 . . . . .53Wb 113
Opie Ho. NW8 . . . . .1D 214
Opossum Way TW4: Houn 55Y 107
Oppenheim Rd. SE13 . . . . .54Ec 114
Oppidan Apartments NW6 . . . . .38Cb 69
(off Netherwood St.)
Oppidans Rd. NW3 . . . . .38Hb 69
Optima Pk. DA1: Cray 54Jd 118
Opulens Pl. HA6: Nwood 24S 44
Opus Ct. WD6: Bore 13Qa 29
Oram Pl. HP3: Hem H 5M 3
Orange Ct. La. BR6: Downe 81Qc 180
Orange Gro. E11 . . . . .34Gc 73
IG7: Chig 23Sc 54
Orange Hill Rd. HA8: Edg 24Sa 47
Orange Pl. SE16 . . . . .48Yb 92
Orangery, The TW10: Ham 61La 130
Orangery Gallery, The 47Bb 89
Orangery La. SE9 . . . . .57Pc 116
Orange St. WC2 . . . . .5E 222 (45Mb 90)
Orange Tree Ct. SE5 . . . . .52Ub 113
(off Havil St.)
Orange Tree Hill RM4: Have B 22Fd 56
Orange Tree Theatre 56Na 109
Orange Yd. W1 . . . . .3E 222
Oransay Rd. N1 . . . . .37Sb 71
Oratory La. SW3 . . . . .7D 226 (50Fb 89)
Orbain Rd. SW6 . . . . .52Ab 110
Orbel St. SW11 . . . . .53Gb 111
Orbis Wharf SW11 . . . . .55Fb 111
Orbit, The 38Dc 72
Orbital 25 Bus. Pk. WD18: Wat 17T 26
Orbital Bus. Cen. EN9: Walt A 6Ec 20
Orbital Cen. IG8: Wfd G 26Mc 53
Orbital Cres. WD25: Wat 7V 12
Orbital One DA1: Dart 61Rd 141
Orbital One Ind. Est. DA1: Dart 61Qd 141
Orb St. SE17 . . . . .6F 231 (49Tb 91)
Orchard, The BR8: Swan 68Fd 140
GU21: Wok .8M 167
GU22: Wok .94A 188
GU25: Vir W 71A 148
KT13: Weyb 77R 150
KT17: Ewe .80Va 154
(Meadow Wlk.)
KT17: Ewe .82Va 174
(Tayles Hill Dr.)
N14 . . . . .15Kb 32
N20 . . . . .18Db 31
N21 . . . . .16Tb 33
NW11 . . . . .29Cb 49
SE3 . . . . .54Fc 115
SM7: Bans .87Cb 175
TN13: Dun G 93Gd 202
TW3: Houn 54Ea 108
W4 . . . . .49Ta 87
W5 . . . . .43Ma 87
(off Montpelier Rd.)
WD4: K Lan .1Q 12
WD17: Wat 9U 12
Orchard Av. CM13: B'wood 20Be 41
CR0: C'don 75Ac 158
CR4: Mitc .74Jb 156
DA1: Dart .59Kd 119
DA11: Grav'nd 4D 144
DA17: Belv 51Ad 117
KT3: N Mald 68Ua 132
KT7: T Ditt 74Ja 152
KT15: Wdhm 83H 169
N3 . . . . .27Cb 49
N14 . . . . .16Lb 32
N20 . . . . .19Fb 31
RM13: Rain 42Ld 97
SL1: Slou 3B 80
SL4: Wind .3E 102
TW5: Hest .52Aa 107
TW14: Felt .57T 106
TW15: Ashf 65S 128
UB1: S'hall 46Ba 85
WD25: Wat .4X 13
Orchard Bldg. E14 . . . . .44Gc 93
Orchard Bungs. SL2: Farn C 8D 60
Orchard Bus. Cen. SE26 . . . . .64Bc 136
Orchard Cl. AL1: St A 3D 6
DA3: Lfield 68De 143
DA7: Bex 53Ad 117
E4 . . . . .21Cc 52
E11 . . . . .28Kc 53
GU22: Wok .88D 168
GU24: W End 5B 166
HA0: Wemb 39Na 67
HA4: Ruis 31S 64
HA8: Edg 23Na 47
HP2: Hem H .1P 3
KT6: Surb .74Ka 152
KT12: Walt T 73X 151
KT19: Ewe .79Ra 153
KT22: Fet .94Fa 192
KT22: Lea .91Ha 192
KT24: E Hor 96V 190
N1 . . . . .38Sb 71
NW2 . . . . .34Wa 68
RM15: S Ock 42Yd 98
SE23 . . . . .58Yb 114
SL1: Burn 2A 80
SM7: Bans 86Db 175
SW20 . . . . .70Ya 132
TN14: S'oaks 92Ld 203
TW15: Ashf 65S 128
TW20: Egh .64D 126
UB5: N'olt .37Ea 66
UB9: Den 37K 63
W10 . . . . .43Bb 89
WD3: Chor 14F 24
WD6: E'tree 14Pa 29
WD7: R'lett .9Ga 14
WD17: Wat .12V 26
WD23: B Hea 18Fa 28
Orchard Cotts. KT2: King T 67Pa 131
UB3: Hayes .47U 84
Orchard Ct. CR3: Cat'm 96Vb 197
E10 . . . . .32Dc 72
EN5: New Bar 13Db 31
EN6: Pot B .3Cb 17
HA8: Edg 22Pa 47
HP3: Bov 9C 2
KT4: Wor Pk 74Wa 154
KT12: Walt T 74V 150
(off Bridge St.)
N14 . . . . .16Lb 32
SE26 . . . . .63Bc 136
SM6: Wall .78Kb 156
TW2: Twick 61Fa 130
TW7: Isle .53Fa 108
UB7: Lford .52L 105
UB8: Uxb 40N 63
(off The Greenway)
W1 . . . . .2H 221
Orchard Cres. EN1: Enf 11Vb 33
HA8: Edg 22Sa 47
Orchard Dene KT14: W Byf 85J 169
(off Madeira Rd.)
Orchard Dr. AL2: Park 9P 5
CM16: They B 8Uc 22
DA13: Meop 10B 144
GU21: Wok 87A 168
HA8: Edg 22Pa 47
KT21: Asht 92Ma 193
RM17: Grays 47Ce 99
SE3 . . . . .54Fc 115
TW17: Shep 69U 128
UB8: Cowl .42M 83
WD3: Chor .13E 24
WD17: Wat .11V 26
Orchard End CR3: Cat'm 94Ub 197
KT13: Weyb 75U 150
KT22: Fet .96Ea 192
Orchard Gdns.
EN9: Walt A 6Ec 20
KT9: Chess 77Na 153
KT18: Eps .86Sa 173
KT24: Eff 100Aa 191
SM1: Sutt .78Cb 155
Orchard Ga. KT10: Esh 74Fa 152
NW9 . . . . .28Ua 48
SL2: Farn C .6G 60
UB6: G'frd .37Ka 66
Orchard Grn. BR6: Orp 75Uc 160

Orchard Gro.—Outgate Rd.

Orchard Gro. BR6: Orp 75Vc 161
CR0: C'don 73Ac 158
HA3: Kenton 29Pa 47
HA8: Edg 25Qa 47
SE20 66Wb 135
Orchard Hgts. CM16: Epp 5Vc 23
Orchard Hill DA1: Cray 57Gd 118
GU20: W'sham 10B 146
SE13 54Dc 114
SM5: Cars 78Hb 155
Orchard Ho. DA8: Erith 53Hd 118
SE5 53Sb 113
(off County Gro.)
SE16 48Yb 92
SW6 52Bb 111
(off Varna Rd.)
W12 46Wa 88
Orchard Ho. La. AL1: St A 3B 6
Orchard La. CM15: Pil H 15Vd 40
IG8: Wfd G 21Lc 53
KT8: E Mos 72Fa 152
RH9: G'stone 2P 209
SW20 67Xa 132
Orchard Lea DA13: Sflt 64Be 143
Orchard Lea Cl. GU22: Pyr 87G 168
Orchardleigh KT22: Lea 94Ka 192
Orchardleigh Av. EN3: Enf H 12Yb 34
Orchard Lodge SL1: Slou 6C 80
(off Streamside)
Orchard Mains GU22: Wok 1N 187
Orchard Mead Ho. NW2 33Cb 69
Orchardmede N21 16Tb 33
Orchard M. GU21: Knap 10F 166
N1 38Tb 71
N6 31Kb 70
SW17 62Eb 133
Orchard on the Grn., The
WD3: Crox G 15P 25
Orchard Pde. EN6: Pot B 3Za 16
Orchard Pl. BR2: Kes 81Lc 179
BR5: St P 69Yc 139
E5 36Xb 71
E14 45Gc 93
(not continuous)
EN8: Chesh 2Zb 20
N17 24Vb 51
TN14: Sund 96Ad 201
UB8: Uxb 38M 63
W4 49Ua 88
Orchard Ri. CR0: C'don 74Ac 158
HA5: Eastc 27V 44
KT2: King T 67Sa 131
TW10: Rich 56Ra 109
Orchard Ri. E. DA15: Sidc 57Vc 117
Orchard Ri. W. DA15: Sidc 57Uc 116
Orchard Rd. BR1: Brom 67Lc 137
BR6: Farnb 78Rc 160
BR6: Prat B 82Yc 181
CR2: Sande 86Xb 177
CR4: Mitc 74Jb 156
DA10: Swans 57Ae 121
DA11: Nflt 61Ee 143
DA14: Sidc 63Uc 138
DA16: Well 55Xc 117
DA17: Belv 49Cd 96
EN3: Pond E 15Yb 34
EN5: Barn 14Bb 31
KT1: King T 68Na 131
KT9: Chess 77Na 153
N6 31Kb 70
RH2: Reig 6K 207
RM7: Mawney 25Dd 56
RM10: Dag 39Cd 76
RM15: S Ock 42Yd 98
SE3 54Gc 115
SE18 49Tc 94
SL4: Old Win 8M 103
SM1: Sutt 78Cb 155
TN13: Riv 94Gd 202
TN14: Otf 88Hd 182
TW1: Twick 57Ja 108
TW4: Houn 57Ba 107
TW8: Bford 51La 108
TW9: Rich 55Qa 109
TW12: Hamp 66Ba 129
TW13: Felt 60W 106
TW16: Sun 66X 129
UB3: Hayes 45W 84
Orchards, The CM16: Epp 4Wc 23
Orchards Cvn. Site, The
WD3: Chal P 24D 42
Orchards Cl. KT14: W Byf 86J 169
Orchardson Ho. NW8 6B 214
Orchardson St. NW8 6B 214 (42Fb 89)
Orchard Sq. SW1 7J 227 (50Jb 90)
W14 50Bb 89
Orchards Res. Pk. SL3: L'ly 46B 82
Orchards Shop. Cen. DA1: Dart 58Nd 119
Orchard St. AL3: St A 3A 6
DA1: Dart 58Nd 119
E17 28Ac 52
HP3: Hem H 5M 3
W1 3H 221 (44Jb 90)
Orchard Studios W6 49Za 88
(off Brook Grn.)
Orchard Ter. DA9: Ghithe 57Ud 120
EN1: Enf 16Wb 33
NW10 35Va 68
Orchard Theatre, The 58Nd 119
Orchard Vw. KT16: Chert 72J 149
UB8: Cowl 42M 83
Orchard Vs. DA14: Sidc 65Yc 139
Orchardville SL1: Burn 2A 80
Orchard Wlk. KT2: King T 67Qa 131
(off Gordon Rd.)
Orchard Way BR3: Beck 73Cc 158
(Monks Orchard Rd.)
BR3: Beck 73Ac 158
(Orchard Av.)
CR0: C'don 73Ac 158
DA2: Wilm 62Md 141
EN1: Enf 13Ub 33
EN6: Pot B 10K 9
GU3: Worp 6H 187
GU23: Send 97E 188
HP3: Bov 10C 2
IG7: Chig 20Wc 37
KT10: Esh 79Ea 152
KT15: Add 78K 149
KT20: Lwr K 98Bb 195
RH2: Reig 9K 207
RH8: Oxt 5L 211
SL3: L'ly 46A 82
SM1: Sutt 77Fb 155
TN15: Kems'g 89Qd 183
TW15: Ashf 61P 127
WD3: Rick 17J 25
Orchard Waye UB8: Uxb 40M 63
Orchard Wharf E14 45Gc 93
(off Orchard Pl.)
Orchehill Av. SL9: Ger X 28A 42
Orchehill Ct. SL9: Ger X 29A 42
Orchehill Ri. SL9: Ger X 29A 42
Orchestra Ct. HA8: Edg 24Ra 47
Orchid Cl. E6 43Nc 94
EN7: G Oak 2Sb 19
KT9: Chess 80La 152
RM4: Abr 13Xc 37
SE13 57Fc 115
UB1: S'hall 45Aa 85
Orchid Ct. HA9: Wemb 33Na 67
TW20: Egh 63D 126
Orchid Dr. GU24: Bisl 7E 166
HP2: Hem H 3M 3
Orchid Gdns. TW3: Houn 56Ba 107
Orchid Grange N14 17Lb 32
Orchid Mead SM7: Bans 86Db 175
Orchid Rd. N14 17Lb 32
Orchid St. W12 45Wa 88
Orchis Gro. RM17: Grays 50Be 99
Orchis Way RM3: Rom 23Pd 57
Orde NW9 25Va 48
Orde Hall St. WC1 6H 217 (42Pb 90)
Ordell Ct. E3 40Bc 72
(off Ordell Rd.)
Ordell Rd. E3 40Bc 72
Ordnance Cl. TW13: Felt 61W 128
Ordnance Cres. SE10 47Gc 93
Ordnance Dock Pl. UB2: S'hall 49Z 85
Ordnance Hill NW8 1C 214 (39Fb 69)
Ordnance M. NW8 1C 214 (40Fb 69)
Ordnance Rd. DA12: Grav'nd 8E 122
E16 43Hc 93
EN3: Enf L, Enf W 9Zb 20
SE18 51Qc 116
Oregano Cl. UB7: Yiew 44N 83
Oregano Dr. E14 44Fc 93
Oregon Av. E12 35Pc 74
Oregon Bldg. SE13 53Dc 114
(off Deal's Gateway)
Oregon Cl. KT3: N Mald 70Sa 131
Oregon M. W5 43La 86
Oregon Sq. BR6: Orp 74Tc 160
Oreily St. SE1 5K 231
Orestan La. KT24: Eff 99X 191
Orestes M. NW6 36Cb 69
Oreston Rd. RM13: Rain 41Md 97
Orewell Gdns. RH2: Reig 8K 207
Orford Ct. DA2: Dart 58Rd 119
(off Osbourne Rd.)
HA7: Stan 23La 46
SE27 61Rb 135
Orford Gdns. TW1: Twick 61Ha 130
Orford Rd. E17 29Cc 52
E18 27Kc 53
SE6 62Dc 136
ORGAN CROSSROADS 80Wa 154
Organ Hall Rd. WD6: Bore 11Na 29
Organ La. E4 19Ec 34
Oriana Ho. E10 33Dc 72
(off Grange Pk. Rd.)
E14 45Bc 92
(off Victory Pl.)
Oriel Cl. CR4: Mitc 70Mb 134
Oriel Ct. AL1: St A 1C 6
CR0: C'don 74Tb 157
NW3 35Eb 69
Oriel Dr. SW13 51Ya 110
Oriel Gdns. IG5: Ilf 27Pc 54
Oriel Ho. NW6 39Cb 69
(off Priory Pk. Rd.)
RM7: Rom 30Fd 56
Oriel M. E18 26Jc 53
Oriel Pl. NW3 35Eb 69
(off Heath St.)
Oriel Rd. E9 37Zb 72
Oriel Way UB5: N'olt 38Da 65
Oriens M. E20 36Ec 72
Oriental Cl. GU22: Wok 89B 168
Oriental Rd. E16 46Mc 93
GU22: Wok 89B 168
SL5: S'hill 10B 124
Oriental St. E14 45Cc 92
(off Pennyfields)
Orient Cl. AL1: St A 4C 6
Orient Ho. SW6 53Eb 111
(off Station Ct.)
Orient Ind. Pk. E10 33Cc 72
Orient St. SE11 5B 230 (49Rb 91)
Orient Way E5 34Zb 72
E10 32Ac 72
Orient Wharf E1 46Xb 91
(off Wapping High St.)
Origin Bus. Pk. NW10 41Qa 87
Oriole Cl. WD5: Ab L 3W 12
Oriole Way SE28 45Xc 95
Orion E14 49Cc 92
(off Crews St.)
Orion Bus. Cen. SE14 50Zb 92
Orion Cen., The CR0: Bedd 75Nb 156
Orion Ho. E1 42Xb 91
(off Coventry Rd.)
Orion M. SM4: Mord 70Cb 133
Orion Pk. RM9: Dag 40Bd 75
Orion Rd. N11 24Jb 50
Orion Way HA6: Nwood 21V 44
Orissa Rd. SE18 50Uc 94
Orkney Ct. E1 43Ac 92
(off Ocean Est.)
Orkney Ho. N1 39Pb 70
(off Bemerton Est.)
WD18: Wat 15V 26
(off Himalayan Way)
Orkney St. SW11 54Jb 112
Orlando Gdns. KT19: Ewe 82Ta 173
Orlando Rd. SW4 55Lb 112
Orleans Cl. KT10: Esh 75Fa 152
Orleans Ct. KT12: Walt T 75Y 151
TW1: Twick 59Ka 108
Orleans House Gallery 60Ka 108
Orleans Pk. School Sports Cen. 59Ka 108
Orleans Rd. SE19 65Tb 135
TW1: Twick 59Ka 108
Orlestone Gdns. BR6: Chels 78Ad 161
Orleston M. N7 37Qb 70
Orleston Rd. N7 37Qb 70
Orley Ct. HA1: Harr 35Ha 66
Orley Farm Rd. HA1: Harr 34Ga 66
Orlick Rd. DA12: Grav'nd 10K 123
Orlop St. SE10 50Gc 93
Ormanton Rd. SE26 63Wb 135
Orme Ct. W2 45Db 89
Orme Ct. M. W2 45Db 89
(off Orme La.)
Orme Ho. E8 39Vb 71
Orme La. W2 45Db 89
Ormeley Rd. SW12 60Kb 112
Orme Rd. KT1: King T 68Ra 131
SM1: Sutt 79Db 155
Ormerod Gdns. CR4: Mitc 68Jb 134
Ormesby Cl. SE28 45Zc 95
Ormesby Dr. EN6: Pot B 4Za 16
Ormesby Way
HA3: Kenton 30Pa 47
Orme Sq. W2 45Db 89
Ormiston Gro. W12 46Xa 88
Ormiston Rd. SE10 50Jc 93
Ormond Av. TW10: Rich 57Ma 109
TW12: Hamp 67Da 129
Ormond Cl. RM3: Hrld W 26Md 57
WC1 7G 217 (43Nb 90)
Ormond Cres.
TW12: Hamp 67Da 129
Ormond Dr. TW12: Hamp 66Da 129
Ormonde Av. BR6: Farnb 75Sc 160
KT19: Ewe 82Ta 173
Ormonde Ct. NW8 1F 215
RM11: Horn 31Hd 76
(off Clydesdale Rd.)
SW15 56Ya 110
Ormonde Ga. SW3 50Hb 89
(not continuous)
Ormonde Mans. WC1 7G 217
Ormonde Pl. KT13: Weyb 79T 150
SW1 6J 227 (49Jb 90)
Ormonde Ri. IG9: Buck H 18Lc 35
Ormonde Rd. GU21: Wok 8N 167
HA6: Nwood 21T 44
SW14 55Sa 109
Ormonde Ter. NW8 1F 215 (39Hb 69)
Ormond Ho. N16 33Tb 71
Ormond M. WC1 6G 217 (42Nb 90)
Ormond Rd. N19 32Nb 70
TW10: Rich 57Ma 109
Ormond Yd. SW1 6C 222 (46Lb 90)
Ormrod Ct. W11 44Bb 88
(off Westbourne Pk. Rd.)
Ormsby SM2: Sutt 80Db 155
Ormsby Gdns. UB6: G'frd 40Ea 66
Ormsby Lodge W4 48Ua 88
Ormsby Pl. N16 34Vb 71
Ormsby Point SE18 49Rc 94
(off Vincent Rd.)
Ormsby St. E2 1K 219 (40Vb 71)
Ormside St. SE15 51Yb 114
Ormside Way RH1: Redh 2B 208
Ormskirk Rd. WD19: Wat 21Z 45
Ornan Rd. NW3 36Gb 69
Oronsay HP3: Hem H 4B 4
Orpen Ho. SW5 49Cb 89
(off Trebovir Rd.)
Orpen Wlk. N16 34Ub 71
Orphanage Rd. WD17: Wat 12Y 27
WD24: Wat 12Y 27
Orpheus Cen., The 2N 209
Orpheus Ho. W10 42Bb 89
(off Harrow Rd.)
Orpheus St. SE5 53Tb 113
ORPINGTON 74Wc 161
Orpington Bus. Pk.
BR5: St M Cry 70Xc 139
Orpington By-Pass
BR6: Chels, Orp 75Xc 161
Orpington By-Pass Rd.
TN14: Bad M 81Bd 181
Orpington Gdns. N18 20Ub 33
Orpington Mans. N21 18Rb 33
Orpington Retail Pk.
BR5: St M Cry 70Yc 139
Orpington Rd. BR7: Chst 69Uc 138
N21 18Rb 33
Orpington Superbowl 74Wc 161
Orpington Trade Cen. BR5: St P 69Xc 139
Orpin Rd. RH1: Mers 2B 208
Orpwood Cl. TW12: Hamp 65Ba 129
ORSETT 3C 100
Orsett Golf Course 5G 100
ORSETT HEATH 7B 100
Orsett Heath Cres. RM16: Grays 8C 100
Orsett Ind. Pk. RM16: Ors 3H 101
Orsett M. W2 44Db 89
(not continuous)
Orsett Rd. RM16: Ors 2E 100
RM17: Grays 50De 99
SS17: Horn H 1G 100
Orsett St. SE11 7J 229 (50Pb 90)
Orsett Ter. IG8: Wfd G 24Lc 53
W2 2A 220 (44Db 89)
Orsman Rd. N1 39Ub 71
Ortman Cl. SL9: Ger X 31A 62
Orton Gro. EN1: Enf 11Wb 33
Orton Ho. RM3: Rom 24Nd 57
(off Leyburn Rd.)
Orton Pl. SW19 66Db 133
Orton St. E1 46Wb 91
Orville Rd. SW11 54Fb 111
Orwell RM18: E Til 9L 101
Orwell Cl. RM13: Rain 43Fd 96
SL4: Wind 5H 103
UB3: Hayes 45U 84
Orwell Ct. E8 39Wb 71
(off Pownall Rd.)
N5 35Sb 71
SE13 55Dc 114
SW17 62Fb 133
(off Grosvenor Way)
WD24: Wat 13Z 27
Orwell Rd. E13 40Lc 73
Osbaldeston Rd. N16 33Wb 71
Osberton Rd. SE12 57Jc 115
Osbert St. SW1 6D 228 (49Mb 90)
Osborn Cl. E8 39Wb 71
Osborne Av. TW19: Stanw 60N 105
Osborne Cl. BR3: Beck 70Ac 136
EN4: Cockf 13Hb 31
KT17: Eps 84Va 174
RM11: Horn 30Kd 57
TW13: Hanw 64Z 129
Osborne Ct. E10 31Dc 72
EN6: Pot B 1Db 17
HA2: Harr 28Da 45
SL4: Wind 4G 102
W5 43Na 87
WD6: Bore 15Sa 29
(off Sandringham Cl.)
Osborne Gdns. CR7: Thor H 68Sb 135
EN6: Pot B 2Db 17
Osborne Gro. E17 28Bc 52
Osborne Hgts. CM14: W'ley 21Xd 58
Osborne Ho. E16 46Jc 93
(off Wesley Av.)
Osborne M. E17 28Bc 52
SL4: Wind 4G 102
Osborne Pl. SM1: Sutt 78Fb 155
Osborne Rd. CM15: Pil H 16Wd 40
CR7: Thor H 68Sb 135
DA17: Belv 50Bd 95
E7 36Kc 73
E9 37Bc 72
E10 33Dc 72
EN3: Enf H 12Ac 34
EN6: Pot B 2Db 17
IG9: Buck H 18Kc 35
KT2: King T 66Na 131
KT12: Walt T 74W 150
N4 32Qb 70
N13 20Qb 32
NW2 37Xa 68
RH1: Redh 3A 208
RM9: Dag 36Bd 75
RM11: Horn 30Kd 57
SL4: Wind 4G 102
TW3: Houn 55Ba 107
TW20: Egh 65B 126
UB1: S'hall 44Ea 86
UB8: Uxb 38L 63
W3 48Ra 87
WD24: Wat 10Y 13
Osborne Sq. RM9: Dag 35Bd 75
Osborne St. SL1: Slou 7K 81
Osborne Ter. SW17 64Hb 133
(off Church La.)
Osborne Way KT9: Chess 78Pa 153
KT19: Eps 84Na 173
Osborn Gdns. NW7 24Za 48
Osborn La. SE23 59Ac 114
Osborn St. E1 43Vb 91
Osborn Ter. SE3 56Hc 115
Osbourne Av. WD4: K Lan 10P 3
Osbourne Ho. IG8: Wfd G 24Qc 54
TW2: Twick 61Ea 130
Osbourne Rd. DA2: Dart 58Rd 119
Oscar Cl. CR8: Purl 82Qb 176
Oscar Ct. SE16 47Ac 92
Oscar Faber Pl. N1 38Ub 71
Oscar St. SE8 54Cc 114
(not continuous)
Oseney Cres. NW5 36Lb 70
Osgood Av. BR6: Chels 78Vc 161
Osgood Gdns. BR6: Chels 78Vc 161
OSIDGE 18Kb 32
Osidge La. N14 18Jb 32
Osier Ct. E1 42Zb 92
(off Osier St.)
RM7: Rom 30Fd 56
TW8: Bford 51Na 109
(off Ealing Rd.)
Osier Cres. N10 25Hb 49
Osier La. SE10 48Hc 93
Osier M. W4 51Ua 110
Osier Pl. TW20: Egh 65E 126
Osiers, The WD3: Crox G 16S 26
Osiers Ct. KT1: King T 67Ma 131
(off Steadfast Rd.)
Osiers Rd. SW18 56Cb 111
Osiers Twr. SW18 56Cb 111
(off Enterprise Way)
Osier St. E1 42Yb 92
Osier Way CR4: Mitc 71Hb 155
E10 34Dc 72
SM7: Bans 86Ab 174
Oslac Rd. SE6 64Dc 136
Oslo Ct. NW8 2D 214
Oslo Ho. E9 37Bc 72
(off Felstead St.)
SE5 54Sb 113
(off Carew St.)
Oslo Sq. SE16 48Ac 92
Oslo Twr. SE8 49Ac 92
(off Naomi St.)
Osman Cl. N15 30Tb 51
Osmani Youth Cen. 43Wb 91
Osman Rd. N9 20Wb 33
W6 48Ya 88
Osmington Ho. SW8 52Pb 112
(off Dorset Rd.)
Osmond Cl. HA2: Harr 33Ea 66
Osmond Gdns. SM6: Wall 78Lb 156
Osmunda Ct. E1 44Wb 91
(off Myrdle St.)
Osmund St. W12 43Va 88
Osnaburgh St. NW1 6A 216 (42Kb 90)
(Euston Rd.)
NW1 4A 216
(Robert St.)
Osnaburgh Ter. NW1 5A 216 (42Kb 90)
Osney Ho. SE2 47Zc 95
Osney Wlk. SM5: Cars 72Fb 155
Osney Way DA12: Grav'nd 1H 145
Osprey NW9 25Va 48
Osprey Cl. BR2: Brom 74Nc 160
E6 43Nc 94
E11 28Jc 53
E17 24Ac 52
HP3: Hem H 7P 3
KT22: Fet 94Ea 192
SM1: Sutt 78Bb 155
UB7: W Dray 47N 83
WD25: Wat 6Aa 13
Osprey Ct. BR3: Beck 66Cc 136
CM14: B'wood 20Xd 40
CR0: C'don 76Sb 157
(off Innes Yd.)
E1 45Wb 91
(off Star Pl.)
EN9: Walt A 6Jc 21
Osprey Dr. KT18: Tatt C 89Xa 174
Osprey Est. SE16 49Zb 92
Osprey Gdns. CR2: Sels 82Ac 178
Osprey Ho. E14 45Ac 92
(off Victory Pl.)
SE1 50Xb 91
(off Lynton Rd.)
Osprey La. HA2: Harr 33Da 65
Osprey M. EN3: Pond E 15Yb 34
Osprey Rd. EN9: Walt A 6Jc 21
Ospringe Cl. SE20 66Yb 136
Ospringe Ct. SE9 58Tc 116
Ospringe Ho. SE1 1A 230
Ospringe Rd. NW5 35Lb 70
Osram Ct. W6 48Ya 88
Osram Rd. HA9: Wemb 34Ma 67
Osric Path N1 2H 219 (40Ub 71)
Ossel Ct. SE10 49Gc 93
Ossian M. N4 31Pb 70
Ossian Rd. N4 31Pb 70
OSSIE GARVIN RDBT. 45X 85
Ossington Bldgs. W1 7H 215 (43Jb 90)
Ossington Cl. W2 45Cb 89
Ossington St. W2 45Cb 89
Ossory Rd. SE1 51Wb 113
Ossulston St. NW1 2D 216 (40Mb 70)
Ossulton Pl. N2 27Eb 49
Ossulton Way N2 28Eb 49
Ostade Rd. SW2 59Pb 112
Ostell Cres. EN3: Enf L 10Cc 20
Ostend Pl. SE1 5D 230 (49Sb 91)
Osten M. SW7 48Db 89
Osterberg Rd. DA1: Dart 56Pd 119
OSTERLEY 52Fa 108
Osterley Av. TW7: Isle 52Fa 108
Osterley Cl. BR5: St P 67Wc 139
Osterley Ct. TW7: Isle 53Fa 108
UB5: N'olt 41Y 85
(off Canberra Dr.)
Osterley Cres. TW7: Isle 53Ga 108
Osterley Gdns. CR7: Thor H 68Sb 135
UB2: S'hall 47Ea 86
Osterley Ho. E14 44Dc 92
(off Giraud St.)
Osterley La. TW7: Isle 49Ea 86
UB2: S'hall 50Ca 85
Osterley Lodge TW7: Isle 52Ga 108
(off Church Rd.)
Osterley Pk. 51Ea 108
Osterley Pk. House 51Ea 108
Osterley Pk. Rd. UB2: S'hall 48Ba 85
Osterley Pk. Vw. Rd. W7 47Ga 86
Osterley Rd. N16 35Ub 71
TW7: Isle 52Ga 108
Osterley Sports & Athletics Cen.
52Ga 108
Osterley Sports Club 48Da 85
Osterley Views UB2: S'hall 47Fa 86
Oster St. AL3: St A 1A 6
Oster Ter. E17 29Zb 52
Ostlers Cl. HP3: Hem H 3D 4
Ostlers Dr. TW15: Ashf 64S 128
Ostliffe Rd. N13 22Sb 51
Oswald Bldg. SW8 51Kb 112
Oswald Cl. KT22: Fet 94Ea 192
RM12: Horn 36Hd 76
Oswald Rd. AL1: St A 3C 6
KT22: Fet 94Ea 192
UB1: S'hall 46Aa 85
Oswald's Mead E9 35Ac 72
Oswald St. E5 34Zb 72
Oswald Ter. NW2 34Ya 68
Osward CR0: Sels 81Bc 178
(not continuous)
Osward Pl. N9 19Xb 33
Osward Rd. SW17 61Hb 133
Oswell Ho. E1 46Xb 91
(off Farthing Flds.)
Oswin Cl. BR5: St M Cry 71Xc 161
Oswin St. SE11 5C 230 (49Rb 91)
Oswyth Rd. SE5 54Ub 113
OTFORD 88Kd 183
Otford Cl. BR1: Brom 69Qc 138
DA5: Bexl 58Dd 118
SE20 67Yb 136
Otford Cres. SE4 58Bc 114
Otford Heritage Cen. 88Kd 183
Otford Ho. SE1 2G 231
SE15 51Yb 114
(off Lovelinch Cl.)
Otford La. TN14: Hals 84Bd 181
Otford Rd. TN14: S'oaks 91Kd 203
Othello Cl. SE11 7B 230 (50Rb 91)
Otho Ct. TW8: Bford 52Ma 109
Otis St. E3 41Ec 92
Otium Leisure Club
St Albans 9M 5
Otley App. IG2: Ilf 30Rc 54
Otley Dr. IG2: Ilf 29Rc 54
Otley Ho. N5 34Qb 70
Otley Rd. E16 44Lc 93
Otley Ter. E5 34Zb 72
Otley Way WD19: Wat 20Y 27
Otlinge Rd. BR5: St M Cry 70Zc 139
Ottawa Gdns. RM10: Dag 38Fd 76
Ottawa Ho. SE16 47Yb 92
(off Province Dr.)
UB4: Yead 41X 85
(off Ayles Rd.)
Ottawa Rd. RM18: Tilb 4C 122
Ottaway St. E5 34Wb 71
Otterbourne Rd. CR0: C'don 75Sb 157
E4 20Fc 35
Otterburn Gdns. TW7: Isle 52Ja 108
Otterburn Ho. SE5 52Sb 113
(off Sultan St.)
Otterburn St. SW17 65Hb 133
Otter Cl. E15 39Ec 72
KT16: Ott 79D 148
Otterden Cl. BR6: Orp 76Uc 160
Otterden St. SE6 63Cc 136
Otterden Ter. SE1 6K 231
Otter Dr. SM5: Cars 74Hb 155
Otterfield Rd. UB7: Yiew 45N 83
Otter Gdns. AL10: Hat 1D 8
Ottermead La. KT16: Ott 79E 148
Otter Mdw. KT22: Lea 91Ha 192
Otter Rd. UB6: G'frd 42Ea 86
Otters Cl. BR5: St P 70Zc 139
OTTERSHAW 79E 148
Ottershaw Pk. KT16: Ott 80C 148
(not continuous)
Otterspool La. WD25: A'ham 10Aa 13
(not continuous)
Otterspool Way WD25: A'ham 10Ba 13
(not continuous)
Otter Way UB7: Yiew 46N 83
Ottley Dr. SE3 56Lc 115
Otto Cl. SE26 62Xb 135
Ottoman Ter. WD17: Wat 13Y 27
Otto St. SE17 51Rb 113
Ott's Yard N19 35Lb 70
(off Southcote Rd.)
Ottway's Av. KT21: Asht 91Ma 193
Otways La. KT21: Asht 92Ma 193
Otway Gdns. WD23: Bush 17Ga 28
Otways Cl. EN6: Pot B 4Db 17
Oulton Cl. E5 33Yb 72
SE28 44Yc 95
Oulton Cres. EN6: Pot B 3Za 16
IG11: Bark 36Vc 75
Oulton Rd. N15 29Tb 51
Oulton Way WD19: Wat 21Ba 45
Oundle Av. WD23: Bush 16Ea 28
Oundle Ho. RM3: Rom 23Md 57
(off Montgomery Cres.)
Ousden Cl. EN8: Chesh 2Ac 20
Ousden Dr. EN8: Chesh 2Ac 20
Ouseley Lodge SL4: Old Win 9N 103
Ouseley Rd. SL4: Old Win 9N 103
SW12 60Hb 111
TW19: Wray 9N 103
Outer Circ. NW1 2E 214 (41Gb 89)
Outgate Rd. NW10 38Va 68

Outlook Pl.—Palmers Dr.

Outlook Pl. WD17: Wat 11W 26
Outram Pl. KT13: Weyb 78S 150
N1 39Nb 70
Outram Rd. CR0: C'don 75Vb 157
E6 39Nc 74
N22 25Mb 50
Outwich St. EC3 2J 225
Outwood Ho. SW2 59Pb 112
(off Deepdene Gdns.)
Outwood La. CR5: Chip, Kgswd 92Gb 195
KT20: Kgswd 94Db 195
RH1: Blet, S Nut 10K 209
Oval, The 51Pb 112
Oval, The DA3: Lfield 69Ee 143
DA15: Sidc 59Wc 117
E2 40Xb 71
SM7: Bans 86Cb 175
Oval Ct. HA8: Edg 24Sa 47
Oval Gdns. RM17: Grays 48Ee 99
Oval Ho. CR0: C'don 74Ub 157
(off Oval Rd.)
Ovalhouse Theatre 51Qb 112
Oval Mans. SE11 51Pb 112
Oval Pl. SW8 52Pb 112
Oval Rd. CR0: C'don 75Tb 157
NW1 39Kb 70
Oval Rd. Nth. RM10: Dag 39Dd 76
Oval Rd. Sth. RM10: Dag 40Dd 76
Ovaltine Ct. WD4: K Lan 1R 12
Ovaltine Dr. WD4: K Lan 1R 12
Oval Way SE11 50Pb 90
SL9: Ger X 28A 42
Ovanna M. N1 37Ub 71
Ovenden Rd. TN14: Chev, Sund 92Zc 201
Overbrae BR3: Beck 65Cc 136
Overbrook KT24: W Hor 100R 190
Overbrook Wlk. HA8: Edg 24Qa 47
(not continuous)
Overbury Av. BR3: Beck 69Dc 136
Overbury Cres. CR0: New Ad 82Ec 178
Overbury Rd. N15 30Tb 51
Overbury St. E5 35Zb 72
Overchess Ridge WD3: Chor 13H 25
Overcliffe DA11: Grav'nd 8C 122
Overcliff Rd. RM17: Grays 49Fe 99
(not continuous)
SE13 55Cc 114
Overcourt Cl. DA15: Sidc 58Xc 117
Overdale KT21: Asht 87Na 173
RH1: Blet 5J 209
Overdale Av. KT3: N Mald 68Sa 131
Overdale Rd. W5 48La 86
Overdown Rd. SE6 63Cc 136
Overhill CR6: W'ham 91Yb 198
Overhill Rd. CR8: Purl 81Qb 176
SE22 59Wb 113
Overhill Way BR3: Beck 71Fc 159
Overlea Rd. E5 31Wb 71
Overlord Ct. KT22: Fet 93Fa 192
Overmead BR8: Swan 71Gd 162
DA15: Sidc 59Tc 116
Over Minnis DA3: Nw A G 76Be 165
Oversley Ho. W2 43Cb 89
(off Alfred Rd.)
Overstand Cl. BR3: Beck 71Cc 158
Overstone Gdns. CR0: C'don 73Bc 158
Overstone Ho. E14 44Cc 92
(off E. India Dock Rd.)
Overstone Rd. W6 48Ya 88
Overstrand Ho. RM12: Horn 34Kd 77
Overstrand Mans. SW11 53Hb 111
Overstream WD3: Loud 14K 25
Over The Misbourne Rd.
SL9: Ger X 30C 42
UB9: Den 30D 42
Overthorpe Cl. GU21: Knap 9J 167
Overton Cl. NW10 37Sa 67
TW7: Isle 53Ha 108
Overton Ct. E11 31Jc 73
SM2: Sutt 80Cb 155
Overton Dr. E11 31Jc 73
RM6: Chad H 31Yc 75
Overton Ho. SW15 59Va 110
(off Tangley Gro.)
Overton Rd. E10 32Ac 72
N14 15Nb 32
SE2 48Yc 95
SM2: Sutt 79Cb 155
SW9 54Qb 112
Overton Rd. E. SE2 48Zc 95
Overton's Yd. CR0: C'don 76Sb 157
Overy Ho. SE1 2B 230 (47Rb 91)
Overy Liberty DA1: Dart 59Nd 119
Overy St. DA1: Dart 58Nd 119
Ovesdon Av. HA2: Harr 32Ba 65
Oveton Way KT23: Bookh 98Ca 191
Ovett Cl. SE19 65Ub 135
Ovex Cl. E14 47Ec 92
Ovington Ct. GU21: Wok 8K 167
SW3 4E 226
Ovington Gdns. SW3 4E 226 (48Gb 89)
Ovington M. SW3 4E 226
Ovington Sq. SW3 4E 226 (48Gb 89)
Ovington St. SW3 4E 226 (49Gb 89)
Owen Cl. CR0: C'don 72Tb 157
RM5: Col R 23Dd 56
SE28 46Yc 95
SL3: L'ly 50B 82
TW16: Sun 67U 128
UB5: N'olt 37Aa 65
(Arnold Rd.)
UB5: N'olt 41X 85
(Attlee Rd.)
Owen Gdns. IG8: Wfd G 23Nc 54
Owen Ho. TW1: Twick 59Ka 108
TW14: Felt 59W 106
Owenite St. SE2 49Xc 95
Owen Mans. W14 51Ab 110
(off Queen's Club Gdns.)
Owen Pl. KT22: Lea 94Ka 192
Owen Rd. GU20: W'sham 8B 146
N13 22Sb 51
UB4: Yead 41X 85
Owens M. E11 33Gc 73
Owen Sq. WD19: Wat 16Z 27
(off Pinner Rd.)
Owen's Row EC1 3B 218 (41Rb 91)
Owen St. EC1 2B 218 (40Rb 71)
Owens Way SE23 59Ac 114
WD3: Crox G 15Q 26
Owen Wlk. SE20 67Wb 135
Owen Way NW10 37Sa 67
Owgan Cl. SE5 52Tb 113
Owl Cl. CR2: Sels 82Zb 178
Owlets Hall Cl.
RM11: Horn, Hrld W 27Pd 57
Owletts 9H 145
Owl Pk. IG10: Lough 13Hc 35
Ownstead Gdns. CR2: Sande 83Vb 177
Ownsted Hill CR0: New Ad 82Ec 178
Oxberry Av. SW6 54Ab 110
Oxborough Ho. SW18 56Eb 111
(off Eltringham St.)
Oxdowne Cl. KT11: Stoke D 86Da 171
Oxenden Wood Rd.
BR6: Chels 79Xc 161
Oxendon St. SW1 5D 222 (45Mb 90)
Oxenford St. SE15 55Vb 113
Oxenham Ho. SE8 51Cc 114
(off Benbow St.)
Oxenhill Rd. TN15: Kems'g 89Nd 183
Oxenhoath Rd. TN11: Roug 100Fe 205
Oxenholme NW1 2C 216
Oxenpark Av. HA9: Wemb 31Na 67
Oxestall's Rd. SE8 50Ac 92
Oxford & Cambridge Mans.
NW1 1E 220
Oxford Av. AL1: St A 3G 6
N14 18Lb 32
RM11: Horn 28Qd 57
RM16: Grays 9C 100
SL1: Burn 10A 60
SL1: Slou 3D 80
SW20 68Ab 132
TW5: Hest 50Ca 85
UB3: Harl 52V 106
Oxford Cir. W1 3B 222
Oxford Cir. Av. W1 3B 222 (44Lb 90)
Oxford Cl. CR4: Mitc 69Lb 134
DA12: Grav'nd 1H 145
EN8: Chesh 1Zb 20
HA6: Nwood 21T 44
N9 19Xb 33
RM2: Rom 29Jd 56
TW15: Ashf 66S 128
Oxford Ct. CM14: W'ley 21Zd 59
EC4 4F 225
KT6: Surb 71Na 153
(off Avenue Elmers)
KT18: Eps 86Ua 174
TW13: Hanw 63Z 129
W3 44Qa 87
W4 50Ra 87
W7 43Ha 86
(off Copley Cl.)
W9 43Cb 89
(off Elmfield Way)
Oxford Cres. KT3: N Mald 72Ta 153
Oxford Dr. HA4: Ruis 33Y 65
SE1 7H 225 (46Ub 91)
Oxford Gdns. N20 18Fb 31
N21 17Sb 33
UB9: Den 34H 63
W4 50Qa 87
W10 44Ya 88
Oxford Ga. W6 49Za 88
Oxford Ho. BR2: Brom 72Mc 159
(off Wells Vw. Dr.)
E3 43Bc 92
(off William Whiffin Sq.)
NW6 40Cb 69
(off Oxford Rd.)
RM8: Dag 35Wc 75
WD6: Bore 12Qa 29
(off Stratfield Rd.)
Oxford M. DA5: Bexl 59Cd 118
Oxford Pl. NW10 34Ta 67
(off Press Rd.)
Oxford Rd. DA14: Sidc 64Xc 139
E15 37Fc 73
(not continuous)
EN3: Pond E 15Xb 33
HA1: Harr 30Ea 46
HA3: W'stone 27Ha 46
IG1: Ilf 36Sc 74
IG8: Wfd G 22Mc 53
N4 32Qb 70
N9 19Xb 33
NW6 40Cb 69
RH1: Redh 5N 207
RM3: Rom 23Pd 57
SE19 65Tb 135
SL4: Wind 3G 102
SL9: Ger X 30A 42
SM5: Cars 79Gb 155
SM6: Wall 78Lb 156
SS17: Stan H 2K 101
SW15 56Ab 110
TW11: Tedd 64Fa 130
UB8: Uxb 36K 63
UB9: Den 33F 62
W5 45Ma 87
Oxford Rd. E. SL4: Wind 3G 102
Oxford Rd. Nth. W4 50Ra 87
Oxford Rd. Sth. W4 50Qa 87
Oxford Row TW16: Sun 69Y 129
Oxford Sq. W2 3E 220 (44Gb 89)
Oxford St. W1 3G 221 (44Jb 90)
WD18: Wat 15X 27
Oxford Ter. NW6 40Db 69
(off Oxford Rd.)
Oxford Wlk. UB1: S'hall 46Ba 85
Oxford Way TW13: Hanw 63Z 129
Oxgate Cen. NW2 33Xa 68
Oxgate Ct. NW2 33Wa 68
Oxgate Ct. Pde. NW2 33Wa 68
Oxgate Gdns. NW2 34Xa 68
Oxgate La. NW2 33Xa 68
Oxgate Pde. NW2 33Wa 68
Oxhawth Cres. BR2: Brom 71Qc 160
OXHEY 16Y 27
Oxhey Av. WD19: Wat 17Z 27
Oxhey Dr. HA6: Nwood 21X 45
WD19: Wat 21X 45
Oxhey Dr. Sth. HA6: Nwood 22X 45
Oxhey La. HA3: Hrw W 18Aa 27
HA5: Hat E 18Aa 27
WD19: Wat 18Aa 27
Oxhey Pk. 16Y 27
Oxhey Pk. Golf Course 19Z 27
Oxhey Ridge Cl. HA6: Nwood 21X 45
Oxhey Rd. WD19: Wat 17Y 27
Oxhey Woods Local Nature Reserve
21W 44
Oxlade Dr. SL3: L'ly 9N 81
Ox La. KT17: Ewe 81Wa 174
Oxleas E6 44Rc 94
Oxleas Cl. DA16: Well 54Tc 116
OXLEASE 1C 8
Oxlease Dr. AL10: Hat 1D 8
Oxleay Rd. HA2: Harr 32Ca 65
Oxleigh Cl. KT3: N Mald 71Ua 154
Oxley Cl. RM2: Rom 26Ld 57
SE1 7K 231 (50Vb 91)
Oxley Sq. E3 42Dc 92
(off Truman Wlk.)
Oxleys Rd. EN9: Walt A 4Jc 21
NW2 34Xa 68
Oxlip Cl. CR0: C'don 74Zb 158
Oxlow La. RM9: Dag 35Bd 75
RM10: Dag 35Bd 75
Oxonian St. SE22 56Vb 113
Oxo Tower Wharf SE1 5A 224 (45Qb 90)
OXSHOTT 85Fa 172
Oxshott Lodge KT22: Oxs 86Fa 172
Oxshott Ri. KT11: Cobh 85Z 171
Oxshott Rd. KT22: Lea 88Ga 172
Oxshott Village Sports Club 86Ea 172
Oxshott Way KT11: Cobh 87Aa 171
OXTED 1J 211
Oxted Cl. CR4: Mitc 69Fb 133
Oxted Ct. RH1: Redh 4B 208
(off Reynolds Av.)
Oxted Ho. RM3: Rom 22Pd 57
(off Redcar Rd.)
Oxted Pl. RH8: Oxt 99Fc 199
Oxted Rd. RH9: G'stone 2A 210
Oxtoby Way SW16 67Mb 134
Oxygen, The E16 45Jc 93
OYO Bus. Units DA17: Belv 47Ed 96
RM9: Dag 42Bd 95
Oystercatcher Cl. E16 44Kc 93
Oyster Cl. EN5: Barn 16Ab 30
Oyster Ct. SE17 6D 230
Oysterfields AL3: St A 1P 5
Oystergate Wlk. EC4 5F 225
Oyster La. KT14: Byfl 82M 169
Oyster M. E7 37Mc 73
Oyster Row E1 44Yb 92
Oyster Wharf SW11 54Fb 111
Ozolins Way E16 44Jc 93

P

Pablo Neruda Cl. SE24 56Rb 113
Paceheath Cl.
RM5: Col R 23Fd 56
Pace Pl. E1 44Xb 91
Pachesham Dr. KT22: Lea 88Ha 172
PACHESHAM PARK 88Ja 172
Pachesham Pk. KT22: Lea 88Ja 172
Pachesham Pk. Golf Course 90Ga 172
Pacific Cl. DA10: Swans 57Ae 121
TW14: Felt 60V 106
Pacific Ct. E1 43Yb 92
Pacific Ho. E1 42Zb 92
(off Ernest St.)
Pacific M. SW9 56Qb 112
Pacific Rd. E16 44Jc 93
Pacific Wharf SE16 46Zb 92
Packenham Ho. E2 41Vb 91
(off Wellington Row)
W10 45Za 88
(off Shalfleet Dr.)
Packet Boat La. UB8: Cowl 44K 83
Packet Boat Marina UB8: Yiew 44L 83
Packham Cl. BR6: Chels 75Yc 161
Packham Ct. KT4: Wor Pk 76Ya 154
Packham Rd. DA11: Nflt 2B 144
Packhorse La. EN6: Ridge 2Ta 15
WD6: Bore 9Ua 16
Packhorse Rd. SL9: Ger X 28A 42
TN13: Bes G 95Ed 202
Packington Rd. W3 48Sa 87
Packington Sq. N1 1D 218 (39Sb 71)
(not continuous)
Packington St. N1 39Rb 71
Packmores Rd. SE9 57Tc 116
Packwell Pl. TW5: Hest 51Y 107
Padbrook RH8: Limp 1L 211
(not continuous)
Padbrook Cl. RH8: Limp 1M 211
Padbury SE17 7H 231
Padbury Cl. TW14: Bedf 60T 106
Padbury Ct. E2 4K 219 (41Vb 91)
Padbury Ho. NW8 5E 214
Padbury Oaks UB7: Lford 53K 105
Padcroft Rd. UB7: Yiew 46M 83
Paddenswick Rd. W6 48Wa 88
PADDINGTON 3B 220 (44Fb 89)
Paddington Cl. UB4: Yead 42Z 85
Paddington Ct. W7 43Ha 86
(off Copley Cl.)
Paddington Grn. W2 7C 214 (43Fb 89)
Paddington Sports Club 42Db 89
Paddington St. W1 7H 215 (43Jb 90)
Paddock, The DA2: Dart 61Ud 142
GU18: Light 3A 166
N10 27Jb 50
NW9 29Qa 47
SL3: Dat 3M 103
SL4: Wink 10A 102
SL9: Chal P 22A 42
TN16: Westrm 98Sc 200
UB10: Ick 35R 64
Paddock Cl. BR6: Farnb 77Rc 160
DA4: S Dar 67Sd 142
KT4: Wor Pk 74Ua 154
RH8: Oxt 3K 211
RM16: Ors 3D 100
SE3 54Jc 115
SE26 63Zb 136
SL4: Wind 3D 102
TN15: Plat 93Ee 205
UB5: N'olt 40Ca 65
WD19: Wat 16Aa 27
Paddock Gdns. SE19 65Ub 135
Paddock Ho. DA11: Grav'nd 4E 144
Paddock La. EN5: Ark 13Ua 30
Paddock Lodge EN1: Enf 15Ub 33
(off Village Rd.)
Paddock Mobile Home Pk.
BR2: Kes 81Nc 180
Paddock Pas. SE19 65Ub 135
(off Paddock Gdns.)
Paddock Rd. DA6: Bex 56Ad 117
HA4: Ruis 34Z 65
NW2 34Wa 68
Paddocks, The AL4: St A 4L 7
BR8: Swan 67Ld 141
CR0: Addtn 79Cc 158
EN4: Cockf 13Hb 31
GU25: Vir W 72A 148
HA9: Wemb 33Ra 67
KT13: Weyb 76U 150
KT15: New H 82K 169
KT23: Bookh 98Da 191
RM4: Stap A 16Hd 38
RM16: Ors 3D 100
TN13: S'oaks 96Md 203
W5 48Ma 87
(off Popes La.)
WD3: Chor 14H 25
Paddocks Cl. BR5: Orp 75Zc 161
HA2: Harr 35Da 65
KT11: Cobh 86Y 171
KT21: Asht 90Na 173
Paddocks Grn. NW9 32Ra 67
Paddocks Mead
GU21: Wok 8J 167
Paddocks Way KT16: Chert 74K 149
KT21: Asht 90Na 173
Paddock Vw. WD7: R'lett 5Ja 14
Paddock Wlk. CR6: W'ham 91Xb 197
Paddock Way BR7: Chst 66Tc 138
GU21: Wok 86D 168
HP1: Hem H 2G 2
RH8: Oxt 3K 211
SW15 59Ya 110
Padelford La. HA7: Stan 19Ja 28
Padfield Ct. HA9: Wemb 34Pa 67
Padfield Rd. SE5 55Sb 113
Padgate Ho. WD19: Wat 20Y 27
Padgets, The EN9: Walt A 6Gc 21
Padley Cl. KT9: Chess 78Pa 153
Padnall Ct. RM6: Chad H 27Zc 55
Padnall Rd. RM6: Chad H 27Zc 55
Padstone Ho. E3 41Dc 92
(off Talwin St.)
Padstow Cl. BR6: Chels 77Vc 161
SL3: L'ly 47A 82
Padstow Ho. E14 45Bc 92
(off Three Colt St.)
Padstow Rd. EN2: Enf 11Rb 33
Padstow Wlk. TW14: Felt 60V 106
Padua Rd. SE20 67Yb 136
Pagden St. SW8 53Kb 112
Pageant Av. NW9 25Ta 47
Pageant Cl. RM18: Tilb 3E 122
Pageant Cres. SE16 46Ac 92
Pageantmaster Ct. EC4 3B 224
Pageant Rd. AL1: St A 3B 6
Pageant Wlk. CR0: C'don 76Ub 157
Page Av. HA9: Wemb 34Sa 67
Page Cl. DA2: Bean 62Yd 142
HA3: Kenton 30Pa 47
RM9: Dag 36Ad 75
TW12: Hamp 65Aa 129
Page Ct. NW7 24Xa 48
Page Cres. CR0: Wadd 78Rb 157
DA8: Erith 52Hd 118
Page Cft. KT15: Add 75K 149
Page Grn. Rd. N15 29Wb 51
Page Grn. Ter. N15 29Vb 51
Page Heath La. BR1: Brom 69Mc 137
Page Heath Vs. BR1: Brom 69Mc 137
Page High N22 26Qb 50
(off Lymington Av.)
Page Ho. SE10 51Ec 114
(off Welland St.)
Pagehurst Rd. CR0: C'don 73Xb 157
Page Mdw. NW7 24Xa 48
Page M. SW11 54Jb 112
Page Pl. AL2: F'mre 10C 6
Page Rd. TW14: Bedf 58T 106
Pages Hill N10 26Jb 50
Pages La. N10 26Jb 50
RM3: Hrld W 26Rd 57
UB8: Uxb 37L 63
Page St. NW7 25Wa 48
SW1 5E 228 (49Mb 90)
Page's Wlk. SE1 5H 231 (49Ub 91)
Pages Yd. W4 51Va 110
Paget Av. SM1: Sutt 76Fb 155
Paget Cl. TW12: Hamp H 63Fa 130
Paget Gdns. BR7: Chst 67Rc 138
Paget Ho. E2 40Yb 72
(off Bishop's Way)
SL9: Chal P 21A 42
(off Micholls Av.)
Paget La. TW7: Isle 55Fa 108
Paget Pl. KT2: King T 65Sa 131
KT7: T Ditt 74Ha 152
Paget Ri. SE18 51Qc 116
Paget Rd. IG1: Ilf 35Rc 74
N16 32Tb 71
SL3: L'ly 49B 82
UB10: Hil 42S 84
Paget St. EC1 3B 218 (41Rb 91)
Paget Ter. SE18 51Rc 116
Pagette Way RM17: Grays 50Ce 99
Pagham Ho. W10 42Ya 88
(off Sutton Way)
Pagin Ho. N15 29Ub 51
(off Braemar Rd.)
Pagitts Gro. EN4: Had W 11Db 31
Paglesfield CM13: Hut 16Ee 41
Pagnell St. SE14 52Bc 114
Pagoda Av. TW9: Rich 55Pa 109
Pagoda Gdns. SE3 54Fc 115
Pagoda Gro. SE27 61Sb 135
Paignton Cl. RM3: Rom 25Md 57
Paignton Rd. HA4: Ruis 34W 64
N15 30Ub 51
Paines Brook Ct. RM3: Rom 23Pd 57
Paines Brook Rd. RM3: Rom 23Pd 57
Paines Brook Way RM3: Rom 23Pd 57
Paines Cl. HA5: Pinn 27Aa 45
Painesfield Dr. KT16: Chert 74J 149
Paines La. HA5: Pinn 25Aa 45
Pain's Cl. CR4: Mitc 68Kb 134
PAINS HILL
KT11 86V 170
RH8 3N 211
PAINSHILL 85V 170
Pains Hill RH8: Limp 4N 211
Pains Hill Ho. KT11: Cobh 86V 170
Painshill Pk. 86V 170
Painsthorpe Rd. N16 34Ub 71
Painted Hall
Greenwich 51Ec 114
Painters Ash La. DA11: Nflt 62Fe 143
Painters La. EN3: Enf W 7Ac 20
Painters M. SE16 49Wb 91
Painters Rd. IG2: Ilf 27Vc 55
Paisley Rd. N22 25Rb 51
SM5: Cars 74Fb 155
Paisley Ter. SM5: Cars 73Fb 155
Pakefield M. SW2 60Pb 112
Pakeman Ho. SE1 1C 230
Pakeman St. N7 35Pb 70
Pakenham Cl. SW12 60Jb 112
Pakenham St. WC1 4J 217 (41Pb 90)
Pakes Way CM16: They B 9Uc 22
Pakington Ho. SW9 54Nb 112
(off Stockwell Gdns. Est.)
Palace Av. W8 47Db 89
Palace Bingo Club 5D 230
Palace Cl. E9 37Bc 72
SL1: Slou 6D 80
WD4: K Lan 2P 11
Palace Ct. BR1: Brom 67Kc 137
(off Palace Gro.)
GU21: Wok 88C 168
(off Maybury Rd.)
HA3: Kenton 30Na 47
NW3 36Db 69
W2 45Db 89
(not continuous)
Palace Ct. Gdns. N10 27Lb 50
Palace Dr. KT13: Weyb 76R 150
Palace Exchange EN2: Enf 14Tb 33
Palace Gdns. IG9: Buck H 18Mc 35
Palace Gdns. M. W8 46Db 89
Palace Gdns. Shop. Cen.
EN2: Enf 14Tb 33
Palace Gdns. Ter. W8 45Cb 89
Palace Ga. W8 2A 226 (47Eb 89)
Palace Gates M. N8 28Nb 50
(off The Campsbourne)
Palace Gates Rd. N22 25Mb 50
Palace Grn. CR0: Sels 80Bc 158
W8 46Db 89
Palace Gro. BR1: Brom 67Kc 137
SE19 66Vb 135
Palace Ice Rink, The 26Mb 50
Palace Mans. KT1: King T 70Ma 131
(off Palace Rd.)
W14 49Ab 88
(off Hammersmith Rd.)
Palace M. E17 28Bc 52
EN2: Enf 13Tb 33
SW1 6J 227
SW6 52Bb 111
Palace Pde. E17 28Bc 52
Palace Pl. SW1 3B 228 (48Lb 90)
Palace Pl. Mans. W8 47Db 89
(off Kensington Ct.)
Palace Rd. BR1: Brom 67Kc 137
HA4: Ruis 35Aa 65
KT1: King T 70Ma 131
KT8: E Mos 69Ea 130
N8 29Mb 50
(not continuous)
N11 24Nb 50
SE19 66Vb 135
SW2 60Pb 112
TN16: Westrm 93Qc 200
Palace Sq. SE19 66Vb 135
Palace St. SW1 3B 228 (48Lb 90)
Palace Superbowl 5C 230
Palace Theatre
Soho 3E 222
Palace Vw. BR1: Brom 69Kc 137
(not continuous)
CR0: C'don 77Bc 158
SE12 61Jc 137
Palace Vw. Rd. E4 22Dc 52
Palace Way GU22: Wok 92D 188
KT13: Weyb 76R 150
Palace Wharf W6 52Ya 110
(off Rainville Rd.)
Palamos Rd. E10 32Cc 72
Palatine Av. N16 35Ub 71
Palatine Rd. N16 35Ub 71
Palazzo Apartments N1 38Ub 71
(off Ardleigh Rd.)
Palemead Cl. SW6 53Za 110
Palermo Rd. NW10 40Wa 68
Palestine Gro. SW19 67Fb 133
Palestra Ho. SE1 7B 224
Palewell Cl. BR5: St P 68Xc 139
Palewell Comn. Dr. SW14 57Ta 109
Palewell Pk. SW14 57Ta 109
Paley Gdns. IG10: Lough 13Rc 36
Palfrey Cl. AL3: St A 1B 6
Palfrey Pl. SW8 52Pb 112
Palgrave Av. UB1: S'hall 45Ca 85
Palgrave Ct. TW11: Hamp W 66La 130
Palgrave Gdns. NW1 5E 214 (42Gb 89)
Palgrave Ho. SE5 52Sb 113
(off Wyndham Est.)
TW2: Whitt 59Ea 108
Palgrave Rd. W12 48Va 88
Palins Way RM16: Grays 46Ce 99
Palissy St. E2 4K 219 (41Vb 91)
(not continuous)
Palladian Cir. DA9: Ghithe 56Yd 120
Palladino Ho. SW17 64Gb 133
(off Laurel Cl.)
Palladio Ct. SW18 58Db 111
(off Mapleton Cres.)
Palladium Ct. E8 38Vb 71
(off Queensbridge Rd.)
Pallant Ho. SE1 4G 231
Pallant Way BR6: Farnb 76Qc 160
Pallet Way SE18 53Nc 116
Palliser Ct. W14 50Ab 88
(off Palliser Rd.)
Palliser Dr. RM13: Rain 43Jd 96
Palliser Ho. E1 42Zb 92
(off Ernest St.)
SE10 51Fc 115
(off Trafalgar Rd.)
Palliser Rd. W14 50Ab 88
Pallister Ter. SW15 62Va 132
Pall Mall SW1 7C 222 (46Lb 90)
Pall Mall E. SW1 6E 222 (46Mb 90)
Pall Mall Pl. SW1 7C 222
Palmadium Ct. N13 20Qb 32
Palmar Cres. DA7: Bex 55Cd 118
Palmar Rd. DA7: Bex 54Cd 118
Palmarsh Rd. BR5: St M Cry 70Zc 139
Palm Av. DA14: Sidc 65Zc 139
Palm Cl. E10 34Dc 72
Palm Ct. SE15 52Vb 113
(off Garnies Cl.)
Palmeira Rd. DA7: Bex 55Zc 117
Palmer Av. DA12: Grav'nd 3F 144
SM3: Cheam 77Ya 154
WD23: Bush 15Da 27
Palmer Cl. BR4: W W'ck 76Fc 159
RH1: Redh 7A 208
TW5: Hest 53Ca 107
UB5: N'olt 37Aa 65
Palmer Cres. KT1: King T 69Na 131
KT16: Ott 79F 148
Palmer Dr. BR1: Brom 70Rc 138
Palmer Gdns. EN5: Barn 15Za 30
Palmer Ho. SE14 52Zb 114
(off Lubbock St.)
Palmer Pl. N7 36Qb 70
Palmer Rd. E13 42Kc 93
RM8: Dag 32Zc 75
Palmers SS17: Stan H 1P 101
Palmers Av. RM17: Grays 50Ee 99
Palmer's Ct. N11 22Lb 50
(off Palmer's Rd.)
Palmers Dr. RM17: Grays 49Ee 99

Palmersfield Rd.—Parkleys

Palmersfield Rd. SM7: Bans 86Cb **175**
PALMERS GREEN 20Qb 32
Palmers Gro. KT8: W Mole 70Ca **129**
Palmers Hill CM16: Epp 1Wc **23**
Palmers La. EN1: Enf 11Xb **33**
EN3: Enf H 11Xb **33**
Palmer's Moor La. SL0: Iver 42J **83**
Palmers Orchard
TN14: S'ham 83Hd **182**
Palmers Pas. *SW14 . . . . .55Sa 109*
(off Little St Leonard's)
Palmer's Rd. E2 . . . . .40Zb **72**
N11 . . . . .22Lb **50**
Palmers Rd. SW14 . . . . .55Sa **109**
SW16 .68Pb **134**
WD6: Bore 11Ra **29**
Palmer's Sports & Fitness Cen. 9A 100
Palmerston Av. SL3: Slou 8M **81**
Palmerston Cen. HA3: W'stone 27Ha **46**
Palmerston Cl. GU21: Wok 86C **168**
RH1: Redh 9A **208**
Palmerston Ct. *E3 . . . . .40Zb 72*
(off Old Ford Rd.)
IG9: Buck H 18Lc **35**
KT6: Surb 73Ma **153**
Palmerston Cres. N13 . . . . .22Pb **50**
SE18 . . . . .51Sc **116**
Palmerstone Ct. *GU25: Vir W 71A 148*
(off Ridge Way)
Palmerston Gdns. RM20: Grays 50Zd **99**
Palmerston Gro. SW19 . . . . .66Cb **133**
Palmerston Ho. SE1 . . . . .2K **229**
SM7: Bans 87Bb 175
(off Basing Rd.)
W8 . . . . .46Cb 89
(off Kensington Pl.)
Palmerston Mans. *W14 . . . . .51Ab 110*
(off Queen's Club Gdns.)
Palmerston Rd. BR6: Farnb 77Sc **160**
CR0: C'don 71Tb **157**
E7 . . . . .37Kc **73**
E17 . . . . .27Bc **52**
HA3: W'stone 27Ga **46**
IG9: Buck H 19Kc **35**
N22 . . . . .24Pb **50**
NW6 . . . . .38Bb **69**
(not continuous)
RM13: Rain 40Ld **77**
RM20: Grays 51Zd **121**
SM1: Sutt 78Eb **155**
SM5: Cars 77Hb **155**
SW14 .56Sa **109**
SW19 .66Cb **133**
TW2: Twick 58Ga **108**
TW3: Houn 53Ea **108**
W3 . . . . .48Sa **87**
Palmerston Way SW8 . . . . .52Kb **112**
Palmer St. SW1 . . . . .3D **228** (48Mb **90**)
(not continuous)
Palmers Way EN8: Chesh 1Ac **20**
Palmers Wharf *KT1: King T 68Ma 131*
(off Emms Pas.)
Palm Gro. W5 . . . . .48Na **87**
Palm Rd. RM7: Rom 29Ed **56**
Palyn Ho. EC1 . . . . .4E **218**
Pamela Av. HP3: Hem H 5P **3**
Pamela Ct. N12 . . . . .23Db **49**
Pamela Gdns. HA5: Eastc 29X **45**
Pamela St. E8 . . . . .39Vb **71**
Pamela Wlk. *E8 . . . . .39Wb 71*
(off Marlborough Av.)
Pampisford Rd. CR2: S Croy 81Rb **177**
CR8: Purl 83Qb **176**
Pams Way KT19: Ewe 78Ta **153**
Panama Ho. *E1 . . . . .43Zb 92*
(off Beaumont Sq.)
Pancake La. HP2: Hem H 3D **4**
Pancras La. EC4 . . . . .3E **224** (44Sb **91**)
Pancras Rd. N1 . . . . .1E **216** (40Nb **70**)
NW1 . . . . .1D **216** (40Mb **70**)
Pancras Sq. N1 . . . . .1F **217** (40Nb **70**)
Pancras Square Leisure Cen.
. . . . .1F 217 (40Nb 70)
Pancras Way E3 . . . . .40Cc **72**
Pancroft RM4: Abr 13Xc **37**
Pandangle Ho. *E8 . . . . .39Vb 71*
(off Kingsland Rd.)
Pandian Way NW1 . . . . .37Mb **70**
Pandora Ct. *E16 . . . . .43Jc 93*
(off Robertson Rd.)
Pandora Rd. NW6 . . . . .37Cb **69**
'Pan' (Epstein) *47Hb 89*
(within Hyde Pk.)
Panfield M. IG2: Ilf 30Qc **54**
Panfield Rd. SE2 . . . . .48Wc **95**
Pangbourne NW1 . . . . .4B **216**
Pangbourne Av. W10 . . . . .43Ya **88**
Pangbourne Dr. HA7: Stan 22Ma **47**
Panhard Pl. UB1: S'hall 45Da **85**
Pank Av. EN5: New Bar 15Eb **31**
Pankhurst Av. E16 . . . . .46Kc **93**
Pankhurst Cl. SE14 . . . . .52Zb **114**
TW7: Isle 55Ha **108**
Pankhurst Ho. W12 . . . . .44Xa **88**
Pankhurst Pl. WD24: Wat 13Y **27**
Pankhurst Rd. KT12: Walt T 73Y **151**
Pankridge WD19: Wat 18Z **27**
Panmuir Rd. SW20 . . . . .67Xa **132**
Panmure Cl. N5 . . . . .35Rb **71**
Panmure Ct. SE26 . . . . .62Xb **135**
UB1: S'hall 44Ea 86
(off Osborne Rd.)
Panmure Rd. SE26 . . . . .62Xb **135**
Pannells Cl. KT16: Chert 74H **149**
Pannells Ct. TW5: Hest 51Ca **107**
Panorama Ct. N6 . . . . .30Lb **50**
Panoramic Twr. *E14 . . . . .44Dc 92*
(off Burcham St.)
Pan Peninsula Sq. E14 . . . . .47Dc **92**
Pansy Gdns. W12 . . . . .45Wa **88**
Panter's BR8: Hext 66Hd **140**
Panther Dr. NW10 . . . . .36Ta **67**
Pantile Cotts. RM14: Upm 29Td **58**
Pantile Rd. KT13: Weyb 77T **150**
Pantile Row SL3: L'ly 49C **82**
Pantiles, The BR1: Brom 69Nc **138**
DA7: Bex 52Bd **117**
NW11 . . . . .28Bb **49**
WD23: B Hea 18Fa **28**
Pantiles Cl. GU21: Wok 10M **167**
N13 . . . . .22Rb **51**
Pantile Wlk. *UB8: Uxb 38L 63*
(off The Pavilions)
Panton Cl. CR0: C'don 74Rb **157**
Panton St. SW1 . . . . .5D **222** (45Mb **90**)
Panxworth Rd. HP3: Hem H 4M **3**
Panyer All. EC1 . . . . .2D **224**
Panyers Gdns. RM10: Dag 34Dd **76**
Paper Bldgs. EC4 . . . . .4A **224**
Papercourt La. GU23: Rip 94H **189**
Papercourt Sailing Club 94H 189
Papermill Cl. SM5: Cars 77Jb **156**
Paper Mill La. DA1: Dart 56Md **119**
Paper Mill M. DA9: Ghithe 56Yd **120**
Papermill Pl. E17 . . . . .26Ac **52**
Paper Mill Wharf E14 . . . . .45Ac **92**
Papillons Wlk. SE3 . . . . .54Jc **115**
Papworth Gdns. N7 . . . . .36Pb **70**
Papworth Way SW2 . . . . .59Qb **112**
Papyrus Ho. N1 . . . . .3D **218** (41Sb **91**)
Parabola Ct. KT8: E Mos 70Ea **130**
Parade, The
CM14: B'wood 20Yd **40**
CR0: C'don 72Nb **156**
DA1: Cray 57Hd **118**
DA3: Hartl 71Ae **165**
DA10: Swans 57Be **121**
DA12: Grav'nd 1F **144**
GU25: Vir W 2P **147**
KT2: King T 68Na 131
(off London Rd.)
KT4: Wor Pk 77Va **154**
KT10: Clay 79Ga **152**
KT17: Eps 85Ua **174**
KT18: Eps 86Qa 173
(off Spa Dr.)
KT18: Eps 85Ta **173**
(Ashley Rd.)
KT20: Tad 91Ab **194**
KT22: Lea 92Ja 192
(off Kingston Rd.)
N4 . . . . .32Qb **70**
RH1: Redh 7A **208**
RM3: Hrld W 23Rd **57**
RM15: Avel 47Sd **98**
SE4 . . . . .54Bc 114
(off Up. Brockley Rd.)
SE26 . . . . .62Xb 135
(off Wells Pk. Rd.)
SM1: Sutt 76Bb **155**
SM5: Cars 78Hb 155
(off Beynon Rd.)
SW11 . . . . .52Hb **111**
TN15: Kems'g 89Nd **183**
TN16: Tats 93Lc 199
(off Ship Hill)
TW12: Hamp H 64Fa **130**
TW16: Sun 66V **128**
TW18: Staines 64F 126
(off Meadow Gdns.)
UB6: G'frd 36Ka **66**
WD17: Wat 13X **27**
WD19: Wat 20Z **27**
(Prestwick Rd.)
WD19: Wat 20Aa **27**
(The Mead)
Parade Ct. KT24: E Hor 98U **190**
Parade Gdns. E4 . . . . .24Dc **52**
Parade Ground Path SE18 . . . . .52Pc **116**
Parade Mans. NW4 . . . . .29Xa **48**
Parade M. SE27 . . . . .61Rb **135**
PARADISE 3M 3
Paradise HP2: Hem H 3M **3**
Paradise Ind. Est. HP2: Hem H 3M **3**
Paradise Pas. N7 . . . . .36Qb **70**
Paradise Path SE28 . . . . .46Wc **95**
Paradise Pl. SE18 . . . . .49Nc **94**
Paradise Rd. EN9: Walt A 6Ec **20**
SW4 . . . . .54Nb **112**
TW9: Rich 57Ma **109**
Paradise Row E2 . . . . .41Xb **91**
Paradise St. SE16 . . . . .47Xb **91**
Paradise Wlk. SW3 . . . . .51Hb **111**
Paragon *TW8: Bford 50La 86*
(off Boston Pk. Rd.)
Paragon, The SE3 . . . . .54Hc **115**
Paragon Cl. E16 . . . . .44Jc **93**
Paragon Gro. KT5: Surb 72Pa **153**
Paragon M. SE1 . . . . .5G **231** (49Tb **91**)
Paragon Pl. KT5: Surb 72Pa **153**
SE3 . . . . .54Hc **115**
Paragon Rd. E9 . . . . .37Yb **72**
Paramount Bldg. EC1 . . . . .5B **218**
Paramount Ct. WC1 . . . . .6C **216**
Paramount Ind. Est. *WD24: Wat 10Y 13*
(off Sandown Rd.)
Parbury Ri. KT9: Chess 79Na **153**
Parbury Rd. SE23 . . . . .58Ac **114**
Parchmore Rd. CR7: Thor H 68Rb **135**
Parchmore Way CR7: Thor H 68Rb **135**
Pardoe Rd. E10 . . . . .31Dc **72**
Pardoner Ho. SE1 . . . . .3G **231**
Pardoner St. SE1 . . . . .3G **231** (48Tb **91**)
(not continuous)
Pardon St. EC1 . . . . .5C **218** (42Rb **91**)
Parent Shop. Mall *E18 . . . . .26Jc 53*
(off Marlborough Rd.)
Parents Paradise
Watford .13Z 27
Pares Cl. GU21: Wok 8P **167**
Parfett St. E1 . . . . .43Wb **91**
(not continuous)
Parfitt Cl. NW3 . . . . .32Eb **69**
Parfour Dr. CR8: Kenley 88Sb **177**
Parfrey St. W6 . . . . .51Ya **110**
Pargraves Ct. HA9: Wemb 33Qa **67**
Parham Dr. IG2: Ilf 30Rc **54**
Parham Way N10 . . . . .26Lb **50**
Paris Corte *SE13 . . . . .55Dc 114*
(off Loampit Va.)
Paris Gdn. SE1 . . . . .6B **224** (46Rb **91**)
Parish Cl. RM11: Horn 33Kd **77**
WD25: Wat 6Y **13**
Parish Ct. KT6: Surb 71Na **153**
Parish Ga. Dr. DA15: Sidc 58Uc **116**
Parish La. SE20 . . . . .65Zb **136**
SL2: Farn C 3F **60**
Parish M. SE20 . . . . .66Zb **136**
Paris Ho. *E2 . . . . .40Xb 71*
(off Old Bethnal Grn. Rd.)
Parish Wharf Pl. SE18 . . . . .49Nc **94**
Parison Cl. TW9: Rich 55Qa **109**
Park & Ride
Windsor, Home Park 1J 103
Windsor, Legoland 7C 102
Park, The DA14: Sidc 64Wc **139**
HA1: Harr 32Ga **66**
KT23: Bookh 95Ca **191**
N6 . . . . .30Jb **50**
NW11 . . . . .32Db **69**
SE23 . . . . .60Yb **114**
SL9: Ger X 28B **42**
SM5: Cars 78Hb **155**
W5 . . . . .46Ma **87**
Park App. DA16: Well 56Xc **117**
SE16 . . . . .48Xb **91**
Park Av. AL1: St A 1E **6**
BR1: Brom 65Hc **137**
BR4: W W'ck 75Ec **158**
BR6: Chels 75Wc **161**
BR6: Farnb 76Pc **160**
CM13: Hut 18Ee **41**
CR3: Cat'm 96Ub **197**
CR4: Mitc 66Kb **134**
DA11: Nflt 10A **122**
DA12: Grav'nd 10E **122**
E6 . . . . .39Qc **74**
E15 . . . . .37Gc **73**
EN1: Enf 15Tb **33**
EN6: Pot B 6Eb **17**
HA4: Ruis 30T **44**
IG1: Ilf 32Qc **74**
IG8: Wfd G 22Kc **53**
IG11: Bark 37Sc **74**
N3 . . . . .25Db **49**
N13 . . . . .20Qb **32**
N18 . . . . .21Wb **51**
N22 . . . . .26Nb **50**
NW2 . . . . .36Xa **68**
NW10 . . . . .40Pa **67**
(Brent Cres., not continuous)
NW10 . . . . .36Xa **68**
(Park Av. Nth.)
NW11 . . . . .32Db **69**
RM14: Upm 31Ud **78**
RM20: W Thur 51Wd **120**
SM5: Cars 79Jb **156**
SW14 . . . . .56Ta **109**
TW3: Houn 58Da **107**
TW17: Shep 69U **128**
TW18: Staines 65H **127**
TW19: Wray 7P **103**
TW20: Egh 65E **126**
UB1: S'hall 47Ba **85**
WD3: Chor 15J **25**
WD7: R'lett 5Ka **14**
WD18: Wat 14W **26**
WD23: Bush 12Aa **27**
Park Av. E. KT17: Ewe 79Wa **154**
Park Av. Maisonettes
WD23: Bush 12Ba **27**
Park Av. M. CR4: Mitc 66Kb **134**
Park Av. Nth. N8 . . . . .28Mb **50**
NW10 . . . . .36Xa **68**
Park Av. Rd. N17 . . . . .24Xb **51**
Park Av. Sth. N8 . . . . .28Mb **50**
Park Av. W. KT17: Ewe 79Wa **154**
Park Blvd. RM2: Rom 25Hd **56**
Park Central Bldg. E3 . . . . .40Cc **72**
Park Chase HA9: Wemb 35Pa **67**
Park Cliff Rd. DA9: Ghithe 56Yd **120**
Park Cl. AL9: Brk P 8J **9**
E9 . . . . .39Yb **72**
HA3: Hrw W 25Ga **46**
KT2: King T 67Qa **131**
KT10: Esh 79Ca **151**
KT12: Walt T 75V **150**
KT14: Byfl 85M **169**
KT15: New H 82K **169**
KT22: Fet 96Fa **192**
N12 . . . . .20Fb **31**
NW2 . . . . .34Xa **68**
NW10 . . . . .41Pa **87**
RH8: Oxt 100Hc **199**
SL4: Wind 4H **103**
SM5: Cars 79Hb **155**
SW1 . . . . .2F **227** (47Hb **89**)
TW3: Houn 57Ea **108**
TW12: Hamp 67Ea **130**
W4 . . . . .51Ta **109**
W14 . . . . .48Bb **89**
WD3: Rick 21R **44**
WD23: Bush 13Z **27**
Park Club, The
Acton .46Ua 88
PARK CORNER 4M 7
Park Cnr. SL4: Wind 5C **102**
Park Cnr. Dr. KT24: E Hor 100U **190**
Park Cnr. Rd. DA13: Sflt 63Be **143**
Park Ct. *CR2: S Croy 78Sb 157*
(off Warham Rd.)
E4 . . . . .19Ec **34**
E17 . . . . .29Dc **52**
GU22: Wok 90B **168**
HA3: Kenton 31Na **67**
HA9: Wemb 36Na **67**
KT1: Hamp W 67La **130**
KT3: N Mald 70Ta **131**
KT14: W Byf 85J **169**
N11 . . . . .24Mb **50**
N17 . . . . .24Wb **51**
SE21 . . . . .62Sb **135**
SE26 . . . . .65Xb **135**
SM6: Wall 78Nb **156**
SW11 . . . . .53Kb **112**
UB8: Uxb 39M **63**
W6 . . . . .49Wa **88**
Park Cres. DA8: Erith 51Ed **118**
EN2: Enf 14Tb **33**
HA3: Hrw W 25Ga **46**
N3 . . . . .24Eb **49**
RM11: Horn 31Jd **76**
SL5: S'dale 2D **146**
TW2: Twick 60Fa **108**
W1 . . . . .6K **215** (42Kb **90**)
WD6: E'tree 13Pa **29**
Park Cres. M. E. W1 . . . . . .6A **216** (42Kb **90**)
Park Cres. M. W. W1 . . . . . .6K **215** (42Kb **90**)
Park Cres. Rd. DA8: Erith 51Fd **118**
Park Cft. HA8: Edg 25Sa **47**
Parkcroft Rd. SE12 . . . . .59Hc **115**
Parkdale N11 . . . . .23Mb **50**
Parkdale Cres. KT4: Wor Pk 76Ta **153**
Parkdale Rd. SE18 . . . . .50Uc **94**
Park Dr. DA3: Lfield 69Ae **143**
EN6: Pot B 3Db **17**
GU22: Wok 90B **168**
HA2: Harr 31Ca **65**
HA3: Hrw W 23Fa **46**
KT13: Weyb 78R **150**
KT21: Asht 90Qa **173**
N21 . . . . .16Sb **33**
NW11 . . . . .32Db **69**
RM1: Rom 28Fd **56**
RM10: Dag 34Ed **76**
RM14: Upm 35Rd **77**
SE7 . . . . .51Nc **116**
SL5: S'dale 2D **146**
SW14 . . . . .57Ta **109**
W3 . . . . .48Qa **87**
Park Driving Range, The 3L 81
Park Dwellings NW3 . . . . .36Hb **69**
Park E. Bldg. *E3 . . . . .40Cc 72*
(off Fairfield Rd.)
Park End BR1: Brom 67Hc **137**
NW3 . . . . .35Gb **69**
Park End Rd. RM1: Rom 28Gd **56**
Parker Av. RM18: Tilb 3E **122**
Parker Bldg. *SE16 . . . . .48Wb 91*
(off Old Jamaica Rd.)
Parker Cl. E16 . . . . .46Nc **94**
SM5: Cars 79Hb **155**
Parker Ct. *N1 . . . . .39Sb 71*
(off Basire St.)
Parker Gdns. SL4: Old Win 8M **103**
Parker Ho. *E14 . . . . .47Cc 92*
(off Admirals Way)
Parker Ind. Cen. DA2: Dart 59Sd **120**
Parker M. WC2 . . . . .2G **223** (44Nb **90**)
Parke Rd. SW13 . . . . .53Wa **110**
TW16: Sun 70W **128**
Parker Rd. CR0: C'don 77Sb **157**
RM17: Grays 50Be **99**
Parker's Cl. KT21: Asht 91Na **193**
Parker's Hill KT21: Asht 91Na **193**
Parker's La. KT21: Asht 91Na **193**
Parkers Row SE1 . . . . .47Wb **91**
Parker St. E16 . . . . .46Nc **94**
WC2 . . . . .2G **223** (44Nb **90**)
WD24: Wat 11X **27**
Parkes Rd. IG7: Chig 22Uc **54**
Parkes St. E20 . . . . .37Cc **72**
Park Farm Cl. HA5: Eastc 29X **45**
N2 . . . . .27Eb **49**
Park Farm Ct. UB3: Hayes 45U **84**
Park Farm Rd. BR1: Brom 67Mc **137**
KT2: King T 66Na **131**
RM14: Upm 36Pd **77**
PARKFIELD .3Db 17
Parkfield DA3: Hartl 70Ae **143**
TN15: Seal, S'oaks 95Nd **203**
TW7: Isle 53Ga **108**
WD3: Chor 14H **25**
Parkfield Av. HA2: Harr 26Ea **46**
SW14 . . . . .56Ua **110**
TW13: Felt 62W **128**
UB5: N'olt 40Z **65**
UB10: Hil 41R **84**
Parkfield Cl. HA8: Edg 23Ra **47**
UB5: N'olt 40Aa **65**
Parkfield Ct. *SE14 . . . . .53Bc 114*
(off Parkfield Rd.)
Parkfield Cres. HA2: Harr 26Ea **46**
HA4: Ruis 33Aa **65**
TW13: Felt 62W **128**
Parkfield Dr. UB5: N'olt 40Z **65**
Parkfield Gdns. HA2: Harr 27Da **45**
Parkfield Ho. HA2: Harr 25Da **45**
Parkfield Ind. Est. SW11 . . . . .54Jb **112**
Parkfield Pde. TW13: Felt 62W **128**
Parkfield Rd. HA2: Harr 34Ea **66**
NW10 . . . . .38Xa **68**
SE14 . . . . .53Bc **114**
SW4 . . . . .58Mb **112**
(not continuous)
TW13: Felt 62W **128**
UB5: N'olt 40Aa **65**
UB10: Ick 33R **64**
Parkfields CR0: C'don 74Bc **158**
KT22: Oxs 83Fa **172**
SW15 . . . . .56Ya **110**
Parkfields Av. NW9 . . . . .32Ta **67**
SW20 . . . . .67Xa **132**
Parkfields Cl. SM5: Cars 77Jb **156**
Parkfields Rd. KT2: King T 64Pa **131**
Parkfield St. N1 . . . . .1A **218** (40Qb **70**)
Parkfield Vw. EN6: Pot B 4Db **17**
Parkfield Way BR2: Brom 72Pc **160**
Park Gdns. DA8: Erith 49Fd **96**
E10 . . . . .32Cc **72**
KT2: King T 64Pa **131**
NW9 . . . . .27Ra **47**
Park Ga. N2 . . . . .27Fb **49**
N21 . . . . .17Pb **32**
W5 . . . . .43Ma **87**
Parkgate *N1 . . . . .39Tb 71*
(off Southgate Rd.)
SE3 . . . . .55Hc **115**
SL1: Burn 2A **80**
Parkgate Av. EN4: Had W 11Eb **31**
Parkgate Cl. KT2: King T 65Ra **131**
Park Ga. Ct. GU22: Wok 90A **168**
TW12: Hamp H 65Ea **130**
Parkgate Cres. EN4: Had W 11Eb **31**
Parkgate Gdns. SW14 . . . . .57Ta **109**
Parkgate M. N6 . . . . .31Lb **70**
Parkgate Rd. BR6: Well H 77Dd **162**
RH2: Reig 7K **207**
SM6: Wall 78Jb **156**
SW11 . . . . .52Gb **111**
WD24: Wat 9Y **13**
Park Gates HA2: Harr 35Ca **65**
Park Grange IG7: Chig 22Tc **54**
Park Grange Gdns. TN13: S'oaks 99Ld **203**
Park Grn. KT23: Bookh 96Ca **191**
Park Gro. BR1: Brom 67Kc **137**
DA7: Bex 56Ed **118**
E15 . . . . .39Jc **73**
HA8: Edg 22Pa **47**
HP8: Chal G 13A **24**
N11 . . . . .24Mb **50**
Park Gro. Rd. E11 . . . . .33Gc **73**
Park Hall *SE10 . . . . .52Fc 115*
(off Croom's Hill)
Park Hall Rd. N2 . . . . .28Gb **49**
RH2: Reig .4J **207**
SE21 . . . . .62Sb **135**
Park Hall Trad. Est. SE21 . . . . .62Sb **135**
Parkham Ct. BR2: Brom 68Gc **137**
Parkham Ho. *RH1: Redh 4B 208*
(off Reynolds Av.)
Parkham St. SW11 . . . . .53Gb **111**
Park Hgts. *GU22: Wok 90A 168*
(off Constitution Hill)
KT18: Eps 86Ta **173**
Park Hgts. Ct. *E14 . . . . .44Bc 92*
(off Wharf La.)
Park Hill BR1: Brom 70Nc **138**
DA13: Meop 10A **144**
IG10: Lough 15Mc **35**
SE23 . . . . .61Xb **135**
SM5: Cars 79Gb **155**
SW4 . . . . .57Mb **112**
TW10: Rich 58Pa **109**
W5 . . . . .43Ma **87**
Parkhill KT10: Esh 77Ea **152**
Park Hill Cl. SM5: Cars 78Gb **155**
Parkhill Cl. RM12: Horn 33Ld **77**
Park Hill Ct. SW17 . . . . .62Hb **133**
Park Hill Dr. KT11: Cobh 87Aa **171**
Park Hill M. CR2: S Croy 78Tb **157**
Park Hill Ri. CR0: C'don 75Ub **157**
Park Hill Rd. BR2: Brom 68Gc **137**
CR0: C'don 75Ub **157**
HP1: Hem H 2K **3**
KT17: Ewe 83Va **174**
SM6: Wall 80Kb **156**
TN14: Otf 89Nd **183**
Parkhill Rd. DA5: Bexl 59Bd **117**
DA14: Sidc 62Tc **138**
DA15: Sidc 62Tc **138**
E4 . . . . .18Ec **34**
NW3 . . . . .36Hb **69**
Parkhill Wlk. NW3 . . . . .36Hb **69**
Parkholme Rd. E8 . . . . .37Wb **71**
Park Homes AL2: Lon C 8G **6**
Park Ho. *E9 . . . . .38Yb 72*
(off Shore Rd.)
N21 . . . . .17Pb **32**
SE5 . . . . .53Tb 113
(off Camberwell Grn.)
TN13: S'oaks 94Ld **203**
W1 . . . . .3H **221**
Park Ho. Dr. RH2: Reig 8H **207**
Park Ho. Gdns. TW1: Twick 57La **108**
Park Ho. Pas. N6 . . . . .31Jb **70**
Parkhouse St. SE5 . . . . .52Tb **113**
Parkhurst KT19: Eps 82Sa **173**
Parkhurst Ct. N7 . . . . .35Nb **70**
Parkhurst Gdns. DA5: Bexl 59Cd **118**
Parkhurst Rd. DA5: Bexl 59Cd **118**
E12 . . . . .35Qc **74**
E17 . . . . .28Ac **52**
N7 . . . . .35Nb **70**
N11 . . . . .23Jb **50**
N17 . . . . .26Wb **51**
N22 . . . . .23Pb **50**
SM1: Sutt 77Fb **155**
Park Ind. Est. AL2: F'mre 9C **6**
Parkinson Ct. N1 . . . . .4G **219**
Parkinson Ho. *E9 . . . . .38Yb 72*
(off Frampton Pk. Rd.)
SW1 . . . . .6C **228**
Parkland Av. RM1: Rom 27Gd **56**
RM14: Upm 36Rd **77**
SL3: L'ly .9P **81**
Parkland Cl. IG7: Chig 20Sc **36**
TN13: S'oaks 100Ld **203**
Parkland Ct. *E15 . . . . .36Gc 73*
(off Maryland Pk.)
W14 . . . . .47Ab 88
(off Holland Pk. Av.)
Parkland Dr. AL3: St A 3N **5**
Parkland Gdns. SW19 . . . . .60Za **110**
Parkland Gro. TW15: Ashf 62Q **128**
Parkland Mead BR1: Brom 69Rc **138**
(not continuous)
Parkland M. BR7: Chst 66Tc **138**
Parkland Rd. IG8: Wfd G 24Kc **53**
N22 . . . . .26Pb **50**
TW15: Ashf 63Q **128**
Parklands CM16: Coop 1Zc **23**
(not continuous)
EN9: Walt A 4Fc **21**
IG7: Chig 20Sc **36**
KT5: Surb 71Pa **153**
KT15: Add 78L **149**
KT23: Bookh 95Ca **191**
N6 . . . . .31Kb **70**
RH1: Redh 4A **208**
RH8: Oxt .3J **211**
WD23: Bush 16Ea **28**
Parklands Cl. EN4: Had W 10Fb **17**
IG2: Ilf 31Sc **74**
SW14 . . . . .57Sa **109**
Parklands Ct. KT19: Eps 84Na **173**
TW5: Hest 54Z **107**
Parklands Dr. N3 . . . . .27Ab **48**
Parklands Gro. TW7: Isle 53Ha **108**
Parklands Pde. *TW5: Hest 54Z 107*
(off Parklands Ct.)
Parklands Rd. SW16 . . . . .64Kb **134**
Parklands Way KT4: Wor Pk 75Ua **154**
Parkland Walk Local Nature Reserve
. . . . .31Nb 70
Park La. AL4: Col H 5M **7**
BR8: Swan 68Ld **141**
CM13: Heron 24Fe **59**
CR0: C'don 76Tb **157**
CR5: Coul 93Mb **196**
CR6: W'ham 89Zb **178**
DA9: Ghithe 58Wd **120**
E15 . . . . .39Fc **73**
EN8: Walt C 5Yb **20**
HA2: Harr 34Da **65**
HA7: Stan 20Ja **28**
HA9: Wemb 36Na **67**
HP1: Hem H 3M **3**
HP2: Hem H 3M **3**
KT21: Asht 90Pa **173**
N9 . . . . .20Ub **33**
(not continuous)
N17 . . . . .24Vb **51**
(not continuous)
RH2: Reig 7G **206**
RM6: Chad H 30Zc **55**
RM11: Horn 30Hd **56**
RM12: Horn 37Kd **77**
RM15: Avel 46Td **98**
(not continuous)
SL1: Burn .3C **60**
SL3: Hort 55C **104**
SL3: Slou .8M **81**
SL4: Wink 10A **102**
SM3: Cheam 79Ab **154**
SM5: Cars 77Jb **156**
SM6: Wall 78Jb **156**
TN13: S'oaks 96Ld **203**
TN15: God G, Seal 93Qd **203**
TN15: Kems'g 90Qd **183**
TW5: Cran 52W **106**
TW9: Rich 56Ma **109**
TW11: Tedd 65Ha **130**
UB4: Hayes 43U **84**
UB9: Hare 25J **43**
W1 . . . . .4G **221** (45Hb **89**)
Park La. Cl. N17 . . . . .24Wb **51**
Park La. E. RH2: Reig 9H **207**
Park La. Mans. *CR0: C'don 76Tb 157*
(off Park La.)
PARK LANGLEY 70Ec 136
Parklangley Club, The 70Ec 136
Park Lawn SL2: Farn R 1G **80**
Parklawn Av. KT18: Eps 85Ra **173**
Park Lawn Rd. KT13: Weyb 77S **150**
Parklea Cl. NW9 . . . . .25Ua **48**
Park Lee Ct. N16 . . . . .31Ub **71**
Parkleigh Rd. SW19 . . . . .68Db **133**
Park Ley Rd. CR3: Wold 92Zb **198**
Parkleys TW10: Ham 63Ma **131**

Parkleys Pde.—Patrol Pl.

Parkleys Pde. TW10: Ham 63Ma **131**
Park Lodge NW8 . . . . .38Fb **69**
W14 . . . . .48Bb 89
(off Melbury Rd.)
Park Lodge Av. UB7: W Dray 47P **83**
Park Lofts *SW2 . . . . .57Nb 112*
(off Lyham Rd.)
Park Lorne NW8 . . . . .4E **214**
Park Mnr. *SM2: Sutt 80Eb 155*
(off Christchurch Pk.)
Park Mans. HA6: Nwood 19S **26**
NW4 .29Xa **48**
NW8 .2D **214**
SW1 . . . . .2F **227**
SW8 .51Nb **112**
SW11 . . . . .53Hb 111
(off Prince of Wales Dr.)
Park Mead DA15: Sidc 57Xc **117**
HA2: Harr 34Da **65**
Parkmead IG10: Lough 15Qc **36**
SW15 .58Xa **110**
Parkmead Cl. CR0: C'don 72Zb **158**
Parkmead Gdns. NW7 . . . . .23Va **48**
Park M. BR7: Chst 65Rc **138**
N8 . . . . .30Nb **50**
RH8: Oxt 100Hc **199**
RM13: Rain 37Jd **76**
RM15: Avel 46Td **98**
SE10 . . . . .50Hc **93**
SE24 .59Sb **113**
TW19: Stanw 59P **105**
W10 . . . . .40Ab **68**
Parkmore Cl. IG8: Wfd G 21Jc **53**
Pk. Nook Gdns. EN2: Enf 9Tb **19**
Park Pale DA12: Shorne 7M **145**
ME2: Strood 7M **145**
Pk. Pale Bri. ME2: Strood 7N **145**
Park Pde. NW10 . . . . .40Va **68**
UB3: Hayes 44U **84**
W3 . . . . .48Qa **87**
Park Piazza SE13 . . . . .58Fc **115**
Park Pl. AL2: Park 9B **6**
BR1: Brom 67Kc 137
(off Park Rd.)
DA12: Grav'nd 8E **122**
E14 . . . . .46Cc **92**
GU22: Wok 90B 168
(off Hill Vw. Rd.)
HA9: Wemb 35Pa **67**
N1 . . . . .38Tb 71
(off Downham Rd.)
SW1 . . . . .7B **222** (46Lb **90**)
TN13: Bes G 95Fd **202**
TW12: Hamp H 65Ea **130**
UB9: Hare 25L **43**
W3 . . . . .49Qa **87**
W5 . . . . .46Ma **87**
Park Pl. Dr. W3 . . . . .48Qa **87**
Park Pl. Vs. W2 . . . . .7A **214** (43Eb **89**)
Park Plaza EN8: Walt C 6Yb **20**
Park Ride SL4: Wind 9B **102**
Park Ridings N8 . . . . .27Qb **50**
Park Ri. HA3: Hrw W 25Ga **46**
KT22: Lea 93Ka **192**
SE23 . . . . .60Ac **114**
Park Ri. Cl. KT22: Lea 93Ka **192**
Park Ri. Rd. SE23 . . . . .60Ac **114**
Park Rd. BR1: Brom 67Kc **137**
BR3: Beck 66Bc **136**
BR5: St M Cry 71Yc **161**
BR7: Chst 65Rc **138**
BR8: Swan 70Hd **140**
CM14: B'wood 18Xd **40**
CR3: Cat'm 95Ub **197**
CR6: W'ham 86Gc **179**
CR8: Kenley 87Rb **177**
DA1: Dart 59Qd **119**
DA10: Swans 58Ae **121**
DA11: Grav'nd 10Dd **122**
E6 . . . . .39Lc **73**
E10 . . . . .32Cc **72**
E12 . . . . .32Kc **73**
E15 . . . . .39Jc **73**
E17 . . . . .29Bc **52**
EN3: Enf W 8Ac **20**
EN4: E Barn 14Fb **31**
EN5: Barn 14Bb **31**
EN6: N'thaw 2Jb **18**
EN8: Walt C 5Zb **20**
GU22: Wok 89B **168**
(not continuous)
HA0: Wemb 37Na **67**
HP1: Hem H 4L **3**
IG1: Ilf .34Tc **74**
KT1: Hamp W 67La **130**
KT2: King T 64Pa **131**
KT3: N Mald 70Ta **131**
KT5: Surb 72Pa **153**
KT8: E Mos 70Ea **130**
KT10: Esh 77Da **151**
KT21: Asht 90Na **173**
N2 . . . . .27Fb **49**
N8 . . . . .28Lb **50**
N11 . . . . .24Mb **50**
N14 . . . . .18Mb **32**
N15 . . . . .28Rb **51**
N18 . . . . .21Vb **51**
NW1 . . . . .4E **214** (42Hb **89**)
NW4 . . . . .31Wa **68**
NW8 . . . . .4E **214** (41Gb **89**)
NW9 . . . . .31Ta **67**
NW10 . . . . .39Ua **68**
RH1: Redh 4P **207**
(not continuous)
RH8: Oxt 100Hc **199**
RM17: Grays 50De **99**
SE25 . . . . .70Ub **135**
SL2: Farn R, Stoke P 10G **60**
SM3: Cheam 79Ab **154**
SM6: Wall 78Kb **156**
(Clifton Rd.)
SM6: Wall 75Kb **156**
(Elmwood Cl.)
SM7: Bans 87Db **175**
SS17: Stan H 2K **101**
SW19 . . . . .65Fb **133**
TW1: Twick 58La **108**
TW3: Houn 57Da **107**
TW7: Isle 53Ka **108**
TW10: Rich 58Pa **109**
TW11: Tedd 65Ha **130**
TW12: Hamp H 63Da **129**
TW13: Hanw 63Z **129**
TW15: Ashf 64R **128**
TW16: Sun 66X **129**
TW17: Shep 74Q **150**
TW19: Stanw, Stanw M 58K **105**
TW20: Egh 63C **126**
Park Rd. UB4: Hayes 43U **84**
UB8: Uxb 38N **63**
W4 . . . . .52Sa **109**
W7 . . . . .45Ha **86**
WD3: Rick 17M **25**
WD7: R'lett 7Ja **14**
WD17: Wat 11W **26**
WD23: Bush 16Ca **27**
Park Rd. E. UB10: Uxb 40M **63**
W3 . . . . .47Ra **87**
Park Rd. Ho.
KT2: King T 66Qa **131**
Park Rd. Ind. Est.
BR8: Swan 69Hd **140**
Pk. Road Leisure Cen. 29Mb **50**
Park Rd. Nth. W3 . . . . .47Ra **87**
W4 . . . . .50Ta **87**
Park Row SE10 . . . . .51Fc **115**
SW2 . . . . .58Qb **112**
PARK ROYAL 41Ra **87**
Park Royal NW10 . . . . .41Qa **87**
PARK ROYAL JUNC. 39Qa **67**
Park Royal Metro Cen.
NW10 . . . . .42Ra **87**
Pk. Royal Rd. NW10 . . . . .41Sa **87**
W3 . . . . .41Sa **87**
Pk. St James NW8 . . . . .1F **215**
Parkshot TW9: Rich 56Ma **109**
Park Side CM16: Epp 1Xc **23**
NW2 . . . . .34Wa **68**
Parkside DA14: Sidc 61Xc **139**
EN6: Pot B 4Eb **17**
EN8: Walt C 6Ac **20**
HP3: Hem H 9A **4**
IG9: Buck H 19Kc **35**
KT15: New H 83K **169**
N3 . . . . .25Db **49**
NW7 . . . . .23Wa **48**
RM16: Grays 48Fe **99**
SE3 . . . . .52Hc **115**
SL9: Ger X 29B **42**
SM3: Cheam 79Ab **154**
SW1 . . . . .1G **227**
SW19 . . . . .62Za **132**
TN14: Hals 85Bd **181**
TW12: Hamp H 64Fa **130**
UB3: Hayes 45U **84**
W3 . . . . .46Ua **88**
W5 . . . . .45Na **87**
WD19: Wat 16Y **27**
Parkside Av. BR1: Brom 70Nc **138**
DA7: Bex 54Fd **118**
RM1: Rom 27Fd **56**
RM18: Tilb 4D **122**
(not continuous)
SE10 . . . . .53Ec **114**
SW19 . . . . .64Za **132**
Parkside Bus. Est. SE8 . . . . .51Ac **114**
Parkside Cl. KT24: E Hor 97V **190**
SE20 . . . . .66Yb **136**
Parkside Ct. *E11 . . . . .30Jc 53*
(off Wanstead Pl.)
E16 . . . . .47Lc 93
(off Booth Rd.)
KT13: Weyb 77Q **150**
N22 . . . . .23Pb **50**
RH1: Redh 2P **207**
Parkside Cres. KT5: Surb 72Sa **153**
N7 . . . . .34Qb **70**
Parkside Cross DA7: Bex 54Gd **118**
Parkside Dr. HA8: Edg 20Qa **29**
WD17: Wat 12U **26**
Parkside Est. E9 . . . . .39Yb **72**
(not continuous)
Parkside Gdns. CR5: Coul 89Kb **176**
EN4: E Barn 18Hb **31**
SW19 . . . . .63Za **132**
Parkside Ho. RM10: Dag 34Ed **76**
Parkside Lodge
DA17: Belv 50Ed **96**
SL3: Slou 8L 81
(off Upton Ct. Rd.)
Parkside M. CR6: W'ham 88Cc **178**
Parkside Pde. *DA1: Erith 54Hd 118*
(off Northend Rd.)
Parkside Pl. KT24: E Hor 97V **190**
TW18: Staines 65J **127**
Parkside Rd. DA17: Belv 49Dd **96**
HA6: Nwood 22V **44**
SL5: S'dale 1E **146**
SW11 . . . . .53Jb **112**
TW3: Houn 57Da **107**
Parkside Sq. E14 . . . . .47Ec **92**
SE10 . . . . .53Ec **114**
Parkside Ter. *BR6: Farnb 76Rc 160*
(off Willow Wlk.)
N18 . . . . .21Tb **51**
Parkside Wlk. SL1: Slou 8L **81**
Parkside Way HA2: Harr 28Da **45**
Parks Info. Cen. 6E **220** (46Gb **89**)
Park Sth. *SW11 . . . . .53Jb 112*
(off Austin Rd.)
Park Sq. KT10: Esh 77Da **151**
RM4: Abr 16Zc **37**
Park Sq. E. NW1 . . . . .5K **215** (42Kb **90**)
Park Sq. M.
NW1 . . . . .6K **215** (42Kb **90**)
Park Sq. W. NW1 . . . . .5K **215** (42Kb **90**)
Parkstead Rd. SW15 . . . . .57Wa **110**
Park Steps W2 . . . . .4E **220**
Parkstone Av. N18 . . . . .23Vb **51**
RM11: Horn 30Nd **57**
Parkstone Rd. E17 . . . . .27Ec **52**
SE15 . . . . .54Wb **113**
PARK STREET 8B **6**
Park St. AL2: Park 8B **6**
CR0: C'don 75Sb **157**
SE1 . . . . .6D **224** (46Sb **91**)
SL1: Slou .8K **81**
SL3: Coln 53F **104**
SL4: Wind 3H **103**
SW6 . . . . .53Eb **111**
TW11: Tedd 65Ga **130**
W1 . . . . .4H **221** (45Jb **90**)
Park St. La. AL2: Park 2Da **13**
Park Ter. DA9: Ghithe 57Yd **120**
EN3: Enf H 10Ac **20**
KT4: Wor Pk 74Wa **154**
SM5: Cars 76Gb **155**
TN14: Sund 96Zc **201**
WD25: Wat 5Z **13**
Park Theatre 33Qb **70**
Parkthorne Cl. HA2: Harr 30Da **45**
Parkthorne Dr. HA2: Harr 30Ca **45**
Parkthorne Rd. SW12 . . . . .59Mb **112**
Park Towers W1 . . . . .7K **221**
Park Va. Ct.
CM14: B'wood 18Yd **40**
Park Vw. BR6: Orp 73Xc **161**
CR3: Cat'm 97Wb **197**
DA10: Swans 59Be **121**
EN6: Pot B 5Eb **17**
(not continuous)
HA5: Hat E 25Ba **45**
HA9: Wemb 36Ra **67**
KT3: N Mald 69Va **132**
KT12: Hers 78Y **151**
KT15: Add 78L 149
(off Bourne Way)
KT23: Bookh 97Ca **191**
N5 . . . . .35Sb **71**
N21 . . . . .17Pb **32**
RM6: Chad H 30Zc **55**
RM15: Avel 46Td **98**
SE8 . . . . .50Zb 92
(off Trundleys Rd.)
TN13: S'oaks 96Ld **203**
TN15: Hod S 81Ee **185**
UB7: Yiew 45N **83**
W3 . . . . .43Sa **87**
Parkview DA18: Erith 48Zc **95**
UB6: G'frd 41Ja 86
(off Perivale La.)
WD25: Wat 4Aa **13**
Pk. View Academy Sports Cen. 28Sb **51**
Park Vw. Apartments *SE16 . . . . . . .48Xb 91*
(off Banyard Rd.)
Parkview Apartments *E14 . . . . .44Dc 92*
(off Chrisp St.)
Parkview Chase SL1: Slou 4C **80**
Park Vw. Cl. AL1: St A 3E **6**
Parkview Cl. SM5: Cars 80Hb **155**
Park Vw. Ct. E3 . . . . .43Cc **92**
GU22: Wok 91B **188**
N12 . . . . .21Gb **49**
SE12 . . . . .62Lc **137**
SE20 . . . . .67Xb **135**
Parkview Ct. HA3: Hrw W 24Ga **46**
IG2: Ilf 30Uc **54**
SW6 . . . . .54Ab **110**
SW18 . . . . .58Cb **111**
Park Vw. Cres. N11 . . . . .21Kb **50**
Parkview Cres. KT4: Wor Pk 73Ya **154**
Park Vw. Dr. CR4: Mitc 68Fb **133**
Park Vw. Est. E2 . . . . .40Zb **72**
Park Vw. Gdns. IG4: Ilf 28Pc **54**
N22 . . . . .25Qb **50**
NW4 . . . . .29Ya **48**
RM17: Grays 50De **99**
Park Vw. Ho. E4 . . . . .22Cc **52**
SE24 . . . . .58Rb 113
(off Hurst St.)
Parkview Ho. N9 . . . . .17Xb **33**
RM12: Horn 33Kd **77**
WD19: Wat 16Z **27**
Park Vw. Mans. *E20 . . . . .36Dc 72*
(off Olympic Pk. Av.)
N4 . . . . .30Rb **51**
Park Vw. M. SW9 . . . . .54Pb **112**
Parkview M. RM13: Rain 43Kd **97**
Park View Road 55Yc **117**
Park Vw. Rd. CR3: Wold 94Ac **198**
DA16: Well 55Yc **117**
HA5: Pinn 24X **45**
KT22: Lea 92Ha **192**
N3 . . . . .25Db **49**
N17 . . . . .27Wb **51**
NW10 . . . . .35Va **68**
UB1: S'hall 46Ca **85**
UB8: Hil .44P **83**
W5 . . . . .43Na **87**
Parkview Rd. CR0: C'don 74Wb **157**
SE9 . . . . .60Rc **116**
Parkview Way KT19: Eps 82Ta **173**
Pk. Village E. NW1 . . . . . . .1K **215** (40Kb **70**)
Pk. Village W. NW1 . . . . . . .1K **215** (40Kb **70**)
Park Vs. RM6: Chad H 30Zc **55**
Parkville Rd. SW6 . . . . .52Bb **111**
Park Vista SE10 . . . . .51Fc **115**
Park Wlk. EN4: Cockf 13Fb **31**
IG1: Ilf .33Rc 74
(within The Exchange)
KT21: Asht 91Pa **193**
N6 . . . . .31Jb **70**
SE10 . . . . .52Fc **115**
SW10 . . . . .51Eb **111**
Park Way CM15: Shenf 18Be **41**
DA5: Bexl 62Gd **140**
EN2: Enf 12Qb **32**
HA4: Ruis 32W **64**
HA8: Edg 25Ra **47**
KT8: W Mole 69Da **129**
KT23: Bookh 95Ca **191**
N20 . . . . .21Hb **49**
NW11 . . . . .29Ab **48**
TW14: Felt 59X **107**
W3 . . . . .48Qa **87**
WD3: Rick 18L **25**
Parkway CR0: New Ad 81Dc **178**
DA18: Erith 48Ad **95**
IG3: Ilf .34Vc **75**
IG8: Wfd G 22Lc **53**
KT13: Weyb 77T **150**
N14 . . . . .19Nb **32**
NW1 . . . . .1K **215** (39Kb **70**)
RM2: Rom 26Hd **56**
RM13: Rain 42Jd **96**
RM16: Ors 3C **100**
SW20 . . . . .70Za **132**
UB10: Hil 38Q **64**
Parkway, The SL0: Iver H 40E **62**
TW4: Cran 54X **107**
TW5: Cran 50W **84**
UB2: S'hall 50W **84**
UB3: Hayes 48X **85**
UB4: Yead 44Y **85**
UB5: N'olt 40Z **65**
Pk. Way Ct. HA4: Ruis 32V **64**
Parkway Ct. AL1: St A 5F **6**
Parkway Cres. E15 . . . . .36Ec **72**
Parkway Trad. Est. TW5: Hest 51Y **107**
Park W. W2 . . . . .2E **220**
Park W. Bldg. E3 . . . . .40Cc **72**
Park W. Pl. W2 . . . . .2E **220** (44Gb **89**)
Park Wharf *SE8 . . . . .50Ac 92*
(off Evelyn St.)
Parkwood BR3: Beck 66Cc **136**
CM15: Dodd 11Zd **41**
N20 . . . . .20Jb **32**
NW8 . . . . .1F **215**
Parkwood Av. KT10: Esh 74Ea **152**
Parkwood Cl. KT22: Fet 95Ea **192**
SM7: Bans 87Za **174**
Pk. Wood Ct. HA4: Ruis 28S **44**
Parkwood Dr. HP1: Hem H 2H **3**
Parkwood Flats N20 . . . . .20Hb **31**
Park Wood Golf Course 94Nc **200**
Parkwood Gro. TW16: Sun 69W **128**
Parkwood Health & Fitness Cen. 3Cb **17**
Parkwood M. N6 . . . . .30Kb **50**
Parkwood Rd. DA5: Bexl 59Bd **117**
RH1: Nutf 5E **208**
SM7: Bans 87Za **174**
SW19 . . . . .64Bb **133**
TN16: Tats 93Nc **200**
TW7: Isle 53Ha **108**
Parkwood Vw. SM7: Bans 88Ya **174**
Pk. Works Rd. RH1: Nutf 5F **208**
Parlaunt Rd. SL3: L'ly 49C **82**
Parley Dr. GU21: Wok 9N **167**
Parliament Ct. E1 . . . . .1J **225**
Parliament Hill 34Hb **69**
Parliament Hill NW3 . . . . .35Gb **69**
Parliament Hill Fields 34Jb **70**
Parliament Hill Lido 35Jb **70**
Parliament Hill Mans. NW5 . . . . .35Jb **70**
Parliament M. SW14 . . . . .54Sa **109**
Parliament Sq. SW1 . . . . .2F **229** (47Nb **90**)
Parliament St. SW1 . . . . . .2F **229** (47Nb **90**)
Parliament Vw. SE1 . . . . .5H **229** (49Pb **90**)
Parma Cres. SW11 . . . . .56Hb **111**
Parmiter St. E2 . . . . .40Xb **71**
Parmoor Ct. EC1 . . . . .5D **218**
Parndon Ho. IG10: Lough 17Nc **36**
Parnell Cl. HA8: Edg 21Ra **47**
RM16: Chaf H 50Yd **98**
W12 . . . . .48Xa **88**
WD5: Ab L 2V **12**
Parnell Gdns. KT13: Weyb 83Q **170**
Parnell Ho. WC1 . . . . .2E **222** (43Mb **90**)
Parnelli Ho. *N1 . . . . .37Rb 71*
(off Canonbury Rd.)
Parnell Rd. E3 . . . . .39Bc **72**
Parnell Way HA3: Stan 25Ka **46**
Parnham Av. GU18: Light 3B **166**
Parnham Cl. BR1: Brom 69Rc **138**
Parnham St. E14 . . . . .44Ac **92**
(not continuous)
Parolles Rd. N19 . . . . .32Lb **70**
Paroma Rd. DA17: Belv 49Cd **96**
Parpins WD4: K Lan 10N **3**
Parr Av. KT17: Ewe 81Xa **174**
Parr Cl. KT22: Lea 92Ha **192**
N9 . . . . .21Xb **51**
N18 . . . . .21Xb **51**
RM16: Chaf H 49Yd **98**
Parr Ct. *GU21: Knap 1G 186*
(off Tudor Way)
N1 . . . . .1F **219**
TW13: Hanw 63Y **129**
Parr Ho. *E16 . . . . .46Kc 93*
(off Beaulieu Av.)
Parrington Ho. SW4 . . . . .58Mb **112**
Parritt Rd. RH1: Redh 4B **208**
Parrock, The DA12: Grav'nd 10E **122**
Parrock Av. DA12: Grav'nd 10E **122**
PARROCK FARM 2F **144**
Parrock Rd. DA12: Grav'nd 8D **122**
Parrock St. DA12: Grav'nd 8D **122**
Parrotts Cl. WD3: Crox G 14Q **26**
Parr Rd. E6 . . . . .39Mc **73**
HA7: Stan 25Ma **47**
Parrs Cl. CR2: Sande 81Tb **177**
Parrs Pl. TW12: Hamp 66Ca **129**
Parr St. N1 . . . . .1F **219** (40Tb **71**)
Parrs Way W6 . . . . .51Ya **110**
Parry Av. E6 . . . . .44Pc **94**
Parry Cl. KT17: Ewe 80Xa **154**
SS17: Stan H 1M **101**
Parry Cotts. *SL9: Chal P 21A 42*
(off Chesham La.)
Parry Dr. KT13: Weyb 82Q **170**
Parry Grn. Nth. SL3: L'ly 49B **82**
Parry Grn. Sth. SL3: L'ly 49C **82**
Parry Ho. *E1 . . . . .46Xb 91*
(off Green Bank)
Parry Pl. SE18 . . . . .49Rc **94**
Parry Rd. SE25 . . . . .69Ub **135**
W10 . . . . .41Ab **88**
Parry St. SW8 . . . . .51Nb **112**
Parsifal Rd. NW6 . . . . .36Cb **69**
Parsley Gdns. CR0: C'don 74Zb **158**
Parsloes Av. RM9: Dag 35Zc **75**
Parsonage Bank *DA4: Eyns 75Nd 163*
(off Edwards Ct.)
Parsonage Cl. CR6: W'ham 88Bc **178**
UB3: Hayes 44V **84**
WD5: Ab L 2U **12**
Parsonage Ct. IG10: Lough 13Rc **36**
Parsonage Farm WD3: Rick 17L **25**
Parsonage Gdns. EN2: Enf 12Sb **33**
Parsonage La. AL9: Wel G 5D **8**
DA2: Sut H 65Rd **141**
DA4: Sut H 65Rd **141**
DA14: Sidc 63Bd **139**
EN1: Enf 12Sb **33**
EN2: Enf 12Sb **33**
SL2: Farn C, Farn R 7G **60**
SL4: Wind 3E **102**
Parsonage Manorway
DA17: Belv 51Cd **118**
Parsonage Rd. AL9: Wel G 5D **8**
RM13: Rain 40Ld **77**
RM20: Grays 51Yd **120**
TW20: Eng G 4P **125**
WD3: Rick 17M **25**
Parsonage St. E14 . . . . .49Ec **92**
Parsons Cl. DA3: Lfield 69Be **143**
SM1: Sutt 76Db **155**
Parsons Ct. WD18: Wat 16W **26**
Parson's Cres. HA8: Edg 20Qa **29**
Parsonsfield Cl. SM7: Bans 87Za **174**
Parsonsfield Rd. SM7: Bans 88Za **174**
Parsons Ga. M. SW6 . . . . .54Cb **111**
PARSONS GREEN 54Bb **111**
Parson's Grn. SW6 . . . . .53Cb **111**
Parson's Grn. La. SW6 . . . . .53Cb **111**
Parson's Gro. HA8: Edg 20Qa **29**
Parsons Hill *SE18 . . . . .48Qc 94*
(off Powis St.)
Parsons Ho. W2 . . . . .6B **214**
Parsons La. DA2: Wilm 62Kd **141**
TN15: Stans 82Ae **185**
Parsons Lodge *NW6 . . . . .38Db 69*
(off Priory Rd.)
Parson's Mead CR0: C'don 74Rb **157**
Parsons Mead KT8: E Mos 69Ea **130**
Parsons M. SW18 . . . . .57Eb **111**
Parson's Rd. E13 . . . . .40Lc **73**
Parsons Rd. SL3: L'ly 50B **82**
Parson St. NW4 . . . . .28Ya **48**
Parson's Wood La. SL2: Farn C 8H **61**
Parthenia Dr. TW7: Isle 55Ja **108**
Parthenia Rd. SW6 . . . . .53Cb **111**
Parthia Cl. KT20: Tad 91Xa **194**
Partingdale La. NW7 . . . . .22Za **48**
Partington Cl. N19 . . . . .32Mb **70**
Partridge Cl. E16 . . . . .43Mc **93**
EN5: Barn 16Ya **30**
HA7: Stan 21Na **47**
UB10: Uxb 39P **63**
WD23: Bush 18Ea **28**
Partridge Ct. EC1 . . . . .5B **218**
Partridge Dr. BR6: Farnb 76Sc **160**
Partridge Grn. SE9 . . . . .62Qc **138**
Partridge Ho. *E3 . . . . .40Bc 72*
(off Stafford Rd.)
Partridge Knoll CR8: Purl 84Rb **177**
Partridge La. RM3: Hrld W 26Nd **57**
Partridge Mead SM7: Bans 87Ya **174**
Partridge Rd. DA14: Sidc 62Uc **138**
TW12: Hamp 65Ba **129**
Partridges, The HP3: Hem H 4A **4**
Partridge Sq. E6 . . . . .43Nc **94**
Partridge Way N22 . . . . .25Nb **50**
Parvills EN9: Walt A 4Fc **21**
Parvis Rd. KT14: W Byf, Byfl 85K **169**
Pasadena Cl. UB3: Hayes 47W **84**
Pasadena Cl. Trad. Est.
UB3: Hayes 47X **85**
Pasadena Pk. TN15: Knat 82Rd **183**
Pascall Ho. *SE17 . . . . .51Sb 113*
(off Draco St.)
Pascal M. SE19 . . . . .66Wb **135**
Pascal Rd. UB1: S'hall 44Da **85**
Pascal St. SW8 . . . . .52Mb **112**
Pascoe Rd. SE13 . . . . .57Fc **115**
Pasfield Cl. EN9: Walt A 5Fc **21**
Pasley Cl. SE17 . . . . .7D **230** (50Rb **91**)
Pasquier Rd. E17 . . . . .27Ac **52**
Passage, The TW9: Rich 57Na **109**
Passey Pl. SE9 . . . . .58Pc **116**
Passfield Dr. E14 . . . . .43Dc **92**
Passfield Hall WC1 . . . . .5E **216**
Passfield Path SE28 . . . . .45Xc **95**
Passfields SE6 . . . . .62Dc **136**
W14 . . . . .50Bb 89
(off Star Rd.)
Passing All. EC1 . . . . .6C **218**
PASSINGFORD BRIDGE 12Ed **38**
Passingham Ho. TW5: Hest 51Ca **107**
Passive Cl. RM13: Rain 42Hd **96**
Passmore Ct. *E14 . . . . .44Cc 92*
(off New Festival Av.)
Passmore Edwards Ho. N11 . . . . . . .23Mb **50**
SL9: Chal P 22A **42**
Passmore Gdns. N11 . . . . .23Mb **50**
Passmore Ho. E2 . . . . .1K **219**
Passmore St. SW1 . . . . . . .6H **227** (50Jb **90**)
Pastel Ct. *E1 . . . . .43Zb 92*
(off Shandy St.)
Pastens Rd. RH8: Limp 3N **211**
Pasteur Cl. NW9 . . . . .26Ua **48**
Pasteur Ct. HA1: Harr 32Ka **66**
Pasteur Dr. RM3: Hrld W 26Md **57**
Pasteur Gdns. N18 . . . . .22Rb **51**
Paston Cl. E5 . . . . .34Zb **72**
SM6: Wall 76Lb **156**
Paston Cres. SE12 . . . . .59Kc **115**
Pastoral Way CM14: W'ley 22Xd **58**
Pastor Ct. N6 . . . . .30Lb **50**
Pastor St. SE11 . . . . .5C **230** (49Rb **91**)
Pasture Cl. HA0: Wemb 34Ka **66**
WD23: Bush 17Ea **28**
Pasture Rd. HA0: Wemb 33Ka **66**
RM9: Dag 36Bd **75**
SE6 . . . . .60Hc **115**
Pastures, The AL2: Chis G 6N **5**
AL10: Hat 1D **8**
HP1: Hem H 1G **2**
N20 . . . . .18Bb **31**
WD19: Wat 17Y **27**
Pastures Mead UB10: Hil 37Q **64**
Pastures Path E11 . . . . .32Hc **73**
Pasture Vw. AL4: S'ford 1L **7**
Patch, The TN13: Riv 94Gd **202**
Patcham Ter. SW8 . . . . .53Kb **112**
Patch Cl. UB10: Uxb 39P **63**
PATCHETTS GREEN 11Ea **28**
Patching Way UB4: Yead 43Aa **85**
Patent Ho. *E14 . . . . .43Dc 92*
(off Morris Rd.)
Paternoster Cl. EN9: Walt A 5Hc **21**
Paternoster Hill EN9: Walt A 4Hc **21**
Paternoster La. EC4 . . . . . .3C **224** (44Rb **91**)
Paternoster Row EC4 . . . . .3D **224** (44Sb **91**)
RM4: Noak H 18Ld **39**
Paternoster Sq. EC4 . . . . . .3C **224** (44Rb **91**)
Paterson Ct. EC1 . . . . .4F **219**
Paterson Rd. TW15: Ashf 64M **127**
Pater St. W8 . . . . .48Cb **89**
Pates Mnr. Dr. TW14: Bedf 59T **106**
Path, The SW19 . . . . .67Db **133**
Pathfield Rd. SW16 . . . . .65Mb **134**
Pathway, The GU23: Send 97H **189**
WD7: R'lett 8Ha **14**
WD19: Wat 18Z **27**
Patience Rd. SW11 . . . . .54Gb **111**
Patina Mans. *E20 . . . . .36Ec 72*
(off Mirabelle Gdns.)
Patio Cl. SW4 . . . . .58Mb **112**
Pat Larner Ho. *AL1: St A 3B 6*
(off Belmont Hill)
Patmore Est. SW8 . . . . .53Lb **112**
Patmore Ho. N16 . . . . .36Ub **71**
Patmore La. KT12: Hers 79V **150**
Patmore Link Rd. HP2: Hem H 2C **4**
Patmore Rd. EN9: Walt A 6Gc **21**
Patmore St. SW8 . . . . .53Lb **112**
Patmore Way RM5: Col R 22Dd **56**
Patmos Lodge *SW9 . . . . .53Rb 113*
(off Elliott Rd.)
Patmos Rd. SW9 . . . . .52Rb **113**
Paton Cl. E3 . . . . .41Cc **92**
Paton Ho. *SW9 . . . . .54Pb 112*
(off Stockwell Rd.)
Paton St. EC1 . . . . .4D **218** (41Sb **91**)
Patricia Cl. SL1: Slou 5C **80**
Patricia Ct. BR7: Chst 67Tc **138**
DA16: Well 52Xc **117**
Patricia Dr. RM11: Horn 32Nd **77**
Patricia Gdns. SM2: Sutt 83Cb **175**
Patrick Coman Ho. EC1 . . . . .4B **218**
Patrick Connolly Gdns. E3 . . . . .41Dc **92**
Patrick Ct. SE1 . . . . .2C **230**
Patrick Cres. RM8: Dag 32Ad **75**
Patrick Gro. EN9: Walt A 5Dc **20**
Patrick Pas. SW11 . . . . .54Gb **111**
Patrick Rd. E13 . . . . .41Lc **93**
Patrington Cl. UB8: Cowl 41L **83**
Patriot Sq. E2 . . . . .40Xb **71**
Patrol Pl. SE6 . . . . .58Dc **114**

Patroni Ct.—Pembury Pl.

Patroni Ct. *E15* ... 41Gc **93**
(off Durban Rd.)
Patrons Way E. UB9: Den ... 30H **43**
Patrons Way W. UB9: Den ... 29H **43**
Pat Shaw Ho. *E1* ... 42Zb **92**
(off Globe Rd.)
Patshull Pl. NW5 ... 37Lb **70**
Patshull Rd. NW5 ... 37Lb **70**
Patten All. TW10: Rich ... 57Ma **109**
Pattenden Rd. SE6 ... 60Bc **114**
Patten Ho. N4 ... 32Sb **71**
Patten Rd. SW18 ... 59Gb **111**
Patterdale NW1 ... 4A **216**
Patterdale Cl.
BR1: Brom ... 65Hc **137**
Patterdale Rd.
DA2: Dart ... 60Td **120**
SE15 ... 52Yb **114**
Pattern Ho. EC1 ... 5B **218** (42Rb **91**)
Patterson Ct. DA1: Dart ... 57Qd **119**
SE19 ... 66Vb **135**
Patterson Rd. SE19 ... 65Vb **135**
Pattina Wlk. *SE16* ... 46Ac **92**
(off Silver Wlk.)
Pattison Ho. *E1* ... 44Zb **92**
(off Wellesley St.)
SE1 ... 1E **230**
Pattison Rd. NW2 ... 34Cb **69**
Pattison Wlk. SE18 ... 50Sc **94**
Paul Byrne Ho. N2 ... 27Eb **49**
Paul Cl. E15 ... 39Gc **73**
Paul Ct. *N18* ... 21Wb **51**
(off Fairfield Rd.)
RM7: Rom ... 29Ed **56**
TW20: Egh ... 65F **126**
Paul Daisley Ct. *NW6* ... 38Ab **68**
(off Christchurch Av.)
Paulet Rd. SE5 ... 54Rb **113**
Paulet Way NW10 ... 38Ua **68**
Paul Gdns. CR0: C'don ... 75Vb **157**
Paul Greengrass Cinema
DA12: Grav'nd ... 9D **122**
(off Woodville Pl.)
Paulhan Rd. HA3: Kenton ... 28Ma **47**
Paul Ho. *W10* ... 42Ab **88**
(off Ladbroke Gro.)
Paulin Dr. N21 ... 17Qb **32**
Pauline Cres.
TW2: Whitt ... 60Ea **108**
Pauline Ho. *E1* ... 43Wb **91**
(off Old Montague St.)
Paulinus Cl. BR5: St P ... 68Yc **139**
Paul Julius Cl. E14 ... 45Fc **93**
Paul Robeson Cl. E6 ... 41Qc **94**
Paul Robeson Ho. WC1 ... 2J **217**
Paul Robeson Theatre, The ... 55Da **107**
Pauls Grn. EN8: Walt C ... 5Ac **20**
Paul's Nursery Rd.
IG10: H Beech ... 11Kc **35**
Paul's Pl. KT21: Asht ... 91Ra **193**
Paul St. E15 ... 39Gc **73**
EC2 ... 6G **219** (42Tb **91**)
Paul's Wlk. EC4 ... 4C **224** (45Sb **91**)
Paultons Ho. *SW3* ... 51Fb **111**
(off Paultons Sq.)
Paultons Sq. SW3 ... 51Fb **111**
Paultons St. SW3 ... 51Fb **111**
Paul Vanson Ct.
KT12: Hers ... 79Z **151**
Pauntley St. N19 ... 32Lb **70**
Pavan Ct. *E2* ... 41Yb **92**
(off Sceptre Rd.)
Paved Ct. TW9: Rich ... 57Ma **109**
Paveley Ct. *NW7* ... 24Ab **48**
(off Langstone Way)
Paveley Dr. SW11 ... 52Gb **111**
Paveley Ho. N1 ... 2H **217**
Paveley St. NW8 ... 4D **214** (41Gb **89**)
Pavement, The *E11* ... 32Ec **72**
(off Hainault Rd.)
SW4 ... 56Lb **112**
SW19 ... 65Bb **133**
(off Worple Rd.)
TW7: Isle ... 55Ja **108**
(off South St.)
TW11: Tedd ... 66Ka **130**
W5 ... 48Na **87**
Pavement M. RM6: Chad H ... 31Zc **75**
Pavement Sq. CR0: C'don ... 74Wb **157**
Pavet Cl. RM10: Dag ... 37Dd **76**
Pavilion, The KT20: Kgswd ... 95Eb **195**
RH2: Reig ... 4N **207**
SW8 ... 52Mb **112**
Pavilion Apartments
NW8 ... 4C **214** (41Fb **89**)
Pavilion Ct. *NW6* ... 41Cb **89**
(off Stafford Rd.)
Pavilion Gdns. TN13: S'oaks ... 96Kd **203**
TW18: Staines ... 66K **127**
Pavilion La. BR3: Beck ... 65Bc **136**
Pavilion Leisure Cen. ... 68Jc **137**
Pavilion Lodge HA2: Harr ... 32Fa **66**
Pavilion M. N3 ... 27Cb **49**
Pavilion Pde. *W12* ... 44Ya **88**
(off Wood La.)
Pavilion Rd. IG1: Ilf ... 31Pc **74**
SW1 ... 2G **227** (48Hb **89**)
SW3 ... 49Hb **89**
Pavilions, The EN3: Enf L ... 8Bc **20**
KT14: Byfl ... 83M **169**
SL4: Wind ... 3F **102**
UB8: Uxb ... 38L **63**
Pavilion Sports & Fitness Club, The
... 69Ea **130**
Pavilion Sq. SW17 ... 62Hb **133**
Pavilions Shop. Cen. EN8: Walt C ... 5Ac **20**
Pavilion St. E13 ... 40Lc **73**
SW1 ... 4G **227** (48Hb **89**)
Pavilion Ter. IG2: Ilf ... 29Uc **54**
W12 ... 44Ya **88**
(off Wood La.)
Pavilion Way HA4: Ruis ... 33Y **65**
HA8: Edg ... 24Ra **47**
SE10 ... 47Gc **93**
Pavillion Ho. *SE16* ... 47Zb **92**
(off Water Gdns. Sq.)
Pavillion M. *N4* ... 33Pb **70**
(off Tollington Pl.)
Pawleyne Cl. SE20 ... 66Yb **136**
Pawsey Cl. E13 ... 39Kc **73**
Pawsons Rd.
CR0: C'don ... 72Sb **157**
Paxfold HA7: Stan ... 22Ma **47**
Paxford Rd.
HA0: Wemb ... 33Ka **66**
Paxton Av. SL1: Slou ... 8G **80**
Paxton Cl. KT12: Walt T ... 73Y **151**
TW9: Kew ... 54Pa **109**
Paxton Ct. *CR4: Mitc* ... 68Hb **133**
(off Armfield Cres.)
N7 ... 37Qb **70**
(off Westbourne Rd.)
SE12 ... 62Lc **137**
SE26 ... 63Ac **136**
(off Adamsrill Rd.)
WD6: Bore ... 14Sa **29**
Paxton Gdns. GU21: Wok ... 84F **168**
Paxton Gro. CR5: Coul ... 88Lb **176**
Paxton Ho. SE17 ... 7E **230**
Paxton M. *SE19* ... 66Ub **135**
(off Westow St.)
Paxton Pl. SE27 ... 63Ub **135**
Paxton Point SE10 ... 52Dc **114**
Paxton Rd. AL1: St A ... 3C **6**
BR1: Brom ... 66Jc **137**
HP4: Berk ... 1A **2**
N17 ... 24Vb **51**
SE23 ... 62Ac **136**
W4 ... 51Ua **110**
Paxton Ter. SW1 ... 51Kb **112**
Paymal Ho. *E1* ... 43Yb **92**
(off Stepney Way)
Payne Cl. IG11: Bark ... 38Uc **74**
Payne Ho. N1 ... 1J **217**
Paynell Ct. SE3 ... 55Gc **115**
Payne Rd. E3 ... 40Dc **72**
Paynes Cotts. TN13: Dun G ... 90Fd **182**
Paynesfield Av. SW14 ... 55Ta **109**
Paynesfield Rd.
TN16: Tats ... 93Lc **199**
(not continuous)
WD23: B Hea ... 17Ha **28**
Payne St. SE8 ... 52Bc **114**
Paynes Wlk. W6 ... 51Ab **110**
Paynetts Ct. KT13: Weyb ... 78T **150**
Payzes Gdns. IG8: Wfd G ... 23Hc **53**
Peaberry Ct. NW4 ... 27Wa **48**
Peabody Av. SW1 ... 7K **227** (50Kb **90**)
Peabody Bldgs. *E1* ... 45Wb **91**
(off John Fisher St.)
EC1 ... 6E **218**
SW3 ... 51Gb **111**
(off Cheyne Row)
Peabody Cl. CR0: C'don ... 74Yb **158**
SE10 ... 53Dc **114**
SW1 ... 50Kb **90**
Peabody Cotts. N17 ... 25Ub **51**
Peabody Ct. EC1 ... 6E **218**
SE5 ... 53Tb **113**
(off Kimpton Rd.)
Peabody Est. *E1* ... 45Zb **92**
(off Brodlove La.)
E2 ... 40Xb **71**
(off Minerva St.)
EC1 ... 6E **218**
(Dufferin St., not continuous)
EC1 ... 6A **218**
(Farringdon La.)
N1 ... 39Sb **71**
SE1 ... 7A **224** (46Qb **90**)
(Duchy St.)
SE1 ... 1E **230**
(Marshalsea Rd.)
SE1 ... 7D **224** (46Sb **91**)
(Southwark St.)
SE5 ... 53Tb **113**
(off Camberwell Grn.)
SE24 ... 59Rb **113**
SW1 ... 5C **228**
SW3 ... 51Gb **111**
SW6 ... 51Cb **111**
(off Lillie Rd.)
SW11 ... 56Gb **111**
W6 ... 50Ya **88**
W10 ... 43Ya **88**
Peabody Hill SE21 ... 60Rb **113**
Peabody Ho. *N1* ... 39Sb **71**
(off Greenman St.)
Peabody Sq. SE1 ... 2B **230** (47Rb **91**)
(not continuous)
Peabody Ter. EC1 ... 6A **218**
Peabody Twr. EC1 ... 6E **218**
Peabody Trust SE17 ... 6F **231** (49Tb **91**)
Peabody Yd. N1 ... 39Sb **71**
Peace Cl. EN7: Chesh ... 1Xb **19**
N14 ... 15Kb **32**
SE25 ... 70Ub **135**
UB6: G'frd ... 39Fa **66**
Peace Ct. *SE1* ... 50Wb **91**
(off Harmony Pl.)
Peace Dr. WD17: Wat ... 13W **26**
Peace Gro. HA9: Wemb ... 34Ra **67**
Peace Prospect WD17: Wat ... 13W **26**
Peace Rd. SL0: Iver H ... 39C **62**
SL3: Ful, Wex ... 41B **82**
Peace St. SE18 ... 51Qc **116**
Peach Cft. DA11: Nflt ... 2A **144**
Peaches Cl. SM2: Cheam ... 80Ab **154**
Peachey Cl. UB8: Cowl ... 44M **83**
Peachey Ho. *SW18* ... 56Eb **111**
(off Eltringham St.)
Peachey La. UB8: Cowl ... 43M **83**
Peach Gro. E11 ... 34Fc **73**
Peach Rd. TW13: Felt ... 60W **106**
W10 ... 41Za **88**
Peach Tree Av. UB7: Yiew ... 44P **83**
Peachum Rd. SE3 ... 51Hc **115**
Peachwalk M. E3 ... 40Zb **72**
Peachy Cl. HA8: Edg ... 23Qa **47**
Peacock Av. TW14: Bedf ... 60T **106**
Peacock Cl. E4 ... 24Bc **52**
KT19: Eps ... 84Pa **173**
NW7 ... 22Ab **48**
RM8: Dag ... 32Yc **75**
RM11: Horn ... 28Nd **57**
Peacock Gdns.
CR2: Sels ... 82Ac **178**
Peacock Ho. *SE5* ... 53Ub **113**
(off St Giles Rd.)
Peacock Ind. Est. N17 ... 24Vb **51**
Peacock Pl. N1 ... 37Qb **70**
Peacocks Shop. Cen., The
GU21: Wok ... 89A **168**
Peacock St. DA12: Grav'nd ... 9E **122**
SE17 ... 6C **230** (49Rb **91**)
Peacock Theatre ... 3H **223**
Peacock Wlk. *E16* ... 44Kc **93**
(off Mortlake Rd.)
N6 ... 31Kb **70**
WD5: Ab L ... 3W **12**
Peacock Yd. SE17 ... 6C **230**
Peak, The SE26 ... 62Yb **136**
Peake Pl. KT15: Wdhm ... 83J **169**
Peakes Pl. *AL1: St A* ... 2D **6**
(off Granville Rd.)
Peaketon Av. IG4: Ilf ... 28Mc **53**
Peak Fitness
Woking ... 89B **168**
(off Chertsey Rd.)
Peak Hill SE26 ... 63Yb **136**
Peak Hill Av. SE26 ... 63Yb **136**
Peak Hill Gdns. SE26 ... 63Yb **136**
Peaks Hill CR8: Purl ... 82Mb **176**
Peaks Hill Ri. CR8: Purl ... 82Nb **176**
Pea La. RM14: Upm ... 37Wd **78**
Peal Gdns. W13 ... 42Ja **86**
Peall Rd. CR0: C'don ... 72Pb **156**
Peall Rd. Ind. Est. CR0: C'don ... 72Pb **156**
Pearce Cl. CR4: Mitc ... 68Jb **134**
Pearcefield Av. SE23 ... 60Yb **114**
Pearce Ho. SW1 ... 6E **228**
Pearces Wlk. *AL1: St A* ... 3B **6**
(off Albert St.)
Pear Cl. NW9 ... 28Ta **47**
SE14 ... 52Ac **114**
Pear Ct. *SE15* ... 52Vb **113**
(off Thruxton Way)
Pearcroft Rd. E11 ... 33Fc **73**
Pearcy Cl. RM3: Rom ... 24Nd **57**
Peardon St. SW8 ... 54Kb **112**
Peareswood Gdns. HA7: Stan ... 25Ma **47**
Peareswood Rd. DA8: Erith ... 53Hd **118**
Pearfield Rd. SE23 ... 62Ac **136**
Pearing Cl. KT4: Wor Pk ... 75Za **154**
Pearl Cl. E6 ... 44Qc **94**
NW2 ... 31Za **68**
Pearl Ct. GU21: Wok ... 8J **167**
Pearl Gdns. SL1: Slou ... 6F **80**
Pearl Rd. E17 ... 27Cc **52**
Pearl St. E1 ... 46Xb **91**
Pearmain Cl. TW17: Shep ... 71R **150**
Pearman Ho. *SL9: Chal P* ... 21A **42**
(off Micholls Av.)
Pearman St. SE1 ... 3A **230** (48Qb **90**)
Pear Pl. SE1 ... 1K **229** (47Qb **90**)
Pear Rd. E11 ... 34Fc **73**
Pears Av. TW17: Shep ... 69U **128**
Pearscroft Ct. SW6 ... 53Db **111**
Pearscroft Rd. SW6 ... 53Db **111**
Pearse St. SE15 ... 51Ub **113**
Pearson Cl. CR8: Purl ... 83Rb **177**
EN5: New Bar ... 13Db **31**
SE5 ... 53Sb **113**
(off Camberwell New Rd.)
Pearson M. *SW4* ... 55Mb **112**
(off Edgeley Rd.)
Pearson's Av. SE14 ... 53Cc **114**
Pearson Sq. W1 ... 1C **222** (43Lb **90**)
Pearson St. E2 ... 1K **219** (40Vb **71**)
Pearson Way CR4: Mitc ... 67Jb **134**
DA1: Dart ... 61Pd **141**
Pears Rd. TW3: Houn ... 55Ea **108**
Peartree SE26 ... 64Ac **136**
Pear Tree Av. UB7: Yiew ... 44P **83**
Peartree Av. SW17 ... 62Eb **133**
Pear Tree Cl. BR2: Brom ... 71Mc **159**
BR8: Swan ... 68Fd **140**
CR4: Mitc ... 68Gb **133**
E2 ... 1K **219** (39Vb **71**)
KT9: Chess ... 78Qa **153**
KT15: Add ... 78J **149**
KT19: Eps ... 81Ta **173**
Peartree Cl. CR2: Sande ... 86Xb **177**
DA8: Erith ... 53Fd **118**
HP1: Hem H ... 1J **3**
RM15: S Ock ... 40Yd **78**
SL1: Slou ... 6D **80**
Pear Tree Ct. E18 ... 25Kc **53**
EC1 ... 6A **218** (42Qb **90**)
SE26 ... 62Bc **136**
Peartree Ct. WD25: Wat ... 8Z **13**
Peartree Gdns. RM7: Mawney ... 26Dd **56**
RM8: Dag ... 35Xc **75**
Pear Tree Ho. SE4 ... 55Bc **114**
Pear Tree La.
DA12: High'm, Shorne ... 6N **145**
RM13: Rain ... 40Fd **76**
Peartree La. E1 ... 45Yb **92**
Pear Tree Rd. KT15: Add ... 78J **149**
TW15: Ashf ... 64S **128**
Peartree Rd. EN1: Enf ... 13Ub **33**
HP1: Hem H ... 1J **3**
Pear Trees CM13: Ingve ... 23Ee **59**
Peartrees UB7: Yiew ... 45M **83**
Pear Tree St. EC1 ... 5C **218** (42Sb **91**)
Peartree Way SE10 ... 49Jc **93**
Peary Ho. NW10 ... 38Ta **67**
Peary Mead DA1: Dart ... 57Pd **119**
Peary Pl. E2 ... 41Yb **92**
Peascod Pl. *SL4: Wind* ... 3H **103**
(off Peascod St.)
Peascod St. SL4: Wind ... 3G **102**
Peascroft Rd. HP3: Hem H ... 5A **4**
Pease Cl. RM12: Horn ... 38Kd **77**
Pease Hill TN15: Ash ... 79Ae **165**
Peasmead Ter. E4 ... 21Ec **52**
Peatfield Cl. DA15: Sidc ... 62Uc **138**
Peatmore Av. GU22: Pyr ... 88J **169**
Peatmore Cl. GU22: Pyr ... 88J **169**
Peatmore Dr. GU24: Brkwd ... 3A **186**
Pebble Cl. KT20: Walt H ... 1A **206**
Pebblehill Rd. RH3: Bet ... 1A **206**
Pebble La. KT18: Eps D ... 94Qa **193**
KT22: Lea ... 96Pa **193**
Pebble Way *W3* ... 46Ra **87**
(off Steyne Rd.)
Pebworth Ct. RH1: Redh ... 4A **208**
Pebworth Rd. HA1: Harr ... 33Ja **66**
Peche Way BR5: Orp ... 74Zc **161**
Peckarmans Wood SE26 ... 62Wb **135**
Peckett Sq. N5 ... 35Sb **71**
Peckford Pl. SW9 ... 54Qb **112**
PECKHAM ... 53Wb **113**
Peckham Gro. SE15 ... 52Ub **113**
Peckham High St. SE15 ... 53Wb **113**
Peckham Hill St. SE15 ... 52Wb **113**
Peckham Hurst Rd. TN11: Roug ... 100Fe **205**
Peckham Pk. Rd. SE15 ... 52Wb **113**
Peckham Pulse Health & Leisure Cen.
... 53Wb **113**
Peckham Rd. SE5 ... 53Ub **113**
SE15 ... 53Ub **113**
Peckham Rye SE15 ... 55Wb **113**
SE22 ... 56Wb **113**
Peckham Sq. SE15 ... 53Wb **113**
Peckham Wlk. Av. TN15: Plax ... 100Zd **205**
Pecks Yd. E1 ... 7K **219**
Peckwater St. NW5 ... 36Lb **70**
Pedham Place Golf Course ... 72Ld **163**
Pedham Pl. Ind. Est. BR8: Swan ... 71Jd **162**
Pedlar's Wlk. N7 ... 36Pb **70**
Pedley Rd. RM8: Dag ... 32Yc **75**
Pedley St. E1 ... 42Wb **91**
(not continuous)
Pedro St. E5 ... 34Zb **72**
Pedworth Gdns. SE16 ... 49Yb **92**
Peebles Ct. *UB1: S'hall* ... 44Ea **86**
(off Haldane Rd.)
Peebles Ho. *NW6* ... 40Db **69**
(off Carlton Vale)
Peek Cres. SW19 ... 64Za **132**
Peel Cl. E4 ... 19Dc **34**
N9 ... 20Wb **33**
SL4: Wind ... 5F **102**
Peel Ct. SL1: Slou ... 3F **80**
Peel Dr. IG5: Ilf ... 27Nc **54**
NW9 ... 27Va **48**
Peel Gro. E2 ... 40Yb **72**
Peel Pas. W8 ... 46Cb **89**
Peel Pl. IG5: Ilf ... 26Nc **54**
SE18 ... 53Pc **116**
SW6 ... 51Cb **111**
Peel Pct. NW6 ... 40Cb **69**
Peel Rd. BR6: Farnb ... 78Sc **160**
E18 ... 25Hc **53**
HA3: W'stone ... 27Ha **46**
HA9: Wemb ... 34Ma **67**
Peel St. W8 ... 46Cb **89**
Peel Way RM3: Hrld W ... 26Pd **57**
UB8: Hil ... 43N **83**
Peerage Way RM11: Horn ... 31Nd **77**
Peerglow Est. EN3: Pond E ... 15Yb **34**
Peerglow Ind. Est. WD18: Wat ... 18R **26**
Peerless Dr. UB9: Hare ... 29L **43**
Peerless St. EC1 ... 4F **219** (41Tb **91**)
Pegamoid Rd. N18 ... 20Yb **34**
Pegasus Cl. N16 ... 35Tb **71**
Pegasus Ct. CR3: Cat'm ... 95Vb **197**
DA12: Grav'nd ... 2E **144**
KT1: King T ... 69Ma **131**
KT22: Lea ... 93La **192**
(off Epsom Rd.)
N21 ... 17Sb **33**
NW10 ... 41Xa **88**
(off Trenmar Gdns.)
SM7: Bans ... 87Cb **175**
TW8: Bford ... 50Pa **87**
TW20: Egh ... 64D **126**
W3 ... 44Sa **87**
(off Horn La.)
WD5: Ab L ... 4V **12**
Pegasus Ho. *E1* ... 42Zb **92**
(off Beaumont Sq.)
E13 ... 41Kc **93**
Pegasus Pl. AL3: St A ... 1B **6**
SE11 ... 51Qb **112**
SW6 ... 53Cb **111**
Pegasus Rd. CR0: Wadd ... 79Qb **156**
Pegasus Way N11 ... 23Kb **50**
Pegelm Gdns. RM11: Horn ... 31Pd **77**
Peggotty Way UB8: Hil ... 44R **84**
Pegg Rd. TW5: Hest ... 52Z **107**
Peggy Bond Cl. KT16: Chert ... 74K **149**
Pegley Gdns. SE12 ... 61Jc **137**
Pegmire La. WD25: A'ham ... 11Ea **28**
Pegrum Dr. AL2: Lon C ... 9F **6**
Pegswood Ct. *E1* ... 45Wb **91**
(off Cable St.)
Pegwell St. SE18 ... 52Uc **116**
Peket Cl. TW18: Staines ... 67G **126**
Pekin Cl. *E14* ... 44Cc **92**
(off Pekin St.)
Pekin St. E14 ... 44Cc **92**
Pelabon Ho. *TW1: Twick* ... 58Ma **109**
(off Clevedon Rd.)
Peldon Ct. TW9: Rich ... 56Pa **109**
Peldon Pas. TW10: Rich ... 56Pa **109**
Peldon Wlk. *N1* ... 39Rb **71**
(off Popham St.)
Pelham Av. IG11: Bark ... 39Vc **75**
Pelham Cl. SE5 ... 55Ub **113**
Pelham Cotts. DA5: Bexl ... 60Dd **118**
Pelham Ct. DA14: Sidc ... 62Wc **139**
HP2: Hem H ... 2C **4**
SW3 ... 6D **226**
TW18: Staines ... 64K **127**
(off Kingston Rd.)
Pelham Cres. SW7 ... 6D **226** (49Gb **89**)
Pelham Ho. CR3: Cat'm ... 96Vb **197**
SW1 ... 4E **228**
W14 ... 49Bb **89**
(off Mornington Av.)
Pelham La. WD25: A'ham ... 8Da **13**
Pelham Pl. SW7 ... 5D **226** (49Gb **89**)
W13 ... 42Ha **86**
Pelham Rd. BR3: Beck ... 68Yb **136**
DA7: Bex ... 55Cd **118**
DA11: Grav'nd ... 10B **122**
E18 ... 27Kc **53**
IG1: Ilf ... 33Tc **74**
N15 ... 28Vb **51**
N22 ... 26Qb **50**
SW19 ... 66Cb **133**
Pelham Rd. Sth.
DA11: Grav'nd, Nflt ... 10B **122**
Pelhams, The WD25: Wat ... 7Z **13**
Pelham's Cl. KT10: Esh ... 77Ca **151**
Pelham St. SW7 ... 5C **226** (49Fb **89**)
Pelham's Wlk. KT10: Esh ... 77Ca **151**
Pelham Ter. DA11: Grav'nd ... 9B **122**
Pelham Towers DA11: Grav'nd ... 9B **122**
Pelham Way KT23: Bookh ... 98Da **191**
Pelican Dr. HA2: Harr ... 33Da **65**
Pelican Est. SE15 ... 53Vb **113**
Pelican Ho. SE5 ... 53Vb **113**
SE8 ... 49Bc **92**
Pelican Pas. E1 ... 42Yb **92**
Pelican Wlk. SW9 ... 56Rb **113**
Pelican Wharf *E1* ... 46Yb **92**
(off Wapping Wall)
Pelier St. SE17 ... 51Sb **113**
Pelinore Rd. SE6 ... 61Gc **137**
Pella Ho. SE11 ... 7J **229** (50Pb **90**)
Pellant Rd. SW6 ... 52Ab **110**
Pellatt Gro. N22 ... 25Qb **50**
Pellatt Rd. HA9: Wemb ... 33Ma **67**
SE22 ... 57Vb **113**
Pellerin Rd. N16 ... 36Ub **71**
Pellew Ho. *E1* ... 42Xb **91**
(off Somerford St.)
Pelling Hill SL4: Old Win ... 9M **103**
Pellings Cl. BR2: Brom ... 69Gc **137**
Pelling St. E14 ... 44Cc **92**
Pellipar Cl. N13 ... 20Qb **32**
Pellipar Gdns. SE18 ... 50Pc **94**
Pellipar Rd. SE18 ... 50Pc **94**
Pellow Cl. EN5: Barn ... 16Bb **31**
Pells La. TN15: W King ... 84Wd **184**
Pell St. SE8 ... 49Ac **92**
Pelly Ct. CM16: Epp ... 3Vc **23**
Pelly Rd. E13 ... 39Jc **73**
(not continuous)
Pelman Ho. KT19: Eps ... 82Ra **173**
Pelman Way KT19: Eps ... 82Ra **173**
Peloton Av. E20 ... 36Dc **72**
Pelter St. E2 ... 3K **219** (41Vb **91**)
Pelton Av. SM2: Sutt ... 82Db **175**
Pelton Rd. SE10 ... 50Gc **93**
Pembar Av. E17 ... 27Ac **52**
Pemberley Apartments
RM2: Rom ... 26Ld **57**
Pemberley Chase KT19: Ewe ... 78Ra **153**
Pemberley Cl. KT19: Ewe ... 78Ra **153**
Pemberley Ho. *KT19: Ewe* ... 78Ra **153**
(off Pemberley Chase)
Pemberley Lodge SL4: Wind ... 5E **102**
Pember Rd. NW10 ... 41Za **88**
Pemberton Almshouses *AL1: St A* ... 1B **6**
(off St Peter's St.)
Pemberton Av. RM2: Rom ... 27Kd **57**
Pemberton Cl. AL1: St A ... 5B **6**
TW19: Stanw ... 60N **105**
Pemberton Ct. *E1* ... 41Zb **92**
(off Portelet Rd.)
EN1: Enf ... 13Ub **33**
Pemberton Gdns. BR8: Swan ... 69Gd **140**
N19 ... 34Lb **70**
RM6: Chad H ... 29Ad **55**
Pemberton Ho. *SE26* ... 63Wb **135**
(off High Level Dr.)
Pemberton Pl. E8 ... 38Xb **71**
KT10: Esh ... 76Ea **152**
Pemberton Rd. KT8: E Mos ... 70Ea **130**
N4 ... 29Qb **50**
SL2: Slou ... 2C **80**
Pemberton Row EC4 ... 2A **224** (44Qb **90**)
Pemberton Ter. N19 ... 34Lb **70**
Pembrey Way RM12: Horn ... 37Ld **77**
Pembridge Av. TW2: Whitt ... 60Ba **107**
Pembridge Chase HP3: Bov ... 10B **2**
Pembridge Cl. HP3: Bov ... 10B **2**
Pembridge Cres. W11 ... 45Cb **89**
Pembridge Gdns. W2 ... 45Cb **89**
Pembridge M. W11 ... 45Cb **89**
Pembridge Pl. SW15 ... 57Cb **111**
W2 ... 45Cb **89**
Pembridge Rd. HP3: Bov ... 10C **2**
W11 ... 45Cb **89**
Pembridge Sq. W2 ... 45Cb **89**
Pembridge Studios *W11* ... 45Cb **89**
(off Pembridge Vs.)
Pembridge Vs. W2 ... 45Cb **89**
W11 ... 45Cb **89**
Pembroke *W14* ... 49Bb **89**
(off Kensington Village)
Pembroke Av. EN1: Enf ... 10Xb **19**
HA3: Kenton ... 27Ja **46**
HA5: Pinn ... 32Z **65**
KT5: Surb ... 71Ra **153**
KT12: Hers ... 77Z **151**
N1 ... 39Nb **70**
Pembroke Bldgs. NW10 ... 41Wa **88**
Pembroke Bus. Cen. BR8: Swan ... 67Fd **140**
Pembroke Cen., The HA4: Ruis ... 32V **64**
Pembroke Cl. RM11: Horn ... 28Pd **57**
SL5: S'hill ... 1B **146**
SM7: Bans ... 89Db **175**
SW1 ... 2J **227** (47Jb **90**)
Pembroke Cotts. *W8* ... 48Cb **89**
(off Pembroke Sq.)
Pembroke Ct. *W7* ... 44Ha **86**
(off Copley Cl.)
W8 ... 48Cb **89**
(off Sth. Edwardes Sq.)
Pembroke Dr. EN7: G Oak ... 1Rb **19**
RM15: Avel ... 47Sd **98**
Pembroke Gdns. GU22: Wok ... 90C **168**
HA4: Ruis ... 32V **64**
RM10: Dag ... 34Dd **76**
SW14 ... 56Ra **109**
W8 ... 49Bb **89**
Pembroke Gdns. Cl. W8 ... 48Cb **89**
Pembroke Hall *NW4* ... 27Ya **48**
(off Mulberry Cl.)
Pembroke Ho. RM8: Dag ... 36Wc **75**
SW1 ... 4H **227**
W2 ... 44Db **89**
(off Hallfield Est.)
W3 ... 47Sa **87**
(off Park Rd. E.)
WD6: Bore ... 14Qa **29**
(off Academy Ct.)
Pembroke Lodge HA7: Stan ... 23Ma **47**
Pembroke Mans. *NW6* ... 37Eb **69**
(off Canfield Gdns.)
Pembroke M. E3 ... 41Ac **92**
N10 ... 25Jb **50**
SL5: S'hill ... 1B **146**
TN13: S'oaks ... 97Kd **203**
W8 ... 48Cb **89**
Pembroke Pde. DA8: Erith ... 50Ed **96**
Pembroke Pl. DA4: Sut H ... 67Rd **141**
HA8: Edg ... 24Qa **47**
TW7: Isle ... 54Ga **108**
W8 ... 48Cb **89**
Pembroke Rd. BR1: Brom ... 68Lc **137**
CR4: Mitc ... 68Jb **134**
DA8: Erith ... 50Ed **96**
E6 ... 43Pc **94**
E17 ... 29Dc **52**
GU22: Wok ... 90C **168**
HA4: Ruis ... 32V **64**
HA6: Nwood ... 20S **26**
HA9: Wemb ... 34Ma **67**
IG3: Ilf ... 32Vc **75**
N8 ... 28Nb **50**
N10 ... 25Jb **50**
N13 ... 20Sb **33**
N15 ... 29Vb **51**
SE25 ... 70Ub **135**
TN13: S'oaks ... 97Kd **203**
UB6: G'frd ... 42Da **85**
W8 ... 49Bb **89**
Pembroke Sq. W8 ... 48Cb **89**
Pembroke St. N1 ... 38Nb **70**
(not continuous)
Pembroke Studios W8 ... 48Bb **89**
Pembroke Ter. NW8 ... 1B **214**
Pembroke Vs. TW9: Rich ... 56Ma **109**
W8 ... 49Cb **89**
Pembroke Wlk. W8 ... 49Cb **89**
Pembroke Way UB3: Harl ... 48S **84**
Pembrook M. SW11 ... 56Fb **111**
Pembry Cl. SW9 ... 53Qb **112**
Pembury Av. KT4: Wor Pk ... 74Wa **154**
Pembury Cl. BR2: Hayes ... 73Hc **159**
CR5: Coul ... 86Jb **176**
E5 ... 36Xb **71**
Pembury Ct. UB3: Harl ... 51T **106**
Pembury Cres. DA14: Sidc ... 61Ad **139**
Pembury Pl. E5 ... 36Xb **71**

Pembury Rd. DA7: Bex 52Ad 117
E5 36Xb 71
N17 25Vb 51
SE25 70Wb 135
Pemdevon Rd. CR0: C'don 73Qb 156
Pemell Cl. E1 42Yb 92
Pemell Ho. *E1* 42Yb 92
(off Pemell Cl.)
Pemerich Cl. UB3: Harl 50V 84
Pempath Pl. HA9: Wemb 33Ma 67
Pemsel Ct. HP3: Hem H 4M 3
Penally Pl. N1 39Tb 71
Penang Ho. *E1* 46Xb 91
(off Prusom St.)
Penang St. E1 46Xb 91
Penard Rd. UB2: S'hall 48Da 85
Penart Ct. SM2: Sutt 80Eb 155
Penarth Cen. SE15 51Yb 114
Penarth St. SE15 51Yb 114
Penates KT10: Esh 77Fa 152
Penberth Rd. SE6 61Ec 136
Penbury Rd. UB2: S'hall 49Ba 85
Pencombe M. W11 45Bb 89
Pencraig Way SE15 51Xb 113
Pencroft Dr. DA1: Dart 59Ld 119
Pendall Cl. EN4: E Barn 14Gb 31
Penda Rd. DA8: Erith 52Dd 118
Pendarves Rd. SW20 67Ya 132
Penda's Mead E9 35Ac 72
Pendeen Ct. SL1: Slou 6E 80
Pendell Av. UB3: Harl 52V 106
Pendell Rd. RH1: Blet 3H 209
Pendennis Cl. KT14: W Byf 86J 169
Pendennis Ho. SE8 49Ac 92
Pendennis Rd. BR6: Chels 75Yc 161
N17 27Tb 51
SW16 63Nb 134
TN13: S'oaks 95Kd 203
Pendenza KT11: Cobh 88Aa 171
Penderel Rd. TW3: Houn 57Ca 107
Penderry Ri. SE6 61Fc 137
Penderyn Way N7 35Mb 70
Pendlebury Ct. *KT5: Surb* 70Na 131
(off Cranes Pk.)
Pendle Ct. UB10: Hil 39R 64
Pendle Ho. SE26 62Wb 135
Pendle Rd. SW16 65Kb 134
Pendlestone Rd. E17 29Dc 52
Pendleton Cl. RH1: Redh 7P 207
Pendleton Rd. RH1: Redh 9L 207
RH2: Reig 9L 207
Pendlewood Cl. W5 43La 86
Pendley Ho. *E2* 39Wb 71
(off Whiston Rd.)
Pendolino Way NW10 38Qa 67
Pendragon Rd. BR1: Brom 62Hc 137
Pendragon Wlk. NW9 30Ua 48
Pendrell Ho. WC2 3E 222
Pendrell Rd. SE4 54Ac 114
Pendrell St. SE18 51Tc 116
Pendula Dr. UB4: Yead 42Z 85
Pendulum M. E8 36Vb 71
Penenden DA3: Nw A G 75Be 165
Penerley Rd. RM13: Rain 43Kd 97
SE6 60Dc 114
Penfield Lodge *W9* 43Cb 89
(off Admiral Wlk.)
Penfields Ho. *N7* 37Nb 70
(off York Way Est.)
Penfold Cl. CR0: Wadd 76Qb 156
Penfold La. DA5: Bexl 61Zc 139
(not continuous)
Penfold Pl. NW1 7D 214 (43Gb 89)
Penfold Rd. N9 18Zb 34
Penfold St. NW1 6C 214 (42Fb 89)
NW8 6C 214 (42Fb 89)
Penfold Trad. Est. WD24: Wat 11Y 27
Penford Gdns. SE9 55Mc 115
Penford St. SE5 54Rb 113
Pengarth Rd. DA5: Bexl 57Zc 117
PENGE 66Yb 136
Penge Ho. SW11 55Fb 111
Penge La. SE20 66Yb 136
Pengelly Apartments *E14* 50Dc 92
(off Bartlett M.)
Pengelly Cl. EN7: Chesh 2Xb 19
Penge Rd. E13 39Lc 73
SE20 69Wb 135
SE25 69Wb 135
Penhale Cl. BR6: Chels 77Wc 161
Penhale Pl. SL1: Burn 3A 80
Penhall Rd. SE7 49Mc 93
Pen Haven SL9: Ger X 29B 42
Penhill Rd. DA5: Bexl 58Yc 117
Penhurst GU21: Wok 86B 168
Penhurst Mans. *SW6* 53Bb 111
(off Rostrevor Rd.)
Penhurst Pl. SE1 4J 229
Penhurst Rd. IG6: Ilf 24Rc 54
Penifather La. UB6: G'frd 41Fa 86
Peninsula Apartments *N1* 39Sb 71
(off Basire St.)
W2 1C 220
Peninsula Ct. *E14* 48Dc 92
(off E. Ferry Rd.)
N1 39Sb 71
(off Basire St.)
Peninsula Hgts. SE1 7G 229 (50Nb 90)
Peninsular Cl. NW7 22Ab 48
TW14: Felt 58T 106
Peninsular Pk. SE7 49Jc 93
Peninsular Pk. Rd. SE7 49Jc 93
Peninsula Sq. SE10 47Gc 93
Penistone Rd. SW16 66Nb 134
Penistone Wlk. RM3: Rom 23Ld 57
Penketh Dr. HA1: Harr 34Fa 66
Penley Ct. WC2 4J 223 (45Pb 90)
Penman Cl. AL2: Chis G 9N 5
Penman's Grn. WD4: Bucks 5H 11
Penman's Hill WD4: Bucks 5H 11
Penmayne Ho. SE11 7A 230
Penmon Rd. SE2 48Wc 95
Pennack Rd. SE15 51Vb 113
Penn Almshouses *SE10* 53Ec 114
(off Greenwich Sth. St.)
Pennant M. W8 49Db 89
Pennant Ter. E17 26Bc 52
Pennard Ho. WD19: Wat 20Z 27
Pennard Mans. *W12* 47Ya 88
(off Goldhawk Rd.)
Pennard Rd. W12 47Ya 88
Pennards, The TW16: Sun 69Y 129
Penn Cl. HA3: Kenton 28La 46
RM16: Ors 2D 100
UB6: G'frd 40Da 65
UB8: Cowl 42M 83
WD3: Chor 16F 24
Penn Ct. NW9 27Ta 47
Penn Dr. UB9: Den 30H 43
Penne Cl. WD7: R'lett 6Ha 14
Penner Cl. SW19 61Ab 132
Penners Gdns.
KT6: Surb 73Na 153
Pennethorne Cl. E9 39Yb 72
Pennethorne Ho. SW11 55Fb 111
Pennethorne Rd. SE15 52Xb 113
Penney Cl. DA1: Dart 59Md 119
Penney Gro. DA11: Nflt 61De 143
Penn Gdns. BR7: Chst 68Rc 138
RM5: Col R 24Cd 56
Penn Gaskell La.
SL9: Chal P 22B 42
Penn Ho. HA6: Nwood 20T 26
NW8 6D 214
SL1: Burn 1A 80
SL4: Eton 10H 81
(off Common La.)
SL9: Chal P 22A 42
WD19: Wat 20Y 27
Pennine Dr. NW2 33Za 68
Pennine Ho. *N9* 20Wb 33
(off Plevna Rd.)
Pennine La. NW2 33Ab 68
Pennine Pde. NW2 33Ab 68
Pennine Rd. SL2: Slou 3E 80
Pennine Way DA7: Bex 53Gd 118
DA11: Nflt 2A 144
UB3: Harl 52T 106
Pennington Cl. RM5: Col R 22Cd 56
SE27 63Tb 135
Pennington Ct. SE16 46Ac 92
Pennington Dr. KT13: Weyb 76Q 150
N21 15Nb 32
Pennington Lodge
KT5: Surb 71Na 153
(off Cranes Dr.)
Pennington St. E1 45Xb 91
Pennington Way SE12 61Kc 137
Pennis La. DA3: Fawk 72Zd 165
Penniston Cl. N17 26Sb 51
Penniwell Cl. HA8: Edg 21Pa 47
Penn La. DA5: Bexl 57Zc 117
TN14: Ide H, Sund 99Ad 201
Penn Mdw.
SL2: Stoke P 9K 61
Penn Pl. WD3: Rick 17M 25
Penn Rd. AL2: Park 9A 6
N7 36Nb 70
SL2: Slou 2H 81
SL3: Dat 3P 103
SL9: Chal P 25A 42
WD3: Rick 18H 25
WD24: Wat 11X 27
Penn St. N1 1G 219 (39Tb 71)
Penn Way WD3: Chor 16F 24
Penny Brookes St. E15 37Ec 72
E20 37Ec 72
Penny Cl. E4 20Gc 35
RM13: Rain 41Kd 97
Penny Ct. *AL3: St A* 1B 6
(off Worley Rd.)
WD17: Wat 12X 27
(off Westland Rd.)
Pennycroft CR0: Sels 81Ac 178
Pennyfather La. EN2: Enf 13Sb 33
Pennyfield KT11: Cobh 85W 170
Pennyfields CM14: W'ley 21Yd 58
E14 45Cc 92
(not continuous)
Penny Flds. Ho. *SE8* 53Bc 114
(off Francis Harvey Way)
Pennyford Ct. NW8 5B 214
Penny La. TW17: Shep 73U 150
Pennylets Grn. SL2: Stoke P 8K 61
Pennymead Dr. KT24: E Hor 99V 190
Pennymead Pl. KT10: Esh 79Ba 151
Pennymead Ri. KT24: E Hor 99V 190
Penny M. SW12 59Kb 112
Pennymoor Wlk. *W9* 42Bb 89
(off Fernhead Rd.)
PENNY POT 4G 166
Pennypot La. GU24: Chob 5F 166
Penny Rd. NW10 41Ra 87
Penny Royal SM6: Wall 79Mb 156
Pennyroyal Av. E6 44Qc 94
Pennyroyal Dr. UB7: W Dray 47P 83
Penpoll Rd. E8 37Xb 71
Penpool La. DA16: Well 55Xc 117
Penrhyn Av. E17 25Bc 52
Penrhyn Cl. CR3: Cat'm 92Tb 197
Penrhyn Cres. E17 25Cc 52
SW14 56Sa 109
Penrhyn Gdns. KT1: King T 70Ma 131
Penrhyn Gro. E17 25Cc 52
Penrhyn Rd. KT1: King T 70Na 131
Penrith Cl. BR3: Beck 67Dc 136
RH2: Reig 5N 207
SW15 57Ab 110
UB8: Uxb 38M 63
Penrith Cres. RM13: Rain 36Jd 76
Penrith Pl. SE27 61Rb 135
Penrith Rd. CR7: Thor H 68Sb 135
IG6: Ilf 23Vc 55
KT3: N Mald 70Ta 131
N15 29Tb 51
RM3: Rom 22Pd 57
Penrith St. SW16 65Lb 134
Penrose Av. WD19: Wat 19Z 27
Penrose Ct. SW12 60Jb 112
TW20: Eng G 5N 125
(not continuous)
Penrose Dr. KT19: Eps 83Qa 173
Penrose Gro. SE17 7D 230 (50Sb 91)
Penrose Ho. N21 15Pb 32
SE17 7D 230 (50Sb 91)
Penrose Rd. KT22: Fet 94Ea 192
Penrose St. SE17 7D 230 (50Sb 91)
Penrose Way SE10 46Gc 93
Penryn Ho. *RH1: Redh* 4A 208
(off London Rd.)
SE11 7B 230
Penryn St. NW1 1D 216 (40Mb 70)
Penry St. SE1 6J 231 (49Ub 91)
Pensbury Pl. SW8 54Lb 112
Pensbury St. SW8 54Lb 112
Penscroft Gdns. WD6: Bore 14Ta 29
Pensford Av. TW9: Kew 54Qa 109
Penshurst NW5 37Jb 70
Penshurst Av. DA15: Sidc 58Wc 117
Penshurst Cl. DA3: Lfield 68Fe 143
SL9: Chal P 26A 42
TN15: W King 79Ud 164
Penshurst Gdns. HA8: Edg 22Ra 47
Penshurst Grn. BR2: Brom 71Hc 159
Penshurst Ho. *SE15* 51Yb 114
(off Lovelinch Cl.)
Penshurst Rd. CR7: Thor H 71Rb 157
DA7: Bex 53Bd 117
E9 38Zb 72
EN6: Pot B 3Fb 17
N17 24Vb 51
Penshurst Wlk. BR2: Brom 71Hc 159
Penshurst Way
BR5: St M Cry 70Yc 139
SM2: Sutt 80Cb 155
Pensilver Cl. EN4: E Barn 14Gb 31
Penstemon Cl. N3 23Cb 49
Penstock Footpath N8 27Pb 50
N22 27Pb 50
Penta Ct. *WD6: Bore* 14Qa 29
(off Station Rd.)
Pentagram Yd. *W11* 44Cb 89
(off Needham Rd.)
Pentavia Retail Pk. NW7 24Va 48
Pentelow Gdns. TW14: Felt 58W 106
Pentire Cl. GU21: Wok 86A 168
RM14: Upm 30Ud 58
Pentire Rd. E17 25Fc 53
Pentland Av. HA8: Edg 19Ra 29
TW17: Shep 71Q 150
Pentland Cl. N9 19Yb 34
NW11 33Ab 68
Pentland Gdns. SW18 58Eb 111
Pentland Pl. UB5: N'olt 39Aa 65
Pentland Rd. NW6 41Cb 89
SL2: Slou 3E 80
WD23: Bush 16Ea 28
Pentlands Cl. CR4: Mitc 69Kb 134
Pentland St. SW18 58Eb 111
Pentland Way UB10: Ick 34S 64
Pentlow St. SW15 55Ya 110
Pentlow Way IG9: Buck H 17Nc 36
Pentney Rd. E4 18Fc 35
SW12 60Lb 112
SW19 67Ab 132
Penton Av. TW18: Staines 66H 127
Penton Ct. TW18: Staines 65H 127
Penton Dr. EN8: Chesh 1Zb 20
Penton Gro. N1 2K 217 (40Qb 70)
Penton Hall TW18: Staines 67J 127
Penton Hall Dr.
TW18: Staines 67J 127
Penton Hook Marina 68H 127
Penton Hook Rd. TW18: Staines 66J 127
Penton Hook Yacht Club 69J 127
Penton Ho. N1 2K 217
SE2 46Zc 95
Penton Pk. KT16: Chert 69K 127
Penton Pl. SE17 6C 230 (50Rb 91)
Penton Ri. WC1 3J 217 (41Pb 90)
Penton Rd. TW18: Staines 66H 127
Penton St. N1 1K 217 (40Qb 70)
PENTONVILLE 2H 217 (40Pb 70)
Pentonville Rd. N1 3G 217 (40Nb 70)
Pentrich Av. EN1: Enf 10Wb 19
Pentridge St. SE15 52Vb 113
Pentstemon Dr. DA10: Swans 57Ae 121
Pentyre Av. N18 22Tb 51
Penventon Ct. *RM18: Tilb* 4C 122
(off Dock Rd.)
Penwerris Av. TW7: Isle 52Ea 108
Penwerris Ct. TW5: Hest 52Ea 108
Penwith Rd. SW18 61Cb 133
Penwith Wlk. GU22: Wok 1P 187
Penwood Ct. HA5: Pinn 28Ba 45
Penwood End GU22: Wok 3M 187
Penwood Ho. SW15 58Va 110
Penwortham Ct. *N22* 26Qb 50
(off Mayes Rd.)
Penwortham Rd. CR2: Sande 82Sb 177
SW16 65Kb 134
Penylan Pl. HA8: Edg 24Qa 47
Penywern Rd. SW5 50Cb 89
Penzance Cl. UB9: Hare 25M 43
Penzance Gdns. RM3: Rom 23Qd 57
(not continuous)
Penzance Pl. W11 46Ab 88
Penzance Rd. RM3: Rom 23Qd 57
Penzance Spur SL2: Slou 2F 80
Penzance St. W11 46Ab 88
Peony Cl. CM15: Pil H 16Xd 40
Peony Ct. IG8: Wfd G 24Gc 53
SW10 51Eb 111
Peony Gdns. W12 45Wa 88
Peoplebuilding HP2: Hem H 1B 4
Peperfield WC1 4H 217
Pepler Ho. *W10* 42Ab 88
(off Wornington Rd.)
Pepler M. SE5 50Vb 91
Pepler Way SL1: Burn 1A 80
Peplins Cl. AL9: Brk P 8G 8
Peplins Way AL9: Brk P 7G 8
Peploe Rd. NW6 40Za 68
Peplow Cl. UB7: Yiew 46M 83
Pepper All. IG10: Lough 12Hc 35
Pepper Cl. CR3: Cat'm 97Ub 197
E6 43Pc 94
Peppercorn Cl. CR7: Thor H 68Tb 135
PEPPER HILL 62Fe 143
Pepper Hill DA11: Nflt 62Ee 143
Pepperhill La. DA11: Nflt 62Ee 143
Peppermead Sq. SE13 57Cc 114
Peppermint Cl. CR0: C'don 73Nb 156
Peppermint Pl. E11 34Gc 73
Pepper St. E14 48Dc 92
SE1 1D 230 (47Sb 91)
Peppie Cl. N16 33Ub 71
Pepys Cl. DA1: Dart 56Qd 119
DA11: Nflt 62Fe 143
KT21: Asht 89Qa 173
RM18: Tilb 3E 122
SL3: L'ly 51D 104
UB10: Ick 35R 64
Pepys Cres. E16 46Jc 93
EN5: Barn 15Ya 30
Pepys Ho. *E2* 41Yb 92
(off Kirkwall Pl.)
Pepys Ri. BR6: Orp 74Vc 161
Pepys Rd. SE14 53Zb 114
SW20 67Ya 132
Pepys St. EC3 4J 225 (45Ub 91)
Perceval Av. NW3 36Gb 69
Perceval Ct. UB5: N'olt 36Ca 65
Perceval Ho. W5 45La 86
Percheron Cl. TW7: Isle 55Ha 108
Percheron Dr. GU21: Knap 1G 186
Percheron Rd. WD6: Bore 16Ta 29
Perch St. E8 35Vb 71
Percival Av. NW9 26Va 48
Percival Cl. KT22: Oxs 83Da 171
Percival Ct. EN8: Chesh 2Ac 20
N17 24Vb 51
Percival Gdns. RM6: Chad H 30Yc 55
Percival M. SE11 51Pb 112
Percival Rd. BR6: Farnb 75Rc 160
EN1: Enf 14Vb 33
RM11: Horn 30Ld 57
SW14 56Sa 109
TW13: Felt 61V 128
Percival St. EC1 5B 218 (42Rb 91)
Percival Way KT19: Ewe 77Ta 153
Percy Av. TW15: Ashf 64Q 128
Percy Bilton Ct. *TW5: Hest* 53Da 107
(off Skinners La.)
Percy Bryant Rd. TW16: Sun 66U 128
Percy Bush Rd. UB7: W Dray 48P 83
Percy Cir. WC1 3J 217 (41Pb 90)
Percy Ct. WD18: Wat 14X 27
Percy Gdns. EN3: Pond E 15Zb 34
KT4: Wor Pk 74Ta 153
TW7: Isle 55Ka 108
UB4: Hayes 41U 84
Percy Laurie Ho. *SW15* 56Za 110
(off Nursery Cl.)
Percy M. W1 1D 222
Percy Pas. W1 1D 222
Percy Pl. SL3: Dat 3M 103
Percy Rd. CR4: Mitc 73Jb 156
DA7: Bex 54Ad 117
E11 31Gc 73
E16 43Gc 93
IG3: Ilf 31Wc 75
N12 22Eb 49
N21 17Sb 33
RM7: Mawney 27Dd 56
SE20 67Zb 136
SE25 71Wb 157
TW2: Whitt 60Da 107
TW7: Isle 56Ja 108
TW12: Hamp 66Ca 129
W12 47Wa 88
WD18: Wat 14X 27
Percy St. RM17: Grays 51Ee 121
W1 1D 222 (43Mb 90)
Percy Ter. BR1: Brom 69Rc 138
Percy Way TW2: Whitt 60Ea 108
Percy Yd. WC1 3J 217 (41Pb 90)
Peregrine Cl. NW10 36Ta 67
WD25: Wat 6Aa 13
Peregrine Ct. DA16: Well 53Vc 117
SE8 51Cc 114
(off Edward St.)
SW16 63Pb 134
Peregrine Gdns. CR0: C'don 75Ac 158
Peregrine Ho. EC1 3C 218
Peregrine Rd. EN9: Walt A 6Jc 21
IG6: Ilf 22Xc 55
N17 25Sb 51
TW16: Sun 68V 128
Peregrine Wlk. RM12: Horn 37Kd 77
Peregrine Way AL10: Hat 1C 8
SW19 66Ya 132
Perendale Dr. TW17: Shep 67S 128
Perham Rd. W14 50Ab 88
Perham Way AL2: Lon C 8H 7
Peridot Ct. E2 4K 219
Peridot St. E6 43Nc 94
Perifield SE21 60Sb 113
Perilla Ho. *E1* 44Wb 91
(off Boulevard Walkway)
Perimeade Rd. UB6: G'frd 40La 66
Periton Rd. SE9 56Mc 115
PERIVALE 39La 66
Perivale Gdns. W13 42Ka 86
WD25: Wat 6X 13
Perivale Grange UB6: G'frd 41Ja 86
Perivale La. UB6: G'frd 41Ja 86
Perivale Lodge *UB6: G'frd* 41Ja 86
(off Perivale La.)
Perivale New Bus. Cen.
UB6: G'frd 40La 66
Perivale Pk. UB6: G'frd 40Ka 66
Perivale Pk. Athletics Track 41Ga 86
Perivale Pk. Golf Course 41Ga 86
Perivale Wood Local Nature Reserve
39Ha 66
Periwood Cres. UB6: G'frd 39Ja 66
Perkin Cl. HA0: Wemb 36Ka 66
TW3: Houn 56Ca 107
Perkins Cl. DA9: Ghithe 57Vd 120
Perkins Ct. TW15: Ashf 64P 127
Perkins Gdns. UB10: Ick 33S 64
Perkins Ho. *E14* 43Bc 92
(off Wallwood St.)
Perkin's Rents SW1 3D 228 (48Mb 90)
Perkins Rd. IG2: Ilf 29Tc 54
Perkins Sq. SE1 6E 224 (46Sb 91)
Perks Cl. SE3 55Gc 115
Perkyn Sq. N17 27Xb 51
Perleybrooke La. GU21: Wok 9L 167
Perley Ho. *E3* 43Bc 92
(off Weatherley Cl.)
Permain Cl. WD7: Shenl 5Na 15
Perpins Rd. SE9 58Uc 116
Perran Cl. DA3: Hartl 70Be 143
Perran Rd. SW2 60Rb 113
Perran Wlk. TW8: Bford 50Na 87
Perren St. NW5 37Kb 70
Perrers Rd. W6 49Xa 88
Perrin Apartments *N1* 38Nb 70
(off Caledonian Rd.)
Perrin Cl. TW15: Ashf 64P 127
WD23: B Hea 18Ga 28
Perrin Ct. GU21: Wok 87D 168
TW15: Ashf 63Q 128
Perring Est. *E3* 43Cc 92
(off Gale St.)
Perrin Ho. NW6 41Cb 89
Perrin Rd. DA1: Dart 57Pd 119
HA0: Wemb 35Ka 66
Perrin's Ct. NW3 35Eb 69
Perrin's La. NW3 35Eb 69
Perrin's Wlk. NW3 35Eb 69
Perronet Ho. SE1 4C 230
Perrott St. SE18 49Sc 94
Perry Av. W3 44Ta 87
Perry Cl. IG2: Ilf 30Tc 54
UB8: Hil 44R 84
Perry Ct. *E14* 50Cc 92
(off Maritime Quay)
KT1: King T 68Na 131
(off Old London Rd.)
N15 30Ub 51
Perrycroft SL4: Wind 5C 102
Perryfields Way SL1: Burn 2A 80
Perryfield Way NW9 30Va 48
TW10: Ham 62Ka 130
Perry Gdns. N9 20Tb 33
Perry Gth. UB5: N'olt 39Y 65
Perry Gro. DA1: Dart 56Qd 119
Perry Hall Cl. BR6: St M Cry 73Wc 161
Perry Hall Rd. BR6: St M Cry 72Vc 161
Perry Hill GU3: Worp 9J 187
(not continuous)
SE6 62Bc 136
Perry Ho. SL1: Burn 2A 80
Perry How KT4: Wor Pk 74Va 154
Perry Lodge E12 32Mc 73
Perryman Ho. *IG11: Bark* 39Sc 74
(off The Shaftesburys)
Perrymans Farm Rd. IG2: Ilf 30Tc 54
Perryman Way SL2: Slou 1D 80
(not continuous)
Perry Mead EN2: Enf 12Rb 33
WD23: Bush 16Ea 28
Perrymead St. SW6 53Cb 111
Perryn Ct. TW1: Twick 58Ja 108
Perryn Ho. W3 45Ua 88
Perryn Rd. SE16 48Xb 91
W3 46Ta 87
Perry Ri. SE23 62Ac 136
Perry Rd. RM9: Dag 43Bd 95
Perrys La. BR6: Prat B 85Xc 181
Perry's Pl. W1 2D 222 (44Mb 90)
PERRY STREET 10B 122
Perry St. BR7: Chst 65Tc 138
DA1: Cray 56Gd 118
DA11: Nflt 10A 122
Perry St. Gdns. BR7: Chst 65Uc 138
Perry St. Shaw BR7: Chst 66Uc 138
Perry's Way RM15: S Ock 43Yd 98
Perry Va. SE23 61Yb 136
Perry Way RM15: Avel 45Sd 98
Persant Rd. SE6 61Gc 137
Perseverance Cotts. GU23: Rip 93L 189
Perseverance Pl. SW9 52Qb 112
TW9: Rich 56Na 109
Perseverance Works E2 3J 219
Persfield Cl. KT17: Ewe 82Va 174
Persfield M. KT17: Ewe 82Va 174
Pershore Cl. IG2: Ilf 29Rc 54
Pershore Gro. SM5: Cars 72Fb 155
Pershore Ho. *W13* 46Ja 86
(off Singapore Rd.)
Pert Cl. N10 24Kb 50
Perth Av. NW9 31Ta 67
SL1: Slou 4G 80
UB4: Yead 42Y 85
Perth Cl. SE5 56Tb 113
SW20 68Va 132
UB5: N'olt 36Ca 65
Perth Ho. *N1* 38Pb 70
(off Bemerton Est.)
RM18: Tilb 4C 122
Perth Rd. BR3: Beck 68Ec 136
E10 32Ac 72
E13 40Kc 73
IG2: Ilf 30Qc 54
IG11: Bark 40Tc 74
N4 32Qb 70
N22 25Rb 51
Perth Ter. IG2: Ilf 31Sc 74
Perth Trad. Est. SL1: Slou 3F 80
Perwell Av. HA2: Harr 32Ba 65
Perystreete SE23 61Yb 136
Pescot Av. DA3: Lfield 69Ce 143
Petands Ct. *RM12: Horn* 34Md 77
(off Randall Dr.)
Petavel Rd. TW11: Tedd 65Ga 130
Peter Av. NW10 38Xa 68
RH8: Oxt 1H 211
Peter Best Ho. *E1* 44Xb 91
(off Nelson St.)
Peterboat Cl. SE10 49Gc 93
Peterborough Av. RM14: Upm 32Ud 78
Peterborough Ct. EC4 3A 224 (44Qb 90)
Peterborough Gdns. IG1: Ilf 31Nc 74
Peterborough Ho. *WD6: Bore* 12Qa 29
(off Stratfield Rd.)
Peterborough M. SW6 54Cb 111
Peterborough Rd. E10 29Ec 52
HA1: Harr 32Ga 66
SM5: Cars 72Gb 155
SW6 54Cb 111
Peterborough Vs. SW6 53Db 111
Peter Butler Ho. *SE1* 47Wb 91
(off Wolseley St.)
Peterchurch Ho. *SE15* 51Xb 113
(off Commercial Way)
Petergate SW11 56Eb 111
Peter Harrison Planetarium 52Fc 115
Peterhead Ct. *UB1: S'hall* 44Ea 86
(off Osborne Rd.)
Peterhead M. SL3: L'ly 50C 82
Peter Heathfield Ho. *E15* 39Fc 73
(off Wise Rd.)
Peterhill Cl. SL9: Chal P 22A 42
Peter Hills Ho. *SE16* 49Wb 91
(off Alexis St.)
Peter Ho. *SW8* 52Nb 112
(off Luscombe Way)
Peter James Bus. Cen.
UB3: Hayes 47W 84
Peter James Ent. Cen. NW10 41Sa 87
Peter Kennedy Ct. CR0: C'don 72Bc 158
Peterley Bus. Cen. E2 40Xb 71
Peter Lyell Ct. HA4: Ruis 33X 65
Peter May Sports Cen. 24Ec 52
Peter Pan Statue 6B 220 (46Fb 89)
Peters Av. AL2: Lon C 8G 6
Peters Cl. DA16: Well 54Uc 116
HA7: Stan 23Ma 47
RM8: Dag 32Zc 75
Peters Ct. *W2* 44Db 89
(off Porchester Rd.)
Petersfield Av. RM3: Rom 23Nd 57
SL2: Slou 6L 81
TW18: Staines 64L 127
Petersfield Cl. N18 22Sb 51
RM3: Rom 23Qd 57
Petersfield Cres. CR5: Coul 87Nb 176
Petersfield Ri. SW15 60Xa 110
Petersfield Rd.
TW18: Staines 64L 127
W3 47Sa 87
Petersgate *KT2: King T* 65Sa 131
(off Warren Rd.)
PETERSHAM 60Na 109
Petersham Av. KT14: Byfl 84N 169
Petersham Cl. KT14: Byfl 84N 169
SM1: Sutt 78Cb 155
TW10: Ham 61Ma 131
Petersham Dr. BR5: St P 68Vc 139
Petersham Gdns. BR5: St P 68Vc 139
Petersham Ho. SW7 5B 226
Petersham La. SW7 3A 226 (48Eb 89)
Petersham M. SW7 4A 226 (48Eb 89)
Petersham Pl. SW7 3A 226 (48Eb 89)
Petersham Rd.
TW10: Rich, Ham 58Ma 109

Petersham Ter.—Pinkerton Pl.

Petersham Ter. CR0: Bedd 76Nb 156
(off Richmond Grn.)
Peter's Hill EC4 4D 224 (45Sb 91)
Peter Shore Ct. E1 43Zb 92
(off Beaumont Sq.)
Peter's La. EC1 7C 218 (43Rb 91)
(not continuous)
Peterslea WD4: K Lan 1R 12
Petersmead Cl. KT20: Tad 95Ya 194
Peterson Ct. IG10: Lough 12Qc 36
Peter's Path SE26 63Xb 135
Peterstone Rd. SE2 47Xc 95
Peterstow Cl. SW19 61Ab 132
Peter St. DA12: Grav'nd 9D 122
W1 4D 222 (45Mb 90)
Peterwood Pk. CR0: Wadd 75Pb 156
Peterwood Way CR0: Wadd 75Pb 156
Petham Ct. BR8: Crock 72Hd 162
Petherton Ct. HA1: Harr 30Ha 46
(off Gayton Rd.)
NW10 39Za 68
(off Tiverton Rd.)
Petherton Rd. N5 36Sb 71
Petiver Cl. E9 38Yb 72
Petley Rd. W6 51Za 110
Peto Pl. NW1 5A 216 (42Kb 90)
Peto St. Nth. E16 44Hc 93
Petre Cl. CM13: W H'dn 30Ee 59
Petresfield Way CM13: W H'dn 30Ee 59
Petridge Rd. RH1: Redh 10P 207
PETRIDGE WOOD COMMON 10P 207
Petrie Cl. NW2 37Ab 68
Petrie Ho. SE18 51Qc 116
(off Woolwich Comn.)
Petrie Mus. of Egyptian Archaeology 6D 216 (42Mb 90)
Petros Gdns. NW3 37Db 69
Pettacre Cl. SE28 48Sc 94
Pett Cl. RM11: Horn 33Kd 77
Petten Cl. BR5: Orp 74Zc 161
Petten Gro. BR5: Orp 74Yc 161
Petters Rd. KT21: Asht 88Pa 173
Petticoat La. E1 1K 225 (43Ub 91)
Petticoat Lane Market 1J 225
(off Middlesex St.)
Petticoat Sq. E1 2K 225 (44Vb 91)
Petticoat Twr. E1 2K 225
PETTINGS 80De 165
Pettits Blvd. RM1: Rom 25Gd 56
Pettits Cl. RM1: Rom 26Gd 56
Pettits La. RM1: Rom 26Gd 56
Pettits La. Nth. RM1: Rom 25Fd 56
Pettits Pl. RM10: Dag 36Cd 76
Pettits Rd. RM10: Dag 36Cd 76
Pettiward Cl. SW15 56Ya 110
Pettley Gdns. RM7: Rom 29Fd 56
Pettman Cres. SE28 48Tc 94
Pettsgrove Av. HA0: Wemb 36La 66
Pett's Hill UB5: N'olt 36Da 65
Petts La. TW17: Shep 70Q 128
Pett St. SE18 49Nc 94
PETTS WOOD 71Tc 160
Petts Wood Rd. BR5: Pet W 71Sc 160
Petty Cross SL1: Slou 4C 80
Petty France SW1 3C 228 (48Lb 90)
Pettys Cl. EN8: Chesh 1Zb 20
Petty Wales EC3 5J 225 (45Ub 91)
Petworth Cl. CR5: Coul 91Lb 196
UB5: N'olt 38Ba 65
Petworth Ct. SL4: Wind 3E 102
Petworth Gdns. SW20 69Xa 132
UB10: Hil 39S 64
Petworth Rd. DA6: Bex 57Cd 118
N12 22Gb 49
Petworth St. SW11 53Gb 111
Petworth Way RM12: Horn 35Hd 76
Petyt Pl. SW3 51Gb 111
Petyward SW3 6E 226 (49Gb 89)
Pevensey Av. EN1: Enf 12Ub 33
N11 22Mb 50
Pevensey Cl. TW7: Isle 52Ea 108
Pevensey Ct. SW16 62Qb 134
W3 47Ra 87
Pevensey Ho. E1 43Zb 92
(off Ben Jonson Rd.)
Pevensey Rd. E7 35Hc 73
SL2: Slou 3E 80
SW17 63Fb 133
TW13: Felt 60Aa 107
Pevensey Way WD3: Crox G 14R 26
Peverel E6 44Qc 94
Peverel Ho. RM10: Dag 33Cd 76
Peveret Cl. N11 22Kb 50
Peveril Ct. DA2: Dart 58Rd 119
(off Osbourne Rd.)
Peveril Dr. TW11: Tedd 64Fa 130
Peveril Ho. SE1 4G 231
Pewsey Cl. E4 22Cc 52
Peyton Pl. SE10 52Ec 114
Peyton's Cotts. RH1: Nutf 4F 208
Pharamond NW2 37Za 68
Pharaoh Cl. CR4: Mitc 73Hb 155
Pharaoh's Island TW17: Shep 75P 149
Pheasant Cl. CR8: Purl 85Rb 177
E16 44Kc 93
Pheasant Ct. WD25: Wat 7Y 13
Pheasantry Ho. SW3 7E 226
Pheasantry Welcome Cen., The 67Ha 130
Pheasants Way WD3: Rick 17K 25
Pheasant Wlk. SL9: Chal P 21A 42
Phelps Cl. TN15: W King 79Ud 164
Phelps La. NW7 22Ab 48
Phelps Lodge N1 39Pb 70
Phelp St. SE17 51Tb 113
Phelps Way UB3: Harl 49V 84
Phene St. SW3 51Gb 111
Philadelphia Ct. SW10 52Eb 111
(off Uverdale Rd.)
Philanthropic Rd. RH1: Redh 7A 208
Philan Way RM5: Col R 23Fd 56
Philbeach Gdns. SW5 50Cb 89
Phil Brown Pl. SW8 55Kb 112
(off Daley Thompson Way)
Philbye M. SL1: Slou 7D 80
Philchurch Pl. E1 44Wb 91
Philia Ho. NW1 38Lb 70
(off Farrier St.)
Philimore Cl. SE18 50Uc 94
Philip Av. BR8: Swan 70Fd 140
RM7: Rush G 32Fd 76
Philip Cl. CM15: Pil H 16Xd 40
RM7: Rush G 32Fd 76
Philip Ct. W2 7B 214
Philip Gdns. CR0: C'don 75Bc 158
Philip Ho. NW6 39Db 69
(off Mortimer Pl.)
Philip Jones Ct. N4 32Pb 70
Philip La. N15 28Tb 51
Philip Mole Ho. W9 42Cb 89
(off Chippenham Rd.)
Philipot Path SE9 58Pc 116
Philippa Gdns. SE9 57Mc 115
Philippa Way RM16: Grays 9D 100
Philip Rd. N15 28Tb 51
RM13: Rain 41Gd 96
TW18: Staines 65M 127
Philips Cl. SM5: Cars 74Jb 156
Philip Sidney Ct. RM16: Chaf H 50Zd 99
(off Philip Sidney Rd.)
Philip Sq. SW8 54Kb 112
Philip St. E13 42Jc 93
Philip Sydney Rd. RM16: Chaf H 50Zd 99
Philip Wlk. SE15 55Wb 113
(not continuous)
Phillida Rd. RM3: Hrld W 26Qd 57
Phillimore Ct. W8 47Cb 89
(off Kensington High St.)
WD7: R'lett 8Ga 14
Phillimore Gdns. NW10 39Ya 68
W3 46Qa 87
W8 47Cb 89
Phillimore Gdns. Cl. W8 48Cb 89
Phillimore Pl. W8 47Cb 89
WD7: R'lett 8Ga 14
Phillimore Ter. W8 48Cb 89
(off Allen St.)
Phillimore Wlk. W8 48Cb 89
Phillipers WD25: Wat 8Z 13
Phillip Ho. E1 43Vb 91
(off Heneage St.)
Phillippines Shaw TN14: Ide H 100Yc 201
Phillipp St. N1 1H 219 (39Ub 71)
Phillips Cl. DA1: Dart 58Kd 119
Phillips Ct. HA8: Edg 23Qa 47
Phillip's Quad. GU22: Wok 90A 168
Philpot La. EC3 4H 225 (45Ub 91)
GU24: Chob 5M 167
Philpot Path IG1: Ilf 34Sc 74
Philpots Cl. UB7: Yiew 45M 83
Philpot Sq. SW6 55Db 111
Philpot St. E1 44Xb 91
Phineas Pett Rd. SE9 55Nc 116
Phipps Bri. Rd. CR4: Mitc 69Fb 133
SW19 68Eb 133
Phipps Hatch La. EN2: Enf 10Sb 19
Phipps Ho. SE7 50Kc 93
(off Woolwich Rd.)
W12 45Xa 88
(off White City Est.)
Phipp's M. SW1 4A 228
Phipps Rd. SL1: Slou 3B 80
(not continuous)
Phipp St. EC2 5H 219 (42Ub 91)
Phoebeth Rd. SE4 57Cc 114
Phoebe Wlk. E16 44Kc 93
Phoenix Apartments WD17: Wat 15Z 27
(off Lwr. High St.)
Phoenix Av. SE10 47Gc 93
Phoenix Cen. 80Nb 156
Phoenix Cinema
East Finchley 28Gb 49
Phoenix Cl. BR4: W W'ck 75Ec 159
CR4: Mitc 69Fb 133
E8 39Vb 71
E17 26Bc 52
HA6: Nwood 21V 44
KT19: Eps 84Qa 173
W12 45Xa 88
Phoenix Ct. CR2: S Croy 78Vb 157
DA11: Nflt 57Ce 121
E1 42Xb 91
(off Buckhurst St.)
E4 20Dc 34
E14 49Cc 92
KT3: N Mald 69Va 132
KT17: Eps 85Ua 174
(off Depot Rd.)
NW1 2E 216
SE14 51Ac 114
(off Chipley St.)
TW3: Houn 55Ca 107
TW4: Houn 57Z 107
TW8: Bford 50Na 87
TW13: Felt 63U 128
Phoenix Dr. BR2: Kes 77Mc 159
Phoenix Hgts. E. E14 47Cc 92
(off Byng St.)
Phoenix Hgts. W. E14 47Cc 92
(off Mastmaker Ct.)
Phoenix Ho. AL1: St A 3E 6
(off Campfield Rd.)
SM1: Sutt 77Db 155
Phoenix Ind. Est. HA1: Harr 28Ha 46
Phoenix Lodge Mans. W6 49Za 88
(off Brook Grn.)
Phoenix Pk. NW2 33Wa 68
Phoenix Pl. DA1: Dart 59Md 119
WC1 5J 217 (42Pb 90)
Phoenix Point SE28 46Yc 95
Phoenix Rd. NW1 3D 216 (41Mb 90)
SE20 65Yb 136
Phoenix Sports Cen.
Hammersmith 45Wa 88
Phoenix St. WC2 3E 222 (44Mb 90)
Phoenix Theatre 3E 222
Phoenix Trad. Est. UB6: G'frd 39La 66
Phoenix Trad. Pk. TW8: Bford 50Ma 87
Phoenix Way E16 43Hc 93
(off Barking Rd.)
SW18 57Eb 111
TW5: Hest 51Z 107
Phoenix Wharf E1 46Xb 91
(off Wapping High St.)
Phoenix Wharf Rd. SE1 2K 231
Phoenix Yd. WC1 4J 217
Photographers Gallery 3B 222
Phygtle, The SL9: Chal P 23A 42
Phyllis Av. KT3: N Mald 71Xa 154
Phyllis Hodges Ho. NW1 2D 216
(off Aldenham St.)
Phyllis Ho. CR0: Wadd 77Rb 157
(off Ashley La.)
Physical Energy Statue 7A 220 (46Eb 89)
Physic Pl. SW3 51Hb 111
Piano La. N16 34Tb 71
Piano Works IG11: Bark 38Sc 74
(off Ripple Rd.)
Piano Yd. NW5 36Kb 70
Piazza, The UB8: Uxb 38M 63
WC2 4G 223
(not continuous)
Piazza Wlk. E1 44Wb 91
Picardy Ho. EN2: Enf 10Sb 19
Picardy Manorway DA17: Belv 48Dd 96
Picardy Rd. DA17: Belv 50Cd 96
Picardy St. DA17: Belv 48Cd 96
Picasso Ct. WD24: Wat 8W 12
Piccadilly W1 1K 227 (46Kb 90)
Piccadilly Arc. SW1 6B 222
Piccadilly Circus 5D 222 (45Mb 90)
Piccadilly Cir. W1 5D 222 (45Mb 90)
Piccadilly Ct. N7 37Pb 70
(off Caledonian Rd.)
Piccadilly Pl. W1 5C 222
Piccadilly Theatre 4C 222
Piccotts End HP1: Hem H 1L 3
Pickard Cl. N14 18Mb 32
Pickard Gdns. E3 43Bc 92
Pickard St. EC1 3C 218 (41Rb 91)
Pickering Av. E6 40Qc 74
Pickering Cl. E9 38Zb 72
Pickering Ct. DA2: Dart 58Rd 119
(off Osbourne Rd.)
Pickering Gdns.
CR0: C'don 72Vb 157
N11 23Jb 50
Pickering Ho. W2 44Eb 89
(off Hallfield Est.)
W5 49La 86
(off Windmill Rd.)
Pickering La. BR5: Farnb 74Tc 160
Pickering M. W2 44Db 89
Pickering Pl. SW1 7C 222
Pickering Rd. IG11: Bark 37Sc 74
Pickering St. N1 39Rb 71
Pickets Cl. WD23: B Hea 18Fa 28
Pickets St. SW12 59Kb 112
Pickett Cft. HA7: Stan 25Ma 47
Picketts Lock La. N9 19Yb 34
Picketts Lock La. Ind. Est. N9 19Ac 34
Picketts Ter. SE22 57Wb 113
Pickford Cl. DA7: Bex 54Ad 117
Pickford Dr. SL3: L'ly 46A 82
Pickford La. DA7: Bex 54Ad 117
Pickford Rd. AL1: St A 2F 6
DA7: Bex 55Ad 117
Pickfords Gdns. SL1: Slou 6J 81
Pickfords Wharf N1 2D 218 (40Sb 71)
SE1 6F 225 (46Tb 91)
Pick Hill EN9: Walt A 4Hc 21
Pickhurst Grn. BR2: Hayes 73Hc 159
Pickhurst La. BR2: Hayes 71Gc 159
BR4: W W'ck 71Gc 159
Pickhurst Mead BR2: Hayes 73Hc 159
Pickhurst Pk. BR2: Brom 71Gc 159
Pickhurst Ri. BR4: W W'ck 73Ec 158
Pickins Piece SL3: Hort 54C 104
Pickle M. SW9 52Qb 112
Pickmoss La. TN14: Otf 88Jd 182
Pickwick Cl. TW4: Houn 57Aa 107
Pickwick Ct. SE9 60Nc 116
Pickwick Gdns. DA11: Nflt 62Fe 143
Pickwick Ho. DA11: Nflt 62Fe 143
SE16 47Wb 91
(off George Row)
W11 46Za 88
(off St Ann's Rd.)
Pickwick M. N18 21Ub 51
Pickwick Pl. HA1: Harr 31Ga 66
Pickwick Rd. SE21 59Tb 113
Pickwick St. SE1 2D 230 (47Sb 91)
Pickwick Way BR7: Chst 65Sc 138
Pickworth Cl. SW8 52Nb 112
Picquets Way SM7: Bans 88Ab 174
Picton Mt. CR6: W'ham 91Wb 197
Picton Pl. KT6: Surb 74Qa 153
W1 3J 221 (44Jb 90)
Picton St. SE5 52Tb 113
Picture Ho. SW16 61Nb 134
Picturehouse Central 5D 222
Pied Bull Ct. WC1 1G 223
Pied Bull Yd. N1 39Rb 71
(off Theberton St.)
WC1 1F 223
Piedmont Rd. SE18 50Tc 94
(not continuous)
PIELD HEATH 42P 83
Pield Heath Av. UB8: Hil 42Q 84
Pield Heath Rd. UB8: Cowl, Hil 42N 83
Pierce Campion Ct. E17 27Bc 52
Piercing Hill CM16: They B 7Tc 22
Pier Head E1 46Xb 91
(not continuous)
Pierhead Wharf E1 46Xb 91
(off Wapping High St.)
Pier Ho. SW3 51Gb 111
Pierian Spring HP1: Hem H 1K 3
Pieris Ho. TW13: Felt 61W 128
(off High St.)
Piermont Grn. SE22 57Xb 113
Piermont Pl. BR1: Brom 68Nc 138
Piermont Rd. SE22 57Xb 113
Pier Pde. E16 46Qc 94
(off Pier Rd.)
Pierpoint Bldg. E14 47Bc 92
Pierrepoint Rd. W3 45Ra 87
Pierrepont Arc. N1 1B 218
Pierrepont Row N1 1B 218
Pier Rd. DA8: Erith 51Gd 118
(not continuous)
DA9: Ghithe 56Xd 120
DA11: Nflt 8B 122
E16 46Qc 94
TW14: Felt 57X 107
Pierson Rd. SL4: Wind 3B 102
Pier St. E14 49Ec 92
(not continuous)
Pier Ter. SW18 56Db 111
Pier Wlk. SE10 47Gc 93
Pier Way SE28 47Sc 94
Pier Wharf RM17: Grays 52Ce 121
Pietra Lara Bldg. EC1 5D 218
Pigeon Ho. La. CR5: Coul 97Eb 195
Pigeon La. TW12: Hamp 63Ca 129
Piggott Ho. E2 40Zb 72
(off Sewardstone Rd.)
Piggs Cnr. RM17: Grays 48Ee 99
Piggy La. WD3: Chor 16D 24
Pigott St. E14 44Cc 92
Pike Cl. BR1: Brom 64Kc 137
UB10: Uxb 39P 63
Pike La. RM14: Upm 36Vd 78
Pikemans Ct. SW5 49Cb 89
(off W. Cromwell Rd.)
Pike Rd. NW7 21Ta 47
Pikes Cotts. EN5: Ark 14Ya 30
Pike's End HA5: Eastc 28X 45
Pikes Hill KT17: Eps 85Ua 174
Pikestone Cl. UB4: Yead 42Aa 85
Pikethorne SE23 61Zb 136
Pilgrimage St. SE1 2F 231 (47Tb 91)
Pilgrim Cl. AL2: Park 9A 6
SM4: Mord 73Db 155
Pilgrim Hill SE27 63Sb 135
Pilgrim Ho. SE1 4G 231
SE16 47Yb 92
(off Brunel Rd.)
Pilgrim M. RH2: Reig 6J 207
Pilgrims Cloisters SE5 52Ub 113
(off Sedgmoor Pl.)
Pilgrim's Cl. CM15: Pil H 15Vd 40
Pilgrims Cl. N13 21Pb 50
UB5: N'olt 36Ea 66
WD25: Wat 5Z 13
Pilgrims Cnr. NW6 40Cb 69
(off Chichester Rd.)
Pilgrim's Ct. DA1: Dart 57Qd 119
Pilgrims Ct. EN1: Enf 12Tb 33
PILGRIMS HATCH 16Xd 40
Pilgrim's La. NW3 35Fb 69
Pilgrims La. CM14: Pil H 14Td 40
RH8: T'sey 97Kc 199
RM16: Chaf H 48Zd 99
RM16: N Stif 46Yd 98
TN16: Westrm 97Kc 199
Pilgrims' La. CR3: Cat'm 98Pb 196
Pilgrims M. E14 45Gc 93
Pilgrim's Pl. NW3 35Fb 69
Pilgrims Pl. RH2: Reig 4J 207
Pilgrims Ri. EN4: E Barn 15Gb 31
Pilgrims Rd.
DA10: Nflt, Swans 56Ae 121
PILGRIMS RDBT. 47Yd 98
Pilgrim St. EC4 3B 224 (44Rb 91)
Pilgrims Vw. DA9: Ghithe 58Yd 120
Pilgrim's Way GU24: Bisl 8E 166
HA9: Wemb 32Ra 67
TN13: Dun G 89Ed 182
(not continuous)
Pilgrims Way
CR2: S Croy 79Vb 157
DA1: Dart 60Qd 119
E6 39Nc 74
ME19: Tros 86Fe 185
N19 32Mb 70
RH2: Reig 4H 207
TN14: Otf 88Md 183
TN14: Sund 94Wc 201
TN15: Kems'g 88Md 183
TN15: Wro 88Be 185
(not continuous)
TN16: Westrm, Bras 95Pc 200
Pilgrims Way Cotts.
TN15: Kems'g 89Qd 183
Pilgrims Way E. TN14: Otf 87Ld 183
Pilgrims Way W. TN14: Otf 89Fd 182
Pilkington Rd.
BR6: Farnb 76Sc 160
SE15 54Xb 113
Pillar Box La. TN15: Seal 94Ud 204
Pill Box Studios E2 42Xb 91
(off Coventry Rd.)
Pillfold Ho. SE11 5H 229
Pillions La. UB4: Hayes 42T 84
Pilot Cl. SE8 51Bc 114
Pilot Ind. Cen. NW10 42Ta 87
Pilots Pl. DA12: Grav'nd 8E 122
Pilot Wlk. SE10 48Hc 93
Pilsdon Cl. SW19 60Za 110
Piltdown Rd. WD19: Wat 21Z 45
Pilton Est., The CR0: C'don 75Rb 157
Pilton Pl. SE17 7E 230 (50Sb 91)
Pimento Ct. W5 48Ma 87
PIMLICO
HP3 6E 4
SW1 7B 228 (50Lb 90)
Pimlico Ho. SW1 7K 227
Pimlico Rd. SW1 7H 227 (50Jb 90)
Pimlico Sq. SW1 7H 227 (50Jb 90)
Pimlico Wlk. N1 3H 219
Pimpernel Way RM3: Rom 23Md 57
Pimp Hall Nature Reserve 19Ec 35
Pinchbeck Rd. BR6: Chels 79Vc 161
Pinchfield WD3: Map C 22F 42
Pinchin & Johnsons Yd. E1 45Wb 91
(off Pinchin St.)
Pinchin St. E1 45Wb 91
Pincombe Ho. SE17 7F 231
Pincott La. KT24: W Hor 100R 190
Pincott Pl. SE4 55Zb 114
Pincott Rd. DA6: Bex 57Cd 118
SW19 66Eb 133
Pincroft Wood DA3: Lfield 69Ee 143
Pindar St. EC2 7H 219 (43Ub 91)
PINDEN 68Yd 142
Pindock M. W9 42Db 89
Pindoria M. E1 6K 219
Pineapple Ct. SW1 3B 228
Pine Av. BR4: W W'ck 74Dc 158
DA12: Grav'nd 10F 122
E15 36Fc 73
Pine Cl. BR8: Swan 70Hd 140
CR8: Kenley 89Tb 177
E10 33Dc 72
EN8: Chesh 1Zb 20
GU21: Wok 8N 167
HA7: Stan 21Ka 46
KT15: New H 83K 169
KT19: Eps 81Sa 173
N14 17Lb 32
N19 33Lb 70
SE20 67Yb 136
Pine Coombe CR0: C'don 77Zb 158
Pinecote Dr. SL5: S'dale 3D 146
Pine Ct. CM14: Gt War 23Xd 58
KT13: Weyb 78S 150
KT15: Add 77K 149
(off Church Rd.)
N21 15Pb 32
RM14: Upm 35Rd 77
UB5: N'olt 42Aa 85
Pine Cres. CM13: Hut 14Fe 41
SM5: Cars 83Fb 175
Pinecrest Gdns. BR6: Farnb 77Rc 160
Pine Cft. KT13: Weyb 79T 150
(off St George's Rd.)
Pinecroft CM13: Hut 17De 41
HP3: Hem H 6P 3
RM2: Rom 28Ld 57
Pinecroft Ct. DA16: Well 52Wc 117
HP3: Hem H 6P 3
Pinecroft Cres.
EN5: Barn 14Ab 30
Pine Dean KT23: Bookh 97Da 191
Pinedene SE15 53Xb 113
Pinefield Cl. E14 45Cc 92
Pinefields KT15: Add 77K 149
(off Church Rd.)
Pine Gdns. HA4: Ruis 32X 65
KT5: Surb 72Qa 153
Pinegate KT23: Bookh 97Da 191
Pine Glade BR6: Farnb 77Pc 160
Pine Gro. AL2: Brick W 2Ba 13
AL9: Brk P 9K 9
GU20: W'sham 9B 146
KT13: Weyb 78R 150
N4 33Nb 70
N20 18Bb 31
SW19 64Bb 133
WD23: Bush 12Ba 27
Pine Gro. M. KT13: Weyb 78S 150
Pine Hill KT18: Eps 87Ta 173
Pine Ho. E3 39Ac 72
(off Barge La.)
SE16 47Yb 92
(off Ainsty Est.)
W10 42Ab 88
(off Droop St.)
Pinehurst GU22: Wok 90B 168
(off Park Dr.)
SL5: S'hill 1B 146
TN14: S'oaks 93Nd 203
TW20: Eng G 6N 125
Pinehurst Cl. KT20: Kgswd 94Cb 195
SS17: Stan H 3K 101
WD5: Ab L 4U 12
Pinehurst Ct. W11 44Bb 89
(off Colville Gdns.)
Pinehurst Gdns. KT14: W Byf 84L 169
Pinehurst Wlk. BR6: Orp 74Tc 160
Pinelands Cl. SE3 52Hc 115
Pinel Cl. GU25: Vir W 70A 126
Pine Lodge KT11: Cobh 87Y 171
(off Leigh Cnr.)
Pine Lodge Way KT19: Eps 83Qa 173
Pinemartin Cl. NW2 34Ya 68
Pine M. NW10 40Za 68
(off Clifford Gdns.)
Pineneedle La. TN13: S'oaks 95Kd 203
Pine Pl. SM7: Bans 86Za 174
UB4: Hayes 42V 84
Piner Cotts. SL4: Wind 5C 102
Pine Ridge AL1: St A 5E 6
SM5: Cars 80Jb 156
Pineridge Cl. KT13: Weyb 77U 150
Pineridge Ct. EN5: Barn 14Za 30
Pine Rd. GU22: Wok 2N 187
N11 19Jb 32
NW2 35Ya 68
Pines, The CR5: Coul 90Kb 176
CR8: Purl 85Sb 177
GU21: Wok 86B 168
HP3: Hem H 6H 3
IG8: Wfd G 20Hc 35
KT9: Chess 76Na 153
N14 15Lb 32
RM16: Grays 46De 99
SE19 65Rb 135
SL2: Wex 3M 81
SL3: L'ly 46B 82
TN14: S'oaks 93Md 203
TW16: Sun 69W 128
WD6: Bore 12Pa 29
Pines Av. EN1: Enf 8Yb 20
Pines Cl. HA6: Nwood 23U 44
Pines Rd. BR1: Brom 68Nc 138
Pine St. EC1 5K 217 (42Qb 90)
Pine Tops KT22: Oxs 86Ea 172
Pine Tree Cl. HP2: Hem H 1M 3
TW5: Cran 53X 107
Pinetree Gdns. HP3: Hem H 4N 3
Pine Tree Hill GU22: Pyr 88F 168
Pinetree Ho. WD25: Wat 8Aa 13
Pine Tree La. TN15: Ivy H 97Wd 204
Pine Tree Lodge BR2: Brom 70Hc 137
Pine Trees Bus. Pk.
TW18: Staines 64G 126
Pine Trees Dr. UB10: Ick 35N 63
Pine Tree Way SE13 55Dc 114
Pine Vw. TN15: Plat 92Ee 205
Pineview Ct. E4 18Ec 34
Pine Vw. Mnr. CM16: Epp 2Wc 23
Pine Wlk. CR3: Cat'm 94Ub 197
KT5: Surb 72Qa 153
KT11: Cobh 86Z 171
KT23: Bookh 97Da 191
KT24: E Hor 100V 190
SM5: Cars 82Fb 175
SM7: Bans 89Hb 175
Pine Wlk. E. SM5: Cars 83Fb 175
Pine Wlk. W. SM5: Cars 82Fb 175
Pine Way TW20: Eng G 5M 125
Pine Wood TW16: Sun 67W 128
Pinewood Av. DA15: Sidc 60Uc 116
HA5: Hat E 23Da 45
KT15: New H 81L 169
RM13: Rain 42Kd 97
TN14: S'oaks 93Md 203
UB8: Hil 44P 83
Pinewood Cl. AL4: St A 2G 6
BR6: Orp 74Tc 160
CR0: C'don 76Ac 158
GU21: Wok 87C 168
HA5: Hat E 23Da 45
HA6: Nwood 22W 44
SL0: Iver H 38E 62
SL9: Ger X 31A 62
SS17: Linf 8K 101
WD6: Bore 11Ta 29
WD17: Wat 11W 26
Pinewood Ct. EN2: Enf 13Rb 33
KT15: Add 77M 149
SW4 58Mb 112
Pinewood Dr. BR6: Orp 78Uc 160
EN6: Pot B 3Bb 17
KT15: New H 82L 169
TW18: Staines 64J 127
Pinewood Film Studios 38D 62
Pinewood Gdns. HP1: Hem H 2K 3
Pinewood Grn. SL0: Iver H 38E 62
Pinewood Gro. KT15: New H 82K 169
W5 44La 86
Pinewood Lodge WD23: B Hea 18Fa 28
Pinewood M. TW19: Stanw 58M 105
Pinewood Pk. KT15: New H 83K 169
Pinewood Pl. DA2: Wilm 61Gd 140
(not continuous)
KT19: Ewe 77Ta 153
Pinewood Rd. BR2: Brom 70Jc 137
GU25: Vir W 10L 125
RM4: Have B 21Ed 56
SE2 51Zc 117
SL0: Iver H 37D 62
TW13: Felt 62X 129
Pinewood Way CM13: Hut 15Fe 41
Pinfold Rd. SW16 63Nb 134
WD23: Bush 12Ba 27
Pinglestone Cl. UB7: Harm 52N 105
Pinkcoat Cl. TW13: Felt 62X 129
Pinkerton Pl. SW16 63Mb 134

Pinkham Mans.—Pool End Cl.

Pinkham Mans. W4 50Qa 87
Pinkham Way N11 24Jb 50
Pink La. SL1: Burn 10A 60
Pinks Farm WD7: Shenl 3Sa 15
Pink's Hill BR8: Swan 71Gd 162
Pinkwell Av. UB3: Harl 49T 84
Pinkwell La. UB3: Harl 49S 84
Pinley Gdns. RM9: Dag 39Xc 75
Pinnace Ho. E14 48Ec 92
(off Manchester Rd.)
Pinnacle, The 3H 225
Pinnacle, The TN13: S'oaks 96Jd 222
Pinnacle Apartments CR0: C'don 74Sb 157
(off Saffron Central Sq.)
Pinnacle Hill DA7: Bex 56Dd 118
Pinnacle Hill Nth. DA7: Bex 56Dd 118
Pinnacle Ho. BR5: St M Cry 70Yc 139
(off Ridge Pl.)
EN1: Enf 13Ub 33
(off Colman Pde.)
NW9 26Va 48
(off Heritage Av.)
SW18 56Eb 111
Pinnacle Pl. HA7: Stan 21Ka 46
Pinnacles EN9: Walt A 6Gc 21
Pinnacle Way E14 44Ac 92
(off Commercial Rd.)
Pinnata Cl. EN2: Enf 11Sb 33
Pinn Cl. UB8: Cowl 44M 83
Pinnell Rd. SE9 56Mc 115
PINNER 28Aa 45
Pinner Ct. HA5: Pinn 28Ca 45
NW8 5B 214
PINNER GREEN 26Y 45
Pinner Grn. HA5: Pinn 26Y 45
Pinner Gro. HA5: Pinn 28Aa 45
Pinner Hill HA5: Pinn 24X 45
Pinner Hill Farm HA5: Pinn 25X 45
Pinner Hill Golf Course 23X 45
Pinner Hill Rd. HA5: Pinn 24X 45
Pinner Pk. 25Ca 45
Pinner Pk. HA5: Pinn 26Ca 45
Pinner Pk. Av. HA2: Harr 27Da 45
Pinner Pk. Gdns. HA2: Harr 26Ea 46
Pinner Rd. HA1: Harr 28Ca 45
HA2: Harr 28Ca 45
HA5: Pinn 28Ba 45
HA6: Nwood, Pinn 25V 44
HA6: Pinn 25V 44
WD19: Wat 16Z 27
Pinners Cl. SM5: Cars 75Gb 155
Pinners Pas. EC2 2G 225
Pinner Vw. HA1: Harr 28Ea 46
HA2: Harr 28Ea 46
PINNERWOOD PARK 25Y 45
Pinnocks Av. DA11: Grav'nd 10D 122
Pinn Way HA4: Ruis 31T 64
Pinson Way BR5: Orp 74Zc 161
Pinstone Way SL9: Ger X 33D 62
Pintail Ct. E6 43Nc 94
Pintail Ct. SE8 51Bc 114
(off Pilot Cl.)
Pintail Rd. IG8: Wfd G 24Kc 53
Pintail Way UB4: Yead 43Z 85
Pinter Ho. SW9 54Nb 112
(off Grantham Rd.)
Pinto Cl. WD6: Bore 16Ta 29
Pinto Way SE3 56Kc 115
Pioneer Cen., The SE15 53Yb 114
Pioneer Cl. E14 43Dc 92
Pioneer Ct. E16 43Jc 93
(off Hammersley Rd.)
Pioneer Ho. WC1 3H 217
Pioneer Pl. CR0: Sels 81Cc 178
Pioneer Point IG1: Ilf 34Rc 74
Pioneers Ind. Pk. CR0: Bedd 74Nb 156
Pioneer St. SE15 53Wb 113
Pioneer Way BR8: Swan 69Gd 140
W12 44Xa 88
WD18: Wat 16V 26
Piper Bldg., The SW6 55Db 111
Piper Cl. N7 37Pb 70
Piper Rd. KT1: King T 69Qa 131
Pipers Cl. KT11: Cobh 87Z 171
SL1: Burn 1A 80
Piper's End GU25: Vir W 9P 125
Piper's Gdns. CR0: C'don 73Ac 158
Pipers Grn. NW9 29Sa 47
Pipers Grn. La. HA8: Edg 20Na 29
(not continuous)
Piper's Grn. Rd. TN16: B Char 100Wc 201
Pipers Ho. SE10 50Fc 93
(off Collington St.)
Pipers La. TN16: B Char 99Wc 201
Pipers Rd. CR5: Coul 88Mb 176
Piper Way IG1: Ilf 32Tc 74
Pipewell Rd. SM5: Cars 72Gb 155
Pipit Dr. SW15 58Ya 110
Pippenhall SE9 58Rc 116
Pippin Cl. CR0: C'don 74Bc 158
NW2 34Wa 68
SL2: Slou 3H 81
TW13: Hanw 62Ba 129
WD7: Shenl 5Na 15
Pippin Ct. SW8 51Pb 112
(off Vauxhall Gro.)
Pippin Ho. W10 45Za 88
(off Freston Rd.)
Pippin Mans. E20 36Ec 72
(off Mirabelle Gdns.)
Pippins, The SL3: L'ly 46B 82
WD25: Wat 6Y 13
Pippins Cl. UB7: W Dray 48M 83
Pippins Ct. TW15: Ashf 65R 128
Pique M. E1 45Zb 92
(off Glasshouse Flds.)
Piquet Rd. SE20 68Yb 136
Pirate Cove Adventure Pk. 59Wd 120
PIRBRIGHT 5D 186
PIRBRIGHT CAMP 3A 186
Pirbright Cres. CR0: New Ad 79Ec 158
Pirbright Golf Course 3B 186
Pirbright Grn. GU24: Pirb 5D 186
Pirbright Rd. GU3: Norm 10A 186
SW18 60Bb 111
Pirbright Ter. GU24: Pirb 5D 186
Pirie Cl. SE5 55Tb 113
Pirie St. E16 46Kc 93
Pirin Ct. E4 21Cc 52
Pirrip Cl. DA12: Grav'nd 10H 123
Pirton Ct. HP2: Hem H 1P 3
Pisa Pl. WD18: Wat 13U 26
Pisces Ct. HA8: Edg 24Qa 47
Pissaro Ho. N1 38Qb 70
(off Augustas La.)
Pitcairn Cl. RM7: Mawney 28Cd 56
Pitcairn Ho. E9 38Yb 72
Pitcairn Rd. CR4: Mitc 66Hb 133
Pitcairn's Path HA2: Harr 34Ea 66
Pitcher Ct. DA11: Nflt 61Ee 143
Pitchfont La. RH8: Limp, T'sey 97Hc 199
Pitchford St. E15 38Fc 73
PITCH PLACE 10L 187
Pitfield DA3: Hartl 70Be 143
Pitfield Cres. SE28 46Wc 95
Pitfield Est. N1 3H 219 (41Ub 91)
Pitfield St. N1 4H 219 (41Ub 91)
Pitfield Way EN3: Enf H 11Yb 34
NW10 37Sa 67
Pitfold Cl. SE12 58Kc 115
Pitfold Rd. SE12 58Jc 115
Pitlake CR0: C'don 75Rb 157
Pitlochry Ho. SE27 61Rb 135
(off Elmcourt Rd.)
Pitman Bldg. SE16 48Wb 91
(off Old Jamaica Rd.)
Pitman Ho. SE8 53Cc 114
Pitman St. SE5 52Sb 113
Pitmaston Ho. SE13 54Ec 114
(off Lewisham Rd.)
Pitmaston Rd. SE13 54Ec 114
Pitsea Pl. E1 44Zb 92
Pitsea St. E1 44Zb 92
Pitshanger La. W5 42Ka 86
Pitson Cl. KT15: Add 77M 149
Pitt Cres. SW19 63Db 133
Pitt Dr. AL4: St A 5G 6
Pittman Cl. CM13: Ingve 22Ee 59
Pittman Gdns. IG1: Ilf 36Sc 74
Pitt Pl. KT17: Eps 86Ua 174
Pitt Rd. BR6: Farnb 77Sc 160
CR0: C'don 71Sb 157
CR7: Thor H 71Sb 157
HA2: Harr 33Ea 66
KT17: Eps 86Ua 174
Pitt's Head M. W1 7J 221 (46Jb 90)
Pittsmead Av. BR2: Hayes 73Jc 159
Pitts Rd. SL1: Slou 6G 80
Pitt St. W8 47Cb 89
Pittville Gdns. SE25 69Wb 135
Pittwood CM15: Shenf 18Ce 41
Pitwell M. E8 37Wb 71
Pitwood Grn. KT20: Tad 92Ya 194
Pitwood Pk. Ind. Est. KT20: Tad 92Xa 194
Pix Farm La. HP1: Hem H 3D 2
Pixfield Ct. BR2: Brom 68Hc 137
(off Beckenham La.)
Pixies Hill Cres. HP1: Hem H 4H 3
(not continuous)
Pixies Hill Rd. HP1: Hem H 3H 3
Pixley M. GU24: Bisl 9E 166
Pixley St. E14 44Bc 92
Pixton Way CR0: Sels 81Ac 178
Place, The 4E 216 (41Mb 90)
Place, The SE1 7G 225 (46Tb 91)
Place Farm Av. BR6: Orp 74Tc 160
Place Farm Rd. RH1: Blet 2K 209
Placehouse La. CR5: Coul 91Pb 196
Plackett Way SL1: Slou 6B 80
Plain, The CM16: Epp 1Xc 23
Plaines Cl. SL1: Slou 6D 80
Plain Ride SL4: Wind 10A 102
Plaisterers Highwalk EC2 1D 224
PLAISTOW
BR1 66Jc 137
E13 40Jc 73
Plaistow Cl. SS17: Stan H 1M 101
Plaistow Gro. BR1: Brom 66Kc 137
E15 39Hc 73
Plaistow La. BR1: Brom 66Jc 137
Plaistow Pk. Rd. E13 40Kc 73
(not continuous)
Plaistow Rd. E13 39Hc 73
E15 39Hc 73
Plaistow Wharf E16 47Jc 93
Plaitford Cl. WD3: Rick 19N 25
Plane Av. DA11: Nflt 59Fe 121
Plane Ho. BR2: Brom 68Gc 137
Planes, The KT16: Chert 73L 149
Plane St. SE26 62Xb 135
Planet Ice
Hemel Hempstead 3P 3
Planetree Ct. W6 49Za 88
(off Brook Grn.)
Plane Tree Cres. TW13: Felt 62X 129
Plane Tree Ho. SE8 51Ac 114
(off Etta St.)
W8 47Bb 89
(off Duchess of Bedford's Wlk.)
Plane Tree Wlk. N2 27Gb 49
SE19 65Ub 135
Plantaganet Pl. EN9: Walt A 5Dc 20
Plantagenet Cl. KT4: Wor Pk 77Ta 153
Plantagenet Gdns. RM6: Chad H 31Zc 75
Plantagenet Ho. SE18 48Pc 94
(off Leda Rd.)
Plantagenet Pl. RM6: Chad H 31Zc 75
Plantagenet Rd. EN5: New Bar 14Eb 31
Plantain Gdns. E11 34Fc 73
(off Hollydown Way)
Plantain Pl. SE1 1F 231 (47Tb 91)
Plantation, The SE3 54Jc 115
Plantation Cl. DA9: Ghithe 58Vd 120
SW4 57Nb 112
WD23: Bush 15Z 27
Plantation Dr. BR5: Orp 74Zc 161
Plantation La.
CR3: W'ham, Wold 91Ac 198
CR6: W'ham 91Ac 198
EC3 4H 225
Plantation Pl. EC3 4H 225
Plantation Rd. BR8: Hext 66Jd 140
DA8: Erith 53Jd 118
Plantation Wharf SW11 55Eb 111
Plantree Path E17 28Cc 52
(off Selborne Rd.)
Plasel Ct. E13 39Kc 73
(off Pawsey Cl.)
PLASHET 37Nc 74
Plashet Cl. SS17: Stan H 1M 101
Plashet Gdns. CM13: B'wood 21Ce 59
Plashet Gro. E6 39Lc 73
Plashet Rd. E13 39Jc 73
Plassy Rd. SE6 59Dc 114
Plate Ho. E14 50Dc 92
(off Burrells Wharf Sq.)
Platford Grn. RM11: Horn 28Nd 57
Platform Theatre 39Nb 70
Platina St. EC2 5G 219
Platinum Ct. E1 42Yb 92
(off Cephas Av.)
RM7: Mawney 27Dd 56
Platinum M. N15 29Vb 51
Platinum Way TN15: Plat 92Ee 205
Plato Rd. SW2 56Nb 112
Platt, The SW15 55Za 110
Platt Comn. TN15: Plat 92Ee 205
Platt Ct. AL1: St A 2C 6
(off Hatfield Rd.)
Platt Halls NW9 26Va 48
Platt Ho. La. TN15: Fair, Wro 85Ee 185
Platt Ind. Est. TN15: Plat 91De 205
Platt Mill Cl. TN15: Plat 92De 205
Platt Mill Ter. TN15: Plat 92De 205
Platt's Eyot TW12: Hamp 68Ca 129
Platt's La. NW3 35Cb 69
Platts Rd. EN3: Enf H 11Yb 34
Platt St. NW1 1D 216 (40Mb 70)
Plawsfield Rd. BR3: Beck 67Zb 136
Plaxdale Grn. Rd. TN15: Stans 85Zd 185
Plaxdale Ho. SE17 6H 231
PLAXTOL 99Ae 205
Plaxtol Cl. BR1: Brom 67Lc 137
Plaxtol La. TN15: Plax 99Yd 204
Plaxtol Rd. DA8: Erith 52Cd 118
PLAXTOL SPOUTE 99Ce 205
Plaxton Ct. E11 34Hc 73
Playfair Ho. E14 44Cc 92
(off Saracen St.)
Playfair Mans. W14 51Ab 110
(off Queen's Club Gdns.)
Playfair St. W6 50Ya 88
Playfield Av. RM5: Col R 25Ed 56
Playfield Cres. SE22 57Vb 113
Playfield Rd. HA8: Edg 26Sa 47
Playford Rd. N4 33Pb 70
(not continuous)
Playgreen Way SE6 62Cc 136
Playground Cl. BR3: Beck 68Zb 136
Playhouse Ct. SE1 7D 224
Playhouse Theatre 6G 223
Playhouse Yd. EC4 3B 224 (44Rb 91)
Plaza DA9: Bluew 60Vd 120
Plaza Bus. Cen. EN3: Brim 12Bc 34
Plaza Gdns. SW15 57Ab 110
Plaza Hgts. E10 34Ec 72
Plaza Pde. HA0: Wemb 37Na 67
(off Ealing Rd.)
NW6 40Db 69
Plaza Shop. Cen., The
W1 2C 222 (44Lb 90)
Plaza Wlk. NW9 27Sa 47
Pleasance, The SW15 56Xa 110
Pleasance Rd. BR5: St P 68Xc 139
SW15 57Xa 110
Pleasance Theatre
London 37Nb 70
(off Carpenters M.)
Pleasant Gro. CR0: C'don 76Bc 158
Pleasant Pl. KT12: Hers 79Y 151
N1 38Rb 71
WD3: W Hyd 24G 42
Pleasant Row NW1 39Kb 70
Pleasant Vw. DA8: Erith 50Gd 96
Pleasant Vw. Pl. BR6: Farnb 78Rc 160
Pleasant Way HA0: Wemb 40La 66
Pleasaunce Mans. SE10 50Jc 93
(off Halstow Rd.)
Pleasure Pit Rd. KT21: Asht 90Ra 173
Plender Ct. NW1 39Lb 70
(off College Pl.)
Plender St. NW1 1B 216 (39Lb 70)
Pleshey Rd. N7 35Mb 70
Plesman Way SM6: Wall 81Nb 176
Plessey Bldg. E14 44Cc 92
(off Dod St.)
Plevna Cres. N15 30Ub 51
Plevna Rd. N9 20Wb 33
TW12: Hamp 67Da 129
Plevna St. E14 48Ec 92
Pleydell Av. SE19 66Vb 135
W6 49Va 88
Pleydell Ct. EC4 3A 224
Pleydell Est. EC1 4E 218
Pleydell Gdns. SE19 65Vb 135
(off Anerley Hill)
Pleydell Ho. EC4 3A 224
(off Pleydell St.)
Pleydell St. EC4 3A 224
Plimley Pl. W12 47Za 88
(off Shepherd's Bush Pl.)
Plimsoll Cl. E14 44Dc 92
Plimsoll Rd. N4 34Qb 70
Plough Cl. NW10 41Xa 88
Plough Ct. EC3 4G 225 (45Tb 91)
RM13: Rain 40Fd 76
(off Broadis Way)
Plough Farm Cl. HA4: Ruis 30T 44
Plough Hill EN6: Cuff 1Nb 18
TN15: Bor G 95Be 205
Plough Ind. Est. KT22: Lea 92Ja 192
Plough La. CR8: Purl 81Nb 176
KT11: Cobh 89W 170
SE22 58Vb 113
SL2: Stoke P 9M 61
SM6: Bedd, Wall 77Nb 156
SW17 64Db 133
SW19 64Db 133
TW11: Tedd 64Ja 130
UB9: Hare 23L 43
WD3: Sarr 5H 11
Plough La. Cl. SM6: Bedd 78Nb 156
Ploughlees La. SL1: Slou 5J 81
Ploughmans Cl. NW1 39Mb 70
Ploughmans End TW7: Isle 57Fa 108
Ploughmans Wlk. N2 26Eb 49
(off Long La.)
Plough M. SW11 56Fb 111
Plough Pl. EC4 2A 224 (44Qb 90)
Plough Ri. RM14: Upm 31Ud 78
Plough Rd. KT19: Ewe 81Ta 173
SW11 55Fb 111
Plough St. E1 44Vb 91
(off Buckle St.)
Plough Ter. SW11 56Fb 111
Plough Way SE16 49Zb 92
Plough Yd. EC2 6J 219 (42Ub 91)
Plover Cl. TW18: Staines 62H 127
Plover Gdns. RM14: Upm 32Vd 78
Plover Ho. SW9 52Qb 112
(off Brixton Rd.)
Plovers Ri. GU24: Brkwd 2C 186
Plover Way SE16 48Ac 92
UB4: Yead 44Z 85
Plowden Bldgs. EC4 4K 223
(off Middle Temple La.)
Plowman Cl. N18 22Tb 51
Plowman Way RM8: Dag 32Yc 75
Plumber's Row E1 43Wb 91
Plumbridge St. SE10 53Ec 114
Plum Cl. TW13: Felt 60W 106
Plume Ho. SE10 51Dc 114
(off Creek Rd.)
Plum Gth. TW8: Bford 49Ma 87
Plum La. RM13: Rain 40Fd 76
SE18 52Rc 116
Plummer La. CR4: Mitc 68Hb 133
Plummer Rd. SW4 59Mb 112
Plummers Cft. TN13: Dun G 93Gd 202
Plumpton Av. RM12: Horn 35Nd 77
Plumpton Cl. UB5: N'olt 37Ca 65
Plumpton Way SM5: Cars 76Gb 155
PLUMSTEAD 49Uc 94
PLUMSTEAD COMMON 51Rc 116
Plumstead Comn. Rd. SE18 51Rc 116
Plumstead High St. SE18 49Tc 94
Plumstead Rd. SE18 49Rc 94
(not continuous)
Plumtree Cl. RM10: Dag 37Dd 76
SM6: Wall 80Mb 156
Plum Tree Ct. RM3: Rom 21Nd 57
Plumtree Ct. EC4 2B 224 (44Rb 91)
Plumtree Mead IG10: Lough 13Qc 36
Pluto Cl. SL1: Slou 7C 80
Pluto Ri. HP2: Hem H 1N 3
Plymen Ho. KT8: W Mole 71Ca 151
Plymouth Ct. KT5: Surb 70Na 131
(off Cranes Pk. Av.)
Plymouth Dr. TN13: S'oaks 96Ld 203
Plymouth Ho. IG11: Bark 38Wc 75
(off Margaret Bondfield Av.)
SE10 53Dc 114
(off Devonshire Dr.)
Plymouth Pk. TN13: S'oaks 96Ld 203
Plymouth Rd. BR1: Brom 67Kc 137
E16 43Jc 93
RM16: Chaf H 49Yd 98
SL1: Slou 3C 80
Plymouth Ter. NW2 37Ya 68
(off Sidmouth Rd.)
Plymouth Wharf E14 49Fc 93
Plympton Av. NW6 38Bb 69
Plympton Cl. DA17: Belv 48Ad 95
Plympton Pl. NW8 6D 214 (42Gb 89)
Plympton Rd. NW6 38Bb 69
Plympton St. NW8 6D 214 (42Gb 89)
Plymstock Rd. DA16: Well 52Yc 117
PM Gallery & House 46Ma 87
Pocahontas Memorial 8D 122
(off Church St.)
Pocket Hill TN13: S'oaks 100Jd 202
Pocketsdell La. HP3: Bov 10A 2
Pocklington Cl. NW9 26Ua 48
W12 48Wa 88
(off Ashchurch Pk. Vs.)
Pocklington Ct. SW15 60Wa 110
Pocklington Lodge W12 48Wa 88
Pocock Av. UB7: W Dray 48P 83
Pococks La. SL4: Eton 10J 81
Pocock St. SE1 1B 230 (47Rb 91)
Podmore Rd. SW18 56Eb 111
Poet Ct. E1 43Zb 92
(off Shandy St.)
Poets Chase HP1: Hem H 1K 3
Poets Ct. SE25 70Wb 135
W3 46Sa 87
Poet's Rd. N5 36Tb 71
Poets Way HA1: Harr 28Ga 46
Point, The 13Qa 29
Point, The E17 28Cc 52
(off Tower M.)
GU21: Wok 88B 168
(off Chertsey Rd.)
HA4: Ruis 35W 64
W2 1B 220
Pointalls Cl. N3 26Eb 49
Point Cl. SE10 53Ec 114
Pointer Cl. SE28 44Zc 95
Pointers, The KT21: Asht 92Na 193
Pointers Cl. E14 50Dc 92
Pointers Cotts. TW10: Ham 61La 130
POINTERS GREEN 90W 170
Pointers Rd. KT11: Cobh 88S 170
Point Hill SE10 52Ec 114
Point Pl. HA9: Wemb 38Ra 67
Point Pleasant SW18 56Cb 111
Point Ter. E7 36Kc 73
(off Claremont Rd.)
Point W. SW7 49Db 89
Point Wharf TW8: Bford 52Na 109
Point Wharf La. TW8: Bford 52Ma 109
Poland St. W1 2C 222 (44Lb 90)
Polar Pk. UB7: Harm 52P 105
Poldo Ho. SE10 49Gc 93
(off Cable Wlk.)
Polebrook Rd. SE3 55Lc 115
Pole Cat All. BR2: Hayes 75Hc 159
Polecroft La. SE6 61Bc 136
Polehamptons, The
TW12: Hamp 66Ea 130
Pole Hill Rd. E4 17Ec 34
UB4: Hayes 41S 84
UB10: Hil 42R 84
Polesden Gdns. SW20 68Xa 132
Polesden La. GU23: Rip 95H 189
Polesden Rd. KT23: Bookh 100Da 191
Polesden Vw. KT23: Bookh 99Da 191
Poles Hill WD3: Sarr 5G 10
Polesteeple Hill TN16: Big H 89Mc 179
Polesworth Ho. W2 43Cb 89
(off Alfred Rd.)
Polesworth Rd. RM9: Dag 38Zc 75
Poley Rd. SS17: Stan H 2L 101
Polhill TN14: Hals 87Ed 182
Polhill Pk. TN14: Hals 88Fd 182
Police Sta. La.
WD23: Bush 17Da 27
Police Sta. Rd. KT12: Hers 79Y 151
POLISH WAR MEMORIAL 38Y 65
Polka Theatre for Children 65Db 133
Pollard Av. UB9: Den 30H 43
Pollard Cl. E16 45Jc 93
IG7: Chig 22Wc 55
N7 35Pb 70
SL4: Old Win 7M 103
Pollard Ho. KT4: Wor Pk 77Ya 154
N1 2H 217
SE16 48Vb 91
(off Spa Rd.)
Pollard Rd. GU22: Wok 88D 168
N20 19Gb 31
SM4: Mord 71Fb 155
Pollard Row E2 41Wb 91
Pollards WD3: Map C 22F 42
Pollards Cl. EN7: G Oak 1Sb 19
IG10: Lough 15Lc 35
Pollards Cres. SW16 69Nb 134
Pollards Hill E. SW16 69Pb 134
Pollards Hill Nth. SW16 69Nb 134
Pollards Hill Sth. SW16 69Nb 134
Pollards Hill W. SW16 69Pb 134
Pollards Oak Cres. RH8: Oxt 4L 211
Pollards Oak Rd. RH8: Oxt 4L 211
Pollard St. E2 41Wb 91
Pollardswood Grange
HP8: Chal G 14A 24
Pollards Wood Hill RH8: Oxt 2M 211
Pollards Wood Rd. RH8: Oxt 3M 211
SW16 69Nb 134
Pollard Wlk. DA14: Sidc 65Yc 139
Pollen St. W1 3A 222 (44Lb 90)
Pollitt Dr. NW8 5B 214 (42Fb 89)
Pollock Ho. W10 42Ab 88
(off Kensal Rd.)
Pollock's Toy Mus. 7C 216 (43Lb 90)
Pollyhaugh DA4: Eyns 76Nd 163
Polo Cen., The SL5: S'hill 9G 124
Polo M. BR7: Chst 64Tc 138
Polperro Cl. BR6: St M Cry 72Vc 161
Polperro Ho. W2 43Cb 89
(off Westbourne Pk. Rd.)
Polperro M. SE11 5A 230 (49Rb 91)
Polsted Rd. SE6 59Bc 114
Polsten M. EN3: Enf L 9Cc 20
Polthorne Est. SE18 49Tc 94
(off Polthorne Gro.)
Polthorne Gro. SE18 49Sc 94
Polworth Rd. SW16 64Nb 134
Polychrome Ct. SE1 2B 230
Polydamas Cl. E3 40Cc 72
Polygon, The NW8 39Fb 69
(off Avenue Rd.)
SW4 56Lb 112
Polygon Bus. Cen. SL3: Poyle 54H 105
Polygon Rd. NW1 2D 216 (40Mb 70)
(not continuous)
Polytechnic St. SE18 49Qc 94
Pomell Way E1 2K 225 (44Vb 91)
Pomeroy Cl. TW1: Twick 56Ka 108
Pomeroy Cres. WD24: Wat 8X 13
Pomeroy Ho. E2 40Zb 72
(off St James's Av.)
W11 44Ab 88
(off Lancaster Rd.)
Pomeroy St. SE14 52Yb 114
Pomfret Pl. E14 45Ec 92
(off Bullivant St.)
Pomfret Rd. SE5 55Rb 113
Pomoja La. N19 33Nb 70
Pomona Ho. SE8 49Ac 92
(off Evelyn St.)
Pompadour Cl. CM14: W'ley 22Yd 58
Pompadour Way IG11: Bark 40Xc 75
Pond Cl. CR8: Kenley 88Rb 177
KT12: Hers 79V 150
(not continuous)
N12 23Gb 49
SE3 54Jc 115
UB9: Hare 26L 43
Pond Cott. La. BR4: W W'ck 74Cc 158
Pond Cotts. SE21 60Ub 113
PONDERS END 15Yb 34
Ponders End Ind. Est.
EN3: Pond E 15Ac 34
Ponder St. N7 38Pb 70
Pond Farm Cl. KT20: Walt H 96Xa 194
Pond Farm Est. E5 34Yb 72
Pond Fld. End IG10: Lough 16Lc 35
Pondfield Ho. SE27 64Sb 135
Pondfield La. CM13: B'wood 21Ce 59
DA12: Shorne 6N 145
Pondfield Rd. BR2: Hayes 74Gc 159
BR6: Farnb 76Rc 160
CR8: Kenley 88Rb 177
RM10: Dag 36Dd 76
Pond Grn. HA4: Ruis 33U 64
Pond Hill Gdns. SM3: Cheam 79Ab 154
Pond Ho. HA7: Stan 23Ka 46
KT16: Chert 73K 149
SW3 6D 226 (49Gb 89)
Pond La. TN15: Ivy H 97Ud 204
Pond Lees Cl. RM10: Dag 38Fd 76
Pond Mead SE21 58Tb 113
Pond Path BR7: Chst 65Rc 138
Pond Piece KT22: Oxs 85Da 171
Pond Pl. KT21: Asht 89Na 173
SW3 6D 226 (49Gb 89)
Pond Rd. E15 40Gc 73
GU22: Wok 2L 187
HP3: Hem H 7A 4
SE3 54Hc 115
TW20: Egh 65E 126
Ponds, The KT13: Weyb 79T 150
Pondside Av. KT4: Wor Pk 74Ya 154
Pondside Cl. UB3: Harl 51T 106
Pond Sq. N6 32Jb 70
Pond St. NW3 36Gb 69
Pond Wlk. RM14: Upm 33Ud 78
Pond Way TW11: Tedd 65La 130
Pondwicks Cl. AL1: St A 3A 6
Pondwood Ri. BR6: Orp 73Uc 160
Ponler St. E1 44Xb 91
Ponsard Rd. NW10 41Xa 88
Ponsford St. E9 37Yb 72
Ponsonby Ho. E2 40Yb 72
(off Bishop's Way)
Ponsonby Pl. SW1 7E 228 (50Mb 90)
Ponsonby Rd. SW15 59Xa 110
Ponsonby Ter. SW1 7E 228 (50Mb 90)
Ponsonby Vs. E2 40Yb 72
(off Lark Row)
Pontefract Ct. UB5: N'olt 36Da 65
(off Newmarket Av.)
Pontefract Rd. BR1: Brom 64Hc 137
Pontes Av. TW3: Houn 56Ba 107
Pontifex Apartments SE1 6F 225
(off Stoney St.)
Pontoise Cl. TN13: S'oaks 94Hd 202
Ponton Rd. SW8 51Mb 112
Pontoon Rd. E16 46Kc 93
Pont St. SW1 4F 227 (48Hb 89)
Pont St. M. SW1 4F 227 (48Hb 89)
Pontypool Pl. SE1 1B 230 (47Rb 91)
Pontypool Wlk.
RM3: Rom 23Ld 57
Pony Chase KT11: Cobh 85Ba 171
Pooja Ct. NW1 38Lb 70
(off Agar Gro.)
Pool Cl. BR3: Beck 64Cc 136
KT8: W Mole 71Ba 151
Pool Ct. SE6 61Cc 136
Poole Cl. HA4: Ruis 35U 64
Poole Ct. N1 38Ub 71
(off St Peter's Way)
TW4: Houn 54Aa 107
Poole Ct. Rd. TW4: Houn 54Aa 107
Poole Ho. RM16: Grays 7E 100
SE11 5J 229
POOL END 71Q 150
Pool End Cl. TW17: Shep 71Q 150

Poole Rd.—Prescott Grn.

Poole Rd. E9 .37Zb 72
GU21: Wok .90A 168
KT19: Ewe .79Ta 153
RM11: Horn .31Pd 77
Pooles Bldgs. WC1 .6K 217
Pooles Cotts. TW10: Ham .61Ma 131
Pooles La. RM9: Dag .40Ad 75
SW10 .52Eb 111
Pooles Pk. N4 .33Qb 70
Poole St. N1 .1F 219 (39Tb 71)
Poole Way UB4: Hayes .41U 84
Pooley Av. TW20: Egh .64D 126
Pooley Dr. SW14 .55Sa 109
POOLEY GREEN .64E 126
Pooley Grn. Cl. TW20: Egh .64E 126
Pooley Grn. Rd. TW20: Egh .64D 126
Pooley Ho. E1 .41Zb 92
E18 .25Jc 53
Pooleys La. AL9: Wel G .5D 8
Pool Ho. NW8 .7C 214
Pool in the Pk. .91B 188
Pool La. SL1: Slou .5J 81
Poolmans Rd. SL4: Wind .5B 102
Poolmans St. SE16 .47Zb 92
Pool Rd. HA1: Harr .31Fa 66
KT8: W Mole .71Ba 151
Poolsford Rd. NW9 .28Ua 48
Poolside Manor .25Bb 49
Pools on the Pk. .56Ma 109
Pool St. E20 .38Ec 72
Poonah St. E1 .44Yb 92
Pope Cl. SW19 .65Fb 133
TW14: Felt .60V 106
Pope Ct. CM14: W'ley .22Xd 58
Pope Ho. SE5 .52Tb 113
(off Elmington Est.)
SE16 .49Xb 91
(off Manor Est.)
Pope Rd. BR2: Brom .71Mc 159
Popes Av. TW2: Twick .61Ga 130
Popes Cl. SL3: Coln .52D 104
Pope's Ct. WD5: Ab L .3U 12
Popes Ct. TW2: Twick .61Ga 130
Popes Dr. N3 .25Cb 49
Popes Gro. CR0: C'don .76Bc 158
TW1: Twick .61Ha 130
TW2: Twick .61Ha 130
Pope's Head All. EC3 .3G 225 (44Tb 91)
Popes La. RH8: Oxt .6J 211
W5 .48Ma 87
WD24: Wat .9X 13
Pope's Rd. SW9 .55Qb 112
WD5: Ab L .3U 12
Pope St. SE1 .2J 231 (47Ub 91)
Popham Cl. TW13: Hanw .62Ba 129
Popham Gdns. TW9: Rich .55Qa 109
Popham Rd. N1 .39Sb 71
Popham St. N1 .39Rb 71
(not continuous)
Pop in Commercial Cen.
HA9: Wemb .36Ra 67
Popinjays Row SM3: Cheam .78Za 154
(off Netley Cl.)
POPLAR .45Dc 92
Poplar Av. AL10: Hat .1P 7
BR6: Farnb .75Rc 160
CR4: Mitc .67Hb 133
DA12: Grav'nd .3E 144
KT22: Lea .94Ka 192
UB2: S'hall .48Da 85
UB7: Yiew .45P 83
Poplar Bath St. E14 .44Dc 92
Poplar Bus. Pk. E14 .45Ec 92
Poplar Cl. E9 .36Bc 72
HA5: Pinn .25Z 45
KT17: Eps D .87Xa 174
RM15: S Ock .42Zd 99
SL3: Poyle .53G 104
Poplar Ct. SW19 .64Cb 133
TW1: Twick .58La 108
UB5: N'olt .40Y 65
Poplar Cres. KT19: Ewe .79Sa 153
Poplar Dr. CM13: Hut .16Ee 41
SM7: Bans .86Za 174
Poplar Farm Cl. KT19: Ewe .79Sa 153
Poplar Gdns. KT3: N Mald .68Ta 131
SE28 .45Yc 95
Poplar Gro. GU22: Wok .91A 188
HA9: Wemb .34Sa 67
KT3: N Mald .68Ta 131
N11 .23Jb 50
W6 .47Ya 88
Poplar High St. E14 .45Dc 92
Poplar Ho. KT19: Eps .81Ta 173
SE4 .56Bc 114
(off Wickham Rd.)
SE16 .47Zb 92
(off Woodland Cres.)
SL3: L'ly .50B 82
Poplar Leisure Cen. .45Dc 92
Poplar M. W12 .46Ya 88
Poplar Mt. DA17: Belv .49Dd 96
Poplar Pl. SE28 .45Yc 95
UB3: Hayes .45W 84
W2 .45Db 89
Poplar Rd. KT10: Surb .76Ka 152
KT22: Lea .94Ka 192
SE24 .56Sb 113
SM3: Sutt .74Bb 155
SW19 .68Cb 133
TW15: Ashf .64S 128
UB9: Den .36L 63
Poplar Rd. Sth. SW19 .69Cb 133
Poplar Row CM16: They B .9Uc 22
Poplars, The AL1: St A .6F 6
DA12: Grav'nd .9G 122
EN9: Walt A .7Lc 21
HP1: Hem H .3K 3
N14 .15Kb 32
RM4: Abr .13Xc 37
UB9: Hare .25L 43
WD6: Bore .11Qa 29
Poplars Av. NW2 .37Ya 68
Poplars Cl. AL10: Hat .1P 7
DA3: Lfield .69Ee 143
HA4: Ruis .32U 64
WD25: Wat .4X 13
Poplar Shaw EN9: Walt A .5Hc 21
Poplars Rd. E17 .30Dc 52
Poplar St. RM7: Rom .28Ed 56
Poplar Vw. HA9: Wemb .33Ma 67
Poplar Wlk. CR0: C'don .75Sb 157
CR3: Cat'm .95Ub 197
SE24 .55Sb 113
(not continuous)
Poplar Way IG6: Ilf .28Sc 54
TW13: Felt .62W 128
Poppins Ct. EC4 .3B 224 (44Rb 91)
Poppleton Rd. E11 .30Gc 53
Poppy Cl. CM15: Pil H .15Xd 40
DA17: Belv .48Dd 96
EN5: New Bar .16Eb 31
HP1: Hem H .1G 2
SL3: L'ly .9N 81
SM6: Wall .74Jb 156
UB5: N'olt .37Ba 65
Poppy Dr. EN3: Pond E .14Xb 33
Poppy La. CR0: C'don .73Yb 158
Poppy M. SE22 .57Wb 113
Porchester Cl. DA3: Hartl .70Be 143
RM11: Horn .30Nd 57
SE5 .56Sb 113
Porchester Ct. W2 .45Db 89
(off Porchester Gdns.)
Porchester Gdns. W2 .45Db 89
Porchester Gdns. M. W2 .44Db 89
Porchester Ga. W2 .5A 220
Porchester Ho. E1 .44Xb 91
(off Philpot St.)
Porchester Leisure Cen. .44Db 89
Porchester Mead
BR3: Beck .65Dc 136
Porchester Pl. W2 .3E 220 (44Gb 89)
Porchester Rd.
KT1: King T .68Ra 131
W2 .44Db 89
Porchester Sq. W2 .44Db 89
Porchester Sq. M. W2 .44Db 89
Porchester Ter. W2 .4A 220 (45Eb 89)
Porchester Ter. Nth. W2 .44Db 89
Porchester Wlk. W2 .44Db 89
(off Porchester Ter. Nth.)
Porchfield Cl. DA12: Grav'nd .1E 144
SM2: Sutt .82Db 175
Porch Way N20 .20Hb 31
Porcupine Cl. SE9 .61Nc 138
Porden Rd. SW2 .56Pb 112
Porlock Av. HA2: Harr .32Ea 66
Porlock Ho. SE26 .62Wb 135
Porlock Rd. EN1: Enf .17Vb 33
Porlock St. SE1 .1G 231 (47Tb 91)
Porrington Cl.
BR7: Chst .67Pc 138
Portal Cl. HA4: Ruis .35W 64
SE27 .62Qb 134
UB10: Uxb .38N 63
Portal Way W3 .43Ta 87
Port Av. DA9: Ghithe .58Xd 120
Portbury Cl. SE15 .53Wb 113
Port Cres. E13 .42Kc 93
Portcullis Ho. SW1 .2F 229
Portcullis Lodge Rd. EN1: Enf .13Tb 33
Port East Apartments E14 .45Cc 92
(off Hertsmere Rd.)
Portelet Ct. N1 .39Ub 71
(off De Beauvoir Est.)
Portelet Rd. E1 .41Zb 92
Porten Ho's. W14 .48Ab 88
(off Porten Rd.)
Porten Rd. W14 .48Ab 88
Porter Cl. RM20: Grays .51Yd 120
Porter Rd. E6 .44Pc 94
Porters & Walters Almshouses
N22 .24Pb 50
(off Nightingale Rd.)
Porters Av. RM8: Dag .37Xc 75
RM9: Dag .37Xc 75
Porters Cl. CM14: B'wood .18Wd 40
Porters Lodge, The SW10 .52Eb 111
(off Coleridge Gdns.)
Porters M. RM9: Dag .37Xc 75
Porters Pk. Dr. WD7: Shenl .5Ma 15
Porters Pk. Golf Course .6La 14
Porter Sq. N19 .32Nb 70
Porter St. SE1 .6E 224 (46Sb 91)
W1 .7G 215 (43Hb 89)
Porters Wlk. E1 .45Xb 91
(off Tobacco Dock)
Porters Way N12 .23Gb 49
UB7: W Dray .48P 83
Porteus Pl. SW4 .55Lb 112
Porteus Rd. W2 .7A 214 (43Eb 89)
Portfleet Pl. N1 .39Ub 71
(off De Beauvoir Rd.)
Portgate Cl. W9 .42Bb 89
Porthallow Cl. BR6: Chels .77Vc 161
Porthcawe Rd. SE26 .63Ac 136
Port Hill BR6: Prat B .84Xc 181
Porthkerry Av. DA16: Well .56Wc 117
Port Ho. E14 .50Dc 92
(off Burrells Wharf Sq.)
Portia Ct. IG11: Bark .38Wc 75
SE11 .7B 230
Portia Way E3 .42Bc 92
Porticos, The SW3 .51Fb 111
(off King's Rd.)
Portinscale Rd. SW15 .57Ab 110
Portishead Ho. W2 .43Cb 89
(off Westbourne Pk. Rd.)
Portland Av. DA12: Grav'nd .1D 144
DA15: Sidc .58Wc 117
KT3: N Mald .73Va 154
N16 .31Vb 71
Portland Bus. Cen. SL3: Dat .3M 103
Portland Cl. KT4: Wor Pk .73Xa 154
RM6: Chad H .29Ad 55
SL2: Slou .2B 80
Portland Commercial Est.
IG11: Bark .40Yc 75
Portland Cotts. CR0: Bedd .73Mb 156
Portland Ct. N1 .38Ub 71
(off St Peter's Way)
SE1 .3F 231
SE14 .51Ac 114
(off Whitcher Cl.)
Portland Cres. HA7: Stan .26Ma 47
SE9 .61Nc 138
TW13: Felt .63T 128
UB6: G'frd .42Da 85
Portland Dr. EN2: Enf .10Ub 19
EN7: Chesh .3Wb 19
RH1: Mers .1D 208
Portland Gdns. N4 .30Rb 51
RM6: Chad H .29Zc 55
Portland Gro. SW8 .53Pb 112
Portland Hgts. HA6: Nwood .21V 44
Portland Ho. RH1: Mers .1D 208
SL9: Ger X .29B 42
SW1 .4B 228
SW15 .57Za 110
Portland Ho. M. KT18: Eps .86Ta 173
(off Caithness Dr.)
Portland Mans. W14 .49Bb 89
(off Addison Bri. Pl.)
Portland M. W1 .3C 222 (44Lb 90)
Portland Pk. SL9: Ger X .30A 42
Portland Pl. DA3: Lfield .69Ae 143
(off Park Dr.)
DA9: Ghithe .56Yd 120
KT17: Eps .84Ua 174
SE25 .70Wb 135
(off Sth. Norwood Hill)
W1 .6K 215 (43Kb 90)
Portland Ri. N4 .32Rb 71
(not continuous)
Portland Rd. BR1: Brom .63Lc 137
CR4: Mitc .68Gb 133
DA11: Nflt .58Fe 121
DA12: Grav'nd .10D 122
KT1: King T .69Na 131
N15 .28Vb 51
SE9 .61Nc 138
SE25 .70Wb 135
TW15: Ashf .62N 127
UB2: S'hall .48Ba 85
UB4: Hayes .41U 84
W11 .45Ab 88
Portlands SL9: Ger X .30A 42
Portland Sq. E1 .46Xb 91
Portland St. AL3: St A .2A 6
SE17 .7F 231 (50Tb 91)
Portland Ter. HA8: Edg .24Qa 47
TW9: Rich .56Ma 109
Portland Wlk. SE17 .51Tb 113
Portley La. CR3: Cat'm .93Ub 197
Portley Wood Rd. CR3: Whyt .92Vb 197
Portmadoc Ho. RM3: Rom .21Nd 57
(off Broseley Rd.)
Portman Av. SW14 .55Ta 109
Portman Cl. DA5: Bexl .60Gd 118
DA7: Bex .55Ad 117
W1 .2G 221 (44Hb 89)
Portman Dr. IG8: Wfd G .26Mc 53
Portman Gdns. NW9 .26Ta 47
UB10: Hil .38Q 64
Portman Ga. NW1 .6E 214 (42Gb 89)
Portman Mans. W1 .7G 215
Portman M. Sth. W1 .3H 221 (44Jb 90)
Portman Pl. E2 .41Yb 92
Portman Rd. KT1: King T .68Pa 131
Portman Sq. W1 .2H 221 (44Jb 90)
Portman St. W1 .3H 221 (44Jb 90)
Portman Towers W1 .2G 221 (44Hb 89)
Portmeadow Wlk. SE2 .47Zc 95
Portmeers Cl. E17 .30Bc 52
Portmore Gdns. RM5: Col R .22Cd 56
Portmore Pk. Rd. KT13: Weyb .77Q 150
Portmore Pl. KT13: Weyb .76T 150
(off Oatlands Dr.)
Portmore Quays KT13: Weyb .77P 149
Portmore Way KT13: Weyb .76Q 150
Portnall Dr. GU25: Vir W .10K 125
Portnall Ho. W9 .41Bb 89
(off Portnall Rd.)
Portnall Ri. GU25: Vir W .1K 147
Portnall Rd. GU25: Vir W .1K 147
W9 .40Bb 69
Portnalls Cl. CR5: Coul .88Kb 176
Portnalls Ri. CR5: Coul .88Lb 176
Portnalls Rd. CR5: Coul .90Kb 176
Portnoi Cl. RM1: Rom .26Fd 56
Portobello Ct. W11 .44Bb 89
Portobello Grn. W10 .43Ab 88
(off Portobello Rd.)
Portobello Ho. BR2: Brom .72Mc 159
Portobello Lofts W10 .42Ab 88
(off Kensal Rd.)
Portobello M. W11 .45Cb 89
Portobello Pde. TN15: W King .81Wd 184
Portobello Rd. W10 .43Ab 88
W11 .44Bb 89
Portobello Road Market .45Bb 89
(off Portobello Rd.)
Porton Ct. KT6: Surb .72La 152
Portpool La. EC1 .7K 217 (43Qb 90)
Portree Cl. N22 .24Pb 50
Portree St. E14 .44Fc 93
Portrush Ct. UB1: S'hall .44Ea 86
(off Whitecote Rd.)
Portsdown HA8: Edg .22Qa 47
Portsdown Av. NW11 .30Bb 49
Portsdown M. NW11 .30Bb 49
Portsea Hall W2 .3E 220
Portsea M. W2 .3E 220
Portsea Pl. W2 .3E 220 (44Gb 89)
Portsea Rd. RM18: Tilb .3E 122
Portslade Rd. SW8 .54Lb 112
Portsmouth Av. KT7: T Ditt .73Ja 152
Portsmouth Ct. SL1: Slou .5J 81
Portsmouth M. E16 .46Kc 93
Portsmouth Rd. GU23: Rip, Wis .93M 189
GU23: Send, Rip .97H 189
KT1: King T .73Ja 152
KT6: Surb .73Ja 152
KT7: T Ditt .73Ja 152
KT10: Esh .79Ca 151
(Hawkshill Cl.)
KT10: Esh .77Ea 152
(Sandown Rd.)
KT10: Esh .85V 170
(Seven Hills Rd. Sth.)
KT11: Cobh .85V 170
SW15 .59Xa 110
Portsmouth St. WC2 .2H 223 (44Pb 90)
Portsoken St. E1 .4K 225 (45Vb 91)
Portswood Pl. SW15 .58Va 110
Portugal Gdns. TW2: Twick .61Ea 130
Portugal Rd. GU21: Wok .88B 168
Portugal St. WC2 .3H 223 (44Pb 90)
Port Way GU24: Bisl .8E 166
Portway E15 .39Hc 73
KT17: Ewe .81Wa 174
RM13: Rain .39Jd 76
Portway Cres. KT17: Ewe .81Wa 174
Portway Gdns. SE18 .52Mc 115
Pory Ho. SE11 .6J 229 (49Pb 90)
Poseidon Ct. E14 .49Cc 92
(off Homer Dr.)
POSK .49Wa 88
(off King St.)
Postal Mus., The .5J 217 (42Pb 90)
Post Boys Row KT11: Cobh .86W 170
Postern, The EC2 .1E 224
Postern Grn. EN2: Enf .12Qb 32
Post Ho. La. KT23: Bookh .97Ca 191
Post La. TW2: Twick .60Fa 108
Postmasters Lodge HA5: Pinn .31Aa 65
Post Mdw. SL0: Iver H .41F 82
Postmill Cl. CR0: C'don .76Yb 158
RM5: Col R .23Cd 56
Post Office All. W4 .51Ra 109
(off Thames Rd.)
Post Office App. E7 .36Kc 73
Post Office Ct. EC3 .3G 225
Post Office La.
SL3: Geor G .4P 81
Post Office Way SW8 .52Mb 112
Post Rd. UB2: S'hall .48Da 85
Postway M. IG1: Ilf .34Rc 74
(not continuous)
Potash La. TN15: Plat .93Ee 205
Potbury Cl. SL4: Wink .5A 124
Potier St. SE1 .4G 231 (48Tb 91)
Potiphar Pl. CM14: W'ley .21Xd 58
Potter Cl. CR4: Mitc .68Kb 134
SE15 .52Ub 113
Potterells AL9: N Mym .7F 8
Potter Ho. E1 .43Zb 92
(off Beaufort Gdns.)
Potteries, The EN5: Barn .15Cb 31
KT16: Ott .79G 148
Potterne Cl. SW19 .59Za 110
POTTERS BAR .4Bb 17
Potters Bar Golf Course .3Cb 17
Potters Bar Mus. .4Bb 17
Potters Bar Station Yd.
EN6: Pot B .4Cb 17
(off Darkes La.)
Potters Cl. CR0: C'don .74Ac 158
IG10: Lough .12Nc 36
Potters Ct. EN6: Pot B .4Cb 17
SM1: Sutt .79Bb 155
(off Rosebery Rd.)
Potters Cross SL0: Iver H .41G 82
POTTERS CROUCH .6K 5
Potterscrouch La. AL2: Pot C .6K 5
AL3: St A .6K 5
Potters Fld. HA5: Pinn .23X 45
Potters Fld. EN1: Enf .14Ub 33
(off Lincoln Rd.)
Potters Flds. SE1 .7J 225 (46Ub 91)
Potters Gro. KT3: N Mald .70Sa 131
Potters Hgts. Cl.
HA5: Pinn .24X 45
Potter's La. SW16 .65Mb 134
Potters La.
EN5: New Bar .14Cb 31
GU23: Send .95D 188
WD6: Bore .11Sa 29
Potters Lodge E14 .50Ec 92
(off Ferry St.)
Potters M. WD6: E'tree .16Ma 29
Potter's Rd.
EN5: New Bar .14Db 31
Potters Rd. SW6 .54Eb 111
Potters Row E20 .36Dc 72
(off Keirin Rd.)
Potter St. HA5: Pinn .25X 45
HA6: Nwood .25W 44
Potter St. Hill HA5: Pinn .23X 45
Potters Way RH2: Reig .10L 207
Pottery Cl. SE25 .69Wb 135
Pottery Ga. N11 .23Mb 50
Pottery La. W11 .46Ab 88
Pottery Rd. DA5: Bexl .61Ed 140
TW8: Bford .51Na 109
Pottery St. SE16 .47Xb 91
Pott St. E2 .41Xb 91
POUCHEN END .3F 2
Pouchen End La. HP1: Hem H .1F 2
Poulcott TW19: Wray .58A 104
Poulett Gdns. TW1: Twick .60Ja 108
Poulett Rd. E6 .40Pc 74
Poulter Ct. DA10: Swans .59Be 121
Poulter Pk. .72Gb 155
Poulters Wood BR2: Kes .78Mc 159
Poultney Cl. WD7: Shenl .4Pa 15
Poulton Av. SM1: Sutt .76Fb 155
Poulton Cl. E8 .37Xb 71
Poulton Ho. W3 .43Ta 87
(off Victoria Rd.)
Poultry EC2 .3F 225 (44Tb 91)
Pound, The SL1: Burn .2B 80
Pound Bank Cl. TN15: W King .81Vd 184
Pound Cl. BR6: Orp .75Tc 160
KT6: Surb .74La 152
KT19: Eps .83Ta 173
Pound Ct. KT21: Asht .90Pa 173
Pound Ct. Dr. BR6: Orp .75Tc 160
Pound Cres. KT22: Fet .93Fa 192
Pound Farm Cl. KT10: Esh .74Fa 152
Poundfield WD25: Wat .7V 12
Poundfield Ct. GU22: Wok .93E 188
Poundfield Gdns. GU22: Wok .92E 188
(not continuous)
Poundfield Rd. IG10: Lough .15Qc 36
Pound Grn. DA5: Bexl .59Cd 118
Pound La. GU20: W'sham .9A 146
KT19: Eps .84Sa 173
NW10 .37Wa 68
RM16: Ors .2C 100
TN13: S'oaks .96Ld 203
TN14: Knock .87Zc 181
WD7: Shenl .5Pa 15
Pound Pk. Rd. SE7 .49Mc 93
Pound Pl. SE9 .58Qc 116
Pound Rd. KT16: Chert .73K 149
SM7: Bans .89Bb 175
Pound St. SM5: Cars .78Hb 155
Pound Way BR7: Chst .66Sc 138
Pounsley Rd. TN13: Dun G .93Gd 202
Pountney Rd. SW11 .55Jb 112
POVEREST .70Wc 139
Poverest Rd.
BR5: St M Cry .71Vc 161
Povey Ho. SE17 .6H 231
Powderham Ct. GU21: Knap .10H 167
Powder Mill La. DA1: Dart .61Nd 141
TW2: Whitt .59Ba 107
Powdermill La. EN9: Walt A .5Dc 20
Powdermill M.
EN9: Walt A .5Dc 20
(off Powdermill La.)
Powell Av. DA2: Dart .61Ud 142
Powell Cl. HA8: Edg .23Pa 47
KT9: Chess .78Ma 153
Powell Ct. CR2: S Croy .77Rb 157
(off Bramley Hill)
E17 .27Dc 52
Powell Dr. E4 .14Dc 34
Powell Gdns. RH1: Redh .4B 208
RM10: Dag .35Cd 76
Powell Ho. EN1: Enf .14Ub 33
(off Dunstan M.)
W2 .4B 220
(off Gloucester Ter.)
Powell Rd. E5 .34Xb 71
IG9: Buck H .17Lc 35
Powell's Wlk. W4 .51Ua 110
Power Dr. EN3: Enf L .8Bc 20
Powergate Bus. Pk. NW10 .41Ta 87
Powerhouse, The .47U 84
Powerleague
Barking .41Sc 94
Colney Hatch .24Jb 50
Croydon .79Pb 156
Ilford .24Vc 55
Mill Hill .24Xa 48
Slough .8H 81
Tottenham .23Xb 51
Watford .13Ca 27
Power Rd. W4 .49Qa 87
Powers Ct. TW1: Twick .59Ma 109
Powerscroft Rd. DA14: Sidc .65Yc 139
(not continuous)
E5 .35Yb 72
Power Works Est. DA8: Erith .53Jd 118
Powis Cl. EN6: Pot B .6Eb 17
W11 .44Bb 89
(off Powis Gdns.)
WD23: B Hea .18Fa 28
(off Rutherford Way)
Powis Gdns. NW11 .31Bb 69
W11 .44Bb 89
Powis Ho. WC2 .2G 223
Powis M. W11 .44Bb 89
Powis Pl. WC1 .6G 217 (42Nb 90)
Powis Rd. E3 .41Dc 92
Powis Sq. W11 .44Bb 89
(not continuous)
Powis St. SE18 .48Qc 94
Powis Ter. W11 .44Bb 89
Powlesland Ct. E1 .44Ac 92
(off White Horse Rd.)
Powlett Ho. NW1 .37Kb 70
(off Powlett Pl.)
Powlett Pl. NW1 .38Jb 70
Pownall Gdns. TW3: Houn .56Da 107
Pownall Rd. E8 .39Vb 71
TW3: Houn .56Da 107
Pownsett Ter. IG1: Ilf .36Sc 74
Powster Rd. BR1: Brom .64Jc 137
Powys Cl. DA7: Bex .51Zc 117
Powys Ct. N11 .22Nb 50
WD6: Bore .13Ta 29
Powys La. N13 .21Nb 50
N14 .21Nb 50
POYLE .53G 104
Poyle Ind. Est. SL3: Poyle .55H 105
Poyle La. SL1: Burn .10A 60
Poyle New Cotts. SL3: Poyle .54H 105
Poyle Pk. SL3: Poyle .55G 104
Poyle Rd. SL3: Poyle .55G 104
Poyle Technical Cen. SL3: Poyle .54G 104
Poyle Trad. Est. SL3: Poyle .55G 104
Poynder Rd. RM18: Tilb .3D 122
Poynders Ct. SW4 .58Lb 112
Poynders Gdns. SW4 .59Lb 112
Poynders Hill HP2: Hem H .3C 4
Poynders Pde. SW4 .58Mb 112
Poynders Rd. SW4 .58Lb 112
Poynings, The SL0: Rich P .49H 83
Poynings Cl. BR6: Chels .75Yc 161
Poynings Rd. N19 .34Lb 70
Poynings Way N12 .22Cb 49
RM3: Hrld W .25Nd 57
Poyntell Cres. BR7: Chst .67Tc 138
Poynter Ct. UB5: N'olt .40Z 65
(off Gallery Gdns.)
Poynter Ho. NW8 .5B 214
W11 .46Za 88
(off Queensdale Cres.)
Poynter Rd. EN1: Enf .15Wb 33
Poynton Rd. N17 .26Wb 51
Poyntz Rd. SW11 .54Hb 111
Poyser St. E2 .40Xb 71
Prado Path TW1: Twick .60Ha 108
(off Laurel Av.)
Prae Cl. AL3: St A .1P 5
Praed M. W2 .2C 220 (44Fb 89)
Praed St. W2 .3B 220 (44Fb 89)
Praetorian Ct. AL1: St A .5A 6
Praetorian Pl. RH1: Redh .3B 208
Pragel St. E13 .40Lc 73
Pragnell Rd. SE12 .61Kc 137
Prague Pl. SW2 .57Nb 112
Prah Rd. N4 .33Qb 70
Prairie Cl. KT15: Add .76K 149
Prairie Rd. KT15: Add .76K 149
Prairie St. SW8 .54Jb 112
Praline Ct. E3 .40Dc 72
(off Taylor Pl.)
Pratchett Ct. WD18: Wat .14U 26
(off Raven Cl.)
Pratt M. NW1 .39Lb 70
PRATT'S BOTTOM .82Yc 181
PRATT'S BOTTOM .81Yc 181
Pratts La. KT12: Hers .77Z 151
Pratts Pas. KT1: King T .68Na 131
Pratt St. NW1 .39Lb 70
Pratt Wlk. SE11 .5J 229 (49Pb 90)
Prayle Gro. NW2 .32Za 68
Preachers Ct. EC1 .6C 218
Prebend Gdns. W4 .49Va 88
W6 .49Va 88
(not continuous)
Prebend Mans. W4 .49Va 88
(off Chiswick High Rd.)
Prebend St. N1 .1D 218 (39Sb 71)
Precinct, The SS17: Stan H .2M 101
TW20: Egh .64C 126
Precinct Rd. UB3: Hayes .45W 84
Precincts, The SL1: Burn .2A 80
SM4: Mord .72Cb 155
Precista Ct. BR6: Orp .73Xc 161
Premier Av. RM16: Grays .47Ee 99
Premier Cinema
Peckham .54Wb 113
Premier Cnr. W9 .40Bb 69
Premier Ct. EN3: Enf W .10Zb 20
Premier Pl. E14 .45Cc 92
Premier Ho. N1 .38Rb 71
(off Waterloo Ter.)
Premier Pk. NW10 .39Ra 67
(not continuous)
Premier Pk. Rd. NW10 .40Ra 67
Premier Pl. SW15 .56Ab 110
WD18: Wat .15V 26
Prendergast Rd. SE3 .55Gc 115
Prentice Ct. SW19 .64Bb 133
Prentis Rd. SW16 .63Mb 134
Prentiss Ct. SE7 .49Mc 93
Presburg Rd. KT3: N Mald .71Ua 154
Presburg St. E5 .34Zb 72
Presbury Ct. GU21: Wok .10L 167
Prescelly Pl. HA8: Edg .25Pa 47
Prescot St. E1 .4K 225 (45Vb 91)
Prescott Av. BR5: Pet W .72Rc 160
Prescott Cl. SW16 .66Nb 134
Prescott Grn. IG10: Lough .13Sc 36

Prescott Ho.—Prospect Bus. Pk.

Prescott Ho. *SE17* .51Rb **113**
(off Hillingdon St.)
Prescott Pl. SW4 .55Mb **112**
Prescott Rd. SL3: Poyle .54G **104**
Presentation M. SW2 .61Pb **134**
Preshaw Cres. CR4: Mitc .69Gb **133**
President Dr. E1 .46Xb **91**
President Ho. EC1 .4C **218** (41Rb **91**)
President Quay *E1* .46Vb **91**
(off St Katherine's Way)
President St. EC1 .3D **218**
Prespa Cl. N9 .19Yb **34**
Press Ct. SE1 .50Wb **91**
Press Ho. BR5: Pet W .71Sc **160**
E1 .43Zb **92**
(off Trafalgar Gdns.)
NW10 .34Ta **67**
Press Rd. NW10 .34Ta **67**
UB8: Uxb .37M **63**
Prestage Way E14 .45Ec **92**
Prestbury Cres. SM7: Bans .88Hb **175**
Prestbury Rd. E7 .38Lc **73**
Prestbury Sq. SE9 .63Pc **138**
Prested Rd. SW11 .56Gb **111**
Prestige Way NW4 .29Ya **48**
PRESTON .32Na 67
Preston Av. E4 .23Fc **53**
Preston Cl. SE1 .5H **231** (49Ub **91**)
TW2: Twick .62Ga **130**
Preston Ct. *DA14: Sidc* .63Vc **139**
(off The Crescent)
EN5: New Bar .14Eb **31**
KT12: Walt T .74Y **151**
Preston Dr. DA7: Bex .53Zc **117**
E11 .29Lc **53**
KT19: Ewe .79Ua **154**
Preston Gdns. EN3: Enf L .9Ac **20**
IG1: Ilf .30Nc **54**
NW10 .37Va **68**
Preston Gro. KT21: Asht .89La **172**
Preston Hill HA3: Kenton .31Na **67**
Preston Ho. *RM10: Dag* .34Cd **76**
(off Uvedale Rd.)
SE1 .5H **231**
(Preston Cl.)
SE1 .3K **231**
(St Saviour's Est.)
Preston La. KT20: Tad .93Xa **194**
Preston Mnr. Rd. KT20: Tad .92Ya **194**
Preston Pl. NW2 .37Wa **68**
TW10: Rich .57Na **109**
Preston Rd. DA11: Nflt .10A **122**
E11 .30Gc **53**
HA3: Kenton .32Na **67**
HA9: Wemb .32Na **67**
RM3: Rom .21Md **57**
SE19 .65Rb **135**
SL2: Slou .5N **81**
SW20 .66Va **132**
TW17: Shep .71Q **150**
Preston's Rd. E14 .45Ec **92**
Prestons Rd. BR2: Hayes .76Jc **159**
Preston St. E2 .40Zb **72**
Preston Waye HA3: Kenton .32Na **67**
Prestwich Ter. SW4 .57Lb **112**
Prestwick Cl. UB2: S'hall .50Aa **85**
Prestwick Ct. *UB1: S'hall* .45Ea **86**
(off Baird Av.)
Prestwick Rd. WD19: Wat .18Y **27**
Prestwick Road Meadows
Local Nature Reserve .22Z 45
Prestwood SL2: Slou .4M **81**
WD19: Wat .19Aa **27**
Prestwood Av. HA3: Kenton .28Ka **46**
Prestwood Cl. HA3: Kenton .28Ka **46**
SE18 .51Wc **117**
Prestwood Dr. RM5: Col R .22Ed **56**
Prestwood Gdns. CR0: C'don .73Sb **157**
Prestwood Ga. AL1: St A .1C **6**
Prestwood Ho. *SE16* .48Xb **91**
(off Drummond Rd.)
Prestwood St. N1 .2E **218** (40Sb **71**)
Pretoria Av. E17 .28Ac **52**
Pretoria Cres. E4 .18Ec **34**
Pretoria Rd. E4 .18Ec **34**
E11 .32Fc **73**
E16 .42Hc **93**
IG1: Ilf .36Rc **74**
KT16: Chert .74H **149**
N17 .24Vb **51**
RM7: Rom .28Ed **56**
SW16 .65Kb **134**
WD18: Wat .14W **26**
Pretoria Rd. Nth. N18 .23Vb **51**
Pretty La. CR5: Coul .93Lb **196**
Prevost Rd. N11 .19Jb **32**
PREY HEATH .5N 187
Prey Heath Cl. GU22: Wok .6N **187**
Prey Heath Rd. GU22: Wok .6M **187**
Priam Ho. *E2* .40Xb **71**
(off Old Bethnal Grn. Rd.)
Price Cl. SW17 .62Hb **133**
Price Ho. *N1* .39Sb **71**
(off Britannia Row)
Price Rd. CR0: Wadd .78Rb **157**
Price's Ct. SW11 .55Fb **111**
Prices La. RH2: Reig .9J **207**
Price's M. N1 .39Pb **70**
Price's St. SE1 .6C **224** (46Rb **91**)
Price Way TW12: Hamp .65Aa **129**
Prichard Ct. N7 .36Pb **70**
Prichard Ho. SE11 .6K **229**
Pricklers Hill EN5: New Bar .16Db **31**
Prickley Wood BR2: Hayes .74Hc **159**
Priddy Pl. RH1: Mers .3C **208**
Priddy's Yd. CR0: C'don .75Sb **157**
Prideaux Ho. WC1 .3J **217**
Prideaux Pl. W3 .45Ta **87**
WC1 .3J **217** (41Pb **90**)
Prideaux Rd. SW9 .55Nb **112**
Pridham Rd. CR7: Thor H .70Tb **135**
Priest Cl. TW12: Hamp .63Ca **129**
Priestfield Rd. SE23 .62Ac **136**
Priest Hill RH8: Limp .1M **211**
SL4: Old Win .2N **125**
TW20: Eng G, Old Win .2N **125**
Priest Hill Cl. KT17: Eps .85Xa **174**
Priestlands Pk. Rd. DA15: Sidc .62Vc **139**
Priest La. GU24: W End .5A **166**
Priestley Cl. N16 .31Vb **71**
Priestley Ct. RM17: Grays .49Ee **99**
Priestley Gdns. RM6: Chad H .30Xc **55**
Priestley Ho. EC1 .5D **218**
HA9: Wemb .34Sa **67**
(off Barnhill Rd.)
Priestley Rd. CR4: Mitc .68Jb **134**
Priestley Way E17 .27Zb **52**
NW2 .32Wa **68**
Priestly Gdns. GU22: Wok .92C **188**
Priestman Point *E3* .41Dc **92**
(off Rainhill Way)
Priest Pk. Av. HA2: Harr .33Ca **65**
Priests Av. RM1: Rom .26Fd **56**
Priests Bri. SW14 .55Ua **110**
SW15 .55Ua **110**
Priest's Ct. EC2 .2D **224**
Priest's Fld. CM13: Ingve .22Ee **59**
Priest's La.
CM15: B'wood, Shenf .17Be **41**
Priest's Wlk. DA12: Grav'nd .1J **145**
Prima Rd. SW9 .52Qb **112**
Primary Rd. SL1: Slou .8H **81**
Prime Meridian Line .52Fc 115
Prime Meridian Wlk. E14 .45Fc **93**
Primeplace M.
CR7: Thor H .68Sb **135**
Primezone M. N8 .30Nb **50**
Primmett Cl. TN15: W King .79Ud **164**
Primrose Av. EN2: Enf .11Tb **33**
RM6: Chad H .31Xc **75**
Primrose Cl. AL10: Hat .1D **8**
E3 .40Cc **72**
HA2: Harr .34Ba **65**
HP1: Hem H .3G **2**
N3 .26Db **49**
SE6 .64Ec **136**
SM6: Wall .73Kb **156**
Primrose Ct.
CM14: B'wood .20Yd **40**
NW8 .1F **215**
SW12 .59Mb **112**
Primrose Dr. GU24: Bisl .7E **166**
UB7: W Dray .49M **83**
Primrose Gdns. HA4: Ruis .36Y **65**
NW3 .37Gb **69**
WD7: R'lett .7Ja **14**
WD23: Bush .17Da **27**
Primrose Glen RM11: Horn .28Nd **57**
PRIMROSE HILL .39Jb 70
Primrose Hill CM14: B'wood .20Yd **40**
EC4 .3A **224** (44Qb **90**)
WD4: K Lan .10B **4**
Primrose Hill Ct. NW3 .38Hb **69**
Primrose Hill Rd. NW3 .38Hb **69**
Primrose Hill Studios NW1 .39Jb **70**
Primrose Ho. *KT18: Eps* .85Sa **173**
(off Dalmeny Way)
SE15 .53Wb **113**
(off Peckham Hill St.)
SE16 .47Ac **92**
(off Blondin Way)
Primrose La. CR0: C'don .74Yb **158**
WD25: A'ham .10Fa **14**
Primrose Mans. SW11 .53Jb **112**
Primrose M. *NW1* .38Hb **69**
(off Sharpleshall St.)
SE3 .52Jc **115**
Primrose Path EN7: Chesh .3Wb **19**
Primrose Pl. TW7: Isle .54Ha **108**
Primrose Rd. E10 .32Dc **72**
E18 .26Kc **53**
KT12: Hers .78Y **151**
Primrose Sq. E9 .38Yb **72**
Primrose St. EC2 .7H **219** (43Ub **91**)
Primrose Ter. DA12: Grav'nd .10E **122**
Primrose Wlk. KT17: Ewe .80Va **154**
SE14 .52Ac **114**
Primrose Way HA0: Wemb .40Ma **67**
SE10 .54Ec **114**
Primula St. W12 .44Wa **88**
Prince Albert Ct. NW8 .1F **215**
TW16: Sun .66V **128**
Prince Albert Rd. NW1 .1J **215**, 3D **214**
NW8 .3D **214** (41Gb **89**)
Prince Albert's Wlk. SL4: Wind .3L **103**
Prince Arthur M. NW3 .35Eb **69**
Prince Arthur Rd. NW3 .36Eb **69**
Prince Charles Av. DA4: S Dar .68Td **142**
RM16: Ors .2D **100**
Prince Charles Cinema .4E 222
Prince Charles Dr. NW4 .31Ya **68**
Prince Charles Rd. SE3 .54Hc **115**
Prince Charles Way SM6: Wall .76Kb **156**
Prince Consort Cotts. SL4: Wind .4H **103**
Prince Consort Dr. BR7: Chst .67Tc **138**
Prince Consort Rd. SW7 .3A **226** (48Eb **89**)
Prince Consort's Dr. SL4: Wind .8D **102**
Princedale Rd. W11 .46Ab **88**
Prince Edward Mans. *W2* .45Cb **89**
(off Moscow Rd.)
Prince Edward Rd. E9 .37Bc **72**
Prince Edward Theatre .3E 222
Prince Eugene Pl. AL1: St A .5A **6**
Prince George Av. N14 .15Mb **32**
Prince George Rd. N16 .35Ub **71**
Prince George's Av. SW20 .68Ya **132**
Prince George's Rd. SW19 .67Fb **133**
Prince Henry Rd. SE7 .52Mc **115**
Prince Imperial Rd. BR7: Chst .67Rc **138**
SE18 .53Pc **116**
Prince John Rd. SE9 .57Nc **116**
Princelet St. E1 .7K **219** (43Vb **91**)
Prince Michael of Kent Ct.
DA1: Cray .54Jd **118**
Prince of Orange Ct. *SE16* .48Yb **92**
(off Lower Rd.)
Prince of Orange La. SE10 .52Ec **114**
Prince of Wales Cl. DA12: Grav'nd .9F **122**
NW4 .28Xa **48**
Prince of Wales Dr. SW8 .52Kb **112**
SW11 .53Gb **111**
Prince of Wales Footpath
EN3: Enf W .10Zb **20**
Prince of Wales Mans. SW11 .53Jb **112**
Prince of Wales Pas. NW1 .4B **216**
Prince of Wales Rd. E16 .44Lc **93**
NW5 .37Jb **70**
SE3 .54Hc **115**
SM1: Sutt .75Fb **155**
Prince of Wales Ter. W4 .50Ua **88**
W8 .47Db **89**
Prince of Wales Theatre .5D 222
Prince Pk. HP1: Hem H .3J **3**
Prince Philip Av. RM16: Grays .46Ce **99**
Prince Regent Ct. NW8 .1E **214**
SE16 .45Ac **92**
(off Edward Sq.)
Prince Regent La. E13 .41Kc **93**
E16 .41Kc **93**
Prince Regent M. NW1 .4B **216**
Prince Regent Rd. TW3: Houn .55Da **107**
Prince Rd. SE25 .71Ub **157**
Prince Rupert Rd. SE9 .56Pc **116**
Princes Arc. SW1 .6C **222**
Prince's Av. UB6: G'frd .44Da **85**
WD18: Wat .15V **26**
Princes Av. BR5: Pet W .71Uc **160**
CR2: Sande .87Xb **177**
DA2: Dart .60Rd **119**
EN3: Enf W .8Ac **20**
IG8: Wfd G .21Kc **53**
KT6: Surb .74Qa **153**
N3 .25Cb **49**
N10 .27Kb **50**
N13 .22Qb **50**
N22 .25Mb **50**
NW9 .28Qa **47**
SM5: Cars .80Hb **155**
W3 .48Qa **87**
Princes Cir. WC2 .2F **223** (44Nb **90**)
Prince's Cl. TW11: Tedd .63Fa **130**
Princes Cl. CR2: Sande .87Xb **177**
DA14: Sidc .62Zc **139**
HA8: Edg .22Qa **47**
N4 .32Rb **71**
NW9 .28Qa **47**
SL4: Eton W .10D **80**
SW4 .55Lb **112**
Prince's Ct. SE16 .48Bc **92**
SW3 .3F **227**
Princes Ct. HA9: Wemb .36Na **67**
HP3: Hem H .5K **3**
KT13: Weyb .78R **150**
(off Princes Rd.)
Princes Ct. Bus. Cen. E1 .45Xb **91**
Prince's Dr. KT22: Oxs .84Ga **172**
Princes Dr. HA1: Harr .27Ga **46**
Princesfield Rd.
EN9: Walt A .5Kc **21**
Prince's Gdns. SW7 .3C **226** (48Fb **89**)
Princes Gdns. W3 .43Qa **87**
W5 .42La **86**
Prince's Ga. SW7 .2C **226** (47Fb **89**)
(not continuous)
Prince's Ga. Ct. SW7 .2C **226** (47Fb **89**)
Prince's Ga. M.
SW7 .3C **226** (48Fb **89**)
Princes Ho. W11 .45Bb **89**
Princes La. N10 .27Kb **50**
Prince's M. W2 .45Db **89**
Princes M. TW3: Houn .56Ca **107**
W6 .50Xa **88**
(off Down Pl.)
Princes Pde. EN6: Pot B .4Db **17**
NW11 .30Ab **48**
(off Golders Grn. Rd.)
Princes Pk. RM13: Rain .38Jd **76**
Princes Pk. Av. NW11 .30Ab **48**
UB3: Hayes .45T **84**
Princes Pk. Circ. UB3: Hayes .45T **84**
Princes Pk. Cl. UB3: Hayes .45T **84**
Princes Pk. Golf Course .60Qd 119
Princes Pk. La. UB3: Hayes .45T **84**
Princes Pk. Pde. UB3: Hayes .45T **84**
Princes Pk. Stadium .60Qd 119
Princes Pl. SW1 .6C **222**
W11 .46Ab **88**
Prince's Plain BR2: Brom .73Nc **160**
Prince's Ri. SE13 .54Ec **114**
Princes Riverside Rd. SE16 .46Zb **92**
Prince's Rd. CM14: Kel C, N'side .11Nd **39**
RM1: Rom .29Jd **56**
SW19 .65Cb **133**
TW11: Tedd .63Fa **130**
Princes Rd. BR8: Hext .65Jd **140**
DA1: Dart .58Jd **118**
DA2: Dart .60Rd **119**
(not continuous)
DA12: Grav'nd .3E **144**
IG6: Ilf .28Tc **54**
IG9: Buck H .19Lc **35**
KT2: King T .66Qa **131**
KT13: Weyb .78R **150**
N18 .21Yb **52**
RH1: Redh .8P **207**
SE20 .65Zb **136**
SW14 .55Ta **109**
TW9: Kew .53Pa **109**
TW10: Rich .57Pa **109**
TW13: Felt .62W **128**
TW15: Ashf .64P **127**
TW20: Egh .65B **126**
W13 .46Ka **86**
PRINCES ROAD INTERCHANGE .60Rd **119**
Princessa Ct. EN2: Enf .15Tb **33**
Princess Alice Ho. W10 .42Ya **88**
Princess Alice Way SE28 .47Tc **94**
Princess Av. HA9: Wemb .33Na **67**
RM18: E Til .9L **101**
SL4: Wind .5F **102**
Princess Av. E. HA9: Wemb .33Na **67**
Princess Cl. SE28 .44Zc **95**
Princess Ct. *KT1: King T* .69Pa **131**
(off Horace Rd.)
N6 .31Lb **70**
NW6 .37Db **69**
(off Compayne Gdns.)
W1 .1F **221**
W2 .45Db **89**
(off Queensway)
Princess Cres. N4 .33Rb **71**
Princess Diana Dr. AL4: St A .3H **7**
Princesses Pde. *DA1: Cray* .57Gd **118**
(off Waterside)
Princess Gdns. GU22: Wok .88D **168**
Princess Ho. RH1: Redh .5A **208**
Princess La. HA4: Ruis .32U **64**
Princess Louise Bldg. *SE8* .52Cc **114**
(off Hales St.)
Princess Louise Cl. W2 .7C **214** (43Fb **89**)
Princess Louise Wlk. W10 .43Za **88**
Princess Margaret Rd. RM18: E Til .8K **101**
SS17: E Til, Linf .8K **101**
Princess Mary Ho. SW1 .5E **228**
Princess Marys Rd. KT15: Add .77L **149**
Princess May Rd. N16 .35Ub **71**
Princess M. KT1: King T .69Pa **131**
NW3 .36Fb **69**
Princess of Wales Ho. SL9: Chal P .21B **42**
Princess of Wales Memorial Fountain
.1C 226 (47Fb 89)
Princess Pde. BR6: Farnb .76Qc **160**
RM10: Dag .40Cd **76**
Princess Pk. KT15: Add .77J **149**
Princess Pk. Mnr. N11 .22Jb **50**
Princes Sq. W2 .45Db **89**
(not continuous)
Princess Rd. CR0: C'don .72Sb **157**
GU22: Wok .88D **168**
NW1 .39Jb **70**
NW6 .40Cb **69**
Princess Sq. KT10: Esh .79Ea **152**
Princess St. SE1 .4C **230** (48Rb **91**)
Prince's St. EC2 .3F **225** (44Tb **91**)
Princes St. DA7: Bex .55Bd **117**
DA11: Grav'nd .8D **122**
N17 .23Ub **51**
SL1: Slou .7M **81**
SM1: Sutt .77Fb **155**
TW9: Rich .56Na **109**
W1 .3A **222** (44Kb **90**)
Princess Way RH1: Redh .5A **208**
Princes Ter. E13 .39Kc **73**
Prince's Twr. *SE16* .47Yb **92**
(off Elephant La.)
Prince St. SE8 .51Bc **114**
WD17: Wat .13Y **27**
Princes Vw. DA1: Dart .60Qd **119**
Princes Way BR4: W W'ck .77Hc **159**
CM13: Hut .19Ce **41**
CR0: Wadd .78Pb **156**
HA4: Ruis .35Aa **65**
IG9: Buck H .19Lc **35**
SW19 .59Za **110**
W3 .48Qa **87**
Prince's Yd. W11 .46Ab **88**
Princethorpe Ho. *W2* .43Db **89**
(off Woodchester Sq.)
Princethorpe Rd. SE26 .63Zb **136**
Princeton Ct. SW15 .55Za **110**
Princeton M. KT2: King T .67Qa **131**
Princeton St. WC1 .1H **223** (43Pb **90**)
Prince William Ct. *TW15: Ashf* .64P **127**
(off Clarendon Rd.)
Principal Cl. N14 .18Lb **32**
Principal Pl. EC2 .6J **219**
Principal Sq. E9 .36Zb **72**
Pringle Gdns. CR8: Purl .82Pb **176**
SW16 .63Lb **134**
(not continuous)
Printers Av. WD18: Wat .15U **26**
Printers Ct. *AL1: St A* .3B **6**
(off Thorpe Rd.)
Printers Inn Ct. EC4 .2K **223** (44Qb **90**)
Printers M. E3 .39Ac **72**
Printers Rd. SW9 .53Pb **112**
Printer St. EC4 .2A **224** (44Qb **90**)
Printing Ho. La. UB3: Hayes .47U **84**
Printing Ho. Yd. E2 .4J **219** (41Ub **91**)
Printon Ho. *E14* .43Bc **92**
(off Wallwood St.)
Print Room, The .44Cb 89
(off Hereford Rd.)
Print Room Cinema, The .46Cb 89
(off Notting Hill Ga.)
Print Village SE15 .54Vb **113**
Printwork Apartments SE1 .3H **231**
SE5 .53Sb **113**
(off Coldharbour La.)
Priolo Rd. SE7 .50Lc **93**
Prior Av. SM2: Sutt .80Gb **155**
Prior Bolton St. N1 .37Rb **71**
Prior Chase RM17: Grays .49Ce **99**
Prior Ct. KT8: W Mole .71Ba **151**
Prioress Cres. DA9: Ghithe .56Yd **120**
Prioress Ho. *E3* .41Dc **92**
(off Bromley High St.)
Prioress Rd. SE27 .62Rb **135**
Prioress St. SE1 .4G **231** (48Ub **91**)
Prior Rd. IG1: Ilf .34Qc **74**
Priors, The KT21: Asht .91Ma **193**
NW3 .34Fb **69**
Priors Cl. SL1: Slou .8L **81**
Priors Ct. GU21: Wok .10L **167**
Prior's Cft. GU22: Wok .92C **188**
Priors Cft. E17 .26Ac **52**
Priors Farm La. UB5: N'olt .37Aa **65**
Priors Fld. UB5: N'olt .37Aa **65**
Priorsford Av. BR5: St M Cry .70Wc **139**
Priors Gdns. HA4: Ruis .36Y **65**
Priors Golf Course, The .16Ld 39
Priors Mead EN1: Enf .11Ub **33**
KT23: Bookh .97Ea **192**
Priors Pk. RM12: Horn .34Ld **77**
Priors Rd. SL4: Wind .5B **102**
Prior St. SE10 .52Ec **114**
Priors Wood KT10: Hin W .75Ha **152**
Priory, The CR0: Wadd .77Qb **156**
KT22: Lea .94Ka **192**
N8 .28Mb **50**
RH9: G'stone .3P **209**
SE3 .56Hc **115**
Priory Apartments, The SE6 .60Dc **114**
Priory Av. BR5: Pet W .72Tc **160**
E4 .20Bc **34**
E17 .29Cc **52**
HA0: Wemb .35Ha **66**
N8 .28Mb **50**
SM3: Cheam .77Za **154**
UB9: Hare .28L **43**
W4 .49Ua **88**
Priory Cl. BR3: Beck .69Ac **136**
BR7: Chst .67Pc **138**
CM15: Pil H .15Wd **40**
DA1: Dart .57Ld **119**
E4 .20Bc **34**
E18 .25Jc **53**
GU21: Wok .85F **168**
HA0: Wemb .35Ha **66**
HA4: Ruis .32V **64**
HA7: Stan .20Ha **28**
KT12: Walt T .76W **150**
N3 .25Bb **49**
N14 .15Kb **32**
N20 .18Bb **31**
SL5: S'dale .3E **146**
SW19 .67Db **133**
TW12: Hamp .67Ba **129**
TW16: Sun .66W **128**
UB3: Hayes .45X **85**
UB9: Den .34J **63**
UB9: Hare .28K **43**
Priory Ct. AL1: St A .3C **6**
DA1: Dart .58Md **119**
E6 .39Lc **73**
E9 .36Zb **72**
E17 .26Bc **52**
EC4 .3C **224**
HA0: Wemb .40Na **67**
KT1: King T .69Na **131**
(off Denmark Rd.)
KT17: Ewe .81Va **174**
SM3: Cheam .77Ab **154**
SW8 .53Mb **112**
TW3: Houn .55Da **107**
TW20: Egh .65E **126**
WD23: Bush .18Ea **28**
(off Sparrows Herne)
Priory Ct. Est. E17 .26Bc **52**
Priory Cres. HA0: Wemb .34Ja **66**
SE19 .66Sb **135**
SM3: Cheam .77Za **154**
Priory Dr. HA7: Stan .20Ha **28**
RH2: Reig .8J **207**
SE2 .50Zc **95**
Priory Fld. Dr. HA8: Edg .21Ra **47**
Priory Flds. DA4: Eyns .75Pd **163**
WD17: Wat .11W **26**
Priory Gdns. .73Xc 161
Priory Gdns. DA1: Dart .57Md **119**
HA0: Wemb .35Ja **66**
N6 .30Kb **50**
NW10 .41Na **87**
SE25 .70Vb **135**
SW13 .55Va **110**
TW12: Hamp .66Ba **129**
TW15: Ashf .64T **128**
UB9: Hare .28L **43**
W4 .49Ua **88**
W5 .41Na **87**
Priory Grange *N2* .27Hb **49**
(off Fortis Grn.)
Priory Grn. N1 .1H **217** (40Pb **70**)
TW18: Staines .64K **127**
Priory Grn. Est. N1 .1J **217** (40Pb **70**)
Priory Gro. EN5: Barn .15Cb **31**
RM3: Rom .20Nd **39**
SW8 .53Nb **112**
Priory Hgts. N1 .1J **217**
Priory Hill DA1: Dart .57Md **119**
HA0: Wemb .35Ja **66**
Priory Ho. E1 .7K **219**
EC1 .5B **218**
SW1 .7D **228**
Priory La. DA4: Eyns .74Pd **163**
KT8: W Mole .70Da **129**
SW15 .58Ua **110**
Priory Leas SE9 .60Nc **116**
Priory Lodge *W4* .50Qa **87**
(off Kew Bri. Ct.)
WD3: Rick .17M **25**
(off Nightingale Pl.)
Priory Mans. SW10 .7A **226**
Priory Mkt. Pl. DA1: Dart .59Nd **119**
Priory M. CR3: Cat'm .97Vb **197**
RM11: Horn .32Kd **77**
SW8 .53Nb **112**
TW18: Staines .64K **127**
Priory Pk. SE3 .55Hc **115**
Priory Pk. Rd. HA0: Wemb .35Ja **66**
NW6 .39Bb **69**
Priory Path RM3: Rom .20Nd **39**
Priory Pl. DA1: Dart .58Md **119**
KT12: Walt T .76W **150**
Priory Retail Pk. SW19 .66Fb **133**
Priory Rd. CR0: C'don .73Qb **156**
E6 .39Mc **73**
IG10: Lough .14Nc **36**
IG11: Bark .38Tc **74**
KT9: Chess .76Na **153**
N8 .28Lb **50**
NW6 .39Db **69**
RH2: Reig .8J **207**
RM3: Rom .20Nd **39**
SL1: Slou .3A **80**
SL5: S'dale .3E **146**
SL9: Chal P .26A **42**
SM3: Cheam .77Za **154**
SS17: Stan H .1N **101**
SW19 .66Fb **133**
TW3: Houn .57Ea **108**
TW9: Kew .51Qa **109**
TW12: Hamp .66Ba **129**
W4 .48Ta **87**
Priory Rd. Nth. DA1: Dart .56Md **119**
Priory Rd. Sth. DA1: Dart .58Md **119**
Priory Shop. Cen. DA1: Dart .58Nd **119**
Priory Sports Cen. .74Yc 161
Priory St. E3 .41Dc **92**
Priory Ter. NW6 .39Db **69**
TW16: Sun .66W **128**
Priory Vw. WD23: B Hea .17Ga **28**
Priory Vs. *N11* .23Hb **49**
(off Colney Hatch La.)
Priory Wlk. AL1: St A .5C **6**
SW10 .7A **226** (50Eb **89**)
TW16: Sun .66W **128**
Priory Way HA2: Harr .28Da **45**
SL3: Dat .2M **103**
UB2: S'hall .48Z **85**
UB7: Harm .51N **105**
Priscilla Cl. N15 .29Sb **51**
Pritchard Ho. *E2* .40Xb **71**
(off Ada Pl.)
Pritchard's Rd. E2 .39Wb **71**
Pritchett Cl. EN3: Enf L .9Cc **20**
Priter Rd. SE16 .48Wb **91**
Priter Rd. Hostel *SE16* .48Wb **91**
(off Dockley Rd.)
Priter Way SE16 .48Wb **91**
Private Rd. EN1: Enf .15Tb **33**
Privet Dr. WD25: Wat .6V **12**
Privet M. CR8: Purl .84Lb **176**
Prize Wlk. E20 .36Ec **72**
Probert Rd. SW2 .57Qb **112**
Probyn Ho. SW1 .5E **228**
Probyn Rd. SW2 .61Rb **135**
Procter Ho. *SE1* .50Wb **91**
(off Avondale Sq.)
SE5 .52Tb **113**
(off Picton St.)
Procter St. WC1 .1H **223** (43Pb **90**)
Proctor Cl. CR4: Mitc .67Jb **134**
Proctor Gdns. KT23: Bookh .97Da **191**
Proctor Pl. RM13: Rain .39Jd **76**
Proctors Cl. TW14: Felt .60W **106**
Proffits Cotts. KT20: Tad .94Za **194**
Profumo Rd. KT12: Hers .78Z **151**
Progress Bus. Cen. SL1: Slou .4B **80**
Progress Bus. Pk.
CR0: Wadd .75Pb **156**
Progress Cen., The
EN3: Pond E .13Zb **34**
Progress Way CR0: Wadd .75Pb **156**
EN1: Enf .15Wb **33**
N22 .25Qb **50**
Project Pk. E16 .42Fc **93**
Prologis Pk. CR0: Bedd .73Mb **156**
E3 .42Ec **92**
TW4: Houn .56Y **107**
Promenade, The HA8: Edg .22Qa **47**
W4 .54Ua **110**
Promenade App. Rd. W4 .52Ua **110**
Promenade de Verdun
CR8: Purl .83Mb **176**
Propeller Cres. CR0: Wadd .78Qb **156**
Propeller Way NW9 .27Wa **48**
Prospect Av. SS17: Stan H .2K **101**
Prospect Bus. Pk.
IG10: Lough .14Tc **36**

Prospect Cl.—Queen Mary Ho.

Prospect Cl. DA17: Belv 49Cd 96
HA4: Ruis 31Z 65
SE26 63Xb 135
TW3: Houn 53Ba 107
WD23: Bush 17Fa 28
Prospect Cotts. SW18 56Cb 111
Prospect Cres. TW2: Whitt 58Ea 108
Prospect Gro.
DA12: Grav'nd 9F 122
Prospect Hill E17 28Dc 52
Prospect Ho. E3 41Cc 92
(off Campbell Rd.)
E17 27Ec 52
(off Prospect Hill)
KT19: Eps 81Ra 173
N1 2K 217
SE1 4B 230
SE16 48Wb 91
(off Frean St.)
SW19 67Fb 133
(off Chapter Way)
W10 44Za 88
(off Bridge Cl.)
Prospect La. TW20: Eng G 4L 125
Prospect Pl. BR2: Brom 69Kc 137
CR2: S Croy 79Sb 157
DA1: Dart 58Nd 119
DA12: Grav'nd 9F 122
E1 46Yb 92
(not continuous)
KT17: Eps 84Ua 174
N2 28Fb 49
N7 35Nb 70
N17 24Ub 51
NW2 34Bb 69
NW3 35Eb 69
RM5: Col R 26Ed 56
RM17: Grays 51De 121
SE8 51Bc 114
(off Evelyn St.)
SL4: Wind 5H 103
(off Osborne Rd.)
SW8 52Kb 112
SW20 66Xa 132
TW18: Staines 64H 127
W4 50Ta 87
Prospect Quay SW18 56Cb 111
(off Lightermans Wlk.)
Prospect Ring N2 27Fb 49
Prospect Rd. AL1: St A 4B 6
EN5: New Bar 14Cb 31
EN8: Chesh 1Yb 20
IG8: Wfd G 23Lc 53
KT6: Surb 72La 152
NW2 34Bb 69
RM11: Horn 27Pd 57
TN13: S'oaks 95Ld 203
Prospect St. SE16 48Xb 91
Prospect Va. SE18 49Nc 94
Prospect Way CM13: Hut 14Fe 41
Prospect Wharf E1 45Yb 92
Prospero Ho. E1 4K 225
Prospero Rd. N19 32Mb 70
Prossers KT20: Tad 93Za 194
Protea Cl. E16 42Hc 93
Protea Pl. E9 38Yb 72
(off Lyme Gro.)
Protheroe Ho. N17 27Vb 51
Prothero Gdns. NW4 29Xa 48
Prothero Ho. NW10 38Ta 67
(off Fawood Av.)
Prothero Rd. SW6 52Ab 110
Proton Twr. E14 45Fc 93
Proud Ho. E1 44Xb 91
(off Amazon St.)
Prout Gro. NW10 35Ua 68
Prout Rd. E5 34Xb 71
Provence St. N1 1D 218 (40Sb 71)
Providence Av. HA2: Harr 32Ca 65
Providence Cl. E9 39Zb 72
Providence Ct. W1 4J 221 (45Jb 90)
Providence Ho. E14 44Bc 92
(off Three Colt St.)
Providence La. UB3: Harl 52T 106
Providence Pl. GU22: Pyr 86J 169
KT17: Eps 84Ua 174
N1 39Rb 71
RM5: Col R 25Bd 55
SE10 50Gc 93
Providence Rd. UB7: Yiew 46N 83
Providence Row N1 2H 217
Providence Row Cl. E2 41Xb 91
Providence Sq. SE1 47Wb 91
Providence St.
DA9: Ghithe 57Wd 120
Providence Twr. E14 45Fc 93
(off Fairmont Av.)
SE16 47Wb 91
(off Bermondsey Wall W.)
Providence Yd. E2 41Wb 91
(off Ezra St.)
Provident Ind. Est.
UB3: Hayes 47W 84
Province Dr. SE16 47Yb 92
Province Sq. E14 46Ec 92
(off Blackwall Way)
Provincial Ter. SE20 66Zb 136
Provost Ct. NW3 37Hb 69
(off Eton Rd.)
Provost Est. N1 3F 219
Provost Rd. NW3 38Hb 69
Provost St. N1 2F 219 (40Tb 71)
Provost Way RM8: Dag 35Wc 75
Prowse Av. WD23: B Hea 18Ea 28
Prowse Ct. N18 22Wb 51
(off Lord Graham M.)
Prowse Pl. NW1 38Lb 70
Proyers Path HA1: Harr 31Ka 66
Prudence La.
BR6: Farnb 77Qc 160
Pruden Cl. N14 19Lb 32
Prudent Pas. EC2 3E 224
Prudhoe Ct. DA2: Dart 58Rd 119
(off Osbourne Rd.)
Prune Hill
TW20: Egh, Eng G 6P 125
Prunus Cl. GU24: W End 5C 166
Prusom's Island E1 46Yb 92
(off Wapping High St.)
Prusom St. E1 46Xb 91
Pryce Ho. E3 41Cc 92
(off Campbell Rd.)
Pryor Cl. WD5: Ab L 4V 12
Puccinia Ct. TW19: Stanw 60N 105
(off Yeoman Dr.)
Puck La. EN9: Walt A 1Fc 21
Pucknells Cl. BR8: Swan 67Ed 140
Pucks Hill GU21: Knap 9H 167
Pudding La. AL3: St A 2B 6
(off Chequer St.)
EC3 5G 225 (45Tb 91)
HP1: Hem H 1J 3
IG7: Chig 16Uc 36
TN15: Seal 93Pd 203
Pudding Mill La. E15 39Dc 72
Puddingstone Dr. AL4: St A 4G 6
PUDDLEDOCK 65Gd 140
Puddle Dock EC4 4C 224 (45Rb 91)
(not continuous)
Puddledock Farm Fishery 32Yd 78
Puddledock La. DA2: Wilm 64Gd 140
PUDDS CROSS 1A 10
Puffin Cl. BR3: Beck 71Zb 158
IG11: Bark 41Xc 95
Pugin Cl. SW19 63Db 133
Pugin Ct. N1 38Qb 70
(off Liverpool Rd.)
Pulborough Ho. RM3: Rom 24Nd 57
(off Kingsbridge Cir.)
Pulborough Rd. SW18 59Bb 111
Pulborough Way
TW4: Houn 56Y 107
Pulford Rd. N15 30Tb 51
Pulham Av. N2 28Eb 49
Pulham Ho. SW8 52Pb 112
(off Dorset Rd.)
Pullen's Bldgs. SE17 7C 230
Puller Rd. EN5: Barn 12Ab 30
HP1: Hem H 3J 3
Pulleyns Av. E6 41Nc 94
Pulleys Cl. HP1: Hem H 1H 3
Pulleys La. HP1: Hem H 1G 2
(not continuous)
Pullman Cl. AL1: St A 4C 6
Pullman Ct. SW2 60Nb 112
Pullman Gdns. SW15 58Ya 110
Pullman M. SE12 62Kc 137
Pullman Pl. RH1: Mers 100Lb 196
(off Station Rd.)
SE9 57Nc 116
Pullmans Pl. TW18: Staines 64J 127
Pullman Sq. GU24: Bisl 9E 166
Pulross Rd. SW9 55Pb 112
Pulse Apartments NW6 36Db 69
(off Lymington Rd.)
Pulse Ct. RM7: Rush G 30Gd 56
Pulteney Cl. E3 39Bc 72
TW7: Isle 55Ja 108
Pulteney Gdns. E18 27Jc 53
Pulteney Rd. E18 27Kc 53
Pulteney Ter. N1 39Pb 70
(not continuous)
Pultney St. N1 1J 217 (39Pb 70)
Pulton Ho. SE4 56Ac 114
(off Turnham Rd.)
Pulton Pl. SW6 52Cb 111
Puma Ct. E1 7K 219 (43Vb 91)
Pump All. TW8: Bford 52Ma 109
Pump Cl. UB5: N'olt 40Ca 65
Pump Ct. EC4 3K 223 (44Qb 90)
Pumphandle Path N2 26Fb 49
(off Oak La.)
Pump Hill IG10: Lough 12Pc 36
Pumphouse, The N8 28Pb 50
Pump Ho. Cl. BR2: Brom 68Gc 137
SE16 47Yb 92
Pump Ho. Cres. TW8: Bford 50Na 87
Pumphouse Cres. WD17: Wat 15Y 27
Pumphouse Educational Mus., The
46Ac 92
Pump House Gallery 52Jb 112
Pump Ho. La. SW8 52Lb 112
Pump Ho. M. E1 45Wb 91
(off Hooper St.)
Pump House Steam & Transport Mus.
30Ac 52
Pump House Theatre & Arts Cen. 15Z 27
Pumping Ho. E14 45Fc 93
(off Naval Row)
Pumping Station Rd. W4 52Ua 110
Pumpkin Hill SL1: Burn 7C 60
Pump La. BR6: Well H 78Dd 162
SE14 52Yb 114
SL5: Asc 7C 124
UB3: Hayes 47W 84
Pump Pail Nth. CR0: C'don 76Sb 157
Pump Pail Sth. CR0: C'don 76Sb 157
Pump St. SS17: Horn H 1J 101
Punchard Cres. EN3: Enf L 10Dc 20
Punch Cft. DA3: Nw A G 76Ae 165
Punderson's Gdns. E2 41Xb 91
Purbeck Av. KT3: N Mald 72Va 154
Purbeck Cl. RH1: Mers 100Mb 196
Purbeck Dr. GU21: Wok 86B 168
NW2 33Za 68
Purbeck Ho. SW8 52Pb 112
(off Bolney St.)
WD18: Wat 16V 26
(off Scammell Way)
Purbeck Rd. RM11: Horn 31Jd 76
Purberry Gro. KT17: Ewe 82Va 174
Purberry Shot KT17: Ewe 82Va 174
Purbrock Av. WD25: Wat 8Y 13
Purbrook Est. SE1 2J 231 (47Ub 91)
Purbrook St. SE1 3J 231 (48Ub 91)
Purcell Cl. CR8: Kenley 86Sb 177
SS17: Stan H 1L 101
WD6: Bore 11Ma 29
Purcell Cres. SW6 52Za 110
Purcell Ho. EN1: Enf 10Wb 19
SW10 51Fb 111
(off Milman's St.)
Purcell Mans. W14 51Ab 110
(off Queen's Club Gdns.)
Purcell M. NW10 38Ua 68
Purcell Rd. UB6: G'frd 43Da 85
Purcell Room 6J 223
Purcells Av. HA8: Edg 22Qa 47
Purcell's Cl. KT21: Asht 90Pa 173
Purcell St. N1 1H 219 (40Ub 71)
Purcell Way SS17: Stan H 1L 101
Purchese St. NW1 1D 216 (40Mb 70)
Purday Ho. W10 41Ab 88
(off Bruckner St.)
Purdon Ho. SE15 53Wb 113
(off Oliver Goldsmith Est.)
Purdy Ct. KT4: Wor Pk 75Wa 154
Purdy St. E3 42Dc 92
PureGym
Bayswater 45Db 89
(off Moscow Pl.)
Canary Wharf 45Cc 92
Hallam St. 7A 216
Holborn 7H 217
Marylebone 7F 215 (43Hb 89)
Piccadilly 6D 222
Purelake M. SE13 55Fc 115
(off Marischal Rd.)
PURFLEET 49Qd 97
Purfleet By-Pass RM19: Purf 49Qd 97
Purfleet Deep Wharf RM19: Purf 51Sd 120
Purfleet Heritage & Military Cen.
49Pd 97
Purfleet Ind. Access Rd.
RM15: Avel 48Qd 97
Purfleet Ind. Pk. RM15: Avel 46Pd 97
(not continuous)
Purfleet Rd. RM15: Avel 47Qd 97
Purfleet Thames Terminal
RM19: Purf 52Sd 120
Purkis Cl. UB8: Hil 45S 84
Purland Cl. RM8: Dag 32Bd 75
Purland Rd. SE28 47Vc 95
(not continuous)
Purleigh Av. IG8: Wfd G 23Nc 54
PURLEY 83Qb 176
Purley Av. NW2 33Ab 68
Purley Bury Av. CR8: Purl 83Sb 177
Purley Bury Cl. CR8: Purl 83Sb 177
Purley Cl. IG5: Ilf 26Qc 54
PURLEY CROSS 83Qb 176
Purley Downs Golf Course 83Tb 177
Purley Downs Rd. CR2: Sande 82Sb 177
CR8: Purl 82Sb 177
Purley Hill CR8: Purl 84Rb 177
Purley Knoll CR8: Purl 83Pb 176
Purley Leisure Cen. 83Qb 176
Purley Oaks Rd. CR2: Sande 81Tb 177
Purley Pde. CR8: Purl 83Qb 176
Purley Pk. Rd. CR8: Purl 82Rb 177
Purley Pl. N1 38Rb 71
Purley Ri. CR8: Purl 84Pb 176
Purley Rd. CR2: S Croy 80Tb 157
CR8: Purl 83Qb 176
N9 20Ub 33
Purley Va. CR8: Purl 85Rb 177
Purley Vw. Ter. CR2: S Croy 80Tb 157
(off Sanderstead Rd.)
Purley Way CR0: C'don, Wadd 73Pb 156
CR8: Purl 82Qb 176
Purley Way Cen., The
CR0: Wadd 75Qb 156
Purley Way Cres. CR0: C'don 73Pb 156
Purlieu Way CM16: They B 7Uc 22
Purlings Rd. WD23: Bush 15Da 27
Purneys Rd. SE9 56Mc 115
Purrett Rd. SE18 50Vc 95
Purser Ho. SW2 58Qb 112
Pursers Ct. SL2: Slou 4J 81
Pursers Cross Rd. SW6 53Bb 111
Pursewardens Cl. W13 46La 86
Pursey Cl. TN15: W King 79Ud 164
Pursley Gdns. WD6: Bore 10Qa 15
Pursley Rd. NW7 24Xa 48
Purton Ct. SL2: Farn R 8G 60
Purton La. SL2: Farn C, Farn R 8G 60
Purves Rd. NW10 41Xa 88
Purvis Ho. CR0: C'don 73Tb 157
Pusey Ho. E14 44Cc 92
(off Saracen St.)
Puteaux Ho. E2 40Zb 72
(off Mace St.)
PUTNEY 56Za 110
Putney Arts Theatre 56Za 110
Putney Bri. SW15 55Ab 110
Putney Bri. App. SW6 55Ab 110
Putney Bri. Rd. SW15 56Ab 110
SW18 56Ab 110
Putney Comn. SW15 55Ya 110
Putney Exchange (Shop. Cen.)
SW15 56Za 110
Putney Gdns. RM6: Chad H 29Xc 55
PUTNEY HEATH 58Ya 110
Putney Heath SW15 59Xa 110
Putney Heath La. SW15 58Za 110
Putney High St. SW15 56Za 110
Putney Hill SW15 59Za 110
(not continuous)
Putney Leisure Cen. 56Ya 110
Putney Pk. Av. SW15 56Wa 110
Putney Pk. La. SW15 56Xa 110
(not continuous)
Putney Rd. EN3: Enf W 8Zb 20
PUTNEY VALE 62Wa 132
Putney Va. Crematorium SW19 61Xa 132
Putney Wharf SW15 55Ab 110
Puttenham Cl. WD19: Wat 19Y 27
Putt in the Pk. 56Bb 111
Puttocks Cl. AL9: Wel G 5E 8
Puttocks Dr. AL9: Wel G 5E 8
Pycroft Way N9 21Vb 51
Pye Cl. CR3: Cat'm 95Tb 197
Pyecombe Cnr. N12 21Bb 49
Pyghtle, The UB9: Den 31J 63
Pyghtle Footpath UB9: Den 32J 63
Pylbrook Rd. SM1: Sutt 76Cb 155
Pyle Cl. KT15: Add 77L 149
PYLE HILL 6P 187
Pyle Hill GU22: Wok 6P 187
Pylon Way CR0: Bedd 74Nb 156
Pym Cl. EN4: E Barn 15Fb 31
Pymers Mead SE21 60Sb 113
Pymmes Brook Dr. EN4: E Barn 14Gb 31
Pymmes Brook Ho. N10 24Jb 50
Pymmes Cl. N13 22Pb 50
N17 25Xb 51
Pymmes Gdns. Nth. N9 20Vb 33
Pymmes Gdns. Sth. N9 20Vb 33
Pymmes Grn. Rd. N11 21Kb 50
Pymmes Rd. N13 23Nb 50
Pym Orchard TN16: Bras 96Yc 201
Pym Pl. RM17: Grays 49Ce 99
Pynchester Cl. UB10: Ick 33Q 64
Pynefield Ho. WD3: Rick 17H 25
Pyne Rd. KT6: Surb 74Qa 153
Pynest Grn. La.
EN9: Lough, Walt A 10Jc 21
Pynfolds SE16 47Xb 91
Pynham Cl. SE2 48Xc 95
Pynnacles Cl. HA7: Stan 22Ka 46
Pynnersmead SE24 57Sb 113
Pyramid Ct. KT1: King T 68Pa 131
(off Cambridge Rd.)
Pyramid Ho. TW4: Houn 54Aa 107
Pyrcroft La. KT13: Weyb 78R 150
Pyrcroft Rd. KT16: Chert 73G 148
PYRFORD 88J 169
Pyrford Comn. Rd. GU22: Pyr 88F 168
Pyrford Ct. GU22: Pyr 89G 168
Pyrford Golf Course 89K 169
PYRFORD GREEN 89K 169
Pyrford Heath GU22: Pyr 88H 169
Pyrford Ho. SW9 56Rb 113
Pyrford Lock GU23: Wis 88L 169
Pyrford Rd. GU22: Pyr 85J 169
KT14: W Byf 85J 169
PYRFORD VILLAGE 90J 169
Pyrford Wood Est. GU22: Pyr 88H 169
Pyrford Woods GU22: Pyr 87G 168
Pyrford Woods Cl. GU22: Pyr 87H 169
Pyrian Cl. GU22: Wok 88F 168
Pyrland Rd. N5 36Tb 71
TW10: Rich 58Pa 109
Pyrles Grn. IG10: Lough 11Rc 36
Pyrles La. IG10: Lough 12Rc 36
Pyrmont Gro. SE27 62Rb 135
Pyrmont Rd. W4 51Qa 109
Pytchley Cres. SE19 65Sb 135
Pytchley Rd. SE22 55Ub 113

Q

Q Bldg., The E15 37Gc 73
(off The Grove)
QED - Queen Elizabeth Distribution Pk.
RM19: Purf 50Td 98
Quad Ct. SE1 3J 231
Quadrangle, The E15 37Gc 73
SE24 57Sb 113
SW6 52Ab 110
SW10 53Eb 111
W2 2D 220 (44Gb 89)
Quadrangle Cl. SE1 5H 231 (49Ub 91)
Quadrangle M. HA7: Stan 24La 46
Quadrant, The DA7: Bex 52Zc 117
HA2: Harr 27Fa 46
HA8: Edg 23Qa 47
(off Manor Pk. Cres.)
KT17: Eps 85Ua 174
NW4 28Ya 48
RM19: Purf 49Sd 98
SM2: Sutt 79Eb 155
SW20 67Ab 132
TW9: Rich 56Ma 109
W10 41Za 88
WD3: Rick 17N 25
Quadrant Arc. RM1: Rom 29Gd 56
W1 5C 222
Quadrant Bus. Cen. NW6 39Ab 68
Quadrant Cl. NW4 29Xa 48
Quadrant Ct. DA9: Ghithe 56Vd 120
HA9: Wemb 35Qa 67
Quadrant Courtyard, The
KT13: Weyb 77Q 150
(off Quadrant Way)
Quadrant Gro. NW5 36Hb 69
Quadrant Ho. E1 45Wb 91
(off Nesham St.)
E15 41Gc 93
(off Durban Rd.)
SE1 7B 224
Quadrant Rd. CR7: Thor H 70Rb 135
TW9: Rich 56Ma 109
Quadrant Wlk. E14 48Dc 92
(off Lanterns Way)
Quadrant Way KT13: Weyb 77Q 150
Quadrivium Point SL1: Slou 6G 80
Quad Rd. HA9: Wemb 34Ma 67
Quaggy Wlk. SE3 56Jc 115
Quail Gdns. CR2: Sels 82Ac 178
Quain Mans. W14 51Ab 110
(off Queen's Club Gdns.)
Quainton St. NW10 34Ta 67
Quaker Cl. TN13: S'oaks 95Md 203
Quaker Ct. E1 6K 219
EC1 5E 218
Quaker Dr. RM3: Rom 22Ld 57
Quaker La. EN9: Walt A 6Ec 20
UB2: S'hall 48Ca 85
Quakers Cl. DA3: Hartl 69Ae 143
Quakers Course NW9 25Va 48
Quakers Hall La. TN13: S'oaks 94Ld 203
Quakers La. EN6: Pot B 2Db 17
TW7: Isle 52Ja 108
Quakers Pl. E7 36Mc 73
Quaker St. E1 6K 219 (42Vb 91)
Quakers Wlk. N21 15Tb 33
Quality Ct. WC2 2K 223
Quality Living Leisure Club 4D 6
Quality St. RH1: Mers 100Kb 196
Quant Bldg. E17 28Cc 52
Quantock Cl. SL3: L'ly 50C 82
UB3: Harl 52T 106
Quantock Dr. KT4: Wor Pk 75Ya 154
Quantock Gdns. NW2 33Za 68
Quantock Ho. N16 32Vb 71
Quantock M. SE15 54Wb 113
Quantock Rd. DA7: Bex 54Gd 118
Quantum Ct. E1 45Yb 92
(off King David La.)
Quarles Cl. RM5: Col R 24Cd 56
Quarles Pk. Rd. RM6: Chad H 30Xc 55
Quarrendon St. SW6 54Cb 111
Quarr Rd. SM5: Cars 72Fb 155
Quarry, The RH3: Bet 4A 206
Quarry Cl. DA11: Grav'nd 9B 122
KT22: Lea 93Ma 193
RH8: Oxt 2J 211
Quarry Cotts. RH2: Reig 3K 207
TN13: S'oaks 95Jd 202
Quarry Gdns. KT22: Lea 93Ma 193
Quarry Hill RM17: Grays 50Ce 99
TN15: S'oaks 95Md 203
Quarry Hill Pk. RH2: Reig 3L 207
Quarry Hill Rd. TN15: Bor G 92Be 205
Quarry M. RM19: Purf 49Qd 97
Quarry Pk. Rd. SM1: Sutt 79Bb 155
Quarry Path RH8: Oxt 3J 211
Quarry Ri. SM1: Sutt 79Bb 155
Quarry Rd. RH8: Oxt 2J 211
RH9: G'stone 100Yb 198
SW18 58Eb 111
Quarryside Bus. Pk. RH1: Redh 3B 208
Quarry Vw. DA9: Ghithe 58Wd 120
(off Woodpecker Dr.)
Quarterdeck, The E14 47Cc 92
Quarter Ho. SW18 56Eb 111
Quartermaine Av. GU22: Wok 94B 188
Quartermass Cl. HP1: Hem H 1J 3
Quartermass Rd. HP1: Hem H 1J 3
Quartermaster La. NW7 22Ab 48
Quarters Apartments CR0: C'don 75Tb 157
(off Wellesley Rd.)
Quartz Ho. HA2: Harr 32Ca 65
Quasar
Hemel Hempstead 3M 3
Quastel Ho. SE1 2F 231
Quatre Ports E4 22Fc 53
Quaves Rd. SL3: Slou 8M 81
Quay Ho. E14 47Cc 92
(off Admirals Way)
Quay La. DA9: Ghithe 56Xd 120
Quayside Cotts. E1 46Wb 91
(off Mews St.)
Quayside Ct. SE16 46Zb 92
(off Abbotshade Rd.)
Quayside Ho. E14 46Bc 92
E16 44Hc 93
(off Tarling Rd.)
W10 42Ab 88
Quayside Wlk. KT1: King T 68Ma 131
(off Wadbrook St.)
Quay Sth. Ct. UB9: Hare 25J 43
Quay Vw. Apartments E14 48Cc 92
(off Arden Cres.)
Quay W. Ct. WD3: W Hyd 24H 43
Quebec Av. TN16: Westrm 98Tc 200
Quebec Cotts. TN16: Westrm 99Tc 200
Quebec House 98Tc 200
Quebec M. W1 3G 221 (44Hb 89)
Quebec Rd. IG1: Ilf 31Rc 74
IG2: Ilf 31Rc 74
RM18: Tilb 4C 122
UB4: Yead 44Y 85
Quebec Sq. TN16: Westrm 98Tc 200
Quebec Way SE16 47Zb 92
Quebec Way Ind. Est. SE16 47Ac 92
(not continuous)
Quebec Wharf E8 39Ub 71
(off Kingsland Rd.)
E14 44Cc 92
Quedgeley Ct. SE15 51Vb 113
(off Ebley Cl.)
Queen Adelaide Ct. SE20 65Yb 136
Queen Adelaide Rd. SE20 65Yb 136
Queen Adelaide's Ride SL4: Wink 8B 102
Queen Alexandra Mans. WC1 3F 217
Queen Alexandra's Ct. SW19 64Bb 133
Queen Alexandra's Way
KT19: Eps 83Qa 173
Queen Anne Alcove 5B 220
Queen Anne Av. BR2: Brom 69Hc 137
Queen Anne Dr. KT10: Clay 80Ga 152
Queen Anne Ho. E16 46Jc 93
(off Hardy Av.)
Queen Anne M. W1 1A 222 (43Kb 90)
Queen Anne Rd. E9 37Zb 72
Queen Anne's Cl. SL4: Wind 2F 124
TW2: Twick 62Fa 130
Queen Anne's Ct. SE10 50Fc 93
(off Park Row)
Queen Anne's Gdns. CR4: Mitc 69Hb 133
EN1: Enf 16Ub 33
KT22: Lea 93Ka 192
W4 48Ua 88
W5 47Na 87
Queen Anne's Ga. DA7: Bex 55Zc 117
SW1 2D 228 (47Mb 90)
Queen Anne's Gro. EN1: Enf 17Tb 33
W4 48Ua 88
W5 47Na 87
Queen Anne's Pl. EN1: Enf 16Ub 33
Queen Anne's Ride SL4: Wind 5E 124
Queen Anne's Rd. SL4: Wind 6G 102
Queen Annes Sq. SE1 49Wb 91
(off Monnow Rd.)
Queen Anne's Ter. KT22: Lea 93Ka 192
Queen Anne St. W1 2K 221 (44Jb 90)
Queen Anne's Wlk. WC1 6G 217
Queen Anne Ter. E1 45Xb 91
(off Sovereign Cl.)
Queen Ann's Ct. SL4: Wind 3H 103
(off Peascod St.)
Queenborough Gdns. BR7: Chst 65Tc 138
IG2: Ilf 28Qc 54
Queenbridge Ind. Pk.
RM20: W Thur 51Wd 120
Queen Caroline St. W6 50Ya 88
Queen Catherine Ho. SW6 52Db 111
(off Wandon Rd.)
Queen Charlotte St. SL4: Wind 3H 103
(off Market St.)
Queen Ct. WC1 6G 217
(off Queen Sq.)
Queendale Ct. GU21: Wok 8K 167
Queen Elizabeth II Bri.
DA1: Dart 55Td 120
RM20: Dart, W Thur 55Td 120
Queen Elizabeth II Stadium 12Vb 33
Queen Elizabeth Av. RM18: E Til 9K 101
Queen Elizabeth Bldgs. EC4 4K 223
Queen Elizabeth Ct. EN5: Barn 13Cb 31
EN9: Walt A 8Ec 20
(off Greenwich Way)
Queen Elizabeth Gdns.
SM4: Mord 70Cb 133
Queen Elizabeth Hall 6H 223 (46Pb 90)
Queen Elizabeth Ho. SW12 59Jb 112
Queen Elizabeth II Conference Cen.
2E 228 (47Mb 90)
Queen Elizabeth Olympic Pk. 38Dc 72
Queen Elizabeth Rd. E17 27Ac 52
KT2: King T 68Pa 131
Queen Elizabeth's Cl. N16 33Tb 71
Queen Elizabeth's Coll. SE10 52Ec 114
Queen Elizabeth's Dr.
CR0: New Ad 81Fc 179
N14 18Nb 32
Queen Elizabeth's Gdns.
CR0: New Ad 82Fc 179
Queen Elizabeth's Hunting Lodge 17Hc 35
Queen Elizabeth Sports Cen. 14Bb 31
Queen Elizabeth St. SE1 1K 231 (47Ub 91)
Queen Elizabeth's Wlk. N16 32Tb 71
SL4: Wind 4J 103
SM6: Bedd 77Mb 156
Queen Elizabeth Wlk. SW13 53Wa 110
Queen Elizabeth Way GU22: Wok 91B 188
SL4: Eton, Wind 3F 102
Queenhill Rd. CR2: Sels 82Xb 177
Queenhithe EC4 4E 224 (45Sb 91)
Queenhythe Cres. GU4: Jac W 10P 187
Queenhythe Rd. GU4: Jac W 10P 187
Queen Isabella Way EC1 2C 224
Queen Margaret Flats E2 41Xb 91
(off St Jude's Rd.)
Queen Margaret's Gro. N1 36Ub 71
Queen Mary Av. E18 25Jc 53
RM18: E Til 9L 101
SM4: Mord 71Za 154
Queen Mary Cl. GU22: Wok 88E 168
KT6: Surb 76Qa 153
RM1: Rom 30Fd 56
Queen Mary Ct.
RM18: E Til 9L 101
TW19: Stanw 60N 105
Queen Mary Ho. E16 46Kc 93
(off Wesley Av.)
E18 25Kc 53

Queen Mary Rd.—Raglan Cl.

Queen Mary Rd. SE19 65Rb 135
TW17: Shep 68S 128
Queen Mary's Av.
SM5: Cars 80Hb 155
WD18: Wat 14U 26
Queen Marys Bldgs. SW1 5C 228
Queen Mary's Ct. *SE10* 51Fc 115
(off Park Row)
Queen Marys Ct. *EN9: Walt A* 7Ec 20
(off Harrison Rd.)
Queen Mary's Dr.
KT15: New H 82H 169
Queen Mary's Ho. SW15 58Wa 110
Queen Mary University of London
Charterhouse Square 6C 218 (42Rb 91)
Lincoln's Inn Fields Campus 2H 223
Mile End Campus 42Ac 92
West Smithfield Campus 1C 224
Queen Mother Memorial 7D 222
Queen Mothers Dr. UB9: Den 30H 43
Queen Mother Sports Cen., The 5B 228
Queen of Denmark Ct.
SE16 48Bc 92
Queens Acre SL4: Wind 6H 103
SM3: Cheam 80Za 154
Queens Acre Ho. SL4: Wind 5H 103
Queens All. CM16: Epp 3Vc 23
Queen's Av. KT14: Byfl 84M 169
UB6: G'frd 44Da 85
WD18: Wat 14V 26
Queens Av. HA7: Stan 27La 46
IG8: Wfd G 22Kc 53
N3 24Eb 49
N10 27Jb 50
N20 19Fb 31
N21 18Rb 33
TW13: Hanw 63Y 129
Queensberry Ho. TW9: Rich 57La 108
Queensberry M. W.
SW7 5B 226 (49Fb 89)
Queensberry Pl. E12 36Mc 73
SW7 5B 226 (49Fb 89)
TW9: Rich 57Ma 109
(off Friars La.)
Queensberry Way SW7 5B 226 (49Fb 89)
Queensborough Ct. *N3* 28Bb 49
(off Tillingbourne Gdns.)
Queensborough M. W2 45Eb 89
Queensborough Pas. *W2* 45Eb 89
(off Queensborough M.)
Queensborough Studios *W2* 45Eb 89
(off Queensborough M.)
Queensborough Ter. W2 45Db 89
Queensbridge Ct. E2 1K 219
Queensbridge Pk. TW7: Isle 57Ga 108
Queensbridge Rd. E2 37Vb 71
E8 37Vb 71
Queensbridge Sports & Community Cen. 38Vb 71
QUEENSBURY 27Na 47
Queensbury Circ. Pde.
HA3: Kenton 27Na 47
HA7: Kenton 27Na 47
Queensbury Rd. HA0: Wemb 40Pa 67
NW9 31Ta 67
Queensbury Sta. Pde. HA8: Edg 27Pa 47
Queensbury St. N1 38Sb 71
Queen's Cir. SW8 52Kb 112
Queen's Cl. KT10: Esh 77Da 151
SL4: Old Win 7L 103
Queens Cl. GU24: Bisl 8E 166
HA8: Edg 22Qa 47
KT20: Walt H 96Wa 194
SM6: Wall 78Kb 156
Queen's Club Gdns. W14 51Ab 110
Queen's Club, The (Tennis Courts) 50Ab 88
Queens Club Ter. *W14* 51Bb 111
(off Normand Rd.)
Queen's Ct. NW8 1B 214
SM2: Sutt 83Cb 175
WD17: Wat 13Y 27
(off Queen's Rd.)
Queens Ct. AL1: St A 2F 6
CR2: S Croy 78Sb 157
(off Warham Rd.)
CR7: Thor H 71Qb 156
E11 31Gc 73
GU22: Wok 90B 168
HA3: Kenton 26Ka 46
IG9: Buck H 19Mc 35
KT13: Weyb 78T 150
KT19: Ewe 82Ua 174
NW6 36Db 69
NW11 29Bb 49
RH1: Redh 5A 208
(off St Anne's Mt.)
RM11: Horn 32Md 77
SE16 48Vb 91
(off Old Jamaica Rd.)
SE23 61Yb 136
SL1: Slou 5K 81
TW10: Rich 58Pa 109
TW18: Staines 65M 127
W2 45Db 89
(off Queensway)
WD6: Bore 11Pa 29
(off Bennington Dr.)
Queenscourt HA9: Wemb 35Na 67
Queens Ct. Ride KT11: Cobh 85W 170
Queen's Cres. NW5 37Jb 70
TW10: Rich 57Pa 109
Queenscroft Rd. SE9 57Mc 115
Queensdale Cres. W11 46Za 88
(not continuous)
Queensdale Pl. W11 46Ab 88
Queensdale Rd. W11 46Za 88
Queensdale Wlk. W11 46Ab 88
Queensdown Rd. E5 35Xb 71
Queen's Dr. EN8: Walt C 6Cc 20
KT5: Surb 73Qa 153
KT7: T Ditt 72Ja 152
KT22: Oxs 83Ea 172
N4 33Rb 71
SL3: Ful, Wex 38B 62
Queens Dr. E10 31Cc 72
TN14: S'oaks 92Ld 203
W3 44Pa 87
W5 44Pa 87
WD5: Ab L 4V 12
Queens Dr., The
WD3: Rick 17H 25
Queen's Elm Pde. *SW3* 7C 226
(off Old Church St.)
Queen's Elm Sq. SW3 7C 226 (50Fb 89)
Queen's Farm DA12: Shorne 10N 123
Queen's Farm Rd.
DA12: Shorne, Grav'nd 1N 145
Queensferry Wlk. N17 28Xb 51
Queensfield Ct. SM3: Cheam 77Ya 154
Queen's Gallery 2A 228 (47Kb 90)
Queen's Gdns. NW4 29Ya 48
RM13: Rain 40Fd 76
TW5: Hest 53Aa 107
W2 4A 220 (45Eb 89)
W5 42La 86
Queens Gdns. DA2: Dart 60Rd 119
RM14: Upm 30Vd 58
Queen's Ga. SW7 2A 226 (47Eb 89)
Queens Ga. *WD17: Wat* 13Y 27
(off Lord St.)
Queensgate EN8: Walt C 6Bc 20
KT11: Cobh 84Z 171
Queensgate Cen. RM17: Grays 50Ce 99
Queens Ga. Cotts. SL4: Wind 6H 103
Queensgate Ct. N12 22Db 49
Queen's Ga. Gdns.
SW7 4A 226 (48Eb 89)
Queens Ga. Gdns.
BR7: Chst 67Tc 138
SW15 56Xa 110
Queensgate Ho. *E3* 40Bc 72
(off Hereford Rd.)
Queen's Ga. M. SW7 2A 226 (48Eb 89)
Queensgate M. BR3: Beck 67Ac 136
Queen's Ga. Pl. SW7 4A 226 (48Eb 89)
Queensgate Pl. NW6 38Cb 69
Queen's Ga. Pl. M.
SW7 4A 226 (48Eb 89)
Queen's Ga. Ter. SW7 3A 226 (48Eb 89)
Queens Ga. Vs. E9 38Ac 72
Queen's Gro. NW8 1B 214 (39Fb 69)
Queens Gro. Rd. E4 18Fc 35
Queen's Gro. Studios
NW8 1B 214 (39Fb 69)
Queen's Head Pas. EC4 2D 224 (44Sb 91)
Queen's Head St. N1 39Rb 71
Queens Head Yd. SE1 7F 225
Queens Hill Ri. SL5: Asc 9A 124
Queen's House, The 51Fc 115
(within National Maritime Mus.)
Queens Ho. *SE17* 51Tb 113
(off Merrow St.)
SW8 52Nb 112
(off Sth. Lambeth Rd.)
TW11: Tedd 65Ha 130
W2 45Db 89
(off Queensway)
Queenshurst Sq. KT2: King T 67Na 131
Queen's Ice & Bowl 45Db 89
Queenside M. RM12: Horn 33Nd 77
Queen's Keep TW1: Twick 58La 108
Queensland Av. N18 23Sb 51
SW19 67Db 133
Queensland Cl. E17 26Bc 52
Queensland Ho. *E16* 46Qc 94
(off Rymill St.)
Queensland Rd. N7 35Qb 70
Queens La. N10 27Kb 50
Queen's Mans. *W6* 49Za 88
(off Brook Grn.)
Queen's Mkt. E13 39Lc 73
Queens Mead HA8: Edg 23Pa 47
Queensmead KT22: Oxs 83Ea 172
NW8 39Fb 69
SL3: Dat 2M 103
Queensmead Av. KT17: Ewe 82Xa 174
Queens Mead Rd. BR2: Brom 68Hc 137
Queensmead Sports Cen. 35Z 65
Queensmere Cl. SW19 61Za 132
Queensmere Ct. SW13 52Va 110
Queensmere Rd. SL1: Slou 7K 81
SW19 61Za 132
Queensmere Shop. Cen. SL1: Slou 7K 81
Queen's M. W2 45Db 89
Queensmill Rd. SW6 52Za 110
Queen's Pde. *N11* 22Hb 49
(off Friern Barnet Rd.)
NW2 37Ya 68
(off Willesden La.)
Queens Pde. N8 28Rb 51
NW4 29Ya 48
(off Queens Rd.)
W5 44Pa 87
Queen's Pde. Cl. N11 22Hb 49
QUEENS PARK 40Ab 68
Queens Pk. Ct. W10 41Za 88
Queen's Pk. Gdns. TW13: Felt 62V 128
Queen's Pk. Rangers FC 46Xa 88
Queen's Pk. Rd. CR3: Cat'm 95Ub 197
RM3: Hrld W 25Qd 57
Queens Pas. BR7: Chst 65Rc 138
Queens Pl. SM4: Mord 70Cb 133
WD17: Wat 13Y 27
Queen's Prom.
KT1: King T, Surb 70Ma 131
Queen Sq. WC1 6G 217 (42Nb 90)
Queen Sq. Pl. WC1 6G 217
Queen's Quay EC4 4E 224
Queens Reach KT1: King T 68Ma 131
KT8: E Mos 70Ga 130
Queens Ride SW13 55Wa 110
SW15 55Wa 110
Queens Ri. TW10: Rich 58Pa 109
Queen's Rd. CR4: Mitc 69Fb 133
DA8: Erith 51Gd 118
DA16: Well 54Xc 117
E17 30Bc 52
EN1: Enf 14Ub 33
EN8: Walt C 5Ac 20
GU21: Knap 10G 166
IG9: Buck H 19Kc 35
IG10: Lough 13Nc 36
KT7: T Ditt 71Ha 152
SE14 53Xb 113
SE15 53Xb 113
SL1: Slou 5K 81
SL3: Dat 2M 103
SL4: Wind 4G 102
SL5: S'hill 1B 146
SM2: Sutt 82Cb 175
SW14 55Ta 109
TW3: Houn 55Da 107
TW10: Rich 59Pa 109
TW11: Tedd 65Ha 130
TW12: Hamp H 63Da 129
TW13: Felt 60X 107
TW20: Egh 64B 126
UB8: Uxb 41L 83
W5 44Na 87
WD17: Wat 14Y 27
(Carey Pl., not continuous)
WD17: Wat 12Y 27
(Orphanage Rd.)
Queens Rd. BR1: Brom 68Jc 137
BR3: Beck 68Ac 136
BR7: Chst 65Rc 138
CM14: B'wood 20Yd 40
CR0: C'don 72Rb 157
DA12: Grav'nd 2E 144
E11 31Fc 73
E13 39Kc 73
EN5: Barn 13Za 30
GU24: Bisl, Brkwd 2C 186
IG11: Bark 37Sc 74
KT2: King T 66Qa 131
KT3: N Mald 70Va 132
KT12: Hers 77V 150
KT13: Weyb 77S 150
N3 25Eb 49
N9 20Xb 33
N11 24Nb 50
NW4 29Ya 48
SL4: Eton W 10D 80
SM4: Mord 70Cb 133
SM6: Wall 78Kb 156
SW19 65Bb 133
TW1: Twick 60Ja 108
UB2: S'hall 47Z 85
UB3: Hayes 44U 84
UB7: W Dray 47P 83
Queens Rd. Est. EN5: Barn 13Za 30
Queens Rd. W. E13 40Jc 73
Queen's Row SE17 51Tb 113
Queen's Square, The
HP2: Hem H 2P 3
Queens St. TW15: Ashf 63P 127
Queen's Ter. E13 39Kc 73
NW8 1B 214 (39Fb 69)
Queens Ter. *E1* 42Yb 92
(off Cephas St.)
KT7: T Ditt 72Ja 152
(off Queens Dr.)
SL4: Wind 5H 103
TW7: Isle 56Ja 108
Queen's Ter. Cotts. W7 47Ga 86
Queen's Theatre
Westminster 4D 222
Queens Theatre
Hornchurch 31Md 77
Queensthorpe M. SE26 63Zb 136
Queensthorpe Rd. SE26 63Zb 136
Queens Tower 3B 226
Queenstown Gdns. RM13: Rain 41Hd 96
Queenstown M. SW8 54Kb 112
Queenstown Rd. SW8 51Kb 112
Queen St. AL3: St A 2A 6
CM14: W'ley 22Yd 58
CR0: C'don 77Sb 157
DA7: Bex 55Bd 118
DA8: Erith 51Gd 118
DA12: Grav'nd 8D 122
EC4 4E 224 (45Sb 91)
(not continuous)
KT16: Chert 74J 149
N17 23Ub 51
RM7: Rom 30Dd 56
W1 6K 221 (46Kb 90)
WD4: Chfd 4J 11
Queen St. Pl. EC4 5E 224 (45Sb 91)
Queensville Rd. SW12 59Mb 112
Queen's Wlk. N5 36Rb 71
SW1 6B 222 (46Lb 90)
TW15: Ashf 63M 127
W5 42La 86
Queen's Wlk., The SE1 5A 224 (45Qb 90)
(Oxo Tower Wharf)
SE1 6G 225 (46Ub 91)
(Tooley St.)
SE1 6J 223 (46Pb 90)
(Waterloo Rd.)
Queens Wlk. E4 18Fc 35
HA1: Harr 28Ga 46
HA4: Ruis 33Y 65
NW9 33Sa 67
Queens Wlk. Ter. HA4: Ruis 34Y 65
Queen's Way GU24: Brkwd 1B 186
NW4 29Ya 48
Queens Way EN8: Walt C 6Bc 20
TW13: Hanw 63Y 129
WD7: Shenl 4Na 15
Queensway BR4: W W'ck 76Gc 159
BR5: Pet W 71Sc 160
CR0: Wadd 79Pb 156
EN3: Pond E 14Xb 33
HP1: Hem H 1L 3
HP2: Hem H 1N 3
RH1: Redh 5P 207
TW16: Sun 68X 129
W2 44Db 89
Queensway, The SL9: Chal P 28A 42
Queensway Bus. Cen.
EN3: Pond E 14Xb 33
Queensway Ind. Est. EN3: Pond E 14Yb 34
Queensway M. *BR1: Brom* 63Ec 136
(off Whitefoot La.)
Queensway Nth. KT12: Hers 77Y 151
Queensway Sth. KT12: Hers 78Y 151
Queenswell Av. N20 20Gb 31
Queenswood Av. CM13: Hut 14Fe 41
CR7: Thor H 71Qb 156
E17 25Ec 52
SM6: Bedd 77Mb 156
TW3: Houn 54Ba 107
TW12: Hamp 65Da 129
Queenswood Ct. KT2: King T 67Qa 131
SE27 63Tb 135
SW4 57Nb 112
Queenswood Cres. TW20: Eng G 6N 125
WD25: Wat 5W 12
Queenswood Gdns. E11 32Kc 73
Queenswood Ho. *CM14: B'wood* 19Zd 41
(off Eastfield Rd.)
Queenswood Lodge RM2: Rom 27Jd 56
Queenswood Pk. N3 26Ab 48
Queens Wood Rd. N10 30Kb 50
Queenswood Rd. DA15: Sidc 57Vc 117
GU21: Wok 1H 187
SE23 62Zb 136
SS17: Stan H 3K 101
Queen's Yd. WC1 6C 216 (43Lb 90)
Queens Yd. E9 37Cc 72
QUEEN VICTORIA 77Za 154
Queen Victoria Av. HA0: Wemb 38Ma 67
Queen Victoria Memorial 2B 228 (47Lb 90)
Queen Victoria Rd. GU24: Brkwd 1B 186
Queen Victoria Seaman's Rest
E14 44Dc 92
(off E. India Dock Rd.)
Queen Victoria Statue 46Db 89
Queen Victoria St. EC4 4B 224 (45Rb 91)
Queen Victoria Ter. *E1* 45Xb 91
(off Sovereign Cl.)
Queen Victoria Wlk. SL4: Wind 3J 103
Queenwood Golf Course 79B 148
Quelmans Head Ride SL4: Wind 1B 124
Quemerford Rd. N7 36Pb 70
Quendell Wlk. HP2: Hem H 2N 3
Quendon Dr. EN9: Walt A 5Fc 21
Quendon Ho. *W10* 42Ya 88
(off Sutton Way)
Quenington Ct. SE15 51Vb 113
Quennell Cl. KT21: Asht 91Pa 193
Quennell Way CM13: Hut 17Ee 41
Quentin Ho. SE1 1B 230
(not continuous)
Quentin Pl. SE13 55Gc 115
Quentin Rd. SE13 55Gc 115
Quentins Dr. TN16: Big H 88Rc 180
Quentins Wlk. *TN16: Big H* 88Rc 180
(off St Anns Way)
Quentin Way GU25: Vir W 10M 125
Quernmore Cl. BR1: Brom 65Jc 137
Quernmore Rd. BR1: Brom 65Jc 137
N4 30Qb 50
Querrin St. SW6 54Eb 111
Quest, The *W11* 45Ab 88
(off Clarendon Rd.)
Quested Ct. *E8* 36Xb 71
(off Brett Rd.)
Questor DA1: Dart 61Nd 141
Questors Theatre, The 45La 86
Quex Ct. *NW6* 39Db 69
(off West End La.)
Quex M. NW6 39Cb 69
Quex Rd. NW6 39Cb 69
Quiberon Ct. TW16: Sun 69W 128
Quickley Brow WD3: Chor 16D 24
Quickley La. WD3: Chor 16D 24
Quickley Ri. WD3: Chor 16E 24
Quickmoor La. WD4: Bucks 5K 11
Quick Rd. W4 50Ua 88
Quicks Rd. SW19 66Db 133
Quick St. N1 2C 218 (40Rb 71)
Quick St. M. N1 2B 218 (40Rb 71)
Quickswood NW3 38Gb 69
Quickwood Cl. WD3: Rick 16J 25
Quiet Cl. KT15: Add 77J 149
Quiet Nook BR2: Hayes 76Mc 159
Quill Ho. *E2* 42Wb 91
(off Cheshire St.)
Quill La. SW15 56Za 110
Quillot, The KT12: Hers 78V 150
Quill St. N4 34Qb 70
W5 41Na 87
Quilp St. SE1 1D 230 (47Sb 91)
(not continuous)
Quilter Gdns. BR5: Orp 74Yc 161
Quilter Rd. BR5: Orp 74Yc 161
Quilters Pl. SE9 60Sc 116
Quilter St. E2 41Wb 91
SE18 50Vc 95
Quilter Way RM3: Rom 22Md 57
Quilting Ct. *SE16* 47Zb 92
(off Garter Way)
Quinbrookes SL2: Slou 4N 81
Quince Cl. SL5: S'hill 10B 124
Quince Dr. GU24: Bisl 7F 166
Quince Ho. *SE13* 54Dc 114
(off Quince Rd.)
Quince Rd. SE13 54Dc 114
Quince Tree Cl. RM15: S Ock 41Yd 98
Quincy Rd. TW20: Egh 64C 126
Quinn Cl. E2 40Yb 72
Quinnell Cl. SE18 50Vc 95
Quinta Dr. EN5: Barn 15Xa 30
Quintain Ho. *KT1: King T* 68Ma 131
(off Wood St.)
Quintet, The KT12: Walt T 74W 150
Quintin Av. SW20 67Bb 133
Quintin Cl. HA5: Eastc 28X 45
Quinton Cl. BR3: Beck 69Ec 136
SM6: Wall 77Kb 156
TW5: Cran 52X 107
Quinton Ct. *SE16* 49Ac 92
(off Plough Way)
Quinton Ho. *SW8* 52Nb 112
(off Wyvil Rd.)
Quinton Rd. KT7: T Ditt 74Ja 152
Quinton St. SW18 61Eb 133
Quintrell Cl. GU21: Wok 9M 167
Quixley St. E14 45Fc 93
Quoin Ho. UB7: Yiew 45M 83
Quorn Rd. SE22 56Ub 113

R

Rabbit La. KT12: Hers 80W 150
Rabbit Row W8 46Cb 89
Rabbits Rd. DA4: S Dar 68Td 142
E12 35Nc 74
Rabbs Mill Ho. UB8: Uxb 40M 63
Rabies Heath Rd. RH1: Blet 5L 209
RABLEY 4Ta 15
Rablus Pl. DA4: Farni 72Pd 163
Rabournmead Dr. UB5: N'olt 36Aa 65
Raby Rd. KT3: N Mald 70Ta 131
Raby St. E14 44Ac 92
Raccoon Way TW4: Houn 54Y 107
Racefield Cl. DA12: Shorne 6N 145
RAC Golf Course 89Sa 173
Rachel Cl. IG6: Ilf 27Tc 54
Racine *SE5* 53Ub 113
(off Sceaux Gdns.)
Rackham Cl. DA16: Well 54Xc 117
Rackham M. SW16 65Lb 134
Rackstraw Ho. NW3 38Hb 69
Racton Rd. SW6 51Cb 111
RADA
Chenies St. 7D 216
Gower St. 7D 216
RADA Studios 7D 216
Radbourne Av. W5 49La 86
Radbourne Cl. E5 35Zb 72
Radbourne Ct. HA3: Kenton 30Ka 46
Radbourne Cres. E17 26Fc 53
Radbourne Rd. SW12 59Lb 112
Radburn Pl. DA10: Swans 57Ae 121
Radcliff Cl. *E3* 42Bc 92
(off Jospeh St.)
Radcliffe Av. EN2: Enf 11Sb 33
NW10 40Wa 68
Radcliffe Gdns. SM5: Cars 81Gb 175
Radcliffe Ho. CM14: B'wood 20Xd 40
SE16 49Xb 91
(off Anchor St.)
SE20 67Wb 135
Radcliffe M. TW12: Hamp H 64Ea 130
Radcliffe Path SW8 54Kb 112
Radcliffe Rd. CR0: C'don 75Vb 157
HA3: W'stone 26Ja 46
N21 18Rb 33
SE1 3J 231 (48Ub 91)
Radcliffe Sq. SW15 58Za 110
Radcliffe Way UB5: N'olt 41Z 85
Radcot Av. SL3: L'ly 48D 82
Radcot Point SE23 62Zb 136
Radcot St. SE11 7A 230 (50Qb 90)
Raddington Rd. W10 43Ab 88
Raddon Twr. *E8* 37Vb 71
(off Dalston Sq.)
Radfield Dr. DA2: Dart 60Sd 120
Radfield Way DA15: Sidc 59Tc 116
Radford Ct. *SE15* 52Xb 113
(off Old Kent Rd.)
Radford Est. NW10 41Ua 88
Radford Ho. *E14* 43Dc 92
(off St Leonard's Rd.)
N7 36Pb 70
Radford Rd. SE13 58Ec 114
Radford Way IG11: Bark 41Vc 95
Radipole Rd. SW6 53Bb 111
Radisson Ct. *SE1* 3H 231
(off Long La.)
Radius Apartments N1 2G 217
Radius Pk. TW14: Felt 56V 106
Radland Rd. E16 44Hc 93
Radleigh Pl. BR3: Beck 65Cc 136
Radlet Av. SE26 62Xb 135
RADLETT 7Ja 14
Radlett Cen., The 8Ja 14
Radlett Cl. E7 37Hc 73
Radlett Golf Academy 4Ja 14
Radlett La. WD7: R'lett, Shenl 6Ma 15
Radlett Pk. Golf Course 13Ma 29
Radlett Pk. Rd. WD7: R'lett 6Ja 14
Radlett Pl. NW8 39Gb 69
Radlett Rd. AL2: Col S, F'mre 10C 6
WD17: Wat 13Y 27
WD24: Wat 13Y 27
WD25: A'ham 11Da 27
Radley Av. IG3: Bark, Ilf 35Wc 75
Radley Cl. TW14: Felt 60V 106
Radley Ct. *AL1: St A* 2C 6
(off Newsome Pl.)
SE16 47Zb 92
Radley Gdns. HA3: Kenton 28Na 47
Radley Ho. NW1 5F 215
SE2 47Zc 95
(off Wolvercote Rd.)
Radley M. W8 48Cb 89
Radley Rd. N17 26Ub 51
Radley's La. E18 26Jc 53
Radleys Mead RM10: Dag 37Dd 76
Radley Sq. E5 33Yb 72
Radley Ter. *E16* 43Hc 93
(off Hermit Rd.)
Radlix Rd. E10 32Cc 72
Radnor Av. DA16: Well 57Xc 117
HA1: Harr 29Ga 46
Radnor Cl. BR7: Chst 65Uc 138
CR4: Mitc 70Nb 134
Radnor Ct. HA3: Hrw W 25Ha 46
RH1: Redh 6N 207
W7 44Ha 86
(off Copley Cl.)
Radnor Cres. IG4: Ilf 29Pc 54
SE18 52Wc 117
Radnor Gdns. EN1: Enf 11Ub 33
TW1: Twick 61Ha 130
Radnor Gro. UB10: Hil 40Q 64
Radnor Ho. EC1 4E 218
SW16 68Pb 134
Radnor Lodge W2 3C 220
Radnor M. W2 3C 220 (44Fb 89)
Radnor Pl. W2 3D 220 (44Gb 89)
Radnor Rd. HA1: Harr 29Fa 46
KT13: Weyb 76Q 150
NW6 39Ab 68
SE15 52Wb 113
TW1: Twick 60Ha 108
Radnor St. EC1 4E 218 (41Sb 91)
Radnor Ter. SM2: Sutt 80Cb 155
W14 49Bb 89
Radnor Wlk. CR0: C'don 72Ac 158
E14 49Cc 92
(off Barnsdale Av.)
SW3 7E 226 (50Gb 89)
Radnor Way NW10 42Ra 87
SL3: L'ly 49A 82
Radolphs KT20: Tad 94Za 194
Radstock Av. HA3: Kenton 27Ja 46
Radstock Cl. N11 23Jb 50
Radstock Ho. *RM3: Rom* 22Md 57
(off Darlington Gdns.)
Radstock St. SW11 52Gb 111
(not continuous)
Radstock Way RH1: Mers 100Mb 196
Radstone Ct. GU22: Wok 90B 168
Radway Ho. *W2* 43Cb 89
(off Alfred Rd.)
Radwin Cl. RM5: Col R 23Fd 56
Radzan Cl. DA2: Wilm 61Gd 140
Raebarn Gdns. EN5: Barn 15Xa 30
Raeburn Av. DA1: Dart 57Kd 119
KT5: Surb 74Ra 153
Raeburn Cl. KT1: Hamp W 66Ma 131
NW11 30Eb 49
Raeburn Ct. GU21: Wok 1L 187
Raeburn Gro. GU21: Wok 10L 167
Raeburn Ho. *UB5: N'olt* 40Z 65
(off Academy Gdns.)
Raeburn Rd. DA15: Sidc 58Uc 116
HA8: Edg 25Qa 47
UB4: Hayes 40T 64
Raeburn St. SW2 56Nb 112
RAF Bomber Command Memorial 1K 227 (47Kb 90)
Rafdene Copse
GU22: Wok 1N 187
Raffles Ho. NW4 28Xa 48
Rafford Way BR1: Brom 68Kc 137
RAF Mus. London 26Wa 48
RAF Northolt Aerodrome 37V 64
RAF Uxbridge, Battle of Britain Bunker 39P 63
Ragged Hall La.
AL2: Chis G, Pot C 6K 5
Ragged School Mus. 43Ac 92
Ragge Way TN15: Seal 92Pd 203
Raggleswood BR7: Chst 67Qc 138
Rag Hill Cl. TN16: Tats 93Nc 200
Rag Hill Rd. TN16: Tats 93Mc 199
Raglan Av. EN8: Walt C 6Zb 20
Raglan Cl. RH2: Reig 4M 207
TW4: Houn 57Ba 107

Raglan Ct.—Rawson St.

Raglan Ct. CR2: S Croy 78Rb 157
E17 29Ec 52
HA9: Wemb 35Pa 67
SE12 57Jc 115
Raglan Gdns. WD19: Wat 18X 27
Raglan Pct. CR3: Cat'm 94Ub 197
Raglan Rd. BR2: Brom 70Lc 137
DA17: Belv 49Bd 95
E17 29Ec 52
EN1: Enf 17Vb 33
GU21: Knap, Wok 10J 167
RH2: Reig 3K 207
SE18 50Sc 94
Raglan St. NW5 37Kb 70
Raglan Ter. HA2: Harr 35Da 65
Raglan Way UB5: N'olt 37Ea 66
Ragley Cl. W3 47Sa 87
Ragstone Rd. SL1: Slou 8J 81
Ragstones TN15: Seal 92Pd 203
Ragwort Ct. SE26 64Xb 135
Rahere Ct. *E1* 42Ac 92
(off Toby La.)
Rahn Rd. CM16: Epp 3Wc 23
Raider Cl. RM7: Mawney 25Cd 56
Railey M. NW5 36Lb 70
Railpit La. CR6: W'ham 87Gc 179
Railshead Rd. TW1: Isle 56Ka 108
TW7: Isle 56Ka 108
Rails La. GU24: Pirb 7A 186
Railton Cl. KT13: Weyb 80Q 150
Railton Rd. SE24 56Qb 112
Railway & Bicycle Apartments, The
TN13: S'oaks 96Jd 202
Railway App. HA1: Harr 28Ha 46
HA3: Harr 28Ha 46
N4 30Qb 50
RM7: Rush G 30Fd 56
SE1 6G 225 (46Tb 91)
(not continuous)
SM6: Wall 78Kb 156
TW1: Twick 59Ja 108
Railway Arches *E1* 44Zb 92
(off Barnardo St.)
E1 45Xb 91
(off Chapman St.)
E2 2K 219
(off Cremer St.)
E2 1K 219
(Geffrye St.)
E2 1K 219
(Laburnum St.)
E3 42Bc 92
(off Cantrell Rd.)
E7 35Jc 73
(off Winchelsea Rd.)
E8 38Xb 71
(off Mentmore Ter.)
E10 32Ec 72
E11 32Fc 73
(off Grove Grn. Rd.)
E16 46Jc 93
W6 48Ya 88
W12 47Ya 88
(off Shepherd's Bush Mkt.)
Railway Av. SE16 47Yb 92
(not continuous)
Railway Children Wlk.
BR1: Brom 61Jc 137
SE12 61Jc 137
Railway Cotts. *E15* 40Gc 73
(off Baker's Row)
SW19 63Db 133
W6 47Ya 88
(off Sulgrave Rd.)
WD4: K Lan 2R 12
WD7: R'lett 7Ka 14
WD24: Wat 11X 27
Railway Fields Local Nature Reserve
30Rb 51
Railway Gro. SE14 52Bc 114
Railway M. W10 44Ab 88
Railway Pde. *CM15: Shenf* 17Ce 41
(off Hutton Rd.)
Railway Pas. TW11: Tedd 65Ja 130
Railway Pl. DA12: Grav'nd 8D 122
DA17: Belv 48Cd 96
Railway Ri. SE22 56Ub 113
Railway Rd. EN8: Walt C 5Bc 20
TW11: Tedd 63Ga 130
Railway Side SW13 55Ua 110
Railway Sidings DA13: Meop 10C 144
Railway Sidings Ind. Est.
DA13: Meop 10C 144
Railway Sidings Rd. SE16 48Wb 91
Railway Sq. CM14: B'wood 20Yd 40
Railway St. DA11: Nflt 57Ce 121
N1 2G 217 (40Nb 70)
RM6: Chad H 31Yc 75
Railway Ter. *CR5: Coul* 87Mb 176
(off Station App.)
E17 25Ec 52
SE13 57Dc 114
SL2: Slou 6K 81
TN16: Westrm 97Tc 200
TW13: Felt 60W 106
TW18: Staines 64F 126
WD4: K Lan 9A 4
WD24: Wat 11X 27
Railway Vw. SL3: Hort 55B 104
Railway Wharf *KT1: King T* 67Ma 131
(off Thames Side)
Rainborough Cl. NW10 37Sa 67
Rainbow Av. E14 50Dc 92
Rainbow Ct. GU21: Wok 8J 167
SE14 51Ac 114
(off Chipley St.)
WD19: Wat 16Y 27
Rainbow Gdns. DA1: Dart 54Pd 119
Rainbow Ind. Est. SW20 68Xa 132
UB7: Yiew 45M 83
Rainbow La. RM18: W Til 9F 100
SS17: Stan H 1P 101
Rainbow Leisure Cen.
Epsom 84Ua 174
Rainbow Quay SE16 48Ac 92
(not continuous)
Rainbow Rd. DA8: Erith 52Jd 118
RM16: Chaf H 49Yd 98
Rainbow St. SE5 52Ub 113
Raine Gdns. IG8: Wfd G 21Jc 53
Rainer Apartment *CR0: C'don* 74Tb 157
(off Cherry Orchard Rd.)
Rainer Cl. EN8: Chesh 1Zb 20
Raines Est. Ct. N16 33Vb 71
Raine St. E1 46Xb 91
RAINHAM 42Jd 96
Rainham Cl. SE9 58Uc 116
SW11 58Gb 111
Rainham Hall 42Jd 96
Rainham Ho. NW1 1C 216
Rainham Marshes 45Jd 96
Rainham Marshes Nature Reserve
48Nd 97
Rainham Marshes Nature Reserve Vis. Cen.
49Pd 97
Rainham Rd. NW10 41Ya 88
RM12: Horn, Rain 36Hd 76
RM13: Rain 38Gd 76
Rainham Rd. Nth. RM10: Dag 33Cd 76
Rainham Rd. Sth. RM10: Dag 35Dd 76
Rainham Trad. Est. RM13: Rain 42Hd 96
Rainhill Way E3 41Cc 92
(not continuous)
Rainsborough Av. SE8 49Ac 92
Rainsborough Ho. *SW15* 57Ab 110
(off Stamford Sq.)
Rainsborough Sq. SW6 51Cb 111
Rainsford Cl. HA7: Stan 22La 46
Rainsford Rd. NW10 41Qa 87
Rainsford St. W2 2D 220 (44Gb 89)
Rainsford Way RM12: Horn 32Jd 76
Rainton Rd. SE7 50Jc 93
Rainville Rd. W6 51Ya 110
Raisins Hill HA5: Eastc 27Y 45
Raith Av. N14 20Mb 32
Rajsee Apartments *E2* 41Wb 91
(off Bethnal Grn. Rd.)
Raleana Rd. E14 46Ec 92
Raleigh Av. SM6: Bedd 77Mb 156
UB4: Yead 43X 85
Raleigh Cl. DA8: Erith 51Hd 118
DA12: Grav'nd 3E 144
HA4: Ruis 33V 64
HA5: Pinn 31Z 65
NW4 29Ya 48
SL1: Slou 6E 80
Raleigh Ct. BR3: Beck 67Dc 136
DA8: Erith 52Hd 118
SE8 50Ac 92
(off Evelyn St.)
SE16 46Zb 92
(off Clarence M.)
SM6: Wall 79Kb 156
TW18: Staines 63J 127
W12 47Ya 88
(off Scott's Rd.)
W13 43Ka 86
Raleigh Dr. KT5: Surb 74Sa 153
KT10: Clay 78Fa 152
N20 20Gb 31
Raleigh Gdns. CR4: Mitc 69Hb 133
(not continuous)
SW2 58Pb 112
Raleigh Ho. *BR1: Brom* 67Jc 137
(off Hammelton Rd.)
CR0: C'don 73Pb 156
(off Mitcham Rd.)
E14 47Dc 92
(off Admirals Way)
SW1 51Mb 112
(off Dolphin Sq.)
Raleigh M. BR6: Chels 78Vc 161
N1 39Rb 71
(off Packington St.)
Raleigh Rd. EN2: Enf 14Tb 33
N8 28Qb 50
SE20 66Zb 136
TW9: Rich 55Pa 109
TW13: Felt 62V 128
UB2: S'hall 50Aa 85
Raleigh St. N1 1C 218 (39Rb 71)
Raleigh Way N14 18Mb 32
TW13: Hanw 64Y 129
Rale La. E4 17Fc 35
Ralliwood Rd. KT21: Asht 91Qa 193
Ralph Bayer Ct. *E3* 43Cc 92
(off Geoff Cade Way)
Ralph Brook Ct. N1 3G 219
Ralph Ct. *W2* 44Db 89
(off Queensway)
Ralph Perring Ct. BR3: Beck 70Cc 136
Ralston Ct. *SL4: Wind* 3H 103
(off Russell St.)
Ralston St. SW3 50Hb 89
Ralston Way WD19: Wat 19Z 27
Ramac Ind. Est. SE7 49Kc 93
Rama Cl. SW16 66Nb 134
Rama Ct. HA1: Harr 33Ga 66
Ramac Way SE7 49Kc 93
Rama La. SE19 66Vb 135
Ramar Ho. *E1* 43Wb 91
(off Hanbury St.)
Rambert 6K 223
Rambler Cl. SL6: Tap 4A 80
SW16 63Lb 134
Rambler La. DA1: Dart 54Pd 119
SL3: L'ly 8N 81
Rame Cl. SW17 64Jb 134
Ramilles Cl. SW2 58Nb 112
Ramillies Pl. W1 3B 222 (44Lb 90)
Ramillies Rd. DA15: Sidc 58Xc 117
NW7 19Ua 30
W4 49Ta 87
Ramillies St. W1 3B 222 (44Lb 90)
Ramney Dr. EN3: Enf L 8Ac 20
Ramones Ter. *CR4: Mitc* 70Nb 134
(off Yorkshire Rd.)
Ramornie Cl. KT12: Hers 77Ba 151
Ramparts, The AL3: St A 3P 5
Rampart St. E1 44Xb 91
Ram Pas. KT1: King T 68Ma 131
Rampayne St. SW1 7D 228 (50Mb 90)
Ram Pl. E9 37Yb 72
Rampton Cl. E4 20Cc 34
Ram Quarter SW18 57Db 111
Ramryge Ct. AL1: St A 4B 6
Ramsay Gdns. RM3: Rom 25Ld 57
Ramsay Ho. NW8 1D 214
Ramsay M. SW3 51Gb 111
Ramsay Rd. E7 35Gc 73
GU20: W'sham 8C 146
W3 48Sa 87
Ramsbury Rd. AL1: St A 3C 6
Ramscroft Cl. N9 17Ub 33
Ramsdale Rd. SW17 64Jb 134
RAMSDEN 74Yc 161
Ramsden Cl. BR5: Orp 74Yc 161
Ramsden Dr. RM5: Col R 24Cd 56
Ramsden Rd. BR5: Orp 74Xc 161
DA8: Erith 52Fd 118
N11 22Hb 49
SW12 58Jb 112
Ramsey Cl. AL1: St A 3A 208
AL9: Brk P 9M 9
NW9 30Va 48
UB6: G'frd 36Fa 66
Ramsey Ct. *CR0: C'don* 75Rb 157
(off Church St.)
SL2: Slou 2B 80
Ramsey Ho. SW9 52Qb 112
Ramsey Lodge Ct. AL1: St A 1C 6
Ramsey Pl. CR3: Cat'm 94Sb 197
Ramsey Rd. CR7: Thor H 72Pb 156
Ramsey St. E2 42Wb 91
Ramsey Wlk. N1 37Tb 71
Ramsey Way N14 17Lb 32
Ramsfort Ho. *SE16* 49Xb 91
(off Camilla Rd.)
Ramsgate Cl. E16 46Kc 93
Ramsgate St. E8 37Vb 71
Ramsgill App. IG2: Ilf 28Vc 55
Ramsgill Dr. IG2: Ilf 29Vc 55
Rams Gro. RM6: Chad H 28Ad 55
Ramson Ri. HP1: Hem H 3G 2
Ram St. SW18 57Db 111
Ram Twr. SW18 57Db 111
Ramulis Dr. UB4: Yead 42Z 85
Ramuswood Av. BR6: Chels 78Uc 160
Rancliffe Gdns. SE9 56Nc 116
Rancliffe Rd. E6 40Nc 74
Randal Cres. RH2: Reig 8J 207
Randall Av. NW2 33Ua 68
Randall Cl. DA8: Erith 51Ed 118
SL3: L'ly 50B 82
SW11 53Gb 111
Randall Ct. NW7 24Wa 48
RM13: Rain 42Kd 97
SL4: Old Win 8L 103
(off Lyndwood Dr.)
Randall Dr. RM12: Horn 35Ld 77
RM16: Ors 3C 100
Randall Hill Rd. TN15: Wro 88Be 185
Randall Pl. SE10 52Ec 114
Randall Rd. SE11 6H 229 (50Pb 90)
Randall Row SE11 6H 229 (49Pb 90)
Randalls Cres. KT22: Lea 92Ja 192
Randalls Dr. CM13: Hut 16Fe 41
Randalls Pk. Av. KT22: Lea 92Ja 192
Randalls Pk. Crematorium (Leatherhead)
KT22: Lea 92Ga 192
Randalls Pk. Dr. KT22: Lea 93Ja 192
Randalls Rents *SE16* 48Bc 92
(off Gulliver St.)
Randalls Ride HP2: Hem H 1M 3
Randalls Rd. KT22: Lea 91Ga 192
Randalls Wlk. AL2: Brick W 2Ba 13
Randalls Way KT22: Lea 93Ja 192
Randell's Rd. N1 39Nb 70
Randisbourne Gdns. SE6 62Dc 136
Randle Rd. TW10: Ham 63La 130
Randlesdown Rd. SE6 63Cc 136
(not continuous)
Randles La. TN14: Knock 87Zc 181
Randolph App. E16 44Lc 93
Randolph Av. W9 4A 214 (40Db 69)
Randolph Cl. DA7: Bex 55Ed 118
GU21: Knap 9J 167
KT2: King T 64Sa 131
KT11: Stoke D 87Ca 171
Randolph Ct. *HA5: Hat E* 24Ca 45
(off The Avenue)
NW8 39Eb 69
Randolph Cres. W9 6A 214 (42Eb 89)
Randolph Gdns. NW6 40Db 69
Randolph Gro. RM6: Chad H 29Yc 55
Randolph Ho. *KT18: Eps* 86Sa 173
(off Dalmeny Way)
Randolph M. W9 6A 214 (42Eb 89)
Randolph Rd. BR2: Brom 74Pc 160
E17 29Dc 52
KT17: Eps 86Va 174
SL3: L'ly 48A 82
UB1: S'hall 47Ba 85
W9 6A 214 (42Eb 89)
Randolph's La. TN16: Westrm 98Rc 200
Randolph St. NW1 38Lb 70
Randon Cl. HA2: Harr 26Da 45
Ranelagh SL4: Wink 1A 124
Ranelagh Av. SW6 55Bb 111
SW13 54Wa 110
Ranelagh Bri. W2 43Db 89
Ranelagh Cl. HA8: Edg 21Qa 47
Ranelagh Cotts. SW1 7J 227
Ranelagh Dr. HA8: Edg 21Qa 47
TW1: Twick 56Ka 108
Ranelagh Gdns. DA11: Nflt 9B 122
E11 29Lc 53
IG1: Ilf 32Pc 74
SW6 55Ab 110
(not continuous)
W4 52Sa 109
W6 49Va 88
Ranelagh Gdns. Mans. *SW6* 55Ab 110
(off Ranelagh Gdns.)
Ranelagh Gro. SW1 7J 227 (50Jb 90)
Ranelagh Ho. SW3 7F 227
Ranelagh M. W5 47Ma 87
Ranelagh Pl. KT3: N Mald 71Ua 154
Ranelagh Rd. E6 39Qc 74
E11 35Gc 73
E15 40Gc 73
HA0: Wemb 37Ma 67
HP2: Hem H 2B 4
N17 27Ub 51
N22 25Pb 50
NW10 40Va 68
RH1: Redh 6N 207
SW1 7C 228 (50Lb 90)
UB1: S'hall 46Z 85
W5 47Ma 87
Ranfurly Rd. SM1: Sutt 75Cb 155
Rangbourne Ho. N7 36Nb 70
Rangefield Rd. BR1: Brom 64Gc 137
Rangemoor Rd. N15 29Vb 51
Range Rd. DA12: Grav'nd 9G 122
Ranger's House 53Fc 115
Ranger's Rd. E4 17Gc 35
IG10: Lough 17Gc 35
Rangers Sq. SE10 53Fc 115
Ranger Wlk. KT15: Add 78K 149
Range Way TW17: Shep 73Q 150
Rangeworth Pl. DA15: Sidc 62Vc 139
Rangoon St. EC3 3K 225
Rankin Cl. NW9 27Ua 48
Rankine Ho. SE1 4D 230
Ranleigh Gdns. DA7: Bex 52Bd 117
Ranmere St. SW12 60Kb 112
Ranmoor Cl. HA1: Harr 28Fa 46
Ranmoor Gdns. HA1: Harr 28Fa 46
Ranmore Av. CR0: C'don 76Vb 157
Ranmore Cl. RH1: Redh 3A 208
Ranmore Ct. KT6: Surb 71Ma 153
Ranmore Path BR5: St M Cry 70Wc 139
Ranmore Pl. KT13: Weyb 78S 150
Ranmore Rd.
SM2: Cheam 81Za 174
Rannoch Cl. HA8: Edg 19Ra 29
Rannoch Rd. W6 51Ya 110
Rannock Av. NW9 31Ta 67
Ranskill Cl. WD6: Bore 11Qa 29
Ranskill Rd. WD6: Bore 11Qa 29
Ransom Cl. WD19: Wat 17Y 27
Ransome's Dock Bus. Cen.
SW11 52Gb 111
Ransom Rd. SE7 49Lc 93
Ranston Cl. UB9: Den 30H 43
Ranston St. NW1 7D 214 (43Gb 89)
Rant Mdw. HP3: Hem H 4A 4
(not continuous)
Ranulf Rd. NW2 35Bb 69
Ranwell Cl. E3 39Bc 72
Ranwell Ho. *E3* 39Bc 72
(off Ranwell Cl.)
Ranworth Cl. DA8: Erith 54Gd 118
HP3: Hem H 4M 3
Ranworth Gdns. EN6: Pot B 3Za 16
Ranworth Rd. N9 19Yb 34
Ranyard Cl. KT9: Chess 76Pa 153
Raphael Av. RM1: Rom 27Hd 56
RM18: Tilb 2C 122
Raphael Cl. KT1: King T 70Ma 131
WD7: Shenl 4Na 15
Raphael Ct. *SE16* 50Xb 91
(off Stubbs Dr.)
Raphael Dr. IG10: Lough 12Rc 36
KT7: T Ditt 73Ha 152
WD24: Wat 12Z 27
Raphael Rd.
DA12: Grav'nd 9F 122
Raphael St. SW7 2F 227 (47Hb 89)
Raphen Apartments *E3* 40Ac 72
(off Medway Rd.)
Rapier Cl. RM19: Purf 49Pd 97
Rapley Ho. *E2* 41Wb 91
(off Turin St.)
Rapley's Fld. GU24: Pirb 5C 186
Rapsley La. GU21: Knap 10F 166
Raquel Ct. SE1 1H 231
Rasehill Cl. WD3: Rick 15L 25
Rashleigh Ct. SW8 54Kb 112
Rashleigh Ho. WC1 4F 217
Rashleigh St. *SW8* 54Kb 112
(off Peardon St.)
Rashleigh Way DA4: Hort K 70Sd 142
Rasper Rd. N20 19Eb 31
Rastell Av. SW2 61Mb 134
RATCLIFF 43Ac 92
Ratcliffe Cl. SE12 59Jc 115
UB8: Cowl 41M 83
Ratcliffe Ct. SE1 2E 230
Ratcliffe Cross St. E1 44Zb 92
Ratcliffe Ho. *E14* 44Ac 92
(off Barnes St.)
Ratcliffe La. E14 44Ac 92
Ratcliffe Orchard E1 45Zb 92
Ratcliff Rd. E7 36Lc 73
Rathbone Ho. *E16* 44Hc 93
(off Rathbone St.)
NW6 39Cb 69
Rathbone Mkt. E16 43Hc 93
Rathbone Pl. W1 1D 222 (43Mb 90)
Rathbone Sq. CR0: C'don 77Sb 157
Rathbone St. E16 44Hc 93
W1 1C 222 (43Lb 90)
Rathcoole Av. N8 29Pb 50
Rathcoole Gdns. N8 29Pb 50
Rathfern Rd. SE6 60Bc 114
Rathgar Av. W13 46Ka 86
Rathgar Cl. N3 26Bb 49
RH1: Redh 10A 208
Rathgar Rd. SW9 55Rb 113
Rathlin HP3: Hem H 5B 4
Rathmell Dr. SW4 58Mb 112
Rathmore Rd. *DA11: Grav'nd* 8D 122
(off New Rathmore Rd.)
SE7 50Kc 93
Rathnew Ct. *E2* 41Zb 92
(off Meath Cres.)
Rathore Cl. RM6: Chad H 29Zc 55
Rats La. IG10: H Beech, Lough 10Kc 21
Rattray Ct. SE6 61Hc 137
Rattray Rd. SW2 56Qb 112
Raul Rd. SE15 54Wb 113
Raveley St. NW5 35Lb 70
(not continuous)
Ravel Gdns. RM15: Avel 44Sd 98
Ravel Rd. RM15: Avel 44Sd 98
Raven Cl. NW9 26Ua 48
RM7: Rush G 31Cd 76
WD3: Rick 17L 25
WD18: Wat 15U 26
Raven Ct. AL10: Hat 1C 8
DA12: Grav'nd 8F 122
(off Admirals Way)
Ravencroft RM16: Grays 7D 100
Ravendale Rd. TW16: Sun 68V 128
Ravenet St. SW8 53Kb 112
SW11 53Kb 112
(not continuous)
Ravenfield TW20: Eng G 5N 125
Ravenfield Rd. SW17 62Hb 133
Ravenhill Rd. E13 40Lc 73
Raven Ho. *SE16* 49Zb 92
(off Tawny Way)
Ravenings Pde. IG3: Ilf 32Wc 75
Ravenna Rd. SW15 57Za 110
Ravenoak Way IG7: Chig 22Uc 54
Ravenor Ct. UB6: G'frd 42Da 85
Ravenor Pk. Rd. UB6: G'frd 41Da 85
Raven Rd. E18 26Lc 53
Raven Row E1 43Xb 91
Raven Row Contemporary Art Cen.
1K 225 (43Vb 91)
Raven's Ait 71Ma 153
Ravensbourne Apartments
SW6 55Eb 111
(off Central Av.)
Ravensbourne Av. BR2: Brom 66Fc 137
BR3: Beck 66Fc 137
TW19: Stanw 60N 105
Ravensbourne Ct. SE6 59Cc 114
Ravensbourne Cres. RM3: Hrld W 27Pd 57
Ravensbourne Gdns. IG5: Ilf 25Qc 54
W13 43Ka 86
Ravensbourne Ho. BR1: Brom 64Fc 137
NW8 7D 214
Ravensbourne Mans. *SE8* 51Cc 114
(off Berthon St.)
Ravensbourne Pk. SE6 59Cc 114
Ravensbourne Pk. Cres. SE6 59Bc 114
Ravensbourne Pl. SE8 53Cc 114
SE13 54Dc 114
Ravensbourne Rd. BR1: Brom 69Jc 137
DA1: Cray 55Jd 118
SE6 59Bc 114
TW1: Twick 58La 108
Ravensbourne Ter. TW19: Stanw 60N 105
Ravensbury Av. SM4: Mord 71Eb 155
Ravensbury Ct. *CR4: Mitc* 70Fb 133
(off Ravensbury Gro.)
Ravensbury Gro. CR4: Mitc 70Fb 133
Ravensbury La. CR4: Mitc 70Fb 133
Ravensbury Path CR4: Mitc 70Fb 133
Ravensbury Rd. BR5: St P 69Vc 139
SW18 61Db 133
Ravensbury Ter. SW18 61Db 133
Ravenscar NW1 1B 216
Ravenscar Rd. BR1: Brom 63Gc 137
KT6: Surb 75Pa 153
Ravens Cl. BR2: Brom 68Hc 137
EN1: Enf 12Ub 33
GU21: Knap 8G 166
KT6: Surb 72Ma 153
RH1: Redh 5P 207
Ravens Ct. *KT1: King T* 71Ma 153
(off Uxbridge Rd.)
Ravenscourt CM15: B'wood 17Yd 40
TW16: Sun 67V 128
Ravenscourt Av. W6 49Wa 88
Ravenscourt Cl. HA4: Ruis 31S 64
RM12: Horn 34Nd 77
Ravenscourt Dr. RM12: Horn 34Nd 77
Ravenscourt Gdns. W6 49Wa 88
Ravenscourt Gro. RM12: Horn 33Nd 77
Ravenscourt Pk. EN5: Barn 14Za 30
W6 48Wa 88
Ravenscourt Pk. Mans. *W6* 48Xa 88
(off Paddenswick Rd.)
Ravenscourt Pl. W6 49Xa 88
Ravenscourt Rd. BR5: St P 69Wc 139
W6 49Xa 88
Ravenscourt Sq. W6 48Wa 88
Ravenscraig Rd. N11 21Lb 50
Ravenscroft WD25: Wat 7Aa 13
Ravenscroft Av. HA9: Wemb 32Na 67
NW11 31Bb 69
(not continuous)
Ravenscroft Cl. E16 43Jc 93
Ravenscroft Cotts. EN5: New Bar 14Cb 31
Ravenscroft Cres. SE9 62Pc 138
Ravenscroft Pk. E2 3K 219
EN5: Barn 13Za 30
Ravenscroft Rd. BR3: Beck 68Yb 136
E16 43Jc 93
KT13: Weyb 83S 170
W4 49Sa 87
Ravenscroft St. E2 2K 219 (40Vb 71)
Ravensdale Av. N12 21Eb 49
Ravensdale Gdns. SE19 66Tb 135
TW4: Houn 55Aa 107
Ravensdale Ind. Est. N16 30Wb 51
Ravensdale Mans. *N8* 30Nb 50
(off Haringey Pk.)
Ravensdale M. TW18: Staines 65K 127
Ravensdale Rd. N16 31Vb 71
TW4: Houn 55Aa 107
Ravensdell HP1: Hem H 1H 3
Ravens Dene BR7: Chst 64Pc 138
Ravensdon St. SE11 7A 230 (50Qb 90)
Ravens Fld. SL3: L'ly 7P 81
Ravensfield Cl. RM9: Dag 35Zc 75
Ravensfield Gdns. KT19: Ewe 78Ua 154
Ravens Ga. M. BR2: Brom 68Gc 137
Ravenshaw St. NW6 36Bb 69
Ravenshead Cl. CR2: Sels 83Yb 178
Ravenshill BR7: Chst 67Rc 138
Ravenshurst Av. NW4 28Ya 48
Ravenside *KT1: King T* 71Ma 153
(off Portsmouth Rd.)
Ravenside Cl. N18 22Zb 52
Ravenside Retail Pk. N18 22Zb 52
Ravens La. HP4: Berk 1A 2
Ravenslea Rd. SW12 59Hb 111
Ravensleigh Gdns. BR1: Brom 64Kc 137
Ravensmead SL9: Chal P 22B 42
Ravensmead Rd. BR2: Brom 66Fc 137
Ravensmede Way W4 49Va 88
Ravensmere CM16: Epp 3Wc 23
Ravens M. SE12 57Jc 115
Ravensquay Bus. Cen.
BR5: St M Cry 71Xc 161
Ravenstone SE17 7J 231 (50Ub 91)
Ravenstone Rd. N8 27Qb 50
NW9 30Va 48
Ravenstone St. SW12 60Jb 112
Ravens Wlk. E20 37Dc 72
Ravens Way SE12 57Jc 115
Ravens Wharf HP4: Berk 1A 2
Ravenswold CR8: Kenley 87Sb 177
Ravenswood DA5: Bexl 60Ad 117
Ravenswood Av. BR4: W W'ck 74Ec 158
KT6: Surb 75Pa 153
Ravenswood Cl. KT11: Cobh 87Z 171
RM5: Col R 22Dd 56
Ravenswood Ct. GU22: Wok 90B 168
KT2: King T 65Ra 131
Ravenswood Cres. BR4: W W'ck 74Ec 158
HA2: Harr 33Ba 65
Ravenswood Gdns. TW7: Isle 53Ga 108
Ravenswood Ind. Est. E17 28Ec 52
Ravenswood Pk. HA6: Nwood 23W 44
Ravenswood Rd. CR0: Wadd 76Rb 157
E17 28Ec 52
SW12 59Kb 112
Ravensworth Ct. *SW6* 52Cb 111
(off Fulham Rd.)
Ravensworth Rd. NW10 41Xa 88
SE9 62Pc 138
SL2: Slou 1E 80
Raven Wharf SE1 1K 231
Ravey St. EC2 5H 219 (42Ub 91)
Ravine Gro. SE18 51Uc 116
Rav Pinter Cl. N16 31Ub 71
Rawchester Cl. SW18 60Bb 111
Rawlings Cl. BR3: Beck 71Ec 158
BR6: Chels 78Vc 161
Rawlings Cres. HA9: Wemb 34Ra 67
Rawlings St. SW3 5F 227 (49Hb 89)
Rawlins Cl. CR2: Sels 80Bc 158
N3 27Ab 48
Rawlinson Ct. NW2 31Ya 68
Rawlinson Ho. *SE13* 56Fc 115
(off Mercator Rd.)
Rawlinson Ter. N17 27Vb 51
Rawlyn Cl. RM16: Chaf H 50Yd 98
Rawnsley Av. CR4: Mitc 71Fb 155
Rawreth Wlk. *N1* 39Sb 71
(off Basire St.)
Rawson St. SW11 53Jb 112
(not continuous)

Rawsthorne Cl.—Regal Row

Rawsthorne Cl. E16 46Pc 94
Rawsthorne Ct. TW4: Houn 56Ba 107
Rawstone Wlk. E13 40Jc 73
Rawstorne Pl. EC1 3B 218 (41Rb 91)
Rawstorne St. EC1 3B 218 (41Rb 91)
(not continuous)
Raybell Ct. TW7: Isle 54Ha 108
Rayburne Ct. IG9: Buck H 18Lc 35
W14 48Ab 88
Rayburn Rd. RM11: Horn 31Qd 77
Ray Cl. KT9: Chess 79La 152
Raydean Rd. EN5: New Bar 15Db 31
Raydon Rd. EN8: Chesh 4Zb 20
Raydons Gdns. RM9: Dag 36Ad 75
Raydons Rd. RM9: Dag 36Ad 75
Raydon St. N19 33Kb 70
Rayfield CM16: Epp 2Wc 23
Rayfield Cl. BR2: Brom 72Nc 160
Rayford Av. SE12 59Hc 115
Rayford Cl. DA1: Dart 57Ld 119
Ray Gdns. HA7: Stan 22Ka 46
IG11: Bark 40Wc 75
Ray Gunter Ho. SE17 7C 230
Ray Ho. *N1* *39Ub 71*
(off Colville Est.)
W10 *44Za 88*
(off Cambridge Gdns.)
Ray Lamb Way DA8: Erith 51Kd 119
Rayleas Cl. SE18 53Rc 116
Rayleigh Av. TW11: Tedd 65Ga 130
Rayleigh Cl. CM13: Hut 16Ee 41
N13 20Tb 33
Rayleigh Ct. KT1: King T 68Qa 131
N22 25Sb 51
Rayleigh Ho. WD5: Ab L 4V 12
Rayleigh Pde. CM13: Hut 16Ee 41
Rayleigh Ri. CR2: S Croy 79Ub 157
Rayleigh Rd. CM13: Hut 16De 41
E16 46Kc 93
IG8: Wfd G 23Lc 53
N13 20Sb 33
SS17: Stan H 2K 101
SW19 67Bb 133
Ray Lodge Rd. IG8: Wfd G 23Lc 53
Ray Massey Way *E6* *39Nc 74*
(off High St. Nth.)
Raymead Av. CR7: Thor H 71Qb 156
Raymead Cl. KT22: Fet 94Ga 192
Raymead Pas. *CR7: Thor H* *71Qb 156*
(off Raymead Av.)
Raymead Way KT22: Fet 94Ga 192
Raymede Towers *W10* *43Za 88*
(off Treverton St.)
Raymer Cl. AL1: St A 1C 6
Raymere Gdns. SE18 52Tc 116
Raymond Av. E18 27Hc 53
W13 48Ja 86
Raymond Bldgs. WC1 7J 217 (43Pb 90)
Raymond Chadburn Ho. E7 35Kc 73
Raymond Cl. SE26 64Yb 136
SL3: Poyle 53G 104
WD5: Ab L 4T 12
Raymond Ct. EN6: Pot B 6Eb 17
N10 24Kb 50
Raymond Gdns. IG7: Chig 20Xc 37
Raymond Postgate Ct. SE28 45Xc 95
Raymond Rd. BR3: Beck 70Ac 136
E13 39Lc 73
IG2: Ilf 31Tc 74
SL3: L'ly 48C 82
SW19 65Ab 132
Raymond Way KT10: Clay 79Ja 152
Raymouth Rd. SE16 49Xb 91
Raynald Ho. SW16 62Nb 134
Rayne Ct. E18 28Hc 53
Rayne Ho. SW12 58Jb 112
W9 *42Db 89*
(off Delaware Rd.)
Rayner Cl. SM5: Cars 78Hb 155
Rayner Ct. *W12* *47Ya 88*
(off Bamborough Gdns.)
Rayners Cl. HA0: Wemb 36Ma 67
SL3: Coln 52E 104
Rayner's Cl. DA11: Nflt 57De 121
Rayners Cres. UB5: N'olt 41X 85
Rayners Gdns. UB5: N'olt 40X 85
RAYNERS LANE 32Ba 65
Rayners La. HA2: Harr 32Ca 65
HA5: Pinn 29Ba 45
Rayners Rd. SW15 57Ab 110
Rayners Ter. *E14* *44Ac 92*
(off Carr St.)
Rayner Towers *E10* *31Cc 72*
(off Albany Rd.)
Raynes Av. E11 31Lc 73
Raynes Cl. GU21: Knap 1F 186
RAYNES PARK 70Ya 132
Raynes Pk. Bri. SW20 68Ya 132
Raynes Pk. School Sports Cen. 69Xa 132
Raynham W2 2E 220
Raynham Av. N18 23Wb 51
Raynham Ho. *E1* *42Zb 92*
(off Harpley Sq.)
Raynham Rd. N18 22Wb 51
W6 49Xa 88
Raynham Ter. N18 22Wb 51
Raynor Cl. UB1: S'hall 46Ba 85
Raynor Pl. N1 38Sb 71
Raynton Cl. HA2: Harr 32Aa 65
UB4: Hayes 42V 84
Raynton Dr. UB4: Hayes 42V 84
Raynton Rd. EN3: Enf W 9Zb 20
Ray Rd. KT8: W Mole 71Da 151
RM5: Col R 22Dd 56
Ray's Av. SL4: Wind 2D 102
Rays Av. N18 21Yb 52
Rays Hill DA4: Hort K 70Sd 142
Rays Rd. BR4: W W'ck 73Ec 158
N18 21Yb 52
Ray St. EC1 6A 218 (42Qb 90)
Ray St. Bri. EC1 6A 218
Ray Wlk. N7 33Pb 70
Raywood Cl. UB3: Harl 52S 106
Raywood Mans. *E20* *37Ec 72*
(off West Pk. Wlk.)
Razia M. E12 36Pc 74
Reachview Cl. NW1 38Lb 70
Read Cl. KT7: T Ditt 73Ja 152
Read Ct. E17 30Cc 52
EN9: Walt A 5Jc 21
Reade Ct. *W3* *48Sa 87*
(off Stanley Rd.)
Readens, The SM7: Bans 88Gb 175
Reader Ho. *SE5* *53Sb 113*
(off Badsworth Rd.)
Read Ho. *SE11* *51Qb 112*
(off Clayton St.)
Reading Arch Rd. RH1: Redh 6P 207
Reading Cl. SE22 58Wb 113
Reading Ho. *SE15* *51Wb 113*
(off Friary Est.)
W2 *44Eb 89*
(off Hallfield Est.)
Reading La. E8 37Xb 71
Reading Rd. SM1: Sutt 78Eb 155
UB5: N'olt 36Da 65
Readings, The WD3: Chor 13H 25
Readman Ct. SE20 67Xb 135
Read Rd. KT21: Asht 89Ma 173
Reads Cl. IG1: Ilf 34Rc 74
Reads Rest La. KT20: Tad 91Bb 195
Read Way DA12: Grav'nd 4F 144
Ream Apartments *SE23* *61Yb 136*
(off Clyde Ter.)
Reapers Cl. NW1 39Mb 70
Reapers Way TW7: Isle 57Fa 108
Reardon Ct. N21 19Rb 33
Reardon Ho. *E1* *46Xb 91*
(off Reardon St.)
Reardon Path E1 46Xb 91
(not continuous)
Reardon St. E1 46Xb 91
Reaston St. SE14 52Zb 114
Rebecca Ct. DA14: Sidc 63Xc 139
Rebecca Ho. *E3* *42Bc 92*
(off Brokesley St.)
N12 *21Db 49*
(off Woodside Pk. Rd.)
Reckitt Rd. W4 50Ua 88
Recognition Ho. SL4: Wind 4E 102
Record St. SE15 51Yb 114
Recovery St. SW17 64Gb 133
Recreation Av. RM3: Hrld W 26Pd 57
RM7: Rom 29Ed 56
Recreation Rd. BR2: Brom 68Hc 137
DA15: Sidc 62Uc 138
SE26 63Zb 136
UB2: S'hall 49Aa 85
Recreation Way CR4: Mitc 69Mb 134
Rector St. N1 39Sb 71
Rectory Bus. Cen. DA14: Sidc 63Xc 139
Rectory Chambers *SW3* *51Gb 111*
(off Old Church St.)
Rectory Chase CM13: L War 28Zd 59
Rectory Cl. DA1: Cray 56Gd 118
DA14: Sidc 63Xc 139
E4 20Cc 34
HA7: Stan 22Ka 46
KT6: Surb 74La 152
KT14: Byfl 85M 169
KT21: Asht 91Pa 193
N3 25Bb 49
SL2: Farn R 1G 80
SL4: Wind 3E 102
SW20 69Ya 132
TW17: Shep 69Q 128
Rectory Ct. E18 25Hc 53
SM6: Wall 77Lb 156
TW13: Felt 63Y 129
Rectory Cres. E11 30Lc 53
(not continuous)
Rectory Farm Rd. EN2: Enf 10Pb 18
(not continuous)
Rectory Field 52Kc 115
Rectory Fld. Cres. SE7 52Lc 115
Rectory Flds. RM16: Ors 3D 100
Rectory Gdns. *BR3: Beck* *67Cc 136*
(off Rectory Rd.)
N8 28Nb 50
RM14: Upm 33Td 78
SW4 55Lb 112
UB5: N'olt 39Ba 65
Rectory Grn. BR3: Beck 67Bc 136
Rectory Gro. CR0: C'don 75Rb 157
SW4 55Lb 112
TW12: Hamp 63Ba 129
Rectory La. CM13: Heron 24Fe 59
DA14: Sidc 63Xc 139
GU20: W'sham 9A 146
HA7: Stan 22Ka 46
HA8: Edg 23Qa 47
IG10: Lough 12Qc 36
KT6: Surb 74Ka 152
KT14: Byfl 85N 169
KT21: Asht 91Pa 193
KT23: Bookh 98Ba 191
RH3: Bkld 3B 206
SM6: Wall 77Lb 156
SM7: Bans 86Hb 175
SW17 65Jb 134
TN13: S'oaks 98Ld 203
TN15: Igh 94Yd 204
TN16: Bras 96Yc 201
TN16: Westrm 95Nc 200
WD3: Rick 18M 25
WD4: K Lan 10A 4
WD7: Shenl 5Pa 15
WD23: Bush 16Ca 27
Rectory Mdw. DA13: Sflt 65Ce 143
Rectory Orchard SW19 63Ab 132
Rectory Pk. CR2: Sande 85Ub 177
Rectory Pk. Av. UB5: N'olt 41Ba 85
Rectory Pl. SE18 49Qc 94
Rectory Rd. BR2: Kes 80Mc 159
BR3: Beck 67Cc 136
CR5: Coul 97Eb 195
DA10: Swans 59Ae 121
E12 36Pc 74
E17 28Dc 52
N16 33Vb 71
RM10: Dag 37Dd 76
RM16: Ors 2C 100
RM17: Grays 48Fe 99
RM18: W Til 1F 122
SM1: Sutt 76Cb 155
SS17: Stan H 2L 101
SW13 54Wa 110
TN15: Ash 78De 165
TW4: Cran 54Y 107
UB2: S'hall 48Ba 85
UB3: Hayes 44W 84
W3 46Ra 87
WD3: Rick 18M 25
Rectory Sq. E1 43Zb 92
Rectory Ter. SS17: Stan H 2L 101
Rectory Way UB10: Ick 33R 64
Reculver Ho. *SE15* *51Yb 114*
(off Lovelinch Cl.)
Reculver M. N18 21Wb 51
Reculver Rd. SE16 50Zb 92
Red Anchor Cl. SW3 51Fb 111
Redan Pl. W2 44Db 89
Redan St. W14 48Za 88
Redan Ter. SE5 54Rb 113
Redbarn Cl. CR8: Purl 83Rb 177
Red Barracks Rd. SE18 49Pc 94
Redberry Gro. SE26 62Yb 136
Redbourne Av. N3 25Cb 49
Redbourne Dr. SE28 44Zc 95
(not continuous)
Redbourne Ho. *E14* *44Bc 92*
(off Norbiton Rd.)
Redbourn Ho. *W10* *42Ya 88*
(off Sutton Way)
Redbourn Rd. AL3: St A 1N 5
REDBRIDGE 30Nc 54
Redbridge Cycling Cen. 23Yc 55
Redbridge Ent. Cen. IG1: Ilf 33Sc 74
Redbridge Foyer *IG1: Ilf* *33Sc 74*
(off Sylvan Rd.)
Redbridge Gdns. SE5 52Ub 113
Redbridge Ho. *E16* *45Rc 94*
(off University Way)
Redbridge La. E. IG4: Ilf 30Mc 53
Redbridge La. W. E11 30Kc 53
REDBRIDGE RDBT. 30Mc 53
Redbridge Sports & Leisure Cen. 25Tc 54
Redbrooke Ct. SS17: Linf 8J 101
Redburn Ind. Est. EN3: Pond E 16Zb 34
Redburn St. SW3 51Hb 111
Redbury Cl. RM13: Rain 42Ld 97
Redcar Cl. UB5: N'olt 36Da 65
Redcar Rd. RM3: Rom 22Pd 57
Redcar St. SE5 52Sb 113
Redcastle Cl. E1 45Yb 92
Red Cedars Rd. BR6: Orp 73Uc 160
Redchurch St. E2 5K 219 (42Vb 91)
Redcliffe Cl. *SW5* *50Db 89*
(off Old Brompton Rd.)
Redcliffe Ct. *E5* *34Xb 71*
(off Napoleon Rd.)
Redcliffe Gdns. IG1: Ilf 32Qc 74
SW10 50Db 89
W4 52Ra 109
Redcliffe M. SW10 50Db 89
Redcliffe Pl. SW10 51Eb 111
Redcliffe Rd. SW10 50Eb 89
Redcliffe Sq. SW10 50Db 89
Redcliffe St. SW10 51Db 111
Redclose Av. SM4: Mord 71Cb 155
Redclyffe Rd. E6 39Lc 73
Redclyf Ho. *E1* *42Yb 92*
(off Cephas St.)
Red Cottage M. SL3: L'ly 8N 81
Red Ct. SL1: Slou 6J 81
Redcourt CR0: C'don 76Ub 157
GU22: Pyr 87F 168
Red Cow La. EC1 5D 218 (42Sb 91)
Redcroft Rd. UB1: S'hall 45Ea 86
Red Cross Cotts. SE1 1E 230
Redcross Way SE1 1E 230 (47Sb 91)
Redden Ct. Rd. RM3: Hrld W 27Nd 57
Redding Cl. DA2: Dart 61Ud 142
Redding Ho. SE18 48Nc 94
WD18: Wat 16U 26
Reddings HP3: Hem H 4A 4
Reddings, The NW7 20Va 30
WD6: Bore 13Pa 29
Reddings Av. WD23: Bush 15Da 27
Reddings Cl. NW7 21Va 48
Reddington Cl. CR2: Sande 81Tb 177
Reddington Dr. SL3: L'ly 48A 82
Redding Way GU21: Knap 1F 186
Reddins Rd. SE15 51Wb 113
Reddons Rd. BR3: Beck 66Ac 136
Reddown Rd. CR5: Coul 90Mb 176
Reddy Rd. DA8: Erith 51Hd 118
Rede Ct. *KT13: Weyb* *76R 150*
(off Old Palace Rd.)
Redenham Ho. *SW15* *59Wa 110*
(off Ellisfield Dr.)
Rede Pl. W2 44Cb 89
Redesdale Gdns. TW7: Isle 52Ja 108
Redesdale St. SW3 51Gb 111
Redfern Av. TW4: Houn 59Ca 107
Redfern Cl. UB8: Uxb 39L 63
Redfern Ct. *WD18: Wat* *15U 26*
(off Whippendell Rd.)
Redfern Gdns. RM2: Rom 26Md 57
Redfern Ho. *E13* *39Hc 73*
(off Redriffe Rd.)
NW8 *39Fb 69*
(off Dorman Way)
Redfern Rd. NW10 38Ua 68
SE6 59Ec 114
Redfield La. SW5 49Cb 89
Redfield M. SW5 49Db 89
Redford Av. CR5: Coul 87Kb 176
CR7: Thor H 70Pb 134
SM6: Wall 79Nb 156
Redford Cl. TW13: Felt 61V 128
Redford Rd. SL4: Wind 3B 102
Redford Wlk. *N1* *39Sb 71*
(off Popham St.)
Redford Way UB8: Uxb 38M 63
Redgate Dr. BR2: Hayes 75Kc 159
Redgate Ter. SW15 58Za 110
Redgrave Cl. CR0: C'don 72Vb 157
Redgrave Ct. UB9: Den 29H 43
Redgrave Rd. SW15 55Za 110
Redgrave Ter. *E2* *41Wb 91*
(off Derbyshire St.)
Redgrove Ho. *CM16: Epp* *1Wc 23*
(off Stonards Hill)
Redhall Cl. AL10: Hat 3B 8
Redhall Ct. CR3: Cat'm 95Tb 197
Redhall Dr. AL10: Hat 4B 8
Redhall End AL4: Col H 4A 8
Redhall La. AL4: Col H 4A 8
WD3: Chan C 11N 25
Redheath Cl. WD25: Wat 7V 12
REDHILL 5P 207
Red Hill BR7: Chst 64Rc 138
UB9: Den 33F 62
Redhill Aerodrome and Heliport 10D 208
Redhill & Reigate Golf Course 9M 207
Redhill Comn. RH1: Redh 7N 207
Redhill Ct. SW2 61Qb 134
Redhill Dr. HA8: Edg 26Ra 47
Redhill Golf Course 10A 208
Redhill Ho. RH1: Redh 4P 207
Redhill Rd. DA3: Nw A G 76Ae 165
KT11: Cobh 84R 170
Redhill St. NW1 2A 216 (40Kb 70)
Redhill Wood DA3: Nw A G 76Ce 165
(not continuous)
Red House 56Ad 117
Red Ho. *SE20* *66Xb 135*
(off Anerley Pk.)
Red Ho. Cotts. TN13: S'oaks 97Ld 203
Red Ho. La. DA6: Bex 56Zc 117
KT12: Walt T 75W 150
Redhouse Rd. CR0: C'don 72Mb 156
TN16: Tats 92Lc 199
Red Ho. Sq. N1 38Sb 71
Redif Ho. RM10: Dag 35Dd 76
Redington Gdns. NW3 35Db 69
Redington Ho. N1 1J 217
Redington Rd. NW3 34Db 69
Redknap Ho. TW10: Ham 62La 130
Redland Gdns.
KT8: W Mole 70Ba 129
Redlands CR5: Coul 88Nb 176
N15 28Tb 51
TW11: Tedd 65Ja 130
Redlands, The BR3: Beck 68Dc 136
Redlands Ct. BR1: Brom 66Hc 137
Redlands Rd. EN3: Enf H 11Ac 34
TN13: S'oaks 96Hd 202
Redlands Way SW2 59Pb 112
Red La. KT10: Clay 79Ja 152
RH8: Oxt 6M 211
Red Leaf Cl. SL3: L'ly 46B 82
Redleaf Cl. DA17: Belv 51Cd 118
KT22: Fet 96Fa 192
Redleaves Av.
TW15: Ashf 65R 128
Redlees Cl. TW7: Isle 56Ja 108
Red Leys UB8: Uxb 38N 63
Redlibbets Golf Course 74Zd 165
Redlin Ct. RH1: Redh 4P 207
Red Lion Bus. Pk.
KT6: Surb 76Pa 153
Red Lion Cl. BR5: St M Cry 72Yc 161
SE17 *51Tb 113*
(off Red Lion Row)
WD25: A'ham 9Ea 14
Red Lion Ct. EC4 3A 224 (44Qb 90)
SE1 6E 224 (46Sb 91)
TW3: Houn *55Da 107*
(off Alexandra Rd.)
Red Lion Hill N2 26Fb 49
(not continuous)
Red Lion La. GU24: Chob 1J 167
HP3: Hem H 8A 4
SE18 52Qc 116
WD3: Sarr 7J 11
Red Lion Pde. HA5: Pinn 27Aa 45
Red Lion Pl. SE18 53Qc 116
Red Lion Rd. GU24: Chob 1J 167
KT6: Surb 75Pa 153
Red Lion Row SE17 51Sb 113
Red Lion Sq. SW18 57Cb 111
WC1 1H 223 (43Pb 90)
Red Lion St. TW9: Rich 57Ma 109
WC1 7H 217 (43Pb 90)
Red Lion Wlk. *TW3: Houn* *55Da 107*
(off High St.)
Red Lion Yd. W1 6K 221
Red Lodge BR4: W W'ck 74Ec 158
WD6: Bore 13Pa 29
Red Lodge Cres. DA5: Bexl 62Fd 140
Red Lodge Rd. BR4: W W'ck 74Ec 158
DA5: Bexl 62Fd 140
Redlynch Ct. *W14* *47Ab 88*
(off Addison Cres.)
Redlynch Ho. *SW9* *53Qb 112*
(off Gosling Way)
Redman Cl. UB5: N'olt 40Y 65
Redman Ho. EC1 7K 217
SE1 2E 230
Redmans La. TN14: S'ham 79Ed 162
Redmans Pl. *TN13: S'oaks* *97Ld 203*
(off Akehurst La.)
Redman's Rd. E1 43Yb 92
Redmead La. E1 46Wb 91
Redmead Rd. UB3: Harl 49U 84
Redmill Ho. *E1* *42Xb 91*
(off Headlam St.)
Redmond Ho. N1 1J 217
Redmore Rd. W6 49Xa 88
Red Oak Cl. BR6: Farnb 76Rc 160
CR0: C'don 75Cc 158
Red Oaks Mead CM16: They B 9Tc 22
Redo Ho. *E12* *36Qc 74*
(off Dore Av.)
Red Path E9 37Ac 72
Redpath Way SE10 47Gc 93
Red Pl. W1 4H 221 (45Jb 90)
Redpoll Way DA18: Erith 48Zc 95
Red Post Hill SE21 56Tb 113
SE24 56Tb 113
Red Post Ho. E6 38Mc 73
Redriffe Rd. E13 39Hc 73
Redriff Est. SE16 48Bc 92
Redriff Rd. RM7: Mawney 26Dd 56
SE16 49Zb 92
Red Rd. CM14: W'ley 21Xd 58
GU18: Light 4A 166
WD6: Bore 13Pa 29
Redroofs Cl. BR3: Beck 67Dc 136
Redrose Trad. Cen. EN4: E Barn 15Fb 31
RED ROVER 56Wa 110
Redrup Ho. *SE14* *51Zb 114*
(off John Williams Cl.)
Redruth Cl. N22 24Pb 50
Redruth Gdns. KT10: Clay 80Ha 152
RM3: Rom 22Pd 57
Redruth Ho. SM2: Sutt 80Db 155
Redruth Rd. E9 39Yb 72
RM3: Rom 22Pd 57
Redruth Wlk. RM3: Rom 22Pd 57
Redsan Cl. CR2: S Croy 80Tb 157
Redshank Ho. *SE1* *50Vb 91*
(off Avocet Cl.)
Red Sq. N16 34Tb 71
Redstart Cl. CR0: New Ad 82Fc 179
E6 43Nc 94
SE14 52Ac 114
Redstart Mans. *IG1: Ilf* *34Qc 74*
(off Mill Rd.)
Redstone Hill RH1: Redh 6A 208
Redstone Hollow RH1: Redh 7A 208
Redstone Mnr. RH1: Redh 6A 208
Redstone Pk. RH1: Redh 6A 208
Redstone Rd. RH1: Redh 7A 208
Redston Rd. N8 28Mb 50
REDSTREET 65De 143
Red St. DA13: Sflt 64Ce 143
Redtiles Gdns. CR8: Kenley 87Rb 177
Redvers Ct. *CR6: W'ham* *90Zb 178*
(off Redvers Rd.)
Redvers Rd. CR6: W'ham 90Zb 178
N22 26Qb 50
Redvers St. N1 3J 219 (41Ub 91)
Redwald Rd. E5 35Zb 72
Redway Dr. TW2: Whitt 59Ea 108
REDWELL 94Yd 204
Redwell Cotts. TN15: Igh 95Yd 204
Redwell Ct. EN8: Walt C 6Bc 20
Redwell La. TN15: Igh 95Xd 204
Redwing Cl. CR2: Sels 83Zb 178
Redwing Ct. *BR6: Orp* *73Wc 161*
(off High St.)
RM3: Rom 25Md 57
SE1 2E 230
Redwing Cres. DA9: Ghithe 58Wd 120
Redwing Gdns. KT14: W Byf 84K 169
Redwing Gro. WD5: Ab L 3W 12
Redwing M. SE5 54Sb 113
Redwing Path SE28 47Tc 94
Redwing Rd. SM6: Wall 80Nb 156
Redwood TW20: Thorpe 68G 126
Redwood Av. RM3: Hrld W 26Nd 57
Redwood Chase RM15: S Ock 42Yd 98
Redwood Cl. AL1: St A 2G 6
CR8: Kenley 86Sb 177
DA15: Sidc 60Wc 117
E3 40Cc 72
N14 17Mb 32
SE16 46Ac 92
UB10: Hil 40R 64
WD19: Wat 21Y 45
Redwood Ct. DA1: Dart 58Qd 119
KT6: Surb 73Ma 153
KT17: Ewe 83Va 174
KT22: Lea *92Ha 192*
(off Park Vw. Rd.)
N19 31Mb 70
NW6 38Ab 68
UB5: N'olt 41Aa 85
Redwood Dr. HP3: Hem H 4N 3
KT19: Eps 82Sa 173
SL5: S'dale 2F 146
Redwood Est. TW5: Cran 51X 107
Redwood Gdns. E4 16Dc 34
IG7: Chig 22Wc 55
SL1: Slou 5H 81
Redwood Gro. W5 48Ka 86
Redwood Ho. EC1 4D 218
TN16: Westrm 95Rc 200
Redwood Mans. *W8* *48Db 89*
(off Chantry Sq.)
Redwood M. SW4 55Kb 112
TW15: Ashf *66T 128*
(off Staines Rd. W.)
Redwood Mt. RH2: Reig 3J 207
Redwood Pl. TN13: S'oaks 95Hd 202
Redwood Ri. WD6: Bore 9Ra 15
Redwoods KT15: Add 79J 149
SW15 60Wa 110
Redwoods, The SL4: Wind 5H 103
Redwoods Cl. IG9: Buck H 19Kc 35
Redwood Wlk. KT6: Surb 74Ma 153
Redwood Way EN5: Barn 15Za 30
Reece M. SW7 6B 226 (49Fb 89)
Reed Av. BR6: Orp 76Uc 160
Reed Cl. AL2: Lon C 9J 7
E16 43Jc 93
SE12 57Jc 115
SL0: Iver 44G 82
Reed Ct. DA9: Ghithe 56Yd 120
Reed Dr. RH1: Redh 9A 208
Reede Gdns. RM10: Dag 36Dd 76
Reede Rd. RM10: Dag 37Cd 76
Reede Way RM10: Dag 37Dd 76
Reedham Cl. AL2: Brick W 1Ca 13
N17 28Xb 51
Reedham Dr. CR8: Purl 85Pb 176
Reedham Pk. Av. CR8: Purl 88Qb 176
Reedham Rd. SL1: Burn 1A 80
Reedham St. SE15 54Wb 113
Reedholm Vs. N16 35Tb 71
Reed Ho. SW19 63Db 133
Reed Pl. KT14: W Byf 85G 168
SW4 56Mb 112
TW17: Shep 74P 149
Reed Pond Wlk. RM2: Rom 26Hd 56
Reed Rd. N17 26Vb 51
Reeds Chapel *WD24: Wat* *12Y 27*
(off Keele Cl.)
Reeds Cres. WD24: Wat 12Y 27
Reedsfield Cl. TW15: Ashf 62R 128
Reedsfield Rd. TW15: Ashf 63R 128
Reeds Mdw. RH1: Mers 2C 208
Reed's Pl. NW1 38Lb 70
Reed St. GU22: Wok 94B 188
Reeds Wlk. WD24: Wat 12Y 27
(not continuous)
Reed Way SL1: Slou 5D 80
SL4: Wind 3B 102
Reedworth St. SE11 6A 230 (49Qb 90)
Reef Ho. *E14* *48Ec 92*
(off Manchester St.)
Reef St. RM9: Dag 41Ad 95
Reel Cinema, The
Borehamwood *13Qa 29*
(within The Point)
Reenglass Rd. HA7: Stan 21Ma 47
Rees Dr. HA7: Stan 21Na 47
Rees Gdns. CR0: C'don 72Vb 157
Reesland Cl. E12 37Qc 74
Rees St. N1 1E 218 (39Sb 71)
Reets Farm Cl. NW9 30Ua 48
Reeve Rd. RH2: Reig 10L 207
Reeves Av. NW9 31Ta 67
Reeves Cnr. CR0: C'don 75Rb 157
Reeves Cres. BR8: Swan 69Fd 140
Reeves Ho. SE1 2K 229
Reeves M. W1 5H 221 (45Jb 90)
Reeves Rd. E3 42Dc 92
SE18 51Rc 116
Reflection, The *E16* *47Rc 94*
(off Woolwich Mnr. Way)
Reflection Ho. *E2* *42Wb 91*
(off Cheshire St.)
Reflex Apartments
BR2: Brom *70Kc 137*
(off Wheeler Pl.)
Reform Row N17 26Vb 51
Reform St. SW11 54Hb 111
Regal Bldg. W10 41Za 88
Regal Cl. E1 43Wb 91
W5 43Ma 87
Regal Ct. CR4: Mitc 69Hb 133
N18 22Vb 51
NW6 *40Bb 69*
(off Malvern Rd.)
SW6 *52Cb 111*
(off Dawes Rd.)
Regal Cres. SM6: Wall 76Kb 156
Regal Dr. N11 22Kb 50
Regal Ho. IG2: Ilf 30Tc 54
Regal Ho., The SW6 54Eb 111
Regalia Point *E2* *41Zb 92*
(off Palmer's Rd.)
Regal La. NW1 1K 215 (39Jb 70)
Regal Pl. E3 41Bc 92
SW6 52Db 111
Regal Row SE15 53Yb 114

Regal Way—Richmond Pk. Golf Course

Regal Way HA3: Kenton 30Na 47
WD24: Wat 10Y 13
Regal Wharf Apartments N1 39Ub 71
(off De Beauvoir Cres.)
Regan Ho. N18 23Vb 51
Regan Way N1 2H 219 (40Ub 71)
Regarder Rd.
IG7: Chig, Ilf 22Wc 55
Regarth Av. RM1: Rom 30Gd 56
Regatta Ho. TW11: Tedd 63Ja 130
Regatta La. W6 51Ya 110
Regatta Point E14 47Cc 92
(off Westferry Rd.)
TW8: Bford 51Pa 109
Regenct Ct. HA7: Stan 24Ma 47
(off Unwin Way)
Regency Cl. IG7: Chig 22Sc 54
TN15: W King 79Ud 164
TW12: Hamp 64Ba 129
W5 44Na 87
Regency Ct. AL1: St A 2F 6
BR2: Brom 72Mc 159
CM14: B'wood 19Yd 40
E3 40Bc 72
(off Norman Gro.)
E9 39Yb 72
(off Park Cl.)
E18 26Jc 53
EN1: Enf 15Tb 33
HP2: Hem H 2M 3
KT15: Add 76M 149
(off Albert Rd.)
SE8 52Bc 114
(off Glenville Gro.)
SM1: Sutt 77Eb 155
TW11: Tedd 65Ka 130
WD17: Wat 11W 26
(off Langley Rd.)
Regency Cres. NW4 26Za 48
Regency Dr. HA4: Ruis 32U 64
KT14: W Byf 85H 169
Regency Gdns. KT12: Walt T 74Y 151
KT13: Weyb 79S 150
RM11: Horn 31Ld 77
Regency Ho. E16 46Jc 93
(off Pepys Cres.)
N3 26Bb 49
SW1 5E 228
SW6 53Eb 111
(off The Boulevard)
Regency Lawn NW5 34Kb 70
Regency Lodge IG9: Buck H 19Mc 35
KT13: Weyb 76U 150
(off Oatlands Chase)
NW3 38Fb 69
(off Adelaide Rd.)
Regency M. BR3: Beck 67Ec 136
NW10 37Wa 68
SW9 52Rb 113
TW7: Isle 57Ga 108
Regency Pde. NW3 38Fb 69
(off Finchley Rd.)
Regency Pl. SW1 5E 228 (49Mb 90)
Regency St. NW10 42Ua 88
SW1 5D 228 (49Mb 90)
Regency Ter. SW7 7B 226
Regency Wlk. CR0: C'don 72Bc 158
TW10: Rich 57Na 109
(off The Vineyard)
Regency Way DA6: Bex 55Zc 117
Regeneration House 1F 217 (39Nb 70)
Regeneration Rd. SE16 49Zb 92
Regent Av. UB10: Hil 38R 64
Regent Bus. Cen. UB3: Hayes 47X 85
Regent Cl. HA3: Kenton 30Na 47
KT15: New H 81M 169
N12 22Eb 49
RH1: Mers 1C 208
RM16: Grays 47Ee 99
TW4: Cran 53X 107
WD4: K Lan 1Q 12
Regent Ct. N3 24Db 49
N20 19Fb 31
NW6 38Bb 69
(off Cavendish Rd.)
NW8 4D 214
RM15: Avel 46Td 98
SL1: Slou 4J 81
SL4: Wind 3H 103
W8 48Db 89
(off Wright's La.)
Regent Cres. RH1: Redh 4P 207
Regent Gdns. IG3: Ilf 31Wc 75
Regent Ga. EN8: Walt C 6Zb 20
Regent Ho. CM14: B'wood 20Xd 40
KT17: Eps 83Ua 174
RH1: Redh 5P 207
W14 49Ab 88
(off Windsor Way)
Regent Pde. SM2: Sutt 79Eb 155
Regent Pk. KT22: Lea 90Ja 172
Regent Pl. CR0: C'don 74Vb 157
SW19 64Eb 133
W1 4C 222 (45Lb 90)
Regent Rd. CM16: Epp 2Vc 23
KT5: Surb 71Pa 153
SE24 58Rb 113
Regents Av. N13 22Qb 50
Regent's Bri. Gdns. SW8 52Nb 112
Regents Canal Ho. E14 44Ac 92
(off Commercial Rd.)
Regents Cl. CR2: S Croy 79Ub 157
CR3: Whyt 90Ub 177
HA8: Edg 21Na 47
UB4: Hayes 43V 84
WD7: R'lett 6Ja 14
Regents Ct. BR1: Brom 66Hc 137
DA11: Grav'nd 7D 122
E8 39Wb 71
HA5: Pinn 26Z 45
KT2: King T 67Na 131
(off Sopwith Way)
KT13: Weyb 79R 150
Regents Dr. BR2: Kes 78Mc 159
IG8: Wfd G 23Qc 54
Regents Ga. Ho. E14 45Ac 92
(off Horseferry Rd.)
Regents Ho. E3 43Cc 92
(off Bow Common La.)
Regents M. NW8 1A 214 (40Eb 69)
REGENT'S PARK 4A 216 (41Kb 90)
Regent's Pk. 2G 215 (40Hb 69)
Regent's Pk. Barracks 2A 216
Regents Pk. Est. NW1 3B 216
Regent's Pk. Gdns. M. NW1 39Hb 69
Regent's Pk. Ho. NW8 4E 214
Regent's Pk. Open Air Theatre
4H 215 (41Jb 90)
Regent's Pk. Rd. NW1 38Hb 69
(not continuous)
Regents Pk. Rd. N3 27Bb 49
Regent's Pk. Ter. NW1 39Kb 70
Regent's Pl. SE3 54Jc 115
Regents Pl. IG10: Lough 17Mc 35
KT12: Walt T 76Y 151
NW1 5B 216 (42Lb 90)
Regent's Pl. Plaza NW1 5B 216 (42Lb 90)
Regents Plaza NW6 40Db 69
(off Kilburn High Rd.)
Regent Sq. DA17: Belv 49Dd 96
E3 41Dc 92
WC1 4G 217 (41Nb 90)
Regent's Row E8 39Wb 71
Regents Studios E8 39Xb 71
Regent St. NW10 41Za 88
SW1 5D 222 (45Mb 90)
W1 2A 222 (44Kb 90)
W4 50Qa 87
WD24: Wat 10X 13
Regent's University London
5H 215 (42Hb 89)
Regents Wlk. SL5: Asc 2A 146
Regents Wharf E2 39Xb 71
(off Wharf Pl.)
N1 1H 217 (40Pb 70)
Regent Ter. SW8 51Nb 112
Regent Way CM14: B'wood 17Xd 40
Regiment Hill NW7 23Ab 48
Regina Cl. EN5: Barn 13Za 30
Regina Ho. SE20 67Zb 136
Reginald Ellingworth St.
RM9: Dag 39Xc 75
Reginald Pl. SE8 52Cc 114
(off Deptford High St.)
Reginald Rd. E7 38Jc 73
HA6: Nwood 25V 44
RM3: Hrld W 25Qd 57
SE8 52Cc 114
Reginald Sorenson Ho. E11 31Fc 73
Reginald Sq. SE8 52Cc 114
Regina Point SE16 48Yb 92
(off Canada Est.)
Regina Rd. N4 32Pb 70
SE25 69Wb 135
UB2: S'hall 49Aa 85
W13 46Ja 86
Regina Ter. W13 46Ka 86
Regis Ct. CR4: Mitc 67Gb 133
N8 28Pb 50
NW1 7F 215
Regis Ho. W1 7J 215
Regis Pl. SW2 56Pb 112
Regis Rd. NW5 36Kb 70
Regna Cl. RM13: Rain 43Kd 97
Regnart Bldgs. NW1 4C 216
Regnas Ho. E15 37Hc 73
(off Carnarvon Rd.)
Regnolruf Ct. KT12: Walt T 73W 150
Regnum Apartments E1 6K 219
Reid Av. CR3: Cat'm 93Tb 197
Reid Bldg. E3 42Bc 92
(off Eric St.)
Reid Cl. CR5: Coul 88Kb 176
HA5: Eastc 28W 44
UB3: Hayes 44U 84
Reidhaven Rd. SE18 49Uc 94
REIDON HILL 10F 166
Reidonhill Cotts. GU21: Knap 10F 166
REIGATE 6J 207
Reigate Av. SM1: Sutt 74Cb 155
Reigate Bus. M. RH2: Reig 5H 207
REIGATE HEATH 6F 206
Reigate Heath Golf Course 6E 206
Reigate Heath (Local Nature Reserve)
6F 206
Reigate Hill RH2: Reig 2L 207
Reigate Hill Cl. RH2: Reig 3J 207
Reigate Hill Golf Course 100Jb 196
REIGATE HILL INTERCHANGE 1K 207
Reigate Priory Mus. 7J 207
Reigate Rd. BR1: Brom 62Hc 137
IG3: Ilf 33Vc 75
KT17: Eps, Ewe, Eps D 82Va 174
KT18: Tatt C 89Za 174
KT20: Tad 89Za 174
KT22: Lea 95La 192
RH1: Redh 6K 207
RH2: Reig 6K 207
(Chart La.)
RH2: Reig 5A 206
(Station Rd.)
RH3: Bet, Bkld 5A 206
Reigate Way SM6: Wall 78Nb 156
Reighton Rd. E5 34Wb 71
Reindeer Cl. E13 39Jc 73
Reinickendorf Av. SE9 58Sc 116
Reis Pl. N15 28Vb 51
(off Blenheim Ri.)
Reizel Cl. N16 32Vb 71
Relf Rd. SE15 55Wb 113
Reliance Arc. SW9 56Qb 112
Reliance Wharf N1 39Ub 71
Relko Ct. KT19: Eps 83Ta 173
Relko Gdns. SM1: Sutt 78Fb 155
Relton M. SW7 3E 226 (48Gb 89)
Rembrandt Cl. E14 48Fc 93
SW1 7H 227
Rembrandt Ct. KT19: Ewe 79Va 154
SE16 50Xb 91
(off Stubbs Dr.)
Rembrandt Dr. DA11: Nflt 62Fe 143
Rembrandt Rd. HA8: Edg 26Qa 47
SE13 56Gc 115
Rembrandt Way KT12: Walt T 75X 151
WD18: Wat 15V 26
Reminder La. SE10 48Hc 93
Remington Rd. E6 44Nc 94
N15 30Tb 51
Remington St. N1 2C 218 (40Rb 71)
Remnant St. WC2 2H 223 (44Pb 90)
Remsted Ho. NW6 39Db 69
(off Mortimer Cres.)
Remus Bldg., The EC1 4A 218
Remus Cl. AL1: St A 6B 6
Remus Rd. E3 38Cc 72
Renaissance KT15: Add 77L 149
(off High St.)
Renaissance Ct. SM1: Sutt 74Eb 155
TW3: Houn 55Ea 108
(off Prince Regent Rd.)
Renaissance Ho. KT17: Eps 85Ua 174
(off Up. High St.)
Renaissance Wlk. SE10 48Hc 93
(off Teal St.)
Renbold Ho. SE10 53Ec 114
(off Blissett St.)
Rendalls HA1: Harr 32Ga 66
(off Grove Hill)
Rendel Ho. SM7: Bans 90Eb 175
Rendle Cl. CR0: C'don 71Vb 157
Rendle Ho. W10 42Ab 88
(off Wornington Rd.)
Rendlesham Av. WD7: R'lett 9Ha 14
Rendlesham Rd. E5 35Wb 71
EN2: Enf 11Rb 33
Rendlesham Way WD3: Chor 16E 24
Renforth St. SE16 48Yb 92
Renfree Way TW17: Shep 73Q 150
Renfrew Cl. E6 45Qc 94
Renfrew Ct. TW4: Houn 54Aa 107
Renfrew Ho. E17 26Bc 52
NW6 40Db 69
(off Carlton Vale)
Renfrew Rd. KT2: King T 66Ra 131
SE11 5B 230 (49Rb 91)
TW4: Houn 54Z 107
Renmans, The KT21: Asht 88Pa 173
Renmuir St. SW17 65Hb 133
Rennell St. SE13 55Ec 114
Rennels Way TW7: Isle 54Ga 108
Renness Rd. E17 27Ac 52
Rennets Cl. SE9 57Uc 116
Rennets Wood Rd. SE9 57Tc 116
Rennie Cl. TW15: Ashf 62M 127
Rennie Cotts. E1 42Yb 92
(off Pemell Cl.)
Rennie Ct. EN3: Enf L 10Cc 20
SE1 6B 224
Rennie Dr. DA1: Dart 54Qd 119
Rennie Est. SE16 49Xb 91
Rennie Ho. SE1 4D 230
Rennie St. SE1 6B 224 (46Rb 91)
(not continuous)
Rennie Ter. RH1: Redh 7A 208
Renoir Ct. SE16 50Xb 91
(off Stubbs Dr.)
Renovation, The E16 47Rc 94
(off Woolwich Mnr. Way)
Renown Cl. CR0: C'don 74Rb 157
RM7: Mawney 25Dd 56
Rensburg Rd. E17 29Zb 52
Renshaw Cl. DA17: Belv 51Bd 117
SE6 59Cc 114
Renshaw Ind. Est. TW18: Staines 63H 127
Renters Av. NW4 30Ya 48
Renton Cl. SW2 58Pb 112
Renton Dr. BR5: Orp, St M Cry 73Zc 161
Renwick Dr. BR2: Brom 72Mc 159
Renwick Ind. Est. IG11: Bark 40Xc 75
Renwick Rd. IG11: Bark 42Xc 95
Repens Way UB4: Yead 42Y 85
Rephidim St. SE1 4H 231 (48Ub 91)
Replingham Rd. SW18 60Bb 111
Reporton Rd. SW6 52Ab 110
Repository Rd. SE18 51Pc 116
Repton Av. HA0: Wemb 35La 66
RM2: Rom 27Jd 56
UB3: Harl 49T 84
Repton Cl. SM5: Cars 78Gb 155
Repton Ct. BR1: Brom 65Mc 137
BR3: Beck 67Dc 136
IG5: Ilf 25Pc 54
Repton Dr. RM2: Rom 28Jd 56
Repton Gdns. RM2: Rom 27Jd 56
Repton Gro. IG5: Ilf 25Pc 54
Repton Ho. E4 23Ec 52
SW1 6C 228
REPTON PARK 24Qc 54
Repton Rd. BR6: Chels 76Wc 161
HA3: Kenton 28Pa 47
Repton St. E14 44Ac 92
Repton Way WD3: Crox G 15Q 26
Repulse Cl. RM5: Col R 25Cd 56
Reservoir Cl. CR7: Thor H 69Tb 135
DA9: Ghithe 58Yd 120
Reservoir Ct. AL10: Hat 1B 8
Reservoir Rd. HA4: Ruis 28S 44
IG10: H Beech 11Kc 35
N14 15Lb 32
SE4 54Ac 114
Reservoir Studios E1 44Zb 92
(off Cable St.)
Reservoir Way IG7: Chig 21Xc 55
Resham Cl. UB2: S'hall 48Y 85
Residence Twr. N4 31Sb 71
(off Goodchild Rd.)
Resolution Plaza E1 2K 225
Resolution Wlk. SE18 48Pc 94
Resolution Way SE8 52Cc 114
(off Deptford High St.)
Reson Way HP1: Hem H 3K 3
Restavon Cvn. Site TN16: Big H 88Rc 180
Restell Cl. SE3 51Gc 115
Restmor Way SM6: Wall 75Jb 156
Reston Cl. WD6: Bore 10Qa 15
Reston Path WD6: Bore 10Qa 15
Reston Pl. SW7 2A 226 (47Eb 89)
Restons Cres. SE9 58Tc 116
Restoration Sq. SW11 53Fb 111
Restormel Cl. TW3: Houn 57Ca 107
Restormel Ho. SE11 6A 230
Retcar Pl. N19 33Kb 70
Retford Cl. RM3: Rom 23Qd 57
WD6: Bore 10Qa 15
Retford Path RM3: Rom 23Qd 57
Retford Rd. RM3: Rom 23Pd 57
Retford St. N1 2J 219 (40Ub 71)
Retingham Way E4 19Dc 34
Retles Ct. HA1: Harr 31Ga 66
Retreat, The BR6: Chels 79Xc 161
CM13: Hut 16De 41
CM14: B'wood 18Xd 40
CR7: Thor H 70Tb 135
HA2: Harr 31Ca 65
HP6: L Chal 11A 24
KT4: Wor Pk 75Xa 154
KT5: Surb 72Pa 153
NW9 29Ta 47
RM17: Grays 51De 121
SW14 55Ua 110
TN13: S'oaks 97Kd 203
TW20: Eng G 4P 125
WD4: K Lan 3S 12
Retreat Cl. HA3: Kenton 29La 46
Retreat Ho. E9 37Yb 72
Retreat Mobile Home Pk., The
IG9: Buck H 19Jc 35
Retreat Pl. E9 37Yb 72
Retreat Rd. TW9: Rich 57Ma 109
Retreat Way IG7: Chig 20Xc 37
Reubens Ct. W4 50Ra 87
(off Chaseley Dr.)
Reubens Rd. CM13: Hut 16De 41
Reunion Row E1 45Xb 91
Reuters Plaza E14 46Dc 92
(off The South Colonnade)
Reveley Cotts. WD23: Bush 16Ca 27
Reveley Sq. SE16 47Ac 92
Revell Cl. KT22: Fet 94Da 191
Revell Dr. KT22: Fet 94Da 191
Revell Ri. SE18 51Vc 117
Revell Rd. KT1: King T 68Ra 131
SM1: Sutt 79Bb 155
Revelon Rd. SE4 56Ac 114
Revelstoke Rd. SW18 61Bb 133
Reventlow Rd. SE9 60Sc 116
Reverdy Rd. SE1 49Wb 91
Reverend Cl. HA2: Harr 34Da 65
Revere Way KT19: Ewe 81Ua 174
Revesby Cl. GU24: W End 5B 166
Revesby Rd. SM5: Cars 72Fb 155
Review Lodge RM10: Dag 39Dd 76
Review Rd. NW2 33Va 68
RM10: Dag 39Dd 76
Rewell St. SW6 52Eb 111
Rewley Rd. SM5: Cars 72Fb 155
Rex Av. TW15: Ashf 65Q 128
Rex Cl. RM5: Col R 24Dd 56
Rex Pl. W1 5J 221 (45Jb 90)
Reydon Av. E11 29Lc 53
Reydon Pl. KT12: Walt T 75X 151
Reynard Bus. Pk. TW8: Bford 50La 86
Reynard Cl. BR1: Brom 69Qc 138
SE4 55Ac 114
Reynard Dr. SE19 66Vb 135
Reynard Pl. SE14 51Ac 114
Reynardson Rd. N17 24Sb 51
Reynards Way AL2: Brick W 1Ba 13
Reynolah Gdns. SE7 50Kc 93
Reynolds Av. E12 36Qc 74
KT9: Chess 80Na 153
RH1: Redh 4B 208
RM6: Chad H 31Yc 75
Reynolds Cl. HP1: Hem H 1J 3
NW11 31Db 69
SM5: Cars 74Hb 155
SW19 67Fb 133
Reynolds Ct. RM6: Chad H 27Zc 55
Reynolds Dr. HA8: Edg 27Pa 47
Reynolds Fitness Spa 61Gd 140
Reynolds Ho. E2 40Yb 72
(off Approach Rd.)
NW8 2C 214
SW1 6E 228
Reynolds Pl. SE3 52Kc 115
TW10: Rich 58Pa 109
Reynolds Rd. KT3: N Mald 73Ta 153
SE15 56Yb 114
UB4: Yead 42Y 85
W4 48Sa 87
Reynolds Sports Cen. 46Qa 87
Reynolds Way CR0: C'don 77Ub 157
Rhapsody Cres. CM14: W'ley 21Xd 58
Rheidol M. N1 1D 218
Rheidol Ter. N1 1C 218 (39Sb 71)
Rheingold Way SM6: Wall 81Nb 176
Rhein Ho. N8 27Nb 50
(off Campsfield Rd.)
Rheola Cl. N17 25Vb 51
Rhoda McGaw Theatre 89A 168
Rhoda St. E2 5K 219 (42Vb 91)
Rhodes Av. N22 25Lb 50
Rhodes Cl. TW20: Egh 64D 126
Rhodes Ct. TW20: Egh 64E 126
(off Rhodes Cl.)
Rhodes Ho. N1 3F 219
Rhodesia Rd. E11 33Fc 73
SW9 54Nb 112
Rhodes Moorhouse Ct.
SM4: Mord 72Cb 155
Rhodes St. N7 36Pb 70
Rhodes Way WD24: Wat 12Z 27
Rhodeswell Rd. E14 43Ac 92
(not continuous)
Rhodium Ct. E14 43Cc 92
(off Thomas Rd.)
Rhododendron Ride TW20: Eng G 5K 125
Rhodrons Av. KT9: Chess 78Na 153
Rhondda Gro. E3 41Ac 92
RHS Garden Wisley 90N 169
Rhyl Rd. UB6: G'frd 40Ha 66
Rhyl St. NW5 37Jb 70
Rhymes, The HP1: Hem H 1K 3
Rhys Av. N11 24Mb 50
Rialto Rd. CR4: Mitc 68Jb 134
Ribble Cl. IG8: Wfd G 23Lc 53
Ribbledale AL2: Lon C 9K 7
Ribblesdale Av. N11 23Jb 50
UB5: N'olt 37Da 65
Ribblesdale Ho. NW6 39Cb 69
(off Kilburn Vale)
Ribblesdale Rd. DA2: Dart 60Sd 120
N8 28Pb 50
SW16 65Kb 134
Ribbon Dance M. SE5 53Tb 113
Ribbons Wlk. E20 36Ec 72
Ribchester Av. UB6: G'frd 41Ha 86
Ribston Cl. BR2: Brom 74Pc 160
WD7: Shenl 5Ma 15
Ricardo Path SE28 46Yc 95
Ricardo Rd. SL4: Old Win 8M 103
Ricardo St. E14 44Dc 92
Ricards Rd. SW19 64Bb 133
Riccall Ct. NW9 25Ua 48
(off Pageant Av.)
Ricebridge La. RH2: Reig 9D 206
Rice Cl. HP2: Hem H 1P 3
Rice Pde. BR5: Pet W 71Tc 160
Riceyman Ho. WC1 4K 217
Richard Anderson Ct. SE14 52Zb 114
(off Monson Rd.)
Richard Blackburn Ho.
RM7: Rush G 33Gd 76
Richard Burbidge Mans. SW13 51Ya 110
(off Brasenose Dr.)
Richard Burton Ct. IG9: Buck H 19Lc 35
(off Palmerston Rd.)
Richard Challoner Sports Cen. 73Ta 153
Richard Cl. SE18 49Nc 94
Richard Fell Ho. E12 35Qc 74
(off Walton Rd.)
Richard Fielden Ho. E1 41Ac 92
Richard Ho. SE16 49Yb 92
(off Silwood St.)
Richard Ho. Dr. E16 44Mc 93
Richard Neale Ho. E1 45Xb 91
(off Cornwall St.)
Richard Neve Ho. SE18 49Uc 94
(off Plumstead High St.)
Richard Robert Residence, The
E15 37Fc 73
(off Salway Rd.)
Richard Ryan Pl. RM9: Dag 39Ad 75
Richards Av. RM7: Rom 30Ed 56
Richards Cl. HA1: Harr 29Ja 46
UB3: Harl 51T 106
UB10: Hil 39Q 64
WD23: Bush 17Fa 28
Richards Fld. KT19: Ewe 81Ta 173
Richard Sharples Ct. SM2: Sutt 80Eb 155
Richardson Cl. AL2: Lon C 9J 7
(not continuous)
DA9: Ghithe 57Vd 120
E8 39Vb 71
Richardson Ct. SW4 54Nb 112
(off Studley Rd.)
Richardson Gdns. RM10: Dag 37Dd 76
Richardson Pl. AL4: Col H 4M 7
Richardson Rd. E15 40Gc 73
Richardson's M. W1 6B 216
Richard's Pl. SW3 5E 226 (49Gb 89)
Richards Pl. E17 27Cc 52
Richards Rd. KT11: Stoke D 86Da 171
Richard Stagg Cl. AL1: St A 4G 6
Richard St. E1 44Xb 91
Richards Way SL1: Slou 6C 80
Richbell WC1 7H 217
Richbell Cl. KT21: Asht 90Ma 173
Richbell Pl. WC1 7H 217 (43Pb 90)
Richborne Ter. SW8 52Pb 112
Richborough Cl. BR5: St M Cry 70Zc 139
Richborough Ho. SE15 51Yb 114
(off Sharratt St.)
Richborough Rd. NW2 35Ab 68
Richbourne Ct. W1 2E 220
(off Harrowby St.)
Richens Cl. TW3: Houn 54Fa 108
Riches Rd. IG1: Ilf 33Sc 74
Richfield Rd. WD23: Bush 17Ea 28
Richford Ga. W6 48Ya 88
Richford Rd. E15 39Hc 73
Richford St. W6 47Ya 88
Rich Ind. Est. SE1 4J 231 (48Ub 91)
SE15 51Xb 113
RICHINGS PARK 48G 82
Richings Pk. Golf Course 49F 82
Richings Pl. SL0: Rich P 48G 82
Richings Way SL0: Rich P 48G 82
(not continuous)
Richland Av. CR5: Coul 86Jb 176
Richland Ho. SE15 53Wb 113
(off Goldsmith Rd.)
Richlands Av. KT17: Ewe 77Wa 154
Rich La. SW5 50Db 89
Richman Ho. SE8 50Bc 92
(off Grove St.)
Richmer Rd. DA8: Erith 52Jd 118
Richmix Sq. E1 5K 219
RICHMOND 57Ma 109
Richmond, The American International
University in London
Kensington Campus -
Ansdell Street 48Db 89
(off Ansdell St.)
St Albans Grove 48Db 89
Young Street 47Db 89
Richmond Hill Campus 59Na 109
Richmond & London Scottish RUFC
55Ma 109
Richmond Athletic Ground 55Ma 109
Richmond Av. CM14: B'wood 18Yd 40
E4 22Fc 53
N1 39Pb 70
NW10 37Ya 68
SW20 67Ab 132
TW14: Felt 58U 106
UB10: Hil 37R 64
Richmond Bri. TW1: Twick 58Ma 109
Richmond Bldgs. W1 3D 222 (44Mb 90)
RICHMOND CIRCUS 56Na 109
Richmond Cl. E17 30Bc 52
EN8: Chesh 1Yb 20
KT18: Eps 86Ua 174
KT22: Fet 96Ea 192
TN16: Big H 91Kc 199
WD6: Bore 15Ta 29
Richmond Cotts. W14 49Ab 88
(off Hammersmith Rd.)
Richmond Ct. AL1: St A 2E 6
AL10: Hat 2D 8
CR4: Mitc 69Fb 133
E8 38Xb 71
(off Mare St.)
EN6: Pot B 3Eb 17
HA9: Wemb 34Pa 67
IG10: Lough 15Mc 35
(off High Rd.)
N11 23Jb 50
(off Pickering Gdns.)
NW6 38Za 68
(off Willesden La.)
SW1 2G 227
W14 49Ab 88
(off Hammersmith Rd.)
Richmond Cres. E4 22Fc 53
KT19: Eps 84Na 173
N1 39Pb 70
N9 18Wb 33
SL1: Slou 6L 81
TW18: Staines 64H 127
Richmond Cricket Ground 55Na 109
Richmond Dr. DA12: Grav'nd 1G 144
IG8: Wfd G 24Qc 54
TW17: Shep 72T 150
WD17: Wat 12U 26
Richmond Gdns. HA3: Hrw W 24Ha 46
NW4 29Wa 48
Richmond Golf Course 61Na 131
Richmond Grn. CR0: Bedd 76Nb 156
Richmond Gro. KT5: Surb 72Pa 153
N1 38Rb 71
(not continuous)
Richmond Hill TW10: Rich 58Na 109
Richmond Hill Ct. TW10: Rich 58Na 109
Richmond Ho. CR3: Cat'm 96Vb 197
E3 43Cc 92
(off Bow Common La.)
NW1 2A 216
SE17 7F 231
Richmond La. DA1: Dart 57Pd 119
Richmond Mans. SW5 50Db 89
(off Old Brompton Rd.)
TW1: Twick 58Ma 109
Richmond M. SE6 60Dc 114
TW11: Tedd 64Ha 130
W1 3D 222 (44Mb 90)
Richmond Pde. TW1: Twick 58La 108
(off Richmond Rd.)
Richmond Pk. IG10: Lough 17Mc 35
Richmond Pk. Golf Course 59Ua 110

Richmond Pk. (National Nature Reserve)—Riverside Ct.

Richmond Pk. (National Nature Reserve) 59Qa 109
Richmond Pk. Rd.
KT2: King T 67Na 131
SW14 .....57Sa 109
Richmond Pl. SE18 .....49Sc 94
SL9: Ger X 3N 61
Richmond Rd. CR0: Bedd 76Nb 156
CR5: Coul 87Kb 176
CR7: Thor H 69Rb 135
E4 .....18Fc 35
E7 .....36Kc 73
E8 .....38Vb 71
E11 .....33Fc 73
EN5: New Bar 15Db 31
EN6: Pot B 3Eb 17
IG1: Ilf 34Sc 74
KT2: King T 64Ma 131
N2 .....26Eb 49
N11 .....23Nb 50
N15 .....30Ub 51
RM1: Rom 30Hd 56
RM17: Grays 51Ee 121
SW20 .....67Xa 132
TW1: Twick 59Ka 108
TW7: Isle 55Ja 108
TW18: Staines 64H 127
W5 .....47Na 87
Richmond St. E13 .....40Jc 73
Richmond Ter. SW1 .....1F 229 (47Nb 90)
Richmond Theatre 56Ma 109
Richmond Way E11 .....33Jc 73
KT22: Fet 95Da 191
(not continuous)
W12 .....47Za 88
W14 .....48Za 88
WD3: Crox G 14S 26
Richmondwood SL5: S'dale 4F 146
Richmount Gdns. SE3 .....55Jc 115
Rich St. E14 .....45Bc 92
Rickard Cl. NW4 .....28Xa 48
SW2 .....60Qb 112
UB7: W Dray 48M 83
Rickards Cl. KT6: Surb 75Na 153
Ricketts Hill Rd. TN16: Tats 90Mc 179
Rickett St. SW6 .....51Cb 111
Rickfield Cl. AL10: Hat 2C 8
Rickford GU3: Worp 8H 187
Rickford Hill GU3: Worp 8H 187
Rickman Ct. KT15: Add 76K 149
Rickman Cres. KT15: Add 76K 149
Rickman Hill CR5: Coul 90Kb 176
Rickman Hill Rd.
CR5: Chip, Coul 90Kb 176
Rickman Ho. *E1* *41Yb 92*
(off Rickman St.)
Rickman's La. SL2: Stoke P 7J 61
Rickman St. E1 .....42Yb 92
RICKMANSWORTH 18M 25
Rickmansworth Golf Course 19P 25
Rickmansworth La. SL9: Chal P 24A 42
Rickmansworth Pk. 17M 25
Rickmansworth Rd. HA5: Pinn 26X 45
HA6: Nwood 22R 44
UB9: Hare 25L 43
WD3: Chor 13J 24
WD17: Wat 14U 26
WD18: Wat 14U 26
Rickmansworth Sailing Club 25H 43
Rick Roberts Way E15 .....39Ec 72
Ricksons La. KT24: W Hor 99R 190
Rickthorne Rd. N19 .....33Nb 70
Rickyard Path SE9 .....56Nc 116
Riddell Ct. SE5 .....7K 231
Ridding La. UB6: G'frd 36Ha 66
Riddings, The CR3: Cat'm 97Vb 197
RIDDLESDOWN 85Sb 177
Riddlesdown Av. CR8: Purl 83Sb 177
Riddlesdown Rd.
CR8: Kenley, Purl 82Sb 177
Riddons Rd. SE12 .....62Lc 137
Ride, The EN3: Pond E 13Yb 34
EN8: Chesh 3Zb 20
TW8: Bford 50Ka 86
Rideout St. SE18 .....49Pc 94
Rider Cl. DA15: Sidc 58Uc 116
Riders Way RH9: G'stone 3A 210
Ride The Hill, Mountainboarding Cen.
.....7D 208
Rideway Dr. W3 .....48Qa 87
Ridgdale St. E3 .....40Dc 72
RIDGE 6Ua 16
Ridge, The BR6: Orp 75Tc 160
CR3: Wold 98Cc 198
CR5: Coul 86Nb 176
CR6: W'ham 97Fc 199
CR8: Purl 82Lb 176
DA5: Bexl 59Bd 117
EN5: Barn 15Bb 31
GU22: Wok 89D 168
HA6: Nwood 24V 44
KT5: Surb 71Qa 153
KT18: Eps 90Sa 173
KT22: Fet 96Fa 192
SL5: S'dale 3E 146
TW2: Whitt 59Fa 108
Ridge Av. DA1: Cray 58Hd 118
N21 .....17Sb 33
Ridgebank SL1: Slou 5D 80
Ridgebrook Rd. SE3 .....55Mc 115
Ridge Cl. GU22: Wok 3M 187
NW4 .....26Za 48
NW9 .....28Ta 47
SE28 .....47Tc 94
Ridge Ct. CR6: W'ham 90Wb 177
SE22 .....59Wb 113
SL4: Wind 5G 102
Ridge Crest EN2: Enf 11Pb 32
Ridgecroft Cl. DA5: Bexl 60Ed 118
Ridgefield WD17: Wat 9U 12
Ridgegate Cl. RH2: Reig 4M 207
RIDGE GREEN 9E 208
Ridge Grn. RH1: S Nut 9E 208
Ridge Grn. Cl. RH1: S Nut 9E 208
RIDGE HILL 2Sa 15
Ridge Hill AL2: Lon C 10L 7
NW11 .....32Ab 68
WD7: Shenl 10L 7
Ridgehurst Av. WD25: Wat 6V 12
Ridgelands KT22: Fet 96Fa 192
Ridge La. WD17: Wat 9V 12
Ridge Langley CR2: Sande 82Wb 177
Ridge Lea HP1: Hem H 2H 3
Ridgemead Cl. N14 .....19Nb 32
Ridgemead Rd. TW20: Eng G 2L 125
Ridgemont Gdns. HA8: Edg 21Sa 47
Ridgemont Pl. RM11: Horn 30Md 57
Ridgemount KT13: Weyb 75U 150
Ridgemount Av. CR0: C'don 74Zb 158
CR5: Coul 89Kb 176
Ridgemount Cl. SE20 .....66Xb 135
Ridgemount End SL9: Chal P 22A 42
Ridgemount Gdns. EN2: Enf 13Rb 33
Ridgemount Rd. SL5: S'dale 5E 146
Ridgemount Way RH1: Redh 8M 207
Ridge Pk. CR8: Purl 82Mb 176
Ridge Pl. BR5: St M Cry 70Yc 139
Ridge Rd. CR4: Mitc 66Kb 134
N8 .....30Pb 50
N21 .....18Sb 33
NW2 .....34Bb 69
SM3: Sutt 74Ab 154
(not continuous)
Ridge St. WD24: Wat 10X 13
Ridges Yd. CR0: C'don 76Rb 157
Ridgeview AL2: Lon C 10K 7
Ridgeview Cl. EN5: Barn 16Za 30
Ridgeview Rd. N20 .....20Db 31
Ridge Way DA1: Cray 58Hd 118
GU25: Vir W 71A 148
SE19 .....65Ub 135
TW13: Hanw 62Aa 129
Ridge Way, The CR2: Sande 81Ub 177
Ridgeway BR2: Hayes 75Jc 159
CM13: Hut 18De 41
DA2: Daren 64Ud 142
GU21: Wok 7P 167
IG8: Wfd G 21Lc 53
KT19: Eps 84Sa 173
RM17: Grays 9A 100
WD3: Rick 17K 25
WD7: Shenl 3La 14
Ridgeway, The CR0: Wadd 76Pb 156
DA12: Shorne 6N 145
E4 .....19Dc 34
EN2: Enf 8Mb 18
EN6: N'thaw, Cuff 10N 9, 1Mb 18
EN6: Pot B 6Fb 17
GU24: Brkwd 2D 186
HA2: Harr 29Ba 45
(not continuous)
HA3: Kenton 30La 46
HA4: Ruis 31W 64
HA7: Stan 23La 46
KT12: Walt T 74V 150
KT22: Fet 95Fa 192
KT22: Oxs 86Ea 172
N3 .....24Db 49
N11 .....21Hb 49
N14 .....19Nb 32
NW7 .....20Wa 30
NW9 .....28Ta 47
NW11 .....31Ab 68
RM2: Rom 28Jd 56
RM3: Hrld W 25Pd 57
SL0: Iver 46G 82
SL9: Chal P 27A 42
W3 .....48Qa 87
WD7: R'lett 9Ha 14
WD17: Wat 9U 12
Ridgeway Av. DA12: Grav'nd 2D 144
EN4: E Barn 16Hb 31
Ridgeway Bungs. DA12: Shorne 6P 145
Ridgeway Cl. GU21: Wok 7P 167
HP3: Hem H 8P 3
KT22: Fet 96Ga 192
KT22: Oxs 86Ea 172
Ridgeway Ct. HA5: Hat E 24Ca 45
RH1: Redh 7P 207
Ridgeway Cres. BR6: Orp 76Uc 160
Ridgeway Cres. Gdns. BR6: Orp 75Uc 160
Ridgeway Dr. BR1: Brom 63Kc 137
Ridgeway E. DA15: Sidc 57Vc 117
Ridgeway Gdns. GU21: Wok 7P 167
IG4: Ilf 29Nc 54
N6 .....31Lb 70
Ridgeway Rd. RH1: Redh 6P 207
TW7: Isle 52Ga 108
Ridgeway Rd. Nth. TW7: Isle 51Ga 108
Ridgeway Trad. Est. SL0: Iver 45H 83
Ridgeway Wlk. *UB5: N'olt* *37Aa 65*
(off Cowings Mead)
Ridgeway W. DA15: Sidc 57Uc 116
Ridgewell Av. RM16: Ors 2C 100
Ridgewell Cl. N1 .....39Sb 71
RM10: Dag 39Dd 76
SE26 .....63Bc 136
Ridgewell Gro. RM12: Horn 38Kd 77
Ridgewood DA3: Lfield 68Ee 143
Ridgmont Rd. AL1: St A 2C 6
(not continuous)
Ridgmount Gdns. WC1 .....6D 216 (43Mb 90)
Ridgmount Pl. WC1 .....7D 216 (43Mb 90)
Ridgmount Rd. SW18 .....57Db 111
Ridgmount St. WC1 .....7D 216 (43Mb 90)
RIDGWAY 87J 169
Ridgway GU22: Pyr 87J 169
SW19 .....66Ya 132
TW10: Rich 58Na 109
Ridgway, The SM2: Sutt 80Fb 155
Ridgway Ct. SW19 .....65Za 132
Ridgway Gdns. SW19 .....66Za 132
Ridgway Pl. SW19 .....65Ab 132
Ridgway Rd. GU22: Pyr 87H 169
SW9 .....55Rb 113
Ridgwell Rd. E16 .....43Lc 93
Ridgy Fld. Cl. TN15: Wro 89Ce 185
Riding, The GU21: Wok 86D 168
NW11 .....31Bb 69
Riding Ct. Farm SL3: Dat 1M 103
Riding Ct. Rd. SL3: Dat, L'ly 2N 103
Riding Hill CR2: Sande 85Wb 177
Riding Ho. St. W1 .....1A 222 (43Kb 90)
Ridings, The E11 .....29Jc 53
EN4: E Barn 17Fb 31
GU23: Rip 95J 189
HP5: Lat 8A 10
IG7: Chig 21Xc 55
KT5: Surb 71Qa 153
KT11: Cobh 84Ca 171
KT15: Add 79G 148
KT17: Ewe 81Va 174
KT18: Eps 87Ua 174
KT20: Tad 92Bb 195
KT21: Asht 89Ma 173
KT24: E Hor 97U 190
RH2: Reig 4M 207
SL0: Rich P 49H 83
SL4: Wind 2A 102
TN16: Big H 89Nc 180
TW16: Sun 67W 128
W5 .....42Pa 87
Ridings Av. N21 .....14Rb 33
Ridings Cl. N6 .....31Lb 70
Ridings La. GU23: Ock 95R 190
Ridlands Gro. RH8: Limp 2P 211
Ridlands La. RH8: Limp 2P 211
Ridlands Ri. RH8: Limp 2P 211
Ridler Rd. EN1: Enf 10Ub 19
RIDLEY 78De 165
Ridley Av. W13 .....48Ka 86
Ridley Cl. IG11: Bark 38Vc 75
RM3: Rom 25Kd 57
Ridley Ct. SW16 .....65Nb 134
Ridley Ho. SW1 .....4E 228
Ridley Rd. BR2: Brom 69Hc 137
CR6: W'ham 90Yb 178
DA16: Well 53Xc 117
E7 .....35Lc 73
E8 .....36Vb 71
NW10 .....40Wa 68
SW19 .....66Db 133
Ridsdale Rd. GU21: Wok 9M 167
SE20 .....66Xb 135
Riefield Rd. SE9 .....56Sc 116
Riesco Dr. CR0: C'don 79Yb 158
Riffel Rd. NW2 .....36Ya 68
Riffhams CM13: B'wood 20De 41
Rifle Butts All.
KT18: Eps 86Va 174
Rifle Ct. SE11 .....51Qb 112
Rifle St. E14 .....43Dc 92
Riga M. *E1* *44Wb 91*
(off Commercial Rd.)
Rigault Rd. SW6 .....54Ab 110
Rigby Cl. CR0: Wadd 76Qb 156
Rigby Gdns.
RM16: Grays 9D 100
Rigby La. UB3: Hayes 47S 84
Rigby Lodge SL1: Slou 4J 81
Rigby M. IG1: Ilf 33Qc 74
Rigby Pl. EN3: Enf L 9Cc 20
Rigden St. E14 .....44Dc 92
Rigeley Rd. NW10 .....41Wa 88
Rigg App. E10 .....32Zb 72
Rigge Pl. SW4 .....56Mb 112
Riggindale Rd. SW16 .....64Mb 134
Riggs Way TN15: Wro 88Be 185
Riley Cl. KT19: Eps 83Ra 173
Riley Ho. *E3* *42Cc 92*
(off Ireton St.)
SW10 .....*52Fb 111*
(off Riley St.)
Riley Rd. EN3: Enf W 10Yb 20
SE1 .....3J 231 (48Vb 91)
Riley St. SW10 .....51Fb 111
Rill Ct. *IG11: Bark* *40Sc 74*
(off Spring Pl.)
Rill Ho. *SE5* *52Tb 113*
(off Harris St.)
Rill La. HA8: Edg 23Ta 47
Rima Ho. *SW3* *51Fb 111*
(off Callow St.)
Rinaldo Rd. SW12 .....59Kb 112
Ring, The SW7 .....2C 226 (47Fb 89)
W2 .....4D 220 (45Fb 89)
Ring Cl. BR1: Brom 66Kc 137
Ring Ct. SE1 .....1B 230
Ringcroft St. N7 .....36Qb 70
Ringers Ct. *BR1: Brom* *69Jc 137*
(off Ringers Rd.)
Ringers Rd. BR1: Brom 69Jc 137
Ringford Rd. SW18 .....57Bb 111
Ring Ho. *E1* *45Yb 92*
(off Sage St.)
Ringles Ct. E6 .....39Pc 74
Ringlet Cl. E16 .....43Kc 93
Ringlewell Cl. EN1: Enf 12Xb 33
Ringley Pk. Av. RH2: Reig 7M 207
Ringley Pk. Rd. RH2: Reig 6L 207
Ringmer Av. SW6 .....53Ab 110
Ringmer Gdns. N19 .....33Nb 70
Ringmer Pl. N21 .....15Tb 33
Ringmer Way BR1: Brom 71Nc 160
Ringmore Ri. SE23 .....59Xb 113
Ringmore Rd. KT12: Walt T 76Y 151
Ringmore Vw. SE23 .....59Xb 113
Ring Rd. W12 .....46Ya 88
(not continuous)
Ringsfield Ho. SE17 .....7E 230
Ringshall Rd. BR5: St P 69Wc 139
Ringside Ct. SE28 .....46Yc 95
Ringslade Rd. N22 .....26Pb 50
Ringstead Rd. SE6 .....59Dc 114
SM1: Sutt 77Fb 155
Ring Way N11 .....23Lb 50
Ringway UB2: S'hall 50Z 85
Ringway Rd. AL2: Park 9P 5
Ringwold Cl. BR3: Beck 66Ac 136
Ringwood Av. BR6: Prat B 82Yc 181
CR0: C'don 73Nb 156
N2 .....26Hb 49
RH1: Redh 3P 207
RM12: Horn 33Md 77
Ringwood Cl. HA5: Pinn 27Y 45
Ringwood Gdns. E14 .....49Cc 92
SW15 .....60Wa 110
Ringwood Lodge RH1: Redh 3A 208
Ringwood Rd. E17 .....30Bc 52
Ringwood Way N21 .....18Rb 33
TW12: Hamp H 63Ca 129
Rio Cinema
Dalston *36Ub 71*
(off Kingsland High St.)
RIPLEY 93L 189
Ripley Av. TW20: Egh 65A 126
Ripley Bldgs. SE1 .....1C 230
Ripley By-Pass GU23: Rip 95L 189
Ripley Cl. BR1: Brom 71Pc 160
CR0: New Ad 79Ec 158
SL3: L'ly 49A 82
Ripley Ct. CR4: Mitc 68Fb 133
IG7: Chig 19Sc 36
Ripley Gdns. SM1: Sutt 77Eb 155
(not continuous)
SW14 .....55Ta 109
Ripley Ho. *SW1* *51Lb 112*
(off Churchill Gdns.)
Ripley La. GU23: Rip 95Nb 189
KT24: W Hor 97Q 190
Ripley M. E11 .....30Gc 53
Ripley Rd. DA17: Belv 49Cd 96
E16 .....44Lc 93
EN2: Enf 11Sb 33
GU4: E Clan 98L 189
GU23: Send 98L 189
IG3: Ilf 33Vc 75
TW12: Hamp 66Ca 129
Ripley's Believe It or Not *5D 222*
(within London Pavilion)
Ripleys Mkt. DA1: Dart 59Nd 119
RIPLEY SPRINGS 65A 126
Ripley Vw. IG10: Lough 10Rc 22
Ripley Vs. W5 .....44La 86
Ripley Way EN7: Chesh 2Xb 19
HP1: Hem H 1G 2
KT19: Eps 83Qa 173
Ripon Cl. UB5: N'olt 36Ca 65
Ripon Ct. *N11* *23Jb 50*
(off Ribblesdale Av.)
Ripon Gdns. IG1: Ilf 30Nc 54
KT9: Chess 78Ma 153
Ripon Ho. *RM3: Rom* *23Md 57*
(off Dartfields)
Ripon Rd. N9 .....17Xb 33
N17 .....27Tb 51
SE18 .....51Rc 116
Ripon Way WD6: Bore 15Ta 29
Rippersley Rd. DA16: Well 53Wc 117
Ripple Nature Reserve, The 41Xc 95
Ripple Rd. IG11: Bark, Dag 38Sc 74
RM9: Dag 39Xc 75
RIPPLESIDE 39Xc 75
Rippleside Commercial Est.
IG11: Bark 40Yc 75
Ripplevale Gro. N1 .....38Pb 70
Rippolson Rd. SE18 .....50Vc 95
Ripston Rd. TW15: Ashf 64T 128
Risborough Cl. N10 .....27Kb 50
Risborough Dr. KT4: Wor Pk 73Wa 154
Risborough Ho. NW8 .....5E 214
Risborough St. SE1 .....1C 230 (47Rb 91)
Risdon Ho. *SE16* *47Yb 92*
(off Risdon St.)
Risdon St. SE16 .....48Yb 92
Rise, The AL2: Park 7B 6
CR2: Sels 81Yb 178
DA1: Cray 56Hd 118
DA5: Bexl 59Yc 117
DA9: Ghithe 58Wd 120
DA12: Grav'nd 3G 144
E11 .....29Jc 53
EN9: Walt A 2Kc 21
HA0: Wemb 36Ja 66
HA8: Edg 22Ra 47
IG9: Buck H 17Mc 35
KT17: Ewe 82Va 174
KT20: Tad 92Ya 194
KT24: E Hor 98U 190
N13 .....21Qb 50
NW7 .....23Va 48
NW10 .....35Ta 67
TN13: S'oaks 100Ld 203
UB6: G'frd 36Ja 66
UB10: Hil 40P 63
WD6: E'tree 15Pa 29
Risebridge Chase RM1: Rom 24Hd 56
Risebridge Golf Course 24Hd 56
Risebridge Rd. RM2: Rom 26Hd 56
Risedale Cl. HP3: Hem H 5N 3
Risedale Hill HP3: Hem H 5N 3
Risedale Rd. DA7: Bex 55Ed 118
HP3: Hem H 5N 3
Riseholme Ct. E9 .....37Bc 72
Riseldine Rd. SE23 .....58Ac 114
RISE PARK 26Gd 56
Rise Pk. Blvd. RM1: Rom 25Hd 56
Rise Pk. Pde. RM1: Rom 26Gd 56
Rise Rd. SL5: S'dale 1C 146
Riseway CM15: B'wood 20Ae 41
Rising Hill Cl. HA6: Nwood 23S 44
Risinghill St. N1 .....1K 217 (40Pb 70)
Risingholme Cl. HA3: Hrw W 25Ga 46
WD23: Bush 17Da 27
Risingholme Rd. HA3: Hrw W 26Ga 46
Risings, The E17 .....28Fc 53
Risings Ter. *RM11: Horn* *27Pd 57*
(off Prospect Rd.)
Rising Sun Ct. EC1 .....1C 224
Risley Av. N17 .....25Sb 51
Risley Cl. SM4: Mord 71Db 155
Rita Rd. SW8 .....51Nb 112
Ritches Rd. N15 .....29Sb 51
Ritchie Ho. *E14* *44Fc 93*
(off Blair St.)
N19 .....32Mb 70
SE16 .....*48Yb 92*
(off Howland Est.)
Ritchie Rd. CR0: C'don 72Xb 157
Ritchie St. N1 .....1A 218 (40Qb 70)
Ritchings Av. E17 .....28Ac 52
Ritcroft Cl. HP3: Hem H 3B 4
Ritcroft Dr. HP3: Hem H 3B 4
Ritcroft St. HP3: Hem H 3B 4
Ritherdon Rd. SW17 .....61Jb 134
Ritson Ho. N1 .....1H 217
Ritson Rd. E8 .....37Wb 71
Ritter St. SE18 .....51Qc 116
Ritz Ct. EN6: Pot B 3Cb 17
Ritz Pde. W5 .....42Pa 87
Ritzy Picturehouse *56Qb 112*
(off Coldharbour La.)
Riva Bldg., The SE13 .....56Fc 115
Rivaz Pl. E9 .....37Yb 72
Riven Ct. *W2* *44Db 89*
(off Inverness Ter.)
Rivenhall Gdns. E18 .....28Hc 53
River App. HA8: Edg 25Sa 47
RIVER ASH ESTATE 73V 150
River Av. KT7: T Ditt 73Ja 152
N13 .....20Rb 33
River Av. Ind. Est. N13 .....22Qb 50
River Bank KT7: T Ditt 71Ha 152
KT8: E Mos 69Ga 130
N21 .....17Sb 33
TW12: Hamp 69Ca 129
Riverbank TW18: Staines 65H 127
Riverbank, The SL4: Wind 2F 102
Riverbank Point UB8: Uxb 37L 63
Riverbank Rd. BR1: Brom 62Jc 137
Riverbank Way TW8: Bford 51La 108
River Barge Cl. E14 .....47Ec 92
River Bourne Health Club 73J 149
River Brent Bus. Pk. W7 .....48Ga 86
River Cl. E11 .....30Lc 53
EN8: Walt C 6Cc 20
HA4: Ruis 30V 44
RM13: Rain 43Kd 97
UB2: S'hall 47Ea 86
River Ct. GU21: Wok 86E 168
KT6: Surb *71Ma 153*
(off Portsmouth Rd.)
RM19: Purf 49Pd 97
SE1 .....5B 224 (45Rb 91)
TN13: Riv 94Gd 202
TW17: Shep 73S 150
Rivercourt Rd. W6 .....49Xa 88
River Crane Way *TW13: Hanw* *61Ba 129*
(off Watermill Way)
Riverdale SE13 .....56Ec 114
Riverdale Cl. IG11: Bark 42Xc 95
Riverdale Ct. N21 .....15Tb 33
Riverdale Dr. GU22: Wok 93B 188
SW18 .....60Db 111
Riverdale Gdns. TW1: Twick 58La 108
Riverdale Ho. SE13 .....56Ec 114
Riverdale Rd. DA5: Bexl 59Bd 117
DA8: Erith 50Dd 96
SE18 .....50Vc 95
TW1: Twick 58La 108
TW13: Hanw 63Aa 129
Riverdale Shop. Cen. SE13 .....55Ec 114
Riverdene HA8: Edg 20Sa 29
Riverdene Ind. Est. KT12: Hers 78Z 151
Riverdene Rd. IG1: Ilf 34Qc 74
River Dr. RM14: Upm 30Sd 58
Riverfield Rd. TW18: Staines 65H 127
Riverfleet WC1 .....3G 217
Riverford Ho. *W2* *43Cb 89*
(off Westbourne Pk. Rd.)
River Front EN1: Enf 13Ub 33
River Gdns. SM5: Cars 75Jb 156
TW14: Felt 57X 107
River Gdns. Bus. Cen. TW14: Felt 57X 107
River Gdns. Wlk. SE10 .....50Gc 93
River Gro. Pk. BR3: Beck 67Bc 136
RIVERHEAD 94Gd 202
Riverhead Cl. E17 .....26Zb 52
Riverhead Dr. SM2: Sutt 82Db 175
Riverhead M. TN13: Riv 95Gd 202
River Hgts. E15 .....39Ec 72
N17 .....25Vb 51
River Hill KT11: Cobh 87X 171
Riverhill KT4: Wor Pk 75Ta 153
Riverhill M. KT4: Wor Pk 76Ta 153
Riverhill Mobile Home Pk.
KT4: Wor Pk 75Ta 153
Riverholme Dr. KT19: Ewe 81Ta 173
Riverhope Mans. SE18 .....48Nc 94
River Ho. SE26 .....62Xb 135
Riverhouse Barn 73V 150
River Island Cl. KT22: Fet 92Fa 192
River La. KT11: Cobh 88Aa 171
KT22: Fet, Lea 93Fa 192
TW10: Ham 59Ma 109
Riverleigh Ct. E4 .....22Bc 52
Riverlight Quay SW8 .....51Lb 112
River Lodge *SW1* *51Lb 112*
(off Grosvenor Rd.)
Rivermead KT1: King T 71Ma 153
KT8: E Mos 69Ea 130
KT14: Byfl 85P 169
Rivermead Cl. KT15: Add 80L 149
TW11: Tedd 64Ka 130
Rivermead Ct. SW6 .....55Bb 111
Rivermead Ho. E9 .....36Ac 72
TW16: Sun *69Y 129*
(off Thames St.)
Rivermeads Rd. N18 .....23Zb 52
River Meads Av. TW2: Twick 62Ca 129
River Mole Bus. Pk. KT10: Esh 75Ca 151
River Mole Local Nature Reserve
.....91Fa 192
River Mt. KT12: Walt T 73V 150
Rivernook Cl. KT12: Walt T 71Y 151
River Pde. TN13: Riv 94Gd 202
River Pk. HP1: Hem H 4J 3
River Pk. Av. TW18: Staines 63F 126
River Pk. Gdns. BR2: Brom 66Fc 137
River Pk. Rd. N22 .....26Pb 50
River Pk. Vw. BR6: Orp 73Xc 161
River Pl. N1 .....38Sb 71
River Reach TW11: Tedd 64La 130
River Rd. CM14: B'wood 21Vd 58
IG9: Buck H 18Nc 36
IG11: Bark 40Uc 74
SL4: Wind 2A 102
TW18: Staines 67H 127
River Rd. Bus. Pk. IG11: Bark 41Vc 95
Rivers Apartments *N17* *23Vb 51*
(off Cannon Rd.)
Riversdale DA11: Nflt 1A 144
Riversdale Gdns. N22 .....25Qb 50
Riversdale Rd. KT7: T Ditt 71Ja 152
N5 .....34Rb 71
RM5: Col R 24Dd 56
Riversdell Cl. KT16: Chert 73H 149
Riversend Rd. HP3: Hem H 5L 3
Riversfield Rd. EN1: Enf 13Ub 33
Rivers Ho. *TW7: Isle* *56Ka 108*
(off Richmond Rd.)
TW8: Bford *50Qa 87*
(off Aitman Dr.)
Riverside AL2: Lon C 9J 7
DA4: Eyns 75Md 163
E3 .....39Cc 72
HP1: Hem H 3M 3
KT16: Chert 68J 127
NW4 .....31Xa 68
SE7 .....48Kc 93
SW11 .....52Gb 111
TW1: Twick 60Ka 108
TW9: Rich 57Ma 109
TW10: Rich 57Ma 109
TW16: Sun 68Z 129
TW17: Shep 73U 150
TW18: Staines 67H 127
TW19: Wray 9N 103
TW20: Egh 62C 126
W6 .....51Ya 110
WC1 .....3G 217
Riverside, The KT8: E Mos 69Fa 130
Riverside Apartments *N4* *31Tb 71*
(off Goodchild Rd.)
N13 .....22Pb 50
Riverside App. RM18: Tilb 6B 122
Riverside Arts Cen. 69Y 129
Riverside Av. GU18: Light 3A 166
KT8: E Mos 71Fa 152
Riverside Bus. Cen. SW18 .....60Db 111
Riverside Bus. Pk. SW19 .....67Eb 133
Riverside Cl. AL1: St A 3C 6
BR5: St P 68Yc 139
E5 .....32Yb 72
GU24: Brkwd 2D 186
KT1: King T 70Ma 131
RM1: Rom 28Fd 56
SM6: Wall 76Kb 156
TW18: Staines 67H 127
W7 .....42Ga 86
WD4: K Lan 1R 12
Riverside Cotts. IG11: Bark 40Tc 74
Riverside Ct. AL1: St A 4C 6
E4 .....16Cc 34
KT22: Fet 94Ja 192
SE3 .....56Hc 115
SW8 .....51Mb 112
TW7: Isle *54Ha 108*
(off Woodlands Rd.)
TW14: Felt 59U 106

Riverside Dr.—Rolland Ho.

Riverside Dr. CR4: Mitc 71Gb 155
KT10: Esh 77Ca 151
NW11 . . . . 30Ab 48
TW10: Ham 62Ka 130
TW18: Staines 64G 126
W4 . . . . 52Ta 109
WD3: Rick 18M 25
Riverside Gdns. EN2: Enf 12Sb 33
GU22: Wok 93D 188
HA0: Wemb 40Na 67
N3 . . . . 27Ab 48
W6 . . . . 50Xa 88
Riverside Hgts. RM18: Tilb 4C 122
Riverside Ho. *N1* *38Sb 71*
(off Canonbury St.)
Riverside Ind. Est. AL2: Lon C 9J 7
DA1: Dart 57Nd 119
EN3: Pond E 16Ac 34
IG11: Bark 41Wc 95
Riverside Leisure Area 8E 122
Riverside Mans. *E1* *46Yb 92*
(off Milk Yd.)
Riverside M. CR0: Bedd 76Nb 156
Riverside Pk. KT13: Weyb 78N 149
SL3: Poyle 54G 104
Riverside Path EN8: Chesh 1Yb 20
Riverside Pl. N11 . . . . 20Lb 32
TW19: Stanw 58M 105
Riverside Rail Freight Terminal
RM18: Tilb 6C 122
Riverside Retail Pk.
TN14: S'oaks 91Ld 203
Riverside Rd. AL1: St A 3C 6
DA14: Sidc 62Ad 139
E15 . . . . 40Ec 72
KT12: Hers 77Z 151
N15 . . . . 30Wb 51
SW17 . . . . 63Db 133
TW18: Staines 66H 127
TW19: Stanw 57M 105
WD19: Wat 16X 27
Riverside Shop. Cen. DA8: Erith . . . 51Hd 118
Riverside Studios 50Ya 88
Riverside Twr. *SW6* *54Eb 111*
(off The Boulevard)
Riverside Vs. KT6: Surb 72La 152
Riverside Wlk. BR4: W W'ck 74Dc 158
EN5: Barn 16Za 30
(not continuous)
KT1: King T 69Ma 131
N12 . . . . 23Cb 49
(not continuous)
N20 . . . . 20Db 31
SL4: Wind 2H 103
SW6 . . . . 55Ab 110
TW7: Isle 55Ga 108
W4 . . . . *51Va 110*
(off Chiswick Wharf)
Riverside Walk Local Nature Reserve
. . . . 1N 147
Riverside Way DA1: Dart 57Nd 119
UB8: Uxb 39K 63
Riverside Way Ind. Est. UB8: Uxb . . . 38K 63
Riverside Wharf DA1: Dart 56Md 119
E3 . . . . 39Cc 72
Riverside Works IG11: Bark 38Rc 74
Riverside Yd. SW17 . . . . 63Eb 133
Riverstone Cl. HA2: Harr 32Fa 66
Riverstone Ct. KT2: King T 67Pa 131
River St. EC1 . . . . 3K 217 (41Qb 90)
SL4: Wind 2H 103
River St. M. EC1 . . . . 3K 217
River Ter. WC2 . . . . 5H 223
River Thames Vis. Cen. 58Ma 109
Riverton Cl. W9 . . . . 41Bb 89
River Twr. SW8 . . . . 51Nb 112
River Vw. *DA1: Dart* *56Rd 119*
(off Shakespeare Rd.)
EN2: Enf 13Sb 33
EN9: Walt A *5Dc 20*
(off Powdermill La.)
KT15: Add 78L 149
RM16: Grays 9C 100
Riverview Ct. E14 . . . . 48Bc 92
Riverview Flats RM19: Purf 50Rd 97
River Vw. Gdns. TW1: Twick 61Ha 130
Riverview Gdns. KT11: Cobh 85W 170
SW13 . . . . 51Xa 110
Riverview Gro. W4 . . . . 51Ra 109
River Vw. Hgts. *SE16* *47Wb 91*
(off Bermondsey Wall W.)
RIVERVIEW PARK 3H 145
Riverview Pk. *DA12: Grav'nd* *3H 145*
(off Whinfell Way)
SE6 . . . . 61Cc 136
Riverview Rd. DA9: Ghithe 57Wd 120
KT19: Ewe 77Sa 153
W4 . . . . 52Ra 109
Riverview Ter. RM19: Purf 50Qd 97
Riverview Wlk. SE6 . . . . 62Bc 136
River Wlk. E4 . . . . 24Ec 52
KT12: Walt T 72W 150
SW6 . . . . 54Eb 111
UB9: Den 36L 63
W6 . . . . 52Ya 110
Riverwalk SW1 . . . . 7F 229 (50Nb 90)
Riverwalk Apartments *SW6* *55Eb 111*
(off Central Av.)
Riverwalk Bus. Pk. EN3: Brim 14Bc 34
River Wlk. Rd. EN3: Brim 14Bc 34
River Way BR3: Beck 74Cc 158
IG10: Lough 16Pc 36
KT19: Ewe 78Ta 153
SE10 . . . . 48Hc 93
TW2: Twick 61Da 129
Riverway N13 . . . . 22Qb 50
TW18: Staines 67K 127
River Wharf Bus. Pk. DA17: Belv 46Fd 96
Riverwood La. BR7: Chst 67Tc 138
Rivet Ho. SE1 . . . . 7K 231
Rivey Cl. KT14: W Byf 86H 169
Riviera Ct. *E1* *46Wb 91*
(off St Katharine's Way)
Rivington Av. IG8: Wfd G 26Mc 53
Rivington Ct. NW10 . . . . 39Wa 68
RM10: Dag 37Dd 76
Rivington Cres. NW7 . . . . 24Va 48
Rivington Pl. EC2 . . . . 4J 219 (41Ub 91)
Rivington St. EC2 . . . . 4H 219 (41Ub 91)
Rivington Wlk. E8 . . . . 39Wb 71
Rivulet Apartments N4 . . . . 31Tb 71
Rivulet Rd. N17 . . . . 24Sb 51
Rixon Cl. SL3: Geor G 44A 82
Rixon Ho. SE18 . . . . 51Rc 116
Rixon St. N7 . . . . 34Qb 70
Rixsen Rd. E12 . . . . 36Nc 74
Roach RM18: E Til 9L 101
Roach Rd. E3 . . . . 38Cc 72
Road Ho. Est. GU22: Wok 93C 188
Roads Pl. N19 . . . . 33Nb 70
Roakes Av. KT15: Add 75J 149
Roan Gdns. CR4: Mitc 67Hb 133
Roan St. SE10 . . . . 51Ec 114
Roasthill La. SL4: Dor 1B 102
Robarts Cl. HA5: Eastc 29X 45
Robbins Hall EN3: Pond E 16Zb 34
Robb Rd. HA7: Stan 23Ja 46
Robe End HP1: Hem H 1H 3
Robert Adam St. W1 . . . . 2H 221 (44Jb 90)
Roberta St. E2 . . . . 41Wb 91
Robert Av. AL1: St A 6P 5
Robert Bell Ho. *SE16* *49Wb 91*
(off Rouel Rd.)
Robert Burns Ho. *N17* *24Xb 51*
(off Northumberland Pk.)
Robert Burns M. SE24 . . . . 57Rb 113
Robert Clack Leisure Cen. 32Cd 76
Robert Cl. EN6: Pot B 5Ab 16
IG7: Chig 22Vc 55
KT12: Hers 78X 151
W9 . . . . 6A 214 (42Eb 89)
WD18: Wat 16V 26
Robert Ct. SE15 . . . . 54Wb 113
Robert Daniels Ct. CM16: They B . . . 9Uc 22
Robert Dashwood Way
SE17 . . . . 6D 230 (49Sb 91)
Robert Gentry Ho. *W14* *50Ab 88*
(off Gledstanes Rd.)
Robert Jones Ho. *SE16* *49Wb 91*
(off Rouel Rd.)
Robert Keen Cl. SE15 . . . . 53Wb 113
Robert Lowe Cl. SE14 . . . . 52Zb 114
Robert Morton Ho. NW8 . . . . 38Eb 69
Roberton Dr. BR1: Brom 67Lc 137
Robert Owen Ho. E2 . . . . 3K 219
N22 . . . . *25Qb 50*
(off Progress Way)
SW6 . . . . 53Za 110
Robert Rd. SL2: Hedg 3H 61
Robert Runcie Ct. SW2 . . . . 56Pb 112
Roberts All. W5 . . . . 47Ma 87
Robertsbridge Rd. SM5: Cars 74Eb 155
Roberts Cl. BR5: St M Cry 71Yc 161
CR7: Thor H 69Tb 135
EN8: Chesh 2Ac 20
IG11: Bark *37Sc 74*
(off Tanner St.)
RM3: Rom 25Kd 57
SE9 . . . . 60Tc 116
SE16 . . . . 47Zb 92
SM3: Cheam 80Za 154
TW19: Stanw 58L 105
UB7: Yiew 46N 83
Roberts Ct. KT9: Chess 78Ma 153
N1 . . . . *39Rb 71*
(off Essex Rd.)
NW10 . . . . 37Ua 68
SE20 . . . . *67Yb 136*
(off Maple Rd.)
Roberts La. SL9: Chal P 22C 42
Roberts M. BR6: Orp 74Wc 161
SW1 . . . . 4H 227 (48Jb 90)
Robertson Ct. GU21: Wok 10J 167
RM17: Grays *49De 99*
(off Hathaway Rd.)
Robertson Gro. SW17 . . . . 64Gb 133
Robertson Rd. E16 . . . . 43Jc 93
HP4: Berk 1A 2
Robertson St. SW8 . . . . 55Kb 112
Roberts Pl. EC1 . . . . 5A 218 (42Qb 90)
RM10: Dag 37Cd 76
Roberts Rd. DA17: Belv 50Cd 96
E17 . . . . 25Dc 52
WD18: Wat 15Y 27
Robert St. CR0: C'don 76Sb 157
E16 . . . . 46Rc 94
NW1 . . . . 4A 216 (41Kb 90)
SE18 . . . . 50Tc 94
(not continuous)
WC2 . . . . 5G 223 (45Nb 90)
Robert Sutton Ho. *E1* *44Yb 92*
(off Tarling St.)
Roberts Way AL10: Hat 2B 8
TW20: Eng G 6N 125
Roberts Wood Dr. SL9: Chal P 22B 42
Robertswood Lodge SL9: Chal P 23B 42
Robeson St. E3 . . . . 43Bc 92
Robeson Way WD6: Bore 11Sa 29
Robina Cl. DA6: Bex 56Zc 117
HA6: Nwood 25V 44
Robina Ct. BR8: Swan 70Jd 140
Robin Cl. KT15: Add 78M 149
NW7 . . . . 20Ua 30
RM5: Col R 24Fd 56
TW12: Hamp 64Aa 129
Robin Ct. E14 . . . . 47Ec 92
SE16 . . . . 49Wb 91
SM6: Wall 78Lb 156
Robin Cres. E6 . . . . 43Mc 93
Robin Gdns. RH1: Redh 4A 208
Robin Gro. HA3: Kenton 30Pa 47
N6 . . . . 33Jb 70
TW8: Bford 51La 108
Robin Hill Dr. BR7: Chst 65Nc 138
ROBIN HOOD 62Ua 132
Robin Hood Cl. GU21: Wok 10K 167
SL1: Slou 6D 80
Robinhood Cl. CR4: Mitc 69Lb 134
Robin Hood Ct. EC4 . . . . 2A 224
Robin Hood Cres. GU21: Knap 9J 167
Robin Hood Dr. HA3: Hrw W 24Ha 46
WD23: Bush 11Ba 27
Robin Hood Gdns. *E14* *45Ec 92*
(off Woolmore St.)
Robin Hood Grn. BR5: St M Cry . . . 71Wc 161
Robin Hood La. DA6: Bex 57Ad 117
E14 . . . . 45Ec 92
GU4: Sut G 96B 188
SM1: Sutt 78Cb 155
SW15 . . . . 62Ua 132
Robinhood La. CR4: Mitc 69Lb 134
Robin Hood Rd. CM15: B'wood 17Xd 40
GU21: Knap, Wok 9H 167
(not continuous)
SW19 . . . . 64Wa 132
Robin Hood Way SW15 . . . . 62Ua 132
SW20 . . . . 62Ua 132
UB6: G'frd 37Ha 66
Robin Hood Works GU21: Knap 9J 167
Robin Ho. NW8 . . . . 2D 214
Robin Howard Dance Theatre 4E 216
Robinia Av. DA11: Nflt 59Fe 121
Robinia Cl. IG6: Ilf 22Uc 54
SE20 . . . . *67Wb 135*
(off Sycamore Gro.)
Robinia Cres. E10 . . . . 33Dc 72
Robinia Ho. *SE16* *47Ac 92*
(off Blondin Way)
Robin La. NW4 . . . . 27Za 48
Robin Pde. SL2: Farn C 6G 60
Robin Pl. WD25: Wat 4X 13
Robins, The RM13: Rain 40Md 77
Robins Cl. AL2: Lon C 9J 7
UB8: Cowl 43L 83
Robin's Ct. BR3: Beck 68Fc 137
Robins Ct. *CR2: S Croy* *77Ub 157*
(off Birdhurst Rd.)
SE12 . . . . 62Lc 137
Robinscroft M. SE10 . . . . 53Ec 114
Robins Dale GU21: Knap 9G 166
Robinsfield HP1: Hem H 2J 3
Robinsfield Gdns. CR3: Cat'm 95Vb 197
Robins Gro. BR4: W W'ck 76Jc 159
Robin's La. CM16: They B 8Sc 22
Robinson Av. EN7: G Oak 1Rb 19
Robinson Cl. E11 . . . . 34Gc 73
EN2: Enf 13Sb 33
GU22: Wok 92E 188
RM12: Horn 38Kd 77
Robinson Ct. CR7: Thor H 72Rb 157
N1 . . . . *39Rb 71*
(off St Mary's Path)
TW9: Rich 56Pa 109
Robinson Cres. WD23: B Hea 18Ea 28
Robinson Ho. *E14* *43Cc 92*
(off Selsey St.)
W10 . . . . *44Za 88*
(off Bramley Rd.)
Robinson Rd. E2 . . . . 40Yb 72
RM10: Dag 35Cd 76
SW17 . . . . 65Gb 133
Robinson's Cl. W13 . . . . 43Ja 86
Robinson St. SW3 . . . . 51Hb 111
Robinson Way DA11: Nflt 57Ce 121
SE14 . . . . 52Zb 114
Robins Orchard SL9: Chal P 23A 42
Robins Rd. HP3: Hem H 4A 4
Robins Way AL10: Hat 3B 8
Robinsway EN9: Walt A 6Gc 21
KT12: Hers 77Y 151
Robinswood Gdns. E17 . . . . 25Bc 52
Robinswood M. N5 . . . . 36Rb 71
Robin Way BR5: St P 69Xc 139
TW18: Staines 62H 127
Robin Willis Way SL4: Old Win 8L 103
Robinwood Dr. TN15: Seal 91Pd 203
Robinwood Gro. UB8: Hil 42P 83
Robinwood Pl. SW15 . . . . 63Ta 131
Roborough Wlk. RM12: Horn 37Ld 77
Robsart St. SW9 . . . . 54Pb 112
Robson Av. NW10 . . . . 38Wa 68
Robson Cl. E6 . . . . 44Nc 94
EN2: Enf 12Rb 33
SL9: Chal P 22A 42
Robson Rd. SE27 . . . . 62Sb 135
Robsons Cl. EN8: Chesh 1Yb 20
Roby Ho. EC1 . . . . 5D 218
Robyns Cft. DA11: Nflt 2A 144
Robyns Way TN13: S'oaks 94Hd 202
Roca Ct. E11 . . . . 29Jc 53
Rocastle Rd. SE4 . . . . 57Ac 114
Roch Av. HA8: Edg 26Pa 47
Rochdale Rd. E17 . . . . 31Cc 72
SE2 . . . . 50Xc 95
Rochdale Way SE8 . . . . 52Cc 114
(not continuous)
Roche Ho. *E14* *45Bc 92*
(off Beccles St.)
Rochelle Cl. SW11 . . . . 56Fb 111
Rochelle St. E2 . . . . 4K 219 (41Vb 91)
(not continuous)
Rochemont Wlk. *E8* *39Wb 71*
(off Pownell Rd.)
Roche Rd. SW16 . . . . 67Pb 134
Rochester & Cobham Pk. Golf Course
. . . . 9N 145
Rochester Av. BR1: Brom 68Kc 137
E13 . . . . 39Lc 73
TW13: Felt 61V 128
Rochester Cl. DA15: Sidc 58Xc 117
EN1: Enf 11Ub 33
SW16 . . . . 66Nb 134
Rochester Ct. *E2* *42Xb 91*
(off Wilmot St.)
NW1 . . . . *38Lb 70*
(off Rochester Sq.)
Rochester Dr. DA5: Bexl 58Bd 117
HA5: Pinn 29Z 45
WD25: Wat 7Y 13
Rochester Gdns. CR0: C'don 76Ub 157
CR3: Cat'm 94Ub 197
IG1: Ilf 31Pc 74
Rochester Ho. SE1 . . . . 2F 231
SE15 . . . . *51Yb 114*
(off Sharratt St.)
Rochester M. NW1 . . . . 38Lb 70
W5 . . . . 49La 86
Rochester Pde. TW13: Felt 61W 128
Rochester Pl. NW1 . . . . 37Lb 70
Rochester Rd. DA1: Dart 59Qd 119
DA12: Grav'nd 9G 122
HA6: Nwood 27V 44
NW1 . . . . 37Lb 70
RM12: Horn 38Kd 77
SM5: Cars 77Hb 155
TW18: Staines 64F 126
Rochester Row SW1 . . . . 5C 228 (49Lb 90)
Rochester Sq. NW1 . . . . 38Lb 70
Rochester St. SW1 . . . . 4D 228 (48Mb 90)
Rochester Ter. NW1 . . . . 37Lb 70
Rochester Wlk. RH2: Reig 10K 207
SE1 . . . . 6F 225 (46Tb 91)
Rochester Way DA1: Dart 59Fd 118
SE3 . . . . 53Kc 115
SE9 . . . . 55Pc 116
WD3: Crox G 14R 26
Rochester Way Relief Rd. SE3 . . . . 53Kc 115
SE9 . . . . 56Lc 115
Roche Wlk. SM5: Cars 72Fb 155
Rochford *N17* *26Ub 51*
(off Griffin Rd.)
Rochford Av. CM15: Shenf 15Ce 41
EN9: Walt A 6Fc 21
IG10: Lough 13Sc 36
RM6: Chad H 29Yc 55
Rochford Cl. E6 . . . . 40Mc 73
RM12: Horn 37Kd 77
Rochford Grn. IG10: Lough 13Sc 36
Rochfords Gdns. SL2: Slou 5N 81
Rochford Wlk. E8 . . . . 38Wb 71
Rochford Way CR0: C'don 72Nb 156
Rochfort Ho. SE8 . . . . 50Bc 92
Rockall Ct. SL3: L'ly 48D 82
Rock Av. SW14 . . . . 55Ta 109
Rockbourne M. SE23 . . . . 60Zb 114
Rockbourne Rd. SE23 . . . . 60Zb 114
Rockchase Gdns. RM11: Horn 30Nd 57
Rock Cl. CR4: Mitc 68Fb 133
Rockdale TN13: S'oaks 97Kd 203
Rockdale Gdns.
TN13: S'oaks 97Kd 203
Rockdale Pleasance
TN13: S'oaks 98Kd 203
Rockdale Rd. TN13: S'oaks 97Ld 203
Rockell's Pl. SE22 . . . . 58Xb 113
Rockfield Cl. RH8: Oxt 3K 211
Rockfield Ho. *NW4* *28Za 48*
(off Belle Vue Est.)
SE10 . . . . *51Ec 114*
(off Welland St.)
Rockfield Rd. RH8: Oxt 1K 211
Rockford Av. UB6: G'frd 40Ja 66
Rock Gdns. RM10: Dag 36Dd 76
Rock Gro. Way SE16 . . . . 49Wb 91
(not continuous)
Rockhall Rd. NW2 . . . . 35Za 68
Rockhall Way NW2 . . . . 34Za 68
Rockhampton Cl. SE27 . . . . 63Qb 134
Rockhampton Rd. CR2: S Croy 79Ub 157
SE27 . . . . 63Qb 134
Rock Hill BR6: Well H 79Dd 162
SE26 . . . . 63Vb 135
(not continuous)
Rockingham Av.
RM11: Horn 30Kd 57
Rockingham Cl. SW15 . . . . 56Va 110
UB8: Uxb 39L 63
Rockingham Ga. WD23: Bush 16Ea 28
Rockingham Pde. UB8: Uxb 38L 63
Rockingham Rd. UB8: Uxb 39K 63
Rockingham St. SE1 . . . . 4D 230 (48Sb 91)
Rockland Rd. SW15 . . . . 56Ab 110
Rocklands Dr. CR2: S Croy 79Tb 157
HA7: Stan 26Ka 46
Rockleigh Ct. CM15: Shenf 17Ce 41
Rockley Ct. *W14* *47Za 88*
(off Rockley Rd.)
Rockley Rd. W14 . . . . 47Za 88
Rockliffe Av. WD4: K Lan 2Q 12
Rockmount Rd. SE18 . . . . 50Vc 95
SE19 . . . . 65Tb 135
Rock Rd. TN15: Bor G 92Be 205
Rockshaw Rd. RH1: Mers 99Lb 196
Rocks La. SW13 . . . . 53Wa 110
Rock St. N4 . . . . 33Qb 70
Rockware Av. UB6: G'frd 39Fa 66
Rockware Av. Bus. Cen.
UB6: G'frd 39Fa 66
Rockways EN5: Ark 16Va 30
Rockwell Ct. WD18: Wat 15U 26
Rockwell Gdns. SE19 . . . . 64Ub 135
Rockwell Rd. RM10: Dag 36Dd 76
Rockwood Pl. W12 . . . . 47Ya 88
Rocky La. RH1: Redh 100Hb 195
RH2: Reig 100Hb 195
Rocliffe St. N1 . . . . 2C 218 (40Rb 71)
Rocombe Cres. SE23 . . . . 59Yb 114
Rocque Ho. *SW6* *52Bb 111*
(off Estcourt Rd.)
Rocque La. SE3 . . . . 55Hc 115
Rodale Mans. SW18 . . . . 58Db 111
Rodborough Ct. *W9* *42Bb 89*
(off Hermes Cl.)
Rodborough Rd. NW11 . . . . 32Cb 69
Rodd Est. TW17: Shep 71S 150
Roden Ct. N6 . . . . 31Mb 70
Roden Gdns. CR0: C'don 72Ub 157
Rodenhurst Rd. SW4 . . . . 58Lb 112
Roden St. IG1: Ilf 34Qc 74
N7 . . . . 34Pb 70
Roden Way *IG1: Ilf* *34Qc 74*
(off Roden St.)
Rodeo Cl. DA8: Erith 53Kd 119
Roderick Ho. *SE16* *49Yb 92*
(off Raymouth Rd.)
Roderick Rd. NW3 . . . . 35Hb 69
Rodgers Cl. WD6: E'tree 16Ma 29
Rodgers Ho. *SW4* *59Mb 112*
(off Clapham Pk. Est.)
Rodin Ct. *N1* *39Rb 71*
(off Essex Rd.)
Roding CM14: B'wood 18Xd 40
Roding Av. IG8: Wfd G 23Nc 54
Roding Gdns. IG10: Lough 16Nc 36
Roding Ho. N1 . . . . 1K 217
Roding La. IG7: Chig 19Qc 36
IG9: Buck H 18Mc 35
Roding La. Nth. IG8: Wfd G 23Nc 54
Roding La. Sth. IG4: Ilf, Wfd G 28Mc 53
(not continuous)
IG8: Wfd G 28Mc 53
Roding M. E1 . . . . 46Wb 91
Roding Rd. E5 . . . . 35Zb 72
E6 . . . . 43Rc 94
IG10: Lough 15Nc 36
Rodings, The IG8: Wfd G 23Lc 53
RM14: Upm 30Td 58
Rodings Row *EN5: Barn* *14Ab 30*
(off Leecroft Rd.)
Roding Trad. Est. IG11: Bark 38Rc 74
Roding Valley Meadows Nature Reserve
. . . . 17Qc 36
Roding Vw. IG9: Buck H 18Mc 35
Roding Way RM13: Rain 40Md 77
Rodmarton St. W1 . . . . 1G 221 (43Hb 89)
Rodmell WC1 . . . . 4G 217
Rodmell Cl. UB4: Yead 42Aa 85
Rodmell Slope N12 . . . . 22Bb 49
Rodmere St. SE10 . . . . 50Gc 93
Rodmill La. SW2 . . . . 59Nb 112
Rodney Av. AL1: St A 4E 6
Rodney Cl. CR0: C'don 74Rb 157
HA5: Pinn 31Aa 65
KT3: N Mald 71Ua 154
KT12: Walt T 74Y 151
Rodney Ct. EN5: Barn 13Bb 31
W9 . . . . 5A 214 (42Eb 89)
Rodney Gdns. BR4: W W'ck 77Jc 159
HA5: Eastc 29X 45
Rodney Grn. KT12: Walt T 75Y 151
Rodney Ho. *E14* *49Dc 92*
(off Cahir St.)
N1 . . . . 2J 217
SW1 . . . . *50Lb 90*
(off Dolphin Sq.)
W11 . . . . *45Cb 89*
(off Pembridge Cres.)
Rodney Pl. E17 . . . . 26Ac 52
SE17 . . . . 5E 230 (49Sb 91)
SW19 . . . . 67Eb 133
Rodney Point *SE16* *47Bc 92*
(off Rotherhithe St.)
Rodney Rd. CR4: Mitc 69Gb 133
E11 . . . . 28Kc 53
KT3: N Mald 71Ua 154
KT12: Walt T 75Y 151
SE17 . . . . 5E 230 (49Sb 91)
(not continuous)
TW2: Whitt 58Ca 107
Rodney St. N1 . . . . 1J 217 (40Pb 70)
Rodney Way RM7: Mawney 25Dd 56
SL3: Poyle 53G 104
Rodona Rd. KT13: Weyb 83T 170
Rodway Rd. BR1: Brom 67Kc 137
SW15 . . . . 59Wa 110
Rodwell Cl. HA4: Ruis 32Y 65
Rodwell Ct. KT12: Walt T 76X 151
KT15: Add 77L 149
Rodwell Pl. HA8: Edg 23Qa 47
Rodwell Rd. SE22 . . . . 58Vb 113
Roe NW9 . . . . 24Va 48
Roebourne Way E16 . . . . 46Qc 94
Roebuck Cl. KT21: Asht 92Na 193
N17 . . . . 23Vb 51
RH2: Reig 6J 207
TW13: Felt 63X 129
Roebuck Grn. SL1: Slou 6C 80
Roebuck Hgts. IG9: Buck H 17Lc 35
Roebuck La. IG9: Buck H 17Lc 35
Roebuck Rd. IG6: Ilf 22Xc 55
KT9: Chess 78Qa 153
Roebuck Rd. Trad. Est. IG6: Ilf 23Xc 55
Roedean Av. EN3: Enf H 11Yb 34
Roedean Cl. BR6: Chels 77Xc 161
EN3: Enf H 11Yb 34
Roedean Cres. SW15 . . . . 58Ua 110
Roedean Dr. RM1: Rom 28Gd 56
Roedean Ho. *WD24: Wat* *12Y 27*
(off Exeter Cl.)
Roe End NW9 . . . . 28Sa 47
Roefields Cl. HP3: Hem H 6J 3
ROE GREEN 28Sa 47
Roe Grn. NW9 . . . . 29Sa 47
Roe Grn. Cl. AL10: Hat 1A 8
ROEHAMPTON 59Wa 110
Roehampton Cl. DA12: Grav'nd 9G 122
SW15 . . . . 56Wa 110
Roehampton Dr. BR7: Chst 65Sc 138
Roehampton Ga. SW15 . . . . 58Ua 110
Roehampton Golf Course 56Va 110
Roehampton High St. SW15 . . . . 59Wa 110
Roehampton Ho. RM8: Dag 36Wc 75
ROEHAMPTON LANE 60Xa 110
Roehampton La. SW15 . . . . 56Wa 110
Roehampton Sport & Fitness Cen.
. . . . 59Wa 110
Roehampton University 58Va 110
Roehampton Va. SW15 . . . . 62Va 132
Roe Hill Cl. AL10: Hat 1B 8
ROEHYDE 2A 8
Roehyde Way AL10: Hat 2A 8
Roe La. NW9 . . . . 28Ra 47
Roesel Pl. BR5: Pet W 71Rc 160
ROESTOCK 5P 7
Roestock Gdns. AL4: Col H 4A 8
Roestock La. AL4: Col H 5P 7
Roe Way SM6: Wall 79Nb 156
Rofant Rd. HA6: Nwood 23U 44
Roffe's La. CR3: Cat'm 96Tb 197
Roffey Cl. CR8: Purl 88Rb 177
Roffey St. E14 . . . . 47Ec 92
Roffo Ct. *SE17* *51Tb 113*
(off Boundary La.)
Roffords GU21: Wok 9M 167
Rogate Ho. E5 . . . . 34Wb 71
Roger Dowley Ct. E2 . . . . 40Yb 72
Roger Harriss Almshouses *E15* *39Hc 73*
(off Gift La.)
Roger Reede's Almshouses
RM1: Rom 28Gd 56
Rogers Cl. CR3: Cat'm 94Xb 197
CR5: Coul 90Rb 177
Rogers Ct. BR8: Swan 70Jd 140
E14 . . . . *45Cc 92*
(off Premiere Pl.)
Rogers Est. E2 . . . . 41Yb 92
(not continuous)
Rogers Gdns. RM10: Dag 36Cd 76
Roger's Ho. RM10: Dag 34Cd 76
Rogers Ho. SW1 . . . . 5E 228
Roger Simmons Ct.
KT23: Bookh 96Ba 191
Rogers La. CR6: W'ham 90Bc 178
SL2: Stoke P 8K 61
Rogers Mead RH9: G'stone 4P 209
Rogers Rd. E16 . . . . 44Hc 93
RM10: Dag 36Cd 76
RM17: Grays 49Ee 99
SW17 . . . . 63Fb 133
Rogers Ruff HA6: Nwood 25S 44
Roger St. WC1 . . . . 6J 217 (42Pb 90)
Rogers Wlk. N12 . . . . 20Db 31
Rogers Wood La. DA3: Fawk 77Wd 164
Rohere Ho. EC1 . . . . 3D 218 (41Sb 91)
Rojack Rd. SE23 . . . . 60Zb 114
Rokeby Ct. GU21: Wok 9K 167
Rokeby Gdns. IG8: Wfd G 25Jc 53
Rokeby Ho. *SW12* *59Kb 112*
(off Lochinvar St.)
WC1 . . . . 6H 217
Rokeby Pl. SW20 . . . . 66Xa 132
Rokeby Rd. HA1: Harr 27Fa 46
SE4 . . . . 54Bc 114
Rokeby St. E15 . . . . 39Fc 73
Roke Cl. CR8: Kenley 86Sb 177
Rokell Ho. *BR3: Beck* *64Dc 136*
(off Beckenham Hill Rd.)
Roke Lodge Rd. CR8: Kenley 85Rb 177
Roke Rd. CR8: Kenley 87Sb 177
Roker Pk. Av. UB10: Ick 35N 63
Rokesby Cl. DA16: Well 54Tc 116
Rokesby Pl. HA0: Wemb 36Ma 67
Rokesby Rd. SL2: Slou 1D 80
Rokesly Av. N8 . . . . 29Nb 50
Rokewood Apartments
BR3: Beck 67Cc 136
Roland Gdns. SW7 . . . . 7A 226 (50Eb 89)
SW10 . . . . 7A 226 (50Eb 89)
Roland Ho. SW7 . . . . 7A 226
Roland Mans. SW7 . . . . 6A 226
Roland M. E1 . . . . 43Zb 92
Roland Rd. E17 . . . . 28Fc 53
Roland St. AL1: St A 2E 6
Roland Way KT4: Wor Pk 75Va 154
SE17 . . . . 50Tb 91
SW7 . . . . 7A 226 (50Eb 89)
Roles Gro. RM6: Chad H 28Zc 55
Rolfe Cl. EN4: E Barn 14Gb 31
Rolinsden Way BR2: Kes 78Mc 159
Rolland Ho. W7 . . . . 43Ga 86

Roshni Ho. SW17 .65Gb 133
Rosie's Way RM15: S Ock .44Zd 99
Rosina St. E9 .37Zb 72
Rosing Apartments
BR2: Brom .70Lc 137
(off Homesdale Rd.)
Roskeen Ct. SW20 .66Ya 132
Roskell Rd. SW15 .55Za 110
Rosken Gro. SL2: Farn R .10F 60
Rosler Bldg. SE1 .7D 224
Roslin Ho. *E1* .45Zb 92
(off Brodlove La.)
Roslin Rd. W3 .48Ra 87
Roslin Way BR1: Brom .64Jc 137
Roslyn Cl. CR4: Mitc .68Fb 133
Roslyn Ct. GU21: Wok .10L 167
Roslyn Gdns. RM2: Rom .26Hd 56
Roslyn Rd. N15 .29Tb 51
Rosmead Rd. W11 .45Ab 88
Rosoman Pl. EC1 .5A 218 (42Qb 90)
Rosoman St. EC1 .4A 218 (41Qb 90)
Rossall Cl. RM11: Horn .30Jd 56
Rossall Cres. NW10 .41Pa 87
Ross Apartments *E16* .45Jc 93
(off Seagull La.)
Ross Av. RM8: Dag .32Bd 75
Ross Cl. HA3: Hrw W .24Ea 46
UB3: Harl .49T 84
UB5: N'olt .35Fa 66
Ross Ct. *E5* .35Xb 71
(off Napoleon Rd.)
NW9 .27Ua 48
SW15 .59Za 110
W13 .43Ka 86
(off Cleveland Rd.)
Rosscourt Mans. SW1 .3A 228
Ross Cres. WD25: Wat .7W 12
Rossdale SM1: Sutt .78Gb 155
Rossdale Dr. N9 .16Yb 34
NW9 .32Sa 67
Rossdale Rd. SW15 .56Ya 110
Rosse Gdns. SE13 .58Fc 115
Rosse M. SE3 .53Kc 115
Rossendale Cl. EN2: Enf .8Rb 19
Rossendale St. E5 .33Xb 71
Rossendale Way NW1 .38Lb 70
Rossetti *CR0: C'don* .74Sb 157
(off Saffron Central Sq.)
Rossetti Ct. WC1 .7D 216
Rossetti Gdn. Mans. *SW3* .51Hb 111
(off Flood St.)
Rossetti Gdns. CR5: Coul .90Pb 176
Rossetti Ho. SW1 .6E 228
Rossetti M. NW8 .1C 214 (39Fb 69)
Rossetti Rd. SE16 .50Xb 91
Rossetti Studios *SW3* .51Gb 111
(off Flood St.)
Ross Haven Pl. HA6: Nwood .25V 44
Ross Ho. *E1* .46Xb 91
(off Prusom St.)
Rossignol Gdns. SM5: Cars .75Jb 156
Rossindel Rd. TW3: Houn .57Ca 107
Rossington Av. WD6: Bore .10Na 15
Rossington Cl. EN1: Enf .10Xb 19
Rossington St. E5 .33Wb 71
Rossiter Cl. SE19 .66Sb 135
SL3: L'ly .49A 82
Rossiter Flds. EN5: Barn .16Ab 30
Rossiter Gro. SW9 .55Qb 112
Rossiter Rd. SW12 .60Kb 112
Rossland Cl. DA6: Bex .57Dd 118
Rosslare Cl. TN16: Westrm .97Tc 200
Rosslyn Av. E4 .19Hc 35
EN4: E Barn .16Gb 31
RM3: Hrld W .26Nd 57
RM8: Dag .31Bd 75
SW13 .55Ua 110
TW14: Felt .58W 106
Rosslyn Cl. BR4: W W'ck .76Hc 159
TW16: Sun .65U 128
UB3: Hayes .43T 84
Rosslyn Cres. HA1: Harr .28Ha 46
HA9: Wemb .35Na 67
Rosslyn Gdns. HA9: Wemb .34Na 67
Rosslyn Hill NW3 .35Fb 69
Rosslyn Mans. *NW6* .38Eb 69
(off Goldhurst Ter.)
Rosslyn M. NW3 .35Fb 69
Rosslyn Pk. KT13: Weyb .77T 150
Rosslyn Pk. M. NW3 .36Fb 69
Rosslyn Rd. E17 .28Ec 52
IG11: Bark .38Tc 74
TW1: Twick .58La 108
WD18: Wat .13X 27
Rossmere M. CM14: B'wood .18Yd 40
Rossmore Cl. EN3: Pond E .14Zb 34
NW1 .6E 214
Rossmore Ct. NW1 .5F 215 (42Hb 89)
Rossmore Rd. NW1 .6E 214 (42Gb 89)
Ross Pde. SM6: Wall .79Kb 156
Ross Rd. DA1: Dart .58Jd 118
KT11: Cobh .85Y 171
SE25 .69Tb 135
SM6: Wall .78Lb 156
TW2: Whitt .60Da 107
Ross Wlk. SE27 .62Tb 135
Ross Way E14 .44Ac 92
HA6: Nwood .21V 44
SE9 .55Nc 116
Rossway Bus. Cen. WD23: Bush .15Fa 28
Rossway Dr. WD23: Bush .15Ea 28
Rosswood Gdns. SM6: Wall .79Lb 156
Rostella Rd. SW17 .63Fb 133
Rostrevor Av. N15 .30Vb 51
Rostrevor Gdns. SL0: Iver H .40F 62
UB2: S'hall .50Aa 85
UB3: Hayes .46U 84
Rostrevor Mans. *SW6* .53Bb 111
(off Rostrevor Rd.)
Rostrevor M. SW6 .53Bb 111
Rostrevor Rd. SW6 .53Bb 111
SW19 .64Cb 133
Roswell Apartments *E3* .43Bc 92
(off Joseph St.)
Roswell Cl. EN8: Chesh .2Ac 20
Rotary Ho. RM17: Grays .48Ee 99
Rotary St. SE1 .3B 230 (48Rb 91)
Rothay NW1 .3A 216
Rothbury Av. RM13: Rain .43Kd 97
Rothbury Cotts. *SE10* .49Gc 93
(off Maritius Rd.)
Rothbury Gdns. TW7: Isle .52Ja 108
Rothbury Rd. E9 .38Bc 72
Rothbury Wlk. N17 .24Wb 51
Roth Dr. CM13: Hut .19De 41
Rotheley Ho. *E9* .38Yb 72
(off Balcorne St.)
Rother Cl. WD25: Wat .6Y 13
Rotherfield Ct. *N1* .38Tb 71
(off Rotherfield St.)
Rotherfield Rd. EN3: Enf W .9Zb 20
SM5: Cars .77Jb 156
Rotherfield St. N1 .38Sb 71
Rotherham Wlk. SE1 .7B 224
Rotherhill Av. SW16 .65Mb 134
ROTHERHITHE .47Yb 92
Rotherhithe Bus. Est. SE16 .49Xb 91
Rotherhithe New Rd. SE16 .50Xb 91
Rotherhithe Old Rd. SE16 .49Zb 92
Rotherhithe St. SE16 .47Yb 92
Rotherhithe Tunnel SE16 .46Zb 92
Rother Ho. SE15 .56Xb 113
Rotherwick Hill W5 .42Pa 87
Rotherwick Ho. *E1* .45Wb 91
(off Thomas More St.)
Rotherwick Rd. NW11 .31Cb 69
Rotherwood Cl. SW20 .67Ab 132
Rotherwood Rd. SW15 .55Za 110
Rothery St. *N1* .39Rb 71
(off St Marys Path)
Rothery Ter. *SW9* .52Rb 113
(off Foxley Rd.)
Rothesay Av. SW20 .68Ab 132
TW10: Rich .56Ra 109
UB6: G'frd .37Ea 66
(not continuous)
Rothesay Ct. *SE6* .61Hc 137
(off Cumberland Pl.)
SE11 .51Qb 112
(off Harleyford St.)
SE12 .62Kc 137
Rothesay Rd. SE25 .70Tb 135
Rothley Ct. NW8 .5B 214
Rothsay Ct. KT13: Weyb .79T 150
Rothsay Rd. E7 .38Lc 73
Rothsay St. SE1 .3H 231 (48Ub 91)
Rothsay Wlk. *E14* .49Cc 92
(off Charnwood Gdns.)
Rothschild Rd. W4 .49Sa 87
Rothschild St. SE27 .63Rb 135
Roth Wlk. N7 .33Pb 70
Rothwell Ct. HA1: Harr .29Ha 46
Rothwell Gdns.
KT15: Add .79H 149
RM9: Dag .38Yc 75
Rothwell Ho. TW5: Hest .51Ca 107
Rothwell Rd. RM9: Dag .39Yc 75
Rothwell St. NW1 .39Hb 69
Rotten Row NW3 .32Eb 69
SW1 .1C 226 (47Fb 89)
SW7 .1C 226 (47Fb 89)
Rotterdam Dr. E14 .48Ec 92
Rotunda, The *RM7: Rom* .29Fd 56
(off Yew Tree Gdns.)
Rotunda Cen., The .68Na 131
Rotunda Ct. *BR1: Brom* .64Kc 137
(off Burnt Ash La.)
Rouel Rd. SE16 .49Wb 91
Rouge La. DA12: Grav'nd .10D 122
Rougemont Av. SM4: Mord .72Cb 155
Rough, The GU22: Wok .89F 168
Roughdown Av. HP3: Hem H .5J 3
Roughdown Rd. HP3: Hem H .5K 3
Roughdown Vs. Rd. HP3: Hem H .5J 3
ROUGHETS, THE .1M 209
Roughets La. RH1: Blet .1L 209
Roughlands GU22: Pyr .87G 168
Rough Rd. GU22: Wok .4G 186
Roughs, The HA6: Nwood .20U 26
ROUGHWAY .100De 205
Roughway La.
TN11: Dun G, Roug .100De 205
Roughwood Cl. WD17: Wat .10U 12
Roughwood Cft. HP8: Chal G .15A 24
Roughwood La. HP8: Chal G .17A 24
Rounce La. GU24: W End .5B 166
Roundabout Ho. HA6: Nwood .25W 44
Roundacre SW19 .61Za 132
Round Ash Way DA3: Hartl .72Ae 165
Roundaway Rd. IG5: Ilf .25Pc 54
Roundburrow Cl. CR6: W'ham .89Wb 177
ROUND BUSH .10Fa 14
Roundbush La. WD25: A'ham .10Ea 14
Roundel Cl. SE4 .56Bc 114
Round Gro. CR0: C'don .73Zb 158
Roundhay Cl. SE23 .61Zb 136
Roundhedge Way EN2: Enf .10Pb 18
Round Hill SE26 .61Yb 136
(not continuous)
Roundhill GU22: Wok .91D 188
Roundhill Dr. EN2: Enf .14Pb 32
GU22: Wok .90D 168
Roundhills EN9: Walt A .6Gc 21
Roundhill Way KT11: Cobh .83Da 171
Roundhouse, The .38Jb 70
Round Ho. Ct. EN8: Chesh .1Zb 20
Roundhouse La. *E20* .37Ec 72
(off International Way)
Roundlyn Gdns. BR5: St M Cry .70Xc 139
Roundmead Av. IG10: Lough .12Qc 36
Roundmead Cl. IG10: Lough .13Qc 36
Roundmoor Dr. EN8: Chesh .1Ac 20
Round Oak Rd. KT13: Weyb .77P 149
ROUNDSHAW .80Nb 156
Roundshaw Downs Local Nature Reserve
.81Pb 176
ROUND STREET .10F 144
Round St. DA13: Sole S .9E 144
Roundtable Rd. BR1: Brom .62Hc 137
Roundthorn Way GU21: Wok .8K 167
Roundtree Rd. HA0: Wemb .36Ka 66
Roundway TN16: Big H .88Lc 179
TW20: Egh .64E 126
Roundway, The KT10: Clay .79Ha 152
N17 .25Sb 51
WD18: Wat .16V 26
Roundways HA4: Ruis .34V 64
Round Wood WD4: K Lan .9N 3
Roundwood BR7: Chst .68Rc 138
Roundwood Av. CM13: Hut .18Ce 41
UB11: Stock P .46S 84
Roundwood Cl. HA4: Ruis .31T 64
Roundwood Ct. E2 .41Zb 92
Roundwood Gro. CM13: Hut .17De 41
Roundwood Lake CM13: Hut .17De 41
Roundwood Rd. NW10 .37Va 68
Roundwood Vw. SM7: Bans .87Za 174
Roundwood Way SM7: Bans .87Za 174
Rounton Cl. WD17: Wat .10V 12
Rounton Rd. E3 .42Cc 92
EN9: Walt A .5Gc 21
Roupell Ho. *KT2: King T* .66Pa 131
(off Florence Rd.)
Roupell Rd. SW2 .60Pb 112
Roupell St. SE1 .7A 224 (46Qb 90)
Rousden St. NW1 .38Lb 70
Rousebarn La.
WD3: Chan C, Crox G .10P 11
Rouse Cl. KT13: Weyb .77V 150
Rouse Cl. SL9: Ger X .29B 42
Rouse Gdns. SE21 .63Ub 135
Rous Rd. IG9: Buck H .18Nc 36
Routemaster Cl. E13 .41Kc 93
Routh Ct. TW14: Bedf .60T 106
Routh Rd. SW18 .59Gb 111
Routh St. E6 .43Pc 94
Rover Av. IG6: Ilf .23Vc 55
Rover Ho. N1 .1J 219
Row, The DA3: Nw A G .75Be 165
Rowallan Rd. SW6 .52Ab 110
Rowallen Pde. RM8: Dag .32Yc 75
Rowan N10 .26Kb 50
Rowan Av. E4 .23Bc 52
TW20: Egh .64E 126
Rowan Cl. AL2: Brick W .3Ca 13
AL4: St A .2J 7
HA0: Wemb .34Ja 66
HA7: Stan .23Ha 46
HP2: Hem H .2P 3
IG1: Ilf .36Tc 74
KT3: N Mald .68Ua 132
RH2: Reig .8L 207
SM7: Bans .87Za 174
SW16 .67Lb 134
TW15: Ashf .63M 127
W5 .47Na 87
WD7: Shenl .5Na 15
Rowan Ct. *E13* .40Kc 73
(off High St.)
SE15 .52Vb 113
(off Garnies Cl.)
SW11 .58Hb 111
WD6: Bore .14Qa 29
Rowan Cres. DA1: Dart .60Ld 119
SW16 .67Lb 134
Rowan Dr. NW9 .27Wa 48
Rowan Gdns. CR0: C'don .76Vb 157
SL0: Iver H .40F 62
Rowan Grn. KT13: Weyb .77T 150
Rowan Grn. E. CM13: B'wood .21Be 59
Rowan Grn. W. CM13: B'wood .20Be 41
Rowan Gro. CR5: Coul .93Kb 196
RM15: Avel .45Sd 98
Rowan Ho. BR2: Brom .68Gc 137
DA14: Sidc .62Vc 139
E3 .39Bc 72
(off Hornbeam Sq.)
IG1: Ilf .36Tc 74
SE16 .47Zb 92
(off Woodland Cres.)
Rowanhurst Dr. SL2: Farn C .6G 60
Rowan Lodge *W8* .48Db 89
(off Chantry Sq.)
Rowan Mead KT20: Tad .91Xa 194
Rowan Pl. UB3: Hayes .45V 84
Rowan Rd. BR8: Swan .69Fd 140
DA7: Bex .55Ad 117
SW16 .68Lb 134
TW8: Bford .52Ka 108
UB7: W Dray .49M 83
W6 .49Za 88
Rowans, The *EN9: Walt A* .7Lc 21
(within Woodbine Cl. Cvn. Pk.)
GU22: Wok .90A 168
HP1: Hem H .2J 3
N13 .20Rb 33
RM15: Avel .46Sd 98
TW16: Sun .64V 128
Rowans Cl. DA3: Lfield .68Zd 143
Rowans Complex .33Qb 70
Rowans Way IG10: Lough .14Pc 36
Rowan Ter. SW19 .66Ab 132
W6 .49Za 88
Rowantree Cl. N21 .18Tb 33
Rowantree Rd. EN2: Enf .12Rb 33
N21 .18Tb 33
Rowan Wlk. AL10: Hat .3C 8
BR2: Brom .76Pc 160
EN5: New Bar .15Db 31
N2 .29Eb 49
N19 .33Lb 70
RM11: Horn .28Md 57
W10 .42Ab 88
Rowan Way RM6: Chad H .27Yc 55
RM15: S Ock .42Yd 98
SL2: Slou .3F 80
Rowanwood Av. DA15: Sidc .60Wc 117
Rowanwood M. EN2: Enf .12Rb 33
Rowben Cl. N20 .18Db 31
Rowberry Cl. SW6 .52Ya 110
Rowbourne Pl. EN6: Cuff .1Mb 18
Rowcroft HP1: Hem H .3G 2
Rowcross St. SE1 .7K 231 (50Vb 91)
Rowdell Rd. UB5: N'olt .39Ca 65
Rowden Pde. *E4* .23Cc 52
(off Chingford Rd.)
Rowden Pk. Gdns. E4 .24Cc 52
Rowden Rd. BR3: Beck .67Ac 136
E4 .23Dc 52
KT19: Ewe .77Ra 153
Rowditch La. SW11 .54Jb 112
Rowdon Av. NW10 .38Xa 68
Row Dow TN14: Otf .88Md 183
Row Dow La. TN15: Knat .85Md 183
Rowdown Cres. CR0: New Ad .81Fc 179
Rowdowns Rd. RM9: Dag .39Bd 75
Rowe Gdns. IG11: Bark .40Vc 75
Rowe Ho. E9 .37Yb 72
Rowe La. E9 .36Yb 72
GU24: Pirb .6E 186
Rowena Cres. SW11 .54Gb 111
Rowenhurst Mans. *NW6* .37Eb 69
(off Canfield Gdns.)
Rowe Wlk. HA2: Harr .34Ca 65
Rowfant Rd. SW17 .60Jb 112
Rowhedge CM13: B'wood .20Ce 41
ROWHILL .79H 149
Rowhill KT15: Add .79H 149
Rowhill Rd. BR8: Hext .65Hd 140
DA2: Wilm .65Hd 140
E5 .35Xb 71
Rowhurst Av. KT15: Add .79K 149
KT22: Lea .89Ha 172
Rowington Cl. W2 .43Db 89
Rowland Av. HA3: Kenton .27La 46
Rowland Cl. SL4: Wind .5B 102
Rowland Ct. E16 .42Hc 93
Rowland Cres. IG7: Chig .21Uc 54
Rowland Gro. SE26 .62Xb 135
(not continuous)
Rowland Hill Almshouses
TW15: Ashf .64Q 128
(off Feltham Hill Rd.)
Rowland Hill Av. N17 .24Sb 51
Rowland Hill Ho. SE1 .1B 230 (47Rb 91)
Rowland Hill St. NW3 .36Gb 69
Rowland Pl. CR8: Purl .88Qb 176
HA6: Nwood .24U 44
Rowlands Av. HA5: Hat E .22Ca 45
Rowlands Cl. EN8: Chesh .2Zb 20
N6 .30Jb 50
NW7 .24Wa 48
Rowlands Ct. *EN8: Chesh* .2Zb 20
(off Rowlandsfields)
Rowlandsfields EN8: Chesh .1Zb 20
Rowlands Rd. RM8: Dag .33Bd 75
Rowland Wlk.
RM4: Have B .20Gd 38
Rowland Way SW19 .67Db 133
TW15: Ashf .66T 128
Rowlatt Cl. DA2: Wilm .63Ld 141
Rowlatt Ct. *AL1: St A* .1C 6
(off Hillside Rd.)
Rowlatt Dr. AL3: St A .4N 5
Rowlatt Rd. DA2: Wilm .63Ld 141
Rowley Av. DA15: Sidc .59Xc 117
Rowley Cl. GU22: Pyr .88K 169
HA0: Wemb .38Pa 67
WD19: Wat .16Aa 27
Rowley Ct. CR3: Cat'm .94Tb 197
EN1: Enf .15Ub 33
(off Wellington Rd.)
Rowley Gdns. EN8: Chesh .1Zb 20
N4 .31Sb 71
ROWLEY GREEN .14Va 30
Rowley Green Common Nature Reserve
.14Va 30
Rowley Grn. Rd. EN5: Ark .15Va 30
Rowley Ho. *SE8* .50Cc 92
(off Watergate St.)
Rowley Ind. Pk. W3 .48Ra 87
Rowley La. EN5: Ark .14Ua 30
SL3: Wex .9N 61
WD6: Bore .11Ta 29
Rowley Lane Golf Course .14Ua 30
Rowley Lane Sports Ground .14Ua 30
Rowley Rd. N15 .29Sb 51
RM16: Ors .3C 100
Rowley Way NW8 .39Db 69
Rowlheys Pl. UB7: W Dray .48N 83
Rowlls Rd. KT1: King T .69Pa 131
Rowlock Ho. UB7: Yiew .45M 83
Rowmarsh Cl. DA11: Nflt .62Fe 143
Rowney Gdns. RM9: Dag .37Xc 75
Rowney Rd. RM9: Dag .37Xc 75
Rowntree Clifford Cl. E13 .42Jc 93
Rowntree Cl. NW6 .37Cb 69
Rowntree M. E17 .25Bc 52
Rowntree Path SE28 .46Xc 95
Rowntree Rd. TW2: Twick .60Ga 108
Rowse Cl. E15 .39Ec 72
Rowsley Av. NW4 .27Ya 48
Rowstock Gdns. N7 .36Mb 70
Rowton Rd. SE18 .52Sc 116
ROW TOWN .79J 149
Row Town KT15: Add .80H 149
Rowzill Rd. BR8: Hext .65Hd 140
Roxborough Av. HA1: Harr .31Fa 66
TW7: Isle .52Ha 108
Roxborough Hgts. *HA1: Harr* .30Ga 46
(off College Rd.)
Roxborough Pk. HA1: Harr .31Ga 66
Roxborough Rd. HA1: Harr .29Fa 46
Roxbourne Cl. UB5: N'olt .37Z 65
Roxbourne Pk. Miniature Railway .33Z 65
Roxburgh Av. RM14: Upm .34Sd 78
Roxburghe Mans. *W8* .47Db 89
(off Kensington Ct.)
Roxburgh Pl. BR1: Brom .67Nc 138
Roxburgh Rd. SE27 .64Rb 135
Roxburn Way HA4: Ruis .34V 64
ROXETH .33Fa 66
Roxeth Ct. TW15: Ashf .64Q 128
Roxeth Grn. Av. HA2: Harr .34Da 65
UB5: N'olt .36Ca 65
Roxeth Gro. HA2: Harr .35Da 65
Roxeth Hill HA2: Harr .33Fa 66
Roxford Cl. TW17: Shep .71U 150
Roxford Ho. *E3* .42Dc 92
(off Devas St.)
Roxley Rd. SE13 .58Dc 114
Roxton Gdns. CR0: Addtn .78Cc 158
Roxwell *NW1* .37Kb 70
(off Hartland Rd.)
Roxwell Cl. SL1: Slou .6C 80
Roxwell Gdns. CM13: Hut .15Ee 41
Roxwell Ho. IG10: Lough .17Nc 36
Roxwell Rd. IG11: Bark .40Wc 75
W12 .47Wa 88
Roxwell Trad. Pk. E10 .31Ac 72
Roxwell Way IG8: Wfd G .24Lc 53
Roxy Av. RM6: Chad H .31Yc 75
Royal Academy of Arts (Burlington House)
.5B 222 (45Lb 90)
Royal Academy of Music Mus. .6J 215
Royal Air Force Memorial
.7G 223 (46Nb 90)
Royal Albert Hall .2B 226 (47Fb 89)
ROYAL ALBERT RDBT. .45Nc 94
(off Royal Albert Way)
Royal Albert Way E16 .45Mc 93
Royal Arc. W1 .5B 222
Royal Archer *SE14* .52Zb 114
(off Egmont St.)
ROYAL ARSENAL WEST .48Rc 94
Royal Ascot Golf Course .7A 124
Royal Av. EN8: Walt C .5Ac 20
KT4: Wor Pk .75Ua 154
SW3 .7F 227 (50Hb 89)
Royal Av. Ho. SW3 .7F 227
Royal Belgrave Ho. SW1 .6A 228
Royal Blackheath Golf Course .59Pc 116
Royal Botanic Gdns.
Kew .53Na 109
Royal Brass Foundry .48Rc 94
Royal Carriage M. SE18 .48Rc 94
Royal Cir. SE27 .62Qb 134
Royal Cl. BR6: Farnb .77Rc 160
IG3: Ilf .31Wc 75
KT4: Wor Pk .75Ua 154
N16 .32Ub 71
SE8 .51Bc 114
SW19 .62Za 132
UB8: Hil .44P 83
Royal College of Art .2A 226 (47Fb 89)
Royal College of Music .3B 226 (48Fb 89)
Royal College of Obstetricians &
Gynaecologists .5F 215 (42Hb 89)
Royal College of Physicians .5A 216
Royal College of Physicians Mus. .5A 216
Royal College of Surgeons .2J 223
Royal Coll. St. NW1 .1D 216 (38Lb 70)
Royal Connaught Apartments
E16 .46Mc 93
(off Connaught Rd.)
Royal Connaught Dr. WD23: Bush .14Ba 27
Royal Connaught Pk. WD23: Bush .14Ba 27
Royal Ct. EC3 .3G 225
EN1: Enf .16Ub 33
HA4: Ruis .30W 44
HP3: Hem H .5N 3
SE9 .60Pc 116
SE16 .48Bc 92
WD18: Wat .14U 26
WD23: Bush .15Aa 27
Royal Courts of Justice .3J 223
Royal Court Theatre .6H 227
Royal Cres. HA4: Ruis .35Aa 65
IG2: Ilf .30Tc 54
W11 .46Za 88
Royal Cres. M. W11 .46Za 88
Royal Docks Rd. E6 .44Rc 94
IG11: Bark .44Rc 94
Royal Dr. KT18: Tatt C .90Xa 174
N11 .22Jb 50
(not continuous)
Royal Duchess M. SW12 .59Kb 112
Royal Earlswood Pk.
RH1: Redh .9A 208
Royale Leisure Pk. W3 .42Qa 87
Royal Engineers Way NW7 .23Ab 48
Royal Epping Forest & Chingford Golf Course
.17Gc 35
Royal Exchange .3G 225 (44Tb 91)
Royal Exchange Av. EC3 .3G 225
Royal Exchange Bldgs. EC3 .3G 225
Royal Festival Hall .7J 223 (46Pb 90)
Royal Free Ct. *SL4: Wind* .3H 103
(off Bachelors Acre)
Royal Fusiliers Mus. .45Vb 91
Royal Gdns. W7 .48Ja 86
Royal Geographical Society .2B 226
Royal George M. SE5 .56Tb 113
Royal Gunpowder Mills .4Dc 20
Royal Herbert Pavilions SE18 .53Pc 116
Royal Hill SE10 .52Ec 114
Royal Hill Ct. *SE10* .52Ec 114
(off Greenwich High St.)
Royal Holloway (University of London)
Egham Hill .5P 125
Gower Street .7E 216
Sports Cen. .66A 126
Royal Horticultural Society Cotts.
GU23: Wis .88N 169
Royal Hospital Chelsea Mus.
.7H 227 (50Jb 90)
Royal Hospital Rd.
SW3 .7G 227 (51Hb 111)
Royal Household Golf Course .3J 103
Royal Institution Mus. .5B 222 (45Lb 90)
Royal Jubilee Ct. RM2: Rom .27Jd 56
Royal La. UB7: Yiew .43P 83
UB8: Hil .43P 83
Royal Langford Apartments
NW6 .40Db 69
(off Greville Rd.)
Royal London Bldgs. *SE15* .51Xb 113
(off Old Kent Rd.)
Royal London Est., The N17 .23Xb 51
Royal London Hospital Archives & Mus.
.43Xb 91
(off Newark St.)
Royal London Ind. Est. NW10 .40Ta 67
Royal Mausoleum
Windsor .5J 103
Royal Mews, The .3A 228 (47Kb 90)
Royal M. KT8: E Mos .69Ga 130
SL4: Wind .3H 103
SW1 .3A 228 (48Kb 90)
Royal Mid-Surrey Golf Course .55Ma 109
Royal Mint Ct. EC3 .5K 225 (45Vb 91)
Royal Mint Pl. E1 .45Wb 91
Royal Mint St. E1 .4K 225 (45Vb 91)
Royal Naval Pl. SE14 .52Bc 114
Royal Oak Cotts. *HP1: Hem H* .1M 3
(off High St.)
Royal Oak Ct. N1 .3H 219
Royal Oak Hill TN14: Knock .90Vc 181
Royal Oak M. TW11: Tedd .64Ja 130
Royal Oak Pl. SE22 .58Xb 113
Royal Oak Rd. DA6: Bex .57Bd 117
(not continuous)
E8 .37Xb 71
GU21: Wok .10N 167
Royal Oak Ter. *DA12: Grav'nd* .10E 122
(off Parrock Rd.)
Royal Oak Yd. SE1 .2H 231 (47Ub 91)
Royal Observatory Greenwich .52Gc 115
Royal Opera Arc. SW1 .6D 222 (46Mb 90)
Royal Opera House .3G 223 (44Nb 90)
Royal Opera House, Bob &
Tamar Manoukian Production Workshop
.50Sd 98
Royal Orchard Cl. SW18 .59Ab 110
Royal Pde. BR7: Chst .66Sc 138
RM10: Dag .37Dd 76
SE3 .54Hc 115
SW6 .52Ab 110
TW9: Kew .53Qa 109
(off Station App.)
W5 .41Na 87
Royal Pde. M. *BR7: Chst* .66Sc 138
(off Royal Pde.)
SE3 .54Hc 115
(off Royal Pde.)
Royal Pier M. DA12: Grav'nd .8E 122
Royal Pier Rd. DA12: Grav'nd .8D 122
Royal Pl. SE10 .52Ec 114
Royal Quarter KT2: King T .67Na 131
Royal Quay UB9: Hare .24J 43
Royal Quay Rd. E16 .45Rc 94
Royal Rd. AL1: St A .2F 6
DA2: Hawl .64Qd 141
DA14: Sidc .62Zc 139
E16 .44Mc 93
SE17 .51Rb 113
TW11: Tedd .64Fa 130
Royal Route HA9: Wemb .35Pa 67
Royal St. SE1 .3J 229 (48Pb 90)
Royal Twr. Lodge *E1* .45Wb 91
(off Cartwright St.)
Royalty Mans. W1 .3D 222
Royalty M. W1 .3D 222 (44Mb 90)
Royalty Studios *W11* .44Ab 88
(off Lancaster Rd.)
Royal Veterinary College
Camden Town .1D 216 (39Mb 70)
Hawkshead Campus -
Boltons Park Site .1Cb 17
Hawkshead La. .10F 8

Royal Victoria Docks Watersports Cen.—Ruxton Ct.

Royal Victoria Docks Watersports Cen. . . . 45Jc 93
Royal Victoria Gdns. SE16 . . . 49Ac 92
(off Whiting Way)
Royal Victoria Patriotic Bldg.
SW18 . . . 58Fb 111
Royal Victoria Pl. E16 . . . 46Kc 93
Royal Victoria Sq. E16 . . . 45Kc 93
Royal Victor Pl. E3 . . . 40Zb 72
Royal Wlk. SM6: Wall . . . 75Kb 156
TW17: Shep . . . 74Q 150
Royal Westminster Lodge SW1 . . . 5D 228
Royal Wimbledon Golf Course . . . 64Xa 132
Royal Windsor Racecourse . . . 1D 102
Royal Windsor Way SL4: Wind . . . 3F 102
Royce Gro. WD25: Wat . . . 6V 12
Roycraft Av. IG11: Bark . . . 40Vc 75
Roycroft Av. IG11: Bark . . . 40Vc 75
Roycroft Cl. E18 . . . 25Kc 53
SW2 . . . 60Qb 112
Roydene Rd. SE18 . . . 51Uc 116
Roydon Cl. IG10: Lough . . . 17Nc 36
SW11 . . . 54Hb 111
(off Battersea Pk. Rd.)
Roydon Ct. KT12: Hers . . . 77W 150
TW20: Egh . . . 65F 126
Royds La. CM14: Kel H . . . 11Td 40
Roy Gdns. IG2: Ilf . . . 28Uc 54
Roy Gro. TW12: Hamp . . . 65Da 129
Royle Bldg. N1 . . . 1D 218
Royle Cl. RM2: Rom . . . 29Kd 57
SL9: Chal P . . . 24B 42
Royle Cres. W13 . . . 42Ja 86
Royley Ho. EC1 . . . 5E 218
Roymount Ct. TW2: Twick . . . 62Ga 130
Roy Richmond Way KT19: Eps . . . 82Ua 174
Roy Rd. HA6: Nwood . . . 24V 44
Roy Sq. E14 . . . 45Ac 92
Royston Av. E4 . . . 22Cc 52
KT14: Byfl . . . 84N 169
SM1: Sutt . . . 76Fb 155
SM6: Bedd . . . 77Mb 156
Royston Cl. KT12: Walt T . . . 74W 150
TW5: Cran . . . 53X 107
Royston Ct. E13 . . . 39Jc 73
(off Stopford Rd.)
KT10: Hin W . . . 75Ha 152
SE24 . . . 58Sb 113
TW9: Kew . . . 53Pa 109
W8 . . . 46Cb 89
(off Kensington Chu. St.)
Royston Gdns. IG1: Ilf . . . 30Mc 53
Royston Gro. HA5: Hat E . . . 23Ca 45
Royston Ho. N11 . . . 21Hb 49
SE15 . . . 51Xb 113
(off Friary Est.)
Royston Pde. IG1: Ilf . . . 30Mc 53
Royston Pk. KT14: Byfl . . . 84N 169
Royston Pk. Rd. HA5: Hat E . . . 23Ba 45
Royston Rd. AL1: St A . . . 3F 6
DA1: Cray . . . 58Hd 118
KT14: Byfl . . . 84N 169
RM3: Hrld W . . . 24Qd 57
SE20 . . . 67Zb 136
TW10: Rich . . . 57Na 109
Roystons, The KT5: Surb . . . 71Ra 153
Royston St. E2 . . . 40Yb 72
Royston Way SL1: Slou . . . 3B 80
Rozel Ct. N1 . . . 39Ub 71
Rozel Rd. SW4 . . . 55Lb 112
Rozel Ter. CR0: C'don . . . 76Sb 157
(off Church Rd.)
RQ33 SW18 . . . 56Cb 111
Rubastic Rd. UB2: S'hall . . . 48Y 85
Rubeck Cl. RH1: Redh . . . 4B 208
Rubens Ct. WD25: Wat . . . 8Z 13
Rubens Gdns. SE22 . . . 59Wb 113
(off Lordship La.)
Rubens Pl. SW4 . . . 56Nb 112
Rubens Rd. UB5: N'olt . . . 40Y 65
Rubens St. SE6 . . . 61Bc 136
Rubicon Ct. N1 . . . 39Nb 70
Rubin Pl. EN3: Enf L . . . 9Cc 20
Rubus Cl. GU24: W End . . . 5C 166
Ruby Cl. E5 . . . 34Zb 72
SL1: Slou . . . 7E 80
Ruby Ct. E15 . . . 39Ec 72
(off Warton Rd.)
RM8: Dag . . . 32Cd 76
(off Emerald Gdns.)
Ruby Rd. E17 . . . 27Cc 52
Ruby St. NW10 . . . 38Sa 67
SE15 . . . 51Xb 113
Ruby Triangle SE15 . . . 51Xb 113
Ruby Tuesday Dr. DA1: Dart . . . 54Pd 119
Ruby Way NW9 . . . 25Va 48
Ruckholt Cl. E10 . . . 34Dc 72
Ruckholt Rd. E10 . . . 35Cc 72
RUCKLERS LANE . . . 9M 3
Rucklers La. WD4: K Lan . . . 10J 3
Rucklidge Av. NW10 . . . 40Va 68
Rucklidge Pas. NW10 . . . 40Va 68
(off Rucklidge Av.)
Rudall Cres. NW3 . . . 35Fb 69
Rudbeck Ho. SE15 . . . 52Wb 113
(off Peckham Pk. Rd.)
Ruddington Cl. E5 . . . 35Ac 72
Ruddlesway SL4: Wind . . . 3B 102
Ruddock Cl. HA8: Edg . . . 24Sa 47
Ruddstreet Cl. SE18 . . . 49Rc 94
Ruddy Way NW7 . . . 23Va 48
Ruden Way KT17: Eps D . . . 88Xa 174
Rudge Ho. SE16 . . . 48Wb 91
(off Jamaica Rd.)
Rudge Ri. KT15: Add . . . 78H 149
Rudgwick Ct. SE18 . . . 49Nc 94
(off Woodville St.)
Rudgwick Ter. NW8 . . . 1E 214 (39Gb 69)
Rudland Rd. DA7: Bex . . . 55Dd 118
Rudloe Rd. SW12 . . . 59Lb 112
Rudolf Pl. SW8 . . . 51Nb 112
Rudolph Rd. E13 . . . 40Hc 73
NW6 . . . 40Cb 69
WD23: Bush . . . 16Ca 27
Rudstone Ho. E3 . . . 41Dc 92
(off Bromley High St.)
Rudsworth Cl. SL3: Coln . . . 53F 104
Rudyard Ct. CM14: W'ley . . . 22Xd 58
SE1 . . . 2G 231
Rudyard Gro. NW7 . . . 23Sa 47
Rue de St Lawrence EN9: Walt A . . . 6Ec 20
Ruegg Ho. SE18 . . . 51Qc 116
(off Woolwich Comn.)
Ruffets Wood DA12: Grav'nd . . . 5E 144
Ruffetts, The CR2: Sels . . . 80Xb 157
Ruffetts Cl. CR2: Sels . . . 80Xb 157
Ruffetts Way KT20: Tad . . . 90Ab 174
Ruffle Cl. UB7: W Dray . . . 47N 83
Rufford Cl. HA3: Kenton . . . 30Ja 46
WD17: Wat . . . 9V 12
Rufford St. N1 . . . 39Nb 70
Rufford St. M. N1 . . . 38Nb 70
Rufford Twr. W3 . . . 46Ra 87
Rufforth Ct. NW9 . . . 25Ua 48
(off Pageant Av.)
Rufus Bus. Cen. SW18 . . . 61Db 133
Rufus Cl. HA4: Ruis . . . 34Aa 65
Rufus Ho. SE1 . . . 3K 231
Rufus St. N1 . . . 4H 219 (41Ub 91)
Rugby Av. HA0: Wemb . . . 36Ka 66
N9 . . . 18Vb 33
UB6: G'frd . . . 37Fa 66
Rugby Cl. HA1: Harr . . . 28Ga 46
Rugby Gdns. RM9: Dag . . . 37Yc 75
Rugby La. SM2: Cheam . . . 81Za 174
Rugby Lodge WD24: Wat . . . 7U 12
Rugby Mans. W14 . . . 49Ab 88
(off Bishop King's Rd.)
Rugby Rd. NW9 . . . 28Ra 47
RM9: Dag . . . 38Xc 75
TW1: Twick . . . 57Ga 108
W4 . . . 47Ua 88
Rugby St. WC1 . . . 6H 217 (42Pb 90)
Rugby Way WD3: Crox G . . . 15R 26
Rugged La. EN9: Walt A . . . 5Mc 21
Ruggles-Brise Rd. TW15: Ashf . . . 64M 127
Rugg St. E14 . . . 45Cc 92
Rugless Ho. E14 . . . 47Ec 92
(off E. Ferry Rd.)
Rugmere NW1 . . . 38Jb 70
(off Ferdinand St.)
Rugosa Rd. GU24: W End . . . 5C 166
RUISLIP . . . 32U 64
Ruislip Cl. UB6: G'frd . . . 42Da 85
RUISLIP COMMON . . . 28S 44
Ruislip Ct. HA4: Ruis . . . 33V 64
RUISLIP GARDENS . . . 34W 64
Ruislip Golf Course . . . 33S 64
Ruislip Lido . . . 28T 44
Ruislip Lido Railway . . . 28T 44
Ruislip Lido Woodlands Cen. . . . 28T 44
RUISLIP MANOR . . . 33W 64
Ruislip Rd. UB5: N'olt . . . 39Y 65
UB6: G'frd . . . 41Ca 85
Ruislip Rd. E. UB6: G'frd . . . 42Fa 86
W7 . . . 42Ga 86
W13 . . . 42Fa 86
Ruislip St. SW17 . . . 63Hb 133
Ruislip Woods (National Nature Reserve) . . . 27S 44
Rumania Wlk. DA12: Grav'nd . . . 2H 145
Rumball Ho. SE5 . . . 52Ub 113
(off Harris St.)
Rumballs Cl. HP3: Hem H . . . 5A 4
Rumballs Rd. HP3: Hem H . . . 5A 4
Rumbold Rd. SW6 . . . 52Db 111
Rum Cl. E1 . . . 45Yb 92
Rumford Ho. SE1 . . . 4D 230
Rumford Shop. Hall RM1: Rom . . . 29Gd 56
Rumney Ct. UB5: N'olt . . . 40Z 65
(off Parkfield Dr.)
Rumsey Cl. TW12: Hamp . . . 65Ba 129
Rumsey M. N4 . . . 34Rb 71
Rumsey Rd. SW9 . . . 55Pb 112
Runacres Ct. SE17 . . . 7D 230 (50Sb 91)
Runbury Circ. NW9 . . . 33Ta 67
Runcie Ct. IG6: Ilf . . . 28Tc 54
Runciman Cl. BR6: Prat B . . . 82Yc 181
Runcorn Cl. N17 . . . 28Xb 51
Runcorn Ho. RM3: Rom . . . 23Nd 57
(off Kingsbridge Cir.)
Runcorn Pl. W11 . . . 45Ab 88
Rundell Cres. NW4 . . . 29Xa 48
Rundell Twr. SW8 . . . 53Pb 112
Runes Cl. CR4: Mitc . . . 70Fb 133
Runham Rd. HP3: Hem H . . . 4N 3
Runnel Ct. IG11: Bark . . . 40Sc 74
(off Spring Pl.)
Runnelfield HA1: Harr . . . 34Ga 66
Runnemede Rd. TW20: Egh . . . 63B 126
Running Horse Yd. TW8: Bford . . . 51Na 109
Running Waters CM13: B'wood . . . 21Ce 59
(not continuous)
RUNNYMEDE . . . 1P 125
Runnymede SW19 . . . 67Eb 133
Runnymede Cl. TW2: Whitt . . . 58Da 107
Runnymede Ct. DA2: Dart . . . 60Sd 120
SM6: Wall . . . 79Kb 156
SS17: Stan H . . . 2L 101
SW15 . . . 60Wa 110
TW20: Egh . . . 63C 126
Runnymede Cres. SW16 . . . 67Mb 134
Runnymede Gdns. TW2: Whitt . . . 58Da 107
UB6: G'frd . . . 40Ga 66
Runnymede Ga. KT15: Add . . . 78J 149
Runnymede Ho. E9 . . . 35Ac 72
KT16: Chert . . . 73J 149
(off London St.)
Runnymede Rd. SS17: Stan H . . . 2L 101
TW2: Whitt . . . 58Da 107
RUNNYMEDE RDBT. . . . 63D 126
Runtley Wood La. GU4: Sut G . . . 97B 188
Runway, The HA4: Ruis . . . 36X 65
Runway Cl. NW9 . . . 26Va 48
Rupack St. SE16 . . . 47Yb 92
Rupert Av. HA9: Wemb . . . 36Na 67
Rupert Ct. KT8: W Mole . . . 70Ca 129
(off St Peter's Rd.)
W1 . . . 4D 222 (45Mb 90)
Rupert Gdns. SW9 . . . 54Rb 113
Rupert Ho. SE11 . . . 7A 230 (49Qb 90)
SW5 . . . 49Cb 89
(off Nevern Sq.)
Rupert Rd. N19 . . . 34Mb 70
(not continuous)
NW6 . . . 40Bb 69
W4 . . . 48Ua 88
Rupert St. W1 . . . 4D 222 (45Mb 90)
Rural Cl. RM11: Horn . . . 32Kd 77
Rural Va. DA11: Nflt . . . 9A 122
Rural Way RH1: Redh . . . 6A 208
SW16 . . . 66Kb 134
Rusbridge Cl. E8 . . . 36Wb 71
Ruscoe Dr. GU22: Wok . . . 89C 168
Ruscoe Rd. E16 . . . 44Hc 93
Ruscombe NW1 . . . 1A 216
Ruscombe Dr. AL2: Park . . . 8A 6
Ruscombe Gdns. SL3: Dat . . . 2L 103
Ruscombe Way TW14: Felt . . . 59V 106
Ruscus Rd. E17 . . . 25Cc 52
Rush, The SW19 . . . 67Bb 133
(off Watery La.)
Rusham Ct. TW20: Egh . . . 65C 126
Rusham Pk. Av. TW20: Egh . . . 65B 126
Rusham Rd. SW12 . . . 58Hb 111
TW20: Egh . . . 65B 126
Rushbridge Cl. CR0: C'don . . . 72Sb 157
Rushbrook Cres. E17 . . . 25Bc 52
Rushbrook Rd. SE9 . . . 61Sc 138
Rushbury Ct. TW12: Hamp . . . 67Ca 129
Rush Comn. M. SW2 . . . 59Pb 112
Rushcroft Rd. E4 . . . 24Dc 52
SW2 . . . 56Qb 112
Rushcutters Ct. SE16 . . . 49Ac 92
(off Boat Lifter Way)
Rushden Cl. SE19 . . . 66Tb 135
Rushdene SE2 . . . 48Zc 95
(not continuous)
Rushdene Av. EN4: E Barn . . . 17Gb 31
Rushdene Cl. UB5: N'olt . . . 40Y 65
Rushdene Cres. UB5: N'olt . . . 40X 65
Rushdene Rd. CM15: B'wood . . . 17Yd 40
HA5: Eastc . . . 30Z 45
Rushdene Wlk. TN16: Big H . . . 89Mc 179
Rushden Gdns. IG5: Ilf . . . 26Qc 54
NW7 . . . 23Ya 48
Rushdon Cl. RM1: Rom . . . 29Jd 56
RM17: Grays . . . 48Ce 99
Rush Dr. EN9: Walt A . . . 8Ec 20
Rushen Wlk. SM5: Cars . . . 74Fb 155
Rushes, The TW18: Staines . . . 64G 126
(off Wapshott Rd.)
Rushes Mead UB8: Uxb . . . 39L 63
Rushet Rd. BR5: St P . . . 68Wc 139
Rushett Cl. KT7: T Ditt . . . 74Ka 152
Rushett La. KT9: Chess . . . 83La 172
KT18: Eps . . . 83La 172
Rushett Rd. KT7: T Ditt . . . 73Ka 152
RUSHETTS FARM . . . 10L 207
Rushetts Rd. RH2: Reig . . . 10L 207
TN15: W King . . . 80Ud 164
Rushey Cl. KT3: N Mald . . . 70Ta 131
Rushey Grn. SE6 . . . 59Dc 114
Rushey Hill EN2: Enf . . . 14Pb 32
Rushey Mead SE4 . . . 57Cc 114
Rushfield EN6: Pot B . . . 4Za 16
Rushford Rd. SE4 . . . 58Bc 114
RUSH GREEN . . . 32Fd 76
Rush Grn. Gdns. RM7: Rush G . . . 32Ed 76
Rush Grn. Rd. RM7: Rush G . . . 32Dd 76
Rushgrove Av. NW9 . . . 29Ua 48
Rushgrove Ct. NW9 . . . 29Ua 48
Rushgrove Pde. NW9 . . . 29Ua 48
Rushgrove St. SE18 . . . 49Pc 94
Rush Hill M. SW11 . . . 55Jb 112
(off Rush Hill Rd.)
Rush Hill Rd. SW11 . . . 55Jb 112
Rushleigh Av. EN8: Chesh . . . 3Zb 20
Rushley Cl. BR2: Kes . . . 77Mc 159
RM16: Grays . . . 46Fe 99
Rush Leys Ct. AL2: Lon C . . . 9E 6
Rushlight M. KT9: Chess . . . 84La 172
Rushmead E2 . . . 41Xb 91
TW10: Ham . . . 62Ka 130
Rushmead Cl. CR0: C'don . . . 77Vb 157
HA8: Edg . . . 19Ra 29
Rushmere Av. RM14: Upm . . . 34Sd 78
Rushmere Ct. HP3: Hem H . . . 6N 3
KT4: Wor Pk . . . 75Wa 154
TN15: Igh . . . 92Zd 205
Rushmere Pl. SW19 . . . 64Za 132
TW20: Eng G . . . 64A 126
Rushmon Gdns. KT12: Walt T . . . 76X 151
Rushmon Pl. SM3: Cheam . . . 79Ab 154
Rushmon Vs. KT3: N Mald . . . 70Va 132
Rushmoor Cl. HA5: Eastc . . . 28X 45
WD3: Rick . . . 19M 25
Rushmoor Ct. WD18: Wat . . . 16S 26
Rushmore Cl. BR1: Brom . . . 69Nc 138
Rushmore Cres. E5 . . . 35Zb 72
Rushmore Hill BR6: Prat B . . . 81Yc 181
TN14: Knock, Prat B . . . 84Zc 181
Rushmore Ho. SW15 . . . 59Wa 110
W14 . . . 48Ab 88
(off Russell Rd.)
Rushmore Rd. E5 . . . 35Yb 72
(not continuous)
Rusholme Av. RM10: Dag . . . 34Cd 76
Rusholme Gro. SE19 . . . 64Ub 135
Rusholme Rd. SW15 . . . 58Za 110
Rushout Av. HA3: Kenton . . . 30Ka 46
Rushton Av. RH9: S God . . . 10A 210
WD25: Wat . . . 7W 12
Rushton Ct. EN8: Chesh . . . 1Zb 20
Rushton Ho. SW8 . . . 54Mb 112
Rushton St. N1 . . . 1G 219 (40Tb 71)
Rushton Wlk. E3 . . . 42Bc 92
(off Hamlets Way)
Rushworth Rd. RH2: Reig . . . 5J 207
Rushworth St. SE1 . . . 1C 230 (47Rb 91)
Rushymead TN15: Kems'g . . . 90Qd 183
Rushy Mdw. La. SM5: Cars . . . 75Gb 155
Ruskin Av. DA16: Well . . . 54Wc 117
E12 . . . 37Nc 74
EN9: Walt A . . . 6Gc 21
RM14: Upm . . . 31Sd 78
TW9: Kew . . . 52Qa 109
TW14: Felt . . . 58V 106
Ruskin Cl. NW11 . . . 30Db 49
Ruskin Ct. N21 . . . 17Pb 32
SE5 . . . 55Tb 113
(off Champion Hill)
Ruskin Dr. BR6: Orp . . . 76Uc 160
DA16: Well . . . 55Wc 117
KT4: Wor Pk . . . 75Xa 154
Ruskin Gdns. HA3: Kenton . . . 29Pa 47
RM3: Rom . . . 24Kd 57
W5 . . . 42Ma 87
Ruskin Gro. DA1: Dart . . . 57Qd 119
DA16: Well . . . 54Wc 117
Ruskin Ho. CR2: S Croy . . . 78Tb 157
(off Selsdon Rd.)
SW1 . . . 6E 228
Ruskin Mans. W14 . . . 51Ab 110
(off Queen's Club Gdns.)
Ruskin Pde. CR2: S Croy . . . 78Tb 157
(off Selsdon Rd.)
HA8: Edg . . . 21Pa 47
Ruskin Pk. Ho. SE5 . . . 55Tb 113
Ruskin Rd. CR0: C'don . . . 75Rb 157
DA17: Belv . . . 49Cd 96
N17 . . . 25Vb 51
RM16: Grays . . . 9C 100
SM5: Cars . . . 78Hb 155
SS17: Stan H . . . 2L 101
TW7: Isle . . . 55Ha 108
TW18: Staines . . . 65H 127
UB1: S'hall . . . 45Aa 85
Ruskin Sq. CR0: C'don . . . 75Tb 157
Ruskin Wlk. BR2: Brom . . . 72Pc 160
N9 . . . 19Wb 33
SE24 . . . 57Sb 113
Ruskin Way SW19 . . . 67Fb 133
Rusland Av. BR6: Orp . . . 76Tc 160
Rusland Hgts. HA1: Harr . . . 28Ga 46
Rusland Pk. Rd. HA1: Harr . . . 28Ga 46
Rusling Ct. WD17: Wat . . . 12X 27
Rusmon Ct. KT16: Chert . . . 73H 149
Rusper Cl. HA7: Stan . . . 21La 46
NW2 . . . 34Ya 68
Rusper Ct. SW9 . . . 54Nb 112
(off Clapham Rd.)
Rusper Rd. N17 . . . 27Sb 51
N22 . . . 26Rb 51
RM9: Dag . . . 37Yc 75
Russell Av. AL3: St A . . . 2B 6
N22 . . . 26Qb 50
Russell Chambers WC1 . . . 1G 223
Russell Cl. BR3: Beck . . . 69Ec 136
CM15: B'wood . . . 17Xd 40
DA1: Cray . . . 56Jd 118
DA7: Bex . . . 56Cd 118
GU21: Wok . . . 7N 167
HA4: Ruis . . . 33Y 65
HA6: Nwood . . . 22S 44
HP6: L Chal . . . 11A 24
KT20: Walt H . . . 97Wa 194
NW10 . . . 38Sa 67
SE7 . . . 52Lc 115
W4 . . . 51Va 110
Russell Ct. AL2: Brick W . . . 2Ca 13
CR8: Purl . . . 82Db 176
E10 . . . 31Dc 72
EN5: New Bar . . . 14Eb 31
KT22: Lea . . . 94Ka 192
N14 . . . 16Mb 32
SE15 . . . 54Xb 113
(off Heaton Rd.)
SM6: Wall . . . 78Lb 156
(off Ross Rd.)
SW1 . . . 7C 222
SW16 . . . 64Pb 134
WC1 . . . 6F 217
Russell Cres. WD25: Wat . . . 7V 12
Russell Dr. TW19: Stanw . . . 58M 105
Russell Flint Ho. E16 . . . 46Kc 93
(off Pankhurst Av.)
Russell Gdns. IG2: Ilf . . . 31Tc 74
N20 . . . 19Gb 31
NW11 . . . 30Ab 48
TW10: Ham . . . 61La 130
UB7: Sip . . . 50Q 84
W14 . . . 48Ab 88
Russell Gdns. M. W14 . . . 47Ab 88
Russell Grn. Cl. CR8: Purl . . . 82Qb 176
Russell Gro. NW7 . . . 22Ua 48
SW9 . . . 52Qb 112
Russell Hill CR8: Purl . . . 82Pb 176
Russell Hill Pl. CR8: Purl . . . 83Qb 176
Russell Hill Rd. CR8: Purl . . . 83Qb 176
Russell Ho. BR2: Brom . . . 72Nc 160
(off Wells Vw. Dr.)
E14 . . . 44Cc 92
(off Saracen St.)
SW1 . . . 7B 228
Russell Kerr Cl. W4 . . . 52Sa 109
Russell La. N20 . . . 19Gb 31
WD17: Wat . . . 8T 12
Russell Lodge E4 . . . 19Ec 34
SE1 . . . 3F 231
Russell Mans. WC1 . . . 7G 217
Russell Mead HA3: Hrw W . . . 25Ha 46
Russell Pde. NW11 . . . 30Ab 48
(off Golders Grn. Rd.)
Russell Pl. DA4: Sut H . . . 67Qd 141
HP3: Hem H . . . 5K 3
NW3 . . . 36Gb 69
SE16 . . . 48Ac 92
SM2: Sutt . . . 80Db 155
Russell Quay DA11: Grav'nd . . . 7C 122
Russell Rd. CR4: Mitc . . . 69Gb 133
DA12: Grav'nd . . . 8F 122
E4 . . . 21Bc 52
E10 . . . 30Dc 52
E16 . . . 44Jc 93
E17 . . . 27Bc 52
EN1: Enf . . . 10Vb 19
GU21: Wok . . . 7N 167
HA6: Nwood . . . 20S 26
IG9: Buck H . . . 18Kc 35
KT12: Walt T . . . 72W 150
N8 . . . 30Mb 50
N13 . . . 23Pb 50
N15 . . . 29Ub 51
N20 . . . 19Gb 31
NW9 . . . 30Va 48
RM17: Grays . . . 49Ce 99
RM18: Tilb . . . 3A 122
SW19 . . . 66Cb 133
TW2: Twick . . . 58Ha 108
TW17: Shep . . . 73S 150
UB5: N'olt . . . 36Ea 66
W14 . . . 48Ab 88
Russells KT20: Tad . . . 94Za 194
Russell's Footpath SW16 . . . 64Nb 134
Russell Sq. DA3: Lfield . . . 69Zd 143
WC1 . . . 6F 217 (43Nb 90)
Russell Sq. Mans. WC1 . . . 7G 217
Russell's Ride EN8: Chesh . . . 3Ac 20
Russell St. SL4: Wind . . . 3H 103
WC2 . . . 4G 223 (45Nb 90)
Russell's Way RM15: S Ock . . . 44Zd 99
Russell's Wharf Flats W10 . . . 42Bb 89
Russell Ter. DA4: Hort K . . . 70Sd 142
Russell Wlk. TW10: Rich . . . 58Pa 109
Russell Way SM1: Sutt . . . 78Db 155
WD19: Wat . . . 17X 27
Russell Wilson Ho. RM3: Hrld W . . . 25Pd 57
Russell Yd. SW15 . . . 56Ab 110
Russet Av. TW17: Shep . . . 69U 128
Russet Cl. KT12: Hers . . . 76Z 151
TW19: Stanw M . . . 58H 105
UB10: Hil . . . 42S 84
Russet Cres. N7 . . . 36Pb 70
Russet Dr. AL4: St A . . . 3G 6
CR0: C'don . . . 74Ac 158
WD7: Shenl . . . 4Na 15
Russet Ho. RM17: Grays . . . 52Ee 121
Russets KT20: Tad . . . 95Ya 194
Russets Cl. E4 . . . 21Fc 53
Russett Cl. BR6: Chels . . . 78Xc 161
Russett Ct. CR3: Cat'm . . . 97Wb 197
Russett Hill SL9: Chal P . . . 27A 42
Russettings HA5: Hat E . . . 24Ba 45
(off Westfield Pk.)
Russetts RM11: Horn . . . 28Nd 57
Russetts Cl. GU21: Wok . . . 87B 168
Russett Way BR8: Swan . . . 68Fd 140
SE13 . . . 54Dc 114
Russia Dock Rd. SE16 . . . 46Ac 92
Russia La. E2 . . . 40Yb 72
Russia Row EC2 . . . 3E 224 (44Sb 91)
Russia Wlk. SE16 . . . 47Ac 92
Russington Rd. TW17: Shep . . . 72T 150
Rusthall Av. W4 . . . 49Ta 87
Rusthall Cl. CR0: C'don . . . 72Yb 158
Rustic Av. SW16 . . . 66Kb 134
Rustic Cl. RM14: Upm . . . 32Ud 78
Rustic Pl. HA0: Wemb . . . 35Ma 67
Rustic Wlk. E16 . . . 44Kc 93
(off Lambert Rd.)
Rustington Wlk. SM4: Mord . . . 73Bb 155
Ruston Av. KT5: Surb . . . 73Ra 153
Ruston Gdns. N14 . . . 16Jb 32
Ruston M. W11 . . . 44Ab 88
Ruston Rd. SE18 . . . 48Nc 94
Ruston St. E3 . . . 39Bc 72
Rust Sq. SE5 . . . 52Tb 113
Rutford Rd. SW16 . . . 64Nb 134
Ruth Cl. HA7: Stan . . . 28Pa 47
Ruth Ct. E3 . . . 40Ac 72
Ruthen Cl. KT18: Eps . . . 86Ra 173
Rutherford Cl. SL4: Wind . . . 3D 102
SM2: Sutt . . . 79Fb 155
UB8: Hil . . . 42P 83
WD6: Bore . . . 12Sa 29
Rutherford Ho. E1 . . . 42Xb 91
(off Brady St.)
HA9: Wemb . . . 34Sa 67
(off Barnhill Rd.)
SL9: Ger X . . . 29A 42
SW11 . . . 54Hb 111
(off Battersea Pk. Rd.)
Rutherford Pl. RM3: Rom . . . 22Ld 57
Rutherford St. SW1 . . . 5D 228 (49Mb 90)
Rutherford Twr. UB1: S'hall . . . 44Da 85
Rutherford Way HA9: Wemb . . . 35Qa 67
WD23: B Hea . . . 18Fa 28
Rutherglen Rd. SE2 . . . 51Wc 117
Rutherwick Ri. CR5: Coul . . . 89Nb 176
Rutherwyke Cl. KT17: Ewe . . . 79Wa 154
Rutherwyk Rd. KT16: Chert . . . 73G 148
Ruth Ho. W10 . . . 42Ab 88
(off Kensal Rd.)
Ruthin Cl. NW9 . . . 30Ua 48
Ruthin Rd. SE3 . . . 51Jc 115
Ruthven Av. EN8: Walt C . . . 5Zb 20
Ruthven St. E9 . . . 39Zb 72
Rutland App. RM11: Horn . . . 29Qd 57
Rutland Av. DA15: Sidc . . . 59Wc 117
SL1: Slou . . . 3G 80
Rutland Cl. DA1: Dart . . . 59Md 119
DA5: Bexl . . . 61Zc 139
KT9: Chess . . . 79Pa 153
KT19: Ewe . . . 82Ta 173
KT21: Asht . . . 89Na 173
RH1: Redh . . . 5P 207
SW14 . . . 55Ra 109
SW19 . . . 66Gb 133
Rutland Ct. BR7: Chst . . . 67Qc 138
EN3: Pond E . . . 15Xb 33
KT1: King T . . . 70Ma 131
(off Palace Rd.)
SE5 . . . 56Tb 113
SE9 . . . 61Sc 138
SW7 . . . 2E 226
W3 . . . 44Qa 87
Rutland Dr. RM11: Horn . . . 29Qd 57
SM4: Mord . . . 72Bb 155
TW10: Ham . . . 60Ma 109
Rutland Gdns. CR0: C'don . . . 77Ub 157
HP2: Hem H . . . 1P 3
N4 . . . 30Rb 51
RM8: Dag . . . 36Yc 75
SW7 . . . 2E 226 (47Gb 89)
W13 . . . 43Ja 86
Rutland Gdns. M. SW7 . . . 2E 226 (47Gb 89)
Rutland Ga. BR2: Brom . . . 70Hc 137
DA17: Belv . . . 50Dd 96
SW7 . . . 2E 226 (47Gb 89)
Rutland Ga. M. SW7 . . . 2D 226
Rutland Gro. W6 . . . 50Xa 88
Rutland Ho. UB5: N'olt . . . 37Ca 65
(off The Farmlands)
W8 . . . 48Db 89
(off Marloes Rd.)
Rutland M. NW8 . . . 39Db 69
Rutland M. E. SW7 . . . 3E 226
Rutland M. Sth. SW7 . . . 3D 226
Rutland M. W. SW7 . . . 3D 226
Rutland Pk. NW2 . . . 37Ya 68
SE6 . . . 61Bc 136
Rutland Pk. Gdns. NW2 . . . 37Ya 68
(off Rutland Pk.)
Rutland Pk. Mans. NW2 . . . 37Ya 68
Rutland Pl. EC1 . . . 7C 218 (42Rb 91)
WD23: B Hea . . . 18Fa 28
Rutland Rd. E7 . . . 38Mc 73
E9 . . . 39Zb 72
E11 . . . 29Kc 53
E17 . . . 30Cc 52
HA1: Harr . . . 30Ea 46
IG1: Ilf . . . 34Rc 74
SW19 . . . 66Gb 133
TW2: Twick . . . 61Fa 130
UB1: S'hall . . . 43Ca 85
UB3: Harl . . . 49T 84
Rutland St. SW7 . . . 3E 226 (48Gb 89)
Rutland Wlk. SE6 . . . 61Bc 136
Rutland Way BR5: St M Cry . . . 72Yc 161
Rutledge Cl. RM16: Ors . . . 3C 100
Rutley Cl. RM3: Hrld W . . . 26Md 57
SE17 . . . 51Rb 113
Rutlish Rd. SW19 . . . 67Cb 133
Rutson Rd. KT14: Byfl . . . 86P 169
Rutter Gdns. CR4: Mitc . . . 70Eb 133
Rutters Cl. UB7: W Dray . . . 47Q 84
Rutts, The WD23: B Hea . . . 18Fa 28
Rutt's Ter. SE14 . . . 53Zb 114
Ruvigny Gdns. SW15 . . . 55Za 110
Ruxbury Ct. TW15: Ashf . . . 62N 127
Ruxbury Rd. KT16: Chert . . . 72E 148
RUXLEY . . . 66Zc 139
Ruxley Cl. DA14: Sidc . . . 65Zc 139
KT19: Ewe . . . 78Ra 153
KT20: Kgswd . . . 93Ab 194
Ruxley Cnr. Ind. Est. DA14: Sidc . . . 65Zc 139
Ruxley Ct. GU22: Wok . . . 1P 187
(off West Hill Rd.)
KT19: Ewe . . . 78Sa 153
Ruxley Cres. KT10: Clay . . . 79Ka 152
Ruxley Gdns. TW17: Shep . . . 71S 150
Ruxley La. KT19: Ewe . . . 79Ra 153
Ruxley M. KT19: Ewe . . . 78Ra 153
Ruxley Pk. Golf Course . . . 67Zc 139
Ruxley Ridge KT10: Clay . . . 80Ja 152
Ruxley Towers KT10: Clay . . . 80Ja 152
Ruxton Cl. BR8: Swan . . . 69Gd 140
CR5: Coul . . . 87Lb 176
Ruxton Ct. BR8: Swan . . . 69Gd 140

Ryall Cl. AL2: Brick W 1Aa 13
Ryalls Ct. N20 20Hb 31
Ryan Cl. HA4: Ruis 32X 65
SE3 56Lc 115
Ryan Ct. RM7: Rom 30Ed 56
SW16 66Nb 134
WD19: Wat 17Aa 27
Ryan Dr. TW8: Bford 51Ja 108
Ryan Way WD24: Wat 11Y 27
Ryarsh Cres. BR6: Orp 77Uc 160
Rybrook Dr. KT12: Walt T 75Y 151
Rycott Path SE22 59Wb 113
Rycroft SL4: Wind 5D 102
Rycroft Way N17 27Vb 51
Ryculff Sq. SE3 54Hc 115
Rydal Cl. CR8: Purl 85Tb 177
NW4 25Ab 48
Rydal Ct. HA8: Edg 22Pa 47
HA9: Wemb 31Pa 67
WD25: Wat 4X 13
Rydal Cres. UB6: G'frd 41Ka 86
Rydal Dr. BR4: W W'ck 75Gc 159
DA7: Bex 53Cd 118
Rydale Ct. TN13: Dun G 93Gd 202
Rydal Gdns.
HA9: Wemb 32La 66
NW9 29Ua 48
SW15 64Ua 132
TW3: Houn 58Da 107
Rydal Mt. BR2: Brom 70Hc 137
EN6: Pot B 5Ab 16
Rydal Rd. SW16 63Mb 134
Rydal Water NW1 4B 216 (41Lb 90)
Rydal Way EN3: Pond E 16Yb 34
HA4: Ruis 35Y 65
TW20: Egh 66D 126
Ryde, The TW18: Staines 67K 127
Ryde Cl. GU23: Rip 93L 189
Ryde Dr. SS17: Stan H 3L 101
Ryde Heron GU21: Knap 9J 167
Ryde Ho. NW6 39Cb 69
(off Priory Pk. Rd.)
RYDENS 76Y 151
Rydens Av. KT12: Walt T 75X 151
Rydens Cl. KT12: Walt T 75Y 151
Rydens Gro. KT12: Hers 77Z 151
Rydens Ho. SE9 62Lc 137
Rydens Pde. GU22: Wok 92D 188
Rydens Pk. KT12: Walt T 75Z 151
Rydens Rd. KT12: Walt T 76X 151
Rydens Way GU22: Wok 92C 188
Ryde Pl. TW1: Twick 58Ma 109
Ryder Av. E10 31Dc 72
Ryder Cl. BR1: Brom 64Kc 137
HP3: Bov 10C 2
WD23: Bush 16Da 27
Ryder Ct. E10 33Dc 72
SW1 6C 222
Ryder Dr. SE16 50Xb 91
Ryder Gdns. RM13: Rain 37Hd 76
Ryder Ho. E1 42Yb 92
(off Colebert Av.)
Ryder M. E9 36Yb 72
Ryders Av. AL4: Col H, S'ford 2A 8
Ryder Seed M. AL1: St A 3B 6
Ryder's Ter. NW8 1A 214 (40Eb 69)
Ryder St. SW1 6C 222 (46Lb 90)
Ryder Yd. SW1 6C 222 (46Lb 90)
Rydes Cl. GU22: Wok 92E 188
Ryde Va. Rd. SW12 61Lb 134
Rydinghurst Ho. SL9: Chal P 22A 42
Rydings SL4: Wind 5D 102
Rydon Bus. Cen. KT22: Lea 92Ka 192
Rydon M. SW19 66Ya 132
Rydons Cl. SE9 55Nc 116
Rydon's La. CR5: Coul 92Sb 197
Rydon St. N1 39Sb 71
Rydons Way RH1: Redh 7P 207
Rydon's Wood Cl. CR5: Coul 92Sb 197
Rydston Cl. N7 38Nb 70
Rye, The N14 17Mb 32
Ryebridge Cl. KT22: Lea 90Ja 172
Ryebrook KT22: Lea 92Ja 192
Ryebrook Rd. KT22: Lea 90Ja 172
Rye Cl. DA5: Bexl 58Dd 118
RM12: Horn 35Ld 77
WD6: Bore 14Ta 29
Ryecotes Mead SE21 60Ub 113
Rye Ct. SL1: Slou 8L 81
Rye Cres. BR5: Orp 74Zc 161
Ryecroft AL10: Hat 2B 8
DA3: Long H 70Fe 143
DA12: Grav'nd 4G 144
Ryecroft Av. IG5: Ilf 26Rc 54
TW2: Whitt 59Da 107
Ryecroft Cl. HP2: Hem H 3C 4
Ryecroft Ct. AL4: St A 2K 7
Ryecroft Cres. EN5: Barn 15Xa 30
Ryecroft Rd. BR5: Pet W 72Tc 160
SE13 57Ec 114
SW16 65Qb 134
TN14: Otf 89Jd 182
Ryecroft St. SW6 53Db 111
Ryedale SE22 58Xb 113
Ryedale Pl. RM3: Rom 24Nd 57
Rye Fld. BR5: Orp 74Zc 161
KT21: Asht 88Ma 173
Ryefield Av. UB10: Hil 38R 64
Ryefield Ct. HA6: Nwood 26W 44
Ryefield Cres. HA6: Nwood 26W 44
Ryefield Pde. HA6: Nwood 26W 44
(off Joel St.)
Ryefield Path SW15 60Wa 110
Ryefield Rd. SE19 65Sb 135
Ryegates SE15 54Xb 113
(off Caulfield Rd.)
Rye Gro. GU18: Light 10D 146
Rye Hill Pk. SE15 56Yb 114
Rye Ho. SE16 47Yb 92
(off Swan Rd.)
SW1 7K 227
Ryeland Cl. UB7: Yiew 44N 83
Ryelands Cl. CR3: Cat'm 93Ub 197
Ryelands Ct. KT22: Lea 90Ja 172
Ryelands Cres. SE12 58Lc 115
Ryelands Pl.
KT13: Weyb 76U 150
Rye La. SE15 53Wb 113
TN14: Dun G, Otf 92Hd 202
Rye Mans. E20 36Ec 72
(off Napa Cl.)
Rye Pas. SE15 55Wb 113
Rye Rd. SE15 56Zb 114
Rye Wlk. SW15 57Za 110
Rye Way HA8: Edg 23Pa 47
Ryfold Rd. SW19 62Cb 133
Ryhope Rd. N11 21Kb 50
Rykhill RM16: Grays 8D 100
Ryland Cl. TW13: Felt 63V 128
Rylandes Rd. CR2: Sels 81Xb 177
NW2 34Wa 68
Ryland Rd. NW5 37Kb 70
Rylett Cres. W12 47Va 88
Rylett Rd. W12 47Va 88
Rylston Rd. N13 20Tb 33
SW6 51Bb 111
Rylton Ho. KT12: Walt T 74W 150
Ryman Ct. WD3: Chor 16E 24
Rymer Rd. CR0: C'don 73Ub 157
Rymer St. SE24 58Rb 113
Rymill Cl. HP3: Bov 10C 2
Rymill St. E16 46Qc 94
Rysbrack St. SW3 3F 227 (48Hb 89)
Rysted La. TN16: Westrm 98Sc 200
Rythe, The KT10: Esh 82Da 171
Rythe Bank Cl. KT7: T Ditt 73Ka 152
Rythe Cl. KT9: Chess 80La 152
KT10: Clay 78Ga 152
Rythe Ct. KT7: T Ditt 73Ja 152
Rythe Rd. KT10: Clay 78Fa 152
Ryvers End SL3: L'ly 48B 82
Ryvers Rd. SL3: L'ly 48B 82

S

Saatchi Gallery 7G 227 (50Hb 89)
Sabah Ct. TW15: Ashf 63Q 128
Sabella Ct. E3 40Bc 72
Sabina Rd. RM16: Grays 9E 100
Sabine Rd. SW11 55Hb 111
SABINE'S GREEN 13Nd 39
Sabine's Rd. CM14: Nave, N'side 12Md 39
RM4: Nave, N'side 12Md 39
Sable Cl. TW4: Houn 55Y 107
Sable Ho. E20 36Dc 72
(off Scarlet Cl.)
Sable St. N1 38Rb 71
Sachfield Dr. RM16: Chaf H 48Ae 99
Sach Rd. E5 33Xb 71
Sackville Av. BR2: Hayes 74Jc 159
Sackville Cl. HA2: Harr 34Fa 66
TN13: S'oaks 94Kd 203
Sackville Cotts. RH1: Blet 5K 209
Sackville Cres. RM3: Hrld W 25Nd 57
Sackville Gdns. IG1: Ilf 32Pc 74
Sackville Ho. SW16 62Nb 134
Sackville Pl. TN13: S'oaks 96Ld 203
Sackville Rd. DA2: Wilm 61Nd 141
SM2: Sutt 80Cb 155
Sackville St. W1 5C 222 (45Lb 90)
Sacombe Rd. HP1: Hem H 1H 3
Saddington St. DA12: Grav'nd 9D 122
Saddleback La. W7 48Ga 86
Saddlebrook Pk. TW16: Sun 63U 128
Saddle M. CR0: C'don 73Sb 157
Saddlers Cl. EN5: Ark 15Xa 30
HA5: Hat E 23Ca 45
WD6: Bore 15Ta 29
Saddlers Ct. KT18: Eps 85Sa 173
Saddlers Ho. E20 36Ec 72
(off Ribbons Wlk.)
Saddlers M. HA0: Wemb 35Ha 66
KT1: Hamp W 67La 130
SW8 53Nb 112
Saddler's Pk. DA4: Eyns 76Md 163
Saddlers Path WD6: Bore 15Ta 29
(off Farriers Way)
Saddlers Pl. TW3: Houn 55Ea 108
Saddlers Wlk. WD4: K Lan 1Q 12
Saddlers Way KT18: Eps D 91Ta 193
Saddlescombe Way N12 22Cb 49
Saddleworth Rd. RM3: Rom 23Ld 57
Saddleworth Sq. RM3: Rom 23Ld 57
Saddle Yd. W1 6K 221 (46Kb 90)
Sadleir Rd. AL1: St A 4C 6
Sadler Cl. CR4: Mitc 68Hb 133
Sadler Hgts. N1 38Pb 70
(off Caledonian Rd.)
Sadler Ho. E3 41Dc 92
(off Bromley High St.)
EC1 3B 218
Sadler Pl. E9 36Ac 72
Sadlers Ct. SE1 3H 231
Sadlers Ga. M. SW15 55Ya 110
Sadlers Ride KT8: W Mole 68Ea 130
Sadler's Wells Theatre 3A 218 (41Qb 90)
Safara Ho. SE5 53Ub 113
(off Dalwood St.)
Saffron Av. E14 45Fc 93
Saffron Central Sq. CR0: C'don 74Sb 157
Saffron Cl. CM13: W H'dn 30Fe 59
CR0: C'don 72Nb 156
NW11 30Bb 49
SL3: Dat 3M 103
SS17: Horn H 1J 101
Saffron Ct. E15 36Gc 73
(off Maryland Pk.)
TW14: Bedf 59S 106
SAFFRON GREEN 11Va 30
Saffron Hill EC1 7A 218 (43Qb 90)
Saffron Ho. SM2: Sutt 80Db 155
TW9: Kew 53Ra 109
Saffron La. HP1: Hem H 1J 3
Saffron M. SW19 66Ab 132
Saffron Rd. RM5: Col R 26Fd 56
RM16: Chaf H 49Yd 98
Saffron St. EC1 7A 218 (43Qb 90)
Saffron Way KT6: Surb 74Ma 153
Saffron Wharf SE1 1K 231
Sage Cl. E6 43Pc 94
Sage M. SE22 57Vb 113
Sage St. E1 45Yb 92
Sage Way WC1 4H 217
Sage Yd. KT6: Surb 74Pa 153
Sahara Ct. UB1: S'hall 45Aa 85
Saigasso Cl. E16 44Mc 93
Sailacre Ho. SE10 50Hc 93
Sail Ct. E14 45Fc 93
(off Newport Av.)
Sailmakers Ct. SW6 55Eb 111
Sail St. SE11 5J 229 (49Pb 90)
Saimet NW9 24Va 48
(off Wiggins Mead)
Sainfoin Rd. SW17 61Jb 134
Sainsbury Cen., The
KT16: Chert 73J 149
Sainsbury Rd. SE19 64Ub 135
Sainsbury Wing 5E 222
St Agatha's Dr. KT2: King T 65Pa 131
St Agatha's Gro. SM5: Cars 74Hb 155
St Agnes Cl. E9 39Yb 72
St Agnes Ho. E3 40Cc 72
(off Ordell Rd.)
St Agnes Pl. SE11 51Rb 113
St Agnes Quad. SE11 51Qb 112
St Agnes Well EC1 5G 219
St Aidans Ct. IG11: Bark 40Xc 75
St Aidan's Rd. SE22 58Xb 113
W13 47Ka 86
St Aidan's Way DA12: Grav'nd 2G 144
ST ALBANS 2B 6
St Alban's Av. E6 41Pc 94
RM14: Upm 33Ud 78
W4 49Ta 87
St Albans Av. KT13: Weyb 76Q 150
TW13: Hanw 64Z 129
St Albans Cathedral 2A 6
St Albans City FC 1D 6
St Albans Clocktower 2B 6
(off High St.)
St Alban's Cl. DA12: Grav'nd 2F 144
SL4: Wind 3H 103
St Albans Cl. NW11 32Cb 69
St Albans Ct. EC2 2E 224
St Alban's Cres. IG8: Wfd G 24Jc 53
N22 25Qb 50
St Albans Farm TW14: Houn 57Y 107
St Alban's Gdns. DA12: Grav'nd 2F 144
TW11: Tedd 64Ja 130
St Alban's Gro. SM5: Cars 73Gb 155
W8 48Db 89
St Albans Hill HP3: Hem H 5N 3
St Alban's La. NW11 32Cb 69
St Albans La. WD5: Bedm 8F 4
St Albans Mans. W8 48Db 89
(off Kensington Ct. Pl.)
St Albans Organ Theatre 3F 6
St Albans Pl. N1 1B 218 (39Rb 71)
St Albans Retail Pk.
AL1: St A 4B 6
St Alban's Rd. CM16: Coop 1Zc 24
DA1: Dart 59Pd 119
IG8: Wfd G 24Jc 53
KT2: King T 65Na 131
RH2: Reig 4J 207
SM1: Sutt 77Bb 155
St Albans Rd. EN5: Barn 7Xa 16
EN6: S Mim 3Ua 16
HP2: Hem H 4M 3
HP3: Hem H 4M 3
IG3: Ilf 32Vc 75
NW5 34Jb 70
NW10 39Ua 68
WD17: Wat 12X 27
WD24: Wat 12X 27
WD25: Wat 8Y 13
St Albans Rd. W.
AL10: Hat 1N 7
(not continuous)
St Albans South Signal Box 3D 6
(off Ridgmont Rd.)
St Alban's St. SL4: Wind 3H 103
SW1 5D 222 (45Mb 90)
St Albans Studios W8 48Db 89
(off St Albans Gro.)
St Albans Sub Aqua Club 3B 6
St Albans Ter. W6 51Ab 110
St Albans Vs. NW5 34Jb 70
St Alfege Pas. SE10 51Ec 114
St Alfege Rd. SE7 51Mc 115
St Alphage Ct. NW9 27Ta 47
St Alphage Gdn. EC2 1E 224 (43Sb 91)
St Alphage Highwalk EC2 1E 224
St Alphage Wlk. HA8: Edg 26Sa 47
St Alphege Rd. N9 17Yb 34
St Alphonsus Rd. SW4 56Lb 112
St Amunds Cl. SE6 63Cc 136
St Andrew's Av. HA0: Wemb 35Ja 66
RM12: Horn 36Hd 76
SL4: Wind 4C 102
St Andrews Chambers W1 1C 222
St Andrew's Cl. HA4: Ruis 33Z 65
HA7: Stan 26La 46
N12 21Eb 49
NW2 34Xa 68
SL4: Old Win 8L 103
TW7: Isle 53Ga 108
TW17: Shep 70T 128
TW19: Wray 58A 104
St Andrews Cl. GU21: Wok 9N 167
KT7: T Ditt 74Ka 152
RH2: Reig 7K 207
SE16 50Xb 91
SE28 44Zc 95
SW19 65Db 133
St Andrews Cotts. SL4: Wind 4E 102
(off Cross Oak)
St Andrew's Ct. DA12: Grav'nd 8D 122
(off Queen St.)
SW18 61Eb 133
St Andrews Ct. BR8: Swan 69Gd 140
E17 26Ac 52
RM18: Tilb 4C 122
SL1: Slou 8J 81
(off Upton Pk.)
SM1: Sutt 76Gb 155
WD17: Wat 11X 27
St Andrew's Cres. SL4: Wind 4D 102
St Andrew's Dr. BR5: St M Cry 72Xc 161
St Andrews Dr. AL1: St A 5F 6
HA7: Stan 25La 46
St Andrews Gdns. KT11: Cobh 85Y 171
St Andrew's Ga. GU22: Wok 90B 168
St Andrew's Gro. N16 32Tb 71
St Andrew's Hill EC4 4C 224 (45Rb 91)
(not continuous)
St Andrews Ho. KT17: Eps 85Ta 173
(off High St.)
RM8: Dag 35Wc 75
SE16 48Xb 91
(off Southwark Pk. Rd.)
St Andrews Mans. W1 1H 221
W14 51Ab 110
(off St Andrew's Rd.)
St Andrew's M. N16 32Ub 71
SE3 52Jc 115
St Andrews M. SW12 60Mb 112
St Andrew's Pl. CM15: Shenf 19Be 41
NW1 5A 216 (42Kb 90)
St Andrew's Rd. CR0: C'don 77Sb 157
CR5: Coul 88Jb 176
DA12: Grav'nd 9D 122
DA14: Sidc 62Zc 139
E11 30Gc 53
E13 41Kc 93
E17 26Zb 52
EN1: Enf 13Tb 33
HP3: Hem H 6M 3
IG1: Ilf 31Pc 74
KT6: Surb 72Ma 153
N9 17Yb 34
NW9 32Ta 67
NW10 37Xa 68
St Andrew's Rd. NW11 30Bb 49
RM7: Rom 30Fd 56
RM18: Tilb 3A 122
SM5: Cars 76Gb 155
UB10: Uxb 39N 63
W3 45Ua 88
W14 51Ab 110
St Andrews Rd. W7 47Ga 86
WD19: Wat 20Z 27
St Andrew's Sq. KT6: Surb 72Ma 153
St Andrews Sq. W11 44Ab 88
St Andrews Ter. WD19: Wat 22Y 45
St Andrew's Twr. UB1: S'hall 45Ea 86
(off Baird Av.)
St Andrew St. EC4 1A 224 (43Qb 90)
St Andrew's Wlk. KT11: Cobh 87X 171
St Andrew's Way SL1: Slou 5B 80
St Andrews Way E3 42Dc 92
SS17: Stan H 3K 101
St Andrew's Wharf SE1 1K 231 (47Vb 91)
St Anna Rd. EN5: Barn 15Za 30
St Anne's Av. TW19: Stanw 59M 105
St Annes Blvd. RH1: Redh 4B 208
St Anne's Cl. N6 34Jb 70
WD19: Wat 21Y 45
St Annes Cl. RM16: Grays 46De 99
St Anne's Ct. BR4: W W'ck 77Gc 159
NW6 39Ab 68
W1 3D 222 (44Mb 90)
St Anne's Dr. RH1: Redh 5A 208
St Annes Dr. Nth. RH1: Redh 4A 208
St Anne's Flats NW1 3D 216
St Anne's Gdns. NW10 41Pa 87
St Annes M. SW20 66Za 132
St Anne's Mt. RH1: Redh 5A 208
St Anne's Pas. E14 44Bc 92
St Anne's Ri. RH1: Redh 5A 208
St Anne's Rd. AL2: Lon C 9H 7
CM15: Mount, Shenf 11Ee 41
E11 33Fc 73
HA0: Wemb 36Ma 67
UB9: Hare 27L 43
St Anne's Row E14 44Bc 92
St Annes Ter. IG6: Ilf 22Uc 54
St Anne's Trad. Est. E14 44Bc 92
(off St Anne's Row)
St Anne St. E14 44Bc 92
St Annes Way RH1: Redh 5A 208
St Ann's IG11: Bark 39Sc 74
St Anns GU22: Wok 90A 168
St Ann's Cl. KT16: Chert 72H 149
St Ann's Ct. NW4 27Xa 48
St Ann's Cres. SW18 58Db 111
St Ann's Gdns. NW5 37Jb 70
St Ann's Hill SW18 57Db 111
St Ann's Hill Rd. KT16: Chert 72E 148
St Ann's Ho. WC1 4K 217
St Ann's La. SW1 4E 228 (48Mb 90)
St Ann's M. KT16: Chert 73G 148
ST ANN'S PARK 70B 126
St Ann's Pk. Rd. SW18 58Eb 111
St Ann's Pas. SW13 55Ua 110
St Ann's Rd. HA1: Harr 30Ga 46
IG11: Bark 39Sc 74
KT16: Chert 72G 148
(not continuous)
N9 19Vb 33
N15 29Rb 51
SW13 54Va 110
W11 45Za 88
St Ann's Shop. Cen. HA1: Harr 30Ga 46
St Ann's St. SW1 3E 228 (48Mb 90)
St Ann's Ter. NW8 1C 214 (40Fb 69)
St Ann's Vs. W11 46Za 88
St Ann's Way CR2: S Croy 79Rb 157
St Anns Way TN16: Big H 88Rc 180
St Anselms Ct. SW16 64Nb 134
St Anselm's Pl. W1 4K 221 (45Kb 90)
St Anselm's Rd. UB3: Hayes 47V 84
St Anthony's Av. IG8: Wfd G 23Lc 53
St Anthonys Av. HP3: Hem H 4B 4
St Anthony's Cl. E1 46Wb 91
E9 37Bc 72
(off Wallis Rd.)
SW17 61Gb 133
St Anthony's Ct. BR6: Farnb 75Rc 160
SW17 61Jb 134
St Anthony's Flats NW1 2D 216
St Anthony's Way TW14: Felt 56V 106
St Antony's Rd. E7 38Kc 73
St Arvan's Cl. CR0: C'don 76Ub 157
St Asaph Rd. SE4 55Zb 114
St Aubins Ct. N1 39Tb 71
St Aubyn's Av. SW19 64Bb 133
TW3: Houn 57Ca 107
St Aubyn's Cl. BR6: Orp 76Vc 161
St Aubyn's Gdns. BR6: Orp 75Vc 161
St Aubyn's Rd. SE19 65Vb 135
St Audrey Av. DA7: Bex 54Cd 118
St Audreys Cl. AL10: Hat 3D 8
St Augustine Rd. RM16: Grays 9D 100
St Augustine's Av. BR2: Brom 71Nc 160
CR2: S Croy 79Sb 157
HA9: Wemb 34Na 67
W5 40Na 67
St Augustine's Ct. SE1 50Xb 91
(off Lynton Rd.)
St Augustine's Ho. NW1 3D 216
St Augustine's Mans. SW1 6C 228
St Augustine's Path N5 35Sb 71
St Augustine's Rd. DA17: Belv 49Bd 95
NW1 38Mb 70
St Augustine's Sports Cen. 40Cb 69
St Austell Cl. HA8: Edg 26Pa 47
St Austell Rd. SE13 54Ec 114
St Awdry's Rd. IG11: Bark 38Tc 74
St Awdry's Wlk. IG11: Bark 38Sc 74
St Barnabas Cl. BR3: Beck 68Ec 136
SE22 57Ub 113
St Barnabas Ct. HA3: Hrw W 25Ea 46
HP2: Hem H 2A 4
St Barnabas Gdns. KT8: W Mole 71Ca 151
St Barnabas M. SW1 7J 227
St Barnabas Rd. CR4: Mitc 66Jb 134
E17 30Cc 52
IG8: Wfd G 25Kc 53
SM1: Sutt 78Fb 155
St Barnabas St. SW1 7J 227 (50Jb 90)
St Barnabas Ter. E9 36Zb 72
St Barnabas Vs. SW8 53Nb 112
St Bartholomew's Cl. SE26 63Xb 135
St Bartholomew's Ct. E6 40Nc 74
(off St Bartholomew's Rd.)
St Bartholomew's Hospital Mus. 1C 224
St Bartholomew's Rd. E6 40Pc 74
St Bart's Cl. AL4: St A 3H 7
St Benedict's Av. DA12: Grav'nd 1F 144
St Benedict's Cl. SW17 64Jb 134
St Benet's Cl. SW17 61Gb 133
St Benet's Gro. SM5: Cars 73Eb 155
St Benet's Pl. EC3 4G 225 (45Tb 91)
St Benjamins Dr. BR6: Prat B 81Yc 181
St Bernards CR0: C'don 76Ub 157
St Bernard's Cl. SE27 63Tb 135
St Bernards Ho. E14 48Ec 92
(off Galbraith St.)
St Bernard's Rd. AL3: St A 1C 6
E6 39Mc 73
St Bernards Rd. SL3: L'ly 8N 81
St Blaise Av. BR1: Brom 68Kc 137
St Botolph Rd. DA11: Nflt 62Fe 143
St Botolph Row EC3 3K 225 (44Vb 91)
St Botolphs E1 2K 225
St Botolph's Av. TN13: S'oaks 96Jd 202
St Botolph's Rd.
TN13: S'oaks 96Kd 203
St Botolph St. EC3 2K 225 (44Vb 91)
St Brelades Ct. N1 39Ub 71
St Bride's Av. EC4 3B 224
HA8: Edg 25Pa 47
St Brides Cl. DA18: Erith 47Zc 95
St Bride's Crypt Mus. 3B 224
St Bride's Ho. E3 40Cc 72
(off Ordell Rd.)
St Bride's Pas. EC4 3B 224
St Bride St. EC4 2B 224 (44Rb 91)
St Catherines GU22: Wok 1N 187
KT13: Weyb 76R 150
(off Thames St.)
St Catherine's Apartments E3 41Dc 92
(off Bow Rd.)
St Catherine's Cl. SW17 61Gb 133
SW20 71Ya 154
St Catherines Cl. KT9: Chess 79Ma 153
St Catherine's Ct. W4 48Ua 88
St Catherines Ct. TW13: Felt 60W 106
TW18: Staines 63J 127
St Catherine's Cross RH1: Blet 6L 209
St Catherine's Dr. SE14 54Zb 114
St Catherine's Farm Ct. HA4: Ruis 30S 44
St Catherines M. SW3 5F 227 (49Hb 89)
St Catherines Pl. TW20: Egh 64C 126
St Catherine's Rd. E4 19Cc 34
HA4: Ruis 30T 44
St Cecelia's Pl. SE3 50Jc 93
St Cecilia Rd. RM16: Grays 9D 100
St Cecilia's Cl. SM3: Sutt 74Ab 154
St Cedd's Ct. RM16: Grays 46De 99
St Chads Cl. KT6: Surb 73La 152
St Chad's Dr. DA12: Grav'nd 2G 144
St Chad's Gdns. RM6: Chad H 31Ad 75
St Chad's Pl. WC1 3G 217 (41Nb 90)
St Chad's Rd. RM6: Chad H 31Ad 75
St Chads Rd. RM16: Grays 4C 122
RM18: Grays, Tilb 4C 122
St Chad's St. WC1 3G 217 (41Nb 90)
(not continuous)
St Charles Ct. KT13: Weyb 78Q 150
St Charles Pl. KT13: Weyb 78Q 150
W10 43Ab 88
St Charles Rd. CM14: B'wood 18Xd 40
St Charles Sq. W10 43Za 88
St Chloe's Ho. E3 40Cc 72
(off Ordell Rd.)
St Christopher Rd. UB8: Cowl 44M 83
St Christopher's Cl. TW7: Isle 53Ga 108
St Christophers Ct. KT12: Walt T 75Y 151
(off Rydens Av.)
WD3: Chor 15F 24
St Christophers Dr. UB3: Hayes 45X 85
St Christopher's Gdns.
CR7: Thor H 69Qb 134
St Christopher's Ho. NW1 2C 216
St Christopher's M. SM6: Wall 78Lb 156
St Christopher's Pl. W1 2J 221 (44Jb 90)
St Clair Cl. IG5: Ilf 26Pc 54
RH2: Reig 6L 207
RH8: Oxt 2G 210
St Clair Dr. KT4: Wor Pk 76Xa 154
St Clair Ho. E3 41Bc 92
(off British St.)
St Clair Rd. E13 40Kc 73
St Clair's Rd. CR0: C'don 75Ub 157
St Clare Bus. Pk. TW12: Hamp H 65Ea 130
St Clare St. EC3 3K 225 (44Vb 91)
St Clement Cl. UB8: Cowl 44M 83
St Clement's Av. RM20: W Thur 51Xd 120
St Clements Av. E3 41Bc 92
RM3: Hrld W 26Nd 57
St Clement's Cl. DA11: Nflt 2B 144
St Clement's Ct. EC4 4G 225
N7 37Qb 70
St Clements Ct. EN9: Walt A 5Ec 20
RM17: Grays 51Be 121
RM19: Purf 49Qd 97
SE14 51Zb 114
(off Myers La.)
W11 45Za 88
(off Stoneleigh St.)
St Clement's Development E3 41Bc 92
St Clements Hgts. SE26 62Wb 135
St Clements Ho. E1 1K 225
St Clements Lakes Development
DA9: Ghithe 57Wd 120
St Clement's La. WC2 3H 223 (44Pb 90)
St Clements Mans. SW6 51Za 110
(off Lillie Rd.)
St Clements Rd. DA9: Ghithe 56Yd 120
RM20: Grays 52Yd 120
St Clements St. N7 37Qb 70
St Clements Way
DA2: Bean, Bluew 57Wd 120
DA9: Bluew, Ghithe 57Wd 120
RM20: W Thur 51Vd 120
St Clements Yd. SE22 56Vb 113
St Clere TN15: Kems'g 88Vd 184
St Clere Hill Rd. TN15: W King 84Vd 184
St Clere's Hall Golf Course 3K 101
St Cloud Rd. SE27 63Sb 135
St Columba's Cl. DA12: Grav'nd 2F 144
(not continuous)
St Columba's Ct. E15 35Gc 73
(off Janson Rd.)
St Columbas Ho. E17 28Dc 52
St Columb's Ho. W10 43Ab 88
(off Blagrove Rd.)
St Crispin's Cl. NW3 35Gb 69
UB1: S'hall 44Ba 85
St Crispins Way KT16: Ott 81E 168
St Cross St. EC1 7A 218 (43Qb 90)
St Cuthbert La. UB8: Cowl 44M 83
St Cuthberts Cl. TW20: Eng G 5P 125
St Cuthberts Gdns. HA5: Hat E 24Ba 45
St Cuthbert's Rd. NW2 37Bb 69
St Cuthberts Rd. N13 23Qb 50
St Cyprian's St. SW17 63Hb 133

St Daniel Ct. BR3: Beck 66Cc 136
(off Brackley Rd.)
St David Cl. UB8: Cowl 43M 83
St David's CR5: Coul 89Pb 176
St David's Cl. BR4: W W'ck 73Dc 158
HA9: Wemb 34Sa 67
HP3: Hem H 3D 4
RH2: Reig 5L 207
SL0: Iver H 39F 62
St Davids Cl. SE16 50Xb 91
(off Masters Dr.)
St David's Ct. BR1: Brom 69Rc 138
E17 27Ec 52
St Davids Ct. TW15: Ashf 61P 127
St David's Cres. DA12: Grav'nd 3F 144
St David's Dr. HA8: Edg 25Pa 47
St Davids Dr. TW20: Eng G 6N 125
St Davids M. E3 41Ac 92
(off Morgan St.)
E18 25Jc 53
St David's Pl. NW4 31Xa 68
St Davids Rd. BR8: Hext 65Hd 140
St Davids Sq. E14 50Dc 92
St Denis Rd. SE27 63Tb 135
St Denys Cl. CR8: Purl 82Rb 177
GU21: Knap 10H 167
St Dionis Rd. SW6 54Bb 111
St Domingo Ho. SE18 48Pc 94
(off Leda Rd.)
St Donatt's Rd. SE14 53Bc 114
ST DUNSTAN'S 79Bb 155
St Dunstan's All. EC3 5H 225
St Dunstans Av. W3 45Ta 87
St Dunstan's Cl. UB3: Harl 50V 84
St Dunstan's Ct. EC4 3A 224 (44Qb 90)
St Dunstan's Dr. DA12: Grav'nd 3G 144
St Dunstan's Enterprises 60Cc 114
St Dunstan's Gdns. W3 45Ta 87
St Dunstan's Hill SM1: Sutt 78Ab 154
St Dunstans Hill EC3 5H 225 (45Ub 91)
St Dunstan's Ho. WC2 2K 223
St Dunstan's La. BR3: Beck 72Ec 158
EC3 5H 225 (45Ub 91)
St Dunstans M. E1 43Ac 92
(off White Horse Rd.)
St Dunstan's Rd. E7 37Kc 73
SE25 70Vb 135
TW4: Cran 54X 107
(not continuous)
TW13: Felt 62V 128
W6 50Za 88
W7 47Ga 86
St Ebbas Way KT19: Eps 81Sa 173
St Edith Cl. KT18: Eps 86Sa 173
St Edith Cotts. TN15: Kems'g 88Xd 184
St Ediths Ct. TN15: Kems'g 89Qd 183
St Edith's Farm Cott.
TN15: Kems'g 90Rd 183
St Edith's Rd. TN15: Kems'g 90Qd 183
St Edmund's Av. HA4: Ruis 30T 44
St Edmund's Cl. NW8 1F 215 (39Hb 69)
SW17 61Gb 133
St Edmunds Cl. DA18: Erith 47Zc 95
St Edmund's Ct. NW8 1F 215
TN15: W King 81Vd 184
St Edmunds Dr. HA7: Stan 25Ja 46
St Edmund's La. TW2: Whitt 59Da 107
St Edmund's Rd. DA1: Dart 56Qd 119
IG1: Ilf 30Pc 54
N9 17Wb 33
St Edmunds Sq. SW13 51Ya 110
St Edmund's Ter. NW8 1E 214 (39Gb 69)
St Edmunds Wlk. AL4: St A 3H 7
St Edward's Cl. CR0: New Ad 83Fc 179
NW11 30Cb 49
St Edwards Ct. NW11 30Cb 49
St Edwards Way RM1: Rom 29Fd 56
St Egberts Way E4 18Ec 34
St Elizabeth Dr. KT18: Eps 86Sa 173
St Elmo Cl. SL2: Slou 2H 81
St Elmo Cres. SL2: Slou 2H 81
St Elmo Rd. W12 46Va 88
St Elmos Rd. SE16 47Ac 92
St Erkenwald M. IG11: Bark 39Tc 74
St Erkenwald Rd. IG11: Bark 39Tc 74
St Ermin's Hill SW1 3D 228
St Ervan's Rd. W10 43Bb 89
St Ethelburga Ct. RM3: Hrld W 26Qd 57
St Eugene Ct. NW6 39Ab 68
(off Salusbury Rd.)
St Faith's Cl. EN2: Enf 11Sb 33
St Faith's Country Pk. 19Wd 40
St Faith's Rd. SE21 60Rb 113
St Fidelis Rd. DA8: Erith 49Fd 96
St Fillans GU22: Wok 88D 168
St Fillans Rd. SE6 60Ec 114
St Francis Av. DA12: Grav'nd 3G 144
St Francis Cl. BR5: Pet W 72Uc 160
EN6: Pot B 6Eb 17
WD19: Wat 18X 27
St Francis' Ho. NW1 2D 216
St Francis Pl. KT17: Ewe 82Wa 174
SW12 58Kb 112
St Francis Rd. DA8: Erith 49Fd 96
SE22 56Ub 113
UB9: Den 30H 43
St Francis Way IG1: Ilf 35Tc 74
RM16: Grays 8E 100
St Frideswide's M. E14 44Ec 92
St Gabriel's Cl. E11 33Kc 73
E14 43Dc 92
St Gabriels Ct. N11 24Mb 50
St Gabriels Mnr. SE5 53Rb 113
(off Cormont Rd.)
St Gabriels Rd. NW2 36Za 68
St Gabriel Wlk. SE1 5C 230
St George Ga. KT15: Add 76M 149
St George's Av. E7 38Kc 73
KT13: Weyb 79R 150
N7 35Mb 70
NW9 28Ta 47
RM11: Horn 31Pd 77
RM17: Grays 49Ee 99
UB1: S'hall 45Ba 85
W5 47Ma 87
St George's Bldgs. SE1 4B 230
St Georges Bus. Pk. KT13: Weyb 81Q 170
St George's Cathedral 3A 216
St George's Cen. DA11: Grav'nd 8D 122
St Georges Chapel
Windsor 2H 103
St George's Cir. SE1 3B 230 (48Rb 91)
St George's Cl. HA0: Wemb 34Ja 66
KT13: Weyb 78S 150
NW11 30Bb 49
SW8 53Lb 112
St Georges Cl. SE28 44Zc 95
SL4: Wind 3C 102
St George's Ct. CM14: B'wood 17Xd 40
E6 42Pc 94
KT13: Weyb 79S 150
SE1 4B 230
SW1 7B 228
SW3 5D 226
SW7 3A 226 (48Eb 89)
SW15 56Bb 111
St Georges Ct. AL1: St A 2C 6
(off Lemsford Rd.)
CM13: Hut 17Ee 41
E17 29Fc 53
EC4 2B 224 (44Rb 91)
HA3: Kenton 30Ja 46
(off Kenton Rd.)
KT15: Add 77L 149
TN15: Wro 88Be 185
St George's Cres. DA12: Grav'nd 3F 144
SL1: Slou 5B 80
St George's Dr. SW1 6A 228 (49Kb 90)
UB10: Ick 34P 63
WD19: Wat 20Aa 27
ST GEORGE'S FIELD 45Gb 89
St George's Flds. W2 3E 220 (44Gb 89)
St George's Gdns. KT6: Surb 75Ra 153
KT17: Eps 86Va 174
St George's Gro. SW17 62Fb 133
ST GEORGE'S HILL 82R 170
St George's Hill Golf Course 83S 170
St George's Ho. NW1 2D 216
St Georges Ho. SW11 53Jb 112
(off Charlotte Despard Av.)
St George's Ind. Est.
KT2: King T 64Ma 131
N22 24Rb 51
St George's La. EC3 4G 225
SL5: Asc 1A 146 (9A 124)
St George's Leisure Cen. 45Xb 91
St George's Mans. SW1 7E 228
St George's M. NW1 38Hb 69
SE1 3A 230
SE8 49Bc 92
St Georges Pde. SE6 61Bc 136
(off Perry Hill)
St George's Path SE4 56Cc 114
(off Adelaide Av.)
St George's Pl. TW1: Twick 60Ja 108
St Georges Pl. KT10: Esh 77Ea 152
St George's RC Cathedral
3A 230 (48Qb 90)
St George's Rd. BR1: Brom 68Pc 138
BR3: Beck 67Dc 136
BR5: Pet W 72Tc 160
CR4: Mitc 69Kb 134
DA14: Sidc 65Zc 139
E7 38Kc 73
E10 34Ec 72
EN1: Enf 10Vb 19
HP3: Hem H 6L 3
IG1: Ilf 31Pc 74
KT2: King T 66Qa 131
KT13: Weyb 79T 150
KT15: Add 77L 149
N13 20Pb 32
NW11 30Bb 49
RM9: Dag 36Ad 75
SE1 3A 230 (48Qb 90)
SM6: Wall 78Kb 156
SW19 66Bb 133
(not continuous)
TN13: S'oaks 94Kd 203
TW1: Twick 57Ka 108
TW13: Hanw 63Z 129
W4 47Ta 87
W7 46Ha 86
WD24: Wat 10X 13
St Georges Rd. BR8: Swan 70Hd 140
(not continuous)
TW9: Rich 55Pa 109
St George's Rd. W. BR1: Brom 67Nc 138
St George's Shop. & Leisure Cen.
HA1: Harr 30Ga 46
St George's Sq. DA3: Lfield 69Ae 143
E7 38Kc 73
KT3: N Mald 69Ua 132
SE8 49Bc 92
(not continuous)
SW1 7D 228 (50Mb 90)
St Georges Sq. DA11: Grav'nd 8D 122
E14 45Ac 92
St George's Sq. M.
SW1 7D 228 (50Mb 90)
St George's Stadium 33V 64
St George's Ter. E6 41Nc 94
(off Masterman Rd.)
NW1 38Hb 69
SE15 52Wb 113
(off Peckham Hill St.)
St George St. W1 3A 222 (45Kb 90)
St George's Wlk. CR0: C'don 76Sb 157
St George's Way SE15 51Ub 113
St George's Wharf SE1 1K 231
St George Wharf SW8 51Nb 112
St Gerards Cl. SW4 57Lb 112
St German's Pl. SE3 53Jc 115
St German's Rd. SE23 60Ac 114
St Giles Av. EN6: S Mim 4Xa 16
RM10: Dag 38Dd 76
UB10: Ick 35S 64
St Giles Cir. W1 2E 222 (44Mb 90)
St Giles Cl. BR6: Farnb 78Tc 160
RM10: Dag 38Dd 76
RM16: Ors 2C 100
TW5: Hest 52Aa 107
St Giles Ct. EN1: Enf 7Yb 20
HP8: Chal G 19C 24
St Giles High St. WC2 2E 222 (44Mb 90)
St Giles Ho. EN5: New Bar 14Eb 31
SE5 53Ub 113
St Giles Pas. WC2 3E 222
St Giles Quad. HP8: Chal G 19C 24
St Giles Rd. SE5 52Ub 113
St Giles Ter. EC2 1E 224
St Giles Twr. SE5 53Ub 113
(off Gables Cl.)
St Gilles Ho. E2 40Zb 72
(off Mace St.)
St Gothard Rd. SE27 63Tb 135
(not continuous)
St Gregory Cl. HA4: Ruis 35Y 65
St Gregory's Ct. DA12: Grav'nd 1G 144
St Gregory's Cres.
DA12: Grav'nd 1G 144
St Helena Ho. WC1 4K 217
St Helena Rd. SE16 49Zb 92
St Helena St. WC1 4K 217 (41Qb 90)
St Helena Ter. TW9: Rich 57Ma 109
St Helens KT7: T Ditt 73Ha 152
St Helen's Cl. KT4: Wor Pk 74Wa 154
St Helens Cl. UB8: Cowl 43M 83
St Helen's Ct. RM13: Rain 42Jd 96
St Helens Ct. CM16: Epp 2Wc 23
St Helen's Cres. SW16 67Pb 134
St Helen's Gdns. W10 43Za 88
St Helen's M.
CM14: B'wood 19Zd 41
St Helen's Pl. EC3 2H 225 (44Ub 91)
St Helens Pl. E10 31Ac 72
St Helen's Rd. DA18: Erith 47Zc 95
IG1: Ilf 30Pc 54
SW16 67Pb 134
W13 46Ka 86
St Helen's Swimming & Fitness Club
23U 44
ST HELIER 73Gb 155
St Helier Av. SM4: Mord 73Eb 155
St Helier Ct. N1 39Ub 71
(off De Beauvoir Est.)
SE16 47Zb 92
(off Poolmans St.)
St Helier's Av. TW3: Houn 57Ca 107
St Helier's Rd. E10 30Ec 52
St Hilary's Ct. BR1: Brom 69Rc 138
St Hildas TN15: Plax 99Be 205
St Hilda's Av. TW15: Ashf 64N 127
St Hilda's Cl. GU21: Knap 9H 167
NW6 38Za 68
SW17 61Gb 133
St Hilda's Rd. SW13 51Xa 110
St Hilda's Way
DA12: Grav'nd 3F 144
St Hilda's Wharf E1 46Yb 92
(off Wapping High St.)
St Huberts Cl. SL9: Ger X 32A 62
St Hubert's Ho. E14 48Cc 92
(off Janet St.)
St Hubert's La. SL9: Ger X 33B 62
St Hughes Cl. SW17 61Gb 133
St Hugh's Rd. SE20 67Xb 135
St Ignatius College Sports Cen. 9Xb 19
St Ives Cl. RM3: Rom 24Pd 57
St Ives Pl. E14 43Ec 92
St Ivian Ct. N10 26Jb 50
St Ivian's Dr. RM2: Rom 27Jd 56
St James SE14 53Ac 114
St James Apartments E17 29Ac 52
(off Pretoria Av.)
St James Av. KT17: Ewe 83Va 174
N20 20Gb 31
SM1: Sutt 78Cb 155
W13 46Ja 86
St James Cl.
EN4: E Barn 14Fb 31
GU21: Wok 10L 167
HA4: Ruis 33Y 65
KT3: N Mald 71Va 154
KT18: Eps 86Ua 174
N20 20Gb 31
SE18 50Sc 94
St James Ct. AL1: St A 3E 6
CR0: C'don 73Rb 157
DA9: Ghithe 58Vd 120
E2 41Wb 91
(off Bethnal Grn. Rd.)
E12 33Lc 73
KT13: Weyb 78S 150
(off York Rd.)
KT21: Asht 89Ma 173
RM1: Rom 28Hd 56
SE3 53Kc 115
St James' Ct. SW1 3C 228 (48Lb 90)
St James Dr. RM3: Rom 23Nd 57
St James Gdns. RM6: Chad H 28Xc 55
St James' Gdns. HA0: Wemb 38Ma 67
St James Ga. IG9: Buck H 18Lc 35
SL5: S'dale 3D 146
St James Gro. SW11 54Hb 111
St James Hall N1 39Sb 71
(off Prebend St.)
St James Ho. RM1: Rom 29Hd 56
(off Eastern Rd.)
St James Ind. M. SE1 50Wb 91
St James La. DA9: Dart, Ghithe 60Ud 120
St James Mans. SE1 3K 229
St James' Mans. NW6 38Cb 69
(off West End La.)
St James M. E14 48Ec 92
E17 29Ac 52
(off St James's St.)
KT13: Weyb 77R 150
St James Oaks DA11: Grav'nd 9C 122
St James Path E17 29Ac 52
St James Pl. DA1: Dart 58Md 119
SL1: Slou 4A 80
St James Residences W1 4D 222
St James Rd. CM14: B'wood 20Yd 40
CR4: Mitc 66Jb 134
CR8: Purl 85Rb 177
SM1: Sutt 78Cb 155
SM5: Cars 76Gb 155
WD18: Wat 15X 27
St James' Rd. E15 36Hc 73
KT6: Surb 72Ma 153
N9 19Xb 33
ST JAMES'S 7C 222 (46Mb 90)
St James's App. EC2 6H 219 (42Ub 91)
St James's Av. BR3: Beck 69Ac 136
DA11: Grav'nd 9C 122
E2 40Yb 72
TW12: Hamp H 64Ea 130
St James's Chambers SW1 6C 222
St James's Cl. NW8 1F 215
SW17 61Hb 133
St James's Cotts.
TW9: Rich 57Ma 109
St James's Ct. HA1: Harr 30Ja 46
KT1: King T 69Na 131
N18 22Wb 51
(off Fore St.)
St James's Cres. SW9 55Qb 112
St James's Dr. SW12 60Hb 111
SW17 60Hb 111
St James's Gdns. W11 46Ab 88
(not continuous)
St James's Ho. SE1 49Wb 91
(off Strathnairn St.)
St James's La. N10 28Kb 50
St James's Mkt. SW1 5D 222 (45Mb 90)
St James's Palace 1C 228 (47Lb 90)
St James's Pk. 1D 228 (47Mb 90)
St James's Pk.
CR0: C'don 73Sb 157
St James's Pas. EC3 3J 225
St James's Pl. SW1 7B 222 (46Lb 90)
St James Sq. DA3: Lfield 69Ae 143
(off Park Dr.)
St James's Rd. CR0: C'don 73Rb 157
DA11: Grav'nd 8C 122
KT1: King T 68Ma 131
SE1 51Wb 113
SE16 48Wb 91
TN13: S'oaks 94Kd 203
TW12: Hamp H 64Da 129
St James's Sq. SW1 6C 222 (46Lb 90)
St James's St. DA11: Grav'nd 8C 122
E17 29Ac 52
SW1 6B 222 (46Lb 90)
St James's Ter. NW8 1F 215
St James's Ter. M. NW8 1F 215 (39Hb 69)
St James St. W6 50Ya 88
St James's Wlk. EC1 5B 218 (42Rb 91)
St James Ter. BR6: Prat B 81Yc 181
(off St Benjamins Dr.)
SW12 60Jb 112
St James Theatre 3B 228
St James Wlk. SL0: Rich P 47G 82
St James Way DA14: Sidc 64Ad 139
St Jeromes Gro. UB3: Hayes 44S 84
St Joan's Ho. NW1 3D 216
St Joan's Rd. N9 19Vb 33
St John Fisher Rd. DA18: Erith 48Zc 95
ST JOHN'S
RH1 8N 207
TN13 94Ld 203
ST JOHNS
GU21 10K 167
SE8 54Cc 114
St John's RH1: Redh 8N 207
St John's Av. CM14: W'ley 21Zd 59
KT17: Eps 84Wa 174
KT22: Lea 93Ka 192
N11 22Hb 49
NW10 39Va 68
SW15 57Za 110
St Johns Cvn. Pk. EN2: Enf 9Rb 19
St Johns Chu. Rd. E9 36Yb 72
St John's Cl. EN6: Pot B 5Eb 17
HA9: Wemb 36Na 67
KT22: Lea 93La 192
N20 20Eb 31
(off Rasper Rd.)
RM13: Rain 38Jd 76
SW6 52Cb 111
St Johns Cl. HP1: Hem H 4K 3
N14 16Lb 32
TN16: Big H 88Rc 180
UB8: Uxb 39K 63
St John's Concert Hall 4F 229
St John's Cnr. RH1: Redh 8P 207
(off St John's Rd.)
St John's Cotts. SE20 66Yb 136
St John's Ct. AL1: St A 1F 6
DA8: Erith 49Fd 96
E1 46Xb 91
(off Scandrett St.)
GU24: Brkwd 2D 186
HA1: Harr 30Ha 46
HA6: Nwood 24U 44
(off Murray Rd.)
IG9: Buck H 18Kc 35
KT1: King T 70Na 131
(off Beaufort Rd.)
N4 33Rb 71
RM17: Grays 49Ee 99
SE13 54Ec 114
TN13: S'oaks 94Ld 203
TW7: Isle 54Ha 108
TW20: Egh 64C 126
W6 49Xa 88
(off Glenthorne Rd.)
St Johns Ct. GU21: Wok 1L 187
RH9: S God 10D 210
SW10 52Eb 111
(off Ashburnham Rd.)
St John's Cres. SW9 55Qb 112
St John's Dr. KT12: Walt T 74Y 151
SL4: Wind 4E 102
St Johns Dr. SW18 60Db 111
St John's Est. N1 2G 219 (40Tb 71)
SE1 1K 231
St John's Gdns. GU21: Wok 10L 167
(off St John's Rd.)
W11 45Ab 88
St John's Gate 6B 218
St John's Gro. N19 33Lb 70
SW13 54Va 110
TW9: Rich 56Na 109
St John's Hill CR5: Coul 89Qb 176
SW11 57Fb 111
TN13: S'oaks 93Ld 203
St John's Hill Gro. SW11 56Fb 111
St John's Hill Rd. GU21: Wok 1L 187
St John's Ho. E14 49Ec 92
(off Pier St.)
St Johns Ho. SE17 51Tb 113
(off Lytham St.)
St John's Jerusalem 66Rd 141
St John's La. DA3: Hartl 72Be 165
EC1 6B 218 (42Rb 91)
St John's Lodge NW3 38Gb 69
(off King Henry's Rd.)
St Johns Lodge GU21: Wok 1L 187
St John's Lye GU21: Wok 1K 187
St John's Mans. EC1 3B 218
St John's M. GU21: Wok 1L 187
KT1: Hamp W 68La 130
W11 44Cb 89
St John's Pde. W13 46Ka 86
St Johns Pde. DA14: Sidc 63Wc 139
(off Sidcup High St.)
St John's Pk. SE3 52Hc 115
St John's Pk. Mans. N19 34Lb 70
St John's Pas. SW19 65Ab 132
St John's Path EC1 6B 218
St Johns Pathway SE23 60Yb 114
St John's Pl. EC1 6B 218 (42Rb 91)
St John's Ri. GU21: Wok 1M 187
St Johns Ri. TN16: Big H 88Rc 180
St John's Rd. BR5: Pet W 72Tc 160
CM16: Epp 2Vc 23
CR0: C'don 76Rb 157
DA2: Dart 59Sd 120
DA8: Erith 50Fd 96
DA12: Grav'nd 9F 122
DA14: Sidc 63Xc 139
(not continuous)
DA16: Well 55Xc 117
E4 21Dc 52
E6 39Nc 74
E16 44Jc 93
E17 26Dc 52
GU21: Wok 1K 187
HA1: Harr 30Ha 46
HA9: Wemb 35Ma 67
St John's Rd. HP1: Hem H 4J 3
IG2: Ilf 31Tc 74
IG10: Lough 12Pc 36
IG11: Bark 39Uc 74
KT1: Hamp W 68La 130
KT3: N Mald 69Sa 131
KT8: E Mos 70Fa 130
KT22: Lea 93La 192
N15 30Ub 51
NW11 30Bb 49
RH1: Redh 8P 207
SE20 65Yb 136
SL4: Wind 4E 102
SM1: Sutt 75Db 155
SM5: Cars 76Gb 155
SW11 56Gb 111
SW19 66Ab 132
TN13: S'oaks 93Kd 203
TW7: Isle 54Ha 108
TW9: Rich 56Na 109
TW13: Hanw 63Aa 129
UB2: S'hall 48Aa 85
UB8: Uxb 39K 63
WD17: Wat 12X 27
St Johns Rd. RM5: Col R 22Ed 56
RM16: Grays 10D 100
SL2: Slou 5L 81
St John's Sq. EC1 6B 218 (42Rb 91)
St Johns Sq. SL4: Eton 1H 103
St John's Ter. E7 37Kc 73
EN2: Enf 9Tb 19
SE18 51Sc 116
SW15 62Ua 132
(off Kingston Va.)
W10 42Za 88
St John's Ter. Rd. RH1: Redh 8P 207
St John St. EC1 2A 218 (40Qb 70)
St John's Va. SE8 54Cc 114
St John's Vs. N11 22Hb 49
(off Friern Barnet Rd.)
N19 33Mb 70
W8 48Db 89
(off St Mary's Pl.)
St Johns Waterside GU21: Wok 10K 167
(off Copse Rd.)
St John's Way KT16: Chert 74J 149
N19 33Lb 70
ST JOHN'S WOOD 2C 214 (40Fb 69)
St John's Wood Ct. NW8 4C 214
St John's Wood High St.
NW8 2C 214 (40Fb 69)
St John's Wood Pk. NW8 39Fb 69
St John's Wood Rd.
NW8 5B 214 (42Fb 89)
St John's Wood Ter.
NW8 1C 214 (40Fb 69)
St John's Yd. N17 24Vb 51
St Josephs Almshouses W6 49Za 88
(off Brook Grn.)
St Joseph's Cl. BR6: Orp 77Vc 161
W10 43Ab 88
St Joseph's College Sports Cen.
65Rb 135
St Joseph's Cotts. SW3 6F 227
St Joseph's Ct. E4 17Fc 35
St Josephs Ct. SE2 51Zc 117
SE7 51Kc 115
St Joseph's Dr. UB1: S'hall 46Aa 85
St Joseph's Flats NW1 3D 216
St Joseph's Gro. NW4 28Xa 48
St Joseph's Ho. W6 49Za 88
(off Brook Grn.)
St Joseph's Rd. EN8: Walt C 5Ac 20
N9 17Xb 33
St Joseph's St. SW8 53Kb 112
St Joseph's Va. SE3 55Fc 115
St Jude's Cl. TW20: Eng G 4N 125
St Jude's Cotts. TW20: Eng G 4N 125
St Judes Ct. IG8: Wfd G 24Nc 54
St Jude's Rd. E2 40Xb 71
St Judes Rd. TW20: Eng G 2N 125
St Jude St. N16 36Ub 71
St Julian Rd.
TN15: S'oaks, Under 100Nd 203
ST JULIANS 5B 6
St Julian's Cl. SW16 63Qb 134
St Julian's Farm Rd. SE27 63Qb 134
St Julian's Rd. AL1: St A 4B 6
NW6 39Cb 69
St Justin Cl. BR5: St P 69Zc 139
St Katharine Docks 5K 225
St Katharine's Pier 46Vb 91
St Katharine's Pct. NW1 1K 215 (40Kb 70)
St Katharine's Way E1 6K 225 (46Vb 91)
(not continuous)
St Katharine's Yacht Haven 46Vb 91
(off St Katharine's Way)
St Katherine's Rd. DA18: Erith 47Zc 95
St Katherines Rd. CR3: Cat'm 97Wb 197
St Katherine's Row EC3 3J 225
St Katherines Wlk. W11 46Za 88
(off St Ann's Rd.)
St Kathryn's Pl. RM14: Upm 33Sd 78
St Keverne Rd. SE9 63Nc 138
St Kilda Rd. BR6: Orp 74Vc 161
W13 46Ja 86
St Kilda's Rd. CM15: B'wood 17Xd 40
HA1: Harr 30Ga 46
N16 32Tb 71
St Kitts Ter. SE19 64Ub 135
St Laurence Cl. BR5: St P 69Zc 139
NW6 39Za 68
UB8: Cowl 43L 83
St Laurence Way SL1: Slou 8L 81
St Lawrence Bus. Cen.
TW13: Felt 61X 129
St Lawrence Cl. HA8: Edg 24Pa 47
HP3: Bov 9C 2
WD5: Ab L 2U 12
St Lawrence Cotts. E14 46Ec 92
(off St Lawrence St.)
St Lawrence Ct. GU24: Chob 3J 167
N1 38Tb 71
WD5: Ab L 2U 12
St Lawrence Dr. HA5: Eastc 29X 45
St Lawrence Ho. GU24: Chob 3J 167
(off Bagshot Rd.)
SE1 3J 231
St Lawrence Rd. RM14: Upm 33Sd 78
St Lawrence St. E14 46Ec 92
St Lawrence's Way RH2: Reig 6J 207
St Lawrence Ter. W10 43Ab 88
St Lawrence Way AL2: Brick W 2Ba 13
CR3: Cat'm 95Sb 197
SW9 53Qb 112
St Leger Ct. NW6 38Za 68
(off Coverdale Rd.)
St Leonard M. N1 1H 219

St Leonard's Av.—St Saviour's Rd.

St Leonard's Av. E4 23Fc 53
HA3: Kenton 29La 46
SL4: Wind 4G 102
St Leonard's Cl. DA16: Well 55Wc 117
WD23: Bush 14Aa 27
St Leonards Cl.
RM17: Grays 51Be 121
St Leonard's Ct. N1 3G 219
St Leonards Ct. SW14 55Sa 109
St Leonard's Gdns. IG1: Ilf 36Sc 74
TW5: Hest 52Aa 107
ST LEONARDS HAMLET 32Kd 77
St Leonard's Hill SL4: Wind 6B 102
St Leonard's Ri. BR6: Orp 77Uc 160
St Leonard's Rd. CR0: Wadd 76Rb 157
E14 43Dc 92
(not continuous)
KT6: Surb 71Ma 153
KT7: T Ditt 72Ja 152
KT10: Clay 79Ha 152
KT18: Tatt C 91Ya 194
NW10 42Ta 87
SL4: Wind 5E 102
(Imperial Rd.)
SL4: Wind 4G 102
(Osborne M.)
SL4: Wink 8A 102
SW14 55Ra 109
W13 45La 86
(not continuous)
St Leonards Sq. KT6: Surb 71Ma 153
NW5 37Jb 70
St Leonard's St. E3 41Dc 92
St Leonard's Studios SW3 7F 227
St Leonard's Ter. SW3 7F 227 (50Hb 89)
St Leonard's Wlk. SW16 66Pb 134
St Leonards Wlk. SL0: Rich P 48H 83
St Leonards Way RM11: Horn 33Kd 77
St Loo Av. SW3 51Gb 111
St Loo Ct. *SW3* *51Gb 111*
(off St Loo Av.)
St Louis Cl. EN6: Pot B 5Eb 17
St Louis Rd. SE27 63Tb 135
St Loy's Rd. N17 26Ub 51
St Lucia Dr. E15 39Hc 73
St Luke Cl. UB8: Cowl 44M 83
ST LUKE'S 5E 218 (42Sb 91)
St Luke's Av. EN2: Enf 10Tb 19
IG1: Ilf 36Rc 74
SW4 56Mb 112
St Luke's Cl. BR8: Swan 68Fd 140
DA2: Daren 64Ud 142
EC1 5E 218 (42Sb 91)
SE25 72Xb 157
St Lukes Ct. *E10* *31Dc 72*
(off Capworth St.)
GU21: Wok 86E 168
W11 *44Bb 89*
(off St Luke's Rd.)
St Luke's Est. EC1 4F 219 (41Tb 91)
St Luke's M. W11 44Bb 89
St Lukes M. *E14* *47Cc 92*
(off Strafford St.)
St Luke's Pas. KT2: King T 67Pa 131
St Luke's Path IG1: Ilf 36Rc 74
St Luke's Rd. CR3: Whyt 90Vb 177
SL4: Old Win 8L 103
UB10: Uxb 39N 63
W11 43Bb 89
St Luke's Sq. E16 44Hc 93
St Luke's St. SW3 7E 226 (50Gb 89)
St Luke's Yd. W9 40Bb 69
(not continuous)
St Magnus Ct. HP3: Hem H 4B 4
St Malo Av. N9 20Yb 34
St Margaret Dr. KT18: Eps 86Sa 173
ST MARGARETS
DA4 66Ud 142
TW1 58Ka 108
St Margaret's IG11: Bark 39Tc 74
KT2: King T 64Sa 131
St Margaret's Av. DA15: Sidc 62Tc 138
HA2: Harr 34Ea 66
N15 28Rb 51
N20 18Eb 31
SM3: Cheam 76Ab 154
SS17: Stan H 3L 101
TW15: Ashf 64R 128
St Margarets Av. TN16: Big H 88Rc 180
UB8: Hil 42Q 84
St Margarets Bus. Cen.
TW1: Twick 58Ka 108
St Margaret's Cl. BR6: Chels 77Xc 161
DA2: Dart 61Td 142
HP4: Berk 2A 2
St Margarets Cl. EC2 2F 225 (44Tb 91)
SL0: Iver H 40F 62
St Margaret's Ct. N11 21Jb 50
St Margarets Ct. HA8: Edg 22Ra 47
SE1 7F 225 (46Sb 91)
SL0: Iver H 40F 62
SW15 56Xa 110
St Margaret's Cres. DA12: Grav'nd 2G 144
SW15 57Xa 110
St Margaret's Dr. TW1: Twick 57Ka 108
St Margarets Ga. SL0: Iver H 40F 62
St Margaret's Gro. E11 34Hc 73
SE18 51Sc 116
TW1: Twick 58Ja 108
St Margaret's Ho. *NW1* *2D 216*
(off Polygon Rd.)
St Margaret's La. W8 48Db 89
St Margaret's M. KT2: King T 64Sa 131
St Margaret's Pas. SE13 55Gc 115
(not continuous)
St Margarets Path SE18 50Sc 94
St Margaret's Rd.
CR5: Coul 93Kb 196
E12 33Lc 73
HA4: Ruis 30T 44
HA8: Edg 22Ra 47
N17 27Ub 51
NW10 41Ya 88
W7 47Ga 86
St Margarets Rd.
DA2: G St G 66Ud 142
DA4: S Dar 66Ud 142
DA11: Nflt 10A 122
SE4 56Bc 114
(not continuous)
TW1: Twick 58Ka 108
TW7: Isle, Twick 56Ka 108
ST MARGARETS RDBT. 58Ka 108
St Margaret's Sports Cen. 18Da 27
St Margaret's Ter. SE18 50Sc 94
St Margaret St. SW1 2F 229 (47Nb 90)
St Margarets Way
HP2: Hem H 2C 4
St Margaret Way *SL1: Slou* *7D 80*
(off Mathecombe Rd.)
St Mark's Av. DA11: Nflt 9A 122
St Mark's Cl. EN5: New Bar 13Db 31
SE10 52Ec 114
W11 44Ab 88
St Marks Cl. AL4: Col H 4M 7
HA1: Harr 31Ka 66
SW6 53Cb 111
St Mark's Ct. *GU22: Wok* *91A 188*
(off Brooklyn Rd.)
St Marks Ct. NW8 2A 214
W7 *47Ga 86*
(off Lwr. Boston Rd.)
St Mark's Cres. NW1 39Jb 70
St Mark's Ga. E9 38Bc 72
St Mark's Gro. SW10 52Db 111
St Mark's Hill KT6: Surb 72Na 153
St Marks Ho. *SE17* *51Tb 113*
(off Lytham St.)
St Marks Ind. Est. E16 46Mc 93
St Mark's Pl. RM10: Dag 37Cd 76
SW19 65Bb 133
W11 44Ab 88
St Marks Pl. SL4: Wind 4G 102
St Mark's Ri. E8 36Vb 71
St Mark's Rd. BR2: Brom 69Jc 137
KT18: Tatt C 90Ya 174
SE25 70Wb 135
TW11: Tedd 66Ka 130
W5 46Na 87
W7 47Ga 86
W10 43Za 88
W11 44Ab 88
St Marks Rd. CR4: Mitc 68Hb 133
EN1: Enf 16Vb 33
SL4: Wind 4G 102
St Mark's Sq. BR2: Brom 69Jc 137
NW1 39Jb 70
St Mark St. E1 44Vb 91
St Mark's Vs. *N4* *33Pb 70*
(off Moray Rd.)
St Martha's Av.
GU22: Wok 93B 188
St Martin Cl. UB8: Cowl 44M 83
St Martin-in-the-Fields Church 5F 223
St Martins HA6: Nwood 22T 44
St Martin's Almshouses
NW1 39Lb 70
St Martin's App.
HA4: Ruis 31U 64
St Martin's Av. E6 40Mc 73
KT18: Eps 86Ua 174
St Martin's Cl. CM13: Hut 19Ee 41
DA18: Erith 47Zc 95
EN1: Enf 11Xb 33
NW1 39Lb 70
UB7: W Dray 48M 83
St Martins Cl. KT17: Eps 85Va 174
KT24: E Hor 100U 190
WD19: Wat 21Y 45
St Martin's Ct. EC4 2D 224
KT24: E Hor 100U 190
TW15: Ashf 64L 127
WC2 4F 223 (45Nb 90)
St Martins Ct. *N1* *39Ub 71*
(off De Beauvoir Est.)
St Martin's Courtyard WC2 4F 223
St Martin's Dr. DA4: Eyns 77Md 163
St Martins Dr.
KT12: Walt T 76Y 151
St Martins Est. SW2 60Qb 112
St Martin's Ho. *NW1* *3D 216*
(off Polygon Rd.)
St Martin's La. BR3: Beck 71Dc 158
WC2 4F 223 (45Nb 90)
St Martin's Le-Grand
EC1 2D 224 (44Sb 91)
St Martins Mdw.
TN16: Bras 95Yc 201
St Martins M. GU22: Pyr 88J 169
St Martin's Pl. WC2 5F 223 (45Nb 90)
St Martin's Rd. DA1: Dart 58Pd 119
N9 19Xb 33
SW9 54Pb 112
UB7: W Dray 48L 83
St Martin's St. WC2 5E 222 (45Mb 90)
(not continuous)
St Martin's Theatre 4F 223
St Martins Way SW17 62Eb 133
St Mary Abbot's Ct. *W14* *48Bb 89*
(off Warwick Gdns.)
St Mary Abbot's Pl. W8 48Bb 89
St Mary Abbot's Ter. W14 48Bb 89
St Mary at Hill EC3 5H 225 (45Ub 91)
St Mary Av. SM6: Wall 76Jb 156
St Mary Axe EC3 3H 225 (44Ub 91)
St Marychurch St. SE16 47Yb 92
ST MARY CRAY 70Yc 139
St Mary Graces Ct. E1 45Vb 91
St Marylebone Cl. NW10 39Ua 68
St Marylebone Crematorium N2 27Db 49
St Mary le-Park Ct. *SW11* *52Gb 111*
(off Parkgate Rd.)
St Mary Magdalene Gdns. N7 37Qb 70
St Mary Newington Cl. SE17 7J 231
St Mary Rd. E17 28Cc 52
St Mary's IG11: Bark 39Tc 74
St Marys KT13: Weyb 76T 150
St Mary's App. E12 36Pc 74
St Mary's Av. BR2: Brom 69Gc 137
CM15: Shenf 15Ce 41
E11 31Kc 73
HA6: Nwood 22U 44
N3 26Ab 48
TW11: Tedd 65Ha 130
TW19: Stanw 59M 105
St Mary's Av. Central UB2: S'hall 49Da 85
St Mary's Av. Nth. UB2: S'hall 49Da 85
St Mary's Av. Sth. UB2: S'hall 49Da 85
St Mary's Chu. Rd. TN14: Sund 97Bd 201
St Mary's Cl. BR5: St P 68Xc 139
DA12: Grav'nd 1E 144
IG10: Lough 14Nc 36
KT9: Chess 80Pa 153
KT17: Ewe 80Va 154
KT22: Fet 95Fa 192
N17 25Wb 51
RH8: Oxt 1J 211
TN15: Plat 92Ee 205
TW16: Sun 70W 128
TW19: Stanw 59M 105
UB9: Hare 27K 43
WD18: Wat *14Y 27*
(off George St.)
St Marys Cl. HP1: Hem H 1L 3
RM17: Grays 51Fe 121
St Mary's Copse KT4: Wor Pk 75Ua 154
St Mary's Ct. *E3* *41Dc 92*
(off Bow Rd.)
E6 42Pc 94
EN6: Pot B 4Db 17
HP2: Hem H 1M 3
KT3: N Mald 69Ua 132
SE7 52Mc 115
SM6: Wall 77Lb 156
TN16: Westrm 98Tc 200
W5 47Ma 87
W6 48Va 88
St Marys Ct. WD3: Rick 18N 25
St Mary's Cres. NW4 27Xa 48
TW7: Isle 52Fa 108
TW19: Stanw 59M 105
UB3: Hayes 45V 84
St Mary's Dr. TN13: Riv 95Gd 202
TW14: Bedf 59S 106
St Mary's Est. *SE16* *47Yb 92*
(off Elephant La.)
St Mary's Flats NW1 3D 216
St Marys Gdn. GU3: Worp 9J 187
St Mary's Gdns. SE11 5A 230 (49Qb 90)
St Mary's Ga. W8 48Db 89
St Mary's Grn. N2 26Eb 49
TN16: Big H 90Lc 179
St Mary's Gro. N1 37Rb 71
SW13 55Xa 110
TN16: Big H 90Lc 179
TW9: Rich 56Pa 109
W4 51Ra 109
St Mary's Hill SL5: S'hill 2A 146
St Mary's Ho. *N1* *39Rb 71*
(off St Mary's Path)
St Mary's La. CM13: W H'dn 31De 79
RM14: Upm 33Qd 77
St Mary's Mans. W2 7B 214 (43Fb 89)
St Mary's M. NW6 38Db 69
St Marys M. TW10: Ham 61La 130
St Mary's Mt. CR3: Cat'm 96Vb 197
St Mary's Path *E1* *44Wb 91*
(off White Church La.)
N1 39Rb 71
St Mary's Pl. SE9 58Pc 116
W5 47Ma 87
W8 48Db 89
ST MARYS PLATT 92Ee 205
St Mary's Rd. BR8: Swan 70Fd 140
CR2: Sande 82Tb 177
DA5: Bexl 60Ed 118
DA9: Ghithe 57Ud 120
E10 34Ec 72
E13 40Kc 73
EN4: E Barn 17Hb 31
EN8: Chesh 1Yb 20
GU21: Wok 9N 167
HP2: Hem H 1M 3
IG1: Ilf 33Sc 74
KT4: Wor Pk 75Ua 154
KT6: Surb 73La 152
(St Chads Cl.)
KT6: Surb 72Ma 153
(Victoria Rd.)
KT8: E Mos 71Fa 152
KT13: Weyb 77T 150
KT22: Lea 94Ka 192
N8 28Nb 50
N9 18Xb 33
(not continuous)
NW10 39Ua 68
NW11 31Ab 68
RH2: Reig 7K 207
RM16: Grays 8D 100
SE15 53Yb 114
SE25 69Ub 135
SL3: L'ly 46A 82
SL5: Asc 3A 146
SW19 64Ab 132
TN15: Wro 89Ce 185
UB3: Hayes 45V 84
UB9: Den 30H 43
UB9: Hare 27K 43
WD18: Wat 14X 27
St Marys Rd. W5 47Ma 87
St Mary's Sq. W2 7B 214 (43Fb 89)
W5 47Ma 87
St Mary's Ter. W2 7A 214 (43Fb 89)
St Mary's Twr. EC1 6E 218
St Mary St. SE18 49Pc 94
St Mary's University College 62Ha 130
St Mary's University College Sports Cen. 63Ha 130
St Mary's Vw. HA3: Kenton 29La 46
WD18: Wat *14Y 27*
(off King St.)
St Mary's Wlk. RH1: Blet 5K 209
SE11 5A 230 (49Qb 90)
UB3: Hayes 45V 84
St Mary's Way DA3: Lfield 69Ae 143
IG7: Chig 22Qc 54
SL9: Chal P 26A 42
St Matthew Cl. UB8: Cowl 44M 83
St Matthew's Av. KT6: Surb 74Na 153
St Matthew's Cl. RM13: Rain 38Jd 76
St Matthews Cl. WD19: Wat 16Z 27
St Matthew's Ct. *TW15: Ashf* *63Q 128*
(off Feltham Rd.)
St Matthews Ct. E10 31Dc 72
N10 26Jb 50
SE1 4D 230
St Matthew's Dr. BR1: Brom 69Pc 138
St Matthews Ho. *SE17* *51Tb 113*
(off Phelp St.)
St Matthew's Lodge NW1 1C 216
St Matthew's Rd. RH1: Redh 5P 207
SW2 56Pb 112
W5 46Na 87
St Matthew's Row E2 41Wb 91
St Matthew St. SW1 4D 228 (48Mb 90)
St Matthias Cl. NW9 29Va 48
St Maur Rd. SW6 53Bb 111
St Mawes Cl. WD3: Crox G 14R 26
St Mellion Cl. SE28 44Zc 95
St Merryn Cl. SE18 52Tc 116
St Merryn Ct. BR3: Beck 66Cc 136
St Michael's RH8: Limp 2L 211
St Michaels AL3: St A 2P 5
St Michael's All. EC3 3G 225 (44Tb 91)
St Michael's Av. HA9: Wemb 37Qa 67
N9 17Yb 34
St Michaels Av. HP3: Hem H 4B 4
St Michael's Cl. BR1: Brom 69Nc 138
DA18: Erith 47Zc 95
KT4: Wor Pk 75Va 154
KT12: Walt T 75Y 151
N3 26Bb 49
N12 22Gb 49
RM15: Avel 45Sd 98
St Michaels Cl. E16 43Mc 93
St Michael's Ct. *CR0: C'don* *74Sb 157*
(off Poplar Wlk.)
KT13: Weyb *78S 150*
(off Pine Gro.)
SE1 2E 230
St Michaels Ct. *E14* *43Ec 92*
(off St Leonard's Rd.)
SL2: Slou 2B 80
St Michael's Cres. HA5: Pinn 30Aa 45
St Michael's Dr. TN14: Otf 88Md 183
St Michaels Dr. WD25: Wat 5X 13
St Michael's Flats NW1 2D 216
St Michael's Gdns. W10 43Ab 88
St Michael's M. SW1 6H 227 (49Jb 90)
St Michael's Pde. WD24: Wat 10X 13
St Michael's Ri. DA16: Well 53Xc 117
St Michael's Rd. CR0: C'don 74Sb 157
CR3: Cat'm 94Tb 197
DA16: Well 55Xc 117
GU21: Wok 86F 168
NW2 35Ya 68
RM16: Grays 10D 100
SM6: Wall 79Lb 156
SW9 54Pb 112
TW15: Ashf 64Q 128
St Michael's St. AL3: St A 2P 5
W2 2C 220 (44Fb 89)
St Michael's Ter. N22 25Nb 50
St Michaels Ter. *N6* *32Jb 70*
(off South Gro.)
St Michaels Way EN6: Pot B 2Db 17
St Mildred's Ct. EC2 3F 225 (44Tb 91)
St Mildreds Rd. SE6 59Gc 115
SE12 59Gc 115
St Mirren Ct. EN5: New Bar 15Eb 31
St Monica's Rd. KT20: Kgswd 93Bb 195
St Nazaire Cl. TW20: Egh 64E 126
St Neots Cl. WD6: Bore 10Qa 15
St Neot's Rd. RM3: Rom 24Pd 57
St Nicholas Av. KT23: Bookh 97Da 191
RM12: Horn 34Jd 76
St Nicholas Cen. SM1: Sutt 78Db 155
St Nicholas Cl. UB8: Cowl 44M 83
WD6: E'tree 16Ma 29
St Nicholas Ct. *KT1: King T* *70Na 131*
(off Surbiton Rd.)
TN13: S'oaks *97Kd 203*
(off Lime Tree Wlk.)
St Nicholas Cres. GU22: Pyr 88J 169
St Nicholas Dr. TN13: S'oaks 98Kd 203
TW17: Shep 73Q 150
St Nicholas' Flats NW1 2D 216
St Nicholas Glebe SW17 64Jb 134
St Nicholas Gro. CM13: Ingve 22Ee 59
St Nicholas Hill KT22: Lea 94Ka 192
St Nicholas Ho. *SE8* *51Cc 114*
(off Deptford Grn.)
St Nicholas Ho's. EN2: Enf 7Jb 18
St Nicholas M. KT7: T Ditt 72Ha 152
St Nicholas Mt. HP1: Hem H 2H 3
St Nicholas Pl. IG10: Lough 14Qc 36
St Nicholas Rd. KT7: T Ditt 72Ha 152
SE18 50Vc 95
SM1: Sutt 78Db 155
St Nicholas St. SE8 53Bc 114
St Nicholas Way SM1: Sutt 77Db 155
St Nicolas La. BR7: Chst 67Nc 138
St Ninian's Ct. N20 20Hb 31
St Norbert Grn. SE4 56Ac 114
St Norbert Rd. SE4 57Zb 114
St Normans Way KT17: Ewe 82Wa 174
St Olaf Ho. SE1 6G 225
St Olaf's Rd. SW6 52Ab 110
St Olaf Stairs SE1 6G 225
St Olaves Cl. TW18: Staines 66H 127
St Olave's Ct. EC2 3F 225 (44Tb 91)
St Olave's Est. SE1 1J 231 (47Ub 91)
St Olave's Gdns. SE11 5K 229 (49Qb 90)
St Olaves Ho. SE11 5K 229
St Olave's Mans. SE11 5K 229
St Olave's Rd. E6 39Qc 74
St Olaves Wlk. SW16 68Lb 134
St Olav's Sq. SE16 47Yb 92
St Onge Pde. *EN1: Enf* *13Tb 33*
(off Southbury Rd.)
St Oswald's Pl. SE11 7H 229 (50Pb 90)
St Oswald's Rd. SW16 67Rb 135
St Oswalds Studios *SW6* *51Cb 111*
(off Sedlescombe Rd.)
St Oswulf St. SW1 6E 228 (49Mb 90)
St Owen Ho. SE1 3J 231
ST PANCRAS 4F 217 (41Nb 90)
St Pancras Commercial Cen.
NW1 *39Lb 70*
(off Pratt St.)
St Pancras Ct. N2 26Fb 49
St Pancras Way NW1 1D 216 (38Lb 70)
St Patrick's Ct. IG8: Wfd G 24Gc 53
St Patrick's Gdns. DA12: Grav'nd 2F 144
St Patrick's Pl. RM16: Grays 9D 100
St Patricks Pl. RM3: Rom 25Kd 57
St Paul Cl. UB8: Cowl 43M 83
St Paulinus Ct. *DA1: Cray* *56Gd 118*
(off Manor Rd.)
St Paul's All. *EC4* *3C 224*
(off St Paul's Chyd.)
St Paul's Av. HA3: Kenton 28Pa 47
NW2 37Ya 68
SE16 46Zb 92
St Pauls Av. SL2: Slou 5K 81
St Paul's Bldgs. EC1 5C 218
St Paul's Cathedral 3D 224 (44Sb 91)
St Paul's Chyd. EC4 3C 224 (44Rb 91)
St Paul's Cl. DA10: Swans 59Ae 121
KT9: Chess 77Ma 153
KT15: Add 78J 149
RM15: Avel 45Sd 98
SM5: Cars 74Gb 155
TW3: Houn 54Aa 107
TW15: Ashf 64S 128
UB3: Harl 50T 84
W5 47Pa 87
St Pauls Cl. SE7 50Mc 93
WD6: Bore 15Sa 29
St Paul's Ct. TW4: Houn 55Aa 107
St Pauls Ct. SW4 57Mb 112
WD4: Bucks 5M 11
WD4: Chfd 3J 11
St Pauls Courtyard *SE8* *52Cc 114*
(off Crossfield St.)
ST PAUL'S CRAY 68Xc 139
St Paul's Cray Rd. BR7: Chst 67Tc 138
St Paul's Cres. NW1 38Mb 70
(not continuous)
St Paul's Dr. E15 36Fc 73
St Pauls Ho. *SE8* *52Cc 114*
(off Market Yd.)
St Paul's M. NW1 38Mb 70
St Paul's Pl. N1 37Tb 71
St Pauls Pl. AL1: St A 2E 6
RM15: Avel 45Sd 98
St Paul's Ri. N13 23Rb 51
St Paul's Rd. CR7: Thor H 69Sb 135
DA8: Erith 52Ed 118
GU22: Wok 89C 168
HP2: Hem H 1M 3
IG11: Bark 39Sc 74
N1 37Rb 71
N17 24Wb 51
TW8: Bford 51Ma 109
TW9: Rich 55Pa 109
TW18: Staines 64F 126
St Paul's Shrubbery N1 37Tb 71
St Paul's Sq. BR2: Brom 68Hc 137
St Paul's Studios *W14* *50Ab 88*
(off Talgarth Rd.)
St Pauls Ter. SE17 51Rb 113
St Paul St. N1 1D 218 (39Sb 71)
(not continuous)
St Pauls Vw. Apartments EC1 4K 217
St Paul's Wlk. KT2: King T 66Qa 131
St Paul's Way E3 43Bc 92
N3 24Db 49
St Pauls Way EN9: Walt A 5Fc 21
WD24: Wat 12Y 27
St Paul's Wood Hill BR5: St P 68Uc 138
St Peter Claver Ct. *BR3: Beck* *67Dc 136*
(off Albemarle Rd.)
St Peters HP8: Chal G 19C 24
KT16: Chert 76E 148
St Peter's All. EC3 3G 225
St Peter's Av. E2 40Wb 71
E17 28Gc 53
N18 21Wb 51
St Peters Av. TN16: Big H 88Rc 180
St Petersburgh M. W2 45Db 89
St Petersburgh Pl. W2 45Db 89
St Peter's Cen. *E1* *46Xb 91*
(off Reardon St.)
St Peter's Chu. Ct. N1 1C 218
St Peter's Cl. AL1: St A 1B 6
BR7: Chst 66Tc 138
DA10: Swans 59Be 121
E2 40Wb 71
EN5: Barn 15Xa 30
GU22: Wok 92E 188
HA4: Ruis 33Z 65
IG2: Ilf 28Uc 54
SL1: Burn 2A 80
SL4: Old Win 7L 103
SW17 61Gb 133
TW18: Staines 65H 127
St Peters Cl. SL9: Chal P 25A 42
WD3: Rick 18K 25
WD23: B Hea 18Fa 28
St Peter's Ct. NW4 29Ya 48
SL9: Chal P 25A 42
WC1 4G 217
St Peters Ct. *E1* *42Yb 92*
(off Cephas St.)
KT8: W Mole 70Ca 129
SE12 57Hc 115
St Peter's Gdns. SE27 62Qb 134
St Peter's Gro. W6 49Wa 88
St Peter's Ho. WC1 4G 217
St Peters Ho. SE17 51Tb 113
St Peter's La. BR5: St P 68Wc 139
St Peter's M. AL1: St A 1B 6
St Peters M. N4 29Rb 51
N8 29Qb 50
St Peter's Path E17 27Gc 53
St Peters Pl. W9 42Db 89
St Peter's Rd. AL1: St A 2C 6
CM14: W'ley 21Xd 58
CR0: C'don 77Tb 157
GU22: Wok 93D 188
KT1: King T 68Qa 131
KT8: W Mole 70Ca 129
N9 18Xb 33
RM16: Grays 9D 100
TW1: Twick 57Ka 108
UB1: S'hall 43Ca 85
W6 50Wa 88
St Peters Rd. SL4: Old Win 7L 103
UB8: Cowl 43M 83
St Peter's Sq. E2 40Wb 71
W6 49Va 88
St Peter's St. AL1: St A 2B 6
(not continuous)
CR2: S Croy 78Tb 157
N1 1C 218 (39Rb 71)
St Peter's St. M. N1 1C 218
St Peter's Ter. SW6 52Bb 111
St Peter's Vs. W6 49Wa 88
St Peter's Way KT15: Add 77F 148
KT16: Chert 77F 148
N1 38Ub 71
W5 43Ma 87
St Peters Way UB3: Harl 50T 84
WD3: Chor 14D 24
St Peter's Wharf W4 50Wa 88
St Philip Ho. WC1 4K 217
St Philip's Av. KT4: Wor Pk 75Xa 154
St Philip's Ga. KT4: Wor Pk 75Xa 154
St Philip Sq. SW8 54Kb 112
St Philip's Rd. E8 37Wb 71
St Philips Rd. KT6: Surb 72Ma 153
St Philip St. SW8 54Kb 112
St Philip's Way N1 39Sb 71
St Pinnock Av. TW18: Staines 67J 127
St Quentin Ho. SW18 58Fb 111
St Quentin Rd. DA16: Well 55Vc 117
St Quintin Av. W10 43Ya 88
St Quintin Gdns. W10 43Ya 88
St Quintin Ho. *W10* *43Za 88*
(off Princess Louise Wlk.)
St Quintin Rd. E13 41Kc 93
St Quintin Vw. W10 43Ya 88
St Raphaels Ct. *AL1: St A* *1C 6*
(off Avenue Rd.)
St Raphael's Way NW10 36Sa 67
St Regis Cl. N10 26Kb 50
St Regis Hgts. NW3 34Db 69
St Richard's Ho. NW1 3D 216
St Ronan's Cl. EN4: Had W 10Fb 17
St Ronan's Cres. IG8: Wfd G 24Jc 53
St Ronans Vw. DA1: Dart 59Pd 119
St Rule St. SW8 54Lb 112
St Saviour's Ct. *CR8: Purl* *85Pb 176*
(off OLd Lodge La.)
St Saviours Ct. HA1: Harr 29Ga 46
N22 26Mb 50
St Saviour's Est. SE1 3K 231 (47Vb 91)
St Saviour's Rd. CR0: C'don 72Rb 157
SW2 57Pb 112

St Saviours Vw.—Sandringham Flats

St Saviours Vw. AL1: St A 1D 6
(off Lemsford Rd.)
St Saviours Wlk. DA1: Dart 58Nd 119
(off Bullace La.)
St Saviour's Wharf SE1 ....47Vb 91
(off Mill St.)
SE1 ....1K 231
(off Shad Thames)
Saints Cl. SE27 ....63Rb 135
Saints Dr. E7 ....36Mc 73
St Silas Pl. NW5 ....37Jb 70
St Simon's Av. SW15 ....57Ya 110
Saints M. CR4: Mitc 69Gb 133
ST STEPHENS 4A 6
St Stephen's Av. AL3: St A 4P 5
E17 ....29Ec 52
KT21: Asht 88Na 173
W12 ....46Xa 88
(not continuous)
W13 ....44Ka 86
St Stephen's Cl. E17 ....29Dc 52
NW8 ....1E 214 (39Gb 69)
UB1: S'hall 43Ca 85
St Stephens Cl. AL3: St A 5P 5
NW5 ....36Hb 69
(off Malden Rd.)
St Stephen's Ct. EN1: Enf 16Ub 33
(off Park Av.)
St Stephens Ct. N8 ....30Pb 50
RH9: S God 10C 210
(off Oaklands)
W13 ....44Ka 86
St Stephen's Cres.
CM13: B'wood 21Ce 59
CR7: Thor H 69Qb 134
W2 ....44Cb 89
St Stephens Cres. RM16: Grays 10D 100
St Stephen's Gdns. SW15 ....57Bb 111
TW1: Twick 58La 108
W2 ....44Cb 89
(not continuous)
St Stephens Gro. SE13 ....55Ec 114
St Stephen's Hill AL1: St A 4A 6
St Stephens Ho. SE17 ....51Tb 113
(off Lytham St.)
St Stephen's M. W2 ....43Cb 89
St Stephens Pde. E7 ....38Lc 73
St Stephen's Pas. TW1: Twick 58La 108
St Stephen's Rd. E3 ....39Ac 72
E6 ....38Lc 73
E17 ....29Dc 52
EN5: Barn 15Za 30
TW3: Houn 58Ca 107
UB7: Yiew 46M 83
W13 ....44Ka 86
St Stephens Rd. EN3: Enf W 9Zb 20
St Stephen's Row EC4 ....3F 225
St Stephen's Ter. SW8 ....52Pb 112
St Stephen's Wlk. SW7 ....5A 226
Saint's Wlk. RM16: Grays 9E 100
St Swithins La. EC4 ....4F 225 (45Tb 91)
St Swithun's Rd. SE13 ....58Fc 115
St Teresa Wlk. RM16: Grays 9D 100
St Theresa Cl. KT18: Eps 86Sa 173
St Theresa Ct. E4 ....17Fc 35
St Theresa's Cl. E9 ....35Cc 72
St Theresa's Rd. TW14: Felt 56V 106
St Thomas' Almshouses
DA11: Grav'nd 10C 122
St Thomas Cl. GU21: Wok 9N 167
KT6: Surb 74Pa 153
St Thomas Ct. DA5: Bexl 59Cd 118
E10 ....31Dc 72
(off Lake Rd.)
HA5: Pinn 25Aa 45
NW1 ....38Lb 70
(off Wrotham Rd.)
St Thomas Dr. BR5: Farnb 74Sc 160
St Thomas' Dr. HA5: Pinn 25Aa 45
St Thomas Gdns. IG1: Ilf 37Sc 74
St Thomas Ho. E1 ....44Zb 92
(off W. Arbour St.)
St Thomas M. SW18 ....57Cb 111
St Thomas Rd. DA11: Nflt 1A 144
DA17: Belv 47Ed 96
E16 ....44Jc 93
N14 ....17Mb 32
W4 ....51Sa 109
St Thomas' Rd. CM14: B'wood 19Zd 41
St Thomas's Av. DA11: Grav'nd 10D 122
St Thomas's Cl. EN9: Walt A 5Kc 21
St Thomas's Gdns. NW5 ....37Jb 70
St Thomas's M. SE7 ....49Nc 94
St Thomas's Pl. E9 ....38Yb 72
RM17: Grays 51De 121
St Thomas's Rd. N4 ....33Qb 70
NW10 ....39Ua 68
St Thomas's Sq. E9 ....38Yb 72
St Thomas St. SE1 ....7F 225 (46Tb 91)
St Thomas's Way SW6 ....52Bb 111
St Thomas Wlk. SL3: Coln 52F 104
St Timothys M. BR1: Brom 67Kc 137
St Ursula Gro. HA5: Pinn 29Z 45
St Ursula Rd. UB1: S'hall 44Ca 85
St Valery Pl. TW5: Hest 52Z 107
St Vincent Cl. SE27 ....64Rb 135
St Vincent De Paul Ho. E1 ....43Yb 92
(off Jubilee St.)
St Vincent Dr. AL1: St A 5E 6
St Vincent Ho. SE1 ....3K 231
St Vincent Rd. KT12: Walt T 76X 151
TW2: Whitt 58Ea 108
St Vincents Av. DA1: Dart 57Qd 119
St Vincent's Cots. WD18: Wat 14X 27
(off Marlborough Rd.)
ST VINCENT'S HAMLET 18Rd 39
St Vincent's La. NW7 ....21Ya 48
St Vincents Rd. DA1: Dart 58Qd 119
St Vincent St. W1 ....1J 221 (43Jb 90)
St Vincents Vs. DA1: Dart 58Pd 119
St Vincents Way EN6: Pot B 6Eb 17
St Wilfrid's Cl. EN4: E Barn 15Gb 31
St Wilfrid's Rd. EN4: E Barn 15Fb 31
St Williams Ct. N1 ....38Nb 70
St Winefride's Av. E12 ....36Pc 74
St Winifreds CR8: Kenley 87Sb 177
St Winifred's Cl. IG7: Chig 22Sc 54
St Winifred's Rd. TN16: Big H 90Pc 180
TW11: Tedd 65Ka 130
St Yon Ct. AL4: St A 2J 7
Sakura Dr. N22 ....25Mb 50
Saladin Dr. RM19: Purf 49Qd 97
Salamanca Pl. IG11: Bark 40Xc 75
SE1 ....6H 229 (49Pb 90)
Salamanca Sq. SE1 ....6H 229
Salamanca St. SE1 ....6H 229 (49Pb 90)
SE11 ....6H 229 (49Pb 90)
Salamander Cl. KT2: King T 64La 130
Salamander Quay KT1: Hamp W 67Ma 131
UB9: Hare 24J 43
Salamons Way RM13: Rain 44Gd 96
Salcombe Ct. E14 ....43Ec 92
(off St Ives Pl.)
Salcombe Dr. RM6: Chad H 30Bd 55
SM4: Mord 74Za 154
Salcombe Gdns. NW7 ....23Ya 48
Salcombe Pk. IG10: Lough 15Mc 35
Salcombe Rd. E17 ....31Bc 72
N16 ....36Ub 71
TW15: Ashf 62N 127
Salcombe Vs. TW10: Rich 57Na 109
Salcombe Way HA4: Ruis 33W 64
UB4: Hayes 41T 84
Salcot Cres. CR0: New Ad 82Ec 178
Salcote Rd. DA12: Grav'nd 4G 144
Salcott Rd. CR0: Bedd 76Nb 156
SW11 ....57Gb 111
Salehurst Cl. HA3: Kenton 29Na 47
Salehurst Rd. SE4 ....58Bc 114
Salem Pl. CR0: C'don 76Sb 157
DA11: Nflt 59Fe 121
Salem Rd. W2 ....45Db 89
Salento Cl. N3 ....24Cb 49
Sale Pl. W2 ....1D 220 (43Gb 89)
Salesian Gdns. KT16: Chert 74J 149
Sale St. E2 ....42Wb 91
Salford Ho. E14 ....49Ec 92
(off Seyssel St.)
Salford Rd. SW2 ....60Mb 112
Salhouse Cl. SE28 ....44Yc 95
Salisbury Av. AL1: St A 1F 6
BR8: Swan 70Jd 140
IG11: Bark 38Tc 74
N3 ....27Bb 49
SL2: Slou 2G 80
SM1: Sutt 79Bb 155
SS17: Stan H 2M 101
Salisbury Cl. EN6: Pot B 4Eb 17
KT4: Wor Pk 76Va 154
RM14: Upm 33Ud 78
SE17 ....5F 231 (49Tb 91)
Salisbury Ct. E9 ....36Ac 72
(off Mabley St.)
EC4 ....3B 224 (44Rb 91)
EN2: Enf 14Tb 33
(off London Rd.)
SE16 ....48Wb 91
(off Stork's Rd.)
SM5: Cars 78Hb 155
UB5: N'olt 36Da 65
(off Newmarket Av.)
Salisbury Cres. EN8: Chesh 4Zb 20
Salisbury Gdns. IG9: Buck H 19Mc 35
SW19 ....66Ab 132
Salisbury Hall Gdns. E4 ....23Cc 52
Salisbury Ho. AL3: St A 3A 6
E14 ....44Dc 92
(off Hobday St.)
EC2 ....1G 225
HA7: Stan 23Ja 46
N1 ....39Rb 71
(off St Mary's Path)
SM6: Wall 78Kb 156
SW1 ....7E 228
SW9 ....52Qb 112
(off Cranmer Rd.)
Salisbury Mans. N15 ....29Rb 51
Salisbury M. SW6 ....52Bb 111
Salisbury Pas. SW6 ....52Bb 111
(off Dawes Rd.)
Salisbury Pavement SW6 ....52Bb 111
(off Dawes Rd.)
Salisbury Pl. KT14: W Byf 83L 169
SW9 ....52Rb 113
W1 ....7F 215 (43Hb 89)
Salisbury Prom. N8 ....29Rb 51
Salisbury Rd. BR2: Brom 71Nc 160
DA2: Dart 60Sd 120
DA5: Bexl 60Cd 118
DA11: Grav'nd 10B 122
E4 ....20Cc 34
E7 ....37Jc 73
E10 ....33Ec 72
E12 ....36Mc 73
E17 ....29Ec 52
EN3: Enf L 9Bc 20
EN5: Barn 13Ab 30
GU22: Wok 91A 188
HA1: Harr 29Fa 46
HA5: Eastc 28W 44
IG3: Ilf 33Uc 74
KT3: N Mald 69Ta 131
KT4: Wor Pk 77Ta 153
N4 ....29Rb 51
N22 ....25Rb 51
RH9: G'stone 3A 210
RM2: Rom 29Kd 57
RM10: Dag 37Dd 76
RM17: Grays 51Ee 121
SE25 ....72Wb 157
SM5: Cars 79Hb 155
SM7: Bans 86Db 175
SW19 ....66Ab 132
TW4: Houn 55Y 107
TW6: H'row A 58S 106
(not continuous)
TW9: Rich 56Na 109
TW13: Felt 60Y 107
UB2: S'hall 49Aa 85
UB8: Uxb 40K 63
W13 ....47Ka 86
WD24: Wat 10X 13
Salisbury Sq. EC4 ....3A 224 (44Qb 90)
Salisbury St. NW8 ....6C 214 (42Gb 89)
W3 ....47Sa 87
Salisbury Ter. SE15 ....55Yb 114
Salisbury Wlk. N19 ....33Lb 70
Salix Cl. KT22: Fet 95Da 191
TW16: Sun 66X 129
Salix Ct. N3 ....23Cb 49
Salix La. IG8: Wfd G 25Nc 54
Salix Rd. RM17: Grays 51Fe 121
Salk Cl. NW9 ....26Ua 48
Salliesfield TW2: Whitt 58Fa 108
Sallow Rd. RM3: Hrld W 26Nd 57
Sallows Shaw DA13: Sole S 10E 144
Sally Murray Cl. E12 ....35Qc 74
Salmen Rd. E13 ....40Hc 73
Salmond Cl. HA7: Stan 23Ja 46
Salmonds Gro. CM13: Ingve 22Ee 59
Salmon La. E14 ....44Ac 92
Salmon Mdw. HP3: Hem H 6M 3
Salmon M. NW6 ....36Cb 69
Salmon Rd. DA1: Dart 55Pd 119
DA17: Belv 50Cd 96
Salmons La. CR3: Whyt, Cat'm 92Ub 197
Salmons La. W. CR3: Cat'm 92Ub 197
Salmons Rd. KT9: Chess 79Na 153
KT24: Eff 100X 191
N9 ....18Wb 33
Salmon St. E14 ....44Bc 92
NW9 ....32Ra 67
Salomons Rd. E13 ....43Lc 93
Salop Rd. E17 ....30Zb 52
Salsabil Apartments E3 ....42Bc 92
Saltash Cl. SM1: Sutt 77Bb 155
Saltash Rd. DA16: Well 53Yc 117
IG6: Ilf 24Tc 54
Salt Box Cotts. GU2: Guild 10L 187
Saltbox Hill TN16: Big H 85Kc 179
Saltbox Hill Nature Reserve 84Kc 179
Salt Box Rd. GU3: Guild 10K 187
GU4: Guild 10K 187
Saltcoats Rd. W4 ....47Ua 88
Saltcote Cl. DA1: Cray 58Gd 118
Saltcroft Cl. HA9: Wemb 32Ra 67
Saltdene N4 ....32Pb 70
Salter Cl. HA2: Harr 35Ba 65
Salterford Rd. SW17 ....65Jb 134
Saltern Ct. IG11: Bark 41Xc 95
(off Galleons Dr.)
Salter Rd. SE16 ....46Zb 92
Salters Cl. WD3: Rick 18N 25
Salters Ct. EC4 ....3E 224
Salters Gdns. WD17: Wat 11W 26
Salter's Hall Ct. EC4 ....4F 225
Salter's Hill SE19 ....64Tb 135
Salters Rd. E17 ....28Fc 53
W10 ....42Za 88
Salters Row N1 ....37Tb 71
(off Tilney Gdns.)
Salter St. E14 ....45Bc 92
(not continuous)
NW10 ....41Wa 88
Salterton Rd. N7 ....34Pb 70
Saltford Cl. DA8: Erith 50Gd 96
SALT HILL 6G 80
Salt Hill Av. SL1: Slou 6G 80
Salt Hill Cl. UB8: Uxb 36N 63
Salt Hill Dr. SL1: Slou 6G 80
Salt Hill Mans. SL1: Slou 6G 80
Salt Hill Way SL1: Slou 6G 80
Saltings, The
DA9: Ghithe 56Yd 120
Saltley Cl. E6 ....44Nc 94
Salton Cl. N3 ....26Cb 49
Salton Sq. E14 ....44Bc 92
Saltoun Rd. SW2 ....56Qb 112
Saltram Cl. N15 ....28Vb 51
Saltram Cres. W9 ....41Bb 89
Saltwell St. E14 ....45Cc 92
Saltwood Cl. BR6: Chels 77Yc 161
Saltwood Gro. SE17 ....7F 231 (50Tb 91)
Saltwood Ho. SE15 ....51Yb 114
(off Lovelinch Cl.)
Salusbury Rd. NW6 ....39Ab 68
Salus Ct. CR0: C'don 77Sb 157
(off Parker Rd.)
Salutation Rd. SE10 ....49Gc 93
Salvador SW17 ....64Hb 133
Salvation Pl. KT22: Fet 96Ja 192
Salvia Ct. GU24: Bisl 8E 166
Salvia Gdns. UB6: G'frd 40Ja 66
Salvin Rd. SW15 ....55Za 110
Salway Cl. IG8: Wfd G 24Jc 53
Salway Pl. E15 ....37Fc 73
Salway Rd. E15 ....37Fc 73
Samantha Cl. E17 ....31Bc 72
Samantha M. RM4: Have B 20Gd 38
Samaras Mans. E20 ....36Ec 72
(off Liberty Bri. Rd.)
Samas Way DA1: Cray 57Jd 118
Sam Bartram Cl. SE7 ....50Lc 93
Sambourne Family Home, The
18 Stafford Terrace 48Cb 89
(off Stafford Ter.)
Sambroke Sq. EN4: E Barn 14Fb 31
Sambrook Ho. E1 ....43Yb 92
(off Jubilee St.)
SE11 ....6K 229
Sambruck M. SE6 ....60Dc 114
Samels Ct. W6 ....50Wa 88
Samford Ho. N1 ....1K 217
Samford St. NW8 ....6D 214 (42Fb 89)
Samian Ga. AL3: St A 4M 5
Samira Cl. E17 ....30Cc 52
Sam King Wlk. SE5 ....52Tb 113
(off Edmund St.)
Sam Manners Ho. SE10 ....50Gc 93
(off Tuskar St.)
Sam March Ho. E14 ....44Fc 93
(off Blair St.)
Sammi Ct. CR7: Thor H 70Sb 135
Samos Rd. SE20 ....68Xb 135
Samphire Ct. RM17: Grays 1A 122
Samphire Hgts. E20 ....36Ec 72
(off Napa Cl.)
Sampson Av. EN5: Barn 15Za 30
Sampson Cl. DA17: Belv 48Zc 95
Sampson Ct. TW17: Shep 71S 150
Sampson Ho. SE1 ....6C 224 (46Rb 91)
Sampson's Grn. SL2: Slou 1D 80
Sampson St. E1 ....46Wb 91
Samsbrooke Ct. EN1: Enf 16Ub 33
Samson St. E13 ....40Lc 73
Samuda Est. E14 ....48Ec 92
Samuel Cl. E8 ....39Vb 71
HA7: Stan 19Ja 28
SE14 ....51Zb 114
SE18 ....49Nc 94
Samuel Ct. N1 ....4H 219
Samuel Ferguson Pl. IG11: Bark 40Vc 75
Samuel Gray Gdns. KT2: King T 67Ma 131
Samuel Ho. E8 ....39Vb 71
(off Clarissa St.)
Samuel Johnson Cl. SW16 ....63Pb 134
Samuel Jones Ct. SE15 ....52Ub 113
Samuel Lewis Bldgs. N1 ....37Qb 70
Samuel Lewis Trust Dwellings
E8 ....36Wb 71
(off Amhurst Rd.)
N16 ....30Ub 51
SW3 ....6D 226 (49Gb 89)
SW6 ....52Cb 111
(off Vanston Pl.)
W14 ....49Bb 89
(off Lisgar Ter.)
Samuel Lewis Trust Est. SE5 ....53Sb 113
(off Warner Rd.)
Samuel Palmer Ct. BR6: Orp 73Wc 161
(off Chislehurst Rd.)
Samuel Richardson Ho. W14 ....49Bb 89
(off North End Cres.)
Samuel's Cl. W6 ....49Ya 88
Samuel Sq. AL1: St A 3B 6
(off Pageant Rd.)
Samuel St. SE15 ....52Vb 113
SE18 ....49Pc 94
Samuel Wallis Lodge SE3 ....55Hc 115
(off Banning St.)
SE10 ....49Gc 93
(off Banning St.)
Sanchia Ct. E2 ....41Wb 91
(off Wellington Row)
Sancroft Cl. NW2 ....34Xa 68
Sancroft Ho. SE11 ....7J 229
Sancroft Rd. HA3: W'stone 26Ha 46
Sancroft St. SE11 ....7J 229 (50Pb 90)
Sanctuary, The DA5: Bexl 58Zc 117
SM4: Mord 72Cb 155
SW1 ....3E 228
Sanctuary Cl. DA1: Dart 58Ld 119
UB9: Hare 24L 43
Sanctuary Gdns. SS17: Stan H 1N 101
Sanctuary M. E8 ....37Vb 71
Sanctuary Rd. TW6: H'row A 58Q 106
Sanctuary St. SE1 ....1E 230 (47Sb 91)
Sandale Cl. N16 ....34Tb 71
Sandall Cl. W5 ....42Na 87
Sandall Ho. E3 ....40Ac 72
Sandall Rd. NW5 ....37Lb 70
W5 ....42Na 87
Sandal Rd. KT3: N Mald 71Ta 153
N18 ....22Wb 51
Sandal St. E15 ....39Gc 73
Sandalwood Av. KT16: Chert 76G 148
Sandalwood Cl. E1 ....42Ac 92
EN5: Ark 15Va 30
Sandalwood Dr. HA4: Ruis 31S 64
Sandalwood Ho. DA15: Sidc 61Vc 139
Sandalwood Mans. W8 ....48Db 89
(off Stone Hall Gdns.)
Sandalwood Rd. TW13: Felt 62X 129
Sanday Cl. HP3: Hem H 4B 4
Sandbach Pl. SE18 ....49Sc 94
Sandbanks TW14: Felt 60U 106
Sandbanks Hill DA2: G St G 65Xd 142
Sandbourne NW8 ....39Db 69
(off Abbey Rd.)
W11 ....44Cb 89
(off Dartmouth Cl.)
Sandbourne Av. SW19 ....68Db 133
Sandbourne Rd. SE4 ....54Ac 114
Sandbrook Cl. NW7 ....23Ta 47
Sandbrook Rd. N16 ....34Ub 71
Sandby Ct. NW10 ....41Xa 88
(off Plough Cl.)
Sandby Grn. SE9 ....55Nc 116
Sandby Ho. NW6 ....39Cb 69
Sandcliff Rd. DA8: Erith 49Fd 96
Sandcroft Cl. N13 ....23Rb 51
Sandcross La. RH2: Reig 9H 207
Sandell's Av. TW15: Ashf 63S 128
Sandell St. SE1 ....1K 229 (47Qb 90)
Sanderling Cl. RM18: E Til 9K 101
Sanderling Ct. SE8 ....51Bc 114
(off Abinger Gro.)
SE28 ....45Yc 95
Sanderling Lodge E1 ....45Vb 91
(off Star Pl.)
Sanderling Way DA9: Ghithe 58Wd 120
Sanders Cl. AL2: Lon C 9H 7
HP3: Hem H 6P 3
TW12: Hamp H 64Ea 130
Sanders Ct. CM14: W'ley 21Yd 58
Sandersfield Gdns. SM7: Bans 87Cb 175
Sandersfield Rd. SM7: Bans 87Db 175
Sanders Ho. WC1 ....3K 217
Sanders La. NW7 ....24Ya 48
(Bittacy Ri.)
NW7 ....24Za 48
(Grants Cl.)
TW4: Houn 57Ba 107
Sanderson Cl. CM13: W H'dn 30Ge 59
NW5 ....35Kb 70
Sanderson Ho. E16 ....43Jc 93
(off Hammersley Rd.)
SE8 ....50Bc 92
(off Grove St.)
Sanderson Rd. UB8: Uxb 37L 63
Sandersons Av. TN14: Bad M 82Cd 182
Sandersons La. W4 ....50Ta 87
(off Chiswick High Rd.)
Sanderson Sq. BR1: Brom 69Qc 138
Sanders Pl. AL1: St A 3E 6
(off Camp Rd.)
Sanders Rd. HP3: Hem H 6A 4
SANDERSTEAD 84Wb 177
Sanderstead Av. NW2 ....33Ab 68
Sanderstead Cl. SW12 ....59Lb 112
Sanderstead Ct. Av.
CR2: Sande 85Wb 177
Sanderstead Hill CR2: Sande 83Ub 177
Sanderstead Rd. BR5: St M Cry 72Xc 161
CR2: Sande, S Croy 80Tb 157
E10 ....32Ac 72
Sanders Way N19 ....32Mb 70
Sandes Ct. CR7: Thor H 69Sb 135
Sandes Pl. KT22: Lea 90Ja 172
Sandfield WC1 ....4G 217
Sandfield Gdns. CR7: Thor H 69Rb 135
Sandfield Pas. CR7: Thor H 69Sb 135
Sandfield Pl. CR7: Thor H 69Sb 135
Sandfield Rd. AL1: St A 2E 6
CR7: Thor H 69Rb 135
Sandfields GU23: Send 96F 188
Sandford Av. IG10: Lough 13Sc 36
N22 ....25Sb 51
Sandford Cl. E6 ....42Pc 94
Sandford Ct. EN5: New Bar 13Db 31
N16 ....32Ub 71
Sandford Rd. BR2: Brom 69Jc 137
DA7: Bex 56Ad 117
E6 ....41Nc 94
Sandford St. SW6 ....52Db 111
Sandgate Cl. RM7: Rush G 31Ed 76
Sandgate Ho. E5 ....36Xb 71
W5 ....43La 86
Sandgate La. SW18 ....60Gb 111
Sandgate Rd. DA16: Well 52Yc 117
Sandgates KT16: Chert 75G 148
Sandgate St. SE15 ....51Xb 113
Sandgate Trad. Est. SE15 ....51Xb 113
(off Sandgate St.)
Sandham Ct. SW4 ....53Nb 112
Sandham Point SE18 ....49Rc 94
(off Vincent Rd.)
Sandhills SM6: Bedd 77Mb 156
Sandhills, The SW10 ....51Eb 111
(off Limerston St.)
Sandhills Ct. GU25: Vir W 71A 148
Sandhills La. GU25: Vir W 71A 148
Sandhills Mdw. TW17: Shep 73S 150
Sandhills Rd. RH2: Reig 7J 207
Sandhurst Av. HA2: Harr 30Da 45
KT5: Surb 73Ra 153
Sandhurst Cl. CR2: Sande 81Ub 177
NW9 ....27Qa 47
Sandhurst Ct. SW2 ....56Nb 112
Sandhurst Dr. IG3: Bark, Ilf 35Vc 75
Sandhurst Ho. E1 ....43Yb 92
(off Wolsy St.)
E17 ....25Bc 52
(off Robinswood Gdns.)
Sandhurst Mkt. SE6 ....60Ec 114
(off Sandhurst Rd.)
Sandhurst Rd. BR6: Chels 76Wc 161
DA5: Bexl 57Zc 117
DA15: Sidc 62Vc 139
N9 ....16Yb 34
NW9 ....27Qa 47
RM18: Tilb 4E 122
SE6 ....60Fc 115
Sandhurst Way CR2: Sande 80Ub 157
Sandifer Dr. NW2 ....34Za 68
Sandifield AL10: Hat 3D 8
Sandiford Rd. SM3: Sutt 75Bb 155
Sandiland Cres. BR2: Hayes 75Hc 159
Sandilands CR0: C'don 75Wb 157
TN13: Chip 94Fd 202
Sandilands Rd. SW6 ....53Db 111
Sandison St. SE15 ....55Wb 113
Sandlands Gro. KT20: Walt H 95Wa 194
Sandlands Rd. KT20: Walt H 95Wa 194
Sandland St. WC1 ....1J 223 (43Pb 90)
Sandlers End SL2: Slou 2F 80
Sandling Ri. SE9 ....62Qc 138
Sandlings, The N22 ....26Qb 50
Sandlings Cl. SE15 ....54Xb 113
Sandmartin Way SM6: Wall 74Jb 156
Sandmere Cl. HP2: Hem H 3A 4
Sandmere Rd. SW4 ....56Nb 112
Sandon Cl. KT10: Esh 73Fa 152
Sandon Rd. EN8: Chesh 2Yb 20
Sandover Ho. SE16 ....48Wb 91
(off Spa Rd.)
Sandow Cres. UB3: Hayes 48V 84
Sandown Av. KT10: Esh 78Ea 152
RM10: Dag 37Ed 76
RM12: Horn 33Md 77
Sandown Cl. RM16: Ors 3G 100
TW5: Cran 53W 106
Sandown Ct. HA7: Stan 22La 46
RH1: Redh 5N 207
(off Station Rd.)
RM10: Dag 37Ed 76
(off Sandown Av.)
SE26 ....62Xb 135
SM2: Sutt 80Db 155
Sandown Dr. SM5: Cars 81Jb 176
Sandown Ga. KT10: Esh 76Fa 152
Sandown Ind. Pk. KT10: Esh 75Ca 151
Sandown Lodge KT18: Eps 86Ta 173
Sandown Pk. Golf Course 76Da 151
Sandown Pk. Racecourse 75Ea 152
Sandown Rd. CR5: Coul 88Jb 176
DA12: Grav'nd 5E 144
KT10: Esh 77Ea 152
RM16: Ors 3G 100
SE25 ....71Xb 157
SL2: Slou 3D 80
WD24: Wat 10Y 13
Sandown Rd. Ind. Est. WD24: Wat 9Y 13
Sandown Sports Club 76Da 151
Sandown Way UB5: N'olt 37Aa 65
Sandpiper Cl. AL10: Hat 1C 8
DA9: Ghithe 58Wd 120
E17 ....24Zb 52
RM18: E Til 9K 101
SE16 ....47Bc 92
Sandpiper Ct. E1 ....45Wb 91
(off Thomas More St.)
E14 ....48Ec 92
(off New Union Cl.)
SE8 ....51Cc 114
(off Edward Pl.)
Sandpiper Dr. DA8: Erith 52Kd 119
HA2: Harr 33Da 65
Sandpiper Ho. UB7: Yiew 45M 83
(off Wraysbury Dr.)
Sandpiper Rd. CR2: Sels 83Zb 178
SM1: Sutt 78Bb 155
Sandpipers, The DA12: Grav'nd 1F 144
Sandpiper Ter. IG5: Ilf 27Rc 54
Sandpiper Way BR5: St P 70Zc 139
Sandpit Cotts. GU24: Pirb 4C 186
Sandpit Hall Rd. GU24: Chob 4L 167
Sandpit La. AL1: St A 1C 6
AL4: St A 1C 6
CM14: Pil H, S Weald 18Vd 40
CM15: Pil H 18Vd 40
GU21: Knap 6F 166
(not continuous)
Sandpit Pl. SE7 ....50Nc 94
Sandpit Rd. BR1: Brom 64Gc 137
DA1: Dart 56Ld 119
RH1: Redh 7N 207
Sandpits Rd. CR0: C'don 77Zb 158
TW10: Ham 61Ma 131
Sandra Cl. N22 ....25Sb 51
TW3: Houn 57Da 107
Sandra Ct. CR4: Mitc 65Hb 133
Sandra Ho. KT8: E Mos 71Fa 152
Sandridge Cl. EN4: Had W 9Gb 17
HA1: Harr 28Ga 46
Sandridge Rd. AL1: St A 1C 6
Sandridge St. N19 ....33Lb 70
Sandringham Av. SW20 ....67Ab 132
Sandringham Bldgs. SE17 ....5F 231
Sandringham Cl. EN1: Enf 12Ub 33
GU22: Pyr 88J 169
IG6: Ilf 27Sc 54
SW19 ....60Za 110
WD6: Bore 15Sa 29
Sandringham Ct. DA15: Sidc 58Vc 117
KT2: King T 67Na 131
(off Skerne Wlk.)
SE16 ....46Zb 92
(off King & Queen Wharf)
SL1: Slou 4B 80
SM2: Sutt 81Cb 175
UB10: Hil 42S 84
W1 ....3C 222
W9 ....4A 214
Sandringham Cres.
HA2: Harr 33Ca 65
Sandringham Dr. DA2: Wilm 61Gd 140
DA16: Well 54Uc 116
TW15: Ashf 63M 127
Sandringham Flats WC2 ....4E 222

Sandringham Gdns. IG6: Ilf 27Sc **54**
KT8: W Mole 70Ca **129**
N8 30Nb **50**
N12 23Fb **49**
TW5: Cran 53W **106**
Sandringham Ho. *W14* *49Ab* ***88***
(off Windsor Way)
Sandringham M. TW12: Hamp 67Ba **129**
W5 45Ma **87**
Sandringham Pk. KT11: Cobh 84Ca **171**
Sandringham Rd. BR1: Brom 64Jc **137**
CM15: Pil H 16Xd **40**
CR7: Thor H 71Sb **157**
E7 36Lc **73**
E8 36Vb **71**
E10 30Fc **53**
EN6: Pot B 2Db **17**
IG11: Bark 36Vc **75**
KT4: Wor Pk 76Wa **154**
N22 27Sb **51**
NW2 37Xa **68**
NW11 31Ab **68**
TW6: H'row A 57N **105**
UB5: N'olt 38Ca **65**
WD24: Wat 9Y **13**
Sandringham Way EN8: Walt C 6Yb **20**
Sandrock Pl. CR0: C'don 77Zb **158**
Sandrock Rd. SE13 55Cc **114**
Sandroyd Way KT11: Cobh 85Ca **171**
SANDS END **53Eb 111**
Sand's End La. SW6 53Db **111**
Sands Farm Dr. SL1: Burn 2A **80**
Sandshaw Ct. DA3: Hartl 71Ae **165**
Sandstone Cl. RH1: Mers 100Nb **196**
Sandstone La. E16 45Kc **93**
Sandstone Pl. N19 33Kb **70**
Sandstone Rd. SE12 61Kc **137**
Sands Way IG8: Wfd G 23Pc **54**
Sandtoft Rd. SE7 51Kc **115**
Sandway Path *BR5: St M Cry* *70Yc* ***139***
(off Okemore Gdns.)
Sandway Rd. BR5: St M Cry 70Yc **139**
Sandwell Cres. NW6 37Cb **69**
Sandwich Ho. *SE16* *47Yb* ***92***
(off Swan Rd.)
WC1 4F **217**
Sandwich St. WC1 4F **217** (41Nb **90**)
Sandwick Cl. NW7 24Wa **48**
Sandy Bank Rd. DA12: Grav'nd 10D **122**
Sandy Bury BR6: Orp 76Tc **160**
Sandy Cl. GU22: Wok 89E **168**
Sandycombe Rd.
TW9: Kew, Rich 55Pa **109**
TW14: Felt 60W **106**
Sandycoombe Rd. TW1: Twick 58La **108**
Sandy Ct. KT11: Cobh 85Ba **171**
Sandy Cft. KT17: Ewe 82Ya **174**
Sandycroft SE2 51Wc **117**
Sandy Dr. KT11: Cobh 83Ca **171**
TW14: Felt 60U **106**
Sandy Gro. WD6: Bore 12Pa **29**
Sandy Hill Av. SE18 50Rc **94**
Sandy Hill Rd. SE18 50Rc **94**
SM6: Wall 81Lb **176**
Sandyhill Rd. IG1: Ilf 35Rc **74**
Sandy Holt KT11: Cobh 85Ba **171**
Sandy La. BR5: St P 68Zc **139**
BR6: Orp 73Wc **161**
CR4: Mitc 67Jb **134**
DA2: Bean, Sflt 61Yd **142**
DA14: Sidc 68Zc **139**
GU22: Pyr 89J **169**
(not continuous)
GU22: Wok 89D **168**
GU23: Send 95E **188**
GU24: Chob 1J **167**
GU25: Vir W 70A **126**
(not continuous)
HA3: Kenton 30Pa **47**
HA6: Nwood 19V **26**
KT1: Hamp W 66Ja **130**
KT11: Cobh 84Ba **171**
KT12: Walt T 72X **151**
KT20: Kgswd 96Bb **195**
KT22: Oxs 84Ca **171**
RH1: Blet 4H **209**
RH1: S Nut 7D **208**
RH2: Reig 7D **206**
RH3: Bet 7A **206**
RH8: Limp 99Kc **199**
RH8: Oxt 1G **210**
RM15: Avel, Wenn 45Pd **97**
RM16: Grays 1D **122**
RM20: W Thur 50Xd **98**
SL5: S'dale 1E **146**
SM2: Cheam 80Ab **154**
SM6: Wall 79Mb **156**
TN13: S'oaks 95Ld **203**
TN15: Ivy H, Igh 97Xd **204**
TN16: Westrm 97Tc **200**
TW10: Ham 61La **130**
TW11: Hamp W, Tedd 66Ja **130**
WD23: Bush 13Ea **28**
WD25: A'ham 13Ea **28**
Sandy La. Cvn. Site WD25: A'ham 13Ea **28**
Sandy La. Nth. SM6: Wall 79Mb **156**
Sandy La. Sth. SM6: Wall 81Lb **176**
Sandy Lodge HA5: Hat E 23Ca **45**
HA6: Nwood 19U **26**
Sandy Lodge Ct. HA6: Nwood 22U **44**
Sandy Lodge Golf Course 19T **26**
Sandy Lodge La. HA6: Nwood 19T **26**
Sandy Lodge Rd. WD3: Rick 19R **26**
Sandy Lodge Way HA6: Nwood 22T **44**
Sandy Mead KT19: Eps 82Qa **173**
Sandymount Av. HA7: Stan 22La **46**
Sandy Ride SL5: S'hill 10C **124**
Sandy Ridge BR7: Chst 65Qc **138**
TN15: Bor G 92Ce **205**
Sandy Ri. SL9: Chal P 25A **42**
Sandy Rd. KT15: Add 79J **149**
NW3 33Db **69**
NW11 33Db **69**
Sandys Row E1 1J **225** (43Ub **91**)
Sandy Way CR0: C'don 76Bc **158**
GU22: Wok 89E **168**
KT11: Cobh 84Ca **171**
KT12: Walt T 74V **150**
Sanford La. N16 34Vb **71**
Sanford St. SE14 51Ac **114**
Sanford Ter. N16 34Vb **71**
Sanford Wlk. N16 33Vb **71**
SE14 51Ac **114**
Sangam Cl. UB2: S'hall 48Aa **85**
Sanger Av. KT9: Chess 78Na **153**
Sanger Dr. GU23: Send 95E **188**
Sangley Rd. SE6 59Dc **114**
SE25 70Ub **135**
Sangora Rd. SW11 56Fb **111**
San Juan Dr. RM16: Chaf H 49Yd **98**
Sankey Ho. *E2* *40Yb* ***72***
(off St James's Av.)
San Luis Dr. RM16: Chaf H 49Yd **98**
San Marcos Dr. RM16: Chaf H 49Yd **98**
Sansom Cl. WD3: Crox G 15T **26**
Sansom Rd. E11 33Hc **73**
Sansom St. SE5 53Tb **113**
Sans Wlk. EC1 5A **218** (42Qb **90**)
Santa Maria Ct. *E1* *43Ac* ***92***
(off Ocean Est.)
Santers La. EN6: Pot B 5Ab **16**
Sant Ho. SE17 6E **230**
Santiago Ct. *E1* *43Ac* ***92***
(off Ocean Est.)
Santiago Way RM16: Chaf H 50Zd **99**
Santina Apartment
CR0: C'don *74Tb* ***157***
(off Cherry Orchard Rd.)
Santley Ho. SE1 2A **230** (47Qb **90**)
Santley St. SW4 56Pb **112**
Santos Rd. SW18 57Cb **111**
Santway, The HA7: Stan 22Ga **46**
SANWAY **86N 169**
Sanway Cl. KT14: Byfl 86N **169**
Sanway Rd. KT14: Byfl 86N **169**
Sapcote Trad. Cen. NW10 37Va **68**
Saperton Wlk. SE11 5J **229**
Saphire Ct. *E15* *39Ec* ***72***
(off Warton Rd.)
Sapho Pk. DA12: Grav'nd 3H **145**
Saphora Cl. BR6: Farnb 78Tc **160**
Sapperton Ct. EC1 5D **218**
Sapperton Ho. *W2* *43Cb* ***89***
(off Westbourne Pk. Rd.)
Sapphire Cl. E6 44Qc **94**
RM8: Dag 32Yc **75**
Sapphire Ct. *E1* *45Wb* ***91***
(off Cable St.)
Sapphire Rd. NW10 38Sa **67**
SE8 49Ac **92**
Sappho Ct. GU21: Wok 8J **167**
Saracen Cl. CR0: C'don 72Tb **157**
Saracen Est. HP2: Hem H 1B **4**
Saracen Ind. Area HP2: Hem H 1A **4**
Saracens Head HP2: Hem H 1A **4**
Saracens Head Yd. AL1: St A 2B **6**
EC3 3K **225**
Saracens RUFC 24Ya **48**
Saracen St. E14 44Cc **92**
Sara Cres. DA9: Ghithe 56Xd **120**
Sarah Ct. UB5: N'olt 39Ba **65**
Sarah Ho. *E1* *44Xb* ***91***
(off Commercial Rd.)
Sarah Swift Ho. SE1 1G **231**
Sara La. Ct. N1 1J **219**
Sara Pk. DA12: Grav'nd 3G **144**
Saratoga Rd. E5 35Yb **72**
Sara Turnbull Ho. SE18 49Pc **94**
Saravia Ct. SE13 58Gc **115**
Sarcus Dean SL9: Chal P 22B **42**
Sardinia St. WC2 3H **223** (44Pb **90**)
Sargeant Cl. UB8: Cowl 41M **83**
Sarita Cl. HA3: Hrw W 26Fa **46**
Sarjant Path *SW19* *61Za* ***132***
(off Blincoe Cl.)
Sarjeant Ct. *BR4: W W'ck* *75Fc* ***159***
(off Bencurtis Pk.)
Sark Cl. TW5: Hest 52Ca **107**
Sark Ho. EN3: Enf W 10Zb **20**
WD18: Wat *16V* ***26***
(off Scammell Way)
Sark Twr. SE28 47Sc **94**
Sark Wlk. E16 44Kc **93**
Sarnes Ct. *N11* *21Kb* ***50***
(off Oakleigh Rd. Sth.)
Sarnesfield Ho. *SE15* *51Xb* ***113***
(off Pencraig Way)
Sarnesfield Rd. EN2: Enf 14Tb **33**
SARRATT 8J **11**
SARRATT BOTTOM 9G **10**
SARRATT HALL 7J **11**
Sarratt Ho. *W10* *43Ya* ***88***
(off Sutton Way)
Sarratt La. WD3: Chor, Loud, Sarr 12K **25**
Sarratt Rd.
WD3: Sarr, Chan C, Crox G 9K **11**
Sarre Av. RM12: Horn 37Ld **77**
Sarre Rd. BR5: St M Cry 71Yc **161**
NW2 36Bb **69**
Sarsby Dr. TW19: Wray 61C **126**
Sarsen Av. TW3: Houn 54Ca **107**
Sarsens Cl. DA12: Cobh 9H **145**
Sarsfeld Rd. SW12 61Hb **133**
Sarsfield Rd. UB6: G'frd 40Ka **66**
Sartor Rd. SE15 56Zb **114**
Sarum Complex UB8: Uxb 41K **83**
Sarum Grn. KT13: Weyb 76U **150**
Sarum Ho. *W11* *45Bb* ***89***
(off Portobello Rd.)
Sarum Ter. E3 42Bc **92**
Sassoon NW9 25Va **48**
Sassoon M. DA11: Nflt 61De **143**
Satanita Cl. E16 44Mc **93**
Satchell Mead NW9 25Va **48**
Satchwell Rd. E2 41Wb **91**
Satchwell St. E2 41Wb **91**
Satin Ho. *E1* *44Wb* ***91***
(off Piazza Wlk.)
Satinwood Ct. HP3: Hem H 4N **3**
Satis Ct. KT17: Ewe 83Va **174**
Satis Ho. SL3: Dat 2N **103**
Sattar M. N16 34Tb **71**
Saturn Ho. *E3* *39Cc* ***72***
(off Garrison Rd.)
E15 *39Fc* ***73***
(off High St.)
Sauls Grn. E11 34Gc **73**
Saundby La. SE3 56Kc **115**
Saunders Apartments *E3* *41Cc* ***92***
(off Marchant St.)
Saunders Cl. DA11: Nflt 1A **144**
E14 *45Bc* ***92***
(off Limehouse C'way.)
IG1: Ilf 32Tc **74**
Saunders Copse GU22: Wok 4M **187**
Saunders Ho. *SE16* *47Zb* ***92***
(off Quebec Way)
Saunders La. GU22: Wok 4J **187**
Saunders Ness Rd. E14 50Ec **92**
Saunders Rd. SE18 50Vc **95**
UB10: Uxb 38P **63**
Saunders St. SE11 5K **229** (49Qb **90**)
Saunders Way DA1: Dart 61Pd **141**
SE28 45Xc **95**
Saunderton Rd.
HA0: Wemb 36Ka **66**
Saunton Av. UB3: Harl 52V **106**
Saunton Ct. *UB1: S'hall* *45Ea* ***86***
(off Haldane Rd.)
Saunton Rd. RM12: Horn 33Jd **76**
Savage Gdns. E6 44Pc **94**
EC3 4J **225** (45Ub **91**)
(not continuous)
Savanna Ct. *WD18: Wat* *14V* ***26***
(off Rickmansworth Rd.)
Savannah Cl. SE15 52Vb **113**
Savay Cl. UB9: Den 31J **63**
Savay La. UB9: Den 30J **43**
Savera Cl. UB2: S'hall 48Y **85**
Savernake Ct. HA7: Stan 23Ka **46**
Savernake Ho. N4 31Sb **71**
Savernake Rd. N9 16Wb **33**
NW3 35Hb **69**
Savery Dr. KT6: Surb 73Ka **152**
Savile Cl. KT3: N Mald 71Ua **154**
KT7: T Ditt 74Ha **152**
Savile Gdns.
CR0: C'don 75Vb **157**
Savile Row W1 4B **222** (45Lb **90**)
Savill Building, The 5K **125**
Saville Cl. KT19: Eps 83Ra **173**
Saville Cres. TW15: Ashf 65T **128**
Saville Pl. TW20: Eng G 4P **125**
Saville Rd. E16 46Nc **94**
RM6: Chad H 30Bd **55**
TW1: Twick 60Ha **108**
W4 48Ta **87**
Saville Row BR2: Hayes 74Hc **159**
EN3: Enf H 12Zb **34**
Savill Garden, The 5J **125**
Savill Gdns. SW20 69Wa **132**
Savill Ho. *E16* *46Rc* ***94***
(off Robert St.)
SW4 58Mb **112**
Savill M. TW20: Eng G 5P **125**
Savill Row IG8: Wfd G 23Hc **53**
Savin Lodge
SM2: Sutt *80Eb* ***155***
(off Walnut M.)
Savona Cl. SW19 66Za **132**
Savona Ho. *SW8* *52Lb* ***112***
(off Savona St.)
Savona St. SW8 52Lb **112**
Savoy Av. UB3: Harl 50U **84**
Savoy Bldgs. WC2 5H **223**
Savoy Chapel 5H **223**
SAVOY CIRCUS **45Va 88**
Savoy Cl. E15 39Gc **73**
HA8: Edg 22Qa **47**
UB9: Hare 26M **43**
Savoy Ct. HA2: Harr 29Da **45**
NW3 34Eb **69**
SW5 *49Cb* ***89***
(off Cromwell Rd.)
WC2 5G **223** (45Pb **90**)
Savoy Gro. RM11: Horn 30Kd **57**
Savoy Hill WC2 5H **223** (45Pb **90**)
Savoy M. AL1: St A 5P **5**
SW9 55Nb **112**
Savoy Pde. EN1: Enf 13Ub **33**
Savoy Pl. W12 46Za **88**
WC2 5G **223** (45Nb **90**)
Savoy Rd.
DA1: Dart 57Md **119**
Savoy Row WC2 4H **223**
Savoy Steps WC2 5H **223**
Savoy St. WC2 4H **223** (45Pb **90**)
Savoy Theatre 5H **223**
Savoy Way WC2 5H **223**
Sawbill Cl. UB4: Yead 43Z **85**
Sawbridgeworth Ct. *WD23: Bush* *15Ea* ***28***
(off Goddard Dr.)
Sawcotts Way RM16: Grays 8A **100**
Sawkins Cl. SW19 61Ab **132**
Sawley Rd. W12 46Wa **88**
Saw Mill Way N16 30Wb **51**
Sawmill Yd. E3 39Ac **72**
Sawston Ct. *RM19: Purf* *50Rd* ***97***
(off Linnet Way)
Sawtry Cl. SM5: Cars 73Gb **155**
Sawtry Way WD6: Bore 10Qa **15**
Sawyer Cl. N9 19Wb **33**
Sawyer Ct. NW10 38Ta **67**
Sawyers Chase RM4: Abr 13Xc **37**
Sawyers Cl. RM10: Dag 37Ed **76**
SL4: Wind 2C **102**
Sawyers Ct. CM15: Shenf 17Be **41**
EN8: Walt C 5Zb **20**
Sawyers Gro. CM15: B'wood 18Zd **41**
Sawyers Hall La. CM15: B'wood 17Yd **40**
Sawyer's Hill TW10: Rich 59Pa **109**
Sawyers La. EN6: Pot B 5Za **16**
Sawyers Lawn W13 44Ja **86**
Sawyer St. SE1 1D **230** (47Sb **91**)
Sawyers Way HP2: Hem H 2P **3**
Saxby Rd. SW2 59Nb **112**
Saxbys Rd. TN15: Seal 94Td **204**
Saxham Rd. IG11: Bark 40Uc **74**
Saxlingham Rd. E4 20Fc **35**
Saxon Av. TW13: Hanw 61Aa **129**
Saxonbury Av. TW16: Sun 69X **129**
Saxonbury Cl. CR4: Mitc 69Fb **133**
Saxonbury Ct. N7 36Nb **70**
Saxonbury Gdns. KT6: Surb 74La **152**
Saxon Bus. Cen. SW19 68Eb **133**
Saxon Chase N8 30Pb **50**
Saxon Cl. CM13: B'wood 20Ce **41**
DA11: Nflt 62Ee **143**
E17 31Cc **72**
KT6: Surb 72Ma **153**
RM3: Hrld W 26Pd **57**
SL3: L'ly 47B **82**
TN14: Otf 89Hd **182**
UB8: Hil 43P **83**
Saxon Ct. HA6: Nwood 24V **44**
N1 39Nb **70**
SL0: Iver 44G **82**
WD6: Bore 11Na **29**
Saxon Dr. W3 44Qa **87**
Saxonfield Cl. SW2 59Pb **112**
Saxon Gdns. UB1: S'hall 45Aa **85**
Saxon Hall *W2* *45Db* ***89***
(off Palace Ct.)
Saxon Ho. E1 1K **225**
KT1: King T 70Pa **131**
SM6: Wall *74Jb* ***156***
(off London Rd.)
TN14: S'oaks 93Md **203**
TW13: Hanw 61Ba **129**
Saxon Lea Ct. *E3* *40Bc* ***72***
(off Saxon Rd.)
Saxon Lodge *CR0: C'don* *74Sb* ***157***
(off Tavistock Rd.)
Saxon Pl. DA4: Hort K 71Sd **164**
Saxon Rd. BR1: Brom 66Hc **137**
DA2: Hawl 63Nd **141**
E3 40Bc **72**
E6 42Pc **94**
HA9: Wemb 34Sa **67**
IG1: Ilf 37Rc **74**
KT2: King T 67Na **131**
KT12: Walt T 76Z **151**
N22 25Rb **51**
SE25 71Tb **157**
TW15: Ashf 65T **128**
UB1: S'hall 45Aa **85**
Saxons KT20: Tad 93Za **194**
Saxon Ter. SE6 61Bc **136**
Saxon Wlk. DA14: Sidc 65Yc **139**
Saxon Way EN9: Walt A 5Ec **20**
N14 16Mb **32**
RH2: Reig 5H **207**
SL4: Old Win 8M **103**
UB7: Harm 51L **105**
Saxon Way Ind. Est. UB7: Harm 51L **105**
Saxony Pde. UB3: Hayes 43S **84**
Saxton Cl. RM17: Grays 51De **121**
SE13 55Fc **115**
Saxton M. WD17: Wat 12W **26**
Saxton Pl. KT8: W Mole 70Ba **129**
Saxville Rd. BR5: St P 69Xc **139**
Sayer Cl. DA9: Ghithe 57Wd **120**
Sayers Cl. KT22: Fet 95Ea **192**
Sayers Ct. W5 47Ma **87**
Sayers Ho. *N2* *26Fb* ***49***
(off The Grange)
Sayer's Wlk. TW10: Rich 59Pa **109**
Sayesbury La. N18 22Wb **51**
Sayes Ct. KT15: Add 78L **149**
SE8 51Bc **114**
Sayes Ct. Farm Dr. KT15: Add 78K **149**
Sayes Ct. Rd. BR5: St P 70Wc **139**
Sayes Ct. St. SE8 51Bc **114**
Scadbury Gdns. BR5: St P 68Wc **139**
Scadbury Pk. (Nature Reserve) **66Vc** 139
Scads Hill Cl. BR6: Pet W 72Vc **161**
Scafell NW1 3B **216**
Scafell Rd. SL2: Slou 2D **80**
Scala *3G 217*
(off Pentonville Rd.)
Scala St. W1 7C **216** (43Lb **90**)
Scales Rd. N17 27Vb **51**
Scalpel, The 3H **225**
Scammell Way WD18: Wat 16V **26**
Scampston M. W10 44Za **88**
Scandrett St. E1 46Xb **91**
Scarab Cl. E16 45Hc **93**
Scarba Wlk. *N1* *37Tb* ***71***
(off Essex Rd.)
Scarborough Cl. SM2: Cheam 83Bb **175**
TN16: Big H 90Lc **179**
Scarborough Dr. WD3: Crox G 14R **26**
Scarborough Rd. E11 32Fc **73**
N4 31Qb **70**
N9 17Yb **34**
TW6: H'row A 58S **106**
Scarborough St. E1 3K **225** (44Vb **91**)
Scarborough Way SL1: Slou 8F **80**
Scarbrook Rd. CR0: C'don 76Sb **157**
Scarle Rd. HA0: Wemb 37Ma **67**
Scarlet Cl. BR5: St P 70Xc **139**
E20 36Dc **72**
Scarlet Rd. DA8: Erith 52Jd **118**
SE6 62Gc **137**
Scarlett Cl. GU21: Wok 10K **167**
Scarlette Mnr. Way SW2 59Qb **112**
Scarlet Wlk. EN3: Pond E 15Zb **34**
Scarsbrook Rd. SE3 55Mc **115**
Scarsdale Pl. W8 48Db **89**
Scarsdale Rd. HA2: Harr 34Ea **66**
Scarsdale Studios *W8* *48Cb* ***89***
(off Stratford Rd.)
Scarsdale Vs. W8 48Cb **89**
Scarth Rd. SW13 55Va **110**
Scatterdells La. WD4: Chfd 2H **11**
Scatterdells Pk. WD4: Chfd 2J **11**
Scawen Cl. SM5: Cars 77Jb **156**
Scawen Rd. SE8 50Ac **92**
Scawfell St. E2 40Vb **71**
SCC Smallholdings Rd.
KT17: Eps 86Ya **174**
(not continuous)
Sceaux Gdns. SE5 53Ub **113**
Sceptre Ct. EC3 4K **225**
Sceptre Ho. *E1* *42Yb* ***92***
(off Malcolm Rd.)
Sceptre Rd. E2 41Yb **92**
Sceynes Link N12 21Cb **49**
Schafer Ho. NW1 5B **216** (41Lb **90**)
Schofield Wlk. SE3 52Jc **115**
Scholars, The *WD18: Wat* *15Y* ***27***
(off Lady's Cl.)
Scholars Cl. EN5: Barn 14Ab **30**
Scholar's Ct. *AL1: St A* *2C* ***6***
(off Newsom Pl.)
Scholars Ct. AL4: Col H 5N **7**
RM2: Rom *29Jd* ***56***
(off Academy Flds. Rd.)
Scholars Ho. *NW6* *39Cb* ***69***
(off Glengall Rd.)
Scholars Pl. KT12: Walt T 74Y **151**
N16 34Ub **71**
Scholars Rd. E4 18Fc **35**
SW12 60Lb **112**
Scholars Vw. KT7: T Ditt 73Ga **152**
Scholars Wlk. AL10: Hat 3C **8**
(not continuous)
SL3: L'ly 47C **82**
SL9: Chal P 23A **42**
Scholars Way RM2: Rom 29Kd **57**
RM8: Dag 35Wc **75**
Scholefield Rd. N19 33Mb **70**
Scholey Ho. SW11 55Gb **111**
Schomberg Ho. SW1 5E **228**
Schonfeld Sq. N16 33Tb **71**
School All. TW1: Twick 60Ja **108**
School Allotment Ride SL4: Wink 9A **102**
School App. E2 3J **219**
TN15: Bor G 92Ce **205**
UB4: Hayes 42V **84**
Schoolbank Rd. SE10 48Hc **93**
Schoolbell M. E3 40Ac **72**
School Cl. GU24: Bisl 7D **166**
School Cotts. *GU22: Wok* *4N* ***187***
(off Mayford Grn.)
School Cres. DA1: Cray 56Hd **118**
Schoolfield Rd. RM20: W Thur 51Wd **120**
Schoolfield Way RM20: W Thur 51Wd **120**
Schoolgate Dr. SM4: Mord 71Db **155**
School Hill RH1: Mers 100Lb **196**
School Ho. SE1 5H **231**
Schoolhouse Gdns. IG10: Lough 14Rc **36**
School Ho. La. NW7 23Ab **48**
TW11: Tedd 66Ka **130**
Schoolhouse La. E1 45Zb **92**
Schoolhouse Yd. SE18 50Rc **94**
School La. AL2: Brick W 6Ba **13**
BR8: Swan 67Kd **141**
CM13: Ingve 23Ee **59**
CR3: Cat'm 98Vb **197**
DA2: Bean 63Yd **142**
DA3: Fawk 71Ud **164**
DA4: Hort K 70Sd **142**
DA16: Well 55Xc **117**
GU20: W'sham 8B **146**
GU23: Ock 94R **190**
GU24: Pirb 4C **186**
HA5: Pinn 28Aa **45**
IG7: Chig 21Vc **55**
KT1: Hamp W 67La **130**
KT6: Surb 74Pa **153**
KT15: Add 78J **149**
KT20: Walt H 97Wa **194**
KT22: Fet 94Fa **192**
KT24: W Hor 100R **190**
RH5: Mick 99La **192**
RM16: Ors 3C **100**
SE23 61Xb **135**
SL2: Slou 5K **81**
SL2: Stoke P 8M **61**
SL9: Chal P 26A **42**
TN11: Plax, S'brne 100Ae **205**
TN15: Plax 100Ae **205**
TN15: Seal 93Pd **203**
TN15: W King 84Ud **184**
TW17: Shep 72R **150**
TW20: Egh 64C **126**
WD23: Bush 17Da **27**
WD25: Wat 6Ba **13**
School Mead WD5: Ab L 4U **12**
School M. *E1* *45Xb* ***91***
(off Hawksmoor M.)
School Nook E5 33Zb **72**
School Pde. UB9: Hare 26L **43**
School Pas. KT1: King T 68Pa **131**
UB1: S'hall 45Ba **85**
School Rd. BR7: Chst 67Sc **138**
DA12: Grav'nd 2E **144**
E12 35Pc **74**
EN6: Pot B 2Eb **17**
GU20: W'sham 8A **146**
KT1: Hamp W 67La **130**
KT8: E Mos 70Fa **130**
NW10 42Ta **87**
RM10: Dag 39Cd **76**
SL5: S'hill 1B **146**
TW3: Houn 55Ea **108**
TW12: Hamp H 65Ea **130**
TW15: Ashf 65R **128**
UB7: Harm 51M **105**
School Rd. Av. TW12: Hamp H 65Ea **130**
SCHOOL ROAD JUNC. **66R 128**
School Row HP1: Hem H 3H **3**
School Sq. SE10 48Hc **93**
School Wlk. SL2: Slou 5M **81**
TW16: Sun 70V **128**
School Way N12 23Fb **49**
RM8: Dag 34Yc **75**
Schooner Cl. E14 48Fc **93**
IG11: Bark 41Xc **95**
SE16 47Zb **92**
Schooner Ct. DA2: Dart 56Sd **120**
Schooner Ho. DA8: Erith 50Gd **96**
Schooner Pk. DA2: Dart 57Sd **120**
Schroder Ct. TW20: Eng G 4M **125**
Schubert Rd. SW15 57Bb **111**
WD6: E'tree 16Ma **29**
Schurlock Pl. TW2: Twick 61Ga **130**
Schwartz Wharf E9 38Cc **72**
Science Mus.
Knightsbridge **4B 226 (48Fb** 89)
Scilla Ct. RM17: Grays 51Fe **121**
SCILLY ISLES **75Ga 152**
Sclater St. E1 5K **219** (42Vb **91**)
Scoble Pl. N16 35Vb **71**
Scoles Cres. SW2 60Rb **113**
Scoop, The **7J 225 (46Ub** 91)
Scope Way KT1: King T 70Na **131**
Score Complex, The
Leyton **34Dc** 72
Scoresby St. SE1 7B **224** (46Rb **91**)
Scorton Av. UB6: G'frd 40Ja **66**
Scorton Ho. N1 1J **219**
Scotch Comn. W13 43Ja **86**
SCOTCH HOUSE **2F 227 (47Hb 89)**
Scoter Cl. IG8: Wfd G 24Kc **53**
Scoter Ct. *SE8* *51Bc* ***114***
(off Abinger Gro.)
Scot Gro. HA5: Pinn 24Z **45**
Scotia Bldg. *E1* *45Zb* ***92***
(off Jardine Rd.)
Scotia Ct. *SE16* *47Yb* ***92***
(off Canada Est.)
Scotia Rd. SW2 59Qb **112**
Scotland Bri. Lock KT15: New H 83J **169**
Scotland Bri. Rd. KT15: New H 83J **169**
Scotland Grn. N17 26Vb **51**
Scotland Grn. Rd. EN3: Pond E 15Zb **34**
Scotland Grn. Rd. Nth.
EN3: Pond E 14Zb **34**
Scotland La. DA12: Cobh 9H **145**
(not continuous)
Scotland Pl. SW1 6F **223** (46Nb **90**)
Scotland Rd. IG9: Buck H 18Lc **35**
Scotlands Dr.
SL2: Farn C 7F **60**
Scotland Yard ***47Nb 90***
(off Victoria Emb.)
Scotney Cl. BR6: Farnb 77Qc **160**
WD3: Crox G 14R **26**
Scotney Ho. E9 37Yb **72**
Scotney Wlk.
RM12: Horn 36Ld **77**
Scots Cl. TW19: Stanw 60M **105**
Scotscraig WD7: R'lett 7Ha **14**
Scotsdale Cl. BR5: Pet W 70Uc **138**
SM3: Cheam 80Ab **154**
Scotsdale Rd. SE12 57Kc **115**
Scotshall La.
CR6: W'ham 87Ec **178**
Scots Hill WD3: Crox G 16P **25**
Scots Hill Cl. WD3: Crox G 16P **25**
Scotsmill La. WD3: Crox G 16P **25**
Scotson Ho. SE11 6K **229**
Scotspine La. RM3: Hrld W 26Nd **57**
Scotswood Pk.
GU21: Wok 86F **168**
Scotswood St. EC1 5A **218** (42Qb **90**)
Scotswood Wlk. N17 24Wb **51**
Scott Av. SW15 58Ab **110**

Scott Cl.—Seymour Cl.

Scott Cl. AL3: St A 4N 5
DA1: Dart 57Pd 119
KT19: Ewe 78Sa 153
SL2: Farn C 6G 60
SW16 67Pb 134
UB7: W Dray 49P 83
Scott Ct. W3 47Ta 87
Scott Cres. DA8: Erith 53Hd 118
HA2: Harr 32Da 65
Scott Ellis Gdns. NW8 4B 214 (41Fb 89)
Scottes La. RM8: Dag 32Zc 75
Scott Farm Cl. KT7: T Ditt 74Ka 152
Scott Gdns. TW5: Hest 52Z 107
Scott Ho. DA17: Belv 50Bd 95
E13 40Jc 73
(off Queens Rd. W.)
E14 47Cc 92
(off Admirals Way)
KT17: Eps 84Ua 174
(off Winter Cl.)
N7 37Pb 70
(off Caledonian Rd.)
N18 22Wb 51
(off Woolmer Rd.)
NW8 6D 214
NW10 38Ta 67
(off Stonebridge Pk.)
RM11: Horn 30Jd 56
(off Benjamin Cl.)
SE8 50Bc 92
(off Grove St.)
Scott Lidgett Cres. SE16 47Wb 91
Scott Rd. DA12: Grav'nd 4F 144
HA8: Edg 26Ra 47
RM16: Grays 9C 100
Scott Russell Pl. E14 50Dc 92
Scotts Av. BR2: Brom 68Fc 137
TW16: Sun 66U 128
Scotts Cl. RM12: Horn 36Ld 77
Scotts Ct. W12 47Ya 88
(off Scott's Rd.)
Scotts Dr. TW12: Hamp 66Da 129
Scotts Farm Rd. KT19: Ewe 79Sa 153
Scott's Gro. Cl. GU24: Chob 5H 167
Scott's Gro. Rd. GU24: Chob 5F 166
Scott's La. BR2: Brom 69Fc 137
Scotts La. KT12: Hers 77Z 151
Scotts Pas. SE18 49Rc 94
Scott's Rd. E10 32Ec 72
UB2: S'hall 48Y 85
W12 47Xa 88
Scotts Rd. BR1: Brom 66Jc 137
Scott's Sufferance Wharf SE1 2K 231
Scotts Ter. SE9 61Nc 138
Scott St. E1 42Xb 91
Scotts Way TN13: Riv 94Gd 202
TW16: Sun 66U 128
Scottswood Cl. WD23: Bush 12Aa 27
Scottswood Rd. WD23: Bush 12Aa 27
Scott's Yd. EC4 4F 225 (45Tb 91)
Scott Trimmer Way TW3: Houn 54Aa 107
Scottwell Dr. NW9 29Ua 48
Scoulding Ho. E14 48Cc 92
(off Mellish St.)
Scoulding Rd. E16 44Jc 93
Scouler St. E14 45Ec 92
Scout App. NW10 35Ua 68
Scout La. SW4 55Lb 112
Scout Pk. 24Mb 50
Scout Way NW7 21Ta 47
Scovell Cres. SE1 2D 230
Scovell Rd. SE1 2D 230 (47Sb 91)
Scratchers La. DA3: Fawk 75Td 164
Scratton Flds. DA12: Sole S 10F 144
Scratton Rd. SS17: Stan H 1M 101
Scrattons Farm Eco-Pk. 40Ad 75
Scrattons Ter. IG11: Bark 40Zc 75
Screen on the Green Cinema 39Rb 71
(off Upper St.)
Screenworks N5 36Sb 71
Scrimgoeur Pl. N4 32Sb 71
Scriven Ct. E8 39Vb 71
Scriveners Cl. HP2: Hem H 2N 3
Scriven St. E8 39Vb 71
Scrooby St. SE6 58Dc 114
Scrope Ho. EC1 7K 217
Scrubbitts Pk. Rd. WD7: R'lett 7Ja 14
Scrubbitts Sq. WD7: R'lett 7Ja 14
Scrubs La. NW10 41Wa 88
W10 41Wa 88
Scrutton Cl. SW12 59Mb 112
Scrutton St. EC2 6H 219 (42Ub 91)
Scudamore La. NW9 28Sa 47
Scudders Hill DA3: Fawk 72Xd 164
Sculpture Ho. E1 43Zb 92
(off Duckett St.)
Scutari Rd. SE22 57Yb 114
Scutley La. GU18: Light 1C 166
GU20: W'sham 1C 166
Scylla Cres. TW6: H'row A 59R 106
(not continuous)
Scylla Pl. GU21: Wok 1L 187
Scylla Rd. SE15 55Wb 113
(not continuous)
TW6: H'row A 58R 106
Seaborne Wharf E3 43Cc 92
(off Invicta Cl.)
Seaborough Rd. RM16: Grays 8E 100
Seabright St. E2 41Xb 91
Seabrook Dr. BR4: W W'ck 75Gc 159
Seabrooke Ri. RM17: Grays 51De 121
Seabrook Gdns. RM7: Rush G 31Cd 76
Seabrook Rd. RM8: Dag 34Zc 75
WD4: K Lan 9D 4
Seaburn Cl. RM13: Rain 40Gd 76
Seacole Cl. W3 44Ta 87
Seacole Ct. N21 15Pb 32
(off Pennington Dr.)
Sea Containers Ho. SE1 5A 224
Seacon Twr. E14 47Bc 92
Seacourt Rd. SE2 47Zc 95
SL3: L'ly 49D 82
Seacroft Gdns. WD19: Wat 20Z 27
Seafarer Way SE16 49Ac 92
Seafield Rd. N11 21Mb 50
Seaford Cl. HA4: Ruis 32T 64
Seaford Ho. SE16 47Yb 92
(off Swan Rd.)
Seaford Rd. E17 27Dc 52
EN1: Enf 14Ub 33
N15 29Tb 51
TW6: H'row A 57M 105
W13 46Ka 86
Seaford St. WC1 4G 217 (41Nb 90)
Seaforth Av. KT3: N Mald 71Xa 154
Seaforth Cl. RM1: Rom 24Gd 56
Seaforth Cres. N5 36Sb 71
Seaforth Dr. EN8: Walt C 6Zb 20
Seaforth Gdns. IG8: Wfd G 22Lc 53
KT19: Ewe 77Va 154
N21 17Pb 32
Seaforth Pl. SW1 3C 228
Seager Pl. SE8 53Cc 114
(off Deptford Bri.)
Seagrave Cl. E1 43Zb 92
Seagrave Lodge SW6 51Cb 111
(off Seagrave Rd.)
Seagrave Rd. SW6 51Cb 111
Seagry Rd. E11 31Jc 73
Seagull Cl. IG11: Bark 41Wc 95
Seagull La. E16 45Jc 93
Seahorse Sailing Club 33Ta 67
SEAL 93Pd 203
Sealand Rd. TW6: H'row A 58Q 106
Sealand Wlk. UB5: N'olt 41Z 85
SEAL CHART 95Sd 204
Sealcroft Cotts. TN15: Seal 91Pd 203
Seal Dr. TN15: Seal 93Pd 203
Seale Hill RH2: Reig 8J 207
Seal Hollow Rd. TN13: S'oaks 96Ld 203
TN15: S'oaks 96Ld 203
Seal Ho. SE1 3G 231
Sea Life London Aquarium
1H 229 (47Pb 90)
Seally Rd. RM17: Grays 50Ce 99
Seal Rd. TN14: S'oaks 93Ld 203
TN15: S'oaks 93Ld 203
Seal St. E8 35Vb 71
Sealy Way HP3: Hem H 6M 3
Seaman Cl. AL2: Park 7B 6
Searches La. WD5: Bedm 9J 5
Searchwood Hgts. CR6: W'ham 90Xb 177
Searchwood Rd. CR6: W'ham 90Xb 177
Searle Ho. NW8 1E 214
SW11 53Jb 112
(off Macduff Rd.)
Searle Pl. N4 32Pb 70
Searles Cl. SW11 52Gb 111
Searles Dr. E6 43Rc 94
Searles Rd. SE1 5G 231 (49Tb 91)
Searlwood Cl. GU24: W End 6D 166
Searson Ho. SE17 6C 230
Sears St. SE5 52Tb 113
Seasalter Ho. SW9 53Qb 112
(off Gosling Way)
Seasons Cl. W7 46Ha 86
Seasons Ho. E20 37Ec 72
(off Mirabelle Gdns.)
Seasprite Cl. UB5: N'olt 41Z 85
Seaton Av. IG3: Ilf 36Vc 75
Seaton Cl. E13 42Jc 93
SE11 7A 230 (50Qb 90)
SW15 60Xa 110
TW2: Whitt 58Fa 108
Seaton Dr. TW15: Ashf 61N 127
Seaton Gdns. HA4: Ruis 34V 64
Seaton Point E5 35Wb 71
Seaton Rd. AL2: Lon C 8H 7
CR4: Mitc 68Gb 133
DA1: Dart 59Jd 118
DA16: Well 52Yc 117
HA0: Wemb 40Na 67
HP3: Hem H 5M 3
TW2: Whitt 58Ea 108
UB3: Harl 49T 84
Seaton Sq. NW7 24Za 48
Seaton St. N18 22Wb 51
Seawell Ct. IG11: Bark 40Sc 74
(off Dock Rd.)
Sebastian Av. CM15: Shenf 16Ce 41
Sebastian Ct. IG11: Bark 39Vc 75
Sebastian Ho. N1 2H 219
Sebastian St. EC1 4C 218 (41Rb 91)
Sebastopol Rd. N9 21Wb 51
Sebbon St. N1 38Rb 71
Sebergham Gro. NW7 24Wa 48
Sebert Rd. E7 36Kc 73
Sebright Ho. E2 40Wb 71
(off Coate St.)
Sebright Pas. E2 40Wb 71
Sebright Rd. EN5: Barn 12Za 30
HP1: Hem H 4J 3
Secker Cres. HA3: Hrw W 25Ea 46
Secker Ho. SW9 54Rb 113
(off Loughborough Est.)
Secker St. SE1 7K 223 (46Qb 90)
Secombe Theatre
Sutton 78Db 155
Second Av. E12 35Nc 74
E13 41Jc 93
E17 29Cc 52
EN1: Enf 15Vb 33
EN9: Walt A 2Kc 21
HA9: Wemb 33Ma 67
KT12: Walt T 72X 151
KT20: Lwr K 97Ab 194
N18 21Yb 52
NW4 28Za 48
RM6: Chad H 29Yc 55
RM10: Dag 40Dd 76
RM20: W Thur 51Wd 120
SS17: Stan H 1M 101
SW14 55Ua 110
UB3: Hayes 46V 84
W3 46Va 88
W10 42Ab 88
WD25: Wat 7Z 13
Second Cl. KT8: W Mole 70Ea 130
Second Cres. SL1: Slou 3G 80
Second Cross Rd. TW2: Twick 61Ga 130
Second Way HA9: Wemb 35Ra 67
Sedan Way SE17 7H 231 (50Ub 91)
Sedcombe Cl. DA14: Sidc 63Xc 139
Sedcote Rd. EN3: Pond E 15Yb 34
Sedding St. SW1 5H 227 (49Jb 90)
Sedding Studios SW1 5H 227
Seddon Highwalk EC2 7D 218
(off Aldersgate St.)
Seddon Ho. EC2 7D 218
Seddon Rd. SM4: Mord 71Fb 155
Seddon St. WC1 4J 217 (41Pb 90)
Sedgebrook Rd. SE3 54Mc 115
Sedgecombe Av. HA3: Kenton 29La 46
Sedge Ct. RM17: Grays 2A 122
Sedgefield Cl. RM3: Rom 21Pd 57
Sedgefield Ct. UB5: N'olt 36Da 65
(off Newmarket Av.)
Sedgefield Cres. RM3: Rom 22Pd 57
Sedgeford Rd. W12 46Va 88
Sedge Gdns. IG11: Bark 41Wc 95
Sedgehill Rd. SE6 63Cc 136
Sedgemere Av. N2 27Eb 49
Sedgemere Rd. SE2 48Yc 95
Sedgemoor Dr. RM10: Dag 35Cd 76
Sedge Rd. N17 24Yb 52
Sedgeway SE6 60Hc 115
Sedgewood Cl. BR2: Hayes 73Hc 159
Sedgmoor Pl. SE5 52Ub 113
Sedgwick Av. UB10: Hil 38R 64
Sedgwick Ho. E3 43Cc 92
(off Gale St.)
Sedgwick Pl. WD17: Wat 15Y 27
Sedgwick Rd. E10 33Ec 72
Sedgwick St. E9 36Zb 72
Sedleigh Rd. SW18 58Bb 111
Sedlescombe Rd. SW6 51Cb 111
Sedley DA13: Sflt 65Ce 143
Sedley Cl. EN1: Enf 10Xb 19
Sedley Ct. SE26 61Xb 135
Sedley Gro. UB9: Hare 28L 43
Sedley Ho. SE11 7K 229
Sedley Pl. W1 3K 221 (44Kb 90)
Sedley Ri. IG10: Lough 12Pc 36
Sedona Ho. E20 37Dc 72
(off Victory Pde.)
Sedum Cl. NW9 29Ra 47
Sedum M. EN2: Enf 13Qb 32
Seedbed Cen., The RM7: Rush G 31Gd 76
Seeley Dr. SE21 63Ub 135
Seelig Av. NW9 31Wa 68
Seely Rd. SW17 65Jb 134
Seetha Ho. IG1: Ilf 33Tc 74
(off High Rd.)
Seething La. EC3 4J 225 (45Ub 91)
SEETHING WELLS 72La 152
Seething Wells La. KT6: Surb 72La 152
Sefton Av. HA3: Hrw W 26Fa 46
NW7 22Ta 47
Sefton Cl. AL1: St A 3F 6
BR5: St M Cry 70Vc 139
GU24: W End 5D 166
SL2: Stoke P 9K 61
Sefton Ct. EN2: Enf 12Rb 33
TW3: Houn 53Da 107
Sefton Paddock SL2: Stoke P 8L 61
Sefton Pk. SL2: Stoke P 8L 61
Sefton Rd. BR5: St M Cry 70Vc 139
CR0: C'don 74Wb 157
KT19: Ewe 82Ta 173
Sefton St. SW15 55Ya 110
Sefton Way UB8: Cowl 44L 83
Segal Cl. SE23 59Ac 114
Segrave Cl. KT13: Weyb 80Q 150
Sejant Ho. RM17: Grays 51De 121
(off Bridge Rd.)
Sekforde St. EC1 6B 218 (42Rb 91)
Sekhon Ter. TW13: Hanw 62Ca 129
Selah Dr. BR8: Swan 67Ed 140
Selan Gdns. UB4: Yead 43X 85
Selbie Av. NW10 36Va 68
Selborne Av. DA5: Bexl 60Ad 117
E12 35Qc 74
Selborne Gdns. NW4 28Wa 48
UB6: G'frd 40Ja 66
Selborne Pl. KT13: Weyb 79T 150
Selborne Rd. CR0: C'don 76Ub 157
DA14: Sidc 63Xc 139
E17 29Bc 52
IG1: Ilf 33Qc 74
KT3: N Mald 68Ua 132
N14 20Nb 32
N22 25Pb 50
SE5 54Tb 113
Selborne Wlk. E17 29Bc 52
Selborne Wlk. Shop. Cen. E17 28Bc 52
Selbourne Av. KT6: Surb 75Pa 153
KT15: New H 81K 169
Selbourne Cl. DA3: Lfield 69Fe 143
KT15: New H 81K 169
Selbourne Ho. SE1 3F 231
Selbourne Sq. RH9: G'stone 2A 210
Selby Av. AL3: St A 2B 6
Selby Cen., The 23Ub 51
Selby Chase HA4: Ruis 33X 65
Selby Cl. BR7: Chst 65Qc 138
E6 43Nc 94
KT9: Chess 80Na 153
Selby Gdns. UB1: S'hall 42Ca 85
Selby Grn. SM5: Cars 73Gb 155
Selby Rd. E11 34Gc 73
E13 43Kc 93
N17 24Ub 51
SE20 68Wb 135
SM5: Cars 73Gb 155
TW15: Ashf 65S 128
W5 42Ka 86
Selby Sq. W10 41Ab 88
(off Dowland St.)
Selby St. E1 42Wb 91
Selby Wlk. GU21: Wok 10M 167
Selcroft Ho. SE10 50Hc 93
(off Glenister Rd.)
Selcroft Rd. CR8: Purl 84Rb 177
Selden Hill HP1: Hem H 3M 3
HP2: Hem H 3M 3
Selden Ho. SE15 54Yb 114
(off Selden Rd.)
Selden Rd. SE15 54Yb 114
Selden Wlk. N7 33Pb 70
Seldon Ho. SW1 50Lb 90
(off Churchill Gdns.)
SW8 52Lb 112
(off Stewart's Rd.)
Selfridges 3J 221
SELHURST 72Ub 157
Selhurst Cl. GU21: Wok 87B 168
SW19 60Za 110
Selhurst New Rd. SE25 72Ub 157
Selhurst Pk. 70Ub 135
Selhurst Pl. SE25 72Ub 157
Selhurst Rd. N9 20Tb 33
SE25 72Ub 157
Selig Ct. NW11 31Ab 68
Selim Ct. SL1: Slou 7M 81
(off Clifton Rd.)
Selina Ho. NW8 5C 214
Selinas La. RM8: Dag 31Ad 75
Selkirk Dr. DA8: Erith 53Gd 118
Selkirk Ho. N1 39Pb 70
(off Bingfield St.)
Selkirk Rd. SW17 63Gb 133
TW2: Twick 61Ea 130
Sellers Cl. WD6: Bore 11Sa 29
Sellers Hall Cl. N3 24Cb 49
Sellincourt Rd. SW17 64Gb 133
Sellindge Cl. BR3: Beck 66Bc 136
Sellons Av. NW10 39Va 68
Sellwood Dr. EN5: Barn 15Za 30
Selman Ho. E9 37Ac 72
SELSDON 82Yb 178
Selsdon Av. CR2: S Croy 79Tb 157
Selsdon Cl. KT6: Surb 71Na 153
RM5: Col R 25Ed 56
Selsdon Cres. CR2: Sels 81Yb 178
Selsdon Pk. Hotel Golf Course 83Yb 178
Selsdon Pk. Rd. CR0: Sels 81Zb 178
CR2: Sels 81Zb 178
Selsdon Rd. CR2: S Croy 78Tb 157
E11 31Jc 73
E13 39Lc 73
KT15: New H 83J 169
NW2 33Va 68
SE27 62Qb 134
Selsdon Way E14 48Dc 92
Selsdon Wood Nature Reserve 83Ac 178
Selsea Pl. N16 36Ub 71
Selsey WC1 4G 217
Selsey Cres. DA16: Well 53Zc 117
Selsey St. E14 43Cc 92
Selvage La. NW7 22Ta 47
Selway Cl. HA5: Eastc 28X 45
Selway Ho. SW8 53Nb 112
(off Sth. Lambeth Rd.)
Selwin Ct. KT12: Walt T 74Y 151
Selwood Cl. TW19: Stanw 58L 105
Selwood Gdns.
TW19: Stanw 58L 105
Selwood Pl. SW7 7B 226 (50Fb 89)
Selwood Rd. CM14: B'wood 20Vd 40
CR0: C'don 75Xb 157
GU22: Wok 92D 188
KT9: Chess 77Ma 153
SM3: Sutt 74Bb 155
Selwoods SW2 59Qb 112
Selwood Ter. SW7 7B 226 (50Fb 89)
Selworthy Cl. E11 29Jc 53
Selworthy Ho. SW11 53Fb 111
(off Battersea Church Rd.)
Selworthy Rd. SE6 62Bc 136
Selwyn Av. AL10: Hat 1P 7
E4 23Ec 52
IG3: Ilf 30Vc 55
TW9: Rich 55Na 109
Selwyn Cl. SL4: Wind 4B 102
TW4: Houn 56Aa 107
Selwyn Ct. E17 29Cc 52
(off Yunus Khan Cl.)
HA8: Edg 24Ra 47
HA9: Wemb 34Sa 67
SE3 55Hc 115
TW10: Rich 57Pa 109
(off Church Rd.)
Selwyn Cres. AL10: Hat 1A 8
DA16: Well 55Xc 117
Selwyn Dr. AL10: Hat 1P 7
Selwyn Pl. BR5: St P 69Xc 139
SL1: Slou 5D 80
Selwyn Rd. E3 40Bc 72
E13 39Kc 73
KT3: N Mald 71Ta 153
NW10 38Ua 68
RM18: Tilb 4B 122
Semley Ga. E9 37Bc 72
(not continuous)
Semley Ho. SW1 6K 227
Semley Pl. SW1 6J 227 (49Jb 90)
Semley Rd. SW16 68Nb 134
Semper Cl. GU21: Knap 9J 167
Semper Rd. RM16: Grays 7E 100
Sempill Rd. HP3: Hem H 5N 3
Semples SS17: Stan H 1P 101
Senate St. SE15 54Yb 114
Senators Lodge E3 40Ac 72
(off Roman Rd.)
Senator Wlk. SE28 48Tc 94
SEND 95F 188
Sendall Ct. SW11 55Fb 111
(off Winstanley Rd.)
Send & Ripley History Society Mus.
93K 189
Send Barns La. GU23: Send 96F 188
Send Cl. GU23: Send 95E 188
Send Hill GU23: Send 97E 188
SEND MARSH 95H 189
Send Marsh Grn. GU23: Rip 95H 189
Send Marsh Rd. GU23: Rip, Send 96F 188
Send Pde. Cl. GU23: Send 95E 188
Send Rd. GU23: Send 95D 188
Seneca Rd. CR7: Thor H 70Sb 135
Sener Ct. CR2: S Croy 79Sb 157
Senga Rd. SM6: Wall 74Jb 156
Senhouse Rd. SM3: Cheam 76Za 154
Senior St. W2 43Db 89
Senlac Rd. SE12 60Kc 115
Sennen Rd. EN1: Enf 17Vb 33
Sennen Wlk. SE9 62Nc 138
Sennocke Ct. TN13: S'oaks 97Kd 203
Senrab St. E1 44Zb 92
Sentamu Cl. SE24 60Rb 113
Sentinel WD17: Wat 12X 27
Sentinel Cl. UB5: N'olt 42Aa 85
Sentinel Sq. NW4 28Ya 48
Sentis Ct. HA6: Nwood 23V 44
September Ct. UB1: S'hall 46Da 85
(off Dormer's Wells La.)
UB8: Uxb 40M 63
September Way HA7: Stan 23Ka 46
Septimus Pl. EN1: Enf 15Wb 33
Sequoia Cl. WD23: B Hea 18Fa 28
Sequoia Gdns. BR6: Orp 73Vc 161
Sequoia Pk. HA5: Hat E 23Da 45
Seraph Ct. EC1 3D 218
Serbin Cl. E10 31Ec 72
Serenaders Rd. SW9 54Qb 112
Serene M. RM3: Rom 23Kd 57
Serenity Apartments E17 29Dc 52
SW11 56Gb 111
(off Monarch Sq.)
Serenity Cl. HA2: Harr 33Da 65
Serenity Ct. DA9: Ghithe 56Wd 120
(off Evelyn Wlk.)
Seren Pk. Gdns. SE3 51Gc 115
Sergeant Ind. Est. SW18 58Db 111
Sergeants Grn. La. EN9: Walt A 5Lc 21
Sergeants Pl. CR3: Cat'm 94Sb 197
Sergehill La. WD5: Bedm 9F 4
Serica Ct. SE10 52Ec 114
Serjeants Inn EC4 3A 224 (44Qb 90)
Serlby Ct. W14 48Bb 89
(off Somerset Sq.)
Serle St. WC2 2J 223 (44Pb 90)
Sermed Ct. SL2: Slou 6N 81
Sermon Dr. BR8: Swan 69Ed 140
Sermon La. EC4 3D 224
Serpentine, The 7D 220 (46Gb 89)
Serpentine Cl. RM6: Chad H 31Yc 75
Serpentine Ct. SE16 47Zb 92
(off Christopher Cl.)
TN13: S'oaks 94Md 203
Serpentine Gallery 7B 220 (47Fb 89)
Serpentine Grn. RH1: Mers 1D 208
Serpentine Rd.
TN13: S'oaks 95Ld 203
W2 7D 220 (46Gb 89)
Serpentine Sackler Gallery
6D 220 (46Fb 89)
Serra Ho. AL1: St A 3D 6
Service Rd., The EN6: Pot B 4Cb 17
Serviden Dr. BR1: Brom 67Mc 137
Servite Ho. BR3: Beck 67Bc 136
GU21: Knap 9H 167
KT4: Wor Pk 75Va 154
(off The Avenue)
N14 15Kb 32
(off Bramley Rd.)
Servius Ct. TW8: Bford 52Ma 109
Setchell Rd. SE1 5K 231 (49Vb 91)
Setchell Way SE1 5K 231 (49Vb 91)
Seth St. SE16 47Yb 92
Seton Gdns. RM9: Dag 38Yc 75
Settle Point E13 40Jc 73
Settle Rd. RM3: Rom 21Qd 57
Settlers Ct. E14 45Fc 93
Settles St. E1 43Wb 91
Settrington Rd. SW6 54Db 111
Seven Acres BR8: Crock 72Fd 162
DA3: Nw A G 76Ae 165
HA6: Nwood 23X 45
SM5: Cars 75Gb 155
Seven Arches App. KT13: Weyb 80P 149
Seven Arches Rd.
CM14: B'wood 20Zd 41
Seven Dials WC2 3F 223 (44Nb 90)
Seven Dials Ct. WC2 3F 223
Sevenex Pde. HA9: Wemb 36Na 67
Seven Hills Cl. KT12: W Vill 81U 170
Seven Hills Rd. KT11: Cobh 82U 170
KT12: Hers, W Vill 81U 170
SL0: Iver H 36D 62
Seven Hills Rd. Sth.
KT11: Cobh 85U 170
Seven Islands Leisure Cen. 48Yb 92
SEVEN KINGS 32Vc 75
Seven Kings Rd. IG3: Ilf 32Uc 74
Seven Kings Way KT2: King T 67Ma 131
SEVENOAKS 97Kd 203
Sevenoaks Bus. Cen.
TN14: S'oaks 93Ld 203
Sevenoaks By-Pass
TN14: Ide H, S'oaks, Sund 95Ed 202
Sevenoaks Cl. DA7: Bex 56Dd 118
RM3: Rom 21Ld 57
SM2: Sutt 82Cb 175
SEVENOAKS COMMON 100Kd 203
Sevenoaks Ct. HA6: Nwood 24S 44
Sevenoaks Leisure Cen. 97Ld 203
Sevenoaks Rd. BR6: Chels, Orp 78Vc 161
BR6: Prat B 80Vc 161
SE4 58Ac 114
TN14: Hals 81Ad 181
TN14: Otf, S'oaks 88Kd 183
TN15: Bor G 92Ae 205
TN15: Igh, Seal 95Vd 204
Sevenoaks Way BR5: St P 66Yc 139
DA14: Sidc 66Yc 139
Sevenoaks Wildlife Reserve 93Hd 202
Seven Sea Gdns. E3 43Dc 92
Sevenseas Rd. TW6: H'row A 58S 106
SEVEN SISTERS 29Vb 51
Seven Sisters Rd. N4 33Qb 70
N7 34Pb 70
N15 33Qb 70
Seven Stars Cnr. W12 48Wa 88
Seven Stars Yd. E1 7K 219
Seventh Av. E12 35Pc 74
KT20: Lwr K 97Ab 194
UB3: Hayes 46W 84
Seven Ways Pde. IG2: Ilf 29Qc 54
Severn RM18: E Til 8K 101
Severnake Cl. E14 49Cc 92
Severn Av. RM2: Rom 27Kd 57
W10 41Ab 88
Severn Ct. KT2: King T 67Ma 131
(off John Williams Cl.)
Severn Cres. SL3: L'ly 50D 82
Severn Dr. EN1: Enf 10Wb 19
KT10: Hin W 75Ja 152
KT12: Walt T 75Z 151
RM14: Upm 30Td 58
Severn Ho. SW18 56Cb 111
(off Enterprise Way)
Severn Rd. RM15: Avel 44Sd 98
Severns Fld. CM16: Epp 1Wc 23
Severnvale AL2: Lon C 9K 7
Severn Way NW10 36Va 68
WD25: Wat 6Y 13
Severus Ho. UB3: Hayes 44T 84
Severus Rd. SW11 56Gb 111
Seville Ho. E1 46Wb 91
(off Wapping High St.)
Seville M. N1 38Ub 71
Seville St. SW1 2G 227 (47Hb 89)
Sevington Rd. NW4 30Xa 48
Sevington St. W9 42Db 89
Seward Rd. BR3: Beck 68Zb 136
W7 47Ja 86
SEWARDSTONE 12Ec 34
SEWARDSTONEBURY 15Gc 35
Sewardstone Cl. E4 11Ec 34
Sewardstone Gdns. E4 15Dc 34
Sewardstone Rd. E2 40Yb 72
E4 17Dc 34
EN9: Walt A 6Ec 20
Sewardstone St.
EN9: Walt A 6Ec 20
Seward St. EC1 5C 218 (41Rb 91)
Sewdley St. E5 34Zb 72
Sewell Cl. AL4: St A 2J 7
RM16: Chaf H 50Yd 98
Sewell Rd. SE2 48Wc 95
Sewell St. E13 41Jc 93
Sextant Av. E14 49Fc 93
Sexton Cl. RM13: Rain 39Hd 76
Sexton Ct. E14 45Fc 93
(off Newport Av.)
Sexton Rd. RM18: Tilb 3B 122
Sextons Ho. SE10 51Ec 114
(off Bardsley La.)
Seymer Rd. RM1: Rom 27Fd 56
Seymore M. SE14 52Bc 114
(off New Cross Rd.)
Seymour Av. CR3: Cat'm 95Sb 197
KT17: Ewe 81Xa 174
N17 26Wb 51
SM4: Mord 73Za 154
Seymour Chase CM16: Epp 1Xc 23
Seymour Cl. HA5: Hat E 25Ba 45
IG10: Lough 16Nc 36
KT8: E Mos 71Ea 152

Seymour Ct. E4 19Hc 35
KT1: Hamp W 67Ma 131
KT11: Cobh 85W 170
KT19: Ewe 81Ua 174
N10 26Jb 50
N21 16Pb 32
NW2 33Xa 68
Seymour Cres. HP2: Hem H 2N 3
Seymour Dr. BR2: Brom 74Pc 160
Seymour Gdns. HA4: Ruis 32Z 65
IG1: Ilf 32Pc 74
KT5: Surb 71Pa 153
SE4 55Ac 114
TW1: Twick 59Ka 108
TW13: Hanw 63Y 129
Seymour Gro. WD19: Wat 17Y 27
Seymour Ho. E16 46Jc 93
(off De Quincey M.)
NW1 3E 216
SL3: L'ly 47A 82
SM2: Sutt 79Db 155
(off Mulgrave Rd.)
WC1 5F 217
Seymour Leisure Cen. 1F 221 (43Hb 89)
Seymour M. KT17: Ewe 82Wa 174
W1 2H 221 (44Jb 90)
Seymour Pl. GU22: Wok 2M 187
KT13: Weyb 76R 150
RM11: Horn 31Md 77
SE25 70Xb 135
W1 7E 214 (43Hb 89)
Seymour Rd. CR4: Mitc 73Jb 156
DA11: Nflt 10B 122
E4 18Dc 34
E6 40Mc 73
E10 32Bc 72
KT1: Hamp W 67Ma 131
KT8: W Mole, E Mos 71Ea 152
N3 24Db 49
N8 29Qb 50
N9 19Xb 33
RM18: Tilb 3B 122
SL1: Slou 7G 80
SM5: Cars 78Jb 156
SW18 59Bb 111
SW19 62Za 132
TW12: Hamp H 64Ea 130
W4 49Sa 87
Seymours, The IG10: Lough 11Qc 36
Seymour St. SE18 48Sc 94
W1 3F 221 (44Hb 89)
W2 3F 221 (44Hb 89)
Seymour Ter. SE20 67Xb 135
Seymour Vs. SE20 67Xb 135
Seymour Wlk. DA10: Swans 59Ae 121
SW10 51Eb 111
Seymour Way TW16: Sun 66V 128
Seyssel St. E14 49Ec 92
Shaa Rd. W3 45Ta 87
Shabana Rd. W12 46Xa 88
Shabden Cotts. CR5: Chip 93Hb 195
Shab Hall Cotts. TN13: Dun G 90Ed 182
Shacklands Rd.
TN14: Bad M, S'ham 83Dd 182
Shackleford Rd. GU22: Wok 92C 188
Shacklegate La. TW11: Tedd 63Ga 130
Shackleton Cl. SE23 61Xb 135
Shackleton Ct. E14 50Cc 92
(off Maritime Quay)
TW19: Stanw 58N 105
(off Whitley Cl.)
W12 47Xa 88
(off Scott's Rd.)
Shackleton Dr. DA1: Dart 57Pd 119
Shackleton Ho. E1 46Yb 92
(off Prusom St.)
NW10 38Ta 67
Shackleton Rd. SL1: Slou 5K 81
UB1: S'hall 45Ba 85
Shackleton Ter. DA12: Grav'nd 3E 144
(off Christian Flds.)
Shackleton Way WD5: Ab L 4W 12
(off Lysander Way)
SHACKLEWELL 35Vb 71
Shacklewell Grn. E8 35Vb 71
Shacklewell Ho. E8 35Vb 71
Shacklewell La. E8 36Vb 71
N16 36Vb 71
Shacklewell Rd. N16 35Vb 71
Shacklewell Row E8 35Vb 71
Shacklewell St. E2 5K 219 (41Vb 91)
Shadbolt Av. E4 22Ac 52
Shadbolt Cl. KT4: Wor Pk 75Va 154
Shad Thames SE1 7K 225 (46Vb 91)
(Anchor Brewhouse)
SE1 2K 231 (47Vb 91)
(Jamaica Rd.)
SHADWELL 45Xb 91
Shadwell Ct. UB5: N'olt 40Ba 65
Shadwell Dr. UB5: N'olt 41Ba 85
Shadwell Gdns. E1 45Yb 92
Shadwell Pierhead E1 45Yb 92
Shadwell Pl. E1 45Yb 92
(off Sutton St.)
Shady Bush Cl. WD23: Bush 17Ea 28
Shady La. WD17: Wat 12X 27
Shaef Way TW11: Tedd 66Ja 130
Shafter Rd. RM10: Dag 37Ed 76
Shaftesbury IG10: Lough 13Mc 35
Shaftesbury Av. EN3: Enf H 12Zb 34
EN5: New Bar 14Eb 31
HA2: Harr 32Da 65
HA3: Kenton 29Ma 47
TW14: Felt 58W 106
UB2: S'hall 49Ca 85
W1 4D 222 (45Mb 90)
WC1 2F 223 (44Nb 90)
WC2 2F 223 (44Nb 90)
Shaftesbury Cen. W10 42Za 88
(off Barlby Rd.)
Shaftesbury Circ. HA2: Harr 32Ea 66
Shaftesbury Ct. E6 44Qc 94
(off Sapphire Cl.)
N1 2F 219
SE1 3F 231
SE5 56Tb 113
SL1: Slou 7J 81
SW6 53Db 111
(off Maltings Pl.)
SW16 62Mb 134
WD3: Crox G 14R 26
Shaftesbury Cres. TW18: Staines 66M 127
Shaftesbury Dr. CR5: Coul 89Lb 176
Shaftesbury Gdns. NW10 42Ua 88
Shaftesbury Ho. CR5: Coul 94Mb 196
Shaftesbury La. DA1: Dart 56Rd 119
Shaftesbury Lodge E14 44Dc 92
(off Upper Nth. St.)
Shaftesbury M. SW4 57Lb 112
W8 48Cb 89
Shaftesbury Pde. HA2: Harr 32Ea 66
Shaftesbury Pl. EC2 1D 224
(off London Wall)
W14 49Bb 89
(off Warwick Rd.)
Shaftesbury Point E13 40Jc 73
(off High St.)
Shaftesbury Rd. BR3: Beck 68Bc 136
CM16: Epp 1Vc 23
E4 18Fc 35
E7 38Lc 73
E10 32Cc 72
E17 30Dc 52
GU22: Wok 89D 168
GU24: Bisl 8D 166
N18 23Ub 51
N19 32Nb 70
RM1: Rom 30Hd 56
SM5: Cars 73Fb 155
TW9: Rich 55Na 109
WD17: Wat 13Y 27
Shaftesbury Row SE8 52Cc 114
(off Speedwell St.)
Shaftesburys, The IG11: Bark 40Sc 74
Shaftesbury St. N1 2E 218 (40Sb 71)
(not continuous)
Shaftesbury Theatre 2F 223
Shaftesbury Vs. W8 48Cb 89
(off Allen St.)
Shaftesbury Way TW2: Twick 62Fa 130
WD4: K Lan 10C 4
Shaftesbury Waye UB4: Yead 43Y 85
Shafto M. SW1 4G 227 (48Hb 89)
Shafton M. E9 39Zb 72
Shafton Rd. E9 39Zb 72
Shaftsbury Ct. DA8: Erith 53Hd 118
(off Selkirk Dr.)
Shafts Ct. EC3 3H 225 (44Ub 91)
Shaftswood Ct. SW17 62Hb 133
(off Lynwood Rd.)
Shaggy Calf La. SL2: Slou 5L 81
Shahjalal Ho. E2 40Wb 71
(off Pritchards Rd.)
Shakespeare Av. N11 22Lb 50
NW10 39Ta 67
RM18: Tilb 4D 122
TW14: Felt 58W 106
UB4: Hayes, Yead 44W 84
(not continuous)
UB4: Yead 42X 85
Shakespeare Cl. HA3: Kenton 31Qa 67
Shakespeare Ct. EN5: New Bar 13Db 31
HA3: Kenton 30Pa 47
NW6 38Eb 69
(off Fairfax Rd.)
Shakespeare Cres. E12 37Pc 74
Shakespeare Dr. HA3: Kenton 30Pa 47
WD6: Bore 14Qa 29
Shakespeare Gdns. N2 28Hb 49
Shakespeare Ho. E9 38Yb 72
(off Lyme Gro.)
N14 19Mb 32
Shakespeare Ind. Est. WD24: Wat 10W 12
Shakespeare Rd. DA1: Dart 56Qd 119
DA7: Bex 53Ad 117
E17 26Zb 52
KT15: Add 77M 149
N3 25Cb 49
NW7 21Va 48
NW10 39Ta 67
RM1: Rom 30Hd 56
SE24 57Rb 113
W3 46Sa 87
W7 45Ha 86
Shakespeare's Globe & Exhibition
5D 224 (46Sb 91)
Shakespeare Sq. IG6: Ilf 23Sc 54
Shakespeare St. WD24: Wat 10X 13
Shakespeare Twr. EC2 7E 218
Shakespeare Way TW13: Hanw 63Y 129
Shakspeare M. N16 35Ub 71
Shakspeare Wlk. N16 35Ub 71
Shalbourne Sq. E9 37Bc 72
Shalcomb St. SW10 51Eb 111
Shalcross Dr. EN8: Chesh 2Bc 20
Shalden Ho. SW15 58Va 110
Shaldon Dr. HA4: Ruis 34Y 65
SM4: Mord 71Ab 154
Shaldon Rd. HA8: Edg 26Pa 47
Shaldon Way KT12: Walt T 76Y 151
Shale Grn. RH1: Mers 1D 208
Shalfleet Dr. W10 45Za 88
Shalford Cl. BR6: Farnb 75Sc 160
Shalford Ct. N1 1B 218 (40Rb 71)
Shalford Ho. SE1 3G 231 (48Tb 91)
Shalimar Gdns. W3 45Sa 87
Shalimar Rd. W3 45Sa 87
Shallcross Cres. AL10: Hat 3C 8
Shallons Rd. SE9 63Rc 138
Shalstone Rd. SW14 55Ra 109
Shalston Vs. KT6: Surb 72Pa 153
Shambles, The TN13: S'oaks 97Ld 203
Shamrock Cl. KT22: Fet 93Fa 192
Shamrock Cotts. GU23: Worp 10M 187
Shamrock Ho. SE26 63Wb 135
(off Talisman Sq.)
Shamrock Rd. CR0: C'don 72Pb 156
DA12: Grav'nd 9G 122
Shamrock St. SW4 55Mb 112
Shamrock Way N14 18Kb 32
Shandon Rd. SW4 58Lb 112
Shand St. SE1 1H 231 (47Ub 91)
Shandy St. E1 43Zb 92
Shan Ho. WC1 6H 217
Shanklin Cl. EN7: Chesh 1Vb 19
Shanklin Gdns. WD19: Wat 21Y 45
Shanklin Ho. E17 26Bc 52
Shanklin Rd. N8 29Mb 50
N15 28Wb 51
Shannon Cl. NW2 34Za 68
UB2: S'hall 50Z 85
Shannon Commercial Cen.
KT3: N Mald 70Wa 132
SHANNON CORNER 70Wa 132
Shannon Cnr. Retail Pk.
KT3: N Mald 70Wa 132
Shannon Ct. CR0: C'don 74Sb 157
(off Tavistock Rd.)
N16 34Ub 71
SE15 52Vb 113
(off Garnies Cl.)
Shannon Gro. SW9 56Pb 112
Shannon M. SE3 56Hc 115
Shannon Pl. NW8 1E 214 (40Gb 69)
Shannon Way BR3: Beck 65Dc 136
RM15: Avel 45Sd 98
Shanti Ct. SW18 60Cb 111
Shantock Hall La. HP3: Bov 1A 10
Shantock La. HP3: Bov 2A 10
Shap Cres. SM5: Cars 74Hb 155
Shapland Way N13 22Pb 50
Shapwick Cl. N11 22Hb 49
Shard, The 7G 225
Shardcroft Av. SE24 57Rb 113
Shardeloes Rd. SE4 55Bc 114
SE14 54Bc 114
Shard's Sq. SE15 51Wb 113
Sharland Cl. CR7: Thor H 72Qb 156
Sharland Rd. DA12: Grav'nd 1E 144
Sharman Ct. DA14: Sidc 63Wc 139
Sharman Row SL3: L'ly 50B 82
Sharnbrooke Cl. DA16: Well 55Yc 117
Sharnbrook Ho. W14 51Cb 111
Sharney Av. SL3: L'ly 48C 82
Sharon Cl. KT6: Surb 74La 152
KT19: Eps 85Sa 173
KT23: Bookh 96Ca 191
Sharon Ct. CR2: S Croy 78Sb 157
(off Warham Rd.)
Sharon Gdns. E9 39Yb 72
Sharon Rd. EN3: Enf H 12Ac 34
W4 50Ta 87
Sharpe Cl. W7 43Ha 86
Sharpes La. HP1: Hem H 4D 2
Sharp Ho. SW8 55Kb 112
TW1: Twick 58Ma 109
Sharpleshall St. NW1 38Hb 69
Sharpley Ct. SE1 1B 230
Sharpness Cl. UB4: Yead 43Aa 85
Sharp's La. HA4: Ruis 31T 64
Sharp Way DA1: Dart 55Pd 119
Sharratt St. SE15 51Yb 114
Sharsted St. SE17 7B 230 (50Rb 91)
Sharvel La. UB5: N'olt 39W 64
Sharwood WC1 2J 217
Shaver's Pl. SW1 5D 222
Shaw, The BR7: Chst 66Sc 138
Shaw Av. IG11: Bark 40Ad 75
Shawbrooke Rd. SE9 57Lc 115
Shawbury Cl. NW9 25Ua 48
Shawbury Rd. SE22 57Vb 113
Shaw Cl. CR2: Sande 84Vb 177
EN8: Chesh 1Yb 20
KT16: Ott 79E 148
KT17: Ewe 83Va 174
RM11: Horn 32Kd 77
SE28 46Xc 95
TW19: Stanw 60N 105
WD23: B Hea 19Ga 28
Shaw Ct. CR3: Cat'm 93Tb 197
SL4: Old Win 7L 103
SM4: Mord 73Eb 155
W3 48Sa 87
(off All Saints Rd.)
Shaw Cres. CM13: Hut 14Fe 41
CR2: Sande 84Vb 177
E14 43Ac 92
RM18: Tilb 3D 122
Shaw Dr. KT12: Walt T 73Y 151
SHAW FARM 6J 103
Shawfield Ct. UB7: W Dray 48N 83
Shawfield Pk. BR1: Brom 68Mc 137
Shawfield St. SW3 7E 226 (50Gb 89)
Shawford Ct. SW15 59Wa 110
Shawford Rd. KT19: Ewe 79Ta 153
Shaw Gdns. IG11: Bark 40Ad 75
SL3: L'ly 50B 82
Shaw Gro. CR5: Coul 92Sb 197
Shaw Ho. DA17: Belv 50Bd 95
E16 46Qc 94
(off Claremont St.)
SM7: Bans 91Eb 195
Shawley Cres. KT18: Tatt C 90Ya 174
Shawley Way KT18: Tatt C 90Xa 174
Shaw Path BR1: Brom 62Hc 137
Shaw Pl. N2 27Jb 50
Shaw Rd. BR1: Brom 62Hc 137
EN3: Enf H 11Zb 34
SE22 56Ub 113
TN16: Tats 92Lc 199
Shaw's Cnr. RH1: Redh 6N 207
Shaws Cotts. SE23 62Ac 136
Shaws Path KT1: Hamp W 67La 130
(off Bennett Cl.)
Shaw Sq. E17 25Ac 52
Shaw Theatre 4E 216 (41Mb 90)
Shaw Way SM6: Wall 80Nb 156
Shaxton Cres. CR0: New Ad 81Ec 178
Shead Ct. E1 44Xb 91
(off James Voller Way)
Sheaf Cotts. KT7: T Ditt 74Ga 152
(off Weston Grn.)
Shearing Dr. SM5: Cars 73Eb 155
Shearling Way N7 37Nb 70
Shearman Rd. SE3 56Hc 115
SHEARS, THE 66U 128
Shears Cl. DA1: Dart 61Ld 141
Shears Ct. TW16: Sun 66U 128
Shears Grn. Ct. DA11: Nflt 1C 144
Shears La. SW16 66Nb 134
Shearsmith Ho. E1 45Wb 91
(off Hindmarsh Cl.)
Shears Way TW16: Sun 67U 128
Shearwater DA3: Lfield 69De 143
Shearwater Av. RM18: E Til 10K 101
Shearwater Cl. IG11: Bark 41Wc 95
Shearwater Ct. DA9: Ghithe 58Wd 120
(off Waterstone Way)
E1 45Wb 91
(off Star Pl.)
SE8 51Bc 114
(off Abinger Gro.)
Shearwater Dr. NW9 31Wa 68
Shearwater Rd. HP3: Hem H 6L 3
SM1: Sutt 78Bb 155
Shearwater Way UB4: Yead 44Z 85
Shearwood Cres. DA1: Cray 55Hd 118
Sheath Cotts. KT7: T Ditt 72Ka 152
(off Ferry Rd.)
Sheath La. KT22: Oxs 85Da 171
Sheaveshill Av. NW9 28Ua 48
Sheaveshill Ct. NW9 28Ta 47
Sheaveshill Pde. NW9 28Ua 48
(off Sheaveshill Av.)
Sheba Ct. N17 23Wb 51
(off Altair Cl.)
Sheba Pl. E1 6K 219 (42Vb 91)
Sheehy Way SL2: Slou 5M 81
Sheen Comn. Dr. TW10: Rich 56Qa 109
Sheen Ct. TW10: Rich 56Qa 109
Sheen Ct. Rd. TW10: Rich 56Qa 109
Sheendale Rd. TW9: Rich 56Pa 109
Sheenewood SE26 63Xb 135
Sheen Ga. Gdns. SW14 56Sa 109
Sheengate Mans. SW14 56Ta 109
Sheen Gro. N1 39Qb 70
Sheen La. SW14 57Sa 109
Sheen Pk. TW9: Rich 56Pa 109
Sheen Rd. BR5: St M Cry 70Vc 139
TW9: Rich 57Na 109
TW10: Rich 57Na 109
Sheen Way SM6: Wall 78Pb 156
Sheen Wood SW14 57Sa 109
Sheepbarn La. CR6: W'ham 84Hc 179
Sheepcot Dr. WD25: Wat 6Y 13
Sheepcote Cl. TW5: Cran 52W 106
Sheepcote Gdns. UB9: Den 30J 43
Sheepcote La. BR5: St M Cry 71Bd 161
BR8: Swan 71Bd 161
SW11 54Hb 111
Sheepcote Rd. HA1: Harr 30Ha 46
HP2: Hem H 2P 3
SL4: Eton W 10E 80
SL4: Wind 4C 102
Sheepcotes Rd. RM6: Chad H 28Ad 55
Sheepcot La. WD25: Wat 5W 12
(not continuous)
Sheephouse Rd. HP3: Hem H 4P 3
Sheephouse Way KT3: N Mald 74Ta 153
Sheep La. E8 39Xb 71
Sheep Wlk. KT18: Eps D 93Ta 193
RH2: Reig 3H 207
TW17: Shep 73P 149
Sheep Wlk., The GU22: Wok 90F 168
Sheep Wlk. M. SW19 65Za 132
Sheerness M. E16 47Rc 94
SHEERWATER 86F 168
Sheerwater Av. KT15: Wdhm 84G 168
Sheerwater Bus. Cen. GU21: Wok 87E 168
Sheerwater Rd. E16 43Mc 93
GU21: Wok 84G 168
KT14: W Byf 84G 168
KT15: Wdhm 84G 168
Sheethanger La. HP3: Hem H 5J 3
SHEET HILL 97Be 205
Sheet Hill TN15: Plax 97Zd 205
SHEET'S HEATH 1D 186
Sheet's Heath La. GU24: Brkwd 1E 186
Sheet St. SL4: Wind 4H 103
Sheet St. Rd. SL4: Wind 3B 124
Sheffield Dr. RM3: Rom 22Qd 57
Sheffield Gdns. RM3: Rom 22Qd 57
Sheffield Rd. SL1: Slou 4G 80
TW6: H'row A 58S 106
Sheffield Sq. E3 41Bc 92
Sheffield St. WC2 3H 223 (44Pb 90)
Sheffield Ter. W8 46Cb 89
Sheffield Way TW6: H'row A 57T 106
Shefton Ri. HA6: Nwood 24W 44
Sheila Cl. RM5: Col R 24Dd 56
Sheila Rd. RM5: Col R 24Dd 56
Sheilings, The RM11: Horn 29Pd 57
TN15: Seal 92Pd 203
Shelbourne Cl. HA5: Pinn 27Ba 45
Shelbourne Pl. BR3: Beck 66Bc 136
Shelbourne Rd. N17 26Xb 51
Shelburne Dr. TW4: Houn 58Ca 107
Shelburne Rd. N7 35Pb 70
Shelbury Cl. DA14: Sidc 62Wc 139
Shelbury Rd. SE22 57Xb 113
Sheldon Av. IG5: Ilf 26Rc 54
N6 31Gb 69
Sheldon Cl. RH2: Reig 7K 207
SE12 57Kc 115
SE20 67Xb 135
Sheldon Ct. EN5: New Bar 14Db 31
RM7: Rush G 30Fd 56
(off Union Rd.)
SW8 52Nb 112
(off Lansdowne Grn.)
Sheldon Hgts. DA12: Grav'nd 6G 144
Sheldon Ho. N1 39Ub 71
(off Kingsland Rd.)
Sheldon Pl. E2 40Wb 71
(not continuous)
Sheldon Rd. DA7: Bex 53Bd 117
N18 21Ub 51
NW2 35Za 68
RM9: Dag 38Ad 75
Sheldon Sq. W2 1A 220 (43Eb 89)
Sheldon St. CR0: C'don 76Sb 157
Sheldrake Cl. E16 46Pc 94
Sheldrake Ct. E6 40Nc 74
(off St Bartholomew's Rd.)
Sheldrake Ho. SE16 49Zb 92
(off Tawny Way)
Sheldrake Pl. W8 47Cb 89
Sheldrick Cl. SW19 68Fb 133
Shelduck Cl. E15 36Hc 73
Shelduck Ct. SE8 51Bc 114
(off Pilot Cl.)
Sheldwich Ter. BR2: Brom 72Nc 160
Shelford KT1: King T 68Qa 131
Shelford Cl. RM16: Ors 3C 100
Shelford Pl. N16 34Tb 71
Shelford Ri. SE19 66Vb 135
Shelford Rd. EN5: Barn 16Ya 30
Shelgate Rd. SW11 57Gb 111
Shellbank La.
DA2: Bean, G St G 65Wd 142
Shell Cen. SE1 7J 223 (46Pb 90)
Shell Cl. BR2: Brom 72Nc 160
Shellduck Cl. NW9 26Ua 48
Shelley N8 27Nb 50
(off Boyton Rd.)
Shelley Av. E12 37Nc 74
RM12: Horn 33Hd 76
UB6: G'frd 41Fa 86
Shelley Cl. BR6: Orp 76Uc 160
CR5: Coul 89Pb 176
HA6: Nwood 22W 44
HA8: Edg 21Qa 47
SE15 54Xb 113
SL3: L'ly 50B 82
SM7: Bans 87Za 174
UB4: Hayes 43W 84
UB6: G'frd 41Fa 86
WD6: Bore 14Qa 29
Shelley Ct. E10 31Dc 72
(off Skelton's La.)
E11 28Kc 53
(off Makepeace Rd.)
EN9: Walt A 5Hc 21
(off Ninefields)
N19 32Pb 70
SW3 51Hb 111
(off Tite St.)
Shelley Cres. TW5: Hest 53Z 107
UB1: S'hall 44Ba 85
Shelley Dr. DA16: Well 53Uc 116
Shelley Gdns. HA0: Wemb 33La 66
Shelley Gro. IG10: Lough 14Pc 36
Shelley Ho. E2 41Yb 92
(off Cornwall Av.)
N16 35Ub 71
SE17 7E 230
SW1 51Lb 112
(off Churchill Gdns.)
Shelley La. UB9: Hare 25J 43
Shelley Lodge EN2: Enf 11Tb 33
Shelley M. HP3: Hem H 5K 3
Shelley Pl. RM18: Tilb 3D 122
Shelley Rd. CM13: Hut 17Fe 41
NW10 39Ta 67
Shelleys La. TN14: Knock 88Vc 181
Shelley Way SW19 64Fb 133
Shellfield Cl. TW19: Stanw M 57J 105
Shellness Rd. E5 36Xb 71
Shell Rd. SE13 55Dc 114
Shellwood Rd. SW11 54Hb 111
Shelmerdine Cl. E3 43Cc 92
Shelson Av. TW13: Felt 62V 128
Shelson Pde. TW13: Felt 62V 128
Shelton Av. CR6: W'ham 89Yb 178
Shelton Cl. CR6: W'ham 89Yb 178
Shelton Ct. SL3: L'ly 8N 81
Shelton Rd. SW19 67Cb 133
Shelton St. WC2 3F 223 (44Nb 90)
(not continuous)
Shelvers Grn. KT20: Tad 93Ya 194
Shelvers Hill KT20: Tad 93Xa 194
Shelvers Spur KT20: Tad 93Ya 194
Shelvers Way KT20: Tad 93Ya 194
Shenden Cl. TN13: S'oaks 99Ld 203
Shenden Way TN13: S'oaks 100Ld 203
Shendish Edge HP3: Hem H 7P 3
Shendish Manor Golf Course 8M 3
Shene Ho. EC1 7K 217
Shene Sports & Fitness Cen. 56Ta 109
SHENFIELD 16Ce 41
Shenfield Cl. CR5: Coul 91Lb 196
Shenfield Cres. CM15: B'wood 19Ae 41
Shenfield Gdns. CM13: Hut 16De 41
Shenfield Grn. CM15: Shenf 17Ce 41
Shenfield Ho. SE18 53Mc 115
(off Portway Gdns.)
Shenfield Pl. CM15: Shenf 17Ae 41
Shenfield Rd.
CM15: B'wood, Shenf 19Zd 41
IG8: Wfd G 24Kc 53
Shenfield St. N1 2J 219 (40Ub 71)
(not continuous)
SHENLEY 6Qa 15
Shenley Av. HA4: Ruis 33V 64
SHENLEYBURY 3Na 15
Shenleybury WD7: Shenl 2Na 15
Shenleybury Cotts. WD7: Shenl 3Na 15
Shenleybury Vs. WD7: Shenl 3Na 15
Shenley Cl. CR2: Sande 82Vb 177
Shenley Hill WD7: R'lett 7Ka 14
Shenley La. AL2: Lon C 7F 6
Shenley Pk. 5Na 15
Shenley Rd. DA1: Dart 58Qd 119
SE5 53Ub 113
TW5: Hest 53Aa 107
WD6: Bore 14Qa 29
WD7: R'lett 6Ka 14
Shen Pl. Almshouses
CM15: B'wood 19Zd 41
Shenston Ct. SL4: Wind 3H 103
(off James St.)
Shenstone W13 46La 86
Shenstone Cl. DA1: Cray 56Fd 118
Shenstone Dr. SL1: Burn 2B 80
Shenstone Gdns. RM3: Rom 25Ld 57
Shenstone Ho. SW16 64Lb 134
Shenstone Pk. SL5: S'hill 10C 124
Shenwood Ct. WD6: Bore 9Qa 15
Shepherd Cl. TW13: Hanw 63Aa 129
WD5: Ab L 2V 12
Shepherdess Pl. N1 3E 218 (41Sb 91)
Shepherdess Wlk. N1 1E 218 (40Sb 71)
Shepherd Ho. E14 44Dc 92
(off Annabel Cl.)
E16 45Rc 94
(off University Way)
Shepherd Mkt. W1 7K 221 (46Kb 90)
SHEPHERD'S BUSH 47Ya 88
Shepherd's Bush Empire Theatre 47Ya 88
Shepherd's Bush Grn. W12 47Ya 88
Shepherd's Bush Mkt. W12 47Ya 88
(not continuous)
Shepherd's Bush Pl. W12 47Za 88
Shepherd's Bush Rd. W6 49Ya 88
Shepherd's Cl. BR6: Orp 76Vc 161
N6 30Kb 50
Shepherds Cl. HA7: Stan 22Ja 46
(not continuous)
RM6: Chad H 29Zc 55
TW17: Shep 72R 150
UB8: Cowl 42L 83
W1 4H 221
Shepherds Ct. SL4: Wind 4C 102
W12 47Za 88
(off Shepherd's Bush Grn.)
Shepherds Farm WD3: Rick 18J 25
Shepherds Grn. BR7: Chst 66Tc 138
HP1: Hem H 3G 2
(not continuous)
Shepherd's Hill N6 30Kb 50
RH1: Mers 98Lb 196
Shepherds Hill RM3: Hrld W 26Qd 57
RM14: Upm 26Qd 57
Shepherd's La. DA1: Dart 60Jd 118
WD3: Chor, Rick 16F 24
Shepherds La. E9 37Zb 72
GU20: W'sham 8D 146
SE28 46Uc 94
Shepherds Leas SE9 56Sc 116
Shepherd's Path CM14: S Weald 17Ud 40
NW3 36Fb 69
(off Lyndhurst Rd.)
Shepherds Path UB5: N'olt 37Aa 65
(off Arnold Rd.)
Shepherds Pl. W1 4H 221 (45Jb 90)
Shepherd's Rd. WD18: Wat 13V 26
Shepherd St. DA11: Nflt 59Fe 121
W1 7K 221 (46Kb 90)
Shepherd's Wlk. KT18: Eps D 93Ra 193
NW3 36Fb 69
Shepherds Wlk. NW2 33Wa 68
WD23: B Hea 19Fa 28
Shepherds Way AL9: Brk P 9L 9
CR2: Sels 80Zb 158
WD3: Rick 17K 25
Shepiston La. UB3: Harl 49R 84
Shepley Cl. SM5: Cars 76Jb 156
Shepley Dr. SL5: S'dale 2G 146
Shepley End SL5: S'dale 1H 147
Shepley M. EN3: Enf L 9Cc 20

Sheppard Cl.—Siding St.

Sheppard Cl. EN1: Enf . . . 11Xb 33
KT1: King T . . . 70Na 131
Sheppard Dr. SE16 . . . 50Xb 91
Sheppard Ho. *E2* . . . *40Wb 71*
(off Warner Pl.)
SW2 . . . 60Qb 112
Sheppards Coll. *BR1: Brom* . . . *67Jc 137*
(off London Rd.)
Sheppard St. E16 . . . 42Hc 93
Sheppards Yd. *HP2: Hem H* . . . *1M 3*
(off Figtree Hill)
SHEPPERTON . . . 72R 150
Shepperton Bus. Pk.
TW17: Shep . . . 71S 150
Shepperton Cl. WD6: Bore . . . 11Ta 29
Shepperton Ct. TW17: Shep . . . 72R 150
Shepperton Ct. Dr.
TW17: Shep . . . 71R 150
Shepperton Film Studios . . . 69P 127
SHEPPERTON GREEN . . . 70Q 128
Shepperton Marina TW17: Shep . . . 72U 150
Shepperton Rd. BR5: Pet W . . . 72Sc 160
N1 . . . 39Sb 71
TW18: Lale, Shep . . . 69L 127
Sheppey Cl. DA8: Erith . . . 52Kd 119
Sheppey Gdns. RM9: Dag . . . 38Yc 75
Sheppey Rd. RM9: Dag . . . 38Xc 75
Sheppey's La. WD4: K Lan . . . 1S 12
WD5: Bedm . . . 1S 12
Sheppy Pl. DA12: Grav'nd . . . 9D 122
Shepton Ho's. *E2* . . . *41Yb 92*
(off Welwyn St.)
Sherard Ct. N7 . . . 34Nb 70
Sherard Ho. *E9* . . . *38Yb 72*
(off Frampton Pk. Rd.)
Sherard Rd. SE9 . . . 57Nc 116
Sheraton Bus. Cen. UB6: G'frd . . . 40Ka 66
Sheraton Cl. WD6: E'tree . . . 15Pa 29
Sheraton Dr. KT19: Eps . . . 85Sa 173
Sheraton Ho. *SW1* . . . *51Kb 112*
(off Churchill Gdns.)
WD3: Chor . . . 14E 24
Sheraton M. WD18: Wat . . . 14U 26
Sheraton St. W1 . . . 3D 222 (44Mb 90)
Sherborne *NW1* . . . *38Mb 70*
(off Agar Gro.)
Sherborne Av. EN3: Enf H . . . 12Yb 34
UB2: S'hall . . . 49Ca 85
Sherborne Cl. KT18: Tatt C . . . 89Ya 174
SL3: Poyle . . . 53G 104
UB4: Yead . . . 44Y 85
Sherborne Cotts. *WD18: Wat* . . . *15Y 27*
(off Muriel Av.)
Sherborne Cres. SM5: Cars . . . 73Gb 155
Sherborne Gdns. NW9 . . . 27Qa 47
RM5: Col R . . . 22Cd 56
W13 . . . 43Ka 86
Sherborne Gro. TN15: Kems'g . . . 89Qd 183
Sherborne Ho. SW1 . . . 7A 228
SW8 . . . *52Pb 112*
(off Bolney St.)
Sherborne La. EC4 . . . 4F 225 (45Tb 91)
Sherborne Pl. HA6: Nwood . . . 23T 44
Sherborne Rd. BR5: St M Cry . . . 70Vc 139
KT9: Chess . . . 78Na 153
SM3: Sutt . . . 75Cb 155
TW14: Bedf . . . 60T 106
(not continuous)
Sherborne St. N1 . . . 39Tb 71
Sherborne Wlk. KT22: Lea . . . 93La 192
Sherborne Way WD3: Crox G . . . 14R 26
Sherboro Rd. N15 . . . 30Vb 51
Sherbourne Cl. HP2: Hem H . . . 3N 3
TN15: W King . . . 79Ud 164
Sherbourne Ct. *AL1: St A* . . . *2D 6*
(off Beaconsfield Rd.)
SM2: Sutt . . . 79Eb 155
SW5 . . . *49Db 89*
(off Cromwell Rd.)
Sherbourne Dr. SL4: Wind . . . 6D 102
SL5: S'dale . . . 1H 147
Sherbourne Gdns. TW17: Shep . . . 73U 150
Sherbourne Ho. WD18: Wat . . . 16T 26
Sherbourne Pl. HA7: Stan . . . 23Ja 46
Sherbourne Wlk. SL2: Farn C . . . 5G 60
Sherbrooke Cl. DA6: Bex . . . 56Cd 118
Sherbrooke Ho. *E2* . . . *40Yb 72*
(off Bonner Rd.)
SW1 . . . 4E 228
Sherbrooke Rd. SW6 . . . 52Ab 110
Sherbrooke Ter. *SW6* . . . *52Ab 110*
(off Sherbrooke Rd.)
Sherbrooke Way KT4: Wor Pk . . . 73Xa 154
Sherbrook Gdns. N21 . . . 17Rb 33
Sherbrook Ho. *SE16* . . . *47Yb 92*
(off Albatross Way)
Shere Av. SM2: Cheam . . . 82Ya 174
Shere Cl. KT9: Chess . . . 78Ma 153
Sheredan Rd. E4 . . . 22Fc 53
Shere Ho. SE1 . . . 3F 231
Shere Rd. IG2: Ilf . . . 29Qc 54
Sherfield Av. WD3: Rick . . . 20M 25
Sherfield Cl. KT3: N Mald . . . 70Ra 131
Sherfield Gdns. SW15 . . . 58Va 110
Sherfield M. UB3: Hayes . . . 44U 84
Sherfield Rd. RM17: Grays . . . 51De 121
Sheridan Bldgs. WC2 . . . 3G 223
Sheridan Cl. BR8: Swan . . . 70Hd 140
HP1: Hem H . . . 3K 3
RM3: Rom . . . 24Ld 57
UB10: Hil . . . 42S 84
Sheridan Ct. *CR0: C'don* . . . *77Ub 157*
(off Coombe Rd.)
DA1: Dart . . . 56Qd 119
HA1: Harr . . . 30Fa 46
NW6 . . . *38Eb 69*
(off Belsize Rd.)
SL1: Slou . . . 5C 80
SW5 . . . *49Db 89*
(off Barkston Gdns.)
TW4: Houn . . . 57Aa 107
UB5: N'olt . . . 36Da 65
W7 . . . *45Ha 86*
(off Milton Rd.)
Sheridan Cres. BR7: Chst . . . 68Rc 138
Sheridan Dr. RH2: Reig . . . 4K 207
Sheridan Gdns. HA3: Kenton . . . 30Ma 47
Sheridan Grange SL5: S'dale . . . 2E 146
Sheridan Hgts. *E1* . . . *44Xb 91*
(off Watney St.)
Sheridan Ho. KT22: Lea . . . 93Ja 192
SE11 . . . 6A 230
Sheridan Lodge *BR2: Brom* . . . *70Lc 137*
(off Homesdale Rd.)
Sheridan M. E11 . . . 30Kc 53
Sheridan Pl. BR1: Brom . . . 68Mc 137
SW13 . . . 55Va 110
TW12: Hamp . . . 67Da 129
Sheridan Rd. DA7: Bex . . . 55Ad 117
DA17: Belv . . . 49Cd 96
E7 . . . 34Hc 73
E12 . . . 36Nc 74
SW19 . . . 67Bb 133
TW10: Ham . . . 62La 130
WD19: Wat . . . 17Z 27
Sheridans Rd. KT23: Bookh . . . 98Ea 192
Sheridan Ter. UB5: N'olt . . . 36Da 65
Sheridan Wlk. NW11 . . . 30Cb 49
SM5: Cars . . . 78Hb 155
Sheridan Way BR3: Beck . . . 67Bc 136
Sheriden Pl. HA1: Harr . . . 31Ga 66
Sheriff Way WD25: Wat . . . 5W 12
Sheringham NW8 . . . 39Fb 69
Sheringham Av. E12 . . . 35Pc 74
N14 . . . 15Mb 32
RM7: Rom . . . 30Ed 56
TW2: Whitt . . . 60Ba 107
Sheringham Ct. *TW13: Felt* . . . *62W 128*
(off Sheringham Av.)
UB3: Hayes . . . 47V 84
Sheringham Dr. IG11: Bark . . . 36Vc 75
Sheringham Ho. NW1 . . . 7D 214
Sheringham Rd. N7 . . . 37Pb 70
SE20 . . . 69Yb 136
Sheringham Twr. UB1: S'hall . . . 45Da 85
Sherington Av. HA5: Hat E . . . 24Ca 45
Sherington Rd. SE7 . . . 51Kc 115
Sherland Ct. *WD7: R'lett* . . . *8Ja 14*
(off The Dell)
Sherland Rd. TW1: Twick . . . 60Ha 108
Sherleys Ct. HA4: Ruis . . . 33U 64
Sherlies Av. BR6: Orp . . . 75Uc 160
Sherlock Cl. SW16 . . . 68Pb 134
Sherlock Ct. *NW8* . . . *39Fb 69*
(off Dorman Way)
Sherlock Holmes Mus. . . . 6G 215
Sherlock M. W1 . . . 7H 215 (43Jb 90)
Shermanbury Cl. DA8: Erith . . . 52Hd 118
Shermanbury Pl. DA8: Erith . . . 52Hd 118
Sherman Gdns. RM6: Chad H . . . 30Yc 55
Sherman Ho. *E14* . . . *44Ec 92*
(off Dee St.)
UB3: Harl . . . *48S 84*
(off Nine Acres Cl.)
Sherman Rd. BR1: Brom . . . 67Jc 137
SL1: Slou . . . 3J 81
Shernbroke Rd. EN9: Walt A . . . 6Hc 21
Shernhall St. E17 . . . 27Ec 52
Sherrard Rd. E7 . . . 37Lc 73
E12 . . . 37Lc 73
Sherrards Way EN5: Barn . . . 15Cb 31
Sherren Ho. E1 . . . 42Yb 92
Sherrick Grn. Rd. NW10 . . . 36Xa 68
Sherriff Cl. KT10: Esh . . . 75Da 151
Sherriff Ct. *NW6* . . . *37Cb 69*
(off Sherriff Rd.)
Sherriff Rd. NW6 . . . 37Cb 69
Sherringham Av. N17 . . . 26Wb 51
TW13: Felt . . . 62W 128
Sherrington Ct. *E16* . . . *43Hc 93*
(off Rathbone St.)
Sherrin Rd. E10 . . . 35Dc 72
Sherrock Gdns. NW4 . . . 28Xa 48
Sherry M. IG11: Bark . . . 38Tc 74
Sherston Ct. SE1 . . . 5C 230
WC1 . . . 4K 217
Sherwin Ho. *SE11* . . . *51Qb 112*
(off Kennington Rd.)
Sherwin Rd. SE14 . . . 53Zb 114
Sherwood KT6: Surb . . . 75Ma 153
NW6 . . . 38Ab 68
RM16: N Stif . . . 46Ae 99
WD18: Wat . . . 15V 26
Sherwood Av. E18 . . . 27Kc 53
EN6: Pot B . . . 4Ab 16
HA4: Ruis . . . 30U 44
SW16 . . . 66Mb 134
UB4: Yead . . . 42X 85
UB6: G'frd . . . 37Ga 66
Sherwood Cl. DA5: Bexl . . . 58Yc 117
E17 . . . 26Bc 52
KT22: Fet . . . 95Ea 192
SL3: L'ly . . . 48A 82
SW13 . . . 55Xa 110
W13 . . . 46Ka 86
Sherwood Ct. *CR2: S Croy* . . . *78Sb 157*
(off Nottingham Rd.)
HA2: Harr . . . 33Da 65
SL3: L'ly . . . 50B 82
SW11 . . . 55Eb 111
W1 . . . 1F 221
WD25: Wat . . . 6V 12
Sherwood Cres. RH2: Reig . . . 10K 207
Sherwood Gdns. E14 . . . 49Cc 92
IG11: Bark . . . 38Tc 74
SE16 . . . 50Wb 91
Sherwood Ho. *WD5: Ab L* . . . *3V 12*
(off College Rd.)
Sherwood Pk. Av. DA15: Sidc . . . 59Wc 117
Sherwood Pk. Rd. CR4: Mitc . . . 70Lb 134
SM1: Sutt . . . 78Cb 155
Sherwood Rd. CR0: C'don . . . 73Xb 157
CR5: Coul . . . 88Lb 176
DA16: Well . . . 54Uc 116
GU21: Knap . . . 9J 167
HA2: Harr . . . 33Ea 66
IG6: Ilf . . . 28Tc 54
NW4 . . . 27Ya 48
SW19 . . . 66Bb 133
TW12: Hamp H . . . 64Ea 130
Sherwoods Rd. WD19: Wat . . . 17Aa 27
Sherwood St. N20 . . . 20Fb 31
W1 . . . 4C 222 (45Lb 90)
Sherwood Ter. *E16* . . . *44Lc 93*
(off Bingley Rd.)
N20 . . . 20Fb 31
Sherwood Way BR4: W W'ck . . . 75Ec 158
KT19: Eps . . . 84Pa 173
Shetland Cl. WD6: Bore . . . 16Ta 29
Shetland Ho. DA17: Belv . . . 47Dd 96
WD18: Wat . . . *16V 26*
(off Pioneer Way)
Shetland Rd. E3 . . . 40Bc 72
TW6: H'row A . . . 58S 106
Shevon Way CM14: B'wood . . . 21Vd 58
Shewens Rd. KT13: Weyb . . . 77T 150
Shey Copse GU22: Wok . . . 89E 168
Shield Dr. TW8: Bford . . . 51Ja 108
Shieldhall St. SE2 . . . 49Xc 95
Shield Rd. TW15: Ashf . . . 63S 128
Shields Ct. *RM18: E Til* . . . *9L 101*
(off Coronation Av.)
Shiers Av. DA1: Dart . . . 55Pd 119
Shifford Path SE23 . . . 62Zb 136
Shilburn Way GU21: Wok . . . 10L 167
Shillaker Ct. W3 . . . 46Va 88
Shillibeer Pl. W1 . . . 1E 220
Shillibeer Wlk. IG7: Chig . . . 20Vc 37
Shillingford Cl. NW7 . . . 24Za 48
Shillingford Ho. *E3* . . . *41Dc 92*
(off Talwin St.)
Shillingford St. N1 . . . 38Rb 71
Shilling Pl. W7 . . . 47Ja 86
Shillingshaw Lodge *E16* . . . *44Jc 93*
(off Butchers Rd.)
Shillingstone Ho. *W14* . . . *48Ab 88*
(off Russell Rd.)
Shillington Gro. WD17: Wat . . . 11W 26
Shillitoe Av. EN6: Pot B . . . 4Za 16
Shinecroft TN14: Otf . . . 88Jd 182
Shinfield St. W12 . . . 44Ya 88
Shingle Ct. EN9: Walt A . . . 5Jc 21
Shinglewell Rd. DA8: Erith . . . 52Cd 118
Shingly Pl. E4 . . . 18Ec 34
Shinners Cl. SE25 . . . 71Wb 157
Ship All. W4 . . . 51Qa 109
Ship & Mermaid Row
SE1 . . . 1G 231 (47Tb 91)
Shipfield Cl. TN16: Tats . . . 93Lc 199
Ship Hill SL1: Burn . . . 2C 60
TN16: Tats . . . 93Lc 199
Shipka Rd. SW12 . . . 60Kb 112
Shiplake Ho. E2 . . . 4K 219
Ship La. BR8: Swan . . . 67Md 141
DA4: Sut H . . . 67Md 141
RM15: Avel, Purf . . . 46Td 98
RM19: Purf . . . 46Td 98
SW14 . . . 55Sa 109
Shipley Hills Rd. DA13: Meop . . . 75Fe 165
Shipman Rd. E16 . . . 44Kc 93
SE23 . . . 61Zb 136
Ship St. SE8 . . . 53Cc 114
Ship Tavern Pas. EC3 . . . 4H 225 (45Ub 91)
Shipton Cl. RM8: Dag . . . 34Zc 75
Shipton Ho. *E2* . . . *40Vb 71*
(off Shipton St.)
Shipton Rd. UB10: Ick . . . 35P 63
Shipton St. E2 . . . 3K 219 (40Vb 71)
Shipwright Rd. SE16 . . . 47Ac 92
Shipwright Yd. SE1 . . . 7H 225 (46Ub 91)
Ship Yd. E14 . . . 50Dc 92
KT13: Weyb . . . 76R 150
Shirburn Cl. SE23 . . . 59Yb 114
Shirebrook Rd. SE3 . . . 55Mc 115
Shire Ct. DA18: Erith . . . 48Zc 95
HP2: Hem H . . . 1A 4
KT17: Ewe . . . 80Va 154
Shirehall Cl. NW4 . . . 30Za 48
Shirehall Gdns. NW4 . . . 30Za 48
Shirehall La. NW4 . . . 30Za 48
Shirehall Pk. NW4 . . . 29Za 48
Shire Hall Rd. DA2: Hawl, Wilm . . . 64Ld 141
Shire Horse Way TW7: Isle . . . 55Ha 108
Shire Ho. *E3* . . . *41Dc 92*
(off Talwin St.)
EC1 . . . 6F 219
Shire La. BR2: Kes . . . 81Nc 180
BR6: Chels, Downe . . . 80Rc 160
(not continuous)
HP8: Chal G . . . 19C 24
SL9: Chal P . . . 20D 24
(not continuous)
WD3: Chor . . . 18C 24
(Bullsland La.)
WD3: Chor . . . 15D 24
(Chalfont La.)
Shire London Golf Course, The . . . 11Za 30
Shiremeade WD6: E'tree . . . 15Pa 29
Shire M. TW2: Whitt . . . 58Ea 108
Shire Pl. RH1: Redh . . . 8P 207
SW18 . . . 59Eb 111
TW8: Bford . . . 52Ma 109
Shires, The TW10: Ham . . . 63Na 131
TW18: Staines . . . *64G 126*
(off Wapshott Rd.)
WD25: Wat . . . 3X 13
Shires Cl. KT21: Asht . . . 91Ma 193
Shires Ho. KT14: Byfl . . . 85N 169
Shirland M. W9 . . . 41Bb 89
Shirland Rd. W9 . . . 41Bb 89
Shirlbutt St. E14 . . . 45Dc 92
SHIRLEY . . . 75Zb 158
Shirley Av. CR0: C'don . . . 74Yb 158
CR5: Coul . . . 91Rb 197
DA5: Bexl . . . 59Zc 117
RH1: Redh . . . 10P 207
SL4: Wind . . . 3D 102
SM1: Sutt . . . 77Fb 155
SM2: Cheam . . . 81Bb 175
Shirley Chu. Rd. CR0: C'don . . . 76Zb 158
Shirley Cl. DA1: Dart . . . 56Ld 119
DA12: Grav'nd . . . 1K 145
E17 . . . 29Dc 52
EN8: Chesh . . . 1Yb 20
TW3: Houn . . . 57Ea 108
Shirley Ct. IG10: Lough . . . 12Pc 36
SW16 . . . 66Nb 134
Shirley Cres. BR3: Beck . . . 70Ac 136
Shirley Dr. TW3: Houn . . . 57Ea 108
Shirley Gdns. IG11: Bark . . . 37Uc 74
RM12: Horn . . . 33Ld 77
W7 . . . 46Ha 86
Shirley Gro. N9 . . . 17Yb 34
SW11 . . . 55Jb 112
Shirley Hgts. SM6: Wall . . . 81Lb 176
Shirley Hills Rd. CR0: C'don . . . 78Yb 158
Shirley Ho. *SE5* . . . *52Tb 113*
(off Picton St.)
Shirley Ho. Dr. SE7 . . . 52Lc 115
Shirleyhyrst KT13: Weyb . . . 79T 150
SHIRLEY OAKS . . . 74Zb 158
Shirley Oaks Rd. CR0: C'don . . . 74Zb 158
Shirley Pk. CR0: C'don . . . 75Yb 158
Shirley Pk. Golf Course . . . 75Xb 157
Shirley Pk. Rd. CR0: C'don . . . 74Xb 157
Shirley Pl. GU21: Knap . . . 9G 166
Shirley Rd. AL1: St A . . . 3D 6
CR0: C'don . . . 73Xb 157
DA15: Sidc . . . 62Uc 138
E15 . . . 38Gc 73
EN2: Enf . . . 13Sb 33
SM6: Wall . . . 81Lb 176
W4 . . . 47Ta 87
WD5: Ab L . . . 4V 12
WD17: Wat . . . 11W 26
Shirley St. E16 . . . 44Hc 93
Shirley Way CR0: C'don . . . 76Ac 158
Shirley Windmill . . . 76Yb 158
Shirlock Rd. NW3 . . . 35Hb 69
Shirwell Cl. NW7 . . . 24Za 48
Shobden Rd. N17 . . . 25Tb 51
Shobroke Cl. NW2 . . . 34Ya 68
Shoebury Rd. E6 . . . 38Pc 74
Shoelands Ct. NW9 . . . 27Ta 47
Shoe La. EC4 . . . 2A 224 (44Qb 90)
Sholden Gdns. BR5: St M Cry . . . 71Yc 161
Sholto Rd. TW6: H'row A . . . 57P 105
Shona Ho. E13 . . . 43Lc 93
Shonks Mill Rd. RM4: Nave . . . 11Kd 39
Shooters Av. HA3: Kenton . . . 28La 46
SHOOTERS HILL . . . 53Qc 116
Shooters Hill DA16: Well . . . 53Pc 116
SE18 . . . 53Pc 116
Shooters Hill Golf Course . . . 53Sc 116
Shooters Hill Rd. SE3 . . . 52Lc 115
SE10 . . . 53Fc 115
SE18 . . . 52Lc 115
Shooters Rd. EN2: Enf . . . 11Rb 33
Shoot Up Hill NW2 . . . 36Ab 68
Shopping Hall, The E6 . . . 39Nc 74
Shop Rd. SL4: Wind . . . 2A 102
Shopwick Pl. WD6: E'tree . . . 16Ma 29
Shord Hill CR8: Kenley . . . 88Tb 177
Shore, The DA11: Nflt . . . 8B 122
(Clifton Marine Pde.)
DA11: Nflt . . . 57Fe 121
(Granby Rd.)
Shore Bus. Cen. E9 . . . 38Yb 72
Shore Cl. TW12: Hamp . . . 65Aa 129
TW14: Felt . . . 59W 106
Shorediche Cl. UB10: Ick . . . 34P 63
SHOREDITCH . . . 3H 219 (41Ub 91)
Shoreditch Ct. *E8* . . . *38Vb 71*
(off Queensbridge Rd.)
Shoreditch High St. E1 . . . 4J 219 (42Ub 91)
Shoreditch Ho. BR2: Brom . . . 72Nc 160
N1 . . . 4G 219
Shore Gro. TW13: Hanw . . . 61Ca 129
SHOREHAM . . . 83Hd 182
Shoreham Aircraft Mus., The . . . 83Hd 182
Shoreham Cl. CR0: C'don . . . 72Yb 158
DA5: Bexl . . . 60Zc 117
SW18 . . . 57Db 111
Shoreham La. BR6: Well H . . . 79Cd 162
TN13: Riv, S'oaks . . . 94Hd 202
TN14: Hals . . . 84Bd 181
Shoreham Pl. TN14: S'ham . . . 84Jd 182
Shoreham Ri. SL2: Slou . . . 2B 80
Shoreham Rd. BR5: St P . . . 67Xc 139
DA4: Eyns . . . 79Ld 163
TN14: Otf, S'ham . . . 83Kd 183
Shoreham Rd. E. TW6: H'row A . . . 57N 105
Shoreham Rd. W. TW6: H'row A . . . 57N 105
Shoreham Way BR2: Hayes . . . 72Jc 159
Shorehill Ct. TN15: Kems'g . . . 89Pd 183
Shorehill La.
TN15: Kems'g, Knat . . . 87Pd 183
Shore Ho. SW8 . . . 55Kb 112
Shore M. *E9* . . . *38Yb 72*
(off Shore Rd.)
Shore Pl. E9 . . . 38Yb 72
Shore Point IG9: Buck H . . . 19Kc 35
Shore Rd. E9 . . . 38Yb 72
Shores Rd. GU21: Wok . . . 86A 168
Shore Way *SW9* . . . *54Qb 112*
(off Crowhurst Cl.)
Shorncliffe Rd. SE1 . . . 7K 231 (50Vb 91)
Shorndean St. SE6 . . . 60Ec 114
SHORNE . . . 4N 145
Shorne Cl. BR5: St M Cry . . . 70Zc 139
DA15: Sidc . . . 58Xc 117
Shornefield Cl. BR1: Brom . . . 69Qc 138
Shorne Ifield Rd. DA12: Shorne . . . 5J 145
Shornells Way SE2 . . . 49Yc 95
SHORNE RIDGEWAY . . . 6N 145
Shorne Woods Country Pk. . . . 6K 145
Shorne Woods Country Pk. Vis. Cen.
. . . 6L 145
Shorrold's Rd. SW6 . . . 52Bb 111
Shortacres RH1: Nutf . . . 5F 208
Short Blue Pl. IG11: Bark . . . 38Sc 74
Shortcroft Rd. KT17: Ewe . . . 80Va 154
Shortcrofts Rd. RM9: Dag . . . 37Bd 75
Shorter Av. CM15: Shenf . . . 17Be 41
Shorter St. E1 . . . 4K 225 (45Vb 91)
Shortfern SL2: Slou . . . 4N 81
Shortgate N12 . . . 21Bb 49
Short Hedges TW3: Houn . . . 53Ca 107
Short Hill HA1: Harr . . . 32Ga 66
SHORTLANDS . . . 68Gc 137
Shortlands UB3: Harl . . . 51T 106
W6 . . . 49Za 88
Shortlands Cl. DA17: Belv . . . 48Bd 95
N18 . . . 20Tb 33
Shortlands Gdns. BR2: Brom . . . 68Gc 137
Shortlands Golf Course . . . 67Gc 137
Shortlands Gro. BR2: Brom . . . 69Fc 137
Shortlands Rd. BR2: Brom . . . 69Fc 137
E10 . . . 31Dc 72
KT2: King T . . . 66Pa 131
Short La. AL2: Brick W . . . 1Aa 13
RH8: Limp . . . 4M 211
TN15: Igh . . . 95Xd 204
TW19: Stanw . . . 59P 105
Shortmead Dr. EN8: Chesh . . . 3Ac 20
Short Path SE18 . . . 51Rc 116
Short Rd. E11 . . . 33Gc 73
TW6: H'row A . . . 58N 105
W4 . . . 51Ua 110
Shorts Cft. NW9 . . . 28Ra 47
Shorts Gdns. WC2 . . . 3F 223 (44Nb 90)
Shorts Rd. SM5: Cars . . . 77Gb 155
Short St. *NW4* . . . *28Ya 48*
(off Foster St.)
SE1 . . . 1A 230 (47Qb 90)
Short Wall E15 . . . 41Ec 92
Shortwave Cinema . . . 3J 231
Short Way N12 . . . 23Gb 49
SE9 . . . 55Nc 116
TW2: Whitt . . . 59Ea 108
Shortwood *GU22: Wok* . . . *1P 187*
(off Mt. Hermon Rd.)
Shortwood Av. TW18: Staines . . . 62K 127
Shortwood Comn. TW18: Staines . . . 63K 127
Shorwell Ct. RM19: Purf . . . 50Rd 97
Shotfield SM6: Wall . . . 79Kb 156
Shothanger Way HP3: Bov . . . 7F 2
Shott Cl. SM1: Sutt . . . 78Eb 155
Shottendane Rd. SW6 . . . 53Cb 111
Shottery Cl. SE9 . . . 62Nc 138
Shottfield Av. SW14 . . . 56Ua 110
Shottsford *W2* . . . *44Cb 89*
(off Talbot Rd.)
Shoulder of Mutton All. E14 . . . 45Ac 92
Shouldham St. W1 . . . 1E 220 (43Gb 89)
Showcase Cinema
Barking . . . 41Tc 94
Bluewater . . . 60Vd 120
Showers Way UB3: Hayes . . . 46W 84
Shrapnel Cl. SE18 . . . 52Nc 116
Shrapnel Rd. SE9 . . . 55Pc 116
SHREDING GREEN . . . 44E 82
Shrek's Adventure! . . . 1H 229 (47Pb 90)
Shrewsbury Av. HA3: Kenton . . . 28Na 47
SW14 . . . 56Sa 109
Shrewsbury Cl. KT6: Surb . . . 75Na 153
Shrewsbury Ct. EC1 . . . 6E 218
Shrewsbury Ho. *SW3* . . . *51Gb 111*
(off Cheyne Wlk.)
SW8 . . . *51Pb 112*
(off Kennington Oval)
Shrewsbury La. SE18 . . . 53Rc 116
Shrewsbury M. *W2* . . . *43Cb 89*
(off Chepstow Rd.)
Shrewsbury Rd. BR3: Beck . . . 69Ac 136
E7 . . . 36Mc 73
N11 . . . 23Lb 50
NW10 . . . 39Ta 67
RH1: Redh . . . 6N 207
SM5: Cars . . . 72Gb 155
TW6: H'row A . . . 58S 106
(not continuous)
W2 . . . 44Cb 89
Shrewsbury St. W10 . . . 42Ya 88
Shrewsbury Wlk. *TW7: Isle* . . . *55Ja 108*
(off Magdala Rd.)
Shrewton Rd. SW17 . . . 66Hb 133
Shri Swaminarayan Mandir
London . . . 37Ta 67
Shroffold Rd. BR1: Brom . . . 63Gc 137
Shropshire Cl. CR4: Mitc . . . 70Nb 134
Shropshire Ct. *W7* . . . *44Ha 86*
(off Copley Cl.)
Shropshire Ho. *N18* . . . *22Xb 51*
(off Cavendish Cl.)
Shropshire Pl. WC1 . . . 6D 216 (42Lb 90)
Shropshire Rd. N22 . . . 24Pb 50
Shroton St. NW1 . . . 7D 214 (43Gb 89)
Shrubberies, The AL1: St A . . . 3B 6
E18 . . . 26Jc 53
IG7: Chig . . . 22Sc 54
Shrubbery, The E11 . . . 29Kc 53
HP1: Hem H . . . 1G 2
KT6: Surb . . . 74Na 153
RM14: Upm . . . 34Sd 78
Shrubbery Cl. N1 . . . 39Sb 71
Shrubbery Gdns. N21 . . . 17Rb 33
Shrubbery Rd. DA4: S Dar . . . 67Td 142
DA12: Grav'nd . . . 10D 122
N9 . . . 20Wb 33
SW16 . . . 63Nb 134
UB1: S'hall . . . 46Ba 85
Shrubbs Hill GU24: Chob . . . 1G 166
Shrubbs Hill La. SL5: S'dale . . . 2G 146
Shrubhill Rd. HP1: Hem H . . . 3H 3
Shrubland Ct. *SM7: Bans* . . . *88Bb 175*
(off Garratts La.)
Shrubland Gro. KT4: Wor Pk . . . 76Ya 154
Shrubland Rd. E8 . . . 39Vb 71
E10 . . . 31Cc 72
E17 . . . 29Cc 52
SM7: Bans . . . 88Bb 175
Shrublands AL9: Brk P . . . 8K 9
Shrublands, The EN6: Pot B . . . 5Ab 16
Shrublands Av. CR0: C'don . . . 76Cc 158
Shrublands Cl. IG7: Chig . . . 23Sc 54
N20 . . . 18Fb 31
SE26 . . . 62Yb 136
Shrubsall Cl. SE9 . . . 60Nc 116
Shrubshall Mdw. TN15: Plax . . . 99Ce 205
SHRUBS HILL . . . 2G 146
Shrubs Rd. UB9: Rick . . . 23P 43
Shuna Wlk. N1 . . . 37Tb 71
Shurland Av. EN4: E Barn . . . 16Fb 31
Shurland Gdns. SE15 . . . 52Vb 113
Shurlock Av. BR8: Swan . . . 68Fd 140
Shurlock Dr. BR6: Farnb . . . 77Sc 160
Shushan Cl. N16 . . . 31Ub 71
Shuters Sq. W14 . . . 50Bb 89
Shuttle Cl. DA15: Sidc . . . 59Vc 117
Shuttlemead DA5: Bexl . . . 59Bd 117
Shuttle Rd. DA1: Cray . . . 55Jd 118
Shuttle St. E1 . . . 42Wb 91
Shuttleworth Rd. SW11 . . . 54Gb 111
Siamese M. N3 . . . 25Cb 49
Siani M. N8 . . . 28Rb 51
Sibella Rd. SW4 . . . 54Mb 112
Sibley Cl. BR1: Brom . . . 71Nc 160
DA6: Bex . . . 57Ad 117
Sibley Ct. BR2: Brom . . . 68Fc 137
UB8: Hil . . . 43S 84
Sibley Gro. E12 . . . 38Nc 74
Sibthorpe Rd. AL9: Wel G . . . 6Kf 8
SE12 . . . 58Kc 115
Sibthorp Rd. CR4: Mitc . . . 68Hb 133
Sibton Rd. SM5: Cars . . . 73Gb 155
Sicilian Av. WC1 . . . 1G 223
Sickle Cnr. RM9: Dag . . . 42Dd 96
Sidbury Cl. SL5: S'dale . . . 1E 146
Sidbury St. SW6 . . . 53Ab 110
SIDCUP . . . 63Wc 139
Sidcup By-Pass BR5: Sidc, St P . . . 65Wc 139
BR7: Chst, Sidc . . . 62Tc 138
DA14: Sidc . . . 65Wc 139
Sidcup Golf Course . . . 60Xc 117
Sidcup High St. DA14: Sidc . . . 63Wc 139
Sidcup Hill DA14: Sidc . . . 63Xc 139
Sidcup Hill Gdns. DA14: Sidc . . . 64Yc 139
Sidcup Leisure Cen. . . . 61Wc 139
Sidcup Place . . . 64Wc 139
Sidcup Pl. DA14: Sidc . . . 64Wc 139
Sidcup Rd. SE9 . . . 58Lc 115
SE12 . . . 58Lc 115
Sidcup Technology Cen.
DA14: Sidc . . . 64Zc 139
Siddeley Dr. TW4: Houn . . . 55Aa 107
Siddeley Rd. DA1: Cray . . . 57Jd 118
E17 . . . 26Ec 52
Siddons Cl. SS17: Linf . . . 8J 101
Siddons La. NW1 . . . 6G 215 (42Hb 89)
Siddons Rd. CR0: Wadd . . . 76Qb 156
N17 . . . 25Wb 51
SE23 . . . 61Ac 136
Side Rd. E17 . . . 29Bc 52
UB9: Den . . . 31F 62
Sidewood Rd. SE9 . . . 60Tc 116
Sidford Cl. HP1: Hem H . . . 2H 3
Sidford Ho. SE1 . . . 4K 229
Sidford Pl. SE1 . . . 4J 229 (48Qb 90)
Sidgwick Ho. *SW9* . . . *54Pb 112*
(off Stockwell Rd.)
Sidi Ct. N15 . . . 27Rb 51
Sidings, The AL10: Hat . . . 1A 8
E11 . . . 32Ec 72
HP2: Hem H . . . 2M 3
IG10: Lough . . . 16Nc 36
TN13: Dun G . . . 92Gd 202
TW18: Staines . . . 63K 127
Sidings Apartments, The E16 . . . 47Qc 94
Sidings M. N7 . . . 34Qb 70
Siding St. E20 . . . 39Dc 72

Siding Way—Smithfield St.

Siding Way AL2: Lon C 8E 6
Sidlaw Ho. N16 32Vb 71
Sidmouth Av. TW7: Isle 54Ga 108
Sidmouth Cl. WD19: Wat 19X 27
Sidmouth Ct. *DA1: Dart* 60Rd 119
(off Churchill Cl.)
Sidmouth Dr. HA4: Ruis 34W 64
Sidmouth Ho. *SE15* 52Wb 113
(off Lindsey Est.)
W1 2E 220
Sidmouth M. WC1 4H 217 (41Pb 90)
Sidmouth Pde. NW2 38Ya 68
Sidmouth Rd.
BR5: St M Cry 71Xc 161
(not continuous)
DA16: Well 52Yc 117
E10 34Ec 72
NW2 38Ya 68
Sidmouth St. WC1 4G 217 (41Nb 90)
Sidney Av. N13 22Pb 50
Sidney Boyd Ct. NW6 38Cb 69
Sidney Cl. UB8: Uxb 38L 63
Sidney Elson Way E6 40Qc 74
Sidney Est. E1 44Yb 92
(Bromhead St.)
E1 43Yb 92
(Lindley St.)
Sidney Gdns. TN14: Otf 88Ld 183
TW8: Bford 51Ma 109
Sidney Godley (VC) Ho. *E2* 41Yb 92
(off Digby St.)
Sidney Gro. EC1 2B 218 (40Rb 71)
Sidney Ho. *E2* 40Zb 72
(off Old Ford Rd.)
Sidney Miller Ct. *W3* 46Ra 87
(off Crown St.)
Sidney Rd. BR3: Beck 68Ac 136
CM16: They B 8Tc 22
E7 34Jc 73
HA2: Harr 27Ea 46
KT12: Walt T 73W 150
N22 24Pb 50
SE25 71Wb 157
SL4: Wind 5A 102
SW9 54Pb 112
TW1: Twick 58Ja 108
TW18: Staines 63J 127
Sidney Sq. E1 43Yb 92
Sidney St. E1 43Xb 91
(not continuous)
Sidney Webb Ho. SE1 3G 231
Sidonie Apartments *SW11* 56Gb 111
(off Danvers Av.)
Sidworth St. E8 38Xb 71
Siebel Ct. TW20: Egh 63D 126
Siebert Rd. SE3 51Jc 115
Siege Ho. *E1* 44Xb 91
(off Sidney St.)
Siemens Brothers Way E16 45Jc 93
Siemens Rd. SE18 48Mc 93
Sienna SE28 48Wc 95
Sienna Alto *SE13* 55Ec 114
(off Cornmill La.)
Sienna Cl. KT9: Chess 79Ma 153
Sienna Ho. *E20* 37Dc 72
(off Victory Pde.)
Sienna Ter. NW2 33Wa 68
Sierra Dr. RM9: Dag 40Dd 76
Sigdon Pas. E8 36Wb 71
Sigdon Rd. E8 36Wb 71
Sigers, The HA5: Eastc 30X 45
Sigmund Freud Statue 37Fb 69
Signal Ho. *E8* 38Xb 71
(off Martello Ter.)
SE1 2D 230
Signal Wlk. E4 23Ec 52
Signmakers Yd. *NW1* 39Kb 70
(off Delancey St.)
Sigrist Sq. KT2: King T 67Na 131
Sikorski Mus. 2C 226 (47Fb 89)
Silas Ct. *WD17: Wat* 11W 26
(off Lockhart Rd.)
Silbury Av. CR4: Mitc 67Gb 133
Silbury Ho. SE26 62Wb 135
Silbury St. N1 3F 219 (41Tb 91)
Silchester Ct. CR7: Thor H 70Qb 134
TW15: Ashf 61N 127
Silchester Rd. W10 44Za 88
Silecroft Rd. DA7: Bex 53Cd 118
Silesia Bldgs. E8 38Xb 71
Silex St. SE1 2C 230 (47Rb 91)
Silicon Bus. Cen. UB6: G'frd 40La 66
Silicon Way N1 4G 219
Silistria Cl. GU21: Knap 10G 166
Silk Cl. SE12 57Jc 115
Silk Ct. *E2* 41Wb 91
(off Squirries St.)
Silkfield Rd. NW9 29Ua 48
Silkham Rd. RH8: Oxt 99Fc 199
Silk Ho. *E1* 44Wb 91
(off Leman St.)
E1 43Zb 92
(off Trafalgar Gdns.)
E2 1K 219
NW9 27Ta 47
Silkin M. SE15 52Wb 113
Silk M. SE11 7A 230
Silk Mill Ct. WD19: Wat 16X 27
Silk Mill Rd. WD19: Wat 17X 27
Silk Mills Cl. TN14: S'oaks 93Ld 203
Silk Mills Pas. SE13 54Dc 114
Silk Mills Path SE13 54Ec 114
(not continuous)
Silk Mills Sq. E9 37Bc 72
Silkmore La. KT24: W Hor 97Q 190
Silks Ct. E11 32Hc 73
Silkstream Pde. HA8: Edg 25Sa 47
Silkstream Rd. HA8: Edg 25Sa 47
Silk St. EC2 7E 218 (43Sb 91)
Silk Weaver Way E2 40Xb 71
Sillitoe Ho. *N1* 39Tb 71
(off Colville Est.)
Silsoe Ho. NW1 2A 216 (40Kb 70)
Silsoe Rd. N22 26Pb 50
Silverbeck Way TW19: Stanw M 57J 105
Silver Birch Av. E4 22Bc 52
Silver Birch Cl. DA2: Wilm 63Gd 140
KT15: Wdhm 84G 168
N11 23Jb 50
SE6 62Bc 136
SE28 46Wc 95
UB10: Ick 35N 63
Silver Birch Ct. EN8: Chesh 3Zb 20
Silver Birches CM13: Hut 18Ce 41
Silver Birch Gdns. E6 42Pc 94
Silver Birch M. IG6: Ilf 23Sc 54
RM14: Upm 32Ud 78
Silverbirch Wlk. NW5 37Jb 70
Silverburn Ho. *SW9* 53Rb 113
(off Lothian Rd.)
Silvercliffe Gdns. EN4: E Barn 14Gb 31
Silver Cl. HA3: Hrw W 24Fa 46
KT20: Kgswd 96Ab 194
SE14 52Ac 114
Silver Ct. KT22: Lea 92Ka 192
Silver Cres. W4 49Ra 87
Silverdale DA3: Hartl 70Be 143
EN2: Enf 14Nb 32
NW1 3B 216
SE26 63Yb 136
Silverdale Av. IG2: Ilf 29Uc 54
KT12: Walt T 75V 150
KT22: Oxs 86Ea 172
Silverdale Cen., The HA0: Wemb 39Pa 67
Silverdale Cl. SM1: Sutt 77Bb 155
UB5: N'olt 36Ba 65
W7 46Ga 86
Silverdale Ct. EC1 5C 218
TW18: Staines 63K 127
Silverdale Dr. RM12: Horn 36Kd 77
SE9 61Nc 138
TW16: Sun 68X 129
Silverdale Factory Cen.
UB3: Hayes 48W 84
Silverdale Gdns. UB3: Hayes 47W 84
Silverdale Ind. Est. UB3: Hayes 47W 84
Silverdale Rd. BR5: Pet W 70Sc 138
BR5: St P 69Wc 139
DA7: Bex 54Dd 118
E4 23Fc 53
UB3: Hayes 47V 84
WD23: Bush 15Aa 27
Silver Dell WD24: Wat 7V 12
Silverdene *N12* 23Db 49
(off Thyra Gro.)
Silvergate KT19: Ewe 78Sa 153
Silverglade Bus. Pk. KT9: Chess 84La 172
Silverhall St. TW7: Isle 55Ja 108
Silver Hill WD6: Bore 8Sa 15
Silverholme Cl. HA3: Kenton 31Na 67
Silver Jubilee Way TW4: Cran 54X 107
Silverlands Cl. KT16: Chert 76F 148
Silverland St. E16 46Pc 94
Silver La. BR4: W W'ck 75Fc 159
CR8: Purl 84Mb 176
Silverleigh Rd. CR7: Thor H 70Pb 134
Silverlocke Rd. RM17: Grays 51Fe 121
Silver Mead E18 25Jc 53
Silvermere Av. RM5: Col R 23Dd 56
Silvermere Ct. CR3: Cat'm 96Vb 197
CR8: Purl 84Qb 176
Silvermere Dr. N18 23Zb 52
Silvermere Golf Course 85S 170
Silvermere Rd. SE6 59Dc 114
Silver Pl. W1 4C 222 (44Lb 90)
WD18: Wat 14U 26
Silver Rd. DA12: Grav'nd 1G 144
SE13 55Dc 114
Silvers *IG9: Buck H* 18Lc 35
(off Palmerston Rd.)
Silversmiths Way GU21: Wok 10N 167
Silver Spring Cl. DA8: Erith 51Dd 118
Silverstead La. TN16: Westrm 93Tc 200
Silverstone Cl. RH1: Redh 4P 207
Silverston Way HA7: Stan 23La 46
Silver St. EN1: Enf 13Tb 33
EN7: Walt C, G Oak 2Rb 19
EN9: Walt A 6Ec 20
N18 21Tb 51
RM4: Abr 13Xc 37
Silverthorn *NW8* 39Db 69
(off Abbey Rd.)
Silverthorn Dr. HP3: Hem H 6B 4
Silverthorne Loft Apartments
SE5 51Tb 113
(off Albany Rd.)
Silverthorne Rd. SW8 54Kb 112
Silverthorn Gdns. E4 19Cc 34
Silverton Rd. W6 51Za 110
SILVERTOWN 46Lc 93
Silvertown Av. SS17: Stan H 1M 101
Silvertown Sq. E16 43Hc 93
Silvertown Viaduct E16 44Hc 93
Silvertown Way E16 44Gc 93
(Clarkson Rd.)
E16 46Jc 93
(Hanover Av.)
Silver Train Gdns. DA1: Dart 54Pd 119
Silver Tree Cl. KT12: Walt T 76W 150
Silvertree La. UB6: G'frd 41Fa 86
Silver Trees AL2: Brick W 2Ba 13
Silver Wlk. SE16 46Ac 92
Silver Way RM7: Mawney 27Dd 56
UB10: Hil 40R 64
Silver Wing Ind. Est. CR0: Wadd 79Pb 156
Silverwood Cl. BR3: Beck 66Cc 136
CR0: Sels 81Bc 178
HA6: Nwood 25S 44
RM16: Grays 45Ce 99
Silverwood Pl. SE10 53Ec 114
Silvester Ho. *E1* 44Xb 91
(off Varden St.)
E2 41Yb 92
(off Sceptre Rd.)
W11 44Bb 89
(off Basing St.)
Silvester Rd. SE22 57Vb 113
Silvester St. SE1 2F 231 (47Tb 91)
Silvocea Way E14 44Fc 93
Silwood Cl. SL5: Asc 8B 124
Silwood Est. SE16 49Yb 92
Silwood Pk. 9C 124
Silwood Rd. SL5: S'dale, S'hill 10D 124
Silwood St. *SE16* 49Yb 92
(off Rotherhithe New Rd.)
Simkins Cl. SW2 56Nb 112
Simla Ct. *N7* 38Nb 70
(off Brewery Rd.)
Simla Ho. SE1 2G 231
Simmil Rd. KT10: Clay 78Ga 152
Simmonds Ct. *SW5* 49Db 89
(off Earl's Ct. Gdns.)
Simmonds Dr. DA3: Hartl 71Ce 165
Simmonds Ho. *TW8: Bford* 50Na 87
(off Clayponds La.)
Simmonds Ri. HP3: Hem H 4M 3
Simmons Cl. KT9: Chess 79La 152
N20 19Gb 31
SL3: L'ly 49C 82
Simmons Dr. RM8: Dag 34Ad 75
Simmons Ga. KT10: Esh 78Ea 152
Simmons La. E4 19Fc 35
Simmons Pl. RM16: Grays 46Ce 99
TW18: Staines 64G 126
Simmons Rd. SE18 50Rc 94
Simmons Way N20 19Gb 31
Simms Cl. SM5: Cars 75Gb 155
Simms Gdns. N2 26Eb 49
Simms Rd. SE1 49Wb 91
Simnel Rd. SE12 59Kc 115
Simon Cl. W11 45Bb 89
Simon Ct. *W9* 41Cb 89
(off Saltram Cres.)
WD23: Bush 16Ca 27
Simon Dean HP3: Bov 9C 2
Simonds Rd. E10 33Cc 72
Simone Cl. BR1: Brom 67Mc 137
Simone Ct. SE26 62Yb 136
Simone Dr. CR8: Kenley 88Sb 177
Simons Cl. KT16: Ott 79E 148
Simons Ct. N16 33Vb 71
Simons Wlk. E15 36Fc 73
TW20: Eng G 6N 125
Simplemarsh Ct. KT15: Add 77K 149
Simplemarsh Rd. KT15: Add 77J 149
Simpson Cl. CR0: C'don 71Sb 157
N21 15Nb 32
Simpson Dr. W3 44Ta 87
Simpson Ho. NW8 4D 214 (42Gb 89)
SE11 7J 229 (50Pb 90)
Simpson Rd. RM13: Rain 37Hd 76
TW4: Houn 58Ba 107
TW10: Ham 63La 130
Simpson's Rd. E14 45Dc 92
Simpson St. SW11 54Gb 111
Simpsons Way SL1: Slou 6H 81
Simpson Way KT6: Surb 72La 152
Simrose Ct. SW18 57Cb 111
Sims Cl. RM1: Rom 28Hd 56
Sims Wlk. SE3 56Hc 115
Sinclair Ct. CR0: C'don 75Ub 157
Sinclair Dr. SM2: Sutt 81Db 175
Sinclair Gdns. W14 47Za 88
Sinclair Gro. NW11 30Za 48
Sinclair Ho. WC1 4F 217
Sinclair Mans. *W12* 47Za 88
(off Richmond Way)
Sinclair Pl. SE4 58Cc 114
Sinclair Rd. E4 22Bc 52
SL4: Wind 5G 102
W14 47Za 88
Sinclairs Ho. *E3* 40Bc 72
(off St Stephen's Rd.)
Sinclair Way DA2: Daren 63Td 142
Sinclare Cl. EN1: Enf 11Vb 33
Sincots Rd. RH1: Redh 6P 207
Sinderby Cl. WD6: Bore 11Pa 29
Sindercombe M. W12 48Wa 88
Singapore Rd. W13 46Ja 86
Singer M. *SW4* 54Nb 112
(off Union Rd.)
Singer St. EC2 4G 219 (41Tb 91)
Singles Cross TN14: Knock 87Zc 181
Singles Cross La. TN14: Knock 86Yc 181
SINGLE STREET 87Rc 180
Single St. TN16: Big H 87Rc 180
Singleton Cl. CR0: C'don 73Sb 157
RM12: Horn 35Hd 76
SW17 66Hb 133
Singleton Rd. RM9: Dag 36Bd 75
Singleton Scarp N12 22Cb 49
SINGLEWELL 4F 144
Singlewell La. DA11: Grav'nd 2D 144
Singlewell Rd. DA11: Grav'nd 2D 144
Singret Pl. UB8: Cowl 42L 83
Sinnott Rd. E17 25Zb 52
Siobhan Davis Dance Studios 4B 230
Sion Ct. TW1: Twick 60Ka 108
Sion Rd. TW1: Twick 60Ka 108
Sippetts Ct. IG1: Ilf 32Tc 74
SIPSON 51Q 106
Sipson Cl. UB7: Sip 51Q 106
Sipson La. UB3: Harl 51Q 106
UB7: Sip 51Q 106
Sipson Rd. UB7: Sip, W Dray 48P 83
(not continuous)
Sipson Way UB7: Sip 52Q 106
Sir Abraham Dawes Cotts.
SW15 56Ab 110
Sir Alexander Cl. W3 46Va 88
Sir Alexander Rd. W3 46Va 88
Sir Christopher France Ho. E1 41Ac 92
Sir Cyril Black Way SW19 66Cb 133
Sirdar Rd. CR4: Mitc 65Jb 134
N22 27Rb 51
W11 45Za 88
Sirdar Strand DA12: Grav'nd 4H 145
Sir Francis Drake Ct. SE10 50Fc 93
Sir Francis Way CM14: B'wood 19Xd 40
Sir Henry Peakes Dr. SL2: Farn C 7E 60
Sirinham Point *SW8* 51Pb 112
(off Meadow Rd.)
Sirius SW11 54Hb 111
Sirius Bldg. *E1* 45Zb 92
(off Jardine Rd.)
Sirius Ho. *SE16* 49Ac 92
(off Seafarer Way)
Sirius Rd. HA6: Nwood 22V 44
Sir James Altham Pool 22Z 45
Sir James Black Ho. *SE5* 54Tb 113
(off Coldharbour La.)
Sir John Kirk Cl. SE5 52Sb 113
Sir John Lyon Ho. EC4 4D 224
Sir John Morden Wlk. SE3 54Jc 115
Sir John Soane's Mus. 2H 223 (44Pb 90)
Sir Nicholas Garrow Ho. *W10* 42Ab 88
(off Kensal Rd.)
Sir Oswald Stoll Foundation, The
SW6 52Db 111
(off Fulham Rd.)
Sir Oswald Stoll Mans. *SW6* 52Db 111
(off Fulham Rd.)
Sir Robert M. SL3: L'ly 50C 82
Sir Sydney Camm Ho. SL4: Wind 3F 102
Sir Walter Raleigh Ct. SE10 50Gc 93
Sir William Atkins Ho.
KT18: Eps 85Ta 173
Sir William Powell's Almshouses
SW6 54Ab 110
Sise La. EC4 3F 225 (44Tb 91)
Siskin Cl. WD6: Bore 14Qa 29
WD23: Bush 14Aa 27
Siskin Dr. DA9: Ghithe 58Wd 120
HP3: Hem H 7M 3
Siskin Ho. *SE16* 49Zb 92
(off Tawny Way)
WD18: Wat 16T 26
Sisley Rd. IG11: Bark 39Uc 74
Sispara Gdns. SW18 58Bb 111
Sissinghurst Cl. BR1: Brom 64Gc 137
Sissinghurst Ho. *SE15* 51Yb 114
(off Sharratt St.)
Sissinghurst Rd. CR0: C'don 73Wb 157
Sissulu Ct. E6 39Lc 73
Sister Mabel's Way SE15 52Wb 113
Sisters Av. SW11 55Hb 111
Sistova Rd. SW12 60Kb 112
Sisulu Pl. SW9 55Qb 112
Sitarey Ct. W12 46Xa 88
Sittingbourne Av. EN1: Enf 16Tb 33
Sitwell Gro. HA7: Stan 22Ha 46
Siverst Cl. UB5: N'olt 37Da 65
Sivill Ho. E2 3K 219
Siviter Way RM10: Dag 38Dd 76
Siward Rd. BR2: Brom 69Kc 137
N17 25Tb 51
SW17 62Eb 133
Six Acres HP3: Hem H 5A 4
Six Acres Est. N4 33Pb 70
Six Bells La. TN13: S'oaks 98Ld 203
Six Bridges Ind. Est. SE1 50Wb 91
(not continuous)
Sixpenny Ct. IG11: Bark 37Sc 74
Sixteenth Av. KT20: Lwr K 98Ab 194
Sixth Av. E12 35Pc 74
KT20: Lwr K 97Ab 194
UB3: Hayes 46V 84
W10 41Ab 88
WD25: Wat 7Z 13
Sixth Cross Rd. TW2: Twick 62Ea 130
Skardu Rd. NW2 36Ab 68
Skarnings Ct. EN9: Walt A 5Jc 21
Skeena Hill SW18 59Ab 110
Skeet Hill La. BR5: Orp 76Cd 162
BR6: Orp 74Ad 161
Skeffington Rd. E6 39Pc 74
Skeffington St. SE18 48Sc 94
Skeggs Ho. *E14* 48Ec 92
(off Glengall St.)
Skegness Ho. *N7* 38Pb 70
(off Sutterton St.)
Skelbrook St. SW18 61Eb 133
Skelgill Rd. SW15 56Bb 111
Skelley Rd. E15 38Hc 73
Skelton Cl. E8 37Vb 71
Skelton Rd. E7 37Jc 73
Skelton's La. E10 31Dc 72
Skelwith Rd. W6 51Ya 110
Skene Cl. GU23: Send 95D 188
Skenfrith Ho. *SE15* 51Xb 113
(off Commercial Way)
Skerne Rd. KT2: King T 67Ma 131
Skerne Wlk. KT2: King T 67Ma 131
Skerries Ct. SL3: L'ly 49C 82
Sketch Apartments *E1* 43Zb 92
(off Shandy St.)
Sketchley Gdns. SE16 50Zb 92
Sketty Rd. EN1: Enf 13Vb 33
Skibbs La. BR5: Orp, St M Cry 75Bd 161
BR6: Chels, Orp 78Ad 161
Skid Hill La. CR6: W'ham 84Hc 179
Skidmore Way WD3: Rick 18N 25
Skiers St. E15 39Gc 73
Skiffington Cl. SW2 60Qb 112
Skillen Lodge HA5: Pinn 25Z 45
Skimmington Cotts. RH2: Reig 7F 206
Skimpans Cl. AL9: Wel G 6F 8
Skinner Ct. *E3* 42Dc 92
(off Barry Blandford Way)
Skinner Pl. SW1 6H 227
Skinners Ct. N13 20Qb 32
Skinners La. EC4 4E 224 (45Sb 91)
KT21: Asht 90Ma 173
TW5: Hest 53Da 107
Skinner's Row SE10 53Dc 114
Skinner St. EC1 4A 218 (41Qb 90)
Skinney La. DA4: Hort K, S Dar 69Td 142
Skip La. UB9: Hare 32M 63
Skipper Ct. IG11: Bark 39Sc 74
Skippers Cl. DA9: Ghithe 57Xd 120
Skipsea Ho. SW18 58Gb 111
Skipsey Av. E6 41Pc 94
Skipton Cl. N11 23Jb 50
Skipton Dr. UB3: Harl 48S 84
Skipton Ho. SE4 56Ac 114
Skipwith Ho. EC1 7K 217
Skipworth Rd. E9 39Yb 72
Skua Ct. *SE8* 51Bc 114
(off Dorking Cl.)
Sky Bus. Pk. TW20: Thorpe 68E 126
Skydmore Path SL2: Slou 1D 80
Skye Ho. WD18: Wat 16V 26
Skye La. HA8: Edg 21Pa 47
Skye Lodge *SL1: Slou* 6J 81
(off Lansdowne Av.)
Sky Gdn. Wlk. EC3 4H 225
Skylark Av. DA9: Ghithe 58Wd 120
Skylark Ct. RM13: Rain 40Fd 76
SE1 2E 230
SW15 58Ya 110
Skylark Gro. RM3: Rom 21Md 57
Skylark Pl. KT17: Ewe 83Wa 174
Skylark Rd. UB9: Den 32E 62
Skyline Apartments *N4* 31Tb 71
(off Devan Gro.)
Skyline Ct. *CR0: C'don* 76Tb 157
(off Park La.)
SE1 4K 231 (48Vb 91)
Skyline Plaza Bldg. *E1* 44Wb 91
(off Commercial Rd.)
Skylines E14 47Ec 92
Skylines Village E14 47Ec 92
Sky Peals Rd. IG8: Wfd G 24Fc 53
Skyport Dr. UB7: Harm 52M 105
Sky Studios E16 47Qc 94
Skyvan Cl. TW6: H'row A 57S 106
Skyview Apartments *CR0: C'don* 75Sb 157
(off Park St.)
Skyway 14 SL3: Poyle 55H 105
Slade, The SE18 51Uc 116
Sladebrook Rd. SE3 55Mc 115
Slade Ct. EN5: New Bar 13Db 31
KT16: Ott 79F 148
WD7: R'lett 7Ja 14
Sladedale Rd. SE18 50Uc 94
Slade End CM16: They B 8Uc 22
Slade Gdns. DA8: Erith 53Hd 118
SLADE GREEN 53Jd 118
Slade Grn. Rd. DA8: Erith 52Kd 119
Slade Ho. TW4: Houn 58Ba 107
Sladen Pl. E5 35Xb 71
Slade Oak La. SL9: Ger X 27D 42
UB9: Den 29E 42
Slade Rd. GU24: Brkwd 2B 186
KT16: Ott 79F 148
Slades Cl. EN2: Enf 13Qb 32
Slades Dr. BR7: Chst 62Sc 138
Slades Gdns. EN2: Enf 12Qb 32
Slades Hill EN2: Enf 13Qb 32
Slades Ri. EN2: Enf 13Qb 32
Slade Twr. *E10* 33Cc 72
(off Leyton Grange Est.)
Slade Wlk. SE17 51Rb 113
Slade Way CR4: Mitc 67Jb 134
Slagrove Pl. SE13 57Cc 114
Slaidburn St. SW10 51Eb 111
Slaithwaite Rd. SE13 56Ec 114
Slaney Ct. NW10 38Ya 68
Slaney Pl. N7 36Qb 70
Slaney Rd. RM1: Rom 29Gd 56
Slapleys GU22: Wok 92A 188
Slater Cl. SE18 50Qc 94
Slater M. *SW4* 55Lb 112
(off Grafton Sq.)
Slatter NW9 24Va 48
Slattery Rd. TW13: Felt 60Z 107
Sleaford Grn. WD19: Wat 20Z 27
Sleaford Ho. *E3* 42Cc 92
(off Fern St.)
Sleaford Ind. Est. SW8 52Lb 112
Sleaford St. SW8 52Lb 112
Sleapcross Gdns. AL4: S'ford 3M 7
SLEAPSHYDE 3M 7
Sleapshyde La. AL4: S'ford 3M 7
Sleat Ho. *E3* 40Bc 72
(off Saxon Rd.)
Sledmere Ct. TW14: Bedf 60U 106
Sleepers Farm Rd. RM16: Grays 7D 100
Sleigh Ho. *E2* 41Yb 92
(off Bacton St.)
Slewins Cl. RM11: Horn 29Ld 57
Slewins La. RM11: Horn 29Ld 57
Slide, The 38Dc 72
Slievemore Cl. SW4 55Mb 112
Sligo Ho. *E1* 42Zb 92
(off Beaumont Gro.)
Slindon Ct. N16 34Vb 71
Slines Oak Rd.
CR3: W'ham, Wold 95Cc 198
CR6: W'ham 91Cc 198
Slingsby Pl. WC2 4F 223 (45Nb 90)
Slip, The TN16: Westrm 98Sc 200
Slippers Hill HP2: Hem H 1M 3
Slippers Pl. SE16 48Xb 91
Slipshatch Rd. RH2: Reig 10F 206
Slipshoe St. RH2: Reig 6H 207
Slipway Ho. *E14* 50Dc 92
(off Burrells Wharf Sq.)
Sloane Av. SW3 6E 226 (49Gb 89)
Sloane Av. Mans. SW3 6F 227 (49Hb 89)
Sloane Ct. TW7: Isle 53Ga 108
Sloane Ct. E. SW3 7H 227 (50Jb 90)
Sloane Ct. W. SW3 7H 227 (50Jb 90)
Sloane Gdns. BR6: Farnb 76Sc 160
SW1 6H 227 (49Jb 90)
Sloane Ga. Mans. SW1 5H 227
Sloane Ho. *E9* 38Yb 72
(off Loddiges Rd.)
Sloane M. N8 29Nb 50
Sloane Sq. DA3: Lfield 69Ae 143
SW1 6G 227 (49Jb 90)
Sloane St. SW1 2G 227 (47Hb 89)
Sloane Ter. SW1 5G 227 (49Jb 90)
Sloane Ter. Mans. SW1 5H 227
Sloane Wlk. CR0: C'don 72Bc 158
Slocock Hill GU21: Wok 9N 167
Slocum Cl. SE28 45Yc 95
SLOUGH 7K 81
Slough Crematorium SL2: Slou 3K 81
Slough Ind. Est. SL1: Slou 3E 80
(not continuous)
Slough Interchange Ind. Est.
SL2: Slou 6L 81
Slough La. KT18: Head 97Sa 193
NW9 29Sa 47
RH3: Bkld 4C 206
Slough Mus. 7K 81
Slough Retail Pk. SL1: Slou 6F 80
Slough Rd. SL0: Iver H 41E 82
SL1: Slou 9J 81
SL3: Dat 10L 81
SL4: Eton 1H 103
Slough Town FC 4L 81
Slough Trad. Est. SL1: Slou 5F 80
(Ajax Av.)
SL1: Slou 4F 80
(Liverpool Rd.)
SL1: Slou 3D 80
(Oxford Av.)
Slowmans Cl. AL2: Park 10A 6
Sly St. E1 44Xb 91
Smaldon Cl. UB7: W Dray 48Q 84
Small Acre HP1: Hem H 2H 3
Smallberry Av. TW7: Isle 54Ha 108
Smallbrook M. W2 3B 220 (44Fb 89)
Smalley Cl. N16 34Vb 71
Smalley Rd. Est. *N16* 34Vb 71
(off Smalley Cl.)
SMALLFORD 2M 7
Smallford La. AL4: S'ford 3M 7
Smallford Works AL4: S'ford 3M 7
Small Grains DA3: Fawk 76Xd 164
Small Heath Av. RM3: Rom 22Ld 57
Smallwood Rd. SW17 63Fb 133
Smarden Cl. DA17: Belv 50Cd 96
Smarden Gro. SE9 63Pc 138
Smart Cl. RM3: Rom 25Kd 57
Smart's Heath La. GU22: Wok 5L 187
Smart's Heath Rd. GU22: Wok 5K 187
Smart's La. IG10: Lough 14Mc 35
Smart's Pl. N18 22Wb 51
WC2 2G 223 (44Nb 90)
Smarts Rd. DA12: Grav'nd 2D 144
Smart St. E2 41Zb 92
Smead Way SE13 55Dc 114
Smeathman Ct. HP1: Hem H 3L 3
Smeaton Cl. EN9: Walt A 4Gc 21
KT9: Chess 79Ma 153
Smeaton Ct. SE1 4D 230 (48Sb 91)
Smeaton Dr. GU22: Wok 92D 188
Smeaton Rd. EN3: Enf L 9Cc 20
IG8: Wfd G 22Pc 54
SW18 59Cb 111
Smeaton St. E1 46Xb 91
Smedley St. SW4 54Mb 112
SW8 54Mb 112
Smeed Rd. E3 38Cc 72
Smikle Ct. *SE14* 53Zb 114
(off Hatcham Pk. M.)
Smiles Pl. GU22: Wok 88D 168
SE13 54Ec 114
Smitham Bottom La. CR8: Purl 83Lb 176
Smitham Downs Rd. CR8: Purl 85Mb 176
Smith Cl. SE16 46Zb 92
Smith Ct. GU21: Wok 85F 168
Smithfield HP2: Hem H 1M 3
Smithfield (Central Markets) 1B 224
Smithfield Ct. *E1* 45Wb 91
(off Cable St.)
Smithfield St. EC1 1B 224 (43Rb 91)

Smith Hill—South Grn.

Smith Hill TW8: Bford 51Na 109
Smithies Rd. SE2 .....49Xc 95
Smith Rd. RH2: Reig 9H 207
Smith's Ct. W1 .....4D 222
Smiths Cres. AL4: S'ford 3M 7
Smithsland Rd. RM3: Rom 22Nd 57
Smith's La. SL4: Wind 4C 102
Smith's Lawn (Polo & Equestrian Grounds) 6J 125
Smithson Rd. N17 .....25Tb 51
Smiths Point E13 .....39Jc 73
(off Brooks Rd.)
Smith Sq. SW1 .....4F 229 (48Nb 90)
Smith St. KT5: Surb 72Pa 153
SW3 .....7F 227 (50Hb 89)
WD18: Wat 14Y 27
Smiths Yd. CR0: C'don 76Sb 157
(off St George's Wlk.)
SW18 .....61Eb 133
Smith Ter. SW3 .....7F 227 (50Hb 89)
Smithwood Cl. SW19 .....60Ab 110
Smithy Cl. KT20: Lwr K 98Bb 195
Smithy La. KT20: Lwr K 99Bb 195
TW3: Houn 55Da 107
Smithy's Grn. GU20: W'sham 9B 146
Smithy St. E1 .....43Yb 92
Smock Wlk. CR0: C'don 72Sb 157
Smokehouse Yd. EC1 .....7C 218
Smoke La. RH2: Reig 8K 207
Smoothfield Ct. TW3: Houn 56Ca 107
Smugglers Wlk. DA9: Ghithe 57Xd 120
Smugglers Way SW18 .....56Db 111
Smugglers Yd. W12 .....46Xa 88
(off Devonport Rd.)
SMUG OAK 2Da 13
Smug Oak Grn. Bus. Cen.
AL2: Brick W 1Da 13
Smug Oak La. AL2: Brick W, Col S 2Da 13
Smyrk's Rd. SE17 .....7J 231 (50Ub 91)
Smyrna Mans. NW6 .....38Cb 69
(off Smyrna Rd.)
Smyrna Rd. NW6 .....38Cb 69
Smythe Cl. N9 .....20Wb 33
Smythe Rd. DA4: Sut H 67Qd 141
Smythe St. E14 .....45Dc 92
Snag La. BR6: Prat B 83Uc 180
TN14: Cud 84Tc 180
Snakes Hill CM14: N'side, Pil H 12Sd 40
Snakes La. N14 .....13Kb 32
Snakes La. E. IG8: Buck H, Wfd G 23Lc 53
Snakes La. W. IG8: Wfd G 22Jc 53
Snakey La. TW13: Felt 63W 128
Snape Spur SL1: Slou 4J 81
SNARESBROOK 29Jc 53
Snaresbrook Dr. HA7: Stan 21Ma 47
Snaresbrook Hall E18 .....28Jc 53
Snaresbrook Ho. E18 .....28Hc 53
Snaresbrook Rd. E11 .....28Gc 53
Snarsgate St. W10 .....43Ya 88
Snatts Hill RH8: Oxt 1K 211
Sneath Av. NW11 .....31Bb 69
Snelling Av. DA11: Nflt 1A 144
Snellings Rd. KT12: Hers 78Y 151
Snells Pk. N18 .....23Vb 51
Sneyd Rd. NW2 .....35Ya 68
Snipe Cl. DA8: Erith 52Kd 119
Snodland Cl. BR6: Downe 82Qc 180
Snowberry Cl. E15 .....35Fc 73
EN5: Barn 13Bb 31
Snowbury Rd. SW6 .....54Db 111
Snow Cen., The 4P 3
Snowcrete SL3: Wex 10N 61
Snowden Av. UB10: Hil 40R 64
Snowden Cl. SL4: Wind 6B 102
Snowden Hill DA11: Nflt 57Ce 121
Snowden St. EC2 .....6H 219 (42Ub 91)
Snowdon Aviary 1G 215
Snowdon Ct. RM2: Rom 28Ld 57
Snowdon Cres. UB3: Harl 48S 84
Snowdon Dr. NW9 .....30Ua 48
Snowdon Rd. TW6: H'row A 58S 106
Snowdown Cl. SE20 .....67Zb 136
Snowdrop Cl. TW12: Hamp 65Ca 129
Snowdrop Ct. RM13: Rain 40Ed 76
Snowdrop M. HA5: Pinn 26Y 45
Snowdrop Path RM3: Rom 24Md 57
Snowdrop Way GU24: Bisl 9E 166
Snowerhill Rd. RH3: Bet 8A 206
Snow Hill EC1 .....1B 224 (43Rb 91)
Snow Hill Ct. EC1 .....2C 224 (44Rb 91)
Snowman Ho. NW6 .....39Db 69
Snowsfields SE1 .....1G 231 (47Tb 91)
Snowshill Rd. E12 .....36Nc 74
Snows Paddock GU20: W'sham 6A 146
Snow's Ride GU20: W'sham 8A 146
Snowy Fielder Waye TW7: Isle 54Ka 108
Soames Pl. EN4: Had W 12Db 31
Soames St. SE15 .....55Vb 113
Soames Wlk. KT3: N Mald 67Ua 132
Soane Cl. W5 .....47Ma 87
Soane Ct. NW1 .....38Lb 70
(off St Pancras Way)
Soane Ho. SE17 .....50Tb 91
(off Roland Way)
Soane Sq. HA7: Stan 20Ga 28
Soap Ho. La. TW8: Bford 52Na 109
Soap Yd. SE1 .....7F 225
Sobell Leisure Cen. 34Pb 70
Sobraon Ho. KT2: King T 66Pa 131
(off Elm Rd.)
Socket La. BR2: Hayes 72Kc 159
Soda Studios E8 .....39Vb 71
(off Kingsland Rd.)
Soham Rd. EN3: Enf L 9Bc 20
SOHO 3D 222 (44Lb 90)
Soho Ho. W12 .....45Ya 88
Soho Sq. W1 .....2D 222 (44Mb 90)
Soho St. W1 .....2D 222 (44Mb 90)
Soho Theatre & Writers Cen. 3D 222
Sojourner Truth Cl. E8 .....37Xb 71
Sola Ct. CR0: C'don 74Tb 157
(off Sydenham Rd.)
Solander Gdns. E1 .....45Xb 91
(off Cable St.)
E1 .....45Yb 92
(The Highway)
Solar Ct. N3 .....24Db 49
SE16 .....47Wb 91
(off Chambers St.)
WD18: Wat 15V 26
Solar Ho. E6 .....43Qc 94
E15 .....37Gc 73
(off Romford Rd.)
Solarium Ct. SE1 .....5K 231
Solar Way EN3: Enf L 8Bc 20
Soldene Ct. N7 .....37Pb 70
Solebay St. E1 .....42Ac 92
Solecote KT23: Bookh 97Ca 191
Sole Farm Av. KT23: Bookh 97Ba 191
Sole Farm Cl. KT23: Bookh 96Ba 191
Sole Farm Rd. KT23: Bookh 97Ba 191
Solefields Rd. TN13: S'oaks 100Kd 203
Solent Ct. SW16 .....68Pb 134
Solent Ho. E1 .....43Ac 92
(off Ben Jonson Rd.)
Solent Ri. E13 .....41Jc 93
Solent Rd. NW6 .....36Cb 69
Soleoak Dr. TN13: S'oaks 99Kd 203
Solesbridge Cl. WD3: Chor 13H 25
Solesbridge La.
WD3: Chor, Sarr 13H 25
SOLE STREET 10F 144
Sole St. DA12: Cobh, Sole S 10F 144
Soley M. WC1 .....3K 217 (41Qb 90)
Solid La. CM15: Dodd, Pil H 11Vd 40
Solna Av. SW15 .....57Ya 110
Solna Rd. N21 .....18Tb 33
Solomon Av. N9 .....21Wb 51
Solomons Ct. N12 .....24Eb 49
Solomon's Hill WD3: Rick 17M 25
Solomon's Pas. SE15 .....56Xb 113
Soloms Ct. Rd. SM7: Bans 89Fb 175
Solon New Rd. SW4 .....56Nb 112
Solon New Rd. Est. SW4 .....56Nb 112
Solon Rd. SW2 .....56Nb 112
Solway RM18: E Til 8L 101
Solway Cl. E8 .....37Vb 71
(off Queensbridge Rd.)
TW4: Houn 55Aa 107
Solway Ho. E1 .....42Zb 92
(off Ernest St.)
Solway Rd. N22 .....25Rb 51
SE22 .....56Wb 113
Somaford Gro. EN4: E Barn 16Fb 31
Somali Rd. NW2 .....35Bb 69
Sombourne Ho. SW15 .....59Wa 110
(off Fontley Way)
Somerby Rd. IG11: Bark 38Tc 74
Somercoates Cl. EN4: Cockf 13Gb 31
Somer Ct. SW6 .....51Cb 111
(off Anselm Rd.)
Somerden Rd. BR5: St M Cry 73Zc 161
Somerfield Cl. KT20: Tad 91Ab 194
Somerfield Rd. N4 .....33Rb 71
(not continuous)
Somerfield St. SE16 .....50Zb 92
Somerford Cl. HA5: Eastc 28W 44
Somerford Gro. N16 .....35Vb 71
N17 .....24Wb 51
(not continuous)
Somerford Gro. Est. N16 .....35Vb 71
Somerford St. E1 .....42Xb 91
Somerford Way SE16 .....47Ac 92
Somerhill Av. DA15: Sidc 59Xc 117
Somerhill Rd. DA16: Well 54Xc 117
Someries Rd. HP1: Hem H 1H 3
Somerleyton Pas. SW9 .....56Rb 113
Somerleyton Rd. SW9 .....56Qb 112
Somersby Gdns. IG4: Ilf 29Pc 54
Somers Cl. NW1 .....1D 216 (40Mb 70)
RH2: Reig 5J 207
Somers Cres. W2 .....3D 220 (44Gb 89)
Somerset Av. DA16: Well 57Vc 117
KT9: Chess 77Ma 153
SW20 .....68Xa 132
Somerset Cl. IG8: Wfd G 25Jc 53
KT3: N Mald 72Ua 154
KT12: Hers 78X 151
KT19: Ewe 81Ta 173
N17 .....26Tb 51
SM3: Wor Pk 77Ya 154
Somerset Ct. IG9: Buck H 19Lc 35
NW1 .....2D 216 (40Mb 70)
TW11: Tedd 64Ga 130
W7 .....44Ha 86
(off Copley Cl.)
Somerset Est. SW11 .....53Fb 111
Somerset Gdns. HA0: Wemb 36La 66
N6 .....31Jb 70
N17 .....24Ub 51
RH1: Redh 8M 207
RM11: Horn 32Qd 77
SE13 .....54Dc 114
SW16 .....69Pb 134
TW11: Tedd 64Ga 130
Somerset Hall N17 .....24Ub 51
Somerset House 4H 223 (45Pb 90)
Somerset Ho. GU22: Wok 89B 168
(off Oriental Rd.)
RH1: Redh 5P 207
SW19 .....62Za 132
Somerset Lodge TW8: Bford 51Ma 109
Somerset Rd. BR6: Orp 73Wc 161
DA1: Dart 58Kd 119
E17 .....29Cc 52
EN3: Enf L 10Cc 20
EN5: New Bar 15Db 31
HA1: Harr 29Ea 46
KT1: King T 68Pa 131
N17 .....27Vb 51
N18 .....22Vb 51
NW4 .....28Ya 48
RH1: Redh 8M 207
SS17: Linf 7J 101
SW19 .....62Za 132
TW8: Bford 51La 108
TW11: Tedd 64Ga 130
UB1: S'hall 43Ba 85
W4 .....48Ta 87
W13 .....46Ka 86
Somerset Sq. W14 .....47Ab 88
Somerset Way SL0: Rich P 47H 83
Somerset Waye TW5: Hest 51Aa 107
Somersham Rd. DA7: Bex 54Ad 117
Somers Pl. RH2: Reig 5J 207
SW2 .....59Pb 112
Somers Rd. AL9: Wel G 6E 8
E17 .....28Bc 52
RH2: Reig 5J 207
SW2 .....58Pb 112
Somers Sq. AL9: Wel G 5E 8
Somerston Ho. NW1 .....39Lb 70
(off St Pancras Way)
SOMERS TOWN 2D 216 (40Mb 70)
Somers Town Community Sports Cen.
.....2D 216 (40Mb 70)
Somers Way WD23: Bush 17Ea 28
Somerton Av. TW9: Rich 55Ra 109
Somerton Cl. CR8: Purl 87Qb 176
Somerton Ho. WC1 .....4E 216
Somerton Rd. NW2 .....34Za 68
SE15 .....56Xb 113
Somertrees Av. SE12 .....61Kc 137
Somervell Rd. HA2: Harr 36Ba 65
Somerville Av. SW13 .....51Xa 110
Somerville Cl. SW9 .....53Pb 112
Somerville Ct. RH1: Redh 5N 207
(off Oxford Rd.)
Somerville Point SE16 .....47Bc 92
Somerville Rd. DA1: Dart 58Pd 119
KT11: Cobh 86Ca 171
RM6: Chad H 30Yc 55
SE20 .....66Zb 136
SL4: Eton 10G 80
Somery Wlk. WD25: A'ham 8Da 13
Sommerville Ct. WD6: Bore 11Pa 29
(off Alconbury Cl.)
Sonderburg Rd. N7 .....33Pb 70
Sondes St. SE17 .....51Tb 113
Sonesta Apartments SE15 .....53Xb 113
Songhurst Cl. CR0: C'don 72Pb 156
Sonia Cl. WD19: Wat 17Y 27
Sonia Ct. HA1: Harr 30Ha 46
HA8: Edg 24Pa 47
Sonia Gdns. N12 .....21Eb 49
NW10 .....35Va 68
TW5: Hest 52Ca 107
Sonnets, The HP1: Hem H 1K 3
Sonnet Wlk. TN16: Big H 90Kc 179
Sonning Gdns.
TW12: Hamp 65Aa 129
Sonning Ho. E2 .....4K 219
Sonning Rd. SE25 .....72Wb 157
Sontan Ct. TW2: Twick 60Fa 108
Soper Cl. E4 .....22Bc 52
SE23 .....60Zb 114
Soper Dr. CR3: Cat'm 95Tb 197
Soper M. EN3: Enf L 10Cc 20
Sophia Rd. EN6: Cuff 1Pb 18
Sophia Cl. N7 .....37Pb 70
Sophia Ho. W6 .....50Ya 88
(off Queen Caroline St.)
Sophia Rd. E10 .....32Dc 72
E16 .....44Kc 93
Sophia Sq. SE16 .....45Ac 92
(off Sovereign Cres.)
Sophie Gdns. SL3: L'ly 7P 81
Sophora Ho. SW8 .....52Kb 112
Soprano Ct. E15 .....39Hc 73
(off Plaistow Rd.)
Soprano Way KT10: Surb 76Ka 152
SOPWELL 5C 6
Sopwell La. AL1: St A 3B 6
Sopwell Nunnery (remains) 4C 6
Sopwith NW9 .....24Va 48
Sopwith Av. E17 .....27Zb 52
KT9: Chess 78Na 153
Sopwith Cl. KT2: King T 64Pa 131
TN16: Big H 88Mc 179
Sopwith Dr. KT13: Weyb 83N 169
Sopwith Rd. TW5: Hest 52Y 107
Sopwith Way KT2: King T 67Na 131
KT15: Add 76M 149
SW8 .....52Kb 112
Sorbie Cl. KT13: Weyb 79T 150
Sorbus Ct. EN2: Enf 12Rb 33
Sorensen Ct. E10 .....33Dc 72
(off Leyton Grange Est.)
Sorrel Bank CR0: Sels 82Ac 178
(not continuous)
Sorrel Cl. SE28 .....46Wc 95
Sorrel Ct. RM17: Grays 51Fe 121
Sorrel Gdns. E6 .....43Nc 94
Sorrel La. E14 .....44Fc 93
Sorrell Cl. SE14 .....52Ac 114
SW9 .....54Qb 112
Sorrells, The SS17: Stan H 1P 101
Sorrel Mead NW9 .....31Wa 68
Sorrel Wlk. RM1: Rom 27Hd 56
Sorrel Way DA11: Nflt 1A 144
Sorrento Rd. SM1: Sutt 76Db 155
Sospel Ct. SL2: Farn R 10G 60
Sotheby Rd. N5 .....34Rb 71
Sotheran Cl. E8 .....39Wb 71
Sotherby Lodge E2 .....40Yb 72
(off Sewardstone Rd.)
Sotheron Pl. SW6 .....52Db 111
Sotheron Rd. WD17: Wat 13Y 27
Soudan Rd. SW11 .....53Hb 111
Souldern Rd. W14 .....48Za 88
Souldern St. WD18: Wat 15X 27
Sounding All. E3 .....39Cc 72
Sounds Lodge BR8: Crock 72Ed 162
Sth. Access Rd. E17 .....31Ac 72
Southacre W2 .....3D 220
Southacre Way HA5: Pinn 25Y 45
SOUTH ACTON 47Sa 87
Sth. Africa Rd. W12 .....46Xa 88
Sth. Albert Rd. RH2: Reig 5H 207
SOUTHALL 46Ba 85
Southall Ct. UB1: S'hall 45Ba 85
Southall Ent. Cen. UB2: S'hall 47Ca 85
SOUTHALL GREEN 48Aa 85
Southall Ho. RM3: Rom 23Nd 57
(off Kingsbridge Cir.)
Southall La. TW5: Cran 51X 107
UB2: S'hall 51X 107
Southall Pl. SE1 .....2F 231 (47Tb 91)
Southall Sports Cen. 46Aa 85
Southall Way CM14: B'wood 21Vd 58
Southam Ho. KT15: Add 78K 149
(off Addlestone Pk.)
W10 .....42Ab 88
(off Southam St.)
Southam M. WD3: Crox G 16R 26
Southampton Bldgs.
WC2 .....1K 223 (43Qb 90)
Southampton Gdns. CR4: Mitc 71Nb 156
Southampton M. E16 .....46Kc 93
Southampton Pl. WC1 .....1G 223 (43Nb 90)
Southampton Rd. NW5 .....36Hb 69
Southampton Rd. E.
TW6: H'row A 58P 105
Southampton Rd. W.
TW6: H'row A 58N 105
Southampton Row WC1 .....7G 217 (43Nb 90)
Southampton St. WC2 .....4G 223 (45Nb 90)
Southampton Way SE5 .....52Tb 113
Southam St. W10 .....42Ab 88
South App. HA6: Nwood 20T 26
SOUTH ASCOT 2A 146
Sth. Ash Rd. TN15: Ash 82Zd 185
Sth. Audley St. W1 .....5J 221 (45Jb 90)
South Av. E4 .....17Dc 34
KT12: W Vill 82U 170
KT13: Weyb 82Q 170
SM5: Cars 80Jb 156
TW9: Kew 54Qa 109
TW20: Egh 65E 126
UB1: S'hall 45Ba 85
South Av. Gdns.
UB1: S'hall 45Ba 85
South Bank KT6: Surb 72Na 153
TN16: Westrm 98Tc 200
Southbank BR8: Hext 66Hd 140
(not continuous)
KT7: T Ditt 73Ka 152
Southbank Bus. Cen. SW11 .....53Hb 111
Southbank Cen. 6J 223 (46Pb 90)
Sth. Bank Ter. KT6: Surb 72Na 153
SOUTH BARNET 18Jb 32
SOUTH BEDDINGTON 79Mb 156
Sth. Birkbeck Rd. E11 .....34Fc 73
Sth. Black Lion La. W6 .....50Wa 88
South Block RM2: Rom 27Md 57
SE1 .....2H 229
Sth. Bolton Gdns. SW5 .....50Db 89
Sth. Border, The CR8: Purl 83Mb 176
SOUTHBOROUGH
BR2 .....71Pc 160
KT6 .....74Na 153
Southborough Cl. KT6: Surb 74Ma 153
Southborough Ho. SE17 .....7H 231
Southborough La. BR2: Brom 71Nc 160
Southborough Rd. BR1: Brom 69Nc 138
E9 .....39Zb 72
KT6: Surb 74Na 153
Southbourne BR2: Hayes 73Jc 159
Southbourne Av. NW9 .....26Sa 47
Southbourne Cl. HA5: Pinn 31Aa 65
Southbourne Ct. NW9 .....26Sa 47
Southbourne Cres. NW4 .....28Ab 48
Southbourne Gdns. HA4: Ruis 32X 65
IG1: Ilf 36Sc 74
SE12 .....57Kc 115
Southbridge Pl. CR0: C'don 77Sb 157
Southbridge Rd. CR0: C'don 77Sb 157
Southbridge Way UB2: S'hall 47Aa 85
SOUTH BROMLEY 45Ec 92
Southbrook M. SE12 .....58Hc 115
Southbrook Rd. SE12 .....58Hc 115
SW16 .....67Nb 134
South Buckinghamshire Academy, The
.....3K 81
South Buckinghamshire Golf Course, The
.....9J 61
Southbury NW8 .....39Eb 69
(off Loudoun Rd.)
Southbury Av. EN1: Enf 14Wb 33
Southbury Cl. RM12: Horn 36Md 77
Southbury Ho. EN8: Walt C 4Zb 20
(off High St.)
Southbury Leisure Cen. 13Wb 33
Southbury Rd. EN1: Enf 13Ub 33
EN3: Pond E 13Ub 33
Sth. Carriage Dr. SW1 .....2C 226 (47Fb 89)
SW7 .....2C 226 (47Fb 89)
SOUTH CHINGFORD 22Bc 52
Southchurch Ct. E6 .....40Pc 74
(off High St. Sth.)
Southchurch Rd. E6 .....40Pc 74
South City Ct. SE15 .....52Ub 113
Southcliffe Dr. SL9: Chal P 22A 42
South Cl. AL2: Chis G 7P 5
DA6: Bex 56Zc 117
EN5: Barn 13Bb 31
GU21: Wok 8N 167
HA5: Pinn 31Ba 65
N6 .....30Kb 50
RM10: Dag 39Cd 76
RM15: S Ock 42Yd 98
SL1: Slou 5B 80
SM4: Mord 72Cb 155
TW2: Twick 62Ca 129
UB7: W Dray 48P 83
South Cl. Grn. RH1: Mers 1B 208
Sth. Colonnade, The E14 .....46Cc 92
(not continuous)
Southcombe St. W14 .....49Ab 88
South Comn. Rd. UB8: Uxb 37N 63
Southcote GU21: Wok 7P 167
Southcote Av. KT5: Surb 73Ra 153
TW13: Felt 61V 128
Southcote Ho. KT15: Add 75M 149
Southcote Ri. HA4: Ruis 31T 64
Southcote Rd. CR2: Sande 82Ub 177
E17 .....29Zb 52
N19 .....35Lb 70
RH1: Mers 2C 208
SE25 .....71Xb 157
Sth. Cottage Dr. WD3: Chor 15H 25
Sth. Cottage Gdns. WD3: Chor 15H 25
Southcott Ho. E3 .....41Dc 92
(off Devons Rd.)
W9 .....6A 214
Southcott M. NW8 .....2D 214 (40Gb 69)
Southcott Rd. TW11: Hamp W 67La 130
Sth. Countess Rd. E17 .....27Bc 52
South Cres. E16 .....42Fc 93
WC1 .....1D 222 (43Mb 90)
Sth. Crescent M. WC1 .....5F 217 (42Nb 90)
Southcroft SL2: Slou 2F 80
TW20: Eng G 4M 125
Southcroft Av. BR4: W W'ck 75Ec 158
DA16: Well 55Uc 116
Southcroft Rd. BR6: Orp 76Uc 160
SW16 .....65Jb 134
SW17 .....65Jb 134
Sth. Cross Rd. IG6: Ilf 29Sc 54
Sth. Croxted Rd. SE21 .....62Tb 135
SOUTH CROYDON 78Tb 157
South Croydon Sports Club 78Ub 157
Southdale IG7: Chig 23Tc 54
SOUTH DARENTH 67Sd 142
Southdean Gdns. SW19 .....61Bb 133
South Dene NW7 .....20Ta 29
Southdene TN14: Hals 85Bd 181
(not continuous)
Southdene Ct. N11 .....20Kb 32
Southdown Av. W7 .....48Ja 86
Southdown Ct. AL10: Hat 3C 8
Southdown Cres. HA2: Harr 32Ea 66
IG2: Ilf 29Uc 54
Southdown Dr. SW20 .....66Za 132
Southdown Rd. AL10: Hat 3C 8
CR3: Wold 94Bc 198
KT12: Hers 77Aa 151
RM11: Horn 31Kd 77
SM5: Cars 81Jb 176
SW20 .....67Za 132
Southdowns DA4: S Dar 68Td 142
South Dr. AL4: St A 2H 7
BR6: Orp 78Uc 160
CM14: W'ley 21Zd 59
CR5: Coul 87Mb 176
EN6: Cuff 2Nb 18
GU24: Brkwd 3A 186
GU25: Vir W 4L 147
HA4: Ruis 32U 64
RM2: Rom 27Ld 57
SM2: Cheam 82Ab 174
SM7: Bans 85Gb 175
Sth. Ealing Rd. W5 .....47Ma 87
South East Dance Studios 67Gd 140
Sth. Eastern Av. N9 .....20Vb 33
Sth. Eaton Pl. SW1 .....5J 227 (49Jb 90)
Sth. Eden Pk. Rd.
BR3: Beck 72Dc 158
Sth. Edwardes Sq. W8 .....48Bb 89
SOUTHEND 63Fc 137
South End CR0: C'don 77Sb 157
CR2: S Croy 77Sb 157
KT23: Bookh 98Da 191
W8 .....48Db 89
Southend Arterial Rd.
CM13: Gt War, L War, W H'dn
.....29Zd 59
RM2: Rom 26Md 57
RM3: Hrld W 26Md 57
RM11: Horn, Upm 26Md 57
RM14: Gt War, Upm 26Md 57
Sth. End Cl. NW3 .....35Gb 69
Southend Cl. SE9 .....58Rc 116
Southend Cres. SE9 .....58Rc 116
Sth. End Grn. NW3 .....35Gb 69
Southend Ho. SS17: Stan H 1N 101
Southend La. EN9: Walt A 6Kc 21
SE6 .....63Bc 136
SE26 .....63Bc 136
Sth. End Rd. NW3 .....35Gb 69
RM12: Horn 37Kd 77
RM13: Horn, Rain 40Jd 76
Southend Rd. BR3: Beck 67Cc 136
E4 .....22Ac 52
E6 .....38Pc 74
E17 .....25Dc 52
E18 .....25Jc 53
IG8: Wfd G 26Lc 53
RM17: Grays 49Ee 99
SS17: Corr, Stan H 1M 101
Sth. End Row W8 .....48Db 89
Southerland Cl. KT13: Weyb 77S 150
Southern Av. SE25 .....69Vb 135
TW14: Felt 60W 106
Southern Cotts. TW19: Stanw M 57J 105
Southern Dr. IG10: Lough 16Pc 36
Southerngate Way SE14 .....52Ac 114
Southern Gro. E3 .....41Bc 92
Southernhay IG10: Lough 14Mc 35
Southern Perimeter Rd.
TW6: H'row A, Stanw 57K 105
(not continuous)
Southern Pl. BR8: Swan 70Fd 140
HA1: Harr 35Ha 66
Southern Rd. E13 .....40Kc 73
N2 .....28Hb 49
Southern Row W10 .....42Ab 88
Southerns La. CR5: Coul 97Eb 195
Southern St. N1 .....1H 217 (40Pb 70)
Southern Ter. W12 .....46Ya 88
Southern Valley Golf Course 3J 145
Southern Way RM7: Rom 30Cd 56
SE10 .....49Hc 93
Southernwood Cl. HP2: Hem H 1A 4
Southernwood Retail Pk.
SE1 .....7K 231 (50Vb 91)
Southerton Rd. W6 .....49Ya 88
Southerton Way WD7: Shenl 5Na 15
Sth. Esk Rd. E7 .....37Lc 73
Sth. Essex Crematorium
RM14: Upm 36Td 78
Southey Cl. KT23: Bookh 96Da 191
Southey Ho. SE17 .....7E 230
Southey M. E16 .....46Jc 93
Southey Rd. N15 .....29Ub 51
SW9 .....53Qb 112
SW19 .....66Cb 133
Southey St. SE20 .....66Zb 136
Southey Wlk. RM18: Tilb 3D 122
Southfield EN5: Barn 16Za 30
Southfield Av. WD24: Wat 10Y 13
Southfield Cl. SL4: Dor 8A 80
UB8: Hil 42Q 84
Southfield Cotts. W7 .....47Ha 86
Southfield Ct. E11 .....34Hc 73
Southfield Gdns. SL1: Burn 3A 80
TW1: Twick 63Ha 130
Southfield Pk. HA2: Harr 28Da 45
Southfield Pl. KT13: Weyb 80R 150
Southfield Rd. BR7: Chst 69Wc 139
EN3: Pond E 16Xb 33
EN8: Walt C 4Ac 20
N17 .....26Ub 51
W4 .....47Ta 87
SOUTHFIELDS
RM16 .....4F 100
SW18 .....60Bb 111
Southfields BR8: Hext 66Gd 140
KT8: E Mos 72Ga 152
NW4 .....27Xa 48
Southfields Av. TW15: Ashf 65R 128
Southfields Ct. SM1: Sutt 75Cb 155
Southfields Grn. DA11: Grav'nd 4D 144
Southfields Ho. DA11: Grav'nd 4D 144
(off Southfields Grn.)
Southfields M. SW18 .....58Cb 111
Southfields Pas. SW18 .....58Cb 111
Southfields Rd. CR3: Wold 94Dc 198
SW18 .....58Cb 111
TN15: W King 80Vd 164
SOUTHFLEET 64Ce 143
Southfleet NW5 .....37Jb 70
Southfleet Av. DA3: Lfield 68De 143
Southfleet Rd. BR6: Orp 76Uc 160
DA2: Bean 63Yd 142
DA10: Swans 59Be 121
DA11: Nflt 10B 122
South Gdns. HA9: Wemb 33Qa 67
SW19 .....66Fb 133
SOUTHGATE 18Mb 32
Southgate RM19: Purf 49Sd 98
Southgate Av. TW13: Felt 63T 128
Southgate Cir. N14 .....18Mb 32
Southgate Cotts.
WD3: Rick 17M 25
Southgate Ct. N1 .....38Tb 71
(off Downham Rd.)
Southgate Gro. N1 .....38Tb 71
Southgate Hockey Cen. 13Kb 32
Southgate Ho. EN8: Chesh 2Ac 20
(off Turner's Hill)
Southgate Leisure Cen. 17Mb 32
Southgate Rd. EN6: Pot B 5Eb 17
N1 .....39Tb 71
Sth. Gipsy Rd. DA16: Well 55Zc 117
Sth. Glade, The DA5: Bexl 60Bd 117
SOUTH GODSTONE 10C 210
South Grn. NW9 .....25Ua 48
(off Parklea Cl.)
SL1: Slou 5J 81

Spinney, The—Stalisfield Pl.

Spinney, The BR8: Swan 68Gd 140
CM13: Hut 16Ee 41
CR8: Purl 83Rb 177
DA14: Sidc 64Ad 139
EN5: New Bar 12Db 31
EN6: Pot B 3Fb 17
EN7: Chesh 2Xb 19
GU23: Send 99L 189
HA0: Wemb 34Ja 66
HA6: Nwood 23W 44
HA7: Stan 21Na 47
IG10: Lough 14Rc 36
KT18: Head 98Sa 193
KT18: Tatt C 91Xa 194
KT22: Oxs 84Ea 172
KT23: Bookh 96Da 191
N21 17Qb 32
RM16: Ors 2C 100
SL5: S'dale 1C 146
SL9: Ger X 2P 61
SM3: Cheam 77Ya 154
SW13 52Xa 110
SW16 62Lb 134
TW16: Sun 67W 128
WD17: Wat 11W 26
WD25: A'ham 10Fa 14
Spinney Cl. BR3: Beck 70Dc 136
KT3: N Mald 71Ua 154
KT4: Wor Pk 75Va 154
KT11: Cobh 83Ca 171
RM13: Rain 40Gd 76
SL5: Asc 8A 124
UB7: Yiew 45N 83
Spinneycroft KT22: Oxs 87Fa 172
Spinney Dr. TW14: Bedf 59S 106
Spinney Gdns. KT10: Esh 76Ca 151
RM9: Dag 36Ad 75
SE19 64Vb 135
Spinney Hill KT15: Add 78G 148
Spinney Oak BR1: Brom 68Nc 138
KT16: Ott 79F 148
Spinney Oaks KT15: Add 78G 148
Spinney Row AL2: Lon C 8F 6
Spinneys, The BR1: Brom 68Pc 138
Spinneys Dr. AL3: St A 4P 5
Spinney Way TN14: Cud 83Tc 180
Spire Cl. DA12: Grav'nd 10D 122
Spire Ct. BR3: Beck 68Dc 136
(off Crescent Rd.)
Spire Ho. W2 4A 220
Spire Pl. CR6: W'ham 90Ac 178
Spires, The
CM14: B'wood 19Zd 41
DA1: Dart 61Md 141
HP2: Hem H 3M 3
Spires Shop. Cen., The
EN5: Barn 13Ab 30
Spirit Quay E1 46Wb 91
SPITAL 6F 102
SPITALFIELDS 7K 219 (43Vb 91)
Spitalfields City Farm 42Wb 91
Spital La. CM14: B'wood 20Vd 40
Spital Sq. E1 7J 219 (43Ub 91)
Spital St. DA1: Dart 58Md 119
E1 43Wb 91
Spital Yd. E1 7J 219 (43Ub 91)
Spitfire Bldg. N1 2H 217
Spitfire Bus. Pk. CR0: Wadd 79Qb 156
Spitfire Cl. SL3: L'ly 49C 82
Spitfire Est., The TW5: Cran 50Y 85
Spitfire Rd. SM6: Wall 80Nb 156
TW6: H'row A 58S 106
Spitfire Way TW5: Cran 50Y 85
Splendour Wlk. SE16 50Yb 92
(off Verney Rd.)
Spode Ho. SE11 4K 229
Spode Wlk. NW6 36Db 69
Spondon Rd. N15 28Wb 51
Spoonbill Way UB4: Yead 43Z 85
Spooner Ho. TW5: Hest 51Ca 107
Spooners Dr. AL2: Park 9A 6
Spooners M. W3 46Ta 87
Spooner Wlk. SM6: Wall 78Nb 156
Sporle Rd. Ct. SW11 55Fb 111
Sportsbank St. SE6 59Ec 114
SportsDock 45Rc 94
Sportsman Pl. E2 39Wb 71
Sportspace
Hemel Hempstead 4L 3
Longdean 5B 4
Sportspace Athletics Track 4P 3
Sports Village, The 74Db 155
Spottiswood Ct. CR0: C'don 72Sb 157
(off Harry Cl.)
Spottons Gro. N17 25Sb 51
Spout Hill CR0: Addtn 78Cc 158
Spout La. TW19: Stanw M 57J 105
Spout La. Nth. TW19: Stanw M 56K 105
Spratt Hall Rd. E11 30Jc 53
Spratts All. KT16: Ott 79G 148
Spratts La. KT16: Ott 79G 148
Spray La. TW2: Whitt 58Ga 108
Spray St. SE18 49Rc 94
Spread Eagle Wlk. KT19: Eps 85Ta 173
Spreighton Rd. KT8: W Mole 70Da 129
Spriggs Ct. CM16: Epp 1Wc 23
(off Palmers Hill)
Spriggs Ho. N1 38Rb 71
(off Canonbury Rd.)
Spriggs Oak CM16: Epp 1Wc 23
(off Palmers Hill)
Sprimont Pl. SW3 7F 227 (50Hb 89)
Springall St. SE15 52Xb 113
Springalls Wharf SE16 47Wb 91
(off Bermondsey Wall W.)
Spring Apartments CR0: C'don 75Tb 157
(off Addiscombe Gro.)
E14 49Ec 92
(off Stebondale St.)
Springate Fld. SL3: L'ly 47A 82
Spring Av. TW20: Egh 65A 126
Springbank N21 16Pb 32
Springbank Av.
RM12: Horn 36Ld 77
Springbank Rd. SE13 58Fc 115
Springbank Wlk. NW1 38Mb 70
Springbottom La. RH1: Blet 99Qb 196
Springbourne Ct. BR3: Beck 67Ec 136
Spring Bri. M. W5 45Ma 87
Spring Bri. Rd. W5 45Ma 87
Spring Cl. EN5: Barn 15Za 30
HP5: Lat 8A 10
RM8: Dag 32Zc 75
UB9: Hare 25M 43
WD6: Bore 11Qa 29
Springclose La.
SM3: Cheam 79Ab 154
Springcopse Rd. RH2: Reig 8L 207
Spring Cnr. TW13: Felt 62W 128
Spring Cotts. KT6: Surb 71Ma 153
Spring Ct. KT17: Ewe 81Va 174
NW6 37Bb 69
W7 45Fa 86
Spring Ct. Rd. EN2: Enf 10Qb 18
Springcroft DA3: Hartl 72Ce 165
Springcroft Av. N2 28Hb 49
Spring Crofts WD23: Bush 15Ca 27
Spring Cross DA3: Nw A G 76Ce 165
(not continuous)
Springdale M. N16 35Tb 71
Springdale Rd. N16 35Tb 71
Spring Dr. HA5: Eastc 30W 44
Springer Ct. E3 42Ec 92
(off Navigation Rd.)
Springett Ho. SW2 57Qb 112
(off St Matthews Rd.)
Springfarm Cl. RM13: Rain 41Md 97
Springfield CM16: Epp 4Vc 23
E5 32Xb 71
GU18: Light 3B 166
RH8: Oxt 2H 211
SE25 69Wb 135
SL1: Slou 8M 81
WD23: B Hea 18Fa 28
Springfield Av. BR8: Swan 70Hd 140
CM13: Hut 17Fe 41
N10 27Lb 50
SW20 69Bb 133
TW12: Hamp 65Da 129
Springfield Cl. EN6: Pot B 3Gb 17
GU21: Knap 10J 167
HA7: Stan 20Ja 28
N12 22Db 49
SL4: Wind 4F 102
WD3: Crox G 15R 26
Springfield Ct. IG1: Ilf 36Rc 74
KT1: King T 69Na 131
(off Springfield Rd.)
NW3 38Gb 69
(off Eton Av.)
RM14: Upm 34Sd 78
SM6: Wall 78Kb 156
WD3: Rick 18K 25
Springfield Dr. IG2: Ilf 29Sc 54
KT22: Lea 91Ga 192
Springfield Gdns. BR1: Brom 70Pc 138
BR4: W W'ck 75Dc 158
E5 32Xb 71
HA4: Ruis 32X 65
IG8: Wfd G 24Lc 53
NW9 29Ta 47
RM14: Upm 34Rd 77
Springfield Gro. SE7 51Lc 115
TW16: Sun 67V 128
Springfield La. KT13: Weyb 77R 150
NW6 39Db 69
Springfield Mdws. KT13: Weyb 77R 150
Springfield Mt. NW9 29Ua 48
Springfield Pde. M. N13 21Qb 50
Springfield Pl. KT3: N Mald 70Sa 131
SL9: Ger X 29A 42
Springfield Ri. SE26 62Xb 135
Springfield Rd. AL1: St A 3E 6
AL4: S'ford 2M 7
BR1: Brom 70Pc 138
CR7: Thor H 67Sb 135
DA7: Bex 56Dd 118
DA16: Well 55Xc 117
E4 18Gc 35
E6 38Pc 74
E15 41Gc 93
E17 30Bc 52
EN8: Chesh 4Ac 20
HA1: Harr 30Ga 46
HP2: Hem H 1P 3
KT1: King T 69Na 131
KT17: Ewe 82Ya 174
KT22: Lea 91Ha 192
N11 22Kb 50
N15 28Wb 51
NW8 39Eb 69
RM16: Grays 47Fe 99
SE26 64Xb 135
SL3: L'ly 52D 104
SL4: Wind 4F 102
SM6: Wall 78Kb 156
SW19 64Bb 133
TW2: Whitt 60Ca 107
TW11: Tedd 64Ja 130
TW15: Ashf 64P 127
UB4: Yead 46Y 85
W7 46Ga 86
WD25: Wat 5X 13
Springfields EN5: New Bar 15Db 31
(off Somerset Rd.)
EN9: Walt A 6Gc 21
Springfields Cl. KT16: Chert 74K 149
Springfield Wlk. BR6: Orp 74Tc 160
(off Place Farm Av.)
NW6 39Db 69
Spring Gdns. BR6: Chels 79Xc 161
IG8: Wfd G 24Lc 53
KT8: W Mole 71Da 151
N5 36Sb 71
RM7: Rom 29Ed 56
RM12: Horn 35Kd 77
SM6: Wall 78Lb 156
SW1 6E 222 (46Mb 90)
(not continuous)
TN16: Big H 90Lc 179
WD25: Wat 7Y 13
Spring Gdns. Bus. Pk. RM7: Rom 30Ed 56
Spring Glen AL10: Hat 1B 8
SPRING GROVE 53Ga 108
Spring Gro. CR4: Mitc 67Jb 134
DA12: Grav'nd 10D 122
IG10: Lough 16Mc 35
KT22: Fet 95Da 191
SE19 66Vb 135
TW12: Hamp 67Da 129
W4 50Qa 87
W7 45Ga 86
Spring Gro. Cres.
TW3: Houn 53Ea 108
Spring Gro. Rd.
TW3: Houn, Isle 53Da 107
TW7: Isle 53Da 107
TW10: Rich 57Pa 109
Spring Head Cl.
TN15: Kems'g 89Pd 183
Springhead Ent. Pk. DA11: Nflt 60De 121
Springhead Parkway
DA11: Nflt 60De 121
Spring Head Rd. TN15: Kems'g 89Pd 183
Springhead Rd. DA8: Erith 51Hd 118
DA11: Nflt 61Ee 143
SpringHealth Leisure Club
Richmond 56Ma 109
(within Pools on the Pk.)
Spring Hill E5 31Wb 71
SE26 63Yb 136
Springhill Cl. SE5 55Tb 113
Springholm Cl. TN16: Big H 90Lc 179
Spring Ho. E17 26Ec 52
(off Fulbourne Rd.)
WC1 4K 217
Springhouse La. SS17: Corr 1P 101
Springhouse Rd. SS17: Corr 1P 101
Springhurst Cl. CR0: C'don 77Bc 158
Spring Lake HA7: Stan 21Ka 46
Spring La. E5 31Xb 71
HP1: Hem H 1H 3
N10 27Jb 50
RH8: Oxt 3H 211
SE25 72Xb 157
SL1: Slou 6D 80
SL2: Farn R 8F 60
TN15: Igh 94Xd 204
Spring M. KT17: Ewe 81Va 174
SE11 7H 229 (50Pb 90)
TW9: Rich 56Na 109
(off Rosedale Rd.)
W1 7G 215 (43Hb 89)
SPRING PARK 76Cc 158
Spring Pk. Av. CR0: C'don 75Zb 158
Spring Pk. Dr. N4 32Sb 71
Springpark Dr. BR3: Beck 69Ec 136
Spring Pk. Rd. CR0: C'don 75Zb 158
Spring Pas. SW15 55Za 110
Spring Path NW3 36Fb 69
Spring Pl. IG11: Bark 40Sc 74
KT11: Cobh 85Aa 171
N3 27Cb 49
NW5 36Kb 70
Springpond Rd. RM9: Dag 36Ad 75
Spring Prom. UB7: W Dray 47P 83
Spring Promenade
UB7: W Dray 47P 83
Springrice Rd. SE13 58Fc 115
Spring Ri. TW20: Egh 65A 126
Spring Rd. TW13: Felt 62V 128
Springs Cl. TW19: Stanw 60N 105
Springshaw Cl. TN13: Bes G 95Fd 202
Spring Shaw Rd. BR5: St P 67Wc 139
Spring St. KT17: Ewe 81Va 174
W2 3B 220 (44Fb 89)
Spring Ter. TW9: Rich 57Na 109
Spring Tide Cl. SE15 53Xb 113
Spring Va. DA7: Bex 56Dd 118
DA9: Ghithe 58Yd 120
Springvale Av. TW8: Bford 50Ma 87
Spring Va. Cl. BR8: Hext 67Hd 140
Springvale Ct. KT23: Bookh 97Da 191
Springvale Ct. DA11: Nflt 61Ee 143
Spring Va. Nth. DA1: Dart 59Md 119
Springvale Retail Pk. BR5: St P 69Yc 139
(not continuous)
Spring Va. Sth. DA1: Dart 59Md 119
Springvale Ter. W14 48Za 88
Springvale Way BR5: St P 69Yc 139
Spring Villa Pk. HA8: Edg 24Qa 47
Spring Villa Rd. HA8: Edg 24Qa 47
Spring Wlk. E1 43Wb 91
Springwater WC1 7H 217
Springwater Cl. SE18 53Qc 116
Spring Way HP2: Hem H 1B 4
SE5 53Sb 113
Springway HA1: Harr 31Fa 66
Springwell Av. NW10 39Va 68
WD3: Rick 19J 25
Springwell Cl. SW16 63Pb 134
Springwell Ct. UB9: Hare 20J 25
Springwell La. UB9: Hare 20J 25
WD3: Rick 20J 25
Springwell Rd. SW16 63Qb 134
TW4: Houn 54Z 107
TW5: Hest 54Z 107
Springwood Cl. E3 40Cc 72
UB9: Hare 25M 43
Springwood Ct. CR2: S Croy 77Ub 157
(off Birdhurst Rd.)
Springwood Cres. HA8: Edg 19Ra 29
Springwood Pl. KT13: Weyb 80R 150
Springwoods GU25: Vir W 10M 125
Springwood Way RM1: Rom 29Jd 56
Sproggit Ind. Est. TW19: Stanw 58P 105
Sprowston M. E7 37Jc 73
Sprowston Rd. E7 36Jc 73
Spruce Cl. RH1: Redh 5P 207
Spruce Ct. SL1: Slou 8K 81
W5 48Na 87
Sprucedale Cl. BR8: Swan 68Gd 140
Sprucedale Gdns. CR0: C'don 77Zb 158
SM6: Wall 81Nb 176
Spruce Hills Rd. E17 26Ec 52
Spruce Ho. SE16 47Zb 92
(off Woodland Cres.)
Spruce Pk. BR2: Brom 70Hc 137
Spruce Rd. TN16: Big H 88Mc 179
Spruce Way AL2: Park 9P 5
Sprules Rd. SE4 54Ac 114
Spur, The GU21: Knap 10F 166
KT12: Walt T 75Y 151
SL1: Slou 3B 80
Spur Cl. RM4: Abr 13Xc 37
WD5: Ab L 5T 12
Spurfield KT8: W Mole 69Da 129
Spurgate CM13: Hut 19Ce 41
Spurgeon Av. SE19 67Tb 135
Spurgeon Cl. RM17: Grays 51Ee 121
Spurgeon Rd. SE19 67Tb 135
Spurgeon St. SE1 3F 231 (48Tb 91)
Spurling Rd. RM9: Dag 37Bd 75
SE22 56Vb 113
Spurrell Av. DA5: Bexl 63Fd 140
Spur Rd. BR6: Orp 75Wc 161
HA8: Edg 21Na 47
N15 28Tb 51
SE1 1K 229 (47Qb 90)
SW1 2B 228 (47Lb 90)
TW7: Isle 52Ka 108
TW14: Felt 56X 107
Spurstowe Rd. E8 37Xb 71
Spurstowe Ter. E8 36Wb 71
Spurway Pde. IG2: Ilf 29Pc 54
(off Woodford Av.)
Spynes Mere Nature Reserve 2F 208
Squadrons App. RM12: Horn 37Ld 77
Square, The BR8: Swan 69Fd 140
CM14: B'wood 19Yd 40
CR3: Cat'm 96Wb 197
E10 34Ec 72
GU18: Light 2A 166
GU23: Wis 88N 169
Square, The HP1: Hem H 2M 3
IG1: Ilf 31Qc 74
IG8: Wfd G 22Jc 53
IG10: Lough 13Rc 36
KT13: Weyb 77S 150
KT22: Lea 92Ja 192
SM5: Cars 78Jb 156
TN13: Riv 94Gd 202
TN16: Tats 92Lc 199
TW9: Rich 57Ma 109
UB2: S'hall 49Y 85
UB7: Lford 53K 105
UB11: Stock P 46T 84
W6 50Ya 88
WD24: Wat 9X 13
Square of Fame 35Qa 67
(off Arena Sq.)
Square Rigger Row SW11 55Eb 111
Squarey St. SW17 62Eb 133
Squerryes 100Sc 200
Squerryes, The CR3: Cat'm 93Ub 197
Squerryes Ct. TN16: Westrm 100Sc 200
Squerryes Mede TN16: Westrm 99Sc 200
Squerryes Pk. Cotts.
TN16: Westrm 99Sc 200
Squire Gdns. NW8 4B 214
Squires, The RM7: Rom 30Ed 56
Squire's Bri. Rd. TW17: Shep 70P 127
Squires Ct. KT16: Chert 74K 149
SW4 53Nb 112
SW19 63Cb 133
Squires Fld. BR8: Hext 67Jd 140
Squires La. N3 26Db 49
Squires Mt. NW3 34Fb 69
Squire's Rd. TW17: Shep 70Q 128
Squires Wlk. TW15: Ashf 66T 128
(not continuous)
Squires Way DA2: Wilm 63Fd 140
Squires Wood Dr. BR7: Chst 66Nc 138
Squirrel Chase HP1: Hem H 1G 2
Squirrel Cl. TW4: Houn 55Y 107
Squirrel Dr. SL4: Wink 10A 102
Squirrel Keep KT14: W Byf 84K 169
Squirrel La. SL4: Wink 10A 102
Squirrel M. W13 45Ha 86
Squirrels, The HA5: Pinn 27Ba 45
SE13 55Fc 115
WD23: Bush 15Ea 28
Squirrels Chase RM16: Ors 7C 100
Squirrels Cl. BR6: Orp 74Uc 160
BR8: Swan 69Hd 140
N12 21Eb 49
UB10: Hil 38Q 64
Squirrels Ct. KT4: Wor Pk 75Va 154
(off The Avenue)
Squirrels Drey BR2: Brom 68Gc 137
(off Park Hill Rd.)
Squirrels Grn. KT4: Wor Pk 75Va 154
KT23: Bookh 95Ca 191
RH1: Redh 5P 207
SQUIRREL'S HEATH 27Md 57
Squirrels Heath Av. RM2: Rom 27Kd 57
Squirrels Heath La.
RM2: Horn, Rom 28Ld 57
RM11: Horn, Rom 28Ld 57
Squirrels Heath Rd. RM3: Hrld W 27Nd 57
Squirrel's La. IG9: Buck H 20Mc 35
Squirrels Trad. Est. UB3: Hayes 48V 84
Squirrels Way KT18: Eps 86Ta 173
Squirrel Wood KT14: W Byf 84K 169
Squirries St. E2 41Wb 91
SSE Arena Wembley, The 35Qa 67
SS Robin 45Kc 93
Stable Block, The RH1: Blet 3K 209
Stable Cl. KT2: King T 65Pa 131
KT18: Eps D 91Ua 194
UB5: N'olt 40Ca 65
Stable Ct. AL1: St A 1C 6
CR3: Cat'm 94Wb 197
EC1 6C 218
SM6: Wall 76Jb 156
TN13: S'oaks 98Ld 203
Stable M. AL1: St A 1C 6
(off Hillside Rd.)
NW5 37Kb 70
RH2: Reig 6J 207
SE6 60Gc 115
TW1: Twick 60Ha 108
Stable Pl. N4 33Rb 71
Stables, The DA3: Nflt G 64Fe 143
IG9: Buck H 17Lc 35
KT11: Cobh 86Ba 171
TN15: Seal 93Pd 203
WD6: E'tree 14Na 29
WD25: A'ham 8Da 13
Stables End BR6: Farnb 76Sc 160
Stables Gallery & Arts Cen. 34Wa 68
Stables Lodge E8 38Xb 71
(off Mare St.)
Stables Mkt., The NW1 38Kb 70
Stables M. AL9: Brk P 10M 9
SE27 64Sb 135
Stables Row E11 29Jc 53
Stable St. N1 1F 217 (39Nb 70)
Stables Way SE11 7K 229 (50Qb 90)
Stables Yd. SW18 58Cb 111
Stable Vs. BR1: Brom 65Mc 137
Stable Wlk. N2 25Fb 49
Stable Way W10 44Ya 88
Stable Yd. SW1 1B 228
SW15 55Ya 110
TN15: Kems'g 89Qd 183
Stableyard, The SW9 54Pb 112
Stableyard M. TW11: Tedd 65Ha 130
Stable Yd. Rd. SW1 7C 222 (47Lb 90)
(not continuous)
Staburn Ct. HA8: Edg 26Sa 47
Stacey Av. N18 21Yb 52
Stacey Cl. DA12: Grav'nd 4G 144
E10 29Fc 53
Stacey Ct. RH1: Mers 1C 208
Stacey St. N7 34Qb 70
WC2 3E 222 (44Mb 90)
Stack Ho. RH8: Oxt 2J 211
SW1 6J 227
Stackhouse St. SW3 3F 227
Stacklands Cl. TN15: W King 79Ud 164
Stack La. DA3: Hartl 71Be 165
Stack Rd. DA4: Hort K 70Td 142
Stacy Path SE5 52Ub 113
Stadbury, The KT13: Weyb 75Q 150
Staddlewood Pl. TN15: Plat 92De 205
Staddon Cl. BR3: Beck 70Ac 136
Stadium, The
AFC Hornchurch 33Qd 77
Stadium Bus. Cen. HA9: Wemb 34Ra 67
Stadium M. N5 34Qb 70
Stadium Retail Pk. HA9: Wemb 34Qa 67
Stadium Rd. SE18 52Nc 116
Stadium Rd. E. NW4 31Xa 68
Stadium St. SW10 52Eb 111
Stadium Way DA1: Cray 57Gd 118
HA9: Wemb 35Pa 67
WD18: Wat 15X 27
Staffa Rd. E10 32Ac 72
Staffhurst Wood Nature Reserve 9N 211
Staffhurst Wood Rd. TN8: Eden 9N 211
Stafford Av. RM11: Horn 27Md 57
SL2: Slou 2G 80
Stafford Cl. CR3: Cat'm 95Vb 197
DA9: Ghithe 57Vd 120
E17 30Bc 52
(not continuous)
EN8: Chesh 1Xb 19
N14 15Lb 32
NW6 41Cb 89
RM16: Chaf H 49Yd 98
SL6: Tap 4A 80
SM3: Cheam 79Ab 154
SS17: Linf 8J 101
Stafford Ct. DA5: Bexl 59Bd 117
SW8 52Nb 112
W7 44Ha 86
(off Copley Cl.)
W8 48Cb 89
Stafford Cripps Ho. E2 41Yb 92
(off Globe Rd.)
SW6 51Bb 111
(off Clem Attlee Ct.)
Stafford Cross Bus. Pk.
CR0: Wadd 78Pb 156
Stafford Gdns. CR0: Wadd 78Pb 156
Stafford Ho. SE1 7K 231
Stafford Ind. Est. RM11: Horn 27Md 57
STAFFORDLAKE 10D 166
Stafford Lake GU21: Knap 10D 166
GU24: Bisl 10D 166
Stafford Mans. SW1 3B 228
SW4 56Nb 112
SW11 52Hb 111
(off Albert Bri. Rd.)
W14 48Za 88
(off Haarlem Rd.)
Stafford Pl. SW1 3B 228 (48Lb 90)
TW10: Rich 59Pa 109
Stafford Ri. CR3: Cat'm 94Wb 197
Stafford Rd. CR0: Wadd 77Qb 156
CR3: Cat'm 95Vb 197
DA14: Sidc 63Uc 138
E3 40Bc 72
E7 38Lc 73
HA3: Hrw W 24Ea 46
HA4: Ruis 35V 64
KT3: N Mald 69Sa 131
NW6 41Cb 89
SM6: Wall 79Lb 156
Staffordshire St. SE15 53Wb 113
Stafford Sq. KT13: Weyb 77T 150
Stafford St. W1 6B 222 (46Lb 90)
Stafford Ter. W8 48Cb 89
Stafford Way TN13: S'oaks 99Ld 203
Staff St. EC1 4G 219 (41Tb 91)
Stagbury Av. CR5: Chip 90Gb 175
Stagbury Cl. CR5: Chip 91Gb 195
Stagbury Ho. CR5: Chip 91Gb 195
Stag Cl. HA8: Edg 26Ra 47
Stag Community Arts Cen. 97Kd 203
Stag Ct. KT2: King T 67Qa 131
(off Coombe Rd.)
Staggart Grn. IG7: Chig, Ilf 22Vc 55
Stagg Hill EN4: Had W 7Fb 17
EN6: Pot B 7Fb 17
STAG LANE 61Va 132
Stag La. HA8: Edg 26Ra 47
IG9: Buck H 19Kc 35
NW9 26Ra 47
SW15 62Va 132
WD3: Chor 16E 24
Stag Leys KT21: Asht 92Na 193
Stag Leys Cl. SM7: Bans 87Gb 175
Stags Way TW7: Isle 51Ha 108
Stainash Cres. TW18: Staines 64K 127
Stainash Pde. TW18: Staines 64K 127
(off Kingston Rd.)
Stainbank Rd. CR4: Mitc 69Kb 134
Stainby Cl. UB7: W Dray 48N 83
Stainby Rd. N15 28Vb 51
Stainer Rd. WD6: Bore 11Ma 29
Stainer St. SE1 7G 225 (46Tb 91)
Staines Av. SM3: Cheam 75Za 154
Staines Boat Club 64G 126
Staines Bri. TW18: Staines 64G 126
Staines By-Pass TW15: Ashf 63K 127
TW18: Staines 63K 127
TW19: Staines 61E 126
Staines La. KT16: Chert 72H 149
Staines La. Cl. KT16: Chert 72H 149
Staines Moor Nature Reserve 60G 104
Staines Rd. IG1: Ilf 36Sc 74
KT16: Chert 68H 127
TW2: Twick 62Ca 129
TW3: Houn 55Da 107
TW4: Houn 58X 107
TW14: Bedf, Felt 60Q 106
TW18: Lale, Staines 67K 127
TW19: Wray 59A 104
Staines Rd. E. TW16: Sun 66W 128
Staines Rd. W.
TW15: Ashf 65R 128
TW16: Sun 65R 128
Staines Town FC 66J 127
STAINES-UPON-THAMES 63H 127
Staines Wlk. DA14: Sidc 65Yc 139
Stainford Cl. TW15: Ashf 64T 128
Stainforth Rd. E17 28Cc 52
IG2: Ilf 31Tc 74
Staining La. EC2 2E 224 (44Sb 91)
Stainmore Cl. BR7: Chst 67Tc 138
Stainsbury St. E2 40Yb 72
Stainsby Rd. E14 44Cc 92
Stains Cl. EN8: Chesh 1Ac 20
Stainton Ct. WD23: Bush 15Da 27
(off Farrington Av.)
Stainton Rd. EN3: Enf H 11Yb 34
SE6 58Fc 115
Stainton Wlk. GU21: Wok 10N 167
Stairfoot La. TN13: Chip 94Ed 202
Staiths Way KT20: Tad 92Xa 194
Stalbridge Flats W1 3J 221
Stalbridge Ho. NW1 2B 216
Stalbridge St. NW1 7E 214 (43Gb 89)
Staleys Acre TN15: Bor G 92Be 205
Staleys Rd. TN15: Bor G 92Ae 205
Stalham St. SE16 48Xb 91
Stalham Way IG6: Ilf 25Rc 54
Stalisfield Pl. BR6: Downe 82Qc 180

Stambourne Way—Station M.

Stambourne Way BR4: W W'ck 75Ec 158
SE19 .66Ub 135
Stambourne Woodland Wlk.
SE19 .66Ub 135
Stamford Bridge 52Db 111
Stamford Bri. Studios SW6 . . . . . . .52Db 111
(off Wandon Rd.)
Stamford Brook Arches W6 . . . . . . .49Wa 88
Stamford Brook Av. W6 . . . . .48Va 88
Stamford Brook Gdns. W6 . . . . .48Va 88
Stamford Brook Mans. W6 . . . . .49Va 88
(off Goldhawk Rd.)
Stamford Brook Rd. W6 . . . . .48Va 88
Stamford Bldgs. SW8 . . . . .52Nb 112
(off Meadow Pl.)
Stamford Cl. EN6: Pot B 4Fb 17
HA3: Hrw W 24Ga 46
N15 . . . . .28Wb 51
NW3 . . . . .34Eb 69
(off Heath St.)
UB1: S'hall 45Ca 85
Stamford Cotts. SW10 . . . . .52Db 111
(off Billing St.)
Stamford Ct. W6 . . . . .49Wa 88
Stamford Dr. BR2: Brom 70Hc 137
Stamford Gdns. RM9: Dag 38Yc 75
Stamford Ga. SW6 . . . . .52Db 111
STAMFORD GREEN 85Ra 173
Stamford Grn. Rd. KT18: Eps 85Ra 173
Stamford Gro. E. N16 . . . . .32Wb 71
Stamford Gro. W. N16 . . . . .32Wb 71
STAMFORD HILL 32Vb 71
Stamford Hill N16 . . . . .33Vb 71
Stamford Ho. GU24: Chob 3J 167
(off Bagshot Rd.)
Stamford Lodge N16 . . . . .31Vb 71
Stamford Rd. E6 . . . . .39Nc 74
KT12: Walt T 76Z 151
N1 . . . . .38Ub 71
N15 . . . . .29Wb 51
RM9: Dag 39Xc 75
WD17: Wat 12X 27
Stamford Sq. SW15 . . . . .57Ab 110
Stamford St. SE1 . . . . .7K 223 (46Qb 90)
Stamp Pl. E2 . . . . .3K 219 (40Vb 71)
Stanacre Ct. KT20: Kgswd 93Bb 195
Stanard Cl. N16 . . . . .31Ub 71
Stanborough Av. WD6: Bore 9Qa 15
Stanborough Cl. TW12: Hamp 65Ba 129
WD6: Bore 10Qa 15
Stanborough Ho. E3 . . . . .42Dc 92
(off Empson St.)
Stanborough Pk. WD25: Wat 7Y 13
Stanborough Pas. E8 . . . . .37Vb 71
Stanborough Rd. TW3: Houn 55Fa 108
Stanbridge Pl. N21 . . . . .19Rb 33
Stanbridge Rd. SW15 . . . . .55Ya 110
Stanbrook Rd. DA11: Grav'nd 10B 122
SE2 . . . . .47Xc 95
Stanbury Av. WD17: Wat 9U 12
Stanbury Ct. NW3 . . . . .37Hb 69
Stanbury Rd. SE15 . . . . .54Xb 113
(not continuous)
Stancroft NW9 . . . . .29Ua 48
Standale Gro. HA4: Ruis 29S 44
Standard Ind. Est. E16 . . . . .47Pc 94
Standard Pl. EC2 . . . . .4J 219
Standard Rd. BR6: Downe 82Qc 180
DA6: Bex 56Ad 117
DA17: Belv 50Cd 96
EN3: Enf W 10Ac 20
NW10 . . . . .42Sa 87
TW4: Houn 55Aa 107
Standcumbe Ct. BR3: Beck 71Bc 158
Standen Av. RM12: Horn 34Nd 77
Standen Rd. SW18 . . . . .59Bb 111
Standfield WD5: Ab L 3U 12
Standfield Gdns. RM10: Dag 37Cd 76
Standfield Rd. RM10: Dag 36Cd 76
Standish Ho. W6 . . . . .49Wa 88
(off St Peter's Gro.)
Standish Rd. W6 . . . . .49Wa 88
Standlake Point SE23 . . . . .62Zb 136
Standring Ri. HP3: Hem H 5K 3
Stane Cl. SW19 . . . . .66Db 133
Stane Gro. SW9 . . . . .54Nb 112
Stanesgate Ho. SE15 . . . . .52Wb 113
(off Friary Est.)
Stane Way KT17: Ewe 82Wa 174
SE18 . . . . .52Mc 115
Stanfield Ho. NW8 . . . . .5C 214
UB5: N'olt 40Z 65
(off Academy Gdns.)
Stanfield Rd. E3 . . . . .40Ac 72
Stanford Cl. HA4: Ruis 30S 44
IG8: Wfd G 22Nc 54
RM7: Rom 30Dd 56
TW12: Hamp 65Ba 129
STANFORD COMMON 8C 186
Stanford Cotts. GU24: Pirb 8C 186
Stanford Ct. EN9: Walt A 5Jc 21
SW6 . . . . .53Db 111
W8 . . . . .48Db 89
(off Cornwall Gdns.)
Stanford Gdns. RM15: Avel 46Ud 98
Stanford Ind. Est. SS17: Stan H 2L 101
STANFORD-LE-HOPE 2M 101
Stanford M. E8 . . . . .36Wb 71
Stanford Pl. SE17 . . . . .6H 231 (49Ub 91)
Stanford Rd. N11 . . . . .22Hb 49
RM16: Grays, Ors 7A 100
SS17: Stan H 4F 100
SW16 . . . . .68Mb 134
W8 . . . . .48Db 89
Stanfords, The KT17: Eps 84Va 174
(off East St.)
Stanford St. SW1 . . . . .6D 228 (49Mb 90)
Stanford Warren Nature Reserve 4M 101
Stanford Way SW16 . . . . .68Mb 134
Stangate SE1 . . . . .3J 229
Stangate Cres. WD6: Bore 15Ta 29
Stangate Gdns. HA7: Stan 21Ka 46
Stangate Lodge N21 . . . . .16Pb 32
Stanger Rd. SE25 . . . . .70Wb 135
Stanham Pl. DA1: Cray 56Jd 118
Stanham Rd. DA1: Dart 57Ld 119
Stanhill Cotts. DA2: Wilm 66Fd 140
Stanhope Av. BR2: Hayes 74Hc 159
HA3: Hrw W 25Fa 46
N3 . . . . .27Bb 49
Stanhope Cl. SE16 . . . . .47Zb 92
Stanhope Gdns. IG1: Ilf 32Pc 74
N4 . . . . .30Rb 51
N6 . . . . .30Kb 50
NW7 . . . . .22Va 48
RM8: Dag 34Bd 75
SW7 . . . . .5A 226 (49Eb 89)
Stanhope Ga. W1 . . . . .7J 221 (46Jb 90)
Stanhope Gro. BR3: Beck 71Bc 158
Stanhope Heath
TW19: Stanw 58L 105
Stanhope Ho. N11 . . . . .21Kb 50
(off Coppies Gro.)
SE8 . . . . .52Bc 114
(off Adolphus St.)
Stanhope Ind. Pk.
SS17: Stan H 4P 101
Stanhope M. E. SW7 . . . . . .5A 226 (49Eb 89)
Stanhope M. Sth. SW7 . . . .6A 226 (49Eb 89)
Stanhope M. W. SW7 . . . . . .5A 226 (49Eb 89)
Stanhope Pde. NW1 . . . . . .3B 216 (41Lb 90)
Stanhope Pk. Rd.
UB6: G'frd 42Ea 86
Stanhope Pl. W2 . . . . .3F 221 (45Hb 89)
Stanhope Rd. AL1: St A 2D 6
CR0: C'don 76Ub 157
DA7: Bex 54Ad 117
DA10: Swans 58Be 121
DA15: Sidc 63Wc 139
E17 . . . . .29Dc 52
EN5: Barn 16Ya 30
EN8: Walt C 5Ac 20
N6 . . . . .30Lb 50
N12 . . . . .22Eb 49
RM8: Dag 33Bd 75
RM13: Rain 40Jd 76
SL1: Slou .4B 80
SM5: Cars 80Jb 156
UB6: G'frd 43Ea 86
Stanhope Row W1 . . . . .7K 221 (46Kb 90)
Stanhopes RH8: Limp 100Kc 199
Stanhope St. NW1 . . . . .2B 216 (40Lb 70)
Stanhope Ter.
TW2: Twick 59Ha 108
W2 . . . . .4C 220 (45Fb 89)
Stanhope Way TN13: Riv 94Fd 202
TW19: Stanw 58L 105
Stanier Cl. W14 . . . . .50Bb 89
Stanier Ho. SW6 . . . . .53Eb 111
(off Station Ct.)
Staniland Dr. KT13: Weyb 83P 169
Stanlake M. W12 . . . . .46Ya 88
Stanlake Rd. W12 . . . . .46Ya 88
Stanlake Vs. W12 . . . . .46Ya 88
Stanley Av. AL2: Chis G 7N 5
BR3: Beck 68Ec 136
HA0: Wemb 38Na 67
IG11: Bark 40Vc 75
KT3: N Mald 71Wa 154
RM2: Rom 28Jd 56
RM8: Dag 32Bd 75
UB6: G'frd 39Ea 66
Stanley Bri. Studios
SW6 . . . . .52Db 111
(off King's Rd.)
Stanley Cl. CR5: Coul 89Pb 176
DA9: Ghithe 57Ud 120
HA0: Wemb 38Na 67
RM2: Rom 28Jd 56
RM12: Horn 33Ld 77
SE9 . . . . .60Sc 116
SW8 . . . . .51Pb 112
UB8: Uxb .40M 63
Stanley Cohen Ho. EC1 . . . . .6D 218
Stanley Cotts. DA2: Daren 64Ud 142
SL2: Slou .6K 81
Stanley Ct. SM2: Sutt 80Db 155
SM5: Cars 80Jb 156
W5 . . . . .43La 86
Stanley Cres. DA12: Grav'nd 4F 144
W11 . . . . .45Bb 89
Stanleycroft Cl. TW7: Isle 53Ga 108
Stanley Dr. AL10: Hat 2D 8
Stanley Gdns. CR2: Sande 84Wb 177
CR4: Mitc 65Jb 134
KT12: Hers 79Y 151
NW2 . . . . .36Ya 68
SM6: Wall 79Lb 156
W3 . . . . .47Ua 88
W11 . . . . .45Bb 89
WD6: Bore 11Na 29
Stanley Gdns. M. W11 . . . . .45Bb 89
(off Kensington Pk. Rd.)
Stanley Gdns. Rd. TW11: Tedd 64Ga 130
Stanley Grn. E. SL3: L'ly 49B 82
Stanley Grn. W. SL3: L'ly 49B 82
Stanley Gro. CR0: C'don 72Qb 156
SW8 . . . . .54Jb 112
Stanley Hill GU24: Pirb 4A 186
Stanley Holloway Ct. E16 . . . . .44Jc 93
(off Coolfin Rd.)
Stanley Ho. E14 . . . . .44Cc 92
(off Saracen St.)
SW10 . . . . .52Eb 111
(off Coleridge Gdns.)
Stanley Mans. SW10 . . . . .51Eb 111
(off Park Wlk.)
Stanley Maude Ho. SL9: Chal P 21A 42
(off Micholls Av.)
Stanley M. SW10 . . . . .52Eb 111
(off Coleridge Gdns.)
Stanley Pk. Dr. HA0: Wemb 39Pa 67
Stanley Pk. Rd. SM5: Cars 80Gb 155
SM6: Wall 79Kb 156
Stanley Picker Gallery 69Na 131
(off Springfield Rd.)
Stanley Rd. BR2: Brom 70Kc 137
BR6: Orp 74Wc 161
CR0: C'don 73Qb 156
CR4: Mitc 66Jb 134
DA10: Swans 58Be 121
DA11: Nflt 1A 144
DA14: Sidc 62Wc 139
E4 . . . . .18Fc 35
E10 . . . . .30Dc 52
E12 . . . . .36Nc 74
E18 . . . . .25Hc 53
EN1: Enf 13Ub 33
GU21: Wok 88B 168
HA2: Harr 33Ea 66
HA6: Nwood 25W 44
HA9: Wemb 37Pa 67
IG1: Ilf 33Tc 74
N2 . . . . .27Fb 49
N9 . . . . .18Vb 33
N10 . . . . .24Kb 50
N11 . . . . .23Mb 50
N15 . . . . .28Rb 51
NW9 . . . . .31Wa 68
RM12: Horn 33Ld 77
RM17: Grays 50De 99
SM2: Sutt 79Db 155
SM4: Mord 70Cb 133
SM5: Cars 80Jb 156
SW14 . . . . .56Ra 109
SW19 . . . . .65Cb 133
Stanley Rd. TW2: Twick 62Fa 130
TW3: Houn 56Ea 108
TW11: Tedd 63Ga 130
TW15: Ashf 64N 127
UB1: S'hall 45Aa 85
W3 . . . . .48Sa 87
WD17: Wat 14Y 27
Stanley Rd. Nth. RM13: Rain 39Gd 76
Stanley Rd. Sth.
RM13: Rain 40Hd 76
Stanley Sq. SM5: Cars 81Hb 175
Stanley St. CR3: Cat'm 94Sb 197
SE8 . . . . .52Bc 114
Stanley Studios SW10 . . . . .51Eb 111
(off Park Wlk.)
Stanley Ter. DA6: Bex 56Cd 118
N19 . . . . .33Nb 70
Stanley Way BR5: St M Cry 71Xc 161
Stanliff Ho. E14 . . . . .48Cc 92
Stanmer St. SW11 . . . . .53Gb 111
STANMORE 22Ka 46
Stanmore & Edgware Golf Cen. . . .20Ma 29
Stanmore Chase AL4: St A 3H 7
Stanmore Common Local Nature Reserve
. . . . .19Ha 28
Stanmore Country Pk.
(Local Nature Reserve) 20La 28
Stanmore Gdns. SM1: Sutt 76Eb 155
TW9: Rich 55Pa 109
Stanmore Golf Course 24Ka 46
Stanmore Hill HA7: Stan 20Ja 28
Stanmore Lodge HA7: Stan 21Ka 46
Stanmore Pl. NW1 . . . . .39Kb 70
Stanmore Rd. DA17: Belv 49Ed 96
E11 . . . . .32Hc 73
N15 . . . . .28Rb 51
TW9: Rich 55Pa 109
WD24: Wat 11X 27
Stanmore St. N1 . . . . .39Pb 70
Stanmore Ter. BR3: Beck 68Cc 136
Stanmore Way IG10: Lough 11Qc 36
Stanmount Rd.
AL2: Chis G 7N 5
Stannard Cotts. E1 . . . . .42Yb 92
(off Fox Cl.)
Stannard Ct. SE6 . . . . .60Dc 114
Stannard Ho. SW19 . . . . .63Eb 133
Stannard M. E8 . . . . .37Wb 71
(off Stannard Rd.)
Stannard Rd. E8 . . . . .37Wb 71
Stannary Pl. SE11 . . . . .50Qb 90
Stannary St. SE11 . . . . .51Qb 112
STANNERS HILL 10P 147
Stannet Way SM6: Wall 77Lb 156
Stannington Path WD6: Bore 11Qa 29
Stansborough Ho. E3 . . . . .42Dc 92
(off Empson St.)
Stansbury Sq. W10 . . . . .41Ab 88
Stansfeld Ho. SE1 . . . . .6K 231
Stansfeld Rd. E6 . . . . .43Mc 93
E16 . . . . .43Mc 93
Stansfield Rd. SW9 . . . . .55Pb 112
TW4: Cran 54X 107
Stansgate Rd. RM10: Dag 33Cd 76
Stanstead WC1 . . . . .4G 217
Stanstead Cl. BR2: Brom 71Hc 159
CR3: Cat'm 96Ub 197
Stanstead Gro. SE6 . . . . .60Bc 114
Stanstead Ho. E3 . . . . .42Ec 92
(off Devas St.)
Stanstead Mnr. SM1: Sutt 79Cb 155
Stanstead Rd. CR3: Cat'm 99Tb 197
E11 . . . . .29Kc 53
SE6 . . . . .60Zb 114
SE23 . . . . .60Zb 114
STANSTED 82Be 185
Stansted Cl. RM12: Horn 37Kd 77
Stansted Cres. DA5: Bexl 60Zc 117
Stansted Hill TN15: Stans 82Be 185
Stansted La. TN15: Ash 82Xd 184
Stansted Rd. TW6: H'row A 58P 105
Stanswood Gdns. SE5 . . . . .52Ub 113
Stanthorpe Cl. SW16 . . . . .64Nb 134
Stanthorpe Rd. SW16 . . . . .64Nb 134
Stanton Av. TW11: Tedd 65Ga 130
Stanton Cl. BR5: Orp 73Yc 161
KT4: Wor Pk 74Za 154
KT19: Ewe 78Ra 153
Stanton Ct. CR2: S Croy 78Ub 157
(off Birdhurst Ri.)
Stanton Ho. SE10 . . . . .51Ec 114
(off Thames St.)
SE16 . . . . .47Bc 92
(off Rotherhithe St.)
Stanton Rd. CR0: C'don 73Sb 157
SE26 . . . . .63Bc 136
SW13 . . . . .54Va 110
SW20 . . . . .67Za 132
Stanton Sq. SE26 . . . . .63Bc 136
Stanton Way SE26 . . . . .63Bc 136
SL3: L'ly .49A 82
Stanway Cl. IG7: Chig 22Uc 54
Stanway Cotts. KT16: Chert 74J 149
Stanway Ct. N1 . . . . .2J 219
(not continuous)
Stanway Gdns. HA8: Edg 22Sa 47
W3 . . . . .46Qa 87
Stanway Rd. EN9: Walt A 5Jc 21
Stanway St. N1 . . . . .1J 219 (40Ub 71)
STANWELL 58M 105
Stanwell Cl. TW19: Stanw 58M 105
Stanwell Gdns. TW19: Stanw 58M 105
STANWELL MOOR 57J 105
Stanwell Moor Rd. TW18: Staines 62J 127
TW19: Staines, Stanw M 62J 127
UB7: Lford 56K 105
Stanwell New Rd. TW18: Staines 62J 127
Stanwell Pl.
TW19: Stanw, Stanw M 58L 105
Stanwell Rd. SL3: Hort, Poyle 55C 104
TW14: Bedf 59R 106
TW15: Ashf 61N 127
Stanwick Rd. W14 . . . . .49Bb 89
Stanworth Ct. TW5: Hest 52Ba 107
Stanworth St. SE1 . . . . .2K 231 (48Vb 91)
Stanwyck Dr. IG7: Chig 22Sc 54
Stanwyck Gdns. RM3: Rom 22Kd 57
Stanyhurst SE23 . . . . .60Ac 114
Stapenhill Rd. HA0: Wemb 34Ka 66
Staplands Mnr. KT13: Weyb 76U 150
Staple Cl. DA5: Bexl 62Fd 140
Staplefield Cl. HA5: Pinn 24Aa 45
SW2 . . . . .60Nb 112
Stapleford N17 . . . . .26Ub 51
(off Willan Rd.)
STAPLEFORD ABBOTTS 15Ed 38
Stapleford Abbotts Golf Course 17Jd 38
Stapleford Av. IG2: Ilf 29Uc 54
Stapleford Cl. E4 . . . . .20Ec 34
KT1: King T 68Qa 131
SW19 . . . . .59Ab 110
Stapleford Ct. TN13: S'oaks 96Hd 202
Stapleford Gdns. RM5: Col R 23Cd 56
Stapleford Rd. HA0: Wemb 38Ma 67
RM4: Stap A, Stap T 14Dd 38
Staple Hill Rd. GU24: Chob 9H 147
Staplehurst Cl. RH2: Reig 10L 207
Staplehurst Rd. RH2: Reig 10L 207
SE13 . . . . .57Fc 115
SM5: Cars 80Gb 155
Staple Inn WC1 . . . . .1K 223
Staple Inn Bldgs. WC1 . . . .1K 223 (43Qb 90)
Staples, The BR8: Swan 67Kd 141
Staples Cl. SE16 . . . . .46Ac 92
STAPLES CORNER 32Xa 68
Staples Cnr. Bus. Pk. NW2 . . . . .32Xa 68
Staples Cnr. Retail Pk. NW2 . . . . . . .32Xa 68
Staples Ho. E6 . . . . .44Qc 94
(off Savage Gdns.)
Staple's Rd. IG10: Lough 13Mc 35
Staple St. SE1 . . . . .2G 231 (47Tb 91)
Stapleton Cl. EN6: Pot B 3Fb 17
Stapleton Cres. RM13: Rain 37Jd 76
Stapleton Gdns. CR0: Wadd 78Qb 156
Stapleton Hall Rd. N4 . . . . .32Pb 70
Stapleton Ho. E2 . . . . .41Xb 91
(off Ellsworth St.)
Stapleton Rd. BR6: Orp 77Vc 161
DA7: Bex 52Bd 117
SW17 . . . . .62Jb 134
WD6: Bore 10Qa 15
Stapleton Vs. N16 . . . . .35Ub 71
(off Wordsworth Rd.)
Stapley Rd. AL3: St A 1B 6
DA17: Belv 50Cd 96
Stapylton Rd. EN5: Barn 13Ab 30
Star All. EC3 . . . . .4J 225
Star & Garter Hill TW10: Rich 60Na 109
Star Apartments KT12: Hers 79Y 151
Starboard Av. DA9: Ghithe 58Xd 120
Starboard Way E14 . . . . .48Cc 92
Starbuck Cl. SE9 . . . . .59Qc 116
Star Bus. Cen. RM13: Rain 43Fd 96
Starch Ho. La. IG6: Ilf 26Tc 54
Star Cl. EN3: Pond E 16Yb 34
Starcross St. NW1 . . . . . . .4C 216 (41Lb 90)
Starfield Rd. W12 . . . . .47Wa 88
Star Hill DA1: Cray 57Gd 118
Star Hill Rd. TN14: Dun G 88Bd 181
Starkey Pl. DA8: Erith 52Gd 118
Star La. BR5: St M Cry, St P 70Yc 139
CM16: Epp 2Wc 23
CR5: Coul 93Jb 196
E16 . . . . .42Gc 93
Starley Cl. E17 . . . . .25Fc 53
Starlight Way AL4: St A 4G 6
TW6: H'row A 57S 106
Starling Cl. CR0: C'don 72Ac 158
DA3: Lfield 69De 143
HA5: Pinn 27Y 45
IG9: Buck H 18Jc 35
Starling Cres. SL3: L'ly 9N 81
Starling Ho. NW8 . . . . .1D 214
Starling La. EN6: Cuff 1Pb 18
Starling Pl. WD25: Wat 4Y 13
Starlings, The KT22: Oxs 85Ea 172
Starling Wlk. TW12: Hamp 64Aa 129
Starmans Cl. RM9: Dag 39Ad 75
Star Path UB5: N'olt 40Ca 65
(off Brabazon Rd.)
Star Pl. E1 .45Vb 91
Star Rd. TW7: Isle 54Fa 108
UB10: Hil .42S 84
W14 . . . . .51Bb 111
Starrock La. CR5: Chip 92Hb 195
Starrock Rd. CR5: Coul 91Kb 196
Star St. W2 . . . . .2C 220 (44Gb 89)
Starts Cl. BR6: Farnb 76Qc 160
Starts Hill Av. BR6: Farnb 77Rc 160
Starts Hill Rd. BR6: Farnb 76Qc 160
Starveall Cl. UB7: W Dray 48P 83
Star Wharf NW1 . . . . .39Lb 70
(off St Pancras Way)
Starwood Cl. KT14: W Byf 83L 169
Starwood Ct. SL3: L'ly 8N 81
Star Yd. WC2 . . . . .2K 223 (44Qb 90)
State Farm Av. BR6: Farnb 77Rc 160
Staten Bldg. E3 . . . . .40Cc 72
(off Fairfield Rd.)
Staten Gdns. TW1: Twick 60Ha 108
State Pde. IG6: Ilf 26Sc 54
Statham Gro. N16 . . . . .35Tb 71
N18 . . . . .22Ub 51
Statham Ho. SW8 . . . . .53Lb 112
(off Wadhurst Rd.)
Station App. BR1: Brom 69Jc 137
(off High St.)
BR2: Hayes 74Jc 159
BR3: Beck 67Cc 136
BR4: W W'ck 73Ec 158
BR5: St M Cry 70Xc 139
BR6: Chels 78Xc 161
BR6: Orp 75Vc 161
BR7: Chst 65Nc 138
(Bennetts Copse)
BR7: Chst 67Qc 138
(Vale Rd.)
BR8: Swan 70Gd 140
CM13: W H'dn 31Ee 79
CM16: They B 8Uc 22
CR0: C'don 75Tb 157
(off Dingwall Rd.)
CR2: Sande 81Tb 177
CR3: Whyt 89Wb 177
CR5: Chip 90Hb 175
CR5: Coul 88Mb 176
CR8: Purl 83Qb 176
DA1: Cray 58Hd 118
DA1: Dart 58Nd 119
DA5: Bexl 60Cd 118
DA7: Bex 54Ed 118
(Barnehurst Rd.)
DA7: Bex 54Ad 117
(Percy Rd.)
DA13: Meop 10C 144
DA16: Well 54Wc 117
E4 . . . . .23Fc 53
E7 . . . . .35Kc 73
E11 . . . . .29Jc 53
E17 . . . . .29Cc 52
E18 . . . . .26Kc 53
EN5: New Bar 14Eb 31
EN8: Walt C 6Ac 20
GU22: Wok 90B 168
GU25: Vir W 10P 125
HA0: Wemb 37Ka 66
Station App. HA1: Harr 31Ga 66
HA4: Ruis 36X 65
(Mahlon Av.)
HA4: Ruis 32U 64
(Pembroke Rd.)
HA5: Pinn 27Aa 45
HA6: Nwood 24U 44
HP3: Hem H 5J 3
IG8: Wfd G 23Kc 53
IG9: Buck H 21Mc 53
IG10: Lough 15Nc 36
(Alderton Hill)
IG10: Lough 14Sc 36
(Torrington Dr.)
KT1: King T 67Qa 131
KT4: Wor Pk 74Wa 154
KT10: Hin W 76Ha 152
KT13: Weyb 79Q 150
KT14: W Byf 84J 169
KT17: Ewe 81Va 174
(Fennells Mead)
KT17: Ewe 82Xa 174
(Nonsuch Ct. Av.)
KT19: Eps 85Ta 173
KT19: Ewe 78Wa 154
KT20: Tad 94Ya 194
KT22: Lea 93Ja 192
KT22: Oxs 84Ea 172
KT24: E Hor 98U 190
N11 . . . . .22Kb 50
N12 . . . . .21Db 49
N16 . . . . .33Vb 71
(off Stamford Hill)
NW1 . . . . .6G 215 (42Hb 89)
NW10 . . . . .41Va 88
NW11 . . . . .31Za 68
RH1: Redh 5A 208
(off Redstone Hill)
RH8: Oxt .1J 211
RM14: Upm 33Sd 78
RM15: S Ock 41Yd 98
RM17: Grays 51Ce 121
RM18: Tilb 6D 122
SE3 . . . . .55Kc 115
SE9 . . . . .61Sc 138
(Bercta Rd.)
SE9 . . . . .60Pc 116
(Crossmead)
SE12 . . . . .58Jc 115
(off Burnt Ash Hill)
SE26 . . . . .63Yb 136
SL3: L'ly .47C 82
SL9: Ger X 29A 42
SM2: Cheam 80Ab 154
SM2: Sutt 82Db 175
SM5: Cars 77Hb 155
SW6 . . . . .55Ab 110
SW14 . . . . .55Sa 109
SW16 . . . . .65Mb 134
(Estreham Rd.)
SW16 . . . . .64Mb 134
(Gleneagle Rd.)
SW20 . . . . .68Xa 132
TN13: Dun G 92Gd 202
TN15: Bor G 92Be 205
TW8: Bford 51La 108
(off Sidney Gdns.)
TW9: Kew 53Qa 109
TW12: Hamp 67Ca 129
TW15: Ashf 63P 127
TW16: Sun 67W 128
TW17: Shep 71S 150
TW18: Staines 64J 127
UB3: Hayes 48V 84
UB6: G'frd 38Ea 66
UB7: Yiew 46N 83
UB9: Den 31F 62
W7 . . . . .46Ga 86
WD3: Chor 14F 24
WD4: K Lan 2R 12
WD7: R'lett 7Ja 14
WD19: Wat 20Z 27
Station App. E. RH1: Redh 8P 207
Station App. Nth.
DA15: Sidc 61Wc 139
Station App. Rd. CR5: Coul 87Mb 176
SE1 . . . . .2K 229 (47Qb 90)
W4 . . . . .52Sa 109
Station App. Sth.
DA15: Sidc 61Wc 139
(off Jubilee Way)
Station App. W. RH1: Redh 8P 207
Station Arc. W1 . . . . .6A 216
Station Av. CR3: Cat'm 96Wb 197
KT3: N Mald 69Ua 132
KT12: Walt T 77W 150
KT19: Ewe 81Ua 174
SW9 . . . . .55Rb 113
TW9: Kew 53Qa 109
Station Bldgs. KT1: King T 68Na 131
(off Fife Rd.)
Station Chambers E6 . . . . .38Nc 74
(off High St. Nth.)
Station Cl. AL9: Brk P 8G 8
EN6: Pot B 3Bb 17
N3 . . . . .25Cb 49
N12 . . . . .21Db 49
TW12: Hamp 67Da 129
Station Cotts. BR6: Orp 75Vc 161
Station Ct. KT12: Hers 77W 150
N15 . . . . .29Vb 51
SW6 . . . . .53Eb 111
TN15: Bor G 91Be 205
Station Cres. HA0: Wemb 37Ka 66
N15 . . . . .28Tb 51
SE3 . . . . .50Jc 93
TW15: Ashf 62M 127
Stationer's Hall Ct.
EC4 . . . . .3C 224 (44Rb 91)
Stationers Pl. HP3: Hem H 7N 3
Station Est. BR3: Beck 69Zb 136
E18 . . . . .26Kc 53
Station Est. Rd.
TW14: Felt 60X 107
Station Footpath WD4: K Lan 2R 12
(not continuous)
Station Forecourt
WD3: Rick 17M 25
(off Homestead Rd.)
Station Garage M. SW16 . . . . .65Mb 134
Station Gdns. W4 . . . . .52Sa 109
Station Gro. HA0: Wemb 37Na 67
Station Hill BR2: Hayes 75Jc 159
Station Ho. SE8 . . . . .52Cc 114
(off Deptford High St.)
Station Ho. M. N9 . . . . .21Wb 51
Station La. RM12: Horn 34Md 77
Station M. EN6: Pot B 3Cb 17

Station Pde.—Stonecroft Way

Station Pde. BR1: Brom 67Jc 137
(off Tweedy Rd.)
DA7: Bex 54Ad 117
(off Pickford La.)
DA15: Sidc 61Wc 139
E6 38Nc 74
E11 29Jc 53
E13 39Lc 73
(off Green St.)
EN4: Cockf 14Jb 32
GU25: Vir W 10P 125
HA2: Harr 35Da 65
HA3: Kenton 26Ja 46
HA4: Ruis 33T 64
HA8: Edg 24Na 47
IG9: Buck H 21Mc 53
IG11: Bark 38Sc 74
KT24: E Hor 98U 190
N14 18Mb 32
NW2 37Ya 68
RM1: Rom 30Gd 56
RM9: Dag 37Cd 76
RM12: Horn 35Kd 77
SL5: S'dale 3E 146
SM2: Sutt 79Eb 155
(off High St.)
SW12 60Jb 112
TN13: S'oaks 96Jd 202
TW9: Kew 53Qa 109
TW14: Felt 60X 107
TW15: Ashf 63P 127
UB5: N'olt 35Da 65
(Accock Gro.)
UB5: N'olt 38Ca 65
(Court Farm Rd.)
UB9: Den 31J 63
W3 44Qa 87
W4 52Sa 109
W5 46Pa 87
Station Pas. E18 26Kc 53
E20 37Ec 72
SE15 53Yb 114
Station Path E8 37Xb 71
(off Graham Rd.)
SW6 55Bb 111
TW18: Staines 63H 127
Station Pl. N4 33Qb 70
Station Ri. SE27 61Rb 135
Station Rd. AL2: Brick W 3Ca 13
AL4: S'ford 1M 7
AL9: Brk P, N Mym, Wel G 6E 8
BR1: Brom 67Jc 137
BR2: Brom 68Gc 137
BR4: W W'ck 75Ec 158
BR5: St P 70Yc 139
BR6: Orp 75Vc 161
BR8: Swan 70Gd 140
CM13: W H'dn 30Ee 59
CM16: Epp 3Vc 23
CR0: C'don 74Sb 157
CR3: Whyt 90Vb 177
CR3: Wold 94Ac 198
CR8: Kenley 86Sb 177
DA1: Cray 59Hd 118
DA3: Lfield 69Ae 143
DA4: Eyns 76Md 163
DA4: S Dar 68Rd 141
DA7: Bex 55Ad 117
DA9: Ghithe 57Wd 120
(not continuous)
DA11: Nflt 58De 121
DA13: Meop 10C 144
DA13: Sflt 63Be 143
DA15: Sidc 61Wc 139
DA17: Belv 48Cd 96
E4 18Fc 35
E7 35Jc 73
E12 35Nc 74
E17 30Ac 52
EN5: New Bar 15Db 31
EN6: Cuff 1Pb 18
EN9: Walt C, Walt A 6Cc 20
GU24: Chob 3K 167
HA1: Harr 28Ha 46
HA2: Harr 29Da 45
HA8: Edg 23Qa 47
HP1: Hem H 4K 3
HP4: Berk 1A 2
IG1: Ilf 34Rc 74
IG6: Ilf 27Tc 54
IG7: Chig 20Rc 36
IG10: Lough 14Nc 36
KT1: Hamp W 67La 130
KT2: King T 67Qa 131
KT3: N Mald 71Xa 154
KT7: T Ditt 73Ha 152
KT9: Chess 78Na 153
KT10: Clay 79Ga 152
KT10: Esh 75Fa 152
KT11: Stoke D 89Aa 171
KT14: W Byf 84J 169
KT15: Add 77L 149
KT16: Chert 73H 149
KT22: Lea 93Ja 192
N3 25Cb 49
N11 22Kb 50
N17 27Wb 51
N19 34Lb 70
N21 18Rb 33
N22 26Nb 50
(not continuous)
NW4 30Wa 48
NW7 23Ua 48
NW10 40Va 68
RH1: Mers 100Lb 196
RH1: Redh 5N 207
RH3: Bet 3A 206
RH9: S God 10C 210
RM2: Rom 28Kd 57
RM3: Hrld W 25Pd 57
RM6: Chad H, Dag 31Zc 75
RM14: Upm 33Sd 78
RM18: E Til, W Til 1H 123
SE13 55Ec 114
SE20 65Yb 136
SE25 70Vb 135
SL1: Slou 4C 80
SL3: L'ly 48C 82
SL5: S'dale 2E 146
SL9: Ger X 29A 42
SM2: Sutt 82Cb 175
SM5: Cars 77Hb 155
SW13 54Va 110
SW19 67Eb 133
TN13: Dun G 92Gd 202
TN14: Hals 82Bd 181
TN14: Otf 88Kd 183
TN14: S'ham 83Jd 182
Station Rd. TN15: Bor G 92Be 205
TN16: Bras 95Xc 201
TW1: Twick 60Ha 108
TW3: Houn 56Da 107
TW11: Tedd 65Ja 130
TW12: Hamp 67Ca 129
TW15: Ashf 63P 127
TW16: Sun 66W 128
TW17: Shep 71S 150
TW19: Wray 58B 104
TW20: Egh 64C 126
UB3: Harl, Hayes 49U 84
(not continuous)
UB7: W Dray 47N 83
UB8: Cowl 42L 83
W5 44Pa 87
W7 46Ga 86
WD3: Rick 17M 25
WD4: K Lan 1R 12
WD6: Bore 14Qa 29
WD7: R'lett 7Ja 14
WD17: Wat 12X 27
Station Rd. E. RH8: Oxt 1J 211
Station Rd. Nth. DA17: Belv 48Dd 96
RH1: Mers 100Lb 196
TW20: Egh 64C 126
Station Rd. Sth. RH1: Mers 100Lb 196
Station Rd. W. RH8: Oxt 1J 211
Station Sq. BR5: Pet W 71Sc 160
RM2: Rom 28Kd 57
Station St. E15 38Fc 73
E16 46Rc 94
Station Ter. AL2: Park 8B 6
NW10 40Za 68
RM19: Purf 50Qd 97
SE5 53Sb 113
Station Ter. M. SE3 50Jc 93
Station Vw. UB6: G'frd 39Fa 66
Station Wlk. IG1: Ilf 33Rc 74
(within The Exchange)
W11 45Za 88
(off Bramley Rd.)
Station Way AL1: St A 2D 6
IG9: Buck H 21Lc 53
KT10: Clay 79Ga 152
KT19: Eps 85Ta 173
SE15 54Wb 113
SE18 48Rc 94
SM3: Cheam 79Ab 154
Station Yd. AL4: S'ford 2M 7
CR8: Purl 84Rb 177
HA4: Ruis 33S 64
KT20: Kgswd 93Bb 195
TW1: Twick 59Ja 108
UB9: Den 31J 63
Staton Ct. E10 31Dc 72
(off Kings Cl.)
Staunton Ho. SE17 6H 231
Staunton Rd. KT2: King T 65Na 131
SL2: Slou 3H 81
Staunton St. SE8 51Bc 114
Stave Hill Ecological Pk. 47Ac 92
Staveley NW1 3B 216
Staveley Cl. E9 36Yb 72
N7 35Nb 70
SE15 53Xb 113
Staveley Ct. E11 29Jc 53
Staveley Gdns. W4 53Ta 109
Staveley Rd. TW15: Ashf 65T 128
W4 51Sa 109
Staveley Way GU21: Knap 9J 167
Stavers Ho. E3 40Bc 72
(off Tredegar Rd.)
Staverton Rd. NW2 38Ya 68
RM11: Horn 30Md 57
Stave Yd. Rd. SE16 46Ac 92
Stavordale Lodge W14 48Bb 89
(off Melbury Rd.)
Stavordale Rd. N5 35Rb 71
SM5: Cars 73Eb 155
Stayne End GU25: Vir W 10L 125
Stayner's Rd. E1 42Zb 92
Stayton Rd. SM1: Sutt 76Cb 155
Stead Cl. BR7: Chst 64Qc 138
Steadfast Rd. KT1: King T 67Ma 131
Steadman Ct. EC1 5E 218
Steadman Ho. RM10: Dag 34Cd 76
(off Uvedale Rd.)
Stead St. SE17 6F 231 (49Tb 91)
Steam Farm La. TW14: Felt 56V 106
Stean St. E8 39Vb 71
Stebbing Ho. W11 46Za 88
(off Queensdale Cres.)
Stebbing Way IG11: Bark 40Wc 75
Stebondale St. E14 49Ec 92
Stedham Pl. WC1 2F 223
Stedman Cl. DA5: Bexl 62Gd 140
UB10: Ick 34Q 64
Steed Cl. RM11: Horn 33Kd 77
Steedman St. SE17 6D 230 (49Sb 91)
Steeds Rd. N10 25Hb 49
Steeds Way IG10: Lough 13Nc 36
Steele Av. DA9: Ghithe 57Vd 120
Steele Ct. TW11: Tedd 66La 130
Steele Ho. E15 40Gc 73
(off Eve Rd.)
Steele Rd. E11 35Gc 73
N17 27Ub 51
NW10 40Sa 67
TW7: Isle 56Ja 108
W4 48Sa 87
Steele's M. Nth. NW3 37Hb 69
Steele's M. Sth. NW3 37Hb 69
Steele's Rd. NW3 37Hb 69
Steele's Studios NW3 37Hb 69
Steele Wlk. DA8: Erith 52Dd 118
Steel's La. E1 44Yb 92
KT22: Oxs 86Da 171
Steelyard Pas. EC4 5F 225
Steen Way SE22 57Ub 113
Steep Cl. BR6: Chels 79Vc 161
Steep Hill CR0: C'don 77Ub 157
GU24: Chob 10G 146
SW16 62Mb 134
Steeplands WD23: Bush 17Da 27
Steeple Cl. SW6 54Ab 110
SW19 64Ab 132
Steeple Ct. E1 42Xb 91
TW20: Egh 64D 126
Steeple Gdns. KT15: Add 78K 149
Steeple Hgts. Dr. TN16: Big H 89Mc 179
Steeple Point SL5: Asc 9A 124
Steeplestone Cl. N18 22Sb 51
Steeple Wlk. N1 39Sb 71
(off New Nth. Rd.)
Steerforth St. SW18 61Eb 133
Steering Cl. N9 18Yb 34
Steers Mead CR4: Mitc 67Hb 133
Steers Way SE16 47Ac 92
Stelfox Ho. WC1 3J 217
Stella Cl. UB8: Hil 43R 84
Stellar Ho. N17 23Vb 51
Stella Rd. SW17 65Hb 133
Stelling Rd. DA8: Erith 52Fd 118
Stellman Cl. E5 34Wb 71
Stembridge Rd. SE20 68Xb 135
Stem Ct. KT16: Chert 74L 149
Sten Cl. EN3: Enf L 9Cc 20
Stenning Av. SS17: Linf 9K 101
Stents La. KT11: Stoke D 92Ba 191
Stepbridge Path GU21: Wok 9P 167
Stepgates KT16: Chert 73K 149
Stepgates Cl. KT16: Chert 73K 149
Stephan Cl. E8 39Wb 71
Stephen Av. RM13: Rain 37Jd 76
Stephen Cl. BR6: Orp 76Uc 160
TW20: Egh 65E 126
Stephendale Rd. SW6 55Db 111
Stephen Fox Ho. W4 50Ua 88
(off Chiswick La.)
Stephen Jewers Gdns. IG11: Bark 38Vc 75
Stephen M. W1 1D 222 (43Mb 90)
Stephen Pl. SW4 55Lb 112
Stephen Rd. DA7: Bex 55Ed 118
Stephens Cl. RM3: Rom 22Ld 57
Stephens Ct. E16 42Hc 93
SE4 55Ac 114
Stephens Lodge N12 20Eb 31
(off Woodside La.)
Stephenson Av. RM18: Tilb 3C 122
Stephenson Cl. DA16: Well 54Wc 117
E3 41Dc 92
Stephenson Ct. SL1: Slou 7K 81
(off Osborne St.)
SM2: Cheam 80Ab 154
(off Station App.)
Stephenson Dr. SL4: Wind 2F 102
Stephenson Ho. SE1 3D 230 (48Sb 91)
Stephenson Pl. RH1: Mers 100Lb 196
(off Station Rd. Nth.)
Stephenson Rd. E17 29Ac 52
TW2: Whitt 59Ca 107
W7 44Ha 86
Stephenson St. E16 42Gc 93
NW10 41Ua 88
Stephenson Way NW1 5C 216 (42Lb 90)
WD23: Bush 13Z 27
Stephenson Wharf HP3: Hem H 7P 3
Stephen's Rd. E15 39Gc 73
Stephen St. W1 1D 222 (43Mb 90)
Stephyns Chambers HP1: Hem H 3M 3
STEPNEY 43Zb 92
Stepney C'way. E1 44Zb 92
Stepney City Apartments E1 43Yb 92
Stepney Cl. CR4: Mitc 67Jb 134
Stepney Grn. E1 43Yb 92
Stepney Grn. Ct. E1 43Zb 92
(off Stepney Grn.)
Stepney High St. E1 43Zb 92
Stepney Way E1 43Xb 91
Stepping City Farm 43Zb 92
Sterling Av. EN8: Walt C 6Zb 20
HA8: Edg 21Pa 47
Sterling Cl. NW10 38Wa 68
Sterling Ct. KT16: Chert 73J 149
Sterling Gdns. SE14 51Ac 114
Sterling Ind. Est. RM10: Dag 35Dd 76
Sterling Pl. KT13: Weyb 77U 150
W5 49Na 87
Sterling Rd. DA7: Bex 56Dd 118
EN2: Enf 11Tb 33
Sterling St. SW7 3E 226 (48Gb 89)
Sterling Way N18 21Tb 51
Sternberg Cen., The 27Cb 49
Stern Cl. IG11: Bark 40Yc 75
Stern Ct. E3 41Ec 92
(off Culvert Dr.)
Sterndale Rd. DA1: Dart 59Pd 119
W14 48Za 88
Sterne St. W12 47Za 88
Sternhall La. SE15 55Wb 113
Sternhold Av. SW2 61Mb 134
Sterry Cres. RM10: Dag 36Cd 76
Sterry Dr. KT7: T Ditt 72Ga 152
KT19: Ewe 77Ua 154
Sterry Gdns. RM10: Dag 37Cd 76
Sterry Rd. IG11: Bark 39Vc 75
RM10: Dag 35Cd 76
Sterry St. SE1 2F 231 (47Tb 91)
Steucers La. SE23 60Ac 114
Stevannie Ct. DA17: Belv 50Bd 95
Steve Biko Ct. W10 42Za 88
(off St John's Ter.)
Steve Biko La. SE6 63Cc 136
Steve Biko Lodge E13 40Jc 73
(off London Rd.)
Steve Biko Rd. N7 34Qb 70
Steve Biko Way TW3: Houn 55Ca 107
Stevedale Rd. DA16: Well 54Yc 117
Stevedore St. E1 46Xb 91
Stevenage Cres. WD6: Bore 11Na 29
Stevenage Rd. E6 37Qc 74
SW6 52Za 110
Stevens Av. E9 37Yb 72
Stevens Cl. BR3: Beck 65Cc 136
DA2: Daren 64Ud 142
DA5: Bexl 63Fd 140
EN6: Pot B 5Za 16
HA5: Eastc 29Y 45
KT17: Eps 84Ua 174
TW12: Hamp 65Ba 129
Stevens Grn. WD23: B Hea 18Ea 28
Stevens La. KT10: Clay 80Ja 152
Stevenson Cl. DA8: Erith 52Kd 119
EN5: New Bar 17Fb 31
Stevenson Ct. CR4: Mitc 69Gb 133
SE6 61Hc 137
Stevenson Cres. SE16 50Wb 91
Stevenson Ho. NW8 39Eb 69
(off Boundary Rd.)
Stevenson Rd. SL2: Hedg 3H 61
Stevens Pl. CR8: Purl 85Rb 177
Stevens Rd. RM8: Dag 33Yc 75
Stevens St. SE1 3J 231 (48Ub 91)
Stevens Way IG7: Chig 21Uc 54
Steventon Rd. W12 45Va 88
Steward Cl. EN8: Chesh 2Ac 20
Steward Ho. E3 41Cc 92
(off Trevithick Way)
Stewards Cl. CM16: Epp 4Wc 23
STEWARD'S GREEN 4Xc 23
Stewards Grn. La. CM16: Epp 4Xc 23
Stewards Grn. Rd.
CM16: Epp, Fidd H 5Wc 23
Stewards Holte Wlk. N11 21Kb 50
Steward St. E1 1J 225 (43Ub 91)
Stewards Wlk. RM1: Rom 29Gd 56
Stewart KT20: Tad 93Za 194
Stewart Av. RM14: Upm 34Rd 77
SL1: Slou 3K 81
TW17: Shep 70Q 128
Stewart Cl. BR7: Chst 64Rc 138
GU21: Wok 9K 167
NW9 30Sa 47
TW12: Hamp 65Aa 129
WD5: Ab L 4V 12
Stewart Ct. CM16: Epp 3Uc 22
UB9: Den 30H 43
Stewart Ho. KT1: King T 69Pa 131
Stewart Quay UB3: Hayes 47U 84
Stewart Rainbird Ho. E12 36Qc 74
(off Parkhurst Rd.)
Stewart Rd. E15 35Fc 73
Stewartsby Cl. N18 22Sb 51
Stewart's Dr. SL2: Farn C 5F 60
Stewarts Gro. SW3 7C 226 (50Fb 89)
Stewarts Lodge WD5: Ab L 3V 12
Stewart's Pl. SW2 58Pb 112
Stewart's Rd. SW8 52Lb 112
Stewart St. E14 47Ec 92
Stew La. EC4 4D 224 (45Sb 91)
Steyne Horn La. W3 46Ra 87
Steyne Ho. W3 46Sa 87
(off Narrow St.)
Steyne Rd. W3 46Ra 87
Steyning Cl. CR8: Kenley 88Rb 177
Steyning Gro. SE9 63Pc 138
Steynings Way N12 22Cb 49
Steyning Way TW4: Houn 56Y 107
Steynton Av. DA5: Bexl 61Zc 139
Stibbington Ho. NW1 1C 216
STICKING HILL 1E 100
Stickland Rd. DA17: Belv 49Cd 96
Stickle Ho. SE8 52Dc 114
(off Creative Rd.)
Stickleton Cl. UB6: G'frd 41Da 85
Stifford Clays Rd.
RM16: N Stif, Grays, Ors 46Be 99
(not continuous)
Stifford Hill RM15: N Stif, S Ock 45Yd 98
RM16: N Stif 46Zd 99
Stifford Ho. E1 43Yb 92
(off Stepney Way)
Stifford Rd. RM15: Avel, S Ock 46Ud 98
Stilecroft Gdns. HA0: Wemb 34Ka 66
Stile Footpath RH1: Redh 6P 207
Stile Hall Gdns. W4 50Qa 87
Stile Hall Mans. W4 50Qa 87
(off Wellesley Rd.)
Stile Hall Pde. W4 50Qa 87
Stileman Ho. E3 43Bc 92
(off Ackroyd Dr.)
Stile Path TW16: Sun 69W 128
Stile Rd. SL3: L'ly 8P 81
Stiles Cl. BR2: Brom 72Pc 160
DA8: Erith 50Dd 96
Stillingfleet Rd. SW13 51Wa 110
Stillington St. SW1 5C 228 (49Lb 90)
Stillness Rd. SE23 58Ac 114
Still Wlk. SE1 7J 225
Stilton Path WD6: Bore 10Qa 15
Stilwell Cl. BR5: St P 67Xc 139
Stilwell Dr. UB8: Hil 42P 83
STILWELL RDBT. 45Q 84
Stipularis Dr. UB4: Yead 42Z 85
Stirling Av. HA5: Pinn 32Z 65
SM6: Wall 80Nb 156
TW17: Shep 69U 128
Stirling Bus. Pk. EN8: Walt C 6Bc 20
Stirling Cl. DA14: Sidc 63Uc 138
RM13: Rain 41Kd 97
SL4: Wind 4B 102
SM7: Bans 89Bb 175
SW16 67Mb 134
UB8: Cowl 41L 83
STIRLING CORNER 16Ta 29
Stirling Cnr. EN5: Ark 16Ta 29
Stirling Ct. EC1 5B 218
W13 45Ka 86
Stirling Dr. BR6: Chels 78Xc 161
CR3: Cat'm 93Sb 197
Stirling Gro. TW3: Houn 54Ea 108
Stirling Ho. RH1: Redh 6P 207
SE18 50Rc 94
WD6: Bore 14Sa 29
Stirling Retail Pk. WD6: Bore 16Ta 29
Stirling Rd. E13 40Kc 73
E17 27Ac 52
HA3: W'stone 27Ha 46
N17 25Wb 51
N22 25Rb 51
SL1: Slou 3E 80
SW9 54Nb 112
TW2: Whitt 59Ca 107
TW6: H'row A 58P 105
UB3: Hayes 45X 85
W3 48Ra 87
Stirling Rd. Path E17 27Ac 52
Stirling Wlk. KT5: Surb 72Ra 153
Stirling Way CR0: Bedd 73Nb 156
WD5: Ab L 4W 12
WD6: Bore 16Ta 29
Stites Hill Rd. CR5: Coul 92Rb 197
Stiven Cres. HA2: Harr 34Ba 65
Stoats Nest Rd. CR5: Coul 86Nb 176
Stoats Nest Village CR5: Coul 87Nb 176
Stockbeck NW1 2C 216
Stockbridge Ho. SW18 56Eb 111
(off Eltringham St.)
Stockbury Rd. CR0: C'don 72Yb 158
Stockdale Rd. RM8: Dag 33Bd 75
Stockdales Rd. SL4: Eton W 9D 80
Stockdove Way UB6: G'frd 41Ha 86
Stocker Gdns. RM9: Dag 38Yc 75
Stockers Farm Rd. WD3: Rick 20M 25
Stocker's Lake (Nature Reserve) 20K 25
Stockers La. GU22: Wok 92B 188
(not continuous)
Stockfield Rd. KT10: Clay 78Ga 152
SW16 62Pb 134
Stockford Av. NW7 24Za 48
Stockham's Cl. CR2: Sande 82Tb 177
Stock Hill TN16: Big H 88Mc 179
Stockholm Apartments NW1 38Jb 70
(off Chalk Farm Rd.)
Stockholm Ho. E1 45Wb 91
(off Swedenborg Gdns.)
Stockholm Rd. SE16 50Yb 92
Stockholm Way E1 46Wb 91
Stockhurst Cl. SW15 54Ya 110
Stockingswater La. EN3: Brim 12Bc 34
Stockland Rd. RM7: Rom 30Fd 56
Stock La. DA2: Wilm 62Ld 141
Stockleigh Hall NW8 1E 214
Stockley Cl. UB7: W Dray 47R 84
Stockley Country Pk. 45Q 84
Stockley Farm Rd. UB7: W Dray 48R 84
STOCKLEY PARK 46R 84
Stockley Pk. Golf Course 45S 84
Stockley Rd. UB7: W Dray 49R 84
UB8: Hil 44Q 84
UB11: Stock P 44Q 84
Stock Orchard Cres. N7 36Pb 70
Stock Orchard St. N7 36Pb 70
Stockport Rd. SW16 67Mb 134
WD3: Herons 17E 24
Stocksfield Rd. E17 27Ec 52
Stocks Mdw. HP2: Hem H 1A 4
Stocks Pl. E14 45Bc 92
UB10: Hil 39Q 64
Stock St. E13 40Jc 73
Stockton Cl. EN5: New Bar 14Eb 31
Stockton Ct. SW1 4D 228
Stockton Gdns. N17 24Sb 51
NW7 20Ua 30
Stockton Ho. E2 41Xb 91
(off Ellsworth St.)
HA2: Harr 32Ca 65
Stockton Rd. N17 24Sb 51
N18 23Wb 51
RH2: Reig 9J 207
STOCKWELL 54Pb 112
Stockwell Av. SW9 55Pb 112
Stockwell Cl. BR1: Brom 68Kc 137
HA8: Edg 26Sa 47
Stockwell Gdns. SW9 53Pb 112
Stockwell Gdns. Est. SW9 54Nb 112
Stockwell Grn. SW9 54Pb 112
Stockwell Grn. Ct. SW9 54Pb 112
Stockwell La. EN7: Chesh 1Xb 19
(not continuous)
SW9 54Pb 112
Stockwell M. SW9 54Pb 112
Stockwell Pk. Cres. SW9 54Pb 112
Stockwell Pk. Est. SW9 54Pb 112
Stockwell Pk. Rd. SW9 53Pb 112
Stockwell Pk. Wlk. SW9 55Qb 112
Stockwell Rd. SW9 54Pb 112
Stockwell St. SE10 51Ec 114
Stockwell Ter. SW9 53Pb 112
Stodart Rd. SE20 67Yb 136
Stoddart Ho. SW8 51Pb 112
Stodmarsh Ho. SW9 53Qb 112
(off Cowley Rd.)
Stofield Gdns. SE9 62Mc 137
Stoford Cl. SW19 59Ab 110
Stoke Av. IG6: Ilf 23Wc 55
Stoke Cl. KT11: Stoke D 88Ba 171
STOKE COMMON 5L 61
Stoke Comn. Rd. SL3: Ful 5L 61
Stoke Cotts. KT22: Fet 93Fa 192
Stoke Ct. Dr. SL2: Stoke P 9J 61
STOKE D'ABERNON 89Aa 171
Stoke Gdns. SL1: Slou 6J 81
STOKE GREEN 2L 81
Stoke Grn. SL2: Stoke P 2L 81
Stokenchurch St. SW6 53Db 111
STOKE NEWINGTON 34Vb 71
Stoke Newington Chu. St. N16 34Tb 71
Stoke Newington Comn. N16 34Vb 71
Stoke Newington High St. N16 34Vb 71
Stoke Newington Rd. N16 36Vb 71
Stoke Pk.
Stoke Poges 8J 61
Stoke Pk. Av. SL2: Farn R 1G 80
Stoke Pl. NW10 41Va 88
STOKE POGES 8L 61
Stoke Poges Golf Course 1H 81
Stoke Poges La. SL1: Slou 6J 81
SL2: Slou, Stoke P 4J 81
Stoke Rd. KT2: King T 66Sa 131
KT11: Cobh, Stoke D 87Y 171
KT12: Walt T 76Y 151
RM13: Rain 40Md 77
SL2: Slou, Stoke P 6K 81
Stokesay SL2: Slou 5K 81
Stokesay Ct. DA2: Dart 58Rd 119
(off Osbourne Rd.)
Stokesby Rd. KT9: Chess 79Pa 153
Stokes Cotts. IG6: Ilf 25Sc 54
Stokes Ct. N2 28Gb 49
Stokes Field (Local Nature Reserve)
75Ka 152
Stokesheath Rd. KT22: Oxs 83Ea 172
Stokesley St. W12 44Va 88
Stokes M. TW11: Tedd 64Ja 130
Stokes Ridings KT20: Tad 95Za 194
Stokes Rd. CR0: C'don 72Zb 158
E6 42Nc 94
Stoke Vw. SL1: Slou 6K 81
Stoke Wood SL2: Stoke P 5K 61
Stokley Ct. N8 28Nb 50
Stoll Cl. NW2 34Ya 68
Stompond La. KT12: Walt T 75W 150
Stomp Rd. SL1: Burn 3A 80
Stoms Path SE6 64Cc 136
(off Maroons Way)
Stonard Rd. N13 20Qb 32
RM8: Dag 36Xc 75
Stonards Hill CM16: Coop, Epp 1Wc 23
IG10: Lough 16Pc 36
Stondon Pk. SE23 58Ac 114
Stondon Wlk. E6 40Mc 73
STONE 57Ud 120
Stonebanks KT12: Walt T 73W 150
STONEBRIDGE 39Ta 67
Stonebridge Cen. N15 29Vb 51
Stonebridge Fld. SL4: Eton 10F 80
Stonebridge M. SE19 66Tb 135
Stonebridge Pk. NW10 38Ta 67
Stonebridge Road 57Ce 121
Stonebridge Rd. DA11: Nflt 57Ce 121
N15 29Vb 51
Stonebridge Way HA9: Wemb 37Ra 67
Stone Bldgs. WC2 1J 223
Stone Castle Dr. DA9: Ghithe 58Wd 120
Stonechat M. DA9: Ghithe 58Wd 120
SW15 56Wa 110
Stonechat Sq. E6 43Nc 94
Stone Cl. RM8: Dag 33Bd 75
SW4 54Lb 112
UB7: Yiew 46P 83
Stonecot Cl. SM3: Sutt 74Ab 154
Stonecot Hill SM3: Sutt 74Ab 154
Stone Ct. CR3: Cat'm 97Ub 197
DA8: Erith 50Hd 96
TN15: Bor G 91Ce 205
Stone Cres. TW14: Felt 59V 106
Stonecroft Av. SL0: Iver 44G 82
Stonecroft Cl. EN5: Ark 14Xa 30
Stonecroft Rd. DA8: Erith 52Ed 118
Stonecroft Way CR0: C'don 73Nb 156

Stonecrop Cl.—Stychens La.

Stonecrop Cl. NW9 27Ta 47
Stonecross AL1: St A 1C 6
Stonecross Cl. AL1: St A 1C 6
Stonecutter St. EC4 2B 224 (44Rb 91)
Stonefield N4 33Pb 70
Stonefield Cl. DA7: Bex 55Cd 118
HA4: Ruis 36Aa 65
Stonefield Mans. N1 39Qb 70
(off Cloudesley St.)
Stonefield St. N1 39Qb 70
Stonefield Way HA4: Ruis 35Aa 65
SE7 52Mc 115
Stonegate Cl. BR5: St P 69Yc 139
Stone Ga. Ct. TW18: Staines 63J 127
STONEGROVE 21Pa 47
Stonegrove HA8: Edg 21Na 47
Stone Gro. Ct. HA8: Edg 22Pa 47
Stonegrove Gdns. HA8: Edg 22Na 47
Stone Hall W8 48Db 89
(off Stone Hall Gdns.)
Stonehall Av. IG1: Ilf 30Nc 54
Stone Hall Gdns. W8 48Db 89
Stone Hall Pl. W8 48Db 89
Stone Hall Rd. N21 17Pb 32
Stoneham Rd. N11 22Lb 50
SS17: Stan H 3K 101
STONEHILL 79A 148
Stonehill Bus. Pk. N18 23Ac 52
Stonehill Cl. KT23: Bookh 97Ca 191
SW14 57Ta 109
Stonehill Ct. E4 17Dc 34
Stonehill Cres. KT16: Ott 79A 148
Stonehill Ga. SL5: S'hill 2B 146
STONEHILL GREEN 66Ed 140
Stonehill Rd. GU24: Chob 2N 167
KT16: Ott 10N 147
SW14 57Sa 109
W4 50Qa 87
Stonehills Ct. SE21 62Ub 135
Stonehill Woods Pk. DA14: Sidc 65Dd 140
Stonehorse Rd. EN3: Pond E 15Yb 34
Stonehouse NW1 1C 216
Stone Ho. Fld. TN15: Plat 92De 205
Stone Ho. Gdns. CR3: Cat'm 97Ub 197
Stonehouse Ho. W2 43Cb 89
(off Westbourne Pk. Rd.)
Stone Ho. La. DA2: Dart 58Sd 120
Stonehouse La. RM19: Purf 50Ud 98
TN14: Hals 81Zc 181
Stonehouse Rd. TN14: Hals 82Yc 181
Stoneings La. TN14: Knock 90Vc 181
Stone Lake Ind. Pk. SE7 49Lc 93
Stone Lake Retail Pk. SE7 49Lc 93
Stonelea Rd. HP3: Hem H 4P 3
STONELEIGH 78Wa 154
Stoneleigh Av. EN1: Enf 10Xb 19
KT4: Wor Pk 77Wa 154
Stoneleigh B'way. KT17: Ewe 78Wa 154
Stoneleigh Cl. EN8: Walt C 5Zb 20
Stoneleigh Ct. IG5: Ilf 27Nc 54
KT11: Stoke D 89Aa 171
Stoneleigh Cres. KT19: Ewe 78Ua 154
Stoneleigh M. E3 40Ac 72
Stoneleigh Pk. KT13: Weyb 78S 150
Stoneleigh Pk. Av. CR0: C'don 72Zb 158
Stoneleigh Pk. Rd. KT4: Wor Pk 79Va 154
KT19: Ewe 79Va 154
Stoneleigh Pl. W11 45Za 88
Stoneleigh Rd. BR1: Brom 69Rc 138
IG5: Ilf 27Nc 54
N17 27Vb 51
RH8: Limp 2P 211
SM5: Cars 73Gb 155
Stoneleigh St. W11 45Za 88
Stoneleigh Ter. N19 33Kb 70
Stonell's Rd. SW11 58Hb 111
Stonely Cres. DA9: Ghithe 56Yd 120
Stonemason Ct. SE1 2D 230
Stonemason Ho. SE14 53Zb 114
(off Fishers Ct.)
Stonemasons Cl. N15 28Tb 51
Stonemasons Yd. SW18 59Fb 111
Stoneness Rd. RM20: W Thur 51Xd 120
Stonenest St. N4 32Pb 70
Stone Pk. Av. BR3: Beck 70Cc 136
Stone Pl. KT4: Wor Pk 75Wa 154
Stone Pl. Rd. DA9: Ghithe 57Ud 120
Stone Rd. BR2: Brom 71Hc 159
Stones All. WD18: Wat 14X 27
Stones Av. DA1: Dart 54Pd 119
Stones Cross Rd. BR8: Crock 71Ed 162
Stones End St. SE1 2D 230 (47Sb 91)
Stone's Rd. KT17: Eps 84Ua 174
STONE STREET 97Vd 204
Stone St. DA11: Grav'nd 9D 122
Stone St. Rd. TN15: Ivy H, Seal 95Sd 204
Stoneswood Rd. RH8: Limp 2M 211
Stonewall E6 43Qc 94
Stonewell Rd. TW19: Stanw 60N 105
Stonewold Ct. W5 44Ma 87
STONEWOOD 62Zd 143
Stonewood DA2: Bean 62Yd 142
Stonewood Rd. DA8: Erith 50Gd 96
Stoney All. SE18 54Qc 116
Stoneyard La. E14 45Dc 92
Stoney Bri. Dr. EN9: Walt A 6Jc 21
Stoney Cft. CR5: Coul 94Lb 196
Stoneycroft HP1: Hem H 2J 3
Stoneycroft Cl. SE12 59Hc 115
Stoneycroft Rd. IG8: Wfd G 23Nc 54
Stoneydeep TW11: Tedd 63Ja 130
Stoneydown E17 28Ac 52
Stoneydown Av. E17 28Ac 52
Stoneydown Ho. E17 28Ac 52
(off Stoneydown)
Stoneyfield SL9: Ger X 2N 61
Stoneyfield Rd. CR5: Coul 89Pb 176
Stoneyfields Gdns. HA8: Edg 21Ta 47
Stoneyfields La. HA8: Edg 22Sa 47
Stoneylands Ct. TW20: Egh 64B 126
Stoneylands Rd. TW20: Egh 64B 126
Stoney La. E1 2J 225 (44Vb 91)
HP1: Hem H 5C 2
HP3: Bov 9D 2
SE19 65Vb 135
SL2: Farn R 9E 60
WD4: Chfd 2G 10
Stoney Meade SL1: Slou 6F 80
Stoney St. SE1 6F 225 (46Tb 91)
Stonhouse St. SW4 56Mb 112
Stonny Cft. KT21: Asht 89Pa 173
Stonor Rd. W14 49Bb 89
Stony Cnr. DA13: Meop 10A 144
Stonycroft Cl. EN3: Enf H 12Ac 34
Stony Hill KT10: Esh 80Ba 151
Stony La. HP6: L Chal 10A 10
Stony Path IG10: Lough 11Pc 36
Stonyshotts EN9: Walt A 6Gc 21
Stoop Ct. KT14: W Byf 84K 169
Stopes St. SE15 52Vb 113
Stopford Rd. E13 39Jc 73
SE17 7C 230 (50Rb 91)
Stopher Ho. SE1 2C 230
Storas Ct. RM19: Purf 50Rd 97
(off Linnet Way)
Storehouse M. E14 45Cc 92
Storer Dr. DA16: Well 55Xc 117
Store Rd. E16 47Qc 94
Storers Quay E14 49Fc 93
Store St. E15 36Fc 73
WC1 1D 222 (43Mb 90)
Storey Cl. UB10: Ick 34S 64
Storey Ct. NW8 4B 214
WD23: Bush 15Da 27
Storey Ho. E14 45Dc 92
(off Cottage St.)
Storey Rd. E17 28Bc 52
N6 30Hb 49
Storey's Ga. SW1 2E 228 (47Mb 90)
Storey St. E16 46Qc 94
HP3: Hem H 6M 3
Stories M. SE5 54Ub 113
Stories Rd. SE5 55Ub 113
Stork Rd. E7 37Hc 73
Storksmead Rd. HA8: Edg 24Ua 48
Stork's Rd. SE16 48Wb 91
Stormont Lawn Tennis & Squash Club 29Hb 49
Stormont Rd. N6 31Hb 69
SW11 55Jb 112
Stormont Way KT9: Chess 78La 152
Stormount Dr. UB3: Harl 47S 84
Stornaway Rd. SL3: L'ly 49E 82
Stornaway Strand DA12: Grav'nd 2H 145
Stornoway HP3: Hem H 4B 4
Storr Gdns. CM13: Hut 15Fe 41
Storrington WC1 4G 217
Storrington Rd. CR0: C'don 74Vb 157
Storr's La. GU3: Worp 6G 186
Storth Oaks Mead BR7: Chst 64Pc 138
Story St. N1 38Pb 70
Stothard Ho. E1 42Yb 92
(off Amiel St.)
Stothard Pl. E1 7J 219 (43Ub 91)
Stothard St. E1 42Yb 92
Stott Cl. SW18 58Fb 111
Stoughton Av. SM3: Cheam 78Ab 155
Stoughton Cl. SE11 6J 229 (49Pb 90)
SW15 60Wa 110
Stour Av. UB2: S'hall 48Ca 85
Stourcliffe Cl. W1 2F 221 (44Hb 89)
Stourcliffe St. W1 3F 221 (44Hb 89)
Stour Cl. BR2: Kes 77Lc 159
SL1: Slou 8F 80
Stourhead Cl. SW19 59Za 110
Stourhead Gdns. SW20 69Wa 132
Stourhead Ho. SW1 7D 228
Stour Rd. DA1: Cray 55Jd 118
E3 38Cc 72
RM10: Dag 33Cd 76
RM16: Grays 10C 100
Stourton Av. TW13: Hanw 63Ba 129
Stour Way RM14: Upm 30Ud 58
Stovell Rd. SL4: Wind 2F 102
Stowage SE8 51Cc 114
Stow Ct. DA2: Dart 59Sd 120
Stow Cres. E17 24Ac 52
Stowe Cres. HA4: Ruis 30R 44
Stowe Gdns. N9 18Vb 33
Stowe Ho. NW11 30Eb 49
Stowell Av. CR0: New Ad 82Fc 179
Stowell Ho. N8 28Nb 50
(off Pembroke Rd.)
Stowe Pl. N15 27Ub 51
Stowe Rd. BR6: Chels 77Xc 161
SL1: Slou 5C 80
W12 47Xa 88
Stowting Rd. BR6: Orp 77Uc 160
Stox Mead HA3: Hrw W 25Fa 46
Stracey Rd. E7 35Jc 73
NW10 39Ta 67
Strachan Pl. SW19 65Ya 132
Stradbroke Dr. IG7: Chig 23Qc 54
Stradbroke Gro. IG5: Ilf 27Nc 54
IG9: Buck H 18Mc 35
Stradbroke Pk. IG7: Chig 23Rc 54
Stradbroke Rd. N5 35Sb 71
Stradbrook Cl. HA2: Harr 34Ba 65
Stradella Rd. SE24 58Sb 113
Strafford Av. IG5: Ilf 26Qc 54
Strafford Cl. EN6: Pot B 4Cb 17
Strafford Ga. EN6: Pot B 4Cb 17
Strafford Ho. SE8 50Bc 92
(off Grove St.)
Strafford Rd. EN5: Barn 13Ab 30
TW1: Twick 59Ja 108
TW3: Houn 55Ba 107
W3 47Sa 87
Strafford St. E14 47Cc 92
Strahan Rd. E3 41Ac 92
Straight, The UB1: S'hall 47Z 85
Straight Mile Pl. KT18: Tatt C 90Ya 174
Straight Rd. RM3: Rom 22Kd 57
SL4: Old Win 7L 103
Straightsmouth SE10 52Ec 114
Strait Rd. E6 45Nc 94
Strakers Rd. SE15 56Xb 113
Strale Ho. N1 1H 219
Strand WC2 6F 223 (45Nb 90)
Strandburgh Pl. HP3: Hem H 4B 4
Strand Cl. KT18: Eps D 91Ta 193
Strand Ct. SE18 50Vc 95
Strand Dr. TW9: Kew 52Ra 109
Strandfield Cl. SE18 50Uc 94
Strand Ho. BR2: Brom 72Mc 159
(off Wells Vw. Dr.)
SE28 46Tc 94
Strand La. WC2 4J 223 (45Pb 90)
STRAND ON THE GREEN 51Qa 109
Strand on the Grn. W4 51Qa 109
Strand Pl. N18 21Ub 51
Strand School App. W4 51Qa 109
Strangeways WD17: Wat 8U 12
Strang Ho. N1 39Sb 71
Strangways Ter. W14 48Bb 89
Stranraer Gdns. SL1: Slou 6J 81
Stranraer Way N1 38Nb 70
TW6: H'row A 58N 105
Strasburg Rd. SW11 53Jb 112
Strata SE1 5D 230
Strata Ct. KT12: Walt T 74V 150
Stratfield Pk. Cl. N21 17Rb 33
Stratfield Rd. SL1: Slou 7L 81
WD6: Bore 13Qa 29
STRATFORD 38Fc 73
Stratford Av. UB10: Hil 40P 63
Stratford Cen., The E15 38Fc 73
Stratford Circus (Performing Arts Cen.) 37Fc 73
Stratford Cl. IG11: Bark 38Wc 75
RM10: Dag 38Ed 76
SL2: Slou 2B 80
Stratford Ct. KT3: N Mald 70Ta 131
WD17: Wat 11X 27
Stratford Eye E15 37Fc 73
Stratford Gdns.
SS17: Stan H 1M 101
Stratford Gro. SW15 56Za 110
Stratford Ho. RM3: Rom 23Md 57
(off Dartfields)
Stratford Ho. Av. BR1: Brom 69Nc 138
STRATFORD NEW TOWN 37Fc 73
Stratford Office Village, The E15 38Gc 73
(off Romford Rd.)
Stratford One E20 37Dc 72
Stratford Picture House
London 37Fc 73
Stratford Pl. E20 37Ec 72
(within Westfield Stratford City Shop. Cen.)
W1 3K 221 (44Kb 90)
Stratford Rd. CR7: Thor H 70Qb 134
E13 39Hc 73
(not continuous)
NW4 28Za 48
TW6: H'row A 58R 106
UB2: S'hall 49Aa 85
UB4: Yead 42X 85
W8 48Cb 89
WD17: Wat 12W 26
Stratford Studios W8 48Cb 89
Stratford Theatre Royal 38Fc 73
Stratford Vs. NW1 38Lb 70
Stratford Way AL2: Brick W 1Ba 13
HP3: Hem H 5K 3
WD17: Wat 12V 26
Stratford Workshops E15 39Fc 73
(off Burford Rd.)
Stratham Ct. N19 34Nb 70
(off Alexander Rd.)
Strathan Cl. SW18 58Ab 110
Strathaven Rd. SE12 58Kc 115
Strathblaine Rd. SW11 57Fb 111
Strathbrook Rd. SW16 66Pb 134
Strathcona Av. KT23: Bookh 100Aa 191
Strathcona Gdns. GU21: Knap 10H 167
(not continuous)
Strathcona Rd. HA9: Wemb 33Ma 67
Strathdale SW16 64Pb 134
Strathdon Dr. SW17 62Fb 133
Strathearn Av. TW2: Whitt 60Da 107
UB3: Harl 52V 106
Strathearn Ho. W2 4D 220
Strathearn Pl. W2 4D 220 (44Gb 89)
Strathearn Rd. SM1: Sutt 78Cb 155
SW19 64Cb 133
Stratheden Pde. SE3 52Jc 115
Stratheden Rd. SE3 53Jc 115
Strathfield Gdns. IG11: Bark 37Tc 74
Strathleven Rd. SW2 57Nb 112
Strathmore RM18: E Til 9L 101
Strathmore Cl. CR3: Cat'm 93Ub 197
Strathmore Ct. NW8 3D 214
Strathmore Gdns. HA8: Edg 26Ra 47
N3 25Db 49
RM12: Horn 32Hd 76
W8 46Cb 89
Strathmore Rd. CR0: C'don 73Tb 157
SW19 62Cb 133
TW11: Tedd 63Ga 130
Strathnairn St. SE1 49Wb 91
(not continuous)
Strathray Gdns. NW3 37Gb 69
Strath Ter. SW11 56Gb 111
Strathville Rd. SW18 61Cb 133
(not continuous)
Strathyre Av. SW16 69Qb 134
Stratosphere Twr. E15 38Fc 73
(off Gt. Eastern Rd.)
STRATTON 4A 210
Stratton Av. EN2: Enf 9Tb 19
SM6: Wall 81Mb 176
Stratton Cl. DA7: Bex 55Ad 117
HA8: Edg 23Pa 47
KT12: Walt T 74Y 151
SW19 68Cb 133
TW3: Houn 53Ca 107
Stratton Ct. HA5: Hat E 24Ba 45
(off Devonshire Rd.)
N1 38Ub 71
(off Hertford Rd.)
Strattondale St. E14 48Ec 92
Stratton Dr. IG11: Bark 36Uc 74
Stratton Gdns. UB1: S'hall 44Ba 85
Stratton Rd. DA7: Bex 55Ad 117
RM3: Rom 22Qd 57
SW19 68Cb 133
TW16: Sun 68V 128
Stratton St. W1 6A 222 (46Kb 90)
Stratton Ter. TN16: Westrm 99Sc 200
Stratton Wlk. RM3: Rom 22Qd 57
Strauss Rd. W4 47Ta 87
Strawberry Cl. GU24: Brkwd 3B 186
Strawberry Cres. AL2: Lon C 8F 6
Strawberry Fld. AL10: Hat 3C 8
Strawberry Flds. BR6: Farnb 78Rc 160
BR8: Swan 67Gd 140
GU24: Bisl 7E 166
KT15: Add 80H 149
STRAWBERRY HILL 62Ha 130
Strawberry Hill 62Ha 130
Strawberry Hill KT9: Chess 79Ma 153
TW1: Twick 62Ha 130
Strawberry Hill Cl. TW1: Twick 62Ha 130
Strawberry Hill Golf Course 62Ga 130
Strawberry Hill Rd. TW1: Twick 62Ha 130
Strawberry La. SM5: Cars 76Jb 156
Strawberry M. HP2: Hem H 2D 4
Strawberry Ri. GU24: Bisl 7E 166
Strawberry Ter. N10 25Hb 49
Strawberry Va. N2 25Fb 49
TW1: Twick 62Ja 130
(not continuous)
Straw Cl. CR3: Cat'm 95Sb 197
Strayfield Rd. EN2: Enf 8Qb 18
Streakes Fld. Rd. NW2 33Wa 68
Stream Cl. KT14: Byfl 84M 169
Streamdale SE2 51Xc 117
Stream La. HA8: Edg 22Ra 47
Streamline Ct. SE22 60Wb 113
(off Streamline M.)
Streamline M. SE22 60Wb 113
Streamside SL1: Slou 6D 80
Streamside Cl. BR2: Brom 70Jc 137
N9 18Vb 33
Streamway DA17: Belv 51Cd 118
Streatfeild Av. E6 39Pc 74
Streatfield Rd. HA3: Kenton 27La 46
STREATHAM 62Nb 134
Streatham Cl. SW16 61Nb 134
STREATHAM COMMON 65Mb 134
Streatham Comn. Nth. SW16 64Nb 134
Streatham Comn. Sth. SW16 65Nb 134
Streatham Ct. SW16 62Nb 134
Streatham High Rd. SW16 63Nb 134
STREATHAM HILL 61Nb 134
Streatham Hill SW2 61Nb 134
Streatham Hub 64Mb 134
STREATHAM PARK 64Lb 134
Streatham Pl. SW2 59Nb 112
Streatham Rd. CR4: Mitc 67Jb 134
SW16 67Jb 134
Streatham St. WC1 2F 223 (44Nb 90)
STREATHAM VALE 66Lb 134
Streatham Va. SW16 67Lb 134
Streathbourne Rd. SW17 61Jb 134
Streatley Pl. NW3 35Eb 69
Streatley Rd. NW6 38Bb 69
Street, The DA4: Hort K 70Rd 141
DA12: Cobh 9H 145
DA12: Shorne 4N 145
E20 37Ec 72
(within Westfield Stratford City Shop. Cen.)
GU4: W Cla 100J 189
KT21: Asht 91Na 193
KT22: Fet 94Fa 192
KT24: Eff 99Z 191
KT24: W Hor 100R 190
RH3: Bet 7A 206
TN15: Ash 78Zd 165
TN15: Igh 93Zd 205
TN15: Plax 99Ae 205
WD4: Chfd 3J 11
Streeters La. SM6: Bedd 76Mb 156
Streetfield M. SE3 55Jc 115
Streets Heath GU24: W End 4D 166
Streimer Rd. E15 40Ec 72
Strelley Way W3 45Ua 88
Stretton Mans. SE8 50Cc 92
Stretton Rd. CR0: C'don 73Ub 157
TW10: Ham 61La 130
Stretton Way WD6: Bore 10Na 15
Strickland Av. DA1: Dart 55Pd 119
(not continuous)
Strickland Ct. SE15 55Wb 113
Strickland Ho. E2 4K 219
Strickland Row SW18 59Fb 111
Strickland St. SE8 54Cc 114
Strickland Way BR6: Orp 77Vc 161
Stride Rd. E13 40Hc 73
Strides Ct. KT16: Ott 79E 148
(off Brox Rd.)
Strimon Cl. N9 19Yb 34
Stringer Ho. N1 1J 219
Stringer's Av. GU4: Jac W 10P 187
STRINGERS COMMON 10N 187
Stringers Cotts. SL9: Chal P 25A 42
(off The Vale)
Stringhams Copse GU23: Rip 96H 189
Stripling Way WD18: Wat 16W 26
Strode Cl. N10 24Jb 50
Strode Rd. E7 35Jc 73
N17 26Ub 51
NW10 37Wa 68
SW6 52Ab 110
Strode's Coll. La. TW20: Egh 64B 126
Strode's Cres. TW18: Staines 64L 127
Strode St. TW20: Egh 63C 126
Stroma Cl. HP3: Hem H 4C 4
Stroma Ct. SL1: Slou 5B 80
Strome Ho. NW6 40Db 69
(off Carlton Vale)
Strone Rd. E7 37Lc 73
E12 37Lc 73
Strone Way UB4: Yead 42Aa 85
Strongbow Cres. SE9 57Pc 116
Strongbow Rd. SE9 57Pc 116
Strongbridge Cl. HA2: Harr 32Ca 65
Stronsa Rd. W12 47Va 88
Stronsay Cl. HP3: Hem H 4C 4
Strood Av. RM7: Rush G 32Fd 76
Strood Ho. SE1 2G 231
Strood La. SL4: Wink 5A 124
Stroud Cl. SL4: Wind 5B 102
Stroud Cres. SW15 62Wa 132
STROUDE 68B 126
Stroude Rd. GU25: Vir W 71A 148
TW20: Egh 65C 126
Stroudes Cl. KT4: Wor Pk 73Ua 154
Stroud Fld. UB5: N'olt 37Aa 65
Stroud Ga. HA2: Harr 35Da 65
STROUD GREEN 31Pb 70
Stroud Grn. Gdns. CR0: C'don 73Yb 158
Stroud Grn. Rd. N4 32Pb 70
Stroud Grn. Way CR0: C'don 73Xb 157
Stroud Ho. RM3: Rom 22Md 57
(off Montgomery Cres.)
Stroudley Ho. SW8 53Lb 112
Stroudley Wlk. E3 41Dc 92
Stroud Rd. SE25 72Wb 157
SW19 62Cb 133
Stroud's Cl. RM6: Chad H 29Xc 55
Stroudwater Pk. KT13: Weyb 79R 150
Stroud Way TW15: Ashf 65R 128
Stroud Wood Bus. Cen. AL2: F'mre 9C 6
Strouts Pl. E2 3K 219 (41Vb 91)
Struan Gdns. GU21: Wok 87A 168
Strudwick Ct. SW4 53Nb 112
(off Binfield Rd.)
Strutton Ct. SW1 4D 228
Strutton Ground SW1 3D 228 (48Mb 90)
Struttons Av. DA11: Nflt 1B 144
Strype St. E1 1K 225 (43Vb 91)
Stuart Av. BR2: Hayes 74Jc 159
HA2: Harr 34Ba 65
KT12: Walt T 74X 151
NW9 31Wa 68
W5 47Pa 87
Stuart Cl. BR8: Hext 66Hd 140
CM15: Pil H 15Xd 40
SL4: Wind 4D 102
UB10: Hil 37Q 64
Stuart Ct. CR0: C'don 76Rb 157
(off St John's Rd.)
RH1: Redh 5A 208
(off St Anne's Ri.)
WD6: E'tree 16Ma 29
Stuart Cres. CR0: C'don 76Bc 158
N22 25Pb 50
RH2: Reig 9J 207
UB3: Hayes 44S 84
Stuart Evans Cl. DA16: Well 55Yc 117
Stuart Gro. TW11: Tedd 64Ga 130
Stuart Ho. E9 37Zb 72
(off Queen Anne Rd.)
E16 46Kc 93
(off Beaulieu Av.)
W14 49Ab 88
(off Windsor Way)
Stuart Lodge KT18: Eps 85Ta 173
(off Ashley Rd.)
Stuart Mantle Way DA8: Erith 52Fd 118
(not continuous)
Stuart Mill Ho. N1 2H 217
Stuart Pl. CR4: Mitc 67Hb 133
Stuart Rd. CR6: W'ham 92Xb 197
CR7: Thor H 70Sb 135
DA11: Grav'nd 8C 122
DA16: Well 53Xc 117
EN4: E Barn 17Gb 31
HA3: W'stone 27Ha 46
IG11: Bark 38Vc 75
NW6 41Cb 89
RH2: Reig 9J 207
RM17: Grays 50De 99
SE15 56Yb 114
SW19 62Cb 133
TW10: Ham 61Ka 130
W3 46Sa 87
Stuarts RM11: Horn 32Pd 77
(off High St.)
Stuarts Cl. HP3: Hem H 4M 3
Stuart Twr. W9 4A 214
Stuart Way EN7: Chesh 3Xb 19
GU25: Vir W 10L 125
SL4: Wind 4C 102
TW18: Staines 65K 127
Stubbers Adventure Cen. 37Ud 78
Stubbers La. RM14: Upm 37Td 78
Stubbings Hall La. EN9: Walt A 1Ec 20
Stubbs Cl. NW9 29Sa 47
Stubbs Ct. W4 50Ra 87
(off Chaseley Dr.)
Stubbs Dr. SE16 50Xb 91
Stubbs Hill BR6: Prat B 85Yc 181
Stubbs Ho. E2 41Zb 92
(off Bonner St.)
SW1 6E 228
Stubbs La. KT20: Lwr K 100Bb 195
Stubbs M. RM8: Dag 35Xc 75
(off Marlborough Rd.)
Stubbs Point E13 42Jc 93
Stubbs Way SW19 67Fb 133
Stucley Pl. NW1 38Kb 70
Stucley Rd. TW5: Hest 52Ea 108
Studdridge St. SW6 54Cb 111
Studd St. N1 39Rb 71
Stud Grn. WD25: Wat 4W 12
Studholme Ct. NW3 35Cb 69
Studholme St. SE15 52Xb 113
Studio Ct. N15 28Ub 51
Studio La. W5 46Ma 87
Studio M. NW4 28Ya 48
Studio Pl. SW1 2G 227
Studio Plaza KT12: Walt T 74W 150
Studios, The DA3: Nw A G 75Be 165
(off The Row)
SW4 56Lb 112
(off Crescent La.)
W8 46Cb 89
(off Edge St.)
WD17: Wat 13X 27
(off The Parade)
WD23: Bush 16Ca 27
Studios Rd. TW17: Shep 69P 127
Studio Theatre
Carshalton 77Jb 156
Studio Theatre, The DA12: Grav'nd 9D 122
(off Woodville Pl.)
Studio Tour Dr. WD25: Wat 6U 12
Studio Way WD6: Bore 12Sa 29
Studland SE17 7F 231
Studland Cl. DA15: Sidc 62Vc 139
Studland Ho. E14 44Ac 92
(off Aston St.)
Studland Rd. KT2: King T 65Na 131
KT14: Byfl 85P 169
SE26 64Zb 136
W7 44Fa 86
Studland St. W6 49Xa 88
Studley Av. E4 24Fc 53
Studley Cl. E5 36Ac 72
Studley Ct. DA14: Sidc 64Xc 139
E14 45Fc 93
(off Jamestown Way)
Studley Cres. DA3: Lfield 68Ee 143
Studley Dr. IG4: Ilf 30Mc 53
Studley Est. SW4 53Nb 112
Studley Grange Rd. W7 47Ga 86
Studley Rd. E7 37Kc 73
RM9: Dag 38Zc 75
SW4 53Nb 112
Stukeley Rd. E7 38Kc 73
Stukeley St. WC2 2G 223 (44Nb 90)
Stumble Hill TN11: S'brne 100Yd 204
Stumps Hill La. BR3: Beck 65Cc 136
Stumps La. CR3: Whyt 89Vb 177
(not continuous)
Stunell Ho. SE14 51Zb 114
(off John Williams Cl.)
Sturdee Ho. E2 40Wb 71
(off Horatio St.)
Sturdy Ho. E3 40Ac 72
(off Gernon Rd.)
Sturdy Rd. SE15 54Xb 113
Sturge Av. E17 26Dc 52
Sturgeon Rd. SE17 7D 230 (50Sb 91)
Sturges Fld. BR7: Chst 65Tc 138
Sturgess Av. NW4 31Xa 68
Sturge St. SE1 1D 230 (47Sb 91)
Sturlas Way EN8: Walt C 5Zb 20
Sturmer Cl. AL4: St A 3G 6
Sturmer Way N7 36Pb 70
Sturminster NW1 38Mb 70
(off Agar Gro.)
Sturminster Cl. UB4: Yead 44Y 85
Sturminster Ho. SW8 52Pb 112
(off Dorset Rd.)
Sturrock Cl. N15 28Tb 51
Sturry St. E14 44Dc 92
Sturts Apartments N1 39Tb 71
(off Branch Pl.)
Sturt's La. KT20: Walt H 99Va 194
Sturt St. N1 2E 218 (40Sb 71)
Stutfield St. E1 44Wb 91
Stuttle Ho. E1 42Wb 91
(off Buxton St.)
STYANTS BOTTOM 94Vd 204
Styants Bottom Rd. TN15: Seal 93Vd 204
Stychens Cl. RH1: Blet 5J 209
Stychens La. RH1: Blet 3J 209

Stylecroft Rd. HP8: Chal G 20A 24
Styles End KT23: Bookh 99Da 191
Styles Gdns. SW9 55Rb 113
Styles Ho. SE1 7B 224
Styles Way BR3: Beck 70Ec 136
Stylus Ho. E1 44Yb 92
Styventon Pl. KT16: Chert 73H 149
Subrosa Dr. RH1: Mers 2B 208
Subrosa Pk. RH1: Mers 2B 208
Success Ho. SE1 7K 231
Succombs Hill CR3: W'ham 92Xb 197
CR6: W'ham 92Xb 197
Succombs Pl. CR6: W'ham 91Xb 197
Sudbourne Rd. SW2 57Nb 112
Sudbrooke Rd. SW12 58Hb 111
Sudbrook Gdns. TW10: Ham 62Ma 131
Sudbrook La. TW10: Ham 60Na 109
SUDBURY 36Ka 66
Sudbury E6 43Qc 94
Sudbury Av. HA0: Wemb 34La 66
Sudbury Cl. RM3: Rom 22Nd 57
RM6: Chad H 29Xc 55
Sudbury Ct. AL1: St A 3C 6
SW8 53Mb 112
(off Allen Edwards Dr.)
Sudbury Ct. Dr. HA1: Harr 34Ha 66
Sudbury Ct. Rd. HA1: Harr 34Ha 66
Sudbury Cres. BR1: Brom 65Jc 137
HA0: Wemb 36Ka 66
Sudbury Cft. HA0: Wemb 35Ha 66
Sudbury Gdns. CR0: C'don 77Ub 157
Sudbury Golf Course 38La 66
Sudbury Hgts. Av. UB6: G'frd 36Ha 66
Sudbury Hill HA1: Harr 33Ga 66
Sudbury Hill Cl. HA0: Wemb 35Ha 66
Sudbury Ho. SW18 57Db 111
Sudbury Rd. IG11: Bark 36Vc 75
Sudeley Ct. *E17* 25Bc 52
(off Broughton Pl.)
Sudeley St. N1 2C 218 (40Rb 71)
Sudicamps Ct. EN9: Walt A 5Jc 21
Sudlow Rd. SW18 57Cb 111
Sudrey St. SE1 2D 230 (47Sb 91)
Suez Av. UB6: G'frd 40Ha 66
Suez Rd. EN3: Brim 14Ac 34
Suffield Cl. CR2: Sels 84Zb 178
SUFFIELD HATCH 21Ec 52
Suffield Ho. SE17 7C 230
Suffield Rd. E4 20Dc 34
N15 29Vb 51
SE20 68Yb 136
Suffolk Cl. AL2: Lon C 7G 6
SL1: Slou 4C 80
WD6: Bore 15Ta 29
Suffolk Ct. E10 31Cc 72
IG3: Ilf 30Uc 54
RM6: Chad H 30Yc 55
Suffolk Ho. *CR0: C'don* 75Tb 157
(off George St.)
KT13: Weyb 78S 150
(off Princes Rd.)
SE20 67Zb 136
(off Croydon Rd.)
Suffolk La. EC4 4F 225 (45Tb 91)
Suffolk Pk. Rd. E17 28Ac 52
Suffolk Pl. SE2 50Yc 95
SW1 6E 222 (46Mb 90)
Suffolk Rd. DA1: Dart 58Nd 119
DA12: Grav'nd 8F 122
DA14: Sidc 65Yc 139
E13 41Jc 93
EN3: Pond E 15Xb 33
EN6: Pot B 4Ab 16
HA2: Harr 30Ba 45
IG3: Ilf 30Uc 54
IG11: Bark 38Tc 74
KT4: Wor Pk 75Va 154
N15 29Tb 51
NW10 38Ua 68
RM10: Dag 36Ed 76
SE25 70Vb 135
SW13 52Va 110
Suffolk St. E7 35Jc 73
SW1 5E 222 (45Mb 90)
Suffolk Way RM11: Horn 28Qd 57
TN13: S'oaks 97Ld 203
Sugar Bakers Ct. EC3 3J 225
Sugar Ho. *E1* 44Wb 91
(off Leman St.)
Sugar Ho. La. E15 40Ec 72
Sugar La. HP1: Hem H 4D 2
Sugar Loaf Wlk. E2 41Yb 92
Sugar Quay EC3 5J 225
Sugar Quay Wlk. EC3 5J 225 (45Ub 91)
Sugden Rd. KT7: T Ditt 74Ka 152
SW11 55Jb 112
Sugden Way IG11: Bark 40Vc 75
Sulby Ho. *SE4* 56Ac 114
(off Turnham Rd.)
Sulgrave Gdns. W6 47Ya 88
Sulgrave Rd. W6 48Ya 88
Sulina Rd. SW2 59Nb 112
Sulivan Ct. SW6 54Cb 111
Sulivan Ent. Cen. SW6 55Db 111
Sulivan Rd. SW6 55Cb 111
Sulkin Ho. *E2* 41Zb 92
(off Knottisford St.)
Sullivan Av. E16 43Mc 93
Sullivan Cl. DA1: Dart 58Kd 119
KT8: W Mole 69Da 129
SW11 55Gb 111
UB4: Yead 43Y 85
Sullivan Ct. *E3* 42Bc 92
(off Eric St.)
N16 31Vb 71
SW5 49Cb 89
(off Earls Ct. Rd.)
Sullivan Cres. UB9: Hare 26M 43
Sullivan Ho. SE11 6J 229
SW1 51Kb 112
(off Churchill Gdns.)
Sullivan Rd. RM18: Tilb 3C 122
SE11 5A 230 (49Qb 90)
Sullivan Row BR2: Brom 72Mc 159
Sullivans Reach KT12: Walt T 73V 150
Sullivan Way WD6: E'tree 16La 28
Sultan Ho. *SE1* 50Wb 91
(off St James's Rd.)
Sultan Rd. E11 28Kc 53
Sultan St. BR3: Beck 68Zb 136
SE5 52Sb 113
Sultan Ter. N22 26Qb 50
Sumatra Rd. NW6 36Cb 69
Sumburgh Rd. SW12 58Jb 112
Sumburgh Way SL1: Slou 3J 81
Sumeria Ct. *SE16* 49Yb 92
(off Rotherhithe New Rd.)
Summer Av. KT8: E Mos 71Ga 152

Summerbee Ho. *SW18* 56Eb 111
(off Eltringham St.)
Summer Cl. KT14: Byfl 86P 169
Summer Ct. HP2: Hem H 1M 3
Summercourt Rd. E1 44Yb 92
Summer Crossing KT7: T Ditt 71Ga 152
Summer Dr. UB7: W Dray 47P 83
Summerene Cl. SW16 66Lb 134
Summerfield AL10: Hat 3C 8
BR1: Brom 67Kc 137
(off Freelands Rd.)
KT21: Asht 91Ma 193
Summerfield Av. NW6 40Ab 68
Summerfield Cl. AL2: Lon C 8G 6
KT15: Add 78H 149
Summerfield La. KT6: Surb 75Ma 153
Summerfield Pl. KT16: Ott 79F 148
Summerfield Rd. IG10: Lough 16Mc 35
W5 42Ka 86
WD25: Wat 7W 12
Summerfields Av. N12 23Gb 49
Summerfield St. SE12 59Hc 115
Summer Gdns. KT8: E Mos 71Ga 152
UB10: Ick 33S 64
Summer Gro. BR4: W W'ck 75Gc 159
WD6: E'tree 16Ma 29
Summerhayes Cl. GU21: Wok 86A 168
Summerhays KT11: Cobh 85Z 171
Summer Hill BR7: Chst 68Qc 138
WD6: E'tree 15Qa 29
Summerhill Cl. BR6: Orp 76Uc 160
Summerhill Ct. *AL1: St A* 1D 6
(off Avenue Rd)
Summerhill Gro. EN1: Enf 16Ub 33
Summerhill Rd. DA1: Dart 59Md 119
N15 28Tb 51
Summerhill Vs. *BR7: Chst* 67Qc 138
(off Susan Wood)
Summerhill Way CR4: Mitc 67Jb 134
Summerhouse Av. TW5: Hest 53Aa 107
Summerhouse Dr. DA2: Wilm 63Fd 140
DA5: Bexl, Dart 63Fd 140
Summerhouse La. UB7: Harm 51M 105
UB9: Hare 24J 43
WD25: A'ham 12Ea 28
Summerhouse Rd. N16 33Ub 71
Summerhouse Way WD5: Ab L 2V 12
Summerland Gdns. N10 27Kb 50
Summerland Grange N10 27Kb 50
Summerlands Av. W3 45Sa 87
Summerlands Lodge BR6: Farnb 77Qc 160
Summerlay Cl. KT20: Tad 92Ab 194
Summerlea SL1: Slou 6F 80
Summerlea Ct. HP2: Hem H 2N 3
Summerlee Av. N2 28Hb 49
Summerlee Gdns. N2 28Hb 49
Summerleigh *KT13: Weyb* 79T 150
(off Gower Rd.)
Summerley St. SW18 61Db 133
Summerly Av. RH2: Reig 5J 207
Summer Pl. WD18: Wat 16V 26
Summer Rd. KT7: T Ditt 71Ga 152
KT8: E Mos 71Fa 152
(not continuous)
Summersby Rd. N6 30Kb 50
Summers Cl. HA9: Wemb 32Ra 67
KT13: Weyb 83Q 170
SM2: Sutt 80Cb 155
Summerskill Cl. SE15 55Xb 113
Summerskille Cl. N9 20Xb 33
Summers La. N12 24Fb 49
Summers Rd. SL1: Burn 1A 80
Summers Row N12 23Hb 49
Summers St. EC1 6K 217 (42Qb 90)
SUMMERSTOWN 62Eb 133
Summerstown SW17 62Eb 133
Summers Way AL2: Lon C 9J 7
Summerswood Cl. CR8: Kenley 88Tb 177
Summerswood La. WD6: Bore 6Ua 16
Summerton Way SE28 44Zc 95
Summer Trees TW16: Sun 67X 129
Summerville Gdns. SM1: Sutt 79Bb 155
Summerwood SL5: S'dale 3D 146
Summerwood Rd. TW7: Isle 57Ha 108
Summit, The IG10: Lough 11Pc 36
Summit Av. NW9 29Ta 47
Summit Bus. Pk. TW16: Sun 66W 128
Summit Cen. EN6: Pot B 2Ab 16
Summit Cl. HA8: Edg 24Qa 47
N14 19Lb 32
NW9 28Ta 47
Summit Ct. NW2 36Ab 68
Summit Dr. IG8: Wfd G 26Mc 53
Summit Est. N16 31Wb 71
Summit Ho. BR4: W W'ck 75Ec 158
Summit Pl. KT13: Weyb 80Q 150
Summit Rd. E17 28Dc 52
EN6: Pot B 2Ab 16
UB5: N'olt 38Ca 65
Summit Way N14 19Kb 32
SE19 66Ub 135
Sumner Av. SE15 53Vb 113
Sumner Bldgs. SE1 6D 224
Sumner Cl. BR6: Farnb 77Sc 160
KT22: Fet 96Fa 192
Sumner Ct. SW8 52Nb 112
Sumner Est. SE15 52Vb 113
Sumner Gdns. CR0: C'don 74Qb 156
Sumner Ho. *E3* 43Dc 92
(off Watts Gro.)
Sumner Pl. KT15: Add 78J 149
SW7 6B 226 (49Fb 89)
Sumner Pl. M. SW7 6C 226 (49Fb 89)
Sumner Rd. CR0: C'don 74Qb 156
HA1: Harr 31Ea 66
SE15 51Vb 113
Sumner Rd. Sth. CR0: C'don 74Qb 156
Sumner St. SE1 6C 224 (46Rb 91)
Sumpter Cl. NW3 37Eb 69
Sumpter Yd. AL1: St A 3B 6
Sun All. TW9: Rich 56Na 109
Sunbeam Cres. W10 42Ya 88
Sunbeam Rd. NW10 42Sa 87
Sunbury Way NW10 42Ta 87
Sunbird Wlk. *HA2: Harr* 33Da 65
(off Sandpiper Dr.)
SUNBURY 69Y 129
Sunbury Av. NW7 22Ta 47
SW14 56Ta 109
Sunbury Av. Pas. SW14 56Ua 110
Sunbury Bus. Cen. TW16: Sun 67W 128
Sunbury Cl. KT12: Walt T 72W 150
SUNBURY COMMON 66V 128
Sunbury Ct. EN5: Barn 14Ab 30
SL4: Eton 1H 103
Sunbury Ct. Island TW16: Sun 69Z 129
Sunbury Ct. M. TW16: Sun 68Z 129
Sunbury Ct. Rd. TW16: Sun 68Y 129

Sunbury Cres. TW13: Felt 63V 128
SUNBURY CROSS 66W 128
Sunbury Cross Cen.
TW16: Sun 66V 128
Sunbury Embroidery Gallery, The
69X 129
Sunbury Gdns. NW7 22Ta 47
Sunbury Golf Course 70T 128
Sunbury Ho. E2 4K 219
SE14 51Zb 114
(off Myers La.)
TW16: Sun 67U 128
(off Brooklands Cl.)
Sunbury La. KT12: Walt T 72W 150
SW11 53Fb 111
(not continuous)
Sunbury Leisure Cen. 67V 128
Sunburylock Ait KT12: Walt T 70X 129
Sunbury Pk. Walled Garden 69X 129
Sunbury Rd. SL4: Eton 1H 103
SM3: Cheam 76Za 154
TW13: Felt 62V 128
Sunbury St. SE18 48Pc 94
Sunbury Way TW13: Hanw 64Y 129
Sunbury Workshops E2 4K 219
Sun Cl. SL4: Eton 1H 103
Sun Ct. DA8: Erith 54Hd 118
E3 42Ec 92
(off Navigation Rd.)
EC3 3G 225
Suncroft Pl. SE26 62Yb 136
Sundale *AL1: St A* 1D 6
(off Althorp Rd.)
Sundale Av. CR2: Sels 82Yb 178
Sundeala Cl. *TW16: Sun* 66W 128
(off Hanworth Rd.)
Sunderland Av. AL1: St A 1E 6
Sunderland Ct. SE22 59Wb 113
TW19: Stanw 58N 105
(off Whitley Cl.)
Sunderland Est. WD4: K Lan 1R 12
Sunderland Gro. WD25: Wat 6V 12
Sunderland Ho. *W2* 43Cb 89
(off Westbourne Pk. Rd.)
Sunderland Mt. SE23 61Zb 136
Sunderland Point E16 46Sc 94
Sunderland Rd. SE23 60Zb 114
W5 48Ma 87
Sunderland Ter. W2 44Db 89
Sunderland Way E12 33Mc 73
Sundew Av. W12 45Wa 88
Sundew Cl. GU18: Light 3B 166
W12 45Wa 88
Sundew Ct. *HA0: Wemb* 40Na 67
(off Elmore Cl.)
RM17: Grays 51Fe 121
Sundew Rd. HP1: Hem H 3G 2
Sundial Av. SE25 69Vb 135
Sundial Ct. EC1 7E 218
Sundon Cres. GU25: Vir W 1M 147
Sundorne Rd. SE7 50Lc 93
Sundown Av. CR2: Sande 83Vb 177
Sundown Rd. TW15: Ashf 64S 128
Sundra Wlk. E1 42Zb 92
SUNDRIDGE
BR1 65Kc 137
TN14 96Ad 201
Sundridge Av. BR1: Brom 67Mc 137
BR7: Chst 67Mc 137
DA16: Well 54Tc 116
Sundridge Cl. DA1: Dart 58Qd 119
Sundridge Hill
TN14: Knock, Sund 90Yc 181
Sundridge Ho. *E9* 38Zb 72
(off Church Cres.)
Sundridge La. TN14: Knock 89Xc 181
Sundridge Pde. BR1: Brom 66Kc 137
SUNDRIDGE PARK 66Kc 137
Sundridge Pk. Golf Course 65Kc 137
Sundridge Pl. CR0: C'don 74Wb 157
Sundridge Rd. CR0: C'don 73Vb 157
GU22: Wok 91C 188
TN14: Dun G 92Cd 202
Sunfields Pl. SE3 52Kc 115
Sunflower Ct. NW2 33Bb 69
RM13: Rain 40Ed 76
Sunflower Way RM3: Hrld W 25Md 57
Sungate Cotts. RM5: Col R 25Bd 55
Sun Ga. Ho. KT3: N Mald 70Ua 132
Sunguard Ct. SE1 6B 224 (46Rb 91)
Sun Hill DA3: Fawk 76Wd 164
GU22: Wok 3L 187
SUN-IN-THE-SANDS 52Kc 115
Sunken Rd. CR0: C'don 78Yb 158
Sunkist Way SM6: Wall 81Nb 176
Sunland Av. DA6: Bex 56Ad 117
Sun La. DA12: Grav'nd 1E 144
SE3 52Kc 115
Sunleigh Rd. HA0: Wemb 39Na 67
Sunley Gdns. UB6: G'frd 39Ja 66
Sun Life Trad. Est. TW14: Felt 55W 106
Sunlight Cl. SW19 65Eb 133
Sunlight M. SW6 54Db 111
Sunlight Sq. E2 41Xb 91
Sunliner Way RM15: S Ock 42Xd 98
Sunmead Cl. KT22: Fet 94Ha 192
Sunmead Rd. HP2: Hem H 1M 3
TW16: Sun 69W 128
Sunna Gdns. TW16: Sun 68X 129
Sunniholme Ct. *CR2: S Croy* 78Sb 157
(off Warham Rd.)
Sunning Av. SL5: S'dale 3C 146
SUNNINGDALE 1E 146
Sunningdale N14 22Mb 50
W13 43Ka 86
(off Hardwick Grn.)
Sunningdale Av. HA4: Ruis 32Y 65
IG11: Bark 39Tc 74
RM13: Rain 42Kd 97
TW13: Hanw 61Aa 129
W3 45Ua 88
Sunningdale Cl. E6 41Pc 94
HA7: Stan 23Ja 46
KT6: Surb 75Na 153
SE16 50Xb 91
SE28 44Ad 95
Sunningdale Ct. *TW7: Isle* 58Fa 108
(off Whitton Dene)
UB1: S'hall 44Ea 86
(off Fleming Rd.)
Sunningdale Gdns. NW9 29Sa 47
W8 48Cb 89
(off Stratford Rd.)
Sunningdale Golf Course 4E 146
Sunningdale Ladies Golf Course 4E 146
Sunningdale Lodge *HA8: Edg* 22Pa 47
(off Stonegrove)
Sunningdale Pk. 1D 146

Sunningdale Rd. BR1: Brom 70Nc 138
RM13: Rain 38Jd 76
SM1: Sutt 76Bb 155
Sunningfields Cres. NW4 26Xa 48
Sunningfields Rd. NW4 26Xa 48
SUNNINGHILL 1B 146
Sunninghill DA11: Nflt 1A 144
Sunninghill Cl. SL5: S'hill 10B 124
Sunninghill Ct. SL5: S'hill 10B 124
W3 47Sa 87
SUNNINGHILL PARK 7A 124
Sunninghill Rd. SE13 54Dc 114
SL4: Wink 4B 124
SL5: Asc 4B 124
SL5: S'hill 1B 146
Sunnings La. RM14: Upm 36Sd 78
Sunningvale Av. TN16: Big H 87Lc 179
Sunningvale Cl. TN16: Big H 88Mc 179
Sunny Bank SE25 69Wb 135
Sunnybank CR6: W'ham 89Ac 178
KT18: Eps 88Sa 173
Sunnybank Rd. EN6: Pot B 5Cb 17
Sunnybank Vs. RH1: Blet 4M 209
Sunny Cres. NW10 38Sa 67
Sunnycroft Gdns. RM14: Upm 31Vd 78
Sunnycroft Rd. SE25 69Wb 135
TW3: Houn 54Da 107
UB1: S'hall 43Ca 85
Sunnydale BR6: Farnb 75Qc 160
Sunnydale Gdns. NW7 23Ta 47
Sunnydale Rd. SE12 57Kc 115
Sunnydell AL2: Chis G 8P 5
Sunnydene Av. E4 22Fc 53
HA4: Ruis 32W 64
Sunnydene Cl. RM3: Hrld W 24Pd 57
Sunnydene Gdns. HA0: Wemb 37La 66
Sunnydene Rd. CR8: Purl 85Rb 177
Sunnydene St. SE26 63Ac 136
Sunnyfield NW7 21Va 48
Sunnyfield Rd. BR7: Chst 69Wc 139
Sunny Gdns. Pde. NW4 26Xa 48
Sunny Gdns. Rd. NW4 26Xa 48
Sunny Hill NW4 27Xa 48
Sunnyhill Cl. E5 35Ac 72
Sunnyhill Rd. HP1: Hem H 2K 3
SW16 63Nb 134
WD3: W Hyd 23F 42
Sunnyhurst Cl. SM1: Sutt 76Cb 155
Sunnymead Av. CR4: Mitc 69Mb 134
Sunnymead Rd. NW9 31Ta 67
SW15 57Xa 110
SUNNYMEADS 56A 104
Sunnymede IG7: Chig 20Xc 37
Sunnymede Av. KT19: Ewe 81Ua 174
SM5: Cars 83Fb 175
Sunnymede Dr. IG2: Ilf 29Rc 54
IG6: Ilf 29Rc 54
Sunny M. NW1 38Jb 70
RM5: Col R 24Ed 56
Sunny Nook Gdns. CR2: S Croy 79Tb 157
Sunny Pl. NW4 28Ya 48
Sunny Ri. CR3: Cat'm 96Tb 197
Sunny Rd., The EN3: Enf H 11Zb 34
Sunnyside GU21: Knap 1F 186
KT12: Walt T 71Y 151
NW2 34Bb 69
SE6 59Bc 114
(off Blythe Hill)
SW19 65Ab 132
Sunnyside Dr. E4 17Ec 34
Sunnyside Gdns. RM14: Upm 34Sd 78
Sunnyside Ho's. *NW2* 34Bb 69
(off Sunnyside)
Sunnyside Pas. SW19 65Ab 132
Sunnyside Pl. SW19 65Ab 132
Sunnyside Rd. CM16: Epp 5Vc 23
E10 32Cc 72
IG1: Ilf 34Sc 74
N19 31Mb 70
TW11: Tedd 63Fa 130
W5 46Ma 87
Sunnyside Rd. E. N9 20Wb 33
Sunnyside Rd. Nth. N9 20Vb 33
Sunnyside Rd. Sth. N9 20Vb 33
Sunnyside Ter. NW9 27Ta 47
Sunny Vw. NW9 29Ta 47
Sunny Way N12 24Gb 49
Sun Pas. *SE16* 48Wb 91
(off Old Jamaica Rd.)
SL4: Wind 3H 103
Sunray Av. BR2: Brom 72Nc 160
CM13: Hut 16Fe 41
KT5: Surb 75Ra 153
SE24 56Tb 113
UB7: W Dray 47M 83
Sunrise Av. RM12: Horn 34Ld 77
Sunrise Cl. E20 36Ec 72
TW13: Hanw 62Ba 129
Sunrise Cotts. TN13: S'oaks 94Hd 202
Sunrise Cres. HP3: Hem H 5N 3
Sunrise Vw. NW7 23Va 48
Sun Rd. DA10: Swans 58Be 121
W14 50Bb 89
Sunset Av. E4 18Dc 34
IG8: Wfd G 21Hc 53
Sunset Cl. DA8: Erith 52Kd 119
Sunset Ct. IG8: Wfd G 24Lc 53
Sunset Dr. RM4: Have B 22Kd 57
Sunset Gdns. SE25 68Vb 135
Sunset Lodge *NW10* 38Ya 68
(off Hanover Rd.)
Sunset M. RM5: Col R 23Ed 56
Sunset Rd. SE5 56Sb 113
SE28 46Wc 95
SW19 64Xa 132
Sunset Vw. EN5: Barn 12Ab 30
Sunshine Way CR4: Mitc 68Hb 133
Sun Sq. *HP1: Hem H* 1M 3
(off Chapel St.)
Sunstone Gro. RH1: Mers 1D 208
Sun St. EC2 7G 219 (43Tb 91)
(Finsbury Sq.)
EC2 7H 219 (43Ub 91)
(Primrose St.)
EN9: Walt A 5Ec 20
Sun St. Pas. EC2 1H 225 (43Ub 91)
Sun Wlk. E1 45Vb 91
Sunwell Cl. SE15 53Xb 113
Sun Wharf *SE8* 52Dc 114
(off Creekside)
Superior Dr. BR6: Chels 79Vc 161
Supreme Court
Westminster 2F 229 (47Nb 90)
Supreme Point *E16* 43Jc 93
(off Butchers Rd.)
SURBITON 72Ma 153
Surbiton Ct. KT6: Surb 72La 152
Surbiton Cres. KT1: King T 70Na 131

Surbiton Golf Course 77Ka 152
Surbiton Hall Cl. KT1: King T 70Na 131
Surbiton Hill Pk. KT5: Surb 71Pa 153
Surbiton Hill Rd. KT6: Surb 70Na 131
Surbiton Pde. KT6: Surb 72Na 153
Surbiton Plaza *KT6: Surb* 72Ma 153
(off St Mary's Rd.)
Surbiton Raceway 76Ta 153
Surbiton Rd. KT1: King T 70Ma 131
Surlingham Cl. SE28 45Zc 95
Surly Hall Wlk. SL4: Wind 3D 102
Surma Cl. E1 42Xb 91
Surman Cres. CM13: Hut 17Ee 41
Surmans Cl. RM9: Dag 39Yc 75
Surrendale Pl. W9 42Cb 89
Surrey Av. SL2: Slou 3C 80
Surrey Canal Rd. SE14 51Yb 114
SE15 51Yb 114
Surrey Canal Trade Pk. SE14 51Zb 114
Surrey Cl. N3 27Ab 48
TN15: W King 80Ud 164
Surrey County Cricket Club 51Pb 112
Surrey Cres. W4 50Qa 87
Surrey Docks Farm 48Bc 92
Surrey Docks Watersports Cen. 48Ac 92
Surrey Downs Golf Course 94Eb 195
Surrey Dr. RM11: Horn 28Qd 57
Surrey Gdns. KT24: Eff J 94W 190
N4 30Sb 51
Surrey Gro. SE17 7H 231 (50Ub 91)
SM1: Sutt 76Fb 155
Surrey Health & Racquets Club, The
79Pb 156
Surrey History Cen. 10P 167
Surrey Ho. *CR0: C'don* 76Sb 157
(off Surrey St.)
SE16 46Zb 92
(off Rotherhithe St.)
Surrey La. SW11 53Gb 111
Surrey La. Est. SW11 53Gb 111
Surrey Lodge *KT12: Hers* 78X 151
(off Queens Rd.)
Surrey M. SE27 63Ub 135
Surrey Mt. SE23 60Xb 113
Surrey National Golf Course 95Rb 197
Surrey Quays Rd. SE16 48Yb 92
Surrey Quays Shop. Cen.
SE16 48Zb 92
Surrey Rd. BR4: W W'ck 74Dc 158
HA1: Harr 29Ea 46
IG11: Bark 38Uc 74
RM10: Dag 36Dd 76
SE15 57Zb 114
Surrey Row SE1 1B 230 (47Rb 91)
Surrey Sq. SE17 7H 231 (50Ub 91)
Surrey Steps WC2 4J 223
Surrey St. CR0: C'don 75Sb 157
E13 41Kc 93
WC2 4J 223 (45Pb 90)
Surrey Ter. SE17 7J 231 (50Ub 91)
Surrey Towers *KT15: Add* 78L 149
(off Bush Cl.)
Surrey Water Rd. SE16 46Zb 92
Surridge Cl. RM13: Rain 41Ld 97
Surridge Ct. *SW9* 54Nb 112
(off Clapham Rd.)
Surridge Gdns. SE19 65Tb 135
Surr St. N7 36Nb 70
Sury Basin KT2: King T 67Na 131
Susan Cl. RM7: Mawney 27Ed 56
Susan Constant Ct. *E14* 45Fc 93
(off Newport Av.)
Susan Edwards Ho. *SL9: Chal P* 21A 42
(off Micholls Av.)
Susan Lawrence Ho. *E3* 40Ac 72
(off Zealand Rd.)
E12 35Qc 74
(off Walton Rd.)
Susannah St. E14 44Dc 92
Susan Rd. SE3 54Kc 115
Susan Wood BR7: Chst 67Qc 138
Sussex Av. RM3: Hrld W 24Pd 57
TW7: Isle 55Ga 108
Sussex Cl. GU21: Knap 10G 166
IG4: Ilf 29Pc 54
KT3: N Mald 70Ua 132
N19 33Nb 70
RH2: Reig 7M 207
SL1: Slou 7M 81
TN15: W King 80Ud 164
TW1: Twick 58Ka 108
Sussex Ct. GU21: Knap 9G 166
KT15: Add 78L 149
KT18: Eps 86Ua 174
(off Downside)
SE10 51Ec 114
(off Roan St.)
W2 3B 220
Sussex Cres. UB5: N'olt 37Ca 65
Sussex Gdns. KT9: Chess 79Ma 153
N4 29Sb 51
N6 29Hb 49
W2 4B 220 (45Fb 89)
Sussex Ga. N6 29Hb 49
Sussex Ho. NW1 1D 216
SL2: Farn C 7G 60
Sussex Keep SL1: Slou 7M 81
Sussex Lodge W2 3C 220
Sussex Mans. SW7 6B 226
WC2 4G 223
Sussex M. SE6 59Cc 114
Sussex M. E. W2 3C 220
Sussex M. W.
W2 4C 220 (45Fb 89)
Sussex Pl. GU21: Knap 10G 166
KT3: N Mald 70Ua 132
NW1 5F 215 (42Hb 89)
SL1: Slou 7L 81
W2 3C 220 (44Fb 89)
W6 50Ya 88
Sussex Ring N12 22Cb 49
Sussex Rd. BR4: W W'ck 74Dc 158
BR5: Orp 72Yc 161
CM14: W'ley 21Xd 58
CR2: S Croy 79Tb 157
CR4: Mitc 71Nb 156
DA1: Dart 59Qd 119
DA8: Erith 52Dd 118
DA14: Sidc 64Xc 139
E6 39Qc 74
GU21: Knap 10G 166
HA1: Harr 29Ea 46
KT3: N Mald 70Ua 132
SM5: Cars 79Hb 155
UB2: S'hall 48Z 85
UB10: Ick 35S 64
WD24: Wat 9W 12
Sussex Sq. W2 4C 220 (45Fb 89)

Sussex St.—Syringa Ct.

Sussex St. E13 41Kc 93
SW1 7A 228 (50Kb 90)
Sussex Ter. RM19: Purf 50Rd 97
SE20 66Yb 136
(off Graveney Gro.)
Sussex Way EN4: Cockf 15Kb 32
N7 33Nb 70
N19 32Mb 70
(not continuous)
Sutcliffe Cl. NW11 29Db 49
WD23: Bush 14Ea 28
Sutcliffe Ho. UB3: Hayes 44W 84
Sutcliffe Pk. Athletics Track 57Lc 115
Sutcliffe Rd. DA16: Well 54Yc 117
SE18 51Uc 116
Sutherland Av. BR5: St M Cry 72Vc 161
DA16: Well 56Uc 116
EN6: Cuff 1Mb 18
GU4: Jac W 100A 188
TN16: Big H 89Mc 179
TW16: Sun 68V 128
UB3: Hayes 49W 84
W9 4A 214 (42Cb 89)
W13 44Ka 86
Sutherland Cl. DA9: Ghithe 57Vd 120
DA12: Grav'nd 1K 145
EN5: Barn 14Ab 30
Sutherland Ct. N16 34Tb 71
NW9 29Ra 47
W9 42Cb 89
(off Marylands Rd.)
WD18: Wat 17S 26
Sutherland Dr. SW19 67Fb 133
Sutherland Gdns. KT4: Wor Pk 74Xa 154
SW14 55Ua 110
TW16: Sun 68V 128
Sutherland Grange SL4: Wind 2B 102
Sutherland Gro. SW18 58Ab 110
TW11: Tedd 64Ga 130
Sutherland Ho. IG8: Wfd G 24Qc 54
W8 48Db 89
Sutherland Pl. W2 44Cb 89
Sutherland Rd. CR0: C'don 73Qb 156
DA17: Belv 48Cd 96
E3 40Bc 72
E17 26Zb 52
EN3: Pond E 16Zb 34
N9 18Xb 33
N17 24Wb 51
UB1: S'hall 44Ba 85
W4 51Ua 110
W13 44Ja 86
Sutherland Rd. Path E17 27Zb 52
Sutherland Row SW1 7A 228 (50Kb 90)
Sutherland Sq. SE17 50Sb 91
Sutherland St. SW1 7K 227 (50Kb 90)
Sutherland Wlk. SE17 7E 230 (50Sb 91)
Sutherland Way EN6: Cuff 1Mb 18
Sutlej Rd. SE7 52Lc 115
Sutterton St. N7 37Pb 70
SUTTON
SL3 50E 82
SM1 78Db 155
Sutton Arena Leisure Cen. 73Eb 155
SUTTON AT HONE 66Rd 141
Sutton Av. GU21: Wok 1J 187
SL3: L'ly 7N 81
Sutton Cl. BR3: Beck 67Dc 136
HA5: Eastc 29W 44
IG10: Lough 17Nc 36
W4 51Sa 109
(off Sutton La. Sth.)
Sutton Comn. Rd. SM1: Sutt 73Bb 155
SM3: Sutt 73Bb 155
Sutton Ct. KT8: W Mole 71Ba 151
SE19 66Vb 135
SM2: Sutt 79Eb 155
W4 51Sa 109
W5 46Na 87
Sutton Ct. Rd. E13 41Lc 93
SM1: Sutt 79Eb 155
UB10: Hil 39R 64
W4 52Sa 109
Sutton Cres. EN5: Barn 15Za 30
Sutton Dene TW3: Houn 53Da 107
Sutton Ecology Cen. 77Hb 155
Sutton Est. EC1 4G 219
SW3 7E 226 (50Gb 89)
W10 43Ya 88
Sutton Est., The N1 38Rb 71
Sutton Gdns. CR0: C'don 71Vb 157
IG11: Bark 39Uc 74
RH1: Mers 1D 208
SUTTON GREEN 98B 188
Sutton Grn. *IG11: Bark* 39Uc 74
(off Sutton Rd.)
Sutton Green Golf Course 95A 188
Sutton Grn. Rd. GU4: Sut G 98A 188
Sutton Gro. SM1: Sutt 77Fb 155
Sutton Hall Rd. TW5: Hest 52Ca 107
Sutton Hgts. SM2: Sutt 80Fb 155
Sutton La. EC1 6C 218
SL3: L'ly 51D 104
SM2: Sutt 83Db 175
SM7: Bans 83Db 175
TW3: Houn 55Ba 107
Sutton La. Nth. W4 50Sa 87
Sutton La. Sth. W4 51Sa 109
Sutton Pde. *NW4* 28Ya 48
(off Church Rd.)
SUTTON PARK 98B 188
Sutton Pk. Rd. SM1: Sutt 79Db 155
Sutton Path WD6: Bore 13Qa 29
Sutton Pl. E9 36Yb 72
SL3: L'ly 51D 104
Sutton Rd. AL1: St A 3F 6
E13 42Hc 93
E17 25Zb 52
IG11: Bark 40Uc 74
N10 25Jb 50
TW5: Hest 53Ca 107
WD17: Wat 13Y 27
(not continuous)
Sutton Row W1 2E 222 (44Mb 90)
Suttons Av. RM12: Horn 34Ld 77
Suttons Bus. Pk. RM13: Rain 41Gd 96
Suttons Gdns. RM12: Horn 34Md 77
Suttons La. RM12: Horn 36Md 77
Sutton Sq. E9 36Yb 72
TW5: Hest 53Ba 107
Sutton St. E1 45Yb 92
Sutton's Way EC1 6E 218
Suttons Wharf E2 41Zb 92
Sutton Tennis Academy 74Db 155
Sutton United FC 77Cb 155
Sutton Wlk. SE1 7J 223 (46Pb 90)
Sutton Way TW5: Hest 53Ba 107
W10 42Ya 88
SW1 Gallery 3B 228 (48Lb 90)
Swabey Rd. SL3: L'ly 49C 82
Swaby Rd. SW18 60Eb 111
Swaffam Ct. RM6: Chad H 30Yc 55
Swaffham Way N22 24Rb 51
Swaffield Rd. SW18 59Db 111
TN13: S'oaks 94Ld 203
Swail Ho. KT18: Eps 85Ta 173
Swain Cl. SW16 65Kb 134
Swain Rd. CR7: Thor H 71Sb 157
Swains Cl. UB7: W Dray 47N 83
Swain's La. N6 32Jb 70
Swainson Rd. W3 47Va 88
Swains Rd. SW17 66Hb 133
Swain St. NW8 5D 214 (42Gb 89)
Swaisland Rd. DA1: Dart 57Kd 119
Swaislands Dr. DA1: Cray 57Hd 118
Swakeleys Dr. UB10: Ick 35Q 64
Swakeleys Rd. UB10: Ick 35N 63
SWAKELEYS RDBT. 35N 63
Swalecliffe Rd. DA17: Belv 50Dd 96
Swale Cl. RM15: Avel 44Sd 98
Swaledale Cl. N11 23Jb 50
Swaledale Rd. DA2: Dart 60Sd 120
Swale Rd. DA1: Cray 56Jd 118
Swaley's Way RM15: S Ock 44Zd 99
Swallands Rd. SE6 62Cc 136
(not continuous)
Swallow Cl. DA8: Erith 53Gd 118
DA9: Ghithe 57Vd 120
RM16: Chaf H 49Yd 98
SE14 53Zb 114
TW18: Staines 63H 127
WD3: Rick 17L 25
WD23: Bush 18Ea 28
Swallow Ct. EN3: Enf W 9Yb 20
HA4: Ruis 32Y 65
IG2: Ilf 29Rc 54
SE1 2E 230
SE12 59Jc 115
W9 43Cb 89
(off Admiral Wlk.)
Swallowdale CR2: Sels 81Zb 178
SL0: Iver H 41F 82
Swallow Dr. NW10 37Ta 67
UB5: N'olt 40Ca 65
Swallowfield NW1 4A 216
TW20: Eng G 5M 125
Swallowfield Rd. SE7 50Kc 93
Swallow Flds. SL0: Iver 42F 82
Swallowfields DA11: Nflt 2A 144
Swallowfield Way UB3: Hayes 47T 84
Swallow Gdns. AL10: Hat 2C 8
SW16 64Mb 134
Swallow Ho. NW8 1D 214
Swallow La. AL1: St A 5F 6
Swallow Pk. KT6: Surb 76Pa 153
Swallow Pk. Cl. KT6: Surb 76Pa 153
Swallow Pas. W1 3B 222
Swallow Pl. *E14* 44Bc 92
(off Newell St.)
KT17: Ewe 82Wa 174
W1 3A 222 (44Kb 90)
Swallow Ri. GU21: Knap 9G 166
Swallows, The *UB9: Den* 29H 43
(off Patrons Way W.)
Swallows Cl. SM1: Sutt 76Cb 155
Swallows Ct. *DA1: Dart* 55Pd 119
(off Vickers La.)
Swallows Oak WD5: Ab L 3V 12
Swallow St. E6 43Nc 94
SL0: Iver, Iver H 41F 82
W1 5C 222 (45Lb 90)
Swallowtail Cl. BR5: St P 70Zc 139
Swallowtail Ho. *E20* 36Ec 72
(off Sunrise Cl.)
Swallow Wlk. HP3: Hem H 6L 3
RM12: Horn 37Kd 77
SWAN, THE 75Ec 158
Swanage Ct. *N1* 38Ub 71
(off Hertford Rd.)
Swanage Ho. *SW8* 52Pb 112
(off Dorset Rd.)
Swanage Rd. E4 24Ec 52
SW18 58Eb 111
Swanage Waye UB4: Yead 44Y 85
Swan & Pike Rd. EN3: Enf L 10Cc 20
Swan App. E6 43Nc 94
Swan Av. RM14: Upm 32Vd 78
Swanbourne Dr. RM12: Horn 36Ld 77
Swanbourne Ho. NW8 5D 214
Swanbridge Rd. DA7: Bex 53Cd 118
Swan Bus. Pk. DA1: Dart 56Md 119
Swan Cen., The KT22: Lea 93Ka 192
SW17 62Db 133
Swan Cl. BR5: St P 69Wc 139
CR0: C'don 73Ub 157
E17 25Ac 52
KT12: Walt T 73V 150
TW13: Hanw 63Aa 129
WD3: Rick 17M 25
Swan Ct. *E1* 45Wb 91
(off Star Pl.)
E14 44Bc 92
(off Agnes St.)
HA4: Ruis 31T 64
HP1: Hem H 3L 3
KT22: Lea 94Ka 192
SW3 50Gb 89
SW6 52Cb 111
(off Fulham Rd.)
TW7: Isle 55Ka 108
(off Swan St.)
Swandon Way SW18 56Db 111
Swandrift TW18: Staines 66H 127
Swan Dr. NW9 26Ua 48
Swan Fld. Ho. WD3: Rick 17M 25
Swanfield Rd. EN8: Walt C 5Ac 20
Swanfield St. E2 4K 219 (41Vb 91)
Swan Ho. *E15* 38Gc 73
(off Broadway)
EN3: Pond E 15Yb 34
N1 38Tb 71
(off Oakley Rd.)
Swan Island TW1: Twick 62Ja 130
Swanland Rd. AL9: N Mym 7D 8
EN6: S Mim 6Xa 16
Swan La. CM14: B'wood 19Yd 40
DA1: Dart 59Hd 118
EC4 5F 225 (45Tb 91)
IG10: Lough 17Lc 35
N4 32Sb 71
N20 20Eb 31
SWANLEY 69Gd 140
SWANLEY BAR 10K 9
Swanley Bar La. EN6: Pot B 10K 9
Swanley By-Pass BR8: Swan 67Dd 140
DA14: Sidc 67Dd 140
Swanley Cen. BR8: Swan 69Gd 140
Swanley Ct. WD24: Wat 9Y 13
Swanley Cres. EN6: Pot B 1Db 17
Swanley Ho. SE17 7J 231
SWANLEY INTERCHANGE 71Kd 163
Swanley La. BR8: Swan 69Hd 140
Swanley Rd. DA16: Well 53Yc 117
SWANLEY VILLAGE 67Kd 141
Swanley Village Rd. BR8: Swan 67Kd 141
Swan Mead HP3: Hem H 7P 3
SE1 4H 231 (48Ub 91)
Swan M. CR4: Mitc 67Hb 133
RM7: Mawney 28Dd 56
SW6 53Bb 111
SW9 54Pb 112
Swann Ct. SL1: Slou 8J 81
TW7: Isle 55Ja 108
(off South St.)
Swanne Ho. *SE10* 52Ec 114
(off Gloucester Cir.)
Swannells Wlk. WD3: Rick 17H 25
Swanns Mdw. KT23: Bookh 98Ca 191
Swan Paddock
CM14: B'wood 19Yd 40
Swan Pas. *E1* 45Vb 91
(off Cartwright St.)
Swan Path KT1: King T 69Pa 131
Swan Pl. SW13 54Va 110
TN16: Westrm 99Tc 200
Swan Rd. EN8: Walt C 6Ac 20
SE16 47Yb 92
SE18 48Mc 93
SL0: Iver 44H 83
TW13: Hanw 64Aa 129
UB1: S'hall 44Da 85
UB7: W Dray 47M 83
Swans, The UB9: Den 29H 43
Swan Sanctuary, The 72U 150
Swans Cl. AL4: St A 3J 7
SWANSCOMBE 57Be 121
Swanscombe Bus. Cen.
DA10: Swans 56Ae 121
Swanscombe Heritage Pk. 58Zd 121
Swanscombe Ho. *W11* 46Za 88
(off St Ann's Rd.)
Swanscombe Leisure Cen. 58Zd 121
Swanscombe Rd. W4 50Ua 88
W11 46Za 88
Swanscombe Skull Site
National Nature Reserve 58Zd 121
Swanscombe St. DA10: Swans 59Ae 121
Swans Ct. EN8: Walt C 6Ac 20
Swansea Cl. RM5: Col R 24Fd 56
Swansea Ct. *E16* 46Rc 94
(off Fishguard Way)
Swansea Rd. EN3: Pond E 14Yb 34
TW14: Felt 58S 106
Swanshope IG10: Lough 12Rc 36
Swansland Gdns. E17 25Ac 52
Swansmere Cl. KT12: Walt T 74Y 151
Swanston Ho. *WD18: Wat* 14W 26
(off Whippendell Rd.)
Swanston Path WD19: Wat 20Y 27
Swan St. SE1 3E 230 (48Sb 91)
TW7: Isle 55Ka 108
Swansway, The KT13: Weyb 76Q 150
Swan Ter. SL4: Wind 2F 102
Swanton Ct. SE13 55Dc 114
Swanton Gdns. SW19 60Za 110
Swanton La. TN11: Roug 100Fe 205
Swanton Rd. DA8: Erith 52Cd 118
Swan Wlk. RM1: Rom 29Gd 56
SW3 51Hb 111
TW17: Shep 73U 150
Swan Way EN3: Enf H 12Zb 34
Swan Wharf Bus. Cen. UB8: Uxb 40K 63
Swanwick Cl. SW15 59Va 110
Swanworth La. RH5: Mick 100Ja 192
Swan Yd. N1 37Rb 71
Swanzy Rd. TN14: S'oaks 92Ld 203
Sward Rd. BR5: St M Cry 72Wc 161
Swathling Ho. *SW15* 58Va 110
(off Tunworth Cres.)
Swaton Rd. E3 42Cc 92
Swaylands Rd. DA17: Belv 51Cd 118
Swaythling Cl. N18 21Xb 51
Swedeland Ct. E1 1J 225
Swedenborg Gdns. E1 45Xb 91
Sweden Ga. SE16 48Ac 92
Swedish Quays SE16 48Ac 92
(not continuous)
Sweeney Cres. SE1 2K 231 (47Vb 91)
Sweeps Ditch Cl. TW18: Staines 66J 127
Sweeps La. BR5: St M Cry 71Zc 161
TW20: Egh 64B 126
Sweetbriar Av. SM5: Cars 74Hb 155
Sweet Briar Grn. N9 20Vb 33
Sweet Briar Gro. N9 20Vb 33
Sweet Briar La. KT18: Eps 86Ta 173
Sweet Briar Wlk. N18 21Vb 51
Sweetcroft La. UB10: Hil 38P 63
Sweetland Ct. RM8: Dag 37Xc 75
Sweetmans Av. HA5: Pinn 27Z 45
Sweets Way N20 19Fb 31
Swell Ct. E17 30Cc 52
Swetenham Wlk. SE18 50Sc 94
Swete St. E13 40Jc 73
Sweyne Rd. DA10: Swans 58Ae 121
Sweyn Pl. SE3 54Jc 115
Swievelands Rd. TN16: Big H 91Kc 199
Swift Cen. CR0: Wadd 80Pb 156
Swift Cl. E17 24Ac 52
HA2: Harr 33Da 65
KT17: Ewe 82Wa 174
RM14: Upm 32Ud 78
SE28 45Xc 95
SL1: Slou 5D 80
UB3: Hayes 44V 84
Swift Ct. SM2: Sutt 80Db 155
TN15: Seal 93Qd 203
Swift Ho. *E3* 39Bc 72
(off Old Ford Rd.)
NW6 40Bb 69
(off Albert Rd.)
Swift Lodge *W9* 43Cb 89
(off Admiral Wlk.)
Swift Rd. TW13: Hanw 62Aa 129
UB2: S'hall 48Ca 85
Swiftsden Way BR1: Brom 65Gc 137
Swiftstone Twr. SE10 48Jc 93
Swift St. SW6 53Bb 111
Swiftsure Rd. RM16: Chaf H 49Yd 98
Swiller's La. DA12: Shorne 4N 145
SWILLET, THE 16D 24
Swimmers La. E2 1K 219 (39Vb 71)
Swinbrook Rd. W10 43Ab 88
Swinburne Ct. *SE5* 56Tb 113
(off Basingdon Way)
Swinburne Cres. CR0: C'don 72Yb 158
Swinburne Gdns. RM18: Tilb 4D 122
Swinburne Ho. *E2* 41Yb 92
(off Roman Rd.)
Swinburne Rd. SW15 56Wa 110
Swinderby Rd. HA0: Wemb 37Na 67
Swindon Cl. IG3: Ilf 33Uc 74
RM3: Rom 22Pd 57
Swindon Gdns. RM3: Rom 22Pd 57
Swindon La. RM3: Rom 22Pd 57
Swindon Rd.
TW6: H'row A 57S 106
Swindon St. W12 46Xa 88
Swinfield Cl. TW13: Hanw 62Aa 129
Swinford Gdns. SW9 55Rb 113
Swingate La. SE18 51Uc 116
Swingfield Ho. *E9* 39Yb 72
(off Templecombe Rd.)
Swing Ga. La. HP4: Berk 3A 2
Swinley Ho. NW1 3A 216
Swinnerton St. E9 36Ac 72
Swinson Ho. N11 22Lb 50
Swinton Cl. HA9: Wemb 32Ra 67
Swinton Pl. WC1 3H 217 (41Pb 90)
Swinton St. WC1 3H 217 (41Pb 90)
Swires Shaw BR2: Kes 77Mc 159
Swiss Av. WD18: Wat 14U 26
Swiss Cl. WD18: Wat 13U 26
SWISS COTTAGE 38Fb 69
Swiss Cott. Pl.
IG10: Lough 15Mc 35
Swiss Cottage Sports Cen. 38Fb 69
Swiss Ct. W1 5E 222
Swiss Ter. NW6 38Fb 69
Switch Ho. E14 45Fc 93
Swithland Gdns. SE9 63Qc 138
Swyncombe Av. W5 49Ka 86
Swynford Gdns. NW4 28Wa 48
Sybil M. N4 30Rb 51
Sybil Phoenix Cl. SE8 50Zb 92
Sybil Thorndike Casson Ho.
SW5 50Cb 89
(off Kramer M.)
Sybourn St. E17 31Bc 72
Sycamore App. WD3: Crox G 15S 26
Sycamore Av. AL10: Hat 1C 8
DA15: Sidc 58Vc 117
E3 39Bc 72
GU22: Wok 92A 188
RM14: Upm 34Qd 77
UB3: Hayes 45U 84
W5 48Ma 87
Sycamore Cl. CM14: Gt War 23Xd 58
CR2: S Croy 78Ub 157
DA12: Grav'nd 9F 122
E16 42Gc 93
EN4: E Barn 16Fb 31
HA8: Edg 21Sa 47
IG10: Lough 12Rc 36
KT19: Ewe 78Ra 153
KT22: Fet 95Ha 192
N9 21Wb 51
RM18: Tilb 4C 122
SE9 61Nc 138
SM5: Cars 77Hb 155
TW13: Felt 62W 128
UB5: N'olt 39Aa 65
UB7: Yiew 45P 83
W3 46Ua 88
WD23: Bush 12Aa 27
WD25: Wat 7X 13
Sycamore Ct. *DA8: Erith* 50Fd 96
(off Sandcliff Rd.)
DA9: Ghithe 59Ud 120
E7 37Jc 73
KT3: N Mald 69Ua 132
KT13: Weyb 76V 150
NW6 39Cb 69
(off Bransdale Cl.)
RH8: Oxt 1J 211
RM12: Horn 32Hd 76
SE1 2H 231
SL4: Wind 5G 102
TW4: Houn 56Aa 107
Sycamore Dr. AL2: Park 9B 6
BR8: Swan 69Gd 140
CM14: B'wood 18Yd 40
Sycamore Gdns. CR4: Mitc 68Fb 133
N15 28Vb 51
W6 47Xa 88
Sycamore Gro. KT3: N Mald 69Ta 131
NW9 31Sa 67
RM2: Rom 26Jd 56
SE6 58Ec 114
SE20 67Wb 135
Sycamore Hill N11 23Jb 50
Sycamore Ho. BR2: Brom 68Gc 137
CR6: W'ham 87Dc 178
IG9: Buck H 19Mc 35
N2 26Fb 49
(off The Grange)
SE16 47Zb 92
(off Woodland Cres.)
W6 47Xa 88
WD23: Bush 15Z 27
(off Plantation Cl.)
Sycamore Lodge BR6: Orp 75Vc 161
TW16: Sun 66V 128
W8 48Db 89
(off Stone Hall Pl.)
Sycamore M. CR3: Cat'm 95Tb 197
DA8: Erith 50Fd 96
(off St John's Rd.)
SW4 55Lb 112
Sycamore Path *E17* 30Dc 52
(off Poplars Rd.)
Sycamore Pl. BR1: Brom 69Qc 138
IG7: Chig 21Tc 54
Sycamore Ri. SM7: Bans 86Za 174
Sycamore Rd. DA1: Dart 60Md 119
SW19 65Ya 132
WD3: Crox G 15S 26
Sycamores, The AL1: St A 3B 6
BR8: Hext 65Hd 140
EN9: Walt A 7Lc 21
HP3: Hem H 5H 3
KT23: Bookh 96Ea 192
RM15: Avel 46Td 98
WD7: R'lett 6Ka 14
Sycamore St. EC1 6D 218 (42Sb 91)
Sycamore Wlk. IG6: Ilf 28Sc 54
RH2: Reig 9L 207
SL3: Geor G 44A 82
TW20: Eng G 5M 125
W10 42Ab 88
Sycamore Way CR7: Thor H 71Qb 156
RM15: S Ock 42Zd 99
TW11: Tedd 65La 130
Sydcote SE21 60Sb 113
SYDENHAM 63Yb 136
Sydenham Av. N21 15Pb 32
SE26 64Xb 135
Sydenham Cl. RM1: Rom 27Hd 56
Sydenham Cotts. SE12 61Lc 137
Sydenham Ct.
CR0: C'don 74Tb 157
(off Sydenham Rd.)
Sydenham Gdns. SL1: Slou 7G 80
Sydenham Hill SE23 60Xb 113
SE26 63Vb 135
Sydenham Hill Local Nature Reserve 61Wb 135
Sydenham Pk. SE26 62Yb 136
Sydenham Pk. Mans. *SE26* 62Yb 136
(off Sydenham Pk.)
Sydenham Pk. Rd. SE26 62Yb 136
Sydenham Pl. SE27 62Rb 135
Sydenham Ri. SE23 61Xb 135
Sydenham Rd. CR0: C'don 74Sb 157
SE26 64Zb 136
Sydmons Ct. SE23 59Yb 114
Sydner M. N16 35Vb 71
Sydner Rd. N16 35Vb 71
Sydney Av. CR8: Purl 84Pb 176
Sydney Chapman Way EN5: Barn 12Bb 31
Sydney Cl. SW3 6C 226 (49Fb 89)
Sydney Ct. UB4: Yead 42Y 85
Sydney Cres. TW15: Ashf 65R 128
Sydney Gro. NW4 29Ya 48
SL1: Slou 4G 80
Sydney M. SW3 6C 226 (49Fb 89)
Sydney Pl. AL3: St A 2A 6
SW7 6C 226 (49Fb 89)
Sydney Rd. DA6: Bex 56Zc 117
DA14: Sidc 63Uc 138
E11 30Kc 53
EN2: Enf 14Tb 33
IG6: Ilf 26Sc 54
IG8: Wfd G 21Jc 53
N8 28Qb 50
N10 25Jb 50
RM18: Tilb 4C 122
SE2 48Yc 95
SM1: Sutt 77Cb 155
SW20 68Za 132
TW9: Rich 56Na 109
TW11: Tedd 64Ha 130
TW14: Felt 60W 106
W13 46Ja 86
WD18: Wat 15U 26
Sydney Russell Leisure Cen. 36Ad 75
Sydney Simmons KT21: Asht 90Pa 173
Sydney St. SW3 6D 226 (50Gb 89)
Sydney Ter. *KT10: Clay* 79Ha 152
(off The Green)
Syke Cluan SL0: Rich P 47G 82
Syke Ings SL0: Rich P 48G 82
Sykes Dr. TW18: Staines 64K 127
Sykes Rd. SL1: Slou 4F 80
Sylva Cotts. SE8 53Cc 114
Sylvana Cl. UB10: Hil 39P 63
Sylvan Av. N3 26Cb 49
N22 24Pb 50
NW7 23Ua 48
RM6: Chad H 30Bd 55
RM11: Horn 30Nd 57
Sylvan Cl. CR2: Sels 82Xb 177
GU22: Wok 89D 168
HP3: Hem H 3A 4
RH8: Limp 1M 211
RM16: Chaf H 49Ae 99
Sylvan Ct. N12 20Db 31
NW6 39Db 69
(off Abbey Rd.)
Sylvan Est. SE19 67Vb 135
Sylvan Gdns. KT6: Surb 73Ma 153
Sylvan Gro. NW2 35Za 68
SE15 51Xb 113
Sylvan Hgts. AL1: St A 4E 6
Sylvan Hill SE19 67Ub 135
Sylvan M. *DA9: Ghithe* 56Xd 120
(off Watermans Way)
Sylvan Rd. E7 37Kc 73
E11 29Jc 53
E17 29Cc 52
IG1: Ilf 33Sc 74
SE19 67Vb 135
Sylvan Ter. *SE15* 51Xb 113
(off Sylvan Gro.)
Sylvan Wlk. BR1: Brom 69Pc 138
Sylvan Way BR4: W W'ck 77Gc 159
IG7: Chig 20Xc 37
RH1: Redh 7A 208
RM8: Dag 35Xc 75
Sylverdale Rd. CR0: C'don 76Rb 157
CR8: Purl 85Rb 177
Sylvester Av. BR7: Chst 65Pc 138
Sylvester Gdns. IG6: Ilf 22Xc 55
Sylvester Path E8 37Xb 71
Sylvester Pl. CR3: Cat'm 95Tb 197
Sylvester Rd. E8 37Xb 71
E17 31Bc 72
HA0: Wemb 36La 66
N2 26Eb 49
Sylvestres TN13: Riv 93Fd 202
Sylvestrian Leisure Cen. 28Gc 53
Sylvestrus Cl. KT1: King T 67Qa 131
Sylvia Av. CM13: Hut 19Ee 41
HA5: Hat E 23Aa 45
Sylvia Ct. HA9: Wemb 38Ra 67
N1 2G 219
Sylvia Gdns. HA9: Wemb 38Ra 67
Sylvia Pankhurst Ho. *RM10: Dag* 34Cd 76
(off Wythenshawe Rd.)
Symes M. NW1 1B 216 (40Lb 70)
Symington Ho. SE1 3F 231
Symington M. E9 36Zb 72
Symister M. N1 4H 219
Symonds Cl. TN15: W King 78Ud 164
Symonds Ct. EN8: Chesh 1Zb 20
Symons Cl. SE15 54Yb 114
Symons St. SW3 6G 227 (49Hb 89)
Sympathy Vale DA1: Dart 54Pd 119
Symphony Cl. HA8: Edg 24Ra 47
Symphony M. W10 41Ab 88
Syon Ct. AL1: St A 3E 6
E11 29Kc 53
Syon Ga. Way TW8: Bford 52Ja 108
Syon House 53La 108
Syon La. TW7: Isle 51Ga 108
Syon Lodge SE12 59Jc 115
Syon Pk. 53Ka 108
Syon Pk. Gdns. TW7: Isle 52Ha 108
Syracuse Av. RM13: Rain 41Nd 97
Syringa Ct. RM17: Grays 52Fe 121

403

Teesdale St.—Thellusson Way

Teesdale St. E2 40Xb 71
Teesdale Yd. E2 40Xb 71
(off Teesdale St.)
Tees Dr. RM3: Rom 20Md 39
Teeswater Ct. DA18: Erith 48Zc 95
Teevan Cl. CR0: C'don 73Wb 157
Teevan Rd. CR0: C'don 74Wb 157
Tegan Cl. SM2: Sutt 80Cb 155
Tegg's La. GU22: Pyr 88H 169
Teign M. SE9 61Nc 138
Teignmouth Cl. HA8: Edg 26Pa 47
SW4 56Mb 112
Teignmouth Gdns.
UB6: G'frd 40Ja 66
Teignmouth Pde. UB6: G'frd 40Ja 66
Teignmouth Rd. DA16: Well 54Yc 117
NW2 36Za 68
Telcon Way SE10 49Gc 93
Telcote Way HA4: Ruis 31Y 65
Telegraph Av. SE10 49Gc 93
Telegraph Hill NW3 34Db 69
Telegraph La. KT10: Clay 77Ha 152
Telegraph M. IG3: Ilf 32Wc 75
Telegraph Pas. SW2 59Nb 112
(off New Pk. Rd.)
Telegraph Path
BR7: Chst 64Rc 138
Telegraph Pl. E14 49Dc 92
Telegraph Rd. SW15 59Xa 110
Telegraph St. EC2 2F 225 (44Tb 91)
Telegraph Track
SM5: Cars 83Jb 176
Telemann Sq. SE3 56Kc 115
Telephone Pl. SW6 51Bb 111
Telfer Cl. W3 47Sa 87
Telfer Ho. EC1 4D 218
Telferscot Rd. SW12 60Mb 112
Telford Av. SW2 60Mb 112
Telford Cl. E17 31Ac 72
SE19 65Vb 135
WD25: Wat 7Z 13
Telford Ct. AL1: St A 3C 6
AL10: Hat 2B 8
Telford Dr. KT12: Walt T 73Y 151
SL1: Slou 7E 80
Telford Ho. SE1 3D 230
W10 43Ab 88
(off Portobello Rd.)
Telford Rd. AL2: Lon C 9G 6
N11 22Lb 50
NW9 30Wa 48
SE9 61Tc 138
TW2: Whitt 59Ca 107
UB1: S'hall 45Da 85
W10 43Ab 88
Telford Sq. DA1: Dart 55Pd 119
Telfords Yd. E1 45Wb 91
Telford Ter. SW1 51Lb 112
Telford Way UB4: Yead 43Aa 85
W3 43Ua 88
Telham Rd. E6 40Qc 74
Tell Gro. SE22 56Vb 113
Tellisford KT10: Esh 77Da 151
Tellson Av. SE18 53Mc 115
Telscombe Cl. BR6: Orp 75Uc 160
Telston La. TN14: Otf 89Gd 182
Temair Ho. SE10 52Dc 114
(off Tarves Way)
Temeraire Pl. TW8: Bford 50Pa 87
Temeraire St. SE16 47Yb 92
Tempelhof Av. NW2 31Ya 68
NW4 31Ya 68
Temperance St. AL3: St A 2A 6
Temperley Rd. SW12 59Jb 112
Tempest Av. EN6: Pot B 4Fb 17
Tempest Rd. TW20: Egh 65E 126
Tempest Way RM13: Rain 37Jd 76
Templar Ct. NW8 4B 214
RM7: Mawney 28Dd 56
Templar Dr. DA11: Grav'nd 4C 144
SE28 44Zc 95
Templar Ho. HA2: Harr 33Ea 66
NW2 37Bb 69
Templar Pl. TW12: Hamp 66Ca 129
Templars Av. NW11 30Bb 49
Templars Ct. DA1: Dart 57Qd 119
Templars Cres. N3 26Cb 49
Templars Dr. HA3: Hrw W 23Fa 46
Templars Ho. E16 45Rc 94
(off University Way)
Templar St. SE5 54Rb 113
Temple Av. CR0: C'don 75Bc 158
EC4 4A 224 (45Qb 90)
N20 17Fb 31
RM8: Dag 32Cd 76
Temple Bar 3K 223
Temple Bar Gate 3C 224
Temple Bar Rd. GU21: Wok 1K 187
Temple Chambers EC4 4A 224
Temple Cl. E11 31Gc 73
EN7: Chesh 3Wb 19
KT19: Eps 84Ta 173
N3 26Bb 49
SE28 48Sc 94
WD17: Wat 12V 26
Templecombe M. GU22: Wok 88D 168
Templecombe Rd. E9 39Yb 72
Templecombe Way SM4: Mord 71Ab 154
Temple Ct. E1 43Zb 92
(off Rectory Sq.)
EN6: Pot B 3Ab 16
KT13: Weyb 77R 150
KT19: Eps 84Ta 173
SW8 52Nb 112
(off Thorncroft St.)
Templecroft TW15: Ashf 65T 128
Templedene Av. TW18: Staines 66K 127
Temple Dwellings E2 40Xb 71
(off Temple St.)
Templefield Cl. KT15: Add 79K 149
TEMPLE FORTUNE 29Bb 49
Temple Fortune Hill NW11 29Cb 49
Temple Fortune La. NW11 30Bb 49
Temple Fortune Pde. NW11 29Bb 49
Temple Gdns. EC4 4K 223
N21 19Rb 33
NW11 30Bb 49
RM8: Dag 34Zc 75
TW18: Staines 67H 127
WD3: Rick 21R 44
Temple Gro. EN2: Enf 12Rb 33
NW11 30Cb 49
Temple Hall Ct. E4 19Fc 35
TEMPLE HILL 57Pd 119
Temple Hill DA1: Dart 58Pd 119
Temple Hill Sq.
DA1: Dart 57Pd 119
Temple Ho. EN7: Walt C 5Wb 19
Temple La. EC4 3A 224 (44Qb 90)
Templeman Cl. CR8: Purl 88Rb 177
Templeman Rd. W7 43Ha 86
Temple Mkt. KT13: Weyb 77R 150
Temple Mead HP2: Hem H 1M 3
Templemead SL9: Ger X 2N 61
Temple Mead Cl.
HA7: Stan 23Ka 46
Templemead Cl. W3 44Ua 88
Templemead Ho. E9 35Ac 72
Templemere KT13: Weyb 76T 150
TEMPLE MILLS 35Dc 72
Temple Mills La. E10 35Dc 72
E15 36Ec 72
E20 35Dc 72
Temple of Mithras (remains) 3F 225
Templepan La.
WD3: Chan C 9N 11
Temple Pde. EN5: New Bar 17Fb 31
(off Netherlands Rd.)
Temple Pk. UB8: Hil 41Q 84
Temple Pl. WC2 4J 223 (45Pb 90)
Templer Av. RM16: Grays 9C 100
Temple Rd. CR0: C'don 77Tb 157
E6 39Nc 74
KT19: Eps 84Ta 173
N8 28Pb 50
NW2 35Ya 68
SL4: Wind 4G 102
TN16: Big H 89Mc 179
TW3: Houn 56Da 107
TW9: Rich 54Pa 109
W4 48Sa 87
W5 48Ma 87
Temple Sheen SW14 56Sa 109
Temple Sheen Rd.
SW14 56Ra 109
Temple St. E2 40Xb 71
Temple Ter. N22 26Qb 50
(off Vincent Rd.)
Templeton Av. E4 21Cc 52
Templeton Cl. N15 30Tb 51
N16 36Ub 71
SE19 67Tb 135
Templeton Ct. AL1: St A 1C 6
(off Newsom Pl.)
EN3: Enf W 10Yb 20
WD6: Bore 11Pa 29
(off Lyndhurst Wlk.)
Templeton Pl. SW5 49Cb 89
Templeton Rd. N15 30Tb 51
Temple Vw. AL3: St A 1A 6
Temple Way SL2: Farn C 6G 60
SM1: Sutt 76Fb 155
Temple W. M. SE11 4B 230 (48Rb 91)
Templewood W13 43Ka 86
Templewood Av. NW3 34Db 69
Temple Wood Dr.
RH1: Redh 3P 207
Templewood Gdns. NW3 34Db 69
Templewood Ga. SL2: Farn C 6G 60
Templewood La.
SL2: Farn C, Stoke P 6G 60
Templewood Point NW2 33Bb 69
(off Granville Rd.)
Temple Yd. E2 40Xb 71
(off Temple St.)
Tempo Ho. UB5: N'olt 40Z 65
Tempsford Av. WD6: Bore 14Ta 29
Tempsford Cl. EN2: Enf 14Sb 33
Tempsford Ct. HA1: Harr 30Ha 46
Tempus Apartments EC1 3B 218
Tempus Ct. E18 25Jc 53
Tempus Wharf SE16 47Wb 91
(off Bermondsey Wall W.)
Temsford Cl. HA2: Harr 26Ea 46
Tenacre GU21: Wok 10L 167
Ten Acre La.
TW20: Thorpe 68E 126
Ten Acres KT22: Fet 96Fa 192
Ten Acres Cl. KT22: Fet 96Fa 192
Tenbury Cl. E7 36Mc 73
Tenbury Ct. SW2 60Mb 112
Tenby Av. HA3: Kenton 26Ka 46
Tenby Cl. N15 28Vb 51
RM6: Chad H 30Ad 55
Tenby Ct. E17 29Ac 52
Tenby Dr. SL5: S'hill 1B 146
Tenby Gdns. UB5: N'olt 37Ca 65
Tenby Ho. UB3: Harl 48S 84
W2 3A 220
Tenby Mans. W1 7J 215
Tenby Rd. DA16: Well 53Zc 117
E17 29Ac 52
EN3: Pond E 14Yb 34
HA8: Edg 25Pa 47
RM6: Chad H 30Ad 55
Tenchley's La. RH8: Limp 3N 211
Tench St. E1 46Xb 91
Tenda Rd. SE16 49Xb 91
Tendring Ct. CM13: Hut 15Fe 41
Tendring Way RM6: Chad H 29Yc 55
Tenham Av. SW2 60Mb 112
Tenison Ct. W1 4B 222 (45Lb 90)
Tenison Way SE1 7K 223
Tennants Row RM18: Tilb 4A 122
Tenniel Cl. W2 45Eb 89
Tennis Ct. La. KT8: E Mos 69Ha 130
Tennison Av. WD6: Bore 15Ra 29
Tennison Cl. CR5: Coul 92Rb 197
Tennison Rd. SE25 70Vb 135
Tennis St. SE1 1F 231 (47Tb 91)
Tenniswood Rd.
EN1: Enf 11Ub 33
Tenny Ho. RM17: Grays 52De 121
Tennyson CR0: C'don 74Sb 157
N8 27Nb 50
(off Boyton Cl.)
Tennyson Av. E11 31Jc 73
E12 38Nc 74
EN9: Walt A 6Gc 21
KT3: N Mald 71Xa 154
NW9 27Sa 47
RM17: Grays 48De 99
TW1: Twick 60Ha 108
Tennyson Cl.
DA16: Well 53Uc 116
EN3: Pond E 15Zb 34
TW14: Felt 58V 106
Tennyson Ct. NW1 6F 215
SW6 53Eb 111
(off Imperial Rd.)
Tennyson Ho. DA17: Belv 50Bd 95
SE17 7E 230
Tennyson Mans. SW3 51Gb 111
(off Lordship Pl.)
W14 51Bb 111
(off Queen's Club Gdns.)
Tennyson Rd. AL2: Chis G 8N 5
CM13: Hut 17Ee 41
DA1: Dart 57Qd 119
E10 32Dc 72
E15 38Gc 73
E17 30Bc 52
KT15: Add 77N 149
NW6 39Bb 69
NW7 22Wa 48
RM3: Rom 24Ld 57
SE20 66Zb 136
SW19 65Eb 133
TW3: Houn 54Ea 108
TW15: Ashf 64N 127
W7 45Ha 86
Tennyson St. SW8 54Kb 112
Tennyson Wlk. DA11: Nflt 62Fe 143
RM18: Tilb 4D 122
Tennyson Way RM12: Horn 33Hd 76
SL2: Slou 2C 80
Tenpin
Acton 42Qa 87
Bexleyheath 56Bd 117
Croydon 75Pb 156
Feltham 61X 129
Kingston upon Thames 68Na 131
(within The Rotunda Cen.)
Tensing Av. DA11: Nflt 2A 144
Tensing Ct. TW19: Stanw 60N 105
Tensing Rd. UB2: S'hall 48Ca 85
Tentelow La. UB2: S'hall 50Ca 85
Tenterden Cl. NW4 27Za 48
SE9 63Pc 138
Tenterden Dr. NW4 27Za 48
Tenterden Gdns. CR0: C'don 73Wb 157
NW4 27Za 48
Tenterden Gro. NW4 27Za 48
Tenterden Ho. SE17 7H 231
Tenterden Rd. CR0: C'don 73Wb 157
N17 24Vb 51
RM8: Dag 33Bd 75
Tenterden St. W1 3A 222 (44Kb 90)
Tenter Ground E1 1K 225 (43Vb 91)
Tenter Pas. E1 3K 225
Tenth Av. KT20: Lwr K 98Ab 194
Tent Peg La. BR5: Pet W 71Sc 160
Tent St. E1 42Xb 91
Tenzing Ct. E14 43Dc 92
(off Hillary M.)
Tenzing Rd. HP2: Hem H 2A 4
Tequila Wharf E14 44Ac 92
Tera 40 UB6: G'frd 38Ea 66
Terborch Way SE22 57Ub 113
Tercel Path IG7: Chig 21Xc 55
Teredo St. SE16 48Zb 92
Terence Cl. DA12: Grav'nd 10H 123
Terence Ct. DA17: Belv 51Bd 117
(off Nuxley Rd.)
Terence McMillan Stadium 42Lc 93
Terence Messenger Twr. E10 33Dc 72
(off Alpine Rd.)
Teresa Gdns. EN8: Walt C 6Yb 20
Teresa M. E17 28Cc 52
Teresa Wlk. N10 29Kb 50
Terling Cl. E11 34Hc 73
Terling Ho. W10 43Ya 88
(off Sutton Way)
Terling Rd. RM8: Dag 33Cd 76
Terlings, The CM14: B'wood 20Wd 40
Terling Wlk. N1 39Sb 71
(off Popham St.)
TERMINAL 4 RDBT. 58S 106
TERMINAL 5 RDBT. 54K 105
Terminal Ho. HA7: Stan 22Ma 47
Terminus Pl. SW1 4A 228 (48Kb 90)
Tern Gdns. RM14: Upm 32Ud 78
Tern Way CM14: B'wood 21Ud 58
Terrace, The DA12: Grav'nd 8D 122
E2 41Yb 92
(off Old Ford Rd.)
E4 20Gc 35
(off Newgate St.)
EC4 3K 223
GU22: Wok 92C 188
(not continuous)
IG8: Wfd G 23Jc 53
KT15: Add 78N 149
N3 26Bb 49
NW6 39Cb 69
SE8 49Bc 92
(off Longshore)
SE23 59Ac 114
SL5: S'hill 1B 146
SW13 54Ua 110
TN13: Riv 94Fd 202
Terrace Apartments N5 36Qb 70
Terrace Gdns. SW13 54Va 110
WD17: Wat 12X 27
Terrace Hill CR0: C'don 76Rb 157
(off Hanover St.)
Terrace La. TW10: Rich 58Na 109
Terrace Rd. E9 38Yb 72
E13 40Jc 73
KT12: Walt T 73W 150
Terraces, The DA2: Dart 59Sd 120
E2 40Wb 71
(off Garner St.)
NW8 1B 214
Terrace St. DA12: Grav'nd 8D 122
(not continuous)
Terrace Wlk. RM9: Dag 36Ad 75
SW11 52Hb 111
Terracotta Rd. RH9: S God 10A 210
Terrano Ho. TW9: Kew 52Ra 109
Terrapin Rd. SW17 62Kb 134
Terrent Ct. SL4: Wind 3E 102
Terretts Pl. N1 38Rb 71
(off Upper St.)
Terrick Rd. N22 25Nb 50
Terrick St. W12 44Xa 88
Terrilands HA5: Pinn 27Ba 45
Territorial Ho. SE11 6A 230
Terront Rd. N15 28Sb 51
Terry Pl. UB8: Cowl 43L 83
Terry's Lodge Rd. TN15: Wro 86Xd 184
Terry Spinks Pl. E16 43Gc 93
(off Barking Rd.)
Tersha St. TW9: Rich 56Pa 109
Tesla Ct. W3 47Ua 88
Tessa Sanderson Pl. SW8 55Kb 112
(off Daley Thompson Way)
Tessa Sanderson Way UB6: G'frd 36Fa 66
Tester's Cl. RH8: Oxt 3M 211
Testerton Rd. W11 45Za 88
(off Hurstway Wlk.)
Testerton Wlk. W11 45Za 88
Testwood Ct. W7 45Ga 86
Testwood Rd. SL4: Wind 3B 102
Tetbury Pl. N1 1B 218 (39Rb 71)
Tetcott Rd. SW10 52Eb 111
(not continuous)
Tetherdown N10 27Jb 50
Tetty Way BR1: Brom 68Jc 137
Tevatree Ho. SE1 50Wb 91
(off Old Kent Rd.)
Teversham La. SW8 53Nb 112
Teviot Av. RM15: Avel 44Sd 98
Teviot Cl. DA16: Well 53Xc 117
Teviot Est. E14 43Dc 92
Teviot St. E14 43Ec 92
Tewin Rd. HP2: Hem H 2C 4
Tewkesbury Av. HA5: Pinn 29Aa 45
SE23 60Xb 113
Tewkesbury Cl.
EN4: E Barn 14Fb 31
IG10: Lough 16Nc 36
KT14: Byfl 83M 169
N15 30Tb 51
Tewkesbury Gdns. NW9 27Ra 47
Tewkesbury Rd. N15 30Tb 51
SM5: Cars 74Fb 155
W13 46Ja 86
Tewkesbury Ter. N11 23Lb 50
Tewson Rd. SE18 50Uc 94
Texcel Bus. Pk. DA1: Erith 54Hd 118
Texryte Ho. N1 39Tb 71
(off Southgate Rd.)
Textile Ho. E1 43Zb 92
(off Duckett St.)
Teynham Av. EN1: Enf 16Tb 33
Teynham Ct. BR3: Beck 69Dc 136
Teynham Grn. BR2: Brom 71Jc 159
Teynham Rd. DA2: Dart 60Sd 120
Teynton Ter. N17 25Sb 51
Thackeray Av. N17 26Wb 51
RM18: Tilb 3D 122
Thackeray Cl. SW19 66Za 132
TW7: Isle 54Ja 108
UB8: Hil 44R 84
Thackeray Ct. NW6 38Eb 69
(off Fairfax Rd.)
SW3 7F 227
W5 44Pa 87
(off Hanger Va. La.)
W14 48Ab 88
(off Blythe Rd.)
Thackeray Dr. DA11: Nflt 61De 143
RM6: Chad H 31Wc 75
Thackeray Ho. WC1 5F 217
Thackeray Lodge TW14: Bedf 58T 106
Thackeray M. E8 37Wb 71
Thackeray Rd. E6 40Mc 73
SW8 54Kb 112
Thackeray St. W8 48Db 89
Thackery Ct. EC1 7B 218
Thackrah Cl. N2 26Eb 49
(off Simms Gdns.)
Thakeham Cl. SE26 63Xb 135
Thalia Cl. SE10 51Fc 115
Thalia Ct. E8 38Vb 71
(off Albion Dr.)
Thalmassing Cl. CM13: Hut 19De 41
Thame Rd. SE16 47Zb 92
Thames Av. KT4: Wor Pk 74Ya 154
KT16: Chert 69J 127
RM9: Dag, Rain 42Dd 96
SL4: Wind 2H 103
SW10 53Eb 111
UB6: G'frd 40Ha 66
Thames Bank SW14 54Sa 109
Thamesbank Pl. SE28 44Yc 95
Thames Barrier 47Mc 93
Thames Barrier Ind. Area SE18 48Mc 93
(off Faraday Way)
Thames Barrier Pk. 47Lc 93
Thames Barrier Vis. Cen. 48Mc 93
Thamesbrook SW3 7D 226
Thames Chase Forest Cen. 34Wd 78
Thames Circ. E14 49Cc 92
Thames Cl. KT16: Chert 73K 149
RM13: Rain 44Kd 97
SS17: Corr 1P 101
TW12: Hamp 68Da 129
Thames Cotts. KT7: T Ditt 72Ka 152
Thames Ct. KT8: W Mole 68Da 129
NW6 40Bb 69
(off Albert Rd.)
SE15 52Vb 113
(off Daniel Gdns.)
W7 44Ga 86
(off Hanway Rd.)
Thames Cres. W4 52Ua 110
Thamesdale AL2: Lon C 9K 7
THAMES DITTON 72Ja 152
Thames Ditton & Esher Golf Course
75Fa 152
Thames Dr. HA4: Ruis 30S 44
RM16: Grays 10C 100
Thames Edge Ct. TW18: Staines 63G 126
(off Clarence St.)
Thames Exchange Bldg. EC4 4E 224
Thames Eyot TW1: Twick 60Ja 108
Thamesfield Ct. TW17: Shep 73S 150
Thamesfield M. TW17: Shep 73S 150
Thames Ga. DA1: Dart 57Qd 119
Thamesgate TW18: Staines 67K 127
Thamesgate Cl. TW10: Ham 63Ka 130
Thamesgate Shop. Cen.
DA11: Grav'nd 8D 122
Thames Gateway RM9: Dag 40Bd 75
RM13: Rain, Wenn 43Gd 96
RM15: Avel, Purf 46Pd 97
Thames Gateway Pk. RM9: Dag 41Bd 95
Thames Haven KT6: Surb 71Ma 153
Thames Hgts. SE1 1K 231
Thameshill Av. RM5: Col R 26Ed 56
Thames Ho. DA1: Cray 55Jd 118
EC4 4E 224
KT1: King T 70Ma 131
(off Surbiton Rd.)
SW1 5F 229
Thameside KT8: W Mole 69Da 129
KT16: Chert 70L 127
TW11: Tedd 66Ma 131
TW18: Lale, Staines 64H 127
(not continuous)
Thameside Aviation Mus. 3M 123
Thameside Cen. TW8: Bford 51Pa 109
Thameside Ind. Est. DA8: Erith 51Md 119
E16 47Mc 93
Thameside Pl. KT1: Hamp W 67Ma 131
Thameside Theatre 50Ce 99
Thameside Wlk. SE28 44Wc 95
Thames Ind. Pk. RM18: E Til 10K 101
Thames Innovation Cen.
DA18: Erith 47Bd 95
Thames Lock KT12: Walt T 69Y 129
KT13: Weyb 76Q 150
THAMESMEAD 46Xc 95
Thames Mead SL4: Wind 3C 102
Thamesmead KT12: Walt T 72W 150
THAMESMEAD CENTRAL 46Wc 95
THAMESMEAD EAST 47Bd 95
THAMESMEAD NORTH 44Zc 95
Thames Mdw. KT8: W Mole 68Ca 129
TW17: Shep 74T 150
THAMESMEAD SOUTH 47Zc 95
THAMESMEAD SOUTH WEST 47Vc 95
THAMESMEAD WEST 48Sc 94
Thamesmere Dr. SE28 45Wc 95
Thamesmere Leisure Cen. 45Wc 95
Thames Path SE7 48Jc 93
SE10 48Jc 93
Thames Pl. SW15 55Za 110
Thames Point SW6 54Eb 111
Thamespoint TW11: Tedd 66Ma 131
Thames Quay E14 47Dc 92
SW10 53Eb 111
(off Chelsea Harbour)
Thames Reach KT1: Hamp W 67Ma 131
SE28 47Uc 94
W6 51Ya 110
(off Rainville Rd.)
Thames Rd. DA1: Cray 54Hd 118
E16 46Mc 93
IG11: Bark 41Vc 95
RM17: Grays 52De 121
SL3: L'ly 49C 82
SL4: Wind 2A 102
W4 51Qa 109
Thames Rd. Ind. Est. E16 46Mc 93
Thames Side KT1: King T 67Ma 131
KT7: T Ditt 72Ka 152
SL4: Wind 2H 103
Thames St. DA9: Ghithe 56Vd 120
KT1: King T 68Ma 131
KT12: Walt T 73V 150
KT13: Weyb 75R 150
SE10 51Dc 114
SL4: Wind 3H 103
TW12: Hamp 67Da 129
TW16: Sun 70W 128
TW18: Staines 64H 127
Thames Tunnel Mills SE16 47Yb 92
Thamesvale Cl. TW3: Houn 55Ca 107
Thames Valley Athletics Cen. 10J 81
Thames Vw. IG1: Ilf 33Sc 74
(off Axon Pl.)
RM16: Grays 10C 100
Thamesview Bus. Cen.
RM13: Rain 43Gd 96
Thamesview Golf Course 44Ad 95
Thames Vw. Ho's. KT12: Walt T 72W 150
Thames Vw. Lodge IG11: Bark 41Uc 94
Thames Village W4 53Sa 109
Thames Wlk. KT12: Walt T 73W 150
(off Manor Rd.)
SW11 52Gb 111
Thames Way DA11: Nflt, Grav'nd 57Ce 121
Thames Wharf Studios W6 51Ya 110
(off Rainville Rd.)
Thamley RM19: Purf 49Qd 97
Thanescroft Gdns. CR0: C'don 76Ub 157
Thanet Ct. W3 44Qa 87
Thanet Dr. BR2: Kes 76Mc 159
Thanet Ho. CR0: C'don 77Sb 157
(off Coombe Rd.)
DA11: Nflt 10B 122
WC1 4F 217
WD18: Wat 16V 26
(off Explorer Dr.)
Thanet Lodge NW2 37Ab 68
(off Mapesbury Rd.)
Thanet Pl. CR0: C'don 77Sb 157
Thanet Rd. DA5: Bexl 59Cd 118
DA8: Erith 52Gd 118
Thanet St. WC1 4F 217 (41Nb 90)
Thanet Wharf SE8 51Dc 114
(off Coppers St.)
Thane Vs. N7 34Pb 70
Thane Works N7 34Pb 70
Thanington Ct. SE9 58Uc 116
Thant Cl. E10 34Dc 72
Tharp Rd. SM6: Wall 78Mb 156
Thatcham Ct. N20 17Eb 31
Thatcham Gdns. N20 17Eb 31
Thatcher Cl. UB7: W Dray 47N 83
Thatcher Ct. DA1: Dart 59Md 119
Thatchers Cl. IG10: Lough 12Sc 36
Thatchers La. GU3: Worp 9H 187
Thatchers Way TW7: Isle 57Fa 108
Thatches Gro. RM6: Chad H 28Ad 55
Thavie's Inn EC4 2A 224 (44Qb 90)
Thaxted Bold CM13: Hut 15Fe 41
Thaxted Ct. N1 2G 219
Thaxted Grn. CM13: Hut 15Ee 41
Thaxted Ho. RM10: Dag 38Dd 76
SE16 49Yb 92
(off Abbeyfield Est.)
Thaxted Pl. SW20 66Za 132
Thaxted Rd. IG9: Buck H 17Nc 36
SE9 62Sc 138
Thaxted Wlk. RM13: Rain 38Gd 76
Thaxted Way EN9: Walt A 5Fc 21
Thaxton Pl. E4 17Fc 35
Thaxton Rd. W14 51Bb 111
Thayers Farm Rd. BR3: Beck 67Ac 136
Thayer St. W1 1J 221 (44Jb 90)
Thaynesfield EN6: Pot B 3Fb 17
The ....
Names prefixed with 'The' for example 'The Acacias,' are indexed under the main name such as 'Acacias, The'
Theatre Bldg. E3 41Cc 92
(off Paton Cl.)
Theatre Ct. KT18: Eps 85Ta 173
Theatre Pl. SE8 52Cc 114
(off Speedwell Ct.)
Theatre-Rites 2B 230
Theatre Royal
Drury Lane 3H 223
Haymarket 5E 222
Stratford 38Fc 73
Windsor 2H 103
Theatre Sq. E15 37Fc 73
Theatre St. SW11 55Hb 111
Theatre Vw. Apartments SE1 1A 230
Theatro Technis 1C 216
Theatro Twr. SE8 51Cc 114
Theberton St. N1 39Qb 70
Theed St. SE1 7K 223 (46Qb 90)
Thelbridge Ho. E3 41Dc 92
(off Bruce Rd.)
Thellusson Way WD3: Rick 18H 25

Thelma Cl.—Thurso St.

Thelma Cl. DA12: Grav'nd 4H 145
Thelma Gdns. SE3 ....53Mc 115
Thelma Gro. TW11: Tedd 65Ja 130
Thelusson Ct. WD7: R'lett 7Ja 14
Theobald Cres. HA3: Hrw W 25Ea 46
Theobald Rd. CR0: C'don 75Rb 157
E17 ....31Bc 72
Theobalds Av. N12 ....21Eb 49
RM17: Grays 50Ee 99
Theobalds Cl. EN6: Cuff 2Pb 18
TN15: Kems'g 90Qd 183
Theobalds Ct. EN8: Chesh 4Zb 20
(off Crossbrook St.)
N4 ....34Sb 71
Theobalds La. EN7: Walt C 4Wb 19
EN8: Chesh 4Wb 19
Theobalds Pk. Rd.
EN2: Crew H, Enf 7Rb 19
Theobald's Rd. WC1 ....1H 223 (43Pb 90)
Theobalds Rd. EN6: Cuff 2Nb 18
Theobald St. SE1 ....4F 231 (48Tb 91)
WD6: Bore 8Ka 14
WD7: R'lett 8Ka 14
Theodora Way HA5: Eastc 27V 44
Theodor Ct. NW9 ....26Ta 47
Theodore Ct. SE13 ....58Fc 115
Theodore Rd. SE13 ....58Fc 115
Thepps Cl. RH1: S Nut 9F 208
Therapia La. CR0: Bedd 73Mb 156
CR0: C'don 72Nb 156
Therapia Rd. SE22 ....58Yb 114
Theresa Rd. W6 ....49Wa 88
Theresa's Wlk. CR2: Sande 81Tb 177
Therfield Ct. N4 ....33Sb 71
Thermopylae Ga. E14 ....49Dc 92
Theseus Wlk. N1 ....2C 218
Thesiger Rd. SE20 ....66Zb 136
Thessaly Ho. SW8 ....52Lb 112
(off Thessaly Rd.)
Thessaly Rd. SW8 ....52Lb 112
(not continuous)
Thesus Ho. E14 ....44Ec 92
(off Blair St.)
Thetford Cl. N13 ....23Rb 51
Thetford Gdns. RM9: Dag 38Ad 75
Thetford Ho. SE1 ....3K 231
Thetford Rd. KT3: N Mald 72Ta 153
RM9: Dag 38Zc 75
TW15: Ashf 63N 127
Thetis Ter. TW9: Kew 51Qa 109
Theven St. E1 ....42Yb 92
THEYDON BOIS 8Uc 22
Theydon Bois Golf Course 6Tc 22
Theydon Bold CM13: Hut 15Fe 41
Theydon Bower CM16: Epp 3Wc 23
Theydon Ct. EN9: Walt A 5Jc 21
Theydon Gdns. RM13: Rain 38Gd 76
THEYDON GARNON 7Yc 23
Theydon Gro. CM16: Epp 2Wc 23
IG8: Wfd G 23Lc 53
THEYDON MOUNT 8Bd 23
Theydon Pk. Rd. CM16: They B 9Uc 22
Theydon Pl. CM16: Epp 3Vc 23
Theydon Rd. CM16: Epp 4Tc 22
E5 ....33Yb 72
Theydon St. E17 ....31Bc 72
Theydon Towers CM16: Epp 5Tc 22
Thicket, The UB7: Yiew 44N 83
Thicket Cres. SM1: Sutt 77Eb 155
Thicket Gro. RM9: Dag 37Yc 75
SE20 ....66Wb 135
Thicket Rd. SE20 ....66Wb 135
SM1: Sutt 77Eb 155
Thicketts TN13: S'oaks 95Ld 203
Thickthorne La. TW18: Staines 66L 127
Third Av. DA11: Nflt 10A 122
E12 ....35Nc 74
E13 ....41Jc 93
E17 ....29Cc 52
EN1: Enf 15Vb 33
EN9: Walt A 2Kc 21
HA9: Wemb 33Ma 67
KT20: Lwr K 97Ab 194
RM6: Chad H 30Yc 55
RM10: Dag 39Dd 76
RM20: W Thur 51Wd 120
UB3: Hayes 46V 84
W3 ....46Wa 88
W10 ....41Ab 88
WD25: Wat 7Z 13
Third Cl. KT8: W Mole 70Ea 130
Third Cres. SL1: Slou 3G 80
Third Cross Rd. TW2: Twick 61Fa 130
Third Way HA9: Wemb 35Ra 67
Thirkleby Cl. SL1: Slou 6G 80
Thirleby Rd. HA8: Edg 25Ta 47
NW7 ....22Ab 48
SW1 ....4C 228 (48Lb 90)
Thirlestane AL1: St A 1D 6
Thirlestane Cl. N10 ....26Jb 50
Thirlmere NW1 ....3A 216
Thirlmere Av. SL1: Slou 3A 80
UB6: G'frd 41La 86
Thirlmere Cl. TW20: Egh 66D 126
Thirlmere Dr. AL1: St A 4F 6
Thirlmere Gdns. HA6: Nwood 22R 44
HA9: Wemb 32La 66
Thirlmere Ho. N16 ....35Tb 71
(off Howard Rd.)
TW7: Isle 57Ha 108
Thirlmere Ri. BR1: Brom 65Hc 137
Thirlmere Rd. DA7: Bex 53Ed 118
N10 ....25Kb 50
SW16 ....63Mb 134
Thirsk Cl. UB5: N'olt 37Ca 65
Thirsk Rd. CR4: Mitc 66Jb 134
SE25 ....70Tb 135
SW11 ....55Jb 112
WD6: Bore 9Qa 15
Thirston Path WD6: Bore 12Qa 29
Thirteenth Av. KT20: Lwr K 98Bb 195
Thirza Ho. E1 ....44Yb 92
(off Devonport St.)
Thirza Rd. DA1: Dart 58Pd 119
Thistlebrook SE2 ....48Yc 95
Thistlebrook Ind. Est. SE2 ....48Yc 95
Thistle Cl. HP1: Hem H 3G 2
Thistle Cl. DA1: Dart 60Rd 119
(off Churchill Cl.)
SE12 ....61Jc 137
Thistlecroft HP1: Hem H 3K 3
Thistlecroft Gdns. HA7: Stan 25Ma 47
Thistlecroft Rd. KT12: Hers 77Y 151
Thistledene KT7: T Ditt 72Ga 152
KT14: W Byf 85H 169
Thistledene Av. HA2: Harr 34Aa 65
RM5: Col R 22Dd 56
Thistledown DA12: Grav'nd 5F 144
Thistlefield Cl. DA5: Bexl 60Zc 117
Thistle Gro. SW10 ....7A 226 (50Eb 89)
Thistle Ho. E14 ....44Ec 92
(off Dee St.)
Thistle Mead IG10: Lough 13Qc 36
Thistlemead BR7: Chst 68Rc 138
Thistle Rd. DA12: Grav'nd 9G 122
Thistles, The HP1: Hem H 1K 3
KT22: Lea 94La 192
Thistlewaite Rd. E5 ....34Xb 71
Thistlewood Cl. N7 ....33Pb 70
Thistlewood Cres. CR0: New Ad 84Fc 179
Thistleworth Cl. TW7: Isle 52Fa 108
Thistleworth Marina TW7: Isle 56Ka 108
(off Railshead Rd.)
Thistley Cl. CR5: Coul 94Mb 196
N12 ....23Gb 49
Thistley Ct. SE8 ....51Dc 114
Thoby La. CM15: Mount 11Ee 41
Thomas A Beckett Cl.
HA0: Wemb 35Ha 66
Thomas Av. CR3: Cat'm 93Sb 197
Thomas Baines Rd. SW11 ....55Fb 111
Thomas Bata Av. RM18: E Til 9K 101
Thomas Burt Ho. E2 ....41Xb 91
(off Canrobert St.)
Thomas Cl. CM15: B'wood 19Ae 41
Thomas Ct. IG6: Ilf 28Sc 54
Thomas Cribb M. E6 ....44Qc 94
Thomas Darby Ct. W11 ....44Ab 88
(off Lancaster Rd.)
Thomas Dean Rd. SE26 ....63Bc 136
Thomas Dinwiddy Rd. SE12 ....61Kc 137
Thomas Doyle St. SE1 ....3C 230 (48Rb 91)
Thomas Dr. DA12: Grav'nd 1F 144
RM2: Rom 28Ld 57
UB8: Uxb 37N 63
Thomas England Ho. RM7: Rom 30Fd 56
(off Waterloo Gdns.)
Thomas Frye Ct. E15 ....40Dc 72
(off High St.)
Thomas Fyre Dr. E3 ....40Cc 72
Thomas Hardy Ho. N22 ....24Pb 50
Thomas Hardy M. SW16 ....64Lb 134
Thomas Hewlett Ho. HA1: Harr 35Ga 66
Thomas Hollywood Ho. E2 ....40Yb 72
(off Approach Rd.)
Thomas Ho. SL2: Stoke P 8L 61
(off Bells Hill Grn.)
SM2: Sutt 80Db 155
Thomas Jacomb Pl. E17 ....28Bc 52
Thomas Joseph Ho. SE4 ....57Zb 114
(off St Norbert Rd.)
Thomas La. SE6 ....59Cc 114
Thomas Lodge E17 ....29Dc 52
Thomas Moore Ho. RH2: Reig 6L 207
(off Reigate Rd.)
Thomas More Gdns. KT10: Esh 76Ca 151
Thomas More Highwalk EC2 ....1D 224
Thomas More Ho. EC2 ....1D 224
HA4: Ruis 32U 64
Thomas More Sq. E1 ....45Wb 91
Thomas More St. E1 ....45Wb 91
Thomas More Way N2 ....27Eb 49
Thomas Neal's Cen.
WC2 ....3F 223 (44Nb 90)
Thomas Parmiter Sports Cen., The 3Z 13
Thomas Pl. W8 ....48Db 89
Thomas Rd. DA1: Cray 55Jd 118
E14 ....44Bc 92
Thomas Rd. Ind. Est. E14 ....43Cc 92
(not continuous)
Thomas Sims Ct. RM12: Horn 37Kd 77
Thomas Spencer Hall of Residence
SE18 ....49Qc 94
(off Grand Depot Rd.)
Thomas St. SE18 ....49Rc 94
Thomas Tallis Sports Cen. 55Kc 115
Thomas Twr. E8 ....37Vb 71
(off Dalston Sq.)
Thomas Turner Path CR0: C'don 75Sb 157
(off George St.)
Thomas Wall Cl. SM1: Sutt 78Db 155
Thomas Watson Cott. Homes
EN5: Barn 14Ab 30
(off Leecroft Rd.)
Thomas Wyatt Way TN15: Wro 88Be 185
Thompkins La. SL2: Farn R 8D 60
Thompson Av. TW9: Rich 55Qa 109
Thompson Cl. IG1: Ilf 33Sc 74
SL3: L'ly 49B 82
SM3: Sutt 74Cb 155
Thompson Ho. SE14 ....51Zb 114
(off John Williams Cl.)
W10 ....42Ab 88
(off Wornington Rd.)
Thompson Rd. RM9: Dag 34Bd 75
SE22 ....58Vb 113
TW3: Houn 56Da 107
UB10: Uxb 38N 63
Thompson's Av. SE5 ....52Sb 113
Thompson's Cl. GU24: Pirb 5B 186
Thompsons Cl. EN7: Chesh 1Vb 19
Thompson's La. GU24: Chob 1H 167
IG10: Lough 10Jc 21
Thompson Way WD3: Rick 18J 25
Thomson Cres. CR0: C'don 74Qb 156
Thomson Ho. E14 ....44Cc 92
(off Saracen St.)
SE17 ....6H 231
SW1 ....7E 228
UB1: S'hall 45Aa 85
(off The Broadway)
Thomson Rd. HA3: W'stone 27Ga 46
THONG 5J 145
Thong La. DA12: Grav'nd, Shorne 3H 145
TN15: Bor G 93Ae 205
Thorburn Ho. SW1 ....2G 227
Thorburn Sq. SE1 ....49Wb 91
Thorburn Way SW19 ....67Fb 133
Thoresby St. N1 ....3E 218 (41Sb 91)
Thorkhill Gdns. KT7: T Ditt 74Ja 152
Thorkhill Rd. KT7: T Ditt 74Ja 152
Thorley Cl. KT14: W Byf 86J 169
Thorley Gdns. GU22: Pyr 87J 169
Thorley Rd. RM16: Grays 46Ce 99
Thornaby Gdns. N18 ....23Wb 51
Thornaby Ho. E2 ....41Xb 91
(off Canrobert St.)
Thorn Apartments E3 ....43Cc 92
(off St Paul's Way)
Thornash Cl. GU21: Wok 7N 167
Thornash Rd. GU21: Wok 7N 167
Thornash Way GU21: Wok 7N 167
Thorn Av. WD23: B Hea 18Ea 28
Thornbank Cl. TW19: Stanw M 55J 105
Thornbill Ho. SE15 ....52Wb 113
(off Bird in Bush Rd.)
Thornbridge Rd. SL0: Iver H 39E 62
Thornbury NW4 ....28Xa 48
(off Prince of Wales Cl.)
Thornbury Av. TW7: Isle 52Fa 108
Thornbury Cl. N16 ....36Ub 71
NW7 ....24Za 48
Thornbury Ct. CR2: S Croy 78Tb 157
(off Blunt Rd.)
CR3: Whyt 92Vb 197
TW7: Isle 52Ga 108
W11 ....45Cb 89
(off Chepstow Vs.)
Thornbury Gdns. WD6: Bore 14Sa 29
Thornbury Ho. RM3: Rom 22Md 57
(off Bridgwater Wlk.)
Thornbury Lodge EN2: Enf 13Rb 33
Thornbury Rd. SW2 ....58Nb 112
TW7: Isle 52Fa 108
Thornbury Sq. N6 ....32Lb 70
Thornbury Way E17 ....25Bc 52
Thornby Rd. E5 ....34Yb 72
Thorncliffe Rd. SW2 ....58Nb 112
UB2: S'hall 50Ba 85
Thorn Cl. BR2: Brom 72Qc 160
UB5: N'olt 41Ba 85
Thorncombe Rd. SE22 ....57Ub 113
Thorncroft HP3: Hem H 4B 4
RM11: Horn 30Kd 57
TW20: Eng G 6N 125
Thorncroft Cl. CR5: Coul 91Qb 196
Thorncroft Dr. KT22: Lea 95Ka 192
Thorncroft Rd. SM1: Sutt 78Db 155
Thorncroft St. SW8 ....52Nb 112
Thorndales CM14: W'ley 21Zd 59
Thorndean St. SW18 ....61Eb 133
Thorndene SE28 ....45Xc 95
Thorndene Av. N11 ....18Jb 32
Thorndike SL2: Slou 3E 80
Thorndike Av. UB5: N'olt 39Z 65
Thorndike Cl. SW10 ....52Eb 111
Thorndike Ho. SW1 ....7D 228
Thorndike Rd. N1 ....37Tb 71
Thorndike St. SW1 ....6D 228 (49Mb 90)
Thorndon App. CM13: Heron 24Ee 59
Thorndon Av. CM13: W H'dn 28Ee 59
Thorndon Cl. BR5: St P 68Vc 139
Thorndon Country Pk. 23Ce 59
Thorndon Country Pk. North 24Be 59
Thorndon Country Pk. South 26Ee 59
Thorndon Countryside Cen. 24Be 59
Thorndon Gdns. KT19: Ewe 78Ua 154
Thorndon Ga. CM13: Ingve 22Ee 59
Thorndon Hall CM13: Ingve 23De 59
Thorndon Pk. Golf Course 23De 59
Thorndon Rd. BR5: St P 68Vc 139
Thorndown La. GU20: W'sham 10B 146
Thorn Dr. SL3: Geor G 44A 82
Thorndyke Ct. HA5: Hat E 23Ba 45
Thorndyke Way TN15: Wro 88Be 185
Thorne Cl. DA8: Erith 51Dd 118
E11 ....35Fc 73
E16 ....44Jc 93
HP1: Hem H 4K 3
KT10: Clay 80Ja 152
TW15: Ashf 66S 128
Thorne Ho. AL1: St A 1C 6
E2 ....41Yb 92
(off Roman Rd.)
E14 ....48Ec 92
(off Launch St.)
Thorneloe Gdns. CR0: Wadd 78Qb 156
Thorne Pas. SW13 ....54Ua 110
Thorne Rd. SW8 ....52Nb 112
Thornes Cl. BR3: Beck 69Ec 136
Thorne St. SW13 ....55Ua 110
Thornet Wood Rd. BR1: Brom 69Qc 138
Thornewill Ho. E1 ....45Yb 92
(off Cable St.)
THORNEY 48K 83
Thorney Bus. Pk. SL0: Iver 47F 82
Thorney Country Pk. 48K 83
Thorney Ct. W8 ....2A 226
Thorney Cres. SW11 ....52Fb 111
Thorneycroft Cl. KT12: Walt T 72Y 151
Thorneycroft Dr. EN3: Enf L 9Cc 20
Thorney Hedge Rd. W4 ....49Ra 87
Thorney La. Nth. SL0: Iver 44H 83
Thorney La. Sth. SL0: Rich P 47H 83
Thorney Mill Rd. SL0: Thorn 48J 83
(not continuous)
UB7: W Dray 48J 83
Thorney Pk. Golf Course 47K 83
Thorney St. SW1 ....5F 229 (49Nb 90)
Thornfield Av. NW7 ....25Ab 48
Thornfield Ct. NW7 ....24Ab 48
Thornfield Ho. E14 ....45Cc 92
(off Rosefield Gdns.)
Thornfield Pde. NW7 ....24Ab 48
(off Holders Hill Rd.)
Thornfield Rd. SM7: Bans 89Cb 175
W12 ....47Xa 88
(not continuous)
Thornford Rd. SE13 ....57Ec 114
Thorngate Rd. W9 ....42Cb 89
Thorngrove Rd. E13 ....39Kc 73
Thornham Gro. E15 ....36Fc 73
Thornham Ind. Est. E15 ....36Fc 73
Thornham St. SE10 ....51Dc 114
Thornhaugh M. WC1 ....6E 216 (42Mb 90)
Thornhaugh St. WC1 ....6E 216 (42Mb 90)
Thornhill Av. KT6: Surb 75Na 153
SE18 ....52Uc 116
Thornhill Bri. N1 ....1H 217
Thornhill Bri. Wharf N1 ....1H 217 (39Pb 70)
Thornhill Cres. N1 ....38Pb 70
Thornhill Gdns. E10 ....33Dc 72
IG11: Bark 38Uc 74
Thornhill Gro. N1 ....38Pb 70
Thornhill Ho. W4 ....50Ua 88
(off Wood St.)
Thornhill Ho's. N1 ....38Qb 70
(off Thornhill Rd.)
Thornhill M. SW15 ....56Bb 111
Thornhill Rd. CR0: C'don 73Sb 157
E10 ....33Dc 72
HA6: Nwood 21S 44
KT6: Surb 75Na 153
N1 ....38Qb 70
UB10: Ick 35P 63
Thornhill Sq. N1 ....38Pb 70
Thornhill Way TW17: Shep 71Q 150
Thorn Ho. WD6: Bore 12Sa 29
(off Elstree Way)
Thornicroft Ho. SW9 ....54Pb 112
(off Stockwell Rd.)
Thorn La. RM13: Rain 40Md 77
Thornlaw Rd. SE27 ....63Qb 134
Thornleas Pl. KT24: E Hor 98U 190
Thornley Cl. N17 ....24Wb 51
Thornley Dr. HA2: Harr 33Da 65
Thornley Pl. SE10 ....50Gc 93
Thornridge CM14: B'wood 18Xd 40
Thorns, The CM15: Kel H 11Ud 40
Thornsbeach Rd. SE6 ....60Ec 114
Thornsett Pl. SE20 ....68Xb 135
Thornsett Rd. SE20 ....68Xb 135
SW18 ....60Db 111
Thornsett Ter. SE20 ....68Xb 135
(off Croydon Rd.)
Thorns Mdw. TN16: Bras 95Yc 201
Thorn Ter. SE15 ....55Yb 114
Thornton Av.
qCR0: C'don 72Pb 156
SW2 ....60Mb 112
UB7: W Dray 48P 83
W4 ....49Ua 88
Thornton Cl. UB7: W Dray 48P 83
Thornton Cres. CR5: Coul 91Qb 196
Thornton Dene BR3: Beck 68Cc 136
Thornton Gdns. SW12 ....60Mb 112
Thornton Gro. HA5: Hat E 23Ca 45
THORNTON HEATH 70Sb 135
Thornton Heath Leisure Cen. 70Sb 135
THORNTON HEATH POND 71Qb 156
Thornton Hill SW19 ....66Ab 132
Thornton Ho. SE17 ....6H 231
Thornton Pl. W1 ....7G 215 (43Hb 89)
Thornton Rd. BR1: Brom 64Jc 137
CR0: C'don 73Pb 156
CR7: Thor H 73Pb 156
DA17: Belv 49Dd 96
E11 ....33Fc 73
EN5: Barn 13Ab 30
EN6: Pot B 2Eb 17
IG1: Ilf 35Rc 74
N18 ....20Yb 34
SM5: Cars 74Fb 155
SW12 ....59Mb 112
SW14 ....56Ta 109
SW19 ....65Za 132
Thornton Rd. E. SW19 ....65Za 132
Thornton Rd. Ind. Est.
CR0: C'don 72Pb 156
Thornton Row CR7: Thor H 71Qb 156
Thorntons CM13: Ingve 23Ee 59
Thornton's Farm Av.
RM7: Rush G 32Ed 76
Thornton Side RH1: Mers 3B 208
Thornton St. AL3: St A 1A 6
E20 ....38Dc 72
SW9 ....54Qb 112
Thornton Way NW11 ....29Db 49
Thorntree Ct. W5 ....43Na 87
Thorntree Rd. SE7 ....50Mc 93
Thornville Gro. CR4: Mitc 68Fb 133
Thornville St. SE8 ....53Cc 114
Thornwell Ct. W7 ....47Ga 86
(off Lwr. Boston Rd.)
Thornwood Cl. E18 ....26Kc 53
Thornwood Gdns. W8 ....47Cb 89
Thornwood Ho. IG9: Buck H 17Nc 36
Thornwood Lodge W8 ....47Cb 89
(off Thornwood Gdns.)
Thornwood Rd. CM16: Epp 1Xc 23
SE13 ....57Gc 115
Thornycroft Ho. W4 ....50Ua 88
(off Fraser St.)
Thorogood Gdns. E15 ....36Gc 73
Thorogood Way RM13: Rain 39Gd 76
Thorold Cl. CR2: Sels 82Zb 178
Thorold Ho. SE1 ....1D 230
Thorold Rd. IG1: Ilf 33Rc 74
N22 ....24Nb 50
Thoroughfare, The
KT20: Walt H 96Wa 194
Thorparch Rd. SW8 ....53Mb 112
THORPE 69E 126
Thorpebank Rd. W12 ....46Wa 88
Thorpe Bold CM13: Hut 15Fe 41
Thorpe By-Pass TW20: Thorpe 68D 126
Thorpe Cl. BR6: Orp 75Uc 160
CR0: New Ad 83Ec 178
SE26 ....63Zb 136
W10 ....44Ab 88
Thorpe Ct. EN2: Enf 13Rb 33
Thorpe Cres. E17 ....26Bc 52
WD19: Wat 17Y 27
Thorpedale Gdns. IG2: Ilf 28Qc 54
IG6: Ilf 28Qc 54
Thorpedale Rd. N4 ....33Nb 70
THORPE GREEN 70C 126
Thorpe Hall Rd. E17 ....25Ec 52
Thorpe Hay Meadow Nature Reserve
....66F 126
Thorpe Ho. N1 ....1J 217
Thorpe Ind. Pk. TW20: Thorpe 67E 126
THORPE LEA 65E 126
Thorpe Lea Rd.
TW20: Egh, Thorpe 65D 126
Thorpe Lodge RM11: Horn 30Nd 57
Thorpe Pk. 70G 126
Thorpe Rd. AL1: St A 3B 6
E6 ....39Pc 74
E7 ....35Hc 73
E17 ....26Ec 52
IG11: Bark 38Tc 74
KT2: King T 66Na 131
KT16: Chert 71F 148
N15 ....30Ub 51
TW18: Staines 65F 126
Thorpeside Cl. TW18: Staines 68G 126
Thorpewood Av. SE26 ....61Xb 135
Thorpland Av. UB10: Ick 34S 64
Thorrington Bold CM13: Hut 15Fe 41
Thorsden Cl. GU22: Wok 91A 188
Thorsden Ct. GU22: Wok 90A 168
Thorsden Way SE19 ....64Ub 135
Thors Oak SS17: Stan H 1N 101
Thorverton Rd. NW2 ....34Ab 68
Thoydon Rd. E3 ....40Ac 72
Thrale Rd. SW16 ....63Lb 134
Thrale St. SE1 ....7E 224 (46Sb 91)
Thrapston Ho. RM3: Rom 22Nd 57
(off Lindfield Rd.)
Thrasher Cl. E8 ....39Vb 71
Thrawl St. E1 ....1K 225 (43Vb 91)
Thrayle Ho. SW9 ....55Pb 112
(off Benedict Rd.)
Threadgold Ho. N1 ....37Tb 71
(off Dovercourt Est.)
Threadneedle St. EC2 ....3F 225 (44Tb 91)
Threadneedle Wlk. EC2 ....2G 225
Three Arch Bus. Pk. RH1: Redh 10A 208
Three Arches Pk. RH1: Redh 10P 207
Three Arch Rd. RH1: Redh 10P 207
Three Barrels Wlk. EC4 ....5E 224
Three Bridges Bus. Cen.
UB2: S'hall 47Ea 86
Three Bridges Path
KT1: King T 69Na 131
(off Bellvue Rd.)
Three Colt Cnr. E2 ....42Wb 91
(off Cheshire St.)
Three Colts La. E2 ....42Xb 91
Three Colt St. E14 ....44Bc 92
Three Corners DA7: Bex 54Dd 118
HP3: Hem H 4A 4
Three Cranes Wlk. EC4 ....5E 224
Three Cups Yd. WC1 ....1J 223
Three Gates Rd. DA3: Fawk 76Vd 164
Three Kings Yd. W1 ....4K 221 (45Kb 90)
Three Meadows M.
HA3: Hrw W 25Ha 46
Three Mill La. E3 ....41Ec 92
Three Mills Studios E3 ....41Ec 92
Three Nun Ct. EC2 ....2E 224
Three Oak La. SE1 ....1K 231 (47Vb 91)
Three Oaks Cl. UB10: Ick 34P 63
Three Quays EC3 ....5J 225
Three Quays Wlk. EC3 ....5J 225 (45Ub 91)
Three Rivers Mus., The 17N 25
Three Valleys Way
WD23: Bush 15Z 27
Threshers Pl. W11 ....45Ab 88
Threshold Way GU24: Chob 82A 168
Thriffwood SE26 ....62Yb 136
Thrift, The DA2: Bean 62Yd 142
Thrift Farm La. WD6: Bore 12Sa 29
Thrift Grn. CM13: B'wood 20Ce 41
Thrift La. TN14: Cud 89Uc 180
Thrifts Hall Farm M.
CM16: They B 9Vc 23
Thrifts Mead CM16: They B 9Uc 22
Thriftwood Holiday Pk.
TN15: Stans 85Ae 185
Thriftwood International Scout Activity Cen.
....19Ce 41
Thrigby Rd. KT9: Chess 79Pa 153
Thring Ho. SW9 ....54Pb 112
(off Stockwell Rd.)
Throckmorton Rd. E16 ....44Kc 93
Throgmorton Av. EC2 ....2G 225 (44Tb 91)
(not continuous)
Throgmorton St. EC2 ....2G 225 (44Tb 91)
Throstle Pl. WD25: Wat 4Y 13
Throwley Cl. SE2 ....48Yc 95
(not continuous)
Throwley Rd. SM1: Sutt 78Db 155
Throwley Way SM1: Sutt 77Db 155
Thrums, The WD24: Wat 9X 13
Thrupp Cl. CR4: Mitc 68Kb 134
Thrupp's Av. KT12: Hers 78Z 151
Thrupp's La. KT12: Hers 78Z 151
Thrush Av. AL10: Hat 2C 8
Thrush Grn. HA2: Harr 28Ca 45
WD3: Rick 17L 25
Thrush St. SE17 ....7C 230 (50Sb 91)
Thumpers HP2: Hem H 1N 3
Thurbarn Rd. SE6 ....64Dc 136
Thurland Ho. SE16 ....49Xb 91
(off Camilla Rd.)
Thurland Rd. SE16 ....48Wb 91
Thurlby Cl. HA1: Harr 30Ja 46
IG8: Wfd G 22Pc 54
Thurlby Cft. NW4 ....27Ya 48
(off Mulberry Cl.)
Thurlby Rd. HA0: Wemb 37Ma 67
SE27 ....63Qb 134
Thurleigh Av. SW12 ....58Jb 112
Thurleigh Ct. SW12 ....58Jb 112
Thurleigh Rd. SW12 ....59Hb 111
Thurleston Av. SM4: Mord 71Ab 154
Thurlestone Av.
IG3: Bark, Ilf 35Vc 75
N12 ....23Hb 49
Thurlestone Cl. TW17: Shep 72S 150
Thurlestone Ct. UB1: S'hall 44Da 85
(off Howard Rd.)
Thurlestone Pde.
TW17: Shep 72S 150
(off High St.)
Thurlestone Rd. SE27 ....62Qb 134
Thurloe Cl. SW7 ....5D 226 (49Gb 89)
Thurloe Ct. SW3 ....6D 226
Thurloe Gdns. RM1: Rom 30Hd 56
Thurloe Pl. SW7 ....5C 226 (49Fb 89)
Thurloe Pl. M. SW7 ....5C 226
Thurloe Sq. SW7 ....5D 226 (49Gb 89)
Thurloe St. SW7 ....5C 226 (49Fb 89)
Thurloe Wlk. RM17: Grays 48Ce 99
Thurlow Cl. E4 ....23Dc 52
Thurlow Gdns. HA0: Wemb 36Ma 67
IG6: Ilf 23Tc 54
Thurlow Hill SE21 ....60Sb 113
Thurlow Ho. SW16 ....62Nb 134
Thurlow Pk. Rd. SE21 ....61Rb 135
Thurlow Rd. NW3 ....36Fb 69
W7 ....47Ja 86
Thurlow St. SE17 ....7G 231 (50Tb 91)
(not continuous)
Thurlow Ter. NW5 ....36Jb 70
Thurlow Wlk. SE17 ....7H 231 (50Ub 91)
(not continuous)
Thurlstone Rd. HA4: Ruis 34W 64
Thurlton Ct. GU21: Wok 88A 168
Thurnby Ct. TW2: Twick 62Ga 130
Thurnham Way KT20: Tad 92Za 194
Thurnscoe NW1 ....1B 216
Thurrock Athletics Stadium 47Fe 99
Thurrock Bus. Cen.
RM20: W Thur 51Vd 120
Thurrock Commercial Cen.
RM15: Avel 47Pd 97
Thurrock Ent. Cen.
RM17: Grays 51Ce 121
THURROCK LAKESIDE 48Wd 98
Thurrock Lakeside (Intu Lakeside)
RM20: W Thur 48Xd 98
Thurrock Mus. 50De 99
Thurrock Pk. Way RM18: Tilb 52Fe 121
THURROCK SERVICE AREA 47Vd 98
Thurrock Trade Pk.
RM20: W Thur 52Wd 120
Thurrock Yacht Club 52Ce 121
Thursby Rd. GU21: Wok 10L 167
Thursland Rd. DA14: Sidc 64Ad 139
Thursley Cres. CR0: New Ad 80Ec 158
Thursley Gdns. SW19 ....61Za 132
Thursley Ho. SW2 ....59Pb 112
(off Holmewood Gdns.)
Thursley Rd. SE9 ....62Pc 138
Thurso Cl. RM3: Hrld W 23Rd 57
Thurso Ho. NW6 ....40Db 69
Thurso St. SW17 ....63Fb 133

Torrington Way—Triangle Ct.

Torrington Way SM4: Mord ... 72Cb 155
Tor Rd. DA16: Well ... 53Yc 117
Torr Rd. SE20 ... 66Zb 136
Tortington Ho. SE15 ... 52Wb 113
(off Friary Est.)
Torver Rd. HA1: Harr ... 28Ga 46
Torver Way BR6: Orp ... 76Tc 160
Torwood La. CR3: Whyt ... 92Vb 197
Torwood Rd. SW15 ... 57Wa 110
Torworth Rd. WD6: Bore ... 11Pa 29
TOT HILL ... 98Sa 193
Tothill Ho. SW1 ... 5E 228
Tot Hill La. KT18: Head ... 98Sa 193
Tothill St. SW1 ... 2D 228 (47Mb 90)
Totnes Rd. DA16: Well ... 52Xc 117
Totnes Vs. N11 ... 22Lb 50
(off Telford Rd.)
Totnes Wlk. N2 ... 28Fb 49
Tottan Ter. E1 ... 44Zb 92
Tottenhall NW1 ... 38Jb 70
(off Ferdinand St.)
Tottenhall Rd. N13 ... 23Qb 50
TOTTENHAM ... 26Vb 51
Tottenham Community Sports Cen.
... 25Vb 51
Tottenham Ct. Rd. W1 ... 6C 216 (42Lb 90)
Tottenham Ent. Cen. N17 ... 26Vb 51
Tottenham Grn. E. N15 ... 28Vb 51
(not continuous)
Tottenham Green Leisure Cen. ... 28Vb 51
TOTTENHAM HALE ... 26Wb 51
TOTTENHAM HALE GYRATORY ... 28Wb 51
Tottenham Hale Retail Pk. N15 ... 28Wb 51
Tottenham Hotspur FC ... 24Wb 51
Tottenham La. N8 ... 30Nb 50
Tottenham M. W1 ... 7C 216 (43Lb 90)
Tottenham Rd. N1 ... 37Ub 71
Tottenham St. W1 ... 1C 222 (43Lb 90)
Totterdown St. SW17 ... 63Hb 133
TOTTERIDGE ... 18Bb 31
Totteridge Comn. N20 ... 19Wa 30
Totteridge Fields Local Nature Reserve
... 18Wa 30
Totteridge Grn. N20 ... 19Cb 31
Totteridge Ho. SW11 ... 54Fb 111
(off Yelverton Rd.)
Totteridge La. N20 ... 19Cb 31
Totteridge Rd. EN3: Enf W ... 9Zb 20
Totteridge Village N20 ... 18Ab 30
Totternhoe Cl. HA3: Kenton ... 29La 46
Totters Ct. SE17 ... 51Tb 113
(off Westmorland Rd.)
Totton Rd. CR7: Thor H ... 69Qb 134
Toucan Cl. NW10 ... 41Qa 87
Touchard Ho. N1 ... 4G 219
Toulmin St. SE1 ... 2D 230 (47Sb 91)
Toulon St. SE5 ... 52Sb 113
Toulouse Ct. SE16 ... 50Xb 91
(off Rossetti Rd.)
Tounson Ct. SW1 ... 6E 228
Tourist Info. Cen.
Bexleyheath ... 56Bd 117
Borehamwood ... 12Ra 29
City of London ... 3D 224 (44Sb 91)
Enfield ... 14Tb 33
Gravesend ... 8D 122
Greenwich ... 51Ec 114
Heathrow Central ... 55R 106
Kingston upon Thames ... 68Ma 131
St Albans ... 2B 6
Swanley ... 69Gd 140
Uxbridge ... 38M 63
Waltham Abbey ... 5Ec 20
Windsor ... 3H 103
Tournay Rd. SW6 ... 52Bb 111
Tours Pas. SW11 ... 56Eb 111
Tourtel Yd. DA11: Nflt ... 60Ee 121
Toussaint Wlk. SE16 ... 48Wb 91
Tovey Cl. AL2: Lon C ... 8H 7
Tovil Cl. SE20 ... 68Xb 135
Tovy Ho. SE1 ... 50Wb 91
(off Avondale Sq.)
Towcester Rd. E3 ... 42Dc 92
Tower, The SW8 ... 51Nb 112
TW8: Bford ... 50Ma 87
(off Ealing Rd.)
Tower 1 SE13 ... 55Ec 114
(off Station Rd.)
Tower 2 SE13 ... 55Ec 114
(off Station Rd.)
Tower 3 SE13 ... 55Ec 114
(off Station Rd.)
Tower 4 SE13 ... 55Ec 114
(off Station Rd.)
Tower 42 ... 2H 225 (44Ub 91)
Tower Bri. SE1 ... 7K 225 (46Vb 91)
Tower Bri. App. E1 ... 6K 225 (46Vb 91)
Tower Bri. Bus. Complex SE16 ... 48Wb 91
Tower Bri. Bus. Sq. SE16 ... 49Xb 91
Tower Bridge Exhibition ... 6K 225
Tower Bri. M. HA1: Harr ... 35Ha 66
Tower Bri. Plaza SE1 ... 7K 225 (46Vb 91)
Tower Bri. Rd. SE1 ... 4H 231 (48Ub 91)
Tower Bri. Sq. SE1 ... 1K 231
Tower Bri. Wharf E1 ... 46Wb 91
Tower Bldgs. E1 ... 46Xb 91
(off Brewhouse La.)
Tower Cl. BR6: Orp ... 75Vc 161
DA12: Grav'nd ... 4G 144
GU21: Wok ... 9P 167
IG6: Ilf ... 23Rc 54
NW3 ... 36Fb 69
SE20 ... 66Xb 135
Tower Ct. CM14: B'wood ... 19Yd 40
E5 ... 31Vb 71
N1 ... 38Sb 71
(off Canonbury St.)
NW8 ... 1E 214
TW20: Egh ... 64C 126
WC2 ... 3F 223
Tower Cft. DA4: Eyns ... 75Nd 163
Tower Gdns.
KT10: Clay ... 80Ja 152
Tower Gdns. Rd. N17 ... 25Sb 51
Towergate SE1 ... 5H 231
Towergate Cl. UB8: Uxb ... 36N 63
Towergate Ho. E3 ... 40Bc 72
(off Ordell Rd.)
Tower Gro. KT13: Weyb ... 75U 150
Tower Hamlets Rd. E7 ... 35Hc 73
E17 ... 27Cc 52
TOWER HILL ... 2H 11
TOWER HILL ... 5K 225 (45Vb 91)
Tower Hill
CM14: B'wood ... 19Yd 40
EC3 ... 5J 225 (45Ub 91)
WD4: Chfd ... 1G 10
Tower Hill Ter. EC3 ... 5J 225
Tower Ho. E1 ... 43Wb 91
(off Fieldgate St.)
KT14: Byfl ... 84N 169
(off High Rd.)
SE13 ... 55Ec 114
SL0: Iver ... 44G 82
SL1: Slou ... 7J 81
UB8: Uxb ... 38L 63
(off High St.)
Tower Ind. Est.
TN15: Wro ... 86Zd 185
Tower La. HA9: Wemb ... 34Ma 67
RH2: Reig ... 100Gb 195
Tower Mans. SE1 ... 4K 231
Tower M. E5 ... 35Ac 72
E17 ... 28Cc 52
Tower Mill Rd. SE15 ... 52Ub 113
Tower of London, The ... 5K 225 (45Vb 91)
Tower of London Welcome Cen.
... 5J 225 (45Ub 91)
Tower Pk. Rd. DA1: Cray ... 57Hd 118
Tower Pl. CR6: W'ham ... 87Cc 178
EC3 ... 5J 225 (45Ub 91)
Tower Pl. E. EC3 ... 5J 225
Tower Pl. W. EC3 ... 5J 225
Tower Point EN2: Enf ... 14Tb 33
Tower Retail Pk. DA1: Cray ... 57Hd 118
Tower Ride SL4: Wind ... 2C 124
Tower Ri. TW9: Rich ... 55Na 109
Tower Rd. BR6: Orp ... 75Vc 161
CM16: Epp ... 2Uc 22
DA1: Dart ... 51Jd 119
DA7: Bex ... 56Cd 118
DA17: Belv ... 49Ed 96
KT20: Tad ... 95Ya 194
NW10 ... 38Wa 68
TW1: Twick ... 62Ha 130
Towers, The CR8: Kenley ... 87Sb 177
Towers Av. UB10: Hil ... 41S 84
Towers Bus. Pk. HA9: Wemb ... 35Sa 67
(off Carey Way)
Towers Ct. UB10: Hil ... 41S 84
Towers Pl. TW9: Rich ... 57Na 109
Towers Rd. HA5: Pinn ... 25Aa 45
HP2: Hem H ... 1N 3
RM17: Grays ... 50Ee 99
UB1: S'hall ... 42Ca 85
Tower St. WC2 ... 3E 222 (44Nb 90)
Towers Wlk. KT13: Weyb ... 79R 150
Towers Wood DA4: S Dar ... 67Td 142
Tower Ter. N22 ... 26Pb 50
Tower Vw. CR0: C'don ... 73Ac 158
WD23: B Hea ... 17Ga 28
Tower Wlk. SE1 ... 5H 231
Tower Wharf DA11: Nflt ... 56De 121
SE1 ... 1K 231
Tower Workshops SE1 ... 2K 231
Tower Yd. TW10: Rich ... 57Pa 109
Towfield Ct. TW13: Hanw ... 61Ba 129
Towfield Rd. TW13: Hanw ... 61Ba 129
Town, The EN2: Enf ... 13Tb 33
Towncourt Cres. BR5: Pet W ... 71Sc 160
Towncourt La. BR5: Pet W ... 72Tc 160
Town Ct. Path N4 ... 32Sb 71
Towneley Cotts. RM4: Stap A ... 18Gd 38
Town End CR3: Cat'm ... 94Ub 197
Town End Cl. CR3: Cat'm ... 94Ub 197
Townend Ct. BR1: Brom ... 67Hc 137
Town End Pde. KT1: King T ... 69Ma 131
(off High St.)
Towney Mead UB5: N'olt ... 40Ba 65
Towney Mead Ct. UB5: N'olt ... 40Ba 65
Town Farm Way TW19: Stanw ... 59M 105
Townfield WD3: Rick ... 17L 25
Townfield Cnr. DA12: Grav'nd ... 10E 122
Townfield Rd. UB3: Hayes ... 46V 84
Townfield Sq. UB3: Hayes ... 45V 84
Town Fld. Way TW7: Isle ... 54Ja 108
Towngate KT11: Cobh ... 87Aa 171
Town Hall App. N16 ... 35Tb 71
(off Albion Rd.)
Town Hall App. Rd. N15 ... 28Vb 51
Town Hall Av. W4 ... 50Ta 87
Town Hall Rd. SW11 ... 55Hb 111
Townhall Sq. DA1: Cray ... 57Hd 118
Townholm Cres. W7 ... 48Ha 86
Town La. TW19: Stanw ... 58M 105
(not continuous)
Townley Ct. E15 ... 37Hc 73
Townley Rd. DA6: Bex ... 57Bd 117
SE22 ... 57Ub 113
Townley St. SE17 ... 7F 231 (50Tb 91)
(not continuous)
Town Mead RH1: Blet ... 5K 209
Townmead Bus. Cen. SW6 ... 55Eb 111
Town Mdw. TW8: Bford ... 51Ma 109
Town Mdw. Rd. TW8: Bford ... 52Ma 109
Townmead Rd. EN9: Walt A ... 6Ec 20
SW6 ... 55Db 111
TW9: Kew ... 54Ra 109
Town Pier DA11: Grav'nd ... 7D 122
Town Quay IG11: Bark ... 39Rc 74
TW18: Lale ... 69K 127
(off Blacksmiths La.)
Town Quay Wharf IG11: Bark ... 39Rc 74
Town Rd. N9 ... 19Xb 33
TOWNSEND ... 1B 6
Townsend HP2: Hem H ... 1M 3
Townsend Av. AL1: St A ... 1C 6
N14 ... 21Mb 50
Townsend Dr. AL3: St A ... 1B 6
Townsend Ga. HP4: Berk ... 2A 2
Townsend Ho. SE1 ... 49Wb 91
(off Strathnairn St.)
Townsend Ind. Est. NW10 ... 40Sa 67
Townsend La. GU22: Wok ... 93D 188
NW9 ... 31Ta 67
Townsend M. SW18 ... 61Eb 133
Townsend Rd. N15 ... 29Vb 51
SE3 ... 56Lc 115
TW15: Ashf ... 64N 127
UB1: S'hall ... 46Aa 85
Townsend St. SE17 ... 6G 231 (49Ub 91)
Townsend Way HA6: Nwood ... 24V 44
Townsend Yd. N6 ... 32Kb 70
Townshend Cl. DA14: Sidc ... 65Xc 139
Townshend Ct. NW8 ... 1E 214
Townshend Est. NW8 ... 1D 214 (40Gb 69)
Townshend Rd. BR7: Chst ... 64Rc 138
NW8 ... 1D 214 (39Gb 69)
(not continuous)
TW9: Rich ... 56Pa 109
Townshend Ter. TW9: Rich ... 56Pa 109
Townshott Cl. KT23: Bookh ... 97Ca 191
Towns Ho. SW4 ... 55Mb 112
Townslow La. GU23: Wis ... 88L 169
Townson Av. UB5: N'olt ... 40W 64
Townson Way UB5: N'olt ... 40W 64
Town Sq. DA8: Erith ... 51Gd 118
GU21: Wok ... 89A 168
IG11: Bark ... 39Sc 74
(off Clockhouse Av.)
SL1: Slou ... 7K 81
TW7: Isle ... 55Ka 108
(off Swan St.)
Town Tree Rd. TW15: Ashf ... 64Q 128
Town Wharf TW7: Isle ... 55Ka 108
Towpath KT12: Walt T ... 71W 150
TW17: Shep ... 74P 149
Towpath, The SW10 ... 53Fb 111
Towpath Rd. N18 ... 23Zb 52
Towpath Wlk. E9 ... 36Bc 72
Towpath Way CR0: C'don ... 72Vb 157
Towton M. N11 ... 23Mb 50
Towton Rd. SE27 ... 61Sb 135
Toynbec Cl. BR7: Chst ... 63Rc 138
Toynbee Rd. SW20 ... 67Ab 132
Toynbee St. E1 ... 1K 225 (43Vb 91)
Toynbee Studios ... 2K 225
Toyne Way N6 ... 30Hb 49
Tozer Wlk. SL4: Wind ... 5B 102
Tracery, The SM7: Bans ... 87Db 175
Tracey Av. NW2 ... 36Ya 68
Tracey Bellamy Ct. E14 ... 44Ac 92
(off Repton St.)
Tracious Cl. GU21: Wok ... 8M 167
Tracious La. GU21: Wok ... 8M 167
Tracy Av. SL3: L'ly ... 50B 82
Tracy Ct. HA7: Stan ... 24La 46
Tracy Ho. E3 ... 41Bc 92
(off Mile End Rd.)
Trade City KT13: Weyb ... 82N 169
Trade City Bus. Pk. TW16: Sun ... 67U 128
UB8: Uxb ... 40L 63
Trade Cl. N13 ... 21Qb 50
Trader Rd. E6 ... 44Rc 94
Tradescant Ho. E9 ... 38Yb 72
(off Frampton Pk. Rd.)
Tradescant Rd. SW8 ... 52Nb 112
Tradewind Hgts. SE16 ... 46Zb 92
(off Rotherhithe St.)
Tradewinds Ct. E1 ... 45Wb 91
Trading Est. Rd. NW10 ... 42Sa 87
Traditions Golf Course ... 87K 169
Trafalgar Av. KT4: Wor Pk ... 74Za 154
N17 ... 23Ub 51
SE15 ... 7K 231 (50Vb 91)
Trafalgar Bldg. KT2: King T ... 67Ma 131
(off Henry Macaulay Av.)
Trafalgar Bus. Cen. IG11: Bark ... 42Vc 95
Trafalgar Chambers SW3 ... 7C 226
Trafalgar Cl. SE16 ... 48Ac 92
Trafalgar Ct. DA8: Erith ... 52Hd 118
(off Frobisher Rd.)
E1 ... 46Yb 92
(off Wapping Wall)
KT11: Cobh ... 85W 170
Trafalgar Dr. KT12: Walt T ... 76X 151
Trafalgar Gdns. E1 ... 43Zb 92
W8 ... 48Db 89
Trafalgar Gro. SE10 ... 51Fc 115
Trafalgar Ho. SE17 ... 7F 231
SW18 ... 56Eb 111
Trafalgar M. E9 ... 37Bc 72
Trafalgar Pl. E11 ... 28Jc 53
N18 ... 22Wb 51
Trafalgar Point N1 ... 38Tb 71
(off Downham Rd.)
Trafalgar Quarters SE10 ... 51Fc 115
(off Park Row)
Trafalgar Rd. DA1: Dart ... 61Nd 141
DA11: Grav'nd ... 9C 122
RM13: Rain ... 40Hd 76
SE10 ... 51Fc 115
SW19 ... 66Db 133
TW2: Twick ... 61Fa 130
Trafalgar Square ... 6E 222 (46Mb 90)
Trafalgar Sq. SW1 ... 6E 222 (46Mb 90)
WC2 ... 6E 222 (46Mb 90)
Trafalgar St. SE17 ... 7F 231 (50Tb 91)
Trafalgar Studios ... 6F 223
Trafalgar Ter. HA1: Harr ... 32Ga 66
Trafalgar Trad. Est. EN3: Brim ... 14Ac 34
Trafalgar Way CR0: Wadd ... 75Qb 156
E14 ... 46Ec 92
Trafford Cl. IG6: Ilf ... 23Vc 55
WD7: Shenl ... 4Na 15
Trafford Ho. N1 ... 2G 219
Trafford Rd. CR7: Thor H ... 71Pb 156
Trafford Way BR3: Beck ... 65Cc 136
Traherne Lodge TW11: Tedd ... 64Ha 130
Trahorn Cl. E1 ... 42Xb 91
Traitors' Gate ... 6K 225
Tralee Ct. SE16 ... 50Xb 91
(off Masters Dr.)
Tram Cl. SE24 ... 55Rb 113
(off Milkwood Rd.)
Tramlink, The SW19 ... 68Eb 133
Tramsheds, The CR0: Bedd ... 73Mb 156
Tramway Av. E15 ... 38Gc 73
N9 ... 17Xb 33
Tramway Cl. SE20 ... 67Yb 136
Tramway Ct. E1 ... 43Ac 92
Tramway Path CR4: Mitc ... 70Gb 133
(not continuous)
Tranby M. E9 ... 36Zb 72
(off Brooksby's Wlk.)
Tranley M. NW3 ... 35Gb 69
(off Fleet Rd.)
Tranmere Ct. SM2: Sutt ... 80Eb 155
Tranmere Rd. N9 ... 17Vb 33
SW18 ... 61Eb 133
TW2: Whitt ... 59Da 107
Tranquil Dale RH3: Bkld ... 4B 206
Tranquil La. HA2: Harr ... 32Da 65
Tranquil Pas. SE3 ... 54Hc 115
(off Montpelier Va.)
Tranquil Ri. DA8: Erith ... 50Gd 96
Tranquil Va. SE3 ... 54Gc 115
Transenna Works N1 ... 37Rb 71
(off Laycock St.)
Transept St. NW1 ... 1E 220 (43Gb 89)
Transmere Cl. BR5: Pet W ... 72Sc 160
Transmere Rd. BR5: Pet W ... 72Sc 160
Transom Cl. SE16 ... 49Ac 92
Transom Sq. E14 ... 50Dc 92
Transport Av. TW8: Bford ... 50Ja 86
Tranton Rd. SE16 ... 48Wb 91
Trappes Ho. SE16 ... 49Xb 91
(off Camilla Rd.)
Trap's Hill IG10: Lough ... 13Pc 36
Traps La. KT3: N Mald ... 67Ua 132
Traq Motor Racing ... 72Lb 156
Travellers Cl. AL9: Wel G ... 5E 8
Travellers La. AL9: Wel G ... 4E 8
AL10: Hat ... 1C 8
Travellers Way TW4: Cran ... 54Y 107
Travers Cl. E17 ... 25Zb 52
Travers Ho. SE10 ... 51Fc 115
(off Trafalgar Gro.)
Travers Rd. N7 ... 34Qb 70
Travic Rd. SL2: Slou ... 1D 80
Travis Ct. SL2: Farn R ... 1F 80
Trayford Ct. RM19: Purf ... 50Rd 97
(off Wingrove Dr.)
TREACLE MINE RDBT. ... 47Be 99
Treacy Cl. WD23: B Hea ... 19Ea 28
Treadgold Ho. W11 ... 45Za 88
(off Bomore Rd.)
Treadgold St. W11 ... 45Za 88
Treadway St. E2 ... 40Xb 71
Treadwell Rd. KT18: Eps ... 88Ua 174
Treasury Cl. SM6: Wall ... 78Mb 156
Treasury M. DA5: Bexl ... 59Dd 118
Treasury Pas. SW1 ... 1F 229
Treaty Cen. TW3: Houn ... 55Da 107
Treaty St. N1 ... 1H 217 (39Pb 70)
Trebble Rd. DA10: Swans ... 58Ae 121
Trebeck St. W1 ... 6K 221 (46Kb 90)
Trebellan Dr. HP2: Hem H ... 1P 3
Trebovir Rd. SW5 ... 50Cb 89
Treby St. E3 ... 42Bc 92
Trecastle Way N7 ... 35Mb 70
Tredegar Ho. E3 ... 41Cc 92
(off Bow Rd.)
Tredegar M. E3 ... 41Bc 92
Tredegar Rd. DA2: Wilm ... 61Jd 140
E3 ... 40Bc 72
N11 ... 24Mb 50
Tredegar Sq. E3 ... 41Bc 92
Tredegar Ter. E3 ... 41Bc 92
Trederwen Rd. E8 ... 39Wb 71
Tredown Rd. SE26 ... 64Yb 136
Tredwell Cl. BR2: Brom ... 70Nc 138
SW2 ... 61Pb 134
Tredwell Rd. SE27 ... 63Rb 135
Treebourne Rd. TN16: Big H ... 89Lc 179
Treebys Av. GU4: Jac W ... 10P 187
Tree Cl. TW10: Ham ... 60Ma 109
Tree La. TN15: Plax ... 99Ae 205
Treemount Ct. KT17: Eps ... 85Ua 174
Treen Av. SW13 ... 55Va 110
Tree Rd. E16 ... 44Lc 93
Treeside Cl. UB7: W Dray ... 49M 83
Treeside Pl. N10 ... 28Kb 50
Treetop Ct. CR7: Thor H ... 71Sb 157
Tree Top M. RM10: Dag ... 37Fd 76
Treetop M. NW6 ... 38Ab 68
Tree Tops CM15: B'wood ... 18Yd 40
SL9: Chal P ... 22A 42
Treetops CR3: W'ham ... 90Wb 177
DA12: Grav'nd ... 4D 144
RH9: S God ... 9C 210
TN15: Kems'g ... 89Qd 183
Treetops Cl. HA6: Nwood ... 22T 44
SE2 ... 50Ad 95
Treetops Vw. IG10: Lough ... 16Mc 35
Tree Vw. Cl. SE19 ... 67Ub 135
Treeview Ct. RH2: Reig ... 6M 207
(off Wray Comn. Rd.)
Treewall Gdns. BR1: Brom ... 63Kc 137
Tree Way RH2: Reig ... 3K 207
Trefgarne Rd. RM10: Dag ... 33Cd 76
Trefil Wlk. N7 ... 35Nb 70
Trefoil Ho. DA18: Erith ... 47Ad 95
(off Kale Rd.)
RM17: Grays ... 52De 121
Trefoil Rd. SW18 ... 57Eb 111
Trefusis Ct. TW5: Cran ... 53X 107
Trefusis Wlk. WD17: Wat ... 11U 26
Tregaron Av. N8 ... 30Nb 50
Tregaron Gdns. KT3: N Mald ... 70Ua 132
Tregarthen Pl. KT22: Lea ... 93La 192
Tregarth Pl. GU21: Wok ... 9K 167
Tregarvon Rd. SW11 ... 56Jb 112
Tregenna Av. HA2: Harr ... 35Ca 65
Tregenna Cl. N14 ... 15Lb 32
Tregenna Ct. HA2: Harr ... 35Ca 65
Treglos Ct. KT13: Weyb ... 74U 150
Tregonwell Ter. SE9 ... 63Rc 138
Tregony Rd. BR6: Chels ... 77Vc 161
Trego Rd. E9 ... 38Cc 72
Tregothnan Rd. SW9 ... 55Nb 112
Tregunter Rd. SW10 ... 7A 226 (51Db 111)
Trehaven Pde. RH2: Reig ... 9K 207
Trehearn Rd. IG6: Ilf ... 24Tc 54
Treherne Ct. SW17 ... 63Jb 134
Trehern Rd. SW14 ... 55Ta 109
Trehurst St. E5 ... 36Ac 72
Trelawn Cl. KT16: Ott ... 80E 148
Trelawney Av. SL3: L'ly ... 8P 81
Trelawney Est. E9 ... 37Yb 72
Trelawney Gro. KT13: Weyb ... 79Q 150
Trelawney Ho. SE1 ... 1D 230
Trelawney Pl. RM16: Chaf H ... 48Yd 98
Trelawney Rd. IG6: Ilf ... 24Tc 54
Trelawn Rd. E10 ... 34Ec 72
SW2 ... 57Qb 112
Trelawny Cl. E17 ... 28Dc 52
Trellick Twr. W10 ... 42Bb 89
(off Golborne Rd.)
Trellis Ho. SW19 ... 66Eb 133
Trellis Sq. E3 ... 41Bc 92
Treloar Gdns. SE19 ... 65Tb 135
Tremadoc Rd. SW4 ... 56Mb 112
Tremaine Cl. SE4 ... 54Cc 114
Tremaine Rd. SE20 ... 68Xb 135
Trematon Bldg. N1 ... 1G 217
Trematon Ho. SE11 ... 7A 230
Trematon M. N1 ... 1G 217 (40Nb 70)
Trematon Pl. TW11: Tedd ... 66La 130
Trematon Wlk. N1 ... 1G 217
Tremelo Grn. RM8: Dag ... 32Ad 75
Tremlett Gro. N19 ... 34Lb 70
Tremlett M. N19 ... 34Lb 70
Trenance GU21: Wok ... 9L 167
Trenance Gdns. IG3: Ilf ... 34Wc 75
Trenchard Av. HA4: Ruis ... 35X 65
Trenchard Cl. HA7: Stan ... 23Ja 46
KT12: Hers ... 78Y 151
NW9 ... 25Ua 48
Trenchard Ct. NW4 ... 29Wa 48
SM4: Mord ... 72Cb 155
Trenchard St. SE10 ... 50Fc 93
Trenches La. SL3: L'ly ... 45C 82
Trenchold St. SW8 ... 51Nb 112
Trendell Ho. E14 ... 44Cc 92
(off Dod St.)
Trenear Cl. BR6: Chels ... 77Wc 161
Trenham Dr. CR6: W'ham ... 88Yb 178
Trenholme Cl. SE20 ... 66Xb 135
Trenholme Ct. CR3: Cat'm ... 95Wb 197
Trenholme Rd. SE20 ... 66Xb 135
Trenholme Ter. SE20 ... 66Xb 135
Trenmar Gdns. NW10 ... 41Xa 88
Trent RM18: E Til ... 9L 101
Trent Av. RM14: Upm ... 30Td 58
W5 ... 48La 86
Trentbridge Cl. IG6: Ilf ... 23Vc 55
Trent Cl. WD7: Shenl ... 4Na 15
Trent Ct. CR2: S Croy ... 78Sb 157
(off Nottingham Rd.)
Trent Gdns. N14 ... 16Kb 32
Trentham Cres.
GU22: Wok ... 93C 188
Trentham Dr. BR5: St M Cry ... 70Wc 139
Trentham Ho. W3 ... 43Ta 87
Trentham Rd. RH1: Redh ... 8P 207
Trentham St. SW18 ... 60Cb 111
Trent Ho. KT2: King T ... 67Ma 131
SE15 ... 56Yb 114
TRENT PARK ... 12Kb 32
Trent Pk. (Country Pk.) ... 11Kb 32
Trent Pk. Golf Course ... 14Lb 32
Trent Rd. IG9: Buck H ... 18Kc 35
SL3: L'ly ... 51D 104
SW2 ... 57Pb 112
Trent Vs. SL3: Dat ... 3M 103
(off Datchet Pl.)
Trent Way KT4: Wor Pk ... 76Ya 154
UB4: Hayes ... 40U 64
Trentwood Side EN2: Enf ... 13Pb 32
Treport St. SW18 ... 59Db 111
Tresco Cl. BR1: Brom ... 65Gc 137
Trescoe Gdns. HA2: Harr ... 31Aa 65
RM5: Col R ... 22Ed 56
Tresco Gdns. IG3: Ilf ... 33Wc 75
Tresco Ho. SE11 ... 7K 229
Tresco Rd. SE15 ... 56Xb 113
Tresham Cres. NW8 ... 5D 214 (42Gb 89)
Tresham Ho. WC1 ... 7H 217
(off Red Lion Sq.)
Tresham Rd. IG11: Bark ... 38Vc 75
Tresham Wlk. E9 ... 36Yb 72
Tresidder Ho. SW4 ... 59Mb 112
Tresilian Av. N21 ... 15Pb 32
Tresillian Way
GU21: Wok ... 8L 167
Tressell Cl. N1 ... 38Rb 71
Tressillian Cres. SE4 ... 55Cc 114
Tressillian Rd. SE4 ... 56Bc 114
Tress Pl. SE1 ... 6B 224
Tresta Wlk. GU21: Wok ... 8L 167
Trestis Cl. UB4: Yead ... 43Z 85
Trestle Theatre ... 3H 7
Treswell Rd. RM9: Dag ... 39Ad 75
Tretawn Gdns. NW7 ... 21Ua 48
Tretawn Pk. NW7 ... 21Ua 48
Trevanion Rd. W14 ... 49Ab 88
Treve Av. HA1: Harr ... 31Fa 66
Trevellance Way WD25: Wat ... 5Z 13
Trevelyan Av. E12 ... 35Pc 74
Trevelyan Cl. DA1: Dart ... 56Pd 119
Trevelyan Ct. KT3: N Mald ... 73Ua 154
SL4: Wind ... 4F 102
Trevelyan Cres. HA3: Kenton ... 31Ma 67
Trevelyan Gdns. NW10 ... 39Ya 68
Trevelyan Ho. E2 ... 41Zb 92
(off Morpeth St.)
SE5 ... 52Rb 113
(off John Ruskin St.)
Trevelyan Pl. AL1: St A ... 4A 6
Trevelyan Rd. E15 ... 35Hc 73
SW17 ... 64Gb 133
Trevenna Ho. SE23 ... 62Zb 136
(off Dacres Rd.)
Trevera Ct. EN3: Pond E ... 14Ac 34
EN8: Walt C ... 5Ac 20
(off Eleanor Rd.)
Treveris St. SE1 ... 7C 224 (46Rb 91)
Treversh Ct. BR1: Brom ... 67Gc 137
Treverton St. W10 ... 42Za 88
Treverton Towers W10 ... 43Za 88
(off Treverton St.)
Treves Cl. N21 ... 15Pb 32
Treves Ho. E1 ... 42Wb 91
(off Vallance Rd.)
Treville St. SW15 ... 59Xa 110
Treviso Rd. SE23 ... 61Zb 136
Trevithick Cl. TW14: Felt ... 60V 106
Trevithick Dr. DA1: Dart ... 56Pd 119
Trevithick Ho. SE16 ... 49Xb 91
(off Rennie Est.)
Trevithick St. SE8 ... 51Cc 114
Trevithick Way E3 ... 41Cc 92
Trevone Gdns. HA5: Pinn ... 30Aa 45
Trevor Cl. BR2: Hayes ... 73Hc 159
EN4: E Barn ... 16Fb 31
HA3: Hrw W ... 24Ha 46
TW7: Isle ... 57Ha 108
UB5: N'olt ... 40Y 65
Trevor Cres. HA4: Ruis ... 35V 64
Trevor Gdns. HA4: Ruis ... 35W 64
HA8: Edg ... 25Ta 47
UB5: N'olt ... 40Y 65
Trevor Pl. SW7 ... 2E 226 (47Gb 89)
Trevor Rd. HA8: Edg ... 25Ta 47
IG8: Wfd G ... 24Jc 53
SW19 ... 66Ab 132
UB3: Hayes ... 47U 84
Trevor Sq. SW7 ... 2F 227 (47Hb 89)
Trevor St. SW7 ... 2E 226 (47Gb 89)
Trevor Wlk. SW7 ... 2F 227
(not continuous)
Trevose Av. KT14: W Byf ... 86H 169
Trevose Ho. SE11 ... 7J 229
SL2: Slou ... 2F 80
Trevose Rd. E17 ... 25Fc 53
Trevose Way WD19: Wat ... 20Y 27
Trewarden Av. SL0: Iver H ... 40F 62
Trewenna Dr. EN6: Pot B ... 4Fb 17
KT9: Chess ... 78Ma 153
Trewince Rd. SW20 ... 67Ya 132
Trewint St. SW18 ... 61Eb 133
Trewsbury Ho. SE2 ... 46Zc 95
Trewsbury Rd. SE26 ... 64Zb 136
Tria Apartments E2 ... 41Wb 91
(off Durant St.)
Triandra Way UB4: Yead ... 43Z 85
Triangle, The DA15: Sidc ... 59Wc 117
(off Burnt Oak La.)
E8 ... 39Xb 71
EC1 ... 5C 218
GU21: Wok ... 10N 167
IG11: Bark ... 37Sc 74
KT1: King T ... 68Ra 131
N13 ... 21Pb 50
Triangle Bus. Cen., The
NW10 ... 41Va 88
Triangle Cen. UB1: S'hall ... 46Fa 86
Triangle Ct. E16 ... 43Mc 93
SE1 ... 7E 224

Triangle Est.—Turnpike M.

Triangle Est. SE11 7K 229
Triangle Ho. SE1 1K 231
Triangle Pas.
EN4: E Barn 14Eb 31
Triangle Pl. SW4 56Mb 112
Triangle Rd. E8 39Xb 71
Triangle Way W3 48Qa 87
Tribeca Apartments *E1* *43Vb 91*
(off Heneage St.)
Trickett Ho. SM2: Sutt 81Db 175
Trico Ho. *TW8: Bford* *50Ma 87*
(off Ealing Rd.)
Tricorn Ho. SE28 46Uc 94
Tricycle Cinema, The 38Bb 69
Tricycle Theatre, The 38Bb 69
Trident Bus. Cen. SW17 64Hb 133
Trident Cen., The
WD24: Wat 11Y 27
Trident Gdns. UB5: N'olt 41Z 85
Trident Ho. *E14* *44Ec 92*
(off Blair St.)
SE28 46Tc 94
TW19: Stanw *59N 105*
(off Clare Rd.)
Trident Ind. Est. SL3: Poyle 55G 104
Trident Pl. *SW3* *51Fb 111*
(off Old Church St.)
Trident Point HA1: Harr 30Fa 46
Trident Rd. WD25: Wat 6V 12
Trident St. SE16 49Zb 92
Trident Way UB2: S'hall 48X 85
Trigg's Cl. GU22: Wok 1P 187
Trigg's La. GU21: Wok 1N 187
GU22: Wok 1N 187
Trig La. EC4 4D 224 (45Sb 91)
Trigo Ct. KT19: Eps 83Ta 173
Trigon Rd. SW8 52Pb 112
Tri Ho. KT12: Hers 77W 150
Trilby Rd. SE23 61Zb 136
Trillo Ct. IG2: Ilf 31Uc 74
Trimdon NW1 1B 216 (39Lb 70)
Trimmer Wlk.
TW8: Bford 51Na 109
Trim St. SE14 51Bc 114
Trinder Gdns. N19 32Nb 70
Trinder M. SW12 60Jb 112
TW11: Tedd 64Ja 130
Trinder Rd. EN5: Barn 15Ya 30
N19 32Nb 70
Trindles Rd. RH1: S Nut 8F 208
Tring Av. HA9: Wemb 37Qa 67
UB1: S'hall 44Ba 85
W5 46Pa 87
Tring Cl. IG2: Ilf 29Tc 54
RM3: Rom 21Pd 57
Tring Ct. TW1: Twick 63Ja 130
Tring Gdns. RM3: Rom 21Nd 57
Tring Grn. RM3: Rom 21Nd 57
Tringham Cl. GU21: Knap 10G 166
KT16: Ott 78E 148
Tringham Cotts. GU24: W End 4D 166
Tring Ho. WD18: Wat 17U 26
Tring Wlk. RM3: Rom 21Nd 57
Trinidad Gdns. RM10: Dag 38Fd 76
Trinidad Ho. *E14* *45Bc 92*
(off Gill St.)
Trinidad St. E14 45Bc 92
Trinity Av. EN1: Enf 16Vb 33
N2 27Fb 49
Trinity Buoy Wharf *E14* *45Gc 93*
(off Orchard Pl.)
Trinity Chu. Pas. SW13 51Xa 110
Trinity Chu. Rd. SW13 51Xa 110
Trinity Chu. Sq. SE1 2E 230 (48Sb 91)
Trinity Cl. BR2: Brom 74Nc 160
CR2: Sande 81Ub 177
E8 37Vb 71
E11 33Gc 73
HA6: Nwood 23U 44
KT20: Tad 91Ya 194
NW3 35Fb 69
SE13 56Fc 115
SW4 56Lb 112
TW4: Houn 56Aa 107
TW19: Stanw 58L 105
Trinity Cotts. TW9: Rich 55Pa 109
Trinity Ct. *AL1: St A* *1C 6*
(off Newsom Pl.)
BR1: Brom *67Hc 137*
(off Highland Rd.)
CR0: C'don 75Sb 157
DA1: Dart *60Rd 119*
(off Churchill Cl.)
DA1: Dart 59Md 119
(Baker Cres.)
EN2: Enf 12Sb 33
N1 *39Ub 71*
(off Downham Rd.)
N18 23Vb 51
NW2 36Ya 68
SE7 49Mc 93
SE8 *50Ac 92*
(off Evelyn St.)
SE25 72Ub 157
SE26 62Yb 136
SL4: Wind *4G 102*
(off Hawtrey Rd.)
SW9 55Pb 112
W2 2A 220
W9 *41Bb 89*
(off Croxley Rd.)
WC1 5J 217
WD3: Rick 19N 25
WD17: Wat 11V 26
Trinity Cres. SL5: S'dale 1E 146
SW17 61Hb 133
Trinity Dr. UB8: Hil 43S 84
Trinity Gdns. DA1: Dart 58Md 119
E16 43Hc 93
(not continuous)
SW9 56Pb 112
Trinity Grn. E1 42Yb 92
Trinity Gro. SE10 53Ec 114
Trinity Hall Cl.
WD24: Wat 13Y 27
Trinity Hospital (Almshouses)
SE10 50Fc 93
Trinity Ho. EC3 4K 225
EN8: Walt C 4Ac 20
RM8: Dag 36Xc 75
RM17: Grays *52De 121*
(off Argent St.)
SE1 3E 230
W14 48Bb 89
WD6: Bore 14Qa 29
Trinity Laban *51Ec 114*
(within Old Royal Naval College)
Trinity La. EN8: Walt C 4Ac 20
Trinity M. *E1* *43Yb 92*
(off Redman's Rd.)
HP2: Hem H 3D 4
SE20 67Xb 135
W10 44Za 88
Trinity Pk. E4 23Bc 52
Trinity Path SE23 62Yb 136
SE26 62Yb 136
Trinity Pl. DA6: Bex 56Bd 117
EC3 5K 225 (45Vb 91)
SL4: Wind 4G 102
Trinity Ri. SW2 60Qb 112
Trinity Rd. DA12: Grav'nd 9E 122
GU21: Knap 10F 166
IG6: Ilf 27Sc 54
N2 27Fb 49
N22 24Nb 50
(not continuous)
SW17 57Fb 111
SW18 56Eb 111
SW19 65Cb 133
TW9: Rich 55Pa 109
UB1: S'hall 46Aa 85
Trinity Sq. E14 44Gc 93
EC3 5J 225 (45Ub 91)
Trinity St. E16 43Hc 93
EN2: Enf 12Sb 33
SE1 2E 230 (47Sb 91)
(not continuous)
Trinity Ter. IG9: Lough 17Kc 35
Trinity Twr. *E1* *45Wb 91*
(off Vaughan Way)
E14 48Dc 92
Trinity Wlk. HP2: Hem H 3D 4
NW3 37Eb 69
Trinity Way E4 23Bc 52
W3 45Ua 88
Trio Pl. SE1 2E 230 (47Sb 91)
Triptych Ho. *SE8* *52Cc 114*
(off Watson's St.)
Triscott Ho. UB3: Hayes 46W 84
Tristan Ct. *SE8* *51Bc 114*
(off Dorking Cl.)
Tristan Lodge WD23: Bush 14Z 27
Tristan Sq. SE3 55Gc 115
Tristram Cl. E17 27Fc 53
Tristram Dr. N9 20Wb 33
Tristram Rd. BR1: Brom 63Hc 137
Triton Ct. *E16* *43Jc 93*
(off Robertson Rd.)
Triton Ho. *E14* *49Dc 92*
(off Cahir St.)
Triton Sq. NW1 5B 216 (42Lb 90)
Triton St. NW1 5A 216 (42Kb 90)
Tritton Av. CR0: Bedd 77Nb 156
Tritton Rd. SE21 62Tb 135
Trittons KT20: Tad 93Za 194
Triumph Cl.
RM16: Chaf H 49Yd 98
UB3: Harl 53S 106
Triumph Ho. IG11: Bark 41Wc 95
TW18: Staines 65K 127
Triumph Rd. E6 44Pc 94
Triumph Trad. Est. N17 23Wb 51
Trivett Cl. DA9: Ghithe 57Wd 120
Trocette Mans. SE1 3H 231
Trojan Ct. NW6 38Ab 68
Trojan Ind. Est. NW10 37Va 68
Trojan M. SW19 66Cb 133
Trojan Way CR0: Wadd 76Pb 156
Troon Cl. SE16 50Xb 91
SE28 44Zc 95
Troon Ct. SL5: S'hill 1A 146
Troon Ho. *E1* *44Ac 92*
(off White Horse Rd.)
Troon St. E1 44Ac 92
Troopers Dr. RM3: Rom 21Md 57
Tropical Ct. *W10* *41Za 88*
(off Kilburn La.)
Trosley Av. DA11: Grav'nd 1D 144
Trosley Country Pk. Vis. Cen. 84Fe 185
Trosley Rd. DA17: Belv 51Cd 118
Trossachs Rd. SE22 57Ub 113
Troston Ct. TW18: Staines 64H 127
Trothy Rd. SE1 49Wb 91
Trotman Ho. *SE14* *53Yb 114*
(off Pomeroy St.)
Trotsworth Av.
GU25: Vir W 70A 126
Trotsworth Ct. GU25: Vir W 10P 125
Trotters Bottom EN5: Barn 9Wa 16
Trotters La. GU24: Chob 4M 167
Trotter Way KT19: Eps 84Qa 173
Trott Rd. N10 24Hb 49
Trotts La. TN16: Westrm 99Sc 200
Trott St. SW11 53Gb 111
Trotwood IG7: Chig 23Tc 54
Trotwood Cl. CM15: Shenf 18Ae 41
Trotwood Ho. *SE16* *47Xb 91*
(off Wilson Gro.)
Troughton Rd. SE7 50Kc 93
Troutbeck NW1 4A 216
Troutbeck Cl. SL2: Slou 5L 81
Troutbeck Rd. SE14 53Ac 114
Trout La. UB7: Yiew 45L 83
Trout Ri. WD3: Loud 13K 25
Trout Rd. UB7: Yiew 46M 83
Troutstream Way
WD3: Loud 14J 25
Trouvere Pk. HP1: Hem H 1K 3
Trouville Rd. SW4 58Lb 112
Trowbridge Est. *E9* *37Bc 72*
(off Osborne Rd.)
Trowbridge Ho. *E9* *37Bc 72*
(off Felstead St.)
Trowbridge Rd. E9 37Bc 72
RM3: Rom 23Md 57
Trowers Way RH1: Redh 3B 208
Trowers Way Cen.
RH1: Redh 3B 208
Trowley Ri. WD5: Ab L 3U 12
Trowlock Av. TW11: Tedd 65La 130
Trowlock Island TW11: Tedd 65Ma 131
Trowlock Way TW11: Tedd 65Ma 131
Troy Cl. KT20: Tad 92Xa 194
Troy Ct. SE18 49Rc 94
W8 *48Cb 89*
(off Kensington High St.)
Troy Ind. Est. HA1: Harr 29Ha 46
Troy Rd. SE19 65Tb 135
Troy Town SE15 55Wb 113
Trubshaw Rd. UB2: S'hall 48Da 85
True Lovers Ct. HA6: Nwood 24T 44
Trueman Cl. HA8: Edg 24Ra 47
Trueman Rd. CR8: Kenley 92Tb 197
Truesdale Dr. UB9: Hare 28L 43
Truesdale Rd. E6 44Pc 94
Truesdales UB10: Ick 33S 64
truGym
Bromley *67Jc 137*
(off East St.)
Crouch End 30Nb 50
Uxbridge *38M 63*
(off Vine St.)
Trulock Ct. N17 24Wb 51
Trulock Rd. N17 24Wb 51
Trumans Rd. N16 36Vb 71
Truman Wlk. E3 42Dc 92
Trumble Gdns. CR7: Thor H 70Sb 135
Trumpers Way W7 48Ga 86
Trumper Way SL1: Slou 6D 80
UB8: Uxb 38L 63
Trumpets Hill Rd. RH2: Reig 7D 206
Trumpington Dr. AL1: St A 5B 6
Trumpington Rd. E7 35Hc 73
TRUMPS GREEN 2P 147
Trumpsgreen Av. GU25: Vir W 2P 147
Trumps Grn. Cl. GU25: Vir W 71A 148
Trumpsgreen Rd. GU25: Vir W 4N 147
Trumps Mill La. GU25: Vir W 72B 148
Trump St. EC2 3E 224 (44Sb 91)
Trundle Ho. SE1 1D 230
Trundlers Way WD23: B Hea 18Ga 28
Trundle St. SE1 1D 230 (47Sb 91)
Trundleys Rd. SE8 50Zb 92
Trundley's Ter. SE8 49Zb 92
Trunks All. BR8: Swan 68Dd 140
Truro Gdns. IG1: Ilf 31Nc 74
Truro Ho. HA5: Hat E 24Ba 45
W2 *43Cb 89*
(off Westbourne Pk. Rd.)
Truro Rd. DA12: Grav'nd 2F 144
E17 28Bc 52
N22 24Nb 50
Truro St. NW5 37Jb 70
Truro Wlk. RM3: Rom 23Ld 57
Truro Way UB4: Hayes 41U 84
Truslove Rd. SE27 64Qb 134
Truss Hill Rd. SL5: S'hill 1A 146
Trussley Rd. W6 48Ya 88
Trustees Cl. UB9: Den 30H 43
Truston's Gdns. RM11: Horn 31Jd 76
Trust Rd. EN8: Walt C 6Ac 20
Trust Wlk. SE21 60Rb 113
Trycewell La. TN15: Igh 93Zd 205
Tryfan Cl. IG4: Ilf 29Mc 53
Tryon Cres. E9 39Yb 72
Tryon St. SW3 7F 227 (50Hb 89)
Trystings Cl. KT10: Clay 79Ja 152
Tuam Rd. SE18 51Tc 116
Tubbenden Cl. BR6: Orp 76Uc 160
Tubbenden Dr. BR6: Orp 77Tc 160
Tubbenden La. BR6: Orp 77Tc 160
Tubbenden La. Sth. BR6: Farnb 78Tc 160
Tubbs Rd. NW10 40Va 68
Tubs Hill TN13: S'oaks 96Kd 203
Tubs Hill Ho. TN13: S'oaks 96Jd 202
Tubs Hill Pde. TN13: S'oaks 96Jd 202
Tubwell Rd. SL2: Stoke P 9M 61
Tucana Ct. *E1* *5K 219*
(off Cygnet St.)
Tucana Hgts. *E20* *36Ec 72*
(off Cheering La.)
Tucker Rd. KT16: Ott 79F 148
Tucker St. WD18: Wat 15Y 27
Tuckey Gro. GU23: Rip 95H 189
Tucklow Wlk. SW15 59Va 110
Tuck Rd. RM13: Rain 37Jd 76
Tudor Av. EN7: Chesh 3Wb 19
KT4: Wor Pk 76Xa 154
RM2: Rom 27Jd 56
TW12: Hamp 66Ca 129
WD24: Wat 10Z 13
Tudor Bus. Cen. KT20: Kgswd 93Bb 195
Tudor Cl. AL10: Hat 3B 8
BR7: Chst 67Pc 138
CM15: Shenf 16Ce 41
CR2: Sande 87Xb 177
CR5: Coul 90Qb 176
DA1: Dart 58Kd 119
DA11: Nflt 10A 122
EN7: Chesh 3Xb 19
GU22: Wok 89C 168
HA5: Eastc 29W 44
IG7: Chig 21Qc 54
IG8: Wfd G 22Kc 53
KT9: Chess 78Na 153
KT11: Cobh 85Ba 171
KT17: Ewe 82Va 174
KT23: Bookh 96Ba 191
(not continuous)
N6 31Lb 70
NW3 36Gb 69
NW7 23Wa 48
NW9 33Sa 67
SM3: Cheam 78Za 154
SM6: Wall 80Lb 156
SM7: Bans 87Ab 174
SW2 58Pb 112
TW12: Hamp H 64Ea 130
TW15: Ashf 63N 127
Tudor Ct. AL2: Lon C 8H 7
BR8: Crock 73Ed 162
CM14: W'ley 22Xd 58
DA14: Sidc 62Wc 139
E17 31Bc 72
GU21: Knap 9H 167
N1 37Ub 71
N22 24Nb 50
RH1: Redh *5A 208*
(off St Anne's Ri.)
RM3: Hrld W 23Rd 57
SE9 56Nc 116
SE16 *46Zb 92*
(off Princes Riverside Rd.)
TN16: Big H 90Nc 180
TW11: Tedd 65Ha 130
TW13: Hanw 63Y 129
TW19: Stanw 58N 105
TW20: Egh 64C 126
W3 47Qa 87
WD3: Rick 18J 25
WD6: Bore 12Na 29
Tudor Ct. Nth. HA9: Wemb 36Qa 67
Tudor Ct. Sth. HA9: Wemb 36Qa 67
Tudor Cres. EN2: Enf 11Sb 33
IG6: Ilf 23Rc 54
TN14: Otf 88Ld 183
Tudor Dr. KT2: King T 64Ma 131
KT12: Walt T 74Z 151
RM2: Rom 28Jd 56
SM4: Mord 72Za 154
TN14: Otf 88Ld 183
WD24: Wat 10Z 13
Tudor Ent. Pk. HA1: Harr 34Ha 66
HA3: W'stone 27Fa 46
Tudor Est. NW10 40Ra 67
Tudor Gdns. BR4: W W'ck 76Ec 158
HA3: Hrw W 26Fa 46
NW9 33Sa 67
RM2: Rom 28Jd 56
RM14: Upm 33Sd 78
SL1: Slou 4A 80
SW13 55Ua 110
TW1: Twick 60Ha 108
W3 43Qa 87
Tudor Grange KT13: Weyb 75U 150
Tudor Gro. E9 38Yb 72
Tudor Ho. E9 38Yb 72
E16 *46Kc 93*
(off Wesley Av.)
HA5: Pinn *26Y 45*
(off Pinner Hill Rd.)
KT13: Weyb 79Q 150
SE1 7K 225
W14 *49Za 88*
(off Windsor Way)
Tudor La. SL4: Old Win 9N 103
Tudor Lodge KT20: Kgswd 93Bb 195
Tudor Mnr. Gdns. WD25: Wat 4Z 13
Tudor M. E17 28Bc 52
RM1: Rom 29Hd 56
Tudor Pde. RM6: Chad H 31Zc 75
SE9 56Nc 116
WD3: Rick 17J 25
Tudor Pl. CR4: Mitc 66Gb 133
IG9: Buck H 19Nc 36
SE19 66Vb 135
Tudor Rd. BR3: Beck 69Ec 136
E4 23Dc 52
E6 39Lc 73
E9 39Xb 71
EN5: New Bar 13Cb 31
HA3: Hrw W, W'stone 26Fa 46
HA5: Pinn 26Y 45
IG11: Bark 39Vc 75
KT2: King T 66Qa 131
N9 17Xb 33
SE19 66Vb 135
SE25 71Xb 157
TW3: Houn 56Fa 108
TW12: Hamp 66Ca 129
TW15: Ashf 65T 128
UB1: S'hall 45Aa 85
UB3: Hayes 44T 84
Tudors, The RH2: Reig 3L 207
Tudor Sq. UB3: Hayes 43T 84
Tudor Stacks SE24 56Sb 113
Tudor St. EC4 4A 224 (45Qb 90)
Tudor Vs. EN7: G Oak 1Ub 19
(not continuous)
Tudor Wlk. DA5: Bexl 58Ad 117
KT13: Weyb 76R 150
KT22: Lea 92Ha 192
WD24: Wat 9Z 13
Tudor Way BR5: Pet W 72Tc 160
EN9: Walt A 5Fc 21
GU21: Knap 1G 186
N14 18Mb 32
SL4: Wind 3C 102
UB10: Hil 37Q 64
W3 47Qa 87
WD3: Rick 18J 25
Tudor Well Cl. HA7: Stan 22Ka 46
Tudor Works UB4: Yead 46Y 85
Tudway Rd. SE3 55Kc 115
Tuffnell Ct. *EN8: Chesh* *1Zb 20*
(off Coopers Wlk.)
Tufnail Rd. DA1: Dart 58Pd 119
Tufnell Ct. *E3* *39Bc 72*
(off Old Ford Rd.)
TUFNELL PARK 35Lb 70
Tufnell Pk. Rd. N7 35Lb 70
N19 35Lb 70
Tufter Rd. IG7: Chig 22Vc 55
Tufton Ct. SW1 4F 229
Tufton Gdns. KT8: W Mole 68Da 129
Tufton Rd. E4 21Cc 52
Tufton St. SW1 3E 228 (48Nb 90)
Tugboat St. SE28 47Uc 94
Tugela Rd. CR0: C'don 72Tb 157
Tugela St. SE6 61Bc 136
Tugmutton Cl. BR6: Farnb 77Rc 160
Tugwood Cl. CR5: Coul 93Mb 196
Tulip Cl. CM15: Pil H 15Xd 40
CR0: C'don 74Zb 158
E6 43Pc 94
RM3: Rom 23Ld 57
TW12: Hamp 65Ba 129
UB2: S'hall 47Ea 86
Tulip Gdns. E4 20Fc 35
IG1: Ilf 37Rc 74
Tulip Tree Ct. SM2: Sutt 83Cb 175
Tulip Way UB7: W Dray 49M 83
Tulk Ho. KT16: Ott 80D 148
Tullis Ho. *E9* *38Yb 72*
(off Frampton Pk. Rd.)
Tull St. CR4: Mitc 73Hb 155
Tulse Cl. BR3: Beck 69Ec 136
TULSE HILL 60Rb 113
Tulse Hill SW2 58Qb 112
Tulse Hill Est. SW2 58Qb 112
Tulse Ho. SW2 58Qb 112
Tulsemere Rd. SE27 61Sb 135
Tulyar Cl. KT20: Tad 92Xa 194
Tumber St. KT18: Head 97Sa 193
Tumblefield Rd.
TN15: Stans, Wro 82Be 185
Tumblewood Rd. SM7: Bans 88Ab 174
Tumbling Bay KT12: Walt T 72W 150
Tumbling Dice M. DA1: Dart 54Pd 119
Tummons Gdns. SE25 68Ub 135
Tump Ho. SE28 46Uc 94
Tunbridge Ct. *AL1: St A* *1D 6*
(off Manor Rd.)
Tunbridge Ho. EC1 3B 218
Tuncombe Rd. N18 21Ub 51
Tunis Rd. W12 46Ya 88
Tunley Grn. E14 43Bc 92
Tunley Rd. NW10 39Ua 68
SW17 60Jb 112
Tunmarsh La. E13 41Kc 93
Tunnan Leys E6 44Qc 94
Tunnel App. E14 45Ac 92
SE10 47Gc 93
SE16 47Yb 92
Tunnel Av. SE10 47Fc 93
Tunnel Av. Trad. Est. SE10 47Fc 93
Tunnel Est. RM20: W Thur 49Vd 98
Tunnel Gdns. N11 24Lb 50
Tunnel Ind. Est. RM20: W Thur 50Vd 98
Tunnel Link Rd. TW6: H'row A 58Q 106
Tunnel Rd. RH2: Reig 6J 207
SE16 47Yb 92
Tunnel Rd. E. TW6: H'row A 53R 106
Tunnel Rd. W. TW6: H'row A 53Q 106
Tunnel Wood Cl. WD17: Wat 9V 12
Tunnel Wood Rd.
WD17: Wat 9V 12
Tuns La. SL1: Slou 8G 80
Tunstall Av. IG6: Ilf 23Wc 55
Tunstall Cl. BR6: Orp 77Uc 160
Tunstall Rd. CR0: C'don 74Ub 157
SW9 56Pb 112
Tunstall Wlk. TW8: Bford 51Na 109
Tunstock Way DA17: Belv 48Ad 95
Tunworth Cl. NW9 30Sa 47
Tunworth Cres. SW15 58Va 110
Tun Yd. *SW8* *54Kb 112*
(off Peardon St.)
Tupelo Rd. E10 33Dc 72
Tupman Ho. *SE16* *47Wb 91*
(off Scott Lidgett Cres.)
Tuppy St. SE28 48Sc 94
Tupwood Ct. CR3: Cat'm 96Wb 197
Tupwood Gdns. CR3: Cat'm 97Wb 197
Tupwood La. CR3: Cat'm 98Wb 197
Tupwood Scrubbs Rd.
CR3: Cat'm 100Wb 197
Turenne Cl. SW18 56Eb 111
Turfhouse La. GU24: Chob 1J 167
Turin Ho. WD18: Wat 14U 26
Turin Rd. N9 17Yb 34
Turin St. E2 41Wb 91
Turkey Oak Cl. SE19 67Ub 135
TURKEY STREET 9Xb 19
Turkey St. EN1: Enf 8Wb 19
EN3: Enf W 9Xb 19
Turks Boatyard KT1: King T 67Ma 131
Turks Cl. UB8: Hil 41Q 84
Turks Head Ct. SL4: Eton 2H 103
Turk's Head Yd. EC1 7B 218 (43Rb 91)
Turk's Row SW3 7G 227 (50Hb 89)
Turle Rd. N4 33Pb 70
SW16 68Nb 134
Turlewray Cl. N4 32Pb 70
Turley Cl. E15 39Gc 73
Turnagain La. EC4 2B 224
Turnage Rd. RM8: Dag 32Ad 75
Turnant Rd. N17 25Sb 51
Turnberry Cl. NW4 26Za 48
SE16 50Xb 91
Turnberry Ct. WD19: Wat 20Y 27
Turnberry Dr. AL2: Brick W 2Aa 13
Turnberry Quay E14 48Dc 92
Turnberry Way BR6: Orp 74Tc 160
Turnbull Cl. DA9: Ghithe 59Ud 120
Turnbull Ho. N1 39Rb 71
Turnbury Cl. SE28 44Zc 95
Turnchapel M. SW4 55Kb 112
Turner Av. CR4: Mitc 67Hb 133
N15 28Ub 51
TN16: Big H 84Lc 179
TW2: Twick 62Ea 130
Turner Cl. HA0: Wemb 37Ma 67
NW11 30Db 49
SW9 52Rb 113
UB4: Hayes 40S 64
Turner Ct. DA1: Dart 57Ld 119
KT22: Lea *93Ja 192*
(off Highbury Dr.)
SE16 *47Yb 92*
(off Albion St.)
Turner Cres. CR0: C'don 72Sb 157
Turner Dr. NW11 30Db 49
Turner Ho. *E14* *47Cc 92*
(off Cassilis Rd.)
NW6 *36Eb 69*
(off Dresden Cl.)
NW8 1D 214
SW1 6E 228
TW1: Twick *58Ma 109*
(off Clevedon Rd.)
Turner M. SM2: Sutt 80Db 155
Turner Pde. *N1* *38Qb 70*
(off Barnsbury Pk.)
Turner Pl. CR5: Coul 88Lb 176
SW11 57Gb 111
Turner Rd. DA2: Bean 62Xd 142
E17 27Ec 52
HA8: Edg 26Na 47
KT3: N Mald 73Ta 153
RM12: Horn 33Hd 76
SL3: L'ly 7N 81
WD23: Bush 14Ea 28
Turners Cl. N20 20Hb 31
TW18: Staines 64K 127
Turners Ct. *E15* *35Ec 72*
(off Drapers Rd.)
EN8: Chesh 3Zb 20
N15 29Tb 51
RM4: Abr 13Xc 37
TN15: W King 79Ud 164
Turners Gdns. TN13: S'oaks 100Ld 203
Turner's Hill EN8: Chesh 1Zb 20
Turners Hill HP2: Hem H 3N 3
Turners La. KT12: Hers 79X 151
Turners Mdw. Way BR3: Beck 67Bc 136
Turners M. EN8: Chesh 2Zb 20
Turners Oak DA3: Nw A G 76Ae 165
Turners Pl. DA4: S Dar 68Sd 142
Turners Rd. E3 43Bc 92
Turner St. E1 43Xb 91
E16 44Hc 93
Turners Way CR0: Wadd 75Qb 156
Turners Wood NW11 31Eb 69
Turneville Rd. W14 51Bb 111
Turney Rd. SE21 59Sb 113
Turneys Orchard WD3: Chor 15F 24
TURNHAM GREEN 49Ua 88
Turnham Grn. Ter. W4 49Ua 88
Turnham Grn. Ter. M. W4 49Ua 88
Turnham Rd. SE4 57Ac 114
Turnmill St. EC1 6A 218 (42Rb 91)
Turnoak Av. GU22: Wok 92A 188
Turnoak La. GU22: Wok 92A 188
Turnoak Pk. SL4: Wind 6C 102
Turnour Ho. *E1* *44Xb 91*
(off Walburgh St.)
Turnpike Cl. DA16: Well 55Wc 117
SE8 52Bc 114
Turnpike Ct. DA6: Bex 56Zc 117
EN8: Walt C 6Ac 20
Turnpike Dr. BR6: Prat B 81Yc 181
Turnpike Ho. EC1 4C 218 (41Rb 91)
Turnpike La. N8 28Pb 50
RM18: W Til 9F 100
SM1: Sutt 78Eb 155
UB10: Uxb 41N 83
Turnpike Link CR0: C'don 75Ub 157
Turnpike M. *N8* *27Qb 50*
(off Turnpike La.)

Turnpike Pde. N15 27Rb 51
(off Green Lanes)
Turnpike Way TW7: Isle 53Ja 108
Turnpin La. SE10 51Ec 114
Turnstone DA3: Lfield 69Ce 143
Turnstone Cl. CR2: Sels 82Ac 178
E13 41Jc 93
NW9 26Ua 48
RM18: E Til 9K 101
UB10: Ick 36R 64
Turnstone Ho. E1 45Wb 91
(off Star Pl.)
Turnstones, The
DA12: Grav'nd 1F 144
WD25: Wat 8Aa 13
Turp Av. RM16: Grays 47Ee 99
Turpentine La. SW1 7A 228 (50Kb 90)
Turpin Av. RM5: Col R 23Cd 56
Turpin Cl. E1 45Zb 92
EN3: Enf L 9Cc 20
Turpin Ct. WD18: Wat 15V 26
Turpington Cl. BR2: Brom 73Nc 160
Turpington La. BR2: Brom 73Nc 160
Turpin Ho. SW11 53Kb 112
Turpin La. DA8: Erith 51Jd 118
Turpin Rd. TW14: Felt 58V 106
Turpin's La. IG8: Wfd G 22Pc 54
Turpins Ri. GU20: W'sham 7A 146
Turpins Yd. NW2 36Za 68
SE10 52Ec 114
Turpin Way N19 33Mb 70
SM6: Wall 80Kb 156
Turquand St. SE17 6E 230 (49Sb 91)
Turret Gro. SW4 55Lb 112
Turton Rd. HA0: Wemb 36Na 67
Turton Way SL1: Slou 8H 81
Turville Ct. KT23: Bookh 97Da 191
Turville Ho. NW8 5D 214
Turville St. E2 5K 219 (42Vb 91)
Tuscan Ho. E2 41Yb 92
(off Knottisford St.)
Tuscan Rd. SE18 50Tc 94
Tuscany Corte SE13 55Dc 114
(off Loampit Va.)
Tuscany Ho. E17 26Bc 52
IG3: Ilf 30Wc 55
Tuskar St. SE10 51Gc 115
Tussah Ho. E2 40Yb 72
(off Russia La.)
Tussauds Cl. WD3: Crox G 15Q 26
Tustin Est. SE15 51Yb 114
Tuttlebee La. IG9: Buck H 19Jc 35
Tuttleby Cotts. RM4: Abr 17Ad 37
Tuttle Ho. SW1 7D 228
Tutton Ho. DA12: Grav'nd 3E 144
Tuxford Cl. WD6: Bore 10Na 15
Twankhams All. CM16: Epp 2Wc 23
Tweed RM18: E Til 9L 101
Tweed Ct. W7 44Ga 86
(off Hanway Rd.)
Tweeddale Gro. UB10: Ick 34S 64
Tweeddale Rd. SM5: Cars 74Fb 155
Tweed Glen RM1: Rom 24Fd 56
Tweed Grn. RM1: Rom 24Fd 56
Tweedmouth Rd. E13 40Kc 73
Tweed Rd. SL3: L'ly 51D 104
Tweed Wlk. E14 42Ec 92
Tweed Way RM1: Rom 24Fd 56
Tweedy Cl. EN1: Enf 15Vb 33
Tweedy Rd. BR1: Brom 67Jc 137
Tweezer's All. WC2 4K 223
Twelfth Av. KT20: Lwr K 98Ab 194
Twelve Acre Cl. KT23: Bookh 96Ba 191
Twelve Acre Ho. E12 34Qc 74
(off Grantham Rd.)
Twelvetrees Bus. Pk. E3 42Fc 93
Twelvetrees Cres. E3 42Ec 92
(not continuous)
E16 42Ec 92
Twentyman Cl. IG8: Wfd G 22Jc 53
TWICKENHAM 60Ja 108
Twickenham Bri. TW1: Twick 57La 108
Twickenham Cl. CR0: Bedd 76Pb 156
Twickenham Gdns. HA3: Hrw W 24Ga 46
UB6: G'frd 36Ja 66
Twickenham Ho. DA1: Dart 54Pd 119
Twickenham Mus. 60Ja 108
(off The Embankment)
Twickenham Pl. KT7: T Ditt 75Ha 152
(off Woodfield Rd.)
Twickenham Rd. E11 33Ec 72
TW7: Isle 57Ja 108
TW9: Rich 56La 108
TW11: Tedd 63Ja 130
(not continuous)
TW13: Hanw 62Ba 129
Twickenham Stadium 58Ga 108
Twickenham Stoop 59Ga 108
Twickenham Trad. Est.
TW1: Twick 58Ha 108
Twig Folly Cl. E2 40Zb 72
Twigg Cl. DA8: Erith 52Gd 118
Twilley St. SW18 59Db 111
Twin Bridges Bus. Pk.
CR2: S Croy 79Tb 157
Twinches La. SL1: Slou 6F 80
Twine Cl. IG11: Bark 41Xc 95
Twine Ct. E1 45Yb 92
Twineham Grn. N12 21Cb 49
Twine Ter. E3 42Bc 92
(off Ropery St.)
Twining Av. TW2: Twick 62Ea 130
Twinoaks KT11: Cobh 85Ca 171
Twin Tumps Way SE28 45Wc 95
Twisden Rd. NW5 35Kb 70
Twist Ho. SE1 4J 231 (48Ub 91)
Twistleton Ct. DA1: Dart 58Md 119
Twist Way SL2: Slou 2D 80
Twitten Gro. BR1: Brom 69Pc 138
TWITTON 88Gd 182
Twitton La. TN14: Otf 87Fd 182
Twitton Mdws. TN14: Otf 88Gd 182
Twitton Stream Cotts.
TN14: Otf 88Gd 182
Two Mile Dr. SL1: Slou 7C 80
Two Oaks KT13: Weyb 77R 150
Two Rivers Retail Pk.
TW18: Staines 63G 126
Two Rivers Shop. Cen.
TW18: Staines 63H 127
TWO WATERS 5M 3
Two Waters Rd. HP3: Hem H 4L 3
Two Waters Way HP3: Hem H 6L 3
Twybridge Way NW10 38Sa 67
Twycross M. SE10 50Gc 93
Twyford Abbey Rd. NW10 41Pa 87
Twyford Av. N2 27Hb 49
W3 45Qa 87
Twyford Ct. HA0: Wemb 40Na 67
(off Vicars Bri. Cl.)
N10 27Jb 50
Twyford Cres. W3 46Qa 87
Twyford Ho. N5 34Rb 71
N15 30Ub 51
(off Chisley Rd.)
Twyford Pl. WC2 2H 223 (44Pb 90)
Twyford Rd. HA2: Harr 32Da 65
IG1: Ilf 36Sc 74
SM5: Cars 74Fb 155
Twyford Sports Cen. 46Ra 87
Twyford St. N1 39Pb 70
Twynersh Av. KT16: Chert 72H 149
Twynholm Mans. SW6 52Ab 110
(off Lillie Rd.)
Twysdens Ter. AL9: Wel G 6E 8
Tyas Rd. E16 42Hc 93
Tybenham Rd. SW19 69Cb 133
Tyberry Rd. EN3: Enf H 13Xb 33
Tyburn Ho. NW8 5C 214
Tyburn La. HA1: Harr 31Ha 66
Tyburns, The CM13: Hut 19Ee 41
Tyburn Tree (site of) 4F 221
Tyburn Way W1 4G 221 (45Hb 89)
Tycehurst Hill IG10: Lough 14Pc 36
Tydcombe Rd. CR6: W'ham 91Yb 198
Tye La. BR6: Farnb 78Sc 160
KT18: Head 99Ua 194
Tyers Est. SE1 1H 231
Tyer's Ga. SE1 2H 231 (47Ub 91)
Tyers St. SE11 7H 229 (50Pb 90)
Tyers Ter. SE11 7J 229 (50Pb 90)
Tyeshurst Cl. SE2 50Ad 95
Tyfield Cl. EN8: Chesh 2Yb 20
Tygan Ho. SM3: Cheam 79Ab 154
(off The Broadway)
Tylecroft Rd. SW16 68Nb 134
Tyle Grn. RM11: Horn 28Nd 57
Tylehurst Dr. RH1: Redh 7P 207
Tylehurst Gdns. IG1: Ilf 36Sc 74
Tyle Pl. SL4: Old Win 7L 103
Tyler Cl. DA8: Erith 52Dd 118
DA11: Nflt 60Ee 121
E2 1K 219 (40Vb 71)
Tyler Ct. SE17 5F 231
Tyler Gdns. KT15: Add 77L 149
Tyler Gro. DA1: Dart 56Pd 119
Tyler Rd. UB2: S'hall 48Da 85
Tylers Cl. IG10: Lough 17Nc 36
RH9: G'stone 2P 209
WD4: K Lan 10N 3
Tyler's Ct. W1 3D 222
Tylers Ct. E17 28Cc 52
(off Westbury Rd.)
HA0: Wemb 40Na 67
Tylers Cres. RM12: Horn 36Ld 77
Tylersfield WD5: Ab L 3V 12
Tylers Ga. HA3: Kenton 30Na 47
TYLER'S GREEN 1P 209
Tylers Grn. Rd. BR8: Crock 72Ed 162
Tylers Path SM5: Cars 77Hb 155
Tyler St. SE10 50Gc 93
(not continuous)
Tylers Way WD25: A'ham 13Ea 28
Tyler Wlk. SL3: L'ly 50B 82
Tyler Way CM14: B'wood 18Xd 40
Tylney Av. SE19 64Vb 135
(not continuous)
Tylney Cl. IG7: Chig 21Vc 55
Tylney Ho. E1 44Xb 91
(off Nelson St.)
Tylney Rd. BR1: Brom 68Mc 137
E7 35Lc 73
Tynamara KT1: King T 70Ma 131
(off Portsmouth Rd.)
Tynan Cl. TW14: Felt 60W 106
Tyndale Ct. E9 37Ac 72
(off Brookfield Rd.)
E14 50Dc 92
(off Transom Sq.)
Tyndale Ho. N1 38Rb 71
(off Tyndale La.)
Tyndale La. N1 38Rb 71
Tyndale Mans. N1 38Rb 71
(off Upper St.)
Tyndale M. SL1: Slou 7F 80
Tyndale Ter. N1 38Rb 71
Tyndall Gdns. E10 33Ec 72
Tyndall Rd. DA16: Well 55Vc 117
E10 33Ec 72
Tyne RM18: E Til 9L 101
Tyne Cl. RM14: Upm 30Td 58
Tyne Ct. W7 44Ga 86
(off Hanway Rd.)
Tynedale AL2: Lon C 9K 7
Tynedale Cl. DA2: Dart 60Td 120
Tyne Gdns. RM15: Avel 45Sd 98
Tyneham Cl. SW11 55Jb 112
Tyneham Rd. SW11 54Jb 112
Tyne Ho. KT2: King T 67Ma 131
Tynemouth Cl. E6 44Rc 94
Tynemouth Dr. EN1: Enf 10Wb 19
Tynemouth Rd. CR4: Mitc 66Jb 134
N15 28Vb 51
SE18 50Uc 94
Tynemouth St. SW6 54Eb 111
Tyne St. E1 2K 225 (44Vb 91)
Tynley Gro. GU4: Jac W 10P 187
Tynsdale Rd. NW10 38Ua 68
Tynte Ct. E9 36Ac 72
(off Mabley St.)
Tynwald Ho. SE26 62Wb 135
Type St. E2 40Zb 72
Typhoon Way SM6: Wall 80Nb 156
Tyrawley Rd. SW6 53Db 111
Tyre La. NW9 28Ua 48
Tyrell Cl. HA1: Harr 35Ga 66
Tyrell Ct. SM5: Cars 77Hb 155
Tyrell Gdns. SL4: Wind 5D 102
Tyrell Ho. BR3: Beck 64Dc 136
(off Beckenham Hill Rd.)
Tyrell Pl. CM15: Shenf 18Be 41
Tyrell Ri. CM14: W'ley 22Yd 58
Tyrells Cl. RM14: Upm 33Rd 77
Tyrian Pl. E1 43Wb 91
Tyrols Rd. SE23 60Zb 114
Tyrone Rd. E6 40Pc 74
Tyron Way DA14: Sidc 63Uc 138
Tyrrell Av. DA16: Well 57Wc 117
Tyrrell Ho. SW1 51Lb 112
(off Churchill Gdns.)
Tyrrell Rd. SE22 56Wb 113
Tyrrells Hall Cl. RM17: Grays 51Fe 121
Tyrrell Sq. CR4: Mitc 67Gb 133
TYRRELL'S WOOD 96Qa 193
Tyrrells Wood Golf Course 96Pa 193
Tyrrel Way NW9 31Wa 68
Tyrsal Cl. RM11: Horn 29Qd 57
Tyrwhitt Rd. SE4 55Cc 114
TYSEA HILL 17Hd 38
Tysea Hill RM4: Noak H, Stap A 18Hd 38
Tysoe Av. EN3: Enf L 8Bc 20
Tysoe St. EC1 4A 218 (41Qb 90)
Tyson Gdns. SE23 59Yb 114
Tyson Rd. SE23 59Yb 114
Tyssen Pas. E8 37Vb 71
Tyssen Pl. RM15: S Ock 41Yd 98
Tyssen Rd. N16 34Vb 71
Tyssen St. E8 37Vb 71
N1 1J 219 (40Ub 71)
Tytherton E2 40Yb 72
(off Cyprus St.)
Tytherton Rd. N19 34Mb 70
TYTTENHANGER 5J 7
Tyttenhanger Grn. AL4: St A 5H 7

U

Uamvar St. E14 43Dc 92
Uber E17 28Bc 52
Uckfield Gro. CR4: Mitc 66Jb 134
Uckfield Rd. EN3: Enf W 9Zb 20
Udall Gdns. RM5: Col R 23Cd 56
Udall St. SW1 6C 228 (49Lb 90)
Udimore Ho. W10 43Ya 88
(off Sutton Way)
Udney Pk. Rd. TW11: Tedd 65Ja 130
Uffington Rd. NW10 39Wa 68
SE27 63Qb 134
Ufford Cl. HA3: Hrw W 24Da 45
Ufford Rd. HA3: Hrw W 24Da 45
Ufford St. SE1 1A 230 (47Qb 90)
Ufton Ct. UB5: N'olt 41Z 85
Ufton Gro. N1 38Tb 71
Ufton Rd. N1 38Tb 71
(not continuous)
UH Gallery 1C 6
Uhura Sq. N16 34Ub 71
Ujima Ct. SW16 63Nb 134
Ullathorne Rd. SW16 63Lb 134
Ulleswater Rd. N14 20Nb 32
Ullin St. E14 43Ec 92
Ullswater E18 26Jc 53
Ullswater Bus. Pk. CR5: Coul 88Nb 176
Ullswater Cl. BR1: Brom 66Gc 137
GU18: Light 2A 166
SL1: Slou 3A 80
SW15 63Ta 131
UB4: Hayes 40U 64
Ullswater Ct. HA2: Harr 31Ca 65
Ullswater Cres. CR5: Coul 88Mb 176
SW15 63Ta 131
Ullswater Ho. SE15 51Yb 114
(off Hillbeck Cl.)
Ullswater Rd. GU18: Light 2A 166
HP3: Hem H 4C 4
SE27 61Rb 135
SW13 52Wa 110
Ullswater Way RM12: Horn 36Jd 76
Ulstan Cl. CR3: Wold 95Cc 198
Ulster Gdns. N13 21Sb 51
Ulster Pl. NW1 6K 215 (42Kb 90)
Ulster Ter. NW1 6K 215 (42Kb 90)
Ulundi Rd. SE3 51Gc 115
Ulva Rd. SW15 57Za 110
Ulverscroft Rd. SE22 57Vb 113
Ulverston RM19: Purf 50Sd 98
Ulverston Cl. AL1: St A 2D 6
Ulverstone Rd. SE27 61Rb 135
Ulverston Ho. RM3: Rom 23Nd 57
(off Kingsbridge Cir.)
Ulverston Rd. E17 26Fc 53
Ulwin Av. KT14: Byfl 85N 169
Ulysses Rd. NW6 36Bb 69
Umberstones GU25: Vir W 2P 147
Umberston St. E1 44Wb 91
Umberville Way SL2: Slou 1D 80
Umbria St. SW15 58Wa 110
Umbriel Pl. E13 40Jc 73
Umfreville Rd. N4 30Rb 51
Underacres Cl. HP2: Hem H 1A 4
Undercliff Rd. SE13 55Cc 114
UNDERHILL 15Cb 31
Underhill EN5: Barn 15Cb 31
Underhill Ct. EN5: Barn 15Cb 31
Underhill Gdns. W5 45La 86
Underhill Ho. E14 43Cc 92
(off Burgess St.)
Underhill Pk. Rd. RH2: Reig 3J 207
Underhill Pas. NW1 39Kb 70
(off Camden High St.)
Underhill Rd. SE22 57Wb 113
Underhill St. NW1 39Kb 70
Underne Av. N14 19Kb 32
Undershaft EC3 3H 225 (44Ub 91)
Undershaw Rd. BR1: Brom 62Hc 137
Underwood CR0: New Ad 78Ec 158
Underwood, The SE9 61Pc 138
Underwood Bldg., The EC1 1D 224
(off Bartholomew Cl.)
Underwood Ct. CR3: Cat'm 97Ub 197
E10 32Dc 72
(off Leyton Grange Est.)
Underwood Ho. KT8: W Mole 71Ca 151
(off Approach Rd.)
W6 48Xa 88
(off Sycamore Gdns.)
Underwood Rd. CR3: Cat'm 98Ub 197
E1 42Wb 91
E4 22Dc 52
IG8: Wfd G 24Lc 53
Underwood Row N1 3E 218 (41Sb 91)
Underwood St. N1 3E 218 (41Sb 91)
Undine Rd. E14 49Dc 92
Undine St. SW17 64Hb 133
Uneeda Dr. UB6: G'frd 39Ea 66
Unex Twr. E15 38Fc 73
(off Station St.)
Unicorn Bldg. E1 45Zb 92
(off Jardine Rd.)
Unicorn Theatre
London 7J 225 (46Ub 91)
Unicorn Vw. EN5: Barn 16Bb 31
Unicorn Wlk. DA9: Ghithe 57Vd 120
Unicorn Works N17 24Yb 52
Union Bus. Pk. UB8: Uxb 38K 63
Union Cl. E11 35Fc 73
Union Cotts. E15 38Gc 73
Union Ct. EC2 2H 225
SW4 54Nb 112
TW9: Rich 57Na 109
W9 43Cb 89
(off Elmfield Way)
Union Dr. E1 42Ac 92
Union Grn. HP2: Hem H 1M 3
Union Gro. SW8 54Mb 112
Union Ho. CR0: C'don 73Sb 157
Union La. TW7: Isle 54Ja 108
Union M. SW4 54Nb 112
Union Pk. SE10 50Hc 93
Union Rd. BR2: Brom 71Mc 159
CR0: C'don 73Sb 157
E17 30Bc 52
HA0: Wemb 37Na 67
N11 23Mb 50
RM7: Rush G 30Fd 56
SW4 54Mb 112
SW8 54Mb 112
UB5: N'olt 40Ca 65
Union Sq. N1 1D 218 (39Sb 71)
Union St. EN5: Barn 13Ab 30
KT1: King T 68Ma 131
SE1 7B 224 (46Rb 91)
Union Theatre 7C 224
Union Wlk. E2 3J 219 (41Ub 91)
Union Wharf N1 1E 218 (39Sb 71)
(Arlington Av.)
N1 2D 218
(Wenlock Rd.)
UB7: Yiew 46M 83
(off Bentinck Rd.)
Union Yd. W1 3A 222 (44Kb 90)
Unitair Cen. TW14: Bedf 58S 106
United Dr. TW14: Felt 59V 106
United Ho. SE16 47Yb 92
(off Brunel Rd.)
Unit Workshops E1 44Wb 91
(off Adler St.)
Unity Cl. CR0: New Ad 81Dc 178
NW10 37Wa 68
SE19 64Sb 135
Unity Ct. SE1 50Vb 91
(off Fortune Pl.)
Unity M. NW1 1D 216 (40Mb 70)
Unity Pl. E17 27Ac 52
Unity Rd. EN3: Enf W 9Yb 20
Unity Ter. HA2: Harr 32Da 65
Unity Trad. Est.
IG8: Wfd G 26Mc 53
Unity Way SE18 48Mc 93
Unity Wharf SE1 1K 231
Universal Ho. UB1: S'hall 45Aa 85
University Cl. NW7 24Va 48
WD23: Bush 14Ca 27
University College London
Art Mus. 5D 216
Bloomsbury Campus
5D 216 (42Mb 90)
Department of Geological Collections
6D 216
Institute of Neurology 6G 217
(off Queen Sq.)
Slade School of Fine Art 5D 216
University for the Creative Arts
Epsom Campus 86Ua 174
University Gdns. DA5: Bexl 59Bd 117
University of East London
Docklands Campus 45Qc 94
Duncan House 39Fc 73
Stratford Campus 37Gc 73
University of Greenwich
Avery Hill Campus 58Sc 116
Greenwich Campus -
King William Wlk. 51Fc 115
Maritime Greenwich Campus 51Ec 114
University of Hertfordshire
Art & Design Gallery 1A 8
College Lane Campus 1B 8
University of London
Birkbeck College 6E 216 (43Mb 90)
Heythrop College 48Db 89
(off Kensington Sq.)
Institute of Education &
Institute of Advanced Legal Studies
6E 216 (42Mb 90)
Observatory 23Va 48
School of Hygiene & Tropical Medicine
7E 216
School of Oriental & African Studies
6E 216
Senate House 7E 216 (43Mb 90)
Warburg Institute 6E 216 (42Mb 90)
University of North London
Hornsey Rd. 35Qb 70
Ladbrooke House 36Sb 71
North London Campus -
Spring House 37Qb 70
University of the Arts London
Camberwell College of Arts -
Peckham Rd. 53Ub 113
Wilson Rd. 53Ub 113
Chelsea College of Art & Design
7E 228 (50Mb 90)
London College of Fashion -
Curtain Rd. 5J 219
Golden La. 6D 218
Mare St. 38Yb 72
Wimbledon College of Art 67Ab 132
University of West London
Brentford Campus 50La 86
Ealing Campus -
Grove House 46Ma 87
Spesom House 45La 86
St Marys Road 46Ma 87
Vestry Hall 47Ma 87
Walpole House 45Ma 87
University of Westminster
Cavendish Campus -
Hanson St. 7B 216 (43Lb 90)
Lit. Titchfield St. 1B 222
Harrow Campus 31Ja 66
Marylebone Campus 7H 215 (43Jb 90)
Regent Campus -
Regent St. 2A 222
Wells St. 1C 222
University Pl. DA8: Erith 52Ed 118
University Rd. SW19 65Fb 133
University St. WC1 6C 216 (42Lb 90)
University Way DA1: Dart 56Rd 119
E16 45Qc 94
Unwin Av. TW14: Felt 57T 106
Unwin Cl. SE15 51Wb 113
Unwin Ct. N2 28Gb 49
Unwin Mans. W14 51Bb 111
(off Queen's Club Gdns.)
Unwin Rd. SW7 3B 226 (48Fb 89)
TW7: Isle 55Ga 108
Unwin Way HA7: Stan 24Ma 47
Up at The O2 46Gc 93
Upbrook M. W2 3A 220 (44Eb 89)
Upcerne Rd. SW10 52Eb 111
Upchurch Cl. SE20 66Xb 135
Upcott Ho. E3 41Dc 92
(off Bruce Rd.)
E9 38Yb 72
(off Frampton Pk. Rd.)
Upcroft SL4: Wind 5F 102
Upcroft Av. HA8: Edg 22Sa 47
Updale Cl. EN6: Pot B 5Ab 16
Updale Rd. DA14: Sidc 63Vc 139
Updown Hill GU20: W'sham 9B 146
Upfield CR0: C'don 76Xb 157
Upfield Rd. W7 43Ha 86
Upgrove Mnr. Way SW2 59Qb 112
Uphall Rd. IG1: Ilf 36Rc 74
Upham Pk. Rd. W4 49Ua 88
Uphavering Ho. RM12: Horn 33Ld 77
Uphill BR2: Brom 70Hc 137
(off Westmoreland Rd.)
Uphill Dr. NW7 22Ua 48
NW9 29Sa 47
Uphill Gro. NW7 21Ua 48
Uphill Rd. NW7 21Ua 48
Upland Ct. HA6: Nwood 21V 44
Upland Ct. Rd. RM3: Hrld W 26Pd 57
Upland Dr. AL9: Brk P 7K 9
KT18: Tatt C 90Ya 174
Upland M. SE22 57Wb 113
Upland Rd. CR2: S Croy 78Tb 157
CR3: W'ham, Wold 92Cc 198
DA7: Bex 55Bd 117
E13 42Jc 93
SE22 57Wb 113
(not continuous)
SM2: Sutt 80Fb 155
Uplands BR3: Beck 68Cc 136
CR6: W'ham 90Bc 178
KT21: Asht 92Ma 193
WD3: Crox G 16P 25
Uplands, The AL2: Brick W 2Aa 13
HA4: Ruis 32W 64
IG10: Lough 13Pc 36
SL9: Ger X 32A 62
Uplands Av. E17 26Zb 52
Uplands Bus. Pk. E17 27Zb 52
Uplands Cl. SE18 50Rc 94
SL9: Ger X 32A 62
SW14 57Ra 109
TN13: Riv 95Hd 202
Uplands Ct. N21 17Qb 32
(off The Green)
Uplands Dr. KT22: Oxs 86Fa 172
Uplands End IG8: Wfd G 24Nc 54
Uplands Est. RM19: Purf 49Sd 98
(off Arterial Rd.)
Uplands Pk. Rd. EN2: Enf 12Qb 32
Uplands Rd. BR6: Orp 74Xc 161
CM14: W'ley 22Ae 59
CR8: Kenley 88Sb 177
EN4: E Barn 18Jb 32
IG8: Wfd G 24Nc 54
N8 29Pb 50
RM6: Chad H 27Zc 55
Uplands Way N21 15Qb 32
TN13: Riv 95Hd 202
Upland Way KT18: Tatt C 90Ya 174
UPMINSTER 33Sd 78
Upminster Golf Course 31Td 78
Upminster Rd. RM11: Horn 33Pd 77
RM12: Horn 33Pd 77
RM14: Upm 33Pd 77
Upminster Rd. Nth.
RM13: Rain 41Ld 97
Upminster Rd. Sth. RM13: Rain 42Jd 96
Upminster Tithe Barn Mus. of Nostalgia
31Td 78
Upminster Trad. Pk.
RM14: Upm 31Zd 79
Upminster Windmill 33Rd 77
Upnall Ho. SE15 51Yb 114
Upney Cl. RM12: Horn 36Md 77
Upney La. IG11: Bark 37Uc 74
Upnor Way SE17 7J 231 (50Ub 91)
Uppark Dr. IG2: Ilf 30Sc 54
Up. Abbey Rd. DA17: Belv 49Bd 95
Up. Addison Gdns. W14 47Ab 88
Up. Austin Lodge Rd.
DA4: Eyns 77Md 163
Upper Av. DA13: Ist R 7A 144
Up. Bank St. E14 46Dc 92
(not continuous)
Up. Bardsey Wlk. N1 37Sb 71
(off Douglas Rd. Nth.)
Upper Barn HP3: Hem H 5P 3
Up. Belgrave St. SW1 3J 227 (48Jb 90)
Up. Berenger Wlk. SW10 52Fb 111
(off Berenger Wlk.)
Up. Berkeley St. W1 3F 221 (44Hb 89)
Up. Beulah Hill SE19 67Ub 135
Up. Blantyre Wlk. SW10 52Fb 111
(off Blantyre Wlk.)
Up. Bourne End La.
HP1: Hem H 6A 2
(not continuous)
Up. Brentwood Rd. RM2: Rom 28Ld 57
Upper Bri. Rd. RH1: Redh 6N 207
Up. Brighton Rd. KT6: Surb 72Ma 153
Up. Brockley Rd. SE4 55Bc 114
(not continuous)
Up. Brook St. W1 5H 221 (45Jb 90)
Upper Butts TW8: Bford 51La 108
Up. Caldy Wlk. N1 37Sb 71
(off Caldy Wlk.)
Up. Camelford Wlk. W11 44Ab 88
(off St Mark's Rd.)
Up. Cavendish Av. N3 27Cb 49
Up. Cheapside Pas. EC2 3D 224
(off Cheapside)
Up. Cheyne Row SW3 51Gb 111
Up. Church Hill
DA9: Ghithe 57Ud 120
UPPER CLAPTON 33Xb 71
Up. Clapton Rd. E5 32Xb 71
Up. Clarendon Wlk. W11 44Ab 88
(off Clarendon Rd.)
Upper Cornsland
CM14: B'wood 20Zd 41
Upper Ct. Rd. CR3: Wold 95Cc 198
KT19: Eps 83Sa 173
Up. Culver Rd. AL1: St A 1C 6
Up. Dagnall St. AL3: St A 2B 6
Up. Dartrey Wlk. SW10 52Eb 111
(off Whistler Wlk.)
Up. Dengie Wlk. N1 39Sb 71
(off Baddow Wlk.)
Upper Dr. TN16: Big H 90Lc 179
Upper Dunnymans
SM7: Bans 86Bb 175
UPPER EDMONTON 22Wb 51
UPPER ELMERS END 71Bc 158

Up. Elmers End Rd.—Venn St.

Up. Elmers End Rd.
BR3: Beck 70Ac **136**
Up. Fairfield Rd. KT22: Lea 93Ka **192**
Up. Farm Rd. KT8: W Mole 70Ba **129**
Upper Feilde W1 ....4H **221**
Upper Fosters *NW4* *28Ya* **48**
(off New Brent St.)
UPPER GATTON 99Fb **195**
Up. Green E. CR4: Mitc 69Hb **133**
Up. Green W. CR4: Mitc 68Hb **133**
(not continuous)
Up. Grosvenor St. W1 ....5H **221** (45Jb **90**)
Up. Grotto Rd. TW1: Twick 61Ha **130**
Upper Ground SE1 ....6K **223** (46Qb **90**)
Upper Gro. SE25 ....70Ub **135**
Up. Grove Rd. DA17: Belv 51Bd **117**
Up. Guild Hall DA9: Bluew 59Vd **120**
Up. Gulland Wlk. *N1* *38Sb* **71**
(off Church Rd.)
UPPER HALLIFORD 70U **128**
Up. Halliford By-Pass
TW17: Shep 70U **128**
Up. Halliford Grn. TW17: Shep 70U **128**
Up. Halliford Rd. TW17: Shep 69U **128**
(not continuous)
Up. Hall Pk. HP4: Berk 2A **2**
Up. Hampstead Wlk. NW3 ....35Eb **69**
Up. Ham Rd. KT2: King T 63Ma **131**
TW10: Ham 63Ma **131**
Up. Handa Wlk. *N1* *37Tb* **71**
(off Handa Wlk.)
Upper Harestone CR3: Cat'm 99Wb **197**
Up. Hawkwell Wlk. *N1* *39Sb* **71**
(off Maldon Cl.)
Up. Heath Rd. AL1: St A 1D **6**
Up. High St. KT17: Eps 85Ua **174**
Upper Highway WD4: Hunt C 4S **12**
WD5: Ab L 4S **12**
Up. Hill Ri. WD3: Rick 16J **25**
Upper Hitch WD19: Wat 18Aa **27**
UPPER HOLLOWAY 33Lb **70**
Up. Holly Hill Rd. DA17: Belv 50Dd **96**
Up. James St. W1 ....4C **222** (45Lb **90**)
Up. John St. W1 ....4C **222** (45Lb **90**)
Up. Lattimore Rd. AL1: St A 2C **6**
Up. Lees Rd. SL2: Slou 1F **80**
Up. Lismore Wlk. *N1* *37Sb* **71**
(off Clephane Rd.)
Upper Lodge *W8* *46Db* **89**
(off Palace Grn.)
Up. Lodge M. TW12: Hamp H 65Fa **130**
Up. Lodge Way CR5: Coul 94Mb **196**
Upper Mall W6 ....50Wa **88**
(not continuous)
Up. Marlborough Rd. AL1: St A 2C **6**
Upper Marsh SE1 ....3J **229** (48Pb **90**)
Upper Mdw. SL9: Ger X 2N **61**
Up. Montagu St. W1 ....7F **215** (43Hb **89**)
Up. Mulgrave Rd. SM2: Cheam 80Ab **154**
Upper Nth. St. E14 ....43Cc **92**
UPPER NORWOOD 67Ub **135**
Upper Nursery SL5: S'dale 1E **146**
Up. Paddock Rd. WD19: Wat 16Aa **27**
Upper Pk. IG10: Lough 14Mc **35**
Upper Pk. Rd. BR1: Brom 67Kc **137**
DA17: Belv 49Dd **96**
KT2: King T 65Qa **131**
N11 ....22Kb **50**
NW3 ....36Hb **69**
Up. Phillimore Gdns. W8 ....47Cb **89**
Up. Pillory Down SM5: Cars 85Jb **176**
Upper Pines SM7: Bans 89Hb **175**
Up. Rainham Rd. RM12: Horn 32Hd **76**
Up. Ramsey Wlk. *N1* *37Tb* **71**
(off Ramsey Wlk.)
Up. Rawreth Wlk. *N1* *39Sb* **71**
(off Basire St.)
Up. Richmond Rd. SW15 ....56Va **110**
Up. Richmond Rd. W. SW14 ....56Qa **109**
TW10: Rich 56Qa **109**
Upper Rd. E13 ....41Jc **93**
SM6: Wall 78Mb **156**
UB9: Den 31F **62**
Up. Rose Gallery DA9: Bluew 59Wd **120**
UPPER RUXLEY 66Cd **140**
Upper Ryle CM14: B'wood 17Xd **40**
Up. St Martin's La. WC2 ....4F **223** (45Nb **90**)
Upper Sales HP1: Hem H 3H **3**
Upper Sawleywood SM7: Bans 86Bb **175**
Up. Selsdon Rd.
CR2: Sande, Sels 80Vb **157**
Up. Sheridan Rd. DA17: Belv 49Cd **96**
UPPER SHIRLEY 77Zb **158**
Up. Shirley Rd. CR0: C'don 75Yb **158**
Up. Spring La. TN15: Igh 94Xd **204**
Upper Sq. TW7: Isle 55Ja **108**
Upper Stanford GU24: Pirb 7D **186**
Up. Station Rd. WD7: R'lett 7Ja **14**
Upper St. N1 ....1A **218** (40Qb **70**)
Upper St. Nth. *DA3: Nw A G* *75Be* **165**
(off The Row)
Upper St. Sth. *DA3: Nw A G* *75Be* **165**
(off The Row)
Up. Sunbury Rd. TW12: Hamp 67Aa **129**
Up. Sutton La. TW5: Hest 52Ca **107**
Upper Swaines CM16: Epp 2Vc **23**
UPPER SYDENHAM 62Xb **135**
Up. Tachbrook St. SW1 ....5B **228** (49Lb **90**)
Upper Tail WD19: Wat 20Aa **27**
Up. Talbot Wlk. *W11* *44Ab* **88**
(off Talbot Wlk.)
Up. Teddington Rd.
KT1: Hamp W 66La **130**
Upper Ter. NW3 ....34Eb **69**
Up. Thames St. EC4 ....4C **224** (45Rb **91**)
Up. Thames Wlk. DA9: Bluew 60Vd **120**
Up. Tollington Pk. N4 ....32Qb **70**
(not continuous)
Upperton Rd. DA14: Sidc 64Vc **139**
Upperton Rd. E. E13 ....41Lc **93**
Upperton Rd. W. E13 ....41Lc **93**
UPPER TOOTING 63Hb **133**
Up. Tooting Pk. SW17 ....61Hb **133**
Up. Tooting Rd. SW17 ....63Hb **133**
Up. Town Rd. UB6: G'frd 42Da **85**
Up. Tulse Hill SW2 ....59Pb **112**
Up. Vernon Rd. SM1: Sutt 78Fb **155**
Up. Village Rd. SL5: S'hill 1A **146**
Upper Wlk. GU25: Vir W 70A **126**
UPPER WALTHAMSTOW 28Fc **53**
Up. Walthamstow Rd. E17 ....28Ec **52**
UPPER WARLINGHAM 89Wb **177**
Up. West St. RH2: Reig 6H **207**
Up. Whistler Wlk. *SW10* *52Eb* **111**
(off Worlds End Est.)
Up. Wickham La.
DA16: Well 52Xc **117**
Up. Wimpole St. W1 ....7J **215** (43Jb **90**)
Up. Woburn Pl. WC1 ....4E **216** (41Mb **90**)
Up. Woodcote Village CR8: Purl 84Mb **176**
Uppingham Av. HA7: Stan 25Ka **46**
Upsdell Av. N13 ....23Qb **50**
UPSHIRE 5Mc **21**
Upshirebury Grn. EN9: Walt A 5Mc **21**
Upshire Ho. E17 ....26Bc **52**
Upshire Rd. EN9: Walt A 4Hc **21**
Upshot La. GU22: Pyr 89H **169**
Upstairs at the Gatehouse Theatre
Highgate 32Jb **70**
Upstall St. SE5 ....53Rb **113**
UPTON
DA6 ....57Zc **117**
E7 ....38Jc **73**
SL1 ....8L **81**
Upton GU21: Wok 9M **167**
Upton Av. AL3: St A 1B **6**
E7 ....38Jc **73**
Upton Cl. AL2: Park 7B **6**
DA5: Bexl 58Bd **117**
NW2 ....34Ab **68**
SL1: Slou 8K **81**
SS17: Stan H 1M **101**
Upton Ct. *SE20* *66Yb* **136**
(off Blean Gro.)
Upton Ct. Rd. SL3: L'ly, Slou 8L **81**
Upton Dene SM2: Sutt 80Db **155**
Upton Gdns. HA3: Kenton 29Ka **46**
Upton Hgts. E7 ....38Jc **73**
Upton Ho. *E9* *36Ac* **72**
(off Ward La.)
RM3: Rom *22Md* **57**
(off Barnstaple Rd.)
Upton La. E7 ....38Jc **73**
Upton Lea Pde. SL2: Slou 5M **81**
Upton Lodge E7 ....37Jc **73**
Upton Lodge Cl. WD23: Bush 17Ea **28**
UPTON PARK
E6 ....39Mc **73**
SL1 ....8K **81**
Upton Pk. SL1: Slou 8J **81**
Upton Pk. Boleyn Cinema 40Mc **73**
Upton Pk. Rd. E7 ....38Kc **73**
Upton Rd. CR7: Thor H 68Tb **135**
DA5: Bexl 56Ad **117**
DA6: Bex 56Ad **117**
N18 ....22Wb **51**
SE18 ....51Sc **116**
SL1: Slou 8L **81**
TW3: Houn 55Ca **107**
WD18: Wat 13X **27**
Upton Rd. Sth. DA5: Bexl 58Bd **117**
Upton Vs. DA6: Bex 56Ad **117**
Upward Ct. RM1: Rom 28Hd **56**
Upway N12 ....23Gb **49**
SL9: Chal P 25B **42**
Upwey Ho. N1 ....39Ub **71**
Upwood Rd. SE12 ....58Jc **115**
SW16 ....67Nb **134**
Uranus Rd. HP2: Hem H 1P **3**
Urban Av. RM12: Horn 34Ld **77**
Urbanest King's Cross N1 ....39Nb **70**
Urban M. N4 ....30Rb **51**
Urdang, The 4A **218**
Urlwin St. SE5 ....51Sb **113**
Urlwin Wlk. SW9 ....53Qb **112**
Urmston Dr. SW19 ....60Ab **110**
Urmston Ho. *E14* *49Ec* **92**
(off Seyssel St.)
Urquhart Ct. BR3: Beck 66Bc **136**
Ursa Mans. *E20* *36Ec* **72**
(off Cheering La.)
Ursula Gould Way E14 ....43Cc **92**
Ursula Lodges DA14: Sidc 64Xc **139**
Ursula M. N4 ....32Sb **71**
Ursula St. SW11 ....53Gb **111**
Urswick Gdns. RM9: Dag 38Ad **75**
Urswick Rd. E9 ....36Yb **72**
RM9: Dag 38Zc **75**
Usborne M. SW8 ....52Pb **112**
Usher Hall *NW4* *28Xa* **48**
(off The Burroughs)
Usher Rd. E3 ....39Bc **72**
(not continuous)
Usk Rd. RM15: Avel 43Sd **98**
SW11 ....56Eb **111**
Usk St. E2 ....41Zb **92**
Utah Bldg. *SE13* *53Dc* **114**
(off Deal's Gateway)
Utopia Village NW1 ....38Jb **70**
Uvedale Cl. CR0: New Ad 83Fc **179**
Uvedale Cres. CR0: New Ad 83Fc **179**
Uvedale Rd. EN2: Enf 15Tb **33**
RH8: Oxt 2K **211**
RM10: Dag 34Cd **76**
Uverdale Rd. SW10 ....52Eb **111**
UXBRIDGE 38M **63**
Uxbridge Ct. *KT1: King T* *71Ma* **153**
(off Uxbridge Rd.)
Uxbridge Golf Course 33N **63**
Uxbridge Ind. Est. UB8: Uxb 40K **63**
Uxbridge Lido 37N **63**
UXBRIDGE MOOR 40K **63**
Uxbridge Moor Nature Reserve 38K **63**
Uxbridge Rd. HA3: Hrw W 24Ea **46**
HA5: Hat E, Pinn 26Y **45**
HA7: Stan 24Ea **46**
KT1: King T 70Ma **131**
SL0: Iver H 7M **81**
SL1: Slou 7L **81**
SL2: Slou 7M **81**
SL3: Geor G, Wex 7L **81**
TW12: Hamp, Hamp H 63Ca **129**
TW13: Felt 61Y **129**
UB1: S'hall 46Ca **85**
UB4: Hayes, Yead 43U **84**
UB10: Hil 41Q **84**
W3 ....45Na **87**
W5 ....45Na **87**
W7 ....46Ha **86**
W12 ....46Wa **88**
W13 ....46Ka **86**
WD3: Rick 20H **25**
Uxbridge Rd. Retail Pk.
UB4: Yead 45Y **85**
Uxbridge St. W8 ....46Cb **89**
Uxendon Cres. HA9: Wemb 32Na **67**
Uxendon Hill HA9: Wemb 32Pa **67**

V

Vaillant Rd. KT13: Weyb 77S **150**
Vaine Ho. E9 ....37Ac **72**
Vaizeys Wharf SE7 ....48Kc **93**
Valance Av. E4 ....18Gc **35**
Valan Leas BR2: Brom 69Gc **137**
Vale, The CM14: B'wood 18Yd **40**
CR0: C'don 75Zb **158**
CR5: Coul 86Mb **176**
HA4: Ruis 35Y **65**
IG8: Wfd G 24Jc **53**
N10 ....25Jb **50**
N14 ....17Mb **32**
NW11 ....34Za **68**
SL9: Chal P 25A **42**
SW3 ....51Fb **111**
TW5: Hest 51Aa **107**
TW14: Felt 58X **107**
TW16: Sun 65W **128**
W3 ....46Ta **87**
Vale Av. WD6: Bore 15Ra **29**
Vale Border CR0: Sels 83Zb **178**
CR2: Sels 83Zb **178**
Vale Cl. BR6: Farnb 77Qc **160**
CM15: Pil H 15Vd **40**
CR5: Coul 86Nb **176**
GU21: Wok 88A **168**
KT13: Weyb 76T **150**
KT18: Eps D 91Ua **194**
N2 ....27Hb **49**
SL9: Chal P 25A **42**
TW1: Twick 62Ja **130**
W9 ....4A **214** (41Eb **89**)
Vale Cotts. SW15 ....62Ua **132**
Vale Ct. EN5: New Bar 14Db **31**
KT13: Weyb 76T **150**
W3 ....46Va **88**
W9 ....4A **214** (41Eb **89**)
Vale Cres. SW15 ....63Ua **132**
Vale Cft. HA5: Pinn 29Aa **45**
KT10: Clay 81Ha **172**
Vale Dr. EN5: Barn 14Bb **31**
Vale End SE22 ....56Vb **113**
Vale Est., The W3 ....46Ua **88**
Va. Farm Rd. GU21: Wok 89A **168**
Vale Farm Sports Cen. 35Ka **66**
Vale Gro. N4 ....31Sb **71**
SL1: Slou 8J **81**
W3 ....47Ta **87**
Vale Ho. GU21: Wok 89A **168**
Vale Ind. Est. WD18: Wat 17R **26**
Vale La. W3 ....43Qa **87**
Vale Lodge SE23 ....61Yb **136**
Valence Av. RM8: Dag 32Zc **75**
Valence Cir. RM8: Dag 34Zc **75**
Valence Dr. EN7: Chesh 1Wb **19**
Valence House Mus. 34Ad **75**
Valence Rd. DA8: Erith 52Fd **118**
Valence Wood Rd. RM8: Dag 34Zc **75**
Valencia Rd. HA7: Stan 21La **46**
Valency Cl. HA6: Nwood 21V **44**
Valency Dr. HA6: Nwood 21V **44**
Valentia Pl. SW9 ....56Qb **112**
Valentina Av. NW9 ....26Va **48**
Valentine Av. DA5: Bexl 61Ad **139**
Valentine Ct. SE23 ....61Zb **136**
(not continuous)
Valentine Ho. *E3* *39Bc* **72**
(off Garrison Rd.)
Valentine Pl. SE1 ....1B **230** (47Rb **91**)
Valentine Rd. E9 ....37Zb **72**
HA2: Harr 34Da **65**
Valentine Row SE1 ....2B **230** (48Rb **91**)
Valentines Mansion & Gdns. 31Qc **74**
Valentines Rd. IG1: Ilf 32Rc **74**
Valentine's Way RM7: Rush G 33Gd **76**
Valentine Vs. RM15: S Ock 43Yd **98**
Valentine Way HP8: Chal G 20A **24**
Valentyne Cl. CR0: New Ad 83Gc **179**
VALE OF HEALTH 34Eb **69**
Vale of Health NW3 ....34Fb **69**
Vale Pde. SW15 ....62Ua **132**
Valerian Wlk. N11 ....19Jb **32**
Valerian Way E15 ....41Gc **93**
Valerie Cl. AL1: St A 2F **6**
Valerie Ct. SM2: Sutt 80Db **155**
WD23: Bush 17Ea **28**
Valerio M. N1 ....37Tb **71**
Vale Ri. NW11 ....32Bb **69**
Vale Rd. BR1: Brom 67Qc **138**
CR4: Mitc 69Mb **134**
DA1: Dart 60Kd **119**
DA11: Nflt 59Fe **121**
E7 ....37Kc **73**
KT4: Wor Pk 76Va **154**
KT10: Clay 81Ga **172**
KT13: Weyb 76T **150**
KT19: Ewe 77Va **154**
N4 ....31Sb **71**
SL4: Wind 2D **102**
SM1: Sutt 77Db **155**
WD23: Bush 15Aa **27**
Vale Rd. Nth. KT6: Surb 75Na **153**
Vale Rd. Sth. KT6: Surb 75Na **153**
Vale Row N5 ....34Rb **71**
Vale Royal N7 ....38Nb **70**
Vale Royal Ho. WC2 ....4E **222**
Valery Pl. TW12: Hamp 66Ca **129**
Valeside Ct. EN5: New Bar 14Db **31**
Vale St. SE27 ....62Tb **135**
Valeswood Rd. BR1: Brom 64Hc **137**
Vale Ter. N4 ....30Sb **51**
Valetta Gro. E13 ....40Jc **73**
Valetta Rd. W3 ....47Ua **88**
Valette Ct. *N10* *28Kb* **50**
(off St James's La.)
Valette Ho. E9 ....37Yb **72**
Valette St. E9 ....37Yb **72**
Valiant Cl. RM7: Mawney 26Dd **56**
UB5: N'olt 41Z **85**
Valiant Ho. *E14* *47Ec* **92**
(off Plevna St.)
SE7 ....50Lc **93**
Valiant Path NW9 ....24Ua **48**
Valiant Way E6 ....43Pc **94**
Vallance Rd. E1 ....41Wb **91**
E2 ....41Wb **91**
N22 ....26Lb **50**
Vallentin Rd. E17 ....28Ec **52**
Valley, The 50Lc **93**
Valley Av. N12 ....21Fb **49**
Valley Cl. DA1: Cray 58Hd **118**
EN9: Walt A 4Ec **20**
HA5: Pinn 26X **45**
IG10: Lough 16Pc **36**
Valley Ct. CR3: Cat'm 94Wb **197**
RH2: Reig 5M **207**
Valley Dr. DA12: Grav'nd 3F **144**
NW9 ....30Qa **47**
TN13: S'oaks 98Kd **203**
VALLEY END 9E **146**
Valley End SL3: Wex 2N **81**
Valley End Rd. GU24: Chob 9E **146**
Valleyfield Rd. SW16 ....64Pb **134**
Valley Flds. Cres. EN2: Enf 12Qb **32**
Valley Gdns., The 8J **125**
Valley Gdns. DA9: Ghithe 58Xd **120**
HA0: Wemb 38Pa **67**
SW19 ....66Fb **133**
Valley Gro. SE7 ....50Lc **93**
Valley Hgts. DA1: Dart 56Pd **119**
Valley Hill IG10: Lough 17Nc **36**
Valley Ho. EN8: Chesh 4Zb **20**
Valley Leisure Pk. CR0: Wadd 74Nb **156**
Valleylink Est. EN3: Pond E 16Ac **34**
Valley Lodge IG10: Lough 16Pc **36**
Valley M. TW1: Twick 61Ha **130**
Valley Pk. BR8: Hext 66Kd **141**
WD18: Wat 17S **26**
Valley Point Ind. Est. CR0: Bedd 73Nb **156**
Valley Ri. WD25: Wat 5X **13**
Valley Rd. BR2: Brom 68Gc **137**
BR5: St P 67Xc **139**
CR8: Kenley 87Tb **177**
DA1: Cray 58Hd **118**
DA3: Fawk 74Xd **164**
DA8: Erith 49Ed **96**
DA17: Belv 49Dd **96**
SW16 ....64Pb **134**
UB10: Uxb 40N **63**
WD3: Rick 15J **25**
Valley Side E4 ....19Cc **34**
SE7 ....50Mc **93**
Valleyside HP1: Hem H 2H **3**
Valley Side Pde. E4 ....19Cc **34**
Valley Vw. DA9: Ghithe 58Xd **120**
EN5: Barn 16Ab **30**
EN7: G Oak 1Sb **19**
TN16: Big H 90Lc **179**
Valley Vw. Gdns. CR8: Kenley 87Ub **177**
Valley Vw. Ter. DA4: Farni 74Pd **163**
Valley Wlk. CR0: C'don 75Yb **158**
WD3: Crox G 15S **26**
Valley Way SL9: Ger X 1N **61**
Valliere Rd. NW10 ....41Wa **88**
Valliers Wood Rd. DA15: Sidc 60Uc **116**
Vallings Pl. KT6: Surb 73Ka **152**
Vallis Way KT9: Chess 77Ma **153**
W13 ....43Ja **86**
Val McKenzie Av. N7 ....34Qb **70**
Valmar Av. SS17: Stan H 2K **101**
Valmar Rd. SE5 ....53Sb **113**
Valmar Trad. Est. SE5 ....53Sb **113**
Valnay St. SW17 ....64Hb **133**
Valognes Av. E17 ....25Ac **52**
Valois Ho. SE1 ....3K **231**
Valonia Gdns. SW18 ....58Bb **111**
Vambery Rd. SE18 ....51Sc **116**
Vanbrough Ct. BR1: Brom 69Jc **137**
V&A Mus. of Childhood 41Yb **92**
Vanbrough Cres. UB5: N'olt 39Y **65**
Vanbrugh Castle *SE10* *51Gc* **115**
(off Maze Hill)
Vanbrugh Cl. E16 ....43Mc **93**
Vanbrugh Ct. SE11 ....6A **230**
Vanbrugh Dr. KT12: Walt T 73Y **151**
Vanbrugh Flds. SE3 ....51Hc **115**
Vanbrugh Hill SE3 ....50Hc **93**
SE10 ....50Hc **93**
Vanbrugh Ho. *E9* *38Yb* **72**
(off Loddiges Rd.)
Vanbrugh M. KT12: Walt T 73Y **151**
Vanbrugh Pk. SE3 ....52Hc **115**
Vanbrugh Pk. Rd. SE3 ....52Hc **115**
Vanbrugh Pk. Rd. W. SE3 ....52Hc **115**
Vanbrugh Rd. W4 ....48Ta **87**
Vanbrugh Ter. SE3 ....53Hc **115**
Vanburgh Cl. BR6: Orp 74Uc **160**
Vanburgh Ho. E1 ....7K **219**
Vancouver Cl. BR6: Chels 77Wc **161**
KT19: Eps 83Sa **173**
Vancouver Ho. *E1* *46Xb* **91**
(off Reardon Path)
SE16 ....*47Zb* **92**
(off Needleman St.)
Vancouver Mans. HA8: Edg 25Ra **47**
Vancouver Rd. HA8: Edg 25Ra **47**
SE23 ....61Ac **136**
TW10: Ham 63La **130**
UB4: Yead 42X **85**
Vanda Cres. AL1: St A 3D **6**
Vanderbilt Rd. SW18 ....60Db **111**
Vanderbilt Vs. *W12* *47Za* **88**
(off Sterne St.)
Vandervell Ct. *W3* *47Ua* **88**
(off Amber Way)
Vanderville Gdns. N2 ....26Fb **49**
Vandome Cl. E16 ....44Kc **93**
Vandon Ct. SW1 ....3C **228**
Vandon Pas. SW1 ....3C **228** (48Lb **90**)
Vandon St. SW1 ....3C **228** (48Lb **90**)
Van Dyck Av. KT3: N Mald 73Ta **153**
Vandyke Cl. RH1: Redh 3P **207**
SW15 ....59Za **110**
Vandyke Cross SE9 ....57Nc **116**
Vandy St. EC2 ....6H **219** (42Ub **91**)
Vane Cl. HA3: Kenton 30Pa **47**
NW3 ....36Fb **69**
Vanessa Cl. DA17: Belv 50Cd **96**
Vanessa Wlk. DA12: Grav'nd 4H **145**
Vanessa Way DA5: Bexl 62Fd **140**
Vane St. SW1 ....5C **228** (49Lb **90**)
Vange Ho. *W10* *43Ya* **88**
(off Sutton Way)
Van Gogh Cl. TW7: Isle 55Ja **108**
Van Gogh Ct. E14 ....48Fc **93**
Vanguard NW9 ....24Ua **48**
Vanguard Bldg. E14 ....47Bc **92**
Vanguard Cl. CR0: C'don 74Rb **157**
E16 ....43Jc **93**
RM7: Mawney 26Cd **56**
Vanguard Ct. SE5 ....53Ub **113**
Vanguard Ho. E8 ....38Xb **71**
Vanguard St. SE8 ....53Cc **114**
Vanguard Way SM6: Wall 80Nb **156**
TW6: H'row A 54U **106**
Vanilla & Sesame Ct. SE1 ....1K **231**
Vanneck Sq. SW15 ....57Wa **110**
Vanners Pde. KT14: Byfl 85N **169**
Vanoc Gdns. BR1: Brom 63Jc **137**
Vanquish Cl. TW2: Whitt 59Ca **107**
Vanquisher Wlk. DA12: Grav'nd 2H **145**
Vanryne Ho. IG10: Lough 13Nc **36**
Vansittart Est. SL4: Wind 2G **102**
Vansittart Rd. E7 ....35Hc **73**
SL4: Wind 3F **102**
Vansittart St. SE14 ....52Ac **114**
Vanstone Ct. *N7* *37Qb* **70**
(off Blackthorn Av.)
Vanston Pl. SW6 ....52Cb **111**
Vantage Bldg. *UB3: Hayes* *48V* **84**
(off Station App.)
Vantage Ct. GU21: Wok 9P **167**
UB3: Harl 52U **106**
Vantage M. *E14* *46Ec* **92**
(off Coldharbour)
HA6: Nwood 23T **44**
Vantage Pl. TW14: Felt 58W **106**
W8 ....48Cb **89**
Vantage Point *BR3: Beck* *67Fc* **137**
(off Albemarle Rd.)
CR2: Sande 81Tb **177**
DA9: Ghithe 59Wd **120**
EN5: Barn *14Bb* **31**
(off Victors Way)
Vantage Rd. SL1: Slou 6F **80**
Vantage W. TW8: Bford 49Pa **87**
Vantrey Ho. SE11 ....6K **229**
Vant Rd. SW17 ....64Hb **133**
Vapery La. GU24: Pirb 3B **186**
Varcoe Gdns. UB3: Hayes 44T **84**
Varcoe Rd. SE16 ....50Xb **91**
Vardens Rd. SW11 ....56Fb **111**
Varden St. E1 ....44Xb **91**
Vardon Cl. W3 ....44Ta **87**
Varley Dr. TW1: Isle 56Ka **108**
Varley Ho. NW6 ....39Cb **69**
SE1 ....4E **230**
Varley Pde. NW9 ....28Ua **48**
Varley Rd. E16 ....44Kc **93**
Varley Way CR4: Mitc 68Fb **133**
Varna Rd. SW6 ....52Ab **110**
TW12: Hamp 67Da **129**
Varndell St. NW1 ....3B **216** (41Lb **90**)
Varney Cl. HP1: Hem H 2H **3**
Varney Rd. HP1: Hem H 2H **3**
Varnishers Yd. N1 ....2G **217**
Varsity Dr. TW1: Twick 57Ga **108**
Varsity Row SW14 ....54Sa **109**
Vartry Rd. N15 ....30Tb **51**
Vascroft Est. NW10 ....42Ra **87**
Vassall Ho. *E3* *41Ac* **92**
(off Antill Rd.)
Vassall Rd. SW9 ....52Qb **112**
Vat Ho. *SW8* *52Nb* **112**
(off Rita Rd.)
Vauban Est. SE16 ....4K **231** (48Vb **91**)
Vauban St. SE16 ....4K **231** (48Vb **91**)
Vaudeville Theatre 5G **223**
Vaughan Almshouses *TW15: Ashf* *64R* **128**
(off Feltham Hill Rd.)
Vaughan Av. DA9: Ghithe 56Yd **120**
NW4 ....29Wa **48**
RM12: Horn 35Md **77**
W6 ....49Va **88**
Vaughan Cl. DA1: Dart 59Md **119**
TW12: Hamp 65Aa **129**
Vaughan Copse SL4: Eton 9H **81**
Vaughan Est. E2 ....3K **219**
Vaughan Gdns. IG1: Ilf 31Pc **74**
SL4: Eton W 9D **80**
Vaughan Ho. SE1 ....1B **230**
SW4 ....59Lb **112**
Vaughan Rd. DA16: Well 54Vc **117**
E15 ....37Hc **73**
HA1: Harr 30Ea **46**
KT7: T Ditt 73Ka **152**
SE5 ....54Sb **113**
Vaughan St. RM8: Dag 32Ad **75**
SE16 ....47Bc **92**
Vaughan Way E1 ....45Wb **91**
SL2: Slou 2C **80**
Vaughan Williams Cl. SE8 ....52Cc **114**
Vaughan Williams Way
CM14: Gt War, W'ley 23Wd **58**
Vaux Cres. KT12: Hers 79X **151**
VAUXHALL 7G **229** (51Nb **112**)
Vauxhall Bri. SW1 ....7E **228** (50Nb **90**)
Vauxhall Bri. Rd. SW1 ....4B **228** (48Lb **90**)
Vauxhall City Farm 7H **229**
Vauxhall Climbing Cen. *51Nb* **112**
(off Sth. Lambeth Rd.)
Vauxhall Cl. DA11: Nflt 9B **122**
VAUXHALL CROSS 50Nb **90**
Vauxhall Gdns. CR2: S Croy 79Sb **157**
Vauxhall Gro. SW8 ....51Pb **112**
Vauxhall Pl. DA1: Dart 59Nd **119**
Vauxhall Road 2A **4**
Vauxhall Rd. HP2: Hem H 2A **4**
Vauxhall St. SE11 ....7J **229** (50Pb **90**)
Vauxhall Wlk. SE11 ....7H **229** (50Pb **90**)
Vawdrey Cl. E1 ....42Yb **92**
Veals Mead CR4: Mitc 67Gb **133**
Vectis Gdns. SW17 ....65Kb **134**
Vectis Rd. SW17 ....65Kb **134**
Veda Rd. SE13 ....56Cc **114**
Vega Cres. HA6: Nwood 22V **44**
Vega Ho. *E20* *36Ec* **72**
(off Prize Wlk.)
Vegal Cres. TW20: Eng G 4M **125**
Vega Rd. WD23: Bush 17Ea **28**
Veitch Cl. TW14: Felt 59V **106**
Veldene Way HA2: Harr 34Ba **65**
Velde Way SE22 ....57Ub **113**
Vellacott Cl. RM19: Purf 51Td **120**
Velletri Ho. *E2* *40Zb* **72**
(off Mace St.)
Vellum Ct. E17 ....26Ac **52**
Vellum Dr. SM5: Cars 76Jb **156**
Velocity Way EN3: Enf L 9Bc **20**
Velodrome
Queen Elizabeth Olympic Pk.
....36Dc **72**
Velo Pl. E20 ....36Dc **72**
Velvet Ho. E2 ....1K **219**
Venables Cl. RM10: Dag 35Dd **76**
Venables St. NW8 ....6C **214** (42Fb **89**)
Vencourt Pl. W6 ....49Wa **88**
Veneer Bldg., The UB3: Hayes 47U **84**
Venerable Ho. *E3* *42Bc* **92**
(off Portia Way)
Venetian Ho. *E20* *37Dc* **72**
(off Victory Pde.)
Venetian Rd. SE5 ....54Sb **113**
Venetia Rd. N4 ....30Rb **51**
W5 ....47Ma **87**
Venette Cl. RM13: Rain 43Kd **97**
Venice Av. WD18: Wat 14U **26**
Venice Corte *SE13* *55Ec* **114**
(off Elmira St.)
Venice Ct. *SE5* *52Sb* **113**
(off Bowyer St.)
Venice Ho. HA0: Wemb 39Na **67**
Venice Wlk. W2 ....1A **220** (43Eb **89**)
Venner Cl. RH1: Redh 5A **208**
Venner Rd. SE26 ....65Yb **136**
(not continuous)
Venners Cl. DA7: Bex 54Gd **118**
Venn Ho. N1 ....1J **217**
Venn St. SW4 ....56Lb **112**

Ventnor Av.—Viking Gdns.

Ventnor Av. HA7: Stan 25Ka 46
Ventnor Dr. N20 .....20Db 31
Ventnor Gdns. IG11: Bark 37Uc 74
Ventnor Rd. SE14 .....52Zb 114
SM2: Sutt 80Db 155
Venton Cl. GU21: Wok 9M 167
Ventura Pk. AL2: Col S 1Ha 14
Venture Cl. DA5: Bexl 59Ad 117
Venture Ct. DA12: Grav'nd 8F 122
SE1 .....3J 231
SE12 .....59Jc 115
Venture Ho. W10 .....44Za 88
(off Bridge Cl.)
Venue, The (Leisure Cen.) 12Sa 29
Venue St. E14 .....43Ec 92
Venus Cl. SL2: Slou 2D 80
VENUS HILL 3C 10
Venus Hill HP3: Bov 3C 10
Venus Ho. E3 .....39Cc 72
(off Garrison Rd.)
E14 .....49Cc 92
(off Westferry Rd.)
Venus M. CR4: Mitc 69Gb 133
Venus Rd. SE18 .....48Pc 94
Veny Cres. RM12: Horn 36Md 77
Vera Av. N21 .....15Qb 32
Vera Ct. E3 .....41Dc 92
(off Grace Pl.)
WD19: Wat 17Z 27
Vera Lynn Cl. E7 .....35Jc 73
Vera Rd. SW6 .....53Ab 110
Verbena Cl. E16 .....42Hc 93
RM15: S Ock 44Yd 98
UB7: W Dray 50M 83
Verbena Gdns. W6 .....50Wa 88
Verdana Ct. WD18: Wat 15U 26
(off Whippendell Rd.)
Verdant Ct. SE6 .....59Gc 115
(off Verdant La.)
Verdant La. SE6 .....59Gc 115
Verdayne Av. CR0: C'don 75Zb 158
Verdayne Gdns. CR6: W'ham 88Yb 178
Verderers Rd. IG7: Chig 22Wc 55
Verdi Cres. W10 .....40Ab 68
Verdon Ct. SL2: Farn R 1F 80
Verdon Roe Ct. E4 .....20Dc 34
Verdun Rd. SE18 .....51Wc 117
SW13 .....51Wa 110
Verdure Cl. WD25: Wat 4Aa 13
Vere Ct. W2 .....44Db 89
(off Westbourne Gdns.)
Vereker Dr. TW16: Sun 69W 128
Vereker Rd. W14 .....50Ab 88
Vere Rd. IG10: Lough 14Sc 36
Vere St. W1 .....3K 221 (44Kb 90)
Veridion Way DA18: Erith 47Bd 95
Verini Cl. WD23: Bush 15Z 27
Veritas Ho. DA14: Sidc 61Wc 139
(off Jubilee Way)
Verity Cl. W11 .....45Ab 88
Verity Ho. E3 .....41Bc 92
(off Merchant St.)
Veritys AL10: Hat 1C 8
Vermeer Ct. E14 .....48Fc 93
Vermeer Gdns. SE15 .....56Yb 114
Vermilion Apartments E3 .....39Ac 72
(off Gunmaker's La.)
Vermont Cl. EN2: Enf 14Rb 33
Vermont Ho. E17 .....26Bc 52
Vermont Rd. SE19 .....65Tb 135
SL2: Slou 2D 80
SM1: Sutt 76Db 155
SW18 .....58Db 111
Verna Ho. E20 .....36Ec 72
(off Sunrise Cl.)
Verne Ct. W3 .....48Sa 87
(off Vincent Rd.)
Verney Gdns. RM9: Dag 35Ad 75
Verney Ho. NW8 .....5D 214
Verney Rd. RM9: Dag 35Ad 75
(not continuous)
SE16 .....51Wb 113
SL3: L'ly 49C 82
Verney St. NW10 .....34Ta 67
Verney Way SE16 .....50Xb 91
Vernham Rd. SE18 .....51Sc 116
Vernon Av. E12 .....35Pc 74
EN3: Enf W 8Ac 20
IG8: Wfd G 24Kc 53
SW20 .....68Za 132
Vernon Cl. AL1: St A 3B 6
BR5: St P 69Xc 139
KT16: Ott 79F 148
KT19: Ewe 79Sa 153
TN15: W King 81Vd 184
TW19: Stanw 60N 105
Vernon Ct. HA7: Stan 25Ka 46
NW2 .....34Bb 69
W5 .....45La 86
Vernon Cres. CM13: B'wood 20Ce 41
EN4: E Barn 16Jb 32
Vernon Dr. CR3: Cat'm 94Sb 197
HA7: Stan 25Ja 46
UB9: Hare 25L 43
Vernon Ho. SE11 .....7J 229
WC1 .....1G 223
Vernon Mans. W14 .....51Bb 111
(off Queen's Club Gdns.)
Vernon M. E17 .....29Bc 52
W14 .....49Ab 88
Vernon Pl. WC1 .....1G 223 (43Nb 90)
Vernon Ri. UB6: G'frd 36Fa 66
WC1 .....3J 217 (41Pb 90)
Vernon Rd. DA10: Swans 58Be 121
E3 .....40Bc 72
E11 .....32Gc 73
E15 .....38Gc 73
E17 .....29Bc 52
IG3: Ilf 32Vc 75
N8 .....27Qb 50
RM5: Col R 22Ed 56
SM1: Sutt 78Eb 155
SW14 .....55Ta 109
TW13: Felt 61V 128
WD23: Bush 15Aa 27
Vernon Sq. WC1 .....3J 217 (41Pb 90)
Vernon St. W14 .....49Ab 88
Vernon Wlk. KT20: Tad 92Za 194
Vernon Yd. W11 .....45Bb 89
Vern Pl. TN16: Tats 93Lc 199
Veroan Rd. DA7: Bex 54Ad 117
Verona Cl. UB8: Cowl 44L 83
Verona Ct. SE14 .....51Zb 114
(off Myers La.)
TW15: Ashf 63R 128
W4 .....50Ua 88
Verona Dr. KT6: Surb 75Na 153
Verona Gdns. DA12: Grav'nd 3G 144
Verona Ho. CR4: Mitc 69Kb 134
(off Aventine Av.)
Verona Rd. E7 .....38Jc 73
Veronica Cl. RM3: Rom 24Ld 57
Veronica Gdns. SW16 .....67Lb 134
Veronica Ho. E3 .....41Dc 92
(off Talwin St.)
SE4 .....55Bc 114
Veronica Rd. SW17 .....61Kb 134
Veronique Gdns. IG6: Ilf 29Sc 54
Verralls GU22: Wok 89D 168
(not continuous)
Verran Rd. SW12 .....59Kb 112
Ver Rd. AL3: St A 2A 6
Versailles Rd. SE20 .....66Wb 135
Vert Ho. RM17: Grays 52Ee 121
Verulam Av. CR8: Purl 84Lb 176
E17 .....30Bc 52
Verulam Bldgs. WC1 .....7J 217
Verulam Ct. NW9 .....31Wa 68
UB1: S'hall 44Ea 86
(off Haldane Rd.)
Verulam Golf Course 4D 6
Verulam Ho. W6 .....47Ya 88
(off Hammersmith Gro.)
Verulam Ind. Est. AL1: St A 4D 6
Verulamium Mus. 2P 5
Verulamium Pk. 3P 5
Verulamium Roman Town 2N 5
Verulam Pas. WD17: Wat 12X 27
Verulam Rd. AL3: St A 1A 6
UB6: G'frd 42Ca 85
Verulam St. WC1 .....7K 217 (43Qb 90)
Vervian Ho. SE15 .....52Wb 113
(off Reddins Rd.)
Verwood Dr. EN4: Cockf 13Hb 31
Verwood Ho. SW8 .....52Pb 112
(off Cobbett St.)
Verwood Lodge E14 .....48Fc 93
(off Manchester Rd.)
Verwood Rd. HA2: Harr 26Ea 46
Veryan GU21: Wok 9L 167
Veryan Cl. BR5: St P 70Yc 139
Veryan Ct. N8 .....29Mb 50
Vesage Ct. EC1 .....1A 224
Vesey Path E14 .....44Dc 92
Vespan Rd. W12 .....47Wa 88
Vesta Av. AL1: St A 5A 6
Vesta Ct. SE1 .....2H 231
Vesta Ho. E3 .....39Cc 72
(off Garrison Rd.)
E20 .....36Ec 72
(off Liberty Bri. Rd.)
Vesta Rd. SE4 .....54Ac 114
Vestris Rd. SE23 .....61Zb 136
Vestry Cotts. DA3: Lfield 70Ee 143
TN14: S'oaks 91Ld 203
Vestry Ct. RM7: Rush G 30Gd 56
SW1 .....4E 228
Vestry House Mus. 28Dc 52
Vestry Ind. Est. TN14: S'oaks 91Ld 203
Vestry M. SE5 .....53Ub 113
SW18 .....57Fb 111
Vestry Rd. E17 .....28Dc 52
SE5 .....53Ub 113
TN14: S'oaks 91Kd 203
Vestry St. N1 .....3F 219 (41Tb 91)
Vesuvius Apartments E3 .....40Bc 72
(off Centurion La.)
Vevers Rd. RH2: Reig 9L 207
Vevey St. SE6 .....61Bc 136
Vexil Cl. RM19: Purf 49Td 98
Veysey Cl. HP1: Hem H 4K 3
Veysey Gdns. RM10: Dag 34Cd 76
Viaduct, The E18 .....26Jc 53
HA0: Wemb 39Na 67
N10 .....28Kb 50
Viaduct Bldgs. EC1 .....1A 224 (43Qb 90)
Viaduct Pl. E2 .....41Xb 91
Viaduct Rd. N2 .....26Fb 49
Viaduct St. E2 .....41Xb 91
Viaduct Ter. DA4: S Dar 68Sd 142
Vian Av. EN3: Enf W 7Ac 20
Vian St. SE13 .....55Dc 114
Viant Ho. NW10 .....38Ta 67
(off Fawood Av.)
Via Romana DA12: Grav'nd 10K 123
Vibart Gdns. SW2 .....59Pb 112
Vibart Wlk. N1 .....39Nb 70
(off Outram Pl.)
Vibeca Apartments E1 .....43Vb 91
(off Chicksand St.)
Vibia Cl. TW19: Stanw 59M 105
Viburnum Ct. GU24: W End 5C 166
Viburnum Ga. WD7: R'lett 9Ha 14
Vicarage Av. SE3 .....52Jc 115
TW20: Egh 64D 126
Vicarage Cl. AL1: St A 5A 6
CM14: B'wood 21Ud 58
DA8: Erith 51Ed 118
EN6: N'thaw 2Hb 17
EN6: Pot B 4Ab 16
HA4: Ruis 31T 64
HP1: Hem H 4L 3
KT4: Wor Pk 74Ua 154
KT20: Kgswd 96Ab 194
KT23: Bookh 97Ca 191
UB5: N'olt 38Ba 65
Vicarage Ct. BR3: Beck 69Ac 136
DA12: Grav'nd 10J 123
EN9: Walt A 6Jc 21
(off Horseshoe Cl.)
IG1: Ilf 36Rc 74
TW14: Bedf 59S 106
TW20: Egh 65D 126
W8 .....47Db 89
Vicarage Cres. SW11 .....53Fb 111
TW20: Egh 64D 126
Vicarage Dr. BR3: Beck 67Cc 136
DA11: Nflt 58Ee 121
IG11: Bark 38Sc 74
SW14 .....57Ta 109
Vicarage Farm Ct. TW5: Hest 52Ba 107
Vicarage Farm Rd.
TW3: Houn 54Aa 107
TW5: Hest 53Aa 107
Vicarage Flds. KT12: Walt T 72Y 151
Vicarage Fld. Shop. Cen.
IG11: Bark 38Sc 74
Vicarage Gdns. CR4: Mitc 69Gb 133
SW14 .....57Sa 109
W8 .....46Cb 89
Vicarage Ga. W8 .....46Db 89
Vicarage Ga. M. KT20: Kgswd 96Ab 194
Vicarage Gro. SE5 .....53Tb 113
Vicarage Hill TN16: Westrm 98Tc 200
Vicarage Ho. KT1: King T 68Pa 131
(off Cambridge Rd.)
Vicarage La. DA12: Grav'nd 1J 145
E6 .....41Pc 94
E15 .....38Gc 73
GU23: Send 98E 188
HP3: Bov 8D 2
IG1: Ilf 32Tc 74
IG7: Chig 19Sc 36
KT17: Ewe 81Wa 174
(not continuous)
KT20: Kgswd 95Ab 194
KT22: Lea 94Ka 192
TN13: Dun G 91Fd 202
TW18: Lale 69L 127
TW19: Wray 60A 104
WD4: K Lan 1P 11
Vicarage M. KT16: Longc 6M 147
NW9 .....33Ta 67
Vicarage Pde. N15 .....28Sb 51
Vicarage Pk. SE18 .....50Sc 94
Vicarage Path N8 .....31Nb 70
Vicarage Rd. CM16: Coop 1Yc 23
CR0: Wadd 76Qb 156
DA5: Bexl 60Dd 118
E10 .....31Cc 72
E15 .....38Hc 73
GU22: Wok 93B 188
GU24: Chob 3H 167
IG8: Wfd G 24Nc 54
KT1: Hamp W 67La 130
KT1: King T 68Ma 131
N17 .....25Wb 51
NW4 .....30Wa 48
RM10: Dag 38Dd 76
RM12: Horn 32Jd 76
SE18 .....50Sc 94
(not continuous)
SM1: Sutt 76Db 155
SW14 .....57Sa 109
TW2: Twick 61Ga 130
TW2: Whitt 58Ea 108
TW11: Tedd 64Ja 130
TW16: Sun 64V 128
TW18: Staines 62G 126
TW20: Egh 64C 126
WD18: Wat 17W 26
Vicarage Rd. Pct. WD18: Wat 14X 27
(off Vicarage Rd.)
Vicarage Road Stadium 15X 27
Vicarage Sq. RM17: Grays 51Ce 121
Vicarage Wlk.
KT12: Walt T 73W 150
SW11 .....53Fb 111
Vicarage Way HA2: Harr 31Ca 65
NW10 .....34Ta 67
SL3: Coln 52E 104
SL9: Ger X 30B 42
Vicars Bri. Cl. HA0: Wemb 40Na 67
Vicar's Cl. E9 .....39Yb 72
Vicars Cl. E15 .....39Jc 73
EN1: Enf 12Ub 33
Vicar's Hill SE13 .....56Dc 114
Vicars Moor La. N21 .....17Qb 32
Vicars Oak Rd. SE19 .....65Ub 135
Vicar's Rd. NW5 .....36Jb 70
Vicars Wlk. RM8: Dag 34Xc 75
Vicary Ho. EC1 .....1D 224
Vicentia Ct. SW11 .....55Eb 111
Viceroy Cl. N2 .....28Gb 49
(off East End Rd.)
Viceroy Ct. CR0: C'don 74Tb 157
HA6: Nwood 23U 44
NW8 .....1E 214
Viceroy Pde. N2 .....28Gb 49
(off High Rd.)
Viceroy Rd. SW8 .....53Nb 112
Vicinity Ho. E14 .....45Cc 92
(off Storehouse M.)
Vic Johnson Ho. E3 .....39Bc 72
(off Armagh Rd.)
Vickers Cl. KT16: Vir W 5L 147
SM6: Wall 80Pb 156
Vickers Ct. N17 .....27Xb 51
SE20 .....66Zb 136
TW19: Stanw 58N 105
(off Whitley Cl.)
Vickers Dr. Nth. KT13: Weyb 82N 169
Vickers Dr. Sth.
KT13: Weyb 83N 169
Vickers La. DA1: Dart 55Qd 119
Vickers Rd. DA8: Erith 50Fd 96
Vickers Way TW4: Houn 57Aa 107
Vickery Ct. EC1 .....5E 218
Vickery's Wharf E14 .....44Cc 92
Victor App. RM12: Horn 32Md 77
Victor Beamish Av. CR3: Cat'm 92Ub 197
Victor Cazalet Ho. N1 .....39Rb 71
(off Gaskin St.)
Victor Cl. RM12: Horn 32Md 77
Victor Ct. RM12: Horn 32Md 77
(off Victor App.)
Victor Gdns. RM12: Horn 32Md 77
Victor Gro. HA0: Wemb 38Na 67
Victor Ho. SE7 .....51Lc 115
Victoria Almshouses RH1: Redh 3A 208
RH2: Reig 6L 207
Victoria & Albert Mus. 4C 226 (48Fb 89)
Victoria Arc. SW1 .....4A 228
Victoria Av. CR2: Sande 82Sb 177
DA12: Grav'nd 9D 122
E6 .....39Mc 73
EC2 .....1J 225 (43Ub 91)
EN4: E Barn 14Fb 31
HA9: Wemb 37Ra 67
KT6: Surb 72Ma 153
KT8: W Mole 69Da 129
N3 .....25Bb 49
RM5: Col R 23Dd 56
RM16: Grays 47Ee 99
SM6: Wall 76Jb 156
TW3: Houn 57Ca 107
UB10: Hil 37R 64
Victoria Bldgs. E8 .....39Xb 71
(off Mare St.)
Victoria Chambers EC2 .....5H 219
Victoria Cl. EN4: E Barn 14Fb 31
EN8: Chesh 2Zb 20
HA1: Harr 30Ha 46
KT8: W Mole 69Ca 129
KT13: Weyb 76T 150
RM16: Grays 47Ee 99
SE22 .....57Wb 113
UB3: Hayes 44T 84
WD3: Rick 17M 25
Victoria Colonnade WC1 .....1G 223
Victoria Cotts. E1 .....43Wb 91
(off Deal St.)
N10 .....26Jb 50
TW9: Kew 53Pa 109
Victoria Ct. CM14: W'ley 21Yd 58
E18 .....27Kc 53
HA7: Stan 24Ma 47
(off Howard Rd.)
HA9: Wemb 37Qa 67
RH1: Redh 9A 208
RM1: Rom 29Jd 56
SE1 .....6J 231
SE26 .....65Yb 136
SL1: Slou 6J 81
(off Blair Rd.)
SS17: Stan H 1L 101
W3 .....47Qa 87
WD17: Wat 13Y 27
Victoria Cres. N15 .....29Ub 51
SE19 .....65Ub 135
SL0: Iver 45H 83
SW19 .....66Bb 133
Victoria Dock Rd. E16 .....45Hc 93
Victoria Dr. DA4: S Dar 68Td 142
SL1: Burn, Farn C 7C 60
SL2: Farn C 7C 60
SW19 .....59Za 110
Victoria Emb. EC4 .....2G 229 (47Nb 90)
SW1 .....2G 229 (47Nb 90)
WC2 .....2G 229 (47Nb 90)
Victoria Gdns.
TN16: Big H 87Lc 179
TW5: Hest 53Aa 107
W11 .....46Cb 89
Victoria Gro. N12 .....22Fb 49
W8 .....3A 226 (48Eb 89)
Victoria Gro. M. W2 .....45Cb 89
Victoria Hall E16 .....46Jc 93
(off Wesley Av.)
Victoria Hill Rd. BR8: Hext 67Hd 140
Victoria Ho. E6 .....44Qc 94
HA8: Edg 23Ra 47
KT22: Lea 93La 192
RM2: Rom 28Ld 57
SE16 .....47Yb 92
(off Surrey Quays Rd.)
SL9: Chal P 21A 42
(off Micholls Av.)
SW1 .....7K 227
(Ebury Bri. Rd.)
SW1 .....5C 228
(Francis St.)
SW8 .....52Nb 112
(off Sth. Lambeth Rd.)
Victoria Ind. Est. W3 .....43Ua 88
Victoria La. EN5: Barn 14Bb 31
UB3: Harl 50T 84
Victoria Mans. NW10 .....38Xa 68
SW8 .....52Nb 112
(off Sth. Lambeth Rd.)
W14 .....51Bb 111
(off Queen's Club Gdns.)
Victoria M. E8 .....37Wb 71
KT13: Weyb 77Q 150
(off Balfour Rd.)
NW6 .....39Cb 69
SW4 .....56Kb 112
SW18 .....60Eb 111
TW20: Eng G 5N 125
Victoria Mills Studios E15 .....39Fc 73
(off Burford Rd.)
Victorian Gro. N16 .....35Ub 71
Victorian Hgts. SW8 .....54Kb 112
(off Thackeray Rd.)
Victorian Rd. N16 .....34Ub 71
Victoria Palace Theatre 4B 228
Victoria Pde. SE10 .....51Dc 114
TW9: Kew 53Qa 109
(off Sandycombe Rd.)
Victoria Pk.
Hackney 39Zb 72
Victoria Pk. Ct. E9 .....38Yb 72
(off Well St.)
Victoria Pk. Ind. Cen. E9 .....38Cc 72
(off Rothbury Rd.)
Victoria Pk. Ind. Est. DA1: Dart 57Nd 119
Victoria Pk. Rd. E9 .....39Yb 72
Victoria Pk. Sq. E2 .....41Yb 92
Victoria Pk. Studios E9 .....37Yb 72
(off Milborne St.)
Victoria Pas. NW8 .....5B 214
WD18: Wat 14X 27
Victoria Pl. GU21: Wok 88C 168
(off North Rd.)
HP2: Hem H 2M 3
KT10: Esh 77Da 151
(off Esher Pk. Av.)
KT11: Cobh 86X 171
KT17: Eps 84Ua 174
TW9: Rich 57Ma 109
Victoria Pl. Shop. Cen. SW1 .....5A 228
Victoria Point E13 .....40Jc 73
(off Victoria Rd.)
Victoria Retail Pk. HA4: Ruis 36Z 65
Victoria Ri. NW6 .....38Eb 69
(off Hilgrove Rd.)
SW4 .....55Kb 112
Victoria Road 36Dd 76
Victoria Rd. BR2: Brom 71Mc 159
BR7: Chst 64Qc 138
CM14: W'ley 21Yd 58
CR4: Mitc 66Gb 133
CR5: Coul 87Mb 176
DA1: Dart 57Md 119
DA6: Bex 56Cd 118
DA8: Erith 51Gd 118
DA11: Nflt 10B 122
DA15: Sidc 62Vc 139
E4 .....18Gc 35
E11 .....35Gc 73
E13 .....40Jc 73
E17 .....26Ec 52
E18 .....26Kc 53
EN4: E Barn 14Fb 31
EN9: Walt A 6Ec 20
GU21: Knap 9H 167
GU22: Wok 89A 168
HA4: Ruis 32W 64
IG9: Buck H 19Mc 35
IG11: Bark 37Rc 74
KT1: King T 68Pa 131
KT6: Surb 72Ma 153
KT13: Weyb 76T 150
KT15: Add 77M 149
N4 .....31Pb 70
N9 .....21Vb 51
N15 .....28Wb 51
N18 .....21Vb 51
N22 .....25Lb 50
NW4 .....28Ya 48
NW6 .....40Bb 69
NW7 .....22Va 48
Victoria Rd. NW10 .....43Ta 87
RH1: Redh 7A 208
RM1: Rom 30Hd 56
RM10: Dag 36Dd 76
SL2: Farn C 7G 60
SL2: Slou 6M 81
SL4: Eton W 9C 80
SL5: Asc 4A 146
SM1: Sutt 78Fb 155
SS17: Horn H 1H 101
SS17: Stan H 2L 101
SW14 .....55Ta 109
TN13: S'oaks 97Kd 203
TW1: Twick 59Ka 108
TW11: Tedd 65Ja 130
TW13: Felt 60X 107
TW18: Staines 62G 126
UB2: S'hall 48Ba 85
UB8: Uxb 38L 63
W3 .....43Ta 87
W5 .....43Ka 86
W8 .....48Eb 89
WD23: Bush 18Da 27
WD24: Wat 10X 13
Victoria Scott Ct.
DA1: Cray 55Hd 118
Victoria Sq. AL1: St A 3D 6
SW1 .....3A 228 (48Kb 90)
Victoria St. AL1: St A 2B 6
DA17: Belv 50Bd 95
E15 .....38Gc 73
SL1: Slou 7K 81
SL4: Wind 3H 103
SW1 .....4A 228 (48Lb 90)
TW20: Eng G 5N 125
Victoria's Way RM15: S Ock 44Yd 98
Victoria Ter. HA1: Harr 32Ga 66
N4 .....32Qb 70
NW10 .....42Va 88
W5 .....46Ma 87
Victoria Vs. TW9: Rich 55Pa 109
Victoria Way GU21: Wok 89A 168
HA4: Ruis 36Z 65
KT13: Weyb 76T 150
SE7 .....50Kc 93
Victoria Wharf E2 .....40Zb 72
(off Palmers Rd.)
E14 .....45Ac 92
SE8 .....50Bc 92
(off Dragoon Rd.)
Victoria Works NW2 .....33Xa 68
Victoria Yd. E1 .....44Wb 91
Victor Rd. HA2: Harr 27Ea 46
NW10 .....41Xa 88
SE20 .....66Zb 136
SL4: Wind 5G 102
TW11: Tedd 63Ga 130
Victor's Cres. CM13: Hut 19De 41
Victors Dr. TW12: Hamp 65Aa 129
Victor Smith Ct. AL2: Brick W 3Ca 13
Victors Way EN5: Barn 13Bb 31
Victor Ter. NW10 .....42Ua 88
Victor Vs. N9 .....20Tb 33
Victor Wlk. NW9 .....26Ua 48
RM12: Horn 32Md 77
Victor Way AL2: Col S 3Ha 14
Victor Wharf SE1 .....6F 225
(off Clink St.)
Victory Av. SM4: Mord 71Eb 155
Victory Bus. Cen. TW7: Isle 56Ha 108
Victory Cl. RM16: Chaf H 49Yd 98
TW19: Stanw 60N 105
Victory Cotts. KT24: Eff 100Aa 191
Victory Ct. DA8: Erith 52Hd 118
(off Frobisher Rd.)
IG11: Bark 42Xc 95
W9 .....42Cb 89
(off Hermes Cl.)
Victory Ho. KT18: Eps 85Sa 173
(off West St.)
Victory M. UB2: S'hall 48Aa 85
Victory Pde. E20 .....37Dc 72
SE18 .....48Rc 94
Victory Pk. HA9: Wemb 34Ma 67
Victory Pk. M. KT15: Add 77L 149
(off Victory Pk. Rd.)
Victory Pk. Rd. KT15: Add 76L 149
Victory Pl. E14 .....45Ac 92
SE17 .....5E 230 (49Tb 91)
SE19 .....66Ub 135
Victory Rd. E11 .....28Jc 53
KT16: Chert 74J 149
RM13: Rain 40Jd 76
SW19 .....66Eb 133
Victory Rd. M. SW19 .....66Eb 133
(off Victory Rd.)
Victory Wlk. SE8 .....53Cc 114
Victory Way DA2: Dart 56Sd 120
RM7: Mawney 26Dd 56
SE16 .....47Ac 92
TW5: Cran 50Y 85
Vida Ho. SE8 .....50Zb 92
Video Ct. N4 .....31Pb 70
Vidler Cl. KT9: Chess 79La 152
Vienna Cl. IG5: Ilf 26Mc 53
View, The SE2 .....50Ad 95
View Cl. HA1: Harr 28Fa 46
IG7: Chig 22Tc 54
N6 .....31Hb 69
TN16: Big H 88Lc 179
View Cres. N8 .....29Mb 50
Viewfield Cl. HA3: Kenton 31Na 67
Viewfield Rd. DA5: Bexl 60Yc 117
SW18 .....58Bb 111
Viewland Rd. SE18 .....50Vc 95
Viewlands Av. TN16: Westrm 92Uc 200
View Rd. EN6: Pot B 4Eb 17
N6 .....31Hb 69
View Tube, The 39Dc 72
(off Greenway)
Viga Rd. N21 .....16Qb 32
Vigerons Way
RM16: Grays 9D 100
Vigers Ct. NW10 .....41Xa 88
(off Harrow Rd.)
Viggory La. GU21: Wok 7N 167
Vigilant Cl. SE26 .....63Wb 135
Vigilant Way DA12: Grav'nd 4H 145
Vignoles Rd. RM7: Rush G 31Cd 76
Vigo Hill ME19: Tros 85Fe 185
Vigo Rd. TN15: Fair 83De 185
Vigors Cft. AL10: Hat 1B 8
Vigo St. W1 .....5B 222 (45Lb 90)
Viking Bus. Cen.
RM7: Rush G 31Ed 76
Viking Cl. E3 .....40Ac 72
Viking Ct. SW6 .....51Cb 111
Viking Gdns. E6 .....42Nc 94

Viking Ho. SE5 54Sb 113
(off Denmark Rd.)
SE18 49Nc 94
(off Pett St.)
Viking Pl. E10 32Bc 72
Viking Rd. DA11: Nflt 62Ee 143
UB1: S'hall 45Aa 85
Viking Way CM15: Pil H 16Xd 40
DA8: Erith 48Ed 96
RM13: Rain 42Jd 96
TN15: W King 78Ud 164
Villa Cl. DA12: Grav'nd 1K 145
Villa Ct. DA1: Dart 61Nd 141
Villacourt Rd. SE18 52Wc 117
VILLAGE, THE 2E 124
Village, The DA9: Bluew 59Vd 120
NW3 33Eb 69
SE7 51Lc 115
W12 46Za 88
Village Arc. AL3: St A 2B 6
(off High St.)
E4 18Fc 35
Village Cen. HP3: Hem H 3C 4
Village Cl. E4 22Ec 52
KT13: Weyb 76T 150
NW3 36Fb 69
(off Belsize La.)
Village Ct. E17 29Dc 52
(off Eden Rd.)
KT13: Weyb 77T 150
(off Oatlands Dr.)
SE3 55Gc 115
(off Hurren Cl.)
Village Cres., The
DA9: Bluew 59Vd 120
Village Gdns. KT17: Ewe 82Va 174
Village Ga. TW17: Shep 71R 150
Village Grn. Av. TN16: Big H 89Nc 180
Village Grn. Rd. DA1: Cray 56Jd 118
Village Grn. Way
TN16: Big H 89Nc 180
Village Health Club, The 94Sb 197
Village Hgts. IG8: Wfd G 22Hc 53
Village La. SL2: Hedg 2H 61
Village M. HP3: Bov 9C 2
NW9 33Ta 67
SL5: S'hill 10A 124
SW18 60Bb 111
(off Elsenham St.)
Village Mt. NW3 35Eb 69
(off Perrins Ct.)
Village Pk. Cl. EN1: Enf 16Ub 33
Village Rd. EN1: Enf 15Ub 33
N3 26Ab 48
SL4: Dor 8A 80
TW20: Thorpe 69E 126
UB9: Den 33H 63
Village Row SM2: Sutt 80Cb 155
Village Shop. Cen. SL1: Slou 7K 81
Village Square, The
CR5: Coul 94Mb 196
Village Way BR3: Beck 68Cc 136
CR2: Sande 85Wb 177
HA5: Pinn 31Aa 65
HP7: L Chal 12A 24
IG6: Ilf 27Sc 54
NW10 35Ta 67
SE21 58Tb 113
TW15: Ashf 63P 127
Village Way E. HA2: Harr 31Ca 65
Villa Rd. SW9 55Qb 112
Villas on the Heath
NW3 34Eb 69
Villas Rd. SE18 50Sc 94
Villa St. SE17 7G 231 (50Tb 91)
Villa Wlk SE17 50Tb 91
(off Villa St.)
Villiers, The
KT13: Weyb 79T 150
Villiers Av. KT5: Surb 71Pa 153
TW2: Whitt 60Ba 107
Villiers Cl. E10 33Cc 72
KT5: Surb 70Pa 131
Villiers Ct. SL4: Wind 2E 102
SW11 53Gb 111
(off Battersea Bri. Rd.)
Villiers Gdns. E20 36Dc 72
Villiers Gro.
SM2: Cheam 81Za 174
Villiers Ho. SL4: Eton 10G 80
(off Common La.)
Villiers M. NW2 37Wa 68
Villiers Path KT6: Surb 71Na 153
Villiers Rd. BR3: Beck 68Zb 136
KT1: King T 70Pa 131
NW2 37Wa 68
SL2: Slou 3H 81
TW7: Isle 54Ga 108
UB1: S'hall 46Ba 85
WD19: Wat 16Aa 27
Villiers St.
WC2 5F 223 (46Nb 90)
Villier St. UB8: Uxb 41M 83
Vimy Cl. TW4: Houn 57Ba 107
Vimy Dr. DA1: Dart 55Pd 119
Vimy Ridge Ct. E3 40Bc 72
(off Festubert Pl.)
Vimy Way DA1: Cray 57Jd 118
Vincam Cl. TW2: Whitt 59Ca 107
Vince Ct. N1 4G 219 (41Tb 91)
Vincennes Est. SE27 63Tb 135
Vincent Av. KT5: Surb 75Sa 153
SM5: Cars 83Fb 175
Vincent Cl.
BR2: Brom 70Kc 137
CR5: Chip 92Hb 195
DA15: Sidc 60Uc 116
EN5: New Bar 13Db 31
EN8: Chesh 1Ac 20
IG6: Ilf 23Sc 54
KT10: Esh 76Da 151
KT16: Chert 73G 148
KT22: Fet 95Da 191
SE16 47Ac 92
UB7: Sip 51Q 106
Vincent Ct. HA6: Nwood 25V 44
N4 32Nb 70
NW4 28Za 48
SW9 53Pb 112
W1 2F 221
Vincent Dr. TW17: Shep 69U 128
UB10: Uxb 39P 63
Vincent Gdns. NW2 34Va 68
Vincent Ho. SW1 5E 228
(Regency St.)
SW1 6D 228
(Vincent Sq.)
Vincent M. E3 40Cc 72
Vincent Rd. CR0: C'don 73Ub 157
CR5: Coul 88Lb 176
E4 23Fc 53
HA0: Wemb 38Pa 67
KT1: King T 69Qa 131
KT11: Stoke D 88Aa 171
KT16: Chert 73G 148
N15 28Sb 51
N22 26Qb 50
RM9: Dag 38Ad 75
RM13: Rain 42Ld 97
SE18 49Rc 94
TW4: Houn 54Z 107
TW7: Isle 53Fa 108
W3 48Sa 87
Vincent Row TW12: Hamp H 65Ea 130
Vincents Path UB5: N'olt 37Aa 65
(off Arnold Rd.)
Vincent Sq. N22 26Qb 50
SW1 5C 228 (49Mb 90)
TN16: Big H 85Lc 179
Vincent Sq. Mans. SW1 5C 228
(off Walcott St.)
Vincent St. E16 43Hc 93
SW1 5D 228 (49Mb 90)
Vincent Ter. N1 1B 218 (40Rb 71)
Vincenzo Cl. AL9: Wel G 5E 8
Vince St. EC1 4G 219 (41Tb 91)
Vine, The TN13: S'oaks 96Kd 203
Vine Av. TN13: S'oaks 96Kd 203
Vine Cl. E5 35Wb 71
GU3: Worp 8H 187
KT5: Surb 72Pa 153
SM1: Sutt 76Eb 155
TW19: Stanw M 57J 105
UB7: W Dray 49Q 84
Vine Cotts. E1 44Yb 92
(off Sidney Sq.)
W7 46Ga 86
Vine Ct. E1 43Wb 91
HA3: Kenton 30Na 47
KT12: Hers 79Y 151
Vine Ct. Rd. TN13: S'oaks 96Ld 203
Vinegar All. E17 28Dc 52
Vine Gdns. IG1: Ilf 36Sc 74
Vinegar St. E1 46Xb 91
Vinegar Yd. SE1 1H 231 (47Ub 91)
Vine Gro. UB10: Hil 38Q 64
Vine Hill EC1 6K 217 (42Qb 90)
Vine La. SE1 7J 225 (46Ub 91)
UB10: Hil 39P 63
Vine Lodge TN13: S'oaks 96Ld 203
Vine Lodge Ct. TN13: S'oaks 96Ld 203
Vine Pl. TW3: Houn 56Da 107
W5 46Na 87
(off St Mark's Rd.)
Viner Cl. KT12: Walt T 72Y 151
Vineries, The EN1: Enf 13Ub 33
N14 16Lb 32
SE6 60Cc 114
Vineries Bank NW7 22Xa 48
Vineries Cl. RM9: Dag 37Bd 75
UB7: Sip 51Q 106
Vine Rd. BR6: Chels 79Vc 161
E15 38Hc 73
KT8: E Mos 70Ea 130
SL2: Stoke P 7K 61
SW13 55Va 110
Vinery, The SW8 52Nb 112
(off Regent's Bri. Gdns.)
Vinery Row W6 48Xa 88
Vines Av. N3 25Db 49
Vine Sq. W14 50Bb 89
(off Star Rd.)
Vine St. E17 28Dc 52
EC3 3K 225 (44Vb 91)
RM7: Rom 28Ed 56
UB8: Uxb 39M 63
W1 5C 222 (45Lb 90)
Vine St. Bri. EC1 6A 218 (42Qb 90)
Vine Tree Ct. WD3: Rick 19K 25
Vine Way CM14: B'wood 18Yd 40
Vine Yd. SE1 1E 230
Vineyard, The TW10: Rich 57Na 109
Vineyard Av. NW7 24Ab 48
Vineyard Cl. KT1: King T 69Pa 131
SE6 60Cc 114
Vineyard Gro. N3 25Db 49
Vineyard Hill EN6: N'thaw 1Jb 18
Vineyard Hill Rd. SW19 63Bb 133
Vineyard M. TW10: Rich 57Na 109
Vineyard Pas. TW10: Rich 57Na 109
Vineyard Path SW14 55Ta 109
Vineyard Rd. TW13: Felt 62W 128
Vineyard Row KT1: Hamp W 67La 130
Vineyards, The TW13: Felt 62W 128
(off High St.)
TW16: Sun 69W 128
Vineyards Rd. EN6: N'thaw 2Hb 17
Vineyard Wlk. EC1 5K 217 (42Qb 90)
Viney Bank CR0: Sels 81Bc 178
Viney Rd. SE13 55Dc 114
Vining St. SW9 56Qb 112
Vinlake Av. UB10: Ick 34P 63
Vinson Cl. BR6: Orp 74Wc 161
Vinson Ho. N1 2G 219
Vintage M. E4 21Cc 52
Vinter Ct. TW17: Shep 71Q 150
Vintner's Ct. EC4 4E 224 (45Sb 91)
Vintner's Pl. EC4 4E 224 (45Sb 91)
Vintry Ct. SE1 2G 231
Vintry M. E17 28Cc 52
Viola Av. SE2 49Xc 95
TW14: Felt 58Y 107
TW19: Stanw 60M 105
Viola Cl. RM15: S Ock 41Yd 98
Viola Sq. W12 45Va 88
Violet Av. EN2: Enf 10Tb 19
UB8: Hil 43P 83
Violet Cl. E16 42Gc 93
SE8 51Bc 114
SM3: Sutt 74Ab 154
SM6: Wall 74Jb 156
Violet Ct. E15 38Gc 73
(off Victoria St.)
NW9 25Ua 48
Violet Gdns. CR0: Wadd 78Rb 157
Violet Hill NW8 2A 214 (40Eb 69)
Violet Hill Ho. NW8 2A 214
Violet La. CR0: Wadd 79Rb 157
Violet Rd. E3 42Dc 92
E17 30Cc 52
E18 26Kc 53
Violet St. E2 42Xb 91
Violet Ter. UB8: Hil 43Q 84
Violet Way WD3: Loud 14L 25
VIP Trading Est. SE7 49Lc 93
Virgil Pl. W1 1F 221 (43Hb 89)
Virgil St. SE1 3J 229 (48Pb 90)
Virgin Active
Bank 3G 225 (44Tb 91)
Barbican 7D 218
Borehamwood 13Qa 29
(within The Point)
Broadgate 7H 219
Bromley 70Mc 137
Chislehurst 64Uc 138
Chiswick 53Ua 110
Chiswick Pk. 49Ra 87
City 1D 224
Cricklewood 34Ab 68
Crouch End 29Nb 50
(off Tottenham La.)
Croydon 76Sb 157
(off Surrey St.)
Ealing 45Ma 87
(within Ealing Broadway Cen.)
Enfield 14Tb 33
Epsom 85Ta 173
(within Ebbisham Cen.)
Friern Barnet 22Jb 50
Fulham 51Ab 110
(within Fulham Pools)
Hammersmith 49Za 88
(off Hammersmith Rd.)
Hemel Hempstead 1C 4
Hendon 29Ya 48
Ilford 34Rc 74
(off Clements Rd.)
Islington -
Essex Road 39Rb 71
Goswell Road 2B 218
Kensington 47Db 89
(off Old Court Pl.)
Kingston upon Thames -
Richmond Rd. 67Na 131
The Bentall Cen. 68Ma 131
(within The Bentall Cen.)
Mayfair 4H 221 (44Jb 90)
Merton 67Fb 133
(off Watermill Way)
Mill Hill East 24Ab 48
Moorgate 6F 219 (42Tb 91)
Northwood 23R 44
Notting Hill 44Ab 88
Putney 56Ab 110
Repton Park 24Qc 54
Romford 29Gd 56
Staines Upon Thames 63G 126
Stockley Park 45S 84
Strand 5G 223 (45Nb 90)
Streatham 62Nb 134
Sunbury 67W 128
Swiss Cottage 37Eb 69
(within O2 Centre)
The Surrey Health & Racquets Club
79Pb 156
The Twickenham Club 58Ga 108
Tower Bridge 4K 225
Walbrook 45Tb 91
Wandsworth -
Smugglers Way 56Db 111
Southside Shop. Cen. 57Db 111
West London 46Ua 88
Wimbledon -
North Rd. 65Eb 133
Worple Rd. 65Bb 133
Virginia Av. GU25: Vir W 1N 147
Virginia Beeches GU25: Vir W 9M 125
Virginia Cl. BR2: Brom 69Gc 137
KT3: N Mald 70Sa 131
KT13: Weyb 79S 150
KT21: Asht 90Ma 173
RM5: Col R 24Ed 56
TW18: Lale 69L 127
Virginia Ct. DA1: Dart 55Qd 119
GU25: Vir W 10P 125
SE16 47Zb 92
(off Eleanor Cl.)
WC1 5E 216
Virginia Dr. GU25: Vir W 1N 147
Virginia Gdns. IG6: Ilf 26Sc 54
Virginia Ho. E14 45Ec 92
(off Newby Pl.)
TW11: Tedd 64Ka 130
Virginia Pk. GU25: Vir W 70A 126
Virginia Pl. KT11: Cobh 86W 170
Virginia Rd. CR7: Thor H 67Rb 135
DA1: Cray 57Jd 118
E2 4K 219 (41Vb 91)
Virginia St. E1 45Wb 91
Virginia Wlk. DA12: Grav'nd 5F 144
SW2 58Pb 112
VIRGINIA WATER 1P 147
Virginia Water 9J 125
Viridian Apartments SW8 52Lb 112
Viridian Rd. BR6: Orp 73Xc 161
Visage NW3 38Fb 69
(off Winchester Rd.)
Viscount Cl. N11 23Kb 50
Viscount Ct. SL4: Wind 3G 102
W2 44Cb 89
(off Pembridge Vs.)
Viscount Dr. E6 43Pc 94
Viscount Gdns. KT14: Byfl 84N 169
Viscount Gro. UB5: N'olt 41Z 85
Viscount Ind. Est. SL3: Poyle 55G 104
Viscount M. BR7: Chst 65Rc 138
Viscount Rd. TW19: Stanw 60N 105
Viscount St. EC1 6D 218 (42Sb 91)
Viscount Way TW6: H'row A 56U 106
Vision 20 IG1: Ilf 33Sc 74
Vision Ind. Pk. W3 43Ra 87
Vista, The DA14: Sidc 64Vc 139
SE9 58Mc 115
Vista Av. EN3: Enf H 12Zb 34
Vista Bldg. E3 41Bc 92
(off Bow Rd.)
SE18 49Qc 94
Vista Ct. E1 42Vb 91
(off Ocean Est.)
Vista Dr. IG4: Ilf 29Mc 53
Vista Ho. N4 33Qb 70
SW19 67Fb 133
(off Chapter Way)
Vista Way HA3: Kenton 30Na 47
Vita Apartments CR0: C'don 75Tb 157
Vitae Apartments W6 48Wa 88
Vita Ho. AL1: St A 3D 6
Vitali Cl. SW15 59Wa 110
Vittoria Ho. N1 1J 217
Viveash Cl. UB3: Hayes 48V 84
Vivenne Ho. TW18: Staines 64J 127
Vivian Av. HA9: Wemb 36Qa 67
NW4 29Xa 48
Vivian Cl. WD19: Wat 18W 26
Vivian Comma Cl. N4 34Rb 71
Vivian Ct. N12 22Db 49
W9 40Db 69
Vivian Gdns. HA9: Wemb 36Qa 67
WD19: Wat 18W 26
Vivian Mans. NW4 29Xa 48
(off Vivian Av.)
Vivian Rd. E3 40Ac 72
Vivian Sq. SE15 55Xb 113
Vivian Way N2 29Fb 49
Vivien Cl. KT9: Chess 80Na 153
Vivienne Cl. TW1: Twick 58Ma 109
Vixen M. E8 38Vb 71
(off Haggerston Rd.)
Voce Rd. SE18 52Tc 116
Voewood Cl. KT3: N Mald 72Va 154
Vogan Cl. RH2: Reig 9K 207
Vogans Mill SE1 1K 231 (47Vb 91)
Vogler Ho. E1 45Yb 92
(off Cable St.)
Vogue Ct. BR1: Brom 67Kc 137
Vollasky Ho. E1 43Wb 91
(off Daplyn St.)
Volta Cl. N9 20Yb 34
Voltaire Rd. SW4 55Mb 112
Voltaire Way UB3: Hayes 45U 84
Volt Av. NW10 41Ta 87
Volta Way CR0: Wadd 74Pb 156
Voluntary Pl. E11 30Jc 53
Vorley Rd. N19 33Lb 70
Voss Ct. SW16 65Nb 134
Voss St. E2 41Wb 91
Voyager Bus. Est. SE16 48Wb 91
(off Spa Rd.)
Voyager Ct. E16 43Jc 93
(off Hammersley Rd.)
Voyagers Cl. SE28 44Yc 95
Voysey Cl. N3 27Ab 48
Vue Cinema
Acton 42Qa 87
Apollo 5D 222
Bromley 69Jc 137
Croydon -
High St. 76Sb 157
Purley Way 74Pb 156
Dagenham 39Ad 75
Fallow Corner 24Fb 49
Finchley Rd. 37Eb 69
(within O2 Centre)
Fulham Broadway 52Cb 111
Harrow 30Ga 46
(within St George's Shop. & Leisure Cen.)
Hayes 47U 84
Islington 1A 218 (40Qb 70)
Leicester Square 4E 222
Romford 30Gd 56
Shepherds Bush 47Za 88
Staines Upon Thames 63G 126
Watford 5Y 13
Westfield 46Ya 88
West Thurrock 48Wd 98
Wood Green 26Qb 50
Vulcan Bus. Cen. CR0: New Ad 81Gc 179
Vulcan Cl. E6 44Qc 94
Vulcan Ga. EN2: Enf 12Qb 32
Vulcan Rd. SE4 54Bc 114
Vulcan Sq. E14 49Dc 92
Vulcan Ter. SE4 54Bc 114
Vulcan Way CR0: New Ad 82Gc 179
N7 37Pb 70
SM6: Wall 81Nb 176
Vulcan Wharf E15 40Dc 72
(off Cook's Rd.)
Vyne, The DA7: Bex 55Dd 118
Vyner Rd. W3 45Ta 87
Vyner St. E2 39Xb 71
Vyners Way UB10: Ick 36Q 64
Vyse Cl. EN5: Barn 14Ya 30

W

Wacky Warehouse 19Y 27
Wadard Ter. BR8: Swan 71Ld 163
Wadbrook St. KT1: King T 68Ma 131
Wadding St. SE17 6F 231 (49Tb 91)
Waddington Av. CR5: Coul 92Qb 196
Waddington Cl. CR5: Coul 91Rb 197
EN1: Enf 14Ub 33
Waddington Rd. AL3: St A 2B 6
E15 36Fc 73
Waddington St. E15 37Fc 73
Waddington Way SE19 66Sb 135
WADDON 76Qb 156
Waddon Cl. CR0: Wadd 76Qb 156
Waddon Ct. Rd. CR0: Wadd 76Qb 156
Waddon Leisure Cen. 78Qb 156
Waddon Marsh Way CR0: Wadd 74Pb 156
Waddon New Rd. CR0: C'don 76Rb 157
Waddon Pk. Av. CR0: Wadd 77Qb 156
Waddon Rd. CR0: C'don, Wadd 76Qb 156
Waddon Way CR0: Wadd 79Qb 156
Wade Av. BR5: Orp 73Zc 161
Wade Ct. N10 24Kb 50
Wade Dr. SL1: Slou 6E 80
Wade Ho. EN1: Enf 15Tb 33
SE1 47Wb 91
(off Parkers Row)
Wades, The AL10: Hat 3C 8
Wades Gro. N21 17Qb 32
Wades Hill N21 16Qb 32
Wades La. TW11: Tedd 64Ja 130
Wades M. N21 17Qb 32
Wadeson St. E2 40Xb 71
Wade's Pl. E14 45Dc 92
Wadeville Av. RM6: Chad H 30Ad 55
Wadeville Cl. DA17: Belv 50Cd 96
Wadham Av. E17 24Dc 52
Wadham Cl. TW17: Shep 73S 150
Wadham Gdns. NW3 39Gb 69
UB6: G'frd 37Fa 66
Wadham Ho. N18 22Vb 51
Wadham M. SW14 54Sa 109
Wadham Rd. E17 24Dc 52
SW15 56Ab 110
WD5: Ab L 3V 12
Wadhurst Cl. SE20 68Xb 135
Wadhurst Rd. SW8 53Lb 112
W4 48Ta 87
Wadley Cl. HP2: Hem H 3P 3
Wadley Rd. E11 31Gc 73
Wadsworth Bus. Cen. UB6: G'frd 40La 66
Wadsworth Cl. EN3: Pond E 15Zb 34
UB6: G'frd 40La 66
Wadsworth Rd. UB6: G'frd 40Ka 66
Wager St. E3 42Bc 92
WAGGONERS RDBT. 53X 107
Waggon La. N17 23Wb 51
Waggon M. N14 18Lb 32
Waghorn Rd. E13 39Lc 73
HA3: Kenton 27Ma 47
Waghorn St. SE15 55Wb 113
Wagner M. KT6: Surb 71Na 153
(off Avenue Elmers)
Wagner St. SE15 52Yb 114
Wagon Rd. EN4: Barn, Had W 7Cb 17
EN5: Barn 7Cb 17
Wagon Way WD3: Loud 13L 25
Wagstaff Gdns. RM9: Dag 38Yc 75
Wagtail Cl. EN1: Enf 11Xb 33
NW9 26Ua 48
Wagtail Ct. SW15 58Ya 110
Wagtail Gdns. CR2: Sels 82Ac 178
Wagtail Rd. TW6: H'row A 54K 105
Wagtail Wlk. BR3: Beck 71Ec 158
Wagtail Way BR5: St P 70Zc 139
Waid Cl. DA1: Dart 58Pd 119
Waight's Ct. KT2: King T 67Na 131
Wain Cl. EN6: Pot B 1Db 17
Wainfleet Av. RM5: Col R 26Ed 56
Wainford Cl. SW19 60Za 110
Wainscot SL5: S'dale 2D 146
Wainwright Av. CM13: Hut 16Fe 41
DA9: Ghithe 56Yd 120
Wainwright Gro. TW7: Isle 56Fa 108
Wainwright Ho. E1 46Yb 92
(off Garnet St.)
Waite Davies Rd. SE12 59Hc 115
Waite Ho. W3 46Va 88
Waite St. SE15 51Vb 113
Waithman St. EC4 3B 224
Wakefield Cl. KT14: Byfl 84N 169
Wakefield Ct. SE26 65Yb 136
Wakefield Cres.
SL2: Stoke P 7K 61
Wakefield Gdns. IG1: Ilf 30Nc 54
SE19 66Ub 135
Wakefield Ho. SE15 53Wb 113
Wakefield M. WC1 4G 217 (41Nb 90)
Wakefield Rd. DA9: Ghithe 57Yd 120
N11 22Mb 50
N15 29Vb 51
TW10: Rich 57Ma 109
Wakefield St. DA11: Grav'nd 8D 122
E6 39Mc 73
N18 22Wb 51
WC1 4G 217 (41Nb 90)
Wakefields Wlk. EN8: Chesh 3Ac 20
Wakeford Cl. DA5: Bexl 60Zc 117
SW4 57Lb 112
Wakehams Hill HA5: Pinn 27Ba 45
Wakeham St. N1 37Tb 71
Wakehurst Path GU21: Wok 86E 168
Wakehurst Rd. SW11 57Gb 111
Wakeling Ct. CR8: Purl 82Nb 176
Wakeling La. HA0: Wemb 34Ka 66
Wakeling Rd. W7 43Ha 86
Wakeling St. E14 44Ac 92
Wakelin Ho. N1 38Rb 71
(off Sebbon St.)
Wakelin Rd. E15 40Gc 73
Wakely Cl. TN16: Big H 90Lc 179
Wakely Ct. AL1: St A 2C 6
(off Hatfield Rd.)
Wakeman Ho. NW10 41Za 88
(off Wakeman Rd.)
Wakeman Rd. NW10 41Ya 88
Wakemans Hill Av. NW9 29Ta 47
Wakerfield Cl. RM11: Horn 29Pd 57
Wakering Rd. IG11: Bark 37Sc 74
(not continuous)
Wakerley Cl. E6 44Pc 94
Wake Rd. IG10: H Beech 10Lc 21
Wakley St. EC1 3B 218 (41Rb 91)
Walberswick St. SW8 52Nb 112
Walbrook EC4 4F 225 (45Tb 91)
(not continuous)
Walbrook Bldg., The EC4 4F 225
Walbrook Ct. N1 1H 219
Walbrook Ho. N9 19Yb 34
(off Huntingdon Rd.)
Walbrook Wharf EC4 5E 224
Walburgh St. E1 44Xb 91
Walburton Rd. CR8: Purl 85Lb 176
Walcorde Av. SE17 6E 230 (49Sb 91)
Walcot Gdns. SE11 5K 229
Walcot Rd. EN3: Brim 12Bc 34
Walcot Sq. SE11 5A 230 (49Qb 90)
Walcott St. SW1 5C 228 (49Lb 90)
Waldair Ct. E16 47Rc 94
Waldeck Gro. SE27 62Rb 135
Waldeck Rd. DA1: Dart 59Pd 119
N15 28Rb 51
SW14 55Sa 109
W4 51Qa 109
W13 44Ka 86
Waldeck Ter. SW14 55Sa 109
(off Waldeck Rd.)
Waldegrave Ct. IG11: Bark 39Tc 74
RM14: Upm 32Rd 77
Waldegrave Gdns. RM14: Upm 32Rd 77
TW1: Twick 61Ha 130
Waldegrave Pk. TW1: Twick 63Ha 130
Waldegrave Rd. BR1: Brom 70Nc 138
N8 27Qb 50
RM8: Dag 33Yc 75
SE19 66Vb 135
TW1: Twick 63Ha 130
TW11: Tedd 63Ha 130
W5 45Pa 87
Waldegrove CR0: C'don 76Vb 157
Waldemar Av. SW6 53Ab 110
W13 46La 86
Waldemar Rd. SW19 64Cb 133
Walden Av. BR7: Chst 63Pc 138
N13 21Sb 51
RM13: Rain 40Fd 76
Walden Cl. DA17: Belv 50Bd 95
Walden Ct. SW8 53Mb 112
Walden Gdns. CR7: Thor H 69Pb 134
Walden Ho. SW1 6J 227
SW11 53Jb 112
(off Dagnall St.)
Waldenhurst Rd. BR5: St M Cry 73Zc 161
Walden Pde. BR7: Chst 65Pc 138
(not continuous)
Walden Rd. BR7: Chst 65Pc 138
N17 25Tb 51
RM11: Horn 30Md 57
Waldens Cl. BR5: St M Cry 73Zc 161
Waldenshaw Rd. SE23 60Yb 114
Waldens Pk. Rd. GU21: Wok 8N 167
Waldens Rd. BR5: St M Cry 73Ad 161
GU21: Wok 9P 167
Walden St. E1 44Xb 91
(not continuous)

Walden Way—Warley St.

Walden Way IG6: Ilf .24Uc 54
NW7 .23Za 48
RM11: Horn .30Md 57
Waldo Cl. SW4 .57Lb 112
Waldo Ho. NW10 .41Xa 88
(off Waldo Rd.)
Waldo Ind. Est. BR1: Brom .69Mc 137
Waldon RM18: E Til .8K 101
Waldo Pl. CR4: Mitc .66Gb 133
Waldorf Cl. CR2: S Croy .81Rb 177
Waldo Rd. BR1: Brom .69Mc 137
NW10 .41Wa 88
Waldram Cres. SE23 .60Yb 114
Waldram Pk. Rd. SE23 .60Zb 114
Waldram Pl. SE23 .60Yb 114
Waldrist Way DA18: Erith .48Bd 95
Waldron Gdns. BR2: Brom .70Fc 137
Waldronhyrst CR2: S Croy .77Rb 157
Waldron M. SW3 .51Fb 111
Waldron Rd. HA1: Harr .32Ga 66
HA2: Harr .32Ga 66
SW18 .62Eb 133
Waldrons, The CR0: C'don .77Rb 157
RH8: Oxt .3K 211
Waldron's Path CR2: S Croy .77Sb 157
Waldrons Yd. HA2: Harr .33Fa 66
Waldstock Rd. SE28 .45Wc 95
Waleran Cl. HA7: Stan .22Ha 46
Walerand Rd. SE13 .54Ec 114
Waleran Flats SE1 .5H 231 (49Ub 91)
Wales Av. SM5: Cars .78Gb 155
Wales Cl. SE15 .51Xb 113
Wales Farm Rd. W3 .43Ta 87
Waleton Acres SM6: Wall .79Lb 156
Waley St. E1 .43Ac 92
Walfield Av. N20 .17Db 31
Walford Ho. E1 .44Xb 91
Walford Rd. N16 .35Ub 71
UB8: Uxb .40L 63
Walfrey Gdns. RM9: Dag .38Bd 75
WALHAM GREEN .53Cb 111
Walham Grn. Ct. SW6 .52Db 111
(off Waterford Rd.)
Walham Gro. SW6 .52Cb 111
Walham Ri. SW19 .65Ab 132
Walham Yd. SW6 .52Cb 111
Walk, The EN6: Pot B .4Cb 17
N13 .20Qb 32
(off Fox La.)
RH8: Tand .5E 210
RM11: Horn .33Pd 77
SL4: Eton W .10E 80
TW16: Sun .66V 128
Walkato Lodge IG9: Buck H .18Lc 35
Walkden Rd. BR7: Chst .64Qc 138
Walker Cl. CR0: New Ad .80Ec 158
DA1: Cray .55Hd 118
DA10: Swans .59Be 121
N11 .21Lb 50
SE18 .49Sc 94
TW12: Hamp .65Ba 129
TW14: Felt .59V 106
W7 .46Ga 86
Walker Cres. SL3: L'ly .50B 82
Walker Ho. NW1 .2D 216 (40Mb 70)
SE16 .48Bc 92
(off Redriff Est.)
Walker M. SW2 .57Qb 112
Walker Pl. TN15: Igh .93Zd 205
Walker's Ct. W1 .4D 222
Walkerscroft Mead SE21 .60Sb 113
Walkers Lodge E14 .47Ec 92
(off Manchester Rd.)
Walkers Pl. SW15 .56Ab 110
Walkers Sq. SS17: Stan H .2M 101
Walkfield Dr. KT18: Tatt C .89Xa 174
Walkie-Talkie, The .4H 225
Walkinshaw Ct. N1 .38Sb 71
(off Rotherfield St.)
Walkley Rd. DA1: Dart .57Kd 119
Walks, The N2 .27Fb 49
Walkynscroft SE15 .54Xb 113
(off Caulfield Rd.)
Wallace Bldg. NW8 .6C 214
Wallace Cl. SE28 .45Zc 95
TW17: Shep .70T 128
UB10: Uxb .40N 63
Wallace Collection .2H 221 (44Jb 90)
Wallace Ct. NW1 .1E 220
SE3 .56Kc 115
Wallace Cres. SM5: Cars .78Hb 155
Wallace Flds. KT17: Eps .84Va 174
Wallace Gdns. DA10: Swans .58Ae 121
Wallace Ho. N7 .37Pb 70
(off Caledonian Rd.)
Wallace Rd. N1 .37Sb 71
RM17: Grays .48Ce 99
Wallace Sq. CR5: Coul .94Mb 196
Wallace Wlk. KT15: Add .77L 149
SL4: Eton .10K 81
Wallace Way N19 .33Mb 70
(off St John's Way)
RM1: Rom .25Fd 56
Wallasey Cres. UB10: Ick .33Q 64
Wallbrook Bus. Cen. TW4: Houn .55X 107
Wallbutton Rd. SE4 .54Ac 114
Wallcote Av. NW2 .32Za 68
Wall Ct. N4 .32Pb 70
(off Stroud Grn. Rd.)
Walled Gdn., The KT20: Tad .94Za 194
RH3: Bet .7A 206
Walled Gdn. Cl. BR3: Beck .70Dc 136
Walled Gdn. Cl. HA7: Stan .20Ga 28
Wallenberg Pl. W1 .3G 221
WALLEND .39Qc 74
Wall End Ct. E6 .39Qc 74
(off Wall End Rd.)
Wall End Rd. E6 .38Qc 74
Wallenger Av. RM2: Rom .27Kd 57
Waller Dr. HA6: Nwood .26W 44
Waller La. CR3: Cat'm .95Vb 197
Waller Rd. SE14 .53Zb 114
Wallers Cl. IG8: Wfd G .23Pc 54
RM9: Dag .39Ad 75
Waller's Hoppet IG10: Lough .12Pc 36
Waller Way SE10 .52Dc 114
Wallfield Pk. RH2: Reig .6H 207
Wallflower St. W12 .45Va 88
Wallgrave Rd. SW5 .49Db 89
Wall Hall WD25: A'ham .9Da 13
Wall Hall Dr. WD25: A'ham .8Da 13
Wallhouse Rd. DA8: Erith .52Kd 119
Wallingford Av. W10 .43Za 88
Wallingford Ho. RM3: Rom .23Nd 57
(off Kingsbridge Rd.)
Wallingford Rd. UB8: Uxb .40K 63
Wallingford Wlk. AL1: St A .3B 6
WALLINGTON .79Kb 156
Wallington Cl. HA4: Ruis .30S 44
Wallington Cnr. SM6: Wall .77Kb 156
(off Manor Rd. Nth.)
Wallington Ct. SM6: Wall .79Kb 156
(off Stanley Pk. Rd.)
WALLINGTON GREEN .77Kb 156
Wallington Rd. IG3: Ilf .31Vc 75
Wallington Sq. SM6: Wall .79Kb 156
Wallis All. SE1 .1E 230
Wallis Cl. DA2: Wilm .62Hd 140
RM11: Horn .32Kd 77
SW11 .55Fb 111
Wallis Ct. SL1: Slou .7L 81
Wallis Ho. HA4: Ruis .32T 64
SE14 .53Ac 114
TW8: Bford .50Na 87
Wallis M. KT22: Lea .94Ja 192
N8 .27Qb 50
(off Courcy Rd.)
Wallis Pk. DA11: Nflt .57De 121
Wallis Rd. E9 .37Bc 72
TW6: H'row A .54K 105
UB1: S'hall .44Db 85
Wallis's Cotts. SW2 .59Nb 112
Wallman Pl. N22 .25Pb 50
Wallorton Gdns. SW14 .56Ta 109
Wallpaper Apartments, The
N1 .38Qb 70
(off Offord Rd.)
Wallside EC2 .1E 224
Wall St. N1 .37Tb 71
Wallwood Rd. E11 .31Fc 73
Wallwood St. E14 .43Bc 92
Walmar Cl. EN4: Had W .11Fb 31
Walmer Cl. BR6: Farnb .77Tc 160
E4 .19Dc 34
RM7: Mawney .26Dd 56
Walmer Ct. KT5: Surb .71Na 153
(off Cranes Pk.)
Walmer Gdns. W13 .47Ja 86
Walmer Ho. W10 .44Za 88
(off Bramley Rd.)
Walmer Pl. W1 .7F 215
Walmer Rd. W10 .44Ya 88
W11 .45Ab 88
Walmers Av.
ME3: High'm .3P 145
Walmer St. W1 .7F 215 (43Hb 89)
Walmer Ter. SE18 .49Sc 94
Walmgate Rd. UB6: G'frd .39Ka 66
Walmington Fold N12 .23Cb 49
Walm La. NW2 .37Ya 68
Walney Wlk. N1 .37Sb 71
Walnut Av. UB7: W Dray .48Q 84
Walnut Cl. AL2: Park .9P 5
DA4: Eyns .76Md 163
IG6: Ilf .28Sc 54
KT18: Eps .87Va 174
SE8 .51Bc 114
SM5: Cars .78Hb 155
UB3: Hayes .45U 84
Walnut Ct. E17 .28Ec 52
W5 .47Na 87
W8 .48Db 89
(off St Mary's Ga.)
Walnut Dr. KT20: Kgswd .96Ab 194
Walnut Flds. KT17: Ewe .81Va 174
Walnut Gdns. E15 .36Gc 73
Walnut Grn. WD23: Bush .12Ba 27
Walnut Gro. EN1: Enf .15Tb 33
HP2: Hem H .2M 3
RM12: Horn .32Md 77
SM7: Bans .86Za 174
Walnut Hill Rd. DA13: Meop, Ist R .9A 144
Walnut Ho. E3 .39Bc 72
(off Barge La.)
RH2: Reig .8L 207
Walnut Lodge SL1: Slou .8H 81
Walnut M. N22 .27Qb 50
(off High Rd.)
SM2: Sutt .80Eb 155
Walnut Rd. E10 .33Cc 72
Walnuts, The BR6: Orp .74Wc 161
Walnuts Leisure Cen. .74Wc 161
Walnuts Rd. BR6: Orp .74Xc 161
Walnut Tree Av. CR4: Mitc .69Gb 133
(off De'Arn Gdns.)
DA1: Dart .61Nd 141
Walnut Tree Cl. BR7: Chst .67Tc 138
EN8: Chesh .3Zb 20
KT23: Fet .97Fa 192
SM7: Bans .84Ab 174
SW13 .53Va 110
TN16: Westrm .98Tc 200
TW17: Shep .69S 128
UB10: Ick .35N 63
Walnut Tree Cotts. SW19 .64Ab 132
Walnut Tree Ho. SW10 .51Db 111
(off Tregunter Rd.)
Walnut Tree La. KT14: Byfl .84M 169
Walnut Tree Pl. GU23: Send .95F 188
Walnut Tree Rd. DA8: Erith .50Gd 96
RM8: Dag .33Ad 75
SE10 .50Gc 93
(not continuous)
TW5: Hest .51Ba 107
TW8: Bford .51Na 109
TW17: Shep .68S 128
Walnut Tree Wlk. SE11 .5K 229 (49Qb 90)
Walnut Way BR8: Swan .68Fd 140
HA4: Ruis .37Y 65
IG9: Buck H .20Mc 35
Walpole Av. CR5: Chip .91Hb 195
TW9: Kew .54Pa 109
Walpole Cl. HA5: Hat E .23Ca 45
RM17: Grays .49Ee 99
W13 .47La 86
Walpole Ct. NW6 .38Eb 69
(off Fairfax Rd.)
TW2: Twick .61Ga 130
W14 .48Za 88
(off Blythe Rd.)
Walpole Cres. TW11: Tedd .64Ha 130
Walpole Gdns. TW2: Twick .61Ga 130
W4 .50Sa 87
Walpole Ho. KT8: W Mole .71Ca 151
(off Approach Rd.)
SE1 .2K 229
SL4: Eton .1G 102
(off Eton Wick Rd.)
SW15 .57Ab 110
(off Plaza Gdns.)
Walpole Lodge W13 .46La 86
Walpole M. NW8 .1B 214 (39Fb 69)
SW19 .65Fb 133
Walpole Pk. KT13: Weyb .80Q 150
Walpole Pl. SE18 .49Rc 94
TW11: Tedd .64Ha 130
Walpole Rd. BR2: Brom .71Mc 159
CR0: C'don .75Tb 157
E6 .38Lc 73
E17 .28Ac 52
E18 .25Hc 53
KT6: Surb .73Na 153
N17 .26Sb 51
(not continuous)
SL1: Slou .4B 80
SL4: Old Win .9M 103
SW19 .65Fb 133
TW2: Twick .61Ga 130
TW11: Tedd .64Ha 130
Walpole St. SW3 .7F 227 (50Hb 89)
Walrond Av. HA9: Wemb .36Na 67
Walsham Cl. N16 .32Wb 71
SE28 .45Zc 95
Walsham Ent. Cen. RM17: Grays .50Ee 99
Walsham Ho. SE14 .54Zb 114
SE17 .7F 231
Walsham M. GU23: Rip .93L 189
Walsham Rd. SE14 .54Zb 114
TW14: Felt .59X 107
Walsh Cres. CR0: New Ad .84Gc 179
Walshford Way WD6: Bore .10Qa 15
Walsingham NW8 .39Fb 69
Walsingham Gdns. KT19: Ewe .77Ua 154
Walsingham Ho. E4 .17Fc 35
Walsingham Lodge SW13 .53Wa 110
Walsingham Mans. SW6 .52Db 111
(off Fulham Rd.)
Walsingham Pk. BR7: Chst .68Tc 138
Walsingham Pl. SW4 .58Jb 112
Walsingham Rd. BR5: St P .67Xc 139
CR0: New Ad .82Ec 178
CR4: Mitc .71Hb 155
E5 .34Wb 71
EN2: Enf .14Tb 33
W13 .46Ja 86
Walsingham Wlk. DA17: Belv .51Cd 118
Walsingham Way AL2: Lon C .9G 6
Walston Ho. SW1 .7D 228
Walter Besant Ho. E1 .41Zb 92
(off Bancroft Rd.)
Walter Ct. W3 .44Sa 87
(off Lynton Ter.)
Walter Grn. Ho. SE15 .53Yb 114
(off Lausanne Rd.)
Walter Ho. SW10 .52Fb 111
(off Riley St.)
Walter Hurford Pde. E12 .35Qc 74
(off Grantham Rd.)
Walter Langley Ct. SE16 .47Yb 92
(off Brunel Rd.)
Walter Rodney Cl. E6 .37Pc 74
Walter Savil Twr. E17 .30Cc 52
(off Colchester Rd.)
Walters Cl. SE17 .6E 230
UB3: Hayes .47V 84
Walters Ct. WD17: Wat .10W 12
Walters Ho. N1 .39Rb 71
(off Essex Rd.)
SE17 .51Rb 113
(off Otto St.)
Walter Sickert Hall N1 .2D 218
Walters Mead KT21: Asht .89Na 173
Walters Rd. EN3: Pond E .14Yb 34
SE25 .70Ub 135
Walter St. E2 .41Zb 92
KT2: King T .67Na 131
Walters Way SE23 .58Zb 114
Walters Yd. BR1: Brom .68Jc 137
Walter Ter. E1 .44Zb 92
Walterton Rd. W9 .42Bb 89
Walter Wlk. HA8: Edg .23Sa 47
WALTHAM ABBEY .5Ec 20
Waltham Abbey Church & Gatehouse
.5Ec 20
Waltham Abbey Sports Cen. .5Gc 21
Waltham Abbey Swimming Pool .7Fc 21
Waltham Av. NW9 .30Qa 47
UB3: Harl .48S 84
Waltham Cl. BR5: Orp .74Zc 161
CM13: Hut .16Ee 41
DA1: Dart .58Jd 118
RM3: Rom .23Pd 57
WALTHAM CROSS .5Ac 20
Waltham Dr. HA8: Edg .26Qa 47
Waltham Forest Pool & Track .26Dc 52
Waltham Gdns. EN3: Enf W .8Yb 20
Waltham Ho. NW8 .39Eb 69
Waltham Pk. Way E17 .25Cc 52
Waltham Rd. CR3: Cat'm .94Xb 197
IG8: Wfd G .23Nc 54
SM5: Cars .73Fb 155
UB2: S'hall .48Aa 85
WALTHAMSTOW .27Cc 52
Walthamstow Av. E4 .23Bc 52
Walthamstow Bus. Cen. E17 .26Ec 52
Walthamstow Leisure Cen. .30Bc 52
Walthamstow Marsh Nature Reserve
.31Xb 71
Waltham Way E4 .21Bc 52
Waltheof Av. N17 .25Tb 51
Waltheof Gdns. N17 .25Tb 51
Walton Av. HA2: Harr .36Ba 65
HA9: Wemb .34Ra 67
KT3: N Mald .70Va 132
SM3: Cheam .76Bb 155
Walton Bri. KT12: Walt T .73U 150
TW17: Shep .73U 150
Walton Bri. Rd. TW17: Shep .73U 150
Walton Cl. E4 .22Cc 52
E5 .34Zb 72
(off Orient Way)
HA1: Harr .28Fa 46
NW2 .33Xa 68
SW8 .52Nb 112
Walton Ct. CR2: S Croy .78Sb 157
(off Warham Rd.)
EN5: New Bar .15Eb 31
GU21: Wok .88C 168
NW6 .38Eb 69
(off Fairfax Rd.)
Walton Cft. HA1: Harr .35Ga 66
Walton Dr. HA1: Harr .28Fa 46
NW10 .37Ta 67
Walton Gdns. CM13: Hut .15Ee 41
EN9: Walt A .5Dc 20
HA9: Wemb .33Na 67
TW13: Felt .63V 128
W3 .43Ra 87
Walton Grn. CR0: New Ad .81Dc 178
Walton Hall Campsite
SS17: Stan H .6J 101
WALTON HEATH .99Va 194
Walton Heath Cl. SS17: Stan H .4K 101
Walton Heath Golf Course .97Xa 194
Walton Ho. E2 .5K 219
E17 .27Dc 52
NW1 .5A 216
SW3 .4F 227
Walton La. KT12: Walt T .75R 150
KT13: Weyb .75R 150
SL2: Farn R .10D 60
TW17: Shep .73T 150
WALTON-ON-THAMES .74W 150
Walton on Thames Camping & Cvn. Site
KT12: Walt T .73Ca 151
WALTON ON THE HILL .96Wa 194
Walton Pk. KT12: Walt T .75Z 151
Walton Pk. La. KT12: Walt T .75Z 151
Walton Pl. SW3 .3F 227 (48Hb 89)
Walton Rd. DA14: Sidc .61Yc 139
E12 .35Qc 74
(not continuous)
E13 .40Lc 73
GU21: Wok .88B 168
HA1: Harr .28Fa 46
KT8: W Mole, E Mos .71Y 151
KT12: Walt T .71Y 151
KT18: Eps D .89Va 174
KT18: Eps D, Head .93Sa 193
N15 .28Vb 51
RM5: Col R .24Bd 55
WD23: Bush .14Z 27
Walton's Hall Rd. SS17: Stan H .7J 101
Walton St. AL1: St A .1D 6
EN2: Enf .11Tb 33
KT20: Walt H .96Wa 194
SW3 .5E 226 (49Gb 89)
Walton Ter. GU21: Wok .87D 168
WD6: E'tree .16Ma 29
(off Watford Rd.)
Walton Vs. N1 .38Ub 71
(off Downham Rd.)
Walton Way CR4: Mitc .70Lb 134
W3 .43Ra 87
Walt Whitman Cl. SE24 .56Rb 113
Walverns Cl. WD19: Wat .16Y 27
WALWORTH .7E 230 (50Sb 91)
Walworth Pl. SE17 .7E 230 (50Sb 91)
Walworth Rd. SE1 .5D 230 (49Sb 91)
SE17 .5D 230 (49Sb 91)
Walwyn Av. BR1: Brom .69Mc 137
Wambrook Cl. CM13: Hut .18Ee 41
Wanborough Dr. SW15 .60Xa 110
Wanderer Dr. IG11: Bark .41Yc 95
Wander Wharf WD4: K Lan .1R 12
Wandle Apartments CR2: S Croy .78Tb 157
Wandle Bank CR0: Bedd .76Nb 156
SW19 .66Fb 133
Wandle Ct. CR0: Bedd .76Nb 156
KT19: Ewe .77Sa 153
Wandle Ct. Gdns. CR0: Bedd .76Nb 156
Wandle Ho. BR1: Brom .64Fc 137
NW8 .7D 214
Wandle Industrial Mus. .69Hb 133
Wandle Meadow Nature Pk. .64Eb 133
Wandle Pk. .75Rb 157
Wandle Pk. Trad. Est., The
CR0: C'don .74Rb 157
Wandle Recreation Cen. .58Db 111
Wandle Rd. CR0: Bedd .76Nb 156
CR0: C'don .76Sb 157
SM4: Mord .70Eb 133
SM6: Wall .76Kb 156
SW17 .61Gb 133
Wandle Side CR0: Wadd .76Pb 156
SM6: Wall .76Kb 156
Wandle Technology Pk.
CR4: Mitc .73Hb 155
Wandle Trad. Est. CR4: Mitc .73Hb 155
Wandle Way CR4: Mitc .71Hb 155
SW18 .60Db 111
Wandon Rd. SW6 .52Db 111
WANDSWORTH .57Db 111
Wandsworth Bri. SW6 .55Db 111
Wandsworth Bri. Rd. SW6 .53Db 111
WANDSWORTH COMMON .60Hb 111
Wandsworth Comn. W. Side
SW18 .57Eb 111
WANDSWORTH GYRATORY .57Db 111
Wandsworth High St. SW18 .57Cb 111
Wandsworth Mus. .57Cb 111
Wandsworth Plain SW18 .57Db 111
Wandsworth Rd. SW8 .55Kb 112
Wangey Rd. RM6: Chad H .31Zc 75
Wangford Ho. SW9 .56Rb 113
(off Loughborough Pk.)
Wanless Rd. SE24 .55Sb 113
Wanley Rd. SE5 .56Tb 113
Wanlip Rd. E13 .42Kc 93
Wanmer Ct. RH2: Reig .5J 207
(off Birkheads Rd.)
Wannock Gdns. IG6: Ilf .24Rc 54
Wansbeck Ct. EN2: Enf .13Rb 33
(off Waverley Rd.)
Wansbeck Rd. E9 .38Bc 72
Wansbury Way BR8: Swan .71Jd 162
Wansdown Pl. SW6 .52Db 111
Wansey St. SE17 .6D 230 (49Sb 91)
Wansford Cl. CM14: B'wood .20Vd 40
Wansford Grn. GU21: Wok .9K 167
Wansford Pk. WD6: Bore .14Ta 29
Wansford Rd. IG8: Wfd G .25Lc 53
WANSTEAD .30Kc 53
Wanstead Cl. BR1: Brom .68Lc 137
Wanstead Gdns. IG4: Ilf .30Mc 53
Wanstead Golf Course .31Lc 73
Wanstead La. IG1: Ilf .30Mc 53
Wanstead Leisure Cen. .30Lc 53
Wanstead Pk. Av. E12 .32Mc 73
Wanstead Pk. Rd. IG1: Ilf .30Mc 53
Wanstead Pl. E11 .30Jc 53
Wanstead Rd. BR1: Brom .68Lc 137
Wansunt Rd. DA5: Bexl .60Ed 118
Wantage Rd. SE12 .57Hc 115
Wantz La. RM13: Rain .42Kd 97
Wantz Rd. RM10: Dag .35Dd 76
Waplings, The KT20: Walt H .96Xa 194
WAPPING .46Xb 91
Wapping Dock St. E1 .46Xb 91
Wapping High St. E1 .46Wb 91
Wapping La. E1 .45Xb 91
Wapping Wall E1 .46Yb 92
Wapses Lodge CR3: Wold .92Xb 197
WAPSES LODGE RDBT. .92Xb 197
Wapseys La. SL2: Hedg .1J 61
Wapshott Rd. TW18: Staines .65G 126
Waratah Dr. BR7: Chst .64Pc 138
Warbank Cl. CR0: New Ad .82Gc 179
Warbank Cres. CR0: New Ad .82Gc 179
Warbank La. KT2: King T .66Va 132
Warbeck Ho. KT13: Weyb .78T 150
(off Queens Rd.)
Warbeck Rd. W12 .47Xa 88
Warberry Rd. N22 .25Pb 50
Warbler Ct. HP3: Hem H .7L 3
Warbler's Grn. KT11: Cobh .86Ba 171
Warboys App. KT2: King T .65Ra 131
Warboys Cres. E4 .22Ec 52
Warboys Rd. KT2: King T .65Ra 131
Warburg Ct. NW9 .27Ua 48
(off Mornington Cl.)
Warburton Cl. HA3: Hrw W .23Fa 46
N1 .37Ub 71
(off Culford Rd.)
Warburton Ct. HA4: Ruis .33W 64
Warburton Ho. E8 .39Xb 71
(off Warburton St.)
Warburton Rd. E8 .39Xb 71
TW2: Whitt .60Da 107
Warburtons SS17: Stan H .1P 101
Warburton St. E8 .39Xb 71
Warburton Ter. E17 .26Dc 52
Warbury La. GU21: Knap .7F 166
War Coppice Rd. CR3: Cat'm .99Tb 197
Wardalls Gro. SE14 .52Yb 114
Wardalls Ho. SE8 .51Bc 114
(off Staunton St.)
Ward Av. RM17: Grays .49Ce 99
Ward Cl. CR2: S Croy .79Ub 157
DA8: Erith .51Fd 118
SL0: Iver .45H 83
Wardell Cl. NW7 .24Ua 48
Wardell Fld. NW9 .25Ua 48
Wardell Ho. SE10 .51Ec 114
(off Welland St.)
Wardell M. SW4 .55Kb 112
Warden Av. HA2: Harr .32Ba 65
RM5: Col R .22Ed 56
Warden Rd. NW5 .37Jb 70
Wardens Fld. Cl. BR6: Chels .79Uc 160
Wardens Gro. SE1 .7D 224 (46Sb 91)
Ward Gdns. RM3: Hrld W .25Md 57
SL1: Slou .5C 80
Ward La. CR6: W'ham .88Yb 178
E9 .36Ac 72
Wardle St. E9 .36Zb 72
Wardley St. SW18 .59Db 111
Wardo Av. SW6 .53Ab 110
Wardona Ct. DA10: Swans .58Be 121
DA11: Nflt .57De 121
Wardona Ho. DA10: Swans .58Be 121
Wardour Ct. DA2: Dart .58Rd 119
(off Bow Arrow La.)
Wardour M. W1 .3C 222
Wardour St. W1 .2C 222 (44Lb 90)
Ward Point SE11 .6K 229 (49Qb 90)
Ward Rd. E15 .39Fc 73
N19 .34Lb 70
SW19 .67Eb 133
WD24: Wat .8W 12
Wardrobe, The TW9: Rich .57Ma 109
(off Old Palace Yd.)
Wardrobe Pl. EC4 .3C 224
Wardrobe Ter. EC4 .4C 224
Wardroper Ho. SE1 .4C 230
Ward Royal SL4: Wind .3G 102
Ward Royal Pde. SL4: Wind .3G 102
(off Alma Rd.)
Wards Dr. WD3: Sarr .8H 11
Wards La. WD6: E'tree .12Ha 28
Ward's Pl. TW20: Egh .65E 126
Wards Rd. IG2: Ilf .31Tc 74
Wards Wharf App. E16 .46Mc 93
Wardur Ho. KT12: Walt T .76W 150
Ware Ct. SM1: Sutt .77Bb 155
Wareham Cl. TW3: Houn .56Da 107
Wareham Ct. N1 .38Ub 71
(off Hertford Rd.)
Wareham Ho. SW8 .52Pb 112
Warehome M. E13 .42Jc 93
(off Jutland Rd.)
Warehouse Ct. SE18 .48Rc 94
Warehouse Sports & Performing Arts Cen., The .50Vc 95
Warehouse Way E16 .45Kc 93
Waremead Rd. IG2: Ilf .29Rc 54
Warenford Way WD6: Bore .11Qa 29
Warenne Hgts. RH1: Redh .8M 207
Warenne Rd. KT22: Fet .94Ea 192
Warepoint Dr. SE28 .47Tc 94
Warescot Cl. CM15: B'wood .17Xd 40
Warescot Rd. CM15: B'wood .17Xd 40
Warfield Rd. NW10 .41Za 88
TW12: Hamp .67Da 129
TW14: Felt .59U 106
Warfield Yd. NW10 .41Za 88
(off Warfield Rd.)
Wargrave Av. N15 .30Vb 51
Wargrave Ho. E2 .4K 219
Wargrave Rd. HA2: Harr .34Ea 66
Warham Rd. CR2: S Croy .78Rb 157
HA3: W'stone .26Ha 46
N4 .29Qb 50
TN14: Otf .88Kd 183
Warham St. SE5 .52Rb 113
Waring & Gillow Est. W3 .42Qa 87
Waring Cl. BR6: Chels .79Vc 161
Waring Dr. BR6: Chels .79Vc 161
Waring Rd. DA14: Sidc .65Yc 139
Waring St. SE27 .63Sb 135
Warkworth Gdns. TW7: Isle .52Ja 108
Warkworth Rd. N17 .24Tb 51
Warland Rd. SE18 .52Tc 116
TN15: W King .81Vd 184
WARLEY .22Yd 58
Warley Av. RM8: Dag .31Bd 75
UB4: Hayes .44W 84
Warley Cl. E10 .32Bc 72
Warley Country Pk. .21Wd 58
Warley Gap
CM13: Gt War, L War .24Xd 58
Warley Hall La. RM14: Upm .31Be 79
Warley Hill
CM13: Gt War, W'ley .23Xd 58
CM14: W'ley .23Xd 58
Warley Hill Bus. Pk., The
CM13: Gt War .23Yd 58
Warley Mt. CM14: W'ley .21Yd 58
Warley Pk. Golf Course .26Zd 59
Warley Place Nature Reserve .24Wd 58
Warley Rd. CM13: Gt War .25Wd 58
IG5: Ilf .25Qc 54
IG8: Wfd G .24Kc 53
N9 .19Yb 34
RM14: Gt War, Upm .26Sd 58
UB4: Hayes .44W 84
Warley St.
CM13: Gt War, Upm .28Yd 58
E2 .41Zb 92
RM14: Upm .28Yd 58

Warleywoods Cres.—Watersplash Ct.

Warleywoods Cres.
CM14: W'ley 21Xd 58
WARLINGHAM 90Zb 178
Warlingham Ct. SE13 58Ec 114
Warlingham Rd. CR7: Thor H 70Rb 135
Warlock Rd. W9 42Bb 89
Warlow Cl. EN3: Enf L 9Cc 20
Warlters Cl. N7 35Nb 70
Warlters Rd. N7 35Nb 70
Warltersville Mans. N19 31Nb 70
Warltersville Rd. N19 31Nb 70
Warmark Rd. HP1: Hem H 1G 2
War Memorial Sports Ground 77Gb 155
Warmington Cl. E5 34Zb 72
Warmington Rd. SE24 58Sb 113
Warmington St. E13 42Jc 93
Warminster Gdns. SE25 68Wb 135
Warminster Ho. *RM3: Rom* 22Pd 57
(off Redcar Rd.)
Warminster Rd. SE25 68Vb 135
Warminster Sq. SE25 68Wb 135
Warminster Way CR4: Mitc 67Kb 134
Warmsworth *NW1* 39Lb 70
(off Pratt St.)
Warmwell Av. NW9 25Ua 48
Warndon St. SE16 49Zb 92
Warneford Pl. WD19: Wat 16Aa 27
Warneford Rd. HA3: Kenton 27Ma 47
TW6: H'row A 54K 105
Warneford St. E9 39Xb 71
Warne Pl. DA15: Sidc 58Xc 117
Warner Av. SM3: Cheam 75Ab 154
Warner Bros. Studios Leavesden 6U 12
Warner Cl. E15 36Gc 73
EN4: Had W 9Gb 17
NW9 31Va 68
SL1: Slou 6C 80
TW12: Hamp 64Ba 129
UB3: Harl 52T 106
Warner Dr. WD25: Wat 5V 12
Warner Ho. BR3: Beck 65Dc 136
NW8 3A 214 (41Eb 89)
SE13 54Dc 114
(off Russett Way)
Warner Pl. E2 40Wb 71
Warner Rd. BR1: Brom 66Hc 137
E17 28Ac 52
N8 28Mb 50
SE5 53Sb 113
Warners Cl. IG8: Wfd G 22Jc 53
WARNERS END 1G 2
Warners End Rd. HP1: Hem H 2J 3
Warners La. KT2: King T 63Ma 131
Warners Path IG8: Wfd G 22Jc 53
Warner St. EC1 6K 217 (42Qb 90)
Warner Ter. *E14* 43Dc 92
(off Broomfield St.)
Warner Yd. EC1 6K 217
Warnford Ct. EC2 2G 225
Warnford Ho. *SW15* 58Ua 110
(off Tunworth Cres.)
Warnford Ind. Est. UB3: Hayes 47U 84
Warnford Rd. BR6: Chels 78Vc 161
Warnham WC1 4H 217
Warnham Ct. Rd. SM5: Cars 80Hb 155
Warnham Gro. BR5: St P 68Yc 139
Warnham Ho. *SW2* 59Pb 112
(off Up. Tulse Hill)
Warnham Rd. N12 22Gb 49
Warple M. W3 47Ua 88
Warple Way W3 47Ua 88
Warre Ho. *SL4: Eton* 10G 80
(off Common La.)
Warren, The 47Y 85
Warren, The AL2: Park 10A 6
DA12: Grav'nd 3F 144
E12 35Nc 74
KT4: Wor Pk 77Ta 153
KT20: Kgswd 95Ab 194
KT21: Asht 91Na 193
KT22: Oxs 84Ea 172
SE7 51Lc 115
SL9: Chal P 24B 42
SM5: Cars 81Fb 175
SS17: Stan H 4N 101
TW5: Hest 52Ba 107
UB4: Hayes 44W 84
WD4: K Lan 1P 11
WD7: R'lett 5Ja 14
Warren Av. BR1: Brom 66Gc 137
BR6: Chels 78Vc 161
CR2: Sels 80Zb 158
E10 34Ec 72
SM2: Cheam 82Bb 175
TW10: Rich 56Ra 109
Warren Cl. DA6: Bex 57Cd 118
HA9: Wemb 33Ma 67
KT10: Esh 77Da 151
N9 17Zb 34
SE21 59Sb 113
SL3: L'ly 48A 82
UB4: Yead 43Y 85
Warren Ct. BR3: Beck 66Cc 136
CR0: C'don 74Ub 157
IG7: Chig 21Tc 54
KT13: Weyb 78Q 150
KT21: Asht 91Na 193
N17 27Wb 51
(off High Cross Rd.)
NW1 5B 216
SL2: Farn C 6G 60
TN13: S'oaks 96Ld 203
W5 43La 86
WD25: Wat 2X 13
Warren Ct. Farm
TN14: Hals 85Ad 181
Warren Cres. N9 17Vb 33
Warren Cutting KT2: King T 66Ta 131
Warrender Rd. N19 34Lb 70
Warrender Way HA4: Ruis 31W 64
Warren Dr. BR6: Chels 78Xc 161
HA4: Ruis 31Z 65
KT20: Kgswd 94Bb 195
RM12: Horn 35Jd 76
UB6: G'frd 42Da 85
Warren Dr., The E11 31Lc 73
Warren Dr. Nth. KT5: Surb 74Ra 153
Warren Dr. Sth. KT5: Surb 74Sa 153
Warrene Cl. SS17: Stan H 2M 101
Warreners La. KT13: Weyb 80T 150
Warren Farm Cl. KT17: Bans 87Ya 174
Warren Farm Cotts.
RM6: Chad H 28Bd 55
Warren Farm Mobile Home Pk.
GU22: Pyr 91K 189
Warren Farm Sports Cen. 48Fa 86
Warren Fld. CM16: Epp 4Wc 23
SL0: Iver H 40E 62
Warrenfield Cl. EN7: Chesh 3Wb 19
Warren Flds. HA7: Stan 21La 46
Warren Footpath TW1: Twick 60La 108
Warren Gdns. BR6: Chels 78Wc 161
E15 36Fc 73
Warrengate La. EN6: S Mim 3Ya 16
Warrengate Rd. AL9: N Mym 8D 8
Warren Gro. WD6: Bore 14Ta 29
Warren Hastings Ct.
DA11: Nflt 8B 122
Warren Hgts. IG10: Lough 15Lc 35
RM16: Chaf H 49Ae 99
Warren Hill IG10: Lough 15Lc 35
KT18: Eps 88Ta 173
Warren Ho. *E3* 41Dc 92
(off Bromley High St.)
N17 27Wb 51
(off High Cross Rd.)
W14 49Bb 89
Warrenhurst Gdns.
KT13: Weyb 79T 150
Warren La. CM15: Dodd, Kel H 11Vd 40
GU22: Pyr 90J 169
HA7: Stan 19Ja 28
KT22: Oxs 83Ea 172
RH8: Oxt 6L 211
RM16: Chaf H 49Zd 99
SE18 48Rc 94
Warren La. Ga. SE18 48Rc 94
Warren Lodge KT20: Kgswd 96Ab 194
Warren Lodge Dr.
KT20: Kgswd 96Ab 194
Warren Mead SM7: Bans 87Ya 174
Warren M. KT13: Weyb 76V 150
W1 6B 216 (42Lb 90)
Warrenne Way RH2: Reig 6J 207
Warren Pde. SL2: Slou 6N 81
Warren Pk. CR6: W'ham 90Zb 178
KT2: King T 65Sa 131
Warren Pk. Rd. SM1: Sutt 79Fb 155
Warren Pl. *E1* 44Zb 92
(off Pitsea St.)
Warren Pond Rd. E4 18Hc 35
Warren Ri. KT3: N Mald 67Ta 131
Warren Rd. AL1: St A 6A 6
BR2: Hayes 75Jc 159
BR6: Chels 78Vc 161
(not continuous)
CR0: C'don 74Ub 157
CR8: Purl 84Rb 177
DA1: Dart 62Nd 141
DA6: Bex 57Cd 118
DA13: Sflt 64De 143
DA14: Sidc 62Yc 139
E4 19Ec 34
E10 34Ec 72
E11 30Lc 53
IG6: Ilf 29Tc 54
KT2: King T 65Sa 131
KT15: New H 82J 169
NW2 33Va 68
RH2: Reig 5K 207
SM7: Bans 86Ya 174
SW19 65Gb 133
TW2: Whitt 58Ea 108
TW15: Ashf 66U 128
UB10: Ick 35N 63
WD23: B Hea 18Ea 28
Warrens, The DA3: Hartl 72Be 165
Warren Sports Cen. 29Bd 55
Warrens Shawe La.
HA8: Edg 19Ra 29
Warren St. W1 6B 216 (42Lb 90)
Warren Ter. RM6: Chad H 28Zc 55
RM16: N Stif 47Zd 99
Warren Vw. DA12: Shorne 4N 145
Warren Wlk. SE7 51Lc 115
Warren Way HA8: Edg 26Ra 47
KT13: Weyb 78S 150
WARREN WOOD 4M 9
Warren Wood Cl.
BR2: Hayes 75Hc 159
Warrenwood M. AL9: Hat 4M 9
Warriner Av. RM12: Horn 33Md 77
Warriner Dr. N9 20Wb 33
Warriner Gdns. SW11 53Hb 111
Warrington Av. SL1: Slou 4G 80
Warrington Ct. *CR0: Wadd* 76Rb 157
(off Warrington Rd.)
Warrington Cres. W9 5A 214 (42Eb 89)
Warrington Gdns.
RM11: Horn 30Ld 57
W9 42Eb 89
(not continuous)
Warrington Rd. CR0: Wadd 76Rb 157
HA1: Harr 29Ga 46
RM8: Dag 33Zc 75
TW10: Rich 57Ma 109
Warrington Spur SL4: Old Win 9M 103
Warrington Sq. RM8: Dag 33Zc 75
Warrior Av. DA12: Grav'nd 3E 144
Warrior Cl. SE28 46Tc 94
Warrior Ct. *SW9* 55Rb 113
(off Coldharbour Rd.)
Warrior Sq. E12 35Qc 74
Warsaw Cl. HA4: Ruis 37X 65
Warspite Ho. *E14* 49Dc 92
(off Cahir St.)
Warspite Rd. SE18 48Nc 94
Warton Ct. *E1* 45Zb 92
(off Cable St.)
W3 48Sa 87
(off All Saints Rd.)
Warton Ho. *E15* 39Ec 72
(off High St.)
Warton Rd. E15 39Ec 72
Warwall E6 44Rc 94
Warwark Ct. KT6: Surb 75Na 153
Warwick *W14* 49Bb 89
(off Kensington Village)
Warwick Av. HA2: Harr 35Ba 65
HA8: Edg 20Ra 29
SL2: Slou 2G 80
TW18: Staines 65L 127
TW20: Egh 67E 126
W2 6A 214 (42Eb 89)
W9 6A 214 (42Eb 89)
Warwick Bldg. SW8 51Kb 112
Warwick Chambers *W8* 48Cb 89
(off Pater St.)
Warwick Cl. BR6: Chels 76Wc 161
DA5: Bexl 59Bd 117
EN4: E Barn 15Fb 31
RM11: Horn 28Pd 57
TW12: Hamp 66Ea 130
W8 48Bb 89
(off Kensington High St.)
WD23: B Hea 17Ga 28
Warwick Ct. BR2: Brom 68Gc 137
DA8: Erith 52Hd 118
EC4 3C 224
EN5: New Bar 15Db 31
(off Station Rd.)
HA1: Harr 27Ga 46
KT13: Weyb 78Q 150
N11 23Mb 50
SL4: Wind 4G 102
(off Queen's Rd.)
TN13: S'oaks 97Kd 203
UB5: N'olt 36Ca 65
(off Newmarket Av.)
W7 44Ha 86
(off Copley Cl.)
WC1 1J 223 (43Pb 90)
WD3: Chor 13H 25
Warwick Cres. UB4: Hayes 42V 84
W2 7A 214 (43Eb 89)
Warwick Deeping KT16: Ott 78E 148
Warwick Dene W5 46Na 87
Warwick Dr. EN8: Chesh 1Zb 20
SW15 55Xa 110
Warwick Est. W2 43Db 89
Warwick Gdns.
CR7: Thor H 69Qb 134
EN5: Barn 10Bb 17
IG1: Ilf 32Rc 74
KT7: T Ditt 71Ha 152
KT21: Asht 89La 172
N4 29Sb 51
RM2: Rom 27Ld 57
W14 48Bb 89
Warwick Gro. E5 32Xb 71
KT5: Surb 73Pa 153
Warwick Ho. *AL1: St A* 2B 6
(off London Rd.)
BR8: Swan 70Gd 140
E16 46Jc 93
(off Wesley Av.)
KT2: King T 67Na 131
(off Acre Rd.)
SW9 54Qb 112
Warwick Ho. St. SW1 6E 222 (46Mb 90)
Warwick La. EC4 2C 224 (44Rb 91)
GU21: Wok 1L 187
RM13: Rain 41Pd 97
RM14: Avel, Upm 41Pd 97
Warwick Lodge TW2: Twick 62Da 129
Warwick Mans. *SW5* 49Cb 89
(off Cromwell Cres.)
Warwick M. WD3: Crox G 16Q 26
Warwick Pde. HA3: Kenton 26Ka 46
Warwick Pas. EC4 2C 224
Warwick Pl. CM14: Pil H 14Sd 40
DA11: Nflt 57De 121
KT7: T Ditt 72Ja 152
RH2: Reig 6M 207
UB8: Uxb 38L 63
W5 47Ma 87
W9 7A 214 (43Eb 89)
WD6: Bore 13Ta 29
Warwick Pl. Nth. SW1 6B 228 (49Lb 90)
Warwick Quad. RH1: Redh 5A 208
Warwick Rd. AL1: St A 1D 6
CR5: Coul 86Lb 176
CR7: Thor H 69Qb 134
DA14: Sidc 64Xc 139
DA16: Well 55Yc 117
E4 22Cc 52
E11 29Kc 53
E12 36Nc 74
E15 37Hc 73
E17 25Bc 52
EN3: Enf L 9Bc 20
EN5: New Bar 14Db 31
KT1: Hamp W 67La 130
KT3: N Mald 69Sa 131
KT7: T Ditt 71Ha 152
N11 23Mb 50
N18 21Ub 51
RH1: Redh 5P 207
RM13: Rain 42Ld 97
SE20 69Xb 135
SM1: Sutt 77Eb 155
SW5 49Bb 89
TW2: Twick 60Ga 108
TW4: Houn 55X 107
TW15: Ashf 64N 127
UB2: S'hall 48Ba 85
UB7: W Dray 47N 83
W5 47Ma 87
W14 49Bb 89
WD6: Bore 13Ta 29
Warwick Row SW1 3A 228 (48Lb 90)
Warwickshire Path SE8 52Bc 114
Warwickshire Rd. N16 35Ub 71
Warwick Sq. EC4 2C 224 (44Rb 91)
SW1 7B 228 (50Lb 90)
(not continuous)
Warwick Sq. M. SW1 6B 228 (49Lb 90)
Warwick St. W1 4C 222 (45Lb 90)
Warwick Ter. *E17* 29Fc 53
(off Lea Bri. Rd.)
SE18 51Tc 116
Warwick Vs. TW20: Egh 67E 126
Warwick Way DA1: Dart 61Nd 141
SW1 7K 227 (50Kb 90)
WD3: Crox G 14S 26
WARWICK WOLD 1G 208
Warwick Wold Rd. RH1: Mers 1G 208
Warwick Yd. EC1 6E 218 (42Sb 91)
Wasdale NW1 4A 216
Washbourne Ct. *N9* 19Wb 33
(off Acton Cl.)
Washbourne Rd. NW10 39Ta 67
Washington Av. E12 35Pc 74
Washington Bldg. *SE13* 53Dc 114
(off Deal's Gateway)
Washington Cl. E3 41Dc 92
RH2: Reig 4J 207
Washington Dr. SL1: Slou 5B 80
SL4: Wind 5C 102
Washington Ho. E17 26Bc 52
SW3 2F 227
WD23: Bush 14Ba 27
(off King Edward Pl.)
Washington Rd. E6 38Lc 73
E18 26Hc 53
KT1: King T 68Qa 131
KT4: Wor Pk 75Xa 154
SW13 52Wa 110
TW6: H'row A 55L 105
Wash La. EN6: S Mim 5Xa 16
WASHMILLS 60Yd 120
Washneys Rd. BR6: Prat B 86Wc 181
Washpond La. CR6: W'ham 90Ec 178
Wash Rd. CM13: Hut, Mount 16Fe 41
Wasp Rd. *TW6: H'row A* 54K 105
(off Welland Rd.)
Wastdale Rd. SE23 60Zb 114
Watch, The N12 21Eb 49
Watchfield Ct. W4 50Sa 87
Watchgate DA2: Daren 64Td 142
(not continuous)
Watcombe Cotts. TW9: Kew 51Qa 109
Watcombe Pl. SE25 71Xb 157
Watcombe Rd. SE25 71Xb 157
Waterbank Ho. *SW18* 60Db 111
(off Knaresborough Dr.)
Waterbank Rd. SE6 62Dc 136
Waterbeach Cl. SL1: Slou 4H 81
Waterbeach Rd. RM9: Dag 37Yc 75
SL1: Slou 4H 81
Waterbourne Way CR8: Kenley 86Tb 177
Water Brook La. NW4 29Ya 48
Watercress Cl. TN14: S'oaks 92Ld 203
Watercress Dr. TN14: S'oaks 92Ld 203
Watercress Pl. N1 38Ub 71
Watercress Way DA11: Nflt 59Fe 121
GU21: Wok 9M 167
Watercroft Rd. TN14: Hals 82Bd 181
WATERDALE 2Y 13
WATERDALE 2Z 13
Waterdale AL2: Brick W 2Aa 13
Waterdale Rd. SE2 51Wc 117
Waterdales DA11: Nflt 61Ee 143
Waterden Ct. W11 46Ab 88
Waterden Rd. E20 36Cc 72
Water Dr. WD3: Rick 18N 25
WATER END 8D 8
Water End Cl. WD6: Bore 12Pa 29
Waterer Gdns. KT20: Tad 90Za 174
Waterer Ho. SE6 63Ec 136
Waterer Ri. SM6: Wall 79Mb 156
Waterers Ri. GU21: Knap 9H 167
Waterfall Cl. GU25: Vir W 9L 125
N14 20Lb 32
Waterfall Cotts. SW19 65Fb 133
Waterfall Rd. N11 21Kb 50
N14 21Kb 50
SW19 65Fb 133
Waterfall Ter. SW17 65Gb 133
Waterfall Wlk. N14 18Kb 32
Waterfield KT20: Tad 92Xa 194
WD3: Herons 17E 24
Waterfield Cl. DA17: Belv 48Cd 96
SE28 46Xc 95
Waterfield Dr. CR6: W'ham 91Yb 198
KT18: Tatt C 91Xa 194
KT20: Tad 91Xa 194
Waterfield Gdns. SE25 70Tb 135
Waterfield Grn. KT20: Tad 92Xa 194
Waterfields KT22: Lea 91Ka 192
Waterfields Shop. Pk. WD17: Wat 14Z 27
Waterfields Way WD17: Wat 14Z 27
Waterford Ct. KT11: Cobh 83Aa 171
Waterford Ho. *BR1: Brom* 67Jc 137
(off Newman Rd.)
UB7: W Dray 48L 83
W11 45Bb 89
(off Kensington Pk. Rd.)
Waterford Rd. SW6 52Db 111
Waterford Way NW10 36Xa 68
Waterfront W6 51Ya 110
Waterfront, The WD6: E'tree 16Ka 28
Waterfront Ho. *E5* 33Yb 72
(off Harry Zeital Way)
Waterfront Leisure Cen.
Woolwich 48Qc 94
Waterfront M. N1 1E 218 (40Sb 71)
Waterfront Studios Bus. Cen.
E16 46Hc 93
(off Dock Rd.)
Water Gdns. HA7: Stan 23Ka 46
Water Gdns., The W2 2E 220 (44Gb 89)
Watergardens, The KT2: King T 65Ta 131
Water Gdns. Sq. SE16 47Zb 92
Watergate EC4 4B 224 (45Rb 91)
Watergate, The WD19: Wat 19Z 27
Watergate St. SE8 51Cc 114
Watergate Wlk. WC2 6G 223 (46Nb 90)
Waterglade Ind. Pk.
RM20: W Thur 51Vd 120
WATERHALES 15Md 39
Waterhall Av. E4 21Gc 53
Waterhall Cl. E17 25Zb 52
Waterhead NW1 3B 216
Waterhouse *CR0: C'don* 74Sb 157
(off Saffron Central Sq.)
Waterhouse, The HP1: Hem H 3L 3
Waterhouse Cl. E16 43Mc 93
NW3 36Fb 69
W6 49Za 88
Waterhouse La. CR8: Kenley 91Sb 197
KT20: Kgswd 93Ab 194
RH1: Blet 4M 209
Waterhouse Sq. EC1 1K 223 (43Qb 90)
Waterhouse St. HP1: Hem H 2L 3
Wateridge Cl. E14 48Cc 92
Wateringbury Cl. BR5: St P 69Xc 139
Water La. AL2: Lon C 10H 7
DA14: Sidc 61Bd 139
E15 37Gc 73
EC3 5J 225 (45Ub 91)
GU24: Bisl 1C 186
GU24: Chob 1F 166
HP3: Bov 1C 10
IG3: Ilf 34Uc 74
KT1: King T 67Ma 131
KT11: Cobh 87Aa 171
KT23: Bookh 97Z 191
N9 18Xb 33
NW1 38Kb 70
RH1: Blet 2H 209
RH8: Limp 98Jc 199
RH9: S God 10B 210
RM19: Purf 49Qd 97
SE14 52Yb 114
TN14: S'ham 84Hd 182
TN16: Westrm 99Tc 200
TW1: Twick 60Ja 108
TW9: Rich 57Ma 109
WD4: K Lan 1R 12
WD17: Wat 14Y 27
Water Lily Cl. UB2: S'hall 47Ea 86
Waterline Ho. W2 1C 220
Waterloo Bri. WC2 5H 223 (45Pb 90)
Waterloo Cl. E9 36Yb 72
TW14: Felt 60V 106
Waterloo Ct. AL1: St A 3F 6
KT12: Hers 77W 150
Waterloo East Theatre 7A 224
Waterloo Gdns. E2 40Yb 72
N1 38Rb 71
RM7: Rom 30Fd 56
Waterloo Pas. NW6 38Bb 69
Waterloo Pl. *SM5: Cars* 76Hb 155
(off Wrythe Grn.)
SW1 6D 222 (46Mb 90)
TW9: Rich 56Na 109
Waterloo Rd. CM14: B'wood 18Yd 40
E6 38Lc 73
E7 36Hc 73
E10 31Cc 72
IG6: Ilf 26Sc 54
KT19: Eps 84Ta 173
NW2 32Wa 68
RM7: Rom, Rush G 30Gd 56
SE1 6J 223 (46Pb 90)
SM1: Sutt 78Fb 155
UB8: Uxb 39L 63
Waterloo St. DA12: Grav'nd 9E 122
Waterloo Ter. *KT13: Weyb* 77R 150
(off Baker St.)
N1 38Rb 71
Waterlow Ct. NW11 31Db 69
Waterlow Pk. Cen. 32Kb 70
Waterlow Rd. N19 32Lb 70
RH2: Reig 7L 207
Waterman Bldg. E14 47Bc 92
Waterman Cl. WD19: Wat 16X 27
Waterman Ct. SL1: Slou 6C 80
Watermans RM1: Rom 29Hd 56
Watermans Art Cen., Cinema & Theatre
51Na 109
Watermans Bus. Pk.
TW18: Staines 63G 126
Watermans Cl. KT2: King T 66Na 131
Watermans Ct. *TW8: Bford* 51Ma 109
(off High St.)
Watermans Ho. *E14* 44Fc 93
(off New Village Av.)
Watermans M. W5 45Na 87
Waterman's Quay SW6 54Eb 111
Waterman St. SW15 55Za 110
Watermans Wlk. SE16 47Ac 92
Watermans Way
DA9: Ghithe 56Xd 120
Waterman Way E1 46Xb 91
Watermark Ct. *RM6: Chad H* 30Xc 55
(off Quarles Pk. Rd.)
Water Mead CR5: Chip 89Hb 175
Watermead GU21: Wok 8K 167
KT20: Tad 93Xa 194
TW14: Felt 60U 106
Watermead Ho. E9 36Ac 72
Watermead La. SM5: Cars 73Hb 155
Watermead Lodge *SE16* 46Zb 92
(off Princes Riverside Rd.)
Watermeadow Cl. DA8: Erith 52Kd 119
Watermeadow La. SW6 54Eb 111
Water Mdws. AL2: F'mre 10B 6
Watermead Rd. SE6 63Ec 136
Watermead Way N17 27Xb 51
Watermen's Sq. SE20 66Yb 136
Water M. SE15 56Yb 114
Watermill Bus. Cen. EN3: Brim 12Bc 34
Watermill Cl. TN16: Bras 96Yc 201
TW10: Ham 62La 130
Water Mill Ho. TW13: Hanw 61Ca 129
Watermill La. N18 22Ub 51
Watermill Pl. KT11: Cobh 86X 171
Water Mill Way DA4: S Dar 68Rd 141
Watermill Way SW19 67Eb 133
TW13: Hanw 61Ba 129
Watermint Cl. BR5: St P 70Zc 139
Watermint Quay N16 31Wb 71
Waterperry La. GU24: Chob 2K 167
Water Rd. HA0: Wemb 39Pa 67
Waters Dr. TW18: Staines 62H 127
Water's Edge *SW6* 53Ya 110
(off Palemead Cl.)
Watersedge KT19: Ewe 77Sa 153
Waters Edge Ct. DA8: Erith 50Hd 96
Watersfield Way HA8: Edg 24Ma 47
Waters Gdns. RM10: Dag 36Cd 76
Waterside AL2: Lon C 9J 7
(not continuous)
BR3: Beck 67Bc 136
DA1: Cray 57Gd 118
DA11: Nflt 8A 122
E17 30Yb 52
HP4: Berk 1A 2
N1 2D 218 (40Sb 71)
TW18: Staines 63G 126
UB7: Harm 52L 105
UB8: Cowl 43L 83
W2 1B 220
WD4: K Lan 1Q 12
WD7: R'lett 6Ka 14
Waterside Apartments *N4* 32Sb 71
(off Goodchild Rd.)
Waterside Av. *BR3: Beck* 71Ec 158
(off Adamson Way)
Waterside Bus. Cen. TW7: Isle 56Ka 108
Waterside Cl. E3 39Bc 72
HA9: Wemb 34Sa 67
IG11: Bark 35Wc 75
KT6: Surb 75Na 153
RM3: Hrld W 24Qd 57
SE16 47Wb 91
SE28 46Vc 95
TW17: Shep 67S 128
UB5: N'olt 41Ba 85
WD4: K Lan 1R 12
Waterside Ct. DA2: Dart 57Td 120
HP3: Hem H 6N 3
SM5: Cars 76Jb 156
(off Millpond Pl.)
Waterside Dr. KT12: Walt T 71W 150
SL3: L'ly 47B 82
Waterside Hgts. *E16* 47Lc 93
(off Booth Rd.)
Waterside M. UB9: Hare 23J 43
Waterside Pl. NW1 39Jb 70
Waterside Point SW11 52Gb 111
Waterside Rd. UB2: S'hall 48Ca 85
Waterside Twr. *SW6* 54Eb 111
(off The Boulevard)
Waterside Trad. Cen. W7 48Ga 86
Waterside Trad. Est. KT15: Add 77N 149
Waterside Way GU21: Wok 10M 167
N17 27Xb 51
SW17 63Eb 133
Waterslade RH1: Redh 6N 207
Watersmeet Pl. N4 32Sb 71
Watersmeet Theatre 18N 25
Watersmeet Way SE28 44Yc 95
Waterson Rd. RM16: Grays 9D 100
Waterson St. E2 3J 219 (41Ub 91)
Waters Pl. SW15 54Ya 110
Watersplash Cl. KT1: King T 69Na 131
Watersplash Ct. AL2: Lon C 9K 7

Watersplash La.—Well Ho.

Watersplash La. SL5: Asc 7B 124
TW5: Cran 50X 85
UB3: Harl 49W 84
Watersplash Rd. TW17: Shep 71Q 150
Watersreach Apartments *N4* *32Sb 71*
(off Kayani Av.)
Waters Rd. KT1: King T 68Ra 131
SE6 . . . . . 62Gc 137
Waters Sq. KT1: King T 69Ra 131
Waterstone Way DA9: Ghithe 58Wd 120
Water St. WC2 . . . . . 4K 223
Waterton BR8: Swan 70Fd 140
Waterton Av. DA12: Grav'nd 9G 122
Water Twr. CM14: W'ley 22Xd 58
Water Twr. Cl. UB8: Uxb 36N 63
Water Twr. Hill CR0: C'don 77Tb 157
Water Twr. Pl. N1 . . . . . 39Qb 70
Water Twr. Rd. CM14: Gt War 22Yd 58
Waterview Cl. DA6: Bex 57Zc 117
Waterview Dr. SE10 . . . . . 46Fc 93
Waterview Ho. *E14* *43Ac 92*
(off Carr St.)
Waterway Av. SE13 . . . . . 55Dc 114
Waterway Pk. UB3: Hayes 47S 84
Waterway Rd. KT22: Lea 94Ja 192
Waterways Bus. Cen. EN3: Enf L 10Bc 20
WATERWORKS CORNER 25Gc 53
Waterworks Golf Course (Nature Reserve)
. . . . . 33Ac 72
Waterworks La. E5 . . . . . 33Zb 72
Waterworks Rd. SW2 . . . . . 58Pb 112
Waterworks Vs. TN13: S'oaks 98Kd 203
Waterworks Vis. Cen. 33Ac 72
Waterworks Yd. *CR0: C'don* *76Sb 157*
(off Charles St.)
Watery La. AL10: Hat 1A 8
DA14: Sidc 65Xc 139
GU24: Chob 2H 167
KT16: Lyne 73F 148
SW19 . . . . . 67Bb 133
SW20 . . . . . 68Bb 133
TN15: Kems'g, Seal 93Sd 204
UB3: Harl 50T 84
UB5: N'olt 40Y 65
Wates Way CM15: B'wood 18Zd 41
CR4: Mitc 72Hb 155
Wateville Rd. N17 . . . . . 25Sb 51
WATFORD 14Y 27
Watford Arches Retail Pk.
WD17: Wat 15Z 27
Watford By-Pass HA8: Edg 19Ma 29
WD6: E'tree 16Ja 28
Watford Cl. SW11 . . . . . 53Gb 111
Watford Ent. Cen. WD18: Wat 16U 26
Watford FC 15X 27
Watford Fld. Rd. WD18: Wat 15Y 27
Watford Health Campus
WD18: Wat 15X 27
WATFORD HEATH 17Z 27
Watford Heath WD19: Wat 17Z 27
Watford Heath Farm WD19: Wat 17Aa 27
Watford Ho. *RM3: Rom* *22Pd 57*
(off Redruth Rd.)
Watford Ho. La. WD17: Wat 13X 27
Watford Indoor Bowls Club 5Y 13
Watford Interchange WD24: Wat 11Y 27
Watford Leisure Cen.
Central 13W 26
Woodside 5Y 13
Watford Mus. 14Y 27
Watford Palace Theatre 13X 27
Watford Rd. AL1: St A 9N 5
AL2: Chis G 9N 5
E16 . . . . . 43Jc 93
HA0: Wemb 34Ja 66
HA1: Harr 31Ja 66
HA6: Nwood 24V 44
WD3: Crox G 16Q 26
WD4: Hunt C, K Lan 2Q 12
WD6: E'tree 16Ka 28
WD7: R'lett 8Ga 14
Watford Way NW4 . . . . . 28Wa 48
NW7 . . . . . 21Ua 48
Watkin M. EN3: Enf L 9Cc 20
Watkin Rd. HA9: Wemb 34Ra 67
Watkins Cl. HA6: Nwood 25V 44
Watkins Ho. *E14* *47Ec 92*
(off Manchester Rd.)
Watkinson Rd. N7 . . . . . 37Pb 70
Watkins Ri. EN6: Pot B 4Db 17
Watkins Way RM8: Dag 32Ad 75
WATLING 24Ta 47
Watling Av. HA8: Edg 25Sa 47
Watling Ct. EC4 . . . . . 3E 224
WD6: E'tree 16Ma 29
Watling Farm Cl. HA7: Stan 18La 28
Watling Gdns. NW2 . . . . . 37Ab 68
Watling Ga. NW9 . . . . . 28Ua 48
Watling Ho. *AL3: St A* *4P 5*
(off King Harry La.)
SE1 . . . . . 5E 230
Watling Knoll WD7: R'lett 5Ha 14
Watling Mans. WD7: R'lett 7Ka 14
Watlings Cl. CR0: C'don 72Ac 158
Watling St. AL1: St A 4A 6
AL2: Park 7B 6
DA1: Cray 57Fd 118
DA1: Dart 59Qd 119
(The Brent)
DA1: Dart 58Kd 119
(Broomhill Rd.)
DA2: Bean, Dart 60Td 120
DA6: Bex 56Dd 118
DA11: Grav'nd 4D 144
DA11: Nflt 61De 143
DA12: Cobh, Grav'nd 7J 145
EC4 . . . . . 3D 224 (44Sb 91)
SE15 . . . . . 51Ub 113
WD6: E'tree 3Ha 14
WD7: R'lett 3Ha 14
(Harper La.)
WD7: R'lett 9Ja 14
(Loom La.)
Watling St. Cvn. Pk. AL2: Park 7A 6
Watlington Gdns. CM14: Gt War 23Xd 58
Watlington Gro. SE26 . . . . . 64Ac 136
Watling Vw. AL1: St A 5A 6
Watney Cl. CR8: Purl 85Pb 176
Watney Cotts. SW14 . . . . . 55Sa 109
Watney Mkt. E1 . . . . . 44Xb 91
Watney Rd. SW14 . . . . . 55Sa 109
Watney's Rd. CR4: Mitc 71Mb 156
Watney St. E1 . . . . . 44Xb 91
Watson Av. E6 . . . . . 38Qc 74
SM3: Cheam 75Ab 154
Watson Cl. N16 . . . . . 36Tb 71
RM20: W Thur 53Wd 120
SW19 . . . . . 65Gb 133
Watson Ct. *E3* *41Cc 92*
(off Campbell Rd.)
WD18: Wat 15X 27
Watson Gdns. RM3: Hrld W 26Md 57
Watson Ho. RH2: Reig 5J 207
Watson Pl. SE25 . . . . . 71Vb 157
Watsons Ho. N1 . . . . . 1J 219
Watson's M. W1 . . . . . 1E 220 (43Gb 89)
Watsons Rd. N22 . . . . . 25Pb 50
Watsons St. SE8 . . . . . 52Cc 114
Watson St. E13 . . . . . 40Kc 73
Watson's Wlk. AL1: St A 3C 6
Watsons Yd. BR6: Orp 73Xc 161
Watt Ct. W3 . . . . . 47Ua 88
Wattendon Rd.
CR8: Kenley 88Rb 177
Wattisfield Rd. E5 . . . . . 34Yb 72
WATTON'S GREEN 16Kd 39
Watts Bri. Rd. DA8: Erith 51Hd 118
Watt's Cl. KT20: Tad 94Za 194
Watts Cl. N15 . . . . . 29Ub 51
Watt's Cres. RM19: Purf 49Sd 98
Wattsdown Cl. E13 . . . . . 39Jc 73
Watts Farm Pde. *GU24: Chob* *2K 167*
(off Barnmead)
Watts Gro. E3 . . . . . 43Cc 92
Watts Ho. *W10* *43Ab 88*
(off Wornington Rd.)
Watt's La. KT20: Tad 94Za 194
Watts La. BR7: Chst 67Rc 138
TW11: Tedd 64Ja 130
Watts Lea GU21: Wok 7L 167
Watt's Mead KT20: Tad 94Za 194
Watts M. IG6: Ilf 27Tc 54
SW16 . . . . . 65Mb 134
Watts Point *E13* *39Jc 73*
(off Brooks Rd.)
Watts Rd. KT7: T Ditt 73Ja 152
Watts St. E1 . . . . . 46Xb 91
SE15 . . . . . 53Vb 113
Wat Tyler Ho. *N8* *27Nb 50*
(off Boyton Rd.)
Wat Tyler Rd. SE3 . . . . . 54Fc 115
SE10 . . . . . 54Ec 114
Wauthier Cl. N13 . . . . . 22Rb 51
Wave Ct. RM7: Rush G 30Gd 56
Wavel Ct. *CR0: C'don* *78Tb 157*
(off Hurst Rd.)
E1 . . . . . *46Yb 92*
(off Garnet St.)
Wavelengths Leisure Cen. 52Cc 114
Wavell Dr. DA15: Sidc 58Uc 116
Wavell Gdns. SL2: Slou 1D 80
Wavell Ho. AL1: St A 4F 6
N6 . . . . . *30Jb 50*
(off Hillcrest)
Wavel M. N8 . . . . . 28Mb 50
NW6 . . . . . 38Db 69
Wavel Pl. SE26 . . . . . 63Vb 135
Wavendene Av. TW20: Egh 66D 126
Wavendon Av. W4 . . . . . 50Ta 87
Waveney Av. SE15 . . . . . 56Xb 113
Waveney Cl. E1 . . . . . 46Wb 91
Waveney Ho. SE15 . . . . . 56Xb 113
Waverley Av. CR8: Kenley 88Ub 177
E4 . . . . . 21Bc 52
E17 . . . . . 27Fc 53
HA9: Wemb 36Pa 67
KT5: Surb 72Ra 153
SM1: Sutt 75Db 155
TW2: Whitt 60Ba 107
Waverley Cl. BR2: Brom 71Mc 159
E18 . . . . . 25Lc 53
KT8: W Mole 71Ca 151
UB3: Harl 49T 84
Waverley Ct. EN2: Enf 13Rb 33
GU22: Wok 90A 168
NW3 . . . . . 37Hb 69
NW6 . . . . . 38Ab 68
SE26 . . . . . 64Yb 136
Waverley Cres. RM3: Rom 24Ld 57
SE18 . . . . . 50Tc 94
Waverley Dr. GU25: Vir W 9L 125
KT16: Chert 76F 148
Waverley Gdns. E6 . . . . . 43Nc 94
HA6: Nwood 25W 44
IG6: Ilf 26Sc 54
IG11: Bark 40Uc 74
NW10 . . . . . 40Pa 67
RM16: Grays 47Ce 99
Waverley Gro. N3 . . . . . 27Za 48
Waverley Ind. Est. HA1: Harr 27Fa 46
Waverley Lodge *AL3: St A* *1B 6*
(off Falmouth Ct.)
E15 . . . . . *37Gc 73*
(off Litchfield Av.)
Waverley Pl. KT22: Lea 94Ka 192
N4 . . . . . 33Rb 71
NW8 . . . . . 1B 214 (40Fb 69)
Waverley Rd. AL3: St A 1B 6
E17 . . . . . 27Ec 52
E18 . . . . . 25Lc 53
EN2: Enf 13Rb 33
HA2: Harr 33Aa 65
KT11: Stoke D, Oxs 86Da 171
KT13: Weyb 78Q 150
KT17: Ewe 78Xa 154
KT22: Oxs 86Da 171
N8 . . . . . 30Nb 50
N17 . . . . . 24Xb 51
RM13: Rain 42Kd 97
SE18 . . . . . 50Sc 94
SE25 . . . . . 70Xb 135
SL1: Slou 3G 80
UB1: S'hall 43Da 85
Waverley Vs. N17 . . . . . 26Vb 51
Waverley Way SM5: Cars 79Gb 155
Waverton Ho. E3 . . . . . 39Bc 72
Waverton Rd. SW18 . . . . . 59Eb 111
Waverton St. W1 . . . . . 6J 221 (46Jb 90)
Wavertree Ct. SW2 . . . . . 60Nb 112
Wavertree Rd. E18 . . . . . 26Jc 53
SW2 . . . . . 60Pb 112
Waxham NW3 . . . . . 36Hb 69
Waxhouse Ga. AL3: St A 2B 6
Waxlow Cres. UB1: S'hall 44Ca 85
Waxlow Ho. UB4: Yead 43Z 85
Waxlow Rd. NW10 . . . . . 40Sa 67
Waxlow Way UB5: N'olt 42Ba 85
Waxwell Cl. HA5: Pinn 26Z 45
Waxwell Farm Ho. HA5: Pinn 26Z 45
Waxwell La. HA5: Pinn 26Z 45
Way, The RH2: Reig 5M 207
Wayborne Gro. HA4: Ruis 30S 44
Waycross Rd. RM14: Upm 31Ud 78
Waye Av. TW5: Cran 53W 106
Wayfarer Rd. TW6: H'row A 54K 105
UB5: N'olt 41Z 85
Wayfaring Grn. RM17: Grays 50Be 99
Wayfield Link SE9 . . . . . 58Tc 116
Wayford St. SW11 . . . . . 54Gb 111
Wayland Av. E8 . . . . . 36Wb 71
Wayland Ho. *SW9* *54Qb 112*
(off Robsart St.)
Waylands BR8: Swan 70Hd 140
TW19: Wray 58A 104
UB3: Hayes 43T 84
Waylands Cl. TN14: Knock 88Ad 181
Waylands Mead BR3: Beck 67Dc 136
Waylen Gdns. DA1: Dart 54Pd 119
Waylett Ho. SE11 . . . . . 7K 229
Waylett Pl. HA0: Wemb 35Ma 67
SE27 . . . . . 62Rb 135
Wayman Ct. E8 . . . . . 37Xb 71
Wayne Cl. BR6: Orp 76Vc 161
Wayneflete M. KT12: Hers 77Aa 151
Wayneflete Pl. KT10: Esh 76Da 151
Wayneflete Twr. Av.
KT10: Esh 76Ca 151
Wayne Kirkum Way NW6 . . . . . 36Bb 69
Waynflete *SL4: Eton* *1G 102*
(off Eton Wick Rd.)
Waynflete Av. CR0: Wadd 76Rb 157
Waynflete Ho. *KT10: Esh* *77Da 151*
(off High St.)
SE1 . . . . . 7D 224
Waynflete Sq. W10 . . . . . 45Za 88
(not continuous)
Waynflete St. SW18 . . . . . 61Eb 133
Wayside CR0: New Ad 79Dc 158
EN6: Pot B 5Fb 17
NW11 . . . . . 32Ab 68
SW14 . . . . . 57Sa 109
WD4: Chfd 2K 11
WD7: Shenl 5Ma 15
Wayside, The HP3: Hem H 3C 4
Wayside Av. RM12: Horn 33Md 77
WD23: Bush 16Fa 28
Wayside Cl. N14 . . . . . 16Lb 32
RM1: Rom 27Hd 56
Wayside Commercial Est.
IG11: Bark 39Vc 75
Wayside Ct. AL2: Brick W 2Ba 13
GU21: Wok 8J 167
HA9: Wemb 34Qa 67
TW1: Twick 56La 108
Wayside Gdns. RM10: Dag 36Cd 76
SL9: Ger X 1P 61
Wayside Gro. SE9 . . . . . 63Pc 138
Wayside M. IG2: Ilf 29Qc 54
Wayville Rd. DA1: Dart 59Rd 119
Way Volante DA12: Grav'nd 3G 144
Weald, The BR7: Chst 65Pc 138
Weald Cl. BR2: Brom 75Nc 160
CM14: B'wood 20Wd 40
DA13: Ist R 6A 144
SE16 . . . . . 50Xb 91
Weald Country Pk. 17Td 40
Weald Country Pk. Vis. Cen. 18Td 40
Wealden Ho. *E3* *41Dc 92*
(off Talwin St.)
Wealden Pl. TN13: S'oaks 93Ld 203
Weald La. HA3: Hrw W 26Fa 46
Weald Pk. Golf Course 15Qd 39
Weald Pk. Way CM14: S Weald 20Ud 40
Weald Ri. HA3: Hrw W 24Ha 46
Weald Rd.
CM14: B'wood, S Weald 18Qd 39
TN13: S'oaks 100Kd 203
UB10: Hil 40Q 64
Weald Sq. E5 . . . . . 33Wb 71
WEALDSTONE 27Ga 46
Wealdstone Cen., The *27Ga 46*
(off High St.)
Wealdstone FC 33V 64
Wealdstone Rd. SM3: Sutt 75Bb 155
Weald Way CR3: Cat'm 100Ub 197
RH2: Reig 10L 207
RM7: Rom 30Dd 56
UB4: Hayes 41U 84
Wealdwood Gdns. HA5: Hat E 23Da 45
Weale Rd. E4 . . . . . 20Fc 35
Weall Cl. CR8: Purl 84Pb 176
Weall Ct. HA5: Pinn 28Aa 45
Weall Grn. WD25: Wat 4X 13
Weardale Av. DA2: Dart 61Sd 142
Weardale Gdns. EN2: Enf 11Tb 33
Weardale Rd. SE13 . . . . . 56Fc 115
Wearmouth Ho. *E3* *42Bc 92*
(off Joseph St.)
Wear Pl. E2 . . . . . 41Xb 91
(not continuous)
Wearside Rd. SE13 . . . . . 56Dc 114
Weasdale Ct. GU21: Wok 8K 167
Weatherall Cl. KT15: Add 78K 149
Weatherbury *W2* *44Cb 89*
(off Talbot Rd.)
Weatherbury Ho. *N19* *34Mb 70*
(off Wedmore St.)
Weatherley Cl. E3 . . . . . 43Bc 92
Weaver Ct. RM1: Rom 29Jd 56
Weaver Cl. CR0: C'don 77Vb 157
E6 . . . . . 45Rc 94
Weaver Ho. *E1* *42Wb 91*
(off Pedley St.)
Weavers Almshouses *E11* *30Hc 53*
(off Cambridge Rd.)
Weavers Cl. DA11: Grav'nd 10C 122
TW7: Isle 56Ga 108
Weavers Ho. *E11* *30Jc 53*
(off New Wanstead)
Weavers La. SE1 . . . . . 7J 225 (46Ub 91)
TN14: S'oaks 93Ld 203
Weavers Orchard
DA13: Sflt 65Ce 143
Weavers Row E20 . . . . . 36Dc 72
Weavers Ter. *SW6* *51Cb 111*
(off Micklethwaite Rd.)
Weaver St. E1 . . . . . 42Wb 91
(not continuous)
Weavers Way NW1 . . . . . 39Mb 70
Weaver Wlk. SE27 . . . . . 63Sb 135
Webb Cl. SL3: L'ly 9P 81
W10 . . . . . 42Ya 88
Webb Ct. *SE28* *45Xc 95*
(off Attlee Rd.)
Webber Cl. DA8: Erith 52Kd 119
WD6: E'tree 16Ma 29
Webber Ho. *IG11: Bark* *38Sc 74*
(off North St.)
Webber Pth. *E14* *45Ec 92*
(off Bullivant St.)
Webber Row SE1 . . . . . 2A 230 (47Rb 91)
Webber St. SE1 . . . . . 1A 230 (47Qb 90)
Webb Est. E5 . . . . . 31Wb 71
Webb Gdns. E13 . . . . . 42Jc 93
Webb Ho. *E3* *41Cc 92*
(off Trevithick Way)
RM10: Dag *34Cd 76*
(off Kershaw Rd.)
SW8 . . . . . 52Mb 112
TW13: Hanw 62Aa 129
Webb Pl. NW10 . . . . . 41Va 88
Webb Rd. SE3 . . . . . 51Hc 115
Webb's All. TN13: S'oaks 97Ld 203
(not continuous)
Webbscroft Rd. RM10: Dag 35Dd 76
Webbs Mdw. TN13: S'oaks 97Ld 203
Webb's Rd. SW11 . . . . . 56Hb 111
Webbs Rd. UB4: Yead 41X 85
Webb St. SE1 . . . . . 4H 231 (48Ub 91)
Webheath NW6 . . . . . 38Bb 69
(not continuous)
Webley Ct. *EN3: Enf L* *9Cc 20*
(off Sten Cl.)
Webster Cl. EN9: Walt A 5Hc 21
KT22: Oxs 86Da 171
RM12: Horn 34Md 77
Webster Ct. WD3: Rick 18N 25
Webster Gdns. W5 . . . . . 46Ma 87
Webster Rd. E11 . . . . . 34Ec 72
SE16 . . . . . 48Wb 91
SS17: Stan H 1N 101
Websters Cl. GU22: Wok 2M 187
Weddell Ho. *E1* *42Zb 92*
(off Duckett St.)
Wedderburn Ho. SW1 . . . . . 7H 227
Wedderburn Rd. IG11: Bark 39Uc 74
NW3 . . . . . 36Fb 69
Wedgewood Cl. CM16: Epp 2Wc 23
HA6: Nwood 24S 44
Wedgewood Ct. *BR2: Brom* *69Hc 137*
(off Cumberland Rd.)
DA5: Bexl 59Cd 118
Wedgewood Ho. *SW1* *50Kb 90*
(off Churchill Gdns.)
Wedgwood Ct. N7 . . . . . 35Pb 70
Wedgwood Ho. *E2* *41Zb 92*
(off Warley St.)
SE11 . . . . . 4K 229
Wedgwood M. W1 . . . . . 3E 222 (44Mb 90)
Wedgwood Pl. KT11: Cobh 85W 170
Wedgwoods TN16: Tats 93Lc 199
Wedgwood Wlk. *NW6* *36Db 69*
(off Dresden Cl.)
Wedgwood Way SE19 . . . . . 66Sb 135
Wedlake Cl. RM11: Horn 32Nd 77
Wedlake St. W10 . . . . . 42Ab 88
Wedmore Av. IG5: Ilf 25Qc 54
Wedmore Gdns. N19 . . . . . 33Mb 70
Wedmore M. N19 . . . . . 34Mb 70
Wedmore Rd. UB6: G'frd 41Fa 86
Wedmore St. N19 . . . . . 34Mb 70
Wednesbury Gdns. RM3: Rom 24Pd 57
Wednesbury Grn. RM3: Rom 24Pd 57
Wednesbury Rd. RM3: Rom 24Pd 57
Weech Rd. NW6 . . . . . 35Cb 69
Weedington Rd. NW5 . . . . . 36Jb 70
Weedon Ho. W12 . . . . . 44Wa 88
Weekes Dr. SL1: Slou 6F 80
Weekley Sq. SW11 . . . . . 55Fb 111
Weelkes Cl. SS17: Stan H 1L 101
Weigall Rd. SE12 . . . . . 57Jc 115
Weighhouse St. W1 . . . . . 4J 221 (44Jb 90)
Weightman Ho. SE16 . . . . . 48Wb 91
Weighton M. SE20 . . . . . 68Xb 135
Weighton Rd. HA3: Hrw W 25Fa 46
SE20 . . . . . 68Xb 135
Weihurst Ct. SM1: Sutt 78Gb 155
Weihurst Gdns. SM1: Sutt 78Fb 155
Weimar St. SW15 . . . . . 55Ab 110
Weind, The CM16: They B 8Uc 22
Weint, The SL3: Coln 52E 104
Weir Ct. KT13: Weyb 75R 150
Weirdale Av. N20 . . . . . 19Hb 31
Weird Wood DA3: Lfield 69Ee 143
Weir Hall Av. N18 . . . . . 23Tb 51
Weir Hall Gdns. N18 . . . . . 22Tb 51
Weir Hall Rd. N17 . . . . . 22Tb 51
N18 . . . . . 22Tb 51
Weir Pl. TW18: Staines 67G 126
Weir Rd. DA5: Bexl 59Dd 118
KT12: Walt T 72W 150
KT16: Chert 73K 149
SW12 . . . . . 59Lb 112
SW19 . . . . . 62Db 133
Weirside Gdns. UB7: W Dray 46M 83
Weir's Pas. NW1 . . . . . 3E 216 (41Mb 90)
Weiss Rd. SW15 . . . . . 55Za 110
Welbeck Av. BR1: Brom 63Jc 137
DA15: Sidc 60Wc 117
UB4: Yead 42X 85
Welbeck Cl. KT3: N Mald 71Va 154
KT17: Ewe 80Wa 154
N12 . . . . . 22Fb 49
WD6: Bore 13Qa 29
Welbeck Ct. UB4: Yead 42X 85
W14 . . . . . *49Bb 89*
(off Addison Bri. Pl.)
Welbeck Ho. W1 . . . . . 2K 221
Welbeck Rd. E6 . . . . . 41Mc 93
EN4: E Barn 16Gb 31
HA2: Harr 32Da 65
SM1: Sutt 75Fb 155
SM5: Cars 75Fb 155
Welbeck St. W1 . . . . . 1J 221 (43Jb 90)
Welbeck Vs. N21 . . . . . 19Sb 33
Welbeck Wlk. SM5: Cars 74Fb 155
Welbeck Way W1 . . . . . 2K 221 (44Kb 90)
Welbury Ct. *E8* *38Ub 71*
(off Kingsland Rd.)
Welby Ho. N19 . . . . . 31Mb 70
Welby St. SE5 . . . . . 53Rb 113
Welch Pl. HA5: Pinn 25Y 45
Welclose St. AL3: St A 2A 6
Welcombes Vw. CR5: Coul 88Kb 176
Welcome Ct. *E17* *31Cc 72*
(off Saxon Cl.)
SS17: Stan H 2L 101
Welcomes Cotts. CR3: Wold 95Cc 198
Welcomes Rd. CR8: Kenley 89Tb 177
Welcomes Ter. CR3: Whyt 88Vb 177
Welcote Dr. HA6: Nwood 23T 44
Welden SL2: Slou 4N 81
Weldin M. *SW18* *57Cb 111*
(off Lebanon Rd.)
WELDON 60Be 121
Weldon Cl. HA4: Ruis 37X 65
Weldon Ct. N21 . . . . . 15Pb 32
Weldon Dr. KT8: W Mole 70Ba 129
Weldon Rd. DA10: Swans 59Be 121
Weldon Way RH1: Mers 1D 208
Weld Pl. N11 . . . . . 22Kb 50
(not continuous)
Weld Works M. SW2 . . . . . 58Pb 112
Welfare Rd. E15 . . . . . 38Gc 73
Welford Cl. E5 . . . . . 34Zb 72
Welford Ct. *NW1* *38Kb 70*
(off Castlehaven Rd.)
SW8 . . . . . 54Lb 112
W9 . . . . . *43Cb 89*
(off Elmfield Way)
Welford Ho. *UB5: N'olt* *42Ba 85*
(off Waxlow Way)
Welford Pl. SW19 . . . . . 63Ab 132
Welham Cl. AL9: Wel G 6E 8
WD6: Bore 11Qa 29
Welham Ct. *AL9: Wel G* *6E 8*
(off Dixons Hill Rd.)
WELHAM GREEN 6E 8
Welham Mnr. AL9: Wel G 6E 8
Welham Rd. SW16 . . . . . 65Kb 134
SW17 . . . . . 64Jb 134
Welhouse Rd. SM5: Cars 74Gb 155
Welkin Grn. HP2: Hem H 1C 4
Wellacre Rd. HA3: Kenton 30Ka 46
Wellan Cl. DA15: Sidc 57Xc 117
Welland RM18: E Til 9L 101
Welland Cl. SL3: L'ly 51D 104
Welland Ct. *SE6* *61Bc 136*
(off Oakham Cl.)
Welland Gdns. UB6: G'frd 40Ha 66
Welland Ho. SE15 . . . . . 56Yb 114
Welland M. E1 . . . . . 46Wb 91
Welland Rd. TW6: H'row A 54K 105
Wellands Cl. BR1: Brom 68Pc 138
Welland St. SE10 . . . . . 51Ec 114
Well App. EN5: Barn 15Ya 30
Wellbrook Rd. BR6: Farnb 77Qc 160
Wellbury Ter. HP2: Hem H 2C 4
Wellby Cl. N9 . . . . . 18Wb 33
Wellby Ct. E13 . . . . . 39Lc 73
Well Cl. GU21: Wok 9N 167
HA4: Ruis 34Aa 65
SW16 . . . . . 63Pb 134
Wellclose Sq. E1 . . . . . 45Wb 91
(not continuous)
Wellclose St. E1 . . . . . 45Wb 91
Wellcome Av. DA1: Dart 56Nd 119
Wellcome Collection 5D 216
Wellcome Mus., The *2J 223*
(within Royal College of Surgeons)
Well Cott. Cl. E11 . . . . . 30Lc 53
Well Ct. EC4 . . . . . 3E 224 (44Sb 91)
(not continuous)
Wellcroft HP1: Hem H 1K 3
Wellcroft Rd. SL1: Slou 6F 80
Wellday Ho. *E9* *37Ac 72*
(off Hedger's Gro.)
Welldon Ct. HA1: Harr 29Ga 46
Welldon Cres. HA1: Harr 29Ga 46
WELL END 10Ta 15
Well End Rd. WD6: Bore 9Sa 15
Wellen Ri. HP3: Hem H 5N 3
Weller Ct. *W11* *46Bb 89*
(off Ladbroke Rd.)
Weller Ho. *SE16* *47Wb 91*
(off George Row)
Weller M. BR2: Brom 70Kc 137
EN2: Enf 11Qb 32
Weller Pl. BR6: Downe 83Qc 180
Wellers Cl. TN16: Westrm 99Sc 200
Weller St. SE1 . . . . . 1D 230 (47Sb 91)
Welles Ct. *E14* *45Cc 92*
(off Premiere Pl.)
Wellesford Cl. SM7: Bans 89Bb 175
Wellesley Av. HA6: Nwood 22V 44
SL0: Rich P 48H 83
W6 . . . . . 48Xa 88
Wellesley Cl. SE7 . . . . . 50Lc 93
Wellesley Cnr. DA11: Nflt 60De 121
Wellesley Ct. NW2 . . . . . 33Wa 68
SE1 . . . . . *4D 230*
(off Rockingham St.)
SL0: Rich P 47H 83
SM3: Sutt 74Ab 154
W9 . . . . . 3A 214 (41Eb 89)
Wellesley Ct. Rd. CR0: C'don 75Tb 157
Wellesley Cres. EN6: Pot B 5Ab 16
TW2: Twick 61Ga 130
Wellesley Gro. CR0: C'don 75Tb 157
Wellesley Ho. NW1 . . . . . 4D 216
SL4: Wind *3F 102*
(off Vansittart Rd.)
SW1 . . . . . 7K 227
Wellesley Mans. *W14* *50Bb 89*
(off Edith Vs.)
Wellesley Pde. TW2: Twick 62Ga 130
Wellesley Pk. M. EN2: Enf 12Rb 33
Wellesley Pas. CR0: C'don 75Sb 157
Wellesley Path SL1: Slou 7L 81
Wellesley Pl. NW1 . . . . . 4D 216 (41Mb 90)
NW5 . . . . . 36Jb 70
Wellesley Rd. CM14: B'wood 18Yd 40
CR0: C'don 74Sb 157
E11 . . . . . 29Jc 53
E17 . . . . . 30Cc 52
HA1: Harr 29Ga 46
IG1: Ilf 33Rc 74
N22 . . . . . 26Qb 50
NW5 . . . . . 36Jb 70
SE18 . . . . . 52Qc 116
SL1: Slou 6L 81
SM2: Sutt 79Eb 155
(not continuous)
TW2: Twick 62Fa 130
W4 . . . . . 50Qa 87
Wellesley St. E1 . . . . . 43Zb 92
Wellesley Ter. N1 . . . . . 3E 218 (41Sb 91)
Welley Av. TW19: Wray 56A 104
Welley Rd. SL3: Hort 58A 104
TW19: Wray 58A 104
Well Farm Hgts.
CR3: Whyt 91Wb 197
Well Farm Rd. CR6: W'ham 91Wb 197
Wellfield DA3: Hartl 70Be 143
Wellfield Av. N10 . . . . . 27Kb 50
Wellfield Gdns. SM5: Cars 81Gb 175
Wellfield Rd. SW16 . . . . . 63Nb 134
Wellfields IG10: Lough 13Qc 36
Wellfield Wlk. SW16 . . . . . 63Pb 134
Wellfit St. SE24 . . . . . 55Rb 113
Wellgarth UB6: G'frd 37Ka 66
Wellgarth Rd. NW11 . . . . . 32Db 69
Well Gro. N20 . . . . . 18Eb 31
Well Hall Pde. SE9 . . . . . 56Pc 116
Well Hall Rd. SE9 . . . . . 55Nc 116
WELL HALL RDBT. 56Nc 116
WELL HILL 79Dd 162
Well Hill BR6: Well H 79Dd 162
Well Hill La. BR6: Well H 79Dd 162
Well Ho. SM7: Bans 87Db 175

Wellhouse La.—Westdene

Wellhouse La. EN5: Barn 14Ya 30
RH3: Bet 10A 206
Wellhouse Rd. BR3: Beck 70Cc 136
Wellhurst Cl. BR6: Chels 80Vc 161
WELLING 55Xc 117
Wellingborough Ho.
RM3: Rom 22Pd 57
(off Redruth Rd.)
Welling High St. DA16: Well 55Xc 117
Welling Rd. RM16: Ors 4E 100
Wellings Ho. UB3: Hayes 46X 85
Wellington N8 28Nb 50
(not continuous)
Wellington Arch 1J 227
Wellington Av. DA15: Sidc 58Wc 117
E4 19Cc 34
GU25: Vir W 1M 147
HA5: Hat E 25Ba 45
KT4: Wor Pk 76Ya 154
N9 20Xb 33
N15 30Vb 51
TW3: Houn 57Ca 107
Wellington Bldgs. E3 41Cc 92
(off Wellington Way)
SW1 50Jb 90
Wellington Cl. KT12: Walt T 74V 150
RM10: Dag 38Ed 76
SE14 53Zb 114
W11 44Cb 89
WD19: Wat 20Ba 27
Wellington Ct. KT19: Eps 84Ta 173
NW8 2B 214
RM16: Grays 46De 99
SW1 2F 227
SW6 53Db 111
(off Maltings Pl.)
TW12: Hamp H 64Fa 130
TW15: Ashf 64N 127
TW19: Stanw 59N 105
Wellington Cres. KT3: N Mald 69Sa 131
Wellington Dr. CR8: Purl 82Pb 176
RM10: Dag 38Ed 76
Wellington Gdns. SE7 51Lc 115
TW2: Twick 63Fa 130
Wellington Gro. SE10 52Fc 115
Wellington Hill
IG10: H Beech, Lough 9Jc 21
Wellington Ho. E16 46Jc 93
(off Pepys Cres.)
NW3 37Hb 69
(off Eton Rd.)
RM2: Rom 28Ld 57
SE17 51Sb 113
(off Arnside St.)
UB5: N'olt 38Ca 65
(off The Farmlands)
W5 41Na 87
WD23: Bush 14Ba 27
WD24: Wat 12Y 27
(off Exeter Cl.)
Wellingtonia Av. RM4: Have B 21Ed 56
Wellingtonia Ho. KT15: Add 78J 149
Wellingtonia Pl. RH2: Reig 5J 207
Wellington Lodge SE1 2A 230
SL4: Wink 1A 124
Wellington Mans. E10 32Cc 72
SE7 50Lc 93
(off Wellington Gdns.)
W14 51Bb 111
(off Queen's Club Gdns.)
Wellington M. N7 37Pb 70
(off Roman Way)
SE7 51Lc 115
SE22 56Wb 113
SW16 62Mb 134
Wellington Monument 1J 227
Wellington Pde. DA15: Sidc 57Wc 117
Wellington Pk. Est. NW2 33Wa 68
Wellington Pas. E11 29Jc 53
Wellington Pl. CM14: W'ley 22Yd 58
KT11: Cobh 84Ca 171
N2 29Gb 49
NW8 3C 214 (41Fb 89)
Wellington Rd. AL1: St A 3F 6
AL2: Lon C 9H 7
BR2: Brom 70Lc 137
BR5: St M Cry 72Xc 161
CR0: C'don 73Rb 157
CR3: Cat'm 94Sb 197
DA1: Dart 58Ld 119
DA5: Bexl 57Zc 117
DA17: Belv 50Bd 95
E6 39Pc 74
E7 35Hc 73
E10 32Ac 72
E11 29Jc 53
E17 28Ac 52
EN1: Enf 15Ub 33
HA3: W'stone 27Ga 46
HA5: Hat E 25Ba 45
NW8 1C 214 (40Fb 69)
NW10 41Za 88
RM18: Tilb 4C 122
SW19 61Cb 133
TW2: Twick 64Fa 130
TW6: H'row A 55L 105
(off Whittle Rd.)
TW12: Hamp H 64Fa 130
TW14: Felt 57U 106
TW15: Ashf 64N 127
UB8: Uxb 39L 63
W5 48La 86
WD17: Wat 12X 27
Wellington Rd. Nth. TW4: Houn 55Ba 107
Wellington Rd. Sth. TW4: Houn 56Ba 107
Wellington Row E2 41Vb 91
Wellington Sq. N1 39Nb 70
SW3 7F 227 (50Hb 89)
Wellington St. DA12: Grav'nd 9E 122
SE18 49Qc 94
SL1: Slou 6K 81
WC2 4G 223 (45Pb 90)
Wellington Ter. E1 46Xb 91
GU21: Knap 10J 167
HA1: Harr 32Fa 66
N8 27Qb 50
(off Turnpike La.)
W2 45Cb 89
Wellington Way E3 41Cc 92
KT13: Weyb 82P 169
Welling United FC 55Yc 117
Welling Way DA16: Well 55Sc 116
SE9 55Sc 116
Well La. CM15: Pil H 13Vd 40
GU21: Wok 9N 167
RM16: N Stif 46Ae 99
SW14 57Sa 109
Wellmeade Dr. TN13: S'oaks 99Kd 203
Wellmeadow Rd. SE6 59Gc 115
SE13 58Gc 115
(not continuous)
W7 49Ja 86
Wellow Wlk. SM5: Cars 74Fb 155
Well Path GU21: Wok 9N 167
Well Pl. NW3 34Fb 69
Well Rd. EN5: Barn 15Ya 30
EN6: N'thaw 10N 9
NW3 34Fb 69
TN14: Otf 88Ld 183
WELLS, THE 86Qa 173
Wells, The N14 17Mb 32
Wells Cl. AL3: St A 1A 6
CR2: S Croy 78Ub 157
KT23: Bookh 96Ea 192
SL4: Wind 3E 102
UB5: N'olt 41Y 85
Wells Ct. BR2: Brom 68Fc 137
DA11: Nflt 60De 121
NW6 40Cb 69
(off Cambridge Av.)
WD17: Wat 15Y 27
Wells Dr. NW9 32Ta 67
Wellsfield WD23: Bush 15Aa 27
Wells Gdns. IG1: Ilf 31Nc 74
RM10: Dag 36Dd 76
RM13: Rain 37Hd 76
Wells Ga. Cl. IG8: Wfd G 21Jc 53
Wells Ho. BR1: Brom 64Kc 137
(off Pike Cl.)
EC1 3A 218
IG11: Bark 38Wc 75
(off Margaret Bondfield Av.)
KT18: Eps 86Qa 173
SE16 48Yb 92
(off Howland Est.)
W5 45Ma 87
(off Grove Rd.)
W10 42Ab 88
(off Wornington Rd.)
Wells Ho. Rd. NW10 43Ua 88
Wellside Cl. EN5: Barn 14Ya 30
Wellside Gdns. SW14 56Sa 109
Wells La. SL5: Asc 9A 124
TW3: Houn 55Da 107
Wells M. W1 1C 222 (43Lb 90)
Wellsmoor Gdns. BR1: Brom 69Qc 138
Wells Pk. Rd. SE26 62Wb 135
Wells Path UB4: Hayes 41U 84
Wells Pl. RH1: Mers 2B 208
SW18 59Eb 111
TN16: Westrm 99Sc 200
Wells Pl. Ind. Est. RH1: Mers 1B 208
Wellspring Cl. E14 43Ec 92
Wellspring Cres. HA9: Wemb 34Ra 67
Wellspring M. SE26 62Xb 135
Wellspring Way WD17: Wat 15Y 27
Wells Ri. NW8 1F 215 (39Hb 69)
Wells Rd. BR1: Brom 68Pc 138
KT18: Eps 86Qa 173
W12 47Ya 88
Wells Sq. WC1 4H 217 (41Pb 90)
Wells St. W1 1B 222 (43Lb 90)
Wellstead Av. N9 17Zb 34
Wellstead Rd. E6 40Qc 74
Wells Ter. N4 33Qb 70
Wellstones WD17: Wat 14X 27
Well St. E9 38Yb 72
E15 37Gc 73
Wells Vw. Dr. BR2: Brom 72Nc 160
Wells Way SE5 51Tb 113
SW7 3B 226 (48Fb 89)
Wellswood SL5: Asc 9A 124
Wellswood Cl. HP2: Hem H 1B 4
Wells Yd. N7 36Qb 70
WD17: Wat 13X 27
Well Wlk. NW3 35Fb 69
Well Way KT18: Eps 87Qa 173
Wellwood Cl. CR5: Coul 86Nb 176
Wellwood Rd. IG3: Ilf 32Wc 75
Welmar M. SW4 57Mb 112
(off Clapham Pk. Rd.)
Welsby Ct. W5 43La 86
Welsford St. SE1 49Wb 91
(not continuous)
Welsh Cl. E13 41Jc 93
Welsh Harp (Brent Reservoir)
Nature Reserve 32Va 68
Welsh Ho. E1 46Xb 91
(off Wapping La.)
Welshpool Ho. E8 39Wb 71
(off Welshpool St.)
Welshpool St. E8 39Wb 71
(not continuous)
Welshside NW9 30Ua 48
(off Ruthin Cl.)
Welshside Wlk. NW9 30Ua 48
Welstead Ho. E1 44Xb 91
(off Cannon St. Rd.)
Welstead Way W4 49Va 88
Weltje Rd. W6 49Wa 88
Welton Ct. SE5 53Ub 113
Welton Ho. E1 43Zb 92
(off Stepney Way)
Welton Rd. SE18 52Uc 116
Welwyn Av. TW14: Felt 58V 106
Welwyn St. E2 41Yb 92
Welwyn Way UB4: Hayes 42U 84
WEMBLEY 36Na 67
Wembley & Sudbury Tennis & Squash Club
36Ma 67
Wembley Cl. RM5: Col R 24Ed 56
Wembley Commercial Cen.
HA9: Wemb 33Ma 67
Wembley Hill Rd. HA9: Wemb 34Pa 67
(East La.)
HA9: Wemb 36Pa 67
(South Way)
WEMBLEY PARK 35Qa 67
Wembley Pk. Blvd. HA9: Wemb 35Qa 67
Wembley Pk. Bus. Cen.
HA9: Wemb 35Ra 67
Wembley Pk. Dr. HA9: Wemb 35Pa 67
Wembley Retail Pk. HA9: Wemb 35Ra 67
Wembley Rd. TW12: Hamp 67Ca 129
Wembley Sailing Club 33Ta 67
Wembley Stadium 35Qa 67
Wembley Stadium Ind. Est.
HA9: Wemb 35Ra 67
Wembley Way HA9: Wemb 37Ra 67
Wemborough Rd. HA7: Stan 25Ka 46
Wembury M. N6 31Lb 70
Wembury Rd. N6 31Kb 70
Wemyss Rd. SE3 54Hc 115
Wend, The CR5: Coul 86Mb 176
Wendela Cl. GU22: Wok 90B 168
Wendela Ct. HA1: Harr 33Ga 66
Wendell M. W12 47Va 88
Wendell Rd. W12 48Va 88
Wenderholme CR2: S Croy 78Tb 157
(off South Pk. Hill Rd.)
Wendle Ct. SW8 51Nb 112
Wendle Sq. SW11 53Gb 111
Wendley Dr. KT15: New H 82H 169
Wendling NW5 36Hb 69
Wendling Rd. SM1: Sutt 74Fb 155
Wendon St. E3 39Bc 72
Wendover SE17 7H 231 (50Ub 91)
(not continuous)
Wendover Cl. UB4: Yead 42Aa 85
Wendover Ct. BR2: Brom 69Kc 137
(off Wendover Rd.)
NW2 34Cb 69
NW10 42Ra 87
W1 1H 221
Wendover Dr. KT3: N Mald 72Va 154
Wendover Gdns. CM13: B'wood 19De 41
Wendover Ho. W1 1H 221
WD18: Wat 17U 26
(off Chenies Way)
Wendover Pl. TW18: Staines 64F 126
Wendover Rd. BR2: Brom 70Kc 137
NW10 40Va 68
SE9 55Mc 115
SL1: Burn 3A 80
TW18: Staines 64E 126
Wendover Way BR6: St M Cry 72Wc 161
DA16: Well 57Wc 117
RM12: Horn 36Ld 77
WD23: Bush 16Ea 28
Wendron Cl. GU21: Wok 10L 167
Wendy Cl. EN1: Enf 16Vb 33
Wendy Way HA0: Wemb 39Na 67
Wenham Gdns. CM13: Hut 16Ee 41
Wenham Ho. SW8 52Lb 112
Wenlack Cl. UB9: Den 34J 63
Wenlake Ho. EC1 5D 218
Wenlock Barn Est. N1 2F 219
Wenlock Ct. N1 2G 219 (40Tb 71)
Wenlock Gdns. NW4 28Xa 48
Wenlock M. E10 31Cc 72
Wenlock Rd. HA8: Edg 24Ra 47
N1 2D 218 (40Sb 71)
Wenlock St. N1 2E 218 (40Sb 71)
WENNINGTON 45Md 97
Wennington Rd. E3 40Zb 72
RM13: Rain, Wenn 42Jd 96
Wensdale Ho. E5 33Wb 71
Wensley Av. IG8: Wfd G 24Hc 53
Wensley Cl. N11 23Jb 50
RM5: Col R 22Cd 56
SE9 58Pc 116
Wensleydale Av. IG5: Ilf 26Nc 54
Wensleydale Gdns.
TW12: Hamp 66Da 129
Wensleydale Pas. TW12: Hamp 67Ca 129
Wensleydale Rd. TW12: Hamp 65Ca 129
Wensley Rd. N18 23Xb 51
Wensum Ct. WD3: Rick 18M 25
Wensum Pl. BR2: Hayes 73Jc 159
Wensum Way WD3: Rick 18M 25
Wenta Bus. Cen., The WD24: Wat 9Z 13
Wentbridge Path WD6: Bore 10Qa 15
Wentland Cl. SE6 61Fc 137
Wentland Rd. SE6 61Fc 137
Wentway Ct. W13 42Ha 86
(off Ruislip Rd. E.)
WENTWORTH 1K 147
Wentworth Av. N3 24Cb 49
SL2: Slou 1E 80
WD6: E'tree 15Pa 29
Wentworth Cl. BR2: Hayes 75Jc 159
BR6: Farnb 78Uc 160
DA11: Grav'nd 4C 144
EN6: Pot B 3Cb 17
GU23: Rip 93K 189
KT6: Surb 75Ma 153
N3 24Db 49
SE28 44Zc 95
SM4: Mord 73Cb 155
TW15: Ashf 63R 128
WD17: Wat 10V 12
Wentworth Ct. SW1 7K 227 (50Kb 90)
SW18 58Db 111
(off Garratt La.)
TW2: Twick 62Ga 130
W6 51Ab 110
(off Paynes Wlk.)
Wentworth Cres. SE15 52Wb 113
UB3: Harl 48T 84
Wentworth Dene KT13: Weyb 78R 150
Wentworth Dr. DA1: Dart 58Jd 118
GU25: Vir W 10K 125
HA5: Eastc 29W 44
TW6: H'row A 54K 105
WD19: Pinn, Wat 22Z 45
Wentworth Dwellings E1 2K 225
Wentworth Flds. UB4: Hayes 40T 64
Wentworth Gdns. N13 20Rb 33
Wentworth Golf Course (East Course)
2M 147
Wentworth Golf Course (Edinburgh Course)
4K 147
Wentworth Golf Course (West Course)
1K 147
Wentworth Hill HA9: Wemb 32Pa 67
Wentworth Ho. IG8: Wfd G 24Qc 54
KT15: Add 77K 149
Wentworth M. E3 42Ac 92
W3 44Ua 88
Wentworth Pk. N3 24Cb 49
Wentworth Pl. HA7: Stan 23Ka 46
RM16: Grays 48Fe 99
Wentworth Rd. CR0: C'don 73Qb 156
E12 35Mc 73
EN5: Barn 13Za 30
NW11 30Bb 49
SS17: Stan H 3K 101
UB2: S'hall 49Y 85
Wentworth St. E1 2K 225 (44Vb 91)
Wentworth Tennis & Health Club, The
1L 147
Wentworth Way CR2: Sande 86Wb 177
HA5: Pinn 28Aa 45
RM13: Rain 41Kd 97
Wenvoe Av. DA7: Bex 54Dd 118
Wepham Cl. UB4: Yead 43Z 85
Wernbrook St. SE18 51Sc 116
Werndee Rd. SE25 70Wb 135
Werneth Hall Rd. IG5: Ilf 27Qc 54
Werrington St. NW1 2C 216 (40Lb 70)
Werter Rd. SW15 56Ab 110
Wesco Ct. GU21: Wok 88C 168
Wescott Way UB8: Uxb 40L 63
Wesleyan Pl. NW5 35Kb 70
Wesley Apartments SW8 53Mb 112
Wesley Av. E16 46Jc 93
NW10 41Ta 87
TW3: Houn 54Aa 107
Wesley Cl. BR5: St P 69Yc 139
EN7: G Oak 1Sb 19
HA2: Harr 33Ea 66
KT19: Ewe 78Sa 153
N7 33Pb 70
RH2: Reig 7H 207
SE17 6C 230 (49Rb 91)
Wesley Ct. SE16 48Xb 91
Wesley Dr. TW20: Egh 65C 126
Wesley Ho. AL1: St A 2B 6
(off Marlborough Rd.)
Wesley Pl.
KT18: Tatt C 90Za 174
SL4: Wink 1A 124
Wesley Rd. E10 31Ec 72
KT22: Lea 95La 192
NW10 39Sa 67
UB3: Hayes 45W 84
Wesley's Chapel & Mus. of Methodism
5G 219 (42Tb 91)
Wesley's House 5G 219 (42Tb 91)
Wesley Sq. W11 44Ab 88
Wesley St. W1 1J 221 (43Jb 90)
Wessels KT20: Tad 93Za 194
Wesses Ter. CR4: Mitc 71Gb 155
Wessex Av. SW19 69Cb 133
Wessex Cl. IG3: Ilf 30Uc 54
KT1: King T 67Ra 131
KT7: T Ditt 75Ha 152
Wessex Ct. BR3: Beck 67Ac 136
EN5: Barn 14Za 30
HA9: Wemb 33Pa 67
TW19: Stanw 58N 105
Wessex Dr. DA8: Erith 54Gd 118
HA5: Hat E 24Aa 45
Wessex Gdns. NW11 32Ab 68
Wessex Ho. SE1 7K 231 (50Vb 91)
WD23: Bush 14Ba 27
Wessex La. RM3: Hrld W 25Pd 57
UB6: G'frd 41Fa 86
Wessex St. E2 41Yb 92
Wessex Wlk.
DA2: Wilm 61Gd 140
Wessex Way NW11 32Ab 68
Wesson Mead SE5 52Sb 113
(off Camberwell Rd.)
West 12 Shop. Cen. W12 47Za 88
Westacott UB4: Hayes 43U 84
Westacott Cl. N19 32Mb 70
West Acre HA2: Harr 33Ga 66
West Acres KT10: Esh 80Ba 151
WEST ACTON 44Qa 87
Westall Rd. IG10: Lough 13Rc 36
West App. BR5: Pet W 71Sc 160
W. Arbour St. E1 44Zb 92
West Av. AL2: Chis G 7P 5
E17 28Dc 52
HA5: Pinn 30Ba 45
KT12: W Vill 82U 170
N3 23Cb 49
NW4 29Za 48
SM6: Wall 78Nb 156
UB1: S'hall 45Ba 85
UB3: Hayes 45V 84
West Av. Rd. E17 28Cc 52
West Bank EN2: Enf 12Sb 33
IG11: Bark 39Rc 74
N16 31Ub 71
Westbank Rd. TW12: Hamp H 65Ea 130
WEST BARNES 71Xa 154
W. Barnes La. KT3: N Mald 69Xa 132
SW20 69Xa 132
WEST BECKTON 44Mc 93
WEST BEDFONT 58P 105
Westbeech Rd. N22 27Qb 50
Westbere Dr. HA7: Stan 22Ma 47
Westbere Rd. NW2 35Ab 68
West Block SE1 2H 229
Westbourne Apartments SW6 55Db 111
Westbourne Av. SM3: Cheam 75Ab 154
W3 44Ta 87
Westbourne Bri. W2 1A 220 (43Eb 89)
Westbourne Cl. UB4: Yead 42Y 85
Westbourne Ct. W2 2A 220 (43Eb 89)
Westbourne Cres. W2 4B 220 (45Fb 89)
Westbourne Cres. M. W2 4B 220
Westbourne Dr. CM14: B'wood 21Vd 58
SE23 61Zb 136
Westbourne Gdns. W2 44Db 89
WESTBOURNE GREEN 43Cb 89
Westbourne Gro. W2 44Cb 89
W11 45Bb 89
Westbourne Gro. M. W11 44Cb 89
Westbourne Gro. Ter. W2 44Db 89
Westbourne Ho. SW1 7K 227
TW5: Hest 51Ca 107
Westbourne M. AL1: St A 2B 6
Westbourne Pde. UB10: Hil 42R 84
Westbourne Pk. Pas. W2 43Cb 89
(off Harrow Rd.)
Westbourne Pk. Rd. W2 43Cb 89
W11 44Ab 88
Westbourne Pk. Vs. W2 43Cb 89
Westbourne Pl. N9 20Xb 33
Westbourne Rd. CR0: C'don 72Vb 157
DA7: Bex 52Zc 117
N7 37Pb 70
SE26 65Zb 136
TW13: Felt 62Y 128
TW18: Staines 66K 127
UB8: Hil 42R 84
Westbourne St. W2 4B 220 (45Fb 89)
Westbourne Ter. SE23 61Zb 136
(off Westbourne Dr.)
W2 2A 220 (44Eb 89)
Westbourne Ter. M. W2 2A 220 (44Eb 89)
Westbourne Ter. Rd.
W2 7A 214 (43Db 89)
Westbourne Ter. Rd. Bri. W2 7A 214
Westbridge Cl. W12 47Wa 88
Westbridge Ho. SW11 53Gb 111
(off Westbridge Rd.)
Westbridge Rd. SW11 53Fb 111
WEST BROMPTON 51Eb 111
Westbrook Av. TW12: Hamp 66Ba 129
Westbrook Cl. EN4: Cockf 13Fb 31
Westbrook Cres. EN4: Cockf 13Fb 31
Westbrook Dr. BR5: Orp 74Zc 161
Westbrooke Cres.
DA16: Well 55Yc 117
Westbrooke Rd. DA15: Sidc 61Tc 138
DA16: Well 55Xc 117
Westbrook Ho. E2 41Yb 92
(off Victoria Pk. Sq.)
Westbrook Rd. CR7: Thor H 67Tb 135
SE3 53Kc 115
TW5: Hest 52Ba 107
TW18: Staines 64H 127
Westbrook Sq. EN4: Cockf 13Fb 31
Westbury EN8: Chesh 2Zb 20
SL4: Eton 1G 102
(off Eton Wick Rd.)
Westbury Av. HA0: Wemb 38Na 67
KT10: Clay 79Ha 152
N22 27Rb 51
UB1: S'hall 42Ca 85
Westbury Cl. CR3: Whyt 90Vb 177
HA4: Ruis 31W 64
TW17: Shep 72R 150
Westbury Ct. IG11: Bark 39Tc 74
(off Ripple Rd.)
Westbury Dr. CM14: B'wood 19Yd 40
Westbury Gro. N12 23Cb 49
Westbury Ho. E17 28Bc 52
W11 43Cb 89
(off Aldridge Rd. Vs.)
Westbury La. IG9: Buck H 19Kc 35
Westbury Lodge Cl.
HA5: Pinn 27Z 45
Westbury Pde. SW12 58Kb 112
(off Balham Hill)
Westbury Pl. TW8: Bford 51Ma 109
Westbury Rd. BR1: Brom 67Mc 137
BR3: Beck 69Ac 136
CM14: B'wood 19Yd 40
CR0: C'don 72Tb 157
E7 37Kc 73
E17 28Bc 52
HA0: Wemb 38Na 67
HA6: Nwood 21U 44
IG1: Ilf 33Qc 74
IG9: Buck H 19Lc 35
IG11: Bark 39Tc 74
KT3: N Mald 70Ta 131
N11 23Nb 50
N12 23Cb 49
SE20 67Zb 136
TW13: Felt 60Z 107
W5 44Na 87
WD18: Wat 15X 27
Westbury Ter. E7 37Kc 73
RM14: Upm 33Ud 78
TN16: Westrm 99Sc 200
Westbush Ct. W12 47Xa 88
(off Goldhawk M.)
WEST BYFLEET 85J 169
West Byfleet Golf Course 85H 169
W. Cadet Apartments SE18 52Qc 116
(off Langhorne St.)
Westcar La. KT12: Hers 79X 151
W. Carriage Dr. W2 5D 220 (45Gb 89)
(North Ride)
W2 1C 226 (47Fb 89)
(Rotten Row)
W. Carriage Ho. SE18 48Rc 94
(off Royal Carriage M.)
W. Central St. WC1 2F 223 (44Nb 90)
West Chantry HA3: Hrw W 25Da 45
Westchester Dr. NW4 27Za 48
WEST CLANDON 100J 189
Westcliffe Apartments
W2 1C 220 (43Fb 89)
West Cl. EN4: Cockf 14Jb 32
EN5: Barn 15Xa 30
HA9: Wemb 32Pa 67
N9 20Vb 33
RM13: Rain 42Kd 97
TW12: Hamp 65Aa 129
TW15: Ashf 63N 127
UB6: G'frd 40Ea 66
Westcombe Av. CR0: C'don 73Nb 156
Westcombe Ct. SE3 52Hc 115
Westcombe Dr. EN5: Barn 15Cb 31
Westcombe Hill SE3 52Jc 115
SE10 52Jc 115
Westcombe Lodge Dr. UB4: Hayes 43U 84
Westcombe Pk. Rd. SE3 51Gc 115
West Comn. SL9: Ger X 29A 42
West Comn. Cl. SL9: Ger X 29A 42
West Comn. Rd.
BR2: Hayes, Kes 74Jc 159
UB8: Uxb 36M 63
Westcoombe Av. SW20 67Va 132
Westcote Ri. HA4: Ruis 31S 64
Westcote Rd. KT19: Eps 83Ra 173
SW16 64Lb 134
West Cotts. NW6 36Cb 69
Westcott Av. DA11: Nflt 2B 144
Westcott Cl. BR1: Brom 71Pc 160
CR0: New Ad 81Dc 178
N15 30Vb 51
Westcott Cres. W7 44Ga 86
Westcott Ho. E14 45Cc 92
Westcott Rd. SE17 51Rb 113
Westcott Way SM2: Cheam 82Ya 174
WESTCOURT 1F 144
West Ct. E17 28Cc 52
HA0: Wemb 33La 66
TW5: Isle 52Ea 108
Westcourt La. DA12: Grav'nd 10H 123
Westcourt Pde.
DA12: Grav'nd 2G 144
West Cres. SL4: Wind 3D 102
West Cres. Rd.
DA12: Grav'nd 8D 122
Westcroft SL2: Slou 2F 80
Westcroft Cl. EN3: Enf W 10Yb 20
NW2 35Ab 68
Westcroft Est. NW2 35Ab 68
Westcroft Gdns.
SM4: Mord 69Bb 133
Westcroft Leisure Cen. 77Jb 156
Westcroft Rd. SM5: Cars 77Jb 156
SM6: Wall 77Jb 156
Westcroft Sq. W6 49Wa 88
Westcroft Way NW2 35Ab 68
W. Cromwell Rd. SW5 50Bb 89
W14 50Bb 89
W. Cross Cen. TW8: Bford 51Ja 108
W. Cross Route W10 45Za 88
W11 45Za 88
W12 45Za 88
W. Cross Way TW8: Bford 51Ka 108
Westdale Pas. SE18 51Rc 116
Westdale Rd. SE18 51Rc 116
Westdean Av. SE12 60Kc 115
Westdean Cl. SW18 58Db 111
West Dene SM3: Cheam 79Ab 154
Westdene CR0: C'don 77Tb 157
(off Chatsworth Rd.)
CR8: Purl 85Pb 176
KT12: Hers 77X 151

W. Dene Dr.—West St.

W. Dene Dr. RM3: Rom 22Md 57
Westdene Way
KT13: Weyb 76U 150
West Down KT23: Bookh 99Da 191
Westdown Rd. E15 35Ec 72
SE6 59Cc 114
WEST DRAYTON 47N 83
W. Drayton Pk. Av.
UB7: W Dray 48N 83
W. Drayton Rd. UB8: Hil 44R 84
West Dr. GU25: Vir W 3J 147
(not continuous)
HA3: Hrw W 23Fa 46
KT15: New H 82K 169
KT20: Tad 90Za 174
SL5: S'dale, Vir W 1H 147
SM2: Cheam 81Za 174
SM5: Cars 82Fb 175
SW16 63Lb 134
WD25: Wat 8X 13
West Dr. Gdns.
HA3: Hrw W 23Fa 46
WEST DULWICH 61Tb 135
WEST EALING 46Ka 86
W. Ealing Bus. Cen. W13 45Ja 86
W. Eaton Pl. SW1 5H 227 (49Jb 90)
W. Eaton Pl. M. SW1 5H 227
Wested La.
BR8: Crock, Swan 73Jd 162
(not continuous)
W. Ella Rd. NW10 38Ua 68
W. Elms Studios SW8 53Lb 112
WEST END
GU24 4D 166
KT10 79Ba 151
UB5 40Z 65
West End TN15: Kems'g 89Pd 183
TN16: Bras 97Xc 201
W. End Av. E10 29Fc 53
HA5: Pinn 28Z 45
W. End Cl. NW10 38Sa 67
West End Common (Local Nature Reserve)
80Aa 151
W. End Ct. HA5: Pinn 28Z 45
NW6 38Db 69
SL2: Stoke P 9K 61
W. End Gdns. KT10: Esh 78Ba 151
UB5: N'olt 40Y 65
W. End La. AL9: Ess, Hat 1L 9
EN5: Barn 14Za 30
HA5: Pinn 27Z 45
KT10: Esh 80Ba 151
NW6 36Cb 69
(not continuous)
SL2: Stoke P 9J 61
UB3: Harl 52S 106
W. End Quay W2 1C 220
W. End Rd. HA4: Ruis 33U 64
UB1: S'hall 46Aa 85
UB5: N'olt 38Y 65
Westerdale Ct. *N5* 35Rb 71
(off Hamilton Pk. W.)
Westerdale Rd. SE10 50Jc 93
Westerfield Rd. N15 29Vb 51
Westerfolds Cl. GU22: Wok 89E 168
Westergate W5 43Na 87
Westergate Ho. *KT1: King T* 70Ma 131
(off Portsmouth Rd.)
Westergate Rd. SE2 51Ad 117
WESTERHAM 98Tc 200
Westerham NW1 1C 216
Westerham Av. N9 20Tb 33
Westerham Cl. KT15: Add 79L 149
SM2: Sutt 82Cb 175
Westerham Dr. DA15: Sidc 58Xc 117
Westerham Golf Course 98Wc 201
WESTERHAM HILL 92Qc 200
Westerham Hill TN16: Westrm 93Rc 200
Westerham Ho. SE1 3G 231
Westerham Lodge *BR3: Beck* 66Cc 136
(off Park Rd.)
Westerham Rd. BR2: Kes 79Mc 159
E10 31Dc 72
RH8: Limp, Oxt 1K 211
TN13: Bes G 95Ed 202
TN14: Sund 95Dd 202
TN16: Westrm 100Nc 200
TN16: Westrm, Bras 97Vc 201
Westerham Trade Cen.
TN16: Westrm 97Tc 200
Westerley Cres. SE26 64Bc 136
Westerley Ware *TW9: Kew* 51Qa 109
(off Kew Grn.)
Westermain KT15: New H 82L 169
Western Av. CM14: B'wood 18Yd 40
CM16: Epp 4Vc 23
HA4: Ruis 37R 64
KT16: Chert 69J 127
NW11 30Za 48
RM2: Rom 26Ld 57
RM10: Dag 37Ed 76
TW20: Thorpe 69D 126
UB5: N'olt 38Z 65
UB6: G'frd 40Fa 66
UB9: Den 35L 63
UB10: Hil, Uxb 36Q 64
W3 42Pa 87
W5 42Pa 87
Western Av. Bus. Pk. W3 42Ra 87
Western Beach Apartments
E16 45Jc 93
Western Cl. KT16: Chert 69J 127
Western Ct. N3 23Cb 49
NW6 40Bb 69
RM1: Rom 29Gd 56
(off Chandlers Way)
W3 44Ta 87
Western Courtyard EC2 1J 225
WESTERN CROSS 60Xd 120
Western Cross Cl.
DA9: Ghithe 58Yd 120
Western Dr. TW17: Shep 72T 150
Western Gdns. CM14: B'wood 19Yd 40
W5 45Qa 87
Western Gateway E16 45Jc 93
Western Intl. Mkt. UB2: S'hall 49X 85
Western La. SW12 59Jb 112
Western Mans.
EN5: New Bar 15Db 31
(off Great Nth. Rd.)
Western M. W9 42Bb 89
Western Pde. EN5: New Bar 15Cb 31
RH2: Reig 9K 207
Western Pathway RM12: Horn 38Kd 77
RM13: Rain 38Kd 77
Western Perimeter Rd.
TW6: H'row A, Lford 54K 105
Western Pl. SE16 47Yb 92
Western Rd. CM14: B'wood 19Yd 40
CM16: Epp 4Vc 23
CR4: Mitc 67Fb 133
E13 40Lc 73
E17 29Ec 52
N2 28Hb 49
N22 26Pb 50
NW10 42Sa 87
RM1: Rom 29Gd 56
SM1: Sutt 78Cb 155
SW9 55Qb 112
SW19 67Fb 133
TN15: Bor G 92Be 205
UB2: S'hall 49Y 85
W5 45Ma 87
Western Ter. DA1: Dart 58Kd 119
W6 50Wa 88
Western Transit Shed
N1 1F 217 (39Nb 70)
Western Vw. UB3: Hayes 47V 84
Westernville Gdns. IG2: Ilf 31Sc 74
Western Way EN5: Barn 16Cb 31
SE28 48Tc 94
West Essex Golf Course 14Gc 35
WEST EWELL 81Ta 173
W. Farm Av. KT21: Asht 90La 172
W. Farm Cl. KT21: Asht 91La 192
W. Farm Dr. KT21: Asht 91Ma 193
Westferry Cir. E14 46Bc 92
Westferry Rd. E14 45Bc 92
WESTFIELD 93A 188
Westfield AL9: Hat 5H 9
DA3: Nw A G 77Be 165
IG10: Lough 15Mc 35
KT21: Asht 90Pa 173
RH2: Reig 3K 207
TN13: S'oaks 94Ld 203
Westfield Av. CR2: Sande 85Tb 177
E20 37Dc 72
GU22: Wok 93A 188
WD24: Wat 9Y 13
Westfield Cl. DA12: Grav'nd 5E 144
EN3: Enf H 13Ac 34
EN8: Walt C 3Bc 20
GU22: Wok 93B 188
NW9 27Sa 47
SM1: Sutt 77Bb 155
SW10 52Eb 111
Westfield Comn. GU22: Wok 94A 188
Westfield Community Sports Cen. 15V 26
Westfield Ct. *KT6: Surb* 71Ma 153
(off Portsmouth Rd.)
NW10 41Za 88
(off Chamberlayne Rd.)
Westfield Dr. HA3: Kenton 28Ma 47
KT23: Bookh 94Ca 191
Westfield Gdns. HA3: Kenton 28Ma 47
RM6: Chad H 30Yc 55
Westfield Gro. GU22: Wok 92A 188
Westfield Ho. *SE16* 49Zb 92
(off Rotherhithe New Rd.)
SW10 52Fb 111
(off Cremorne Est.)
Westfield La. HA3: Kenton 29Ma 47
SL3: Geor G 4P 81
Westfield Pde. KT15: New H 82M 169
Westfield Pk. HA5: Hat E 24Ba 45
Westfield Pk. Dr. IG8: Wfd G 23Nc 54
Westfield Rd. BR3: Beck 68Bc 136
CR0: C'don 75Rb 157
CR4: Mitc 68Gb 133
DA7: Bex 55Ed 118
GU22: Wok 4P 187
KT6: Surb 71Ma 153
KT12: Walt T 73Aa 151
NW7 20Ta 29
RM9: Dag 35Ad 75
SL2: Slou 2F 80
SM1: Sutt 77Bb 155
W13 46Ja 86
Westfields AL3: St A 4N 5
SW13 55Va 110
Westfields Av. SW13 55Ua 110
Westfield Shop. Cen. E20 37Ec 72
W12 46Ya 88
Westfield Sq. GU22: Wok 94A 188
Westfields Rd. W3 43Ra 87
Westfield St. SE18 48Mc 93
Westfield Wlk. EN8: Walt C 3Bc 20
Westfield Way E1 41Ac 92
GU22: Wok 94A 188
HA4: Ruis 34U 64
West Gdn. Pl. W2 3E 220 (44Gb 89)
West Gdns. E1 45Xb 91
KT17: Ewe 82Ua 174
SW17 65Gb 133
Westgate W5 41Na 87
Westgate Apartments *E16* 45Jc 93
(off Western Gateway)
Westgate Cl. KT18: Eps 87Ta 173
Westgate Ct. EN8: Walt C 7Zb 20
SE12 60Jc 115
(off Burnt Ash Hill)
SW9 55Qb 112
(off Canterbury Cres.)
Westgate Cres. SL1: Slou 5D 80
Westgate Est. TW14: Bedf 60R 106
Westgate Ho. *KT18: Eps* 87Ta 173
(off Chalk La.)
TW7: Isle 54Fa 108
TW8: Bford 50Ma 87
(off Ealing Rd.)
West Ga. M. WD18: Wat 15U 26
Westgate M. *W10* 42Ab 88
(off West Row)
Westgate Retail Pk. SL1: Slou 5E 80
Westgate Rd. BR3: Beck 67Ec 136
DA1: Dart 58Md 119
SE25 70Xb 135
Westgate St. E8 39Xb 71
Westgate Ter. SW10 51Db 111
Westglade Ct. HA3: Kenton 29Ma 47
WEST GREEN 28Rb 51
West Grn. Pl. UB6: G'frd 39Fa 66
West Grn. Rd. N15 28Rb 51
West Gro. IG8: Wfd G 23Lc 53
KT12: Hers 78X 151
SE10 53Ec 114
Westgrove La. SE10 53Ec 114
W. Halkin St. SW1 3H 227 (48Jb 90)
West Hall KT14: W Byf 85M 169
West Hallowes SE9 60Mc 115
Westhall Pk. CR6: W'ham 91Yb 198
W. Hall Rd. TW9: Kew 53Ra 109
Westhall Rd. CR6: W'ham 90Wb 177
WEST HAM 39Hc 73
W. Ham La. E15 38Fc 73
WEST HAMPSTEAD 37Db 69
W. Hampstead M. NW6 37Db 69
West Ham Utd FC 39Dc 72
W. Handyside Canopy
N1 1F 217 (39Nb 70)
W. Harding St. EC4 2A 224 (44Qb 90)
West Harold BR8: Swan 69Fd 140
WEST HARROW 31Ea 66
W. Hatch Mnr. HA4: Ruis 32V 64
Westhay Gdns. SW14 57Ra 109
WEST HEATH
RH8 2L 211
SE2 51Zc 117
West Heath GU24: Pirb 5B 186
W. Heath Av. NW11 32Cb 69
W. Heath Cl. DA1: Cray 58Hd 118
NW3 34Cb 69
W. Heath Cotts.
TN13: S'oaks 100Kd 203
W. Heath Ct. NW11 32Cb 69
W. Heath Dr. NW11 32Cb 69
W. Heath Gdns. NW3 33Cb 69
W. Heath La. TN13: S'oaks 100Kd 203
W. Heath Rd. DA1: Cray 58Hd 118
NW3 33Cb 69
SE2 51Yc 117
WEST HENDON 31Wa 68
W. Hendon B'way. NW9 30Wa 48
W. Hertfordshire Crematorium
WD25: Wat 3Z 13
W. Herts Bus. Cen. *WD6: Bore* 13Ra 29
(off Eldon Av.)
West Herts Golf Course 13T 26
WEST HILL 58Bb 111
West Hill BR6: Downe 84Pc 180
CR2: Sande 82Ub 177
DA1: Dart 58Md 119
HA2: Harr 33Ga 66
HA9: Wemb 32Pa 67
KT19: Eps 85Ra 173
RH8: Oxt 2H 211
SW15 59Za 110
SW18 59Za 110
W. Hill Av. KT19: Eps 85Ra 173
West Hill Bank RH8: Oxt 2H 211
W. Hill Cl. GU24: Brkwd 2F 186
Westhill Cl. DA12: Grav'nd 10D 122
W. Hill Ct. *KT19: Eps* 85Sa 173
(off Court La.)
N6 34Jb 70
Westhill Ct. *W11* 45Bb 89
(off Denbigh Rd.)
W. Hill Dr. DA1: Dart 58Ld 119
West Hill Golf Course 2F 186
W. Hill Pk. N6 33Hb 69
(not continuous)
W. Hill Pl. RH8: Oxt 1J 211
Westhill Ri. DA1: Dart 58Md 119
W. Hill Rd. GU22: Wok 1P 187
SW18 58Bb 111
W. Hill Way N20 18Db 31
Westholm NW11 28Db 49
West Holme DA8: Erith 53Ed 118
Westholme BR6: Orp 73Uc 160
Westholme Gdns. HA4: Ruis 32W 64
Westhope Ho. *E2* 42Wb 91
(off Derbyshire St.)
WEST HORNDON 30Fe 59
Westhorne Av. SE9 57Mc 115
SE12 59Jc 115
Westhorpe Gdns. NW4 27Ya 48
Westhorpe Rd. SW15 55Ya 110
WEST HORSLEY 100R 190
West Ho. IG11: Bark 37Rc 74
West Ho. Cl. SW19 60Ab 110
West Ho. Cotts. HA5: Pinn 28Z 45
Westhurst Dr. BR7: Chst 64Rc 138
WEST HYDE 24G 42
West Hyde La. SL9: Chal P 24B 42
W. India Av. E14 46Cc 92
W. India Dock Rd. E14 45Bc 92
W. India Ho. *E14* 45Cc 92
(off W. India Dock Rd.)
WEST KENSINGTON 49Ab 88
W. Kensington Ct. *W14* 50Bb 89
(off Edith Vs.)
W. Kensington Mans. *W14* 50Bb 89
(off Beaumont Cres.)
W. Kent Av. DA11: Nflt 58Ee 121
West Kent Golf Course 84Nc 180
WEST KILBURN 41Bb 89
Westking Pl. WC1 4H 217 (41Pb 90)
WEST KINGSDOWN 79Ud 164
W. Kingsdown Ind. Est.
TN15: W King 81Ud 184
Westlake *SE16* 49Yb 92
(off Rotherhithe New Rd.)
Westlake Cl. N13 20Qb 32
UB4: Yead 42Aa 85
Westlake Rd. HA9: Wemb 33Ma 67
Westland Av. RM11: Horn 32Nd 77
Westland Cl. TW19: Stanw 58N 105
WD25: Wat 6V 12
Westland Ct. *UB5: N'olt* 41Z 85
(off Seasprite Cl.)
Westland Dr. AL9: Brk P 9G 8
BR2: Hayes 75Hc 159
Westland Ho. *E16* 46Qc 94
(off Rymill St.)
Westland Pl. N1 3F 219 (41Tb 91)
Westland Rd. WD17: Wat 12X 27
Westlands Av. SL1: Slou 4A 80
Westlands Cl. SL1: Slou 4A 80
UB3: Harl 49W 84
Westlands Ct. KT8: E Mos 70Fa 130
KT18: Eps 87Sa 173
Westlands Est. UB3: Harl 48U 84
Westlands Ter. SW12 58Lb 112
Westlands Way RH8: Oxt 99Fc 199
Westland Vw. RM16: Grays 46Ce 99
West La. SE16 47Xb 91
West Lawn WD25: A'ham 8Da 13
Westlea Av. WD25: Wat 8Aa 13
Westlea Rd. W7 48Ja 86
Westleigh Av. CR5: Coul 88Jb 176
SW15 57Xa 110
Westleigh Ct. *CR2: S Croy* 77Ub 157
(off Birdhurst Rd.)
E11 29Jc 53
(off Nightingale La.)
Westleigh Dr. BR1: Brom 67Nc 138
Westleigh Gdns. HA8: Edg 25Qa 47
West Links HA0: Wemb 41Ma 87
Westlinton Cl. NW7 23Ab 48
West Lodge *E16* 46Jc 93
(off Britannia Ga.)
W. Lodge Av. W3 46Qa 87
W. Lodge Ct. W3 46Qa 87
W. London Crematorium NW10 42Xa 88
W. London Studios *SW6* 52Db 111
(off Fulham Rd.)
Westlyn Cl. RM13: Rain 42Ld 97
Westmacott Dr. TW14: Felt 60V 106
Westmacott Ho. NW8 6C 214
West Mall N9 20Wb 33
RM17: Grays 51Ce 121
(off Grays Shop. Cen.)
W8 46Cb 89
(off Kensington Mall)
W. Malling Way RM12: Horn 36Ld 77
Westmark Point *SW15* 60Xa 110
(off Norley Va.)
West Mead HA4: Ruis 35Y 65
KT19: Ewe 79Ua 154
Westmead GU21: Wok 9M 167
SL4: Wind 5F 102
SW15 58Xa 110
Westmead Cnr. SM5: Cars 77Gb 155
Westmead Ct. SE6 58Cc 114
Westmeade Cl. EN7: Chesh 1Xb 19
Westmead Ho. SM1: Sutt 77Fb 155
Westmead Rd. SM1: Sutt 77Fb 155
Westmede IG7: Chig 23Sc 54
Westmere Dr. NW7 20Ta 29
W. Mersea Cl. E16 46Kc 93
West M. N17 24Xb 51
SW1 6B 228
West Middlesex Golf Course 45Ea 86
West Mill DA11: Grav'nd 8B 122
WESTMINSTER 2F 229 (47Nb 90)
Westminster Abbey 3F 229 (48Mb 90)
Westminster Abbey Chapter House
3F 229
Westminster Abbey Mus. 3F 229
Westminster Abbey Pyx Chamber 3F 229
Westminster Av. CR7: Thor H 68Rb 135
Westminster Boating Base & Pier
51Mb 112
Westminster Bri. SW1 2G 229 (47Nb 90)
Westminster Bri. Ho. SE1 3B 230
Westminster Bri. Rd.
SE1 2H 229 (47Pb 90)
Westminster Bus. Sq. *SE11* 51Pb 112
(off Durham St.)
Westminster Cl. HA6: Nwood 24S 44
IG6: Ilf 26Tc 54
TW11: Tedd 64Ja 130
TW14: Felt 60W 106
Westminster Ct. AL1: St A 4A 6
E11 30Kc 53
(off Cambridge Pk.)
EN8: Walt C 5Cc 20
GU22: Wok 93D 188
NW8 6B 214
SE16 46Zb 92
(off King & Queen Wharf)
Westminster Dr. N13 22Nb 50
Westminster Gdns. E4 18Gc 35
IG6: Ilf 26Sc 54
IG11: Bark 40Uc 74
SW1 5F 229
Westminster Hall 2F 229
Westminster Ho. *WD24: Wat* 12Y 27
(off Hallam Cl.)
Westminster Ind. Est. SE18 48Mc 93
Westminster Lodge Leisure Cen. 3A 6
Westminster Mans. SW1 3E 228
Westminster Pal. Gdns. SW1 4D 228
Westminster RC Cathedral
4B 228 (48Lb 90)
Westminster Rd. N9 18Xb 33
SM1: Sutt 75Fb 155
W7 46Ga 86
Westmoat Cl. BR3: Beck 66Ec 136
WEST MOLESEY 70Ca 129
Westmont Rd. KT10: Hin W 75Ga 152
Westmoor Gdns. EN3: Enf H 12Zb 34
Westmoor Rd. EN3: Enf H 12Zb 34
Westmoor St. SE7 48Lc 93
Westmore Ct. SW15 57Ab 110
Westmore Grn. TN16: Tats 92Lc 199
Westmoreland Av. DA16: Well 55Uc 116
RM11: Horn 29Ld 57
Westmoreland Dr. SM2: Sutt 80Db 155
Westmoreland Ho. *E16* 46Jc 93
(off Gatcombe Rd.)
Westmoreland Pl. BR1: Brom 69Jc 137
SW1 7A 228 (50Kb 90)
W5 43Ma 87
Westmoreland Rd. BR1: Brom 71Gc 159
BR2: Brom 71Gc 159
NW9 27Pa 47
SE17 51Tb 113
(not continuous)
SW13 53Va 110
Westmoreland St. W1 1J 221 (43Jb 90)
Westmoreland Ter. SE20 66Xb 135
SW1 7A 228 (50Kb 90)
Westmoreland Wlk. SE17 51Tb 113
(not continuous)
Westmore Rd. TN16: Tats 93Lc 199
Westmorland Cl. E12 33Mc 73
KT19: Ewe 82Ua 174
TW1: Twick 58Ka 108
Westmorland Ct. KT6: Surb 73Ma 153
Westmorland Rd. E17 30Cc 52
HA1: Harr 29Da 45
Westmorland Sq. CR4: Mitc 71Nb 156
Westmorland Way CR4: Mitc 70Mb 134
Westmount Apartments
WD18: Wat 14V 26
(off Metropolitan Sta. App.)
Westmount Cen. UB4: Yead 45Z 85
Westmount Cl. KT4: Wor Pk 74Ya 154
Westmount Ct. W5 44Pa 87
Westmount Rd. SE9 54Pc 116
WEST NORWOOD 63Sb 135
West Norwood Crematorium
SE27 62Sb 135
West Oak BR3: Beck 67Fc 137
Westoe Rd. N9 19Xb 33
W. Officers Apartments SE18 52Qc 116
Weston Av. KT7: T Ditt 73Ga 152
KT8: W Mole 69Aa 129
KT15: Add 77K 149
RM20: W Thur 51Vd 120
Westonbirt Ct. *SE15* 51Vb 113
(off Ebley Cl.)
Weston Cl. CM13: Hut 17Ee 41
CR5: Coul 92Pb 196
EN6: Pot B 4Bb 17
KT15: Add 80J 149
Weston Ct. *KT1: King T* 69Na 131
(off Grove Cres.)
N4 34Sb 71
N20 17Eb 31
(off Farnham Cl.)
Weston Dr. CR3: Cat'm 94Sb 197
HA7: Stan 25Ka 46
W. One Ho. W1 1B 222
Westone Mans. *IG11: Bark* 38Vc 75
(off Upney La.)
W. One Shop. Cen. W1 3J 221
Weston Gdns. GU22: Pyr 88G 168
TW7: Isle 53Ga 108
WESTON GREEN 74Ga 152
Weston Grn. KT7: T Ditt 74Ga 152
(Weston Grn. Rd.)
KT7: T Ditt 75Ga 152
(Weston Rd.)
RM9: Dag 35Bd 75
Weston Grn. Rd. KT7: T Ditt 74Ga 152
KT10: Esh 74Fa 152
Weston Gro. BR1: Brom 67Hc 137
Weston Ho. *E9* 39Yb 72
(off King Edward's Rd.)
NW6 38Ab 68
Westonia Ct. EN3: Enf W 8Zb 20
Weston Lea KT24: W Hor 97T 190
Weston Pk. KT1: King T 68Na 131
KT7: T Ditt 74Ga 152
N8 30Nb 50
Weston Pk. Cl. KT7: T Ditt 74Ga 152
Weston Ri. WC1 2J 217 (41Pb 90)
Weston Rd. BR1: Brom 66Hc 137
EN2: Enf 12Tb 33
KT7: T Ditt 74Ga 152
KT17: Eps 83Ua 174
RM9: Dag 35Ad 75
SL1: Slou 3D 80
W4 48Sa 87
Weston St. SE1 7G 225 (47Ub 91)
(not continuous)
Westons Yd. SL4: Eton 1H 103
Weston Wlk. E8 38Xb 71
Weston Way GU22: Pyr 88G 168
Westover Cl. SM2: Sutt 81Db 175
Westover Hill NW3 33Cb 69
Westover Rd. SW18 59Eb 111
Westow Hill SE19 65Ub 135
Westow St. SE19 65Ub 135
West Pal. Gdns. KT13: Weyb 76R 150
West Pk. SE9 61Nc 138
Westpark W5 44Ma 87
West Pk. Av. TW9: Kew 53Qa 109
West Pk. Cl. RM6: Chad H 29Zc 55
TW5: Hest 51Ba 107
West Pk. Hill CM14: B'wood 20Wd 40
West Pk. Rd. KT19: Eps 83Pa 173
TW9: Kew 53Qa 109
UB2: S'hall 46Ea 86
W. Parkside CR6: W'ham 87Cc 178
SE10 47Gc 93
West Pk. Wlk. E20 37Ec 72
West Pl. SW19 64Ya 132
West Plaza TW15: Ashf 61N 127
West Point *E14* 45Bc 92
(off Grenade St.)
KT19: Ewe 81Ua 174
SE1 50Wb 91
SL1: Slou 6B 80
Westpoint Apartments N8 27Pb 50
W. Point Cl. *TW4: Houn* 55Ba 107
(off Grosvenor Rd.)
Westpoint Trad. Est. W3 43Ra 87
Westpole Av. EN4: Cockf 14Jb 32
Westport Ct. UB4: Yead 42Y 85
Westport Rd. E13 42Kc 93
Westport St. E1 44Zb 92
W. Poultry Av. EC1 1B 224 (43Rb 91)
West Quarters W12 44Wa 88
W. Quay SW10 53Eb 111
West Quay Dr. UB4: Yead 43Aa 85
West Quay Wlk. E14 48Dc 92
West Ramp TW6: H'row A 53Q 106
Westray HP3: Hem H 4C 4
West Reservoir Cen. 32Sb 71
Westridge Cl. HP1: Hem H 2H 3
W. Ridge Gdns. UB6: G'frd 40Ea 66
West Riding AL2: Brick W 2Ba 13
West Ri. W2 4E 220
West Rd. E15 39Hc 73
EN4: E Barn 18Jb 32
KT2: King T 67Sa 131
KT9: Chess 84La 172
KT13: Weyb 81R 170
N17 23Xb 51
RH2: Reig 7K 207
RM6: Chad H 30Zc 55
RM7: Rush G 31Fd 76
RM15: S Ock 41Xd 98
SE1 1J 229 (47Pb 90)
SW3 50Hb 89
SW4 57Mb 112
TW14: Bedf 58T 106
UB7: W Dray 48P 83
W5 43Na 87
Westrovia Ct. SW1 6D 228
West Row W10 42Ab 88
Westrow SW15 58Ya 110
Westrow Dr. IG11: Bark 36Wc 75
Westrow Gdns. IG3: Ilf 33Vc 75
WEST RUISLIP 33S 64
W. Ruislip Ct. *HA4: Ruis* 33T 64
(off Ickenham Rd.)
West Shaw DA3: Lfield 68Zd 143
W. Sheen Va. TW9: Rich 56Pa 109
West Side HP3: Hem H 7P 3
Westside N2 27Hb 49
NW4 26Xa 48
Westside Apartments *IG1: Ilf* 34Qc 74
(off Roden St.)
W. Side Comn. SW19 64Ya 132
West Side Ct. *TW16: Sun* 66U 128
(off Scotts Av.)
Westside Ct. GU24: W End 5C 166
W9 42Cb 89
(off Elgin Av.)
W. Smithfield EC1 1B 224 (43Rb 91)
W. Spur Rd. UB8: Cowl 41M 83
West Sq. E10 31Dc 72
SE11 4B 230 (48Rb 91)
SL0: Iver 44H 83
West Stand N5 35Rb 71
West St. BR1: Brom 67Jc 137
CR0: C'don 77Sb 157
DA7: Bex 55Bd 117
DA8: Erith 49Fd 96
DA11: Grav'nd 8C 122
E2 40Xb 71
E11 34Gc 73
E17 29Dc 52
GU21: Wok 89B 168
HA1: Harr 32Fa 66
KT17: Ewe 82Ua 174

West St.—Whitehill Rd.

West St. KT18: Eps . . . 85Sa 173
RH2: Reig . . . 6G 206
RM17: Grays . . . 51Ce 121
SM1: Sutt . . . 78Db 155
SM5: Cars . . . 76Hb 155
TN15: Wro . . . 88Be 185
WC2 . . . 3E 222 (44Mb 90)
WD17: Wat . . . 12X 27
West St. La. SM5: Cars . . . 77Hb 155
West St. Pl. CR0: C'don . . . 77Sb 157
(off West St.)
W. Temple Sheen SW14 . . . 57Ra 109
W. Tenter St. E1 . . . 3K 225 (44Vb 91)
West Ter. DA15: Sidc . . . 60Uc 116
W. Thamesmead Bus. Pk. SE28 . . . 48Uc 94
(not continuous)
WEST THURROCK . . . 51Wd 120
W. Thurrock Way
RM20: Chaf H, Grays, W Thur
. . . 48Vd 98
WEST TILBURY . . . 1G 122
West Twr. E14 . . . 47Dc 92
(off Pan Peninsula Sq.)
West Towers HA5: Pinn . . . 29Z 45
Westvale M. W3 . . . 47Ua 88
W. Valley Rd. HP3: Hem H . . . 7L 3
West Vw. IG10: Lough . . . 13Pc 36
KT21: Asht . . . 91La 192
NW4 . . . 28Ya 48
TW14: Bedf . . . 59S 106
Westview GU22: Wok . . . 90B 168
(off Park Dr.)
W7 . . . 44Ga 86
W. View Apartments N7 . . . 38Nb 70
(off York Way)
Westview Av. CR3: Whyt . . . 90Vb 177
Westview Cl. NW10 . . . 36Va 68
RH1: Redh . . . 8N 207
RM13: Rain . . . 41Ld 97
W10 . . . 44Ya 88
West Vw. Ct. WD6: E'tree . . . 16Ma 29
Westview Ct. N20 . . . 18Eb 31
Westview Cres. N9 . . . 17Ub 33
Westview Dr. IG8: Wfd G . . . 26Mc 53
West Vw. Gdns. WD6: E'tree . . . 16Ma 29
Westview Ri. HP2: Hem H . . . 1M 3
West Vw. Rd. AL3: St A . . . 1B 6
BR8: Crock . . . 72Fd 162
BR8: Swan . . . 70Jd 140
DA1: Dart . . . 58Pd 119
Westview Rd. CR6: W'ham . . . 91Xb 197
Westville Rd. KT7: T Ditt . . . 74Ja 152
W12 . . . 47Wa 88
West Wlk. EN4: E Barn . . . 17Jb 32
UB3: Hayes . . . 46W 84
W5 . . . 43Na 87
Westward Rd. E4 . . . 22Bc 52
(not continuous)
Westward Way HA3: Kenton . . . 30Na 47
W. Warwick Pl. SW1 . . . 6B 228 (49Lb 90)
WEST WATFORD . . . 14W 26
West Way BR4: W W'ck . . . 72Fc 159
BR5: Pet W . . . 71Tc 160
CM14: B'wood . . . 20Wd 40
CR0: C'don . . . 75Ac 158
HA4: Ruis . . . 32V 64
HA5: Pinn . . . 28Z 45
HA8: Edg . . . 23Ra 47
N18 . . . 21Tb 51
NW10 . . . 34Ta 67
SM5: Cars . . . 82Fb 175
TW5: Hest . . . 53Ba 107
TW17: Shep . . . 72T 150
WD3: Rick . . . 18K 25
Westway CR3: Cat'm . . . 94Tb 197
SW20 . . . 69Xa 132
UB6: G'frd . . . 39Ga 66
W2 . . . 1A 220 (43Bb 89)
W9 . . . 43Bb 89
W10 . . . 43Bb 89
W12 . . . 45Va 88
Westway Cl. SW20 . . . 69Xa 132
Westway Ct. CR3: Cat'm . . . 95Tb 197
UB5: N'olt . . . 39Ca 65
Westway Est. W3 . . . 43Ua 88
W. Way Gdns. CR0: C'don . . . 75Zb 158
Westway Gdns. RH1: Redh . . . 3A 208
Westway Lodge W9 . . . 43Cb 89
(off Amberley Rd.)
West Ways HA6: Nwood . . . 26W 44
Westways KT19: Ewe . . . 77Va 154
TN16: Westrm . . . 98Sc 200
Westway Sports Cen. . . . 44Za 88
Westway Travellers Site W12 . . . 45Za 88
(off Stable Way)
Westwell Cl. BR5: Orp . . . 74Zc 161
Westwell M. SW16 . . . 65Nb 134
Westwell Rd. SW16 . . . 65Nb 134
Westwell Rd. App. SW16 . . . 65Nb 134
Westwick KT1: King T . . . 68Qa 131
(off Chesterton Ter.)
Westwick Cl. HP2: Hem H . . . 3D 4
Westwick Gdns. TW4: Cran . . . 54X 107
W14 . . . 47Za 88
WEST WICKHAM . . . 74Ec 158
West Wickham Leisure Cen. . . . 74Ec 158
Westwick Pl. WD25: Wat . . . 6Y 13
Westwick Row HP2: Hem H . . . 2D 4
West Wing DA2: Dart . . . 58Sd 120
West Wing Arts Cen. . . . 4L 81
West Wintergarden . . . 46Dc 92
(off Bank St.)
Westwode Cl. RM5: Col R . . . 23Cd 56
WESTWOOD . . . 66Zd 143
Westwood DA11: Grav'nd . . . 4E 144
Westwood Av. CM14: B'wood . . . 21Wd 58
HA2: Harr . . . 35Da 65
KT15: Wdhm . . . 84H 169
SE19 . . . 67Sb 135
Westwood Bus. Cen. NW10 . . . 42Ua 88
Westwood Cl. BR1: Brom . . . 68Mc 137
EN6: Pot B . . . 2Cb 17
HA4: Ruis . . . 30R 44
HP6: L Chal . . . 11A 24
KT10: Esh . . . 76Fa 152
Westwood Ct. EN1: Enf . . . 16Ub 33
(off Village Rd.)
HA0: Wemb . . . 35Ka 66
UB6: G'frd . . . 36Fa 66
Westwood Dr. HP6: L Chal . . . 11A 24
Westwood Gdns. SW13 . . . 55Va 110
Westwood Hill SE26 . . . 64Wb 135
Westwood Ho. W12 . . . 46Ya 88
(off Wood La.)
Westwood La. DA15: Sidc . . . 57Wc 117
DA16: Well . . . 55Vc 117
Westwood M. E3 . . . 41Cc 92
(off Addington Rd.)
Westwood Pk. SE23 . . . 59Xb 113
Westwood Pk. Trad. Est. W3 . . . 43Ra 87
Westwood Pl. SE26 . . . 63Wb 135
Westwood Rd. CR5: Coul . . . 90Mb 176
DA13: Sflt . . . 66Ae 143
E16 . . . 46Kc 93
GU20: W'sham . . . 5C 146
IG3: Ilf . . . 32Vc 75
SW13 . . . 55Va 110
West Woodside DA5: Bexl . . . 59Ad 117
Westwood Way TN13: S'oaks . . . 94Hd 202
WEST YOKE . . . 76Ae 165
West Yoke TN15: Ash . . . 75Zd 165
W. Yoke Rd. DA3: Nw A G . . . 76Ae 165
Wetheral Dr. HA7: Stan . . . 25Ka 46
Wetherall M. AL1: St A . . . 3C 6
Wetherby Cl. UB5: N'olt . . . 37Da 65
Wetherby Gdns. SW5 . . . 6A 226 (49Eb 89)
Wetherby Mans. SW5 . . . 50Db 89
(off Earls Ct. Sq.)
Wetherby M. SW5 . . . 50Db 89
Wetherby Pl. SW7 . . . 6A 226 (49Eb 89)
Wetherby Rd. EN2: Enf . . . 11Sb 33
WD6: Bore . . . 11Na 29
Wetherby Way KT9: Chess . . . 80Na 153
Wetherden St. E17 . . . 31Bc 72
Wethered Dr. SL1: Burn . . . 3A 80
Wetherell Rd. E9 . . . 39Zb 72
Wetherill Rd. N10 . . . 25Jb 50
Wettern Cl. CR2: Sande . . . 82Ub 177
Wetton Ct. TW20: Egh . . . 64B 126
(off Wetton Pl.)
Wetton Pl. TW20: Egh . . . 64B 126
Wevco Wharf SE15 . . . 51Xb 113
Wexfenne Gdns. GU22: Pyr . . . 88K 169
Wexford Ho. E1 . . . 43Yb 92
(off Sidney St.)
Wexford Rd. SW12 . . . 59Hb 111
WEXHAM . . . 2M 81
WEXHAM COURT . . . 4N 81
Wexham Lodge SL2: Wex . . . 2M 81
Wexham Pk. Golf Course . . . 10N 61
Wexham Pk. La. SL3: Wex . . . 2N 81
Wexham Pl. SL2: Wex . . . 7P 61
Wexham Rd. SL1: Slou . . . 7L 81
SL2: Slou, Wex . . . 4M 81
Wexham Springs SL3: Wex . . . 8P 61
WEXHAM STREET . . . 10N 61
Wexham St. SL3: Stoke P . . . 1M 81
SL3: Stoke P, Wex . . . 1M 81
Wexham Woods SL3: Wex . . . 3N 81
Wexner Bldg. E1 . . . 1K 225
Wey Av. KT16: Chert . . . 69J 127
Weybank GU23: Wis . . . 88N 169
Wey Barton KT14: Byfl . . . 85P 169
Weybourne Pl. CR2: Sande . . . 82Tb 177
Weybourne St. SW18 . . . 61Eb 133
Weybourne Way KT15: New H . . . 81L 169
WEYBRIDGE . . . 77Q 150
Weybridge Bus. Pk. KT15: Add . . . 77N 149
Weybridge Ct. SE16 . . . 50Xb 91
Weybridge Ho. KT13: Weyb . . . 78T 150
Weybridge Lawn Tennis Club . . . 75R 150
Weybridge Pk. KT13: Weyb . . . 78Q 150
Weybridge Point SW11 . . . 54Hb 111
Weybridge Rd. CR7: Thor H . . . 70Qb 134
KT13: Weyb . . . 77N 149
KT15: Add . . . 77N 149
Weybridge Sailing Club . . . 75R 150
Weybrook Dr. GU4: Burp . . . 100E 188
Wey Cl. KT14: W Byf . . . 85K 169
Wey Ct. GU22: Wok . . . 91A 188
(off Claremont Av.)
KT15: New H . . . 81M 169
KT19: Ewe . . . 77Sa 153
Weydown Cl. SW19 . . . 60Ab 110
Weyhill Rd. E1 . . . 44Wb 91
Wey Ho. NW8 . . . 6C 214
UB5: N'olt . . . 42Ba 85
(off Taywood Rd.)
Weylands Cl. KT12: Walt T . . . 74Ba 151
Weylands Ct. KT15: Add . . . 77M 149
(off Corrie Rd.)
Weylands Pk. KT13: Weyb . . . 79T 150
Weylond Rd. RM8: Dag . . . 34Bd 75
Wey Mnr. Rd. KT15: New H . . . 81M 169
Weyman Rd. SE3 . . . 53Lc 115
Weymarks, The N17 . . . 23Tb 51
Weymead Ct. KT16: Chert . . . 74L 149
Wey Mdws. KT13: Weyb . . . 78N 149
Weymede KT14: Byfl . . . 84P 169
Weymouth Av. NW7 . . . 22Ua 48
W5 . . . 48La 86
Weymouth Cl. E6 . . . 44Rc 94
Weymouth Ct. E2 . . . 1K 219 (40Vb 71)
SM2: Sutt . . . 80Cb 155
Weymouth Dr. RM16: Chaf H . . . 50Zd 99
Weymouth Ho. BR2: Brom . . . 68Hc 137
(off Hill Ho. M.)
SW8 . . . 52Pb 112
(off Bolney St.)
Weymouth M. W1 . . . 7K 215 (43Kb 90)
Weymouth Pl. SE2 . . . 48Wc 95
Weymouth Rd. UB4: Hayes . . . 41U 84
Weymouth St. HP3: Hem H . . . 6M 3
W1 . . . 1J 221 (43Jb 90)
Weymouth Ter. E2 . . . 1K 219 (40Vb 71)
Weymouth Vs. N4 . . . 33Pb 70
(off Moray Rd.)
Weymouth Wlk. HA7: Stan . . . 23Ja 46
Wey Retail Pk. KT14: Byfl . . . 84N 169
Wey Rd. KT13: Weyb . . . 76P 149
Weyside Cl. KT14: Byfl . . . 84P 169
Weystone Rd. KT13: Weyb . . . 77P 149
Weyver Ct. AL1: St A . . . 1C 6
(off Avenue Rd.)
Weyview Ct. KT15: New H . . . 80L 149
Whadcoat St. N4 . . . 33Qb 70
Whaddon Ho. SE22 . . . 55Ub 113
Whalebone Av. RM6: Chad H . . . 30Bd 55
Whalebone Ct. EC2 . . . 2F 225
Whalebone Gro. RM6: Chad H . . . 30Bd 55
Whalebone La. E15 . . . 38Gc 73
Whalebone La. Nth.
RM6: Chad H, Col R . . . 24Ad 55
Whalebone La. Sth.
RM6: Chad H, Dag . . . 30Bd 55
RM8: Dag . . . 30Bd 55
Whales Yd. E15 . . . 38Gc 73
(off West Ham La.)
Whaley Rd. EN6: Pot B . . . 5Eb 17
Wharf, The DA9: Ghithe . . . 56Wd 120
(off Evelyn Wlk.)
EC3 . . . 6J 225 (46Vb 91)
KT13: Weyb . . . 75Q 150
Wharf Cl. SS17: Stan H . . . 2M 101
Wharfdale Ct. N11 . . . 23Jb 50
Wharfdale Rd. N1 . . . 1G 217 (40Nb 70)
Wharfedale Ct. E5 . . . 35Zb 72
Wharfedale Gdns. CR7: Thor H . . . 70Pb 134
Wharfedale Ho. NW6 . . . 39Db 69
(off Kilburn Vale)
Wharfedale Rd. DA2: Dart . . . 60Sd 120
Wharfedale St. SW10 . . . 50Db 89
Wharfedale Yd. N1 . . . 1G 217
Wharf Ho. DA8: Erith . . . 50Gd 96
(off West St.)
Wharf La. E14 . . . 44Bc 92
GU23: Rip . . . 90M 169
GU23: Send . . . 95E 188
TW1: Twick . . . 60Ja 108
WD3: Rick . . . 18N 25
Wharf Mill Apartments E2 . . . 1K 219
Wharf Pl. E2 . . . 39Xb 71
Wharf Rd. CM14: B'wood . . . 20Yd 40
DA12: Grav'nd . . . 8G 122
E16 . . . 46Lc 93
EN3: Pond E . . . 16Ac 34
HP1: Hem H . . . 4K 3
N1 . . . 2D 218 (40Sb 71)
(Baldwin Ter.)
N1 . . . 1F 217 (39Nb 70)
(York Way)
RM17: Grays . . . 51Be 121
SS17: Stan H . . . 2M 101
TW19: Wray . . . 9N 103
Wharf Rd. Ind. Est. EN3: Pond E . . . 16Ac 34
Wharf Rd. Sth. RM17: Grays . . . 51Be 121
Wharfside Cl. DA8: Erith . . . 50Hd 96
Wharfside Point Nth. E14 . . . 45Ec 92
(off Poplar High St.)
Wharfside Point Sth. E14 . . . 45Ec 92
Wharfside Rd. E16 . . . 43Gc 93
Wharf St. E16 . . . 43Gc 93
SE8 . . . 50Cc 92
Wharf Vw. Ct. E14 . . . 44Ec 92
(off Blair St.)
Wharf Vs. HP1: Hem H . . . 4K 3
Wharf Way WD4: Hunt C . . . 5S 12
Wharncliffe Dr. UB1: S'hall . . . 46Fa 86
Wharncliffe Gdns. SE25 . . . 68Ub 135
Wharncliffe Rd. SE25 . . . 68Ub 135
Wharnecliffe DA9: Ghithe . . . 58Xd 120
Wharncliffe M. SW4 . . . 58Mb 112
Wharton Cl. NW10 . . . 37Ua 68
Wharton Cotts. WC1 . . . 4K 217 (41Qb 90)
Wharton Ho. E2 . . . 41Zb 92
SE1 . . . 3K 231
Wharton Rd. BR1: Brom . . . 67Kc 137
Wharton St. WC1 . . . 4J 217 (41Pb 90)
Whatcote Cotts. TN15: Plat . . . 92Ee 205
Whatcott's Yd. N16 . . . 35Ub 71
Whateley Rd. SE20 . . . 66Zb 136
SE22 . . . 57Vb 113
Whatley Av. SW20 . . . 69Za 132
Whatman Ho. E14 . . . 44Bc 92
(off Wallwood St.)
Whatman Rd. SE23 . . . 59Zb 114
Whatmore Cl. TW19: Stanw M . . . 58J 105
Wheatash Rd. KT15: Add . . . 75K 149
Wheatbutts, The SL4: Eton W . . . 9D 80
Wheatcroft EN7: Chesh . . . 1Xb 19
Wheatcroft Ct. SM1: Sutt . . . 74Db 155
(off Cleeve Way)
Wheatfield Ho. NW6 . . . 41Cb 89
(off Kilburn Pk. Rd.)
Wheatfields CM14: W'ley . . . 21Yd 58
E6 . . . 44Rc 94
EN3: Enf H . . . 11Ac 34
Wheatfields Ct. EN9: Walt A . . . 6Jc 21
(off Farthingale La.)
Wheatfield Way KT1: King T . . . 68Na 131
Wheathill Ho. SE20 . . . 68Xb 135
(off Penge Rd.)
Wheathill Rd. SE20 . . . 69Xb 135
Wheat Knoll CR8: Kenley . . . 88Sb 177
Wheatland Ho. SE22 . . . 55Ub 113
Wheatlands TW5: Hest . . . 51Ca 107
Wheatlands Rd. SL3: Slou . . . 8M 81
SW17 . . . 62Jb 134
Wheatley Cl. DA9: Ghithe . . . 57Wd 120
NW4 . . . 26Wa 48
RM11: Horn . . . 29Md 57
Wheatley Ct. E3 . . . 41Dc 92
(off Bruce Rd.)
Wheatley Cres. UB3: Hayes . . . 45W 84
Wheatley Dr. WD25: Wat . . . 6Y 13
Wheatley Gdns. N9 . . . 19Ub 33
Wheatley Ho. SW15 . . . 59Wa 110
(off Ellisfield Dr)
Wheatley Mans. IG11: Bark . . . 38Wc 75
(off Lansbury Av.)
Wheatley M. KT8: E Mos . . . 70Fa 130
Wheatley Rd. TW7: Isle . . . 55Ha 108
Wheatley's Eyot TW16: Sun . . . 71W 150
Wheatley St. W1 . . . 1J 221 (43Jb 90)
Wheatley Ter. Rd. DA8: Erith . . . 51Hd 118
Wheatley Way SL9: Chal P . . . 23A 42
Wheat Sheaf Cl. E14 . . . 49Dc 92
Wheatsheaf Cl. GU21: Wok . . . 88A 168
KT16: Ott . . . 79F 148
UB5: N'olt . . . 36Aa 65
Wheatsheaf Hill TN14: Hals . . . 81Bd 181
Wheatsheaf La. SW6 . . . 52Ya 110
SW8 . . . 52Nb 112
TW18: Staines . . . 66H 127
Wheatsheaf Pde. SL4: Old Win . . . 7L 103
(off St Luke's Rd.)
Wheatsheaf Pk. . . . 67J 127
Wheatsheaf Rd. RM1: Rom . . . 30Hd 56
Wheatsheaf Ter. SW6 . . . 52Bb 111
Wheatstone Cl. CR4: Mitc . . . 67Gb 133
SL3: Slou . . . 8M 81
Wheatstone Ho. SE1 . . . 4E 230
W10 . . . 43Ab 88
(off Telford Rd.)
Wheatstone Rd. DA8: Erith . . . 50Fd 96
W10 . . . 43Ab 88
Wheeler Av. RH8: Oxt . . . 1H 211
Wheeler Cl. DA1: Dart . . . 57Pd 119
IG8: Wfd G . . . 23Pc 54
Wheeler Gdns. N1 . . . 39Nb 70
(off Outram Pl.)
Wheeler Pl. BR2: Brom . . . 70Kc 137
Wheelers CM16: Epp . . . 1Vc 23
Wheelers Cross IG11: Bark . . . 40Tc 74
Wheelers Dr. HA4: Ruis . . . 30S 44
Wheelers La. CM14: N'side, Pil H . . . 14Rd 39
HP3: Hem H . . . 4N 3
KT18: Eps . . . 86Ra 173
Wheelers Orchard SL9: Chal P . . . 23A 42
Wheel Farm Dr. RM10: Dag . . . 34Ed 76
Wheel Ho. E14 . . . 50Dc 92
(off Burrells Wharf Sq.)
Wheelock Cl. DA8: Erith . . . 52Dd 118
Wheelwright Cl. WD23: Bush . . . 16Da 27
Wheelwrights TN15: Plax . . . 100Ae 205
Wheelwrights Pl. SL3: Coln . . . 52E 104
Wheelwright St. N7 . . . 38Pb 70
Whelan Way SM6: Bedd . . . 76Mb 156
Wheler Ho. E1 . . . 6K 219
Wheler St. E1 . . . 6K 219 (42Vb 91)
Whellock Rd. W4 . . . 48Ua 88
WHELPLEY HILL . . . 8A 2
Whelpley Hill Pk. HP5: Whel H . . . 8A 2
Whenman Av. DA5: Bexl . . . 61Ed 140
Whernside Cl. SE28 . . . 45Yc 95
WHETSTONE . . . 19Eb 31
Whetstone Cl. N20 . . . 19Fb 31
Whetstone Pk. WC2 . . . 2H 223 (44Pb 90)
Whetstone Rd. SE3 . . . 54Lc 115
Whewell Rd. N19 . . . 33Nb 70
Whidborne Bldgs. WC1 . . . 4G 217
Whidborne Cl. SE8 . . . 54Cc 114
Whidborne St. WC1 . . . 4G 217 (41Nb 90)
(not continuous)
Whidbourne M. SW8 . . . 53Mb 112
Whiffins Orchard CM16: Coop . . . 1Zc 23
Whimbrel Cl. CR2: Sande . . . 83Tb 177
SE28 . . . 45Yc 95
Whimbrel Way UB4: Yead . . . 44Z 85
Whinchat Rd. SE28 . . . 48Tc 94
Whinfell Cl. SW16 . . . 64Mb 134
Whinfell Way DA12: Grav'nd . . . 3H 145
Whinshill Ct. SL5: S'dale . . . 4E 146
Whinyates Rd. SE9 . . . 55Nc 116
Whippendell Cl. BR5: St P . . . 67Xc 139
Whippendell Hill WD4: Chfd . . . 2L 11
Whippendell Rd. WD18: Wat . . . 15U 26
Whippendell Way BR5: St P . . . 67Xc 139
Whippingham Ho. E3 . . . 41Bc 92
(off Merchant St.)
Whipps Cross E17 . . . 29Fc 53
Whipps Cross Ho. E17 . . . 29Fc 53
(off Wood St.)
Whipps Cross Rd. E11 . . . 29Fc 53
(not continuous)
Whiskin St. EC1 . . . 4B 218 (41Rb 91)
Whisper Wood WD3: Loud . . . 13K 25
Whisperwood Cl. HA3: Hrw W . . . 25Ga 46
Whistler Ct. WD25: Wat . . . 8Z 13
Whistler Gdns. HA8: Edg . . . 26Pa 47
Whistler M. RM8: Dag . . . 36Xc 75
(off Fitzstephen Rd.)
SE15 . . . 52Vb 113
Whistlers Av. SW11 . . . 52Fb 111
Whistlers Gro. DA15: Sidc . . . 59Uc 116
Whistler St. N5 . . . 36Rb 71
Whistler Twr. SW10 . . . 52Eb 111
(off Worlds End Est.)
Whistler Wlk. SW10 . . . 52Fb 111
Whiston Ho. N1 . . . 38Rb 71
(off Richmond Gro.)
Whiston Rd. E2 . . . 1K 219 (40Vb 71)
Whitacre M. SE11 . . . 50Qb 90
Whitakers Lodge EN2: Enf . . . 11Tb 33
Whitakers Way IG10: Lough . . . 11Pc 36
Whitbread Cl. N17 . . . 25Wb 51
Whitbread Pl. CM14: B'wood . . . 20Yd 40
(off Rollason Way)
Whitbread Rd. SE4 . . . 56Ac 114
Whitburn Rd. SE13 . . . 56Dc 114
Whitby Av. CM13: Ingve . . . 23Fe 59
NW10 . . . 41Ra 87
Whitby Cl. DA9: Ghithe . . . 57Wd 120
TN16: Big H . . . 91Kc 199
Whitby Ct. N7 . . . 35Nb 70
Whitby Gdns. NW9 . . . 27Qa 47
SM1: Sutt . . . 75Fb 155
Whitby Ho. NW8 . . . 39Eb 69
(off Boundary Rd.)
Whitby Pde. HA4: Ruis . . . 33Y 65
Whitby Rd. HA2: Harr . . . 34Ea 66
HA4: Ruis . . . 34X 65
SE18 . . . 49Pc 94
SL1: Slou . . . 5G 80
SM1: Sutt . . . 75Fb 155
Whitby Rd. Bus. Cen. SL1: Slou . . . 5G 80
Whitby St. E1 . . . 5K 219 (42Vb 91)
(not continuous)
Whitcher Cl. SE14 . . . 51Ac 114
Whitcher Pl. NW1 . . . 37Lb 70
Whitchurch Av. HA8: Edg . . . 24Pa 47
Whitchurch Cl. HA8: Edg . . . 23Pa 47
Whitchurch Gdns. HA8: Edg . . . 23Pa 47
Whitchurch Ho. W10 . . . 44Za 88
(off Kingsdown Cl.)
Whitchurch La. HA8: Edg . . . 24Ma 47
Whitchurch Pde. HA8: Edg . . . 24Qa 47
Whitchurch Rd. RM3: Rom . . . 21Md 57
W11 . . . 45Za 88
Whitcomb Ct. WC2 . . . 5E 222
Whitcombe M. TW9: Kew . . . 53Ra 109
Whitcomb St. WC2 . . . 5E 222 (45Mb 90)
Whitcome M. TW9: Kew . . . 53Ra 109
Whiteadder Way E14 . . . 49Dc 92
Whitear Wlk. E15 . . . 37Fc 73
White Av. DA11: Nflt . . . 2B 144
Whitebarn La. RM10: Dag . . . 39Cd 76
Whitebeam Av. BR2: Brom . . . 73Qc 160
Whitebeam Cl. KT17: Eps D . . . 87Xa 174
SW9 . . . 52Pb 112
TN15: Kems'g . . . 89Qd 183
UB8: Uxb . . . 38L 63
WD7: Shenl . . . 5Pa 15
Whitebeam Dr. RH2: Reig . . . 9K 207
RM15: S Ock . . . 41Yd 98
Whitebeam Ho. E15 . . . 41Gc 93
(off Teasel Way)
Whitebeam Pl. CR3: Whyt . . . 89Wb 177
White Beams AL2: Park . . . 10A 6
Whitebeams AL10: Hat . . . 3C 8
White Beam Way KT20: Tad . . . 93Wa 194
White Bear Pl. NW3 . . . 35Fb 69
White Bear Yd. EC1 . . . 6K 217
White Bri. Av. CR4: Mitc . . . 69Fb 133
Whitebridge Cl. TW14: Felt . . . 58V 106
Whitebroom Rd. HP1: Hem H . . . 1G 2
WHITE BUSHES . . . 10A 208
Whitebushes RH1: Redh . . . 10A 208
White Butts Rd. HA4: Ruis . . . 34Z 65
WHITECHAPEL . . . 43Wb 91
Whitechapel Gallery . . . 44Vb 91
Whitechapel High St. E1 . . . 2K 225 (44Vb 91)
Whitechapel Rd. E1 . . . 43Wb 91
Whitechapel Sports Cen. . . . 43Xb 91
White Church La. E1 . . . 44Wb 91
White Church Pas. E1 . . . 44Wb 91
(off White Church La.)
WHITE CITY . . . 45Xa 88
WHITE CITY . . . 44Ya 88
White City Cl. W12 . . . 45Ya 88
White City Est. W12 . . . 45Xa 88
White City Rd. W12 . . . 45Ya 88
White Cl. SL1: Slou . . . 6H 81
White Conduit St. N1 . . . 1A 218 (40Qb 70)
Whitecote Rd. UB1: S'hall . . . 44Ea 86
White Craig Cl. HA5: Hat E . . . 22Ca 45
Whitecroft AL1: St A . . . 5F 6
BR8: Swan . . . 68Gd 140
Whitecroft Cl. BR3: Beck . . . 70Fc 137
Whitecroft Way BR3: Beck . . . 71Ec 158
Whitecross Pl. EC2 . . . 7G 219 (43Tb 91)
Whitecross St. EC1 . . . 5E 218 (42Sb 91)
Whitefield Av. CR8: Purl . . . 88Qb 176
NW2 . . . 32Ya 68
Whitefield Cl. BR5: St P . . . 69Yc 139
SW15 . . . 58Ab 110
Whitefields CR3: Cat'm . . . 93Ub 197
Whitefields Rd. EN8: Chesh . . . 1Yb 20
Whitefoot La. BR1: Brom . . . 63Ec 136
(not continuous)
Whitefoot Ter. BR1: Brom . . . 62Hc 137
Whiteford Rd. SL2: Slou . . . 3J 81
White Friars TN13: S'oaks . . . 99Jd 202
Whitefriars Av. HA3: W'stone . . . 26Ga 46
Whitefriars Ct. N12 . . . 22Fb 49
Whitefriars Dr. HA3: Hrw W . . . 26Fa 46
Whitefriars St. EC4 . . . 3A 224 (44Qb 90)
Whitefriars Trad. Est.
HA3: W'stone . . . 27Fa 46
White Gables Ct. CR2: S Croy . . . 78Ub 157
White Gdns. RM10: Dag . . . 37Cd 76
White Ga. GU22: Wok . . . 92B 188
Whitegate Gdns. HA3: Hrw W . . . 24Ha 46
White Gates KT7: T Ditt . . . 73Ja 152
RM12: Horn . . . 33Ld 77
Whitegates CR3: W'ham . . . 91Wb 197
Whitegates Av. TN15: W King . . . 79Ud 164
Whitegates Cl. WD3: Crox G . . . 14Q 26
Whitegate Way KT20: Tad . . . 92Xa 194
Whitehall . . . 79Ab 154
White Hall RM4: Abr . . . 13Xc 37
Whitehall SW1 . . . 6F 223 (46Nb 90)
Whitehall Cl. IG7: Chig . . . 20Wc 37
UB8: Uxb . . . 39L 63
WD6: Bore . . . 14Qa 29
Whitehall Ct. SW1 . . . 7F 223 (46Nb 90)
(not continuous)
Whitehall Cres. KT9: Chess . . . 78Ma 153
Whitehall Farm La. GU25: Vir W . . . 68A 126
Whitehall Gdns. E4 . . . 18Gc 35
SW1 . . . 7F 223
W3 . . . 46Qa 87
W4 . . . 51Ra 109
Whitehall La. DA8: Erith . . . 54Hd 118
IG9: Buck H . . . 19Jc 35
RH2: Reig . . . 10H 207
RM17: Grays . . . 50Ee 99
TW19: Wray . . . 58C 104
TW20: Egh . . . 66B 126
Whitehall Lodge N10 . . . 26Jb 50
Whitehall Pde. DA12: Grav'nd . . . 2E 144
Whitehall Pk. N19 . . . 32Lb 70
Whitehall Pk. Rd. W4 . . . 51Ra 109
Whitehall Pl. E7 . . . 36Jc 73
SM6: Wall . . . 77Kb 156
SW1 . . . 7F 223 (46Nb 90)
Whitehall Rd. BR2: Brom . . . 71Mc 159
CR7: Thor H . . . 71Qb 156
E4 . . . 19Gc 35
HA1: Harr . . . 31Ga 66
IG8: Wfd G . . . 19Gc 35
RM17: Grays . . . 49Ee 99
UB8: Uxb . . . 39M 63
W7 . . . 47Ja 86
Whitehall St. N17 . . . 24Vb 51
White Hart Av. SE18 . . . 49Vc 95
SE28 . . . 49Vc 95
White Hart Cl. GU23: Rip . . . 93L 189
TN13: S'oaks . . . 100Ld 203
UB3: Harl . . . 51T 106
White Hart Ct. EC2 . . . 1H 225
EN8: Walt C . . . 5Ac 20
White Hart Dr. HP2: Hem H . . . 3P 3
White Hart Lane . . . 24Wb 51
White Hart La. N17 . . . 24Sb 51
N22 . . . 25Pb 50
NW10 . . . 37Va 68
RM7: Col R, Mawney . . . 25Cd 56
SW13 . . . 54Ua 110
White Hart Lane Community Sports Cen.
. . . 24Rb 51
White Hart Mdws. GU23: Rip . . . 93L 189
White Hart M. KT16: Chert . . . 73J 149
White Hart Pde. TN13: Riv . . . 94Gd 202
White Hart Rd. BR6: Orp . . . 73Wc 161
HP2: Hem H . . . 3A 4
SE18 . . . 49Uc 94
SL1: Slou . . . 8H 81
WHITE HART RDBT. . . . 40Z 65
White Hart Slip BR1: Brom . . . 68Jc 137
White Hart St. EC4 . . . 2C 224 (44Rb 91)
SE11 . . . 7A 230 (50Qb 90)
White Hart Triangle SE28 . . . 47Vc 95
White Hart Triangle Bus. Pk.
SE28 . . . 47Wc 95
White Hart Wood TN13: S'oaks . . . 100Ld 203
White Hart Yd. DA11: Grav'nd . . . 8D 122
(off High St.)
SE1 . . . 7F 225 (46Tb 91)
Whitehaven SL1: Slou . . . 5K 81
Whitehaven Cl. BR2: Brom . . . 70Jc 137
EN7: G Oak . . . 1Ub 19
Whitehaven St. NW8 . . . 6D 214 (42Gb 89)
Whitehead Cl. DA2: Wilm . . . 62Ld 141
N18 . . . 22Tb 51
SW18 . . . 59Eb 111
Whiteheads Gro. SW3 . . . 7E 226 (49Gb 89)
White Heart Av. UB8: Hil . . . 43S 84
Whiteheath Av. HA4: Ruis . . . 31S 64
White Heather Ho. WC1 . . . 4G 217
(off Cromer St.)
White Hedge Dr. AL3: St A . . . 1A 6
White Hermitage SL4: Old Win . . . 7N 103
White Heron M. TW11: Tedd . . . 65Ha 130
White Hill CR2: Sande . . . 82Tb 177
CR5: Chip . . . 95Gb 195
GU20: W'sham . . . 7A 146
HP1: Hem H . . . 3H 3
HP4: Berk . . . 1A 2
TN15: Wro . . . 88De 185
WD3: Rick . . . 23P 43
White Hill Cl. CR3: Cat'm . . . 97Ub 197
White Hill La. RH1: Blet . . . 99Tb 197
Whitehill La. DA12: Grav'nd . . . 2E 144
GU23: Ock . . . 95S 190
Whitehill Pl. GU25: Vir W . . . 71A 148
Whitehill Rd. DA1: Cray . . . 57Jd 118
DA3: Dart, Lfield . . . 68Zd 143
DA12: Grav'nd . . . 1E 144
DA13: Sflt . . . 68Zd 143

Whitehills Rd.—William Ellis Cl.

Whitehills Rd. IG10: Lough . . . 13Qc 36
White Horse All. EC1 . . . 7B 218
White Horse Apartments *N1* . . . *39Qb 70*
(off Liverpool Rd.)
White Horse Dr. KT18: Eps . . . 86Sa 173
White Horse Hill BR7: Chst . . . 63Qc 138
White Horse La. AL2: Lon C . . . 8H 7
E1 . . . 43Zb 92
GU23: Rip . . . 93L 189
Whitehorse La. SE25 . . . 70Tb 135
White Horse M. EN3: Enf H . . . 12Zb 34
Whitehorse M. SE1 . . . 3A 230 (48Qb 90)
White Horse Rd. E1 . . . 44Ac 92
(not continuous)
E6 . . . 41Pc 94
SL4: Wind . . . 5B 102
Whitehorse Rd.
CR0: C'don . . . 73Sb 157
CR7: Thor H . . . 73Sb 157
White Horse St. W1 . . . 7A 222 (46Kb 90)
White Horse Yd. EC2 . . . 2F 225 (44Tb 91)
White Ho. *CR0: C'don* . . . *77Tb 157*
(off Coombe Rd.)
SW4 . . . *59Mb 112*
(off Clapham Pk. Est.)
SW11 . . . 53Fb 111
White Ho., The NW1 . . . 5A 216
Whitehouse *E10* . . . *30Ec 52*
(off Leyton Grn. Rd.)
Whitehouse Apartments
SE1 . . . 7J 223 (46Pb 90)
Whitehouse Av. WD6: Bore . . . 13Ra 29
White Ho. Cl. SL9: Chal P . . . 24A 42
White Ho. Commercial Cen.
EN5: Barn . . . 7Cb 17
White Ho. Ct. N14 . . . 19Nb 32
White Ho. Dr. HA7: Stan . . . 21La 46
IG8: Wfd G . . . 23Hc 53
White Ho. La. EN2: Enf . . . 11Sb 33
GU4: Jac W . . . 10P 187
Whitehouse La. WD5: Bedm . . . 8H 5
White Ho. M. E10 . . . 30Ec 52
White Ho. Rd. EN5: Barn . . . 7Cb 17
Whitehouse Way N14 . . . 19Kb 32
SL0: Iver H . . . 41F 82
SL3: L'ly . . . 8P 81
Whitehurst Dr. N18 . . . 22Zb 52
White Kennett St. E1 . . . 2J 225 (44Vb 91)
White Knights Rd. KT13: Weyb . . . 80S 150
White Knobs Way CR3: Cat'm . . . 97Wb 197
Whitelands Av. WD3: Chor . . . 13D 24
Whitelands Cres. SW18 . . . 59Ab 110
Whitelands Ho. SW3 . . . 7F 227
Whitelands Way RM3: Hrld W . . . 25Md 57
White La. RH8: T'sey . . . 95Kc 199
TN16: Tats, T'sey . . . 95Kc 199
Whiteleaf Rd. HP3: Hem H . . . 5L 3
Whiteledges W13 . . . 44La 86
Whitelegg Rd. E13 . . . 40Hc 73
Whiteley SL4: Wind . . . 2C 102
Whiteley Rd. SE19 . . . 64Tb 135
Whiteleys Cen. (Shop. Cen.)
W2 . . . 44Db 89
Whiteleys Pde. UB10: Hil . . . 42R 84
Whiteley's Way TW13: Hanw . . . 62Ca 129
WHITELEY VILLAGE . . . 81U 170
White Lillies Island SL4: Wind . . . 2E 102
White Lion Ct. EC3 . . . 3H 225
SE15 . . . 51Yb 114
TW7: Isle . . . 55Ka 108
White Lion Ga. KT11: Cobh . . . 86W 170
White Lion Hill EC4 . . . 4C 224 (45Rb 91)
White Lion St. HP3: Hem H . . . 6M 3
N1 . . . 2K 217 (40Qb 70)
White Lodge KT21: Asht . . . 92Na 193
SE19 . . . 66Rb 135
TN13: S'oaks . . . 100Jd 202
W5 . . . 43La 86
White Lodge Cl. KT20: Tad . . . 95Ya 194
N2 . . . 30Fb 49
SM2: Sutt . . . 80Eb 155
TN13: S'oaks . . . 95Kd 203
TW7: Isle . . . 54Ja 108
White Lodge Ct. TW16: Sun . . . 67Y 129
White Lodge Mus. . . . 60Ta 109
White Lyon Ct. EC2 . . . 7D 218
White Lyons Rd. CM14: B'wood . . . 19Yd 40
White Oak Ct. BR8: Swan . . . 69Gd 140
Whiteoak Ct. BR7: Chst . . . 65Qc 138
White Oak Dr. BR3: Beck . . . 68Ec 136
White Oak Gdns. DA15: Sidc . . . 59Vc 117
White Oak Leisure Cen. . . . 68Fd 140
Whiteoaks SM7: Bans . . . 85Db 175
Whiteoaks La. UB6: G'frd . . . 41Fa 86
White Oak Sq. *BR8: Swan* . . . *69Gd 140*
(off London Rd.)
White Orchards HA7: Stan . . . 22Ja 46
N20 . . . 18Bb 31
White Pillars GU22: Wok . . . 2M 187
WHITE POST . . . 5L 209
White Post Hill DA4: Farni . . . 73Qd 163
Whitepost Hill RH1: Redh . . . 6N 207
(not continuous)
White Post La. DA13: Sole S . . . 10D 144
E9 . . . 38Bc 72
Whitepost La. RM13: Rain . . . 40Hd 76
White Post St. SE15 . . . 52Yb 114
White Rd. E15 . . . 38Gc 73
White Rose Ct. E1 . . . 1J 225
White Rose La. GU22: Wok . . . 90B 168
White Rose Lane Local Nature Reserve
. . . 91D 188
Whiterose Trad. Est. *EN4: E Barn* . . . *15Fb 31*
(off Margaret Rd.)
Whites Av. IG2: Ilf . . . 30Uc 54
Whites Cl. DA9: Ghithe . . . 58Yd 120
Whites Grounds SE1 . . . 2J 231 (47Ub 91)
White's Grounds Est. SE1 . . . 1J 231
White Shack La. WD3: Chan C . . . 9P 11
Whites La. GU24: Pirb . . . 6E 186
SL3: Dat . . . 1M 103
White's Mdw. BR1: Brom . . . 70Qc 138
White's Row E1 . . . 1K 225 (43Vb 91)
Whites Sq. SW4 . . . 56Mb 112
Whitestile Rd. TW8: Bford . . . 50La 86
Whitestone Cl. EN4: Had W . . . 10Gb 17
Whitestone La. NW3 . . . 34Eb 69
Whitestone Wlk. NW3 . . . 34Eb 69
Whitestone Way CR0: Wadd . . . 75Qb 156
White St. UB1: S'hall . . . 47Z 85
White Swan M. W4 . . . 50Ua 88
Whitethorn Av. CR5: Coul . . . 87Jb 176
UB7: Yiew . . . 45N 83
Whitethorn Gdns. CR0: C'don . . . 75Xb 157
EN2: Enf . . . 15Tb 33
RM11: Horn . . . 30Ld 57
Whitethorn Ho. *E1* . . . *46Yb 92*
(off Prusom St.)
Whitethorn Pas. *E3* . . . *42Cc 92*
(off Whitethorn St.)
Whitethorn Pl. UB7: Yiew . . . 46P 83
Whitethorn St. E3 . . . 43Cc 92
White Twr. Way E1 . . . 43Ac 92
Whiteway KT23: Bookh . . . 98Da 191
Whiteways Ct. TW18: Staines . . . 66K 127
Whitewebbs Golf Course . . . 9Tb 19
Whitewebbs La. EN2: Enf . . . 7Ub 19
Whitewebbs Mus. of Transport . . . 7Rb 19
Whitewebbs Pk. . . . 8Sb 19
Whitewebbs Rd. EN2: Crew H, Enf . . . 7Rb 19
Whitewebbs Way BR5: St P . . . 67Vc 139
Whitewood Cotts. TN16: Tats . . . 92Lc 199
Whitfield Cl. IG1: Ilf . . . 31Pc 74
Whitfield Cres. DA2: Dart . . . 59Sd 120
Whitfield Ho. NW8 . . . 6D 214
Whitfield Pl. W1 . . . 6B 216
Whitfield Rd. DA7: Bex . . . 52Bd 117
E6 . . . 38Lc 73
Whitfields SS17: Stan H . . . 1P 101
Whitfield St. W1 . . . 6B 216 (42Lb 90)
Whitfield Way WD3: Rick . . . 18H 25
Whitford Gdns. CR4: Mitc . . . 69Hb 133
Whitgift Av. CR2: S Croy . . . 78Rb 157
Whitgift Cen. CR0: C'don . . . 75Sb 157
Whitgift Ct. *CR2: S Croy* . . . *78Sb 157*
(off Nottingham Rd.)
Whitgift Ho. SE11 . . . 5H 229 (49Pb 90)
SW11 . . . 53Gb 111
Whitgift Sq. CR0: C'don . . . 75Sb 157
Whitgift St. CR0: C'don . . . 76Sb 157
SE11 . . . 5H 229 (49Pb 90)
Whit Hern Ct. EN8: Chesh . . . 2Yb 20
Whiting Av. IG11: Bark . . . 38Rc 74
Whitings IG2: Ilf . . . 29Uc 54
Whitings Rd. EN5: Barn . . . 15Ya 30
Whitings Way E6 . . . 43Qc 94
Whiting Way SE16 . . . 49Ac 92
Whitland Rd. SM5: Cars . . . 74Fb 155
Whitlars Dr. WD4: K Lan . . . 10P 3
Whitley Cl. TW19: Stanw . . . 58N 105
WD5: Ab L . . . 4W 12
Whitley Ct. *AL1: St A* . . . *2C 6*
(off Hatfield Rd.)
Whitley Ho. *SW1* . . . *51Lb 112*
(off Churchill Gdns.)
Whitley Rd. N17 . . . 26Ub 51
WHITLEY ROW . . . 100Dd 202
Whitlock Dr. SW19 . . . 59Ab 110
Whitman Ho. *E2* . . . *41Yb 92*
(off Cornwall Av.)
Whitman Rd. E3 . . . 42Ac 92
Whitmead Cl. CR2: S Croy . . . 79Ub 157
Whitmoor & Rickford Commons
Local Nature Reserve . . . 9L 187
WHITMOOR COMMON . . . 8L 187
Whitmoor La. GU4: Sut G . . . 8P 187
Whitmore Av. RM3: Hrld W . . . 26Nd 57
RM16: Grays . . . 46De 99
Whitmore Bldg. SE16 . . . 3K 231
Whitmore Cl. N11 . . . 22Kb 50
RM16: Ors . . . 4G 100
Whitmore Est. N1 . . . 1J 219 (39Ub 71)
Whitmore Gdns. NW10 . . . 40Ya 68
Whitmore Ho. N1 . . . 1J 219
Whitmore La. SL5: S'dale, S'hill . . . 1E 146
Whitmore Rd. BR3: Beck . . . 69Bc 136
HA1: Harr . . . 31Ea 66
N1 . . . 1H 219 (39Ub 71)
Whitmores Cl. KT18: Eps . . . 87Sa 173
Whitmore Sports Cen. . . . 32Ea 66
Whitmores Wood HP2: Hem H . . . 1B 4
Whitnell Way SW15 . . . 57Ya 110
(not continuous)
Whitney Av. IG4: Ilf . . . 28Mc 53
Whitney Rd. E10 . . . 31Dc 72
Whitney Wlk. DA14: Sidc . . . 65Ad 139
Whitstable Cl. BR3: Beck . . . 67Bc 136
HA4: Ruis . . . 33U 64
Whitstable Ho. *W10* . . . *44Za 88*
(off Silchester Rd.)
Whitstable Pl. CR0: C'don . . . 77Sb 157
Whitstone La. BR3: Beck . . . 71Dc 158
Whittaker Av. TW9: Rich . . . 57Ma 109
Whittaker Ct. KT21: Asht . . . 89Ma 173
Whittaker Pl. *TW9: Rich* . . . *57Ma 109*
(off Whittaker Av.)
Whittaker Rd. E6 . . . 38Lc 73
SL2: Slou . . . 2B 80
SM3: Sutt . . . 76Bb 155
Whittaker St. SW1 . . . 6H 227 (49Jb 90)
Whittaker Way SE1 . . . 49Wb 91
Whitta Rd. E12 . . . 35Mc 73
Whittell Gdns. SE26 . . . 62Yb 136
Whittenham Cl. SL2: Slou . . . 6L 81
Whittets Ait KT13: Weyb . . . 75Q 150
Whittingham N17 . . . 24Xb 51
Whittingham Ct. W4 . . . 52Ua 110
Whittingstall Rd. SW6 . . . 53Bb 111
Whittington Apartments *E1* . . . *44Zb 92*
(off E. Arbour St.)
Whittington Av. EC3 . . . 3H 225 (44Ub 91)
UB4: Hayes . . . 43V 84
Whittington Ct. N2 . . . 29Hb 49
Whittington Ho. *N19* . . . *33Mb 70*
(off Holloway Rd.)
Whittington M. N12 . . . 21Eb 49
Whittington Rd. CM13: Hut . . . 16Ee 41
N22 . . . 24Nb 50
Whittington Way HA5: Pinn . . . 29Aa 45
Whittlebury Cl. SM5: Cars . . . 80Hb 155
Whittlebury M. E. NW1 . . . 38Jb 70
Whittlebury M. W. NW1 . . . 38Jb 70
Whittle Cl. E17 . . . 30Ac 52
UB1: S'hall . . . 44Da 85
WD25: Wat . . . 6V 12
Whittle Parkway SL1: Slou . . . 4B 80
Whittle Rd. TW5: Hest . . . 52Y 107
TW6: H'row A . . . 55K 105
UB2: S'hall . . . 47Da 85
Whittlesea Cl. HA3: Hrw W . . . 24Ea 46
Whittlesea Path HA3: Hrw W . . . 25Ea 46
Whittlesea Rd. HA3: Hrw W . . . 24Ea 46
Whittlesey St. SE1 . . . 7K 223 (46Qb 90)
WHITTON . . . 59Ea 108
Whitton NW3 . . . 38Hb 69
Whitton Av. E. UB6: G'frd . . . 36Ga 66
Whitton Av. W. UB5: N'olt . . . 36Da 65
UB6: G'frd . . . 36Da 65
Whitton Cl. UB6: G'frd . . . 37Ka 66
Whitton Dene TW3: Houn, Isle . . . 57Da 107
TW7: Isle . . . 58Fa 108
Whitton Dr. UB6: G'frd . . . 37Ja 66
Whitton Mnr. Rd. TW7: Isle . . . 58Ea 108
Whitton Rd. TW1: Twick . . . 58Ha 108
TW2: Twick . . . 58Ga 108
TW3: Houn . . . 56Da 107
WHITTON ROAD RDBT. . . . 58Ha 108
Whitton Sports & Fitness Cen. . . . 61Da 129
Whitton Wlk. E3 . . . 41Cc 92
(not continuous)
Whitton Waye TW3: Houn . . . 58Ca 107
Whitwell Rd. E13 . . . 41Jc 93
WD25: Wat . . . 7Z 13
Whitworth Av. RM3: Rom . . . 22Ld 57
Whitworth Cres. EN3: Enf L . . . 9Cc 20
Whitworth Ho. SE1 . . . 4E 230 (48Sb 91)
Whitworth Rd. SE18 . . . 52Qc 116
SE25 . . . 69Ub 135
Whitworth St. SE10 . . . 50Gc 93
Whopshott Av. GU21: Wok . . . 8N 167
Whopshott Cl. GU21: Wok . . . 8N 167
Whopshott Dr. GU21: Wok . . . 8N 167
Whorlton Rd. SE15 . . . 55Xb 113
Whybrews SS17: Stan H . . . 1P 101
Whybridge Cl. RM13: Rain . . . 39Hd 76
Whychcote Point *NW2* . . . *32Ya 68*
(off Whitefield Av.)
Whymark Av. N22 . . . 27Qb 50
Whyteacre CR3: W'ham . . . 92Xb 197
Whytebeam Vw. CR3: Whyt . . . 90Vb 177
Whytecliffe Rd. Nth.
CR8: Purl . . . 83Rb 177
Whytecliffe Rd. Sth. CR8: Purl . . . 83Qb 176
Whytecroft TW5: Hest . . . 52Z 107
WHYTELEAFE . . . 90Vb 177
Whyteleafe Bus. Village
CR3: Whyt . . . 89Vb 177
Whyteleafe Hill CR3: Whyt . . . 92Ub 197
Whyteleafe Rd. CR3: Cat'm . . . 92Ub 197
Whyte M. SM3: Cheam . . . 80Ab 154
Whyteville Rd. E7 . . . 37Kc 73
Whytlaw Ho. *E3* . . . *43Bc 92*
(off Baythorne St.)
Wichling Cl. BR5: Orp . . . 74Zc 161
Wickenden Rd. TN13: S'oaks . . . 94Ld 203
Wickens Cvn. Site TN14: Dun G . . . 91Jd 202
Wickens Mdw. TN14: Dun G . . . 91Hd 202
Wickersley Rd. SW11 . . . 54Jb 112
Wickers Oake SE19 . . . 63Vb 135
Wicker St. E1 . . . 44Xb 91
Wicket, The CR0: Addtn . . . 78Cc 158
Wicket Rd. UB6: G'frd . . . 41Ja 86
Wickets, The TW15: Ashf . . . 63N 127
Wickets Cl. BR5: St M Cry . . . 71Yc 161
Wickets End WD7: Shenl . . . 5Na 15
Wickets Way IG6: Ilf . . . 23Vc 55
Wickfield Apartments *E15* . . . *37Fc 73*
(off Grove Cres. Rd.)
Wickfield Ho. *SE16* . . . *47Xb 91*
(off Wilson Gro.)
Wickfields IG7: Chig . . . 23Tc 54
Wickford Cl. RM3: Rom . . . 22Pd 57
Wickford Dr. RM3: Rom . . . 22Pd 57
Wickford Ho. *E1* . . . *42Yb 92*
(off Wickford St.)
Wickford St. E1 . . . 42Yb 92
Wickford Way E17 . . . 28Zb 52
Wickham Av. CR0: C'don . . . 75Ac 158
SM3: Cheam . . . 78Ya 154
Wickham Chase BR4: W W'ck . . . 74Fc 159
Wickham Cl. E1 . . . 43Yb 92
EN3: Enf H . . . 13Xb 33
KT3: N Mald . . . 72Va 154
UB9: Hare . . . 25M 43
Wickham Ct. *KT5: Surb* . . . *71Pa 153*
(off Cranes Pk.)
Wickham Ct. Rd. BR4: W W'ck . . . 75Ec 158
Wickham Cres. BR4: W W'ck . . . 75Ec 158
Wickham Fld. TN14: Otf . . . 88Hd 182
Wickham Gdns. SE4 . . . 55Bc 114
Wickham Ho. *N1* . . . *39Ub 71*
(off Halcomb St.)
Wickham La. DA16: Well . . . 50Wc 95
SE2 . . . 50Wc 95
TW20: Egh . . . 66C 126
Wickham M. SE4 . . . 54Bc 114
Wickham Noakes Ct. BR3: Beck . . . 67Dc 136
Wickham Rd. BR3: Beck . . . 68Dc 136
CR0: C'don . . . 75Zb 158
E4 . . . 24Ec 52
HA3: Hrw W . . . 26Fa 46
RM16: Grays . . . 7E 100
SE4 . . . 56Bc 114
Wickham St. DA16: Well . . . 54Uc 116
SE11 . . . 7H 229 (50Pb 90)
Wickhams Way DA3: Hartl . . . 71Be 165
Wickham Theatre Cen. . . . 75Fc 159
Wickham Way BR3: Beck . . . 70Ec 136
Wick Ho. *KT1: Hamp W* . . . *67Ma 131*
(off Station Rd.)
Wick La. E3 . . . 39Cc 72
TW20: Eng G . . . 5K 125
Wickliffe Av. N3 . . . 26Ab 48
Wickliffe Gdns. HA9: Wemb . . . 33Ra 67
Wicklow Ho. N16 . . . 32Vb 71
Wicklow St. WC1 . . . 3H 217 (41Pb 90)
Wick Rd. E9 . . . 37Zb 72
TW11: Tedd . . . 66Ka 130
TW20: Eng G . . . 7L 125
Wicks Cl. SE9 . . . 63Mc 137
Wicksteed Cl. DA5: Bexl . . . 62Fd 140
Wicksteed Ho. SE1 . . . 4E 230 (48Sb 91)
TW8: Bford . . . 50Pa 87
Wickway Ct. *SE15* . . . *51Vb 113*
(off Cator St.)
Wickwood Ct. AL1: St A . . . 1F 6
Wickwood St. SE5 . . . 54Rb 113
Wid Cl. CM13: Hut . . . 15Fe 41
Widdecombe Av. HA2: Harr . . . 33Aa 65
Widdenham Rd. N7 . . . 35Pb 70
Widdin St. E15 . . . 38Gc 73
Widecombe Cl. RM3: Rom . . . 25Md 57
Widecombe Gdns. IG4: Ilf . . . 28Nc 54
Widecombe Rd. SE9 . . . 62Nc 138
Widecombe Way N2 . . . 29Fb 49
Widecroft Rd. SL0: Iver . . . 44G 82
Widegate St. E1 . . . 1J 225 (43Ub 91)
Widenham Cl. HA5: Eastc . . . 29Y 45
Widewater Pl. UB9: Hare . . . 29L 43
Wide Way CR4: Mitc . . . 69Mb 134
Widewing Cl. TW11: Tedd . . . 66Ma 131
Widford *NW1* . . . *37Kb 70*
(off Lewis St.)
Widford Ho. N1 . . . 2B 218
Widgeon Cl. E16 . . . 44Kc 93
Widgeon Rd. DA8: Erith . . . 52Kd 119
TW6: H'row A . . . 54K 105
Widgeon Way WD25: Wat . . . 9Aa 13
Widley Rd. W9 . . . 41Cb 89
Widmer Ct. TW3: Houn . . . 54Aa 107
WIDMORE . . . 69Lc 137
Widmore Dr. HP2: Hem H . . . 1A 4
WIDMORE GREEN . . . 68Mc 137
Widmore Lodge Rd. BR1: Brom . . . 68Mc 137
Widmore Rd. BR1: Brom . . . 68Jc 137
UB8: Hil . . . 42R 84
Widvale Rd. CM13: Mount . . . 13Fe 41
CM15: Shenf, Mount . . . 13Fe 41
Widworthy Hayes
CM13: Hut . . . 18De 41
Wieland Rd. HA6: Nwood . . . 24W 44
Wigan Ho. E5 . . . 32Xb 71
Wigeon Path SE28 . . . 48Tc 94
Wigeon Way UB4: Yead . . . 44Z 85
Wiggenhall Link Rd.
WD17: Wat . . . 16X 27
WD18: Wat . . . 16X 27
Wiggenhall Rd. WD18: Wat . . . 15X 27
Wiggie La. RH1: Redh . . . 4A 208
Wiggington Ho. *SL4: Eton* . . . *2H 103*
(off High St.)
Wiggins La. TW10: Ham . . . 61La 130
Wiggins Mead NW9 . . . 24Va 48
Wigginton Av. HA9: Wemb . . . 37Ra 67
Wight Ho. *KT1: King T* . . . *69Ma 131*
(off Portsmouth Rd.)
WD18: Wat . . . 15V 26
Wightman Rd. N4 . . . 28Qb 50
N8 . . . 28Qb 50
Wighton M. TW7: Isle . . . 54Ga 108
Wigley Bush La.
CM14: B'wood, S Weald . . . 19Ud 40
Wigley Rd. TW13: Felt . . . 61Z 129
Wigmore Hall . . . 2K 221
Wigmore Pl. E17 . . . 27Ac 52
W1 . . . 2K 221 (44Kb 90)
Wigmore Rd. SM5: Cars . . . 75Fb 155
Wigmore St. W1 . . . 3H 221 (44Jb 90)
Wigmore Wlk. SM5: Cars . . . 75Fb 155
Wigram Ho. *E14* . . . *45Dc 92*
(off Wade's Pl.)
Wigram Rd. E11 . . . 30Lc 53
Wigram Sq. E17 . . . 27Ec 52
Wigston Cl. N18 . . . 22Ub 51
Wigston Rd. E13 . . . 42Kc 93
Wigton Gdns. HA7: Stan . . . 25Na 47
Wigton Pl. SE11 . . . 7A 230 (50Qb 90)
Wigton Rd. E17 . . . 25Bc 52
RM3: Rom . . . 21Nd 57
Wigton Way RM3: Rom . . . 21Nd 57
Wilberforce Ct. BR2: Kes . . . 80Mc 159
HA8: Edg . . . *21Pa 47*
(off King's Dr.)
KT18: Eps . . . *86Ta 173*
(off Heathcote Rd.)
Wilberforce M. SW4 . . . 56Mb 112
Wilberforce Rd. N4 . . . 33Rb 71
NW9 . . . 30Wa 48
Wilberforce Wlk. E15 . . . 36Gc 73
Wilberforce Way DA12: Grav'nd . . . 4F 144
SE25 . . . 70Vb 135
SW19 . . . 65Za 132
Wilbraham Ho. *SW8* . . . *52Nb 112*
(off Wandsworth Rd.)
Wilbraham Mans. *SW1* . . . *5H 227*
(off Wilbraham Pl.)
Wilbraham Pl. SW1 . . . 5G 227 (49Hb 89)
Wilbrahams Almshouses
EN5: Barn . . . 12Bb 31
Wilbrooke Pl. SE3 . . . 53Kc 115
Wilbury Av. SM2: Cheam . . . 82Bb 175
Wilbury Rd. GU21: Wok . . . 9P 167
Wilbury Way N18 . . . 22Tb 51
Wilby M. W11 . . . 46Bb 89
Wilcon Way WD25: Wat . . . 6Z 13
Wilcot Av. WD19: Wat . . . 17Aa 27
Wilcot Cl. GU24: Bisl . . . 8E 166
WD19: Wat . . . 17Aa 27
Wilcot Gdns. GU24: Bisl . . . 8E 166
Wilcox Cl. SW8 . . . 52Nb 112
(not continuous)
WD6: Bore . . . 11Sa 29
Wilcox Gdns. TW17: Shep . . . 69N 127
Wilcox Ho. *E3* . . . *43Bc 92*
(off Ackroyd Dr.)
Wilcox Pl. SW1 . . . 4C 228 (48Lb 90)
Wilcox Rd. SM1: Sutt . . . 77Db 155
SW8 . . . 52Nb 112
TW11: Tedd . . . 63Fa 130
Wildacres HA6: Nwood . . . 21V 44
KT14: W Byf . . . 83L 169
Wildbank Ct. GU22: Wok . . . 90B 168
Wildberry Cl. W7 . . . 49Ja 86
Wildbore Ho. *N1* . . . *38Qb 70*
(off Liverpool Rd.)
Wildcat Rd. *TW6: H'row A* . . . *55K 105*
(off Wayfarer Rd.)
Wild Ct. WC2 . . . 3H 223 (44Pb 90)
Wildcroft Gdns. HA8: Edg . . . 23Ma 47
Wildcroft Mnr. SW15 . . . 59Ya 110
Wildcroft Rd. SW15 . . . 59Ya 110
Wilde Cl. E8 . . . 39Wb 71
RM18: Tilb . . . 4E 122
Wilde Ct. AL2: Lon C . . . 9F 6
Wilde Ho. *W2* . . . *4B 220*
(off Gloucester Ter.)
Wilde Pl. N13 . . . 23Rb 51
SW18 . . . 59Fb 111
Wilder Cl. HA4: Ruis . . . 32X 65
Wilderness, The
KT8: W Mole, E Mos . . . 71Ea 152
TW12: Hamp H . . . 63Da 129
WILDERNESSE . . . 94Nd 203
Wildernesse Av.
TN15: Seal, S'oaks . . . 94Nd 203
Wildernesse Golf Course . . . 94Qd 203
Wildernesse Mt. TN13: S'oaks . . . 94Md 203
Wilderness Island Nature Reserve
. . . 75Jb 156
Wilderness M. SW4 . . . 56Kb 112
Wilderness Rd. BR7: Chst . . . 66Rc 138
RH8: Oxt . . . 2H 211
Wilde Rd. DA8: Erith . . . 52Dd 118
Wilders Cl. GU21: Wok . . . 10N 167
Wilderton Rd. N16 . . . 31Ub 71
Wilder Wlk. W1 . . . 5C 222
Wildfell Rd. SE6 . . . 59Dc 114
Wild Goose Dr. SE14 . . . 53Yb 114
Wild Grn. Nth. SL3: L'ly . . . 49C 82
Wild Grn. Sth. SL3: L'ly . . . 49C 82
Wild Hatch NW11 . . . 30Cb 49
WILDHILL . . . 3M 9
Wildhill Rd. AL9: Hat . . . 5G 8
Wilding Ct. *WD6: Bore* . . . *14Qa 29*
(off Whitehall Cl.)
Wildmarsh Ct. *EN3: Enf W* . . . *9Ac 20*
(off Manly Dixon Dr.)
Wildoaks Cl. HA6: Nwood . . . 23V 44
Wild's Rents SE1 . . . 3H 231 (48Ub 91)
Wild St. WC2 . . . 3G 223 (44Nb 90)
Wildwood HA6: Nwood . . . 23T 44
Wildwood Av. AL2: Brick W . . . 2Ba 13
Wildwood Cl. GU22: Pyr . . . 87H 169
KT24: E Hor . . . 97V 190
SE12 . . . 59Hc 115
Wildwood Ct. CR8: Kenley . . . 87Tb 177
WD3: Chor . . . 14H 25
Wildwood Gro. NW3 . . . 32Eb 69
Wildwood Ri. NW11 . . . 32Eb 69
Wildwood Rd. NW11 . . . 30Db 49
Wildwood Ter. NW3 . . . 32Eb 69
Wilford Cl. EN2: Enf . . . 13Tb 33
HA6: Nwood . . . 24T 44
Wilford Rd. CR0: C'don . . . 72Sb 157
SL3: L'ly . . . 49A 82
Wilfred Av. RM13: Rain . . . 43Jd 96
Wilfred Cl. WD18: Wat . . . 15V 26
Wilfred Ct. *N15* . . . *29Tb 51*
(off South Gro.)
Wilfred Owen Cl. SW19 . . . 65Eb 133
Wilfred St. DA12: Grav'nd . . . 8D 122
GU21: Wok . . . 10P 167
SW1 . . . 3B 228 (48Lb 90)
Wilfred Wood Ct. *W6* . . . *49Ya 88*
(off Samuel's Cl.)
Wilfrid Gdns. W3 . . . 43Sa 87
Wilhelmina Av. CR5: Coul . . . 91Lb 196
Wilkes Cl. NW7 . . . 23Za 48
Wilkes Rd. CM13: Hut . . . 15Fe 41
TW8: Bford . . . 51Na 109
Wilkes St. E1 . . . 7K 219 (43Vb 91)
Wilkie Ho. SW1 . . . 7E 228
Wilkins Cl. CR4: Mitc . . . 67Gb 133
UB3: Harl . . . 50V 84
WILKINS GREEN . . . 1N 7
Wilkin's Grn. La. AL4: S'ford . . . 1N 7
AL10: Hat . . . 2M 7
Wilkins Grn. Ter. AL4: S'ford . . . 2M 7
Wilkins Ho. *SW1* . . . *51Kb 112*
(off Churchill Gdns.)
Wilkinson Cl. DA1: Dart . . . 56Pd 119
UB10: Hil . . . 39R 64
Wilkinson Ct. SW17 . . . 63Fb 133
Wilkinson Gdns. SE25 . . . 67Ub 135
Wilkinson Ho. N1 . . . 2G 219
Wilkinson Rd. E16 . . . 44Lc 93
Wilkinson St. SW8 . . . 52Pb 112
Wilkinson Way HP3: Hem H . . . 6P 3
W4 . . . 47Ta 87
Wilkin St. NW5 . . . 37Jb 70
Wilkin St. M. NW5 . . . 37Kb 70
Wilkins Way TN16: Bras . . . 96Xc 201
Wilks Av. DA1: Dart . . . 61Pd 141
Wilks Gdns. CR0: C'don . . . 74Ac 158
Wilks Pl. N1 . . . 2J 219 (40Ub 71)
Wilks Rd. DA2: Dart . . . 58Rd 119
Willan Rd. N17 . . . 26Tb 51
Willard St. SW8 . . . 55Kb 112
Willats Cl. KT16: Chert . . . 72H 149
Willcocks Cl. KT9: Chess . . . 76Na 153
Willcott Rd. W3 . . . 46Ra 87
Will Crooks Gdns. SE9 . . . 56Lc 115
Willen Fld. Rd. NW10 . . . 40Sa 67
Willenhall Av. EN5: New Bar . . . 16Eb 31
Willenhall Ct. EN5: New Bar . . . 16Eb 31
Willenhall Dr. UB3: Hayes . . . 45U 84
Willenhall Rd. SE18 . . . 50Rc 94
Willersley Av. BR6: Orp . . . 76Tc 160
DA15: Sidc . . . 60Vc 117
Willersley Cl. DA15: Sidc . . . 60Vc 117
Willerton Lodge KT13: Weyb . . . 79T 150
WILLESDEN . . . 37Wa 68
WILLESDEN GREEN . . . 37Ya 68
Willesden Green Cultural Cen. & Mus.
. . . 37Xa 68
Willesden La. NW2 . . . 37Ya 68
NW6 . . . 37Ya 68
Willesden Section Ho. *NW6* . . . *38Za 68*
(off Willesden La.)
Willesden Sports Cen. . . . 39Xa 68
Willesden Sports Stadium . . . 39Xa 68
Willes Rd. NW5 . . . 37Kb 70
Willets Cl. RM3: Rom . . . 24Ld 57
Willett Cl. BR5: Pet W . . . 72Uc 160
UB5: N'olt . . . 41Y 85
Willett Ho. *E13* . . . *40Kc 73*
(off Queens Rd. W.)
Willett Pl. CR7: Thor H . . . 71Qb 156
Willett Rd. CR7: Thor H . . . 71Qb 156
Willetts La. UB9: Den . . . 36H 63
Willett Way BR5: Pet W . . . 71Tc 160
Willey Broom La. CR3: Cat'm . . . 97Qb 196
Willey Farm La. CR3: Cat'm . . . 98Sb 197
Willey La. CR3: Cat'm . . . 97Tb 197
William IV St. WC2 . . . 5F 223 (45Nb 90)
William Allen Ho. HA8: Edg . . . 24Pa 47
William Ash Cl. RM9: Dag . . . 37Xc 75
William Banfield Ho. *SW6* . . . *54Bb 111*
(off Munster Rd.)
William Barefoot Dr. SE9 . . . 63Qc 138
William Blake Ho. SW11 . . . 53Gb 111
William Bonney Est. SW4 . . . 56Mb 112
William Booth Ho. *E14* . . . *44Cc 92*
(off Hind Gro.)
William Booth Rd. SE20 . . . 67Wb 135
William Carey Way HA1: Harr . . . 30Ga 46
William Caslon Ho. *E2* . . . *40Xb 71*
(off Patriot Sq.)
William Channing Ho. *E2* . . . *41Xb 91*
(off Canrobert St.)
William Cl. N2 . . . 26Fb 49
RM5: Col R . . . 25Ed 56
SE13 . . . 55Ec 114
UB2: S'hall . . . 47Ea 86
William Cobbett Ho. *W8* . . . *48Db 89*
(off Scarsdale Pl.)
William Congreve M.
N1 . . . 1D 218 (39Sb 71)
William Cory Prom.
DA8: Erith . . . 50Gd 96
William Cotton Ct. *E14* . . . *43Cc 92*
(off Selsey St.)
William Ct. HP3: Hem H . . . 6M 3
NW8 . . . 3A 214 (41Eb 89)
SE10 . . . *53Dc 114*
(off Greenwich High Rd.)
SE25 . . . *69Vb 135*
(off Chalfont Rd.)
SW16 . . . *66Pb 134*
(off Streatham High Rd.)
W5 . . . 43La 86
William Covell Cl. EN2: Enf . . . 10Pb 18
William Crook Ho.
HP1: Hem H . . . 2H 3
William Dr. HA7: Stan . . . 23Ja 46
William Dromey Ct. NW6 . . . 38Bb 69
William Dunbar Ho. *NW6* . . . *40Bb 69*
(off Albert Rd.)
William Dyce M. SW16 . . . 63Mb 134
William Ellis Cl. SL4: Old Win . . . 7L 103

Winchet Wlk.—Withy La.

Winchet Wlk. CR0: C'don 72Yb 158
Winchfield Cl. HA3: Kenton 30La 46
Winchfield Ho. SW15 . . . . 58Va 110
Winchfield Rd. SE26 . . . . 64Ac 136
Winchfield Way WD3: Rick 17L 25
Winch Ho. E14 . . . . 48Dc 92
(off Tiller Rd.)
SW10 . . . . 52Eb 111
(off King's Rd.)
Winchilsea Cres.
KT8: W Mole 68Ea 130
Winchilsea Ho. NW8 . . . . 4B 214
WINCHMORE HILL 17Ob 32
Winchmore Hill Rd. N14 . . . . 18Mb 32
N21 . . . . 18Mb 32
Winchmore Vs. N21 . . . . 17Pb 32
(off Winchmore Hill Rd.)
Winch's Mdw. SL1: Burn 1A 80
Winchstone Cl. TW17: Shep 70P 127
Winckley Cl. HA3: Kenton 29Pa 47
Winckworth Ct. N1 . . . . 4G 219
Wincott Pde. SE11 . . . . 5A 230
Wincott St. SE11 . . . . 5A 230 (49Qb 90)
Wincrofts Dr. SE9 . . . . 56Tc 116
Windall Cl. SE19 . . . . 67Wb 135
Windborough Rd.
SM5: Cars 80Jb 156
Windermere NW1 . . . . 4A 216
Windermere Av. AL1: St A 4F 6
(not continuous)
HA4: Ruis 31Y 65
HA9: Kenton, Wemb 31La 66
N3 . . . . 27Cb 49
NW6 . . . . 39Ab 68
RM12: Horn 36Jd 76
RM19: Purf 50Sd 98
SW19 . . . . 69Db 133
Windermere Cl. BR6: Farnb 76Rc 160
DA1: Dart 60Kd 119
HP3: Hem H 3C 4
TW14: Felt 60V 106
TW19: Stanw 60N 105
TW20: Egh 66D 126
WD3: Chor 15F 24
Windermere Ct. CR8: Kenley 87Rb 177
GU21: Wok 10L 167
(off St John's Rd.)
HA9: Wemb 31La 66
SM5: Cars 76Jb 156
SW13 . . . . 51Va 110
WD17: Wat 12W 26
Windermere Gdns. IG4: Ilf 29Nc 54
Windermere Gro. HA9: Wemb 32La 66
Windermere Hall HA8: Edg 22Pa 47
Windermere Ho. E3 . . . . 42Bc 92
EN5: New Bar 14Db 31
TW7: Isle 57Ha 108
Windermere Point SE15 . . . . 52Yb 114
(off Old Kent Rd.)
Windermere Rd. BR4: W W'ck 75Gc 159
CR0: C'don 74Vb 157
CR5: Coul 87Nb 176
DA7: Bex 54Ed 118
GU18: Light 2A 166
N10 . . . . 25Kb 50
N19 . . . . 33Lb 70
SW15 . . . . 63Ua 132
SW16 . . . . 67Lb 134
UB1: S'hall 43Ba 85
W5 . . . . 48La 86
Windermere Way RH2: Reig 5N 207
SL1: Slou 3A 80
UB7: Yiew 46N 83
Winders Rd. SW11 . . . . 54Gb 111
(not continuous)
Windfield KT22: Lea 93Ka 192
Windfield Cl. SE26 . . . . 63Zb 136
Windham Av. CR0: New Ad 82Fc 179
Windham Rd. TW9: Rich 55Pa 109
Windhover Way DA12: Grav'nd 3G 144
Windings, The CR2: Sande 83Vb 177
Winding Shot HP1: Hem H 1J 3
Winding Way RM8: Dag 34Yc 75
Windlass Pl. SE8 . . . . 49Ac 92
Windlebrook Pk. KT16: Longc 75B 148
Windle Cl. GU20: W'sham 9B 146
Windlemere Golf Course 3C 166
WINDLESHAM 9B 146
Windlesham Ct. GU20: W'sham 6A 146
Windlesham Ct. Dr. GU20: W'sham . . . 7A 146
Windlesham Gro. SW19 . . . . 60Za 110
Windlesham Ho. SE1 . . . . 7J 225
Windlesham M. TW12: Hamp H 65Ea 130
Windlesham Rd. GU24: Chob 10E 146
GU24: W End 3C 166
Windley Cl. SE23 . . . . 61Yb 136
Windmill WC1 . . . . 7H 217
Windmill Av. KT17: Ewe 83Va 174
UB2: S'hall 46Ea 86
Windmill Bri. Ho. CR0: C'don 74Ub 157
(off Freemasons Rd.)
Windmill Bus. Village TW16: Sun . . . 67U 128
Windmill Cl. CR3: Cat'm 93Sb 197
EN9: Walt A 6Gc 21
KT6: Surb 74La 152
KT17: Eps 84Va 174
RM14: Upm 33Qd 77
SE1 . . . . 49Wb 91
(off Beatrice Rd.)
SE13 . . . . 54Ec 114
SL4: Wind 4F 102
TW16: Sun 66U 128
Windmill Ct. E4 . . . . 19Gc 35
HA4: Ruis 32W 64
NW2 . . . . 37Ab 68
W5 . . . . 49La 86
(off Windmill Rd.)
Windmill Dr. BR2: Kes 77Lc 159
KT22: Lea 95La 192
NW2 . . . . 34Ab 68
RH2: Reig 4M 207
SW4 . . . . 57Kb 112
WD3: Crox G 16P 25
Windmill End KT17: Eps 84Va 174
Windmill Fld. GU20: W'sham 9A 146
Windmill Gdns. EN2: Enf 13Qb 32
Windmill Grange
TN15: W King 80Ud 164
Windmill Grn. TW17: Shep 73U 150
Windmill Gro. CR0: C'don 72Sb 157
Windmill Hill EN2: Enf 13Rb 33
HA4: Ruis 31V 64
NW3 . . . . 34Eb 69
TN15: Wro H 93Fe 205
WD4: Chfd 4H 11
(not continuous)
Windmill Ho. E14 . . . . 49Cc 92
SE1 . . . . 7A 224
Windmill La. E15 . . . . 37Fc 73
EN5: Ark 16Va 30
EN8: Chesh 2Ac 20
KT6: Surb 72Ka 152
KT17: Eps 84Va 174
TW7: Isle 48Ea 86
UB2: S'hall 46Ea 86
UB6: G'frd 44Ea 86
WD23: B Hea 18Ga 28
Windmill M. W4 . . . . 49Ua 88
Windmill Pk. TN15: Wro H 92Fe 205
Windmill Pas. W4 . . . . 49Ua 88
Windmill Pl. UB2: S'hall 46Ea 86
Windmill Ri. KT2: King T 66Ra 131
Windmill Rd. CR0: C'don 73Sb 157
CR4: Mitc 71Lb 156
HP2: Hem H 2N 3
N18 . . . . 21Tb 51
SL1: Slou 6H 81
SL3: Ful 6P 61
SW18 . . . . 58Fb 111
SW19 . . . . 61Xa 132
TW8: Bford 49La 86
TW12: Hamp H 64Da 129
TW16: Sun 67U 128
W4 . . . . 49Ua 88
W5 . . . . 49La 86
Windmill Rd. W.
TW16: Sun 68U 128
Windmill Row SE11 . . . . . 7K 229 (50Qb 90)
Windmills, The KT22: Lea 95La 192
Windmill Shott TW20: Egh 65B 126
Windmill St. DA12: Grav'nd 8D 122
W1 . . . . 1D 222 (43Mb 90)
(not continuous)
WD23: B Hea 18Ga 28
Windmill Ter.
TW17: Shep 73U 150
Windmill Wlk. SE1 . . . . . . 7A 224 (46Qb 90)
Windmill Way HA4: Ruis 32V 64
RH2: Reig 4M 207
Windmore Av. EN6: Pot B 3Ya 16
Windmore Cl. HA0: Wemb 36Ja 66
Windridge Cl. AL3: St A 4N 5
Windrose Cl. SE16 . . . . 47Zb 92
Windrush KT3: N Mald 70Ra 131
SE28 . . . . 46Xc 95
Windrush Av. SL3: L'ly 48B 82
Windrush Cl. E8 . . . . 38Wb 71
N17 . . . . 25Ub 51
SW11 . . . . 56Fb 111
UB10: Ick 35P 63
W4 . . . . 53Sa 109
Windrush Ct. DA8: Erith 50Gd 96
Windrushes CR3: Cat'm 97Wb 197
Windrush Ho. NW8 . . . . 6C 214
Windrush La. SE23 . . . . 62Zb 136
Windrush Rd. NW10 . . . . 39Ta 67
RM18: Tilb 2A 122
Windrush Sq. SW2 . . . . 56Qb 112
Winds End Cl. HP2: Hem H 1A 4
Windsock Cl. SE16 . . . . 49Bc 92
Windsock Way TW6: H'row A 54K 105
WINDSOR 3H 103
Windsor & Royal Borough Mus. 3H 103
Windsor Av. E17 . . . . 26Ac 52
HA8: Edg 21Ra 47
KT3: N Mald 71Sa 153
KT8: W Mole 69Ca 129
RM16: Grays 47De 99
SM3: Cheam 76Ab 154
SW19 . . . . 67Eb 133
UB10: Hil 39R 64
Windsor Boys' School Sports Cen. . . . 3F 102
Windsor Bus. Cen. SL4: Wind 2G 102
Windsor Castle 2J 103
Windsor Cen., The N1 . . . . 39Rb 71
(off Windsor St.)
Windsor Cl. BR7: Chst 64Rc 138
EN7: Chesh 2Wb 19
HA2: Harr 34Ca 65
HA6: Nwood 26W 44
HP2: Hem H 4N 3
HP3: Bov 10C 2
N3 . . . . 26Ab 48
SE27 . . . . 63Sb 135
SL1: Burn 2A 80
TW6: H'row A 55L 105
(off Whittle Rd.)
TW8: Bford 51Ka 108
WD6: Bore 11Qa 29
Windsor Cotts. SE14 . . . . 52Bc 114
(off Amersham Gro.)
Windsor Ct. AL1: St A 3E 6
CR3: Whyt 90Vb 177
E3 . . . . 40Cc 72
(off Mostyn Gro.)
GU24: Chob 1J 167
HA5: Pinn 27Z 45
KT1: King T 70Ma 131
(off Palace Rd.)
KT18: Eps 85Ta 173
(off Ashley Rd.)
N11 . . . . 22Hb 49
N14 . . . . 17Lb 32
NW3 . . . . 35Cb 69
NW11 . . . . 30Ab 48
(off Golders Grn. Rd.)
SE16 . . . . 45Zb 92
(off King & Queen Wharf)
SW3 . . . . 7E 226
SW11 . . . . 54Fb 111
TW16: Sun 66W 128
W2 . . . . 45Db 89
(off Moscow Rd.)
W10 . . . . 44Za 88
(off Bramley Rd.)
WD4: K Lan 1Q 12
WD6: Bore 12Sa 29
WD23: Bush 17Ea 28
(off Catsey La.)
Windsor Ct. Rd. GU24: Chob 1J 167
Windsor Cres. HA2: Harr 34Ca 65
HA9: Wemb 34Ra 67
Windsor Dr. BR6: Chels 79Wc 161
DA1: Dart 58Jd 118
EN4: E Barn 16Hb 31
TW15: Ashf 63M 127
Windsor Fitness Club, The 3F 102
Windsor Gdns. CR0: Bedd 76Nb 156
UB3: Harl 48R 84
W9 . . . . 43Cb 89
Windsor Great Pk. 2F 124
Windsor Gro. SE27 . . . . 63Sb 135
Windsor Hall E16 . . . . 46Kc 93
(off Wesley Av.)
Windsor, Home Park
(Park & Ride) 1J 103
Windsor Ho. E2 . . . . 41Zb 92
(off Knottisford St.)
E20 . . . . 36Dc 72
(off Peloton Av.)
KT16: Chert 72J 149
(off Windsor St.)
N1 . . . . 1E 218 (40Sb 71)
NW1 . . . . 3A 216
NW2 . . . . 37Ab 68
(off Chatsworth Rd.)
UB5: N'olt 37Ca 65
(off The Farmlands)
WD23: Bush 14Ba 27
Windsor La. SL1: Burn 2A 80
Windsor Lawn Tennis Club 3F 102
Windsor, Legoland (Park & Ride) 7C 102
Windsor Leisure Cen. 2F 102
Windsor M. SE6 . . . . 60Ec 114
SE23 . . . . 60Ac 114
Windsor Pk. Rd. UB3: Harl 52V 106
Windsor Pl. KT16: Chert 72J 149
SW1 . . . . 5C 228 (48Lb 90)
Windsor Rd. CM15: Pil H 16Xd 40
CR7: Thor H 68Rb 135
DA6: Bex 56Ad 117
DA12: Grav'nd 2D 144
E4 . . . . 21Dc 52
E7 . . . . 36Kc 73
E10 . . . . 33Dc 72
E11 . . . . 32Jc 73
EN3: Enf W 8Zb 20
EN5: Barn 16Za 30
GU24: Chob 7G 146
HA3: Hrw W 25Ea 46
HP9: Beac 1E 60
IG1: Ilf 35Rc 74
KT2: King T 66Na 131
KT4: Wor Pk 75Wa 154
N3 . . . . 26Ab 48
N7 . . . . 34Nb 70
N13 . . . . 20Qb 32
N17 . . . . 26Wb 51
NW2 . . . . 37Xa 68
RM8: Dag 34Ad 75
RM11: Horn 31Ld 77
SL1: Slou 8J 81
SL2: Ger X, Stoke P 5L 61
SL3: Dat 2L 103
SL4: Old Win 10N 103
SL4: Wat O, Wind 2A 102
SL4: Wink 5A 124
SL9: Ger X 2M 61
TW4: Cran 54X 107
TW9: Kew 54Pa 109
TW11: Tedd 64Fa 130
TW16: Sun 65W 128
TW19: Wray 58A 104
TW20: Egh 10N 103
UB2: S'hall 48Ba 85
W5 . . . . 45Na 87
(not continuous)
WD24: Wat 10Y 13
Windsors, The IG9: Buck H 19Nc 36
Windsor St. KT16: Chert 72J 149
N1 . . . . 39Rb 71
UB8: Uxb 39L 63
Windsor Ter. N1 . . . . 3E 218 (41Sb 91)
Windsor Theatre Royal 2H 103
Windsor Wlk. KT12: Walt T 74Z 151
KT13: Weyb 78R 150
SE5 . . . . 54Tb 113
Windsor Way GU22: Wok 88E 168
W14 . . . . 49Za 88
WD3: Rick 18J 25
Windsor Wharf E9 . . . . 36Bc 72
Windsor Wood EN9: Walt A 5Gc 21
Windspoint Dr. SE15 . . . . 51Xb 113
Winds Ridge GU23: Send 97E 188
Windus M. N16 . . . . 32Vb 71
Windus Rd. N16 . . . . 32Vb 71
Windus Wlk. N16 . . . . 32Vb 71
Windward Cl. EN3: Enf W 7Zb 20
Windward Ct. E16 . . . . 45Rc 94
(off Gallions Rd.)
Windycroft Cl. CR8: Purl 85Mb 176
Windy Hill CM13: Hut 18Ee 41
Windy Ridge BR1: Brom 67Nc 138
Windy Ridge Cl. SW19 . . . . 64Za 132
Wine Cl. E1 . . . . 46Yb 92
(not continuous)
Wine Office Ct. EC4 . . . . . 2A 224 (44Qb 90)
Winern Glebe KT14: Byfl 85M 169
Winery La. KT1: King T 69Pa 131
Winey Cl. KT9: Chess 80La 152
Winfield La. TN15: Bor G 97Ae 205
Winfield Mobile Home Pk.
WD25: A'ham 11Da 27
Winford Ct. SE15 . . . . 53Xb 113
Winford Ho. E3 . . . . 38Bc 72
Winford Pde. UB1: S'hall 44Da 85
(off Marconi Way)
Winforton St. SE10 . . . . 53Ec 114
Winfrith Rd. SW18 . . . . 59Eb 111
Wingate & Finchley FC
Harry Abrahams Stadium 24Fb 49
Wingate Bus. Cen. AL9: Wel G 5E 8
Wingate Cres. CR0: C'don 72Nb 156
Wingate Ho. E3 . . . . 41Dc 92
(off Bruce Rd.)
Wingate Rd. DA14: Sidc 65Yc 139
IG1: Ilf 36Rc 74
W6 . . . . 48Xa 88
Wingate Sq. SW4 . . . . 55Lb 112
Wingate Way AL1: St A 3E 6
Wingfield RM17: Grays 49Ee 99
Wingfield Bank DA11: Nflt 61Ee 143
Wingfield Cl. CM13: B'wood 20Ce 41
KT15: New H 82K 169
Wingfield Ct. DA15: Sidc 61Vc 139
E14 . . . . 45Fc 93
(off Newport Av.)
SM7: Bans 87Cb 175
WD18: Wat 16S 26
Wingfield Ho. RM16: Ors 3C 100
Wingfield Gdns. RM14: Upm 30Ud 58
Wingfield Ho. E2 . . . . 4K 219
Wingfield M. SE15 . . . . 55Wb 113
Wingfield Rd. DA12: Grav'nd 9D 122
E15 . . . . 35Gc 73
E17 . . . . 29Dc 52
KT2: King T 65Pa 131
Wingfield St. SE15 . . . . 55Wb 113
Wingfield Way HA4: Ruis 36X 65
Wingford Rd. SW2 . . . . 58Nb 112
Wingletye La. RM11: Horn 28Pd 57
Wingmore Rd. SE24 . . . . 55Sb 113
Wingrad Ho. E1 . . . . 43Yb 92
(off Jubilee St.)
Wingrave Cres. CM14: B'wood 21Ud 58
Wingrave Rd. W6 . . . . 51Ya 110
Wingreen NW8 . . . . 39Db 69
(off Abbey Rd.)
Wingrove E4 . . . . 17Cc 34
Wingrove Ct. RM7: Rom 29Ed 56
Wingrove Dr. RM19: Purf 50Rd 97
Wingrove Rd. SE6 . . . . 61Gc 137
Wings Cl. SM1: Sutt 77Cb 155
Wings Rd. TW6: H'row A 55K 105
(off Whittle Rd.)
Wingway CM14: B'wood 18Yd 40
Wing Yip Bus. Cen. NW2 . . . . 33Xa 68
Winicotte Ho. W2 . . . . 7C 214
Winifred Av. RM12: Horn 35Md 77
Winifred Cl. EN5: Ark 16Va 30
Winifred Dell Ho. CM13: Gt War 23Yd 58
Winifred Pl. N12 . . . . 22Eb 49
Winifred Rd. CR5: Coul 88Jb 176
DA1: Dart 57Kd 119
DA8: Erith 50Gd 96
HP3: Hem H 6M 3
RM8: Dag 33Ad 75
SW19 . . . . 67Cb 133
TW12: Hamp H 63Ca 129
Winifred St. E16 . . . . 46Pc 94
Winifred Ter. EN1: Enf 17Vb 33
Winkers Cl. SL9: Chal P 25B 42
Winkers La. SL9: Chal P 25B 42
Winkfield Rd. E13 . . . . 40Kc 73
N22 . . . . 25Qb 50
SL4: Wind, Wink 10A 102
SL5: Asc 9A 124
Winkley Ct. HA2: Harr 34Ca 65
N10 . . . . 28Kb 50
(off St James's La.)
Winkley St. E2 . . . . 40Xb 71
WINKWELL 4F 2
Winkwell HP1: Hem H 4F 2
Winkworth Cotts. E1 . . . . 42Yb 92
(off Cephas St.)
Winkworth Pl. SM7: Bans 86Bb 175
Winkworth Rd. SM7: Bans 86Cb 175
Winlaton Rd. BR1: Brom 63Fc 137
Winmill Rd. RM8: Dag 34Bd 75
Winnards GU21: Wok 10L 167
Winnepeg Ho. SE16 . . . . 47Yb 92
(off Province Dr.)
Winnett St. W1 . . . . 4D 222 (45Mb 90)
Winningales Ct. IG5: Ilf 26Nc 54
Winnings Wlk. UB5: N'olt 37Aa 65
Winnington Cl. N2 . . . . 30Fb 49
Winnington Ho. SE5 . . . . 52Sb 113
(off Wyndham Est.)
W10 . . . . 42Ab 88
(off Southern Row)
Winnington Rd. EN3: Enf W 10Yb 20
N2 . . . . 30Fb 49
Winnington Way GU21: Wok 10M 167
Winnipeg Dr. BR6: Chels 79Vc 161
Winnock Rd. UB7: Yiew 46M 83
Winn Rd. SE12 . . . . 60Jc 115
Winns Av. E17 . . . . 27Bc 52
Winns Comn. Rd. SE18 . . . . 51Uc 116
Winns M. N15 . . . . 28Ub 51
Winns Ter. E17 . . . . 27Cc 52
Winsbeach E17 . . . . 26Fc 53
Winscombe Cres. W5 . . . . 42Ma 87
Winscombe St. N19 . . . . 33Kb 70
Winscombe Way HA7: Stan 22Ja 46
Winsford Rd. SE6 . . . . 62Bc 136
Winsford Ter. N18 . . . . 22Tb 51
Winsham Gro. SW11 . . . . 57Jb 112
Winsham Ho. NW1 . . . . 3E 216
Winslade Rd. SW2 . . . . 57Nb 112
Winslade Way SE6 . . . . 59Dc 114
Winsland M. W2 . . . . 2B 220 (44Fb 89)
Winsland St. W2 . . . . 2B 220 (44Fb 89)
Winsley St. W1 . . . . 2B 222 (44Lb 90)
Winslow SE17 . . . . 7H 231 (50Ub 91)
Winslow Cl. HA5: Eastc 30X 45
NW10 . . . . 34Ua 68
Winslow Gro. E4 . . . . 19Gc 35
Winslow Rd. W6 . . . . 51Ya 110
Winslow Way KT12: Walt T 76Y 151
TW13: Hanw 62Z 129
Winsmoor Ct. EN2: Enf 13Rb 33
WINSOR PARK 43Rc 94
Winsor Ter. E6 . . . . 43Qc 94
Winstanley Cl. KT11: Cobh 86X 171
Winstanley Est. SW11 . . . . 55Fb 111
Winstanley Rd. SW11 . . . . 55Fb 111
(not continuous)
Winstanley Wlk. KT11: Cobh 86X 171
(off Winstanley Cl.)
Winstead Gdns. RM10: Dag 36Ed 76
Winston Av. NW9 . . . . 31Ua 68
Winston Churchill School Sports Cen.
. . . . 10J 167
Winston Churchill Way
EN8: Walt C 5Yb 20
Winston Cl. DA9: Ghithe 58Vd 120
HA3: Hrw W 23Ha 46
RM7: Mawney 28Dd 56
Winston Ct. BR1: Brom 67Kc 137
(off Widmore Rd.)
HA3: Hrw W 24Da 45
Winston Dr. KT11: Stoke D 88Aa 171
TN16: Big H 89Mc 179
Winston Ho. W13 . . . . 47Ja 86
(off Balfour Rd.)
WC1 . . . . 5E 216
Winston Rd. N16 . . . . 35Tb 71
Winston Wlk. W4 . . . . 48Ta 87
Winston Way EN6: Pot B 5Cb 17
GU22: Wok 92D 188
IG1: Ilf 34Rc 74
Winstre Rd. WD6: Bore 11Qa 29
Winter Av. E6 . . . . 39Nc 74
Winterborne Av. BR6: Orp 76Tc 160
Winterbourne Gro. KT13: Weyb 79S 150
Winterbourne Ho. W11 . . . . 45Ab 88
(off Portland Rd.)
Winterbourne M. RH8: Oxt 2G 210
Winterbourne Rd. CR7: Thor H 70Qb 134
RM8: Dag 33Yc 75
SE6 . . . . 60Bc 114
Winter Box Wlk. TW10: Rich 57Pa 109
Winterbrook Rd. SE24 . . . . 58Sb 113
Winterburn Cl. N11 . . . . 23Jb 50
Winter Cl. KT17: Eps 84Ua 174
Winterdown Gdns. KT10: Esh 79Ba 151
Winterdown Rd. KT10: Esh 79Ba 151
Winterfold Cl. SW19 . . . . 61Ab 132
Wintergarden DA9: Bluew 59Wd 120
Wintergarden Cres. DA9: Bluew 59Wd 120
Winter Gdns. TW11: Tedd 63Ja 130
Wintergreen Blvd. UB7: W Dray 47P 83
Wintergreen Cl. E6 . . . . 43Nc 94
Winterleys NW6 . . . . 40Bb 69
(off Denmark Rd.)
Winter Lodge SE16 . . . . 50Wb 91
(off Fern Wlk.)
Winter's Ct. E4 . . . . 20Dc 34
Winters Cft. DA12: Grav'nd 5F 144
Wintersells Ind. Est. KT14: Byfl 82N 169
Wintersells Rd. KT14: Byfl 82M 169
Winterslow Ho. SE5 . . . . 54Sb 113
(off Flaxman Rd.)
Winterslow Rd. SW9 . . . . 53Rb 113
Winters Rd. KT7: T Ditt 73Ka 152
Winterstoke Gdns. NW7 . . . . 22Wa 48
Winterstoke Rd. SE6 . . . . 60Bc 114
Winters Way EN9: Walt A 5Jc 21
Winterton Ct. KT1: Hamp W 67Ma 131
(off Lwr. Teddington Rd.)
SE20 . . . . 68Wb 135
TN16: Westrm 99Tc 200
(off Market Sq.)
Winterton Ho. E1 . . . . 44Yb 92
(off Deancross St.)
Winterton Pl. SW10 . . . . 51Eb 111
Winterwell Rd. SW2 . . . . 57Nb 112
Winthorpe Gdns. WD6: Bore 11Pa 29
Winthorpe Rd. SW15 . . . . 56Ab 110
Winthrop Ho. W12 . . . . 45Xa 88
(off White City Est.)
Winthrop St. E1 . . . . 43Xb 91
Winthrop Wlk. HA9: Wemb 34Na 67
(off Everard Way)
Winton App. WD3: Crox G 15S 26
Winton Av. N11 . . . . 24Lb 50
Winton Cl. N9 . . . . 17Zb 34
Winton Ct. BR8: Swan 70Gd 140
N1 . . . . 1H 217
Winton Cres. WD3: Crox G 15R 26
Winton Dr. EN8: Chesh 1Ac 20
WD3: Crox G 16R 26
Winton Gdns. HA8: Edg 24Pa 47
Winton Rd. BR6: Farnb 77Rc 160
Winton Ter. AL1: St A 3C 6
(off Old London Rd.)
Winton Way SW16 . . . . 64Qb 134
Wintoun Path SL2: Slou 2C 80
Winvale SL1: Slou 8J 81
Winwood SL2: Slou 4N 81
SL4: Wind 3C 102
Wireless Rd. TN16: Big H 87Mc 179
Wireworks Ct. SE1 . . . . 2C 230
Wirrall Ho. SE26 . . . . 62Wb 135
Wirral Wood Cl. BR7: Chst 65Qc 138
Wirra Rd. TW6: H'row A 54K 105
(off Wayfarer Rd.)
Wisbeach Rd. CR0: C'don 71Tb 157
Wisbech N4 . . . . 32Pb 70
(off Lorne Rd.)
Wisborough Rd. CR2: Sande 81Vb 177
Wisden Ho. SW8 . . . . 51Pb 112
Wisdom Ct. TW7: Isle 55Ja 108
(off South St.)
Wisdons Cl. RM10: Dag 32Dd 76
Wise Ct. WD18: Wat 14U 26
(off Raven Cl.)
Wise La. NW7 . . . . 22Wa 48
UB7: W Dray 48M 83
Wiseman Rd. E10 . . . . 33Cc 72
Wise Rd. E15 . . . . 39Fc 73
Wise's La. AL9: N Mym 9E 8
TN15: Ash, Stans 81Zd 185
Wiseton Rd. SW17 . . . . 60Gb 111
Wishart Rd. SE3 . . . . 54Mc 115
Wishaw Wlk. N13 . . . . 23Nb 50
Wishbone Way GU21: Wok 8K 167
Wishford Ct. KT21: Asht 90Pa 173
WISLEY 88N 169
WISLEY COMMON 88Q 170
Wisley Common, Ockham & Chatley Heath
Nature Reserve 90S 170
Wisley Ct. CR2: Sande 82Tb 177
RH1: Redh 5P 207
(off Clarendon Rd.)
Wisley Golf Course 89M 169
Wisley Ho. SW1 . . . . 7D 228
WISLEY INTERCHANGE 88S 170
Wisley La. GU23: Wis 88L 169
Wisley Rd. BR5: St P 66Wc 139
SW11 . . . . 57Jb 112
Wistaria Cl. BR6: Farnb 75Rc 160
CM15: Pil H 15Yd 40
Wistaria Dr. AL2: Lon C 8F 6
Wisteria Apartments E9 . . . . 37Yb 72
(off Chatham Pl.)
Wisteria Cl. IG1: Ilf 36Rc 74
NW7 . . . . 23Va 48
Wisteria Gdns. BR8: Swan 68Fd 140
IG8: Wfd G 22Jc 53
Wisteria Rd. SE13 . . . . 56Fc 115
Wistlea Cres. AL4: Col H 4E 6
Wistow Ho. E2 . . . . 39Wb 71
(off Whiston Rd.)
Witanhurst La. N6 . . . . 32Jb 70
Witan St. E2 . . . . 41Xb 91
Witches La. TN13: Riv 94Fd 202
Witchwood Ho. SW9 . . . . 55Qb 112
(off Gresham Rd.)
Witham Cl. IG10: Lough 16Nc 36
Witham Ct. E10 . . . . 34Dc 72
SW17 . . . . 62Hb 133
Witham Gdns. CM13: W H'dn 30Fe 59
Witham Rd. RM2: Rom 29Kd 57
RM10: Dag 36Cd 76
SE20 . . . . 69Yb 136
TW7: Isle 53Fa 108
W13 . . . . 46Ja 86
Withens Cl. BR5: St M Cry 70Yc 139
Witherby Cl. CR0: C'don 78Ub 157
Witherings, The RM11: Horn 29Nd 57
Witherington Rd. N5 . . . . 36Qb 70
Withers Cl. KT9: Chess 79La 152
Withers Mead NW9 . . . . 25Va 48
Withers Pl. EC1 . . . . 5E 218 (42Sb 91)
Witherston Way SE9 . . . . 61Qc 138
Withey Beds Local Nature Reserve, The
. . . . 19R 26
Withey Cl. SL4: Wind 3C 102
Witheygate Av.
TW18: Staines 65K 127
Withies, The GU21: Knap 9J 167
KT22: Lea 92Ka 192
Withybed Cnr. KT20: Walt H 95Xa 194
Withy Cl. GU18: Light 2A 166
Withycombe Rd. SW19 . . . . 59Za 110
Withycroft SL3: Geor G 44A 82
Withy Ho. E1 . . . . 42Zb 92
(off Globe Rd.)
Withy La. HA4: Ruis 29S 44

Withy Mead—Woodlands Gdns.

Withy Mead E4 20Fc 35
Withy Pl. AL2: Park 10A 6
Witley Ct. WC1 6F 217
Witley Cres. CR0: New Ad 79Ec 158
Witley Gdns. UB2: S'hall 49Ba 85
Witley Ho. SW2 59Nb 112
Witley Ind. Est. UB2: S'hall 49Ba 85
Witley Point *SW15* 60Xa 110
(off Wanborough Dr.)
Witley Rd. N19 33Lb 70
Witney Cl. HA5: Hat E 23Ba 45
UB10: Ick 35P 63
Witney Path SE23 62Zb 136
Wittenham Way E4 20Fc 35
Wittering Cl. KT2: King T 64Ma 131
Wittering Wlk. RM12: Horn 37Ld 77
Wittersham Rd.
BR1: Brom 64Hc 137
Witts Ho. *KT1: King T* 69Pa 131
(off Winery La.)
Wivenhoe Cl. SE15 55Xb 113
Wivenhoe Ct. TW3: Houn 56Ba 107
Wivenhoe Rd. IG11: Bark 40Wc 75
Wiverton Rd. SE26 65Yb 136
Wix Rd. RM9: Dag 39Zc 75
Wix's La. SW4 55Kb 112
WLA Community Sports Cen. 39Aa 65
Woburn *W13* 43Ka 86
(off Clivedon Ct.)
Woburn Av. CM16: They B 9Uc 22
CR8: Purl 83Qb 176
RM12: Horn 35Jd 76
Woburn Cl. SE28 44Zc 95
SW19 65Eb 133
WD23: Bush 16Ea 28
Woburn Ct. CR0: C'don 74Sb 157
E18 26Jc 53
SE16 50Xb 91
(off Masters Dr.)
WC1 6F 217
(off Bernard St.)
Woburn Hill KT15: Add 75L 149
Woburn Mans. WC1 7D 216
Woburn M. WC1 5E 216 (42Mb 90)
WOBURN PARK 75L 149
Woburn Pl. WC1 5E 216 (42Nb 90)
Woburn Rd. CR0: C'don 74Sb 157
SM5: Cars 74Gb 155
Woburn Sq. WC1 6E 216 (42Mb 90)
(not continuous)
Woburn Twr. *UB5: N'olt* 41Z 85
(off Broomcroft Av.)
Woburn Wlk. WC1 4E 216 (41Mb 90)
Wodeham Gdns. E1 43Wb 91
Wodehouse Av. SE5 53Vb 113
Wodehouse Ct. *W3* 48Sa 87
(off Vincent Rd.)
Wodehouse Rd. DA1: Dart 56Qd 119
Woffington Cl. KT1: Hamp W 67La 130
Wokindon Rd. RM16: Grays 8D 100
WOKING 89B 168
Woking Bus. Pk. GU21: Wok 87D 168
Woking Cl. SW15 56Va 110
Woking Crematorium GU21: Wok 1J 187
Woking FC 92B 188
Woking Golf Course 2L 187
Woking Leisure Cen. 91B 188
Woking Rd. GU4: Jac W 9N 187
Wolcot Ho. NW1 2C 216
Wold, The CR3: Wold 94Cc 198
Woldham Pl. BR2: Brom 70Lc 137
Woldham Rd. BR2: Brom 70Lc 137
WOLDINGHAM 95Cc 198
WOLDINGHAM GARDEN VILLAGE
92Ac 198
Woldingham Golf Course 92Zb 198
Woldingham Rd. CR3: Wold 92Xb 197
Wolds Dr. BR6: Farnb 77Qc 160
Wolesley Ct. *GU21: Knap* 10G 166
(off Tudor Way)
Wolfe Cl. BR2: Hayes 72Jc 159
UB4: Yead 41X 85
Wolfe Cotts. TN16: Westrm 99Tc 200
Wolfe Cres. SE7 50Mc 93
SE16 47Zb 92
Wolfe Ho. *W12* 45Xa 88
(off White City Est.)
W14 49Bb 89
Wolfendale Cl. RH1: Mers 2C 208
Wolferton Rd. E12 35Pc 74
Wolffe Gdns. E15 37Hc 73
Wolfington Rd. SE27 63Rb 135
Wolf La. SL4: Wind 5B 102
Wolfram Cl. SE13 57Gc 115
Wolf's Hill RH8: Oxt 3L 211
Wolf's Rd. RH8: Limp 2M 211
Wolf's Row RH8: Limp 1M 211
Wolfs Wood RH8: Oxt 4L 211
Wolftencroft Cl. SW11 55Gb 111
Wollaston Cl. SE1 5D 230 (49Sb 91)
Wollaton Ho. N1 1A 218
Wollett Ct. *NW1* 38Lb 70
(off St Pancras Way)
Wollstonecraft St. N1 39Mb 70
Wolmer Cl. HA8: Edg 21Qa 47
Wolmer Gdns. HA8: Edg 20Qa 29
Wolseley Av. SW19 61Cb 133
Wolseley Gdns. W4 51Ra 109
Wolseley Rd. CR4: Mitc 73Jb 156
E7 38Kc 73
HA3: W'stone 27Ga 46
N8 30Mb 50
N22 25Pb 50
RM7: Rush G 31Fd 76
W4 49Sa 87
Wolseley St. SE1 47Wb 91
Wolsey Av. E6 41Qc 94
E17 27Bc 52
EN7: Chesh 1Vb 19
KT7: T Ditt 71Ha 152
Wolsey Bus. Pk. WD18: Wat 17T 26
Wolsey Cl. KT2: King T 67Ra 131
KT4: Wor Pk 77Wa 154
SE2 47Yc 95
SW20 66Xa 132
TW3: Houn 56Ea 108
UB2: S'hall 48Ea 86
Wolsey Ct. NW6 38Eb 69
SE9 58Pc 116
(off Court Rd.)
SW11 53Gb 111
(off Westbridge Rd.)
Wolsey Cres. CR0: New Ad 81Ec 178
DA9: Ghithe 58Wd 120
SM4: Mord 73Ab 154
Wolsey Dr. KT2: King T 64Na 131
KT12: Walt T 74Z 151
Wolsey Gdns. IG6: Ilf 23Rc 54
Wolsey Gro. HA8: Edg 24Ta 47
KT10: Esh 77Da 151
Wolsey M. BR6: Chels 78Vc 161
NW5 37Lb 70
Wolsey Pl. Shop. Cen.
GU21: Wok 89A 168
Wolsey Rd. EN1: Enf 12Xb 33
HA6: Nwood 19S 26
HP2: Hem H 3M 3
KT8: E Mos 70Fa 130
KT10: Esh 77Da 151
N1 36Tb 71
TW12: Hamp H 65Da 129
TW15: Ashf 63N 127
TW16: Sun 66V 128
Wolsey St. E1 43Yb 92
Wolsey Wlk. GU21: Wok 89A 168
Wolsey Way KT9: Chess 78Qa 153
Wolsley Cl. DA1: Cray 57Gd 118
Wolstan Cl. UB9: Den 34J 63
Wolstenholme HA7: Stan 22Ka 46
Wolstonbury N12 22Cb 49
Wolvercote Rd. SE2 47Zc 95
Wolverley St. E2 41Xb 91
Wolverton SE17 7G 231
(not continuous)
Wolverton Av. KT2: King T 67Qa 131
Wolverton Gdns. W5 45Pa 87
W6 49Za 88
Wolverton Ho. *RM3: Rom* 22Nd 57
(off Chudleigh Rd.)
Wolverton Rd. HA7: Stan 23Ka 46
Wolverton Way N14 15Lb 32
Wolves La. N13 24Qb 50
N22 24Qb 50
Wombwell Gdns. DA11: Nflt 1A 144
WOMBWELL PARK 61Fe 143
Womersley Rd. N8 30Pb 50
Womersh Way SM2: Cheam 81Za 174
Wonford Cl. KT2: King T 67Ua 132
KT20: Walt H 98Wa 194
Wonham La. RH3: Bet 7A 206
Wonham Pl. RH9: S God 7D 210
Wonnacott Pl. EN3: Enf W 8Zb 20
Wontford Rd. CR8: Purl 87Qb 176
Wontner Cl. N1 38Sb 71
Wontner Rd. SW17 61Hb 133
Wooburn Cl. UB8: Hil 42R 84
Wooburn Comn. Rd. SL1: Burn 3A 60
Wood, The WD19: Wat 19Aa 27
Woodall Av. EN3: Pond E 16Zb 34
Woodall Cl. E14 45Dc 92
KT9: Chess 80La 152
Woodall Rd. EN3: Pond E 16Zb 34
Wood Av. RM19: Purf 49Sd 98
Woodbank WD3: Rick 16L 25
Woodbank Rd. BR1: Brom 62Hc 137
Woodbastwick Rd. SE26 64Zb 136
Woodberry Av. HA2: Harr 28Da 45
N21 19Qb 32
Woodberry Cl. NW7 24Za 48
TW16: Sun 65W 128
Woodberry Cres. N10 27Kb 50
Woodberry Down CM16: Epp 1Wc 23
N4 31Sb 71
Woodberry Down Est. N4 31Sb 71
(not continuous)
Woodberry Gdns. N12 23Eb 49
Woodberry Gro. DA5: Bexl 62Fd 140
N4 31Sb 71
N12 23Eb 49
Woodberry Way E4 17Ec 34
N12 23Eb 49
Woodbine Cl. EN9: Walt A 7Lc 21
TW2: Twick 61Fa 130
Woodbine Cl. Cvn. Pk. EN9: Walt A 7Lc 21
Woodbine Gro. EN2: Enf 10Tb 19
SE20 66Xb 135
Woodbine La. KT4: Wor Pk 76Xa 154
Woodbine Pl. E11 30Jc 53
Woodbine Rd. DA15: Sidc 60Uc 116
Woodbines Av. KT1: King T 69Ma 131
Woodbine Ter. E9 37Yb 72
Woodborough Rd. SW15 56Xa 110
Woodbourne Av. SW16 62Mb 134
Woodbourne Cl. SW16 62Nb 134
Woodbourne Dr. KT10: Clay 79Ha 152
Woodbourne Gdns. SM6: Wall 80Kb 156
Woodbridge Av. KT22: Lea 90Ja 172
Woodbridge Cl. N7 33Pb 70
NW2 34Wa 68
RM3: Rom 21Md 57
Woodbridge Cnr. KT22: Lea 90Ja 172
Woodbridge Ct. IG8: Wfd G 24Nc 54
Woodbridge Gro. KT22: Lea 90Ja 172
Woodbridge Ho. E11 32Hc 73
Woodbridge La. RM3: Rom 20Md 39
Woodbridge Rd. IG11: Bark 36Vc 75
Woodbridge St. EC1 5B 218 (42Rb 91)
(not continuous)
Woodbridge Ter. RM6: Chad H 30Xc 55
Woodbridge Way SS17: Stan H 3K 101
Woodbrook Gdns. EN9: Walt A 5Gc 21
Woodbrook Rd. SE2 51Wc 117
Woodburn Cl. NW4 29Za 48
Woodbury Cl. CR0: C'don 75Vb 157
E11 28Kc 53
TN16: Big H 90Pc 180
Woodbury Dr. SM2: Sutt 82Eb 175
Woodbury Gdns. SE12 62Kc 137
Woodbury Hill IG10: Lough 13Nc 36
Woodbury Hollow IG10: Lough 12Nc 36
Woodbury Ho. SE26 62Wb 135
Woodbury Pk. Rd. W13 42Ka 86
Woodbury Rd. E17 28Dc 52
Woodbury St. SW17 64Gb 133
Woodby Dr. SL5: S'dale 3D 146
Woodchester Ho. *E14* 48Dc 92
(off Selsdon Way)
Woodchester Sq. W2 43Db 89
Woodchurch Cl. DA14: Sidc 62Tc 138
Woodchurch Dr. BR1: Brom 66Mc 137
Woodchurch Rd. NW6 38Cb 69
Wood Cl. DA5: Bexl 62Gd 140
E2 42Wb 91
HA1: Harr 31Fa 66
NW9 31Ta 67
SL4: Wind 6G 102
Woodclyffe Dr. BR7: Chst 68Qc 138
Woodcock Cl. TW6: H'row A 56K 105
Woodcock Ct. HA3: Kenton 31Na 67
Woodcock Dell Av. HA3: Kenton 31Ma 67
Woodcock Dr. GU24: Chob 10G 146
WOODCOCK HILL 22N 43
Woodcock Hill HA3: Kenton 29La 46
WD3: Rick 22N 43
WD6: E'tree 16Ra 29
Woodcock Hill Est. WD3: Rick 21N 43
Woodcock Ho. *E14* 43Cc 92
(off Burgess St.)
Woodcock La. GU24: Chob 10F 146
Woodcocks E16 43Lc 93
Woodcombe Cres. SE23 60Yb 114
WOODCOTE
CR8 84Mb 176
KT18 87Sa 173
Woodcote Av. CR7: Thor H 70Rb 135
NW7 23Ya 48
RM12: Horn 35Jd 76
SM6: Wall 81Kb 176
Woodcote Cl. EN3: Pond E 16Yb 34
EN8: Chesh 2Yb 20
KT2: King T 64Pa 131
KT18: Eps 86Ta 173
WD23: Bush 16Ea 28
Woodcote Ct. *KT18: Eps* 86Ta 173
(off Dorking Rd.)
Woodcote Dr. BR6: Orp 74Tc 160
CR8: Purl 82Mb 176
Woodcote End KT18: Eps 87Ta 173
WOODCOTE GREEN 81Lb 176
Woodcote Grn. SM6: Wall 81Lb 176
Woodcote Grn. Rd.
KT18: Eps 87Sa 173
WOODCOTE GROVE 85Kb 176
Woodcote Gro. Rd. CR5: Coul 87Mb 176
Woodcote Hall KT18: Eps 86Ta 173
Woodcote Ho. KT18: Eps 87Sa 173
SE8 51Bc 114
(off Prince St.)
Woodcote Ho. Ct. KT18: Eps 87Ta 173
Woodcote Hurst KT18: Eps 88Sa 173
Woodcote La. CR8: Purl 83Mb 176
Woodcote Lodge KT18: Eps 87Sa 173
Woodcote M. IG10: Lough 17Mc 35
SM6: Wall 79Kb 156
WOODCOTE PARK 89Sa 173
Woodcote Pk. Av. CR8: Purl 84Lb 176
Woodcote Pk. Golf Course 86Kb 176
Woodcote Pk. Rd. KT18: Eps 88Sa 173
Woodcote Pl. SE27 64Rb 135
Woodcote Rd. CR8: Purl 79Kb 156
E11 31Jc 73
KT18: Eps 86Ta 173
SM6: Wall 79Kb 156
Woodcote Side KT18: Eps 87Ra 173
Woodcote Valley Rd. CR8: Purl 85Mb 176
Woodcote Vs. *SE27* 64Sb 135
(off Woodcote Pl.)
Wood Ct. DA8: Erith 52Gd 118
Wood Cres. HP3: Hem H 3M 3
Wood Crest *SM2: Sutt* 80Eb 155
(off Christchurch Pk.)
Woodcrest Rd. CR8: Purl 85Nb 176
Woodcrest Wlk. RH2: Reig 4N 207
Woodcroft N21 18Qb 32
SE9 62Pc 138
UB6: G'frd 37Ja 66
Woodcroft Av. HA7: Stan 25Ja 46
NW7 23Ua 48
Woodcroft Cl. SE9 58Qc 116
Woodcroft Cres. UB10: Hil 39R 64
Woodcroft M. SE8 49Ac 92
Woodcroft Rd. CR7: Thor H 71Rb 157
Woodcutter Pl. AL2: Park 9A 6
Woodcutters Av. RM16: Grays 47Ee 99
Woodcutters Cl. RM11: Horn 28Md 57
Wood Dr. BR7: Chst 65Nc 138
TN13: S'oaks 98Hd 202
Woodedge Cl. E4 18Hc 35
WOOD END
SL4 5A 124
UB4 43V 84
UB5 36Ea 66
Wood End AL2: Park 10A 6
BR8: Swan 70Ed 140
UB3: Hayes 44U 84
WD3: Crox G 17R 26
Wood End, The SM6: Wall 81Kb 176
Woodend KT10: Esh 75Ea 152
KT22: Lea 97La 192
SE19 65Sb 135
SM1: Sutt 75Eb 155
Wood End Av. HA2: Harr 35Da 65
UB5: N'olt 35Ea 66
Wood End Cl. HP2: Hem H 1C 4
SL2: Farn C 4H 61
UB5: N'olt 36Fa 66
Woodend Cl. GU21: Wok 1L 187
Woodend Dr. SL5: S'hill 1A 146
Wood End Gdns. UB5: N'olt 36Ea 66
Woodend Gdns. EN2: Enf 14Nb 32
WOOD END GREEN 43T 84
Wood End Grn. Rd. UB3: Hayes 43T 84
Wood End La. UB5: N'olt 37Da 65
Woodend Pk. KT11: Cobh 87Z 171
Woodend Ride SL4: Wink 5A 124
SL5: Asc 5A 124
Wood End Rd. HA1: Harr 35Fa 66
Woodend Rd. E17 26Ec 52
Wood End Way UB5: N'olt 36Ea 66
Wooder Gdns. E7 35Jc 73
Wooderson Cl. SE25 70Ub 135
Woodfall Av. EN5: Barn 15Bb 31
Woodfall Dr. DA1: Cray 56Gd 118
Woodfall Rd. N4 33Qb 70
Woodfall St. SW3 7F 227 (50Hb 89)
Wood Farm Cl. HA7: Stan 19Ka 28
Woodfarm Rd. HP2: Hem H 2N 3
Woodfarrs SE5 56Tb 113
Wood Fld. NW3 36Hb 69
Woodfield KT21: Asht 89Ma 173
Woodfield Av. DA11: Grav'nd 10D 122
HA0: Wemb 34La 66
HA6: Nwood 21U 44
NW9 28Ua 48
SM5: Cars 79Jb 156
SW16 62Mb 134
W5 42La 86
Woodfield Cl. CR5: Coul 91Lb 196
EN1: Enf 14Ub 33
KT21: Asht 89Ma 173
RH1: Redh 4N 207
SE19 66Sb 135
Woodfield Cres. W5 42La 86
Woodfield Dr. EN4: E Barn 18Jb 32
HP3: Hem H 4D 4
RM2: Rom 28Jd 56
Woodfield Gdns. HP3: Hem H 4D 4
KT3: N Mald 71Va 154
Woodfield Gro. SW16 62Mb 134
Woodfield Hill CR5: Coul 91Kb 196
Woodfield Ho. *KT7: T Ditt* 75Ha 152
(off Woodfield Rd.)
SE23 62Zb 136
(off Dacres Rd.)
Woodfield La. AL9: Hat 5M 9
KT21: Asht 89Na 173
SG13: New S 5M 9
SW16 62Mb 134
Woodfield Pl. W9 42Bb 89
Woodfield Ri. WD23: Bush 17Fa 28
Woodfield Rd. KT7: T Ditt 75Ha 152
KT21: Asht 89Ma 173
TW4: Cran 54X 107
W5 42La 86
W9 43Bb 89
WD7: R'lett 8Ja 14
Woodfields TN13: Chip 95Fd 202
WD18: Wat 14Y 27
(off George St.)
Woodfields, The CR2: Sande 83Vb 177
Woodfield Ter. UB9: Hare 26K 43
Woodfield Way N11 24Mb 50
RH1: Redh 4N 207
RM12: Horn 32Md 77
Woodfines, The
RM11: Horn 30Md 57
WOODFORD 23Lc 53
Woodford Av. IG2: Ilf 29Pc 54
IG4: Ilf, Wfd G 27Mc 53
WOODFORD BRIDGE 23Nc 54
Woodford Bri. Rd. IG4: Ilf 27Mc 53
Woodford Ct. EN9: Walt A 5Jc 21
W12 47Za 88
(off Shepherd's Bush Grn.)
Woodford Cres. HA5: Pinn 26X 45
Woodforde Ct. UB3: Harl 50T 84
Woodford Golf Course 22Jc 53
WOODFORD GREEN 23Jc 53
Woodford Green Athletics Club 23Nc 54
Woodford Hall Path E18 25Hc 53
Woodford Ho. E18 28Jc 53
Woodford New Rd. E17 28Gc 53
E18 25Gc 53
IG8: Wfd G 25Gc 53
Woodford Pl. HA9: Wemb 32Na 67
Woodford Rd. E7 34Kc 73
E18 28Jc 53
WD17: Wat 12Y 27
WOODFORD SIDE 22Hc 53
Woodford Trad. Est. IG8: Wfd G 26Mc 53
Woodford Way SL2: Slou 1E 80
WOODFORD WELLS 20Kc 35
Woodgate WD25: Wat 5X 13
Woodgate Av. EN6: N'thaw 5Kb 18
KT9: Chess 78Ma 153
Woodgate Cl. KT11: Cobh 85X 171
Woodgate Ct. RM11: Horn 27Md 57
Woodgate Cres. HA6: Nwood 23W 44
Woodgate Dr. SW16 66Mb 134
Woodgate M. WD17: Wat 11W 26
Woodgates Ho. *DA12: Grav'nd* 4E 144
(off Nursery M.)
Woodgavil SM7: Bans 88Bb 175
Woodger Rd. W12 47Ya 88
Woodgers Gro. BR8: Swan 68Hd 140
Woodget Cl. E6 44Nc 94
Woodgrange Av. EN1: Enf 16Wb 33
HA3: Kenton 29La 46
N12 23Fb 49
W5 46Qa 87
Woodgrange Cl. HA3: Kenton 29Ma 47
Woodgrange Gdns. EN1: Enf 16Wb 33
Woodgrange Ho. *W5* 46Pa 87
(off Woodgrange Av.)
Woodgrange Mans.
HA3: Kenton 29Ma 47
Woodgrange Rd. E7 36Kc 73
Woodgrange Ter. EN1: Enf 16Wb 33
WOOD GREEN
EN9 7Lc 21
N22 26Pb 50
Wood Grn. Hall *N22* 26Pb 50
(off Station Rd.)
Woodgreen Rd. EN9: Walt A 5Kc 21
Wood Grn. Shop. City N22 26Qb 50
Wood Grn. Way EN8: Chesh 3Ac 20
Woodhall NW1 4B 216
Woodhall Av. HA5: Pinn 25Aa 45
SE21 62Vb 135
Woodhall Cl. UB8: Uxb 36M 63
Woodhall Cres. RM11: Horn 31Pd 77
Woodhall Dr. HA5: Pinn 25Z 45
SE21 62Vb 135
Woodhall Ga. HA5: Pinn 24Z 45
Woodhall Ho. SW18 58Fb 111
Woodhall La. HP2: Hem H 1N 3
SL5: S'dale 5C 146
WD7: Shenl 7Na 15
WD19: Wat 20Z 27
Woodhall Rd. HA5: Pinn 24Z 45
WOODHAM 83H 169
Woodham Ct. E18 28Hc 53
Woodham Ga. GU21: Wok 85E 168
Woodham Hall Est. GU21: Wok 86D 168
Woodham La. GU21: Wok 86D 168
KT15: Wdhm, New H 84G 168
Woodham Lock KT14: W Byf 84H 169
Woodham Pk. Rd. KT15: Wdhm 81H 169
Woodham Pk. Way KT15: Wdhm 83H 169
Woodham Pl. GU21: Wok 86B 168
Woodham Ri. GU21: Wok 86B 168
Woodham Rd. GU21: Wok 87A 168
SE6 62Ec 136
Woodham Waye GU21: Wok 85D 168
WOODHATCH 9K 207
Woodhatch Cl. E6 43Nc 94
Woodhatch Rd. RH1: Redh 9K 207
RH2: Reig 9K 207
Woodhatch Spinney CR5: Coul 88Nb 176
Woodhaven Gdns. IG6: Ilf 28Sc 54
Woodhaven M. KT12: Walt T 77W 150
Woodhaw TW20: Egh 63D 126
Woodhayes Rd. SW19 66Ya 132
Woodhead Dr. BR6: Orp 76Uc 160
Woodheyes Rd. NW10 36Ta 67
WOODHILL 5M 9
Woodhill GU23: Send 98F 188
SE18 49Nc 94
Woodhill Av. SL9: Ger X 30C 42
Woodhill Ct. GU23: Send 97F 188
SL9: Ger X 31A 62
Woodhill Cres. HA3: Kenton 30Ma 47
Wood Ho. *NW6* 40Bb 69
(off Albert Rd.)
Woodhouse Av. UB6: G'frd 40Ha 66
Woodhouse Cl. SE22 56Wb 113
UB3: Harl 48U 84
UB6: G'frd 39Ha 66
Woodhouse Eaves HA6: Nwood 22W 44
Woodhouse Gro. E12 37Nc 74
Woodhouse Rd. E11 34Hc 73
N12 23Fb 49
Woodhurst Av. BR5: Pet W 72Sc 160
WD25: Wat 6Z 13
Woodhurst Dr. UB9: Den 29H 43
Woodhurst La. RH8: Oxt 2J 211
Woodhurst Pk. RH8: Oxt 2J 211
Woodhurst Rd. SE2 50Wc 95
W3 45Sa 87
Woodhyrst Gdns. CR8: Kenley 87Rb 177
Woodies La. KT3: N Mald 72Ta 153
Woodin Cl. DA1: Dart 58Md 119
Woodington Cl. SE9 58Qc 116
Woodknoll Dr. BR7: Chst 67Pc 138
Woodland App. UB6: G'frd 37Ja 66
Woodland Av. CM13: Hut 15Ee 41
DA3: Hartl 71Be 165
HP1: Hem H 3K 3
SL1: Slou 5H 81
SL4: Wind 6D 102
Woodland Chase
WD3: Crox G 17R 26
Woodland Cl. CM13: Hut 15Ee 41
DA3: Lfield 69Ee 143
HP1: Hem H 3K 3
IG8: Wfd G 20Kc 35
KT13: Weyb 77T 150
KT19: Ewe 79Ua 154
KT24: E Hor 99V 190
NW9 30Sa 47
SE19 65Ub 135
UB10: Ick 33R 64
Woodland Ct. *E11* 30Jc 53
(off New Wanstead)
KT17: Eps 84Va 174
N7 37Nb 70
RH8: Oxt 100Fc 199
Woodland Cres. SE10 51Gc 115
SE16 47Zb 92
Woodland Dr. AL4: St A 1G 6
KT11: Cobh 83Ba 171
KT24: E Hor 99V 190
WD17: Wat 11V 26
(not continuous)
Woodland Gdns. CR2: Sels 83Yb 178
N10 29Kb 50
TW7: Isle 55Ga 108
Woodland Glade SL2: Farn C 4H 61
Woodland Grange SL0: Rich P 48G 82
Woodland Gro. CM16: Epp 4Wc 23
KT13: Weyb 77T 150
SE10 50Gc 93
Woodland Hill SE19 65Ub 135
Woodland La. WD3: Chor 13F 24
Woodland M. *SE13* 55Dc 114
(off Loampit Hill)
SW16 62Nb 134
Woodland Pl. HP1: Hem H 3K 3
WD3: Chor 14H 25
Woodland Ri. N10 28Kb 50
RH8: Oxt 2J 211
TN15: Seal, S'oaks 95Nd 203
UB6: G'frd 37Ja 66
Woodland Rd. CR7: Thor H 70Qb 134
E4 18Ec 34
IG7: Chig 21Tc 54
IG10: Lough 13Nc 36
N11 22Kb 50
SE19 64Ub 135
TN14: Dun G 93Hd 202
WD3: Map C 22F 42
WOODLANDS
TN15 85Sd 184
TW7 55Ga 108
Woodlands AL2: Park 9A 6
AL9: Brk P 8K 9
BR2: Brom 70Hc 137
CM16: Epp 3Wc 23
DA6: Bex 57Dd 118
GU22: Wok 90B 168
GU23: Send 97H 189
HA2: Harr 28Ca 45
KT15: Add 76K 149
KT21: Asht 90Na 173
NW11 29Ab 48
SL9: Ger X 30B 42
SW20 70Ya 132
WD7: R'lett 6Ja 14
Woodlands, The BR6: Chels 79Xc 161
HA1: Harr 33Ga 66
HA7: Stan 22Ka 46
KT10: Esh 75Ea 152
N5 35Sb 71
N12 23Eb 49
N14 18Kb 32
SE13 59Fc 115
SE19 66Sb 135
SM6: Wall 81Kb 176
SW9 52Rb 113
(off Langton Rd.)
TW7: Isle 54Ha 108
Woodlands Av. DA15: Sidc 60Uc 116
E11 32Kc 73
HA4: Ruis 31Y 65
HP4: Berk 2A 2
KT3: N Mald 67Sa 131
KT4: Wor Pk 75Va 154
KT14: W Byf 85H 169
N3 24Eb 49
RH1: Redh 7P 207
RM6: Chad H 30Ad 55
RM11: Horn 29Md 57
W3 46Ra 87
Woodlands Cl. BR1: Brom 68Pc 138
BR8: Swan 69Hd 140
KT10: Clay 80Ha 152
KT16: Ott 82D 168
NW11 29Ab 48
RH1: Mers 1E 208
RM16: Grays 8A 100
SL9: Ger X 30C 42
WD6: Bore 14Ra 29
Woodlands Copse KT21: Asht 88Ma 173
Woodlands Cotts. SL2: Farn C 6G 60
Woodlands Ct. BR1: Brom 67Hc 137
GU21: Wok 10L 167
GU22: Wok 91A 188
HA1: Harr 29Ha 46
IG10: Lough 15Qc 36
KT12: Walt T 74X 151
NW10 39Za 68
(off Wrentham Av.)
RH1: Redh 8P 207
SE23 59Xb 113
Woodlands Dr. HA7: Stan 23Ha 46
RH9: S God 9C 210
TW16: Sun 68Y 129
WD4: K Lan 10C 4
Woodlands Gdns. E17 28Gc 53
KT18: Tatt C 89Ya 174

Woodlands Ga.—Worple St.

Woodlands Ga. SW15 .57Bb 111
(off Woodlands Way)
Woodlands Gro. CR5: Coul .89Jb 176
TW7: Isle .54Ga 108
Woodlands Hgts. SE3 .51Hc 115
(off Vanburgh Hill)
Woodlands Hill HP9: Beac .1C 60
Woodlands Ho. GU21: Wok .86E 168
Woodlands La. DA12: Shorne .6M 145
GU20: W'sham .9B 146
KT11: Lea, Stoke D .89Ca 171
Woodlands Manor Golf Course .85Td 184
Woodlands Pde. TW15: Ashf .65S 128
Woodlands Pk. DA5: Bexl .63Fd 140
GU21: Wok .86E 168
KT15: Add .78H 149
Woodlands Pk. Rd. N15 .29Rb 51
SE10 .51Gc 115
(not continuous)
Woodlands Pl. CR3: Cat'm .98Xb 197
Woodlands Ri. BR8: Swan .68Hd 140
Woodlands Rd. BR1: Brom .68Nc 138
BR6: Chels .79Wc 161
DA7: Bex .55Ad 117
E11 .33Gc 73
E17 .27Ec 52
EN2: Enf .10Tb 19
GU25: Vir W .10N 125
HA1: Harr .29Ha 46
HP3: Hem H .9A 4
IG1: Ilf .34Sc 74
KT6: Surb .73Ma 153
KT14: W Byf .86H 169
KT18: Eps .87Qa 173
KT22: Lea .89Fa 172
KT23: Bookh .100Aa 191
N9 .18Yb 34
RH1: Redh .8P 207
RM1: Rom .27Hd 56
RM3: Hrld W .25Qd 57
SW13 .55Va 110
TW7: Isle .55Fa 108
UB1: S'hall .46Z 85
WD23: Bush .15Aa 27
Woodlands Rd. E. GU25: Vir W .10N 125
Woodlands Rd. W.
GU25: Vir W .10N 125
Woodlands St. SE13 .59Fc 115
Woodlands Ter. BR8: Crock .72Dd 162
Woodland St. E8 .37Vb 71
Woodlands Vw. TN14: Bad M .82Dd 182
Woodlands Way KT21: Asht .88Qa 173
SW15 .57Bb 111
Woodland Ter. SE7 .49Nc 94
Woodland Wlk. BR1: Brom .63Fc 137
(not continuous)
KT19: Ewe .79Qa 153
NW3 .36Gb 69
SE10 .50Gc 93
Woodland Way BR4: W W'ck .77Dc 158
BR5: Pet W .70Sc 138
CM16: They B .8Tc 22
CR0: C'don .74Ac 158
CR3: Cat'm .100Ub 197
CR4: Mitc .66Jb 134
CR8: Purl .85Qb 176
DA9: Ghithe .57Wd 120
IG8: Wfd G .20Kc 35
KT5: Surb .75Ra 153
KT13: Weyb .78T 150
KT20: Kgswd .94Ab 194
N21 .19Qb 32
NW7 .23Va 48
SE2 .49Zc 95
SM4: Mord .70Bb 133
WD5: Bedm .9F 4
Wood La. CR3: Cat'm .96Tb 197
DA2: Daren .63Td 142
GU21: Knap .10H 167
HA4: Ruis .32T 64
HA7: Stan .20Ja 28
HP2: Hem H .3M 3
IG8: Wfd G .21Hc 53
KT13: Weyb .81S 170
KT20: Tad .89Bb 175
N6 .30Kb 50
NW9 .31Ta 67
RM8: Dag .35Zc 75
RM9: Dag .35Zc 75
RM10: Dag .33Cd 76
RM12: Horn .36Jd 76
SL0: Iver, Iver H .41E 82
SL1: Slou .8D 80
SL2: Hedg .3J 61
TW7: Isle .51Ga 108
W12 .44Ya 88
Wood La. Cl. SL0: Iver H .41D 82
Wood La. End HP2: Hem H .1A 4
Wood La. Studios W12 .44Ya 88
Woodlark Ct. KT10: Clay .79Ha 152
Woodlark Gro. RM3: Rom .21Nd 57
Woodlawn Cl. SW15 .57Bb 111
Woodlawn Cres. TW2: Whitt .61Da 129
Woodlawn Dr. TW13: Felt .61Z 129
Woodlawn Gro. GU21: Wok .87B 168
Woodlawn Rd. SW6 .52Za 110
Woodlawns KT19: Ewe .80Ta 153
Woodlea AL2: Chis G .7N 5
DA3: Lfield .69Ee 143
Woodlea Dr. BR2: Brom .71Gc 159
Woodlea Gro. HA6: Nwood .23T 44
Woodlea Rd. N16 .34Ub 71
Woodlee Cl. GU25: Vir W .8N 125
Woodleigh E18 .25Jc 53
Woodleigh Av. N12 .23Gb 49
Woodleigh Gdns. SW16 .62Nb 134
Woodley Cl. SW17 .66Hb 133
Woodley La. SM5: Cars .76Gb 155
Woodley Rd. BR6: Chels .75Yc 161
Woodlodge KT21: Asht .89Na 173
Wood Lodge Gdns. BR1: Brom .66Nc 138
Wood Lodge Grange
TN13: S'oaks .94Ld 203
Wood Lodge La. BR4: W W'ck .76Ec 158
Woodmancote Gdns. KT14: W Byf .85J 169
Woodman La. E4 .15Gc 35
Woodman M. TW9: Kew .53Ra 109
Woodman Pde. E16 .46Qc 94
(off Woodman St.)
Woodman Path IG6: Ilf .23Uc 54
Woodman Rd. CM14: W'ley .22Yd 58
CR5: Coul .87Lb 176
HP3: Hem H .4N 3
IG6: Ilf .22Uc 54
Woodmans Gro. NW10 .36Va 68
Woodmans Ho. WD17: Wat .14Y 27
Woodman's M. W12 .43Xa 88
WOODMANSTERNE .87Hb 175
Woodmansterne La. SM5: Cars .84Hb 175
SM6: Wall .83Kb 176
SM7: Bans .87Db 175
Woodmansterne Rd. CR5: Coul .84Lb 176
SM5: Cars .84Hb 175
SW16 .66Lb 134
Woodmansterne St. SM7: Bans .87Gb 175
Woodman St. E16 .46Qc 94
Woodman Vs. DA3: Fawk .76Xd 164
Wood Martyn Ct. BR6: Orp .75Wc 161
(off Orchard Gro.)
Wood Mead N17 .23Wb 51
Wood Meads CM16: Epp .1Wc 23
Woodmere SE9 .60Pc 116
Woodmere Av. CR0: C'don .73Yb 158
WD24: Wat .10Z 13
Woodmere Cl. CR0: C'don .73Zb 158
SW11 .55Jb 112
Woodmere Ct. N14 .17Kb 32
Woodmere Gdns. CR0: C'don .73Zb 158
Woodmere Way BR3: Beck .71Fc 159
Woodmill Cl. SW15 .58Wa 110
Woodmill Rd. E5 .33Yb 72
Woodmill St. SE1 .3K 231 (48Vb 91)
Woodmount BR8: Crock .73Fd 162
Woodnook Rd. SW16 .64Kb 134
Woodpecker Cl. AL10: Hat .3B 8
HA3: Hrw W .25Ha 46
KT11: Cobh .84Aa 171
N9 .16Xb 33
WD23: Bush .18Ea 28
Woodpecker Dr. DA9: Ghithe .58Wd 120
Woodpecker M. SE13 .56Fc 115
(off Freshfield Cl.)
Woodpecker Mt. CR0: Sels .81Ac 178
Woodpecker Rd. SE14 .51Ac 114
SE28 .45Yc 95
Woodpeckers, The UB9: Den .29H 43
(off Patrons Way W.)
Woodpecker Way GU22: Wok .6P 187
Woodplace Cl. CR5: Coul .91Lb 196
Woodplace La. CR5: Coul .90Lb 176
Woodquest Av. SE24 .57Sb 113
Woodredon Farm La. EN9: Walt A .7Mc 21
Woodredon Rd. EN9: Walt A .7Mc 21
Wood Retreat SE18 .52Tc 116
Woodridden Hill
EN9: Epp, They B, Walt A .7Mc 21
Wood Ride BR5: Pet W .70Tc 138
EN4: Had W .11Fb 31
Woodridge Cl. EN2: Enf .11Qb 32
Woodridge Way HA6: Nwood .23U 44
Wood Riding GU22: Pyr .87G 168
Woodridings KT13: Weyb .79Q 150
Woodridings Av. HA5: Hat E .25Ba 45
Woodridings Cl. HA5: Hat E .24Aa 45
Woodridings Ct. N22 .25Mb 50
Woodriffe Rd. E11 .31Fc 73
Wood Ri. HA5: Eastc .29W 44
Wood Rd. NW10 .38Sa 67
TN16: Big H .90Lc 179
TW17: Shep .70Q 128
Woodrow SE18 .49Pc 94
Woodrow Av. UB4: Hayes .43V 84
Woodrow Cl. UB6: G'frd .38Ka 66
Woodrow Ct. N17 .24Xb 51
SE5 .53Sb 113
(off Camberwell Sta. Rd.)
Woodrush Cl. SE14 .52Ac 114
Woodrush Way RM6: Chad H .28Zc 55
Woods, The HA6: Nwood .22W 44
UB10: Ick .35R 64
WD7: R'lett .6Ka 14
Woods Av. AL10: Hat .1D 8
Wood's Bldgs. E1 .43Xb 91
(off Winthrop St.)
Woods Cl. TW3: Houn .55Da 107
(off High St.)
Woods Dr. SL2: Farn C .6D 60
Woodseer St. E1 .7K 219 (43Vb 91)
Woodsford SE17 .7F 231
Woodsford Sq. W14 .47Ab 88
Woodshire Rd. RM10: Dag .34Dd 76
Woodshore Cl. GU25: Vir W .2M 147
Woodshots Mdw. WD18: Wat .15T 26
Woods Ho. SW1 .7K 227 (50Kb 90)
SW8 .53Lb 112
(off Wadhurst Rd.)
WOODSIDE
AL9 .3J 9
SE25 .72Wb 157
SL4 .4A 124
WD25 .4X 13
Woodside BR6: Chels .78Wc 161
EN7: Chesh .3Wb 19
IG9: Buck H .19Lc 35
KT12: Walt T .74W 150
KT15: New H .81L 169
KT20: Lwr K .100Bb 195
KT22: Fet .94Da 191
KT24: W Hor .98S 190
N10 .27Jb 50
NW11 .29Cb 49
SW19 .65Bb 133
WD6: E'tree .14Na 29
WD24: Wat .8W 12
Woodside Av. BR7: Chst .64Sc 138
HA0: Wemb .39Na 67
KT10: Esh .73Ga 152
KT12: Hers .77X 151
N6 .29Hb 49
N10 .29Hb 49
N12 .21Db 49
SE25 .72Xb 157
Woodside Cl. CM13: Hut .15Fe 41
CR3: Cat'm .96Ub 197
DA7: Bex .56Fd 118
GU21: Knap .9H 167
HA0: Wemb .39Na 67
HA4: Ruis .30T 44
HA7: Stan .22Ka 46
KT5: Surb .73Sa 153
RM13: Rain .42Ld 97
RM16: Grays .8A 100
SL9: Chal P .26A 42
Woodside Cotts. CR3: Wold .95Cc 198
Woodside Ct. E12 .32Lc 73
N12 .21Db 49
RM7: Mawney .28Cd 56
W5 .46Na 87
WD25: Wat .5Y 13
Woodside Ct. Rd. CR0: C'don .73Wb 157
Woodside Cres. DA15: Sidc .62Uc 138
Woodside Dr. DA2: Wilm .63Gd 140
Woodside End HA0: Wemb .39Na 67
Woodside Gdns. E4 .23Dc 52
N17 .26Ub 51
Woodside Grange Rd. N12 .21Db 49
WOODSIDE GREEN .3K 9
Woodside Grn. SE25 .72Wb 157
Woodside Gro. N12 .20Eb 31
Woodside Hill SL9: Chal P .26A 42
Woodside Ho. SW19 .65Bb 133
Woodside La. AL9: Hat .3H 9
DA5: Bexl .58Zc 117
N12 .20Eb 31
SL4: Wink .4A 124
Woodside Leisure Pk. WD25: Wat .5X 13
Woodside M. SE22 .57Vb 113
Woodside Pde. DA15: Sidc .62Uc 138
WOODSIDE PARK .21Cb 49
Woodside Pk. SE25 .72Xb 157
Woodside Pk. Av. E17 .28Fc 53
Woodside Pk. Rd. N12 .21Db 49
Woodside Pl. AL9: Hat .3J 9
HA0: Wemb .39Na 67
Woodside Rd. AL2: Brick W .2Ba 13
BR1: Brom .71Nc 160
CR8: Purl .85Mb 176
DA7: Bex .56Fd 118
DA15: Sidc .62Uc 138
E13 .42Lc 93
HA6: Nwood .24V 44
IG8: Wfd G .21Jc 53
KT2: King T .66Na 131
KT3: N Mald .68Ta 131
KT11: Cobh .85Ca 171
N22 .24Pb 50
SE25 .72Xb 157
SL4: Wink .4A 124
SM1: Sutt .76Eb 155
TN13: S'oaks .95Jd 202
TN14: Sund .96Ad 201
WD5: Ab L .3W 12
WD25: Wat .3W 12
Woodside Stadium .5Y 13
Woodside Way CR0: C'don .72Yb 158
CR4: Mitc .67Kb 134
GU25: Vir W .9M 125
RH1: Redh .7A 208
Woods M. W1 .4G 221 (45Jb 90)
Woodsome Lodge KT13: Weyb .79S 150
Woodsome Rd. NW5 .34Jb 70
Woods Pl. SE1 .4J 231 (48Ub 91)
Woodspring Rd. SW19 .61Ab 132
Woods Rd. SE15 .53Xb 113
Woodstar Ho. SE15 .52Wb 113
(off Reddins Rd.)
Woodstead Gro. HA8: Edg .23Na 47
WOODSTOCK, THE .73Bb 155
Woodstock GU4: W Cla .100K 189
Woodstock Av. NW11 .31Ab 68
RM3: Rom .22Rd 57
SL3: L'ly .9P 81
SM3: Sutt .73Bb 155
TW7: Isle .57Ja 108
UB1: S'hall .41Ba 85
W13 .48Ja 86
Woodstock Cl. DA5: Bexl .59Bd 117
GU21: Wok .88A 168
HA7: Stan .26Na 47
Woodstock Ct. KT19: Eps .85Ta 173
SE11 .7J 229 (50Pb 90)
SE12 .58Jc 115
Woodstock Cres. N9 .16Xb 33
Woodstock Dr. UB10: Ick .35N 63
Woodstock Gdns. BR3: Beck .67Dc 136
IG3: Ilf .33Wc 75
UB4: Hayes .43V 84
Woodstock Grange W5 .46Na 87
Woodstock Gro. W12 .47Za 88
Woodstock La. KT9: Chess .77Ka 152
Woodstock La. Nth. KT6: Surb .75La 152
Woodstock La. Sth. KT9: Chess .78Ka 152
KT10: Clay .78Ka 152
Woodstock M. W1 .1J 221
Woodstock Ri. SM3: Sutt .73Bb 155
Woodstock Rd. CR0: C'don .76Tb 157
CR5: Coul .88Kb 176
E7 .38Lc 73
E17 .26Fc 53
HA0: Wemb .39Pa 67
N4 .32Qb 70
NW11 .31Bb 69
SM5: Cars .78Jb 156
W4 .49Ua 88
WD23: B Hea .17Ga 28
Woodstock Rd. Nth. AL1: St A .1F 6
Woodstock Rd. Sth. AL1: St A .2F 6
Woodstock St. W1 .3K 221 (44Kb 90)
Woodstock Studios W12 .47Za 88
(off Woodstock Gro.)
Woodstock Ter. E14 .45Dc 92
Woodstock Way CR4: Mitc .68Kb 134
Woodstone Av. KT17: Ewe .78Wa 154
WOOD STREET .27Ec 52
Wood St. BR8: Swan .68Ld 141
CR4: Mitc .73Jb 156
E17 .27Ec 52
EC2 .3E 224 (44Sb 91)
(not continuous)
EN5: Barn .14Za 30
KT1: King T .68Ma 131
RH1: Mers .1C 208
RM17: Grays .51Ee 121
W4 .50Ua 88
Woodsway KT22: Oxs .86Ga 172
Woodsyre SE26 .63Vb 135
Wood Ter. NW2 .34Xa 68
Woodthorpe Rd. SW15 .56Xa 110
TW15: Ashf .65M 127
Woodtree Cl. NW4 .26Za 48
Wood Va. N10 .29Lb 50
SE23 .60Xb 113
Woodvale EN8: Walt C .7Yb 20
Woodvale Av. SE25 .69Vb 135
Woodvale Ct. BR1: Brom .67Kc 137
(off Widmore Rd.)
Wood Va. Est. SE23 .59Yb 114
Woodvale Pk. AL1: St A .2F 6
Woodvale Wlk. SE27 .64Sb 135
Woodvale Way NW11 .34Za 68
Wood Vw. RM16: Grays .48Fe 99
RM17: Grays .48Fe 99
Woodview DA2: G St G .65Wd 142
KT9: Chess .83La 172
Woodview Av. E4 .21Ec 52
Woodview Cl. BR6: Farnb .75Sc 160
CR2: Sande .86Xb 177
KT21: Asht .88Qa 173
N4 .31Rb 71
SW15 .63Ta 131
TN15: W King .79Ud 164
Woodview Ct. KT13: Weyb .78S 150
WD17: Wat .11W 26
(off Grandfield Av.)
Wood Vw. M. RM1: Rom .25Fd 56
Woodview M. SE19 .67Ub 135
Woodview Rd. BR8: Swan .68Ed 140
Woodview Way CR3: Cat'm .95Tb 197
Woodville, The .9D 122
Woodville, The W5 .44Ma 87
(off Woodville Rd.)
Woodville Cl. SE3 .53Kc 115
SE12 .57Jc 115
TW11: Tedd .63Ja 130
Woodville Ct. KT22: Lea .92Ka 192
N14 .15Lb 32
SE10 .53Ec 114
(off Blissett St.)
SE19 .67Vb 135
WD17: Wat .12W 26
Woodville Gdns. HA4: Ruis .31S 64
IG6: Ilf .27Rc 54
KT6: Surb .73Ma 153
NW11 .31Za 68
W5 .44Na 87
Woodville Gro. DA16: Well .55Wc 117
Woodville Ho. SE1 .3K 231
Woodville Pl. DA12: Grav'nd .9D 122
Woodville Rd. CR7: Thor H .70Sb 135
E11 .32Hc 73
E17 .28Bc 52
E18 .26Kc 53
EN5: New Bar .13Db 31
N16 .36Ub 71
NW6 .40Bb 69
NW11 .31Za 68
SM4: Mord .70Cb 133
TW10: Ham .62Ka 130
W5 .44Ma 87
Woodville St. SE18 .49Nc 94
Woodvill Rd. KT22: Lea .92Ka 192
Wood Wlk. WD3: Chor .12G 24
Woodward Av. NW4 .29Wa 48
Woodward Cl. KT10: Clay .79Ha 152
RM17: Grays .49De 99
Woodwarde Rd. SE22 .58Ub 113
Woodward Gdns. HA7: Stan .24Ja 46
RM9: Dag .38Yc 75
Woodward Hgts. RM17: Grays .49De 99
Woodward Rd. RM9: Dag .38Xc 75
Woodward's Footpath
TW2: Whitt .58Ea 108
Woodward Ter. DA9: Ghithe .58Ud 120
Wood Way BR6: Farnb .75Qc 160
Woodway CM13: Hut .18Ce 41
CM15: Hut, Shenf .18Ce 41
Woodway Cres. HA1: Harr .30Ja 46
Woodwaye WD19: Wat .17Y 27
Woodwell St. SW18 .57Eb 111
Wood Wharf SE10 .51Dc 114
Wood Wharf Bus. Pk. E14 .46Dc 92
Woodwicks WD3: Map C .22F 42
Woodyard, The CM16: Epp .1Yc 23
Woodyard Cl. NW5 .36Jb 70
Woodyard La. SE21 .59Ub 113
Woodyates Rd. SE12 .58Jc 115
Woolacombe Rd. SE3 .53Lc 115
Woolacombe Way UB3: Harl .49U 84
Woolaton M. CM14: B'wood .18Yd 40
Woolbrook Rd. DA1: Cray .58Gd 118
Woolcombes Ct. SE16 .46Zb 92
(off Princes Riverside Rd.)
Wooldridge Cl. TW14: Bedf .60S 106
Wooler St. SE17 .7F 231 (50Tb 91)
Woolf Cl. SE28 .46Xc 95
Woolf M. WC1 .5E 216
Woolford Ct. SE5 .54Sb 113
(off Coldharbour La.)
Woolf Wlk. RM18: Tilb .4E 122
(off Brennan Rd.)
Woolgar M. N16 .36Ub 71
(off Gillett St.)
Woolhampton Way IG7: Chig .20Xc 37
Woolhams CR3: Cat'm .98Wb 197
Woolhouse Pl. DA2: Dart .58Rd 119
Woolings Cl. RM16: Ors .5B 100
Woollard St. EN9: Walt A .6Ec 20
Woollaston Rd. N4 .30Rb 51
Woollett Cl. DA1: Cray .56Jd 118
Woolley Ho. SW9 .55Rb 113
(off Loughborough Rd.)
Woollon Ho. E1 .44Yb 92
(off Clark St.)
Woolman Rd. WD17: Wat .10W 12
Woolmead Av. NW9 .31Wa 68
Woolmer Cl. WD6: Bore .10Qa 15
Woolmerdine Ct. WD23: Bush .13Z 27
Woolmer Dr. HP2: Hem H .2C 4
Woolmer Gdns. N18 .23Wb 51
Woolmer Rd. N18 .22Wb 51
Woolmore St. E14 .45Ec 92
Woolneigh St. SW6 .55Db 111
Woolridge Way E9 .38Yb 72
Wool Rd. SW20 .65Xa 132
Woolstaplers Way SE16 .48Wb 91
Woolston Cl. E17 .26Zb 52
Woolstone Ho. E2 .39Wb 71
(off Whiston Rd.)
Woolstone Rd. SE23 .61Ac 136
Woolston Manor Golf Course .15Tc 36
WOOLWICH .48Pc 94
Woolwich Cen., The SE18 .49Qc 94
(off Wellington St.)
Woolwich Chu. St. SE18 .48Nc 94
Woolwich Comn. SE18 .51Qc 116
Woolwich Dockyard Ind. Est.
SE18 .48Nc 94
Woolwich High St. SE18 .48Qc 94
Woolwich Ho. UB3: Harl .48S 84
(off Nine Acres Cl.)
Woolwich Mnr. Way E6 .42Pc 94
E16 .47Rc 94
Woolwich New Rd. SE18 .50Qc 94
Woolwich Rd. DA6: Bex .55Cd 118
DA7: Bex .55Cd 118
DA17: Belv .50Bd 95
SE2 .51Zc 117
SE7 .50Jc 93
SE10 .50Hc 93
Woolwich Trade Pk. SE28 .48Tc 94
Wooster Gdns. E14 .44Fc 93
Wooster M. HA2: Harr .27Ea 46
Wooster Pl. SE1 .5G 231
Wootton Cl. KT18: Eps .88Va 174
RM11: Horn .29Md 57
WD7: R'lett .7Ja 14
Wootton Grange GU22: Wok .91A 188
(off Langley Wlk.)
Wootton Gro. N3 .25Cb 49
Wootton Pl. KT10: Esh .77Ea 152
Wootton St. SE1 .7A 224 (46Qb 90)
Worbeck Rd. SE20 .68Xb 135
Worcester Av. N17 .24Wb 51
RM14: Upm .33Vd 78
Worcester Cl. CR0: C'don .75Cc 158
CR4: Mitc .68Jb 134
DA9: Ghithe .56Xd 120
DA13: Ist R .6B 144
NW2 .34Xa 68
SE20 .67Wb 135
Worcester Ct. AL1: St A .3E 6
HA1: Harr .27Ga 46
KT4: Wor Pk .76Ua 154
KT12: Walt T .75Y 151
N12 .22Db 49
RH1: Redh .4N 207
(off Timperley Gdns.)
W7 .44Ha 86
(off Copley Cl.)
W9 .43Cb 89
(off Elmfield Way)
Worcester Cres. IG8: Wfd G .21Kc 53
NW7 .20Ua 30
Worcester Dr. TW15: Ashf .64R 128
W4 .47Ua 88
Worcester Gdns. IG1: Ilf .31Nc 74
KT4: Wor Pk .76Ua 154
SL1: Slou .7H 81
SW11 .57Hb 111
(off Grandison Rd.)
UB6: G'frd .37Fa 66
Worcester Ho. SE11 .4K 229
SW9 .52Qb 112
(off Cranmer Rd.)
W2 .44Eb 89
(off Hallfield Est.)
WD6: Bore .12Qa 29
(off Stratfield Rd.)
Worcester M. NW6 .37Db 69
WORCESTER PARK .74Wa 154
Worcester Pk. Rd. KT4: Wor Pk .76Ta 153
Worcester Point EC1 .4D 218 (41Sb 91)
Worcester Rd. E12 .35Pc 74
E17 .26Zb 52
RH2: Reig .5H 207
SM2: Sutt .80Cb 155
SW19 .64Bb 133
UB8: Cowl .43L 83
Worcesters Av. EN1: Enf .10Wb 19
Wordsworth Av. CR8: Kenley .87Tb 177
E12 .38Nc 74
E18 .27Hc 53
UB6: G'frd .41Fa 86
Wordsworth Cl. AL3: St A .4P 5
RM3: Rom .25Ld 57
RM18: Tilb .4D 122
Wordsworth Ct. HA1: Harr .31Ga 66
Wordsworth Dr. SM3: Cheam .77Ya 154
Wordsworth Gdns. WD6: Bore .15Qa 29
Wordsworth Ho. NW6 .41Cb 89
(off Stafford Rd.)
SE18 .51Qc 116
(off Woolwich Comn.)
Wordsworth Mans. W14 .51Bb 111
(off Queens Club Gdns.)
Wordsworth Mead RH1: Redh .4A 208
Wordsworth Pde. N8 .28Rb 51
Wordsworth Pl. NW5 .36Hb 69
Wordsworth Rd. DA16: Well .53Uc 116
KT15: Add .77M 149
N16 .35Ub 71
SE1 .6K 231 (49Vb 91)
SE20 .66Zb 136
SL2: Slou .2B 80
SM6: Wall .79Lb 156
TW12: Hamp .63Ba 129
Wordsworth Wlk. NW11 .28Cb 49
Wordsworth Way DA1: Dart .56Qd 119
(not continuous)
UB7: W Dray .49N 83
Worfield St. SW11 .52Gb 111
Worgan St. SE11 .7H 229 (50Pb 90)
SE16 .49Zb 92
Worland Rd. E15 .38Gc 73
World Bus. Cen.
TW6: H'row A .53S 106
World Garden .77Ld 163
World of Golf Cen.
Croydon .71Yb 158
New Malden .69Wa 132
Sidcup .62Sc 138
World Rugby Mus. .58Ga 108
WORLD'S END .13Pb 32
World's End KT11: Cobh .86W 170
Worlds End KT18: Eps .88Ta 173
Worlds End Est. SW10 .52Fb 111
World's End La. EN2: Enf .15Pb 32
N21 .15Pb 32
Worlds End La. BR6: Chels .79Vc 161
World's End Pas. SW10 .52Fb 111
(off Worlds End Est.)
World's End Pl. SW10 .52Fb 111
(off Worlds End Est.)
Worley Rd. AL3: St A .1B 6
Worleys Dr. BR6: Orp .77Tc 160
Worlidge St. W6 .50Ya 88
Worlingham Rd. SE22 .56Vb 113
Wormholt Rd. W12 .45Wa 88
Wormley Ct. EN9: Walt A .5Jc 21
Wormwood Scrubs Pk.
(Local Nature Reserve) .43Va 88
Wormwood St. EC2 .2H 225 (44Ub 91)
Wormyngford Ct.
EN9: Walt A .5Jc 21
Wornington Rd. W10 .42Ab 88
(not continuous)
Woronzow Rd. NW8 .1D 214 (39Fb 69)
Worple, The TW19: Wray .58B 104
Worple Av. SW19 .66Za 132
TW7: Isle .57Ja 108
TW18: Staines .65K 127
Worple Cl. HA2: Harr .32Ba 65
Worple Rd. KT18: Eps .87Ta 173
KT22: Lea .94Ka 192
(not continuous)
SW19 .67Za 132
SW20 .68Ya 132
TW7: Isle .56Ja 108
TW18: Staines .65K 127
(not continuous)
Worple Rd. M. SW19 .65Bb 133
WORPLESDON .9J 187
Worplesdon Golf Course .4J 187
Worplesdon Hill GU22: Wok .4G 186
Worplesdon Hill Ho.
GU22: Wok .4H 187
Worplesdon Rd. GU2: Guild .10J 187
GU3: Guild, Worp .7H 187
Worple St. SW14 .55Ta 109

Worple Way—Yorke Gdns.

Worple Way HA2: Harr ...32Ba 65
TW10: Rich ...57Na 109
Worrall La. UB8: Uxb ...38N 63
Worrin Cl. CM15: Shenf ...18Be 41
Worrin Pl. CM15: Shenf ...19Be 41
Worrin Rd. CM15: Shenf ...19Be 41
Worsfold Cl. GU23: Send ...95D 188
Worships Hill TN13: Riv ...95Gd 202
Worship St. EC2 ...6G 219 (42Tb 91)
(not continuous)
Worslade Rd. SW17 ...63Fb 133
Worsley Bri. Rd. BR3: Beck ...66Cc 136
SE26 ...63Bc 136
Worsley Grange BR7: Chst ...65Sc 138
Worsley Gro. E5 ...35Wb 71
Worsley Ho. SE23 ...61Yb 136
Worsley Rd. E11 ...35Gc 71
Worsopp Dr. SW4 ...57Lb 112
Worsted Grn. RH1: Mers ...1C 208
Worth Cl. BR6: Orp ...77Uc 160
Worthfield Cl. KT19: Ewe ...80Ta 153
Worth Gro. SE17 ...7F 231 (50Tb 91)
Worthing Cl. E15 ...39Gc 73
RM17: Grays ...51Ae 121
Worthing Rd. TW5: Hest ...51Ba 107
Worthington Cl. CR4: Mitc ...70Kb 134
Worthington Ho. EC1 ...3A 218
Worthington Rd. KT6: Surb ...74Pa 153
Wortley Rd. CR0: C'don ...73Qb 156
E6 ...38Mc 73
Worton Ct. TW7: Isle ...56Ga 108
Worton Gdns. TW7: Isle ...54Fa 108
Worton Hall Ind. Est.
TW7: Isle ...56Ga 108
Worton Rd. TW7: Isle ...56Fa 108
Worton Way TW3: Houn ...54Fa 108
TW7: Houn, Isle ...54Fa 108
Wotton Ct. E14 ...45Fc 93
(off Jamestown Way)
Wotton Grn. BR5: St M Cry ...70Zc 139
Wotton Ho. SL4: Eton ...10H 81
(off Common La.)
Wotton Rd. NW2 ...34Ya 68
SE8 ...51Bc 114
Wotton Way SM2: Cheam ...82Ya 174
Wouldham Rd. E16 ...44Hc 93
RM20: Grays ...51Ae 121
Wrabness Way TW18: Staines ...67K 127
Wragby Rd. E11 ...34Gc 73
Wrampling Pl. N9 ...18Wb 33
Wrangley Ct. EN9: Walt A ...5Jc 21
Wranghtorn Wlk. CR0: Wadd ...77Qb 156
Wraxall Rd. E3 ...42Bc 92
(off Hamlets Way)
Wray Av. IG5: Ilf ...27Qc 54
Wrayburn Ho. SE16 ...47Wb 91
(off Llewellyn St.)
Wray Cl. RM11: Horn ...31Ld 77
WRAY COMMON ...5M 207
Wray Comn. Rd. RH2: Reig ...5L 207
Wray Cres. N4 ...33Nb 70
Wrayfield Av. RH2: Reig ...5L 207
Wrayfield Rd. SM3: Cheam ...76Za 154
Wraylands Dr. RH2: Reig ...4M 207
Wray La. RH2: Reig ...2L 207
Wraymead Pl. RH2: Reig ...5K 207
Wraymill Ct. RH2: Reig ...6M 207
(off Wray Comn. Rd.)
Wray Mill Pk. RH2: Reig ...4M 207
Wray Pk. Rd. RH2: Reig ...5K 207
Wray Rd. SM2: Cheam ...81Bb 175
WRAYSBURY ...58B 104
Wraysbury Cl. TW4: Houn ...57Aa 107
Wraysbury Dive Cen. ...58B 104
Wraysbury Dr. UB7: Yiew ...45M 83
Wraysbury Gdns. TW18: Staines ...63G 126
Wraysbury Lake Sailing Club ...57A 104
Wraysbury Rd. TW18: Staines ...62E 126
TW19: Staines ...61D 126
Wrays Way UB4: Hayes ...42U 84
Wrekin Rd. SE18 ...52Sc 116
Wren Av. NW2 ...35Ya 68
UB2: S'hall ...49Ba 85
UB10: Uxb ...39P 63
Wren Cl. BR5: St P ...69Zc 139
CR2: Sels ...81Zb 178
E16 ...44Hc 93
N9 ...18Zb 34
TW6: H'row A ...55K 105
Wren Ct. CR0: C'don ...77Tb 157
(off Coombe Rd.)
SL3: L'ly ...48C 82
Wren Cres. KT15: Add ...78M 149
WD23: Bush ...18Ea 28
Wren Dr. EN9: Walt A ...6Jc 21
UB7: W Dray ...48M 83
Wren Gdns. RM9: Dag ...36Zc 75
RM12: Horn ...32Hd 76
Wren Ho. E3 ...40Ac 72
(off Gernon Rd.)
KT1: Hamp W ...68Ma 131
(off High St.)
SW1 ...7D 228
Wren Landing E14 ...46Cc 92
Wren La. HA4: Ruis ...30X 45
Wren M. SE11 ...6J 229 (49Pb 90)
SE13 ...56Gc 115
Wrenn Ho. SW13 ...51Ya 110
Wren Path SE28 ...48Tc 94
Wren Pl. CM14: B'wood ...20Zd 41
Wren Rd. DA14: Sidc ...63Yc 139
RM9: Dag ...36Zc 75
SE5 ...53Tb 113
Wren's Av. TW15: Ashf ...63S 128
Wrens Cft. DA11: Nflt ...3A 144
Wrensfield HP1: Hem H ...2J 3
Wrensfield Cl. WD17: Wat ...9V 12
Wrens Hill KT22: Oxs ...87Ea 172
Wren's Pk. Ho. E5 ...33Xb 71
Wren St. WC1 ...5J 217 (42Pb 90)
Wren Ter. IG10: Lough ...11Rc 36
Wrentham Av. NW10 ...40Za 68
Wrenthorpe Rd. BR1: Brom ...63Gc 137
Wren Vw. N6 ...31Lb 70
Wren Wlk. RM18: Tilb ...2D 122
Wrenwood Way HA5: Eastc ...28X 45
Wrestlers Ct. EC3 ...2H 225
Wrexham Rd. E3 ...40Cc 72
RM3: Rom ...20Md 39
Wricklemarsh Rd. SE3 ...54Kc 115
(not continuous)
Wrigglesworth St. SE14 ...52Zb 114
Wright SL4: Wind ...5A 102
Wright Cl. DA10: Swans ...58Zd 121
SE13 ...56Fc 115
WD23: Bush ...15Aa 27
Wright Gdns. TW17: Shep ...71Q 150
Wright Rd. TW5: Hest ...52Y 107
Wrights All. SW19 ...65Ya 132
Wrightsbridge Rd.
CM14: S Weald ...18Pd 39
Wright's Bldgs. WD17: Wat ...12X 27
(off St Albans Rd.)
Wrights Cl. RM10: Dag ...35Dd 76
Wright's Cotts. SL9: Chal P ...25A 42
(off Church La.)
Wrights Grn. SW4 ...56Mb 112
Wright's La. W8 ...48Db 89
Wrights Pl. NW10 ...37Sa 67
Wright Sq. SL4: Wind ...5B 102
Wright's Rd. E3 ...40Bc 72
(not continuous)
Wrights Rd. SE25 ...69Ub 135
Wrights Row SM6: Wall ...77Kb 156
Wrights Wlk. SW14 ...55Ta 109
Wright Way SL4: Wind ...5A 102
TW6: H'row A ...54K 105
Wrigley Cl. E4 ...22Fc 53
Wrington Ho. RM3: Rom ...22Pd 57
(off Redruth Rd.)
Wriotsley Way KT15: Add ...79J 149
Writtle Ho. NW9 ...26Va 48
Writtle Wlk. RM13: Rain ...39Gd 76
WROTHAM ...88Ce 185
Wrotham Bus. Pk. EN5: Barn ...9Bb 17
Wrotham By-Pass TN15: Wro ...89Ce 185
WROTHAM HEATH ...90Fe 185
Wrotham Heath Golf Course ...92Fe 205
Wrotham Hill Rd. TN15: Wro ...85Be 185
Wrotham Ho. BR3: Beck ...66Bc 136
(off Sellindge Cl.)
SE1 ...3G 231
Wrotham Pk. ...8Bb 17
Wrotham Rd. DA11: Grav'nd ...3C 144
DA13: Ist R, Meop ...9B 144
DA16: Well ...53Yc 117
EN5: Barn ...12Ab 30
NW1 ...38Lb 70
TN15: Bor G, Wro ...92Be 205
W13 ...46La 86
Wrotham Water La. ME19: Tros ...87Fe 185
Wrotham Water Rd.
TN15: Wro H ...86Fe 185
Wroth's Path IG10: Lough ...11Pc 36
Wrott & Hill Ct. DA4: Sut H ...67Rd 141
Wrottesley Rd. NW10 ...40Wa 68
SE18 ...51Sc 116
Wroughton Rd. SW11 ...57Hb 111
Wroughton Ter. NW4 ...28Xa 48
Wroxall Ct. RM19: Purf ...50Rd 97
(off Linnet Way)
Wroxall Rd. RM9: Dag ...37Yc 75
Wroxham Av. HP3: Hem H ...4M 3
Wroxham Gdns. EN2: Crew H ...7Rb 19
EN6: Pot B ...3Za 16
N11 ...24Mb 50
Wroxham Rd. SE28 ...45Zc 95
Wroxham Way IG6: Ilf ...25Rc 54
Wroxton Rd. SE15 ...54Yb 114
WRYTHE, THE ...76Hb 155
Wrythe Grn. SM5: Cars ...76Hb 155
Wrythe Grn. Rd. SM5: Cars ...76Hb 155
Wrythe La. SM5: Cars ...74Eb 155
Wulfred Way TN15: Kems'g ...90Rd 183
Wulfstan St. W12 ...43Va 88
Wulstan Pk. EN6: Pot B ...4Fb 17
Wyatt Cl. GU24: Bisl ...9E 166
SE16 ...47Bc 92
TN15: Bor G ...92Be 205
TW13: Felt ...60Z 107
UB4: Hayes ...43W 84
WD23: Bush ...17Fa 28
Wyatt Ct. HA0: Wemb ...38Na 67
W3 ...48Sa 87
(off All Saints Rd.)
Wyatt Dr. SW13 ...51Xa 110
Wyatt Ho. NW8 ...6B 214
SE3 ...54Hc 115
TW1: Twick ...58Ma 109
Wyatt Pk. Rd. SW2 ...61Nb 134
Wyatt Point SE28 ...47Sc 94
Wyatt Rd. DA1: Cray ...55Hd 118
E7 ...37Jc 73
N5 ...34Sb 71
SL4: Wind ...5B 102
TW18: Staines ...64J 127
Wyatt's Cl. WD3: Chor ...13J 25
Wyatt's Covert UB9: Den ...28H 43
Wyatts La. E17 ...27Ec 52
Wyatt's Rd. WD3: Chor ...14H 25
Wybert St. NW1 ...5B 216 (42Lb 90)
Wyborne Ho. NW10 ...38Sa 67
Wyborne Way NW10 ...38Sa 67
Wyburn Av. EN5: Barn ...13Bb 31
Wychcombe Studios NW3 ...37Hb 69
Wyche Gro. CR2: S Croy ...80Tb 157
Wych Elm Cl. KT2: King T ...66Pa 131
RM11: Horn ...31Qd 77
Wych Elm Lodge BR1: Brom ...66Hc 137
Wych Elm Pas. KT2: King T ...66Pa 131
Wych Elm Rd. RM11: Horn ...30Qd 57
Wychelm Rd. GU18: Light ...3A 166
Wych Elms AL2: Park ...10P 5
Wycherley Cl. SE3 ...52Hc 115
Wycherley Cres. EN5: New Bar ...16Db 31
Wych Hill GU22: Wok ...1N 187
Wych Hill La. GU22: Wok ...1P 187
Wych Hill Pk. GU22: Wok ...1P 187
Wych Hill Ri. GU22: Wok ...1N 187
Wych Hill Way GU22: Wok ...2P 187
Wychwood Av. CR7: Thor H ...69Sb 135
HA8: Edg ...23Ma 47
Wychwood Cl. HA8: Edg ...23Ma 47
KT22: Oxs ...86Fa 172
TW16: Sun ...65W 128
Wychwood End N6 ...31Lb 70
Wychwood Gdns. IG5: Ilf ...28Pc 54
Wychwood Way HA6: Nwood ...24V 44
SE19 ...65Tb 135
Wyckham Ho. RH8: Oxt ...1J 211
(off Station App.)
Wyclif Ct. EC1 ...4B 218
Wycliffe Av. KT15: Add ...80J 149
Wycliffe Cl. DA16: Well ...53Vc 117
EN8: Chesh ...1Zb 20
Wycliffe Ct. WD5: Ab L ...4U 12
Wycliffe Ho. DA11: Nflt ...10B 122
(off Wycliffe Row)
Wycliffe Rd. SW11 ...54Jb 112
SW19 ...65Db 133
Wycliffe Row DA11: Nflt ...10B 122
(not continuous)
Wyclif St. EC1 ...4B 218 (41Rb 91)
Wycombe Gdns. NW11 ...33Cb 69
Wycombe Ho. NW8 ...5D 214
Wycombe Pl. SW18 ...58Eb 111
Wycombe Rd. HA0: Wemb ...39Qa 67
IG2: Ilf ...29Pc 54
N17 ...25Wb 51
Wycombe Sq. W8 ...46Bb 89
Wydehurst Rd. CR0: C'don ...73Wb 157
Wydell Cl. SM4: Mord ...72Za 154
Wydeville Mnr. Rd. SE12 ...63Kc 137
Wyecliffe Gdns. RH1: Mers ...1C 208
Wye Cl. BR6: Orp ...73Vc 161
HA4: Ruis ...30S 44
TW15: Ashf ...63R 128
Wye Ct. W13 ...43Ka 86
(off Malvern Way)
Wyedale AL2: Lon C ...9K 7
Wyemead Cres. E4 ...19Gc 35
Wye Rd. DA12: Grav'nd ...1F 144
TN15: Bor G ...91Ce 205
Wye St. SW11 ...54Fb 111
Wyeth Cl. SL6: Tap ...5A 80
Wyeths M. KT17: Eps ...85Va 174
Wyeths Rd. KT17: Eps ...85Va 174
Wyevale Cl. HA5: Eastc ...27W 44
Wyfields IG5: Ilf ...25Rc 54
Wyfold Ho. SE2 ...47Zc 95
(off Wolvercote Rd.)
Wyfold Rd. SW6 ...52Ab 110
Wyhill Wlk. RM10: Dag ...37Ed 76
Wyke Cl. TW7: Isle ...51Ha 108
Wyke Gdns. W7 ...48Ja 86
Wyke Green Golf Course ...51Ha 108
Wykeham Av. RM9: Dag ...37Yc 75
RM11: Horn ...30Md 57
Wykeham Cl. DA12: Grav'nd ...5G 144
UB7: Sip ...51Q 106
Wykeham Ct. NW4 ...29Ya 48
(off Wykeham Rd.)
Wykeham Grn. RM9: Dag ...37Yc 75
Wykeham Hill HA9: Wemb ...32Pa 67
Wykeham Ho. SE1 ...7D 224
Wykeham Ri. N20 ...18Ab 30
Wykeham Rd. HA3: Kenton ...28Ka 46
NW4 ...28Ya 48
Wyke Rd. E3 ...38Cc 72
SW20 ...68Ya 132
Wylands Rd. SL3: L'ly ...49C 82
Wylchin Cl. HA5: Eastc ...27V 44
Wyldes Cl. NW11 ...32Eb 69
Wyldewoods SL5: S'hill ...2B 146
Wyldfield Gdns. N9 ...19Vb 33
Wyld Way HA9: Wemb ...37Ra 67
Wyleu St. SE23 ...59Ac 114
Wylie Rd. UB2: S'hall ...48Ca 85
Wyllen Cl. E1 ...42Yb 92
Wyllyotts Cen. ...4Bb 17
Wyllyotts Cl. EN6: Pot B ...4Bb 17
Wyllyotts La. EN6: Pot B ...4Bb 17
Wyllyotts Pl. EN6: Pot B ...4Bb 17
Wyllyotts Theatre ...4Bb 17
Wylo Dr. EN5: Ark ...16Wa 30
Wymark Cl. RM13: Rain ...40Jd 76
Wymering Mans. W9 ...41Cb 89
(off Wymering Rd.)
Wymering Rd. W9 ...41Cb 89
Wymers Cl. SL1: Burn ...10A 60
Wymondham Ct. NW8 ...39Fb 69
(off Queensmead)
Wymond St. SW15 ...55Ya 110
Wynan Rd. E14 ...50Dc 92
Wynash Gdns. SM5: Cars ...78Gb 155
Wynaud Ct. N22 ...23Pb 50
Wyncham Av. DA15: Sidc ...61Uc 116
Wyncham Ho. DA15: Sidc ...61Wc 139
(off Longlands Rd.)
Wynches Farm Dr. AL4: St A ...2H 7
Wynchgate HA3: Hrw W ...24Ga 46
N14 ...18Mb 32
N21 ...18Mb 32
UB5: N'olt ...36Aa 65
Wynchlands Cres. AL4: St A ...2H 7
Wyncote Way CR2: Sels ...81Zb 178
Wyncroft Cl. BR1: Brom ...69Pc 138
Wyndale Av. NW9 ...30Qa 47
Wyndcliff Rd. SE7 ...51Kc 115
Wyndcroft Cl. EN2: Enf ...13Rb 33
Wyndham Av. KT11: Cobh ...85W 170
Wyndham Cl. BR6: Farnb ...74Sc 160
SM2: Sutt ...80Cb 155
Wyndham Ct. W7 ...49Ja 86
Wyndham Cres. N19 ...34Lb 70
SL1: Burn ...10A 60
TW4: Houn ...58Ca 107
Wyndham Deedes Ho. E2 ...40Wb 71
(off Hackney Rd.)
Wyndham Est. SE5 ...52Sb 113
Wyndham Ho. E14 ...47Dc 92
(off Marsh Wall)
SW1 ...6H 227
Wyndham M. W1 ...1F 221 (43Hb 89)
Wyndham Pl. W1 ...1F 221 (43Hb 89)
Wyndham Rd. E6 ...38Mc 73
EN4: E Barn ...18Hb 31
GU21: Wok ...10M 167
KT2: King T ...66Pa 131
SE5 ...52Sb 113
W13 ...48Ka 86
Wyndhams Ct. E8 ...38Vb 71
(off Celandine Dr.)
Wyndham's Theatre ...4F 223
Wyndham St. W1 ...7F 215 (43Hb 89)
Wyndham Yd. W1 ...1F 221 (43Hb 89)
Wyndhurst Cl. CR2: S Croy ...80Rb 157
Wyneham Rd. SE24 ...57Tb 113
Wynell Rd. SE23 ...62Zb 136
Wynford Gro. BR5: St P ...69Xc 139
Wynford Pl. DA17: Belv ...51Cd 118
Wynford Rd. N1 ...1H 217 (40Pb 70)
Wynford Way SE9 ...62Pc 138
Wynlie Gdns. HA5: Pinn ...26X 45
Wynn Bri. Cl. IG8: Wfd G ...25Mc 53
Wynndale Rd. E18 ...25Kc 53
Wynne Ct. WD18: Wat ...15U 26
(off Raven Cl.)
Wynne Rd. SW9 ...54Qb 112
Wynn's Av. DA15: Sidc ...57Vc 117
Wynnstay Gdns. W8 ...48Cb 89
Wynnstow Pk. RH8: Oxt ...3K 211
Wynsham Way GU20: W'sham ...7A 146
Wynter St. SW11 ...56Eb 111
Wynton Gdns. SE25 ...71Vb 157
Wynton Gro. KT12: Walt T ...76W 150
Wynton Pl. W3 ...44Ra 87
Wynyard Cl. WD3: Sarr ...8J 11
Wynyard Ho. SE11 ...7J 229
Wynyard Ter. SE11 ...7J 229 (50Pb 90)
Wynyatt St. EC1 ...4B 218 (41Rb 91)
Wyre Gro. HA8: Edg ...20Ra 29
UB3: Harl ...49W 84
Wyresdale Cres. UB6: G'frd ...41Ha 86
Wyteleaf Cl. HA4: Ruis ...30S 44
Wytham Ho. NW8 ...6C 214
Wythburn Ct. W1 ...2F 221
Wythburn Pl. W1 ...3F 221 (44Hb 89)
Wythegate TW18: Staines ...66H 127
Wythenshawe Rd.
RM10: Dag ...34Cd 76
Wythens Wlk. SE9 ...58Rc 116
Wythes Cl. BR1: Brom ...68Pc 138
Wythes Rd. E16 ...46Nc 94
Wythfield Rd. SE9 ...58Pc 116
Wyvenhoe Rd. HA2: Harr ...35Ea 66
Wyvern Cl. BR6: Chels ...76Xc 161
DA1: Dart ...59Ld 119
Wyvern Est. KT3: N Mald ...70Wa 132
Wyvern Ho. RM17: Grays ...51De 121
(off Bridge Rd.)
Wyvern Pl. KT15: Add ...77K 149
Wyvern Rd. CR8: Purl ...82Rb 177
Wyvern Way UB8: Uxb ...38K 63
Wyvil Rd. SW8 ...52Nb 112
Wyvis St. E14 ...43Dc 92

X

XC
Hemel Hempstead ...3P 3
Xchange, The WD18: Wat ...13X 27
(off Exchange Rd.)
Xylon Ho. KT4: Wor Pk ...75Xa 154

Y

Yabsley St. E14 ...46Ec 92
Yaffle Rd. KT13: Weyb ...82S 170
Yaldham Ho. SE1 ...6H 231
Yaldham Mnr. Dr.
TN15: Kems'g ...89Xd 184
Yalding Gro.
BR5: St M Cry ...70Zc 139
Yalding Rd. SE16 ...48Wb 91
Yale Cl. TW4: Houn ...57Ba 107
Yale Ct. NW6 ...36Db 69
Yale Way RM12: Horn ...35Jd 76
Yarborough Rd. SW19 ...67Fb 133
Yarbridge Cl. SM2: Sutt ...82Db 175
Yard, The N1 ...2G 217
Yardley Cl. E4 ...15Dc 34
RH2: Reig ...4K 207
Yardley Ct. SM3: Cheam ...77Ya 154
Yardley La. E4 ...15Dc 34
Yardleys TW20: Thorpe ...69D 126
Yardley St. WC1 ...4K 217 (41Qb 90)
(not continuous)
Yardmaster Ho. CR0: C'don ...74Tb 157
Yard Mead TW20: Egh ...62C 126
Yarlington Ct. N11 ...22Jb 50
(off Sparkford Gdns.)
Yarm Cl. KT22: Lea ...95La 192
Yarm Ct. Rd. KT22: Lea ...95La 192
Yarm Holt KT22: Lea ...96La 192
Yarmouth Cres. N17 ...29Xb 51
Yarmouth Pl. W1 ...7K 221 (46Kb 90)
Yarmouth Rd. SL1: Slou ...5G 80
WD24: Wat ...10Y 13
Yarm Way KT22: Lea ...95Ma 193
Yarnfield Sq. SE15 ...53Wb 113
Yarnton Way DA18: Belv, Erith ...48Bd 95
SE2 ...47Yc 95
Yarra Ho. AL1: St A ...2C 6
(off Beaconsfield Rd.)
Yarrell Mans. W14 ...51Bb 111
(off Queen's Club Gdns.)
Yarrow Ct. TN14: Dun G ...92Hd 202
Yarrow Cres. E6 ...43Nc 94
Yarrow Ho. E14 ...48Ec 92
(off Stewart St.)
W10 ...43Ya 88
(off Sutton Way)
Yateley Ct. CR8: Kenley ...86Sb 177
Yateley St. SE18 ...48Mc 93
Yatesbury Ct. E5 ...36Ac 72
(off Studley Cl.)
Yates Ct. NW2 ...37Za 68
(off Willesden La.)
SE1 ...47Vb 91
(off Abbey St.)
Yates Ho. E2 ...41Wb 91
(off Roberta St.)
Yatton Ho. W10 ...43Ya 88
(off Sutton Way)
YEADING ...42Y 85
Yeading Av. HA2: Harr ...33Aa 65
Yeading Brook Meadows Nature Reserve
...42W 84
Yeading Ct. UB4: Yead ...42Y 85
Yeading Fork UB4: Yead ...43Y 85
Yeading Gdns. UB4: Yead ...43X 85
Yeading Ho. UB4: Yead ...43Z 85
Yeading La. UB4: Yead ...44X 85
UB5: N'olt ...44X 85
Yeading Wlk. HA2: Harr ...29Ba 45
Yeadon Ho. W10 ...43Ya 88
(off Sutton Way)
Yeames Cl. W13 ...44Ja 86
Yearby Ho. W10 ...42Ya 88
(off Sutton Way)
Yeate St. N1 ...38Tb 71
Yeatman Rd. N6 ...30Hb 49
Yeats Cl. NW10 ...36Ua 68
RH1: Redh ...9L 207
SE13 ...54Fc 115
W7 ...45Ha 86
Yeats Ho. AL3: St A ...4P 5
Ye Corner WD19: Wat ...15Z 27
Yeend Cl. KT8: W Mole ...70Ca 129
Yehudi Menuhin Hall ...91Ca 191
Yeldham Ho. W6 ...50Za 88
(off Yeldham Rd.)
Yeldham Rd. W6 ...50Za 88
Yeldham Vs. W6 ...50Za 88
(off Yeldham Rd.)
Yellowcress Dr. GU24: Bisl ...8E 166
Yellowhammer Ct. NW9 ...26Ua 48
(off Eagle Dr.)
Yellowpine Way IG7: Chig ...21Xc 55
Yellow Stock M. RM14: Upm ...36Wd 78
Yelverton Cl. RM3: Rom ...25Md 57
Yelverton Lodge TW1: Twick ...59La 108
(off Richmond Rd.)
Yelverton Rd. SW11 ...54Fb 111
Ye Market CR2: S Croy ...78Tb 157
(off Selsdon Rd.)
Yenston Cl. SM4: Mord ...72Cb 155
Yeoman Cl. E6 ...45Rc 94
SE27 ...62Rb 135
Yeoman Ct. E14 ...42Ec 92
(off Tweed Wlk.)
KT20: Tad ...91Ab 194
TW5: Hest ...52Ba 107
Yeoman Dr. TW19: Stanw ...60N 105
Yeoman Rd. UB5: N'olt ...38Aa 65
Yeomanry Cl. KT17: Eps ...84Va 174
Yeomans Acre HA4: Ruis ...30W 44
Yeomans Cft. KT23: Bookh ...97Ca 191
Yeomans Keep WD3: Chor ...13H 25
Yeoman's Mdws. TN13: S'oaks ...98Jd 202
Yeomans M. TW7: Isle ...58Fa 108
Yeoman's Row SW3 ...4E 226 (48Gb 89)
Yeoman St. SE8 ...49Ac 92
Yeomans Way EN3: Enf H ...12Yb 34
Yeoman's Yd. E1 ...45Vb 91
(off Chamber St.)
Yeoman Way RH1: Redh ...10B 208
Yeomen Way IG6: Ilf ...23Sc 54
Yeo St. E3 ...43Dc 92
Yeoveney Cl. TW19: Staines ...61F 126
Yeovil Cl. BR6: Orp ...75Uc 160
Yeovil Ent. Cen. SL2: Slou ...3D 80
Yeovil Ho. W10 ...42Ya 88
(off Sutton Way)
Yeovil Rd. SL1: Slou ...3C 80
Yeovilton Pl. KT2: King T ...64La 130
Yerbury Rd. N19 ...34Mb 70
(not continuous)
Yester Dr. BR7: Chst ...66Nc 138
Yester Pk. BR7: Chst ...66Pc 138
Yester Rd. BR7: Chst ...66Nc 138
Yetev Lev Ct. E5 ...32Wb 71
Yevele Way RM11: Horn ...31Nd 77
Yew Av. UB7: Yiew ...45N 83
Yewbank Cl. CR8: Kenley ...87Tb 177
Yew Cl. IG9: Buck H ...19Mc 35
Yewdale Cl. BR1: Brom ...65Gc 137
Yewdells Cl. RH3: Bkld ...5C 206
Yewfield Rd. NW10 ...37Va 68
Yew Gro. NW2 ...35Za 68
Yew Ho. SE16 ...47Zb 92
(off Woodland Cres.)
WD23: Bush ...15Z 27
(off Plantation Cl.)
Yewlands Cl. SM7: Bans ...87Eb 175
Yew Pl. KT13: Weyb ...77V 150
Yews, The DA12: Grav'nd ...1F 144
KT14: Byfl ...84N 169
TW15: Ashf ...63R 128
Yews Av. EN1: Enf ...8Xb 19
Yewsley Ter. SL3: L'ly ...50C 82
Yewstone Ct. WD18: Wat ...13W 26
Yewtree Av. RM10: Dag ...36Ed 76
Yew Tree Bottom Rd.
KT17: Eps D ...88Xa 174
KT18: Tatt C ...88Xa 174
Yew Tree Cl. CM13: Hut ...16De 41
CR5: Chip ...91Hb 195
DA3: Lfield ...68Fe 143
DA16: Well ...53Wc 117
KT4: Wor Pk ...74Ua 154
KT17: Eps D ...88Xa 174
N21 ...17Qb 32
SE13 ...55Ec 114
TN13: Bes G ...95Fd 202
Yewtree Cl. HA2: Harr ...28Da 45
N22 ...25Lb 50
Yew Tree Cotts. TN14: Hals ...84Bd 181
Yew Tree Ct. HP1: Hem H ...4J 3
NW11 ...29Bb 49
(off Bridge La.)
SM2: Sutt ...80Eb 155
(off Walnut M.)
WD6: E'tree ...16Ma 29
Yew Tree Dr. CR3: Cat'm ...97Vb 197
HP3: Bov ...10D 2
Yewtree End AL2: Park ...9A 6
Yew Tree Gdns. KT18: Eps ...87Sa 173
RM6: Chad H ...29Ad 55
RM7: Rom ...29Fd 56
Yew Tree La. RH2: Reig ...3K 207
Yew Tree Lodge HA4: Ruis ...30W 44
RM7: Rom ...29Fd 56
(off Yew Tree Gdns.)
SW16 ...63Lb 134
Yew Tree M. TN16: Westrm ...99Tc 200
(off Market Sq.)
Yew Tree Rd. BR3: Beck ...69Bc 136
SL1: Slou ...8L 81
TN14: Dun G ...93Hd 202
UB10: Uxb ...39P 63
W12 ...45Va 88
Yew Trees TW17: Shep ...70P 127
TW20: Thorpe ...69E 126
Yew Tree Wlk. CR8: Purl ...82Sb 177
KT24: Eff ...99Z 191
TW4: Houn ...57Ba 107
Yew Tree Way CR0: Sels ...82Ac 178
Yew Wlk. HA1: Harr ...32Ga 66
YIEWSLEY ...46N 83
Yiewsley Ct. UB7: Yiew ...46N 83
YMCA
Hawker Cen. ...64Ma 131
Leavesden Country Pk. ...3W 12
YMCA Sports Cen.
Earlswood ...9A 208
Yoakley Rd. N16 ...33Ub 71
Yoga Way KT4: Wor Pk ...75Wa 154
Yoke Cl. N7 ...37Nb 70
Yolande Gdns. SE9 ...57Nc 116
Yonge Pk. N4 ...34Qb 70
YOPPS GREEN ...98Ae 205
Yopps Grn. TN15: Plax ...98Ae 205
York Av. DA15: Sidc ...61Uc 138
HA7: Stan ...25Ka 46
SE17 ...7E 230 (50Sb 91)
SL1: Slou ...4G 80
SL4: Wind ...4F 102
SW14 ...57Sa 109
UB3: Hayes ...43S 84
W7 ...46Ga 86
York Bri. NW1 ...5H 215 (42Jb 90)
York Bldgs. WC2 ...5G 223 (45Nb 90)
York Cl. CM15: Shenf ...17Be 41
E6 ...44Pc 94
KT14: Byfl ...84N 169
SE5 ...54Sb 113
(off Lilford Rd.)
SM4: Mord ...70Db 133
TW18: Staines ...65N 127
W7 ...46Ga 86
WD4: K Lan ...1Q 12
York Ct. KT19: Eps ...84Qa 173
N14 ...20Nb 32
York Cres. IG10: Lough ...13Nc 36
WD6: Bore ...12Ta 29
Yorke Gdns. RH2: Reig ...5J 207

HOSPITALS, HOSPICES and selected HEALTHCARE FACILITIES
covered by this atlas.

N.B. Where it is not possible to name these facilities on the map,
the reference given is for the road in which they are situated.

ABRAHAM COWLEY UNIT 76F **148**
Holloway Hill
Lyne
CHERTSEY
KT16 0QE
Tel: 01932 872010

ALPHA HOSPITAL, WOKING 10H **167**
Redding Way
Knaphill
WOKING
GU21 2QS
Tel: 01483 795100

ASHFORD HOSPITAL 61N **127**
London Road
ASHFORD
TW15 3AA
Tel: 01784 884488

ASHTEAD PRIVATE HOSPITAL 91Na **193**
The Warren
ASHTEAD
KT21 2SB
Tel: 01372 221400

BARKING HOSPITAL 38Vc **75**
Upney Lane
BARKING
IG11 9LX
Tel: 020 3288 2300

BARNES HOSPITAL 55Ua **110**
South Worple Way
LONDON
SW14 8SU
Tel: 020 3513 3600

BARNET HOSPITAL 14Za **30**
Wellhouse Lane
BARNET
EN5 3DJ
Tel: 0845 111 4000

BECKENHAM BEACON 68Bc **136**
379 Croydon Road
BECKENHAM
BR3 3QL
Tel: 01689 866667

BECKTON CYGNET HOSPITAL 44Qc **94**
23 Tunnan Leys
LONDON
E6 6ZB
Tel: 020 7511 2299

BETHLEM ROYAL HOSPITAL 73Cc **158**
Monks Orchard Road
BECKENHAM
BR3 3BX
Tel: 020 3228 6000

BISHOPS WOOD BMI HOSPITAL 23R **44**
Rickmansworth Road
NORTHWOOD
HA6 2JW
Tel: 01923 835814

BLACKHEATH BMI HOSPITAL, THE 55Hc **115**
40-42 Lee Terrace
LONDON
SE3 9UD
Tel: 020 8318 7722

**BLACKHEATH BMI HOSPITAL
(OUTPATIENT DEPARTMENT)** 55Hc **115**
Independents Road
LONDON
SE3 9LF
Tel: 020 8297 4500

BLACKHEATH CYGNET HOSPITAL 53Ec **114**
80 Blackheath Hill
LONDON
SE10 8AB
Tel: 020 8692 4007

BLOOMFIELD COURT HOSPITAL 50Rc **94**
69 Bloomfield Road
LONDON
SE18 7JN
Tel: 01992 785 460

BMI CITY MEDICAL 2H **225**
17 St Helen's Place
LONDON
EC3A 6DG
Tel: 0845 123 5380

BMI EMERGENCY CARE CENTRE 34Ha **66**
The Clementine Hospital
Sudbury Hill
HARROW
HA1 3RX
Tel: 020 8872 3999

BRACTON CENTRE 61Hd **140**
Leyton Cross Road
DARTFORD
DA2 7AF
Tel: 01322 294300

BRENT OLDER PEOPLE DAY HOSPITAL 39Wa **68**
341 Harlesden Road
LONDON
NW10 3RX
Tel: 020 8459 3562

BRENTWOOD COMMUNITY HOSPITAL 18Ae **41**
Crescent Drive
Shenfield
BRENTWOOD
CM15 8DR
Tel: 01277 695000

BRENTWOOD NUFFIELD HEALTH HOSPITAL
................................18Ae **41**
Shenfield Road
Shenfield
BRENTWOOD
CM15 8EH
Tel: 01277 695695

BRIDGEWAYS DAY HOSPITAL 72Nc **160**
Turpington Lane
BROMLEY
BR2 8JA
Tel: 020 8462 0170

BUSHEY SPIRE HOSPITAL 17Ha **28**
Heathbourne Road
Bushey Heath
BUSHEY
WD23 1RD
Tel: 020 8901 5505

CAMDEN MEWS DAY HOSPITAL 38Lb **70**
1-5 Camden Mews
LONDON
NW1 9DB
Tel: 020 3317 4740

CASSEL HOSPITAL 63Ma **131**
1 Ham Common
RICHMOND
TW10 7JF
Tel: 020 8483 2900

CATERHAM DENE HOSPITAL 95Vb **197**
Church Road
CATERHAM
CR3 5RA
Tel: 01883 837500

CAVELL BMI HOSPITAL 12Qb **32**
Cavell Drive
ENFIELD
EN2 7PR
Tel: 020 8366 2122

CENTRAL MIDDLESEX HOSPITAL 41Sa **87**
Acton Lane
LONDON
NW10 7NS
Tel: 020 8965 5733

CHALFONTS & GERRARDS CROSS HOSPITAL
................................25A **42**
Hampden Road
Chalfont St Peter
GERRARDS CROSS
SL9 9DR
Tel: 01753 883821

CHARING CROSS HOSPITAL 51Za **110**
Fulham Palace Road
LONDON
W6 8RF
Tel: 020 3311 1234

CHASE FARM HOSPITAL 10Qb **18**
127 The Ridgeway
ENFIELD
EN2 8JL
Tel: 0845 111 4000

CHELSEA & WESTMINSTER HOSPITAL 51Eb **111**
369 Fulham Road
LONDON
SW10 9NH
Tel: 020 3315 8000

CHELSFIELD PARK BMI HOSPITAL 78Bd **161**
Bucks Cross Road
ORPINGTON
BR6 7RG
Tel: 01689 877855

CHESHUNT COMMUNITY HOSPITAL 3Ac **20**
King Arthur Court
Cheshunt
WALTHAM CROSS
EN8 8XN
Tel: 01992 622157

CHILDREN'S HOSPITAL, THE (LEWISHAM)
................................57Dc **114**
Lewisham University Hospital
Lewisham High Street
LONDON
SE13 6LH
Tel: 020 8333 3000

CHILDREN'S TRUST, THE 93Za **194**
Tadworth Court
TADWORTH
KT20 5RU
Tel: 01737 365000

CHURCHILL CAMBIAN HOSPITAL
................................3A **230** (48Qb **90**)
Barkham Terrace
Lambeth Road
LONDON
SE1 7PW
Tel: 0800 138 1418

CITY & HACKNEY CENTRE FOR MENTAL HEALTH
................................36Zb **72**
Homerton Row
LONDON
E9 6SR
Tel: 020 8510 5000

CLAYPONDS HOSPITAL 49Na **87**
Sterling Place
LONDON
W5 4RN
Tel: 020 8568 0064

CLEMENTINE CHURCHILL BMI HOSPITAL ...33Ha **66**
Sudbury Hill
HARROW
HA1 3RX
Tel: 020 8872 3872

**COBORN CENTRE FOR ADOLESCENT
MENTAL HEALTH, THE** 42Mc **93**
Glen Road
LONDON
E13 8SP
Tel: 020 7540 6789

CROMWELL BUPA HOSPITAL 49Db **89**
162-174 Cromwell Road
LONDON
SW5 0TU
Tel: 020 7460 2000

CROYDON UNIVERSITY HOSPITAL 72Rb **157**
530 London Road
THORNTON HEATH
CR7 7YE
Tel: 020 8401 3000

CYGNET HOSPITAL GODDEN GREEN 97Rd **203**
Godden Green
SEVENOAKS
TN15 0JR
Tel: 01732 763491

CYGNET LODGE 58Ec **114**
44 Lewisham Park
Lewisham
LONDON
SE13 6QZ
Tel: 020 8314 5123

DARENT VALLEY HOSPITAL 60Ud **120**
Darenth Wood Road
DARTFORD
DA2 8DA
Tel: 01322 428100

DEMELZA HOSPICE CARE FOR CHILDREN
................................58Pc **116**
5 Wensley Close
LONDON
SE9 5AB
Tel: 020 8859 9800

DULWICH COMMUNITY HOSPITAL 56Ub **113**
East Dulwich Grove
LONDON
SE22 8PT
Tel: 020 3049 8800

EALING CYGNET HOSPITAL 43Na **87**
22 Corfton Road
LONDON
W5 2HT
Tel: 020 8991 6699

EALING HOSPITAL 46Fa **86**
Uxbridge Road
SOUTHALL
UB1 3HW
Tel: 020 8967 5000

EAST HAM CARE CENTRE & DAY HOSPITAL
................................38Mc **73**
Shrewsbury Road
LONDON
E7 8QP
Tel: 020 8475 2001

EASTMAN DENTAL HOSPITAL & DENTAL INSTITUTE
................................5H **217** (42Pb **90**)
256 Gray's Inn Road
LONDON
WC1X 8LD
Tel: 020 3456 7899

EAST SURREY HOSPITAL 10B **208**
Canada Avenue
REDHILL
RH1 5RH
Tel: 01737 768511

EDGWARE COMMUNITY HOSPITAL 24Ra **47**
Burnt Oak Broadway
EDGWARE
HA8 0AD
Tel: 020 8952 2381

ELLENOR HOSPICE 59Pd **119**
St. Ronans View
East Hill Drive
DARTFORD
DA1 1AE
Tel: 01474 320007

ELLENOR LIONS HOSPICE 3B **144**
Coldharbour Road
Northfleet
GRAVESEND
DA11 7HQ
Tel: 01474 320007

ELTHAM COMMUNITY HOSPITAL 58Pc **116**
Passey Place
LONDON
SE9 5DQ
Tel: 020 3049 0400

EPSOM DAY SURGERY CENTRE 85Va **174**
The Old Cottage Hospital
Alexandra Road
EPSOM
KT17 4BL
Tel: 01372 739002

EPSOM GENERAL HOSPITAL 87Sa **173**
Dorking Road
EPSOM
KT18 7EG
Tel: 01372 735735

ERITH & DISTRICT HOSPITAL 51Fd **118**
Park Crescent
ERITH
DA8 3EE
Tel: 01322 356186

EVELINA CHILDREN'S HOSPITAL 3H **229**
St Thomas' Hospital
Westminster Bridge Road
LONDON
SE1 7EH
Tel: 020 7188 7188

FAWKHAM MANOR BMI HOSPITAL 74Yd **164**
Manor Lane
Fawkham
LONGFIELD
DA3 8ND
Tel: 01474 879900

FINCHLEY MEMORIAL HOSPITAL 24Eb **49**
Granville Road
LONDON
N12 0JE
Tel: 020 8349 7500

FITZROY SQUARE BMI HOSPITAL
................................6B **216** (42Lb **90**)
14 Fitzroy Square
LONDON
W1T 6AH
Tel: 020 7388 4954

GARDEN BMI HOSPITAL, THE 27Ya **48**
46-50 Sunny Gardens Road
LONDON
NW4 1RP
Tel: 020 8457 4500

GATEWAY SURGICAL CENTRE 42Mc **93**
Cherry Tree Way
Glen Road
LONDON
E13 8SL
Tel: 020 7476 4000

**GENERAL MEDICAL WALK-IN CENTRE
(LIVERPOOL STREET)** 7J **219** (43Ub **91**)
Exchange Arcade
Bishopsgate
LONDON
EC2M 3WA
Tel: 0845 437 0691

GOODMAYES HOSPITAL 29Wc **55**
Barley Lane
ILFORD
IG3 8XJ
Tel: 0844 600 1207

GORDON HOSPITAL 6D **228** (49Mb **90**)
Bloomburg Street
LONDON
SW1V 2RH
Tel: 020 8746 8733

GRAVESHAM COMMUNITY HOSPITAL 8C **122**
Bath Street
GRAVESEND
DA11 0DG
Tel: 01474 360500

GRAYS COURT COMMUNITY HOSPITAL 38Dd **76**
John Parker Close
DAGENHAM
RM10 9SR
Tel: 020 8724 1463

GREAT ORMOND STREET HOSPITAL FOR CHILDREN
................................6H **217** (42Nb **90**)
Great Ormond Street
LONDON
WC1N 3JH
Tel: 020 7405 9200

GREENACRES 58Rd **119**
Bow Arrow Lane
DARTFORD
DA2 6PB
Tel: 01322 622222

GREENWICH & BEXLEY COMMUNITY HOSPICE
..............................50Yc **95**
185 Bostall Hill
LONDON
SE2 0GB
Tel: 020 8312 2244

GUY'S HOSPITAL 7F **225** (47Tb **91**)
Great Maze Pond
LONDON
SE1 9RT
Tel: 020 7188 7188

GUY'S NUFFIELD HOUSE 1F **231**
Guy's Hospital
Newcomen Street
LONDON
SE1 1YR
Tel: 020 7188 5282

HAMMERSMITH HOSPITAL 44Wa **88**
Du Cane Road
LONDON
W12 0HS
Tel: 020 3313 1000

HAND CLINIC, THE 3A **102**
Dedworth Road
Oakley Green
WINDSOR
SL4 4LH
Tel: 01753 831333

HAREFIELD HOSPITAL 25L **43**
Hill End Road
Harefield
UXBRIDGE
UB9 6JH
Tel: 01895 823737

HARLEY STREET CLINIC, THE 7K **215** (43Kb **90**)
35 Weymouth Street
LONDON
W1G 8BJ
Tel: 020 7935 7700

HARLINGTON HOSPICE 50T **84**
St. Peters Way
HAYES
UB3 5AB
Tel: 020 8759 0453

HARRIS HOSPISCARE 77Vc **161**
Tregony Road
ORPINGTON
BR6 9XA
Tel: 01689 825755

HARROW CYGNET HOSPITAL 33Ga **66**
London Road
HARROW
HA1 3JL
Tel: 020 8966 7000

HARTSWOOD SPIRE HOSPITAL 23Xd **58**
Eagle Way
Great Warley
BRENTWOOD
CM13 3LE
Tel: 01277 266761

HAVEN HOUSE CHILDREN'S HOSPICE 23Hc **53**
High Road
WOODFORD GREEN
IG8 9LB
Tel: 020 8505 9944

HAYES GROVE PRIORY HOSPITAL 75Jc **159**
Prestons Road
Hayes
BROMLEY
BR2 7AS
Tel: 020 8462 7722

HEART HOSPITAL, THE 1K **221** (43Jb **90**)
16-18 Westmoreland Street
LONDON
W1G 8PH
Tel: 020 3456 7898

HEMEL HEMPSTEAD GENERAL HOSPITAL 3M **3**
Hillfield Road
HEMEL HEMPSTEAD
HP2 4AD
Tel: 01442 213141

HIGHGATE HOSPITAL 30Hb **49**
17- 19 View Road
LONDON
N6 4DJ
Tel: 020 8341 4182

HIGHGATE MENTAL HEALTH CENTRE 33Kb **70**
Dartmouth Park Hill
LONDON
N19 5NX
Tel: 020 7561 4000

HILLINGDON HOSPITAL 43P **83**
Pield Heath Road
UXBRIDGE
UB8 3NN
Tel: 01895 238282

HOLLY HOUSE HOSPITAL 19Kc **35**
High Road
BUCKHURST HILL
IG9 5HX
Tel: 020 8505 3311

HOMERTON UNIVERSITY HOSPITAL 36Zb **72**
Homerton Row
LONDON
E9 6SR
Tel: 020 8510 5555

HOSPITAL FOR TROPICAL DISEASES 6C **216**
Mortimer Market
Capper Street
LONDON
WC1E 6JB
Tel: 020 3456 7891

HOSPITAL OF ST JOHN & ST ELIZABETH
..............................2B **214** (40Fb **69**)
60 Grove End Road
LONDON
NW8 9NH
Tel: 020 7806 4000

JOHN HOWARD CENTRE 36Ac **72**
12 Kenworthy Road
LONDON
E9 5TD
Tel: 020 8510 2003

KING EDWARD VII HOSPITAL 5G **102**
St. Leonard's Road
WINDSOR
SL4 3DP
Tel: 01753 860441

KING EDWARD VII'S HOSPITAL SISTER AGNES
..............................7J **215** (43Jb **90**)
5-10 Beaumont Street
LONDON
W1G 6AA
Tel: 020 7486 4411

KING GEORGE HOSPITAL 28Wc **55**
Barley Lane
ILFORD
IG3 8YB
Tel: 020 8983 8000

KING'S COLLEGE HOSPITAL 54Tb **113**
Denmark Hill
LONDON
SE5 9RS
Tel: 020 3299 9000

KINGSLEY GREEN 3La **14**
Harper Lane
Shenley
RADLETT
WD7 9HQ
Tel: 01923 854861

KING'S OAK BMI HOSPITAL 10Qb **18**
The Ridgeway
ENFIELD
EN2 8SD
Tel: 020 8370 9500

KINGSTON HOSPITAL 67Ra **131**
Galsworthy Road
KINGSTON UPON THAMES
KT2 7QB
Tel: 020 8546 7711

LAMBETH HOSPITAL 55Pb **112**
108 Landor Road
LONDON
SW9 9NU
Tel: 020 3228 6000

LEATHERHEAD COMMUNITY HOSPITAL 94La **192**
Poplar Road
LEATHERHEAD
KT22 8SD
Tel: 01372 384348

LISTER HOSPITAL, THE 50Kb **90**
Chelsea Bridge Road
LONDON
SW1W 8RH
Tel: 020 7730 3417

LITTLE BROOK HOSPITAL 58Sd **120**
Bow Arrow Lane
DARTFORD
DA2 6PB
Tel: 01322 622222

LIVINGSTONE HOSPITAL 59Pd **119**
East Hill
DARTFORD
DA1 1SA
Tel: 01322 622387

LONDON BRIDGE HOSPITAL 6G **225** (46Tb **91**)
27 Tooley Street
LONDON
SE1 2PR
Tel: 0845 602 7906

LONDON CHEST HOSPITAL 40Yb **72**
Bonner Road
LONDON
E2 9JX
Tel: 020 3146 5000

LONDON CLINIC 6J **215** (42Jb **90**)
20 Devonshire Place
LONDON
W1G 6BW
Tel: 020 7935 4444

LONDON EYE HOSPITAL 2K **221**
8-10 Harley Street
LONDON
W1G 9PF
Tel: 0800 612 2021

LONDON INDEPENDENT BMI HOSPITAL ...43Zb **92**
1 Beaumont Square
LONDON
E1 4NL
Tel: 020 7780 2400

LONDON WELBECK HOSPITAL 1K **221**
27 Welbeck Street
LONDON
W1G 8EN
Tel: 020 7224 2242

MAIDENHEAD HUNTERCOMBE HOSPITAL 5A **80**
Huntercombe Lane South
Taplow
MAIDENHEAD
SL6 0PQ
Tel: 01628 667881

MARGARET CENTRE (HOSPICE) 30Gc **53**
Whipps Cross University Hospital
Whipps Cross Road
LONDON
E11 1NR
Tel: 020 8535 6604

MARIE CURIE HOSPICE, HAMPSTEAD 36Fb **69**
11 Lyndhurst Gardens
LONDON
NW3 5NS
Tel: 020 7853 3400

MAUDSLEY HOSPITAL, THE 54Tb **113**
Denmark Hill
LONDON
SE5 8AZ
Tel: 020 3228 6000

MEADOW HOUSE HOSPICE 47Fa **86**
Uxbridge Road
SOUTHALL
UB1 3HW
Tel: 020 8967 5179

MEMORIAL HOSPITAL 54Qc **116**
Shooters Hill
LONDON
SE18 3RG
Tel: 020 8836 8500

MICHAEL SOBELL HOUSE (HOSPICE) 23R **44**
Mount Vernon Hospital
Rickmansworth Road
NORTHWOOD
HA6 2RN
Tel: 01923 844531

MILDMAY HOSPITAL 4K **219** (41Vb **91**)
Tabernacle Gardens
LONDON
E2 7DZ
Tel: 020 7613 6300

MILE END HOSPITAL 42Zb **92**
Bancroft Road
LONDON
E1 4DG
Tel: 020 3416 5000

MINOR INJURIES UNIT (CHESHUNT) 3Ac **20**
within Cheshunt Community Hospital
King Arthur Court
WALTHAM CROSS
EN8 8XN
Tel: 01992 622157

MINOR INJURIES UNIT (DAGENHAM) 38Dd **76**
Grays Court Community Hospital
John Parker Close
DAGENHAM
RM10 9SR
Tel: 020 8724 1463

MINOR INJURIES UNIT (GRAVESHAM) 8C **122**
Gravesham Community Hospital
Bath Street
GRAVESEND
DA11 0DG
Tel: 01474 360500

MINOR INJURIES UNIT (NORTHWOOD) 23R **44**
Mount Vernon Hospital
Rickmansworth Road
NORTHWOOD
HA6 2RN
Tel: 01923 826111

**MINOR INJURIES UNIT
(ORSETT HOSPITAL)** 3C **100**
Rowley Road
Orsett
GRAYS
RM16 3EU
Tel: 01268 592300

**MINOR INJURIES UNIT
(PARKWAY HEALTH CENTRE)** 82Ec **178**
Parkway
New Addington
CROYDON
CR0 0JA
Tel: 01689 808810

MINOR INJURIES UNIT (PURLEY) 83Qb **176**
Purley War Memorial Hospital
856 Brighton Road
PURLEY
CR8 2YL
Tel: 020 8401 3238

MINOR INJURIES UNIT (ROEHAMPTON) ...58Wa **110**
Roehampton Lane
LONDON
SW15 5PN
Tel: 020 8487 6000

MINOR INJURIES UNIT (ST ALBANS) 1A **6**
Waverley Road
ST. ALBANS
AL3 5PN
Tel: 01727 866122

**MINOR INJURIES UNIT
(ST BARTHOLOMEW'S HOSPITAL)**
..............................1C **224** (43Rb **91**)
West Smithfield
LONDON
EC1A 7BE
Tel: 020 3465 6843

MINOR INJURIES UNIT (SILVERTOWN) 46Kc **93**
The Practice
12a Wesley Avenue
LONDON
E16 1RZ
Tel: 020 3040 0100

MOLESEY HOSPITAL 71Ca **151**
High Street
WEST MOLESEY
KT8 2LU
Tel: 020 8941 4481

MOORFIELDS EYE HOSPITAL 4F **219** (41Tb **91**)
162 City Road
LONDON
EC1V 2PD
Tel: 020 7253 3411

MOUNT VERNON HOSPITAL 23R **44**
Rickmansworth Road
NORTHWOOD
HA6 2RN
Tel: 01923 826111

**NATIONAL HOSPITAL FOR NEUROLOGY &
NEUROSURGERY** 6G **217** (42Nb **90**)
Queen Square
LONDON
WC1N 3BG
Tel: 020 3456 7890

NATIONAL SOCIETY FOR EPILEPSY, THE 21B **42**
Chesham Lane
Chalfont St Peter
GERRARDS CROSS
SL9 0RJ
Tel: 01494 601300

NELSON HOSPITAL 68Bb **133**
Kingston Road
LONDON
SW20 8DB
Tel: 020 8296 3795

NEW EPSOM & EWELL COTTAGE HOSPITAL
..............................83Na **173**
West Park Road
Horton Lane
EPSOM
KT19 8PB
Tel: 01372 734845

NEWHAM CENTRE FOR MENTAL HEALTH ...42Mc **93**
Cherry Tree Way
Glen Road
LONDON
E13 8SP
Tel: 020 7540 4380

NEWHAM UNIVERSITY HOSPITAL 42Lc **93**
Glen Road
LONDON
E13 8SL
Tel: 020 7476 4000

NEW VICTORIA HOSPITAL 67Ua **132**
184 Coombe Lane West
KINGSTON UPON THAMES
KT2 7EG
Tel: 020 8949 9000

NHS WALK-IN CENTRE (ALEXANDRA CLINIC, THE)
..............................33Ca **65**
275 Alexandra Avenue
HARROW
HA2 9DX
Tel: 020 8427 2470

NHS WALK-IN CENTRE (ASHFORD) 61N **127**
Ashford Hospital
London Road
ASHFORD
TW15 3AA
Tel: 01784 884488

NHS WALK-IN CENTRE (BARKING HOSPITAL)
..............................38Vc **75**
Upney Lane
BARKING
IG11 9LX
Tel: 020 8924 6262

NHS WALK-IN CENTRE (BOW) 42Dc **92**
St. Andrew's Health Centre
2 Hannaford Walk
LONDON
E3 3FF
Tel:

NHS WALK-IN CENTRE (CHESSINGTON) ...77Na **153**
Gosbury Hill Health Centre
Orchard Gardens
CHESSINGTON
KT9 1AG
Tel: 020 8974 1884

NHS WALK-IN CENTRE (CLAPHAM JUNCTION)
..............................55Gb **111**
The Junction Health Centre
Arches 5-8, Clapham Junction Station
Grant Road
LONDON
SW11 2NU
Tel: 0333 200 1718

**NHS WALK-IN CENTRE
(CRICKLEWOOD HEALTH CENTRE)** 35Za **68**
Britannia Business Centre
Cricklewood Lane
LONDON
NW2 1DZ
Tel: 03000 334335

NHS WALK-IN CENTRE (CROYDON) 76Sb **157**
Impact House
Edridge Road
CROYDON
CR9 1PJ
Tel: 020 3040 0800

NHS WALK-IN CENTRE (EARL'S COURT) 49Db **89**
Earl's Court Health & Wellbeing Centre
2b Hogarth Road
LONDON
SW5 0PT
Tel: 020 7341 0300

NHS WALK-IN CENTRE (EAST SURREY) 10A **208**
Canada Avenue
REDHILL
RH1 5RH
Tel:

NHS WALK-IN CENTRE (EDGWARE) 24Ra **47**
Edgware Community Hospital
Burnt Oak Broadway
EDGWARE
HA8 0AD
Tel: 020 8732 6459

NHS WALK-IN CENTRE (FINCHLEY) 24Eb **49**
Finchley Memorial Hospital
Granville Road
LONDON
N12 0JE
Tel: 020 8349 7470

NHS WALK-IN CENTRE (HAROLD WOOD) ...26Pd **57**
St. Clements Avenue
Harold Wood
ROMFORD
RM3 0FE
Tel: 01708 574000

NHS WALK-IN CENTRE (ISLE OF DOGS) 47Cc **92**
Barkantine Practice
121 Westferry Road
LONDON
E14 8JH
Tel: 020 7791 8080

NHS WALK-IN CENTRE (LEYTON) 34Dc **72**
Oliver Road Medical Centre
75 Oliver Road
LONDON
E10 5LG
Tel: 020 8430 8282

NHS WALK-IN CENTRE (LISTER HEALTH CENTRE)
....53Vb **113**
101 Peckham Road
LONDON
SE15 5LJ
Tel: 020 3049 8430

NHS WALK-IN CENTRE (LOXFORD, ILFORD)
....36Sc **74**
Loxford Practice, The
417 Ilford Lane
ILFORD
IG1 2SN
Tel: 0300 300 1700

NHS WALK-IN CENTRE (MITCHAM) 70Hb **133**
Wilson Health Centre, The
Cranmer Road
MITCHAM
CR4 4TP
Tel: 020 3458 5100

NHS WALK-IN CENTRE (PARSONS GREEN)
....53Cb **111**
5-7 Parsons Green
LONDON
SW6 4UL
Tel: 020 8102 4300

NHS WALK-IN CENTRE (PINNER) 27Aa **45**
Pinn Medical Centre, The
37 Love Lane
PINNER
HA5 3EE
Tel: 020 8866 5766

NHS WALK-IN CENTRE
(RICHIE STREET GROUP PRACTICE)
...............................1A **218** (40Qb **70**)
34 Ritchie Street
LONDON
N1 0DG
Tel: 020 7837 1663

NHS WALK-IN CENTRE (SOHO) 3D **222**
1 Frith Street
LONDON
W1D 3HZ
Tel: 020 7534 6575

NHS WALK-IN CENTRE (SOUTHALL) 48Aa **85**
Featherstone Road Health Centre
Hartington Road
SOUTHALL
UB2 5BQ
Tel: 020 3313 9880

NHS WALK-IN CENTRE (SOUTH HORNCHURCH)
....39Jd **76**
South Hornchurch Health Centre
106 South End Road
RAINHAM
RM13 7XJ
Tel: 01708 576000

NHS WALK-IN CENTRE (STRATFORD) 38Gc **73**
DMC Healthcare One
10 Vicarage Lane
LONDON
E15 4ES
Tel: 020 8536 2277

NHS WALK-IN CENTRE (STREATHAM) 62Nb **134**
Gracefield Gardens Health Centre
Gracefield Gardens
LONDON
SW16 2ST
Tel: 020 3049 4040

NHS WALK-IN CENTRE (TEDDINGTON) 65Ga **130**
Teddington Memorial Hospital
Hampton Road
TEDDINGTON
TW11 0JL
Tel: 020 8714 4004

NHS WALK-IN CENTRE (THAMESMEAD) 47Uc **94**
Thamesmead Health Centre
4-5 Thames Reach
LONDON
SE28 0NY
Tel: 020 8319 5880

NHS WALK-IN CENTRE (WALDRON HEALTH CENTRE)
....52Bc **114**
Amersham Vale
LONDON
SE14 6LD
Tel: 020 3049 2370

NHS WALK-IN CENTRE (WEMBLEY) 37Ma **67**
116 Chaplin Road
WEMBLEY
HA0 4UZ
Tel: 020 8795 6112

NHS WALK-IN CENTRE (WEST KILBURN) ..42Bb **89**
Half Penny Steps Health Centre
427-429 Harrow Road
LONDON
W10 4RE
Tel: 020 8962 8700

NHS WALK-IN CENTRE (WEYBRIDGE) 77Q **150**
Weybridge Community Hospital
22 Church Street
WEYBRIDGE
KT13 8DY
Tel: 01932 826013

NHS WALK-IN CENTRE (WOKING) 90B **168**
Woking Community Hospital
Heathside Road
WOKING
GU22 7HS
Tel: 01483 846209

NHS WALK-IN CENTRE (WOOLWICH) 49Rc **94**
Clover Health Centre
General Gordon Place
LONDON
SE18 6AB
Tel: 020 8331 0567

NIGHTINGALE HOSPITAL 7E **214** (43Gb **89**)
11-19 Lisson Grove
LONDON
NW1 6SH
Tel: 020 7535 7700

NOAH'S ARK CHILDREN'S HOSPICE 14Bb **31**
Beauchamp Court
10 Victors Way
BARNET
EN5 5TZ
Tel: 020 8449 8877

NORTH DOWNS PRIVATE HOSPITAL 97Vb **197**
46 Tupwood Lane
CATERHAM
CR3 6DP
Tel: 01883 348981

NORTH EAST LONDON NHS TREATMENT CENTRE
....28Wc **55**
King George Hospital
Barley Lane
ILFORD
IG3 8YB
Tel: 0333 200 4069

NORTH LONDON CLINIC 19Wb **33**
15 Church Street
LONDON
N9 9DY
Tel: 020 8956 1234

NORTH LONDON HOSPICE (BARNET) 20Eb **31**
47 Woodside Avenue
LONDON
N12 8TT
Tel: 020 8343 8841

NORTH LONDON HOSPICE (ENFIELD) 20Sb **33**
110 Barrowell Green
LONDON
N21 3AY
Tel: 020 8343 8841

NORTH LONDON PRIORY HOSPITAL 18Nb **32**
The Bourne
LONDON
N14 6RA
Tel: 020 8882 8191

NORTH MIDDLESEX UNIVERSITY HOSPITAL
....22Ub **51**
Sterling Way
LONDON
N18 1QX
Tel: 020 8887 2000

NORTHWICK PARK HOSPITAL 31Ja **66**
Watford Road
HARROW
HA1 3UJ
Tel: 020 8864 3232

OLD BROAD STREET PRIVATE MEDICAL CENTRE
....2H **225**
31 Old Broad Street
LONDON
EC2N 1HT
Tel: 020 7496 3555

ORPINGTON HOSPITAL 77Vc **161**
Sevenoaks Road
ORPINGTON
BR6 9JU
Tel: 01689 863000

ORSETT HOSPITAL 3C **100**
Rowley Road
Orsett
GRAYS
RM16 3EU
Tel: 01268 524900

PARK ROYAL CENTRE (FOR MENTAL HEALTH)
....40Sa **67**
Central Way
LONDON
NW10 7NS
Tel: 020 8955 4400

PARKSIDE HOSPITAL 62Za **132**
53 Parkside
LONDON
SW19 5NX
Tel: 020 8971 8000

PEACE HOSPICE 13W **26**
Peace Drive
WATFORD
WD17 3PH
Tel: 01923 330330

PEMBRIDGE PALLIATIVE CARE CENTRE ...43Za **88**
St. Charles Hospital
Exmoor Street
LONDON
W10 6DZ
Tel: 020 8962 4410

PORTLAND HOSPITAL FOR WOMEN & CHILDREN
...............................6A **216** (42Kb **90**)
205-209 Great Portland Street
LONDON
W1W 5AH
Tel: 020 7580 4400

POTTERS BAR COMMUNITY HOSPITAL 6Eb **17**
Barnet Road
POTTERS BAR
EN6 2RY
Tel: 01707 646422

PRINCESS ALICE HOSPICE, THE 78Ca **151**
West End Lane
ESHER
KT10 8NA
Tel: 01372 468811

PRINCESS GRACE HOSPITAL 7H **215** (42Jb **90**)
42-52 Nottingham Place
LONDON
W1M 3FD
Tel: 020 7486 1234

PRINCESS MARGARET BMI HOSPITAL 4H **103**
Osborne Road
WINDSOR
SL4 3SJ
Tel: 01753 743434

PRINCESS ROYAL UNIVERSITY HOSPITAL
....76Qc **160**
Farnborough Common
ORPINGTON
BR6 8ND
Tel: 01689 863000

PRIORY HOSPITAL, HEMEL HEAMPSTEAD 7H **3**
Longcroft Lane
Felden
HEMEL HEMPSTEAD
HP3 0BN
Tel: 01442 255371

PRIORY HOSPITAL STURT HOUSE 99Wa **194**
Sturts Lane
Walton on the Hill
TADWORTH
KT20 7RQ
Tel: 01737 817610

PROSPECT HOUSE 13W **26**
Peace Drive
WATFORD
WD17 3XE
Tel: 01923 693900

PURLEY WAR MEMORIAL HOSPITAL 83Qb **176**
856 Brighton Road
PURLEY
CR8 2YL
Tel: 020 8401 3000

QUEEN CHARLOTTE'S & CHELSEA HOSPITAL
....44Wa **88**
Du Cane Road
LONDON
W12 0HS
Tel: 020 3313 1111

QUEEN ELIZABETH HOSPITAL 52Nc **116**
Stadium Road
LONDON
SE18 4QH
Tel: 020 8836 6000

QUEEN MARY'S HOSPITAL FOR CHILDREN
....74Eb **155**
Wrythe Lane
CARSHALTON
SM5 1AA
Tel: 020 8296 2000

QUEEN MARY'S HOSPITAL, ROEHAMPTON
....58Wa **110**
Roehampton Lane
LONDON
SW15 5PN
Tel: 020 8725 3579

QUEEN MARY'S HOSPITAL, SIDCUP 65Wc **139**
Frognal Avenue
SIDCUP
DA14 6LT
Tel: 020 8302 2678

QUEEN'S HOSPITAL 31Gd **76**
Rom Valley Way
ROMFORD
RM7 0AG
Tel: 01708 435000

RENNIE GROVE HOSPICE 1A **6**
Waverley Road
ST. ALBANS
AL3 5QX
Tel: 01727 731000

RICHARD DESMOND CHILDREN'S EYE CENTRE
....4F **219**
Moorfields Eye Hospital
3 Peerless Street
LONDON
EC1V 9EZ
Tel: 020 7253 3411

RICHARD HOUSE CHILDREN'S HOSPICE
....45Mc **93**
Richard House Drive
LONDON
E16 3RG
Tel: 020 7511 0222

RICHMOND ROYAL HOSPITAL 55Na **109**
Kew Foot Road
RICHMOND
TW9 2TE
Tel: 020 3513 3238

RODING SPIRE HOSPITAL 27Mc **53**
Roding Lane South
ILFORD
IG4 5PZ
Tel: 020 8709 7817

ROEHAMPTON HUNTERCOMBE HOSPITAL
....59Wa **110**
Holybourne Avenue
LONDON
SW15 4JD
Tel: 020 8780 6155

ROEHAMPTON PRIORY HOSPITAL 56Va **110**
Priory Lane
LONDON
SW15 5JJ
Tel: 020 8876 8261

ROYAL BROMPTON HOSPITAL
...............................7D **226** (50Gb **89**)
Sydney Street
LONDON
SW3 6NP
Tel: 020 7352 8121

ROYAL BROMPTON HOSPITAL (OUTPATIENTS)
...............................7C **226** (50Fb **89**)
Fulham Road
LONDON
SW3 6HP
Tel: 020 7351 8011

ROYAL FREE HOSPITAL 36Gb **69**
Pond Street
LONDON
NW3 2QG
Tel: 020 7794 0500

ROYAL HOSPITAL FOR NEURO-DISABILITY
....58Ab **110**
West Hill
LONDON
SW15 3SW
Tel: 020 8780 4500

ROYAL LONDON HOSPITAL, THE
....43Xb **91**
Whitechapel Road
LONDON
E1 1BB
Tel: 020 3416 5000

ROYAL LONDON HOSPITAL FOR
INTEGRATED MEDICINE 6G **217** (42Nb **90**)
60 Great Ormond Street
LONDON
WC1N 3HR
Tel: 020 3456 7890

ROYAL MARSDEN HOSPITAL (FULHAM), THE
...............................7C **226** (50Fb **89**)
Fulham Road
LONDON
SW3 6JJ
Tel: 020 7352 8171

ROYAL MARSDEN HOSPITAL (SUTTON), THE
....82Eb **175**
Downs Road
SUTTON
SM2 5PT
Tel: 020 8642 6011

ROYAL NATIONAL ORTHOPAEDIC HOSPITAL
....19La **28**
Brockley Hill
STANMORE
HA7 4LP
Tel: 020 8954 2300

ROYAL NATIONAL ORTHOPAEDIC HOSPITAL
(CENTRAL LONDON OUTPATIENT DEPT.)
...............................6A **216** (42Kb **90**)
45-51 Bolsover Street
LONDON
W1W 5AQ
Tel: 020 8954 2300

ROYAL NATIONAL THROAT, NOSE & EAR HOSPITAL
.................................3H **217** (41Pb **90**)
330 Gray's Inn Road
LONDON
WC1X 8DA
Tel: 020 3456 7890

RUNNYMEDE BMI HOSPITAL 76F **148**
Guildford Road
Ottershaw
CHERTSEY
KT16 0RQ
Tel: 01932 877800

ST ALBANS CITY HOSPITAL 1A **6**
Waverley Road
ST. ALBANS
AL3 5PN
Tel: 01727 866122

ST ANN'S HOSPITAL 29Sb **51**
St. Ann's Road
LONDON
N15 3TH
Tel: 020 8442 6000

ST ANTHONY'S HOSPITAL 74Za **154**
801 London Road
SUTTON
SM3 9DW
Tel: 020 8337 6691

ST BARTHOLOMEW'S HOSPITAL ...1C **224** (43Rb **91**)
West Smithfield
LONDON
EC1A 7BE
Tel: 020 3416 5000

ST BERNARD'S HOSPITAL 47Fa **86**
Uxbridge Road
SOUTHALL
UB1 3EU
Tel: 020 8354 8354

ST CATHERINE'S HOSPICE (CATERHAM) ...93Ub **197**
Foxon Lane
Dormers
CATERHAM
CR3 5SG
Tel: 01293 447387

ST CHARLES HOSPITAL 43Za **88**
Exmoor Street
LONDON
W10 6DZ
Tel: 020 8206 7343

ST CHRISTOPHER'S HOSPICE 64Yb **136**
51-59 Lawrie Park Road
LONDON
SE26 6DZ
Tel: 020 8768 4500

ST EBBA'S 81Sa **173**
Hook Road
EPSOM
KT19 8QJ
Tel: 01883 388300

ST FRANCIS HOSPICE 20Gd **38**
Broxhill Road
Havering-atte-Bower
ROMFORD
RM4 1QH
Tel: 01708 753319

ST GEORGE'S HOSPITAL (TOOTING) 64Fb **133**
Blackshaw Road
LONDON
SW17 0QT
Tel: 020 8672 1255

ST HELIER HOSPITAL 74Eb **155**
Wrythe Lane
CARSHALTON
SM5 1AA
Tel: 020 8296 2000

ST JOHN'S HOSPICE 2B **214**
Hospital of St John & St Elizabeth
60 Grove End Road
LONDON
NW8 9NH
Tel: 020 7806 4050

ST JOSEPH'S HOSPICE 39Xb **71**
Mare Street
LONDON
E8 4SA
Tel: 020 8525 6047

ST LUKE'S HEALTHCARE FOR THE CLERGY
.................................42Lb **90**
14 Fitzroy Square
LONDON
W1T 6AH
Tel: 020 7388 4954

ST LUKE'S HOSPICE 29Ma **47**
Kenton Road
HARROW
HA3 0YG
Tel: 020 8382 8000

ST MARGARET'S HOSPITAL 1Xc **23**
The Plain
EPPING
CM16 6TN
Tel: 01992 902010

ST MARK'S HOSPITAL 31Ka **66**
Watford Road
HARROW
HA1 3UJ
Tel: 020 8235 4000

ST MARY'S HOSPITAL 2C **220** (44Fb **89**)
Praed Street
LONDON
W2 1NY
Tel: 020 3312 6666

ST MICHAEL'S HOSPITAL 11Tb **33**
Gater Drive
ENFIELD
EN2 0JB
Tel: 020 8375 2941

ST PANCRAS HOSPITAL 1D **216** (39Mb **70**)
4 St Pancras Way
LONDON
NW1 0PE
Tel: 020 7530 3500

ST PETER'S HOSPITAL 76F **148**
Guildford Road
CHERTSEY
KT16 0PZ
Tel: 01932 872000

ST RAPHAEL'S HOSPICE 75Za **154**
London Road
SUTTON
SM3 9DX
Tel: 020 8335 4575

ST THOMAS' HOSPITAL 2H **229** (48Pb **90**)
Westminster Bridge Road
LONDON
SE1 7EH
Tel: 020 7188 7188

SAM BEARE HOSPICE 77Q **150**
Weybridge Community Hospital
22 Church Street
WEYBRIDGE
KT13 8DY
Tel: 01932 826095

SEVENOAKS HOSPITAL 93Ld **203**
Hospital Road
SEVENOAKS
TN13 3PG
Tel: 01732 470200

SHIRLEY OAKS BMI HOSPITAL 73Yb **158**
Poppy Lane
CROYDON
CR9 8AB
Tel: 020 8655 5500

SHOOTING STAR HOUSE, CHILDREN'S HOSPICE
.................................65Ba **129**
The Avenue
HAMPTON
TW12 3RA
Tel: 020 8783 2000

SLOANE BMI HOSPITAL, THE 67Fc **137**
125 Albemarle Road
BECKENHAM
BR3 5HS
Tel: 020 8466 4000

**SOUTH WEST LONDON ELECTIVE
ORTHOPAEDIC CENTRE** 87Sa **173**
Epsom General Hospital
Dorking Road
EPSOM
KT18 7EG
Tel: 01372 735800

SPRINGFIELD UNIVERSITY HOSPITAL 61Gb **133**
61 Glenburnie Road
LONDON
SW17 7DJ
Tel: 020 3513 5000

SUTTON HOSPITAL 82Db **175**
Cotswold Road
SUTTON
SM2 5NF
Tel: 020 8296 2000

TEDDINGTON MEMORIAL HOSPITAL 65Ga **130**
Hampton Road
TEDDINGTON
TW11 0JL
Tel: 020 8714 4000

THAMES HOSPICECARE (WINDSOR) 5E **102**
Pine Lodge
Hatch Lane
WINDSOR
SL4 3RW
Tel: 01753 842121

THAMES VALLEY SPIRE HOSPITAL 9N **61**
Wexham Street
Wexham
SLOUGH
SL3 6NH
Tel: 01753 662241

THORPE COOMBE HOSPITAL 27Ec **52**
714 Forest Road
LONDON
E17 3HP
Tel: 0300 555 1239

THURROCK COMMUNITY HOSPITAL 46Ee **99**
Long Lane
GRAYS
RM16 2PX
Tel: 01375 364412

TOLWORTH HOSPITAL 75Qa **153**
Red Lion Road
SURBITON
KT6 7QU
Tel: 020 8390 0102

TOWER HAMLETS CENTRE FOR MENTAL HEALTH
.................................42Zb **92**
Bancroft Road
LONDON
E1 4DG
Tel: 020 8121 5001

TRINITY HOSPICE 56Kb **112**
30 Clapham Common North Side
LONDON
SW4 0RN
Tel: 020 7787 1000

UCH MACMILLAN CANCER CENTRE
.................................6C **216** (42Lb **90**)
Huntley Street
LONDON
WC1E 6DH
Tel: 020 3456 7016

UNIVERSITY COLLEGE HOSPITAL
.................................5C **216** (42Lb **90**)
235 Euston Road
LONDON
NW1 2BU
Tel: 020 3456 7890

UNIVERSITY HOSPITAL, LEWISHAM 57Dc **114**
Lewisham High Street
LONDON
SE13 6LH
Tel: 020 8333 3000

UPTON CENTRE 56Ad **117**
14 Upton Road
BEXLEYHEATH
DA6 8LQ
Tel: 020 8301 7900

UPTON HOSPITAL 7K **81**
Albert Street
SLOUGH
SL1 2BJ
Tel: 01753 821441

URGENT CARE CENTRE (BARNET) 14Za **30**
Barnet Hospital
Wellhouse Lane
BARNET
EN5 3DJ
Tel: 020 8216 4600

URGENT CARE CENTRE (BECKENHAM BEACON)
.................................68Bc **136**
379 Croydon Road
BECKENHAM
BR3 3QL
Tel: 01689 866037

URGENT CARE CENTRE (CARSHALTON) 74Eb **155**
St. Helier Hospital
Wrythe Lane
CARSHALTON
SM5 1AA
Tel: 020 8296 2000

**URGENT CARE CENTRE
(CENTRAL MIDDLESEX HOSPITAL)** 41Sa **87**
Acton Lane
LONDON
NW10 7NS
Tel: 020 8965 5733

URGENT CARE CENTRE (CHASE FARM HOSPITAL)
.................................11Qb **32**
The Ridgeway
ENFIELD
EN2 8JL
Tel: 020 8375 1010

**URGENT CARE CENTRE
(CHELSEA & WESTMINSTER HOSPITAL)**
.................................51Eb **111**
369 Fulham Road
LONDON
SW10 9NH
Tel: 020 3315 8000

URGENT CARE CENTRE (EALING) 47Fa **86**
Ealing Hospital
Uxbridge Road
SOUTHALL
UB1 3HW
Tel: 0333 999 2577

**URGENT CARE CENTRE
(ERITH & DISTRICT HOSPITAL)** 51Fd **118**
Park Crescent
ERITH
DA8 3EE
Tel: 01322 356116

URGENT CARE CENTRE (FULHAM) 50Za **88**
Charing Cross Hospital
Fulham Palace Road
LONDON
W6 8RF
Tel: 020 8846 1005

URGENT CARE CENTRE (GUY'S HOSPITAL)
.................................1G **231** (47Tb **91**)
Great Maze Pond
LONDON
SE1 9RT
Tel: 020 7188 7188

URGENT CARE CENTRE (HAMMERSMITH HOSPITAL)
.................................44Wa **88**
Du Cane Road
LONDON
W12 0HS
Tel: 020 8383 4103

URGENT CARE CENTRE (HAMPSTEAD) 36Gb **69**
Royal Free Hospital
Pond Street
LONDON
NW3 2QG
Tel: 020 7794 0500

URGENT CARE CENTRE (HEMEL HEMPSTEAD)
.................................2M **3**
Hemel Hempstead Hospital
Hillfield Road
HEMEL HEMPSTEAD
HP2 4AD
Tel: 01442 287452

URGENT CARE CENTRE (HILLINGDON HOSPITAL)
.................................43P **83**
Hillingdon Hospital
Pield Heath Road
UXBRIDGE
UB8 3NN
Tel: 01895 238282

**URGENT CARE CENTRE
(HOMERTON UNIVERSITY HOSPITAL)**
.................................36Zb **72**
Homerton Row
LONDON
E9 6SR
Tel: 020 8510 7120

URGENT CARE CENTRE (KING GEORGE HOSPITAL)
.................................28Wc **55**
Barley Lane
ILFORD
IG3 8YB
Tel: 020 8983 8000

URGENT CARE CENTRE (NEWHAM) 42Lc **93**
Newham University Hospital
Glen Road
LONDON
E13 8SL
Tel: 020 7476 4000

URGENT CARE CENTRE (NORTHFLEET)
.................................60Fe **121**
White Horse Surgery
Vale Road
Northfleet
GRAVESEND
DA11 8BZ
Tel: 0300 0300 000

**URGENT CARE CENTRE
(NORTH MIDDLESEX UNIVERSITY HOSPITAL)**
.................................22Ub **51**
Sterling Way
LONDON
N18 1QX
Tel: 020 8887 2398

**URGENT CARE CENTRE
(NORTHWICK PARK HOSPITAL)** 31Ja **66**
Watford Road
HARROW
HA1 3UJ
Tel: 020 8869 3743

**URGENT CARE CENTRE
(PRINCESS ROYAL UNIVERSITY HOSPITAL)**
.................................77Qc **160**
Farnborough Common
ORPINGTON
BR6 8ND
Tel: 01689 863050

**URGENT CARE CENTRE
(QUEEN ELIZABETH HOSPITAL)** 51Nc **116**
Stadium Road
LONDON
SE18 4QH
Tel: 020 8836 4074

URGENT CARE CENTRE (QUEEN'S HOSPITAL)
.................................31Gd **76**
Rom Valley Way
ROMFORD
RM7 0AG
Tel: 01708 435000

**URGENT CARE CENTRE
(ROYAL LONDON HOSPITAL, THE)**
.................................43Xb **91**
174 Whitechapel Road
LONDON
E1 1BZ
Tel: 020 7377 7000

**URGENT CARE CENTRE
(ST CHARLES CENTRE FOR WELL BEING)**
.................................43Za **88**
Exmoor Street
LONDON
W10 6DZ
Tel: 020 8102 5111

URGENT CARE CENTRE (ST GEORGE'S HOSPITAL)
.................................64Gb **133**
Blackshaw Road
LONDON
SW17 0QT
Tel: 020 8725 1265

URGENT CARE CENTRE (ST MARY'S HOSPITAL)
................................2B **220** (44Fb **89**)
Praed Street
LONDON
W2 1NY
Tel: 020 3312 6666

URGENT CARE CENTRE (SEVENOAKS HOSPITAL)
................................93Ld **203**
Hospital Road
Kent
SEVENOAKS
TN13 3PG
Tel: 01732 470200

URGENT CARE CENTRE (SIDCUP) 65Wc **139**
Queen Mary's Hospital
Frognal Avenue
SIDCUP
DA14 6LT
Tel: 020 8308 5611

URGENT CARE CENTRE (THORNTON HEATH)
................................72Rb **157**
Croydon University Hospital
530 London Road
THORNTON HEATH
CR7 7YE
Tel: 020 8401 3000

**URGENT CARE CENTRE
(UNIVERSITY COLLEGE HOSPITAL)**
................................5C **216** (42Lb **90**)
235 Euston Road
LONDON
NW1 2BU
Tel: 020 3456 7890

**URGENT CARE CENTRE
(UNIVERSITY HOSPITAL LEWISHAM)**
................................57Dc **114**
Lewisham High Street
LONDON
SE13 6LH
Tel: 020 8333 3000

URGENT CARE CENTRE (UPTON HOSPITAL)
................................8K **81**
Albert Street
SLOUGH
SL1 2BJ
Tel: 01753 635505

**URGENT CARE CENTRE
(WALTON COMMUNITY HOSPITAL)** 75Y **151**
Rodney Road
WALTON-ON-THAMES
KT12 3LD
Tel: 01932 414205

**URGENT CARE CENTRE
(WEST MIDDLESEX UNIVERSITY HOSPITAL)**
................................54Ja **108**
Twickenham Road
ISLEWORTH
TW7 6AF
Tel: 020 8560 2121

**URGENT CARE CENTRE
(WHIPPS CROSS UNIVERSITY HOSPITAL)**
................................30Fc **53**
Whipps Cross Road
LONDON
E11 1NR
Tel: 020 3416 5000

URGENT CARE CENTRE (WHITTINGTON HOSPITAL)
................................33Lb **70**
Magdala Avenue
LONDON
N19 5NF
Tel: 020 7288 5216

WALTON COMMUNITY HOSPITAL 75X **151**
Rodney Road
WALTON-ON-THAMES
KT12 3LD
Tel: 01932 414205

WATFORD GENERAL HOSPITAL
................................15X **27**
Vicarage Road
WATFORD
WD18 0HB
Tel: 01923 244366

WELLINGTON HOSPITAL, THE
................................2C **214** (41Fb **89**)
8a Wellington Place
LONDON
NW8 9LE
Tel: 020 7483 5148

WESTERN EYE HOSPITAL 7F **215** (43Hb **89**)
171 Marylebone Road
LONDON
NW1 5QH
Tel: 020 3312 6666

WEST MIDDLESEX UNIVERSITY HOSPITAL
................................54Ja **108**
Twickenham Road
ISLEWORTH
TW7 6AF
Tel: 020 8560 2121

WEXHAM PARK HOSPITAL 2N **81**
Wexham Street
Wexham
SLOUGH
SL2 4HL
Tel: 01753 633000

WEYBRIDGE COMMUNITY HOSPITAL
................................77Q **150**
22 Church Street
WEYBRIDGE
KT13 8DY
Tel: 01932 852931

WEYMOUTH BMI HOSPITAL, THE 7J **215**
42-46 Weymouth Street
LONDON
W1G 6NP
Tel: 020 7935 1200

WHIPPS CROSS UNIVERSITY HOSPITAL
................................29Fc **53**
Whipps Cross Road
LONDON
E11 1NR
Tel: 020 3416 5000

WHITTINGTON HOSPITAL 33Lb **70**
Magdala Avenue
LONDON
N19 5NF
Tel: 020 7272 3070

WILLESDEN CENTRE FOR HEALTH & CARE
................................38Wa **68**
Robson Avenue
LONDON
NW10 3RY
Tel: 020 8438 7006

WILSON HOSPTAL 70Hb **133**
Cranmer Road
MITCHAM
CR4 4TP
Tel: 020 8648 3021

WOKING COMMUNITY HOSPITAL
................................90B **168**
Heathside Road
WOKING
GU22 7HS
Tel: 01483 715911

WOKING HOSPICE 90B **168**
5 Hill View Road
WOKING
GU22 7HW
Tel: 01483 881750

WOKING NUFFIELD HEALTH HOSPITAL
................................86A **168**
Shores Road
WOKING
GU21 4BY
Tel: 01483 227800

WOKING PRIORY HOSPITAL 8G **166**
Chobham Road
Knaphill
WOKING
GU21 2QF
Tel: 01483 489211

WOODBURY UNIT 30Gc **53**
178 James Lane
LONDON
E11 1NR
Tel: 0300 555 1260

RAIL, TRAMLINK, DOCKLANDS LIGHT RAILWAY, RIVER BUS, CABLE CAR, BUS, UNDERGROUND, CROSSRAIL AND OVERGROUND STATIONS

with their map square reference

A

Abbey Road (DLR) 40Gc 73
Abbey Wood (Rail) 48Yc 95
Acton Central (Overground) 46Ta 87
Acton Main Line (Rail) 44Sa 87
Acton Town (Underground) 47Qa 87
Addington Bus Station 79Cc 158
Addington Village Stop (Tramlink) 79Cc 158
Addiscombe Stop (Tramlink) 74Wb 157
Addlestone (Rail) 77M 149
Albany Park (Rail) 61Zc 139
Aldgate (Underground) 3K 225 (44Vb 91)
Aldgate Bus Station 3K 225 (44Vb 91)
Aldgate East (Underground) 2K 225 (44Vb 91)
Alexandra Palace (Rail) 26Nb 50
All Saints (DLR) 45Dc 92
Alperton (Underground) 39Ma 67
Ampere Way Stop (Tramlink) 74Pb 156
Anerley (Rail & Overground) 67Xb 135
Angel (Underground) 1A 218 (40Qb 70)
Angel Road (Rail) 22Yb 52
Apsley (Rail) 7N 3
Archway (Underground) 33Lb 70
Archway Bus Station 33Lb 70
Arena Stop (Tramlink) 71Yb 158
Arnos Grove (Underground) 22Lb 50
Arsenal (Underground) 34Qb 70
Ashford (Rail) 63P 127
Ashtead (Rail) 89Na 173
Avenue Road Stop (Tramlink) 68Zb 136

B

Baker Street (Underground) 6G 215 (42Hb 89)
Balham (Rail & Underground) 60Kb 112
Bank (Underground & DLR) 3F 225 (44Tb 91)
Bankside Pier (River Bus & Tours) 5D 224 (45Sb 91)
Banstead (Rail) 86Bb 175
Barbican (Underground) 7D 218 (43Sb 91)
Barking (Rail, Underground & Overground) 38Sc 74
Barkingside (Underground) 27Tc 54
Barnehurst (Rail) 54Ed 118
Barnes (Rail) 55Wa 110
Barnes Bridge (Rail) 54Va 110
Barons Court (Underground) 50Ab 88
Bat & Ball (Rail) 93Ld 203
Battersea Park (Rail) 52Kb 112
Bayswater (Underground) 45Db 89
Beckenham Hill (Rail) 64Ec 136
Beckenham Junction (Rail & Tramlink) 67Cc 136
Beckenham Road Stop (Tramlink) 67Ac 136
Beckton (DLR) 43Qc 94
Beckton Park (DLR) 45Pc 94
Becontree (Underground) 37Zc 75
Beddington Lane Stop (Tramlink) 72Lb 156
Belgrave Walk Stop (Tramlink) 70Fb 133
Bellingham (Rail) 62Dc 136
Belmont (Rail) 82Db 175
Belsize Park (Underground) 36Gb 69
Belvedere (Rail) 48Dd 96
Bermondsey (Underground) 48Wb 91
Berrylands (Rail) 70Ra 131
Betchworth (Rail) 4A 206
Bethnal Green (Overground) 42Xb 91
Bethnal Green (Underground) 41Yb 92
Bexley (Rail) 60Cd 118
Bexleyheath (Rail) 54Ad 117
Bickley (Rail) 69Nc 138
Birkbeck (Rail & Tramlink) 69Yb 136
Blackfriars (Rail & Underground) 4B 224 (45Rb 91)
Blackfriars Millennium Pier (River Bus) 4C 224 (45Rb 91)
Blackheath (Rail) 55Hc 115
Blackhorse Lane Stop (Tramlink) 73Wb 157
Blackhorse Road (Underground & Overground) 28Zb 52
Blackwall (DLR) 45Ec 92
Bluewater Bus Station 60Wd 120
Bond Street (Underground) 3K 221 (44Kb 90)
Bookham (Rail) 95Ba 191
Borough (Underground) 2E 230 (47Sb 91)
Borough Green & Wrotham (Rail) 92Be 205
Boston Manor (Underground) 49Ja 86
Bounds Green (Underground) 23Mb 50
Bow Church (DLR) 41Cc 92
Bowes Park (Rail) 24Nb 50
Bow Road (Underground) 41Cc 92
Brent Cross (Underground) 31Za 68
Brent Cross Bus Station 31Ya 68
Brentford (Rail) 51La 108
Brentwood (Rail & Crossrail) 20Yd 40
Bricket Wood (Rail) 2Ca 13
Brimsdown (Rail) 13Ac 34
Brixton (Rail & Underground) 56Qb 112
Brockley (Rail & Overground) 55Ac 114
Bromley-by-Bow (Underground) 41Dc 92
Bromley North (Rail) 67Jc 137
Bromley South (Rail) 69Jc 137
Brondesbury (Overground) 38Bb 69
Brondesbury Park (Overground) 39Ab 68
Brookmans Park (Rail) 9G 8
Brookwood (Rail) 3E 186
Bruce Grove (Overground) 26Vb 51
Buckhurst Hill (Underground) 19Mc 35
Burnham (Rail) 4B 80
Burnt Oak (Underground) 25Sa 47
Bushey (Rail & Overground) 16Z 27
Bush Hill Park (Overground) 16Vb 33
Byfleet & New Haw (Rail) 82M 169

C

Cadogan Pier (River Bus) 51Gb 111
Caledonian Road (Underground) 37Pb 70
Caledonian Road & Barnsbury (Overground) 38Pb 70
Cambridge Heath (Overground) 40Xb 71
Camden Road (Overground) 38Lb 70
Camden Town (Underground) 39Kb 70
Canada Water Bus Station *47Yb 92*
(off Surrey Quays)
Canada Water (Underground & Overground) 47Yb 92
Canary Wharf (Underground & DLR) 46Cc 92
Canary Wharf Pier (River Bus) 46Bc 92
Canning Town (Underground & DLR) 44Gc 93
Canning Town Bus Station 44Gc 93
Cannon Street (Rail & Underground) 4F 225 (45Tb 91)
Canonbury (Overground) 36Sb 71
Canons Park (Underground) 24Na 47
Carpenders Park (Overground) 20Z 27
Carshalton (Rail) 77Hb 155
Carshalton Beeches (Rail) 79Hb 155
Castle Bar Park (Rail) 43Ha 86
Caterham (Rail) 96Wb 197
Catford (Rail) 59Cc 114
Catford Bridge (Rail) 59Cc 114
Centrale Stop (Tramlink) 75Sb 157
Chadwell Heath (Rail & Crossrail) 31Zc 75
Chafford Hundred (Rail) 49Xd 98
Chalk Farm (Underground) 38Jb 70
Chancery Lane (Underground) 1K 223 (43Qb 90)
Charing Cross (Rail & Underground) 6F 223 (46Nb 90)
Charlton (Rail) 50Lc 93
Cheam (Rail) 80Ab 154
Chelsea Harbour Pier (River Bus) 53Fb 111
Chelsfield (Rail) 78Xc 161
Chertsey (Rail) 74H 149
Cheshunt (Rail) 2Bc 20
Chessington North (Rail) 78Na 153
Chessington South (Rail) 80Ma 153
Chigwell (Underground) 20Rc 36
Chingford (Overground) 17Gc 35
Chingford Bus Station 17Gc 35
Chipstead (Rail) 90Hb 175
Chislehurst (Rail) 68Qc 138
Chiswick (Rail) 52Sa 109
Chiswick Park (Underground) 49Sa 87
Chorleywood (Rail & Underground) 14F 24
Church Street Stop (Tramlink) 75Sb 157
City Thameslink (Rail) 2B 224 (44Rb 91)
Clandon (Rail) 100K 189
Clapham Common (Underground) 56Lb 112
Clapham High Street (Overground) 55Mb 112
Clapham Junction (Rail & Overground) 55Gb 111
Clapham North (Underground) 55Nb 112
Clapham South (Underground) 58Kb 112
Clapton (Overground) 33Xb 71
Claygate (Rail) 79Ga 152
Clock House (Rail) 67Ac 136
Cobham & Stoke D'Abernon (Rail) 89Aa 171
Cockfosters (Underground) 14Jb 32
Colindale (Underground) 27Ua 48
Colliers Wood (Underground) 66Fb 133
Coombe Lane Stop (Tramlink) 78Yb 158
Coulsdon South (Rail) 88Mb 176
Coulsdon Town (Rail) 87Nb 176
Covent Garden (Underground) 3G 223 (45Nb 90)
Crayford (Rail) 58Gd 118
Crews Hill (Rail) 6Pb 18
Cricklewood (Rail) 35Za 68
Crofton Park (Rail) 57Bc 114
Cromwell Road Bus Station 67Na 131
Crossharbour (Underground & DLR) 48Dc 92
Crouch Hill (Overground) 31Pb 70
Croxley (Underground) 16R 26
Crystal Palace (Rail & Overground) 65Wb 135
Cuffley (Rail) 1Pb 18
Custom House for ExCeL (DLR) 45Kc 93
Cutty Sark for Maritime Greenwich (DLR) 51Ec 114
Cyprus (DLR) 45Qc 94

D

Dagenham Dock (Rail) 40Bd 75
Dagenham East (Underground) 36Ed 76
Dagenham Heathway (Underground) 37Bd 75
Dalston Junction (Overground) 37Vb 71
Dalston Kingsland (Overground) 36Ub 71
Dartford (Rail) 58Nd 119
Datchet (Rail) 3M 103
Debden (Underground) 14Sc 36
Denham (Rail) 31J 63
Denham Golf Club (Rail) 31F 62
Denmark Hill (Rail & Overground) 54Tb 113
Deptford (Rail) 52Cc 114
Deptford Bridge (DLR) 53Cc 114
Devons Road (DLR) 42Dc 92
Dollis Hill (Underground) 36Wa 68
Drayton Green (Rail) 44Ha 86
Drayton Park (Rail) 35Qb 70
Dundonald Road Stop (Tramlink) 66Bb 133
Dunton Green (Rail) 91Gd 202

E

Ealing Broadway (Rail & Underground) 45Ma 87
Ealing Common (Underground) 46Pa 87
Earl's Court (Underground) 49Cb 89
Earlsfield (Rail) 60Eb 111
Earlswood (Rail) 8P 207
East Acton (Underground) 44Va 88
East Beckton Bus Station 44Qc 94
Eastcote (Underground) 31Y 65
East Croydon (Rail & Tramlink) 75Tb 157
East Dulwich (Rail) 56Ub 113
East Finchley (Underground) 28Gb 49
East Ham (Underground) 38Nc 74
East India (DLR) 45Fc 93
East Putney (Underground) 57Ab 110
East Tilbury (Rail) 9K 101
Ebbsfleet International (Rail) 58Ce 121
Eden Park (Rail) 71Cc 158
Edgware (Underground) 23Ra 47
Edgware Bus Station 23Ra 47
Edgware Road (Underground) 1D 220 (43Gb 89)
Edmonton Bus Station 19Xb 33
Edmonton Green (Overground) 19Wb 33
Effingham Junction (Rail) 95W 190
Egham (Rail) 64C 126
Elephant & Castle (Rail & Underground) 5D 230 (49Sb 91)
Elmers End (Rail & Tramlink) 70Zb 136
Elm Park (Underground) 35Kd 77
Elmsleigh Bus Station 64H 127
Elmstead Woods (Rail) 65Nc 138
Elstree & Borehamwood (Rail) 14Qa 29
Eltham (Rail) 57Pc 116
Elverson Road (DLR) 54Dc 114
Embankment (Underground) 6G 223 (46Nb 90)
Embankment Pier (River Bus & Tours) 6G 223 (46Nb 90)
Emerson Park (Rail) 31Nd 77
Emirates Greenwich Peninsula 47Hc 93
Emirates Royal Docks 45Jc 93
Enfield Chase (Rail) 13Sb 33
Enfield Lock (Rail) 9Ac 20
Enfield Town (Overground) 13Ub 33
Epping (Underground) 3Wc 23
Epsom (Rail) 85Ta 173
Epsom Downs (Rail) 87Xa 174
Erith (Rail) 50Gd 96
Esher (Rail) 75Fa 152
Essex Road (Rail) 38Sb 71
Euston (Rail, Underground & Overground) 4D 216 (41Lb 90)
Euston Square (Underground) 5C 216 (42Lb 90)
Ewell East (Rail) 82Xa 174
Ewell West (Rail) 81Ua 174
Eynsford (Rail) 77Md 163

F

Fairfield Road Bus Station 68Na 131
Fairlop (Underground) 25Tc 54
Falconwood (Rail) 56Tc 116
Farningham Road (Rail) 68Rd 141
Farringdon (Rail & Underground) 7B 218 (43Rb 91)
Feltham (Rail) 60X 107
Fenchurch Street (Rail) 4J 225 (45Vb 91)
Festival Pier (River Tours) 6H 223 (46Pb 90)
Fieldway Stop (Tramlink) 80Dc 158
Finchley Central (Underground) 25Cb 49
Finchley Road (Underground) 37Eb 69
Finchley Road & Frognal (Overground) 36Eb 69
Finsbury Park (Rail & Underground) 33Qb 70
Finsbury Park Interchange (Bus) 33Qb 70
Forest Gate (Rail & Crossrail) 36Jc 73
Forest Hill (Rail & Overground) 61Yb 136
Fulham Broadway (Underground) 52Cb 111
Fulwell (Rail) 63Fa 130

G

Gallions Reach (DLR) 45Rc 94
Gants Hill (Underground) 30Qc 54
Garston (Rail) 7Z 13
George Street Stop (Tramlink) 75Sb 157
Gerrards Cross (Rail) 29A 42
Gidea Park (Rail & Crossrail) 28Kd 57
Gipsy Hill (Rail) 64Ub 135
Gloucester Road (Underground) 5A 226 (49Eb 89)
Godstone (Rail) 10C 210
Golders Green (Underground) 32Cb 69
Goldhawk Road (Underground) 47Ya 88
Goodge Street (Underground) 7D 216 (43Mb 90)
Goodmayes (Rail & Crossrail) 32Wc 75
Gordon Hill (Rail) 11Rb 33
Gospel Oak (Overground) 35Jb 70
Grange Hill (Underground) 21Tc 54
Grange Park (Rail) 15Rb 33
Gravel Hill Stop (Tramlink) 79Ac 158
Gravesend (Rail) 8D 122
Grays (Rail) 51Ce 121
Great Portland Street (Underground) 6A 216 (42Kb 90)
Greenford (Rail & Underground) 39Fa 66
Greenhithe for Bluewater (Rail) 57Wd 120
Greenland Pier (River Bus) 48Bc 92
Green Line Coach Station 6A 228
Green Park (Underground) 6A 222 (46Lb 90)
Greenwich (Rail & DLR) 52Dc 114
Greenwich Pier (River Bus & Tours) 50Ec 92
Grove Park (Rail) 62Kc 137
Gunnersbury (Underground & Overground) 50Ra 87

H

Hackbridge (Rail) 75Kb 156
Hackney Central (Overground) 37Xb 71
Hackney Downs (Overground) 36Xb 71

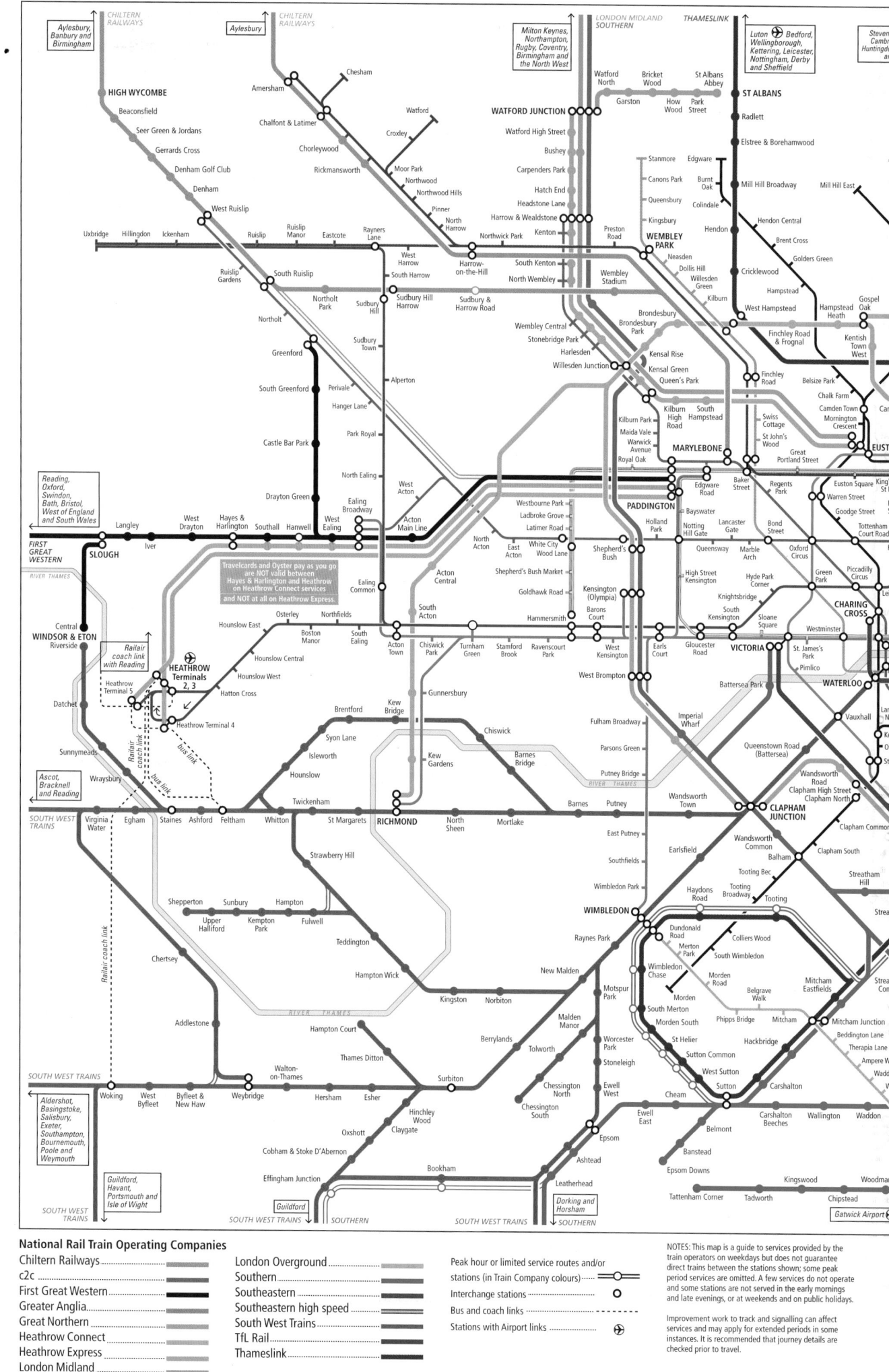

National Rail Train Operating Companies

Chiltern Railways	London Overground
c2c	Southern
First Great Western	Southeastern
Greater Anglia	Southeastern high speed
Great Northern	South West Trains
Heathrow Connect	TfL Rail
Heathrow Express	Thameslink
London Midland	

Peak hour or limited service routes and/or stations (in Train Company colours)

Interchange stations

Bus and coach links

Stations with Airport links

NOTES: This map is a guide to services provided by the train operators on weekdays but does not guarantee direct trains between the stations shown; some peak period services are omitted. A few services do not operate and some stations are not served in the early mornings and late evenings, or at weekends and on public holidays.

Improvement work to track and signalling may affect services and may apply for extended periods in some instances. It is recommended that journey details are checked prior to travel.

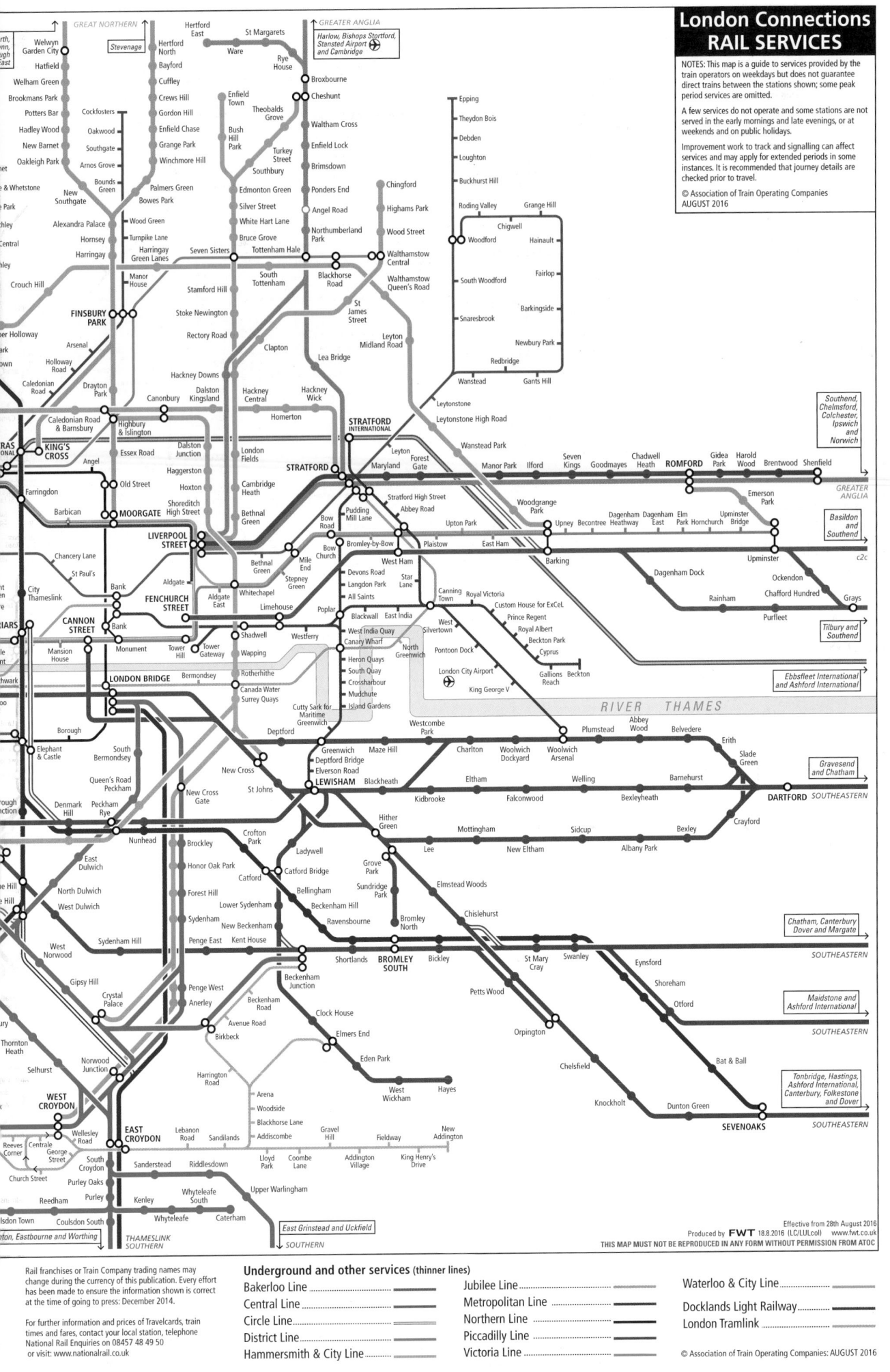

London Connections
RAIL SERVICES

NOTES: This map is a guide to services provided by the train operators on weekdays but does not guarantee direct trains between the stations shown; some peak period services are omitted.

A few services do not operate and some stations are not served in the early mornings and late evenings, or at weekends and on public holidays.

Improvement work to track and signalling can affect services and may apply for extended periods in some instances. It is recommended that journey details are checked prior to travel.

© Association of Train Operating Companies
AUGUST 2016

GREAT NORTHERN
GREATER ANGLIA
Harlow, Bishops Stortford, Stansted Airport and Cambridge

Stevenage

Welwyn Garden City
Hatfield
Welham Green
Brookmans Park
Potters Bar
Hadley Wood
New Barnet
Oakleigh Park

Cockfosters
Oakwood
Southgate
Arnos Grove
Bounds Green

Alexandra Palace
Hornsey
Harringay

Hertford East
St Margarets
Ware
Rye House
Broxbourne
Cheshunt

Hertford North
Bayford
Cuffley
Crews Hill
Gordon Hill
Enfield Chase
Grange Park
Winchmore Hill

Enfield Town
Theobalds Grove
Waltham Cross
Enfield Lock
Brimsdown
Ponders End
Angel Road
Northumberland Park

Epping
Theydon Bois
Debden
Loughton
Buckhurst Hill
Roding Valley
Grange Hill
Chigwell
Hainault
Fairlop
Barkingside
Newbury Park
Redbridge
Gants Hill

Woodford
South Woodford
Snaresbrook
Wanstead

New Southgate
Bowes Park
Palmers Green
Wood Green
Turnpike Lane
Harringay Green Lanes

Edmonton Green
Silver Street
White Hart Lane
Bruce Grove
Seven Sisters

Chingford
Highams Park
Wood Street
Walthamstow Central
Walthamstow Queen's Road

FINSBURY PARK
Manor House
Arsenal
Holloway Road
Caledonian Road
Drayton Park

Stamford Hill
Stoke Newington
Rectory Road
Clapton

South Tottenham
Blackhorse Road
St James Street
Leyton Midland Road

Tottenham Hale

Lea Bridge
Leytonstone
Leytonstone High Road

Caledonian Road & Barnsbury
KING'S CROSS
Angel
Farringdon
Barbican
MOORGATE
Chancery Lane
St Paul's
City Thameslink
Bank
LIVERPOOL STREET
Aldgate
FENCHURCH STREET
CANNON STREET
Bank
Monument
Mansion House

Highbury & Islington
Essex Road
Old Street

Haggerston
Hoxton
Shoreditch High Street
Bethnal Green

Dalston Kingsland
Dalston Junction
Canonbury

London Fields
Cambridge Heath

Hackney Downs
Hackney Central
Homerton
Hackney Wick

STRATFORD INTERNATIONAL
STRATFORD

Leyton
Maryland
Forest Gate
Manor Park
Ilford
Seven Kings
Goodmayes
Chadwell Heath
ROMFORD
Gidea Park
Harold Wood
Brentwood
Shenfield

Wanstead Park

Southend, Chelmsford, Colchester, Ipswich and Norwich

GREATER ANGLIA

Stratford High Street
Abbey Road
Woodgrange Park

Emerson Park

Basildon and Southend

Pudding Mill Lane
Bow Road
Bromley-by-Bow
Bow Church
Upton Park
Plaistow
East Ham

Upney
Becontree
Dagenham Heathway
Dagenham East
Elm Park
Hornchurch
Upminster Bridge

c2c

Bethnal Green
Mile End
Stepney Green
Devons Road
Langdon Park
All Saints

Barking
Upminster
Dagenham Dock
Ockendon
Chafford Hundred
Grays
Rainham
Purfleet

Tilbury and Southend

Aldgate East
Whitechapel
Limehouse
Poplar

Canning Town
Royal Victoria
Custom House for ExCeL
Prince Regent
Royal Albert
Beckton Park
Cyprus
Gallions Reach
Beckton

Shadwell
Wapping
Tower Hill
Tower Gateway

Westferry
Canary Wharf
West India Quay
Blackwall
East India
West Silvertown
Pontoon Dock
London City Airport
King George V

Ebbsfleet International and Ashford International

Heron Quays
South Quay
Crossharbour
Mudchute
Island Gardens

North Greenwich

LONDON BRIDGE
Bermondsey
Rotherhithe
Canada Water
Surrey Quays

Cutty Sark for Maritime Greenwich

RIVER THAMES

Borough
Elephant & Castle
South Bermondsey
Queen's Road Peckham
Denmark Hill
Peckham Rye
Nunhead
Brockley

Deptford
Greenwich
Deptford Bridge
Elverson Road
LEWISHAM
Maze Hill
Westcombe Park
Charlton
Blackheath
Woolwich Dockyard
Woolwich Arsenal
Plumstead
Abbey Wood
Belvedere
Erith
Slade Green

New Cross
New Cross Gate
St Johns
Eltham
Welling
Barnehurst
Kidbrooke
Falconwood
Bexleyheath
Crayford

Gravesend and Chatham

DARTFORD SOUTHEASTERN

East Dulwich
North Dulwich
West Dulwich
Forest Hill
Sydenham
New Cross

Ladywell
Catford
Catford Bridge
Bellingham

Hither Green
Lee
Mottingham
Grove Park
New Eltham
Sidcup
Bexley
Albany Park

West Norwood
Gipsy Hill
Crystal Palace

Sydenham Hill
Penge East
Kent House
Lower Sydenham
New Beckenham
Beckenham Hill
Ravensbourne
Sundridge Park
Bromley North

Elmstead Woods
Chislehurst

Chatham, Canterbury Dover and Margate

Thornton Heath
Selhurst

Penge West
Anerley
Norwood Junction

Beckenham Junction
Beckenham Road
Clock House
Elmers End
Eden Park
West Wickham
Hayes

Shortlands
BROMLEY SOUTH
Bickley
Petts Wood
Orpington
Chelsfield

St Mary Cray
Swanley
Eynsford
Shoreham
Otford

SOUTHEASTERN

Maidstone and Ashford International

SOUTHEASTERN

Harrington Road
Avenue Road
Birkbeck

Arena
Woodside
Blackhorse Lane
Addiscombe
Lebanon Road
Sandilands
Lloyd Park
Coombe Lane
Addington Village
King Henry's Drive

Bat & Ball

Tonbridge, Hastings, Ashford International, Canterbury, Folkestone and Dover

WEST CROYDON
Reeves Corner
Centrale
Wellesley Road
George Street
Church Street

EAST CROYDON
South Croydon
Sanderstead
Purley Oaks
Purley
Reedham

Gravel Hill
Fieldway
New Addington

Knockholt
Dunton Green

SEVENOAKS SOUTHEASTERN

Kenley
Whyteleafe South
Upper Warlingham
Coulsdon South
Whyteleafe
Caterham
Riddlesdown

East Grinstead and Uckfield

THAMESLINK SOUTHERN
SOUTHERN

Eastbourne and Worthing

Effective from 28th August 2016
Produced by FWT 18.8.2016 (LC/LULcol)   www.fwt.co.uk
THIS MAP MUST NOT BE REPRODUCED IN ANY FORM WITHOUT PERMISSION FROM ATOC

Rail franchises or Train Company trading names may change during the currency of this publication. Every effort has been made to ensure the information shown is correct at the time of going to press: December 2014.

For further information and prices of Travelcards, train times and fares, contact your local station, telephone National Rail Enquiries on 08457 48 49 50 or visit: www.nationalrail.co.uk

Underground and other services (thinner lines)

Bakerloo Line
Central Line
Circle Line
District Line
Hammersmith & City Line
Jubilee Line
Metropolitan Line
Northern Line
Piccadilly Line
Victoria Line
Waterloo & City Line
Docklands Light Railway
London Tramlink

© Association of Train Operating Companies: AUGUST 2016

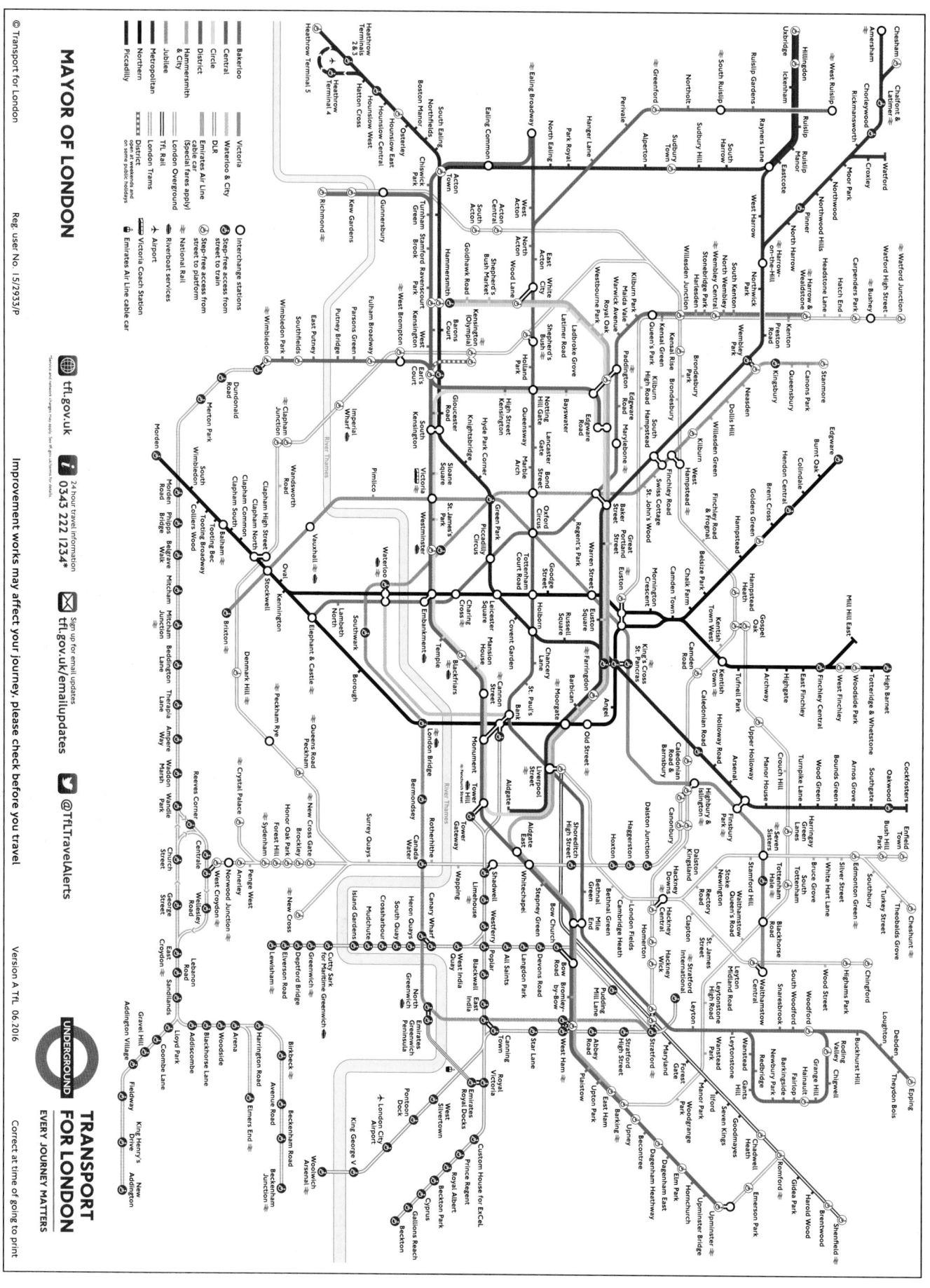

Bakerloo
Central
Circle
District
Hammersmith & City
Jubilee
Metropolitan
Northern
Piccadilly
Victoria
Waterloo & City
DLR
Emirates Air Line cable car (Special fares apply)
London Overground
TfL Rail
London Trams
District open at weekends and on some public holidays
Interchange stations
Step-free access from street to train
Step-free access from street to platform
National Rail
Riverboat services
Airport
Victoria Coach Station
Emirates Air Line cable car
MAYOR OF LONDON
tfl.gov.uk
24 hour travel information
0343 222 1234*
Sign up for email updates
tfl.gov.uk/emailupdates
@TfLTravelAlerts
UNDERGROUND
TRANSPORT FOR LONDON
EVERY JOURNEY MATTERS
© Transport for London
Reg. user No. 15/2933/P
Improvement works may affect your journey, please check before you travel
Version A TfL 06.2016
Correct at time of going to print
River Thames

ADMINISTRATIVE BOUNDARIES
County or Unitary Authority Boundary
Local Authoritory Boundary
SCALE
0 1 2 3 4 Miles
0 1 2 3 4 5 Kilometres
AYLESBURY VALE
Wendover
BERKHAMSTED
DACORUM
HEMEL HEMPSTEAD
ST. ALBANS
HATFIELD
WELWYN
Welham Green
HATFIELD
Brookmans Park
HERTFORDSHIRE
Cuffley
POTTERS BAR
ST. ALBANS
Chiswell Green
London Colney
Colney Heath
Frogmore
Colney Street
Shenleybury
South Mimms
SOUTH MIMMS
Ridge
Ashley Green
Bovingdon
Chipperfield
Kings Langley
Abbots Langley
Bricket Wood
CHESHAM
Great Missenden
CHILTERN
Latimer
Sarratt
Chenies
Chandler's Cross
WATFORD
RADLETT
Aldenham
Shenley
Green Street
HERTSMERE
Bentley Heath
Hadley Wood
Botany Bay
AMERSHAM
Little Chalfont
CHORLEYWOOD
THREE RIVERS
WATFORD
Patchetts Green
BOREHAMWOOD
Monken Hadley
EAST BARNET
Cockfosters
BUCKINGHAMSHIRE
Heronsgate
RICKMANSWORTH
Batchworth
BUSHEY
Oxhey
Bushey Heath
Elstree
Arkley
BARNET
Totteridge
LONDON GATEWAY
Whetstone
SOUTHGATE
FRIERN BARNET
BARNET
WYCOMBE
HIGH WYCOMBE
Chalfont St. Giles
Chalfont Common
Maple Cross
Eastbury
South Oxhey
Hatch End
STANMORE
EDGWARE
Mill Hill
FINCHLEY
WOOD GREEN
BEACONSFIELD
Chalfont St. Peter
West Hyde
Harefield
NORTHWOOD
HARROW
Wooburn Green
BEACONSFIELD
Gerrards Cross
Denham Green
Ruislip Common
KENTON
HENDON
Muswell Hill
Wooburn
Hedgerley
Denham
PINNER
HARROW
Kingsbury
Golders Green
Bourne End
SOUTH BUCKS
Tatling End
Ickenham
Eastcote
RUISLIP
Harrow on the Hill
Rayners Lane
Neasden
Cricklewood
Highgate
HAMPSTEAD
Cookham
Egypt
New Denham
HILLINGDON
BRENT
CAMDEN
Farnham Common
Farnham Royal
Stoke Poges
UXBRIDGE
NORTHOLT
WEMBLEY
WILLESDEN
CAMDEN TOWN
Kilburn
Burnham
Hillingdon
Iver Heath
Taplow
SLOUGH
George Green
Cowley
GREENFORD
Yeading
EALING
MARYLEBONE
FINSBURY
MAIDENHEAD
SLOUGH
A404(M)
Bray
Cippenham
Upton
Langley
Richings Park
Yiewsley
West Drayton
HAYES
SOUTHALL
Hanwell
ACTON
Shepherd's Bush
HAMMERSMITH
KENSINGTON & CHELSEA
PADDINGTON
CITY OF WESTMINSTER
KENSINGTON
WESTMINSTER
CHELSEA
Eton Wick
Eton
Harmondsworth
Sipson
Harlington
HESTON
Heston
Brentford
Osterley
CHISWICK
Kew
HAMMERSMITH
HAMMERSMITH & FULHAM
BATTERSEA
WINDSOR & MAIDENHEAD
WINDSOR
Datchet
Colnbrook
Horton
Poyle
LONDON HEATHROW AIRPORT
Cranford
HOUNSLOW
ISLEWORTH
North Sheen
BARNES
FULHAM
PUTNEY
Old Windsor
Wraysbury
Stanwell Moor
Stanwell
Hatton
HOUNSLOW
RICHMOND
Roehampton
WANDSWORTH
WANDSWORTH
CLAPHAM
Cranbourne
Windsor Great Park
SPELTHORNE
East Bedfont
RICHMOND UPON THAMES
Richmond Park
BRACKNELL FOREST
Winkfield
Winkfield Row
Woodside
Englefield Green
Hythe End
STAINES
ASHFORD
FELTHAM
TWICKENHAM
Ham
WIMBLEDON
STREATHAM
BRACKNELL
North Ascot
Ascot
RUNNYMEDE
EGHAM
Egham Hythe
Thorpe
Felthamhill
Hanworth
Hampton
TEDDINGTON
Hampton Wick
KINGSTON UPON THAMES
MERTON
NEW MALDEN
MERTON
MORDEN
MITCHAM
South Ascot
Sunningdale
Virginia Water
Laleham
Littleton
SUNBURY
Upper Halliford
West Molesey
East Molesey
SURBITON
Sunninghill
Broomhall
Lyne
CHERTSEY
Shepperton
WALTON-ON-THAMES
Thames Ditton
Long Ditton
Beddington
Windlesham
Addlestone
WEYBRIDGE
Hersham
ESHER
Worcester Park
SUTTON
CARSHALTON
SUTTON
Bagshot
Ottershaw
New Haw
Row Town
ELMBRIDGE
Claygate
KINGSTON UPON THAMES
Hook
Chessington
Cheam
EPSOM
WALLINGTON
SURREY HEATH
Lightwater
CAMBERLEY
Chobham
Woodham
Whiteley Village
EPSOM
EWELL
EPSOM & EWELL
PURLEY
West Byfleet
Byfleet
Fairmile
Malden Rushett
Horsell
Sheerwater
Bisley
Knaphill
WOKING
Pyrford
Wisley
Cobham
Stoke D'Abernon
Oxshott
Pachesham
Ashtead
Woodmansterne
BANSTEAD
COULSDON
Frimley
WOKING
COBHAM
Brookwood
Old Woking
Ripley
Ockham
Effingham Common
LEATHERHEAD
Burgh Heath
Chipstead
Tadworth
Hooley
Mayford
Send Marsh
Kingswood
Pirbright
Send
Fetcham
REIGATE
Lower Kingswood
Chaldon
FARNBOROUGH
Little Bookham
Headley
Worplesdon
Sutton Green
SURREY
East Horsley
Effingham
Great Bookham
Mickleham
Walton on the Hill
REIGATE & BANSTEAD
Gatton
Merstham
ALDERSHOT
West Clandon
East Clandon
West Horsley
MOLE VALLEY
Buckland
BANSTEAD
REDHILL
Normandy
GUILDFORD
Ranmore Common
Ash
Betchworth
Tongham
GUILDFORD
Westcott
Brockham
REIGATE
Nutfield
South Nutfield
Gomshall
DORKING
FARNHAM
Puttenham
Compton
Shalford
Shere
M1
M25
M40
M4
M3
A1(M)